WISDEN

PUBLISHED EVERY YEAR SINCE 1864

www.wisden.com

139TH YEAR

WISDEN
CRICKETERS' ALMANACK

2002

EDITED BY GRAEME WRIGHT

PUBLISHED BY JOHN WISDEN & CO LTD
13 OLD AYLESFIELD, FROYLE ROAD
GOLDEN POT, ALTON, HAMPSHIRE GU34 4BY

Cased edition ISBN 0 947766 70 7 £35
Soft cover edition ISBN 0 947766 71 5 £35
Leatherbound edition ISBN 0 947766 72 3 £225

Published in 2002 by
JOHN WISDEN & CO LTD
13 Old Aylesfield, Froyle Road, Golden Pot, Alton, Hampshire GU34 4BY
Tel: 01420 83415 Fax: 01420 83056
E-mail: wisden@ndirect.co.uk
Website: www.wisden.com

WISDEN CRICKETERS' ALMANACK

Deputy editor: Harriet Monkhouse
Managing editor: Hugh Chevallier
Production co-ordinator: Peter Bather
Chief typesetter: Mike Smith
Proofreader: Gordon Burling
Advertisement sales: Colin Ackehurst
Managing director: Christopher Lane

Computer typeset by LazerType, Colchester

Printed and bound in Great Britain by Clays Ltd, St Ives plc
Distributed by The Penguin Group
Distributed in Australia by Hardie Grant Books, Melbourne

PREFACE

Just as the presses were ready to print last year's *Wisden*, Sir Donald Bradman died. It was too late to do full justice to a great cricketer and his life, in and for the game; our printer held back a section, which allowed us to turn the Preface into a special tribute. In this edition, we have been able to reflect at some length on the man, his career and his legacy.

The speed with which we were able to substitute a page at the last minute was an example of how new technologies have altered our lives. Another instance, less than three weeks afterwards, was following V. V. S. Laxman's innings on the internet as he revived India's fortunes in their Second Test against Australia at Kolkata. Initially his mission seemed impossible; after a while it had become unbelievable. "You have seen people bat that well for a session, or even two," said Rahul Dravid, who stayed with him throughout the fourth day. "But he just went on and on." For Laxman, it was the innings of a lifetime; for many, it was the innings of 2001. Despite the tradition that *Wisden's* Cricketers of the Year have played in England during the year under review, Laxman immediately became an exception.

So, in a different way, did Andy Flower, Zimbabwe's wicket-keeper/batsman. As we married Test match reports to scorecards, checked and subbed, Flower's run of scores embedded themselves in the consciousness. With Laxman, selection was based on an innings; with Flower, it was a year. The other three Cricketers of the Year, Adam Gilchrist, Jason Gillespie and Damien Martyn, simply confirm that Australia's cricket in 2001 was superior to England's.

Wisden is fortunate in its network of correspondents, statisticians and informants: I would like to thank them all for their ready assistance in my two years back in office. In particular, I am grateful to Matthew Engel for looking after the obituaries for the 2001 Almanack, and to Eric Midwinter, who took charge for this edition.

Finally, my special thanks go to those most closely involved with the preparation and publishing of this *Wisden*: Harriet Monkhouse, Hugh Chevallier and Christopher Lane at John Wisden; Peter Bather, Dave Clark and Mike Smith at LazerType, our typesetter; Stephen Mitchell at our printer, Clays; Gordon Burling, the Almanack's estimable and long-serving proof-reader; and Philip Bailey, who provided extensive statistical help. Christine Forrest, as she has every year since retiring, smoothed the way in the feverish weeks leading up to the deadline and has everyone's gratitude.

GRAEME WRIGHT

Eastcote, Middlesex
February 2002

CONTRIBUTORS

Kamran Abbasi
Tanya Aldred
Andy Arlidge
Chris Aspin
Philip Bailey
Peter Bather
Greg Baum
Edward Bevan
Paul Bolton
Lawrence Booth
Simon Briggs
Kip Brook
Robert Brooke
Colin Bryden
Don Cameron
Tony Cozier
John Curtis
Gareth Davies
Geoffrey Dean
Ralph Dellor
Norman de Mesquita
Philip Eden
Clive Ellis
Matthew Engel
John Etheridge
Colin Evans
Stephen Fay
Paul Fearn
David Foot
Neville Foulger
David Frith
Nigel Fuller
Andrew Gidley
Julian Guyer
Gideon Haigh
David Hallett
Catherine Hanley
David Hardy
Peter S. Hargreaves
Norman Harris
Les Hatton
Roy Hattersley
Simon Heffer
Richard Hobson
Myles Hodgson
Jim Holden
Grenville Holland
Richard Holt
Simon Hughes
Abid Ali Kazi
Christopher Lane
Neil Leitch
David Llewellyn
Steven Lynch
John MacKinnon
Neil Manthorp
Keith Meadows
Mohandas Menon
Eric Midwinter
R. Mohan
Gerald Mortimer
Francis Payne
Gordon Phillips
Derek Pringle
Andrew Radd
Mark Ray
Peter Roebuck
Graham Russell
Dicky Rutnagur
Carol Salmon·
Samiul Hasan
Andrew Samson
Derek Scott
Utpal Shuvro
Jasmer Singh
Anirban Sircar
Rob Steen
John Stern
E. W. Swanton
Pat Symes
Sa'adi Thawfeeq
Gerry Vaidyasekera
Gordon Vince
John Ward
David Warner
Tim Wellock
Francis Wheen
Steve Whiting

Photographers: Hamish Blair, Gordon Brooks, Val Corbett, Ian Dobson, Ben Duffy, Duif du Toit, Patrick Eagar, Mike Finn-Kelcey, Laurence Griffiths, Huw John, Kamal Kishore, Richard Lewis, Alain Lockyer, Terry Mahoney, Graham Morris, Mueen ud din Hameed, Pete Norton, Roger Ockenden, David Pillinger, Mike Pollard, Craig Prentis, Tom Shaw, Bill Smith and John Woodcock.

Round the World: Anthony Adams, Musaji Banah, Saleh Banah, Alum Bati, Asad Beig, E. J. Cartledge, Kevin Chant, Michel Cogne, John Cribbin, Peter D. Eckersley, Geoff Edwards, Brian Fell, Tom Finlayson, Chris Frean, Simone Gambino, Bob Gibb, Ram Hiralal, Richard Illingworth, Norman M. Langer, John McKillop, Arfat Malik, Phil Marsdale, Basil Mathura, Pierre Naudi, Patrick Opara, David Parsons, Stanley Perlman, Laurie Pieters, Venu Ramadass, Bryan Rouse, Naoaki Saida, Fraser M. Simm, Mark Stafford, Derek Thursby, Mike Tsesmelis, Benedikt Waage, Colin Wolfe and Clive Woodbridge.

Thanks are accorded to the following for checking the scorecards of county and tourist matches: Keith Booth, John Brown, Len Chandler, Byron Denning, Jack Foley, Keith Gerrish, Sam Hale, Neil Harris, Brian Hunt, Vic Isaacs, David Kendix, Tony Kingston, David Norris, John Potter, Gerry Stickley, Gordon Stringfellow, David Wainwright, Alan West, Roy Wilkinson and Graham York.

The editor also acknowledges with gratitude assistance from the following: David Rayvern Allen, Neville Birch, Martin Braybrook, Carl Bridge, Gerry Byrne, Lynda Cole, Marion Collin, Brian Croudy, Prakash Dahatonde, Frank Duckworth, Robert Eastaway, M. L. Fernando, Ric Finlay, Christine Forrest, Bill Frindall, Ghulam Mustafa Khan, Ray Goble, Kate Hanson, Col. Malcolm Havergal, Keith Hayhurst, Brian Heald, Murray Hedgcock, Kay Hewat, Andrew Hignell, Robin Isherwood, Mohammad Ali Jafri, Emma John, Alan Jones, Rajesh Kumar, Stephanie Lawrence, Tessa Lecomber, Nirav Malavi, Mahendra Mapagunaratne, Ray Markham, William Martin, Jack Miller, Pamela Monkhouse, Diana Morris, Charles Oliver, Em Parkinson, John Plummer, S. Pervez Qaiser, John Ramsden, Huw Richards, Major R. W. K. Ross-Hurst, Chris Scott, Damian Sharp, Karen Spink, Bruce Talbot, Ivo Tennant, Charlie Wat, Wendy Wimbush, Danny Window and Peter Wynne-Thomas.

The production of *Wisden* would not be possible without the support and co-operation of many other cricket officials, writers and lovers of the game. To them all, many thanks.

CONTENTS

Part One: Comment

Part Two: The Players

Part Three: Records

Part Four: English Cricket in 2001

Part Five: Overseas Cricket in 2000-01 and 2001

Part Six: Administration and Laws

Part Seven: Miscellaneous

PART ONE: COMMENT

NOTES BY THE EDITOR

Some years have passed since the baby and its bathwater appeared in these Notes. Contrary to the warning of the saw-sayers, the time may have come to throw them both out. It is not only that the water is cold; the baby is old and should have been lifted out long ago.

Which is a long-winded way of saying that the time is approaching to reform the first-class county structure, as opposed to merely meddling with the cricket and the fixture list. Not that a little meddling would go amiss: the passing of the Benson and Hedges Cup this summer provides just the opportunity for fewer games, less travelling and more preparation. But I would like these Notes to open a wider-ranging, longer-term debate, aimed at revivifying professional cricket. And however loath I am to say it, I believe the county system runs counter to a positive future for English cricket at the highest level.

What we have at the moment is a Victorian institution that resisted reform in the 20th century and struggled into the 21st on subsidies rather than public support. It isn't that the counties haven't changed. A number have become like businesses rather than members' clubs, which is not to say they have become more businesslike. To be commercially viable, they have to satisfy their dual market needs. Because professional sport is essentially in the entertainment game, they should be able to attract and entertain an audience; and, such is the framework of English cricket, they must provide the right players for the national teams that generate much of the ECB's income. This is a well-rehearsed argument; it hardly requires repeating any more than the fact that many counties no longer seem capable of fulfilling these conditions. The system survives on a confederacy of mediocrity.

It is easy to understand, to sympathise even, with resistance to radical reform. There are livelihoods and grand traditions at stake. But if 18 counties cannot pay their way without subsidy, and if they fail the needs of the national team, do we need so many? What happens if the subsidy dries up? If nothing else, it might be prudent for county cricket to reform its structure before circumstances force it to change.

Some 60 per cent of the ECB's revenue comes from television. Government and lottery funding are essential for many projects, in particular the much vaunted National Cricket Academy. Cricket, compared with other sports, does well out of the lottery. This suggests that it still has a place in national life, but that place depends on the profile of the national team. Unlike football clubs, the counties have little national reference; rather, for much of the population and the media, county cricket drifts along in a backwater. Without the annual injection of more than a million pounds each, most counties would be further up the creek without a paddle.

Changes have been introduced in attempts to improve standards: among them, four-day matches, two divisions, pitch penalties and smaller-seamed balls. But they have not brought spectators to first-class cricket and they have not provided the core of players able to step up to international level. Some argue that the gap between county and Test cricket is so wide that another tier, regional cricket, is needed. It seems unlikely to happen, but its very presence in the debate is further confirmation that the county structure is failing England. An England squad system, giving players more time to practise and work together as a team, would be more worth while than a regional tier. The success England have enjoyed abroad these past few winters is a strong argument in favour of developing the squad system at home.

In fairness to the counties, there are simply not enough good young English players coming into professional cricket to sustain an environment that produces Test cricketers. The Australian board are able to put 25 cricketers under contract; the ECB manage just a dozen. That can't only be a matter of economics; England would be hard pushed to name 25 ready for international cricket. Take out the centrally contracted bowlers – six last year, three from Yorkshire – and the standard of county bowling is deplorably low. Batsmen hit 118 more centuries in 2001 than in the previous year and twice the number of double-hundreds. The other counties can only envy Yorkshire's bowling depth; England are merely covetous.

The counties themselves acknowledge the paucity of home-grown talent by increasing the intake of overseas players with British passports or flying the European Union's flag of convenience. There were ten in 2001; the Professional Cricketers' Association estimate a 150 per cent increase in 2002. Many come from South Africa, where political decrees on team selection and the country's changing economic circumstances hamper the career prospects of young white cricketers. They won't be able to play for England without meeting the ECB's qualification requirements, but they will have their salaries subsidised by income generated by Team England.

All aboard the academy express

In the meantime, seven counties are receiving £50,000 each towards accredited local academies that will identify players aged between 13 and 18, and help them become first-class cricketers. The need for these academies is a sorry commentary on the way sport, especially cricket, has been downgraded in schools by greater emphasis on exams, the selling-off of sports grounds and the paperwork that absorbs teachers' time, energy and desire. The problem is not new but it has taken cricket time to address it.

It was not so long ago that Lord MacLaurin, chairman of the ECB, was calling the counties themselves English cricket's 18 academies. This was back when the media wanted a national academy along Australian lines; last year their demand was met. It had become so apparent that the so-called "academies" were not producing the right calibre of cricketer to mix it with the best that the board bowed to the inevitable and hired an Australian to do the job properly. Admittedly, they didn't have any premises at the time; happily Rod Marsh, the man they appointed, knew just the place and so England's National Cricket Academy began life at the Australian Academy in Adelaide, where Marsh had previously been director. New Labour are trying something similar with the National Health Service, sending patients abroad for treatment.

Living on borrowed time

In the same way that the board chairman called the counties "academies", his chief executive Tim Lamb took to calling them "centres of excellence", which did nothing for the counties but made him sound like one of those well-spun politicians whose peculiar notion of excellence is applied in defence of failing institutions. Last year he took to describing the counties as "businesses". But, as the farming industry is currently debating, what happens to the business if the subsidy diminishes or disappears?

Given that the ECB's television agreement expires in 2005, this is not idle speculation. Channel 4's viewing figures for cricket have dropped each year since they began to televise the game in 1999. They put a brave face on this, comparing reductions in audiences for other sports. But however the numbers are interpreted, they mean fewer people have been watching cricket on television, and falling figures are anathema to any broadcaster dependent on advertising income. Cricket may not be living on borrowed time; some counties clearly are. I suspect there is already a tendency to let the weakest go to the wall. Natural wastage, businessmen call it.

Cities, not counties

Maybe that's the answer; it is pragmatic, and lately English cricket has been learning to live with pragmatism. But it would add interest to the debate to hear something more radical being discussed; something that would take into account England in the 21st century rather than the 19th. It has become an urban society, built on cities and conurbations. Why not a professional circuit based on these, rather than on shires and counties, however romantically their names resonate? The grounds are already firmly established in cities.

It is a given that cricket does not exist on membership and gate money. Total membership for the 18 counties in 2001 was 128,234, with Yorkshire attracting 15,331 and Derbyshire 1,877 (including 16 dogs), a fair reflection of their Championship positions if ever there was. But one in every 330 adults in England and Wales belonging to a county cricket club is not a fair reflection of the national interest in cricket. It demonstrates mostly the extent to which professional cricket has to market itself. Becoming part of a city's life by name as well as location would assist this process. The cricket club could incorporate civic identity, and benefit from the commercial and sponsorship opportunities such an association would provide. Yorkshire would doubtless claim to be an exception.

Assuming the globalisation of cricket continues apace, it will be only a matter of time before there is a television-driven demand for international inter-city tournaments. Cities are marketable commodities in a way that counties, states and provinces are not. This may seem fanciful now, but looking ahead often does. Cricket may never have the lion's share of the television sports market in England, but it has immense potential elsewhere. English cricket should not simply be aware of this potential but positioned to exploit it when the opportunity arises. Cricket has trundled along traditional lines for a long time, but the pace of change and growth is faster now than it has ever been.

Australia show the way

England's showing against Australia last summer, along with the record of Australians in county cricket, offered ample evidence of the gap that has opened between the two countries. Since England relinquished the Ashes in 1989, six more series have passed and, generally speaking, they have been overwhelmed in each one. But last summer's Australians drove home a further message. Players have to give the public cricket that is entertaining as well as motivated: maybe the two are linked more than is appreciated.

At the end of last season there was a game at Cardiff that was neither. Surrey's first innings lasted from the second day until the last afternoon, by which time they had 701 on the board and were 443 runs ahead. True, it rained, but it is a harder truth that there are days when players do not deserve the efforts of the ECB and the counties to keep them in employment. A strategic aberration at Chelmsford apart, what made Steve Waugh's Australians so exciting was the way they went about their cricket. It's a tired old refrain, but playing cricket has to be more than a job. Sadly, not all cricketers appreciate this as obviously as the former England and Lancashire opening batsman, Winston Place, who died in January 2002. Asked on the last day of his first season what he was doing for a holiday, Place replied, "This is the last day of my holiday." And when, many years later, he was told that Lancashire no longer required him, he wept.

The holiday comment brought to mind a review of Peter Carey's *30 Days in Sydney*. What emerges from this book, wrote reviewer Phillip Knightley, "is a hymn to all those characteristics that make Australians what they are: collectivism, mateship, courage, disdain for authority and love of life, a people forever on holiday". There is enough there to describe the way Australians play their cricket; enough to explain why people turned out in their thousands to see them, whether for a Test match or a game in a park against an MCC invitation eleven. They enjoyed the feeling of being on holiday as well; going to the cricket wasn't just something to do. It showed that there is still a healthy appetite for cricket in England, but it will not be satisfied if players treat the game with disdain.

To bore or not to bore

What confuses the issue is that cricket has always been more than entertainment alone. It is a game of tactics and psychological pressures, on the individual and the team. There are situations in which tactics are in opposition to entertainment; captains will argue that winning (or not losing) comes before crowd-pleasing. England's victories in Pakistan and Sri Lanka in 2000-01 were not always pretty to watch. They resulted from attritional passages of play intended to wear down their opponents' resolve. But if England's cricket was not always fun, it was intriguing and, in retrospect, intelligent. Being boring paid dividends, as Steve Waugh acknowledged in a back-handed way when he spun England's winter strength into a spring insult. Nasser Hussain rose to the bait at Edgbaston: England tried to play a game they were inexperienced at, went one down and never recovered. Back on the subcontinent last winter, England put attrition ahead of attractiveness, made few friends but made up lost ground after losing the First Test to India.

In order to frustrate the supremely gifted Sachin Tendulkar, Ashley Giles bowled his left-arm spin down a leg-side line and to a leg-side field until Tendulkar became so bored (or insulted) that he chanced his arm against the odds, failed and was stumped for the first time in 89 Tests. The Englishmen danced about in unashamed delight but the Bangalore weather gods rained on their parade. The game, almost deservedly so, was drawn. Whether England's tactics were within the letter of the Law, let alone the spirit, is debatable. Obviously the umpires chose to think so, despite the ICC's most recent playing condition that "For bowlers whom umpires consider to be bowling down the leg side as a negative tactic, the strict limited-overs wide interpretation shall be applied."

This condition, or more expressly that particular wording, took effect from September 2001; too late to bring Pakistan to book for employing similar leg-side tactics against England's batsmen at Old Trafford last June. Mind you, even if the new regulation had come in, any oversight by the umpires would have been lost in the furore over dismissals shown by television to result from no-balls.

An atmosphere of lawlessness

All in all, 2001 was not a good year for umpires. But you have to sympathise with them; these days they bear the responsibility for maintaining not just the Laws but the order. The word "anarchy" appeared in cricket headlines a few times in 2001; not something anyone should be proud of. An atmosphere of lawlessness hung over the first two Tests between Sri Lanka and England in March; by November, India and South Africa had taken the law into their own hands. In Sri Lanka, the umpires were under siege – psychologically if not physically; in South Africa it was the match referee, Mike Denness.

Denness was officiating at the Second Test between South Africa and India at Port Elizabeth when he imposed penalties on six Indian players and incurred the wrath of a nation. It would be unfair to say he brought the game to the brink of schism; others did that, among them Jagmohan Dalmiya, former president of the ICC and, since September 2001, president of the Indian board. When India took umbrage at Denness's penalties and insisted he be removed as referee for the final Test – otherwise the team would go home and take their lucrative television purse with them – the South African board buckled under the threat of lost revenue. Denness was denied access to the Third Test, at Centurion, and the ICC withdrew their imprimatur. For the time being anyway: past experience warns that one should never take any ICC ruling for granted. But as things stand, the match at Centurion does not count as an official Test.

Viewed dispassionately, it was difficult to gauge what grieved the Indians more: the fact that prime among the penalised was Tendulkar, accorded god-like status by his millions of adoring fans, or that Denness, white and British, a former England captain, was a representative of the old colonial power. Accusations of racism, because he took no action against the South Africans' appeals and sledging, muddied the waters further.

Tendulkar (we'll come to the other five) was caught up in the catch-all crime of bringing the game into disrepute, fined 75 per cent of his match fee and given a one-match suspended ban. Denness, watching on television, had caught him interfering with the ball "by himself and without the on-field umpire's supervision under Law 42.3 (a)(ii) and Law 42.3 (b)". The umpires appear not to have noticed anything untoward, and the condition of the ball had not changed sufficiently to attract their attention, or the statutory five-run penalty. In fact, Tendulkar was most likely cleaning the seam and guilty on a technicality at worst. By the time the headline writers had put their slant on it, the crime was ball-tampering and the incendiaries were burning effigies of Denness.

In another year, the matter might have ended with the unofficial Test. But Denness, as well as fining captain Sourav Ganguly, Virender Sehwag, Harbhajan Singh, Deep Dasgupta and Shiv Sunder Das for other breaches of the Code of Conduct, also handed out a one-Test suspension to Sehwag, who had earlier hit a hundred on debut at Bloemfontein. In happier circumstances, that would have been the Centurion match. Now, however, India's next Test, as far as the ICC were concerned, was against England at Mohali in December. India, who had not played Sehwag at Centurion, argued otherwise and a period of brinkmanship followed. The Indian selectors included Sehwag in their squad; the ICC's new chief executive, Malcolm Speed, warned in no uncertain manner that the council would not give the Test official status if he played; the ECB said England would not take part in an unofficial match. For a day or two there was the threat of an international split. One deadline passed but eventually, perhaps inevitably, India accepted Speed's offer to set up a "referees commission" to investigate whether Denness had acted in accordance with the Code of Conduct, the role of referees generally and whether players should have a right of appeal. Given that the ICC executive board had already agreed to strengthen the disciplinary power of referees from April 2002, the commission looked like being about as sabre-toothed as its name.

ICC call the shots

A year or two earlier, the Indians would have headed off the ICC well before the impasse. What this eyeballing emphasised was the confidence with which the new administration had grasped authority, following universal acceptance of recommendations in the Condon Report on cricket corruption. Sir Paul (later Lord) Condon's report was considered by many to be a damp squib. There were no disclosures; no sacrificial names from which to hang headlines. But it did challenge the ICC to put their house in order and, given the context of the report, the member countries had little option but to strengthen the executives' role. For that alone, Condon has influenced the way cricket moves forward. But the stand-off also reminded the cricket world that India, through her cricket-crazy population and television's immense marketing potential, has an economic clout no other country can match. Cricket's old establishment may be undecided whether Dalmiya is a smoking gun or a loose cannon, but he epitomises the progressive, post-imperial, nuclear India.

He is both poker player and politician. At the eleventh hour, he knew he couldn't trust his hand against Speed's, but he knew he held the better cards when he wagered an extra India–England one-day international against this summer's Oval Test. It may not have been a gentleman's bet; the ECB had, after all, agreed terms with the pre-Dalmiya administration. But such is the precarious nature of their finances that they could not afford to lose the income the Oval Test would generate. They agreed to the extra one-day game in India (the Indians had initially wanted two), which ironically allowed England to draw the series 3–3.

It is as great an irony that Dalmiya's business acumen, when ICC president, provided the council with the financial muscle to stand up to India. Through television rights to the World Cup and interim knockout tournaments, he showed how cricket could be enriched beyond previous imagination. He may not always have won friends, but he knew how to influence people. He knew, too, how to nurse a grudge, for he had been sorely hurt by the peremptory way the ICC had dropped their pilot once they were in secure waters. When the opportunity came to rock their boat, he was hardly likely to resist it. Dalmiya aside, old attitudes towards India will have to change.

Give them the gizmos

It is so obvious that it bears repeating: umpires are only human and, being human, can always make mistakes. This is not to say that umpiring should be hit or miss; simply that, when they do err, umpires deserve better than histrionics from the players and opprobrium from the media. Similarly, the players deserve the best umpires. They have not always had them. Back in 1987, *Wisden's* Notes advocated an independent panel of leading umpires, appointed by and responsible to the ICC, which in turn would have to show a more positive attitude in supporting them. Fifteen years later we are about to get it. In the interim, we have had that constant companion of cricket administration, compromise, along with the usual diet of fudge.

Having one ICC umpire in a Test match was a start, but it neither tackled the problem of erratic standards nor eradicated the cause of so much player dissent – the suspicion that, deep down, the home umpire was biased. Referees were a recognition of the problem without solving it. They focused on player behaviour in order to sustain the shibboleth that the umpire is always right. Television has thrown that into confusion, and an elite panel will not solve the problem unless cricketers – and this applies at every level – accept that the umpire is integral to the game, not as an authority figure but an arbiter.

So it was worrying when the chairman of the first-class umpires' association, Allan Jones, complained that their representations to the ECB over increasing incidents of dissent were falling on deaf ears. New regulations were introduced last season to stop intimidatory appealing, but umpires feel these were toothless. When they reported players to the board, there was no indication what penalty, if any, had been imposed. "Youngsters see these things taking place on the field and, when nothing is done, they think it's appropriate behaviour," Jones said. It would help if the board dealt out the penalties, but they leave this to the county that employs the offender. It's the procedure, apparently – and very convenient it is, too.

Meanwhile the debate rumbles on over television's role as an umpiring aid. Is there any reason why the talking should not be replaced by trials? For cricket and television to have a meaningful relationship, cricket has to keep up with television. Already there are virtually two games: one watched by those at the ground, the other dissected by millions getting all the gizmos. The technological wizardry does not provide all the answers, but used intelligently it could help umpires avoid errors. Maybe there can never be certitude that a ball would have gone on to hit the stumps, but the umpire could receive advice on where the ball pitched and where the pad was when it was struck. Similarly with catches: it does not matter if there is doubt. The Laws cater for that; if in doubt, not out. Television's opponents argue that it will slow the game, but there is already a hiatus after every delivery during which the umpire could phone a friend, let alone receive a word in his ear from a colleague in the techno-trailer, with immediate access to different camera angles and replays. No-balls could be scrutinised this way, and a larger penalty – four runs or even six – would concentrate bowlers' minds wonderfully.

And now for your bonus point

Give a cricketer a chance to stretch the rules and regulations and, it seems, he'll take it nine times out of ten. Last year, to help avoid predictability in one-day internationals, the ICC introduced bonus points for tournaments involving three or more teams. As an incentive for sides to maintain positive, attacking cricket throughout a game, and prevent crowds from drifting off during the longueurs, the winners now earn a point when their final run-rate is 1.25 times that of their opponents. But the 2001-02 VB triangular series in Australia threw up an unexpected ramification. Once it became obvious to New Zealand that they could not win their last qualifying game, against South Africa, their best route to the finals lay in conceding the bonus point that would guarantee South Africa's progress. Australia would then have to beat the South Africans *and* earn a bonus point to displace the New Zealanders. Victory without the bonus point would leave Australia with the same qualifying points as New Zealand, who had the better head-to-head record. Chasing 271 against South Africa, New Zealand calculated they must not reach 217 – and didn't. Nor did Australia get the bonus point in their last match and so, for only the third time in 23 seasons, they failed to contest the final series. It cost Steve Waugh the captaincy of, and his place in, their one-day side; as ramifications go, it was totally unexpected.

Avarice and averages

For something like 20 years, *Wisden* has liaised with other cricket reference books and the county scorers to ensure accurate scorecards and averages. By way of appreciation, we gave the scorers a small honorarium and a complimentary Almanack. Last season, we heard that the ECB were prohibiting the scorers from checking *Wisden's* scores. Rather than put the scorers in an intolerable position, and not wanting to compromise the accuracy of the scores we publish, we followed the course offered by the ECB. We purchased the scores from them, via the Press Association, which in turn took the scores from the county scorers. This added more than 50 per cent to our costs for English (and Welsh) scores and averages.

Despite some trepidation on our part, the provision of scores and averages worked satisfactorily: the proof, however, is in the publication. Of more concern now is the apparent intention of the ECB and PA to create their scores from a "down-the-line" commentary, rather than using the county scorers. This could lead to two sets of scores with, if I understand the Laws of Cricket correctly, the county scorers' version being the official one. I do not see how a "down-the-line" commentator falls within the requirements of Law 4.

The reason for all this, of course, is money. The ECB can't get enough of it. One sympathises with their need to protect valuable rights, so that cricket benefits from the anticipated wealth that the new technologies might create. It is thought, for example, that the sale of scores, statistics and images to mobile phone users could be worth as much as £25 million over five years. Bothering about the accuracy of *Wisden's* scores must seem small beer in comparison – but it remains essential to us.

SIR DONALD BRADMAN, AC

1908–2001

A PERSONAL RECOLLECTION

By E. W. SWANTON

Jim Swanton followed Don Bradman's progression from his first appearance at Worcester in April 1930 through his four tours of England and MCC's first post-war tour of Australia. After Bradman's retirement in 1948 they developed a friendship and maintained a correspondence that lasted until Swanton's death in January 2000. Written in 1996, this recollection was commissioned to appear in Wisden *after Sir Donald Bradman's death.*

In estimating Don Bradman's cricket and his personality, one is confronted by a dichotomy between public acclaim and private qualification. Whereas his batting in the English summer of 1930 lifted him swiftly to a pinnacle of achievement beyond compare, he was simultaneously imprisoned by fame to a degree he could not readily accept. His own country, a young nation in search of home-grown idols, found in him something of a reluctant hero.

His impact on the English scene always remained clear in the memory, for in 1930 I was in my early years as a cricket writer, and the Lord's Test that summer was the first I reported. My late-April impression at Worcester was of a dapper little man, well-sweatered against the cold, nimble of foot, amazingly quick between the wickets, tirelessly ticking up 236 runs at almost a run a minute. So his batting continued throughout the tour: prolific, almost chanceless, an ever-growing monument to concentration and fitness. By mid-July, by which time 131 in the First Test had been followed by 254 in the Second and 334 in the Third, the image of a phenomenon without parallel was clear to see. A brief glimpse of fallibility on a damp pitch at Old Trafford was followed in the Fifth Test by 232, ended by a deplorable caught-behind decision: 974 runs in the series and an average of 139.14.

The command performance that hoisted him to a status of his own was without doubt the 254 at Lord's. At half-past three of a sunny Saturday afternoon, with Australia 162 for no wicket in answer to England's 425, King George V in grey bowler hat, with walking stick and buttonhole, inspected the teams lined at the Pavilion gate. Fifth ball afterwards, Ponsford was caught at slip by Hammond off White and in came the 21-year-old from Bowral. He was not normally a spectacular starter, but now he moved swiftly out to his first ball and hit it on the full up to the Nursery seats. As White had pinned down the Australians with marvellous skill in 1928-29, this was a strategic blow as well as the opening stroke of his first 50 in 45 minutes. At close of play Don was 155 not out, scored at exactly a run a minute. On the Monday, and more sedately, he completed what he always rated his finest innings – despite what came next.

His 309 not out on the first day of the Third Test at Headingley not only beat R. E. Foster's 287 at Sydney, hitherto the highest in England–Australia

Tests, but also was 95 runs more than anyone (Foster, again) had scored in a day's Test cricket. It commenced with a hundred before lunch. By chance, I shared a cab back to the Queen's Hotel in Leeds that evening with two or three of the Australians and so had an insight into Don's relationship with the rest of the team. "Now we'll be good for a drink from the little beggar," was the comment, but no such luck. At the hotel desk there he was, asking that a pot of tea be brought to his room. I cannot claim to have known him then, but it is well established that he showed no inclination for the company off the field of his colleagues. He was teetotal, a young country boy in a touring party most of whom were not only older but came from the more sophisticated background of the city. Yet, while he did not put his hand in his pocket or in any way court popularity with them, he was alive from the first to the financial opportunities that fame was bringing. Depression was deep in Australia. His ambition was to achieve a degree of security that would enable him to marry his childhood friend, Jessie Menzies.

What turned the coolness of most of his fellow-players to indignation and worse was the decision of his employers, the Sydney sports goods firm of Mick Simmons, to transport their celebrity from Perth to Sydney by rail and air, ahead of the team who continued their homeward journey by ship. Australia had found a hero beyond all imagination, and his arrival in turn at Adelaide, Melbourne and Sydney brought scenes of utmost hysteria. Don found himself enveloped in mayoral welcomes, presentations and dinners that had been arranged to greet the team, whose feelings, as they trailed unheralded in his wake, can be easily imagined. It meant nothing to them that in every impromptu speech Don paid warm tribute to his captain, Billy Woodfull, and to the team. He has always stressed in his writings how embarrassing he found this triumphal cavalcade; apart from the embarrassment, the episode permanently damaged relationships with his contemporaries.

When I next encountered the Don, on the Australian tour of 1934, contact between the countries had been scarred by Bodyline, from which he emerged toughened mentally but with his playing reputation almost unscathed. He was the appointed vice-captain, clearly in line for the succession, but his recuperation from a critical operation for appendicitis and peritonitis after the tour kept him out of cricket for a year. Vic Richardson took the Australians to South Africa in 1935-36, and when Don was promoted to the captaincy, for the 1936-37 tour of G. O. Allen's side, he knew that several under his command would have preferred playing for the popular, outgoing Richardson.

This element, headed by Bill O'Reilly and Jack Fingleton, was still with him in the side he brought to England in 1938. The bowling in support of O'Reilly was too weak for Australia to do better than halve the rubber, but with 13 hundreds in 26 innings – one every other! – the captain could well be said to have led by example, until he broke his ankle at The Oval. What richer irony could be imagined than, after congratulating Len Hutton on surpassing his record 334, Bradman should turn his ankle over in the deep bowling-mark dug by O'Reilly? My belief is that he did not have an Australian side solidly behind him until after those two Irish-Australians retired.

Don Bradman's war is an unhappy chapter in his life, not only because he suffered a health breakdown that culminated in his being invalided out

[*Getty Images*

The Bradman touch: his footwork, judgment and execution were as much his signature in his 40th year as in his 20th. Wicket-keeper Godfrey Evans and Bill Edrich remain silent witnesses.

of the armed forces after 12 months. His transfer from the RAAF, in which he volunteered as an observer, to a physical-training job in the Army soon became the subject of criticism. The MCC party were made aware of this feeling on arriving in Australia in 1946-47. On the face of it, he had opted to exchange a non-commissioned combatant role for one carrying a commission supposedly behind the lines, although his unit was shortly due overseas. In fact, Don had privately sought the advice of Lord Gowrie, the Governor-General, who, he told me, strongly advised him to accept the Army offer. His lordship should have known his Australians better.

The Bradman who emerged after the war was a more mature citizen with a broader vision than one had known before. His handling of an almost unfledged Test side earned their friendship as well as their admiration. On a personal level, once one had gained his trust he was the most reliable and understanding of friends. He was quick to see the benefit to the game of co-operation with a responsible press when the 14 correspondents who accompanied MCC to Australia in 1946-47 formed the Cricket Writers' Club. It was thanks to his influence, as a member of the Australian Board of Control – inclined in the past to hold the press very much at arm's length – that our club's invitation to the 1948 Australians enabled us to stage their

BRADMAN'S TEST RECORD

	Score	Career Avge
1928-29 v England		
Brisbane	18	18.00
	1	9.50
Melbourne	79	32.66
	112	52.50
Adelaide	40	50.00
	58	51.33
Melbourne	123	61.57
	37*	66.85
1930 v England		
Nottingham	8	59.50
	131	67.44
Lord's	254	86.10
	1	78.36
Leeds	334	99.66
Manchester	14	93.07
The Oval	232	103.00
1930-31 v West Indies		
Adelaide	4	96.40
Sydney	25	91.93
Brisbane	223	99.64
Melbourne	152	102.55
Sydney	43	99.42
	0	94.45
1931-32 v South Africa		
Brisbane	226	100.71
Sydney	112	101.22
Melbourne	2	96.91
	167	99.83
Adelaide	299*	112.29
Melbourne	dnb	112.29

	Score	Career Avge
1932-33 v England		
Melbourne	0	107.80
	103*	111.92
Adelaide	8	107.92
	66	106.37
Brisbane	76	105.28
	24	102.48
Sydney	48	100.66
	71	99.70
1934 v England		
Nottingham	29	97.50
	25	95.30
Lord's	36	93.55
	13	91.25
Manchester	30	89.55
Leeds	304	95.35
The Oval	244	99.26
	77	98.69
1936-37 v England		
Brisbane	38	97.17
	0	94.80
Sydney	0	92.54
	82	92.30
Melbourne	13	90.50
	270	94.48
Adelaide	26	93.00
	212	95.53
Melbourne	169	97.06
1938 v England		
Nottingham	51	96.12
	144*	99.06

	Score	Career Avge
Lord's	18	97.44
	102*	99.48
Leeds	103	99.54
	16	97.94
The Oval	dnb	97.94
1946-47 v England		
Brisbane	187	99.62
Sydney	234	102.11
Melbourne	79	101.69
	49	100.75
Adelaide	0	98.98
	56*	99.96
Sydney	12	98.44
	63	97.84
1947-48 v India		
Brisbane	185	99.30
Sydney	13	97.88
Melbourne	132	98.43
	127*	100.48
Adelaide	201	102.07
Melbourne	57*	102.98
1948 v England		
Nottingham	138	103.53
	0	101.93
Lord's	38	100.96
	89	100.79
Manchester	7	99.41
	30*	99.85
Leeds	33	98.88
	173*	101.39
The Oval	0	99.94

Research: Christopher Lane

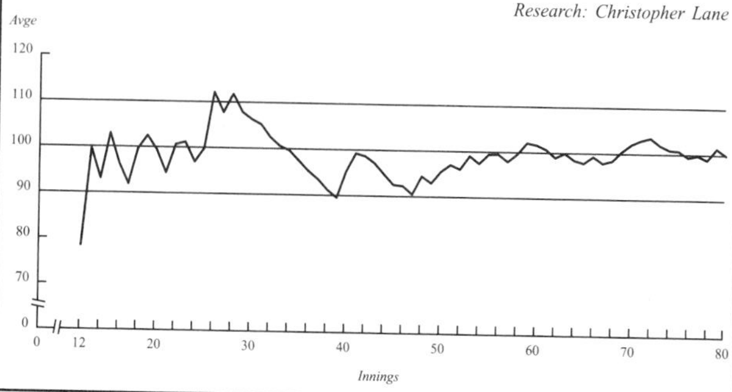

first dinner engagement of the tour; incidentally, it was about the first post-war cricket dinner possible under food rationing. In the presence of the recently married Prince Philip, whose first cricket occasion this certainly was, Don Bradman made a speech rich in sentiment and humour, expressive of shared perils and the renewed fellowship of cricket. It was the speech of a statesman which the nation heard in full because the BBC held back the nine o'clock news.

The only shadow of that summer was that English cricket was not strong enough to extend the powerful side Don had welded together. If he, who celebrated his 40th birthday on August 27 by making 150 at Lord's against the Gentlemen, was a shade less dominant with the bat than heretofore, it was because he did not need to be. When at The Oval, needing just four runs to average 100 in Test cricket, he was bowled by Eric Hollies for a duck, there were two Australians in the press box who nearly died laughing. They were, of course, O'Reilly and Fingleton.

After his retirement, Don retained a perpetual personal involvement in the game, as administrator, selector, author and journalist. He had two spells as chairman of the Australian Cricket Board – the only Test cricketer ever so honoured – and served it almost continuously for 30 years. There is no book of its kind to beat his *The Art of Cricket*, and his commentaries on the England–Australia series of 1953 and 1956 for the *Daily Mail* were models of their kind. His only other visits to England were to the historic ICC meeting of 1960 on the throwing crisis, and for a charity dinner for the benefit of the Lord's Taverners Fund in 1974.

Don's influence behind the scenes in the matter of suspect actions was never made public. Convinced by filmed evidence of its seriousness – "the most complex problem I have known in cricket because it was not a matter of fact but of opinion" – he went along with the dubious decision that, for the visit of Australia to England in 1961, there should be a moratorium for the first few weeks on throwing. But he returned to Australia with a personal solution in mind. He obtained from the state captains a confidential list of suspects and was able to see to it that none of them was selected. *Finis*. As to the Lord's Taverners dinner, he was assured that his presence would produce a £10,000 windfall. It did: there were 900 present, he spoke brilliantly, and he had spent the previous day signing every individual menu. The Don never gave less than 100 per cent.

Nor, as the years went by, did he decline help to any organisation or individual who solicited it. Forewords flowed from his pen, and every personal letter was answered by return post in his own hand. The healthy evolution of cricket depends on old players giving their services to the game in any of the ways open to them. Sir Donald left the field at the peak of his fame: yet in a sense he never retired, for his experience, his intellect and his time were always at cricket's disposal.

BRADMAN AND THE BRITISH

By RICHARD HOLT

Batting statistics, as readers of *Wisden* know only too well, put Sir Donald Bradman in a league of his own. Yet his records, his scoring speed, even his double and triple Test hundreds do not alone explain his special relationship with the British public. Runs were a necessary but not a sufficient condition of Bradman's heroic status in Britain. His batting explains the awe and admiration in which he was held. But it does not explain the remarkable affection of the British public for a man who, as the *Daily Mail* observed in 1930, "was a menace to English cricket".

His four tours of England between 1930 and 1948 gave the public enough time to get to know him – and for many to see him – but not enough to tire of him or take him for granted. In 1948 he was said to be the best-known public figure after King George VI and Churchill. Presenting him with a replica of the Warwick Vase, donated by public subscription to its "Bradman Fund", *The People* claimed Bradman had been "honoured in a way that no other overseas sportsman has enjoyed". This adulation spread beyond the heartlands of English cricket, spanning social classes and generations, cutting across the regions and nations of Great Britain. He played his last competitive matches in Scotland and was asked for his autograph 25 times on a short walk in Aberdeen.

Why did the British public come to *like* Bradman so much? Being an Australian of English descent was, of course, an advantage. Bradman's career, however, also happened to coincide with the inter-war boom in radio broadcasting and the rise of the cinema newsreel. The press, especially mass circulation "Sundays" such as *The People* and the *News of the World*, whose joint circulation reached 30 million by the time Bradman retired, gave extensive coverage to Test cricket, especially the Australian tours. His first autobiography, *My Cricketing Life*, was serialised in the *News of the World* in 1938. Never had so much been known by so many about so few, as Churchill might have said when he bumped into Bradman at Victoria station in 1934 and had the *Daily Mail* photograph the two of them shaking hands.

For all its subsequent warmth, the British relationship with Bradman got off to a cool start. His assault on England and the English counties in 1930 left the public awe-struck and a little resentful. This was not just a matter of his treatment of the local bowlers. His natural reticence and puritan instincts irritated his own team and the English public after his record Test innings of 334. Twenty years later, he was still wondering if he was expected to parade through the streets of Leeds. The press had mistaken his youthful shyness for petulance. It took time for him to realise that he needed, and lacked, the common touch.

When Bradman next appeared in England in 1934, it was in the wake of the Bodyline tour of Australia in 1932-33. By then, the English public – and MCC – were having second thoughts about the tactics of physical intimidation employed by Jardine to stop Bradman. England had not emerged well out of their bowling war. Shared values of sportsmanship were more important

[*Getty Images*

A lone figure in a Headingley throng brimming with warmth and congratulations, Don Bradman makes his way back to the pavilion after his 334 in 1930. Four years later, he treated the Leeds crowd to another triple-hundred.

than winning at all costs; there was an unspoken guilt of which Bradman was the chief beneficiary. He had, moreover, stood up well to the battering – he still had the highest average for the series – and emerged from it with some dignity. J. M. Kilburn caught the new public enthusiasm for Bradman, which was especially strong in Yorkshire: "The crowd raced to the pavilion and made a lane halfway to the wicket." As he went in, "there was a silence of suspense; a murmur of 'He's here,' swelling to a roar of welcome". He went on to score 304.

That summer of 1934 was the turning-point in Bradman's relationship with the British. Fair play was part of the national self-image, and it would have been perverse and petty to deny Bradman his laurels. Then fate intervened. At the end of the series, he was suddenly rushed into hospital with peritonitis. For a day or two his life was in danger. The public suddenly saw this remarkable run-making machine in a new light as a young man with a new bride, whose dash from Sydney to Perth to get the first boat caught the popular imagination. The *Daily Mail*, one of Britain's biggest-selling newspapers, kept up the bulletins from his bedside, reporting the Don wisecracking with the nurses: "What's the score? Is it over 100?" To general relief, he not only recovered quickly, but had also shown the first signs of a sense of humour. He spent a pleasant time in England convalescing with his wife. "Don and Jessie", as they were now affectionately known, fell in love with the English countryside. "Nothing in the world ever appealed to me more than England as nature made her," he wrote later of that time; and nothing could have pleased Stanley Baldwin and the majority of Englishmen more.

Bradman began to apply the same meticulous thoroughness to answering the thousands of letters he received that he took to his batting. He was captain for the next tour of England in 1938, and this gave him a new and much wider public platform. Cricket captains were expected to be sporting ambassadors, attending endless public functions and making polite speeches. Bradman, the plain country boy turned stockbroker, had to learn the etiquette of representing his country in the "mother country". In fact, Bradman mastered the art of being a gentleman so well that some of his Australian team-mates never forgave him. His new gentility, however, went down very well in Britain.

History, too, was running his way. Anglo-Australian relations had sunk to a low ebb in the early 1930s, but by 1938 both countries were anxious to reinforce the imperial bond in the face of mounting international tension. Britain feared Germany; Australia feared Germany's new ally, Japan. Bradman was a firm believer in the British Empire; he was a Protestant, a Freemason, an imperialist and a conservative who strongly opposed what he saw as the anti-British tendency of Irish Catholics in Australian cricket. Indeed, Bradman's bitter dispute with Bill O'Reilly, Jack Fingleton and others did him no harm in England. Britain saw the best side of Bradman. His integrity, his respect for the monarchy, his generosity when Hutton broke his record in the final Test at The Oval in 1938 were music to the British ear. As a captain, he endorsed the values of sportsmanship – "the very essence of this great game" as he later wrote in *The Art of Cricket* – which had a profound resonance with a broad swathe of the British public.

World War II strengthened a bond that was already strong. Hence when Bradman arrived for his final series in 1948, Britain rolled out the red carpet. R. C. Robertson-Glasgow set the tone. "We want him to do well," he chirped, "we feel we have a share in him." And he did do well. The Australians were unbeaten. Bradman's was a triumphal progress to Balmoral, "cherishing the friendly, homely manner" of the royal family. Getting a duck in his final innings against England and missing his century Test average by a decimal point oddly enhanced his status. When he received his knighthood, he was suitably modest, claiming he saw it as "the medium through which England's appreciation of what Australian cricket had meant to the British Empire" could be expressed.

The knighthood also holds the key to another aspect of his appeal. Like the bulk of the British, he believed in both meritocracy *and* deference. He respected hierarchy so long as talent was properly recognised. Like Hobbs and Sutcliffe, Woolley and Compton, Bradman's own life reflected a wider pattern of upward mobility. "I could not help thinking that this knighthood was a sporting example to the world of true democracy," he wrote in *A Farewell to Cricket*, adding that "the same opportunity exists for every Australian boy". To the middle classes, Donald Bradman, batsman and stockbroker, stood for suburban virtue rewarded. To the working man, his blend of virtuosity and grit struck a chord, especially in the North, where his professionalism was more appreciated than in the South. Physically he

[*Getty Images*

No question who the hero is for these London schoolboys as Jack Fingleton and Don Bradman step out along The Strand in 1938.

was slight, with the deceptive frailty of that other great sporting hero of the time, Stanley Matthews. Bradman was treated like an honorary Northerner and was "greeted like an emperor by the crowd" at Headingley in 1948. On retirement he was made an honorary member of both Lancashire and Yorkshire.

"If statistics were the last word in cricket it would be easy to prove that Donald George Bradman was the greatest cricketer who ever lived," *The Times* wrote in a farewell leader, adding tartly, "happily they are not." And there were still a few reservations around the Long Room at Lord's about "the little robot under the green peaked cap". Where was the fun, the bravura or the classicism in Bradman? Yet even his few critics had to admit that "no one has contributed more to the game". *The Times* closed on an elegiac note, imagining a future "Australian batsman… piling up a century" – a Steve Waugh perhaps – while "old stagers who watch him will be able, however finely he plays, to murmur: 'Ah, but you should have seen Bradman.'"

Richard Holt is research professor at the International Centre for Sports History and Culture at De Montfort University, Leicester, and author of Sport and the British.

BEYOND THE LEGEND

By GIDEON HAIGH

The story of Sir Donald Bradman always involved more than cricket – more even than sport. One can only marvel at the statistics, and the one batting average that nobody need ever look up. Yet, in its degree and duration, especially in Australia, Bradman's renown is as much a source of wonder: he was, as Pope wrote of Cromwell, "damned to everlasting fame".

Few figures, sporting or otherwise, have remained an object of reverence for more than half a century after the deeds that formed the basis of their reputation. Fewer still can have justified an autobiography at the age of 21, and the last of many biographies at the age of 87, without surfeiting or even satisfying public curiosity. But with Bradman's death on February 25, 2001 comes a question: what difference will it make to his legend now that, for the first time, it has obtained a life independent of his corporeal existence?

On the face of it, the answer appears to be: not much. In Australia, the Bradman story detached from the Bradman reality some time ago, taking on the qualities of myth: as defined by Georges Sorel, a faith independent of fact or fiction, where the normal processes of attestation and falsification are suspended by unconscious agreement. In the 1990s, in particular, a sort of cultural elision turned Bradman from great batsman to great man: by Prime Minister John Howard's lights, "the greatest living Australian", elevated not merely by his feats but by "the quality of the man himself". Inspired by Bradman, Howard claimed, Australians could make "any dream come true", and "not just in cricket but in life".

This was a new experience for Australians. Poet and critic Max Harris once declared that "the Australian world is peopled by good blokes and bastards, but not heroes". Yet, by the end of his life, Bradman was not merely a "hero"; he had also been, in effect, retrofitted as a "good bloke" – that peculiarly Australian formulation implying, essentially, someone like everybody else. The actuality is, of course, that Bradman was an individual to whom few beyond his immediate family circle were close, whose private life was sedulously guarded, and whose innermost convictions went mostly unaired; his "good blokeness" is, accordingly, more or less unascertainable. But, as Sorel observed: "People who are living in this world of myths are secure from all refutation."

Why this happened can only be conjectured. Perhaps it was the self-image as a sports-loving nation to which Australians cling with such tenacity. Perhaps it was part of the recrudescence of Australian conservatism (it's hard to imagine Howard's republican predecessor, Paul Keating, singling Bradman out as the "greatest living Australian"; indeed, perhaps that partly accounts for his electoral failure). It may be as simple as Bradman keeping his head while all about him were losing theirs. He avoided the public eye, courted no controversies and scorned fame's usual accoutrements. It would be an exaggeration to describe him as an outstanding citizen, at least as this is commonly understood: he was not a conspicuous philanthropist or supporter of causes, and the duty to which he devoted himself most diligently was

[*Courtesy of the Bradman Museum*

Shrine and archive: the Bradman Museum at Bowral ensures that the legend lives on.

simply being Donald Bradman, tirelessly tending his mountainous correspondence and signing perhaps more autographs than anyone in history. But there is no doubt that, standing aloof from modern celebrity culture, he retained a dignity and stature that most public figures sacrifice.

This being the case, it may be that the "greatest living Australian" segues smoothly into becoming the greatest dead one: Bradman certainly won't be doing anything controversial now. But there are reasons against this progression: countries move on, palates jade, reputations are reassessed. There is already something anomalous about Bradman's standing in Australia. National heredity and heritage during his playing career were almost exclusively British; as Dr Greg Manning has noted, Australia's cultural homogeneity in the 1930s and 1940s was a precondition of the Bradman phenomenon. But since the late 1980s, British and old Australian components have accounted for less than half Australia's population. Even the idea of a monolithic Australian mourning of Bradman's death was mostly a media assumption. *The Chaser*, a satirical newspaper, expressed this drolly with a story headlined: "Woman unmoved by Bradman's death". This fantasised about a 42-year-old woman who "surprised reporters when she was unable to recite Bradman's famous batting average or other miscellaneous statistics", who "denied suggestions the cricketer had been an inspiring influence on her life, and said she had no regrets whatsoever that she never saw him play".

A significant role in the ongoing Bradman story will be played by the Bradman Museum at the cricketer's boyhood home of Bowral in the New South Wales southern highlands. So far, the museum is a success story, as unique as its eponymous inspiration: a collecting institution for cricket that is largely self-funding, thanks partly to royalties from the Bradman name, worth between a quarter and half a million Australian dollars annually. And for this, Bradman himself can take a deal of credit. It was he, says the museum's thoughtful curator, Richard Mulvaney, who "recognised that the museum would always have problems getting enough money to do the things it wanted to do", and ten years ago vouchsafed the commercial rights to his name and image. "We wouldn't have dared ask," says Mulvaney.

The museum's future financial security was consolidated in August 2000 by an unforeseen consequence of the South Australian government's decision to rename an Adelaide thoroughfare in honour of its favourite adopted son. When several businesses in the new Sir Donald Bradman Drive proposed exploiting their location in advertising, the Bradman family sought government intervention.

A sex shop provided, as it were, the most convincing argument for prophylaxis. "When the sex shop registered as Erotica on Bradman," Mulvaney recalls, "we couldn't have had a better example of the ways the name could be misused." The subsequent amendment to Australia's Corporations Law – preventing businesses from registering names that suggested a connection with Bradman where it did not exist – invested the Don with a commercial status previously the preserve of members of the royal family. But there was some sense to it, and the amendment has already proved its worth in the relative scarcity of necrodreck in Australia after Bradman's death. In the longer term, too, it should secure for cricket the financial fruits of the Don's legacy, for which the game can be grateful.

Enhanced power over the Bradman franchise sets the museum challenges. Its charter is to be "a museum of Australian cricket commemorating Sir Donald Bradman". The legislation, explicit acknowledgment that Bradman's name is a commodity with commercial value, subtly firms the emphasis on the latter role – something the museum recently recognised by signing an agency agreement for the exploitation of the name with Elite Sports Properties, a six-year-old sports management group now owned by London-based Sportsworld Media plc.

To be fair, Mulvaney perceives the dilemma. He is adamant that the museum will not, in his watch, become a one-man hall of fame: "While it's in my interest to continue putting Bradman's name forward, we shouldn't take his name out of context. We have to be careful that we don't allow excesses where the name takes on a completely different meaning." The responsibilities inherent in ESP's role also weigh heavily on their Andrew Stevens. "We feel very honoured to be representing the greatest Australian icon who ever lived," he says. "And protecting it, which is quite daunting. It's very precious. In fact, if someone strikes out at it, or is reckless with it, you tend to feel quite aggrieved."

To how much protection, though, is Bradman entitled? And what constitutes "recklessness" where the name is concerned? These questions were raised in

2001 in an episode involving two letters, from Bradman to Greg Chappell, dating from the World Series Cricket schism in 1977. After defecting to Kerry Packer's enterprise, Chappell found himself *persona non grata* in his adopted state of Queensland, and confided to a *Brisbane Telegraph* journalist some disparagements of the quality of local cricket administrators that Bradman had made to him some years earlier. When these were published, however, Chappell received a letter of rebuke for what Bradman viewed as a breach of trust. An exchange of correspondence followed in which Bradman enlarged on certain personal philosophies, as well as lamenting the frequent press misrepresentation to which he had been subject.

These were important artefacts. They evoked both the passion of the moment – for this was a time when tempers in cricket were frayed on all sides – and the personality of the writer. In some respects, it is from such flashes of candour that biographies are built; thus Plutarch's famous remark in his life of Alexander the Great that "very often an action of small note, a short saying, or jest, will distinguish a person's real character more than the greatest sieges or the most important battles". But when the letters were auctioned by Christie's in July 2001, Chappell was roundly censured for another breach of trust, that of Bradman's privacy. An anonymous consortium of businessmen styling themselves SAVE – Some Australians Value Ethics – intervened to purchase the letters, plus three others, for $A25,870. They were presented to Mulvaney at the MCG on what would have been the Don's 93rd birthday.

Even ignoring the question of whether it is possible to breach the privacy of the dead, it was a curious interlude. It went unremarked, for example, that the letters had previously been quoted from, without protest, in Adrian McGregor's excellent 1985 Chappell biography. At best, SAVE's intercession was a well-meaning attempt to avoid media sensationalising, which perversely made the letters' contents seem more sensational than they were; at worst, it evinced a disconcerting cultural timidity in Australia, a squeamishness about anything other than the "approved" version of the Bradman story. In an interview with *Sporting Collector*, Mulvaney was quoted as saying that the Museum "considered the contents not necessarily to be in the public interest" and that it had "no option but to keep them private" – which made it sound like an issue of national security.

In an interview for this article, Mulvaney said that the magazine had misrepresented his views: his concern was purely with copyright, which he felt Christie's had breached by reproducing the letters in its catalogue, and he insisted that the museum had no wish to inhibit study of Bradman material. However, when permission was sought to quote from the letters here, Sir Donald's son, John, withheld it; he stated, albeit politely, that this was his present policy on all such enquiries.

One can sympathise with John Bradman's position. No policy will satisfy everyone. Permission for all will invite excess and exploitation; permission for some will smack of favouritism; permission for none will be construed as censorship. Yet attempting to control what is published about Bradman in such a way will carry risks. Revisionists will move in regardless; indeed, they already are. In November 2001, *The Australian* published two articles concerning "The Don We Never Knew", the work of a foot-slogging journalist, David Nason. One revealed what appeared as vestiges of a family rift between the Don and his Bowral kin, disclosing the view of Bradman's nephew that "Don Bradman only ever cared about Don Bradman"; the second examined how the alacrity with which Bradman took over the defunct stockbroking firm of the disgraced Harry Hodgetts antagonised Adelaide's establishment.

Much the same criticisms of invasiveness were advanced as in the Chappell case. Mike Gibson, a columnist for Sydney's *Sunday Telegraph*, thought the first article "pathetic", "despicable", "bitter and twisted"; the second he dismissed as lese-majesty: "You know, I couldn't be bothered reading it. First, his family. Then, his finances. I couldn't stomach any more smears against someone who cannot answer back because he's dead."

Yet what was truly noteworthy about the articles was not that they appeared, but that nothing resembling them had appeared before, that none of Bradman's soi-disant "biographers" had treated his family and financial lives other than perfunctorily. Indeed, it may be that Bradman's most ardent apologists end up doing him the gravest disservice. Identifying a great sportsman isn't difficult: the criteria are relatively simple. Designating a great man entails rather more than a decree, even prime ministerial; some intellectual and historical contestation must be involved. Credulity invites scepticism – and, unlike trade names, reputations cannot be declared off limits by the wave of a legislative wand.

Gideon Haigh edited Wisden Cricketers' Almanack Australia *from 1999 to 2001; he is the author of the award-winning* Mystery Spinner: The Story of Jack Iverson, *and the acclaimed* The Big Ship: Warwick Armstrong and the Making of Modern Cricket *(see Cricket Books).*

TO BE DISLIKED AGAIN

REFLECTIONS ON YORKSHIRE CRICKET

By ROY HATTERSLEY

On a warm afternoon in the late summer of 1946, my father – normally the most reticent of men – danced a little jig on the promenade in Morecambe. He had, as was his invariable summer habit, bought an evening paper to find out the cricket scores. To his delight he discovered that Yorkshire, already the county champions, had lost to Hampshire. He addressed my mother and me in a voice of triumph. "At least they haven't gone all season without being beaten." It was then that I realised that the Yorkshire County Cricket Club attracted the animosity that goes with near invincibility. With any luck, we will soon begin to attract it again.

The complaint, in those days of constant Championships, was that the three Ridings were so big that the county club had a bottomless pool of talent from which to choose. Now, the contract system, which regrettably grows ever more like the football transfer racket, has ended all that. But when I first watched Yorkshire, there was an abundance, in a way an excess, of potential first-class players within the Broad Acres. In 1946, a 43-year-old spin bowler called Arthur Booth took a hundred wickets and topped the national averages. Before the war he had played only the occasional game when Hedley Verity was on Test match duty. But he had soldiered on in the Yorkshire Colts without a thought of playing for another county.

For years, Yorkshire ignored cricketers of the highest quality. Bob Appleyard took 200 wickets in his first full season with the county, 1951, and, as he was a "mature" man at the time, John Arlott (commentating later on a Test in which Appleyard was playing) wondered aloud how he had spent his summers during his early twenties. Long after his retirement, I met the overnight sensation and asked him the same question. "Bowling myself silly in the Bradford League," he told me. Nobody has been able to explain why it took the Yorkshire committee so long to discover him.

League cricket – particularly the Bradford League – was half the secret of Yorkshire's success. Hundreds of tributaries flowed from the club grounds towards Headingley. The two Pudseys – one produced Sir Leonard Hutton, the other Raymond Illingworth – are the most famous examples of that secret strength. But there were dozens of other clubs that thought it their duty to prepare players for the county. In Sheffield, border country in the far south, we always suspected the northern leagues were as far as the county committee ever looked. The prejudice, if it ever existed, has clearly passed – though the young Darren Gough and Michael Vaughan were far too good to be ignored whatever part of the county they came from. What a pity that, now there are South Yorkshire players in the county team, the county team never plays in South Yorkshire.

Perhaps the idea that South Yorkshire got a raw deal was always a myth. But we certainly believed it. In the week that I was born, my father, a temporary Labour Exchange clerk after years of unemployment, was sent to

Yorkshire's 1946 Championship-winning team. *Back:* B. Heyhirst (*masseur*), Ellis Robinson, Len Hutton, Alec Coxon, Frank Smailes, Willie Watson, Harold Beaumont, Arthur Booth, H. Walker (*scorer*). *Front:* Wilf Barber, Bill Bowes, Brian Sellers, Paul Gibb, Maurice Leyland.

work in Wath upon Dearne. Eating his midday sandwiches in the deserted cricket ground, he fell into conversation with the groundsman and naturally told him about the baby boy at home. "He'll never play for Yorkshire," the groundsman said. Thinking the dismissal of my cricketing ability a little premature, my father asked why he was so certain. The reply allowed no contradiction. "Comes from South Yorkshire." The pessimist's name was Turner, and his boy, Cyril, was finding it hard to break into the team. He became a regular member of the side that won the Championship four times before the war and once immediately afterwards.

Sixteen years on, when I was batting in the nets behind Spion Kop at Bramall Lane, the anti-Leeds feeling still persisted. There were rumours that a great fast bowler, a colliery electrician by profession, was about to emerge from Maltby and there were dark suspicions that "the committee" would not do him justice. But nothing could hold Fred Trueman back. To the day of his death, my father (a Nottinghamshire man) argued that Harold Larwood was both more accurate and more aggressive. Filial piety requires me to conclude that Larwood and Trueman were the two greatest English fast bowlers of all time. Neither of them should be anything other than flattered by the comparison.

In the years that followed the war, we Yorkshire members grew used to success. Indeed, in the 1950s, when the team began to fail, we felt that the natural order of things had been disrupted. In 1958, when we came 11th in the Championship, Johnny Wardle, an ingenious spin bowler, prehensile close fielder and irresponsibly entertaining batsman, was sacked for defending himself from committee criticism in a newspaper. I attended the annual meeting with the intention of causing trouble about his treatment. The chairman welcomed members to the "AGM of the champion county" and added, "We know which the champion county is, whichever team happens to be at the top of the table at the end of any one year." After that, no criticism was possible.

After the 1950s the county recovered but continued in its profligate ways. Ray Illingworth left for Leicestershire – and became a highly successful England captain – following an argument about his contract. The accusation was that he was disloyal because he did not regard a year with Yorkshire as better than three with any other county. Brian Close, who led the last Championship-winning team, moved on to Somerset. Bill Athey went to Gloucestershire, and dozens of other players, less talented but highly able, drifted away. For a time it seemed that nothing could go right for Yorkshire. After the pride of a century was forgotten and an overseas player recruited, two of the world's greatest batsmen wore the white rose for a single season. Neither Sachin Tendulkar nor Richie Richardson was a success. Yorkshire remained in the wilderness.

Perhaps, even in the early 1990s, Yorkshire were still suffering from the repercussions of "the Boycott affair". Whatever the merits of the argument – Boycott versus the committee – the damage that the conflict did to the county was immense. In 1978, members were asked to vote on what some thought were rival propositions: endorse sacking Boycott as captain or ask the committee to resign. I voted "yes" to both, hoping that a clearout would put the damaging disputes behind us. It dragged on for year after year, making life impossible for some of the best Yorkshire cricketers of the age, John Hampshire, captain in impossible circumstances, amongst them.

It was all desperately different from 1938 when, as well as winning the Championship, Yorkshire provided five players for the final Test at The Oval. More than half of England's highest-ever total of 903 for seven was made by Len Hutton, with his record-beating 364, and Maurice Leyland, whose century he overshadowed. Hutton, the greatest English batsman of his time, remains the example of what Yorkshire cricketers should be. Genius is not enough. Determination and dedication are equally essential. When I read of Yorkshire fast bowlers who worry about the strains of playing two Championship matches in a week, I wonder if they recall that Hutton lost two inches of bone from his arm in a wartime accident, came back to first-class cricket and almost immediately faced Ray Lindwall and Keith Miller.

Not all the Yorkshire fast bowlers whine about being over-worked. Much to his credit, Matthew Hoggard, asked if he had fears about touring India, replied that he wanted to play for England and therefore had never considered refusing to go. Suddenly – partly owing to their academy and the new coaching regime – Yorkshire have a surfeit of fast bowlers and enough batting strength to make a second successive Championship a strong prospect. I still regret that Darren Lehmann, the star batsman of 2001's success, is Australian, and I wish that Michael Vaughan had been born in Yorkshire as well as being a clear candidate to succeed Nasser Hussain as England's captain. But the clock cannot be turned back – except in one particular. There is a real hope that Yorkshire will become so successful that we are really disliked again.

Lord Hattersley was deputy leader of the Labour Party from 1983 to 1992. His many books include A Yorkshire Boyhood.

UNTOUCHED BY FORTUNE

By PETER ROEBUCK

Throughout the 1990s Michael Atherton was the face of English cricket. Head still, eyes wary, left elbow high and feet moving neatly into position, he dedicated himself to the tasks of scoring runs, resisting bowlers and protecting his team's position. For beneath his pale, youthful and sometimes defiantly stubbled exterior could be found a wilful man blessed with skill and determination. What was wanting were the particular abilities needed by the hour; he lacked the sparkle and drive required to rouse a team from its slumbers, and if ever a team needed rousing during his years as Test cricketer and captain, it was England. But it was not his way to intone "Awake, arise, or be for ever fallen!" He was more inclined to say, in his suburban way, "Come on, lads, let's get stuck in."

In every respect Atherton remained untouched by the vicissitudes of fortune and the ravages of time. Stoicism was his most obvious quality – he played for a decade on constant medication for an inflammatory condition affecting his spine – and there was a dryness of outlook that made him as much an observer as a participant. He was tough, though, and did not flinch in the face of furious bowling or allow his spirit to wilt in adversity. Indeed he was in his element in these circumstances, as the ingredients of his Lancastrian character came together to produce a towering effort.

Just as he did not strive to appease his opponents, nor did he seek to impress the baying public, even if in time the public took him to its heart and claimed him intimately as "Athers". Not that this affected him; proud and private, he performed his duties on the field and then withdrew. Atherton enjoyed the community of the dressing-room and the fellowship of the football crowd, but otherwise he was content to be alone, reading, fishing or looking for a pair of socks in a bulging drawer.

He was a tidy cricketer, and yet also expressive, for he did not depend entirely on the regimented. There was a touch of subcontinental subtlety in a manly Anglo-Saxon game, a thinness of the arm, a hint of wrist as he stroked the ball through point off back or front foot, sending it skimming to the boundary. None the less he regarded himself as a craftsman, not an entertainer, and he did not listen to the whispers of indulgence. His northern common sense outweighed the delicacies he had learnt and occasionally studied at Cambridge.

It was Mike Atherton's fate, though not his fault, to represent his country when its fortunes were at a low ebb. England had been unable to find any cricketers of Ken Barrington or Graham Gooch's calibre, players capable of dictating terms in any arena. Atherton did his utmost, especially against the Australians, whose directness stirred him: he later made friends with Ian Chappell, the most abrasive of them all. But he could not put the matter right. He worked hard, fought hard, told the unpalatable truth, and still England did not improve; so it was that his career ended as it had begun, with heavy and unavenged defeat by the Australians. Perhaps he lacked a

[*Patrick Eagar*

Trademark Atherton.

clarity of character needed to provoke change. He was a wanderer and not a man of action.

Atherton averaged 37.69 in Test cricket and would have hoped for a little more. The top three England run-makers ahead of him – Gooch, Gower and Boycott – as well as Cowdrey, whom he passed in his farewell summer, all averaged more than 40. But, towards the end, his form fell away as his mind grew weary and his body made its complaints. It is the record of an accomplished cricketer whose contribution might be better judged from the stability he brought to the batting order during a long career that produced 7,728 runs in 115 Tests, and 16 centuries, none of them easily compiled.

It was also his fate that his generation threw up some of the great bowlers of any age. There wasn't much relief. Whereas batsmen of previous generations could hope to take advantage of humdrum attacks fielded by weaker nations, Atherton was confronted by Marshall, Ambrose and Walsh, Waqar and Wasim, Donald and Pollock, McGrath and Warne. No wonder he soon lost the carefree approach sometimes seen in his early days. In Sri Lanka in 2001, where unrelenting pace is not an option, he had particular difficulty against Chaminda Vaas as a weakness against left-arm swing bowling was released – precisely the failing that had tormented Geoff Boycott many years earlier. Both men remained classically side-on till the last moment and often seemed locked in this position as the ball darted back and thudded into their pads. Boycott was the consummate technician whose game didn't change much over the years. Atherton was more graceful and inclined to tinker, especially with the placement of his back foot, whose errant ways often brought unwanted trouble. Both were single-minded and watchful in the great tradition of opening batsmen.

Better than most thoughtful men, Atherton could withdraw into a cocoon of concentration, an asset as a batsman but not necessarily as a captain. He was intelligent rather than intellectual and made his decisions easily, at the crease anyhow. A purposeful man with strong opinions and principles, he did not allow his career to fritter away; instead, after last summer's Oval Test, he cut it short in the belief that his battles had been lost and won, and it is for the defiant innings he played in his country's colours that he will be remembered. His duels with Allan Donald and Glenn McGrath were cricket played at its highest pitch. These bowlers strove for his wicket because they knew it was resourcefully protected. Atherton did not give in, his wicket had to be taken from him. He had the heart for the fight regardless of conditions and obstacles.

Donald sometimes prevailed, whereupon he wore a surprised and delighted look. Sometimes the batsman had the better of him, most notably in his unbeaten 185 at Johannesburg in 1995-96, an innings spanning three weeks, or so it seemed, an effort of mind and body that saved a Test match. It was the innings that secured for Atherton the respect and national affection he had not sought through any artificial means.

The seeds had been sown the previous year, another South African series, when the chairman of selectors, Raymond Illingworth, fined him for not being honest with the match referee about having dirt – an "illegal" substance – in his pocket to dry his sweaty hands. The press magnified the incident

MIKE ATHERTON'S TEST CAREER

Season	*Opposition*	*T*	*I*	*NO*	*R*	*HS*	*100s*	*50s*	*SR*	*Avge*
1989	v Australia	2	4	0	73	47	0	0	34	18.25
1990	v New Zealand .	3	5	0	357	151	1	3	42	71.40
1990	v India	3	6	0	378	131	1	3	43	63.00
1990-91	in Australia	5	10	1	279	105	1	1	28	31.00
1991	v West Indies. . .	5	9	0	79	32	0	0	36	8.77
1992	v Pakistan	3	5	0	145	76	0	2	35	29.00
1992-93	in India.	1	2	0	48	37	0	0	35	24.00
1992-93	in Sri Lanka . . .	1	2	0	15	13	0	0	25	7.50
1993	v Australia	6	12	0	553	99	0	6	40	46.08
1993-94	in West Indies . .	5	9	0	510	144	2	2	40	56.66
1994	v New Zealand .	3	4	0	273	111	2	0	40	68.25
1994	v South Africa . .	3	6	0	207	99	0	2	43	34.50
1994-95	in Australia	5	10	0	407	88	0	4	35	40.70
1995	v West Indies. . .	6	12	0	488	113	1	2	40	40.66
1995-96	in South Africa .	5	8	1	390	185*	1	2	32	55.71
1996	v India	3	5	1	263	160	1	1	41	65.75
1996	v Pakistan	3	5	0	162	64	0	1	35	32.40
1996-97	in Zimbabwe . . .	2	4	0	34	16	0	0	32	8.50
1996-97	in New Zealand .	3	4	1	325	118	1	2	39	108.33
1997	v Australia	6	12	1	257	77	0	2	41	23.36
1997-98	in West Indies . .	6	11	0	199	64	0	1	31	18.09
1998	v South Africa . .	5	10	1	493	103	1	3	34	54.77
1998-99	in Australia	4	8	0	110	41	0	0	37	13.75
1999	v New Zealand .	2	4	0	133	64	0	1	32	33.25
1999-2000	in South Africa .	5	8	0	225	108	1	1	39	28.12
2000	v Zimbabwe . . .	2	3	0	225	136	1	1	41	75.00
2000	v West Indies. . .	5	9	0	311	108	1	1	33	34.55
2000-01	in Pakistan	3	6	1	341	125	1	2	34	68.20
2000-01	in Sri Lanka . . .	3	6	0	129	44	0	0	28	21.50
2001	v Pakistan	2	3	0	98	51	0	1	36	32.66
2001	v Australia	5	10	0	221	57	0	2	45	22.10
Totals		**115**	**212**	**7**	**7,728**	**185***	**16**	**46**	**37**	**37.69**

MIKE ATHERTON'S RECORD AGAINST EACH TEST OPPONENT

	T	*I*	*NO*	*R*	*HS*	*100s*	*50s*	*SR*	*Avge*
v Australia	33	66	2	1,900	105	1	15	37	29.68
v South Africa	18	32	2	1,315	185*	3	8	35	43.83
v West Indies.	27	50	0	1,587	144	4	6	37	31.74
v New Zealand.	11	17	1	1,088	151	4	6	39	68.00
v India	7	13	1	689	160	2	4	42	57.41
v Pakistan	11	19	1	746	125	1	6	35	41.44
v Sri Lanka	4	8	0	144	44	0	0	28	18.00
v Zimbabwe	4	7	0	259	136	1	1	39	37.00
Totals	**115**	**212**	**7**	**7,728**	**185***	**16**	**46**	**37**	**37.69**

* *Signifies not out.*
SR = strike-rate, given as runs per 100 balls.

Research: Philip Bailey

into a *cause célèbre*; Atherton went to ground and considered resigning the England captaincy. He didn't, and when he walked out to open the innings in the next Test, the Headingley crowd gave him a roaring reception. In similar circumstances, Fortune would have favoured lesser men with a century. Atherton was dismissed for 99.

McGrath was his nemesis. More than anyone else the Australian understood Atherton's game and knew how to pierce his defences. Atherton liked to wait till the ball was under his nose, choosing his stroke at the last, often playing with soft hands, absorbing the ball like a sponge. McGrath would relentlessly pitch on exactly the right length, moving his deliveries around unpredictably and bouncing the ball steeply so that edges would carry. Repeatedly Atherton was pushed back and, trying to adjust his stroke, often succeeded only in touching a ball others might have missed. He'd leave with a shrug and a sigh, and the Australians, respecting a fighter, were pleased to see him go. But he refused to change his game; it had been tried and tested over the years and had not let him down. He could not bring himself to chance his arm because it would be a betrayal of everything he knew and the team he represented.

Atherton was the finest English batsman of his generation, and captain in 54 Tests, a record for England. He was an even-tempered cricketer, a fierce patriot and a man prepared to fight his corner, popular with team-mates and, eventually, with distant observers. Yet he could seem aloof, even arrogant, to those who occasionally crossed his path. His retirement was well timed and he'll be able to relax now, writing books and articles, voicing his concerns, telling amusing stories and generally confirming that he is better company than he sometimes cared to show. He made an outstanding contribution to his country's cricket and his only regret must be that greatness did not bestow its largesse upon him.

Peter Roebuck is a cricket writer for the Sydney Morning Herald *and* Melbourne Age.

A GAME IN FLUX
AS VIEWED FROM THE BOUNDARY

By SIMON HEFFER

It is easy to forget this, but professional cricket in England took off in the 19th century because people were prepared to pay to watch it. In those days, spectators – whether club members, or people charged at the gate – provided the revenues to pay the players. Now, television companies and corporate sponsors perform that function. Therefore, it might be argued, the public deserves no consideration when it comes to the scheduling of matches, or the composition of the teams that participate in them.

That is certainly how a great many county members have come, in recent years, to regard the cricket authorities' attitude to the sides they support, and the first-class competition in which those sides play. True, it would seem eccentric now to attempt to market county cricket as a viable leisure activity. But first-class county cricket has been changed to an extent at which it seems designed actively to drive spectators away. If this was the plan, it is working brilliantly.

The first step was to play county cricket over four days instead of three. With slow over-rates – why bowl 20 an hour when you can get away with bowling 15 or 16? – and four days to fill, the play became attritional. Only the retired have the time, and then not always the inclination, to watch such a contest. It is a contest made all the more soporific and irrelevant in recent seasons by the introduction of central contracts for England players and an extended international programme. This means that the best English players hardly ever appear for their clubs – and then, for good measure, they complain about the "lack of support" given them by their county committees. The two-division County Championship has suspended some ancient rivalries, an important ingredient of any sporting fixture list, added to which games are often either not scheduled for, or have finished by, the weekend, when people might have time to watch.

Indeed, all the major changes in the last 15 years have been made with complete disregard for the paying public. No doubt this reflects how little cash they actually bring into the game, but there is more to it than that. When counties have tried to stand up for their members' interests, they have been castigated for obstructing "progress". It is a chicken-and-egg argument. The public drifted away from cricket because it became progressively more unattractive as a spectacle. First-class county cricket is nigh unwatchable: it almost beggars belief that anybody should find it a recreation preferable to, say, sitting in his or her own garden and watching the flowers grow.

The county supporter's emotional tie to his or her side is considered sentimental and uncommercial. It seems to be the view of the ECB that the counties exist solely to breed England players. As soon as they are bred they are whisked off, not to be seen again until they have proved inadequate for the international task, returning to their counties in a useful state of demoralisation. This shows contempt for the counties themselves, for the

[*Graham Morris*

A timeless summer scene at Hove – or deckchairs waiting to be rearranged?

players and for the paying public. The ECB don't appear to realise that if the last of those is a far smaller constituency than it used to be – and it is – it is largely the board's own fault, and that of their forerunner. Moreover, this decline matters. Those who lose the habit of paying to watch county cricket will in time lose the habit of paying to watch Test cricket, too.

The way the ECB treat the counties is reckless. At the going rate, there will be hardly any paying supporters for first-class cricket, and greatly reduced county memberships, before the end of the decade. After all, why should members pay to see boring cricket, played (by definition) by those who are not especially good cricketers? And just as this is driving away individuals, so it is driving away the corporate clients who were so in evidence in the 1980s and 1990s. The fewer people who go into county grounds, the less money that will be spent there. The begging bowl, which counties already hold out to the ECB, will be thrust more and more aggressively and desperately in the board's face. The choice will be either to pump more money into these loss-making enterprises, or accept blithely that a club or two will go bankrupt.

The counties have behaved stupidly themselves. Large staffs packed with mediocrities are simply not acceptable. Too many cricketers make it quite clear they hate playing cricket, and the game should not tolerate them. Their attitude is like a cancer dragging down the professional game, while reliance on subsidy has prevented some clubs from challenging the forces of decline head-on.

It does not, however, need to be like that. The board should realise, first, that their greed in scheduling so much international cricket – and thereby taking county players away for so much of the season – will in time prove counterproductive, as the currency of such contests is devalued. They should also realise that they achieve little by demanding that England-contracted players "rest" from matches in between Tests, thereby missing opportunities to stay in or get back into form, while at the same time entertaining county supporters. They should see, too, that four-day cricket is not working. If those with an interest in cricket were told that first-class matches would be played over three days, on uncovered wickets, featuring the best players in between an old-style international programme, then first-class county cricket might become attractive to them again.

At the moment, it is dying a painful death because of the attitude that counties, in return for providing international players, deserve no consideration other than the regular filling of the begging bowl. Yet it is madness to let what, in many cases, could be viable businesses go into terminal decline. We must not expect the ECB to be vulnerable to sentimental arguments about the place of county clubs in the history of English cricket. We might, though, expect the board to want to maximise the appeal of cricket and to make these clubs strong. After all, they are not just a source of players for England, but also of generating interest in English cricket: without such interest the game dies altogether. Furthermore, the more money they make themselves, the less they need from the begging bowl, which in turn means more for the ECB to invest in the game in ways that improve its asset base.

For all the changes that have been made, England are still not an especially good side; they would be unlikely to supply any player to the mythical World XI. It might just be that some of the reasons for the low calibre of the international team are to be found in the neglect of the game at the level that supplies the players. After all, who is to say that if radical changes were introduced, making the county game more attractive and more watchable, these would not cause an infectious spirit of improvement that, as in any successful business, would spread right to the top?

Simon Heffer is a columnist on the Daily Mail.

AN EYE TO THE FUTURE

By SIMON HUGHES

Reruns of Botham's Ashes, broadcast to coincide with the arrival of Steve Waugh's Australians for the 2001 series, made enjoyable, revealing watching. Enjoyable for the sheer satisfaction of seeing rampant Aussies for once cut down to size; revealing because they brought the great advances of television technology into sharp focus. Those pictures from 20 years ago looked so primitive: single-end coverage, so that every other over was viewed from behind the wicket-keeper; four cameras at most; grainy, jerky replays; and stationary shots of scoreboards to update the match situation.

Compare that with what we take for granted now. More than 30 cameras, some in stumps that can pan with the bowler as he's running in, some capable of zooming in so close you can see the stubble a player missed when he shaved that morning, one on rails that whizzes up and down the boundary like a dog-track hare. Countless (sometimes too many) replays of a wicket, the pictures pin-sharp, stump microphones, Snickometers, clever graphics that superimpose red mats on the pitch, statistics galore and the score permanently displayed in the top corner of the screen. The viewer is left in no doubt as to what has occurred, and why, from ten different angles.

Britain had already established itself as a world leader in sports television broadcasting before last summer's revolutionary, and controversial, development: the introduction of Hawk-Eye on Channel 4 and Sky Scope. Based on missile guidance systems, Hawk-Eye uses six small cameras positioned round the ground to monitor the flight, trajectory, speed and movement of the ball, both out of the bowler's hand and off the pitch. This information is then fed into a computer that almost instantly produces an exact replay of the ball in virtual reality, adding in the ball's predicted path if it hadn't cannoned into the batsman's pad, or been hit by his bat.

Suddenly television was not only relaying what *had* happened in explicit detail, but also what *would* have happened in different circumstances (i.e. if the batsman hadn't been there). It was predicting a probability as well as portraying the past. This was very new and very daring and not everyone liked it, fearing it would irreparably damage the fabric of the game, remove its glorious uncertainty. Umpires cowered in dark corners muttering, "Soon I'll only be there to count to six… it'll be the death of us."

They are anticipating the day when there will be cameras in the bats, balls and fielders' helmets, and a speaker in the stumps delivering a computer-generated "That's out" verdict (in a North Country accent if so desired) to send the batsman on his way. In fact, an electronic device, similar to the bleeper in tennis, that signals instantly to the players that a no-ball has just been bowled is already available. Paradoxically, it would probably pose more problems than it solved: "Wasn't that a no-ball then?" "No, it was a car horn in St John's Wood Road." Reassuringly, from an aesthetic point of view, it will be a while before cricket's international body feel they can sanction its use.

But are the umpires' fears justified? Is cricket soon to be presided over only by wired-up men in little boxes? Will bowlers of the future be yelling

[*Courtesy of Hawk-Eye Innovations Ltd*

Hawk-Eye brought a new dimension to watching cricket on television, but opinions were divided as to whether projecting a probability was undermining the umpire. Hawk-Eye would have given Alec Stewart lbw to Shane Warne; the umpire did not.

"Howzat?" to a set of traffic lights rather than an umpire? Well, Hawk-Eye hasn't yet been programmed to see that far ahead. But the short answer to the umpires' understandable worry is that they are likely to be there, doing roughly the same job, 20 years from now. In the same way that closed-circuit TV hasn't made the local bobby redundant, so too television's all-seeing eye does not spell the end of the umpire.

As the technological side of TV coverage develops further, it will just alter the style of his decision-making. Instead of him making instant, hairline judgments, a voice in his headset will give him a bit of guidance. "Pitched outside leg," the voice will say, or "a bit high". These morsels from the third umpire in the TV control unit will take less than five seconds to transmit; the delay will be imperceptible. In fact, the umpire will probably have made up his mind a good deal quicker than Steve Bucknor usually does. But most importantly, the umpire in the middle will still have the final say. It will be up to him to sift all the information he receives, as he does now, and then make his decision. Machines are supplying the information, but, vitally, humans are still interpreting and applying it.

Many supporters of the game will find this scenario disturbing. But you can't turn the clock back. Technological aids generally enhance the viewer's appreciation of the event and will increase in number and sophistication as rival television companies joust for reputation and airtime. For the viewer to have seen exactly what has happened, while the umpire remains more or less in the dark, is unacceptable. Players, too, expect every decision to be as right as it can possibly be.

One problem that needs addressing immediately is the way officials are allowed to use technology. At the moment, cameras can be used to arbitrate whether a ball has gone for four or six, but not whether it has hit the batsman's glove or elbow before being caught. In other words, a relatively minor decision in the scheme of things – deciding whether the ball cleared the rope – is made to appear more significant than a potentially vital one, namely a batsman's dismissal. With more appropriate use of technology, Mike Atherton would have been reprieved in both innings at Trent Bridge last summer (he was given out caught off his arm guard to the second ball of the match) and Australia might not have taken an unassailable 3–0 lead.

The ICC's decision to declare a shortlist of elite umpires worldwide and to employ members of that panel whenever possible is absolutely the right approach. Because one thing Hawk-Eye, the Snickometer, the Red Zone and all the other gimmicks reaffirmed was the supreme quality of the best officials. Men like Peter Willey, David Shepherd, Steve Bucknor and Rudi Koertzen get 95 per cent of the hairline decisions right, often under extreme provocation. They should be paid a prince's ransom and then supplied – as subtly and quickly as possible – with all the televisual information necessary to ensure they aren't made to look fools to the viewer at home.

Television has illuminated and enhanced cricket. All the intricate skills and mysterious strategies of the game have been explained and explored, making it easier to understand and appreciate. Players young and old have benefited from the highlighting of their art. Ultimately, umpires will as well. They think they're the fall guys, but television should help them become even better snap-decision makers.

The technology people are on their side. The men in white coats are part of the fabric of cricket, maintaining its human factor. The day umpires are abolished, leaving the running of the game to people watching monitors, is the day cricket ceases to be sport and becomes, instead, more closely associated with the security industry. Law suits would be filed for "wrongful dismissal" and Test matches would be sponsored by legal firms rather than finance houses and power companies.

It will never happen. It is vital for cricket's credibility that the game played by highly paid international stars is still vaguely recognisable as the same recreation that 22 players indulge in come Saturday afternoon on Putney Common or beside the M62 at Milnrow. What would life be without the sight of a batsman staring incredulously at the umpire's raised finger? Or the bowler glaring at the umpire's implacable gaze and grunting, "But it were knocking all three down." A game without emotion is no game at all.

Simon Hughes writes for the Daily Telegraph *and is the match analyst for Channel 4's cricket coverage.*

SECOND STRING, FIRST CHOICE

By CATHERINE HANLEY

Northamptonshire hardly sprang a surprise when they appointed Mike Hussey as captain, making him the third Australian, along with Somerset's Jamie Cox and Yorkshire's Darren Lehmann, to lead a county in 2002. In addition to scoring most runs in English first-class cricket in 2001, he had impressed members by his positive attitude and approach on and off the field. Yet when Northamptonshire originally announced that he was replacing Matthew Hayden as their overseas player, there weren't many who didn't ask, "Mike who?" It would not have been the first time cricket followers around the country had raised their eyes from the morning newspaper on reading of a county's choice to fill a vacant overseas slot.

It is not surprising, then, that the debate about overseas players, something of a perennial topic, has recently concerned not so much their presence as their quality. Certainly the argument that overseas players take places that could go to aspiring youngsters has become less tenable. Receiving more credence is the view that their presence gives county cricketers the chance to pit themselves against quality opposition – something often lacking now that centrally contracted England players make ever more fleeting appearances for their counties.

During the last ten to 15 years, though, there has been a shift in the type of visitor plying his trade in county cricket. Where once world-class names with established Test pedigrees could be found in every shire, the increasing demands of international cricket mean that such cricketers no longer have the time, or the energy, to commit themselves to a full English season. Counties are now faced with the reality that the days of fielding an international star for a whole season have gone.

Two ways round the problem have emerged, polarising the counties into two groups: a diminishing faction who sign a major star and accept he will not be available for the whole term, and an increasing number who opt for a lesser-known name – good players, but ones who are not proven at international level. The 2001 cohort of overseas players illustrates the point. Test spinners Muttiah Muralitharan and Saqlain Mushtaq were available for barely half of Lancashire's and Surrey's games, while New Zealand captain Stephen Fleming was absent from Middlesex for the middle period of the season. Meanwhile, the Ashes summer meant that the top 16 Australians were otherwise engaged, forcing the counties to examine the next tier and sign names unfamiliar to many English supporters. Michael Di Venuto, Martin Love, Jimmy Maher, Ian Harvey, Andrew Symonds, Dan Marsh, Hussey and Cox had no Test caps, while a further three – Stuart Law, Andy Bichel and Lehmann – had five or less.

This dichotomy can only become more distinct. Under the newly implemented ICC Test Championship cycle, more international cricket will be played between May and September, traditionally the exclusive preserve of English cricket. Test stars will be more jealously guarded by their national boards. Those counties who have not already followed the trend for fringe players will be forced to reconsider their positions.

[*Graham Morris*

[*Pete Norton, Getty Images*

Two Australians to have made a mark in county cricket: Somerset's Jamie Cox and Mike Hussey of Northamptonshire.

This is why the questions regarding the employment of overseas players have become more insistent, with critics suggesting that, if the best are not available, the practice should be scrapped. This fails to take into account the full nature of the overseas player's role. Although it might be pleasant for county members to watch a world-class cricketer at their local ground, the responsibilities of the modern overseas professional are far more wide-ranging. Tom Moody, a former overseas player himself and now director of cricket at Worcestershire, believes that the job is not just about runs and wickets. "One of the most important roles is leading by example, and showing professionalism both on and off the field. But more than this, the overseas professional should have the ability to finish games, to turn games and, most importantly, make the team operate as a team."

A side effect of signing a star name is that it promotes individualism in the game and complacency in other players. It is right to place a large burden of expectation on the player concerned, but not to the extent that the team find it difficult to function without him. Consider the Somerset side of the post-Richards and Garner era, or the more recent example of Sussex. Michael Bevan produced outstanding individual performances throughout the 2000 season, but the side faltered during his absence on international duty. They performed better collectively a year later when he was unavailable and replaced by the lower-profile Murray Goodwin, topping Division Two of the County Championship.

Cricket is, after all, a team game, so the ideal overseas cricketer is not the star who – inadvertently or otherwise – individualises it; rather, he is the man who fits in and helps his county do well. The overseas player who leaves the field with a century or five wickets and considers his job done is not taking his responsibilities seriously. He has to make contributions off the field as well, by acting as an unofficial coach, for example, aiding those very same young hopefuls whose progress he is accused of thwarting. The situation is succinctly encapsulated by Andy Bichel, Worcestershire's overseas player: "You only get out of this job what you put in, and if you're not putting in, then what are you doing here in the first place?"

If the overseas player is to be judged on how well his side performs, the so-called "second stringer" often makes the greatest contribution. As Jamie Cox points out, the international stars may not be concentrating exclusively on their county games. "The temptation might be there to start thinking about a forthcoming Test match, whereas if counties sign somebody who doesn't have any international commitments they can get more out of him, as his focus remains with the club." Cox himself is a good example: unheard-of in many English quarters before arriving at Somerset, he led them to their most successful season in 2001.

Although there have been murmurings that a minimum standard of international experience should be set for overseas players, the question is a thorny one. Such a criterion might have worked a few years ago but, owing to international demands, it is now unfeasible. Nor is it necessarily desirable. Ask the members of Yorkshire, Somerset and Northamptonshire whether they would implement such a system, so denying themselves the services of their present incumbents, and the reply would surely be in the negative.

Another point to consider is the cyclical nature of national cricketing strength. If one country is so strong that it has a surplus of good players who are not required for the national team, why not take advantage of the situation by having them play in England? After all, many of these players would be automatic selections for the Test teams of other countries, or in another era. Their presence in county cricket could only be beneficial, apart from being valuable for the player himself. It would encourage spectators through the gates by providing them with the opportunity to see more high-class performers, a commodity often in short supply.

There is a future for the overseas player in county cricket, but his role will continue to evolve away from the model of the latter part of the 20th century, and the type of player will change. "Different", however, does not equate with "inferior". As Tom Moody points out, there is more to an overseas professional than just his name or profile. "Whoever he is, he can offer a lot, and help the club forge ahead very quickly if you get the right type. County cricket would be very much poorer without overseas players."

Catherine Hanley is a post-doctoral research associate at the University of Sheffield, a Somerset supporter and a contributor to Wisden.com.

A SIMPLE PLEASURE

[*Tom Shaw, Getty Images*

It is easy to forget, in these days of sponsorship, advanced television technology and non-stop international matches, that cricket remains at heart a game that people anywhere can "adventure forth to play, And all be Ranjitsinhjis".

ENGLAND'S UNLUCKY BREAK

[*Graham Morris*

Even before the 2001 Ashes series began, England's prospects had been damaged when captain Nasser Hussain's right hand was broken by Shoaib Akhtar at Lord's. By the time he returned, England's renaissance was on the wane.

UP FROM DOWN UNDER

[*Patrick Eagar*

Steve Waugh, unbeaten and unsponsored, acknowledges the ovation for his hundred at The Oval. After missing the Headingley Test with a calf injury, the Australian captain had fought his way back to semi-fitness, and was still too good for England's bowlers.

500 HIGH

[*Brooks Latouche Photography*

Courtney Walsh appeals for lbw against South Africa's Jacques Kallis at Port-of-Spain; the umpire's confirmation made him the first bowler to capture 500 Test wickets. When Walsh retired three Tests later, on his home ground at Kingston, he had extended his world record to 519.

V

THE HIGH FIVE

[*Patrick Eagar*

Bowlers often feel overlooked; in 2001, Glenn McGrath and his fellow-Australians put that right by introducing a new ritual to a game hardly devoid of them. On taking five wickets in an innings, the bowler held the ball high in response to – or expectation of – the crowd's applause.

THE LOVELIEST GROUND

[*Val Corbett*

Wisden Cricket Monthly launched an annual competition in 2001 to find the loveliest cricket ground in the British Isles. First prize went to the Keswick club, whose ground at Fitz Park in the Lake District lies in the lee of Skiddaw.

[*Ben Duffy, SWpix*

Glares, stares and flying stumps became a feature of Yorkshire's Championship-winning campaign once they called up Steve Kirby as a mid-match replacement for England fast bowler Matthew Hoggard in June.

Advertisement

[*Hamish Blair, Getty Images*

Above: Shane Warne, Steve Waugh and Adam Gilchrist with the ICC Test Championship Trophy after its presentation to first-time holders Australia at Edgbaston. The silver and gold-leaf mace is held by the leading country on the World Championship table.

Below: Captain David Byas and captain-in-waiting Darren Lehmann display the Lord's Taverners Trophy as Yorkshire celebrate their first County Championship for 33 years.

[*Mike Finn-Kelcey, Getty Images*

Advertisement

TOUGH-TALKING HEADS

[*Kamal Kishore, Popperfoto/Reuters*

Cricket found itself at crisis-point late in 2001 when India reacted furiously to penalties imposed on their players by ICC referee Mike Denness. Indian board president Jagmohan Dalmiya (*above*) pushed their protests to the limit; the ICC's recently appointed chief executive, Malcolm Speed (*below*), refuted them with a purpose that firmly fixed the power base of cricket's governing body.

[*Richard Lewis, Associated Press*

FIVE CRICKETERS OF THE YEAR

[*Patrick Eagar*

ADAM GILCHRIST

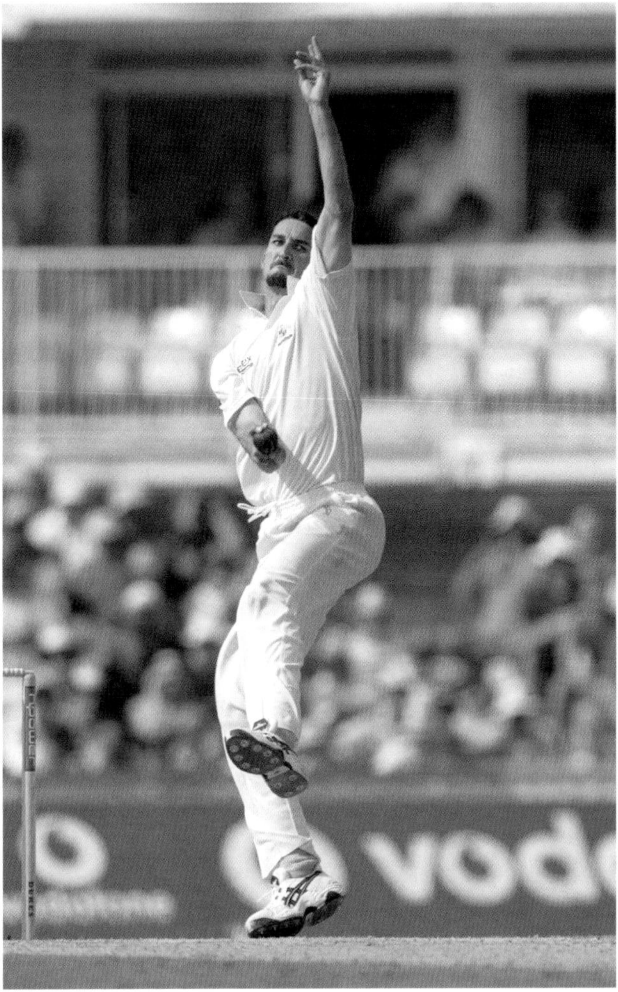

[*Patrick Eagar*

JASON GILLESPIE

[*Graham Morris*

V. V. S. LAXMAN

FIVE CRICKETERS OF THE YEAR

[*Patrick Eagar*

DAMIEN MARTYN

FIVE CRICKETERS OF THE YEAR

[*Patrick Eagar*

ANDY FLOWER

FIVE CRICKETERS OF THE YEAR

ANDY FLOWER

In a country whose descent into anarchy has almost reached terminal velocity, it is hard to keep one's eye on the ball. In a perfect world, a profile of a cricketer would not carry the baggage of politics. But Zimbabwe is not like other Test-playing nations; there is not a man, woman or child there who has been unaffected by events unravelling in a land once called "a jewel in Africa". The bewildering machinations of politicians and their lackeys have permeated every fabric of society, and cricket has not been excluded.

So there was something especially piquant in Andy Flower's regeneration since being stripped of Zimbabwe's captaincy on his return from the tour of England in July 2000; a sacking that came as a "complete bolt from the blue". Lesser men might have quit. Instead, while around him his country and as often as not his team crumbled, Zimbabwe's 32-year-old left-handed wicket-keeper/batsman went about his cricketing business with his usual tight-lipped determination. Twelve months later, the Federation of International Cricketers' Associations named him International Cricketer of the Year.

ANDREW FLOWER was born on the stroke of midnight of April 28/29, 1968 in the Cape coastal hamlet of Fish Hoek, South Africa, the third-born of three brothers and a sister. Brother Grant was born some two and a half years later. Their father, a keen sports enthusiast and an accountant, traversed southern Africa in the course of his career, family in tow, and Andy was ten before the family finally settled in what was then Rhodesia. He excelled at sport throughout his schooldays, being awarded colours for hockey, tennis and cricket, and in 1986, his last year at Vainona High School in northern Harare, he toured England with the Stragglers club. They played 16 games in three weeks, and the seeds of a life in pursuit of the cricketing sun were sown.

The following year, he commenced work at the Anglo American Corporation, but after 16 months returned to England to play for Barnt Green in the Birmingham League, where he met his future wife, Rebecca Hampson. A spell in the Lancashire leagues came next, at Heywood, and he was already playing in The Netherlands, for Voorburg in The Hague, when Zimbabwe selected him for the 1990 ICC Trophy there. Grant, playing for Winscombe in the Somerset League, was also in the squad, and the brothers' contribution to Zimbabwe's successful tournament – they beat Holland in the final – was not inconsequential. Andy scored 311 runs at an average of 77.75, and Grant 253 at just over 63.

Vital as it was to Zimbabwe's quest for Test status, this third successive ICC Trophy win also meant a place at the 1991-92 World Cup in Australasia. Against Sri Lanka at New Plymouth, Andy celebrated his senior international debut in fair style, keeping wicket and batting throughout the innings for an unbeaten 115 – only the third player to score a century on one-day debut. But while it earned him the match award, it didn't result in a Zimbabwe victory, a portent of the way things would be for the rest of the decade.

Zimbabwe's captain for two tenures, Andy Flower led them to their first Test win, a triumphant innings victory over Pakistan at Harare in February

1995. It was only their 11th Test, and saw the Flowers' stand of 269 transcend the fraternal partnership record set by Ian and Greg Chappell against New Zealand in 1973-74. Grant was not out 201, his maiden Test century, while Andy made 156, his second. Zimbabwe's inaugural Test had been against India in October 1992. From then until breaking his thumb on the last day of their Test victory over India, at Harare in June 2001 – he hit the winning boundary – Andy Flower played in every one of his country's 52 Tests and 172 one-day internationals.

He had scored 3,908 runs in the Tests at 51.42, with nine hundreds, as well as making 143 dismissals; in the one-day games, he was averaging 33.54 from 5,267 runs, with two hundreds and 44 half-centuries, and had made 124 catches and 30 stumpings. His highest score, an unbeaten 232 at Nagpur in November 2000, was the best by any wicket-keeper in Tests, and the crowning achievement in a glorious run of nine post-captaincy Tests that brought 1,066 runs at 88.83. In India alone, highlighting his aptitude against spin, his scores in the two Tests were 183 not out, 70, 55 and 232 not out. A seventh consecutive Test fifty, against Bangladesh at Bulawayo, set him alongside Everton Weekes in the record books.

In his earlier years especially, commentators noted Andy Flower's obduracy. These days the talk is more about his mental stamina. "When I started taking cricket seriously," he explained, "I never actually had a high regard for whatever talent I had. Seeing the ball, hitting it, there were plenty of other cricketers who did that far better than I did. But I thought one area where I could be better than them was to be more determined, more hungry, and not give anything away." He may not be the prettiest batsman to watch, building his game around back-foot strokes square of the wicket, but he is considered by some to be the finest exponent of the reverse sweep, having added his own subtleties to that shot.

Returning after injury to play South Africa in September 2001, he did not concede a bye in an innings that lasted ten hours. He followed that up by becoming the first keeper to make hundreds in each innings of a Test, batting for almost 15 hours. His 142 and 199 not out took him to No. 1 in the PwC rankings, the first Zimbabwean and the first wicket-keeper/batsman to top the world list. Still Zimbabwe lost. No wonder Andy Flower is thought of as "The Rock" in some circles – and the patron saint of lost causes in others. – KEITH MEADOWS.

ADAM GILCHRIST

Adam Gilchrist had never been so nervous at the start of a Test as he was at Edgbaston last summer. This was his Ashes debut and he had always been keen to excel in England, where he had played as a young man and enjoyed himself. The nerves showed; he dropped two straightforward catches in the first session. Gilchrist has an equable nature, but he felt he had let himself down and reparation was required. Two days later he came in to bat when Australia were 336 for five. It was a crucial moment. If England could get rid of the tail quickly, they might make a game of it. The left-handed Gilchrist transformed that hope into fantasy. He put on 160 with his Western Australian mate Damien Martyn; his own hundred came up with an unorthodox flick over the keeper's head off glove and bat. When he was last out, having hit five sixes and 20 fours in his highest Test score of 152, Australia were 576. He had humiliated the opposition, and set a pattern that was to repeat itself through the series, except at Headingley where Gilchrist, as stand-in captain, allowed the game to slip away from Australia. That was the only dark shadow over a memorable summer. England's fans, and no doubt their cricketers, felt contradictory sensations of fear and expectation each time he strode to the crease, but he soon became the Australian the crowd most enjoyed watching.

ADAM CRAIG GILCHRIST was born on November 14, 1971 in the small New South Wales town of Bellingen. His father taught in another small town, Deniliquin, before moving into schools administration at Lismore, a town, in the north of the state, that was not much larger. To the outsider, such places may not have had much to offer, but, for an aspiring cricketer, Gilchrist had a privileged upbringing. His father Stan had been a good enough leggie, when a student in Sydney, to play for New South Wales seconds and he nurtured his son's ambitions. So did his mother, who bought him a pair of wicket-keeper's gloves for Christmas before he was ten. The first time he kept with them he broke his nose, but he made the best of it. When told that Rod Marsh had also broken his nose as a boy, Gilchrist declared this proved that it was his destiny to keep wicket for Australia. (Marsh later informed him that there was no truth in the story.)

As a batsman, he was taught by his father to watch the ball, give himself time, and play naturally. "I suppose that's the way I have always thought about it. Just try to hit the ball. That's what the game's about," he says. He decided he would be a professional cricketer at the age of 17 when he had to choose between university entrance exams and a cricket scholarship to England. He chose England, and played a summer for Richmond in the Middlesex League.

His higher education was in the Australian Under-19 team that swaggered through England in 1991, with Martyn as captain and 2001 team manager Steve Bernard as coach, and at the Academy in Adelaide, where he adopted his high-on-the-handle grip. He was promising, though not a prodigy like Martyn. Moreover, he was conscious he was not a natural keeper, and when he made his debut for New South Wales, aged 21, it was as a batsman, not an all-rounder. When he failed to score many runs, Gilchrist wondered whether he should give up keeping; he decided, sensibly as it turned out, that by not keeping he would only increase the pressure on his batting.

It was clear, however, that he would have to leave his home state if he was to get on. In the mid-1990s, Australian professional cricketers could make a decent living only if they played Test cricket, and the first requirement was a secure place in a state side. In 1994-95, he found one in Perth, with his mates Martyn and Justin Langer. He succeeded a popular Test keeper in Tim Zoehrer, but he soon established a reputation as a cheerful colleague and a relentless competitor. He had to learn patience, too. Although he deputised for the injured Ian Healy in Australia's one-day side in 1996-97, and emerged a year later as a dashing opening bat, Healy still wore the gloves in the Tests.

Gilchrist's inexperience let him down in the 1999 World Cup in England, where his free style was undone by seam and swing until the final, when he scored 54. But this didn't prevent the selectors from dumping Healy in November 1999. Batting at No. 7, Gilchrist scored 149 not out in only his second Test, putting on 238 with Langer to provide an improbable win against Pakistan. He became a fixture straightaway; within nine months he was Steve Waugh's vice-captain.

The significance of Gilchrist's batting is that, after the specialist batsmen have established a platform, he is capable of putting Australia's score out of reach of the opposition. He is a breaker of wills. Of course, he knows failure, having scored two runs in four consecutive innings against India in March 2001 after starting the series with a century. But at the end of the Ashes summer his average was 51.30 from 22 Tests; against England, he had just averaged 68.00. He had also taken 94 catches and made seven stumpings – more dismissals per game than Healy, the record-holder.

However, the Ashes series also revealed a flaw. To combine batting, keeping and the captaincy has stretched the talent of cricketers like Alec Stewart too far. The evidence of the Headingley Test, when Gilchrist's slack tactics on the field allowed England an easy victory, suggested that captaincy may be a step too far for him as well. He need not worry. Name a wicket-keeper who has played as many match-winning Test innings. Adam Gilchrist has already come a very long way. – STEPHEN FAY.

JASON GILLESPIE

It was the night the Third Test at Chennai had ended in a close two-wicket win for the home side. India had taken the series 2–1, after being thrashed in the First Test within three days, and Steve Waugh's ambition of leading Australia to a series win in India had been thwarted. But not before a monumental physical and mental effort from one of Waugh's favourite players, Jason Gillespie.

That day he almost dragged the Australians to victory with his second great spell of the match, both of which came towards the end of enervating days in the field under a fierce sun, and on a lifeless pitch. In the second innings, with India cruising to victory, Gillespie responded to the situation – and to the roared encouragement of the pocket of Australian fans in the stand behind him – by digging as deep as cricketers are asked to go. He had Sachin Tendulkar caught off an edge, for the second time in the match, then Sourav Ganguly five balls later. The pressure was back on the Indians, but they scraped home in the end. Gillespie's best was not quite enough to drag his side over the line.

That night he staggered out of a lift on to the Australians' hotel floor, looking as if all he could do next was fall on his bed and sleep for days. The Test, like the First and Second, had been a wonderful event – many rated the series the best three-match rubber ever – but even some journalists had suffered heat exhaustion watching from the open-air press box. No wonder Gillespie was a spent force. The next day it was announced that he was going home to recuperate, instead of staying for the one-day series.

No player on that tour deserved an early respite more than the 25-year-old South Australian fast bowler. Contrary to accepted wisdom, Australia had placed more faith in pace than spin, reasoning that the Indians never cope well with aggressive, high-class fast bowling. But with Brett Lee unavailable through injury, the burden of that game-plan fell on Glenn McGrath and Gillespie. Both accepted it superbly, taking 17 and 13 wickets respectively. Yet, to those watching, Gillespie's rewards had fallen short of his performances, repeating a worrying career pattern. And this after the injuries and accidents that had interrupted a Test career which began against West Indies at Sydney in November 1996, and revealed its full threat when he took seven for 37 against England at Headingley the following year.

He missed most of the 1997-98 season with spinal stress fractures, and most of 1999-2000 with a broken leg and fractured wrist after that calamitous fielding collision with Steve Waugh at Kandy in September 1999. When a badly strained hamstring stopped him in November 2000, his whole career seemed threatened, not just his roles in the coming tours to India and England. Yet by the time he arrived in England six months later, he had formed a formidable new-ball pairing with McGrath.

JASON NEIL GILLESPIE was born on April 19, 1975 in the bohemian inner Sydney suburb of Darlinghurst and, when ten, moved with his family to Adelaide. There, his natural athleticism and easy pace helped him progress quickly through the ranks, culminating in national Under-19 representation and a stint at the Cricket Academy. In 2001, Gillespie's Aboriginal heritage – through his paternal great-great-grandfather – became widely known when he was named captain of an Aboriginal team to play a Prime Minister's XI in a match to mark an increased effort by the Australian Cricket Board to promote the game in the athletically gifted indigenous community.

His early years in first-class cricket were notable for an honest approach to the hard work of fast bowling and a somewhat unconventional lifestyle. He wore a long ponytail, had a daughter named Sapphire and professed a liking for rock music of the more raucous variety. The ponytail eventually went in the interests of simplicity. His bowling continued to be refined, until he landed in England last summer with one of the more efficient, shorter run-ups in the game, and an ability to bowl with the seam so upright so often that he was able to move the ball either way on all surfaces.

In the First Test at Edgbaston, where he took a wicket with his first ball, he made a far-reaching impact when he produced a sharp lifter that smashed the little finger on Nasser Hussain's left hand. The England captain missed the next two Tests, by which time Australia had retained the Ashes with three consecutive wins and Gillespie had taken 17 wickets at 20.47. At Trent Bridge, after Shane Warne had turned and tormented England's second-innings batting, Gillespie put it out of its misery with three wickets in 14 balls. His form faded in the last two Tests, but his influence on those early matches had severely damaged whatever hopes England had harboured of making a contest of the series. Mark Waugh, Australia's brilliant second slip, said that Gillespie was the most difficult bowler to catch to because of his pace and lift off the pitch. But it was not just his speed that marked his performances against England in 2001. He combined high pace with such incisive accuracy and pronounced seam movement that there were times when he was unplayable.

At Trent Bridge, Gillespie reached 100 Test wickets, and his strike-rate of 48 at the end of the series was in the top bracket. Allan Donald's, for example, was 46, McGrath's 50. Steve Waugh has often said that, at his best, Gillespie is as good as any fast bowler Australia has produced. High praise from a captain who knows his cricket history. Yet Waugh is not the only Australian to enjoy Gillespie's success. The lanky fast bowler's dry-humoured modesty and wholehearted approach have made him a most popular player. Moreover, behind his shy, often monosyllabic public utterances lies the sharp mind of a fiercely dedicated cricketer. His best is still ahead of him. – MARK RAY.

V. V. S. LAXMAN

For two reasons at least, the Second Test of the 2000-01 series between India and Australia, at Eden Gardens, will stand out among the most prominent landmarks in the game's history. India's win brought to an end Australia's awesome run of 16 wins, the longest ever, and no side following on as far behind as 274 runs had previously come back to win a Test match.

Victory against such heavy odds was too large a feat to be accomplished by just one man. Indeed, three architects went into shaping it: off-spinner Harbhajan Singh, whose 13 wickets included a first-innings hat-trick, V. V. S. Laxman and Rahul Dravid. To weigh importance of the roles played by each of them might seem unfair, but in truth India owed the largest debt to Laxman. First, he kept the jaws of defeat wrenched apart until they ached and became too weak to snap; and secondly, he scored his epic 281 in the second innings at a rate that left enough time for Harbhajan and his fellow-bowlers to finish the job.

The First Test at Mumbai had been won by Australia in three days. And when India were 317 behind with only two wickets standing at the end of the second day in Kolkata, the prospects of another premature finish were writ large. Laxman was 26 not out that evening. He was unbeaten also – albeit now in the second innings – on the following evening, and again on the one after, this time with 275, the highest Test score by an Indian. By then, it was India whose nostrils were filled with the scent of victory. Haste required by the impending declaration deprived Laxman of further personal glory, but his partnership of 376 with Dravid was India's largest for any wicket against Australia, and their second-highest ever.

VANGIPURAPPU VENKATA SAI LAXMAN was born on November 1, 1974 in Hyderabad, to parents who are both doctors – his father a general practitioner and his mother a radiologist. It was taken for granted that Laxman, like almost all members of his near family, would take up a profession that required academic excellence, and he was therefore sent to an appropriate school, Little Flower. His father was Laxman's role model and he always assumed he would become a doctor as well. But medicine receded into stand-by mode once he fell under cricket's spell.

Yet with sport not figuring in Little Flower's curriculum, Laxman's talent could easily have remained latent. It was spotted by a cricket-playing uncle during family games in his grandparents' back yard. Having learnt the basics from this uncle, he then went to St John's Coaching Foundation for more advanced tutoring, and from there graduated to playing age-group cricket for Hyderabad, beginning with the Under-13s.

As Laxman approached his 18th birthday, his head and his heart were both telling him that his future lay in cricket. The defining moment arrived when he had to choose between exams for entrance to medical school, or a place at an Under-19 national coaching camp. Looking back to that fateful day, he said: "I decided to give myself four years to make it in cricket, knowing that if I didn't, I could always go for medicine. My parents must have had many misgivings about my decision, but they gave me their fullest support."

He did not have to wait long to reassure his parents that he had chosen wisely. Already a full state player, he was picked for India in an Under-19 Test series against Australia, who had Jason Gillespie, Brett Lee, Matthew Nicholson and Andrew Symonds in their ranks. He made four big scores against them, with 151 not out his best, giving early evidence of his taste for Australian bowling (his average against Australia is currently 56.00). A call to full colours was only a matter of time, and while he waited he had an extremely successful Under-19 tour of England. He began the "Test" series with a century on a blissful Taunton pitch.

As Laxman grew to full strength, tall and elegant, and big scores became more frequent, his batting acquired a captivating splendour. His driving possessed a Dexterian majesty and his flicked drive through mid-wicket stirred the senses. He was capped in 1996-97, a winter in which India played home-and-away series against South Africa, followed by five Tests in the West Indies. Laxman played eight Tests during this span and passed 50 three times. Indeed, he was given a fair run, but without being allowed a secure place in the batting order; in the Caribbean, he found himself opening, a role for which he had no taste.

His Test career went into a trough and might well have ended on the Australian tour of 1999-2000, when India were whitewashed 0–3. But in his final innings there, at Sydney, he hit a sumptuous 167 out of a total of 261, from only 198 balls. It was, one thought at the time, the sort of innings a batsman plays once in a lifetime. And so it seemed it would be when he was dropped after India's Mumbai defeat by South Africa not quite two months later. His volume of runs in that season's Ranji Trophy, a record 1,415 with a record eight hundreds, might almost have been mocking him. In Hyderabad's semi-final against Karnataka, he made 353, his fourth score at the time over 200.

Laxman achieved little in his one Test when Zimbabwe visited, or for that matter in the First Test against the Australians. That Sydney century seemed a long time ago. But promoted to his favourite No. 3 position for the second innings at Eden Gardens, he bettered it handsomely, sustaining his brilliance for ten and a half hours, during which he faced 452 balls. Half-centuries in both innings of the final Test helped India take the series 2–1; they also took his aggregate for the three matches to 503 at an average of 83.83. Medicine would just have to wait a while longer for V. V. S. Laxman. – DICKY RUTNAGUR.

DAMIEN MARTYN

Of all the Australian cricketers who swatted aside England during last summer's Ashes series, Damien Martyn was easily the least well known. Others, such as the Waugh twins, Shane Warne and Glenn McGrath, had been plying their golden standards of Pommie torture for years. Yet Martyn, and in particular his graceful and uncluttered strokeplay, seemed to arrive almost without warning.

To be bracketed among such elite company is the apogee of praise, even in Australia. It may have helped that England's bowlers were rarely at their best as a unit, but Martyn made the most of his opportunities, scoring his maiden Test century in the opening match at Edgbaston and adding another in Australia's shock defeat at Headingley. In a rubber Australia took 4–1, he finished the series with 382 runs and an average of 76.40. Yet impressive as his figures were, and they were pretty eye-catching, it was Martyn's back-foot cover-driving that was the sight of the summer, each stroke a perfect marriage of minimal effort and maximum timing. Because he was brought up on the true, high-bouncing pitches of Perth, his instinct is to stand tall and hit through the line, an action that, despite a distinct lack of footwork, brought him sundry boundaries in the arc between cover and mid-off.

This facility, as well as his impressive nose for a partnership, gave many in England the impression that here was a fully fledged batsman arrived from thin air. In some senses, the perception was accurate. Although he was not some strutting stripling a year out of school – though the description could have applied nine years previously, when Martyn made his Test debut at Brisbane against West Indies – the player himself had been reborn, following a turbulent period when he almost gave up the professional game for good.

DAMIEN RICHARD MARTYN was born in Darwin on October 21, 1971. A tropical city, Darwin is a cricketing backwater. But if a life of obscurity beckoned, Cyclone Tracy, which flattened Darwin on Christmas Eve 1974, killing more than 60 people, changed all that. Surviving the five-hour ordeal by sheltering under the dining table, the Martyn family were later evacuated by military plane to Perth where the change of scenery, if at first daunting (the family had lost everything), proved a godsend for young Damien.

Glorying in its isolation, Perth has always tried that little bit harder to impress the rest of Australia, particularly on the cricket field. Its grade competition is felt to be the strongest club competition in the world – a weekend ritual of cut-throat cricket, strong language and even stronger drink. For the teenage Martyn, who felt stifled by the pressed shorts and long sock-culture of Girrawheen High School, it was Elysium, and it wasn't long before he progressed through its ranks to make his first-class debut for Western Australia.

Strong off back foot and front, he quickly developed into the most promising batsman of his generation, with a bullet-proof cockiness to go with it. Australia does not tend to suppress confidence, however misplaced, and Martyn, who had already captained Australia Under-19, suddenly found himself part of the much vaunted Academy, alongside Warne and Justin Langer. A year after leaving, he made his Test debut at the age of 21, and a long and glittering career for state and country looked certain. The portents proved inaccurate, and instead of sailing past the 50-cap mark, like his close friend Warne, Martyn had played just 16 Tests up to the end of the 2001 Ashes series. If that spread is not uncommon in England, where players tend to mature much later, it is a rarity in Australia, where wasted talent is scorned and rarely given a second chance.

The reasons for his lack of progress were mainly self-inflicted, and Martyn freely admits to squandering his early years upon the altar of fast living and an even faster mouth. It was just such a combination that led to a brawl in a Brighton nightclub during the 1993 Ashes tour, an incident that saw him sport a shiner for the rest of the trip. "Playing for Australia at 21, you can go where you want and you get looked after, so there are a lot of late nights," he admitted. "The excesses got worse and worse and you can't get away with that in sport. It took me three or four years to wake up to that fact."

Racy lifestyles will always be correlated with performance, and in the Second Test against South Africa, early in 1994, his critics got their chance to establish a link. It was the middle match of the series and Australia needed 117 to go one up. Instead a parochial Sydney crowd saw them lose by five runs. Martyn's role in the failure was centre stage. Having scored just six runs in an hour and three-quarters, he succumbed to the pressure, lofting a loose drive to cover with just seven runs needed. As mistakes go it was a howler, but the six-year snub that followed cannot have been entirely due to the stroke. He had, after all, scored 59 in the first innings.

A period of self-pity began, and it was during this interval, as his form for Western Australia declined, that he set up a travel company and almost quit the game. Fortunately, a double-century against Tasmania in March 1996, along with the careful cajolings of Wayne Clark, then the Western Australia coach and now in charge at Yorkshire, rekindled his desire. When he did get picked again for Australia, for the 1999-2000 series against New Zealand, his mother had to rummage around in the attic to find his baggy green cap. On the form he showed last summer, it should be some time before it goes back there. – DEREK PRINGLE.

PART TWO: THE PLAYERS

TEST CRICKETERS

Full list from 1877 to September 2, 2001

These lists have been compiled on a home and abroad basis, appearances abroad being printed in *italics*.

Abbreviations. E: England. A: Australia. SA: South Africa. WI: West Indies. NZ: New Zealand. In: India. P: Pakistan. SL: Sri Lanka. Z: Zimbabwe. B: Bangladesh.

All appearances are placed in this order of seniority. Hence, any England cricketer playing against Australia in England has that achievement recorded first and the remainder of his appearances at home (if any) set down before passing to matches abroad. The figures immediately following each name represent the total number of appearances in *all* Tests.

The Test played between Pakistan and Bangladesh in August 2001 has been included.

Where the season embraces two different years, the first year is given; i.e. 1876 indicates 1876-77.

ENGLAND

Number of Test cricketers: 607

Abel, R. 13: v A 1888 (3) 1896 (3) 1902 (2); *v A 1891 (3); v SA 1888 (2)*

Absolom, C. A. 1: *v A 1878*

Adams, C. J. 5: *v SA 1999 (5)*

Afzaal, U. 3: v A 2001 (3)

Agnew, J. P. 3: v A 1985 (1); v WI 1984 (1); v SL 1984 (1)

Allen, D. A. 39: v A 1961 (4) 1964 (1); v SA 1960 (2); v WI 1963 (2) 1966 (1); v P 1962 (4); *v A 1962 (1) 1965 (4); v SA 1964 (4); v WI 1959 (5); v NZ 1965 (3); v In 1961 (5); v P 1961 (3)*

Allen, G. O. B. 25: v A 1930 (1) 1934 (2); v WI 1933 (1); v NZ 1931 (3); v In 1936 (3); *v A 1932 (5) 1936 (5); v WI 1947 (3); v NZ 1932 (2)*

Allom, M. J. C. 5: *v SA 1930 (1); v NZ 1929 (4)*

Allott, P. J. W. 13: v A 1981 (1) 1985 (4); v WI 1984 (3); v In 1982 (2); v SL 1984 (1); *v In 1981 (1); v SL 1981 (1)*

Ames, L. E. G. 47: v A 1934 (5) 1938 (2); v SA 1929 (1) 1935 (4); v WI 1933 (3); v NZ 1931 (3) 1937 (3); v In 1932 (1); *v A 1932 (5) 1936 (5); v SA 1938 (5); v WI 1929 (4) 1934 (4); v NZ 1932 (2)*

Amiss, D. L. 50: v A 1968 (1) 1975 (2) 1977 (2); v WI 1966 (1) 1973 (3) 1976 (1); v NZ 1973 (3); v In 1967 (2) 1971 (1) 1974 (3); v P 1967 (1) 1971 (3) 1974 (3); *v A 1974 (5) 1976 (1); v WI 1973 (5); v NZ 1974 (2); v In 1972 (3) 1976 (5); v P 1972 (3)*

Andrew, K. V. 2: v WI 1963 (1); *v A 1954 (1)*

Appleyard, R. 9: v A 1956 (1); v SA 1955 (1); v P 1954 (1); *v A 1954 (4); v NZ 1954 (2)*

Archer, A. G. 1: *v SA 1898*

Armitage, T. 2: *v A 1876 (2)*

Arnold, E. G. 10: v A 1905 (4); v SA 1907 (2); *v A 1903 (4)*

Arnold, G. G. 34: v A 1972 (3) 1975 (1); v WI 1973 (3); v NZ 1969 (1) 1973 (3); v In 1974 (2); v P 1967 (2) 1974 (3); *v A 1974 (4); v WI 1973 (3); v NZ 1974 (2); v In 1972 (4); v P 1972 (3)*

Arnold, J. 1: v NZ 1931

Astill, W. E. 9: *v SA 1927 (5); v WI 1929 (4)*

Atherton, M. A. 115: v A 1989 (2) 1993 (6) 1997 (6) 2001 (5); v SA 1994 (3) 1998 (5); v WI 1991 (5) 1995 (6) 2000 (5); v NZ 1990 (3) 1994 (3) 1999 (2); v In 1990 (3) 1996 (3); v P 1992 (3) 1996 (3) 2001 (2); v Z 2000 (2); *v A 1990 (5) 1994 (5) 1998 (4); v SA 1995 (5) 1999 (5); v WI 1993 (5) 1997 (6); v NZ 1996 (3); v In 1992 (1); v P 2000 (3); v SL 1992 (1) 2000 (3); v Z 1996 (2)*

Athey, C. W. J. 23: v A 1980 (1); v WI 1988 (1); v NZ 1986 (3); v In 1986 (2); v P 1987 (4); *v A 1986 (5) 1987 (1); v WI 1980 (2); v NZ 1987 (1); v P 1987 (3)*

Attewell, W. 10: v A 1890 (1); *v A 1884 (5) 1887 (1) 1891 (3)*

Bailey, R. J. 4: v WI 1988 (1); *v WI 1989 (3)*

Bailey, T. E. 61: v A 1953 (5) 1956 (4); v SA 1951 (2) 1955 (5); v WI 1950 (2) 1957 (4); v NZ 1949 (4) 1958 (4); v P 1954 (3); *v A 1950 (4) 1954 (5) 1958 (5); v SA 1956 (5); v WI 1953 (5); v NZ 1950 (2) 1954 (2)*

Bairstow, D. L. 4: v A 1980 (1); v WI 1980 (1); v In 1979 (1); *v WI 1980 (1)*

Bakewell, A. H. 6: v SA 1935 (2); v WI 1933 (1); v NZ 1931 (2); *v In 1933 (1)*

Balderstone, J. C. 2: v WI 1976 (2)

Barber, R. W. 28: v A 1964 (1) 1968 (1); v SA 1960 (1) 1965 (3); v WI 1966 (2); v NZ 1965 (3); *v A 1965 (5); v SA 1964 (4); v In 1961 (5); v P 1961 (3)*

Barber, W. 2: v SA 1935 (2)

Barlow, G. D. 3: v A 1977 (1); *v In 1976 (2)*

Barlow, R. G. 17: v A 1882 (1) 1884 (3) 1886 (3); *v A 1881 (4) 1882 (4) 1886 (2)*

Barnes, S. F. 27: v A 1902 (1) 1909 (3) 1912 (3); v SA 1912 (3); *v A 1901 (3) 1907 (5) 1911 (5); v SA 1913 (4)*

Barnes, W. 21: v A 1880 (1) 1882 (1) 1884 (2) 1886 (2) 1888 (3) 1890 (2); *v A 1882 (4) 1884 (5) 1886 (1)*

Barnett, C. J. 20: v A 1938 (3) 1948 (1); v SA 1947 (3); v WI 1933 (1); v NZ 1937 (3); v In 1936 (1); *v A 1936 (5); v In 1933 (3)*

Barnett, K. J. 4: v A 1989 (3); v SL 1988 (1)

Barratt, F. 5: v SA 1929 (1); *v NZ 1929 (4)*

Barrington, K. F. 82: v A 1961 (5) 1964 (5) 1968 (3); v SA 1955 (2) 1960 (4) 1965 (3); v WI 1963 (5) 1966 (2); v NZ 1965 (2); v In 1959 (5) 1967 (3); v P 1962 (4) 1967 (3); *v A 1962 (5) 1965 (5); v SA 1964 (5); v WI 1959 (5) 1967 (5); v NZ 1962 (3); v In 1961 (5) 1963 (1); v P 1961 (2)*

Barton, V. A. 1: *v SA 1891*

Bates, W. 15: *v A 1881 (4) 1882 (4) 1884 (5) 1886 (2)*

Bean, G. 3: *v A 1891 (3)*

Bedser, A. V. 51: v A 1948 (5) 1953 (5); v SA 1947 (2) 1951 (5) 1955 (1); v WI 1950 (3); v NZ 1949 (2); v In 1946 (3) 1952 (4); v P 1954 (2); *v A 1946 (5) 1950 (5) 1954 (1); v SA 1948 (5); v NZ 1946 (1) 1950 (2)*

Benjamin, J. E. 1: v SA 1994

Benson, M. R. 1: v In 1986

Berry, R. 2: v WI 1950 (2)

Bicknell, M. P. 2: v A 1993 (2)

Binks, J. G. 2: *v In 1963 (2)*

Bird, M. C. 10: *v SA 1909 (5) 1913 (5)*

Birkenshaw, J. 5: *v WI 1973 (2); v In 1972 (2); v P 1972 (1)*

Blakey, R. J. 2: *v In 1992 (2)*

Bligh, Hon. I. F. W. 4: *v A 1882 (4)*

Blythe, C. 19: v A 1905 (1) 1909 (2); v SA 1907 (3); *v A 1901 (5) 1907 (1); v SA 1905 (5) 1909 (2)*

Board, J. H. 6: *v SA 1898 (2) 1905 (4)*

Bolus, J. B. 7: v WI 1963 (2); *v In 1963 (5)*

Booth, M. W. 2: *v SA 1913 (2)*

Bosanquet, B. J. T. 7: v A 1905 (3); *v A 1903 (4)*

Botham, I. T. 102: v A 1977 (2) 1980 (1) 1981 (6) 1985 (6) 1989 (3); v WI 1980 (5) 1984 (5) 1991 (1); v NZ 1978 (3) 1983 (4) 1986 (1); v In 1979 (4) 1982 (3); v P 1978 (3) 1982 (3) 1987 (5) 1992 (2); v SL 1984 (1) 1991 (1); *v A 1978 (6) 1979 (3) 1982 (5) 1986 (4); v WI 1980 (4) 1985 (5); v NZ 1977 (3) 1983 (3) 1991 (1); v In 1979 (1) 1981 (6); v P 1983 (1); v SL 1981 (1)*

Bowden, M. P. 2: *v SA 1888 (2)*

Bowes, W. E. 15: v A 1934 (3) 1938 (2); v SA 1935 (4); v WI 1939 (2); v In 1932 (1) 1946 (1); *v A 1932 (1); v NZ 1932 (1)*

Bowley, E. H. 5: v SA 1929 (2); *v NZ 1929 (3)*

Boycott, G. 108: v A 1964 (4) 1968 (3) 1972 (2) 1977 (3) 1980 (1) 1981 (6); v SA 1965 (2); v WI 1966 (4) 1969 (3) 1973 (3) 1980 (5); v NZ 1965 (2) 1969 (3) 1973 (3) 1978 (2); v In 1967 (2) 1971 (1) 1974 (1) 1979 (4); v P 1967 (1) 1971 (2); *v A 1965 (5) 1970 (5) 1978 (6) 1979 (3); v SA 1964 (5); v WI 1967 (5) 1973 (5) 1980 (4); v NZ 1965 (2) 1977 (3); v In 1979 (1) 1981 (4); v P 1977 (3)*

Bradley, W. M. 2: v A 1899 (2)
Braund, L. C. 23: v A 1902 (5); v SA 1907 (3); *v A 1901 (5) 1903 (5) 1907 (5)*
Brearley, J. M. 39: v A 1977 (5) 1981 (4); v WI 1976 (2); v NZ 1978 (3); v In 1979 (4); v P 1978 (3); *v A 1976 (1) 1978 (6) 1979 (3); v In 1976 (5) 1979 (1); v P 1977 (2)*
Brearley, W. 4: v A 1905 (2) 1909 (1); v SA 1912 (1)
Brennan, D. V. 2: v SA 1951 (2)
Briggs, John 33: v A 1886 (3) 1888 (3) 1893 (2) 1896 (1) 1899 (1); *v A 1884 (5) 1886 (2) 1887 (1) 1891 (3) 1894 (5) 1897 (5); v SA 1888 (2)*
Broad, B. C. 25: v A 1989 (2); v WI 1984 (4) 1988 (2); v P 1987 (4); v SL 1984 (1); *v A 1986 (5) 1987 (1); v NZ 1987 (3); v P 1987 (3)*
Brockwell, W. 7: v A 1893 (1) 1899 (1); *v A 1894 (5)*
Bromley-Davenport, H. R. 4: *v SA 1895 (3) 1898 (1)*
Brookes, D. 1: *v WI 1947*
Brown, A. 2: *v In 1961 (1); v P 1961 (1)*
Brown, D. J. 26: v A 1968 (4); v SA 1965 (2); v WI 1966 (1) 1969 (3); v NZ 1969 (1); v In 1967 (2): *v A 1965 (4); v WI 1967 (4); v NZ 1965 (2); v P 1968 (3)*
Brown, F. R. 22: v A 1953 (1); v SA 1951 (5); v WI 1950 (1); v NZ 1931 (2) 1937 (1) 1949 (2); v In 1932 (1); *v A 1950 (5); v NZ 1932 (2) 1950 (2)*
Brown, G. 7: v A 1921 (3); *v SA 1922 (4)*
Brown, J. T. 8: v A 1896 (2) 1899 (1); *v A 1894 (5)*
Brown, S. J. E. 1: v P 1996
Buckenham, C. P. 4: *v SA 1909 (4)*
Butcher, A. R. 1: v In 1979
Butcher, M. A. 32: v A 1997 (5) 2001 (5); v SA 1998 (3); v NZ 1999 (3); v SL 1998 (1); *v A 1998 (5); v SA 1999 (5); v WI 1997 (5)*
Butcher, R. O. 3: *v WI 1980 (3)*
Butler, H. J. 2: v SA 1947 (1); *v WI 1947 (1)*
Butt, H. R. 3: *v SA 1895 (3)*

Caddick, A. R. 50: v A 1993 (4) 1997 (5) 2001 (5); v WI 2000 (5); v NZ 1999 (4); v P 1996 (1) 2001 (2); v Z 2000 (2); *v SA 1999 (5); v WI 1993 (4) 1997 (5); v NZ 1996 (2); v P 2000 (3); v SL 2000 (3)*
Calthorpe, Hon. F. S. G. 4: *v WI 1929 (4)*
Capel, D. J. 15: v A 1989 (1); v WI 1988 (2); v P 1987 (1); *v A 1987 (1); v WI 1989 (4); v NZ 1987 (3); v P 1987 (3)*
Carr, A. W. 11: v A 1926 (4); v SA 1929 (2); *v SA 1922 (5)*
Carr, D. B. 2: *v In 1951 (2)*
Carr, D. W. 1: v A 1909
Cartwright, T. W. 5: v A 1964 (2); v SA 1965 (1); v NZ 1965 (1); *v SA 1964 (1)*
Chapman, A. P. F. 26: v A 1926 (4) 1930 (4); v SA 1924 (2); v WI 1928 (3); *v A 1924 (4) 1928 (4); v SA 1930 (5)*
Charlwood, H. R. J. 2: *v A 1876 (2)*
Chatterton, W. 1: *v SA 1891*
Childs, J. H. 2: v WI 1988 (2)
Christopherson, S. 1: v A 1884
Clark, E. W. 8: v A 1934 (2); v SA 1929 (1); v WI 1933 (2); *v In 1933 (3)*
Clay, J. C. 1: v SA 1935
Close, D. B. 22: v A 1961 (1); v SA 1955 (1); v WI 1957 (2) 1963 (5) 1966 (1) 1976 (3); v NZ 1949 (1); v In 1959 (1) 1967 (3); v P 1967 (3); *v A 1950 (1)*
Coldwell, L. J. 7: v A 1964 (2); v P 1962 (2); *v A 1962 (2); v NZ 1962 (1)*
Compton, D. C. S. 78: v A 1938 (4) 1948 (5) 1953 (5) 1956 (1); v SA 1947 (5) 1951 (4) 1955 (5); v WI 1939 (3) 1950 (1); v NZ 1937 (1) 1949 (4); v In 1946 (3) 1952 (2); v P 1954 (4); *v A 1946 (5) 1950 (4) 1954 (4); v SA 1948 (5) 1956 (5); v WI 1953 (5); v NZ 1946 (1) 1950 (2)*
Cook, C. 1: v SA 1947
Cook, G. 7: v In 1982 (3); *v A 1982 (3); v SL 1981 (1)*
Cook, N. G. B. 15: v A 1989 (3); v WI 1984 (3); v NZ 1983 (2); *v NZ 1983 (1); v P 1983 (3) 1987 (3)*
Cope, G. A. 3: *v P 1977 (3)*
Copson, W. H. 3: v SA 1947 (1); v WI 1939 (2)
Cork, D. G. 34: v A 2001 (1); v SA 1998 (5); v WI 1995 (5) 2000 (4); v In 1996 (3); v P 1996 (3) 2001 (2); v SL 1998 (1); *v A 1998 (2); v SA 1995 (5); v NZ 1996 (3)*

Cornford, W. L. 4: *v NZ 1929 (4)*
Cottam, R. M. H. 4: *v In 1972 (2); v P 1968 (2)*
Coventry, Hon. C. J. 2: *v SA 1888 (2)*
Cowans, N. G. 19: v A 1985 (1); v WI 1984 (1); v NZ 1983 (4); *v A 1982 (4); v NZ 1983 (2); v In 1984 (5); v P 1983 (2)*
Cowdrey, C. S. 6: v WI 1988 (1); *v In 1984 (5)*
Cowdrey, M. C. 114: v A 1956 (5) 1961 (4) 1964 (3) 1968 (4); v SA 1955 (1) 1960 (5) 1965 (3); v WI 1957 (5) 1963 (2) 1966 (4); v NZ 1958 (4) 1965 (3); v In 1959 (5); v P 1962 (4) 1967 (2) 1971 (1); *v A 1954 (5) 1958 (5) 1962 (5) 1965 (4) 1970 (3) 1974 (5); v SA 1956 (5); v WI 1959 (5) 1967 (5); v NZ 1954 (2) 1958 (2) 1962 (3) 1965 (3) 1970 (1); v In 1963 (3); v P 1968 (3)*
Coxon, A. 1: v A 1948
Cranston, J. 1: v A 1890
Cranston, K. 8: v A 1948 (1); v SA 1947 (3); *v WI 1947 (4)*
Crapp, J. F. 7: v A 1948 (3); *v SA 1948 (4)*
Crawford, J. N. 12: v SA 1907 (2); *v A 1907 (5); v SA 1905 (5)*
Crawley, J. P. 29: v A 1997 (5); v SA 1994 (3); v WI 1995 (3); v P 1996 (2); v SL 1998 (1); *v A 1994 (3) 1998 (3); v SA 1995 (1); v WI 1997 (3); v NZ 1996 (3); v Z 1996 (2)*
Croft, R. D. B. 21: v A 1997 (5) 2001 (1); v SA 1998 (3); v WI 2000 (2); v P 1996 (1); *v A 1998 (1); v WI 1997 (1); v NZ 1996 (2); v SL 2000 (3); v Z 1996 (2)*
Curtis, T. S. 5: v A 1989 (3); v WI 1988 (2)
Cuttell, W. R. 2: *v SA 1898 (2)*

Dawson, E. W. 5: *v SA 1927 (1); v NZ 1929 (4)*
Dean, H. 3: v A 1912 (2); v SA 1912 (1)
DeFreitas, P. A. J. 44: v A 1989 (1) 1993 (1); v SA 1994 (3); v WI 1988 (3) 1991 (5) 1995 (1); v NZ 1990 (2) 1994 (3); v P 1987 (1) 1992 (2); v SL 1991 (1); *v A 1986 (4) 1990 (3) 1994 (4); v WI 1989 (2); v NZ 1987 (2) 1991 (3); v In 1992 (1); v P 1987 (2)*
Denness, M. H. 28: v A 1975 (1); v NZ 1969 (1); v In 1974 (3); v P 1974 (3); *v A 1974 (5); v WI 1973 (5); v NZ 1974 (2); v In 1972 (5); v P 1972 (3)*
Denton, D. 11: v A 1905 (1); *v SA 1905 (5) 1909 (5)*
Dewes, J. G. 5: v A 1948 (1); v WI 1950 (2); *v A 1950 (2)*
Dexter, E. R. 62: v A 1961 (5) 1964 (5) 1968 (2); v SA 1960 (5); v WI 1963 (5); v NZ 1958 (1) 1965 (2); v In 1959 (2); v P 1962 (5); *v A 1958 (2) 1962 (5); v SA 1964 (5); v WI 1959 (5); v NZ 1958 (2) 1962 (3); v In 1961 (5); v P 1961 (3)*
Dilley, G. R. 41: v A 1981 (3) 1989 (2); v WI 1980 (3) 1988 (4); v NZ 1983 (1) 1986 (2); v In 1986 (2); v P 1987 (4); *v A 1979 (2) 1986 (4) 1987 (1); v WI 1980 (4); v NZ 1987 (3); v In 1981 (4); v P 1983 (1) 1987 (1)*
Dipper, A. E. 1: v A 1921
Doggart, G. H. G. 2: v WI 1950 (2)
D'Oliveira, B. L. 44: v A 1968 (2) 1972 (5); v WI 1966 (4) 1969 (3); v NZ 1969 (3); v In 1967 (2) 1971 (3); v P 1967 (3) 1971 (3); *v A 1970 (6); v WI 1967 (5); v NZ 1970 (2); v P 1968 (3)*
Dollery, H. E. 4: v A 1948 (2); v SA 1947 (1); v WI 1950 (1)
Dolphin, A. 1: *v A 1920*
Douglas, J. W. H. T. 23: v A 1912 (1) 1921 (5); v SA 1924 (1); *v A 1911 (5) 1920 (5) 1924 (1); v SA 1913 (5)*
Downton, P. R. 30: v A 1981 (1) 1985 (6); v WI 1984 (5) 1988 (3); v In 1986 (1); v SL 1984 (1); *v WI 1980 (3) 1985 (5); v In 1984 (5)*
Druce, N. F. 5: *v A 1897 (5)*
Ducat, A. 1: v A 1921
Duckworth, G. 24: v A 1930 (5); v SA 1924 (1) 1929 (4) 1935 (1); v WI 1928 (1); v In 1936 (3); *v A 1928 (5); v SA 1930 (3); v NZ 1932 (1)*
Duleepsinhji, K. S. 12: v A 1930 (4); v SA 1929 (1); v NZ 1931 (3); *v NZ 1929 (4)*
Durston, F. J. 1: v A 1921

Ealham, M. A. 8: v A 1997 (4); v SA 1998 (2); v In 1996 (1); v P 1996 (1)
Edmonds, P. H. 51: v A 1975 (2) 1985 (5); v NZ 1978 (3) 1983 (2) 1986 (3); v In 1979 (4) 1982 (3) 1986 (2); v P 1978 (3) 1987 (5); *v A 1978 (1) 1986 (5); v WI 1985 (3); v NZ 1977 (3); v In 1984 (5); v P 1977 (2)*

Edrich, J. H. 77: v A 1964 (3) 1968 (5) 1972 (5) 1975 (4); v SA 1965 (1); v WI 1963 (3) 1966 (1) 1969 (3) 1976 (2); v NZ 1965 (1) 1969 (3); v In 1967 (2) 1971 (3) 1974 (3); v P 1971 (3) 1974 (3); *v A 1965 (5) 1970 (6) 1974 (4); v WI 1967 (5); v NZ 1965 (3) 1970 (2) 1974 (2); v In 1963 (2); v P 1968 (3)*

Edrich, W. J. 39: v A 1938 (4) 1948 (5) 1953 (3); v SA 1947 (4); v WI 1950 (2); v NZ 1949 (4); v In 1946 (1); v P 1954 (1); *v A 1946 (5) 1954 (4); v SA 1938 (5); v NZ 1946 (1)*

Elliott, H. 4: v WI 1928 (1); *v SA 1927 (1); v In 1933 (2)*

Ellison, R. M. 11: v A 1985 (2); v WI 1984 (1); v In 1986 (1); v SL 1984 (1); *v WI 1985 (3); v In 1984 (3)*

Emburey, J. E. 64: v A 1980 (1) 1981 (4) 1985 (6) 1989 (3) 1993 (1); v WI 1980 (3) 1988 (3) 1995 (1); v NZ 1978 (1) 1986 (2); v In 1986 (3); v P 1987 (4); v SL 1988 (1); *v A 1978 (4) 1986 (5) 1987 (1); v WI 1980 (4) 1985 (4); v NZ 1987 (3); v In 1979 (1) 1981 (3) 1992 (1); v P 1987 (3); v SL 1981 (1) 1992 (1)*

Emmett, G. M. 1: v A 1948

Emmett, T. 7: *v A 1876 (2) 1878 (1) 1881 (4)*

Evans, A. J. 1: v A 1921

Evans, T. G. 91: v A 1948 (5) 1953 (5) 1956 (5); v SA 1947 (5) 1951 (3) 1955 (3); v WI 1950 (3) 1957 (5); v NZ 1949 (4) 1958 (5); v In 1946 (1) 1952 (4) 1959 (2); v P 1954 (4); *v A 1946 (4) 1950 (5) 1954 (4) 1958 (3); v SA 1948 (3) 1956 (5); v WI 1947 (4) 1953 (4); v NZ 1946 (1) 1950 (2) 1954 (2)*

Fagg, A. E. 5: v WI 1939 (1); v In 1936 (2); *v A 1936 (2)*

Fairbrother, N. H. 10: v NZ 1990 (3); v P 1987 (1); *v NZ 1987 (2); v In 1992 (2); v P 1987 (1); v SL 1992 (1)*

Fane, F. L. 14: *v A 1907 (4); v SA 1905 (5) 1909 (5)*

Farnes, K. 15: v A 1934 (2) 1938 (4); *v A 1936 (2); v SA 1938 (5); v WI 1934 (2)*

Farrimond, W. 4: v SA 1935 (1); *v SA 1930 (2); v WI 1934 (1)*

Fender, P. G. H. 13: v A 1921 (2); v SA 1924 (2) 1929 (1); *v A 1920 (3); v SA 1922 (5)*

Ferris, J. J. 1: *v SA 1891*

Fielder, A. 6: *v A 1903 (2) 1907 (4)*

Fishlock, L. B. 4: v In 1936 (2) 1946 (1); *v A 1946 (1)*

Flavell, J. A. 4: v A 1961 (2) 1964 (2)

Fletcher, K. W. R. 59: v A 1968 (1) 1972 (1) 1975 (2); v WI 1973 (3); v NZ 1969 (2) 1973 (3); v In 1971 (2) 1974 (3); v P 1974 (3); *v A 1970 (5) 1974 (5) 1976 (1); v WI 1973 (4); v NZ 1970 (1) 1974 (2); v In 1972 (5) 1976 (3) 1981 (6); v P 1968 (3) 1972 (3); v SL 1981 (1)*

Flintoff, A. 9: v SA 1998 (2); v WI 2000 (1); v Z 2000 (2); *v SA 1999 (4)*

Flowers, W. 8: v A 1893 (1); *v A 1884 (5) 1886 (2)*

Ford, F. G. J. 5: *v A 1894 (5)*

Foster, F. R. 11: v A 1912 (3); v SA 1912 (3); *v A 1911 (5)*

Foster, N. A. 29: v A 1985 (1) 1989 (3) 1993 (1); v WI 1984 (1) 1988 (2); v NZ 1983 (1) 1986 (1); v In 1986 (1); v P 1987 (5); v SL 1988 (1); *v A 1987 (1); v WI 1985 (3); v NZ 1983 (2); v In 1984 (2); v P 1983 (2) 1987 (2)*

Foster, R. E. 8: v SA 1907 (3); *v A 1903 (5)*

Fothergill, A. J. 2: *v SA 1888 (2)*

Fowler, G. 21: v WI 1984 (5); v NZ 1983 (2); v P 1982 (1); v SL 1984 (1); *v A 1982 (3); v NZ 1983 (2); v In 1984 (5); v P 1983 (2)*

Fraser, A. R. C. 46: v A 1989 (3) 1993 (1); v SA 1994 (2) 1998 (5); v WI 1995 (5); v NZ 1994 (3); v In 1990 (3); v SL 1998 (1); *v A 1990 (3) 1994 (3) 1998 (2); v SA 1995 (3); v WI 1989 (2) 1993 (4) 1997 (6)*

Freeman, A. P. 12: v SA 1929 (3); v WI 1928 (3); *v A 1924 (2); v SA 1927 (4)*

French, B. N. 16: v NZ 1986 (3); v In 1986 (2); v P 1987 (4); *v A 1987 (1); v NZ 1987 (3); v P 1987 (3)*

Fry, C. B. 26: v A 1899 (5) 1902 (3) 1905 (4) 1909 (3) 1912 (3); v SA 1907 (3) 1912 (3); *v SA 1895 (2)*

Gallian, J. E. R. 3: v WI 1995 (2); *v SA 1995 (1)*

Gatting, M. W. 79: v A 1980 (1) 1981 (6) 1985 (6) 1989 (1) 1993 (2); v WI 1980 (4) 1984 (1) 1988 (2); v NZ 1983 (2) 1986 (3); v In 1986 (3); v P 1982 (3) 1987 (5); *v A 1986 (5) 1987 (1) 1994 (5); v WI 1980 (1) 1985 (1); v NZ 1977 (1) 1983 (2) 1987 (3); v In 1981 (5) 1984 (5) 1992 (3); v P 1977 (1) 1983 (3) 1987 (3); v SL 1992 (1)*

Gay, L. H. 1: *v A 1894*

Geary, G. 14: v A 1926 (2) 1930 (1) 1934 (2); v SA 1924 (1) 1929 (2); *v A 1928 (4); v SA 1927(2)*
Gibb, P. A. 8: v In 1946 (2); *v A 1946 (1); v SA 1938 (5)*
Giddins, E. S. H. 4: v WI 2000 (1); v NZ 1999 (1); v Z 2000 (2)
Gifford, N. 15: v A 1964 (2) 1972 (3); v NZ 1973 (2); v In 1971 (2); v P 1971 (2); *v In 1972 (2); v P 1972 (2)*
Giles, A. F. 8: v A 2001 (1); v SA 1998 (1); *v P 2000 (3); v SL 2000 (3)*
Gilligan, A. E. R. 11: v SA 1924 (4); *v A 1924 (5); v SA 1922 (2)*
Gilligan, A. H. H. 4: *v NZ 1929 (4)*
Gimblett, H. 3: v WI 1939 (1); v In 1936 (2)
Gladwin, C. 8: v SA 1947 (2); v NZ 1949 (1); *v SA 1948 (5)*
Goddard, T. W. 8: v A 1930 (1); v WI 1939 (2); v NZ 1937 (2); *v SA 1938 (3)*
Gooch, G. A. 118: v A 1975 (2) 1980 (1) 1981 (5) 1985 (6) 1989 (5) 1993 (6); v SA 1994 (3); v WI 1980 (5) 1988 (5) 1991 (5); v NZ 1978 (3) 1986 (3) 1990 (3) 1994 (3); v In 1979 (4) 1986 (3) 1990 (3); v P 1978 (2) 1992 (5); v SL 1988 (1) 1991 (1); *v A 1978 (6) 1979 (2) 1990 (4) 1994 (5); v WI 1980 (4) 1985 (5) 1989 (2); v NZ 1991 (3); v In 1979 (1) 1981 (6) 1992 (2); v P 1987 (3); v SL 1981 (1)*
Gough, D. 56: v A 1997 (4) 2001 (5); v SA 1994 (3) 1998 (4); v WI 1995 (3) 2000 (5); v NZ 1994 (1); v P 2001 (2); v SL 1998 (1); v Z 2000 (2); *v A 1994 (3) 1998 (5); v SA 1995 (2) 1999 (5); v NZ 1996 (3); v P 2000 (3); v SL 2000 (3); v Z 1996 (2)*
Gover, A. R. 4: v NZ 1937 (2); v In 1936 (1) 1946 (1)
Gower, D. I. 117: v A 1980 (1) 1981 (5) 1985 (6) 1989 (6); v WI 1980 (1) 1984 (5) 1988 (4); v NZ 1978 (3) 1983 (4) 1986 (3); v In 1979 (4) 1982 (3) 1986 (2) 1990 (3); v P 1978 (3) 1982 (3) 1987 (5) 1992 (3); v SL 1984 (1); *v A 1978 (6) 1979 (3) 1982 (5) 1986 (5) 1990 (5); v WI 1980 (4) 1985 (5); v NZ 1983 (3); v In 1979 (1) 1981 (6) 1984 (5); v P 1983 (3); v SL 1981 (1)*
Grace, E. M. 1: v A 1880
Grace, G. F. 1: v A 1880
Grace, W. G. 22: v A 1880 (1) 1882 (1) 1884 (3) 1886 (3) 1888 (3) 1890 (2) 1893 (2) 1896 (3) 1899 (1); *v A 1891 (3)*
Graveney, T. W. 79: v A 1953 (5) 1956 (2) 1968 (5); v SA 1951 (1) 1955 (5); v WI 1957 (4) 1966 (4) 1969 (1); v NZ 1958 (4); v In 1952 (4) 1967 (3); v P 1954 (3) 1962 (4) 1967 (3); *v A 1954 (2) 1958 (5) 1962 (3); v WI 1953 (5) 1967 (5); v NZ 1954 (2) 1958 (2); v In 1951 (4); v P 1968 (3)*
Greenhough, T. 4: v SA 1960 (1); v In 1959 (3)
Greenwood, A. 2: *v A 1876 (2)*
Greig, A. W. 58: v A 1972 (5) 1975 (4) 1977 (5); v WI 1973 (3) 1976 (5); v NZ 1973 (3); v In 1974 (3); v P 1974 (3); *v A 1974 (6) 1976 (1); v WI 1973 (5); v NZ 1974 (2); v In 1972 (5) 1976 (5); v P 1972 (3)*
Greig, I. A. 2: v P 1982 (2)
Grieve, B. A. F. 2: *v SA 1888 (2)*
Griffith, S. C. 3: *v SA 1948 (2); v WI 1947 (1)*
Gunn, G. 15: v A 1909 (1); *v A 1907 (5) 1911 (5); v WI 1929 (4)*
Gunn, J. 6: v A 1905 (1); *v A 1901 (5)*
Gunn, W. 11: v A 1888 (2) 1890 (2) 1893 (3) 1896 (1) 1899 (1); *v A 1886 (2)*

Habib, A. 2: v NZ 1999 (2)
Haig, N. E. 5: v A 1921 (1); *v WI 1929 (4)*
Haigh, S. 11: v A 1905 (2) 1909 (1) 1912 (1); *v SA 1898 (2) 1905 (5)*
Hallows, C. 2: v A 1921 (1); v WI 1928 (1)
Hamilton, G. M. 1: *v SA 1999*
Hammond, W. R. 85: v A 1930 (5) 1934 (5) 1938 (4); v SA 1929 (4) 1935 (5); v WI 1928 (3) 1933 (3) 1939 (3); v NZ 1931 (3) 1937 (3); v In 1932 (1) 1936 (2) 1946 (3); *v A 1928 (5) 1932 (5) 1936 (5) 1946 (4); v SA 1927 (5) 1930 (5) 1938 (5); v WI 1934 (4); v NZ 1932 (2) 1946 (1)*
Hampshire, J. H. 8: v A 1972 (1) 1975 (1); v WI 1969 (2); *v A 1970 (2); v NZ 1970 (2)*
Hardinge, H. T. W. 1: v A 1921
Hardstaff, J. 5: *v A 1907 (5)*
Hardstaff, J. jun. 23: v A 1938 (2) 1948 (1); v SA 1935 (1); v WI 1939 (3); v NZ 1937 (3); v In 1936 (2) 1946 (2); *v A 1936 (5) 1946 (1); v WI 1947 (3)*
Harris, Lord 4: v A 1880 (1) 1884 (2); *v A 1878 (1)*
Hartley, J. C. 2: *v SA 1905 (2)*
Hawke, Lord 5: *v SA 1895 (3) 1898 (2)*

Hayes, E. G. 5: v A 1909 (1); v SA 1912 (1); *v SA 1905 (3)*
Hayes, F. C. 9: v WI 1973 (3) 1976 (2); *v WI 1973 (4)*
Hayward, T. W. 35: v A 1896 (2) 1899 (5) 1902 (1) 1905 (5) 1909 (1); v SA 1907 (3); *v A 1897 (5) 1901 (5) 1903 (5); v SA 1895 (3)*
Headley, D. W. 15: v A 1997 (3); v SA 1998 (1); v NZ 1999 (2); *v A 1998 (3); v WI 1997 (6)*
Hearne, A. 1: *v SA 1891*
Hearne, F. 2: *v SA 1888 (2)*
Hearne, G. G. 1: *v SA 1891*
Hearne, J. T. 12: v A 1896 (3) 1899 (3); *v A 1897 (5); v SA 1891 (1)*
Hearne, J. W. 24: v A 1912 (3) 1921 (1) 1926 (1); v SA 1912 (2) 1924 (3); *v A 1911 (5) 1920 (2) 1924 (4); v SA 1913 (3)*
Hegg, W. K. 2: *v A 1998 (2)*
Hemmings, E. E. 16: v A 1989 (1); v NZ 1990 (3); v In 1990 (3); v P 1982 (2); *v A 1982 (3) 1987 (1) 1990 (1); v NZ 1987 (1); v P 1987 (1)*
Hendren, E. H. 51: v A 1921 (2) 1926 (5) 1930 (2) 1934 (4); v SA 1924 (5) 1929 (4); v WI 1928 (1); *v A 1920 (5) 1924 (5) 1928 (5); v SA 1930 (5); v WI 1929 (4) 1934 (4)*
Hendrick, M. 30: v A 1977 (3) 1980 (1) 1981 (2); v WI 1976 (2) 1980 (2); v NZ 1978 (2); v In 1974 (3) 1979 (4); v P 1974 (2); *v A 1974 (2) 1978 (5); v NZ 1974 (1) 1977 (1)*
Heseltine, C. 2: *v SA 1895 (2)*
Hick, G. A. 65: v A 1993 (3); v SA 1994 (3) 1998 (2); v WI 1991 (4) 1995 (5) 2000 (4); v NZ 1994 (3) 1999 (1); v In 1996 (3); v P 1992 (4) 1996 (1); v SL 1998 (1); v Z 2000 (2); *v A 1994 (3) 1998 (4); v SA 1995 (5); v WI 1993 (5); v NZ 1991 (3); v In 1992 (3); v P 2000 (3); v SL 1992 (1) 2000 (2)*
Higgs, K. 15: v A 1968 (1); v WI 1966 (5); v SA 1965 (1); v In 1967 (1); v P 1967 (3); *v A 1965 (1); v NZ 1965 (3)*
Hill, A. 2: *v A 1876 (2)*
Hill, A. J. L. 3: *v SA 1895 (3)*
Hilton, M. J. 4: v SA 1951 (1); v WI 1950 (1); *v In 1951 (2)*
Hirst, G. H. 24: v A 1899 (1) 1902 (4) 1905 (3) 1909 (4); v SA 1907 (3); *v A 1897 (4) 1903 (5)*
Hitch, J. W. 7: v A 1912 (1) 1921 (1); v SA 1912 (1); *v A 1911 (3) 1920 (1)*
Hobbs, J. B. 61: v A 1909 (3) 1912 (3) 1921 (1) 1926 (5) 1930 (5); v SA 1912 (3) 1924 (4) 1929 (1); v WI 1928 (2); *v A 1907 (4) 1911 (5) 1920 (5) 1924 (5) 1928 (5); v SA 1909 (5) 1913 (5)*
Hobbs, R. N. S. 7: v In 1967 (3); v P 1967 (1) 1971 (1); *v WI 1967 (1); v P 1968 (1)*
Hoggard, M. J. 2: v WI 2000 (1); v P 2001 (1)
Hollies, W. E. 13: v A 1948 (1); v SA 1947 (3); v WI 1950 (2); v NZ 1949 (4); *v WI 1934 (3)*
Hollioake, A. J. 4: v A 1997 (2); *v WI 1997 (2)*
Hollioake, B. C. 2: v A 1997 (1); v SL 1998 (1)
Holmes, E. R. T. 5: v SA 1935 (1); *v WI 1934 (4)*
Holmes, P. 7: v A 1921 (1); v In 1932 (1); *v SA 1927 (5)*
Hone, L. 1: *v A 1878*
Hopwood, J. L. 2: v A 1934 (2)
Hornby, A. N. 3: v A 1882 (1) 1884 (1); *v A 1878 (1)*
Horton, M. J. 2: v In 1959 (2)
Howard, N. D. 4: *v In 1951 (4)*
Howell, H. 5: v A 1921 (1); v SA 1924 (1); *v A 1920 (3)*
Howorth, R. 5: v SA 1947 (1); *v WI 1947 (4)*
Humphries, J. 3: *v A 1907 (3)*
Hunter, J. 5: *v A 1884 (5)*
Hussain, N. 63: v A 1993 (4) 1997 (6) 2001 (3); v SA 1998 (5); v WI 2000 (4); v NZ 1999 (3); v In 1996 (3); v P 1996 (2) 2001 (1); v Z 2000 (2); *v A 1998 (5); v SA 1999 (5); v WI 1989 (3) 1997 (6); v NZ 1996 (3); v P 2000 (3); v SL 2000 (3); v Z 1996 (2)*
Hutchings, K. L. 7: v A 1909 (2); *v A 1907 (5)*
Hutton, L. 79: v A 1938 (3) 1948 (4) 1953 (5); v SA 1947 (5) 1951 (5); v WI 1939 (3) 1950 (3); v NZ 1937 (3) 1949 (4); v In 1946 (3) 1952 (4); v P 1954 (2); *v A 1946 (5) 1950 (5) 1954 (5); v SA 1938 (4) 1948 (5); v WI 1947 (2) 1953 (5); v NZ 1950 (2) 1954 (2)*
Hutton, R. A. 5: v In 1971 (3); v P 1971 (2)

Iddon, J. 5: v SA 1935 (1); *v WI 1934 (4)*
Igglesden, A. P. 3: v A 1989 (1); *v WI 1993 (2)*
Ikin, J. T. 18: v SA 1951 (3) 1955 (1); v In 1946 (2) 1952 (2); *v A 1946 (5); v NZ 1946 (1); v WI 1947 (4)*

Illingworth, R. 61: v A 1961 (2) 1968 (3) 1972 (5); v SA 1960 (4); v WI 1966 (2) 1969 (3) 1973 (3); v NZ 1958 (1) 1965 (1) 1969 (3) 1973 (3); v In 1959 (2) 1967 (3) 1971 (3); v P 1962 (1) 1967 (1) 1971 (3); *v A 1962 (2) 1970 (6); v WI 1959 (5); v NZ 1962 (3) 1970 (2)*

Illingworth, R. K. 9: v WI 1991 (2) 1995 (4); *v SA 1995 (3)*

Ilott, M. C. 5: v A 1993 (3); *v SA 1995 (2)*

Insole, D. J. 9: v A 1956 (1); v SA 1955 (1); v WI 1950 (1) 1957 (1); *v SA 1956 (5)*

Irani, R. C. 3: v NZ 1999 (1); v In 1996 (2)

Jackman, R. D. 4: v P 1982 (2); *v WI 1980 (2)*

Jackson, F. S. 20: v A 1893 (2) 1896 (3) 1899 (5) 1902 (5) 1905 (5)

Jackson, H. L. 2: v A 1961 (1); v NZ 1949 (1)

James, S. P. 2: v SA 1998 (1); v SL 1998 (1)

Jameson, J. A. 4: v In 1971 (2); *v WI 1973 (2)*

Jardine, D. R. 22: v WI 1928 (2) 1933 (2); v NZ 1931 (3); v In 1932 (1); *v A 1928 (5) 1932 (5); v NZ 1932 (1); v In 1933 (3)*

Jarvis, P. W. 9: v A 1989 (2); v WI 1988 (2); *v NZ 1987 (2); v In 1992 (2); v SL 1992 (1)*

Jenkins, R. O. 9: v WI 1950 (2); v In 1952 (2); *v SA 1948 (5)*

Jessop, G. L. 18: v A 1899 (1) 1902 (4) 1905 (1) 1909 (2); v SA 1907 (3) 1912 (2); *v A 1901 (5)*

Jones, A. O. 12: v A 1899 (1) 1905 (2) 1909 (2); *v A 1901 (5) 1907 (2)*

Jones, I. J. 15: v WI 1966 (2); *v A 1965 (4); v WI 1967 (5); v NZ 1965 (3); v In 1963 (1)*

Jupp, H. 2: *v A 1876 (2)*

Jupp, V. W. C. 8: v A 1921 (2); v WI 1928 (2); *v SA 1922 (4)*

Keeton, W. W. 2: v A 1934 (1); v WI 1939 (1)

Kennedy, A. S. 5: *v SA 1922 (5)*

Kenyon, D. 8: v A 1953 (2); v SA 1955 (3); *v In 1951 (3)*

Killick, E. T. 2: v SA 1929 (2)

Kilner, R. 9: v A 1926 (4); v SA 1924 (2); *v A 1924 (3)*

King, J. H. 1: v A 1909

Kinneir, S. P. 1: *v A 1911*

Knight, A. E. 3: *v A 1903 (3)*

Knight, B. R. 29: v A 1968 (2); v WI 1966 (1) 1969 (3); v NZ 1969 (2); v P 1962 (2); *v A 1962 (1) 1965 (2); v NZ 1962 (3) 1965 (2); v In 1961 (4) 1963 (5); v P 1961 (2)*

Knight, D. J. 2: v A 1921 (2)

Knight, N. V. 17: v SA 1998 (1); v WI 1995 (2) 2000 (2); v In 1996 (1); v P 1996 (3) 2001 (1); v Z 2000 (2); *v NZ 1996 (3); v Z 1996 (2)*

Knott, A. P. E. 95: v A 1968 (5) 1972 (5) 1975 (4) 1977 (5) 1981 (2); v WI 1969 (3) 1973 (3) 1976 (5) 1980 (4); v NZ 1969 (3) 1973 (3); v In 1971 (3) 1974 (3); v P 1967 (2) 1971 (3) 1974 (3); *v A 1970 (6) 1974 (6) 1976 (1); v WI 1967 (2) 1973 (5); v NZ 1970 (1) 1974 (2); v In 1972 (5) 1976 (5); v P 1968 (3) 1972 (3)*

Knox, N. A. 2: v SA 1907 (2)

Laker, J. C. 46: v A 1948 (3) 1953 (3) 1956 (5); v SA 1951 (2) 1955 (1); v WI 1950 (1) 1957 (4); v NZ 1949 (1) 1958 (4); v In 1952 (4); v P 1954 (1); *v A 1958 (4); v SA 1956 (5); v WI 1947 (4) 1953 (4)*

Lamb, A. J. 79: v A 1985 (6) 1989 (1); v WI 1984 (5) 1988 (4) 1991 (4); v NZ 1983 (4) 1986 (1) 1990 (3); v In 1982 (3) 1986 (2) 1990 (3); v P 1982 (3) 1992 (2); v SL 1984 (1) 1988 (1); *v A 1982 (5) 1986 (5) 1990 (3); v WI 1985 (5) 1989 (4); v NZ 1983 (3) 1991 (3); v In 1984 (5); v P 1983 (3)*

Langridge, James 8: v SA 1935 (1); v WI 1933 (2); v In 1936 (1) 1946 (1); *v In 1933 (3)*

Larkins, W. 13: v A 1981 (1); v WI 1980 (3); *v A 1979 (1) 1990 (3); v WI 1989 (4); v In 1979 (1)*

Larter, J. D. F. 10: v SA 1965 (2); v NZ 1965 (1); v P 1962 (1); *v NZ 1962 (3); v In 1963 (3)*

Larwood, H. 21: v A 1926 (2) 1930 (3); v SA 1929 (3); v WI 1928 (2); v NZ 1931 (1); *v A 1928 (5) 1932 (5)*

Lathwell, M. N. 2: v A 1993 (2)

Lawrence, D. V. 5: v WI 1991 (2); v SL 1988 (1) 1991 (1); *v NZ 1991 (1)*

Leadbeater, E. 2: *v In 1951 (2)*

Lee, H. W. 1: *v SA 1930*

Lees, W. S. 5: *v SA 1905 (5)*

Legge, G. B. 5: *v SA 1927 (1); v NZ 1929 (4)*

Leslie, C. F. H. 4: *v A 1882 (4)*

Lever, J. K. 21: v A 1977 (3); v WI 1980 (1); v In 1979 (1) 1986 (1); *v A 1976 (1) 1978 (1) 1979 (1); v NZ 1977 (1); v In 1976 (5) 1979 (1) 1981 (2); v P 1977 (3)*
Lever, P. 17: v A 1972 (1) 1975 (1); v In 1971 (1); v P 1971 (3); *v A 1970 (5) 1974 (2); v NZ 1970 (2) 1974 (2)*
Leveson Gower, H. D. G. 3: *v SA 1909 (3)*
Levett, W. H. V. 1: *v In 1933*
Lewis, A. R. 9: v NZ 1973 (1); *v In 1972 (5); v P 1972 (3)*
Lewis, C. C. 32: v A 1993 (2); v WI 1991 (2); v NZ 1990 (1); v In 1990 (2) 1996 (3); v P 1992 (5) 1996 (2); v SL 1991 (1); *v A 1990 (1) 1994 (2); v WI 1993 (5); v NZ 1991 (2); v In 1992 (3); v SL 1992 (1)*
Leyland, M. 41: v A 1930 (3) 1934 (5) 1938 (1); v SA 1929 (5) 1935 (4); v WI 1928 (1) 1933 (1); v In 1936 (2); *v A 1928 (1) 1932 (5) 1936 (5); v SA 1930 (5); v WI 1934 (3)*
Lilley, A. A. 35: v A 1896 (3) 1899 (4) 1902 (5) 1905 (5) 1909 (5); v SA 1907 (3); *v A 1901 (5) 1903 (5)*
Lillywhite, James jun. 2: *v A 1876 (2)*
Lloyd, D. 9: v In 1974 (2); v P 1974 (3); *v A 1974 (4)*
Lloyd, T. A. 1: v WI 1984
Loader, P. J. 13: v SA 1955 (1); v WI 1957 (2); v NZ 1958 (3); v P 1954 (1); *v A 1958 (2); v SA 1956 (4)*
Lock, G. A. R. 49: v A 1953 (2) 1956 (4) 1961 (3); v SA 1955 (3); v WI 1957 (3) 1963 (3); v NZ 1958 (5); v In 1952 (2); v P 1962 (3); *v A 1958 (4); v SA 1956 (1); v WI 1953 (5) 1967 (2); v NZ 1958 (2); v In 1961 (5); v P 1961 (2)*
Lockwood, W. H. 12: v A 1893 (2) 1899 (1) 1902 (4); *v A 1894 (5)*
Lohmann, G. A. 18: v A 1886 (3) 1888 (3) 1890 (2) 1896 (1); *v A 1886 (2) 1887 (1) 1891 (3); v SA 1895 (3)*
Lowson, F. A. 7: v SA 1951 (2) 1955 (1); *v In 1951 (4)*
Lucas, A. P. 5: v A 1880 (1) 1882 (1) 1884 (2); *v A 1878 (1)*
Luckhurst, B. W. 21: v A 1972 (4); v WI 1973 (2); v In 1971 (3); v P 1971 (3); *v A 1970 (5) 1974 (2); v NZ 1970 (2)*
Lyttelton, Hon. A. 4: v A 1880 (1) 1882 (1) 1884 (2)

Macaulay, G. G. 8: v A 1926 (1); v SA 1924 (1); v WI 1933 (2); *v SA 1922 (4)*
MacBryan, J. C. W. 1: v SA 1924
McCague, M. J. 3: v A 1993 (2); *v A 1994 (1)*
McConnon, J. E. 2: v P 1954 (2)
McGahey, C. P. 2: *v A 1901 (2)*
MacGregor, G. 8: v A 1890 (2) 1893 (3); *v A 1891 (3)*
McIntyre, A. J. W. 3: v SA 1955 (1); v WI 1950 (1); *v A 1950 (1)*
MacKinnon, F. A. 1: *v A 1878*
MacLaren, A. C. 35: v A 1896 (2) 1899 (4) 1902 (5) 1905 (4) 1909 (5); *v A 1894 (5) 1897 (5) 1901 (5)*
McMaster, J. E. P. 1: *v SA 1888*
Maddy, D. L. 3: v NZ 1999 (1); *v SA 1999 (2)*
Makepeace, J. W. H. 4: *v A 1920 (4)*
Malcolm, D. E. 40: v A 1989 (1) 1993 (1) 1997 (4); v SA 1994 (1); v WI 1991 (2) 1995 (2); v NZ 1990 (3) 1994 (1); v In 1990 (3); v P 1992 (3); *v A 1990 (5) 1994 (4); v SA 1995 (2); v WI 1989 (4) 1993 (1); v In 1992 (2); v SL 1992 (1)*
Mallender, N. A. 2: v P 1992 (2)
Mann, F. G. 7: v NZ 1949 (2); *v SA 1948 (5)*
Mann, F. T. 5: *v SA 1922 (5)*
Marks, V. J. 6: v NZ 1983 (1); v P 1982 (1); *v NZ 1983 (1); v P 1983 (3)*
Marriott, C. S. 1: v WI 1933
Martin, F. 2: v A 1890 (1); *v SA 1891 (1)*
Martin, J. W. 1: v SA 1947
Martin, P. J. 8: v A 1997 (1); v WI 1995 (3); v In 1996 (1); *v SA 1995 (3)*
Mason, J. R. 5: *v A 1897 (5)*
Matthews, A. D. G. 1: v NZ 1937
May, P. B. H. 66: v A 1953 (2) 1956 (5) 1961 (4); v SA 1951 (2) 1955 (5); v WI 1957 (5); v NZ 1958 (5); v In 1952 (4) 1959 (3); v P 1954 (4); *v A 1954 (5) 1958 (5); v SA 1956 (5); v WI 1953 (5) 1959 (3); v NZ 1954 (2) 1958 (2)*
Maynard, M. P. 4: v A 1993 (2); v WI 1988 (1); *v WI 1993 (1)*

Mead, C. P. 17: v A 1921 (2); *v A 1911 (4) 1928 (1); v SA 1913 (5) 1922 (5)*
Mead, W. 1: v A 1899
Midwinter, W. E. 4: *v A 1881 (4)*
Milburn, C. 9: v A 1968 (2); v WI 1966 (4); v In 1967 (1); v P 1967 (1); *v P 1968 (1)*
Miller, A. M. 1: *v SA 1895*
Miller, G. 34: v A 1977 (2); v WI 1976 (1) 1984 (2); v NZ 1978 (2); v In 1979 (3) 1982 (1); v P 1978 (3) 1982 (1); *v A 1978 (6) 1979 (1) 1982 (5); v WI 1980 (1); v NZ 1977 (3); v P 1977 (3)*
Milligan, F. W. 2: *v SA 1898 (2)*
Millman, G. 6: v P 1962 (2); *v In 1961 (2); v P 1961 (2)*
Milton, C. A. 6: v NZ 1958 (2); v In 1959 (2); *v A 1958 (2)*
Mitchell, A. 6: v SA 1935 (2); v In 1936 (1); *v In 1933 (3)*
Mitchell, F. 2: *v SA 1898 (2)*
Mitchell, T. B. 5: v A 1934 (2); v SA 1935 (1); *v A 1932 (1); v NZ 1932 (1)*
Mitchell-Innes, N. S. 1: v SA 1935
Mold, A. W. 3: v A 1893 (3)
Moon, L. J. 4: *v SA 1905 (4)*
Morley, F. 4: v A 1880 (1); *v A 1882 (3)*
Morris, H. 3: v WI 1991 (2); v SL 1991 (1)
Morris, J. E. 3: v In 1990 (3)
Mortimore, J. B. 9: v A 1964 (1); v In 1959 (2); *v A 1958 (1); v NZ 1958 (2); v In 1963 (3)*
Moss, A. E. 9: v A 1956 (1); v SA 1960 (2); v In 1959 (3); *v WI 1953 (1) 1959 (2)*
Moxon, M. D. 10: v A 1989 (1); v WI 1988 (2); v NZ 1986 (2); v P 1987 (1); *v A 1987 (1); v NZ 1987 (3)*
Mullally, A. D. 19: v A 2001 (1); v NZ 1999 (3); v In 1996 (3); v P 1996 (3); *v A 1998 (4); v SA 1999 (2); v NZ 1996 (1); v Z 1996 (2)*
Munton, T. A. 2: v P 1992 (2)
Murdoch, W. L. 1: *v SA 1891*
Murray, J. T. 21: v A 1961 (5); v WI 1966 (1); v In 1967 (3); v P 1962 (3) 1967 (1); *v A 1962 (1); v SA 1964 (1); v NZ 1962 (1) 1965 (1); v In 1961 (3); v P 1961 (1)*

Newham, W. 1: *v A 1887*
Newport, P. J. 3: v A 1989 (1); v SL 1988 (1); *v A 1990 (1)*
Nichols, M. S. 14: v A 1930 (1); v SA 1935 (4); v WI 1933 (1) 1939 (1); *v NZ 1929 (4); v In 1933 (3)*

Oakman, A. S. M. 2: v A 1956 (2)
O'Brien, Sir T. C. 5: v A 1884 (1) 1888 (1); *v SA 1895 (3)*
O'Connor, J. 4: v SA 1929 (1); *v WI 1929 (3)*
Old, C. M. 46: v A 1975 (3) 1977 (2) 1980 (1) 1981 (2); v WI 1973 (1) 1976 (2) 1980 (1); v NZ 1973 (2) 1978 (1); v In 1974 (3); v P 1974 (3) 1978 (3); *v A 1974 (2) 1976 (1) 1978 (1); v WI 1973 (4) 1980 (1); v NZ 1974 (1) 1977 (2); v In 1972 (4) 1976 (4); v P 1972 (1) 1977 (1)*
Oldfield, N. 1: v WI 1939
Ormond, J. 1: v A 2001

Padgett, D. E. V. 2: v SA 1960 (2)
Paine, G. A. E. 4: *v WI 1934 (4)*
Palairet, L. C. H. 2: v A 1902 (2)
Palmer, C. H. 1: *v WI 1953*
Palmer, K. E. 1: *v SA 1964*
Parfitt, P. H. 37: v A 1964 (4) 1972 (3); v SA 1965 (2); v WI 1969 (1); v NZ 1965 (2); v P 1962 (5); *v A 1962 (2); v SA 1964 (5); v NZ 1962 (3) 1965 (3); v In 1961 (2) 1963 (3); v P 1961 (2)*
Parker, C. W. L. 1: v A 1921
Parker, P. W. G. 1: v A 1981
Parkhouse, W. G. A. 7: v WI 1950 (2); v In 1959 (2); *v A 1950 (2); v NZ 1950 (1)*
Parkin, C. H. 10: v A 1921 (4); v SA 1924 (1); *v A 1920 (5)*
Parks, J. H. 1: v NZ 1937
Parks, J. M. 46: v A 1964 (5); v SA 1960 (5) 1965 (3); v WI 1963 (4) 1966 (4); v NZ 1965 (3); v P 1954 (1); *v A 1965 (5); v SA 1964 (5); v WI 1959 (1) 1967 (3); v NZ 1965 (2); v In 1963 (5)*
Pataudi sen., Nawab of, 3: v A 1934 (1); *v A 1932 (2)*
Patel, M. M. 2: v In 1996 (2)

Paynter, E. 20: v A 1938 (4); v WI 1939 (2); v NZ 1931 (1) 1937 (2); v In 1932 (1); *v A 1932 (3); v SA 1938 (5); v NZ 1932 (2)*
Peate, E. 9: v A 1882 (1) 1884 (3) 1886 (1); *v A 1881 (4)*
Peebles, I. A. R. 13: v A 1930 (2); v NZ 1931 (3); *v SA 1927 (4) 1930 (4)*
Peel, R. 20: v A 1888 (3) 1890 (1) 1893 (1) 1896 (1); *v A 1884 (5) 1887 (1) 1891 (3) 1894 (5)*
Penn, F. 1: v A 1880
Perks, R. T. D. 2: v WI 1939 (1); *v SA 1938 (1)*
Philipson, H. 5: *v A 1891 (1) 1894 (4)*
Pigott, A. C. S. 1: *v NZ 1983*
Pilling, R. 8: v A 1884 (1) 1886 (1) 1888 (1); *v A 1881 (4) 1887 (1)*
Place, W. 3: *v WI 1947 (3)*
Pocock, P. I. 25: v A 1968 (1); v WI 1976 (2) 1984 (2); v SL 1984 (1); *v WI 1967 (2) 1973 (4); v In 1972 (4) 1984 (5); v P 1968 (1) 1972 (3)*
Pollard, R. 4: v A 1948 (2); v In 1946 (1); *v NZ 1946 (1)*
Poole, C. J. 3: *v In 1951 (3)*
Pope, G. H. 1: v SA 1947
Pougher, A. D. 1: *v SA 1891*
Price, J. S. E. 15: v A 1964 (2) 1972 (1); v In 1971 (3); v P 1971 (1); *v SA 1964 (4); v In 1963 (4)*
Price, W. F. F. 1: v A 1938
Prideaux, R. M. 3: v A 1968 (1); *v P 1968 (2)*
Pringle, D. R. 30: v A 1989 (2); v WI 1984 (3) 1988 (4) 1991 (4); v NZ 1986 (1); v In 1982 (3) 1986 (3); v P 1982 (1) 1992 (3); v SL 1988 (1); *v A 1982 (3); v NZ 1991 (2)*
Pullar, G. 28: v A 1961 (5); v SA 1960 (3); v In 1959 (3); v P 1962 (2); *v A 1962 (4); v WI 1959 (5); v In 1961 (3); v P 1961 (3)*

Quaife, W. G. 7: v A 1899 (2); *v A 1901 (5)*

Radford, N. V. 3: v NZ 1986 (1); v In 1986 (1); *v NZ 1987 (1)*
Radley, C. T. 8: v NZ 1978 (3); v P 1978 (3); *v NZ 1977 (2)*
Ramprakash, M. R. 46: v A 1993 (1) 1997 (1) 2001 (4); v SA 1998 (5); v WI 1991 (5) 1995 (2) 2000 (2); v NZ 1999 (4); v P 1992 (3); v SL 1991 (1) 1998 (1); v Z 2000 (2); *v A 1994 (1) 1998 (5); v WI 1993 (4) 1997 (3); v SA 1995 (2)*
Randall, D. W. 47: v A 1977 (5); v WI 1984 (1); v NZ 1983 (3); v In 1979 (3) 1982 (3); v P 1982 (3); *v A 1976 (1) 1978 (6) 1979 (2) 1982 (4); v NZ 1977 (3) 1983 (3); v In 1976 (4); v P 1977 (3) 1983 (3)*
Ranjitsinhji, K. S. 15: v A 1896 (2) 1899 (5) 1902 (3); *v A 1897 (5)*
Read, C. M. W. 3: v NZ 1999 (3)
Read, H. D. 1: v SA 1935
Read, J. M. 17: v A 1882 (1) 1890 (2) 1893 (1); *v A 1884 (5) 1886 (2) 1887 (1) 1891 (3); v SA 1888 (2)*
Read, W. W. 18: v A 1884 (2) 1886 (3) 1888 (3) 1890 (2) 1893 (2); *v A 1882 (4) 1887 (1); v SA 1891 (1)*
Reeve, D. A. 3: *v NZ 1991 (3)*
Relf, A. E. 13: v A 1909 (1); *v A 1903 (2); v SA 1905 (5) 1913 (5)*
Rhodes, H. J. 2: v In 1959 (2)
Rhodes, S. J. 11: v SA 1994 (3); v NZ 1994 (3); *v A 1994 (5)*
Rhodes, W. 58: v A 1899 (3) 1902 (5) 1905 (4) 1909 (4) 1912 (3) 1921 (1) 1926 (1); v SA 1912 (3); *v A 1903 (5) 1907 (5) 1911 (5) 1920 (5); v SA 1909 (5) 1913 (5); v WI 1929 (4)*
Richards, C. J. 8: v WI 1988 (2); v P 1987 (1); *v A 1986 (5)*
Richardson, D. W. 1: v WI 1957
Richardson, P. E. 34: v A 1956 (5); v WI 1957 (5) 1963 (1); v NZ 1958 (4); *v A 1958 (4); v SA 1956 (5); v NZ 1958 (2); v In 1961 (5); v P 1961 (3)*
Richardson, T. 14: v A 1893 (1) 1896 (3); *v A 1894 (5) 1897 (5)*
Richmond, T. L. 1: v A 1921
Ridgway, F. 5: *v In 1951 (5)*
Robertson, J. D. 11: v SA 1947 (1); v NZ 1949 (1); *v WI 1947 (4); v In 1951 (5)*
Robins, R. W. V. 19: v A 1930 (2); v SA 1929 (1) 1935 (3); v WI 1933 (2); v NZ 1931 (1) 1937 (3); v In 1932 (1) 1936 (2); *v A 1936 (4)*
Robinson, R. T. 29: v A 1985 (6) 1989 (1); v In 1986 (1); v P 1987 (5); v SL 1988 (1); *v A 1987 (1); v WI 1985 (4); v NZ 1987 (3); v In 1984 (5); v P 1987 (2)*

Roope, G. R. J. 21: v A 1975 (1) 1977 (2); v WI 1973 (1); v NZ 1973 (3) 1978 (1); v P 1978 (3); *v NZ 1977 (3); v In 1972 (2); v P 1972 (2) 1977 (3)*
Root, C. F. 3: v A 1926 (3)
Rose, B. C. 9: v WI 1980 (3); *v WI 1980 (1); v NZ 1977 (2); v P 1977 (3)*
Royle, V. P. F. A. 1: *v A 1878*
Rumsey, F. E. 5: v A 1964 (1); v SA 1965 (1); v NZ 1965 (3)
Russell, A. C. 10: v A 1921 (2); *v A 1920 (4); v SA 1922 (4)*
Russell, R. C. 54: v A 1989 (6); v WI 1991 (4) 1995 (3); v NZ 1990 (3); v In 1990 (3) 1996 (3); v P 1992 (3) 1996 (2); v SL 1988 (1) 1991 (1); *v A 1990 (3); v SA 1995 (5); v WI 1989 (4) 1993 (5) 1997 (5); v NZ 1991 (3)*
Russell, W. E. 10: v SA 1965 (1); v WI 1966 (2); v P 1967 (1); *v A 1965 (1); v NZ 1965 (3); v In 1961 (1); v P 1961 (1)*

Salisbury, I. D. K. 15: v SA 1994 (1) 1998 (2); v P 1992 (2) 1996 (2); v SL 1998 (1); *v WI 1993 (2); v In 1992 (2); v P 2000 (3)*
Sandham, A. 14: v A 1921 (1); v SA 1924 (2); *v A 1924 (2); v SA 1922 (5); v WI 1929 (4)*
Schofield, C. P. 2: v Z 2000 (2)
Schultz, S. S. 1: *v A 1878*
Scotton, W. H. 15: v A 1884 (1) 1886 (3); *v A 1881 (4) 1884 (5) 1886 (2)*
Selby, J. 6: *v A 1876 (2) 1881 (4)*
Selvey, M. W. W. 3: v WI 1976 (2); *v In 1976 (1)*
Shackleton, D. 7: v SA 1951 (1); v WI 1950 (1) 1963 (4); *v In 1951 (1)*
Sharp, J. 3: v A 1909 (3)
Sharpe, J. W. 3: v A 1890 (1); *v A 1891 (2)*
Sharpe, P. J. 12: v A 1964 (2); v WI 1963 (3) 1969 (3); v NZ 1969 (3); *v In 1963 (1)*
Shaw, A. 7: v A 1880 (1); *v A 1876 (2) 1881 (4)*
Sheppard, Rev. D. S. 22: v A 1956 (2); v WI 1950 (1) 1957 (2); v In 1952 (2); v P 1954 (2) 1962 (2); *v A 1950 (2) 1962 (5); v NZ 1950 (1) 1962 (3)*
Sherwin, M. 3: v A 1888 (1); *v A 1886 (2)*
Shrewsbury, A. 23: v A 1884 (3) 1886 (3) 1890 (2) 1893 (3); *v A 1881 (4) 1884 (5) 1886 (2) 1887 (1)*
Shuter, J. 1: v A 1888
Shuttleworth, K. 5: v P 1971 (1); *v A 1970 (2); v NZ 1970 (2)*
Sidebottom, A. 1: v A 1985
Sidebottom, R. J. 1: v P 2001
Silverwood, C. E. W. 5: *v SA 1999 (4); v Z 1996 (1)*
Simpson, R. T. 27: v A 1953 (3); v SA 1951 (3); v WI 1950 (3); v NZ 1949 (2); v In 1952 (2); v P 1954 (3); *v A 1950 (5) 1954 (1); v SA 1948 (1); v NZ 1950 (2) 1954 (2)*
Simpson-Hayward, G. H. 5: *v SA 1909 (5)*
Sims, J. M. 4: v SA 1935 (1); v In 1936 (1); *v A 1936 (2)*
Sinfield, R. A. 1: v A 1938
Slack, W. N. 3: v In 1986 (1); *v WI 1985 (2)*
Smailes, T. F. 1: v In 1946
Small, G. C. 17: v A 1989 (1); v WI 1988 (1); v NZ 1986 (2) 1990 (3); *v A 1986 (2) 1990 (4); v WI 1989 (4)*
Smith, A. C. 6: *v A 1962 (4); v NZ 1962 (2)*
Smith, A. M. 1: v A 1997
Smith, C. A. 1: *v SA 1888*
Smith, C. I. J. 5: v NZ 1937 (1); *v WI 1934 (4)*
Smith, C. L. 8: v NZ 1983 (2); v In 1986 (1); *v NZ 1983 (2); v P 1983 (3)*
Smith, D. 2: v SA 1935 (2)
Smith, D. M. 2: *v WI 1985 (2)*
Smith, D. R. 5: *v In 1961 (5)*
Smith, D. V. 3: v WI 1957 (3)
Smith, E. J. 11: v A 1912 (3); v SA 1912 (3); *v A 1911 (4); v SA 1913 (1)*
Smith, H. 1: v WI 1928
Smith, M. J. K. 50: v A 1961 (1) 1972 (3); v SA 1960 (4) 1965 (3); v WI 1966 (1); v NZ 1958 (3) 1965 (3); v In 1959 (2); *v A 1965 (5); v SA 1964 (5); v WI 1959 (5); v NZ 1965 (3); v In 1961 (4) 1963 (5); v P 1961 (3)*

Smith, R. A. 62: v A 1989 (5) 1993 (5); v WI 1988 (2) 1991 (4) 1995 (4); v NZ 1990 (3) 1994 (3); v In 1990 (3); v P 1992 (5); v SL 1988 (1) 1991 (1); *v A 1990 (5); v SA 1995 (5); v WI 1989 (4) 1993 (5); v NZ 1991 (3); v In 1992 (3); v SL 1992 (1)*

Smith, T. P. B. 4: v In 1946 (1); *v A 1946 (2); v NZ 1946 (1)*

Smithson, G. A. 2: *v WI 1947 (2)*

Snow, J. A. 49: v A 1968 (5) 1972 (5) 1975 (4); v SA 1965 (1); v WI 1966 (3) 1969 (3) 1973 (1) 1976 (3); v NZ 1965 (1) 1969 (2) 1973 (3); v In 1967 (3) 1971 (2); v P 1967 (1); *v A 1970 (6); v WI 1967 (4); v P 1968 (2)*

Southerton, J. 2: *v A 1876 (2)*

Spooner, R. H. 10: v A 1905 (2) 1909 (2) 1912 (3); v SA 1912 (3)

Spooner, R. T. 7: v SA 1955 (1); *v In 1951 (5); v WI 1953 (1)*

Stanyforth, R. T. 4: *v SA 1927 (4)*

Staples, S. J. 3: *v SA 1927 (3)*

Statham, J. B. 70: v A 1953 (1) 1956 (3) 1961 (4); v SA 1951 (2) 1955 (4) 1960 (5) 1965 (1); v WI 1957 (3) 1963 (2); v NZ 1958 (2); v In 1959 (3); v P 1954 (4) 1962 (3); *v A 1954 (5) 1958 (4) 1962 (5); v SA 1956 (4); v WI 1953 (4) 1959 (3); v NZ 1950 (1) 1954 (2); v In 1951 (5)*

Steel, A. G. 13: v A 1880 (1) 1882 (1) 1884 (3) 1886 (3) 1888 (1); *v A 1882 (4)*

Steele, D. S. 8: v A 1975 (3); v WI 1976 (5)

Stephenson, J. P. 1: v A 1989

Stevens, G. T. S. 10: v A 1926 (2); *v SA 1922 (1) 1927 (5); v WI 1929 (2)*

Stevenson, G. B. 2: *v WI 1980 (1); v In 1979 (1)*

Stewart, A. J. 115: v A 1993 (6) 1997 (6) 2001 (5); v SA 1994 (3) 1998 (5); v WI 1991 (1) 1995 (3) 2000 (5); v NZ 1990 (3) 1994 (3) 1999 (4); v In 1996 (2); v P 1992 (5) 1996 (3) 2001 (2); v SL 1991 (1) 1998 (1); v Z 2000 (2); *v A 1990 (5) 1994 (2) 1998 (5); v SA 1995 (5) 1999 (5); v WI 1989 (4) 1993 (5) 1997 (6); v NZ 1991 (3) 1996 (3); v In 1992 (3); v P 2000 (3); v SL 1992 (1) 2000 (3); v Z 1996 (2)*

Stewart, M. J. 8: v WI 1963 (4); v P 1962 (2); *v In 1963 (2)*

Stoddart, A. E. 16: v A 1893 (3) 1896 (2); *v A 1887 (1) 1891 (3) 1894 (5) 1897 (2)*

Storer, W. 6: v A 1899 (1); *v A 1897 (5)*

Street, G. B. 1: *v SA 1922*

Strudwick, H. 28: v A 1921 (2) 1926 (5); v SA 1924 (1); *v A 1911 (1) 1920 (4) 1924 (5); v SA 1909 (5) 1913 (5)*

Studd, C. T. 5: v A 1882 (1); *v A 1882 (4)*

Studd, G. B. 4: *v A 1882 (4)*

Subba Row, R. 13: v A 1961 (5); v SA 1960 (4); v NZ 1958 (1); v In 1959 (1); *v WI 1959 (2)*

Such, P. M. 11: v A 1993 (5); v NZ 1994 (3) 1999 (1); *v A 1998 (2)*

Sugg, F. H. 2: v A 1888 (2)

Sutcliffe, H. 54: v A 1926 (5) 1930 (4) 1934 (4); v SA 1924 (5) 1929 (5) 1935 (2); v WI 1928 (3) 1933 (2); v NZ 1931 (2); v In 1932 (1); *v A 1924 (5) 1928 (4) 1932 (5); v SA 1927 (5); v NZ 1932 (2)*

Swetman, R. 11: v In 1959 (3); *v A 1958 (2); v WI 1959 (4); v NZ 1958 (2)*

Tate, F. W. 1: v A 1902

Tate, M. W. 39: v A 1926 (5) 1930 (5); v SA 1924 (5) 1929 (3) 1935 (1); v WI 1928 (3); v NZ 1931 (1); *v A 1924 (5) 1928 (5); v SA 1930 (5); v NZ 1932 (1)*

Tattersall, R. 16: v A 1953 (1); v SA 1951 (5); v P 1954 (1); *v A 1950 (2); v NZ 1950 (2); v In 1951 (5)*

Tavaré, C. J. 31: v A 1981 (2) 1989 (1); v WI 1980 (2) 1984 (1); v NZ 1983 (4); v In 1982 (3); v P 1982 (3); v SL 1984 (1); *v A 1982 (5); v NZ 1983 (2); v In 1981 (6); v SL 1981 (1)*

Taylor, J. P. 2: v NZ 1994 (1); *v In 1992 (1)*

Taylor, K. 3: v A 1964 (1); v In 1959 (2)

Taylor, L. B. 2: v A 1985 (2)

Taylor, R. W. 57: v A 1981 (3); v NZ 1978 (3) 1983 (4); v In 1979 (3) 1982 (3); v P 1978 (3) 1982 (3); *v A 1978 (6) 1979 (3) 1982 (5); v NZ 1970 (1) 1977 (3) 1983 (3); v In 1979 (1) 1981 (6); v P 1977 (3) 1983 (3); v SL 1981 (1)*

Tennyson, Hon. L. H. 9: v A 1921 (4); *v SA 1913 (5)*

Terry, V. P. 2: v WI 1984 (2)

Thomas, J. G. 5: v NZ 1986 (1); *v WI 1985 (4)*

Thompson, G. J. 6: v A 1909 (1); *v SA 1909 (5)*

Thomson, N. I. 5: *v SA 1964 (5)*

Thorpe, G. P. 69: v A 1993 (3) 1997 (6) 2001 (1); v SA 1994 (2) 1998 (3); v WI 1995 (6) 2000 (3); v NZ 1999 (4); v In 1996 (3); v P 1996 (3) 2001 (2); *v A 1994 (5) 1998 (1); v SA 1995 (5); v WI 1993 (5) 1997 (6); v NZ 1996 (3); v P 2000 (3); v SL 2000 (3); v Z 1996 (2)*

Titmus, F. J. 53: v A 1964 (5); v SA 1955 (2) 1965 (3); v WI 1963 (4) 1966 (3); v NZ 1965 (3); v P 1962 (2) 1967 (2); *v A 1962 (5) 1965 (5) 1974 (4); v SA 1964 (5); v WI 1967 (2); v NZ 1962 (3); v In 1963 (5)*

Tolchard, R. W. 4: *v In 1976 (4)*

Townsend, C. L. 2: v A 1899 (2)

Townsend, D. C. H. 3: *v WI 1934 (3)*

Townsend, L. F. 4: *v WI 1929 (1); v In 1933 (3)*

Tremlett, M. F. 3: *v WI 1947 (3)*

Trescothick, M. E. 16: v A 2001 (5); v WI 2000 (3); v P 2001 (2); *v P 2000 (3); v SL 2000 (3)*

Trott, A. E. 2: *v SA 1898 (2)*

Trueman, F. S. 67: v A 1953 (1) 1956 (2) 1961 (4) 1964 (4); v SA 1955 (1) 1960 (5); v WI 1957 (5) 1963 (5); v NZ 1958 (5) 1965 (2); v In 1952 (4) 1959 (5); v P 1962 (4); *v A 1958 (3) 1962 (5); v WI 1953 (3) 1959 (5); v NZ 1958 (2) 1962 (2)*

Tudor, A. J. 5: v A 2001 (2); v NZ 1999 (1); *v A 1998 (2)*

Tufnell, N. C. 1: *v SA 1909*

Tufnell, P. C. R. 42: v A 1993 (2) 1997 (1) 2001 (1); v SA 1994 (1); v WI 1991 (1); v NZ 1999 (4); v P 1992 (1); v SL 1991 (1); *v A 1990 (4) 1994 (4); v SA 1999 (3); v WI 1993 (2) 1997 (6); v NZ 1991 (3) 1996 (3); v In 1992 (2); v SL 1992 (1); v Z 1996 (2)*

Turnbull, M. J. 9: v WI 1933 (2); v In 1936 (1); *v SA 1930 (5); v NZ 1929 (1)*

Tyldesley, E. 14: v A 1921 (3) 1926 (1); v SA 1924 (1); v WI 1928 (3); *v A 1928 (1); v SA 1927 (5)*

Tyldesley, J. T. 31: v A 1899 (2) 1902 (5) 1905 (5) 1909 (4); v SA 1907 (3); *v A 1901 (5) 1903 (5); v SA 1898 (2)*

Tyldesley, R. K. 7: v A 1930 (2); v SA 1924 (4); *v A 1924 (1)*

Tylecote, E. F. S. 6: v A 1886 (2); *v A 1882 (4)*

Tyler, E. J. 1: *v SA 1895*

Tyson, F. H. 17: v A 1956 (1); v SA 1955 (2); v P 1954 (1); *v A 1954 (5) 1958 (2); v SA 1956 (2); v NZ 1954 (2) 1958 (2)*

Ulyett, G. 25: v A 1882 (1) 1884 (3) 1886 (3) 1888 (2) 1890 (1); *v A 1876 (2) 1878 (1) 1881 (4) 1884 (5) 1887 (1); v SA 1888 (2)*

Underwood, D. L. 86: v A 1968 (4) 1972 (2) 1975 (4) 1977 (5); v WI 1966 (2) 1969 (2) 1973 (3) 1976 (5) 1980 (1); v NZ 1969 (3) 1973 (1); v In 1971 (1) 1974 (3); v P 1967 (2) 1971 (1) 1974 (3); *v A 1970 (5) 1974 (5) 1976 (1) 1979 (3); v WI 1973 (4); v NZ 1970 (2) 1974 (2); v In 1972 (4) 1976 (5) 1979 (1) 1981 (6); v P 1968 (3) 1972 (2); v SL 1981 (1)*

Valentine, B. H. 7: *v SA 1938 (5); v In 1933 (2)*

Vaughan, M. P. 11: v WI 2000 (4); v P 2001 (2); *v SA 1999 (4); v SL 2000 (1)*

Verity, H. 40: v A 1934 (5) 1938 (4); v SA 1935 (4); v WI 1933 (2) 1939 (1); v NZ 1931 (2) 1937 (1); v In 1936 (3); *v A 1932 (4) 1936 (5); v SA 1938 (5); v NZ 1932 (1); v In 1933 (3)*

Vernon, G. F. 1: *v A 1882*

Vine, J. 2: *v A 1911 (2)*

Voce, W. 27: v NZ 1931 (1) 1937 (1); v In 1932 (1) 1936 (1) 1946 (1); *v A 1932 (4) 1936 (5) 1946 (2); v SA 1930 (5); v WI 1929 (4); v NZ 1932 (2)*

Waddington, A. 2: *v A 1920 (2)*

Wainwright, E. 5: v A 1893 (1); *v A 1897 (4)*

Walker, P. M. 3: v SA 1960 (3)

Walters, C. F. 11: v A 1934 (5); v WI 1933 (3); *v In 1933 (3)*

Ward, A. 5: v WI 1976 (1); v NZ 1969 (3); v P 1971 (1)

Ward, A. 7: v A 1893 (2); *v A 1894 (5)*

Ward, I. J. 5: v A 2001 (3); v P 2001 (2)

Wardle, J. H. 28: v A 1953 (3) 1956 (1); v SA 1951 (2) 1955 (3); v WI 1950 (1) 1957 (1); v P 1954 (4); *v A 1954 (4); v SA 1956 (4); v WI 1947 (1) 1953 (2); v NZ 1954 (2)*

Warner, P. F. 15: v A 1909 (1) 1912 (1); v SA 1912 (1); *v A 1903 (5); v SA 1898 (2) 1905 (5)*

Warr, J. J. 2: *v A 1950 (2)*

Warren, A. R. 1: v A 1905

Washbrook, C. 37: v A 1948 (4) 1956 (3); v SA 1947 (5); v WI 1950 (2); v NZ 1937 (1) 1949 (2); v In 1946 (3); *v A 1946 (5) 1950 (5); v SA 1948 (5); v NZ 1946 (1) 1950 (1)*

Watkin, S. L. 3: v A 1993 (1); v WI 1991 (2)
Watkins, A. J. 15: v A 1948 (1); v NZ 1949 (1); v In 1952 (3); *v SA 1948 (5); v In 1951 (5)*
Watkinson, M. 4: v WI 1995 (3); *v SA 1995 (1)*
Watson, W. 23: v A 1953 (3) 1956 (2); v SA 1951 (5) 1955 (1); v NZ 1958 (2); v In 1952 (1); *v A 1958 (2); v WI 1953 (5); v NZ 1958 (2)*
Webbe, A. J. 1: *v A 1878*
Wellard, A. W. 2: v A 1938 (1); v NZ 1937 (1)
Wells, A. P. 1: v WI 1995
Wharton, A. 1: v NZ 1949
Whitaker, J. J. 1: *v A 1986*
White, C. 21: v A 2001 (3); v SA 1994 (1); v WI 1995 (2) 2000 (4); v NZ 1994 (3); *v NZ 1996 (1); v P 2000 (3); v SL 2000 (3); v Z 1996 (1)*
White, D. W. 2: *v P 1961 (2)*
White, J. C. 15: v A 1921 (1) 1930 (1); v SA 1929 (3); v WI 1928 (1); *v A 1928 (5); v SA 1930 (4)*
Whysall, W. W. 4: v A 1930 (1); *v A 1924 (3)*
Wilkinson, L. L. 3: *v SA 1938 (3)*
Willey, P. 26: v A 1980 (1) 1981 (4) 1985 (1); v WI 1976 (2) 1980 (5); v NZ 1986 (1); v In 1979 (1); *v A 1979 (3); v WI 1980 (4) 1985 (4)*
Williams, N. F. 1: v In 1990
Willis, R. G. D. 90: v A 1977 (5) 1981 (6); v WI 1973 (1) 1976 (2) 1980 (4) 1984 (3); v NZ 1978 (3) 1983 (4); v In 1974 (1) 1979 (3) 1982 (3); v P 1974 (1) 1978 (3) 1982 (2); *v A 1970 (4) 1974 (5) 1976 (1) 1978 (6) 1979 (3) 1982 (5); v WI 1973 (3); v NZ 1970 (1) 1977 (3) 1983 (3); v In 1976 (5) 1981 (5); v P 1977 (3) 1983 (1); v SL 1981 (1)*
Wilson, C. E. M. 2: *v SA 1898 (2)*
Wilson, D. 6: *v NZ 1970 (1); v In 1963 (5)*
Wilson, E. R. 1: *v A 1920*
Wood, A. 4: v A 1938 (1); v WI 1939 (3)
Wood, B. 12: v A 1972 (1) 1975 (3); v WI 1976 (1); v P 1978 (1); *v NZ 1974 (2); v In 1972 (3); v P 1972 (1)*
Wood, G. E. C. 3: v SA 1924 (3)
Wood, H. 4: v A 1888 (1); *v SA 1888 (2) 1891 (1)*
Wood, R. 1: *v A 1886*
Woods S. M. J. 3: *v SA 1895 (3)*
Woolley, F. E. 64: v A 1909 (1) 1912 (3) 1921 (5) 1926 (5) 1930 (2) 1934 (1); v SA 1912 (3) 1924 (5) 1929 (3); v NZ 1931 (1); v In 1932 (1); *v A 1911 (5) 1920 (5) 1924 (5); v SA 1909 (5) 1913 (5) 1922 (5); v NZ 1929 (4)*
Woolmer, R. A. 19: v A 1975 (2) 1977 (5) 1981 (2); v WI 1976 (5) 1980 (2); *v A 1976 (1); v In 1976 (2)*
Worthington, T. S. 9: v In 1936 (2); *v A 1936 (3); v NZ 1929 (4)*
Wright, C. W. 3: *v SA 1895 (3)*
Wright, D. V. P. 34: v A 1938 (3) 1948 (1); v SA 1947 (4); v WI 1939 (3) 1950 (1); v NZ 1949 (1); v In 1946 (2); *v A 1946 (5) 1950 (5); v SA 1938 (3) 1948 (3); v NZ 1946 (1) 1950 (2)*
Wyatt, R. E. S. 40: v A 1930 (1) 1934 (4); v SA 1929 (2) 1935 (5); v WI 1933 (2); v In 1936 (1); *v A 1932 (5) 1936 (2); v SA 1927 (5) 1930 (5); v WI 1929 (2) 1934 (4); v NZ 1932 (2)*
Wynyard, E. G. 3: v A 1896 (1); *v SA 1905 (2)*

Yardley, N. W. D. 20: v A 1948 (5); v SA 1947 (5); v WI 1950 (3); *v A 1946 (5); v SA 1938 (1); v NZ 1946 (1)*
Young, H. I. 2: v A 1899 (2)
Young, J. A. 8: v A 1948 (3); v SA 1947 (1); v NZ 1949 (2); *v SA 1948 (2)*
Young, R. A. 2: *v A 1907 (2)*

AUSTRALIA

Number of Test cricketers: 384

a'Beckett, E. L. 4: v E 1928 (2); v SA 1931 (1); *v E 1930 (1)*
Alderman, T. M. 41: v E 1982 (1) 1990 (4); v WI 1981 (2) 1984 (3) 1988 (2); v NZ 1989 (1); v P 1981 (3) 1989 (2); v SL 1989 (2); *v E 1981 (6) 1989 (6); v WI 1983 (3) 1990 (1); v NZ 1981 (3) 1989 (1); v P 1982 (1)*

Alexander, G. 2: v E 1884 (1); *v E 1880 (1)*
Alexander, H. H. 1: v E 1932
Allan, F. E. 1: v E 1878
Allan, P. J. 1: v E 1965
Allen, R. C. 1: v E 1886
Andrews, T. J. E. 16: v E 1924 (3); *v E 1921 (5) 1926 (5); v SA 1921 (3)*
Angel, J. 4: v E 1994 (1); v WI 1992 (1); *v P 1994 (2)*
Archer, K. A. 5: v E 1950 (3); v WI 1951 (2)
Archer, R. G. 19: v E 1954 (4); v SA 1952 (1); *v E 1953 (3) 1956 (5); v WI 1954 (5); v P 1956 (1)*
Armstrong, W. W. 50: v E 1901 (4) 1903 (3) 1907 (5) 1911 (5) 1920 (5); v SA 1910 (5); *v E 1902 (5) 1905 (5) 1909 (5) 1921 (5); v SA 1902 (3)*

Badcock, C. L. 7: v E 1936 (3); *v E 1938 (4)*
Bannerman, A. C. 28: v E 1878 (1) 1881 (3) 1882 (4) 1884 (4) 1886 (1) 1887 (1) 1891 (3); *v E 1880 (1) 1882 (1) 1884 (3) 1888 (3) 1893 (3)*
Bannerman, C. 3: v E 1876 (2) 1878 (1)
Bardsley, W. 41: v E 1911 (4) 1920 (5) 1924 (3); v SA 1910 (5); *v E 1909 (5) 1912 (3) 1921 (5) 1926 (5); v SA 1912 (3) 1921 (3)*
Barnes, S. G. 13: v E 1946 (4); v In 1947 (3); *v E 1938 (1) 1948 (4); v NZ 1945 (1)*
Barnett, B. A. 4: *v E 1938 (4)*
Barrett, J. E. 2: *v E 1890 (2)*
Beard, G. R. 3: *v P 1979 (3)*
Benaud, J. 3: v P 1972 (2); *v WI 1972 (1)*
Benaud, R. 63: v E 1954 (5) 1958 (5) 1962 (5); v SA 1952 (4) 1963 (4); v WI 1951 (1) 1960 (5); *v E 1953 (3) 1956 (5) 1961 (4); v SA 1957 (5); v WI 1954 (5); v In 1956 (3) 1959 (5); v P 1956 (1) 1959 (3)*
Bennett, M. J. 3: v WI 1984 (2); *v E 1985 (1)*
Bevan, M. G. 18: v E 1994 (3); v SA 1997 (1); v WI 1996 (4); *v E 1997 (3); v SA 1996 (3); v In 1996 (1); v P 1994 (3)*
Bichel, A. J. 5: v SA 1997 (1); v WI 1996 (2) 2000 (2)
Blackham, J. McC. 35: v E 1876 (2) 1878 (1) 1881 (4) 1882 (4) 1884 (2) 1886 (1) 1887 (1) 1891 (3) 1894 (1); *v E 1880 (1) 1882 (1) 1884 (3) 1886 (3) 1888 (3) 1890 (2) 1893 (3)*
Blackie, D. D. 3: v E 1928 (3)
Blewett, G. S. 46: v E 1994 (2); v SA 1997 (3); v WI 1996 (4); v NZ 1997 (3); v In 1999 (3); v P 1995 (3) 1999 (3); *v E 1997 (6); v SA 1996 (3); v WI 1994 (4) 1998 (3); v NZ 1999 (2); v In 1997 (3); v SL 1999 (3); v Z 1999 (1)*
Bonnor, G. J. 17: v E 1882 (4) 1884 (3); *v E 1880 (1) 1882 (1) 1884 (3) 1886 (2) 1888 (3)*
Boon, D. C. 107: v E 1986 (4) 1987 (1) 1990 (5) 1994 (5); v SA 1993 (3); v WI 1984 (3) 1988 (5) 1992 (5); v NZ 1985 (3) 1987 (3) 1989 (1) 1993 (3); v In 1985 (3) 1991 (5); v P 1989 (2) 1995 (3); v SL 1987 (1) 1989 (2) 1995 (3); *v E 1985 (4) 1989 (6) 1993 (6); v SA 1993 (3); v WI 1990 (5) 1994 (4); v NZ 1985 (3) 1989 (1) 1992 (3); v In 1986 (3); v P 1988 (3) 1994 (3); v SL 1992 (3)*
Booth, B. C. 29: v E 1962 (5) 1965 (3); v SA 1963 (4); v P 1964 (1); *v E 1961 (2) 1964 (5); v WI 1964 (5); v In 1964 (3); v P 1964 (1)*
Border, A. R. 156: v E 1978 (3) 1979 (3) 1982 (5) 1986 (5) 1987 (1) 1990 (5); v SA 1993 (3); v WI 1979 (3) 1981 (3) 1984 (5) 1988 (5) 1992 (5); v NZ 1980 (3) 1985 (3) 1987 (3) 1989 (1) 1993 (3); v In 1980 (3) 1985 (3) 1991 (5); v P 1978 (2) 1981 (3) 1983 (5) 1989 (3); v SL 1987 (1) 1989 (2); *v E 1980 (1) 1981 (6) 1985 (6) 1989 (6) 1993 (6); v SA 1993 (3); v WI 1983 (5) 1990 (5); v NZ 1981 (3) 1985 (3) 1989 (1) 1992 (3); v In 1979 (6) 1986 (3); v P 1979 (3) 1982 (3) 1988 (3); v SL 1982 (1) 1992 (3)*
Boyle, H. F. 12: v E 1878 (1) 1881 (4) 1882 (1) 1884 (1); *v E 1880 (1) 1882 (1) 1884 (3)*
Bradman, D. G. 52: v E 1928 (4) 1932 (4) 1936 (5) 1946 (5); v SA 1931 (5); v WI 1930 (5); v In 1947 (5); *v E 1930 (5) 1934 (5) 1938 (4) 1948 (5)*
Bright, R. J. 25: v E 1979 (1); v WI 1979 (1); v NZ 1985 (1); v In 1985 (3); *v E 1977 (3) 1980 (1) 1981 (5); v NZ 1985 (2); v In 1986 (3); v P 1979 (3) 1982 (2)*
Bromley, E. H. 2: v E 1932 (1); *v E 1934 (1)*
Brown, W. A. 22: v E 1936 (2); v In 1947 (3); *v E 1934 (5) 1938 (4) 1948 (2); v SA 1935 (5); v NZ 1945 (1)*
Bruce, W. 14: v E 1884 (2) 1891 (3) 1894 (4); *v E 1886 (2) 1893 (3)*

Burge, P. J. 42: v E 1954 (1) 1958 (1) 1962 (3) 1965 (4); v SA 1963 (5); v WI 1960 (2); *v E 1956 (3) 1961 (5) 1964 (5); v SA 1957 (1); v WI 1954 (1); v In 1956 (3) 1959 (2) 1964 (3); v P 1959 (2) 1964 (1)*
Burke, J. W. 24: v E 1950 (2) 1954 (2) 1958 (5); v WI 1951 (1); *v E 1956 (5); v SA 1957 (5); v In 1956 (3); v P 1956 (1)*
Burn, K. E. 2: *v E 1890 (2)*
Burton, F. J. 2: v E 1886 (1) 1887 (1)

Callaway, S. T. 3: v E 1891 (2) 1894 (1)
Callen, I. W. 1: v In 1977
Campbell, G. D. 4: v P 1989 (1); v SL 1989 (1); *v E 1989 (1); v NZ 1989 (1)*
Carkeek, W. 6: *v E 1912 (3); v SA 1912 (3)*
Carlson, P. H. 2: v E 1978 (2)
Carter, H. 28: v E 1907 (5) 1911 (5) 1920 (2); v SA 1910 (5); *v E 1909 (5) 1921 (4); v SA 1921 (2)*
Chappell, G. S. 87: v E 1970 (5) 1974 (6) 1976 (1) 1979 (3) 1982 (5); v WI 1975 (6) 1979 (3) 1981 (3); v NZ 1973 (3) 1980 (3); v In 1980 (3); v P 1972 (3) 1976 (3) 1981 (3) 1983 (5); *v E 1972 (5) 1975 (4) 1977 (5) 1980 (1); v WI 1972 (5); v NZ 1973 (3) 1976 (2) 1981 (3); v P 1979 (3); v SL 1982 (1)*
Chappell, I. M. 75: v E 1965 (2) 1970 (6) 1974 (6) 1979 (2); v WI 1968 (5) 1975 (6) 1979 (1); v NZ 1973 (3); v In 1967 (4); v P 1964 (1) 1972 (3); *v E 1968 (5) 1972 (5) 1975 (4); v SA 1966 (5) 1969 (4); v WI 1972 (5); v NZ 1973 (3); v In 1969 (5)*
Chappell, T. M. 3: *v E 1981 (3)*
Charlton, P. C. 2: *v E 1890 (2)*
Chipperfield, A. G. 14: v E 1936 (3); *v E 1934 (5) 1938 (1); v SA 1935 (5)*
Clark, W. M. 10: v In 1977 (5); v P 1978 (1); *v WI 1977 (4)*
Colley, D. J. 3: *v E 1972 (3)*
Collins, H. L. 19: v E 1920 (5) 1924 (5); *v E 1921 (3) 1926 (3); v SA 1921 (3)*
Coningham, A. 1: v E 1894
Connolly, A. N. 29: v E 1965 (1) 1970 (1); v SA 1963 (3); v WI 1968 (5); v In 1967 (3); *v E 1968 (5); v SA 1969 (4); v In 1964 (2) 1969 (5)*
Cook, S. H. 2: v NZ 1997 (2)
Cooper, B. B. 1: v E 1876
Cooper, W. H. 2: v E 1881 (1) 1884 (1)
Corling, G. E. 5: *v E 1964 (5)*
Cosier, G. J. 18: v E 1976 (1) 1978 (2); v WI 1975 (3); v In 1977 (4); v P 1976 (3); *v WI 1977 (3); v NZ 1976 (2)*
Cottam, J. T. 1: v E 1886
Cotter, A. 21: v E 1903 (2) 1907 (2) 1911 (4); v SA 1910 (5); *v E 1905 (3) 1909 (5)*
Coulthard, G. 1: v E 1881
Cowper, R. M. 27: v E 1965 (4); v In 1967 (4); v P 1964 (1); *v E 1964 (1) 1968 (4); v SA 1966 (5); v WI 1964 (5); v In 1964 (2); v P 1964 (1)*
Craig, I. D. 11: v SA 1952 (1); *v E 1956 (2); v SA 1957 (5); v In 1956 (2); v P 1956 (1)*
Crawford, P. 4: *v E 1956 (1); v In 1956 (3)*

Dale, A. C. 2: *v WI 1998 (1); v In 1997 (1)*
Darling, J. 34: v E 1894 (5) 1897 (5) 1901 (3); *v E 1896 (3) 1899 (5) 1902 (5) 1905 (5); v SA 1902 (3)*
Darling, L. S. 12: v E 1932 (2) 1936 (1); *v E 1934 (4); v SA 1935 (5)*
Darling, W. M. 14: v E 1978 (4); v In 1977 (1); v P 1978 (1); *v WI 1977 (3); v In 1979 (5)*
Davidson, A. K. 44: v E 1954 (3) 1958 (5) 1962 (5); v WI 1960 (4); *v E 1953 (5) 1956 (2) 1961 (5); v SA 1957 (5); v In 1956 (1) 1959 (5); v P 1956 (1) 1959 (3)*
Davis, I. C. 15: v E 1976 (1); v NZ 1973 (3); v P 1976 (3); *v E 1977 (3); v NZ 1973 (3) 1976 (2)*
Davis, S. P. 1: *v NZ 1985*
De Courcy, J. H. 3: *v E 1953 (3)*
Dell, A. R. 2: v E 1970 (1); v NZ 1973 (1)
Dodemaide, A. I. C. 10: v E 1987 (1); v WI 1988 (2); v NZ 1987 (1); v SL 1987 (1); *v P 1988 (3); v SL 1992 (2)*
Donnan, H. 5: v E 1891 (2); *v E 1896 (3)*
Dooland, B. 3: v E 1946 (2); v In 1947 (1)
Duff, R. A. 22: v E 1901 (4) 1903 (5); *v E 1902 (5) 1905 (5); v SA 1902 (3)*
Duncan, J. R. F. 1: v E 1970

Dyer, G. C. 6: v E 1986 (1) 1987 (1); v NZ 1987 (3); v SL 1987 (1)
Dymock, G. 21: v E 1974 (1) 1978 (3) 1979 (3); v WI 1979 (2); v NZ 1973 (1); v P 1978 (1); *v NZ 1973 (2); v In 1979 (5); v P 1979 (3)*
Dyson, J. 30: v E 1982 (5); v WI 1981 (2) 1984 (3); v NZ 1980 (3); v In 1977 (3) 1980 (3); *v E 1981 (5); v NZ 1981 (3); v P 1982 (3)*

Eady, C. J. 2: v E 1901 (1); *v E 1896 (1)*
Eastwood, K. H. 1: v E 1970
Ebeling, H. I. 1: *v E 1934*
Edwards, J. D. 3: *v E 1888 (3)*
Edwards, R. 20: v E 1974 (5); v P 1972 (2); *v E 1972 (4) 1975 (4); v WI 1972 (5)*
Edwards, W. J. 3: v E 1974 (3)
Elliott, M. T. G. 20: v SA 1997 (3); v WI 1996 (2); v NZ 1997 (3); *v E 1997 (6); v SA 1996 (3); v WI 1998 (3)*
Emery, P. A. 1: *v P 1994*
Emery, S. H. 4: *v E 1912 (2); v SA 1912 (2)*
Evans, E. 6: v E 1881 (2) 1882 (1) 1884 (1); *v E 1886 (2)*

Fairfax, A. G. 10: v E 1928 (1); v WI 1930 (5); *v E 1930 (4)*
Favell, L. E. 19: v E 1954 (4) 1958 (2); v WI 1960 (4); *v WI 1954 (2); v In 1959 (4); v P 1959 (3)*
Ferris, J. J. 8: v E 1886 (2) 1887 (1); *v E 1888 (3) 1890 (2)*
Fingleton, J. H. 18: v E 1932 (3) 1936 (5); v SA 1931 (1); *v E 1938 (4); v SA 1935 (5)*
Fleetwood-Smith, L. O'B. 10: v E 1936 (3); *v E 1938 (4); v SA 1935 (3)*
Fleming, D. W. 20: v E 1994 (3) 1998 (4); v In 1999 (3); v P 1999 (3); *v In 2000 (1); v P 1994 (1) 1998 (2); v SL 1999 (2); v Z 1999 (1)*
Francis, B. C. 3: *v E 1972 (3)*
Freeman, E. W. 11: v WI 1968 (4); v In 1967 (2); *v E 1968 (2); v SA 1969 (2); v In 1969 (1)*
Freer, F. W. 1: v E 1946

Gannon, J. B. 3: v In 1977 (3)
Garrett, T. W. 19: v E 1876 (2) 1878 (1) 1881 (3) 1882 (3) 1884 (3) 1886 (2) 1887 (1); *v E 1882 (1) 1886 (3)*
Gaunt, R. A. 3: v SA 1963 (1); *v E 1961 (1); v SA 1957 (1)*
Gehrs, D. R. A. 6: v E 1903 (1); v SA 1910 (4); *v E 1905 (1)*
Giffen, G. 31: v E 1881 (3) 1882 (4) 1884 (3) 1891 (3) 1894 (5); *v E 1882 (1) 1884 (3) 1886 (3) 1893 (3) 1896 (3)*
Giffen, W. F. 3: v E 1886 (1) 1891 (2)
Gilbert, D. R. 9: v NZ 1985 (3); v In 1985 (2); *v E 1985 (1); v NZ 1985 (1); v In 1986 (2)*
Gilchrist, A. C. 22: v WI 2000 (5); v In 1999 (3); v P 1999 (3); *v E 2001 (5); v NZ 1999 (3); v In 2000 (3)*
Gillespie, J. N. 26: v E 1998 (1); v WI 1996 (2) 2000 (4); *v E 1997 (4) 2001 (5); v SA 1996 (3); v WI 1998 (3); v In 2000 (3); v SL 1999 (1)*
Gilmour, G. J. 15: v E 1976 (1); v WI 1975 (5); v NZ 1973 (2); v P 1976 (3); *v E 1975 (1); v NZ 1973 (1) 1976 (2)*
Gleeson, J. W. 29: v E 1970 (5); v WI 1968 (5); v In 1967 (4); *v E 1968 (5) 1972 (3); v SA 1969 (4); v In 1969 (3)*
Graham, H. 6: v E 1894 (2); *v E 1893 (3) 1896 (1)*
Gregory, D. W. 3: v E 1876 (2) 1878 (1)
Gregory, E. J. 1: v E 1876
Gregory, J. M. 24: v E 1920 (5) 1924 (5) 1928 (1); *v E 1921 (5) 1926 (5); v SA 1921 (3)*
Gregory, R. G. 2: v E 1936 (2)
Gregory, S. E. 58: v E 1891 (1) 1894 (5) 1897 (5) 1901 (5) 1903 (4) 1907 (2) 1911 (1); *v E 1890 (2) 1893 (3) 1896 (3) 1899 (5) 1902 (5) 1905 (3) 1909 (5) 1912 (3); v SA 1902 (3) 1912 (3)*
Grimmett, C. V. 37: v E 1924 (1) 1928 (5) 1932 (3); v SA 1931 (5); v WI 1930 (5); *v E 1926 (3) 1930 (5) 1934 (5); v SA 1935 (5)*
Groube, T. U. 1: *v E 1880*
Grout, A. T. W. 51: v E 1958 (5) 1962 (2) 1965 (5); v SA 1963 (5); v WI 1960 (5); *v E 1961 (5) 1964 (5); v SA 1957 (5); v WI 1964 (5); v In 1959 (4) 1964 (1); v P 1959 (3) 1964 (1)*
Guest, C. E. J. 1: v E 1962

Hamence, R. A. 3: v E 1946 (1); v In 1947 (2)

Hammond, J. R. 5: *v WI 1972 (5)*
Harry, J. 1: v E 1894
Hartigan, R. J. 2: v E 1907 (2)
Hartkopf, A. E. V. 1: v E 1924
Harvey, M. R. 1: v E 1946
Harvey, R. N. 79: v E 1950 (5) 1954 (5) 1958 (5) 1962 (5); v SA 1952 (5); v WI 1951 (5) 1960 (4); v In 1947 (2); *v E 1948 (2) 1953 (5) 1956 (5) 1961 (5); v SA 1949 (5) 1957 (4); v WI 1954 (5); v In 1956 (3) 1959 (5); v P 1956 (1) 1959 (3)*
Hassett, A. L. 43: v E 1946 (5) 1950 (5); v SA 1952 (5); v WI 1951 (4); v In 1947 (4); *v E 1938 (4) 1948 (5) 1953 (5); v SA 1949 (5); v NZ 1945 (1)*
Hawke, N. J. N. 27: v E 1962 (1) 1965 (4); v SA 1963 (4); v In 1967 (1); v P 1964 (1); *v E 1964 (5) 1968 (2); v SA 1966 (2); v WI 1964 (5); v In 1964 (1); v P 1964 (1)*
Hayden, M. L. 21: v WI 1996 (3) 2000 (5); *v E 2001 (5); v SA 1993 (1) 1996 (3); v NZ 1999 (1); v In 2000 (3)*
Hazlitt, G. R. 9: v E 1907 (2) 1911 (1); *v E 1912 (3); v SA 1912 (3)*
Healy, I. A. 119: v E 1990 (5) 1994 (5) 1998 (5); v SA 1993 (3) 1997 (3); v WI 1988 (5) 1992 (5) 1996 (5); v NZ 1989 (1) 1993 (3) 1997 (3); v In 1991 (5); v P 1989 (3) 1995 (3); v SL 1989 (2) 1995 (3); *v E 1989 (6) 1993 (6) 1997 (6); v SA 1993 (3) 1996 (3); v WI 1990 (5) 1994 (4) 1998 (4); v NZ 1989 (1) 1992 (3); v In 1996 (1) 1997 (3); v P 1988 (3) 1994 (2) 1998 (3); v SL 1992 (3) 1999 (3); v Z 1999 (1)*
Hendry, H. L. 11: v E 1924 (1) 1928 (4); *v E 1921 (4); v SA 1921 (2)*
Hibbert, P. A. 1: v In 1977
Higgs, J. D. 22: v E 1978 (5) 1979 (1); v WI 1979 (1); v NZ 1980 (3); v In 1980 (2); *v WI 1977 (4); v In 1979 (6)*
Hilditch, A. M. J. 18: v E 1978 (1); v WI 1984 (2); v NZ 1985 (1); v P 1978 (2); *v E 1985 (6); v In 1979 (6)*
Hill, C. 49: v E 1897 (5) 1901 (5) 1903 (5) 1907 (5) 1911 (5); v SA 1910 (5); *v E 1896 (3) 1899 (3) 1902 (5) 1905 (5); v SA 1902 (3)*
Hill, J. C. 3: *v E 1953 (2); v WI 1954 (1)*
Hoare, D. E. 1: v WI 1960
Hodges, J. 2: v E 1876 (2)
Hogan, T. G. 7: v P 1983 (1); *v WI 1983 (5); v SL 1982 (1)*
Hogg, G. B. 1: *v In 1996*
Hogg, R. M. 38: v E 1978 (6) 1982 (3); v WI 1979 (2) 1984 (4); v NZ 1980 (2); v In 1980 (2); v P 1978 (2) 1983 (4); *v E 1981 (2); v WI 1983 (4); v In 1979 (6); v SL 1982 (1)*
Hohns, T. V. 7: v WI 1988 (2); *v E 1989 (5)*
Hole, G. B. 18: v E 1950 (1) 1954 (3); v SA 1952 (4); v WI 1951 (5); *v E 1953 (5)*
Holland, R. G. 11: v WI 1984 (3); v NZ 1985 (3); v In 1985 (1); *v E 1985 (4)*
Hookes, D. W. 23: v E 1976 (1) 1982 (5); v WI 1979 (1); v NZ 1985 (2); v In 1985 (2); *v E 1977 (5); v WI 1983 (5); v P 1979 (1); v SL 1982 (1)*
Hopkins, A. J. 20: v E 1901 (2) 1903 (5); *v E 1902 (5) 1905 (3) 1909 (2); v SA 1902 (3)*
Horan, T. P. 15: v E 1876 (1) 1878 (1) 1881 (4) 1882 (4) 1884 (4); *v E 1882 (1)*
Hordern, H. V. 7: v E 1911 (5); v SA 1910 (2)
Hornibrook, P. M. 6: v E 1928 (1); *v E 1930 (5)*
Howell, W. P. 18: v E 1897 (3) 1901 (4) 1903 (3); *v E 1899 (5) 1902 (1); v SA 1902 (2)*
Hughes, K. J. 70: v E 1978 (6) 1979 (3) 1982 (5); v WI 1979 (3) 1981 (3) 1984 (4); v NZ 1980 (3); v In 1977 (2) 1980 (3); v P 1978 (2) 1981 (3) 1983 (5); *v E 1977 (1) 1980 (1) 1981 (6); v WI 1983 (5); v NZ 1981 (3); v In 1979 (6); v P 1979 (3) 1982 (3)*
Hughes, M. G. 53: v E 1986 (4) 1990 (4); v WI 1988 (4) 1992 (5); v NZ 1987 (1) 1989 (1); v In 1985 (1) 1991 (5); v P 1989 (3); v SL 1987 (1) 1989 (2); *v E 1989 (6) 1993 (6); v SA 1993 (2); v WI 1990 (5); v NZ 1992 (3)*
Hunt, W. A. 1: v SA 1931
Hurst, A. G. 12: v E 1978 (6); v NZ 1973 (1); v In 1977 (1); v P 1978 (2); *v In 1979 (2)*
Hurwood, A. 2: v WI 1930 (2)

Inverarity, R. J. 6: v WI 1968 (1); *v E 1968 (2) 1972 (3)*
Iredale, F. A. 14: v E 1894 (5) 1897 (4); *v E 1896 (2) 1899 (3)*
Ironmonger, H. 14: v E 1928 (2) 1932 (4); v SA 1931 (4); v WI 1930 (4)
Iverson, J. B. 5: v E 1950 (5)

Jackson, A. A. 8: v E 1928 (2); v WI 1930 (4); *v E 1930 (2)*

Jarman, B. N. 19: v E 1962 (3); v WI 1968 (4); v In 1967 (4); v P 1964 (1); *v E 1968 (4); v In 1959 (1) 1964 (2)*
Jarvis, A. H. 11: v E 1884 (3) 1894 (4); *v E 1886 (2) 1888 (2)*
Jenner, T. J. 9: v E 1970 (2) 1974 (2); v WI 1975 (1); *v WI 1972 (4)*
Jennings, C. B. 6: *v E 1912 (3); v SA 1912 (3)*
Johnson I. W. 45: v E 1946 (4) 1950 (5) 1954 (4); v SA 1952 (1); v WI 1951 (4); v In 1947 (4); *v E 1948 (4) 1956 (5); v SA 1949 (5); v WI 1954 (5); v NZ 1945 (1); v In 1956 (2); v P 1956 (1)*
Johnson, L. J. 1: v In 1947
Johnston, W. A. 40: v E 1950 (5) 1954 (4); v SA 1952 (5); v WI 1951 (5); v In 1947 (4); *v E 1948 (5) 1953 (3); v SA 1949 (5); v WI 1954 (4)*
Jones, D. M. 52: v E 1986 (5) 1987 (1) 1990 (5); v WI 1988 (3); v NZ 1987 (3) 1989 (1); v In 1991 (5); v P 1989 (3); v SL 1987 (1) 1989 (2); *v E 1989 (6); v WI 1983 (2) 1990 (5); v NZ 1989 (1); v In 1986 (3); v P 1988 (3); v SL 1992 (3)*
Jones, E. 19: v E 1894 (1) 1897 (5) 1901 (2); *v E 1896 (3) 1899 (5) 1902 (2); v SA 1902 (1)*
Jones, S. P. 12: v E 1881 (2) 1884 (4) 1886 (1) 1887 (1); *v E 1882 (1) 1886 (3)*
Joslin, L. R. 1: v In 1967
Julian, B. P. 7: v SL 1995 (1); *v E 1993 (2); v WI 1994 (4)*

Kasprowicz, M. S. 17: v E 1998 (1); v SA 1997 (2); v WI 1996 (2); v NZ 1997 (3); v In 1999 (1); v P 1999 (1); *v E 1997 (3); v In 1997 (3) 2000 (1)*
Katich, S. M. 1: *v E 2001*
Kelleway, C. 26: v E 1911 (4) 1920 (5) 1924 (5) 1928 (1); v SA 1910 (5); *v E 1912 (3); v SA 1912 (3)*
Kelly, J. J. 36: v E 1897 (5) 1901 (5) 1903 (5); *v E 1896 (3) 1899 (5) 1902 (5) 1905 (5); v SA 1902 (3)*
Kelly, T. J. D. 2: v E 1876 (1) 1878 (1)
Kendall, T. 2: v E 1876 (2)
Kent, M. F. 3: *v E 1981 (3)*
Kerr, R. B. 2: v NZ 1985 (2)
Kippax, A. F. 22: v E 1924 (1) 1928 (5) 1932 (1); v SA 1931 (4); v WI 1930 (5); *v E 1930 (5) 1934 (1)*
Kline L. F. 13: v E 1958 (2); v WI 1960 (2); *v SA 1957 (5); v In 1959 (3); v P 1959 (1)*

Laird, B. M. 21: v E 1979 (2); v WI 1979 (3) 1981 (3); v P 1981 (3); *v E 1980 (1); v NZ 1981 (3); v P 1979 (3) 1982 (3)*
Langer, J. L. 42: v E 1998 (5); v WI 1992 (2) 1996 (2) 2000 (5); v In 1999 (3); v P 1999 (3); *v E 2001 (1); v WI 1998 (4); v NZ 1992 (3) 1999 (3); v In 2000 (3); v P 1994 (1) 1998 (3); v SL 1999 (3); v Z 1999 (1)*
Langley, G. R. A. 26: v E 1954 (2); v SA 1952 (5); v WI 1951 (5); *v E 1953 (4) 1956 (3); v WI 1954 (4); v In 1956 (2); v P 1956 (1)*
Laughlin, T. J. 3: v E 1978 (1); *v WI 1977 (2)*
Laver, F. 15: v E 1901 (1) 1903 (1); *v E 1899 (4) 1905 (5) 1909 (4)*
Law, S. G. 1: v SL 1995
Lawry, W. M. 67: v E 1962 (5) 1965 (5) 1970 (5); v SA 1963 (5); v WI 1968 (5); v In 1967 (4); v P 1964 (1); *v E 1961 (5) 1964 (5) 1968 (4); v SA 1966 (5) 1969 (4); v WI 1964 (5); v In 1964 (3) 1969 (5); v P 1964 (1)*
Lawson, G. F. 46: v E 1982 (5) 1986 (1); v WI 1981 (1) 1984 (5) 1988 (1); v NZ 1980 (1) 1985 (2) 1989 (1); v P 1983 (5); v SL 1989 (1); *v E 1981 (3) 1985 (6) 1989 (6); v WI 1983 (5); v P 1982 (3)*
Lee, B. 12: v WI 2000 (2); v In 1999 (2); *v E 2001 (5); v NZ 1999 (3)*
Lee, P. K. 2: v E 1932 (1); v SA 1931 (1)
Lehmann, D. S. 5: v E 1998 (2); *v In 1997 (1); v P 1998 (2)*
Lillee, D. K. 70: v E 1970 (2) 1974 (6) 1976 (1) 1979 (3) 1982 (1); v WI 1975 (5) 1979 (3) 1981 (3); v NZ 1980 (3); v In 1980 (3); v P 1972 (3) 1976 (3) 1981 (3) 1983 (5); *v E 1972 (5) 1975 (4) 1980 (1) 1981 (6); v WI 1972 (1); v NZ 1976 (2) 1981 (3); v P 1979 (3); v SL 1982 (1)*
Lindwall, R. R. 61: v E 1946 (4) 1950 (5) 1954 (4) 1958 (2); v SA 1952 (4); v WI 1951 (5); v In 1947 (5); *v E 1948 (5) 1953 (5) 1956 (4); v SA 1949 (4); v WI 1954 (5); v NZ 1945 (1); v In 1956 (3) 1959 (2); v P 1956 (1) 1959 (2)*
Love, H. S. B. 1: v E 1932
Loxton, S. J. E. 12: v E 1950 (3); v In 1947 (1); *v E 1948 (3); v SA 1949 (5)*
Lyons, J. J. 14: v E 1886 (1) 1891 (3) 1894 (3) 1897 (1); *v E 1888 (1) 1890 (2) 1893 (3)*

McAlister, P. A. 8: v E 1903 (2) 1907 (4); *v E 1909 (2)*

Macartney, C. G. 35: v E 1907 (5) 1911 (1) 1920 (2); v SA 1910 (4); *v E 1909 (5) 1912 (3) 1921 (5) 1926 (5); v SA 1912 (3) 1921 (2)*

McCabe, S. J. 39: v E 1932 (5) 1936 (5); v SA 1931 (5); v WI 1930 (5); *v E 1930 (5) 1934 (5) 1938 (4); v SA 1935 (5)*

McCool, C. L. 14: v E 1946 (5); v In 1947 (3); *v SA 1949 (5); v NZ 1945 (1)*

McCormick, E. L. 12: v E 1936 (4); *v E 1938 (3); v SA 1935 (5)*

McCosker, R. B. 25: v E 1974 (3) 1976 (1) 1979 (2); v WI 1975 (4) 1979 (1); v P 1976 (3); *v E 1975 (4) 1977 (5); v NZ 1976 (2)*

McDermott, C. J. 71: v E 1986 (1) 1987 (1) 1990 (2) 1994 (5); v SA 1993 (3); v WI 1984 (2) 1988 (2) 1992 (5); v NZ 1985 (2) 1987 (3) 1993 (3); v In 1985 (2) 1991 (5); v P 1995 (3); v SL 1987 (1) 1995 (3); *v E 1985 (6) 1993 (2); v SA 1993 (3); v WI 1990 (5); v NZ 1985 (2) 1992 (3); v In 1986 (2); v P 1994 (2); v SL 1992 (3)*

McDonald, C. C. 47: v E 1954 (2) 1958 (5); v SA 1952 (5); v WI 1951 (1) 1960 (5); *v E 1956 (5) 1961 (3); v SA 1957 (5); v WI 1954 (5); v In 1956 (2) 1959 (5); v P 1956 (1) 1959 (3)*

McDonald, E. A. 11: v E 1920 (3); *v E 1921 (5); v SA 1921 (3)*

McDonnell, P. S. 19: v E 1881 (4) 1882 (3) 1884 (2) 1886 (2) 1887 (1); *v E 1880 (1) 1884 (3) 1888 (3)*

MacGill, S. C. G. 16: v E 1998 (4); v SA 1997 (1); v WI 2000 (4); *v WI 1998 (4); v P 1998 (3)*

McGrath, G. D. 75: v E 1994 (2) 1998 (5); v SA 1993 (1) 1997 (2); v WI 1996 (5) 2000 (5); v NZ 1993 (2) 1997 (1); v In 1999 (3); v P 1995 (3) 1999 (3); v SL 1995 (3); *v E 1997 (6) 2001 (5); v SA 1993 (2) 1996 (3); v WI 1994 (4) 1998 (4); v NZ 1999 (3); v In 1996 (1) 2000 (3); v P 1994 (2) 1998 (3); v SL 1999 (3); v Z 1999 (1)*

McIlwraith, J. 1: *v E 1886*

McIntyre, P. E. 2: v E 1994 (1); *v In 1996 (1)*

Mackay, K. D. 37: v E 1958 (5) 1962 (3); v WI 1960 (5); *v E 1956 (3) 1961 (5); v SA 1957 (5); v In 1956 (3) 1959 (5); v P 1959 (3)*

McKenzie, G. D. 60: v E 1962 (5) 1965 (4) 1970 (3); v SA 1963 (5); v WI 1968 (5); v In 1967 (2); v P 1964 (1); *v E 1961 (3) 1964 (5) 1968 (5); v SA 1966 (5) 1969 (3); v WI 1964 (5); v In 1964 (3) 1969 (5); v P 1964 (1)*

McKibbin, T. R. 5: v E 1894 (1) 1897 (2); *v E 1896 (2)*

McLaren, J. W. 1: v E 1911

Maclean, J. A. 4: v E 1978 (4)

McLeod, C. E. 17: v E 1894 (1) 1897 (5) 1901 (2) 1903 (3); *v E 1899 (1) 1905 (5)*

McLeod, R. W. 6: v E 1891 (3); *v E 1893 (3)*

McShane, P. G. 3: v E 1884 (1) 1886 (1) 1887 (1)

Maddocks, L. V. 7: v E 1954 (3); *v E 1956 (2); v WI 1954 (1); v In 1956 (1)*

Maguire, J. N. 3: v P 1983 (1); *v WI 1983 (2)*

Mailey, A. A. 21: v E 1920 (5) 1924 (5); *v E 1921 (3) 1926 (5); v SA 1921 (3)*

Mallett, A. A. 38: v E 1970 (2) 1974 (5) 1979 (1); v WI 1968 (1) 1975 (6) 1979 (1); v NZ 1973 (3); v P 1972 (2); *v E 1968 (1) 1972 (2) 1975 (4) 1980 (1); v SA 1969 (1); v NZ 1973 (3); v In 1969 (5)*

Malone, M. F. 1: *v E 1977*

Mann, A. L. 4: v In 1977 (4)

Marr, A. P. 1: v E 1884

Marsh, G. R. 50: v E 1986 (5) 1987 (1) 1990 (5); v WI 1988 (5); v NZ 1987 (3); v In 1985 (3) 1991 (4); v P 1989 (2); v SL 1987 (1); *v E 1989 (6); v WI 1990 (5); v NZ 1985 (3) 1989 (1); v In 1986 (3); v P 1988 (3)*

Marsh, R. W. 96: v E 1970 (6) 1974 (6) 1976 (1) 1979 (3) 1982 (5); v WI 1975 (6) 1979 (3) 1981 (3); v NZ 1973 (3) 1980 (3); v In 1980 (3); v P 1972 (3) 1976 (3) 1981 (3) 1983 (5); *v E 1972 (5) 1975 (4) 1977 (5) 1980 (1) 1981 (6); v WI 1972 (5); v NZ 1973 (3) 1976 (2) 1981 (3); v P 1979 (3) 1982 (3)*

Martin, J. W. 8: v SA 1963 (1); v WI 1960 (3); *v SA 1966 (1); v In 1964 (2); v P 1964 (1)*

Martyn, D. R. 16: v SA 1993 (2); v WI 1992 (4) 2000 (1); *v E 2001 (5); v NZ 1992 (1) 1999 (3)*

Massie, H. H. 9: v E 1881 (4) 1882 (3) 1884 (1); *v E 1882 (1)*

Massie, R. A. L. 6: v P 1972 (2); *v E 1972 (4)*

Matthews, C. D. 3: v E 1986 (2); v WI 1988 (1)

Matthews, G. R. J. 33: v E 1986 (4) 1990 (5); v WI 1984 (1) 1992 (2); v NZ 1985 (3); v In 1985 (3); v P 1983 (2); *v E 1985 (1); v WI 1983 (1) 1990 (2); v NZ 1985 (3); v In 1986 (3); v SL 1992 (3)*

Matthews, T. J. 8: v E 1911 (2); *v E 1912 (3); v SA 1912 (3)*

May, T. B. A. 24: v E 1994 (3); v SA 1993 (3); v WI 1988 (3) 1992 (1); v NZ 1987 (1) 1993 (2); *v E 1993 (5); v SA 1993 (1); v P 1988 (3) 1994 (2)*

Mayne, E. R. 4: *v E 1912 (1); v SA 1912 (1) 1921 (2)*

Mayne, L. C. 6: *v SA 1969 (2); v WI 1964 (3); v In 1969 (1)*
Meckiff, I. 18: v E 1958 (4); v SA 1963 (1); v WI 1960 (2); *v SA 1957 (4); v In 1959 (5); v P 1959 (2)*
Meuleman, K. D. 1: *v NZ 1945*
Midwinter, W. E. 8: v E 1876 (2) 1882 (1) 1886 (2); *v E 1884 (3)*
Miller, C. R. 18: v E 1998 (3); v WI 2000 (3); *v WI 1998 (1); v NZ 1999 (3); v In 2000 (1); v P 1998 (3); v SL 1999 (3); v Z 1999 (1)*
Miller, K. R. 55: v E 1946 (5) 1950 (5) 1954 (4); v SA 1952 (4); v WI 1951 (5); v In 1947 (5); *v E 1948 (5) 1953 (5) 1956 (5); v SA 1949 (5); v WI 1954 (5); v NZ 1945 (1); v P 1956 (1)*
Minnett, R. B. 9: v E 1911 (5); *v E 1912 (1); v SA 1912 (3)*
Misson, F. M. 5: v WI 1960 (3); *v E 1961 (2)*
Moody, T. M. 8: v NZ 1989 (1); v In 1991 (1); v P 1989 (1); v SL 1989 (2); *v SL 1992 (3)*
Moroney, J. 7: v E 1950 (1); v WI 1951 (1); *v SA 1949 (5)*
Morris, A. R. 46: v E 1946 (5) 1950 (5) 1954 (4); v SA 1952 (5); v WI 1951 (4); v In 1947 (4); *v E 1948 (5) 1953 (5); v SA 1949 (5); v WI 1954 (4)*
Morris, S. 1: v E 1884
Moses, H. 6: v E 1886 (2) 1887 (1) 1891 (2) 1894 (1)
Moss, J. K. 1: v P 1978
Moule, W. H. 1: *v E 1880*
Muller, S. A. 2: v P 1999 (2)
Murdoch, W. L. 18: v E 1876 (1) 1878 (1) 1881 (4) 1882 (4) 1884 (1); *v E 1880 (1) 1882 (1) 1884 (3) 1890 (2)*
Musgrove, H. 1: v E 1884

Nagel, L. E. 1: v E 1932
Nash, L. J. 2: v E 1936 (1); v SA 1931 (1)
Nicholson, M. J. 1: v E 1998
Nitschke, H. C. 2: v SA 1931 (2)
Noble, M. A. 42: v E 1897 (4) 1901 (5) 1903 (5) 1907 (5); *v E 1899 (5) 1902 (5) 1905 (5) 1909 (5); v SA 1902 (3)*
Noblet, G. 3: v SA 1952 (1); v WI 1951 (1); *v SA 1949 (1)*
Nothling, O. E. 1: v E 1928

O'Brien, L. P. J. 5: v E 1932 (2) 1936 (1); *v SA 1935 (2)*
O'Connor, J. D. A. 4: v E 1907 (3); *v E 1909 (1)*
O'Donnell, S. P. 6: v NZ 1985 (1); *v E 1985 (5)*
Ogilvie, A. D. 5: v In 1977 (3); *v WI 1977 (2)*
O'Keeffe, K. J. 24: v E 1970 (2) 1976 (1); v NZ 1973 (3); v P 1972 (2) 1976 (3); *v E 1977 (3); v WI 1972 (5); v NZ 1973 (3) 1976 (2)*
Oldfield, W. A. 54: v E 1920 (3) 1924 (5) 1928 (5) 1932 (4) 1936 (5); v SA 1931 (5); v WI 1930 (5); *v E 1921 (1) 1926 (5) 1930 (5) 1934 (5); v SA 1921 (1) 1935 (5)*
O'Neill, N. C. 42: v E 1958 (5) 1962 (5); v SA 1963 (4); v WI 1960 (5); *v E 1961 (5) 1964 (4); v WI 1964 (4); v In 1959 (5) 1964 (2); v P 1959 (3)*
O'Reilly, W. J. 27: v E 1932 (5) 1936 (5); v SA 1931 (2); *v E 1934 (5) 1938 (4); v SA 1935 (5); v NZ 1945 (1)*
Oxenham, R. K. 7: v E 1928 (3); v SA 1931 (1); v WI 1930 (3)

Palmer, G. E. 17: v E 1881 (4) 1882 (4) 1884 (2); *v E 1880 (1) 1884 (3) 1886 (3)*
Park, R. L. 1: v E 1920
Pascoe, L. S. 14: v E 1979 (2); v WI 1979 (1) 1981 (1); v NZ 1980 (3); v In 1980 (3); *v E 1977 (3) 1980 (1)*
Pellew, C. E. 10: v E 1920 (4); *v E 1921 (5); v SA 1921 (1)*
Phillips, W. B. 27: v WI 1984 (2); v NZ 1985 (3); v In 1985 (3); v P 1983 (5); *v E 1985 (6); v WI 1983 (5); v NZ 1985 (3)*
Phillips, W. N. 1: v In 1991
Philpott, P. I. 8: v E 1965 (3); *v WI 1964 (5)*
Ponsford, W. H. 29: v E 1924 (5) 1928 (2) 1932 (3); v SA 1931 (4); v WI 1930 (5); *v E 1926 (2) 1930 (4) 1934 (4)*
Ponting, R. T. 47: v E 1998 (3); v SA 1997 (3); v WI 1996 (2) 2000 (5); v NZ 1997 (3); v In 1999 (3); v P 1999 (3); v SL 1995 (3); *v E 1997 (3) 2001 (5); v WI 1998 (2); v In 1996 (1) 1997 (3) 2000 (3); v P 1998 (1); v SL 1999 (3); v Z 1999 (1)*

Pope, R. J. 1: v E 1884

Rackemann, C. G. 12: v E 1982 (1) 1990 (1); v WI 1984 (1); v NZ 1989 (1); v P 1983 (2) 1989 (3); v SL 1989 (1); *v WI 1983 (1); v NZ 1989 (1)*
Ransford, V. S. 20: v E 1907 (5) 1911 (5); v SA 1910 (5); *v E 1909 (5)*
Redpath, I. R. 66: v E 1965 (1) 1970 (6) 1974 (6); v SA 1963 (1); v WI 1968 (5) 1975 (6); v In 1967 (3); v P 1972 (3); *v E 1964 (5) 1968 (5); v SA 1966 (5) 1969 (4); v WI 1972 (5); v NZ 1973 (3); v In 1964 (2) 1969 (5); v P 1964 (1)*
Reedman, J. C. 1: v E 1894
Reid, B. A. 27: v E 1986 (5) 1990 (4); v WI 1992 (1); v NZ 1987 (2); v In 1985 (3) 1991 (2); *v WI 1990 (2); v NZ 1985 (3); v In 1986 (2); v P 1988 (3)*
Reiffel, P. R. 35: v SA 1993 (2) 1997 (2); v WI 1996 (3); v NZ 1993 (2) 1997 (3); v In 1991 (1); v P 1995 (3); v SL 1995 (2); *v E 1993 (3) 1997 (4); v SA 1993 (1); v WI 1994 (4); v NZ 1992 (3); v In 1996 (1) 1997 (1)*
Renneberg, D. A. 8: v In 1967 (3); *v SA 1966 (5)*
Richardson, A. J. 9: v E 1924 (4); *v E 1926 (5)*
Richardson, V. Y. 19: v E 1924 (3) 1928 (2) 1932 (5); *v E 1930 (4); v SA 1935 (5)*
Rigg, K. E. 8: v E 1936 (3); v SA 1931 (4); v WI 1930 (1)
Ring, D. T. 13: v SA 1952 (5); v WI 1951 (5); v In 1947 (1); *v E 1948 (1) 1953 (1)*
Ritchie, G. M. 30: v E 1986 (4); v WI 1984 (1); v NZ 1985 (3); v In 1985 (2); *v E 1985 (6); v WI 1983 (5); v NZ 1985 (3); v In 1986 (3); v P 1982 (3)*
Rixon, S. J. 13: v WI 1984 (3); v In 1977 (5); *v WI 1977 (5)*
Robertson, G. R. 4: *v In 1997 (3); v P 1998 (1)*
Robertson, W. R. 1: v E 1884
Robinson, R. D. 3: *v E 1977 (3)*
Robinson, R. H. 1: v E 1936
Rorke, G. F. 4: v E 1958 (2); *v In 1959 (2)*
Rutherford, J. W. 1: *v In 1956*
Ryder, J. 20: v E 1920 (5) 1924 (3) 1928 (5); *v E 1926 (4); v SA 1921 (3)*

Saggers, R. A. 6: *v E 1948 (1); v SA 1949 (5)*
Saunders, J. V. 14: v E 1901 (1) 1903 (2) 1907 (5); *v E 1902 (4); v SA 1902 (2)*
Scott, H. J. H. 8: v E 1884 (2); *v E 1884 (3) 1886 (3)*
Sellers, R. H. D. 1: *v In 1964*
Serjeant, C. S. 12: v In 1977 (4); *v E 1977 (3); v WI 1977 (5)*
Sheahan, A. P. 31: v E 1970 (2); v WI 1968 (5); v NZ 1973 (2); v In 1967 (4); v P 1972 (2); *v E 1968 (5) 1972 (2); v SA 1969 (4); v In 1969 (5)*
Shepherd, B. K. 9: v E 1962 (2); v SA 1963 (4); v P 1964 (1); *v WI 1964 (2)*
Sievers, M. W. 3: v E 1936 (3)
Simpson, R. B. 62: v E 1958 (1) 1962 (5) 1965 (3); v SA 1963 (5); v WI 1960 (5); v In 1967 (3) 1977 (5); v P 1964 (1); *v E 1961 (5) 1964 (5); v SA 1957 (5) 1966 (5); v WI 1964 (5) 1977 (5); v In 1964 (3); v P 1964 (1)*
Sincock, D. J. 3: v E 1965 (1); v P 1964 (1); *v WI 1964 (1)*
Slater, K. N. 1: v E 1958
Slater, M. J. 74: v E 1994 (5) 1998 (5); v SA 1993 (3); v WI 2000 (5); v NZ 1993 (3); v In 1999 (3); v P 1995 (3) 1999 (3); v SL 1995 (3); *v E 1993 (6) 2001 (4); v SA 1993 (3); v WI 1994 (4) 1998 (4); v NZ 1999 (3); v In 1996 (1) 1997 (3) 2000 (3); v P 1994 (3) 1998 (3); SL 1999 (3); v Z 1999 (1)*
Sleep, P. R. 14: v E 1986 (3) 1987 (1); v NZ 1987 (3); v P 1978 (1) 1989 (1); v SL 1989 (1); *v In 1979 (2); v P 1982 (1) 1988 (1)*
Slight, J. 1: *v E 1880*
Smith, D. B. M. 2: *v E 1912 (2)*
Smith, S. B. 3: *v WI 1983 (3)*
Spofforth, F. R. 18: v E 1876 (1) 1878 (1) 1881 (1) 1882 (4) 1884 (3) 1886 (1); *v E 1882 (1) 1884 (3) 1886 (3)*
Stackpole, K. R. 43: v E 1965 (2) 1970 (6); v WI 1968 (5); v NZ 1973 (3); v P 1972 (1); *v E 1972 (5); v SA 1966 (5) 1969 (4); v WI 1972 (4); v NZ 1973 (3); v In 1969 (5)*
Stevens, G. B. 4: *v In 1959 (2); v P 1959 (2)*

Taber, H. B. 16: v WI 1968 (1); *v E 1968 (1); v SA 1966 (5) 1969 (4); v In 1969 (5)*
Tallon, D. 21: v E 1946 (5) 1950 (5); v In 1947 (5); *v E 1948 (4) 1953 (1); v NZ 1945 (1)*

Taylor, J. M. 20: v E 1920 (5) 1924 (5); *v E 1921 (5) 1926 (3); v SA 1921 (2)*

Taylor, M. A. 104: v E 1990 (5) 1994 (5) 1998 (5); v SA 1993 (3) 1997 (3); v WI 1988 (2) 1992 (4) 1996 (5); v NZ 1989 (1) 1993 (3) 1997 (3); v In 1991 (5); v P 1989 (3) 1995 (3); v SL 1989 (2) 1995 (3); *v E 1989 (6) 1993 (6) 1997 (6); v SA 1993 (2) 1996 (3); v WI 1990 (5) 1994 (4); v NZ 1989 (1) 1992 (3); v In 1996 (1) 1997 (3); v P 1994 (3) 1998 (3); v SL 1992 (3)*

Taylor, P. L. 13: v E 1986 (1) 1987 (1); v WI 1988 (2); v In 1991 (2); v P 1989 (2); v SL 1987 (1); *v WI 1990 (1); v NZ 1989 (1); v P 1988 (2)*

Thomas, G. 8: v E 1965 (3); *v WI 1964 (5)*

Thoms, G. R. 1: v WI 1951

Thomson, A. L. 4: v E 1970 (4)

Thomson, J. R. 51: v E 1974 (5) 1979 (1) 1982 (4); v WI 1975 (6) 1979 (1) 1981 (2); v In 1977 (5); v P 1972 (1) 1976 (1) 1981 (3); *v E 1975 (4) 1977 (5) 1985 (2); v WI 1977 (5); v NZ 1981 (3); v P 1982 (3)*

Thomson, N. F. D. 2: v E 1876 (2)

Thurlow, H. M. 1: v SA 1931

Toohey, P. M. 15: v E 1978 (5) 1979 (1); v WI 1979 (1); v In 1977 (5); *v WI 1977 (3)*

Toshack, E. R. H. 12: v E 1946 (5); v In 1947 (2); *v E 1948 (4); v NZ 1945 (1)*

Travers, J. P. F. 1: v E 1901

Tribe, G. E. 3: v E 1946 (3)

Trott, A. E. 3: v E 1894 (3)

Trott, G. H. S. 24: v E 1891 (3) 1894 (5) 1897 (5); *v E 1888 (3) 1890 (2) 1893 (3) 1896 (3)*

Trumble, H. 32: v E 1894 (1) 1897 (5) 1901 (5) 1903 (4); *v E 1890 (2) 1893 (3) 1896 (3) 1899 (5) 1902 (3); v SA 1902 (1)*

Trumble, J. W. 7: v E 1884 (4); *v E 1886 (3)*

Trumper, V. T. 48: v E 1901 (5) 1903 (5) 1907 (5) 1911 (5); v SA 1910 (5); *v E 1899 (5) 1902 (5) 1905 (5) 1909 (5); v SA 1902 (3)*

Turner, A. 14: v WI 1975 (6); v P 1976 (3); *v E 1975 (3); v NZ 1976 (2)*

Turner, C. T. B. 17: v E 1886 (2) 1887 (1) 1891 (3) 1894 (3); *v E 1888 (3) 1890 (2) 1893 (3)*

Veivers, T. R. 21: v E 1965 (4); v SA 1963 (3); v P 1964 (1); *v E 1964 (5); v SA 1966 (4); v In 1964 (3); v P 1964 (1)*

Veletta, M. R. J. 8: v E 1987 (1); v WI 1988 (2); v NZ 1987 (3); v P 1989 (1); v SL 1987 (1)

Waite, M. G. 2: *v E 1938 (2)*

Walker, M. H. N. 34: v E 1974 (6) 1976 (1); v WI 1975 (3); v NZ 1973 (1); v P 1972 (2) 1976 (2); *v E 1975 (4) 1977 (5); v WI 1972 (5); v NZ 1973 (3) 1976 (2)*

Wall, T. W. 18: v E 1928 (1) 1932 (4); v SA 1931 (3); v WI 1930 (1); *v E 1930 (5) 1934 (4)*

Walters, F. H. 1: v E 1884

Walters, K. D. 74: v E 1965 (5) 1970 (6) 1974 (6) 1976 (1); v WI 1968 (4); v NZ 1973 (3) 1980 (3); v In 1967 (2) 1980 (3); v P 1972 (1) 1976 (3); *v E 1968 (5) 1972 (4) 1975 (4) 1977 (5); v SA 1969 (4); v WI 1972 (5); v NZ 1973 (3) 1976 (2); v In 1969 (5)*

Ward, F. A. 4: v E 1936 (3); *v E 1938 (1)*

Warne, S. K. 92: v E 1994 (5) 1998 (1); v SA 1993 (3) 1997 (3); v WI 1992 (4) 1996 (5); v NZ 1993 (3) 1997 (3); v In 1991 (2) 1999 (3); v P 1995 (3) 1999 (3); v SL 1995 (3); *v E 1993 (6) 1997 (6) 2001 (5); v SA 1993 (3) 1996 (3); v WI 1994 (4) 1998 (3); v NZ 1992 (3) 1999 (3); v In 1997 (3) 2000 (3); v P 1994 (3); v SL 1992 (2) 1999 (3); v Z 1999 (1)*

Watkins, J. R. 1: v P 1972

Watson, G. D. 5: *v E 1972 (2); v SA 1966 (3)*

Watson, W. J. 4: v E 1954 (1); *v WI 1954 (3)*

Waugh, M. E. 116: v E 1990 (2) 1994 (5) 1998 (5); v SA 1993 (3) 1997 (3); v WI 1992 (5) 1996 (5) 2000 (5); v NZ 1993 (3) 1997 (3); v In 1991 (4) 1999 (3); v P 1995 (3) 1999 (3); v SL 1995 (3); *v E 1993 (6) 1997 (6) 2001 (5); v SA 1993 (3) 1996 (3); v WI 1990 (5) 1994 (4) 1998 (4); v NZ 1992 (2) 1999 (3); v In 1996 (1) 1997 (3) 2000 (3); v P 1994 (3) 1998 (3); v SL 1992 (3) 1999 (3); v Z 1999 (1)*

Waugh, S. R. 139: v E 1986 (5) 1987 (1) 1990 (3) 1994 (5) 1998 (5); v SA 1993 (1) 1997 (3); v WI 1988 (5) 1992 (5) 1996 (4) 2000 (4); v NZ 1987 (3) 1989 (1) 1993 (3) 1997 (3); v In 1985 (2) 1999 (3); v P 1989 (3) 1995 (3) 1999 (3); v SL 1987 (1) 1989 (2) 1995 (2); *v E 1989 (6) 1993 (6) 1997 (6) 2001 (4); v SA 1993 (3) 1996 (3); v WI 1990 (2) 1994 (4) 1998 (4); v NZ 1985 (3) 1989 (1) 1992 (3) 1999 (3); v In 1986 (3) 1996 (1) 1997 (2) 2000 (3); v P 1988 (3) 1994 (2) 1998 (3); SL 1999 (3); v Z 1999 (1)*

Wellham, D. M. 6: v E 1986 (1); v WI 1981 (1); v P 1981 (2); *v E 1981 (1) 1985 (1)*

Wessels, K. C. 24: v E 1982 (4); v WI 1984 (5); v NZ 1985 (1); v P 1983 (5); *v E 1985 (6); v WI 1983 (2); v SL 1982 (1)*
Whatmore, D. F. 7: v P 1978 (2); *v In 1979 (5)*
Whitney, M. R. 12: v WI 1988 (1) 1992 (1); v NZ 1987 (1); v In 1991 (3); *v E 1981 (2); v WI 1990 (2); v SL 1992 (2)*
Whitty, W. J. 14: v E 1911 (2); v SA 1910 (5); *v E 1909 (1) 1912 (3); v SA 1912 (3)*
Wiener, J. M. 6: v E 1979 (2); v WI 1979 (2); *v P 1979 (2)*
Wilson, J. W. 1: *v In 1956*
Wilson, P. 1: *v In 1997*
Wood, G. M. 59: v E 1978 (6) 1982 (1); v WI 1981 (3) 1984 (5) 1988 (3); v NZ 1980 (3); v In 1977 (1) 1980 (3); v P 1978 (1) 1981 (3); *v E 1980 (1) 1981 (6) 1985 (5); v WI 1977 (5) 1983 (1); v NZ 1981 (3); v In 1979 (2); v P 1982 (3) 1988 (3); v SL 1982 (1)*
Woodcock, A. J. 1: v NZ 1973
Woodfull, W. M. 35: v E 1928 (5) 1932 (5); v SA 1931 (5); v WI 1930 (5); *v E 1926 (5) 1930 (5) 1934 (5)*
Woods, S. M. J. 3: *v E 1888 (3)*
Woolley, R. D. 2: *v WI 1983 (1); v SL 1982 (1)*
Worrall, J. 11: v E 1884 (1) 1887 (1) 1894 (1) 1897 (1); *v E 1888 (3) 1899 (4)*
Wright, K. J. 10: v E 1978 (2); v P 1978 (2); *v In 1979 (6)*

Yallop, G. N. 39: v E 1978 (6); v WI 1975 (3) 1984 (1); v In 1977 (1); v P 1978 (1) 1981 (1) 1983 (5); *v E 1980 (1) 1981 (6); v WI 1977 (4); v In 1979 (6); v P 1979 (3); v SL 1982 (1)*
Yardley, B. 33: v E 1978 (4) 1982 (5); v WI 1981 (3); v In 1977 (1) 1980 (2); v P 1978 (1) 1981 (3); *v WI 1977 (5); v NZ 1981 (3); v In 1979 (3); v P 1982 (2); v SL 1982 (1)*
Young, S. 1: *v E 1997*

Zoehrer, T. J. 10: v E 1986 (4); *v NZ 1985 (3); v In 1986 (3)*

SOUTH AFRICA

Number of Test cricketers: 279

Ackerman, H. D. 4: v P 1997 (2); v SL 1997 (2)
Adams, P. R. 34: v E 1995 (2) 1999 (4); v A 1996 (2); v WI 1998 (2); v In 1996 (2); v P 1997 (1); v SL 1997 (2); v Z 1999 (1); *v E 1998 (4); v A 1997 (1); v WI 2000 (1); v NZ 1998 (3); v In 1996 (3); v P 1997 (2); v SL 2000 (3); v Z 1999 (1)*
Adcock, N. A. T. 26: v E 1956 (5); v A 1957 (5); v NZ 1953 (5) 1961 (2); *v E 1955 (4) 1960 (5)*
Anderson, J. H. 1: v A 1902
Ashley, W. H. 1: v E 1888

Bacher, A. 12: v A 1966 (5) 1969 (4); *v E 1965 (3)*
Bacher, A. M. 19: v A 1996 (2); v WI 1998 (1); v In 1996 (3); v P 1997 (3); v SL 1997 (1); v Z 1999 (1); *v E 1998 (1); v A 1997 (3); v P 1997 (3); v Z 1999 (1)*
Balaskas, X. C. 9: v E 1930 (2) 1938 (1); v A 1935 (3); *v E 1935 (1); v NZ 1931 (2)*
Barlow, E. J. 30: v E 1964 (5); v A 1966 (5) 1969 (4); v NZ 1961 (5); *v E 1965 (3); v A 1963 (5); v NZ 1963 (3)*
Baumgartner, H. V. 1: v E 1913
Beaumont, R. 5: v E 1913 (2); *v E 1912 (1); v A 1912 (2)*
Begbie, D. W. 5: v E 1948 (3); v A 1949 (2)
Bell, A. J. 16: v E 1930 (3); *v E 1929 (3) 1935 (3); v A 1931 (5); v NZ 1931 (2)*
Bisset, M. 3: v E 1898 (2) 1909 (1)
Bissett, G. F. 4: v E 1927 (4)
Blanckenberg, J. M. 18: v E 1913 (5) 1922 (5); v A 1921 (3); *v E 1924 (5)*
Bland, K. C. 21: v E 1964 (5); v A 1966 (1); v NZ 1961 (5); *v E 1965 (3); v A 1963 (4); v NZ 1963 (3)*
Bock, E. G. 1: v A 1935
Boje, N. 15: v NZ 2000 (3); v SL 2000 (3); *v WI 2000 (4); v In 1999 (2); v SL 2000 (3)*

Bond, G. E. 1: v E 1938
Bosch, T. 1: *v WI 1991*
Botten, J. T. 3: *v E 1965 (3)*
Boucher, M. V. 42: v E 1999 (5); v WI 1998 (5); v NZ 2000 (3); v P 1997 (3); v SL 1997 (2) 2000 (3); v Z 1999 (1); *v E 1998 (5); v WI 2000 (5); v NZ 1998 (3); v In 1999 (2); v P 1997 (1); v SL 2000 (3); v Z 1999 (1)*
Brann, W. H. 3: v E 1922 (3)
Briscoe, A. W. 2: v E 1938 (1); v A 1935 (1)
Bromfield, H. D. 9: v E 1964 (3); v NZ 1961 (5); *v E 1965 (1)*
Brown, L. S. 2: *v A 1931 (1); v NZ 1931 (1)*
Burger, C. G. de V. 2: v A 1957 (2)
Burke, S. F. 2: v E 1964 (1); v NZ 1961 (1)
Buys, I. D. 1: v E 1922

Cameron, H. B. 26: v E 1927 (5) 1930 (5); *v E 1929 (4) 1935 (5); v A 1931 (5); v NZ 1931 (2)*
Campbell, T. 5: v E 1909 (4); *v E 1912 (1)*
Carlstein, P. R. 8: v A 1957 (1); *v E 1960 (5); v A 1963 (2)*
Carter, C. P. 10: v E 1913 (2); v A 1921 (3); *v E 1912 (2) 1924 (3)*
Catterall, R. H. 24: v E 1922 (5) 1927 (5) 1930 (4); *v E 1924 (5) 1929 (5)*
Chapman, H. W. 2: v E 1913 (1); v A 1921 (1)
Cheetham, J. E. 24: v E 1948 (1); v A 1949 (3); v NZ 1953 (5); *v E 1951 (5) 1955 (3); v A 1952 (5); v NZ 1952 (2)*
Chevalier, G. A. 1: v A 1969
Christy, J. A. J. 10: v E 1930 (1); *v E 1929 (2); v A 1931 (5); v NZ 1931 (2)*
Chubb, G. W. A. 5: *v E 1951 (5)*
Cochran, J. A. K. 1: v E 1930
Coen, S. K. 2: v E 1927 (2)
Commaille, J. M. M. 12: v E 1909 (5) 1927 (2); *v E 1924 (5)*
Commins, J. B. 3: v NZ 1994 (2); v P 1994 (1)
Conyngham, D. P. 1: v E 1922
Cook, F. J. 1: v E 1895
Cook, S. J. 3: v In 1992 (2); *v SL 1993 (1)*
Cooper, A. H. C. 1: v E 1913
Cox, J. L. 3: v E 1913 (3)
Cripps, G. 1: v E 1891
Crisp, R. J. 9: v A 1935 (4); *v E 1935 (5)*
Cronje, W. J. 68: v E 1995 (5) 1999 (5); v A 1993 (3) 1996 (3); v WI 1998 (5); v NZ 1994 (3); v In 1992 (3) 1996 (3); v P 1994 (1) 1997 (2); v SL 1997 (2); v Z 1999 (1); *v E 1994 (3) 1998 (5); v A 1993 (3) 1997 (3); v WI 1991 (1); v NZ 1994 (1) 1998 (3); v In 1996 (3) 1999 (2); v P 1997 (3); v SL 1993 (3); v Z 1995 (1) 1999 (1)*
Cullinan, D. J. 70: v E 1995 (5) 1999 (5); v A 1996 (3); v WI 1998 (5); v NZ 1994 (3) 2000 (3); v In 1992 (1) 1996 (3); v P 1994 (1) 1997 (1); v SL 1997 (2) 2000 (3); v Z 1999 (1); *v E 1994 (1) 1998 (5); v A 1993 (3) 1997 (1); v WI 2000 (5); v NZ 1994 (1) 1998 (3); v In 1996 (3) 1999 (1); v P 1997 (3); v SL 1993 (3) 2000 (3); v Z 1995 (1) 1999 (1)*
Curnow, S. H. 7: v E 1930 (3); *v A 1931 (4)*

Dalton, E. L. 15: v E 1930 (1) 1938 (4); v A 1935 (1); *v E 1929 (1) 1935 (4); v A 1931 (2); v NZ 1931 (2)*
Davies, E. Q. 5: v E 1938 (3); v A 1935 (2)
Dawson, O. C. 9: v E 1948 (4); *v E 1947 (5)*
Deane, H. G. 17: v E 1927 (5) 1930 (2); *v E 1924 (5) 1929 (5)*
de Villiers, P. S. 18: v A 1993 (3); v NZ 1994 (3); v P 1994 (1) 1997 (2); *v E 1994 (3); v A 1993 (3); v NZ 1994 (1); v In 1996 (2)*
Dippenaar, H. H. 7: v NZ 2000 (3); v SL 2000 (2); v Z 1999 (1); *v Z 1999 (1)*
Dixon, C. D. 1: v E 1913
Donald, A. A. 69: v E 1995 (5) 1999 (4); v A 1993 (3) 1996 (3); v WI 1998 (5); v NZ 2000 (2); v In 1992 (4) 1996 (3); v P 1994 (1) 1997 (3); v SL 1997 (2) 2000 (1); v Z 1999 (1); *v E 1994 (3) 1998 (5); v A 1993 (3) 1997 (2); v WI 1991 (1) 2000 (4); v NZ 1994 (1) 1998 (2); v In 1996 (2) 1999 (2); v P 1997 (2); v SL 1993 (3); v Z 1995 (1) 1999 (1)*
Dower, R. R. 1: v E 1898
Draper, R. G. 2: v A 1949 (2)

Duckworth, C. A. R. 2: v E 1956 (2)
Dumbrill, R. 5: v A 1966 (2); *v E 1965 (3)*
Duminy, J. P. 3: v E 1927 (2); *v E 1929 (1)*
Dunell, O. R. 2: v E 1888 (2)
Du Preez, J. H. 2: v A 1966 (2)
Du Toit, J. F. 1: v E 1891
Dyer, D. V. 3: *v E 1947 (3)*

Eksteen, C. E. 7: v E 1995 (1); v NZ 1994 (2); v P 1994 (1); *v NZ 1994 (1); v In 1999 (1); v SL 1993 (1)*
Elgie, M. K. 3: v NZ 1961 (3)
Elworthy, S. 2: *v E 1998 (1); v NZ 1998 (1)*
Endean, W. R. 28: v E 1956 (5); v A 1957 (5); v NZ 1953 (5); *v E 1951 (1) 1955 (5); v A 1952 (5); v NZ 1952 (2)*

Farrer, W. S. 6: v NZ 1961 (3); *v NZ 1963 (3)*
Faulkner, G. A. 25: v E 1905 (5) 1909 (5); *v E 1907 (3) 1912 (3) 1924 (1); v A 1910 (5) 1912 (3)*
Fellows-Smith, J. P. 4: *v E 1960 (4)*
Fichardt, C. G. 2: v E 1891 (1) 1895 (1)
Finlason, C. E. 1: v E 1888
Floquet, C. E. 1: v E 1909
Francis, H. H. 2: v E 1898 (2)
Francois, C. M. 5: v E 1922 (5)
Frank, C. N. 3: v A 1921 (3)
Frank, W. H. B. 1: v E 1895
Fuller, E. R. H. 7: v A 1957 (1); *v E 1955 (2); v A 1952 (2); v NZ 1952 (2)*
Fullerton, G. M. 7: v A 1949 (2); *v E 1947 (2) 1951 (3)*
Funston, K. J. 18: v E 1956 (3); v A 1957 (5); v NZ 1953 (3); *v A 1952 (5); v NZ 1952 (2)*

Gamsy, D. 2: v A 1969 (2)
Gibbs, H. H. 28: v E 1999 (5); v A 1996 (1); v WI 1998 (4); v In 1996 (1); v P 1997 (1); v SL 2000 (2); *v A 1997 (2); v WI 2000 (5); v NZ 1998 (3); v In 1996 (2) 1999 (2)*
Gleeson, R. A. 1: v E 1895
Glover, G. K. 1: v E 1895
Goddard, T. L. 41: v E 1956 (5) 1964 (5); v A 1957 (5) 1966 (5) 1969 (3); *v E 1955 (5) 1960 (5); v A 1963 (5); v NZ 1963 (3)*
Gordon, N. 5: v E 1938 (5)
Graham, R. 2: v E 1898 (2)
Grieveson, R. E. 2: v E 1938 (2)
Griffin, G. M. 2: *v E 1960 (2)*

Hall, A. E. 7: v E 1922 (4) 1927 (2) 1930 (1)
Hall, G. G. 1: v E 1964
Halliwell, E. A. 8: v E 1891 (1) 1895 (3) 1898 (1); v A 1902 (3)
Halse, C. G. 3: *v A 1963 (3)*
Hands, P. A. M. 7: v E 1913 (5); v A 1921 (1); *v E 1924 (1)*
Hands, R. H. M. 1: v E 1913
Hanley, M. A. 1: v E 1948
Harris, T. A. 3: v E 1948 (1); *v E 1947 (2)*
Hartigan, G. P. D. 5: v E 1913 (3); *v E 1912 (1); v A 1912 (1)*
Harvey, R. L. 2: v A 1935 (2)
Hathorn, C. M. H. 12: v E 1905 (5); v A 1902 (3); *v E 1907 (3); v A 1910 (1)*
Hayward, M. 6: v E 1999 (3); *v In 1999 (1); v SL 2000 (2)*
Hearne, F. 4: v E 1891 (1) 1895 (3)
Hearne, G. A. L. 3: v E 1922 (2); *v E 1924 (1)*
Heine, P. S. 14: v E 1956 (5); v A 1957 (4); v NZ 1961 (1); *v E 1955 (4)*
Henry, O. 3: v In 1992 (3)
Hime, C. F. W. 1: v E 1895
Hudson, A. C. 35: v E 1995 (5); v A 1993 (3) 1996 (1); v NZ 1994 (2); v In 1992 (4) 1996 (3); v P 1997 (3); *v E 1994 (2); v A 1993 (3); v WI 1991 (1); v NZ 1994 (1); v In 1996 (3); v SL 1993 (3); v Z 1995 (1)*
Hutchinson, P. 2: v E 1888 (2)

Ironside, D. E. J. 3: v NZ 1953 (3)
Irvine, B. L. 4: v A 1969 (4)

Jack, S. D. 2: v NZ 1994 (2)
Johnson, C. L. 1: v E 1895

Kallis, J. H. 50: v E 1995 (2) 1999 (5); v A 1996 (3); v WI 1998 (5); v NZ 2000 (3); v P 1997 (3); v SL 1997 (2) 2000 (3); v Z 1999 (1); *v E 1998 (5); v A 1997 (3); v WI 2000 (5); v NZ 1998 (3); v In 1999 (2); v P 1997 (1); v SL 2000 (3); v Z 1999 (1)*
Keith, H. J. 8: v E 1956 (3); *v E 1955 (4); v A 1952 (1)*
Kemp, J. M. 3: v SL 2000 (1); *v WI 2000 (2)*
Kempis, G. A. 1: v E 1888
Kirsten, G. 73: v E 1995 (5) 1999 (5); v A 1993 (3) 1996 (3); v WI 1998 (5); v NZ 1994 (3) 2000 (3); v In 1996 (3); v P 1994 (1) 1997 (3); v SL 1997 (2) 2000 (2); *v E 1994 (3) 1998 (5); v A 1993 (3) 1997 (3); v WI 2000 (5); v NZ 1994 (1) 1998 (3); v In 1996 (3) 1999 (2); v P 1997 (3); v SL 2000 (3); v Z 1995 (1)*
Kirsten, P. N. 12: v A 1993 (3); v In 1992 (4); *v E 1994 (3); v A 1993 (1); v WI 1991 (1)*
Klusener, L. 42: v E 1999 (5); v A 1996 (2); v WI 1998 (1); v NZ 2000 (3); v In 1996 (3); v P 1997 (2); v SL 2000 (2); v Z 1999 (1); *v E 1998 (3); v A 1997 (2); v WI 2000 (5); v NZ 1998 (3); v In 1996 (2) 1999 (2); v P 1997 (2); v SL 2000 (3); v Z 1999 (1)*
Kotze, J. J. 3: v A 1902 (2); *v E 1907 (1)*
Kuiper, A. P. 1: *v WI 1991*
Kuys, F. 1: v E 1898

Lance, H. R. 13: v A 1966 (5) 1969 (3); v NZ 1961 (2); *v E 1965 (3)*
Langton, A. B. C. 15: v E 1938 (5); v A 1935 (5); *v E 1935 (5)*
Lawrence, G. B. 5: v NZ 1961 (5)
le Roux, F. L. 1: v E 1913
Lewis, P. T. 1: v E 1913
Liebenberg, G. F. J. 5: v SL 1997 (1); *v E 1998 (4)*
Lindsay, D. T. 19: v E 1964 (3); v A 1966 (5) 1969 (2); *v E 1965 (3); v A 1963 (3); v NZ 1963 (3)*
Lindsay, J. D. 3: *v E 1947 (3)*
Lindsay, N. V. 1: v A 1921
Ling, W. V. S. 6: v E 1922 (3); v A 1921 (3)
Llewellyn, C. B. 15: v E 1895 (1) 1898 (1); v A 1902 (3); *v E 1912 (3); v A 1910 (5) 1912 (2)*
Lundie, E. B. 1: v E 1913

Macaulay, M. J. 1: v E 1964
McCarthy, C. N. 15: v E 1948 (5); v A 1949 (5); *v E 1951 (5)*
McGlew, D. J. 34: v E 1956 (1); v A 1957 (5); v NZ 1953 (5) 1961 (5); *v E 1951 (2) 1955 (5) 1960 (5); v A 1952 (4); v NZ 1952 (2)*
McKenzie, N. D. 14: v NZ 2000 (3); v SL 2000 (3); *v WI 2000 (5); v SL 2000 (3)*
McKinnon, A. H. 8: v E 1964 (2); v A 1966 (2); v NZ 1961 (1); *v E 1960 (1) 1965 (2)*
McLean, R. A. 40: v E 1956 (5) 1964 (2); v A 1957 (4); v NZ 1953 (4) 1961 (5); *v E 1951 (3) 1955 (5) 1960 (5); v A 1952 (5); v NZ 1952 (2)*
McMillan, B. M. 38: v E 1995 (5); v A 1993 (3) 1996 (2); v NZ 1994 (3); v In 1992 (4) 1996 (3); v P 1994 (1); *v E 1994 (3) 1998 (1); v A 1993 (1) 1997 (3); v In 1996 (3); v P 1997 (3); v SL 1993 (2); v Z 1995 (1)*
McMillan, Q. 13: v E 1930 (5); *v E 1929 (2); v A 1931 (4); v NZ 1931 (2)*
Mann, N. B. F. 19: v E 1948 (5); v A 1949 (5); *v E 1947 (5) 1951 (4)*
Mansell, P. N. F. 13: *v E 1951 (2) 1955 (4); v A 1952 (5); v NZ 1952 (2)*
Markham, L. A. 1: v E 1948
Marx, W. F. E. 3: v A 1921 (3)
Matthews, C. R. 18: v E 1995 (3); v A 1993 (3); v NZ 1994 (2); v In 1992 (3); *v E 1994 (3); v A 1993 (2); v NZ 1994 (1); v Z 1995 (1)*
Meintjes, D. J. 2: v E 1922 (2)
Melle, M. G. 7: v A 1949 (2); *v E 1951 (1); v A 1952 (4)*
Melville, A. 11: v E 1938 (5) 1948 (1); *v E 1947 (5)*
Middleton, J. 6: v E 1895 (2) 1898 (2); v A 1902 (2)
Mills, C. 1: v E 1891
Milton, W. H. 3: v E 1888 (2) 1891 (1)

Mitchell, B. 42: v E 1930 (5) 1938 (5) 1948 (5); v A 1935 (5); *v E 1929 (5) 1935 (5) 1947 (5); v A 1931 (5); v NZ 1931 (2)*
Mitchell, F. 3: *v E 1912 (1); v A 1912 (2)*
Morkel, D. P. B. 16: v E 1927 (5); *v E 1929 (5); v A 1931 (5); v NZ 1931 (1)*
Murray, A. R. A. 10: v NZ 1953 (4); *v A 1952 (4); v NZ 1952 (2)*

Nel, J. D. 6: v A 1949 (5) 1957 (1)
Newberry, C. 4: v E 1913 (4)
Newson, E. S. 3: v E 1930 (1) 1938 (2)
Ngam, M. 3: v NZ 2000 (1); v SL 2000 (2)
Nicholson, F. 4: v A 1935 (4)
Nicolson, J. F. W. 3: v E 1927 (3)
Norton, N. O. 1: v E 1909
Nourse, A. D. 34: v E 1938 (5) 1948 (5); v A 1935 (5) 1949 (5); *v E 1935 (4) 1947 (5) 1951 (5)*
Nourse, A. W. 45: v E 1905 (5) 1909 (5) 1913 (5) 1922 (5); v A 1902 (3) 1921 (3); *v E 1907 (3) 1912 (3) 1924 (5); v A 1910 (5) 1912 (3)*
Ntini, M. 15: v NZ 2000 (3); v SL 1997 (2) 2000 (3); *v E 1998 (2); v WI 2000 (4); v SL 2000 (1)*
Nupen, E. P. 17: v E 1922 (4) 1927 (5) 1930 (3); v A 1921 (2) 1935 (1); *v E 1924 (2)*

Ochse, A. E. 2: v E 1888 (2)
Ochse, A. L. 3: v E 1927 (1); *v E 1929 (2)*
O'Linn, S. 7: v NZ 1961 (2); *v E 1960 (5)*
Owen-Smith, H. G. 5: *v E 1929 (5)*

Palm, A. W. 1: v E 1927
Parker, G. M. 2: *v E 1924 (2)*
Parkin, D. C. 1: v E 1891
Partridge, J. T. 11: v E 1964 (3); *v A 1963 (5); v NZ 1963 (3)*
Pearse, O. C. 3: *v A 1910 (3)*
Pegler, S. J. 16: v E 1909 (1); *v E 1912 (3) 1924 (5); v A 1910 (4) 1912 (3)*
Pithey, A. J. 17: v E 1956 (3) 1964 (5); *v E 1960 (2); v A 1963 (4); v NZ 1963 (3)*
Pithey, D. B. 8: v A 1966 (2); *v A 1963 (3); v NZ 1963 (3)*
Plimsoll, J. B. 1: *v E 1947*
Pollock, P. M. 28: v E 1964 (5); v A 1966 (5) 1969 (4); v NZ 1961 (3); *v E 1965 (3); v A 1963 (5); v NZ 1963 (3)*
Pollock, R. G. 23: v E 1964 (5); v A 1966 (5) 1969 (4); *v E 1965 (3); v A 1963 (5); v NZ 1963 (1)*
Pollock, S. M. 56: v E 1995 (5) 1999 (5); v A 1996 (2); v WI 1998 (5); v NZ 2000 (3); v In 1996 (3); v P 1997 (3); v SL 1997 (2) 2000 (3); v Z 1999 (1); *v E 1998 (4); v A 1997 (3); v WI 2000 (5); v NZ 1998 (3); v In 1999 (2); v P 1997 (3); v SL 2000 (3); v Z 1999 (1)*
Poore, R. M. 3: v E 1895 (3)
Pothecary, J. E. 3: *v E 1960 (3)*
Powell, A. W. 1: v E 1898
Prince, C. F. H. 1: v E 1898
Pringle, M. W. 4: v E 1995 (1); v In 1992 (2); *v WI 1991 (1)*
Procter, M. J. 7: v A 1966 (3) 1969 (4)
Promnitz, H. L. E. 2: v E 1927 (2)

Quinn, N. A. 12: v E 1930 (1); *v E 1929 (4); v A 1931 (5); v NZ 1931 (2)*

Reid, N. 1: v A 1921
Rhodes, J. N. 52: v E 1995 (5) 1999 (3); v A 1993 (3) 1996 (1); v WI 1998 (5); v NZ 1994 (3); v In 1992 (4); v P 1994 (1); v Z 1999 (1); *v E 1994 (3) 1998 (5); v A 1993 (3) 1997 (1); v NZ 1994 (1) 1998 (3); v In 1996 (1); v P 1997 (1); v SL 1993 (3) 2000 (3); v Z 1995 (1) 1999 (1)*
Richards, A. R. 1: v E 1895
Richards, B. A. 4: v A 1969 (4)
Richards, W. H. 1: v E 1888
Richardson, D. J. 42: v E 1995 (5); v A 1993 (3) 1996 (3); v NZ 1994 (3); v In 1992 (4) 1996 (3); v P 1994 (1); *v E 1994 (3); v A 1993 (3) 1997 (3); v WI 1991 (1); v NZ 1994 (1); v In 1996 (3); v P 1997 (2); v SL 1993 (3); v Z 1995 (1)*
Robertson, J. B. 3: v A 1935 (3)
Rose-Innes, A. 2: v E 1888 (2)

Routledge, T. W. 4: v E 1891 (1) 1895 (3)
Rowan, A. M. B. 15: v E 1948 (5); *v E 1947 (5) 1951 (5)*
Rowan, E. A. B. 26: v E 1938 (4) 1948 (4); v A 1935 (3) 1949 (5); *v E 1935 (5) 1951 (5)*
Rowe, G. A. 5: v E 1895 (2) 1898 (2); v A 1902 (1)
Rushmere, M. W. 1: *v WI 1991*

Samuelson, S. V. 1: v E 1909
Schultz, B. N. 9: v E 1995 (1); v A 1996 (1); v In 1992 (2); *v P 1997 (1); v SL 1993 (3); v Z 1995 (1)*
Schwarz, R. O. 20: v E 1905 (5) 1909 (4); *v E 1907 (3) 1912 (1); v A 1910 (5) 1912 (2)*
Seccull, A. W. 1: v E 1895
Seymour, M. A. 7: v E 1964 (2); v A 1969 (1); *v A 1963 (4)*
Shalders, W. A. 12: v E 1898 (1) 1905 (5); v A 1902 (3); *v E 1907 (3)*
Shepstone, G. H. 2: v E 1895 (1) 1898 (1)
Sherwell, P. W. 13: v E 1905 (5); *v E 1907 (3); v A 1910 (5)*
Siedle, I. J. 18: v E 1927 (1) 1930 (5); v A 1935 (5); *v E 1929 (3) 1935 (4)*
Sinclair, J. H. 25: v E 1895 (3) 1898 (2) 1905 (5) 1909 (4); v A 1902 (3); *v E 1907 (3); v A 1910 (5)*
Smith, C. J. E. 3: v A 1902 (3)
Smith, F. W. 3: v E 1888 (2) 1895 (1)
Smith, V. I. 9: v A 1949 (3) 1957 (1); *v E 1947 (4) 1955 (1)*
Snell, R. P. 5: v NZ 1994 (1); *v A 1993 (1); v WI 1991 (1); v SL 1993 (2)*
Snooke, S. D. 1: *v E 1907*
Snooke, S. J. 26: v E 1905 (5) 1909 (5) 1922 (3); *v E 1907 (3) 1912 (3); v A 1910 (5) 1912 (2)*
Solomon, W. R. 1: v E 1898
Stewart, R. B. 1: v E 1888
Steyn, P. J. R. 3: v NZ 1994 (1); v P 1994 (1); *v NZ 1994 (1)*
Stricker, L. A. 13: v E 1909 (4); *v E 1912 (2); v A 1910 (5) 1912 (2)*
Strydom, P. C. 2: v E 1999 (1); *v In 1999 (1)*
Susskind, M. J. 5: *v E 1924 (5)*
Symcox, P. L. 20: v A 1996 (1); v WI 1998 (3); v P 1997 (1); *v A 1993 (2) 1997 (3); v In 1996 (3); v P 1997 (3); v SL 1993 (3); v Z 1995 (1)*

Taberer, H. M. 1: v A 1902
Tancred, A. B. 2: v E 1888 (2)
Tancred, L. J. 14: v E 1905 (5) 1913 (1); v A 1902 (3); *v E 1907 (1) 1912 (2); v A 1912 (2)*
Tancred, V. M. 1: v E 1898
Tapscott, G. L. 1: v E 1913
Tapscott, L. E. 2: v E 1922 (2)
Tayfield, H. J. 37: v E 1956 (5); v A 1949 (5) 1957 (5); v NZ 1953 (5); *v E 1955 (5) 1960 (5); v A 1952 (5); v NZ 1952 (2)*
Taylor, A. I. 1: v E 1956
Taylor, D. 2: v E 1913 (2)
Taylor, H. W. 42: v E 1913 (5) 1922 (5) 1927 (5) 1930 (4); v A 1921 (3); *v E 1912 (3) 1924 (5) 1929 (3); v A 1912 (3) 1931 (5); v NZ 1931 (1)*
Terbrugge, D. J. 4: v WI 1998 (4)
Theunissen, N. H. 1: v E 1888
Thornton, P. G. 1: v A 1902
Tomlinson, D. S. 1: *v E 1935*
Traicos, A. J. 3: v A 1969 (3)
Trimborn, P. H. J. 4: v A 1966 (3) 1969 (1)
Tuckett, L. 9: v E 1948 (4); *v E 1947 (5)*
Tuckett, L. R. 1: v E 1913
Twentyman-Jones, P. S. 1: v A 1902

van der Bijl, P. G. V. 5: v E 1938 (5)
Van der Merwe, E. A. 2: v A 1935 (1); *v E 1929 (1)*
Van der Merwe, P. L. 15: v E 1964 (2); v A 1966 (5); *v E 1965 (3); v A 1963 (3); v NZ 1963 (2)*
Van Ryneveld, C. B. 19: v E 1956 (5); v A 1957 (4); v NZ 1953 (5); *v E 1951 (5)*
Varnals, G. D. 3: v E 1964 (3)
Viljoen, K. G. 27: v E 1930 (3) 1938 (4) 1948 (2); v A 1935 (4); *v E 1935 (4) 1947 (5); v A 1931 (4); v NZ 1931 (1)*
Vincent, C. L. 25: v E 1927 (5) 1930 (5); *v E 1929 (4) 1935 (4); v A 1931 (5); v NZ 1931 (2)*

Vintcent, C. H. 3: v E 1888 (2) 1891 (1)
Vogler, A. E. E. 15: v E 1905 (5) 1909 (5); *v E 1907 (3); v A 1910 (2)*

Wade, H. F. 10: v A 1935 (5); *v E 1935 (5)*
Wade, W. W. 11: v E 1938 (3) 1948 (5); v A 1949 (3)
Waite, J. H. B. 50: v E 1956 (5) 1964 (2); v A 1957 (5); v NZ 1953 (5) 1961 (5); *v E 1951 (4) 1955 (5) 1960 (5); v A 1952 (5) 1963 (4); v NZ 1952 (2) 1963 (3)*
Walter, K. A. 2: v NZ 1961 (2)
Ward, T. A. 23: v E 1913 (5) 1922 (5); v A 1921 (3); *v E 1912 (2) 1924 (5); v A 1912 (3)*
Watkins, J. C. 15: v E 1956 (2); v A 1949 (3); v NZ 1953 (3); *v A 1952 (5); v NZ 1952 (2)*
Wesley, C. 3: *v E 1960 (3)*
Wessels, K. C. 16: v A 1993 (3); v In 1992 (4); *v E 1994 (3); v A 1993 (2); v WI 1991 (1); SL 1993 (3)*
Westcott, R. J. 5: v A 1957 (2); v NZ 1953 (3)
White, G. C. 17: v E 1905 (5) 1909 (4); *v E 1907 (3) 1912 (2); v A 1912 (3)*
Willoughby, J. T. 2: v E 1895 (2)
Wimble, C. S. 1: v E 1891
Winslow, P. L. 5: v A 1949 (2); *v E 1955 (3)*
Wynne, O. E. 6: v E 1948 (3); v A 1949 (3)

Zulch, J. W. 16: v E 1909 (5) 1913 (3); v A 1921 (3); *v A 1910 (5)*

WEST INDIES

Number of Test cricketers: 240

Achong, E. 6: v E 1929 (1) 1934 (2); *v E 1933 (3)*
Adams, J. C. 54: v E 1993 (5) 1997 (4); v A 1994 (4) 1998 (4); v SA 1991 (1); v NZ 1995 (2); v P 1999 (3); v Z 1999 (2); *v E 1995 (4) 2000 (5); v A 1992 (3) 1996 (5) 2000 (5); v NZ 1994 (2) 1999 (2); v In 1994 (3)*
Alexander, F. C. M. 25: v E 1959 (5); v P 1957 (5); *v E 1957 (2); v A 1960 (5); v In 1958 (5); v P 1958 (3)*
Ali, Imtiaz 1: v In 1975
Ali, Inshan 12: v E 1973 (2); v A 1972 (3); v In 1970 (1); v P 1976 (1); v NZ 1971 (3); *v E 1973 (1); v A 1975 (1)*
Allan, D. W. 5: v A 1964 (1); v In 1961 (2); *v E 1966 (2)*
Allen, I. B. A. 2: *v E 1991 (2)*
Ambrose, C. E. L. 98: v E 1989 (3) 1993 (5) 1997 (6); v A 1990 (5) 1994 (4) 1998 (4); v SA 1991 (1); v NZ 1995 (2); v In 1988 (4) 1996 (5); v P 1987 (3) 1992 (3) 1999 (3); v SL 1996 (2); v Z 1999 (2); *v E 1988 (5) 1991 (5) 1995 (5) 2000 (5); v A 1988 (5) 1992 (5) 1996 (4); v SA 1998 (4); v NZ 1994 (2); v P 1990 (3) 1997 (2); v SL 1993 (1)*
Arthurton, K. L. T. 33: v E 1993 (5); v A 1994 (3); v SA 1991 (1); v In 1988 (4); v P 1992 (3); *v E 1988 (1) 1995 (5); v A 1992 (5); v NZ 1994 (2); v In 1994 (3); v SL 1993 (1)*
Asgarali, N. 2: *v E 1957 (2)*
Atkinson, D. St E. 22: v E 1953 (4); v A 1954 (4); v P 1957 (1); *v E 1957 (2); v A 1951 (2); v NZ 1951 (1) 1955 (4); v In 1948 (4)*
Atkinson, E. St E. 8: v P 1957 (3); *v In 1958 (3); v P 1958 (2)*
Austin, R. A. 2: v A 1977 (2)

Bacchus, S. F. A. F. 19: v A 1977 (2); *v E 1980 (5); v A 1981 (2); v In 1978 (6); v P 1980 (4)*
Baichan, L. 3: *v A 1975 (1); v P 1974 (2)*
Baptiste, E. A. E. 10: v E 1989 (1); v A 1983 (3); *v E 1984 (5); v In 1983 (1)*
Barrett, A. G. 6: v E 1973 (2); v In 1970 (2); *v In 1974 (2)*
Barrow, I. 11: v E 1929 (1) 1934 (1); *v E 1933 (3) 1939 (1); v A 1930 (5)*
Bartlett, E. L. 5: *v E 1928 (1); v A 1930 (4)*
Benjamin, K. C. G. 26: v E 1993 (5) 1997 (2); v A 1994 (4); v SA 1991 (1); *v E 1995 (5); v A 1992 (1) 1996 (3); v NZ 1994 (2); v In 1994 (3)*
Benjamin, W. K. M. 21: v E 1993 (5); v A 1994 (4); v In 1988 (1); v P 1987 (3) 1992 (2); *v E 1988 (3); v NZ 1994 (1); v In 1987 (1); v SL 1993 (1)*

Best, C. A. 8: v E 1985 (3) 1989 (3); *v P 1990 (2)*
Betancourt, N. 1: v E 1929
Binns, A. P. 5: v A 1954 (1); v In 1952 (1); *v NZ 1955 (3)*
Birkett, L. S. 4: *v A 1930 (4)*
Bishop, I. R. 43: v E 1989 (4) 1997 (3); v NZ 1995 (2); v In 1988 (4) 1996 (4); v P 1992 (2); v SL 1996 (2); *v E 1995 (6); v A 1992 (5) 1996 (5); v P 1990 (3) 1997 (3)*
Black, M. I. 4: *v A 2000 (3); v Z 2001 (1)*
Boyce, K. D. 21: v E 1973 (4); v A 1972 (4); v In 1970 (1); *v E 1973 (3); v A 1975 (4); v In 1974 (3); v P 1974 (2)*
Browne, C. O. 14: v A 1994 (1); v NZ 1995 (2); v In 1996 (3); v SL 1996 (2); *v E 1995 (2); v A 1996 (3); v Z 2001 (1)*
Browne, C. R. 4: v E 1929 (2); *v E 1928 (2)*
Butcher, B. F. 44: v E 1959 (2) 1967 (5); v A 1964 (5); *v E 1963 (5) 1966 (5) 1969 (3); v A 1968 (5); v NZ 1968 (3); v In 1958 (5) 1966 (3); v P 1958 (3)*
Butler, L. 1: v A 1954
Butts, C. G. 7: v NZ 1984 (1); *v NZ 1986 (1); v In 1987 (3); v P 1986 (2)*
Bynoe, M. R. 4: *v In 1966 (3); v P 1958 (1)*

Camacho, G. S. 11: v E 1967 (5); v In 1970 (2); *v E 1969 (2); v A 1968 (2)*
Cameron, F. J. 5: *v In 1948 (5)*
Cameron, J. H. 2: *v E 1939 (2)*
Campbell, S. L. 51: v E 1997 (4); v A 1994 (1) 1998 (4); v NZ 1995 (2); v In 1996 (5); v P 1999 (3); v SL 1996 (2); v Z 1999 (2); *v E 1995 (6) 2000 (5); v A 1996 (5) 2000 (5); v NZ 1994 (2) 1999 (2); v P 1997 (3)*
Carew, G. M. 4: v E 1934 (1) 1947 (2); *v In 1948 (1)*
Carew, M. C. 19: v E 1967 (1); v NZ 1971 (3); v In 1970 (3); *v E 1963 (2) 1966 (1) 1969 (1); v A 1968 (5); v NZ 1968 (3)*
Challenor, G. 3: *v E 1928 (3)*
Chanderpaul, S. 49: v E 1993 (4) 1997 (6); v SA 2000 (2); v NZ 1995 (2); v In 1996 (5); v P 1999 (3); v Z 1999 (2); *v E 1995 (2) 2000 (2); v A 1996 (5) 2000 (1); v SA 1998 (5); v NZ 1994 (2) 1999 (2); v In 1994 (1); v P 1997 (3); v Z 2001 (2)*
Chang, H. S. 1: *v In 1978*
Christiani, C. M. 4: v E 1934 (4)
Christiani, R. J. 22: v E 1947 (4) 1953 (1); v In 1952 (2); *v E 1950 (4); v A 1951 (5); v NZ 1951 (1); v In 1948 (5)*
Clarke, C. B. 3: *v E 1939 (3)*
Clarke, S. T. 11: v A 1977 (1); *v A 1981 (1); v In 1978 (5); v P 1980 (4)*
Collins, P. T. 4: v A 1998 (3); *v Z 2001 (1)*
Collymore, C. D. 1: v A 1998
Constantine, L. N. 18: v E 1929 (3) 1934 (3); *v E 1928 (3) 1933 (1) 1939 (3); v A 1930 (5)*
Croft, C. E. H. 27: v E 1980 (4); v A 1977 (2); v P 1976 (5); *v E 1980 (3); v A 1979 (3) 1981 (3); v NZ 1979 (3); v P 1980 (4)*
Cuffy, C. E. 5: v SA 2000 (2); *v A 1996 (1); v In 1994 (2)*
Cummins, A. C. 5: v P 1992 (2); *v A 1992 (1); v In 1994 (2)*

Da Costa, O. C. 5: v E 1929 (1) 1934 (1); *v E 1933 (3)*
Daniel, W. W. 10: v A 1983 (2); v In 1975 (1); *v E 1976 (4); v In 1983 (3)*
Davis, B. A. 4: v A 1964 (4)
Davis, C. A. 15: v A 1972 (2); v NZ 1971 (5); v In 1970 (4); *v E 1969 (3); v A 1968 (1)*
Davis, W. W. 15: v A 1983 (1); v NZ 1984 (2); v In 1982 (1); *v E 1984 (1); v In 1983 (6) 1987 (4)*
De Caires, F. I. 3: v E 1929 (3)
Depeiza, C. C. 5: v A 1954 (3); *v NZ 1955 (2)*
Dewdney, T. 9: v A 1954 (2); v P 1957 (3); *v E 1957 (1); v NZ 1955 (3)*
Dhanraj, R. 4: v NZ 1995 (1); *v E 1995 (1); v NZ 1994 (1); v In 1994 (1)*
Dillon, M. 16: v A 1998 (1); v SA 2000 (5); v In 1996 (2); *v A 2000 (4); v SA 1998 (3); v P 1997 (1)*
Dowe, U. G. 4: v A 1972 (1); v NZ 1971 (1); v In 1970 (2)
Dujon, P. J. L. 81: v E 1985 (4) 1989 (4); v A 1983 (5) 1990 (5); v NZ 1984 (4); v In 1982 (5) 1988 (4); v P 1987 (3); *v E 1984 (5) 1988 (5) 1991 (5); v A 1981 (3) 1984 (5) 1988 (5); v NZ 1986 (3); v In 1983 (6) 1987 (4); v P 1986 (3) 1990 (3)*

Edwards, R. M. 5: *v A 1968 (2); v NZ 1968 (3)*

Ferguson, W. 8: v E 1947 (4) 1953 (1); *v In 1948 (3)*
Fernandes, M. P. 2: v E 1929 (1); *v E 1928 (1)*
Findlay, T. M. 10: v A 1972 (1); v NZ 1971 (5); v In 1970 (2); *v E 1969 (2)*
Foster, M. L. C. 14: v E 1973 (1); v A 1972 (4) 1977 (1); v NZ 1971 (3); v In 1970 (2); v P 1976 (1); *v E 1969 (1) 1973 (1)*
Francis, G. N. 10: v E 1929 (1); *v E 1928 (3) 1933 (1); v A 1930 (5)*
Frederick, M. 1: v E 1953
Fredericks, R. C. 59: v E 1973 (5); v A 1972 (5); v NZ 1971 (5); v In 1970 (4) 1975 (4); v P 1976 (5); *v E 1969 (3) 1973 (3) 1976 (5); v A 1968 (4) 1975 (6); v NZ 1968 (3); v In 1974 (5); v P 1974 (2)*
Fuller, R. L. 1: v E 1934
Furlonge, H. A. 3: v A 1954 (1); *v NZ 1955 (2)*

Ganga, D. 10: *v A 2000 (4); v SA 1998 (3); v NZ 1999 (1); v Z 2001 (2)*
Ganteaume, A. G. 1: v E 1947
Garner, J. 58: v E 1980 (4) 1985 (5); v A 1977 (2) 1983 (5); v NZ 1984 (4); v In 1982 (4); v P 1976 (5); *v E 1980 (5) 1984 (5); v A 1979 (3) 1981 (3) 1984 (5); v NZ 1979 (3) 1986 (2); v P 1980 (3)*
Garrick, L. V. 1: v SA 2000
Gaskin, B. B. M. 2: v E 1947 (2)
Gayle, C. H. 11: v SA 2000 (5); v P 1999 (1); v Z 1999 (2); *v E 2000 (1); v Z 2001 (2)*
Gibbs, G. L. 1: v A 1954
Gibbs, L. R. 79: v E 1967 (5) 1973 (5); v A 1964 (5) 1972 (5); v NZ 1971 (2); v In 1961 (5) 1970 (1); v P 1957 (4); *v E 1963 (5) 1966 (5) 1969 (3) 1973 (3); v A 1960 (3) 1968 (5) 1975 (6); v NZ 1968 (3); v In 1958 (1) 1966 (3) 1974 (5); v P 1958 (3) 1974 (2)*
Gibson, O. D. 2: *v E 1995 (1); v SA 1998 (1)*
Gilchrist, R. 13: v P 1957 (5); *v E 1957 (4); v In 1958 (4)*
Gladstone, G. 1: v E 1929
Goddard, J. D. C. 27: v E 1947 (4); *v E 1950 (4) 1957 (5); v A 1951 (4); v NZ 1951 (2) 1955 (3); v In 1948 (5)*
Gomes, H. A. 60: v E 1980 (4) 1985 (5); v A 1977 (3) 1983 (2); v NZ 1984 (4); v In 1982 (5); *v E 1976 (2) 1984 (5); v A 1981 (3) 1984 (5); v NZ 1986 (3); v In 1978 (6) 1983 (6); v P 1980 (4) 1986 (3)*
Gomez, G. E. 29: v E 1947 (4) 1953 (4); v In 1952 (4); *v E 1939 (2) 1950 (4); v A 1951 (5); v NZ 1951 (1); v In 1948 (5)*
Grant, G. C. 12: v E 1934 (4); *v E 1933 (3); v A 1930 (5)*
Grant, R. S. 7: v E 1934 (4); *v E 1939 (3)*
Gray, A. H. 5: *v NZ 1986 (2); v P 1986 (3)*
Greenidge, A. E. 6: v A 1977 (2); *v In 1978 (4)*
Greenidge, C. G. 108: v E 1980 (4) 1985 (5) 1989 (4); v A 1977 (2) 1983 (5) 1990 (5); v NZ 1984 (4); v In 1982 (5) 1988 (4); v P 1976 (5) 1987 (3); *v E 1976 (5) 1980 (5) 1984 (5) 1988 (4); v A 1975 (2) 1979 (3) 1981 (2) 1984 (5) 1988 (5); v NZ 1979 (3) 1986 (3); v In 1974 (5) 1983 (6) 1987 (3); v P 1986 (3) 1990 (3)*
Greenidge, G. A. 5: v A 1972 (3); v NZ 1971 (2)
Grell, M. G. 1: v E 1929
Griffith, A. F. G. 14: v A 1998 (2); v P 1999 (3); v Z 1999 (2); *v E 2000 (4); v A 1996 (1); v NZ 1999 (2)*
Griffith, C. C. 28: v E 1959 (1) 1967 (4); v A 1964 (5); *v E 1963 (5) 1966 (5); v A 1968 (3); v NZ 1968 (2); v In 1966 (3)*
Griffith, H. C. 13: v E 1929 (3); *v E 1928 (3) 1933 (2); v A 1930 (5)*
Guillen, S. C. 5: *v A 1951 (3); v NZ 1951 (2)*

Hall, W. W. 48: v E 1959 (5) 1967 (4); v A 1964 (5); v In 1961 (5); *v E 1963 (5) 1966 (5); v A 1960 (5) 1968 (2); v NZ 1968 (1); v In 1958 (5) 1966 (3); v P 1958 (3)*
Harper, R. A. 25: v E 1985 (2); v A 1983 (4); v NZ 1984 (1); *v E 1984 (5) 1988 (3); v A 1984 (2) 1988 (1); v In 1983 (2) 1987 (1); v P 1986 (3); v SL 1993 (1)*
Haynes, D. L. 116: v E 1980 (4) 1985 (5) 1989 (4) 1993 (4); v A 1977 (2) 1983 (5) 1990 (5); v SA 1991 (1); v NZ 1984 (4); v In 1982 (5) 1988 (4); v P 1987 (3) 1992 (3); *v E 1980 (5) 1984 (5) 1988 (4) 1991 (5); v A 1979 (3) 1981 (3) 1984 (5) 1988 (5) 1992 (5); v NZ 1979 (3) 1986 (3); v In 1983 (6) 1987 (4); v P 1980 (4) 1986 (3) 1990 (3); v SL 1993 (1)*

Headley, G. A. 22: v E 1929 (4) 1934 (4) 1947 (1) 1953 (1); *v E 1933 (3) 1939 (3); v A 1930 (5); v In 1948 (1)*
Headley, R. G. A. 2: *v E 1973 (2)*
Hendriks, J. L. 20: v A 1964 (4); v In 1961 (1); *v E 1966 (3) 1969 (1); v A 1968 (5); v NZ 1968 (3); v In 1966 (3)*
Hinds, W. W. 18: v SA 2000 (4); v P 1999 (3); v Z 1999 (2); *v E 2000 (5); v A 2000 (4)*
Hoad, E. L. G. 4: v E 1929 (1); *v E 1928 (1) 1933 (2)*
Holder, R. I. C. 11: v E 1997 (2); v A 1998 (1); v In 1996 (5); v SL 1996 (2); *v P 1997 (1)*
Holder, V. A. 40: v E 1973 (1); v A 1972 (3) 1977 (3); v NZ 1971 (4); v In 1970 (3) 1975 (1); v P 1976 (1); *v E 1969 (3) 1973 (2) 1976 (4); v A 1975 (3); v In 1974 (4) 1978 (6); v P 1974 (2)*
Holding, M. A. 60: v E 1980 (4) 1985 (4); v A 1983 (3); v NZ 1984 (3); v In 1975 (4) 1982 (5); *v E 1976 (4) 1980 (5) 1984 (4); v A 1975 (5) 1979 (3) 1981 (3) 1984 (3); v NZ 1979 (3) 1986 (1); v In 1983 (6)*
Holford, D. A. J. 24: v E 1967 (4); v NZ 1971 (5); v In 1970 (1) 1975 (2); v P 1976 (1); *v E 1966 (5); v A 1968 (2); v NZ 1968 (3); v In 1966 (1)*
Holt, J. K. 17: v E 1953 (5); v A 1954 (5); *v In 1958 (5); v P 1958 (2)*
Hooper, C. L. 87: v E 1989 (3) 1997 (6); v A 1990 (5) 1994 (4) 1998 (2); v SA 2000 (5); v In 1996 (5); v P 1987 (3) 1992 (3); v SL 1996 (2); *v E 1988 (5) 1991 (5) 1995 (5); v A 1988 (5) 1992 (4) 1996 (5); v SA 1998 (5); v In 1987 (3) 1994 (3); v P 1990 (3) 1997 (3); v SL 1993 (1); v Z 2001 (2)*
Howard, A. B. 1: v NZ 1971
Hunte, C. C. 44: v E 1959 (5); v A 1964 (5); v In 1961 (5); v P 1957 (5); *v E 1963 (5) 1966 (5); v A 1960 (5); v In 1958 (5) 1966 (3); v P 1958 (1)*
Hunte, E. A. C. 3: v E 1929 (3)
Hylton, L. G. 6: v E 1934 (4); *v E 1939 (2)*

Jacobs, R. D. 32: v A 1998 (4); v SA 2000 (5); v P 1999 (3); v Z 1999 (2); *v E 2000 (5); v A 2000 (5); v SA 1998 (5); v NZ 1999 (2); v Z 2001 (1)*
Johnson, H. H. H. 3: v E 1947 (1); *v E 1950 (2)*
Johnson, T. F. 1: *v E 1939*
Jones, C. M. 4: v E 1929 (1) 1934 (3)
Jones, P. E. 9: v E 1947 (1); *v E 1950 (2); v A 1951 (1); v In 1948 (5)*
Joseph, D. R. E. 4: v A 1998 (4)
Julien, B. D. 24: v E 1973 (5); v In 1975 (4); v P 1976 (1); *v E 1973 (3) 1976 (2); v A 1975 (3); v In 1974 (4); v P 1974 (2)*
Jumadeen, R. R. 12: v A 1972 (1) 1977 (2); v NZ 1971 (1); v In 1975 (4); v P 1976 (1); *v E 1976 (1); v In 1978 (2)*

Kallicharran, A. I. 66: v E 1973 (5); v A 1972 (5) 1977 (5); v NZ 1971 (2); v In 1975 (4); v P 1976 (5); *v E 1973 (3) 1976 (3) 1980 (5); v A 1975 (6) 1979 (3); v NZ 1979 (3); v In 1974 (5) 1978 (6); v P 1974 (2) 1980 (4)*
Kanhai, R. B. 79: v E 1959 (5) 1967 (5) 1973 (5); v A 1964 (5) 1972 (5); v In 1961 (5) 1970 (5); v P 1957 (5); *v E 1957 (5) 1963 (5) 1966 (5) 1973 (3); v A 1960 (5) 1968 (5); v In 1958 (5) 1966 (3); v P 1958 (3)*
Kentish, E. S. M. 2: v E 1947 (1) 1953 (1)
King, C. L. 9: v P 1976 (1); *v E 1976 (3) 1980 (1); v A 1979 (1); v NZ 1979 (3)*
King, F. M. 14: v E 1953 (3); v A 1954 (4); v In 1952 (5); *v NZ 1955 (2)*
King, L. A. 2: v E 1967 (1); v In 1961 (1)
King, R. D. 14: v P 1999 (3); v Z 1999 (2); *v E 2000 (4); v SA 1998 (1); v NZ 1999 (2); v Z 2001 (2)*

Lambert, C. B. 5: v E 1997 (2); *v E 1991 (1); v SA 1998 (2)*
Lara, B. C. 80: v E 1993 (5) 1997 (6); v A 1994 (4) 1998 (4); v SA 1991 (1) 2000 (5); v NZ 1995 (2); v In 1996 (5); v P 1992 (3); v SL 1996 (2); *v E 1995 (6) 2000 (5); v A 1992 (5) 1996 (5) 2000 (5); v SA 1998 (5); v NZ 1994 (2) 1999 (2); v In 1994 (3); v P 1990 (1) 1997 (3); v SL 1993 (1)*
Lashley, P. D. 4: *v E 1966 (2); v A 1960 (2)*
Legall, R. 4: v In 1952 (4)
Lewis, D. M. 3: v In 1970 (3)
Lewis, R. N. 3: *v SA 1998 (2); v P 1997 (1)*

Lloyd, C. H. 110: v E 1967 (5) 1973 (5) 1980 (4); v A 1972 (3) 1977 (2) 1983 (4); v NZ 1971 (2); v In 1970 (5) 1975 (4) 1982 (5); v P 1976 (5); *v E 1969 (3) 1973 (3) 1976 (5) 1980 (4) 1984 (5); v A 1968 (4) 1975 (6) 1979 (2) 1981 (3) 1984 (5); v NZ 1968 (3) 1979 (3); v In 1966 (3) 1974 (5) 1983 (6); v P 1974 (2) 1980 (4)*

Logie, A. L. 52: v E 1989 (3); v A 1983 (1) 1990 (5); v NZ 1984 (4); v In 1982 (5) 1988 (4); v P 1987 (3); *v E 1988 (5) 1991 (4); v A 1988 (5); v NZ 1986 (3); v In 1983 (3) 1987 (4); v P 1990 (3)*

McGarrell, N. C. 3: v SA 2000 (1); *v Z 2001 (2)*

McLean, N. A. M. 19: v E 1997 (4); v SA 2000 (2); v P 1999 (2); *v E 2000 (2); v A 2000 (5); v SA 1998 (4)*

McMorris, E. D. A. St J. 13: v E 1959 (4); v In 1961 (4); v P 1957 (1); *v E 1963 (2) 1966 (2)*

McWatt, C. A. 6: v E 1953 (5); v A 1954 (1)

Madray, I. S. 2: v P 1957 (2)

Marshall, M. D. 81: v E 1980 (1) 1985 (5) 1989 (2); v A 1983 (4) 1990 (5); v NZ 1984 (4); v In 1982 (5) 1988 (3); v P 1987 (2); *v E 1980 (4) 1984 (4) 1988 (5) 1991 (5); v A 1984 (5) 1988 (5); v NZ 1986 (3); v In 1978 (3) 1983 (6); v P 1980 (4) 1986 (3) 1990 (3)*

Marshall, N. E. 1: v A 1954

Marshall, R. E. 4: *v A 1951 (2); v NZ 1951 (2)*

Martin, F. R. 9: v E 1929 (1); *v E 1928 (3); v A 1930 (5)*

Martindale, E. A. 10: v E 1934 (4); *v E 1933 (3) 1939 (3)*

Mattis, E. H. 4: v E 1980 (4)

Mendonca, I. L. 2: v In 1961 (2)

Merry, C. A. 2: *v E 1933 (2)*

Miller, R. 1: v In 1952

Moodie, G. H. 1: v E 1934

Moseley, E. A. 2: v E 1989 (2)

Murray, D. A. 19: v E 1980 (4); v A 1977 (3); *v A 1981 (2); v In 1978 (6); v P 1980 (4)*

Murray, D. L. 62: v E 1967 (5) 1973 (5); v A 1972 (4) 1977 (2); v In 1975 (4); v P 1976 (5); *v E 1963 (5) 1973 (3) 1976 (5) 1980 (5); v A 1975 (6) 1979 (3); v NZ 1979 (3); v In 1974 (5); v P 1974 (2)*

Murray, J. R. 31: v E 1993 (5) 1997 (1); v A 1994 (3); v In 1996 (2); v P 1992 (3); *v E 1995 (4); v A 1992 (3) 1996 (2); v SA 1998 (2); v NZ 1994 (2); v In 1994 (3); v SL 1993 (1)*

Nagamootoo, M. V. 2: *v E 2000 (1); v A 2000 (1)*

Nanan, R. 1: *v P 1980*

Neblett, J. M. 1: v E 1934

Noreiga, J. M. 4: v In 1970 (4)

Nunes, R. K. 4: v E 1929 (1); *v E 1928 (3)*

Nurse, S. M. 29: v E 1959 (1) 1967 (5); v A 1964 (4); v In 1961 (1); *v E 1966 (5); v A 1960 (3) 1968 (5); v NZ 1968 (3); v In 1966 (2)*

Padmore, A. L. 2: v In 1975 (1); *v E 1976 (1)*

Pairaudeau, B. H. 13: v E 1953 (2); v In 1952 (5): *v E 1957 (2); v NZ 1955 (4)*

Parry, D. R. 12: v A 1977 (5); *v NZ 1979 (1); v In 1978 (6)*

Passailaigue, C. C. 1: v E 1929

Patterson, B. P. 28: v E 1985 (5) 1989 (1); v A 1990 (5); v SA 1991 (1); v P 1987 (1); *v E 1988 (2) 1991 (3); v A 1988 (4) 1992 (1); v In 1987 (4); v P 1986 (1)*

Payne, T. R. O. 1: v E 1985

Perry, N. O. 4: v A 1998 (3); *v NZ 1999 (1)*

Phillip, N. 9: v A 1977 (3); *v In 1978 (6)*

Pierre, L. R. 1: v E 1947

Powell, R. L. 1: *v NZ 1999*

Rae, A. F. 15: v In 1952 (2); *v E 1950 (4); v A 1951 (3); v NZ 1951 (1); v In 1948 (5)*

Ragoonath, S. 2: v A 1998 (2)

Ramadhin, S. 43: v E 1953 (5) 1959 (4); v A 1954 (4); v In 1952 (4); *v E 1950 (4) 1957 (5); v A 1951 (5) 1960 (2); v NZ 1951 (2) 1955 (4); v In 1958 (2); v P 1958 (2)*

Ramnarine, D. 8: v E 1997 (2); v SA 2000 (5); *v NZ 1999 (1)*

Reifer, F. L. 4: v SL 1996 (2); *v SA 1998 (2)*

Richards, I. V. A. 121: v E 1980 (4) 1985 (5) 1989 (3); v A 1977 (2) 1983 (5) 1990 (5); v NZ 1984 (4); v In 1975 (4) 1982 (5) 1988 (4); v P 1976 (5) 1987 (2); *v E 1976 (4) 1980 (5) 1984 (5) 1988 (5) 1991 (5); v A 1975 (6) 1979 (3) 1981 (3) 1984 (5) 1988 (5); v NZ 1986 (3); v In 1974 (5) 1983 (6) 1987 (4); v P 1974 (2) 1980 (4) 1986 (3)*

Richardson, R. B. 86: v E 1985 (5) 1989 (4) 1993 (4); v A 1983 (5) 1990 (5) 1994 (4); v SA 1991 (1); v NZ 1984 (4); v In 1988 (4); v P 1987 (3) 1992 (3); *v E 1988 (3) 1991 (5) 1995 (6); v A 1984 (5) 1988 (5) 1992 (5); v NZ 1986 (3); v In 1983 (1) 1987 (4); v P 1986 (3) 1990 (3); v SL 1993 (1)*

Rickards, K. R. 2: v E 1947 (1); *v A 1951 (1)*

Roach, C. A. 16: v E 1929 (4) 1934 (1); *v E 1928 (3) 1933 (3); v A 1930 (5)*

Roberts, A. M. E. 47: v E 1973 (1) 1980 (3); v A 1977 (2); v In 1975 (2) 1982 (5); v P 1976 (5); *v E 1976 (5) 1980 (3); v A 1975 (5) 1979 (3) 1981 (2); v NZ 1979 (2); v In 1974 (5) 1983 (2); v P 1974 (2)*

Roberts, A. T. 1: *v NZ 1955*

Roberts, L. A. 1: v A 1998

Rodriguez, W. V. 5: v E 1967 (1); v A 1964 (1); v In 1961 (2); *v E 1963 (1)*

Rose, F. A. 19: v E 1997 (1); v In 1996 (5); v P 1999 (1); v SL 1996 (2); v Z 1999 (2); *v E 2000 (3); v SA 1998 (1); v NZ 1999 (2); v P 1997 (2)*

Rowe, L. G. 30: v E 1973 (5); v A 1972 (3); v NZ 1971 (4); v In 1975 (4); *v E 1976 (2); v A 1975 (6) 1979 (3); v NZ 1979 (3)*

St Hill, E. L. 2: v E 1929 (2)

St Hill, W. H. 3: v E 1929 (1); *v E 1928 (2)*

Samuels, M. N. 9: v SA 2000 (4); *v A 2000 (3); v Z 2001 (2)*

Samuels, R. G. 6: v NZ 1995 (2); *v A 1996 (4)*

Sarwan, R. R. 14: v SA 2000 (4); v P 1999 (2); *v E 2000 (3); v A 2000 (3); v Z 2001 (2)*

Scarlett, R. O. 3: v E 1959 (3)

Scott, A. P. H. 1: v In 1952

Scott, O. C. 8: v E 1929 (1); *v E 1928 (2); v A 1930 (5)*

Sealey, B. J. 1: *v E 1933*

Sealy, J. E. D. 11: v E 1929 (2) 1934 (4); *v E 1939 (3); v A 1930 (2)*

Shepherd, J. N. 5: v In 1970 (2); *v E 1969 (3)*

Shillingford, G. C. 7: v NZ 1971 (2); v In 1970 (3); *v E 1969 (2)*

Shillingford, I. T. 4: v A 1977 (1); v P 1976 (3)

Shivnarine, S. 8: v A 1977 (3); *v In 1978 (5)*

Simmons, P. V. 26: v E 1993 (2); v SA 1991 (1); v NZ 1995 (2); v P 1987 (1) 1992 (3); *v E 1991 (5); v A 1992 (5) 1996 (1); v In 1987 (1) 1994 (3); v P 1997 (1); v SL 1993 (1)*

Singh, C. K. 2: v E 1959 (2)

Small, J. A. 3: v E 1929 (1); *v E 1928 (2)*

Small, M. A. 2: v A 1983 (1); *v E 1984 (1)*

Smith, C. W. 5: v In 1961 (1); *v A 1960 (4)*

Smith, O. G. 26: v A 1954 (4); v P 1957 (5); *v E 1957 (5); v NZ 1955 (4); v In 1958 (5); v P 1958 (3)*

Sobers, G. S. 93: v E 1953 (1) 1959 (5) 1967 (5) 1973 (4); v A 1954 (4) 1964 (5); v NZ 1971 (5); v In 1961 (5) 1970 (5); v P 1957 (5); *v E 1957 (5) 1963 (5) 1966 (5) 1969 (3) 1973 (3); v A 1960 (5) 1968 (5); v NZ 1955 (4) 1968 (3); v In 1958 (5) 1966 (3); v P 1958 (3)*

Solomon, J. S. 27: v E 1959 (2); v A 1964 (4); v In 1961 (4); *v E 1963 (5); v A 1960 (5); v In 1958 (4); v P 1958 (3)*

Stayers, S. C. 4: v In 1961 (4)

Stollmeyer, J. B. 32: v E 1947 (2) 1953 (5); v A 1954 (2); v In 1952 (5); *v E 1939 (3) 1950 (4); v A 1951 (5); v NZ 1951 (2); v In 1948 (4)*

Stollmeyer, V. H. 1: *v E 1939*

Stuart, C. E. L. 4: *v A 2000 (2); v Z 2001 (2)*

Taylor, J. 3: v P 1957 (1); *v In 1958 (1); v P 1958 (1)*

Thompson, P. I. C. 2: v NZ 1995 (1); *v A 1996 (1)*

Trim, J. 4: v E 1947 (1); *v A 1951 (1); v In 1948 (2)*

Valentine, A. L. 36: v E 1953 (3); v A 1954 (3); v In 1952 (5) 1961 (2); v P 1957 (1); *v E 1950 (4) 1957 (2); v A 1951 (5) 1960 (5); v NZ 1951 (2) 1955 (4)*

Valentine, V. A. 2: *v E 1933 (2)*

Walcott, C. L. 44: v E 1947 (4) 1953 (5) 1959 (2); v A 1954 (5); v In 1952 (5); v P 1957 (4); *v E 1950 (4) 1957 (5); v A 1951 (3); v NZ 1951 (2); v In 1948 (5)*
Walcott, L. A. 1: v E 1929
Wallace, P. A. 7: v E 1997 (2); *v SA 1998 (4); v P 1997 (1)*
Walsh, C. A. 132: v E 1985 (1) 1989 (3) 1993 (5) 1997 (6); v A 1990 (5) 1994 (4) 1998 (4); v SA 1991 (1) 2000 (5); v NZ 1984 (1) 1995 (2); v In 1988 (4) 1996 (4); v P 1987 (3) 1992 (3) 1999 (3); v SL 1996 (2); v Z 1999 (2); *v E 1988 (5) 1991 (5) 1995 (6) 2000 (5); v A 1984 (5) 1988 (5) 1992 (5) 1996 (5) 2000 (5); v SA 1998 (4); v NZ 1986 (3) 1994 (2) 1999 (2); v In 1987 (4) 1994 (3); v P 1986 (3) 1990 (3) 1997 (3); v SL 1993 (1)*
Watson, C. 7: v E 1959 (5); v In 1961 (1); *v A 1960 (1)*
Weekes, E. D. 48: v E 1947 (4) 1953 (4); v A 1954 (5); v In 1952 (5); v P 1957 (5); *v E 1950 (4) 1957 (5); v A 1951 (5); v NZ 1951 (2) 1955 (4); v In 1948 (5)*
Weekes, K. H. 2: *v E 1939 (2)*
White, W. A. 2: v A 1964 (2)
Wight, C. V. 2: v E 1929 (1); *v E 1928 (1)*
Wight, G. L. 1: v In 1952
Wiles, C. A. 1: *v E 1933*
Willett, E. T. 5: v A 1972 (3); *v In 1974 (2)*
Williams, A. B. 7: v A 1977 (3); *v In 1978 (4)*
Williams, D. 11: v E 1997 (5); v SA 1991 (1); *v A 1992 (2); v P 1997 (3)*
Williams, E. A. V. 4: v E 1947 (3); *v E 1939 (1)*
Williams, S. C. 28: v E 1993 (1) 1997 (4); v A 1994 (4); v In 1996 (5); v SL 1996 (2); *v E 1995 (2); v SA 1998 (2); v NZ 1994 (2); v In 1994 (3); v P 1997 (3)*
Wishart, K. L. 1: v E 1934
Worrell, F. M. M. 51: v E 1947 (3) 1953 (4) 1959 (4); v A 1954 (4); v In 1952 (5) 1961 (5); *v E 1950 (4) 1957 (5) 1963 (5); v A 1951 (5) 1960 (5); v NZ 1951 (2)*

NEW ZEALAND

Number of Test cricketers: 215

Alabaster, J. C. 21: v E 1962 (2); v WI 1955 (1); v In 1967 (4); *v E 1958 (2); v SA 1961 (5); v WI 1971 (2); v In 1955 (4); v P 1955 (1)*
Allcott, C. F. W. 6: v E 1929 (2); v SA 1931 (1); *v E 1931 (3)*
Allott, G. I. 10: v E 1996 (2); v SA 1998 (2); v Z 1995 (2); *v E 1999 (2); v A 1997 (2)*
Anderson, R. W. 9: v E 1977 (3); *v E 1978 (3); v P 1976 (3)*
Anderson, W. M. 1: v A 1945
Andrews, B. 2: *v A 1973 (2)*
Astle, N. J. 46: v E 1996 (3); v A 1999 (3); v SA 1998 (3); v WI 1999 (2); v In 1998 (1); v P 2000 (3); v SL 1996 (2); v Z 1995 (2) 1997 (2) 2000 (1); *v E 1999 (4); v A 1997 (3); v SA 2000 (3); v WI 1995 (2); v In 1999 (3); v P 1996 (2); v SL 1997 (3); v Z 1997 (2) 2000 (2)*

Badcock, F. T. 7: v E 1929 (3) 1932 (2); v SA 1931 (2)
Barber, R. T. 1: v WI 1955
Bartlett, G. A. 10: v E 1965 (2); v In 1967 (2); v P 1964 (1); *v SA 1961 (5)*
Barton, P. T. 7: v E 1962 (3); *v SA 1961 (4)*
Beard, D. D. 4: v WI 1951 (2) 1955 (2)
Beck, J. E. F. 8: v WI 1955 (4); *v SA 1953 (4)*
Bell, M. D. 11: v SA 1998 (1); v In 1998 (2); v P 2000 (3); *v E 1999 (3); In 1999 (2)*
Bell, W. 2: *v SA 1953 (2)*
Bilby, G. P. 2: v E 1965 (2)
Blain, T. E. 11: v A 1992 (2); v P 1993 (3); *v E 1986 (1); v A 1993 (3); v In 1988 (2)*
Blair, R. W. 19: v E 1954 (1) 1958 (2) 1962 (2); v SA 1952 (2) 1963 (3); v WI 1955 (2); *v E 1958 (3); v SA 1953 (4)*
Blunt, R. C. 9: v E 1929 (4); v SA 1931 (2); *v E 1931 (3)*
Bolton, B. A. 2: v E 1958 (2)
Boock, S. L. 30: v E 1977 (3) 1983 (2) 1987 (1); v WI 1979 (3) 1986 (2); v P 1978 (3) 1984 (2) 1988 (1); *v E 1978 (3); v A 1985 (1); v WI 1984 (3); v P 1984 (3); v SL 1983 (3)*
Bracewell, B. P. 6: v P 1978 (1) 1984 (1); *v E 1978 (3); v A 1980 (1)*

Bracewell, J. G. 41: v E 1987 (3); v A 1985 (2) 1989 (1); v WI 1986 (3); v In 1980 (1) 1989 (2); v P 1988 (2); *v E 1983 (4) 1986 (3) 1990 (3); v A 1980 (3) 1985 (2) 1987 (3); v WI 1984 (1); v In 1988 (3); v P 1984 (2); v SL 1983 (2) 1986 (1)*

Bradburn, G. E. 7: v P 2000 (2); v SL 1990 (1); *v P 1990 (3); v SL 1992 (1)*

Bradburn, W. P. 2: v SA 1963 (2)

Brown, V. R. 2: *v A 1985 (2)*

Burgess, M. G. 50: v E 1970 (1) 1977 (3); v A 1973 (1) 1976 (2); v WI 1968 (2); v In 1967 (4) 1975 (3); v P 1972 (3) 1978 (3); *v E 1969 (2) 1973 (3) 1978 (3); v A 1980 (3); v WI 1971 (5); v In 1969 (3) 1976 (3); v P 1969 (3) 1976 (3)*

Burke, C. 1: v A 1945

Burtt, T. B. 10: v E 1946 (1) 1950 (2); v SA 1952 (1); v WI 1951 (2); *v E 1949 (4)*

Butterfield, L. A. 1: v A 1945

Cairns, B. L. 43: v E 1974 (1) 1977 (1) 1983 (3); v A 1976 (1) 1981 (3); v WI 1979 (3); v In 1975 (1) 1980 (3); v P 1978 (3) 1984 (3); v SL 1982 (2); *v E 1978 (2) 1983 (4); v A 1973 (1) 1980 (3) 1985 (1); v WI 1984 (2); v In 1976 (2); v P 1976 (2); v SL 1983 (2)*

Cairns, C. L. 49: v E 1991 (3) 1996 (3); v A 1992 (2) 1999 (3); v WI 1999 (2); v In 1998 (2); v P 1993 (1) 1995 (1); v SL 1990 (1) 1996 (2); v Z 1995 (2) 1997 (2); *v E 1999 (4); v A 1989 (1) 1993 (2) 1997 (3); v In 1995 (3) 1999 (3); v P 1996 (2); v SL 1997 (3); v Z 1997 (2) 2000 (2)*

Cameron, F. J. 19: v E 1962 (3); v SA 1963 (3); v P 1964 (3); *v E 1965 (2); v SA 1961 (5); v In 1964 (1); v P 1964 (2)*

Cave, H. B. 19: v E 1954 (2); v WI 1955 (3); *v E 1949 (4) 1958 (2); v In 1955 (5); v P 1955 (3)*

Chapple, M. E. 14: v E 1954 (1) 1965 (1); v SA 1952 (1) 1963 (3); v WI 1955 (1); *v SA 1953 (5) 1961 (2)*

Chatfield, E. J. 43: v E 1974 (1) 1977 (1) 1983 (3) 1987 (3); v A 1976 (2) 1981 (1) 1985 (3); v WI 1986 (3); v P 1984 (3) 1988 (2); v SL 1982 (2); *v E 1983 (3) 1986 (1); v A 1985 (2) 1987 (2); v WI 1984 (4); v In 1988 (3); v P 1984 (1); v SL 1983 (2) 1986 (1)*

Cleverley, D. C. 2: v SA 1931 (1); v A 1945 (1)

Collinge, R. O. 35: v E 1970 (2) 1974 (2) 1977 (3); v A 1973 (3); v In 1967 (2) 1975 (3); v P 1964 (3) 1972 (2); *v E 1965 (3) 1969 (1) 1973 (3) 1978 (1); v In 1964 (2) 1976 (1); v P 1964 (2) 1976 (2)*

Colquhoun, I. A. 2: v E 1954 (2)

Coney, J. V. 52: v E 1983 (3); v A 1973 (2) 1981 (3) 1985 (3); v WI 1979 (3) 1986 (3); v In 1980 (3); v P 1978 (3) 1984 (3); v SL 1982 (2); *v E 1983 (4) 1986 (3); v A 1973 (2) 1980 (2) 1985 (3); v WI 1984 (4); v P 1984 (3); v SL 1983 (3)*

Congdon, B. E. 61: v E 1965 (3) 1970 (2) 1974 (2) 1977 (3); v A 1973 (3) 1976 (2); v WI 1968 (3); v In 1967 (4) 1975 (3); v P 1964 (3) 1972 (3); *v E 1965 (3) 1969 (3) 1973 (3) 1978 (3); v A 1973 (3); v WI 1971 (5); v In 1964 (3) 1969 (3); v P 1964 (1) 1969 (3)*

Cowie, J. 9: v E 1946 (1); v A 1945 (1); *v E 1937 (3) 1949 (4)*

Cresswell G. F. 3: v E 1950 (2); *v E 1949 (1)*

Cromb, I. B. 5: v SA 1931 (2); *v E 1931 (3)*

Crowe, J. J. 39: v E 1983 (3) 1987 (2); v A 1989 (1); v WI 1986 (3); v P 1984 (3) 1988 (2); v SL 1982 (2); *v E 1983 (2) 1986 (3); v A 1985 (3) 1987 (3) 1989 (1); v WI 1984 (4); v P 1984 (3); v SL 1983 (3) 1986 (1)*

Crowe, M. D. 77: v E 1983 (3) 1987 (3) 1991 (3); v A 1981 (3) 1985 (3) 1992 (3); v SA 1994 (1); v WI 1986 (3); v In 1989 (3); v P 1984 (3) 1988 (2); v SL 1990 (2); *v E 1983 (4) 1986 (3) 1990 (3) 1994 (3); v A 1985 (3) 1987 (3) 1989 (1) 1993 (1); v SA 1994 (3); v WI 1984 (4); v In 1995 (3); v P 1984 (3) 1990 (3); v SL 1983 (3) 1986 (1) 1992 (2); v Z 1992 (2)*

Cunis, R. S. 20: v E 1965 (3) 1970 (2); v SA 1963 (1); v WI 1968 (3); *v E 1969 (1); v WI 1971 (5); v In 1969 (3); v P 1969 (2)*

D'Arcy, J. W. 5: *v E 1958 (5)*

Davis, H. T. 5: v E 1996 (1); v SL 1996 (2); *v E 1994 (1); v Z 1997 (1)*

de Groen, R. P. 5: v P 1993 (2); *v A 1993 (2); v SA 1994 (1)*

Dempster, C. S. 10: v E 1929 (4) 1932 (2); v SA 1931 (2); *v E 1931 (2)*

Dempster, E. W. 5: v SA 1952 (1); *v SA 1953 (4)*

Dick, A. E. 17: v E 1962 (3); v SA 1963 (2); v P 1964 (2); *v E 1965 (2); v SA 1961 (5); v P 1964 (3)*

Dickinson, G. R. 3: v E 1929 (2); v SA 1931 (1)

Donnelly, M. P. 7: *v E 1937 (3) 1949 (4)*

Doull, S. B. 32: v E 1996 (3); v A 1999 (2); v SA 1998 (3); v WI 1994 (2); v In 1998 (2); v P 1993 (3); v SL 1996 (2); v Z 1997 (2); *v E 1999 (1); v A 1993 (2) 1997 (3); v SA 1994 (3); v P 1996 (2); v SL 1997 (1); v Z 1992 (1)*
Dowling, G. T. 39: v E 1962 (3) 1970 (2); v SA 1963 (1); v WI 1968 (3); v In 1967 (4); v P 1964 (2); *v E 1965 (3) 1969 (3); v SA 1961 (4); v WI 1971 (2); v In 1964 (4) 1969 (3); v P 1964 (2) 1969 (3)*
Drum, C. J. 1: v P 2000
Dunning, J. A. 4: v E 1932 (1); *v E 1937 (3)*

Edgar, B. A. 39: v E 1983 (3); v A 1981 (3) 1985 (3); v WI 1979 (3); v In 1980 (3); v P 1978 (3); v SL 1982 (2); *v E 1978 (3) 1983 (4) 1986 (3); v A 1980 (3) 1985 (3); v P 1984 (3)*
Edwards, G. N. 8: v E 1977 (1); v A 1976 (2); v In 1980 (3); *v E 1978 (2)*
Emery, R. W. G. 2: v WI 1951 (2)

Fisher, F. E. 1: v SA 1952
Fleming, S. P. 60: v E 1996 (3); v A 1999 (3); v SA 1994 (1); v WI 1994 (2) 1999 (2); v In 1993 (1) 1998 (2); v P 1995 (1) 2000 (3); v SL 1994 (2) 1996 (2); v Z 1995 (2) 1997 (2) 2000 (1); *v E 1994 (3) 1999 (4); v A 1997 (3); SA 1994 (3) 2000 (3); v WI 1995 (2); v In 1995 (3) 1999 (3); v P 1996 (2); v SL 1997 (3); v Z 1997 (2) 2000 (2)*
Foley, H. 1: v E 1929
Franklin, J. E. C. 2: v P 2000 (2)
Franklin, T. J. 21: v E 1987 (3); v A 1985 (1) 1989 (1); v In 1989 (3); v SL 1990 (3); *v E 1983 (1) 1990 (3); v In 1988 (3); v P 1990 (3)*
Freeman, D. L. 2: v E 1932 (2)

Gallichan, N. 1: *v E 1937*
Gedye, S. G. 4: v SA 1963 (3); v P 1964 (1)
Germon, L. K. 12: v E 1996 (2); v P 1995 (1); v Z 1995 (2); *v WI 1995 (2); v In 1995 (3); v P 1996 (2)*
Gillespie, S. R. 1: v A 1985
Gray, E. J. 10: *v E 1983 (2) 1986 (3); v A 1987 (1); v In 1988 (1); v P 1984 (2); v SL 1986 (1)*
Greatbatch, M. J. 41: v E 1987 (2) 1991 (1); v A 1989 (1) 1992 (3); v In 1989 (3) 1993 (1); v P 1988 (1) 1992 (1) 1993 (3); v SL 1990 (2) 1994 (2); *v E 1990 (3) 1994 (1); v A 1989 (1) 1993 (3); v In 1988 (3) 1995 (3); v P 1990 (3) 1996 (2); v Z 1992 (2)*
Guillen, S. C. 3: v WI 1955 (3)
Guy, J. W. 12: v E 1958 (2); v WI 1955 (2); *v SA 1961 (2); v In 1955 (5); v P 1955 (1)*

Hadlee, D. R. 26: v E 1974 (2) 1977 (1); v A 1973 (3) 1976 (1); v In 1975 (3); v P 1972 (2); *v E 1969 (2) 1973 (3); v A 1973 (3); v In 1969 (3); v P 1969 (3)*
Hadlee, R. J. 86: v E 1977 (3) 1983 (3) 1987 (1); v A 1973 (2) 1976 (2) 1981 (3) 1985 (3) 1989 (1); v WI 1979 (3) 1986 (3); v In 1975 (2) 1980 (3) 1989 (3); v P 1972 (1) 1978 (3) 1984 (3) 1988 (2); v SL 1982 (2); *v E 1973 (1) 1978 (3) 1983 (4) 1986 (3) 1990 (3); v A 1973 (3) 1980 (3) 1985 (3) 1987 (3); v WI 1984 (4); v In 1976 (3) 1988 (3); v P 1976 (3); v SL 1983 (3) 1986 (1)*
Hadlee, W. A. 11: v E 1946 (1) 1950 (2); v A 1945 (1); *v E 1937 (3) 1949 (4)*
Harford, N. S. 8: *v E 1958 (4); v In 1955 (2); v P 1955 (2)*
Harford, R. I. 3: v In 1967 (3)
Harris, C. Z. 19: v A 1992 (1); v SA 1998 (3); v P 1992 (1); *v E 1999 (1); v A 1993 (1) 1997 (1); v WI 1995 (2); v In 1999 (1); v P 1996 (2); v SL 1992 (2) 1997 (2); v Z 1997 (2)*
Harris, P. G. Z. 9: v P 1964 (1); *v SA 1961 (5); v In 1955 (1); v P 1955 (2)*
Harris, R. M. 2: v E 1958 (2)
Hart, M. N. 14: v SA 1994 (1); v WI 1994 (2); v In 1993 (1); v P 1993 (2); *v E 1994 (3); v SA 1994 (3); v In 1995 (2)*
Hartland, B. R. 9: v E 1991 (3); v In 1993 (1); v P 1992 (1) 1993 (1); *v E 1994 (1); v SL 1992 (2)*
Haslam, M. J. 4: *v In 1995 (2); v Z 1992 (2)*
Hastings, B. F. 31: v E 1974 (2); v A 1973 (3); v WI 1968 (3); v In 1975 (1); v P 1972 (3); *v E 1969 (3) 1973 (3); v A 1973 (3); v WI 1971 (5); v In 1969 (2); v P 1969 (3)*
Hayes, J. A. 15: v E 1950 (2) 1954 (1); v WI 1951 (2); *v E 1958 (4); v In 1955 (5); v P 1955 (1)*
Henderson, M. 1: v E 1929
Horne, M. J. 29: v E 1996 (1); v A 1999 (3); v SA 1998 (3); v WI 1999 (1); v In 1998 (2); v SL 1996 (2); v Z 1997 (2) 2000 (1); *v E 1999 (4); v A 1997 (1); v In 1999 (3); v SL 1997 (3); v Z 1997 (2) 2000 (1)*

Horne, P. A. 4: v WI 1986 (1); *v A 1987 (1); v P 1990 (1); v SL 1986 (1)*
Hough, K. W. 2: v E 1958 (2)
Howarth, G. P. 47: v E 1974 (2) 1977 (3) 1983 (3); v A 1976 (2) 1981 (3); v WI 1979 (3); v In 1980 (3); v P 1978 (3) 1984 (3); v SL 1982 (2); *v E 1978 (3) 1983 (4); v A 1980 (2); v WI 1984 (4); v In 1976 (2); v P 1976 (2); v SL 1983 (3)*
Howarth, H. J. 30: v E 1970 (2) 1974 (2); v A 1973 (3) 1976 (2); v In 1975 (2); v P 1972 (3); *v E 1969 (3) 1973 (2); v WI 1971 (5); v In 1969 (3); v P 1969 (3)*

James, K. C. 11: v E 1929 (4) 1932 (2); v SA 1931 (2); *v E 1931 (3)*
Jarvis, T. W. 13: v E 1965 (1); v P 1972 (3); *v WI 1971 (4); v In 1964 (2); v P 1964 (3)*
Jones, A. H. 39: v E 1987 (1) 1991 (3); v A 1989 (1) 1992 (3); v WI 1994 (2); v In 1989 (3); v P 1988 (2) 1992 (1) 1993 (3); v SL 1990 (3); *v E 1990 (3); v A 1987 (3) 1993 (3); v In 1988 (3); v SL 1986 (1) 1992 (2); v Z 1992 (2)*

Kennedy, R. J. 4: v Z 1995 (2); *v WI 1995 (2)*
Kerr, J. L. 7: v E 1932 (2); v SA 1931 (1); *v E 1931 (2) 1937 (2)*
Kuggeleijn, C. M. 2: *v In 1988 (2)*

Larsen, G. R. 8: v SA 1994 (1); v P 1995 (1); v SL 1994 (2); v Z 1995 (1); *v E 1994 (1); v WI 1995 (2)*
Latham, R. T. 4: v E 1991 (1); v P 1992 (1); *v Z 1992 (2)*
Lees, W. K. 21: v E 1977 (2); v A 1976 (1); v WI 1979 (3); v P 1978 (3); v SL 1982 (2); *v E 1983 (2); v A 1980 (2); v In 1976 (3); v P 1976 (3)*
Leggat, I. B. 1: *v SA 1953*
Leggat, J. G. 9: v E 1954 (1); v SA 1952 (1); v WI 1951 (1) 1955 (1); *v In 1955 (3); v P 1955 (2)*
Lissette, A. F. 2: v WI 1955 (2)
Loveridge, G. R. 1: v Z 1995
Lowry, T. C. 7: v E 1929 (4); *v E 1931 (3)*

McEwan, P. E. 4: v WI 1979 (1); *v A 1980 (2); v P 1984 (1)*
MacGibbon, A. R. 26: v E 1950 (2) 1954 (2); v SA 1952 (1); v WI 1955 (3); *v E 1958 (5); v SA 1953 (5); v In 1955 (5); v P 1955 (3)*
McGirr, H. M. 2: v E 1929 (2)
McGregor, S. N. 25: v E 1954 (2) 1958 (2); v SA 1963 (3); v WI 1955 (4); v P 1964 (2); *v SA 1961 (5); v In 1955 (4); v P 1955 (3)*
McLeod, E. G. 1: v E 1929
McMahon, T. G. 5: v WI 1955 (1); *v In 1955 (3); v P 1955 (1)*
McMillan, C. D. 31: v A 1999 (3); v SA 1998 (1); v WI 1999 (2); v In 1998 (2); v P 2000 (3); v Z 1997 (2) 2000 (1); *v E 1999 (4); v A 1997 (3); v SA 2000 (3); v In 1999 (2); v SL 1997 (3); v Z 2000 (2)*
McRae, D. A. N. 1: v A 1945
Marshall, H. J. H. 1: *v SA 2000*
Martin, C. S. 7: v P 2000 (3); v Z 2000 (1); *v SA 2000 (3)*
Matheson, A. M. 2: v E 1929 (1); *v E 1931 (1)*
Meale, T. 2: *v E 1958 (2)*
Merritt, W. E. 6: v E 1929 (4); *v E 1931 (2)*
Meuli, E. M. 1: v SA 1952
Milburn, B. D. 3: v WI 1968 (3)
Miller, L. S. M. 13: v SA 1952 (2); v WI 1955 (3); *v E 1958 (4); v SA 1953 (4)*
Mills, J. E. 7: v E 1929 (3) 1932 (1); *v E 1931 (3)*
Moir, A. M. 17: v E 1950 (2) 1954 (2) 1958 (2); v SA 1952 (1); v WI 1951 (2) 1955 (1); *v E 1958 (2); v In 1955 (2); v P 1955 (3)*
Moloney D. A. R. 3: *v E 1937 (3)*
Mooney, F. L. H. 14: v E 1950 (2); v SA 1952 (2); v WI 1951 (2); *v E 1949 (3); v SA 1953 (5)*
Morgan, R. W. 20: v E 1965 (2) 1970 (2); v WI 1968 (1); v P 1964 (2); *v E 1965 (3); v WI 1971 (3); v In 1964 (4); v P 1964 (3)*
Morrison, B. D. 1: v E 1962
Morrison, D. K. 48: v E 1987 (3) 1991 (3) 1996 (1); v A 1989 (1) 1992 (3); v SA 1994 (1); v WI 1994 (2); v In 1989 (3) 1993 (1); v P 1988 (1) 1992 (1) 1993 (2) 1995 (1); v SL 1990 (3) 1994 (1); *v E 1990 (3); v A 1987 (3) 1989 (1) 1993 (3); v SA 1994 (2); v WI 1995 (2); v In 1988 (1) 1995 (3); v P 1990 (3)*

Morrison, J. F. M. 17: v E 1974 (2); v A 1973 (3) 1981 (3); v In 1975 (3); *v A 1973 (3); v In 1976 (1); v P 1976 (2)*

Motz, R. C. 32: v E 1962 (2) 1965 (3); v SA 1963 (2); v WI 1968 (3); v In 1967 (4); v P 1964 (3); *v E 1965 (3) 1969 (3); v SA 1961 (5); v In 1964 (3); v P 1964 (1)*

Murray, B. A. G. 13: v E 1970 (1); v In 1967 (4); *v E 1969 (2); v In 1969 (3); v P 1969 (3)*

Murray, D. J. 8: v SA 1994 (1); v WI 1994 (2); v SL 1994 (2); *v SA 1994 (3)*

Nash, D. J. 31: v SA 1994 (1) 1998 (3); v WI 1994 (1) 1999 (2); v In 1993 (1) 1998 (2); v P 1995 (1); v SL 1994 (1); v Z 1997 (2); *v E 1994 (3) 1999 (4); v SA 1994 (1); v In 1995 (3) 1999 (3); v SL 1992 (1); v Z 1992 (1) 2000 (1)*

Newman J. 3: v E 1932 (2); v SA 1931 (1)

O'Connor, S. B. 18: v A 1999 (2); v SA 1998 (1); v WI 1999 (1); v Z 1997 (1) 2000 (1); *v E 1999 (1); v A 1997 (2); v SA 2000 (3); v In 1999 (1); v SL 1997 (1); v Z 1997 (2) 2000 (2)*

O'Sullivan, D. R. 11: v In 1975 (1); v P 1972 (1); *v A 1973 (3); v In 1976 (3); v P 1976 (3)*

Overton, G. W. F. 3: *v SA 1953 (3)*

Owens, M. B. 8: v A 1992 (2); v P 1992 (1) 1993 (1); *v E 1994 (2); v SL 1992 (2)*

Page, M. L. 14: v E 1929 (4) 1932 (2); v SA 1931 (2); *v E 1931 (3) 1937 (3)*

Parker, J. M. 36: v E 1974 (2) 1977 (3); v A 1973 (3) 1976 (2); v WI 1979 (3); v In 1975 (3); v P 1972 (1) 1978 (2); *v E 1973 (3) 1978 (2); v A 1973 (3) 1980 (3); v In 1976 (3); v P 1976 (3)*

Parker, N. M. 3: *v In 1976 (2); v P 1976 (1)*

Parore, A. C. 70: v E 1991 (1) 1996 (3); v A 1992 (1) 1999 (3); v SA 1994 (1) 1998 (3); v WI 1994 (2) 1999 (2); v In 1993 (1) 1998 (2); v P 1992 (1) 1995 (1) 2000 (3); v SL 1994 (2) 1996 (2); v Z 1995 (2) 1997 (2) 2000 (1); *v E 1990 (1) 1994 (3) 1999 (4); v A 1997 (3); v SA 1994 (3) 2000 (3); v WI 1995 (1); v In 1995 (3) 1999 (3); v P 1996 (2); v SL 1992 (2) 1997 (3); v Z 1992 (2) 1997 (2) 2000 (2)*

Patel, D. N. 37: v E 1991 (3) 1996 (2); v A 1992 (3); v SA 1994 (1); v WI 1986 (3); v P 1988 (1) 1992 (1) 1995 (1); v SL 1990 (2) 1994 (1) 1996 (2); v Z 1995 (2); *v A 1987 (3) 1989 (1) 1993 (3); v WI 1995 (1); v P 1990 (3) 1996 (2); v Z 1992 (2)*

Petherick, P. J. 6: v A 1976 (1); *v In 1976 (3); v P 1976 (2)*

Petrie, E. C. 14: v E 1958 (2) 1965 (3); *v E 1958 (5); v In 1955 (2); v P 1955 (2)*

Playle, W. R. 8: v E 1962 (3); *v E 1958 (5)*

Pocock, B. A. 15: v E 1996 (3); v P 1993 (2); v SL 1996 (2); *v E 1994 (1); v A 1993 (3) 1997 (2); v Z 1997 (2)*

Pollard, V. 32: v E 1965 (3) 1970 (1); v WI 1968 (3); v In 1967 (4); v P 1972 (1); *v E 1965 (3) 1969 (3) 1973 (3); v In 1964 (4) 1969 (1); v P 1964 (3) 1969 (3)*

Poore, M. B. 14: v E 1954 (1); v SA 1952 (1); *v SA 1953 (5); v In 1955 (4); v P 1955 (3)*

Priest, M. W. 3: v Z 1997 (1); *v E 1990 (1); v SL 1997 (1)*

Pringle, C. 14: v E 1991 (1); v In 1993 (1); v P 1993 (1); v SL 1990 (2) 1994 (1); *v E 1994 (2); v SA 1994 (2); v P 1990 (3); v SL 1992 (1)*

Puna, N. 3: v E 1965 (3)

Rabone, G. O. 12: v E 1954 (2); v SA 1952 (1); v WI 1951 (2); *v E 1949 (4); v SA 1953 (3)*

Redmond, R. E. 1: v P 1972

Reid, J. F. 19: v A 1985 (3); v In 1980 (3); v P 1978 (1) 1984 (3); *v A 1985 (3); v P 1984 (3); v SL 1983 (3)*

Reid, J. R. 58: v E 1950 (2) 1954 (2) 1958 (2) 1962 (3); v SA 1952 (2) 1963 (3); v WI 1951 (2) 1955 (4); v P 1964 (3); *v E 1949 (2) 1958 (5) 1965 (3); v SA 1953 (5) 1961 (5); v In 1955 (5) 1964 (4); v P 1955 (3) 1964 (3)*

Richardson, M. H. 9: v P 2000 (3); v Z 2000 (1); *v SA 2000 (3); v Z 2000 (2)*

Roberts, A. D. G. 7: v In 1975 (2); *v In 1976 (3); v P 1976 (2)*

Roberts, A. W. 5: v E 1929 (1); v SA 1931 (2); *v E 1937 (2)*

Robertson, G. K. 1: v A 1985

Rowe, C. G. 1: v A 1945

Rutherford, K. R. 56: v E 1987 (2) 1991 (2); v A 1985 (3) 1989 (1) 1992 (3); v SA 1994 (1); v WI 1986 (2) 1994 (2); v In 1989 (3) 1993 (1); v P 1992 (1) 1993 (3); v SL 1990 (3) 1994 (2); *v E 1986 (1) 1990 (2) 1994 (3); v A 1987 (1) 1993 (3); v SA 1994 (3); v WI 1984 (4); v In 1988 (2); v P 1990 (3); v SL 1986 (1) 1992 (2); v Z 1992 (2)*

Scott, R. H. 1: v E 1946

Scott, V. J. 10: v E 1946 (1) 1950 (2); v A 1945 (1); v WI 1951 (2); *v E 1949 (4)*
Sewell, D. G. 1: *v Z 1997*
Shrimpton, M. J. F. 10: v E 1962 (2) 1965 (3) 1970 (2); v SA 1963 (1); *v A 1973 (2)*
Sinclair, B. W. 21: v E 1962 (3) 1965 (3); v SA 1963 (3); v In 1967 (2); v P 1964 (2); *v E 1965 (3); v In 1964 (2); v P 1964 (3)*
Sinclair, I. M. 2: v WI 1955 (2)
Sinclair, M. S. 13: v A 1999 (3); v WI 1999 (1); v P 2000 (3); v Z 2000 (1); *v SA 2000 (3); v Z 2000 (2)*
Smith, F. B. 4: v E 1946 (1); v WI 1951 (1); *v E 1949 (2)*
Smith, H. D. 1: v E 1932
Smith, I. D. S. 63: v E 1983 (3) 1987 (3) 1991 (2); v A 1981 (3) 1985 (3) 1989 (1); v WI 1986 (3); v In 1980 (3) 1989 (3); v P 1984 (3) 1988 (2); v SL 1990 (3); *v E 1983 (2) 1986 (2) 1990 (2); v A 1980 (1) 1985 (3) 1987 (3) 1989 (1); v WI 1984 (4); v In 1988 (3); v P 1984 (3) 1990 (3); v SL 1983 (3) 1986 (1)*
Snedden, C. A. 1: v E 1946
Snedden, M. C. 25: v E 1983 (1) 1987 (2); v A 1981 (3) 1989 (1); v WI 1986 (1); v In 1980 (3) 1989 (3); v SL 1982 (2); *v E 1983 (1) 1990 (3); v A 1985 (1) 1987 (1) 1989 (1); v In 1988 (1); v SL 1986 (1)*
Sparling, J. T. 11: v E 1958 (2) 1962 (1); v SA 1963 (2); *v E 1958 (3); v SA 1961 (3)*
Spearman, C. M. 19: v A 1999 (3); v WI 1999 (2); v P 1995 (1); v Z 1995 (2); *v SA 2000 (2); v WI 1995 (2); v In 1999 (3); v SL 1997 (1); v Z 1997 (2) 2000 (1)*
Stead, G. R. 5: v SA 1998 (2); v WI 1999 (2); *v In 1999 (1)*
Stirling, D. A. 6: *v E 1986 (2); v WI 1984 (1); v P 1984 (3)*
Su'a, M. L. 13: v E 1991 (2); v A 1992 (2); v WI 1994 (1); v P 1992 (1); v SL 1994 (1); *v A 1993 (2); v SL 1992 (2); v Z 1992 (2)*
Sutcliffe, B. 42: v E 1946 (1) 1950 (2) 1954 (2) 1958 (2); v SA 1952 (2); v WI 1951 (2) 1955 (2); *v E 1949 (4) 1958 (4) 1965 (1); v SA 1953 (5); v In 1955 (5) 1964 (4); v P 1955 (3) 1964 (3)*

Taylor, B. R. 30: v E 1965 (1); v WI 1968 (3); v In 1967 (3); v P 1972 (3); *v E 1965 (2) 1969 (2) 1973 (3); v WI 1971 (4); v In 1964 (3) 1969 (2); v P 1964 (3) 1969 (1)*
Taylor, D. D. 3: v E 1946 (1); v WI 1955 (2)
Thomson, K. 2: v In 1967 (2)
Thomson, S. A. 19: v E 1991 (1); v WI 1994 (2); v In 1989 (1) 1993 (1); v P 1993 (3); v SL 1990 (2) 1994 (1); *v E 1994 (3); v SA 1994 (3); v In 1995 (2)*
Tindill, E. W. T. 5: v E 1946 (1); v A 1945 (1); *v E 1937 (3)*
Troup, G. B. 15: v A 1981 (2) 1985 (2); v WI 1979 (3); v In 1980 (2); v P 1978 (2); *v A 1980 (2); v WI 1984 (1); v In 1976 (1)*
Truscott, P. B. 1: v P 1964
Tuffey, D. R. 6: v A 1999 (1); v P 2000 (3); *v SA 2000 (2)*
Turner, G. M. 41: v E 1970 (2) 1974 (2); v A 1973 (3) 1976 (2); v WI 1968 (3); v In 1975 (3); v P 1972 (3); v SL 1982 (2); *v E 1969 (2) 1973 (3); v A 1973 (2); v WI 1971 (5); v In 1969 (3) 1976 (3); v P 1969 (1) 1976 (2)*
Twose, R. G. 16: v SA 1998 (3); v In 1998 (1); v P 1995 (1); v Z 1995 (2); *v E 1999 (4); v A 1997 (1); v WI 1995 (2); v In 1995 (2)*

Vance, R. H. 4: v E 1987 (1); v P 1988 (2); *v A 1989 (1)*
Vaughan, J. T. C. 6: v E 1996 (1); *v WI 1995 (2); v P 1996 (2); v SL 1992 (1)*
Vettori, D. L. 31: v E 1996 (2); v A 1999 (2); v SA 1998 (3); v WI 1999 (2); v In 1998 (2); v SL 1996 (2); v Z 1997 (2); *v E 1999 (4); v A 1997 (3); v In 1999 (3); v SL 1997 (3); v Z 1997 (2) 2000 (1)*
Vivian, G. E. 5: *v WI 1971 (4); v In 1964 (1)*
Vivian, H. G. 7: v E 1932 (1); v SA 1931 (1); *v E 1931 (2) 1937 (3)*

Wadsworth, K. J. 33: v E 1970 (2) 1974 (2); v A 1973 (3); v In 1975 (3); v P 1972 (3); *v E 1969 (3) 1973 (3); v A 1973 (3); v WI 1971 (5); v In 1969 (3); v P 1969 (3)*
Walker, B. G. K. 4: v Z 2000 (1); *v SA 2000 (3)*
Wallace, W. M. 13: v E 1946 (1) 1950 (2); v A 1945 (1); v SA 1952 (2); *v E 1937 (3) 1949 (4)*
Walmsley, K. P. 3: v SL 1994 (2); *v SA 2000 (1)*
Ward, J. T. 8: v SA 1963 (1); v In 1967 (1); v P 1964 (1); *v E 1965 (1); v In 1964 (4)*

Watson, W. 15: v E 1991 (1); v A 1992 (2); v SL 1990 (3); *v E 1986 (2); v A 1989 (1) 1993 (1); v P 1990 (3); v Z 1992 (2)*
Watt, L. 1: v E 1954
Webb, M. G. 3: v E 1970 (1); v A 1973 (1); *v WI 1971 (1)*
Webb, P. N. 2: v WI 1979 (2)
Weir, G. L. 11: v E 1929 (3) 1932 (2); v SA 1931 (2); *v E 1931 (3) 1937 (1)*
White, D. J. 2: *v P 1990 (2)*
Whitelaw, P. E. 2: v E 1932 (2)
Wiseman, P. J. 14: v A 1999 (2); v WI 1999 (1); v In 1998 (2); v P 2000 (1); v Z 2000 (1); *v In 1999 (2); v SL 1997 (3); v Z 2000 (2)*
Wright, J. G. 82: v E 1977 (3) 1983 (3) 1987 (3) 1991 (3); v A 1981 (3) 1985 (2) 1989 (1) 1992 (3); v WI 1979 (3) 1986 (3); v In 1980 (3) 1989 (3); v P 1978 (3) 1984 (3)1988 (2); v SL 1982 (2) 1990 (3); *v E 1978 (2) 1983 (3) 1986 (3) 1990 (3); v A 1980 (3) 1985 (3) 1987 (3) 1989 (1); v WI 1984 (4); v In 1988 (3); v P 1984 (3); v SL 1983 (3) 1992 (2)*

Young, B. A. 35: v E 1996 (3); v SA 1994 (1) 1998 (2); v WI 1994 (2); v In 1993 (1); v P 1993 (3) 1995 (1); v SL 1994 (2) 1996 (2); v Z 1997 (2); *v E 1994 (3); v A 1993 (1) 1997 (3); v SA 1994 (3); v In 1995 (1); v P 1996 (2); v SL 1997 (3)*
Yuile, B. W. 17: v E 1962 (2); v WI 1968 (3); v In 1967 (1); v P 1964 (3); *v E 1965 (1); v In 1964 (3) 1969 (1); v P 1964 (1) 1969 (2)*

INDIA

Number of Test cricketers: 237

Abid Ali, S. 29: v E 1972 (4); v A 1969 (1); v WI 1974 (2); v NZ 1969 (3); *v E 1971 (3) 1974 (3); v A 1967 (4); v WI 1970 (5); v NZ 1967 (4)*
Adhikari, H. R. 21: v E 1951 (3); v A 1956 (2); v WI 1948 (5) 1958 (1); v P 1952 (2); *v E 1952 (3); v A 1947 (5)*
Agarkar, A. B. 10: v A 2000 (1); v SA 1999 (1); v Z 2000 (2); *v A 1999 (3); v Z 1998 (1) 2001 (1); v B 2000 (1)*
Amarnath, L. 24: v E 1933 (3) 1951 (3); v WI 1948 (5); v P 1952 (5); *v E 1946 (3); v A 1947 (5)*
Amarnath, M. 69: v E 1976 (2) 1984 (5); v A 1969 (1) 1979 (1) 1986 (3); v WI 1978 (2) 1983 (3) 1987 (3); v NZ 1976 (3); v P 1983 (2) 1986 (5); v SL 1986 (2); *v E 1979 (2) 1986 (2); v A 1977 (5) 1985 (3); v WI 1975 (4) 1982 (5); v NZ 1975 (3); v P 1978 (3) 1982 (6) 1984 (2); v SL 1985 (2)*
Amarnath, S. 10: v E 1976 (2): *v WI 1975 (2); v NZ 1975 (3); v P 1978 (3)*
Amar Singh 7: v E 1933 (3); *v E 1932 (1) 1936 (3)*
Amir Elahi 1: *v A 1947*
Amre, P. K. 11: v E 1992 (3); v Z 1992 (1); *v SA 1992 (4); v SL 1993 (3)*
Ankola, S. A. 1: *v P 1989*
Apte, A. L. 1: *v E 1959*
Apte, M. L. 7: v P 1952 (2); *v WI 1952 (5)*
Arshad Ayub 13: v WI 1987 (4); v NZ 1988 (3); *v WI 1988 (4); v P 1989 (2)*
Arun, B. 2: v SL 1986 (2)
Arun Lal 16: v WI 1987 (4); v NZ 1988 (3); v P 1986 (1); v SL 1982 (1); *v WI 1988 (4); v P 1982 (3)*
Azad, K. 7: v E 1981 (3); v WI 1983 (2); v P 1983 (1); *v NZ 1980 (1)*
Azharuddin, M. 99: v E 1984 (3) 1992 (3); v A 1986 (3) 1996 (1) 1997 (3); v SA 1996 (3) 1999 (1); v WI 1987 (3) 1994 (3); v NZ 1988 (3) 1995 (3); v P 1986 (5) 1998 (3); v SL 1986 (1) 1990 (1) 1993 (3) 1997 (3); v Z 1992 (1); *v E 1986 (3) 1990 (3) 1996 (3); v A 1985 (3) 1991 (5); v SA 1992 (4) 1996 (3); v WI 1988 (3) 1996 (5); v NZ 1989 (3) 1993 (1) 1998 (2); v P 1989 (4); v SL 1985 (3) 1993 (3) 1997 (2) 1998 (1); v Z 1992 (1) 1998 (1)*

Badani, H. K. 4: *v SL 2001 (3); v Z 2001 (1)*
Bahutule, S. V. 2: v A 2000 (1); *v SL 2001 (1)*
Baig, A. A. 10: v A 1959 (3); v WI 1966 (2); v P 1960 (3); *v E 1959 (2)*
Banerjee, S. A. 1: v WI 1948
Banerjee, S. N. 1: v WI 1948

Banerjee, S. T. 1: *v A 1991*
Baqa Jilani, M. 1: *v E 1936*
Bedi, B. S. 67: v E 1972 (5) 1976 (5); v A 1969 (5); v WI 1966 (2) 1974 (4) 1978 (3); v NZ 1969 (3) 1976 (3); *v E 1967 (3) 1971 (3) 1974 (3) 1979 (3); v A 1967 (2) 1977 (5); v WI 1970 (5) 1975 (4); v NZ 1967 (4) 1975 (2); v P 1978 (3)*
Bhandari, P. 3: v A 1956 (1); v NZ 1955 (1); *v P 1954 (1)*
Bharadwaj, R. V. 3: v NZ 1999 (2); *v A 1999 (1)*
Bhat, A. R. 2: v WI 1983 (1); v P 1983 (1)
Binny, R. M. H. 27: v E 1979 (1); v WI 1983 (6); v P 1979 (6) 1983 (2) 1986 (3); *v E 1986 (3); v A 1980 (1) 1985 (2); v NZ 1980 (1); v P 1984 (1); v SL 1985 (1)*
Borde, C. G. 55: v E 1961 (5) 1963 (5); v A 1959 (5) 1964 (3) 1969 (1); v WI 1958 (4) 1966 (3); v NZ 1964 (4); v P 1960 (5); *v E 1959 (4) 1967 (3); v A 1967 (4); v WI 1961 (5); v NZ 1967 (4)*

Chandrasekhar, B. S. 58: v E 1963 (4) 1972 (5) 1976 (5); v A 1964 (2); v WI 1966 (3) 1974 (4) 1978 (4); v NZ 1964 (2) 1976 (3); *v E 1967 (3) 1971 (3) 1974 (2) 1979 (1); v A 1967 (2) 1977(5); v WI 1975 (4); v NZ 1975 (3); v P 1978 (3)*
Chauhan, C. P. S. 40: v E 1972 (2); v A 1969 (1) 1979 (6); v WI 1978 (6); v NZ 1969 (2); v P 1979 (6); *v E 1979 (4); v A 1977 (4) 1980 (3); v NZ 1980 (3); v P 1978 (3)*
Chauhan, R. K. 21: v E 1992 (3); v A 1997 (2); v WI 1994 (2); v NZ 1995 (2); v SL 1993 (3) 1997 (3); v Z 1992 (1); *v NZ 1993 (1); v SL 1993 (3) 1997 (1)*
Chopra, N. 1: v SA 1999
Chowdhury, N. R. 2: v E 1951 (1); v WI 1948 (1)
Colah, S. H. M. 2: v E 1933 (1); *v E 1932 (1)*
Contractor, N. J. 31: v E 1961 (5); v A 1956 (1) 1959 (5); v WI 1958 (5); v NZ 1955 (4); v P 1960 (5); *v E 1959 (4); v WI 1961 (2)*

Dahiya, V. 2: v Z 2000 (2)
Dani, H. T. 1: v P 1952
Das, S. S. 11: v A 2000 (3); v Z 2000 (2); *v SL 2001 (3); v Z 2001 (2); v B 2000 (1)*
Desai, R. B. 28: v E 1961 (4) 1963 (2); v A 1959 (3); v WI 1958 (1); v NZ 1964 (3); v P 1960 (5); *v E 1959 (5); v A 1967 (1); v WI 1961 (3); v NZ 1967 (1)*
Dighe, S. S. 6: v A 2000 (1); *v SL 2001 (3); v Z 2001 (2)*
Dilawar Hussain 3: v E 1933 (2); *v E 1936 (1)*
Divecha, R. V. 5: v E 1951 (2); v P 1952 (1); *v E 1952 (2)*
Doshi, D. R. 33: v E 1979 (1) 1981 (6); v A 1979 (6); v P 1979 (6) 1983 (1); v SL 1982 (1); *v E 1982 (3); v A 1980 (3); v NZ 1980 (2); v P 1982 (4)*
Dravid, R. 48: v A 1996 (1) 1997 (3) 2000 (3); v SA 1996 (3) 1999 (2); v NZ 1999 (3); v P 1998 (3); v SL 1997 (3); v Z 2000 (2); *v E 1996 (2); v A 1999 (3); v SA 1996 (3); v WI 1996 (5); v NZ 1998 (2); v SL 1997 (2) 1998 (1) 2001 (3); v Z 1998 (1) 2001 (2); v B 2000 (1)*
Durani, S. A. 29: v E 1961 (5) 1963 (5) 1972 (3); v A 1959 (1) 1964 (3); v WI 1966 (1); v NZ 1964 (3); *v WI 1961 (5) 1970 (3)*

Engineer, F. M. 46: v E 1961 (4) 1972 (5); v A 1969 (5); v WI 1966 (1) 1974 (5); v NZ 1964 (4) 1969 (2); *v E 1967 (3) 1971 (3) 1974 (3); v A 1967 (4); v WI 1961 (3); v NZ 1967 (4)*

Gadkari, C. V. 6: *v WI 1952 (3); v P 1954 (3)*
Gaekwad, A. D. 40: v E 1976 (4) 1984 (3); v WI 1974 (3) 1978 (5) 1983 (6); v NZ 1976 (3); v P 1983 (3); *v E 1979 (2); v A 1977 (1); v WI 1975 (3) 1982 (5); v P 1984 (2)*
Gaekwad, D. K. 11: v WI 1958 (1); v P 1952 (2) 1960 (1); *v E 1952 (1) 1959 (4); v WI 1952 (2)*
Gaekwad, H. G. 1: v P 1952
Gandhi, D. J. 4: v NZ 1999 (3); *v A 1999 (1)*
Gandotra, A. 2: v A 1969 (1); v NZ 1969 (1)
Ganesh, D. 4: *v SA 1996 (2); v WI 1996 (2)*
Ganguly, S. C. 46: v A 1996 (1) 1997 (3) 2000 (3); v SA 1996 (2) 1999 (2); v NZ 1999 (3); v P 1998 (3); v SL 1997 (3); v Z 2000 (2); *v E 1996 (2); v A 1999 (3); v SA 1996 (3); v WI 1996 (4); v NZ 1998 (2); v SL 1997 (2) 1998 (1) 2001 (3); v Z 1998 (1) 2001 (2); v B 2000 (1)*
Gavaskar, S. M. 125: v E 1972 (5) 1976 (5) 1979 (1) 1981 (6) 1984 (5); v A 1979 (6) 1986 (3); v WI 1974 (2) 1978 (6) 1983 (6); v NZ 1976 (3); v P 1979 (6) 1983 (3) 1986 (4); v SL 1982 (1) 1986 (3); *v E 1971 (3) 1974 (3) 1979 (4) 1982 (3) 1986 (3); v A 1977 (5) 1980 (3) 1985 (3); v WI 1970 (4) 1975 (4) 1982 (5); v NZ 1975 (3) 1980 (3); v P 1978 (3) 1982 (6) 1984 (2); v SL 1985 (3)*

Ghavri, K. D. 39: v E 1976 (3) 1979 (1); v A 1979 (6); v WI 1974 (3) 1978 (6); v NZ 1976 (2); v P 1979 (6); *v E 1979 (4); v A 1977 (3) 1980 (3); v NZ 1980 (1); v P 1978 (1)*
Ghorpade, J. M. 8: v A 1956 (1); v WI 1958 (1); v NZ 1955 (1); *v E 1959 (3); v WI 1952 (2)*
Ghulam Ahmed 22: v E 1951 (2); v A 1956 (2); v WI 1948 (3) 1958 (2); v NZ 1955 (1); v P 1952 (4); *v E 1952 (4); v P 1954 (4)*
Gopalan, M. J. 1: v E 1933
Gopinath, C. D. 8: v E 1951 (3); v A 1959 (1); v P 1952 (1); *v E 1952 (1); v P 1954 (2)*
Guard, G. M. 2: v A 1959 (1); v WI 1958 (1)
Guha, S. 4: v A 1969 (3); *v E 1967 (1)*
Gul Mahomed 8: v P 1952 (2); *v E 1946 (1); v A 1947 (5)*
Gupte, B. P. 3: v E 1963 (1); v NZ 1964 (1); v P 1960 (1)
Gupte, S. P. 36: v E 1951 (1) 1961 (2); v A 1956 (3); v WI 1958 (5); v NZ 1955 (5); v P 1952 (2) 1960 (3); *v E 1959 (5); v WI 1952 (5); v P 1954 (5)*
Gursharan Singh 1: *v NZ 1989*

Hafeez, A. 3: *v E 1946 (3)*
Hanumant Singh 14: v E 1963 (2); v A 1964 (3); v WI 1966 (2); v NZ 1964 (4) 1969 (1); *v E 1967 (2)*
Harbhajan Singh 16: v A 1997 (1) 2000 (3); v NZ 1999 (2); v P 1998 (2); *v NZ 1998 (1); v SL 1998 (1) 2001 (3); v Z 1998 (1) 2001 (2)*
Hardikar, M. S. 2: v WI 1958 (2)
Harvinder Singh 3: v A 1997 (2); *v SL 2001 (1)*
Hazare, V. S. 30: v E 1951 (5); v WI 1948 (5); v P 1952 (3); *v E 1946 (3) 1952 (4); v A 1947 (5); v WI 1952 (5)*
Hindlekar, D. D. 4: *v E 1936 (1) 1946 (3)*
Hirwani, N. D. 17: v SA 1996 (2); v WI 1987 (1); v NZ 1988 (3) 1995 (1); v SL 1990 (1); *v E 1990 (3); v WI 1988 (3); v NZ 1989 (3)*

Ibrahim, K. C. 4: v WI 1948 (4)
Indrajitsinhji, K. S. 4: v A 1964 (3); v NZ 1969 (1)
Irani, J. K. 2: *v A 1947 (2)*

Jadeja, A. 15: v SA 1999 (1); v NZ 1995 (3) 1999 (1); *v E 1996 (2); v SA 1992 (3); v WI 1996 (2); v NZ 1998 (2); v SL 1997 (1)*
Jahangir Khan, M. 4: *v E 1932 (1) 1936 (3)*
Jai, L. P. 1: v E 1933
Jaisimha, M. L. 39: v E 1961 (5) 1963 (5); v A 1959 (1) 1964 (3); v WI 1966 (2); v NZ 1964 (4) 1969 (1); v P 1960 (4); *v E 1959 (1); v A 1967 (2); v WI 1961 (4) 1970 (3); v NZ 1967 (4)*
Jamshedji, R. J. 1: v E 1933
Jayantilal, K. 1: *v WI 1970*
Johnson, D. J. 2: v A 1996 (1); *v SA 1996 (1)*
Joshi, P. G. 12: v E 1951 (2); v A 1959 (1); v WI 1958 (1); v P 1952 (1) 1960 (1); *v E 1959 (3); v WI 1952 (3)*
Joshi, S. B. 15: v A 1996 (1); v SA 1996 (3); v NZ 1999 (2); v P 1998 (1); v Z 2000 (2); *v E 1996 (1); v WI 1996 (4); v B 2000 (1)*

Kaif, M. 4: v SA 1999 (1); *v SL 2001 (3)*
Kambli, V. G. 17: v E 1992 (3); v WI 1994 (3); v NZ 1995 (3); v SL 1993 (3); v Z 1992 (1); *v NZ 1993 (1); v SL 1993 (3)*
Kanitkar, H. H. 2: *v A 1999 (2)*
Kanitkar, H. S. 2: v WI 1974 (2)
Kapil Dev 131: v E 1979 (1) 1981 (6) 1984 (4) 1992 (3); v A 1979 (6) 1986 (3); v WI 1978 (6) 1983 (6) 1987 (4); v NZ 1988 (3); v P 1979 (6) 1983 (3) 1986 (5); v SL 1982 (1) 1986 (3) 1990 (1) 1993 (3); v Z 1992 (1); *v E 1979 (4) 1982 (3) 1986 (3) 1990 (3); v A 1980 (3) 1985 (3) 1991 (5); v SA 1992 (4); v WI 1982 (5) 1988 (4); v NZ 1980 (3) 1989 (3) 1993 (1); v P 1978 (3) 1982 (6) 1984 (2) 1989 (4); v SL 1985 (3) 1993 (3); v Z 1992 (1)*
Kapoor, A. R. 4: v A 1996 (1); v SA 1996 (1); v WI 1994 (1); v NZ 1995 (1)
Kardar, A. H. (*see* Hafeez)
Karim, S. S. 1: *v B 2000*
Kartik, M. 4: v SA 1999 (2); v Z 2000 (1); *v B 2000 (1)*
Kenny, R. B. 5: v A 1959 (4); v WI 1958 (1)

Kirmani, S. M. H. 88: v E 1976 (5) 1979 (1) 1981 (6) 1984 (5); v A 1979 (6); v WI 1978 (6) 1983 (6); v NZ 1976 (3); v P 1979 (6) 1983 (3); v SL 1982 (1); *v E 1982 (3); v A 1977 (5) 1980 (3) 1985 (3); v WI 1975 (4) 1982 (5); v NZ 1975 (3) 1980 (3); v P 1978 (3) 1982 (6) 1984 (2)*
Kischenchand, G. 5: v P 1952 (1); *v A 1947 (4)*
Kripal Singh, A. G. 14: v E 1961 (3) 1963 (2); v A 1956 (2) 1964 (1); v WI 1958 (1); v NZ 1955 (4); *v E 1959 (1)*
Krishnamurthy, P. 5: *v WI 1970 (5)*
Kulkarni, N. M. 3: v A 2000 (1); v SL 1997 (1); *v SL 1997 (1)*
Kulkarni, R. R. 3: v A 1986 (1); v P 1986 (2)
Kulkarni, U. N. 4: *v A 1967 (3); v NZ 1967 (1)*
Kumar, V. V. 2: v E 1961 (1); v P 1960 (1)
Kumble, A. 61: v E 1992 (3); v A 1996 (1) 1997 (3); v SA 1996 (3) 1999 (2); v WI 1994 (3); v NZ 1995 (3) 1999 (3); v P 1998 (3); v SL 1993 (3) 1997 (3); v Z 1992 (1); *v E 1990 (1) 1996 (3); v A 1999 (3); v SA 1992 (4) 1996 (3); v WI 1996 (5); v NZ 1993 (1) 1998 (2); v SL 1993 (3) 1997 (2) 1998 (1); v Z 1992 (1) 1998 (1)*
Kunderan, B. K. 18: v E 1961 (1) 1963 (5); v A 1959 (3); v WI 1966 (2); v NZ 1964 (1); v P 1960 (2); *v E 1967 (2); v WI 1961 (2)*
Kuruvilla, A. 10: v SL 1997 (3); *v WI 1996 (5); v SL 1997 (2)*

Lall Singh 1: *v E 1932*
Lamba, R. 4: v WI 1987 (1); v SL 1986 (3)
Laxman, V. V. S. 24: v A 1997 (2) 2000 (3); v SA 1996 (2) 1999 (1); v P 1998 (3); v Z 2000 (1); *v A 1999 (3); v SA 1996 (2); v WI 1996 (4); v SL 1998 (1); v Z 2001 (2)*

Madan Lal 39: v E 1976 (2) 1981 (6); v WI 1974 (2) 1983 (3); v NZ 1976 (1); v P 1983 (3); v SL 1982 (1); *v E 1974 (2) 1982 (3) 1986 (1); v A 1977 (2); v WI 1975 (4) 1982 (2); v NZ 1975 (3); v P 1982 (3) 1984 (1)*
Maka, E. S. 2: v P 1952 (1); *v WI 1952 (1)*
Malhotra, A. 7: v E 1981 (2) 1984 (1); v WI 1983 (3); *v E 1982 (1)*
Maninder Singh 35: v A 1986 (3); v WI 1983 (4) 1987 (3); v P 1986 (4); v SL 1986 (3); v Z 1992 (1); *v E 1986 (3); v WI 1982 (3); v P 1982 (5) 1984 (1) 1989 (3); v SL 1985 (2)*
Manjrekar, S. V. 37: v SA 1996 (1); v WI 1987 (1) 1994 (3); v NZ 1995 (1); v SL 1990 (1) 1993 (3); *v E 1990 (3) 1996 (2); v A 1991 (5); v SA 1992 (4); v WI 1988 (4); v NZ 1989 (3) 1993 (1); v P 1989 (4); v Z 1992 (1)*
Manjrekar, V. L. 55: v E 1951 (2) 1961 (5) 1963 (4); v A 1956 (3) 1964 (3); v WI 1958 (4); v NZ 1955 (5) 1964 (1); v P 1952 (3) 1960 (5); *v E 1952 (4) 1959 (2); v WI 1952 (4) 1961 (5); v P 1954 (5)*
Mankad, A. V. 22: v E 1976 (1); v A 1969 (5); v WI 1974 (1); v NZ 1969 (2) 1976 (3); *v E 1971 (3) 1974 (1); v A 1977 (3); v WI 1970 (3)*
Mankad, V. 44: v E 1951 (5); v A 1956 (3); v WI 1948 (5) 1958 (2); v NZ 1955 (4); v P 1952 (4); *v E 1946 (3) 1952 (3); v A 1947 (5); v WI 1952 (5); v P 1954 (5)*
Mansur Ali Khan (*see* Pataudi)
Mantri, M. K. 4: v E 1951 (1); *v E 1952 (2); v P 1954 (1)*
Meherhomji, K. R. 1: *v E 1936*
Mehra, V. L. 8: v E 1961 (1) 1963 (2); v NZ 1955 (2); *v WI 1961 (3)*
Merchant, V. M. 10: v E 1933 (3) 1951 (1); *v E 1936 (3) 1946 (3)*
Mhambrey, P. L. 2: *v E 1996 (2)*
Milkha Singh, A. G. 4: v E 1961 (1); v A 1959 (1); v P 1960 (2)
Modi, R. S. 10: v E 1951 (1); v WI 1948 (5); v P 1952 (1); *v E 1946 (3)*
Mohanty, D. S. 2: v SL 1997 (1); *v SL 1997 (1)*
Mongia, N. R. 44: v A 1996 (1) 1997 (3) 2000 (2); v SA 1996 (3) 1999 (2); v WI 1994 (3); v NZ 1995 (3); v P 1998 (3); v SL 1993 (3) 1997 (3); *v E 1996 (3); v SA 1996 (3); v WI 1996 (5); v NZ 1993 (1) 1998 (2); v SL 1997 (2) 1998 (1); v Z 1998 (1)*
More, K. S. 49: v E 1992 (3); v A 1986 (2); v WI 1987 (4); v NZ 1988 (3); v P 1986 (5); v SL 1986 (3) 1990 (1); *v E 1986 (3) 1990 (3); v A 1991 (3); v SA 1992 (4); v WI 1988 (4); v NZ 1989 (3); v P 1989 (4); v SL 1993 (3); v Z 1992 (1)*
Muddiah, V. M. 2: v A 1959 (1); v P 1960 (1)
Mushtaq Ali, S. 11: v E 1933 (2) 1951 (1); v WI 1948 (3); *v E 1936 (3) 1946 (2)*

Nadkarni, R. G. 41: v E 1961 (1) 1963 (5); v A 1959 (5) 1964 (3); v WI 1958 (1) 1966 (1); v NZ 1955 (1) 1964 (4); v P 1960 (4); *v E 1959 (4); v A 1967 (3); v WI 1961 (5); v NZ 1967 (4)*
Naik, S. S. 3: v WI 1974 (2); *v E 1974 (1)*
Naoomal Jeoomal 3: v E 1933 (2); *v E 1932 (1)*
Narasimha Rao, M. V. 4: v A 1979 (2); v WI 1978 (2)
Navle, J. G. 2: v E 1933 (1); *v E 1932 (1)*
Nayak, S. V. 2: *v E 1982 (2)*
Nayudu, C. K. 7: v E 1933 (3); *v E 1932 (1) 1936 (3)*
Nayudu, C. S. 11: v E 1933 (2) 1951 (1); *v E 1936 (2) 1946 (2); v A 1947 (4)*
Nazir Ali, S. 2: v E 1933 (1); *v E 1932 (1)*
Nehra, A. 3: *v SL 1998 (1); v Z 2001 (2)*
Nissar, Mahomed 6: v E 1933 (2); *v E 1932 (1) 1936 (3)*
Nyalchand, S. 1: v P 1952

Pai, A. M. 1: v NZ 1969
Palia, P. E. 2: *v E 1932 (1) 1936 (1)*
Pandit, C. S. 5: v A 1986 (2); *v E 1986 (1); v A 1991 (2)*
Parkar, G. A. 1: *v E 1982*
Parkar, R. D. 2: v E 1972 (2)
Parsana, D. D. 2: v WI 1978 (2)
Patankar, C. T. 1: v NZ 1955
Pataudi sen., Nawab of, 3: *v E 1946 (3)*
Pataudi jun., Nawab of (now Mansur Ali Khan) 46: v E 1961 (3) 1963 (5) 1972 (3); v A 1964 (3) 1969 (5); v WI 1966 (3) 1974 (4); v NZ 1964 (4) 1969 (3); *v E 1967 (3); v A 1967 (3); v WI 1961 (3); v NZ 1967 (4)*
Patel, B. P. 21: v E 1976 (5); v WI 1974 (3); v NZ 1976 (3); *v E 1974 (2); v A 1977 (2); v WI 1975 (3); v NZ 1975 (3)*
Patel, J. M. 7: v A 1956 (2) 1959 (3); v NZ 1955 (1); *v P 1954 (1)*
Patel, R. 1: v NZ 1988
Patiala, Yuvraj of, 1: v E 1933
Patil, S. M. 29: v E 1979 (1) 1981 (4) 1984 (2); v WI 1983 (2); v P 1979 (2) 1983 (3); v SL 1982 (1); *v E 1982 (2); v A 1980 (3); v NZ 1980 (3); v P 1982 (4) 1984 (2)*
Patil, S. R. 1: v NZ 1955
Phadkar, D. G. 31: v E 1951 (4); v A 1956 (1); v WI 1948 (4) 1958 (1); v NZ 1955 (4); v P 1952 (2); *v E 1952 (4); v A 1947 (4); v WI 1952 (4); v P 1954 (3)*
Prabhakar, M. 39: v E 1984 (2) 1992 (3); v WI 1994 (3); v NZ 1995 (3); v SL 1990 (1) 1993 (3); v Z 1992 (1); *v E 1990 (3); v A 1991 (5); v SA 1992 (4); v NZ 1989 (3); v P 1989 (4); v SL 1993 (3); v Z 1992 (1)*
Prasad, B. K. V. 33: v A 1996 (1) 2000 (1); v SA 1996 (3); v NZ 1999 (2); v P 1998 (3); v SL 1997 (1); *v E 1996 (3); v A 1999 (3); v SA 1996 (3); v WI 1996 (5); v NZ 1998 (2); v SL 1997 (2) 1998 (1) 2001 (3)*
Prasad, M. S. K. 6: v NZ 1999 (3); *v A 1999 (3)*
Prasanna, E. A. S. 49: v E 1961 (1) 1972 (3) 1976 (4); v A 1969 (5); v WI 1966 (1) 1974 (5); v NZ 1969 (3); *v E 1967 (3) 1974 (2); v A 1967 (4) 1977 (4); v WI 1961 (1) 1970 (3) 1975 (1); v NZ 1967 (4) 1975 (3); v P 1978 (2)*
Punjabi, P. H. 5: *v P 1954 (5)*

Rai Singh, K. 1: *v A 1947*
Rajinder Pal 1: v E 1963
Rajindernath, V. 1: v P 1952
Rajput, L. S. 2: *v SL 1985 (2)*
Raju, S. L. V. 28: v E 1992 (3); v A 1997 (3) 2000 (1); v WI 1994 (3); v NZ 1995 (2); v SL 1990 (1) 1993 (3); *v E 1996 (1); v A 1991 (4); v SA 1992 (2); v NZ 1989 (2) 1993 (1); v SL 1993 (1); v Z 1992 (1)*
Raman, W. V. 11: v SA 1996 (1); v WI 1987 (1); v NZ 1988 (1); *v SA 1992 (1) 1996 (2); v WI 1988 (1); v NZ 1989 (3); v Z 1992 (1)*
Ramaswami, C. 2: *v E 1936 (2)*
Ramchand, G. S. 33: v A 1956 (3) 1959 (5); v WI 1958 (3); v NZ 1955 (5); v P 1952 (3); *v E 1952 (4); v WI 1952 (5); v P 1954 (5)*
Ramesh, S. 19: v A 2000 (3); v NZ 1999 (3); v P 1998 (3); v Z 2000 (2); *v A 1999 (2); v SL 1998 (1) 2001 (3); v Z 2001 (1); v B 2000 (1)*

Ramji, L. 1: v E 1933
Rangachari, C. R. 4: v WI 1948 (2); *v A 1947 (2)*
Rangnekar, K. M. 3: *v A 1947 (3)*
Ranjane, V. B. 7: v E 1961 (3) 1963 (1); v A 1964 (1); v WI 1958 (1); *v WI 1961 (1)*
Rathore, V. 6: v A 1996 (1); *v E 1996 (3); v SA 1996 (2)*
Razdan, V. 2: *v P 1989 (2)*
Reddy, B. 4: *v E 1979 (4)*
Rege, M. R. 1: v WI 1948
Roy, A. 4: v A 1969 (2); v NZ 1969 (2)
Roy, Pankaj 43: v E 1951 (5); v A 1956 (3) 1959 (5); v WI 1958 (5); v NZ 1955 (3); v P 1952 (3) 1960 (1); *v E 1952 (4) 1959 (5); v WI 1952 (4); v P 1954 (5)*
Roy, Pranab 2: v E 1981 (2)

Sandhu, B. S. 8: v WI 1983 (1); *v WI 1982 (4); v P 1982 (3)*
Sanghvi, R. L. 1: v A 2000
Sarandeep Singh 1: v Z 2000
Sardesai, D. N. 30: v E 1961 (1) 1963 (5) 1972 (1); v A 1964 (3) 1969 (1); v WI 1966 (2); v NZ 1964 (3); *v E 1967 (1) 1971 (3); v A 1967 (2); v WI 1961 (3) 1970 (5)*
Sarwate, C. T. 9: v E 1951 (1); v WI 1948 (2); *v E 1946 (1); v A 1947 (5)*
Saxena, R. C. 1: *v E 1967*
Sekar, T. A. P. 2: *v P 1982 (2)*
Sen, P. 14: v E 1951 (2); v WI 1948 (5); v P 1952 (2); *v E 1952 (2); v A 1947 (3)*
Sen Gupta, A. K. 1: v WI 1958
Sharma, Ajay 1: v WI 1987
Sharma, Chetan 23: v E 1984 (3); v A 1986 (2); v WI 1987 (3); v SL 1986 (2); *v E 1986 (2); v A 1985 (2); v WI 1988 (4); v P 1984 (2); v SL 1985 (3)*
Sharma, Gopal 5: v E 1984 (1); v P 1986 (2); v SL 1990 (1); *v SL 1985 (1)*
Sharma, P. 5: v E 1976 (2); v WI 1974 (2); *v WI 1975 (1)*
Sharma, Sanjeev 2: v NZ 1988 (1); *v E 1990 (1)*
Shastri, R. J. 80: v E 1981 (6) 1984 (5); v A 1986 (3); v WI 1983 (6) 1987 (4); v NZ 1988 (3); v P 1983 (2) 1986 (5); v SL 1986 (3) 1990 (1); *v E 1982 (3) 1986 (3) 1990 (3); v A 1985 (3) 1991 (3); v SA 1992 (3); v WI 1982 (5) 1988 (4); v NZ 1980 (3); v P 1982 (2) 1984 (2) 1989 (4); v SL 1985 (3); v Z 1992 (1)*
Shinde, S. G. 7: v E 1951 (3); v WI 1948 (1); *v E 1946 (1) 1952 (2)*
Shodhan, R. H. 3: v P 1952 (1); *v WI 1952 (2)*
Shukla, R. C. 1: v SL 1982
Sidhu, N. S. 51: v E 1992 (3); v A 1997 (3); v WI 1983 (2) 1994 (3); v NZ 1988 (3) 1995 (2); v SL 1993 (3) 1997 (3); v Z 1992 (1); *v E 1990 (3); v A 1991 (3); v WI 1988 (4) 1996 (4); v NZ 1989 (1) 1993 (1) 1998 (2); v P 1989 (4); v SL 1993 (3) 1997 (2); v Z 1998 (1)*
Singh, R. 1: *v NZ 1998*
Singh, R. R. 1: *v Z 1998*
Sivaramakrishnan, L. 9: v E 1984 (5); *v A 1985 (2); v WI 1982 (1); v SL 1985 (1)*
Sohoni, S. W. 4: v E 1951 (1); *v E 1946 (2); v A 1947 (1)*
Solkar, E. D. 27: v E 1972 (5) 1976 (1); v A 1969 (4); v WI 1974 (4); v NZ 1969 (1); *v E 1971 (3) 1974 (3); v WI 1970 (5) 1975 (1)*
Sood, M. M. 1: v A 1959
Srikkanth, K. 43: v E 1981 (4) 1984 (2); v A 1986 (3); v WI 1987 (4); v NZ 1988 (3); v P 1986 (5); v SL 1986 (3); *v E 1986 (3); v A 1985 (3) 1991 (4); v P 1982 (2) 1989 (4); v SL 1985 (3)*
Srinath, J. 53: v A 1997 (2) 2000 (1); v SA 1996 (3) 1999 (2); v WI 1994 (3); v NZ 1995 (3) 1999 (3); v P 1998 (3); v SL 1997 (3); v Z 2000 (2); *v E 1996 (3); v A 1991 (5) 1999 (3); v SA 1992 (3) 1996 (3); v NZ 1993 (1) 1998 (2); v SL 1993 (2) 2001 (1); v Z 1992 (1) 1998 (1) 2001 (2); v B 2000 (1)*
Srinivasan, T. E. 1: *v NZ 1980*
Subramanya, V. 9: v WI 1966 (2); v NZ 1964 (1); *v E 1967 (2); v A 1967 (2); v NZ 1967 (2)*
Sunderram, G. 2: v NZ 1955 (2)
Surendranath, R. 11: v A 1959 (2); v WI 1958 (2); v P 1960 (2); *v E 1959 (5)*
Surti, R. F. 26: v E 1963 (1); v A 1964 (2) 1969 (1); v WI 1966 (2); v NZ 1964 (1) 1969 (2); v P 1960 (2); *v E 1967 (2); v A 1967 (4); v WI 1961 (5); v NZ 1967 (4)*
Swamy, V. N. 1: v NZ 1955

Tamhane, N. S. 21: v A 1956 (3) 1959 (1); v WI 1958 (4); v NZ 1955 (4); v P 1960 (2); *v E 1959 (2); v P 1954 (5)*
Tarapore, K. K. 1: v WI 1948
Tendulkar, S. R. 84: v E 1992 (3); v A 1996 (1) 1997 (3) 2000 (3); v SA 1996 (3) 1999 (2); v WI 1994 (3); v NZ 1995 (3) 1999 (3); v P 1998 (3); v SL 1990 (1) 1993 (3) 1997 (3); v Z 1992 (1) 2000 (2); *v E 1990 (3) 1996 (3); v A 1991 (5) 1999 (3); v SA 1992 (4) 1996 (3); v WI 1996 (5); v NZ 1989 (3) 1993 (1) 1998 (2); v P 1989 (4); v SL 1993 (3) 1997 (2) 1998 (1); v Z 1992 (1) 1998 (1) 2001 (2); v B 2000 (1)*

Umrigar, P. R. 59: v E 1951 (5) 1961 (4); v A 1956 (3) 1959 (3); v WI 1948 (1) 1958 (5); v NZ 1955 (5); v P 1952 (5) 1960 (5); *v E 1952 (4) 1959 (4); v WI 1952 (5) 1961 (5); v P 1954 (5)*

Vengsarkar, D. B. 116: v E 1976 (1) 1979 (1) 1981 (6) 1984 (5); v A 1979 (6) 1986 (2); v WI 1978 (6) 1983 (5) 1987 (3); v NZ 1988 (3); v P 1979 (5) 1983 (1) 1986 (5); v SL 1982 (1) 1986 (3) 1990 (1); *v E 1979 (4) 1982 (3) 1986 (3) 1990 (3); v A 1977 (5) 1980 (3) 1985 (3) 1991 (5); v WI 1975 (2) 1982 (5) 1988 (4); v NZ 1975 (3) 1980 (3) 1989 (2); v P 1978 (3) 1982 (6) 1984 (2); v SL 1985 (3)*
Venkataraghavan, S. 57: v E 1972 (2) 1976 (1); v A 1969 (5) 1979 (3); v WI 1966 (2) 1974 (2) 1978 (6); v NZ 1964 (4) 1969 (2) 1976 (3); v P 1983 (2); *v E 1967 (1) 1971 (3) 1974 (2) 1979 (4); v A 1977 (1); v WI 1970 (5) 1975 (3) 1982 (5); v NZ 1975 (1)*
Venkataramana, M. 1: *v WI 1988*
Viswanath, G. R. 91: v E 1972 (5) 1976 (5) 1979 (1) 1981 (6); v A 1969 (4) 1979 (6); v WI 1974 (5) 1978 (6); v NZ 1976 (3); v P 1979 (6); v SL 1982 (1); *v E 1971 (3) 1974 (3) 1979 (4) 1982 (3); v A 1977 (5) 1980 (3); v WI 1970 (3) 1975 (4); v NZ 1975 (3) 1980 (3); v P 1978 (3) 1982 (6)*
Viswanath, S. 3: *v SL 1985 (3)*
Vizianagram, Maharaj Kumar of, Sir Vijay A. 3: *v E 1936 (3)*

Wadekar, A. L. 37: v E 1972 (5); v A 1969 (5); v WI 1966 (2); v NZ 1969 (3); *v E 1967 (3) 1971 (3) 1974 (3); v A 1967 (4); v WI 1970 (5); v NZ 1967 (4)*
Wasim Jaffer 2: v SA 1999 (2)
Wassan, A. S. 4: *v E 1990 (1); v NZ 1989 (3)*
Wazir Ali, S. 7: v E 1933 (3); *v E 1932 (1) 1936 (3)*

Yadav, N. S. 35: v E 1979 (1) 1981 (1) 1984 (4); v A 1979 (5) 1986 (3); v WI 1983 (3); v P 1979 (5) 1986 (4); v SL 1986 (2); *v A 1980 (2) 1985 (3); v NZ 1980 (1); v P 1984 (1)*
Yadav, V. S. 1: v Z 1992
Yajurvindra Singh 4: v E 1976 (2); v A 1979 (1); *v E 1979 (1)*
Yashpal Sharma 37: v E 1979 (1) 1981 (2); v A 1979 (6); v WI 1983 (1); v P 1979 (6) 1983 (3); v SL 1982 (1); *v E 1979 (3) 1982 (3); v A 1980 (3); v WI 1982 (5); v NZ 1980 (1); v P 1982 (2)*
Yograj Singh 1: *v NZ 1980*

Zaheer Khan 8: v A 2000 (2); v Z 2000 (1); *v SL 2001 (3); v Z 2001 (1); v B 2000 (1)*

Note: Hafeez, on going later to Oxford University, took his correct name, Kardar.

PAKISTAN

Number of Test cricketers: 170

Aamer Malik 14: v E 1987 (2); v A 1988 (1) 1994 (1); v WI 1990 (1); v In 1989 (4); *v A 1989 (2); v WI 1987 (1); v NZ 1988 (2)*
Aamir Nazir 6: v SL 1995 (1); *v SA 1994 (1); v WI 1992 (1); v NZ 1993 (1); v Z 1994 (2)*
Aamir Sohail 47: v A 1994 (3) 1998 (3); v SA 1997 (1); v WI 1997 (3); v SL 1995 (3) 1999 (2); v Z 1993 (3) 1996 (2) 1998 (1); *v E 1992 (5) 1996 (2); v A 1995 (3); v SA 1994 (1) 1997 (3); v WI 1992 (2); v NZ 1992 (1) 1993 (3) 1995 (1); v SL 1994 (2); v Z 1994 (3)*
Abdul Kadir 4: v A 1964 (1); *v A 1964 (1); v NZ 1964 (2)*
Abdul Qadir 67: v E 1977 (3) 1983 (3) 1987 (3); v A 1982 (3) 1988 (3); v WI 1980 (2) 1986 (3) 1990 (2); v NZ 1984 (3) 1990 (2); v In 1982 (5) 1984 (1) 1989 (4); v SL 1985 (3); *v E 1982 (3) 1987 (4); v A 1983 (5); v WI 1987 (3); v NZ 1984 (2) 1988 (2); v In 1979 (3) 1986 (3); v SL 1985 (2)*

Abdur Razzaq 15: v E 2000 (3); v SL 1999 (2); v B 2001 (1); *v E 2001 (2); v A 1999 (1); v WI 1999 (3); v SL 2000 (3)*
Afaq Hussain 2: v E 1961 (1); *v A 1964 (1)*
Aftab Baloch 2: v WI 1974 (1); v NZ 1969 (1)
Aftab Gul 6: v E 1968 (2); v NZ 1969 (1); *v E 1971 (3)*
Agha Saadat Ali 1: v NZ 1955
Agha Zahid 1: v WI 1974
Akram Raza 9: v A 1994 (2); v WI 1990 (1); v In 1989 (1); v SL 1991 (1); *v NZ 1993 (2); v SL 1994 (1); v Z 1994 (1)*
Ali Hussain Rizvi 1: v SA 1997
Alim-ud-Din 25: v E 1961 (2); v A 1956 (1) 1959 (1); v WI 1958 (1); v NZ 1955 (3); v In 1954 (5); *v E 1954 (3) 1962 (3); v WI 1957 (5); v In 1960 (1)*
Ali Naqvi 5: v SA 1997 (3); *v Z 1997 (2)*
Amir Elahi 5: *v In 1952 (5)*
Anil Dalpat 9: v E 1983 (3); v NZ 1984 (3); *v NZ 1984 (3)*
Anwar Hussain 4: *v In 1952 (4)*
Anwar Khan 1: *v NZ 1978*
Aqib Javed 22: v A 1994 (1); v NZ 1990 (3); v SL 1991 (3) 1995 (3); v Z 1998 (1); *v E 1992 (5); v A 1989 (1); v SA 1994 (1); v NZ 1988 (1) 1992 (1); v Z 1994 (2)*
Arif Butt 3: *v A 1964 (1); v NZ 1964 (2)*
Arshad Khan 8: v E 2000 (1); v A 1998 (1); v WI 1997 (1); v SL 1999 (1); *v SL 1998 (1) 2000 (3)*
Ashfaq Ahmed 1: v Z 1993
Ashraf Ali 8: v E 1987 (3); v In 1984 (2); v SL 1981 (2) 1985 (1)
Asif Iqbal 58: v E 1968 (3) 1972 (3); v A 1964 (1); v WI 1974 (2); v NZ 1964 (3) 1969 (3) 1976 (3); v In 1978 (3); *v E 1967 (3) 1971 (3) 1974 (3); v A 1964 (1) 1972 (3) 1976 (3) 1978 (2); v WI 1976 (5); v NZ 1964 (3) 1972 (3) 1978 (2); v In 1979 (6)*
Asif Masood 16: v E 1968 (2) 1972 (1); v WI 1974 (2); v NZ 1969 (1); *v E 1971 (3) 1974 (3); v A 1972 (3) 1976 (1)*
Asif Mujtaba 25: v E 1987 (1); v WI 1986 (2); v Z 1993 (3); *v E 1992 (5) 1996 (2); v SA 1994 (1); v WI 1992 (3); v NZ 1992 (1) 1993 (2); v SL 1994 (2) 1996 (2); v Z 1994 (1)*
Ata-ur-Rehman 13: v SL 1995 (1); v Z 1993 (3); *v E 1992 (1) 1996 (2); v WI 1992 (3); v NZ 1993 (2) 1995 (1)*
Atif Rauf 1: *v NZ 1993*
Atiq-uz-Zaman 1: v SL 1999
Azam Khan 1: v Z 1996
Azeem Hafeez 18: v E 1983 (2); v NZ 1984 (3); v In 1984 (2); *v A 1983 (5); v NZ 1984 (3); v In 1983 (3)*
Azhar Khan 1: v A 1979
Azhar Mahmood 21: v A 1998 (2); v SA 1997 (3); v WI 1997 (3); v Z 1998 (1); *v E 2001 (2); v A 1999 (3); v SA 1997 (3); v In 1998 (1); v SL 2000 (1); v Z 1997 (2)*
Azmat Rana 1: v A 1979

Basit Ali 19: v A 1994 (2); v SL 1995 (1); v Z 1993 (3); *v A 1995 (3); v WI 1992 (3); v NZ 1993 (3) 1995 (1); v SL 1994 (2); v Z 1994 (1)*
Burki, J. 25: v E 1961 (3); v A 1964 (1); v NZ 1964 (3) 1969 (1); *v E 1962 (5) 1967 (3); v A 1964 (1); v NZ 1964 (3); v In 1960 (5)*

Danish Kaneria 3: v E 2000 (2); v B 2001 (1)
D'Souza, A. 6: v E 1961 (2); v WI 1958 (1); *v E 1962 (3)*

Ehtesham-ud-Din 5: v A 1979 (1); *v E 1982 (1); v In 1979 (3)*

Faisal Iqbal 5: v B 2001 (1); *v E 2001 (1); v NZ 2000 (3)*
Farooq Hamid 1: *v A 1964*
Farrukh Zaman 1: v NZ 1976
Fazal Mahmood 34: v E 1961 (1); v A 1956 (1) 1959 (2); v WI 1958 (3); v NZ 1955 (2); v In 1954 (4); *v E 1954 (4) 1962 (2); v WI 1957 (5); v In 1952 (5) 1960 (5)*
Fazl-e-Akbar 4: v SL 1998 (1); *v SA 1997 (1); v NZ 2000 (2)*

Ghazali, M. E. Z. 2: *v E 1954 (2)*
Ghulam Abbas 1: *v E 1967*

Gul Mahomed 1: v A 1956

Hanif Mohammad 55: v E 1961 (3) 1968 (3); v A 1956 (1) 1959 (3) 1964 (1); v WI 1958 (1); v NZ 1955 (3) 1964 (3) 1969 (1); v In 1954 (5); *v E 1954 (4) 1962 (5) 1967 (3); v A 1964 (1); v WI 1957 (5); v NZ 1964 (3); v In 1952 (5) 1960 (5)*
Haroon Rashid 23: v E 1977 (3); v A 1979 (2) 1982 (3); v In 1982 (1); v SL 1981 (2); *v E 1978 (3) 1982 (1); v A 1976 (1) 1978 (1); v WI 1976 (5); v NZ 1978 (1)*
Hasan Raza 2: v Z 1996 (1) 1998 (1)
Haseeb Ahsan 12: v E 1961 (2); v A 1959 (1); v WI 1958 (1); *v WI 1957 (3); v In 1960 (5)*
Humayun Farhat 1: *v NZ 2000*

Ibadulla, K. 4: v A 1964 (1); *v E 1967 (2); v NZ 1964 (1)*
Ijaz Ahmed, sen. 60: v E 1987 (3); v A 1988 (3) 1994 (1) 1998 (2); v SA 1997 (3); v WI 1990 (3) 1997 (3); v NZ 1996 (2); v SL 1999 (1); v Z 1996 (2) 1998 (2); *v E 1987 (4) 1996 (3); v A 1989(3) 1995 (2) 1999 (3); v SA 1994 (1) 1997 (3); v WI 1987 (2); v NZ 1995 (1) 2000 (2); v In 1986 (1) 1998 (3); v SL 1996 (2) 1998 (1); v Z 1994 (3) 1997 (1)*
Ijaz Ahmed, jun. 2: v SL 1995 (2)
Ijaz Butt 8: v A 1959 (2); v WI 1958 (3); *v E 1962 (3)*
Ijaz Faqih 5: v WI 1980 (1); *v A 1981 (1); v WI 1987 (2); v In 1986 (1)*
Imran Farhat 3: *v NZ 2000 (3)*
Imran Khan 88: v A 1979 (2) 1982 (3); v WI 1980 (4) 1986 (3) 1990 (3); v NZ 1976 (3); v In 1978 (3) 1982 (6) 1989 (4); v SL 1981 (1) 1985 (3) 1991 (3); *v E 1971 (1) 1974 (3) 1982 (3) 1987 (5); v A 1976 (3) 1978 (2) 1981 (3) 1983 (2) 1989 (3); v WI 1976 (5) 1987 (3); v NZ 1978 (2) 1988 (2); v In 1979 (5) 1986 (5); v SL 1985 (3)*
Imran Nazir 5: v E 2000 (1); v SL 1998 (1); *v WI 1999 (2); v SL 2000 (1)*
Imtiaz Ahmed 41: v E 1961 (3); v A 1956 (1) 1959 (3); v WI 1958 (3); v NZ 1955 (3); v In 1954 (5); *v E 1954 (4) 1962 (4); v WI 1957 (5); v In 1952 (5) 1960 (5)*
Intikhab Alam 47: v E 1961 (2) 1968 (3) 1972 (3); v A 1959 (1) 1964 (1); v WI 1974 (2); v NZ 1964 (3) 1969 (3) 1976 (3); *v E 1962 (3) 1967 (3) 1971 (3) 1974 (3); v A 1964 (1) 1972 (3); v WI 1976 (1); v NZ 1964 (3) 1972 (3); v In 1960 (3)*
Inzamam-ul-Haq 75: v E 2000 (3); v A 1994 (3) 1998 (3); v SA 1997 (3); v WI 1997 (3); v NZ 1996 (2); v SL 1995 (3) 1998 (1) 1999 (3); v Z 1993 (3) 1998 (1); v B 2001 (1); *v E 1992 (4) 1996 (3) 2001 (2); v A 1995 (3) 1999 (3); v SA 1994 (1) 1997 (2); v WI 1992 (3) 1999 (3); v NZ 1992 (1) 1993 (3) 1995 (1) 2000 (2); v In 1998 (2); v SL 1994 (2) 1996 (2) 1998 (1) 2000 (3); v Z 1994 (3) 1997 (2)*
Iqbal Qasim 50: v E 1977 (3) 1987 (3); v A 1979 (3) 1982 (2) 1988 (3); v WI 1980 (4); v NZ 1984 (3); v In 1978 (3) 1982 (2); v SL 1981 (3); *v E 1978 (3); v A 1976 (3) 1981 (2); v WI 1976 (2); v NZ 1984 (1); v In 1979 (6) 1983 (1) 1986 (3)*
Irfan Fazil 1: v SL 1999
Israr Ali 4: v A 1959 (2); *v In 1952 (2)*

Jalal-ud-Din 6: v A 1982 (1); v In 1982 (2) 1984 (2); v SL 1985 (1)
Javed Akhtar 1: *v E 1962*
Javed Miandad 124: v E 1977 (3) 1987 (3); v A 1979 (3) 1982 (3) 1988 (3); v WI 1980 (4) 1986 (3) 1990 (2); v NZ 1976 (3) 1984 (3) 1990 (3); v In 1978 (3) 1982 (6) 1984 (2) 1989 (4); v SL 1981 (3) 1985 (3) 1991 (3); v Z 1993 (3); *v E 1978 (3) 1982 (3) 1987 (5) 1992 (5); v A 1976 (3) 1978 (2) 1981 (3) 1983 (5) 1989 (3); v WI 1976 (1) 1987 (3) 1992 (3); v NZ 1978 (3) 1984 (3) 1988 (2) 1992 (1); v In 1979 (6) 1983 (3) 1986 (4); v SL 1985 (3)*

Kabir Khan 4: *v SA 1994 (1); v SL 1994 (1); v Z 1994 (2)*
Kardar, A. H. 23: v A 1956 (1); v NZ 1955 (3); v In 1954 (5); *v E 1954 (4); v WI 1957 (5); v In 1952 (5)*
Khalid Hassan 1: *v E 1954*
Khalid Wazir 2: *v E 1954 (2)*
Khan Mohammad 13: v A 1956 (1); v NZ 1955 (3); v In 1954 (4); *v E 1954 (2); v WI 1957 (2); v In 1952 (1)*

Liaqat Ali 5: v E 1977 (2); v WI 1974 (1); *v E 1978 (2)*

Mahmood Hussain 27: v E 1961 (1); v WI 1958 (3); v NZ 1955 (1); v In 1954 (5); *v E 1954 (2) 1962 (3); v WI 1957 (3); v In 1952 (4) 1960 (5)*

Majid Khan 63: v E 1968 (3) 1972 (3); v A 1964 (1) 1979 (3); v WI 1974 (2) 1980 (4); v NZ 1964 (3) 1976 (3); v In 1978 (3) 1982 (1); v SL 1981 (1); *v E 1967 (3) 1971 (2) 1974 (3) 1982 (1); v A 1972 (3) 1976 (3) 1978 (2) 1981 (3); v WI 1976 (5); v NZ 1972 (3) 1978 (2); v In 1979 (6)*

Mansoor Akhtar 19: v A 1982 (3); v WI 1980 (2); v In 1982 (3); v SL 1981 (1); *v E 1982 (3) 1987 (5); v A 1981 (1) 1989 (1)*

Manzoor Elahi 6: v NZ 1984 (1); v In 1984 (1); *v In 1986 (2); v Z 1994 (2)*

Maqsood Ahmed 16: v NZ 1955 (2); v In 1954 (5); *v E 1954 (4); v In 1952 (5)*

Masood Anwar 1: v WI 1990

Mathias, Wallis 21: v E 1961 (1); v A 1956 (1) 1959 (2); v WI 1958 (3); v NZ 1955 (1); *v E 1962 (3); v WI 1957 (5); v In 1960 (5)*

Miran Bux 2: v In 1954 (2)

Misbah-ul-Haq 1: *v NZ 2000*

Mohammad Akram 9: v NZ 1996 (1); v SL 1995 (2) 1999 (1); *v E 1996 (1); v A 1995 (2) 1999 (1); v NZ 2000 (1)*

Mohammad Aslam 1: *v E 1954*

Mohammad Farooq 7: v NZ 1964 (3); *v E 1962 (2); v In 1960 (2)*

Mohammad Hussain 2: v A 1998 (1); v Z 1996 (1)

Mohammad Ilyas 10: v E 1968 (2); v NZ 1964 (3); *v E 1967 (1); v A 1964 (1); v NZ 1964 (3)*

Mohammad Munaf 4: v E 1961 (2); v A 1959 (2)

Mohammad Nazir 14: v E 1972 (1); v WI 1980 (4); v NZ 1969 (3)*; v A 1983 (3); v In 1983 (3)*

Mohammad Ramzan 1: v SA 1997

Mohammad Sami 2: *v NZ 2000 (2)*

Mohammad Wasim 18: v A 1998 (1); v SA 1997 (2); v WI 1997 (3); v NZ 1996 (2); *v A 1999 (2); v SA 1997 (2); v WI 1999 (3); v SL 2000 (2); v Z 1997 (1)*

Mohammad Zahid 4: v A 1998 (1); v NZ 1996 (1); *v SL 1996 (2)*

Mohsin Kamal 9: v E 1983 (1); v A 1994 (2); v SL 1985 (1); *v E 1987 (4); v SL 1985 (1)*

Mohsin Khan 48: v E 1977 (1) 1983 (3); v A 1982 (3); v WI 1986 (3); v NZ 1984 (2); v In 1982 (6) 1984 (2); v SL 1981 (2) 1985 (2); *v E 1978 (3) 1982 (3); v A 1978 (1) 1981 (2) 1983 (5); v NZ 1978 (1) 1984 (3); v In 1983 (3); v SL 1985 (3)*

Moin Khan 63: v E 2000 (3); v A 1994 (1) 1998 (3); v SA 1997 (3); v WI 1990 (2) 1997 (3); v NZ 1996 (2); v SL 1991 (3) 1995 (3) 1998 (1) 1999 (2); v Z 1996 (2) 1998 (2); *v E 1992 (4) 1996 (2); v A 1995 (2) 1999 (3); v SA 1994 (1) 1997 (3); v WI 1992 (2) 1999 (3); v NZ 2000 (2); v In 1998 (3); v SL 1996 (2) 1998 (1) 2000 (3); v Z 1997 (2)*

Mudassar Nazar 76: v E 1977 (3) 1983 (1) 1987 (3); v A 1979 (3) 1982 (3) 1988 (3); v WI 1986 (2); v NZ 1984 (3); v In 1978 (2) 1982 (6) 1984 (2); v SL 1981 (1) 1985 (3) ; *v E 1978 (3) 1982 (3) 1987 (5); v A 1976 (1) 1978 (1) 1981 (3) 1983 (5); v WI 1987 (3); v NZ 1978 (1) 1984 (3) 1988 (2); v In 1979 (5) 1983 (3); v SL 1985 (3)*

Mufasir-ul-Haq 1: *v NZ 1964*

Munir Malik 3: v A 1959 (1); *v E 1962 (2)*

Mushtaq Ahmed 50: v E 2000 (1); v A 1994 (3) 1998 (2); v SA 1997 (3); v WI 1990 (2) 1997 (3); v NZ 1996 (2); v Z 1993 (2) 1998 (1); *v E 1992 (5) 1996 (3); v A 1989 (1) 1995 (2) 1999 (1); v SA 1997 (3); v WI 1992 (1) 1999 (3); v NZ 1992 (1) 1993 (1) 1995 (1) 2000 (1); v In 1998 (1); v SL 1994 (2) 1996 (2) 2000 (2); v Z 1997 (1)*

Mushtaq Mohammad 57: v E 1961 (3) 1968 (3) 1972 (3); v WI 1958 (1) 1974 (2); v NZ 1969 (2) 1976 (3); v In 1978 (3); *v E 1962 (5) 1967 (3) 1971 (3) 1974 (3); v A 1972 (3) 1976 (3) 1978 (2); v WI 1976 (5); v NZ 1972 (2) 1978 (3); v In 1960 (5)*

Nadeem Abbasi 3: v In 1989 (3)

Nadeem Ghauri 1: *v A 1989*

Nadeem Khan 2: *v WI 1992 (1); v In 1998 (1)*

Nasim-ul-Ghani 29: v E 1961 (2); v A 1959 (2) 1964 (1); v WI 1958 (3); *v E 1962 (5) 1967 (2); v A 1964 (1) 1972 (1); v WI 1957 (5); v NZ 1964 (3); v In 1960 (4)*

Naushad Ali 6: v NZ 1964 (3); *v NZ 1964 (3)*

Naved Anjum 2: v NZ 1990 (1); v In 1989 (1)

Naved Ashraf 2: v SL 1999 (1); v Z 1998 (1)

Nazar Mohammad 5: *v In 1952 (5)*

Nazir Junior (*see* Mohammad Nazir)

Niaz Ahmed 2: v E 1968 (1); *v E 1967 (1)*

Pervez Sajjad 19: v E 1968 (1) 1972 (2); v A 1964 (1); v NZ 1964 (3) 1969 (3); *v E 1971 (3); v NZ 1964 (3) 1972 (3)*

Qaiser Abbas 1: v E 2000

Qasim Omar 26: v E 1983 (3); v WI 1986 (3); v NZ 1984 (3); v In 1984 (2); v SL 1985 (3); *v A 1983 (5); v NZ 1984 (3); v In 1983 (1); v SL 1985 (3)*

Ramiz Raja 57: v E 1983 (2) 1987 (3); v A 1988 (3); v WI 1986 (3) 1990 (2); v NZ 1990 (3); v In 1989 (4); v SL 1985 (1) 1991 (3) 1995 (3); *v E 1987 (2) 1992 (5); v A 1989 (2) 1995 (3); v WI 1987 (3) 1992 (3); v NZ 1992 (1) 1995 (1); v In 1986 (5); v SL 1985 (3) 1996 (2)*

Rashid Khan 4: v SL 1981 (2); *v A 1983 (1); v NZ 1984 (1)*

Rashid Latif 25: v A 1994 (2); v Z 1993 (3); v B 2001 (1); *v E 1992 (1) 1996 (1) 2001 (2); v A 1995 (1); v SA 1997 (1); v WI 1992 (1); v NZ 1992 (1) 1993 (3) 1995 (1); v SL 1994 (2); v Z 1994 (3) 1997 (2)*

Rehman, S. F. 1: *v WI 1957*

Rizwan-uz-Zaman 11: v WI 1986 (1); v SL 1981 (2); *v A 1981 (1); v NZ 1988 (2); v In 1986 (5)*

Sadiq Mohammad 41: v E 1972 (3) 1977 (2); v WI 1974 (1) 1980 (3); v NZ 1969 (3) 1976 (3); v In 1978 (1); *v E 1971 (3) 1974 (3) 1978 (3); v A 1972 (3) 1976 (2); v WI 1976 (5); v NZ 1972 (3); v In 1979 (3)*

Saeed Ahmed 41: v E 1961 (3) 1968 (3); v A 1959 (3) 1964 (1); v WI 1958 (3); v NZ 1964 (3); *v E 1962 (5) 1967 (3) 1971 (1); v A 1964 (1) 1972 (2); v WI 1957 (5); v NZ 1964 (3); v In 1960 (5)*

Saeed Anwar 55: v E 2000 (3); v A 1994 (3) 1998 (2); v SA 1997 (3); v WI 1990 (1) 1997 (3); v NZ 1996 (2); v SL 1995 (2) 1998 (1) 1999 (2); v Z 1996 (2) 1998 (2); v B 2001 (1); *v E 1996 (3) 2001 (2); v A 1999 (3); v SA 1994 (1) 1997 (3); v NZ 1993 (3); v In 1998 (3); v SL 1994 (2) 1998 (1) 2000 (3); v Z 1994 (2) 1997 (2)*

Salah-ud-Din 5: v E 1968 (1); v NZ 1964 (3) 1969 (1)

Saleem Jaffer 14: v E 1987 (1); v A 1988 (2); v WI 1986 (1); v NZ 1990 (2); v In 1989 (1); v SL 1991 (2); *v WI 1987 (1); v NZ 1988 (2); v In 1986 (2)*

Salim Altaf 21: v E 1972 (3); v NZ 1969 (2); v In 1978 (1); *v E 1967 (2) 1971 (2); v A 1972 (3) 1976 (2); v WI 1976 (3); v NZ 1972 (3)*

Salim Elahi 9: v E 2000 (3); *v E 2001 (1); v A 1995 (2); v NZ 2000 (1); v SL 1996 (2)*

Salim Malik 103: v E 1983 (3) 1987 (3); v A 1988 (3) 1994 (3) 1998 (3); v WI 1986 (1) 1990 (3); v NZ 1984 (3) 1990 (3) 1996 (2); v In 1982 (6) 1984 (2) 1989 (4); v SL 1981 (2) 1985 (3) 1991 (3); v Z 1996 (2) 1998 (1); *v E 1987 (5) 1992 (5) 1996 (3); v A 1983 (3) 1989 (1) 1995 (2); v SA 1994 (1); v WI 1987 (3); v NZ 1984 (3) 1988 (2) 1992 (1) 1993 (3) 1995 (1); v In 1983 (2) 1986 (5) 1998 (3); v SL 1985 (3) 1994 (2) 1996 (2); v Z 1994 (3)*

Salim Yousuf 32: v A 1988 (3); v WI 1986 (3) 1990 (1); v NZ 1990 (3); v In 1989 (1); v SL 1981 (1) 1985 (2); *v E 1987 (5); v A 1989 (3); v WI 1987 (3); v NZ 1988 (2); v In 1986 (5)*

Saqlain Mushtaq 35: v E 2000 (3); v A 1998 (1); v SA 1997 (3); v WI 1997 (1); v NZ 1996 (1); v SL 1995 (2) 1998 (1) 1999 (1); v Z 1996 (2) 1998 (1); *v E 2000 (1); v A 1995 (2) 1999 (2); v SA 1997 (1); v WI 1999 (3); v NZ 2000 (3); v In 1998 (3); v SL 1996 (2) 1998 (1); v Z 1997 (1)*

Sarfraz Nawaz 55: v E 1968 (1) 1972 (2) 1977 (2) 1983 (3); v A 1979 (3); v WI 1974 (2) 1980 (2); v NZ 1976 (3); v In 1978 (3) 1982 (6); *v E 1974 (3) 1978 (2) 1982 (1); v A 1972 (2) 1976 (2) 1978 (2) 1981 (3) 1983 (3); v WI 1976 (4); v NZ 1972 (3) 1978 (3)*

Shadab Kabir 3: v Z 1996 (1); *v E 1996 (2)*

Shafiq Ahmed 6: v E 1977 (3); v WI 1980 (2); *v E 1974 (1)*

Shafqat Rana 5: v E 1968 (2); v A 1964 (1); v NZ 1969 (2)

Shahid Afridi 11: v E 2000 (3); v A 1998 (1); v SL 1998 (1) 1999 (2); *v In 1998 (3); v SL 1998 (1)*

Shahid Israr 1: v NZ 1976

Shahid Mahboob 1: v In 1989

Shahid Mahmood 1: *v E 1962*

Shahid Nazir 8: v WI 1997 (1); v NZ 1996 (2); v SL 1998 (1); v Z 1996 (2); *v SL 1996 (2)*

Shahid Saeed 1: v In 1989

Shakeel Ahmed, sen. 1: v A 1998

Shakeel Ahmed, jun. 3: *v WI 1992 (1); v Z 1994 (2)*

Sharpe, D. 3: v A 1959 (3)

Shoaib Akhtar 16: v A 1998 (2); v WI 1997 (1); v SL 1999 (2); v Z 1998 (1); *v E 2001 (1); v A 1999 (3); v SA 1997 (3); v In 1998 (1); v SL 1998 (1); v Z 1997 (1)*

Shoaib Malik 1: v B 2001
Shoaib Mohammad 45: v E 1983 (1) 1987 (1); v A 1988 (3); v WI 1990 (3); v NZ 1984 (1) 1990 (3); v In 1989 (4); v SL 1985 (1) 1991 (3) 1995 (3); v Z 1993 (3); *v E 1987 (4) 1992 (1); v A 1989 (3); v WI 1987 (3); v NZ 1984 (1) 1988 (2); v In 1983 (2) 1986 (3)*
Shuja-ud-Din 19: v E 1961 (2); v A 1959 (3); v WI 1958 (3); v NZ 1955 (3); v In 1954 (5); *v E 1954 (3)*
Sikander Bakht 26: v E 1977 (2); v WI 1980 (1); v NZ 1976 (1); v In 1978 (2) 1982 (1); *v E 1978 (3) 1982 (2); v A 1978 (2) 1981 (3); v WI 1976 (1); v NZ 1978 (3); v In 1979 (5)*

Tahir Naqqash 15: v A 1982 (3); v In 1982 (2); v SL 1981 (3); *v E 1982 (2); v A 1983 (1); v NZ 1984 (1); v In 1983 (3)*
Talat Ali 10: v E 1972 (3); *v E 1978 (2); v A 1972 (1); v NZ 1972 (1) 1978 (3)*
Taslim Arif 6: v A 1979 (3); v WI 1980 (2); *v In 1979 (1)*
Taufeeq Umar 1: v B 2001
Tauseef Ahmed 34: v E 1983 (2) 1987 (2); v A 1979 (3) 1988 (3); v WI 1986 (3); v NZ 1984 (1) 1990 (2); v In 1984 (1); v SL 1981 (3) 1985 (1); v Z 1993 (1); *v E 1987 (2); v A 1989 (3); v NZ 1988 (1); v In 1986 (4); v SL 1985 (2)*

Wajahatullah Wasti 6: v SL 1998 (1) 1999 (1); *v A 1999 (1); v WI 1999 (1); v In 1998 (1); v SL 1998 (1)*
Waqar Hassan 21: v A 1956 (1) 1959 (1); v WI 1958 (1); v NZ 1955 (3); v In 1954 (5); *v E 1954 (4); v WI 1957 (1); v In 1952 (5)*
Waqar Younis 74: v E 2000 (1); v A 1994 (2); v SA 1997 (2); v WI 1990 (3) 1997 (2); v NZ 1990 (3) 1996 (1); v In 1989 (2); v SL 1991 (3) 1995 (1) 1999 (3); v Z 1993 (3) 1996 (2) 1998 (2); v B 2001 (1); *v E 1992 (5) 1996 (3) 2001 (2); v A 1989 (3) 1995 (3) 1999 (1); v SA 1997 (3); v WI 1992 (3) 1999 (3); v NZ 1992 (1) 1993 (3) 1995 (1) 2000 (3); v In 1998 (2); v SL 1994 (2) 2000 (3); v Z 1997 (2)*
Wasim Akram 103: v E 1987 (2) 2000 (2); v A 1994 (2) 1998 (2); v SA 1997 (2); v WI 1986 (2) 1990 (3) 1997 (3); v NZ 1990 (2); v In 1989 (4); v SL 1985 (3) 1991 (3) 1995 (2) 1998 (1) 1999 (1); v Z 1993 (2) 1996 (2) 1998 (2); v B 2001 (1); *v E 1987 (5) 1992 (4) 1996 (3) 2001 (2); v A 1989 (3) 1995 (3) 1999 (3); v SA 1994 (1) 1997 (1); v WI 1987 (3) 1992 (3) 1999 (3); v NZ 1984 (2) 1992 (1) 1993 (3) 1995 (1); v In 1986 (5) 1998 (3); v SL 1985 (3) 1994 (2) 1998 (1) 2000 (3); v Z 1994 (3) 1997 (1)*
Wasim Bari 81: v E 1968 (3) 1972 (3) 1977 (3); v A 1982 (3); v WI 1974 (2) 1980 (2); v NZ 1969 (3) 1976 (2); v In 1978 (3) 1982 (6); *v E 1967 (3) 1971 (3) 1974 (3) 1978 (3) 1982 (3); v A 1972 (3) 1976 (3) 1978 (2) 1981 (3) 1983 (5); v WI 1976 (5); v NZ 1972 (3) 1978 (3); v In 1979 (6) 1983 (3)*
Wasim Raja 57: v E 1972 (1) 1977 (3) 1983 (3); v A 1979 (3); v WI 1974 (2) 1980 (4); v NZ 1976 (1) 1984 (1); v In 1982 (1) 1984 (1); v SL 1981 (3); *v E 1974 (2) 1978 (3) 1982 (1); v A 1978 (1) 1981 (3) 1983 (2); v WI 1976 (5); v NZ 1972 (3) 1978 (3) 1984 (2); v In 1979 (6) 1983 (3)*
Wazir Mohammad 20: v A 1956 (1) 1959 (1); v WI 1958 (3); v NZ 1955 (2); v In 1954 (5); *v E 1954 (2); v WI 1957 (5); v In 1952 (1)*

Younis Ahmed 4: v NZ 1969 (2); *v In 1986 (2)*
Younis Khan 14: v SL 1999 (3); *v E 2001 (2); v WI 1999 (3); v NZ 2000 (3); v SL 2000 (3)*
Yousuf Youhana 33: v E 2000 (3); v A 1998 (2); v SL 1998 (1) 1999 (3); v Z 1998 (2); v B 2001 (1); *v E 2001 (2); v A 1999 (3); v SA 1997 (1); v WI 1999 (3); v NZ 2000 (3); v In 1998 (3); v SL 1998 (1) 2000 (3); v Z 1997 (2)*

Zaheer Abbas 78: v E 1972 (2) 1983 (3); v A 1979 (2) 1982 (3); v WI 1974 (2) 1980 (3); v NZ 1969 (1) 1976 (3) 1984 (3); v In 1978 (3) 1982 (6) 1984 (2); v SL 1981 (1) 1985 (2); *v E 1971 (3) 1974 (3) 1982 (3); v A 1972 (3) 1976 (3) 1978 (2) 1981 (2) 1983 (5); v WI 1976 (3); v NZ 1972 (3) 1978 (2) 1984 (2); v In 1979 (5) 1983 (3)*
Zahid Fazal 9: v A 1994 (2); v WI 1990 (3); v SL 1991 (3) 1995 (1)
Zahoor Elahi 2: v NZ 1996 (2)
Zakir Khan 2: v In 1989 (1); *v SL 1985 (1)*
Zulfiqar Ahmed 9: v A 1956 (1); v NZ 1955 (3); *v E 1954 (2); v In 1952 (3)*
Zulqarnain 3: v SL 1985 (3)

SRI LANKA

Number of Test cricketers: 86

Ahangama, F. S. 3: v In 1985 (3)
Amalean, K. N. 2: v P 1985 (1); *v A 1987 (1)*
Amerasinghe, A. M. J. G. 2: v NZ 1983 (2)
Anurasiri, S. D. 18: v A 1992 (3); v WI 1993 (1); v NZ 1986 (1) 1992 (2); v P 1985 (2); v Z 1997 (1); *v E 1991 (1); v In 1986 (1) 1993 (3); v P 1991 (3)*
Arnold, R. P. 30: v E 2000 (3); v A 1999 (3); v SA 2000 (3); v In 1998 (1) 2001 (3); v P 1996 (2) 2000 (3); *v SA 2000 (3); v WI 1996 (1); v P 1998 (2) 1999 (3); v Z 1999 (3)*
Atapattu, M. S. 47: v E 2000 (3); v A 1992 (1) 1999 (3); v SA 2000 (3); v NZ 1997 (3); v In 1997 (2) 1998 (1) 2001 (3); v P 1996 (2) 2000 (3); v Z 1997 (2); *v E 1998 (1); v SA 1997 (2) 2000 (3); v WI 1996 (1); v NZ 1996 (1); v In 1990 (1) 1993 (1) 1997 (3); v P 1998 (2) 1999 (3); v Z 1999 (3)*

Bandara, C. M. 1: v NZ 1997
Bandaratilleke, M. R. C. N. 4: v NZ 1997 (3); *v P 1998 (1)*

Chandana, U. D. U. 5: v A 1999 (1); v SA 2000 (3); *v P 1998 (1)*

Dassanayake, P. B. 11: v SA 1993 (3); v WI 1993 (1); v P 1994 (2); *v In 1993 (3); v Z 1994 (2)*
de Alwis, R. G. 11: v A 1982 (1); v NZ 1983 (3); v P 1985 (2); *v A 1987 (1); v NZ 1982 (1); v In 1986 (3)*
de Mel, A. L. F. 17: v E 1981 (1); v A 1982 (1); v In 1985 (3); v P 1985 (3); *v E 1984 (1); v In 1982 (1) 1986 (1); v P 1981 (3) 1985 (3)*
de Saram, S. I. 4: *v P 1999 (1); v Z 1999 (3)*
de Silva, A. M. 3: v E 1992 (1); v In 1993 (2)
de Silva, D. S. 12: v E 1981 (1); v A 1982 (1); v NZ 1983 (3); *v E 1984 (1); v NZ 1982 (2); v In 1982 (1); v P 1981 (3)*
de Silva, E. A. R. 10: v In 1985 (1); v P 1985 (1); *v A 1989 (2); v NZ 1990 (3); v In 1986 (3)*
de Silva, G. R. A. 4: v E 1981 (1); *v In 1982 (1); v P 1981 (2)*
de Silva, K. S. C. 8: v In 1997 (1); v P 1996 (1); *v WI 1996 (2); v NZ 1996 (1); v In 1997 (1); v P 1998 (2)*
de Silva, P. A. 89: v E 1992 (1) 2000 (3); v A 1992 (3) 1999 (3); v SA 1993 (3) 2000 (1); v WI 1993 (1); v NZ 1992 (2) 1997 (3); v In 1985 (3) 1993 (3) 1997 (2) 1998 (1); v P 1985 (3) 1994 (2) 1996 (2) 2000 (3); v Z 1996 (2) 1997 (2); *v E 1984 (1) 1988 (1) 1991 (1) 1998 (1); v A 1987 (1) 1989 (2) 1995 (3); v SA 1997 (2) 2000 (1); v WI 1996 (2); v NZ 1990 (3) 1994 (2) 1996 (2); v In 1986 (3) 1990 (1) 1993 (3) 1997 (3); v P 1985 (3) 1991 (3) 1995 (2) 1998 (1) 1999 (2); v Z 1994 (3)*
de Silva, S. K. L. 3: *v In 1997 (3)*
Dharmasena, H. D. P. K. 25: v E 2000 (2); v SA 1993 (2) 2000 (2); v NZ 1997 (2); v P 1994 (2) 1996 (1) 2000 (1); v Z 1996 (1); *v E 1998 (1); v A 1995 (2); v WI 1996 (2); v NZ 1996 (1); v In 1997 (2); v P 1995 (2); v Z 1994 (2)*
Dias, R. L. 20: v E 1981 (1); v A 1982 (1); v NZ 1983 (2) 1986 (1); v In 1985 (3); v P 1985 (1); *v E 1984 (1); v In 1982 (1) 1986 (3); v P 1981 (3) 1985 (3)*
Dilshan, T. M. 10: v E 2000 (3); *v SA 2000 (2); v P 1999 (2); v Z 1999 (3)*
Dunusinghe, C. I. 5: *v NZ 1994 (2); v P 1995 (3)*

Fernando, E. R. N. S. 5: v A 1982 (1); v NZ 1983 (2); *v NZ 1982 (2)*
Fernando, C. R. D. 9: v E 2000 (2); v In 2001 (3); v P 2000 (1); *v SA 2000 (3)*

Gallage, I. S. 1: *v Z 1999*
Goonatillake, H. M. 5: v E 1981 (1); *v In 1982 (1); v P 1981 (3)*
Gunasekera, Y. 2: *v NZ 1982 (2)*
Gunawardene, D. A. 3: *v SA 2000 (1); v P 1998 (2)*
Guneratne, R. P. W. 1: v A 1982
Gurusinha, A. P. 41: v E 1992 (1); v A 1992 (3); v SA 1993 (1); v NZ 1986 (1) 1992 (2); v In 1993 (3); v P 1985 (2) 1994 (1); v Z 1996 (2); *v E 1991 (1); v A 1989 (2) 1995 (3); v NZ 1990 (3) 1994 (2); v In 1986 (3) 1990 (1); v P 1985 (1) 1991 (3) 1995 (3); v Z 1994 (3)*

Hathurusinghe, U. C. 26: v E 1992 (1); v A 1992 (3); v SA 1993 (3); v NZ 1992 (2); v In 1993 (3) 1998 (1); *v E 1991 (1); v A 1995 (3); v NZ 1990 (2); v P 1991 (3) 1995 (3) 1998 (1)*
Herath, H. M. R. K. B. 3: v A 1999 (2); v P 2000 (1)
Hettiarachchi, D. 1: v E 2000

Jayasekera, R. S. A. 1: *v P 1981*
Jayasuriya S. T. 62: v E 1992 (1) 2000 (3); v A 1992 (2) 1999 (3); v SA 1993 (2) 2000 (3); v WI 1993 (1); v NZ 1997 (3); v In 1993 (1) 1997 (2) 2001 (3); v P 1994 (1) 1996 (2) 2000 (3); v Z 1996 (2) 1997 (2); *v E 1991 (1) 1998 (1); v A 1995 (1); v SA 1997 (2) 2000 (3); v WI 1996 (2); v NZ 1990 (2) 1996 (2); v In 1993 (1) 1997 (3); v P 1991 (3) 1999 (3); v Z 1994 (1) 1999 (3)*
Jayawardene, D. P. M. D. 33: v E 2000 (3); v A 1999 (3); v SA 2000 (3); v NZ 1997 (3); v In 1997 (2) 1998 (1) 2001 (3); v P 2000 (3); *v E 1998 (1); v SA 2000 (3); v P 1998 (2) 1999 (3); v Z 1999 (3)*
Jayawardene, H. A. P. W. 1: v P 2000
Jeganathan, S. 2: *v NZ 1982 (2)*
John, V. B. 6: v NZ 1983 (3); *v E 1984 (1); v NZ 1982 (2)*
Jurangpathy, B. R. 2: v In 1985 (1); *v In 1986 (1)*

Kalpage, R. S. 11: v SA 1993 (1); v WI 1993 (1); v NZ 1997 (1); v In 1993 (1); v P 1994 (1) 1996 (1); *v In 1993 (3); v P 1998 (1); v Z 1994 (1)*
Kaluperuma, L. W. 2: v E 1981 (1); *v P 1981 (1)*
Kaluperuma, S. M. S. 4: v NZ 1983 (3); *v A 1987 (1)*
Kaluwitharana, R. S. 40: v A 1992 (2) 1999 (3); v NZ 1997 (3); v In 1993 (1) 1997 (2) 1998 (1); v P 1996 (2) 2000 (2); v Z 1996 (2) 1997 (2); *v E 1998 (1); A 1995 (3); v SA 1997 (2) 2000 (2); v WI 1996 (2); v NZ 1996 (2); v P 1998 (2) 1999 (3); v Z 1999 (3)*
Kuruppu, D. S. B. P. 4: v NZ 1986 (1); *v E 1988 (1) 1991 (1); v A 1987 (1)*
Kuruppuarachchi, A. K. 2: v NZ 1986 (1); v P 1985 (1)

Labrooy, G. F. 9: *v E 1988 (1); v A 1987 (1) 1989 (2); v NZ 1990 (3); v In 1986 (1) 1990 (1)*
Liyanage, D. K. 9: v A 1992 (2); v SA 1993 (1); v NZ 1992 (2); v In 1993 (2) 2001 (1); *v In 1993 (1)*

Madugalle, R. S. 21: v E 1981 (1); v A 1982 (1); v NZ 1983 (3) 1986 (1); v In 1985 (3); *v E 1984 (1) 1988 (1); v A 1987 (1); v NZ 1982 (2); v In 1982 (1); v P 1981 (3) 1985 (3)*
Madurasinghe, A. W. R. 3: v A 1992 (1); *v E 1988 (1); v In 1990 (1)*
Mahanama, R. S. 52: v E 1992 (1); v A 1992 (3); v SA 1993 (3); v WI 1993 (1); v NZ 1986 (1) 1992 (2); v In 1993 (3) 1997 (2); v P 1985 (2) 1994 (2); v Z 1996 (2) 1997 (2); *v E 1991 (1); v A 1987 (1) 1989 (2) 1995 (2); v SA 1997 (2); v WI 1996 (2); v NZ 1990 (1) 1996 (2); v In 1990 (1) 1993 (3) 1997 (3); v P 1991 (2) 1995 (3); v Z 1994 (3)*
Mendis, L. R. D. 24: v E 1981 (1); v A 1982 (1); v NZ 1983 (3) 1986 (1); v In 1985 (3); v P 1985 (3); *v E 1984 (1) 1988 (1); v In 1982 (1) 1986 (3); v P 1981 (3) 1985 (3)*
Muralitharan, M. 65: v E 1992 (1) 2000 (3); v A 1992 (2) 1999 (3); v SA 1993 (3) 2000 (3); v WI 1993 (1); v NZ 1992 (1) 1997 (3); v In 1993 (2) 1997 (2) 2001 (3); v P 1994 (1) 1996 (1) 2000 (3); v Z 1996 (2) 1997 (2); *v E 1998 (1); v A 1995 (2); v SA 1997 (2) 2000 (2); v WI 1996 (2); v NZ 1994 (2) 1996 (2); v In 1993 (3) 1997 (2); v P 1995 (3) 1999 (3); v Z 1994 (2) 1999 (3)*

Perera, A. S. A. 3: v In 2001 (2); *v E 1998 (1)*
Perera, P. D. R. L. 5: v SA 2000 (1); v In 1998 (1) 2001 (2); *v SA 2000 (1)*
Pushpakumara, K. R. 22: v In 1997 (2); v P 1994 (1) 2000 (1); v Z 1996 (1) 1997 (2); *v A 1995 (1); v SA 1997 (2); v WI 1996 (2); v NZ 1994 (2); v In 1997 (2); v P 1995 (1) 1999 (2); v Z 1994 (2) 1999 (1)*

Ramanayake, C. P. H. 18: v E 1992 (1); v A 1992 (3); v SA 1993 (2); v NZ 1992 (1); v In 1993 (1); *v E 1988 (1) 1991 (1); v A 1987 (1) 1989 (2); v NZ 1990 (3); v P 1991 (2)*
Ranasinghe, A. N. 2: *v In 1982 (1); v P 1981 (1)*
Ranatunga, A. 93: v E 1981 (1) 1992 (1); v A 1982 (1) 1992 (3) 1999 (3) ; v SA 1993 (3) 2000 (3); v WI 1993 (1); v NZ 1983 (3) 1986 (1) 1992 (2) 1997 (3); v In 1985 (3) 1993 (3) 1997 (2) 1998 (1); v P 1985 (3) 1994 (2) 1996 (2) 2000 (3); v Z 1996 (2) 1997 (2); *v E 1984 (1) 1988 (1) 1998 (1); v A 1987 (1) 1989 (2) 1995 (2); v SA 1997 (2); v WI 1996 (2); v NZ 1990 (3) 1994 (2) 1996 (2); v In 1982 (1) 1986 (3) 1990 (1) 1993 (3) 1997 (3); v P 1981 (2) 1985 (3) 1991 (3) 1995 (3) 1999 (1); v Z 1994 (3)*
Ranatunga, D. 2: *v A 1989 (2)*

Ranatunga, S. 9: v P 1994 (1); *v A 1995 (1); v WI 1996 (1); v NZ 1994 (2); v P 1995 (1); v Z 1994 (3)*
Ratnayake, R. J. 23: v A 1982 (1); v NZ 1983 (1) 1986 (1); v In 1985 (3); v P 1985 (1); *v E 1991 (1); v A 1989 (1); v NZ 1982 (2) 1990 (3); v In 1986 (2) 1990 (1); v P 1985 (3) 1991 (3)*
Ratnayeke, J. R. 22: v NZ 1983 (2) 1986 (1); v P 1985 (3); *v E 1984 (1) 1988 (1); v A 1987 (1) 1989 (2); v NZ 1982 (2); v In 1982 (1) 1986 (3); v P 1981 (2) 1985 (3)*

Samarasekera, M. A. R. 4: *v E 1988 (1); v A 1989 (1); v In 1990 (1); v P 1991 (1)*
Samaraweera, D. P. 7: v WI 1993 (1); v P 1994 (1); *v NZ 1994 (2); v In 1993 (3)*
Samaraweera, T. T. 1: v In 2001
Sangakkara, K. 12: v E 2000 (3); v SA 2000 (3); v In 2001 (3); *v SA 2000 (3)*
Senanayake, C. P. 3: *v NZ 1990 (3)*
Silva, K. J. 7: v In 1997 (1); v P 1996 (1); v Z 1996 (2) 1997 (1); *v A 1995 (1); v In 1997 (1)*
Silva, S. A. R. 9: v In 1985 (3); v P 1985 (1); *v E 1984 (1) 1988 (1); v NZ 1982 (1); v P 1985 (2)*

Tillekeratne, H. P. 59: v E 1992 (1); v A 1992 (1); v SA 1993 (3); v WI 1993 (1); v NZ 1992 (2) 1997 (2); v In 1993 (3) 1998 (1) 2001 (3); v P 1994 (2) 1996 (2); v Z 1996 (2) 1997 (2); *v E 1991 (1) 1998 (1); v A 1989 (1) 1995 (3); v SA 1997 (2); v WI 1996 (1); v NZ 1990 (3) 1994 (2) 1996 (2); v In 1990 (1) 1993 (3) 1997 (3); v P 1991 (3) 1995 (3) 1998 (2); v Z 1994 (3)*

Upashantha, K. E. A. 1: v In 1998

Vaas, W. P. U. J. C. 51: v E 2000 (3); v A 1999 (3); v SA 2000 (3); v In 1997 (2) 1998 (1) 2001 (3); v P 1994 (1) 1996 (2) 2000 (3); v Z 1996 (2) 1997 (2); *v A 1995 (3); v SA 1997 (1) 2000 (2); v NZ 1994 (2) 1996 (2); v In 1997 (3); v P 1995 (3) 1998 (1) 1999 (3); v Z 1994 (3) 1999 (3)*

Warnapura, B. 4: v E 1981 (1); *v In 1982 (1); v P 1981 (2)*
Warnaweera, K. P. J. 10: v E 1992 (1); v NZ 1992 (2); v In 1993 (3); v P 1985 (1) 1994 (1); *v NZ 1990 (1); v In 1990 (1)*
Weerasinghe, C. D. U. S. 1: v In 1985
Wettimuny, M. D. 2: *v NZ 1982 (2)*
Wettimuny, S. 23: v E 1981 (1); v A 1982 (1); v NZ 1983 (3); v In 1985 (3); v P 1985 (3); *v E 1984 (1); v NZ 1982 (2); v In 1986 (3); v P 1981 (3) 1985 (3)*
Wickremasinghe, A. G. D. 3: v NZ 1992 (2); *v A 1989 (1)*
Wickremasinghe, G. P. 40: v A 1992 (1); v SA 1993 (2); v WI 1993 (1); v NZ 1997 (3); v In 1993 (2); v P 1994 (1); *v E 1998 (1); v A 1995 (3); v SA 1997 (2) 2000 (1); v NZ 1994 (2) 1996 (1); v In 1993 (3) 1997 (1); v P 1991 (3) 1995 (3) 1998 (2) 1999 (3); v Z 1994 (2) 1999 (3)*
Wijegunawardene, K. I. W. 2: *v E 1991 (1); v P 1991 (1)*
Wijesuriya, R. G. C. E. 4: *v P 1981 (1) 1985 (3)*
Wijetunge, P. K. 1: v SA 1993

Zoysa, D. N. T. 17: v E 2000 (1); v A 1999 (3); v SA 2000 (2); v P 1996 (1) 2000 (2); *v SA 1997 (1) 2000 (3); v NZ 1996 (2); v P 1999 (1); v Z 1999 (1)*

ZIMBABWE

Number of Test cricketers: 53

Arnott, K. J. 4: v NZ 1992 (2); v In 1992 (1); *v In 1992 (1)*

Blignaut, A. M. 6: v WI 2001 (2); v In 2001 (2); v B 2000 (2)
Brain, D. H. 9: v NZ 1992 (1); v P 1994 (3); v SL 1994 (2); *v In 1992 (1); v P 1993 (2)*
Brandes, E. A. 10: v E 1996 (1); v NZ 1992 (1); v In 1992 (1); v SL 1999 (1); *v NZ 1995 (2); v In 1992 (1); v P 1993 (3)*
Brent, G. B. 2: v SL 1999 (2)
Briant, G. A. 1: *v In 1992*
Bruk-Jackson, G. K. 2: *v P 1993 (2)*

Burmester, M. G. 3: v NZ 1992 (2); v In 1992 (1)
Butchart, I. P. 1: v P 1994

Campbell, A. D. R. 54: v E 1996 (2); v A 1999 (1); v SA 1995 (1) 1999 (1); v WI 2001 (2); v NZ 1992 (2) 1997 (2) 2000 (2); v In 1992 (1) 1998 (1) 2001 (2); v P 1994 (3) 1997 (2); v SL 1994 (3) 1999 (3); v B 2000 (2); *v E 2000 (2); v SA 1999 (1); v WI 1999 (2); v NZ 1995 (2) 1997 (2) 2000 (1); v In 1992 (1) 2000 (2); v P 1993 (3) 1996 (2) 1998 (2); v SL 1996 (2) 1997 (2)*
Carlisle, S. V. 19: v E 1996 (1); v WI 2001 (1); v NZ 2000 (2); v In 2001 (2); v P 1994 (3); v B 2000 (2); *v E 2000 (1); v WI 1999 (2); v NZ 1995 (2) 2000 (1); v In 2000 (2)*
Crocker, G. J. 3: v NZ 1992 (2); v In 1992 (1)

Dekker, M. H. 14: v E 1996 (1); v SA 1995 (1); v P 1994 (2); v SL 1994 (3); *v P 1993 (3) 1996 (2); v SL 1996 (2)*

Ebrahim, D. D. 6: v WI 2001 (2); v In 2001 (2); v B 2000 (2)
Evans, C. N. 2: v In 1998 (1); *v SL 1996 (1)*

Flower, A. 52: v E 1996 (2); v A 1999 (1); v SA 1995 (1) 1999 (1); v NZ 1992 (2) 1997 (2) 2000 (2); v In 1992 (1) 1998 (1) 2001 (2); v P 1994 (3) 1997 (2); v SL 1994 (3) 1999 (3); v B 2000 (2); *v E 2000 (2); v SA 1999 (1); v WI 1999 (2); v NZ 1995 (2) 1997 (2) 2000 (1); v In 1992 (1) 2000 (2); v P 1993 (3) 1996 (2) 1998 (2); v SL 1996 (2) 1997 (2)*
Flower, G. W. 52: v E 1996 (2); v A 1999 (1); v SA 1995 (1) 1999 (1); v WI 2001 (2); v NZ 1992 (2) 1997 (2) 2000 (2); v In 1992 (1) 2001 (2); v P 1994 (3) 1997 (2); v SL 1994 (3) 1999 (3); v B 2000 (2); *v E 2000 (2); v SA 1999 (1); v WI 1999 (2); v NZ 1995 (2) 1997 (2); v In 1992 (1) 2000 (2); v P 1993 (3) 1996 (2) 1998 (2); v SL 1996 (2) 1997 (2)*
Friend, T. J. 1: v In 2001

Goodwin, M. W. 19: v A 1999 (1); v SA 1999 (1); v In 1998 (1); v P 1997 (2); v SL 1999 (3); *v E 2000 (2); v SA 1999 (1); v WI 1999 (2); v NZ 1997 (2); v P 1998 (2); v SL 1997 (2)*
Gripper, T. R. 7: v A 1999 (1); v SA 1999 (1); v SL 1999 (1); *v E 2000 (1); v SA 1999 (1); v WI 1999 (2)*

Houghton, D. L. 22: v E 1996 (2); v SA 1995 (1); v NZ 1992 (2) 1997 (2); v In 1992 (1); v P 1994 (3); v SL 1994 (3); *v NZ 1995 (2); v In 1992 (1); v P 1993 (3) 1996 (2)*
Huckle, A. G. 8: v NZ 1997 (2); v In 1998 (1); v P 1997 (1); *v NZ 1997 (2); v P 1998 (1); v SL 1997 (1)*

James, W. R. 4: v SL 1994 (3); *v P 1993 (1)*
Jarvis, M. P. 5: v NZ 1992 (1); v In 1992 (1); v SL 1994 (3)
Johnson, N. C. 13: v A 1999 (1); v SA 1999 (1); v In 1998 (1); v SL 1999 (3); *v E 2000 (2); v SA 1999 (1); v WI 1999 (2); v P 1998 (2)*

Lock, A. C. I. 1: v SA 1995

Madondo, T. N. 3: v P 1997 (2); *v NZ 2000 (1)*
Marillier, D. A. 1: *v NZ 2000*
Masakadza, H. 1: v WI 2001
Matambanadzo, E. Z. 3: v NZ 1997 (1); v SL 1999 (1); *v P 1996 (1)*
Mbangwa, M. 15: v SA 1999 (1); v NZ 2000 (1); v In 1998 (1); v P 1997 (2); *v E 2000 (2); v SA 1999 (1); v WI 1999 (1); v NZ 1997 (2); v P 1996 (1) 1998 (2); v SL 1997 (1)*
Murphy, B. A. 10: v In 2001 (2); v B 2000 (1); *v E 2000 (2); v WI 1999 (2); v NZ 2000 (1); v In 2000 (2)*
Mutendera, D. T. 1: v NZ 2000

Nkala, M. L. 6: v NZ 2000 (2); v B 2000 (2); *v E 2000 (1); v In 2000 (1)*

Olonga, H. K. 23: v E 1996 (2); v A 1999 (1); v SA 1999 (1); v NZ 2000 (1); v In 1998 (1) 2001 (1); v P 1994 (1); v SL 1999 (3); *v SA 1999 (1); v WI 1999 (2); v NZ 1995 (1) 2000 (1); v In 2000 (2); v P 1996 (1) 1998 (2); v SL 1996 (2)*

Peall, S. G. 4: v SL 1994 (2); *v P 1993 (2)*

Price, R. W. 4: v WI 2001 (2); v SL 1999 (1); v B 2000 (1)
Pycroft, A. J. 3: v NZ 1992 (2); v In 1992 (1)

Ranchod, U. 1: *v In 1992*
Rennie, G. J. 19: v A 1999 (1); v SA 1999 (1); v NZ 1997 (2) 2000 (2); v In 1998 (1); v P 1997 (1); v SL 1999 (1); *v SA 1999 (1); v NZ 1997 (2) 2000 (1); v In 2000 (2); v P 1998 (2); v SL 1997 (2)*
Rennie, J. A. 4: v NZ 1997 (1); v SL 1994 (1); *v P 1993 (2)*

Shah, A. H. 3: v NZ 1992 (1); *v In 1992 (1); v SL 1996 (1)*
Strang, B. C. 26: v E 1996 (1); v A 1999 (1); v SA 1995 (1) 1999 (1); v WI 2001 (2); v NZ 1997 (2) 2000 (1); v P 1994 (2) 1997 (1); v SL 1999 (3); *v E 2000 (1); v SA 1999 (1); v WI 1999 (1); v NZ 1995 (2) 2000 (1); v In 2000 (1); v P 1996 (2); v SL 1996 (1) 1997 (1)*
Strang, P. A. 23: v E 1996 (2); v SA 1995 (1); v NZ 1997 (2) 2000 (2); v P 1994 (3) 1997 (1); v SL 1994 (1); *v NZ 1995 (2) 1997 (2); v In 2000 (1); v P 1996 (2); v SL 1996 (2) 1997 (2)*
Streak, H. H. 42: v E 1996 (2); v A 1999 (1); v SA 1995 (1); v WI 2001 (2); v NZ 1997 (2) 2000 (2); v In 1998 (1) 2001 (2); v P 1994 (3) 1997 (2); v SL 1994 (3); v B 2000 (2); *v E 2000 (2); v WI 1999 (2); v NZ 1995 (2) 1997 (2) 2000 (1); v In 2000 (2); v P 1993 (3) 1998 (2); v SL 1996 (1) 1997 (2)*

Taibu, T. 2: v WI 2001 (2)
Traicos, A. J. 4: v NZ 1992 (2); v In 1992 (1); *v In 1992 (1)*

Viljoen, D. P. 2: v P 1997 (1); *v In 2000 (1)*

Waller, A. C. 2: v E 1996 (2)
Watambwa, B. T. 4: v In 2001 (2); v B 2000 (2)
Whittall, A. R. 10: v P 1997 (1); v SL 1999 (1); *v NZ 1997 (2); v P 1996 (1) 1998 (1); v SL 1996 (2) 1997 (2)*
Whittall, G. J. 43: v E 1996 (2); v A 1999 (1); v SA 1995 (1) 1999 (1); v WI 2001 (2); v NZ 1997 (2) 2000 (1); v In 2001 (2); v P 1994 (3) 1997 (2); v SL 1994 (3) 1999 (3); v B 2000 (2); *v E 2000 (2); v SA 1999 (1); v NZ 1995 (2) 1997 (2) 2000 (1); v In 2000 (2); v P 1993 (3) 1996 (2); v SL 1996 (2) 1997 (1)*
Wishart, C. B. 15: v SA 1995 (1); v WI 2001 (2); v NZ 2000 (1); v In 1998 (1); v SL 1999 (1); *v NZ 1995 (1); v P 1996 (2) 1998 (2); v SL 1996 (2) 1997 (2)*

BANGLADESH

Number of Test cricketers: 16

Akram Khan 4: v In 2000 (1); *v P 2001 (1); v Z 2000 (2)*
Al-Shahriar Rokon 2: v In 2000 (1); *v Z 2000 (1)*
Aminul Islam, sen. 4: v In 2000 (1); *v P 2001 (1); v Z 2000 (2)*
Bikash Ranjan Das 1: v In 2000
Enamul Haque 2: *v P 2001 (1); v Z 2000 (1)*
Habibul Bashar 4: v In 2000 (1); *v P 2001 (1); v Z 2000 (2)*
Hasibul Hussain 3: v In 2000 (1); *v P 2001 (1); v Z 2000 (1)*
Javed Omar 3: *v P 2001 (1); v Z 2000 (2)*
Khaled Masud 3: v In 2000 (1); *v P 2001 (1); v Z 2000 (1)*
Manjurul Islam 3: *v P 2001 (1); v Z 2000 (2)*
Mehrab Hossain 4: v In 2000 (1); *v P 2001 (1); v Z 2000 (2)*
Mohammad Rafiq 1: v In 2000
Mohammad Sharif 3: *v P 2001 (1); v Z 2000 (2)*
Mushfiqur Rehman 2: *v Z 2000 (2)*
Naimur Rahman 4: v In 2000 (1); *v P 2001 (1); v Z 2000 (2)*
Shahriar Hossain 1: v In 2000

TWO COUNTRIES

Fourteen cricketers have appeared for two countries in Test matches, namely:

Amir Elahi, *India and Pakistan.*
J. J. Ferris, *Australia and England.*
S. C. Guillen, *West Indies and NZ.*
Gul Mahomed, *India and Pakistan.*
F. Hearne, *England and South Africa.*
A. H. Kardar, *India and Pakistan.*
W. E. Midwinter, *England and Australia.*
F. Mitchell, *England and South Africa.*
W. L. Murdoch, *Australia and England.*
Nawab of Pataudi, sen., *England and India.*
A. J. Traicos, *South Africa and Zimbabwe.*
A. E. Trott, *Australia and England.*
K. C. Wessels, *Australia and South Africa.*
S. M. J. Woods, *Australia and England.*

ENGLAND v REST OF THE WORLD

In 1970, owing to the cancellation of the South African tour to England, a series of matches was arranged, with the trappings of a full Test series, between England and the Rest of the World. It was played for the Guinness Trophy.

The following were awarded England caps for playing against the Rest of the World in that series, although the five matches played are now generally considered not to have rated as full Tests: D. L. Amiss (1), G. Boycott (2), D. J. Brown (2), M. C. Cowdrey (4), M. H. Denness (1), B. L. D'Oliveira (4), J. H. Edrich (2), K. W. R. Fletcher (4), A. W. Greig (3), R. Illingworth (5), A. Jones (1), A. P. E. Knott (5), P. Lever (1), B. W. Luckhurst (5), C. M. Old (2), P. J. Sharpe (1), K. Shuttleworth (1), J. A. Snow (5), D. L. Underwood (3), A. Ward (1), D. Wilson (2).

The following players represented the Rest of the World: E. J. Barlow (5), F. M. Engineer (2), L. R. Gibbs (4), Intikhab Alam (5), R. B. Kanhai (5), C. H. Lloyd (5), G. D. McKenzie (3), D. L. Murray (3), Mushtaq Mohammad (2), P. M. Pollock (1), R. G. Pollock (5), M. J. Procter (5), B. A. Richards (5), G. S. Sobers (5).

LIMITED-OVERS INTERNATIONAL CRICKETERS

The following players have appeared for Test-playing countries in limited-overs internationals but had not represented their countries in Test matches by September 2, 2001:

England M. W. Alleyne, I. D. Austin, A. D. Brown, D. R. Brown, M. V. Fleming, P. J. Franks, I. J. Gould, A. P. Grayson, G. W. Humpage, T. E. Jesty, G. D. Lloyd, J. D. Love, M. A. Lynch, M. J. Smith, N. M. K. Smith, V. S. Solanki, G. P. Swann, S. D. Udal, C. M. Wells, V. J. Wells.

Australia G. A. Bishop, N. W. Bracken, M. J. Di Venuto, S. F. Graf, B. J. Haddin, I. J. Harvey, S. Lee, R. J. McCurdy, K. H. MacLeay, J. P. Maher, G. D. Porter, J. D. Siddons, A. M. Stuart, A. Symonds, G. S. Trimble, B. E. Young, A. K. Zesers.

South Africa S. Abrahams, D. M. Benkenstein, R. E. Bryson, D. J. Callaghan, D. N. Crookes, A. C. Dawson, A. J. Hall, L. J. Koen, P. V. Mpitsang, A. Nel, J. L. Ontong, S. J. Palframan, N. Pothas, C. E. B. Rice, M. J. R. Rindel, D. B. Rundle, T. G. Shaw, E. O. Simons, E. L. R. Stewart, R. Telemachus, C. J. P. G. van Zyl, H. S. Williams, C. M. Willoughby, M. Yachad.

West Indies H. A. G. Anthony, B. St A. Browne, H. R. Bryan, V. C. Drakes, R. S. Gabriel, R. C. Haynes, K. C. B. Jeremy, S. C. Joseph, M. R. Pydanna, K. F. Semple, C. M. Tuckett, L. R. Williams.

New Zealand A. R. Adams, M. D. Bailey, B. R. Blair, C. E. Bulfin, P. G. Coman, M. W. Douglas, B. G. Hadlee, R. T. Hart, R. L. Hayes, L. G. Howell, B. J. McKechnie, E. B. McSweeney, J. P. Millmow, K. D. Mills, C. J. Nevin, J. D. P. Oram, A. J. Penn, R. G. Petrie, R. B. Reid, S. J. Roberts, L. W. Stott, S. B. Styris, G. P. Sulzberger, A. R. Tait, L. Vincent, R. J. Webb, J. W. Wilson, W. A. Wisneski.

India A. C. Bedade, A. Bhandari, Bhupinder Singh, sen., G. Bose, V. B. Chandrasekhar, U. Chatterjee, N. A. David, P. Dharmani, R. S. Ghai, S. C. Khanna, G. K. Khoda, A. R. Khurasiya, T. Kumaran, J. J. Martin, D. Mongia, S. P. Mukherjee, G. K. Pandey, J. V. Paranjpe, A. K. Patel, Randhir Singh, S. S. Raul, V. Sehwag, L. R. Shukla, R. P. Singh, R. S. Sodhi, S. Somasunder, S. Sriram, Sudhakar Rao, P. S. Vaidya, Yuvraj Singh.

Pakistan Aamer Hameed, Aamer Hanif, Akhtar Sarfraz, Arshad Pervez, Asif Mahmood, Ghulam Ali, Haafiz Shahid, Hasan Jamil, Imran Abbas, Iqbal Sikandar, Irfan Bhatti, Javed Qadir, Kashif Raza, Mahmood Hamid, Mansoor Rana, Manzoor Akhtar, Maqsood Rana, Masood Iqbal, Moin-ul-Atiq, Mujahid Jamshed, Naeem Ahmed, Naeem Ashraf, Naseer Malik, Parvez Mir, Saadat Ali, Saeed Azad, Sajid Ali, Sajjad Akbar, Salim Pervez, Shabbir Ahmed, Shahid Anwar, Shakil Khan, Sohail Fazal, Tanvir Mehdi, Wasim Haider, Yasir Arafat, Zafar Iqbal, Zahid Ahmed.

Sri Lanka J. W. H. D. Boteju, D. L. S. de Silva, G. N. de Silva, E. R. Fernando, T. L. Fernando, U. N. K. Fernando, J. C. Gamage, W. C. A. Ganegama, F. R. M. Goonatillake, A. A. W. Gunawardene, P. D. Heyn, S. A. Jayasinghe, S. H. U. Karnain, C. Mendis, A. M. N. Munasinghe, M. N. Nawaz, A. R. M. Opatha, S. P. Pasqual, K. G. Perera, H. S. M. Pieris, S. K. Ranasinghe, N. Ranatunga, N. L. K. Ratnayake, L. P. C. Silva, A. P. B. Tennekoon, M. H. Tissera, D. M. Vonhagt, A. P. Weerakkody, K. Weeraratne, S. R. de S. Wettimuny, R. P. A. H. Wickremaratne.

Zimbabwe R. D. Brown, K. M. Curran, S. G. Davies, K. G. Duers, E. A. Essop-Adam, D. A. G. Fletcher, J. G. Heron, V. R. Hogg, A. J. Mackay, G. C. Martin, M. A. Meman, G. A. Paterson, G. E. Peckover, P. W. E. Rawson, M. A. Vermeulen.

Bangladesh Ahmed Kamal, Alam Talukdar, Aminul Islam, jun., Anisur Rahman, Ather Ali Khan, Azhar Hussain, Faruq Ahmed, Faruq Chowdhury, Gazi Ashraf, Ghulam Faruq, Ghulam Nausher, Hafizur Rahman, Harunur Rashid, Jahangir Alam, Jahangir Badshah, Khaled Mahmud, Mafizur Rahman, Mahbubur Rahman, Minhazul Abedin, Mohammad Ashraful, Morshed Ali Khan, Nasir Ahmed, Neeyamur Rashid, Nurul Abedin, Rafiqul Alam, Raqibul Hassan, Saiful Islam, Sajjad Ahmed, Samiur Rahman, Sanuar Hossain, Shafiuddin Ahmed, Shahidur Rahman, Shariful Haq, Sheikh Salahuddin, Wahidul Gani, Zahid Razzak, Zakir Hassan.

A. C. Gilchrist appeared for Australia in 76 limited-overs internationals before making his Test debut.

SIR PAUL GETTY'S XI RESULTS, 2001

Matches 11: Won 6, Lost 1, Drawn 4. Abandoned 1.

May 6	Eton Ramblers	Drawn
May 13	Cambridge University	Won by four wickets
May 27	Oxford UCCE	Won by 43 runs
June 5	Honourable Artillery Company	Won by six wickets
June 13	Pilgrims	Abandoned
July 1	Arabs	Drawn
July 11	MCC	Won by seven wickets
July 25	Melbourne CC	Drawn
July 29	I Zingari	Won by two wickets
August 12	Combined Services	Drawn
September 9	Willow Warblers	Lost by 92 runs
September 16	Gaieties	Won by 107 runs

At Wormsley on July 17, Old England drew with Old Australia.

BIRTHS AND DEATHS OF PAST CRICKETERS

Details of current first-class players are no longer listed in this section but may be found in the Register of Players on pages 164–184.

The qualifications for inclusion are as follows:

1. All players who have appeared in a Test match and are no longer playing first-class cricket.

2. All players who have appeared in a one-day international for a Test-match playing country and are no longer playing first-class cricket.

3. County players who appeared in 200 or more first-class matches during their careers, or 100 after the Second World War, and are no longer playing first-class cricket.

4. English county captains who captained their county in three seasons or more since 1890 and are no longer playing first-class cricket.

5. All *Wisden* Cricketers of the Year who are no longer playing first-class cricket, including the Public Schoolboys chosen for the 1918 and 1919 Almanacks. Cricketers of the Year are identified by the italic notation *CY* and year of appearance. A list of the Cricketers of the Year from 1889 to 2002 appears on pages 185–187.

6. Players or personalities not otherwise qualified who are thought to be of sufficient interest to merit inclusion.

Key to abbreviations and symbols

CU – Cambridge University, OU – Oxford University.

Australian states: NSW – New South Wales, Qld – Queensland, S. Aust. – South Australia, Tas. – Tasmania, Vic. – Victoria, W. Aust. – Western Australia.

Indian teams: Eur. – Europeans, Guj. – Gujarat, H'bad – Hyderabad, H. Pradesh – Himachal Pradesh, Ind. Rlwys – Indian Railways, Ind. Serv. – Indian Services, J/K – Jammu and Kashmir, Karn. – Karnataka (Mysore to 1972-73), M. Pradesh – Madhya Pradesh (Central India [C. Ind.] to 1939-40, Holkar to 1954-55, Madhya Bharat to 1956-57), M'tra – Maharashtra, Naw. – Nawanagar, Raja. – Rajasthan, S'tra – Saurashtra (West India [W. Ind.] to 1945-46, Kathiawar to 1949-50), S. Punjab – Southern Punjab (Patiala to 1958-59, Punjab since 1968-69), TC – Travancore-Cochin (Kerala since 1956-57), TN – Tamil Nadu (Madras to 1959-60), U. Pradesh – Uttar Pradesh (United Provinces [U. Prov.] to 1948-49), Vidarbha (CP & Berar to 1949-50, Madhya Pradesh to 1956-57).

New Zealand provinces: Auck. – Auckland, Cant. – Canterbury, C. Dist. – Central Districts, N. Dist. – Northern Districts, Wgtn – Wellington.

Pakistani teams: ADBP – Agricultural Development Bank of Pakistan, B'pur – Bahawalpur, Customs – Pakistan Customs, F'bad – Faisalabad, HBFC – House Building Finance Corporation, HBL – Habib Bank Ltd, I'bad – Islamabad, IDBP – Industrial Development Bank of Pakistan, Kar. – Karachi, KRL – Khan Research Laboratories, MCB – Muslim Commercial Bank, NBP – National Bank of Pakistan, NWFP – North-West Frontier Province, PACO – Pakistan Automobile Corporation, Pak. Rlwys – Pakistan Railways, Pak. Us – Pakistan Universities, PIA – Pakistan International Airlines, PNSC – Pakistan National Shipping Corporation, PWD – Public Works Department, R'pindi – Rawalpindi, UBL – United Bank Ltd, WAPDA – Water and Power Development Authority.

South African provinces: E. Prov. – Eastern Province, E. Tvl – Eastern Transvaal (Easterns since 1995-96), Griq. W. – Griqualand West, N. Tvl – Northern Transvaal (Northerns since 1997-98), NE Tvl – North-Eastern Transvaal, OFS – Orange Free State (Free State [FS] since 1995-96), Rhod. – Rhodesia, Tvl – Transvaal (Gauteng since 1997-98), W. Prov. – Western Province, W. Tvl – Western Transvaal (North West since 1996-97).

Sri Lankan teams: Ant. – Antonians, Bloom. – Bloomfield Cricket and Athletic Club, BRC – Burgher Recreation Club, CCC – Colombo Cricket Club, Mor. – Moratuwa Sports Club, NCC – Nondescripts Cricket Club, Pan. – Panadura Sports Club, Seb. – Sebastianites, SLAF – Air Force, SSC – Sinhalese Sports Club, TU – Tamil Union Cricket and Athletic Club, Under-23 – Board Under-23 XI, WPC – Western Province (City), WPN – Western Province (North), WPS – Western Province (South).

West Indies islands: B'dos – Barbados, BG – British Guiana (Guyana since 1966), Comb. Is. – Combined Islands, Jam. – Jamaica, T/T – Trinidad & Tobago.

Zimbabwean teams: Mash. – Mashonaland, Mat. – Matabeleland, MCD – Mashonaland Country Districts, Under-24 – Mashonaland Under-24, Zimb. – Zimbabwe.

* *Denotes Test player.* ** *Denotes appeared for two countries. There is a list of Test players country by country on pages 58–118.*
† *Denotes also played for team under its previous name.*

Aamer Hameed (Pak. Us, Lahore, Punjab & OU) b Oct. 18, 1954
*Aamer Malik (ADBP, PIA, Multan & Lahore) b Jan. 3, 1963
Abberley, R. N. (Warwicks) b April 22, 1944
*a'Beckett, E. L. (Vic.) b Aug. 11, 1907, d June 2, 1989
*Abdul Kadir (Kar. & NBP) b May 10, 1944
*Abdul Qadir (HBL, Lahore & Punjab) b Sept. 15, 1955
*Abel, R. (Surrey; *CY 1890*) b Nov. 30, 1857, d Dec. 10, 1936
*Abid Ali, S. (H'bad) b Sept. 9, 1941
Abrahams, J. (Lancs) b July 21, 1952
*Absolom, C. A. (CU & Kent) b June 7, 1846, d July 30, 1889
Acfield, D. L. (CU & Essex) b July 24, 1947
*Achong, E. (T/T) b Feb. 16, 1904, d Aug. 29, 1986
Ackerman, H. M. (Border, NE Tvl, Northants, Natal & W. Prov.) b April 28, 1947
Adams, P. W. (Cheltenham & Sussex; *CY 1919*) b Sept. 5, 1900, d Sept. 28, 1962
*Adcock, N. A. T. (Tvl & Natal; *CY 1961*) b March 8, 1931
*Adhikari, H. R. (Guj., Baroda & Ind. Serv.) b July 31, 1919
*Afaq Hussain (Kar., Pak Us, PIA & PWD) b Dec. 31, 1939
Afford, J. A. (Notts) b May 12, 1964
*Aftab Baloch (PWD, Kar., Sind, NBP & PIA) b April 1, 1953
*Aftab Gul (Punjab U., Pak. Us & Lahore) b March 31, 1946
*Agha Saadat Ali (Pak. Us, Punjab, B'pur & Lahore) b June 21, 1929, d Oct. 26, 1995
*Agha Zahid (Pak Us, Punjab, Lahore & HBL) b Jan. 7, 1953
*Agnew, J. P. (Leics; *CY 1988;* broadcaster) b April 4, 1960
*Ahangama, F. S. (SSC) b Sept. 14, 1959
Aird, R. (CU & Hants; Sec. MCC 1953–62, Pres. MCC 1968–69) b May 4, 1902, d Aug. 16, 1986
Aislabie, B. (Surrey, Hants, Kent & Sussex; Sec. MCC 1822–42) b Jan. 14, 1774, d June 2, 1842
Aitchison, Rev. J. K. (Scotland) b May 26, 1920, d Feb. 13, 1994
*Alabaster, J. C. (Otago) b July 11, 1930
Alcock, C. W. (Sec. Surrey CCC 1872–1907; Editor *Cricket* 1882–1907) b Dec. 2, 1842, d Feb. 26, 1907
Alderman, A. E. (Derbys) b Oct. 30, 1907, d June 4, 1990
*Alderman, T. M. (W. Aust., Kent & Glos; *CY 1982*) b June 12, 1956
*Alexander, F. C. M. (CU & Jam.) b Nov. 2, 1928
*Alexander, G. (Vic.) b April 22, 1851, d Nov. 6, 1930
*Alexander, H. H. (Vic.) b June 9, 1905, d April 15, 1993
Alexander, Lord (Pres. MCC 2000–01) b Sept. 5, 1936
*Ali Hussain Rizvi (Kar. & Customs) by Jan. 6, 1974
Alikhan, R. I. (Sussex, PIA, Surrey & PNSC) b Dec. 28, 1962
*Alim-ud-Din (Rajputana, Guj., Sind, B'pur, Kar. & PWD) b Dec. 15, 1930
*Allan, D. W. (B'dos) b Nov. 5, 1937
*Allan, F. E. (Vic.) b Dec. 2, 1849, d Feb. 9, 1917
Allan, J. M. (OU, Kent, Warwicks & Scotland) b April 2, 1932
*Allan, P. J. (Qld) b Dec. 31, 1935
*Allcott, C. F. W. (Auck.) b Oct. 7, 1896, d Nov. 19, 1973
Allen, B. O. (CU & Glos) b Oct. 13, 1911, d May 1, 1981
*Allen, D. A. (Glos) b Oct. 29, 1935
*Allen, Sir George O. B. (CU & Middx; Pres. MCC 1963–64) b July 31, 1902, d Nov. 29, 1989
*Allen, I. B. A. (Windwards) b Oct. 6, 1965
Allen, M. H. J. (Northants & Derbys) b Jan. 7, 1933, d Oct. 6, 1995
*Allen, R. C. (NSW) b July 2, 1858, d May 2, 1952

Alletson, E. B. (Notts) b March 6, 1884, d July 5, 1963
Alley, W. E. (NSW & Som; Test umpire; *CY 1962*) b Feb. 3, 1919
*Allom, M. J. C. (CU & Surrey; Pres. MCC 1969–70) b March 23, 1906, d April 8, 1995
*Allott, P. J. W. (Lancs & Wgtn) b Sept. 14, 1956
Altham, H. S. CBE (OU, Surrey & Hants; historian; Pres. MCC 1959–60) b Nov. 30, 1888, d March 11, 1965
*Amalean, K. N. (SL) b April 7, 1965
*Amarnath, Lala (N. B.) (N. Ind., S. Punjab, Guj., Patiala, U. Pradesh & Ind. Rlwys) b Sept. 11, 1911, d Aug. 5, 2000
*Amarnath, M. (Punjab & Delhi; *CY 1984*) b Sept. 24, 1950
*Amarnath, S. (Punjab & Delhi) b Dec. 30, 1948
*Amar Singh, L. (Patiala, W. Ind. & Naw.) b Dec. 4, 1910, d May 20, 1940
*Ambrose, C. E. L. (Leewards & Northants; *CY 1992*) b Sept. 21, 1963
*Amerasinghe, A. M. J. G. (Nomads & Ant.) b Feb. 2, 1954
*Ames, L. E. G. CBE (Kent; *CY 1929*) b Dec. 3, 1905, d Feb. 26, 1990
**Amir Elahi (Baroda, N. Ind., S. Punjab & B'pur) b Sept. 1, 1908, d Dec. 28, 1980
*Amiss, D. L. MBE (Warwicks; *CY 1975*) b April 7, 1943
Anderson, I. S. (Derbys & Boland) b April 24, 1960
*Anderson, J. H. (W. Prov.) b April 26, 1874, d March 11, 1926
*Anderson, R. W. (Cant., N. Dist., Otago & C. Dist.) b Oct. 2, 1948
*Anderson, W. M. (Cant.) b Oct. 8, 1919, d Dec. 21, 1979
*Andrew, K. V. (Northants) b Dec. 15, 1929
Andrew, S. J. W. (Hants & Essex) b Jan. 27, 1966
*Andrews, B. (Cant., C. Dist. & Otago) b April 4, 1945
*Andrews, T. J. E. (NSW) b Aug. 26, 1890, d Jan. 28, 1970
Andrews, W. H. R. (Som) b April 14, 1908, d Jan. 9, 1989
Angell, F. L. (Som) b June 29, 1922
*Anil Dalpat (Kar. & PIA) b Sept. 20, 1963
Anisur Rehman (Bangladesh) b March 1, 1971
*Ankola, S. A. (M'tra & †Mumbai) b March 1, 1968
Anthony, H. A. G. (Leewards & Glam) b Jan 16, 1971
*Anurasiri, S. D. (Pan. & WPS) b Feb. 25, 1966
*Anwar Hussain (N. Ind., Bombay, Sind & Kar.) b July 16, 1920
*Anwar Khan (Kar., Sind & NBP) b Dec. 24, 1955
*Appleyard, R. (Yorks; *CY 1952*) b June 27, 1924
*Apte, A. L. (Ind. Us, Bombay & Raja.) b Oct. 24, 1934
*Apte, M. L. (Bombay & Bengal) b Oct. 5, 1932
*Archer, A. G. (Worcs) b Dec. 6, 1871, d July 15, 1935
Archer, G. F. (Notts) b Sept. 26, 1970
*Archer, K. A. (Qld) b Jan. 17, 1928
*Archer, R. G. (Qld) b Oct. 25, 1933
*Arif Butt (Lahore & Pak. Rlwys) b May 17, 1944
Arlott, John OBE (Writer & broadcaster) b Feb. 25, 1914, d Dec. 14, 1991
*Armitage, T. (Yorks) b April 25, 1848, d Sept. 21, 1922
Armstrong, N. F. (Leics) b Dec. 22, 1892, d Jan. 19, 1990
*Armstrong, W. W. (Vic.; *CY 1903*) b May 22, 1879, d July 13, 1947
Arnold, A. P. (Cant. & Northants) b Oct. 16, 1926
*Arnold, E. G. (Worcs) b Nov. 7, 1876, d Oct. 25, 1942
*Arnold, G. G. (Surrey & Sussex; *CY 1972*) b Sept. 3, 1944
*Arnold, J. (Hants) b Nov. 30, 1907, d April 4, 1984
Arnott, D. B. (Rhod.; ICC referee) b March 3, 1936
*Arnott, K. J. (MCD) b March 8, 1961
Arnott, T. (Glam) b Feb. 16, 1902, d Feb. 2, 1975
*Arshad Ayub (H'bad) b Aug. 2, 1958
Arshad Pervez (Sargodha, Lahore, Pak. Us, Servis Ind., HBL & Punjab) b Oct. 1, 1952
*Arthurton, K. L. T. MBE (Leewards) b Feb. 21, 1965
*Arun, B. (TN) b Dec. 14, 1962
*Arun Lal (Delhi & Bengal) b Aug. 1, 1955
*Asgarali, N. (T/T) b Dec. 28, 1920
Ashdown, W. H. (Kent) b Dec. 27, 1898, d Sept. 15, 1979
*Ashley, W. H. (W. Prov.) b Feb. 10, 1862, d July 14, 1930
*Ashraf Ali (Lahore, Income Tax, Pak. Us, Pak. Rlways & UBL) b April 22, 1958
Ashton, C. T. (CU & Essex) b Feb. 19, 1901, d Oct. 31, 1942
Ashton, G. (CU & Worcs) b Sept. 27, 1896, d Feb. 6, 1981
Ashton, Sir Hubert (CU & Essex; *CY 1922;* Pres. MCC 1960–61) b Feb. 13, 1898, d June 17, 1979
Asif Din, M. (Warwicks) b Sept. 21, 1960
*Asif Iqbal (H'bad, Kar., Kent, PIA & NBP; *CY 1968*) b June 6, 1943
*Asif Masood (Lahore, Punjab U. & PIA) b Jan. 23, 1946
Aslett, D. G. (Kent) b Feb. 12, 1958

*Astill, W. E. (Leics; *CY 1933*) b March 1, 1888, d Feb. 10, 1948
Athar Zaidi (Test umpire) b Nov. 12, 1946
Ather Ali Khan (Bangladesh) b Feb. 10, 1962
*Athey, C. W. J. (Yorks, Glos & Sussex) b Sept. 27, 1957
*Atif Rauf (Lahore, I'bad & ADBP) b March 3, 1964
Atkinson, C. R. M. CBE (Som) b July 23, 1931, d June 25, 1991
*Atkinson, D. St E. (B'dos & T/T) b Aug. 9, 1926, d Nov. 9, 2001
*Atkinson, E. St E. (B'dos) b Nov. 6, 1927, d May 29, 1998
Atkinson, G. (Som & Lancs) b March 29, 1938
*Attewell, W. (Notts; *CY 1892*) b June 12, 1861, d June 11, 1927
Austin, Sir Harold B. G. (B'dos) b July 15, 1877, d July 27, 1943
Austin, I. D. (Lancs; *CY 1999*) b May 30, 1966
*Austin, R. A. (Jam.) b Sept. 5, 1954
Avery, A. V. (Essex) b Dec. 19, 1914, d May 10, 1997
Aylward, James (Hants & All-England) b 1741, *buried* Dec. 27, 1827
*Azad, K. (Delhi) b Jan. 2, 1959
*Azeem Hafeez (Kar., Allied Bank & PIA) b July 29, 1963
*Azhar Khan (Lahore, Punjab, Pak. Us, PIA & HBL) b Sept. 7, 1955
*Azharuddin, M. (H'bad & Derbys; *CY 1991*) b Feb. 8, 1963
*Azmat Rana (B'pur, PIA, Punjab, Lahore & MCB) b Nov. 3, 1951

*Bacchus, S. F. A. F. (Guyana, W. Prov. & Border) b Jan. 31, 1954
*Bacher, Dr A. (Tvl; Managing Director UCBSA) b May 24, 1942
*Badcock, C. L. (Tas. & S. Aust.) b April 10, 1914, d Dec. 13, 1982
*Badcock, F. T. (Wgtn & Otago) b Aug. 9, 1897, d Sept. 19, 1982
Baggallay, R. R. C. (Derbys) b May 4, 1884, d Dec. 12, 1975
*Baichan, L. (Guyana) b May 12, 1946
*Baig, A. A. (H'bad, OU & Som) b March 19, 1939
Bailey, J. (Hants) b April 6, 1908, d Feb. 9, 1988
Bailey, J. A. (Essex & OU; Sec. MCC 1974–87) b June 22, 1930
*Bailey, T. E. CBE (Essex & CU; *CY 1950*) b Dec. 3, 1923
Baillie, A. W. (Sec. MCC 1858–63) b June 22, 1830, d May 10, 1867
Bainbridge, H. W. (Surrey, CU & Warwicks) b Oct. 29, 1862, d March 3, 1940
Bainbridge, P. (Glos & Durham; *CY 1986*) b April 16, 1958
*Bairstow, D. L. (Yorks & Griq. W.) b Sept. 1, 1951, d Jan. 5, 1998
Baker, C. S. (Warwicks) b Jan. 5, 1883, d Dec. 16, 1976
Baker, G. R. (Yorks & Lancs) b April 18, 1862, d Dec. 6, 1938
*Bakewell, A. H. (Northants; *CY 1934*) b Nov. 2, 1908, d Jan. 23, 1983
*Balaskas, X. C. (Griq. W., Border, W. Prov., Tvl & NE Tvl) b Oct. 15, 1910, d May 12, 1994
*Balderstone, J. C. (Yorks & Leics) b Nov. 16, 1940, d March 6, 2000
Baldry, D. O. (Middx & Hants) b Dec. 26, 1931
*Banerjee, S. A. (Bengal & Bihar) b Nov. 1, 1919, d Sept. 14, 1992
*Banerjee, S. N. (Bengal, Naw., Bihar & M. Pradesh) b Oct. 3, 1911, d Oct. 14, 1980
*Banerjee, S. T. (Bihar & Bengal) b Feb. 13, 1969
*Bannerman, A. C. (NSW) b March 22, 1854, d Sept. 19, 1924
*Bannerman, Charles (NSW) b July 23, 1851, d Aug. 20, 1930
Bannister, J. D. (Warwicks) b Aug. 23, 1930
*Baqa Jilani, M. (N. Ind.) b July 20, 1911, d July 2, 1941
*Barber, R. T. (Wgton & C. Dist.) b June 3, 1925
*Barber, R. W. (Lancs, CU & Warwicks; *CY 1967*) b Sept. 26, 1935
*Barber, W. (Yorks) b April 18, 1901, d Sept. 10, 1968
Barclay, J. R. T. (Sussex & OFS) b Jan. 22, 1954
*Bardsley, W. (NSW; *CY 1910*) b Dec. 6, 1882, d Jan. 20, 1954
Barker, G. (Essex) b July 6, 1931
Barling, T. H. (Surrey) b Sept. 1, 1906, d Jan. 2, 1993
*Barlow, E. J. (Tvl, E. Prov., W. Prov., Derbys & Boland) b Aug. 12, 1940
*Barlow, G. D. (Middx) b March 26, 1950
*Barlow, R. G. (Lancs) b May 28, 1851, d July 31, 1919
Barnard, H. M. (Hants) b July 18, 1933
*Barnes, S. F. (Warwicks & Lancs; *CY 1910*) b April 19, 1873, d Dec. 26, 1967
*Barnes, S. G. (NSW) b June 5, 1916, d Dec. 16, 1973
*Barnes, W. (Notts; *CY 1890*) b May 27, 1852, d March 24, 1899
*Barnett, B. A. (Vic.) b March 23, 1908, d June 29, 1979
*Barnett, C. J. (Glos; *CY 1937*) b July 3, 1910, d May 28, 1993
Baroda, Maharaja of (Manager, Ind. in Eng. 1959) b April 2, 1930, d Sept. 1, 1988

*Barratt, F. (Notts) b April 12, 1894, d Jan. 29, 1947
*Barrett, A. G. (Jam.) b April 5, 1942
*Barrett, Dr J. E. (Vic.) b Oct. 15, 1866, d Feb. 6, 1916
Barrick, D. W. (Northants) b April 28, 1926
*Barrington, K. F. (Surrey; *CY 1960*) b Nov. 24, 1930, d March 14, 1981
Barron, W. (Lancs & Northants) b Oct. 26, 1917
*Barrow, I. (Jam.) b Jan. 6, 1911, d April 2, 1979
*Bartlett, E. L. (B'dos) b March 10, 1906, d Dec. 21, 1976
*Bartlett, G. A. (C. Dist. & Cant.) b Feb. 3, 1941
Bartlett, H. T. (CU, Surrey & Sussex; *CY 1939*) b Oct. 7, 1914, d June 26, 1988
Bartley, T. J. (Test umpire) b March 19, 1908, d April 2, 1964
Barton, M. R. (OU & Surrey) b Oct. 14, 1914
*Barton, P. T. (Wgtn) b Oct. 9, 1935
*Barton, V. A. (Kent & Hants) b Oct. 6, 1867, d March 23, 1906
Barwick, S. R. (Glam) b Sept. 6, 1960
Base, S. J. (W. Prov., Glam, Boland, Derbys & Border) b Jan. 2, 1960
*Basit Ali (Kar. & UBL) b Dec. 13, 1970
Bates, D. L. (Sussex) b May 10, 1933
Bates, L. A. (Warwicks) b March 20, 1895, d March 11, 1971
*Bates, W. (Yorks) b Nov. 19, 1855, d Jan. 8, 1900
Bates, W. E. (Yorks & Glam) b March 5, 1884, d Jan. 17, 1957
*Baumgartner, H. V. (OFS & Tvl) b Nov. 17, 1883, d April 8, 1938
*Bean, G. (Notts & Sussex) b March 7, 1864, d March 16, 1923
Bear, M. J. (Essex & Cant.) b Feb. 23, 1934, d April 7, 2000
*Beard, D. D. (C. Dist. & N. Dist.) b Jan. 14, 1920, d July 15, 1982
*Beard, G. R. (NSW) b Aug. 19, 1950
Beauclerk, Lord Frederick (Middx, Surrey & MCC) b May 8, 1773, d April 22, 1850
*Beaumont, R. (Tvl) b Feb. 4, 1884, d May 25, 1958
*Beck, J. E. F. (Wgtn) b Aug. 1, 1934, d April 23, 2000
*Bedi, B. S. (N. Punjab, Delhi & Northants) b Sept. 25, 1946
*Bedser, Sir Alec V. (Surrey; *CY 1947*) b July 4, 1918
Bedser, E. A. (Surrey) b July 4, 1918
Beet, G. (Derbys; Test umpire) b April 24, 1886, d Dec. 13, 1946
*Begbie, D. W. (Tvl) b Dec. 12, 1914
Beldam, W. (Hambledon & Surrey) b Feb. 5, 1766, d Feb. 20, 1862
*Bell, A. J. (W. Prov. & Rhod.) b April 15, 1906, d Aug. 1, 1985
Bell, R. V. (Middx & Sussex) b Jan. 7, 1931, d Oct. 26, 1989
*Bell, W. (Cant.) b Sept. 5, 1931
Bellamy, B. W. (Northants) b April 22, 1891, d Dec. 22, 1985
*Benaud, J. (NSW) b May 11, 1944
*Benaud, R. OBE (NSW; *CY 1962;* broadcaster) b Oct. 6, 1930
*Benjamin, J. E. (Warwicks & Surrey) b Feb. 2, 1961
*Benjamin, W. K. M. (Leewards, Leics & Hants) b Dec. 31, 1964
Bencraft, Sir H. W. Russell (Hants) b March 4, 1858, d Dec. 25, 1943
Bennett, D. (Middx) b Dec. 18, 1933
*Bennett, M. J. (NSW) b Oct. 6, 1956
*Benson, M. R. (Kent) b July 6, 1958
Berry, L. G. (Leics) b April 28, 1906, d Feb. 5, 1985
*Berry, R. (Lancs, Worcs & Derbys) b Jan. 29, 1926
Berry, Scyld (Writer) b April 28, 1954
*Best, C. A. (B'dos & W. Prov.) b May 14, 1959
Bestwick, W. (Derbys) b Feb. 24, 1875, d May 2, 1938
*Betancourt, N. (T/T) b June 4, 1887, d Oct. 12, 1947
Bhalekar, R. B. (M'tra) b Feb. 17, 1952
*Bhandari, P. (Delhi & Bengal) b Nov. 27, 1935
*Bhat, A. R. (Karn.) b April 16, 1958
Bhupinder Singh (Punjab) b April 1, 1965
Bick, D. A. (Middx) b Feb. 22, 1936, d Jan. 13, 1992
*Bilby, G. P. (Wgtn) b May 7, 1941
*Binks, J. G. (Yorks; *CY 1969*) b Oct. 5, 1935
*Binns, A. P. (Jam.) b July 24, 1929
*Binny, R. M. H. (Karn.) b July 19, 1955
Birch, J. D. (Notts) b June 18, 1955
Bird, H. D. MBE (Yorks & Leics; Test umpire) b April 19, 1933
*Bird, M. C. (Lancs & Surrey) b March 25, 1888, d Dec. 9, 1933
Bird, R. E. (Worcs) b April 4, 1915, d Feb. 20, 1985
*Birkenshaw, J. (Yorks, Leics & Worcs) b Nov. 13, 1940
*Birkett, L. S. (B'dos, BG & T/T) b April 14, 1904, d Jan. 16, 1998
Bishop, G. A. (S. Aust.) b Feb. 25, 1960
*Bishop, I. R. (T/T & Derbys) b Oct. 24, 1967
*Bisset, Sir Murray (M.) (W. Prov.) b April 14, 1876, d Oct. 24, 1931
*Bissett, G. F. (Griq. W., W. Prov. & Tvl) b Nov. 5, 1905, d Nov. 14, 1965
Bissex, M. (Glos) b Sept. 28, 1944
*Blackham, J. McC. (Vic; *CY 1891*) b May 11, 1854, d Dec. 28, 1932

*Blackie, D. D. (Vic.) b April 5, 1882, d April 18, 1955
*Blain, T. E. (C. Dist.) b Feb. 17, 1962
Blair, B. R. (Otago) b Dec. 27, 1957
*Blair, R. W. (Wgtn & C. Dist.) b June 23, 1932
*Blanckenberg, J. M. (W. Prov. & Natal) b Dec. 31, 1892, dead
*Bland, K. C. (Rhod., E. Prov. & OFS; *CY 1966*) b April 5, 1938
Blenkiron, W. (Warwicks) b July 21, 1942
*Bligh, Hon. Ivo (I. F. W.) (8th Earl of Darnley) (CU & Kent; Pres. MCC 1900) b March 13, 1859, d April 10, 1927
Blofeld, H. C. (CU; writer & broadcaster) b Sept. 23, 1939
*Blunt, R. C. MBE (Cant. & Otago; *CY 1928*) b Nov. 3, 1900, d June 22, 1966
*Blythe, C. (Kent; *CY 1904*) b May 30, 1879, d Nov. 8, 1917
*Board, J. H. (Glos) b Feb. 23, 1867, d April 15, 1924
*Bock, E. G. (Griq. W., Tvl & W. Prov.) b Sept. 17, 1908, d Sept. 5, 1961
*Bolton, B. A. (Cant. & Wgtn) b May 31, 1935
*Bolus, J. B. (Yorks, Notts & Derbys) b Jan. 31, 1934
*Bond, G. E. (W. Prov.) b April 5, 1909, d Aug. 27, 1965
Bond, J. D. (Lancs & Notts; *CY 1971*) b May 6, 1932
*Bonnor, G. J. (Vic. & NSW) b Feb. 25, 1855, d June 27, 1912
*Boock, S. L. (Otago & Cant.) b Sept. 20, 1951
*Boon, D. C. MBE (Tas. & Durham; *CY 1994*) b Dec. 29, 1960
Boon, T. J. (Leics) b Nov. 1, 1961
*Booth, B. C. MBE (NSW) b Oct. 19, 1933
Booth, B. J. (Lancs & Leics) b Dec. 3, 1935
Booth, C. (CU & Hants) b May 11, 1842, d July 14, 1926
*Booth, M. W. (Yorks; *CY 1914*) b Dec. 10, 1886, d July 1, 1916
Booth, R. (Yorks & Worcs) b Oct. 1, 1926
*Borde, C. G. (Baroda & M'tra) b July 21, 1933
*Border, A. R. (NSW, Glos, Qld & Essex; *CY 1982*) b July 27, 1955
Bore, M. K. (Yorks & Notts) b June 2, 1947
Borrington, A. J. (Derbys) b Dec. 8, 1948
*Bosanquet, B. J. T. (OU & Middx; *CY 1905*) b Oct. 13, 1877, d Oct. 12, 1936
*Bosch, T. (N. Tvl & Natal) b March 14, 1966, d Feb. 13, 2000
Bose, G. (Bengal) b May 20, 1947
Boshier, B. S. (Leics) b March 6, 1932
*Botham, I. T. OBE (Som, Worcs, Durham & Qld; *CY 1978*) b Nov. 24, 1955
*Botten, J. T. (NE Tvl & N. Tvl) b June 21, 1938
Boucher, J. C. (Ireland) b Dec. 22, 1910, d Dec. 25, 1995
Bowden, J. (Derbys) b Oct. 8, 1884, d March 1, 1958
*Bowden, M. P. (Surrey & Tvl) b Nov. 1, 1865, d Feb. 19, 1892
Bowell, A. (Hants) b April 27, 1880, d Aug. 28, 1957
*Bowes, W. E. (Yorks; *CY 1932*) b July 25, 1908, d Sept. 5, 1987
*Bowley, E. H. (Sussex & Auck.; *CY 1930*) b June 6, 1890, d July 9, 1974
Bowley, F. L. (Worcs) b Nov. 9 1873, d May 31, 1943
Box, T. (Sussex) b Feb. 7, 1808, d July 12, 1876
*Boyce, K. D. (B'dos & Essex; *CY 1974*) b Oct. 11, 1943, d Oct. 11, 1996
*Boycott, G. OBE (Yorks & N. Tvl; *CY 1965*) b Oct. 21, 1940
Boyd-Moss, R. J. (CU & Northants) b Dec. 16, 1959
Boyes, G. S. (Hants) b March 31, 1899, d Feb. 11, 1973
*Boyle, H. F. (Vic.) b Dec. 10, 1847, d Nov. 21, 1907
*Bracewell, B. P. (C. Dist., Otago & N. Dist.) b Sept. 14, 1959
*Bracewell, J. G. (Otago & Auck.) b April 15, 1958
*Bradburn, W. P. (N. Dist.) b Nov. 24, 1938
*Bradley, W. M. (Kent) b Jan. 2, 1875, d June 19, 1944
*Bradman, Sir Donald G. (NSW & S. Aust.; *CY 1931*) b Aug. 27, 1908, d Feb. 25, 2001
Brain, B. M. (Worcs & Glos) b Sept. 13, 1940
*Brain, D. H. (Mash.) b Oct. 4, 1964
Brann, G. (Sussex) b April 23, 1865, d June 14, 1954
*Brann, W. H. (E. Prov.) b April 4, 1899, d Sept. 22, 1953
Brassington, A. J. (Glos) b Aug. 9, 1954
*Braund, L. C. (Surrey & Som; *CY 1902*) b Oct. 18, 1875, d Dec. 23, 1955
Bray, C. (Essex) b April 6, 1898, d Sept. 12, 1993
Brayshaw, I. J. (W. Aust.) b Jan. 14, 1942
Breakwell, D. (Northants & Som) b July 2, 1948
*Brearley, J. M. OBE (CU & Middx; *CY 1977*) b April 28, 1942
*Brearley, W. (Lancs; *CY 1909*) b March 11, 1876, d Jan. 13, 1937
*Brennan, D. V. (Yorks) b Feb. 10, 1920, d Jan. 9, 1985
*Briant, G. A. (Mash.) b April 11, 1969
Bridges, J. J. (Som) b June 28, 1887, d Sept. 26, 1966
Brierley, T. L. (Glam, Lancs & Canada) b June 15, 1910, d Jan. 7, 1989
Briers, N. E. (Leics; *CY 1993*) b Jan. 15, 1955

*Briggs, John (Lancs; *CY 1889*) b Oct. 3, 1862, d Jan. 11, 1902
*Bright, R. J. (Vic.) b July 13, 1954
*Briscoe, A. W. (Tvl) b Feb. 6, 1911, d April 22, 1941
*Broad, B. C. (Glos & Notts) b Sept. 29, 1957
Broadbent, R. G. (Worcs) b June 21, 1924, d April 26, 1993
*Brockwell, W. (Surrey & Kimberley; *CY 1895*) b Jan. 21, 1865, d June 30, 1935
Broderick, V. (Northants) b Aug. 17, 1920
*Bromfield, H. D. (W. Prov.) b June 26, 1932
*Bromley, E. H. (W. Aust. & Vic.) b Sept. 2, 1912, d Feb. 1, 1967
*Bromley-Davenport, H. R. (CU, Eur., & Middx) b Aug. 18, 1870, d May 23, 1954
*Brookes, D. (Northants; *CY 1957*) b Oct. 29, 1915
Brookes, Wilfrid H. (Editor of *Wisden* 1936–39) b Dec. 5, 1894, d May 28, 1955
*Brown, A. (Kent) b Oct. 17, 1935
Brown, A. S. (Glos) b June 24, 1936
*Brown, D. J. (Warwicks) b Jan. 30, 1942
*Brown, F. R. MBE (CU, Surrey & Northants; *CY 1933;* Pres. MCC 1971–72) b Dec. 16, 1910, d July 24, 1991
*Brown, G. (Hants) b Oct. 6, 1887, d Dec. 3, 1964
Brown, J. MBE (Scotland) b Sept. 24, 1931
*Brown, J. T. (Yorks; *CY 1895*) b Aug. 20, 1869, d Nov. 4, 1904
Brown, K. R. (Middx) b March 18, 1963
*Brown, L. S. (Tvl, NE Tvl & Rhod.) b Nov. 24, 1910, d Sept. 1, 1983
Brown, R. D. (Mash.) b March 11, 1951
Brown, S. M. (Middx) b Dec. 8, 1917, d Dec. 28, 1987
*Brown, V. R. (Cant. & Auck.) b Nov. 3, 1959
*Brown, W. A. (NSW & Qld; *CY 1939; oldest and last surviving pre-war CY at end of 2001*) b July 31, 1912
Brown, W. C. (Northants) b Nov. 13, 1900, d Jan. 20, 1986
Browne, B. St A. (Guyana) b Sept. 16, 1967
*Browne, C. R. (B'dos & BG) b Oct. 8, 1890, d Jan. 12, 1964
*Bruce, W. (Vic.) b May 22, 1864, d Aug. 3, 1925
*Bruk-Jackson, G. K. (MCD & Mash.) b April 25, 1969
Bryan, G. J. CBE (Kent) b Dec. 29, 1902, d April 4, 1991
Bryan, J. L. (CU & Kent; *CY 1922*) b May 26, 1896, d April 23, 1985
Bryan, R. T. (Kent) b July 30, 1898, d July 27, 1970
*Buckenham, C. P. (Essex) b Jan. 16, 1876, d Feb. 23, 1937
Bucknor, S. A. (Test umpire) b May 31, 1946
Buckston, R. H. R. (Derbys) b Oct. 10, 1908, d May 16, 1967
Budd, E. H. (Middx & All-England) b Feb. 23, 1785, d March 29, 1875
Budd, W. L. (Hants; Test umpire) b Oct. 25, 1913, d Aug. 23, 1986
Bull, F. G. (Essex; *CY 1898*) b April 2, 1875, d Sept. 16, 1910
Buller, J. S. MBE (Yorks & Worcs; Test umpire) b Aug. 23, 1909, d Aug. 7, 1970
Burden, M. D. (Hants) b Oct. 4, 1930, d Nov. 9, 1987
*Burge, P. J. (Qld; *CY 1965;* ICC referee) b May 17, 1932, d Oct. 5, 2001
*Burger, C. G. de V. (Natal) b July 12, 1935
Burgess, G. I. (Som) b May 5, 1943
*Burgess, M. G. (Auck.) b July 17, 1944
*Burke, C. (Auck.) b March 22, 1914, d Aug. 4, 1997
*Burke, J. W. (NSW; *CY 1957*) b June 12, 1930, d Feb. 2, 1979
*Burke, S. F. (NE Tvl & OFS) b March 11, 1934
*Burki, Javed (Pak. Us, OU, Punjab, Lahore, Kar., R'pindi & NWFP; ICC referee) b May 8, 1938
*Burn, K. E. (Tas.) b Sept. 17, 1862, d July 20, 1956
Burns, W. B. (Worcs) b Aug. 29, 1883, d July 7, 1916
Burnup, C. J. (CU & Kent; *CY 1903*) b Nov. 21, 1875, d April 5, 1960
Burrough, H. D. (Som) b Feb. 6, 1909, d April 9, 1994
Burrows, R. D. (Worcs) b June 6, 1871, d Feb. 12, 1943
Burton, D. C. F. (Yorks) b Sept. 13, 1887, d Sept. 24, 1971
*Burton, F. J. (Vic. & NSW) b Nov. 2, 1865, d Aug. 25, 1929
*Burtt, T. B. (Cant.) b Jan. 22, 1915, d May 24, 1988
Buse, H. T. F. (Som) b Aug. 5, 1910, d Feb. 23, 1992
Buss, A. (Sussex) b Sept. 1, 1939
Buss, M. A. (Sussex & OFS) b Jan. 24, 1944
*Butchart, I. P. (MCD) b May 9, 1960
*Butcher, A. R. (Surrey & Glam; *CY 1991*) b Jan. 7, 1954
*Butcher, B. F. (Guyana; *CY 1970*) b Sept. 3, 1933
Butcher, I. P. (Leics & Glos) b July 1, 1962
*Butcher, R. O. (Middx, B'dos & Tas.) b Oct. 14, 1953
*Butler, H. J. (Notts) b March 12, 1913, d July 17, 1991
*Butler, L. (T/T) b Feb. 9, 1929
*Butt, H. R. (Sussex) b Dec. 27, 1865, d Dec. 21, 1928
*Butterfield, L. A. (Cant.) b Aug. 29, 1913, d July 7, 1999
*Butts, C. G. (Guyana) b July 8, 1957
Buxton, I. R. (Derbys) b April 17, 1938

*Buys, I. D. (W. Prov.) b Feb. 3, 1895, dead
*Bynoe, M. R. (B'dos) b Feb. 23, 1941
Byrne, J. F. (Warwicks) b June 19, 1871, d May 10, 1954

Cadman, S. (Derbys) b Jan. 29, 1877, d May 6, 1952
Caesar, Julius (Surrey & All-England) b March 25, 1830, d March 6, 1878
Caffyn, W. (Surrey & NSW) b Feb. 2, 1828, d Aug. 28, 1919
Caine, C. Stewart (Editor of *Wisden* 1926–33) b Oct. 28, 1861, d April 15, 1933
*Cairns, B. L. (C. Dist., Otago & N. Dist.) b Oct. 10, 1949
Calder, H. L. (Cranleigh; *CY 1918*) b Jan. 24, 1901, d Sept. 15, 1995
*Callaway, S. T. (NSW & Cant.) b Feb. 6, 1868, d Nov. 25, 1923
*Callen, I. W. (Vic. & Boland) b May 2, 1955
*Calthorpe, Hon. F. S. Gough- (CU, Sussex & Warwicks) b May 27, 1892, d Nov. 19, 1935
*Camacho, G. S. (Guyana; Chief Exec. WICB) b Oct. 15, 1945
*Cameron, F. J. (Jam.) b June 22, 1923, d Feb. 1995
*Cameron, F. J. MBE (Otago) b June 1, 1932
*Cameron, H. B. (Tvl, E. Prov. & W. Prov.; *CY 1936*) b July 5, 1905, d Nov. 2, 1935
*Cameron, J. H. (CU, Jam. & Som) b April 8, 1914, d Feb. 13, 2000
*Campbell, G. D. (Tas.) b March 10, 1964
*Campbell, T. (Tvl) b Feb. 9, 1882, d Oct. 5, 1924
Cannings, V. H. D. (Warwicks & Hants) b April 3, 1919
*Capel, D. J. (Northants & E. Prov.) b Feb. 6, 1963
Cardus, Sir Neville (Writer) b April 3, 1888, d Feb. 27, 1975
*Carew, G. M. (B'dos) b June 4, 1910, d Dec. 9, 1974
*Carew, M. C. (T/T) b Sept. 15, 1937
*Carkeek, W. (Vic.) b Oct. 17, 1878, d Feb. 20, 1937
*Carlson, P. H. (Qld) b Aug. 8, 1951
*Carlstein, P. R. (OFS, Tvl, Natal & Rhod.) b Oct. 28, 1938
Carpenter, D. (Glos) b Sept. 12, 1935
Carpenter, H. A. (Essex) b July 12, 1869, d Dec. 12, 1933
Carpenter, R. (Cambs & Utd England XI) b Nov. 18, 1830, d July 13, 1901
*Carr, A. W. (Notts; *CY 1923*) b May 21, 1893, d Feb. 7, 1963
*Carr, D. B. OBE (OU & Derbys; *CY 1960;* Sec. TCCB 1974–86) b Dec. 28, 1926
*Carr, D. W. (Kent; *CY 1910*) b March 17, 1872, d March 23, 1950
Carr, J. D. (OU & Middx) b June 15, 1963
Carrick, P. (Yorks & E. Prov.) b July 16, 1952, d Jan. 11, 2000
*Carter, C. P. (Natal & Tvl) b April 23, 1881, d Nov. 8, 1952
*Carter, H. (NSW) b March 15, 1878, d June 8, 1948
Carter, R. G. M. (Worcs) b July 11, 1937
*Cartwright, T. W. (Warwicks, Som & Glam) b July 22, 1935
Case, C. C. C. (Som) b Sept. 7, 1895, d Nov. 11, 1969
Cass, G. R. (Essex, Worcs & Tas.) b April 23, 1940
Catt, A. W. (Kent & W. Prov.) b Oct. 2, 1933
*Catterall, R. H. (Tvl, Rhod., Natal & OFS; *CY 1925*) b July 10, 1900, d Jan. 3, 1961
*Cave, H. B. (Wgtn & C. Dist.) b Oct. 10, 1922, d Sept. 15, 1989
Chalk, F. G. H. (OU & Kent) b Sept. 7, 1910, d Feb. 17, 1943
*Challenor, G. (B'dos) b June 28, 1888, d July 30, 1947
Chamberlain, W. R. F. (Northants; Chairman TCCB 1990–94) b April 13, 1925
*Chandrasekhar, B. S. (†Karn.; *CY 1972*) b May 17, 1945
Chandrasekhar, V. B. (Goa) b Aug. 21, 1961
*Chang, H. S. (Jam.) b July 22, 1952
Chaplin, H. P. (Sussex & Eur.) b March 1, 1883, d March 6, 1970
*Chapman, A. P. F. (Uppingham, CU & Kent; *CY 1919*) b Sept. 3, 1900, d Sept. 16, 1961
*Chapman, H. W. (Natal) b June 30, 1890, d Dec. 1, 1941
Chapman, J. (Derbys) b March 11, 1877, d Aug. 12, 1956
*Chappell, G. S. MBE (S. Aust., Som & Qld; *CY 1973*) b Aug. 7, 1948
*Chappell, I. M. (S. Aust. & Lancs; *CY 1976;* broadcaster) b Sept. 26, 1943
*Chappell, T. M. (S. Aust., W. Aust. & NSW) b Oct. 21, 1952
*Chapple, M. E. (Cant. & C. Dist.) b July 25, 1930, d July 31, 1985
Charlesworth, C. (Warwicks) b Feb. 12, 1875, d June 15, 1953
*Charlton, P. C. (NSW) b April 9, 1867, d Sept. 30, 1954
*Charlwood, H. R. J. (Sussex) b Dec. 19, 1846, d June 6, 1888
*Chatfield, E. J. MBE (Wgtn) b July 3, 1950
*Chatterton, W. (Derbys) b Dec. 27, 1861, d March 19, 1913
*Chauhan, C. P. S. (M'tra & Delhi) b July 21, 1947
*Cheetham, J. E. (W. Prov.) b May 26, 1920, d Aug. 21, 1980
Chester, F. (Worcs; Test umpire) b Jan. 20, 1895, d April 8, 1957
*Chevalier, G. A. (W. Prov.) b March 9, 1937

*Childs, J. H. (Glos & Essex; *CY 1987*) b Aug. 15, 1951
*Chipperfield, A. G. (NSW) b Nov. 17, 1905, d July 29, 1987
Chisholm, R. H. E. (Scotland) b May 22, 1927
*Chowdhury, N. R. (Bihar & Bengal) b May 23, 1923, d Dec. 14, 1979
*Christiani, C. M. (BG) b Oct. 28, 1913, d April 4, 1938
*Christiani, R. J. (BG) b July 19, 1920
*Christopherson, S. (Kent; Pres. MCC 1939–45) b Nov. 11, 1861, d April 6, 1949
*Christy, J. A. J. (Tvl & Qld) b Dec. 12, 1904, d Feb. 1, 1971
*Chubb, G. W. A. (Border & Tvl) b April 12, 1911, d Aug. 28, 1982
Clark, D. G. (Kent; Pres. MCC 1977–78) b Jan. 27, 1919
Clark, E. A. (Middx) b April 15, 1937
*Clark, E. W. (Northants) b Aug. 9, 1902, d April 28, 1982
Clark, T. H. (Surrey) b Oct. 5, 1924, d June 14, 1981
*Clark, W. M. (W. Aust.) b Sept. 19, 1953
*Clarke, Dr C. B. OBE (B'dos, Northants & Essex) b April 7, 1918, d Oct. 14, 1993
Clarke, R. W. (Northants) b April 22, 1924, d Aug. 3, 1981
*Clarke, S. T. (B'dos, Surrey, Tvl, OFS & N. Tvl) b Dec. 11, 1954, d Dec. 4, 1999
Clarke, William (Notts; founded All-England XI & Trent Bridge ground) b Dec. 24, 1798, d Aug. 25, 1856
Clarkson, A. (Yorks & Som) b Sept. 5, 1939
*Clay, J. C. (Glam) b March 18, 1898, d Aug. 12, 1973
Clay, J. D. (Notts) b Oct. 15, 1924
Clayton, G. (Lancs & Som) b Feb. 3, 1938
*Cleverley, D. C. (Auck.) b Dec. 23, 1909
Clift, Patrick B. (Rhod., Leics & Natal) b July 14, 1953, d Sept. 3, 1996
Clift, Phil B. (Glam) b Sept. 3, 1918
Clinton, G. S. (Kent, Surrey & Zimb.-Rhod.) b May 5, 1953
*Close, D. B. CBE (Yorks & Som; *CY 1964*) b Feb. 24, 1931
Cobb, R. A. (Leics & N. Tvl) b May 18, 1961
Cobham, 10th Visct (Hon. C. J. Lyttelton) (Worcs; Pres. MCC 1954) b Aug. 8, 1909, d March 20, 1977
*Cochrane, J. A. K. (Tvl & Griq. W.) b July 15, 1909, d June 15, 1987
Coe, S. (Leics) b June 3, 1873, d Nov. 4, 1955
*Coen, S. K. (OFS, W. Prov., Tvl & Border) b Oct. 14, 1902, d Jan. 28, 1967
*Colah, S. M. H. (Bombay, W. Ind. & Naw.) b Sept. 22, 1902, d Sept. 11, 1950
Colchin, Robert ("Long Robin") (Kent & All-England) b Nov. 1713, d April 1750
*Coldwell, L. J. (Worcs) b Jan. 10, 1933, d Aug. 6, 1996
*Colley, D. J. (NSW) b March 15, 1947
*Collinge, R. O. (C. Dist., Wgtn & N. Dist.) b April 2, 1946
Collins, A. E. J. (Clifton Coll. & Royal Engineers) b Aug. 18, 1885, d Nov. 11, 1914
Collins, G. C. (Kent) b Sept. 21, 1889, d Jan. 23, 1949
*Collins, H. L. (NSW) b Jan. 21, 1888, d May 28, 1959
Collins, R. (Lancs) b March 10, 1934
*Colquhoun, I. A. (C. Dist.) b June 8, 1924
Coman, P. G. (Cant.) b April 13, 1943
*Commaille, J. M. M. (W. Prov., Natal, OFS & Griq. W.) b Feb. 21, 1883, d July 28, 1956
*Commins, J. B. (Boland & W. Prov.) b Feb. 19, 1965
*Compton, D. C. S. CBE (Middx & Holkar; *CY 1939*) b May 23, 1918, d April 23, 1997
Compton, L. H. (Middx) b Sept. 12, 1912, d Dec. 27, 1984
*Coney, J. V. MBE (Wgtn; *CY 1984*) b June 21, 1952
*Congdon, B. E. OBE (C. Dist., Wgtn, Otago & Cant.; *CY 1974*) b Feb. 11, 1938
*Coningham, A. (NSW & Qld) b July 14, 1863, d June 13, 1939
*Connolly, A. N. (Vic. & Middx) b June 29, 1939
Connor, C. A. (Hants) b March 24, 1961
Constable, B. (Surrey) b Feb. 19, 1921, d May 15, 1997
Constant, D. J. (Kent & Leics; Test umpire) b Nov. 9, 1941
*Constantine, L. N. (later Baron Constantine of Maraval and Nelson) (T/T & B'dos; *CY 1940*) b Sept. 21, 1901, d July 1, 1971
Constantine, L. S. (T/T) b May 25, 1874, d Jan. 5, 1942
*Contractor, N. J. (Guj. & Ind. Rlwys) b March 7, 1934
*Conyngham, D. P. (Natal, Tvl & W. Prov.) b May 10, 1897, d July 7, 1979
*Cook, C. (Glos) b Aug. 23, 1921, d Sept. 4, 1996
*Cook, F. J. (E. Prov.) b 1870, d Nov. 30, 1914
*Cook, G. (Northants & E. Prov.) b Oct. 9, 1951
Cook, L. W. (Lancs) b March 28, 1885, d Dec. 2, 1933
*Cook, N. G. B. (Leics & Northants) b June 17, 1956
*Cook, S. J. (Tvl & Som; *CY 1990*) b July 31, 1953
Cook, T. E. R. (Sussex) b Jan. 5, 1901, d Jan. 15, 1950
*Cooper, A. H. C. (Tvl) b Sept. 2, 1893, d July 18, 1963
*Cooper, B. B. (Middx, Kent & Vic.) b March 15, 1844, d Aug. 7, 1914

Cooper, E. (Worcs) b Nov. 30, 1915, d Oct. 29, 1968
Cooper, F. S. Ashley- (Historian) b March 22, 1877, d Jan. 31, 1932
Cooper, G. C. (Sussex) b Sept. 2, 1936
Cooper, K. E. (Notts & Glos) b Dec. 27, 1957
*Cooper, W. H. (Vic.) b Sept. 11, 1849, d April 5, 1939
Cooray, B. C. (Test umpire) b May 15, 1941
*Cope, G. A. (Yorks) b Feb. 23, 1947
*Copson, W. H. (Derbys; *CY 1937*) b April 27, 1908, d Sept. 14, 1971
Cordle, A. E. (Glam) b Sept. 21, 1940
*Corling, G. E. (NSW) b July 13, 1941
Cornford, J. H. (Sussex) b Dec. 9, 1911, d June 17, 1985
*Cornford, W. L. (Sussex) b Dec. 25, 1900, d Feb. 6, 1964
Cornwallis, W. S. (later 2nd Baron) (Kent) b March 14, 1892, d Jan. 4, 1982
Corrall, P. (Leics) b July 16, 1906, d Feb. 1994
Corran, A. J. (OU & Notts) b Nov. 25, 1936
*Cosier, G. J. (Vic., S. Aust. & Qld) b April 25, 1953
*Cottam, J. T. (NSW) b Sept. 5, 1867, d Jan. 30, 1897
*Cottam, R. M. H. (Hants & Northants) b Oct. 16, 1944
*Cotter, A. (NSW) b Dec. 3, 1884, d Oct. 31, 1917
Cotton, J. (Notts & Leics) b Nov. 7, 1940
*Coulthard, G. (Vic.; Test umpire) b Aug. 1, 1856, d Oct. 22, 1883
*Coventry, Hon. C. J. (Worcs) b Feb. 26, 1867, d June 2, 1929
*Cowans, N. G. (Middx & Hants) b April 17, 1961
*Cowdrey, C. S. (Kent & Glam) b Oct. 20, 1957
Cowdrey, G. R. (Kent) b June 27, 1964
*Cowdrey, M. C. (later Baron Cowdrey of Tonbridge) (OU & Kent; *CY 1956;* Pres. MCC 1986–87) b Dec. 24, 1932, d Dec. 4, 2000
Cowie, D. B. (Test umpire) b Dec. 2, 1946
*Cowie, J. OBE (Auck.) b March 30, 1912, d June 3, 1994
Cowley, N. G. (Hants & Glam) b March 1, 1953
*Cowper, R. M. (Vic. & W. Aust.) b Oct. 5, 1940
Cox, A. L. (Northants) b July 22, 1907, d Nov. 13, 1986
Cox, G., jun. (Sussex) b Aug. 23, 1911, d March 30, 1985
Cox, G., sen. (Sussex) b Nov. 29, 1873, d March 24, 1949
*Cox, J. L. (Natal) b June 28, 1886, d July 4, 1971
*Coxon, A. (Yorks) b Jan. 18, 1916
Cozier, Tony (Writer & broadcaster) b July 10, 1940
*Craig, I. D. (NSW) b June 12, 1935
Cranfield, L. M. (Glos) b Aug. 29, 1909, d Nov. 18, 1993
Cranmer, P. (Warwicks & Eur.) b Sept. 10, 1914, d May 29, 1994
*Cranston, J. (Glos) b Jan. 9, 1859, d Dec. 10, 1904
*Cranston, K. (Lancs) b Oct. 20, 1917
*Crapp, J. F. (Glos; Test umpire) b Oct. 14, 1912, d Feb. 15, 1981
*Crawford, J. N. (Surrey, S. Aust., Wgtn & Otago; *CY 1907*) b Dec. 1, 1886, d May 2, 1963
*Crawford, P. (NSW) b Aug. 3, 1933
Crawford, V. F. S. (Surrey & Leics) b April 11, 1879, d Aug. 21, 1922
Crawley, A. M. MBE (OU & Kent; Pres. MCC 1972–73) b April 10, 1908, d Nov. 3, 1993
Cray, S. J. (Essex) b May 29, 1921
Creese, W. L. (Hants) b Dec. 27, 1907, d March 9, 1974
*Cresswell, G. F. (Wgtn & C. Dist.) b March 22, 1915, d Jan. 10, 1966
*Cripps, G. (W. Prov.) b Oct. 19, 1865, d July 27, 1943
*Crisp, R. J. (Rhod., W. Prov. & Worcs) b May 28, 1911, d March 3, 1994
*Crocker, G. J. (MCD) b May 16, 1962
*Croft, C. E. H. (Guyana & Lancs) b March 15, 1953
*Cromb, I. B. (Cant.) b June 25, 1905, d March 6, 1984
*Cronje, W. J. (†FS & Leics) b Sept. 25, 1969
Croom, A. J. (Warwicks) b May 23, 1896, d Aug. 16, 1947
*Crowe, J. J. (S. Aust. & Auck.) b Sept. 14, 1958
*Crowe, M. D. MBE (Auck., C. Dist., Som & Wgtn; *CY 1985*) b Sept. 22, 1962
Crump, B. S. (Northants) b April 25, 1938
Cuffe, J. A. (NSW & Worcs) b June 26, 1880, d May 16, 1931
Cumbes, J. (Lancs, Surrey, Worcs & Warwicks) b May 4, 1944
*Cummins, A. C. (B'dos & Durham) b May 7, 1966
*Cunis, R. S. (Auck. & N. Dist.) b Jan. 5, 1941
*Curnow, S. H. (Tvl) b Dec. 16, 1907, d July 28, 1986
Curran, K. M. (Zimb., Glos, Natal, Northants, Boland) b Sept. 7, 1959
*Curtis, T. S. (Worcs & CU) b Jan. 15, 1960
Cutmore, J. A. (Essex) b Dec. 28, 1898, d Nov. 30, 1985
*Cuttell, W. R. (Lancs; *CY 1898*) b Sept. 13, 1864, d Dec. 9, 1929

*Da Costa, O. C. (Jam.) b Sept. 11, 1907, d Oct. 1, 1936

Dacre, C. C. (Auck. & Glos) b May 15, 1899, d Nov. 2, 1975
Daft, H. B. (Notts) b April 5, 1866, d Jan. 12, 1945
Daft, Richard (Notts & All-England) b Nov. 2, 1835, d July 18, 1900
Dalmeny, Lord (later 6th Earl of Rosebery) (Middx, Surrey & Scotland) b Jan. 8, 1882, d May 30, 1974
Dalmiya, J. (President ICC 1997–2000) b May 30, 1940
*Dalton, E. L. (Natal) b Dec. 2, 1906, d June 3, 1981
*Dani, H. T. (M'tra & Ind. Serv.) b May 24, 1933, d Dec. 19, 1999
*Daniel, W. W. (B'dos, Middx & W. Aust.) b Jan. 16, 1956
*D'Arcy, J. W. (Cant., Wgtn & Otago) b April 23, 1936
Dare, R. (Hants) b Nov. 26, 1921
*Darling, J. (S. Aust.; *CY 1900*) b Nov. 21, 1870, d Jan. 2, 1946
*Darling, L. S. (Vic.) b Aug. 14, 1909, d June 24, 1992
*Darling, W. M. (S. Aust.) b May 1, 1957
Davey, J. (Glos) b Sept. 4, 1944
David, N. A. (H'bad) b Feb. 26, 1971
*Davidson, A. K. OBE (NSW; *CY 1962*) b June 14, 1929
Davidson, G. (Derbys) b June 29, 1866, d Feb. 8, 1899
Davies, Dai (Glam; Test umpire) b Aug. 26, 1896, d July 16, 1976
Davies, Emrys (Glam; Test umpire) b June 27, 1904, d Nov. 10, 1975
*Davies, E. Q. (E. Prov., Tvl & NE Tvl) b Aug. 26, 1909, d Nov. 11, 1976
Davies, H. G. (Glam) b April 23, 1912, d Sept. 4, 1993
Davies, J. G. W. OBE (CU & Kent; Pres. MCC 1985–86) b Sept. 10, 1911, d Nov. 5, 1992
Davies, S. G. (Mat.) b May 12, 1977
Davies, T. (Glam) b Oct. 25, 1960
*Davis, B. A. (T/T & Glam) b May 2, 1940
*Davis, C. A. (T/T) b Jan. 1, 1944
Davis, E. (Northants) b March 8, 1922
*Davis, H. T. (Wgtn) b Nov. 30, 1971
*Davis, I. C. (NSW & Qld) b June 25, 1953
Davis, C. P. (Northants) b May 24, 1915, d July 4, 2001
Davis, R. C. (Glam) b Jan. 15, 1946
*Davis, S. P. (Vic.) b Nov. 8, 1959
*Davis, W. W. (Windwards, Glam, Tas., Northants & Wgtn) b Sept. 18, 1958
Davison, B. F. (Rhod., Leics, Tas. & Glos) b Dec. 21, 1946
Davison, I. J. (Notts) b Oct. 4, 1937
Dawkes, G. O. (Leics & Derbys) b July 19, 1920
*Dawson, E. W. (CU & Leics) b Feb. 13, 1904, d June 4, 1979
*Dawson, O. C. (Natal & Border) b Sept. 1, 1919
Day, A. P. (Kent; *CY 1910*) b April 10, 1885, d Jan. 22, 1969
*de Alwis, R. G. (SSC) b Feb. 15, 1959
*Dean, H. (Lancs) b Aug. 13, 1884, d March 12, 1957
Dean, J., sen. (Sussex) b Jan. 4, 1816, d Dec. 25, 1881
*Deane, H. G. (Natal & Tvl) b July 21, 1895, d Oct. 21, 1939
*De Caires, F. I. (BG) b May 12, 1909, d Feb. 2, 1959
*De Courcy, J. H. (NSW) b April 18, 1927, d June 20, 2000
*de Groen, R. P. (Auck. & N. Dist.) b Aug. 5, 1962
*Dekker, M. H. (Mat.) b Dec. 5, 1969
*Dell, A. R. (Qld) b Aug. 6, 1947
*de Mel, A. L. F. (SL) b May 9, 1959
*Dempster, C. S. (Wgtn, Leics, Scotland & Warwicks; *CY 1932*) b Nov. 15, 1903, d Feb. 14, 1974
*Dempster, E. W. (Wgtn) b Jan. 25, 1925
*Denness, M. H. (Scotland, Kent & Essex; *CY 1975;* ICC referee) b Dec. 1, 1940
Dennett, G. (Glos) b April 27, 1880, d Sept. 14, 1937
Denning, P. W. (Som) b Dec. 16, 1949
Dennis, F. (Yorks) b June 11, 1907, d Dec. 21, 2000
Dennis, S. J. (Yorks, OFS & Glam) b Oct. 18, 1960
*Denton, D. (Yorks; *CY 1906*) b July 4, 1874, d Feb. 16, 1950
Deodhar, D. B. (M'tra) b Jan. 14, 1892, d Aug. 24, 1993
*Depeiza, C. C. (B'dos) b Oct. 10, 1927, d Nov. 10, 1995
*Desai, R. B. (Bombay) b June 20, 1939, d April 27, 1998
*de Silva, A. M. (CCC) b Dec. 3, 1963
de Silva, D. L. S. (SL) b Nov. 17, 1956, d April 12, 1980
*de Silva, D. S. (Bloom.) b June 11, 1942
*de Silva, E. A. R. (NCC & Galle; Test umpire) b March 28, 1956
de Silva, G. N. (SL) b March 12, 1955
*de Silva, G. R. A. (SL) b Dec. 12, 1952
de Smidt, R. W. (W. Prov.) b Nov. 24, 1883, d Aug. 3, 1986
De Trafford, C. E. (Lancs & Leics) b May 21, 1864, d Nov. 11, 1951
Devereux, L. N. (Middx, Worcs & Glam) b Oct. 20, 1931
*de Villiers, P. S. (Northerns, N. Tvl & Kent) b Oct. 13, 1964
*Dewdney, C. T. (Jam.) b Oct. 23, 1933
*Dewes, J. G. (CU & Middx) b Oct. 11, 1926

Dews, G. (Worcs) b June 5, 1921
*Dexter, E. R. (CU & Sussex; *CY 1961;* Pres. MCC 2001–02) b May 15, 1935
*Dias, R. L. (CCC; ICC referee) b Oct. 18, 1952
*Dick, A. E. (Otago & Wgtn) b Oct. 10, 1936
*Dickinson, G. R. (Otago) b March 11, 1903, d March 17, 1978
*Dilawar Hussain (C. Ind. and U. Prov.) b March 19, 1907, d Aug. 26, 1967
*Dilley, G. R. (Kent, Natal & Worcs) b May 18, 1959
Dillon, E. W. (Kent & OU) b Feb. 15, 1881, d April 20, 1941
*Dipper, A. E. (Glos) b Nov. 9, 1885, d Nov. 7, 1945
*Divecha, R. V. (Bombay, OU, Northants, Vidarbha & S'tra) b Oct. 18, 1927
Diver, A. J. D. (Cambs., Middx, Notts & All-England) b June 6, 1824, d March 25, 1876
Diver, E. J. (Surrey & Warwicks) b March 20, 1861, d Dec. 27, 1924
Dixon, A. L. (Kent) b Nov. 27, 1933
*Dixon, C. D. (Tvl) b Feb. 12, 1891, d Sept. 9, 1969
Dixon, J. A. (Notts) b May 27, 1861, d June 8, 1931
Dodds, T. C. (Essex) b May 29, 1919, d Sept. 17, 2001
*Dodemaide, A. I. C. (Vic. & Sussex) b Oct. 5, 1963
*Doggart, G. H. G. OBE (CU & Sussex; Pres. MCC 1981–82) b July 18, 1925
*D'Oliveira, B. L. OBE (Worcs; *CY 1967*) b Oct. 4, 1931
D'Oliveira, D. B. (Worcs) b Oct. 19, 1960
*Dollery, H. E. (Warwicks & Wgtn; *CY 1952*) b Oct. 15, 1914, d Jan. 20, 1987
*Dolphin, A. (Yorks) b Dec. 24, 1885, d Oct. 23, 1942
*Donnan, H. (NSW) b Nov. 12, 1864, d Aug. 13, 1956
*Donnelly, M. P. (Wgtn, Cant., OU, Middx & Warwicks; *CY 1948*) b Oct. 17, 1917, d Oct. 22, 1999
*Dooland, B. (S. Aust. & Notts; *CY 1955*) b Nov. 1, 1923, d Sept. 8, 1980
Dorrinton, W. (Kent & All-England) b April 29, 1809, d Nov. 8, 1848
Dorset, 3rd Duke of (Kent) b March 24, 1745, d July 19, 1799
*Doshi, D. R. (Bengal, Notts, Warwicks & S'tra) b Dec. 22, 1947
*Douglas, J. W. H. T. (Essex; *CY 1915*) b Sept. 3, 1882, d Dec. 19, 1930
Dovey, R. R. (Kent) b July 18, 1920, d Dec. 27, 1974
*Dowe, U. G. (Jam.) b March 29, 1949
*Dower, R. R. (E. Prov.) b June 4, 1876, d Sept. 15, 1964
*Dowling, G. T. OBE (Cant.; ICC referee) b March 4, 1937
*Downton, P. R. (Kent & Middx) b April 4, 1957
*Draper, R. G. (E. Prov. & Griq. W.) b Dec. 24, 1926
Dredge, C. H. (Som) b Aug. 4, 1954
*Druce, N. F. (CU & Surrey; *CY 1898*) b Jan. 1, 1875, d Oct. 27, 1954
Drybrough, C. D. (OU & Middx) b Aug. 31, 1938
*D'Souza, A. (Kar., Peshawar & PIA) b Jan. 17, 1939
*Ducat, A. (Surrey; *CY 1920*) b Feb. 16, 1886, d July 23, 1942
*Duckworth, C. A. R. (Natal & Rhod.) b March 22, 1933
*Duckworth, G. (Lancs; *CY 1929*) b May 9, 1901, d Jan. 5, 1966
Dudleston, B. (Leics, Glos & Rhod.; Test umpire) b July 16, 1945
Duers, K. G. (Mash.) b June 30, 1960
*Duff, R. A. (NSW) b Aug. 17, 1878, d Dec. 13, 1911
*Dujon, P. J. L. (Jam.; *CY 1989*) b May 28, 1956
*Duleepsinhji, K. S. (CU & Sussex; *CY 1930*) b June 13, 1905, d Dec. 5, 1959
*Dumbrill, R. (Natal & Tvl) b Nov. 19, 1938
*Duminy, J. P. (OU, W. Prov. & Tvl) b Dec. 16, 1897, d Jan. 31, 1980
*Duncan, J. R. F. (Qld & Vic.) b March 25, 1944
*Dunell, O. R. (E. Prov.) b July 15, 1856, d Oct. 21, 1929
Dunne, R. S. (Otago; Test umpire) b April 22, 1943
*Dunning, J. A. (Otago & OU) b Feb. 6, 1903, d June 24, 1971
*Dunusinghe, C. I. (Ant. & NCC) b Oct. 19, 1970
*Du Preez, J. H. (Rhod. & Zimb.) b Nov. 14, 1942
*Durani, S. A. (S'tra, Guj. & Raja.) b Dec. 11, 1934
*Durston, F. J. (Middx) b July 11, 1893, d April 8, 1965
*Du Toit, J. F. (SA) b April 5, 1868, d July 10, 1909
Dye, J. C. J. (Kent, Northants & E. Prov.) b July 24, 1942
*Dyer, D. V. (Natal) b May 2, 1914, d June 18, 1990
*Dyer, G. C. (NSW) b March 16, 1959
*Dymock, G. (Qld) b July 21, 1945
Dyson, A. H. (Glam) b July 10, 1905, d June 7, 1978
Dyson, Jack (Lancs) b July 8, 1934, d Nov. 16, 2000
*Dyson, John (NSW) b June 11, 1954

*Eady, C. J. (Tas.) b Oct. 29, 1870, d Dec. 20, 1945
Eagar, E. D. R. (OU, Glos & Hants) b Dec. 8, 1917, d Sept. 13, 1977
Ealham, A. G. E. (Kent) b Aug. 30, 1944
East, D. E. (Essex) b July 27, 1959
East, R. E. (Essex) b June 20, 1947
Eastman, L. C. (Essex & Otago) b June 3, 1897, d April 17, 1941
*Eastwood, K. H. (Vic.) b Nov. 23, 1935
*Ebeling, H. I. MBE (Vic.) b Jan. 1, 1905, d Jan. 12, 1980
Ebrahim, Ahmed (ICC referee) b Dec. 2, 1937
Eckersley, P. T. (Lancs) b July 2, 1904, d Aug. 13, 1940
*Edgar, B. A. (Wgtn) b Nov. 23, 1956
Edinburgh, HRH Duke of (Pres. MCC 1948–49, 1974–75) b June 10, 1921
Edmeades, B. E. A. (Essex) b Sept. 17, 1941
*Edmonds, P. H. (CU, Middx & E. Prov.) b March 8, 1951
Edrich, B. R. (Kent & Glam) b Aug. 18, 1922
Edrich, E. H. (Lancs) b March 27, 1914, d July 9, 1993
Edrich, G. A. (Lancs) b July 13, 1918
*Edrich, J. H. MBE (Surrey; *CY 1966*) b June 21, 1937
*Edrich, W. J. (Middx; *CY 1940*) b March 26, 1916, d April 24, 1986
*Edwards, G. N. (C. Dist.) b May 27, 1955
*Edwards, J. D. (Vic.) b June 12, 1862, d July 31, 1911
Edwards, M. J. (CU & Surrey) b March 1, 1940
*Edwards, R. (W. Aust. & NSW) b Dec. 1, 1942
*Edwards, R. M. (B'dos) b June 3, 1940
*Edwards, W. J. (W. Aust.) b Dec. 23, 1949
*Ehtesham-ud-Din (Lahore, Punjab, PIA, NBP & UBL) b Sept. 4, 1950
*Elgie, M. K. (Natal) b March 6, 1933
Elliott, C. S. MBE (Derbys; Test umpire) b April 24, 1912
Elliott, Harold (Lancs; Test umpire) b June 15, 1904, d April 15, 1969
*Elliott, Harry (Derbys) b Nov. 2, 1891, d Feb. 2, 1976
*Ellison, R. M. (Kent & Tas.; *CY 1986*) b Sept. 21, 1959
*Emburey, J. E. (Middx, W. Prov. & Northants; *CY 1984*) b Aug. 20, 1952
*Emery, P. A. (NSW) b June 25, 1964
*Emery, R. W. G. (Auck. & Cant.) b March 28, 1915, d Dec. 18, 1982
*Emery, S. H. (NSW) b Oct. 16, 1885, d Jan. 7, 1967
*Emmett, G. M. (Glos) b Dec. 2, 1912, d Dec. 18, 1976
*Emmett, T. (Yorks) b Sept. 3, 1841, d June 30, 1904
*Endean, W. R. (Tvl) b May 31, 1924
Engel, Matthew L. (Editor of *Wisden* 1993–2000) b June 11, 1951
*Engineer, F. M. (Bombay & Lancs) b Feb. 25, 1938
Enthoven, H. J. (CU & Middx) b June 4, 1903, d June 29, 1975
Essop-Adam, E. A. (Mash.) b Nov. 16, 1968
*Evans, A. J. (OU, Hants & Kent) b May 1, 1889, d Sept. 18, 1960
Evans, D. G. L. (Glam; Test umpire) b July 27, 1933, d March 25, 1990
*Evans, E. (NSW) b March 26, 1849, d July 2, 1921
*Evans, K. P. (Notts) b Sept. 10, 1963
*Evans, T. G. CBE (Kent; *CY 1951*) b Aug. 18, 1920, d May 3, 1999
Evershed, Sir Sydney H. (Derbys) b Jan. 13, 1861, d March 7, 1937
Every, T. (Glam) b Dec. 19, 1909, d Jan. 20, 1990
Eyre, T. J. P. (Derbys) b Oct. 17, 1939

*Fagg, A. E. (Kent; Test umpire) b June 18, 1915, d Sept. 13, 1977
*Fairfax, A. G. (NSW) b June 16, 1906, d May 17, 1955
Fairservice, W. J. (Kent) b May 16, 1881, d June 26, 1971
*Fane, F. L. (OU & Essex) b April 27, 1875, d Nov. 27, 1960
*Farnes, K. (CU & Essex; *CY 1939*) b July 8, 1911, d Oct. 20, 1941
*Farooq Hamid (Lahore & PIA) b March 3, 1945
*Farrer, W. S. (Border) b Dec. 8, 1936
*Farrimond, W. (Lancs) b May 23, 1903, d Nov. 14, 1979
*Farrukh Zaman (Peshawar, NWFP, Punjab & MCB) b April 2, 1956
*Faulkner, G. A. (Tvl) b Dec. 17, 1881, d Sept. 10, 1930
*Favell, L. E. MBE (S. Aust.) b Oct. 6, 1929, d June 14, 1987
*Fazal Mahmood (N. Ind., Punjab & Lahore; *CY 1955*) b Feb. 18, 1927
Fearnley, C. D. (Worcs; bat-maker) b April 12, 1940
Featherstone, N. G. (Tvl, N. Tvl, Middx & Glam) b Aug. 20, 1949
'Felix', N. (Wanostrocht) (Kent, Surrey & All-England) b Oct. 4, 1804, d Sept. 3, 1876
*Fellows-Smith, J. P. (OU, Tvl & Northants) b Feb. 3, 1932
Feltham, M. A. (Surrey & Middx) b June 26, 1963
Felton, N. A. (Som & Northants) b Oct. 24, 1960
*Fender, P. G. H. (Sussex & Surrey; *CY 1915*) b Aug. 22, 1892, d June 15, 1985
*Ferguson, W. (T/T) b Dec. 14, 1917, d Feb. 23, 1961

Ferguson, W. H. BEM (Scorer) b June 6, 1880, d Sept. 22, 1957
*Fernandes, M. P. (BG) b Aug. 12, 1897, d May 8, 1981
Fernando, E. R. (SL) b Feb. 22, 1944
*Fernando, E. R. N. S. (SLAF) b Dec. 19, 1955
Fernando, T. L. (Colts & BRC) b Dec. 27, 1962
Fernando, U. N. K. (SSC & BRC) b March 10, 1970
Ferreira, A. M. (N. Tvl & Warwicks) b April 13, 1955
**Ferris, J. J. (NSW, Glos & S. Aust.; *CY 1889*) b May 21, 1867, d Nov. 21, 1900
*Fichardt, C. G. (OFS) b March 20, 1870, d May 30, 1923
Fiddling, K. (Yorks & Northants) b Oct. 13, 1917, d June 19, 1992
Field, F. E. (Warwicks) b Sept. 23, 1874, d Aug. 25, 1934
*Fielder, A. (Kent; *CY 1907*) b July 19, 1877, d Aug. 30, 1949
*Findlay, T. M. MBE (Comb. Is. & Windwards) b Oct. 19, 1943
Findlay, W. (OU & Lancs; Sec. Surrey CCC 1907–19; Sec. MCC 1926–36) b June 22, 1880, d June 19, 1953
*Fingleton, J. H. OBE (NSW; writer) b April 28, 1908, d Nov. 22, 1981
*Finlason, C. E. (Tvl & Griq. W.) b Feb. 19, 1860, d July 31, 1917
Finney, R. J. (Derbys) b Aug. 2, 1960
Firth, Canon J. D'E. E. (Winchester, OU & Notts; *CY 1918*) b Jan. 21, 1900, d Sept. 21, 1957
Firth, J. (Yorks & Leics) b June 27, 1917, d Sept. 7, 1981
*Fisher, F. E. (Wgtn & C. Dist.) b July 28, 1924, d June 19, 1996
*Fishlock, L. B. (Surrey; *CY 1947*) b Jan. 2, 1907, d June 26, 1986
Fishwick, T. S. (Warwicks) b July 24, 1876, d Feb. 21, 1950
Fitzgerald, R. A. (CU & Middx; Sec. MCC 1863–76) b Oct. 1, 1834, d Oct. 28, 1881
Fitzroy-Newdegate, Hon. J. M. (Northants) b March 20, 1897, d May 7, 1976
*Flavell, J. A. (Worcs; *CY 1965*) b May 15, 1929
*Fleetwood-Smith, L. O'B. (Vic.) b March 30, 1908, d March 16, 1971
Fletcher, D. A. G. (Rhod. & Zimb.) b Sept. 27, 1948
Fletcher, D. G. W. (Surrey) b July 6, 1924
*Fletcher, K. W. R. OBE (Essex; *CY 1974*) b May 20, 1944
Fletcher, S. D. (Yorks & Lancs) b June 8, 1964
*Floquet, C. E. (Tvl) b Nov. 3, 1884, d Nov. 22, 1963
*Flowers, W. (Notts) b Dec. 7, 1856, d Nov. 1, 1926
*Foley, H. (Wgtn) b Jan. 28, 1906, d Oct. 16, 1948
Folley, I. (Lancs & Derbys) b Jan. 9, 1963, d Aug. 30, 1993
Forbes, C. (Notts) b Aug. 9, 1936
*Ford, F. G. J. (CU & Middx) b Dec. 14, 1866, d Feb. 7, 1940
Fordham, A. (Northants) b Nov. 9, 1964
Foreman, D. J. (W. Prov. & Sussex) b Feb. 1, 1933
*Foster, F. R. (Warwicks; *CY 1912*) b Jan. 31, 1889, d May 3, 1958
Foster, G. N. (OU, Worcs & Kent) b Oct. 16, 1884, d Aug. 11, 1971
Foster, H. K. (OU & Worcs; *CY 1911*) b Oct. 30, 1873, d June 23, 1950
Foster, M. K. (Worcs) b Jan. 1, 1889, d Dec. 3, 1940
*Foster, M. L. C. (Jam.) b May 9, 1943
*Foster, N. A. (Essex & Tvl; *CY 1988*) b May 6, 1962
*Foster, R. E. (OU & Worcs; *CY 1901*) b April 16, 1878, d May 13, 1914
*Fothergill, A. J. (Som) b Aug. 26, 1854, d Aug. 1, 1932
Fowke, G. H. S. (Leics) b Oct. 14, 1880, d June 24, 1946
*Fowler, G. (Lancs & Durham) b April 20, 1957
*Francis, B. C. (NSW & Essex) b Feb. 18, 1948
Francis, D. A. (Glam) b Nov. 29, 1953
*Francis, G. N. (B'dos) b Dec. 11, 1897, d Jan. 7, 1942
*Francis, H. H. (Glos & W. Prov.) b May 26, 1868, d Jan. 7, 1936
Francis, K. T. (Test umpire) b Oct. 15, 1949
Francke, F. M. (SL & Qld) b March 29, 1941
*Francois, C. M. (Griq. W.) b June 20, 1897, d May 26, 1944
*Frank, C. N. (Tvl) b Jan. 27, 1891, d Dec. 25, 1961
*Frank, W. H. B. (SA) b Nov. 23, 1872, d Feb. 16, 1945
*Franklin, T. J. (Auck.) b March 18, 1962
*Frederick, M. (B'dos, Derbys & Jam.) b May 6, 1927
*Fredericks, R. C. (†Guyana & Glam; *CY 1974*) b Nov. 11, 1942, d Sept. 5, 2000
*Freeman, A. P. (Kent; *CY 1923*) b May 17, 1888, d Jan. 28, 1965
*Freeman, D. L. (Wgtn) b Sept. 8, 1914, d May 31, 1994
*Freeman, E. W. (S. Aust.) b July 13, 1944
Freeman, J. R. (Essex) b Sept. 3, 1883, d Aug. 8, 1958
*Freer, F. W. (Vic.) b Dec. 4, 1915, d Nov. 2 1998
*French, B. N. (Notts) b Aug. 13, 1959
Frost, G. (Notts) b Jan. 15, 1947

*Fry, C. B. (OU, Sussex & Hants; *CY 1895*) b April 25, 1872, d Sept. 7, 1956
*Fuller, E. R. H. (W. Prov.) b Aug. 2, 1931
*Fuller, R. L. (Jam.) b Jan. 30, 1913, d May 3, 1987
*Fullerton, G. M. (Tvl) b Dec. 8, 1922
*Funston, K. J. (NE Tvl, OFS & Tvl) b Dec. 3, 1925
*Furlonge, H. A. (T/T) b June 19, 1934

Gabriel, R. S. (T/T) b June 5, 1952
*Gadkari, C. V. (M'tra & Ind. Serv.) b Feb. 3, 1928, d Jan. 11, 1998
*Gaekwad, A. D. (Baroda) b Sept. 23, 1952
*Gaekwad, D. K. (Baroda) b Oct. 27, 1928
*Gaekwad, H. G. (†M. Pradesh) b Aug. 29, 1923
Gale, R. A. (Middx) b Dec. 10, 1933
*Gallichan, N. (Wgtn) b June 3, 1906, d March 25, 1969
Gamage, J. C. (Colts & Galle) b April 17, 1964
*Gamsy, D. (Natal) b Feb. 17, 1940
*Gandotra, A. (Delhi & Bengal) b Nov. 24, 1948
*Gannon, J. B. (W. Aust.) b Feb. 8, 1947
*Ganteaume, A. G. (T/T) b Jan. 22, 1921
Gard, T. (Som) b June 2, 1957
Gardiner, Howard (ICC referee) b Jan. 1, 1944
Gardner, F. C. (Warwicks) b June 4, 1922, d Jan. 12, 1979
Gardner, L. R. (Leics) b Feb. 23, 1934
Garland-Wells, H. M. (OU & Surrey) b Nov. 14, 1907, d May 28, 1993
Garlick, R. G. (Lancs & Northants) b April 11, 1917, d May 16, 1988
*Garner, J. MBE (B'dos, Som & S. Aust.; *CY 1980*) b Dec. 16, 1952
Garnham, M. A. (Glos, Leics & Essex) b Aug. 20, 1960
*Garrett, T. W. (NSW) b July 26, 1858, d Aug. 6, 1943
*Gaskin, B. B. M. (BG) b March 21, 1908, d May 1, 1979
*Gatting, M. W. OBE (Middx; *CY 1984*) b June 6, 1957
*Gaunt, R. A. (W. Aust. & Vic.) b Feb. 26, 1934
*Gavaskar, S. M. (Bombay & Som; *CY 1980*) b July 10, 1949
*Gay, L. H. (CU, Hants & Som) b March 24, 1871, d Nov. 1, 1949
*Geary, G. (Leics; *CY 1927*) b July 9, 1893, d March 6, 1981
*Gedye, S. G. (Auck.) b May 2, 1929
*Gehrs, D. R. A. (S. Aust.) b Nov. 29, 1880, d June 25, 1953
*Germon, L. K. (Cant.) b Nov. 4, 1968
Ghai, R. S. (Punjab) b June 12, 1960
*Ghavri, K. D. (S'tra & Bombay) b Feb. 28, 1951
*Ghazali, M. E. Z. (M'tra & Pak. Serv.) b June 15, 1924
*Ghorpade, J. M. (Baroda) b Oct. 2, 1930, d March 29, 1978
*Ghulam Abbas (Kar., NBP & PIA) b May 1, 1947
*Ghulam Ahmed (H'bad) b July 4, 1922, d Oct. 28, 1998
*Gibb, P. A. (CU, Scotland, Yorks & Essex) b July 11, 1913, d Dec. 7, 1977
Gibbons, H. H. (Worcs) b Oct. 10, 1904, d Feb. 16, 1973
*Gibbs, G. L. (BG) b Dec. 27, 1925, d Feb. 21, 1979
*Gibbs, L. R. (†Guyana, S. Aust. & Warwicks; *CY 1972*) b Sept. 29, 1934
Gibbs, P. J. K. (OU & Derbys) b Aug. 17, 1944
Gibson, C. H. (Eton, CU & Sussex; *CY 1918*) b Aug. 23, 1900, d Dec. 31, 1976
Gibson, D. (Surrey) b May 1, 1936
*Giffen, G. (S. Aust.; *CY 1894*) b March 27, 1859, d Nov. 29, 1927
*Giffen, W. F. (S. Aust.) b Sept. 20, 1861, d June 29, 1949
*Gifford, N. MBE (Worcs & Warwicks; *CY 1975*) b March 30, 1940
*Gilbert, D. R. (NSW, Tas. & Glos) b Dec. 29, 1960
*Gilchrist, R. (Jam. & H'bad) b June 28, 1934, d July 18, 2001
Giles, R. J. (Notts) b Oct. 17, 1919
Gilhouley, K. (Yorks & Notts) b Aug. 8, 1934
*Gillespie, S. R. (Auck.) b March 2, 1957
Gilliat, R. M. C. (OU & Hants) b May 20, 1944
*Gilligan, A. E. R. (CU, Surrey & Sussex; *CY 1924;* Pres. MCC 1967–68) b Dec. 23, 1894, d Sept. 5, 1976
*Gilligan, A. H. H. (Sussex) b June 29, 1896, d May 5, 1978
Gilligan, F. W. (OU & Essex) b Sept. 20, 1893, d May 4, 1960
Gillingham, Canon F. H. (Essex) b Sept. 6, 1875, d April 1, 1953
*Gilmour, G. J. (NSW) b June 26, 1951
*Gimblett, H. (Som; *CY 1953*) b Oct. 19, 1914, d March 30, 1978
*Gladstone, G. (*see* Marais, G. G.)
*Gladwin, Cliff (Derbys) b April 3, 1916, d April 10, 1988
*Gleeson, J. W. (NSW & E. Prov.) b March 14, 1938
*Gleeson, R. A. (E. Prov.) b Dec. 6, 1873, d Sept. 27, 1919
Glover, A. C. S. (Warwicks) b April 19, 1872, d May 22, 1949
*Glover, G. K. (Kimberley & Griq. W.) b May 13, 1870, d Nov. 15, 1938
*Goddard, J. D. C. OBE (B'dos) b April 21, 1919, d Aug. 26, 1987

*Goddard, T. L. (Natal & NE Tvl) b Aug. 1, 1931
*Goddard, T. W. (Glos; *CY 1938*) b Oct. 1, 1900, d May 22, 1966
Goel, R. (Patiala & Haryana) b Sept. 29, 1942
*Gomes, H. A. (T/T & Middx; *CY 1985*) b July 13, 1953
*Gomez, G. E. (T/T) b Oct. 10, 1919, d Aug. 6, 1996
*Gooch, G. A. OBE (Essex & W. Prov.; *CY 1980*) b July 23, 1953
Goodwin, K. (Lancs) b June 25, 1938
Goodwin, T. J. (Leics) b Jan. 22, 1929
Goonatillake, F. R. M. de S. (SL) b Aug. 15, 1951
*Goonatillake, H. M. (SL) b Aug. 16, 1952
Goonesena, G. (Ceylon, Notts, CU & NSW) b Feb. 16, 1931
*Gopalan, M. J. (Madras) b June 6, 1909
*Gopinath, C. D. (Madras) b March 1, 1930
*Gordon, N. (Tvl) b Aug. 6, 1911
Gore, A. C. (Eton & Army; *CY 1919*) b May 14, 1900, d June 7, 1990
Gould, I. J. (Middx, Auck. & Sussex) b Aug. 19, 1957
*Gover, A. R. MBE (Surrey; *CY 1937*) b Feb. 29, 1908, d Oct. 7, 2001
*Gower, D. I. OBE (Leics & Hants; *CY 1979*) b April 1, 1957
Grace, C. B. (London County; son of W. G.) b March 1882, d June 6, 1938
*Grace, Dr E. M. (Glos; brother of W. G.) b Nov. 28, 1841, d May 20, 1911
*Grace, G. F. (Glos; brother of W. G.) b Dec. 13, 1850, d Sept. 22, 1880
Grace, Dr Henry (Glos; brother of W. G.) b Jan. 31, 1833, d Nov. 15, 1895
Grace, Dr H. M. (father of W. G.) b Feb. 21, 1808, d Dec. 23, 1871
Grace, Mrs H. M. (mother of W. G.) b July 18, 1812, d July 25, 1884
*Grace, Dr W. G. (Glos; *CY 1896*) b July 18, 1848, d Oct. 23, 1915
Grace, W. G., jun. (CU & Glos; son of W. G.) b July 6, 1874, d March 2, 1905
Graf, S. F. (Vic., W. Aust. & Hants) b May 19, 1957
*Graham, H. (Vic. & Otago) b Nov. 22, 1870, d Feb. 7, 1911
Graham, J. N. (Kent) b May 8, 1943
*Graham, R. (W. Prov.) b Sept. 16, 1877, d April 21, 1946
*Grant, G. C. (CU, T/T & Rhod.) b May 9, 1907, d Oct. 26, 1978
*Grant, R. S. (CU & T/T) b Dec. 15, 1909, d Oct. 18, 1977
Graveney, D. A. (Glos, Som & Durham) b Jan. 2, 1953
Graveney, J. K. (Glos) b Dec. 16, 1924
*Graveney, T. W. OBE (Glos, Worcs & Qld; *CY 1953*) b June 16, 1927
Graves, P. J. (Sussex & OFS) b May 19, 1946
*Gray, A. H. (T/T, Surrey & W. Tvl) b May 23, 1963
*Gray, E. J. (Wgtn) b Nov. 18, 1954
Gray, J. R. (Hants) b May 19, 1926
Gray, L. H. (Middx) b Dec. 15, 1915, d Jan. 3, 1983
Gray, M. A. (President ICC 2000–) b May 30, 1940
*Greatbatch, M. J. (C. Dist.) b Dec. 11, 1963
Green, A. M. (Sussex & OFS) b May 28, 1960
Green, D. M. (OU, Lancs & Glos; *CY 1969*) b Nov. 10, 1939
Green, Major L. (Lancs) b Feb. 1, 1890, d March 2, 1963
*Greenhough, T. (Lancs) b Nov. 9, 1931
*Greenidge, A. E. (B'dos) b Aug. 20, 1956
*Greenidge, C. G. MBE (Hants & B'dos; *CY 1977*) b May 1, 1951
*Greenidge, G. A. (B'dos & Sussex) b May 26, 1948
Greensmith, W. T. (Essex) b Aug. 16, 1930
*Greenwood, A. (Yorks) b Aug. 20, 1847, d Feb. 12, 1889
Greetham, C. (Som) b Aug. 28, 1936
*Gregory, D. W. (NSW; first Australian captain) b April 15, 1845, d Aug. 4, 1919
*Gregory, E. J. (NSW) b May 29, 1839, d April 22, 1899
*Gregory, J. M. (NSW; *CY 1922*) b Aug. 14, 1895, d Aug. 7, 1973
*Gregory, R. G. (Vic.) b Feb. 28, 1916, d June 10, 1942
Gregory, R. J. (Surrey) b Aug. 26, 1902, d Oct. 6, 1973
*Gregory, S. E. (NSW; *CY 1897*) b April 14, 1870, d Aug. 1, 1929
*Greig, A. W. (Border, E. Prov. & Sussex; *CY 1975*) b Oct. 6, 1946
*Greig, I. A. (CU, Border, Sussex & Surrey) b Dec. 8, 1955
*Grell, M. G. (T/T) b Dec. 18, 1899, d Jan. 11, 1976
*Grieve, B. A. F. (Eng.) b May 28, 1864, d Nov. 19, 1917
Grieves, K. J. (NSW & Lancs) b Aug. 27, 1925, d Jan. 3, 1992
*Grieveson, R. E. OBE (Tvl) b Aug. 24, 1909, d July 24, 1998
*Griffin, G. M. (Natal & Rhod.) b June 12, 1939
*Griffith, C. C. (B'dos; *CY 1964*) b Dec. 14, 1938
Griffith, G. ("Ben") (Surrey & Utd England XI) b Dec. 20, 1833, d May 3, 1879
*Griffith, H. C. (B'dos) b Dec. 1, 1893, d March 18, 1980
Griffith, M. G. (CU & Sussex) b Nov. 25, 1943

*Griffith, S. C. CBE (CU, Surrey & Sussex; Sec. MCC 1962–74; Pres. MCC 1979–80) b June 16, 1914, d April 7, 1993
Griffiths, B. J. (Northants) b June 13, 1949
*Grimmett, C. V. (Wgtn, Vic., & S. Aust.; *CY 1931*) b Dec. 25, 1891, d May 2, 1980
*Groube, T. U. (Vic.) b Sept. 2, 1857, d Aug. 5, 1927
*Grout, A. T. W. (Qld) b March 30, 1927, d Nov. 9, 1968
Grove, C. W. (Warwicks & Worcs) b Dec. 16, 1912, d Feb. 15, 1982
Grundy, James (Notts & Utd England XI) b March 5, 1824, d Nov. 24, 1873
*Guard, G. M. (Bombay & Guj.) b Dec. 12, 1925, d March 13, 1978
*Guest, C. E. J. (Vic. & W. Aust.) b Oct. 7, 1937
*Guha, S. (Bengal) b Jan. 31, 1946
**Guillen, S. C. (T/T & Cant.) b Sept. 24, 1924
**Gul Mahomed (N. Ind., Baroda, H'bad, Punjab & Lahore) b Oct. 15, 1921, d May 8, 1992
*Gunasekera, Y. (SL) b Nov. 8, 1957
Gunawardene, A. A. W. (SSC & Moors) b March 31, 1969
*Guneratne, R. P. W. (Nomads) b Jan. 26, 1962
*Gunn, G. (Notts; *CY 1914*) b June 13, 1879, d June 29, 1958
Gunn, G. V. (Notts) b June 21, 1905, d Oct. 14, 1957
*Gunn, J. (Notts; *CY 1904*) b July 19, 1876, d Aug. 21, 1963
*Gunn, W. (Notts; *CY 1890*) b Dec. 4, 1858, d Jan. 29, 1921
*Gupte, B. P. (Bombay, Bengal & Ind. Rlwys) b Aug. 30, 1934
*Gupte, S. P. (Bombay, Bengal, Raja. & T/T) b Dec. 11, 1929
*Gursharan Singh (Punjab) b March 8, 1963
*Gurusinha, A. P. (SSC & NCC) b Sept. 16, 1966
*Guy, J. W. (C. Dist., Wgtn, Northants, Cant., Otago & N. Dist.) b Aug. 29, 1934

Haafiz Shahid (WAPDA) b May 10, 1963
Hadlee, B. G. (Cant.) b Dec. 14, 1941
*Hadlee, D. R. (Cant.) b Jan. 6, 1948
*Hadlee, Sir Richard J. (Cant., Notts & Tas.; *CY 1982*) b July 3, 1951
*Hadlee, W. A. CBE (Cant. & Otago) b June 4, 1915
*Hafeez, A. (*see* Kardar)
*Haig, N. E. (Middx) b Dec. 12, 1887, d Oct. 27, 1966
*Haigh, S. (Yorks; *CY 1901*) b March 19, 1871, d Feb. 27, 1921
Hair, D. B. (Test umpire) b Sept. 30, 1952
Halfyard, D. J. (Kent & Notts) b April 3, 1931, d Aug. 23, 1996
*Hall, A. E. (Tvl & Lancs) b Jan. 23, 1896, d Jan. 1, 1964
*Hall, G. G. (NE Tvl & E. Prov.) b May 24, 1938, d June 26, 1987
Hall, I. W. (Derbys) b Dec. 27, 1939
Hall, L. (Yorks; *CY 1890*) b Nov. 1, 1852, d Nov. 19, 1915
*Hall, W. W. (B'dos, T/T & Qld) b Sept. 12, 1937
Hallam, A. W. (Lancs & Notts; *CY 1908*) b Nov. 12, 1869, d July 24, 1940
Hallam, M. R. (Leics) b Sept. 10, 1931, d Jan. 1, 2000
Halliday, H. (Yorks) b Feb. 9, 1920, d Aug. 27, 1967
*Halliwell, E. A. (Tvl & Middx; *CY 1905*) b Sept. 7, 1864, d Oct. 2, 1919
*Hallows, C. (Lancs; *CY 1928*) b April 4, 1895, d Nov. 10, 1972
Hallows, J. (Lancs; *CY 1905*) b Nov. 14, 1873, d May 20, 1910
*Halse, C. G. (Natal) b Feb. 28, 1935
*Hamence, R. A. (S. Aust.) b Nov. 25, 1915
Hamer, A. (Yorks & Derbys) b Dec. 8, 1916, d Nov. 3, 1993
Hammond, H. E. (Sussex) b Nov. 7, 1907, d June 16, 1985
*Hammond, J. R. (S. Aust.) b April 19, 1950
*Hammond, W. R. (Glos; *CY 1928*) b June 19, 1903, d July 1, 1965
*Hampshire, J. H. (Yorks, Derbys & Tas.; Test umpire) b Feb. 10, 1941
Hampton, G. S. (Auck.; *believed to be oldest living first-class cricketer at end of 2001*) b Aug. 31, 1905
*Hands, P. A. M. (W. Prov.) b March 18, 1890, d April 27, 1951
*Hands, R. H. M. (W. Prov.) b July 26, 1888, d April 20, 1918
*Hanif Mohammad (B'pur, Kar. & PIA; *CY 1968*) b Dec. 21, 1934
*Hanley, M. A. (Border & W. Prov.) b Nov. 10, 1918, d June 2, 2000
*Hanumant Singh (M. Pradesh & Raja.; ICC referee) b March 29, 1939
Harden, R. J. (Som, Yorks & C. Dist.) b Aug. 16, 1965
Hardie, B. R. (Scotland & Essex) b Jan. 14, 1950
*Hardikar, M. S. (Bombay) b Feb. 8, 1936, d Feb. 4, 1995
*Hardinge, H. T. W. (Kent; *CY 1915*) b Feb. 25, 1886, d May 8, 1965
*Hardstaff, J. (Notts; Test umpire) b Nov. 9, 1882, d April 2, 1947
*Hardstaff, J., jun. (Notts & Auck.; *CY 1938*) b July 3, 1911, d Jan. 1, 1990
Hardy, J. J. E. (Hants, Som, W. Prov. & Glos) b Oct. 2, 1960
*Harford, N. S. (C. Dist. & Auck.) b Aug. 30, 1930, d March 30, 1981

*Harford, R. I. (Auck.) b May 30, 1936
Hargreave, S. (Warwicks) b Sept. 22, 1875, d Jan. 1, 1929
Harman, R. (Surrey) b Dec. 28, 1941
*Haroon Rashid (Kar., Sind, NBP, PIA & UBL) b March 25, 1953
*Harper, D. J. (Test umpire) b Oct. 23, 1951
*Harper, R. A. (Guyana & Northants) b March 17, 1963
*Harris, 4th Lord (OU & Kent; Pres. MCC 1895) b Feb. 3, 1851, d March 24, 1932
Harris, C. B. (Notts) b Dec. 6, 1907, d Aug. 8, 1954
Harris, David (Hants & All-England) b 1755, d May 19, 1803
Harris, J. H. (Som; umpire) b Feb. 13, 1936
Harris, M. J. (Middx, Notts, E. Prov. & Wgtn) b May 25, 1944
*Harris, P. G. Z. (Cant.) b July 18, 1927, d Dec. 1, 1991
*Harris, R. M. (Auck.) b July 27, 1933
*Harris, T. A. (Griq. W. & Tvl) b Aug. 27, 1916, d March 7, 1993
Harrison, L. (Hants) b June 8, 1922
*Harry, J. (Vic.) b Aug. 1, 1857, d Oct. 27, 1919
Hart, R. T. (C. Dist. & Wgtn) b Nov. 7, 1961
*Hartigan, G. P. D. (Border) b Dec. 30, 1884, d Jan. 7, 1955
*Hartigan, R. J. (NSW & Qld) b Dec. 12, 1879, d June 7, 1958
*Hartkopf, A. E. V. (Vic.) b Dec. 28, 1889, d May 20, 1968
*Hartland, B. R. (Cant.) b Oct. 22, 1966
Hartley, A. (Lancs; *CY 1911*) b April 11, 1879, d Oct. 9, 1918
*Hartley, J. C. (OU & Sussex) b Nov. 15, 1874, d March 8, 1963
Hartley, P. J. (Warwicks, Yorks & Hants) b April 18, 1960
Hartley, S. N. (Yorks & OFS) b March 18, 1956
Harvey, J. F. (Derbys) b Sept. 27, 1939
*Harvey, M. R. (Vic.) b April 29, 1918, d March 20, 1995
Harvey, P. F. (Notts) b Jan. 15, 1923
*Harvey, R. L. (Natal) b Sept. 14, 1911, d July 20, 2000
*Harvey, R. N. MBE (Vic. & NSW; *CY 1954*) b Oct. 8, 1928
Hasan Jamil (Kalat, Kar., Pak. Us & PIA) b July 25, 1952
*Haseeb Ahsan (Peshawar, Pak. Us, Kar. & PIA) b July 15, 1939
Hassan, B. (Notts) b March 24, 1944
*Hassett, A. L. MBE (Vic.; *CY 1949*) b Aug. 28, 1913, d June 16, 1993
*Hastings, B. F. (Wgtn, C. Dist. & Cant.; ICC referee) b March 23, 1940
*Hathorn, C. M. H. (Tvl) b April 7, 1878, d May 17, 1920
*Hawke, 7th Lord (CU & Yorks; *CY 1909;* Pres. MCC 1914–18) b Aug. 16, 1860, d Oct. 10, 1938
*Hawke, N. J. N. (W. Aust., S. Aust. & Tas.) b June 27, 1939, d Dec. 25, 2000
Hawkins, D. G. (Glos) b May 18, 1935
*Hayes, E. G. (Surrey & Leics; *CY 1907*) b Nov. 6, 1876, d Dec. 2, 1953
*Hayes, F. C. (Lancs) b Dec. 6, 1946
*Hayes, J. A. (Auck. & Cant.) b Jan. 11, 1927
Hayes, R. L. (N. Dist.) b May 9, 1971
Haygarth, A. (Sussex; Historian) b Aug. 4, 1825, d May 1, 1903
Hayhurst, A. N. (Lancs, Som & Derbys) b Nov. 23, 1962
*Haynes, D. L. (B'dos, Middx & W. Prov.; *CY 1991*) b Feb. 15, 1956
Haynes, G. R. (Worcs) b Sept. 29, 1969
Haynes, R. C. (Jam.) b Nov. 2, 1964
Hayward, T. (Cambs. & All-England) b March 21, 1835, d July 21, 1876
*Hayward, T. W. (Surrey; *CY 1895*) b March 29, 1871, d July 19, 1939
*Hazare, V. S. (M'tra, C. Ind. & Baroda) b March 11, 1915
Hazell, H. L. (Som) b Sept. 30, 1909, d March 31, 1990
Hazlerigg, Sir A. G. Bt (later 1st Lord) (Leics) b Nov. 17, 1878, d May 25, 1949
Hazlitt, G. R. (Vic. & NSW) b Sept. 4, 1888, d Oct. 30, 1915
*Headley, D. W. (Middx & Kent) b Jan. 27, 1970
*Headley, G. A. MBE (Jam.; *CY 1934*) b May 30, 1909, d Nov. 30, 1983
*Headley, R. G. A. (Worcs & Jam.) b June 29, 1939
*Healy, I. A. (Qld; *CY 1994*) b April 30, 1964
Heane, G. F. H. (Notts) b Jan. 2, 1904, d Oct. 24, 1969
Heap, J. S. (Lancs) b Aug. 12, 1882, d Jan. 30, 1951
Hearn, P. (Kent) b Nov. 18, 1925
*Hearne, A. (Kent; *CY 1894*) b July 22, 1863, d May 16, 1952
**Hearne, F. (Kent & W. Prov.) b Nov. 23, 1858, d July 14, 1949
*Hearne, G. A. L. (W. Prov.) b March 27, 1888, d Nov. 13, 1978
*Hearne, G. G. (Kent) b July 7, 1856, d Feb. 13, 1932
*Hearne, J. T. (Middx; *CY 1892*) b May 3, 1867, d April 17, 1944
*Hearne, J. W. (Middx; *CY 1912*) b Feb. 11, 1891, d Sept. 14, 1965
Hearne, T. (Middx) b Sept. 4, 1826, d May 13, 1900
Heath, G. E. M. (Hants) b Feb. 20, 1913, d March 6, 1994
Heath, M. (Hants) b March 9, 1934
Hedges, B. (Glam) b Nov. 10, 1927

Hedges, L. P. (Tonbridge, OU, Kent & Glos; *CY 1919*) b July 13, 1900, d Jan. 12, 1933
*Heine, P. S. (NE Tvl, OFS & Tvl) b June 28, 1928
*Hemmings, E. E. (Warwicks, Notts & Sussex) b Feb. 20, 1949
Hemsley, E. J. O. (Worcs) b Sept. 1, 1943
*Henderson, M. (Wgtn) b Aug. 2, 1895, d June 17, 1970
Henderson, R. (Surrey; *CY 1890*) b March 30, 1865, d Jan. 29, 1931
*Hendren, E. H. (Middx; *CY 1920*) b Feb. 5, 1889, d Oct. 4, 1962
*Hendrick, M. (Derbys & Notts; *CY 1978*) b Oct. 22, 1948
*Hendriks, J. L. (Jam.; ICC referee) b Dec. 21, 1933
*Hendry, H. L. (NSW & Vic.) b May 24, 1895, d Dec. 16, 1988
*Henry, O. (W. Prov., Boland, OFS & Scotland) b Jan. 23, 1952
Herman, O. W. (Hants) b Sept. 18, 1907, d June 24, 1987
Herman, R. S. (Middx, Border, Griq. W. & Hants) b Nov. 30, 1946
Heron, J. G. (Zimb.) b Nov. 8, 1948
*Heseltine, C. (Hants) b Nov. 26, 1869, d June 13, 1944
Hever, N. G. (Middx & Glam) b Dec. 17, 1924, d Sept. 11, 1987
Hewett, H. T. (OU & Som; *CY 1893*) b May 25, 1864, d March 4, 1921.
Heyhoe-Flint, Rachael (England Women) b June 11, 1939
Heyn, P. D. (SL) b June 26, 1945
*Hibbert, P. A. (Vic.) b July 23, 1952
Hide, M. E. (Molly) (England Women) b Oct. 24, 1913, d Sept. 10, 1995
*Higgs, J. D. (Vic.) b July 11, 1950
*Higgs, K. (Lancs & Leics; *CY 1968*) b Jan. 14, 1937
Hignell, A. J. (CU & Glos) b Sept. 4, 1955
*Hilditch, A. M. J. (NSW & S. Aust.) b May 20, 1956
Hill, Alan (Derbys & OFS) b June 29, 1950
*Hill, Allen (Yorks) b Nov. 14, 1843, d Aug. 29, 1910
*Hill, A. J. L. (CU & Hants) b July 26, 1871, d Sept. 6, 1950
*Hill, C. (S. Aust.; *CY 1900*) b March 18, 1877, d Sept. 5, 1945
Hill, E. (Som) b July 9, 1923
Hill, G. (Hants) b April 15, 1913
*Hill, J. C. (Vic.) b June 25, 1923, d Aug. 11, 1974
Hill, M. (Notts, Derbys & Som) b Sept. 14, 1935
Hill, N. W. (Notts) b Aug. 22, 1935
Hill, W. A. (Warwicks) b April 27, 1910, d Aug. 11, 1995
Hill-Wood, Sir Samuel H. (Derbys) b March 21, 1872, d Jan. 4, 1949
Hillyer, W. R. (Kent & Surrey) b March 5, 1813, d Jan. 8, 1861
Hilton, C. (Lancs & Essex) b Sept. 26, 1937
*Hilton, M. J. (Lancs; *CY 1957*) b Aug. 2, 1928, d July 8, 1990
*Hime, C. F. W. (Natal) b Oct. 24, 1869, d Dec. 6, 1940
*Hindlekar, D. D. (Bombay) b Jan. 1, 1909, d March 30, 1949
Hinks, S. G. (Kent & Glos) b Oct. 12, 1960
Hipkin, A. B. (Essex) b Aug. 8, 1900, d Feb. 11, 1957
*Hirst, G. H. (Yorks; *CY 1901*) b Sept. 7, 1871, d May 10, 1954
*Hitch, J. W. (Surrey; *CY 1914*) b May 7, 1886, d July 7, 1965
Hitchcock, R. E. (Cant. & Warwicks) b Nov. 28, 1929
*Hoad, E. L. G. (B'dos) b Jan. 29, 1896, d March 5, 1986
*Hoare, D. E. (W. Aust.) b Oct. 19, 1934
*Hobbs, Sir John B. "Jack" (Surrey; *CY 1909, special portrait 1926*) b Dec. 16, 1882, d Dec. 21, 1963
*Hobbs, R. N. S. (Essex & Glam) b May 8, 1942
*Hodges, J. (Vic.) b Aug. 11, 1855, death unknown
Hodgson, A. (Northants) b Oct. 27, 1951
Hodgson, G. D. (Glos) b Oct. 22, 1966
*Hogan, T. G. (W. Aust.) b Sept. 23, 1956
*Hogg, R. M. (S. Aust.) b March 5, 1951
Hogg, V. R. (Zimb.) b July 3, 1952
*Hohns, T. V. (Qld) b Jan. 23, 1954
Holder, J. W. (Hants; Test umpire) b March 19, 1945
*Holder, V. A. (B'dos, Worcs & OFS) b Oct. 8, 1945
*Holding, M. A. (Jam., Lancs, Derbys, Tas. & Cant.; *CY 1977*) b Feb. 16, 1954
*Hole, G. B. (NSW & S. Aust.) b Jan. 6, 1931, d Feb. 14, 1990
*Holford, D. A. J. (B'dos & T/T) b April 16, 1940
Holland, F. C. (Surrey) b Feb. 10, 1876, d Feb. 5, 1957
*Holland, R. G. (NSW & Wgtn) b Oct. 19, 1946
*Hollies, W. E. (Warwicks; *CY 1955*) b June 5, 1912, d April 16, 1981
Holmes, Gp Capt. A. J. (Sussex) b June 30, 1899, d May 21, 1950
*Holmes, E. R. T. (OU & Surrey; *CY 1936*) b Aug. 21, 1905, d Aug. 16, 1960
Holmes, G. C. (Glam) b Sept. 16, 1958
*Holmes, P. (Yorks; *CY 1920*) b Nov. 25, 1886, d Sept. 3, 1971
Holt, A. G. (Hants) b April 8, 1911, d July 28, 1994

*Holt, J. K., jun. (Jam.) b Aug. 12, 1923, d July 2, 1997
Home of the Hirsel, Lord (Middx; Pres. MCC 1966–67) b July 2, 1903, d Oct. 9, 1995
*Hone, L. (MCC) b Jan. 30, 1853, d Dec. 31, 1896
Hooker, R. W. (Middx) b Feb. 22, 1935
*Hookes, D. W. (S. Aust.) b May 3, 1955
*Hopkins, A. J. (NSW) b May 3, 1874, d April 25, 1931
Hopkins, J. A. (Glam & E. Prov.) b June 16, 1953
Hopkins, V. (Glos) b Jan. 21, 1911, d Aug. 6, 1984
*Hopwood, J. L. (Lancs) b Oct. 30, 1903, d June 15, 1985
*Horan, T. P. (Vic.) b March 8, 1854, d April 16, 1916
*Hordern, Dr H. V. (NSW & Philadelphia) b Feb. 10, 1884, d June 17, 1938
Hornby, A. H. (CU & Lancs) b July 29, 1877, d Sept. 6, 1952
*Hornby, A. N. (Lancs) b Feb. 10, 1847, d Dec. 17, 1925
*Horne, P. A. (Auck.) b Jan. 21, 1960
Horner, N. F. (Yorks & Warwicks) b May 10, 1926
*Hornibrook, P. M. (Qld) b July 27, 1899, d Aug. 25, 1976
Horsfall, R. (Essex & Glam) b June 26, 1920, d Aug. 25, 1981
Horton, H. (Worcs & Hants) b April 18, 1923, d Nov. 2, 1998
*Horton, M. J. (Worcs & N. Dist.) b April 21, 1934
*Hough, K. W. (Auck.) b Oct. 24, 1928
*Houghton, D. L. (Mash.) b June 23, 1957
*Howard, A. B. (B'dos) b Aug. 27, 1946
*Howard, N. D. (Lancs) b May 18, 1925, d May 31, 1979
Howard, Major R. (Lancs; MCC Team Manager) b April 17, 1890, d Sept. 10, 1967
*Howarth, G. P. OBE (Auck., Surrey & N. Dist.) b March 29, 1951
*Howarth, H. J. (Auck.) b Dec. 25, 1943
*Howell, H. (Warwicks) b Nov. 29, 1890, d July 9, 1932
Howell, L. G. (Cant. & Auck.) b July 8, 1972
*Howell, W. P. (NSW) b Dec. 29, 1869, d July 14, 1940
*Howorth, R. (Worcs) b April 26, 1909, d April 2, 1980
Hubble, J. C. (Kent) b Feb. 10, 1881, d Feb. 26, 1965
*Huckle, A. G. (Mat.) b Sept. 21, 1971
Huggins, H. J. (Glos) b March 15, 1877, d Nov. 20, 1942
Hughes, D. P. (Lancs & Tas.; *CY 1988*) b May 13, 1947
*Hughes, K. J. (W. Aust. & Natal; *CY 1981*) b Jan. 26, 1954
*Hughes, M. G. (Vic. & Essex; *CY 1994*) b Nov. 23, 1961
Hughes, S. P. (Middx, N. Tvl & Durham) b Dec. 20, 1959
Huish, F. H. (Kent) b Nov. 15, 1869, d March 16, 1957
Hulme, J. H. A. (Middx) b Aug. 26, 1904, d Sept. 26, 1991
Humpage, G. W. (Warwicks & OFS; *CY 1985*) b April 24, 1954
Humphrey, T. (Surrey) b Jan. 16, 1839, d Sept. 3, 1878
Humphreys, E. (Kent & Cant.) b Aug. 24, 1881, d Nov. 6, 1949
Humphreys, W. A. (Sussex & Hants) b Oct. 28, 1849, d March 23, 1924
Humphries, D. J. (Leics & Worcs) b Aug. 6, 1953
*Humphries, J. (Derbys) b May 19, 1876, d May 7, 1946
Hunt, A. V. (Scotland & Bermuda) b Oct. 1, 1910, d March 3, 1999
Hunt, G. E. (Som) b Sept. 30, 1896, d Jan. 22, 1959
*Hunt, W. A. (NSW) b Aug. 26, 1908, d Dec. 30, 1983
*Hunte, Sir Conrad C. (B'dos; *CY 1964*) b May 9, 1932, d Dec. 3, 1999
*Hunte, E. A. C. (T/T) b Oct. 3, 1905, d June 26, 1967
Hunter, D. (Yorks) b Feb. 23, 1860, d Jan. 11, 1927
*Hunter, J. (Yorks) b Aug. 3, 1855, d Jan. 4, 1891
*Hurst, A. G. (Vic.) b July 15, 1950
Hurst, R. J. (Middx) b Dec. 29, 1933, d Feb. 10, 1996
*Hurwood, A. (Qld) b June 17, 1902, d Sept. 26, 1982
*Hutchings, K. L. (Kent; *CY 1907*) b Dec. 7, 1882, d Sept. 3, 1916
Hutchinson, J. M. (Derbys; *believed to be longest-lived first-class cricketer at 103 years 344 days*) b Nov. 29, 1896, d Nov. 7, 2000
*Hutchinson, P. (SA) b Jan. 26, 1862, d Sept. 30, 1925
*Hutton, Sir Leonard (Yorks; *CY 1938*) b June 23, 1916, d Sept. 6, 1990
*Hutton, R. A. (CU, Yorks & Tvl) b Sept. 6, 1942
*Hylton, L. G. (Jam.) b March 29, 1905, d May 17, 1955

*Ibadulla, K. (Punjab, Warwicks, Tas. & Otago) b Dec. 20, 1935
*Ibrahim, K. C. (Bombay) b Jan. 26, 1919
Iddison, R. (Yorks & Lancs) b Sept. 15, 1834, d March 19, 1890

*Iddon, J. (Lancs) b Jan. 8, 1902, d April 17, 1946
*Igglesden, A. P. (Kent & W. Prov.) b Oct. 8, 1964
*Ijaz Butt (Pak. Us, Punjab, Lahore, R'pindi & Multan) b March 10, 1938
*Ijaz Faqih (Kar., Sind, PWD & MCB) b March 24, 1956
*Ikin, J. T. (Lancs) b March 7, 1918, d Sept. 15, 1984
*Illingworth, R. CBE (Yorks & Leics; *CY 1960*) b June 8, 1932
*Imran Khan (Lahore, Dawood, Worcs, OU, PIA, Sussex & NSW; *CY 1983*) b Nov. 25, 1952
*Imtiaz Ahmed (N. Ind., Comb. Us, NWFP, Pak. Servs, Peshawar & PAF) b Jan. 5, 1928
*Imtiaz Ali (T/T) b July 28, 1954
Inchmore, J. D. (Worcs & N. Tvl) b Feb. 22, 1949
*Indrajitsinhji, K. S. (S'tra & Delhi) b June 15, 1937
Ingle, R. A. (Som) b Nov. 5, 1903, d Dec. 19, 1992
Ingleby-Mackenzie, A. C. D. (Hants; Pres. MCC 1996–98) b Sept. 15, 1933
Inman, C. C. (Ceylon & Leics) b Jan. 29, 1936
*Inshan Ali (T/T) b Sept. 25, 1949, d June 24, 1995
*Insole, D. J. CBE (CU & Essex; *CY 1956;* Chairman TCCB 1975–78) b April 18, 1926
*Intikhab Alam (Kar., PIA, Surrey, PWD, Sind, Punjab; ICC referee) b Dec. 28, 1941
*Inverarity, R. J. (W. Aust. & S. Aust.) b Jan. 31, 1944
*Iqbal Qasim (Kar., Sind & NBP) b Aug. 6, 1953
Iqbal Sikandar (PIA, Kar. & H'bad) b Dec. 19, 1958
*Irani, J. K. (Sind) b Aug. 18, 1923, d Feb. 25, 1982
*Iredale, F. A. (NSW) b June 19, 1867, d April 15, 1926
Iremonger, J. (Notts; *CY 1903*) b March 5, 1876, d March 25, 1956
*Ironmonger, H. (Qld & Vic.) b April 7, 1882, d June 1, 1971
*Ironside, D. E. J. (Tvl) b May 2, 1925
*Irvine, B. L. (W. Prov., Natal, Essex & Tvl) b March 9, 1944
Isaacs, E. (ICC referee) b Jan. 26, 1945
*Israr Ali (S. Punjab, B'pur & Multan) b May 1, 1927
*Iverson, J. B. (Vic.) b July 27, 1915, d Oct. 24, 1973

*Jack, S. D. (Tvl) b Aug. 4, 1970
*Jackman, R. D. (Surrey, W. Prov. & Rhod.; *CY 1981*) b Aug. 13, 1945
*Jackson, A. A. (NSW) b Sept. 5, 1909, d Feb. 16, 1933
Jackson, A. B. (Derbys) b Aug. 21, 1933
*Jackson, Rt Hon. Sir F. Stanley (CU & Yorks; *CY 1894;* Pres. MCC 1921) b Nov. 21, 1870, d March 9, 1947
Jackson, G. R. (Derbys) b June 23, 1896, d Feb. 21, 1966
*Jackson, H. L. (Derbys; *CY 1959*) b April 5, 1921
Jackson, J. (Notts & All-England) b May 21, 1833, d Nov. 4, 1901
Jackson, P. F. (Worcs) b May 11, 1911, d April 27, 1999
Jackson, V. E. (NSW & Leics) b Oct. 25, 1916, d Jan. 30, 1965
*Jahangir Khan (N. Ind. & CU) b Feb. 1, 1910, d July 23, 1988
*Jai, L. P. (Bombay) b April 1, 1902, d Jan. 29, 1968
*Jaisimha, M. L. (H'bad) b March 3, 1939, d July 6, 1999
Jakeman, F. (Yorks & Northants) b Jan. 10, 1920, d May 18, 1986
*Jalal-ud-Din (PWD, Kar., IDBP & Allied Bank) b June 12, 1959
James, A. E. (Sussex) b Aug. 7, 1924
James, C. L. R. (Writer) b Jan. 4, 1901, d May 31, 1989
*James, K. C. (Wgtn & Northants) b March 12, 1904, d Aug. 21, 1976
James, K. D. (Middx, Wgtn & Hants) b March 18, 1961
*James, W. R. (Mat.) b Aug. 27, 1965
*Jameson, J. A. (Warwicks) b June 30, 1941
*Jamshedji, R. J. (Bombay) b Nov. 18, 1892, d April 5, 1976
*Jardine, D. R. (OU & Surrey; *CY 1928*) b Oct. 23, 1900, d June 18, 1958
*Jarman, B. N. (S. Aust.; ICC referee) b Feb. 17, 1936
*Jarvis, A. H. (S. Aust.) b Oct. 19, 1860, d Nov. 15, 1933
Jarvis, K. B. S. (Kent & Glos) b April 23, 1953
*Jarvis, M. P. (Mash.) b Dec. 6, 1955
*Jarvis, P. W. (Yorks, Sussex & Som) b June 29, 1965
*Jarvis, T. W. (Auck. & Cant.) b July 29, 1944
*Javed Akhtar (R'pindi & Pak. Serv.; Test umpire) b Nov. 21, 1940
*Javed Miandad (Kar., Sind, Sussex, HBL & Glam; *CY 1982*) b June 12, 1957
*Jayantilal, K. (H'bad) b Jan. 13, 1948
Jayaprakash, A. V. (Test umpire) b March 14, 1950
*Jayasekera, R. S. A. (SL) b Dec. 7, 1957
Jayasinghe, S. (Ceylon & Leics) b Jan. 19, 1931
Jayasinghe, S. A. (SL) b July 15, 1955, d April 20, 1995
Jeeves, P. (Warwicks) b March 5, 1888, d July 22, 1916

Jefferies, S. T. (W. Prov., Derbys, Lancs, Hants & Boland) b Dec. 8, 1959
*Jeganathan, S. (SL) b July 11, 1951, d May 14, 1996
*Jenkins, R. O. (Worcs; *CY 1950*) b Nov. 24, 1918, d July 21, 1995
*Jenner, T. J. (W. Aust. & S. Aust.) b Sept. 8, 1944
*Jennings, C. B. (S. Aust. & Qld) b June 5, 1884, d June 20, 1950
Jennings, R. V. (Tvl & N. Tvl) b Aug. 9, 1954
Jephson, D. L. A. (CU & Surrey) b Feb. 23, 1871, d Jan. 19, 1926
Jepson, A. (Notts; Test umpire) b July 12, 1915, d July 17, 1997
*Jessop, G. L. (CU & Glos; *CY 1898*) b May 19, 1874, d May 11, 1955
Jesty, T. E. (Hants, Border, Griq. W., Cant., Surrey & Lancs; *CY 1983*) b June 2, 1948
Jewell, Major M. F. S. (Worcs & Sussex) b Sept. 15, 1885, d May 28, 1978
*John, V. B. (SL) b May 27, 1960
*Johnson, C. L. (Tvl) b 1871, d May 31, 1908
*Johnson, D. J. (Karn.) b Oct. 16, 1971
Johnson, G. W. (Kent & Tvl) b Nov. 8, 1946
*Johnson, H. H. H. (Jam.) b July 13, 1910, d June 24, 1987
Johnson, H. L. (Derbys) b Nov. 8, 1927
*Johnson, I. W. OBE (Vic.) b Dec. 8, 1917, d Oct. 9, 1998
Johnson, L. A. (Northants) b Aug. 12, 1936
*Johnson, L. J. (Qld) b March 18, 1919, d April 20, 1977
Johnson, P. R. (CU & Som) b Aug. 5, 1880, d July 1, 1959
*Johnson, T. F. (T/T) b Jan. 10, 1917, d April 5, 1985
Johnston, Brian A. CBE (Broadcaster) b June 24, 1912, d Jan. 5, 1994
*Johnston, W. A. (Vic.; *CY 1949*) b Feb. 26, 1922
Jones, A. MBE (Glam, W. Aust., N. Tvl & Natal; *CY 1978*) b Nov. 4, 1938
Jones, A. A. (Sussex, Som, Middx, Glam, N. Tvl & OFS) b Dec. 9, 1947
*Jones, A. H. (Wgtn & C. Dist.) b May 9, 1959
Jones, A. L. (Glam) b June 1, 1957
Jones, A. N. (Sussex, Border & Som) b July 22, 1961
*Jones, A. O. (Notts & CU; *CY 1900*) b Aug. 16, 1872, d Dec. 21, 1914
*Jones, C. M. (BG) b Nov. 3, 1902, d Dec. 10, 1959
*Jones, D. M. (Vic., Durham & Derbys; *CY 1990*) b March 24, 1961
*Jones, Ernest (S. Aust. & W. Aust.) b Sept. 30, 1869, d Nov. 23, 1943
Jones, E. C. (Glam) b Dec. 14, 1911, d April 14, 1989
Jones, E. W. (Glam) b June 25, 1942
*Jones, I. J. (Glam) b Dec. 10, 1941
Jones, K. V. (Middx) b March 28, 1942
*Jones, P. E. (T/T) b June 6, 1917, d Nov. 21, 1991
Jones, P. H. (Kent) b June 19, 1935
*Jones, S. P. (NSW, Qld & Auck.) b Aug. 1, 1861, d July 14, 1951
Jones, W. E. (Glam) b Oct. 31, 1916, d July 25, 1996
Jordon, R. C. (Vic.) b Feb. 17, 1937
*Joseph, D. R. E. (Leewards) b Nov. 15, 1969
*Joshi, P. G. (M'tra) b Oct. 27, 1926, d Jan. 8, 1987
Joshi, U. C. (S'tra, Ind. Rlwys, Guj. & Sussex) b Dec. 23, 1944
*Joslin, L. R. (Vic.) b Dec. 13, 1947
Julian, R. (Leics) b Aug. 23, 1936
*Julien, B. D. (T/T & Kent) b March 13, 1950
*Jumadeen, R. R. (T/T) b April 12, 1948
*Jupp, H. (Surrey) b Nov. 19, 1841, d April 8, 1889
*Jupp, V. W. C. (Sussex & Northants; *CY 1928*) b March 27, 1891, d July 9, 1960
*Jurangpathy, B. R. (CCC) b June 25, 1967

*Kallicharran, A. I. (Guyana, Warwicks, Qld, Tvl & OFS; *CY 1983*) b March 21, 1949
*Kaluperuma, L. W. (SL) b May 25, 1949
*Kaluperuma, S. M. S. (SL) b Oct. 22, 1961
*Kanhai, R. B. (†Guyana, T/T, W. Aust., Warwicks & Tas.; *CY 1964*) b Dec. 26, 1935
*Kanitkar, H. S. (M'tra) b Dec. 8, 1942
*Kapil Dev (Haryana, Northants & Worcs; *CY 1983*) b Jan. 6, 1959
**Kardar, A. H. (formerly Abdul Hafeez) (N. Ind., OU, Warwicks & Pak. Serv.) b Jan. 17, 1925, d April 21, 1996
Karnain, S. H. U. (NCC & Moors) b Aug. 11, 1962
*Keeton, W. W. (Notts; *CY 1940*) b April 30, 1905, d Oct. 10, 1980
*Keith, H. J. (Natal) b Oct. 25, 1927, d Nov. 17, 1997
*Kelleway, C. (NSW) b April 25, 1886, d Nov. 16, 1944
*Kelly, J. J. (NSW; *CY 1903*) b May 10, 1867, d Aug. 14, 1938
Kelly, J. M. (Lancs & Derbys) b March 19, 1922, d Nov. 13, 1979
*Kelly, T. J. D. (Vic.) b May 3, 1844, d July 20, 1893
*Kempis, G. A. (Natal) b Aug. 4, 1865, d May 19, 1890
*Kendall, T. (Vic. & Tas.) b Aug. 24, 1851, d Aug. 17, 1924
Kennedy, A. (Lancs) b Nov. 4, 1949
*Kennedy, A. S. (Hants; *CY 1933*) b Jan. 24, 1891, d Nov. 15, 1959
*Kennedy, R. J. (Otago & Wgtn) b June 3, 1972

*Kenny, R. B. (Bombay & Bengal) b Sept. 29, 1930, d Nov. 21, 1985
*Kent, M. F. (Qld) b Nov. 23, 1953
*Kentish, E. S. M. (Jam. & OU) b Nov. 21, 1916
*Kenyon, D. (Worcs; *CY 1963*) b May 15, 1924, d Nov. 12, 1996
Kenyon, M. N. (Lancs) b Dec. 25, 1886, d Nov. 21, 1960
*Kerr, J. L. (Cant.) b Dec. 28, 1910
*Kerr, R. B. (Qld) b June 16, 1961
Key, Sir Kingsmill J. (Surrey & OU) b Oct. 11, 1864, d Aug. 9, 1932
*Khalid Hassan (Punjab & Lahore) b July 14, 1937
*Khalid Wazir (Pak.) b April 27, 1936
*Khan Mohammad (N. Ind., Pak. Us, Som, B'pur, Sind, Kar. & Lahore) b Jan. 1, 1928
Khanna, S. C. (Delhi) b June 3, 1956
Killick, E. H. (Sussex) b Jan. 17, 1875, d Sept. 29, 1948
*Killick, Rev. E. T. (CU & Middx) b May 9, 1907, d May 18, 1953
Kilner, N. (Yorks & Warwicks) b July 21, 1895, d April 28, 1979
*Kilner, R. (Yorks; *CY 1924*) b Oct. 17, 1890, d April 5, 1928
King, B. P. (Worcs & Lancs) b April 22, 1915, d March 31, 1970
*King, C. L. (B'dos, Glam, Worcs & Natal) b June 11, 1951
*King, F. M. (B'dos) b Dec. 8, 1926, d Dec. 23, 1990
King, J. B. (Philadelphia) b Oct. 19, 1873, d Oct. 17, 1965
*King, J. H. (Leics) b April 16, 1871, d Nov. 18, 1946
*King, L. A. (Jam. & Bengal) b Feb. 27, 1939, d July 9, 1998
*Kinneir, S. P. (Warwicks; *CY 1912*) b May 13, 1871, d Oct. 16, 1928
*Kippax, A. F. (NSW) b May 25, 1897, d Sept. 4, 1972
Kirby, D. (CU & Leics) b Jan. 18, 1939
*Kirmani, S. M. H. (†Karn.) b Dec. 29, 1949
*Kirsten, P. N. (W. Prov., Sussex, Derbys & Border) b May 14, 1955
*Kischenchand, G. (W. Ind., Guj. & Baroda) b April 14, 1925, d April 16, 1997
Kitchen, M. J. (Som; Test umpire) b Aug. 1, 1940
*Kline, L. F. (Vic.) b Sept. 29, 1934
*Knight, A. E. (Leics; *CY 1904*) b Oct. 8, 1872, d April 25, 1946
*Knight, B. R. (Essex & Leics) b Feb. 18, 1938
*Knight, D. J. (OU & Surrey; *CY 1915*) b May 12, 1894, d Jan. 5, 1960
Knight, R. D. V. (CU, Surrey, Glos & Sussex; Sec. MCC 1994–) b Sept. 6, 1946
Knight, W. H. (Editor of *Wisden* 1870–79) b Nov. 29, 1812, d Aug. 16, 1879
*Knott, A. P. E. (Kent & Tas.; *CY 1970*) b April 9, 1946
Knott, C. J. (Hants) b Nov. 26, 1914
Knowles, J. (Notts) b March 25, 1910
*Knox, N. A. (Surrey; *CY 1907*) b Oct. 10, 1884, d March 3, 1935
Koertzen, R. E. (Test umpire) b March 26, 1949
Kortright, C. J. (Essex) b Jan. 9, 1871, d Dec. 12, 1952
*Kotze, J. J. (Tvl & W. Prov.) b Aug. 7, 1879, d July 7, 1931
*Kripal Singh, A. G. (Madras & H'bad) b Aug. 6, 1933, d July 23, 1987
*Krishnamurthy, P. (H'bad) b July 12, 1947, d Jan. 28, 1999
*Kuggeleijn, C. M. (N. Dist.) b May 10, 1956
*Kuiper, A. P. (W. Prov., Derbys & Boland) b Aug. 24, 1959
*Kulkarni, R. R. (Bombay) b Sept. 25, 1962
*Kulkarni, U. N. (Bombay) b March 7, 1942
*Kumar, V. V. (†TN) b June 22, 1935
*Kunderan, B. K. (Ind. Rlwys & Mysore) b Oct. 2, 1939
*Kuruppu, D. S. B. P. (BRC) b Jan. 5, 1962
*Kuruppuarachchi, A. K. (NCC) b Nov. 1, 1964
*Kuruvilla, A. (†Mumbai) b Aug. 8, 1968
*Kuys, F. (W. Prov.) b March 21, 1870, d Sept. 12, 1953
Kynaston, R. (Middx; Sec. MCC 1846–58) b Nov. 5, 1805, d June 21, 1874

*Labrooy, G. F. (CCC) b June 7, 1964
Lacey, Sir Francis E. (CU & Hants; Sec. MCC 1898–1926) b Oct. 19, 1859, d May 26, 1946
*Laird, B. M. (W. Aust.) b Nov. 21, 1950
*Laker, J. C. (Surrey, Auck. & Essex; *CY 1952*) b Feb. 9, 1922, d April 23, 1986
*Lall Singh (S. Punjab) b Dec. 16, 1909, d Nov. 19, 1985
*Lamb, A. J. (W. Prov., Northants & OFS; *CY 1981*) b June 20, 1954
Lamb, T. M. (OU, Middx & Northants; Chief Exec. ECB, 1997–) b March 24, 1953
*Lamba, R. (Delhi) b Jan. 2, 1960, d Feb. 23, 1998
*Lambert, C. B. (Guyana & N. Tvl) b Feb. 10, 1962
Lambert, G. E. (Glos & Som) b May 11, 1918, d Oct. 31, 1991
Lambert, R. H. (Ireland) b July 18, 1874, d March 24, 1956
Lambert, Wm (Surrey) b 1779, d April 19, 1851
*Lance, H. R. (NE Tvl & Tvl) b June 6, 1940
Langdon, T. (Glos) b Jan. 8, 1879, d Nov. 30, 1944
Langford, B. A. (Som) b Dec. 17, 1935
*Langley, G. R. A. (S. Aust.; *CY 1957*) b Sept. 14, 1919, d May 14, 2001

*Langridge, James (Sussex; *CY 1932*) b July 10, 1906, d Sept. 10, 1966
Langridge, John G. MBE (Sussex; Test umpire; *CY 1950*) b Feb. 10, 1910, d June 27, 1999
Langridge, R. J. (Sussex) b April 13, 1939
*Langton, A. B. C. (Tvl) b March 2, 1912, d Nov. 27, 1942
*Larkins, W. (Northants, E. Prov. & Durham) b Nov. 22, 1953
*Larsen, G. R. (Wgtn) b Sept. 27, 1962
*Larter, J. D. F. (Northants) b April 24, 1940
*Larwood, H. MBE (Notts; *CY 1927*) b Nov. 14, 1904, d July 22, 1995
*Lashley, P. D. (B'dos) b Feb. 11, 1937
Latchman, H. C. (Middx & Notts) b July 26, 1943
*Latham, R. T. (Cant.) b June 12, 1961
*Laughlin, T. J. (Vic.) b Jan. 30, 1951
*Laver, F. (Vic.) b Dec. 7, 1869, d Sept. 24, 1919
Lavis, G. (Glam) b Aug. 17, 1908, d July 29, 1956
*Lawrence, D. V. (Glos) b Jan. 28, 1964
*Lawrence, G. B. (Rhod. & Natal) b March 31, 1932
Lawrence, J. (Som) b March 29, 1914, d Dec. 10, 1988
*Lawry, W. M. (Vic.; *CY 1962*) b Feb. 11, 1937
*Lawson, G. F. (NSW & Lancs) b Dec. 7, 1957
Lawton, A. E. (Derbys & Lancs) b March 31, 1879, d Dec. 25, 1955
Leach, G. (Sussex) b July 18, 1881, d Jan. 10, 1945
Leadbeater, B. (Yorks) b Aug. 14, 1943
*Leadbeater, E. (Yorks & Warwicks) b Aug. 15, 1927
Leary, S. E. (Kent) b April 30, 1933, d Aug. 21, 1988
Lee, C. (Yorks & Derbys) b March 17, 1924, d Sept. 3, 1999
Lee, F. S. (Middx & Som; Test umpire) b July 24, 1905, d March 30, 1982
Lee, G. M. (Notts & Derbys) b June 7, 1887, d Feb. 29, 1976
*Lee, H. W. (Middx) b Oct. 26, 1890, d April 21, 1981
Lee, J. W. (Middx & Som) b Feb. 1, 1904, d June 20, 1944
Lee, P. G. (Northants & Lancs; *CY 1976*) b Aug. 27, 1945
*Lee, P. K. (S. Aust.) b Sept. 15, 1904, d Aug. 9, 1980
*Lees, W. K. MBE (Otago) b March 19, 1952
*Lees, W. S. (Surrey; *CY 1906*) b Dec. 25, 1875, d Sept. 10, 1924
Lefebvre, R. P. (Holland, Som, Cant. & Glam) b Feb. 7, 1963
*Legall, R. (B'dos & T/T) b Dec. 1, 1925
*Leggat, I. B. (C. Dist.) b June 7, 1930
*Leggat, J. G. (Cant.) b May 27, 1926, d March 9, 1973
*Legge, G. B. (OU & Kent) b Jan. 26, 1903, d Nov. 21, 1940
Lenham, L. J. (Sussex) b May 24, 1936
Lenham, N. J. (Sussex) b Dec. 17, 1965
*le Roux, F. L. (Tvl & E. Prov.) b Feb. 5, 1882, d Sept. 22, 1963
le Roux, G. S. (W. Prov. & Sussex) b Sept. 4, 1955
*Leslie, C. F. H. (OU & Middx) b Dec. 8, 1861, d Feb. 12, 1921
Lester, E. (Yorks) b Feb. 18, 1923
Lester, G. (Leics) b Dec. 27, 1915, d Jan. 26, 1998
Lester, Dr J. A. (Philadelphia) b Aug. 1, 1871, d Sept. 3, 1969
*Lever, J. K. MBE (Essex & Natal; *CY 1979*) b Feb. 24, 1949
*Lever, P. (Lancs & Tas.) b Sept. 17, 1940
*Leveson Gower, Sir H. D. G. (OU & Surrey) b May 8, 1873, d Feb. 1, 1954
*Levett, W. H. V. (Kent) b Jan. 25, 1908, d Nov. 30, 1995
*Lewis, A. R. CBE (Glam & CU; Pres. MCC 1998–2000; writer & broadcaster) b July 6, 1938
Lewis, A. E. (Som) b Jan. 20, 1877, d Feb. 22, 1956
Lewis, C. BEM (Kent) b July 27, 1908, d April 26, 1993
*Lewis, C. C. (Leics, Notts & Surrey) b Feb. 14, 1968
*Lewis, D. M. (Jam.) b Feb. 21, 1946
Lewis, E. J. (Glam & Sussex) b Jan. 31, 1942
*Lewis, P. T. (W. Prov.) b Oct. 2, 1884, d Jan. 30, 1976
*Leyland, M. (Yorks; *CY 1929*) b July 20, 1900, d Jan. 1, 1967
*Liaqat Ali (Kar., Sind, HBL & PIA) b May 21, 1955
Lightfoot, A. (Northants) b Jan. 8, 1936
*Lillee, D. K. MBE (W. Aust., Tas. & Northants; *CY 1973*) b July 18, 1949
*Lilley, A. A. (Warwicks; *CY 1897*) b Nov. 28, 1866, d Nov. 17, 1929
Lilley, A. W. (Essex) b May 8, 1959
Lilley, B. (Notts) b Feb. 11, 1895, d Aug. 4, 1950
Lillywhite, Fred (Sussex; Editor of *Lillywhite's Guide to Cricketers*) b July 23, 1829, d Sept. 15, 1866
Lillywhite, F. W. ("William") (Sussex) b June 13, 1792, d Aug. 21, 1854
*Lillywhite, James, jun. (Sussex) b Feb. 23, 1842, d Oct. 25, 1929
*Lindsay, D. T. (NE Tvl, N. Tvl & Tvl; ICC referee) b Sept. 4, 1939
*Lindsay, J. D. (Tvl & NE Tvl) b Sept. 8, 1908, d Aug. 31, 1990

*Lindsay, N. V. (Tvl & OFS) b July 30, 1886, d Feb. 2, 1976
*Lindwall, R. R. MBE (NSW & Qld; *CY 1949*) b Oct. 3, 1921, d June 22, 1996
*Ling, W. V. S. (Griq. W. & E. Prov.) b Oct. 3, 1891, d Sept. 26, 1960
*Lissette, A. F. (Auck. & N. Dist.) b Nov. 6, 1919, d Jan. 24, 1973
Lister, W. H. L. (CU & Lancs) b Oct. 7, 1911, d July 29, 1998
Livingston, L. (NSW & Northants) b May 3, 1920, d Jan. 16, 1998
Livingstone, D. A. (Hants) b Sept. 21, 1933, d Sept. 8, 1988
Livsey, W. H. (Hants) b Sept. 23, 1893, d Sept. 12, 1978
*Llewellyn, C. B. (Natal & Hants; *CY 1911*) b Sept. 26, 1876, d June 7, 1964
Llewellyn, M. J. (Glam) b Nov. 27, 1953
Lloyd, B. J. (Glam) b Sept. 6, 1953
*Lloyd, C. H. OBE (†Guyana & Lancs; *CY 1971*) b Aug. 31, 1944
*Lloyd, D. (Lancs) b March 18, 1947
*Lloyd, T. A. (Warwicks & OFS) b Nov. 5, 1956
Lloyds, J. W. (Som, OFS & Glos) b Nov. 17, 1954
*Loader, P. J. (Surrey & W. Aust.; *CY 1958*) b Oct. 25, 1929
Lobb, B. (Warwicks & Som) b Jan. 11, 1931, d May 3, 2000
*Lock, A. C. I. (Mash.) b Sept. 10, 1962
*Lock, G. A. R. (Surrey, W. Aust. & Leics; *CY 1954*) b July 5, 1929, d March 29, 1995
Lock, H. C. (Surrey; first TCCB pitch inspector) b May 8, 1903, d May 19, 1978
Lockwood, Ephraim (Yorks) b April 4, 1845, d Dec. 19, 1921
*Lockwood, W. H. (Notts & Surrey; *CY 1899*) b March 25, 1868, d April 26, 1932
Lockyer, T. (Surrey & All-England) b Nov. 1, 1826, d Dec. 22, 1869
Logan, J. D., jun. (SA) b June 24, 1880, d Jan. 3, 1960
*Logie, A. L. (T/T) b Sept. 28, 1960
*Lohmann, G. A. (Surrey, W. Prov. & Tvl; *CY 1889*) b June 2, 1865, d Dec. 1, 1901
Lomax, J. G. (Lancs & Som) b May 5, 1925, d May 21, 1992
Long, A. (Surrey & Sussex) b Dec. 18, 1940
Longrigg, E. F. (Som & CU) b April 16, 1906, d July 23, 1974
Lord, Thomas (Middx; founder of Lord's) b Nov. 23, 1755, d Jan. 13, 1832
*Love, H. S. B. (NSW & Vic.) b Aug. 10, 1895, d July 22, 1969
Love, J. D. (Yorks) b April 22, 1955
*Lowry, T. C. (Wgtn, CU & Som) b Feb. 17, 1898, d July 20, 1976
*Lowson, F. A. (Yorks) b July 1, 1925, d Sept. 8, 1984
*Loxton, S. J. E. (Vic.) b March 29, 1921
*Lucas, A. P. (CU, Surrey, Middx & Essex) b Feb. 20, 1857, d Oct. 12, 1923
Luckes, W. T. (Som) b Jan. 1, 1901, d Oct. 27, 1982
*Luckhurst, B. W. (Kent; *CY 1971*) b Feb. 5, 1939
Lumb, R. G. (Yorks) b Feb. 27, 1950
*Lundie, E. B. (E. Prov., W. Prov. & Tvl) b March 15, 1888, d Sept. 12, 1917
Lupton, A. W. (Yorks) b Feb. 23, 1879, d April 14, 1944
Lynch, M. A. (Surrey, Glos & Guyana) b May 21, 1958
Lyon, B. H. (OU & Glos; *CY 1931*) b Jan. 19, 1902, d June 22, 1970
Lyon, M. D. (CU & Som) b April 22, 1898, d Feb. 17, 1964
*Lyons, J. J. (S. Aust.) b May 21, 1863, d July 21, 1927
*Lyttelton, Hon. Alfred (CU & Middx; Pres. MCC 1898) b Feb. 7, 1857, d July 5, 1913
Lyttelton, Rev. Hon. C. F. (CU & Worcs) b Jan. 26, 1887, d Oct. 3, 1931
Lyttelton, Hon. C. G. (CU) b Oct. 27, 1842, d June 9, 1922
Lyttelton, Hon. C. J. (*see* 10th Visct Cobham)

*McAlister, P. A. (Vic.) b July 11, 1869, d May 10, 1938
*Macartney, C. G. (NSW & Otago; *CY 1922*) b June 27, 1886, d Sept. 9, 1958
*Macaulay, G. G. (Yorks; *CY 1924*) b Dec. 7, 1897, d Dec. 13, 1940
*Macaulay, M. J. (Tvl, W. Prov., OFS, NE Tvl & E. Prov.) b April 1939
*MacBryan, J. C. W. (CU & Som; *CY 1925*) b July 22, 1892, d July 14, 1983
*McCabe, S. J. (NSW; *CY 1935*) b July 16, 1910, d Aug. 25, 1968
*McCarthy, C. N. (Natal & CU) b March 24, 1929, d Aug. 14, 2000
*McConnon, J. E. (Glam) b June 21, 1922
*McCool, C. L. (NSW, Qld & Som) b Dec. 9, 1916, d April 5, 1986
McCorkell, N. (Hants) b March 23, 1912
*McCormick, E. L. (Vic.) b May 16, 1906, d June 28, 1991
*McCosker, R. B. (NSW; *CY 1976*) b Dec. 11, 1946
McCurdy, R. J. (Vic., Derbys, S. Aust., E. Prov. & Natal) b Dec. 30, 1959
*McDermott, C. J. (Qld; *CY 1986*) b April 14, 1965
*McDonald, C. C. (Vic.) b Nov. 17, 1928
*McDonald, E. A. (Tas., Vic. & Lancs; *CY 1922*) b Jan. 6, 1891, d July 22, 1937
*McDonnell, P. S. (Vic., NSW & Qld) b Nov. 13, 1858, d Sept. 24, 1896
McEwan, K. S. (E. Prov., W. Prov., Essex & W. Aust.; *CY 1978*) b July 16, 1952

*McEwan, P. E. (Cant.) b Dec. 19, 1953
*McGahey, C. P. (Essex; *CY 1902*) b Feb. 12, 1871, d Jan. 10, 1935
*MacGibbon, A. R. (Cant.) b Aug. 28, 1924
McGilvray, A. D. (NSW; broadcaster) b Dec. 6, 1909, d July 16, 1996
*McGirr, H. M. (Wgtn) b Nov. 5, 1891, d April 14, 1964
*McGlew, D. J. (Natal; *CY 1956*) b March 11, 1929, d June 9, 1998
*MacGregor, G. (CU & Middx; *CY 1891*) b Aug. 31, 1869, d Aug. 20, 1919
*McGregor, S. N. (Otago) b Dec. 18, 1931
*McIlwraith, J. (Vic.) b Sept. 7, 1857, d July 5, 1938
*McIntyre, A. J. (Surrey; *CY 1958*) b May 14, 1918
*Mackay, K. D. MBE (Qld) b Oct. 24, 1925, d June 13, 1982
McKechnie, B. J. (Otago) b Nov. 6, 1953
*McKenzie, G. D. (W. Aust. & Leics; *CY 1965*) b June 24, 1941
*McKibbin, T. R. (NSW) b Dec. 10, 1870, d Dec. 15, 1939
*McKinnon, A. H. (E. Prov. & Tvl) b Aug. 20, 1932, d Dec. 1, 1983
*MacKinnon, F. A. (CU & Kent; *believed to be longest-lived Test cricketer*) b April 9, 1848, d Feb. 27, 1947
*MacLaren, A. C. (Lancs; *CY 1895*) b Dec. 1, 1871, d Nov. 17, 1944
*McLaren, J. W. (Qld) b Dec. 24, 1886, d Nov. 17, 1921
MacLaurin of Knebworth, Lord (Chairman ECB 1997–) b March 30, 1937
*Maclean, J. A. (Qld) b April 27, 1946
*McLean, R. A. (Natal; *CY 1961*) b July 9, 1930
MacLeay, K. H. (W. Aust. & Som) b April 2, 1959
*McLeod, C. E. (Vic.) b Oct. 24, 1869, d Nov. 26, 1918
*McLeod, E. G. (Auck. & Wgtn) b Oct. 14, 1900, d Sept. 14, 1989
*McLeod, R. W. (Vic.) b Jan. 19, 1868, d June 14, 1907
McMahon, J. W. (Surrey & Som) b Dec. 28, 1919, d May 8, 2001
*McMahon, T. G. (Wgtn) b Nov. 8, 1929
*McMaster, J. E. P. (Eng.) b March 16, 1861, d June 7, 1929
*McMillan, B. M. (Tvl, W. Prov. & Warwicks) b Dec. 22, 1963
*McMillan, Q. (Tvl) b June 23, 1904, d July 3, 1948
*McMorris, E. D. A. (Jam.) b April 4, 1935
*McRae, D. A. N. (Cant.) b Dec. 25, 1912, d Aug. 10, 1986
*McShane, P. G. (Vic.) b April 18, 1858, d Dec. 11, 1903
McSweeney, E. B. (C. Dist. & Wgtn) b March 8, 1957
McVicker, N. M. (Warwicks & Leics) b Nov. 4, 1940
*McWatt, C. A. (BG) b Feb. 1, 1922, d July 12, 1997
*Madan Lal (Punjab & Delhi) b March 20, 1951
*Maddocks, L. V. (Vic. & Tas.) b May 24, 1926
*Madondo, T. N. (Mash.) b Nov. 22, 1976, d June 11, 2001
*Madray, I. S. (BG) b July 2, 1934
*Madugalle, R. S. (NCC; ICC referee) b April 22, 1959
*Madurasinghe, M. A. W. R. (Kurunegala) b Jan. 30, 1961
Mafizur Rehman (Bangladesh) b Nov. 10, 1978
*Maguire, J. N. (Qld, E. Prov. & Leics) b Sept. 15, 1956
*Mahanama, R. S. (CCC & Bloom.) b May 31, 1966
Maher, B. J. M. (Derbys) b Feb. 11, 1958
*Mahmood Hussain (Pak. Us, Punjab, Kar., E. Pak. & NTB) b April 2, 1932, d Dec. 25, 1991
*Mailey, A. A. (NSW; writer) b Jan. 3, 1886, d Dec. 31, 1967
*Majid Khan (Lahore, Pak. Us, CU, Glam, PIA, Qld, Punjab; *CY 1970*) b Sept. 28, 1946
*Maka, E. S. (Bombay) b March 5, 1922, dead
*Makepeace, H. (Lancs) b Aug. 22, 1881, d Dec. 19, 1952
*Malhotra, A. (Haryana, Bengal & Delhi) b Jan. 26, 1957
*Mallender, N. A. (Northants, Otago & Som) b Aug. 13, 1961
*Mallett, A. A. (S. Aust.) b July 13, 1945
*Malone, M. F. (W. Aust. & Lancs) b Oct. 9, 1950
*Maninder Singh (Delhi) b June 13, 1965
*Manjrekar, V. L. (Bombay, Bengal, Andhra, U. Pradesh, Raja. & M'tra) b Sept. 26, 1931, d Oct. 18, 1983
*Manjrekar, S. V. (†Mumbai) b July 12, 1965
*Mankad, A. V. (Bombay) b Oct. 12, 1946
*Mankad, V. (M. H.) (W. Ind., Naw., M'tra, Guj., Bengal, Bombay & Raja.; *CY 1947*) b April 12, 1917, d Aug. 21, 1978
*Mann, A. L. (W. Aust.) b Nov. 8, 1945
*Mann, F. G. CBE (CU & Middx; Chairman TCCB 1978–83; Pres. MCC 1984–85) b Sept. 6, 1917, d Aug. 8, 2001
*Mann, F. T. (CU & Middx) b March 3, 1888, d Oct. 6, 1964
*Mann, N. B. F. (Natal & E. Prov.) b Dec. 28, 1920, d July 31, 1952
Manning, J. S. (S. Aust. & Northants) b June 11, 1924, d May 5, 1988

Manning, T. E. (Northants) b Sept. 2, 1884, d Nov. 22, 1975
*Mansell, P. N. F. MBE (Rhod.) b March 16, 1920, d May 9, 1995
*Mansoor Akhtar (Kar., UBL & Sind) b Dec. 25, 1957
Mansur Ali Khan (*see* Pataudi, Mansur Ali, Nawab of)
*Mantri, M. K. (Bombay & M'tra) b Sept. 1, 1921
Manuel, P. (Test umpire) b Nov. 18, 1950
*Maqsood Ahmed (S. Punjab, R'pindi, B'pur & Kar.) b March 26, 1925, d Jan. 4, 1999
Maqsood Rana (Lahore, R'pindi & NBP) b Aug. 1, 1972
*Marais, G. G. ("G. Gladstone") (Jam.) b Jan. 14, 1901, d May 19, 1978
Marchant, F. (Kent & CU) b May 22, 1864, d April 13, 1946
*Markham, L. A. (Natal) b Sept. 12, 1924, d Aug. 5, 2000
*Marks, V. J. (OU, Som & W. Aust.; writer) b June 25, 1955
Marlar, R. G. (CU & Sussex; writer) b Jan. 2, 1931
Marlow, F. W. (Sussex) b Oct. 8, 1867, d Aug. 7, 1952
Marner, P. T. (Lancs & Leics) b March 31, 1936
*Marr, A. P. (NSW) b March 28, 1862, d March 15, 1940
*Marriott, C. S. (CU, Lancs & Kent) b Sept. 14, 1895, d Oct. 13, 1966
Marsden, Tom (Eng.) b 1805, d Feb. 27, 1843
*Marsh, G. R. (W. Aust.) b Dec. 31, 1958
*Marsh, R. W. MBE (W. Aust.; *CY 1982*) b Nov. 4, 1947
Marsh, S. A. (Kent) b Jan. 27, 1961
Marshal, Alan (Qld & Surrey; *CY 1909*) b June 12, 1883, d July 23, 1915
*Marshall, M. D. (B'dos, Hants & Natal; *CY 1983*) b April 18, 1958, d Nov. 4, 1999
*Marshall, N. E. (B'dos & T/T) b Feb. 27, 1924
*Marshall, R. E. (B'dos & Hants; *CY 1959*) b April 25, 1930, d Oct. 27, 1992
Marsham, C. H. B. (OU & Kent) b Feb. 10, 1879, d July 19, 1928
Martin, E. J. (Notts) b Aug. 17, 1925
*Martin, F. (Kent; *CY 1892*) b Oct. 12, 1861, d Dec. 13, 1921
*Martin, F. R. (Jam.) b Oct. 12, 1893, d Nov. 23, 1967
Martin, G. C. (Mash.) b May 30, 1966
*Martin, J. W. (NSW & S. Aust.) b July 28, 1931, d July 16, 1992
*Martin, J. W. (Kent) b Feb. 16, 1917, d Jan. 4, 1987
Martin, S. H. (Worcs, Natal & Rhod.) b Jan. 11, 1909, d Feb. 17, 1988
*Martindale, E. A. (B'dos) b Nov. 25, 1909, d March 17, 1972
Martin-Jenkins, Christopher (Writer & broadcaster) b Jan. 20, 1945
Maru, R. J. (Middx & Hants) b Oct. 28, 1962
*Marx, W. F. E. (Tvl) b July 4, 1895, d June 2, 1974
*Mason, J. R. (Kent; *CY 1898*) b March 26, 1874, d Oct. 15, 1958
*Masood Anwar (UBL, Multan, F'bad & Lahore) b Dec. 12, 1967
Masood Iqbal (Lahore, Punjab U., Pak. Us & HBL) b April 17, 1952
*Massie, H. H. (NSW) b April 11, 1854, d Oct. 12, 1938
*Massie, R. A. L. (W. Aust.; *CY 1973*) b April 14, 1947
*Matheson, A. M. (Auck.) b Feb. 27, 1906, d Dec. 31, 1985
*Mathias, Wallis (Sind, Kar. & NBP) b Feb. 4, 1935, d Sept. 1, 1994
*Matthews, A. D. G. (Northants & Glam) b May 3, 1904, d July 29, 1977
*Matthews, C. D. (W. Aust. & Lancs) b Sept. 22, 1962
*Matthews, C. R. (W. Prov.) b Feb. 15, 1965
*Matthews, G. R. J. (NSW) b Dec. 15, 1959
*Matthews, T. J. (Vic.) b April 3, 1884, d Oct. 14, 1943
*Mattis, E. H. (Jam.) b April 11, 1957
*May, P. B. H. CBE (CU & Surrey; *CY 1952;* Pres. MCC 1980–81) b Dec. 31, 1929, d Dec. 27, 1994
*May, T. B. A. (S. Aust.) b Jan. 26, 1962
Mayer, J. H. (Warwicks) b March 2, 1902, d Sept. 6, 1981
Maynard, C. (Warwicks & Lancs) b April 8, 1958
*Mayne, E. R. (S. Aust. & Vict.) b July 2, 1882, d Oct. 26, 1961
*Mayne, L. C. (W. Aust.) b Jan. 23, 1942
*Mead, C. P. (Hants; *CY 1912*) b March 9, 1887, d March 26, 1958
*Mead, W. (Essex; *CY 1904*) b April 1, 1868, d March 18, 1954
Meads, E. A. (Notts) b Aug. 17, 1916
*Meale, T. (Wgtn) b Nov. 11, 1928
*Meckiff, I. (Vic.) b Jan. 6, 1935
Medlycott, K. T. (Surrey & N. Tvl) b May 12, 1965
*Meherhomji, K. R. (W. Ind. & Bombay) b Aug. 9, 1911, d Feb. 10, 1982
*Mehra, V. L. (E. Punjab, Ind. Rlwys & Delhi) b March 12, 1938
*Meintjes, D. J. (Tvl) b June 9, 1890, d July 17, 1979
*Melle, M. G. (Tvl & W. Prov.) b June 3, 1930
*Melville, A. (OU, Sussex, Natal & Tvl; *CY 1948*) b May 19, 1910, d April 18, 1983
Meman, M. A. (Zimb.) b June 26, 1952
Mendis, G. D. (Sussex & Lancs) b April 20, 1955
*Mendis, L. R. D. (SSC) b Aug. 25, 1952

Mendis, M. C. (Colts) b Dec. 28, 1968
*Mendonca, I. L. (BG) b July 13, 1934
Mercer, J. (Sussex, Glam & Northants; *CY 1927*) b April 22, 1895, d Aug. 31, 1987
*Merchant, V. M. (Bombay; *CY 1937*) b Oct. 12, 1911, d Oct. 27, 1987
*Merritt, W. E. (Cant. & Northants) b Aug. 18, 1908, d June 9, 1977
*Merry, C. A. (T/T) b Jan. 20, 1911, d April 19, 1964
Metcalfe, A. A. (Yorks & Notts) b Dec. 25, 1963
Metson, C. P. (Middx & Glam) b July 2, 1963
*Meuleman, K. D. (Vic. & W. Aust.) b Sept. 5, 1923
*Meuli, E. M. (C. Dist.) b Feb. 20, 1926
Meyer, B. J. (Glos; Test umpire) b Aug. 21, 1932
Meyer, R. J. O. OBE (CU, Som & W. Ind.) b March 15, 1905, d March 9, 1991
Mian Mohammad Aslam (Test umpire) b April 1, 1949
Mian Mohammed Saeed (N. India, Patiala & S. Punjab) b Aug. 31, 1910, d Aug. 23, 1979
*Middleton, J. (W. Prov.) b Sept. 30, 1865, d Dec. 23, 1913
Middleton, T. C. (Hants) b Feb. 1, 1964
**Midwinter, W. E. (Vic. & Glos) b June 19, 1851, d Dec. 3, 1890
*Milburn, B. D. (Otago) b Nov. 24, 1943
*Milburn, C. (Northants & W. Aust.; *CY 1967*) b Oct. 23, 1941, d Feb. 28, 1990
*Milkha Singh, A. G. (Madras) b Dec. 31, 1941
*Miller, A. M. (Eng.) b Oct. 19, 1869, d June 26, 1959
Miller, F. P. (Surrey) b July 29, 1828, d Nov. 22, 1875
*Miller, G. (Derbys, Natal & Essex) b Sept. 8, 1952
*Miller, K. R. MBE (Vic., NSW & Notts; *CY 1954*) b Nov. 28, 1919
*Miller, L. S. M. (C. Dist. & Wgtn) b March 31, 1923, d Dec. 17, 1996
Miller, R. (Warwicks) b Jan. 6, 1941, d May 7, 1996
*Miller, R. C. (Jam.) b Dec. 24, 1924
*Milligan, F. W. (Yorks) b March 19, 1870, d March 31, 1900
*Millman, G. (Notts) b Oct. 2, 1934
Millmow, J. P. (Wgtn) b Sept. 22, 1967
*Mills, C. H. (Surrey, Kimberley & W. Prov.) b Nov. 26, 1867, d July 26, 1948
*Mills, J. E. (Auck.) b Sept. 3, 1905, d Dec. 11, 1972
Mills, P. T. (Glos) b May 7, 1879, d Dec. 8, 1950
*Milton, C. A. (Glos; *CY 1959*) b March 10, 1928
*Milton, Sir William H. (W. Prov.) b Dec. 3, 1854, d March 6, 1930
*Minnett, R. B. (NSW) b June 13, 1888, d Oct. 21, 1955
Minshull, John (scorer of first recorded century) b *circa* 1741, d Oct. 1793
*Miran Bux (Pak. Serv., Punjab & R'pindi) b April 20, 1907, d Feb. 8, 1991
*Misson, F. M. (NSW) b Nov. 19, 1938
*Mitchell, A. (Yorks) b Sept. 13, 1902, d Dec. 25, 1976
*Mitchell, B. (Tvl; *CY 1936*) b Jan. 8, 1909, d July 2, 1995
**Mitchell, F. (CU, Yorks & Tvl; *CY 1902*) b Aug. 13, 1872, d Oct. 11, 1935
*Mitchell, T. B. (Derbys) b Sept. 4, 1902, d Jan. 27, 1996
*Mitchell-Innes, N. S. (OU & Som) b Sept. 7, 1914
Mitchley, C. J. (Tvl; Test umpire & ICC referee) b July 4, 1938
*Modi, R. S. (Bombay) b Nov. 11, 1924, d May 17, 1996
*Mohammad Aslam (N. Ind. & Pak. Rlwys) b Jan. 5, 1920
*Mohammad Farooq (Kar.) b April 8, 1938
*Mohammad Ilyas (Lahore & PIA) b March 19, 1946
*Mohammad Munaf (Sind, E. Pak., Kar. & PIA) b Nov. 2, 1935
*Mohammad Nazir (Pak. Rlwys) b March 8, 1946
*Mohammad Zahid (PIA) b Aug. 2, 1976
*Mohsin Kamal (Lahore, Allied Bank & PNSC) b June 16, 1963
*Mohsin Khan (Pak. Rlwys, Kar., Sind, Pak. Us & HBL) b March 15, 1955
*Moir, A. M. (Otago) b July 17, 1919, d June 17, 2000
*Mold, A. (Lancs; *CY 1892*) b May 27, 1863, d April 29, 1921
Moles, A. J. (Warwicks & Griq. W.) b Feb. 12, 1961
*Moloney, D. A. R. (Wgtn, Otago & Cant.) b Aug. 11, 1910, d July 15, 1942
*Moodie, G. H. (Jam.) b Nov. 25, 1915
*Moon, L. J. (CU & Middx) b Feb. 9, 1878, d Nov. 23, 1916
*Mooney, F. L. H. (Wgtn) b May 26, 1921
Moore, H. I. (Notts) b Feb. 28, 1941
Moore, R. H. (Hants) b Nov. 14, 1913
Moores, P. (Worcs & Sussex) b Dec. 18, 1962
Moorhouse, R. (Yorks) b Sept. 7, 1866, d Jan. 7, 1921
*More, K. S. (Baroda) b Sept. 4, 1962
Morgan, D. C. (Derbys) b Feb. 26, 1929
*Morgan, R. W. (Auck.) b Feb. 12, 1941
*Morkel, D. P. B. (W. Prov.) b Jan. 25, 1906, d Oct. 6, 1980
*Morley, F. (Notts) b Dec. 16, 1850, d Sept. 28, 1884
*Moroney, J. (NSW) b July 24, 1917, d July 1, 1999

*Morris, A. R. MBE (NSW; *CY 1949*) b Jan. 19, 1922
*Morris, H. (Glam) b Oct. 5, 1963
Morris, H. M. (Essex & CU) b April 16, 1898, d Nov. 18, 1984
*Morris, S. (Vic.) b June 22, 1855, d Sept. 20, 1931
*Morrison, B. D. (Wgtn) b Dec. 17, 1933
*Morrison, D. K. (Auck. & Lancs) b Feb. 3, 1966
*Morrison, J. F. M. (C. Dist. & Wgtn) b Aug. 27, 1947
Morshed Ali Khan (Bangladesh) b May 14, 1972
Mortensen, O. H. (Denmark & Derbys) b Jan. 29, 1958
*Mortimore, J. B. (Glos) b May 14, 1933
Mortlock, W. (Surrey & Utd Eng. XI) b July 18, 1832, d Jan. 23, 1884
Morton, A., jun. (Derbys) b May 7, 1883, d Dec. 19, 1935
*Moseley, E. A. (B'dos, Glam, E. Prov. & N. Tvl) b Jan. 5, 1958
Moseley, H. R. (B'dos & Som) b May 28, 1948
*Moses, H. (NSW) b Feb. 13, 1858, d Dec. 7, 1938
*Moss, A. E. (Middx) b Nov. 14, 1930
*Moss, J. K. (Vic.) b June 29, 1947
*Motz, R. C. (Cant.; *CY 1966*) b Jan. 12, 1940
*Moule, W. H. (Vic.) b Jan. 31, 1858, d Aug. 24, 1939
*Moxon, M. D. (Yorks & Griq. W.; *CY 1993*) b May 4, 1960
*Mudassar Nazar (Lahore, Punjab, Pak. Us, HBL, PIA & UBL) b April 6, 1956
*Muddiah, V. M. (Mysore & Ind. Servs) b June 8, 1929
*Mufasir-ul-Haq (Kar., Dacca, PWD, E. Pak. & NBP) b Aug. 16, 1944, d July 27, 1983
Mukherjee, S. P. (Bengal) b Oct. 5, 1964
*Muller, S. A. (Qld) b July 11, 1971
Munasinghe, A. M. N. (SSC) b Dec. 10, 1971
Muncer, B. L. (Glam & Middx) b Oct. 23, 1913, d Jan. 18, 1982
Munden, V. S. (Leics) b Jan. 2, 1928
*Munir Malik (Punjab, R'pindi, Pak. Serv. & Kar.) b July 10, 1934
**Murdoch, W. L. (NSW & Sussex) b Oct. 18, 1854, d Feb. 18, 1911
*Murray, A. R. A. (E. Prov.) b April 30, 1922, d April 17, 1995
*Murray, B. A. G. (Wgtn) b Sept. 18, 1940
*Murray, D. A. (B'dos) b Sept. 29, 1950
*Murray, D. J. (Cant.) b Sept. 4, 1967
*Murray, D. L. (T/T, CU, Notts & Warwicks) b May 20, 1943
*Murray, J. T. MBE (Middx; *CY 1967*) b April 1, 1935
Murray-Wood, W. (OU & Kent) b June 30, 1917, d Dec. 21, 1968
Murrell, H. R. (Kent & Middx) b Nov. 19, 1879, d Aug. 15, 1952
*Musgrove, H. (Vic.) b Nov. 27, 1860, d Nov. 2, 1931
*Mushtaq Ali, S. (C. Ind., Guj., †M. Pradesh & U. Pradesh) b Dec. 17, 1914
*Mushtaq Mohammad (Kar., Northants & PIA; *CY 1963*) b Nov. 22, 1943
Mynn, Alfred (Kent & All-Eng.) b Jan. 19, 1807, d Nov. 1, 1861

*Nadeem Ghauri (Lahore, Pak. Rlwys & HBL) b Oct. 12, 1962
*Nadkarni, R. G. (M'tra & Bombay) b April 4, 1932
Naeem Ahmed (Kar., Pak Us, NBP, UBL & PIA) b Sept. 20, 1952
*Nagel, L. E. (Vic.) b March 6, 1905, d Nov. 23, 1971
*Naik, S. S. (Bombay) b Feb. 21, 1945
*Nanan, R. (T/T) b May 29, 1953
*Naoomal Jeoomal, M. (N. Ind. & Sind) b April 17, 1904, d July 18, 1980
*Narasimha Rao, M. V. (H'bad) b Aug. 11, 1954
Naseer Malik (Khairpair & NBP) b Feb. 1, 1950, d Aug. 1, 1999
*Nash, L. J. (Tas. & Vic.) b May 2, 1910, d July 24, 1986
Nash, M. A. (Glam) b May 9, 1945
*Nasim-ul-Ghani (Kar., Pak. Us, Dacca, E. Pak., PWD & NBP) b May 14, 1941
*Naushad Ali (Kar., E. Pak., R'pindi, Peshawar, NWFP, Punjab & Pak. Serv.; ICC referee) b Oct. 1, 1943
*Naved Anjum (Railways, Lahore, UBL & HBL) b July 27, 1963
*Navle, J. G. (Rajputana, C. Ind., Holkar & Gwalior) b Dec. 7, 1902, d Sept. 7, 1979
*Nayak, S. V. (Bombay) b Oct. 20, 1954
*Nayudu, Col. C. K. (C. Ind., Andhra, U. Pradesh & Holkar; *CY 1933*) b Oct. 31, 1895, d Nov. 14, 1967
*Nayudu, C. S. (C. Ind., Holkar, Baroda, Bengal, Andhra & U. Pradesh) b April 18, 1914
*Nazar Mohammad (N. Ind. & Punjab) b March 5, 1921, d July 12, 1996
*Nazir Ali, S. (S. Punjab & Sussex) b Jan. 8, 1906, d Feb. 18, 1975
Neale, P. A. (Worcs; *CY 1989*) b June 5, 1954
Neale, W. L. (Glos) b March 3, 1904, d Oct. 26, 1955
*Neblett, J. M. (B'dos & BG) b Nov. 13, 1901, d March 28, 1959
Needham, A. (Surrey & Middx) b March 23, 1957
*Nel, J. D. (W. Prov.) b July 10, 1928
Nelson, R. P. (Middx, CU & Northants) b Aug. 7, 1912, d Oct. 29, 1940
*Newberry, C. (Tvl) b 1889, d Aug. 1, 1916

Newell, M. (Notts) b Feb. 25, 1965
*Newham, W. (Sussex) b Dec. 12, 1860, d June 26, 1944
Newland, Richard (Sussex) b *circa* 1718, d May 29, 1791
*Newman, Sir Jack (Wgtn & Cant.) b July 3, 1902, d Sept. 23, 1996
Newman, J. A. (Hants & Cant.) b Nov. 12, 1884, d Dec. 21, 1973
Newman, P. G. (Derbys) b Jan. 10, 1959
*Newport, P. J. (Worcs. Boland & N. Tvl) b Oct. 11, 1962
*Newson, E. S. OBE (Tvl & Rhod.) b Dec. 2, 1910, d April 24, 1988
Newstead, J. T. (Yorks; *CY 1909*) b Sept. 8, 1877, d March 25, 1952
Newton, A. E. (OU & Som) b Sept. 12, 1862, d Sept. 15, 1952
*Niaz Ahmed (Dacca, E. Pak., PWD & Pak. Rlwys) b Nov. 11, 1945
Nicholas, M. C. J. (Hants) b Sept. 29, 1957
Nicholls, D. (Kent) b Dec. 8, 1943
Nicholls, E. A. (Test umpire) b Dec. 10, 1947
Nicholls, R. B. (Glos) b Dec. 4, 1933, d July 21, 1994
*Nichols, M. S. (Essex; *CY 1934*) b Oct. 6, 1900, d Jan. 26, 1961
Nicholson, A. G. (Yorks) b June 25, 1938, d Nov. 4, 1985
*Nicholson, F. (Griq. W.) b Sept. 17, 1909, d July 30, 1982
*Nicolson, J. F. W. (Natal & OU) b July 19, 1899, d Dec. 13, 1935
*Nissar, Mahomed (Patiala, S. Punjab & U. Pradesh) b Aug. 1, 1910, d March 11, 1963
*Nitschke, H. C. (S. Aust.) b April 14, 1905, d Sept. 29, 1982
*Noble, M. A. (NSW; *CY 1900*) b Jan. 28, 1873, d June 22, 1940
*Noblet, G. (S. Aust.) b Sept. 14, 1916
*Noreiga, J. M. (T/T) b April 15, 1936
Norman, M. E. J. C. (Northants & Leics) b Jan. 19, 1933
*Norton, N. O. (W. Prov. & Border) b May 11, 1881, d June 27, 1968
*Nothling, O. E. (NSW & Qld) b Aug. 1, 1900, d Sept. 26, 1965
*Nourse, A. D. ("Dudley") (Natal; *CY 1948*) b Nov. 12, 1910, d Aug. 14, 1981
*Nourse, A. W. ("Dave") (Natal, Tvl & W. Prov.) b Jan. 26, 1878, d July 8, 1948
*Nunes, R. K. (Jam.) b June 7, 1894, d July 22, 1958
*Nupen, E. P. (Tvl) b Jan. 1, 1902, d Jan. 29, 1977
*Nurse, S. M. (B'dos; *CY 1967*) b Nov. 10, 1933
Nutter, A. E. (Lancs & Northants) b June 28, 1913, d June 3, 1996
*Nyalchand, S. (W. Ind., Kathiawar, Guj., & S'tra) b Sept. 14, 1919, d Jan. 3, 1997
Nyren, John (Hants) b Dec. 15, 1764, d June 28, 1837
Nyren, Richard (Hants & Sussex; Proprietor Bat & Ball Inn, Broadhalfpenny Down) b 1734, d April 25, 1797

Oakes, C. (Sussex) b Aug. 10, 1912
Oakes, J. (Sussex) b March 3, 1916, d July 4, 1997
*Oakman, A. S. M. (Sussex) b April 20, 1930
Oates, T. W. (Notts) b Aug. 9, 1875, d June 18, 1949
Oates, W. F. (Yorks & Derbys) b June 11, 1929, d May 15, 2001
*O'Brien, L. P. J. (Vic.) b July 2, 1907, d March 13, 1997
*O'Brien, Sir Timothy C. (OU & Middx) b Nov. 5, 1861, d Dec. 9, 1948
*Ochse, A. E. (Tvl) b March 11, 1870, d April 11, 1918
*Ochse, A. L. (E. Prov.) b Oct. 11, 1899, d May 5, 1949
*O'Connor, J. (Essex) b Nov. 6, 1897, d Feb. 22, 1977
*O'Connor, J. D. A. (NSW & S. Aust.) b Sept. 9, 1875, d Aug. 23, 1941
*O'Donnell, S. P. (Vic.) b Jan. 26, 1963
*Ogilvie, A. D. (Qld) b June 3, 1951
O'Gorman, T. J. G. (Derbys) b May 15, 1967
*O'Keeffe, K. J. (NSW & Som) b Nov. 25, 1949
*Old, C. M. (Yorks, Warwicks & N. Tvl; *CY 1979*) b Dec. 22, 1948
*Oldfield, N. (Lancs & Northants; Test umpire) b May 5, 1911, d April 19, 1996
Oldfield, W. A. MBE (NSW; *CY 1927*) b Sept. 9, 1894, d Aug. 10, 1976
Oldham, S. (Yorks & Derbys) b July 26, 1948
Oldroyd, E. (Yorks) b Oct. 1, 1888, d Dec. 27, 1964
*O'Linn, S. (Kent, W. Prov. & Tvl) b May 5, 1927
Oliver, L. (Derbys) b Oct. 18, 1886, d Jan. 22, 1948
*O'Neill, N. C. (NSW; *CY 1962*) b Feb. 19, 1937
Ontong, R. C. (Border, Tvl, N. Tvl & Glam) b Sept. 9, 1955
Onyango, L. (Kenya) b Sept. 22, 1973
Opatha, A. R. M. (SL) b Aug. 5, 1947
Orchard, D. L. (Natal; Test umpire) b June 24, 1948
Ord, J. S. (Warwicks) b July 12, 1912, d Jan. 14, 2001
*O'Reilly, W. J. OBE (NSW; *CY 1935*) b Dec. 20, 1905, d Oct. 6, 1992
Ormrod, J. A. (Worcs & Lancs) b Dec. 22, 1942
Oscroft, W. (Notts) b Dec. 16, 1843, d Oct. 10, 1905

O'Shaughnessy, S. J. (Lancs & Worcs) b Sept. 9, 1961
Oslear, D. O. (Test umpire) b March 3, 1929
*O'Sullivan, D. R. (C. Dist. & Hants) b Nov. 16, 1944
Outschoorn, L. (Worcs) b Sept. 26, 1918, d Jan. 9, 1994
*Overton, G. W. F. (Otago) b June 8, 1919, d Sept. 7, 1993
Owen, H. G. P. (CU & Essex) b May 19, 1859, d Oct. 20, 1912
*Owens, M. B. (Cant.) b Nov. 11, 1969
*Owen-Smith, H. G. (W. Prov., OU & Middx; *CY 1930*) b Feb. 18, 1909, d Feb. 28, 1990
Owen-Thomas, D. R. (CU & Surrey) b Sept. 20, 1948
*Oxenham, R. K. (Qld) b July 28, 1891, d Aug. 16, 1939

*Padgett, D. E. V. (Yorks) b July 20, 1934
*Padmore, A. L. (B'dos) b Dec. 17, 1946
Page, J. C. T. (Kent) b May 20, 1930, d Dec. 14, 1990
Page, M. H. (Derbys) b June 17, 1941
*Page, M. L. (Cant.) b May 8, 1902, d Feb. 13, 1987
*Pai, A. M. (Bombay) b April 28, 1945
*Paine, G. A. E. (Middx & Warwicks; *CY 1935*) b June 11, 1908, d March 30, 1978
*Pairaudeau, B. H. (BG & N. Dist.) b April 14, 1931
*Palairet, L. C. H. (OU & Som; *CY 1893*) b May 27, 1870, d March 27, 1933
Palairet, R. C. N. (OU & Som) b June 25, 1871, d Feb. 11, 1955
*Palia, P. E. (Parsis, Madras, U. Prov., Bombay, Mysore & Bengal) b Sept. 5, 1910, d Sept. 9, 1981
*Palm, A. W. (W. Prov.) b June 8, 1901, d Aug. 17, 1966
*Palmer, C. H. CBE (Worcs & Leics; Pres. MCC 1978–79; Chairman TCCB 1983–85) b May 15, 1919
*Palmer, G. E. (Vic. & Tas.) b Feb. 22, 1859, d Aug. 22, 1910
*Palmer, K. E. (Som; Test umpire) b April 22, 1937
Palmer, R. (Som; Test umpire) b July 12, 1942
Pardon, Charles F. (Editor of *Wisden* 1887–90) b March 28, 1850, d April 18, 1890
Pardon, Sydney H. (Editor of *Wisden* 1891–1925) b Sept. 23, 1855, d Nov. 20, 1925
*Parfitt, P. H. (Middx; *CY 1963*) b Dec. 8, 1936
Paris, C. G. A. (Hants; Chairman TCCB 1968–75; Pres. MCC 1975–76) b Aug. 20, 1911, d April 4, 1998
Parish, R. J. (Aust. Administrator) b May 7, 1916
*Park, Dr R. L. (Vic.) b July 30, 1892, d Jan. 23, 1947
*Parkar, G. A. (Bombay) b Oct. 24, 1955
*Parkar, R. D. (Bombay) b Oct. 31, 1946, d Aug. 11, 1999
Parkar, Z. (Bombay) b Nov. 22, 1957
*Parker, C. W. L. (Glos; *CY 1923*) b Oct. 14, 1882, d July 11, 1959
*Parker, G. M. (SA) b May 27, 1899, d May 1, 1969
Parker, J. F. (Surrey) b April 23, 1913, d Jan. 27, 1983
*Parker, J. M. (N. Dist. & Worcs) b Feb. 21, 1951
*Parker, N. M. (Otago & Cant.) b Aug. 28, 1948
*Parker, P. W. G. (CU, Sussex, Natal & Durham) b Jan. 15, 1956
*Parkhouse, W. G. A. (Glam) b Oct. 12, 1925, d Aug. 10, 2000
*Parkin, C. H. (Yorks & Lancs; *CY 1924*) b Feb. 18, 1886, d June 15, 1943
*Parkin, D. C. (E. Prov., Tvl & Griq. W.) b Feb. 20, 1873, d March 20, 1936
Parks, H. W. (Sussex) b July 18, 1906, d May 7, 1984
*Parks, J. H. (Sussex & Cant.; *CY 1938*) b May 12, 1903, d Nov. 21, 1980
*Parks, J. M. (Sussex & Som; *CY 1968*) b Oct. 21, 1931
Parks, R. J. (Hants & Kent) b June 15, 1959
Parr, George (Notts & All-England) b May 22, 1826, d June 23, 1891
*Parry, D. R. (Comb. Is. & Leewards) b Dec. 22, 1954
*Parsana, D. D. (S'tra, Ind. Rlwys & Guj.) b Dec. 2, 1947
Parsons, A. B. D. (CU & Surrey) b Sept. 20, 1933, d Feb. 11, 1999
Parsons, G. J. (Leics, Warwicks, Boland, Griq. W. & OFS) b Oct. 17, 1959
Parsons, Canon J. H. (Warwicks) b May 30, 1890, d Feb. 2, 1981
*Partridge, J. T. (Rhod.) b Dec. 9, 1932, d June 7, 1988
Partridge, N. E. (Malvern, CU & Warwicks; *CY 1919*) b Aug. 10, 1900, d March 10, 1982
Partridge, R. J. (Northants) b Feb. 11, 1912, d Feb. 1, 1997
Parvez Mir (R'pindi, Lahore, Punjab, Pak. Us, Derbys, HBL & Glam) b Sept. 24, 1953
*Pascoe, L. S. (NSW) b Feb. 13, 1950
Pasqual, S. P. (SL) b Oct. 15, 1961
*Passailaigue, C. C. (Jam.) b Aug. 1902, d Jan. 7, 1972
*Patankar, C. T. (Bombay) b Nov. 24, 1930
**Pataudi, Iftiqar Ali, Nawab of (OU, Worcs, Patiala, N. Ind. & S. Punjab; *CY 1932*) b March 16, 1910, d Jan. 5, 1952
*Pataudi, Mansur Ali, Nawab of (Sussex, OU, Delhi & H'bad; *CY 1968*) b Jan. 5, 1941
Patel, A. K. (S'tra) b March 6, 1957
*Patel, B. P. (Karn.) b Nov. 24, 1952

*Patel, D. N. (Worcs & Auck.) b Oct. 25, 1958
*Patel, J. M. (Guj.) b Nov. 26, 1924, d Dec. 12, 1992
*Patel, R. G. M. (Baroda) b June 1, 1964
Paterson, G. A. (Zimb.) b June 9, 1960
*Patiala, Maharaja of (N. Ind., Patiala & S. Punjab) b Jan. 17, 1913, d June 17, 1974
*Patil, S. M. (Bombay & M. Pradesh) b Aug. 18, 1956
*Patil, S. R. (M'tra) b Oct. 10, 1933
*Patterson, B. P. (Jam., Tas. & Lancs) b Sept. 15, 1961
Patterson, W. H. (OU & Kent) b March 11, 1859, d May 3, 1946
*Payne, T. R. O. (B'dos) b Feb. 13, 1957
*Paynter, E. (Lancs; *CY 1938*) b Nov. 5, 1901, d Feb. 5, 1979
Payton, W. R. D. (Notts) b Feb. 13, 1882, d May 2, 1943
Peach, H. A. (Surrey) b Oct. 6, 1890, d Oct. 8, 1961
*Peall, S. G. (MCD) b Sept. 2, 1969
Pearce, T. N. (Essex) b Nov. 3, 1905, d April 10, 1994
*Pearse, O. C. (Natal) b Oct. 10, 1884, d May 7, 1953
Pearson, F. (Worcs & Auck.) b Sept. 23, 1880, d Nov. 10, 1963
*Peate, E. (Yorks) b March 2, 1855, d March 11, 1900
Peckover, G. E. (Zimb.) b June 2, 1955
*Peebles, I. A. R. (OU, Middx & Scotland; writer; *CY 1931*) b Jan. 20, 1908, d Feb. 28, 1980
*Peel, R. (Yorks; *CY 1889*) b Feb. 12, 1857, d Aug. 12, 1941
*Pegler, S. J. (Tvl) b July 28, 1888, d Sept. 10, 1972
*Pellew, C. E. (S. Aust.) b Sept. 21, 1893, d May 9, 1981
Penn, C. (Kent) b June 19, 1963
*Penn, F. (Kent) b March 7, 1851, d Dec. 26, 1916
Pepper, C. G. (NSW & Aust. Serv.; umpire) b Sept. 15, 1916, d March 24, 1993
Perkins, H. (CU & Cambs; Sec. MCC 1876–97) b Dec. 10, 1832, d May 6, 1916
*Perks, R. T. D. (Worcs) b Oct. 4, 1911, d Nov. 22, 1977
Perrin, P. A. (Essex; *CY 1905*) b May 26, 1876, d Nov. 20, 1945
Perryman, S. P. (Warwicks & Worcs) b Oct. 22, 1955
*Pervez Sajjad (Lahore, PIA & Kar.) b Aug. 30, 1942
*Petherick, P. J. (Otago & Wgtn) b Sept. 25, 1942
*Petrie, E. C. (Auck. & N. Dist.) b May 22, 1927
Petrie, R. G. (Wgtn) b Aug. 23, 1967
Pettiford, J. (NSW & Kent) b Nov. 29, 1919, d Oct. 11, 1964
*Phadkar, D. G. (M'tra, Bombay, Bengal & Ind. Rlwys) b Dec. 10, 1925, d March 17, 1985
Phebey, A. H. (Kent) b Oct. 1, 1924, d June 28, 1998
Phelan, P. J. (Essex) b Feb. 9, 1938
*Philipson, H. (OU & Middx) b June 8, 1866, d Dec. 4, 1935
*Phillip, N. (Comb. Is., Windwards & Essex) b June 12, 1948
Phillips, H. (Sussex) b Oct. 14, 1844, d July 3, 1919
Phillips, R. B. (NSW & Qld) b May 23, 1954
*Phillips, W. B. (S. Aust.) b March 1, 1958
*Phillips, W. N. (Vic.) b Nov. 7, 1962
Phillipson, C. P. (Sussex) b Feb. 10, 1952
Phillipson, W. E. (Lancs; Test umpire) b Dec. 3, 1910, d Aug. 24, 1991
*Philpott, P. I. (NSW) b Nov. 21, 1934
Pick, R. A. (Notts & Wgtn) b Nov. 19, 1963
Pienaar, R. F. (Tvl, †Northerns, W. Prov & Kent) b July 17, 1961
Pieris, H. S. M. (SL) b Feb. 16, 1946
*Pierre, L. R. (T/T) b June 5, 1921, d April 14, 1989
*Pigott, A. C. S. (Sussex, Wgtn & Surrey) b June 4, 1958
Pilch, Fuller (Norfolk & Kent) b March 17, 1804, d May 1, 1870
Pilling, H. (Lancs) b Feb. 23, 1943
*Pilling, R. (Lancs; *CY 1891*) b July 5, 1855, d March 28, 1891
*Pithey, A. J. (Rhod. & W. Prov.) b July 17, 1933
*Pithey, D. B. (Rhod., OU, Northants, W. Prov., Natal & Tvl) b Oct. 4, 1936
*Place, W. (Lancs) b Dec. 7, 1914, d Jan. 25, 2002
Platt, R. K. (Yorks & Northants) b Dec. 21, 1932
*Playle, W. R. (Auck. & W. Aust.) b Dec. 1, 1938
Pleass, J. E. (Glam) b May 21, 1923
Plews, N. T. (Test umpire) b Sept. 5, 1934
*Plimsoll, J. B. (W. Prov. & Natal) b Oct. 27, 1917, d Nov. 11, 1999
Pocock, N. E. J. (Hants) b Dec. 15, 1951
*Pocock, P. I. (Surrey & N. Tvl) b Sept. 24, 1946
*Pollard, R. (Lancs) b June 19, 1912, d Dec. 16, 1985
*Pollard, V. (C. Dist. & Cant.) b Sept. 7, 1945
*Pollock, P. M. (E. Prov.; *CY 1966*) b June 30, 1941
*Pollock, R. G. (E. Prov. & Tvl; *CY 1966*) b Feb. 27, 1944
*Ponsford, W. H. MBE (Vic.; *CY 1935*) b Oct. 19, 1900, d April 6, 1991
Pont, K. R. (Essex) b Jan. 16, 1953

*Poole, C. J. (Notts) b March 13, 1921, d Feb. 11, 1996
Pooley, E. (Surrey & first England tour) b Feb. 13, 1842, d July 18, 1907
*Poore, M. B. (Cant.) b June 1, 1930
*Poore, Brig-Gen. R. M. (Hants & SA; *CY 1900*) b March 20, 1866, d July 14, 1938
Pope, A. V. (Derbys) b Aug. 15, 1909, d May 11, 1996
*Pope, G. H. (Derbys) b Jan. 27, 1911, d Oct. 29, 1993
*Pope, Dr R. J. (NSW) b Feb. 18, 1864, d July 27, 1952
Popplewell, N. F. M. (CU & Som) b Aug. 8, 1957
Popplewell, Hon. Sir Oliver B. (CU; Pres. MCC 1994–96) b Aug. 15, 1927
Porter, G. D. (W. Aust.) b March 18, 1955
Pothecary, A. E. (Hants) b March 1, 1906, d May 21, 1991
*Pothecary, J. E. (W. Prov.) b Dec. 6, 1933
Potter, L. (Kent, Griq. W., Leics & OFS) b Nov. 7, 1962
*Pougher, A. D. (Leics) b April 19, 1865, d May 20, 1926
*Powell, A. W. (Griq. W.) b July 18, 1873, d Sept. 11, 1948
*Prabhakar, M. (Delhi & Durham) b April 15, 1963
*Prasad, M. S. K. (Andhra) b April 24, 1975
*Prasanna, E. A. S. (†Karn.) b May 22, 1940
Prentice, F. T. (Leics) b April 22, 1912, d July 10, 1978
Pressdee, J. S. (Glam & NE Tvl) b June 19, 1933
Preston, Hubert (Editor of *Wisden* 1944–51) b Dec. 16, 1868, d Aug. 6, 1960
Preston, K. C. (Essex) b Aug. 22, 1925
Preston, Norman MBE (Editor of *Wisden* 1952–80) b March 18, 1903, d March 6, 1980
Pretlove, J. F. (CU & Kent) b Nov. 23, 1932
*Price, J. S. E. (Middx) b July 22, 1937
*Price, W. F. (Middx; Test umpire) b April 25, 1902, d Jan. 13, 1969
*Prideaux, R. M. (CU, Kent, Northants, Sussex & OFS) b July 31, 1939
Pridgeon, A. P. (Worcs) b Feb. 22, 1954
*Priest, M. W. (Cant.) b Aug. 12, 1961
*Prince, C. F. H. (W. Prov., Border & E. Prov.) b Sept. 11, 1874, d Feb. 2, 1949
*Pringle, C. (Auck.) b Jan. 26, 1968
*Pringle, D. R. (CU & Essex) b Sept. 18, 1958
Pritchard, T. L. (Wgtn, Warwicks & Kent) b March 10, 1917
*Procter, M. J. (Glos, Natal, W. Prov., Rhod. & OFS; *CY 1970*) b Sept. 15, 1946
Prodger, J. M. (Kent) b Sept. 1, 1935
*Promnitz, H. L. E. (Border, Griq. W. & OFS) b Feb. 23, 1904, d Sept. 7, 1983
*Pullar, G. (Lancs & Glos; *CY 1960*) b Aug. 1, 1935
*Puna, N. (N. Dist.) b Oct. 28, 1929, d June 7, 1996
*Punjabi, P. H. (Sind & Guj.) b Sept. 20, 1921
*Pycroft, A. J. (Zimb.) b June 6, 1956
Pydanna, M. R. (Guyana) b Jan. 27, 1950

*Qasim Omar (Kar. & MCB) b Feb. 9, 1957
Quaife, B. W. (Warwicks & Worcs) b Nov. 24, 1899, d Nov. 28, 1984
Quaife, Walter (Sussex & Warwicks) b April 1, 1864, d Jan. 18, 1943
*Quaife, William (W. G.) (Warwicks & Griq. W.; *CY 1902*) b March 17, 1872, d Oct. 13, 1951
*Quinn, N. A. (Griq. W. & Tvl) b Feb. 21, 1908, d Aug. 5, 1934

*Rabone, G. O. (Wgtn & Auck.) b Nov. 6, 1921
*Rackemann, C. G. (Qld & Surrey) b June 3, 1960
Radcliffe, Sir Everard J. Bt (Yorks) b Jan. 27, 1884, d Nov. 23, 1969
*Radford, N. V. (Lancs, Tvl & Worcs; *CY 1986*) b June 7, 1957
*Radley, C. T. (Middx; *CY 1979*) b May 13, 1944
*Rae, A. F. (Jam.) b Sept. 30, 1922
Raees Mohammad (Kar.) b Dec. 24, 1932
*Rai Singh, K. (S. Punjab & Ind. Serv.) b Feb. 24, 1922
Rait Kerr, Col. R. S. (Eur.; Sec. MCC 1936–52) b April 13, 1891, d April 2, 1961
Rajab Ali (Kenya) b Nov. 19, 1965
Rajadurai, B. E. A. (SSC) b Aug. 24, 1965
*Rajindernath, V. (N. Ind., U. Prov., S. Punjab, Bihar & E. Punjab) b Jan. 7, 1928, d Nov. 22, 1989
*Rajinder Pal (Delhi, S. Punjab & Punjab) b Nov. 18, 1937
*Rajput, L. S. (Bombay & Vidarbha) b Dec. 18, 1961
Ralph, L. H. R. (Essex) b May 22, 1920
*Ramadhin, S. (T/T & Lancs; *CY 1951*) b May 1, 1929
*Raman, W. V. (TN) b May 23, 1965
*Ramaswami, C. (Madras) b June 18, 1896, presumed dead.
Ramaswamy, V. K. (Test umpire) b April 26, 1946
*Ramchand, G. S. (Sind, Bombay & Raja.) b July 26, 1927
*Ramiz Raja (Lahore, Allied Bank, PNSC & I'bad) b Aug. 14, 1962
*Ramji, L. (W. Ind.) b Oct. 2, 1902, d Dec. 20, 1948
*Ranasinghe, A. N. (BRC) b Oct. 13, 1956, d Nov. 9, 1998
Ranasinghe, S. K. (SL) b July 4, 1962
*Ranatunga, D. (SSC) b Oct. 12, 1962

Ranatunga, N. (Colts & WPN) b Jan. 22, 1966
*Ranchod, U. (Mash.) b May 17, 1969
*Randall, D. W. (Notts; *CY 1980*) b Feb. 24, 1951
Randhir Singh (Orissa & Bihar) b Aug. 16, 1957
*Rangachari, C. R. (Madras) b April 14, 1916, d Oct. 9, 1993
*Rangnekar, K. M. (M'tra, Bombay & †M. Pradesh) b June 27, 1917, d Oct. 11, 1984
*Ranjane, V. B. (M'tra & Ind. Rlwys) b July 22, 1937
*Ranjitsinhji, K. S., (later H. H. the Jam Sahib of Nawanagar) (CU & Sussex; *CY 1897*) b Sept. 10, 1872, d April 2, 1933
*Ransford, V. S. (Vic.; *CY 1910*) b March 20, 1885, d March 19, 1958
*Rashid Khan (PWD, Kar. & PIA) b Dec. 15, 1959
Ratcliffe, J. D. (Warwicks & Surrey) b June 19, 1969
Ratnayake, N. L. K. (SSC) b Nov. 22, 1968
*Ratnayake, R. J. (NCC) b Jan. 2, 1964
*Ratnayeke, J. R. (NCC) b May 2, 1960
Rawlin, J. T. (Yorks & Middx) b Nov. 10, 1856, d Jan. 19, 1924
Rawson, P. W. E. (Zimb. & Natal) b May 25, 1957
Rayment, A. W. H. (Hants) b May 29, 1928
*Razdan, V. (Delhi) b Aug. 25, 1969
*Read, H. D. (Surrey & Essex) b Jan. 28, 1910, d Jan. 5, 2000
*Read, J. M. (Surrey; *CY 1890*) b Feb. 9, 1859, d Feb. 17, 1929
*Read, W. W. (Surrey; *CY 1893*) b Nov. 23, 1855, d Jan. 6, 1907
*Reddy, B. (TN) b Nov. 12, 1954
*Redmond, R. E. (Wgtn & Auck.) b Dec. 29, 1944
*Redpath, I. R. MBE (Vic.) b May 11, 1941
Reed, B. L. (Hants) b Sept. 17, 1937
*Reedman, J. C. (S. Aust.) b Oct. 9, 1865, d March 25, 1924
Rees, A. (Glam) b Feb. 17, 1938
*Reeve, D. A. OBE (Sussex & Warwicks; *CY 1996*) b April 2, 1963
Reeves, W. (Essex; Test umpire) b Jan. 22, 1875, d March 22, 1944
*Rege, M. R. (M'tra) b March 18, 1924
*Rehman, S. F. (Punjab, Pak. Us & Lahore) b June 11, 1935
*Reid, B. A. (W. Aust.) b March 14, 1963
*Reid, J. F. (Auck.) b March 3, 1956
*Reid, J. R. OBE (Wgtn & Otago; *CY 1959;* ICC referee) b June 3, 1928
*Reid, N. (W. Prov.) b Dec. 26, 1890, d June 6, 1947
Reid, R. B. (Wgtn & Auck.) b Dec. 3, 1958
Reidy, B. W. (Lancs) b Sept. 18, 1953
*Relf, A. E. (Sussex & Auck.; *CY 1914*) b June 26, 1874, d March 26, 1937
Relf, R. R. (Sussex) b Sept. 1, 1883, d April 28, 1965
*Renneberg, D. A. (NSW) b Sept. 23, 1942
Revill, A. C. (Derbys & Leics) b March 27, 1923, d July 6, 1998
Reynolds, B. L. (Northants) b June 10, 1932
Rhodes, A. E. G. (Derbys; Test umpire) b Oct. 10, 1916, d Oct. 18, 1983
*Rhodes, H. J. (Derbys) b July 22, 1936
*Rhodes, W. (Yorks; *CY 1899*) b Oct. 29, 1877, d July 8, 1973
Riazuddin (Test umpire) b Dec. 15, 1958
Rice, C. E. B. (Tvl & Notts; *CY 1981*) b July 23, 1949
Rice, J. M. (Hants) b Oct. 23, 1949
*Richards, A. R. (W. Prov.) b Dec. 14, 1867, d Jan. 9, 1904
*Richards, B. A. (Natal, Glos, Hants & S. Aust.; *CY 1969*) b July 21, 1945
*Richards, C. J. (Surrey & OFS) b Aug. 10, 1958
Richards, D. L. (Chief Exec. ICC 1993–2001) b July 28, 1946
Richards, G. (Glam) b Nov. 29, 1951
*Richards, Sir Vivian (I. V. A.) OBE (Comb. Is., Leewards, Som, Qld & Glam; *CY 1977*) b March 7, 1952
*Richards, W. H. (SA) b March 26, 1862, d Jan. 4, 1903
*Richardson, A. J. (S. Aust.) b July 24, 1888, d Dec. 23, 1973
Richardson, A. W. (Derbys) b March 4, 1907, d July 29, 1983
*Richardson, D. J. (E. Prov & N. Tvl) b Sept. 16, 1959
*Richardson, D. W. (Worcs) b Nov. 3, 1934
*Richardson, P. E. (Worcs & Kent; *CY 1957*) b July 4, 1931
*Richardson, T. (Surrey & Som; *CY 1897*) b Aug. 11, 1870, d July 2, 1912
*Richardson, V. Y. (S. Aust.) b Sept. 7, 1894, d Oct. 29, 1969
Riches, N. V. H. (Glam) b June 9, 1883, d Nov. 6, 1975
*Richmond, T. L. (Notts) b June 23, 1890, d Dec. 29, 1957
*Rickards, K. R. (Jam. & Essex) b Aug. 23, 1923, d Aug. 21, 1995
Riddington, A. (Leics) b Dec. 22, 1911, d Feb. 25, 1998
*Ridgway, F. (Kent) b Aug. 10, 1923
*Rigg, K. E. (Vic.) b May 21, 1906, d Feb. 28, 1995
*Ring, D. T. (Vic.) b Oct. 14, 1918
*Ritchie, G. M. (Qld) b Jan. 23, 1960
*Rixon, S. J. (NSW) b Feb. 25, 1954
*Rizwan-uz-Zaman (Kar. & PIA) b Sept. 4, 1961
*Roach, C. A. (T/T) b March 13, 1904, d April 16, 1988

*Roberts, A. D. G. (N. Dist.) b May 6, 1947, d Oct. 26, 1989
*Roberts, A. M. E. CBE (Comb. Is., Leewards, Hants, NSW & Leics; *CY 1975*) b Jan. 29, 1951
*Roberts, A. T. (Windwards & T/T) b Sept. 18, 1937, d July 24, 1996
*Roberts, A. W. (Cant. & Otago) b Aug. 20, 1909, d May 13, 1978
Roberts, B. (Tvl & Derbys) b May 30, 1962
Roberts, F. G. (Glos) b April 1, 1862, d April 7, 1936
Roberts, S. J. (Cant.) b March 22, 1965
Roberts, W. B. (Lancs & Victory Tests) b Sept. 27, 1914, d Aug. 24, 1951
*Robertson, G. K. (C. Dist.) b July 15, 1960
*Robertson, G. R. (NSW) b May 28, 1966
*Robertson, J. B. (W. Prov.) b June 5, 1906, d July 5, 1985
*Robertson, J. D. (Middx; *CY 1948*) b Feb. 22, 1917, d Oct. 12, 1996
*Robertson, W. R. (Vic.) b Oct. 6, 1861, d June 24, 1938
Robertson-Glasgow, R. C. (OU & Som; writer) b July 15, 1901, d March 4, 1965
Robins, D. H. (Warwicks) b June 26, 1914
*Robins, R. W. V. (CU & Middx; *CY 1930*) b June 3, 1906, d Dec. 12, 1968
Robinson, D. C. (Glos & Essex) b April 20, 1884, d July 29, 1963
Robinson, E. (Yorks) b Nov. 16, 1883, d Nov. 17, 1969
Robinson, E. P. (Yorks & Som) b Aug. 10, 1911, d Nov. 10, 1998
Robinson, Sir Foster G. (Glos) b Sept. 19, 1880, d Oct. 31, 1967
Robinson, I. D. (Test umpire) b March 11, 1947
Robinson, P. E. (Yorks & Leics) b Aug. 3, 1963
Robinson, P. J. (Worcs & Som) b Feb. 9, 1943
*Robinson, R. D. (Vic.) b June 8, 1946
*Robinson, R. H. (NSW, S. Aust. & Otago) b March 26, 1914, d Aug. 10, 1965
*Robinson, R. T. (Notts; *CY 1986*) b Nov. 21, 1958
Robson, C. (Hants) b June 20, 1859, d Sept. 27, 1943
Robson, E. (Som) b May 1, 1870, d May 23, 1924
*Rodriguez, W. V. (T/T) b June 25, 1934
Roe, B. (Som) b Jan. 27, 1939
Roebuck, P. M. (CU & Som; *CY 1988*) b March 6, 1956
Rogers, N. H. (Hants) b March 9, 1918
Rogers, S. S. (Eur. & Som) b March 18, 1923, d Nov. 6, 1969
Romaines, P. W. (Northants, Glos & Griq. W.) b Dec. 25, 1955
*Roope, G. R. J. (Surrey & Griq. W.) b July 12, 1946
*Root, C. F. (Derbys & Worcs) b April 16, 1890, d Jan. 20, 1954
*Rorke, G. F. (NSW) b June 27, 1938
*Rose, B. C. (Som; *CY 1980*) b June 4, 1950
*Rose-Innes, A. (Kimberley & Tvl) b Feb. 16, 1868, d Nov. 22, 1946
Rotherham, G. A. (Rugby, CU, Warwicks & Wgtn.; *CY 1918*) b May 28, 1899, d Jan. 31, 1985
Rouse, S. J. (Warwicks) b Jan. 20, 1949
*Routledge, T. W. (W. Prov. & Tvl) b April 18, 1867, d May 9, 1927
*Rowan, A. M. B. (Tvl) b Feb. 7, 1921, d Feb. 21, 1998
*Rowan, E. A. B. (Tvl; *CY 1952*) b July 20, 1909, d April 30, 1993
Rowbotham, J. (Yorks; Test umpire) b July 8, 1831, d Dec. 22, 1899
*Rowe, C. G. (Wgtn & C. Dist.) b June 30, 1915, d June 9, 1995
Rowe, C. J. C. (Kent & Glam) b Nov. 11, 1951
Rowe, E. J. (Notts) b July 21, 1920, d Dec. 17, 1989
*Rowe, G. A. (W. Prov.) b June 15, 1874, d Jan. 8, 1950
*Rowe, L. G. (Jam. & Derbys) b Jan. 8, 1949
*Roy, A. (Bengal) b June 5, 1945, d Sept. 19, 1997
*Roy, Pankaj (Bengal) b May 31, 1928, d Feb. 4, 2001
*Roy, Pranab (Bengal) b Feb. 10, 1957
*Royle, Rev. V. P. F. A. (OU & Lancs) b Jan. 29, 1854, d May 21, 1929
*Rumsey, F. E. (Worcs, Som & Derbys) b Dec. 4, 1935
Rundle, D. B. (W. Prov.) b Sept. 25, 1965
Rushby, T. (Surrey) b Sept. 6, 1880, d July 13, 1962
*Rushmere, M. W. (E. Prov & Tvl) b Jan. 7, 1965
*Russell, A. C. (Essex; *CY 1923*) b Oct. 7, 1887, d March 23, 1961
Russell, P. E. (Derbys) b May 9, 1944
Russell, S. E. J. (Middx & Glos) b Oct. 4, 1937, d June 18, 1994
*Russell, W. E. (Middx) b July 3, 1936
*Rutherford, J. W. (W. Aust.) b Sept. 25, 1929
*Rutherford, K. R. (Otago & †Gauteng) b Oct. 26, 1965
Ryan, F. (Hants & Glam) b Nov. 14, 1888, d Jan. 5, 1954
Ryan, M. (Yorks) b June 23, 1933
*Ryder, J. (Vic.) b Aug. 8, 1889, d April 3, 1977

Saadat Ali (Lahore, UBL & HBFC) b Feb. 6, 1955
*Sadiq Mohammad (Kar., PIA, Tas., Essex, Glos & UBL) b May 3, 1945

*Saeed Ahmed (Punjab, Pak. Us, Lahore, PIA, Kar., PWD & Sind) b Oct. 1, 1937
*Saggers, R. A. (NSW) b May 15, 1917, d March 17, 1987
Saiful Islam (Bangladesh) b April 14, 1969
Sainsbury, P. J. (Hants; *CY 1974*) b June 13, 1934
*St Hill, E. L. (T/T) b March 9, 1904, d May 21, 1957
*St Hill, W. H. (T/T) b July 6, 1893, d *circa* 1957
*Salah-ud-Din (Kar., PIA & Pak. Us) b Feb. 14, 1947
*Saleem Altaf (Lahore & PIA) b April 19, 1944
*Saleem Jaffer (Kar. & UBL) b Nov. 19, 1962
Salim Badar (Test umpire) b May 16, 1953
*Salim Malik (Lahore, HBL & Essex; *CY 1988*) b April 16, 1963
Salim Pervez (NBP) b Sept. 9, 1947
*Salim Yousuf (Sind, Kar., IDBP, Allied Bank & Customs) b Dec. 7, 1959
Samaranayake, A. D. A. (SL) b Feb. 25, 1962
*Samarasekera, M. A. R. (CCC) b Aug. 5, 1961
Sampson, H. (Yorks & All-England) b March 13, 1813, d March 29, 1885
*Samuelson, S. V. (Natal) b Nov. 21, 1883, d Nov. 18, 1958
*Sandham, A. (Surrey; *CY 1923*) b July 6, 1890, d April 20, 1982
*Sandhu, B. S. (Bombay) b Aug. 3, 1956
Santall, F. R. (Warwicks) b July 12, 1903, d Nov. 3, 1950
Santall, S. (Warwicks) b June 10, 1873, d March 19, 1957
Sanuar Hossain (Bangladesh) b Aug. 5, 1973
*Sardesai, D. N. (Bombay) b Aug. 8, 1940
*Sarfraz Nawaz (Lahore, Punjab, Northants, Pak. Rlwys & UBL) b Dec. 1, 1948
*Sarwate, C. T. (CP & B, M'tra, Bombay & †M. Pradesh) b June 22, 1920
*Saunders, J. V. (Vic. & Wgtn) b March 21, 1876, d Dec. 21, 1927
Savage, J. S. (Leics & Lancs) b March 3, 1929
Savill, L. A. (Essex) b June 30, 1935
Saville, G. J. (Essex) b Feb. 5, 1944
Saxelby, K. (Notts) b Feb. 23, 1959
*Saxena, R. C. (Delhi & Bihar) b Sept. 20, 1944
Sayer, D. M. (OU & Kent) b Sept. 19, 1936
*Scarlett, R. O. (Jam.) b Aug. 15, 1934
*Schultz, B. N. (E. Prov. & W. Prov) b Aug. 26, 1970
*Schultz, S. S. (CU & Lancs) b Aug. 29, 1857, d Dec. 18, 1937
*Schwarz, R. O. (Middx & Natal; *CY 1908*) b May 4, 1875, d Nov. 18, 1918
*Scott, A. P. H. (Jam.) b July 29, 1934
Scott, C. J. (Glos) b May 1, 1919, d Nov. 22, 1992
Scott, C. W. (Notts & Durham) b Jan. 23, 1964
*Scott, H. J. H. (Vic.) b Dec. 26, 1858, d Sept. 23, 1910
Scott, M. E. (Northants) b May 8, 1936
*Scott, O. C. (Jam.) b Aug. 14, 1892, d June 15, 1961
*Scott, R. H. (Cant.) b March 6, 1917
Scott, S. W. (Middx; *CY 1893*) b March 24, 1854, d Dec. 8, 1933
*Scott, V. J. (Auck.) b July 31, 1916, d Aug. 2, 1980
*Scotton, W. H. (Notts) b Jan. 15, 1856, d July 9, 1893
*Sealey, B. J. (T/T) b Aug. 12, 1899, d Sept. 12, 1963
*Sealy, J. E. D. (B'dos & T/T) b Sept. 11, 1912, d Jan. 3, 1982
*Seccull, A. W. (Kimberley, W. Prov. & Tvl) b Sept. 14, 1868, d July 20, 1945
*Sekar, T. A. P. (TN) b March 28, 1955
*Selby, J. (Notts) b July 1, 1849, d March 11, 1894
Sellers, A. B. MBE (Yorks; *CY 1940*) b March 5, 1907, d Feb. 20, 1981
*Sellers, R. H. D. (S. Aust.) b Aug. 20, 1940
*Selvey, M. W. W. (CU, Surrey, Middx, Glam & OFS; writer) b April 25, 1948
*Sen, P. (Bengal) b May 31, 1926, d Jan. 27, 1970
*Sen Gupta, A. K. (Ind. Serv.) b Aug. 3, 1939
*Senanayake, C. P. (CCC) b Dec. 19, 1962
*Serjeant, C. S. (W. Aust.) b Nov. 1, 1951
Seymour, James (Kent) b Oct. 25, 1879, d Sept. 30, 1930
*Seymour, M. A. (W. Prov.) b June 5, 1936
*Shackleton, D. (Hants; *CY 1959*) b Aug. 12, 1924
*Shafiq Ahmed (Lahore, Punjab, NBP & UBL) b March 28, 1949
*Shafqat Rana (Lahore & PIA) b Aug. 10, 1943
*Shah, A. H. (Mash.) b Aug. 7, 1959
*Shahid Israr (Kar. & Sind) b March 1, 1950
*Shahid Mahboob (Kar., Quetta, R'pindi, I'bad, PACO & Allied Bank) b Aug. 25, 1962
*Shahid Mahmoud (Kar., Pak. Us & PWD) b March 17, 1939
*Shahid Saeed (HBFC, Lahore & PACO) b Jan. 6, 1966
*Shakeel Ahmed, jun. (R'pindi, Peshawar, HBL, Gujranwala & Easterns) b Nov. 12, 1971
Shakeel Khan (WAPDA, HBL, R'pindi & I'bad) b May 28, 1968
*Shalders, W. A. (Griq. W. & Tvl) b Feb. 12, 1880, d March 18, 1917
Shariful Haq (Bangladesh) b Jan. 15, 1976
*Sharma, Chetan (Haryana & Bengal) b Jan. 3, 1966
*Sharma, Gopal (U. Pradesh) b Aug. 3, 1960
*Sharma, P. (Raja.) b Jan. 5, 1948

Sharp, G. (Northants; Test umpire) b March 12, 1950
Sharp, H. P. (Middx) b Oct. 6, 1917, d Jan. 15, 1995
*Sharp, J. (Lancs) b Feb. 15, 1878, d Jan. 28, 1938
Sharp, K. (Yorks & Griq. W.) b April 6, 1959
*Sharpe, D. (Punjab, Pak. Rlwys, Lahore & S. Aust.) b Aug. 3, 1937
*Sharpe, J. W. (Surrey & Notts; *CY 1892*) b Dec. 9, 1866, d June 19, 1936
*Sharpe, P. J. (Yorks & Derbys; *CY 1963*) b Dec. 27, 1936
*Shastri, R. J. (Bombay & Glam) b May 27, 1962
*Shaw, Alfred (Notts & Sussex) b Aug. 29, 1842, d Jan. 16, 1907
Shaw, T. G. (E. Prov.) b July 5, 1959
*Sheahan, A. P. (Vic.) b Sept. 30, 1946
Sheffield, J. R. (Essex & Wgtn) b Nov. 19, 1906, d Nov. 16, 1997
Sheikh Salahuddin (Bangladesh) b Feb. 10, 1969
*Shepherd, B. K. (W. Aust.) b April 23, 1937, d Sept. 17, 2001
Shepherd, D. J. (Glam; *CY 1970*) b Aug. 12, 1927
Shepherd, D. R. MBE (Glos; Test umpire) b Dec. 27, 1940
*Shepherd, J. N. (B'dos, Kent, Rhod. & Glos; *CY 1979*) b Nov. 9, 1943
Shepherd, T. F. (Surrey) b Dec. 5, 1889, d Feb. 13, 1957
*Sheppard, Rt Rev. D. S. (Bishop of Liverpool; later Baron Sheppard) (CU & Sussex; *CY 1953*) b March 6, 1929
*Shepstone, G. H. (Tvl) b April 9, 1876, d July 3, 1940
*Sherwell, P. W. (Tvl) b Aug. 17, 1880, d April 17, 1948
*Sherwin, M. (Notts; *CY 1891*) b Feb. 26, 1851, d July 3, 1910
Shields, J. (Leics) b Feb. 1, 1882, d May 11, 1960
*Shillingford, G. C. (Comb. Is. & Windwards) b Sept. 25, 1944
*Shillingford, I. T. (Comb. Is. & Windwards) b April 18, 1944
*Shinde, S. G. (Baroda, M'tra & Bombay) b Aug. 18, 1923, d June 22, 1955
Shine, K. J. (Hants, Middx & Somerset) b Feb. 22, 1969
Shipman, A. W. (Leics) b March 7, 1901, d Dec. 12, 1979
Shipston, F. W. (Notts; *believed to be oldest living first-class county cricketer at end of 2001*) b July 29, 1906
Shirreff, A. C. (CU, Hants, Kent & Som) b Feb. 12, 1919
*Shivnarine, S. (Guyana) b May 13, 1952
*Shodhan, R. H. (Guj. & Baroda) b Oct. 18, 1928
*Shrewsbury, A. (Notts; *CY 1890*) b April 11, 1856, d May 19, 1903
*Shrimpton, M. J. F. (C. Dist. & N. Dist.) b June 23, 1940
*Shuja-ud-Din, Col. (N. Ind., Pak. Us, Pak. Serv., B'pur & R'pindi) b April 10, 1930
*Shukla, R. C. (Bihar & Delhi) b Feb. 4, 1948
*Shuter, J. (Kent & Surrey) b Feb. 9, 1855, d July 5, 1920
*Shuttleworth, K. (Lancs & Leics) b Nov. 13, 1944
Sibbles, F. M. (Lancs) b March 15, 1904, d July 20, 1973
Siddons, J. D. (Vic & S. Aust.) b April 25, 1964
*Sidebottom, A. (Yorks & OFS) b April 1, 1954
*Sidhu, N. S. (Punjab) b Oct. 20, 1963
Sidwell, T. E. (Leics) b Jan. 30, 1888, d Dec. 8, 1958
*Siedle, I. J. (Natal) b Jan. 11, 1903, d Aug. 24, 1982
*Sievers, M. W. (Vic.) b April 13, 1912, d May 10, 1968
*Sikander Bakht (PWD, PIA, Sind, Kar. & UBL) b Aug. 25, 1957
Silk, D. R. W. CBE (CU & Som; Pres. MCC 1992–94; Chairman TCCB 1994–96) b Oct. 8, 1931
*Silva, K. J. (Bloom. & SSC) b June 2, 1973
*Silva, S. A. R. (NCC) b Dec. 12, 1960
Sime, W. A. MBE (OU & Notts) b Feb. 8, 1909, d May 5, 1983
Simmons, J. MBE (Lancs & Tas.; *CY 1985*) b March 28, 1941
Simons, E. O. (W. Prov. & N. Tvl) b March 9, 1962
*Simpson, R. B. (NSW & W. Aust.; *CY 1965*) b Feb. 3, 1936
*Simpson, R. T. (Sind & Notts; *CY 1950*) b Feb. 27, 1920
*Simpson-Hayward, G. H. (Worcs) b June 7, 1875, d Oct. 2, 1936
Sims, Sir Arthur (Cant.) b July 22, 1877, d April 27, 1969
*Sims, J. M. (Middx) b May 13, 1903, d April 27, 1973
*Sinclair, B. W. (Wgtn) b Oct. 23, 1936
*Sinclair, I. M. (Cant.) b June 1, 1933
*Sinclair, J. H. (Tvl) b Oct. 16, 1876, d Feb. 23, 1913
*Sincock, D. J. (S. Aust.) b Feb. 1, 1942
*Sinfield, R. A. (Glos) b Dec. 24, 1900, d March 17, 1988
*Singh, Charan K. (T/T) b Nov. 27, 1935
Singh, R. P. (U. Pradesh) b Jan. 6, 1963
Singleton, A. P. (OU, Worcs & Rhod.) b Aug. 5, 1914, d March 22, 1999

*Sivaramakrishnan, L. (TN & Baroda) b Dec. 31, 1965
Skelding, A. (Leics; umpire) b Sept. 5, 1886, d April 17, 1960
*Slack, W. N. (Middx & Windwards) b Dec. 12, 1954, d Jan. 15, 1989
Slade, D. N. F. (Worcs) b Aug. 24, 1940
Slater, A. G. (Derbys) b Nov. 22, 1890, d July 22, 1949
*Slater, K. N. (W. Aust.) b March 12, 1935
*Sleep, P. R. (S. Aust.) b May 4, 1957
*Slight, J. (Vic.) b Oct. 20, 1855, d Dec. 9, 1930
Slocombe, P. A. (Som) b Sept. 6, 1954
*Smailes, T. F. (Yorks) b March 27, 1910, d Dec. 1, 1970
Smales, K. (Yorks & Notts) b Sept. 15, 1927
*Small, G. C. (Warwicks & S. Aust.) b Oct. 18, 1961
Small, John, sen. (Hants & All-England) b April 19, 1737, d Dec. 31, 1826
*Small, J. A. (T/T) b Nov. 3, 1892, d April 26, 1958
*Small, M. A. (B'dos) b Feb. 12, 1964
Smart, C. C. (Warwicks & Glam) b July 23, 1898, d May 21, 1975
Smart, J. A. (Warwicks) b April 12, 1891, d Oct. 3, 1979
Smedley, M. J. (Notts) b Oct. 28, 1941
*Smith, A. C. CBE (OU & Warwicks; Chief Exec. TCCB 1987–96; ICC referee) b Oct. 25, 1936
*Smith, Sir C. Aubrey (CU, Sussex & Tvl) b July 21, 1863, d Dec. 20, 1948
*Smith, C. I. J. (Middx; *CY 1935*) b Aug. 25, 1906, d Feb. 9, 1979
*Smith, C. J. E. (Tvl) b Dec. 25, 1872, d March 27, 1947
*Smith, C. L. (Natal, Glam & Hants; *CY 1984*) b Oct. 15, 1958
Smith, C. L. A. (Sussex) b Jan. 1, 1879, d Nov. 22, 1949
Smith, C. S. (later Sir Colin Stansfield-) (CU & Lancs) b Oct. 1, 1932
*Smith, C. W. (B'dos; ICC referee) b July 29, 1933
*Smith, Denis (Derbys; *CY 1936*) b Jan. 24, 1907, d Sept. 12, 1979
*Smith, D. B. M. (Vic.) b Sept. 14, 1884, d July 29, 1963
Smith, D. H. K. (Derbys & OFS) b June 29, 1940
*Smith, D. M. (Surrey, Worcs & Sussex) b Jan. 9, 1956
*Smith, D. R. (Glos) b Oct. 5, 1934
*Smith, D. V. (Sussex) b June 14, 1923
Smith, Edwin (Derbys) b Jan. 2, 1934
Smith, Ernest (OU & Yorks) b Oct. 19, 1869, d April 9, 1945
*Smith, E. J. (Warwicks) b Feb. 6, 1886, d Aug. 31, 1979
*Smith, F. B. (Cant.) b March 13, 1922, d July 6, 1997
*Smith, F. W. (Tvl) b unknown, d April 17, 1914, aged 53
Smith, G. J. (Essex) b April 2, 1935
*Smith, Harry (Glos) b May 21, 1890, d Nov. 12, 1937
Smith, H. A. (Leics) b March 29, 1901, d Aug. 7, 1948
*Smith, H. D. (Otago & Cant.) b Jan. 8, 1913, d Jan. 25, 1986
*Smith, I. D. S. MBE (C. Dist. & Auck.) b Feb. 28, 1957
Smith, K. D. (Warwicks) b July 9, 1956
Smith, M. J. (Middx) b Jan. 4, 1942
*Smith, M. J. K. OBE (Leics, OU & Warwicks; *CY 1960*) b June 30, 1933
Smith, N. (Yorks & Essex) b April 1, 1949
*Smith, O. G. ("Collie") (Jam.; *CY 1958*) b May 5, 1933, d Sept. 9, 1959
Smith, P. A. (Warwicks) b April 5, 1964
Smith, Ray (Essex) b Aug. 10, 1914, d Feb. 21, 1996
Smith, Roy (Som) b April 14, 1930
Smith, R. C. (Leics) b Aug. 3, 1935, d Dec. 12, 2001
*Smith, S. B. (NSW & Tvl) b Oct. 18, 1961
Smith, S. G. (T/T, Northants & Auck.; *CY 1915*) b Jan. 15, 1881, d Oct. 25, 1963
*Smith, T. P. B. (Essex; *CY 1947*) b Oct. 30, 1908, d Aug. 4, 1967
*Smith, V. I. (Natal) b Feb. 23, 1925
Smith, W. A. (Surrey) b Sept. 15, 1937
Smith, W. C. (Surrey; *CY 1911*) b Oct. 4, 1877, d July 16, 1946
*Smithson, G. A. (Yorks & Leics) b Nov. 1, 1926, d Sept. 6, 1970
*Snedden, C. A. (Auck.) b Jan. 7, 1918
*Snedden, M. C. (Auck.) b Nov. 23, 1958
*Snell, R. P. (Natal, Tvl, Somerset & Gauteng) b Sept. 12, 1968
Snellgrove, K. L. (Lancs) b Nov. 12, 1941
*Snooke, S. D. (W. Prov. & Tvl) b Nov. 11, 1878, d April 6, 1959
*Snooke, S. J. (Border, W. Prov. & Tvl) b Feb. 1, 1881, d Aug. 14, 1966
*Snow, J. A. (Sussex; *CY 1973*) b Oct. 13, 1941
*Sobers, Sir Garfield S. (B'dos, S. Aust. & Notts; *CY 1964*) b July 28, 1936
Sohail Fazal (HBL) b Nov. 11, 1967
*Sohoni, S. W. (M'tra, Baroda & Bombay) b March 5, 1918, d May 19, 1993
*Solkar, E. D. (Bombay & Sussex) b March 18, 1948
*Solomon, J. S. (BG) b Aug. 26, 1930
*Solomon, W. R. (Tvl & E. Prov.) b April 23, 1872, d July 12, 1964
*Sood, M. M. (Delhi) b July 6, 1939
Southern, J. W. (Hants) b Sept. 2, 1952

*Southerton, James (Surrey, Hants & Sussex) b Nov. 16, 1827, d June 16, 1880
Southerton, S. J. (Editor of *Wisden* 1934–35) b July 7, 1874, d March 12, 1935
*Sparling, J. T. (Auck.) b July 24, 1938
Speed, M. W. (Chief Exec. ICC 2001–) b Sept. 14, 1948
Spencer, C. T. (Leics) b Aug. 18, 1931
Spencer, J. (CU & Sussex) b Oct. 6, 1949
Spencer, T. W. OBE (Kent; Test umpire) b March 22, 1914
Sperry, J. (Leics) b March 19, 1910, d April 21, 1997
*Spofforth, F. R. (NSW & Vic.) b Sept. 9, 1853, d June 4, 1926
*Spooner, R. H. (Lancs; *CY 1905*) b Oct. 21, 1880, d Oct. 2, 1961
*Spooner, R. T. (Warwicks) b Dec. 30, 1919, d Dec. 20, 1997
Springall, J. D. (Notts) b Sept. 19, 1932
Sprot, E. M. (Hants) b Feb. 4, 1872, d Oct. 8, 1945
Squires, H. S. (Surrey) b Feb. 22, 1909, d Jan. 24, 1950
*Srikkanth, K. (TN) b Dec. 21, 1959
*Srinivasan, T. E. (TN) b Oct. 26, 1950
*Stackpole, K. R. MBE (Vic.; *CY 1973*) b July 10, 1940
Standen, J. A. (Worcs) b May 30, 1935
*Stanyforth, Lt-Col. R. T. (Yorks) b May 30, 1892, d Feb. 20, 1964
Staples, A. (Notts) b Feb. 4, 1899, d Sept. 9, 1965
*Staples, S. J. (Notts; *CY 1929*) b Sept. 18, 1892, d June 4, 1950
*Statham, J. B. CBE (Lancs; *CY 1955*) b June 17, 1930, d June 10, 2000
*Stayers, S. C. (†Guyana & Bombay) b June 9, 1937
Stead, B. (Yorks, Essex, Notts & N. Tvl) b June 21, 1939, d April 15, 1980
*Steel, A. G. (CU & Lancs; Pres. MCC 1902) b Sept. 24, 1858, d June 15, 1914
*Steele, D. S. OBE (Northants & Derbys; *CY 1976*) b Sept. 29, 1941
Steele, J. F. (Leics, Natal & Glam) b July 23, 1946
Stephens, E. J. (Glos) b March 23, 1909, d April 3, 1983
Stephenson, F. D. (B'dos, Glos, Tas., Notts, Sussex & †FS; *CY 1989*) b April 8, 1959
Stephenson, G. R. (Derbys & Hants) b Nov. 19, 1942
Stephenson, H. H. (Surrey & All-England) b May 3, 1832, d Dec. 17, 1896
Stephenson, H. W. (Som) b July 18, 1920
Stephenson, Lt-Col. J. R. CBE (Sec. MCC 1987–93) b Feb. 25, 1931
Stephenson, Lt-Col. J. W. A. (Essex, Worcs, Army, Europeans & Victory Tests) b Aug. 1, 1907, d May 20, 1982
Stevens, Edward ("Lumpy") (Hants) b *circa* 1735, d Sept. 7, 1819
*Stevens, G. B. (S. Aust.) b Feb. 29, 1932
*Stevens, G. T. S. (UCS, OU & Middx; *CY 1918*) b Jan. 7, 1901, d Sept. 19, 1970
*Stevenson, G. B. (Yorks & Northants) b Dec. 16, 1955
Stevenson, K. (Derbys & Hants) b Oct. 6, 1950
*Stewart, M. J. OBE (Surrey; *CY 1958*) b Sept. 16, 1932
*Stewart, R. B. (SA) b Sept. 3, 1856, d Sept. 12, 1913
Stewart, W. J. (Warwicks & Northants) b Oct. 31, 1934
*Stirling, D. A. (C. Dist.) b Oct. 5, 1961
Stocks, F. W. (Notts) b Nov. 6, 1918, d Feb. 23, 1996
*Stoddart, A. E. (Middx; *CY 1893*) b March 11, 1863, d April 3, 1915
*Stollmeyer, J. B. (T/T) b April 11, 1921, d Sept. 10, 1989
*Stollmeyer, V. H. (T/T) b Jan. 24, 1916, d Sept. 21, 1999
Stone, J. (Hants & Glam) b Nov. 29, 1876, d Nov. 15, 1942
Storer, H. jun. (Derbys) b Feb. 2, 1898, d Sept. 1, 1967
*Storer, W. (Derbys; *CY 1899*) b Jan. 25, 1867, d Feb. 28, 1912
Storey, S. J. (Surrey & Sussex) b Jan. 6, 1941
Stott, L. W. (Auck.) b Dec. 8, 1946
Stott, W. B. (Yorks) b July 18, 1934
Stovold, A. W. (Glos & OFS) b March 19, 1953
*Street, G. B. (Sussex) b Dec. 6, 1889, d April 24, 1924
*Stricker, L. A. (Tvl) b May 26, 1884, d Feb. 5, 1960
*Strudwick, H. (Surrey; *CY 1912*) b Jan. 28, 1880, d Feb. 14, 1970
Stuart, A. M. (NSW) b Jan. 2, 1970
*Studd, C. T. (CU & Middx) b Dec. 2, 1860, d July 16, 1931
*Studd, G. B. (CU & Middx) b Oct. 20, 1859, d Feb. 13, 1945
Studd, Sir J. E. Kynaston (Middx & CU; Pres. MCC 1930) b July 26, 1858, d Jan. 14, 1944
*Su'a, M. L. (N. Dist. & Auck.) b Nov. 7, 1966
*Subba Row, R. CBE (CU, Surrey & Northants; *CY 1961;* Chairman TCCB 1985–90; ICC referee) b Jan. 29, 1932
*Subramanya, V. (Mysore) b July 16, 1936
Sudhakar Rao, R. (Karn.) b Aug. 8, 1952
Sueter, T. (Hants & Surrey) b *circa* 1749, d Feb. 17, 1827
*Sugg, F. H. (Yorks, Derbys & Lancs; *CY 1890*) b Jan. 11, 1862, d May 29, 1933
Sullivan, J. (Lancs) b Feb. 5, 1945
Sully, H. (Som & Northants) b Nov. 1, 1939

*Sunderram, G. (Bombay & Raja.) b March 29, 1930
*Surendranath, R. (Ind. Serv.) b Jan. 4, 1937
Surridge, W. S. (Surrey; *CY 1953*) b Sept. 3, 1917, d April 13, 1992
*Surti, R. F. (Guj., Raja., & Qld) b May 25, 1936
*Susskind, M. J. (CU, Middx & Tvl) b June 8, 1891, d July 9, 1957
*Sutcliffe, B. MBE (Auck., Otago & N. Dist.; *CY 1950*) b Nov. 17, 1923, d April 20, 2001
*Sutcliffe, H. (Yorks; *CY 1920*) b Nov. 24, 1894, d Jan. 22, 1978
Sutcliffe, W. H. H. (Yorks) b Oct. 10, 1926, d Sept. 16, 1998
Suttle, K. G. (Sussex) b Aug. 25, 1928
*Swamy, V. N. (Ind. Serv.) b May 23, 1924, d May 1, 1983
Swanton, E. W. CBE (Middx; writer & broadcaster) b Feb. 11, 1907, d Jan. 22, 2000
Swarbrook, F. W. (Derbys, Griq. W. & OFS) b Dec. 17, 1950
Swart, P. D. (Rhod., W. Prov., Glam & Boland) b April 27, 1946, d March 13, 2000
*Swetman, R. (Surrey, Notts & Glos) b Oct. 25, 1933
Sydenham, D. A. D. (Surrey) b April 6, 1934
*Symcox, P. L. (Griq. W., Natal & N. Tvl) b April 14, 1960

*Taber, H. B. (NSW) b April 29, 1940
*Taberer, H. M. (OU & Natal) b Oct. 7, 1870, d June 5, 1932
*Tahir Naqqash (Servis Ind., MCB, Punjab & Lahore) b July 6, 1959
*Talat Ali (Lahore, PIA & UBL; ICC referee) b May 29, 1950
*Tallon, D. (Qld; *CY 1949*) b Feb. 17, 1916, d Sept. 7, 1984
*Tamhane, N. S. (Bombay) b Aug. 4, 1931
*Tancred, A. B. (Kimberley, Griq. W. & Tvl) b Aug. 20, 1865, d Nov. 23, 1911
*Tancred, L. J. (Tvl) b Oct. 7, 1876, d July 28, 1934
*Tancred, V. M. (Tvl) b July 7, 1875, d June 3, 1904
Tanvir Mehdi (Lahore & UBL) b Nov. 7, 1972
*Tapscott, G. L. (Griq. W.) b Nov. 7, 1889, d Dec. 13, 1940
*Tapscott, L. E. (Griq. W.) b March 18, 1894, d July 7, 1934
*Tarapore, K. K. (Bombay) b Dec. 17, 1910, d June 15, 1986
Tarbox, C. V. (Worcs) b July 2, 1891, d June 15, 1978
Tarrant, F. A. (Vic., Middx & Patiala; *CY 1908*) b Dec. 11, 1880, d Jan. 29, 1951
Tarrant, G. F. (Cambs. & All-England) b Dec. 7, 1838, d July 2, 1870
*Taslim Arif (Kar., Sind & NBP) b May 1, 1954
*Tate, F. W. (Sussex) b July 24, 1867, d Feb. 24, 1943
*Tate, M. W. (Sussex; *CY 1924*) b May 30, 1895, d May 18, 1956
*Tattersall, R. (Lancs) b Aug. 17, 1922
*Tauseef Ahmed (PWD, UBL, Kar. & Customs) b May 10, 1958
*Tavaré, C. J. (OU, Kent & Som) b Oct. 27, 1954
*Tayfield, H. J. (Natal, Rhod. & Tvl; *CY 1956*) b Jan. 30, 1929, d Feb. 25, 1994
*Taylor, A. I. (Tvl) b July 25, 1925
Taylor, B. (Essex; *CY 1972*) b June 19, 1932
*Taylor, B. R. (Cant. & Wgtn) b July 12, 1943
Taylor, C. G. (CU & Sussex) b Nov. 21, 1816, d Sept. 10, 1869
*Taylor, Daniel (Natal) b Jan. 9, 1887, d Jan. 24, 1957
*Taylor, D. D. (Auck. & Warwicks) b March 2, 1923, d Dec. 5, 1980
Taylor, D. J. S. (Surrey, Som & Griq. W.) b Nov. 12, 1942
*Taylor, H. W. (Natal, Tvl & W. Prov.; *CY 1925*) b May 5, 1889, d Feb. 8, 1973
*Taylor, J. (T/T) b Jan. 3, 1932, d Nov. 13, 1999
*Taylor, J. M. (NSW) b Oct. 10, 1895, d May 12, 1971
*Taylor, K. (Yorks & Auck.) b Aug. 21, 1935
*Taylor, L. B. (Leics & Natal) b Oct. 25, 1953
*Taylor, M. A. (NSW; *CY 1990*) b Oct. 27, 1964
Taylor, M. N. S. (Notts & Hants) b Nov. 12, 1942
Taylor, N. R. (Kent & Sussex) b July 21, 1959
*Taylor, P. L. (NSW & Qld) b Aug. 22, 1956
Taylor, R. M. (Essex) b Nov. 30, 1909, d Jan. 7, 1984
*Taylor, R. W. MBE (Derbys; *CY 1977*) b July 17, 1941
Taylor, T. L. (CU & Yorks; *CY 1901*) b May 25, 1878, d March 16, 1960
Tennekoon, A. P. B. (SL) b Oct. 29, 1946
*Tennyson, 3rd Lord (Hon. L. H.) (Hants; *CY 1914*) b Nov. 7, 1889, d June 6, 1951
*Terry, V. P. (Hants) b Jan. 14, 1959
*Theunissen, N. H. (W. Prov.) b May 4, 1867, d Nov. 9, 1929
Thomas, A. E. (Northants) b June 7, 1893, d March 21, 1965
Thomas, D. J. (Surrey, N. Tvl, Natal & Glos) b June 30, 1959
*Thomas, G. (NSW) b March 21, 1938
*Thomas, J. G. (Glam, Border, E. Prov. & Northants) b Aug. 12, 1960
Thompson, A. W. (Middx) b April 17, 1916, d Jan. 13, 2001
*Thompson, G. J. (Northants; Test umpire; *CY 1906*) b Oct. 27, 1877, d March 3, 1943
*Thompson, P. I. C. (B'dos) b Sept. 26, 1971
Thompson, R. G. (Warwicks) b Sept. 26, 1932
*Thoms, G. R. (Vic.) b March 22, 1927

*Thomson, A. L. (Vic.) b Dec. 2, 1945
*Thomson, J. R. (NSW, Qld & Middx) b Aug. 16, 1950
*Thomson, K. (Cant.) b Feb. 26, 1941
*Thomson, N. F. D. (NSW) b May 29, 1839, d Sept. 2, 1896
*Thomson, N. I. (Sussex) b Jan. 23, 1929
*Thomson, S. A. (N. Dist.) b Jan. 27, 1969
Thornton, C. I. (CU, Kent & Middx) b March 20, 1850, d Dec. 10, 1929
*Thornton, Dr P. G. (Yorks, Middx & SA) b Dec. 24, 1867, d Jan. 31, 1939
*Thurlow, H. M. (Qld) b Jan. 10, 1903, d Dec. 3, 1975
Tiffin, R. B. (Test umpire) b June 4, 1959
Timms, B. S. V. (Hants & Warwicks) b Dec. 17, 1940
Timms, J. E. (Northants) b Nov. 3, 1906, d May 18, 1980
Tindall, R. A. E. (Surrey) b Sept. 23, 1935
*Tindill, E. W. T. (Wgtn) b Dec. 18, 1910
Tissera, M. H. (SL) b March 23, 1939
*Titmus, F. J. MBE (Middx, Surrey & OFS; *CY 1963*) b Nov. 24, 1932
Todd, L. J. (Kent) b June 19, 1907, d Aug. 20, 1967
Todd, P. A. (Notts & Glam) b March 12, 1953
*Tolchard, R. W. (Leics) b June 15, 1946
Tomlins, K. P. (Middx & Glos) b Oct. 23, 1957
*Tomlinson, D. S. (Rhod. & Border) b Sept. 4, 1910, d July 11, 1993
Tompkin, M. (Leics) b Feb. 17, 1919, d Sept. 27, 1956
*Toohey, P. M. (NSW) b April 20, 1954
Topley, T. D. (Surrey, Essex & Griq. W.) b Feb. 25, 1964
*Toshack, E. R. H. (NSW) b Dec. 15, 1914
Townsend, A. (Warwicks) b Aug. 26, 1921
Townsend, A. F. (Derbys) b March 29, 1912, d Feb. 25, 1994
*Townsend, C. L. (Glos; *CY 1899*) b Nov. 7, 1876, d Oct. 17, 1958
*Townsend, D. C. H. (OU) b April 20, 1912, d Jan. 27, 1997
*Townsend, L. F. (Derbys & Auck.; *CY 1934*) b June 8, 1903, d Feb. 17, 1993
**Traicos, A. J. (Rhod. & Mash.) b May 17, 1947
*Travers, J. P. F. (S. Aust.) b Jan. 10, 1871, d Sept. 15, 1942
*Tremlett, M. F. (Som & C. Dist.) b July 5, 1923, d July 30, 1984
Tremlett, T. M. (Hants) b July 26, 1956
*Tribe, G. E. (Vic. & Northants; *CY 1955*) b Oct. 4, 1920
*Trim, J. (BG) b Jan. 25, 1915, d Nov. 12, 1960
Trimble, G. S. (Qld) b Jan. 1, 1963
*Trimborn, P. H. J. (Natal) b May 18, 1940
**Trott, A. E. (Vic., Middx & Hawkes Bay; *CY 1899*) b Feb. 6, 1873, d July 30, 1914
*Trott, G. H. S. (Vic.; *CY 1894*) b Aug. 5, 1866, d Nov. 10, 1917
Troughton, L. H. W. (Kent) b May 17, 1879, d Aug. 31, 1933
*Troup, G. B. (Auck.) b Oct. 3, 1952
*Trueman, F. S. OBE (Yorks; *CY 1953*) b Feb. 6, 1931
*Trumble, H. (Vic.; *CY 1897*) b May 12, 1867, d Aug. 14, 1938
*Trumble, J. W. (Vic.) b Sept. 16, 1863, d Aug. 17, 1944
*Trumper, V. T. (NSW; *CY 1903*) b Nov. 2, 1877, d June 28, 1915
*Truscott, P. B. (Wgtn) b Aug. 14, 1941
*Tuckett, L. (OFS) b Feb. 6, 1919
*Tuckett, L. R. (Natal & OFS) b April 19, 1885, d April 8, 1963
*Tufnell, N. C. (CU & Surrey) b June 13, 1887, d Aug. 3, 1951
Tunnicliffe, C. J. (Derbys) b Aug. 11, 1951
Tunnicliffe, J. (Yorks; *CY 1901*) b Aug. 26, 1866. d July 11, 1948
*Turnbull, M. J. (CU & Glam; *CY 1931*) b March 16, 1906, d Aug. 5, 1944
*Turner, A. (NSW) b July 23, 1950
Turner, C. (Yorks) b Jan. 11, 1902, d Nov. 19, 1968
*Turner, C. T. B. (NSW; *CY 1889*) b Nov. 16, 1862, d Jan. 1, 1944
Turner, D. R. (Hants & W. Prov.) b Feb. 5, 1949
Turner, F. M. MBE (Leics) b Aug. 8, 1934
*Turner, G. M. (Otago, N. Dist. & Worcs; *CY 1971*) b May 26, 1947
Turner, S. (Essex & Natal) b July 18, 1943
*Twentyman-Jones, Sir Percy S. (W. Prov.) b Sept. 13, 1876, d March 8, 1954
*Tyldesley, E. (Lancs; *CY 1920*) b Feb. 5, 1889, d May 5, 1962
*Tyldesley, J. T. (Lancs; *CY 1902*) b Nov. 22, 1873, d Nov. 27, 1930
*Tyldesley, R. K. (Lancs; *CY 1925*) b March 11, 1897, d Sept. 17, 1943
*Tylecote, E. F. S. (OU & Kent) b June 23, 1849, d March 15, 1938
*Tyler, E. J. (Som) b Oct. 13, 1864, d Jan. 25, 1917
*Tyson, F. H. (Northants; *CY 1956*) b June 6, 1930

Ufton, D. G. (Kent) b May 31, 1928
*Ulyett, G. (Yorks) b Oct. 21, 1851, d June 18, 1898
*Umrigar, P. R. (Bombay & Guj.) b March 28, 1926
*Underwood, D. L. MBE (Kent; *CY 1969*) b June 8, 1945

Vaidya, P. S. (Bengal) b Sept. 23, 1967
*Valentine, A. L. (Jam.; *CY 1951*) b April 28, 1930

*Valentine, B. H. (CU & Kent) b Jan. 17, 1908, d Feb. 2, 1983
*Valentine, V. A. (Jam.) b April 4, 1908, d July 6, 1972
*Vance, R. H. (Wgtn) b March 31, 1955
*van der Bijl, P. G. (W. Prov. & OU) b Oct. 21, 1907, d Feb. 16, 1973
van der Bijl, V. A. P. (Natal, Middx & Tvl; *CY 1981*) b March 19, 1948
*Van der Merwe, E. A. (Tvl) b Nov. 9, 1904, d Feb. 26, 1971
*Van der Merwe, P. L. (W. Prov. & E. Prov.; ICC referee) b March 14, 1937
van Geloven, J. (Yorks & Leics) b Jan. 4, 1934
*Van Ryneveld, C. B. (W. Prov. & OU) b March 19, 1928
van Zyl, C. J. P. G. (OFS & Glam) b Oct. 1, 1961
*Varnals, G. D. (E. Prov., Tvl & Natal) b July 24, 1935
*Vaughan, J. T. C. (Auck.) b Aug. 30, 1967
*Veivers, T. R. (Qld) b April 6, 1937
*Veletta, M. R. J. (W. Aust.) b Oct. 30, 1963
*Vengsarkar, D. B. (Bombay; *CY 1987*) b April 6, 1956
*Venkataraghavan, S. (†TN & Derbys; Test umpire) b April 21, 1946
*Venkataramana, M. (TN) b April 24, 1966
*Verity, H. (Yorks; *CY 1932*) b May 18, 1905, d July 31, 1943
*Vernon, G. F. (Middx) b June 20, 1856, d Aug. 10, 1902
Vials, G. A. T. (Northants) b March 18, 1887, d April 26, 1974
Vigar, F. H. (Essex) b July 7, 1917
*Viljoen, K. G. (Griq. W., OFS & Tvl) b May 14, 1910, d Jan. 21, 1974
*Vincent, C. L. (Tvl) b Feb. 16, 1902, d Aug. 24, 1968
*Vine, J. (Sussex; *CY 1906*) b May 15, 1875, d April 25, 1946
*Vintcent, C. H. (Tvl & Griq. W.) b Sept. 2, 1866, d Sept. 28, 1943
Virgin, R. T. (Som, Northants & W. Prov.; *CY 1971*) b Aug. 26, 1939
*Viswanath, G. R. (†Karn.; ICC referee) b Feb. 12, 1949
*Viswanath, S. (Karn.) b Nov. 29, 1962
*Vivian, G. E. (Auck.) b Feb. 28, 1946
*Vivian, H. G. (Auck.) b Nov. 4, 1912, d Aug. 12, 1983
*Vizianagram, Maharaj Kumar of, Sir Vijay A., (U. Prov.) b Dec. 28, 1905, d Dec. 2, 1965
*Voce, W. (Notts; *CY 1933*) b Aug. 8, 1909, d June 6, 1984
*Vogler, A. E. E. (Middx, Natal, Tvl & E. Prov.; *CY 1908*) b Nov. 28, 1876, d Aug. 9, 1946
Vonhagt, D. M. (Moors) b March 31, 1965

*Waddington, A. (Yorks) b Feb. 4, 1893, d Oct. 28, 1959
*Wade, H. F. (Natal) b Sept. 14, 1905, d Nov. 23, 1980
Wade, T. H. (Essex) b Nov. 24, 1910, d July 25, 1987
*Wade, W. W. (Natal) b June 18, 1914
*Wadekar, A. L. (Bombay) b April 1, 1941
*Wadsworth, K. J. (C. Dist. & Cant.) b Nov. 30, 1946, d Aug. 19, 1976
*Wainwright, E. (Yorks; *CY 1894*) b April 8, 1865, d Oct. 28, 1919
*Waite, J. H. B. (E. Prov. & Tvl) b Jan. 19, 1930
*Waite, M. G. (S. Aust.) b Jan. 7, 1911, d Dec. 16, 1985
*Walcott, Sir Clyde L. (B'dos & BG; *CY 1958;* Chairman ICC 1993–97) b Jan. 17, 1926
*Walcott, L. A. (B'dos) b Jan. 18, 1894, d Feb. 27, 1984
Walden, F. (Northants; Test umpire) b March 1, 1888, d May 3, 1949
Walker, A. (Northants & Durham) b July 7, 1962
Walker, C. (Yorks & Hants) b June 27, 1919, d Dec. 3, 1992
Walker, I. D. (Middx) b Jan. 8, 1844, d July 6, 1898
*Walker, M. H. N. (Vic.) b Sept. 12, 1948
*Walker, P. M. (Glam, Tvl & W. Prov.) b Feb. 17, 1936
Walker, V. E. (Middx) b April 20, 1837, d Jan. 3, 1906
Walker, W. (Notts) b Nov. 24, 1892, d Dec. 3, 1991
*Wall, T. W. (S. Aust.) b May 13, 1904, d March 25, 1981
*Wallace, W. M. (Auck.) b Dec. 19, 1916
*Waller, A. C. (Mash.) b Sept. 25, 1959
Waller, C. E. (Surrey & Sussex) b Oct. 3, 1948
Walsh, J. E. (NSW & Leics) b Dec. 4, 1912, d May 20, 1980
*Walter, K. A. (Tvl) b Nov. 5, 1939
*Walters, C. F. (Glam & Worcs; *CY 1934*) b Aug. 28, 1905, d Dec. 23, 1992
*Walters, F. H. (Vic. & NSW) b Feb. 9, 1860, d June 1, 1922
*Walters, K. D. MBE (NSW) b Dec. 21, 1945
*Waqar Hassan (Pak. Us, Punjab, Pak. Serv. & Kar.) b Sept. 12, 1932
*Ward, Alan (Derbys, Leics & Border) b Aug. 10, 1947
*Ward, Albert (Yorks & Lancs; *CY 1890*) b Nov. 21, 1865, d Jan. 6, 1939
Ward, B. (Essex) b Feb. 28, 1944
Ward, D. (Glam) b Aug. 30, 1934
Ward, D. M. (Surrey) b Feb. 10, 1961
*Ward, F. A. (S. Aust.) b Feb. 23, 1906, d March 25, 1974
*Ward, J. T. (Cant.) b March 11, 1937
*Ward, T. A. (Tvl) b Aug. 2, 1887, d Feb. 16, 1936

Ward, William (MCC & Hants) b July 24, 1787, d June 30, 1849
*Wardle, J. H. (Yorks; *CY 1954*) b Jan. 8, 1923, d July 23, 1985
*Warnapura, B. (SL; ICC referee) b March 1, 1953
*Warnaweera, K. P. J. (Galle & Singha) b Nov. 23, 1960
Warner, A. E. (Worcs & Derbys) b May 12, 1959
*Warner, Sir Pelham F. (OU & Middx; *CY 1904, special portrait 1921;* Pres. MCC 1950–51) b Oct. 2, 1873, d Jan. 30, 1963
*Warr, J. J. (CU & Middx; Pres. MCC 1987–88) b July 16, 1927
*Warren, A. R. (Derbys) b April 2, 1875, d Sept. 3, 1951
*Washbrook, C. CBE (Lancs; *CY 1947*) b Dec. 6, 1914, d April 27, 1999
*Wasim Bari (Kar., PIA & Sind) b March 23, 1948
Wasim Haider (PIA & F'bad) b June 6, 1967
*Wasim Raja (Lahore, Sargodha, Pak. Us, PIA, Punjab & NBP) b July 3, 1952
Wass, T. G. (Notts; *CY 1908*) b Dec. 26, 1873, d Oct. 27, 1953
*Wassan, A. S. (Delhi) b March 23, 1968
Wassell, A. (Hants) b April 15, 1940
*Watkins, A. J. (Glam) b April 21, 1922
*Watkins, J. C. (Natal) b April 10, 1923
*Watkins, J. R. (NSW) b April 16, 1943
*Watkinson, M. (Lancs) b Aug. 1, 1961
Watson, A. (Lancs) b Nov. 4, 1844, d Oct. 26, 1920
*Watson, C. (Jam. & Delhi) b July 1, 1938
Watson, F. (Lancs) b Sept. 17, 1898, d Feb. 1, 1976
*Watson, G. D. (Vic., W. Aust. & NSW) b March 8, 1945
Watson, G. S. (Kent & Leics) b April 10, 1907, d April 1, 1974
*Watson, W. (Yorks & Leics; *CY 1954*) b March 7, 1920
*Watson, W. (Auck.) b Aug. 31, 1965
*Watson, W. J. (NSW) b Jan. 31, 1931
Watt, A. E. (Kent) b June 19, 1907, d Feb. 3, 1974
*Watt, L. (Otago) b Sept. 17, 1924, d Nov. 15, 1996
Watts, E. A. (Surrey) b Aug. 1, 1911, d May 2, 1982
Watts, P. D. (Northants & Notts) b March 31, 1938
Watts, P. J. (Northants) b June 16, 1940
*Wazir, Ali, S. (C. Ind., S. Punjab & Patiala) b Sept. 15, 1903, d June 17, 1950
*Wazir Mohammad (B'pur & Kar.) b Dec. 22, 1929
*Webb, M. G. (Otago & Cant.) b June 22, 1947
*Webb, P. N. (Auck.) b July 14, 1957
Webb, R. J. (Otago) b Sept. 15, 1952
Webb, R. T. (Sussex) b July 11, 1922
*Webbe, A. J. (OU & Middx) b Jan. 16, 1855, d Feb. 19, 1941
Webber, Roy (Statistician) b July 23, 1914, d Nov. 14, 1962
*Weekes, Sir Everton D. (B'dos; *CY 1951*) b Feb. 26, 1925
*Weekes, K. H. (Jam.) b Jan. 24, 1912, d Feb. 9, 1998
Weeks, R. T. (Warwicks) b April 30, 1930
Weerakkody, A. P. (NCC) b Oct. 1, 1970
*Weerasinghe, C. D. U. S. (TU & NCC) b March 1, 1968
Weigall, G. J. V. (CU & Kent) b Oct. 19, 1870, d May 17, 1944
*Weir, G. L. (Auck.; *oldest living Test cricketer at end of 2001*) b June 2, 1908
*Wellard, A. W. (Som; *CY 1936*) b April 8, 1902, d Dec. 31, 1980
*Wellham, D. M. (NSW, Tas. & Qld) b March 13, 1959
*Wells, A. P. (Sussex, Border & Kent) b Oct. 2, 1961
Wells, B. D. (Glos & Notts) b July 27, 1930
Wells, C. M. (Sussex, Border, W. Prov. & Derbys) b March 3, 1960
Wells, W. (Northants) b March 14, 1881, d March 18, 1939
Wenman, E. G. (Kent & England) b Aug. 18, 1803, d Dec. 31, 1879
Wensley, A. F. (Sussex, Auck., Naw. & Eur.) b May 23, 1898, d June 17, 1970
*Wesley, C. (Natal) b Sept. 5, 1937
**Wessels, K. C. (OFS, W. Prov., N. Tvl, Sussex, Qld, E. Prov. & Griq. W.; *CY 1995*) b Sept 14, 1957
West, G. H. (Editor of *Wisden* 1880–86) b 1851, d Oct. 6, 1896
*Westcott, R. J. (W. Prov.) b Sept. 19, 1927
Weston, M. J. (Worcs) b April 8, 1959
*Wettimuny, M. D. (SL) b June 11, 1951
*Wettimuny, S. (SL; *CY 1985;* ICC referee) b Aug. 12, 1956
Wettimuny, S. R. de S. (SL) b Feb. 7, 1949
*Wharton, A. (Lancs & Leics) b April 30, 1923, d Aug. 26, 1993
*Whatmore, D. F. (Vic.) b March 16, 1954
Wheatley, O. S. CBE (CU, Warwicks & Glam; *CY 1969*) b May 28, 1935
Whitaker, Haddon OBE (Editor of *Wisden* 1940–43) b Aug. 30, 1908, d Jan. 5, 1982
*Whitaker, J. J. (Leics; *CY 1987*) b May 5, 1962
White, A. F. T. (CU, Warwicks & Worcs) b Sept. 5, 1915, d March 16, 1993
White, Sir Archibald W. 4th Bt (Yorks) b Oct. 14, 1877, d Dec. 16, 1945
*White, D. J. (N. Dist.) b June 26, 1961
*White, D. W. (Hants & Glam) b Dec. 14, 1935
*White, G. C. (Tvl) b Feb. 5, 1882, d Oct. 17, 1918

*White, J. C. (Som; *CY 1929*) b Feb. 19, 1891, d May 2, 1961
White, Hon. L. R. (5th Lord Annaly) (Middx & Victory Test) b March 15, 1927, d Sept. 30, 1990
White, R. A. (Middx & Notts) b Oct. 6, 1936
White, R. C. (CU, Glos & Tvl) b Jan. 29, 1941
*White, W. A. (B'dos) b Nov. 20, 1938
Whitehead, A. G. T. (Som; Test umpire) b Oct. 28, 1940
Whitehead, H. (Leics) b Sept. 19, 1874, d Sept. 14, 1944
Whitehouse, J. (Warwicks) b April 8, 1949
*Whitelaw, P. E. (Auck.) b Feb. 10, 1910, d Aug. 28, 1988
Whiteside, J. P. (Lancs & Leics) b June 11, 1861, d March 8, 1946
Whitfield, E. W. (Surrey & Northants) b May 31, 1911, d Aug. 10, 1996
Whitington, R. S. (S. Aust. & Victory Tests; writer) b June 30, 1912, d March 13, 1984
*Whitney, M. R. (NSW & Glos) b Feb. 24, 1959
Whittaker, G. J. (Surrey) b May 29, 1916, d April 20, 1997
*Whittall, A. R. (CU & Mat.) b March 28, 1973
Whitticase, P. (Leics) b March 15, 1965
Whittingham, N. B. (Notts) b Oct. 22, 1940
*Whitty, W. J. (S. Aust.) b Aug. 15, 1886, d Jan. 30, 1974
*Whysall, W. W. (Notts; *CY 1925*) b Oct. 31, 1887, d Nov. 11, 1930
*Wickremasinghe, A. G. D. (NCC) b Dec. 27, 1965
*Wiener, J. M. (Vic.) b May 1, 1955
*Wight, C. V. (BG) b July 28, 1902, d Oct. 4, 1969
*Wight, G. L. (BG) b May 28, 1929
Wight, P. B. (BG, Som & Cant.) b June 25, 1930
*Wijegunawardene, K. I. W. (CCC) b Nov. 23, 1964
*Wijesuriya, R. G. C. E. (Mor. & Colts) b Feb. 18, 1960
*Wijetunge, P. K. (SSC & Moors) b Aug. 6, 1971
Wilcox, D. R. (Essex & CU) b June 4, 1910, d Feb. 6, 1953
Wild, D. J. (Northants) b Nov. 28, 1962
*Wiles, C. A. (B'dos & T/T) b Aug. 11, 1892, d Nov. 4, 1957
Wilkins, C. P. (Derbys, Border, E. Prov. & Natal) b July 31, 1944
Wilkinson, C. T. A. (Surrey) b Oct. 4, 1884, d Dec. 16, 1970
*Wilkinson, L. L. (Lancs) b Nov. 5, 1916
Willatt, G. L. (CU, Notts & Derbys) b May 7, 1918
*Willett, E. T. (Comb. Is. & Leewards) b May 1, 1953
Willett, M. D. (Surrey) b April 21, 1933, d Jan. 24, 2002
*Willey, P. (Northants, E. Prov. & Leics; Test umpire) b Dec. 6, 1949
*Williams, A. B. (Jam.) b Nov. 21, 1949
*Williams, D. (T/T) b Nov. 4, 1963
Williams, D. L. (Glam) b Nov. 20, 1946
*Williams, E. A. V. (B'dos) b April 10, 1914, d April 13, 1997
*Williams, N. F. (Middx, Essex, Windwards & Tas.) b July 2, 1962
Williams, R. G. (Northants) b Aug. 10, 1957
*Willis, R. G. D. MBE (Surrey, Warwicks & N. Tvl; *CY 1978*) b May 30, 1949
*Willoughby, J. T. (SA) b Nov. 7, 1874, d March 11, 1952
Willsher, E. (Kent & All-England) b Nov. 22, 1828, d Oct. 7, 1885
Wilson, A. (Lancs) b April 24, 1921
Wilson, A. E. (Middx & Glos) b May 18, 1910
*Wilson, Rev. C. E. M. (CU & Yorks) b May 15, 1875, d Feb. 8, 1944
*Wilson, D. (Yorks) b Aug. 7, 1937
Wilson, E. R. (Betty) (Australia Women) b Nov. 21, 1921
*Wilson, E. R. (CU & Yorks) b March 25, 1879, d July 21, 1957
Wilson, G. (CU & Yorks) b Aug. 21, 1895, d Nov. 29, 1960
Wilson, H. L. (Sussex) b June 27, 1881, d March 15, 1937
Wilson, J. V. (Yorks; *CY 1961*) b Jan. 17, 1921
Wilson, J. W. (Otago) b Oct. 24, 1973
*Wilson, J. W. (Vic. & S. Aust.) b Aug. 20, 1921, d Oct. 13, 1985
Wilson, M. R. (E. Prov.; ICC referee) b Sept. 8, 1944
Wilson, R. C. (Kent) b Feb. 18, 1928
*Wimble, C. S. (Tvl) b April 22, 1861, d Jan. 28, 1930
Windows, A. R. (Glos & CU) b Sept. 25, 1942
Winfield, H. M. (Notts) b June 13, 1933
Winrow, H. F. (Notts) b Jan. 17, 1916, d Aug. 19, 1973
*Winslow, P. L. (Sussex, Tvl & Rhod.) b May 21, 1929
Wisden, John (Sussex; founder John Wisden & Co and *Wisden's Cricketers' Almanack; special portrait 1913*) b Sept. 5, 1826, d April 5, 1884
*Wishart, K. L. (BG) b Nov. 28, 1908, d Oct. 18, 1972
Wolton, A. V. (Warwicks) b June 12, 1919, d Sept. 9, 1990
*Wood, A. (Yorks; *CY 1939*) b Aug. 25, 1898, d April 1, 1973
*Wood, B. (Yorks, Lancs, Derbys & E. Prov.) b Dec. 26, 1942

Wood, C. J. B. (Leics) b Nov. 21, 1875, d June 5, 1960
Wood, D. J. (Sussex) b May 19, 1914, d March 12, 1989
*Wood, G. E. C. (CU & Kent) b Aug. 22, 1893, d March 18, 1971
*Wood, G. M. (W. Aust.) b Nov. 6, 1956
*Wood, H. (Kent & Surrey; *CY 1891*) b Dec. 14, 1854, d April 30, 1919
*Wood, R. (Lancs & Vic.) b March 7, 1860, d Jan. 6, 1915
*Woodcock, A. J. (S. Aust.) b Feb. 27, 1948
Woodcock, John C. OBE (Writer; Editor of *Wisden* 1981–86) b Aug. 7, 1926
*Woodfull, W. M. OBE (Vic.; *CY 1927*) b Aug. 22, 1897, d Aug. 11, 1965
Woodhead, F. G. (Notts) b Oct. 30, 1912, d May 24, 1991
**Woods, S. M. J. (CU & Som; *CY 1889*) b April 13, 1867, d April 30, 1931
Wooller, W. (CU & Glam) b Nov. 20, 1912, d March 10, 1997
Woolley, C. N. (Glos & Northants) b May 5, 1886, d Nov. 3, 1962
*Woolley, F. E. (Kent; *CY 1911*) b May 27, 1887, d Oct. 18, 1978
*Woolley, R. D. (Tas.) b Sept. 16, 1954
*Woolmer, R. A. (Kent, Natal & W. Prov.; *CY 1976*) b May 14, 1948
*Worrall, J. (Vic.) b June 21, 1860, d Nov. 17, 1937
*Worrell, Sir Frank M. M. (B'dos & Jam.; *CY 1951*) b Aug. 1, 1924, d March 13, 1967
Worsley, D. R. (OU & Lancs) b July 18, 1941
*Worthington, T. S. (Derbys; *CY 1937*) b Aug. 21, 1905, d Aug. 31, 1973
Wrathall, H. (Glos) b Feb. 1, 1869, d June 1, 1944
Wright, A. C. (Kent) b April 4, 1895, d May 26, 1959
Wright, A. J. (Glos) b June 27, 1962
*Wright, C. W. (CU & Notts) b May 27, 1863, d Jan. 10, 1936
*Wright, D. V. P. (Kent; *CY 1940*) b Aug. 21, 1914, d Nov. 13, 1998
Wright, Graeme A. (Editor of *Wisden* 1987–92 & 2001–02) b April 23, 1943
*Wright, J. G. MBE (N. Dist., Derbys, Cant. & Auck.) b July 5, 1954
*Wright, K. J. (W. Aust. & S. Aust.) b Dec. 27, 1953
Wright, L. G. (Derbys; *CY 1906*) b June 15, 1862, d Jan. 11, 1953
Wright, W. (Notts & Kent) b Feb. 29, 1856, d March 22, 1940
*Wyatt, R. E. S. (Warwicks & Worcs; *CY 1930*) b May 2, 1901, d April 20, 1995
*Wynne, O. E. (Tvl & W. Prov.) b June 1, 1919, d July 13, 1975
*Wynyard, E. G. (Hants) b April 1, 1861, d Oct. 30, 1936

Yachad, M. (Tvl) b Nov. 17, 1960
*Yadav, N. S. (H'bad) b Jan. 26, 1957
*Yadav, V. S. (Haryana) b March 14, 1967
*Yajurvindra Singh (M'tra & S'tra) b Aug. 1, 1952
*Yallop, G. N. (Vic.) b Oct. 7, 1952
*Yardley, B. (W. Aust.) b Sept. 5, 1947
*Yardley, N. W. D. (CU & Yorks; *CY 1948*) b March 19, 1915, d Oct. 4, 1989
Yardley, T. J. (Worcs & Northants) b Oct. 27, 1946
Yarnold, H. (Worcs) b July 6, 1917, d Aug. 13, 1974
*Yashpal Sharma (Punjab) b Aug. 11, 1954
Yawar Saeed (Som & Punjab) b Jan. 22, 1935
*Yograj Singh (Haryana & Punjab) b March 25, 1958
Young, A. (Som) b Nov. 6, 1890, d April 2, 1936
*Young, B. A. (N. Dist. & Auck.) b Nov. 3, 1964
Young, D. M. (Worcs & Glos) b April 15, 1924, d June 18, 1993
Young, H. I. (Essex) b Feb. 5, 1876, d Dec. 12, 1964
*Young, J. A. (Middx) b Oct. 14, 1912, d Feb. 5, 1993
*Young, R. A. (CU & Sussex) b Sept. 16, 1885, d July 1, 1968
*Younis Ahmed (Lahore, Kar., Surrey, PIA, S. Aust., Worcs & Glam) b Oct. 20, 1947
*Yuile, B. W. (C. Dist.) b Oct. 29, 1941

Zafar Iqbal (Kar. & NBP) b March 6, 1969
*Zaheer Abbas (Kar., Glos, PWD, Dawood Ind., Sind & PIA; *CY 1972*) b July 24, 1947
Zahid Ahmed (PIA & H'bad) b Nov. 15, 1961
Zakir Hassan (Bangladesh) b Dec. 1, 1972
*Zakir Khan (Sind, Peshawar & ADBP) b April 3, 1963
Zesers, A. K. (S. Aust.) b March 11, 1967
*Zoehrer, T. J. (W. Aust.) b Sept. 25, 1961
*Zulch, J. W. (Tvl) b Jan. 2, 1886, d May 19, 1924
*Zulfiqar Ahmed (B'pur & PIA) b Nov. 22, 1926
*Zulqarnain (Pak. Rlwys, Lahore, HBFC & PACO) b May 25, 1962

REGISTER OF CURRENT PLAYERS

The qualifications for inclusion are as follows:

1. All players who appeared in Tests or one-day internationals for a Test-playing country in 2000-01 or 2001.
2. All players who appeared in the County Championship in 2001.
3. All players who appeared in the Pura Cup, Supersport Series, Busta Cup and Duleep Trophy in 2000-01.
4. All players who appeared in first-class domestic cricket in 2000-01 or 2001, who have also played in Tests or one-day international cricket.
5. All players who appeared in one-day internationals for Kenya in 2000-01 and 2001.
6. All players who appeared in first-class cricket for their national A-team in 2000-01.

Notes: The forename by which the player is known is underlined if it is not his first name.

Teams are those played for in 2000-01 and/or 2001, or the last domestic team for which that player appeared.

Countries are those for which players are qualified.

The country of birth is given if it is not the one for which a player is qualified. It is also given to differentiate between nations in the Leeward and Windward Islands, and where it is essential for clarity.

* *Denotes Test player.*

	Team	*Country*	*Born*	*Birthplace*
Aamer Hanif	Karachi/Allied Bank	P	4.10.71	*Karachi*
***Aamir Nazir**	Islamabad/Allied Bank	P	2.1.71	*Lahore*
***Aamir Sohail**	Lahore City/A. Bank/Som	P	14.9.66	*Lahore*
Ababu Josephat Sorongo	Kenya	K	15.4.80	*Kenya*
***Abdur Razzaq**	Lahore City	P	2.12.79	*Lahore*
Abrahams Shafiek	Eastern Province	SA	4.3.68	*Port Elizabeth*
Abrahams Umar	Eastern Province	SA	7.2.81	*Port Elizabeth*
Abrahim Zahir Ahmed	Griqualand West	SA	5.6.72	*Robertson*
***Ackerman** Hylton Deon	Western Province	SA	14.2.73	*Cape Town*
***Adams** Andre Ryan	Auckland	NZ	17.7.75	*Auckland*
***Adams** Christopher John	Sussex	E	6.5.70	*Whitwell*
Adams Fabian Alex	Leeward Islands	WI	7.1.75	*The Valley, Anguilla*
***Adams** James Clive	Jamaica	WI	9.1.68	*Port Maria*
***Adams** Paul Regan	Western Province	SA	20.1.77	*Cape Town*
***Adcock** Nathan Tennyson	South Australia	A	22.4.78	*Campbelltown*
***Afzaal** Usman	Nottinghamshire	E	9.6.77	*Rawalpindi, Pakistan*
***Agarkar** Ajit Bhalchandra	Mumbai	I	4.12.77	*Bombay*
Ahmed Kamal	Khulna	B	28.12.77	*Court Para*
Akhtar Sarfraz	Peshawar/National Bank	P	20.2.76	*Peshawar*
***Akram Khan**	Chittagong	B	1.11.68	*Chittagong*
***Akram Raza**	Sargodha/Habib Bank	P	22.11.64	*Lahore*
Aldred Paul	Derbyshire	E	4.2.69	*Chellaston*
Alexander Camilus Christopher	West Indies B	WI	20.10.81	*Grenada*
Ali Kabir	Worcestershire	E	24.11.80	*Moseley*
Ali Kadeer	Worcestershire	E	7.3.83	*Moseley*
Ali Zaheer Reaz	West Indies B	WI	17.1.81	*Bamboo Village, Trinidad*
***Ali Naqvi**	Islamabad/Customs	P	19.3.77	*Lahore*
Alleyne David	Middlesex	E	17.4.76	*York*
Alleyne Mark Wayne	Gloucestershire	E	23.5.68	*Tottenham*
***Allott** Geoffrey Ian	Canterbury	NZ	24.12.71	*Christchurch*
***Al-Shahriar Rokon**	Dhaka Metropolis	B	23.4.78	*Dhaka*
Ambrose Timothy Raymond	Sussex	E	1.12.82	*Newcastle, Australia*
Amerasinghe Merenna Koralage Don Ishara	Nondescripts	SL	5.3.78	*Colombo*
Amin Rupesh Mahesh	Surrey	E	20.8.77	*Clapham*
Aminul Islam, jun.	Rajshahi	B	1.4.75	*Rajshahi*
***Aminul Islam**, sen.	Biman	B	2.2.68	*Dhaka*

	Team	Country	Born	Birthplace
Amla Ahmed Mahomed	KwaZulu-Natal	SA	15.9.79	*Durban*
* **Amre** Pravin Kalyan	Goa	I	14.8.68	*Bombay*
Anderson Matthew Allan	Queensland	A	10.11.76	*Darwin*
Anderson Ricaldo Sherman Glenroy	Essex	E	22.9.76	*Hammersmith*
Angara Joseph Oduol	Kenya	K	8.11.71	*Nairobi*
* **Angel** Jo	Western Australia	A	22.4.68	*Mount Lawley*
Anisur Rahman	Chittagong	B	1.3.71	*Dhaka*
* **Aqib Javed**	Sheikhupura/Allied Bank	P	5.8.72	*Sheikhupura*
Armstrong Sean Hussain	Barbados	WI	11.5.73	*Bayfield*
Arnberger Jason Lee	Victoria	A	18.11.72	*Penrith*
* **Arnold** Russel Premakumaran	Nondescripts	SL	25.10.73	*Colombo*
* **Arshad Khan**	Peshawar/Allied Bank	P	22.3.71	*Peshawar*
Arthur John Michael	Griqualand West	SA	17.5.68	*Johannesburg*
* **Ashfaq Ahmed**	PIA	P	6.6.73	*Lahore*
Asif Mahmood	Rawalpindi/KRL	P	18.12.75	*Rawalpindi*
* **Asif Mujtaba**	Karachi/PIA	P	4.11.67	*Karachi*
* **Astle** Nathan John	Canterbury	NZ	15.9.71	*Christchurch*
* **Atapattu** Marvan Samson	Sinhalese	SL	22.11.70	*Kalutara*
* **Ata-ur-Rehman**	Allied Bank	P	28.3.75	*Lahore*
* **Atherton** Michael Andrew	Lancashire	E	23.3.68	*Manchester*
* **Atiq-uz-Zaman**	Karachi/Habib Bank	P	20.7.75	*Karachi*
Austin Ryan Anthony	Barbados	WI	15.11.81	*Arima, Trinidad*
Averis James Maxwell Michael	Gloucestershire	E	28.5.74	*Bristol*
Aymes Adrian Nigel	Hampshire	E	4.6.64	*Southampton*
Azam Hussain	Karachi	P	7.9.85	*Karachi*
* **Azam Khan**	Karachi/Customs	P	1.3.69	*Karachi*
* **Azhar Mahmood**	PIA	P	28.2.75	*Rawalpindi*
* **Bacher** Adam Marc	Gauteng	SA	29.10.73	*Johannesburg*
* **Badani** Hemang Kamal	Tamil Nadu	I	14.11.76	*Madras*
* **Bahutule** Sairaj Vasant	Mumbai	I	6.1.73	*Bombay*
Bailey Mark David	Northern Districts	NZ	26.11.70	*Hamilton*
* **Bailey** Robert John	Derbyshire	E	28.10.63	*Biddulph*
Bailey Tobin Michael Barnaby	Northamptonshire	E	28.8.76	*Kettering*
Baker Orlando	Jamaica	WI	15.9.79	*St Catherine*
Bakkes Herman Charles	Free State	SA	24.12.69	*Port Elizabeth*
Balaji Rao Wandavasi Dorakanti	Tamil Nadu	I	4.3.78	*Madras*
Ball Martyn Charles John	Gloucestershire	E	26.4.70	*Bristol*
* **Bandara** Charitha Malinga	Nondescripts	SL	31.12.79	*Kalutara*
* **Bandaratilleke** Mapa Rallage Chandima Niroshan	Tamil Union	SL	16.5.75	*Colombo*
Bangar Sanjay Bapusaheb	Railways	I	11.10.72	*Beed*
Banks Omari Ahmed Clemente	Leeward Islands/Leics	WI	17.7.82	*Anguilla*
* **Baptiste** Eldine Ashworth Elderfield	KwaZulu-Natal	WI	12.3.60	*Liberta, Antigua*
Barnard Pieter Hendrik	Boland	SA	8.5.70	*Nelspruit*
* **Barnett** Kim John	Gloucestershire	E	17.7.60	*Stoke-on-Trent*
Bassano Christopher Warwick Godfrey	Derbyshire	E	11.9.75	*East London, SA*
Bastow Jonathan Edward	KwaZulu-Natal	SA	12.2.74	*Pietermaritzburg*
Batty Gareth Jon	Surrey	E	13.10.77	*Bradford*
Batty Jonathan Neil	Surrey	E	18.4.74	*Chesterfield*
Baugh Carlton	Jamaica	WI	26.6.82	*Kingston*
Bazil Kevin Fabian	Guyana	WI	18.5.82	*Guyana*
Bedade Atul Chandrakant	Baroda	I	24.9.66	*Bombay*
Bell Ian Ronald	Warwickshire	E	11.4.82	*Walsgrave*
* **Bell** Matthew David	Wellington	NZ	25.2.77	*Dunedin*
Benfield Mark Rowland	Eastern Province	SA	3.12.76	*Potgietersrus*
* **Benjamin** Kenneth Charlie Griffith	Easterns	WI	8.4.67	*St John's, Antigua*
Benkenstein Dale Martin	KwaZulu-Natal	SA	9.6.74	*Salisbury, Rhodesia*

	Team	*Country*	*Born*	*Birthplace*
Benn Sulieman Jamaal	West Indies B	WI	22.7.81	*Haynesville*
Bernard David Eddison	West Indies B	WI	19.7.81	*Kingston, Jamaica*
Berry Darren Shane	Victoria	A	10.12.69	*Melbourne*
Betts Melvyn Morris	Warwickshire	E	26.3.75	*Sacriston*
Beukes Jonathan Alan	Free State	SA	15.3.79	*Kimberley*
* **Bevan** Michael Gwyl	New South Wales	A	8.5.70	*Belconnen*
Bhandari Amit	Delhi	I	1.10.78	*Delhi*
* **Bharadwaj** Raghvendrarao Vijay	Karnataka	I	15.8.75	*Bangalore*
* **Bichel** Andrew John	Queensland/Worcestershire	A	27.8.70	*Laidley*
Bicknell Darren John	Nottinghamshire	E	24.6.67	*Guildford*
* **Bicknell** Martin Paul	Surrey	E	14.1.69	*Guildford*
* **Bikash Ranjan Das**	Dhaka Division	B	14.7.82	*Dhaka*
Bishop Justin Edward	Essex	E	4.1.82	*Bury St Edmunds*
* **Black** Marlon Ian	Trinidad & Tobago	WI	7.6.75	*Trinidad*
Blackwell Ian David	Somerset	E	10.6.78	*Chesterfield*
Blain John Angus Rae	Northamptonshire	S	4.1.79	*Edinburgh*
* **Blakey** Richard John	Yorkshire	E	15.1.67	*Huddersfield*
* **Blewett** Gregory Scott	South Australia/Notts	A	29.10.71	*Adelaide*
* **Blignaut** Arnoldus Mauritius	Mashonaland A	Z	1.8.78	*Salisbury*
Bloomfield Timothy Francis	Middlesex	E	31.5.73	*Ashford, Middlesex*
Bodi Ghulam Hussain	KwaZulu-Natal	SA	4.1.79	*Hathuran, India*
* **Boje** Nico	Free State	SA	20.3.73	*Bloemfontein*
Borgas Cameron James	South Australia	A	1.9.83	*Melrose Park*
Bosman Lungile Loots	Griqualand West	SA	14.4.77	*Kimberley*
Bossenger Wendell	Griqualand West	SA	23.10.76	*Cape Town*
Boswell Scott Antony John	Leicestershire	E	11.9.74	*Fulford*
Boteju Jayawardene Welathanthrige Hemantha Devapriya	Colombo	SL	3.11.77	*Colombo*
Botha Anthony Greyvensteyn	Easterns	SA	17.11.76	*Pretoria*
Botha Johan	Eastern Province	SA	2.5.82	*Johannesburg*
Botha Peterus Johannes	Border	SA	28.9.66	*Vereeniging*
* **Boucher** Mark Verdon	Border	SA	3.12.76	*East London*
Boulton Nicholas Ross	Worcestershire	E	22.3.79	*Johannesburg, SA*
Bowler Peter Duncan	Somerset	E	30.7.63	*Plymouth*
Bracken Nathan Wade	New South Wales	A	12.9.77	*Penrith*
* **Bradburn** Grant Eric	Northern Districts	NZ	26.5.66	*Hamilton*
Bradfield Carl Crispin	Eastern Province	SA	18.1.75	*Grahamstown*
Bradshaw Ian David Russell	Barbados	WI	9.7.74	*Hopewell*
Bradstreet Shawn David	New South Wales	A	28.2.72	*Wollongong*
Brand Derek	Easterns	SA	29.5.75	*Bellville*
* **Brandes** Eddo Andre	Mashonaland	Z	5.3.63	*Port Shepstone, SA*
Breese Gareth Rohan	Jamaica	WI	9.1.76	*Montego Bay*
* **Brent** Gary Bazil	Manicaland	Z	13.1.76	*Sinoia*
Bressington Alastair Nigel	Gloucestershire	E	28.11.79	*Bristol*
Bridge Graeme David	Durham	E	4.9.80	*Sunderland*
Brinkley James Edward	Durham	E	13.3.74	*Helensburgh*
Brooker Finley Clint	Northerns	SA	26.12.72	*Kimberley*
Brooker Jason	Griqualand West	SA	16.1.77	*Kimberley*
Brophy Gerard Louis	Free State	SA	26.11.75	*Welkom*
Brouwers Nigel Grant	Northerns	SA	4.9.76	*Port Elizabeth*
Brown Alistair Duncan	Surrey	E	11.2.70	*Beckenham*
Brown Darryl	Trinidad & Tobago	WI	18.12.73	*McBean*
Brown Douglas Robert	Warwickshire	E	29.10.69	*Stirling, Scotland*
Brown Jason Fred	Northamptonshire	E	10.10.74	*Newcastle-under-Lyme*
Brown Michael James	Middlesex/Durham UCCE	E	9.2.80	*Burnley*
* **Brown** Simon John Emmerson	Durham	E	29.6.69	*Cleadon*
* **Browne** Courtney Oswald	Barbados	WI	7.12.70	*Lambeth, England*
Bruyns Mark Lloyd	KwaZulu-Natal	SA	8.11.73	*Pietermaritzburg*
Bryan Henderson Ricardo	Barbados	WI	21.3.70	*Salmonds*
Bryant James Douglas Campbell	Eastern Province	SA	4.2.76	*Durban*

	Team	*Country*	*Born*	*Birthplace*
Bryson Rudi Edwin	Northerns	SA	25.7.68	*Springs*
Buch Valmik Nalinkant	Baroda	I	29.8.75	*Rajkot*
Bulbeck Matthew Paul Leonard	Somerset	E	8.11.79	*Taunton*
Bulfin Carl Edwin	Wellington	NZ	19.8.73	*Blenheim*
Bundela Devendra Singh	Madhya Pradesh	I	22.2.77	*Indore*
* **Burmester** Mark Greville	Manicaland	Z	24.1.68	*Durban, South Africa*
Burns Michael	Somerset	E	6.2.69	*Barrow-in-Furness*
Burns Neil David	Leicestershire	E	19.9.65	*Chelmsford*
Butcher Gary Paul	Surrey	E	11.3.75	*Clapham*
* **Butcher** Mark Alan	Surrey	E	23.8.72	*Croydon*
Butler Deighton Calvin	Windward Islands	WI	14.7.74	*St Vincent*
Byas David	Yorkshire	E	26.8.63	*Kilham*
* **Caddick** Andrew Richard	Somerset	E	21.11.68	*Christchurch, NZ*
* **Cairns** Christopher Lance	Canterbury	NZ	13.6.70	*Picton*
Callaghan David John	Eastern Province	SA	1.2.65	*Queenstown*
* **Campbell** Alistair Douglas Ross	Mashonaland	Z	23.9.72	*Salisbury*
Campbell Donald James Ross	Mashonaland	Z	24.6.74	*Salisbury*
Campbell Ryan John	Western Australia	A	7.2.72	*Osborne Park*
* **Campbell** Sherwin Legay	Barbados	WI	1.11.70	*Bridgetown*
Cannonier Colin Darren	Leeward Islands	WI	22.5.73	*St Kitts*
Carberry Michael Alexander	Surrey	E	29.9.80	*Croydon*
* **Carlisle** Stuart Vance	Mashonaland	Z	10.5.72	*Salisbury*
Carseldine Lee Andrew	Queensland	A	17.11.75	*Nambour*
Carter Neil Miller	Boland/Warwickshire	E	29.1.75	*Cape Town, South Africa*
Cary Sean Ross	Western Australia	A	10.3.71	*Subiaco*
Casimir Kirsten Nicole	Windward Islands	WI	28.5.78	*Dominica*
Cassar Matthew Edward	Northamptonshire	E	16.10.72	*Sydney, Australia*
Cassell Jerry Lee	Queensland	A	12.1.75	*Mona Vale*
Cawdron Michael John	Gloucestershire	E	7.10.74	*Luton*
Chan Navin Indaraj	Trinidad & Tobago	WI	29.12.78	*Port of Spain*
Chandana Samarasinghage	Antonians	SL	1.5.77	*Padukka*
* **Chandana** Umagiliya Durage Upul	Tamil Union	SL	7.5.72	*Galle*
* **Chanderpaul** Shivnarine	Guyana	WI	18.8.74	*Unity Village*
Chapple Glen	Lancashire	E	23.1.74	*Skipton*
Chattergoon Sewnarine	Guyana	WI	3.4.81	*Fyrish*
Chatterjee Utpal	Bengal	I	13.7.64	*Calcutta*
* **Chauhan** Rajesh Kumar	Madhya Pradesh	I	19.12.66	*Ranchi*
Chilton Mark James	Lancashire	E	2.10.76	*Sheffield*
Chopra Akash	Delhi	I	19.9.77	*Agra*
* **Chopra** Nikhil	Delhi	I	26.12.73	*Allahabad*
Christopher Ricky Joseph	Leeward Islands	WI	26.3.75	*Antigua*
Clark Anthony Michael	New South Wales	A	23.3.77	*St Leonards*
Clark Stuart Rupert	New South Wales	A	28.9.75	*Sutherland*
Clarke Michael John	New South Wales	A	2.4.81	*Liverpool*
Clarke Shirley MacDonald	Barbados	WI	21.1.77	*Baywoods*
Clingeleffer Sean Geoffrey	Tasmania	A	9.5.80	*Hobart*
Clinton Richard Selvey	Essex	E	1.9.81	*Sidcup*
Clough Gareth David	Nottinghamshire	E	23.5.78	*Leeds*
Colegrave Mark David	Tasmania	A	1.7.68	*Hobart*
Collingwood Paul David	Durham	E	26.5.76	*Shotley Bridge*
* **Collins** Pedro Tyrone	Barbados	WI	12.8.76	*Boscobelle*
* **Collymore** Corey Dalanelo	Barbados	WI	21.12.77	*Boscobelle*
Cook Jeffrey William	Northamptonshire	E	2.2.72	*Sydney, Australia*
Cook Stephen Craig	Gauteng	SA	29.11.82	*Johannesburg*
* **Cook** Simon Hewitt	New South Wales	A	29.1.72	*Hastings*
Cook Simon James	Middlesex	E	15.1.77	*Oxford*
Copeland Craig Anthony	Griqualand West	SA	2.1.77	*Cape Town*
* **Cork** Dominic Gerald	Derbyshire	E	7.8.71	*Newcastle-under-Lyme*
Cornwall Wilden Winston	Leeward Islands	WI	29.4.73	*Liberta, Antigua*

	Team	Country	Born	Birthplace
Cosker Dean Andrew	Glamorgan	E	7.1.78	*Weymouth*
Cottey Phillip Anthony	Sussex	E	2.6.66	*Swansea*
Cousins Darren Mark	Northamptonshire	E	24.9.71	*Cambridge*
Cowan Ashley Preston	Essex	E	7.5.75	*Hitchin*
Cox Jamie	Tasmania/Somerset	A	15.10.69	*Burnie*
Craig Shawn Andrew Jacob	Victoria	A	23.6.73	*Carlton*
Crandon Esuan Asqui	Guyana	WI	17.12.81	*Rose Hall*
Craven Victor John	Yorkshire	E	31.7.80	*Harrogate*
***Crawley** John Paul	Lancashire	E	21.9.71	*Maldon*
Creed Murray Wayne	Eastern Province	SA	5.3.79	*Port Elizabeth*
Creevey Brendan Neville	Queensland	A	18.2.70	*Charleville*
***Croft** Robert Damien Bale	Glamorgan	E	25.5.70	*Morriston*
Crookes Derek Norman	Easterns	SA	5.3.69	*Mariannhill*
Crowe Carl Daniel	Leicestershire	E	25.11.75	*Leicester*
Croxford Guy Mark	Zimbabwe Academy	Z	2.6.81	*Harare*
Cuff Wayne Everton	Jamaica	WI	26.12.71	*Kingston*
***Cuffy** Cameron Eustace	Windward Islands	WI	8.2.70	*South Rivers, St Vincent*
Cullen Geoffrey Ian	Western Australia	A	16.3.77	*Cottesloe*
***Cullinan** Daryll John	Gauteng/Kent	SA	4.3.67	*Kimberley*
Cunliffe Robert John	Gloucestershire	E	8.11.73	*Oxford*
Cunningham Ryan Orlando	Jamaica	WI	29.5.78	*Kingston*
Currency Romel Kwesi	Windward Islands	WI	7.5.82	*St Vincent*
Cush Lennox Joseph	Guyana	WI	12.12.74	*Georgetown*
Cyster Andrew William	Boland	SA	31.3.79	*Stellenbosch*
Dagnall Charles Edward	Warwickshire	E	10.7.76	*Bury*
***Dahiya** Vijay	Delhi	I	10.5.73	*Delhi*
Dakin Jonathan Michael	Leicestershire	E	28.2.73	*Hitchin*
***Dale** Adam Craig	Queensland	A	30.12.68	*Ivanhoe*
Dale Adrian	Glamorgan	E	24.10.68	*Germiston, South Africa*
Daley James Arthur	Durham	E	24.9.73	*Sunderland*
Dalrymple James William Murray	Middx/Oxford UCCE	E	21.1.81	*Nairobi, Kenya*
Daniel Gerald Ian	Sinhalese	SL	17.8.81	*Colombo*
***Danish Kaneria**	Karachi/Habib Bank	P	16.12.80	*Karachi*
Darlington Kevin Godfrey	Guyana	WI	26.4.72	*Guyana*
***Das** Shiv Sunder	Orissa	I	5.11.77	*Bhubaneshwar*
Dasgupta Deep	Bengal	I	7.6.77	*Calcutta*
***Dassanayake** Pubudu Bathiya	Bloomfield	SL	11.7.70	*Kandy*
Davids Henry	Boland	SA	19.1.80	*Stellenbosch*
Davies Andrew Philip	Glamorgan	E	7.11.76	*Neath*
Davies Christopher James	South Australia	A	15.11.78	*Adelaide*
Davies Michael Kenton	Essex	E	17.7.76	*Ashby-de-la-Zouch*
Davis Mark Jeffrey Gronow	Sussex	E	10.10.71	*Port Elizabeth, SA*
Davis Richard Peter	Leicestershire	E	18.3.66	*Westbrook*
Davison John Michael	Victoria	A	9.5.70	*Campbell River, Canada*
Dawes Joseph Henry	Queensland	A	29.8.70	*Herston*
Dawson Alan Charles	Western Province	SA	27.11.69	*Cape Town*
Dawson Richard Kevin James	Yorkshire	E	4.8.80	*Doncaster*
Dean Kevin James	Derbyshire	E	16.10.75	*Derby*
de Bruyn Pierre	Easterns	SA	31.3.77	*Pretoria*
de Bruyn Zander	Gauteng	SA	5.7.75	*Johannesburg*
***DeFreitas** Phillip Anthony Jason	Leicestershire	E	18.2.66	*Scotts Head, Dominica*
De Groot Nicholas Alexander	Guyana	WI	22.10.75	*Ontario, Canada*
Deitz Shane Andrew	South Australia	A	4.5.75	*Bankstown*
de Kock Manfred Stephen	Boland	SA	3.2.75	*Paarl*
de Lange Con de Wet	Boland	SA	11.2.81	*Bellville*
Denton Gerard John	Tasmania	A	7.8.75	*Mount Isa*
Deonarine Narsingh	West Indies B	WI	8.8.83	*New Amsterdam, Guyana*
***de Saram** Samantha Indika	Tamil Union	SL	2.9.73	*Matara*
***de Silva** Karunakalage Sajeewa Chanaka	Burgher	SL	11.1.71	*Kalutara*

	Team	Country	Born	Birthplace
***de Silva** Pinnaduwage Aravinda	Nondescripts	SL	17.10.65	*Colombo*
***de Silva** Sanjeewa Kumara Lanka	Colombo	SL	29.7.75	*Kurunegala*
***de Silva** Weddikkara Ruwan Sujeewa	Sebastianites	SL	7.10.79	*Beruwala*
de Vos Dirk Johannes Jacobus	Northerns	SA	15.6.75	*Pretoria*
de Vos Hendrik Moller	North West	SA	5.10.69	*Klerksdorp*
de Wett Burton Christopher	North West	SA	25.12.80	*East London*
***Dhanraj** Rajindra	Trinidad & Tobago	WI	6.2.69	*Barrackpore*
Dharmani Pankaj	Punjab	I	27.9.74	*Delhi*
***Dharmasena** Handunnettige Deepthi Priyantha Kumar	Bloomfield	SL	24.4.71	*Colombo*
***Dighe** Samir Sudhakar	Mumbai	I	8.10.68	*Bombay*
***Dillon** Mervyn	Trinidad & Tobago	WI	5.6.74	*Toco*
***Dilshan** Tillekeratne Mudiyanselage	Bloomfield	SL	14.10.76	*Kalutara*
***Dippenaar** Hendrik Human	Free State	SA	14.6.77	*Kimberley*
Di Venuto Michael James	Tasmania/Derbyshire	A	12.12.73	*Hobart*
Diwakar Mihir	Bihar	I	10.12.82	*Siwan*
***Donald** Allan Anthony	Free State	SA	20.10.66	*Bloemfontein*
Douglas Mark William	Central Districts	NZ	20.10.68	*Nelson*
***Doull** Simon Blair	Northern Districts	NZ	6.8.69	*Pukekohe*
Dowlin Travis Montague	Guyana	WI	24.2.77	*Georgetown*
Dowman Mathew Peter	Derbyshire	E	10.5.74	*Grantham*
Downton Andrew Graham	Tasmania	A	17.7.77	*Auburn*
Drakes Vasbert Conniel	Border/Warwickshire	WI	5.8.69	*Springhead*
***Dravid** Rahul	Karnataka	I	11.1.73	*Indore*
Dreyer Jan Nicolaas	North West	SA	9.9.76	*Amanzimtoti*
Driver Ryan Craig	Lancashire	E	30.4.79	*Truro*
Dros Gerald	Northerns	SA	2.4.73	*Pretoria*
***Drum** Christopher James	Auckland	NZ	10.7.74	*Auckland*
Dry Willem Moolman	Griqualand West	SA	9.1.71	*Vryburg*
Dumelow Nathan Robert Charles	Derbyshire	E	30.4.81	*Derby*
Dutch Keith Philip	Somerset	E	21.3.73	*Harrow*
du Toit Willem Johannes	Boland	SA	18.3.81	*Cape Town*
Dykes James Andrew	Tasmania	A	15.11.71	*Hobart*
***Ealham** Mark Alan	Kent	E	27.8.69	*Willesborough*
***Ebrahim** Dion Digby	Mashonaland A	Z	7.8.80	*Bulawayo*
Edwards Alexander David	Derbyshire	E	2.8.75	*Cuckfield*
***Eksteen** Clive Edward	Gauteng	SA	2.12.66	*Johannesburg*
Elliott Grant David	Griqualand West	SA	21.3.79	*Johannesburg*
***Elliott** Matthew Thomas Gray	Victoria	A	28.9.71	*Chelsea*
***Elworthy** Steven	Northerns	SA	23.2.65	*Bulawayo, Rhodesia*
***Enamul Haque**	Chittagong	B	27.2.67	*Comilla*
Eugene John	Windward Islands	WI	16.8.70	*St Lucia*
Evans Alun Wyn	Glamorgan	E	20.8.75	*Glanamman*
***Evans** Craig Neil	Mashonaland	Z	29.11.69	*Salisbury*
***Fairbrother** Neil Harvey	Lancashire	E	9.9.63	*Warrington*
***Faisal Iqbal**	Karachi/PIA	P	30.12.81	*Karachi*
Faisal Naved	ADBP	P	2.3.80	*Sialkot*
Faruq Ahmed	Biman	B	24.7.66	*Dhaka*
***Fazl-e-Akbar**	Peshawar/PIA	P	20.10.80	*Peshawar*
Fellows Gary Matthew	Yorkshire	E	30.7.78	*Halifax*
***Fernando** Conganige Randhi Dilhara	Sinhalese	SL	19.7.79	*Colombo*
Fernando Kandana Aratchchige Dinusha Manoj	Sebastianites	SL	10.8.79	*Panadura*
Fernando Upekha Ashantha	Sinhalese	SL	17.12.79	*Colombo*
Ferreira Lloyd Douglas	Western Province	SA	6.5.74	*Johannesburg*
Fisher Ian Douglas	Yorkshire	E	31.5.76	*Bradford*
Fitzgerald David Andrew	South Australia	A	30.11.72	*Osborne Park*
***Fleming** Damien William	Victoria	A	24.4.70	*Bentley*
Fleming Matthew Valentine	Kent	E	12.12.64	*Macclesfield*

	Team	Country	Born	Birthplace
***Fleming** Stephen Paul	Canterbury/Middlesex	NZ	1.4.73	*Christchurch*
***Flintoff** Andrew	Lancashire	E	6.12.77	*Preston*
***Flower** Andrew	Mashonaland	Z	28.4.68	*Cape Town, SA*
***Flower** Grant William	Mashonaland	Z	20.12.70	*Salisbury*
Flusk Gareth Edward	Easterns	SA	8.11.74	*Johannesburg*
Foster James Savin	Essex/Durham UCCE	E	15.4.80	*Whipps Cross*
Francis John Daniel	Hampshire	E	13.11.80	*Bromley*
***Franklin** James Edward Charles	Wellington	NZ	7.11.80	*Wellington*
Franks Paul John	Nottinghamshire	E	3.2.79	*Mansfield*
***Fraser** Angus Robert Charles	Middlesex	E	8.8.65	*Billinge*
***Friend** Travis John	Midlands	Z	7.1.81	*Kwekwe*
Fulton David Paul	Kent	E	15.11.71	*Lewisham*
Fusedale Neil Andrew	Gauteng	SA	11.11.67	*Hendon, England*
Gaffaney Christopher Blair	Otago	NZ	30.11.75	*Dunedin*
Gagandeep Singh	Punjab	I	3.10.81	*Ludhiana*
Gait Andrew Ian	Free State	SA	19.12.78	*Bulawayo, Rhodesia*
***Gallage** Indika Sanjeewa	Colombo	SL	22.11.75	*Panadura*
***Gallian** Jason Edward Riche	Nottinghamshire	E	25.6.71	*Sydney, Australia*
Gamiet Laden Liep	Border	SA	23.1.78	*East London*
***Gandhi** Devang Jayant	Bengal	I	6.9.71	*Bhavnagar*
Ganegama Withanaarchchige Chamara Akalanka	Nondescripts	SL	29.3.81	*Colombo*
***Ganesh** Doddanarasiah	Karnataka	I	30.6.73	*Bangalore*
***Ganga** Daren	Trinidad & Tobago	WI	14.1.79	*Barrackpore*
***Ganguly** Sourav Chandidas	Bengal	I	8.7.72	*Calcutta*
Gannon Benjamin Ward	Gloucestershire	E	5.9.75	*Oxford*
***Garrick** Leon Vivian	Jamaica	WI	11.11.76	*St Ann*
Gavaskar Rohan Sunil	Bengal	I	20.2.76	*Kanpur*
***Gayle** Christopher Henry	Jamaica	WI	21.9.79	*Kingston*
George Mulligan Frank	Gauteng	SA	10.9.76	*Cape Town*
Ghag Sudhakar Vishwanath	Services	I	25.2.74	*Bombay*
Ghulam Ali	Karachi/PIA	P	8.9.66	*Karachi*
***Gibbs** Herschelle Herman	Western Province	SA	23.2.74	*Cape Town*
***Gibson** Ottis Delroy	Gauteng	WI	16.3.69	*Sion Hill, Barbados*
***Giddins** Edward Simon Hunter	Surrey	E	20.7.71	*Eastbourne*
Gidley Martyn Ian	Griqualand West	SA	30.9.68	*Leicester, England*
***Gilchrist** Adam Craig	Western Australia	A	14.11.71	*Bellingen*
Gilder Gary Michael	KwaZulu-Natal	SA	6.7.74	*Salisbury, Rhodesia*
***Giles** Ashley Fraser	Warwickshire	E	19.3.73	*Chertsey*
***Gillespie** Jason Neil	South Australia	A	19.4.75	*Darlinghurst*
Glasgow Corey Anderson	Barbados	WI	20.3.79	*Bairds Village*
Golding James Mathew	Kent	E	19.7.77	*Canterbury*
Gonsalves Andrew	West Indies B	WI	31.5.78	*Suddie*
***Goodwin** Murray William	W. Australia/Sussex	Z	11.12.72	*Salisbury, Rhodesia*
***Gough** Darren	Yorkshire	E	18.9.70	*Barnsley*
Gough Michael Andrew	Durham	E	18.12.79	*Hartlepool*
Gowda Yere	Railways	I	27.11.71	*Raichur*
Grace Graham Vernon	Eastern Province	SA	16.8.75	*Salisbury, Rhodesia*
Graham Liam	Border	SA	16.3.76	*Johannesburg*
Grant Joseph Benjamin	Essex	WI	17.12.68	*Montego Bay, Jamaica*
Gray Andrew Kenneth Donovan	Yorkshire	E	19.5.74	*Armadale*
Grayson Adrian Paul	Essex	E	31.3.71	*Ripon*
***Griffith** Adrian Frank Gordon	Barbados	WI	19.11.71	*Holders Hill*
Griffith Reon	West Indies B	WI	8.1.79	*Guyana*
***Gripper** Trevor Raymond	Mashonaland A	Z	28.12.75	*Salisbury*
Grove Jamie Oliver	Somerset	E	3.7.79	*Bury St Edmunds*
***Gunawardene** Dihan Avishka	Sinhalese	SL	26.5.77	*Colombo*
Gupta Sandeep Kumar	Kenya	K	7.4.67	*Nairobi*
Guy Simon Mark	Yorkshire	E	17.11.78	*Rotherham*

	Team	Country	Born	Birthplace
***Habib** Aftab	Leicestershire	E	7.2.72	*Reading*
***Habibul Bashar**	Biman	B	17.8.72	*Kushtia*
Haddin Bradley James	New South Wales	A	23.10.77	*Cowra*
Haldipur Nikhil	Bengal	I	19.12.77	*Calcutta*
Hall Andrew James	Gauteng	SA	31.7.75	*Johannesburg*
Hamblin James Rupert Christopher	Hampshire	E	16.8.78	*Pembury*
***Hamilton** Gavin Mark	Yorkshire	E	16.9.74	*Broxburn*
Hancock Timothy Harold Coulter	Gloucestershire	E	20.4.72	*Reading*
Haniff Azeemul	Guyana	WI	24.10.77	*Hampton Court*
***Harbhajan Singh**	Punjab	I	3.7.80	*Jullundur*
Hardinges Mark Andrew	Gloucestershire	E	5.2.78	*Gloucester*
Harmison Stephen James	Durham	E	23.10.78	*Ashington*
Harris Andrew James	Nottinghamshire	E	26.6.73	*Ashton-under-Lyne*
***Harris** Chris Zinzan	Canterbury	NZ	20.11.69	*Christchurch*
Harris Paul Lee	Western Province	SA	2.11.78	*Salisbury, Rhodesia*
Harrity Mark Andrew	South Australia	A	9.3.74	*Semaphore*
***Hart** Matthew Norman	Northern Districts	NZ	16.5.72	*Hamilton*
Harunur Rashid	Dhaka Division	B	30.11.68	*Mymensingh*
Harvey Ian Joseph	Victoria/Gloucestershire	A	10.4.72	*Wonthaggi*
***Harvinder Singh**	Railways	I	23.12.77	*Amritsar*
***Hasan Raza**	Karachi/Habib Bank	P	11.3.82	*Karachi*
***Hasibul Hussain**	Sylhet	B	3.6.77	*Dhaka*
***Haslam** Mark James	Auckland	NZ	26.9.72	*Bury, England*
Hatch Nicholas Guy	Durham	E	21.4.79	*Darlington*
***Hathurusinghe** Upul Chandika	Moors	SL	13.9.68	*Colombo*
***Hayden** Matthew Lawrence	Queensland	A	29.10.71	*Kingaroy*
Haynes Jamie Jonathan	Lancashire	E	5.7.74	*Bristol*
***Hayward** Mornantau	Eastern Province	SA	6.3.77	*Uitenhage*
***Hegg** Warren Kevin	Lancashire	E	23.2.68	*Whitefield*
Hemp David Lloyd	Warwickshire	E	8.11.70	*Hamilton, Bermuda*
Henderson Claude William	Western Province	SA	14.6.72	*Worcester*
Henderson James Michael	Boland	SA	6.8.75	*Worcester*
Henderson Tyron	Border	SA	1.8.74	*Durban*
***Herath** Herath Mudiyanselage Rangana Keerthi Bandara	Moors	SL	19.3.78	*Kurunegala*
Herbst Francois	Gauteng	SA	17.7.77	*Boksburg*
***Hettiarachchi** Dinuka	Colts	SL	15.7.76	*Colombo*
Hewitt Glen Michael	North West	SA	16.4.73	*Johannesburg*
Hewitt James Peter	Middlesex	E	26.2.76	*Southwark*
Hewson Dominic Robert	Gloucestershire	E	3.10.74	*Cheltenham*
Hibbert Keith Hugh	Jamaica	WI	14.6.80	*St Catherine*
***Hick** Graeme Ashley	Worcestershire	E	23.5.66	*Salisbury, Rhodesia*
Higgins Benjamin Hugh	South Australia	A	8.3.72	*Adelaide*
Higgs Mark Anthony	New South Wales	A	30.6.76	*Queanbeyan*
Hills Dene Fleetwood	Tasmania	A	27.8.70	*Wynyard*
Hinds Ryan O'Neal	Barbados	WI	17.2.81	*Holders Hill*
***Hinds** Wavell Wayne	Jamaica	WI	7.9.76	*Kingston*
***Hirwani** Narendra Deepchand	Madhya Pradesh	I	18.10.68	*Gorakhpur*
Hockley James Bernard	Kent	E	16.4.79	*Beckenham*
Hodge Bradley John	Victoria	A	29.12.74	*Sandringham*
***Hogg** George Bradley	Western Australia	A	6.2.71	*Narrogin*
***Hoggard** Matthew James	Yorkshire/Free State	E	31.12.76	*Leeds*
***Holder** Roland Irwin Christopher	Barbados	WI	22.12.67	*Port-of-Spain, Trinidad*
***Hollioake** Adam John	Surrey	E	5.9.71	*Melbourne, Australia*
***Hollioake** Benjamin Caine	Surrey	E	11.11.77	*Melbourne, Australia*
Holloway Piran Charles Laity	Somerset	E	1.10.70	*Helston*
***Hooper** Carl Llewellyn	Guyana	WI	15.12.66	*Georgetown*
Horan Brendan Patrick	Gauteng	SA	17.9.74	*Cape Town*
***Horne** Matthew Jeffery	Otago	NZ	5.12.70	*Takapuna*
Horsley Daniel Anthony	New South Wales	A	20.7.72	*St Leonards*

	Team	Country	Born	Birthplace
House William John	Sussex	E	16.3.76	*Sheffield*
How Jamie Michael	Central Districts	NZ	19.5.81	*New Plymouth*
***Hudson** Andrew Charles	KwaZulu-Natal	SA	17.3.65	*Eshowe*
Hughes Jonathan	Glamorgan	E	30.6.81	*Pontypridd*
***Humayun Farhat**	Lahore City/Allied Bank	P	24.1.81	*Lahore*
Hunter Ian David	Durham	E	11.9.79	*Durham*
***Hussain** Nasser	Essex	E	28.3.68	*Madras, India*
Hussey Michael Edward Killeen	W. Australia/Northants	A	27.5.75	*Morley*
Hutchison Paul Michael	Yorkshire	E	9.6.77	*Leeds*
Hutton Benjamin Leonard	Middlesex	E	29.1.77	*Johannesburg, S. Africa*
Hyam Barry James	Essex	E	9.9.75	*Romford*
***Ijaz Ahmed**, sen.	Islamabad/Habib Bank	P	20.9.68	*Sialkot*
***Ijaz Ahmed**, jun.	Faisalabad/Allied Bank	P	2.2.69	*Lyallpur*
***Illingworth** Richard Keith	Derbyshire	E	23.8.63	*Bradford*
***Ilott** Mark Christopher	Essex	E	27.8.70	*Watford*
Imran Abbas	Gujranwala/ADBP	P	25.3.78	*Gujranwala*
***Imran Farhat**	Lahore City/Biman	P	20.5.82	*Lahore*
***Imran Nazir**	Sheikhupura/National Bank	P	16.12.81	*Gujranwala*
Innes Kevin John	Northamptonshire	E	24.9.75	*Wellingborough*
Iness Mathew William Hunter	Victoria	A	13.1.78	*East Melbourne*
***Inzamam-ul-Haq**	Faisalabad	P	3.3.70	*Multan*
***Irani** Ronald Charles	Essex	E	26.10.71	*Leigh, Lancashire*
Irfan Bhatti	Islamabad	P	28.9.64	*Peshawar*
***Irfan Fazil**	Lahore City/Habib Bank	P	2.11.81	*Lahore*
Jackson Andy	Trinidad & Tobago	WI	4.3.79	*Trinidad*
Jackson Ivan Orlanzo	Windward Islands	WI	16.6.74	*St Vincent*
Jackson Kenneth Charles	Boland	SA	16.8.64	*Kitwe, Zambia*
Jacobs Arno	North West	SA	13.3.77	*Potchefstroom*
***Jacobs** Ridley Detamore	Leeward Islands	WI	26.11.67	*Swetes Village, Antigua*
***Jadeja** Ajaysinhji	Jammu and Kashmir	I	1.2.71	*Jamnagar*
Jahangir Alam	Chittagong	B	5.3.73	*Narayanganj*
Jahangir Alam Talukdar	Biman	B	4.12.68	*Dhaka*
***James** Stephen Peter	Glamorgan	E	7.9.67	*Lydney*
Jan Imran Haniff	Trinidad & Tobago	WI	11.2.79	*Mafeking Village*
Jaques Philip Anthony	New South Wales	A	3.5.79	*Wollongong*
***Javed Omar**	Biman	B	25.11.76	*Dhaka*
Javed Qadir	PIA	P	25.8.76	*Karachi*
Javed Zaman	Assam	I	8.8.76	*Dhubri*
Jayachandra Pinninti	Orissa	I	3.9.76	*Bhubaneshwar*
***Jayasuriya** Sanath Teran	Bloomfield	SL	30.6.69	*Matara*
***Jayawardene** Denagamage Proboth Mahela De Silva	Sinhalese	SL	27.5.77	*Colombo*
***Jayawardene** Hewasandatchige Asiri Prasanna Wishwanath	Sinhalese	SL	10.9.79	*Colombo*
Jefferson William Ingleby	Essex/Durham UCCE	E	25.10.79	*Derby*
Jennings Dylan	Easterns	SA	14.9.79	*Johannesburg*
Jeremy Kerry Clifford Bryan	Leeward Islands	WI	6.2.80	*Antigua*
Jhalani Rohit Banwarilal	Rajasthan	I	1.9.78	*Jaipur*
Johnson Benjamin Andrew	South Australia	A	1.8.73	*Naracoorte*
***Johnson** Neil Clarkson	W. Province/Hants	Z	24.1.70	*Salisbury*
Johnson Paul	Nottinghamshire	E	24.4.65	*Newark*
Johnson Richard Leonard	Somerset	E	29.12.74	*Chertsey*
Jones Geraint Owen	Kent	E	14.7.76	*Kundiawa, Papua N.G.*
Jones Philip Steffan	Somerset	E	9.2.74	*Llanelli*
Jones Richard Andrew	Wellington	NZ	22.10.73	*Auckland*
Jones Simon Philip	Glamorgan	E	25.12.78	*Swansea*
Jordaan Deon	Easterns	SA	3.12.70	*Bloemfontein*
Jordaan Lucas Cornelius Rudolph	North West	SA	20.7.63	*Johannesburg*

	Team	Country	Born	Birthplace
Joseph Sylvester Cleofoster	Leeward Islands	WI	5.9.78	*New Winthorpes, Antigua*
* **Joshi** Sunil Bandacharya	Karnataka	I	6.6.69	*Gadag*
Joubert Pierre	Northerns	SA	2.5.78	*Pretoria*
Joyce Edmund Christopher	Middlesex	E	22.9.78	*Dublin, Ireland*
* **Julian** Brendon Paul	Western Australia	A	10.8.70	*Hamilton, New Zealand*
Jurgensen Shane John	Tasmania	A	28.4.76	*Redcliffe*
* **Kabir Khan**	Peshawar/Habib Bank	P	12.4.74	*Peshawar*
* **Kaif** Mohammad	Uttar Pradesh	I	1.12.80	*Allahabad*
Kalawithigoda Shantha	Colts	SL	23.12.77	*Colombo*
Kale Abhijit Vasant	Maharashtra	I	3.7.73	*Ahmednagar*
* **Kallis** Jacques Henry	Western Province	SA	16.10.75	*Cape Town*
* **Kalpage** Ruwan Senani	Nondescripts	SL	19.2.70	*Kandy*
* **Kaluwitharana** Romesh Shantha	Colts	SL	24.11.69	*Colombo*
Kamande James Kabatha	Kenya	K	12.12.78	*Muranga*
* **Kambli** Vinod Ganpat	Mumbai	I	18.1.72	*Bombay*
* **Kanitkar** Hrishikesh Hemant	Maharashtra	I	14.11.74	*Poona*
Kanwat Rahul Jagdish	Rajasthan	I	21.10.74	*Jaipur*
* **Kapoor** Aashish Rakesh	Tamil Nadu	I	25.3.71	*Madras*
* **Karim** Syed Saba	Bengal	I	14.11.67	*Patna*
Karppinen Stuart James	Western Australia	A	13.6.73	*Townsville*
* **Kartik** Murali	Railways	I	11.9.76	*Madras*
Kashif Raza	Sheikhupura/WAPDA	P	26.12.79	*Sheikhupura*
* **Kasprowicz** Michael Scott	Queensland	A	10.2.72	*South Brisbane*
Katchay Eion	Guyana	WI	8.12.77	*Demerara*
* **Katich** Simon Mathew	Western Australia	A	21.8.75	*Middle Swan*
Keedy Gary	Lancashire	E	27.11.74	*Wakefield*
Keegan Chad Blake	Middlesex	E	30.7.79	*Santon, South Africa*
* **Kemp** Justin Miles	Eastern Province	SA	2.10.77	*Queenstown*
Kendall William Salwey	Hampshire	E	18.12.73	*Wimbledon*
Kent John Carter	KwaZulu-Natal	SA	7.5.79	*Cape Town*
Kenway Derek Anthony	Hampshire	E	12.6.78	*Fareham*
Kerr Jason Ian Douglas	Somerset	E	7.4.74	*Bolton*
Key Robert William Trevor	Kent	E	12.5.79	*East Dulwich*
Khaled Mahmud	Dhaka Metropolis	B	26.7.71	*Dhaka*
* **Khaled Masud**	Rajshahi	B	8.2.76	*Rajshahi*
Khan Rawait Mahmood	Derbyshire	E	5.4.82	*Birmingham*
Khan Wasim Gulzar	Derbyshire	E	26.2.71	*Birmingham*
Khoda Gagan Kishanlal	Rajasthan	I	24.10.74	*Barmer*
Khurasiya Amay Ramsevak	Madhya Pradesh	I	18.5.72	*Jabalpur*
Kidwell Errol Wayne	Griqualand West	SA	6.6.75	*Vereeniging*
Killeen Neil	Durham	E	17.10.75	*Shotley Bridge*
* **King** Reon Dane	Guyana	WI	6.10.75	*Georgetown*
Kirby Steven Paul	Yorkshire	E	4.10.77	*Bury*
* **Kirsten** Gary	Western Province	SA	23.11.67	*Cape Town*
Kirtley Robert James	Sussex	E	10.1.75	*Eastbourne*
Klinger Michael	Victoria	A	4.7.80	*Kew*
Klopper Johan Wilhelm Francois	Border	SA	4.10.72	*Grahamstown*
* **Klusener** Lance	KwaZulu-Natal	SA	4.9.71	*Durban*
* **Knight** Nicholas Verity	Warwickshire	E	28.11.69	*Watford*
Koen Louis Johannes	Boland	SA	28.3.67	*Paarl*
Koenig Sven Gaetan	Gauteng	SA	9.12.73	*Durban*
Koortzen Pieter Petrus Johannes	Griqualand West	SA	24.9.79	*Kimberley*
Kremerskothen Scott Paul	Tasmania	A	5.1.79	*Launceston*
Krikken Karl Matthew	Derbyshire	E	9.4.69	*Bolton*
Kruger Garnett John-Peter	Eastern Province	SA	5.1.77	*Port Elizabeth*
Kruis Gideon Jacobus	Griqualand West	SA	9.5.74	*Pretoria*
Kulatunga Hettiarachchi Gamage Jeevantha Mahesh	Colts	SL	2.11.73	*Kurunegala*
* **Kulkarni** Nilesh Moreshwar	Mumbai	I	3.4.73	*Dombivili*

	Team	*Country*	*Born*	*Birthplace*
Kumaran Thirunavukkarasu	Tamil Nadu	I	30.12.75	*Madras*
***Kumble** Anil	Karnataka	I	17.10.70	*Bangalore*
Lamb Gregory Arthur	Mashonaland A	Z	4.3.80	*Harare*
Lampitt Stuart Richard	Worcestershire	E	29.7.66	*Wolverhampton*
Laney Jason Scott	Hampshire	E	27.4.73	*Winchester*
***Langer** Justin Lee	Western Australia	A	21.11.70	*Perth*
Langeveldt Charl Kenneth	Boland	SA	17.12.74	*Stellenbosch*
***Lara** Brian Charles	Trinidad & Tobago	WI	2.5.69	*Santa Cruz*
Laraman Aaron William	Middlesex	E	10.1.79	*Enfield*
***Lathwell** Mark Nicholas	Somerset	E	26.12.71	*Bletchley*
Lavine Mark John *Died May 12, 2001.*	North West	SA	4.3.73	*Black Bess, Barbados*
Law Danny Richard	Durham	E	15.7.75	*Lambeth*
***Law** Stuart Grant	Queensland/Essex	A	18.10.68	*Herston*
Lawson Andrew Grant	North West	SA	4.3.67	*Durban*
Lawson Jermaine Jay Charles	West Indies B	WI	13.1.82	*Spanish Town, Jamaica*
***Laxman** Vangipurappu Venkata Sai	Hyderabad	I	1.11.74	*Hyderabad*
Leatherdale David Antony	Worcestershire	E	26.11.67	*Bradford*
***Lee** Brett	New South Wales	A	8.11.76	*Wollongong*
Lee Shane	New South Wales	A	8.8.73	*Wollongong*
***Lehmann** Darren Scott	South Australia/Yorkshire	A	5.2.70	*Gawler*
Lewis Jonathan	Gloucestershire	E	26.8.75	*Aylesbury*
Lewis Jonathan James Benjamin	Durham	E	21.5.70	*Isleworth*
Lewis Michael Llewellyn	Victoria	A	29.6.74	*Greensborough*
Lewis Mohammad Rasheed	Free State	SA	24.4.75	*Cape Town*
***Lewis** Rawl Nicholas	Windward Islands	WI	5.9.74	*Union Village, Grenada*
Lewry Jason David	Sussex	E	2.4.71	*Worthing*
***Liebenberg** Gerhardus Frederick Johannes	Free State	SA	7.4.72	*Upington*
Light Craig	North West	SA	23.9.72	*Randburg*
Liptrot Christopher George	Worcestershire	E	13.2.80	*Wigan*
***Liyanage** Dulip Kapila	Colts	SL	6.6.72	*Kalutara*
Lloyd Graham David	Lancashire	E	1.7.69	*Accrington*
Logan Richard James	Nottinghamshire	E	28.1.80	*Stone*
Louw Johann	Griqualand West	SA	12.4.79	*Cape Town*
Love Geoff Terry	Border	SA	19.9.76	*Port Elizabeth*
Love Martin Lloyd	Queensland/Durham	A	30.3.74	*Mundubbera*
***Loveridge** Greg Riaka	Central Districts	NZ	15.1.75	*Palmerston North*
Loye Malachy Bernard	Northamptonshire	E	27.9.72	*Northampton*
Lucas David Scott	Nottinghamshire	E	19.8.78	*Nottingham*
Lumb Michael John	Yorkshire	E	12.2.80	*Johannesburg*
Lungley Tom	Derbyshire	E	25.7.79	*Derby*
Mabhena Elite Funyana	Easterns	SA	14.5.80	*Alexandra, Johannesburg*
***McCague** Martin John	Kent	E	24.5.69	*Larne, N. Ireland*
***McGarrell** Neil Christopher	Guyana	WI	12.7.72	*Georgetown*
McGarry Andrew Charles	Essex	E	8.11.81	*Basildon*
***MacGill** Stuart Charles Glyndwr	New South Wales	A	25.2.71	*Mount Lawley*
McGrath Anthony	Yorkshire	E	6.10.75	*Bradford*
***McGrath** Glenn Donald	New South Wales	A	9.2.70	*Dubbo*
***McIntyre** Peter Edward	South Australia	A	27.4.66	*Gisborne*
Mackay Angus James	Mashonaland	Z	13.6.67	*Salisbury*
McKenzie Denville St Delmo	Jamaica	WI	4.12.75	*Little London*
***McKenzie** Neil Douglas	Northerns	SA	24.11.75	*Johannesburg*
McLaren Adrian Peter	Griqualand West	SA	21.4.80	*Kimberley*
***McLean** Nixon Alexei McNamara	Windward Islands	WI	20.7.73	*Stubbs, St Vincent*
***McMillan** Craig Douglas	Canterbury	NZ	13.9.76	*Christchurch*
MacQueen Robert Bruce	KwaZulu-Natal	SA	6.9.77	*Durban*

	Team	*Country*	*Born*	*Birthplace*
* **Maddy** Darren Lee	Leicestershire	E	23.5.74	*Leicester*
* **Madondo** Trevor Nyasha *Died June 11, 2001.*	Mashonaland	Z	22.11.76	*Mount Darwin*
Mafa Johnson Tumelo	Gauteng	SA	5.2.78	*Johannesburg*
Mahabir Ganesh	Trinidad & Tobago	WI	18.1.81	*Trinidad*
Mahbubur Rahman	Dhaka Division	B	1.2.69	*Mymensingh*
Maher James Patrick	Queensland/Glamorgan	A	27.2.74	*Innistail*
Mahmood Hamid	Karachi/PIA	P	19.1.69	*Karachi*
Mail Gregory John	New South Wales	A	29.4.78	*Penrith*
Makalima Dumisa Liko	Border	SA	29.12.80	*King William's Town*
* **Malcolm** Devon Eugene	Leicestershire	E	22.2.63	*Kingston, Jamaica*
Malik Muhammad Nadeem	Nottinghamshire	E	6.10.82	*Nottingham*
Mall Ashraf	KwaZulu-Natal	SA	8.10.78	*Durham*
Manack Hussein Ahmed	Gauteng	SA	10.4.68	*Pretoria*
* **Manjurul Islam**	Khulna	B	7.11.79	*Khulna*
Manou Graham Allan	South Australia	A	23.4.79	*Modbury*
Mansoor Rana	ADBP	P	27.12.62	*Lahore*
Manzoor Akhtar	Allied Bank/Biman	P	16.4.68	*Karachi*
* **Manzoor Elahi**	ADBP	P	15.4.63	*Sahiwal*
Maqsood Rana	National Bank/Lahore City	P	1.8.72	*Lahore*
* **Marillier** Douglas Anthony	Midlands	Z	24.6.78	*Salisbury*
Marsh Daniel James	Tasmania/Leicestershire	A	14.6.73	*Subiaco*
Marsh Shaun Edward	Western Australia	A	9.7.83	*Narrogin*
Marshall Dave Kerwin	Barbados	WI	24.5.72	*Barbados*
* **Marshall** Hamish John Hamilton	Northern Districts	NZ	15.2.79	*Warkworth*
* **Martin** Christopher Stewart	Canterbury	NZ	10.12.74	*Christchurch*
Martin Jacob Joseph	Baroda	I	11.5.72	*Baroda*
Martin Kenroy Denroy	Windward Islands	WI	18.1.79	*St Vincent*
* **Martin** Peter James	Lancashire	E	15.11.68	*Accrington*
Martin-Jenkins Robin Simon Christopher	Sussex	E	28.10.75	*Guildford*
* **Martyn** Damien Richard	Western Australia	A	21.10.71	*Darwin*
* **Masakadza** Hamilton	Mashonaland	Z	9.8.83	*Harare*
Mascarenhas Adrian Dimitri	Hampshire	E	30.10.77	*Chiswick*
Masimula Walter Bafana	Gauteng	SA	23.10.75	*Johannesburg*
Mason Keno Anthony	Trinidad & Tobago	WI	13.11.72	*Trinidad*
Mason Scott Robert	Tasmania	A	27.7.76	*Launceston*
Mason Timothy James	Essex	E	12.4.75	*Leicester*
Masters David Daniel	Kent	E	22.4.78	*Chatham*
Mataboge Tshepo Khotso	Gauteng	SA	18.11.78	*Soweto*
* **Matambanadzo** Everton Zvikomborero	Mashonaland A	Z	13.4.76	*Salisbury*
Matsikenyeri Stuart	Manicaland	Z	3.5.83	*Harare*
Matthews Ron Samuel	Guyana	WI	11.1.83	*Georgetown*
Maynard Dayne Romano	Barbados	WI	1.4.69	*Barbados*
* **Maynard** Matthew Peter	Glamorgan	E	21.3.66	*Oldham*
* **Mbangwa** Mpumelelo	Matabeleland	Z	26.6.76	*Plumtree*
* **Mehrab Hossain**	Dhaka Metropolis	B	22.9.78	*Dhaka*
Mendis Chaminda	Colts	SL	28.12.68	*Galle*
Meuleman Scott William	Western Australia	A	17.7.80	*Subiaco*
* **Mhambrey** Paras Laxmikant	Mumbai	I	20.6.72	*Bombay*
Middlebrook James Daniel	Yorkshire	E	13.5.77	*Leeds*
* **Miller** Colin Reid	Victoria	A	6.2.64	*Footscray*
Miller Michael Christian	South Australia	A	30.5.79	*Toowoomba*
Millns David James	Nottinghamshire	E	27.2.65	*Clipstone*
Mills Kyle David	Auckland	NZ	15.3.79	*Auckland*
Minhazul Abedin	Chittagong	B	25.9.65	*Chittagong*
* **Misbah-ul-Haq**	Sargodha/KRL	P	28.5.74	*Mianwali*
Mitchell Ian	Border	SA	14.12.77	*Johannesburg*
Mitchum Junie Alexander	Leeward Islands	WI	22.11.73	*St Kitts*

	Team	Country	Born	Birthplace
Modeste Theodore	Trinidad & Tobago	WI	4.7.79	*Trinidad*
Modi Hitesh Subhash	Kenya	K	13.10.71	*Kisumu*
***Mohammad Akram**	Rawalpindi/Allied Bank	P	10.9.74	*Islamabad*
Mohammad Ashraful	Dhaka Metropolis	B	9.9.84	*Dhaka*
***Mohammad Hussain**	Lahore City	P	8.10.76	*Lahore*
***Mohammad Rafiq**	Sylhet	B	15.5.70	*Dhaka*
***Mohammad Ramzan**	Faisalabad	P	25.12.70	*Lyallpur*
***Mohammad Sami**	Karachi	P	24.2.81	*Karachi*
***Mohammad Sharif**	Biman	B	12.12.85	*Narayanganj*
Mohammad Sheikh	Kenya	K	29.8.80	*Nairobi*
***Mohammad Wasim**	Rawalpindi/KRL	P	8.8.77	*Rawalpindi*
Mohammed Dave	Trinidad & Tobago	WI	8.10.79	*Trinidad*
***Mohanty** Debasis Sarbeswar	Orissa	I	20.7.76	*Bhubaneshwar*
***Moin Khan**	Karachi	P	23.9.71	*Rawalpindi*
Moin-ul-Atiq	Habib Bank	P	5.8.64	*Karachi*
Mokoenanyana Tseko Johannes	Free State	SA	5.12.77	*Bloemfontein*
Mokoenenyana Ernst Teboho	Easterns	SA	15.8.76	*Bloemfontein*
Mongia Dinesh	Punjab	I	17.4.77	*Chandigarh*
***Mongia** Nayan Ramlal	Baroda	I	19.12.69	*Baroda*
Montgomerie Richard Robert	Sussex	E	3.7.71	*Rugby*
***Moody** Thomas Masson	Western Australia	A	2.10.65	*Adelaide*
Morgan McNeil Junior	Windward Islands	WI	18.10.70	*St Vincent*
Morkel Johannes Albertus	Easterns	SA	10.6.81	*Vereeniging*
Morris Alexander Corfield	Hampshire	E	4.10.76	*Barnsley*
***Morris** John Edward	Nottinghamshire	E	1.4.64	*Crewe*
Morshed Ali Khan	Dhaka Metropolis	B	14.5.72	*Faridpur*
Morton Runako Shaku	Leeward Islands	WI	22.7.68	*Nevis*
Moss Jonathon	Victoria	A	4.5.75	*Manly*
Mott Matthew Peter	Victoria	A	3.10.73	*Charleville*
Mpitsang Phenyo Victor	Free State	SA	28.3.80	*Kimberley*
Mubarak Jehan	Colombo	SL	10.1.81	*Washington*
Mujahid Jamshed	Sheikhupura/Habib Bank	P	1.12.71	*Muredke*
***Mullally** Alan David	Hampshire	E	12.7.69	*Southend-on-Sea*
Munnik Renier	Western Province	SA	7.1.78	*Cape Town*
***Munton** Timothy Alan	Derbyshire	E	30.7.65	*Melton Mowbray*
***Muralitharan** Muttiah	Tamil Union/Lancashire	SL	17.4.72	*Kandy*
***Murphy** Brian Andrew	Mashonaland A	Z	1.12.76	*Salisbury, Rhodesia*
Murray Denys Wayne	Eastern Province	SA	29.7.77	*Graaff-Reinet*
***Murray** Junior Randalph	Windward Islands	WI	20.1.68	*St Georges, Grenada*
Murtagh Timothy James	Surrey	E	2.8.81	*Lambeth*
***Mushfiqur Rehman**	Rajshahi	B	1.1.80	*Rajshahi*
***Mushtaq Ahmed**	Lahore City	P	28.6.70	*Sahiwal*
***Mutendera** David Travolta	Mashonaland A	Z	25.1.79	*Salisbury*
Myburgh Johannes Gerhardus	Northerns	SA	22.10.80	*Pretoria*
***Nadeem Abbasi**	Rawalpindi/KRL	P	15.4.64	*Rawalpindi*
***Nadeem Khan**	PIA	P	10.12.69	*Rawalpindi*
Naeem Ashraf	Lahore City	P	10.11.72	*Lahore*
***Nagamootoo** Mahendra Veeren	Guyana	WI	9.10.75	*Whim*
Nagamootoo Vishal	Guyana	WI	7.1.77	*Whim*
Naidu Venatswamy Suryaprakash Thilak	Karnataka	I	27.1.78	*Bangalore*
***Naimur Rahman**	Dhaka Metropolis	B	19.9.74	*Dhaka*
Najaf Shah	Rawalpindi/PIA	P	17.12.84	*Gujranwala*
Nandakishore Ammanabrole	Hyderabad	I	10.7.70	*Warangal*
Napier Graham Richard	Essex	E	6.1.80	*Colchester*
Nash Brendan Paul	Queensland	A	14.12.77	*Attadale*
Nash Donald Anthony	New South Wales	A	29.3.78	*Dubbo*
Nash David Charles	Middlesex	E	19.1.78	*Chertsey*
***Nash** Dion Joseph	Auckland	NZ	20.11.71	*Auckland*

	Team	Country	Born	Birthplace
* **Naved Ashraf**	Rawalpindi/KRL	P	4.9.74	*Rawalpindi*
Nawaz Mohamed Naveed	Nondescripts	SL	20.9.73	*Colombo*
Nayyar Rajiv	Himachal Pradesh	I	28.3.70	*Delhi*
Ndima Solomzi Solomon	Gauteng	SA	16.5.77	*Johannesburg*
Neeyamur Rashid	Dhaka Metropolis	B	1.1.75	*Pabna*
* **Nehra** Ashish	Delhi	I	29.4.79	*Delhi*
Nel Andre	Easterns	SA	15.7.77	*Germiston*
Nevin Christopher John	Wellington	NZ	3.8.75	*Dunedin*
Newell Keith	Glamorgan	E	25.3.72	*Crawley*
* **Ngam** Mfuneko	Eastern Province	SA	29.1.79	*Middledrift*
* **Nicholson** Matthew James	Western Australia	A	2.10.74	*St Leonards*
Niewoudt Riaan	North West	SA	8.5.76	*Cradock*
Nixon Paul Andrew	Kent	E	21.10.70	*Carlisle*
* **Nkala** Mluleki Luke	Matabeleland	Z	1.4.81	*Bulawayo*
Noffke Ashley Allan	Queensland	A	30.4.77	*Nambour*
North Marcus James	Western Australia	A	28.7.79	*Pakenham*
* **Ntini** Makhaya	Border	SA	6.7.77	*Zwelitsha*
Obuya Collins Omondi	Kenya	K	27.7.81	*Nairobi*
Also known as C. O. Otieno.				
Obuya David Oluoch	Kenya	K	14.8.79	*Nairobi*
Also known as D. O. Otieno				
Obuya Kennedy Otieno (*see K. O. Otieno*)				
Ochieng Peter	Kenya	K	2.2.77	*Kenya*
Also known as P. J. C. Ongondo.				
* **O'Connor** Shayne Barry	Otago	NZ	15.11.73	*Hastings*
Odoyo Thomas Migai	Kenya	K	12.5.78	*Nairobi*
Odumbe Maurice Omondi	Kenya	K	15.6.69	*Nairobi*
Oldroyd Bradley John	Western Australia	A	5.11.73	*Bentley*
O'Leary Scott James	Queensland	A	17.12.77	*Herston*
* **Olonga** Henry Khaaba	Matabeleland	Z	3.7.76	*Lusaka, Zambia*
Ondik Otieno Suji (*see T. O. Suji*)				
Ongondo Peter Jimmy Carter (*see P. Ochieng*)				
Ontong Justin Lee	Boland	SA	4.1.80	*Paarl*
Onyango Lameck Ngoche	Kenya	K	22.9.73	*Nairobi*
Oram Jacob David Philip	Central Districts	NZ	28.7.78	*Palmerston North*
* **Ormond** James	Leicestershire	E	20.8.77	*Walsgrave*
Ostler Dominic Piers	Warwickshire	E	15.7.70	*Solihull*
Otieno Collins Omondi (*see C. O. Obuya*)				
Otieno David Oluoch (*see D. O. Obuya*)				
Otieno Kennedy Obuya	Kenya	K	11.3.72	*Nairobi*
Also known as K. O. Obuya.				
Otto Johannes Marthinus	Gauteng	SA	4.9.80	*Pretoria*
Outram Gary	North West	SA	13.2.76	*Johannesburg*
Pagnis Amit Anil	Railways	I	18.9.78	*Bombay*
Paleker Allahudien	Northerns	SA	1.1.78	*Cape Town*
Palframan Steven John	Boland	SA	12.5.70	*East London*
Pandey Gyanendrakumar Kedarnath	Uttar Pradesh	I	12.8.72	*Lucknow*
* **Pandit** Chandrakant Sitaram	Madhya Prasesh	I	30.9.61	*Bombay*
Panesar Mudhsuden Singh	Northamptonshire	E	25.4.82	*Luton*
Paranjpe Jatin Vasudeo	Mumbai	I	17.4.72	*Bombay*
Parchment Brenton Anthony	Jamaica	WI	24.6.82	*St Elizabeth*
Parida Kulamani Shankar	Railways	I	9.3.77	*Cuttack*
Parida Rashmi Ranjan	Orissa	I	7.9.74	*Bhubaneshwar*
Parkin Owen Thomas	Glamorgan	E	24.9.72	*Coventry*
* **Parore** Adam Craig	Auckland	NZ	23.1.71	*Auckland*
Parsons Keith Alan	Somerset	E	2.5.73	*Taunton*
Pascoe Matthew David	Queensland	A	10.1.77	*Camperdown*

	Team	*Country*	*Born*	*Birthplace*
Patel Brijal Jagdish	Kenya	K	14.11.77	*Nairobi*
Patel Lalit Amrutlal	Gujarat	I	25.9.77	*Magdalla*
* **Patel** Minal Mahesh	Kent	E	7.7.70	*Bombay, India*
Patel Niraj Kanubhai	Gujarat	I	26.3.81	*Ahmedabad*
Peake Clinton John	Victoria	A	25.3.77	*Geelong*
Peiris Gorakanage Ruwin Prasantha	Tamil Union	SL	9.8.70	*Colombo*
Penberthy Anthony Leonard	Northamptonshire	E	1.9.69	*Troon, Cornwall*
Peng Nicky	Durham	E	18.9.82	*Newcastle upon Tyne*
Penn Andrew Jonathan	Wellington	NZ	27.7.74	*Wanganui*
Penney Trevor Lionel	Warwicks/Mashonaland	E	12.6.68	*Salisbury, Rhodesia*
* **Perera** Anhettige Suresh Asanka	Sinhalese	SL	16.2.78	*Colombo*
Perera Kahawelage Gamini	Galle	SL	22.5.64	*Colombo*
* **Perera** Panagodage Don Ruchira Laksiri	Sinhalese	SL	6.4.77	*Colombo*
Perren Clinton Terrence	Queensland	A	22.2.75	*Herston*
* **Perry** Nehemiah Odolphus	Jamaica	WI	16.6.68	*Jamaica*
Persad Mukesh	Trinidad & Tobago	WI	1.5.70	*Trinidad*
Peters Keon Kenroy	West Indies B	WI	24.2.82	*St Vincent*
Peters Stephen David	Essex	E	10.12.78	*Harold Wood*
Petersen Alviro Nathan	Northerns	SA	25.11.80	*Port Elizabeth*
Peterson Robin John	Eastern Province	SA	4.8.79	*Port Elizabeth*
Pettini Mark Lewis	Essex	E	2.8.83	*Brighton*
Phelps Matthew James	New South Wales	A	1.9.72	*Lismore*
Phillip Wayne	West Indies B	WI	25.11.77	*Grandfond, Dominica*
Phillips Nicholas Charles	Durham	E	10.5.74	*Pembury*
Phillips Timothy James	Essex/Durham UCCE	E	13.3.81	*Cambridge*
Pierson Adrian Roger Kirshaw	Derbyshire	E	21.7.63	*Enfield, Middlesex*
Pietersen Kevin Peter	Nottinghamshire	E	27.6.80	*Pietermaritzburg, SA*
Pilon Nathan Steven	New South Wales	A	27.10.76	*Bulli*
Pinnington Todd Andrew	Tasmania	A	21.3.73	*Hobart*
Pipe David James	Worcestershire	E	16.12.77	*Bradford*
Piper Keith John	Warwickshire	E	18.12.69	*Leicester*
Player Bradley Thomas	Boland	SA	18.1.67	*Benoni*
* **Pocock** Blair Andrew	Auckland	NZ	18.6.71	*Papakura*
Pollard Paul Raymond	Worcestershire	E	24.9.68	*Nottingham*
* **Pollock** Shaun Maclean	KwaZulu-Natal	SA	16.7.73	*Port Elizabeth*
* **Ponting** Ricky Thomas	Tasmania	A	19.12.74	*Launceston*
Poole Ezra Glynn	North West	SA	10.2.75	*Cape Town*
Pope Steven Charles	Border	SA	15.11.72	*East London*
Pothas Nic	Gauteng	SA	18.11.73	*Johannesburg*
Powar Ramesh Rajaram	Mumbai	I	20.5.78	*Bombay*
Powell Darren Brentlyle	Jamaica	WI	15.4.78	*Jamaica*
Powell Michael James	Warwickshire	E	5.4.75	*Bolton*
Powell Michael John	Glamorgan	E	3.2.77	*Abergavenny*
* **Powell** Ricardo Lloyd	Jamaica	WI	16.12.78	*St Elizabeth*
* **Prasad** Bapu Krishnarao Venkatesh	Karnataka	I	5.8.69	*Bangalore*
Pratt Andrew	Durham	E	4.3.75	*Helmington Row*
Pratt Gary Joseph	Durham	E	22.12.81	*Bishop Auckland*
Pretorius Dewald	Free State	SA	6.12.77	*Pretoria*
* **Price** Raymond William	Midlands	Z	12.6.76	*Salisbury*
Prichard Paul John	Essex	E	7.1.65	*Billericay*
Prince Ashwell Gavin	Western Province	SA	28.5.77	*Port Elizabeth*
Prince Goldwyn Terrence	Leeward Islands	WI	18.6.74	*Antigua*
Pringle Andrew Alexander Welsh	Boland	SA	7.2.78	*Bedford*
* **Pringle** Meyrick Wayne	Eastern Province	SA	22.6.66	*Adelaide*
Prior Matthew James	Sussex	E	26.2.82	*Johannesburg, SA*
Prittipaul Lawrence Roland	Hampshire	E	19.10.79	*Portsmouth*
* **Pushpakumara** Karuppiahyage Ravindra	Nondescripts	SL	21.7.75	*Panadura*
Puttick Andrew George	Western Province	SA	11.12.80	*Cape Town*

	Team	*Country*	*Born*	*Birthplace*
***Qaiser Abbas**	Sheikhupura/N. Bank	P	7.5.82	*Muredke*
***Ragoonath** Suruj	Trinidad & Tobago	WI	22.3.68	*Chaguanus*
Raja Ali	Railways	I	5.7.76	*Bhopal*
Rajiv Kumar	Bihar	I	2.12.76	*Patna*
***Raju** Sagi Lakshmi Venkatapathy	Hyderabad	I	9.7.69	*Hyderabad*
***Ramanayake** Champaka Priyadarshana Hewage	Galle	SL	8.1.65	*Colombo*
***Ramesh** Sadagoppan	Tamil Nadu	I	16.10.75	*Madras*
***Ramnarine** Dinanath	Trinidad & Tobago	WI	4.6.75	*Chaguanus*
Rampersad Denis	Trinidad & Tobago	WI	22.9.74	*Couva*
***Ramprakash** Mark Ravin	Surrey	E	5.9.69	*Bushey*
***Ranatunga** Arjuna	Sinhalese	SL	1.12.63	*Colombo*
***Ranatunga** Sanjeeva	Sinhalese	SL	25.4.69	*Colombo*
Randall Stephen John	Nottinghamshire	E	9.6.80	*Nottingham*
***Ranjan Das** (*see Bikash Ranjan Das*)				
***Rashid Latif**	Karachi/Allied Bank	P	14.10.68	*Karachi*
Rashid Umar Bin Abdul	Sussex	E	6.2.76	*Southampton*
***Rathore** Vikram	Punjab	I	26.3.69	*Jullundur*
Ratra Ajay	Haryana	I	13.12.81	*Faridabad*
Raul Sanjay Susanta	Orissa	I	6.10.76	*Cuttack*
Rawnsley Matthew James	Worcestershire	E	8.6.76	*Birmingham*
***Read** Christopher Mark Wells	Nottinghamshire	E	10.8.78	*Paignton*
Reddy Brendon Leigh	Easterns	SA	6.11.83	*Durban*
***Reifer** Floyd Lamonte	Barbados	WI	23.7.72	*Parish Land*
***Reiffel** Paul Ronald	Victoria	A	19.4.66	*Box Hill*
***Rennie** Gavin James	Mashonaland	Z	12.1.76	*Fort Victoria*
***Rennie** John Alexander	Matabeleland	Z	29.7.70	*Fort Victoria*
***Rhodes** Jonathan Neil	KwaZulu-Natal	SA	27.7.69	*Pietermaritzburg*
***Rhodes** Steven John	Worcestershire	E	17.6.64	*Bradford*
Richards Corey John	New South Wales	A	25.8.75	*Camden*
Richardson Alan	Warwickshire	E	6.5.75	*Newcastle-under-Lyme*
***Richardson** Mark Hunter	Otago	NZ	11.6.71	*Hastings*
***Richardson** Richard Benjamin	West Indies B	WI	12.1.62	*Five Islands Vill., Antigua*
Richardson Scott Andrew	Yorkshire	E	5.9.77	*Oldham*
Rindel Michael John Raymond	Easterns	SA	9.2.63	*Durban*
Ripley David	Northamptonshire	E	13.9.66	*Leeds*
Roach Peter John	Victoria	A	19.5.75	*Kew*
***Roberts** Lincoln Abraham	Trinidad & Tobago	WI	4.9.74	*Accord, Antigua*
Roberts Timothy William	Lancashire	E	4.3.78	*Kettering*
Robinson Darren David John	Essex	E	2.3.73	*Braintree*
Robinson Mark Andrew	Sussex	E	23.11.66	*Hull*
Roe Garth Anthony	North West	SA	9.7.73	*Port Elizabeth*
Rofe Paul Cameron	South Australia	A	16.1.81	*Adelaide*
Rogers Barney Guy	Zimbabwe Academy	Z	20.8.82	*Harare*
Rollins Adrian Stewart	Northamptonshire	E	8.2.72	*Barking*
Romero Leon Constantine	Trinidad & Tobago	WI	29.12.74	*Trinidad*
***Rose** Franklyn Albert	Jamaica	WI	1.2.72	*St Ann's Bay*
Rose Graham David	Somerset	E	12.4.64	*Tottenham*
Roseberry Michael Anthony	Middlesex	E	28.11.66	*Sunderland*
Rudolph Jacobus Andries	Northerns	SA	4.5.81	*Springs*
Rummans Graeme Clifford	New South Wales	A	13.12.76	*Camperdown*
***Russell** Robert Charles	Gloucestershire	E	15.8.63	*Stroud*
***Saeed Anwar**	Lahore City	P	6.9.68	*Karachi*
Saeed Azad	Karachi/National Bank	P	14.8.66	*Karachi*
Saggers Martin John	Kent	E	23.5.72	*King's Lynn*
Sahabuddin Khatib Syeb	Andhra	I	1.1.79	*Kadiri*
Saiful Islam	Dhaka Division	B	14.4.69	*Mymensingh*
Sajid Ali	National Bank	P	1.7.63	*Karachi*

	Team	Country	Born	Birthplace
Sajjad Ahmed	Dhaka Metropolis	B	20.5.74	*Dhaka*
Sajjad Akbar	Sargodha	P	1.3.61	*Lahore*
Saker David James	Tasmania	A	29.5.66	*Oakleigh*
† **Sales** David John	Northamptonshire	E	3.12.77	*Carshalton*
* **Salim Elahi**	Lahore City	P	21.11.76	*Sahiwal*
* **Salisbury** Ian David Kenneth	Surrey	E	21.1.70	*Northampton*
Salman Butt	Lahore City	P	7.10.84	*Lahore*
* **Samaraweera** Dulip Prasanna	Colts	SL	12.2.72	*Colombo*
* **Samaraweera** Thilan Thusara	Sinhalese	SL	22.9.76	*Colombo*
* **Samuels** Marlon Nathaniel	Jamaica	WI	5.1.81	*Kingston*
* **Samuels** Robert George	Jamaica	WI	13.3.71	*Kingston*
* **Sangakkara** Kumar	Nondescripts	SL	27.10.77	*Colombo*
* **Sanghvi** Rahul Laxman	Delhi	I	3.9.74	*Surat*
Sanson Audley Algan	Jamaica	WI	5.11.74	*Clarendon*
Sanuar Hossain	Biman	B	5.8.73	*Mymensingh*
* **Saqlain Mushtaq**	Surrey	P	29.12.76	*Lahore*
* **Sarandeep Singh**	Punjab	I	21.10.79	*Amritsar*
* **Sarwan** Ramnaresh Ronnie	Guyana	WI	23.6.80	*Wakeanam*
Saxena Santosh Ramesh	Mumbai	I	20.4.76	*Bombay*
* **Schofield** Christopher Paul	Lancashire	E	6.10.78	*Rochdale*
Schofield James Edward Knowle	Hampshire	E	1.11.78	*Blackpool*
Schorn James Robin	Free State	SA	2.4.82	*Pietermaritzberg*
Scott Gary Michael	Durham	E	21.7.84	*Sunderland*
Scuderi Joseph Charles	Lancashire	E	24.12.68	*Ingham, Australia*
Seccombe Wade Anthony	Queensland	A	30.10.71	*Murgon*
Sehwag Virender	Delhi	I	20.10.78	*Delhi*
Selwood Steven Andrew	Derbyshire	E	24.11.79	*Barnet*
Semple Keith Fitzpatrick	Guyana	WI	21.8.70	*Georgetown*
Senekal Dewald Meyer	Eastern Province	SA	12.1.81	*Uitenhage*
* **Sewell** David Graham	Otago	NZ	20.10.77	*Christchurch*
Seymore Andre Johan	Gauteng/Easterns	SA	16.2.75	*Rustenburg*
Shabbir Ahmed	National Bank	P	21.4.76	*Khanewal*
* **Shadab Kabir**	Karachi	P	12.11.77	*Karachi*
Shafayat Bilal Mustafa	Nottinghamshire	E	10.7.84	*Nottingham*
Shafiuddin Ahmed	Chittagong	B	1.6.73	*Dhaka*
Shah Owais Alam	Middlesex	E	22.10.78	*Karachi, Pakistan*
Shah Ravindu Dhirajlal	Kenya	K	28.8.72	*Nairobi*
Shahid Nadeem	Surrey	E	23.4.69	*Karachi, Pakistan*
* **Shahid Afridi**	Karachi/Habib Bank/Leics	P	1.3.80	*Khyber Agency*
Shahid Anwar	Lahore City/National Bank	P	5.7.68	*Multan*
* **Shahid Nazir**	Faisalabad/Habib Bank	P	4.12.77	*Faisalabad*
* **Shahriar Hossain**	Dhaka Division	B	1.6.76	*Narayangonj*
* **Shakeel Ahmed**, sen.	Rawalpindi/KRL	P	12.2.66	*Kuwait City, Kuwait*
Sharif Zoheb Khalid	Essex	E	22.2.83	*Leytonstone*
Shariful Haq	Biman	B	15.1.76	*Mymensingh*
Sharma Abhay	Railways	I	30.4.69	*Delhi*
* **Sharma** Ajay	Himachal Pradesh	I	3.4.64	*Delhi*
* **Sharma** Sanjeev	Rajasthan	I	25.8.65	*Delhi*
Shaw Adrian David	Glamorgan	E	17.2.72	*Neath*
Sheikh Mohamed Avez	Warwickshire	E	2.7.73	*Birmingham*
Sheriyar Alamgir	Worcestershire	E	15.11.73	*Birmingham*
Shillingford Shane	Windward Islands	WI	23.2.83	*Dominica*
* **Shoaib Akhtar**	Somerset	P	13.8.75	*Rawalpindi*
* **Shoaib Malik**	PIA	P	1.2.82	*Sialkot*
* **Shoaib Mohammad**	PIA	P	8.1.61	*Karachi*
Shukla Laxmi Ratan	Bengal	I	6.5.81	*Howrah*
Siddiqui Iqbal	Maharashtra	I	26.12.74	*Aurangabad*
* **Sidebottom** Ryan Jay	Yorkshire	E	15.6.78	*Huddersfield*

† *Sales did not play in 2001, but was expected to return in 2002.*

	Team	Country	Born	Birthplace
Sillence Roger John	Gloucestershire	E	29.6.77	*Salisbury*
Silva Lindamlilage Prageeth Chamara	Panadura	SL	14.12.79	*Panadura*
* **Silverwood** Christopher Eric Wilfred	Yorkshire	E	5.3.75	*Pontefract*
Simmonds Joel McKenzie	Leeward Islands	WI	27.1.76	*Nevis*
* **Simmons** Philip Verant	Trinidad & Tobago	WI	18.4.63	*Arima*
* **Sinclair** Mathew Stuart	Central Districts	NZ	9.11.75	*Katherine, Australia*
Singh Anurag	Worcestershire	E	9.9.75	*Kanpur, India*
* **Singh** Rabindra Ramanarayan (Robin)	Tamil Nadu	I	14.9.63	*Princes Town, Trinidad*
* **Singh** Robin	Delhi	I	1.1.70	*Delhi*
* **Slater** Michael Jonathon	New South Wales	A	21.2.70	*Wagga Wagga*
Smethurst Michael Paul	Lancashire	E	11.10.76	*Oldham*
Smit Willem Johannes	Free State	SA	1.8.74	*Calvinia*
* **Smith** Andrew Michael	Gloucestershire	E	1.10.67	*Dewsbury*
Smith Benjamin Francis	Leics/Central Districts	E	3.4.72	*Corby*
Smith Devon Sheldon	Windward Islands	WI	21.10.81	*Grenada*
Smith Edward Thomas	Kent	E	19.7.77	*Pembury*
Smith Graeme Craig	Western Province	SA	1.2.81	*Johannesburg*
Smith Gregory James	Northerns/Notts	E	30.10.71	*Pretoria, SA*
Smith Michael John	South Australia	A	17.7.73	*Rose Park*
Smith Neil Michael Knight	Warwickshire	E	27.7.67	*Birmingham*
Smith Richard Andrew Mortimer	Trinidad & Tobago	WI	17.7.71	*Trinidad*
* **Smith** Robin Arnold	Hampshire	E	13.9.63	*Durban, South Africa*
Smith Trevor Mark	Derbyshire	E	18.1.77	*Derby*
Snape Jeremy Nicholas	Gloucestershire	E	27.4.73	*Stoke-on-Trent*
Sodhi Reetinder Singh	Punjab	I	18.10.80	*Patiala*
Solanki Vikram Singh	Worcestershire	E	1.4.76	*Udaipur, India*
Somasunder Sujith	Karnataka	I	2.12.72	*Bangalore*
Sooklal Rodney Ian	West Indies B	WI	21.12.80	*Freeport*
Speak Nicholas Jason	Durham	E	21.11.66	*Manchester*
* **Spearman** Craig Murray	Central Districts	NZ	4.7.72	*Auckland*
Speight Martin Peter	Durham	E	24.10.67	*Walsall*
Spires James Ashley	Warwickshire	E	12.11.79	*Solihull*
* **Srinath** Javagal	Karnataka	I	31.8.69	*Mysore*
Sriram Sridharan	Tamil Nadu	I	21.2.76	*Madras*
Srivastava Shalabh Jagdishprasad	Uttar Pradesh	I	22.9.81	*Allahabad*
* **Stead** Gary Raymond	Canterbury	NZ	9.1.72	*Christchurch*
Stemp Richard David	Nottinghamshire	E	11.12.67	*Birmingham*
* **Stephenson** John Patrick	Hampshire	E	14.3.65	*Stebbing*
Stevens Darren Ian	Leicestershire	E	30.4.76	*Leicester*
* **Stewart** Alec James	Surrey	E	8.4.63	*Merton*
Stewart Errol Leslie Rae	KwaZulu-Natal	SA	30.7.69	*Durban*
Stewart James	New South Wales	A	22.8.70	*East Fremantle*
* **Steyn** Philippus Jeremia Rudolf	Northerns	SA	30.6.67	*Kimberley*
Still Quentin Raxham	Northerns	SA	8.8.74	*Pietermaritzburg*
* **Strang** Bryan Colin	Mashonaland	Z	9.6.72	*Bulawayo*
* **Strang** Paul Andrew	Mashonaland	Z	28.7.70	*Bulawayo*
Strauss Andrew John	Middlesex	E	2.3.77	*Johannesburg, SA*
* **Streak** Heath Hilton	Matabeleland	Z	16.3.74	*Bulawayo*
Strong Michael Richard	Northamptonshire	E	28.6.74	*Cuckfield*
Strydom Johannes Gerhardus	Boland	SA	6.9.79	*Cape Town*
Strydom Morne	North West	SA	20.2.74	*Port Elizabeth*
* **Strydom** Pieter Coenraad	Border	SA	10.6.69	*Somerset East*
* **Stuart** Colin Ellsworth Laurie	Guyana	WI	28.9.73	*Georgetown*
Stubbings Stephen David	Derbyshire	E	31.3.78	*Huddersfield*
Styris Scott Bernard	Northern Districts	NZ	10.7.75	*Brisbane, Australia*
* **Such** Peter Mark	Essex	E	12.6.64	*Helensburgh, Scotland*
Sudarshana Tuduwa Kankanamge Dhammika	Galle	SL	19.6.76	*Galle*

	Team	*Country*	*Born*	*Birthplace*
Sugden Craig Brian	Border	SA	7.3.74	*Durban*
Suji Martin Armon	Kenya	K	2.6.71	*Nairobi*
Suji Tony Ondik	Kenya	K	5.2.76	*Nairobi*
Also known as O. S. Ondik.				
Sukhbinder Singh	Assam	I	23.2.67	*Jullundur*
Sulzberger Glen Paul	Central Districts	NZ	14.3.73	*Kaponga*
Surendra Singh	Jammu and Kashmir	I	1.3.74	*Jammu*
Sutcliffe Iain John	Leicestershire	E	20.12.74	*Leeds*
Sutton Luke David	Derbyshire	E	4.10.76	*Keynsham*
Swain Brett Andrew	South Australia	A	14.2.74	*Stirling*
Swan Gavin Graham	Western Australia	A	30.10.70	*Subiaco*
Swann Alec James	Northamptonshire	E	26.10.76	*Northampton*
Swann Graeme Peter	Northamptonshire	E	24.3.79	*Northampton*
Sylvester John Anthony Rodney	Windward Islands	WI	6.10.69	*Grenada*
Symonds Andrew	Queensland/Kent	A	9.6.75	*Birmingham, England*
* **Taibu** Tatenda	Mashonaland A	Z	14.5.83	*Harare*
Tait Alex Ross	Northern Districts	NZ	13.6.72	*Paparoa*
Targett Benjamin Stuart	Tasmania	A	27.12.72	*Paddington*
Tatton Craig Ross	Griqualand West	SA	29.1.75	*Bulawayo, Rhodesia*
* **Taufeeq Umar**	Lahore City/Habib Bank	P	20.6.81	*Lahore*
Taylor Billy Victor	Sussex	E	11.1.77	*Southampton*
Taylor Christopher Glyn	Gloucestershire	E	27.9.76	*Bristol*
Taylor Christopher Robert	Yorkshire	E	21.2.81	*Pudsey*
* **Taylor** Jonathan Paul	Northamptonshire	E	8.8.64	*Ashby-de-la-Zouch*
Telemachus Roger	Western Province	SA	27.3.73	*Stellenbosch*
* **Tendulkar** Sachin Ramesh	Mumbai	I	24.4.73	*Bombay*
* **Terbrugge** David John	Gauteng	SA	31.1.77	*Ladysmith*
Thomas Alfonso Clive	North West	SA	9.2.77	*Cape Town*
Thomas Fernix	Windward Islands	WI	26.9.80	*Dominica*
Thomas Ian James	Glamorgan	E	9.5.79	*Newport*
Thomas Stuart Darren	Glamorgan	E	25.1.75	*Morriston*
* **Thorpe** Graham Paul	Surrey	E	1.8.69	*Farnham*
Tikolo Stephen Ogomji	Kenya	K	25.6.71	*Nairobi*
* **Tillekeratne** Hashan Prasantha	Nondescripts	SL	14.7.67	*Colombo*
Titchard Stephen Paul	Derbyshire	E	17.12.67	*Warrington*
Tolley Christopher Mark	Nottinghamshire	E	30.12.67	*Kidderminster*
Townsend David Hume	Northerns	SA	22.12.77	*Port Elizabeth*
Toyana Geoffrey	Gauteng	SA	27.2.74	*Soweto*
Tredwell James Cullum	Kent	E	27.2.82	*Ashford*
Trego Peter David	Somerset	E	12.6.81	*Weston-super-Mare*
Tremlett Christopher Timothy	Hampshire	E	2.9.81	*Southampton*
* **Trescothick** Marcus Edward	Somerset	E	25.12.75	*Keynsham*
Trott Benjamin James	Kent	E	14.3.75	*Wellington*
Trott Ian Jonathan Leonard	Boland	SA	22.4.81	*Cape Town*
Troughton Jamie Oliver	Warwichshire	E	2.3.79	*Camden*
Tsolekile Thami Lungisa	Western Province	SA	9.10.80	*Cape Town*
Tubb Shannon Ben	Tasmania	A	11.5.80	*Launceston*
Tucker Brett Hurst	Griqualand West	SA	4.4.79	*Johannesburg*
Tucker Joseph Peter	Somerset	E	14.9.79	*Bath*
Tuckett Carl McArthur	Leeward Islands	WI	18.5.70	*Nevis*
* **Tudor** Alex Jeremy	Surrey	E	23.10.77	*Kensington*
* **Tuffey** Daryl Raymond	Northern Districts	NZ	11.6.78	*Milton*
* **Tufnell** Philip Charles Roderick	Middlesex	E	29.4.66	*Barnet*
Turner Robert Julian	Somerset	E	25.11.67	*Malvern*
Tweedie Andrew Neil Walter	KwaZulu-Natal	SA	27.11.75	*Durban*
* **Twose** Roger Graham	Wellington	NZ	17.4.68	*Torquay, England*
Udal Shaun David	Hampshire	E	18.3.69	*Farnborough, Hants*
* **Upashantha** Kalutarage Eric Amila	Colts	SL	10.6.72	*Kurunegala*
Uys Johannes	Easterns	SA	14.2.78	*Benoni*

	Team	*Country*	*Born*	*Birthplace*
* **Vaas** Warnakulasuriya Patabendige Ushantha Joseph Chaminda	Colts	SL	27.1.74	*Mattumagala*
van Deinsen Brett Paul	New South Wales	A	28.12.77	*Camperdown*
van den Berg Adolf Matthys	Easterns	SA	9.3.78	*Randfontein*
van der Merwe Francois	North West	SA	5.7.76	*Kempton Park*
van der Wath Johannes Jacobus	Free State	SA	10.1.78	*Newcastle*
van Dort Michael Graydon	Colombo	SL	19.1.80	*Colombo*
van Jaarsveld Martin	Northerns	SA	18.6.74	*Klerksdorp*
van Wyk Cornelius Francois Kruger	Northerns	SA	2.7.80	*Wolmaransstad*
van Wyk Morne Nico	Free State	SA	20.3.79	*Bloemfontein*
Vaughan Jeffrey Mark	South Australia	A	26.3.74	*Blacktown*
* **Vaughan** Michael Paul	Yorkshire	E	29.10.74	*Manchester*
Veenstra Ross Edward	KwaZulu-Natal	SA	22.4.72	*Estcourt*
Venter Jacobus Francois	Free State	SA	1.10.69	*Bloemfontein*
Venter Martin Colin	North West	SA	12.12.68	*East London*
Vermeulen Mark Andrew	Matabeleland	Z	2.3.79	*Salisbury*
* **Vettori** Daniel Luca	Northern Districts	NZ	27.1.79	*Auckland*
* **Viljoen** Dirk Peter	Mashonaland A	Z	11.3.77	*Salisbury*
Vimpani Graeme Ronald	Victoria	A	27.1.72	*Herston*
Vincent Lou	Auckland	NZ	12.11.78	*Auckland*
Wagh Mark Anant	Warwickshire	E	20.10.76	*Birmingham*
* **Wajahatullah Wasti**	Peshawar/Allied Bank	P	11.11.74	*Peshawar*
* **Walker** Brooke Graeme Keith	Auckland	NZ	25.3.77	*Auckland*
Walker Matthew Jonathan	Kent	E	2.1.74	*Gravesend*
Wallace Mark Alexander	Glamorgan	E	19.11.81	*Abergavenny*
* **Wallace** Philo Alphonso	Barbados	WI	2.8.70	*Haynesville*
* **Walmsley** Kerry Peter	Otago	NZ	23.8.73	*Dunedin*
* **Walsh** Courtney Andrew	Jamaica	WI	30.10.62	*Kingston*
Walsh Mark Jason	Western Australia	A	28.4.72	*Townsville*
Wanasinghe Wasala Mudiyanselage Pasan Nirmitha	Galle	SL	30.9.70	*Colombo*
* **Waqar Younis**	Lahore City	P	16.11.71	*Vehari*
* **Ward** Ian James	Surrey	E	30.9.72	*Plymouth*
Ward Trevor Robert	Leicestershire	E	18.1.68	*Farningham*
Warnapura Basnayake Shalith Malinda	Burgher	SL	26.5.79	*Colombo*
* **Warne** Shane Keith	Victoria	A	13.9.69	*Ferntree Gully*
Warren Russell John	Northamptonshire	E	10.9.71	*Northampton*
* **Wasim Akram**	Lahore City	P	3.6.66	*Lahore*
Wasim Haider	Faisalabad	P	6.6.67	*Lyallpur*
* **Wasim Jaffer**	Mumbai	I	16.2.78	*Bombay*
* **Watambwa** Brighton Tonderai	Mashonaland A	Z	9.6.77	*Salisbury*
* **Watkin** Steven Llewellyn	Glamorgan	E	15.9.64	*Maesteg*
Watson Douglas James	KwaZulu-Natal	SA	15.5.73	*Pietermaritzburg*
Watson Shane Robert	Tasmania	A	17.6.81	*Ipswich*
Watt Balthazar Michael	Windward Islands	WI	12.4.75	*Dominica*
* **Waugh** Mark Edward	New South Wales	A	2.6.65	*Sydney*
* **Waugh** Stephen Rodger	New South Wales	A	2.6.65	*Sydney*
Weekes Lesroy Charlesworth	Northamptonshire	WI	19.7.71	*Montserrat*
Weekes Paul Nicholas	Middlesex	E	8.7.69	*Hackney*
Weerakoon Sajeewa	Burgher	SL	17.2.78	*Galle*
Weeraratne Kaushalya	Nondescripts	SL	29.1.81	*Gampola*
Welch Graeme	Derbyshire	E	21.3.72	*Durham*
Wells Vincent John	Leicestershire	E	6.8.65	*Dartford*
Welton Guy Edward	Nottinghamshire	E	4.5.78	*Grimsby*
Weston Robin Michael Swann	Middlesex	E	7.6.75	*Durham*
Weston William Philip Christopher	Worcestershire	E	16.6.73	*Durham*
Wharf Alexander George	Glamorgan	E	4.6.75	*Bradford*
Wharton Lian James	Derbyshire	E	21.2.77	*Holbrook*
Whiley Matthew Jeffrey Allen	Leicestershire	E	6.5.80	*Nottingham*

	Team	Country	Born	Birthplace
White Brad Middleton	Easterns	SA	15.5.70	*Johannesburg*
***White** Craig	Yorkshire	E	16.12.69	*Morley*
White Cameron Leon	Victoria	A	18.8.83	*Bairnsdale*
White Giles William	Hampshire	E	23.3.72	*Barnstaple*
White Robert Allan	Northamptonshire	E	15.10.79	*Chelmsford*
***Whittall** Guy James	Manicaland	Z	5.9.72	*Chipinga*
Wiblin Wayne	Border	SA	13.2.69	*Grahamstown*
Wickremaratne Ranasinghe Pattikirikoralalage Aruna Hemantha	Sinhalese	SL	21.2.71	*Colombo*
***Wickremasinghe** Gallage Pramodya	Sinhalese	SL	14.8.71	*Matara*
Widdup Simon	Yorkshire	E	10.11.77	*Doncaster*
Wilkinson Kurt Jason	West Indies B	WI	14.8.81	*Applethwaites, Barbados*
Wilkinson Louis Johannes	Free State	SA	19.11.66	*Vereeniging*
Willett Tonito Akanni	West Indies B	WI	6.2.83	*Nevis*
Williams Brad Andrew	Western Australia	A	20.11.74	*Frankston*
Williams Connor Cecil	Baroda	I	7.8.73	*Baroda*
Williams Davon Alphonso	Leeward Islands	WI	27.5.72	*Montserrat*
Williams Henry Smith	Boland	SA	11.6.67	*Stellenbosch*
Williams Jody Wendell	Easterns	SA	9.1.80	*Johannesburg*
Williams Luke	South Australia	A	24.12.79	*Henley Beach*
Williams Laurie Rohan	Jamaica	WI	12.12.68	*Jamaica*
Williams Richard Charles James	Gloucestershire	E	8.8.69	*Southmead*
***Williams** Stuart Clayton	Leeward Islands	WI	12.8.69	*Government Road, Nevis*
Willoughby Charl Myles	Western Province	SA	3.12.74	*Cape Town*
***Wilson** Paul	South Australia	A	12.1.72	*Newcastle*
Wilson Sheldon Greg	Windward Islands	WI	23.8.72	*St Lucia*
Windows Matthew Guy Norman	Gloucestershire	E	5.4.73	*Bristol*
Wingfield Wade Richard	KwaZulu-Natal	SA	17.12.77	*Scottburgh*
***Wiseman** Paul John	Otago	NZ	4.5.70	*Auckland*
***Wishart** Craig Brian	Midlands	Z	9.1.74	*Salisbury*
Wisneski Warren Anthony	Canterbury	NZ	19.2.69	*New Plymouth*
Wood John	Lancashire	E	22.7.70	*Crofton*
Wood Matthew James	Yorkshire	E	6.4.77	*Huddersfield*
Wood Matthew James	Somerset	E	30.9.80	*Exeter*
Wright Damien Geoffrey	Tasmania	A	25.7.75	*Casino*
Yadav Jai Prakash	Madhya Pradesh	I	7.8.74	*Bhopal*
Yardy Michael Howard	Sussex	E	27.11.80	*Pembury*
Yasir Arafat	Rawalpindi/KRL	P	12.3.82	*Rawalpindi*
Yates Gary	Lancashire	E	20.9.67	*Ashton-under-Lyne*
Young Bradley Evan	South Australia	A	23.2.73	*Semaphore*
***Young** Shaun	Tasmania	A	13.6.70	*Burnie*
***Younis Khan**	Peshawar/Habib Bank	P	29.11.77	*Mardan*
***Yousuf Youhana**	Lahore City	P	27.8.74	*Lahore*
Yuvraj Singh	Punjab	I	12.12.81	*Chandigarh*
***Zaheer Khan**	Baroda	I	7.10.78	*Shrirampur*
***Zahid Fazal**	Grujanwala/PIA	P	10.11.73	*Sialkot*
***Zahoor Elahi**	Lahore City/ADBP/ Dhaka Metropolis	P	1.3.71	*Sahiwal*
Zaidi Ashish Winston	Uttar Pradesh	I	16.9.71	*Allahabad*
Zakir Hassan	Dhaka Division	B	1.12.72	*Mymensingh*
***Zoysa** Demuni Nuwan Tharanga	Sinhalese	SL	13.5.78	*Colombo*
Zuffri Syed Zakaria	Assam	I	12.10.75	*Guwahati*
Zuiderent Bastiaan	Sussex	E	3.3.77	*Utrecht, Holland*

CRICKETERS OF THE YEAR, 1889–2002

1889 *Six Great Bowlers of the Year:* J. Briggs, J. J. Ferris, G. A. Lohmann, R. Peel, C. T. B. Turner, S. M. J. Woods.

1890 *Nine Great Batsmen of the Year:* R. Abel, W. Barnes, W. Gunn, L. Hall, R. Henderson, J. M. Read, A. Shrewsbury, F. H. Sugg, A. Ward.

1891 *Five Great Wicket-Keepers:* J. McC. Blackham, G. MacGregor, R. Pilling, M. Sherwin, H. Wood.

1892 *Five Great Bowlers:* W. Attewell, J. T. Hearne, F. Martin, A. W. Mold, J. W. Sharpe.

1893 *Five Batsmen of the Year:* H. T. Hewett, L. C. H. Palairet, W. W. Read, S. W. Scott, A. E. Stoddart.

1894 *Five All-Round Cricketers:* G. Giffen, A. Hearne, F. S. Jackson, G. H. S. Trott, E. Wainwright.

1895 *Five Young Batsmen of the Season:* W. Brockwell, J. T. Brown, C. B. Fry, T. W. Hayward, A. C. MacLaren.

1896 W. G. Grace.

1897 *Five Cricketers of the Season:* S. E. Gregory, A. A. Lilley, K. S. Ranjitsinhji, T. Richardson, H. Trumble.

1898 *Five Cricketers of the Year:* F. G. Bull, W. R. Cuttell, N. F. Druce, G. L. Jessop, J. R. Mason.

1899 *Five Great Players of the Season:* W. H. Lockwood, W. Rhodes, W. Storer, C. L. Townsend, A. E. Trott.

1900 *Five Cricketers of the Season:* J. Darling, C. Hill, A. O. Jones, M. A. Noble, Major R. M. Poore.

1901 *Mr R. E. Foster and Four Yorkshiremen:* R. E. Foster, S. Haigh, G. H. Hirst, T. L. Taylor, J. Tunnicliffe.

1902 L. C. Braund, C. P. McGahey, F. Mitchell, W. G. Quaife, J. T. Tyldesley.

1903 W. W. Armstrong, C. J. Burnup, J. Iremonger, J. J. Kelly, V. T. Trumper.

1904 C. Blythe, J. Gunn, A. E. Knight, W. Mead, P. F. Warner.

1905 B. J. T. Bosanquet, E. A. Halliwell, J. Hallows, P. A. Perrin, R. H. Spooner.

1906 D. Denton, W. S. Lees, G. J. Thompson, J. Vine, L. G. Wright.

1907 J. N. Crawford, A. Fielder, E. G. Hayes, K. L. Hutchings, N. A. Knox.

1908 A. W. Hallam, R. O. Schwarz, F. A. Tarrant, A. E. E. Vogler, T. G. Wass.

1909 *Lord Hawke and Four Cricketers of the Year:* W. Brearley, Lord Hawke, J. B. Hobbs, A. Marshal, J. T. Newstead.

1910 W. Bardsley, S. F. Barnes, D. W. Carr, A. P. Day, V. S. Ransford.

1911 H. K. Foster, A. Hartley, C. B. Llewellyn, W. C. Smith, F. E. Woolley.

1912 *Five Members of the MCC's Team in Australia:* F. R. Foster, J. W. Hearne, S. P. Kinneir, C. P. Mead, H. Strudwick.

1913 John Wisden: Personal Recollections.

1914 M. W. Booth, G. Gunn, J. W. Hitch, A. E. Relf, Hon. L. H. Tennyson.

1915 J. W. H. T. Douglas, P. G. H. Fender, H. T. W. Hardinge, D. J. Knight, S. G. Smith.

1916–17 No portraits appeared.

1918 *School Bowlers of the Year:* H. L. Calder, J. E. D'E. Firth, C. H. Gibson, G. A. Rotherham, G. T. S. Stevens.

1919 *Five Public School Cricketers of the Year:* P. W. Adams, A. P. F. Chapman, A. C. Gore, L. P. Hedges, N. E. Partridge.

1920 *Five Batsmen of the Year:* A. Ducat, E. H. Hendren, P. Holmes, H. Sutcliffe, E. Tyldesley.

1921 P. F. Warner.

1922 H. Ashton, J. L. Bryan, J. M. Gregory, C. G. Macartney, E. A. McDonald.

1923 A. W. Carr, A. P. Freeman, C. W. L. Parker, A. C. Russell, A. Sandham.

1924 *Five Bowlers of the Year:* A. E. R. Gilligan, R. Kilner, G. G. Macaulay, C. H. Parkin, M. W. Tate.

1925 R. H. Catterall, J. C. W. MacBryan, H. W. Taylor, R. K. Tyldesley, W. W. Whysall.

1926 J. B. Hobbs.

1927	G. Geary, H. Larwood, J. Mercer, W. A. Oldfield, W. M. Woodfull.
1928	R. C. Blunt, C. Hallows, W. R. Hammond, D. R. Jardine, V. W. C. Jupp.
1929	L. E. G. Ames, G. Duckworth, M. Leyland, S. J. Staples, J. C. White.
1930	E. H. Bowley, K. S. Duleepsinhji, H. G. Owen-Smith, R. W. V. Robins, R. E. S. Wyatt.
1931	D. G. Bradman, C. V. Grimmett, B. H. Lyon, I. A. R. Peebles, M. J. Turnbull.
1932	W. E. Bowes, C. S. Dempster, James Langridge, Nawab of Pataudi sen., H. Verity.
1933	W. E. Astill, F. R. Brown, A. S. Kennedy, C. K. Nayudu, W. Voce.
1934	A. H. Bakewell, G. A. Headley, M. S. Nichols, L. F. Townsend, C. F. Walters.
1935	S. J. McCabe, W. J. O'Reilly, G. A. E. Paine, W. H. Ponsford, C. I. J. Smith.
1936	H. B. Cameron, E. R. T. Holmes, B. Mitchell, D. Smith, A. W. Wellard.
1937	C. J. Barnett, W. H. Copson, A. R. Gover, V. M. Merchant, T. S. Worthington.
1938	T. W. J. Goddard, J. Hardstaff jun., L. Hutton, J. H. Parks, E. Paynter.
1939	H. T. Bartlett, W. A. Brown, D. C. S. Compton, K. Farnes, A. Wood.
1940	L. N. Constantine, W. J. Edrich, W. W. Keeton, A. B. Sellers, D. V. P. Wright.
1941–46	No portraits appeared.
1947	A. V. Bedser, L. B. Fishlock, V. (M. H.) Mankad, T. P. B. Smith, C. Washbrook.
1948	M. P. Donnelly, A. Melville, A. D. Nourse, J. D. Robertson, N. W. D. Yardley.
1949	A. L. Hassett, W. A. Johnston, R. R. Lindwall, A. R. Morris, D. Tallon.
1950	T. E. Bailey, R. O. Jenkins, John Langridge, R. T. Simpson, B. Sutcliffe.
1951	T. G. Evans, S. Ramadhin, A. L. Valentine, E. D. Weekes, F. M. M. Worrell.
1952	R. Appleyard, H. E. Dollery, J. C. Laker, P. B. H. May, E. A. B. Rowan.
1953	H. Gimblett, T. W. Graveney, D. S. Sheppard, W. S. Surridge, F. S. Trueman.
1954	R. N. Harvey, G. A. R. Lock, K. R. Miller, J. H. Wardle, W. Watson.
1955	B. Dooland, Fazal Mahmood, W. E. Hollies, J. B. Statham, G. E. Tribe.
1956	M. C. Cowdrey, D. J. Insole, D. J. McGlew, H. J. Tayfield, F. H. Tyson.
1957	D. Brookes, J. W. Burke, M. J. Hilton, G. R. A. Langley, P. E. Richardson.
1958	P. J. Loader, A. J. McIntyre, O. G. Smith, M. J. Stewart, C. L. Walcott.
1959	H. L. Jackson, R. E. Marshall, C. A. Milton, J. R. Reid, D. Shackleton.
1960	K. F. Barrington, D. B. Carr, R. Illingworth, G. Pullar, M. J. K. Smith.
1961	N. A. T. Adcock, E. R. Dexter, R. A. McLean, R. Subba Row, J. V. Wilson.
1962	W. E. Alley, R. Benaud, A. K. Davidson, W. M. Lawry, N. C. O'Neill.
1963	D. Kenyon, Mushtaq Mohammad, P. H. Parfitt, P. J. Sharpe, F. J. Titmus.
1964	D. B. Close, C. C. Griffith, C. C. Hunte, R. B. Kanhai, G. S. Sobers.
1965	G. Boycott, P. J. Burge, J. A. Flavell, G. D. McKenzie, R. B. Simpson.
1966	K. C. Bland, J. H. Edrich, R. C. Motz, P. M. Pollock, R. G. Pollock.
1967	R. W. Barber, B. L. D'Oliveira, C. Milburn, J. T. Murray, S. M. Nurse.
1968	Asif Iqbal, Hanif Mohammad, K. Higgs, J. M. Parks, Nawab of Pataudi jun.
1969	J. G. Binks, D. M. Green, B. A. Richards, D. L. Underwood, O. S. Wheatley.
1970	B. F. Butcher, A. P. E. Knott, Majid Khan, M. J. Procter, D. J. Shepherd.
1971	J. D. Bond, C. H. Lloyd, B. W. Luckhurst, G. M. Turner, R. T. Virgin.
1972	G. G. Arnold, B. S. Chandrasekhar, L. R. Gibbs, B. Taylor, Zaheer Abbas.
1973	G. S. Chappell, D. K. Lillee, R. A. L. Massie, J. A. Snow, K. R. Stackpole.
1974	K. D. Boyce, B. E. Congdon, K. W. R. Fletcher, R. C. Fredericks, P. J. Sainsbury.
1975	D. L. Amiss, M. H. Denness, N. Gifford, A. W. Greig, A. M. E. Roberts.
1976	I. M. Chappell, P. G. Lee, R. B. McCosker, D. S. Steele, R. A. Woolmer.
1977	J. M. Brearley, C. G. Greenidge, M. A. Holding, I. V. A. Richards, R. W. Taylor.
1978	I. T. Botham, M. Hendrick, A. Jones, K. S. McEwan, R. G. D. Willis.
1979	D. I. Gower, J. K. Lever, C. M. Old, C. T. Radley, J. N. Shepherd.
1980	J. Garner, S. M. Gavaskar, G. A. Gooch, D. W. Randall, B. C. Rose.
1981	K. J. Hughes, R. D. Jackman, A. J. Lamb, C. E. B. Rice, V. A. P. van der Bijl.
1982	T. M. Alderman, A. R. Border, R. J. Hadlee, Javed Miandad, R. W. Marsh.
1983	Imran Khan, T. E. Jesty, A. I. Kallicharran, Kapil Dev, M. D. Marshall.
1984	M. Amarnath, J. V. Coney, J. E. Emburey, M. W. Gatting, C. L. Smith.
1985	M. D. Crowe, H. A. Gomes, G. W. Humpage, J. Simmons, S. Wettimuny.
1986	P. Bainbridge, R. M. Ellison, C. J. McDermott, N. V. Radford, R. T. Robinson.
1987	J. H. Childs, G. A. Hick, D. B. Vengsarkar, C. A. Walsh, J. J. Whitaker.
1988	J. P. Agnew, N. A. Foster, D. P. Hughes, P. M. Roebuck, Salim Malik.
1989	K. J. Barnett, P. J. L. Dujon, P. A. Neale, F. D. Stephenson, S. R. Waugh.

1990 S. J. Cook, D. M. Jones, R. C. Russell, R. A. Smith, M. A. Taylor.
1991 M. A. Atherton, M. Azharuddin, A. R. Butcher, D. L. Haynes, M. E. Waugh.
1992 C. E. L. Ambrose, P. A. J. DeFreitas, A. A. Donald, R. B. Richardson, Waqar Younis.
1993 N. E. Briers, M. D. Moxon, I. D. K. Salisbury, A. J. Stewart, Wasim Akram.
1994 D. C. Boon, I. A. Healy, M. G. Hughes, S. K. Warne, S. L. Watkin.
1995 B. C. Lara, D. E. Malcolm, T. A. Munton, S. J. Rhodes, K. C. Wessels.
1996 D. G. Cork, P. A. de Silva, A. R. C. Fraser, A. Kumble, D. A. Reeve.
1997 S. T. Jayasuriya, Mushtaq Ahmed, Saeed Anwar, P. V. Simmons, S. R. Tendulkar.
1998 M. T. G. Elliott, S. G. Law, G. D. McGrath, M. P. Maynard, G. P. Thorpe.
1999 I. D. Austin, D. Gough, M. Muralitharan, A. Ranatunga, J. N. Rhodes.
2000 C. L. Cairns, R. Dravid, L. Klusener, T. M. Moody, Saqlain Mushtaq.
Cricketers of the Century D. G. Bradman, G. S. Sobers, J. B. Hobbs, S. K. Warne, I. V. A. Richards.
2001 M. W. Alleyne, M. P. Bicknell, A. R. Caddick, J. L. Langer, D. S. Lehmann.
2002 A. Flower, A. C. Gilchrist, J. N. Gillespie, V. V. S. Laxman, D. R. Martyn.

CRICKETERS OF THE YEAR: AN ANALYSIS

The five players selected to be Cricketers of the Year for 2002 bring the number chosen since selection began in 1889 to 517. They have been chosen from 37 different teams as follows:

Derbyshire	13	Nottinghamshire	25	South Africans	21	Eton College	2
Essex	22	Somerset	17	West Indians	23	Malvern College	1
Glamorgan	10	Surrey	47	New Zealanders	8	Rugby School	1
Gloucestershire	16	Sussex	20	Indians	13	Tonbridge School	1
Hampshire	14	Warwickshire	19	Pakistanis	11	Univ. Coll. School	1
Kent	25	Worcestershire	15	Sri Lankans	4	Uppingham School	1
Lancashire	31	Yorkshire	40	Zimbabweans	1	Winchester College	1
Leicestershire	8	Oxford Univ.	6	Staffordshire	1		
Middlesex	26	Cambridge Univ.	10	Cheltenham College	1		
Northants	13	Australians	66	Cranleigh School	1		

Notes: Schoolboys were chosen in 1918 and 1919 when first-class cricket was suspended due to war. The total of sides comes to 535 because 18 players played regularly for two teams (England excluded) in the year for which they were chosen. John Wisden, listed as a Sussex player, retired 50 years before his posthumous selection.

Types of Players

Of the 517 Cricketers of the Year, 260 are best classified as batsmen, 148 as bowlers, 75 as all-rounders and 34 as wicket-keepers or wicket-keeper/batsmen.

Nationalities

At the time they were chosen, 326 players (63.05 per cent) were qualified to play for England, 77 for Australia, 36 West Indies, 31 South Africa, 14 Pakistan, 14 India, 12 New Zealand, 5 Sri Lanka and 2 Zimbabwe.

Note: Nationalities and teams are not necessarily identical.

Ages

On April 1 in the year of selection

Youngest: 17 years 67 days H. L. Calder, 1918. The youngest first-class cricketer was Mushtaq Mohammad, 19 years 130 days in 1963.

Oldest: 48 years 228 days Lord Hawke, 1909. (This excludes John Wisden, whose portrait appeared 87 years after his birth and 29 years after his death.)

An analysis of post-war Cricketers of the Year may be found in Wisden *1998, page 174.*

Research: Robert Brooke

PART THREE: RECORDS

CRICKET RECORDS

First-class and limited-overs records by PHILIP BAILEY
Test match records by PHILIP BAILEY and GORDON VINCE

All records are amended to the end of the 2001 season in England, including those matches played in Sri Lanka and Zimbabwe after their 2000-01 seasons. These are designated 2001 (SL) and 2001 (Z). The Test between Pakistan and Bangladesh which ended on August 31, 2001, two days before the end of the 2001 (SL) series between Sri Lanka and India, is also included.

Updated Test records can be found on the Wisden website, www.wisden.com.

Unless otherwise stated, all records apply only to first-class cricket. This is considered to have started in 1815, after the Napoleonic War.
* Denotes not out or an unbroken partnership.
(E), (A), (SA), (WI), (NZ), (I), (P), (SL), (Z) or (B) indicates either the nationality of the player, or the country in which the record was made.

FIRST-CLASS RECORDS

BATTING RECORDS

BOWLING RECORDS

ALL-ROUND RECORDS

WICKET-KEEPING RECORDS

FIELDING RECORDS

TEAM RECORDS

TEST RECORDS

BATTING RECORDS

BOWLING RECORDS

ALL-ROUND RECORDS

WICKET-KEEPING RECORDS

FIELDING RECORDS

TEAM RECORDS

PLAYERS

UMPIRES

TEST SERIES

LIMITED-OVERS INTERNATIONAL RECORDS

MISCELLANEOUS

FIRST-CLASS RECORDS

BATTING RECORDS

HIGHEST INDIVIDUAL INNINGS

501*	B. C. Lara	Warwickshire v Durham at Birmingham	1994
499	Hanif Mohammad	Karachi v Bahawalpur at Karachi	1958-59
452*	D. G. Bradman	NSW v Queensland at Sydney	1929-30
443*	B. B. Nimbalkar	Maharashtra v Kathiawar at Poona	1948-49
437	W. H. Ponsford	Victoria v Queensland at Melbourne	1927-28
429	W. H. Ponsford	Victoria v Tasmania at Melbourne	1922-23
428	Aftab Baloch	Sind v Baluchistan at Karachi	1973-74
424	A. C. MacLaren	Lancashire v Somerset at Taunton	1895
405*	G. A. Hick	Worcestershire v Somerset at Taunton	1988
394	Naved Latif	Sargodha v Gujranwala at Gujranwala	2000-01
385	B. Sutcliffe	Otago v Canterbury at Christchurch	1952-53
383	C. W. Gregory	NSW v Queensland at Brisbane	1906-07
377	S. V. Manjrekar	Bombay v Hyderabad at Bombay	1990-91
375	B. C. Lara	West Indies v England at St John's	1993-94
369	D. G. Bradman	South Australia v Tasmania at Adelaide	1935-36
366	N. H. Fairbrother	Lancashire v Surrey at The Oval	1990
366	M. V. Sridhar	Hyderabad v Andhra at Secunderabad	1993-94
365*	C. Hill	South Australia v NSW at Adelaide	1900-01
365*	G. S. Sobers	West Indies v Pakistan at Kingston	1957-58
364	L. Hutton	England v Australia at The Oval	1938
359*	V. M. Merchant	Bombay v Maharashtra at Bombay	1943-44
359	R. B. Simpson	NSW v Queensland at Brisbane	1963-64
357*	R. Abel	Surrey v Somerset at The Oval	1899
357	D. G. Bradman	South Australia v Victoria at Melbourne	1935-36
356	B. A. Richards	South Australia v Western Australia at Perth	1970-71
355*	G. R. Marsh	Western Australia v South Australia at Perth	1989-90
355	B. Sutcliffe	Otago v Auckland at Dunedin	1949-50
353	V. V. S. Laxman	Hyderabad v Karnataka at Bangalore	1999-2000
352	W. H. Ponsford	Victoria v NSW at Melbourne	1926-27
350	Rashid Israr	Habib Bank v National Bank at Lahore	1976-77
345	C. G. Macartney	Australians v Nottinghamshire at Nottingham	1921
344*	G. A. Headley	Jamaica v Lord Tennyson's XI at Kingston	1931-32
344	W. G. Grace	MCC v Kent at Canterbury	1876
343*	P. A. Perrin	Essex v Derbyshire at Chesterfield	1904
341	G. H. Hirst	Yorkshire v Leicestershire at Leicester	1905
340*	D. G. Bradman	NSW v Victoria at Sydney	1928-29
340	S. M. Gavaskar	Bombay v Bengal at Bombay	1981-82
340	S. T. Jayasuriya	Sri Lanka v India at Colombo	1997-98
338*	R. C. Blunt	Otago v Canterbury at Christchurch	1931-32
338	W. W. Read	Surrey v Oxford University at The Oval	1888
337*	Pervez Akhtar	Railways v Dera Ismail Khan at Lahore	1964-65
337*	D. J. Cullinan	Transvaal v Northern Transvaal at Johannesburg	1993-94
337	Hanif Mohammad	Pakistan v West Indies at Bridgetown	1957-58
336*	W. R. Hammond	England v New Zealand at Auckland	1932-33
336	W. H. Ponsford	Victoria v South Australia at Melbourne	1927-28
334*	M. A. Taylor	Australia v Pakistan at Peshawar	1998-99
334	D. G. Bradman	Australia v England at Leeds	1930
333	K. S. Duleepsinhji	Sussex v Northamptonshire at Hove	1930
333	G. A. Gooch	England v India at Lord's	1990
332	W. H. Ashdown	Kent v Essex at Brentwood	1934
331*	J. D. Robertson	Middlesex v Worcestershire at Worcester	1949
329*	M. E. K. Hussey	Northamptonshire v Essex at Northampton	2001
325*	H. L. Hendry	Victoria v New Zealanders at Melbourne	1925-26

325	A. Sandham	England v West Indies at Kingston	1929-30
325	C. L. Badcock	South Australia v Victoria at Adelaide	1935-36
324*	D. M. Jones	Victoria v South Australia at Melbourne	1994-95
324	J. B. Stollmeyer	Trinidad v British Guiana at Port-of-Spain	1946-47
324	Waheed Mirza	Karachi Whites v Quetta at Karachi	1976-77
323	A. L. Wadekar	Bombay v Mysore at Bombay	1966-67
323	D. Gandhi	Bengal v Assam at Gauhati	1998-99
322*	M. B. Loye	Northamptonshire v Glamorgan at Northampton	1998
322	E. Paynter	Lancashire v Sussex at Hove	1937
322	I. V. A. Richards	Somerset v Warwickshire at Taunton	1985
321	W. L. Murdoch	NSW v Victoria at Sydney	1881-82
320	R. Lamba	North Zone v West Zone at Bhilai	1987-88
319	Gul Mahomed	Baroda v Holkar at Baroda	1946-47
318*	W. G. Grace	Gloucestershire v Yorkshire at Cheltenham	1876
317	W. R. Hammond	Gloucestershire v Nottinghamshire at Gloucester	1936
317	K. R. Rutherford	New Zealanders v D. B. Close's XI at Scarborough	1986
316*	J. B. Hobbs	Surrey v Middlesex at Lord's	1926
316*	V. S. Hazare	Maharashtra v Baroda at Poona	1939-40
316	R. H. Moore	Hampshire v Warwickshire at Bournemouth	1937
315*	T. W. Hayward	Surrey v Lancashire at The Oval	1898
315*	P. Holmes	Yorkshire v Middlesex at Lord's	1925
315*	A. F. Kippax	NSW v Queensland at Sydney	1927-28
315	M. A. Wagh	Warwickshire v Middlesex at Lord's	2001
314*	C. L. Walcott	Barbados v Trinidad at Port-of-Spain	1945-46
314*	Wasim Jaffer	Mumbai v Saurashtra at Rajkot	1996-97
313*	S. J. Cook	Somerset v Glamorgan at Cardiff	1990
313	H. Sutcliffe	Yorkshire v Essex at Leyton	1932
313	W. V. Raman‡	Tamil Nadu v Goa at Panjim	1988-89
312*	W. W. Keeton	Nottinghamshire v Middlesex at The Oval†	1939
312*	J. M. Brearley	MCC Under-25 v North Zone at Peshawar	1966-67
312	R. Lamba	Delhi v Himachal Pradesh at Delhi	1994-95
312	J. E. R. Gallian	Lancashire v Derbyshire at Manchester	1996
311*	G. M. Turner	Worcestershire v Warwickshire at Worcester	1982
311	J. T. Brown	Yorkshire v Sussex at Sheffield	1897
311	R. B. Simpson	Australia v England at Manchester	1964
311	Javed Miandad	Karachi Whites v National Bank at Karachi	1974-75
310*	J. H. Edrich	England v New Zealand at Leeds	1965
310	H. Gimblett	Somerset v Sussex at Eastbourne	1948
309*	S. P. James	Glamorgan v Sussex at Colwyn Bay	2000
309	V. S. Hazare	The Rest v Hindus at Bombay	1943-44
308*	F. M. M. Worrell	Barbados v Trinidad at Bridgetown	1943-44
308*	D. Mongia	Punjab v Jammu and Kashmir at Jullundur	2000-01
307*	T. N. Lazard	Boland v W. Province at Worcester, Cape Province	1993-94
307	M. C. Cowdrey	MCC v South Australia at Adelaide	1962-63
307	R. M. Cowper	Australia v England at Melbourne	1965-66
306*	A. Ducat	Surrey v Oxford University at The Oval	1919
306*	E. A. B. Rowan	Transvaal v Natal at Johannesburg	1939-40
306*	D. W. Hookes	South Australia v Tasmania at Adelaide	1986-87
306	M. H. Richardson	New Zealanders v Zimbabwe A at Kwekwe	2000-01
305*	F. E. Woolley	MCC v Tasmania at Hobart	1911-12
305*	F. R. Foster	Warwickshire v Worcestershire at Dudley	1914
305*	W. H. Ashdown	Kent v Derbyshire at Dover	1935
305*	P. Dharmani	Punjab v Jammu and Kashmir at Ludhiana	1999-2000
304*	A. W. Nourse	Natal v Transvaal at Johannesburg	1919-20
304*	P. H. Tarilton	Barbados v Trinidad at Bridgetown	1919-20
304*	E. D. Weekes	West Indians v Cambridge University at Cambridge	1950
304	R. M. Poore	Hampshire v Somerset at Taunton	1899
304	D. G. Bradman	Australia v England at Leeds	1934
303*	W. W. Armstrong	Australians v Somerset at Bath	1905
303*	Mushtaq Mohammad	Karachi Blues v Karachi University at Karachi	1967-68
303*	Abdul Azeem	Hyderabad v Tamil Nadu at Hyderabad	1986-87

303*	S. Chanderpaul	Guyana v Jamaica at Kingston	1995-96
303*	G. A. Hick	Worcestershire v Hampshire at Southampton	1997
303*	D. J. Sales	Northamptonshire v Essex at Northampton	1999
302*	P. Holmes	Yorkshire v Hampshire at Portsmouth	1920
302*	W. R. Hammond	Gloucestershire v Glamorgan at Bristol	1934
302*	Arjan Kripal Singh‡	Tamil Nadu v Goa at Panjim	1988-89
302	W. R. Hammond	Gloucestershire v Glamorgan at Newport	1939
302	L. G. Rowe	West Indies v England at Bridgetown	1973-74
301*	E. H. Hendren	Middlesex v Worcestershire at Dudley	1933
301*	V. V. S. Laxman	Hyderabad v Bihar at Jamshedpur	1997-98
301	W. G. Grace	Gloucestershire v Sussex at Bristol	1896
300*	V. T. Trumper	Australians v Sussex at Hove	1899
300*	F. B. Watson	Lancashire v Surrey at Manchester	1928
300*	Imtiaz Ahmed	PM's XI v Commonwealth XI at Bombay	1950-51
300*	G. K. Khoda	Central Zone v South Zone at Panaji	2000-01
300	J. T. Brown	Yorkshire v Derbyshire at Chesterfield	1898
300	D. C. S. Compton	MCC v N. E. Transvaal at Benoni	1948-49
300	R. Subba Row	Northamptonshire v Surrey at The Oval	1958
300	Ramiz Raja	Allied Bank v Habib Bank at Lahore	1994-95

† *Played at The Oval because Lord's was required for Eton v Harrow.*

‡ *In the same innings, a unique occurrence.*

DOUBLE-HUNDRED ON DEBUT

227	T. Marsden	Sheffield & Leicester v Nottingham at Sheffield	1826
207	N. F. Callaway†	New South Wales v Queensland at Sydney	1914-15
240	W. F. E. Marx	Transvaal v Griqualand West at Johannesburg	1920-21
200*	A. Maynard	Trinidad v MCC at Port-of-Spain	1934-35
232*	S. J. E. Loxton	Victoria v Queensland at Melbourne	1946-47
215*	G. H. G. Doggart	Cambridge University v Lancashire at Cambridge	1948
202	J. Hallebone	Victoria v Tasmania at Melbourne	1951-52
230	G. R. Viswanath	Mysore v Andhra at Vijayawada	1967-68
260	A. A. Muzumdar	Bombay v Haryana at Faridabad	1993-94
209*	A. Pandey	Madhya Pradesh v Uttar Pradesh at Bhilai	1995-96
210*	D. J. Sales	Northants v Worcestershire at Kidderminster	1996
200*	M. J. Powell	Glamorgan v Oxford University at Oxford	1997

† *In his only first-class innings. He was killed in action in France in 1917.*

TWO SEPARATE HUNDREDS ON DEBUT

148 and 111	A. R. Morris	New South Wales v Queensland at Sydney	1940-41
152 and 102*	N. J. Contractor	Gujarat v Baroda at Baroda	1952-53
132* and 110	Aamer Malik	Lahore A v Railways at Lahore	1979-80

HUNDRED ON DEBUT IN ENGLAND

This does not include players who have previously appeared in first-class cricket outside the British Isles. The following have achieved the feat since 1990. For fuller lists please see earlier *Wisdens*.

116*	J. J. B. Lewis	Essex v Surrey at The Oval	1990
117	J. D. Glendenen	Durham v Oxford University at Oxford	1992
109	J. R. Wileman	Nottinghamshire v Cambridge University at Nottingham	1992
123	A. J. Hollioake†	Surrey v Derbyshire at Ilkeston	1993
101	E. T. Smith	Cambridge University v Glamorgan at Cambridge	1996
110	S. D. Peters	Essex v Cambridge University at Cambridge	1996
210*	D. J. Sales†	Northamptonshire v Worcestershire at Kidderminster	1996
200*	M. J. Powell	Glamorgan v Oxford University at Oxford	1997
104	C. G. Taylor	Gloucestershire v Middlesex at Lord's	2000

† *In his second innings.*

TWO DOUBLE-HUNDREDS IN A MATCH

A. E. Fagg	244	202*	Kent v Essex at Colchester	1938

TRIPLE-HUNDRED AND HUNDRED IN A MATCH

G. A. Gooch	333	123	England v India at Lord's	1990

DOUBLE-HUNDRED AND HUNDRED IN A MATCH

C. B. Fry	125	229	Sussex v Surrey at Hove	1900
W. W. Armstrong	157*	245	Victoria v South Australia at Melbourne	1920-21
H. T. W. Hardinge	207	102*	Kent v Surrey at Blackheath	1921
C. P. Mead	113	224	Hampshire v Sussex at Horsham	1921
K. S. Duleepsinhji	115	246	Sussex v Kent at Hastings	1929
D. G. Bradman	124	225	Woodfull's XI v Ryder's XI at Sydney	1929-30
B. Sutcliffe	243	100*	New Zealanders v Essex at Southend	1949
M. R. Hallam	210*	157	Leicestershire v Glamorgan at Leicester	1959
M. R. Hallam	203*	143*	Leicestershire v Sussex at Worthing	1961
Hanumant Singh	109	213*	Rajasthan v Bombay at Bombay	1966-67
Salah-ud-Din	256	102*	Karachi v East Pakistan at Karachi	1968-69
K. D. Walters	242	103	Australia v West Indies at Sydney	1968-69
S. M. Gavaskar	124	220	India v West Indies at Port-of-Spain	1970-71
L. G. Rowe	214	100*	West Indies v New Zealand at Kingston	1971-72
G. S. Chappell	247*	133	Australia v New Zealand at Wellington	1973-74
L. Baichan	216*	102	Berbice v Demerara at Georgetown	1973-74
Zaheer Abbas	216*	156*	Gloucestershire v Surrey at The Oval	1976
Zaheer Abbas	230*	104*	Gloucestershire v Kent at Canterbury	1976
Zaheer Abbas	205*	108*	Gloucestershire v Sussex at Cheltenham	1977
Saadat Ali	141	222	Income Tax v Multan at Multan	1977-78
Talat Ali	214*	104	PIA v Punjab at Lahore	1978-79
Shafiq Ahmad	129	217*	National Bank v MCB at Karachi	1978-79
D. W. Randall	209	146	Nottinghamshire v Middlesex at Nottingham	1979
Zaheer Abbas	215*	150*	Gloucestershire v Somerset at Bath	1981
Qasim Omar	210*	110	MCB v Lahore at Lahore	1982-83
A. I. Kallicharran	200*	117*	Warwickshire v Northants at Birmingham	1984
Rizwan-uz-Zaman	139	217*	PIA v PACO at Lahore	1989-90
G. A. Hick	252*	100*	Worcestershire v Glamorgan at Abergavenny	1990
N. R. Taylor	204	142	Kent v Surrey at Canterbury	1990
N. R. Taylor	111	203*	Kent v Sussex at Hove	1991
W. V. Raman	226	120	Tamil Nadu v Haryana at Faridabad	1991-92
A. J. Lamb	209	107	Northants v Warwicks at Northampton	1992
G. A. Gooch	101	205	Essex v Worcestershire at Worcester	1994
P. A. de Silva	255	116	Kent v Derbyshire at Maidstone	1995
M. C. Mendis	111	200*	Colts CC v Singha SC at Colombo	1995-96
A. M. Bacher	210	112*	Transvaal v Griqualand West at Kimberley	1996-97
H. H. Gibbs	200*	171	South Africans v India A at Nagpur	1996-97
M. L. Hayden	235*	119	Hampshire v Warwickshire at Southampton	1997
G. S. Blewett	169*	213*	Australian XI v England XI at Hobart	1998-99
A. Jadeja	136	202*	Haryana v Saurashtra at Rajkot	1998-99
J. Cox	216	129*	Somerset v Hampshire at Southampton	1999
Mohammad Ramzan	205	102*	Faisalabad v Sargodha at Faisalabad	2000-01
M. W. Goodwin	115	203*	Sussex v Nottinghamshire at Nottingham	2001
D. P. Fulton	208*	104*	Kent v Somerset at Canterbury	2001

TWO SEPARATE HUNDREDS IN A MATCH

Eight times: Zaheer Abbas.
Seven times: W. R. Hammond.
Six times: J. B. Hobbs, G. M. Turner.
Five times: C. B. Fry, G. A. Gooch.
Four times: D. G. Bradman, G. S. Chappell, J. Cox, J. H. Edrich, L. B. Fishlock, T. W. Graveney, C. G. Greenidge, H. T. W. Hardinge, E. H. Hendren, G. A. Hick, Javed Miandad, G. L. Jessop, H. Morris, M. H. Parmar, P. A. Perrin, R. T. Ponting, M. R. Ramprakash, B. Sutcliffe, H. Sutcliffe.
Three times: Agha Zahid, L. E. G. Ames, Basit Ali, G. Boycott, I. M. Chappell, D. C. S. Compton, S. J. Cook, M. C. Cowdrey, D. Denton, P. A. de Silva, K. S. Duleepsinhji, R. E. Foster, R. C. Fredericks, S. M. Gavaskar, W. G. Grace, G. Gunn, M. R. Hallam, Hanif Mohammad, M. J. Harris, M. L. Hayden, T. W. Hayward, V. S. Hazare, D. W. Hookes, L. Hutton, A. Jones, D. M. Jones, P. N. Kirsten, R. B. McCosker, P. B. H. May, C. P. Mead, T. M. Moody, Rizwan-uz-Zaman, R. T. Robinson, A. C. Russell, Sadiq Mohammad, J. T. Tyldesley, K. C. Wessels.

Notes: W. Lambert scored 107 and 157 for Sussex v Epsom at Lord's in 1817, and it was not until W. G. Grace made 130 and 102* for South of the Thames v North of the Thames at Canterbury in 1868 that the feat was repeated.

C. J. B. Wood, 107* and 117* for Leicestershire v Yorkshire at Bradford in 1911, and S. J. Cook, 120* and 131* for Somerset v Nottinghamshire at Nottingham in 1989, are alone in carrying their bats and scoring hundreds in each innings.

FOUR HUNDREDS OR MORE IN SUCCESSION

Six in succession: D. G. Bradman 1938-39; C. B. Fry 1901; M. J. Procter 1970-71.
Five in succession: B. C. Lara 1993-94/1994; E. D. Weekes 1955-56.
Four in succession: C. W. J. Athey 1987; M. Azharuddin 1984-85; M. G. Bevan 1990-91; G. S. Blewett 1998-99; A. R. Border 1985; D. G. Bradman 1931-32, 1948/1948-49; D. C. S. Compton 1946-47; N. J. Contractor 1957-58; S. J. Cook 1989; K. S. Duleepsinhji 1931; C. B. Fry 1911; C. G. Greenidge 1986; W. R. Hammond 1936-37, 1945/1946; H. T. W. Hardinge 1913; T. W. Hayward 1906; G. A. Hick 1998; J. B. Hobbs 1920, 1925; D. W. Hookes 1976-77; Ijaz Ahmed, jun. 1994-95; R. S. Kaluwitharana 1996-97; P. N. Kirsten 1976-77; J. G. Langridge 1949; C. G. Macartney 1921; K. S. McEwan 1977; P. B. H. May 1956-57; V. M. Merchant 1941-42; A. Mitchell 1933; Nawab of Pataudi sen. 1931; Rizwan-uz-Zaman 1989-90; L. G. Rowe 1971-72; Pankaj Roy 1962-63; Sadiq Mohammad 1976; Saeed Ahmed 1961-62; M. V. Sridhar 1990-91/1991-92; H. Sutcliffe 1931, 1939; S. R. Tendulkar 1994-95; E. Tyldesley 1926; W. W. Whysall 1930; F. E. Woolley 1929; Younis Khan 1999-2000; Zaheer Abbas 1970-71, 1982-83.

Notes: T. W. Hayward (Surrey v Nottinghamshire and Leicestershire) and D. W. Hookes (South Australia v Queensland and New South Wales) are the only players listed above to score two hundreds in two successive matches. Hayward scored his in six days, June 4-9, 1906.

The most fifties in consecutive innings is ten – by E. Tyldesley in 1926, by D. G. Bradman in the 1947-48 and 1948 seasons and by R. S. Kaluwitharana in 1994-95.

MOST HUNDREDS IN A SEASON

Eighteen: D. C. S. Compton 1947.
Sixteen: J. B. Hobbs 1925.
Fifteen: W. R. Hammond 1938.
Fourteen: H. Sutcliffe 1932.
Thirteen: G. Boycott 1971, D. G. Bradman 1938, C. B. Fry 1901, W. R. Hammond 1933 and 1937, T. W. Hayward 1906, E. H. Hendren 1923, 1927 and 1928, C. P. Mead 1928, H. Sutcliffe 1928 and 1931.

Since 1969 (excluding G. Boycott – above)

Twelve: G. A. Gooch 1990.
Eleven: S. J. Cook 1991, Zaheer Abbas 1976.
Ten: G. A. Hick 1988, H. Morris 1990, M. R. Ramprakash 1995, G. M. Turner 1970, Zaheer Abbas 1981.

Note: The most achieved outside England is eight by D. G. Bradman in Australia (1947-48), D. C. S. Compton (1948-49), R. N. Harvey and A. R. Morris (both 1949-50) in South Africa, M. D. Crowe in New Zealand (1986-87), Asif Mujtaba in Pakistan (1995-96) and V. V. S. Laxman in India (1999-2000).

MOST DOUBLE-HUNDREDS IN A SEASON

Six: D. G. Bradman 1930.
Five: K. S. Ranjitsinhji 1900; E. D. Weekes 1950.
Four: Arun Lal 1986-87; C. B. Fry 1901; W. R. Hammond 1933, 1934; E. H. Hendren 1929-30; V. M. Merchant 1944-45; G. M. Turner 1971-72.
Three: L. E. G. Ames 1933; Arshad Pervez 1977-78; D. G. Bradman 1930-31, 1931-32, 1934, 1935-36, 1936-37, 1938, 1939-40; W. J. Edrich 1947; C. B. Fry 1903, 1904; M. W. Gatting 1994; G. A. Gooch 1994; W. R. Hammond 1928, 1928-29, 1932-33, 1938; J. Hardstaff jun. 1937, 1947; V. S. Hazare 1943-44; E. H. Hendren 1925; J. B. Hobbs 1914, 1926; M. E. K. Hussey 2001; L. Hutton 1949; D. M. Jones 1991-92; A. I. Kallicharran 1982; V. G. Kambli 1992-93; P. N. Kirsten 1980; R. S. Modi 1944-45; D. Mongia 2000-01; Nawab of Pataudi sen. 1933; W. H. Ponsford 1927-28, 1934; W. V. Raman 1988-89; M. R. Ramprakash 1995; K. S. Ranjitsinhji 1901; I. V. A. Richards 1977; R. B. Simpson 1963-64; P. R. Umrigar 1952, 1959; F. B. Watson 1928.

MOST HUNDREDS IN A CAREER

(35 or more)

		Total	Total Inns	100th 100 Season	100th 100 Inns	400s	300s	200s
1	J. B. Hobbs	197	1,315	1923	821	0	1	15
2	E. H. Hendren	170	1,300	1928-29	740	0	1	21
3	W. R. Hammond	167	1,005	1935	679	0	4	32
4	C. P. Mead	153	1,340	1927	892	0	0	13
5	G. Boycott	151	1,014	1977	645	0	0	10
6	H. Sutcliffe	149	1,088	1932	700	0	1	16
7	F. E. Woolley	145	1,532	1929	1,031	0	1	8
8	L. Hutton	129	814	1951	619	0	1	10
9	G. A. Gooch	128	990	1992-93	820	0	1	12
10	W. G. Grace	126	1,493	1895	1,113	0	3	10
11	D. C. S. Compton	123	839	1952	552	0	1	8
12	T. W. Graveney	122	1,223	1964	940	0	0	7
13	D. G. Bradman	117	338	1947-48	295	1	5	31
	G. A. Hick	**117**	**695**	**1998**	**574**	**1**	**1**	**11**
15	I. V. A. Richards	114	796	1988-89	658	0	1	9
16	Zaheer Abbas	108	768	1982-83	658	0	0	10
17	A. Sandham	107	1,000	1935	871	0	1	10
	M. C. Cowdrey	107	1,130	1973	1,035	0	1	2
19	T. W. Hayward	104	1,138	1913	1,076	0	1	7
20	G. M. Turner	103	792	1982	779	0	1	9
	J. H. Edrich	103	979	1977	945	0	1	3
22	L. E. G. Ames	102	951	1950	915	0	0	9
	E. Tyldesley	102	961	1934	919	0	0	7
	D. L. Amiss	102	1,139	1986	1,081	0	0	3

E. H. Hendren, D. G. Bradman and I. V. A. Richards scored their 100th hundreds in Australia; G. A. Gooch scored his in India. His record includes his century in South Africa in 1981-82, which is no longer accepted by ICC. Zaheer Abbas scored his 100th in Pakistan. Zaheer Abbas and G. Boycott did so in Test matches.

Most double-hundreds scored by batsmen not included in the above list:

Sixteen: C. B. Fry. **Fourteen:** C. G. Greenidge, K. S. Ranjitsinhji. **Thirteen:** W. H. Ponsford (including two 400s and two 300s), J. T. Tyldesley. **Twelve:** P. Holmes, Javed Miandad, R. B. Simpson. **Eleven:** J. W. Hearne, V. M. Merchant. **Ten:** S. M. Gavaskar, J. Hardstaff, jun., V. S. Hazare, A. Shrewsbury, R. T. Simpson.

J. W. Hearne 96
C. B. Fry 94
M. W. Gatting 94
C. G. Greenidge 92
A. J. Lamb 89
A. I. Kallicharran 87
W. J. Edrich 86
G. S. Sobers 86
J. T. Tyldesley 86
P. B. H. May 85
R. E. S. Wyatt 85
J. Hardstaff, jun. 83
R. B. Kanhai 83
S. M. Gavaskar 81
Javed Miandad 80
M. Leyland 80
B. A. Richards 80
C. H. Lloyd 79
M. E. Waugh 78
K. F. Barrington 76
J. G. Langridge 76
C. Washbrook 76
H. T. W. Hardinge 75
R. Abel 74
G. S. Chappell 74
D. Kenyon 74
K. S. McEwan 74
Majid Khan 73
Mushtaq Mohammad 72
J. O'Connor 72
W. G. Quaife 72
K. S. Ranjitsinhji 72
D. Brookes 71
M. D. Crowe 71
A. C. Russell 71
A. R. Border 70
D. Denton 69
M. J. K. Smith 69
D. C. Boon 68
R. E. Marshall 68
R. N. Harvey 67
P. Holmes 67
J. D. Robertson 67
P. A. Perrin 66
S. R. Waugh 66
K. C. Wessels 66
S. J. Cook 64
T. M. Moody 64
R. G. Pollock 64
R. T. Simpson 64
K. W. R. Fletcher 63
R. T. Robinson 63
G. Gunn 62
D. L. Haynes 61
V. S. Hazare 60
G. H. Hirst 60
R. B. Simpson 60
P. F. Warner 60
I. M. Chappell 59
A. L. Hassett 59
W. Larkins 59
A. Shrewsbury 59
R. A. Smith 59
J. G. Wright 59
K. J. Barnett 58
A. E. Fagg 58
P. H. Parfitt 58
W. Rhodes 58
P. N. Kirsten 57
L. B. Fishlock 56
A. Jones 56
C. A. Milton 56
C. W. J. Athey 55
C. Hallows 55
Hanif Mohammad 55
D. M. Jones 55
M. R. Ramprakash 55
D. B. Vengsarkar 55
W. Watson 55
M. A. Atherton 54
M. Azharuddin 54
C. L. Hooper 54
D. J. Insole 54
W. W. Keeton 54
S. G. Law 54
D. S. Lehmann 54
W. Bardsley 53
B. F. Davison 53
A. E. Dipper 53
D. I. Gower 53
G. L. Jessop 53
H. Morris 53
James Seymour 53
Shafiq Ahmad 53
E. H. Bowley 52
D. B. Close 52
A. Ducat 52
J. E. Morris 52
D. W. Randall 52
E. R. Dexter 51
J. M. Parks 51
W. W. Whysall 51
B. C. Broad 50
G. Cox, jun. 50
H. E. Dollery 50
K. S. Duleepsinhji 50
H. Gimblett 50
W. M. Lawry 50
Sadiq Mohammad 50
F. B. Watson 50
M. G. Bevan 49
J. L. Langer 49
C. G. Macartney 49
M. J. Stewart 49
K. G. Suttle 49
P. R. Umrigar 49
W. M. Woodfull 49
C. J. Barnett 48
M. R. Benson 48
W. Gunn 48
M. L. Hayden 48
E. G. Hayes 48
B. W. Luckhurst 48
M. P. Maynard 48
M. J. Procter 48
C. E. B. Rice 48
C. J. Tavaré 48
S. R. Tendulkar 48
R. J. Bailey 47
A. C. MacLaren 47
P. W. G. Parker 47
W. H. Ponsford 47
C. L. Smith 47
A. J. Stewart 47
A. R. Butcher 46
N. H. Fairbrother 46
J. Iddon 46
A. R. Morris 46
C. T. Radley 46
A. P. Wells 46
Younis Ahmed 46
W. W. Armstrong 45
Asif Iqbal 45
L. G. Berry 45
J. M. Brearley 45
A. W. Carr 45
C. Hill 45
M. D. Moxon 45
N. C. O'Neill 45
E. Paynter 45
Rev. D. S. Sheppard 45
N. R. Taylor 45
K. D. Walters 45
H. H. Gibbons 44
N. Hussain 44
V. M. Merchant 44
A. Mitchell 44
P. E. Richardson 44
B. Sutcliffe 44
G. R. Viswanath 44
P. Willey 44
E. J. Barlow 43
T. S. Curtis 43
B. L. D'Oliveira 43
J. H. Hampshire 43
S. P. James 43
A. F. Kippax 43
J. W. H. Makepeace 43
Rizwan-uz-Zaman 43
Salim Malik 43
Asif Mujtaba 42
P. D. Bowler 42
James Langridge 42
B. C. Lara 42
Mudassar Nazar 42
H. W. Parks 42
T. F. Shepherd 42
V. T. Trumper 42
J. Cox 41
M. J. Harris 41
G. D. Mendis 41
K. R. Miller 41
A. D. Nourse 41
J. H. Parks 41
R. M. Prideaux 41
G. Pullar 41

W. E. Russell	41	P. J. Burge	38	**R. B. Richardson**	**37**
M. A. Taylor	41	J. F. Crapp	38	**Shoaib Mohammad**	**37**
J. P. Crawley	**40**	**D. J. Cullinan**	**38**	H. S. Squires	37
P. A. de Silva	**40**	D. Lloyd	38	R. T. Virgin	37
R. C. Fredericks	40	V. L. Manjrekar	38	C. J. B. Wood	37
J. Gunn	40	A. W. Nourse	38	N. F. Armstrong	36
P. Johnson	**40**	N. Oldfield	38	G. Fowler	36
M. J. Smith	40	Rev. J. H. Parsons	38	M. C. J. Nicholas	36
G. P. Thorpe	**40**	W. W. Read	38	E. Oldroyd	36
C. L. Walcott	40	**Ajay Sharma**	**38**	W. Place	36
D. M. Young	40	J. Sharp	38	A. L. Wadekar	36
Arshad Pervez	39	V. P. Terry	38	E. D. Weekes	36
W. H. Ashdown	39	L. J. Todd	38	**G. S. Blewett**	**35**
J. B. Bolus	39	J. J. Whitaker	38	C. S. Dempster	35
W. A. Brown	39	J. Arnold	37	**Inzamam-ul-Haq**	**35**
R. J. Gregory	39	**D. J. Bicknell**	**37**	D. R. Jardine	35
M. A. Lynch	39	G. Brown	37	T. E. Jesty	35
W. R. D. Payton	39	G. Cook	37	K. R. Rutherford	35
J. R. Reid	39	G. M. Emmett	37	**Sajid Ali**	**35**
F. M. M. Worrell	39	H. W. Lee	37	J. D. Siddons	35
I. T. Botham	38	M. A. Noble	37	B. H. Valentine	35
F. L. Bowley	38	B. P. Patel	37	G. M. Wood	35

Bold type denotes those who played in 2000-01 and 2001 seasons.

MOST RUNS IN A SEASON

	Season	*I*	*NO*	*R*	*HS*	*100s*	*Avge*
D. C. S. Compton	1947	50	8	3,816	246	18	90.85
W. J. Edrich	1947	52	8	3,539	267*	12	80.43
T. W. Hayward	1906	61	8	3,518	219	13	66.37
L. Hutton	1949	56	6	3,429	269*	12	68.58
F. E. Woolley	1928	59	4	3,352	198	12	60.94
H. Sutcliffe	1932	52	7	3,336	313	14	74.13
W. R. Hammond	1933	54	5	3,323	264	13	67.81
E. H. Hendren	1928	54	7	3,311	209*	13	70.44
R. Abel	1901	68	8	3,309	247	7	55.15

Notes: 3,000 in a season has been surpassed on 19 other occasions (a full list can be found in *Wisden* 1999 and earlier editions). W. R. Hammond, E. H. Hendren and H. Sutcliffe are the only players to achieve the feat three times. M. J. K. Smith (3,245 in 1959) and W. E. Alley (3,019 in 1961) are the only players except those listed above to have reached 3,000 since World War II.

2,000 RUNS IN A SEASON

(Since reduction of Championship matches in 1969)

Five times: G. A. Gooch 2,746 (1990), 2,559 (1984), 2,324 (1988), 2,208 (1985), 2,023 (1993).
Three times: D. L. Amiss 2,239 (1984), 2,110 (1976), 2,030 (1978); S. J. Cook 2,755† (1991), 2,608 (1990), 2,241 (1989); M. W. Gatting 2,257 (1984), 2,057 (1991), 2,000 (1992); G. A. Hick 2,713 (1988), 2,347 (1990), 2,004 (1986); G. M. Turner 2,416 (1973), 2,379 (1970), 2,101 (1981).
Twice: G. Boycott 2,503 (1971), 2,051 (1970); J. H. Edrich 2,238 (1969), 2,031 (1971); A. I. Kallicharran 2,301 (1984), 2,120 (1982); Zaheer Abbas 2,554 (1976), 2,306 (1981).
Once: M. Azharuddin 2,016 (1991); J. B. Bolus 2,143 (1970); P. D. Bowler 2,044 (1992); B. C. Broad 2,226 (1990); A. R. Butcher 2,116 (1990); C. G. Greenidge 2,035 (1986); M. J. Harris 2,238 (1971); D. L. Haynes 2,346 (1990); M. E. K. Hussey 2,055 (2001); Javed Miandad 2,083 (1981); A. J. Lamb 2,049 (1981); B. C. Lara 2,066 (1994); K. S. McEwan 2,176 (1983); Majid Khan 2,074 (1972); A. A. Metcalfe 2,047 (1990); H. Morris 2,276 (1990); M. R. Ramprakash 2,258 (1995); D. W. Randall 2,151 (1985); I. V. A. Richards 2,161 (1977); R. T. Robinson 2,032 (1984); M. A. Roseberry 2,044 (1992); C. L. Smith 2,000 (1985); R. T. Virgin 2,223 (1970); D. M. Ward 2,072 (1990); M. E. Waugh 2,072 (1990).

Notes: W. G. Grace scored 2,739 runs in 1871 – the first batsman to reach 2,000 runs in a season. He made ten hundreds and twice exceeded 200, with an average of 78.25 in all first-class matches.

† *Highest since the reduction of Championship matches in 1969.*

1,000 RUNS IN A SEASON MOST TIMES

(Includes overseas tours and seasons)

28 times: W. G. Grace 2,000 (6); F. E. Woolley 3,000 (1), 2,000 (12).
27 times: M. C. Cowdrey 2,000 (2); C. P. Mead 3,000 (2), 2,000 (9).
26 times: G. Boycott 2,000 (3); J. B. Hobbs 3,000 (1), 2,000 (16).
25 times: E. H. Hendren 3,000 (3), 2,000 (12).
24 times: D. L. Amiss 2,000 (3); W. G. Quaife 2,000 (1); H. Sutcliffe 3,000 (3), 2,000 (12).
23 times: A. Jones.
22 times: T. W. Graveney 2,000 (7); W. R. Hammond 3,000 (3), 2,000 (9).
21 times: D. Denton 2,000 (5); J. H. Edrich 2,000 (6); G. A. Gooch 2,000 (5); W. Rhodes 2,000 (2).
20 times: D. B. Close; K. W. R. Fletcher; M. W. Gatting 2,000 (3); G. Gunn; T. W. Hayward 3,000 (2), 2,000 (8); James Langridge 2,000 (1); J. M. Parks 2,000 (3); A. Sandham 2,000 (8); M. J. K. Smith 3,000 (1), 2,000 (5); C. Washbrook 2,000 (2).
19 times: J. W. Hearne 2,000 (4); G. H. Hirst 2,000 (3); D. Kenyon 2,000 (7); E. Tyldesley 3,000 (1), 2,000 (5); J. T. Tyldesley 3,000 (1), 2,000 (4).
18 times: L. G. Berry 2,000 (1); H. T. W. Hardinge 2,000 (5); R. E. Marshall 2,000 (6); P. A. Perrin; G. M. Turner 2,000 (3); R. E. S. Wyatt 2,000 (5).
17 times: L. E. G. Ames 3,000 (1), 2,000 (5); T. E. Bailey 2,000 (1); D. Brookes 2,000 (6); D. C. S. Compton 3,000 (1), 2,000 (5); C. G. Greenidge 2,000 (1); G. A. Hick 2,000 (3); L. Hutton 3,000 (1), 2,000 (8); J. G. Langridge 2,000 (11); M. Leyland 2,000 (3); I. V. A. Richards 2,000 (1); K. G. Suttle 2,000 (1); Zaheer Abbas 2,000 (2).
16 times: K. J. Barnett; D. G. Bradman 2,000 (4); D. E. Davies 2,000 (1); E. G. Hayes 2,000 (2); C. A. Milton 2,000 (1); J. O'Connor 2,000 (4); C. T. Radley; James Seymour 2,000 (1); C. J. Tavaré.
15 times: G. Barker; K. F. Barrington 2,000 (3); E. H. Bowley 2,000 (4); M. H. Denness; A. E. Dipper 2,000 (5); H. E. Dollery 2,000 (2); W. J. Edrich 3,000 (1), 2,000 (8); J. H. Hampshire; P. Holmes 2,000 (7); Mushtaq Mohammad; R. B. Nicholls 2,000 (1); P. H. Parfitt 2,000 (3); W. G. A. Parkhouse 2,000 (1); B. A. Richards 2,000 (1); J. D. Robertson 2,000 (9); G. S. Sobers; M. J. Stewart 2,000 (1).

Notes: F. E. Woolley reached 1,000 runs in 28 consecutive seasons (1907-1938), C. P. Mead in 27 (1906-1936).

Outside England, 1,000 runs in a season has been reached most times by D. G. Bradman (in 12 seasons in Australia).

Three batsmen have scored 1,000 runs in a season in each of four different countries: G. S. Sobers in West Indies, England, India and Australia; M. C. Cowdrey and G. Boycott in England, South Africa, West Indies and Australia.

HIGHEST AGGREGATES OUTSIDE ENGLAND

	Season	*I*	*NO*	*R*	*HS*	*100s*	*Avge*
In Australia							
D. G. Bradman	1928-29	24	6	1,690	340*	7	93.88
In South Africa							
J. R. Reid	1961-62	30	2	1,915	203	7	68.39
In West Indies							
E. H. Hendren	1929-30	18	5	1,765	254*	6	135.76
In New Zealand							
M. D. Crowe	1986-87	21	3	1,676	175*	8	93.11
In India							
C. G. Borde	1964-65	28	3	1,604	168	6	64.16
In Pakistan							
Saadat Ali	1983-84	27	1	1,649	208	4	63.42

	Season	I	NO	R	HS	100s	Avge
In Sri Lanka							
R. P. Arnold	1995-96	24	3	1,475	217*	5	70.23
In Zimbabwe							
G. W. Flower	1994-95	20	3	983	201*	4	57.82

Note: In more than one country, the following aggregates of over 2,000 runs have been recorded:

	Season	I	NO	R	HS	100s	Avge
M. Amarnath (P/I/WI)	1982-83	34	6	2,234	207	9	79.78
J. R. Reid (SA/A/NZ)	1961-62	40	2	2,188	203	7	57.57
S. M. Gavaskar (I/P)	1978-79	30	6	2,121	205	10	88.37
R. B. Simpson (I/P/A/WI)	1964-65	34	4	2,063	201	8	68.76
M. H. Richardson (Z/SA/NZ)	2000-01	34	3	2,030	306	4	65.48

LEADING BATSMEN IN AN ENGLISH SEASON

(Qualification: 8 completed innings)

Season	Leading scorer	Runs	Avge	Top of averages	Runs	Avge
1946	D. C. S. Compton	2,403	61.61	W. R. Hammond	1,783	84.90
1947	D. C. S. Compton	3,816	90.85	D. C. S. Compton	3,816	90.85
1948	L. Hutton	2,654	64.73	D. G. Bradman	2,428	89.92
1949	L. Hutton	3,429	68.58	J. Hardstaff	2,251	72.61
1950	R. T. Simpson	2,576	62.82	E. Weekes	2,310	79.65
1951	J. D. Robertson	2,917	56.09	P. B. H. May	2,339	68.79
1952	L. Hutton	2,567	61.11	D. S. Sheppard	2,262	64.62
1953	W. J. Edrich	2,557	47.35	R. N. Harvey	2,040	65.80
1954	D. Kenyon	2,636	51.68	D. C. S. Compton	1,524	58.61
1955	D. J. Insole	2,427	42.57	D. J. McGlew	1,871	58.46
1956	T. W. Graveney	2,397	49.93	K. Mackay	1,103	52.52
1957	T. W. Graveney	2,361	49.18	P. B. H. May	2,347	61.76
1958	P. B. H. May	2,231	63.74	P. B. H. May	2,231	63.74
1959	M. J. K. Smith	3,245	57.94	V. L. Manjrekar	755	68.63
1960	M. J. K. Smith	2,551	45.55	R. Subba Row	1,503	55.66
1961	W. E. Alley	3,019	56.96	W. M. Lawry	2,019	61.18
1962	J. H. Edrich	2,482	51.70	R. T. Simpson	867	54.18
1963	J. B. Bolus	2,190	41.32	G. S. Sobers	1,333	47.60
1964	T. W. Graveney	2,385	54.20	K. F. Barrington	1,872	62.40
1965	J. H. Edrich	2,319	62.67	M. C. Cowdrey	2,093	63.42
1966	A. R. Lewis	2,198	41.47	G. S. Sobers	1,349	61.31
1967	C. A. Milton	2,089	46.42	K. F. Barrington	2,059	68.63
1968	B. A. Richards	2,395	47.90	G. Boycott	1,487	64.65
1969	J. H. Edrich	2,238	69.93	J. H. Edrich	2,238	69.93
1970	G. M. Turner	2,379	61.00	G. S. Sobers	1,742	75.73
1971	G. Boycott	2,503	100.12	G. Boycott	2,503	100.12
1972	Majid Khan	2,074	61.00	G. Boycott	1,230	72.35
1973	G. M. Turner	2,416	67.11	G. M. Turner	2,416	67.11
1974	R. T. Virgin	1,936	56.94	C. H. Lloyd	1,458	63.39
1975	G. Boycott	1,915	73.65	R. B. Kanhai	1,073	82.53
1976	Zaheer Abbas	2,554	75.11	Zaheer Abbas	2,554	75.11
1977	I. V. A. Richards	2,161	65.48	G. Boycott	1,701	68.04
1978	D. L. Amiss	2,030	53.42	C. E. B. Rice	1,871	66.82
1979	K. C. Wessels	1,800	52.94	G. Boycott	1,538	102.53
1980	P. N. Kirsten	1,895	63.16	A. J. Lamb	1,797	66.55
1981	Zaheer Abbas	2,306	88.69	Zaheer Abbas	2,306	88.69
1982	A. I. Kallicharran	2,120	66.25	G. M. Turner	1,171	90.07
1983	K. S. McEwan	2,176	64.00	I. V. A. Richards	1,204	75.25
1984	G. A. Gooch	2,559	67.34	C. G. Greenidge	1,069	82.23
1985	G. A. Gooch	2,208	71.22	I. V. A. Richards	1,836	76.50
1986	C. G. Greenidge	2,035	67.83	C. G. Greenidge	2,035	67.83

Season	*Leading scorer*	*Runs*	*Avge*	*Top of averages*	*Runs*	*Avge*
1987	G. A. Hick	1,879	52.19	M. D. Crowe	1,627	67.79
1988	G. A. Hick	2,713	77.51	R. A. Harper	622	77.75
1989	S. J. Cook	2,241	60.56	D. M. Jones	1,510	88.82
1990	G. A. Gooch	2,746	101.70	G. A. Gooch	2,746	101.70
1991	S. J. Cook	2,755	81.02	C. L. Hooper	1,501	93.81
1992	P. D. Bowler	2,044	65.93	Salim Malik	1,184	78.93
	M. A. Roseberry	2,044	56.77			
1993	G. A. Gooch	2,023	63.21	D. C. Boon	1,437	75.63
1994	B. C. Lara	2,066	89.82	J. D. Carr	1,543	90.76
1995	M. R. Ramprakash	2,258	77.86	M. R. Ramprakash	2,258	77.86
1996	G. A. Gooch	1,944	67.03	S. C. Ganguly	762	95.25
1997	S. P. James	1,775	68.26	G. A. Hick	1,524	69.27
1998	J. P. Crawley	1,851	74.04	J. P. Crawley	1,851	74.04
1999	S. G. Law	1,833	73.32	S. G. Law	1,833	73.32
2000	D. S. Lehmann	1,477	67.13	M. G. Bevan	1,124	74.93
2001	M. E. K. Hussey	2,055	79.03	D. R. Martyn	942	104.66

Notes: The highest average recorded in an English season was 115.66 (2,429 runs, 26 innings) by D. G. Bradman in 1938.

In 1953, W. A. Johnston averaged 102.00 from 17 innings, 16 not out.

25,000 RUNS

Dates in italics denote the first half of an overseas season; i.e. *1945* denotes the 1945-46 season.

		Career	*R*	*I*	*NO*	*HS*	*100s*	*Avge*
1	J. B. Hobbs	1905-34	61,237	1,315	106	316*	197	50.65
2	F. E. Woolley	1906-38	58,969	1,532	85	305*	145	40.75
3	E. H. Hendren	1907-38	57,611	1,300	166	301*	170	50.80
4	C. P. Mead	1905-36	55,061	1,340	185	280*	153	47.67
5	W. G. Grace	1865-1908	54,896	1,493	105	344	126	39.55
6	W. R. Hammond	1920-51	50,551	1,005	104	336*	167	56.10
7	H. Sutcliffe	1919-45	50,138	1,088	123	313	149	51.95
8	G. Boycott	1962-86	48,426	1,014	162	261*	151	56.83
9	T. W. Graveney	1948-*71*	47,793	1,223	159	258	122	44.91
10	G. A. Gooch	1973-2000	44,846	990	75	333	128	49.01
11	T. W. Hayward	1893-1914	43,551	1,138	96	315*	104	41.79
12	D. L. Amiss	1960-87	43,423	1,139	126	262*	102	42.86
13	M. C. Cowdrey	1950-76	42,719	1,130	134	307	107	42.89
14	A. Sandham	1911-*37*	41,284	1,000	79	325	107	44.82
15	L. Hutton	1934-60	40,140	814	91	364	129	55.51
16	M. J. K. Smith	1951-75	39,832	1,091	139	204	69	41.84
17	W. Rhodes	1898-1930	39,802	1,528	237	267*	58	30.83
18	J. H. Edrich	1956-78	39,790	979	104	310*	103	45.47
19	R. E. S. Wyatt	1923-57	39,405	1,141	157	232	85	40.04
20	D. C. S. Compton	1936-64	38,942	839	88	300	123	51.85
21	E. Tyldesley	1909-36	38,874	961	106	256*	102	45.46
22	J. T. Tyldesley	1895-1923	37,897	994	62	295*	86	40.66
23	K. W. R. Fletcher	1962-88	37,665	1,167	170	228*	63	37.77
24	C. G. Greenidge	1970-92	37,354	889	75	273*	92	45.88
25	J. W. Hearne	1909-36	37,252	1,025	116	285*	96	40.98
26	L. E. G. Ames	1926-51	37,248	951	95	295	102	43.51
27	D. Kenyon	1946-67	37,002	1,159	59	259	74	33.63
28	W. J. Edrich	1934-58	36,965	964	92	267*	86	42.39
29	J. M. Parks	1949-76	36,673	1,227	172	205*	51	34.76
30	M. W. Gatting	1975-98	36,549	861	123	258	94	49.52
31	D. Denton	1894-1920	36,479	1,163	70	221	69	33.37
32	G. H. Hirst	1891-1929	36,323	1,215	151	341	60	34.13
33	I. V. A. Richards	*1971*-93	36,212	796	63	322	114	49.40
34	A. Jones	1957-83	36,049	1,168	72	204*	56	32.89
35	W. G. Quaife	1894-1928	36,012	1,203	185	255*	72	35.37

		Career	*R*	*I*	*NO*	*HS*	*100s*	*Avge*
36	R. E. Marshall	*1945*-72	35,725	1,053	59	228*	68	35.94
37	G. Gunn	1902-32	35,208	1,061	82	220	62	35.96
38	D. B. Close	1949-86	34,994	1,225	173	198	52	33.26
39	Zaheer Abbas	*1965-86*	34,843	768	92	274	108	51.54
40	J. G. Langridge	1928-55	34,380	984	66	250*	76	37.45
41	G. M. Turner	*1964-82*	34,346	792	101	311*	103	49.70
42	C. Washbrook	1933-64	34,101	906	107	251*	76	42.67
43	**G. A. Hick**	***1983*-2001**	**33,793**	**695**	**65**	**405***	**117**	**53.63**
44	M. Leyland	1920-48	33,660	932	101	263	80	40.50
45	H. T. W. Hardinge	1902-33	33,519	1,021	103	263*	75	36.51
46	R. Abel	1881-1904	33,124	1,007	73	357*	74	35.46
47	A. I. Kallicharran	*1966*-90	32,650	834	86	243*	87	43.64
48	A. J. Lamb	*1972*-95	32,502	772	108	294	89	48.94
49	C. A. Milton	1948-74	32,150	1,078	125	170	56	33.73
50	J. D. Robertson	1937-59	31,914	897	46	331*	67	37.50
51	J. Hardstaff, jun.	1930-55	31,847	812	94	266	83	44.35
52	James Langridge	1924-53	31,716	1,058	157	167	42	35.20
53	K. F. Barrington	1953-68	31,714	831	136	256	76	45.63
54	C. H. Lloyd	*1963*-86	31,232	730	96	242*	79	49.26
55	Mushtaq Mohammad	*1956*-85	31,091	843	104	303*	72	42.07
56	C. B. Fry	1892-*1921*	30,886	658	43	258*	94	50.22
57	D. Brookes	1934-59	30,874	925	70	257	71	36.10
58	P. Holmes	1913-35	30,573	810	84	315*	67	42.11
59	R. T. Simpson	*1944*-63	30,546	852	55	259	64	38.32
60	L. G. Berry	1924-51	30,225	1,056	57	232	45	30.25
	K. G. Suttle	1949-71	30,225	1,064	92	204*	49	31.09
62	P. A. Perrin	1896-1928	29,709	918	91	343*	66	35.92
63	P. F. Warner	1894-1929	29,028	875	75	244	60	36.28
64	R. B. Kanhai	*1954-81*	28,774	669	82	256	83	49.01
65	J. O'Connor	1921-39	28,764	903	79	248	72	34.90
66	Javed Miandad	*1973-93*	28,647	631	95	311	80	53.44
67	T. E. Bailey	1945-67	28,641	1,072	215	205	28	33.42
68	D. W. Randall	1972-93	28,456	827	81	237	52	38.14
69	E. H. Bowley	1912-34	28,378	859	47	283	52	34.94
70	B. A. Richards	*1964-82*	28,358	576	58	356	80	54.74
71	G. S. Sobers	*1952*-74	28,315	609	93	365*	86	54.87
72	A. E. Dipper	1908-32	28,075	865	69	252*	53	35.27
73	D. G. Bradman	*1927-48*	28,067	338	43	452*	117	95.14
74	J. H. Hampshire	1961-84	28,059	924	112	183*	43	34.55
75	**K. J. Barnett**	**1979-2001**	**27,952**	**769**	**73**	**239***	**58**	**40.16**
76	P. B. H. May	1948-63	27,592	618	77	285*	85	51.00
77	R. T. Robinson	1978-99	27,571	739	85	220*	63	42.15
78	B. F. Davison	*1967-87*	27,453	766	79	189	53	39.96
79	Majid Khan	*1961-84*	27,444	700	62	241	73	43.01
80	A. C. Russell	1908-30	27,358	717	59	273	71	41.57
81	E. G. Hayes	1896-1926	27,318	896	48	276	48	32.21
82	A. E. Fagg	1932-57	27,291	803	46	269*	58	36.05
83	James Seymour	1900-26	27,237	911	62	218*	53	32.08
84	W. Larkins	1972-95	27,142	842	54	252	59	34.44
85	A. R. Border	*1976-95*	27,131	625	97	205	70	51.38
86	P. H. Parfitt	1956-*73*	26,924	845	104	200*	58	36.33
87	G. L. Jessop	1894-1914	26,698	855	37	286	53	32.63
88	K. S. McEwan	*1972-91*	26,628	705	67	218	74	41.73
89	D. E. Davies	1924-54	26,564	1,032	80	287*	32	27.90
90	A. Shrewsbury	1875-1902	26,505	813	90	267	59	36.65
91	M. J. Stewart	1954-72	26,492	898	93	227*	49	32.90
92	C. T. Radley	1964-87	26,441	880	134	200	46	35.44
93	D. I. Gower	1975-93	26,339	727	70	228	53	40.08
94	C. E. B. Rice	*1969-93*	26,331	766	123	246	48	40.95
95	Younis Ahmed	*1961-86*	26,073	762	118	221*	46	40.48
96	P. E. Richardson	1949-65	26,055	794	41	185	44	34.60

		Career	R	I	NO	HS	100s	Avge
97	D. L. Haynes	1976-96	26,030	639	72	255*	61	45.90
98	M. H. Denness	1959-80	25,886	838	65	195	33	33.48
99	S. M. Gavaskar	*1966*-87	25,834	563	61	340	81	51.46
100	J. W. H. Makepeace	1906-30	25,799	778	66	203	43	36.23
101	W. Gunn	1880-1904	25,691	850	72	273	48	33.02
102	W. Watson	1939-64	25,670	753	109	257	55	39.86
103	G. Brown	1908-33	25,649	1,012	52	232*	37	26.71
104	G. M. Emmett	1936-59	25,602	865	50	188	37	31.41
105	J. B. Bolus	1956-75	25,598	833	81	202*	39	34.03
106	W. E. Russell	1956-72	25,525	796	64	193	41	34.87
107	C. W. J. Athey	1976-97	25,453	784	71	184	55	35.69
108	C. J. Barnett	1927-*53*	25,389	821	45	259	48	32.71
109	L. B. Fishlock	1931-52	25,376	699	54	253	56	39.34
110	D. J. Insole	1947-63	25,241	743	72	219*	54	37.61
111	J. M. Brearley	1961-83	25,185	768	102	312*	45	37.81
112	J. Vine	1896-1922	25,171	920	79	202	34	29.92
113	R. M. Prideaux	1958-*74*	25,136	808	75	202*	41	34.29
114	J. H. King	1895-1925	25,122	988	69	227*	34	27.33
115	J. G. Wright	*1975-92*	25,073	636	44	192	59	42.35

Bold type denotes those who played in 2000-01 and 2001 seasons.

Note: Some works of reference provide career figures which differ from those in this list, owing to the exclusion or inclusion of matches recognised or not recognised as first-class by *Wisden*.

Current Players with 20,000 Runs

	Career	R	I	NO	HS	100s	Avge
R. A. Smith	*1980*-2001	24,801	677	85	209*	59	41.89
M. E. Waugh	*1985*-2001	24,632	532	70	229*	78	53.31
A. J. Stewart	1981-2001	24,334	689	75	271*	47	39.63
M. A. Atherton	1987-2001	21,929	584	47	268*	54	40.83
R. J. Bailey	1982-2001	21,844	628	89	224*	47	40.52
J. E. Morris	1982-2001	21,539	612	35	229	52	37.32
M. P. Maynard	1985-2001	21,518	569	56	243	48	41.94
T. M. Moody	*1985-2000*	21,001	501	47	272	64	46.25
S. R. Waugh	*1984*-2001	20,707	471	79	216*	66	52.82
N. H. Fairbrother	1982-2001	20,206	561	79	366	46	41.92
M. R. Ramprakash	1987-2001	20,142	495	62	235	55	46.51

CAREER AVERAGE OVER 50

(Qualification: 10,000 runs)

Avge		*Career*	*I*	*NO*	*R*	*HS*	*100s*
95.14	D. G. Bradman	*1927-48*	338	43	28,067	452*	117
71.22	V. M. Merchant	*1929-51*	229	43	13,248	359*	44
67.46	**Ajay Sharma**	***1984-2000***	**166**	**16**	**10,120**	**259***	**38**
65.18	W. H. Ponsford	*1920-34*	235	23	13,819	437	47
64.99	W. M. Woodfull	*1921-34*	245	39	13,388	284	49
62.04	**S. R. Tendulkar**	***1988-2001 (Z)***	**265**	**28**	**14,705**	**233***	**48**
58.24	A. L. Hassett	*1932-53*	322	32	16,890	232	59
58.19	V. S. Hazare	*1934-66*	365	45	18,621	316*	60
57.40	**R. Dravid**	***1990-2001 (SL)***	**245**	**35**	**12,056**	**215**	**33**
57.22	A. F. Kippax	*1918-35*	256	33	12,762	315*	43
56.83	G. Boycott	1962-86	1,014	162	48,426	261*	151
56.55	C. L. Walcott	*1941-63*	238	29	11,820	314*	40
56.37	K. S. Ranjitsinhji	1893-1920	500	62	24,692	285*	72
56.22	R. B. Simpson	*1952-77*	436	62	21,029	359	60
56.11	**D. S. Lehmann**	***1987*-2001**	**323**	**22**	**16,890**	**255**	**54**

Avge		Career	I	NO	R	HS	100s
56.10	W. R. Hammond	1920-51	1,005	104	50,551	336*	167
56.02	M. D. Crowe	*1979-95*	412	62	19,608	299	71
55.51	L. Hutton	1934-60	814	91	40,140	364	129
55.46	**M. G. Bevan**	***1989*-2001**	**316**	**56**	**14,420**	**203***	**49**
55.34	E. D. Weekes	*1944*-64	241	24	12,010	304*	36
55.11	S. V. Manjrekar	*1984-97*	217	31	10,252	377	31
54.87	G. S. Sobers	*1952*-74	609	93	28,315	365*	86
54.74	B. A. Richards	*1964-82*	576	58	28,358	356	80
54.67	R. G. Pollock	*1960-86*	437	54	20,940	274	64
54.24	F. M. M. Worrell	*1941*-64	326	49	15,025	308*	39
53.78	R. M. Cowper	*1959-69*	228	31	10,595	307	26
53.67	A. R. Morris	*1940-63*	250	15	12,614	290	46
53.63	**G. A. Hick**	***1983*-2001**	**695**	**65**	**33,793**	**405***	**117**
53.44	Javed Miandad	*1973-93*	631	95	28,647	311	80
53.31	**M. E. Waugh**	***1985*-2001**	**532**	**70**	**24,632**	**229***	**78**
53.27	**R. T. Ponting**	***1992*-2001**	**219**	**31**	**10,016**	**233**	**34**
52.86	D. B. Vengsarkar	*1975-91*	390	52	17,868	284	55
52.82	**S. R. Waugh**	***1984*-2001**	**471**	**79**	**20,707**	**216***	**66**
52.32	Hanif Mohammad	*1951-75*	371	45	17,059	499	55
52.27	P. R. Umrigar	*1944-67*	350	41	16,154	252*	49
52.20	G. S. Chappell	*1966-83*	542	72	24,535	247*	74
51.98	M. Azharuddin	*1981-99*	343	38	15,855	226	54
51.95	H. Sutcliffe	1919-45	1,088	123	50,138	313	149
51.85	D. M. Jones	*1981-97*	415	45	19,188	324*	55
51.85	D. C. S. Compton	1936-64	839	88	38,942	300	123
51.81	**M. L. Hayden**	***1991*-2001**	**338**	**34**	**15,752**	**235***	**48**
51.54	Zaheer Abbas	*1965-86*	768	92	34,843	274	108
51.53	A. D. Nourse	*1931-52*	269	27	12,472	260*	41
51.46	S. M. Gavaskar	*1966*-87	563	61	25,834	340	81
51.44	W. A. Brown	*1932-49*	284	15	13,838	265*	39
51.38	A. R. Border	*1976-95*	625	97	27,131	205	70
51.00	P. B. H. May	1948-63	618	77	27,592	285*	85
50.95	N. C. O'Neill	*1955-67*	306	34	13,859	284	45
50.93	R. N. Harvey	*1946-62*	461	35	21,699	231*	67
50.90	W. M. Lawry	*1955-71*	417	49	18,734	266	50
50.90	A. V. Mankad	*1963-82*	326	71	12,980	265	31
50.80	E. H. Hendren	1907-38	1,300	166	57,611	301*	170
50.65	J. B. Hobbs	1905-34	1,315	106	61,237	316*	197
50.58	K. C. Wessels	*1973-99*	539	50	24,738	254	66
50.58	S. J. Cook	*1972-94*	475	57	21,143	313*	64
50.57	**Inzamam-ul-Haq**	***1985-2001***	**296**	**46**	**12,644**	**201***	**35**
50.52	**J. L. Langer**	***1991*-2001**	**346**	**37**	**15,612**	**274***	**49**
50.40	**S. G. Law**	***1988*-2001**	**390**	**41**	**17,590**	**263**	**54**
50.22	C. B. Fry	1892-*1921*	658	43	30,886	258*	94
50.17	**Asif Mujtaba**	***1984*-2001**	**395**	**77**	**15,956**	**208**	**42**

Note: G. A. Headley (*1927*-1954) scored 9,921 runs, average 69.86.

Bold type denotes those who played in 2000-01 and 2001 seasons.

FASTEST FIFTIES

Minutes			
11	C. I. J. Smith (66)	Middlesex v Gloucestershire at Bristol	1938
13	Khalid Mahmood (56)	Gujranwala v Sargodha at Gujranwala	2000-01
14	S. J. Pegler (50)	South Africans v Tasmania at Launceston	1910-11
14	F. T. Mann (53)	Middlesex v Nottinghamshire at Lord's	1921
14	H. B. Cameron (56)	Transvaal v Orange Free State at Johannesburg	1934-35
14	C. I. J. Smith (52)	Middlesex v Kent at Maidstone	1935

Note: The following fast fifties were scored in contrived circumstances when runs were given from full tosses and long hops to expedite a declaration: C. C. Inman (8 minutes), Leicestershire v

Nottinghamshire at Nottingham, 1965; G. Chapple (10 minutes), Lancashire v Glamorgan at Manchester, 1993; T. M. Moody (11 minutes), Warwickshire v Glamorgan at Swansea, 1990; A. J. Stewart (14 minutes), Surrey v Kent at Dartford, 1986; M. P. Maynard (14 minutes), Glamorgan v Yorkshire at Cardiff, 1987.

FASTEST HUNDREDS

Minutes			
35	P. G. H. Fender (113*)	Surrey v Northamptonshire at Northampton	1920
40	G. L. Jessop (101)	Gloucestershire v Yorkshire at Harrogate	1897
40	Ahsan-ul-Haq (100*)	Muslims v Sikhs at Lahore	1923-24
42	G. L. Jessop (191)	Gentlemen of South v Players of South at Hastings	1907
43	A. H. Hornby (106)	Lancashire v Somerset at Manchester	1905
43	D. W. Hookes (107)	South Australia v Victoria at Adelaide	1982-83
44	R. N. S. Hobbs (100)	Essex v Australians at Chelmsford	1975

Notes: The fastest recorded authentic hundred in terms of balls received was scored off 34 balls by D. W. Hookes (above).

Research of the scorebook has shown that P. G. H. Fender scored his hundred from between 40 and 46 balls. He contributed 113 to an unfinished sixth-wicket partnership of 171 in 42 minutes with H. A. Peach.

E. B. Alletson (Nottinghamshire) scored 189 out of 227 runs in 90 minutes against Sussex at Hove in 1911. It has been estimated that his last 139 runs took 37 minutes.

The following fast hundreds were scored in contrived circumstances when runs were given from full tosses and long hops to expedite a declaration: G. Chapple (21 minutes), Lancashire v Glamorgan at Manchester, 1993; T. M. Moody (26 minutes), Warwickshire v Glamorgan at Swansea, 1990; S. J. O'Shaughnessy (35 minutes), Lancashire v Leicestershire at Manchester, 1983; C. M. Old (37 minutes), Yorkshire v Warwickshire at Birmingham, 1977; N. F. M. Popplewell (41 minutes), Somerset v Gloucestershire at Bath, 1983.

FASTEST DOUBLE-HUNDREDS

Minutes			
113	R. J. Shastri (200*)	Bombay v Baroda at Bombay	1984-85
120	G. L. Jessop (286)	Gloucestershire v Sussex at Hove	1903
120	C. H. Lloyd (201*)	West Indians v Glamorgan at Swansea	1976
130	G. L. Jessop (234)	Gloucestershire v Somerset at Bristol	1905
131	V. T. Trumper (293)	Australians v Canterbury at Christchurch	1913-14

FASTEST TRIPLE-HUNDREDS

Minutes			
181	D. C. S. Compton (300)	MCC v N. E. Transvaal at Benoni	1948-49
205	F. E. Woolley (305*)	MCC v Tasmania at Hobart	1911-12
205	C. G. Macartney (345)	Australians v Nottinghamshire at Nottingham	1921
213	D. G. Bradman (369)	South Australia v Tasmania at Adelaide	1935-36

300 RUNS IN A DAY

390*	B. C. Lara	Warwickshire v Durham at Birmingham	1994
345	C. G. Macartney	Australians v Nottinghamshire at Nottingham	1921
334	W. H. Ponsford	Victoria v New South Wales at Melbourne	1926-27
333	K. S. Duleepsinhji	Sussex v Northamptonshire at Hove	1930
331*	J. D. Robertson	Middlesex v Worcestershire at Worcester	1949
325*	B. A. Richards	S. Australia v W. Australia at Perth	1970-71
322†	E. Paynter	Lancashire v Sussex at Hove	1937
322	I. V. A. Richards	Somerset v Warwickshire at Taunton	1985
318	C. W. Gregory	New South Wales v Queensland at Brisbane	1906-07
317	K. R. Rutherford	New Zealanders v D. B. Close's XI at Scarborough	1986

316†	R. H. Moore	Hampshire v Warwickshire at Bournemouth	1937
315*	R. C. Blunt	Otago v Canterbury at Christchurch	1931-32
312*	J. M. Brearley	MCC Under-25 v North Zone at Peshawar	1966-67
311*	G. M. Turner	Worcestershire v Warwickshire at Worcester	1982
311*	N. H. Fairbrother	Lancashire v Surrey at The Oval	1990
309*	D. G. Bradman	Australia v England at Leeds	1930
307*	W. H. Ashdown	Kent v Essex at Brentwood	1934
306*	A. Ducat	Surrey v Oxford University at The Oval	1919
305*	F. R. Foster	Warwickshire v Worcestershire at Dudley	1914

† *E. Paynter's 322 and R. H. Moore's 316 were scored on the same day: July 28, 1937.*

These scores do not necessarily represent the complete innings. See pages 193–195.

LONGEST INNINGS

Mins			
1,015	R. Nayyar (271)	Himachal Pradesh v Jammu and Kashmir at Chamba	1999-2000
970	Hanif Mohammad (337)	Pakistan v West Indies at Bridgetown	1957-58
	Hanif believes he batted 999 minutes.		
878	G. Kirsten (275)	South Africa v England at Durban	1999-2000
799	S. T. Jayasuriya (340)	Sri Lanka v India at Colombo	1997-98
797	L. Hutton (364)	England v Australia at The Oval	1938

1,000 RUNS IN MAY

	Runs	*Avge*
W. G. Grace, May 9 to May 30, 1895 (22 days):		
13, 103, 18, 25, 288, 52, 257, 73*, 18, 169	1,016	112.88
Grace was within two months of completing his 47th year.		
W. R. Hammond, May 7 to May 31, 1927 (25 days):		
27, 135, 108, 128, 17, 11, 99, 187, 4, 30, 83, 7, 192, 14	1,042	74.42
Hammond scored his 1,000th run on May 28, thus equalling Grace's record of 22 days.		
C. Hallows, May 5 to May 31, 1928 (27 days):		
100, 101, 51*, 123, 101*, 22, 74, 104, 58, 34*, 232	1,000	125.00

1,000 RUNS IN APRIL AND MAY

	Runs	*Avge*
T. W. Hayward, April 16 to May 31, 1900:		
120*, 55, 108, 131*, 55, 193, 120, 5, 6, 3, 40, 146, 92	1,074	97.63
D. G. Bradman, April 30 to May 31, 1930:		
236, 185*, 78, 9, 48*, 66, 4, 44, 252*, 32, 47*	1,001	143.00
On April 30 Bradman was 75 not out.		
D. G. Bradman, April 30 to May 31, 1938:		
258, 58, 137, 278, 2, 143, 145*, 5, 30*	1,056	150.85
Bradman scored 258 on April 30, and his 1,000th run on May 27.		
W. J. Edrich, April 30 to May 31, 1938:		
104, 37, 115, 63, 20*, 182, 71, 31, 53*, 45, 15, 245, 0, 9, 20*	1,010	84.16
Edrich was 21 not out on April 30. All his runs were scored at Lord's.		
G. M. Turner, April 24 to May 31, 1973:		
41, 151*, 143, 85, 7, 8, 17*, 81, 13, 53, 44, 153*, 3, 2, 66*, 30, 10*, 111	1,018	78.30
G. A. Hick, April 17 to May 29, 1988:		
61, 37, 212, 86, 14, 405*, 8, 11, 6, 7, 172	1,019	101.90
Hick scored a record 410 runs in April, and his 1,000th run on May 28.		

1,000 RUNS IN TWO SEPARATE MONTHS

Only four batsmen, C. B. Fry, K. S. Ranjitsinhji, H. Sutcliffe and L. Hutton, have scored over 1,000 runs in each of two months in the same season. L. Hutton, by scoring 1,294 in June 1949, made more runs in a single month than anyone else. He also made 1,050 in August 1949.

MOST RUNS SCORED OFF AN OVER

(All instances refer to six-ball overs)

36	G. S. Sobers	off M. A. Nash, Nottinghamshire v Glamorgan at Swansea (six sixes)	1968
36	R. J. Shastri	off Tilak Raj, Bombay v Baroda at Bombay (six sixes)	1984-85
34	E. B. Alletson	off E. H. Killick, Nottinghamshire v Sussex at Hove (46604446; including two no-balls)	1911
34	F. C. Hayes	off M. A. Nash, Lancashire v Glamorgan at Swansea (646666)	1977
34†	A. Flintoff	off A. J. Tudor, Lancashire v Surrey at Manchester (64444660; including two no-balls)	1998
32	I. T. Botham	off I. R. Snook, England XI v Central Districts at Palmerston North (466466)	1983-84
32	P. W. G. Parker	off A. I. Kallicharran, Sussex v Warwickshire at Birmingham (466664)	1982
32	I. R. Redpath	off N. Rosendorff, Australians v Orange Free State at Bloemfontein (666644)	1969-70
32	C. C. Smart	off G. Hill, Glamorgan v Hampshire at Cardiff (664664)	1935
32	Khalid Mahmood	off Naved Latif, Gujranwala v Sargodha at Gujranwala (666662)	2000-01

† *Altogether 38 runs were scored off this over, the two no-balls counting for two extra runs each under ECB regulations.*

Notes: The following instances have been excluded from the above table because of the bowlers' compliance: 34 – M. P. Maynard off S. A. Marsh, Glamorgan v Kent at Swansea, 1992; 34 – G. Chapple off P. A. Cottey, Lancashire v Glamorgan at Manchester, 1993; 34 – F. B. Touzel off F. J. J. Viljoen, Western Province B v Griqualand West at Kimberley, 1993-94; 32 – C. C. Inman off N. W. Hill, Leicestershire v Nottinghamshire at Nottingham, 1965; 32 – T. E. Jesty off R. J. Boyd-Moss, Hampshire v Northamptonshire at Southampton, 1984; 32 – M. A. Ealham off G. D. Hodgson, Kent v Gloucestershire at Bristol, 1992; 32 – G. Chapple off P. A. Cottey, Lancashire v Glamorgan at Manchester, 1993. Chapple's 34 and 32 came off successive overs from Cottey.

There were 35 runs off an over received by A. T. Reinholds off H. T. Davis, Auckland v Wellington at Auckland 1995-96, but this included six no-balls (counting as two runs each), four byes and only 19 off the bat.

In a Shell Trophy match against Canterbury at Christchurch in 1989-90, R. H. Vance (Wellington), acting on the instructions of his captain, deliberately conceded 77 runs in an over of full tosses which contained 17 no-balls and, owing to the umpire's understandable miscalculation, only five legitimate deliveries.

The greatest number of runs scored off an eight-ball over is 34 (40446664) by R. M. Edwards off M. C. Carew, Governor-General's XI v West Indians at Auckland, 1968-69.

MOST SIXES IN AN INNINGS

16	A. Symonds (254*)	Gloucestershire v Glamorgan at Abergavenny	1995
15	J. R. Reid (296)	Wellington v Northern Districts at Wellington	1962-63
14	Shakti Singh (128)	Himachal Pradesh v Haryana at Dharmsala	1990-91
13	Majid Khan (147*)	Pakistanis v Glamorgan at Swansea	1967
13	C. G. Greenidge (273*)	D. H. Robins' XI v Pakistanis at Eastbourne	1974
13	C. G. Greenidge (259)	Hampshire v Sussex at Southampton	1975
13	G. W. Humpage (254)	Warwickshire v Lancashire at Southport	1982
13	R. J. Shastri (200*)	Bombay v Baroda at Bombay	1984-85
12	Gulfraz Khan (207)	Railways v Universities at Lahore	1976-77
12	I. T. Botham (138*)	Somerset v Warwickshire at Birmingham	1985

12	R. A. Harper (234)	Northamptonshire v Gloucestershire at Northampton	1986
12	D. M. Jones (248)	Australians v Warwickshire at Birmingham	1989
12	U. N. K. Fernando (160)	Sinhalese SC v Sebastianites C and AC at Colombo	1990-91
12	D. N. Patel (204)	Auckland v Northern Districts at Auckland	1991-92
12	W. V. Raman (206)	Tamil Nadu v Kerala at Madras	1991-92
12	G. D. Lloyd (241)	Lancashire v Essex at Chelmsford	1996
12	Wasim Akram (257*)	Pakistan v Zimbabwe at Sheikhupura	1996-97
11	C. K. Nayudu (153)	Hindus v MCC at Bombay	1926-27
11	C. J. Barnett (194)	Gloucestershire v Somerset at Bath	1934
11	R. Benaud (135)	Australians v T. N. Pearce's XI at Scarborough	1953
11	R. Bora (126)	Assam v Tripura at Gauhati	1987-88
11	G. A. Hick (405*)	Worcestershire v Somerset at Taunton	1988
11	A. S. Jayasinghe (183)	Tamil Union v Burgher RC at Colombo	1996-97

Note: F. B. Touzel (128*) hit 13 sixes for Western Province B v Griqualand West in contrived circumstances at Kimberley in 1993-94.

MOST SIXES IN A MATCH

20	A. Symonds (254*, 76)	Gloucestershire v Glamorgan at Abergavenny	1995
17	W. J. Stewart (155, 125)	Warwickshire v Lancashire at Blackpool	1959

MOST SIXES IN A SEASON

80	I. T. Botham	1985
66	A. W. Wellard	1935
57	A. W. Wellard	1936
57	A. W. Wellard	1938
51	A. W. Wellard	1933
49	I. V. A. Richards	1985
48	A. W. Carr	1925
48	J. H. Edrich	1965
48	A. Symonds	1995

MOST BOUNDARIES IN AN INNINGS

	4s/6s			
72	62/10	B. C. Lara (501*)	Warwickshire v Durham at Birmingham	1994
68	68/–	P. A. Perrin (343*)	Essex v Derbyshire at Chesterfield	1904
65	64/1	A. C. MacLaren (424)	Lancashire v Somerset at Taunton	1895
64	64/–	Hanif Mohammad (499)	Karachi v Bahawalpur at Karachi	1958-59
57	52/5	J. H. Edrich (310*)	England v New Zealand at Leeds	1965
57	52/5	Naved Latif (394)	Sargodha v Gujranwala at Gujranwala	2000-01
55	55/–	C. W. Gregory (383)	NSW v Queensland at Brisbane	1906-07
55	51/3†	S. V. Manjrekar (377)	Bombay v Hyderabad at Bombay	1990-91
55	53/2	G. R. Marsh (355*)	W. Australia v S. Australia at Perth	1989-90
54	53/1	G. H. Hirst (341)	Yorkshire v Leicestershire at Leicester	1905
53	51/2	V. V. S. Laxman (353)	Hyderabad v Karnataka at Bangalore	1999-2000
53	53/–	A. W. Nourse (304*)	Natal v Transvaal at Johannesburg	1919-20
53	45/8	K. R. Rutherford (317)	New Zealanders v D. B. Close's XI at Scarborough	1986
52	47/5	N. H. Fairbrother (366)	Lancashire v Surrey at The Oval	1990
51	51/–	W. G. Grace (344)	MCC v Kent at Canterbury	1876
51	47/4	C. G. Macartney (345)	Australians v Notts at Nottingham	1921
51	50/1	B. B. Nimbalkar (443*)	Maharashtra v Kathiawar at Poona	1948-49
50	46/4	D. G. Bradman (369)	S. Australia v Tasmania at Adelaide	1935-36
50	47/–‡	A. Ducat (306*)	Surrey v Oxford U. at The Oval	1919
50	35/15	J. R. Reid (296)	Wellington v N. Districts at Wellington	1962-63
50	42/8	I. V. A. Richards (322)	Somerset v Warwickshire at Taunton	1985

† *Plus one five.*
‡ *Plus three fives.*

PARTNERSHIPS OVER 500

577	V. S. Hazare (288) and Gul Mahomed (319), fourth wicket, Baroda v Holkar at Baroda	1946-47
576	S. T. Jayasuriya (340) and R. S. Mahanama (225), second wicket, Sri Lanka v India at Colombo	1997-98
574*	F. M. M. Worrell (255*) and C. L. Walcott (314*), fourth wicket, Barbados v Trinidad at Port-of-Spain	1945-46
561	Waheed Mirza (324) and Mansoor Akhtar (224*), first wicket, Karachi Whites v Quetta at Karachi	1976-77
555	P. Holmes (224*) and H. Sutcliffe (313), first wicket, Yorkshire v Essex at Leyton	1932
554	J. T. Brown (300) and J. Tunnicliffe (243), first wicket, Yorkshire v Derbyshire at Chesterfield	1898
502*	F. M. M. Worrell (308*) and J. D. C. Goddard (218*), fourth wicket, Barbados v Trinidad at Bridgetown	1943-44

HIGHEST PARTNERSHIPS FOR EACH WICKET

The following lists include all stands above 400; otherwise the top ten for each wicket.

First Wicket

561	Waheed Mirza and Mansoor Akhtar, Karachi Whites v Quetta at Karachi	1976-77
555	P. Holmes and H. Sutcliffe, Yorkshire v Essex at Leyton	1932
554	J. T. Brown and J. Tunnicliffe, Yorkshire v Derbyshire at Chesterfield	1898
490	E. H. Bowley and J. G. Langridge, Sussex v Middlesex at Hove	1933
464	R. Sehgal and R. Lamba, Delhi v Himachal Pradesh at Delhi	1994-95
459	Wasim Jaffer and S. K. Kulkarni, Mumbai v Saurashtra at Rajkot	1996-97
456	E. R. Mayne and W. H. Ponsford, Victoria v Queensland at Melbourne	1923-24
451*	S. Desai and R. M. H. Binny, Karnataka v Kerala at Chikmagalur	1977-78
431	M. R. J. Veletta and G. R. Marsh, Western Australia v South Australia at Perth	1989-90
428	J. B. Hobbs and A. Sandham, Surrey v Oxford University at The Oval	1926
425*	L. V. Garrick and C. H. Gayle, Jamaica v West Indies B at Montego Bay	2000-01
424	I. J. Siedle and J. F. W. Nicolson, Natal v Orange Free State at Bloemfontein	1926-27
421	S. M. Gavaskar and G. A. Parkar, Bombay v Bengal at Bombay	1981-82
418	Kamal Najamuddin and Khalid Alvi, Karachi v Railways at Karachi	1980-81
413	V. Mankad and Pankaj Roy, India v New Zealand at Madras	1955-56
406*	D. J. Bicknell and G. E. Welton, Notts v Warwickshire at Birmingham	2000
405	C. P. S. Chauhan and M. S. Gupte, Maharashtra v Vidarbha at Poona	1972-73
403	Rizwan-uz-Zaman and Shoaib Mohammad, PIA v Hyderabad at Hyderabad	1999-2000

Second Wicket

576	S. T. Jayasuriya and R. S. Mahanama, Sri Lanka v India at Colombo	1997-98
475	Zahir Alam and L. S. Rajput, Assam v Tripura at Gauhati	1991-92
465*	J. A. Jameson and R. B. Kanhai, Warwicks v Gloucestershire at Birmingham	1974
455	K. V. Bhandarkar and B. B. Nimbalkar, Maharashtra v Kathiawar at Poona	1948-49
451	W. H. Ponsford and D. G. Bradman, Australia v England at The Oval	1934
446	C. C. Hunte and G. S. Sobers, West Indies v Pakistan at Kingston	1957-58
429*	J. G. Dewes and G. H. G. Doggart, Cambridge U. v Essex at Cambridge	1949
426	Arshad Pervez and Mohsin Khan, Habib Bank v Income Tax at Lahore	1977-78
417	K. J. Barnett and T. A. Tweats, Derbyshire v Yorkshire at Derby	1997
415	A. Jadeja and S. V. Manjrekar, Indians v Bowl XI at Springs	1992-93
403	G. A. Gooch and P. J. Prichard, Essex v Leicestershire at Chelmsford	1990

Third Wicket

467	A. H. Jones and M. D. Crowe, New Zealand v Sri Lanka at Wellington	1990-91
456	Khalid Irtiza and Aslam Ali, United Bank v Multan at Karachi	1975-76
451	Mudassar Nazar and Javed Miandad, Pakistan v India at Hyderabad	1982-83
445	P. E. Whitelaw and W. N. Carson, Auckland v Otago at Dunedin	1936-37
438*	G. A. Hick and T. M. Moody, Worcestershire v Hampshire at Southampton	1997
434	J. B. Stollmeyer and G. E. Gomez, Trinidad v British Guiana at Port-of-Spain	1946-47
424*	W. J. Edrich and D. C. S. Compton, Middlesex v Somerset at Lord's	1948
413	D. J. Bicknell and D. M. Ward, Surrey v Kent at Canterbury	1990
410*	R. S. Modi and L. Amarnath, India in England v The Rest at Calcutta	1946-47
409	V. V. S. Laxman and R. Dravid, South Zone v West Zone at Surat	2000-01
406*	R. S. Gavaskar and S. J. Kalyani, Bengal v Tripura at Agartala	1999-2000
405	A. Jadeja and A. S. Kaypee, Haryana v Services at Faridabad	1991-92

Fourth Wicket

577	V. S. Hazare and Gul Mahomed, Baroda v Holkar at Baroda	1946-47
574*	C. L. Walcott and F. M. M. Worrell, Barbados v Trinidad at Port-of-Spain	1945-46
502*	F. M. M. Worrell and J. D. C. Goddard, Barbados v Trinidad at Bridgetown	1943-44
470	A. I. Kallicharran and G. W. Humpage, Warwicks v Lancs at Southport	1982
462*	D. W. Hookes and W. B. Phillips, South Australia v Tasmania at Adelaide	1986-87
448	R. Abel and T. W. Hayward, Surrey v Yorkshire at The Oval	1899
436	S. Abbas Ali and P. K. Dwevedi, Madhya Pradesh v Railways at Indore	1997-98
425*	A. Dale and I. V. A. Richards, Glamorgan v Middlesex at Cardiff	1993
424	I. S. Lee and S. O. Quin, Victoria v Tasmania at Melbourne	1933-34
411	P. B. H. May and M. C. Cowdrey, England v West Indies at Birmingham	1957
410	G. Abraham and P. Balan Pandit, Kerala v Andhra at Palghat	1959-60
402	W. Watson and T. W. Graveney, MCC v British Guiana at Georgetown	1953-54
402	R. B. Kanhai and K. Ibadulla, Warwicks v Notts at Nottingham	1968

Fifth Wicket

464*	M. E. Waugh and S. R. Waugh, New South Wales v Western Australia at Perth	1990-91
405	S. G. Barnes and D. G. Bradman, Australia v England at Sydney	1946-47
401	M. B. Loye and D. Ripley, Northamptonshire v Glamorgan at Northampton	1998
397	W. Bardsley and C. Kelleway, New South Wales v South Australia at Sydney	1920-21
393	E. G. Arnold and W. B. Burns, Worcestershire v Warwickshire at Birmingham	1909
391	A. Malhotra and S. Dogra, Delhi v Services at Delhi	1995-96
385	S. R. Waugh and G. S. Blewett, Australia v South Africa at Johannesburg	1996-97
381	R. Nayyar and V. Sehwag, North Zone v South Zone at Agartala	1999-2000
377*	G. P. Thorpe and M. R. Ramprakash, England XI v South Australia at Adelaide	1998-99
376	V. V. S. Laxman and R. Dravid, India v Australia at Kolkata	2000-01

Sixth Wicket

487*	G. A. Headley and C. C. Passailaigue, Jamaica v Lord Tennyson's XI at Kingston	1931-32
428	W. W. Armstrong and M. A. Noble, Australians v Sussex at Hove	1902
411	R. M. Poore and E. G. Wynyard, Hampshire v Somerset at Taunton	1899
376	R. Subba Row and A. Lightfoot, Northamptonshire v Surrey at The Oval	1958
372*	K. P. Pietersen and J. E. Morris, Nottinghamshire v Derbyshire at Derby	2001
371	V. M. Merchant and R. S. Modi, Bombay v Maharashtra at Bombay	1943-44
365	B. C. Lara and R. D. Jacobs, West Indians v Australia A at Hobart	2000-01
356	W. V. Raman and A. Kripal Singh, Tamil Nadu v Goa at Panjim	1988-89
353	Salah-ud-Din and Zaheer Abbas, Karachi v East Pakistan at Karachi	1968-69
346	J. H. W. Fingleton and D. G. Bradman, Australia v England at Melbourne	1936-37

Seventh Wicket

460	Bhupinder Singh, jun. and P. Dharmani, Punjab v Delhi at Delhi	1994-95
347	D. St E. Atkinson and C. C. Depeiza, West Indies v Australia at Bridgetown	1954-55
344	K. S. Ranjitsinhji and W. Newham, Sussex v Essex at Leyton	1902
340	K. J. Key and H. Philipson, Oxford University v Middlesex at Chiswick Park	1887
336	F. C. W. Newman and C. R. N. Maxwell, Sir J. Cahn's XI v Leicestershire at Nottingham	1935
335	C. W. Andrews and E. C. Bensted, Queensland v New South Wales at Sydney	1934-35
325	G. Brown and C. H. Abercrombie, Hampshire v Essex at Leyton	1913
323	E. H. Hendren and L. F. Townsend, MCC v Barbados at Bridgetown	1929-30
308	Waqar Hassan and Imtiaz Ahmed, Pakistan v New Zealand at Lahore	1955-56
301	C. C. Lewis and B. N. French, Nottinghamshire v Durham at Chester-le-Street	1993

Eighth Wicket

433	V. T. Trumper and A. Sims, A. Sims' Aust. XI v Canterbury at Christchurch	1913-14
313	Wasim Akram and Saqlain Mushtaq, Pakistan v Zimbabwe at Sheikhupura	1996-97
292	R. Peel and Lord Hawke, Yorkshire v Warwickshire at Birmingham	1896
270	V. T. Trumper and E. P. Barbour, New South Wales v Victoria at Sydney	1912-13
263	D. R. Wilcox and R. M. Taylor, Essex v Warwickshire at Southend	1946
255	E. A. V. Williams and E. A. Martindale, Barbados v Trinidad at Bridgetown	1935-36
249*	Shaukat Mirza and Akram Raza, Habib Bank v PNSC at Lahore	1993-94
246	L. E. G. Ames and G. O. B. Allen, England v New Zealand at Lord's	1931
243	R. J. Hartigan and C. Hill, Australia v England at Adelaide	1907-08
242*	T. J. Zoehrer and K. H. MacLeay, W. Australia v New South Wales at Perth	1990-91

Ninth Wicket

283	J. Chapman and A. Warren, Derbyshire v Warwickshire at Blackwell	1910
268	J. B. Commins and N. Boje, South Africa A v Mashonaland at Harare	1994-95
251	J. W. H. T. Douglas and S. N. Hare, Essex v Derbyshire at Leyton	1921
249*†	A. S. Srivastava and K. Seth, Madhya Pradesh v Vidarbha at Indore	2000-01
245	V. S. Hazare and N. D. Nagarwalla, Maharashtra v Baroda at Poona	1939-40
244*	Arshad Ayub and M. V. Ramanamurthy, Hyderabad v Bihar at Hyderabad	1986-87
239	H. B. Cave and I. B. Leggat, Central Districts v Otago at Dunedin	1952-53
232	C. Hill and E. Walkley, South Australia v New South Wales at Adelaide	1900-01
231	P. Sen and J. Mitter, Bengal v Bihar at Jamshedpur	1950-51
230	D. A. Livingstone and A. T. Castell, Hampshire v Surrey at Southampton	1962

† 276 unbeaten runs were scored for this wicket in two separate partnerships; after Srivastava retired hurt, Seth and N. D. Hirwani added 27.

Tenth Wicket

307	A. F. Kippax and J. E. H. Hooker, New South Wales v Victoria at Melbourne	1928-29
249	C. T. Sarwate and S. N. Banerjee, Indians v Surrey at The Oval	1946
235	F. E. Woolley and A. Fielder, Kent v Worcestershire at Stourbridge	1909
233	Ajay Sharma and Maninder Singh, Delhi v Bombay at Bombay	1991-92
230	R. W. Nicholls and W. Roche, Middlesex v Kent at Lord's	1899
228	R. Illingworth and K. Higgs, Leicestershire v Northamptonshire at Leicester	1977
218	F. H. Vigar and T. P. B. Smith, Essex v Derbyshire at Chesterfield	1947
211	M. Ellis and T. J. Hastings, Victoria v South Australia at Melbourne	1902-03
196*	Nadim Yousuf and Maqsood Kundi, MCB v National Bank at Lahore	1981-82
192	H. A. W. Bowell and W. H. Livsey, Hampshire v Worcs at Bournemouth	1921

UNUSUAL DISMISSALS

Handled the Ball

J. Grundy	MCC v Kent at Lord's	1857
G. Bennett	Kent v Sussex at Hove	1872
W. H. Scotton	Smokers v Non-Smokers at East Melbourne	1886-87
C. W. Wright	Nottinghamshire v Gloucestershire at Bristol	1893
E. Jones	South Australia v Victoria at Melbourne	1894-95
A. W. Nourse	South Africans v Sussex at Hove	1907
E. T. Benson	MCC v Auckland at Auckland	1929-30
A. W. Gilbertson	Otago v Auckland at Auckland	1952-53
W. R. Endean	South Africa v England at Cape Town	1956-57
P. J. Burge	Queensland v New South Wales at Sydney	1958-59
Dildar Awan	Services v Lahore at Lahore	1959-60
M. Mehra	Railways v Delhi at Delhi	1959-60
Mahmood-ul-Hasan	Karachi University v Railways-Quetta at Karachi	1960-61
Ali Raza	Karachi Greens v Hyderabad at Karachi	1961-62
Mohammad Yusuf	Rawalpindi v Peshawar at Peshawar	1962-63
A. Rees	Glamorgan v Middlesex at Lord's	1965
Pervez Akhtar	Multan v Karachi Greens at Sahiwal	1971-72
Javed Mirza	Railways v Punjab at Lahore	1972-73
R. G. Pollock	Eastern Province v Western Province at Cape Town	1973-74
C. I. Dey	Northern Transvaal v Orange Free State at Bloemfontein	1973-74
Nasir Valika	Karachi Whites v National Bank at Karachi	1974-75
Haji Yousuf	National Bank v Railways at Lahore	1974-75
Masood-ul-Hasan	PIA v National Bank B at Lyallpur	1975-76
Hanif Solangi	Hyderabad v Karachi B at Hyderabad	1977-78
D. K. Pearse	Natal v Western Province at Cape Town	1978-79
A. M. J. Hilditch	Australia v Pakistan at Perth	1978-79
Musleh-ud-Din	Railways v Lahore at Lahore	1979-80
Jalal-ud-Din	IDBP v Habib Bank at Bahawalpur	1981-82
Mohsin Khan	Pakistan v Australia at Karachi	1982-83
D. L. Haynes	West Indies v India at Bombay	1983-84
K. Azad	Delhi v Punjab at Amritsar	1983-84
Athar A. Khan	Allied Bank v HBFC at Sialkot	1983-84
A. N. Pandya	Saurashtra v Baroda at Baroda	1984-85
G. L. Linton	Barbados v Windward Islands at Bridgetown	1985-86
R. B. Gartrell	Tasmania v Victoria at Melbourne	1986-87
R. Nayyar	Himachal Pradesh v Punjab at Una	1988-89
R. Weerawardene	Moratuwa v Nomads SC at Colombo	1988-89
A. M. Kane	Vidarbha v Railways at Nagpur	1989-90
P. Bali	Jammu and Kashmir v Services at Delhi	1991-92
M. J. G. Davis	Northern Transvaal B v OFS B at Bloemfontein	1991-92
J. T. C. Vaughan	Emerging Players v England XI at Hamilton	1991-92
G. A. Gooch	England v Australia at Manchester	1993
A. C. Waller	Mashonaland CD v Mashonaland Under-24 at Harare	1994-95
K. M. Krikken	Derbyshire v Indians at Derby	1996
A. Badenhorst	Eastern Province B v North West at Fochville	1998-99
S. R. Waugh	Australia v India at Chennai	2000-01

Obstructing the Field

C. A. Absolom	Cambridge University v Surrey at The Oval	1868
T. Straw	Worcestershire v Warwickshire at Worcester	1899
T. Straw	Worcestershire v Warwickshire at Birmingham	1901
J. P. Whiteside	Leicestershire v Lancashire at Leicester	1901
L. Hutton	England v South Africa at The Oval	1951
J. A. Hayes	Canterbury v Central Districts at Christchurch	1954-55
D. D. Deshpande	Madhya Pradesh v Uttar Pradesh at Benares	1956-57
K. Ibadulla	Warwickshire v Hampshire at Coventry	1963
Qaiser Khan	Dera Ismail Khan v Railways at Lahore	1964-65

Ijaz Ahmed	Lahore Greens v Lahore Blues at Lahore	1973-74
Qasim Feroze	Bahawalpur v Universities at Lahore	1974-75
T. Quirk	Northern Transvaal v Border at East London	1978-79
Mahmood Rashid	United Bank v Muslim Commercial Bank at Bahawalpur	1981-82
Arshad Ali	Sukkur v Quetta at Quetta	1983-84
H. R. Wasu	Vidarbha v Rajasthan at Akola	1984-85
Khalid Javed	Railways v Lahore at Lahore	1985-86
C. Binduhewa	Singha SC v Sinhalese SC at Colombo	1990-91
S. J. Kalyani	Bengal v Orissa at Calcutta	1994-95

Hit the Ball Twice

G. Rawlins	Sheffield v Nottingham at Nottingham	1827
H. E. Bull	MCC v Oxford University at Lord's	1864
H. R. J. Charlwood	Sussex v Surrey at Hove	1872
R. G. Barlow	North v South at Lord's	1878
P. S. Wimble	Transvaal v Griqualand West at Kimberley	1892-93
G. B. Nicholls	Somerset v Gloucestershire at Bristol	1896
A. A. Lilley	Warwickshire v Yorkshire at Birmingham	1897
J. H. King	Leicestershire v Surrey at The Oval	1906
A. P. Binns	Jamaica v British Guiana at Georgetown	1956-57
K. Bhavanna	Andhra v Mysore at Guntur	1963-64
Zaheer Abbas	PIA A v Karachi Blues at Karachi	1969-70
Anwar Miandad	IDBP v United Bank at Lahore	1979-80
Anwar Iqbal	Hyderabad v Sukkur at Hyderabad	1983-84
Iqtidar Ali	Allied Bank v Muslim Commercial Bank at Lahore	1983-84
Aziz Malik	Lahore Division v Faisalabad at Sialkot	1984-85
Javed Mohammad	Multan v Karachi Whites at Sahiwal	1986-87
Shahid Pervez	Jammu and Kashmir v Punjab at Srinagar	1986-87
Ali Naqvi	PNSC v National Bank at Faisalabad	1998-99
A. George	Tamil Nadu v Maharashtra at Pune	1998-99
Maqsood Raza	Lahore Division v PNSC at Sheikhupura	1999-2000

Timed Out

H. Yadav	Tripura v Orissa at Cuttack	1997-98

BOWLING RECORDS

TEN WICKETS IN AN INNINGS

	O	*M*	*R*		
E. Hinkly (Kent)				v England at Lord's	1848
*J. Wisden (North)				v South at Lord's	1850
V. E. Walker (England)	43	17	74	v Surrey at The Oval	1859
V. E. Walker (Middlesex)	44.2	5	104	v Lancashire at Manchester	1865
G. Wootton (All England)	31.3	9	54	v Yorkshire at Sheffield	1865
W. Hickton (Lancashire)	36.2	19	46	v Hampshire at Manchester	1870
S. E. Butler (Oxford)	24.1	11	38	v Cambridge at Lord's	1871
James Lillywhite (South)	60.2	22	129	v North at Canterbury	1872
A. Shaw (MCC)	36.2	8	73	v North at Lord's	1874
E. Barratt (Players)	29	11	43	v Australians at The Oval	1878
G. Giffen (Australian XI)	26	10	66	v The Rest at Sydney	1883-84
W. G. Grace (MCC)	36.2	17	49	v Oxford University at Oxford	1886
G. Burton (Middlesex)	52.3	25	59	v Surrey at The Oval	1888
†A. E. Moss (Canterbury)	21.3	10	28	v Wellington at Christchurch	1889-90
S. M. J. Woods (Cambridge U.)	31	6	69	v Thornton's XI at Cambridge	1890
T. Richardson (Surrey)	15.3	3	45	v Essex at The Oval	1894
H. Pickett (Essex)	27	11	32	v Leicestershire at Leyton	1895

	O	*M*	*R*		
E. J. Tyler (Somerset)	34.3	15	49	v Surrey at Taunton	1895
W. P. Howell (Australians)	23.2	14	28	v Surrey at The Oval	1899
C. H. G. Bland (Sussex)	25.2	10	48	v Kent at Tonbridge	1899
J. Briggs (Lancashire)	28.5	7	55	v Worcestershire at Manchester	1900
A. E. Trott (Middlesex)	14.2	5	42	v Somerset at Taunton	1900
A. Fielder (Players)	24.5	1	90	v Gentlemen at Lord's	1906
E. G. Dennett (Gloucestershire)	19.4	7	40	v Essex at Bristol	1906
A. E. E. Vogler (E. Province)	12	2	26	v Griqualand W. at Johannesburg	1906-07
C. Blythe (Kent)	16	7	30	v Northants at Northampton	1907
J. B. King (Philadelphia)	18.1	7	53	v Ireland at Haverford‡	1909
A. Drake (Yorkshire)	8.5	0	35	v Somerset at Weston-s-Mare	1914
W. Bestwick (Derbyshire)	19	2	40	v Glamorgan at Cardiff	1921
A. A. Mailey (Australians)	28.4	5	66	v Gloucestershire at Cheltenham	1921
C. W. L. Parker (Glos.)	40.3	13	79	v Somerset at Bristol	1921
T. Rushby (Surrey)	17.5	4	43	v Somerset at Taunton	1921
J. C. White (Somerset)	42.2	11	76	v Worcestershire at Worcester	1921
G. C. Collins (Kent)	19.3	4	65	v Nottinghamshire at Dover	1922
H. Howell (Warwickshire)	25.1	5	51	v Yorkshire at Birmingham	1923
A. S. Kennedy (Players)	22.4	10	37	v Gentlemen at The Oval	1927
G. O. B. Allen (Middlesex)	25.3	10	40	v Lancashire at Lord's	1929
A. P. Freeman (Kent)	42	9	131	v Lancashire at Maidstone	1929
G. Geary (Leicestershire)	16.2	8	18	v Glamorgan at Pontypridd	1929
C. V. Grimmett (Australians)	22.3	8	37	v Yorkshire at Sheffield	1930
A. P. Freeman (Kent)	30.4	8	53	v Essex at Southend	1930
H. Verity (Yorkshire)	18.4	6	36	v Warwickshire at Leeds	1931
A. P. Freeman (Kent)	36.1	9	79	v Lancashire at Manchester	1931
V. W. C. Jupp (Northants)	39	6	127	v Kent at Tunbridge Wells	1932
H. Verity (Yorkshire)	19.4	16	10	v Nottinghamshire at Leeds	1932
T. W. Wall (South Australia)	12.4	2	36	v New South Wales at Sydney	1932-33
T. B. Mitchell (Derbyshire)	19.1	4	64	v Leicestershire at Leicester	1935
J. Mercer (Glamorgan)	26	10	51	v Worcestershire at Worcester	1936
T. W. J. Goddard (Glos.)	28.4	4	113	v Worcestershire at Cheltenham	1937
T. F. Smailes (Yorkshire)	17.1	5	47	v Derbyshire at Sheffield	1939
E. A. Watts (Surrey)	24.1	8	67	v Warwickshire at Birmingham	1939
*W. E. Hollies (Warwickshire)	20.4	4	49	v Notts at Birmingham	1946
J. M. Sims (East)	18.4	2	90	v West at Kingston	1948
T. E. Bailey (Essex)	39.4	9	90	v Lancashire at Clacton	1949
J. K. Graveney (Glos.)	18.4	2	66	v Derbyshire at Chesterfield	1949
R. Berry (Lancashire)	36.2	9	102	v Worcestershire at Blackpool	1953
S. P. Gupte (President's XI)	24.2	7	78	v Combined XI at Bombay	1954-55
J. C. Laker (Surrey)	46	18	88	v Australians at The Oval	1956
J. C. Laker (England)	51.2	23	53	v Australia at Manchester	1956
G. A. R. Lock (Surrey)	29.1	18	54	v Kent at Blackheath	1956
K. Smales (Nottinghamshire)	41.3	20	66	v Gloucestershire at Stroud	1956
P. M. Chatterjee (Bengal)	19	11	20	v Assam at Jorhat	1956-57
J. D. Bannister (Warwickshire)	23.3	11	41	v Comb. Services at Birmingham§	1959
A. J. G. Pearson (Cambridge U.)	30.3	8	78	v Leics at Loughborough	1961
N. I. Thomson (Sussex)	34.2	19	49	v Warwickshire at Worthing	1964
P. J. Allan (Queensland)	15.6	3	61	v Victoria at Melbourne	1965-66
I. J. Brayshaw (W. Australia)	17.6	4	44	v Victoria at Perth	1967-68
Shahid Mahmood (Karachi Whites)	25	5	58	v Khairpur at Karachi	1969-70
E. E. Hemmings (International XI)	49.3	14	175	v West Indies XI at Kingston	1982-83
P. Sunderam (Rajasthan)	22	5	78	v Vidarbha at Jodhpur	1985-86
S. T. Jefferies (W. Province)	22.5	7	59	v Orange Free State at Cape Town	1987-88
Imran Adil (Bahawalpur)	22.5	3	92	v Faisalabad at Faisalabad	1989-90
G. P. Wickremasinghe (Sinhalese)	19.2	5	41	v Kalutara at Colombo	1991-92
R. L. Johnson (Middlesex)	18.5	6	45	v Derbyshire at Derby	1994
Naeem Akhtar (Rawalpindi B)	21.3	10	28	v Peshawar at Peshawar	1995-96
A. Kumble (India)	26.3	9	74	v Pakistan at Delhi	1998-99
D. S. Mohanty (East Zone)	19	5	46	v South Zone at Agartala	2000-01

Note: The following instances were achieved in 12-a-side matches:

	O	M	R		
E. M. Grace (MCC)	32.2	7	69	v Gents of Kent at Canterbury	1862
W. G. Grace (MCC)	46.1	15	92	v Kent at Canterbury	1873
†D. C. S. Hinds (A. B. St Hill's XII)	19.1	6	36	v Trinidad at Port-of-Spain	1900-01

* *J. Wisden and W. E. Hollies achieved the feat without the direct assistance of a fielder. Wisden's ten were all bowled; Hollies bowled seven and had three lbw.*
† *On debut in first-class cricket.* ‡ *Pennsylvania.* § *Mitchells & Butlers Ground.*

OUTSTANDING BOWLING ANALYSES

	O	M	R	W		
H. Verity (Yorkshire)	19.4	16	10	10	v Nottinghamshire at Leeds	1932
G. Elliott (Victoria)	19	17	2	9	v Tasmania at Launceston	1857-58
Ahad Khan (Railways)	6.3	4	7	9	v Dera Ismail Khan at Lahore	1964-65
J. C. Laker (England)	14	12	2	8	v The Rest at Bradford	1950
D. Shackleton (Hampshire)	11.1	7	4	8	v Somerset at Weston-s-Mare	1955
E. Peate (Yorkshire)	16	11	5	8	v Surrey at Holbeck	1883
F. R. Spofforth (Australians)	8.3	6	3	7	v England XI at Birmingham	1884
W. A. Henderson (North-Eastern Transvaal)	9.3	7	4	7	v Orange Free State at Bloemfontein	1937-38
Rajinder Goel (Haryana)	7	4	4	7	v Jammu and Kashmir at Chandigarh	1977-78
V. I. Smith (South Africans)	4.5	3	1	6	v Derbyshire at Derby	1947
S. Cosstick (Victoria)	21.1	20	1	6	v Tasmania at Melbourne	1868-69
Israr Ali (Bahawalpur)	11	10	1	6	v Dacca U. at Bahawalpur	1957-58
A. D. Pougher (MCC)	3	3	0	5	v Australians at Lord's	1896
G. R. Cox (Sussex)	6	6	0	5	v Somerset at Weston-s-Mare	1921
R. K. Tyldesley (Lancashire)	5	5	0	5	v Leicestershire at Manchester	1924
P. T. Mills (Gloucestershire)	6.4	6	0	5	v Somerset at Bristol	1928

MOST WICKETS IN A MATCH

19-90	J. C. Laker	England v Australia at Manchester	1956
17-48†	C. Blythe	Kent v Northamptonshire at Northampton	1907
17-50	C. T. B. Turner	Australians v England XI at Hastings	1888
17-54	W. P. Howell	Australians v Western Province at Cape Town	1902-03
17-56	C. W. L. Parker	Gloucestershire v Essex at Gloucester	1925
17-67	A. P. Freeman	Kent v Sussex at Hove	1922
17-89	W. G. Grace	Gloucestershire v Nottinghamshire at Cheltenham	1877
17-89	F. C. L. Matthews	Nottinghamshire v Northants at Nottingham	1923
17-91	H. Dean	Lancashire v Yorkshire at Liverpool	1913
17-91†	H. Verity	Yorkshire v Essex at Leyton	1933
17-92	A. P. Freeman	Kent v Warwickshire at Folkestone	1932
17-103	W. Mycroft	Derbyshire v Hampshire at Southampton	1876
17-106	G. R. Cox	Sussex v Warwickshire at Horsham	1926
17-106†	T. W. J. Goddard	Gloucestershire v Kent at Bristol	1939
17-119	W. Mead	Essex v Hampshire at Southampton	1895
17-137	W. Brearley	Lancashire v Somerset at Manchester	1905
17-159	S. F. Barnes	England v South Africa at Johannesburg	1913-14
17-201	G. Giffen	South Australia v Victoria at Adelaide	1885-86
17-212	J. C. Clay	Glamorgan v Worcestershire at Swansea	1937

† *Achieved in a single day.*

FOUR WICKETS WITH CONSECUTIVE BALLS

J. Wells	Kent v Sussex at Brighton	1862
G. Ulyett	Lord Harris's XI v New South Wales at Sydney	1878-79
G. Nash	Lancashire v Somerset at Manchester	1882
J. B. Hide	Sussex v MCC and Ground at Lord's	1890
F. J. Shacklock	Nottinghamshire v Somerset at Nottingham	1893
A. D. Downes	Otago v Auckland at Dunedin	1893-94
F. Martin	MCC and Ground v Derbyshire at Lord's	1895
A. W. Mold	Lancashire v Nottinghamshire at Nottingham	1895
W. Brearley†	Lancashire v Somerset at Manchester	1905
S. Haigh	MCC v Army XI at Pretoria	1905-06
A. E. Trott‡	Middlesex v Somerset at Lord's	1907
F. A. Tarrant	Middlesex v Gloucestershire at Bristol	1907
A. Drake	Yorkshire v Derbyshire at Chesterfield	1914
S. G. Smith	Northamptonshire v Warwickshire at Birmingham	1914
H. A. Peach	Surrey v Sussex at The Oval	1924
A. F. Borland	Natal v Griqualand West at Kimberley	1926-27
J. E. H. Hooker†	New South Wales v Victoria at Sydney	1928-29
R. K. Tyldesley†	Lancashire v Derbyshire at Derby	1929
R. J. Crisp	Western Province v Griqualand West at Johannesburg	1931-32
R. J. Crisp	Western Province v Natal at Durban	1933-34
A. R. Gover	Surrey v Worcestershire at Worcester	1935
W. H. Copson	Derbyshire v Warwickshire at Derby	1937
W. A. Henderson	N.E. Transvaal v Orange Free State at Bloemfontein	1937-38
F. Ridgway	Kent v Derbyshire at Folkestone	1951
A. K. Walker§	Nottinghamshire v Leicestershire at Leicester	1956
D. Robins†	South Australia v New South Wales at Adelaide	1965-66
S. N. Mohol	President's XI v Combined XI at Poona	1965-66
P. I. Pocock	Surrey v Sussex at Eastbourne	1972
S. S. Saini†	Delhi v Himachal Pradesh at Delhi	1988-89
D. Dias	W. Province (Suburbs) v Central Province at Colombo	1990-91
Ali Gauhar	Karachi Blues v United Bank at Peshawar	1994-95
K. D. James**	Hampshire v Indians at Southampton	1996
G. P. Butcher	Surrey v Derbyshire at The Oval	2000

† *Not all in the same innings.*
‡ *Trott achieved another hat-trick in the same innings of this, his benefit match.*
§ *Having bowled Firth with the last ball of the first innings, Walker achieved a unique feat by dismissing Lester, Tompkin and Smithson with the first three balls of the second.*
** *James also scored a century, a unique double.*

Notes: In their match with England at The Oval in 1863, Surrey lost four wickets in the course of a four-ball over from G. Bennett.

Sussex lost five wickets in the course of the final (six-ball) over of their match with Surrey at Eastbourne in 1972. P. I. Pocock, who had taken three wickets in his previous over, captured four more, taking in all seven wickets with 11 balls, a feat unique in first-class matches. (The eighth wicket fell to a run-out.)

HAT-TRICKS

Double Hat-Trick

Besides Trott's performance, which is given in the preceding section, the following instances are recorded of players having performed the hat-trick twice in the same match, Rao doing so in the same innings.

A. Shaw	Nottinghamshire v Gloucestershire at Nottingham	1884
T. J. Matthews	Australia v South Africa at Manchester	1912
C. W. L. Parker	Gloucestershire v Middlesex at Bristol	1924
R. O. Jenkins	Worcestershire v Surrey at Worcester	1949
J. S. Rao	Services v Northern Punjab at Amritsar	1963-64
Amin Lakhani	Combined XI v Indians at Multan	1978-79

Five Wickets in Six Balls

W. H. Copson	Derbyshire v Warwickshire at Derby	1937
W. A. Henderson	N.E. Transvaal v Orange Free State at Bloemfontein	1937-38
P. I. Pocock	Surrey v Sussex at Eastbourne	1972

Most Hat-Tricks

Seven times: D. V. P. Wright.
Six times: T. W. J. Goddard, C. W. L. Parker.
Five times: S. Haigh, V. W. C. Jupp, A. E. G. Rhodes, F. A. Tarrant.
Four times: R. G. Barlow, A. P. Freeman, J. T. Hearne, J. C. Laker, G. A. R. Lock, G. G. Macaulay, T. J. Matthews, M. J. Procter, T. Richardson, F. R. Spofforth, F. S. Trueman.
Three times: W. M. Bradley, H. J. Butler, S. T. Clarke, W. H. Copson, R. J. Crisp, J. W. H. T. Douglas, J. A. Flavell, G. Giffen, D. W. Headley, K. Higgs, A. Hill, W. A. Humphreys, R. D. Jackman, R. O. Jenkins, A. S. Kennedy, W. H. Lockwood, E. A. McDonald, T. L. Pritchard, J. S. Rao, A. Shaw, J. B. Statham, M. W. Tate, H. Trumble, Wasim Akram, D. Wilson, G. A. Wilson.
Twice (current players only): D. G. Cork, K. J. Dean, D. Gough, A. Kumble, J. D. Lewry, A. Sheriyar, Waqar Younis.

Hat-Trick on Debut

H. Hay	South Australia v Lord Hawke's XI at Unley, Adelaide	1902-03
H. A. Sedgwick	Yorkshire v Worcestershire at Hull	1906
R. Wooster	Northamptonshire v Dublin University at Northampton	1925
J. C. Treanor	New South Wales v Queensland at Brisbane	1954-55
V. B. Ranjane	Maharashtra v Saurashtra at Poona	1956-57
N. Frederick	Ceylon v Madras at Colombo	1963-64
J. S. Rao	Services v Jammu and Kashmir at Delhi	1963-64
Mehboodullah	Uttar Pradesh v Madhya Pradesh at Lucknow	1971-72
R. O. Estwick	Barbados v Guyana at Bridgetown	1982-83
S. A. Ankola	Maharashtra v Gujarat at Poona	1988-89
J. Srinath	Karnataka v Hyderabad at Secunderabad	1989-90
S. P. Mukherjee	Bengal v Hyderabad at Secunderabad	1989-90

Notes: R. R. Phillips (Border) took a hat-trick in his first over in first-class cricket (v Eastern Province at Port Elizabeth, 1939-40) having previously played in four matches without bowling.

J. S. Rao took two more hat-tricks in his next match.

250 WICKETS IN A SEASON

	Season	*O*	*M*	*R*	*W*	*Avge*
A. P. Freeman	1928	1,976.1	423	5,489	304	18.05
A. P. Freeman	1933	2,039	651	4,549	298	15.26
T. Richardson	1895‡	1,690.1	463	4,170	290	14.37
C. T. B. Turner	1888†	2,427.2	1,127	3,307	283	11.68
A. P. Freeman	1931	1,618	360	4,307	276	15.60
A. P. Freeman	1930	1,914.3	472	4,632	275	16.84
T. Richardson	1897‡	1,603.4	495	3,945	273	14.45
A. P. Freeman	1929	1,670.5	381	4,879	267	18.27
W. Rhodes	1900	1,553	455	3,606	261	13.81
J. T. Hearne	1896‡	2,003.1	818	3,670	257	14.28
A. P. Freeman	1932	1,565.5	404	4,149	253	16.39
W. Rhodes	1901	1,565	505	3,797	251	15.12

† *Indicates 4-ball overs.* ‡ *5-ball overs.*

Notes: In four consecutive seasons (1928-31), A. P. Freeman took 1,122 wickets, and in eight consecutive seasons (1928-35), 2,090 wickets. In each of these eight seasons he took over 200 wickets.

T. Richardson took 1,005 wickets in four consecutive seasons (1894-97).

In 1896, J. T. Hearne took his 100th wicket as early as June 12. In 1931, C. W. L. Parker did the same and A. P. Freeman obtained his 100th wicket a day later.

LEADING BOWLERS IN AN ENGLISH SEASON

(Qualification: 10 wickets in 10 innings)

Season	*Leading wicket-taker*	*Wkts*	*Avge*	*Top of averages*	*Wkts*	*Avge*
1946	W. E. Hollies	184	15.60	A. Booth	111	11.61
1947	T. W. J. Goddard	238	17.30	J. C. Clay	65	16.44
1948	J. E. Walsh	174	19.56	J. C. Clay	41	14.17
1949	R. O. Jenkins	183	21.19	T. W. J. Goddard	160	19.18
1950	R. Tattersall	193	13.59	R. Tattersall	193	13.59
1951	R. Appleyard	200	14.14	R. Appleyard	200	14.14
1952	J. H. Wardle	177	19.54	F. S. Trueman	61	13.78
1953	B. Dooland	172	16.58	C. J. Knott	38	13.71
1954	B. Dooland	196	15.48	J. B. Statham	92	14.13
1955	G. A. R. Lock	216	14.49	R. Appleyard	85	13.01
1956	D. J. Shepherd	177	15.36	G. A. R. Lock	155	12.46
1957	G. A. R. Lock	212	12.02	G. A. R. Lock	212	12.02
1958	G. A. R. Lock	170	12.08	H. L. Jackson	143	10.99
1959	D. Shackleton	148	21.55	J. B. Statham	139	15.01
1960	F. S. Trueman	175	13.98	J. B. Statham	135	12.31
1961	J. A. Flavell	171	17.79	J. A. Flavell	171	17.79
1962	D. Shackleton	172	20.15	C. Cook	58	17.13
1963	D. Shackleton	146	16.75	C. C. Griffith	119	12.83
1964	D. Shackleton	142	20.40	J. A. Standen	64	13.00
1965	D. Shackleton	144	16.08	H. J. Rhodes	119	11.04
1966	D. L. Underwood	157	13.80	D. L. Underwood	157	13.80
1967	T. W. Cartwright	147	15.52	D. L. Underwood	136	12.39
1968	R. Illingworth	131	14.36	O. S. Wheatley	82	12.95
1969	R. M. H. Cottam	109	21.04	A. Ward	69	14.82
1970	D. J. Shepherd	106	19.16	Majid Khan	11	18.81
1971	L. R. Gibbs	131	18.89	G. G. Arnold	83	17.12
1972	T. W. Cartwright	98	18.64	I. M. Chappell	10	10.60
	B. Stead	98	20.38			
1973	B. S. Bedi	105	17.94	T. W. Cartwright	89	15.84
1974	A. M. E. Roberts	119	13.62	A. M. E. Roberts	119	13.62
1975	P. G. Lee	112	18.45	A. M. E. Roberts	57	15.80
1976	G. A. Cope	93	24.13	M. A. Holding	55	14.38
1977	M. J. Procter	109	18.04	R. A. Woolmer	19	15.21
1978	D. L. Underwood	110	14.49	D. L. Underwood	110	14.49
1979	D. L. Underwood	106	14.85	J. Garner	55	13.83
	J. K. Lever	106	17.30			
1980	R. D. Jackman	121	15.40	J. Garner	49	13.93
1981	R. J. Hadlee	105	14.89	R. J. Hadlee	105	14.89
1982	M. D. Marshall	134	15.73	R. J. Hadlee	61	14.57
1983	J. K. Lever	106	16.28	Imran Khan	12	7.16
	D. L. Underwood	106	19.28			
1984	R. J. Hadlee	117	14.05	R. J. Hadlee	117	14.05
1985	N. V. Radford	101	24.68	R. M. Ellison	65	17.20
1986	C. A. Walsh	118	18.17	M. D. Marshall	100	15.08
1987	N. V. Radford	109	20.81	R. J. Hadlee	97	12.64
1988	F. D. Stephenson	125	18.31	M. D. Marshall	42	13.16
1989	D. R. Pringle	94	18.64	T. M. Alderman	70	15.64
	S. L. Watkin	94	25.09			
1990	N. A. Foster	94	26.61	I. R. Bishop	59	19.05
1991	Waqar Younis	113	14.65	Waqar Younis	113	14.65
1992	C. A. Walsh	92	15.96	C. A. Walsh	92	15.96
1993	S. L. Watkin	92	22.80	Wasim Akram	59	19.27
1994	M. M. Patel	90	22.86	C. E. L. Ambrose	77	14.45
1995	A. Kumble	105	20.40	A. A. Donald	89	16.07

Season	*Leading wicket-taker*	*Wkts*	*Avge*	*Top of averages*	*Wkts*	*Avge*
1996	C. A. Walsh	85	16.84	C. E. L. Ambrose	43	16.67
1997	A. M. Smith	83	17.63	A. A. Donald	60	15.63
1998	C. A. Walsh	106	17.31	V. J. Wells	36	14.27
1999	A. Sheriyar	92	24.70	Saqlain Mushtaq	58	11.37
2000	G. D. McGrath	80	13.21	C. A. Walsh	40	11.42
2001	R. J. Kirtley	75	23.32	G. D. McGrath	40	15.60

100 WICKETS IN A SEASON

(Since reduction of Championship matches in 1969)

Five times: D. L. Underwood 110 (1978), 106 (1979), 106 (1983), 102 (1971), 101 (1969).
Four times: J. K. Lever 116 (1984), 106 (1978), 106 (1979), 106 (1983).
Twice: B. S. Bedi 112 (1974), 105 (1973); T. W. Cartwright 108 (1969), 104 (1971); N. A. Foster 105 (1986), 102 (1991); N. Gifford 105 (1970), 104 (1983); R. J. Hadlee 117 (1984), 105 (1981); P. G. Lee 112 (1975), 101 (1973); M. D. Marshall 134 (1982), 100 (1986); M. J. Procter 109 (1977), 108 (1969); N. V. Radford 109 (1987), 101 (1985); F. J. Titmus 105 (1970), 104 (1971); C. A. Walsh 118 (1986), 106 (1998).
Once: J. P. Agnew 101 (1987); I. T. Botham 100 (1978); A. R. Caddick 105 (1998); K. E. Cooper 101 (1988); R. M. H. Cottam 109 (1969); D. R. Doshi 101 (1980); J. E. Emburey 103 (1983); L. R. Gibbs 131 (1971); R. N. S. Hobbs 102 (1970); Intikhab Alam 104 (1971); R. D. Jackman 121 (1980); A. Kumble 105 (1995); A. M. E. Roberts 119 (1974); P. J. Sainsbury 107 (1971); Sarfraz Nawaz 101 (1975); M. W. W. Selvey 101 (1978); D. J. Shepherd 106 (1970); F. D. Stephenson 125 (1988); Waqar Younis 113 (1991); D. Wilson 102 (1969).

100 WICKETS IN A SEASON MOST TIMES

(Includes overseas tours and seasons)

23 times: W. Rhodes 200 wkts (3).
20 times: D. Shackleton (In successive seasons – 1949 to 1968 inclusive).
17 times: A. P. Freeman 300 wkts (1), 200 wkts (7).
16 times: T. W. J. Goddard 200 wkts (4), C. W. L. Parker 200 wkts (5), R. T. D. Perks, F. J. Titmus.
15 times: J. T. Hearne 200 wkts (3), G. H. Hirst 200 wkts (1), A. S. Kennedy 200 wkts (1).
14 times: C. Blythe 200 wkts (1), W. E. Hollies, G. A. R. Lock 200 wkts (2), M. W. Tate 200 wkts (3), J. C. White.
13 times: J. B. Statham.
12 times: J. Briggs, E. G. Dennett 200 wkts (1), C. Gladwin, D. J. Shepherd, N. I. Thomson, F. S. Trueman.
11 times: A. V. Bedser, G. Geary, S. Haigh, J. C. Laker, M. S. Nichols, A. E. Relf.
10 times: W. Attewell, W. G. Grace, R. Illingworth, H. L. Jackson, V. W. C. Jupp, G. G. Macaulay 200 wkts (1), W. Mead, T. B. Mitchell, T. Richardson 200 wkts (3), J. Southerton 200 wkts (1), R. K. Tyldesley, D. L. Underwood, J. H. Wardle, T. G. Wass, D. V. P. Wright.

100 WICKETS IN A SEASON OUTSIDE ENGLAND

W		*Season*	*Country*	*R*	*Avge*
116	M. W. Tate	1926-27	India/Ceylon	1,599	13.78
113	Kabir Khan	1998-99	Pakistan	1,706	15.09
107	Ijaz Faqih	1985-86	Pakistan	1,719	16.06
106	C. T. B. Turner	1887-88	Australia	1,441	13.59
106	R. Benaud	1957-58	South Africa	2,056	19.39
105	Murtaza Hussain	1995-96	Pakistan	1,882	17.92
104	S. F. Barnes	1913-14	South Africa	1,117	10.74
104	Sajjad Akbar	1989-90	Pakistan	2,328	22.38
103	Abdul Qadir	1982-83	Pakistan	2,367	22.98

1,500 WICKETS

Dates in italics denote the first half of an overseas season; i.e. *1970* denotes the 1970-71 season.

		Career	*W*	*R*	*Avge*
1	W. Rhodes	1898-1930	4,187	69,993	16.71
2	A. P. Freeman	1914-36	3,776	69,577	18.42
3	C. W. L. Parker	1903-35	3,278	63,817	19.46
4	J. T. Hearne	1888-1923	3,061	54,352	17.75
5	T. W. J. Goddard	1922-52	2,979	59,116	19.84
6	W. G. Grace	1865-1908	2,876	51,545	17.92
7	A. S. Kennedy	1907-36	2,874	61,034	21.23
8	D. Shackleton	1948-69	2,857	53,303	18.65
9	G. A. R. Lock	1946-*70*	2,844	54,709	19.23
10	F. J. Titmus	1949-82	2,830	63,313	22.37
11	M. W. Tate	1912-37	2,784	50,571	18.16
12	G. H. Hirst	1891-1929	2,739	51,282	18.72
13	C. Blythe	1899-1914	2,506	42,136	16.81
14	D. L. Underwood	1963-87	2,465	49,993	20.28
15	W. E. Astill	1906-39	2,431	57,783	23.76
16	J. C. White	1909-37	2,356	43,759	18.57
17	W. E. Hollies	1932-57	2,323	48,656	20.94
18	F. S. Trueman	1949-69	2,304	42,154	18.29
19	J. B. Statham	1950-68	2,260	36,999	16.37
20	R. T. D. Perks	1930-55	2,233	53,770	24.07
21	J. Briggs	1879-1900	2,221	35,431	15.95
22	D. J. Shepherd	1950-72	2,218	47,302	21.32
23	E. G. Dennett	1903-26	2,147	42,571	19.82
24	T. Richardson	1892-1905	2,104	38,794	18.43
25	T. E. Bailey	1945-67	2,082	48,170	23.13
26	R. Illingworth	1951-83	2,072	42,023	20.28
27	N. Gifford	1960-88	2,068	48,731	23.56
27	F. E. Woolley	1906-38	2,068	41,066	19.85
29	G. Geary	1912-38	2,063	41,339	20.03
30	D. V. P. Wright	1932-57	2,056	49,307	23.98
31	J. A. Newman	1906-30	2,032	51,111	25.15
32	†A. Shaw	1864-97	2,027	24,580	12.12
33	S. Haigh	1895-1913	2,012	32,091	15.94
34	H. Verity	1930-39	1,956	29,146	14.90
35	W. Attewell	1881-1900	1,951	29,896	15.32
36	J. C. Laker	1946-*64*	1,944	35,791	18.41
37	A. V. Bedser	1939-60	1,924	39,279	20.41
38	W. Mead	1892-1913	1,916	36,388	18.99
39	A. E. Relf	1900-21	1,897	39,724	20.94
40	P. G. H. Fender	1910-36	1,894	47,458	25.05
41	J. W. H. T. Douglas	1901-30	1,893	44,159	23.32
42	J. H. Wardle	1946-*67*	1,846	35,027	18.97
43	G. R. Cox	1895-1928	1,843	42,136	22.86
44	G. A. Lohmann	1884-97	1,841	25,295	13.73
45	J. W. Hearne	1909-36	1,839	44,926	24.42
46	G. G. Macaulay	1920-35	1,837	32,440	17.65
47	M. S. Nichols	1924-39	1,833	39,666	21.63
48	J. B. Mortimore	1950-75	1,807	41,904	23.18
48	**C. A. Walsh**	***1981-2000***	**1,807**	**39,233**	**21.71**
50	C. Cook	1946-64	1,782	36,578	20.52
51	R. Peel	1882-99	1,752	28,442	16.23
52	H. L. Jackson	1947-63	1,733	30,101	17.36
53	J. K. Lever	1967-89	1,722	41,772	24.25
54	T. P. B. Smith	1929-52	1,697	45,059	26.55
55	J. Southerton	1854-79	1,681	24,290	14.44
56	A. E. Trott	*1892*-1911	1,674	35,317	21.09

		Career	W	R	Avge
57	A. W. Mold	1889-1901	1,673	26,010	15.54
58	T. G. Wass	1896-1920	1,666	34,092	20.46
59	V. W. C. Jupp	1909-38	1,658	38,166	23.01
60	C. Gladwin	1939-58	1,653	30,265	18.30
61	M. D. Marshall	*1977-95*	1,651	31,548	19.10
62	W. E. Bowes	1928-47	1,639	27,470	16.76
63	A. W. Wellard	1927-50	1,614	39,302	24.35
64	J. E. Emburey	1973-97	1,608	41,958	26.09
65	P. I. Pocock	1964-86	1,607	42,648	26.53
66	N. I. Thomson	1952-72	1,597	32,867	20.58
67	J. Mercer	1919-47	1,591	37,210	23.38
	G. J. Thompson	1897-1922	1,591	30,058	18.89
69	J. M. Sims	1929-53	1,581	39,401	24.92
70	T. Emmett	1866-88	1,571	21,314	13.56
	Intikhab Alam	*1957-82*	1,571	43,474	27.67
72	B. S. Bedi	*1961-81*	1,560	33,843	21.69
73	W. Voce	1927-52	1,558	35,961	23.08
74	A. R. Gover	1928-48	1,555	36,753	23.63
75	T. W. Cartwright	1952-77	1,536	29,357	19.11
	K. Higgs	1958-86	1,536	36,267	23.61
77	James Langridge	1924-53	1,530	34,524	22.56
78	J. A. Flavell	1949-67	1,529	32,847	21.48
79	E. E. Hemmings	1966-95	1,515	44,403	29.30
80	C. F. Root	1910-33	1,512	31,933	21.11
	F. A. Tarrant	*1898-1936*	1,512	26,450	17.49
82	R. K. Tyldesley	1919-35	1,509	25,980	17.21

Bold type denotes those who played in 2000-01 and 2001 seasons.

† *The figures for A. Shaw exclude one wicket for which no analysis is available.*

Note: Some works of reference provide career figures which differ from those in this list, owing to the exclusion or inclusion of matches recognised or not recognised as first-class by *Wisden*.

Current Players with 1,000 Wickets

	Career	W	R	Avge
A. A. Donald	*1985-2000*	1,169	26,177	22.39
P. A. J. DeFreitas	1985-2001	1,094	30,302	27.69
P. C. R. Tufnell	1986-2001	1,012	29,636	29.28
Wasim Akram	*1984-2001*	1,011	21,935	21.69

ALL-ROUND RECORDS

HUNDRED AND TEN WICKETS IN AN INNINGS

V. E. Walker, England v Surrey at The Oval; 20*, 108, ten for 74, and four for 17 . . 1859
W. G. Grace, MCC v Oxford University at Oxford; 104, two for 60, and ten for 49 . . 1886

Note: E. M. Grace, for MCC v Gentlemen of Kent in a 12-a-side match at Canterbury in 1862, scored 192* and took five for 77 and ten for 69.

DOUBLE-HUNDRED AND 16 WICKETS

G. Giffen, South Australia v Victoria at Adelaide; 271, nine for 96, and seven for 70 . . 1891-92

HUNDRED IN EACH INNINGS AND FIVE WICKETS TWICE

G. H. Hirst, Yorkshire v Somerset at Bath; 111, 117*, six for 70, and five for 45 . . . 1906

HUNDRED IN EACH INNINGS AND TEN WICKETS

B. J. T. Bosanquet, Middlesex v Sussex at Lord's; 103, 100*, three for 75, and eight for 53. 1905
F. D. Stephenson, Nottinghamshire v Yorkshire at Nottingham; 111, 117, four for 105, and seven for 117 1988

HUNDRED AND FOUR WICKETS WITH CONSECUTIVE BALLS

K. D. James, Hampshire v Indians at Southampton; 103 and five for 74 including four wickets with consecutive balls. 1996

HUNDRED AND HAT-TRICK

G. Giffen, Australians v Lancashire at Manchester 1884
W. E. Roller, Surrey v Sussex at The Oval. *Unique instance of 200 and hat-trick*. . . 1885
W. B. Burns, Worcestershire v Gloucestershire at Worcester. 1913
V. W. C. Jupp, Sussex v Essex at Colchester. 1921
R. E. S. Wyatt, MCC v Ceylon at Colombo 1926-27
L. N. Constantine, West Indians v Northamptonshire at Northampton. 1928
D. E. Davies, Glamorgan v Leicestershire at Leicester. 1937
V. M. Merchant, Dr C. R. Pereira's XI v Sir Homi Mehta's XI at Bombay 1946-47
M. J. Procter, Gloucestershire v Essex at Westcliff-on-Sea. 1972
M. J. Procter, Gloucestershire v Leicestershire at Bristol. 1979

SEASON DOUBLES

2,000 Runs and 200 Wickets

1906 G. H. Hirst 2,385 runs and 208 wickets

3,000 Runs and 100 Wickets

1937 J. H. Parks 3,003 runs and 101 wickets

2,000 Runs and 100 Wickets

	Season	*R*	*W*
W. G. Grace	1873	2,139	106
W. G. Grace	1876	2,622	130
C. L. Townsend	1899	2,440	101
G. L. Jessop	1900	2,210	104
G. H. Hirst	1904	2,501	132
G. H. Hirst	1905	2,266	110
W. Rhodes	1909	2,094	141
W. Rhodes	1911	2,261	117
F. A. Tarrant	1911	2,030	111
J. W. Hearne	1913	2,036	124
J. W. Hearne	1914	2,116	123
F. E. Woolley	1914	2,272	125
J. W. Hearne	1920	2,148	142
V. W. C. Jupp	1921	2,169	121
F. E. Woolley	1921	2,101	167
F. E. Woolley	1922	2,022	163
F. E. Woolley	1923	2,091	101
L. F. Townsend	1933	2,268	100
D. E. Davies	1937	2,012	103
James Langridge	1937	2,082	101
T. E. Bailey	1959	2,011	100

1,000 Runs and 200 Wickets

	Season	R	W
A. E. Trott	1899	1,175	239
A. E. Trott	1900	1,337	211
A. S. Kennedy	1922	1,129	205
M. W. Tate	1923	1,168	219
M. W. Tate	1924	1,419	205
M. W. Tate	1925	1,290	228

1,000 Runs and 100 Wickets

Sixteen times: W. Rhodes.
Fourteen times: G. H. Hirst.
Ten times: V. W. C. Jupp.
Nine times: W. E. Astill.
Eight times: T. E. Bailey, W. G. Grace, M. S. Nichols, A. E. Relf, F. A. Tarrant, M. W. Tate†, F. J. Titmus, F. E. Woolley.
Seven times: G. E. Tribe.

† *M. W. Tate also scored 1,193 runs and took 116 wickets for MCC in first-class matches on the 1926-27 MCC tour of India and Ceylon.*

Note: R. J. Hadlee (1984) and F. D. Stephenson (1988) are the only players to perform the feat since the reduction of County Championship matches. A complete list of those performing the feat before then will be found on page 202 of the 1982 *Wisden*.

Wicket-Keeper's Double

	Season	R	D
L. E. G. Ames	1928	1,919	122
L. E. G. Ames	1929	1,795	128
L. E. G. Ames	1932	2,482	104
J. T. Murray	1957	1,025	104

20,000 RUNS AND 2,000 WICKETS

	Career	R	Avge	W	Avge	Doubles
W. E. Astill	1906-39	22,731	22.55	2,431	23.76	9
T. E. Bailey	1945-67	28,641	33.42	2,082	23.13	8
W. G. Grace	1865-1908	54,896	39.55	2,876	17.92	8
G. H. Hirst	1891-1929	36,323	34.13	2,739	18.72	14
R. Illingworth	1951-83	24,134	28.06	2,072	20.28	6
W. Rhodes	1898-1930	39,802	30.83	4,187	16.71	16
M. W. Tate	1912-37	21,717	25.01	2,784	18.16	8†
F. J. Titmus	1949-82	21,588	23.11	2,830	22.37	8
F. E. Woolley	1906-38	58,969	40.75	2,068	19.85	8

† *Plus one double overseas (see above).*

WICKET-KEEPING RECORDS

MOST DISMISSALS IN AN INNINGS

9 (8ct, 1st)	Tahir Rashid	Habib Bank v PACO at Gujranwala	1992-93
9 (7ct, 2st)	W. R. James*	Matabeleland v Mashonaland CD at Bulawayo	1995-96
8 (all ct)	A. T. W. Grout	Queensland v Western Australia at Brisbane	1959-60
8 (all ct)†	D. E. East	Essex v Somerset at Taunton	1985
8 (all ct)	S. A. Marsh‡	Kent v Middlesex at Lord's	1991

8 (6ct, 2st)	T. J. Zoehrer	Australians v Surrey at The Oval	1993
8 (7ct, 1st)	D. S. Berry	Victoria v South Australia at Melbourne	1996-97
8 (7ct, 1st)	Y. S. S. Mendis	Bloomfield v Kurunegala Youth at Colombo	2000-01
7 (4ct, 3st)	E. J. Smith	Warwickshire v Derbyshire at Birmingham	1926
7 (6ct, 1st)	W. Farrimond	Lancashire v Kent at Manchester	1930
7 (all ct)	W. F. F. Price	Middlesex v Yorkshire at Lord's	1937
7 (3ct, 4st)	D. Tallon	Queensland v Victoria at Brisbane	1938-39
7 (all ct)	R. A. Saggers	New South Wales v Combined XI at Brisbane	1940-41
7 (1ct, 6st)	H. Yarnold	Worcestershire v Scotland at Dundee	1951
7 (4ct, 3st)	J. Brown	Scotland v Ireland at Dublin	1957
7 (6ct, 1st)	N. Kirsten	Border v Rhodesia at East London	1959-60
7 (all ct)	M. S. Smith	Natal v Border at East London	1959-60
7 (all ct)	K. V. Andrew	Northamptonshire v Lancashire at Manchester	1962
7 (all ct)	A. Long	Surrey v Sussex at Hove	1964
7 (all ct)	R. M. Schofield	Central Districts v Wellington at Wellington	1964-65
7 (all ct)	R. W. Taylor	Derbyshire v Glamorgan at Derby	1966
7 (6ct, 1st)	H. B. Taber	New South Wales v South Australia at Adelaide	1968-69
7 (6ct, 1st)	E. W. Jones	Glamorgan v Cambridge University at Cambridge	1970
7 (6ct, 1st)	S. Benjamin	Central Zone v North Zone at Bombay	1973-74
7 (all ct)	R. W. Taylor	Derbyshire v Yorkshire at Chesterfield	1975
7 (6ct, 1st)	Shahid Israr	Karachi Whites v Quetta at Karachi	1976-77
7 (4ct, 3st)	Wasim Bari	PIA v Sind at Lahore	1977-78
7 (all ct)	J. A. Maclean	Queensland v Victoria at Melbourne	1977-78
7 (5ct, 2st)	Taslim Arif	National Bank v Punjab at Lahore	1978-79
7 (all ct)	Wasim Bari	Pakistan v New Zealand at Auckland	1978-79
7 (all ct)	R. W. Taylor	England v India at Bombay	1979-80
7 (all ct)	D. L. Bairstow	Yorkshire v Derbyshire at Scarborough	1982
7 (6ct, 1st)	R. B. Phillips	Queensland v New Zealanders at Bundaberg	1982-83
7 (3ct, 4st)	Masood Iqbal	Habib Bank v Lahore at Lahore	1982-83
7 (3ct, 4st)	Arif-ud-Din	United Bank v PACO at Sahiwal	1983-84
7 (6ct, 1st)	R. J. East	OFS v Western Province B at Cape Town	1984-85
7 (all ct)	B. A. Young	Northern Districts v Canterbury at Christchurch	1986-87
7 (all ct)	D. J. Richardson	Eastern Province v OFS at Bloemfontein	1988-89
7 (6ct, 1st)	Dildar Malik	Multan v Faisalabad at Sahiwal	1988-89
7 (all ct)	W. K. Hegg	Lancashire v Derbyshire at Chesterfield	1989
7 (all ct)	Imran Zia	Bahawalpur v Faisalabad at Faisalabad	1989-90
7 (all ct)	I. D. S. Smith	New Zealand v Sri Lanka at Hamilton	1990-91
7 (all ct)	J. F. Holyman	Tasmania v Western Australia at Hobart	1990-91
7 (all ct)	P. J. L. Radley	OFS v Western Province at Cape Town	1990-91
7 (all ct)	C. P. Metson	Glamorgan v Derbyshire at Chesterfield	1991
7 (all ct)	H. M. de Vos	W. Transvaal v E. Transvaal at Potchefstroom	1993-94
7 (all ct)	P. Kirsten	Griqualand West v W. Transvaal at Potchefstroom	1993-94
7 (6ct, 1st)	S. A. Marsh	Kent v Durham at Canterbury	1994
7 (all ct)	K. J. Piper	Warwickshire v Essex at Birmingham	1994
7 (6ct, 1st)	K. J. Piper	Warwickshire v Derbyshire at Chesterfield	1994
7 (all ct)	H. H. Devapriya	Colts v Sinhalese at Colombo	1995-96
7 (all ct)	D. J. R. Campbell	Mashonaland CD v Matabeleland at Bulawayo	1995-96
7 (all ct)	A. C. Gilchrist	Western Australia v South Australia at Perth	1995-96
7 (all ct)	C. W. Scott	Durham v Yorkshire at Chester-le-Street	1996
7 (all ct)	Zahid Umar	WAPDA v Habib Bank at Sheikhupura	1997-98
7 (all ct)	K. S. M. Iyer	Vidarbha v Uttar Pradesh at Allahabad	1997-98
7 (all ct)	W. M. Noon	Nottinghamshire v Kent at Nottingham	1999
7 (all ct)	Aamer Iqbal	Pakistan Customs v Karachi Whites at Karachi	1999-2000
7 (all ct)	H. A. P. W. Jayawardene	Sebastianites v Sinhalese at Colombo	1999-2000
7 (all ct)	R. D. Jacobs	West Indies v Australia at Melbourne	2000-01
7 (all ct)	N. D. Burns	Leicestershire v Somerset at Leicester	2001
7 (all ct)	R. J. Turner	Somerset v Northamptonshire at Taunton	2001

* *W. R. James also scored 99 and 99 not out.*
† *The first eight wickets to fall.*
‡ *S. A. Marsh also scored 108 not out.*

WICKET-KEEPERS' HAT-TRICKS

W. H. Brain, Gloucestershire v Somerset at Cheltenham, 1893 – three stumpings off successive balls from C. L. Townsend.

G. O. Dawkes, Derbyshire v Worcestershire at Kidderminster, 1958 – three catches off successive balls from H. L. Jackson.

R. C. Russell, Gloucestershire v Surrey at The Oval, 1986 – three catches off successive balls from C. A. Walsh and D. V. Lawrence (2).

MOST DISMISSALS IN A MATCH

13 (11ct, 2st)	W. R. James*	Matabeleland v Mashonaland CD at Bulawayo	1995-96
12 (8ct, 4st)	E. Pooley	Surrey v Sussex at The Oval	1868
12 (9ct, 3st)	D. Tallon	Queensland v New South Wales at Sydney	1938-39
12 (9ct, 3st)	H. B. Taber	New South Wales v South Australia at Adelaide	1968-69
11 (all ct)	A. Long	Surrey v Sussex at Hove	1964
11 (all ct)	R. W. Marsh	Western Australia v Victoria at Perth	1975-76
11 (all ct)	D. L. Bairstow	Yorkshire v Derbyshire at Scarborough	1982
11 (all ct)	W. K. Hegg	Lancashire v Derbyshire at Chesterfield	1989
11 (all ct)	A. J. Stewart	Surrey v Leicestershire at Leicester	1989
11 (all ct)	T. J. Nielsen	South Australia v Western Australia at Perth	1990-91
11 (10ct, 1st)	I. A. Healy	Australians v N. Transvaal at Verwoerdburg	1993-94
11 (10ct, 1st)	K. J. Piper	Warwickshire v Derbyshire at Chesterfield	1994
11 (all ct)	D. S. Berry	Victoria v Pakistanis at Melbourne	1995-96
11 (10ct, 1st)	W. A. Seccombe	Queensland v Western Australia at Brisbane	1995-96
11 (all ct)	R. C. Russell	England v South Africa (2nd Test) at Johannesburg	1995-96
11 (10ct, 1st)	D. S. Berry	Victoria v South Australia at Melbourne	1996-97
11 (all ct)	Wasim Yousufi	Peshawar v Bahawalpur at Peshawar	1997-98
11 (all ct)	Aamer Iqbal	Pakistan Customs v Karachi Whites at Karachi	1999-2000

* *W. R. James also scored 99 and 99 not out.*

100 DISMISSALS IN A SEASON

128 (79ct, 49st)	L. E. G. Ames	1929
122 (70ct, 52st)	L. E. G. Ames	1928
110 (63ct, 47st)	H. Yarnold	1949
107 (77ct, 30st)	G. Duckworth	1928
107 (96ct, 11st)	J. G. Binks	1960
104 (40ct, 64st)	L. E. G. Ames	1932
104 (82ct, 22st)	J. T. Murray	1957
102 (69ct, 33st)	F. H. Huish	1913
102 (95ct, 7st)	J. T. Murray	1960
101 (62ct, 39st)	F. H. Huish	1911
101 (85ct, 16st)	R. Booth	1960
100 (91ct, 9st)	R. Booth	1964

1,000 DISMISSALS

Dates in italics denote the first half of an overseas season; i.e. *1914* denotes the 1914-15 season.

		Career	*M*	*Ct*	*St*
1,649	R. W. Taylor	1960-88	639	1,473	176
1,527	J. T. Murray	1952-75	635	1,270	257
1,497	H. Strudwick	1902-27	675	1,242	255
1,344	A. P. E. Knott	1964-85	511	1,211	133
1,310	F. H. Huish	1895-1914	497	933	377
1,294	B. Taylor	1949-73	572	1,083	211
1,253	D. Hunter	1889-1909	548	906	347
1,241	**R. C. Russell**	**1981-2001**	**435**	**1,119**	**122**
1,228	H. R. Butt	1890-1912	550	953	275
1,207	J. H. Board	1891-*1914*	525	852	355
1,206	H. Elliott	1920-47	532	904	302
1,181	J. M. Parks	1949-76	739	1,088	93
1,134	**S. J. Rhodes**	**1981-2001**	**397**	**1,020**	**114**

		Career	M	Ct	St
1,126	R. Booth	1951-70	468	948	178
1,121	L. E. G. Ames	1926-51	593	703	418†
1,099	D. L. Bairstow	1970-90	459	961	138
1,096	G. Duckworth	1923-47	504	753	343
1,082	H. W. Stephenson	1948-64	462	748	334
1,071	J. G. Binks	1955-75	502	895	176
1,066	T. G. Evans	1939-69	465	816	250
1,046	A. Long	1960-80	452	922	124
1,043	G. O. Dawkes	1937-61	482	895	148
1,037	R. W. Tolchard	1965-83	483	912	125
1,017	W. L. Cornford	1921-47	496	675	342

Bold type denotes those who played in 2000-01 and 2001 seasons.

† *Record.*

Current Players with 500 Dismissals

		Career	M	Ct	St
777	W. K. Hegg	1986-2001	288	698	79
772	R. J. Blakey	1985-2001	319	717	55
763	D. Ripley	1984-2001	307	678	85
616	P. A. Nixon	1989-2001	220	570	46
612	C. P. Metson	1981-2001	232	561	51
544	R. J. Turner	1988-2001	193	505	39
543	A. N. Aymes	1987-2001	210	500	43
530	K. M. Krikken	*1988*-2001	204	499	31
510	D. S. Berry	*1989-2000*	128	468	42
508	K. J. Piper	1989-2001	187	476	32

Note: In 417 matches since 1981, A. J. Stewart has achieved 635 catches and 27 stumpings, but 213 of his catches were taken as a fielder.

FIELDING RECORDS

(Excluding wicket-keepers)

MOST CATCHES IN AN INNINGS

7	M. J. Stewart	Surrey v Northamptonshire at Northampton	1957
7	A. S. Brown	Gloucestershire v Nottinghamshire at Nottingham	1966

MOST CATCHES IN A MATCH

10	W. R. Hammond†	Gloucestershire v Surrey at Cheltenham	1928
8	W. B. Burns	Worcestershire v Yorkshire at Bradford	1907
8	F. G. Travers	Europeans v Parsees at Bombay	1923-24
8	A. H. Bakewell	Northamptonshire v Essex at Leyton	1928
8	W. R. Hammond	Gloucestershire v Worcestershire at Cheltenham	1932
8	K. J. Grieves	Lancashire v Sussex at Manchester	1951
8	C. A. Milton	Gloucestershire v Sussex at Hove	1952
8	G. A. R. Lock	Surrey v Warwickshire at The Oval	1957
8	J. M. Prodger	Kent v Gloucestershire at Cheltenham	1961
8	P. M. Walker	Glamorgan v Derbyshire at Swansea	1970
8	Masood Anwar	Rawalpindi v Lahore Division at Rawalpindi	1983-84
8	M. C. J. Ball	Gloucestershire v Yorkshire at Cheltenham	1994
8	J. D. Carr	Middlesex v Warwickshire at Birmingham	1995

† *Hammond also scored a hundred in each innings.*

MOST CATCHES IN A SEASON

78	W. R. Hammond	1928	69	P. M. Walker	1960
77	M. J. Stewart	1957	66	J. Tunnicliffe	1895
73	P. M. Walker	1961	65	W. R. Hammond	1925
71	P. J. Sharpe	1962	65	P. M. Walker	1959
70	J. Tunnicliffe	1901	65	D. W. Richardson	1961
69	J. G. Langridge	1955			

Note: The most catches by a fielder since the reduction of County Championship matches in 1969 is 49 by C. J. Tavaré in 1978.

750 CATCHES

Dates in italics denote the first half of an overseas season; i.e. *1970* denotes the 1970-71 season.

			M				*M*
1,018	F. E. Woolley	1906-38	979	784	J. G. Langridge	1928-55	574
887	W. G. Grace	1865-1908	879	764	W. Rhodes	1898-1930	1,107
830	G. A. R. Lock	1946-*70*	654	758	C. A. Milton	1948-74	620
819	W. R. Hammond	1920-51	634	754	E. H. Hendren	1907-38	833
813	D. B. Close	1949-86	786				

Note: The most catches by a current player is 522 by G. A. Hick (*1983*-2001).

TEAM RECORDS

HIGHEST INNINGS TOTALS

1,107	Victoria v New South Wales at Melbourne	1926-27
1,059	Victoria v Tasmania at Melbourne	1922-23
952-6 dec.	Sri Lanka v India at Colombo	1997-98
951-7 dec.	Sind v Baluchistan at Karachi	1973-74
944-6 dec.	Hyderabad v Andhra at Secunderabad	1993-94
918	New South Wales v South Australia at Sydney	1900-01
912-8 dec.	Holkar v Mysore at Indore	1945-46
912-6 dec.†	Tamil Nadu v Goa at Panjim	1988-89
910-6 dec.	Railways v Dera Ismail Khan at Lahore	1964-65
903-7 dec.	England v Australia at The Oval	1938
887	Yorkshire v Warwickshire at Birmingham	1896
868†	North Zone v West Zone at Bhilai	1987-88
863	Lancashire v Surrey at The Oval	1990
855-6 dec.†	Bombay v Hyderabad at Bombay	1990-91
849	England v West Indies at Kingston	1929-30
843	Australians v Oxford & Cambridge U P & P at Portsmouth	1893
839	New South Wales v Tasmania at Sydney	1898-99
826-4	Maharashtra v Kathiawar at Poona	1948-49
824	Lahore Greens v Bahawalpur at Lahore	1965-6
821-7 dec.	South Australia v Queensland at Adelaide	1939-40
815	New South Wales v Victoria at Sydney	1908-09
811	Surrey v Somerset at The Oval	1899
810-4 dec.	Warwickshire v Durham at Birmingham	1994
807	New South Wales v South Australia at Adelaide	1899-1900
805	New South Wales v Victoria at Melbourne	1905-06
803-4 dec.	Kent v Essex at Brentwood	1934

803	Non-Smokers v Smokers at East Melbourne	1886-87
802-8 dec.	Karachi Blues v Lahore City at Peshawar	1994-95
802	New South Wales v South Australia at Sydney	1920-21
801	Lancashire v Somerset at Taunton	1895
798	Maharashtra v Northern India at Poona	1940-41
793	Victoria v Queensland at Melbourne	1927-28
791-6 dec.	Karnataka v Bengal at Calcutta	1990-91
790-3 dec.	West Indies v Pakistan at Kingston	1957-58
786	New South Wales v South Australia at Adelaide	1922-23
784	Baroda v Holkar at Baroda	1946-47
783-8 dec.	Hyderabad v Bihar at Secunderabad	1986-87
781-7 dec.	Northamptonshire v Nottinghamshire at Northampton	1995
780-8	Punjab v Delhi at Delhi	1994-95
777	Canterbury v Otago at Christchurch	1996-97
775	New South Wales v Victoria at Sydney	1881-82

† *Tamil Nadu's total of 912-6 dec. included 52 penalty runs from their opponents' failure to meet the required bowling rate. North Zone's total of 868 included 68, and Bombay's total of 855-6 dec. included 48.*

HIGHEST FOURTH-INNINGS TOTALS

(Unless otherwise stated, the side making the runs won the match.)

654-5	England v South Africa at Durban *After being set 696 to win. The match was left drawn on the tenth day.*	1938-39
604	Maharashtra (*set 959 to win*) v Bombay at Poona	1948-49
576-8	Trinidad (*set 672 to win*) v Barbados at Port-of-Spain	1945-46
572	New South Wales (*set 593 to win*) v South Australia at Sydney	1907-08
529-9	Combined XI (*set 579 to win*) v South Africans at Perth	1963-64
518	Victoria (*set 753 to win*) v Queensland at Brisbane	1926-27
507-7	Cambridge University v MCC and Ground at Lord's	1896
506-6	South Australia v Queensland at Adelaide	1991-92
502-6	Middlesex v Nottinghamshire at Nottingham	1925
502-8	Players v Gentlemen at Lord's	1900
500-7	South African Universities v Western Province at Stellenbosch	1978-79

HIGHEST AGGREGATES IN A MATCH

Runs	*Wkts*		
2,376	37	Maharashtra v Bombay at Poona	1948-49
2,078	40	Bombay v Holkar at Bombay	1944-45
1,981	35	England v South Africa at Durban	1938-39
1,945	18	Canterbury v Wellington at Christchurch	1994-95
1,929	39	New South Wales v South Australia at Sydney	1925-26
1,911	34	New South Wales v Victoria at Sydney	1908-09
1,905	40	Otago v Wellington at Dunedin	1923-24

In Britain

Runs	Wkts		
1,808	20	Sussex v Essex at Hove	1993
1,795	34	Somerset v Northamptonshire at Taunton	2001
1,723	31	England v Australia at Leeds	1948
1,706	23	Hampshire v Warwickshire at Southampton	1997
1,655	25	Derbyshire v Nottinghamshire at Derby	2001
1,650	19	Surrey v Lancashire at The Oval	1990
1,642	29	Nottinghamshire v Kent at Nottingham	1995
1,641	16	Glamorgan v Worcestershire at Abergavenny	1990
1,614	30	England v India at Manchester	1990
1,606	34	Somerset v Derbyshire at Taunton	1996
1,603	28	England v India at Lord's	1990
1,601	29	England v Australia at Lord's	1930
1,601	35	Kent v Surrey at Canterbury	1995

LOWEST INNINGS TOTALS

12	Oxford University v MCC and Ground at Oxford	†1877
12	Northamptonshire v Gloucestershire at Gloucester	1907
13	Auckland v Canterbury at Auckland	1877-78
13	Nottinghamshire v Yorkshire at Nottingham	1901
14	Surrey v Essex at Chelmsford	1983
15	MCC v Surrey at Lord's	1839
15	Victoria v MCC at Melbourne	†1903-04
15	Northamptonshire v Yorkshire at Northampton	†1908
15	Hampshire v Warwickshire at Birmingham	1922
	Following on, Hampshire scored 521 and won by 155 runs.	
16	MCC and Ground v Surrey at Lord's	1872
16	Derbyshire v Nottinghamshire at Nottingham	1879
16	Surrey v Nottinghamshire at The Oval	1880
16	Warwickshire v Kent at Tonbridge	1913
16	Trinidad v Barbados at Bridgetown	1942-43
16	Border v Natal at East London (first innings)	1959-60
17	Gentlemen of Kent v Gentlemen of England at Lord's	1850
17	Gloucestershire v Australians at Cheltenham	1896
18	The Bs v England at Lord's	1831
18	Kent v Sussex at Gravesend	†1867
18	Tasmania v Victoria at Melbourne	1868-69
18	Australians v MCC and Ground at Lord's	†1896
18	Border v Natal at East London (second innings)	1959-60
19	Sussex v Surrey at Godalming	1830
19	Sussex v Nottinghamshire at Hove	†1873
19	MCC and Ground v Australians at Lord's	1878
19	Wellington v Nelson at Nelson	1885-86
19	Matabeleland v Mashonaland at Harare	2000-01

† *Signifies that one man was absent.*

Note: At Lord's in 1810, The Bs, with one man absent, were dismissed by England for 6.

LOWEST TOTALS IN A MATCH

34	(16 and 18) Border v Natal at East London	1959-60
42	(27 and 15) Northamptonshire v Yorkshire at Northampton	1908

Note: Northamptonshire batted one man short in each innings.

LOWEST AGGREGATE IN A COMPLETED MATCH

Runs	*Wkts*		
105	31	MCC v Australians at Lord's	1878

Note: The lowest aggregate since 1900 is 157 for 22 wickets, Surrey v Worcestershire at The Oval, 1954.

LARGEST VICTORIES

Largest Innings Victories

Inns and 851 runs:	Railways (910-6 dec.) v Dera Ismail Khan at Lahore	1964-65
Inns and 666 runs:	Victoria (1,059) v Tasmania at Melbourne	1922-23
Inns and 656 runs:	Victoria (1,107) v New South Wales at Melbourne	1926-27
Inns and 605 runs:	New South Wales (918) v South Australia at Sydney	1900-01
Inns and 579 runs:	England (903-7 dec.) v Australia at The Oval	1938
Inns and 575 runs:	Sind (951-7 dec.) v Baluchistan at Karachi	1973-74
Inns and 527 runs:	New South Wales (713) v South Australia at Adelaide	1908-09
Inns and 517 runs:	Australians (675) v Nottinghamshire at Nottingham	1921

Largest Victories by Runs Margin

685 runs:	New South Wales (235 and 761-8 dec.) v Queensland at Sydney	1929-30
675 runs:	England (521 and 342-8 dec.) v Australia at Brisbane	1928-29
638 runs:	New South Wales (304 and 770) v South Australia at Adelaide	1920-21
609 runs:	Muslim Commercial Bank (575 and 282-0 dec.) v WAPDA at Lahore	1977-78
585 runs:	Sargodha (336 and 416) v Lahore Municipal Corporation at Faisalabad	1978-79
573 runs:	Sinhalese SC (395-7 dec. and 350-2 dec.) v Sebastianites C and AC at Colombo	1990-91
571 runs:	Victoria (304 and 649) v South Australia at Adelaide	1926-27
562 runs:	Australia (701 and 327) v England at The Oval	1934
556 runs:	Nondescripts (397-8 dec. and 313-6 dec.) v Matara at Colombo	1998-99

Victory Without Losing a Wicket

Lancashire (166-0 dec. and 66-0) beat Leicestershire by ten wickets at Manchester	1956
Karachi A (277-0 dec.) beat Sind A by an innings and 77 runs at Karachi	1957-58
Railways (236-0 dec. and 16-0) beat Jammu and Kashmir by ten wickets at Srinagar	1960-61
Karnataka (451-0 dec.) beat Kerala by an innings and 186 runs at Chikmagalur	1977-78

TIED MATCHES

Since 1948 a tie has been recognised only when the scores are level with all the wickets down in the fourth innings.

The following are the instances since then:

Hampshire v Kent at Southampton	1950
Sussex v Warwickshire at Hove	1952
Essex v Lancashire at Brentwood	1952
Northamptonshire v Middlesex at Peterborough	1953
Yorkshire v Leicestershire at Huddersfield	1954
Sussex v Hampshire at Eastbourne	1955
Victoria v New South Wales at Melbourne	1956-57
T. N. Pearce's XI v New Zealanders at Scarborough	1958
Essex v Gloucestershire at Leyton	1959
Australia v West Indies (First Test) at Brisbane	1960-61
Bahawalpur v Lahore B at Bahawalpur	1961-62
Hampshire v Middlesex at Portsmouth	1967
England XI v England Under-25 XI at Scarborough	1968

Yorkshire v Middlesex at Bradford	1973
Sussex v Essex at Hove	1974
South Australia v Queensland at Adelaide	1976-77
Central Districts v England XI at New Plymouth	1977-78
Victoria v New Zealanders at Melbourne	1982-83
Muslim Commercial Bank v Railways at Sialkot	1983-84
Sussex v Kent at Hastings	1984
Northamptonshire v Kent at Northampton	1984
Eastern Province B v Boland at Albany SC, Grahamstown	1985-86
Natal B v Eastern Province B at Pietermaritzburg	1985-86
India v Australia (First Test) at Madras	1986-87
Gloucestershire v Derbyshire at Bristol	1987
Bahawalpur v Peshawar at Bahawalpur	1988-89
Wellington v Canterbury at Wellington	1988-89
Sussex v Kent at Hove	†1991
Nottinghamshire v Worcestershire at Nottingham	1993

† *Sussex (436) scored the highest total to tie a first-class match.*

MATCHES COMPLETED ON FIRST DAY

(Since 1946)

Derbyshire v Somerset at Chesterfield, June 11	1947
Lancashire v Sussex at Manchester, July 12	1950
Surrey v Warwickshire at The Oval, May 16	1953
Somerset v Lancashire at Bath, June 6 (H. F. T. Buse's benefit)	1953
Kent v Worcestershire at Tunbridge Wells, June 15	1960

THE ASHES

"In affectionate remembrance of English cricket which died at The Oval, 29th August, 1882. Deeply lamented by a large circle of sorrowing friends and acquaintances, R.I.P.
N.B. The body will be cremated and the Ashes taken to Australia."

Australia's first victory on English soil over the full strength of England, on August 29, 1882, inspired a young London journalist, Reginald Shirley Brooks, to write this mock "obituary". It appeared in the *Sporting Times*.

Before England's defeat at The Oval, by seven runs, arrangements had already been made for the Hon. Ivo Bligh, afterwards Lord Darnley, to lead a team to Australia. Three weeks later they set out, now with the popular objective of recovering the Ashes. In the event, Australia won the First Test by nine wickets, but with England winning the next two it became generally accepted that they brought back the Ashes.

It was long believed that the real Ashes – a small urn thought to contain the ashes of a bail used in the third match – were presented to Bligh by a group of Melbourne women. In 1998, Lord Darnley's 82-year-old daughter-in-law said they were the remains of her mother-in-law's veil, not a bail. Other evidence suggests a ball. The certain origin of the Ashes, therefore, is the subject of some dispute.

After Lord Darnley's death in 1927, the urn was given to MCC by Lord Darnley's Australian-born widow, Florence. It can be seen in the cricket museum at Lord's, together with a red and gold velvet bag, made specially for it, and the scorecard of the 1882 match.

TEST RECORDS

Note: This section covers all Tests up to September 2, 2001.

BATTING RECORDS

HIGHEST INDIVIDUAL INNINGS

375	B. C. Lara	West Indies v England at St John's	1993-94
365*	G. S. Sobers	West Indies v Pakistan at Kingston	1957-58
364	L. Hutton	England v Australia at The Oval	1938
340	S. T. Jayasuriya	Sri Lanka v India at Colombo (RPS)	1997-98
337	Hanif Mohammad	Pakistan v West Indies at Bridgetown	1957-58
336*	W. R. Hammond	England v New Zealand at Auckland	1932-33
334*	M. A. Taylor	Australia v Pakistan at Peshawar	1998-99
334	D. G. Bradman	Australia v England at Leeds	1930
333	G. A. Gooch	England v India at Lord's	1990
325	A. Sandham	England v West Indies at Kingston	1929-30
311	R. B. Simpson	Australia v England at Manchester	1964
310*	J. H. Edrich	England v New Zealand at Leeds	1965
307	R. M. Cowper	Australia v England at Melbourne	1965-66
304	D. G. Bradman	Australia v England at Leeds	1934
302	L. G. Rowe	West Indies v England at Bridgetown	1973-74
299*	D. G. Bradman	Australia v South Africa at Adelaide	1931-32
299	M. D. Crowe	New Zealand v Sri Lanka at Wellington	1990-91
291	I. V. A. Richards	West Indies v England at The Oval	1976
287	R. E. Foster	England v Australia at Sydney	1903-04
285*	P. B. H. May	England v West Indies at Birmingham	1957
281	V. V. S. Laxman	India v Australia at Kolkata	2000-01
280*	Javed Miandad	Pakistan v India at Hyderabad	1982-83
278	D. C. S. Compton	England v Pakistan at Nottingham	1954
277	B. C. Lara	West Indies v Australia at Sydney	1992-93
275*	D. J. Cullinan	South Africa v New Zealand at Auckland	1998-99
275	G. Kirsten	South Africa v England at Durban	1999-2000
274	R. G. Pollock	South Africa v Australia at Durban	1969-70
274	Zaheer Abbas	Pakistan v England at Birmingham	1971
271	Javed Miandad	Pakistan v New Zealand at Auckland	1988-89
270*	G. A. Headley	West Indies v England at Kingston	1934-35
270	D. G. Bradman	Australia v England at Melbourne	1936-37
268	G. N. Yallop	Australia v Pakistan at Melbourne	1983-84
267*	B. A. Young	New Zealand v Sri Lanka at Dunedin	1996-97
267	P. A. de Silva	Sri Lanka v New Zealand at Wellington	1990-91
266	W. H. Ponsford	Australia v England at The Oval	1934
266	D. L. Houghton	Zimbabwe v Sri Lanka at Bulawayo	1994-95
262*	D. L. Amiss	England v West Indies at Kingston	1973-74
261	F. M. M. Worrell	West Indies v England at Nottingham	1950
260	C. C. Hunte	West Indies v Pakistan at Kingston	1957-58
260	Javed Miandad	Pakistan v England at The Oval	1987
259	G. M. Turner	New Zealand v West Indies at Georgetown	1971-72
258	T. W. Graveney	England v West Indies at Nottingham	1957
258	S. M. Nurse	West Indies v New Zealand at Christchurch	1968-69
257*	Wasim Akram	Pakistan v Zimbabwe at Sheikhupura	1996-97
256	R. B. Kanhai	West Indies v India at Calcutta	1958-59
256	K. F. Barrington	England v Australia at Manchester	1964
255*	D. J. McGlew	South Africa v New Zealand at Wellington	1952-53
254	D. G. Bradman	Australia v England at Lord's	1930
251	W. R. Hammond	England v Australia at Sydney	1928-29
250	K. D. Walters	Australia v New Zealand at Christchurch	1976-77
250	S. F. A. F. Bacchus	West Indies v India at Kanpur	1978-79

Note: The highest individual innings for Bangladesh is 145 by Aminul Islam against India at Dhaka in 2000-01.

HUNDRED ON TEST DEBUT

C. Bannerman (165*)	Australia v England at Melbourne	1876-77
W. G. Grace (152)	England v Australia at The Oval	1880
H. Graham (107)	Australia v England at Lord's	1893
†K. S. Ranjitsinhji (154*)	England v Australia at Manchester	1896
†P. F. Warner (132*)	England v South Africa at Johannesburg	1898-99
†R. A. Duff (104)	Australia v England at Melbourne	1901-02
R. E. Foster (287)	England v Australia at Sydney	1903-04
G. Gunn (119)	England v Australia at Sydney	1907-08
†R. J. Hartigan (116)	Australia v England at Adelaide	1907-08
†H. L. Collins (104)	Australia v England at Sydney	1920-21
W. H. Ponsford (110)	Australia v England at Sydney	1924-25
A. A. Jackson (164)	Australia v England at Adelaide	1928-29
†G. A. Headley (176)	West Indies v England at Bridgetown	1929-30
J. E. Mills (117)	New Zealand v England at Wellington	1929-30
Nawab of Pataudi sen. (102)	England v Australia at Sydney	1932-33
B. H. Valentine (136)	England v India at Bombay	1933-34
†L. Amarnath (118)	India v England at Bombay	1933-34
†P. A. Gibb (106)	England v South Africa at Johannesburg	1938-39
S. C. Griffith (140)	England v West Indies at Port-of-Spain	1947-48
A. G. Ganteaume (112)	West Indies v England at Port-of-Spain	1947-48
†J. W. Burke (101*)	Australia v England at Adelaide	1950-51
P. B. H. May (138)	England v South Africa at Leeds	1951
R. H. Shodhan (110)	India v Pakistan at Calcutta	1952-53
B. H. Pairaudeau (115)	West Indies v India at Port-of-Spain	1952-53
†O. G. Smith (104)	West Indies v Australia at Kingston	1954-55
A. G. Kripal Singh (100*)	India v New Zealand at Hyderabad	1955-56
C. C. Hunte (142)	West Indies v Pakistan at Bridgetown	1957-58
C. A. Milton (104*)	England v New Zealand at Leeds	1958
†A. A. Baig (112)	India v England at Manchester	1959
Hanumant Singh (105)	India v England at Delhi	1963-64
Khalid Ibadulla (166)	Pakistan v Australia at Karachi	1964-65
B. R. Taylor (105)	New Zealand v India at Calcutta	1964-65
K. D. Walters (155)	Australia v England at Brisbane	1965-66
J. H. Hampshire (107)	England v West Indies at Lord's	1969
†G. R. Viswanath (137)	India v Australia at Kanpur	1969-70
G. S. Chappell (108)	Australia v England at Perth	1970-71
‡L. G. Rowe (214, 100*)	West Indies v New Zealand at Kingston	1971-72
A. I. Kallicharran (100*)	West Indies v New Zealand at Georgetown	1971-72
R. E. Redmond (107)	New Zealand v Pakistan at Auckland	1972-73
†F. C. Hayes (106*)	England v West Indies at The Oval	1973
†C. G. Greenidge (107)	West Indies v India at Bangalore	1974-75
†L. Baichan (105*)	West Indies v Pakistan at Lahore	1974-75
G. J. Cosier (109)	Australia v West Indies at Melbourne	1975-76
S. Amarnath (124)	India v New Zealand at Auckland	1975-76
Javed Miandad (163)	Pakistan v New Zealand at Lahore	1976-77
†A. B. Williams (100)	West Indies v Australia at Georgetown	1977-78
†D. M. Wellham (103)	Australia v England at The Oval	1981
†Salim Malik (100*)	Pakistan v Sri Lanka at Karachi	1981-82
K. C. Wessels (162)	Australia v England at Brisbane	1982-83
W. B. Phillips (159)	Australia v Pakistan at Perth	1983-84
§M. Azharuddin (110)	India v England at Calcutta	1984-85
D. S. B. P. Kuruppu (201*)	Sri Lanka v New Zealand at Colombo (CCC)	1986-87
†M. J. Greatbatch (107*)	New Zealand v England at Auckland	1987-88
M. E. Waugh (138)	Australia v England at Adelaide	1990-91
A. C. Hudson (163)	South Africa v West Indies at Bridgetown	1991-92
R. S. Kaluwitharana (132*)	Sri Lanka v Australia at Colombo (SSC)	1992-93
D. L. Houghton (121)	Zimbabwe v India at Harare	1992-93
P. K. Amre (103)	India v South Africa at Durban	1992-93

†G. P. Thorpe (114*)	England v Australia at Nottingham	1993
G. S. Blewett (102*)	Australia v England at Adelaide	1994-95
S. C. Ganguly (131)	India v England at Lord's	1996
†Mohammad Wasim (109*)	Pakistan v New Zealand at Lahore	1996-97
Ali Naqvi (115)	Pakistan v South Africa at Rawalpindi	1997-98
Azhar Mahmood (128*)	Pakistan v South Africa at Rawalpindi	1997-98
M. S. Sinclair (214)	New Zealand v West Indies at Wellington	1999-2000
†Younis Khan (107)	Pakistan v Sri Lanka at Rawalpindi	1999-2000
Aminul Islam (145)	Bangladesh v India at Dhaka	2000-01
†H. Masakadza (119)	Zimbabwe v West Indies at Harare	2001
T. T. Samaraweera (103*)	Sri Lanka v India at Colombo (SSC)	2001
Taufeeq Umar (104)	Pakistan v Bangladesh at Multan	2001-02

† *In his second innings of the match.*
‡ *L. G. Rowe is the only batsman to score a hundred in each innings on debut.*
§ *M. Azharuddin is the only batsman to score hundreds in each of his first three Tests.*

Notes: L. Amarnath and S. Amarnath were father and son.
Ali Naqvi and Azhar Mahmood achieved the feat in the same innings.
Only Bannerman, Houghton and Aminul Islam scored hundreds in their country's first Test.

300 RUNS IN FIRST TEST

314	L. G. Rowe (214, 100*)	West Indies v New Zealand at Kingston	1971-72
306	R. E. Foster (287, 19)	England v Australia at Sydney	1903-04

TRIPLE-HUNDRED AND HUNDRED IN A TEST

G. A. Gooch (England)	333 and 123 v India at Lord's	1990

The only instance in first-class cricket. M. A. Taylor (Australia) scored 334 and 92 v Pakistan at Peshawar in 1998-99.*

DOUBLE-HUNDRED AND HUNDRED IN A TEST

K. D. Walters (Australia)	242 and 103 v West Indies at Sydney	1968-69
S. M. Gavaskar (India)	124 and 220 v West Indies at Port-of-Spain	1970-71
†L. G. Rowe (West Indies)	214 and 100* v New Zealand at Kingston	1971-72
G. S. Chappell (Australia)	247* and 133 v New Zealand at Wellington	1973-74

† *On Test debut.*

TWO SEPARATE HUNDREDS IN A TEST

Three times: S. M. Gavaskar.
Twice in one series: C. L. Walcott v Australia (1954-55).
Twice: †A. R. Border; G. S. Chappell; ‡P. A. de Silva; G. A. Headley; H. Sutcliffe.
Once: W. Bardsley; D. G. Bradman; I. M. Chappell; D. C. S. Compton; R. Dravid; G. W. Flower; G. A. Gooch; C. G. Greenidge; A. P. Gurusinha; W. R. Hammond; Hanif Mohammad; V. S. Hazare; G. P. Howarth; Javed Miandad; A. H. Jones; D. M. Jones; R. B. Kanhai; G. Kirsten; A. Melville; L. R. D. Mendis; B. Mitchell; J. Moroney; A. R. Morris; E. Paynter; §L. G. Rowe; A. C. Russell; R. B. Simpson; G. S. Sobers; A. J. Stewart; G. M. Turner; Wajahatullah Wasti; K. D. Walters; S. R. Waugh; E. D. Weekes.

† *A. R. Border scored 150* and 153 against Pakistan in 1979-80 to become the first to score 150 in each innings of a Test match.*
‡ *P. A. de Silva scored 138* and 103* against Pakistan in 1996-97 to become the first to score two not out hundreds in a Test match.*
§ *L. G. Rowe's two hundreds were on his Test debut.*

MOST HUNDREDS

				Opponents									
	Total	*200+*	*Inns*	*E*	*A*	*SA*	*WI*	*NZ*	*I*	*P*	*SL*	*Z*	*B*
S. M. Gavaskar (I)	34	4	214	4	8	–	13	2	–	5	2	–	–
D. G. Bradman (A)	29	12	80	19	–	4	2	–	4	–	–	–	–
A. R. Border (A)	27	2	265	8	–	0	3	5	4	6	1	–	–
S. R. Waugh (A)	**27**	**1**	**220**	**9**	–	**2**	**6**	**2**	**2**	**2**	**3**	**1**	–
G. S. Sobers (WI)	26	2	160	10	4	–	–	1	8	3	–	–	–
S. R. Tendulkar (I)	**25**	**2**	**135**	**4**	**6**	**2**	**1**	**3**	–	**1**	**6**	**2**	**0**
G. S. Chappell (A)	24	4	151	9	–	–	5	3	1	6	0	–	–
I. V. A. Richards (WI)	24	3	182	8	5	–	–	1	8	2	–	–	–
Javed Miandad (P)	23	6	189	2	6	–	2	7	5	–	1	–	–
M. Azharuddin (I)	22	0	147	6	2	4	0	2	–	3	5	0	–
G. Boycott (E)	22	1	193	–	7	1	5	2	4	3	–	–	–
M. C. Cowdrey (E)	22	0	188	–	5	3	6	2	3	3	–	–	–
W. R. Hammond (E)	22	7	140	–	9	6	1	4	2	–	–	–	–
D. C. Boon (A)	21	1	190	7	–	–	3	3	6	1	1	–	–
R. N. Harvey (A)	21	2	137	6	–	8	3	–	4	0	–	–	–
K. F. Barrington (E)	20	1	131	–	5	2	3	3	3	4	–	–	–
G. A. Gooch (E)	20	2	215	–	4	–	5	4	5	1	1	–	–
M. E. Waugh (A)	**20**	**0**	**192**	**6**	–	**4**	**4**	**1**	**1**	**3**	**1**	**0**	–

Notes: The most hundreds for Sri Lanka is 19 by **P. A. de Silva** in 153 innings, for New Zealand 17 by M. D. Crowe in 131 innings, for South Africa 14 by **D. J. Cullinan** in 115 innings, for Zimbabwe 9 by **A. Flower** in 92 innings, and for Bangladesh 1 by **Aminul Islam** in 8 innings.

The most double-hundreds by batsmen not qualifying for the above list is four by M. S. Atapattu (Sri Lanka), C. G. Greenidge (West Indies), L. Hutton (England) and Zaheer Abbas (Pakistan). In 2001-02, after the deadline for this section, Atapattu hit a fifth double-hundred.

Bold type denotes those who played Test cricket in 2000-01 and 2001 seasons. Dashes indicate that a player did not play against the country concerned.

CARRYING BAT THROUGH TEST INNINGS

(Figures in brackets show side's total.)

A. B. Tancred	26*	(47)	South Africa v England at Cape Town	1888-89
J. E. Barrett	67*	(176)†	Australia v England at Lord's	1890
R. Abel	132*	(307)	England v Australia at Sydney	1891-92
P. F. Warner	132*	(237)†	England v South Africa at Johannesburg	1898-99
W. W. Armstrong	159*	(309)	Australia v South Africa at Johannesburg	1902-03
J. W. Zulch	43*	(103)	South Africa v England at Cape Town	1909-10
W. Bardsley	193*	(383)	Australia v England at Lord's	1926
W. M. Woodfull	30*	(66)§	Australia v England at Brisbane	1928-29
W. M. Woodfull	73*	(193)‡	Australia v England at Adelaide	1932-33
W. A. Brown	206*	(422)	Australia v England at Lord's	1938
L. Hutton	202*	(344)	England v West Indies at The Oval	1950
L. Hutton	156*	(272)	England v Australia at Adelaide	1950-51
Nazar Mohammad¶	124*	(331)	Pakistan v India at Lucknow	1952-53
F. M. M. Worrell	191*	(372)	West Indies v England at Nottingham	1957
T. L. Goddard	56*	(99)	South Africa v Australia at Cape Town	1957-58
D. J. McGlew	127*	(292)	South Africa v New Zealand at Durban	1961-62
C. C. Hunte	60*	(131)	West Indies v Australia at Port-of-Spain	1964-65
G. M. Turner	43*	(131)	New Zealand v England at Lord's	1969
W. M. Lawry	49*	(107)	Australia v India at Delhi	1969-70
W. M. Lawry	60*	(116)‡	Australia v England at Sydney	1970-71

G. M. Turner	223* (386)	New Zealand v West Indies at Kingston	1971-72
I. R. Redpath	159* (346)	Australia v New Zealand at Auckland	1973-74
G. Boycott	99* (215)	England v Australia at Perth	1979-80
S. M. Gavaskar	127* (286)	India v Pakistan at Faisalabad	1982-83
Mudassar Nazar¶	152* (323)	Pakistan v India at Lahore	1982-83
S. Wettimuny	63* (144)	Sri Lanka v New Zealand at Christchurch	1982-83
D. C. Boon	58* (103)	Australia v New Zealand at Auckland	1985-86
D. L. Haynes	88* (211)	West Indies v Pakistan at Karachi	1986-87
G. A. Gooch	154* (252)	England v West Indies at Leeds	1991
D. L. Haynes	75* (176)	West Indies v England at The Oval	1991
A. J. Stewart	69* (175)	England v Pakistan at Lord's	1992
D. L. Haynes	143* (382)	West Indies v Pakistan at Port-of-Spain	1992-93
M. H. Dekker	68* (187)	Zimbabwe v Pakistan at Rawalpindi	1993-94
M. A. Atherton	94* (228)	England v New Zealand at Christchurch	1996-97
G. Kirsten	100* (239)	South Africa v Pakistan at Faisalabad	1997-98
M. A. Taylor	169* (350)	Australia v South Africa at Adelaide	1997-98
G. W. Flower	156* (321)	Zimbabwe v Pakistan at Bulawayo	1997-98
Saeed Anwar	188* (316)	Pakistan v India at Calcutta	1998-99
M. S. Atapattu	216* (428)	Sri Lanka v Zimbabwe at Bulawayo	1999-2000
R. P. Arnold	104* (231)	Sri Lanka v Zimbabwe at Harare	1999-2000
Javed Omar	85* (168)†‡	Bangladesh v Zimbabwe at Bulawayo	2000-01

† On debut. ‡ One man absent. § Two men absent. ¶ Father and son.

Notes: G. M. Turner (223*) holds the record for the highest score by a player carrying his bat through a Test innings. He is also the youngest player to do so, being 22 years 63 days old when he first achieved the feat (1969).

D. L. Haynes, who is alone in achieving this feat on three occasions, also opened the batting and was last man out in each innings for West Indies v New Zealand at Dunedin, 1979-80.

750 RUNS IN A SERIES

	T	*I*	*NO*	*R*	*HS*	*100s*	*Avge*		
D. G. Bradman	5	7	0	974	334	4	139.14	A v E	1930
W. R. Hammond	5	9	1	905	251	4	113.12	E v A	1928-29
M. A. Taylor	6	11	1	839	219	2	83.90	A v E	1989
R. N. Harvey	5	9	0	834	205	4	92.66	A v SA	1952-53
I. V. A. Richards	4	7	0	829	291	3	118.42	WI v E	1976
C. L. Walcott	5	10	0	827	155	5	82.70	WI v A	1954-55
G. S. Sobers	5	8	2	824	365*	3	137.33	WI v P	1957-58
D. G. Bradman	5	9	0	810	270	3	90.00	A v E	1936-37
D. G. Bradman	5	5	1	806	299*	4	201.50	A v SA	1931-32
B. C. Lara	5	8	0	798	375	2	99.75	WI v E	1993-94
E. D. Weekes	5	7	0	779	194	4	111.28	WI v I	1948-49
†S. M. Gavaskar	4	8	3	774	220	4	154.80	I v WI	1970-71
B. C. Lara	6	10	1	765	179	3	85.00	WI v E	1995
Mudassar Nazar	6	8	2	761	231	4	126.83	P v I	1982-83
D. G. Bradman	5	8	0	758	304	2	94.75	A v E	1934
D. C. S. Compton	5	8	0	753	208	4	94.12	E v SA	1947
‡G. A. Gooch	3	6	0	752	333	3	125.33	E v I	1990

† Gavaskar's aggregate was achieved in his first Test series.
‡ G. A. Gooch is alone in scoring 1,000 runs in Test cricket during an English season with 1,058 runs in 11 innings against New Zealand and India in 1990.

1,200 RUNS IN A CALENDAR YEAR

	T	*I*	*NO*	*R*	*HS*	*100s*	*Avge*	*Year*
I. V. A. Richards (WI)	11	19	0	1,710	291	7	90.00	1976
S. M. Gavaskar (I)	18	27	1	1,555	221	5	59.80	1979
G. R. Viswanath (I)	17	26	3	1,388	179	5	60.34	1979
R. B. Simpson (A)	14	26	3	1,381	311	3	60.04	1964
D. L. Amiss (E)	13	22	2	1,379	262*	5	68.95	1974
S. M. Gavaskar (I)	18	32	4	1,310	236*	5	46.78	1983
S. T. Jayasuriya (SL)	11	19	0	1,271	340	3	66.89	1997
G. A. Gooch (E)	9	17	1	1,264	333	4	79.00	1990
D. C. Boon (A)	16	25	5	1,241	164*	4	62.05	1993
B. C. Lara (WI)	12	20	2	1,222	179	4	67.88	1995
A. J. Stewart (E)	16	31	3	1,222	164	2	43.64	1998
P. A. de Silva (SL)	11	19	3	1,220	168	7	76.25	1997
M. A. Taylor (A)	11	20	1	1,219	219	4	64.15	1989†

† *The year of his debut.*

Notes: M. Amarnath reached 1,000 runs in 1983 on May 3.

The only batsman to score 1,000 runs in a year before World War II was C. Hill of Australia: 1,061 in 1902.

2,500 RUNS

ENGLAND

		T	*I*	*NO*	*R*	*HS*	*100s*	*Avge*
1	G. A. Gooch	118	215	6	8,900	333	20	42.58
2	D. I. Gower	117	204	18	8,231	215	18	44.25
3	G. Boycott	108	193	23	8,114	246*	22	47.72
4	**M. A. Atherton**	**115**	**212**	**7**	**7,728**	**185***	**16**	**37.69**
5	M. C. Cowdrey	114	188	15	7,624	182	22	44.06
6	**A. J. Stewart**	**115**	**207**	**17**	**7,469**	**190**	**14**	**39.31**
7	W. R. Hammond	85	140	16	7,249	336*	22	58.45
8	L. Hutton	79	138	15	6,971	364	19	56.67
9	K. F. Barrington	82	131	15	6,806	256	20	58.67
10	D. C. S. Compton	78	131	15	5,807	278	17	50.06
11	J. B. Hobbs	61	102	7	5,410	211	15	56.94
12	I. T. Botham	102	161	6	5,200	208	14	33.54
13	J. H. Edrich	77	127	9	5,138	310*	12	43.54
14	T. W. Graveney	79	123	13	4,882	258	11	44.38
15	A. J. Lamb	79	139	10	4,656	142	14	36.09
16	H. Sutcliffe	54	84	9	4,555	194	16	60.73
17	P. B. H. May	66	106	9	4,537	285*	13	46.77
18	E. R. Dexter	62	102	8	4,502	205	9	47.89
19	**G. P. Thorpe**	**69**	**126**	**16**	**4,498**	**138**	**9**	**40.89**
20	M. W. Gatting	79	138	14	4,409	207	10	35.55
21	A. P. E. Knott	95	149	15	4,389	135	5	32.75
22	R. A. Smith	62	112	15	4,236	175	9	43.67
23	D. L. Amiss	50	88	10	3,612	262*	11	46.30
24	A. W. Greig	58	93	4	3,599	148	8	40.43
25	**N. Hussain**	**63**	**113**	**12**	**3,535**	**207**	**9**	**35.00**
26	E. H. Hendren	51	83	9	3,525	205*	7	47.63
27	**G. A. Hick**	**65**	**114**	**6**	**3,383**	**178**	**6**	**31.32**
28	F. E. Woolley	64	98	7	3,283	154	5	36.07
29	K. W. R. Fletcher	59	96	14	3,272	216	7	39.90
30	M. Leyland	41	65	5	2,764	187	9	46.06
31	C. Washbrook	37	66	6	2,569	195	6	42.81

AUSTRALIA

		T	*I*	*NO*	*R*	*HS*	*100s*	*Avge*
1	A. R. Border	156	265	44	11,174	205	27	50.56
2	**S. R. Waugh**	**139**	**220**	**41**	**9,286**	**200**	**27**	**51.87**
3	M. A. Taylor	104	186	13	7,525	334*	19	43.49
4	**M. E. Waugh**	**116**	**192**	**17**	**7,511**	**153***	**20**	**42.92**
5	D. C. Boon	107	190	20	7,422	200	21	43.65
6	G. S. Chappell	87	151	19	7,110	247*	24	53.86
7	D. G. Bradman	52	80	10	6,996	334	29	99.94
8	R. N. Harvey	79	137	10	6,149	205	21	48.41
9	K. D. Walters	74	125	14	5,357	250	15	48.26
10	I. M. Chappell	75	136	10	5,345	196	14	42.42
11	**M. J. Slater**	**74**	**131**	**7**	**5,312**	**219**	**14**	**42.83**
12	W. M. Lawry	67	123	12	5,234	210	13	47.15
13	R. B. Simpson	62	111	7	4,869	311	10	46.81
14	I. R. Redpath	66	120	11	4,737	171	8	43.45
15	K. J. Hughes	70	124	6	4,415	213	9	37.41
16	I. A. Healy	119	182	23	4,356	161*	4	27.39
17	R. W. Marsh	96	150	13	3,633	132	3	26.51
18	D. M. Jones	52	89	11	3,631	216	11	46.55
19	A. R. Morris	46	79	3	3,533	206	12	46.48
20	C. Hill	49	89	2	3,412	191	7	39.21
21	G. M. Wood	59	112	6	3,374	172	9	31.83
22	V. T. Trumper	48	89	8	3,163	214*	8	39.04
23	C. C. McDonald	47	83	4	3,107	170	5	39.32
24	A. L. Hassett	43	69	3	3,073	198*	10	46.56
25	K. R. Miller	55	87	7	2,958	147	7	36.97
26	W. W. Armstrong	50	84	10	2,863	159*	6	38.68
27	G. R. Marsh	50	93	7	2,854	138	4	33.18
28	**R. T. Ponting**	**47**	**74**	**8**	**2,830**	**197**	**8**	**42.87**
29	K. R. Stackpole	43	80	5	2,807	207	7	37.42
30	N. C. O'Neill	42	69	8	2,779	181	6	45.55
31	G. N. Yallop	39	70	3	2,756	268	8	41.13
32	S. J. McCabe	39	62	5	2,748	232	6	48.21
33	**J. L. Langer**	**42**	**69**	**3**	**2,679**	**223**	**8**	**40.59**
34	G. S. Blewett	46	79	4	2,552	214	4	34.02

SOUTH AFRICA

		T	*I*	*NO*	*R*	*HS*	*100s*	*Avge*
1	**G. Kirsten**	**73**	**129**	**10**	**4,806**	**275**	**12**	**40.38**
2	**D. J. Cullinan**	**70**	**115**	**12**	**4,554**	**275***	**14**	**44.21**
3	W. J. Cronje	68	111	9	3,714	135	6	36.41
4	B. Mitchell	42	80	9	3,471	189*	8	48.88
5	A. D. Nourse	34	62	7	2,960	231	9	53.81
6	**J. H. Kallis**	**50**	**81**	**9**	**2,952**	**160**	**7**	**41.00**
7	H. W. Taylor	42	76	4	2,936	176	7	40.77
8	J. N. Rhodes	52	80	9	2,532	117	3	35.66
9	E. J. Barlow	30	57	2	2,516	201	6	45.74
9	T. L. Goddard	41	78	5	2,516	112	1	34.46

Note: K. C. Wessels scored 2,788 runs in 40 Tests: 1,761 (average 42.95) in 24 Tests for Australia, and 1,027 (average 38.03) in 16 Tests for South Africa.

WEST INDIES

		T	*I*	*NO*	*R*	*HS*	*100s*	*Avge*
1	I. V. A. Richards	121	182	12	8,540	291	24	50.23
2	G. S. Sobers	93	160	21	8,032	365*	26	57.78
3	C. G. Greenidge	108	185	16	7,558	226	19	44.72
4	C. H. Lloyd	110	175	14	7,515	242*	19	46.67
5	D. L. Haynes	116	202	25	7,487	184	18	42.29
6	**B. C. Lara**	**80**	**141**	**4**	**6,533**	**375**	**15**	**47.68**
7	R. B. Kanhai	79	137	6	6,227	256	15	47.53
8	R. B. Richardson	86	146	12	5,949	194	16	44.39
9	**C. L. Hooper**	**87**	**148**	**14**	**4,699**	**178***	**10**	**35.06**
10	E. D. Weekes	48	81	5	4,455	207	15	58.61
11	A. I. Kallicharran	66	109	10	4,399	187	12	44.43
12	R. C. Fredericks	59	109	7	4,334	169	8	42.49
13	F. M. M. Worrell	51	87	9	3,860	261	9	49.48
14	C. L. Walcott	44	74	7	3,798	220	15	56.68
15	P. J. L. Dujon	81	115	11	3,322	139	5	31.94
16	C. C. Hunte	44	78	6	3,245	260	8	45.06
17	H. A. Gomes	60	91	11	3,171	143	9	39.63
18	B. F. Butcher	44	78	6	3,104	209*	7	43.11
19	**J. C. Adams**	**54**	**90**	**17**	**3,012**	**208***	**6**	**41.26**
20	**S. L. Campbell**	**51**	**91**	**4**	**2,856**	**208**	**4**	**32.82**
21	**S. Chanderpaul**	**49**	**81**	**9**	**2,833**	**137***	**2**	**39.34**
22	S. M. Nurse	29	54	1	2,523	258	6	47.60

NEW ZEALAND

		T	*I*	*NO*	*R*	*HS*	*100s*	*Avge*
1	M. D. Crowe	77	131	11	5,444	299	17	45.36
2	J. G. Wright	82	148	7	5,334	185	12	37.82
3	**S. P. Fleming**	**60**	**104**	**7**	**3,596**	**174***	**2**	**37.07**
4	B. E. Congdon	61	114	7	3,448	176	7	32.22
5	J. R. Reid	58	108	5	3,428	142	6	33.28
6	R. J. Hadlee	86	134	19	3,124	151*	2	27.16
7	G. M. Turner	41	73	6	2,991	259	7	44.64
8	A. H. Jones	39	74	8	2,922	186	7	44.27
9	B. Sutcliffe	42	76	8	2,727	230*	5	40.10
10	M. G. Burgess	50	92	6	2,684	119*	5	31.20
11	J. V. Coney	52	85	14	2,668	174*	3	37.57
12	**A. C. Parore**	**70**	**117**	**16**	**2,613**	**100***	**1**	**25.87**
13	**N. J. Astle**	**46**	**79**	**6**	**2,576**	**141**	**6**	**35.28**
14	**C. L. Cairns**	**49**	**83**	**4**	**2,572**	**126**	**4**	**32.55**
15	G. P. Howarth	47	83	5	2,531	147	6	32.44

INDIA

		T	*I*	*NO*	*R*	*HS*	*100s*	*Avge*
1	S. M. Gavaskar	125	214	16	10,122	236*	34	51.12
2	**S. R. Tendulkar**	**84**	**135**	**14**	**6,919**	**217**	**25**	**57.18**
3	D. B. Vengsarkar	116	185	22	6,868	166	17	42.13
4	M. Azharuddin	99	147	9	6,215	199	22	45.03
5	G. R. Viswanath	91	155	10	6,080	222	14	41.93
6	Kapil Dev	131	184	15	5,248	163	8	31.05
7	M. Amarnath	69	113	10	4,378	138	11	42.50
8	**R. Dravid**	**48**	**84**	**9**	**4,033**	**200***	**9**	**53.77**
9	R. J. Shastri	80	121	14	3,830	206	11	35.79
10	P. R. Umrigar	59	94	8	3,631	223	12	42.22

		T	I	NO	R	HS	100s	Avge
11	V. L. Manjrekar	55	92	10	3,208	189*	7	39.12
12	N. S. Sidhu	51	78	2	3,202	201	9	42.13
13	C. G. Borde	55	97	11	3,061	177*	5	35.59
14	**S. C. Ganguly**	**46**	**79**	**7**	**2,997**	**173**	**7**	**41.62**
15	Nawab of Pataudi jun.	46	83	3	2,793	203*	6	34.91
16	S. M. H. Kirmani	88	124	22	2,759	102	2	27.04
17	F. M. Engineer	46	87	3	2,611	121	2	31.08

PAKISTAN

		T	I	NO	R	HS	100s	Avge
1	Javed Miandad	124	189	21	8,832	280*	23	52.57
2	Salim Malik	103	154	22	5,768	237	15	43.69
3	**Inzamam-ul-Haq**	**75**	**124**	**13**	**5,299**	**200***	**15**	**47.73**
4	Zaheer Abbas	78	124	11	5,062	274	12	44.79
5	Mudassar Nazar	76	116	8	4,114	231	10	38.09
6	**Saeed Anwar**	**55**	**91**	**2**	**4,052**	**188***	**11**	**45.52**
7	Majid Khan	63	106	5	3,931	167	8	38.92
8	Hanif Mohammad	55	97	8	3,915	337	12	43.98
9	Imran Khan	88	126	25	3,807	136	6	37.69
10	Mushtaq Mohammad	57	100	7	3,643	201	10	39.17
11	Asif Iqbal	58	99	7	3,575	175	11	38.85
12	**Ijaz Ahmed, sen.**	**60**	**92**	**4**	**3,315**	**211**	**12**	**37.67**
13	Saeed Ahmed	41	78	4	2,991	172	5	40.41
14	**Wasim Akram**	**103**	**147**	**19**	**2,898**	**257***	**3**	**22.64**
15	Ramiz Raja	57	94	5	2,833	122	2	31.83
16	Aamir Sohail	47	83	3	2,823	205	5	35.28
17	Wasim Raja	57	92	14	2,821	125	4	36.16
18	Mohsin Khan	48	79	6	2,709	200	7	37.10
19	Shoaib Mohammad	45	68	7	2,705	203*	7	44.34
20	Sadiq Mohammad	41	74	2	2,579	166	5	35.81

SRI LANKA

		T	I	NO	R	HS	100s	Avge
1	**P. A. de Silva**	**89**	**153**	**11**	**5,952**	**267**	**19**	**41.91**
2	A. Ranatunga	93	155	12	5,105	135*	4	35.69
3	**S. T. Jayasuriya**	**62**	**106**	**10**	**3,760**	**340**	**8**	**39.16**
4	**H. P. Tillekeratne**	**59**	**95**	**15**	**3,145**	**136***	**7**	**39.31**
5	**M. S. Atapattu**	**47**	**83**	**8**	**2,644**	**223**	**7**	**35.25**
6	R. S. Mahanama	52	89	1	2,576	225	4	29.27

ZIMBABWE

		T	I	NO	R	HS	100s	Avge
1	**A. Flower**	**52**	**92**	**16**	**3,908**	**232***	**9**	**51.42**
2	**G. W. Flower**	**52**	**96**	**4**	**2,835**	**201***	**6**	**30.81**
3	**A. D. R. Campbell**	**54**	**97**	**4**	**2,509**	**103**	**2**	**26.97**

BANGLADESH: The highest aggregate is 334 (average 47.71) by **Habibul Bashar** in 4 Tests.

Bold type denotes those who played Test cricket in 2000-01 and 2001 seasons.

CAREER AVERAGE OVER 50

(Qualification: 20 innings)

Avge		*T*	*I*	*NO*	*R*	*HS*	*100s*
99.94	D. G. Bradman (A)	52	80	10	6,996	334	29
60.97	R. G. Pollock (SA)	23	41	4	2,256	274	7
60.83	G. A. Headley (WI)	22	40	4	2,190	270*	10
60.73	H. Sutcliffe (E)	54	84	9	4,555	194	16
59.23	E. Paynter (E)	20	31	5	1,540	243	4
58.67	K. F. Barrington (E)	82	131	15	6,806	256	20
58.61	E. D. Weekes (WI)	48	81	5	4,455	207	15
58.45	W. R. Hammond (E)	85	140	16	7,249	336*	22
57.78	G. S. Sobers (WI)	93	160	21	8,032	365*	26
57.18	**S. R. Tendulkar (I)**	**84**	**135**	**14**	**6,919**	**217**	**25**
56.94	J. B. Hobbs (E)	61	102	7	5,410	211	15
56.68	C. L. Walcott (WI)	44	74	7	3,798	220	15
56.67	L. Hutton (E)	79	138	15	6,971	364	19
55.00	E. Tyldesley (E)	14	20	2	990	122	3
54.20	C. A. Davis (WI)	15	29	5	1,301	183	4
54.20	V. G. Kambli (I)	17	21	1	1,084	227	4
53.86	G. S. Chappell (A)	87	151	19	7,110	247*	24
53.81	A. D. Nourse (SA)	34	62	7	2,960	231	9
53.77	**R. Dravid (I)**	**48**	**84**	**9**	**4,033**	**200***	**9**
52.57	Javed Miandad (P)	124	189	21	8,832	280*	23
51.87	**S. R. Waugh (A)**	**139**	**220**	**41**	**9,286**	**200**	**27**
51.62	J. Ryder (A)	20	32	5	1,394	201*	3
51.42	**A. Flower (Z)**	**52**	**92**	**16**	**3,908**	**232***	**9**
51.30	**A. C. Gilchrist (A)**	**22**	**30**	**4**	**1,334**	**152**	**3**
51.21	**M. S. Sinclair (NZ)**	**13**	**23**	**4**	**973**	**214**	**3**
51.12	S. M. Gavaskar (I)	125	214	16	10,122	236*	34
51.00	**D. R. Martyn (A)**	**16**	**27**	**7**	**1,020**	**118**	**2**
50.56	A. R. Border (A)	156	265	44	11,174	205	27
50.23	I. V. A. Richards (WI)	121	182	12	8,540	291	24
50.06	D. C. S. Compton (E)	78	131	15	5,807	278	17

Bold type denotes those who played Test cricket in 2000-01 and 2001 seasons.

FASTEST FIFTIES

Minutes			
28	J. T. Brown	England v Australia at Melbourne	1894-95
29	S. A. Durani	India v England at Kanpur	1963-64
30	E. A. V. Williams	West Indies v England at Bridgetown	1947-48
30	B. R. Taylor	New Zealand v West Indies at Auckland	1968-69
33	C. A. Roach	West Indies v England at The Oval	1933
34	C. R. Browne	West Indies v England at Georgetown	1929-30

The fastest fifties in terms of balls received (where recorded) are:

Balls			
26	I. T. Botham	England v India at Delhi	1981-82
30	Kapil Dev	India v Pakistan at Karachi (2nd Test)	1982-83
31	W. J. Cronje	South Africa v Sri Lanka at Centurion	1997-98
32	I. V. A. Richards	West Indies v India at Kingston	1982-83
32	I. T. Botham	England v New Zealand at The Oval	1986
33	R. C. Fredericks	West Indies v Australia at Perth	1975-76
33	Kapil Dev	India v Pakistan at Karachi	1978-79
33	Kapil Dev	India v England at Manchester	1982
33	A. J. Lamb	England v New Zealand at Auckland	1991-92

FASTEST HUNDREDS

Minutes			
70	J. M. Gregory	Australia v South Africa at Johannesburg	1921-22
75	G. L. Jessop	England v Australia at The Oval	1902
78	R. Benaud	Australia v West Indies at Kingston	1954-55
80	J. H. Sinclair	South Africa v Australia at Cape Town	1902-03
81	I. V. A. Richards	West Indies v England at St John's	1985-86
86	B. R. Taylor	New Zealand v West Indies at Auckland	1968-69

The fastest hundreds in terms of balls received (where recorded) are:

Balls			
56	I. V. A. Richards	West Indies v England at St John's	1985-86
67	J. M. Gregory	Australia v South Africa at Johannesburg	1921-22
71	R. C. Fredericks	West Indies v Australia at Perth	1975-76
74	Majid Khan	Pakistan v New Zealand at Karachi	1976-77
74	Kapil Dev	India v Sri Lanka at Kanpur	1986-87
74	M. Azharuddin	India v South Africa at Calcutta	1996-97
76	G. L. Jessop	England v Australia at The Oval	1902

FASTEST DOUBLE-HUNDREDS

Minutes			
214	D. G. Bradman	Australia v England at Leeds	1930
223	S. J. McCabe	Australia v England at Nottingham	1938
226	V. T. Trumper	Australia v South Africa at Adelaide	1910-11
234	D. G. Bradman	Australia v England at Lord's	1930
240	W. R. Hammond	England v New Zealand at Auckland	1932-33
241	S. E. Gregory	Australia v England at Sydney	1894-95
245	D. C. S. Compton	England v Pakistan at Nottingham	1954

The fastest double-hundreds in terms of balls received (where recorded) are:

Balls			
220	I. T. Botham	England v India at The Oval	1982
232	C. G. Greenidge	West Indies v England at Lord's	1984
240	C. H. Lloyd	West Indies v India at Bombay	1974-75
241	Zaheer Abbas	Pakistan v India at Lahore	1982-83
242	D. G. Bradman	Australia v England at The Oval	1934
242	I. V. A. Richards	West Indies v Australia at Melbourne	1984-85

FASTEST TRIPLE-HUNDREDS

Minutes			
288	W. R. Hammond	England v New Zealand at Auckland	1932-33
336	D. G. Bradman	Australia v England at Leeds	1930

MOST RUNS IN A DAY

309	D. G. Bradman	Australia v England at Leeds	1930
295	W. R. Hammond	England v New Zealand at Auckland	1932-33
273	D. C. S. Compton	England v Pakistan at Nottingham	1954
271	D. G. Bradman	Australia v England at Leeds	1934

SLOWEST INDIVIDUAL BATTING

0 in 101 minutes	G. I. Allott, New Zealand v South Africa at Auckland	1998-99
5 in 102 minutes	Nawab of Pataudi jun., India v England at Bombay	1972-73
6 in 106 minutes	D. R. Martyn, Australia v South Africa at Sydney	1993-94
7 in 123 minutes	G. Miller, England v Australia at Melbourne	1978-79
9 in 132 minutes	R. K. Chauhan, India v Sri Lanka at Ahmedabad	1993-94
10* in 133 minutes	T. G. Evans, England v Australia at Adelaide	1946-47
14* in 165 minutes	D. K. Morrison, New Zealand v England at Auckland	1996-97
18 in 194 minutes	W. R. Playle, New Zealand v England at Leeds	1958
19 in 217 minutes	M. D. Crowe, New Zealand v Sri Lanka at Colombo (SSC)	1983-84
25 in 242 minutes	D. K. Morrison, New Zealand v Pakistan at Faisalabad	1990-91
29* in 277 minutes	R. C. Russell, England v South Africa at Johannesburg	1995-96
35 in 332 minutes	C. J. Tavaré, England v India at Madras	1981-82
60 in 390 minutes	D. N. Sardesai, India v West Indies at Bridgetown	1961-62
62 in 408 minutes	Ramiz Raja, Pakistan v West Indies at Karachi	1986-87
68 in 458 minutes	T. E. Bailey, England v Australia at Brisbane	1958-59
99 in 505 minutes	M. L. Jaisimha, India v Pakistan at Kanpur	1960-61
105 in 575 minutes	D. J. McGlew, South Africa v Australia at Durban	1957-58
114 in 591 minutes	Mudassar Nazar, Pakistan v England at Lahore	1977-78
146* in 635 minutes	N. Hussain, England v South Africa at Durban	1999-2000
163 in 720 minutes	Shoaib Mohammad, Pakistan v New Zealand at Wellington	1988-89
201* in 777 minutes	D. S. B. P. Kuruppu, Sri Lanka v New Zealand at Colombo (CCC)	1986-87
275 in 878 minutes	G. Kirsten, South Africa v England at Durban	1999-2000
337 in 970 minutes	Hanif Mohammad, Pakistan v West Indies at Bridgetown	1957-58

SLOWEST HUNDREDS

557 minutes	Mudassar Nazar, Pakistan v England at Lahore	1977-78
545 minutes	D. J. McGlew, South Africa v Australia at Durban	1957-58
535 minutes	A. P. Gurusinha, Sri Lanka v Zimbabwe at Harare	1994-95
516 minutes	J. J. Crowe, New Zealand v Sri Lanka at Colombo (CCC)	1986-87
500 minutes	S. V. Manjrekar, India v Zimbabwe at Harare	1992-93
488 minutes	P. E. Richardson, England v South Africa at Johannesburg	1956-57

Notes: The slowest hundred for any Test in England is 458 minutes (329 balls) by K. W. R. Fletcher, England v Pakistan, The Oval, 1974.

The slowest double-hundred in a Test was scored in 777 minutes (548 balls) by D. S. B. P. Kuruppu for Sri Lanka v New Zealand at Colombo (CCC), 1986-87, on his debut. It is also the slowest-ever first-class double-hundred.

MOST DUCKS

C. A. Walsh (West Indies) 43; C. E. L. Ambrose (West Indies) 26; S. K. Warne (Australia) 25; D. K. Morrison (New Zealand) 24; B. S. Chandrasekhar (India) 23; G. D. McGrath (Australia) 22.

PARTNERSHIPS OVER 400

576	for 2nd	S. T. Jayasuriya (340)/R. S. Mahanama (225)	SL v I	Colombo (RPS)	1997-98
467	for 3rd	A. H. Jones (186)/M. D. Crowe (299)	NZ v SL	Wellington	1990-91
451	for 2nd	W. H. Ponsford (266)/D. G. Bradman (244)	A v E	The Oval	1934
451	for 3rd	Mudassar Nazar (231)/Javed Miandad (280*)	P v I	Hyderabad	1982-83
446	for 2nd	C. C. Hunte (260)/G. S. Sobers (365*)	WI v P	Kingston	1957-58
413	for 1st	V. Mankad (231)/Pankaj Roy (173)	I v NZ	Madras	1955-56
411	for 4th	P. B. H. May (285*)/M. C. Cowdrey (154)	E v WI	Birmingham	1957
405	for 5th	S. G. Barnes (234)/D. G. Bradman (234)	A v E	Sydney	1946-47

Note: 415 runs were scored for the third wicket for India v England at Madras in 1981-82 between D. B. Vengsarkar (retired hurt), G. R. Viswanath and Yashpal Sharma.

HIGHEST PARTNERSHIPS FOR EACH WICKET

The following lists include all stands above 300; otherwise the top ten for each wicket.

First Wicket

413	V. Mankad (231)/Pankaj Roy (173)	I v NZ	Madras	1955-56
387	G. M. Turner (259)/T. W. Jarvis (182)	NZ v WI	Georgetown	1971-72
382	W. M. Lawry (210)/R. B. Simpson (201)	A v WI	Bridgetown	1964-65
359	L. Hutton (158)/C. Washbrook (195)	E v SA	Johannesburg	1948-49
335	M. S. Atapattu (207*)/S. T. Jayasuriya (188)	SL v P	Kandy	2000 (SL)
329	G. R. Marsh (138)/M. A. Taylor (219)	A v E	Nottingham	1989
323	J. B. Hobbs (178)/W. Rhodes (179)	E v A	Melbourne	1911-12
298	C. G. Greenidge (149)/D. L. Haynes (167)	WI v E	St John's	1989-90
298	Aamir Sohail (160)/Ijaz Ahmed, sen. (151)	P v WI	Karachi	1997-98
296	C. G. Greenidge (154*)/D. L. Haynes (136)	WI v I	St John's	1982-83

Second Wicket

576	S. T. Jayasuriya (340)/R. S. Mahanama (225)	SL v I	Colombo (RPS)	1997-98
451	W. H. Ponsford (266)/D. G. Bradman (244)	A v E	The Oval	1934
446	C. C. Hunte (260)/G. S. Sobers (365*)	WI v P	Kingston	1957-58
382	L. Hutton (364)/M. Leyland (187)	E v A	The Oval	1938
369	J. H. Edrich (310*)/K. F. Barrington (163)	E v NZ	Leeds	1965
351	G. A. Gooch (196)/D. I. Gower (157)	E v A	The Oval	1985
344*	S. M. Gavaskar (182*)/D. B. Vengsarkar (157*)	I v WI	Calcutta	1978-79
331	R. T. Robinson (148)/D. I. Gower (215)	E v A	Birmingham	1985
315*	H. H. Gibbs (211*)/J. H. Kallis (148*)	SA v NZ	Christchurch	1998-99
301	A. R. Morris (182)/D. G. Bradman (173*)	A v E	Leeds	1948

Third Wicket

467	A. H. Jones (186)/M. D. Crowe (299)	NZ v SL	Wellington	1990-91
451	Mudassar Nazar (231)/Javed Miandad (280*)	P v I	Hyderabad	1982-83
397	Qasim Omar (206)/Javed Miandad (203*)	P v SL	Faisalabad	1985-86
370	W. J. Edrich (189)/D. C. S. Compton (208)	E v SA	Lord's	1947
352*‡	Ijaz Ahmed, sen. (211)/Inzamam-ul-Haq (200*)	P v SL	Dhaka	1998-99
341	E. J. Barlow (201)/R. G. Pollock (175)	SA v A	Adelaide	1963-64
338	E. D. Weekes (206)/F. M. M. Worrell (167)	WI v E	Port-of-Spain	1953-54
323	Aamir Sohail (160)/Inzamam-ul-Haq (177)	P v WI	Rawalpindi	1997-98
319	A. Melville (189)/A. D. Nourse (149)	SA v E	Nottingham	1947
316†	G. R. Viswanath (222)/Yashpal Sharma (140)	I v E	Madras	1981-82
308	R. B. Richardson (154)/I. V. A. Richards (178)	WI v A	St John's	1983-84
308	G. A. Gooch (333)/A. J. Lamb (139)	E v I	Lord's	1990
303	I. V. A. Richards (232)/A. I. Kallicharran (97)	WI v E	Nottingham	1976
303	M. A. Atherton (135)/R. A. Smith (175)	E v WI	St John's	1993-94

† 415 runs were scored for this wicket in two separate partnerships; D. B. Vengsarkar retired hurt when he and Viswanath had added 99 runs.
‡ 366 runs were scored for this wicket in two separate partnerships; Inzamam retired ill when he and Ijaz had added 352 runs.

Fourth Wicket

411	P. B. H. May (285*)/M. C. Cowdrey (154)	E v WI	Birmingham	1957
399	G. S. Sobers (226)/F. M. M. Worrell (197*)	WI v E	Bridgetown	1959-60
388	W. H. Ponsford (181)/D. G. Bradman (304)	A v E	Leeds	1934

350	Mushtaq Mohammad (201)/Asif Iqbal (175)	P v NZ	Dunedin	1972-73
336	W. M. Lawry (151)/K. D. Walters (242)	A v WI	Sydney	1968-69
322	Javed Miandad (153*)/Salim Malik (165)	P v E	Birmingham	1992
288	N. Hussain (207)/G. P. Thorpe (138)	E v A	Birmingham	1997
287	Javed Miandad (126)/Zaheer Abbas (168)	P v I	Faisalabad	1982-83
283	F. M. M. Worrell (261)/E. D. Weekes (129)	WI v E	Nottingham	1950
281	S. R. Tendulkar (217)/S. C. Ganguly (125)	I v NZ	Ahmedabad	1999-2000

Fifth Wicket

405	S. G. Barnes (234)/D. G. Bradman (234)	A v E	Sydney	1946-47
385	S. R. Waugh (160)/G. S. Blewett (214)	A v SA	Johannesburg	1996-97
376	V. V. S. Laxman (281)/R. Dravid (180)	I v A	Kolkata	2000-01
332*	A. R. Border (200*)/S. R. Waugh (157*)	A v E	Leeds	1993
327	J. L. Langer (144)/R. T. Ponting (197)	A v P	Perth	1999-2000
322†	B. C. Lara (213)/J. C. Adams (94)	WI v A	Kingston	1998-99
281	Javed Miandad (163)/Asif Iqbal (166)	P v NZ	Lahore	1976-77
281	S. R. Waugh (199)/R. T. Ponting (104)	A v WI	Bridgetown	1998-99
277*	M. W. Goodwin (166*)/A. Flower (100*)	Z v P	Bulawayo	1997-98
268	M. T. G. Elliott (199)/R. T. Ponting (127)	A v E	Leeds	1997

† 344 runs were scored for this wicket in two separate partnerships; P. T. Collins retired hurt when he and Lara had added 22 runs.

Sixth Wicket

346	J. H. Fingleton (136)/D. G. Bradman (270)	A v E	Melbourne	1936-37
298*	D. B. Vengsarkar (164*)/R. J. Shastri (121*)	I v A	Bombay	1986-87
274*	G. S. Sobers (163*)/D. A. J. Holford (105*)	WI v E	Lord's	1966
272	M. Azharuddin (199)/Kapil Dev (163)	I v SL	Kanpur	1986-87
260*	D. M. Jones (118*)/S. R. Waugh (134*)	A v SL	Hobart	1989-90
254	C. A. Davis (183)/G. S. Sobers (142)	WI v NZ	Bridgetown	1971-72
250	C. H. Lloyd (242*)/D. L. Murray (91)	WI v I	Bombay	1974-75
246*	J. J. Crowe (120*)/R. J. Hadlee (151*)	NZ v SL	Colombo (CCC)	1986-87
240	P. H. Parfitt (131*)/B. R. Knight (125)	E v NZ	Auckland	1962-63
238	J. L. Langer (127)/A. C. Gilchrist (149*)	A v P	Hobart	1999-2000

Seventh Wicket

347	D. St E. Atkinson (219)/C. C. Depeiza (122)	WI v A	Bridgetown	1954-55
308	Waqar Hassan (189)/Imtiaz Ahmed (209)	P v NZ	Lahore	1955-56
248	Yousuf Youhana (203)/Saqlain Mushtaq (101*)	P v NZ	Christchurch	2000-01
246	D. J. McGlew (255*)/A. R. A. Murray (109)	SA v NZ	Wellington	1952-53
235	R. J. Shastri (142)/S. M. H. Kirmani (102)	I v E	Bombay	1984-85
221	D. T. Lindsay (182)/P. L. van der Merwe (76)	SA v A	Johannesburg	1966-67
217	K. D. Walters (250)/G. J. Gilmour (101)	A v NZ	Christchurch	1976-77
197	M. J. K. Smith (96)/J. M. Parks (101*)	E v WI	Port-of-Spain	1959-60
194*	H. P. Tillekeratne (136*)/T. T. Samaraweera (103*)	SL v I	Colombo (SSC)	2001 (SL)
186	D. N. Sardesai (150)/E. D. Solkar (65)	I v WI	Bridgetown	1970-71
186	W. K. Lees (152)/R. J. Hadlee (87)	NZ v P	Karachi	1976-77

Eighth Wicket

313	Wasim Akram (257*)/Saqlain Mushtaq (79)	P v Z	Sheikhupura	1996-97
246	L. E. G. Ames (137)/G. O. B. Allen (122)	E v NZ	Lord's	1931
243	R. J. Hartigan (116)/C. Hill (160)	A v E	Adelaide	1907-08
217	T. W. Graveney (165)/J. T. Murray (112)	E v WI	The Oval	1966
173	C. E. Pellew (116)/J. M. Gregory (100)	A v E	Melbourne	1920-21

168	R. Illingworth (107)/P. Lever (88*)	E v I	Manchester	1971
161	M. Azharuddin (109)/A. Kumble (88)	I v SA	Calcutta	1996-97
154	G. J. Bonnor (128)/S. P. Jones (40)	A v E	Sydney	1884-85
154	C. W. Wright (71)/H. R. Bromley-Davenport (84)	E v SA	Johannesburg	1895-96
154	D. Tallon (92)/R. R. Lindwall (100)	A v E	Melbourne	1946-47

Ninth Wicket

195	M. V. Boucher (78)/P. L. Symcox (108)	SA v P	Johannesburg	1997-98
190	Asif Iqbal (146)/Intikhab Alam (51)	P v E	The Oval	1967
163*	M. C. Cowdrey (128*)/A. C. Smith (69*)	E v NZ	Wellington	1962-63
161	C. H. Lloyd (161*)/A. M. E. Roberts (68)	WI v I	Calcutta	1983-84
161	Zaheer Abbas (82*)/Sarfraz Nawaz (90)	P v E	Lahore	1983-84
154	S. E. Gregory (201)/J. McC. Blackham (74)	A v E	Sydney	1894-95
151	W. H. Scotton (90)/W. W. Read (117)	E v A	The Oval	1884
150	E. A. E. Baptiste (87*)/M. A. Holding (69)	WI v E	Birmingham	1984
149	P. G. Joshi (52*)/R. B. Desai (85)	I v P	Bombay	1960-61
147	Mohammad Wasim (192)/Mushtaq Ahmed (57)	P v Z	Harare	1997-98

Tenth Wicket

151	B. F. Hastings (110)/R. O. Collinge (68*)	NZ v P	Auckland	1972-73
151	Azhar Mahmood (128*)/Mushtaq Ahmed (59)	P v SA	Rawalpindi	1997-98
133	Wasim Raja (71)/Wasim Bari (60*)	P v WI	Bridgetown	1976-77
130	R. E. Foster (287)/W. Rhodes (40*)	E v A	Sydney	1903-04
128	K. Higgs (63)/J. A. Snow (59*)	E v WI	The Oval	1966
127	J. M. Taylor (108)/A. A. Mailey (46*)	A v E	Sydney	1924-25
124	J. G. Bracewell (83*)/S. L. Boock (37)	NZ v A	Sydney	1985-86
120	R. A. Duff (104)/W. W. Armstrong (45*)	A v E	Melbourne	1901-02
117*	P. Willey (100*)/R. G. D. Willis (24*)	E v WI	The Oval	1980
109	H. R. Adhikari (81*)/Ghulam Ahmed (50)	I v P	Delhi	1952-53

BOWLING RECORDS

MOST WICKETS IN AN INNINGS

10-53	J. C. Laker	England v Australia at Manchester	1956
10-74	A. Kumble	India v Pakistan at Delhi	1998-99
9-28	G. A. Lohmann	England v South Africa at Johannesburg	1895-96
9-37	J. C. Laker	England v Australia at Manchester	1956
9-52	R. J. Hadlee	New Zealand v Australia at Brisbane	1985-86
9-56	Abdul Qadir	Pakistan v England at Lahore	1987-88
9-57	D. E. Malcolm	England v South Africa at The Oval	1994
9-65	M. Muralitharan	Sri Lanka v England at The Oval	1998
9-69	J. M. Patel	India v Australia at Kanpur	1959-60
9-83	Kapil Dev	India v West Indies at Ahmedabad	1983-84
9-86	Sarfraz Nawaz	Pakistan v Australia at Melbourne	1978-79
9-95	J. M. Noreiga	West Indies v India at Port-of-Spain	1970-71
9-102	S. P. Gupte	India v West Indies at Kanpur	1958-59
9-103	S. F. Barnes	England v South Africa at Johannesburg	1913-14
9-113	H. J. Tayfield	South Africa v England at Johannesburg	1956-57
9-121	A. A. Mailey	Australia v England at Melbourne	1920-21
8-7	G. A. Lohmann	England v South Africa at Port Elizabeth	1895-96
8-11	J. Briggs	England v South Africa at Cape Town	1888-89
8-29	S. F. Barnes	England v South Africa at The Oval	1912
8-29	C. E. H. Croft	West Indies v Pakistan at Port-of-Spain	1976-77
8-31	F. Laver	Australia v England at Manchester	1909

8-31	F. S. Trueman	England v India at Manchester	1952
8-34	I. T. Botham	England v Pakistan at Lord's	1978
8-35	G. A. Lohmann	England v Australia at Sydney	1886-87
8-38	L. R. Gibbs	West Indies v India at Bridgetown	1961-62
8-38	G. D. McGrath	Australia v England at Lord's	1997
8-43†	A. E. Trott	Australia v England at Adelaide	1894-95
8-43	H. Verity	England v Australia at Lord's	1934
8-43	R. G. D. Willis	England v Australia at Leeds	1981
8-45	C. E. L. Ambrose	West Indies v England at Bridgetown	1989-90
8-51	D. L. Underwood	England v Pakistan at Lord's	1974
8-52	V. Mankad	India v Pakistan at Delhi	1952-53
8-53	G. B. Lawrence	South Africa v New Zealand at Johannesburg	1961-62
8-53†	R. A. L. Massie	Australia v England at Lord's	1972
8-53	A. R. C. Fraser	England v West Indies at Port-of-Spain	1997-98
8-55	V. Mankad	India v England at Madras	1951-52
8-56	S. F. Barnes	England v South Africa at Johannesburg	1913-14
8-58	G. A. Lohmann	England v Australia at Sydney	1891-92
8-58	Imran Khan	Pakistan v Sri Lanka at Lahore	1981-82
8-59	C. Blythe	England v South Africa at Leeds	1907
8-59	A. A. Mallett	Australia v Pakistan at Adelaide	1972-73
8-60	Imran Khan	Pakistan v India at Karachi	1982-83
8-61†	N. D. Hirwani	India v West Indies at Madras	1987-88
8-64†	L. Klusener	South Africa v India at Calcutta	1996-97
8-65	H. Trumble	Australia v England at The Oval	1902
8-68	W. Rhodes	England v Australia at Melbourne	1903-04
8-69	H. J. Tayfield	South Africa v England at Durban	1956-57
8-69	Sikander Bakht	Pakistan v India at Delhi	1979-80
8-70	S. J. Snooke	South Africa v England at Johannesburg	1905-06
8-71	G. D. McKenzie	Australia v West Indies at Melbourne	1968-69
8-71	S. K. Warne	Australia v England at Brisbane	1994-95
8-71	A. A. Donald	South Africa v Zimbabwe at Harare	1995-96
8-72	S. Venkataraghavan	India v New Zealand at Delhi	1964-65
8-75†	N. D. Hirwani	India v West Indies at Madras	1987-88
8-75	A. R. C. Fraser	England v West Indies at Bridgetown	1993-94
8-76	E. A. S. Prasanna	India v New Zealand at Auckland	1975-76
8-79	B. S. Chandrasekhar	India v England at Delhi	1972-73
8-81	L. C. Braund	England v Australia at Melbourne	1903-04
8-83	J. R. Ratnayeke	Sri Lanka v Pakistan at Sialkot	1985-86
8-84†	R. A. L. Massie	Australia v England at Lord's	1972
8-84	Harbhajan Singh	India v Australia at Chennai	2000-01
8-85	Kapil Dev	India v Pakistan at Lahore	1982-83
8-86	A. W. Greig	England v West Indies at Port-of-Spain	1973-74
8-86	J. Srinath	India v Pakistan at Calcutta	1998-99
8-87	M. G. Hughes	Australia v West Indies at Perth	1988-89
8-87	M. Muralitharan	Sri Lanka v India at Colombo (SSC)	2001 (SL)
8-92	M. A. Holding	West Indies v England at The Oval	1976
8-94	T. Richardson	England v Australia at Sydney	1897-98
8-97	C. J. McDermott	Australia v England at Perth	1990-91
8-103	I. T. Botham	England v West Indies at Lord's	1984
8-104†	A. L. Valentine	West Indies v England at Manchester	1950
8-106	Kapil Dev	India v Australia at Adelaide	1985-86
8-107	B. J. T. Bosanquet	England v Australia at Nottingham	1905
8-107	N. A. Foster	England v Pakistan at Leeds	1987
8-109	P. A. Strang	Zimbabwe v New Zealand at Bulawayo	2000-01
8-112	G. F. Lawson	Australia v West Indies at Adelaide	1984-85
8-126	J. C. White	England v Australia at Adelaide	1928-29
8-141	C. J. McDermott	Australia v England at Manchester	1985
8-143	M. H. N. Walker	Australia v England at Melbourne	1974-75
8-164	Saqlain Mushtaq	Pakistan v England at Lahore	2000-01

† *On Test debut.*

Note: The best for Bangladesh is 6-81 by Manjurul Islam against Zimbabwe at Bulawayo in 2000-01.

OUTSTANDING BOWLING ANALYSES

	O	M	R	W		
J. C. Laker (E)	51.2	23	53	10	v Australia at Manchester	1956
A. Kumble (I)	26.3	9	74	10	v Pakistan at Delhi	1998-99
G. A. Lohmann (E)	14.2	6	28	9	v South Africa at Johannesburg	1895-96
J. C. Laker (E)	16.4	4	37	9	v Australia at Manchester	1956
G. A. Lohmann (E)	9.4	5	7	8	v South Africa at Port Elizabeth	1895-96
J. Briggs (E)	14.2	5	11	8	v South Africa at Cape Town	1888-89
J. Briggs (E)	19.1	11	17	7	v South Africa at Cape Town	1888-89
M. A. Noble (A)	7.4	2	17	7	v England at Melbourne	1901-02
W. Rhodes (E)	11	3	17	7	v Australia at Birmingham	1902
A. E. R. Gilligan (E)	6.3	4	7	6	v South Africa at Birmingham	1924
S. Haigh (E)	11.4	6	11	6	v South Africa at Cape Town	1898-99
D. L. Underwood (E)	11.6	7	12	6	v New Zealand at Christchurch	1970-71
S. L. V. Raju (I)	17.5	13	12	6	v Sri Lanka at Chandigarh	1990-91
H. J. Tayfield (SA)	14	7	13	6	v New Zealand at Johannesburg	1953-54
C. T. B. Turner (A)	18	11	15	6	v England at Sydney	1886-87
M. H. N. Walker (A)	16	8	15	6	v Pakistan at Sydney	1972-73
E. R. H. Toshack (A)	2.3	1	2	5	v India at Brisbane	1947-48
H. Ironmonger (A)	7.2	5	6	5	v South Africa at Melbourne	1931-32
T. B. A. May (A)	6.5	3	9	5	v West Indies at Adelaide	1992-93
Pervez Sajjad (P)	12	8	5	4	v New Zealand at Rawalpindi	1964-65
K. Higgs (E)	9	7	5	4	v New Zealand at Christchurch	1965-66
P. H. Edmonds (E)	8	6	6	4	v Pakistan at Lord's	1978
J. C. White (E)	6.3	2	7	4	v Australia at Brisbane	1928-29
J. H. Wardle (E)	5	2	7	4	v Australia at Manchester	1953
R. Appleyard (E)	6	3	7	4	v New Zealand at Auckland	1954-55
R. Benaud (A)	3.4	3	0	3	v India at Delhi	1959-60

WICKET WITH FIRST BALL IN TEST CRICKET

	Batsman dismissed			
A. Coningham	A. C. MacLaren	A v E	Melbourne	1894-95
W. M. Bradley	F. Laver	E v A	Manchester	1899
E. G. Arnold	V. T. Trumper	E v A	Sydney	1903-04
G. G. Macaulay	G. A. L. Hearne	E v SA	Cape Town	1922-23
M. W. Tate	M. J. Susskind	E v SA	Birmingham	1924
M. Henderson	E. W. Dawson	NZ v E	Christchurch	1929-30
H. D. Smith	E. Paynter	NZ v E	Christchurch	1932-33
T. F. Johnson	W. W. Keeton	WI v E	The Oval	1939
R. Howorth	D. V. Dyer	E v SA	The Oval	1947
Intikhab Alam	C. C. McDonald	P v A	Karachi	1959-60
R. K. Illingworth	P. V. Simmons	E v WI	Nottingham	1991
N. M. Kulkarni	M. S. Atapattu	I v SL	Colombo (RPS)	1997-98

HAT-TRICKS

F. R. Spofforth	Australia v England at Melbourne	1878-79
W. Bates	England v Australia at Melbourne	1882-83
J. Briggs	England v Australia at Sydney	1891-92
G. A. Lohmann	England v South Africa at Port Elizabeth	1895-96
J. T. Hearne	England v Australia at Leeds	1899
H. Trumble	Australia v England at Melbourne	1901-02
H. Trumble	Australia v England at Melbourne	1903-04
T. J. Matthews† / T. J. Matthews	Australia v South Africa at Manchester	1912
M. J. C. Allom‡	England v New Zealand at Christchurch	1929-30
T. W. J. Goddard	England v South Africa at Johannesburg	1938-39

P. J. Loader	England v West Indies at Leeds	1957
L. F. Kline	Australia v South Africa at Cape Town	1957-58
W. W. Hall	West Indies v Pakistan at Lahore	1958-59
G. M. Griffin	South Africa v England at Lord's	1960
L. R. Gibbs	West Indies v Australia at Adelaide	1960-61
P. J. Petherick‡	New Zealand v Pakistan at Lahore	1976-77
C. A. Walsh§	West Indies v Australia at Brisbane	1988-89
M. G. Hughes§	Australia v West Indies at Perth	1988-89
D. W. Fleming‡	Australia v Pakistan at Rawalpindi	1994-95
S. K. Warne	Australia v England at Melbourne	1994-95
D. G. Cork	England v West Indies at Manchester	1995
D. Gough	England v Australia at Sydney	1998-99
Wasim Akram¶	Pakistan v Sri Lanka at Lahore	1998-99
Wasim Akram¶	Pakistan v Sri Lanka at Dhaka	1998-99
D. N. T. Zoysa	Sri Lanka v Zimbabwe at Harare	1999-2000
Abdur Razzaq	Pakistan v Sri Lanka at Galle	2000 (SL)
G. D. McGrath	Australia v West Indies at Perth	2000-01
Harbhajan Singh	India v Australia at Kolkata	2000-01

† *T. J. Matthews did the hat-trick in each innings of the same match.*
‡ *On Test debut.*
§ *Not all in the same innings.*
¶ *Wasim Akram did the hat-trick in successive matches.*

FOUR WICKETS IN FIVE BALLS

M. J. C. Allom	England v New Zealand at Christchurch *On debut, in his eighth over: W-WWW*	1929-30
C. M. Old	England v Pakistan at Birmingham *Sequence interrupted by a no-ball: WW-WW*	1978
Wasim Akram	Pakistan v West Indies at Lahore (*WW-WW*)	1990-91

MOST WICKETS IN A TEST

19-90	J. C. Laker	England v Australia at Manchester	1956
17-159	S. F. Barnes	England v South Africa at Johannesburg	1913-14
16-136†	N. D. Hirwani	India v West Indies at Madras	1987-88
16-137†	R. A. L. Massie	Australia v England at Lord's	1972
16-220	M. Muralitharan	Sri Lanka v England at The Oval	1998
15-28	J. Briggs	England v South Africa at Cape Town	1888-89
15-45	G. A. Lohmann	England v South Africa at Port Elizabeth	1895-96
15-99	C. Blythe	England v South Africa at Leeds	1907
15-104	H. Verity	England v Australia at Lord's	1934
15-123	R. J. Hadlee	New Zealand v Australia at Brisbane	1985-86
15-124	W. Rhodes	England v Australia at Melbourne	1903-04
15-217	Harbhajan Singh	India v Australia at Chennai	2000-01
14-90	F. R. Spofforth	Australia v England at The Oval	1882
14-99	A. V. Bedser	England v Australia at Nottingham	1953
14-102	W. Bates	England v Australia at Melbourne	1882-83
14-116	Imran Khan	Pakistan v Sri Lanka at Lahore	1981-82
14-124	J. M. Patel	India v Australia at Kanpur	1959-60
14-144	S. F. Barnes	England v South Africa at Durban	1913-14
14-149	M. A. Holding	West Indies v England at The Oval	1976
14-149	A. Kumble	India v Pakistan at Delhi	1998-99
14-199	C. V. Grimmett	Australia v South Africa at Adelaide	1931-32

† *On Test debut.*

Note: The best for South Africa is 13-165 by H. J. Tayfield against Australia at Melbourne, 1952-53, for Zimbabwe 11-255 by A. G. Huckle v New Zealand at Bulawayo, 1997-98, and for Bangladesh 6-81 by Manjurul Islam v Zimbabwe at Bulawayo, 2000-01.

MOST BALLS BOWLED IN A TEST

S. Ramadhin (West Indies) sent down 774 balls in 129 overs against England at Birmingham, 1957. It was the most delivered by any bowler in a Test, beating H. Verity's 766 for England against South Africa at Durban, 1938-39. In this match Ramadhin also bowled the most balls (588) in a Test or first-class innings, since equalled by Arshad Ayub, Hyderabad v Madhya Pradesh at Secunderabad, 1991-92.

MOST WICKETS IN A SERIES

	T	*R*	*W*	*Avge*		
S. F. Barnes	4	536	49	10.93	England v South Africa	1913-14
J. C. Laker	5	442	46	9.60	England v Australia	1956
C. V. Grimmett	5	642	44	14.59	Australia v South Africa	1935-36
T. M. Alderman	6	893	42	21.26	Australia v England	1981
R. M. Hogg	6	527	41	12.85	Australia v England	1978-79
T. M. Alderman	6	712	41	17.36	Australia v England	1989
Imran Khan	6	558	40	13.95	Pakistan v India	1982-83
A. V. Bedser	5	682	39	17.48	England v Australia	1953
D. K. Lillee	6	870	39	22.30	Australia v England	1981
M. W. Tate	5	881	38	23.18	England v Australia	1924-25
W. J. Whitty	5	632	37	17.08	Australia v South Africa	1910-11
H. J. Tayfield	5	636	37	17.18	South Africa v England	1956-57
A. E. E. Vogler	5	783	36	21.75	South Africa v England	1909-10
A. A. Mailey	5	946	36	26.27	Australia v England	1920-21
G. D. McGrath	6	701	36	19.47	Australia v England	1997
G. A. Lohmann	3	203	35	5.80	England v South Africa	1895-96
B. S. Chandrasekhar	5	662	35	18.91	India v England	1972-73
M. D. Marshall	5	443	35	12.65	West Indies v England	1988

Notes: The most for New Zealand is 33 by R. J. Hadlee against Australia in 1985-86, for Sri Lanka 26 by M. Muralitharan against Pakistan in 1999-2000 and against South Africa in 2000 (SL), for Zimbabwe 22 by H. H. Streak against Pakistan in 1994-95, and for Bangladesh 6 by Naimur Rahman against India in 2000-01 and by Manjurul Islam against Zimbabwe in 2000-01.

70 WICKETS IN A CALENDAR YEAR

	T	*R*	*W*	*Avge*	*5W/i*	*10W/m*	*Year*
D. K. Lillee (A)	13	1,781	85	20.95	5	2	1981
A. A. Donald (SA)	14	1,571	80	19.63	7	–	1998
J. Garner (WI)	15	1,604	77	20.83	4	–	1984
Kapil Dev (I)	18	1,739	75	23.18	5	1	1983
M. Muralitharan (SL)	10	1,463	75	19.50	7	3	2000
Kapil Dev (I)	18	1,720	74	23.24	5	–	1979
M. D. Marshall (WI)	13	1,471	73	20.15	9	1	1984
S. K. Warne (A)	16	1,697	72	23.56	2	–	1993
G. D. McKenzie (A)	14	1,737	71	24.46	4	1	1964
S. K. Warne (A)	10	1,274	70	18.20	6	2	1994

100 WICKETS

ENGLAND

		T	Balls	R	W	Avge	5W/i	10W/m
1	I. T. Botham	102	21,815	10,878	383	28.40	27	4
2	R. G. D. Willis	90	17,357	8,190	325	25.20	16	–
3	F. S. Trueman	67	15,178	6,625	307	21.57	17	3
4	D. L. Underwood	86	21,862	7,674	297	25.83	17	6
5	J. B. Statham	70	16,056	6,261	252	24.84	9	1
6	A. V. Bedser	51	15,918	5,876	236	24.89	15	5
7	**D. Gough**	**56**	**11,503**	**6,288**	**228**	**27.57**	**9**	–
8	J. A. Snow	49	12,021	5,387	202	26.66	8	1
9	J. C. Laker	46	12,027	4,101	193	21.24	9	3
10	S. F. Barnes	27	7,873	3,106	189	16.43	24	7
11	**A. R. Caddick**	**50**	**10,728**	**5,392**	**181**	**29.79**	**10**	–
12	A. R. C. Fraser	46	10,876	4,836	177	27.32	13	2
13	G. A. R. Lock	49	13,147	4,451	174	25.58	9	3
14	M. W. Tate	39	12,523	4,055	155	26.16	7	1
15	F. J. Titmus	53	15,118	4,931	153	32.22	7	–
16	J. E. Emburey	64	15,391	5,646	147	38.40	6	–
17	H. Verity	40	11,173	3,510	144	24.37	5	2
18	C. M. Old	46	8,858	4,020	143	28.11	4	–
19	A. W. Greig	58	9,802	4,541	141	32.20	6	2
20	P. A. J. DeFreitas	44	9,838	4,700	140	33.57	4	–
21	G. R. Dilley	41	8,192	4,107	138	29.76	6	–
22	T. E. Bailey	61	9,712	3,856	132	29.21	5	1
23	D. E. Malcolm	40	8,480	4,748	128	37.09	5	2
24	W. Rhodes	58	8,231	3,425	127	26.96	6	1
25	P. H. Edmonds	51	12,028	4,273	125	34.18	2	–
26	**D. G. Cork**	**34**	**7,195**	**3,647**	**124**	**29.41**	**5**	–
27	D. A. Allen	39	11,297	3,779	122	30.97	4	–
	R. Illingworth	61	11,934	3,807	122	31.20	3	–
29	**P. C. R. Tufnell**	**42**	**11,288**	**4,560**	**121**	**37.68**	**5**	**2**
30	J. Briggs	33	5,332	2,095	118	17.75	9	4
31	G. G. Arnold	34	7,650	3,254	115	28.29	6	–
32	G. A. Lohmann	18	3,821	1,205	112	10.75	9	5
33	D. V. P. Wright	34	8,135	4,224	108	39.11	6	1
34	J. H. Wardle	28	6,597	2,080	102	20.39	5	1
35	R. Peel	20	5,216	1,715	101	16.98	5	1
36	C. Blythe	19	4,546	1,863	100	18.63	9	4

AUSTRALIA

		T	Balls	R	W	Avge	5W/i	10W/m
1	**S. K. Warne**	**92**	**25,587**	**10,590**	**407**	**26.01**	**19**	**5**
2	**G. D. McGrath**	**75**	**17,950**	**7,620**	**358**	**21.28**	**22**	**3**
3	D. K. Lillee	70	18,467	8,493	355	23.92	23	7
4	C. J. McDermott	71	16,586	8,332	291	28.63	14	2
5	R. Benaud	63	19,108	6,704	248	27.03	16	1
6	G. D. McKenzie	60	17,681	7,328	246	29.78	16	3
7	R. R. Lindwall	61	13,650	5,251	228	23.03	12	–
8	C. V. Grimmett	37	14,513	5,231	216	24.21	21	7
9	M. G. Hughes	53	12,285	6,017	212	28.38	7	1
10	J. R. Thomson	51	10,535	5,601	200	28.00	8	–
11	A. K. Davidson	44	11,587	3,819	186	20.53	14	2
12	G. F. Lawson	46	11,118	5,501	180	30.56	11	2
13	K. R. Miller	55	10,461	3,906	170	22.97	7	1
	T. M. Alderman	41	10,181	4,616	170	27.15	14	1

		T	*Balls*	*R*	*W*	*Avge*	*5W/i*	*10W/m*
15	W. A. Johnston	40	11,048	3,826	160	23.91	7	–
16	W. J. O'Reilly	27	10,024	3,254	144	22.59	11	3
17	H. Trumble	32	8,099	3,072	141	21.78	9	3
18	M. H. N. Walker	34	10,094	3,792	138	27.47	6	–
19	A. A. Mallett	38	9,990	3,940	132	29.84	6	1
20	B. Yardley	33	8,909	3,986	126	31.63	6	1
21	R. M. Hogg	38	7,633	3,503	123	28.47	6	2
22	M. A. Noble	42	7,159	3,025	121	25.00	9	2
23	B. A. Reid	27	6,244	2,784	113	24.63	5	2
24	I. W. Johnson	45	8,780	3,182	109	29.19	3	–
25	P. R. Reiffel	35	6,403	2,804	104	26.96	5	–
26	G. Giffen	31	6,457	2,791	103	27.09	7	1
27	A. N. Connolly	29	7,818	2,981	102	29.22	4	–
	J. N. Gillespie	**26**	**4,875**	**2,522**	**102**	**24.72**	**6**	–
29	C. T. B. Turner	17	5,179	1,670	101	16.53	11	2

SOUTH AFRICA

		T	*Balls*	*R*	*W*	*Avge*	*5W/i*	*10W/m*
1	**A. A. Donald**	**69**	**15,037**	**7,034**	**325**	**21.64**	**20**	**3**
2	**S. M. Pollock**	**56**	**12,428**	**4,694**	**231**	**20.32**	**12**	–
3	H. J. Tayfield	37	13,568	4,405	170	25.91	14	2
4	T. L. Goddard	41	11,736	3,226	123	26.22	5	–
5	P. M. Pollock	28	6,522	2,806	116	24.18	9	1
6	N. A. T. Adcock	26	6,391	2,195	104	21.10	5	–

WEST INDIES

		T	*Balls*	*R*	*W*	*Avge*	*5W/i*	*10W/m*
1	**C. A. Walsh**	**132**	**30,019**	**12,688**	**519**	**24.44**	**22**	**3**
2	C. E. L. Ambrose	98	22,103	8,501	405	20.99	22	3
3	M. D. Marshall	81	17,584	7,876	376	20.94	22	4
4	L. R. Gibbs	79	27,115	8,989	309	29.09	18	2
5	J. Garner	58	13,169	5,433	259	20.97	7	–
6	M. A. Holding	60	12,680	5,898	249	23.68	13	2
7	G. S. Sobers	93	21,599	7,999	235	34.03	6	–
8	A. M. E. Roberts	47	11,136	5,174	202	25.61	11	2
9	W. W. Hall	48	10,421	5,066	192	26.38	9	1
10	I. R. Bishop	43	8,407	3,909	161	24.27	6	–
11	S. Ramadhin	43	13,939	4,579	158	28.98	10	1
12	A. L. Valentine	36	12,953	4,215	139	30.32	8	2
13	C. E. H. Croft	27	6,165	2,913	125	23.30	3	–
14	V. A. Holder	40	9,095	3,627	109	33.27	3	–

NEW ZEALAND

		T	*Balls*	*R*	*W*	*Avge*	*5W/i*	*10W/m*
1	R. J. Hadlee	86	21,918	9,612	431	22.29	36	9
2	**C. L. Cairns**	**49**	**9,381**	**4,995**	**171**	**29.21**	**10**	**1**
3	D. K. Morrison	48	10,064	5,549	160	34.68	10	–
4	B. L. Cairns	43	10,628	4,280	130	32.92	6	1
5	E. J. Chatfield	43	10,360	3,958	123	32.17	3	1
6	R. O. Collinge	35	7,689	3,392	116	29.24	3	–
7	B. R. Taylor	30	6,334	2,953	111	26.60	4	–
8	**D. L. Vettori**	**31**	**8,295**	**3,458**	**106**	**32.62**	**5**	**1**
9	J. G. Bracewell	41	8,403	3,653	102	35.81	4	1
10	R. C. Motz	32	7,034	3,148	100	31.48	5	–

INDIA

		T	*Balls*	*R*	*W*	*Avge*	*5W/i*	*10W/m*
1	Kapil Dev	131	27,740	12,867	434	29.64	23	2
2	A. Kumble	61	19,115	7,728	276	28.00	16	3
3	B. S. Bedi	67	21,364	7,637	266	28.71	14	1
4	B. S. Chandrasekhar	58	15,963	7,199	242	29.74	16	2
5	**J. Srinath**	**53**	**12,278**	**5,899**	**197**	**29.94**	**8**	**1**
6	E. A. S. Prasanna	49	14,353	5,742	189	30.38	10	2
7	V. Mankad	44	14,686	5,236	162	32.32	8	2
8	S. Venkataraghavan	57	14,877	5,634	156	36.11	3	1
9	R. J. Shastri	80	15,751	6,185	151	40.96	2	–
10	S. P. Gupte	36	11,284	4,403	149	29.55	12	1
11	D. R. Doshi	33	9,322	3,502	114	30.71	6	–
12	K. D. Ghavri	39	7,042	3,656	109	33.54	4	–
13	N. S. Yadav	35	8,349	3,580	102	35.09	3	–

PAKISTAN

		T	*Balls*	*R*	*W*	*Avge*	*5W/i*	*10W/m*
1	**Wasim Akram**	**103**	**22,611**	**9,774**	**414**	**23.60**	**25**	**5**
2	Imran Khan	88	19,458	8,258	362	22.81	23	6
3	**Waqar Younis**	**74**	**14,361**	**7,643**	**332**	**23.02**	**21**	**5**
4	Abdul Qadir	67	17,126	7,742	236	32.80	15	5
5	**Mushtaq Ahmed**	**50**	**12,226**	**5,901**	**183**	**32.24**	**10**	**3**
6	Sarfraz Nawaz	55	13,927	5,798	177	32.75	4	1
7	Iqbal Qasim	50	13,019	4,807	171	28.11	8	2
8	**Saqlain Mushtaq**	**35**	**10,698**	**4,447**	**151**	**29.45**	**11**	**2**
9	Fazal Mahmood	34	9,834	3,434	139	24.70	13	4
10	Intikhab Alam	47	10,474	4,494	125	35.95	5	2

SRI LANKA

		T	*Balls*	*R*	*W*	*Avge*	*5W/i*	*10W/m*
1	**M. Muralitharan**	**65**	**21,361**	**8,567**	**340**	**25.19**	**26**	**6**
2	**W. P. U. J. C. Vaas**	**51**	**11,026**	**4,671**	**153**	**30.52**	**5**	**1**

Note: In 2001-02, after the deadline for this section, Muralitharan became the seventh bowler to take 4000 Test wickets.

ZIMBABWE

		T	*Balls*	*R*	*W*	*Avge*	*5W/i*	*10W/m*
1	**H. H. Streak**	**42**	**9,382**	**4,021**	**163**	**24.66**	**6**	–

BANGLADESH: The highest aggregate is 9 wickets, average 41.44, by **Naimur Rahman** in 4 Tests.

Bold type denotes those who played Test cricket in 2000-01 and 2001 seasons.

BEST CAREER AVERAGES

(Qualification: 75 wickets)

Avge		*T*	*W*	*BB*	*5W/i*	*10W/m*	*SR*
10.75	G. A. Lohmann (E)	18	112	9-28	9	5	34.11
16.43	S. F. Barnes (E)	27	189	9-103	24	7	41.65
16.53	C. T. B. Turner (A)	17	101	7-43	11	2	51.27
16.98	R. Peel (E).	20	101	7-31	5	1	51.64
17.75	J. Briggs (E).	33	118	8-11	9	4	45.18
18.41	F. R. Spofforth (A)	18	94	7-44	7	4	44.52
18.56	F. H. Tyson (E).	17	76	7-27	4	1	45.42
18.63	C. Blythe (E)	19	100	8-59	9	4	45.46
20.32	**S. M. Pollock (SA)**	**56**	**231**	**7-87**	**12**	–	**53.80**
20.39	J. H. Wardle (E)	28	102	7-36	5	1	64.67
20.53	A. K. Davidson (A).	44	186	7-93	14	2	62.29
20.94	M. D. Marshall (WI)	81	376	7-22	22	4	46.76
20.97	J. Garner (WI)	58	259	6-56	7	–	50.84
20.99	C. E. L. Ambrose (WI). . .	98	405	8-45	22	3	54.57
21.10	N. A. T. Adcock (SA). . . .	26	104	6-43	5	–	61.45
21.24	J. C. Laker (E)	46	193	10-53	9	3	62.31
21.28	**G. D. McGrath (A)**.	**75**	**358**	**8-38**	**22**	**3**	**50.13**
21.51	G. E. Palmer (A).	17	78	7-65	6	2	57.91
21.57	F. S. Trueman (E)	67	307	8-31	17	3	49.43
21.64	**A. A. Donald (SA)**	**69**	**325**	**8-71**	**20**	**3**	**46.26**
21.78	H. Trumble (A).	32	141	8-65	9	3	57.43
22.29	R. J. Hadlee (NZ)	86	431	9-52	36	9	50.85
22.59	W. J. O'Reilly (A)	27	144	7-54	11	3	69.61
22.73	J. V. Saunders (A)	14	79	7-34	6	–	45.12
22.81	Imran Khan (P).	88	362	8-58	23	6	53.75
22.97	K. R. Miller (A)	55	170	7-60	7	1	61.53

BEST CAREER STRIKE-RATES

(Qualification: 75 wickets)

SR		*T*	*W*	*Avge*	*BB*	*5W/i*	*10W/m*
34.11	G. A. Lohmann (E)	18	112	10.75	9-28	9	5
41.65	S. F. Barnes (E)	27	189	16.43	9-103	24	7
43.25	**Waqar Younis (P)**.	**74**	**332**	**23.02**	**7-76**	**21**	**5**
44.52	F. R. Spofforth (A)	18	94	18.41	7-44	7	4
45.12	J. V. Saunders (A)	14	79	22.73	7-34	6	–
45.18	J. Briggs (E).	33	118	17.75	8-11	9	4
45.42	F. H. Tyson (E).	17	76	18.56	7-27	4	1
45.46	C. Blythe (E)	19	100	18.63	8-59	9	4
46.26	**A. A. Donald (SA)**	**69**	**325**	**21.64**	**8-71**	**20**	**3**
46.76	M. D. Marshall (WI)	81	376	20.94	7-22	22	4
47.79	**J. N. Gillespie (A)**	**26**	**102**	**24.72**	**7-37**	**6**	–
49.32	C. E. H. Croft (WI).	27	125	23.30	8-29	3	–
49.43	F. S. Trueman (E)	67	307	21.57	8-31	17	3
49.96	**S. C. G. MacGill (A)** . . .	**16**	**75**	**25.02**	**7-50**	**4**	**1**
50.13	**G. D. McGrath (A)**.	**75**	**358**	**21.28**	**8-38**	**22**	**3**
50.45	**D. Gough (E)**.	**56**	**228**	**27.57**	**6-42**	**9**	–
50.84	J. Garner (WI)	58	259	20.97	6-56	7	–
50.85	R. J. Hadlee (NZ)	86	431	22.29	9-52	36	9
51.10	T. Richardson (E)	14	88	25.22	8-94	11	4

SR		*T*	*W*	*Avge*	*BB*	*5W/i*	*10W/m*
51.16	M. A. Holding (WI).	60	249	23.68	8-92	13	2
51.27	C. T. B. Turner (A)	17	101	16.53	7-43	11	2
51.54	G. A. Faulkner (SA).	25	82	26.58	7-84	4	–
51.64	R. Peel (E).	20	101	16.98	7-31	5	1
51.92	B. P. Patterson (WI).	28	93	30.90	5-24	5	–
52.01	D. K. Lillee (A)	70	355	23.92	7-83	23	7
52.05	A. Cotter (A)	21	89	28.64	7-148	7	–
52.21	I. R. Bishop (WI)	43	161	24.27	6-40	6	–
52.67	J. R. Thomson (A).	51	200	28.01	6-46	8	–
53.40	R. G. D. Willis (E)	90	325	25.20	8-43	16	–
53.75	Imran Khan (P).	88	362	22.81	8-58	23	6
53.80	**S. M. Pollock (SA)**	**56**	**231**	**20.32**	**7-87**	**12**	–
54.14	G. O. B. Allen (E).	25	81	29.37	7-80	5	1
54.27	W. W. Hall (WI)	48	192	26.38	7-69	9	1
54.57	C. E. L. Ambrose (WI). . .	98	405	20.99	8-45	22	3
54.61	**Wasim Akram (P)**	**103**	**414**	**23.60**	**7-119**	**25**	**5**
54.85	**C. L. Cairns (NZ)**	**49**	**171**	**29.21**	**7-27**	**10**	**1**

ALL-ROUND RECORDS

HUNDRED AND FIVE WICKETS IN AN INNINGS

England					
A. W. Greig	148	6-164	v West Indies. .	Bridgetown . . .	1973-74
I. T. Botham	103	5-73	v New Zealand	Christchurch . .	1977-78
I. T. Botham	108	8-34	v Pakistan	Lord's.	1978
I. T. Botham	114	6-58 } 7-48 }	v India	Bombay	1979-80
I. T. Botham	149*	6-95	v Australia. . . .	Leeds	1981
I. T. Botham	138	5-59	v New Zealand	Wellington. . . .	1983-84
Australia					
C. Kelleway	114	5-33	v South Africa .	Manchester . . .	1912
J. M. Gregory	100	7-69	v England	Melbourne. . . .	1920-21
K. R. Miller	109	6-107	v West Indies. .	Kingston	1954-55
R. Benaud	100	5-84	v South Africa .	Johannesburg . .	1957-58
South Africa					
J. H. Sinclair	106	6-26	v England	Cape Town . . .	1898-99
G. A. Faulkner	123	5-120	v England	Johannesburg . .	1909-10
J. H. Kallis	110	5-90	v West Indies. .	Cape Town . . .	1998-99
West Indies					
D. St E. Atkinson	219	5-56	v Australia. . . .	Bridgetown . . .	1954-55
O. G. Smith	100	5-90	v India	Delhi	1958-59
G. S. Sobers	104	5-63	v India	Kingston	1961-62
G. S. Sobers	174	5-41	v England	Leeds	1966
New Zealand					
B. R. Taylor†	105	5-86	v India	Calcutta	1964-65
India					
V. Mankad	184	5-196	v England	Lord's.	1952
P. R. Umrigar	172*	5-107	v West Indies. .	Port-of-Spain . .	1961-62

Pakistan					
Mushtaq Mohammad	201	5-49	v New Zealand	Dunedin	1972-73
Mushtaq Mohammad	121	5-28	v West Indies	Port-of-Spain	1976-77
Imran Khan	117	6-98 } 5-82 }	v India	Faisalabad	1982-83
Wasim Akram	123	5-100	v Australia	Adelaide	1989-90
Zimbabwe					
P. A. Strang	106*	5-212	v Pakistan	Sheikhupura	1996-97

† *On debut.*

HUNDRED AND FIVE DISMISSALS IN AN INNINGS

D. T. Lindsay	182	6ct	SA v A	Johannesburg	1966-67
I. D. S. Smith	113*	4ct, 1st	NZ v E	Auckland	1983-84
S. A. R. Silva	111	5ct	SL v I	Colombo (PSS)	1985-86

100 RUNS AND TEN WICKETS IN A TEST

A. K. Davidson	44 80	5-135 } 6-87 }	A v WI	Brisbane	1960-61
I. T. Botham	114	6-58 } 7-48 }	E v I	Bombay	1979-80
Imran Khan	117	6-98 } 5-82 }	P v I	Faisalabad	1982-83

1,000 RUNS AND 100 WICKETS

	Tests	*Runs*	*Wkts*	*Tests for Double*
England				
T. E. Bailey	61	2,290	132	47
†I. T. Botham	102	5,200	383	21
J. E. Emburey	64	1,713	147	46
A. W. Greig	58	3,599	141	37
R. Illingworth	61	1,836	122	47
W. Rhodes	58	2,325	127	44
M. W. Tate	39	1,198	155	33
F. J. Titmus	53	1,449	153	40
Australia				
R. Benaud	63	2,201	248	32
A. K. Davidson	44	1,328	186	34
G. Giffen	31	1,238	103	30
M. G. Hughes	53	1,032	212	52
I. W. Johnson	45	1,000	109	45
R. R. Lindwall	61	1,502	228	38
K. R. Miller	55	2,958	170	33
M. A. Noble	42	1,997	121	27
S. K. Warne	**92**	**1,676**	**407**	**58**
South Africa				
T. L. Goddard	41	2,516	123	36
S. M. Pollock	**56**	**2,015**	**231**	**26**

	Tests	Runs	Wkts	Tests for Double
West Indies				
C. E. L. Ambrose	98	1,439	405	69
M. D. Marshall	81	1,810	376	49
†G. S. Sobers	93	8,032	235	48
New Zealand				
J. G. Bracewell	41	1,001	102	41
C. L. Cairns	**49**	**2,572**	**171**	**33**
R. J. Hadlee	86	3,124	431	28
India				
Kapil Dev	131	5,248	434	25
A. Kumble	61	1,192	276	56
V. Mankad	44	2,109	162	23
R. J. Shastri	80	3,830	151	44
Pakistan				
Abdul Qadir	67	1,029	236	62
Imran Khan	88	3,807	362	30
Intikhab Alam	47	1,493	125	41
Sarfraz Nawaz	55	1,045	177	55
Wasim Akram	**103**	**2,898**	**414**	**45**
Sri Lanka				
W. P. U. J. C. Vaas	**51**	**1,104**	**153**	**47**
Zimbabwe				
H. H. Streak	**42**	**1,133**	**163**	**40**

Bold type denotes those who played Test cricket in 2000-01 and 2001 seasons.

† I. T. Botham (120 catches) and G. S. Sobers (109) are the only players to have achieved the treble of 1,000 runs, 100 wickets and 100 catches.

WICKET-KEEPING RECORDS

MOST DISMISSALS IN AN INNINGS

7 (all ct)	Wasim Bari	Pakistan v New Zealand at Auckland	1978-79
7 (all ct)	R. W. Taylor	England v India at Bombay	1979-80
7 (all ct)	I. D. S. Smith	New Zealand v Sri Lanka at Hamilton	1990-91
7 (all ct)	R. D. Jacobs	West Indies v Australia at Melbourne	2000-01
6 (all ct)	A. T. W. Grout	Australia v South Africa at Johannesburg	1957-58
6 (all ct)	D. T. Lindsay	South Africa v Australia at Johannesburg	1966-67
6 (all ct)	J. T. Murray	England v India at Lord's	1967
6 (5ct, 1st)	S. M. H. Kirmani	India v New Zealand at Christchurch	1975-76
6 (all ct)	R. W. Marsh	Australia v England at Brisbane	1982-83
6 (all ct)	S. A. R. Silva	Sri Lanka v India at Colombo (SSC)	1985-86
6 (all ct)	R. C. Russell	England v Australia at Melbourne	1990-91
6 (all ct)	R. C. Russell	England v South Africa at Johannesburg	1995-96
6 (all ct)	I. A. Healy	Australia v England at Birmingham	1997
6 (all ct)	A. J. Stewart	England v Australia at Manchester	1997
6 (all ct)	M. V. Boucher	South Africa v Pakistan at Port Elizabeth	1997-98
6 (all ct)	Rashid Latif	Pakistan v Zimbabwe at Bulawayo	1997-98
6 (all ct)	M. V. Boucher	South Africa v Sri Lanka at Cape Town	1997-98
6 (5ct, 1st)	†C. M. W. Read	England v New Zealand at Birmingham	1999

† *On debut.*

Note: The most stumpings in an innings is 5 by K. S. More for India v West Indies at Madras in 1987-88.

MOST DISMISSALS IN A TEST

11 (all ct)	R. C. Russell	England v South Africa at Johannesburg	1995-96
10 (all ct)	R. W. Taylor	England v India at Bombay	1979-80
10 (all ct)	A. C. Gilchrist	Australia v New Zealand at Hamilton	1999-2000
9 (8ct, 1st)	G. R. A. Langley	Australia v England at Lord's	1956
9 (all ct)	D. A. Murray	West Indies v Australia at Melbourne	1981-82
9 (all ct)	R. W. Marsh	Australia v England at Brisbane	1982-83
9 (all ct)	S. A. R. Silva	Sri Lanka v India at Colombo (SSC)	1985-86
9 (8ct, 1st)	S. A. R. Silva	Sri Lanka v India at Colombo (PSS)	1985-86
9 (all ct)	D. J. Richardson	South Africa v India at Port Elizabeth	1992-93
9 (all ct)	Rashid Latif	Pakistan v New Zealand at Auckland	1993-94
9 (all ct)	I. A. Healy	Australia v England at Brisbane	1994-95
9 (all ct)	C. O. Browne	West Indies v England at Nottingham	1995
9 (7ct, 2st)	R. C. Russell	England v South Africa at Port Elizabeth	1995-96
9 (8ct, 1st)	M. V. Boucher	South Africa v Pakistan at Port Elizabeth	1997-98
9 (8ct, 1st)	R. D. Jacobs	West Indies v Australia at Melbourne	2000-01

Notes: S. A. R. Silva made 18 dismissals in two successive Tests.

The most stumpings in a match is 6 by K. S. More for India v West Indies at Madras in 1987-88.

J. J. Kelly (8ct) for Australia v England in 1901-02 and L. E. G. Ames (6ct, 2st) for England v West Indies in 1933 were the only wicket-keepers to make eight dismissals in a Test before World War II.

MOST DISMISSALS IN A SERIES

(Played in 5 Tests unless otherwise stated)

28 (all ct)	R. W. Marsh	Australia v England	1982-83
27 (25ct, 2st)	R. C. Russell	England v South Africa	1995-96
27 (25ct, 2st)	I. A. Healy	Australia v England (6 Tests)	1997
26 (23ct, 3st)	J. H. B. Waite	South Africa v New Zealand	1961-62
26 (all ct)	R. W. Marsh	Australia v West Indies (6 Tests)	1975-76
26 (21ct, 5st)	I. A. Healy	Australia v England (6 Tests)	1993
26 (25ct, 1st)	M. V. Boucher	South Africa v England	1998
26 (24ct, 2st)	A. C. Gilchrist	Australia v England	2001
25 (23ct, 2st)	I. A. Healy	Australia v England	1994-95

Notes: S. A. R. Silva made 22 dismissals (21ct, 1st) in three Tests for Sri Lanka v India in 1985-86.

H. Strudwick, with 21 (15ct, 6st) for England v South Africa in 1913-14, was the only wicket-keeper to make as many as 20 dismissals in a series before World War II.

100 DISMISSALS

		T	*Ct*	*St*
395	I. A. Healy (Australia)	119	366	29
355	R. W. Marsh (Australia)	96	343	12
272	P. J. L. Dujon (West Indies)	81	267	5
269	A. P. E. Knott (England)	95	250	19
231	**A. J. Stewart (England)**	**115**	**220**	**11**
228	Wasim Bari (Pakistan)	81	201	27
219	T. G. Evans (England)	91	173	46
198	S. M. H. Kirmani (India)	88	160	38
189	D. L. Murray (West Indies)	62	181	8
187	A. T. W. Grout (Australia)	51	163	24
183	**A. C. Parore (New Zealand)**	**70**	**176**	**7**

		T	Ct	St
176	I. D. S. Smith (New Zealand)	63	168	8
174	R. W. Taylor (England)	57	167	7
167	**M. V. Boucher (South Africa)**	**42**	**163**	**4**
165	R. C. Russell (England)	54	153	12
152	D. J. Richardson (South Africa)	42	150	2
143	**A. Flower (Zimbabwe)**	**52**	**136**	**7**
141	J. H. B. Waite (South Africa)	50	124	17
134	**Moin Khan (Pakistan)**	**63**	**114**	**20**
130	K. S. More (India)	49	110	20
130	W. A. S. Oldfield (Australia)	54	78	52
122	**R. D. Jacobs (West Indies)**	**32**	**118**	**4**
114	J. M. Parks (England)	46	103	11
107	**N. R. Mongia (India)**	**44**	**99**	**8**
104	Salim Yousuf (Pakistan)	32	91	13
101	**A. C. Gilchrist (Australia)**	**22**	**94**	**7**

Notes: The records for P. J. L. Dujon and J. M. Parks each include two catches taken when not keeping wicket in two and three Tests respectively. A. J. Stewart's record includes 36 catches taken in 51 Tests when not keeping wicket; A. C. Parore's includes three in 11 Tests, A. Flower's five in four Tests and Moin Khan's one in three Tests when not keeping wicket.

The most wicket-keeping dismissals for Sri Lanka is 94 (**R. S. Kaluwitharana** 74ct, 20st in 40 Tests) and for Bangladesh is 3 (**Khaled Masud** 3ct in three Tests). H. P. Tillekeratne (Sri Lanka) has made 95 dismissals (93ct, 2st) but only 35 (33ct, 2st) in ten Tests as wicket-keeper.

Bold type denotes those who played Test cricket in 2000-01 and 2001 seasons.

FIELDING RECORDS

(Excluding wicket-keepers)

MOST CATCHES IN AN INNINGS

5	V. Y. Richardson	Australia v South Africa at Durban	1935-36
5	Yajurvindra Singh	India v England at Bangalore	1976-77
5	M. Azharuddin	India v Pakistan at Karachi	1989-90
5	K. Srikkanth	India v Australia at Perth	1991-92
5	S. P. Fleming	New Zealand v Zimbabwe at Harare	1997-98

MOST CATCHES IN A TEST

7	G. S. Chappell	Australia v England at Perth	1974-75
7	Yajurvindra Singh	India v England at Bangalore	1976-77
7	H. P. Tillekeratne	Sri Lanka v New Zealand at Colombo (SSC)	1992-93
7	S. P. Fleming	New Zealand v Zimbabwe at Harare	1997-98
6	A. Shrewsbury	England v Australia at Sydney	1887-88
6	A. E. E. Vogler	South Africa v England at Durban	1909-10
6	F. E. Woolley	England v Australia at Sydney	1911-12
6	J. M. Gregory	Australia v England at Sydney	1920-21
6	B. Mitchell	South Africa v Australia at Melbourne	1931-32
6	V. Y. Richardson	Australia v South Africa at Durban	1935-36
6	R. N. Harvey	Australia v England at Sydney	1962-63
6	M. C. Cowdrey	England v West Indies at Lord's	1963
6	E. D. Solkar	India v West Indies at Port-of-Spain	1970-71
6	G. S. Sobers	West Indies v England at Lord's	1973
6	I. M. Chappell	Australia v New Zealand at Adelaide	1973-74
6	A. W. Greig	England v Pakistan at Leeds	1974
6	D. F. Whatmore	Australia v India at Kanpur	1979-80
6	A. J. Lamb	England v New Zealand at Lord's	1983
6	G. A. Hick	England v Pakistan at Leeds	1992
6	B. A. Young	New Zealand v Pakistan at Auckland	1993-94

6	J. C. Adams	West Indies v England at Kingston	1993-94
6	S. P. Fleming	New Zealand v Australia at Brisbane	1997-98
6	D. P. M. D. Jayawardene	Sri Lanka v Pakistan at Peshawar	1999-2000
6	M. E. Waugh	Australia v India at Chennai	2000-01

MOST CATCHES IN A SERIES

15	J. M. Gregory	Australia v England	1920-21
14	G. S. Chappell	Australia v England (6 Tests)	1974-75
13	R. B. Simpson	Australia v South Africa	1957-58
13	R. B. Simpson	Australia v West Indies	1960-61
13	B. C. Lara	West Indies v England (6 Tests)	1997-98

100 CATCHES

Ct	*T*		*Ct*	*T*	
161	**116**	**M. E. Waugh (Australia)**	110	85	W. R. Hammond (England)
157	104	M. A. Taylor (Australia)	109	93	G. S. Sobers (West Indies)
156	156	A. R. Border (Australia)	108	125	S. M. Gavaskar (India)
122	87	G. S. Chappell (Australia)	106	80	B. C. Lara (West Indies)
122	121	I. V. A. Richards (West Indies)	105	75	I. M. Chappell (Australia)
120	102	I. T. Botham (England)	105	99	M. Azharuddin (India)
120	114	M. C. Cowdrey (England)	103	118	G. A. Gooch (England)
110	62	R. B. Simpson (Australia)	102	87	C. L. Hooper (West Indies)

Note: The most catches in the field for other countries are South Africa **67** in 70 Tests (**D. J. Cullinan**); New Zealand **91** in 60 Tests (**S. P. Fleming**); Pakistan 93 in 124 Tests (Javed Miandad); Sri Lanka **60** in 49 Tests (**H. P. Tillekeratne**); Zimbabwe **53** in 54 Tests (**A. D. R. Campbell**); Bangladesh **3** in 2 Tests (**Al-Shahriar Rokon**) and **3** in 3 Tests (**Mohammad Sharif**).

Bold type denotes those who played Test cricket in 2000-01 and 2001 seasons.

TEAM RECORDS

HIGHEST INNINGS TOTALS

952-6 dec.	Sri Lanka v India at Colombo (RPS)	1997-98
903-7 dec.	England v Australia at The Oval	1938
849	England v West Indies at Kingston	1929-30
790-3 dec.	West Indies v Pakistan at Kingston	1957-58
758-8 dec.	Australia v West Indies at Kingston	1954-55
729-6 dec.	Australia v England at Lord's	1930
708	Pakistan v England at The Oval	1987
701	Australia v England at The Oval	1934
699-5	Pakistan v India at Lahore	1989-90
695	Australia v England at The Oval	1930
692-8 dec.	West Indies v England at The Oval	1995
687-8 dec.	West Indies v England at The Oval	1976
681-8 dec.	West Indies v England at Port-of-Spain	1953-54
676-7	India v Sri Lanka at Kanpur	1986-87
674-6	Pakistan v India at Faisalabad	1984-85
674	Australia v India at Adelaide	1947-48
671-4	New Zealand v Sri Lanka at Wellington	1990-91
668	Australia v West Indies at Bridgetown	1954-55
660-5 dec.	West Indies v New Zealand at Wellington	1994-95

The highest innings for the countries not mentioned above are:

622-9 dec.	South Africa v Australia at Durban	1969-70
563-9 dec.	Zimbabwe v West Indies at Harare	2001 (Z)
400	Bangladesh v India at Dhaka	2000-01

HIGHEST FOURTH-INNINGS TOTALS

To win

406-4	India (needing 403) v West Indies at Port-of-Spain	1975-76
404-3	Australia (needing 404) v England at Leeds	1948
369-6	Australia (needing 369) v Pakistan at Hobart	1999-2000
362-7	Australia (needing 359) v West Indies at Georgetown	1977-78
348-5	West Indies (needing 345) v New Zealand at Auckland	1968-69
344-1	West Indies (needing 342) v England at Lord's	1984

To tie

347	India v Australia at Madras	1986-87

To draw

654-5	England (needing 696 to win) v South Africa at Durban	1938-39
429-8	India (needing 438 to win) v England at The Oval	1979
423-7	South Africa (needing 451 to win) v England at The Oval	1947
408-5	West Indies (needing 836 to win) v England at Kingston	1929-30

To lose

445	India (lost by 47 runs) v Australia at Adelaide	1977-78
440	New Zealand (lost by 38 runs) v England at Nottingham	1973
417	England (lost by 45 runs) v Australia at Melbourne	1976-77
411	England (lost by 193 runs) v Australia at Sydney	1924-25
402	Australia (lost by 103 runs) v England at Manchester	1981

MOST RUNS IN A DAY (BOTH SIDES)

588	England (398-6), India (190-0) at Manchester (2nd day)	1936
522	England (503-2), South Africa (19-0) at Lord's (2nd day)	1924
508	England (221-2), South Africa (287-6) at The Oval (3rd day)	1935

MOST RUNS IN A DAY (ONE SIDE)

503	England (503-2) v South Africa at Lord's (2nd day)	1924
494	Australia (494-6) v South Africa at Sydney (1st day)	1910-11
475	Australia (475-2) v England at The Oval (1st day)	1934
471	England (471-8) v India at The Oval (1st day)	1936
458	Australia (458-3) v England at Leeds (1st day)	1930
455	Australia (455-1) v England at Leeds (2nd day)	1934
450	Australia (450) v South Africa at Johannesburg (1st day)	1921-22

MOST WICKETS IN A DAY

27	England (18-3 to 53 all out and 62) v Australia (60) at Lord's (2nd day)	1888
25	Australia (112 and 48-5) v England (61) at Melbourne (1st day)	1901-02

HIGHEST AGGREGATES IN A TEST

Runs	*Wkts*			*Days played*
1,981	35	South Africa v England at Durban	1938-39	10†
1,815	34	West Indies v England at Kingston	1929-30	9‡
1,764	39	Australia v West Indies at Adelaide	1968-69	5
1,753	40	Australia v England at Adelaide	1920-21	6
1,723	31	England v Australia at Leeds	1948	5
1,661	36	West Indies v Australia at Bridgetown	1954-55	6

† *No play on one day.* ‡ *No play on two days.*

LOWEST INNINGS TOTALS

26	New Zealand v England at Auckland	1954-55
30	South Africa v England at Port Elizabeth	1895-96
30	South Africa v England at Birmingham	1924
35	South Africa v England at Cape Town	1898-99
36	Australia v England at Birmingham	1902
36	South Africa v Australia at Melbourne	1931-32
42	Australia v England at Sydney	1887-88
42	New Zealand v Australia at Wellington	1945-46
42†	India v England at Lord's	1974
43	South Africa v England at Cape Town	1888-89
44	Australia v England at The Oval	1896
45	England v Australia at Sydney	1886-87
45	South Africa v Australia at Melbourne	1931-32
46	England v West Indies at Port-of-Spain	1993-94
47	South Africa v England at Cape Town	1888-89
47	New Zealand v England at Lord's	1958

The lowest innings for the countries not mentioned above are:

51	West Indies v Australia at Port-of-Spain	1998-99
62	Pakistan v Australia at Perth	1981-82
63	Zimbabwe v West Indies at Port-of-Spain	1999-2000
71	Sri Lanka v Pakistan at Kandy	1994-95
91	Bangladesh v India at Dhaka	2000-01

† *Batted one man short.*

FEWEST RUNS IN A FULL DAY'S PLAY

95	Australia (80), Pakistan (15-2) at Karachi (1st day, 5½ hours)	1956-57
104	Pakistan (0-0 to 104-5) v Australia at Karachi (4th day, 5½ hours)	1959-60
106	England (92-2 to 198) v Australia at Brisbane (4th day, 5 hours). *England were dismissed five minutes before the close of play, leaving no time for Australia to start their second innings.*	1958-59
111	South Africa (48-2 to 130-6 dec.), India (29-1) at Cape Town (5th day, 5½ hours)	1992-93
112	Australia (138-6 to 187), Pakistan (63-1) at Karachi (4th day, 5½ hours)	1956-57
115	Australia (116-7 to 165 and 66-5 after following on) v Pakistan at Karachi (4th day, 5½ hours)	1988-89
117	India (117-5) v Australia at Madras (1st day, 5½ hours)	1956-57
117	New Zealand (6-0 to 123-4) v Sri Lanka at Colombo (SSC) (5th day, 5¾ hours)	1983-84

In England

151	England (175-2 to 289), New Zealand (37-7) at Lord's (3rd day, 6 hours)	1978
158	England (211-2 to 369-9) v South Africa at Manchester (5th day, 6 hours)	1998
159	Pakistan (208-4 to 350), England (17-1) at Leeds (3rd day, 6 hours)	1971

LOWEST AGGREGATES IN A COMPLETED TEST

Runs	*Wkts*			*Days played*
234	29	Australia v South Africa at Melbourne	1931-32	3†
291	40	England v Australia at Lord's	1888	2
295	28	New Zealand v Australia at Wellington	1945-46	2
309	29	West Indies v England at Bridgetown	1934-35	3
323	30	England v Australia at Manchester	1888	2

† *No play on one day.*

PLAYERS

YOUNGEST TEST PLAYERS

Years	*Days*			
14	227†	Hasan Raza	Pakistan v Zimbabwe at Faisalabad	1996-97
15	124	Mushtaq Mohammad	Pakistan v West Indies at Lahore	1958-59
15	128	Mohammad Sharif	Bangladesh v Zimbabwe at Bulawayo	2000-01
16	189	Aqib Javed	Pakistan v New Zealand at Wellington	1988-89
16	205	S. R. Tendulkar	India v Pakistan at Karachi	1989-90
16	221	Aftab Baloch	Pakistan v New Zealand at Dacca	1969-70
16	248	Nasim-ul-Ghani	Pakistan v West Indies at Bridgetown	1957-58
16	352	Khalid Hassan	Pakistan v England at Nottingham	1954
17	5	Zahid Fazal	Pakistan v West Indies at Karachi	1990-91
17	69	Ata-ur-Rehman	Pakistan v England at Birmingham	1992
17	78	Imran Nazir	Pakistan v Sri Lanka at Lahore	1998-99
17	118	L. Sivaramakrishnan	India v West Indies at St John's	1982-83
17	122	J. E. D. Sealy	West Indies v England at Bridgetown	1929-30
17	129	Fazl-e-Akbar	Pakistan v South Africa at Durban	1997-98
17	189	C. D. U. S. Weerasinghe	Sri Lanka v India at Colombo (PSS)	1985-86
17	193	Maninder Singh	India v Pakistan at Karachi	1982-83
17	239	I. D. Craig	Australia v South Africa at Melbourne	1952-53
17	245	G. S. Sobers	West Indies v England at Kingston	1953-54
17	265	V. L. Mehra	India v New Zealand at Bombay	1955-56
17	265	Harbhajan Singh	India v Australia at Bangalore	1997-98
17	300	Hanif Mohammad	Pakistan v India at Delhi	1952-53
17	341	Intikhab Alam	Pakistan v Australia at Karachi	1959-60
17	352	H. Masakadza	Zimbabwe v West Indies at Harare	2001 (Z)
17	364	Waqar Younis	Pakistan v India at Karachi	1989-90

† *Hasan Raza's age is in dispute and has been rejected by the Pakistan Cricket Board.*

Note: The youngest Test players for countries not mentioned above are: England – D. B. Close, 18 years 149 days, v New Zealand at Manchester, 1949; New Zealand – D. L. Vettori, 18 years 10 days, v England at Wellington, 1996-97; South Africa – P. R. Adams, 18 years 340 days v England at Port Elizabeth, 1995-96.

OLDEST PLAYERS ON TEST DEBUT

Years	*Days*			
49	119	J. Southerton	England v Australia at Melbourne	1876-77
47	284	Miran Bux	Pakistan v India at Lahore	1954-55
46	253	D. D. Blackie	Australia v England at Sydney	1928-29
46	237	H. Ironmonger	Australia v England at Brisbane	1928-29
42	242	N. Betancourt	West Indies v England at Port-of-Spain	1929-30
41	337	E. R. Wilson	England v Australia at Sydney	1920-21
41	27	R. J. D. Jamshedji	India v England at Bombay	1933-34
40	345	C. A. Wiles	West Indies v England at Manchester	1933
40	295	O. Henry	South Africa v India at Durban	1992-93
40	216	S. P. Kinneir	England v Australia at Sydney	1911-12
40	110	H. W. Lee	England v South Africa at Johannesburg	1930-31
40	56	G. W. A. Chubb	South Africa v England at Nottingham	1951
40	37	C. Ramaswami	India v England at Manchester	1936

Note: The oldest Test player on debut for New Zealand was H. M. McGirr, 38 years 101 days, v England at Auckland, 1929-30; for Sri Lanka, D. S. de Silva, 39 years 251 days, v England at Colombo (PSS), 1981-82; for Zimbabwe, A. C. Waller, 37 years 84 days, v England at Bulawayo, 1996-97; for Bangladesh, Aminul Islam, 32 years 282 days, v India at Dhaka, 2000-01. A. J. Traicos was 45 years 154 days old when he made his debut for Zimbabwe (v India at Harare, 1992-93) having played three Tests for South Africa in 1969-70.

OLDEST TEST PLAYERS

(Age on final day of their last Test match)

Years	*Days*			
52	165	W. Rhodes	England v West Indies at Kingston	1929-30
50	327	H. Ironmonger	Australia v England at Sydney	1932-33
50	320	W. G. Grace	England v Australia at Nottingham	1899
50	303	G. Gunn	England v West Indies at Kingston	1929-30
49	139	J. Southerton	England v Australia at Melbourne	1876-77
47	302	Miran Bux	Pakistan v India at Peshawar	1954-55
47	249	J. B. Hobbs	England v Australia at The Oval	1930
47	87	F. E. Woolley	England v Australia at The Oval	1934
46	309	D. D. Blackie	Australia v England at Adelaide	1928-29
46	206	A. W. Nourse	South Africa v England at The Oval	1924
46	202	H. Strudwick	England v Australia at The Oval	1926
46	41	E. H. Hendren	England v West Indies at Kingston	1934-35
45	304	A. J. Traicos	Zimbabwe v India at Delhi	1992-93
45	245	G. O. B. Allen	England v West Indies at Kingston	1947-48
45	215	P. Holmes	England v India at Lord's	1932
45	140	D. B. Close	England v West Indies at Manchester	1976

100 TEST APPEARANCES

156	A. R. Border (Australia)
139	**S. R. Waugh (Australia)**
132	**C. A. Walsh (West Indies)**
131	Kapil Dev (India)
125	S. M. Gavaskar (India)
124	Javed Miandad (Pakistan)
121	I. V. A. Richards (West Indies)
119	I. A. Healy (Australia)
118	G. A. Gooch (England)
117	D. I. Gower (England)
116	D. L. Haynes (West Indies)
116	D. B. Vengsarkar (India)
116	**M. E. Waugh (Australia)**
115	**M. A. Atherton (England)**
115	**A. J. Stewart (England)**
114	M. C. Cowdrey (England)
110	C. H. Lloyd (West Indies)
108	G. Boycott (England)
108	C. G. Greenidge (West Indies)
107	D. C. Boon (Australia)
104	M. A. Taylor (Australia)
103	Salim Malik (Pakistan)
103	**Wasim Akram (Pakistan)**
102	I. T. Botham (England)

Note: The most appearances for Sri Lanka is 93 by A. Ranatunga, for New Zealand 86 by R. J. Hadlee, for South Africa 73 by **G. Kirsten**, for Zimbabwe 54 by **A. D. R. Campbell** and for **Bangladesh** 4 by **Akram Khan, Aminul Islam, Habibul Bashar, Mehrab Hossain** and **Naimur Rahman**.

Bold type denotes those who played Test cricket in 2000-01 and 2001 seasons.

MOST CONSECUTIVE TEST APPEARANCES

153	A. R. Border (Australia)	March 1979 to March 1994
106	S. M. Gavaskar (India)	January 1975 to February 1987
95	M. E. Waugh (Australia)	June 1993 to August 2001
87	G. R. Viswanath (India)	March 1971 to February 1983
85	G. S. Sobers (West Indies)	April 1955 to April 1972
84†	S. R. Tendulkar (India)	November 1989 to June 2001
72	D. L. Haynes (West Indies)	December 1979 to June 1988
71	I. M. Chappell (Australia)	January 1966 to February 1976
69	M. Azharuddin (India)	April 1989 to February 1999
66	Kapil Dev (India)	October 1978 to December 1984
65	I. T. Botham (England)	February 1978 to March 1984
65	Kapil Dev (India)	January 1985 to March 1994
65	A. P. E. Knott (England)	March 1971 to August 1977

The most consecutive Test appearances for the countries not mentioned on the previous page are:

58†	J. R. Reid (New Zealand)	July 1949 to July 1965
53	Javed Miandad (Pakistan)	December 1977 to January 1984
53	G. Kirsten (South Africa)	December 1993 to March 1999
54†	A. D. R. Campbell (Zimbabwe)	October 1992 to July 2001
41	M. S. Atapattu (Sri Lanka)	June 1997 to September 2001

By February 21, 2002, after the deadline for this section, M. E. Waugh had extended his sequence of consecutive Test appearances to 101, and Atapattu to 48. A. D. R. Campbell's sequence ended at 56 in September 2001.

† *Indicates complete Test career.*

MOST TESTS AS CAPTAIN

	P	*W*	*L*	*D*
A. R. Border (A)	93	32	22	38*
C. H. Lloyd (WI)	74	36	12	26
A. Ranatunga (SL)	56	12	19	25
M. A. Atherton (E)	**54**	**13**	**21**	**20**
W. J. Cronje (SA)	53	27	11	15
I. V. A. Richards (WI)	50	27	8	15
M. A. Taylor (A)	50	26	13	11
G. S. Chappell (A)	48	21	13	14
Imran Khan (P)	48	14	8	26
M. Azharuddin (I)	47	14	14	19
S. M. Gavaskar (I)	47	9	8	30
P. B. H. May (E)	41	20	10	11
Nawab of Pataudi jun. (I)	40	9	19	12
R. B. Simpson (A)	39	12	12	15
G. S. Sobers (WI)	39	9	10	20
S. P. Fleming (NZ)	**36**	**13**	**13**	**10**
G. A. Gooch (E)	34	10	12	12
Javed Miandad (P)	34	14	6	14
Kapil Dev (I)	34	4	7	22*
J. R. Reid (NZ)	34	3	18	13
D. I. Gower (E)	32	5	18	9
J. M. Brearley (E)	31	18	4	9
R. Illingworth (E)	31	12	5	14
I. M. Chappell (A)	30	15	5	10
E. R. Dexter (E)	30	9	7	14
G. P. Howarth (NZ)	30	11	7	12

* *One match tied.*

Most Tests as captain of other countries:

	P	*W*	*L*	*D*
A. Flower (Z)	20	1	10	9
Naimur Rahman (B)	**4**	**0**	**4**	**0**

Notes: A. R. Border captained Australia in 93 consecutive Tests.

W. W. Armstrong (Australia) captained his country in the most Tests without being defeated: ten matches with eight wins and two draws.

I. T. Botham (England) captained his country in the most Tests without ever winning: 12 matches with eight draws and four defeats.

Bold type denotes those who were captains in 2000-01 and 2001 seasons.

UMPIRES

MOST TESTS

		First Test	*Last Test*
66	H. D. Bird (England)	1973	1996
60	**S. A. Bucknor (West Indies)**	**1988-89**	**2001 (SL)**
57	**D. R. Shepherd (England)**	**1985**	**2001**
48	F. Chester (England)	1924	1955
47	**S. Venkataraghavan (India)**	**1992-93**	**2001**
42	C. S. Elliott (England)	1957	1974
39	**D. B. Hair (Australia)**	**1991-92**	**2001-02**
38	**R. S. Dunne (New Zealand)**	**1988-89**	**2000-01**
36	D. J. Constant (England)	1971	1988
36	S. G. Randell (Australia)	1984-85	1997-98
34	Khizar Hayat (Pakistan)	1979-80	1996-97
33	J. S. Buller (England)	1956	1969
33	A. R. Crafter (Australia)	1978-79	1991-92
32	R. W. Crockett (Australia)	1901-02	1924-25
31	D. Sang Hue (West Indies)	1961-62	1980-81

Bold type indicates umpires who stood in 2000-01 or 2001 seasons.

SUMMARY OF TESTS

To September 2, 2001

	Opponents	*Tests*	*Won by* E	A	SA	WI	NZ	I	P	SL	Z	B	*Tied*	*Drawn*
England	Australia	**301**	94	121	–	–	–	–	–	–	–	–	–	86
	South Africa	**120**	50	–	23	–	–	–	–	–	–	–	–	47
	West Indies	**126**	31	–	–	52	–	–	–	–	–	–	–	43
	New Zealand	**82**	37	–	–	–	6	–	–	–	–	–	–	39
	India	**84**	32	–	–	–	–	14	–	–	–	–	–	38
	Pakistan	**60**	16	–	–	–	–	–	10	–	–	–	–	34
	Sri Lanka	**9**	5	–	–	–	–	–	–	3	–	–	–	1
	Zimbabwe	**4**	1	–	–	–	–	–	–	–	0	–	–	3
Australia	South Africa	**65**	–	34	14	–	–	–	–	–	–	–	–	17
	West Indies	**95**	–	42	–	31	–	–	–	–	–	–	1	21
	New Zealand	**38**	–	18	–	–	7	–	–	–	–	–	–	13
	India	**60**	–	29	–	–	–	13	–	–	–	–	1	17
	Pakistan	**46**	–	18	–	–	–	–	11	–	–	–	–	17
	Sri Lanka	**13**	–	7	–	–	–	–	–	1	–	–	–	5
	Zimbabwe	**1**	–	1	–	–	–	–	–	–	0	–	–	0
South Africa	West Indies	**11**	–	–	7	2	–	–	–	–	–	–	–	2
	New Zealand	**27**	–	–	15	–	3	–	–	–	–	–	–	9
	India	**12**	–	–	6	–	–	2	–	–	–	–	–	4
	Pakistan	**7**	–	–	3	–	–	–	1	–	–	–	–	3
	Sri Lanka	**11**	–	–	6	–	–	–	–	1	–	–	–	4
	Zimbabwe	**3**	–	–	3	–	–	–	–	–	0	–	–	0
West Indies	New Zealand	**30**	–	–	–	10	6	–	–	–	–	–	–	14
	India	**70**	–	–	–	28	–	7	–	–	–	–	–	35
	Pakistan	**37**	–	–	–	13	–	–	10	–	–	–	–	14
	Sri Lanka	**3**	–	–	–	1	–	–	–	0	–	–	–	2
	Zimbabwe	**4**	–	–	–	3	–	–	–	–	0	–	–	1
New Zealand	India	**40**	–	–	–	–	7	14	–	–	–	–	–	19
	Pakistan	**42**	–	–	–	–	6	–	19	–	–	–	–	17
	Sri Lanka	**18**	–	–	–	–	7	–	–	4	–	–	–	7
	Zimbabwe	**11**	–	–	–	–	5	–	–	–	0	–	–	6
India	Pakistan	**47**	–	–	–	–	–	5	9	–	–	–	–	33
	Sri Lanka	**23**	–	–	–	–	–	8	–	3	–	–	–	12
	Zimbabwe	**7**	–	–	–	–	–	3	–	–	2	–	–	2
	Bangladesh	**1**	–	–	–	–	–	1	–	–	–	0	–	0
Pakistan	Sri Lanka	**27**	–	–	–	–	–	–	13	5	–	–	–	9
	Zimbabwe	**12**	–	–	–	–	–	–	6	–	2	–	–	4
	Bangladesh	**1**	–	–	–	–	–	–	1	–	–	0	–	0
Sri Lanka	Zimbabwe	**10**	–	–	–	–	–	–	–	5	0	–	–	5
Zimbabwe	Bangladesh	**2**	–	–	–	–	–	–	–	–	2	0	–	0
		1,560	266	270	77	140	47	67	80	22	6	0	2	583

	Tests	*Won*	*Lost*	*Drawn*	*Tied*	*Toss Won*
England	786	266	229	291	–	379
Australia	619	270	171	176	2	316
South Africa	256	77	93	86	–	118
West Indies	376	140	103	132	1	198
New Zealand	288	47	117	124	–	144
India	344	67	116	160	1	177
Pakistan	279	80	68	131	–	133
Sri Lanka	114	22	47	45	–	63
Zimbabwe	54	6	27	21	–	30
Bangladesh	4	0	4	0	–	2

ENGLAND v AUSTRALIA

	Captains					
Season	*England*	*Australia*	*T*	*E*	*A*	*D*
1876-77	James Lillywhite	D. W. Gregory	2	1	1	0
1878-79	Lord Harris	D. W. Gregory	1	0	1	0
1880	Lord Harris	W. L. Murdoch	1	1	0	0
1881-82	A. Shaw	W. L. Murdoch	4	0	2	2
1882	A. N. Hornby	W. L. Murdoch	1	0	1	0

THE ASHES

	Captains						
Season	*England*	*Australia*	*T*	*E*	*A*	*D*	*Held by*
1882-83	Hon. Ivo Bligh	W. L. Murdoch	4*	2	2	0	E
1884	Lord Harris[1]	W. L. Murdoch	3	1	0	2	E
1884-85	A. Shrewsbury	T. P. Horan[2]	5	3	2	0	E
1886	A. G. Steel	H. J. H. Scott	3	3	0	0	E
1886-87	A. Shrewsbury	P. S. McDonnell	2	2	0	0	E
1887-88	W. W. Read	P. S. McDonnell	1	1	0	0	E
1888	W. G. Grace[3]	P. S. McDonnell	3	2	1	0	E
1890†	W. G. Grace	W. L. Murdoch	2	2	0	0	E
1891-92	W. G. Grace	J. McC. Blackham	3	1	2	0	A
1893	W. G. Grace[4]	J. McC. Blackham	3	1	0	2	E
1894-95	A. E. Stoddart	G. Giffen[5]	5	3	2	0	E
1896	W. G. Grace	G. H. S. Trott	3	2	1	0	E
1897-98	A. E. Stoddart[6]	G. H. S. Trott	5	1	4	0	A
1899	A. C. MacLaren[7]	J. Darling	5	0	1	4	A
1901-02	A. C. MacLaren	J. Darling[8]	5	1	4	0	A
1902	A. C. MacLaren	J. Darling	5	1	2	2	A
1903-04	P. F. Warner	M. A. Noble	5	3	2	0	E
1905	Hon. F. S. Jackson	J. Darling	5	2	0	3	E
1907-08	A. O. Jones[9]	M. A. Noble	5	1	4	0	A
1909	A. C. MacLaren	M. A. Noble	5	1	2	2	A
1911-12	J. W. H. T. Douglas	C. Hill	5	4	1	0	E
1912	C. B. Fry	S. E. Gregory	3	1	0	2	E
1920-21	J. W. H. T. Douglas	W. W. Armstrong	5	0	5	0	A
1921	Hon. L. H. Tennyson[10]	W. W. Armstrong	5	0	3	2	A
1924-25	A. E. R. Gilligan	H. L. Collins	5	1	4	0	A
1926	A. W. Carr[11]	H. L. Collins[12]	5	1	0	4	E
1928-29	A. P. F. Chapman[13]	J. Ryder	5	4	1	0	E
1930	A. P. F. Chapman[14]	W. M. Woodfull	5	1	2	2	A
1932-33	D. R. Jardine	W. M. Woodfull	5	4	1	0	E
1934	R. E. S. Wyatt[15]	W. M. Woodfull	5	1	2	2	A
1936-37	G. O. B. Allen	D. G. Bradman	5	2	3	0	A
1938†	W. R. Hammond	D. G. Bradman	4	1	1	2	A
1946-47	W. R. Hammond[16]	D. G. Bradman	5	0	3	2	A
1948	N. W. D. Yardley	D. G. Bradman	5	0	4	1	A
1950-51	F. R. Brown	A. L. Hassett	5	1	4	0	A
1953	L. Hutton	A. L. Hassett	5	1	0	4	E
1954-55	L. Hutton	I. W. Johnson[17]	5	3	1	1	E
1956	P. B. H. May	I. W. Johnson	5	2	1	2	E
1958-59	P. B. H. May	R. Benaud	5	0	4	1	A
1961	P. B. H. May[18]	R. Benaud[19]	5	1	2	2	A
1962-63	E. R. Dexter	R. Benaud	5	1	1	3	A
1964	E. R. Dexter	R. B. Simpson	5	0	1	4	A
1965-66	M. J. K. Smith	R. B. Simpson[20]	5	1	1	3	A
1968	M. C. Cowdrey[21]	W. M. Lawry[22]	5	1	1	3	A
1970-71†	R. Illingworth	W. M. Lawry[23]	6	2	0	4	E
1972	R. Illingworth	I. M. Chappell	5	2	2	1	E
1974-75	M. H. Denness[24]	I. M. Chappell	6	1	4	1	A

	Captains						
Season	*England*	*Australia*	*T*	*E*	*A*	*D*	*Held by*
1975	A. W. Greig[25]	I. M. Chappell	4	0	1	3	A
1976-77‡	A. W. Greig	G. S. Chappell	1	0	1	0	—
1977	J. M. Brearley	G. S. Chappell	5	3	0	2	E
1978-79	J. M. Brearley	G. N. Yallop	6	5	1	0	E
1979-80‡	J. M. Brearley	G. S. Chappell	3	0	3	0	—
1980‡	I. T. Botham	G. S. Chappell	1	0	0	1	—
1981	J. M. Brearley[26]	K. J. Hughes	6	3	1	2	E
1982-83	R. G. D. Willis	G. S. Chappell	5	1	2	2	A
1985	D. I. Gower	A. R. Border	6	3	1	2	E
1986-87	M. W. Gatting	A. R. Border	5	2	1	2	E
1987-88‡	M. W. Gatting	A. R. Border	1	0	0	1	—
1989	D. I. Gower	A. R. Border	6	0	4	2	A
1990-91	G. A. Gooch[27]	A. R. Border	5	0	3	2	A
1993	G. A. Gooch[28]	A. R. Border	6	1	4	1	A
1994-95	M. A. Atherton	M. A. Taylor	5	1	3	1	A
1997	M. A. Atherton	M. A. Taylor	6	2	3	1	A
1998-99	A. J. Stewart	M. A. Taylor	5	1	3	1	A
2001	N. Hussain[29]	S. R. Waugh[30]	5	1	4	0	A
	In Australia		155	53	76	26	
	In England		146	41	45	60	
Totals			301	94	121	86	

** The Ashes were awarded in 1882-83 after a series of three matches which England won 2–1. A fourth match was played and this was won by Australia.*
† The matches at Manchester in 1890 and 1938 and at Melbourne (Third Test) in 1970-71 were abandoned without a ball being bowled and are excluded.
‡ The Ashes were not at stake in these series.

Notes: The following deputised for the official touring captain or were appointed by the home authority for only a minor proportion of the series:

[1]A. N. Hornby (First). [2]W. L. Murdoch (First), H. H. Massie (Third), J. McC. Blackham (Fourth). [3]A. G. Steel (First). [4]A. E. Stoddart (First). [5]J. McC. Blackham (First). [6]A. C. MacLaren (First, Second and Fifth). [7]W. G. Grace (First). [8]H. Trumble (Fourth and Fifth). [9]F. L. Fane (First, Second and Third). [10]J. W. H. T. Douglas (First and Second). [11]A. P. F. Chapman (Fifth). [12]W. Bardsley (Third and Fourth). [13]J. C. White (Fifth). [14]R. E. S. Wyatt (Fifth). [15]C. F. Walters (First). [16]N. W. D. Yardley (Fifth). [17]A. R. Morris (Second). [18]M. C. Cowdrey (First and Second). [19]R. N. Harvey (Second). [20]B. C. Booth (First and Third). [21]T. W. Graveney (Fourth). [22]B. N. Jarman (Fourth). [23]I. M. Chappell (Seventh). [24]J. H. Edrich (Fourth). [25]M. H. Denness (First). [26]I. T. Botham (First and Second). [27]A. J. Lamb (First). [28]M. A. Atherton (Fifth and Sixth). [29]M. A. Atherton (Second and Third). [30]A. C. Gilchrist (Fourth).

HIGHEST INNINGS TOTALS

For England	in England: 903-7 dec. at The Oval	1938
	in Australia: 636 at Sydney	1928-29
For Australia	in England: 729-6 dec. at Lord's	1930
	in Australia: 659-8 dec. at Sydney	1946-47

LOWEST INNINGS TOTALS

For England	in England: 52 at The Oval	1948
	in Australia: 45 at Sydney	1886-87
For Australia	in England: 36 at Birmingham	1902
	in Australia: 42 at Sydney	1887-88

INDIVIDUAL HUNDREDS

For England (208)

R. Abel (1)
132*‡ Sydney 1891-92
L. E. G. Ames (1)
120 Lord's..... 1934
M. A. Atherton (1)
105 Sydney 1990-91
R. W. Barber (1)
185 Sydney 1965-66
W. Barnes (1)
134 Adelaide ... 1884-85
C. J. Barnett (2)
129 Adelaide ... 1936-37
126 Nottingham . 1938
K. F. Barrington (5)
132* Adelaide ... 1962-63
101 Sydney 1962-63
256 Manchester. . 1964
102 Adelaide ... 1965-66
115 Melbourne . . 1965-66
I. T. Botham (4)
119* Melbourne . . 1979-80
149* Leeds 1981
118 Manchester. . 1981
138 Brisbane ... 1986-87
G. Boycott (7)
113 The Oval ... 1964
142* Sydney 1970-71
119* Adelaide ... 1970-71
107 Nottingham . 1977
191 Leeds 1977
128* Lord's..... 1980
137 The Oval ... 1981
L. C. Braund (2)
103* Adelaide ... 1901-02
102 Sydney 1903-04
J. Briggs (1)
121 Melbourne . . 1884-85
B. C. Broad (4)
162 Perth...... 1986-87
116 Adelaide ... 1986-87
112 Melbourne . . 1986-87
139 Sydney 1987-88
J. T. Brown (1)
140 Melbourne . . 1894-95
M. A. Butcher (2)
116 Brisbane ... 1998-99
173* Leeds 2001
A. P. F. Chapman (1)
121 Lord's..... 1930
D. C. S. Compton (5)
102† Nottingham . 1938
147 } Adelaide ... 1946-47
103*} Adelaide ... 1946-47
184 Nottingham . 1948
145* Manchester. . 1948
M. C. Cowdrey (5)
102 Melbourne . . 1954-55
100* Sydney 1958-59
113 Melbourne . . 1962-63
104 Melbourne . . 1965-66
104 Birmingham . 1968
M. H. Denness (1)
188 Melbourne . . 1974-75
E. R. Dexter (2)
180 Birmingham . 1961
174 Manchester. . 1964
B. L. D'Oliveira (2)
158 The Oval ... 1968
117 Melbourne . . 1970-71
K. S. Duleepsinhji (1)
173† Lord's..... 1930
J. H. Edrich (7)
120† Lord's..... 1964
109 Melbourne . . 1965-66
103 Sydney 1965-66
164 The Oval ... 1968
115* Perth...... 1970-71
130 Adelaide ... 1970-71
175 Lord's..... 1975
W. J. Edrich (2)
119 Sydney 1946-47
111 Leeds 1948
K. W. R. Fletcher (1)
146 Melbourne . . 1974-75
R. E. Foster (1)
287† Sydney 1903-04
C. B. Fry (1)
144 The Oval ... 1905
M. W. Gatting (4)
160 Manchester. . 1985
100* Birmingham . 1985
100 Adelaide ... 1986-87
117 Adelaide ... 1994-95
G. A. Gooch (4)
196 The Oval ... 1985
117 Adelaide ... 1990-91
133 Manchester. . 1993
120 Nottingham . 1993
D. I. Gower (9)
102 Perth...... 1978-79
114 Adelaide ... 1982-83
166 Nottingham . 1985
215 Birmingham . 1985
157 The Oval ... 1985
136 Perth...... 1986-87
106 Lord's..... 1989
100 Melbourne . . 1990-91
123 Sydney 1990-91
W. G. Grace (2)
152† The Oval ... 1880
170 The Oval ... 1886
T. W. Graveney (1)
111 Sydney 1954-55
A. W. Greig (1)
110 Brisbane ... 1974-75
G. Gunn (2)
119† Sydney 1907-08
122* Sydney 1907-08
W. Gunn (1)
102* Manchester. . 1893
W. R. Hammond (9)
251 Sydney 1928-29
200 Melbourne . . 1928-29
119*} Adelaide ... 1928-29
177 } Adelaide ... 1928-29
113 Leeds 1930
112 Sydney 1932-33
101 Sydney 1932-33
231* Sydney 1936-37
240 Lord's..... 1938
J. Hardstaff jun. (1)
169* The Oval ... 1938
T. W. Hayward (2)
130 Manchester. . 1899
137 The Oval ... 1899
J. W. Hearne (1)
114 Melbourne . . 1911-12
E. H. Hendren (3)
127* Lord's..... 1926
169 Brisbane ... 1928-29
132 Manchester. . 1934
J. B. Hobbs (12)
126* Melbourne . . 1911-12
187 Adelaide ... 1911-12
178 Melbourne . . 1911-12
107 Lord's..... 1912
122 Melbourne . . 1920-21
123 Adelaide ... 1920-21
115 Sydney 1924-25
154 Melbourne . . 1924-25
119 Adelaide ... 1924-25
119 Lord's..... 1926
100 The Oval ... 1926
142 Melbourne . . 1928-29
N. Hussain (2)
207 Birmingham . 1997
105 Leeds 1997
K. L. Hutchings (1)
126 Melbourne . . 1907-08
L. Hutton (5)
100† Nottingham . 1938
364 The Oval ... 1938
122* Sydney 1946-47
156*‡ Adelaide ... 1950-51
145 Lord's..... 1953
Hon. F. S. Jackson (5)
103 The Oval ... 1893
118 The Oval ... 1899
128 Manchester. . 1902
144* Leeds 1905
113 Manchester. . 1905

G. L. Jessop (1)
104 The Oval . . . 1902
A. P. E. Knott (2)
106* Adelaide . . . 1974-75
135 Nottingham . 1977
A. J. Lamb (1)
125 Leeds 1989
M. Leyland (7)
137† Melbourne . . 1928-29
109 Lord's 1934
153 Manchester . . 1934
110 The Oval . . . 1934
126 Brisbane . . . 1936-37
111* Melbourne . . 1936-37
187 The Oval . . . 1938
B. W. Luckhurst (2)
131 Perth 1970-71
109 Melbourne . . 1970-71
A. C. MacLaren (5)
120 Melbourne . . 1894-95
109 Sydney 1897-98
124 Adelaide . . . 1897-98
116 Sydney 1901-02
140 Nottingham . 1905
J. W. H. Makepeace (1)
117 Melbourne . . 1920-21
P. B. H. May (3)
104 Sydney 1954-55
101 Leeds 1956
113 Melbourne . . 1958-59
C. P. Mead (1)
182* The Oval . . . 1921
Nawab of Pataudi sen. (1)
102† Sydney 1932-33
E. Paynter (1)
216* Nottingham . 1938
M. R. Ramprakash (1)
133 The Oval . . . 2001
D. W. Randall (3)
174† Melbourne . . 1976-77
150 Sydney 1978-79
115 Perth 1982-83
K. S. Ranjitsinhji (2)
154*† Manchester . . 1896
175 Sydney 1897-98
W. W. Read (1)
117 The Oval . . . 1884
W. Rhodes (1)
179 Melbourne . . 1911-12
C. J. Richards (1)
133 Perth 1986-87
P. E. Richardson (1)
104 Manchester . . 1956
R. T. Robinson (2)
175† Leeds 1985
148 Birmingham . 1985
A. C. Russell (3)
135* Adelaide . . . 1920-21
101 Manchester . . 1921
102* The Oval . . . 1921
R. C. Russell (1)
128* Manchester . . 1989
J. Sharp (1)
105 The Oval . . . 1909
Rev. D. S. Sheppard (2)
113 Manchester . . 1956
113 Melbourne . . 1962-63
A. Shrewsbury (3)
105* Melbourne . . 1884-85
164 Lord's 1886
106 Lord's 1893
R. T. Simpson (1)
156* Melbourne . . 1950-51
R. A. Smith (2)
143 Manchester . . 1989
101 Nottingham . 1989
A. G. Steel (2)
135* Sydney 1882-83
148 Lord's 1884
A. J. Stewart (1)
107 Melbourne . . 1998-99
A. E. Stoddart (2)
134 Adelaide . . . 1891-92
173 Melbourne . . 1894-95
R. Subba Row (2)
112† Birmingham . 1961
137 The Oval . . . 1961
H. Sutcliffe (8)
115† Sydney 1924-25
176 } Melbourne . . 1924-25
127 }
143 Melbourne . . 1924-25
161 The Oval . . . 1926
135 Melbourne . . 1928-29
161 The Oval . . . 1930
194 Sydney 1932-33
G. P. Thorpe (3)
114*† Nottingham . 1993
123 Perth 1994-95
138 Birmingham . 1997
J. T. Tyldesley (3)
138 Birmingham . 1902
100 Leeds 1905
112* The Oval . . . 1905
G. Ulyett (1)
149 Melbourne . . 1881-82
A. Ward (1)
117 Sydney 1894-95
C. Washbrook (2)
112 Melbourne . . 1946-47
143 Leeds 1948
W. Watson (1)
109† Lord's 1953
F. E. Woolley (2)
133* Sydney 1911-12
123 Sydney 1924-25
R. A. Woolmer (3)
149 The Oval . . . 1975
120 Lord's 1977
137 Manchester . . 1977

† *Signifies hundred on first appearance in England–Australia Tests.*
‡ *Carried his bat.*

For Australia (256)

W. W. Armstrong (4)
133* Melbourne . . 1907-08
158 Sydney 1920-21
121 Adelaide . . . 1920-21
123* Melbourne . . 1920-21
C. L. Badcock (1)
118 Melbourne . . 1936-37
C. Bannerman (1)
165*† Melbourne . . 1876-77
W. Bardsley (3)
136 } The Oval . . . 1909
130 }
193*‡ Lord's 1926
S. G. Barnes (2)
234 Sydney 1946-47
141 Lord's 1948
G. S. Blewett (3)
102*† Adelaide . . . 1994-95
115 Perth 1994-95
125 Birmingham . 1997
G. J. Bonnor (1)
128 Sydney 1884-85
D. C. Boon (7)
103 Adelaide . . . 1986-87
184* Sydney 1987-88
121 Adelaide . . . 1990-91
164* Lord's 1993
101 Nottingham . 1993
107 Leeds 1993
131 Melbourne . . 1994-95
B. C. Booth (2)
112 Brisbane . . . 1962-63
103 Melbourne . . 1962-63
A. R. Border (8)
115 Perth 1979-80
123* Manchester . . 1981
106* The Oval . . . 1981
196 Lord's 1985
146* Manchester . . 1985
125 Perth 1986-87
100* Adelaide . . . 1986-87
200* Leeds 1993
D. G. Bradman (19)
112 Melbourne . . 1928-29
123 Melbourne . . 1928-29

131 Nottingham 1930
254 Lord's 1930
334 Leeds 1930
232 The Oval 1930
103* Melbourne 1932-33
304 Leeds 1934
244 The Oval 1934
270 Melbourne 1936-37
212 Adelaide 1936-37
169 Melbourne 1936-37
144* Nottingham 1938
102* Lord's 1938
103 Leeds 1938
187 Brisbane 1946-47
234 Sydney 1946-47
138 Nottingham 1948
173* Leeds 1948

W. A. Brown (3)
105 Lord's 1934
133 Nottingham 1938
206*‡ Lord's 1938

P. J. Burge (4)
181 The Oval 1961
103 Sydney 1962-63
160 Leeds 1964
120 Melbourne 1965-66

J. W. Burke (1)
101*† Adelaide 1950-51

G. S. Chappell (9)
108† Perth 1970-71
131 Lord's 1972
113 The Oval 1972
144 Sydney 1974-75
102 Melbourne 1974-75
112 Manchester 1977
114 Melbourne 1979-80
117 Perth 1982-83
115 Adelaide 1982-83

I. M. Chappell (4)
111 Melbourne 1970-71
104 Adelaide 1970-71
118 The Oval 1972
192 The Oval 1975

H. L. Collins (3)
104† Sydney 1920-21
162 Adelaide 1920-21
114 Sydney 1924-25

R. M. Cowper (1)
307 Melbourne 1965-66

J. Darling (3)
101 Sydney 1897-98
178 Adelaide 1897-98
160 Sydney 1897-98

R. A. Duff (2)
104† Melbourne 1901-02
146 The Oval 1905

J. Dyson (1)
102 Leeds 1981

R. Edwards (2)
170* Nottingham 1972
115 Perth 1974-75

M. T. G. Elliott (2)
112 Lord's 1997
199 Leeds 1997

J. H. Fingleton (2)
100 Brisbane 1936-37
136 Melbourne 1936-37

G. Giffen (1)
161 Sydney 1894-95

A. C. Gilchrist (1)
152† Birmingham 2001

H. Graham (2)
107† Lord's 1893
105 Sydney 1894-95

J. M. Gregory (1)
100 Melbourne 1920-21

S. E. Gregory (4)
201 Sydney 1894-95
103 Lord's 1896
117 The Oval 1899
112 Adelaide 1903-04

R. J. Hartigan (1)
116† Adelaide 1907-08

R. N. Harvey (6)
112† Leeds 1948
122 Manchester 1953
162 Brisbane 1954-55
167 Melbourne 1958-59
114 Birmingham 1961
154 Adelaide 1962-63

A. L. Hassett (4)
128 Brisbane 1946-47
137 Nottingham 1948
115 Nottingham 1953
104 Lord's 1953

I. A. Healy (2)
102* Manchester 1993
134 Brisbane 1998-99

H. L. Hendry (1)
112 Sydney 1928-29

A. M. J. Hilditch (1)
119 Leeds 1985

C. Hill (4)
188 Melbourne 1897-98
135 Lord's 1899
119 Sheffield 1902
160 Adelaide 1907-08

T. P. Horan (1)
124 Melbourne 1881-82

K. J. Hughes (3)
129 Brisbane 1978-79
117 Lord's 1980
137 Sydney 1982-83

F. A. Iredale (2)
140 Adelaide 1894-95
108 Manchester 1896

A. A. Jackson (1)
164† Adelaide 1928-29

D. M. Jones (3)
184* Sydney 1986-87
157 Birmingham 1989
122 The Oval 1989

C. Kelleway (1)
147 Adelaide 1920-21

A. F. Kippax (1)
100 Melbourne 1928-29

J. L. Langer (2)
179* Adelaide 1998-99
102* The Oval 2001

W. M. Lawry (7)
130 Lord's 1961
102 Manchester 1961
106 Manchester 1964
166 Brisbane 1965-66
119 Adelaide 1965-66
108 Melbourne 1965-66
135 The Oval 1968

R. R. Lindwall (1)
100 Melbourne 1946-47

J. J. Lyons (1)
134 Sydney 1891-92

C. G. Macartney (5)
170 Sydney 1920-21
115 Leeds 1921
133* Lord's 1926
151 Leeds 1926
109 Manchester 1926

S. J. McCabe (4)
187* Sydney 1932-33
137 Manchester 1934
112 Melbourne 1936-37
232 Nottingham 1938

C. L. McCool (1)
104* Melbourne 1946-47

R. B. McCosker (2)
127 The Oval 1975
107 Nottingham 1977

C. C. McDonald (2)
170 Adelaide 1958-59
133 Melbourne 1958-59

P. S. McDonnell (3)
147 Sydney 1881-82
103 The Oval 1884
124 Adelaide 1884-85

C. E. McLeod (1)
112 Melbourne 1897-98

G. R. Marsh (2)
110† Brisbane 1986-87
138 Nottingham 1989

R. W. Marsh (1)
110* Melbourne 1976-77

D. R. Martyn (2)
105† Birmingham 2001
118 Leeds 2001

G. R. J. Matthews (1)
128 Sydney 1990-91

K. R. Miller (3)
141* Adelaide 1946-47
145* Sydney 1950-51
109 Lord's 1953

A. R. Morris (8)
155 Melbourne . . 1946-47
122 } Adelaide . . . 1946-47
124*}
105 Lord's 1948
182 Leeds 1948
196 The Oval . . . 1948
206 Adelaide . . . 1950-51
153 Brisbane . . . 1954-55
W. L. Murdoch (2)
153* The Oval . . . 1880
211 The Oval . . . 1884
M. A. Noble (1)
133 Sydney 1903-04
N. C. O'Neill (2)
117 The Oval . . . 1961
100 Adelaide . . . 1962-63
C. E. Pellew (2)
116 Melbourne . . 1920-21
104 Adelaide . . . 1920-21
W. H. Ponsford (5)
110† Sydney 1924-25
128 Melbourne . . 1924-25
110 The Oval . . . 1930
181 Leeds 1934
266 The Oval . . . 1934
R. T. Ponting (2)
127† Leeds 1997
144 Leeds 2001
V. S. Ransford (1)
143* Lord's 1909
I. R. Redpath (2)
171 Perth 1970-71
105 Sydney 1974-75
A. J. Richardson (1)
100 Leeds 1926
V. Y. Richardson (1)
138 Melbourne . . 1924-25
G. M. Ritchie (1)
146 Nottingham . 1985
J. Ryder (2)
201* Adelaide . . . 1924-25
112 Melbourne . . 1928-29
H. J. H. Scott (1)
102 The Oval . . . 1884
R. B. Simpson (2)
311 Manchester . . 1964
225 Adelaide . . . 1965-66
M. J. Slater (7)
152 Lord's 1993
176 Brisbane . . . 1994-95
103 Sydney 1994-95
124 Perth 1994-95
113 Brisbane . . . 1998-99
103 Adelaide . . . 1998-99
123 Sydney 1998-99
K. R. Stackpole (3)
207 Brisbane . . . 1970-71
136 Adelaide . . . 1970-71
114 Nottingham . 1972
J. M. Taylor (1)
108 Sydney 1924-25
M. A. Taylor (6)
136† Leeds 1989
219 Nottingham . 1989
124 Manchester . . 1993
111 Lord's 1993
113 Sydney 1994-95
129 Birmingham . 1997
G. H. S. Trott (1)
143 Lord's 1896
V. T. Trumper (6)
135* Lord's 1899
104 Manchester . . 1902
185* Sydney 1903-04
113 Adelaide . . . 1903-04
166 Sydney 1907-08
113 Sydney 1911-12
K. D. Walters (4)
155† Brisbane . . . 1965-66
115 Melbourne . . 1965-66
112 Brisbane . . . 1970-71
103 Perth 1974-75
M. E. Waugh (6)
138† Adelaide . . . 1990-91
137 Birmingham . 1993
140 Brisbane . . . 1994-95
121 Sydney 1998-99
108 Lord's 2001
120 The Oval . . . 2001
S. R. Waugh (9)
177* Leeds 1989
152* Lord's 1989
157* Leeds 1993
108 } Manchester . . 1997
116 }
112 Brisbane . . . 1998-99
122* Melbourne . . 1998-99
105 Birmingham . 2001
157* The Oval . . . 2001
D. M. Wellham (1)
103† The Oval . . . 1981
K. C. Wessels (1)
162† Brisbane . . . 1982-83
G. M. Wood (3)
100 Melbourne . . 1978-79
112 Lord's 1980
172 Nottingham . 1985
W. M. Woodfull (6)
141 Leeds 1926
117 Manchester . . 1926
111 Sydney 1928-29
107 Melbourne . . 1928-29
102 Melbourne . . 1928-29
155 Lord's 1930
G. N. Yallop (3)
102† Brisbane . . . 1978-79
121 Sydney 1978-79
114 Manchester . . 1981

† *Signifies hundred on first appearance in England–Australia Tests.*
‡ *Carried his bat.*

RECORD PARTNERSHIPS FOR EACH WICKET

For England

323 for 1st	J. B. Hobbs and W. Rhodes at Melbourne	1911-12
382 for 2nd†	L. Hutton and M. Leyland at The Oval	1938
262 for 3rd	W. R. Hammond and D. R. Jardine at Adelaide	1928-29
288 for 4th	N. Hussain and G. P. Thorpe at Birmingham	1997
206 for 5th	E. Paynter and D. C. S. Compton at Nottingham	1938
215 for 6th	L. Hutton and J. Hardstaff jun. at The Oval	1938
	G. Boycott and A. P. E. Knott at Nottingham	1977
143 for 7th	F. E. Woolley and J. Vine at Sydney	1911-12
124 for 8th	E. H. Hendren and H. Larwood at Brisbane	1928-29
151 for 9th	W. H. Scotton and W. W. Read at The Oval	1884
130 for 10th†	R. E. Foster and W. Rhodes at Sydney	1903-04

For Australia

329 for 1st	G. R. Marsh and M. A. Taylor at Nottingham	1989
451 for 2nd†	W. H. Ponsford and D. G. Bradman at The Oval	1934
276 for 3rd	D. G. Bradman and A. L. Hassett at Brisbane	1946-47
388 for 4th†	W. H. Ponsford and D. G. Bradman at Leeds	1934
405 for 5th†	S. G. Barnes and D. G. Bradman at Sydney	1946-47
346 for 6th†	J. H. Fingleton and D. G. Bradman at Melbourne	1936-37
165 for 7th	C. Hill and H. Trumble at Melbourne	1897-98
243 for 8th†	R. J. Hartigan and C. Hill at Adelaide	1907-08
154 for 9th†	S. E. Gregory and J. McC. Blackham at Sydney	1894-95
127 for 10th†	J. M. Taylor and A. A. Mailey at Sydney	1924-25

† *Denotes record partnership against all countries.*

MOST RUNS IN A SERIES

England in England	732 (average 81.33)	D. I. Gower	1985
England in Australia	905 (average 113.12)	W. R. Hammond	1928-29
Australia in England	974 (average 139.14)	D. G. Bradman	1930
Australia in Australia	810 (average 90.00)	D. G. Bradman	1936-37

TEN WICKETS OR MORE IN A MATCH

For England (37)

13-163 (6-42, 7-121)	S. F. Barnes, Melbourne	1901-02
14-102 (7-28, 7-74)	W. Bates, Melbourne	1882-83
10-105 (5-46, 5-59)	A. V. Bedser, Melbourne	1950-51
14-99 (7-55, 7-44)	A. V. Bedser, Nottingham	1953
11-102 (6-44, 5-58)	C. Blythe, Birmingham	1909
11-176 (6-78, 5-98)	I. T. Botham, Perth	1979-80
10-253 (6-125, 4-128)	I. T. Botham, The Oval	1981
11-74 (5-29, 6-45)	J. Briggs, Lord's	1886
12-136 (6-49, 6-87)	J. Briggs, Adelaide	1891-92
10-148 (5-34, 5-114)	J. Briggs, The Oval	1893
10-104 (6-77, 4-27)†	R. M. Ellison, Birmingham	1985
10-179 (5-102, 5-77)†	K. Farnes, Nottingham	1934
10-60 (6-41, 4-19)	J. T. Hearne, The Oval	1896
11-113 (5-58, 6-55)	J. C. Laker, Leeds	1956
19-90 (9-37, 10-53)	J. C. Laker, Manchester	1956
10-124 (5-96, 5-28)	H. Larwood, Sydney	1932-33
11-76 (6-48, 5-28)	W. H. Lockwood, Manchester	1902
12-104 (7-36, 5-68)	G. A. Lohmann, The Oval	1886
10-87 (8-35, 2-52)	G. A. Lohmann, Sydney	1886-87
10-142 (8-58, 2-84)	G. A. Lohmann, Sydney	1891-92
12-102 (6-50, 6-52)†	F. Martin, The Oval	1890
11-68 (7-31, 4-37)	R. Peel, Manchester	1888
15-124 (7-56, 8-68)	W. Rhodes, Melbourne	1903-04
10-156 (5-49, 5-107)†	T. Richardson, Manchester	1893
11-173 (6-39, 5-134)	T. Richardson, Lord's	1896
13-244 (7-168, 6-76)	T. Richardson, Manchester	1896
10-204 (8-94, 2-110)	T. Richardson, Sydney	1897-98

11-228 (6-130, 5-98)†	M. W. Tate, Sydney	1924-25
11-88 (5-58, 6-30)	F. S. Trueman, Leeds	1961
11-93 (7-66, 4-27)	P. C. R. Tufnell, The Oval	1997
10-130 (4-45, 6-85)	F. H. Tyson, Sydney	1954-55
10-82 (4-37, 6-45)	D. L. Underwood, Leeds	1972
11-215 (7-113, 4-102)	D. L. Underwood, Adelaide	1974-75
15-104 (7-61, 8-43)	H. Verity, Lord's	1934
10-57 (6-41, 4-16)	W. Voce, Brisbane	1936-37
13-256 (5-130, 8-126)	J. C. White, Adelaide	1928-29
10-49 (5-29, 5-20)	F. E. Woolley, The Oval	1912

For Australia (41)

10-151 (5-107, 5-44)	T. M. Alderman, Leeds	1989
10-239 (4-129, 6-110)	L. O'B. Fleetwood-Smith, Adelaide	1936-37
10-160 (4-88, 6-72)	G. Giffen, Sydney	1891-92
11-82 (5-45, 6-37)†	C. V. Grimmett, Sydney	1924-25
10-201 (5-107, 5-94)	C. V. Grimmett, Nottingham	1930
10-122 (5-65, 5-57)	R. M. Hogg, Perth	1978-79
10-66 (5-30, 5-36)	R. M. Hogg, Melbourne	1978-79
12-175 (5-85, 7-90)†	H. V. Hordern, Sydney	1911-12
10-161 (5-95, 5-66)	H. V. Hordern, Sydney	1911-12
10-164 (7-88, 3-76)	E. Jones, Lord's	1899
11-134 (6-47, 5-87)	G. F. Lawson, Brisbane	1982-83
10-181 (5-58, 5-123)	D. K. Lillee, The Oval	1972
11-165 (6-26, 5-139)	D. K. Lillee, Melbourne	1976-77
11-138 (6-60, 5-78)	D. K. Lillee, Melbourne	1979-80
11-159 (7-89, 4-70)	D. K. Lillee, The Oval	1981
11-85 (7-58, 4-27)	C. G. Macartney, Leeds	1909
11-157 (8-97, 3-60)	C. J. McDermott, Perth	1990-91
12-107 (5-57, 7-50)	S. C. G. MacGill, Sydney	1998-99
10-302 (5-160, 5-142)	A. A. Mailey, Adelaide	1920-21
13-236 (4-115, 9-121)	A. A. Mailey, Melbourne	1920-21
16-137 (8-84, 8-53)†	R. A. L. Massie, Lord's	1972
10-152 (5-72, 5-80)	K. R. Miller, Lord's	1956
13-77 (7-17, 6-60)	M. A. Noble, Melbourne	1901-02
11-103 (5-51, 6-52)	M. A. Noble, Sheffield	1902
10-129 (5-63, 5-66)	W. J. O'Reilly, Melbourne	1932-33
11-129 (4-75, 7-54)	W. J. O'Reilly, Nottingham	1934
10-122 (5-66, 5-56)	W. J. O'Reilly, Leeds	1938
11-165 (7-68, 4-97)	G. E. Palmer, Sydney	1881-82
10-126 (7-65, 3-61)	G. E. Palmer, Melbourne	1882-83
13-148 (6-97, 7-51)	B. A. Reid, Melbourne	1990-91
13-110 (6-48, 7-62)	F. R. Spofforth, Melbourne	1878-79
14-90 (7-46, 7-44)	F. R. Spofforth, The Oval	1882
11-117 (4-73, 7-44)	F. R. Spofforth, Sydney	1882-83
10-144 (4-54, 6-90)	F. R. Spofforth, Sydney	1884-85
12-89 (6-59, 6-30)	H. Trumble, The Oval	1896
10-128 (4-75, 6-53)	H. Trumble, Manchester	1902
12-173 (8-65, 4-108)	H. Trumble, The Oval	1902
12-87 (5-44, 7-43)	C. T. B. Turner, Sydney	1887-88
10-63 (5-27, 5-36)	C. T. B. Turner, Lord's	1888
11-110 (3-39, 8-71)	S. K. Warne, Brisbane	1994-95
11-229 (7-165, 4-64)	S. K. Warne, The Oval	2001

† *Signifies ten wickets or more on first appearance in England–Australia Tests.*

Note: J. Briggs, J. C. Laker, T. Richardson in 1896, R. M. Hogg, A. A. Mailey, H. Trumble and C. T. B. Turner took ten wickets or more in successive Tests. J. Briggs was omitted, however, from the England team for the first Test match in 1893.

MOST WICKETS IN A SERIES

England in England	46 (average 9.60)	J. C. Laker	1956
England in Australia	38 (average 23.18)	M. W. Tate	1924-25
Australia in England	42 (average 21.26)	T. M. Alderman (6 Tests)	1981
Australia in Australia	41 (average 12.85)	R. M. Hogg (6 Tests)	1978-79

WICKET-KEEPING – MOST DISMISSALS

	M	*Ct*	*St*	*Total*
†R. W. Marsh (Australia)	42	141	7	148
I. A. Healy (Australia)	33	123	12	135
A. P. E. Knott (England)	34	97	8	105
†W. A. Oldfield (Australia)	38	59	31	90
A. A. Lilley (England)	32	65	19	84
A. T. W. Grout (Australia)	22	69	7	76
T. G. Evans (England)	31	64	12	76

† The number of catches by R. W. Marsh (141) and stumpings by W. A. Oldfield (31) are respective records in England–Australia Tests.

SCORERS OF OVER 2,000 RUNS

	T	*I*	*NO*	*R*	*HS*	*Avge*
D. G. Bradman	37	63	7	5,028	334	89.78
J. B. Hobbs	41	71	4	3,636	187	54.26
A. R. Border	47	82	19	3,548	200*	56.31
D. I. Gower	42	77	4	3,269	215	44.78
G. Boycott	38	71	9	2,945	191	47.50
S. R. Waugh	41	65	18	2,895	177*	61.59
W. R. Hammond	33	58	3	2,852	251	51.85
H. Sutcliffe	27	46	5	2,741	194	66.85
C. Hill	41	76	1	2,660	188	35.46
J. H. Edrich	32	57	3	2,644	175	48.96
G. A. Gooch	42	79	0	2,632	196	33.31
G. S. Chappell	35	65	8	2,619	144	45.94
M. A. Taylor	33	61	2	2,496	219	42.30
M. C. Cowdrey	43	75	4	2,433	113	34.26
L. Hutton	27	49	6	2,428	364	56.46
R. N. Harvey	37	68	5	2,416	167	38.34
V. T. Trumper	40	74	5	2,263	185*	32.79
D. C. Boon	31	57	8	2,237	184	45.65
W. M. Lawry	29	51	5	2,233	166	48.54
M. E. Waugh	29	51	7	2,204	140	50.09
S. E. Gregory	52	92	7	2,193	201	25.80
W. W. Armstrong	42	71	9	2,172	158	35.03
I. M. Chappell	30	56	4	2,138	192	41.11
K. F. Barrington	23	39	6	2,111	256	63.96
A. R. Morris	24	43	2	2,080	206	50.73

BOWLERS WITH 100 WICKETS

	T	*Balls*	*R*	*W*	*5W/i*	*Avge*
D. K. Lillee	29	8,516	3,507	167	11	21.00
I. T. Botham	36	8,479	4,093	148	9	27.65
H. Trumble	31	7,895	2,945	141	9	20.88
R. G. D. Willis	35	7,294	3,346	128	7	26.14
S. K. Warne	23	7,005	2,693	118	7	22.82
M. A. Noble	39	6,845	2,860	115	9	24.86
R. R. Lindwall	29	6,728	2,559	114	6	22.44
W. Rhodes	41	5,791	2,616	109	6	24.00
S. F. Barnes	20	5,749	2,288	106	12	21.58
C. V. Grimmett	22	9,224	3,439	106	11	32.44
D. L. Underwood	29	8,000	2,770	105	4	26.38
A. V. Bedser	21	7,065	2,859	104	7	27.49
G. Giffen	31	6,457	2,791	103	7	27.09
W. J. O'Reilly	19	7,864	2,587	102	8	25.36
R. Peel	20	5,216	1,715	101	5	16.98
C. T. B. Turner	17	5,195	1,670	101	11	16.53
T. M. Alderman	17	4,717	2,117	100	11	21.17
J. R. Thomson	21	4,951	2,418	100	5	24.18

RESULTS ON EACH GROUND

In England

THE OVAL (33)

England (15) 1880, 1886, 1888, 1890, 1893, 1896, 1902, 1912, 1926, 1938, 1953, 1968, 1985, 1993, 1997.
Australia (6) 1882, 1930, 1934, 1948, 1972, 2001.
Drawn (12) 1884, 1899, 1905, 1909, 1921, 1956, 1961, 1964, 1975, 1977, 1981, 1989.

MANCHESTER (27)

England (7) 1886, 1888, 1905, 1956, 1972, 1977, 1981.
Australia (7) 1896, 1902, 1961, 1968, 1989, 1993, 1997.
Drawn (13) 1884, 1893, 1899, 1909, 1912, 1921, 1926, 1930, 1934, 1948, 1953, 1964, 1985.

The scheduled matches in 1890 and 1938 were abandoned without a ball bowled and are excluded.

LORD'S (32)

England (5) 1884, 1886, 1890, 1896, 1934.
Australia (13) 1888, 1899, 1909, 1921, 1930, 1948, 1956, 1961, 1972, 1985, 1989, 1993, 2001.
Drawn (14) 1893, 1902, 1905, 1912, 1926, 1938, 1953, 1964, 1968, 1975, 1977, 1980, 1981, 1997.

NOTTINGHAM (19)

England (3) 1905, 1930, 1977.
Australia (7) 1921, 1934, 1948, 1981, 1989, 1997, 2001.
Drawn (9) 1899, 1926, 1938, 1953, 1956, 1964, 1972, 1985, 1993.

LEEDS (23)

England (7) 1956, 1961, 1972, 1977, 1981, 1985, 2001.
Australia (8) 1909, 1921, 1938, 1948, 1964, 1989, 1993, 1997.
Drawn (8) 1899, 1905, 1926, 1930, 1934, 1953, 1968, 1975.

BIRMINGHAM (11)

England (4) 1909, 1981, 1985, 1997.

Australia (3) 1975, 1993, 2001.

Drawn (4) 1902, 1961, 1968, 1989.

SHEFFIELD (1)

Australia (1) 1902.

In Australia

MELBOURNE (51)

England (19) *1876*, *1882*, *1884*(2), *1894*(2), *1903*, *1907*, *1911*(2), *1924*, *1928*, *1950*, *1954*, *1962*, *1974*, *1982*, *1986*, *1998*.

Australia (25) *1876*, *1878*, *1882*, *1891*, *1897*(2), *1901*(2), *1903*, *1907*, *1920*(2), *1924*, *1928*, *1932*, *1936*(2), *1950*, *1958*(2), *1976*, *1978*, *1979*, *1990*, *1994*.

Drawn (7) *1881*(2), *1946*, *1965*(2), *1970*, *1974*.

One scheduled match in 1970-71 was abandoned without a ball bowled and is excluded.

SYDNEY (51)

England (20) *1882*, *1886*(2), *1887*, *1894*, *1897*, *1901*, *1903*(2), *1911*, *1928*, *1932*(2), *1936*, *1954*, *1965*, *1970*(2), *1978*(2).

Australia (24) *1881*(2), *1882*, *1884*(2), *1891*, *1894*, *1897*, *1901*, *1907*(2), *1911*, *1920*(2), *1924*(2), *1946*(2), *1950*, *1962*, *1974*, *1979*, *1986*, *1998*.

Drawn (7) *1954*, *1958*, *1962*, *1982*, *1987*, *1990*, *1994*.

ADELAIDE (27)

England (8) *1884*, *1891*, *1911*, *1928*, *1932*, *1954*, *1978*, *1994*.

Australia (14) *1894*, *1897*, *1901*, *1903*, *1907*, *1920*, *1924*, *1936*, *1950*, *1958*, *1965*, *1974*, *1982*, *1998*.

Drawn (5) *1946*, *1962*, *1970*, *1986*, *1990*.

BRISBANE Exhibition Ground (1)

England (1) *1928*.

BRISBANE Woolloongabba (16)

England (4) *1932*, *1936*, *1978*, *1986*.

Australia (8) *1946*, *1950*, *1954*, *1958*, *1974*, *1982*, *1990*, *1994*.

Drawn (4) *1962*, *1965*, *1970*, *1998*.

PERTH (9)

England (1) *1978*.

Australia (5) *1974*, *1979*, *1990*, *1994*, *1998*.

Drawn (3) *1970*, *1982*, *1986*.

For Tests in Australia the first year of the season is given in italics; i.e. *1876* denotes the 1876-77 season.

ENGLAND v SOUTH AFRICA

	Captains					
Season	*England*	*South Africa*	*T*	*E*	*SA*	*D*
1888-89	C. A. Smith[1]	O. R. Dunell[2]	2	2	0	0
1891-92	W. W. Read	W. H. Milton	1	1	0	0
1895-96	Lord Hawke[3]	E. A. Halliwell[4]	3	3	0	0
1898-99	Lord Hawke	M. Bisset	2	2	0	0
1905-06	P. F. Warner	P. W. Sherwell	5	1	4	0
1907	R. E. Foster	P. W. Sherwell	3	1	0	2
1909-10	H. D. G. Leveson Gower[5]	S. J. Snooke	5	2	3	0
1912	C. B. Fry	F. Mitchell[6]	3	3	0	0
1913-14	J. W. H. T. Douglas	H. W. Taylor	5	4	0	1
1922-23	F. T. Mann	H. W. Taylor	5	2	1	2
1924	A. E. R. Gilligan[7]	H. W. Taylor	5	3	0	2
1927-28	R. T. Stanyforth[8]	H. G. Deane	5	2	2	1
1929	J. C. White[9]	H. G. Deane	5	2	0	3
1930-31	A. P. F. Chapman	H. G. Deane[10]	5	0	1	4
1935	R. E. S. Wyatt	H. F. Wade	5	0	1	4
1938-39	W. R. Hammond	A. Melville	5	1	0	4
1947	N. W. D. Yardley	A. Melville	5	3	0	2
1948-49	F. G. Mann	A. D. Nourse	5	2	0	3
1951	F. R. Brown	A. D. Nourse	5	3	1	1
1955	P. B. H. May	J. E. Cheetham[11]	5	3	2	0
1956-57	P. B. H. May	C. B. van Ryneveld[12]	5	2	2	1
1960	M. C. Cowdrey	D. J. McGlew	5	3	0	2
1964-65	M. J. K. Smith	T. L. Goddard	5	1	0	4
1965	M. J. K. Smith	P. L. van der Merwe	3	0	1	2
1994	M. A. Atherton	K. C. Wessels	3	1	1	1
1995-96	M. A. Atherton	W. J. Cronje	5	0	1	4
1998	A. J. Stewart	W. J. Cronje	5	2	1	2
1999-2000	N. Hussain	W. J. Cronje	5	1	2	2
	In South Africa		68	26	16	26
	In England		52	24	7	21
	Totals		120	50	23	47

Notes: The following deputised for the official touring captain or were appointed by the home authority for only a minor proportion of the series:

[1]M. P. Bowden (Second). [2]W. H. Milton (Second). [3]Sir T. C. O'Brien (First). [4]A. R. Richards (Third). [5]F. L. Fane (Fourth and Fifth). [6]L. J. Tancred (Second and Third). [7]J. W. H. T. Douglas (Fourth). [8]G. T. S. Stevens (Fifth). [9]A. W. Carr (Fourth and Fifth). [10]E. P. Nupen (First), H. B. Cameron (Fourth and Fifth). [11]D. J. McGlew (Third and Fourth). [12]D. J. McGlew (Second).

HIGHEST INNINGS TOTALS

For England in England: 554-8 dec. at Lord's 1947
in South Africa: 654-5 at Durban 1938-39

For South Africa in England: 552-5 dec. at Manchester 1998
in South Africa: 572-7 at Durban 1999-2000

LOWEST INNINGS TOTALS

For England in England: 76 at Leeds 1907
in South Africa: 92 at Cape Town 1898-99

For South Africa in England: 30 at Birmingham 1924
in South Africa: 30 at Port Elizabeth 1895-96

INDIVIDUAL HUNDREDS

For England (96)

R. Abel (1)
120 Cape Town . . 1888-89
L. E. G. Ames (2)
148* The Oval . . . 1935
115 Cape Town . . 1938-39
M. A. Atherton (3)
185* Johannesburg 1995-96
103 Birmingham . 1998
108 Port Elizabeth 1999-00
K. F. Barrington (2)
148* Durban 1964-65
121 Johannesburg 1964-65
G. Boycott (1)
117 Port Elizabeth 1964-65
L. C. Braund (1)
104† Lord's 1907
M. A. Butcher (1)
116 Leeds 1998
D. C. S. Compton (7)
163† Nottingham . 1947
208 Lord's 1947
115 Manchester . . 1947
113 The Oval . . . 1947
114 Johannesburg 1948-49
112 Nottingham . 1951
158 Manchester . . 1955
M. C. Cowdrey (3)
101 Cape Town . . 1956-57
155 The Oval . . . 1960
105 Nottingham . 1965
D. Denton (1)
104 Johannesburg 1909-10
E. R. Dexter (1)
172 Johannesburg 1964-65
J. W. H. T. Douglas (1)
119† Durban 1913-14
W. J. Edrich (3)
219 Durban 1938-39
189 Lord's 1947
191 Manchester . . 1947
F. L. Fane (1)
143 Johannesburg 1905-06
C. B. Fry (1)
129 The Oval . . . 1907
P. A. Gibb (2)
106† Johannesburg 1938-39
120 Durban 1938-39
W. R. Hammond (6)
138* Birmingham . 1929
101* The Oval . . . 1929
136* Durban 1930-31
181 Cape Town . . 1938-39
120 Durban 1938-39
140 Durban 1938-39
T. W. Hayward (1)
122 Johannesburg 1895-96
E. H. Hendren (2)
132 Leeds 1924
142 The Oval . . . 1924
G. A. Hick (2)
110 Leeds 1994
141 Centurion . . . 1995-96
A. J. L. Hill (1)
124 Cape Town . . 1895-96
J. B. Hobbs (2)
187 Cape Town . . 1909-10
211 Lord's 1924
N. Hussain (2)
105 Lord's 1998
146* Durban 1999-00
L. Hutton (4)
100 Leeds 1947
158 Johannesburg 1948-49
123 Johannesburg 1948-49
100 Leeds 1951
D. J. Insole (1)
110* Durban 1956-57
M. Leyland (2)
102 Lord's 1929
161 The Oval . . . 1935
F. G. Mann (1)
136* Port Elizabeth 1948-49
P. B. H. May (3)
138† Leeds 1951
112 Lord's 1955
117 Manchester . . 1955
C. P. Mead (3)
102 Johannesburg 1913-14
117 Port Elizabeth 1913-14
181 Durban 1922-23
P. H. Parfitt (1)
122* Johannesburg 1964-65
J. M. Parks (1)
108* Durban 1964-65
E. Paynter (3)
117* }
100 } †Johannesburg 1938-39
243 Durban 1938-39
G. Pullar (1)
175 The Oval . . . 1960
W. Rhodes (1)
152 Johannesburg 1913-14
P. E. Richardson (1)
117† Johannesburg 1956-57
R. W. V. Robins (1)
108 Manchester . . 1935
A. C. Russell (2)
140 }
111 } Durban 1922-23
R. T. Simpson (1)
137 Nottingham . 1951
M. J. K. Smith (1)
121 Cape Town . . 1964-65
R. H. Spooner (1)
119† Lord's 1912
A. J. Stewart (1)
164 Manchester . . 1998
H. Sutcliffe (6)
122 Lord's 1924
102 Johannesburg 1927-28
114 Birmingham . 1929
100 Lord's 1929
104 }
109* } The Oval . . . 1929
M. W. Tate (1)
100* Lord's 1929
E. Tyldesley (2)
122 Johannesburg 1927-28
100 Durban 1927-28
J. T. Tyldesley (1)
112 Cape Town . . 1898-99
B. H. Valentine (1)
112 Cape Town . . 1938-39
P. F. Warner (1)
132*†‡ Johannesburg 1898-99
C. Washbrook (1)
195 Johannesburg 1948-49
A. J. Watkins (1)
111 Johannesburg 1948-49
H. Wood (1)
134* Cape Town . . 1891-92
F. E. Woolley (3)
115* Johannesburg 1922-23
134* Lord's 1924
154 Manchester . . 1929
R. E. S. Wyatt (2)
113 Manchester . . 1929
149 Nottingham . 1935

For South Africa (72)

E. J. Barlow (1)
138 Cape Town. . 1964-65
K. C. Bland (2)
144* Johannesburg 1964-65
127 The Oval . . . 1965
M. V. Boucher (1)
108 Durban 1999-00
R. H. Catterall (3)
120 Birmingham . 1924
120 Lord's 1924
119 Durban 1927-28
W. J. Cronje (1)
126 Nottingham . 1998
D. J. Cullinan (2)
108 Johannesburg 1999-00
120 Cape Town. . 1999-00
E. L. Dalton (2)
117 The Oval . . . 1935
102 Johannesburg 1938-39
W. R. Endean (1)
116* Leeds 1955
G. A. Faulkner (1)
123 Johannesburg 1909-10
T. L. Goddard (1)
112 Johannesburg 1964-65
C. M. H. Hathorn (1)
102 Johannesburg 1905-06
J. H. Kallis (2)
132 Manchester. . 1998
105 Cape Town. . 1999-00
G. Kirsten (3)
110 Johannesburg 1995-96
210 Manchester. . 1998
275 Durban 1999-00
P. N. Kirsten (1)
104 Leeds 1994
L. Klusener (1)
174 Port Elizabeth 1999-00
D. J. McGlew (2)
104* Manchester. . 1955
133 Leeds 1955
R. A. McLean (3)
142 Lord's 1955
100 Durban 1956-57
109 Manchester. . 1960
B. M. McMillan (1)
100* Johannesburg 1995-96
A. Melville (4)
103 Durban 1938-39
189 } 104* } Nottingham . 1947
117 Lord's 1947
B. Mitchell (7)
123 Cape Town. . 1930-31
164* Lord's 1935
128 The Oval . . . 1935
109 Durban 1938-39
120 } 189* } The Oval . . . 1947
120 Cape Town. . 1948-49
A. D. Nourse (7)
120 Cape Town. . 1938-39
103 Durban 1938-39
149 Nottingham . 1947
115 Manchester. . 1947
112 Cape Town. . 1948-49
129* Johannesburg 1948-49
208 Nottingham . 1951
H. G. Owen-Smith (1)
129 Leeds 1929
A. J. Pithey (1)
154 Cape Town. . 1964-65
R. G. Pollock (2)
137 Port Elizabeth 1964-65
125 Nottingham . 1965
J. N. Rhodes (1)
117 Lord's 1998
E. A. B. Rowan (2)
156* Johannesburg 1948-49
236 Leeds 1951
P. W. Sherwell (1)
115 Lord's 1907
I. J. Siedle (1)
141 Cape Town. . 1930-31
J. H. Sinclair (1)
106 Cape Town. . 1898-99
H. W. Taylor (7)
109 Durban 1913-14
176 Johannesburg 1922-23
101 Johannesburg 1922-23
102 Durban 1922-23
101 Johannesburg 1927-28
121 The Oval . . . 1929
117 Cape Town. . 1930-31
P. G. V. van der Bijl (1)
125 Durban 1938-39
K. G. Viljoen (1)
124 Manchester. . 1935
W. W. Wade (1)
125 Port Elizabeth 1948-49
J. H. B. Waite (1)
113 Manchester. . 1955
K. C. Wessels (1)
105† Lord's 1994
G. C. White (2)
147 Johannesburg 1905-06
118 Durban 1909-10
P. L. Winslow (1)
108 Manchester. . 1955

† *Signifies hundred on first appearance in England–South Africa Tests. K. C. Wessels had earlier scored 162 on his Test debut for Australia against England at Brisbane in 1982-83.*
‡ *P. F. Warner carried his bat through the second innings.*

Notes: A. Melville's four hundreds were made in successive Test innings. H. Wood scored the only hundred of his career in a Test match.

RECORD PARTNERSHIPS FOR EACH WICKET

For England

359	for 1st†	L. Hutton and C. Washbrook at Johannesburg	1948-49
280	for 2nd	P. A. Gibb and W. J. Edrich at Durban	1938-39
370	for 3rd†	W. J. Edrich and D. C. S. Compton at Lord's	1947
197	for 4th	W. R. Hammond and L. E. G. Ames at Cape Town	1938-39
237	for 5th	D. C. S. Compton and N. W. D. Yardley at Nottingham	1947
206*	for 6th	K. F. Barrington and J. M. Parks at Durban	1964-65
115	for 7th	J. W. H. T. Douglas and M. C. Bird at Durban	1913-14
154	for 8th	C. W. Wright and H. R. Bromley-Davenport at Johannesburg	1895-96
71	for 9th	H. Wood and J. T. Hearne at Cape Town	1891-92
92	for 10th	A. C. Russell and A. E. R. Gilligan at Durban	1922-23

For South Africa

260	for 1st†	B. Mitchell and I. J. Siedle at Cape Town	1930-31
238	for 2nd	G. Kirsten and J. H. Kallis at Manchester	1998
319	for 3rd	A. Melville and A. D. Nourse at Nottingham	1947
214	for 4th†	H. W. Taylor and H. G. Deane at The Oval	1929
192	for 5th†	G. Kirsten and M. V. Boucher at Durban	1999-2000
171	for 6th	J. H. B. Waite and P. L. Winslow at Manchester	1955
123	for 7th	H. G. Deane and E. P. Nupen at Durban	1927-28
119	for 8th	L. Klusener and M. V. Boucher at Port Elizabeth	1999-2000
137	for 9th	E. L. Dalton and A. B. C. Langton at The Oval	1935
103	for 10th†	H. G. Owen-Smith and A. J. Bell at Leeds	1929

† *Denotes record partnership against all countries.*

MOST RUNS IN A SERIES

England in England	753 (average 94.12)	D. C. S. Compton	1947
England in South Africa	653 (average 81.62)	E. Paynter	1938-39
South Africa in England	621 (average 69.00)	A. D. Nourse	1947
South Africa in South Africa	582 (average 64.66)	H. W. Taylor	1922-23

TEN WICKETS OR MORE IN A MATCH

For England (25)

11-110 (5-25, 6-85)†	S. F. Barnes, Lord's	1912
10-115 (6-52, 4-63)	S. F. Barnes, Leeds	1912
13-57 (5-28, 8-29)	S. F. Barnes, The Oval	1912
10-105 (5-57, 5-48)	S. F. Barnes, Durban	1913-14
17-159 (8-56, 9-103)	S. F. Barnes, Johannesburg	1913-14
14-144 (7-56, 7-88)	S. F. Barnes, Durban	1913-14
12-112 (7-58, 5-54)	A. V. Bedser, Manchester	1951
11-118 (6-68, 5-50)	C. Blythe, Cape Town	1905-06
15-99 (8-59, 7-40)	C. Blythe, Leeds	1907
10-104 (7-46, 3-58)	C. Blythe, Cape Town	1909-10
15-28 (7-17, 8-11)	J. Briggs, Cape Town	1888-89
13-91 (6-54, 7-37)†	J. J. Ferris, Cape Town	1891-92
10-122 (5-60, 5-62)	A. R. C. Fraser, Nottingham	1998
10-207 (7-115, 3-92)	A. P. Freeman, Leeds	1929
12-171 (7-71, 5-100)	A. P. Freeman, Manchester	1929
12-130 (7-70, 5-60)	G. Geary, Johannesburg	1927-28
11-90 (6-7, 5-83)	A. E. R. Gilligan, Birmingham	1924
10-119 (4-64, 6-55)	J. C. Laker, The Oval	1951
15-45 (7-38, 8-7)†	G. A. Lohmann, Port Elizabeth	1895-96
12-71 (9-28, 3-43)	G. A. Lohmann, Johannesburg	1895-96
10-138 (1-81, 9-57)	D. E. Malcolm, The Oval	1994
11-97 (6-63, 5-34)	J. B. Statham, Lord's	1960
12-101 (7-52, 5-49)	R. Tattersall, Lord's	1951
12-89 (5-53, 7-36)	J. H. Wardle, Cape Town	1956-57
10-175 (5-95, 5-80)	D. V. P. Wright, Lord's	1947

For South Africa (7)

11-127 (6-53, 5-74)	A. A. Donald, Johannesburg	1999-2000
11-112 (4-49, 7-63)†	A. E. Hall, Cape Town	1922-23
11-150 (5-63, 6-87)	E. P. Nupen, Johannesburg	1930-31
10-87 (5-53, 5-34)	P. M. Pollock, Nottingham	1965
12-127 (4-57, 8-70)	S. J. Snooke, Johannesburg	1905-06

13-192 (4-79, 9-113)	H. J. Tayfield, Johannesburg	1956-57
12-181 (5-87, 7-94)	A. E. E. Vogler, Johannesburg	1909-10

† *Signifies ten wickets or more on first appearance in England–South Africa Tests.*

Notes: S. F. Barnes took ten wickets or more in his first five Tests v South Africa and in six of his seven Tests v South Africa. A. P. Freeman and G. A. Lohmann took ten wickets or more in successive matches.

MOST WICKETS IN A SERIES

England in England	34 (average 8.29)	S. F. Barnes	1912
England in South Africa	49 (average 10.93)	S. F. Barnes	1913-14
South Africa in England	33 (average 19.78)	A. A. Donald	1998
South Africa in South Africa	37 (average 17.18)	H. J. Tayfield	1956-57

ENGLAND v WEST INDIES

Captains

Season	*England*	*West Indies*	*T*	*E*	*WI*	*D*
1928	A. P. F. Chapman	R. K. Nunes	3	3	0	0
1929-30	Hon. F. S. G. Calthorpe	E. L. G. Hoad[1]	4	1	1	2
1933	D. R. Jardine[2]	G. C. Grant	3	2	0	1
1934-35	R. E. S. Wyatt	G. C. Grant	4	1	2	1
1939	W. R. Hammond	R. S. Grant	3	1	0	2
1947-48	G. O. B. Allen[3]	J. D. C. Goddard[4]	4	0	2	2
1950	N. W. D. Yardley[5]	J. D. C. Goddard	4	1	3	0
1953-54	L. Hutton	J. B. Stollmeyer	5	2	2	1
1957	P. B. H. May	J. D. C. Goddard	5	3	0	2
1959-60	P. B. H. May[6]	F. C. M. Alexander	5	1	0	4

THE WISDEN TROPHY

Captains

Season	*England*	*West Indies*	*T*	*E*	*WI*	*D*	*Held by*
1963	E. R. Dexter	F. M. M. Worrell	5	1	3	1	WI
1966	M. C. Cowdrey[7]	G. S. Sobers	5	1	3	1	WI
1967-68	M. C. Cowdrey	G. S. Sobers	5	1	0	4	E
1969	R. Illingworth	G. S. Sobers	3	2	0	1	E
1973	R. Illingworth	R. B. Kanhai	3	0	2	1	WI
1973-74	M. H. Denness	R. B. Kanhai	5	1	1	3	WI
1976	A. W. Greig	C. H. Lloyd	5	0	3	2	WI
1980	I. T. Botham	C. H. Lloyd[8]	5	0	1	4	WI
1980-81†	I. T. Botham	C. H. Lloyd	4	0	2	2	WI
1984	D. I. Gower	C. H. Lloyd	5	0	5	0	WI
1985-86	D. I. Gower	I. V. A. Richards	5	0	5	0	WI
1988	J. E. Emburey[9]	I. V. A. Richards	5	0	4	1	WI
1989-90‡	G. A. Gooch[10]	I. V. A. Richards[11]	4	1	2	1	WI
1991	G. A. Gooch	I. V. A. Richards	5	2	2	1	WI
1993-94	M. A. Atherton	R. B. Richardson[12]	5	1	3	1	WI
1995	M. A. Atherton	R. B. Richardson	6	2	2	2	WI
1997-98	M. A. Atherton	B. C. Lara	6	1	3	2	WI
2000	N. Hussain[13]	J. C. Adams	5	3	1	1	E
	In England		70	21	29	20	
	In West Indies		56	10	23	23	
	Totals		126	31	52	43	

† *The Second Test, at Georgetown, was cancelled owing to political pressure and is excluded.*
‡ *The Second Test, at Georgetown, was abandoned without a ball being bowled and is excluded.*

Notes: The following deputised for the official touring captain or were appointed by the home authority for only a minor proportion of the series:

[1]N. Betancourt (Second), M. P. Fernandes (Third), R. K. Nunes (Fourth). [2]R. E. S. Wyatt (Third). [3]K. Cranston (First). [4]G. A. Headley (First), G. E. Gomez (Second). •[5]F. R. Brown (Fourth). [6]M. C. Cowdrey (Fourth and Fifth). [7]M. J. K. Smith (First), D. B. Close (Fifth). [8]I. V. A. Richards (Fifth). [9]M. W. Gatting (First), C. S. Cowdrey (Fourth), G. A. Gooch (Fifth). [10]A. J. Lamb (Fourth and Fifth). [11]D. L. Haynes (Third). [12]C. A. Walsh (Fifth). [13]A. J. Stewart (Second).

HIGHEST INNINGS TOTALS

For England in England: 619-6 dec. at Nottingham		1957
	in West Indies: 849 at Kingston	1929-30
For West Indies in England: 692-8 dec. at The Oval		1995
	in West Indies: 681-8 dec. at Port-of-Spain	1953-54

LOWEST INNINGS TOTALS

For England in England: 71 at Manchester		1976
	in West Indies: 46 at Port-of-Spain	1993-94
For West Indies in England: 54 at Lord's		2000
	in West Indies: 102 at Bridgetown	1934-35

INDIVIDUAL HUNDREDS

For England (100)

L. E. G. Ames (3)		
105	Port-of-Spain	1929-30
149	Kingston	1929-30
126	Kingston	1934-35
D. L. Amiss (4)		
174	Port-of-Spain	1973-74
262*	Kingston	1973-74
118	Georgetown	1973-74
203	The Oval	1976
M. A. Atherton (4)		
144	Georgetown	1993-94
135	St John's	1993-94
113	Nottingham	1995
108	The Oval	2000
A. H. Bakewell (1)		
107†	The Oval	1933
K. F. Barrington (3)		
128†	Bridgetown	1959-60
121	Port-of-Spain	1959-60
143	Port-of-Spain	1967-68
G. Boycott (5)		
116	Georgetown	1967-68
128	Manchester	1969
106	Lord's	1969
112	Port-of-Spain	1973-74
104*	St John's	1980-81
D. C. S. Compton (2)		
120†	Lord's	1939
133	Port-of-Spain	1953-54
M. C. Cowdrey (6)		
154†	Birmingham	1957
152	Lord's	1957
114	Kingston	1959-60
119	Port-of-Spain	1959-60
101	Kingston	1967-68
148	Port-of-Spain	1967-68
E. R. Dexter (2)		
136*†	Bridgetown	1959-60
110	Georgetown	1959-60
J. H. Edrich (1)		
146	Bridgetown	1967-68
T. G. Evans (1)		
104	Manchester	1950
K. W. R. Fletcher (1)		
129*	Bridgetown	1973-74
G. Fowler (1)		
106	Lord's	1984
G. A. Gooch (5)		
123	Lord's	1980
116	Bridgetown	1980-81
153	Kingston	1980-81
146	Nottingham	1988
154*‡	Leeds	1991
D. I. Gower (1)		
154*	Kingston	1980-81
T. W. Graveney (5)		
258	Nottingham	1957
164	The Oval	1957
109	Nottingham	1966
165	The Oval	1966
118	Port-of-Spain	1967-68
A. W. Greig (3)		
148	Bridgetown	1973-74
121	Georgetown	1973-74
116	Leeds	1976
S. C. Griffith (1)		
140†	Port-of-Spain	1947-48
W. R. Hammond (1)		
138	The Oval	1939
J. H. Hampshire (1)		
107†	Lord's	1969
F. C. Hayes (1)		
106*†	The Oval	1973
E. H. Hendren (2)		
205*	Port-of-Spain	1929-30
123	Georgetown	1929-30
G. A. Hick (1)		
118*	Nottingham	1995
J. B. Hobbs (1)		
159	The Oval	1928
N. Hussain (1)		
106	St John's	1997-98
L. Hutton (5)		
196†	Lord's	1939
165*	The Oval	1939
202*‡	The Oval	1950
169	Georgetown	1953-54
205	Kingston	1953-54

R. Illingworth (1)
113 Lord's. 1969
D. R. Jardine (1)
127 Manchester. . 1933
A. P. E. Knott (1)
116 Leeds 1976
A. J. Lamb (6)
110 Lord's. 1984
100 Leeds 1984
100* Manchester. . 1984
113 Lord's. 1988
132 Kingston . . . 1989-90
119 Bridgetown . 1989-90
P. B. H. May (3)
135 Port-of-Spain 1953-54
285* Birmingham . 1957
104 Nottingham . 1957
C. Milburn (1)
126* Lord's. 1966
J. T. Murray (1)
112† The Oval . . . 1966
J. M. Parks (1)
101*† Port-of-Spain 1959-60
W. Place (1)
107 Kingston . . . 1947-48
M. R. Ramprakash (1)
154 Bridgetown . 1997-98
P. E. Richardson (2)
126 Nottingham . 1957
107 The Oval . . . 1957
J. D. Robertson (1)
133 Port-of-Spain 1947-48
A. Sandham (2)
152† Bridgetown . 1929-30
325 Kingston . . . 1929-30
M. J. K. Smith (1)
108 Port-of-Spain 1959-60
R. A. Smith (3)
148* Lord's. 1991
109 The Oval . . . 1991
175 St John's . . . 1993-94
D. S. Steele (1)
106† Nottingham . 1976
A. J. Stewart (3)
118 } 143 } Bridgetown . 1993-94
105 Manchester. . 2000
R. Subba Row (1)
100† Georgetown . 1959-60
G. P. Thorpe (1)
103 Bridgetown . 1997-98
E. Tyldesley (1)
122† Lord's. 1928
C. Washbrook (2)
114† Lord's. 1950
102 Nottingham . 1950
W. Watson (1)
116† Kingston . . . 1953-54
P. Willey (2)
100* The Oval . . . 1980
102* St John's . . . 1980-81

For West Indies (111)

J. C. Adams (1)
137 Georgetown . 1993-94
K. L. T. Arthurton (1)
126 Kingston . . . 1993-94
I. Barrow (1)
105 Manchester. . 1933
C. A. Best (1)
164 Bridgetown . 1989-90
B. F. Butcher (2)
133 Lord's. 1963
209* Nottingham . 1966
G. M. Carew (1)
107 Port-of-Spain 1947-48
S. Chanderpaul (1)
118 Georgetown . 1997-98
C. A. Davis (1)
103 Lord's. 1969
P. J. L. Dujon (1)
101 Manchester. . 1984
R. C. Fredericks (3)
150 Birmingham . 1973
138 Lord's. 1976
109 Leeds 1976
A. G. Ganteaume (1)
112† Port-of-Spain 1947-48
H. A. Gomes (2)
143 Birmingham . 1984
104* Leeds 1984
C. G. Greenidge (7)
134 } 101 } Manchester. . 1976
115 Leeds 1976
214* Lord's. 1984
223 Manchester. . 1984
103 Lord's. 1988
149 St John's . . . 1989-90
D. L. Haynes (5)
184 Lord's. 1980
125 The Oval . . . 1984
131 St John's . . . 1985-86
109 Bridgetown . 1989-90
167 St John's . . . 1989-90
G. A. Headley (8)
176† Bridgetown . 1929-30
114 } 112 } Georgetown . 1929-30
223 Kingston . . . 1929-30
169* Manchester. . 1933
270* Kingston . . . 1934-35
106 } 107 } Lord's. 1939
D. A. J. Holford (1)
105* Lord's. 1966
J. K. Holt (1)
166 Bridgetown . 1953-54
C. L. Hooper (3)
111 Lord's. 1991
127 The Oval . . . 1995
108* St John's . . . 1997-98
C. C. Hunte (3)
182 Manchester. . 1963
108* The Oval . . . 1963
135 Manchester. . 1966
B. D. Julien (1)
121 Lord's. 1973
A. I. Kallicharran (2)
158 Port-of-Spain 1973-74
119 Bridgetown . 1973-74
R. B. Kanhai (5)
110 Port-of-Spain 1959-60
104 The Oval . . . 1966
153 Port-of-Spain 1967-68
150 Georgetown . 1967-68
157 Lord's. 1973
C. B. Lambert (1)
104 St John's . . . 1997-98
B. C. Lara (6)
167 Georgetown . 1993-94
375 St John's . . . 1993-94
145 Manchester. . 1995
152 Nottingham . 1995
179 The Oval . . . 1995
112 Manchester. . 2000
C. H. Lloyd (5)
118† Port-of-Spain 1967-68
113* Bridgetown . 1967-68
132 The Oval . . . 1973
101 Manchester. . 1980
100 Bridgetown . 1980-81
S. M. Nurse (2)
137 Leeds 1966
136 Port-of-Spain 1967-68
A. F. Rae (2)
106 Lord's. 1950
109 The Oval . . . 1950
I. V. A. Richards (8)
232† Nottingham . 1976
135 Manchester. . 1976
291 The Oval . . . 1976
145 Lord's. 1980
182* Bridgetown . 1980-81
114 St John's . . . 1980-81
117 Birmingham . 1984
110* St John's . . . 1985-86
R. B. Richardson (4)
102 Port-of-Spain 1985-86
160 Bridgetown . 1985-86
104 Birmingham . 1991
121 The Oval . . . 1991

C. A. Roach (2)
122 Bridgetown . 1929-30
209 Georgetown . 1929-30
L. G. Rowe (3)
120 Kingston . . . 1973-74
302 Bridgetown . 1973-74
123 Port-of-Spain 1973-74
O. G. Smith (2)
161† Birmingham . 1957
168 Nottingham . 1957
G. S. Sobers (10)
226 Bridgetown . 1959-60
147 Kingston . . . 1959-60
145 Georgetown . 1959-60
102 Leeds 1963
161 Manchester. . 1966
163* Lord's 1966
174 Leeds 1966
113* Kingston . . . 1967-68
152 Georgetown . 1967-68
150* Lord's 1973
C. L. Walcott (4)
168* Lord's 1950
220 Bridgetown . 1953-54
124 Port-of-Spain 1953-54
116 Kingston . . . 1953-54
E. D. Weekes (3)
141 Kingston . . . 1947-48
129 Nottingham . 1950
206 Port-of-Spain 1953-54
K. H. Weekes (1)
137 The Oval . . . 1939
F. M. M. Worrell (6)
131* Georgetown . 1947-48
261 Nottingham . 1950
138 The Oval . . . 1950
167 Port-of-Spain 1953-54
191*‡ Nottingham . 1957
197* Bridgetown . 1959-60

† *Signifies hundred on first appearance in England–West Indies Tests. S. C. Griffith provides the only instance for England of a player hitting his maiden century in first-class cricket in his first Test.*
‡ *Carried his bat.*

RECORD PARTNERSHIPS FOR EACH WICKET

For England

212	for 1st	C. Washbrook and R. T. Simpson at Nottingham	1950
266	for 2nd	P. E. Richardson and T. W. Graveney at Nottingham	1957
303	for 3rd	M. A. Atherton and R. A. Smith at St John's	1993-94
411	for 4th†	P. B. H. May and M. C. Cowdrey at Birmingham	1957
150	for 5th	A. J. Stewart and G. P. Thorpe at Bridgetown	1993-94
205	for 6th	M. R. Ramprakash and G. P. Thorpe at Bridgetown	1997-98
197	for 7th†	M. J. K. Smith and J. M. Parks at Port-of-Spain	1959-60
217	for 8th	T. W. Graveney and J. T. Murray at The Oval	1966
109	for 9th	G. A. R. Lock and P. I. Pocock at Georgetown	1967-68
128	for 10th	K. Higgs and J. A. Snow at The Oval	1966

For West Indies

298	for 1st†	C. G. Greenidge and D. L. Haynes at St John's	1989-90
287*	for 2nd	C. G. Greenidge and H. A. Gomes at Lord's	1984
338	for 3rd†	E. D. Weekes and F. M. M. Worrell at Port-of-Spain	1953-54
399	for 4th†	G. S. Sobers and F. M. M. Worrell at Bridgetown	1959-60
265	for 5th	S. M. Nurse and G. S. Sobers at Leeds	1966
274*	for 6th†	G. S. Sobers and D. A. J. Holford at Lord's	1966
155*	for 7th‡	G. S. Sobers and B. D. Julien at Lord's	1973
99	for 8th	C. A. McWatt and J. K. Holt at Georgetown	1953-54
150	for 9th	E. A. E. Baptiste and M. A. Holding at Birmingham	1984
70	for 10th	I. R. Bishop and D. Ramnarine at Georgetown	1997-98

† *Denotes record partnership against all countries.*
‡ *231 runs were added for this wicket in two separate partnerships: G. S. Sobers retired ill and was replaced by K. D. Boyce when 155 had been added.*

TEN WICKETS OR MORE IN A MATCH

For England (12)

11-98 (7-44, 4-54)	T. E. Bailey, Lord's	1957
11-110 (8-53, 3-57)	A. R. C. Fraser, Port-of-Spain	1997-98
10-93 (5-54, 5-39)	A. P. Freeman, Manchester	1928
13-156 (8-86, 5-70)	A. W. Greig, Port-of-Spain	1973-74

11-48 (5-28, 6-20)	G. A. R. Lock, The Oval	1957
10-137 (4-60, 6-77)	D. E. Malcolm, Port-of-Spain	1989-90
11-96 (5-37, 6-59)†	C. S. Marriott, The Oval	1933
10-142 (4-82, 6-60)	J. A. Snow, Georgetown	1967-68
10-195 (5-105, 5-90)†	G. T. S. Stevens, Bridgetown	1929-30
11-152 (6-100, 5-52)	F. S. Trueman, Lord's	1963
12-119 (5-75, 7-44)	F. S. Trueman, Birmingham	1963
11-149 (4-79, 7-70)	W. Voce, Port-of-Spain	1929-30

For West Indies (15)

10-127 (2-82, 8-45)	C. E. L. Ambrose, Bridgetown	1989-90
11-84 (5-60, 6-24)	C. E. L. Ambrose, Port-of-Spain	1993-94
10-174 (5-105, 5-69)	K. C. G. Benjamin, Nottingham	1995
11-147 (5-70, 6-77)†	K. D. Boyce, The Oval	1973
11-229 (5-137, 6-92)	W. Ferguson, Port-of-Spain	1947-48
11-157 (5-59, 6-98)†	L. R. Gibbs, Manchester	1963
10-106 (5-37, 5-69)	L. R. Gibbs, Manchester	1966
14-149 (8-92, 6-57)	M. A. Holding, The Oval	1976
10-96 (5-41, 5-55)†	H. H. H. Johnson, Kingston	1947-48
10-92 (6-32, 4-60)	M. D. Marshall, Lord's	1988
11-152 (5-66, 6-86)	S. Ramadhin, Lord's	1950
10-123 (5-60, 5-63)	A. M. E. Roberts, Lord's	1976
11-204 (8-104, 3-100)†	A. L. Valentine, Manchester	1950
10-160 (4-121, 6-39)	A. L. Valentine, The Oval	1950
10-117 (4-43, 6-74)	C. A. Walsh, Lord's	2000

† *Signifies ten wickets or more on first appearance in England–West Indies Tests.*

Note: F. S. Trueman took ten wickets or more in successive matches.

ENGLAND v NEW ZEALAND

	Captains					
Season	*England*	*New Zealand*	*T*	*E*	*NZ*	*D*
1929-30	A. H. H. Gilligan	T. C. Lowry	4	1	0	3
1931	D. R. Jardine	T. C. Lowry	3	1	0	2
1932-33	D. R. Jardine[1]	M. L. Page	2	0	0	2
1937	R. W. V. Robins	M. L. Page	3	1	0	2
1946-47	W. R. Hammond	W. A. Hadlee	1	0	0	1
1949	F. G. Mann[2]	W. A. Hadlee	4	0	0	4
1950-51	F. R. Brown	W. A. Hadlee	2	1	0	1
1954-55	L. Hutton	G. O. Rabone	2	2	0	0
1958	P. B. H. May	J. R. Reid	5	4	0	1
1958-59	P. B. H. May	J. R. Reid	2	1	0	1
1962-63	E. R. Dexter	J. R. Reid	3	3	0	0
1965	M. J. K. Smith	J. R. Reid	3	3	0	0
1965-66	M. J. K. Smith	B. W. Sinclair[3]	3	0	0	3
1969	R. Illingworth	G. T. Dowling	3	2	0	1
1970-71	R. Illingworth	G. T. Dowling	2	1	0	1
1973	R. Illingworth	B. E. Congdon	3	2	0	1
1974-75	M. H. Denness	B. E. Congdon	2	1	0	1
1977-78	G. Boycott	M. G. Burgess	3	1	1	1
1978	J. M. Brearley	M. G. Burgess	3	3	0	0
1983	R. G. D. Willis	G. P. Howarth	4	3	1	0
1983-84	R. G. D. Willis	G. P. Howarth	3	0	1	2
1986	M. W. Gatting	J. V. Coney	3	0	1	2
1987-88	M. W. Gatting	J. J. Crowe[4]	3	0	0	3
1990	G. A. Gooch	J. G. Wright	3	1	0	2

Season	*England*	*New Zealand*	*T*	*E*	*NZ*	*D*
1991-92	G. A. Gooch	M. D. Crowe	3	2	0	1
1994	M. A. Atherton	K. R. Rutherford	3	1	0	2
1996-97	M. A. Atherton	L. K. Germon[5]	3	2	0	1
1999	N. Hussain[6]	S. P. Fleming	4	1	2	1
	In New Zealand		38	15	2	21
	In England		44	22	4	18
	Totals		82	37	6	39

Notes: The following deputised for the official touring captain or were appointed by the home authority for only a minor proportion of the series:

[1]R. E. S. Wyatt (Second). [2]F. R. Brown (Third and Fourth). [3]M. E. Chapple (First). [4]J. G. Wright (Third). [5]S. P. Fleming (Third). [6]M. A. Butcher (Third).

HIGHEST INNINGS TOTALS

For England in England: 567-8 dec. at Nottingham 1994
in New Zealand: 593-6 dec. at Auckland 1974-75

For New Zealand in England: 551-9 dec. at Lord's 1973
in New Zealand: 537 at Wellington 1983-84

LOWEST INNINGS TOTALS

For England in England: 126 at Birmingham 1999
in New Zealand: 64 at Wellington 1977-78

For New Zealand in England: 47 at Lord's 1958
in New Zealand: 26 at Auckland 1954-55

INDIVIDUAL HUNDREDS

For England (83)

G. O. B. Allen (1)
122† Lord's 1931
L. E. G. Ames (2)
137† Lord's 1931
103 Christchurch . 1932-33
D. L. Amiss (2)
138*† Nottingham . 1973
164* Christchurch . 1974-75
M. A. Atherton (4)
151† Nottingham . 1990
101 Nottingham . 1994
111 Manchester . . 1994
118 Christchurch . 1996-97

T. E. Bailey (1)
134* Christchurch . 1950-51
K. F. Barrington (3)
126† Auckland . . . 1962-63
137 Birmingham . 1965
163 Leeds 1965
I. T. Botham (3)
103 Christchurch . 1977-78
103 Nottingham . 1983
138 Wellington . . 1983-84
E. H. Bowley (1)
109 Auckland . . . 1929-30

G. Boycott (2)
115 Leeds 1973
131 Nottingham . 1978
B. C. Broad (1)
114† Christchurch . 1987-88
D. C. S. Compton (2)
114 Leeds 1949
116 Lord's 1949
M. C. Cowdrey (2)
128* Wellington . . 1962-63
119 Lord's 1965
M. H. Denness (1)
181 Auckland . . . 1974-75

E. R. Dexter (1)
141 Christchurch. 1958-59
B. L. D'Oliveira (1)
100 Christchurch. 1970-71
K. S. Duleepsinhji (2)
117 Auckland... 1929-30
109 The Oval... 1931
J. H. Edrich (3)
310*† Leeds..... 1965
115 Lord's..... 1969
155 Nottingham . 1969
W. J. Edrich (1)
100 The Oval... 1949
K. W. R. Fletcher (2)
178 Lord's..... 1973
216 Auckland... 1974-75
G. Fowler (1)
105† The Oval... 1983
M. W. Gatting (1)
121 The Oval... 1986
G. A. Gooch (4)
183 Lord's..... 1986
154 Birmingham. 1990
114 Auckland... 1991-92
210 Nottingham . 1994
D. I. Gower (4)
111† The Oval... 1978
112* Leeds..... 1983
108 Lord's..... 1983
131 The Oval... 1986

A. W. Greig (1)
139† Nottingham . 1973
W. R. Hammond (4)
100* The Oval... 1931
227 Christchurch. 1932-33
336* Auckland... 1932-33
140 Lord's..... 1937
J. Hardstaff jun. (2)
114† Lord's..... 1937
103 The Oval... 1937
L. Hutton (3)
100 Manchester.. 1937
101 Leeds..... 1949
206 The Oval... 1949
B. R. Knight (1)
125† Auckland... 1962-63
A. P. E. Knott (1)
101 Auckland... 1970-71
A. J. Lamb (3)
102*† The Oval... 1983
137* Nottingham . 1983
142 Wellington.. 1991-92
G. B. Legge (1)
196 Auckland... 1929-30
P. B. H. May (3)
113* Leeds..... 1958
101 Manchester.. 1958
124* Auckland... 1958-59
C. A. Milton (1)
104*† Leeds..... 1958

P. H. Parfitt (1)
131*† Auckland... 1962-63
C. T. Radley (1)
158 Auckland... 1977-78
D. W. Randall (2)
164 Wellington.. 1983-84
104 Auckland... 1983-84
P. E. Richardson (1)
100† Birmingham. 1958
J. D. Robertson (1)
121† Lord's..... 1949
P. J. Sharpe (1)
111 Nottingham . 1969
R. T. Simpson (1)
103† Manchester.. 1949
A. J. Stewart (4)
148 Christchurch. 1991-92
107 Wellington.. 1991-92
119 Lord's..... 1994
173 Auckland... 1996-97
H. Sutcliffe (2)
117† The Oval... 1931
109* Manchester.. 1931
C. J. Tavaré (1)
109† The Oval... 1983
G. P. Thorpe (2)
119† Auckland... 1996-97
108 Wellington.. 1996-97
C. Washbrook (1)
103* Leeds..... 1949

For New Zealand (43)

N. J. Astle (2)
102*† Auckland... 1996-97
101 Manchester.. 1999
J. G. Bracewell (1)
110 Nottingham . 1986
M. G. Burgess (2)
104 Auckland... 1970-71
105 Lord's..... 1973
J. V. Coney (1)
174* Wellington.. 1983-84
B. E. Congdon (3)
104 Christchurch. 1965-66
176 Nottingham . 1973
175 Lord's..... 1973
J. J. Crowe (1)
128 Auckland... 1983-84
M. D. Crowe (5)
100 Wellington.. 1983-84
106 Lord's..... 1986
143 Wellington.. 1987-88
142 Lord's..... 1994
115 Manchester.. 1994
C. S. Dempster (2)
136 Wellington.. 1929-30
120 Lord's..... 1931

M. P. Donnelly (1)
206 Lord's..... 1949
S. P. Fleming (1)
129 Auckland... 1996-97
T. J. Franklin (1)
101 Lord's..... 1990
M. J. Greatbatch (1)
107*† Auckland... 1987-88
W. A. Hadlee (1)
116 Christchurch. 1946-47
M. J. Horne (1)
100 Lord's..... 1999
G. P. Howarth (3)
122 } Auckland... 1977-78
102 }
123 Lord's..... 1978
A. H. Jones (1)
143 Wellington.. 1991-92
C. D. McMillan (1)
107* Manchester.. 1999
J. E. Mills (1)
117† Wellington.. 1929-30

M. L. Page (1)
104 Lord's..... 1931
J. M. Parker (1)
121 Auckland... 1974-75
V. Pollard (2)
116 Nottingham . 1973
105* Lord's..... 1973
J. R. Reid (1)
100 Christchurch. 1962-63
K. R. Rutherford (1)
107* Wellington.. 1987-88
B. W. Sinclair (1)
114 Auckland... 1965-66
I. D. S. Smith (1)
113* Auckland... 1983-84
B. Sutcliffe (2)
101 Manchester.. 1949
116 Christchurch. 1950-51
J. G. Wright (4)
130 Auckland... 1983-84
119 The Oval... 1986
103 Auckland... 1987-88
116 Wellington.. 1991-92

† *Signifies hundred on first appearance in England–New Zealand Tests.*

RECORD PARTNERSHIPS FOR EACH WICKET

For England

223	for 1st	G. Fowler and C. J. Tavaré at The Oval	1983
369	for 2nd	J. H. Edrich and K. F. Barrington at Leeds	1965
245	for 3rd	J. Hardstaff jun. and W. R. Hammond at Lord's	1937
266	for 4th	M. H. Denness and K. W. R. Fletcher at Auckland	1974-75
242	for 5th	W. R. Hammond and L. E. G. Ames at Christchurch	1932-33
240	for 6th†	P. H. Parfitt and B. R. Knight at Auckland	1962-63
149	for 7th	A. P. E. Knott and P. Lever at Auckland	1970-71
246	for 8th†	L. E. G. Ames and G. O. B. Allen at Lord's	1931
163*	for 9th†	M. C. Cowdrey and A. C. Smith at Wellington	1962-63
59	for 10th	A. P. E. Knott and N. Gifford at Nottingham	1973

For New Zealand

276	for 1st	C. S. Dempster and J. E. Mills at Wellington	1929-30
241	for 2nd†	J. G. Wright and A. H. Jones at Wellington	1991-92
210	for 3rd	B. A. Edgar and M. D. Crowe at Lord's	1986
155	for 4th	M. D. Crowe and M. J. Greatbatch at Wellington	1987-88
180	for 5th	M. D. Crowe and S. A. Thomson at Lord's	1994
141	for 6th	M. D. Crowe and A. C. Parore at Manchester	1994
117	for 7th	D. N. Patel and C. L. Cairns at Christchurch	1991-92
104	for 8th	D. A. R. Moloney and A. W. Roberts at Lord's	1937
118	for 9th	J. V. Coney and B. L. Cairns at Wellington	1983-84
106*	for 10th	N. J. Astle and D. K. Morrison at Auckland	1996-97

† *Denotes record partnership against all countries.*

TEN WICKETS OR MORE IN A MATCH

For England (8)

11-140 (6-101, 5-39)	I. T. Botham, Lord's	1978
10-149 (5-98, 5-51)	A. W. Greig, Auckland	1974-75
11-65 (4-14, 7-51)	G. A. R. Lock, Leeds	1958
11-84 (5-31, 6-53)	G. A. R. Lock, Christchurch	1958-59
11-147 (4-100, 7-47)†	P. C. R. Tufnell, Christchurch	1991-92
11-70 (4-38, 7-32)†	D. L. Underwood, Lord's	1969
12-101 (6-41, 6-60)	D. L. Underwood, The Oval	1969
12-97 (6-12, 6-85)	D. L. Underwood, Christchurch	1970-71

For New Zealand (5)

10-144 (7-74, 3-70)	B. L. Cairns, Leeds	1983
10-140 (4-73, 6-67)	J. Cowie, Manchester	1937
10-100 (4-74, 6-26)	R. J. Hadlee, Wellington	1977-78
10-140 (6-80, 4-60)	R. J. Hadlee, Nottingham	1986
11-169 (6-76, 5-93)	D. J. Nash, Lord's	1994

† *Signifies ten wickets or more on first appearance in England–New Zealand Tests.*

Note: D. L. Underwood took 12 wickets in successive matches against New Zealand in 1969 and 1970-71.

ENGLAND v INDIA

	Captains					
Season	*England*	*India*	*T*	*E*	*I*	*D*
1932	D. R. Jardine	C. K. Nayudu	1	1	0	0
1933-34	D. R. Jardine	C. K. Nayudu	3	2	0	1
1936	G. O. B. Allen	Maharaj of Vizianagram	3	2	0	1
1946	W. R. Hammond	Nawab of Pataudi sen.	3	1	0	2
1951-52	N. D. Howard[1]	V. S. Hazare	5	1	1	3
1952	L. Hutton	V. S. Hazare	4	3	0	1
1959	P. B. H. May[2]	D. K. Gaekwad[3]	5	5	0	0
1961-62	E. R. Dexter	N. J. Contractor	5	0	2	3
1963-64	M. J. K. Smith	Nawab of Pataudi jun.	5	0	0	5
1967	D. B. Close	Nawab of Pataudi jun.	3	3	0	0
1971	R. Illingworth	A. L. Wadekar	3	0	1	2
1972-73	A. R. Lewis	A. L. Wadekar	5	1	2	2
1974	M. H. Denness	A. L. Wadekar	3	3	0	0
1976-77	A. W. Greig	B. S. Bedi	5	3	1	1
1979	J. M. Brearley	S. Venkataraghavan	4	1	0	3
1979-80	J. M. Brearley	G. R. Viswanath	1	1	0	0
1981-82	K. W. R. Fletcher	S. M. Gavaskar	6	0	1	5
1982	R. G. D. Willis	S. M. Gavaskar	3	1	0	2
1984-85	D. I. Gower	S. M. Gavaskar	5	2	1	2
1986	M. W. Gatting[4]	Kapil Dev	3	0	2	1
1990	G. A. Gooch	M. Azharuddin	3	1	0	2
1992-93	G. A. Gooch[5]	M. Azharuddin	3	0	3	0
1996	M. A. Atherton	M. Azharuddin	3	1	0	2
	In England		41	22	3	16
	In India		43	10	11	22
	Totals.		84	32	14	38

Notes: The 1932 Indian touring team was captained by the Maharaj of Porbandar but he did not play in the Test match.

The following deputised for the official touring captain or were appointed by the home authority for only a minor proportion of the series:

[1]D. B. Carr (Fifth). [2]M. C. Cowdrey (Fourth and Fifth). [3]Pankaj Roy (Second). [4]D. I. Gower (First). [5]A. J. Stewart (Second).

HIGHEST INNINGS TOTALS

For England in England: 653-4 dec. at Lord's. 1990
in India: 652-7 dec. at Madras 1984-85

For India in England: 606-9 dec. at The Oval. 1990
in India: 591 at Bombay 1992-93

LOWEST INNINGS TOTALS

For England in England: 101 at The Oval 1971
in India: 102 at Bombay 1981-82

For India in England: 42 at Lord's 1974
in India: 83 at Madras 1976-77

INDIVIDUAL HUNDREDS

For England (76)

D. L. Amiss (2)
188 Lord's 1974
179 Delhi 1976-77
M. A. Atherton (2)
131 Manchester . . 1990
160 Nottingham . 1996
K. F. Barrington (3)
151* Bombay 1961-62
172 Kanpur 1961-62
113* Delhi 1961-62
I. T. Botham (5)
137 Leeds 1979
114 Bombay 1979-80
142 Kanpur 1981-82
128 Manchester . . 1982
208 The Oval . . . 1982
G. Boycott (4)
246*† Leeds 1967
155 Birmingham . 1979
125 The Oval . . . 1979
105 Delhi 1981-82
M. C. Cowdrey (3)
160 Leeds 1959
107 Calcutta 1963-64
151 Delhi 1963-64
M. H. Denness (2)
118 Lord's 1974
100 Birmingham . 1974
E. R. Dexter (1)
126* Kanpur 1961-62
B. L. D'Oliveira (1)
109† Leeds 1967
J. H. Edrich (1)
100* Manchester . . 1974
T. G. Evans (1)
104 Lord's 1952
K. W. R. Fletcher (2)
113 Bombay 1972-73
123* Manchester . . 1974
G. Fowler (1)
201 Madras 1984-85
M. W. Gatting (3)
136 Bombay 1984-85
207 Madras 1984-85
183* Birmingham . 1986
G. A. Gooch (5)
127 Madras 1981-82
114 Lord's 1986
333 } Lord's 1990
123 }
116 Manchester . . 1990
D. I. Gower (2)
200*† Birmingham . 1979
157* The Oval . . . 1990
T. W. Graveney (2)
175† Bombay 1951-52
151 Lord's 1967
A. W. Greig (3)
148 Bombay 1972-73
106 Lord's 1974
103 Calcutta 1976-77
W. R. Hammond (2)
167 Manchester . . 1936
217 The Oval . . . 1936
J. Hardstaff jun. (1)
205* Lord's 1946
G. A. Hick (1)
178 Bombay 1992-93
N. Hussain (2)
128† Birmingham . 1996
107* Nottingham . 1996
L. Hutton (2)
150 Lord's 1952
104 Manchester . . 1952
R. Illingworth (1)
107 Manchester . . 1971
B. R. Knight (1)
127 Kanpur 1963-64
A. J. Lamb (3)
107 The Oval . . . 1982
139 Lord's 1990
109 Manchester . . 1990
A. R. Lewis (1)
125 Kanpur 1972-73
C. C. Lewis (1)
117 Madras 1992-93
D. Lloyd (1)
214* Birmingham . 1974
B. W. Luckhurst (1)
101 Manchester . . 1971
P. B. H. May (1)
106 Nottingham . 1959
P. H. Parfitt (1)
121 Kanpur 1963-64
G. Pullar (2)
131 Manchester . . 1959
119 Kanpur 1961-62
D. W. Randall (1)
126 Lord's 1982
R. T. Robinson (1)
160 Delhi 1984-85
R. C. Russell (1)
124 Lord's 1996
D. S. Sheppard (1)
119 The Oval . . . 1952
M. J. K. Smith (1)
100† Manchester . . 1959
R. A. Smith (2)
100*† Lord's 1990
121* Manchester . . 1990
C. J. Tavaré (1)
149 Delhi 1981-82
B. H. Valentine (1)
136† Bombay 1933-34
C. F. Walters (1)
102 Madras 1933-34
A. J. Watkins (1)
137*† Delhi 1951-52
T. S. Worthington (1)
128 The Oval . . . 1936

For India (64)

L. Amarnath (1)
118† Bombay 1933-34
M. Azharuddin (6)
110† Calcutta 1984-85
105 Madras 1984-85
122 Kanpur 1984-85
121 Lord's 1990
179 Manchester . . 1990
182 Calcutta 1992-93
A. A. Baig (1)
112† Manchester . . 1959
F. M. Engineer (1)
121 Bombay 1972-73
S. C. Ganguly (2)
131† Lord's 1996
136 Nottingham . 1996
S. M. Gavaskar (4)
101 Manchester . . 1974
108 Bombay 1976-77
221 The Oval . . . 1979
172 Bangalore . . 1981-82
Hanumant Singh (1)
105† Delhi 1963-64
V. S. Hazare (2)
164* Delhi 1951-52
155 Bombay 1951-52
M. L. Jaisimha (2)
127 Delhi 1961-62
129 Calcutta 1963-64
V. G. Kambli (1)
224 Bombay 1992-93
Kapil Dev (2)
116 Kanpur 1981-82
110 The Oval . . . 1990
S. M. H. Kirmani (1)
102 Bombay 1984-85
B. K. Kunderan (2)
192 Madras 1963-64
100 Delhi 1963-64

V. L. Manjrekar (3)
133 Leeds 1952
189* Delhi 1961-62
108 Madras 1963-64
V. Mankad (1)
184 Lord's 1952
V. M. Merchant (3)
114 Manchester. . 1936
128 The Oval . . . 1946
154 Delhi 1951-52
Mushtaq Ali (1)
112 Manchester. . 1936
R. G. Nadkarni (1)
122* Kanpur 1963-64
Nawab of Pataudi jun. (3)
103 Madras 1961-62
203* Delhi 1963-64
148 Leeds 1967

S. M. Patil (1)
129* Manchester. . 1982
D. G. Phadkar (1)
115 Calcutta. . . . 1951-52
Pankaj Roy (2)
140 Bombay. . . . 1951-52
111 Madras 1951-52
R. J. Shastri (4)
142 Bombay. . . . 1984-85
111 Calcutta. . . . 1984-85
100 Lord's 1990
187 The Oval . . . 1990
N. S. Sidhu (1)
106 Madras 1992-93
S. R. Tendulkar (4)
119* Manchester. . 1990
165 Madras 1992-93
122 Birmingham . 1996
177 Nottingham . 1996

P. R. Umrigar (3)
130* Madras 1951-52
118 Manchester. . 1959
147* Kanpur 1961-62
D. B. Vengsarkar (5)
103 Lord's 1979
157 Lord's 1982
137 Kanpur 1984-85
126* Lord's 1986
102* Leeds 1986
G. R. Viswanath (4)
113 Bombay. . . . 1972-73
113 Lord's 1979
107 Delhi 1981-82
222 Madras 1981-82
Yashpal Sharma (1)
140 Madras 1981-82

† *Signifies hundred on first appearance in England–India Tests.*

Notes: G. A. Gooch's match aggregate of 456 (333 and 123) for England at Lord's in 1990 is the record in Test matches and provides the only instance of a batsman scoring a triple-hundred and a hundred in the same first-class match. His 333 is the highest innings in any match at Lord's.

M. Azharuddin scored hundreds in each of his first three Tests.

RECORD PARTNERSHIPS FOR EACH WICKET

For England

225 for 1st	G. A. Gooch and M. A. Atherton at Manchester	1990
241 for 2nd	G. Fowler and M. W. Gatting at Madras	1984-85
308 for 3rd	G. A. Gooch and A. J. Lamb at Lord's	1990
266 for 4th	W. R. Hammond and T. S. Worthington at The Oval	1936
254 for 5th†	K. W. R. Fletcher and A. W. Greig at Bombay	1972-73
171 for 6th	I. T. Botham and R. W. Taylor at Bombay	1979-80
125 for 7th	D. W. Randall and P. H. Edmonds at Lord's	1982
168 for 8th	R. Illingworth and P. Lever at Manchester	1971
83 for 9th	K. W. R. Fletcher and N. Gifford at Madras	1972-73
70 for 10th	P. J. W. Allott and R. G. D. Willis at Lord's	1982

For India

213 for 1st	S. M. Gavaskar and C. P. S. Chauhan at The Oval	1979
192 for 2nd	F. M. Engineer and A. L. Wadekar at Bombay	1972-73
316 for 3rd†‡	G. R. Viswanath and Yashpal Sharma at Madras	1981-82
222 for 4th	V. S. Hazare and V. L. Manjrekar at Leeds	1952
214 for 5th	M. Azharuddin and R. J. Shastri at Calcutta	1984-85
130 for 6th	S. M. H. Kirmani and Kapil Dev at The Oval	1982
235 for 7th†	R. J. Shastri and S. M. H. Kirmani at Bombay	1984-85
128 for 8th	R. J. Shastri and S. M. H. Kirmani at Delhi	1981-82
104 for 9th	R. J. Shastri and Madan Lal at Delhi	1981-82
51 for 10th	R. G. Nadkarni and B. S. Chandrasekhar at Calcutta	1963-64
	S. M. H. Kirmani and Chetan Sharma at Madras	1984-85

† *Denotes record partnership against all countries.*
‡ *415 runs were added between the fall of the 2nd and 3rd wickets: D. B. Vengsarkar retired hurt when he and Viswanath had added 99 runs.*

TEN WICKETS OR MORE IN A MATCH

For England (7)

10-78 (5-35, 5-43)†	G. O. B. Allen, Lord's	1936
11-145 (7-49, 4-96)†	A. V. Bedser, Lord's	1946
11-93 (4-41, 7-52)	A. V. Bedser, Manchester	1946
13-106 (6-58, 7-48)	I. T. Botham, Bombay	1979-80
11-163 (6-104, 5-59)†	N. A. Foster, Madras	1984-85
10-70 (7-46, 3-24)†	J. K. Lever, Delhi	1976-77
11-153 (7-49, 4-104)	H. Verity, Madras	1933-34

For India (4)

10-177 (6-105, 4-72)	S. A. Durani, Madras	1961-62
12-108 (8-55, 4-53)	V. Mankad, Madras	1951-52
10-188 (4-130, 6-58)	Chetan Sharma, Birmingham	1986
12-181 (6-64, 6-117)†	L. Sivaramakrishnan, Bombay	1984-85

† *Signifies ten wickets or more on first appearance in England–India Tests.*

Note: A. V. Bedser took 11 wickets in a match in each of the first two Tests of his career.

ENGLAND v PAKISTAN

	Captains					
Season	*England*	*Pakistan*	*T*	*E*	*P*	*D*
1954	L. Hutton[1]	A. H. Kardar	4	1	1	2
1961-62	E. R. Dexter	Imtiaz Ahmed	3	1	0	2
1962	E. R. Dexter[2]	Javed Burki	5	4	0	1
1967	D. B. Close	Hanif Mohammad	3	2	0	1
1968-69	M. C. Cowdrey	Saeed Ahmed	3	0	0	3
1971	R. Illingworth	Intikhab Alam	3	1	0	2
1972-73	A. R. Lewis	Majid Khan	3	0	0	3
1974	M. H. Denness	Intikhab Alam	3	0	0	3
1977-78	J. M. Brearley[3]	Wasim Bari	3	0	0	3
1978	J. M. Brearley	Wasim Bari	3	2	0	1
1982	R. G. D. Willis[4]	Imran Khan	3	2	1	0
1983-84	R. G. D. Willis[5]	Zaheer Abbas	3	0	1	2
1987	M. W. Gatting	Imran Khan	5	0	1	4
1987-88	M. W. Gatting	Javed Miandad	3	0	1	2
1992	G. A. Gooch	Javed Miandad	5	1	2	2
1996	M. A. Atherton	Wasim Akram	3	0	2	1
2000-01	N. Hussain	Moin Khan	3	1	0	2
2001	N. Hussain[6]	Waqar Younis	2	1	1	0
	In England		39	14	8	17
	In Pakistan		21	2	2	17
	Totals		60	16	10	34

Notes: The following deputised for the official touring captain or were appointed by the home authority for only a minor proportion of the series:

[1]D. S. Sheppard (Second and Third). [2]M. C. Cowdrey (Third). [3]G. Boycott (Third). [4]D. I. Gower (Second). [5]D. I. Gower (Second and Third). [6]A. J. Stewart (Second).

HIGHEST INNINGS TOTALS

For England in England:	558-6 dec. at Nottingham	1954
in Pakistan:	546-8 dec. at Faisalabad	1983-84
For Pakistan in England:	708 at The Oval	1987
in Pakistan:	569-9 dec. at Hyderabad	1972-73

LOWEST INNINGS TOTALS

For England in England: 130 at The Oval . . . 1954
in Pakistan: 130 at Lahore . . . 1987-88

For Pakistan in England: 87 at Lord's . . . 1954
in Pakistan: 158 at Karachi . . . 2000-01

INDIVIDUAL HUNDREDS

For England (52)

D. L. Amiss (3)
112 Lahore 1972-73
158 Hyderabad . . 1972-73
183 The Oval . . . 1974
M. A. Atherton (1)
125 Karachi 2000-01
C. W. J. Athey (1)
123 Lord's 1987
K. F. Barrington (4)
139† Lahore 1961-62
148 Lord's 1967
109* Nottingham . 1967
142 The Oval . . . 1967
I. T. Botham (2)
100† Birmingham . 1978
108 Lord's 1978
G. Boycott (3)
121* Lord's 1971
112 Leeds 1971
100* Hyderabad . . 1977-78
B. C. Broad (1)
116 Faisalabad . . 1987-88
D. C. S. Compton (1)
278 Nottingham . 1954
M. C. Cowdrey (3)
159† Birmingham . 1962
182 The Oval . . . 1962
100 Lahore 1968-69
J. P. Crawley (1)
106 The Oval . . . 1996
E. R. Dexter (2)
205 Karachi 1961-62
172 The Oval . . . 1962
B. L. D'Oliveira (1)
114* Dacca 1968-69
K. W. R. Fletcher (1)
122 The Oval . . . 1974
M. W. Gatting (2)
124 Birmingham . 1987
150* The Oval . . . 1987
G. A. Gooch (1)
135 Leeds 1992
D. I. Gower (2)
152 Faisalabad . . 1983-84
173* Lahore 1983-84
T. W. Graveney (3)
153 Lord's 1962
114 Nottingham . 1962
105 Karachi 1968-69
N. V. Knight (1)
113 Leeds 1996
A. P. E. Knott (1)
116 Birmingham . 1971
B. W. Luckhurst (1)
108*† Birmingham . 1971
C. Milburn (1)
139 Karachi 1968-69
P. H. Parfitt (4)
111 Karachi 1961-62
101* Birmingham . 1962
119 Leeds 1962
101* Nottingham . 1962
G. Pullar (1)
165 Dacca 1961-62
C. T. Radley (1)
106† Birmingham . 1978
D. W. Randall (1)
105 Birmingham . 1982
R. T. Robinson (1)
166† Manchester . . 1987
R. T. Simpson (1)
101 Nottingham . 1954
R. A. Smith (1)
127† Birmingham . 1992
A. J. Stewart (2)
190† Birmingham . 1992
170 Leeds 1996
G. P. Thorpe (2)
118 Lahore 2000-01
138 Manchester . . 2001
M. E. Trescothick (1)
117 Manchester . . 2001
M. P. Vaughan (1)
120 Manchester . . 2001

For Pakistan (43)

Aamir Sohail (1)
205 Manchester . . 1992
Abdur Razzaq (1)
100* Faisalabad . . 2000-01
Alim-ud-Din (1)
109 Karachi 1961-62
Asif Iqbal (3)
146 The Oval . . . 1967
104* Birmingham . 1971
102 Lahore 1972-73
Hanif Mohammad (3)
111 } Dacca 1961-62
104 }
187* Lord's 1967
Haroon Rashid (2)
122† Lahore 1977-78
108 Hyderabad . . 1977-78
Ijaz Ahmed, sen. (1)
141 Leeds 1996
Imran Khan (1)
118 The Oval . . . 1987
Intikhab Alam (1)
138 Hyderabad . . 1972-73
Inzamam-ul-Haq (3)
148 Lord's 1996
142 Karachi 2000-01
114 Manchester . . 2001
Javed Burki (3)
138† Lahore 1961-62
140 Dacca 1961-62
101 Lord's 1962
Javed Miandad (2)
260 The Oval . . . 1987
153* Birmingham . 1992
Mohsin Khan (2)
200 Lord's 1982
104 Lahore 1983-84
Moin Khan (1)
105 Leeds 1996
Mudassar Nazar (3)
114† Lahore 1977-78

124	Birmingham.	1987
120	Lahore	1987-88
Mushtaq Mohammad (3)		
100*	Nottingham .	1962
100	Birmingham.	1971
157	Hyderabad ..	1972-73
Nasim-ul Ghani (1)		
101	Lord's.....	1962
Sadiq Mohammad (1)		
119	Lahore	1972-73
Saeed Anwar (1)		
176	The Oval...	1996
Salim Malik (4)		
116	Faisalabad ..	1983-84
102	The Oval...	1987
165	Birmingham.	1992
100*	The Oval...	1996
Wasim Raja (1)		
112	Faisalabad ..	1983-84
Yousuf Youhana (2)		
124†	Lahore	2000-01
117	Karachi....	2000-01
Zaheer Abbas (2)		
274†	Birmingham.	1971
240	The Oval...	1974

† *Signifies hundred on first appearance in England–Pakistan Tests.*

Note: Three batsmen – Majid Khan, Mushtaq Mohammad and D. L. Amiss – were dismissed for 99 at Karachi, 1972-73: the only instance in Test matches.

RECORD PARTNERSHIPS FOR EACH WICKET

For England

198	for 1st	G. Pullar and R. W. Barber at Dacca	1961-62
248	for 2nd	M. C. Cowdrey and E. R. Dexter at The Oval	1962
267	for 3rd	M. P. Vaughan and G. P. Thorpe at Manchester	2001
188	for 4th	E. R. Dexter and P. H. Parfitt at Karachi	1961-62
192	for 5th	D. C. S. Compton and T. E. Bailey at Nottingham	1954
166	for 6th	G. P. Thorpe and C. White at Lahore	2000-01
167	for 7th	D. I. Gower and V. J. Marks at Faisalabad	1983-84
99	for 8th	P. H. Parfitt and D. A. Allen at Leeds	1962
76	for 9th	T. W. Graveney and F. S. Trueman at Lord's	1962
79	for 10th	R. W. Taylor and R. G. D. Willis at Birmingham	1982

For Pakistan

173	for 1st	Mohsin Khan and Shoaib Mohammad at Lahore	1983-84
291	for 2nd†	Zaheer Abbas and Mushtaq Mohammad at Birmingham	1971
180	for 3rd	Mudassar Nazar and Haroon Rashid at Lahore	1977-78
322	for 4th	Javed Miandad and Salim Malik at Birmingham	1992
197	for 5th	Javed Burki and Nasim-ul-Ghani at Lord's	1962
145	for 6th	Mushtaq Mohammad and Intikhab Alam at Hyderabad	1972-73
112	for 7th	Asif Mujtaba and Moin Khan at Leeds	1996
130	for 8th	Hanif Mohammad and Asif Iqbal at Lord's	1967
190	for 9th†	Asif Iqbal and Intikhab Alam at The Oval	1967
62	for 10th	Sarfraz Nawaz and Asif Masood at Leeds	1974

† *Denotes record partnership against all countries.*

TEN WICKETS OR MORE IN A MATCH

For England (2)

11-83 (6-65, 5-18)†	N. G. B. Cook, Karachi	1983-84
13-71 (5-20, 8-51)	D. L. Underwood, Lord's	1974

For Pakistan (6)

10-194 (5-84, 5-110)	Abdul Qadir, Lahore	1983-84
10-211 (7-96, 3-115)	Abdul Qadir, The Oval	1987
13-101 (9-56, 4-45)	Abdul Qadir, Lahore	1987-88
10-186 (5-88, 5-98)	Abdul Qadir, Karachi	1987-88
12-99 (6-53, 6-46)	Fazal Mahmood, The Oval	1954
10-77 (3-37, 7-40)	Imran Khan, Leeds	1987

† *Signifies ten wickets or more on first appearance in England–Pakistan Tests.*

ENGLAND v SRI LANKA

Season	Captains England	Sri Lanka	T	E	SL	D
1981-82	K. W. R. Fletcher	B. Warnapura	1	1	0	0
1984	D. I. Gower	L. R. D. Mendis	1	0	0	1
1988	G. A. Gooch	R. S. Madugalle	1	1	0	0
1991	G. A. Gooch	P. A. de Silva	1	1	0	0
1992-93	A. J. Stewart	A. Ranatunga	1	0	1	0
1998	A. J. Stewart	A. Ranatunga	1	0	1	0
2000-01	N. Hussain	S. T. Jayasuriya	3	2	1	0
	In England		4	2	1	1
	In Sri Lanka		5	3	2	0
	Totals		9	5	3	1

HIGHEST INNINGS TOTALS

For England in England: 445 at The Oval 1998
in Sri Lanka: 387 at Kandy 2000-01

For Sri Lanka in England: 591 at The Oval 1998
in Sri Lanka: 470-5 dec. at Galle 2000-01

LOWEST INNINGS TOTALS

For England in England: 181 at The Oval 1998
in Sri Lanka: 189 at Galle 2000-01

For Sri Lanka in England: 194 at Lord's 1988
in Sri Lanka: 81 at Colombo (SSC) 2000-01

INDIVIDUAL HUNDREDS

For England (9)

J. P. Crawley (1)
156*† The Oval . . . 1998
G. A. Gooch (1)
174 Lord's 1991
G. A. Hick (1)
107 The Oval . . . 1998
N. Hussain (1)
109 Kandy 2000-01
A. J. Lamb (1)
107† Lord's 1984
R. A. Smith (1)
128 Colombo (SSC) 1992-93
A. J. Stewart (1)
113*† Lord's 1991
G. P. Thorpe (1)
113* Colombo (SSC) 2000-01
M. E. Trescothick (1)
122† Galle 2000-01

For Sri Lanka (8)

M. S. Atapattu (1)
201* Galle 2000-01
P. A. de Silva (2)
152 The Oval . . . 1998
106 Galle 2000-01
S. T. Jayasuriya (1)
213 The Oval . . . 1998
D. P. M. D. Jayawardene (1)
101 Kandy 2000-01
L. R. D. Mendis (1)
111 Lord's 1984
S. A. R. Silva (1)
102*† Lord's 1984
S. Wettimuny (1)
190 Lord's 1984

† Signifies hundred on first appearance in England–Sri Lanka Tests.

RECORD PARTNERSHIPS FOR EACH WICKET

For England

101 for 1st	M. A. Atherton and M. E. Trescothick at Galle	2000-01
139 for 2nd	G. A. Gooch and A. J. Stewart at Lord's	1991
167 for 3rd	N. Hussain and G. P. Thorpe at Kandy	2000-01
128 for 4th	G. A. Hick and M. R. Ramprakash at The Oval	1998
86 for 5th	G. P. Thorpe and M. P. Vaughan at Colombo (SSC)	2000-01
87 for 6th	A. J. Lamb and R. M. Ellison at Lord's	1984
	A. J. Stewart and C. White at Kandy	2000-01
63 for 7th	A. J. Stewart and R. C. Russell at Lord's	1991
28 for 8th	G. P. Thorpe and R. D. B. Croft at Colombo (SSC)	2000-01
53 for 9th	M. R. Ramprakash and D. Gough at The Oval	1998
89 for 10th	J. P. Crawley and A. R. C. Fraser at The Oval	1998

For Sri Lanka

99 for 1st	R. S. Mahanama and U. C. Hathurusinghe at Colombo (SSC)	1992-93
92 for 2nd	M. S. Atapattu and K. Sangakkara at Galle	2000-01
243 for 3rd†	S. T. Jayasuriya and P. A. de Silva at The Oval	1998
148 for 4th	S. Wettimuny and A. Ranatunga at Lord's	1984
150 for 5th†	S. Wettimuny and L. R. D. Mendis at Lord's	1984
138 for 6th	S. A. R. Silva and L. R. D. Mendis at Lord's	1984
93 for 7th	K. Sangakkara and H. D. P. K. Dharmasena at Kandy	2000-01
53 for 8th	H. D. P. K. Dharmasena and W. P. U. J. C. Vaas at Kandy	2000-01
83 for 9th†	H. P. Tillekeratne and M. Muralitharan at Colombo (SSC)	1992-93
64 for 10th	J. R. Ratnayeke and G. F. Labrooy at Lord's	1988

† *Denotes record partnership against all countries.*

TEN WICKETS OR MORE IN A MATCH

For Sri Lanka (1)

16-220 (7-155, 9-65)	M. Muralitharan at The Oval	1998

Note: The best match figures by an England bowler are 8-95 (5-28, 3-67) by D. L. Underwood at Colombo (PSS), 1981-82.

ENGLAND v ZIMBABWE

	Captains					
Season	*England*	*Zimbabwe*	*T*	*E*	*Z*	*D*
1996-97	M. A. Atherton	A. D. R. Campbell	2	0	0	2
2000	N. Hussain	A. Flower	2	1	0	1
	In England		2	1	0	1
	In Zimbabwe		2	0	0	2
	Totals		4	1	0	3

HIGHEST INNINGS TOTALS

For England in England: 415 at Lord's	2000
in Zimbabwe: 406 at Bulawayo	1996-97
For Zimbabwe in England: 285-4 dec. at Nottingham	2000
in Zimbabwe: 376 at Bulawayo	1996-97

LOWEST INNINGS TOTALS

For England in England: 147 at Nottingham 2000
in Zimbabwe 156 at Harare 1996-97

For Zimbabwe in England: 83 at Lord's 2000
in Zimbabwe: 215 at Harare 1996-97

INDIVIDUAL HUNDREDS

For England (6)

M. A. Atherton (1)
136 Nottingham . 2000
J. P. Crawley (1)
112† Bulawayo . . . 1996-97

G. Hick (1)
101† Lord's 2000
N. Hussain (1)
113† Bulawayo . . . 1996-97

A. J. Stewart (2)
101* Harare 1996-97
124* Lord's 2000

For Zimbabwe (2)

A. Flower (1)
112† Bulawayo . . . 1996-97

M. W. Goodwin (1)
148* Nottingham . 2000

† *Signifies hundred on first appearance in England–Zimbabwe Tests.*

HUNDRED PARTNERSHIPS

For England

121	for 1st	M. A. Atherton and M. R. Ramprakash at Nottingham	2000
137	for 2nd	N. V. Knight and A. J. Stewart at Bulawayo	1996-97
149	for 4th	G. A. Hick and A. J. Stewart at Lord's	2000
106*	for 4th	A. J. Stewart and G. P. Thorpe at Harare	1996-97
148	for 5th	N. Hussain and J. P. Crawley at Bulawayo	1996-97
114	for 5th	A. J. Stewart and N. V. Knight at Lord's	2000

For Zimbabwe

127	for 2nd	G. W. Flower and A. D. R. Campbell at Bulawayo	1996-97
129	for 3rd	M. W. Goodwin and N. C. Johnson at Nottingham	2000
122	for 4th	M. W. Goodwin and A. Flower at Nottingham	2000

BEST MATCH BOWLING ANALYSES

For England

7-42 (5-15, 2-27)†	E. S. H. Giddins, Lord's	2000

For Zimbabwe

7-186 (5-123, 2-63)†	P. A. Strang, Bulawayo	1996-97

† *Signifies on first appearance in England–Zimbabwe Tests.*

AUSTRALIA v SOUTH AFRICA

Season	Captains: Australia	Captains: South Africa	*T*	*A*	*SA*	*D*
1902-03*S*	J. Darling	H. M. Taberer[1]	3	2	0	1
1910-11*A*	C. Hill	P. W. Sherwell	5	4	1	0
1912*E*	S. E. Gregory	F. Mitchell[2]	3	2	0	1
1921-22*S*	H. L. Collins	H. W. Taylor	3	1	0	2
1931-32*A*	W. M. Woodfull	H. B. Cameron	5	5	0	0
1935-36*S*	V. Y. Richardson	H. F. Wade	5	4	0	1
1949-50*S*	A. L. Hassett	A. D. Nourse	5	4	0	1
1952-53*A*	A. L. Hassett	J. E. Cheetham	5	2	2	1
1957-58*S*	I. D. Craig	C. B. van Ryneveld[3]	5	3	0	2
1963-64*A*	R. B. Simpson[4]	T. L. Goddard	5	1	1	3
1966-67*S*	R. B. Simpson	P. L. van der Merwe	5	1	3	1
1969-70*S*	W. M. Lawry	A. Bacher	4	0	4	0
1993-94*A*	A. R. Border	K. C. Wessels[5]	3	1	1	1
1993-94*S*	A. R. Border	K. C. Wessels	3	1	1	1
1996-97*S*	M. A. Taylor	W. J. Cronje	3	2	1	0
1997-98*A*	M. A. Taylor	W. J. Cronje	3	1	0	2
	In South Africa		36	18	9	9
	In Australia		26	14	5	7
	In England		3	2	0	1
	Totals		65	34	14	17

S Played in South Africa. A Played in Australia. E Played in England.

Notes: The following deputised for the official touring captain or were appointed by the home authority for only a minor proportion of the series:
[1]J. H. Anderson (Second), E. A. Halliwell (Third). [2]L. J. Tancred (Third). [3]D. J. McGlew (First). [4]R. Benaud (First). [5]W. J. Cronje (Third).

HIGHEST INNINGS TOTALS

For Australia in Australia: 578 at Melbourne 1910-11
in South Africa: 628-8 dec. at Johannesburg 1996-97

For South Africa in Australia: 595 at Adelaide 1963-64
in South Africa: 622-9 dec. at Durban 1969-70

LOWEST INNINGS TOTALS

For Australia in Australia: 111 at Sydney 1993-94
in South Africa: 75 at Durban 1949-50

For South Africa in Australia: 36† at Melbourne 1931-32
in South Africa: 85‡ at Johannesburg 1902-03
85‡ at Cape Town 1902-03

† *Scored 45 in the second innings giving the smallest aggregate of 81 (12 extras) in Test cricket.*
‡ *In successive innings.*

INDIVIDUAL HUNDREDS

For Australia (65)

W. W. Armstrong (2)
159*‡ Johannesburg 1902-03
132 Melbourne 1910-11
W. Bardsley (3)
132† Sydney 1910-11
121 Manchester 1912
164 Lord's 1912
R. Benaud (2)
122 Johannesburg 1957-58
100 Johannesburg 1957-58
G. S. Blewett (1)
214† Johannesburg 1996-97
B. C. Booth (2)
169† Brisbane 1963-64
102* Sydney 1963-64
D. G. Bradman (4)
226† Brisbane 1931-32
112 Sydney 1931-32
167 Melbourne 1931-32
299* Adelaide 1931-32
W. A. Brown (1)
121 Cape Town 1935-36
J. W. Burke (1)
189 Cape Town 1957-58
A. G. Chipperfield (1)
109† Durban 1935-36
H. L. Collins (1)
203 Johannesburg 1921-22
J. H. Fingleton (3)
112 Cape Town 1935-36
108 Johannesburg 1935-36
118 Durban 1935-36
J. M. Gregory (1)
119 Johannesburg 1921-22
R. N. Harvey (8)
178 Cape Town 1949-50
151* Durban 1949-50
100 Johannesburg 1949-50
116 Port Elizabeth 1949-50
109 Brisbane 1952-53
190 Sydney 1952-53
116 Adelaide 1952-53
205 Melbourne 1952-53
A. L. Hassett (3)
112† Johannesburg 1949-50
167 Port Elizabeth 1949-50
163 Adelaide 1952-53
C. Hill (3)
142† Johannesburg 1902-03
191 Sydney 1910-11
100 Melbourne 1910-11
C. Kelleway (2)
114 Manchester 1912
102 Lord's 1912
W. M. Lawry (1)
157 Melbourne 1963-64
S. J. E. Loxton (1)
101† Johannesburg 1949-50
C. G. Macartney (2)
137 Sydney 1910-11
116 Durban 1921-22
S. J. McCabe (2)
149 Durban 1935-36
189* Johannesburg 1935-36
C. C. McDonald (1)
154 Adelaide 1952-53
J. Moroney (2)
118 } Johannesburg 1949-50
101* }
A. R. Morris (2)
111 Johannesburg 1949-50
157 Port Elizabeth 1949-50
R. T. Ponting (1)
105† Melbourne 1997-98
K. E. Rigg (1)
127† Sydney 1931-32
J. Ryder (1)
142 Cape Town 1921-22
R. B. Simpson (1)
153 Cape Town 1966-67
K. R. Stackpole (1)
134 Cape Town 1966-67
M. A. Taylor (2)
170† Melbourne 1993-94
169*‡ Adelaide 1997-98
V. T. Trumper (2)
159 Melbourne 1910-11
214* Adelaide 1910-11
M. E. Waugh (4)
113* Durban 1993-94
116 Port Elizabeth 1996-97
100 Sydney 1997-98
115* Adelaide 1997-98
S. R. Waugh (2)
164† Adelaide 1993-94
160 Johannesburg 1996-97
W. M. Woodfull (1)
161 Melbourne 1931-32

For South Africa (40)

E. J. Barlow (5)
114† Brisbane 1963-64
109 Melbourne 1963-64
201 Adelaide 1963-64
127 Cape Town 1969-70
110 Johannesburg 1969-70
K. C. Bland (1)
126 Sydney 1963-64
W. J. Cronje (1)
122 Johannesburg 1993-94
W. R. Endean (1)
162* Melbourne 1952-53
G. A. Faulkner (3)
204 Melbourne 1910-11
115 Adelaide 1910-11
122* Manchester 1912
C. N. Frank (1)
152 Johannesburg 1921-22
A. C. Hudson (1)
102 Cape Town 1993-94
B. L. Irvine (1)
102 Port Elizabeth 1969-70
J. H. Kallis (1)
101 Melbourne 1997-98
G. Kirsten (1)
108* Adelaide 1997-98
D. T. Lindsay (3)
182 Johannesburg 1966-67
137 Durban 1966-67
131 Johannesburg 1966-67
D. J. McGlew (2)
108 Johannesburg 1957-58
105 Durban 1957-58
A. D. Nourse (2)
231 Johannesburg 1935-36
114 Cape Town 1949-50
A. W. Nourse (1)
111 Johannesburg 1921-22
R. G. Pollock (5)
122 Sydney 1963-64
175 Adelaide 1963-64
209 Cape Town 1966-67
105 Port Elizabeth 1966-67
274 Durban 1969-70
B. A. Richards (2)
140 Durban 1969-70
126 Port Elizabeth 1969-70

E. A. B. Rowan (1)		
143	Durban	1949-50
J. H. Sinclair (2)		
101	Johannesburg	1902-03
104	Cape Town	1902-03
S. J. Snooke (1)		
103	Adelaide	1910-11
K. G. Viljoen (1)		
111	Melbourne	1931-32
J. H. B. Waite (2)		
115	Johannesburg	1957-58
134	Durban	1957-58
J. W. Zulch (2)		
105	Adelaide	1910-11
150	Sydney	1910-11

† *Signifies hundred on first appearance in Australia–South Africa Tests.*
‡ *Carried his bat.*

RECORD PARTNERSHIPS FOR EACH WICKET

For Australia

233 for 1st	J. H. Fingleton and W. A. Brown at Cape Town	1935-36
275 for 2nd	C. C. McDonald and A. L. Hassett at Adelaide	1952-53
242 for 3rd	C. Kelleway and W. Bardsley at Lord's	1912
169 for 4th	M. A. Taylor and M. E. Waugh at Melbourne	1993-94
385 for 5th	S. R. Waugh and G. S. Blewett at Johannesburg	1996-97
108 for 6th	S. R. Waugh and I. A. Healy at Cape Town	1993-94
160 for 7th	R. Benaud and G. D. McKenzie at Sydney	1963-64
83 for 8th	A. G. Chipperfield and C. V. Grimmett at Durban	1935-36
78 for 9th	D. G. Bradman and W. J. O'Reilly at Adelaide	1931-32
78 for 9th	K. D. Mackay and I. Meckiff at Johannesburg	1957-58
82 for 10th	V. S. Ransford and W. J. Whitty at Melbourne	1910-11

For South Africa

176 for 1st	D. J. McGlew and T. L. Goddard at Johannesburg	1957-58
173 for 2nd	L. J. Tancred and C. B. Llewellyn at Johannesburg	1902-03
341 for 3rd†	E. J. Barlow and R. G. Pollock at Adelaide	1963-64
206 for 4th	C. N. Frank and A. W. Nourse at Johannesburg	1921-22
129 for 5th	J. H. B. Waite and W. R. Endean at Johannesburg	1957-58
200 for 6th†	R. G. Pollock and H. R. Lance at Durban	1969-70
221 for 7th	D. T. Lindsay and P. L. van der Merwe at Johannesburg	1966-67
124 for 8th	A. W. Nourse and E. A. Halliwell at Johannesburg	1902-03
85 for 9th	R. G. Pollock and P. M. Pollock at Cape Town	1966-67
74 for 10th	B. M. McMillan and P. L. Symcox at Adelaide	1997-98

† *Denotes record partnership against all countries.*

TEN WICKETS OR MORE IN A MATCH

For Australia (7)

14-199 (7-116, 7-83)	C. V. Grimmett, Adelaide	1931-32
10-88 (5-32, 5-56)	C. V. Grimmett, Cape Town	1935-36
10-110 (3-70, 7-40)	C. V. Grimmett, Johannesburg	1935-36
13-173 (7-100, 6-73)	C. V. Grimmett, Durban	1935-36
11-24 (5-6, 6-18)	H. Ironmonger, Melbourne	1931-32
12-128 (7-56, 5-72)	S. K. Warne, Sydney	1993-94
11-109 (5-75, 6-34)	S. K. Warne, Sydney	1997-98

For South Africa (3)

10-123 (4-80, 6-43)	P. S. de Villiers, Sydney	1993-94
10-116 (5-43, 5-73)	C. B. Llewellyn, Johannesburg	1902-03
13-165 (6-84, 7-81)	H. J. Tayfield, Melbourne	1952-53

Note: C. V. Grimmett took ten wickets or more in three consecutive matches in 1935-36.

AUSTRALIA v WEST INDIES

Season	Captains Australia	West Indies	T	A	WI	T	D
1930-31*A*	W. M. Woodfull	G. C. Grant	5	4	1	0	0
1951-52*A*	A. L. Hassett[1]	J. D. C. Goddard[2]	5	4	1	0	0
1954-55*W*	I. W. Johnson	D. St E. Atkinson[3]	5	3	0	0	2

THE FRANK WORRELL TROPHY

Season	Captains Australia	West Indies	T	A	WI	T	D	Held by
1960-61*A*	R. Benaud	F. M. M. Worrell	5	2	1	1	1	A
1964-65*W*	R. B. Simpson	G. S. Sobers	5	1	2	0	2	WI
1968-69*A*	W. M. Lawry	G. S. Sobers	5	3	1	0	1	A
1972-73*W*	I. M. Chappell	R. B. Kanhai	5	2	0	0	3	A
1975-76*A*	G. S. Chappell	C. H. Lloyd	6	5	1	0	0	A
1977-78*W*	R. B. Simpson	A. I. Kallicharran[4]	5	1	3	0	1	WI
1979-80*A*	G. S. Chappell	C. H. Lloyd[5]	3	0	2	0	1	WI
1981-82*A*	G. S. Chappell	C. H. Lloyd	3	1	1	0	1	WI
1983-84*W*	K. J. Hughes	C. H. Lloyd[6]	5	0	3	0	2	WI
1984-85*A*	A. R. Border[7]	C. H. Lloyd	5	1	3	0	1	WI
1988-89*A*	A. R. Border	I. V. A. Richards	5	1	3	0	1	WI
1990-91*W*	A. R. Border	I. V. A. Richards	5	1	2	0	2	WI
1992-93*A*	A. R. Border	R. B. Richardson	5	1	2	0	2	WI
1994-95*W*	M. A. Taylor	R. B. Richardson	4	2	1	0	1	A
1996-97*A*	M. A. Taylor	C. A. Walsh	5	3	2	0	0	A
1998-99*W*	S. R. Waugh	B. C. Lara	4	2	2	0	0	A
2000-01*A*	S. R. Waugh[8]	J. C. Adams	5	5	0	0	0	A
	In Australia		57	30	18	1	8	
	In West Indies		38	12	13	0	13	
	Totals		95	42	31	1	21	

A Played in Australia. W Played in West Indies.

Notes: The following deputised for the official touring captain or were appointed by the home authority for only a minor proportion of the series:

[1]A. R. Morris (Third). [2]J. B. Stollmeyer (Fifth). [3]J. B. Stollmeyer (Second and Third). [4]C. H. Lloyd (First and Second). [5]D. L. Murray (First). [6]I. V. A. Richards (Second). [7]K. J. Hughes (First and Second). [8]A. C. Gilchrist (Third).

HIGHEST INNINGS TOTALS

For Australia in Australia: 619 at Sydney . . . 1968-69
in West Indies: 758-8 dec. at Kingston . . . 1954-55

For West Indies in Australia: 616 at Adelaide . . . 1968-69
in West Indies: 573 at Bridgetown . . . 1964-65

LOWEST INNINGS TOTALS

For Australia in Australia: 76 at Perth . . . 1984-85
in West Indies: 90 at Port-of-Spain . . . 1977-78

For West Indies in Australia: 78 at Sydney . . . 1951-52
in West Indies: 51 at Port-of-Spain . . . 1998-99

INDIVIDUAL HUNDREDS

For Australia (86)

R. G. Archer (1)
128 Kingston . . . 1954-55
R. Benaud (1)
121 Kingston . . . 1954-55
D. C. Boon (3)
149 Sydney 1988-89
109* Kingston . . . 1990-91
111 Brisbane . . . 1992-93
B. C. Booth (1)
117 Port-of-Spain 1964-65
A. R. Border (3)
126 Adelaide . . . 1981-82
100* Port-of-Spain 1983-84
110 Melbourne . . 1992-93
D. G. Bradman (2)
223 Brisbane . . . 1930-31
152 Melbourne . . 1930-31
G. S. Chappell (5)
106 Bridgetown . 1972-73
123 }
109* } ‡Brisbane . . . 1975-76
182* Sydney 1975-76
124 Brisbane . . . 1979-80
I. M. Chappell (5)
117† Brisbane . . . 1968-69
165 Melbourne . . 1968-69
106* Bridgetown . 1972-73
109 Georgetown . 1972-73
156 Perth. 1975-76
G. J. Cosier (1)
109† Melbourne . . 1975-76
R. M. Cowper (2)
143 Port-of-Spain 1964-65
102 Bridgetown . 1964-65
J. Dyson (1)
127*† Sydney 1981-82
R. N. Harvey (3)
133 Kingston . . . 1954-55
133 Port-of-Spain 1954-55
204 Kingston . . . 1954-55
A. L. Hassett (2)
132 Sydney 1951-52
102 Melbourne . . 1951-52
M. L. Hayden (1)
125 Adelaide . . . 1996-97
I. A. Healy (1)
161* Brisbane . . . 1996-97
A. M. J. Hilditch (1)
113† Melbourne . . 1984-85
K. J. Hughes (2)
130*† Brisbane . . . 1979-80
100* Melbourne . . 1981-82
D. M. Jones (1)
216 Adelaide . . . 1988-89
A. F. Kippax (1)
146† Adelaide . . . 1930-31
J. L. Langer (1)
127 St John's . . . 1998-99
W. M. Lawry (4)
210 Bridgetown . 1964-65
105 Brisbane . . . 1968-69
205 Melbourne . . 1968-69
151 Sydney 1968-69
R. R. Lindwall (1)
118 Bridgetown . 1954-55
R. B. McCosker (1)
109* Melbourne . . 1975-76
C. C. McDonald (2)
110 Port-of-Spain 1954-55
127 Kingston . . . 1954-55
K. R. Miller (4)
129 Sydney 1951-52
147 Kingston . . . 1954-55
137 Bridgetown . 1954-55
109 Kingston . . . 1954-55
A. R. Morris (1)
111 Port-of-Spain 1954-55
N. C. O'Neill (1)
181† Brisbane . . . 1960-61
W. B. Phillips (1)
120 Bridgetown . 1983-84
W. H. Ponsford (2)
183 Sydney 1930-31
109 Brisbane . . . 1930-31
R. T. Ponting (1)
104 Bridgetown . 1998-99
I. R. Redpath (4)
132 Sydney 1968-69
102 Melbourne . . 1975-76
103 Adelaide . . . 1975-76
101 Melbourne . . 1975-76
C. S. Serjeant (1)
124 Georgetown . 1977-78
R. B. Simpson (1)
201 Bridgetown . 1964-65
M. J. Slater (1)
106 Port-of-Spain 1998-99
K. R. Stackpole (1)
142 Kingston . . . 1972-73
M. A. Taylor (1)
144 St John's . . . 1990-91
P. M. Toohey (1)
122 Kingston . . . 1977-78
A. Turner (1)
136 Adelaide . . . 1975-76
K. D. Walters (6)
118 Sydney 1968-69
110 Adelaide . . . 1968-69
242 }
103 } Sydney 1968-69
102* Bridgetown . 1972-73
112 Port-of-Spain 1972-73
M. E. Waugh (4)
139* St John's . . . 1990-91
112 Melbourne . . 1992-93
126 Kingston . . . 1994-95
119 Perth. 2000-01
S. R. Waugh (6)
100 Sydney 1992-93
200 Kingston . . . 1994-95
100 Kingston . . . 1998-99
199 Bridgetown . 1998-99
121* Melbourne . . 2000-01
103 Sydney 2000-01
K. C. Wessels (1)
173 Sydney 1984-85
G. M. Wood (2)
126 Georgetown . 1977-78
111 Perth. 1988-89

For West Indies (86)

F. C. M. Alexander (1)
108 Sydney 1960-61
K. L. T. Arthurton (1)
157*† Brisbane . . . 1992-93
D. St E. Atkinson (1)
219 Bridgetown . 1954-55
B. F. Butcher (3)
117 Port-of-Spain 1964-65
101 Sydney 1968-69
118 Adelaide . . . 1968-69
S. L. Campbell (2)
113 Brisbane . . . 1996-97
105 Bridgetown . 1998-99
C. C. Depeiza (1)
122 Bridgetown . 1954-55
P. J. L. Dujon (2)
130 Port-of-Spain 1983-84
139 Perth. 1984-85
M. L. C. Foster (1)
125† Kingston . . . 1972-73
R. C. Fredericks (1)
169 Perth. 1975-76
H. A. Gomes (6)
101† Georgetown . 1977-78
115 Kingston . . . 1977-78
126 Sydney 1981-82
124* Adelaide . . . 1981-82
127 Perth. 1984-85
120* Adelaide . . . 1984-85

C. G. Greenidge (4)
120* Georgetown . 1983-84
127 Kingston . . . 1983-84
104 Adelaide . . . 1988-89
226 Bridgetown . 1990-91
D. L. Haynes (5)
103* Georgetown . 1983-84
145 Bridgetown . 1983-84
100 Perth. 1988-89
143 Sydney 1988-89
111 Georgetown . 1990-91
G. A. Headley (2)
102* Brisbane . . . 1930-31
105 Sydney 1930-31
C. L. Hooper (1)
102 Brisbane . . . 1996-97
C. C. Hunte (1)
110 Melbourne . . 1960-61
A. I. Kallicharran (4)
101 Brisbane . . . 1975-76
127 Port-of-Spain 1977-78
126 Kingston . . . 1977-78
106 Adelaide . . . 1979-80
R. B. Kanhai (5)
117 } 115 } Adelaide . . . 1960-61
129 Bridgetown . 1964-65
121 Port-of-Spain 1964-65
105 Bridgetown . 1972-73

B. C. Lara (6)
277 Sydney 1992-93
132 Perth. 1996-97
213 Kingston . . . 1998-99
153* Bridgetown . 1998-99
100 St John's . . . 1998-99
182 Adelaide . . . 2000-01
C. H. Lloyd (6)
129† Brisbane . . . 1968-69
178 Georgetown . 1972-73
149 Perth. 1975-76
102 Melbourne . . 1975-76
121 Adelaide . . . 1979-80
114 Brisbane . . . 1984-85
F. R. Martin (1)
123* Sydney 1930-31
S. M. Nurse (2)
201 Bridgetown . 1964-65
137 Sydney 1968-69
I. V. A. Richards (5)
101 Adelaide . . . 1975-76
140 Brisbane . . . 1979-80
178 St John's . . . 1983-84
208 Melbourne . . 1984-85
146 Perth. 1988-89
R. B. Richardson (9)
131* Bridgetown . 1983-84
154 St John's . . . 1983-84
138 Brisbane . . . 1984-85
122 Melbourne . . 1988-89
106 Adelaide . . . 1988-89
104* Kingston . . . 1990-91
182 Georgetown . 1990-91
109 Sydney 1992-93
100 Kingston . . . 1994-95
L. G. Rowe (1)
107 Brisbane . . . 1975-76
P. V. Simmons (1)
110 Melbourne . . 1992-93
O. G. Smith (1)
104† Kingston . . . 1954-55
G. S. Sobers (4)
132 Brisbane . . . 1960-61
168 Sydney 1960-61
110 Adelaide . . . 1968-69
113 Sydney 1968-69
J. B. Stollmeyer (1)
104 Sydney 1951-52
C. L. Walcott (5)
108 Kingston . . . 1954-55
126 } 110 } Port-of-Spain 1954-55
155 } 110 } Kingston . . . 1954-55
E. D. Weekes (1)
139 Port-of-Spain 1954-55
A. B. Williams (1)
100† Georgetown . 1977-78
F. M. M. Worrell (1)
108 Melbourne . . 1951-52

† *Signifies hundred on first appearance in Australia–West Indies Tests.*
‡ *G. S. Chappell is the only player to score hundreds in both innings of his first Test as captain.*

Note: F. C. M. Alexander and C. C. Depeiza scored the only hundreds of their first-class careers in a Test match.

RECORD PARTNERSHIPS FOR EACH WICKET

For Australia

382 for 1st†	W. M. Lawry and R. B. Simpson at Bridgetown	1964-65
298 for 2nd	W. M. Lawry and I. M. Chappell at Melbourne	1968-69
295 for 3rd†	C. C. McDonald and R. N. Harvey at Kingston	1954-55
336 for 4th	W. M. Lawry and K. D. Walters at Sydney	1968-69
281 for 5th	S. R. Waugh and R. T. Ponting at Bridgetown	1998-99
206 for 6th	K. R. Miller and R. G. Archer at Bridgetown	1954-55
134 for 7th	A. K. Davidson and R. Benaud at Brisbane	1960-61
137 for 8th	R. Benaud and I. W. Johnson at Kingston	1954-55
114 for 9th	D. M. Jones and M. G. Hughes at Adelaide	1988-89
97 for 10th	T. G. Hogan and R. M. Hogg at Georgetown	1983-84

For West Indies

250*	for 1st	C. G. Greenidge and D. L. Haynes at Georgetown	1983-84
297	for 2nd	D. L. Haynes and R. B. Richardson at Georgetown	1990-91
308	for 3rd	R. B. Richardson and I. V. A. Richards at St John's	1983-84
198	for 4th	L. G. Rowe and A. I. Kallicharran at Brisbane	1975-76
322	for 5th†‡	B. C. Lara and J. C. Adams at Kingston	1998-99
165	for 6th	R. B. Kanhai and D. L. Murray at Bridgetown	1972-73
347	for 7th†	D. St E. Atkinson and C. C. Depeiza at Bridgetown	1954-55
87	for 8th	P. J. L. Dujon and C. E. L. Ambrose at Port-of-Spain	1990-91
122	for 9th	D. A. J. Holford and J. L. Hendriks at Adelaide	1968-69
56	for 10th	J. Garner and C. E. H. Croft at Brisbane	1979-80

† Denotes record partnership against all countries.
‡ 344 runs were added between the fall of the 4th and 5th wickets: P. T. Collins retired hurt when he and Lara had added 22 runs.

TEN WICKETS OR MORE IN A MATCH

For Australia (15)

10-113 (4-31, 6-82)	M. G. Bevan, Adelaide	1996-97
11-96 (7-46, 4-50)	A. R. Border, Sydney	1988-89
11-222 (5-135, 6-87)†	A. K. Davidson, Brisbane	1960-61
11-183 (7-87, 4-96)†	C. V. Grimmett, Adelaide	1930-31
10-115 (6-72, 4-43)	N. J. N. Hawke, Georgetown	1964-65
10-144 (6-54, 4-90)	R. G. Holland, Sydney	1984-85
13-217 (5-130, 8-87)	M. G. Hughes, Perth	1988-89
11-79 (7-23, 4-56)	H. Ironmonger, Melbourne	1930-31
11-181 (8-112, 3-69)	G. F. Lawson, Adelaide	1984-85
10-127 (7-83, 3-44)	D. K. Lillee, Melbourne	1981-82
10-78 (5-50, 5-28)	G. D. McGrath, Port-of-Spain	1998-99
10-27 (6-17, 4-10)	G. D. McGrath, Brisbane	2000-01
10-159 (8-71, 2-88)	G. D. McKenzie, Melbourne	1968-69
10-113 (5-81, 5-32)	C. R. Miller, Adelaide	2000-01
10-185 (3-87, 7-98)	B. Yardley, Sydney	1981-82

For West Indies (4)

10-120 (6-74, 4-46)	C. E. L. Ambrose, Adelaide	1992-93
10-113 (7-55, 3-58)	G. E. Gomez, Sydney	1951-52
11-107 (5-45, 6-62)	M. A. Holding, Melbourne	1981-82
10-107 (5-69, 5-38)	M. D. Marshall, Adelaide	1984-85

† Signifies ten wickets or more on first appearance in Australia–West Indies Tests.

AUSTRALIA v NEW ZEALAND

	Captains					
Season	*Australia*	*New Zealand*	*T*	*A*	*NZ*	*D*
1945-46*N*	W. A. Brown	W. A. Hadlee	1	1	0	0
1973-74*A*	I. M. Chappell	B. E. Congdon	3	2	0	1
1973-74*N*	I. M. Chappell	B. E. Congdon	3	1	1	1
1976-77*N*	G. S. Chappell	G. M. Turner	2	1	0	1
1980-81*A*	G. S. Chappell	G. P. Howarth[1]	3	2	0	1
1981-82*N*	G. S. Chappell	G. P. Howarth	3	1	1	1

TRANS-TASMAN TROPHY

	Captains						
Season	*Australia*	*New Zealand*	*T*	*A*	*NZ*	*D*	*Held by*
1985-86*A*	A. R. Border	J. V. Coney	3	1	2	0	NZ
1985-86*N*	A. R. Border	J. V. Coney	3	0	1	2	NZ
1987-88*A*	A. R. Border	J. J. Crowe	3	1	0	2	A
1989-90*A*	A. R. Border	J. G. Wright	1	0	0	1	A
1989-90*N*	A. R. Border	J. G. Wright	1	0	1	0	NZ
1992-93*N*	A. R. Border	M. D. Crowe	3	1	1	1	NZ
1993-94*A*	A. R. Border	M. D. Crowe[2]	3	2	0	1	A
1997-98*A*	M. A. Taylor	S. P. Fleming	3	2	0	1	A
1999-2000*N*	S. R. Waugh	S. P. Fleming	3	3	0	0	A
	In Australia		19	10	2	7	
	In New Zealand		19	8	5	6	
	Totals		38	18	7	13	

A Played in Australia. N Played in New Zealand.

Notes: The following deputised for the official touring captain: [1]M. G. Burgess (Second). [2]K. R. Rutherford (Second and Third).

HIGHEST INNINGS TOTALS

For Australia in Australia: 607-6 dec. at Brisbane 1993-94
in New Zealand: 552 at Christchurch 1976-77

For New Zealand in Australia: 553-7 dec. at Brisbane 1985-86
in New Zealand: 484 at Wellington. 1973-74

LOWEST INNINGS TOTALS

For Australia in Australia: 162 at Sydney. 1973-74
in New Zealand: 103 at Auckland 1985-86

For New Zealand in Australia: 121 at Perth 1980-81
in New Zealand: 42 at Wellington 1945-46

INDIVIDUAL HUNDREDS

For Australia (35)

D. C. Boon (3)
143 Brisbane . . . 1987-88
200 Perth. 1989-90
106 Hobart 1993-94

A. R. Border (5)
152* Brisbane . . . 1985-86
140 }
114* } Christchurch. 1985-86
205 Adelaide . . . 1987-88
105 Brisbane . . . 1993-94

G. S. Chappell (3)
247* }
133 } Wellington . . 1973-74
176 Christchurch. 1981-82

I. M. Chappell (2)
145 }
121 } Wellington . . 1973-74

M. T. G. Elliott (1)
114 Hobart 1997-98

G. J. Gilmour (1)
101 Christchurch. 1976-77

I. A. Healy (1)
113* Perth. 1993-94

J. L. Langer (1)
122* Hamilton . . . 1999-00

G. R. Marsh (1)
118 Auckland. . . 1985-86

R. W. Marsh (1)
132 Adelaide . . . 1973-74

G. R. J. Matthews (2)
115† Brisbane . . . 1985-86
130 Wellington . . 1985-86

I. R. Redpath (1)
159*‡ Auckland. . . 1973-74

M. J. Slater (2)
168 Hobart 1993-94
143 Wellington . . 1999-00

K. R. Stackpole (1)
122† Melbourne . . 1973-74

M. A. Taylor (2)
142* Perth. 1993-94
112 Brisbane . . . 1997-98

K. D. Walters (3)
104* Auckland. . . 1973-74
250 Christchurch. 1976-77
107 Melbourne . . 1980-81

M. E. Waugh (1)
111 Hobart 1993-94

S. R. Waugh (2)
147* Brisbane . . . 1993-94
151* Wellington . . 1999-00

G. M. Wood (2)
111† Brisbane . . . 1980-81
100 Auckland. . . 1981-82

For New Zealand (21)

C. L. Cairns (1)
109 Wellington . . 1999-00
J. V. Coney (1)
101* Wellington . . 1985-86
B. E. Congdon (2)
132 Wellington . . 1973-74
107* Christchurch. 1976-77
M. D. Crowe (3)
188 Brisbane . . . 1985-86
137 Christchurch. 1985-86
137 Adelaide . . . 1987-88
B. A. Edgar (1)
161 Auckland. . . 1981-82

M. J. Greatbatch (1)
146*† Perth. 1989-90
B. F. Hastings (1)
101 Wellington . . 1973-74
M. J. Horne (1)
133† Hobart 1997-98
A. H. Jones (2)
150 Adelaide . . . 1987-88
143 Perth. 1993-94
J. F. M. Morrison (1)
117 Sydney 1973-74
J. M. Parker (1)
108 Sydney 1973-74

J. F. Reid (1)
108† Brisbane . . . 1985-86
K. R. Rutherford (1)
102 Christchurch. 1992-93
G. M. Turner (2)
101 }
110* } Christchurch. 1973-74
J. G. Wright (2)
141 Christchurch. 1981-82
117* Wellington . . 1989-90

† *Signifies hundred on first appearance in Australia–New Zealand Tests.*
‡ *Carried his bat.*

Note: G. S. and I. M. Chappell at Wellington in 1973-74 provide the only instance in Test matches of brothers both scoring a hundred in each innings and in the same Test.

RECORD PARTNERSHIPS FOR EACH WICKET

For Australia

198 for 1st	M. J. Slater and M. A. Taylor at Perth	1993-94
235 for 2nd	M. J. Slater and D. C. Boon at Hobart	1993-94
264 for 3rd	I. M. Chappell and G. S. Chappell at Wellington	1973-74
153 for 4th	M. E. Waugh and S. R. Waugh at Perth	1997-98
213 for 5th	G. M. Ritchie and G. R. J. Matthews at Wellington	1985-86
197 for 6th	A. R. Border and G. R. J. Matthews at Brisbane	1985-86
217 for 7th†	K. D. Walters and G. J. Gilmour at Christchurch	1976-77
93 for 8th	G. J. Gilmour and K. J. O'Keeffe at Auckland	1976-77
69 for 9th	I. A. Healy and C. J. McDermott at Perth	1993-94
60 for 10th	K. D. Walters and J. D. Higgs at Melbourne	1980-81

For New Zealand

111 for 1st	M. J. Greatbatch and J. G. Wright at Wellington	1992-93
132 for 2nd	M. J. Horne and A. C. Parore at Hobart	1997-98
224 for 3rd	J. F. Reid and M. D. Crowe at Brisbane	1985-86
229 for 4th	B. E. Congdon and B. F. Hastings at Wellington	1973-74
88 for 5th	J. V. Coney and M. G. Burgess at Perth	1980-81
110 for 6th	S. P. Fleming and C. L. Cairns at Wellington	1999-2000
132* for 7th	J. V. Coney and R. J. Hadlee at Wellington	1985-86
88* for 8th	M. J. Greatbatch and M. C. Snedden at Perth	1989-90
73 for 9th	H. J. Howarth and D. R. Hadlee at Christchurch	1976-77
124 for 10th	J. G. Bracewell and S. L. Boock at Sydney	1985-86

† *Denotes record partnership against all countries.*

TEN WICKETS OR MORE IN A MATCH

For Australia (2)

10-174 (6-106, 4-68)	R. G. Holland, Sydney	1985-86
11-123 (5-51, 6-72)	D. K. Lillee, Auckland	1976-77

For New Zealand (5)

10-106 (4-74, 6-32)	J. G. Bracewell, Auckland	1985-86
15-123 (9-52, 6-71)	R. J. Hadlee, Brisbane	1985-86
11-155 (5-65, 6-90)	R. J. Hadlee, Perth	1985-86
10-176 (5-109, 5-67)	R. J. Hadlee, Melbourne	1987-88
12-149 (5-62, 7-87)	D. L. Vettori, Auckland	1999-2000

AUSTRALIA v INDIA

	Captains						
Season	*Australia*	*India*	*T*	*A*	*I*	*T*	*D*
1947-48*A*	D. G. Bradman	L. Amarnath	5	4	0	0	1
1956-57*I*	I. W. Johnson[1]	P. R. Umrigar	3	2	0	0	1
1959-60*I*	R. Benaud	G. S. Ramchand	5	2	1	0	2
1964-65*I*	R. B. Simpson	Nawab of Pataudi jun.	3	1	1	0	1
1967-68*A*	R. B. Simpson[2]	Nawab of Pataudi jun.[3]	4	4	0	0	0
1969-70*I*	W. M. Lawry	Nawab of Pataudi jun.	5	3	1	0	1
1977-78*A*	R. B. Simpson	B. S. Bedi	5	3	2	0	0
1979-80*I*	K. J. Hughes	S. M. Gavaskar	6	0	2	0	4
1980-81*A*	G. S. Chappell	S. M. Gavaskar	3	1	1	0	1
1985-86*A*	A. R. Border	Kapil Dev	3	0	0	0	3
1986-87*I*	A. R. Border	Kapil Dev	3	0	0	1	2
1991-92*A*	A. R. Border	M. Azharuddin	5	4	0	0	1

THE BORDER–GAVASKAR TROPHY

	Captains							
Season	*Australia*	*India*	*T*	*A*	*I*	*T*	*D*	*Held by*
1996-97*I*	M. A. Taylor	S. R. Tendulkar	1	0	1	0	0	I
1997-98*I*	M. A. Taylor	M. Azharuddin	3	1	2	0	0	I
1999-2000*A*	S. R. Waugh	S. R. Tendulkar	3	3	0	0	0	A
2000-01*I*	S. R. Waugh	S. C. Ganguly	3	1	2	0	0	I
	In Australia		28	19	3	0	6	
	In India		32	10	10	1	11	
	Totals		60	29	13	1	17	

A Played in Australia. I Played in India.

Notes: The following deputised for the official touring captain or were appointed by the home authority for only a minor proportion of the series:

[1]R. R. Lindwall (Second). [2]W. M. Lawry (Third and Fourth). [3]C. G. Borde (First).

HIGHEST INNINGS TOTALS

For Australia in Australia: 674 at Adelaide	1947-48
in India: 574-7 dec. at Madras	1986-87
For India in Australia: 600-4 dec. at Sydney	1985-86
in India: 657-7 dec. at Kolkata	2000-01

LOWEST INNINGS TOTALS

For Australia in Australia: 83 at Melbourne	1980-81
in India: 105 at Kanpur	1959-60
For India in Australia: 58 at Brisbane	1947-48
in India: 135 at Delhi	1959-60

INDIVIDUAL HUNDREDS

For Australia (61)

S. G. Barnes (1)
112 Adelaide . . . 1947-48
D. C. Boon (6)
123† Adelaide . . . 1985-86
131 Sydney 1985-86
122 Madras 1986-87
129* Sydney 1991-92
135 Adelaide . . . 1991-92
107 Perth. 1991-92
A. R. Border (4)
162† Madras 1979-80
124 Melbourne . . 1980-81
163 Melbourne . . 1985-86
106 Madras 1986-87
D. G. Bradman (4)
185† Brisbane . . . 1947-48
132 } Melbourne . . 1947-48
127* }
201 Adelaide . . . 1947-48
J. W. Burke (1)
161 Bombay. . . . 1956-57
G. S. Chappell (1)
204† Sydney 1980-81
I. M. Chappell (2)
151 Melbourne . . 1967-68
138 Delhi 1969-70
R. M. Cowper (2)
108 Adelaide . . . 1967-68
165 Sydney 1967-68
L. E. Favell (1)
101 Madras 1959-60
A. C. Gilchrist (1)
122 Mumbai. . . . 2000-01

R. N. Harvey (4)
153 Melbourne . . 1947-48
140 Bombay. . . . 1956-57
114 Delhi 1959-60
102 Bombay. . . . 1959-60
A. L. Hassett (1)
198* Adelaide . . . 1947-48
M. L. Hayden (2)
119† Mumbai. . . . 2000-01
203 Chennai. . . . 2000-01
K. J. Hughes (2)
100 Madras 1979-80
213 Adelaide . . . 1980-81
D. M. Jones (2)
210† Madras 1986-87
150* Perth. 1991-92
J. L. Langer (1)
223 Sydney 1999-00
W. M. Lawry (1)
100 Melbourne . . 1967-68
A. L. Mann (1)
105 Perth. 1977-78
G. R. Marsh (1)
101 Bombay. . . . 1986-87
G. R. J. Matthews (1)
100* Melbourne . . 1985-86
T. M. Moody (1)
101† Perth. 1991-92
A. R. Morris (1)
100* Melbourne . . 1947-48

N. C. O'Neill (2)
163 Bombay. . . . 1959-60
113 Calcutta. . . . 1959-60
R. T. Ponting (2)
125 Adelaide . . . 1999-00
141* Sydney 1999-00
G. M. Ritchie (1)
128† Adelaide . . . 1985-86
A. P. Sheahan (1)
114 Kanpur 1969-70
R. B. Simpson (4)
103 Adelaide . . . 1967-68
109 Melbourne . . 1967-68
176 Perth. 1977-78
100 Adelaide . . . 1977-78
K. R. Stackpole (1)
103† Bombay. . . . 1969-70
M. A. Taylor (2)
100 Adelaide . . . 1991-92
102* Bangalore . . 1997-98
K. D. Walters (1)
102 Madras 1969-70
M. E. Waugh (1)
153* Bangalore . . 1997-98
S. R. Waugh (2)
150 Adelaide . . . 1999-00
110 Kolkata 2000-01
G. M. Wood (1)
125 Adelaide . . . 1980-81
G. N. Yallop (2)
121† Adelaide . . . 1977-78
167 Calcutta. . . . 1979-80

For India (44)

M. Amarnath (2)
100 Perth. 1977-78
138 Sydney 1985-86
M. Azharuddin (2)
106 Adelaide . . . 1991-92
163* Calcutta. . . . 1997-98
N. J. Contractor (1)
108 Bombay. . . . 1959-60
R. Dravid (1)
180 Kolkata 2000-01
S. M. Gavaskar (8)
113† Brisbane . . . 1977-78
127 Perth. 1977-78
118 Melbourne . . 1977-78
115 Delhi 1979-80
123 Bombay. . . . 1979-80
166* Adelaide . . . 1985-86
172 Sydney 1985-86

103 Bombay. . . . 1986-87
V. S. Hazare (2)
116 } Adelaide . . . 1947-48
145 }
M. L. Jaisimha (1)
101 Brisbane . . . 1967-68
Kapil Dev (1)
119 Madras 1986-87
S. M. H. Kirmani (1)
101* Bombay. . . . 1979-80
V. V. S. Laxman (2)
167 Sydney 1999-00
281 Kolkata 2000-01
V. Mankad (2)
116 Melbourne . . 1947-48
111 Melbourne . . 1947-48
N. R. Mongia (1)
152† Delhi 1996-97

Nawab of Pataudi jun. (1)
128*† Madras 1964-65
S. M. Patil (1)
174 Adelaide . . . 1980-81
D. G. Phadkar (1)
123 Adelaide . . . 1947-48
G. S. Ramchand (1)
109 Bombay. . . . 1956-57
R. J. Shastri (2)
121* Bombay. . . . 1986-87
206 Sydney 1991-92
K. Srikkanth (1)
116 Sydney 1985-86
S. R. Tendulkar (6)
148* Sydney 1991-92
114 Perth. 1991-92
155* Chennai. . . . 1997-98
177 Bangalore . . 1997-98

116	Melbourne	1999-00	164*	Bombay	1986-87	131	Delhi	1979-80
126	Chennai	2000-01	**G. R. Viswanath** (4)			114	Melbourne	1980-81
D. B. Vengsarkar (2)			137†	Kanpur	1969-70	**Yashpal Sharma** (1)		
112	Bangalore	1979-80	161*	Bangalore	1979-80	100*	Delhi	1979-80

† *Signifies hundred on first appearance in Australia–India Tests.*

RECORD PARTNERSHIPS FOR EACH WICKET

For Australia

217	for 1st	D. C. Boon and G. R. Marsh at Sydney	1985-86
236	for 2nd	S. G. Barnes and D. G. Bradman at Adelaide	1947-48
222	for 3rd	A. R. Border and K. J. Hughes at Madras	1979-80
178	for 4th	D. M. Jones and A. R. Border at Madras	1986-87
239	for 5th	S. R. Waugh and R. T. Ponting at Adelaide	1999-2000
197	for 6th	M. L. Hayden and A. C. Gilchrist at Mumbai	2000-01
108	for 7th	S. R. Waugh and S. K. Warne at Adelaide	1999-2000
73	for 8th	T. R. Veivers and G. D. McKenzie at Madras	1964-65
133	for 9th	S. R. Waugh and J. N. Gillespie at Kolkata	2000-01
77	for 10th	A. R. Border and D. R. Gilbert at Melbourne	1985-86

For India

192	for 1st	S. M. Gavaskar and C. P. S. Chauhan at Bombay	1979-80
224	for 2nd	S. M. Gavaskar and M. Amarnath at Sydney	1985-86
159	for 3rd	S. M. Gavaskar and G. R. Viswanath at Delhi	1979-80
159	for 4th	D. B. Vengsarkar and G. R. Viswanath at Bangalore	1979-80
376	for 5th†	V. V. S. Laxman and R. Dravid at Kolkata	2000-01
298*	for 6th†	D. B. Vengsarkar and R. J. Shastri at Bombay	1986-87
132	for 7th	V. S. Hazare and H. R. Adhikari at Adelaide	1947-48
127	for 8th	S. M. H. Kirmani and K. D. Ghavri at Bombay	1979-80
81	for 9th	S. R. Tendulkar and K. S. More at Perth	1991-92
94	for 10th	S. M. Gavaskar and N. S. Yadav at Adelaide	1985-86

† *Denotes record partnership against all countries.*

TEN WICKETS OR MORE IN A MATCH

For Australia (12)

11-105 (6-52, 5-53)	R. Benaud, Calcutta	1956-57
12-124 (5-31, 7-93)	A. K. Davidson, Kanpur	1959-60
12-166 (5-99, 7-67)	G. Dymock, Kanpur	1979-80
10-168 (5-76, 5-92)	C. J. McDermott, Adelaide	1991-92
10-103 (5-48, 5-55)	G. D. McGrath, Sydney	1999-2000
10-91 (6-58, 4-33)†	G. D. McKenzie, Madras	1964-65
10-151 (7-66, 3-85)	G. D. McKenzie, Melbourne	1967-68
10-144 (5-91, 5-53)	A. A. Mallett, Madras	1969-70
10-249 (5-103, 5-146)	G. R. J. Matthews, Madras	1986-87
12-126 (6-66, 6-60)	B. A. Reid, Melbourne	1991-92
11-31 (5-2, 6-29)†	E. R. H. Toshack, Brisbane	1947-48
11-95 (4-68, 7-27)	M. R. Whitney, Perth	1991-92

For India (8)

10-194 (5-89, 5-105)	B. S. Bedi, Perth	1977-78
12-104 (6-52, 6-52)	B. S. Chandrasekhar, Melbourne	1977-78
10-130 (7-49, 3-81)	Ghulam Ahmed, Calcutta	1956-57
13-196 (7-123, 6-73)	Harbhajan Singh, Kolkata	2000-01
15-217 (7-133, 8-84)	Harbhajan Singh, Chennai	2000-01
11-122 (5-31, 6-91)	R. G. Nadkarni, Madras	1964-65
14-124 (9-69, 5-55)	J. M. Patel, Kanpur	1959-60
10-174 (4-100, 6-74)	E. A. S. Prasanna, Madras	1969-70

† *Signifies ten wickets or more on first appearance in Australia–India Tests.*

AUSTRALIA v PAKISTAN

	Captains					
Season	*Australia*	*Pakistan*	*T*	*A*	*P*	*D*
1956-57*P*	I. W. Johnson	A. H. Kardar	1	0	1	0
1959-60*P*	R. Benaud	Fazal Mahmood[1]	3	2	0	1
1964-65*P*	R. B. Simpson	Hanif Mohammad	1	0	0	1
1964-65*A*	R. B. Simpson	Hanif Mohammad	1	0	0	1
1972-73*A*	I. M. Chappell	Intikhab Alam	3	3	0	0
1976-77*A*	G. S. Chappell	Mushtaq Mohammad	3	1	1	1
1978-79*A*	G. N. Yallop[2]	Mushtaq Mohammad	2	1	1	0
1979-80*P*	G. S. Chappell	Javed Miandad	3	0	1	2
1981-82*A*	G. S. Chappell	Javed Miandad	3	2	1	0
1982-83*P*	K. J. Hughes	Imran Khan	3	0	3	0
1983-84*A*	K. J. Hughes	Imran Khan[3]	5	2	0	3
1988-89*P*	A. R. Border	Javed Miandad	3	0	1	2
1989-90*A*	A. R. Border	Imran Khan	3	1	0	2
1994-95*P*	M. A. Taylor	Salim Malik	3	0	1	2
1995-96*A*	M. A. Taylor	Wasim Akram	3	2	1	0
1998-99*P*	M. A. Taylor	Aamir Sohail	3	1	0	2
1999-2000*A*	S. R. Waugh	Wasim Akram	3	3	0	0
	In Pakistan		20	3	7	10
	In Australia		26	15	4	7
	Totals		46	18	11	17

A Played in Australia. P Played in Pakistan.

Notes: The following deputised for the official touring captain or were appointed by the home authority for only a minor proportion of the series:

[1]Imtiaz Ahmed (Second). [2]K. J. Hughes (Second). [3]Zaheer Abbas (First, Second and Third).

HIGHEST INNINGS TOTALS

For Australia	in Australia: 585 at Adelaide	1972-73
	in Pakistan: 617 at Faisalabad	1979-80
For Pakistan	in Australia: 624 at Adelaide	1983-84
	in Pakistan: 580-9 dec. at Peshawar	1998-99

LOWEST INNINGS TOTALS

For Australia	in Australia: 125 at Melbourne	1981-82
	in Pakistan: 80 at Karachi	1956-57
For Pakistan	in Australia: 62 at Perth	1981-82
	in Pakistan: 134 at Dacca	1959-60

INDIVIDUAL HUNDREDS

For Australia (53)

J. Benaud (1)
142 Melbourne . . 1972-73
D. C. Boon (1)
114* Karachi 1994-95
A. R. Border (6)
105† Melbourne . . 1978-79
150* } Lahore 1979-80
153 }
118 Brisbane . . . 1983-84
117* Adelaide . . . 1983-84
113* Faisalabad . . 1988-89
G. S. Chappell (6)
116* Melbourne . . 1972-73
121 Melbourne . . 1976-77
235 Faisalabad . . 1979-80
201 Brisbane . . . 1981-82
150* Brisbane . . . 1983-84
182 Sydney 1983-84
I. M. Chappell (1)
196 Adelaide . . . 1972-73
G. J. Cosier (1)
168 Melbourne . . 1976-77
I. C. Davis (1)
105† Adelaide . . . 1976-77
A. C. Gilchrist (1)
149* Hobart 1999-00
K. J. Hughes (2)
106 Perth. 1981-82
106 Adelaide . . . 1983-84
D. M. Jones (2)
116 } Adelaide . . . 1989-90
121* }
J. L. Langer (3)
116 Peshawar . . . 1998-99
127 Hobart 1999-00
144 Perth. 1999-00
R. B. McCosker (1)
105 Melbourne . . 1976-77
R. W. Marsh (1)
118† Adelaide . . . 1972-73
N. C. O'Neill (1)
134 Lahore 1959-60
W. B. Phillips (1)
159† Perth. 1983-84
R. T. Ponting (1)
197 Perth. 1999-00
I. R. Redpath (1)
135 Melbourne . . 1972-73
G. M. Ritchie (1)
106* Faisalabad . . 1982-83
A. P. Sheahan (1)
127 Melbourne . . 1972-73
R. B. Simpson (2)
153 } †Karachi 1964-65
115 }
M. J. Slater (3)
110 Rawalpindi . . 1994-95
108 Rawalpindi . . 1998-99
169 Brisbane . . . 1999-00
M. A. Taylor (4)
101† Melbourne . . 1989-90
101* Sydney 1989-90
123 Hobart 1995-96
334* Peshawar . . . 1998-99
K. D. Walters (1)
107 Adelaide . . . 1976-77
M. E. Waugh (3)
116 Sydney 1995-96
117 Karachi 1998-99
100 Brisbane . . . 1999-00
S. R. Waugh (2)
112* Brisbane . . . 1995-96
157 Rawalpindi . . 1998-99
K. C. Wessels (1)
179 Adelaide . . . 1983-84
G. M. Wood (1)
100 Melbourne . . 1981-82
G. N. Yallop (3)
172 Faisalabad . . 1979-80
141 Perth. 1983-84
268 Melbourne . . 1983-84

For Pakistan (44)

Aamir Sohail (2)
105 Lahore 1994-95
133 Karachi 1998-99
Asif Iqbal (3)
152* Adelaide . . . 1976-77
120 Sydney 1976-77
134* Perth. 1978-79
Hanif Mohammad (2)
101* Karachi 1959-60
104 Melbourne . . 1964-65
Ijaz Ahmed, sen. (6)
122 Faisalabad . . 1988-89
121 Melbourne . . 1989-90
137 Sydney 1995-96
155 Peshawar . . . 1998-99
120* Karachi 1998-99
115 Perth. 1999-00
Imran Khan (1)
136 Adelaide . . . 1989-90
Inzamam-ul-Haq (1)
118 Hobart 1999-00
Javed Miandad (6)
129* Perth. 1978-79
106* Faisalabad . . 1979-80
138 Lahore 1982-83
131 Adelaide . . . 1983-84
211 Karachi 1988-89
107 Faisalabad . . 1988-89
Khalid Ibadulla (1)
166† Karachi 1964-65
Majid Khan (3)
158 Melbourne . . 1972-73
108 Melbourne . . 1978-79
110* Lahore 1979-80
Mansoor Akhtar (1)
111 Faisalabad . . 1982-83
Mohsin Khan (3)
135 Lahore 1982-83
149 Adelaide . . . 1983-84
152 Melbourne . . 1983-84
Moin Khan (1)
115*† Lahore 1994-95
Mushtaq Mohammad (1)
121 Sydney 1972-73
Qasim Omar (1)
113 Adelaide . . . 1983-84
Sadiq Mohammad (2)
137 Melbourne . . 1972-73
105 Melbourne . . 1976-77
Saeed Ahmed (1)
166 Lahore 1959-60
Saeed Anwar (3)
145 Rawalpindi . . 1998-99
126 Peshawar . . . 1998-99
119 Brisbane . . . 1999-00
Salim Malik (2)
237 Rawalpindi . . 1994-95
143 Lahore 1994-95
Taslim Arif (1)
210* Faisalabad . . 1979-80
Wasim Akram (1)
123 Adelaide . . . 1989-90
Zaheer Abbas (2)
101 Adelaide . . . 1976-77
126 Faisalabad . . 1982-83

† *Signifies hundred on first appearance in Australia–Pakistan Tests.*

RECORD PARTNERSHIPS FOR EACH WICKET

For Australia

269 for 1st	M. J. Slater and G. S. Blewett at Brisbane	1999-2000
279 for 2nd	M. A. Taylor and J. L. Langer at Peshawar	1998-99
203 for 3rd	G. N. Yallop and K. J. Hughes at Melbourne	1983-84
217 for 4th	G. S. Chappell and G. N. Yallop at Faisalabad	1979-80
327 for 5th	J. L. Langer and R. T. Ponting at Perth	1999-2000
238 for 6th	J. L. Langer and A. C. Gilchrist at Hobart	1999-2000
185 for 7th	G. N. Yallop and G. R. J. Matthews at Melbourne	1983-84
117 for 8th	G. J. Cosier and K. J. O'Keeffe at Melbourne	1976-77
83 for 9th	J. R. Watkins and R. A. L. Massie at Sydney	1972-73
86 for 10th	S. K. Warne and S. A. Muller at Brisbane	1999-2000

For Pakistan

249 for 1st	Khalid Ibadulla and Abdul Kadir at Karachi	1964-65
233 for 2nd	Mohsin Khan and Qasim Omar at Adelaide	1983-84
223* for 3rd	Taslim Arif and Javed Miandad at Faisalabad	1979-80
177 for 4th	Saeed Anwar and Yousuf Youhana at Brisbane	1999-2000
186 for 5th	Javed Miandad and Salim Malik at Adelaide	1983-84
196 for 6th	Salim Malik and Aamir Sohail at Lahore	1994-95
104 for 7th	Intikhab Alam and Wasim Bari at Adelaide	1972-73
111 for 8th	Majid Khan and Imran Khan at Lahore	1979-80
120 for 9th	Saeed Anwar and Mushtaq Ahmed at Rawalpindi	1998-99
87 for 10th	Asif Iqbal and Iqbal Qasim at Adelaide	1976-77

TEN WICKETS OR MORE IN A MATCH

For Australia (4)

10-111 (7-87, 3-24)†	R. J. Bright, Karachi	1979-80
10-135 (6-82, 4-53)	D. K. Lillee, Melbourne	1976-77
11-118 (5-32, 6-86)†	C. G. Rackemann, Perth	1983-84
11-77 (7-23, 4-54)	S. K. Warne, Brisbane	1995-96

For Pakistan (6)

11-218 (4-76, 7-142)	Abdul Qadir, Faisalabad	1982-83
13-114 (6-34, 7-80)†	Fazal Mahmood, Karachi	1956-57
12-165 (6-102, 6-63)	Imran Khan, Sydney	1976-77
11-118 (4-69, 7-49)	Iqbal Qasim, Karachi	1979-80
11-125 (2-39, 9-86)	Sarfraz Nawaz, Melbourne	1978-79
11-160 (6-62, 5-98)†	Wasim Akram, Melbourne	1989-90

† *Signifies ten wickets or more on first appearance in Australia–Pakistan Tests.*

AUSTRALIA v SRI LANKA

Season	Captains Australia	Sri Lanka	T	A	SL	D
1982-83*S*	G. S. Chappell	L. R. D. Mendis	1	1	0	0
1987-88*A*	A. R. Border	R. S. Madugalle	1	1	0	0
1989-90*A*	A. R. Border	A. Ranatunga	2	1	0	1
1992-93*S*	A. R. Border	A. Ranatunga	3	1	0	2
1995-96*A*	M. A. Taylor	A. Ranatunga[1]	3	3	0	0
1999-2000*S*	S. R. Waugh	S. T. Jayasuriya	3	0	1	2
	In Australia		6	5	0	1
	In Sri Lanka		7	2	1	4
	Totals		13	7	1	5

A Played in Australia. *S Played in Sri Lanka.*

Note: The following deputised for the official touring captain:
[1]P. A. de Silva (Third).

HIGHEST INNINGS TOTALS

For Australia in Australia: 617-5 dec. at Perth 1995-96
in Sri Lanka: 514-4 dec. at Kandy 1982-83

For Sri Lanka in Australia: 418 in Brisbane. 1989-90
in Sri Lanka: 547-8 dec. at Colombo (SSC). 1992-93

LOWEST INNINGS TOTALS

For Australia in Australia: 224 at Hobart 1989-90
in Sri Lanka: 140 at Kandy 1999-2000

For Sri Lanka in Australia: 153 at Perth 1987-88
in Sri Lanka: 164 at Colombo (SSC) 1992-93

INDIVIDUAL HUNDREDS

For Australia (16)

D. C. Boon (1)
110 Melbourne . . 1995-96
A. R. Border (1)
106 Moratuwa . . 1992-93
D. W. Hookes (1)
143*† Kandy. 1982-83
D. M. Jones (3)
102† Perth. 1987-88
118* Hobart 1989-90
100* Colombo (KS) 1992-93
T. M. Moody (1)
106† Brisbane . . . 1989-90
R. T. Ponting (1)
105* Colombo (SSC) 1999-00
M. J. Slater (1)
219† Perth. 1995-96
M. A. Taylor (2)
164† Brisbane . . . 1989-90
108 Hobart 1989-90
M. E. Waugh (1)
111 Perth. 1995-96
S. R. Waugh (3)
134* Hobart 1989-90
131* Melbourne . . 1995-96
170 Adelaide . . . 1995-96
K. C. Wessels (1)
141† Kandy. 1982-83

For Sri Lanka (7)

P. A. de Silva (1)	**S. T. Jayasuriya** (1)	**A. Ranatunga** (1)
167 Brisbane . . . 1989-90	112 Adelaide . . . 1995-96	127 Colombo (SSC) 1992-93
A. P. Gurusinha (2)	**R. S. Kaluwitharana** (1)	**H. P. Tillekeratne** (1)
137 Colombo (SSC) 1992-93	132*† Colombo (SSC) 1992-93	119 Perth. 1995-96
143 Melbourne . . 1995-96		

† *Signifies hundred on first appearance in Australia–Sri Lanka Tests.*

RECORD PARTNERSHIPS FOR EACH WICKET

For Australia

228	for 1st	M. J. Slater and M. A. Taylor at Perth	1995-96
170	for 2nd	K. C. Wessels and G. N. Yallop at Kandy	1982-83
158	for 3rd	T. M. Moody and A. R. Border at Brisbane	1989-90
163	for 4th	M. A. Taylor and A. R. Border at Hobart	1989-90
155*	for 5th	D. W. Hookes and A. R. Border at Kandy	1982-83
260*	for 6th	D. M. Jones and S. R. Waugh at Hobart	1989-90
129	for 7th	G. R. J. Matthews and I. A. Healy at Moratuwa	1992-93
107	for 8th	R. T. Ponting and J. N. Gillespie at Kandy	1999-2000
45	for 9th	I. A. Healy and S. K. Warne at Colombo (SSC)	1992-93
49	for 10th	I. A. Healy and M. R. Whitney at Colombo (SSC)	1992-93

For Sri Lanka

110	for 1st	R. S. Mahanama and U. C. Hathurusinghe at Colombo (KS)	1992-93
92	for 2nd	R. S. Mahanama and A. P. Gurusinha at Colombo (SSC)	1992-93
125	for 3rd	S. T. Jayasuriya and S. Ranatunga at Adelaide	1995-96
230	for 4th	A. P. Gurusinha and A. Ranatunga at Colombo (SSC)	1992-93
116	for 5th	H. P. Tillekeratne and A. Ranatunga at Moratuwa	1992-93
96	for 6th	A. P. Gurusinha and R. S. Kaluwitharana at Colombo (SSC)	1992-93
144	for 7th	P. A. de Silva and J. R. Ratnayeke at Brisbane	1989-90
33	for 8th	A. Ranatunga and C. P. H. Ramanayake at Perth	1987-88
46	for 9th	H. D. P. K. Dharmasena and G. P. Wickremasinghe at Perth	1995-96
27	for 10th	P. A. de Silva and C. P. H. Ramanayake at Brisbane	1989-90

BEST MATCH BOWLING ANALYSES

For Australia

8-156 (3-68, 5-88)	M. G. Hughes, Hobart	1989-90

For Sri Lanka

8-157 (5-82, 3-75)	C. P. H. Ramanayake, Moratuwa	1992-93

AUSTRALIA v ZIMBABWE

	Captains					
Season	*Australia*	*Zimbabwe*	*T*	*A*	*Z*	*D*
1999-2000Z	S. R. Waugh	A. D. R. Campbell	1	1	0	0

Z Played in Zimbabwe.

HIGHEST INNINGS TOTALS

For Australia: 422 at Harare 1999-2000

For Zimbabwe: 232 at Harare 1999-2000

INDIVIDUAL HUNDRED

For Australia (1)

S. R. Waugh (1)
151*† Harare. 1999-00

Highest score for Zimbabwe: 91 by M. W. Goodwin at Harare, 1999-2000.

† *Signifies hundred on first appearance in Australia–Zimbabwe Tests.*

HIGHEST PARTNERSHIPS

For Australia

114 for 8th S. R. Waugh and D. W. Fleming at Harare 1999-2000

For Zimbabwe

98 for 2nd T. R. Gripper and M. W. Goodwin at Harare. 1999-2000

BEST MATCH BOWLING ANALYSES

For Australia

6-90 (3-44, 3-46) G. D. McGrath, Harare. 1999-2000

For Zimbabwe

5-93 (5-93) H. H. Streak, Harare 1999-2000

SOUTH AFRICA v WEST INDIES

	Captains					
Season	*South Africa*	*West Indies*	*T*	*SA*	*WI*	*D*
1991-92*W*	K. C. Wessels	R. B. Richardson	1	0	1	0
1998-99*S*	W. J. Cronje	B. C. Lara	5	5	0	0

SIR VIVIAN RICHARDS TROPHY

	Captains						
Season	*South Africa*	*West Indies*	*T*	*SA*	*WI*	*D*	*Held by*
2000-01*W*	S. M. Pollock	C. L. Hooper	5	2	1	2	SA
	In South Africa		5	5	0	0	
	In West Indies		6	2	2	2	
	Totals		11	7	2	2	

S Played in South Africa. W Played in West Indies.

HIGHEST INNINGS TOTALS

For South Africa	in South Africa: 406-8 dec. at Cape Town	1998-99
	in West Indies: 454 at Bridgetown	2000-01
For West Indies	in South Africa: 271 at Cape Town	1998-99
	in West Indies: 387 at Bridgetown	2000-01

LOWEST INNINGS TOTALS

For South Africa	in South Africa: 195 at Port Elizabeth	1998-99
	in West Indies: 141 at Kingston	2000-01
For West Indies	in South Africa: 121 at Port Elizabeth	1998-99
	in West Indies: 140 at St John's	2000-01

INDIVIDUAL HUNDREDS

For South Africa (10)

M. V. Boucher (1)
100 Centurion . . . 1998-99

D. J. Cullinan (3)
168 Cape Town . . 1998-99
103 Port-of-Spain 2000-01
134 Bridgetown . 2000-01

A. C. Hudson (1)
163† Bridgetown . 1991-92

J. H. Kallis (1)
110 Cape Town . . 1998-99

G. Kirsten (2)
134 Centurion . . 1998-99
150 Georgetown . 2000-01

S. M. Pollock (1)
106* Bridgetown . 2000-01

J. N. Rhodes (1)
103* Centurion . . 1998-99

For West Indies (1)

R. D. Jacobs (1)
113* Bridgetown . 2000-01

† *Signifies hundred on first appearance in South Africa–West Indies Tests.*

RECORD PARTNERSHIPS FOR EACH WICKET

For South Africa

97 for 1st	G. Kirsten and H. H. Gibbs at Durban	1998-99
146 for 2nd	G. Kirsten and J. H. Kallis at Georgetown	2000-01
235 for 3rd	J. H. Kallis and D. J. Cullinan at Cape Town	1998-99
149 for 4th	D. J. Cullinan and N. D. McKenzie at Bridgetown	2000-01
115 for 5th	G. Kirsten and J. N. Rhodes at Centurion	1998-99
92 for 6th	J. N. Rhodes and S. M. Pollock at Port Elizabeth	1998-99
92 for 7th	J. H. Kallis and M. V. Boucher at Centurion	1998-99
75 for 8th	S. M. Pollock and N. Boje at St John's	2000-01
132 for 9th	S. M. Pollock and A. A. Donald at Bridgetown	2000-01
25 for 10th	P. L. Symcox and D. J. Terbrugge at Johannesburg	1998-99

For West Indies

99 for 1st	D. L. Haynes and P. V. Simmons at Bridgetown	1991-92
88 for 2nd	C. H. Gayle and M. N. Samuels at Georgetown	2000-01
160 for 3rd	S. Chanderpaul and B. C. Lara at Durban	1998-99
91 for 4th	S. Chanderpaul and C. L. Hooper at Johannesburg	1998-99
116 for 5th	B. C. Lara and C. L. Hooper at Bridgetown	2000-01
92 for 6th	R. R. Sarwan and C. L. Hooper at Port-of-Spain	2000-01
81 for 7th	R. D. Jacobs and N. A. M. McLean at Centurion	1998-99
65 for 8th	R. D. Jacobs and N. A. M. McLean at Cape Town	1998-99
71 for 9th	R. D. Jacobs and M. Dillon at Port-of-Spain	2000-01
64 for 10th	R. D. Jacobs and M. Dillon at Cape Town	1998-99

BEST MATCH BOWLING ANALYSES

For South Africa

9-94 (5-28, 4-66) S. M. Pollock, Kingston 2000-01

For West Indies

8-79 (2-28, 6-51) C. E. L. Ambrose, Port Elizabeth 1998-99

SOUTH AFRICA v NEW ZEALAND

	Captains					
Season	*South Africa*	*New Zealand*	*T*	*SA*	*NZ*	*D*
1931-32*N*	H. B. Cameron	M. L. Page	2	2	0	0
1952-53*N*	J. E. Cheetham	W. M. Wallace	2	1	0	1
1953-54*S*	J. E. Cheetham	G. O. Rabone[1]	5	4	0	1
1961-62*S*	D. J. McGlew	J. R. Reid	5	2	2	1
1963-64*N*	T. L. Goddard	J. R. Reid	3	0	0	3
1994-95*S*	W. J. Cronje	K. R. Rutherford	3	2	1	0
1994-95*N*	W. J. Cronje	K. R. Rutherford	1	1	0	0
1998-99*N*	W. J. Cronje	D. J. Nash	3	1	0	2
2000-01*S*	S. M. Pollock	S. P. Fleming	3	2	0	1
	In New Zealand		11	5	0	6
	In South Africa		16	10	3	3
	Totals		27	15	3	9

N Played in New Zealand. S Played in South Africa.

Note: The following deputised for the official touring captain:
[1]B. Sutcliffe (Fourth and Fifth).

HIGHEST INNINGS TOTALS

For South Africa in South Africa: 471-9 dec. at Bloemfontein 2000-01
in New Zealand: 621-5 dec. at Auckland 1998-99

For New Zealand in South Africa: 505 at Cape Town 1953-54
in New Zealand: 364 at Wellington 1931-32

LOWEST INNINGS TOTALS

For South Africa in South Africa: 148 at Johannesburg 1953-54
in New Zealand: 223 at Dunedin 1963-64

For New Zealand in South Africa: 79 at Johannesburg 1953-54
in New Zealand: 138 at Dunedin 1963-64

INDIVIDUAL HUNDREDS

For South Africa (23)

X. C. Balaskas (1)
122* Wellington . . 1931-32
J. A. J. Christy (1)
103† Christchurch. 1931-32
W. J. Cronje (2)
112 Cape Town. . 1994-95
101 Auckland. . . 1994-95
D. J. Cullinan (2)
275* Auckland. . . 1998-99
152 Wellington . . 1998-99
H. H. Dippenaar (1)
100 Johannesburg 2000-01
W. R. Endean (1)
116 Auckland. . . 1952-53

H. H. Gibbs (2)
211* Christchurch. 1998-99
120 Wellington . . 1998-99
J. H. Kallis (2)
148* Christchurch. 1998-99
160 Bloemfontein 2000-01
G. Kirsten (1)
128 Auckland. . . 1998-99
D. J. McGlew (3)
255*† Wellington . . 1952-53
127*‡ Durban 1961-62
120 Johannesburg 1961-62
N. D. McKenzie (1)
120 Port Elizabeth 2000-01

R. A. McLean (2)
101 Durban 1953-54
113 Cape Town. . 1961-62
B. Mitchell (1)
113† Christchurch. 1931-32
A. R. A. Murray (1)
109† Wellington . . 1952-53
D. J. Richardson (1)
109 Cape Town. . 1994-95
J. H. B. Waite (1)
101 Johannesburg 1961-62

For New Zealand (8)

P. T. Barton (1)
109 Port Elizabeth 1961-62
P. G. Z. Harris (1)
101 Cape Town. . 1961-62
G. O. Rabone (1)
107 Durban 1953-54

J. R. Reid (2)
135 Cape Town. . 1953-54
142 Johannesburg 1961-62
B. W. Sinclair (1)
138 Auckland. . . 1963-64

M. S. Sinclair (1)
150 Port Elizabeth 2000-01
H. G. Vivian (1)
100† Wellington . . 1931-32

† *Signifies hundred on first appearance in South Africa–New Zealand Tests.*
‡ *Carried his bat.*

RECORD PARTNERSHIPS FOR EACH WICKET

For South Africa

196	for 1st	J. A. J. Christy and B. Mitchell at Christchurch	1931-32
315*	for 2nd†	H. H. Gibbs and J. H. Kallis at Christchurch	1998-99
183	for 3rd	G. Kirsten and D. J. Cullinan at Auckland	1998-99
145	for 4th	D. J. Cullinan and W. J. Cronje at Wellington	1998-99
141	for 5th	D. J. Cullinan and J. N. Rhodes at Auckland	1998-99
126*	for 6th	D. J. Cullinan and S. M. Pollock at Auckland	1998-99
246	for 7th†	D. J. McGlew and A. R. A. Murray at Wellington	1952-53
136	for 8th	N. D. McKenzie and N. Boje at Port Elizabeth	2000-01
60	for 9th	P. M. Pollock and N. A. T. Adcock at Port Elizabeth	1961-62
47	for 10th	D. J. McGlew and H. D. Bromfield at Port Elizabeth	1961-62

For New Zealand

126	for 1st	G. O. Rabone and M. E. Chapple at Cape Town	1953-54
90	for 2nd	M. J. Horne and N. J. Astle at Auckland	1998-99
94	for 3rd	M. B. Poore and B. Sutcliffe at Cape Town	1953-54
171	for 4th	B. W. Sinclair and S. N. McGregor at Auckland	1963-64
176	for 5th	J. R. Reid and J. E. F. Beck at Cape Town	1953-54
100	for 6th	H. G. Vivian and F. T. Badcock at Wellington	1931-32
84	for 7th	J. R. Reid and G. A. Bartlett at Johannesburg	1961-62
74	for 8th	S. A. Thomson and D. J. Nash at Johannesburg	1994-95
69	for 9th	C. F. W. Allcott and I. B. Cromb at Wellington	1931-32
57	for 10th	S. B. Doull and R. P. de Groen at Johannesburg	1994-95

† *Denotes record partnership against all countries.*

TEN WICKETS OR MORE IN A MATCH

For South Africa (1)

11-196 (6-128, 5-68)† S. F. Burke, Cape Town 1961-62

† *Signifies ten wickets or more on first appearance in South Africa–New Zealand Tests.*

Note: The best match figures for New Zealand are 8-134 (3-57, 5-77) by M. N. Hart at Johannesburg, 1994-95.

SOUTH AFRICA v INDIA

	Captains					
Season	*South Africa*	*India*	*T*	*SA*	*I*	*D*
1992-93*S*	K. C. Wessels	M. Azharuddin	4	1	0	3
1996-97*I*	W. J. Cronje	S. R. Tendulkar	3	1	2	0
1996-97*S*	W. J. Cronje	S. R. Tendulkar	3	2	0	1
1999-2000*I*	W. J. Cronje	S. R. Tendulkar	2	2	0	0
	In South Africa		7	3	0	4
	In India		5	3	2	0
	Totals.		12	6	2	4

S Played in South Africa. I Played in India.

HIGHEST INNINGS TOTALS

For South Africa in South Africa: 529-7 dec. at Cape Town 1996-97
in India: 479 at Bangalore 1999-2000

For India in South Africa: 410 at Johannesburg 1996-97
in India: 400-7 dec. at Kanpur. 1996-97

LOWEST INNINGS TOTALS

For South Africa in South Africa: 235 at Durban 1996-97
in India: 105 at Ahmedabad 1996-97

For India in South Africa: 66 at Durban. 1996-97
in India: 113 at Mumbai 1999-2000

INDIVIDUAL HUNDREDS

For South Africa (10)

W. J. Cronje (1)
135 Port Elizabeth 1992-93

D. J. Cullinan (2)
153* Calcutta. . . . 1996-97
122* Johannesburg 1996-97

A. C. Hudson (1)
146 Calcutta. . . . 1996-97

G. Kirsten (3)
102 } Calcutta. . . . 1996-97
133 }
103 Cape Town. . 1996-97

L. Klusener (1)
102* Cape Town. . 1996-97

B. M. McMillan (1)
103* Cape Town. . 1996-97

K. C. Wessels (1)
118† Durban 1992-93

For India (9)

P. K. Amre (1)

103†	Durban	1992-93

M. Azharuddin (4)

109	Calcutta	1996-97
163*	Kanpur	1996-97
115	Cape Town	1996-97
102	Bangalore	1999-00

R. Dravid (1)

148	Johannesburg	1996-97

Kapil Dev (1)

129	Port Elizabeth	1992-93

S. R. Tendulkar (2)

111	Johannesburg	1992-93
169	Cape Town	1996-97

† *Signifies hundred on first appearance in South Africa–India Tests.*

RECORD PARTNERSHIPS FOR EACH WICKET

For South Africa

236	for 1st	A. C. Hudson and G. Kirsten at Calcutta	1996-97
212	for 2nd	G. Kirsten and D. J. Cullinan at Calcutta	1996-97
114	for 3rd	G. Kirsten and D. J. Cullinan at Cape Town	1996-97
94	for 4th	A. C. Hudson and D. J. Cullinan at Cape Town	1996-97
164	for 5th	J. H. Kallis and L. Klusener at Bangalore	1999-2000
112	for 6th	B. M. McMillan and S. M. Pollock at Johannesburg	1996-97
101*	for 7th	B. M. McMillan and S. M. Pollock at Cape Town	1996-97
147*	for 8th	B. M. McMillan and L. Klusener at Cape Town	1996-97
60	for 9th	P. S. de Villiers and A. A. Donald at Ahmedabad	1996-97
74	for 10th	B. M. McMillan and A. A. Donald at Durban	1996-97

For India

90	for 1st	V. Rathore and N. R. Mongia at Johannesburg	1996-97
85	for 2nd	M. Prabhakar and S. V. Manjrekar at Cape Town	1992-93
54	for 3rd	R. Dravid and S. R. Tendulkar at Johannesburg	1996-97
145	for 4th	R. Dravid and S. C. Ganguly at Johannesburg	1996-97
87	for 5th	M. Azharuddin and P. K. Amre at Durban	1992-93
222	for 6th	S. R. Tendulkar and M. Azharuddin at Cape Town	1996-97
76	for 7th	R. Dravid and J. Srinath at Johannesburg	1996-97
161	for 8th†	M. Azharuddin and A. Kumble at Calcutta	1996-97
77	for 9th	Kapil Dev and A. Kumble at Port Elizabeth	1992-93
52	for 10th	A. B. Agarkar and M. Kartik at Mumbai	1999-2000

† *Denotes record partnership against all countries.*

TEN WICKETS OR MORE IN A MATCH

For South Africa (1)

12-139 (5-55, 7-84)	A. A. Donald, Port Elizabeth	1992-93

For India (1)

10-153 (5-60, 5-93)	B. K. V. Prasad, Durban	1996-97

SOUTH AFRICA v PAKISTAN

	Captains					
Season	*South Africa*	*Pakistan*	*T*	*SA*	*P*	*D*
1994-95*S*	W. J. Cronje	Salim Malik	1	1	0	0
1997-98*P*	W. J. Cronje	Saeed Anwar	3	1	0	2
1997-98*S*	W. J. Cronje[1]	Rashid Latif[2]	3	1	1	1
	In South Africa		4	2	1	1
	In Pakistan		3	1	0	2
	Totals		7	3	1	3

S Played in South Africa. P Played in Pakistan.

Notes: The following deputised for the official touring captain or were appointed by the home authority for only a minor proportion of the series:
[1]G. Kirsten (First). [2]Aamir Sohail (First and Second).

HIGHEST INNINGS TOTALS

For South Africa: 460 at Johannesburg 1994-95

For Pakistan: 456 at Rawalpindi 1997-98

LOWEST INNINGS TOTALS

For South Africa: 214 at Faisalabad 1997-98

For Pakistan: 92 at Faisalabad 1997-98

INDIVIDUAL HUNDREDS

For South Africa (3)

G. Kirsten (1)
100*‡ Faisalabad .. 1997-98

B. M. McMillan (1)
113† Johannesburg 1994-95

P. L. Symcox (1)
108 Johannesburg 1997-98

For Pakistan (5)

Ali Naqvi (1)
115† Rawalpindi .. 1997-98

Azhar Mahmood (3)
128*† Rawalpindi .. 1997-98
136 Johannesburg 1997-98
132 Durban 1997-98

Saeed Anwar (1)
118 Durban 1997-98

† *Signifies hundred on first appearance in South Africa–Pakistan Tests.*
‡ *Carried his bat.*

RECORD PARTNERSHIPS FOR EACH WICKET

For South Africa

135 for 1st	G. Kirsten and A. M. Bacher at Sheikhupura	1997-98
114 for 2nd	G. Kirsten and J. H. Kallis at Rawalpindi	1997-98
83 for 3rd	J. H. Kallis and H. D. Ackerman at Durban	1997-98
79 for 4th	G. Kirsten and W. J. Cronje at Johannesburg	1994-95
43 for 5th	P. L. Symcox and W. J. Cronje at Faisalabad	1997-98

157 for 6th	J. N. Rhodes and B. M. McMillan at Johannesburg	1994-95
106 for 7th	S. M. Pollock and D. J. Richardson at Rawalpindi	1997-98
124 for 8th	G. Kirsten and P. L. Symcox at Faisalabad	1997-98
195 for 9th†	M. V. Boucher and P. L. Symcox at Johannesburg	1997-98
71 for 10th	P. S. de Villiers and A. A. Donald at Johannesburg	1994-95

For Pakistan

101 for 1st	Saeed Anwar and Aamir Sohail at Durban	1997-98
69 for 2nd	Ali Naqvi and Mohammad Ramzan at Rawalpindi	1997-98
72 for 3rd	Ijaz Ahmed, sen. and Mohammad Wasim at Johannesburg	1997-98
93 for 4th	Asif Mujtaba and Inzamam-ul-Haq at Johannesburg	1994-95
44 for 5th	Ali Naqvi and Mohammad Wasim at Rawalpindi	1997-98
144 for 6th	Inzamam-ul-Haq and Moin Khan at Faisalabad	1997-98
35 for 7th	Salim Malik and Wasim Akram at Johannesburg	1994-95
40 for 8th	Inzamam-ul-Haq and Kabir Khan at Johannesburg	1994-95
80 for 9th	Azhar Mahmood and Shoaib Akhtar at Durban	1997-98
151 for 10th†	Azhar Mahmood and Mushtaq Ahmed at Rawalpindi	1997-98

† *Denotes record partnership against all countries.*

TEN WICKETS OR MORE IN A MATCH

For South Africa (1)

10-108 (6-81, 4-27)†	P. S. de Villiers, Johannesburg	1994-95

For Pakistan (1)

10-133 (6-78, 4-55)	Waqar Younis, Port Elizabeth	1997-98

† *Signifies ten wickets or more on first appearance in South Africa–Pakistan Tests.*

SOUTH AFRICA v SRI LANKA

	Captains					
Season	*South Africa*	*Sri Lanka*	*T*	*SA*	*SL*	*D*
1993-94*SL*	K. C. Wessels	A. Ranatunga	3	1	0	2
1997-98*SA*	W. J. Cronje	A. Ranatunga	2	2	0	0
2000*SL*	S. M. Pollock	S. T. Jayasuriya	3	1	1	1
2000-01*SA*	S. M. Pollock	S. T. Jayasuriya	3	2	0	1
	In South Africa		5	4	0	1
	In Sri Lanka		6	2	1	3
	Totals		11	6	1	4

SA Played in South Africa. SL Played in Sri Lanka.

HIGHEST INNINGS TOTALS

For South Africa in South Africa: 504-7 dec. at Cape Town	2000-01
in Sri Lanka: 495 at Colombo (SSC)	1993-94
For Sri Lanka in South Africa: 306 at Cape Town (in each innings)	1997-98
in Sri Lanka: 522 at Galle	2000

LOWEST INNINGS TOTALS

For South Africa	in South Africa: 200 at Centurion	1997-98
	in Sri Lanka: 231 at Kandy	2000
For Sri Lanka	in South Africa: 95 at Cape Town	2000-01
	in Sri Lanka: 119 at Colombo (SSC)	1993-94

INDIVIDUAL HUNDREDS

For South Africa (11)

W. J. Cronje (1)
122 Colombo (SSC) 1993-94

D. J. Cullinan (5)
102 Colombo (PSS) 1993-94
113 Cape Town 1997-98
103 Centurion 1997-98
114* Galle 2000
112 Cape Town 2000-01

G. Kirsten (1)
180 Durban 2000-01

L. Klusener (1)
118* Kandy 2000

N. D. McKenzie (1)
103 Centurion 2000-01

S. M. Pollock (1)
111 Centurion 2000-01

J. N. Rhodes (1)
101*† Moratuwa 1993-94

For Sri Lanka (5)

M. S. Atapattu (1)
120 Kandy 2000

S. T. Jayasuriya (1)
148 Galle 2000

D. P. M. D. Jayawardene (2)
167† Galle 2000
101* Colombo (SSC) 2000

A. Ranatunga (1)
131† Moratuwa 1993-94

† *Signifies hundred on first appearance in South Africa–Sri Lanka Tests.*

RECORD PARTNERSHIPS FOR EACH WICKET

For South Africa

137 for 1st	K. C. Wessels and A. C. Hudson at Colombo (SSC)	1993-94
96 for 2nd	G. Kirsten and J. H. Kallis at Cape Town	2000-01
116 for 3rd	J. H. Kallis and D. J. Cullinan at Cape Town	1997-98
116 for 4th	G. Kirsten and W. J. Cronje at Centurion	1997-98
86 for 5th	D. J. Cullinan and M. V. Boucher at Cape Town	2000-01
124 for 6th	L. Klusener and M. V. Boucher at Kandy	2000
95 for 7th	S. M. Pollock and M. V. Boucher at Cape Town	1997-98
150 for 8th†	N. D. McKenzie and S. M. Pollock at Centurion	2000-01
45 for 9th	N. Boje and P. R. Adams at Kandy	2000
43 for 10th	L. Klusener and M. Hayward at Kandy	2000

For Sri Lanka

193 for 1st	M. S. Atapattu and S. T. Jayasuriya at Galle	2000
103 for 2nd	S. T. Jayasuriya and R. P. Arnold at Colombo (SSC)	2000
168 for 3rd	K. Sangakkara and D. P. M. D. Jayawardene at Durban	2000-01
118 for 4th	R. S. Mahanama and A. Ranatunga at Centurion	1997-98
121 for 5th	P. A. de Silva and A. Ranatunga at Moratuwa	1993-94
103 for 6th	A. Ranatunga and H. P. Tillekeratne at Moratuwa	1993-94
43 for 7th	P. A. de Silva and G. P. Wickremasinghe at Centurion	1997-98
117 for 8th†	D. P. M. D. Jayawardene and W. P. U. J. C. Vaas at Galle	2000
48 for 9th	G. P. Wickremasinghe and M. Muralitharan at Cape Town	1997-98
22 for 10th	W. P. U. J. C. Vaas and M. Muralitharan at Galle	2000

† *Denotes record partnership against all countries.*

TEN WICKETS OR MORE IN A MATCH

For Sri Lanka (2)

13-171 (6-87, 7-84)	M. Muralitharan at Galle	2000
11-161 (5-122, 6-39)	M. Muralitharan at Durban	2000-01

Note: The best match figures for South Africa are 9-106 (5-48, 4-58) by B. N. Schultz at Colombo (SSC), 1993-94.

SOUTH AFRICA v ZIMBABWE

	Captains					
Season	*South Africa*	*Zimbabwe*	*T*	*SA*	*Z*	*D*
1995-96*Z*	W. J. Cronje	A. Flower	1	1	0	0
1999-2000*S*	W. J. Cronje	A. D. R. Campbell	1	1	0	0
1999-2000*Z*	W. J. Cronje	A. Flower	1	1	0	0
	In Zimbabwe		2	2	0	0
	In South Africa		1	1	0	0
	Totals		3	3	0	0

S Played in South Africa. Z Played in Zimbabwe.

HIGHEST INNINGS TOTALS

For South Africa: 462-9 dec. at Harare . . . 1999-2000

For Zimbabwe: 283 at Harare . . . 1995-96

LOWEST INNINGS TOTALS

For South Africa: 346 at Harare . . . 1995-96

For Zimbabwe: 102 at Harare . . . 1999-2000

INDIVIDUAL HUNDREDS

For South Africa (3)

M. V. Boucher (1)
125 Harare . . . 1999-00

A. C. Hudson (1)
135† Harare . . . 1995-96

J. H. Kallis (1)
115 Harare . . . 1999-00

Highest score for Zimbabwe: 85 by G. J. Whittall at Bloemfontein, 1999-2000.

† *Signifies hundred on first appearance in South Africa–Zimbabwe Tests.*

HUNDRED PARTNERSHIPS

For South Africa

100 for 4th	J. H. Kallis and W. J. Cronje at Harare	1999-2000
101 for 6th	A. C. Hudson and B. M. McMillan at Harare	1995-96
148 for 8th	M. V. Boucher and S. M. Pollock at Harare	1999-2000

Note: The highest partnership for Zimbabwe is 97 for the 5th wicket between A. Flower and G. J. Whittall at Harare, 1995-96.

TEN WICKETS OR MORE IN A MATCH

For South Africa (1)

11-113 (3-42, 8-71)† A. A. Donald, Harare 1995-96

Note: The best match figures for Zimbabwe are 5-105 (3-68, 2-37) by A. C. I. Lock at Harare, 1995-96.

† *Signifies ten wickets or more on first appearance in South Africa–Zimbabwe Tests.*

WEST INDIES v NEW ZEALAND

	Captains					
Season	*West Indies*	*New Zealand*	*T*	*WI*	*NZ*	*D*
1951-52*N*	J. D. C. Goddard	B. Sutcliffe	2	1	0	1
1955-56*N*	D. St E. Atkinson	J. R. Reid[1]	4	3	1	0
1968-69*N*	G. S. Sobers	G. T. Dowling	3	1	1	1
1971-72*W*	G. S. Sobers	G. T. Dowling[2]	5	0	0	5
1979-80*N*	C. H. Lloyd	G. P. Howarth	3	0	1	2
1984-85*W*	I. V. A. Richards	G. P. Howarth	4	2	0	2
1986-87*N*	I. V. A. Richards	J. V. Coney	3	1	1	1
1994-95*N*	C. A. Walsh	K. R. Rutherford	2	1	0	1
1995-96*W*	C. A. Walsh	L. K. Germon	2	1	0	1
1999-2000*N*	B. C. Lara	S. P. Fleming	2	0	2	0
	In New Zealand		19	7	6	6
	In West Indies		11	3	0	8
	Totals		30	10	6	14

N Played in New Zealand. W Played in West Indies.

Notes: The following deputised for the official touring captain or were appointed by the home authority for only a minor proportion of the series:
[1]H. B. Cave (First). [2]B. E. Congdon (Third, Fourth and Fifth).

HIGHEST INNINGS TOTALS

For West Indies in West Indies: 564-8 at Bridgetown. 1971-72
in New Zealand: 660-5 dec. at Wellington. 1994-95

For New Zealand in West Indies: 543-3 dec. at Georgetown 1971-72
in New Zealand: 518-9 dec. at Wellington. 1999-2000

LOWEST INNINGS TOTALS

For West Indies in West Indies: 133 at Bridgetown 1971-72
in New Zealand: 77 at Auckland 1955-56

For New Zealand in West Indies: 94 at Bridgetown. 1984-85
in New Zealand: 74 at Dunedin 1955-56

INDIVIDUAL HUNDREDS

By West Indies (33)

J. C. Adams (2)
151 Wellington . . 1994-95
208* St John's . . . 1995-96
S. L. Campbell (2)
208 Bridgetown . 1995-96
170 Hamilton . . . 1999-00
M. C. Carew (1)
109† Auckland . . . 1968-69
C. A. Davis (1)
183 Bridgetown . 1971-72
R. C. Fredericks (1)
163 Kingston . . . 1971-72
C. G. Greenidge (2)
100 Port-of-Spain 1984-85
213 Auckland . . . 1986-87
A. F. G. Griffith (1)
114† Hamilton . . . 1999-00
D. L. Haynes (3)
105† Dunedin . . . 1979-80
122 Christchurch . 1979-80
121 Wellington . . 1986-87
A. I. Kallicharran (2)
100*† Georgetown . 1971-72
101 Port-of-Spain 1971-72
C. L. King (1)
100* Christchurch . 1979-80
B. C. Lara (1)
147 Wellington . . 1994-95
J. R. Murray (1)
101* Wellington . . 1994-95
S. M. Nurse (2)
168† Auckland . . . 1968-69
258 Christchurch . 1968-69
I. V. A. Richards (1)
105 Bridgetown . 1984-85
R. B. Richardson (1)
185 Georgetown . 1984-85
L. G. Rowe (3)
214 } †Kingston . . . 1971-72
100* }
100 Christchurch . 1979-80
R. G. Samuels (1)
125 St John's . . . 1995-96
G. S. Sobers (1)
142 Bridgetown . 1971-72
J. B. Stollmeyer (1)
152 Auckland . . . 1951-52
C. L. Walcott (1)
115 Auckland . . . 1951-52
E. D. Weekes (3)
123 Dunedin . . . 1955-56
103 Christchurch . 1955-56
156 Wellington . . 1955-56
F. M. M. Worrell (1)
100 Auckland . . . 1951-52

By New Zealand (21)

N. J. Astle (2)
125† Bridgetown . 1995-96
103 St John's . . . 1995-96
M. G. Burgess (1)
101 Kingston . . . 1971-72
B. E. Congdon (2)
166* Port-of-Spain 1971-72
126 Bridgetown . 1971-72
J. J. Crowe (1)
112 Kingston . . . 1984-85
M. D. Crowe (3)
188 Georgetown . 1984-85
119 Wellington . . 1986-87
104 Auckland . . . 1986-87
B. A. Edgar (1)
127 Auckland . . . 1979-80
R. J. Hadlee (1)
103 Christchurch . 1979-80
B. F. Hastings (2)
117* Christchurch . 1968-69
105 Bridgetown . 1971-72
G. P. Howarth (1)
147 Christchurch . 1979-80
T. W. Jarvis (1)
182 Georgetown . 1971-72
A. C. Parore (1)
100*† Christchurch . 1994-95
M. S. Sinclair (1)
214† Wellington . . 1999-00
B. R. Taylor (1)
124† Auckland . . . 1968-69
G. M. Turner (2)
223*‡ Kingston . . . 1971-72
259 Georgetown . 1971-72
J. G. Wright (1)
138 Wellington . . 1986-87

† *Signifies hundred on first appearance in West Indies–New Zealand Tests.*
‡ *Carried his bat.*

Notes: E. D. Weekes in 1955-56 made three hundreds in consecutive innings.

L. G. Rowe and A. I. Kallicharran each scored hundreds in their first two innings in Test cricket, Rowe being the only batsman to do so in his first match.

RECORD PARTNERSHIPS FOR EACH WICKET

For West Indies

276 for 1st	A. F. G. Griffith and S. L. Campbell at Hamilton	1999-2000
269 for 2nd	R. C. Fredericks and L. G. Rowe at Kingston	1971-72
221 for 3rd	B. C. Lara and J. C. Adams at Wellington	1994-95
162 for 4th	E. D. Weekes and O. G. Smith at Dunedin	1955-56
	C. G. Greenidge and A. I. Kallicharran at Christchurch	1979-80
189 for 5th	F. M. M. Worrell and C. L. Walcott at Auckland	1951-52
254 for 6th	C. A. Davis and G. S. Sobers at Bridgetown	1971-72
143 for 7th	D. St E. Atkinson and J. D. C. Goddard at Christchurch	1955-56
83 for 8th	I. V. A. Richards and M. D. Marshall at Bridgetown	1984-85
70 for 9th	M. D. Marshall and J. Garner at Bridgetown	1984-85
31 for 10th	T. M. Findlay and G. C. Shillingford at Bridgetown	1971-72

For New Zealand

387	for 1st†	G. M. Turner and T. W. Jarvis at Georgetown	1971-72
210	for 2nd	G. P. Howarth and J. J. Crowe at Kingston	1984-85
241	for 3rd	J. G. Wright and M. D. Crowe at Wellington	1986-87
189	for 4th	M. S. Sinclair and N. J. Astle at Wellington	1999-2000
144	for 5th	N. J. Astle and J. T. C. Vaughan at Bridgetown	1995-96
220	for 6th	G. M. Turner and K. J. Wadsworth at Kingston	1971-72
143	for 7th	M. D. Crowe and I. D. S. Smith at Georgetown	1984-85
136	for 8th	B. E. Congdon and R. S. Cunis at Port-of-Spain	1971-72
62*	for 9th	V. Pollard and R. S. Cunis at Auckland	1968-69
45	for 10th	D. K. Morrison and R. J. Kennedy at Bridgetown	1995-96

† *Denotes record partnership against all countries.*

TEN WICKETS OR MORE IN A MATCH

For West Indies (2)

11-120 (4-40, 7-80)	M. D. Marshall, Bridgetown	1984-85
13-55 (7-37, 6-18)	C. A. Walsh, Wellington	1994-95

For New Zealand (4)

10-100 (3-73, 7-27)†	C. L. Cairns, Hamilton	1999-2000
10-124 (4-51, 6-73)†	E. J. Chatfield, Port-of-Spain	1984-85
11-102 (5-34, 6-68)†	R. J. Hadlee, Dunedin	1979-80
10-166 (4-71, 6-95)	G. B. Troup, Auckland	1979-80

† *Signifies ten wickets or more on first appearance in West Indies–New Zealand Tests.*

WEST INDIES v INDIA

	Captains					
Season	*West Indies*	*India*	*T*	*WI*	*I*	*D*
1948-49*I*	J. D. C. Goddard	L. Amarnath	5	1	0	4
1952-53*W*	J. B. Stollmeyer	V. S. Hazare	5	1	0	4
1958-59*I*	F. C. M. Alexander	Ghulam Ahmed[1]	5	3	0	2
1961-62*W*	F. M. M. Worrell	N. J. Contractor[2]	5	5	0	0
1966-67*I*	G. S. Sobers	Nawab of Pataudi jun.	3	2	0	1
1970-71*W*	G. S. Sobers	A. L. Wadekar	5	0	1	4
1974-75*I*	C. H. Lloyd	Nawab of Pataudi jun.[3]	5	3	2	0
1975-76*W*	C. H. Lloyd	B. S. Bedi	4	2	1	1
1978-79*I*	A. I. Kallicharran	S. M. Gavaskar	6	0	1	5
1982-83*W*	C. H. Lloyd	Kapil Dev	5	2	0	3
1983-84*I*	C. H. Lloyd	Kapil Dev	6	3	0	3
1987-88*I*	I. V. A. Richards	D. B. Vengsarkar[4]	4	1	1	2
1988-89*W*	I. V. A. Richards	D. B. Vengsarkar	4	3	0	1
1994-95*I*	C. A. Walsh	M. Azharuddin	3	1	1	1
1996-97*W*	C. A. Walsh[5]	S. R. Tendulkar	5	1	0	4
	In India		37	14	5	18
	In West Indies		33	14	2	17
	Totals		70	28	7	35

I Played in India. W Played in West Indies.

Notes: The following deputised for the official touring captain or were appointed by the home authority for only a minor proportion of the series:

[1]P. R. Umrigar (First), V. Mankad (Fourth), H. R. Adhikari (Fifth). [2]Nawab of Pataudi jun. (Third, Fourth and Fifth). [3]S. Venkataraghavan (Second). [4]R. J. Shastri (Fourth). [5]B. C. Lara (Third).

HIGHEST INNINGS TOTALS

For West Indies in West Indies: 631-8 dec. at Kingston 1961-62
in India: 644-8 dec. at Delhi 1958-59

For India in West Indies: 469-7 at Port-of-Spain 1982-83
in India: 644-7 dec. at Kanpur 1978-79

LOWEST INNINGS TOTALS

For West Indies in West Indies: 140 at Bridgetown 1996-97
in India: 127 at Delhi. 1987-88

For India in West Indies: 81 at Bridgetown. 1996-97
in India: 75 at Delhi. 1987-88

INDIVIDUAL HUNDREDS

For West Indies (82)

J. C. Adams (2)		
125*	Nagpur	1994-95
174*	Mohali	1994-95
S. F. A. F. Bacchus (1)		
250	Kanpur	1978-79
B. F. Butcher (2)		
103	Calcutta. . . .	1958-59
142	Madras	1958-59
S. Chanderpaul (1)		
137*	Bridgetown .	1996-97
R. J. Christiani (1)		
107†	Delhi	1948-49
C. A. Davis (2)		
125*	Georgetown .	1970-71
105	Port-of-Spain	1970-71
P. J. L. Dujon (1)		
110	St John's . . .	1982-83
R. C. Fredericks (2)		
100	Calcutta. . . .	1974-75
104	Bombay. . . .	1974-75
H. A. Gomes (1)		
123	Port-of-Spain	1982-83
G. E. Gomez (1)		
101†	Delhi	1948-49
C. G. Greenidge (5)		
107†	Bangalore . .	1974-75
154*	St John's . . .	1982-83
194	Kanpur	1983-84
141	Calcutta. . . .	1987-88
117	Bridgetown .	1988-89
D. L. Haynes (2)		
136	St John's . . .	1982-83
112*	Bridgetown .	1988-89
J. K. Holt (1)		
123	Delhi	1958-59
C. L. Hooper (2)		
100*	Calcutta. . . .	1987-88
129	Kingston . . .	1996-97
C. C. Hunte (1)		
101	Bombay. . . .	1966-67
A. I. Kallicharran (3)		
124†	Bangalore . .	1974-75
103*	Port-of-Spain	1975-76
187	Bombay. . . .	1978-79
R. B. Kanhai (4)		
256	Calcutta. . . .	1958-59
138	Kingston . . .	1961-62
139	Port-of-Spain	1961-62
158*	Kingston . . .	1970-71
B. C. Lara (1)		
103	St John's . . .	1996-97
C. H. Lloyd (7)		
163	Bangalore . .	1974-75
242*	Bombay. . . .	1974-75
102	Bridgetown .	1975-76
143	Port-of-Spain	1982-83
106	St John's . . .	1982-83
103	Delhi	1983-84
161*	Calcutta. . . .	1983-84
A. L. Logie (2)		
130	Bridgetown .	1982-83
101	Calcutta. . . .	1987-88
E. D. A. McMorris (1)		
125†	Kingston . . .	1961-62
B. H. Pairaudeau (1)		
115†	Port-of-Spain	1952-53
A. F. Rae (2)		
104	Bombay. . . .	1948-49
109	Madras	1948-49
I. V. A. Richards (8)		
192*	Delhi	1974-75
142	Bridgetown .	1975-76
130	Port-of-Spain	1975-76
177	Port-of-Spain	1975-76
109	Georgetown .	1982-83
120	Bombay. . . .	1983-84
109*	Delhi	1987-88
110	Kingston . . .	1988-89
R. B. Richardson (2)		
194	Georgetown .	1988-89
156	Kingston . . .	1988-89
O. G. Smith (1)		
100	Delhi	1958-59
G. S. Sobers (8)		
142*†	Bombay. . . .	1958-59
198	Kanpur	1958-59
106*	Calcutta. . . .	1958-59
153	Kingston . . .	1961-62
104	Kingston . . .	1961-62
108*	Georgetown .	1970-71
178*	Bridgetown .	1970-71
132	Port-of-Spain	1970-71
J. S. Solomon (1)		
100*	Delhi	1958-59
J. B. Stollmeyer (2)		
160	Madras	1948-49
104*	Port-of-Spain	1952-53
C. L. Walcott (4)		
152†	Delhi	1948-49
108	Calcutta. . . .	1948-49
125	Georgetown .	1952-53
118	Kingston . . .	1952-53
E. D. Weekes (7)		
128†	Delhi	1948-49
194	Bombay. . . .	1948-49
162 101	} Calcutta. . . .	1948-49
207	Port-of-Spain	1952-53
161	Port-of-Spain	1952-53
109	Kingston . . .	1952-53
A. B. Williams (1)		
111	Calcutta. . . .	1978-79
S. C. Williams (1)		
128	Port-of-Spain	1996-97
F. M. M. Worrell (1)		
237	Kingston . . .	1952-53

For India (59)

H. R. Adhikari (1)
114*† Delhi 1948-49

M. Amarnath (3)
101* Kanpur 1978-79
117 Port-of-Spain 1982-83
116 St John's . . . 1982-83

M. L. Apte (1)
163* Port-of-Spain 1952-53

C. G. Borde (3)
109 Delhi 1958-59
121 Bombay. . . . 1966-67
125 Madras 1966-67

S. A. Durani (1)
104 Port-of-Spain 1961-62

F. M. Engineer (1)
109 Madras 1966-67

A. D. Gaekwad (1)
102 Kanpur 1978-79

S. M. Gavaskar (13)
116 Georgetown . 1970-71
117* Bridgetown . 1970-71
124 } 220 } Port-of-Spain 1970-71
156 Port-of-Spain 1975-76
102 Port-of-Spain 1975-76
205 Bombay. . . . 1978-79
107 } 182* } Calcutta. . . . 1978-79
120 Delhi 1978-79
147* Georgetown . 1982-83
121 Delhi 1983-84
236* Madras 1983-84

V. S. Hazare (2)
134* Bombay. . . . 1948-49
122 Bombay. . . . 1948-49

Kapil Dev (3)
126* Delhi 1978-79
100* Port-of-Spain 1982-83
109 Madras 1987-88

S. V. Manjrekar (1)
108 Bridgetown . 1988-89

V. L. Manjrekar (1)
118 Kingston . . . 1952-53

R. S. Modi (1)
112 Bombay. . . . 1948-49

Mushtaq Ali (1)
106† Calcutta. . . . 1948-49

B. P. Patel (1)
115* Port-of-Spain 1975-76

M. Prabhakar (1)
120 Mohali 1994-95

Pankaj Roy (1)
150 Kingston . . . 1952-53

D. N. Sardesai (3)
212 Kingston . . . 1970-71
112 Port-of-Spain 1970-71
150 Bridgetown . 1970-71

R. J. Shastri (2)
102 St John's . . . 1982-83
107 Bridgetown . 1988-89

N. S. Sidhu (3)
116 Kingston . . . 1988-89
107 Nagpur 1994-95
201 Port-of-Spain 1996-97

E. D. Solkar (1)
102 Bombay. . . . 1974-75

S. R. Tendulkar (1)
179 Nagpur 1994-95

P. R. Umrigar (3)
130 Port-of-Spain 1952-53
117 Kingston . . . 1952-53
172* Port-of-Spain 1961-62

D. B. Vengsarkar (6)
157* Calcutta. . . . 1978-79
109 Delhi 1978-79
159 Delhi 1983-84
100 Bombay. . . . 1983-84
102 Delhi 1987-88
102* Calcutta. . . . 1987-88

G. R. Viswanath (4)
139 Calcutta. . . . 1974-75
112 Port-of-Spain 1975-76
124 Madras 1978-79
179 Kanpur 1978-79

† *Signifies hundred on first appearance in West Indies–India Tests.*

RECORD PARTNERSHIPS FOR EACH WICKET

For West Indies

296	for 1st	C. G. Greenidge and D. L. Haynes at St John's	1982-83
255	for 2nd	E. D. A. McMorris and R. B. Kanhai at Kingston	1961-62
220	for 3rd	I. V. A. Richards and A. I. Kallicharran at Bridgetown	1975-76
267	for 4th	C. L. Walcott and G. E. Gomez at Delhi	1948-49
219	for 5th	E. D. Weekes and B. H. Pairaudeau at Port-of-Spain	1952-53
250	for 6th	C. H. Lloyd and D. L. Murray at Bombay	1974-75
130	for 7th	C. G. Greenidge and M. D. Marshall at Kanpur	1983-84
124	for 8th	I. V. A. Richards and K. D. Boyce at Delhi	1974-75
161	for 9th†	C. H. Lloyd and A. M. E. Roberts at Calcutta	1983-84
98*	for 10th	F. M. M. Worrell and W. W. Hall at Port-of-Spain	1961-62

For India

153	for 1st	S. M. Gavaskar and C. P. S. Chauhan at Bombay	1978-79
344*	for 2nd†	S. M. Gavaskar and D. B. Vengsarkar at Calcutta	1978-79
177	for 3rd	N. S. Sidhu and S. R. Tendulkar at Nagpur	1994-95
172	for 4th	G. R. Viswanath and A. D. Gaekwad at Kanpur	1978-79
204	for 5th	S. M. Gavaskar and B. P. Patel at Port-of-Spain	1975-76
170	for 6th	S. M. Gavaskar and R. J. Shastri at Madras	1983-84
186	for 7th	D. N. Sardesai and E. D. Solkar at Bridgetown	1970-71
107	for 8th	Yashpal Sharma and B. S. Sandhu at Kingston	1982-83
143*	for 9th	S. M. Gavaskar and S. M. H. Kirmani at Madras	1983-84
64	for 10th	J. Srinath and S. L. V. Raju at Mohali	1994-95

† *Denotes record partnership against all countries.*

TEN WICKETS OR MORE IN A MATCH

For West Indies (4)

11-126 (6-50, 5-76)	W. W. Hall, Kanpur	1958-59
11-89 (5-34, 6-55)	M. D. Marshall, Port-of-Spain	1988-89
12-121 (7-64, 5-57)	A. M. E. Roberts, Madras	1974-75
10-101 (6-62, 4-39)	C. A. Walsh, Kingston	1988-89

For India (4)

11-235 (7-157, 4-78)†	B. S. Chandrasekhar, Bombay	1966-67
10-223 (9-102, 1-121)	S. P. Gupte, Kanpur	1958-59
16-136 (8-61, 8-75)†	N. D. Hirwani, Madras	1987-88
10-135 (1-52, 9-83)	Kapil Dev, Ahmedabad	1983-84

† *Signifies ten wickets or more on first appearance in West Indies–India Tests.*

WEST INDIES v PAKISTAN

	Captains					
Season	*West Indies*	*Pakistan*	*T*	*WI*	*P*	*D*
1957-58*W*	F. C. M. Alexander	A. H. Kardar	5	3	1	1
1958-59*P*	F. C. M. Alexander	Fazal Mahmood	3	1	2	0
1974-75*P*	C. H. Lloyd	Intikhab Alam	2	0	0	2
1976-77*W*	C. H. Lloyd	Mushtaq Mohammad	5	2	1	2
1980-81*P*	C. H. Lloyd	Javed Miandad	4	1	0	3
1986-87*P*	I. V. A. Richards	Imran Khan	3	1	1	1
1987-88*W*	I. V. A. Richards[1]	Imran Khan	3	1	1	1
1990-91*P*	D. L. Haynes	Imran Khan	3	1	1	1
1992-93*W*	R. B. Richardson	Wasim Akram	3	2	0	1
1997-98*P*	C. A. Walsh	Wasim Akram	3	0	3	0
1999-2000*W*	J. C. Adams	Moin Khan	3	1	0	2
	In West Indies		19	9	3	7
	In Pakistan		18	4	7	7
	Totals		37	13	10	14

P Played in Pakistan. W Played in West Indies.

Note: The following was appointed by the home authority for only a minor proportion of the series:

[1]C. G. Greenidge (First).

HIGHEST INNINGS TOTALS

For West Indies	in West Indies: 790-3 dec. at Kingston	1957-58
	in Pakistan: 493 at Karachi	1974-75
For Pakistan	in West Indies: 657-8 dec. at Bridgetown	1957-58
	in Pakistan: 471 at Rawalpindi	1997-98

LOWEST INNINGS TOTALS

For West Indies	in West Indies: 127 at Port-of-Spain	1992-93
	in Pakistan: 53 at Faisalabad	1986-87
For Pakistan	in West Indies: 106 at Bridgetown	1957-58
	in Pakistan: 77 at Lahore	1986-87

INDIVIDUAL HUNDREDS

For West Indies (26)

L. Baichan (1)
105*† Lahore 1974-75
P. J. L. Dujon (1)
106* Port-of-Spain 1987-88
R. C. Fredericks (1)
120 Port-of-Spain 1976-77
C. G. Greenidge (1)
100 Kingston ... 1976-77
D. L. Haynes (3)
117 Karachi 1990-91
143*‡ Port-of-Spain 1992-93
125 Bridgetown . 1992-93
W. W. Hinds (1)
165 Bridgetown . 1999-00
C. L. Hooper (3)
134 Lahore 1990-91
178* St John's ... 1992-93
106 Karachi 1997-98
C. C. Hunte (3)
142† Bridgetown . 1957-58
260 Kingston ... 1957-58
114 Georgetown . 1957-58
B. D. Julien (1)
101 Karachi 1974-75
A. I. Kallicharran (1)
115 Karachi 1974-75
R. B. Kanhai (1)
217 Lahore 1958-59
C. H. Lloyd (1)
157 Bridgetown . 1976-77
I. V. A. Richards (2)
120* Multan 1980-81
123 Port-of-Spain 1987-88
I. T. Shillingford (1)
120 Georgetown . 1976-77
G. S. Sobers (3)
365* Kingston ... 1957-58
125 }
109* } Georgetown . 1957-58
C. L. Walcott (1)
145 Georgetown . 1957-58
E. D. Weekes (1)
197† Bridgetown . 1957-58

For Pakistan (26)

Aamir Sohail (2)
160 Rawalpindi . . 1997-98
160 Karachi 1997-98
Asif Iqbal (1)
135 Kingston ... 1976-77
Hanif Mohammad (2)
337† Bridgetown . 1957-58
103 Karachi 1958-59
Ijaz Ahmed, sen. (1)
151 Karachi 1997-98
Imran Khan (1)
123 Lahore 1980-81
Imran Nazir (1)
131† Bridgetown . 1999-00
Imtiaz Ahmed (1)
122 Kingston ... 1957-58
Inzamam-ul-Haq (3)
123 St John's ... 1992-93
177 Rawalpindi . . 1997-98
135 Georgetown . 1999-00
Javed Miandad (2)
114 Georgetown . 1987-88
102 Port-of-Spain 1987-88
Majid Khan (2)
100 Karachi 1974-75
167 Georgetown . 1976-77
Mushtaq Mohammad (2)
123 Lahore 1974-75
121 Port-of-Spain 1976-77
Saeed Ahmed (1)
150 Georgetown . 1957-58
Salim Malik (1)
102 Karachi 1990-91
Wasim Raja (2)
107* Karachi 1974-75
117* Bridgetown . 1976-77
Wazir Mohammad (2)
106 Kingston ... 1957-58
189 Port-of-Spain 1957-58
Yousuf Youhana (2)
115 Bridgetown . 1999-00
103* St John's ... 1999-00

† *Signifies hundred on first appearance in West Indies–Pakistan Tests.*
‡ *Carried his bat.*

RECORD PARTNERSHIPS FOR EACH WICKET

For West Indies

182	for 1st	R. C. Fredericks and C. G. Greenidge at Kingston	1976-77
446	for 2nd†	C. C. Hunte and G. S. Sobers at Kingston	1957-58
169	for 3rd	D. L. Haynes and B. C. Lara at Port-of-Spain	1992-93
188*	for 4th	G. S. Sobers and C. L. Walcott at Kingston	1957-58
185	for 5th	E. D. Weekes and O. G. Smith at Bridgetown	1957-58
151	for 6th	C. H. Lloyd and D. L. Murray at Bridgetown	1976-77
74	for 7th	S. Chanderpaul and N. A. M. McLean at Georgetown	1999-2000
60	for 8th	C. L. Hooper and A. C. Cummins at St John's	1992-93
61*	for 9th	P. J. L. Dujon and W. K. M. Benjamin at Bridgetown	1987-88
106	for 10th†	C. L. Hooper and C. A. Walsh at St John's	1992-93

For Pakistan

298	for 1st†	Aamir Sohail and Ijaz Ahmed, sen. at Karachi	1997-98
178	for 2nd	Hanif Mohammad and Saeed Ahmed at Karachi	1958-59
323	for 3rd	Aamir Sohail and Inzamam-ul-Haq at Rawalpindi	1997-98
174	for 4th	Shoaib Mohammad and Salim Malik at Karachi	1990-91

88	for 5th	Basit Ali and Inzamam-ul-Haq at St John's	1992-93
206	for 6th	Inzamam-ul-Haq and Abdur Razzaq at Georgetown	1999-2000
128	for 7th[1]	Wasim Raja and Wasim Bari at Karachi	1974-75
94	for 8th	Salim Malik and Salim Yousuf at Port-of-Spain	1987-88
96	for 9th	Inzamam-ul-Haq and Nadeem Khan at St John's	1992-93
133	for 10th	Wasim Raja and Wasim Bari at Bridgetown	1976-77

† Denotes record partnership against all countries.

[1]Although the seventh wicket added 168 runs against West Indies at Lahore in 1980-81, this comprised two partnerships with Imran Khan adding 72 with Abdul Qadir (retired hurt) and a further 96 with Sarfraz Nawaz.*

TEN WICKETS OR MORE IN A MATCH

For Pakistan (4)

12-100 (6-34, 6-66)	Fazal Mahmood, Dacca	1958-59
11-121 (7-80, 4-41)	Imran Khan, Georgetown	1987-88
10-106 (5-35, 5-71)	Mushtaq Ahmed, Peshawar	1997-98
11-110 (6-61, 5-49)	Wasim Akram, St John's	1999-2000

Note: The best match figures for West Indies are 9-95 (8-29, 1-66) by C. E. H. Croft at Port-of-Spain, 1976-77.

WEST INDIES v SRI LANKA

Season	*Captains* *West Indies*	*Sri Lanka*	*T*	*WI*	*SL*	*D*
1993-94*S*	R. B. Richardson	A. Ranatunga	1	0	0	1
1996-97*W*	C. A. Walsh	A. Ranatunga	2	1	0	1
	In West Indies		2	1	0	1
	In Sri Lanka		1	0	0	1
	Totals		3	1	0	2

W Played in West Indies. S Played in Sri Lanka.

HIGHEST INNINGS TOTALS

For West Indies: 343 at St Vincent 1996-97

For Sri Lanka: 233-8 at St Vincent 1996-97

LOWEST INNINGS TOTALS

For West Indies: 147 at St Vincent 1996-97

For Sri Lanka: 152 at St John's 1996-97

INDIVIDUAL HUNDRED

For West Indies (1)

B. C. Lara (1)
115 St Vincent . . 1996-97

Highest score for Sri Lanka: 90 by S. T. Jayasuriya at St Vincent, 1996-97

HUNDRED PARTNERSHIPS

For West Indies

160 for 1st S. L. Campbell and S. C. Williams at St John's. 1996-97

For Sri Lanka

110 for 4th S. T. Jayasuriya and A. Ranatunga at St John's 1996-97

BEST MATCH BOWLING ANALYSES

For West Indies

8-78 (5-37, 3-41) C. E. L. Ambrose, St John's. 1996-97

For Sri Lanka

8-106 (5-34, 3-72) M. Muralitharan, St John's. 1996-97

WEST INDIES v ZIMBABWE

	Captains					
Season	*West Indies*	*Zimbabwe*	*T*	*WI*	*Z*	*D*
1999-2000*W*	J. C. Adams	A. Flower	2	2	0	0
2001*Z*	C. L. Hooper	H. H. Streak	2	1	0	1
	In West Indies.		2	2	0	0
	In Zimbabwe.		2	1	0	1
	Totals		4	3	0	1

W Played in West Indies. Z Played in Zimbabwe.

HIGHEST INNINGS TOTALS

For West Indies in West Indies: 339 at Kingston 1999-2000
in Zimbabwe: 559-6 dec. at Bulawayo 2001

For Zimbabwe in West Indies: 308 at Kingston 1999-2000
in Zimbabwe: 563-9 dec. at Harare 2001

LOWEST INNINGS TOTALS

For West Indies in West Indies: 147 at Port-of-Spain. 1999-2000
in Zimbabwe: 347 at Harare. 2001

For Zimbabwe in West Indies: 63 at Port-of-Spain 1999-2000
in Zimbabwe: 131 at Harare. 2001

INDIVIDUAL HUNDREDS

For West Indies (3)

J. C. Adams (1)
101* Kingston . . . 1999-00

C. H. Gayle (1)
175 Bulawayo. . . 2001

C. L. Hooper (1)
149† Bulawayo. . . 2001

For Zimbabwe (4)

A. D. R. Campbell (1)
103 Bulawayo. . . 2001

A. Flower (1)
113*† Port-of-Spain 1999-00

M. W. Goodwin (1)
113 Kingston . . . 1999-00

H. Masakadza (1)
119† Harare. 2001

† *Signifies hundred on first appearance in West Indies–Zimbabwe Tests.*

RECORD PARTNERSHIPS FOR EACH WICKET

For West Indies

214 for 1st	D. Ganga and C. H. Gayle at Bulawayo	2001
100 for 2nd	D. Ganga and S. Chanderpaul at Harare	2001
37 for 3rd	S. L. Campbell and S. Chanderpaul at Port-of-Spain	1999-2000
131 for 4th	R. R. Sarwan and C. L. Hooper at Bulawayo	2001
100 for 5th	C. L. Hooper and M. N. Samuels at Bulawayo	2001
39 for 6th	J. C. Adams and R. D. Jacobs at Kingston	1999-2000
50 for 7th	R. R. Sarwan and N. C. McGarrell at Harare	2001
147 for 8th†	J. C. Adams and F. A. Rose at Kingston	1999-2000
12 for 9th	W. W. Hinds and R. D. King at Port-of-Spain	1999-2000
26 for 10th	W. W. Hinds and C. A. Walsh at Port-of-Spain	1999-2000

For Zimbabwe

164 for 1st†	D. D. Ebrahim and A. D. R. Campbell at Bulawayo	2001
91 for 2nd	A. D. R. Campbell and H. Masakadza at Harare	2001
169 for 3rd	H. Masakadza and C. B. Wishart at Harare	2001
176 for 4th	M. W. Goodwin and A. Flower at Kingston	1999-2000
25 for 5th	G. J. Whittall and G. W. Flower at Bulawayo	2001
34 for 6th	G. W. Flower and H. H. Streak at Harare	2001
154 for 7th†	H. H. Streak and A. M. Blignaut at Harare	2001
23 for 8th	G. J. Whittall and T. Taibu at Harare	2001
28 for 9th	H. H. Streak and B. C. Strang at Harare	2001
54 for 10th	S. V. Carlisle and H. K. Olonga at Kingston	1999-2000

† *Denotes record partnership against all countries.*

BEST MATCH BOWLING ANALYSES

For West Indies

7-50 (4-42, 3-8)	C. E. L. Ambrose, Port-of-Spain	1999-2000

For Zimbabwe

9-72 (4-45, 5-27)	H. H. Streak, Port-of-Spain	1999-2000

NEW ZEALAND v INDIA

Captains

Season	*New Zealand*	*India*	*T*	*NZ*	*I*	*D*
1955-56*I*	H. B. Cave	P. R. Umrigar[1]	5	0	2	3
1964-65*I*	J. R. Reid	Nawab of Pataudi jun.	4	0	1	3
1967-68*N*	G. T. Dowling[2]	Nawab of Pataudi jun.	4	1	3	0
1969-70*I*	G. T. Dowling	Nawab of Pataudi jun.	3	1	1	1
1975-76*N*	G. M. Turner	B. S. Bedi[3]	3	1	1	1
1976-77*I*	G. M. Turner	B. S. Bedi	3	0	2	1
1980-81*N*	G. P. Howarth	S. M. Gavaskar	3	1	0	2
1988-89*I*	J. G. Wright	D. B. Vengsarkar	3	1	2	0
1989-90*N*	J. G. Wright	M. Azharuddin	3	1	0	2
1993-94*N*	K. R. Rutherford	M. Azharuddin	1	0	0	1
1995-96*I*	L. K. Germon	M. Azharuddin	3	0	1	2
1998-99*N*†	S. P. Fleming	M. Azharuddin	2	1	0	1
1999-2000*I*	S. P. Fleming	S. R. Tendulkar	3	0	1	2
	In India		24	2	10	12
	In New Zealand		16	5	4	7
	Totals		40	7	14	19

I Played in India. N Played in New Zealand.

† *The First Test at Dunedin was abandoned without a ball being bowled and is excluded.*

Notes: The following deputised for the official touring captain or were appointed by the home authority for a minor proportion of the series:
[1]Ghulam Ahmed (First). [2]B. W. Sinclair (First). [3]S. M. Gavaskar (First).

HIGHEST INNINGS TOTALS

For New Zealand in New Zealand: 502 at Christchurch . . . 1967-68
in India: 462-9 dec. at Calcutta . . . 1964-65

For India in New Zealand: 482 at Auckland . . . 1989-90
in India: 583-7 dec. at Ahmedabad . . . 1999-2000

LOWEST INNINGS TOTALS

For New Zealand in New Zealand: 100 at Wellington . . . 1980-81
in India: 124 at Hyderabad . . . 1988-89

For India in New Zealand: 81 at Wellington . . . 1975-76
in India: 83 at Mohali . . . 1999-2000

INDIVIDUAL HUNDREDS

For New Zealand (22)

C. L. Cairns (1)
126 Hamilton . . . 1998-99
M. D. Crowe (1)
113 Auckland . . . 1989-90
G. T. Dowling (3)
129 Bombay . . . 1964-65
143 Dunedin . . . 1967-68
239 Christchurch . 1967-68
J. W. Guy (1)
102† Hyderabad . . 1955-56
G. P. Howarth (1)
137* Wellington . . 1980-81
A. H. Jones (1)
170* Auckland . . . 1989-90
J. M. Parker (1)
104 Bombay 1976-77
J. F. Reid (1)
123* Christchurch . 1980-81
J. R. Reid (2)
119* Delhi 1955-56
120 Calcutta 1955-56

I. D. S. Smith (1)

173 Auckland . . . 1989-90

B. Sutcliffe (3)

137*† Hyderabad . . 1955-56

230* Delhi 1955-56

151* Calcutta. . . . 1964-65

B. R. Taylor (1)

105† Calcutta. . . . 1964-65

G. M. Turner (2)

117 Christchurch. 1975-76

113 Kanpur 1976-77

J. G. Wright (3)

110 Auckland. . . 1980-81

185 Christchurch. 1989-90

113* Napier. 1989-90

For India (32)

S. Amarnath (1)

124† Auckland. . . 1975-76

M. Azharuddin (2)

192 Auckland. . . 1989-90

103* Wellington . . 1998-99

C. G. Borde (1)

109 Bombay. . . . 1964-65

R. Dravid (3)

190 } Hamilton . . . 1998-99

103* } Hamilton . . . 1998-99

144 Mohali 1999-00

S. C. Ganguly (2)

101* Hamilton . . . 1998-99

125 Ahmedabad . 1999-00

S. M. Gavaskar (2)

116† Auckland. . . 1975-76

119 Bombay. . . . 1976-77

A. G. Kripal Singh (1)

100*† Hyderabad . . 1955-56

V. L. Manjrekar (3)

118† Hyderabad . . 1955-56

177 Delhi 1955-56

102* Madras 1964-65

V. Mankad (2)

223 Bombay. . . . 1955-56

231 Madras 1955-56

Nawab of Pataudi jun. (2)

153 Calcutta. . . . 1964-65

113 Delhi 1964-65

G. S. Ramchand (1)

106* Calcutta. . . . 1955-56

S. Ramesh (1)

110 Ahmedabad . 1999-00

Pankaj Roy (2)

100 Calcutta. . . . 1955-56

173 Madras 1955-56

D. N. Sardesai (2)

200* Bombay. . . . 1964-65

106 Delhi 1964-65

N. S. Sidhu (1)

116† Bangalore . . 1988-89

S. R. Tendulkar (3)

113 Wellington . . 1998-99

126* Mohali 1999-00

217 Ahmedabad . 1999-00

P. R. Umrigar (1)

223† Hyderabad . . 1955-56

G. R. Viswanath (1)

103* Kanpur 1976-77

A. L. Wadekar (1)

143 Wellington . . 1967-68

† *Signifies hundred on first appearance in New Zealand–India Tests. B. R. Taylor provides the only instance for New Zealand of a player scoring his maiden hundred in first-class cricket in his first Test.*

RECORD PARTNERSHIPS FOR EACH WICKET

For New Zealand

149	for 1st	T. J. Franklin and J. G. Wright at Napier	1989-90
155	for 2nd	G. T. Dowling and B. E. Congdon at Dunedin	1967-68
222*	for 3rd	B. Sutcliffe and J. R. Reid at Delhi	1955-56
160	for 4th	R. G. Twose and C. D. McMillan at Hamilton	1998-99
140	for 5th	C. D. McMillan and A. C. Parore at Hamilton	1998-99
137	for 6th	C. D. McMillan and C. L. Cairns at Wellington	1998-99
163	for 7th	B. Sutcliffe and B. R. Taylor at Calcutta	1964-65
137	for 8th	D. J. Nash and D. L. Vettori at Wellington	1998-99
136	for 9th†	I. D. S. Smith and M. C. Snedden at Auckland	1989-90
61	for 10th	J. T. Ward and R. O. Collinge at Madras	1964-65

For India

413	for 1st†	V. Mankad and Pankaj Roy at Madras	1955-56
204	for 2nd	S. M. Gavaskar and S. Amarnath at Auckland	1975-76
238	for 3rd	P. R. Umrigar and V. L. Manjrekar at Hyderabad	1955-56
281	for 4th†	S. R. Tendulkar and S. C. Ganguly at Ahmedabad	1999-2000
127	for 5th	V. L. Manjrekar and G. S. Ramchand at Delhi	1955-56
193*	for 6th	D. N. Sardesai and Hanumant Singh at Bombay	1964-65
128	for 7th	S. R. Tendulkar and K. S. More at Napier	1989-90
144	for 8th	R. Dravid and J. Srinath at Hamilton	1998-99
105	for 9th	S. M. H. Kirmani and B. S. Bedi at Bombay	1976-77
		S. M. H. Kirmani and N. S. Yadav at Auckland	1980-81
57	for 10th	R. B. Desai and B. S. Bedi at Dunedin	1967-68

† *Denotes record partnership against all countries.*

TEN WICKETS OR MORE IN A MATCH

For New Zealand (2)

11-58 (4-35, 7-23)	R. J. Hadlee, Wellington	1975-76
10-88 (6-49, 4-39)	R. J. Hadlee, Bombay	1988-89

For India (3)

10-134 (4-67, 6-67)	A. Kumble, Kanpur	1999-2000
11-140 (3-64, 8-76)	E. A. S. Prasanna, Auckland	1975-76
12-152 (8-72, 4-80)	S. Venkataraghavan, Delhi	1964-65

NEW ZEALAND v PAKISTAN

	Captains					
Season	*New Zealand*	*Pakistan*	*T*	*NZ*	*P*	*D*
1955-56*P*	H. B. Cave	A. H. Kardar	3	0	2	1
1964-65*N*	J. R. Reid	Hanif Mohammad	3	0	0	3
1964-65*P*	J. R. Reid	Hanif Mohammad	3	0	2	1
1969-70*P*	G. T. Dowling	Intikhab Alam	3	1	0	2
1972-73*N*	B. E. Congdon	Intikhab Alam	3	0	1	2
1976-77*P*	G. M. Turner[1]	Mushtaq Mohammad	3	0	2	1
1978-79*N*	M. G. Burgess	Mushtaq Mohammad	3	0	1	2
1984-85*P*	J. V. Coney	Zaheer Abbas	3	0	2	1
1984-85*N*	G. P. Howarth	Javed Miandad	3	2	0	1
1988-89*N*†	J. G. Wright	Imran Khan	2	0	0	2
1990-91*P*	M. D. Crowe	Javed Miandad	3	0	3	0
1992-93*N*	K. R. Rutherford	Javed Miandad	1	0	1	0
1993-94*N*	K. R. Rutherford	Salim Malik	3	1	2	0
1995-96*N*	L. K. Germon	Wasim Akram	1	0	1	0
1996-97*P*	L. K. Germon	Saeed Anwar	2	1	1	0
2000-01*N*	S. P. Fleming	Moin Khan[2]	3	1	1	1
	In Pakistan		20	2	12	6
	In New Zealand		22	4	7	11
	Totals		42	6	19	17

N Played in New Zealand. P Played in Pakistan.

† The First Test at Dunedin was abandoned without a ball being bowled and is excluded.

Note: The following deputised for the official touring captain:
[1]J. M. Parker (Third). [2]Inzamam-ul-Haq (Third).

HIGHEST INNINGS TOTALS

For New Zealand in New Zealand: 492 at Wellington	1984-85
in Pakistan: 482-6 dec. at Lahore	1964-65
For Pakistan in New Zealand: 616-5 dec. at Auckland	1988-89
in Pakistan: 565-9 dec. at Karachi	1976-77

LOWEST INNINGS TOTALS

For New Zealand in New Zealand: 93 at Hamilton	1992-93
in Pakistan: 70 at Dacca	1955-56
For Pakistan in New Zealand: 104 at Hamilton	2000-01
in Pakistan: 102 at Faisalabad	1990-91

INDIVIDUAL HUNDREDS

For New Zealand (24)

M. D. Bell (1)
105 Hamilton . . . 2000-01
M. G. Burgess (2)
119* Dacca 1969-70
111 Lahore 1976-77
J. V. Coney (1)
111* Dunedin . . . 1984-85
M. D. Crowe (2)
174 Wellington . . 1988-89
108* Lahore 1990-91
B. A. Edgar (1)
129† Christchurch. 1978-79
M. J. Greatbatch (1)
133 Hamilton . . . 1992-93
B. F. Hastings (1)
110 Auckland. . . 1972-73
G. P. Howarth (1)
114 Napier. 1978-79
W. K. Lees (1)
152 Karachi 1976-77
S. N. McGregor (1)
111 Lahore 1955-56
R. E. Redmond (1)
107† Auckland. . . 1972-73
J. F. Reid (3)
106 Hyderabad . . 1984-85
148 Wellington . . 1984-85
158* Auckland. . . 1984-85
J. R. Reid (1)
128 Karachi 1964-65
M. H. Richardson (1)
106 Hamilton . . . 2000-01
B. W. Sinclair (1)
130 Lahore 1964-65
M. S. Sinclair (1)
204* Christchurch. 2000-01
S. A. Thomson (1)
120* Christchurch. 1993-94
G. M. Turner (1)
110† Dacca 1969-70
J. G. Wright (1)
107 Karachi 1984-85
B. A. Young (1)
120 Christchurch. 1993-94

For Pakistan (45)

Asif Iqbal (3)
175 Dunedin . . . 1972-73
166 Lahore 1976-77
104 Napier. 1978-79
Basit Ali (1)
103 Christchurch. 1993-94
Hanif Mohammad (3)
103 Dacca 1955-56
100* Christchurch. 1964-65
203* Lahore 1964-65
Ijaz Ahmed, sen. (2)
103 Christchurch. 1995-96
125 Rawalpindi. . 1996-97
Imtiaz Ahmed (1)
209 Lahore 1955-56
Inzamam-ul-Haq (2)
135* Wellington . . 1993-94
130 Christchurch. 2000-01
Javed Miandad (7)
163† Lahore 1976-77
206 Karachi 1976-77
160* Christchurch. 1978-79
104 }
103* } Hyderabad . . 1984-85
118 Wellington . . 1988-89
271 Auckland. . . 1988-89
Majid Khan (3)
110 Auckland. . . 1972-73
112 Karachi 1976-77
119* Napier. 1978-79
Mohammad Ilyas (1)
126 Karachi 1964-65
Mohammad Wasim (1)
109*† Lahore 1996-97
Mudassar Nazar (1)
106 Hyderabad . . 1984-85
Mushtaq Mohammad (3)
201 Dunedin . . . 1972-73
101 Hyderabad . . 1976-77
107 Karachi 1976-77
Sadiq Mohammad (2)
166 Wellington . . 1972-73
103* Hyderabad . . 1976-77
Saeed Ahmed (1)
172 Karachi 1964-65
Saeed Anwar (2)
169 Wellington . . 1993-94
149 Rawalpindi. . 1996-97
Salim Malik (2)
119* Karachi 1984-85
140 Wellington . . 1993-94
Saqlain Mushtaq (1)
101* Christchurch. 2000-01
Shoaib Mohammad (5)
163 Wellington . . 1988-89
112 Auckland. . . 1988-89
203* Karachi 1990-91
105 Lahore 1990-91
142 Faisalabad . . 1990-91
Waqar Hassan (1)
189 Lahore 1955-56
Younis Khan (1)
149*† Auckland. . . 2000-01
Yousuf Youhana (1)
203 Christchurch. 2000-01
Zaheer Abbas (1)
135 Auckland. . . 1978-79

† *Signifies hundred on first appearance in New Zealand–Pakistan Tests.*

Note: Mushtaq and Sadiq Mohammad, at Hyderabad in 1976-77, provide the fourth instance in Test matches, after the Chappells (thrice), of brothers each scoring hundreds in the same innings.

RECORD PARTNERSHIPS FOR EACH WICKET

For New Zealand

181 for 1st	M. H. Richardson and M. D. Bell at Hamilton	2000-01
195 for 2nd	J. G. Wright and G. P. Howarth at Napier	1978-79
178 for 3rd	B. W. Sinclair and J. R. Reid at Lahore.	1964-65

147 for 4th	C. D. McMillan and S. P. Fleming at Hamilton	2000-01
183 for 5th	M. G. Burgess and R. W. Anderson at Lahore	1976-77
145 for 6th	J. F. Reid and R. J. Hadlee at Wellington	1984-85
186 for 7th†	W. K. Lees and R. J. Hadlee at Karachi	1976-77
100 for 8th	B. W. Yuile and D. R. Hadlee at Karachi	1969-70
96 for 9th	M. G. Burgess and R. S. Cunis at Dacca	1969-70
151 for 10th†	B. F. Hastings and R. O. Collinge at Auckland	1972-73

For Pakistan

172 for 1st	Ramiz Raja and Shoaib Mohammad at Karachi	1990-91
262 for 2nd	Saeed Anwar and Ijaz Ahmed, sen. at Rawalpindi	1996-97
248 for 3rd	Shoaib Mohammad and Javed Miandad at Auckland	1988-89
350 for 4th†	Mushtaq Mohammad and Asif Iqbal at Dunedin	1972-73
281 for 5th†	Javed Miandad and Asif Iqbal at Lahore	1976-77
217 for 6th†	Hanif Mohammad and Majid Khan at Lahore	1964-65
308 for 7th†	Waqar Hassan and Imtiaz Ahmed at Lahore	1955-56
89 for 8th	Anil Dalpat and Iqbal Qasim at Karachi	1984-85
52 for 9th	Intikhab Alam and Arif Butt at Auckland	1964-65
	Moin Khan and Mushtaq Ahmed at Auckland	2000-01
65 for 10th	Salah-ud-Din and Mohammad Farooq at Rawalpindi	1964-65

† *Denotes record partnership against all countries.*

TEN WICKETS OR MORE IN A MATCH

For New Zealand (1)

11-152 (7-52, 4-100)	C. Pringle, Faisalabad	1990-91

For Pakistan (10)

10-182 (5-91, 5-91)	Intikhab Alam, Dacca	1969-70
11-130 (7-52, 4-78)	Intikhab Alam, Dunedin	1972-73
11-130 (4-64, 7-66)†	Mohammad Zahid, Rawalpindi	1996-97
10-171 (3-115, 7-56)	Mushtaq Ahmed, Christchurch	1995-96
10-143 (4-59, 6-84)	Mushtaq Ahmed, Lahore	1996-97
10-106 (3-20, 7-86)	Waqar Younis, Lahore	1990-91
12-130 (7-76, 5-54)	Waqar Younis, Faisalabad	1990-91
10-128 (5-56, 5-72)	Wasim Akram, Dunedin	1984-85
11-179 (4-60, 7-119)	Wasim Akram, Wellington	1993-94
11-79 (5-37, 6-42)†	Zulfiqar Ahmed, Karachi	1955-56

† *Signifies ten wickets or more on first appearance in New Zealand–Pakistan Tests.*

Note: Waqar Younis's performances were in successive matches.

NEW ZEALAND v SRI LANKA

	Captains					
Season	*New Zealand*	*Sri Lanka*	*T*	*NZ*	*SL*	*D*
1982-83*N*	G. P. Howarth	D. S. de Silva	2	2	0	0
1983-84*S*	G. P. Howarth	L. R. D. Mendis	3	2	0	1
1986-87*S*†	J. J. Crowe	L. R. D. Mendis	1	0	0	1
1990-91*N*	M. D. Crowe[1]	A. Ranatunga	3	0	0	3

	Captains					
Season	*New Zealand*	*Sri Lanka*	*T*	*NZ*	*SL*	*D*
1992-93*S*	M. D. Crowe	A. Ranatunga	2	0	1	1
1994-95*N*	K. R. Rutherford	A. Ranatunga	2	0	1	1
1996-97*N*	S. P. Fleming	A. Ranatunga	2	2	0	0
1997-98*S*	S. P. Fleming	A. Ranatunga	3	1	2	0
	In New Zealand		9	4	1	4
	In Sri Lanka		9	3	3	3
	Totals		18	7	4	7

N Played in New Zealand. S Played in Sri Lanka.

† *The Second and Third Tests were cancelled owing to civil disturbances.*

Note: The following was appointed by the home authority for only a minor proportion of the series:
[1]I. D. S. Smith (Third).

HIGHEST INNINGS TOTALS

For New Zealand in New Zealand: 671-4 at Wellington 1990-91
in Sri Lanka: 459 at Colombo (CCC) 1983-84

For Sri Lanka in New Zealand: 497 at Wellington 1990-91
in Sri Lanka: 397-9 dec. at Colombo (CCC) 1986-87

LOWEST INNINGS TOTALS

For New Zealand in New Zealand: 109 at Napier 1994-95
in Sri Lanka: 102 at Colombo (SSC) 1992-93

For Sri Lanka in New Zealand: 93 at Wellington 1982-83
in Sri Lanka: 97 at Kandy 1986-87

INDIVIDUAL HUNDREDS

For New Zealand (13)

J. J. Crowe (1)
120* Colombo (CCC) 1986-87

M. D. Crowe (2)
299 Wellington . . 1990-91
107 Colombo (SSC) 1992-93

S. P. Fleming (1)
174* Colombo (RPS) 1997-98

R. J. Hadlee (1)
151* Colombo (CCC) 1986-87

A. H. Jones (3)
186 Wellington . . 1990-91
122 } 100* } Hamilton . . . 1990-91

C. D. McMillan (1)
142† Colombo (RPS) 1997-98

J. F. Reid (1)
180 Colombo (CCC) 1983-84

K. R. Rutherford (1)
105 Moratuwa . . 1992-93

J. G. Wright (1)
101 Hamilton . . . 1990-91

B. A. Young (1)
267* Dunedin . . . 1996-97

For Sri Lanka (12)

P. A. de Silva (2)
267† Wellington . . 1990-91
123 Auckland . . . 1990-91
R. L. Dias (1)
108† Colombo (SSC) 1983-84
A. P. Gurusinha (3)
119 } Hamilton . . . 1990-91
102 }
127 Dunedin . . . 1994-95
D. P. M. D. Jayawardene (1)
167 Galle. 1997-98
R. S. Kaluwitharana (1)
103† Dunedin . . . 1996-97
D. S. B. P. Kuruppu (1)
201*† Colombo (CCC) 1986-87
R. S. Mahanama (2)
153 Moratuwa . . 1992-93
109 Colombo (SSC) 1992-93
H. P. Tillekeratne (1)
108 Dunedin . . . 1994-95

† *Signifies hundred on first appearance in New Zealand–Sri Lanka Tests.*

Note: A. P. Gurusinha and A. H. Jones at Hamilton in 1990-91 provided the second instance of a player on each side hitting two separate hundreds in a Test match.

RECORD PARTNERSHIPS FOR EACH WICKET

For New Zealand

161	for 1st	T. J. Franklin and J. G. Wright at Hamilton	1990-91
140	for 2nd	B. A. Young and M. J. Horne at Dunedin	1996-97
467	for 3rd†‡	A. H. Jones and M. D. Crowe at Wellington	1990-91
240	for 4th	S. P. Fleming and C. D. McMillan at Colombo (RPS)	1997-98
151	for 5th	K. R. Rutherford and C. Z. Harris at Moratuwa	1992-93
246*	for 6th†	J. J. Crowe and R. J. Hadlee at Colombo (CCC)	1986-87
47	for 7th	D. N. Patel and M. L. Su'a at Dunedin	1994-95
79	for 8th	J. V. Coney and W. K. Lees at Christchurch	1982-83
43	for 9th	A. C. Parore and P. J. Wiseman at Galle	1997-98
52	for 10th	W. K. Lees and E. J. Chatfield at Christchurch	1982-83

For Sri Lanka

102	for 1st	R. S. Mahanama and U. C. Hathurusinghe at Colombo (SSC)	1992-93
138	for 2nd	R. S. Mahanama and A. P. Gurusinha at Moratuwa	1992-93
159*	for 3rd[1]	S. Wettimuny and R. L. Dias at Colombo (SSC)	1983-84
192	for 4th	A. P. Gurusinha and H. P. Tillekeratne at Dunedin	1994-95
130	for 5th	R. S. Madugalle and D. S. de Silva at Wellington	1982-83
109*	for 6th[2]	R. S. Madugalle and A. Ranatunga at Colombo (CCC)	1983-84
137	for 7th	R. S. Kaluwitharana and W. P. U. J. C. Vaas at Dunedin	1996-97
73	for 8th	H. P. Tillekeratne and G. P. Wickremasinghe at Dunedin	1996-97
31	for 9th	G. F. Labrooy and R. J. Ratnayake at Auckland	1990-91
		S. T. Jayasuriya and R. J. Ratnayake at Auckland	1990-91
71	for 10th	R. S. Kaluwitharana and M. Muralitharan at Colombo (SSC)	1997-98

† *Denotes record partnership against all countries.*
‡ *Record third-wicket partnership in first-class cricket.*
[1] *163 runs were added for this wicket in two separate partnerships: S. Wettimuny retired hurt and was replaced by J. R. Ratnayeke when 159 had been added.*
[2] *119 runs were added for this wicket in two separate partnerships: R. S. Madugalle retired hurt and was replaced by D. S. de Silva when 109 had been added.*

TEN WICKETS OR MORE IN A MATCH

For New Zealand (1)

10-102 (5-73, 5-29) R. J. Hadlee, Colombo (CCC) . . . 1983-84

For Sri Lanka (1)

10-90 (5-47, 5-43)† W. P. U. J. C. Vaas, Napier . . . 1994-95

† *Signifies ten wickets or more on first appearance in New Zealand–Sri Lanka Tests.*

NEW ZEALAND v ZIMBABWE

	Captains					
Season	*New Zealand*	*Zimbabwe*	*T*	*NZ*	*Z*	*D*
1992-93*Z*	M. D. Crowe	D. L. Houghton	2	1	0	1
1995-96*N*	L. K. Germon	A. Flower	2	0	0	2
1997-98*Z*	S. P. Fleming	A. D. R. Campbell	2	0	0	2
1997-98*N*	S. P. Fleming	A. D. R. Campbell	2	2	0	0
2000-01*Z*	S. P. Fleming	H. H. Streak	2	2	0	0
2000-01*N*	S. P. Fleming	H. H. Streak	1	0	0	1
	In New Zealand		5	2	0	3
	In Zimbabwe		6	3	0	3
	Totals		11	5	0	6

N Played in New Zealand. Z Played in Zimbabwe.

HIGHEST INNINGS TOTALS

For New Zealand in New Zealand: 487-7 dec. at Wellington 2000-01
in Zimbabwe: 465 at Harare 2000-01

For Zimbabwe in New Zealand: 340-6 dec. at Wellington 2000-01
in Zimbabwe: 461 at Bulawayo 1997-98

LOWEST INNINGS TOTALS

For New Zealand in New Zealand: 251 at Auckland 1995-96
in Zimbabwe: 207 at Harare 1997-98

For Zimbabwe in New Zealand: 170 at Auckland 1997-98
in Zimbabwe: 119 at Bulawayo 2000-01

INDIVIDUAL HUNDREDS

For New Zealand (11)

N. J. Astle (2)
114 Auckland . . . 1997-98
141 Wellington . . 2000-01

C. L. Cairns (2)
120 Auckland . . . 1995-96
124 Harare 2000-01

M. D. Crowe (1)
140 Harare 1992-93

M. J. Horne (2)
157 Auckland . . . 1997-98
110 Bulawayo . . . 2000-01

R. T. Latham (1)
119† Bulawayo . . . 1992-93

C. D. McMillan (2)
139† Wellington . . 1997-98
142 Wellington . . 2000-01

C. M. Spearman (1)
112 Auckland . . . 1995-96

For Zimbabwe (6)

K. J. Arnott (1)
101*† Bulawayo . . . 1992-93

G. W. Flower (2)
104, 151 } Harare 1997-98

D. L. Houghton (1)
104* Auckland . . . 1995-96

G. J. Whittall (2)
203* Bulawayo . . . 1997-98
188* Harare 2000-01

† *Signifies hundred on first appearance in New Zealand–Zimbabwe Tests.*

RECORD PARTNERSHIPS FOR EACH WICKET

For New Zealand

214	for 1st	C. M. Spearman and R. G. Twose at Auckland	1995-96
127	for 2nd	R. T. Latham and A. H. Jones at Bulawayo	1992-93
71	for 3rd	A. H. Jones and M. D. Crowe at Bulawayo	1992-93
243	for 4th†	M. J. Horne and N. J. Astle at Auckland	1997-98
222	for 5th†	N. J. Astle and C. D. McMillan at Wellington	2000-01
82*	for 6th	A. C. Parore and L. K. Germon at Hamilton	1995-96
108	for 7th	C. D. McMillan and D. J. Nash at Wellington	1997-98
144	for 8th†	C. L. Cairns and D. J. Nash at Harare	2000-01
78	for 9th	A. C. Parore and D. L. Vettori at Bulawayo	2000-01
27	for 10th	C. D. McMillan and S. B. Doull at Auckland	1997-98

For Zimbabwe

156	for 1st	G. J. Rennie and G. W. Flower at Harare	1997-98
107	for 2nd	K. J. Arnott and A. D. R. Campbell at Harare	1992-93
70	for 3rd	A. Flower and G. J. Whittall at Bulawayo	1997-98
130	for 4th	G. J. Rennie and A. Flower at Wellington	2000-01
131	for 5th	A. Flower and G. J. Whittall at Harare	2000-01
151	for 6th	G. J. Whittall and H. H. Streak at Harare	2000-01
91	for 7th	G. J. Whittall and P. A. Strang at Hamilton	1995-96
94	for 8th	A. D. R. Campbell and H. H. Streak at Wellington	1997-98
46	for 9th	G. J. Crocker and M. G. Burmester at Harare	1992-93
40	for 10th	G. J. Whittall and E. Z. Matambanadzo at Bulawayo	1997-98

† *Denotes record partnership against all countries.*

TEN WICKETS OR MORE IN A MATCH

For Zimbabwe (2)

11-255 (6-109, 5-146)	A. G. Huckle, Bulawayo	1997-98
10-158 (8-109, 2-49)	P. A. Strang, Bulawayo	2000-01

Note: The best match figures for New Zealand are 8-85 (4-35, 4-50) by S. B. Doull at Auckland, 1997-98.

INDIA v PAKISTAN

	Captains					
Season	*India*	*Pakistan*	*T*	*I*	*P*	*D*
1952-53*I*	L. Amarnath	A. H. Kardar	5	2	1	2
1954-55*P*	V. Mankad	A. H. Kardar	5	0	0	5
1960-61*I*	N. J. Contractor	Fazal Mahmood	5	0	0	5
1978-79*P*	B. S. Bedi	Mushtaq Mohammad	3	0	2	1
1979-80*I*	S. M. Gavaskar[1]	Asif Iqbal	6	2	0	4
1982-83*P*	S. M. Gavaskar	Imran Khan	6	0	3	3
1983-84*I*	Kapil Dev	Zaheer Abbas	3	0	0	3
1984-85*P*	S. M. Gavaskar	Zaheer Abbas	2	0	0	2
1986-87*I*	Kapil Dev	Imran Khan	5	0	1	4
1989-90*P*	K. Srikkanth	Imran Khan	4	0	0	4
1998-99*I*	M. Azharuddin	Wasim Akram	2	1	1	0
1998-99*I*†	M. Azharuddin	Wasim Akram	1	0	1	0
	In India		27	5	4	18
	In Pakistan		20	0	5	15
	Totals		47	5	9	33

I Played in India. P Played in Pakistan.

† *This Test was part of the Asian Test Championship and was not counted as part of the preceding bilateral series.*

Note: The following was appointed by the home authority for only a minor proportion of the series:
[1]G. R. Viswanath (Sixth).

HIGHEST INNINGS TOTALS

For India in India: 539-9 dec. at Madras	1960-61
in Pakistan: 509 at Lahore	1989-90
For Pakistan in India: 487-9 dec. at Madras	1986-87
in Pakistan: 699-5 at Lahore	1989-90

LOWEST INNINGS TOTALS

For India in India: 106 at Lucknow	1952-53
in Pakistan: 145 at Karachi	1954-55
For Pakistan in India: 116 at Bangalore	1986-87
in Pakistan: 158 at Dacca	1954-55

INDIVIDUAL HUNDREDS

For India (32)

M. Amarnath (4)		
109*	Lahore	1982-83
120	Lahore	1982-83
103*	Karachi	1982-83
101*	Lahore	1984-85
M. Azharuddin (3)		
141	Calcutta	1986-87
110	Jaipur	1986-87
109	Faisalabad	1989-90
C. G. Borde (1)		
177*	Madras	1960-61
A. D. Gaekwad (1)		
201	Jullundur	1983-84
S. M. Gavaskar (5)		
111 } 137 }	Karachi	1978-79
166	Madras	1979-80
127*‡	Faisalabad	1982-83
103*	Bangalore	1983-84
V. S. Hazare (1)		
146*	Bombay	1952-53
S. V. Manjrekar (2)		
113*†	Karachi	1989-90
218	Lahore	1989-90
S. M. Patil (1)		
127	Faisalabad	1984-85
R. J. Shastri (3)		
128	Karachi	1982-83
139	Faisalabad	1984-85
125	Jaipur	1986-87
R. H. Shodhan (1)		
110†	Calcutta	1952-53
K. Srikkanth (1)		
123	Madras	1986-87
S. R. Tendulkar (1)		
136	Chennai	1998-99
P. R. Umrigar (5)		
102	Bombay	1952-53
108	Peshawar	1954-55
115	Kanpur	1960-61
117	Madras	1960-61
112	Delhi	1960-61
D. B. Vengsarkar (2)		
146*	Delhi	1979-80
109	Ahmedabad	1986-87
G. R. Viswanath (1)		
145†	Faisalabad	1978-79

For Pakistan (43)

Aamer Malik (2)		
117	Faisalabad	1989-90
113	Lahore	1989-90
Alim-ud-Din (1)		
103*	Karachi	1954-55
Asif Iqbal (1)		
104†	Faisalabad	1978-79
Hanif Mohammad (2)		
142	Bahawalpur	1954-55
160	Bombay	1960-61
Ijaz Faqih (1)		
105†	Ahmedabad	1986-87
Imran Khan (3)		
117	Faisalabad	1982-83
135*	Madras	1986-87
109*	Karachi	1989-90
Imtiaz Ahmed (1)		
135	Madras	1960-61
Javed Miandad (5)		
154*†	Faisalabad	1978-79
100	Karachi	1978-79
126	Faisalabad	1982-83
280*	Hyderabad	1982-83
145	Lahore	1989-90
Mohsin Khan (1)		
101*†	Lahore	1982-83
Mudassar Nazar (6)		
126	Bangalore	1979-80
119	Karachi	1982-83
231	Hyderabad	1982-83
152*‡	Lahore	1982-83
152	Karachi	1982-83
199	Faisalabad	1984-85
Mushtaq Mohammad (1)		
101	Delhi	1960-61
Nazar Mohammad (1)		
124*‡	Lucknow	1952-53
Qasim Omar (1)		
210	Faisalabad	1984-85
Ramiz Raja (1)		
114	Jaipur	1986-87
Saeed Ahmed (2)		
121†	Bombay	1960-61
103	Madras	1960-61
Saeed Anwar (1)		
188*‡	Calcutta	1998-99
Salim Malik (3)		
107	Faisalabad	1982-83
102*	Faisalabad	1984-85
102*	Karachi	1989-90
Shahid Afridi (1)		
141†	Chennai	1998-99
Shoaib Mohammad (2)		
101	Madras	1986-87
203*	Lahore	1989-90
Wasim Raja (1)		
125	Jullundur	1983-84
Zaheer Abbas (6)		
176†	Faisalabad	1978-79
235*	Lahore	1978-79
215	Lahore	1982-83
186	Karachi	1982-83
168	Faisalabad	1982-83
168*	Lahore	1984-85

† *Signifies hundred on first appearance in India–Pakistan Tests.*
‡ *Carried his bat.*

RECORD PARTNERSHIPS FOR EACH WICKET

For India

200 for 1st	S. M. Gavaskar and K. Srikkanth at Madras	1986-87
135 for 2nd	N. S. Sidhu and S. V. Manjrekar at Karachi	1989-90
190 for 3rd	M. Amarnath and Yashpal Sharma at Lahore	1982-83
186 for 4th	S. V. Manjrekar and R. J. Shastri at Lahore	1989-90
200 for 5th	S. M. Patil and R. J. Shastri at Faisalabad	1984-85
143 for 6th	M. Azharuddin and Kapil Dev at Calcutta	1986-87
155 for 7th	R. M. H. Binny and Madan Lal at Bangalore	1983-84
122 for 8th	S. M. H. Kirmani and Madan Lal at Faisalabad	1982-83
149 for 9th†	P. G. Joshi and R. B. Desai at Bombay	1960-61
109 for 10th†	H. R. Adhikari and Ghulam Ahmed at Delhi	1952-53

For Pakistan

162 for 1st	Hanif Mohammad and Imtiaz Ahmed at Madras	1960-61
250 for 2nd	Mudassar Nazar and Qasim Omar at Faisalabad	1984-85
451 for 3rd†	Mudassar Nazar and Javed Miandad at Hyderabad	1982-83
287 for 4th	Javed Miandad and Zaheer Abbas at Faisalabad	1982-83
213 for 5th	Zaheer Abbas and Mudassar Nazar at Karachi	1982-83
207 for 6th	Salim Malik and Imran Khan at Faisalabad	1982-83
154 for 7th	Imran Khan and Ijaz Faqih at Ahmedabad	1986-87
112 for 8th	Imran Khan and Wasim Akram at Madras	1986-87
60 for 9th	Wasim Bari and Iqbal Qasim at Bangalore	1979-80
104 for 10th	Zulfiqar Ahmed and Amir Elahi at Madras	1952-53

† *Denotes record partnership against all countries.*

TEN WICKETS OR MORE IN A MATCH

For India (5)

11-146 (4-90, 7-56)	Kapil Dev, Madras	1979-80
14-149 (4-75, 10-74)	A. Kumble, Delhi	1998-99
10-126 (7-27, 3-99)	Maninder Singh, Bangalore	1986-87
13-131 (8-52, 5-79)†	V. Mankad, Delhi	1952-53
13-132 (5-46, 8-86)	J. Srinath, Calcutta	1998-99

For Pakistan (7)

12-94 (5-52, 7-42)	Fazal Mahmood, Lucknow	1952-53
11-79 (3-19, 8-60)	Imran Khan, Karachi	1982-83
11-180 (6-98, 5-82)	Imran Khan, Faisalabad	1982-83
10-175 (4-135, 6-40)	Iqbal Qasim, Bombay	1979-80
10-187 (5-94, 5-93)†	Saqlain Mushtaq, Chennai	1998-99
10-216 (5-94, 5-122)	Saqlain Mushtaq, Delhi	1998-99
11-190 (8-69, 3-121)	Sikander Bakht, Delhi	1979-80

† *Signifies ten wickets or more on first appearance in India–Pakistan Tests.*

INDIA v SRI LANKA

	Captains					
Season	*India*	*Sri Lanka*	*T*	*I*	*SL*	*D*
1982-83*I*	S. M. Gavaskar	B. Warnapura	1	0	0	1
1985-86*S*	Kapil Dev	L. R. D. Mendis	3	0	1	2
1986-87*I*	Kapil Dev	L. R. D. Mendis	3	2	0	1
1990-91*I*	M. Azharuddin	A. Ranatunga	1	1	0	0
1993-94*S*	M. Azharuddin	A. Ranatunga	3	1	0	2
1993-94*I*	M. Azharuddin	A. Ranatunga	3	3	0	0
1997-98*S*	S. R. Tendulkar	A. Ranatunga	2	0	0	2
1997-98*I*	S. R. Tendulkar	A. Ranatunga	3	0	0	3
1998-99*S*†	M. Azharuddin	A. Ranatunga	1	0	0	1
2001*S*	S. C. Ganguly	S. T. Jayasuriya	3	1	2	0
	In India		11	6	0	5
	In Sri Lanka		12	2	3	7
	Totals		23	8	3	12

I Played in India. S Played in Sri Lanka.

† This Test was part of the Asian Test Championship.

HIGHEST INNINGS TOTALS

For India in India: 676-7 at Kanpur 1986-87
in Sri Lanka: 537-8 dec. at Colombo (RPS) 1997-98

For Sri Lanka in India: 420 at Kanpur 1986-87
in Sri Lanka: 952-6 dec. at Colombo (RPS) 1997-98

LOWEST INNINGS TOTALS

For India in India: 288 at Chandigarh 1990-91
in Sri Lanka: 180 at Galle 2001

For Sri Lanka in India: 82 at Chandigarh 1990-91
in Sri Lanka: 198 at Kandy 1985-86

INDIVIDUAL HUNDREDS

For India (30)

M. Amarnath (2)
116* Kandy 1985-86
131 Nagpur 1986-87

M. Azharuddin (5)
199 Kanpur 1986-87
108 Bangalore . . 1993-94
152 Ahmedabad . 1993-94
126 Colombo (RPS) 1997-98
108* Colombo (SSC) 1997-98

R. Dravid (1)
107 Colombo (SSC) 1998-99

S. C. Ganguly (3)
147 Colombo (SSC) 1997-98
109 Mohali 1997-98
173 Mumbai. . . . 1997-98

S. M. Gavaskar (2)
155† Madras 1982-83
176 Kanpur 1986-87

V. G. Kambli (2)
125 Colombo (SSC) 1993-94
120 Colombo (PSS) 1993-94

Kapil Dev (1)
163 Kanpur 1986-87

S. M. Patil (1)
114*† Madras 1982-83

S. Ramesh (1)
143† Colombo (SSC) 1998-99

N. S. Sidhu (4)
104 Colombo (SSC) 1993-94
124 Lucknow . . . 1993-94
111 Colombo (RPS) 1997-98
131 Mohali 1997-98

S. R. Tendulkar (6)
104* Colombo (SSC) 1993-94
142 Lucknow . . . 1993-94
143 Colombo (RPS) 1997-98
139 Colombo (SSC) 1997-98
148 Mumbai. . . . 1997-98
124* Colombo (SSC) 1998-99

D. B. Vengsarkar (2)
153 Nagpur 1986-87
166 Cuttack 1986-87

For Sri Lanka (25)

M. S. Atapattu (2)
108 Mohali 1997-98
108 Colombo (SSC) 2001
P. A. de Silva (5)
148 Colombo (PSS) 1993-94
126 Colombo (RPS) 1997-98
146 } Colombo (SSC) 1997-98
120 }
110* Mohali 1997-98
R. L. Dias (1)
106 Kandy. 1985-86
S. T. Jayasuriya (3)
340 Colombo (RPS) 1997-98
199 Colombo (SSC) 1997-98
111 Galle. 2001
D. P. M. D. Jayawardene (3)
242 Colombo (SSC) 1998-99
104 Kandy. 2001
139 Colombo (SSC) 2001
R. S. Madugalle (1)
103 Colombo (SSC) 1985-86
R. S. Mahanama (2)
151 Colombo (PSS) 1993-94
225 Colombo (RPS) 1997-98
L. R. D. Mendis (3)
105 } †Madras 1982-83
105 }
124 Kandy. 1985-86
A. Ranatunga (1)
111 Colombo (SSC) 1985-86
T. T. Samaraweera (1)
103*† Colombo (SSC) 2001
K. Sangakkara (1)
105*† Galle. 2001
S. A. R. Silva (1)
111 Colombo (PSS) 1985-86
H. P. Tillekeratne (1)
136* Colombo (SSC) 2001

† *Signifies hundred on first appearance in India–Sri Lanka Tests.*

RECORD PARTNERSHIPS FOR EACH WICKET

For India

171	for 1st	M. Prabhakar and N. S. Sidhu at Colombo (SSC)	1993-94
232	for 2nd	S. Ramesh and R. Dravid at Colombo (SSC)	1998-99
173	for 3rd	M. Amarnath and D. B. Vengsarkar at Nagpur	1986-87
256	for 4th	S. C. Ganguly and S. R. Tendulkar at Mumbai	1997-98
150	for 5th	S. R. Tendulkar and S. C. Ganguly at Colombo (SSC)	1997-98
272	for 6th	M. Azharuddin and Kapil Dev at Kanpur	1986-87
78*	for 7th	S. M. Patil and Madan Lal at Madras	1982-83
70	for 8th	Kapil Dev and L. Sivaramakrishnan at Colombo (PSS)	1985-86
89	for 9th	S. C. Ganguly and A. Kuruvilla at Mohali	1997-98
30	for 10th	Zaheer Khan and B. K. V. Prasad at Colombo (SSC)	2001

For Sri Lanka

159	for 1st	S. Wettimuny and J. R. Ratnayeke at Kanpur	1986-87
576	for 2nd†	S. T. Jayasuriya and R. S. Mahanama at Colombo (RPS)	1997-98
218	for 3rd	S. T. Jayasuriya and P. A. de Silva at Colombo (SSC)	1997-98
216	for 4th	R. L. Dias and L. R. D. Mendis at Kandy	1985-86
144	for 5th[1]	R. S. Madugalle and A. Ranatunga at Colombo (SSC)	1985-86
103	for 6th	P. A. de Silva and H. D. P. K. Dharmasena at Mohali	1997-98
194*	for 7th†	H. P. Tillekeratne and T. T. Samaraweera at Colombo (SSC)	2001
48	for 8th	P. A. de Silva and M. Muralitharan at Colombo (SSC)	1997-98
60	for 9th	H. P. Tillekeratne and A. W. R. Madurasinghe at Chandigarh	1990-91
64	for 10th	M. Muralitharan and P. D. R. L. Perera at Kandy	2001

† *Denotes record partnership against all countries.*

[1] *Although the fifth wicket added 176 runs against India at Colombo (SSC) in 1998-99, this comprised two partnerships with D. P. M. D. Jayawardene adding 115* with A. Ranatunga (retired hurt) and a further 61 with H. P. Tillekeratne.*

TEN WICKETS OR MORE IN A MATCH

For India (3)

11-128 (4-69, 7-59)	A. Kumble, Lucknow	1993-94
10-107 (3-56, 7-51)	Maninder Singh, Nagpur	1986-87
11-125 (5-38, 6-87)	S. L. V. Raju, Ahmedabad	1993-94

For Sri Lanka (1)

11-196 (8-87, 3-109)	M. Muralitharan, Colombo (SSC)	2001

INDIA v ZIMBABWE

Season	*Captains* India	*Captains* Zimbabwe	*T*	*I*	*Z*	*D*
1992-93*Z*	M. Azharuddin	D. L. Houghton	1	0	0	1
1992-93*I*	M. Azharuddin	D. L. Houghton	1	1	0	0
1998-99*Z*	M. Azharuddin	A. D. R. Campbell	1	0	1	0
2000-01*I*	S. C. Ganguly	H. H. Streak	2	1	0	1
2001*Z*	S. C. Ganguly	H. H. Streak	2	1	1	0
	In India		3	2	0	1
	In Zimbabwe		4	1	2	1
	Totals		7	3	2	2

I Played in India. Z Played in Zimbabwe.

HIGHEST INNINGS TOTALS

For India in India: 609-6 dec. at Nagpur 2000-01
in Zimbabwe: 318 at Bulawayo 2001

For Zimbabwe in India: 503-6 at Nagpur 2000-01
in Zimbabwe: 456 at Harare 1992-93

LOWEST INNINGS TOTALS

For India in India: No completed innings
in Zimbabwe: 173 at Harare 1998-99

For Zimbabwe in India: 201 at Delhi 1992-93
in Zimbabwe: 173 at Bulawayo 2001

INDIVIDUAL HUNDREDS

For India (8)

S. S. Das (1)
110 Nagpur 2000-01
R. Dravid (3)
118† Harare 1998-99
200* Delhi 2000-01
162 Nagpur 2000-01
V. G. Kambli (1)
227† Delhi 1992-93
S. V. Manjrekar (1)
104† Harare 1992-93
S. R. Tendulkar (2)
122 Delhi 2000-01
201* Nagpur 2000-01

For Zimbabwe (6)

A. D. R. Campbell (1)
102 Nagpur 2000-01
A. Flower (3)
115 Delhi 1992-93
183* Delhi 2000-01
232* Nagpur 2000-01
G. W. Flower (1)
106* Nagpur 2000-01
D. L. Houghton (1)
121† Harare 1992-93

† *Signifies hundred on first appearance in India–Zimbabwe Tests.*

RECORD PARTNERSHIPS FOR EACH WICKET

For India

72	for 1st	S. S. Das and S. Ramesh at Nagpur	2000-01
155	for 2nd	S. S. Das and R. Dravid at Nagpur	2000-01
249	for 3rd	R. Dravid and S. R. Tendulkar at Nagpur	2000-01
110*	for 4th	R. Dravid and S. C. Ganguly at Delhi	2000-01
67	for 5th	R. Dravid and S. C. Ganguly at Harare	1998-99
96	for 6th	S. V. Manjrekar and Kapil Dev at Harare	1992-93
44	for 7th	R. Dravid and R. R. Singh at Harare	1998-99
72	for 8th	S. S. Dighe and Harbhajan Singh at Bulawayo	2001
19	for 9th	H. K. Badani and J. Srinath at Harare	2001
40	for 10th	J. Srinath and Harbhajan Singh at Harare	1998-99

For Zimbabwe

138	for 1st	G. J. Rennie and C. B. Wishart at Harare	1998-99
101	for 2nd	G. J. Whittall and S. V. Carlisle at Nagpur	2000-01
119	for 3rd	S. V. Carlisle and A. D. R. Campbell at Delhi	2000-01
209	for 4th	A. D. R. Campbell and A. Flower at Nagpur	2000-01
96	for 5th	A. Flower and G. W. Flower at Nagpur	2000-01
165	for 6th†	D. L. Houghton and A. Flower at Harare	1992-93
98*	for 7th	A. Flower and H. H. Streak at Nagpur	2000-01
46	for 8th	A. Flower and B. A. Murphy at Delhi	2000-01
33	for 9th	H. K. Olonga and A. G. Huckle at Harare	1998-99
97*	for 10th†	A. Flower and H. K. Olonga at Delhi	2000-01

† *Denotes record partnership against all countries.*

BEST MATCH BOWLING ANALYSES

For India

9-141 (4-81, 5-60) J. Srinath, Delhi 2000-01

For Zimbabwe

7-115 (3-69, 4-46) H. H. Streak, Harare 2001

INDIA v BANGLADESH

	Captains					
Season	*India*	*Bangladesh*	*T*	*I*	*B*	*D*
2000-01*B*	S. C. Ganguly	Naimur Rahman	1	1	0	0

B Played in Bangladesh.

HIGHEST INNINGS TOTALS

For India: 429 at Dhaka 2000-01

For Bangladesh: 400 at Dhaka 2000-01

INDIVIDUAL HUNDRED

For Bangladesh (1)

Aminul Islam (1)
145† Dhaka. 2000-01

Highest score for India: 92 by S. B. Joshi at Dhaka, 2000-01.

† *Signifies hundred on first appearance in India–Bangladesh Tests.*

HIGHEST PARTNERSHIPS

For India

121 for 7th S. C. Ganguly and S. B. Joshi at Dhaka 2000-01

For Bangladesh

93 for 7th Aminul Islam and Khaled Masud at Dhaka 2000-01

BEST MATCH BOWLING ANALYSES

For India

8-169 (5-142, 3-27) S. B. Joshi, Dhaka 2000-01

For Bangladesh

6-154 (6-132, 0-22) Naimur Rahman, Dhaka. 2000-01

PAKISTAN v SRI LANKA

	Captains					
Season	*Pakistan*	*Sri Lanka*	*T*	*P*	*SL*	*D*
1981-82*P*	Javed Miandad	B. Warnapura[1]	3	2	0	1
1985-86*P*	Javed Miandad	L. R. D. Mendis	3	2	0	1
1985-86*S*	Imran Khan	L. R. D. Mendis	3	1	1	1
1991-92*P*	Imran Khan	P. A. de Silva	3	1	0	2
1994-95*S*†	Salim Malik	A. Ranatunga	2	2	0	0
1995-96*P*	Ramiz Raja	A. Ranatunga	3	1	2	0
1996-97*S*	Ramiz Raja	A. Ranatunga	2	0	0	2
1998-99*P*‡	Wasim Akram	H. P. Tillekeratne	1	0	0	1
1998-99*B*‡	Wasim Akram	P. A. de Silva	1	1	0	0
1999-2000*P*	Saeed Anwar[2]	S. T. Jayasuriya	3	1	2	0
2000*S*	Moin Khan	S. T. Jayasuriya	3	2	0	1
	In Pakistan		16	7	4	5
	In Sri Lanka		10	5	1	4
	In Bangladesh		1	1	0	0
	Totals.		27	13	5	9

P Played in Pakistan. S Played in Sri Lanka. B Played in Bangladesh.

† *One Test was cancelled owing to the threat of civil disturbances following a general election.*
‡ *These two Tests were part of the Asian Test Championship.*

Note: The following deputised for the official touring captain or were appointed by the home authority for only a minor proportion of the series:
[1]L. R. D. Mendis (Second). [2]Moin Khan (Third).

HIGHEST INNINGS TOTALS

For Pakistan in Pakistan: 555-3 at Faisalabad	1985-86
in Sri Lanka: 600-8 dec. at Galle	2000
in Bangladesh: 594 at Dhaka	1998-99
For Sri Lanka in Pakistan: 479 at Faisalabad	1985-86
in Sri Lanka: 467-5 at Kandy	2000

LOWEST INNINGS TOTALS

For Pakistan in Pakistan: 182 at Rawalpindi	1999-2000
in Sri Lanka: 132 at Colombo (CCC)	1985-86
For Sri Lanka in Pakistan: 149 at Karachi	1981-82
in Sri Lanka: 71 at Kandy	1994-95

INDIVIDUAL HUNDREDS

For Pakistan (23)

Haroon Rashid (1)
153† Karachi 1981-82
Ijaz Ahmed, sen. (2)
113† Colombo (RPS) 1996-97
211 Dhaka 1998-99
Inzamam-ul-Haq (4)
100* Kandy 1994-95
200* Dhaka 1998-99
138 Karachi 1999-00
112 Galle 2000
Javed Miandad (1)
203* Faisalabad . . 1985-86
Mohsin Khan (1)
129 Lahore 1981-82
Moin Khan (1)
117* Sialkot 1995-96
Qasim Omar (1)
206† Faisalabad . . 1985-86
Ramiz Raja (1)
122 Colombo (PSS) 1985-86
Saeed Anwar (2)
136† Colombo (PSS) 1994-95
123 Galle 2000
Salim Malik (3)
100*† Karachi 1981-82
101 Sialkot 1991-92
155 Colombo (SSC) 1996-97
Wajahatullah Wasti (2)
133 }
121* } †Lahore 1998-99
Wasim Akram (1)
100 Galle 2000
Younis Khan (2)
107† Rawalpindi . . 1999-00
116 Galle 2000
Zaheer Abbas (1)
134† Lahore 1981-82

For Sri Lanka (19)

R. P. Arnold (1)
123 Lahore 1998-99
M. S. Atapattu (1)
207* Kandy 2000
P. A. de Silva (8)
122† Faisalabad . . 1985-86
105 Karachi 1985-86
127 Colombo (PSS) 1994-95
105 Faisalabad . . 1995-96
168 Colombo (RPS) 1996-97
138* }
103* } Colombo (SSC) 1996-97
112 Rawalpindi . . 1999-00
R. L. Dias (1)
109 Lahore 1981-82
A. P. Gurusinha (1)
116* Colombo (PSS) 1985-86
S. T. Jayasuriya (2)
113 Colombo (SSC) 1996-97
188 Kandy 2000
R. S. Kaluwitharana (1)
100 Lahore 1998-99
A. Ranatunga (1)
135* Colombo (PSS) 1985-86
H. P. Tillekeratne (2)
115 Faisalabad . . 1995-96
103 Colombo (RPS) 1996-97
S. Wettimuny (1)
157 Faisalabad . . 1981-82

† *Signifies hundred on first appearance in Pakistan–Sri Lanka Tests.*

RECORD PARTNERSHIPS FOR EACH WICKET

For Pakistan

156 for 1st	Wajahatullah Wasti and Shahid Afridi at Lahore	1998-99
151 for 2nd	Mohsin Khan and Majid Khan at Lahore	1981-82
397 for 3rd	Qasim Omar and Javed Miandad at Faisalabad	1985-86
178 for 4th	Wajahatullah Wasti and Yousuf Youhana at Lahore	1998-99
132 for 5th	Salim Malik and Imran Khan at Sialkot	1991-92
124 for 6th	Inzamam-ul-Haq and Younis Khan at Karachi	1999-2000
120 for 7th	Younis Khan and Wasim Akram at Galle	2000
88 for 8th	Moin Khan and Waqar Younis at Karachi	1999-2000
145 for 9th	Younis Khan and Wasim Akram at Rawalpindi	1999-2000
90 for 10th	Wasim Akram and Arshad Khan at Colombo (SSC)	2000

For Sri Lanka

335 for 1st†	M. S. Atapattu and S. T. Jayasuriya at Kandy	2000
217 for 2nd	S. Wettimuny and R. L. Dias at Faisalabad	1981-82
176 for 3rd	U. C. Hathurusinghe and P. A. de Silva at Faisalabad	1995-96
240* for 4th†	A. P. Gurusinha and A. Ranatunga at Colombo (PSS)	1985-86
143 for 5th	R. P. Arnold and R. S. Kaluwitharana at Lahore	1998-99
121 for 6th	A. Ranatunga and P. A. de Silva at Faisalabad	1985-86
131 for 7th	H. P. Tillekeratne and R. S. Kalpage at Kandy	1994-95
76 for 8th	P. A. de Silva and W. P. U. J. C. Vaas at Colombo (SSC)	1996-97
52 for 9th	P. A. de Silva and R. J. Ratnayake at Faisalabad	1985-86
73 for 10th†	H. P. Tillekeratne and K. S. C. de Silva at Dhaka	1998-99

† Denotes record partnership against all countries.

TEN WICKETS OR MORE IN A MATCH

For Pakistan (2)

14-116 (8-58, 6-58)	Imran Khan, Lahore	1981-82
11-119 (6-34, 5-85)	Waqar Younis, Kandy	1994-95

For Sri Lanka (1)

10-148 (4-77, 6-71)	M. Muralitharan, Peshawar	1999-2000

PAKISTAN v ZIMBABWE

	Captains					
Season	*Pakistan*	*Zimbabwe*	*T*	*P*	*Z*	*D*
1993-94*P*	Wasim Akram[1]	A. Flower	3	2	0	1
1994-95*Z*	Salim Malik	A. Flower	3	2	1	0
1996-97*P*	Wasim Akram	A. D. R. Campbell	2	1	0	1
1997-98*Z*	Rashid Latif	A. D. R. Campbell	2	1	0	1
1998-99*P*†	Aamir Sohail[2]	A. D. R. Campbell	2	0	1	1
	In Pakistan		7	3	1	3
	In Zimbabwe		5	3	1	1
	Totals		12	6	2	4

P Played in Pakistan. Z Played in Zimbabwe.

† The Third Test at Faisalabad was abandoned without a ball being bowled and is excluded.

Notes: The following were appointed by the home authority for only a minor proportion of the series:

[1]Waqar Younis (First). [2]Moin Khan (Second).

HIGHEST INNINGS TOTALS

For Pakistan	in Pakistan: 553 at Sheikhupura	1996-97
	in Zimbabwe: 354 at Harare	1997-98
For Zimbabwe	in Pakistan: 375 at Sheikhupura	1996-97
	in Zimbabwe: 544-4 dec. at Harare	1994-95

LOWEST INNINGS TOTALS

For Pakistan	in Pakistan: 103 at Peshawar	1998-99
	in Zimbabwe: 158 at Harare	1994-95
For Zimbabwe	in Pakistan: 133 at Faisalabad	1996-97
	in Zimbabwe: 139 at Harare	1994-95

INDIVIDUAL HUNDREDS

For Pakistan (4)

Inzamam-ul-Haq (1)
101 Harare. 1994-95
Mohammad Wasim (1)
192† Harare. 1997-98
Wasim Akram (1)
257* Sheikhupura . 1996-97
Yousuf Youhana (1)
120* Lahore 1998-99

For Zimbabwe (9)

A. Flower (2)
156 Harare. 1994-95
100* Bulawayo. . . 1997-98
G. W. Flower (3)
201* Harare. 1994-95
110 Sheikhupura . 1996-97
156*‡ Bulawayo. . . 1997-98
M. W. Goodwin (1)
166*† Bulawayo. . . 1997-98
N. C. Johnson (1)
107† Peshawar . . . 1998-99
P. A. Strang (1)
106* Sheikhupura . 1996-97
G. J. Whittall (1)
113* Harare. 1994-95

† *Signifies hundred on first appearance in Pakistan–Zimbabwe Tests.*
‡ *Carried his bat.*

RECORD PARTNERSHIPS FOR EACH WICKET

For Pakistan

95	for 1st	Aamir Sohail and Shoaib Mohammad at Karachi (DS)	1993-94
118*	for 2nd	Shoaib Mohammad and Asif Mujtaba at Lahore	1993-94
83	for 3rd	Shoaib Mohammad and Javed Miandad at Karachi (DS)	1993-94
118	for 4th	Ijaz Ahmed, sen. and Yousuf Youhana at Peshawar	1998-99
110	for 5th	Yousuf Youhana and Moin Khan at Bulawayo	1997-98
96	for 6th	Inzamam-ul-Haq and Rashid Latif at Harare	1994-95
120	for 7th	Ijaz Ahmed, sen. and Inzamam-ul-Haq at Harare	1994-95
313	for 8th†	Wasim Akram and Saqlain Mushtaq at Sheikhupura	1996-97
147	for 9th	Mohammad Wasim and Mushtaq Ahmed at Harare	1997-98
50*	for 10th	Yousuf Youhana and Waqar Younis at Lahore	1998-99

For Zimbabwe

48*	for 1st	G. J. Rennie and G. W. Flower at Lahore	1998-99
135	for 2nd†	M. H. Dekker and A. D. R. Campbell at Rawalpindi	1993-94
84	for 3rd	G. W. Flower and D. L. Houghton at Sheikhupura	1996-97
269	for 4th†	G. W. Flower and A. Flower at Harare	1994-95
277*	for 5th†	M. W. Goodwin and A. Flower at Bulawayo	1997-98
72	for 6th	M. H. Dekker and G. J. Whittall at Rawalpindi	1993-94
131	for 7th	G. W. Flower and P. A. Strang at Sheikhupura	1996-97
110	for 8th†	G. J. Whittall and B. C. Strang at Harare	1997-98
87	for 9th†	P. A. Strang and B. C. Strang at Sheikhupura	1996-97
29	for 10th	E. A. Brandes and S. G. Peall at Rawalpindi	1993-94

† *Denotes record partnership against all countries.*

TEN WICKETS OR MORE IN A MATCH

For Pakistan (2)

13-135 (7-91, 6-44)†	Waqar Younis, Karachi (DS)	1993-94
10-106 (6-48, 4-58)	Wasim Akram, Faisalabad	1996-97

Note: The best match figures for Zimbabwe are 9-105 (6-90, 3-15) by H. H. Streak at Harare, 1994-95.

† *Signifies ten wickets or more on first appearance in Pakistan–Zimbabwe Tests.*

PAKISTAN v BANGLADESH

	Captains					
Season	*Pakistan*	*Bangladesh*	*T*	*P*	*B*	*D*
2001-02*P*†	Waqar Younis	Naimur Rahman	1	1	0	0

P Played in Pakistan.

† *This Test was part of the Asian Test Championship.*

HIGHEST INNINGS TOTALS

For Pakistan: 546-3 dec. at Multan 2001-02

For Bangladesh: 148 at Multan 2001-02

INDIVIDUAL HUNDREDS

For Pakistan (5)

Abdur Razzaq (1)
110*† Multan 2001-02

Inzamam-ul-Haq (1)
105*† Multan 2001-02

Saeed Anwar (1)
101† Multan 2001-02

Taufeeq Umar (1)
104† Multan 2001-02

Yousuf Youhana (1)
102*† Multan 2001-02

Highest score for Bangladesh: 56* by Habibul Bashar at Multan, 2001-02.

† *Signifies hundred on first appearance in Pakistan–Bangladesh Tests.*

HIGHEST PARTNERSHIPS

For Pakistan

168	for 1st	Saeed Anwar and Taufeeq Umar at Multan	2001-02
165*	for 4th‡	Yousuf Youhana and Abdur Razzaq at Multan	2001-02
123*	for 4th‡	Inzamam-ul-Haq and Yousuf Youhana at Multan	2001-02

‡ *A total of 288 runs was added between the fall of the 3rd wicket and the end of the innings: Inzamam-ul-Haq retired hurt when he and Yousuf Youhana had added 123 runs.*

For Bangladesh

45	for 8th	Habibul Bashar and Hasibul Hussain at Multan	2001-02

TEN WICKETS OR MORE IN A MATCH

For Pakistan (1)

12-94 (6-42, 6-52)†	Danish Kaneria, Multan	2001-02

Note: The best match figures for Bangladesh are 2-110 by Mohammad Sharif at Multan, 2001-02.

† *Signifies ten wickets or more on first appearance in Pakistan–Bangladesh Tests.*

SRI LANKA v ZIMBABWE

	Captains					
Season	*Sri Lanka*	*Zimbabwe*	*T*	*SL*	*Z*	*D*
1994-95*Z*	A. Ranatunga	A. Flower	3	0	0	3
1996-97*S*	A. Ranatunga	A. D. R. Campbell	2	2	0	0
1997-98*S*	A. Ranatunga	A. D. R. Campbell	2	2	0	0
1999-2000*Z*	S. T. Jayasuriya	A. Flower	3	1	0	2
	In Sri Lanka		4	4	0	0
	In Zimbabwe		6	1	0	5
	Totals		10	5	0	5

S Played in Sri Lanka. Z Played in Zimbabwe.

HIGHEST INNINGS TOTALS

For Sri Lanka	in Sri Lanka:	469-9 dec. at Kandy	1997-98
	in Zimbabwe:	432 at Harare	1999-2000
For Zimbabwe	in Sri Lanka:	338 at Kandy	1997-98
	in Zimbabwe:	462-9 dec. at Bulawayo	1994-95

LOWEST INNINGS TOTALS

For Sri Lanka	in Sri Lanka:	225 at Colombo (SSC)	1997-98
	in Zimbabwe:	218 at Bulawayo	1994-95
For Zimbabwe	in Sri Lanka:	127 at Colombo (RPS)	1996-97
	in Zimbabwe:	174 at Harare	1999-2000

INDIVIDUAL HUNDREDS

For Sri Lanka (10)

R. P. Arnold (1)
104*‡ Harare 1999-00

M. S. Atapattu (2)
223† Kandy 1997-98
216*‡ Bulawayo . . . 1999-00

P. A. de Silva (1)
143* Colombo (SSC) 1997-98

T. M. Dilshan (1)
163* Harare 1999-00

A. P. Gurusinha (1)
128† Harare 1994-95

S. Ranatunga (2)
118† Harare 1994-95
100* Bulawayo . . . 1994-95

H. P. Tillekeratne (2)
116 Harare 1994-95
126* Colombo (SSC) 1996-97

For Zimbabwe (4)

A. Flower (2)
105* Colombo (SSC) 1997-98
129 Harare 1999-00

D. L. Houghton (2)
266 Bulawayo . . . 1994-95
142 Harare 1994-95

† *Signifies hundred on first appearance in Sri Lanka–Zimbabwe Tests.*
‡ *Carried his bat.*

RECORD PARTNERSHIPS FOR EACH WICKET

For Sri Lanka

85	for 1st	M. S. Atapattu and S. T. Jayasuriya at Bulawayo	1999-2000
217	for 2nd	A. P. Gurusinha and S. Ranatunga at Harare	1994-95
140	for 3rd	M. S. Atapattu and P. A. de Silva at Kandy	1997-98
178	for 4th	D. P. M. D. Jayawardene and T. M. Dilshan at Harare	1999-2000
114	for 5th	A. P. Gurusinha and H. P. Tillekeratne at Colombo (SSC)	1996-97
189*	for 6th†	P. A. de Silva and A. Ranatunga at Colombo (SSC)	1997-98
57	for 7th	M. S. Atapattu and W. P. U. J. C. Vaas at Kandy	1997-98
73	for 8th	H. D. P. K. Dharmasena and W. P. U. J. C. Vaas at Colombo (RPS)	1996-97
30	for 9th	R. P. Arnold and G. P. Wickremasinghe at Harare	1999-2000
25	for 10th	H. D. P. K. Dharmasena and M. Muralitharan at Bulawayo	1994-95

For Zimbabwe

113	for 1st	G. W. Flower and M. H. Dekker at Harare	1994-95
40	for 2nd	G. J. Rennie and M. W. Goodwin at Colombo (SSC)	1997-98
194	for 3rd†	A. D. R. Campbell and D. L. Houghton at Harare	1994-95
121	for 4th	D. L. Houghton and A. Flower at Bulawayo	1994-95
101	for 5th	M. W. Goodwin and A. Flower at Harare	1999-2000
100	for 6th	D. L. Houghton and W. R. James at Bulawayo	1994-95
125	for 7th	A. Flower and G. J. Whittall at Harare	1999-2000
84	for 8th	D. L. Houghton and J. A. Rennie at Bulawayo	1994-95
43	for 9th	J. A. Rennie and S. G. Peall at Bulawayo	1994-95
34	for 10th	P. A. Strang and H. K. Olonga at Colombo (SSC)	1996-97

† *Denotes record partnership against all countries.*

TEN WICKETS OR MORE IN A MATCH

For Sri Lanka (1)

12-117 (5-23, 7-94) M. Muralitharan, Kandy 1997-98

Note: The best match figures for Zimbabwe are 6-112 (2-28, 4-84) by H. H. Streak at Colombo (SSC), 1997-98.

ZIMBABWE v BANGLADESH

	Captains					
Season	*Zimbabwe*	*Bangladesh*	*T*	*Z*	*B*	*D*
2000-01Z	H. H. Streak	Naimur Rahman	2	2	0	0

Z Played in Zimbabwe.

HIGHEST INNINGS TOTALS

For Zimbabwe: 457 at Bulawayo 2000-01

For Bangladesh: 266 at Harare 2000-01

LOWEST INNINGS TOTAL

For Bangladesh: 168 at Bulawayo 2000-01

INDIVIDUAL HUNDRED

For Zimbabwe (1)

G. J. Whittall (1)
119† Bulawayo. . . 2000-01

Highest score for Bangladesh: 85* by Javed Omar at Bulawayo, 2000-01.

† *Signifies hundred on first appearance in Zimbabwe–Bangladesh Tests.*

HUNDRED PARTNERSHIPS

For Zimbabwe

149 for 4th	G. J. Whittall and A. Flower at Bulawayo	2000-01
133 for 6th	G. W. Flower and H. H. Streak at Harare	2000-01
120 for 6th	G. W. Flower and H. H. Streak at Bulawayo.	2000-01

For Bangladesh

114 for 4th†	Mehrab Hossain and Habibul Bashar at Harare.	2000-01

† *Denotes Bangladesh's only hundred partnership in Test cricket.*

BEST MATCH BOWLING ANALYSES

For Zimbabwe

8-110 (5-73, 3-37)	A. M. Blignaut, Bulawayo	2000-01

For Bangladesh

6-81 (6-81)	Manjurul Islam, Bulawayo	2000-01

TEST GROUNDS

In Chronological Sequence

	City and Ground	*First Test Match*		*Tests*
1	Melbourne, Melbourne Cricket Ground	March 15, 1877	A v E	93
2	London, Kennington Oval	September 6, 1880	E v A	84
3	Sydney, Sydney Cricket Ground (No. 1)	February 17, 1882	A v E	87
4	Manchester, Old Trafford	July 11, 1884	E v A	67
5	London, Lord's	July 21, 1884	E v A	102
6	Adelaide, Adelaide Oval	December 12, 1884	A v E	59
7	Port Elizabeth, St George's Park	March 12, 1889	SA v E	19
8	Cape Town, Newlands	March 25, 1889	SA v E	33
9	Johannesburg, Old Wanderers	March 2, 1896	SA v E	22
	Now the site of Johannesburg Railway Station.			
10	Nottingham, Trent Bridge	June 1, 1899	E v A	48
11	Leeds, Headingley	June 29, 1899	E v A	62
12	Birmingham, Edgbaston	May 29, 1902	E v A	37
13	Sheffield, Bramall Lane	July 3, 1902	E v A	1
	Sheffield United Football Club have built a stand over the cricket pitch.			
14	Durban, Lord's	January 21, 1910	SA v E	4
	Ground destroyed and built on.			
15	Durban, Kingsmead	January 18, 1923	SA v E	28
16	Brisbane, Exhibition Ground	November 30, 1928	A v E	2
	No longer used for cricket.			
17	Christchurch, Lancaster Park	January 10, 1930	NZ v E	37
	Ground also known under sponsors' names.			
18	Bridgetown, Kensington Oval	January 11, 1930	WI v E	37
19	Wellington, Basin Reserve	January 24, 1930	NZ v E	37
20	Port-of-Spain, Queen's Park Oval	February 1, 1930	WI v E	50
21	Auckland, Eden Park	February 17, 1930	NZ v E	43
22	Georgetown, Bourda	February 21, 1930	WI v E	27
23	Kingston, Sabina Park	April 3, 1930	WI v E	36
24	Brisbane, Woolloongabba	November 27, 1931	A v SA	43
25	Bombay, Gymkhana Ground	December 15, 1933	I v E	1
	No longer used for first-class cricket.			
26	Calcutta (*now Kolkata*), Eden Gardens	January 5, 1934	I v E	31
27	Madras (*now Chennai*), Chepauk (Chidambaram Stadium)	February 10, 1934	I v E	25
28	Delhi, Feroz Shah Kotla	November 10, 1948	I v WI	26
29	Bombay, Brabourne Stadium	December 9, 1948	I v WI	17
	Rarely used for first-class cricket.			
30	Johannesburg, Ellis Park	December 27, 1948	SA v E	6
	Mainly a rugby stadium, no longer used for cricket.			
31	Kanpur, Green Park (Modi Stadium)	January 12, 1952	I v E	18
32	Lucknow, University Ground	October 25, 1952	I v P	1
	Ground destroyed, now partly under a river bed.			
33	Dacca (*now Dhaka*), Dacca (now Bangabandhu) Stadium	January 1, 1955	P v I	9
	Originally in East Pakistan, now Bangladesh.			
34	Bahawalpur, Dring (now Bahawal) Stadium	January 15, 1955	P v I	1
	Still used for first-class cricket.			
35	Lahore, Lawrence Gardens (Bagh-i-Jinnah)	January 29, 1955	P v I	3
	Still used for club and occasional first-class matches.			
36	Peshawar, Services Ground	February 13, 1955	P v I	1
	Superseded by new stadium.			
37	Karachi, National Stadium	February 26, 1955	P v I	35
38	Dunedin, Carisbrook	March 11, 1955	NZ v E	10
39	Hyderabad, Fateh Maidan (Lal Bahadur Stadium)	November 19, 1955	I v NZ	3

	City and Ground	*First Test Match*		*Tests*
40	Madras, Corporation Stadium	January 6, 1956	I v NZ	9
	Superseded by rebuilt Chepauk Stadium.			
41	Johannesburg, Wanderers	December 24, 1956	SA v E	22
42	Lahore, Gaddafi Stadium	November 21, 1959	P v A	31
43	Rawalpindi, Pindi Club Ground	March 27, 1965	P v NZ	1
	Superseded by new stadium.			
44	Nagpur, Vidarbha C.A. Ground	October 3, 1969	I v NZ	6
45	Perth, Western Australian C.A. Ground	December 11, 1970	A v E	28
46	Hyderabad, Niaz Stadium	March 16, 1973	P v E	5
47	Bangalore, Karnataka State C.A. Ground (Chinnaswamy Stadium)	November 22, 1974	I v WI	13
48	Bombay (*now Mumbai*), Wankhede Stadium	January 23, 1975	I v WI	18
49	Faisalabad, Iqbal Stadium	October 16, 1978	P v I	20
50	Napier, McLean Park	February 16, 1979	NZ v P	3
51	Multan, Ibn-e-Qasim Bagh Stadium	December 30, 1980	P v WI	1
52	St John's (Antigua), Recreation Ground	March 27, 1981	WI v E	16
53	Colombo, P. Saravanamuttu Stadium	February 17, 1982	SL v E	6
54	Kandy, Asgiriya Stadium	April 22, 1983	SL v A	12
55	Jullundur, Burlton Park	September 24, 1983	I v P	1
56	Ahmedabad, Gujarat Stadium	November 12, 1983	I v WI	5
57	Colombo, Sinhalese Sports Club Ground	March 16, 1984	SL v NZ	18
58	Colombo, Colombo Cricket Club Ground	March 24, 1984	SL v NZ	3
59	Sialkot, Jinnah Stadium	October 27, 1985	P v SL	4
60	Cuttack, Barabati Stadium	January 4, 1987	I v SL	2
61	Jaipur, Sawai Mansingh Stadium	February 21, 1987	I v P	1
62	Hobart, Bellerive Oval	December 16, 1989	A v SL	5
63	Chandigarh, Sector 16 Stadium	November 23, 1990	I v SL	1
	Superseded by Mohali ground.			
64	Hamilton, Seddon Park	February 22, 1991	NZ v SL	9
	Ground also known under various sponsors' names.			
65	Gujranwala, Municipal Stadium	December 20, 1991	P v SL	1
66	Colombo, R. Premadasa (Khettarama) Stadium	August 28, 1992	SL v A	5
67	Moratuwa, Tyronne Fernando Stadium	September 8, 1992	SL v A	4
68	Harare, Harare Sports Club	October 18, 1992	Z v I	19
69	Bulawayo, Bulawayo Athletic Club	November 1, 1992	Z v NZ	1
	Superseded by Queens Sports Club ground.			
70	Karachi, Defence Stadium	December 1, 1993	P v Z	1
71	Rawalpindi, Rawalpindi Cricket Stadium	December 9, 1993	P v Z	7
72	Lucknow, K. D. "Babu" Singh Stadium	January 18, 1994	I v SL	1
73	Bulawayo, Queens Sports Club	October 20, 1994	Z v SL	10
74	Mohali, Punjab Cricket Association Stadium	December 10, 1994	I v WI	3
75	Peshawar, Arbab Niaz Stadium	September 8, 1995	P v SL	5
76	Centurion (*formerly Verwoerdburg*), Centurion Park	November 16, 1995	SA v E	6
77	Sheikhupura, Municipal Stadium	October 17, 1996	P v Z	2
78	St Vincent, Arnos Vale	June 20, 1997	WI v SL	1
79	Galle, International Stadium	June 3, 1998	SL v NZ	6
80	Springbok Park, Bloemfontein	October 29, 1999	SA v Z	2
	Ground also known under sponsor's name.			
81	Multan, Multan Cricket Stadium	August 29, 2001	P v B	1

FAMILIES IN TEST CRICKET

GRANDFATHER, FATHER AND SON

G. A. Headley (West Indies, 22 Tests, 1929-30–1953-54), R. G. A. Headley (West Indies, 2 Tests, 1973) and D. W. Headley (England, 15 Tests, 1997–1999).

FATHERS AND SONS

England
A. R. Butcher (1 Test, 1979) and M. A. Butcher (32 Tests, 1997–2001).
M. C. Cowdrey (114 Tests, 1954-55–1974-75) and C. S. Cowdrey (6 Tests, 1984-85–1988).
J. Hardstaff (5 Tests, 1907-08) and J. Hardstaff jun. (23 Tests, 1935–1948).
L. Hutton (79 Tests, 1937–1954-55) and R. A. Hutton (5 Tests, 1971).
F. T. Mann (5 Tests, 1922-23) and F. G. Mann (7 Tests, 1948-49–1949).
J. H. Parks (1 Test, 1937) and J. M. Parks (46 Tests, 1954–1967-68).
A. Sidebottom (1 Test, 1985) and R. J. Sidebottom (1 Test, 2001).
M. J. Stewart (8 Tests, 1962–1963-64) and A. J. Stewart (115 Tests, 1989-90–2001).
F. W. Tate (1 Test, 1902) and M. W. Tate (39 Tests, 1924–1935).
C. L. Townsend (2 Tests, 1899) and D. C. H. Townsend (3 Tests, 1934-35).

Australia
E. J. Gregory (1 Test, 1876-77) and S. E. Gregory (58 Tests, 1890–1912).

South Africa
F. Hearne (4 Tests, 1891-92–1895-96) and G. A. L. Hearne (3 Tests, 1922-23–1924).
F. Hearne also played 2 Tests for England in 1888-89.
J. D. Lindsay (3 Tests, 1947) and D. T. Lindsay (19 Tests, 1963-64–1969-70).
A. W. Nourse (45 Tests, 1902-03–1924) and A. D. Nourse (34 Tests, 1935–1951).
P. M. Pollock (28 Tests, 1961-62–1969-70) and S. M. Pollock (56 Tests, 1995-96–2000-01).
L. R. Tuckett (1 Test, 1913-14) and L. Tuckett (9 Tests, 1947–1948-49).

West Indies
O. C. Scott (8 Tests, 1928–1930-31) and A. P. H. Scott (1 Test, 1952-53).

New Zealand
W. M. Anderson (1 Test, 1945-46) and R. W. Anderson (9 Tests, 1976-77–1978).
W. P. Bradburn (2 Tests, 1963-64) and G. E. Bradburn (7 Tests, 1990-91–2000-01).
B. L. Cairns (43 Tests, 1973-74–1985-86) and C. L. Cairns (49 Tests, 1989-90–2000-01).
W. A. Hadlee (11 Tests, 1937–1950-51) and D. R. Hadlee (26 Tests, 1969–1977-78); R. J. Hadlee (86 Tests, 1972-73–1990).
P. G. Z. Harris (9 Tests, 1955-56–1964-65) and C. Z. Harris (19 Tests, 1993-94–1999-2000).
H. G. Vivian (7 Tests, 1931–1937) and G. E. Vivian (5 Tests, 1964-65–1971-72).

India
L. Amarnath (24 Tests, 1933-34–1952-53) and M. Amarnath (69 Tests, 1969-70–1987-88); S. Amarnath (10 Tests, 1975-76–1978-79).
D. K. Gaekwad (11 Tests, 1952–1960-61) and A. D. Gaekwad (40 Tests, 1974-75–1984-85).
H. S. Kanitkar (2 Tests, 1974-75) and H. H. Kanitkar (2 Tests, 1999-2000).
Nawab of Pataudi (Iftikhar Ali Khan) (3 Tests, 1946) and Nawab of Pataudi (Mansur Ali Khan) (46 Tests, 1961-62–1974-75).
Nawab of Pataudi sen. also played 3 Tests for England, 1932-33–1934.
V. L. Manjrekar (55 Tests, 1951-52–1964-65) and S. V. Manjrekar (37 Tests, 1987-88–1996-97).
V. Mankad (44 Tests, 1946–1958-59) and A. V. Mankad (22 Tests, 1969-70–1977-78).
Pankaj Roy (43 Tests, 1951-52–1960-61) and Pranab Roy (2 Tests, 1981-82).

India and Pakistan
M. Jahangir Khan (4 Tests, 1932–1936) and Majid Khan (63 Tests, 1964-65–1982-83).
S. Wazir Ali (7 Tests, 1932–1936) and Khalid Wazir (2 Tests, 1954).

Pakistan
Hanif Mohammad (55 Tests, 1952-53–1969-70) and Shoaib Mohammad (45 Tests, 1983-84–1995-96).
Nazar Mohammad (5 Tests, 1952-53) and Mudassar Nazar (76 Tests, 1976-77–1988-89).

GRANDFATHER AND GRANDSONS

Australia
V. Y. Richardson (19 Tests, 1924-25–1935-36) and G. S. Chappell (87 Tests, 1970-71–1983-84); I. M. Chappell (75 Tests, 1964-65–1979-80); T. M. Chappell (3 Tests, 1981).

GREAT-GRANDFATHER AND GREAT-GRANDSON

Australia
W. H. Cooper (2 Tests, 1881-82 and 1884-85) and A. P. Sheahan (31 Tests, 1967-68–1973-74).

BROTHERS IN SAME TEST TEAM

England
E. M., G. F. and W. G. Grace: 1 Test, 1880; C. T. and G. B. Studd: 4 Tests, 1882-83; A. and G. G. Hearne: 1 Test, 1891-92. *F. Hearne, their brother, played in this match for South Africa*; D. W. and P. E. Richardson: 1 Test, 1957; A. J. and B. C. Hollioake: 1 Test, 1997.

Australia
E. J. and D. W. Gregory: 1 Test, 1876-77; C. and A. C. Bannerman: 1 Test, 1878-79; G. and W. F. Giffen: 2 Tests, 1891-92; G. H. S. and A. E. Trott: 3 Tests, 1894-95; I. M. and G. S. Chappell: 43 Tests, 1970-71–1979-80; S. R. and M. E. Waugh: 96 Tests, 1990-91–2001 – the only instance of twins appearing together.

South Africa
S. J. and S. D. Snooke: 1 Test, 1907; D. and H. W. Taylor: 2 Tests, 1913-14; R. H. M. and P. A. M. Hands: 1 Test, 1913-14; E. A. B. and A. M. B. Rowan: 9 Tests, 1948-49–1951; P. M. and R. G. Pollock: 23 Tests, 1963-64–1969-70; A. J. and D. B. Pithey: 5 Tests, 1963-64; P. N. and G. Kirsten (half-brothers): 7 Tests, 1993-94–1994.

West Indies
G. C. and R. S. Grant: 4 Tests, 1934-35; J. B. and V. H. Stollmeyer: 1 Test, 1939; D. St E. and E. St E. Atkinson: 1 Test, 1957-58.

New Zealand
D. R. and R. J. Hadlee: 10 Tests, 1973–1977-78; H. J. and G. P. Howarth: 4 Tests, 1974-75–1976-77; J. M. and N. M. Parker: 3 Tests, 1976-77; B. P. and J. G. Bracewell: 1 Test, 1980-81; J. J. and M. D. Crowe: 34 Tests, 1983–1989-90.

India
S. Wazir Ali and S. Nazir Ali: 2 Tests, 1932–1933-34; L. Ramji and Amar Singh: 1 Test, 1933-34; C. K. and C. S. Nayudu: 4 Tests, 1933-34–1936; A. G. Kripal Singh and A. G. Milkha Singh: 1 Test, 1961-62; S. and M. Amarnath: 8 Tests, 1975-76–1978-79.

Pakistan
Wazir and Hanif Mohammad: 18 Tests, 1952-53–1959-60; Wazir and Mushtaq Mohammad: 1 Test, 1958-59; Hanif and Mushtaq Mohammad: 19 Tests, 1960-61–1969-70; Hanif, Mushtaq and Sadiq Mohammad: 1 Test, 1969-70; Mushtaq and Sadiq Mohammad: 26 Tests, 1969-70–1978–79; Wasim and Ramiz Raja: 2 Tests, 1983-84; Moin and Nadeem Khan: 1 Test, 1998-99; Humayun and Imran Farhat: 1 Test, 2000-01.

Sri Lanka
M. D. and S. Wettimuny: 2 Tests, 1982-83; A. and D. Ranatunga: 2 Tests, 1989-90; A. and S. Ranatunga: 8 Tests, 1994-95–1996-97.

Zimbabwe
A. and G. W. Flower: 50 Tests, 1992-93–2001 (Z); J. A. and G. J. Rennie: 1 Test, 1997-98; P. A. and B. C. Strang: 14 Tests, 1994-95–2000-01.

LIMITED-OVERS INTERNATIONAL RECORDS

Limited-overs international matches do not have first-class status.

SUMMARY OF LIMITED-OVERS INTERNATIONALS

1970-71 to August 19, 2001

	Opponents	*Matches*					*Won by*							*Tied*	*NR*
			E	*A*	*SA*	*WI*	*NZ*	*I*	*P*	*SL*	*Z*	*B*	*Ass*		
England	Australia	**70**	31	37	–	–	–	–	–	–	–	–	–	1	1
	South Africa	**23**	7	–	16	–	–	–	–	–	–	–	–	–	–
	West Indies	**61**	26	–	–	32	–	–	–	–	–	–	–	–	3
	New Zealand	**47**	23	–	–	–	20	–	–	–	–	–	–	1	3
	India	**36**	19	–	–	–	–	16	–	–	–	–	–	–	1
	Pakistan	**49**	28	–	–	–	–	–	20	–	–	–	–	–	1
	Sri Lanka	**23**	13	–	–	–	–	–	–	10	–	–	–	–	–
	Zimbabwe	**16**	9	–	–	–	–	–	–	–	7	–	–	–	–
	Bangladesh	**1**	1	–	–	–	–	–	–	–	–	0	–	–	–
	Associates	**5**	5	–	–	–	–	–	–	–	–	–	0	–	–
Australia	South Africa	**45**	–	21	22	–	–	–	–	–	–	–	–	2	–
	West Indies	**98**	–	43	–	52	–	–	–	–	–	–	–	2	1
	New Zealand	**80**	–	55	–	–	22	–	–	–	–	–	–	–	3
	India	**67**	–	39	–	–	–	25	–	–	–	–	–	–	3
	Pakistan	**60**	–	33	–	–	–	–	24	–	–	–	–	1	2
	Sri Lanka	**43**	–	28	–	–	–	–	–	13	–	–	–	–	2
	Zimbabwe	**19**	–	18	–	–	–	–	–	–	1	–	–	–	–
	Bangladesh	**2**	–	2	–	–	–	–	–	–	–	0	–	–	–
	Associates	**3**	–	3	–	–	–	–	–	–	–	–	0	–	–
South Africa	West Indies	**25**	–	–	17	8	–	–	–	–	–	–	–	–	–
	New Zealand	**27**	–	–	17	–	7	–	–	–	–	–	–	–	3
	India	**38**	–	–	24	–	–	13	–	–	–	–	–	–	1
	Pakistan	**29**	–	–	19	–	–	–	10	–	–	–	–	–	–
	Sri Lanka	**25**	–	–	14	–	–	–	–	10	–	–	–	–	1
	Zimbabwe	**12**	–	–	9	–	–	–	–	–	2	–	–	–	1
	Associates	**5**	–	–	5	–	–	–	–	–	–	–	0	–	–
West Indies	New Zealand	**30**	–	–	–	19	9	–	–	–	–	–	–	–	2
	India	**66**	–	–	–	41	–	23	–	–	–	–	–	1	1
	Pakistan	**95**	–	–	–	59	–	–	34	–	–	–	–	2	–
	Sri Lanka	**32**	–	–	–	21	–	–	–	10	–	–	–	–	1
	Zimbabwe	**17**	–	–	–	13	–	–	–	–	4	–	–	–	–
	Bangladesh	**3**	–	–	–	3	–	–	–	–	–	0	–	–	–
	Associates	**5**	–	–	–	4	–	–	–	–	–	–	1*	–	–
New Zealand	India	**61**	–	–	–	–	27	31	–	–	–	–	–	–	3
	Pakistan	**59**	–	–	–	–	22	–	35	–	–	–	–	1	1
	Sri Lanka	**50**	–	–	–	–	26	–	–	21	–	–	–	1	2
	Zimbabwe	**25**	–	–	–	–	16	–	–	–	7	–	–	1	1
	Bangladesh	**2**	–	–	–	–	2	–	–	–	–	0	–	–	–
	Associates	**4**	–	–	–	–	4	–	–	–	–	–	0	–	–
India	Pakistan	**85**	–	–	–	–	–	29	52	–	–	–	–	–	4
	Sri Lanka	**70**	–	–	–	–	–	36	–	29	–	–	–	–	5
	Zimbabwe	**36**	–	–	–	–	–	28	–	–	6	–	–	2	–
	Bangladesh	**8**	–	–	–	–	–	8	–	–	–	0	–	–	–
	Associates	**9**	–	–	–	–	–	8	–	–	–	–	1†	–	–
Pakistan	Sri Lanka	**87**	–	–	–	–	–	–	54	30	–	–	–	1	2
	Zimbabwe	**22**	–	–	–	–	–	–	19	–	2	–	–	1	–
	Bangladesh	**8**	–	–	–	–	–	–	7	–	–	1	–	–	–
	Associates	**6**	–	–	–	–	–	–	6	–	–	–	0	–	–
Sri Lanka	Zimbabwe	**23**	–	–	–	–	–	–	–	17	5	–	–	–	1
	Bangladesh	**6**	–	–	–	–	–	–	–	6	–	0	–	–	–
	Associates	**3**	–	–	–	–	–	–	–	3	–	–	0	–	–
Zimbabwe	Bangladesh	**7**	–	–	–	–	–	–	–	–	7	0	–	–	–
	Associates	**11**	–	–	–	–	–	–	–	–	10	–	0	–	1
Bangladesh	Associates	**7**	–	–	–	–	–	–	–	–	–	2	5‡	–	–
Associates	Associates	**1**	–	–	–	–	–	–	–	–	–	–	1§	–	–
		1,747	162	279	143	252	155	217	261	149	51	3	8	17	50

* *Kenya beat West Indies in the 1996 World Cup.*
† *Kenya beat India at Gwalior, 1997-98 and 1998-99.*
‡ *Kenya beat Bangladesh five times in 1997-98 and 1998-99.*
§ *United Arab Emirates beat Holland in the 1996 World Cup.*

Note: Current Associate Members of ICC who have played one-day internationals are Canada, East Africa, Holland, Kenya, Scotland and United Arab Emirates. Sri Lanka, Zimbabwe and Bangladesh also played one-day internationals before being given Test status; these are not included among the Associates' results.

RESULTS SUMMARY OF LIMITED-OVERS INTERNATIONALS

1970-71 to 2001 (1,747 matches)

	Matches	*Won*	*Lost*	*Tied*	*No Result*	*% Won (excl. NR)*
South Africa	229	143	78	2	6	64.12
West Indies	432	252	167	5	8	59.43
Australia	487	279	190	6	12	58.73
Pakistan	500	261	223	6	10	53.26
England	331	162	158	2	9	50.31
India	476	217	238	3	18	47.37
Sri Lanka	362	149	197	2	14	42.81
New Zealand	385	155	208	4	18	42.23
Zimbabwe	188	51	129	4	4	27.71
Kenya	37	7	29	–	1	19.44
United Arab Emirates	7	1	6	–	–	14.28
Bangladesh	44	3	41	–	–	6.81
Canada	3	–	3	–	–	–
East Africa	3	–	3	–	–	–
Holland	5	–	5	–	–	–
Scotland	5	–	5	–	–	–

Note: Matches abandoned without a ball bowled are not included. Those called off after play began are counted as official internationals in their own right, even when replayed, according to the ICC's ruling.

5,000 RUNS

	M	*I*	*NO*	*R*	*HS*	*100s*	*Avge*
S. R. Tendulkar (India)	273	266	25	10,461	186*	29	43.40
M. Azharuddin (India)	334	308	54	9,378	153*	7	36.92
D. L. Haynes (West Indies)	238	237	28	8,648	152*	17	41.37
P. A. de Silva (Sri Lanka)	275	266	26	8,430	145	11	35.12
M. E. Waugh (Australia)	237	229	19	8,374	173	18	39.87
Saeed Anwar (Pakistan)	228	225	17	8,282	194	19	39.81
Inzamam-ul-Haq (Pakistan)	248	234	34	8,028	137*	7	40.14
A. Ranatunga (Sri Lanka)	269	255	47	7,456	131*	4	35.84
S. R. Waugh (Australia)	317	281	57	7,382	120*	3	32.95
Javed Miandad (Pakistan)	233	218	41	7,381	119*	8	41.70
B. C. Lara (West Indies)	190	186	17	7,171	169	14	42.43
Salim Malik (Pakistan)	283	256	38	7,170	102	5	32.88
S. T. Jayasuriya (Sri Lanka)	242	234	8	6,906	189	11	30.55
I. V. A. Richards (West Indies)	187	167	24	6,721	189*	11	47.00
S. C. Ganguly (India)	174	169	14	6,717	183	16	43.33

	M	*I*	*NO*	*R*	*HS*	*100s*	*Avge*
Ijaz Ahmed, sen. (Pakistan). . . .	250	232	29	6,564	139*	10	32.33
A. R. Border (Australia).	273	252	39	6,524	127*	3	30.62
R. B. Richardson (West Indies) .	224	217	30	6,249	122	5	33.41
D. M. Jones (Australia)	164	161	25	6,068	145	7	44.61
D. C. Boon (Australia).	181	177	16	5,964	122	5	37.04
Ramiz Raja (Pakistan)	198	197	15	5,841	119*	9	32.09
G. Kirsten (South Africa)	154	154	14	5,700	188*	10	40.71
W. J. Cronje (South Africa). . . .	188	175	31	5,565	112	2	38.64
M. G. Bevan (Australia).	164	145	51	5,384	108*	5	57.27
A. Jadeja (India).	196	179	36	5,359	119	6	37.47
A. Flower (Zimbabwe)	172	169	12	5,267	120*	2	33.54
R. S. Mahanama (Sri Lanka). . .	213	198	23	5,162	119*	4	29.49
C. G. Greenidge (West Indies). .	128	127	13	5,134	133*	11	45.03
C. L. Hooper (West Indies). . . .	197	180	37	5,006	113*	6	35.00

Note: The leading aggregates for other Test-playing countries are:

	M	*I*	*NO*	*R*	*HS*	*100s*	*Avge*
M. D. Crowe (New Zealand) . . .	143	140	18	4,704	107*	4	38.55
G. A. Gooch (England)	125	122	6	4,290	142	8	36.98
Akram Khan (Bangladesh)	38	38	2	857	65	0	23.80

HIGHEST INDIVIDUAL INNINGS

194	Saeed Anwar	Pakistan v India at Chennai	1996-97
189*	I. V. A. Richards	West Indies v England at Manchester	1984
189	S. T. Jayasuriya	Sri Lanka v India at Sharjah.	2000-01
188*	G. Kirsten	South Africa v UAE at Rawalpindi.	1995-96
186*	S. R. Tendulkar	India v New Zealand at Hyderabad	1999-2000
183	S. C. Ganguly	India v Sri Lanka at Taunton	1999
181	I. V. A. Richards	West Indies v Sri Lanka at Karachi	1987-88
175*	Kapil Dev	India v Zimbabwe at Tunbridge Wells.	1983
173	M. E. Waugh	Australia v West Indies at Melbourne	2000-01
171*	G. M. Turner	New Zealand v East Africa at Birmingham	1975
169*	D. J. Callaghan	South Africa v New Zealand at Verwoerdburg	1994-95
169	B. C. Lara	West Indies v Sri Lanka at Sharjah	1995-96
167*	R. A. Smith	England v Australia at Birmingham	1993
161	A. C. Hudson	South Africa v Holland at Rawalpindi.	1995-96
158	D. I. Gower	England v New Zealand at Brisbane.	1982-83
154	A. C. Gilchrist	Australia v Sri Lanka at Melbourne	1998-99
153*	I. V. A. Richards	West Indies v Australia at Melbourne	1979-80
153*	M. Azharuddin	India v Zimbabwe at Cuttack	1997-98
153*	S. C. Ganguly	India v New Zealand at Gwalior	1999-2000
153	B. C. Lara	West Indies v Pakistan at Sharjah	1993-94
153	R. Dravid	India v New Zealand at Hyderabad	1999-2000
152*	D. L. Haynes	West Indies v India at Georgetown.	1988-89
152	C. H. Gayle	West Indies v Kenya at Nairobi.	2001 (K)
151*	S. T. Jayasuriya	Sri Lanka v India at Mumbai	1996-97
150	S. Chanderpaul	West Indies v South Africa at East London	1998-99

Note: The highest individual scores for other Test-playing countries are:

142*	G. W. Flower	Zimbabwe v Bangladesh at Bulawayo	2000-01
142	D. L. Houghton	Zimbabwe v New Zealand at Hyderabad, India. . . .	1987-88
101	Mehrab Hossain	Bangladesh v Zimbabwe at Dhaka	1998-99

TEN HUNDREDS

		Opponents										
Total		*E*	*A*	*SA*	*WI*	*NZ*	*I*	*P*	*SL*	*Z*	*B*	*Ass*
29	S. R. Tendulkar (India)	0	6	2	2	3	–	2	6	5	0	3
19	Saeed Anwar (Pakistan)	0	1	0	2	4	3	–	7	2	0	0
18	M. E. Waugh (Australia)	1	–	2	3	3	3	1	1	3	0	1
17	D. L. Haynes (West Indies)	2	6	0	–	2	2	4	1	0	–	–
16	S. C. Ganguly (India)	0	1	2	0	3	–	2	4	3	1	0
14	B. C. Lara (West Indies)	1	3	2	–	2	0	4	1	0	1	0
11	N. J. Astle (New Zealand)	1	1	1	0	–	4	2	0	2	0	0
11	P. A. de Silva (Sri Lanka)	0	2	0	0	0	3	3	–	2	0	1
11	C. G. Greenidge (West Indies)	0	1	–	–	3	3	2	1	1	–	–
11	S. T. Jayasuriya (Sri Lanka)	0	0	0	0	3	4	2	–	1	1	0
11	I. V. A. Richards (West Indies)	3	3	–	–	1	3	0	1	0	–	–
10	Ijaz Ahmed, sen. (Pakistan)	1	1	2	0	0	2	–	1	2	1	0
10	G. Kirsten (South Africa)	1	2	–	0	2	3	1	0	0	–	1

Note: Ass = Associate Members.

HIGHEST PARTNERSHIP FOR EACH WICKET

252	for 1st	S. C. Ganguly and S. R. Tendulkar	I v SL	Colombo (RPS)	1997-98
331	for 2nd	S. R. Tendulkar and R. Dravid	I v NZ	Hyderabad	1999-2000
237*	for 3rd	R. Dravid and S. R. Tendulkar	I v K	Bristol	1999
275*	for 4th	M. Azharuddin and A. Jadeja	I v Z	Cuttack	1997-98
223	for 5th	M. Azharuddin and A. Jadeja	I v SL	Colombo (RPS)	1997-98
161	for 6th	M. O. Odumbe and A. V. Vadher	K v SL	Southampton	1999
124	for 7th	Yousuf Youhana and Rashid Latif	P v A	Cardiff	2001
119	for 8th	P. R. Reiffel and S. K. Warne	A v SA	Port Elizabeth	1993-94
126*	for 9th	Kapil Dev and S. M. H. Kirmani	I v Z	Tunbridge Wells	1983
106*	for 10th	I. V. A. Richards and M. A. Holding	WI v E	Manchester	1984

Note: Ganguly and Tendulkar raised their first-wicket record to 258 v Kenya at Paarl in 2001-02, after the deadline for this section.

150 WICKETS

	M	*Balls*	*R*	*W*	*BB*	*4W/i*	*Avge*
Wasim Akram (Pakistan)	319	16,369	10,581	440	5-15	21	24.04
Waqar Younis (Pakistan)	215	10,586	8,147	348	7-36	25	23.41
A. Kumble (India)	208	11,167	7,827	274	6-12	9	28.56
S. K. Warne (Australia)	167	9,237	6,541	262	5-33	12	24.96
J. Srinath (India)	192	10,035	7,462	261	5-23	7	28.59
Saqlain Mushtaq (Pakistan)	144	7,537	5,370	257	5-20	16	20.89
Kapil Dev (India)	225	11,202	6,945	253	5-43	4	27.45
M. Muralitharan (Sri Lanka)	174	9,552	6,332	250	7-30	10	25.32
C. A. Walsh (West Indies)	205	10,822	6,918	227	5-1	7	30.47
A. A. Donald (South Africa)	136	7,125	4,835	226	6-23	12	21.39
C. E. L. Ambrose (West Indies)	176	9,353	5,429	225	5-17	10	24.12
G. D. McGrath (Australia)	140	7,512	5,002	212	5-14	10	23.59
W. P. U. J. C. Vaas (Sri Lanka)	166	8,067	5,715	207	5-14	4	27.60
C. J. McDermott (Australia)	138	7,461	5,018	203	5-44	5	24.71
S. T. Jayasuriya (Sri Lanka)	242	8,974	7,176	203	6-29	8	35.34
S. R. Waugh (Australia)	317	8,823	6,702	195	4-33	3	34.36
B. K. V. Prasad (India)	159	8,037	6,236	193	5-27	4	32.31
S. M. Pollock (South Africa)	132	6,936	4,380	190	6-35	9	23.05
Aqib Javed (Pakistan)	163	8,012	5,721	182	7-37	6	31.43
Imran Khan (Pakistan)	175	7,461	4,845	182	6-14	4	26.62
C. Z. Harris (New Zealand)	188	8,533	6,098	173	5-42	3	35.24
C. L. Hooper (West Indies)	197	8,239	5,999	171	4-34	3	35.08

	M	*Balls*	*R*	*W*	*BB*	*4W/i*	*Avge*
Mushtaq Ahmed (Pakistan)	143	7,483	5,296	161	5-36	4	32.89
R. J. Hadlee (New Zealand)	115	6,182	3,407	158	5-25	6	21.56
M. Prabhakar (India)	130	6,360	4,535	157	5-33	6	28.88
M. D. Marshall (West Indies)	136	7,175	4,233	157	4-18	6	26.96
H. H. Streak (Zimbabwe)	128	6,449	4,825	156	5-32	4	30.92

Note: The most wickets for other Test-playing countries are:

	M	*Balls*	*R*	*W*	*BB*	*4W/i*	*Avge*
D. Gough (England)	95	5,244	3,661	147	5-44	8	24.90
Hasibul Hussain (Bangladesh)	27	1,219	1,160	28	4-56	1	41.42

BEST BOWLING ANALYSES

7-30	M. Muralitharan	Sri Lanka v India at Sharjah	2000-01
7-36	Waqar Younis	Pakistan v England at Leeds	2001
7-37	Aqib Javed	Pakistan v India at Sharjah	1991-92
7-51	W. W. Davis	West Indies v Australia at Leeds	1983
6-12	A. Kumble	India v West Indies at Calcutta	1993-94
6-14	G. J. Gilmour	Australia v England at Leeds	1975
6-14	Imran Khan	Pakistan v India at Sharjah	1984-85
6-15	C. E. H. Croft	West Indies v England at St Vincent	1980-81
6-18	Azhar Mahmood	Pakistan v West Indies at Sharjah	1999-2000
6-19	H. K. Olonga	Zimbabwe v England at Cape Town	1999-2000
6-20	B. C. Strang	Zimbabwe v Bangladesh at Nairobi (Aga Khan)	1997-98
6-23	A. A. Donald	South Africa v Kenya at Nairobi (Gymkhana)	1996-97
6-26	Waqar Younis	Pakistan v Sri Lanka at Sharjah	1989-90
6-29	B. P. Patterson	West Indies v India at Nagpur	1987-88
6-29	S. T. Jayasuriya	Sri Lanka v England at Moratuwa	1992-93
6-30	Waqar Younis	Pakistan v New Zealand at Auckland	1993-94
6-35	S. M. Pollock	South Africa v West Indies at East London	1998-99
6-39	K. H. MacLeay	Australia v India at Nottingham	1983
6-41	I. V. A. Richards	West Indies v India at Delhi	1989-90
6-44	Waqar Younis	Pakistan v New Zealand at Sharjah	1996-97
6-49	L. Klusener	South Africa v Sri Lanka at Lahore	1997-98
6-50	A. H. Gray	West Indies v Australia at Port-of-Spain	1990-91
6-59	Waqar Younis	Pakistan v Australia at Nottingham	2001

Notes: W. P. U. J. C. Vaas took 8-19, including a hat-trick, for Sri Lanka against Zimbabwe in 2001-02, after the deadline for this section.

The best analyses for other Test-playing countries are:

5-15	M. A. Ealham	England v Zimbabwe at Kimberley	1999-2000
5-22	M. N. Hart	New Zealand v West Indies at Margao	1994-95
4-36	Saiful Islam	Bangladesh v Sri Lanka at Sharjah	1994-95

HAT-TRICKS

Jalal-ud-Din	Pakistan v Australia at Hyderabad	1982-83
B. A. Reid	Australia v New Zealand at Sydney	1985-86
Chetan Sharma	India v New Zealand at Nagpur	1987-88
Wasim Akram	Pakistan v West Indies at Sharjah	1989-90
Wasim Akram	Pakistan v Australia at Sharjah	1989-90
Kapil Dev	India v Sri Lanka at Calcutta	1990-91
Aqib Javed	Pakistan v India at Sharjah	1991-92
D. K. Morrison	New Zealand v India at Napier	1993-94
Waqar Younis	Pakistan v New Zealand at East London	1994-95
Saqlain Mushtaq†	Pakistan v Zimbabwe at Peshawar	1996-97
E. A. Brandes	Zimbabwe v England at Harare	1996-97
A. M. Stuart	Australia v Pakistan at Melbourne	1996-97
Saqlain Mushtaq	Pakistan v Zimbabwe at The Oval	1999

† *Four wickets in five balls.*

SIX DISMISSALS IN AN INNINGS

6 (all ct)	A. C. Gilchrist	Australia v South Africa at Cape Town	1999-2000
6 (all ct)	A. J. Stewart	England v Zimbabwe at Manchester	2000

100 DISMISSALS

		M	*Ct*	*St*
257	Moin Khan (Pakistan)	190	191	66
234	I. A. Healy (Australia)	168	195	39
204	P. J. L. Dujon (West Indies)	169	183	21
189	R. S. Kaluwitharana (Sri Lanka)	167	119	70
182	A. C. Gilchrist (Australia)	119	153	29
165	D. J. Richardson (South Africa)	122	148	17
154	A. Flower (Zimbabwe)	172	124	30
154	N. R. Mongia (India)	140	110	44
147	A. J. Stewart (England)	146	136	11
137	M. V. Boucher (South Africa)	91	132	5
129	Rashid Latif (Pakistan)	107	100	29
128	R. D. Jacobs (West Indies)	84	108	20
125	A. C. Parore (New Zealand)	169	100	25
124	R. W. Marsh (Australia)	92	120	4
103	Salim Yousuf (Pakistan)	86	81	22

Notes: The most for Bangladesh is 32 (25 ct, 7 st) in 34 matches by Khaled Masud.

A. J. Stewart's record includes 11 catches taken in 32 limited-overs internationals when not keeping wicket; A. C. Parore's includes 5 in 29; A. Flower's 4 in 7; and R. S. Kaluwitharana's 1 in 3.

FOUR CATCHES IN AN INNINGS

(Excluding wicket-keepers)

5	J. N. Rhodes	South Africa v West Indies at Bombay	1993-94
4	Salim Malik	Pakistan v New Zealand at Sialkot	1984-85
4	S. M. Gavaskar	India v Pakistan at Sharjah	1984-85
4	R. B. Richardson	West Indies v England at Birmingham	1991
4	K. C. Wessels	South Africa v West Indies at Kingston	1991-92
4	M. A. Taylor	Australia v West Indies at Sydney	1992-93
4	C. L. Hooper	West Indies v Pakistan at Durban	1992-93
4	K. R. Rutherford	New Zealand v India at Napier	1994-95
4	P. V. Simmons	West Indies v Sri Lanka at Sharjah	1995-96
4	M. Azharuddin	India v Pakistan at Toronto	1997-98
4	S. R. Tendulkar	India v Pakistan at Dhaka	1997-98
4	R. Dravid	India v West Indies at Toronto	1999-2000
4	G. J. Whittall	Zimbabwe v England at The Oval	2000
4	C. Z. Harris	New Zealand v India at Colombo (RPS)	2001 (SL)

Note: While fielding as substitute, J. G. Bracewell held 4 catches for New Zealand v Australia at Adelaide, 1980-81.

75 CATCHES

Ct	M	
156	334	M. Azharuddin (India)
127	273	A. R. Border (Australia)
109	213	R. S. Mahanama (Sri Lanka)
108	317	S. R. Waugh (Australia)
105	237	M. E. Waugh (Australia)
101	187	I. V. A. Richards (West Indies)
93	197	C. L. Hooper (West Indies)
91	200	J. N. Rhodes (South Africa)
90	250	Ijaz Ahmed, sen. (Pakistan)
88	273	S. R. Tendulkar (India)
86	275	P. A. de Silva (Sri Lanka)
85	242	S. T. Jayasuriya (Sri Lanka)
84	319	Wasim Akram (Pakistan)
82	190	B. C. Lara (West Indies)
81	283	Salim Malik (Pakistan)
78	174	M. Muralitharan (Sri Lanka)
75	248	Inzamam-ul-Haq (Pakistan)
75	224	R. B. Richardson (West Indies)

Most catches for other Test-playing countries:

Ct	M	
70	156	S. P. Fleming (New Zealand)
65	164	A. D. R. Campbell (Zimbabwe)
64	120	G. A. Hick (England)
13	38	Aminul Islam (Bangladesh)

2,000 RUNS AND 100 WICKETS

	M	R	W
I. T. Botham (England)	116	2,113	145
C. L. Cairns (New Zealand)	137	3,216	131
W. J. Cronje (South Africa)	188	5,565	114
C. Z. Harris (New Zealand)	188	3,349	173
C. L. Hooper (West Indies)	197	5,006	171
Imran Khan (Pakistan)	175	3,709	182
S. T. Jayasuriya (Sri Lanka)	242	6,906	203
J. H. Kallis (South Africa)	126	4,379	117
Kapil Dev (India)	225	3,783	253
L. Klusener (South Africa)	113	2,562	137
Mudassar Nazar (Pakistan)	122	2,653	111
I. V. A. Richards (West Indies)	187	6,721	118
R. J. Shastri (India)	150	3,108	129
S. R. Tendulkar (India)	273	10,461	101
Wasim Akram (Pakistan)	319	3,328	440
S. R. Waugh (Australia)	317	7,382	195

1,000 RUNS AND 100 DISMISSALS

	M	R	W
P. J. L. Dujon (West Indies)	169	1,945	204
A. Flower (Zimbabwe)	172	5,267	154
A. C. Gilchrist (Australia)	119	3,848	182
I. A. Healy (Australia)	168	1,764	234
R. D. Jacobs (West Indies)	84	1,334	128
R. S. Kaluwitharana (Sri Lanka)	167	3,339	189
R. W. Marsh (Australia)	92	1,225	124
Moin Khan (Pakistan)	190	2,853	257
N. R. Mongia (India)	140	1,272	154
A. C. Parore (New Zealand)	169	3,205	125
A. J. Stewart (England)	146	4,100	147

HIGHEST INNINGS TOTALS

398-5	(50 overs)	Sri Lanka v Kenya at Kandy	1995-96
376-2	(50 overs)	India v New Zealand at Hyderabad	1999-2000
373-6	(50 overs)	India v Sri Lanka at Taunton	1999
371-9	(50 overs)	Pakistan v Sri Lanka at Nairobi (Gymkhana)	1996-97
363-7	(55 overs)	England v Pakistan at Nottingham	1992
360-4	(50 overs)	West Indies v Sri Lanka at Karachi	1987-88
349-6	(50 overs)	Australia v New Zealand at Auckland	1999-2000
349-9	(50 overs)	Sri Lanka v Pakistan at Singapore	1995-96
349-9	(50 overs)	New Zealand v India at Rajkot	1999-2000
348-8	(50 overs)	New Zealand v India at Nagpur	1995-96
347-3	(50 overs)	Kenya v Bangladesh at Nairobi (Gymkhana)	1997-98
339-4	(50 overs)	Sri Lanka v Pakistan at Mohali	1996-97
338-4	(50 overs)	New Zealand v Bangladesh at Sharjah	1989-90
338-4	(50 overs)	Australia v India at Vishakhapatnam	2000-01
338-5	(60 overs)	Pakistan v Sri Lanka at Swansea	1983
337-7	(50 overs)	Australia v Pakistan at Sydney	1999-2000

Note: The highest totals by other Test-playing countries are:

328-3	(50 overs)	South Africa v Holland at Rawalpindi	1995-96
325-6	(50 overs)	Zimbabwe v Kenya at Dhaka	1998-99
272-8	(50 overs)	Bangladesh v Zimbabwe at Bulawayo	2000-01

HIGHEST TOTALS BATTING SECOND

329	(49.3 overs)	Sri Lanka v West Indies at Sharjah (*Lost by 4 runs*)	1995-96
316-7	(47.5 overs)	India v Pakistan at Dhaka (*Won by 3 wickets*)	1997-98
316-4	(48.5 overs)	Australia v Pakistan at Lahore (*Won by 6 wickets*)	1998-99
315	(49.4 overs)	Pakistan v Sri Lanka at Singapore (*Lost by 34 runs*)	1995-96
313-7	(49.2 overs)	Sri Lanka v Zimbabwe at New Plymouth (*Won by 3 wickets*)	1991-92
310	(48.5 overs)	India v South Africa at Nagpur (*Lost by 10 runs*)	1999-2000

HIGHEST MATCH AGGREGATES

664-19	(99.4 overs)	Pakistan v Sri Lanka at Singapore	1995-96
662-17	(99.3 overs)	Sri Lanka v West Indies at Sharjah	1995-96
660-19	(99.5 overs)	Pakistan v Sri Lanka at Nairobi (Gymkhana)	1996-97
655-19	(97 overs)	India v New Zealand at Rajkot	1999-2000
652-12	(100 overs)	Sri Lanka v Kenya at Kandy	1995-96
650-15	(100 overs)	New Zealand v Australia at Auckland	1999-2000

LOWEST INNINGS TOTALS

43	(19.5 overs)	Pakistan v West Indies at Cape Town	1992-93
45	(40.3 overs)	Canada v England at Manchester	1979
54	(26.3 overs)	India v Sri Lanka at Sharjah	2000-01
55	(28.3 overs)	Sri Lanka v West Indies at Sharjah	1986-87
63	(25.5 overs)	India v Australia at Sydney	1980-81

64	(35.5 overs)	New Zealand v Pakistan at Sharjah	1985-86
68	(31.3 overs)	Scotland v West Indies at Leicester	1999
69	(28 overs)	South Africa v Australia at Sydney	1993-94
70	(25.2 overs)	Australia v England at Birmingham	1977
70	(26.3 overs)	Australia v New Zealand at Adelaide	1985-86

Notes: Zimbabwe were dismissed for 38 (15.4 overs) by Sri Lanka at Colombo (SSC) in 2001-02, after the deadline for this section.

This section does not take into account those matches in which the number of overs was reduced.

The lowest totals by other Test-playing countries are:

86	(32.4 overs)	England v Australia at Manchester	2001
87	(29.3 overs)	West Indies v Australia at Sydney	1992-93
87	(34.2 overs)	Bangladesh v Pakistan at Dhaka	1999-2000
94	(31.4 overs)	Zimbabwe v Pakistan at Sharjah	1996-97

LARGEST VICTORIES

245 runs	Sri Lanka (299-5 in 50 overs) v India (54 in 26.3 overs) at Sharjah	2000-01
233 runs	Pakistan (320-3 in 50 overs) v Bangladesh (87 in 34.2 overs) at Dhaka	1999-2000
232 runs	Australia (323-2 in 50 overs) v Sri Lanka (91 in 35.5 overs) at Adelaide	1984-85
206 runs	New Zealand (276-7 in 50 overs) v Australia (70 in 26.3 overs) at Adelaide	1985-86
202 runs	England (334-4 in 60 overs) v India (132-3 in 60 overs) at Lord's	1975
202 runs	South Africa (305-8 in 50 overs) v Kenya (103 in 25.1 overs) at Nairobi	1996-97

By ten wickets: there have been 15 instances of victory by ten wickets.

TIED MATCHES

West Indies 222-5 (50 overs) v Australia 222-9 (50 overs) at Melbourne	1983-84
England 226-5 (55 overs) v Australia 226-8 (55 overs) at Nottingham	1989
West Indies 186-5 (39 overs) v Pakistan 186-9 (39 overs) at Lahore	1991-92
India 126 (47.4 overs) v West Indies 126 (41 overs) at Perth	1991-92
Australia 228-7 (50 overs) v Pakistan 228-9 (50 overs) at Hobart	1992-93
Pakistan 244-6 (50 overs) v West Indies 244-5 (50 overs) at Georgetown	1992-93
India 248-5 (50 overs) v Zimbabwe 248 (50 overs) at Indore	1993-94
Pakistan 161-9 (50 overs) v New Zealand 161 (49.4 overs) at Auckland	1993-94
Zimbabwe 219-9 (50 overs) v Pakistan 219 (49.5 overs) at Harare	1994-95
New Zealand 169-8 (50 overs) v Sri Lanka 169 (48 overs) at Sharjah	1996-97
Zimbabwe 236-8 (50 overs) v India 236 (49.5 overs) at Paarl	1996-97
New Zealand 237 (49.4 overs) v England 237-8 (50 overs) at Napier	1996-97
Zimbabwe 233-8 (50 overs) v New Zealand 233-9 (50 overs) at Bulawayo	1997-98
West Indies 173-5 (30 overs) v Australia 173-7 (30 overs) at Georgetown	1998-99
Australia 213 (49.2 overs) v South Africa 213 (49.4 overs) at Birmingham	1999
Pakistan 196 (49.4 overs) v Sri Lanka 196 (49.1 overs) at Sharjah	1999-2000
South Africa 226 (50 overs) v Australia 226-9 (50 overs) at Melbourne (CS)	2000 (A)

200 APPEARANCES

	Total	*E*	*A*	*SA*	*WI*	*NZ*	*I*	*P*	*SL*	*Z*	*B*	*Ass*
M. Azharuddin (I)	334	24	43	33	43	40	–	64	53	22	7	5
Wasim Akram (P)	319	31	43	19	63	34	47	–	51	21	6	4
S. R. Waugh (A)	317	30	–	43	50	56	53	43	24	14	2	2
Salim Malik (P)	283	26	26	16	46	43	52	–	53	13	3	5
P. A. de Silva (SL)	275	13	30	18	27	36	55	72	–	15	6	3
A. R. Border (A)	273	43	–	15	61	52	38	34	23	5	1	1

	Total	E	A	SA	WI	NZ	I	P	SL	Z	B	Ass
S. R. Tendulkar (I) . .	273	14	33	36	29	31	–	43	45	30	6	6
A. Ranatunga (SL) . .	269	18	33	16	22	35	56	67	–	15	4	3
Ijaz Ahmed, sen. (P) .	250	19	34	20	38	27	53	–	39	13	4	3
Inzamam-ul-Haq (P) .	248	18	22	22	35	31	44	–	49	17	6	4
S. T. Jayasuriya (SL).	242	13	25	24	20	30	46	56	–	21	4	3
D. L. Haynes (WI) . .	238	35	64	8	–	13	36	65	14	3	–	–
M. E. Waugh (A) . . .	237	21	–	39	47	35	27	29	23	13	1	2
Javed Miandad (P) . .	233	27	35	3	64	24	35	–	35	6	1	3
Saeed Anwar (P) . . .	228	10	25	23	17	32	49	–	48	13	6	5
Kapil Dev (I).	225	23	41	13	42	29	–	32	34	9	2	–
R. B. Richardson (WI)	224	35	51	9	–	11	32	61	21	3	–	1
Waqar Younis (P) . . .	215	13	23	25	40	32	25	–	42	11	1	3
R. S. Mahanama (SL)	213	11	26	15	22	22	45	52	–	14	4	2
A. Kumble (I)	208	15	21	32	21	26	–	30	36	18	4	5
C. A. Walsh (WI) . . .	205	31	36	5	–	38	16	52	22	2	1	2
J. N. Rhodes (SA) . .	200	21	44	–	23	23	26	23	25	11	–	4

Note: The most appearances for other Test-playing countries are:

	Total	E	A	SA	WI	NZ	I	P	SL	Z	B	Ass
C. Z. Harris (NZ). . .	188	17	27	24	14	–	27	29	28	19	1	2
A. Flower (Z)	172	16	15	12	13	23	30	22	23	–	7	11
A. J. Stewart (E) . . .	146	–	23	15	25	19	14	21	15	10	1	3
Akram Khan (B) . . .	38	1	2	–	1	2	6	7	5	7	–	7
Aminul Islam (B) . . .	38	1	2	–	3	2	8	7	5	4	–	6

CAPTAINS

England (331 matches; 22 captains)

G. A. Gooch 50; M. A. Atherton 43; A. J. Stewart 40; M. W. Gatting 37; R. G. D. Willis 29; J. M. Brearley 25; D. I. Gower 24; N. Hussain 18; A. J. Hollioake 14; M. H. Denness 12; I. T. Botham 9; K. W. R. Fletcher 5; J. E. Emburey 4; A. J. Lamb 4; D. B. Close 3; R. Illingworth 3; G. P. Thorpe 3; G. Boycott 2; N. Gifford 2; A. W. Greig 2; J. H. Edrich 1; A. P. E. Knott 1.

Australia (487 matches; 15 captains)

A. R. Border 178; S. R. Waugh 98; M. A. Taylor 67; G. S. Chappell 49; K. J. Hughes 49; I. M. Chappell 11; S. K. Warne 11; I. A. Healy 8; G. R. Marsh 4; G. N. Yallop 4; A. C. Gilchrist 3; R. B. Simpson 2; R. J. Bright 1; D. W. Hookes 1; W. M. Lawry 1.

South Africa (229 matches; 4 captains)

W. J. Cronje 138; K. C. Wessels 52; S. M. Pollock 36; C. E. B. Rice 3.

West Indies (432 matches; 15 captains)

I. V. A. Richards 108; R. B. Richardson 87; C. H. Lloyd 81; B. C. Lara 44; C. A. Walsh 43; J. C. Adams 26; C. L. Hooper 19; C. G. Greenidge 8; D. L. Haynes 7; M. A. Holding 2; R. B. Kanhai 2; D. L. Murray 2; S. L. Campbell 1; P. J. L. Dujon 1; A. I. Kallicharran 1.

New Zealand (385 matches; 15 captains)

S. P. Fleming 96; G. P. Howarth 60; M. D. Crowe 44; K. R. Rutherford 37; L. K. Germon 36; J. G. Wright 31; J. V. Coney 25; J. J. Crowe 16; M. G. Burgess 8; G. M. Turner 8; D. J. Nash 7; B. E. Congdon 6; C. D. McMillan 6; G. R. Larsen 3; A. H. Jones 2.

India (476 matches; 16 captains)

M. Azharuddin 174; Kapil Dev 74; S. R. Tendulkar 73; S. C. Ganguly 45; S. M. Gavaskar 37; D. B. Vengsarkar 18; A. Jadeja 13; K. Srikkanth 13; R. J. Shastri 11; S. Venkataraghavan 7; B. S. Bedi 4; R. Dravid 2; A. L. Wadekar 2; M. Amarnath 1; S. M. H. Kirmani 1; G. R. Viswanath 1.

Pakistan (500 matches; 18 captains)

Imran Khan 139; Wasim Akram 110; Javed Miandad 62; Moin Khan 34; Salim Malik 34; Aamir Sohail 22; Ramiz Raja 22; Waqar Younis 15; Rashid Latif 13; Zaheer Abbas 13; Saeed Anwar 10; Asif Iqbal 6; Abdul Qadir 5; Wasim Bari 5; Mushtaq Mohammad 4; Intikhab Alam 3; Majid Khan 2; Sarfraz Nawaz 1.

Sri Lanka (362 matches; 11 captains)

A. Ranatunga 193; L. R. D. Mendis 61; S. T. Jayasuriya 60; P. A. de Silva 18; R. S. Madugalle 13; B. Warnapura 8; A. P. B. Tennekoon 4; R. S. Mahanama 2; M. S. Atapattu 1; D. S. de Silva 1; J. R. Ratnayeke 1.

Zimbabwe (188 matches; 8 captains)

A. D. R. Campbell 76; A. Flower 52; H. H. Streak 29; D. L. Houghton 17; D. A. G. Fletcher 6; A. J. Traicos 6; G. W. Flower 1; G. J. Whittall 1.

Bangladesh (44 matches; 5 captains)

Aminul Islam 16; Akram Khan 15; Gazi Ashraf 7; Naimur Rahman 4; Minhazul Abedin 2.

Associate Members (60 matches; 8 captains)

A. Y. Karim (Kenya) 21; M. O. Odumbe (Kenya) 16; Sultan M. Zarawani (UAE) 7; G. Salmond (Scotland) 5; S. W. Lubbers (Holland) 4; B. M. Mauricette (Canada) 3; Harilal R. Shah (East Africa) 3; R. P. Lefebvre (Holland) 1.

WORLD CUP FINALS

1975	WEST INDIES (291-8) beat Australia (274) by 17 runs	Lord's
1979	WEST INDIES (286-9) beat England (194) by 92 runs	Lord's
1983	INDIA (183) beat West Indies (140) by 43 runs	Lord's
1987-88	AUSTRALIA (253-5) beat England (246-8) by seven runs	Calcutta
1991-92	PAKISTAN (249-6) beat England (227) by 22 runs	Melbourne
1995-96	SRI LANKA (245-3) beat Australia (241-7) by seven wickets	Lahore
1999	AUSTRALIA (133-2) beat Pakistan (132) by eight wickets	Lord's

MISCELLANEOUS

LARGE ATTENDANCES

Test Series

943,000	Australia v England (5 Tests)	1936-37
In England		
549,650	England v Australia (5 Tests)	1953

Test Matches

†‡465,000	India v Pakistan, Calcutta	1998-99
350,534	Australia v England, Melbourne (Third Test)	1936-37

Note: Attendance at India v England at Calcutta in 1981-82 may have exceeded 350,000.

In England		
158,000+	England v Australia, Leeds	1948
137,915	England v Australia, Lord's	1953

Test Match Day

‡100,000	India v Pakistan, Calcutta (first four days)	1998-99
90,800	Australia v West Indies, Melbourne (Fifth Test, second day)	1960-61

Other First-Class Matches in England

93,000	England v Australia, Lord's (Fourth Victory Match, 3 days)	1945
80,000+	Surrey v Yorkshire, The Oval (3 days)	1906
78,792	Yorkshire v Lancashire, Leeds (3 days)	1904
76,617	Lancashire v Yorkshire, Manchester (3 days)	1926

Limited-Overs Internationals

‡100,000	India v South Africa, Calcutta	1993-94
‡100,000	India v West Indies, Calcutta	1993-94
‡100,000	India v West Indies, Calcutta	1994-95
‡100,000	India v Sri Lanka, Calcutta (World Cup semi-final)	1995-96
‡90,000	India v Pakistan, Calcutta	1986-87
‡90,000	India v South Africa, Calcutta	1991-92
87,182	England v Pakistan, Melbourne (World Cup final)	1991-92
86,133	Australia v West Indies, Melbourne	1983-84

† *Estimated.*
‡ *No official attendance figures were issued for these games, but capacity is believed to have reached 100,000 following rebuilding in 1993.*

LORD'S CRICKET GROUND

Lord's and the Marylebone Cricket Club were founded in 1787. The Club has enjoyed an uninterrupted career since that date, but there have been three grounds known as Lord's. The first (1787–1810) was situated where Dorset Square now is; the second (1809–13), at North Bank, had to be abandoned owing to the cutting of the Regent's Canal; and the third, opened in 1814, is the present one at St John's Wood. It was not until 1866 that the freehold of Lord's was secured by MCC. The present pavilion was erected in 1890 at a cost of £21,000.

HIGHEST INDIVIDUAL SCORES MADE AT LORD'S

333	G. A. Gooch	England v India	1990
316*	J. B. Hobbs	Surrey v Middlesex	1926
315*	P. Holmes	Yorkshire v Middlesex	1925
315	M. A. Wagh	Warwickshire v Middlesex	2001

Notes: The longest innings in a first-class match at Lord's was played by S. Wettimuny (636 minutes, 190 runs) for Sri Lanka v England, 1984. Wagh batted for 630 minutes.

HIGHEST TOTALS AT LORD'S

First-Class Matches

729-6 dec.	Australia v England	1930
665	West Indians v Middlesex	1939
653-4 dec.	England v India	1990
652-8 dec.	West Indies v England	1973

Minor Match

735-9 dec.	MCC and Ground v Wiltshire	1888

BIGGEST HIT AT LORD'S

The only known instance of a batsman hitting a ball over the present pavilion at Lord's occurred when A. E. Trott, appearing for MCC against Australians on July 31, August 1, 2, 1899, drove M. A. Noble so far and high that the ball struck a chimney pot and fell behind the building.

MINOR CRICKET

HIGHEST INDIVIDUAL SCORES

628*	A. E. J. Collins, Clark's House v North Town at Clifton College. *A junior house match. His innings of 6 hours 50 minutes was spread over four afternoons*	1899
566	C. J. Eady, Break-o'-Day v Wellington at Hobart	1901-02
515	D. R. Havewalla, B. B. and C. I. Railways v St Xavier's at Bombay	1933-34
506*	J. C. Sharp, Melbourne GS v Geelong College at Melbourne	1914-15
502*	Chaman Lal, Mehandra Coll., Patiala v Government Coll., Rupar at Patiala	1956-57
485	A. E. Stoddart, Hampstead v Stoics at Hampstead	1886
475*	Mohammad Iqbal, Muslim Model HS v Islamia HS, Sialkot at Lahore	1958-59
466*	G. T. S. Stevens, Beta v Lambda (University College School house match) at Neasden	1919
459	J. A. Prout, Wesley College v Geelong College at Geelong	1908-09

Note: The highest score in a Minor County match is 323* by F. E. Lacey for Hampshire v Norfolk at Southampton in 1887; the highest in the Minor Counties Championship is 282 by E. Garnett for Berkshire v Wiltshire at Reading in 1908.

HIGHEST PARTNERSHIP

664* for 3rd	V. G. Kambli and S. R. Tendulkar, Sharadashram Vidyamandir School v St Xavier's High School at Bombay	1987-88

RECORD HIT

The Rev. W. Fellows, while at practice on the Christ Church ground at Oxford in 1856, drove a ball bowled by Charles Rogers 175 yards from hit to pitch.

THROWING THE CRICKET BALL

140 yards 2 feet, Robert Percival, on the Durham Sands racecourse, Co. Durham	c1882
140 yards 9 inches, Ross Mackenzie, at Toronto	1872
140 yards, "King Billy" the Aborigine, at Clermont, Queensland	1872

Note: Extensive research by David Rayvern Allen has shown that these traditional records are probably authentic, if not necessarily wholly accurate. Modern competitions have failed to produce similar distances although Ian Pont, the Essex all-rounder who also played baseball, was reported to have thrown 138 yards in Cape Town in 1981. There have been speculative reports attributing throws of 150 yards or more to figures as diverse as the South African Test player Colin Bland, the Latvian javelin thrower Janis Lusis, who won a gold medal for the Soviet Union in the 1968 Olympics, and the British sprinter Charley Ransome. The definitive record is still awaited.

COUNTY CHAMPIONSHIP

MOST APPEARANCES

762	W. Rhodes	Yorkshire	1898-1930
707	F. E. Woolley	Kent	1906-38
668	C. P. Mead	Hampshire	1906-36
617	N. Gifford	Worcestershire (484), Warwickshire (133)	1960-88
611	W. G. Quaife	Warwickshire	1895-1928
601	G. H. Hirst	Yorkshire	1891-1921

MOST CONSECUTIVE APPEARANCES

423	K. G. Suttle	Sussex	1954-69
412	J. G. Binks	Yorkshire	1955-69

Notes: J. Vine made 417 consecutive appearances for Sussex in all first-class matches (399 of them in the Championship) between July 1900 and September 1914.

J. G. Binks did not miss a Championship match for Yorkshire between making his debut in June 1955 and retiring at the end of the 1969 season.

UMPIRES

MOST COUNTY CHAMPIONSHIP APPEARANCES

569	T. W. Spencer	1950-1980	481	P. B. Wight	1966-1995
533	F. Chester	1922-1955	462	J. Moss	1899-1929
516	H. G. Baldwin	1932-1962	457	A. Skelding	1931-1958

MOST SEASONS ON FIRST-CLASS LIST

33	**D. J. Constant**	**1969-2001**	28	F. Chester	1922-1955
32	**A. G. T. Whitehead**	**1970-2001**	27	J. Moss	1899-1929
31	T. W. Spencer	1950-1980	26	W. A. J. West	1896-1925
30	**R. Julian**	**1972-2001**	25	H. G. Baldwin	1932-1962
30	**K. E. Palmer**	**1972-2001**	25	A. Jepson	1960-1984
30	P. B. Wight	1966-1995	25	J. G. Langridge	1956-1980
29	H. D. Bird	1970-1998	25	B. J. Meyer	1973-1997

Bold type denotes umpires who stood in the 2001 season.

WOMEN'S TEST RECORDS

Amended by MARION COLLIN to the end of the 2001 season in England

HIGHEST INDIVIDUAL SCORES

209*	K. L. Rolton	Australia v England at Leeds	2001
204	K. E. Flavell	New Zealand v England at Scarborough	1996
204	M. A. J. Goszko	Australia v England at Shenley Park	2001
200	J. Broadbent	Australia v England at Guildford	1998
193	D. A. Annetts	Australia v England at Collingham	1987
190	S. Agarwal	India v England at Worcester	1986
189	E. A. Snowball	England v New Zealand at Christchurch	1934-35
179	R. Heyhoe-Flint	England v Australia at The Oval	1976
176*	K. L. Rolton	Australia v England at Worcester	1998

1,000 RUNS IN A CAREER

R	T		R	T	
1,935	27	J. A. Brittin (England)	1,110	13	S. Agarwal (India)
1,594	22	R. Heyhoe-Flint (England)	1,078	12	E. Bakewell (England)
1,301	19	D. A. Hockley (New Zealand)	1,007	14	M. E. Maclagan (England)
1,164	18	C. A. Hodges (England)			

BEST BOWLING ANALYSES

8-53	N. David	India v England at Jamshedpur	1995-96
7-6	M. B. Duggan	England v Australia at Melbourne	1957-58
7-7	E. R. Wilson	Australia v England at Melbourne	1957-58
7-10	M. E. Maclagan	England v Australia at Brisbane	1934-35
7-18	A. Palmer	Australia v England at Brisbane	1934-35

11 WICKETS IN A MATCH

11-16	E. R. Wilson	Australia v England at Melbourne	1957-58
11-63	J. Greenwood	England v West Indies at Canterbury	1979

50 WICKETS IN A CAREER

W	T		W	T	
77	17	M. B. Duggan (England)	57	16	R. H. Thompson (Australia)
68	11	E. R. Wilson (Australia)	55	15	J. Lord (New Zealand)
63	20	D. F. Edulji (India)	50	12	E. Bakewell (England)
60	14	M. E. Maclagan (England)			

SIX DISMISSALS IN AN INNINGS

8 (6ct, 2st)	L. Nye	England v New Zealand at New Plymouth	1991-92
6 (2ct, 4st)	B. Brentnall	New Zealand v South Africa at Johannesburg	1971-72

EIGHT DISMISSALS IN A MATCH

9 (8ct, 1st)	C. Matthews	Australia v India at Adelaide	1990-91
8 (6ct, 2st)	L. Nye	England v New Zealand at New Plymouth	1991-92

25 DISMISSALS IN A CAREER

		T	Ct	St
58	C. Matthews (Australia)	20	46	12
36	S. A. Hodges (England)	11	19	17
28	B. Brentnall (New Zealand)	10	16	12

HIGHEST INNINGS TOTALS

569-6 dec.	Australia v England at Guildford	1998
525	Australia v India at Ahmedabad	1983-84
517-8	New Zealand v England at Scarborough	1996
503-5 dec.	England v New Zealand at Christchurch	1934-35

LOWEST INNINGS TOTALS

35	England v Australia at Melbourne	1957-58
38	Australia v England at Melbourne	1957-58
44	New Zealand v England at Christchurch	1934-35
47	Australia v England at Brisbane	1934-35

PART FOUR: ENGLISH CRICKET IN 2001

FEATURES OF 2001

Double-Hundreds (19)

329*†‡	M. E. K. Hussey	Northamptonshire v Essex at Northampton.
315	M. A. Wagh	Warwickshire v Middlesex at Lord's.
280	J. P. Crawley	Lancashire v Northamptonshire at Manchester.
252	D. S. Lehmann	Yorkshire v Lancashire at Leeds.
236	M. J. Powell	Warwickshire v Oxford UCCE at Oxford.
232‡	M. E. K. Hussey	Northamptonshire v Leicestershire at Northampton.
230	M. A. Butcher	Surrey v Glamorgan at Cardiff.
221	M. Burns	Somerset v Yorkshire at Bath.
218*	K. P. Pietersen	Nottinghamshire v Derbyshire at Derby.
217	J. P. Maher	Glamorgan v Essex at Cardiff.
208*	D. P. Fulton	Kent v Somerset at Canterbury.
208‡	M. E. K. Hussey	Northamptonshire v Somerset at Taunton.
204	A. Dale	Glamorgan v Northamptonshire at Northampton.
203*	M. W. Goodwin	Sussex v Nottinghamshire at Nottingham.
203	O. A. Shah	Middlesex v Derbyshire at Southgate.
203	I. J. Sutcliffe	Leicestershire v Glamorgan at Cardiff.
201‡	G. A. Hick	Worcestershire v Warwickshire at Birmingham.
201	Saeed Anwar	Pakistanis v Kent at Canterbury.
200*‡	G. A. Hick	Worcestershire v Durham at Chester-le-Street.

† *County record.* ‡ *Hussey scored three double-hundreds, and Hick two.*

Three Hundreds in Successive Innings

D. P. Fulton (Kent)	208* and 104* v Somerset at Canterbury; 197 v Northamptonshire at Northampton.
B. F. Smith (Leicestershire)	179 v Surrey at Leicester; 117 v Glamorgan at Cardiff; 111 v Kent at Leicester.

Hundred in Each Innings of a Match

C. W. G. Bassano†	186*	106	Derbyshire v Gloucestershire at Derby.
I. D. Blackwell	103	122	Somerset v Northamptonshire at Northampton.
D. P. Fulton	208*	104*	Kent v Somerset at Canterbury.
M. W. Goodwin	115	203*	Sussex v Nottinghamshire at Nottingham.
A. P. Grayson	173	149	Essex v Northamptonshire at Northampton.
S. G. Law	116*	123*	Essex v Lancashire at Manchester.
J. E. Morris	170	136*	Nottinghamshire v Derbyshire at Derby.
D. D. J. Robinson	102	118*	Essex v Leicestershire at Chelmsford.

† *On Championship debut.*

Carrying Bat through Completed Innings

S. A. A. Block	56*	Cambridge UCCE (129) v Kent at Cambridge.
M. A. Butcher	145*	Surrey (281) v Glamorgan at The Oval.
M. K. Floyd	128*	Oxford University (325) v Cambridge University at Cambridge.
S. P. James	61*	Glamorgan (146) v Leicestershire at Leicester.
M. H. Richardson	64*	MCC (124) v Australians at Arundel.
A. J. Strauss	112*	Middlesex (253) v Hampshire at Southampton.
L. D. Sutton	140*	Derbyshire (263) v Sussex at Derby.

Sutton was last man out in the second innings for 54 out of 117.

Fastest Hundred

I. J. Harvey . . . . 61 balls Gloucestershire v Derbyshire at Bristol.

Hundred before Lunch

A. P. Grayson. . . . . . 114* Essex v Cambridge UCCE at Cambridge (1st day).

First to 1,000 Runs

D. P. Fulton (Kent) on July 4.

First to 2,000 Runs

M. E. K. Hussey (Northamptonshire) on September 13.

Long Innings

Mins		
630	M. A. Wagh (315).	Warwickshire v Middlesex at Lord's.
615	M. E. K. Hussey (329*).	Northamptonshire v Essex at Northampton.

An Hour without Scoring a Run

A. L. Penberthy (20) 60 mins on 20 Northamptonshire v Essex at Chelmsford.

First-Wicket Partnership of 100 in Each Innings

163 147. . . . . J. Cox/M. J. Wood, Somerset v Northamptonshire at Taunton.

Highest Partnerships

First Wicket

372* M. W. Goodwin/R. R. Montgomerie, Sussex v Nottinghamshire at Nottingham.
343 M. J. Powell/I. R. Bell, Warwickshire v Oxford UCCE at Oxford.
309 C. White/M. J. Wood, Yorkshire v Lancashire at Manchester.
307 Saeed Anwar/Salim Elahi, Pakistanis v Kent at Canterbury.

Second Wicket

258† J. J. B. Lewis/M. L. Love, Durham v Nottinghamshire at Chester-le-Street.

Third Wicket

306 M. G. N. Windows/C. G. Taylor, Gloucestershire v Nottinghamshire at Bristol.
300 B. F. Smith/A. Habib, Leicestershire v Somerset at Taunton.
287 M. E. K. Hussey/R. J. Warren, Northamptonshire v Somerset at Taunton.
284 J. P. Maher/M. J. Powell, Glamorgan v Essex at Cardiff.
267 M. P. Vaughan/G. P. Thorpe, England v Pakistan (Second Test) at Manchester.

Fourth Wicket

316 U. Afzaal/J. E. Morris, Nottinghamshire v Derbyshire at Derby.
292 O. A. Shah/B. L. Hutton, Middlesex v Derbyshire at Southgate.

Fifth Wicket
248 A. Dale/K. Newell, Glamorgan v Northamptonshire at Northampton.

Sixth Wicket
372*† K. P. Pietersen/J. E. Morris, Nottinghamshire v Derbyshire at Derby.
251* D. R. Martyn/A. C. Gilchrist, Australians v Essex at Chelmsford.
250 R. J. Warren/A. L. Penberthy, Northamptonshire v Glamorgan at Northampton.

Seventh Wicket
222 R. J. Turner/K. P. Dutch, Somerset v Essex at Taunton.
206 A. J. Stewart/A. J. Tudor, Surrey v Essex at The Oval.
199 K. P. Pietersen/P. J. Franks, Nottinghamshire v Middlesex at Lord's.
190 S. M. Katich/S. K. Warne, Australians v MCC at Arundel.
182 I. D. Blackwell/K. P. Dutch, Somerset v Northamptonshire at Northampton.
163 A. Dale/S. D. Thomas, Glamorgan v Essex at Chelmsford.

Eighth Wicket
161 A. L. Penberthy/D. Ripley, Northamptonshire v Somerset at Northampton.
152 V. J. Wells/P. A. J. DeFreitas, Leicestershire v Yorkshire at Leicester.

Tenth Wicket
135 C. M. W. Read/R. D. Stemp, Nottinghamshire v Hampshire at Southampton.
129 G. Chapple/G. Keedy, Lancashire v Somerset at Manchester.
109* M. P. Bicknell/I. D. K. Salisbury, Surrey v Leicestershire at Leicester.
107 I. D. Blackwell/J. O. Grove, Somerset v Surrey at Taunton.
103 A. J. Stewart/A. R. Caddick, England v Australia (First Test) at Birmingham.

† *County record.*

Eight Wickets in an Innings (5)

8-49	Mushtaq Ahmed.	Pakistanis v British Universities at Nottingham.
8-63	D. E. Malcolm.	Leicestershire v Surrey at Leicester.
8-90	A. D. Mullally	Hampshire v Warwickshire at Southampton.
8-102	D. M. Cousins	Northamptonshire v Yorkshire at Leeds.
8-119	M. M. Patel	Kent v Somerset at Canterbury.

Twelve Wickets in a Match (3)

13-79	J. D. Lewry.	Sussex v Hampshire at Hove.
12-72	S. P. Kirby	Yorkshire v Leicestershire at Leeds.
12-144	M. M. Patel	Kent v Somerset at Canterbury.

Hat-Tricks (2)

J. D. Lewry.	Sussex v Hampshire at Hove.
Waqar Younis.	Pakistanis v Leicestershire at Leicester.

Wicket with First Ball in First-Class Cricket

J. E. K. Schofield. . . . Hampshire v Australians at Southampton.

100 Wickets

No bowler took 100 wickets. The highest aggregate was 75 by R. J. Kirtley (Sussex).

Six Wicket-Keeping Dismissals in an Innings

7 ct.	N. D. Burns	Leicestershire v Somerset at Leicester.
7 ct†	R. J. Turner	Somerset v Northamptonshire at Taunton.
6 ct.	N. D. Burns	Leicestershire v Yorkshire at Leicester.
6 ct.	N. D. Burns	Leicestershire v Glamorgan at Leicester.
6 ct.	C. M. W. Read	Nottinghamshire v Middlesex at Nottingham.
6 ct.	R. J. Turner	Somerset v Surrey at Taunton.

† *County record.*

Nine Wicket-Keeping Dismissals in a Match

9 ct.	N. D. Burns	Leicestershire v Somerset at Leicester.
8 ct, 1 st	N. D. Burns	Leicestershire v Yorkshire at Leicester.
9 ct.	R. J. Turner	Somerset v Surrey at Taunton.

Five Catches in an Innings in the Field

M. J. Di Venuto . . . . Derbyshire v Durham at Chester-le-Street.

Seven Catches in a Match in the Field

D. P. Fulton . . . . Kent v Somerset at Canterbury.

No Byes Conceded in a Total of 500 or More

T. M. B. Bailey	Northamptonshire v Surrey (607) at Northampton.
D. Ripley	Northamptonshire v Kent (576-8 dec.) at Canterbury.
R. J. Turner	Somerset v Northamptonshire (567) at Northampton.

Highest Innings Totals

701-9 dec.	Surrey v Glamorgan at Cardiff.
650	Somerset v Northamptonshire at Taunton.
641-4 dec.	Australia v England (Fifth Test) at The Oval.
633-6 dec.	Northamptonshire v Essex at Northampton.
631-6 dec.	Worcestershire v Durham UCCE at Worcester.
631-9 dec.	Warwickshire v Middlesex at Lord's.
612-8 dec.	Leicestershire v Kent at Canterbury.
608-8 dec.	Gloucestershire v Nottinghamshire at Bristol.
607	Surrey v Northamptonshire at Northampton.
600-6 dec.	Lancashire v Northamptonshire at Manchester.
600-8 dec.	Somerset v Glamorgan at Taunton.

Lowest Innings Totals

67	Durham UCCE v Durham at Chester-le-Street.
68	Essex v Kent at Tunbridge Wells.
74	British Universities v Pakistanis at Nottingham.

Highest Fourth-Innings Totals

478-9	Surrey v Leicestershire at Leicester (set 536).
461-3	Nottinghamshire v Worcestershire at Worcester (set 458).
403-7	Kent v Leicestershire at Leicester (set 401).

Match Aggregate of 1,500 Runs

1,795 for 34 . . . . . . Somerset (650 and 250-6) v Northamptonshire (463-9 dec. and 432-9 dec.) at Taunton.
1,655 for 25 . . . . . . Derbyshire (572) v Nottinghamshire (526 and 557-5) at Derby.
1,583 for 34 . . . . . . Leicestershire (425 and 365-7 dec.) v Kent (390 and 403-7) at Leicester.

Most Extras in an Innings

	b	*l-b*	*w*	*n-b*	
68	23	31	10	4	Surrey (478-9) v Leicestershire at Leicester.
66	8	24	20	14	Sussex (404) v Nottinghamshire at Hove. *Sussex gained another 56 extras in their second innings.*
61	16	13	6	26	Gloucestershire (520) v Sussex at Cheltenham.

There were 13 further instances of 50 extras in an innings, including the one mentioned above.

Career Aggregate Milestones

20,000 runs . . . . N. H. Fairbrother, M. R. Ramprakash.
15,000 runs . . . . D. J. Bicknell.
10,000 runs . . . . M. A. Butcher, A. Dale, N. V. Knight, D. R. Martyn, R. T. Ponting.
1,000 wickets. . . . . . P. C. R. Tufnell, Wasim Akram.
500 wickets . . . . V. C. Drakes, P. J. Martin.
500 dismissals . . . . . A. N. Aymes, K. M. Krikken, K. J. Piper, R. J. Turner.

PROFESSIONAL CRICKETERS' ASSOCIATION AWARDS

At the Professional Cricketers' Association annual dinner in September 2001, David Fulton of Kent was named Fleming Player of the Year for 2001. Nicky Peng of Durham was the Costcutter PCA Young Player of the Year. Mike Atherton, who had just retired, received a special ECB award. Glamorgan were named the MCC Spirit of Cricket County Team. Mark Butcher won the Slazenger Sheer Instinct Award, for his match-winning century during the fourth Ashes Test at Leeds. The npower Contribution to Cricket Award went to England captain Nasser Hussain. Marcus Trescothick of Somerset and England was voted Sports.com Cricketer of the Year via the internet. The Fleming Woman Cricketer of the Year Award was won by Claire Taylor. Neil Mallender received the Accenture PCA Umpire of the Year Award. The Jardine Lloyd Thompson Special Merit Award went to Vic Cook, the long-serving chairman of the Middlesex County Cricket Development Association, who was responsible for the creation of the Wilf Slack Memorial Ground in Finchley.

FIRST-CLASS AVERAGES, 2001

BATTING

(Qualification: 8 completed innings)

* *Signifies not out.* † *Denotes a left-handed batsman.*

		M	I	NO	R	HS	100s	50s	Avge	Ct/St
1	D. R. Martyn (*Australians*)	9	14	5	942	176*	5	3	104.66	3
2	†D. S. Lehmann (*Yorks*)	13	19	2	1,416	252	5	5	83.29	6
3	†A. C. Gilchrist (*Australians*)	8	10	2	663	152	3	2	82.87	28/4
4	†M. E. K. Hussey (*Northants*)	16	30	4	2,055	329*	5	9	79.03	19
5	D. P. Fulton (*Kent*)	18	27	2	1,892	208*	9	3	75.68	27
6	M. E. Waugh (*Australians*)	9	15	6	644	120	2	2	71.55	12
7	S. G. Law (*Essex*)	13	23	3	1,311	153	4	8	65.55	18
8	S. R. Waugh (*Australians*)	7	11	2	583	157*	3	0	64.77	5
9	I. R. Bell (*Warwicks*)	11	16	3	836	135	3	4	64.30	11
10	†N. H. Fairbrother (*Lancs*)	12	19	4	939	179*	4	1	62.60	16
11	M. W. Goodwin (*Sussex*)	17	32	5	1,654	203*	7	5	61.25	8
12	R. T. Ponting (*Australians*)	9	15	1	844	147*	3	5	60.28	11
13	R. R. Montgomerie (*Sussex*)	18	33	4	1,704	160*	8	5	58.75	17
14	M. A. Wagh (*Warwicks*)	16	24	2	1,277	315	3	6	58.04	4
15	K. P. Pietersen (*Notts*)	15	26	4	1,275	218*	4	6	57.95	14
16	J. Cox (*Somerset*)	15	25	3	1,264	186	1	9	57.45	6
17	†M. A. Butcher (*Surrey*)	15	25	2	1,300	230	3	6	56.52	15
18	G. A. Hick (*Worcs*)	17	28	3	1,409	201	6	3	56.36	19
19	M. B. Loye (*Northants*)	12	21	3	1,003	197	3	4	55.72	4
20	R. J. Warren (*Northants*)	16	27	3	1,303	194	4	7	54.29	8
21	†J. P. Maher (*Glam*)	14	23	2	1,133	217	4	3	53.95	13
22	P. D. Collingwood (*Durham*)	13	24	3	1,108	153	3	6	52.76	10
23	M. P. Vaughan (*Yorks*)	9	16	0	839	133	3	4	52.43	8
24	†S. P. Fleming (*Middx*)	14	23	2	1,091	151	4	6	51.95	22
25	C. J. Adams (*Sussex*)	15	23	2	1,086	192	3	7	51.71	28
26	A. Dale (*Glam*)	15	23	3	1,026	204	3	4	51.30	9
27	M. L. Love (*Durham*)	15	29	2	1,364	149*	1	13	50.51	21
28	M. R. Ramprakash (*Surrey*)	13	22	0	1,094	146	4	4	49.72	7
29	†I. D. Blackwell (*Somerset*)	11	17	0	839	122	4	3	49.35	5
30	†D. L. Hemp (*Warwicks*)	17	25	5	987	186*	4	2	49.35	12
31	A. P. Grayson (*Essex*)	16	29	3	1,275	189	6	1	49.03	7
32	W. K. Hegg (*Lancs*)	13	20	4	782	133	2	5	48.87	35/3
33	J. N. Snape (*Glos*)	14	21	3	868	131	3	5	48.22	10
34	M. J. Wood (*Yorks*)	14	23	1	1,060	124	4	6	48.18	10
35	G. S. Blewett (*Notts*)	16	30	3	1,292	137*	5	5	47.85	24
36	R. S. C. Martin-Jenkins (*Sussex*)	9	15	4	524	113	1	3	47.63	4
37	S. P. James (*Glam*)	9	15	3	568	156	1	4	47.33	5
38	D. P. Ostler (*Warwicks*)	10	12	1	520	121	2	2	47.27	22
39	A. Symonds (*Kent*)	8	12	0	563	131	2	2	46.91	13
40	M. P. Bicknell (*Surrey*)	15	22	6	748	110*	1	4	46.75	5
41	C. G. Taylor (*Glos*)	12	20	0	930	196	3	4	46.50	6
42	D. J. Marsh (*Leics*)	9	16	3	600	138*	1	5	46.15	13
43	T. R. Ward (*Leics*)	12	21	2	872	160*	4	2	45.89	7
44	R. W. T. Key (*Kent*)	18	28	0	1,281	132	4	7	45.75	7
45	J. E. Morris (*Notts*)	8	16	2	640	170	2	4	45.71	3
46	†M. J. Di Venuto (*Derbys*)	14	25	1	1,082	165	4	5	45.08	15
47	†D. Byas (*Yorks*)	16	24	5	853	110*	4	2	44.89	38
48	A. J. Strauss (*Middx*)	17	28	1	1,211	176	3	6	44.85	7
49	†M. J. Walker (*Kent*)	17	25	3	985	124	4	3	44.77	9
50	K. J. Barnett (*Glos*)	14	25	2	1,029	114	1	7	44.73	10
51	†N. C. Johnson (*Hants*)	17	27	3	1,073	105*	2	8	44.70	28
52	†N. V. Knight (*Warwicks*)	13	19	2	759	140	2	3	44.64	18

		M	I	NO	R	HS	100s	50s	Avge	Ct/St
53	M. J. Wood (*Somerset*)	7	12	0	529	122	1	4	44.08	2
54	B. F. Smith (*Leics*)	17	30	2	1,222	180*	5	2	43.64	19
55	C. W. G. Bassano (*Derbys*)	8	14	2	523	186*	2	2	43.58	5
56	R. M. S. Weston (*Middx*)	10	17	1	671	135*	3	1	41.93	5
57	†W. P. C. Weston (*Worcs*)	18	31	4	1,132	192	2	7	41.92	11
58	O. A. Shah (*Middx*)	15	25	0	1,040	203	3	4	41.60	14
59	P. D. Bowler (*Somerset*)	14	22	2	827	164	2	4	41.35	14
60	†M. E. Trescothick (*Somerset*)	10	17	0	700	147	2	3	41.17	9
61	†N. D. Burns (*Leics*)	17	28	7	862	111	1	6	41.04	65/3
62	A. Habib (*Leics*)	13	21	2	779	153	3	3	41.00	8
63	†A. L. Penberthy (*Northants*)	15	24	1	942	132*	3	5	40.95	11
64	A. N. Aymes (*Hants*)	16	19	5	572	112*	1	4	40.85	43/2
65	I. J. Harvey (*Glos*)	10	15	2	531	130*	2	1	40.84	8
66	J. P. Crawley (*Lancs*)	14	24	2	898	280	2	5	40.81	4
67	A. J. Hollioake (*Surrey*)	13	20	1	758	97	0	7	39.89	15
68	†M. L. Hayden (*Australians*)	10	17	1	636	142	1	3	39.75	6
69	†B. L. Hutton (*Middx*)	14	22	2	786	139	3	2	39.30	20
70	D. R. Brown (*Warwicks*)	16	20	3	666	104	1	6	39.17	16
71	E. T. Smith (*Kent*)	18	28	1	1,054	116	3	4	39.03	5
72	A. J. Stewart (*Surrey*)	12	18	3	581	106	1	2	38.73	36/1
73	†P. A. Nixon (*Kent*)	18	24	7	651	87*	0	4	38.29	44/4
74	†U. Afzaal (*Notts*)	15	28	1	1,011	138	1	8	37.44	9
75	†R. C. Russell (*Glos*)	10	12	2	373	91*	0	2	37.30	42/2
76	A. Singh (*Worcs*)	18	31	2	1,054	168	2	4	36.34	5
77	†D. J. Bicknell (*Notts*)	16	29	0	1,050	167	3	3	36.20	8
78	Shahid Afridi (*MCC & Leics*)	6	9	0	325	164	1	1	36.11	8
79	M. Burns (*Somerset*)	17	28	1	961	221	1	7	35.59	13
80	K. J. Piper (*Warwicks*)	15	17	5	426	92*	0	2	35.50	39/1
81	D. R. Hewson (*Glos*)	14	25	2	816	168	2	4	35.47	6
82	M. N. Lathwell (*Somerset*)	13	21	1	702	99	0	8	35.10	9
83	M. G. N. Windows (*Glos*)	16	27	3	840	174	3	3	35.00	6
84	M. H. Yardy (*Sussex*)	17	29	6	796	87*	0	5	34.60	9
85	D. A. Kenway (*Hants*)	16	30	3	932	166	2	4	34.51	16
86	S. J. Rhodes (*Worcs*)	15	20	7	442	52	0	1	34.00	51/1
86	N. Hussain (*Essex*)	6	10	1	306	64	0	3	34.00	0
88	†S. D. Stubbings (*Derbys*)	17	31	0	1,047	127	3	6	33.77	6
89	†I. J. Sutcliffe (*Leics*)	17	31	1	1,004	203	2	5	33.46	5
90	R. J. Turner (*Somerset*)	17	26	3	761	115*	1	3	33.08	59
91	D. D. J. Robinson (*Essex*)	18	31	2	955	118*	3	4	32.93	11
92	K. Newell (*Glam*)	7	11	2	296	103	1	1	32.88	5
93	D. C. Nash (*Middx*)	15	19	5	458	103*	1	4	32.71	39/4
94	†P. N. Weekes (*Middx*)	17	27	5	719	107	1	5	32.68	15
95	†C. P. Schofield (*Lancs*)	9	14	2	390	80*	0	4	32.50	8
96	M. A. Atherton (*Lancs*)	11	21	1	649	160	1	3	32.45	17
97	A. McGrath (*Yorks*)	9	15	2	417	116*	1	2	32.07	6
98	C. White (*Yorks*)	12	21	2	605	186	2	0	31.84	6
99	A. J. Tudor (*Surrey*)	9	14	1	413	116	1	1	31.76	2
100	†J. L. Langer (*Australians*)	6	11	2	285	104*	2	0	31.66	5
101	G. R. Napier (*Essex*)	10	16	0	506	104	1	2	31.62	4
102	R. L. Johnson (*Somerset*)	13	15	3	379	68	0	2	31.58	3
103	A. D. Brown (*Surrey*)	13	20	0	630	122	3	2	31.50	3
104	M. J. Powell (*Warwicks*)	17	24	0	755	236	2	2	31.45	14
105	J. J. B. Lewis (*Durham*)	17	32	0	1,000	129	3	3	31.25	6
106	M. W. Alleyne (*Glos*)	16	26	3	718	136	2	2	31.21	12/1
107	A. Flintoff (*Lancs*)	14	23	1	686	120	1	2	31.18	17
108	†M. A. Carberry (*Surrey*)	6	10	0	311	84	0	1	31.10	6
109	P. Johnson (*Notts*)	13	24	2	684	149	2	2	31.09	7
110	G. Chapple (*Lancs*)	13	19	3	497	155	1	2	31.06	3
111	M. P. Maynard (*Glam*)	13	20	0	621	145	1	3	31.05	6
112	B. C. Hollioake (*Surrey*)	12	19	0	586	118	1	4	30.84	18
113	C. M. W. Read (*Notts*)	16	27	5	666	78	0	5	30.27	43/1
114	V. J. Wells (*Leics*)	13	22	1	628	138	2	2	29.90	8

		M	I	NO	R	HS	100s	50s	Avge	Ct/St
115	M. J. Chilton (*Lancs*)	14	24	1	684	104	1	4	29.73	10
116	S. K. Warne (*Australians*)	8	10	2	237	69	0	2	29.62	13
117	M. J. Powell (*Glam*)	15	25	2	681	108	2	4	29.60	12
118	J. C. Scuderi (*Lancs*)	12	17	2	444	89	0	3	29.60	2
119	†S. D. Thomas (*Glam*)	15	21	2	562	138	1	4	29.57	5
120	S. J. Cook (*Middx*)	10	11	3	236	93*	0	1	29.50	3
121	K. P. Dutch (*Somerset*)	16	22	4	530	118	1	3	29.44	19
122	M. C. J. Ball (*Glos*)	12	16	3	379	68	0	3	29.15	21
123	R. C. Irani (*Essex*)	17	29	2	779	119	1	6	28.85	4
124	L. D. Sutton (*Derbys*)	15	27	3	688	140*	2	1	28.66	9
125	J. A. Daley (*Durham*)	9	16	1	428	128*	1	1	28.53	1
126	G. M. Fellows (*Yorks*)	12	17	1	455	63	0	3	28.43	4
127	M. J. Slater (*Australians*)	8	13	1	341	77	0	2	28.41	1
128	†P. C. L. Holloway (*Somerset*)	12	21	1	567	85	0	4	28.35	3
129	†P. R. Pollard (*Worcs*)	10	12	1	309	131*	1	0	28.09	5
130	M. A. Roseberry (*Middx*)	11	17	2	420	87	0	2	28.00	9
131	V. S. Solanki (*Worcs*)	18	29	0	802	112	3	2	27.65	17
132	R. D. B. Croft (*Glam*)	10	15	2	353	93	0	3	27.15	6
133	R. J. Blakey (*Yorks*)	15	21	6	405	78*	0	3	27.00	49/5
134	J. S. Foster (*Durham UCCE & Essex*)	16	25	0	664	103	1	4	26.56	31/8
135	†I. J. Ward (*Surrey*)	16	27	1	690	79	0	4	26.53	6
136	G. W. White (*Hants*)	17	32	4	739	141	2	1	26.39	17/2
137	N. Peng (*Durham*)	13	23	2	551	101	1	3	26.23	8
138	A. J. Bichel (*Worcs*)	16	24	0	627	78	0	3	26.12	5
139	†J. W. Cook (*Northants*)	9	16	1	391	88	0	4	26.06	5
140	I. D. K. Salisbury (*Surrey*)	15	21	4	440	54	0	1	25.88	9
141	S. R. Lampitt (*Worcs*)	10	13	5	205	42*	0	0	25.62	4
142	M. J. Brown (*Durham UCCE & Middx*)	5	10	2	203	60*	0	2	25.37	2
143	M. P. Speight (*Durham*)	8	15	3	304	67*	0	1	25.33	3
144	D. Ripley (*Northants*)	15	25	6	481	95	0	2	25.31	45/3
145	R. A. Smith (*Hants*)	16	26	2	598	118	3	1	24.91	4
146	†A. C. Morris (*Hants*)	16	19	2	423	65	0	3	24.88	10
147	A. D. Mascarenhas (*Hants*)	15	23	5	447	104	1	1	24.83	8
148	M. J. G. Davis (*Sussex*)	15	22	4	439	52	0	1	24.38	5
149	S. A. Richardson (*Yorks*)	7	11	2	215	69	0	2	23.88	6
150	D. G. Cork (*Derbys*)	7	11	0	262	128	1	0	23.81	6
151	B. Zuiderent (*Sussex*)	17	27	1	619	122	1	3	23.80	18
152	A. S. Rollins (*Northants*)	6	10	1	214	65	0	1	23.77	3
153	D. A. Leatherdale (*Worcs*)	17	27	3	570	93	0	2	23.75	7
154	W. S. Kendall (*Hants*)	17	30	3	638	94	0	3	23.62	11
155	D. R. Law (*Durham*)	16	26	1	586	103	1	1	23.44	10
156	S. D. Udal (*Hants*)	16	20	2	414	81	0	3	23.00	5
156	M. A. Ealham (*Kent*)	12	15	2	299	153*	1	0	23.00	8
158	†M. P. Dowman (*Derbys*)	14	26	1	567	145*	1	1	22.68	4
159	J. W. M. Dalrymple (*Oxford UCCE & Middx*)	5	10	1	203	70	0	1	22.55	8
160	†M. A. Wallace (*Glam*)	10	16	3	290	80*	0	2	22.30	27/1
161	S. D. Peters (*Essex*)	15	26	3	508	56*	0	1	22.08	6
162	D. Gough (*Yorks*)	9	15	5	219	96	0	1	21.90	0
163	M. V. Fleming (*Kent*)	17	23	5	393	59	0	1	21.83	6
164	A. J. Swann (*Northants*)	13	22	0	479	113	1	2	21.77	9
165	K. M. Krikken (*Derbys*)	14	25	5	435	93*	0	3	21.75	33/1
165	Yousuf Youhana (*Pakistanis*)	6	8	0	174	80	0	1	21.75	0
167	G. P. Swann (*Northants*)	15	25	0	543	61	0	3	21.72	9
168	N. R. C. Dumelow (*Derbys*)	9	15	1	304	61	0	2	21.71	2
169	D. I. Stevens (*Leics*)	8	14	2	259	63	0	1	21.58	2
170	R. J. Bailey (*Derbys*)	14	25	1	515	136*	1	2	21.45	8
171	N. M. K. Smith (*Warwicks*)	14	14	2	254	54	0	1	21.16	2
172	T. H. C. Hancock (*Glos*)	6	11	0	230	55	0	1	20.90	7
173	V. C. Drakes (*Warwicks*)	14	13	3	209	50	0	1	20.90	1

		M	*I*	*NO*	*R*	*HS*	*100s*	*50s*	*Avge*	*Ct/St*
174	J. P. Pyemont (*Camb. UCCE*)	5	9	1	167	70	0	1	20.87	4
	C. E. W. Silverwood (*Yorks*)	8	9	1	167	70	0	1	20.87	2
176	†R. S. Clinton (*Essex*)	8	15	1	283	58*	0	1	20.21	2
177	†A. Pratt (*Durham*)	16	28	4	476	68*	0	3	19.83	49/7
178	P. A. J. DeFreitas (*Leics*)	9	14	1	256	97	0	2	19.69	0
179	M. J. Prior (*Sussex*)	16	24	2	433	66	0	1	19.68	39/2
180	M. A. Gough (*Durham*)	13	23	0	450	79	0	1	19.56	8
181	†J. P. Taylor (*Northants*)	12	17	3	273	53	0	1	19.50	3
182	†I. J. Thomas (*Glam*)	6	11	1	194	59	0	1	19.40	2
183	J. Ormond (*Leics*)	12	18	5	251	42	0	0	19.30	2
184	†J. M. Dakin (*Leics*)	7	11	0	211	69	0	1	19.18	1
185	G. Welch (*Derbys*)	16	29	2	511	64	0	1	18.92	3
186	S. L. Watkin (*Glam*)	15	17	7	188	38	0	0	18.80	5
187	P. J. Martin (*Lancs*)	9	12	3	169	51*	0	1	18.77	2
188	D. L. Maddy (*Leics*)	17	29	1	521	111	1	2	18.60	15
189	†U. B. A. Rashid (*Sussex*)	14	21	1	367	106	1	0	18.35	1
190	L. R. Prittipaul (*Hants*)	7	9	0	165	84	0	1	18.33	6
191	P. J. Prichard (*Essex*)	7	11	0	201	111	1	0	18.27	1
192	D. S. Lucas (*Notts*)	5	8	0	145	41	0	0	18.12	0
193	I. D. Hunter (*Durham*)	8	14	3	199	37	0	0	18.09	4
194	G. J. Smith (*Notts*)	15	20	9	195	44*	0	0	17.72	3
195	N. Shahid (*Surrey*)	7	12	0	208	65	0	1	17.33	8
196	A. P. Cowan (*Essex*)	15	24	3	360	68	0	2	17.14	8
197	†M. C. Ilott (*Essex*)	10	12	1	186	34	0	0	16.90	6
198	J. J. Haynes (*Lancs*)	5	8	0	133	57	0	1	16.62	7
199	P. S. Jones (*Somerset*)	16	16	5	180	29*	0	0	16.36	3
200	N. G. Hatch (*Durham*)	9	16	8	129	24	0	0	16.12	1
201	J. N. Batty (*Surrey*)	10	16	1	239	59	0	1	15.93	26/2
202	D. A. Cosker (*Glam*)	11	15	4	175	35	0	0	15.90	10
203	M. M. Patel (*Kent*)	17	19	3	247	38	0	0	15.43	9
204	G. E. Welton (*Notts*)	12	22	0	337	61	0	2	15.31	5
205	†J. D. Lewry (*Sussex*)	17	18	4	202	47	0	0	14.42	7
206	J. Wood (*Lancs*)	8	10	1	127	35	0	0	14.11	0
207	R. S. G. Anderson (*Essex*)	8	11	0	154	45	0	0	14.00	2
208	J. B. Hockley (*Kent*)	7	13	1	166	29	0	0	13.83	6
209	Saqlain Mushtaq (*Pakistanis & Surrey*)	13	18	6	164	38	0	0	13.66	2
	†R. C. J. Williams (*Glos*)	5	9	0	123	33	0	0	13.66	15/1
211	M. J. Rawnsley (*Worcs*)	15	21	5	210	39	0	0	13.12	7
212	C. G. Liptrot (*Worcs*)	12	14	4	128	22	0	0	12.80	4
213	†G. M. Hamilton (*Yorks*)	8	9	0	114	34	0	0	12.66	1
214	R. J. Logan (*Notts*)	10	15	2	162	37*	0	0	12.46	4
215	A. R. C. Fraser (*Middx*)	13	12	0	149	41	0	0	12.41	4
216	M. J. Saggers (*Kent*)	17	20	5	185	61*	0	1	12.33	1
217	†M. R. Strong (*Northants*)	9	13	4	110	34	0	0	12.22	2
218	T. A. Munton (*Derbys*)	9	13	1	145	50	0	1	12.08	2
219	†K. J. Dean (*Derbys*)	8	12	2	117	23	0	0	11.70	2
220	†R. C. Driver (*Lancs*)	5	8	0	93	35	0	0	11.62	5
221	M. M. Betts (*Warwicks*)	12	11	3	92	19	0	0	11.50	9
222	G. D. Bridge (*Durham*)	7	13	2	125	39*	0	0	11.36	5
223	A. R. Caddick (*Somerset*)	9	15	4	122	49*	0	0	11.09	1
224	R. J. Kirtley (*Sussex*)	16	24	6	196	51*	0	1	10.88	8
225	P. M. Such (*Essex*)	15	20	9	117	25	0	0	10.63	7
226	A. D. Mullally (*Hants*)	14	13	5	82	36	0	0	10.25	4
227	J. E. Brinkley (*Durham*)	10	13	2	111	65	0	1	10.09	4
228	P. Aldred (*Derbys*)	8	13	1	120	35	0	0	10.00	5
	†T. J. Phillips (*Durham UCCE & Essex*)	6	8	0	80	27	0	0	10.00	0
230	†T. M. Smith (*Derbys*)	6	10	2	79	19	0	0	9.87	4
231	S. J. Harmison (*Durham*)	12	14	4	97	27	0	0	9.70	0
232	R. K. J. Dawson (*Yorks*)	9	11	1	95	37	0	0	9.50	6
233	D. E. Malcolm (*Leics*)	16	21	7	126	50	0	1	9.00	1

		M	I	NO	R	HS	100s	50s	Avge	Ct/St
234	S. P. Jones (*Glam*)	8	11	1	83	46	0	0	8.30	0
235	Kadeer Ali (*Worcs*)	5	8	0	65	38	0	0	8.12	2
236	C. D. Crowe (*Leics*)	7	10	1	73	42	0	0	8.11	4
237	†J. E. Bishop (*Essex*)	8	12	2	74	18	0	0	7.40	0
238	T. F. Bloomfield (*Middx*)	16	16	4	85	28	0	0	7.08	2
239	A. Sheriyar (*Worcs*)	16	19	8	71	20	0	0	6.45	3
240	S. P. Kirby (*Yorks*)	10	10	2	49	15*	0	0	6.12	4
241	A. J. Harris (*Notts*)	9	15	2	79	20*	0	0	6.07	0
242	B. J. Trott (*Kent*)	14	13	3	57	13	0	0	5.70	3
243	C. B. Keegan (*Middx*)	7	10	2	45	30*	0	0	5.62	1
244	P. C. R. Tufnell (*Middx*)	17	20	8	52	11*	0	0	4.33	0
245	M. A. Robinson (*Sussex*)	14	15	7	32	10	0	0	4.00	1
246	†L. J. Wharton (*Derbys*)	11	18	9	29	13*	0	0	3.22	1
247	J. M. M. Averis (*Glos*)	15	19	3	35	7*	0	0	2.18	3

BOWLING

(Qualification: 10 wickets)

		Style	O	M	R	W	BB	5W/i	Avge
1	C. J. Adams (*Sussex*)	RM	40.2	6	111	10	4-28	0	11.10
2	Mushtaq Ahmed (*Pakistanis*)	LBG	69.2	18	176	14	8-49	1	12.57
3	G. D. McGrath (*Australians*)	RFM	234.5	74	624	40	7-76	4	15.60
4	Kabir Ali (*Worcs*)	RFM	84.2	18	253	14	5-22	1	18.07
5	A. D. Mullally (*Hants*)	LFM	477.4	151	1,184	64	8-90	6	18.50
6	S. K. Warne (*Australians*)	LBG	263	56	784	42	7-165	3	18.66
7	I. J. Harvey (*Glos*)	RM	288.4	92	773	41	5-33	2	18.85
8	M. A. Robinson (*Sussex*)	RM	415.4	125	1,083	56	5-35	3	19.33
9	M. Muralitharan (*Lancs*)	OB	484.5	159	971	50	6-53	5	19.42
10	C. E. W. Silverwood (*Yorks*)	RF	209.1	42	644	33	5-20	3	19.51
11	R. S. G. Anderson (*Essex*)	RFM	231.1	54	699	35	5-21	3	19.97
12	C. T. Tremlett (*Hants*)	RFM	131.2	37	401	20	4-34	0	20.05
13	N. Killeen (*Durham*)	RFM	89	29	222	11	3-14	0	20.18
14	D. W. Fleming (*Australians*)	RFM	138	32	390	19	6-59	1	20.52
15	Saqlain Mushtaq (*Pakistanis & Surrey*)	OB	567.2	157	1,286	62	7-58	5	20.74
16	S. P. Kirby (*Yorks*)	RFM	280.3	60	980	47	7-50	3	20.85
17	M. P. Bicknell (*Surrey*)	RFM	541.5	132	1,538	72	7-60	3	21.36
18	J. E. Brinkley (*Durham*)	RFM	222.1	57	663	31	6-14	2	21.38
19	J. Lewis (*Glos*)	RFM	175.4	56	454	21	5-71	1	21.61
20	J. E. K. Schofield (*Hants*)	RFM	89.1	17	285	13	4-51	0	21.92
21	G. Chapple (*Lancs*)	RFM	379.2	87	1,174	53	6-46	4	22.15
22	Waqar Younis (*Pakistanis*)	RFM	119.1	23	399	18	5-23	1	22.16
23	M. J. Hoggard (*Yorks*)	RFM	240	58	733	32	6-51	2	22.90
24	G. D. Bridge (*Durham*)	SLA	172	48	413	18	6-84	1	22.94
25	M. A. Ealham (*Kent*)	RM	226.5	68	574	25	6-64	2	22.96
26	C. E. Dagnall (*Warwicks*)	RFM	83	16	279	12	6-50	1	23.25
27	R. J. Kirtley (*Sussex*)	RFM	566.3	135	1,749	75	6-34	5	23.32
28	R. L. Johnson (*Somerset*)	RFM	463.2	89	1,474	62	5-40	5	23.77
29	S. J. E. Brown (*Durham*)	LFM	115	29	333	14	6-70	1	23.78
30	M. J. Saggers (*Kent*)	RFM	512.3	118	1,551	64	6-92	3	24.23
31	G. J. Smith (*Notts*)	LFM	446.2	103	1,256	50	5-37	3	25.12
32	A. Sheriyar (*Worcs*)	LFM	536.1	125	1,795	71	6-88	3	25.28
33	A. D. Mascarenhas (*Hants*)	RM	399.3	112	1,015	40	6-26	2	25.37
34	Wasim Akram (*Pakistanis*)	LFM	153	44	385	15	4-18	0	25.66
35	G. M. Hamilton (*Yorks*)	RFM	211.2	43	672	26	5-27	1	25.84
36	M. C. J. Ball (*Glos*)	OB	349.3	94	879	34	6-23	2	25.85
37	K. J. Dean (*Derbys*)	LFM	250.5	58	888	34	6-73	2	26.11
38	J. D. Lewry (*Sussex*)	LFM	512.1	126	1,548	59	7-42	3	26.23
39	M. W. Alleyne (*Glos*)	RM	372.4	86	1,076	41	5-50	1	26.24

		Style	O	M	R	W	BB	5W/i	Avge
40	D. R. Law (*Durham*)	RFM	351	70	1,103	42	6-53	3	26.26
41	B. J. Trott (*Kent*)	RFM	372.5	68	1,235	47	6-13	4	26.27
42	R. J. Sidebottom (*Yorks*)	LFM	278.2	75	710	27	4-49	0	26.29
43	M. M. Betts (*Warwicks*)	RFM	308.2	72	979	37	5-22	2	26.45
44	J. M. Dakin (*Leics*)	RM	122.3	22	427	16	4-53	0	26.68
45	A. Richardson (*Warwicks*)	RFM	395.5	111	983	36	5-89	1	27.30
46	A. J. Bichel (*Worcs*)	RFM	555.5	137	1,804	66	6-44	4	27.33
47	P. A. J. DeFreitas (*Leics*)	RM	303	66	934	34	6-65	1	27.47
48	C. G. Liptrot (*Worcs*)	RFM	308.4	80	966	35	3-12	0	27.60
49	J. N. Gillespie (*Australians*)	RF	228	54	801	29	5-37	2	27.62
50	V. J. Wells (*Leics*)	RM	181	47	498	18	5-36	1	27.66
51	S. R. Lampitt (*Worcs*)	RM	203.2	49	669	24	5-22	1	27.87
52	A. C. Morris (*Hants*)	RFM	472	106	1,428	51	5-39	2	28.00
53	A. K. D. Gray (*Yorks*)	OB	92	23	281	10	4-128	0	28.10
54	D. E. Malcolm (*Leics*)	RFM	545.1	94	1,944	68	8-63	4	28.58
55	P. C. R. Tufnell (*Middx*)	SLA	690	166	1,721	60	6-44	3	28.68
56	D. L. Maddy (*Leics*)	RM	237.3	45	804	28	5-67	1	28.71
57	J. Ormond (*Leics*)	RFM	486.4	113	1,421	49	5-71	2	29.00
58	A. R. Caddick (*Somerset*)	RFM	351.2	53	1,376	47	5-81	4	29.27
59	P. J. Martin (*Lancs*)	RFM	322.3	86	969	33	5-52	1	29.36
60	S. D. Udal (*Hants*)	OB	566.1	143	1,610	54	7-74	1	29.81
61	P. N. Weekes (*Middx*)	OB	439.5	100	1,198	40	5-90	1	29.95
62	T. C. Hicks (*Oxford UCCE*)	OB	143	30	394	13	5-77	1	30.30
63	D. R. Brown (*Warwicks*)	RFM	472.1	123	1,284	42	6-60	1	30.57
64	D. S. Lehmann (*Yorks*)	SLA	139.1	33	368	12	3-13	0	30.66
65	M. M. Patel (*Kent*)	SLA	524.2	158	1,228	40	8-119	1	30.70
66	D. Gough (*Yorks*)	RF	321.4	55	1,212	39	5-61	2	31.07
67	R. K. Illingworth (*Derbys*)	SLA	126.4	39	316	10	4-37	0	31.60
68	R. S. C. Martin-Jenkins (*Sussex*)	RFM	248	63	764	24	4-18	0	31.83
69	R. J. Logan (*Notts*)	RFM	329.1	53	1,375	43	6-93	3	31.97
70	A. G. Wharf (*Glam*)	RM	127.4	19	448	14	5-63	1	32.00
71	M. A. Gough (*Durham*)	OB	157.3	34	449	14	5-66	1	32.07
72	R. C. Irani (*Essex*)	RFM	354.5	97	1,040	32	6-79	3	32.50
73	N. M. K. Smith (*Warwicks*)	OB	314	75	813	25	4-76	0	32.52
74	M. S. Panesar (*Northants*)	SLA	101.3	28	358	11	4-11	0	32.54
75	C. R. Miller (*Australians*)	OB	157.2	37	586	18	4-41	0	32.55
76	S. L. Watkin (*Glam*)	RFM	472.4	113	1,400	43	6-67	1	32.55
77	N. M. Carter (*Warwicks*)	LFM	120	12	456	14	5-78	1	32.57
78	D. M. Cousins (*Northants*)	RFM	333.4	54	1,176	36	8-102	2	32.66
78	C. B. Keegan (*Middx*)	RFM	170	38	588	18	4-54	0	32.66
80	P. J. Franks (*Notts*)	RFM	149.1	33	429	13	4-65	0	33.00
81	G. M. Fellows (*Yorks*)	RM	156	43	398	12	3-23	0	33.16
82	A. Symonds (*Kent*)	RM/OB	106.2	23	333	10	3-28	0	33.30
83	N. G. Hatch (*Durham*)	RM	248.4	43	867	26	3-42	0	33.34
84	R. K. J. Dawson (*Yorks*)	OB	315.5	69	1,014	30	6-82	2	33.80
85	M. C. Ilott (*Essex*)	LFM	287	65	921	27	5-85	1	34.11
86	P. S. Jones (*Somerset*)	RFM	560	100	2,015	59	5-115	1	34.15
87	T. F. Bloomfield (*Middx*)	RFM	479.4	79	1,709	50	5-58	2	34.18
88	T. A. Munton (*Derbys*)	RFM	242.1	61	659	19	5-85	1	34.68
89	S. J. Cook (*Middx*)	RFM	218.1	47	696	20	3-10	0	34.80
90	T. M. Smith (*Derbys*)	RFM	91.3	15	383	11	4-61	0	34.81
91	C. White (*Yorks*)	RFM	214.1	52	599	17	4-57	0	35.23
92	A. J. Tudor (*Surrey*)	RFM	251.1	53	927	26	5-44	2	35.65
93	A. F. Giles (*Warwicks*)	SLA	154.5	41	429	12	5-46	1	35.75
94	Abdur Razzaq (*Pakistanis*)	RFM	105.3	19	359	10	3-61	0	35.90
95	S. J. Harmison (*Durham*)	RF	419.5	86	1,262	35	6-111	2	36.05
96	A. N. Bressington (*Glos*)	RFM	120.4	31	397	11	3-42	0	36.09
97	U. B. A. Rashid (*Sussex*)	SLA	134.2	38	398	11	4-9	0	36.18
98	K. P. Dutch (*Somerset*)	OB	367	64	1,268	35	4-32	0	36.22
99	D. A. Leatherdale (*Worcs*)	RM	158	39	580	16	4-70	0	36.25

		Style	O	M	R	W	BB	5W/i	Avge
100	M. A. Wagh (*Warwicks*)	OB	184	37	473	13	3-3	0	36.38
101	V. C. Drakes (*Warwicks*)	RFM	505.2	107	1,537	42	5-37	1	36.59
102	E. S. H. Giddins (*Surrey*)	RFM	352.5	83	1,102	30	5-48	1	36.73
103	G. Welch (*Derbys*)	RFM	502.3	108	1,631	44	6-30	3	37.06
104	A. R. C. Fraser (*Middx*)	RFM	469.4	140	1,204	32	3-46	0	37.62
105	J. M. M. Averis (*Glos*)	RFM	463.2	100	1,621	43	5-52	1	37.69
106	G. R. Napier (*Essex*)	RM	104.1	15	453	12	3-55	0	37.75
107	J. E. Bishop (*Essex*)	LFM	224	39	915	24	5-148	1	38.12
108	J. P. Hewitt (*Middx*)	RFM	83	8	386	10	3-72	0	38.60
109	R. D. B. Croft (*Glam*)	OB	328.3	86	927	24	5-95	2	38.62
110	A. Flintoff (*Lancs*)	RFM	245.3	48	736	19	3-36	0	38.73
111	A. J. Harris (*Notts*)	RFM	330.4	84	1,097	28	6-98	1	39.17
112	J. A. R. Blain (*Northants*)	RFM	153	16	673	17	6-42	1	39.58
113	N. C. Johnson (*Hants*)	RFM	252.5	42	911	23	4-20	0	39.60
114	M. J. G. Davis (*Sussex*)	OB	349.3	82	956	24	6-116	1	39.83
115	A. L. Penberthy (*Northants*)	RM	339.2	70	1,019	25	4-39	0	40.76
116	N. C. Phillips (*Durham*)	OB	285.5	60	939	23	5-64	1	40.82
117	G. Keedy (*Lancs*)	SLA	387.1	76	1,150	28	5-73	2	41.07
118	M. V. Fleming (*Kent*)	RM	302.4	59	910	22	4-53	0	41.36
119	M. N. Malik (*Notts*)	RFM	104	21	414	10	5-57	1	41.40
120	M. J. Cawdron (*Glos*)	RM	168	50	498	12	4-79	0	41.50
121	D. A. Cosker (*Glam*)	SLA	423.5	84	1,390	33	4-48	0	42.12
122	I. D. K. Salisbury (*Surrey*)	LBG	396.2	72	1,151	27	5-95	1	42.62
123	I. D. Hunter (*Durham*)	RM	181.3	27	700	16	4-55	0	43.75
124	Shahid Afridi (*MCC & Leics*)	LBG	166.1	41	569	13	5-84	1	43.76
125	T. Lungley (*Derbys*)	RFM	115.4	14	527	12	3-58	0	43.91
126	R. D. Stemp (*Notts*)	SLA	244.4	51	707	16	3-39	0	44.18
127	B. Lee (*Australians*)	RF	186.5	30	752	17	3-17	0	44.23
128	I. D. Blackwell (*Somerset*)	SLA	291.4	72	896	20	5-122	1	44.80
129	M. J. Rawnsley (*Worcs*)	SLA	446.2	122	1,211	27	3-55	0	44.85
130	M. Burns (*Somerset*)	RM	138.5	23	539	12	6-54	1	44.91
131	G. P. Swann (*Northants*)	OB	422.3	87	1,365	30	5-34	1	45.50
132	A. P. Cowan (*Essex*)	RFM	461.5	103	1,518	33	3-64	0	46.00
133	J. P. Taylor (*Northants*)	LFM	379.2	49	1,345	29	4-100	0	46.37
134	J. F. Brown (*Northants*)	OB	473.5	102	1,407	28	5-107	1	50.25
135	S. D. Thomas (*Glam*)	RFM	420.1	56	1,668	33	4-54	0	50.54
136	J. P. Pyemont (*Camb. UCCE*)	OB	146	31	512	10	4-101	0	51.20
137	D. G. Cork (*Derbys*)	RFM	206.5	44	618	12	4-122	0	51.50
138	N. R. C. Dumelow (*Derbys*)	OB	185.5	34	723	14	4-81	0	51.64
139	S. P. Jones (*Glam*)	RF	198.2	29	887	17	3-36	0	52.17
140	M. R. Strong (*Northants*)	RFM	256.3	46	992	19	3-98	0	52.21
141	C. P. Schofield (*Lancs*)	LBG	252.1	52	757	14	3-53	0	54.07
142	P. M. Such (*Essex*)	OB	433	98	1,362	24	5-131	1	56.75
143	P. Aldred (*Derbys*)	RM	189.3	30	742	13	3-102	0	57.07
144	J. W. M. Dalrymple (*Oxford UCCE & Middx*)	OB	203.3	47	578	10	4-86	0	57.80
145	U. Afzaal (*Notts*)	SLA	158.2	29	579	10	3-88	0	57.90
146	A. C. McGarry (*Essex*)	RFM	148	19	637	10	3-77	0	63.70

BOWLING STYLES

LBG Leg-breaks and googlies (5)
LFM Left-arm fast-medium (12)
OB Off-breaks (23)
RF Right-arm fast (6)
RFM Right-arm fast-medium (64)
RM Right-arm medium (23)
SLA Slow left-arm (14)

Note: The total comes to 147, because A. Symonds has two styles of bowling.

INDIVIDUAL SCORES OF 100 AND OVER

There were 314 three-figure innings in 168 first-class matches in 2001, 118 more than in 2000 when 182 matches were played. Of these, 19 were double-hundreds, compared with nine in 2000. The list includes 264 hundreds hit in the County Championship, compared with 154 in 2000.

* *Signifies not out.*

D. P. Fulton (9)
120 Kent v Cambridge UCCE, Cambridge
111 Kent v Surrey, The Oval
140 Kent v Somerset, Taunton
179 Kent v Essex, Tunbridge Wells
107 Kent v Leics, Canterbury
208* }
104* } Kent v Somerset, Canterbury
197 Kent v Northants, Northampton
196 Kent v Northants, Canterbury

R. R. Montgomerie (8)
116 Sussex v Warwicks, Hove
112 Sussex v Worcs, Horsham
160* Sussex v Notts, Nottingham
116 Sussex v Middx, Lord's
156 Sussex v Durham, Chester-le-Street
107 Sussex v Glos, Cheltenham
157 Sussex v Australians, Hove
121 Sussex v Warwicks, Birmingham

M. W. Goodwin (7)
195 Sussex v Hants, Southampton
109 Sussex v Worcs, Horsham
115 }
203* } Sussex v Notts, Nottingham
127 Sussex v Middx, Hove
105 Sussex v Australians, Hove
150 Sussex v Warwicks, Birmingham

A. P. Grayson (6)
127 Essex v Cambridge UCCE, Cambridge
115 Essex v Surrey, The Oval
189 Essex v Glam, Chelmsford
173 }
149 } Essex v Northants, Northampton
186* Essex v Lancs, Colchester

G. A. Hick (6)
120 Worcs v Hants, Southampton
124 Worcs v Warwicks, Worcester
123 Worcs v Notts, Worcester
171 Worcs v Derbys, Derby
201 Worcs v Warwicks, Birmingham
200* Worcs v Durham, Chester-le-Street

G. S. Blewett (5)
133 Notts v Durham, Nottingham
137* Notts v Durham, Chester-le-Street
134* Notts v Worcs, Worcester
108 Notts v Worcs, Nottingham
106* Notts v Derbys, Nottingham

M. E. K. Hussey (5)
159 Northants v Glam, Cardiff
122 Northants v Yorks, Northampton
329* Northants v Essex, Northampton
232 Northants v Leics, Northampton
208 Northants v Somerset, Taunton

D. S. Lehmann (5)
187* Yorks v Somerset, Bath
104 Yorks v Leics, Leeds
252 Yorks v Lancs, Leeds
106* Yorks v Surrey, Leeds
193 Yorks v Leics, Leicester

D. R. Martyn (5)
108 Australians v Worcs, Worcester
114* Australians v Essex, Chelmsford
105 Australia v England, Birmingham
176* Australians v Somerset, Taunton
118 Australia v England, Leeds

B. F. Smith (5)
110 Leics v Kent, Canterbury
179 Leics v Surrey, Leicester
117 Leics v Glam, Cardiff
111 Leics v Kent, Leicester
180* Leics v Somerset, Taunton

I. D. Blackwell (4)
103 }
122 } Somerset v Northants, Northampton
102 Somerset v Glam, Taunton
120 Somerset v Surrey, Taunton

D. Byas (4)
105* Yorks v Glam, Swansea
110* Yorks v Northants, Northampton
100 Yorks v Leics, Leicester
104 Yorks v Glam, Scarborough

M. J. Di Venuto (4)
108 Derbys v Worcs, Worcester
109 Derbys v Warwicks, Birmingham
111* Derbys v Durham, Chester-le-Street
165 Derbys v Notts, Nottingham

N. H. Fairbrother (4)
179* Lancs v Somerset, Taunton
101 Lancs v Leics, Manchester
158 Lancs v Glam, Colwyn Bay
132 Lancs v Essex, Colchester

S. P. Fleming (4)
121* Middx v Glos, Bristol
114 Middx v Durham, Chester-le-Street
151 Middx v Notts, Nottingham
102 Middx v Warwicks, Lord's

D. L. Hemp (4)
100* Warwicks v Oxford UCCE, Oxford
105 Warwicks v Middx, Birmingham
105 Warwicks v Notts, Birmingham
186* Warwicks v Worcs, Birmingham

R. W. T. Key (4)
101 Kent v Surrey, The Oval
119 Kent v Pakistanis, Canterbury
123 Kent v Essex, Southend
132 Kent v Lancs, Manchester

S. G. Law (4)
153 Essex v Surrey, The Oval
116* } 123* } Essex v Lancs, Manchester
115 Essex v Leics, Chelmsford

J. P. Maher (4)
123* Glam v Kent, Maidstone
150 Glam v Northants, Cardiff
217 Glam v Essex, Cardiff
100 Glam v Leics, Leicester

K. P. Pietersen (4)
165* Notts v Middx, Lord's
103* Notts v Worcs, Worcester
218* Notts v Derbys, Derby
150 Notts v Derbys, Nottingham

M. R. Ramprakash (4)
146 Surrey v Kent, The Oval
143 Surrey v Somerset, The Oval
133 England v Australia, The Oval
131 Surrey v Yorks, The Oval

M. J. Walker (4)
105 Kent v Surrey, The Oval
112* Kent v Glam, Swansea
124 Kent v Essex, Tunbridge Wells
120* Kent v Leics, Leicester

T. R. Ward (4)
119 Leics v Somerset, Leicester
160* Leics v Northants, Leicester
109 Leics v Glam, Cardiff
110 Leics v Kent, Leicester

R. J. Warren (4)
175 Northants v Glam, Northampton
194 Northants v Lancs, Manchester
104 Northants v Kent, Canterbury
144 Northants v Somerset, Taunton

M. J. Wood (4)
124 Yorks v Somerset, Bath
102 Yorks v Leics, Leeds
115 Yorks v Lancs, Manchester
124 Yorks v Glam, Scarborough

C. J. Adams (3)
192 Sussex v Derbys, Arundel
123 Sussex v Glos, Cheltenham
139 Sussex v Warwicks, Birmingham

I. R. Bell (3)
130 Warwicks v Oxford UCCE, Oxford
103 Warwicks v Notts, Birmingham
135 Warwicks v Derbys, Derby

D. J. Bicknell (3)
167 Notts v Warwicks, Nottingham
123 Notts v Sussex, Nottingham
104 Notts v Worcs, Worcester

A. D. Brown (3)
122 Surrey v Northants, Northampton
103 Surrey v Northants, Guildford
115 Surrey v Glam, Cardiff

M. A. Butcher (3)
145* Surrey v Glam, The Oval
173* England v Australia, Leeds
230 Surrey v Glam, Cardiff

P. D. Collingwood (3)
130 Durham v Durham UCCE, Chester-le-Street
153 Durham v Warwicks, Birmingham
103 Durham v Worcs, Chester-le-Street

A. Dale (3)
204 Glam v Northants, Northampton
113 Glam v Essex, Chelmsford
140 Glam v Lancs, Colwyn Bay

A. C. Gilchrist (3)
150* Australians v Essex, Chelmsford
152 Australia v England, Birmingham
114 Australians v Sussex, Hove

A. Habib (3)
153 Leics v Kent, Leicester
124 Leics v Essex, Chelmsford
149 Leics v Somerset, Taunton

B. L. Hutton (3)
133 Middx v Oxford UCCE, Oxford
139 Middx v Derbys, Southgate
120 Middx v Durham, Lord's

J. J. B. Lewis (3)
110 Durham v Durham UCCE, Chester-le-Street
112 Durham v Notts, Chester-le-Street
129 Durham v Worcs, Chester-le-Street

M. B. Loye (3)
167* Northants v Surrey, Northampton
177 Northants v Lancs, Northampton
197 Northants v Somerset, Northampton

A. L. Penberthy (3)
132* Northants v Glam, Northampton
101 Northants v Essex, Northampton
101 Northants v Somerset, Taunton

R. T. Ponting (3)
128 Australians v Somerset, Taunton
147* Australians v Sussex, Hove
144 Australia v England, Leeds

D. D. J. Robinson (3)
109 Essex v Cambridge UCCE, Cambridge
102 } 118* } Essex v Leics, Chelmsford

O. A. Shah (3)
190 Middx v Durham, Chester-le-Street
203 Middx v Derbys, Southgate
144 Middx v Notts, Nottingham

E. T. Smith (3)
103* Kent v Yorks, Canterbury
116 Kent v Glam, Maidstone
107 Kent v Leics, Leicester

R. A. Smith (3)
118 Hants v Warwicks, Birmingham
102* Hants v Glos, Southampton
113 Hants v Australians, Southampton

J. N. Snape (3)
119 Glos v Derbys, Derby
131 Glos v Sussex, Cheltenham
100* Glos v Notts, Bristol

V. S. Solanki (3)
106 Worcs v Durham UCCE, Worcester
109 Worcs v Derbys, Derby
112 Worcs v Warwicks, Birmingham

A. J. Strauss (3)
125 Middx v Worcs, Lord's
176 Middx v Durham, Lord's
112* Middx v Hants, Southampton

S. D. Stubbings (3)
126 Derbys v Glos, Derby
127 Derbys v Notts, Derby
120 Derbys v Glos, Bristol

C. G. Taylor (3)
196 Glos v Notts, Nottingham
140 Glos v Sussex, Cheltenham
148 Glos v Notts, Bristol

M. P. Vaughan (3)
133 Yorks v Northants, Leeds
120 England v Pakistan, Manchester
113 Yorks v Essex, Scarborough

M. A. Wagh (3)
104 Warwicks v Durham, Birmingham
112 Warwicks v Durham, Chester-le-Street
315 Warwicks v Middx, Lord's

S. R. Waugh (3)
105 Australians v MCC, Arundel
105 Australia v England, Birmingham
157* Australia v England, The Oval

R. M. S. Weston (3)
135* Middx v Hants, Southgate
100 Middx v Warwicks, Birmingham
106 Middx v Worcs, Worcester

M. G. N. Windows (3)
106* Glos v Middx, Bristol
123 Glos v Middx, Lord's
174 Glos v Notts, Bristol

M. W. Alleyne (2)
132 Glos v Durham, Gloucester
136 Glos v Derbys, Derby

C. W. G. Bassano (2)
186* } 106 } Derbys v Glos, Derby

P. D. Bowler (2)
138* Somerset v Leics, Leicester
164 Somerset v Glam, Taunton

J. P. Crawley (2)
113 Lancs v Yorks, Leeds
280 Lancs v Northants, Manchester

I. J. Harvey (2)
130* Glos v Middx, Lord's
104 Glos v Derbys, Bristol

W. K. Hegg (2)
107* Lancs v Northants, Northampton
133 Lancs v Essex, Manchester

D. R. Hewson (2)
100* Glos v Derbys, Derby
168 Glos v Derbys, Bristol

N. C. Johnson (2)
103 Hants v Worcs, Worcester
105* Hants v Notts, Nottingham

P. Johnson (2)
109 Notts v Durham, Chester-le-Street
149 Notts v Glos, Bristol

E. C. Joyce (2)
104 Middx v Warwicks, Lord's
108* Middx v Worcs, Worcester

D. A. Kenway (2)
131 Hants v Glos, Southampton
166 Hants v Notts, Southampton

N. V. Knight (2)
140 Warwicks v Hants, Birmingham
124 Warwicks v Derbys, Derby

J. L. Langer (2)
104* Australians v Somerset, Taunton
102* Australia v England, The Oval

J. E. Morris (2)
170 }
136* } Notts v Derbys, Derby

D. P. Ostler (2)
119 Warwicks v Hants, Birmingham
121 Warwicks v Durham, Chester-le-Street

M. J. Powell (2)
133 Warwicks v Glos, Birmingham
236 Warwicks v Oxford UCCE, Oxford

M. J. Powell (2)
106 Glam v Northants, Northampton
108 Glam v Essex, Cardiff

A. Singh (2)
128 Worcs v Durham UCCE, Worcester
168 Worcs v Middx, Worcester

I. J. Sutcliffe (2)
203 Leics v Glam, Cardiff
165 Leics v Essex, Chelmsford

L. D. Sutton (2)
110* Derbys v Warwicks, Birmingham
140* Derbys v Sussex, Derby

A. Symonds (2)
125 Kent v Leics, Leicester
131 Kent v Northants, Northampton

G. P. Thorpe (2)
148 Surrey v Northants, Northampton
138 England v Pakistan, Manchester

M. E. Trescothick (2)
147 Somerset v Glam, Cardiff
117 England v Pakistan, Manchester

M. E. Waugh (2)
108 Australia v England, Lord's
120 Australia v England, The Oval

V. J. Wells (2)
138 Leics v Kent, Canterbury
133 Leics v Yorks, Leicester

W. P. C. Weston (2)
192 Worcs v Notts, Worcester
102* Worcs v Warwicks, Birmingham

C. White (2)
186 Yorks v Lancs, Manchester
183 Yorks v Glam, Scarborough

G. W. White (2)
141 Hants v Sussex, Southampton
112 Hants v Notts, Nottingham

The following each played one three-figure innings:

U. Afzaal, 138, Notts v Derbys, Derby; M. A. Atherton, 160, Lancs v Essex, Manchester; A. N. Aymes, 112*, Hants v Notts, Southampton.

R. J. Bailey, 136*, Derbys v Worcs, Derby; K. J. Barnett, 114, Glos v Notts, Nottingham; M. P. Bicknell, 110*, Surrey v Kent, Canterbury; D. R. Brown, 104, Warwicks v Notts, Birmingham; M. Burns, 221, Somerset v Yorks, Bath; N. D. Burns, 111, Leics v Glam, Leicester.

G. Chapple, 155, Lancs v Somerset, Manchester; M. J. Chilton, 104, Lancs v Northants, Northampton; D. G. Cork, 128, Derbys v Notts, Derby; J. Cox, 186, Somerset v Essex, Chelmsford.

J. A. Daley, 128*, Durham v Durham UCCE, Chester-le-Street; M. P. Dowman, 145*, Derbys v Pakistanis, Derby; K. P. Dutch, 118, Somerset v Essex, Taunton.

M. A. Ealham, 153*, Kent v Northants, Canterbury.

A. Flintoff, 120, Lancs v Durham UCCE, Durham; M. K. Floyd, 128*, Oxford U. v Cambridge U., Cambridge; J. S. Foster, 103, Durham UCCE v Worcs, Worcester.

M. L. Hayden, 142, Australians v Hants, Southampton; B. C. Hollioake, 118, Surrey v Yorks, The Oval.

Inzamam-ul-Haq, 114, Pakistan v England, Manchester; R. C. Irani, 119, Essex v Surrey, Ilford.

S. P. James, 156, Glam v Essex, Chelmsford.

S. M. Katich, 168*, Australians v MCC, Arundel.

D. R. Law, 103, Durham v Hants, Chester-le-Street; M. L. Love, 149*, Durham v Notts, Chester-le-Street; M. J. Lumb, 122, Yorks v Leics, Leeds.

A. McGrath, 116*, Yorks v Surrey, The Oval; D. L. Maddy, 111, Leics v Kent, Leicester; D. J. Marsh, 138*, Leics v Somerset, Leicester; R. S. C. Martin-Jenkins, 113, Sussex v Glos, Hove; A. D. Mascarenhas, 104, Hants v Worcs, Southampton; M. P. Maynard, 145, Glam v Lancs, Colwyn Bay.

G. R. Napier, 104, Essex v Cambridge UCCE, Cambridge; D. C. Nash, 103*, Middx v Warwicks, Lord's; K. Newell, 103, Glam v Northants, Northampton.

K. A. Parsons, 139, Somerset v Northants, Taunton; N. Peng, 101, Durham v Middx, Chester-le-Street; P. R. Pollard, 131*, Worcs v Durham UCCE, Worcester; P. J. Prichard, 111, Essex v Cambridge UCCE, Cambridge.

U. B. A. Rashid, 106, Sussex v Durham, Chester-le-Street.

Saeed Anwar, 201, Pakistanis v Kent, Canterbury; Shahid Afridi, 164, Leics v Northants, Northampton; A. J. Stewart, 106, Surrey v Essex, The Oval; A. J. Swann, 113, Northants v Leics, Northampton.

S. D. Thomas, 138, Glam v Essex, Chelmsford; A. J. Tudor, 116, Surrey v Essex, The Oval; R. J. Turner, 115*, Somerset v Essex, Taunton.

P. N. Weekes, 107, Middx v Warwicks, Lord's; M. J. Wood, 122, Somerset v Northants, Taunton.

B. Zuiderent, 122, Sussex v Notts, Hove.

TEN WICKETS IN A MATCH

There were 18 instances of bowlers taking ten or more wickets in a match in first-class cricket in 2001, nine fewer than in 2000. The list includes 16 in the County Championship.

R. J. Kirtley (2)
10-95, Sussex v Durham, Hove; 10-93, Sussex v Glos, Hove.

A. J. Bichel, 10-86, Worcs v Glos, Worcester; M. P. Bicknell, 11-117, Surrey v Glam, The Oval; D. R. Brown, 10-80, Warwicks v Derbys, Derby.

A. R. Caddick, 10-173, Somerset v Yorks, Leeds; R. D. B. Croft, 10-191, Glam v Northants, Cardiff.

K. J. Dean, 10-105, Derbys v Durham, Chester-le-Street.

S. P. Kirby, 12-72, Yorks v Leics, Leeds.

J. D. Lewry, 13-79, Sussex v Hants, Hove.

D. E. Malcolm, 10-187, Leics v Surrey, Leicester; M. Muralitharan, 10-123, Lancs v Essex, Manchester; Mushtaq Ahmed, 10-51, Pakistanis v British Universities, Nottingham.

M. M. Patel, 12-144, Kent v Somerset, Canterbury.

G. J. Smith, 10-101, Notts v Sussex, Hove.

B. J. Trott, 11-78, Kent v Essex, Tunbridge Wells; P. C. R. Tufnell, 10-133, Middx v Derbys, Southgate.

S. K. Warne, 11-229, Australia v England, The Oval.

WOMBWELL CRICKET LOVERS' SOCIETY AWARDS, 2001

Darren Lehmann, the Australian batsman who helped Yorkshire to the County Championship, was voted George Spofforth Cricketer of the Year by members of the Wombwell Cricket Lovers' Society. Lehmann also won the Dr Leslie Taylor Award for Best Performance in the Roses Matches. Other award-winners were: C. B. Fry Young Cricketer of the Year – Nicky Peng; Brian Sellers Captain of the Year – David Byas; Les Bailey Best Yorkshire Newcomer – Steve Kirby; Learie Constantine Best Fielder in C&G Final – Rob Turner; Denis Compton Memorial Award for Flair – Shane Warne; J. M. Kilburn Cricket Writer of the Year – Malcolm Lorimer, for *Glory Lightly Worn*; Ted Umbers Services to Yorkshire Cricket – Philip Akroyd.

THE PAKISTANIS IN ENGLAND, 2001

Review by KAMRAN ABBASI

It is always hasty to write off a Pakistan tour as a non-event – however short. In the end, this 11th visit to England, excluding World Cups, turned out to be one of their more memorable, but for all the wrong reasons. The 1999 World Cup had delivered a new breed of Asian cricket fan: young, assertive, and passionate in support of a faraway land. But whereas those fans complemented the vigour of their heroes, the class of 2001 wrenched the limelight from the cricketers, against a background of racial violence spreading through England's northern cities.

Between sharing a Test series in New Zealand and arriving in England, Pakistan had managed to change their captain, coach and manager; the touring party was announced barely 72 hours before the flight to London. Moin Khan, captain and wicket-keeper when England won their series in Pakistan several months earlier, was excluded on fitness grounds, even though he was playing domestic cricket. Wasim Akram needed a casting vote from the chairman of Pakistan's cricket board to secure his place, and then had to accept the captaincy of Waqar Younis, his one-time friend and long-term adversary. Just as intriguingly, whistleblower-in-chief and former captain Rashid Latif was back as sole wicket-keeper, playing alongside five of the men – among them the new captain – who had been fined by Justice Qayyum's match-fixing inquiry.

The tourists were a curious blend of youth and experience, either under-cooked or over-seasoned. Shoaib Akhtar and the new pace-bowling sensation, Mohammad Sami, who had a match-winning five-wicket haul against New Zealand on his Test debut, backed Wasim and Waqar, and it was hoped that all-rounders Abdur Razzaq, only 21, and Azhar Mahmood would feature prominently in English conditions. Inzamam-ul-Haq's broad shoulders carried the batting, along with the silkier touch of Saeed Anwar and Yousuf Youhana. But if Pakistan held an advantage, it was not in their fast-bowling champions or their enigmatic batsmen. It lay in the spinning wrists of Saqlain Mushtaq and Mushtaq Ahmed.

With doubts still voiced about his action, Shoaib was fortunate to make the squad at all. However, he had convinced the ICC (with help from the University of Western Australia) that the kink in his action was unavoidable because of hyper-extensible joints. This did not breach the spirit of the law, argued Shoaib's defence, even though it might breach the letter of the law. Perhaps the ICC was too confused to make a fuss.

As often in the past, the Pakistan squad was ripe for discord, but the management launched an extraordinary campaign when the team arrived in England, claiming that their disagreements were history and should be forgotten. Indeed, Pakistan spent more time playing down rumours of internal bickering than focusing on the First Test, which should have begun on May 17, the coldest Test match day in the history of English cricket. But it was rain and not the temperature, a chilly 7°C (45°F), that prevented any play.

THE PAKISTANI TOURING PARTY

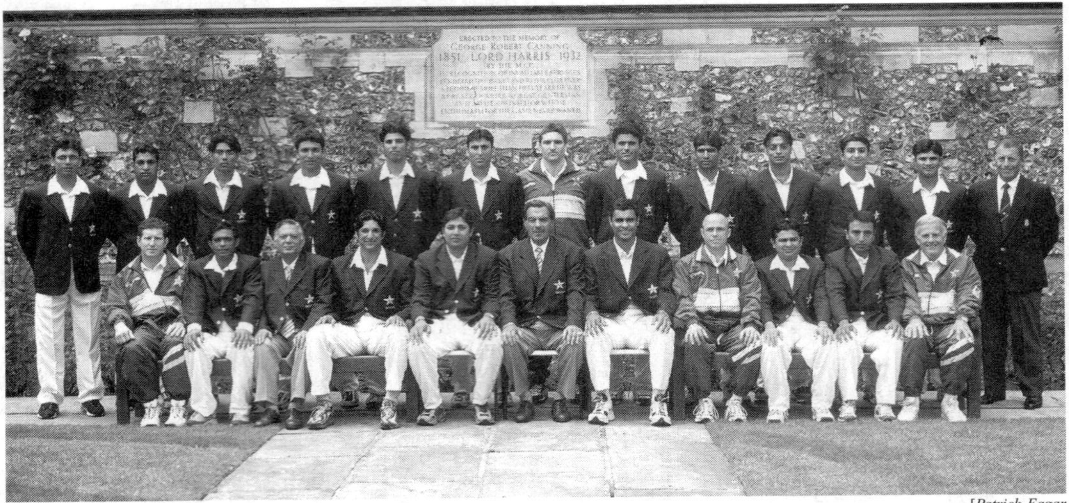

[*Patrick Eagar*

Standing: Saqlain Mushtaq, Salim Elahi, Mohammad Sami, Azhar Mahmood, Mohammad Wasim, Younis Khan, N. Walker (*physiotherapist*), Abdur Razzaq, Yousuf Youhana, Shoaib Akhtar, Faisal Iqbal, Imran Farhat, R. Hobley (*media liaison officer*). *Seated:* D. Naylor (*trainer*), Rashid Latif, Mohammad Ahmad (*assistant manager*), Wasim Akram, Inzamam-ul-Haq, Yawar Saeed (*manager*), Waqar Younis (*captain*), R. A. Pybus (*coach*), Mushtaq Ahmed, Saeed Anwar, D. H. Foster (*bowling coach*).

England, meanwhile, were riding a wave of optimism, created by the force of successive victories over Zimbabwe, West Indies, Pakistan and Sri Lanka. Nasser Hussain starred in television advertisements and Darren "Dazzler" Gough launched his rather premature autobiography to widespread acclaim. England's players could do no wrong, it seemed; when Lord's in May followed the script to perfection, the odds narrowed further on Australia being humbled again after their Indian hiccup.

Pakistan were brushed aside as Andrew Caddick rediscovered his liking for English conditions and Gough just dazzled, securing his first five-wicket Test haul at Lord's. Rashid Latif, in the process of stylishly resurrecting his international career, became Gough's 200th Test victim. Graham Thorpe neutered Pakistan's bowlers as he had in the winter. But if the visitors were ill prepared, the crisis was partly of their own making. In the previous county game, they foolishly allowed Kent to bat first and lost an ideal practice opportunity. The First Test arrived too soon, with most of the batsmen woefully out of touch. So, too, was Shoaib, who had missed the first few days of the tour because of a stomach complaint. Still clearly unfit, he somehow managed to be selected ahead of Saqlain – and he dealt the decisive blow of the series when a lightning-fast, rising delivery broke Hussain's right thumb, putting him out of the match and the series.

Before he left Lord's, the England captain expressed dismay at the number of young Asian Britons baying for Pakistan. He was right to ask for support from all sections of the community, but his comments were ill judged as northern towns struggled to defuse racial tension sparked by provocative posturing from the National Front and the British National Party. Nor did the organisers of the Old Trafford Test agree with Hussain's analysis. Fearing empty stands and coffers, they marketed it as a home game for Pakistan, and their policy worked. Fans wearing and bearing green and white dominated the ground on all five days as Old Trafford's stewards ensured that the threatened racial violence did not occur.

In Hussain's absence, Alec Stewart again added the captaincy to his other duties of batsman and wicket-keeper, and, after England lost their tenth toss in 11 Tests, Pakistan batted first, fresh from a day out on the rollercoasters and donkeys of Blackpool's pleasure beach. Enjoying the country is an important part of touring, but to choose the day before a Test smacked of carelessness. Luckily, the pitch played as if it had been flown in from Lahore, and Pakistan rattled up 403 runs in the first innings, 370 of them on the first day. Inzamam bludgeoned 199 runs in the match, including a first-innings hundred and his 5,000th Test run.

England responded with resilience, even arrogance, as Thorpe and Michael Vaughan took them to 282 for two; Thorpe matched his highest score in Tests and Vaughan stroked his maiden Test century. Then Thorpe, overconfident, chanced a single to Wasim, who ran him out by a distance. It would be the turning-point of England's summer. They raided their memory bank to conjure a remarkable collapse: eight wickets for 75 runs. Was this a blip or the beginning of a prolonged relapse? The second innings gave the answer. Chasing 285 on the final day, Stewart's troops played for a draw when Hussain's boys would have dared to win. By mid-afternoon, England had blocked themselves out of the game, and an unlikely alignment of fates conspired in Pakistan's favour.

[*Patrick Eagar*

How the Test was won – and a series squared. The opening day at Old Trafford was all about Inzamam-ul-Haq's savagery and the slaughter of an England attack that put Pakistan to the sword at Lord's. The last day belonged, in the end, to Saqlain Mushtaq, who slipped and slid the ball past England's defences. Ten men crowded around the bat to see how Matthew Hoggard would cope.

[*Patrick Eagar*

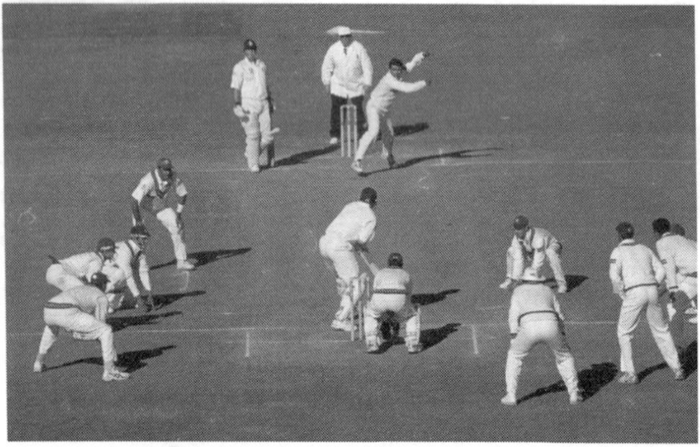

Waqar ran in as if his captaincy and his career depended on the result, his fury such that he crossed the line between banter and intimidation. He also worked hard on the ball, illegally if some camera shots were to be believed, and it began to reverse-swing. Saqlain twirled away, bowling no-ball after no-ball and getting away with it. Umpires David Shepherd and Eddie Nicholls squinted so hard at glove, bat and pad that the popping-crease was forgotten. As England surrendered eight wickets for 60 runs, four of those dismissals were clear no-balls, and were shown again and again by the television networks. Marcus Trescothick's century was in vain; Pakistan romped home, a fitting farewell to Old Trafford for Wasim, and their players prayed in gratitude on the outfield. England rued their lack of ambition – and the no-balls. The debate about umpiring and technology was alive again.

The NatWest one-day series had a familiar pattern to it. Pakistan were too good for England, Australia were too good for both, and the final was a carbon copy of the 1999 World Cup final, with Pakistan all a-quiver on the big day. But the tournament was overshadowed by the behaviour of their fans, whose constant pitch invasions began as over-enthusiasm and ended as defiance. It was clear that the ECB and the ground authorities were woefully unready for the persistence of the running classes. And the security measures, belatedly introduced after a steward was injured at Headingley and Stewart conceded the match, were inadequate and half-heartedly implemented. The British media, relieved to be distracted from England's dismal performances, heightened the tension by labelling Pakistan's fans as thugs and undesirables.

The tourists returned home blaming the media for diverting attention from their success. This was a moot point. Pakistan had last failed to win a series in England in 1982, and Australia thoroughly outplayed them in the one-day competition. The young pace bowlers had been a disappointment: shin problems ruled out Sami before the Manchester Test and Shoaib never seemed fit. Against Australia at Cardiff, Shoaib was recorded at 97.7mph, the fastest recorded since Jeff Thomson, but he left the field after bowling five overs, vomiting blood, and within days he was tactlessly dumped from the tour. In batsmanship, Inzamam was peerless; Saeed Anwar roused himself in the one-day series, but he had other things on his mind. His three-year-old daughter had a major operation during the tour and she died in September.

For England, Gough and Caddick shone at Lord's but dented their growing reputation by bowling bewilderingly short at Old Trafford. Of the back-up Yorkshiremen, first Ryan Sidebottom and then Matthew Hoggard, the latter impressed more, though mostly through honest effort and perseverance rather than control and movement. Craig White's reverse-swing was missed at Old Trafford, as was a quality spinner. Indeed, it was difficult to see how England could challenge Australia with such poor support for their opening bowlers. But Stewart's captaincy was the weakest link when England rolled back the years in the Second Test and revived their house-of-cards act. Hussain's injuries would haunt them throughout the summer, as would those to Thorpe and Vaughan ahead of the Ashes series. Thorpe, especially, was at the peak of his considerable powers until that fateful run-out. England's resolve and confidence were terminally shaken at Old Trafford, and by the end of the NatWest Series the team was in disarray. Australia were circling for the kill. It was not the script that was promised at the start of the summer.

PAKISTANI TOURING PARTY

Waqar Younis (Lahore Blues) (*captain*), Inzamam-ul-Haq (Faisalabad) (*vice-captain*), Abdur Razzaq (Lahore Blues), Azhar Mahmood (PIA), Faisal Iqbal (Karachi Blues/PIA), Imran Farhat (Lahore Blues), Mohammad Sami (Karachi Whites), Mohammad Wasim (Rawalpindi/KRL), Mushtaq Ahmed (Lahore Blues), Rashid Latif (Karachi Blues/Allied Bank), Saeed Anwar (Lahore Blues), Salim Elahi (Lahore Whites), Saqlain Mushtaq (PIA), Shoaib Akhtar (KRL), Wasim Akram (Lahore Blues), Younis Khan (Peshawar/Habib Bank), Yousuf Youhana (Lahore Blues).

Imran Nazir (Sheikhupura/National Bank), Shahid Afridi (Karachi Whites/Habib Bank) and Shoaib Malik (PIA) replaced Imran Farhat, Mohammad Wasim and Mushtaq Ahmed for the one-day tournament that followed the Tests. Mohammad Sami remained in England for treatment of his shin injury. He and the unfit Shoaib Akhtar were released from the tour; Fazl-e-Akbar (Peshawar/PIA) briefly joined the squad.

Manager: Yawar Saeed. *Assistant manager:* Mohammad Ahmad. *Coach:* R. A. Pybus. *Bowling coach/consultant:* D. H. Foster. *Physiotherapist:* N. Walker. *Trainer:* D. Naylor.

PAKISTANI TOUR RESULTS

Test matches – Played 2: Won 1, Lost 1.
First-class matches – Played 6: Won 3, Lost 1, Drawn 2.
Wins – England, British Universities, Leicestershire.
Loss – England.
Draws – Derbyshire, Kent.
One-day internationals – Played 7: Won 4, Lost 2, No result 1. *Wins* – England (3), Australia. *Losses* – Australia (2). *No result* – Australia.
Other non-first-class match – Won v Leicestershire.

TEST MATCH AVERAGES

ENGLAND – BATTING

	T	*I*	*NO*	*R*	*HS*	*100s*	*50s*	*Avge*	*Ct*
G. P. Thorpe	2	3	0	228	138	1	1	76.00	5
M. P. Vaughan	2	3	0	166	120	1	0	55.33	2
M. E. Trescothick	2	3	0	163	117	1	0	54.33	2
A. J. Stewart	2	3	1	102	44	0	0	51.00	10
M. A. Atherton	2	3	0	98	51	0	1	32.66	6
I. J. Ward	2	3	0	61	39	0	0	20.33	1
D. Gough	2	3	1	28	23	0	0	14.00	0
D. G. Cork	2	3	0	31	25	0	0	10.33	1
A. R. Caddick	2	3	0	6	5	0	0	2.00	0

Played in one Test: M. J. Hoggard 0, 0*; N. Hussain 64; N. V. Knight 15, 0 (2 ct); R. J. Sidebottom 4.

* *Signifies not out.*

BOWLING

	O	*M*	*R*	*W*	*BB*	*5W/i*	*Avge*
D. Gough	78.3	13	280	14	5-61	1	20.00
A. R. Caddick	85	12	309	14	4-52	0	22.07
M. J. Hoggard	48	8	172	6	3-79	0	28.66
D. G. Cork	72.3	17	200	5	3-41	0	40.00

Also bowled: R. J. Sidebottom 20–2–64–0; M. E. Trescothick 5–1–16–0; M. P. Vaughan 3–0–33–0.

PAKISTAN – BATTING

	T	*I*	*NO*	*R*	*HS*	*100s*	*50s*	*Avge*	*Ct*
Inzamam-ul-Haq	2	4	0	232	114	1	1	58.00	1
Younis Khan	2	4	0	141	65	0	2	35.25	1
Rashid Latif	2	4	0	134	71	0	1	33.50	9
Wasim Akram	2	4	1	83	36	0	0	27.66	0
Abdur Razzaq	2	4	0	98	53	0	1	24.50	2
Azhar Mahmood	2	4	0	89	37	0	0	22.25	1
Yousuf Youhana	2	4	0	85	49	0	0	21.25	0
Saeed Anwar	2	4	0	61	29	0	0	15.25	1
Waqar Younis	2	4	1	40	21	0	0	13.33	0

Played in one Test: Faisal Iqbal 16, 14; Salim Elahi 0, 0; Saqlain Mushtaq 21*, 5; Shoaib Akhtar 0, 2*.

* *Signifies not out.*

BOWLING

	O	*M*	*R*	*W*	*BB*	*5W/i*	*Avge*
Azhar Mahmood	34	12	85	4	4-50	0	21.25
Saqlain Mushtaq	77.2	27	154	6	4-74	0	25.66
Abdur Razzaq	53	9	162	5	3-61	0	32.40
Waqar Younis	71.1	11	249	7	3-85	0	35.57
Wasim Akram	87	20	247	5	2-59	0	49.40

Also bowled: Shoaib Akhtar 19–4–64–1; Younis Khan 5–0–27–0.

PAKISTANI TOUR AVERAGES – FIRST-CLASS AVERAGES

BATTING

	M	*I*	*NO*	*R*	*HS*	*100s*	*50s*	*Avge*	*Ct/St*
Saeed Anwar	4	6	0	351	201	1	1	58.50	1
Salim Elahi	3	4	1	172	94*	0	2	57.33	1
Faisal Iqbal	4	4	0	178	83	0	2	44.50	0
Inzamam-ul-Haq	6	7	0	299	114	1	1	42.71	4
Azhar Mahmood	3	5	1	169	80*	0	1	42.25	1
Younis Khan	4	6	0	185	65	0	2	30.83	1
Rashid Latif	5	6	0	137	71	0	1	22.83	15/1
Abdur Razzaq	5	7	1	133	53	0	1	22.16	2
Yousuf Youhana	6	8	0	174	80	0	1	21.75	0
Waqar Younis	5	7	2	105	50*	0	1	21.00	1
Wasim Akram	5	6	1	93	36	0	0	18.60	2
Saqlain Mushtaq	4	4	1	33	21*	0	0	11.00	1
Shoaib Akhtar	3	4	2	19	16	0	0	9.50	1

Played in three matches: Mohammad Wasim 27, 15, 36 (2 ct); Mushtaq Ahmed 0, 0. Played in two matches: Mohammad Sami 15. Played in one match: Imran Farhat 46, 23* (2 ct).

* *Signifies not out.*

BOWLING

	O	M	R	W	BB	5W/i	Avge
Mushtaq Ahmed	69.2	18	176	14	8-49	1	12.57
Saqlain Mushtaq	156	48	334	19	6-34	1	17.57
Waqar Younis	119.1	23	399	18	5-23	1	22.16
Mohammad Sami	45	8	148	6	2-27	0	24.66
Wasim Akram	153	44	385	15	4-18	0	25.66
Abdur Razzaq	105.3	19	359	10	3-61	0	35.90

Also bowled: Azhar Mahmood 54–15–152–4; Faisal Iqbal 3–0–19–0; Imran Farhat 7–0–48–1; Mohammad Wasim 2–0–5–0; Shoaib Akhtar 55–9–174–3; Younis Khan 8–1–42–0.

Note: Matches in this section which were not first-class are signified by a dagger.

BRITISH UNIVERSITIES v PAKISTANIS

At Nottingham, May 4, 5. Pakistanis won by an innings and 87 runs. Toss: British Universities.

Batting first was not a good move for the Universities, captained by Pyemont after Yorkshire off-spinner Richard Dawson had broken his hand. Wasim Akram removed the Durham trio of Brown, Banes and Jefferson (playing no stroke) with his fourth, fifth and seventh deliveries, and later added Porter, his 1,000th first-class wicket; 64 for nine at lunch was akin to a recovery. In contrast, the tourists' experienced strokeplayers graced the afternoon, although Murtagh demonstrated, with late movement and clever changes of pace, how different the morning might have been had the students bowled first. Next day, he finished with six wickets, but not before the last pair, Waqar Younis and Mohammad Sami, had reversed a Pakistani collapse in which five wickets fell for six runs. Batting again, Jefferson and Brown put up 50 in ten overs before they, and those who followed, were bewitched by Mushtaq Ahmed's bag of tricks. Match figures of ten for 51 gave the leg-spinner and his team-mates a day off but were no guarantee of a Test place.

Close of play: First day, Pakistanis 224-4 (Salim Elahi 67*, Younis Khan 23*).

British Universities

M. J. Brown (*Durham*) b Wasim Akram	0	(2) c Wasim Akram b Mushtaq Ahmed	19
W. I. Jefferson (*Durham*) b Wasim Akram	5	(1) lbw b Mushtaq Ahmed	40
M. J. Banes (*Durham*) lbw b Wasim Akram	0	b Mushtaq Ahmed	19
*J. P. Pyemont (*Cambridge*) c sub b Waqar Younis	18	b Mushtaq Ahmed	4
J. J. Porter (*Oxford Brookes*) b Wasim Akram	14	lbw b Mushtaq Ahmed	10
J. W. M. Dalrymple (*Oxford*) c Mohammad Wasim b Mohammad Sami	3	lbw b Mushtaq Ahmed	0
†J. S. Foster (*Durham*) c Rashid Latif b Waqar Younis	0	c Waqar Younis b Mushtaq Ahmed	17
R. S. Ferley (*Durham*) c Wasim Akram b Waqar Younis	15	c sub b Mushtaq Ahmed	0
T. J. Murtagh (*St Mary's UC*) b Mushtaq Ahmed	0	not out	22
C. J. Elstub (*Leeds Metropolitan*) not out	6	b Mohammad Sami	0
M. A. Tournier (*Loughborough*) lbw b Mushtaq Ahmed	0	lbw b Mohammad Sami	13
B 5, l-b 3, w 2, n-b 3	13	B 1, l-b 3, w 3, n-b 4	11
1/0 2/0 3/5 4/30 5/38 6/48 7/53 8/56 9/64	74	1/51 2/71 3/78 4/100 5/100 6/107 7/113 8/124 9/125	155

Bowling: *First Innings*—Wasim Akram 11–5–18–4; Waqar Younis 9–2–30–3; Mohammad Sami 8–2–16–1; Mushtaq Ahmed 4.2–2–2–2. *Second Innings*—Wasim Akram 9–3–31–0; Waqar Younis 8–3–29–0; Mohammad Sami 14–6–27–2; Mushtaq Ahmed 24–10–49–8; Younis Khan 3–1–15–0.

Pakistanis

Saeed Anwar c Jefferson b Murtagh	89
Mohammad Wasim c Foster b Murtagh	27
Salim Elahi c Foster b Murtagh	78
Inzamam-ul-Haq b Murtagh	18
Yousuf Youhana c Foster b Murtagh	0
Younis Khan c Dalrymple b Elstub	32
†Rashid Latif b Ferley	2
Wasim Akram c Porter b Ferley	3
*Waqar Younis not out	50
Mushtaq Ahmed c Dalrymple b Elstub	0
Mohammad Sami c Jefferson b Murtagh	15
L-b 1, w 1	2
1/48 2/171 3/189 4/189 5/244 6/244 7/249 8/249 9/250	316

Bowling: Tournier 19–6–67–0; Elstub 17–4–65–2; Murtagh 22.5–3–86–6; Ferley 18–7–66–2; Dalrymple 9–2–31–0.

Umpires: J. H. Evans and V. A. Holder.

DERBYSHIRE v PAKISTANIS

At Derby, May 8, 9, 10. Drawn. Toss: Derbyshire. First-class debuts: C. W. G. Bassano, N. R. C. Dumelow.

Shoaib Akhtar, having arrived from Pakistan the previous day, bowled tentatively and did not appear ready for the next week's Test. While Derbyshire handled Saqlain Mushtaq better than at The Oval the previous August, when he took seven for 11 in their second innings, he still caused constant problems and polished off the tail with three wickets in seven balls. Nathan Dumelow, on first-class debut, took four wickets with his more orthodox off-spin before Azhar Mahmood's composed batting built on the lead in a last-wicket stand of 80 with Shoaib. Dowman celebrated his 27th birthday with a century of much charm. He had to work hard for two sessions but could be more expansive after tea, ending with two sixes and 20 fours as the match drifted away. Cork, playing at the selectors' request, satisfied them that he was fit enough to take up his England contract. A minor disturbance on the second day resulted in a group of Pakistan supporters being ejected.

Close of play: First day, Pakistanis 4-0 (Mohammad Wasim 1*, Imran Farhat 2*); Second day, Derbyshire 66-2 (Sutton 25*, Dowman 15*).

Derbyshire

L. D. Sutton c Imran Farhat b Saqlain Mushtaq	26	– (2) c Rashid Latif b Abdur Razzaq	34
S. D. Stubbings c Inzamam-ul-Haq b Waqar Younis	8	– (1) run out	15
S. P. Titchard b Abdur Razzaq	11	– b Waqar Younis	0
M. P. Dowman b Shoaib Akhtar	36	– not out	145
C. W. G. Bassano lbw b Shoaib Akhtar	17	– lbw b Waqar Younis	13
*D. G. Cork lbw b Saqlain Mushtaq	27	– lbw b Imran Farhat	15
†K. M. Krikken c Rashid Latif b Saqlain Mushtaq	0	– not out	10
N. R. C. Dumelow c Imran Farhat b Saqlain Mushtaq	6		
T. M. Smith not out	14		
T. Lungley b Saqlain Mushtaq	0		
L. J. Wharton lbw b Saqlain Mushtaq	0		
B 5, l-b 10, n-b 6	21	B 2, l-b 7, n-b 6	15
1/17 2/44 3/61 4/102 5/107 6/114 7/131 8/158 9/158	166	1/25 2/25 3/111 4/164 5/189 (5 wkts dec.)	247

Bowling: *First Innings*—Waqar Younis 7–1–25–1; Shoaib Akhtar 12–0–31–2; Abdur Razzaq 11–2–36–1; Azhar Mahmood 7–1–21–0; Saqlain Mushtaq 21.1–9–34–6; Imran Farhat 1–0–4–0. *Second Innings*—Waqar Younis 12–4–33–2; Shoaib Akhtar 11–2–31–0; Saqlain Mushtaq 14.2–2–35–0; Azhar Mahmood 13–2–46–0; Abdur Razzaq 11–4–25–1; Imran Farhat 6–0–44–1; Mohammad Wasim 2–0–5–0; Faisal Iqbal 3–0–19–0.

Pakistanis

Mohammad Wasim b Smith	15		
Imran Farhat c Bassano b Dumelow	46	– not out	23
Faisal Iqbal c Cork b Smith	65		
Yousuf Youhana c Stubbings b Dumelow	5	– (1) lbw b Smith	4
Inzamam-ul-Haq c and b Dumelow	13		
Abdur Razzaq b Dumelow	0	– (3) not out	34
†Rashid Latif b Smith	1		
Azhar Mahmood not out	80		
*Waqar Younis c Stubbings b Lungley	7		
Saqlain Mushtaq lbw b Lungley	0		
Shoaib Akhtar c Cork b Lungley	16		
L-b 3, w 7, n-b 4	14	L-b 1, n-b 1	2
1/28 2/101 3/113 4/142 5/142 6/153 7/154 8/172 9/182	262	1/5	(1 wkt) 63

Bowling: *First Innings*—Cork 16–4–34–0; Smith 16–3–50–3; Wharton 9–2–36–0; Lungley 15.3–1–58–3; Dumelow 22–4–81–4. *Second Innings*—Cork 5–2–10–0; Smith 5–1–14–1; Lungley 3–1–20–0; Dumelow 5–2–10–0; Wharton 2–0–8–0.

Umpires: A. Clarkson and P. Willey.

KENT v PAKISTANIS

At Canterbury, May 12, 13, 14. Drawn. Toss: Pakistanis. First-class debut: A. Khan.

Rain washed out the last day and the prospect of Kent setting the Pakistanis a challenging target in their final game before Lord's. By putting Kent in, they had wasted the chance of valuable batting practice, even if Mohammad Sami's two quick wickets momentarily made it look a good decision. Key and Walker then put on 207 in 53 overs, with Key hitting his second hundred of the season, off 194 balls including 16 fours, and Walker going close to his third before playing on to Saqlain Mushtaq via his elbow. On the second day, Saeed Anwar and Salim Elahi produced a batting masterclass against an inexperienced attack. Their 307 was the highest partnership by any touring side for any wicket against Kent. Acting-captain Patel conceded five sixes towards Anwar's third double-hundred – his second in England – which came in 278 minutes and 230 balls and also contained 27 fours. His wicket gave Amjad Khan a memorable scalp on first-class debut, and the young Danish-born seam bowler also benefited from a net session with Waqar Younis.

Close of play: First day, Pakistanis 41-0 (Saeed Anwar 32*, Salim Elahi 4*); Second day, Kent 94-3 (Hockley 6*).

Kent

D. P. Fulton c Salim Elahi b Mohammad Sami	3	– c Rashid Latif b Abdur Razzaq	40
R. W. T. Key c Inzamam-ul-Haq b Wasim Akram	119	– c Rashid Latif b Mohammad Sami	21
E. T. Smith b Mohammad Sami	0	– st Rashid Latif b Saqlain Mushtaq	17
M. J. Walker b Saqlain Mushtaq	98		
J. B. Hockley c Rashid Latif b Saqlain Mushtaq	0	– (4) not out	6
†P. A. Nixon not out	42		
J. M. Golding not out	21		
L-b 4, w 4, n-b 22	30	L-b 2, w 6, n-b 2	10
1/9 2/9 3/216 4/217 5/250	(5 wkts dec.) 313	1/58 2/77 3/94	(3 wkts) 94

M. J. McCague, *M. M. Patel, A. Khan and B. J. Trott did not bat.

Bowling: *First Innings*—Wasim Akram 18–5–34–1; Mohammad Sami 14–0–74–2; Abdur Razzaq 14–2–59–0; Mushtaq Ahmed 18–1–74–0; Saqlain Mushtaq 21–2–68–2. *Second Innings*—Wasim Akram 10–1–31–0; Mohammad Sami 9–0–31–1; Mushtaq Ahmed 8–2–10–0; Abdur Razzaq 5–1–14–1; Saqlain Mushtaq 3.4–1–6–1.

Pakistanis

Saeed Anwar c Golding b Khan	201
Salim Elahi not out	94
L-b 7, n-b 5	12
1/307 (1 wkt dec.)	307

Abdur Razzaq, *Inzamam-ul-Haq, Yousuf Youhana, Faisal Iqbal, Wasim Akram, †Rashid Latif, Saqlain Mushtaq, Mushtaq Ahmed and Mohammad Sami did not bat.

Bowling: Khan 8.2–2–46–1; Trott 20–4–66–0; McCague 9–2–35–0; Patel 14–0–83–0; Golding 12–2–32–0; Hockley 7–0–38–0.

Umpires: R. Palmer and D. R. Shepherd.

ENGLAND v PAKISTAN

First npower Test

At Lord's, May 17, 18, 19, 20. England won by an innings and nine runs. Toss: Pakistan. Test debuts: R. J. Sidebottom, I. J. Ward.

Sustained inaccuracy and total breakdown on Saturday afternoon from usually reliable Lord's performers marred this match. Clearly, it was time for MCC's electronic scoreboards to be centrally contracted. Gough and Caddick, who between them took 16 for 207, were persuasive advocates for the virtues of being fresh for the big occasion. This was the 12th time in their 24 Tests together that England had won, a testament to their combined potency and a record that, temporarily at least, compared favourably with Trueman and Statham (13 from 35). They were ably supported by assured close catching, notably from Thorpe, while a solid all-round batting effort gave the new-ball duo the platform they required.

As usual, fortune favoured the victors. Law 13 certainly proved unlucky for Pakistan when, after Thursday's total washout, the follow-on lead was reduced from 200 runs to 150; as it was, they struggled to close the gap to 188. Overcast skies had encouraged Waqar Younis to bowl first, and the England openers received some testing overs from him and Wasim Akram that they did well to survive. Contrastingly, Shoaib Akhtar, playing his first Test in more than a year after injuries and investigations into his action, looked short of match fitness. Abdur Razzaq made the initial breakthrough, but it was Azhar Mahmood, the sixth bowler used, who stood out. Bowling from close to the stumps, he pitched the ball up, giving it every chance to swing and seam around the batsmen's off stump; his whippy action meant he was just quick enough not to be hit off his good length.

Vaughan, promoted to No. 3 ahead of Hussain, struck 26 elegant runs in boundaries before Mahmood "strangled" him down the leg side. And when the same bowler ended Atherton's 200th Test innings, bowling him between bat and pad for 42, England were 114 for three. Then came the stand of the match, a mixture of attack and attrition. Thorpe did most of the former, Hussain the latter, and, as they added 132 in 46 overs, Pakistan had cause to regret following England's example in omitting a specialist spinner. Thorpe moved serenely to 50 for the 36th time in Tests but, frustratingly, there was no ninth hundred.

His exit brought in Ryan Sidebottom, making his debut only because of back injuries to Yorkshire colleagues White and Hoggard. He and his father, Arnie, were the tenth such pairing to play for England but, with his corn-dolly locks tumbling from under his helmet, hair rather than heredity informed most discussion of the night-watchman. More importantly, he saw out the day. Even better for England was that Hussain was still there, too, his near-four-hour vigil yielding a gutsy 53 not out. But their progress was checked the following morning when Shoaib fractured the captain's right thumb. Next over, clearly in pain, he was caught behind off Mahmood for 64. Two years earlier

THE ENGLAND SQUAD FOR THE LORD'S TEST

[*Patrick Eagar*

Back row: R. D. B. Croft, M. J. Hoggard, A. F. Giles, M. P. Vaughan, R. J. Sidebottom, C. White, I. J. Ward. *Middle row:* D. O. Conway (*physiotherapist*), R. M. H. Cottam (*assistant coach*), D. G. Cork, A. R. Caddick, M. E. Trescothick, N. P. Stockill (*physiologist*), P. A. Neale (*manager*). *Front row:* D. Gough, M. A. Atherton, N. Hussain (*captain*), D. A. G. Fletcher (*coach*), A. J. Stewart, G. P. Thorpe.

[*Patrick Eagar*

No flying stumps, but Rashid Latif's leg-side flick to keeper Alec Stewart suits Darren Gough just as well: Test wicket 200 is in the bank. Taking out the tail soon after gave him his first, much cherished, five-wicket return at Lord's.

at Lord's, he broke his right middle finger while fielding against New Zealand, and in June 2000 he broke his left thumb fielding for Essex.

Few England batsmen have enjoyed the luxury of playing their first innings with more than 300 on the board. Even so, Ian Ward was admirably serene. Only the arrival of No. 11 Gough prompted rashness, rather as the appearance of Gough's fast-bowling partner, Caddick, prompted indiscretion from Pakistan's top order. Striding in from the Nursery End so the Lord's slope complemented his out-swing, he struck with his third ball, Salim Elahi edging to first slip for a duck. Fellow-opener Saeed Anwar followed soon afterwards, also well taken by Atherton, this time off Gough. When Caddick had Inzamam-ul-Haq and Razzaq caught behind, Pakistan were 60 for four in 18 overs. But without White, the gap between the strike bowlers and the support looked worryingly wide. Left-armer Sidebottom bowled as if conscious that, like his father, this might be his only Test, while Cork frequently pitched too short.

Pakistan lost Yousuf Youhana first thing on Sunday morning, but Younis Khan, severe on anything short and seizing on anything overpitched, remained defiant. His fifty came from 78 balls, including eight fours; one, straight-driven off Caddick, was as good as any shot in the match. It was a surprise to see him misjudge a rare good-length ball from Cork, and with him went Pakistan's chance of avoiding the follow-on. Gough mopped up the tail in four balls either side of lunch, becoming in his 50th Test the eighth England bowler to take 200 Test wickets when he dismissed Rashid Latif; his five for 61 gave him the place on the Lord's honours board that he craved even more.

An excited crowd was lifted further when Thorpe, diving full length to his right at third slip, took a superlative one-handed catch off Caddick's fifth ball to dismiss the luckless Elahi for a pair. Despite the disappointment of three near dismissals, Caddick never flagged and deservedly claimed the match award after twice routing the top order. Only Razzaq showed any inclination to hit back. Wasim and Waqar, in what seemed certain to be their last Lord's Test, tried to resist but were powerless. When Cork finished the match by dismissing Waqar, England had taken 16 wickets in the day. Their overall performance – their first innings victory over Pakistan since Ian Botham's one-man show at Lord's 23 years earlier – was worthy of their 100th Test here and the first of the new World Test Championship. On the debit side, Thursday's abandonment had cost £400,000 in ticket refunds, and yet again revenue was lost from the lack of a fifth day. Wise heads agreed that things could not go on like this, but, dared their supporters hope, could England? – JULIAN GUYER.

Man of the Match: A. R. Caddick. *Attendance:* 80,559; *receipts* £1,661,047.

Close of play: First day, No play; Second day, England 254-4 (Hussain 53*, Sidebottom 4*); Third day, Pakistan 115-4 (Yousuf Youhana 26*, Younis Khan 32*).

England

M. A. Atherton b Azhar Mahmood	42
M. E. Trescothick c Azhar Mahmood b Abdur Razzaq	36
M. P. Vaughan c Rashid Latif b Azhar Mahmood	32
*N. Hussain c Rashid Latif b Azhar Mahmood	64
G. P. Thorpe c Abdur Razzaq b Waqar Younis	80
R. J. Sidebottom c Inzamam-ul-Haq b Wasim Akram	4
†A. J. Stewart lbw b Shoaib Akhtar	44
I. J. Ward c Abdur Razzaq b Waqar Younis	39
D. G. Cork c Younis Khan b Wasim Akram	25
A. R. Caddick b Azhar Mahmood	5
D. Gough not out	5
B 1, l-b 5, w 1, n-b 8	15
1/60 (2) 2/105 (3) 3/114 (1) 4/246 (5) 5/254 (6) 6/307 (4) 7/317 (7) 8/365 (9) 9/385 (10) 10/391 (8)	391

Bowling: Wasim Akram 34–9–99–2; Waqar Younis 25–5–77–2; Shoaib Akhtar 19–4–64–1; Abdur Razzaq 21–2–68–1; Younis Khan 5–0–27–0; Azhar Mahmood 26–12–50–4.

Pakistan

Saeed Anwar c Atherton b Gough	12	– c Thorpe b Caddick	8
Salim Elahi c Atherton b Caddick	0	– c Thorpe b Caddick	0
Abdur Razzaq c Stewart b Caddick	22	– c Atherton b Caddick	53
Inzamam-ul-Haq c Stewart b Caddick	13	– c Stewart b Cork	20
Yousuf Youhana lbw b Gough	26	– c Vaughan b Gough	6
Younis Khan b Cork	58	– lbw b Cork	1
Azhar Mahmood c Trescothick b Caddick	14	– c Stewart b Caddick	24
†Rashid Latif c Stewart b Gough	18	– c Stewart b Gough	20
Wasim Akram not out	19	– c Thorpe b Gough	12
*Waqar Younis c Thorpe b Gough	0	– c Stewart b Cork	21
Shoaib Akhtar b Gough	0	– not out	2
B 1, l-b 7, n-b 13	21	L-b 6, n-b 6	12
1/4 (2) 2/21 (1) 3/37 (4) 4/60 (3) 5/116 (5) 6/153 (7) 7/167 (6) 8/203 (8) 9/203 (10) 10/203 (11)	203	1/2 (2) 2/30 (1) 3/67 (4) 4/84 (5) 5/87 (6) 6/121 (3) 7/122 (7) 8/147 (9) 9/167 (8) 10/179 (10)	179

Bowling: *First Innings*—Gough 16–5–61–5; Caddick 17–3–52–4; Sidebottom 11–0–38–0; Cork 11–3–42–1; Trescothick 2–1–2–0. *Second Innings*—Gough 16–4–40–3; Caddick 18–3–54–4; Sidebottom 9–2–26–0; Cork 15.3–3–41–3; Vaughan 1–0–12–0.

Umpires: D. B. Hair (Australia) and P. Willey.
Third umpire: B. Dudleston. Referee: B. F. Hastings (New Zealand).

†LEICESTERSHIRE v PAKISTANIS

At Leicester, May 23. Pakistanis won by seven wickets. Toss: Leicestershire.

Salim Elahi put his Lord's pair behind him with a fluent century off 114 balls that enabled the tourists to cruise home with seven overs to spare. Smith, captaining the county, had revived his side after the top order was blown away in Shoaib Akhtar's opening overs. He shared stands of 65 and 108 with Maddy and Sutcliffe, and his 105 from 116 balls contained 12 fours, some hit straight with real authority. Even so, Elahi shaded him and, as he added 112 in 19 overs with Yousuf Youhana, under-strength Leicestershire were bereft of options.

Leicestershire

J. M. Dakin b Shoaib Akhtar	0
D. I. Stevens c and b Shoaib Akhtar	9
T. R. Ward lbw b Shoaib Akhtar	8
*B. F. Smith c Imran Farhat b Saqlain Mushtaq	105
D. L. Maddy lbw b Mushtaq Ahmed	40
I. J. Sutcliffe b Shoaib Akhtar	46
A. S. Wright c Salim Elahi b Saqlain Mushtaq	3
C. D. Crowe not out	7
†S. J. Adshead not out	2
L-b 2, w 3	5
1/0 2/18 3/30 4/95 5/203 6/215 7/215 (7 wkts, 50 overs)	225

S. A. J. Boswell and M. J. A. Whiley did not bat.

Bowling: Shoaib Akhtar 10–1–37–4; Azhar Mahmood 10–3–29–0; Saqlain Mushtaq 10–0–47–2; Mushtaq Ahmed 10–0–47–1; Imran Farhat 8–0–45–0; Younis Khan 1–0–6–0; Mohammad Wasim 1–0–12–0.

Pakistanis

Imran Farhat c Adshead b Whiley	7
Salim Elahi not out	108
Faisal Iqbal c Wright b Dakin	26
Yousuf Youhana c Smith b Stevens	40
Younis Khan not out	15
B 2, l-b 5, w 22, n-b 3	32
1/8 2/94 3/206 (3 wkts, 42.4 overs)	228

Azhar Mahmood, *†Rashid Latif, Mushtaq Ahmed, Mohammad Wasim, Saqlain Mushtaq and Shoaib Akhtar did not bat.

Bowling: Boswell 7–0–26–0; Whiley 10–0–68–1; Dakin 6–1–27–1; Maddy 5–0–19–0; Crowe 10–0–41–0; Stevens 4.4–0–40–1.

Umpires: M. J. Kitchen and A. G. T. Whitehead.

LEICESTERSHIRE v PAKISTANIS

At Leicester, May 24, 25. Pakistanis won by an innings and 26 runs. Toss: Leicestershire. First-class debut: A. S. Wright. County debut: O. A. C. Banks.

Scheduled for four days, the match was over in two as the tourists' pace and spin had Leicestershire in complete disarray. First, after Smith had elected to bat on a good-looking pitch, Wasim Akram and Waqar Younis bowled them out for just 96: Wasim took the first four, starting with his second ball, and when Waqar replaced Shoaib Akhtar he saw off Burns, DeFreitas and Leewards all-rounder Omari Banks with a hat-trick in his second over. Only Sutcliffe, batting through the innings for 55, offered any resistance. The tourists then gained a lead of 198, despite losing their last six wickets for 49 to the county's second-string attack. Maddy again failed to survive Wasim's opening over, but this time Ashley Wright stayed with Sutcliffe to put on 71. After tea, Saqlain Mushtaq and Mushtaq Ahmed picked off the remaining eight wickets for 84 in 24 overs.

Close of play: First day, Pakistanis 201-3 (Faisal Iqbal 81*, Yousuf Youhana 38*).

Leicestershire

D. L. Maddy lbw b Wasim Akram	0	– lbw b Wasim Akram	0
I. J. Sutcliffe c Shoaib Akhtar b Abdur Razzaq	55	– b Saqlain Mushtaq	38
A. S. Wright b Wasim Akram	0	– c Inzamam-ul-Haq b Abdur Razzaq	30
D. I. Stevens lbw b Wasim Akram	17	– b Saqlain Mushtaq	24
*B. F. Smith c Saqlain Mushtaq b Wasim Akram	7	– lbw b Saqlain Mushtaq	18
†N. D. Burns lbw b Waqar Younis	0	– not out	28
P. A. J. DeFreitas b Waqar Younis	0	– lbw b Mushtaq Ahmed	1
O. A. C. Banks b Waqar Younis	0	– lbw b Mushtaq Ahmed	4
C. D. Crowe lbw b Waqar Younis	2	– c Mohammad Wasim b Mushtaq Ahmed	0
S. A. J. Boswell b Waqar Younis	4	– b Mushtaq Ahmed	0
P. Griffiths not out	4	– lbw b Saqlain Mushtaq	1
N-b 7	7	B 16, l-b 6, n-b 6	28
1/0 2/0 3/24 4/40 5/41 6/41 7/41 8/70 9/92	96	1/0 2/71 3/88 4/118 5/134 6/141 7/161 8/163 9/171	172

Bowling: *First Innings*—Wasim Akram 12–6–19–4; Shoaib Akhtar 7–1–28–0; Waqar Younis 9–1–23–5; Abdur Razzaq 4.3–0–26–1. *Second Innings*—Wasim Akram 6–4–5–1; Shoaib Akhtar 6–2–20–0; Abdur Razzaq 7–1–37–1; Waqar Younis 3–1–10–0; Saqlain Mushtaq 18.3–7–37–4; Mushtaq Ahmed 15–3–41–4.

Pakistanis

†Mohammad Wasim lbw b Maddy	36
Abdur Razzaq c and b Boswell	1
Faisal Iqbal lbw b Griffiths	83
Inzamam-ul-Haq b Crowe	36
Yousuf Youhana c Crowe b Boswell	80
Younis Khan c Boswell b Maddy	12
Wasim Akram lbw b Griffiths	7
*Waqar Younis c Burns b Boswell	8
Saqlain Mushtaq lbw b DeFreitas	7
Mushtaq Ahmed b DeFreitas	0
Shoaib Akhtar not out	1
L-b 13, w 1, n-b 9	23
1/8 2/57 3/127 4/215 5/245 6/261 7/272 8/292 9/292	294

Bowling: Boswell 28.3–5–87–3; Griffiths 20–7–51–2; DeFreitas 18–4–41–2; Maddy 13–4–27–2; Crowe 10–0–34–1; Banks 9–0–38–0; Sutcliffe 1–0–3–0.

Umpires: M. J. Harris and N. J. Llong.

ENGLAND v PAKISTAN

Second npower Test

At Manchester, May 31, June 1, 2, 3, 4. Pakistan won by 108 runs. Toss: Pakistan.

This was Test cricket at its twisting, turning best. At tea on the last day, England were 196 for two and on course for the draw that would have brought them a fifth consecutive series win for the first time in 30 years. But eight wickets fell in a frantic, fractious final session, sparking scenes of jubilation from Pakistan's horn-blowing, flag-waving fans. Four batsmen were dismissed by no-balls which, amid the flurry of appeals, the umpires failed to spot. This was bad luck for England, but it couldn't detract from the truth: the better side had won, extending England's dismal record at Old Trafford to a solitary victory since 1981.

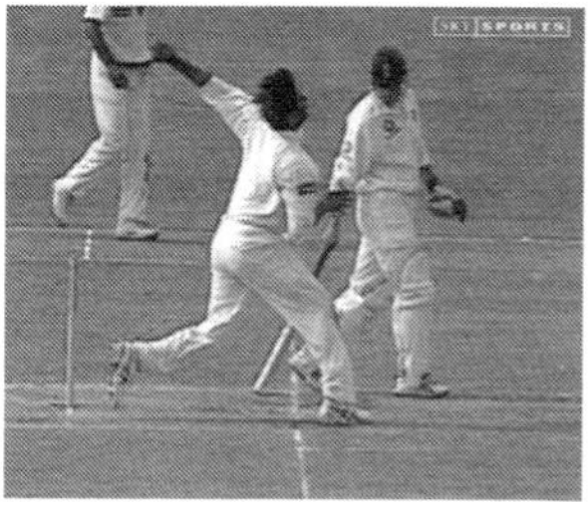

[*Sky Sports*

The TV talking point that turned England's summer. Caught by the camera, unnoticed by the umpire's eye, Wasim Akram (*left*) and Saqlain Mushtaq were both over the mark when they dismissed Nick Knight and Ian Ward on the last day. England not only lost the Test; they rediscovered a losing habit.

The star of the show was Inzamam-ul-Haq, who came within 15 runs of emulating Steve Waugh's twin hundreds here in 1997 as he toyed with the bowlers like a cuddly lion pawing a mouse. He inspired Pakistan on the opening day, first keeping his head above water while the ship threatened to go down, then powering full steam ahead to leave England floundering; he averted another mini-crisis in the second innings; and he moved into third place on Pakistan's all-time run-list, ahead of Zaheer Abbas.

England weren't helped by Hussain's absence. The captaincy passed to Stewart, and Knight came into the middle order; in the only other change from Lord's, Hoggard – winning his second cap almost a year after his first – replaced fellow-Yorkshireman Sidebottom. Pakistan, who warmed up for the game with a trip to Blackpool's pleasure beach, brought in off-spinner Saqlain Mushtaq for Shoaib Akhtar, and Faisal Iqbal for Salim Elahi.

Under heaving skies, the match got off to a breathless start. Caddick reduced Pakistan to 92 for four, only for Inzamam, caught behind off a Cork no-ball on 31, to throw his weight around. England's bowlers were hindered by a strong wind, but that only partly explained the long-hops and leg-stump half-volleys now served up. Inzamam greedily tucked in, working anything on his stumps through mid-wicket and biffing the short stuff over square leg *en route* to his 14th Test century. He added 141 for the fifth wicket with Younis Khan – an aesthetic mixture of subcontinental wrists and MCC left elbow – before Hoggard trapped Younis leg-before on the stroke of tea. When Inzamam slashed Hoggard to gully, England sensed an opening. Rashid Latif had other ideas. Stealing singles and whipping balls off his pads with panache, he helped the score to 370 for eight by the close. Not since 1992, when Pakistan themselves hit 388 for three, also at Old Trafford, had any side scored so heavily on the opening day of a Test in England.

England wrapped up the innings next morning for 403, Latif reaching a Test-best 71, but lost both openers at 15. Now Thorpe and Vaughan embarked on the most thrilling partnership by two English batsmen since Thorpe himself and Hussain slew Australia at Edgbaston in 1997. In the form of his life, Thorpe cut with great certainty, while Vaughan was masterful off front and back foot, especially through the off. Early on the third morning, Thorpe moved to his ninth Test hundred, and Vaughan followed him to his first – getting there in bizarre fashion with a six that included four overthrows.

The game now turned on its head. Having equalled his Test-best 138, Thorpe hustled for one single too many and was beaten by Wasim's athleticism to end a record all-wicket partnership for England against Pakistan (267). When Vaughan gloved Waqar Younis down the leg side five balls later, the floodgates opened. Ward was caught red-handed trying to pinch a second run after a misfield, Knight nibbled at an out-swinger, and then Cork flapped feebly to mid-off to begin a procession of four wickets in four overs. Stewart was left unbeaten on 39 after failing to protect the tail.

Pakistan led by 46, but lost three for 63 and again turned to Inzamam for salvation. Dropped at second slip on 36 – Knight's third miss of the match – Inzamam shared in another stand of 141, this time with Yousuf Youhana. They fell in consecutive overs, Youhana given out caught at slip off the peak of his helmet, but England again failed to run through the lower order and were left with a target of 370 in 112 overs. Atherton and Trescothick gave them a rollicking start and reduced the equation to 285 off 90 overs by stumps. A nation speculated excitedly.

On the final morning, England made a cautious 64 runs for the loss of Atherton, bowled through the gate after his fourth century opening stand with Trescothick. But straight after lunch they were outmanoeuvred. Saqlain – the key player on a pitch now providing turn and bounce – bowled into the rough outside Trescothick's leg stump; in ten overs England managed just ten runs. Having bored them out of the game, Waqar could now attack at leisure. Trescothick reached his second Test century, Vaughan fell soon after, and at tea England, with eight wickets in hand, needed 174 off 32 overs.

A draw looked on the cards, but the second new ball triggered another England collapse. Waqar skittled Thorpe, Trescothick touched a leg-side bouncer from Wasim, and Stewart padded up to a straight one from the tireless Saqlain. Then the controversy began. Wasim trapped Knight with a huge no-ball that went uncalled by umpire Nicholls, and with successive deliveries Saqlain had Ward caught behind cutting and Caddick dumbfounded by the "doosra". On both occasions, he had overstepped; more to the point, England had lost four for one in 13 balls. Cork and Gough dug in, but with barely seven overs left Cork fell to yet another Saqlain no-ball. Gough slashed to point next over and the Pakistani fans rushed on to the pitch. They could hardly believe their luck; nor could the Australians, watching in London on television. – LAWRENCE BOOTH.

Man of the Match: Inzamam-ul-Haq. *Attendance:* 63,502; *receipts* £644,795.

Men of the Series: England – G. P. Thorpe; Pakistan – Inzamam-ul-Haq.

Close of play: First day, Pakistan 370-8 (Rashid Latif 64*, Saqlain Mushtaq 2*); Second day, England 204-2 (Vaughan 84*, Thorpe 98*); Third day, Pakistan 87-3 (Inzamam-ul-Haq 25*, Yousuf Youhana 3*); Fourth day, England 85-0 (Atherton 30*, Trescothick 47*).

Pakistan

Saeed Anwar c Atherton b Caddick	29	– c Thorpe b Gough	12
Abdur Razzaq b Caddick	1	– c Cork b Hoggard	22
Faisal Iqbal c Vaughan b Gough	16	– c Stewart b Caddick	14
Inzamam-ul-Haq c Ward b Hoggard	114	– c Trescothick b Hoggard	85
Yousuf Youhana c Knight b Caddick	4	– c Atherton b Caddick	49
Younis Khan lbw b Hoggard	65	– lbw b Cork	17
Azhar Mahmood c Knight b Hoggard	37	– b Caddick	14
†Rashid Latif run out	71	– c Atherton b Hoggard	25
Wasim Akram c Stewart b Gough	16	– b Gough	36
Saqlain Mushtaq not out	21	– c Stewart b Gough	5
*Waqar Younis lbw b Gough	5	– not out	14
L-b 9, n-b 15	24	L-b 11, n-b 19	30
1/6 (2) 2/39 (3) 3/86 (1) 4/92 (5) 5/233 (6) 6/255 (4) 7/308 (7) 8/357 (9) 9/380 (8) 10/403 (11)	403	1/24 (1) 2/41 (2) 3/63 (3) 4/204 (4) 5/208 (5) 6/232 (6) 7/241 (7) 8/300 (8) 9/306 (9) 10/323 (10)	323

Bowling: *First Innings*—Gough 23.4–2–94–3; Caddick 28–2–111–3; Hoggard 19–4–79–3; Cork 21–2–75–0; Trescothick 3–0–14–0; Vaughan 2–0–21–0. *Second Innings*—Gough 22.5–2–85–3; Caddick 22–4–92–3; Hoggard 29–4–93–3; Cork 25–9–42–1.

England

M. A. Atherton c Rashid Latif b Waqar Younis	5	– b Waqar Younis	51
M. E. Trescothick b Wasim Akram	10	– c Rashid Latif b Wasim Akram	117
M. P. Vaughan c Rashid Latif b Waqar Younis	120	– c Rashid Latif b Abdur Razzaq	14
G. P. Thorpe run out	138	– b Waqar Younis	10
*†A. J. Stewart not out	39	– lbw b Saqlain Mushtaq	19
I. J. Ward run out	12	– c Rashid Latif b Saqlain Mushtaq	10
N. V. Knight c Rashid Latif b Abdur Razzaq	15	– lbw b Wasim Akram	0
D. G. Cork c Saeed Anwar b Abdur Razzaq	2	– lbw b Saqlain Mushtaq	4
A. R. Caddick c Rashid Latif b Saqlain Mushtaq	1	– b Saqlain Mushtaq	0
D. Gough b Abdur Razzaq	0	– c sub (Imran Nazir) b Waqar Younis	23
M. J. Hoggard b Saqlain Mushtaq	0	– not out	0
L-b 5, w 2, n-b 8	15	B 6, l-b 4, w 1, n-b 2	13
1/15 (2) 2/15 (1) 3/282 (4) 4/283 (3) 5/309 (6) 6/348 (7) 7/353 (8) 8/354 (9) 9/356 (10) 10/357 (11)	357	1/146 (1) 2/174 (3) 3/201 (4) 4/213 (2) 5/229 (5) 6/230 (7) 7/230 (6) 8/230 (9) 9/261 (8) 10/261 (10)	261

Bowling: *First Innings*—Wasim Akram 30–7–89–1; Waqar Younis 24–3–87–2; Azhar Mahmood 8–0–35–0; Saqlain Mushtaq 30.2–7–80–2; Abdur Razzaq 19–2–61–3. *Second Innings*—Wasim Akram 23–4–59–2; Waqar Younis 22.1–3–85–3; Saqlain Mushtaq 47–20–74–4; Abdur Razzaq 13–5–33–1.

Umpires: E. A. Nicholls (West Indies) and D. R. Shepherd.
Third umpire: R. Julian. Referee: B. F. Hastings (New Zealand).

Pakistan's matches v England and Australia in the NatWest Series (June 7–23) may be found in that section.

VODAFONE ENGLAND PLAYER OF THE YEAR AWARDS

The Vodafone England Cricketer of the Year Award was won in May 2001 by Darren Gough of Yorkshire. He received £15,000 at a dinner, during which players, officials and journalists voted Graham Thorpe's unbeaten 113 and 32 in the Third Test against Sri Lanka, at Colombo in March 2001, the Vodafone Outstanding Individual Performance of the Year. The award for the Outstanding Individual Performance for England Women went to Clare Taylor, for her figures of three for 30 against Australia in the World Cup at Lincoln, New Zealand in December 2000. Thorpe and Taylor received £5,000 each.

THE AUSTRALIANS IN ENGLAND, 2001

Review by DAVID FRITH

Seldom has such high expectation before an Ashes series ended in such summary demolition. Peter May's 1958-59 England team, which had a truly formidable look about it, was crushed 4–0 by Richie Benaud's eager combination, yet it was 63 days into the series before the Ashes were relinquished. In 2001, with its compressed schedule (five Tests within 54 days), Steve Waugh's Australians made sure of retention in only 31, framing a mere 11 days of combat; Benaud's needed 22. After emphatic defeat in seven successive Ashes series, will deflated England ever be equipped to challenge the Baggy Green brigade seriously? Contrariwise, will Australia be capable of introducing reliable talent after the likes of the Waughs, Glenn McGrath and even Shane Warne (whom Heaven protect) are gone? This side's average age was 30, Australia's ripest since 1948.

They arrived in England as outstanding favourites, notwithstanding their reversals at Kolkata and Chennai and the revival in England's performances under Nasser Hussain and coach Duncan Fletcher. England had crushed Zimbabwe and West Indies the previous summer, and their winter tour had returned notable successes in Pakistan and Sri Lanka. They had then won at Lord's against Pakistan, before slipping up at Old Trafford. At the outset, Steve Waugh knew England were stronger than in recent years, and acknowledged that forecasting was fraught with difficulties. But he did add ominously, "If we can get on top early, we can open up some old scars."

English optimists felt that the rubber might be decided by whoever benefited more from the luck that forever swirls about cricket. The toss, the weather, injuries, umpiring errors? As it transpired, these factors nearly all went against England from the start, the most serious being the absence through injury of three first-choice batsmen in Graham Thorpe (for four Tests), captain Hussain (two) and Michael Vaughan (all five), as well as left-arm spinner Ashley Giles (four). When this ill-fortune was overtaken by some dismal cricket from England, particularly the inept catching at Lord's, the outcome was inescapable.

It remained for us to try to assess whether we had been watching the best cricket team of all time. Wasted though the exercise may be, the man in the traffic jam or the halted railway carriage was eager for debate about the relative qualities of the 1902, 1921, 1948 and 1975 Australians, the 1950s England sides, South Africa 1969-70, the West Indies combination of 1984.

None of these teams had thought to start a tour with a side-trip deep into emotional territory, as Steve Waugh and his men did by their visit to Gallipoli, the battleground where thousands of Anzacs (many British-born, let it be remembered) fought a hopeless contest in 1915 against the Turks. Unself-consciously, the cricketers donned Diggers' slouch hats, and acknowledged how deeply touching and inspirational the excursion had been. Days later, they were singing *Waltzing Matilda* with gusto and surprising euphony on stage at an official Australia House reception, where Waugh spoke of his desire for the team not to be one-dimensional but, instead, men whose

THE AUSTRALIAN TOURING PARTY

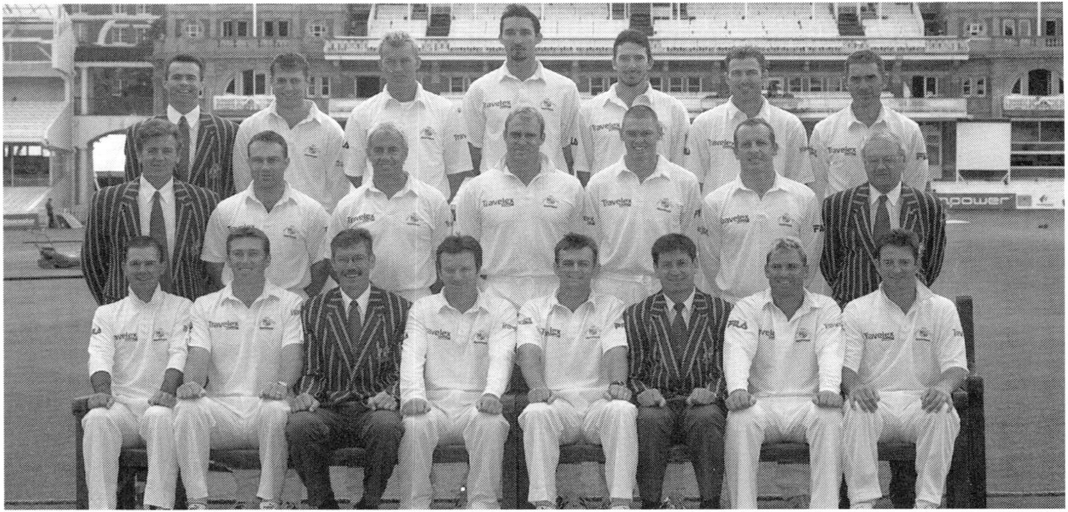

[*Craig Prentis, Getty Images*

Back row: J. A. Campbell (*physical performance manager*), S. M. Katich, B. Lee, J. N. Gillespie, D. W. Fleming, D. R. Martyn, J. L. Langer. *Middle row:* E. L. Alcott (*physiotherapist*), M. J. Slater, C. R. Miller, M. L. Hayden, A. A. Noffke, W. A. Seccombe, M. K. Walsh (*video analyst/assistant manager*). *Front row:* R. T. Ponting, G. D. McGrath, J. M. Buchanan (*coach*), S. R. Waugh (*captain*), A. C. Gilchrist (*vice-captain*), S. R. Bernard (*team manager*), S. K. Warne, M. E. Waugh.

understanding of real war broadened their vision, enhanced them as people, bonded them and toughened them. Waugh was to become a walking – or limping – materialisation of all this when he batted for five hours with a gammy leg in the final Test.

The first stage of the campaign embraced the NatWest one-day series, for which the tourists called on the limited-overs skills of Michael Bevan, Ian Harvey and Andrew Symonds; later, Simon Katich, Justin Langer, Colin Miller and Michael Slater replaced them in the Test squad. Brett Lee had been chosen only for the Tests but was brought into the one-day reckoning when Nathan Bracken injured a shoulder. Bracken's replacement, Ashley Noffke, was himself soon repatriated after damaging ankle ligaments at practice.

The Worcester fixture was happily restored as the three-day tour opener and saw Damien Martyn make a hundred that presaged a stream of runs from his cultured bat. His sound technique would show up starkly the flawed, angled-batted efforts of some home batsmen throughout the summer. But the day after England lost the Old Trafford Test to Pakistan, the Australians managed to lose against a young Middlesex side in a one-day match, the county's first victory over an Australian touring team and one that gave some encouragement to the bar-room pundits. Two days later, the visitors tied with Northamptonshire, and the optimism swelled further. None of it was of the slightest significance.

Australia cruised to the one-day trophy, playing excellently according to the specialist requirements, stunning England – particularly at Old Trafford, where they bowled them out for 86 – with aggressive field placings more usually identified with Test cricket, and losing only one of their six preliminaries, to Pakistan at Trent Bridge. Here, Waugh took his team off the field for 20 minutes after a firecracker was thrown near to Lee in the outfield. There had already been crowd disorder and stampeding on to the field by Pakistani spectators at Edgbaston and Headingley, and the Australians were puzzled and disgusted that such incursions apparently could not be prevented. The ultimate blot on the tournament came at Lord's following their victory in the final: objects were thrown at the Pavilion balcony during the presentation ceremony, and a full beer can struck Bevan on the jaw. Australia's nine-wicket win, with 23.3 overs to spare, was as emphatic as their victory over Pakistan in the World Cup final here two years earlier. With Adam Gilchrist, the Waughs, Ricky Ponting and Martyn all finely tuned, and the bowlers on song, the sense of Australian insuperability was firmly in place.

As June faded, Katich announced his presence by hitting a strong century at Arundel against a multinational MCC attack, but Langer and Slater struggled. At Chelmsford, Martyn and Gilchrist foreshadowed their momentous deeds in the First Test with a blistering unbeaten 251 for the sixth wicket, Jason Gillespie showed his sharp teeth with five wickets, and then the Australians batted again – on and on, well past 500 on the last day, to cries of frustration from the Essex supporters, some of it on behalf of Hussain, who would have relished a second innings with the Test coming up.

Hussain had crafted a double-century at Edgbaston in 1997, when England won the opening encounter by nine wickets. But Australia were not being

[*Patrick Eagar*

Third day, Third Test, and Australians on the Trent Bridge balcony celebrate settling the serious business of the tour. England have been beaten 3–0 (in just 11 match days) and the Ashes retained with embarrassing ease.

caught cold this time. Rather it was England who were in disarray, summoning 17 players to Birmingham at some stage or other as injuries carved a swathe through their ranks. Still, they began well after losing the statuesque Marcus Trescothick for a duck, only to subside before Alec Stewart and Andrew Caddick compiled a riotous century for the tenth wicket. Matthew Hayden and Slater pulled back the initiative with 98 that evening – 16 from Slater's sizzling bat off Darren Gough's opening over – and thereafter the match ran away from England. Four hours of Steve Waugh preceded hundreds from Martyn and Gilchrist. At the precise moment Waugh was out, having made his 26th Test century and passed 9,000 runs, Joe Roff in Melbourne levelled the score against the British Lions with a try for the Wallabies, who went on to win. It seemed then that Australian sports ruled the world.

Gilchrist's nervousness with the gloves on the opening day had surprised his team-mates, but now he batted with his usual destructive power, lashing five sixes to equal Sam Loxton's Australian Ashes record, and taking 22 off a Mark Butcher over. He and Martyn increased the number of centuries scored by Australians in their first Test against England to 21 (against England's 16 in reply), and it was a further measure of Australia's recent domination that nine of their batsmen had done it since 1981 – against only Tim Robinson and Thorpe for England. Trescothick warmed English hearts with his 76, but the innings defeat was deeply demoralising. So, too, was Hussain's second fracture of the summer, his little finger broken by Gillespie. When one of Trescothick's sixes was pouched by a spectator, a suggestion that the catcher be enlisted by England was nullified by the thought that he was probably one of the numerous Australian visitors. A letter in *The Times* proposed that a more interesting contest might be staged between England's men and the Australian women, also in England and currently thrashing their counterparts.

Somerset omitted some key players and recruited two Pakistani guests, raising fresh cries for regional selections to play touring teams. But it didn't bother the Australians. They cruised to victory, while wondering what had happened to the John Bull spirit as several England players stated that they had no desire to captain their country in Hussain's absence. Atherton reluctantly took the reins for the next two Tests, which Australia won with ease.

McGrath, Gillespie, Lee and Warne had gelled as the established attack for the series, and were to finish with all but two of the 93 English wickets which fell. At Lord's they rolled England over again for under 200. Mark Waugh made an enchanting century before overtaking Mark Taylor's record tally of Test catches, Gilchrist a robust 90, while the tinkle of England's dropped catches echoed. In contrast, Australia swallowed just about everything going behind the stumps, seemingly willing edge after edge to come. And Thorpe, having missed the NatWest Series and the First Test through a calf-muscle strain, now had his hand broken by Lee. It was wondered if the pressure on the National Health Service was chiefly attributable to England's walking wounded.

Hampshire's two-wicket victory on the eve of the Third Test worried the tourists not in the least; as if handing over a wartime food parcel, it suited them to field an under-strength batting side. During the match, however, the distribution of coach John Buchanan's battle dossier to the wrong rooms at the team's Southampton hotel was seen as psychological warfare. Buchanan ("I am not a devious person") denied the error was deliberate, but his quotations from ancient Chinese warlord Sun Tzu, and his assertion that England were "hanging on to excuses", received wide publicity.

England won the first day at Trent Bridge, their fast attack, Alex Tudor prominent, slightly outdoing McGrath and company on a sporty pitch. Significantly, the catches were held. But Australia's tail wagged, and then Warne, the peroxide blond whose best days were said to be behind him, spun six out, leaving Australia to make 158 to retain the Ashes. A Caddick no-ball – yet another symbol of poor English professional standards through the series – signalled the moment at four o'clock on the third day. Australia's ecstasy was diminished only by their captain's ruptured calf – suffered in a freak injury. Gilchrist, the deputy, politely acknowledged that England had repeatedly put them under pressure, but they had stood up to it. He said he had been standing at the toilet when, through a window, he saw his captain on a crutch, hobbling to a car to take him to hospital: "I can't wait to give him a big hug" – a further expression of the side's solidarity.

There remained the prospect of a 5–0 "greenwash" and, after Sussex had amassed a lot of runs, only to be shown who was boss, and a rain-ruined visit to Belfast, Australia went to Headingley set on writing more history. This time, the weather upset the strategy. Ponting's attractive 144 and 72 dominated the Australian scorecard in this 300th England–Australia Test, and England were always running behind – until rain halted Australia's progress towards setting an unattainable target. Keen to win, Gilchrist made what still seemed a fairly one-sided declaration and, after half an hour of the fifth day, victory seemed assured as McGrath and Gillespie removed the openers and bowled many nasty deliveries. Then, against the tide, Butcher, back in the colours because of the pre-Edgbaston withdrawals, put on a memorable 181 with Hussain and smashed his way to a match-winning 173 not out, lodging his name in the Hall of Fame with an innings Gilchrist generously acknowledged as "one of the great Ashes knocks of all time". Having secured their second-highest target ever to beat Australia, England caused the land to be awash with "if onlys".

That reaction was just one huge red rag to the Australian bull. Conspicuously sporting in their reaction to England's astounding Leeds victory, within a week they had smothered local euphoria. Slater, averaging 24 and with personal problems, was dropped for The Oval; Langer, after a poor tour, came in as opener and sweated his way to a hundred before taking a sickening blow to the head; the Waughs made glorious centuries, Steve limping most of the way (to finish the series with an average of 107.00); and Warne bagged 11 wickets in 72.2 overs, including his 400th. Four years earlier, it had been 11 wickets to Phil Tufnell, who now managed only one. It was a decisive note on which to finish, for England had been close to full strength. Indeed, Ramprakash, his 133 poignantly impressive, a treat to the eye, might not have been playing had Thorpe and Vaughan been fit.

All was triumph for the Australians, whose image had been enhanced by their demeanour. McGrath had passed Dennis Lillee's 355 Test wickets, Gilchrist had his 100th dismissal in a record 22 Tests, the Waughs now stood with 47 Test centuries between them, and Australia had won 20 of their last 23 Tests, all of which had had positive conclusions, another record. And still their captain claimed they were a team without stars. They were responsible, too, for yet another innovation: a bowler, on taking his fifth wicket, held the ball high in response to the applause. How could it have taken such a natural gesture so long to be adopted? McGrath, Warne and Gillespie performed it eight times between them; Gough and Caddick, such an incisive pair against West Indies the year before, and Tudor could manage only one five-wicket return apiece for England.

But if the final measure of supremacy came with the appointment of an Aussie battler, Rod Marsh, to head England's new cricket academy, the touring team went home with one sore point unresolved. What did they have to do to get Lord's to return the little 1883 Ashes urn to Melbourne, its place of origin?

AUSTRALIAN TOUR PARTY

S. R. Waugh (New South Wales) (*captain*), A. C. Gilchrist (Western Australia) (*vice-captain*), M. G. Bevan (New South Wales), N. W. Bracken (New South Wales), D. W. Fleming (Victoria), J. N. Gillespie (South Australia), I. J. Harvey (Victoria), M. L. Hayden (Queensland), S. M. Katich (Western Australia), J. L. Langer (Western Australia), B. Lee (New South Wales), G. D. McGrath (New South Wales), D. R. Martyn (Western Australia), C. R. Miller (Victoria), R. T. Ponting (Tasmania), W. A. Seccombe (Queensland), M. J. Slater (New South Wales), A. Symonds (Queensland), S. K. Warne (Victoria), M. E. Waugh (New South Wales).

Bevan, Harvey and Symonds were replaced by Katich, Langer, Miller and Slater after the NatWest Series. Seccombe was added to the party after the original selection. A. A. Noffke (Queensland) replaced the injured Bracken and returned home himself after being injured.

Manager: S. R. Bernard. *Coach:* J. M. Buchanan. *Physiotherapists:* P. Farhart and E. L. Alcott. *Video analyst/assistant manager:* M. K. Walsh. *Physical performance manager:* J. A. Campbell. *Masseur:* R. Lauder. *Media manager:* B. H. Murgatroyd.

AUSTRALIAN TOUR RESULTS

Test matches – Played 5: Won 4, Lost 1.
First-class matches – Played 11: Won 8, Lost 2, Drawn 1.
Wins – England (4), Worcestershire, MCC, Somerset, Sussex.
Losses – England, Hampshire.
Draw – Essex.
One-day internationals – Played 6: Won 5, Lost 1. Abandoned 1. *Wins* – Pakistan (2), England (3). *Loss* – Pakistan. *Abandoned* – Pakistan.
Other non-first-class matches – Played 3: Lost 1, Tied 1, No result 1. *Loss* – Middlesex. *Tie* – Northamptonshire. *No result* – Ireland.

TEST MATCH AVERAGES

ENGLAND – BATTING

	T	*I*	*NO*	*R*	*HS*	*100s*	*50s*	*Avge*	*Ct*
M. A. Butcher	5	10	1	456	173*	1	1	50.66	4
M. R. Ramprakash	4	8	0	318	133	1	0	39.75	3
N. Hussain	3	6	1	177	55	0	2	35.40	0
A. J. Stewart	5	9	1	283	76*	0	2	35.37	13
M. E. Trescothick	5	10	0	321	76	0	3	32.10	4
M. A. Atherton	5	10	0	221	57	0	2	22.10	7
U. Afzaal	3	6	1	83	54	0	1	16.60	0
A. R. Caddick	5	9	2	101	49*	0	0	14.42	1
D. Gough	5	9	3	82	39*	0	0	13.66	0
I. J. Ward	3	6	1	68	23*	0	0	13.60	0
C. White	3	6	1	38	27*	0	0	7.60	1

Played in two Tests: A. J. Tudor 3, 9, 2. Played in one Test: D. G. Cork 24, 2; R. D. B. Croft 3, 0; A. F. Giles 7, 0; A. D. Mullally 0; J. Ormond 18, 17; G. P. Thorpe 20, 2 (1 ct); P. C. R. Tufnell 7*, 0.

* *Signifies not out.*

BOWLING

	O	*M*	*R*	*W*	*BB*	*5W/i*	*Avge*
A. J. Tudor	44.5	7	195	7	5-44	1	27.85
D. Gough	155.1	24	657	17	5-103	1	38.64
A. R. Caddick	177.4	24	748	15	5-101	1	49.86

Also bowled: U. Afzaal 9–0–49–1; M. A. Butcher 14–4–63–4; D. G. Cork 23–3–84–1; R. D. B. Croft 3–0–10–1; A. F. Giles 25–0–108–1; A. D. Mullally 30.3–10–99–2; J. Ormond 34–4–115–1; M. R. Ramprakash 8–0–31–0; P. C. R. Tufnell 39–2–174–1; C. White 46.4–7–189–1.

AUSTRALIA – BATTING

	T	*I*	*NO*	*R*	*HS*	*100s*	*50s*	*Avge*	*Ct/St*
S. R. Waugh	4	5	2	321	157*	2	0	107.00	2
M. E. Waugh	5	8	3	430	120	2	1	86.00	9
D. R. Martyn	5	7	2	382	118	2	2	76.40	0
A. C. Gilchrist	5	5	0	340	152	1	2	68.00	24/2
R. T. Ponting	5	8	0	338	144	1	2	42.25	7
M. L. Hayden	5	8	1	234	68	0	1	33.42	4
M. J. Slater	4	7	0	170	77	0	1	24.28	1
J. N. Gillespie	5	4	1	41	27*	0	0	13.66	2
G. D. McGrath	5	4	3	11	8*	0	0	11.00	1
B. Lee	5	4	0	24	20	0	0	6.00	0
S. K. Warne	5	4	0	13	8	0	0	3.25	6

Played in one Test: S. M. Katich 15, 0* (1 ct); J. L. Langer 102* (1 ct).

* *Signifies not out.*

BOWLING

	O	*M*	*R*	*W*	*BB*	*5W/i*	*Avge*
G. D. McGrath	194.2	56	542	32	7-76	4	16.93
S. K. Warne	195.2	41	580	31	7-165	3	18.70
J. N. Gillespie	174	42	652	19	5-53	1	34.31
B. Lee	120.5	18	496	9	2-37	0	55.11

Also bowled: R. T. Ponting 4–0–8–0; M. E. Waugh 13–1–69–1.

AUSTRALIAN TOUR AVERAGES – FIRST-CLASS MATCHES

BATTING

	M	*I*	*NO*	*R*	*HS*	*100s*	*50s*	*Avge*	*Ct/St*
D. R. Martyn	9	14	5	942	176*	5	3	104.66	3
A. C. Gilchrist	8	10	2	663	152	3	2	82.87	28/4
S. M. Katich	5	7	3	288	168*	1	1	72.00	7
M. E. Waugh	9	15	6	644	120	2	2	71.55	12
S. R. Waugh	7	11	2	583	157*	3	0	64.77	5
R. T. Ponting	9	15	1	844	147*	3	5	60.28	11
M. L. Hayden	10	17	1	636	142	1	3	39.75	6
J. L. Langer	6	11	2	285	104*	2	0	31.66	5
W. A. Seccombe	4	5	0	157	76	0	1	31.40	8/2
S. K. Warne	8	10	2	237	69	0	2	29.62	13
M. J. Slater	8	13	1	341	77	0	2	28.41	1
C. R. Miller	5	4	1	68	62	0	1	22.66	2
B. Lee	8	7	0	127	79	0	1	18.14	0
G. D. McGrath	7	6	3	53	38	0	0	17.66	1
J. N. Gillespie	8	9	3	94	27*	0	0	15.66	3
D. W. Fleming	5	6	0	49	20	0	0	8.16	0

Played in three matches: A. A. Noffke 22, 28, 19 (1 ct). Played in one match: M. G. Bevan 33, 34; N. W. Bracken 1*, 9* (1 ct).

* *Signifies not out.*

BOWLING

	O	*M*	*R*	*W*	*BB*	*5W/i*	*Avge*
N. W. Bracken	24	5	61	5	3-29	0	12.20
G. D. McGrath.	234.5	74	624	40	7-76	4	15.60
S. K. Warne.	263	56	784	42	7-165	3	18.66
D. W. Fleming	138	32	390	19	6-59	1	20.52
J. N. Gillespie	228	54	801	29	5-37	2	27.62
C. R. Miller.	157.2	37	586	18	4-41	0	32.55
A. A. Noffke	67.4	16	258	6	3-66	0	43.00
B. Lee	186.5	30	752	17	3-17	0	44.23

Also bowled: M. G. Bevan 5–0–28–0; M. L. Hayden 11–2–44–0; S. M. Katich 24–2–106–4; J. L. Langer 2–0–5–0; D. R. Martyn 9–1–53–2; R. T. Ponting 7.3–1–15–0; M. J. Slater 3.2–0–23–1; M. E. Waugh 24–2–121–2.

Note: Matches in this section which were not first-class are signified by a dagger.

WORCESTERSHIRE v AUSTRALIANS

At Worcester, June 1, 2, 3. Australians won by 360 runs. Toss: Australians.

The Australians, running up 711 in their two innings at more than four and a half an over, brought a limited-overs approach to the three-day game as they tuned up for the NatWest Series. Despite the absence of Bichel and Lampitt, Worcestershire's young pace men Liptrot and Kabir Ali had them 178 for six. But Martyn and Warne then added 148 in 30 overs, the elegant Martyn hitting 88 of his 108 in boundaries, to the generous appreciation of a capacity crowd. McGrath, who enjoyed a successful 2000 season at New Road, removed Weston before stumps, and next day the Australian fast bowlers encountered resistance only from Singh. Steve Waugh did not enforce the follow-on and, once his main batsmen had used their time profitably, he declared with a lead of 548, shortly before lunch on the final day. That left sufficient time for the Australians to win with 45 minutes to spare.

Close of play: First day, Worcestershire 50-1 (Singh 25*, Hick 19*); Second day, Australians 236-4 (S. R. Waugh 15*, Gilchrist 7*).

Australians

M. L. Hayden c Pipe b Kabir Ali	20	– (2) b Rawnsley.	65
M. E. Waugh c Singh b Sheriyar	13	– (1) b Sheriyar	48
R. T. Ponting lbw b Liptrot	24	– c Sheriyar b Solanki	65
M. G. Bevan c Weston b Kabir Ali	33	– c Kadeer Ali b Solanki	34
*S. R. Waugh b Liptrot.	30	– b Rawnsley	32
D. R. Martyn lbw b Rawnsley	108	– (7) st Pipe b Rawnsley.	28
†A. C. Gilchrist c Leatherdale b Liptrot	21	– (6) lbw b Kabir Ali.	13
S. K. Warne lbw b Rawnsley	68	– (9) not out.	41
D. W. Fleming b Rawnsley.	11	– (8) lbw b Liptrot	20
N. W. Bracken not out	1	– not out	9
G. D. McGrath c Leatherdale b Kabir Ali.	4		
B 9, l-b 7, n-b 2.	18	L-b 4, n-b 1	5
1/29 2/55 3/59 4/109 5/134 6/178 7/326 8/333 9/342	351	1/103 2/143 3/189 4/218 5/254 6/266 7/305 8/309 (8 wkts dec.)	360

Bowling: *First Innings*—Sheriyar 20–3–86–1; Kabir Ali 12.2–1–43–3; Liptrot 17–3–37–3; Leatherdale 5–0–46–0; Rawnsley 23–4–90–3; Solanki 10–3–33–0. *Second Innings*—Sheriyar 12–1–78–1; Kabir Ali 11–1–55–1; Liptrot 11–0–74–1; Rawnsley 24–3–108–3; Solanki 9–1–41–2.

Worcestershire

W. P. C. Weston c Warne b McGrath	6	– lbw b Bracken	22
A. Singh c Gilchrist b McGrath	62	– c M. E. Waugh b Fleming	11
*G. A. Hick c Warne b McGrath	19	– c Warne b Fleming	0
V. S. Solanki lbw b Fleming	3	– c Warne b McGrath	15
D. A. Leatherdale c Gilchrist b Bracken	22	– b Bracken	72
Kadeer Ali lbw b Bracken	5	– b McGrath	2
†D. J. Pipe b Warne	5	– c Bracken b Warne	8
Kabir Ali lbw b Bracken	11	– lbw b McGrath	39
M. J. Rawnsley b Fleming	8	– b McGrath	1
C. G. Liptrot not out	13	– not out	4
A. Sheriyar st Gilchrist b Warne	3	– run out	5
L-b 3, n-b 3	6	B 1, l-b 4, w 2, n-b 2	9
1/6 2/50 3/67 4/109 5/115 6/120 7/134 8/138 9/143	163	1/18 2/20 3/40 4/52 5/56 6/99 7/165 8/174 9/178	188

Bowling: *First Innings*—McGrath 13–6–31–3; Fleming 15–3–47–2; Warne 18.4–7–38–2; Bracken 13–2–29–3; Martyn 4–1–15–0. *Second Innings*—McGrath 12.3–4–31–4; Fleming 12–1–39–2; Bracken 11–3–32–2; Bevan 5–0–28–0; Warne 12–3–34–1; M. E. Waugh 5–0–19–0.

Umpires: M. Dixon and A. A. Jones.

†MIDDLESEX v AUSTRALIANS

At Lord's, June 5. Middlesex won by six wickets. Toss: Middlesex. First-team debut: T. A. Hunt.

The absence of McGrath, Lee and Gilchrist from the touring team could not detract from an excellent win for Middlesex, who were themselves without four regulars. Ponting showed his class with 57 off 47 balls, and Harvey bludgeoned 84 off 65. But against keen bowling and sharp fielding, inspired by acting-captain Weekes's three wickets and three catches, the Australians succumbed inside 45 overs. When Middlesex replied, Shah and Hutton added 113 in 25 overs. Hutton was run out backing up for the second time in three days, but Cook contributed a quickfire 20, then Roseberry's swept boundary clinched a historic victory with 17 balls to spare. Previously, Middlesex had played the Australians in 30 first-class matches and two limited-overs games without beating them.

Australians

M. L. Hayden c Weekes b Hewitt	3	S. K. Warne c Nash b Weekes	7
M. E. Waugh c Hutton b Hewitt	14	J. N. Gillespie not out	19
R. T. Ponting c Nash b Weekes	57	N. W. Bracken b Hunt	1
*S. R. Waugh c Weekes b Keegan	4	L-b 4, w 3, n-b 4	11
D. R. Martyn c Nash b Cook	19		
A. Symonds lbw b Cook	4	1/17 2/36 3/43 (44.2 overs)	232
I. J. Harvey b Cook	84	4/78 5/106 6/108	
†W. A. Seccombe c and b Weekes	9	7/141 8/154 9/229	

Bowling: Hewitt 9–2–43–2; Keegan 10–2–57–1; Hunt 4.2–0–32–1; Cook 8–0–39–3; Weekes 10–0–36–3; Hutton 3–0–21–0.

Middlesex

A. J. Strauss c Harvey b Bracken	15	M. A. Roseberry not out	11
B. L. Hutton run out	73	B 3, l-b 5, w 15, n-b 5	28
O. A. Shah st Seccombe b Warne	50		
R. M. S. Weston not out	36	1/33 2/146 (4 wkts, 47.1 overs)	233
S. J. Cook c Martyn b Harvey	20	3/170 4/204	

*P. N. Weekes, †D. C. Nash, C. B. Keegan, J. P. Hewitt and T. A. Hunt did not bat.

Bowling: Gillespie 9–0–38–0; Bracken 8–0–47–1; Warne 10–1–39–1; Harvey 10–1–36–1; Symonds 8.1–0–54–0; Martyn 2–0–11–0.

Umpires: B. Leadbeater and A. G. T. Whitehead.

†NORTHAMPTONSHIRE v AUSTRALIANS

At Northampton, June 7. Tied. Toss: Northamptonshire.

Northamptonshire wasted a golden opportunity to emulate Middlesex. They needed three off the final over, from Harvey, with three wickets in hand. Weekes hit the first ball for two, but was run out off the next; Cousins was caught behind two balls later; and last man Brown was run out attempting an impossible bye. Older spectators remembered a similar finish in 1961, when Albert Lightfoot's failure to run left the county's three-day match against the Australians drawn, with the scores level. That Northamptonshire came so close this time owed much to Hussey, who scored a determined half-century against his compatriots, and useful middle-order contributions. The Australians' total resulted from an unbroken 157 in 27 overs between Martyn (131 balls, five fours) and Mark Waugh (89 balls, eight fours). In the end, though, it was Harvey's one-day nous that saved them from going into the NatWest Series on the back of two county defeats.

Australians

*†A. C. Gilchrist b Cousins	19
D. R. Martyn not out	101
A. Symonds lbw b Cousins	0
M. G. Bevan c G. P. Swann b Penberthy	19
M. E. Waugh not out	88
L-b 3, w 1, n-b 3	7
1/38 2/38 3/77 (3 wkts, 50 overs)	234

M. L. Hayden, I. J. Harvey, W. A. Seccombe, J. N. Gillespie, D. W. Fleming and G. D. McGrath did not bat.

Bowling: Weekes 10–0–57–0; Cousins 10–3–27–2; Penberthy 10–0–41–1; Brown 10–0–41–0; Innes 7–0–46–0; G. P. Swann 3–0–19–0.

Northamptonshire

M. E. K. Hussey b Bevan	73
M. B. Loye b McGrath	18
J. W. Cook b Gillespie	12
G. P. Swann lbw b Gillespie	20
A. J. Swann c Gilchrist b Bevan	24
A. L. Penberthy run out	22
K. J. Innes c Gilchrist b Symonds	9
*†D. Ripley not out	23
L. C. Weekes run out	11
D. M. Cousins c Gilchrist b Harvey	0
J. F. Brown run out	0
B 1, l-b 12, w 6, n-b 3	22
1/29 2/56 3/91 4/155 5/156 6/173 7/217 8/234 9/234 (50 overs)	234

Bowling: McGrath 10–2–39–1; Fleming 4–0–19–0; Gillespie 10–0–51–2; Harvey 10–0–31–1; Symonds 10–0–43–1; Martyn 2–0–14–0; Bevan 4–0–24–2.

Umpires: N. G. Cowley and D. R. Shepherd.

Australia's matches v Pakistan and England in the NatWest Series (June 9–23) may be found in that section.

MCC v AUSTRALIANS

At Arundel, June 25, 26, 27. Australians won by 280 runs. Toss: Australians.

Queenslander Dawes, leading wicket-taker in the 2000-01 Pura Cup, gave his countrymen a hurry-up with four wickets before lunch. When Willoughby, the Western Province left-armer, had Steve Waugh playing on first ball after the interval, the big crowd stirred at the prospect of an upset. Instead, they were treated to a dazzling century from left-hander Katich: his unbeaten 168 from 167 balls, in his second game for his country, contained 101 between lunch and tea, 27 fours and a six. Warne helped him add 190 in under two hours. MCC lost six for 82 before the close. Next morning, New Zealand opener Richardson carried his bat; otherwise, it was a poor response. Waugh and Martyn added 158 after Slater and Langer (first ball) disappointed again. Waugh reached his hundred with two sixes and a four off successive balls from Asif Mujtaba. On the final day, Ward, formerly of Surrey and now coach at Whitgift School, rollicked to 57 with 18, including two sixes, from a Warne over. Shahid Afridi smashed three sixes and two fours in his 14-ball stay, and Adams kept the Australians in the field for almost two and a half hours.

Close of play: First day, MCC 82-6 (Richardson 31*, Metson 0*); Second day, Australians 294-8 (Warne 30*, Gillespie 2*).

Australians

M. J. Slater lbw b Dawes	7	– (2) c Aminul Islam b Azhar Mahmood	17
M. L. Hayden c Kruis b Dawes	31	– (1) c Kruis b Willoughby	16
J. L. Langer c Adams b Dawes	4	– b Dawes	0
*S. R. Waugh b Willoughby	45	– c Asif Mujtaba b Kruis	105
D. R. Martyn b Dawes	8	– lbw b Shahid Afridi	80
S. M. Katich not out	168		
†W. A. Seccombe c Metson b Willoughby	17	– (6) c Ward b Willoughby	20
S. K. Warne c Shahid Afridi b Adams	69	– not out	30
J. N. Gillespie c Ward b Aminul Islam	1	– (10) not out	2
D. W. Fleming c and b Aminul Islam	6	– (7) c and b Shahid Afridi	1
C. R. Miller c Adams b Aminul Islam	4	– (9) b Willoughby	0
B 4, l-b 12, w 7, n-b 7	30	B 10, l-b 7, w 1, n-b 5	23
1/11 2/27 3/54 4/64 5/126 6/175 7/365 8/378 9/386	390	1/29 2/30 3/55 4/213 5/251 6/253 7/259 8/273 (8 wkts dec.)	294

Bowling: *First Innings*—Dawes 19–5–74–4; Willoughby 14–4–43–2; Azhar Mahmood 14–2–76–0; Kruis 10–2–56–0; Shahid Afridi 3–0–28–0; Asif Mujtaba 6–0–38–0; Adams 6–0–45–1; Aminul Islam 2.5–0–14–3. *Second Innings*—Dawes 12–1–51–1; Willoughby 21–4–66–3; Azhar Mahmood 9–2–31–1; Kruis 13–1–52–1; Asif Mujtaba 10–1–39–0; Aminul Islam 3–0–8–0; Shahid Afridi 10–2–30–2.

MCC

M. H. Richardson not out	64	– b Gillespie	17
Asif Mujtaba lbw b Fleming	0	– lbw b Miller	22
Aminul Islam lbw b Fleming	1	– (4) c Seccombe b Martyn	20
D. M. Ward c Warne b Gillespie	4	– (3) c Waugh b Warne	57
*J. C. Adams lbw b Miller	0	– not out	81
Shahid Afridi c Warne b Miller	2	– c Katich b Martyn	28
Azhar Mahmood lbw b Warne	30	– run out	10
†C. P. Metson lbw b Gillespie	0	– lbw b Miller	3
G. J. Kruis lbw b Warne	2	– c Hayden b Miller	0
J. H. Dawes b Miller	1	– b Slater	10
C. M. Willoughby b Miller	0	– run out	8
B 1, l-b 12, n-b 7	20	B 2, l-b 14, w 1, n-b 7	24
1/2 2/12 3/29 4/33 5/35 6/82 7/95 8/115 9/124	124	1/33 2/109 3/109 4/155 5/193 6/215 7/232 8/232 9/253	280

Bowling: *First Innings*—Gillespie 11–2–32–2; Fleming 12–4–28–2; Miller 8.3–2–41–4; Warne 7–2–10–2. *Second Innings*—Gillespie 10–3–24–1; Fleming 10–4–17–0; Miller 23–3–87–3; Hayden 6–2–12–0; Warne 12–1–48–1; Martyn 5–0–38–2; Katich 3–0–15–0; Slater 3.2–0–23–1.

Umpires: N. L. Bainton and A. Clarkson.

ESSEX v AUSTRALIANS

At Chelmsford, June 29, 30, July 1. Drawn. Toss: Australians.

Ilott and Bishop extracted enough bounce to put the tourists on the back foot in the first hour, but they were revived initially by Ponting, then by Martyn and Gilchrist, who added 251 in 49 overs. Gilchrist struck 102 of his 150 in boundaries, Martyn's 114 contained 16 fours and a six. Essex lost half their side for 79 before 21-year-olds Foster and Napier put on 104, Napier's 59 coming from 63 balls with ten fours and two sixes. When Gillespie removed him, then added Bishop and Such without scoring, Foster looked like missing out on a deserved fifty; instead, he went from 47 to 74 while last man McGarry stood firm for 22 minutes. Hayden and Slater launched the Australians' second innings with a confident century stand. The tourists were 362 ahead at the close but, to the crowd's annoyance, batted throughout the final day – denying Hussain the opportunity of a morale-boosting innings before the forthcoming Test. All three days were watched by crowds of 5,000 plus.

Close of play: First day, Essex 16-1 (Hussain 7*, Robinson 8*); Second day, Australians 188-2 (Langer 10*, Lee 7*).

Australians

M. J. Slater c Foster b Ilott	15	– (2) c Ilott b McGarry	58
M. L. Hayden c Foster b Bishop	23	– (1) c Grayson b Such	98
J. L. Langer c Foster b Ilott	0	– b Such	17
M. E. Waugh c Napier b Bishop	25	– (6) lbw b Bishop	0
R. T. Ponting b Such	63	– (7) st Foster b Such	79
D. R. Martyn not out	114	– (10) not out	46
*†A. C. Gilchrist not out	150	– (11) not out	25
B. Lee (did not bat)		– (4) st Foster b Such	79
J. N. Gillespie (did not bat)		– (5) c Foster b Such	22
G. D. McGrath (did not bat)		– (8) c McGarry b Clinton	38
C. R. Miller (did not bat)		– (9) c Ilott b Clinton	62
B 4, l-b 10, n-b 1	15	B 14, l-b 16, n-b 15	45
1/36 2/36 3/46 4/108 5/154 (5 wkts dec.)	405	1/138 2/175 3/210 4/271 5/272 6/372 7/379 8/477 9/490 (9 wkts dec.)	569

Bowling: *First Innings*—Ilott 19–4–83–2; Irani 8–3–11–0; Bishop 18–5–70–2; McGarry 11–0–86–0; Such 23–3–99–1; Grayson 8–2–42–0. *Second Innings*—Ilott 13–2–62–0; Bishop 15–0–80–1; McGarry 19–2–121–1; Such 39–11–131–5; Grayson 13–2–54–0; Robinson 10–0–54–0; Clinton 8–0–30–2; Foster 2–0–6–0; Hussain 1–0–1–0.

Essex

N. Hussain c Langer b Gillespie	16
A. P. Grayson c Gilchrist b McGrath	0
D. D. J. Robinson st Gilchrist b Miller	34
R. S. Clinton lbw b Gillespie	0
*R. C. Irani c Ponting b Miller	18
†J. S. Foster c Gillespie b Lee	74
G. R. Napier c Miller b Gillespie	59
J. E. Bishop c Martyn b Gillespie	0
M. C. Ilott lbw b Miller	7
P. M. Such lbw b Gillespie	0
A. C. McGarry not out	0
L-b 7, n-b 16	23
1/7 2/29 3/33 4/74 5/79 6/183 7/183 8/190 9/202	231

Bowling: McGrath 15–8–20–1; Gillespie 16–5–37–5; Lee 7–1–41–1; Miller 21–4–94–3; Hayden 5–0–32–0.

Umpires: I. J. Gould and T. E. Jesty.

ENGLAND v AUSTRALIA

First npower Test

At Birmingham, July 5, 6, 7, 8. Australia won by an innings and 118 runs. Toss: Australia. Test debut: U. Afzaal.

One session was all Australia needed to settle into their defence of the Ashes. When England were 106 for one with an over to lunch, pre-match fears for Hussain's reconstructed team looked overblown. Then Steve Waugh introduced Warne. Butcher pushed a pad at his second ball and gloved a catch to Ponting, diving forward from short cover. It was the beginning of the end. When, in the second innings, Gillespie broke Hussain's little finger with a startling delivery, England's whole campaign was threatened.

Butcher had been called up, along with debutant Usman Afzaal, when injuries ruled out Thorpe (calf), Vaughan (knee) and Thorpe's cover, Ramprakash (hamstring), from the original 14. White and Giles, having missed the Pakistan series, returned but were still feeling their way back to full match fitness. Australia omitted the out-of-form Langer, promoted Ponting to No. 3 and slotted Martyn in for his 12th Test in eight and a half years.

The opening day provided exhilarating cricket. The sun beat down on a full house and runs blazed off the bat: between them, the teams scored 427 at almost five an over, including 236 after tea. Century stands topped and tailed England's innings: Atherton and Butcher put on 104 after Trescothick had edged Gillespie's first ball to first slip, and Stewart and Caddick whacked a merry 103 for the tenth wicket. Caddick struck seven fours and a six in his 40-ball 49 not out, his best score in Tests and the second-best by an England No. 11 after John Snow's unbeaten 59 against West Indies in 1966. But in between it was an old story. After Atherton, rapped on the fingers by Gillespie, had edged his next ball to second slip, Hussain padded up to McGrath, who then had Ward playing on from a nothing defensive stroke. Warne, meanwhile, had been stock-bowling at the other end, but a trademark leg-break out of the rough – an off-break to the left-handed Afzaal – opened up the lower order. In seven overs either side of tea, four wickets fell for 21 as Warne claimed his 17th five-wicket return in Tests – his fifth against England.

Slater launched Australia's reply by crashing Gough's first two deliveries (one a no-ball) behind point for four, then taking another two fours in an opening over that cost 18. Hayden caught his mood and they had put on 98 in 15 overs when White, twisting to his left in mid-air, intercepted Hayden's mid-wicket flick off Giles. Gough, albeit overstepping, had Ponting lbw before the close, then bowled Slater with his first ball next morning. But if the game appeared nicely poised at 134 for three, Steve Waugh's 26th Test hundred, and some ill-judged England seam bowling in helpful conditions, tipped it Australia's way.

Waugh was unforgiving as he stamped his authority on England's ambitions, drilling fours through Hussain's attacking fields – 13 all told in 181 balls – and becoming the third, after Allan Border (11,174) and Sunil Gavaskar (10,122) to reach 9,000 Test runs. While he and twin Mark were adding 133, it seemed unimportant that Mark's form was sketchy. Giving Mark two lives mattered more to England psychologically, however, than it had meant to Australia when they missed two catches the previous morning. Australia simply rectified the fault; England's errors – up to half a dozen chances went begging – opened a confidence fault line.

Martyn, often sublime in partnerships with his captain and Gilchrist, confirmed Australia's depth and shut the door on England. Had bad light and rain not limited Friday's final session to two balls, and taken the equivalent of a session out of Saturday, the match might not have entered the fourth day. Yet England had openings. Gough trapped Steve Waugh first thing Saturday with a ball that kept low and, immediately after a two-hour stoppage either side of lunch, had Martyn, 65 at the time, dropped by Stewart as he dived in front of first slip. He and Gilchrist added another 109 after

Playing the short-pitched ball: Adam Gilchrist goes to his first Ashes hundred by scooping Andrew Caddick's bouncer over the wicket-keeper's head for four. Caddick (*below*) resorts to the tailenders' time-honoured method, swinging hard and hoping for contact. Brett Lee won this duel; Caddick, 49 not out in a last-wicket stand of 103 with Alec Stewart, finished well ahead on points.

[*Patrick Eagar*

that. Martyn went to tea on 99; soon after he was caught at cover off Butcher as he tried to repeat the sumptuous cover drive with which he celebrated his maiden Test century. He faced 165 balls and hit 15 fours.

For a brief moment, Butcher's part-time swing bowling seemed unplayable. He capped Martyn's wicket with three more in five balls; four wickets for five runs. But it was an illusion. Gilchrist, 93 when joined by last man McGrath, reached his hundred in 118 balls by anticipating Caddick's bouncer, stooping and scooping it inventively over the wicket-keeper for four. Then he went into overdrive, upping his boundary tally to 20 fours and five sixes, including 22 runs off Butcher, which equalled the most expensive over in Ashes history. By the time Gilchrist was caught at long-on for 152 off 143 balls, the last wicket had added 63. McGrath's contribution was a single; when he had Atherton prodding to second slip, dismissing him for the 14th time in 26 innings, his day was complete.

MOST EXPENSIVE OVERS IN ASHES TESTS

22 (613642)	D. K. Lillee to I. T. Botham/C. J. Tavaré, A v E at Manchester	1981
22 (224644)	M. G. Hughes to I. T. Botham, A v E at Brisbane	1986-87
22 (440446)	C. J. McDermott to P. A. J. DeFreitas, A v E at Adelaide	1994-95
22 (606460)	**M. A. Butcher to A. C. Gilchrist, E v A at Birmingham**	**2001**

Research: Charlie Wat

LOWEST SCORES BY NO. 11 IN A TEST 50 PARTNERSHIP

1*	**G. D. McGrath**	**63 with A. C. Gilchrist, A v E at Birmingham**	**2001**
2*	P. C. R. Tufnell	68 with G. A. Hick, E v I at Bombay	1992-93
2*	T. M. Alderman	63 with W. B. Phillips, A v WI at Bridgetown	1983-84
2*	C. E. H. Croft	56 with J. Garner, WI v A at Brisbane	1979-80
3*	W. W. Davis	51 with P. J. L. Dujon, WI v I at Ahmedabad	1983-84
4	Iqbal Qasim	87 with Asif Iqbal, P v A at Adelaide	1976-77
4*	Asif Masood	62 with Sarfraz Nawaz, P v E at Leeds	1974
4	T. W. Wall	55 with S. J. McCabe, A v E at Sydney	1932-33
4	B. K. Kunderan	51 with P. R. Umrigar, I v WI at Port-of-Spain	1961-62
5*	L. O'B. Fleetwood-Smith	77 with S. J. McCabe, A v E at Nottingham	1938

Research: Gordon Vince

England resumed on Sunday 234 runs behind. Again Butcher was solid, adding 95 with Trescothick until Lee undid him with a ball that reared from just short of a length. Gillespie found something more damaging for the hapless Hussain – trapping his left hand against the bat handle and forcing him to retire – then blew away England's middle order with fast bowling of frightening intensity. He should also have had Giles first ball after lunch. Mark Waugh uncharacteristically dropped the slip chance but quickly helped Warne account for Trescothick and Giles, moving to within one catch of Mark Taylor's Test-record 157. Warne, meanwhile, went ahead of Ian Botham to become the sixth-highest wicket-taker in Tests.

For England, Trescothick's defiant 76, containing 11 fours and one six apiece off McGrath and Lee, offered a solitary silver lining. For Australia, there was a lap of honour and the prospect of Monday at Wimbledon to support fellow-countryman Pat Rafter in the men's final. – GRAEME WRIGHT.

Man of the Match: A. C. Gilchrist. *Attendance:* 78,225; *receipts* £1,778,631.

Close of play: First day, Australia 133-2 (Slater 76*, M. E. Waugh 0*); Second day, Australia 332-4 (S. R. Waugh 101*, Martyn 34*); Third day, England 48-1 (Trescothick 21*, Butcher 15*).

England

M. A. Atherton c M. E. Waugh b Gillespie	57	– c M. E. Waugh b McGrath	4
M. E. Trescothick c Warne b Gillespie	0	– c M. E. Waugh b Warne	76
M. A. Butcher c Ponting b Warne	38	– c Gilchrist b Lee	41
*N. Hussain lbw b McGrath	13	– retired hurt	9
I. J. Ward b McGrath	23	– b Lee	3
†A. J. Stewart lbw b McGrath	65	– c Warne b Gillespie	5
U. Afzaal b Warne	4	– lbw b Gillespie	2
C. White lbw b Warne	4	– b Gillespie	0
A. F. Giles c Gilchrist b Warne	7	– c M. E. Waugh b Warne	0
D. Gough c Gillespie b Warne	0	– lbw b Warne	0
A. R. Caddick not out	49	– not out	6
B 10, l-b 8, n-b 16	34	B 1, l-b 5, n-b 12	18
1/2 (2) 2/106 (3) 3/123 (1) 4/136 (4) 5/159 (5) 6/170 (7) 7/174 (8) 8/191 (9) 9/191 (10) 10/294 (6)	294	1/4 (1) 2/99 (3) 3/142 (5) 4/148 (6) 5/150 (7) 6/154 (8) 7/155 (2) 8/155 (10) 9/164 (9)	164

In the second innings Hussain retired hurt at 117.

Bowling: *First Innings*—McGrath 17.3–2–67–3; Gillespie 17–3–67–2; Lee 12–2–71–0; Warne 19–4–71–5. *Second Innings*—McGrath 13–5–34–1; Gillespie 11–2–52–3; Warne 10.1–4–29–3; M. E. Waugh 1–0–6–0; Lee 7–0–37–2.

Australia

M. J. Slater b Gough	77
M. L. Hayden c White b Giles	35
R. T. Ponting lbw b Gough	11
M. E. Waugh c Stewart b Caddick	49
*S. R. Waugh lbw b Gough	105
D. R. Martyn c Trescothick b Butcher	105
†A. C. Gilchrist c Caddick b White	152
S. K. Warne c Atherton b Butcher	8
B. Lee c Atherton b Butcher	0
J. N. Gillespie lbw b Butcher	0
G. D. McGrath not out	1
B 3, l-b 7, n-b 23	33
1/98 (2) 2/130 (3) 3/134 (1) 4/267 (4) 5/336 (5) 6/496 (6) 7/511 (8) 8/513 (9) 9/513 (10) 10/576 (7)	576

Bowling: Gough 33–6–152–3; Caddick 36–0–163–1; White 26.4–5–101–1; Giles 25–0–108–1; Butcher 9–3–42–4.

Umpires: S. A. Bucknor (West Indies) and G. Sharp.
Third umpire: K. E. Palmer. Referee: Talat Ali (Pakistan).

SOMERSET v AUSTRALIANS

At Taunton, July 13, 14, 15, 16. Australians won by 176 runs. Toss: Australians. County debuts: Aamir Sohail, Shoaib Akhtar.

Even without the Australians' Test attack, there was never much doubt about the result once Ponting set Somerset an unattainable 417, and left his bowlers more than a day to dismiss them. Standing in for the first time as Australian captain, he had hit a lively, attractive 128 in 130 balls on the opening day, with 20 fours and two sixes. Langer, while more circumspect, helped him put on 168, then added a further 118 with Mark Waugh as he moved to his own century. In the second innings it was the turn of Martyn, backed by Seccombe. On the final day, Wood compiled an assured half-century, his third in five first-class innings as he sought an extended run with Somerset. Fleming, meanwhile, sought a Test recall with match figures of eight for 97. Whether the guest appearances for Somerset of the Pakistan pair, Shoaib Akhtar and Aamir Sohail, contributed to the 4,000 spectators on the opening day, it was hard to tell. Shoaib worked up a fair pace with unexceptional success; Sohail scored a tentative first-innings 50, with not too much support.

Close of play: First day, Australians 348-3 (Langer 104*, Waugh 55*); Second day, Somerset 267; Third day, Somerset 52-1 (Aamir Sohail 20*, Burns 19*).

Australians

M. L. Hayden c Parsons b Grove	6		
M. J. Slater lbw b Kerr	28		
*R. T. Ponting b Shoaib Akhtar	128		
J. L. Langer not out	104	– (1) lbw b Shoaib Akhtar	10
M. E. Waugh not out	55	– (6) not out	41
S. M. Katich (did not bat)		– (2) c Turner b Shoaib Akhtar	3
D. R. Martyn (did not bat)		– (3) not out	176
†W. A. Seccombe (did not bat)		– (4) c Holloway b Blackwell	76
A. A. Noffke (did not bat)		– (5) c and b Blackwell	22
L-b 15, w 2, n-b 10	27	L-b 3, w 2, n-b 2	7
1/9 2/62 3/230 (3 wkts dec.)	348	1/12 2/15 3/171 4/213 (4 wkts dec.)	335

D. W. Fleming and C. R. Miller did not bat.

Bowling: *First Innings*—Shoaib Akhtar 14–0–81–1; Grove 16–0–96–1; Kerr 17–3–52–1; Parsons 9–1–42–0; Blackwell 8–0–25–0; Burns 7–1–21–0; Aamir Sohail 3–0–16–0. *Second Innings*—Shoaib Akhtar 7–3–9–2; Grove 14–1–77–0; Kerr 19–0–89–0; Parsons 13–1–61–0; Burns 4–1–8–0; Blackwell 24–3–88–2.

Somerset

Aamir Sohail c Hayden b Noffke	50	– c Ponting b Miller	36
P. C. L. Holloway c Katich b Fleming	0	– c Ponting b Noffke	7
*M. Burns c Miller b Fleming	9	– lbw b Fleming	59
P. D. Bowler b Fleming	2	– (7) not out	26
M. J. Wood c Katich b Miller	39	– (4) lbw b Miller	51
K. A. Parsons c Martyn b Waugh	38	– (5) lbw b Fleming	3
†R. J. Turner c Langer b Fleming	42	– (6) lbw b Noffke	9
I. D. Blackwell c Ponting b Fleming	30	– c Noffke b Katich	28
J. I. D. Kerr c Seccombe b Fleming	13	– c Martyn b Katich	0
J. O. Grove c Waugh b Miller	6	– c Katich b Miller	0
Shoaib Akhtar not out	4	– st Seccombe b Katich	10
B 6, l-b 3, w 13, n-b 12	34	W 5, n-b 6	11
1/1 2/15 3/33 4/111 5/132 6/189 7/243 8/250 9/263	267	1/13 2/93 3/118 4/122 5/173 6/175 7/228 8/228 9/229	240

Bowling: *First Innings*—Fleming 17–2–59–6; Noffke 15–1–71–1; Miller 27.2–2–90–2; Ponting 3–1–5–0; Waugh 6–1–33–1. *Second Innings*—Fleming 19–6–38–2; Noffke 22–3–92–2; Miller 25–10–89–3; Katich 4–0–21–3.

Umpires: M. Dixon and M. J. Kitchen.

ENGLAND v AUSTRALIA

Second npower Test

At Lord's, July 19, 20, 21, 22. Australia won by eight wickets. Toss: Australia.

Australia ended England's run of three Lord's victories with a display of all-round brilliance that approached perfection. For the home side, events had a depressing familiarity. As in the First Test, the batting, notably the middle order, fractured – quite literally – under pressure. At Edgbaston, Hussain broke a finger: at Lord's, Thorpe a bone in his right hand. Once again, only the weather dragged play into a fourth day. And so, for the fifth time in seven Ashes series, England found themselves 2–0 down after two Tests. In theory, they could still reclaim the Ashes, though, with the gulf between the teams yawning wide, no one paid heed to theory. Quite simply, Australia looked insuperable. To begin to compete, England needed more runs and, as importantly, quality support for Gough and Caddick.

Beforehand, though, England's quest was for a locum captain to replace the brittle-boned Hussain: Stewart declined the post after leading them to seven straight international defeats, while Butcher, dropped after his only foray into Test captaincy in 1999, ruled himself out. Gough optimistically volunteered his services, but Atherton, for a record 53rd time, was preferred. Despite Hussain's injury, England's selection worries had eased slightly. Fit again were Surrey colleagues Ramprakash and Thorpe, the one home batsman averaging 40 or more in Tests (Australia boasted seven). It meant the entire middle order, from Nos 3 to 7, came from one county, an unprecedented event. Selected more for his Lord's record than current form, Cork ousted left-arm spinner Giles.

It was all much easier for Steve Waugh, who named an unchanged team and won Australia's 13th toss in 14 Ashes contests, England's ninth consecutive reversal since winning at Lahore the previous November. Cricket began 90 minutes late because of rain, whose return, abetted by intermittent bad light and an unreschedulable visit from the Queen, played merry hell with the timetable for the rest of the day, preventing batsman or bowler from finding rhythm. Given the conditions, England did well to pick their way to 121 for three. Atherton had contributed a phlegmatic 37, Butcher a steady 21, and Thorpe and Ramprakash were constructing a useful stand. But before the weather closed in for the last time, Lee, disappointing hitherto, castled Ramprakash with a majestic ball that swung away then seamed up the slope between bat and pad. It gave Australia an initiative they never relinquished.

Under Friday's brighter skies, England withered in the face of a devastating McGrath onslaught. Immediately finding an exacting length, he took three for one in 20 pitch-perfect deliveries, starting with Stewart and ending with White, both for nought. Stewart's was his first Lord's duck in 29 Test innings, White's his fifth in eight international innings. The prize catch, though, came sandwiched between the two, Thorpe wafting his bat at one better ignored. Ward grittily hung on till the end which, despite an unconvincing hooked six by Cork, came – unlike Edgbaston – with a whimper.

A take-no-hostages opening salvo from Gough and Caddick briefly fostered hopes that 187 was not, after all, quite so feeble. But a diet of deliveries pitching on middle or leg – especially from Cork and White – fed Mark Waugh's insatiable appetite for on-side runs. In the most eloquent style, he revived Australia from a troubled 27 for two. Even so, had Gough held a sharp return catch from Steve Waugh, on 14, they would have been 136 for four. Instead, the Waughs powered on, adding 107 for the fourth wicket. Mark eventually went for a cultured 108, run out by a direct hit from Gough at mid-on. By the close, Edgbaston centurions Martyn and Gilchrist had given Australia a lead of 68.

Desperate for an early breakthrough, England's prayers seemed answered next morning when Gilchrist, 13, edged Gough's first ball straight to second slip – where it bounced out of Butcher's hands, leaving him a distraught, crumpled heap. It set an ugly trend. Atherton spilled the simplest of Gilchrist's four reprieves – all off Gough – allowing him to make a typically aggressive 90 before he swished at a short ball, by now the sole weapon in the English armoury. Australia, dismissed for 401, their first-innings score at Headingley precisely 20 years earlier, were 214 ahead.

With few signs of deterioration in the pitch, there were runs to be had, provided batsmen kept their heads. The Australians, however, were masters in exploiting the merest weaknesses. Every lapse cost an England wicket. Gillespie had Trescothick caught behind for the second time, Warne bowled Atherton (who had just crawled to tenth in the list of Test run-scorers, one ahead of Colin Cowdrey's 7,624) round his legs, and Lee, having already broken Thorpe's right hand, had him lbw to leave England 50 for three at tea.

[*Graham Morris*

How you do it, how you don't. Mark Waugh, with 157 Test catches to his credit, makes it look so simple as he pouches a world-record 158th to wrap up England's second innings. Mike Atherton, no mean slip himself, was one of several offenders on a nightmare Saturday morning for England – and bowler Darren Gough in particular. To add insult to injury, Gough became Waugh's world-record victim.

Butcher, combining patience and courage with good fortune, led an overdue fightback with Ramprakash, whose 40 was his best score in 13 unhappy Test innings at Lord's, the ground he had left for The Oval earlier in the year. Together, they added 96 for the fourth wicket. Incorrigible optimists thought back to the derring-do of Botham and Willis, but these Australians were never going to buckle like their predecessors of 1981. On the fourth morning, McGrath, summoning an array of devastating deliveries with apparent ease, snuffed out the daydream with three for four in 11 balls. The *coup de grâce* came when Mark Waugh held a record 158th catch to dismiss Gough. Many of the other 157 had been more difficult, but it was just the kind of chance England had grassed the previous morning. Australia made a pig's ear of reaching 14, but their overall performance was phenomenal. – HUGH CHEVALLIER.

Man of the Match: G. D. McGrath. *Attendance:* 109,116; *receipts* £2,995,294.

Close of play: First day, England 121-4 (Thorpe 16*, Stewart 0*); Second day, Australia 255-5 (Martyn 24*, Gilchrist 10*); Third day, England 163-4 (Butcher 73*, Stewart 13*).

England

*M. A. Atherton lbw b McGrath	37	– b Warne	20
M. E. Trescothick c Gilchrist b Gillespie	15	– c Gilchrist b Gillespie	3
M. A. Butcher c M. E. Waugh b McGrath	21	– c Gilchrist b Gillespie	83
G. P. Thorpe c Gilchrist b McGrath	20	– lbw b Lee	2
M. R. Ramprakash b Lee	14	– lbw b Gillespie	40
†A. J. Stewart c Gilchrist b McGrath	0	– lbw b McGrath	28
I. J. Ward not out	23	– c Ponting b McGrath	0
C. White c Hayden b McGrath	0	– not out	27
D. G. Cork c Ponting b Gillespie	24	– c Warne b McGrath	2
A. R. Caddick b Warne	0	– c Gilchrist b Gillespie	7
D. Gough b Warne	5	– c M. E. Waugh b Gillespie	1
B 7, l-b 8, w 2, n-b 11	28	L-b 3, w 2, n-b 9	14
1/33 (2) 2/75 (3) 3/96 (1) 4/121 (5) 5/126 (6) 6/129 (4) 7/131 (8) 8/178 (9) 9/181 (10) 10/187 (11)	187	1/8 (2) 2/47 (1) 3/50 (4) 4/146 (5) 5/188 (6) 6/188 (7) 7/188 (3) 8/193 (9) 9/225 (10) 10/227 (11)	227

Bowling: *First Innings*—McGrath 24–9–54–5; Gillespie 18–6–56–2; Lee 16–3–46–1; Warne 5.3–0–16–2. *Second Innings*—McGrath 19–4–60–3; Gillespie 16–4–53–5; Lee 9–1–41–1; Warne 20–4–58–1; M. E. Waugh 2–1–12–0.

Australia

M. J. Slater c Stewart b Caddick	25	– (2) c Butcher b Caddick	4
M. L. Hayden c Butcher b Caddick	0	– (1) not out	6
R. T. Ponting c Thorpe b Gough	14	– lbw b Gough	4
M. E. Waugh run out	108	– not out	0
*S. R. Waugh c Stewart b Cork	45		
D. R. Martyn c Stewart b Caddick	52		
†A. C. Gilchrist c Stewart b Gough	90		
S. K. Warne c Stewart b Caddick	5		
B. Lee b Caddick	20		
J. N. Gillespie b Gough	9		
G. D. McGrath not out	0		
L-b 9, w 1, n-b 23	33		
1/5 (2) 2/27 (3) 3/105 (1) 4/212 (4) 5/230 (5) 6/308 (6) 7/322 (8) 8/387 (7) 9/401 (10) 10/401 (9)	401	1/6 (2) 2/13 (3)	(2 wkts) 14

Bowling: *First Innings*—Gough 25–3–115–3; Caddick 32.1–4–101–5; White 18–1–80–0; Cork 23–3–84–1; Butcher 3–1–12–0. *Second Innings*—Gough 2–0–5–1; Caddick 1.1–0–9–1.

Umpires: S. A. Bucknor (West Indies) and J. W. Holder.
Third umpire: J. W. Lloyds. Referee: Talat Ali (Pakistan).

HAMPSHIRE v AUSTRALIANS

At Southampton, July 28, 29, 30. Hampshire won by two wickets. Toss: Hampshire. First-team debut: J. E. K. Schofield.

The last time Hampshire beat the Australians was in 1912, the year the *Titanic* left nearby Southampton Docks. So there was understandable jubilation when Brunnschweiler, in his second match, swept Miller to the fine-leg boundary for the winning runs with nine balls remaining. Waugh's surprising declaration had left Hampshire 26 overs to score 133. During the run-chase, Warne took four wickets against his old county to jangle their nerves, but Hampshire held on to inflict the Australians' first first-class defeat of the tour. Going into the game with only four specialist batsmen, they had been bowled out in the first session by Mullally and debutant James Schofield, who dismissed Hayden with his first ball in first-class cricket. But there was quality batting later from Kenway, Smith and Johnson and, for the Australians, Hayden and Katich. The Hampshire management could celebrate more than victory; the Rose Bowl attracted 13,000 spectators over three days, bringing receipts of more than £100,000.

Close of play: First day, Hampshire 238-3 (Smith 79*, Johnson 64*); Second day, Australians 176-1 (Hayden 92*, Katich 49*).

Australians

M. L. Hayden c Johnson b Schofield	1	– c Johnson b Udal	142
J. L. Langer lbw b Schofield	2	– c Kenway b Johnson	30
S. M. Katich c Prittipaul b Mullally	3	– c sub (J. D. Francis) b Udal	59
*S. R. Waugh c Johnson b Schofield	10	– c and b White	40
†W. A. Seccombe c Kenway b Mullally	13	– b Udal	31
S. K. Warne c Brunnschweiler b Mullally	1	– c Brunnschweiler b Schofield	15
B. Lee c Brunnschweiler b Mascarenhas	22	– c Brunnschweiler b Johnson	2
A. A. Noffke c Brunnschweiler b Mullally	28	– (10) c Prittipaul b Schofield	19
J. N. Gillespie b Mullally	1	– (8) not out	27
D. W. Fleming c Johnson b Udal	6	– (9) c sub (J. D. Francis) b Udal	5
C. R. Miller not out	2		
B 4, l-b 2, w 1, n-b 1	8	B 10, l-b 8, w 1	19
1/1 2/10 3/16 4/20 5/23 6/47 7/63 8/72 9/95	97	1/72 2/198 3/271 4/283 5/321 6/333 7/333 8/345 9/389 (9 wkts dec.)	389

Bowling: *First Innings*—Mullally 11.4–3–18–5; Schofield 6–2–25–3; Mascarenhas 8–2–17–1; Johnson 4–0–25–0; Udal 1–0–6–1. *Second Innings*—Mullally 8–3–20–0; Schofield 28.1–3–106–2; Mascarenhas 1.5–0–8–0; Udal 47.1–10–149–4; Johnson 16–4–50–2; White 8–0–38–1.

Hampshire

D. A. Kenway c Waugh b Warne	70	– (2) c Katich b Lee	22
G. W. White c Seccombe b Lee	0	– (1) c Seccombe b Lee	8
W. S. Kendall lbw b Lee	0	– b Warne	9
*R. A. Smith lbw b Noffke	113	– (6) c Langer b Miller	10
N. C. Johnson b Gillespie	88	– lbw b Warne	37
L. R. Prittipaul c Seccombe b Gillespie	10	– (4) b Lee	0
A. D. Mascarenhas c Seccombe b Noffke	10	– b Warne	14
S. D. Udal c Warne b Noffke	15	– b Warne	2
†I. Brunnschweiler c Waugh b Miller	1	– not out	10
J. E. K. Schofield c Katich b Miller	0	– not out	1
A. D. Mullally not out	4		
B 7, l-b 22, w 2, n-b 12	43	B 3, l-b 10, w 5, n-b 3	21
1/13 2/14 3/116 4/298 5/321 6/328 7/339 8/350 9/350	354	1/27 2/38 3/42 4/90 5/99 6/111 7/121 8/128 (8 wkts)	134

Bowling: *First Innings*—Lee 19–6–54–2; Fleming 21–6–53–0; Noffke 22.1–11–66–3; Gillespie 14–2–37–2; Miller 21–8–55–2; Warne 13–2–43–1; Katich 4–0–17–0. *Second Innings*—Lee 7–2–17–3; Fleming 4–0–22–0; Gillespie 3–0–19–0; Miller 5.3–0–32–1; Warne 5–0–31–4.

Umpires: J. F. Steele and R. A. White.

ENGLAND v AUSTRALIA

Third npower Test

At Nottingham, August 2, 3, 4. Australia won by seven wickets. Toss: England.

Australia won their seventh consecutive Ashes series at four o'clock on August 4, by which time their successful defence of the trophy had taken not quite 4,000 deliveries, or just over a week in actual playing time. Victory at Trent Bridge was a testament to their resourcefulness, for England at two stages held the upper hand. Australia trailed by 80 runs with three first-innings wickets remaining at the end of the first day, and England led by 110 with eight second-innings wickets remaining late on the second: the visitors regrouped on both occasions in dynamic fashion, led first by Gilchrist, then by Warne. England, meanwhile, experienced their usual quota of misfortune and miscellaneous acts of God.

First of these was the loss of their captain, Atherton, moments after he had won England's first toss in ten attempts. McGrath's second delivery looped from Atherton's forearm guard to second slip, and umpire Hampshire upheld the appeal for a catch, a decision greeted with hoots of dismay when the big screen replayed the contact. It went down as Atherton's 20th Test duck, an England record. The pitch, recently relaid,

MOST TEST DUCKS FOR ENGLAND

	Ducks	*Tests*		*Ducks*	*Tests*
M. A. Atherton	**20**	**115**	J. E. Emburey	16	64
D. L. Underwood	19	86	M. W. Gatting	16	79
J. A. Snow	17	49	**P. C. R. Tufnell**	**15**	**42**
T. G. Evans	17	91	D. W. Randall	14	47
D. E. Malcolm	16	40	**D. Gough**	**14**	**56**
A. R. Caddick	**16**	**50**	I. T. Botham	14	102

Research: Gordon Vince

offered bowlers discomfiting bounce and sideways movement, and England might have been dismissed before lunch had it not been for the stoical Trescothick: he did not make a mistake for more than two hours, striking 13 emphatic boundaries, including three sumptuous pull shots from Lee. Otherwise, Stewart aside, McGrath encountered little resistance from batsmen frankly overawed by both his craft and his reputation. The narrow man from Narromine claimed five wickets in a Test innings for the 20th time, and the fifth time against England. The wider Warne snuck in to claim his 100th Ashes wicket, having Croft taken at silly point.

It appeared business as usual when Hayden and Slater steered Australia to 48 without loss in 55 minutes against some rather ragged new-ball bowling from Caddick and Gough. But Tudor made it seem like two weeks since his last Test, rather than two years, as he trapped Hayden lbw. A remarkable 93 minutes followed in which Australia lost seven for 54 in less than 20 overs, with Gough and Caddick also profiting from the conditions; Steve Waugh's snick to slip seemed to send a tremor through their dressing-room. Gilchrist, however, remained, by now perhaps a wicket more coveted than that of his captain.

The sun broke through on the second morning, but England, after removing Lee, did not. Gilchrist bolted to his half-century from 47 deliveries with ten boundaries, twice edging to fine leg within a breath of leg stump but otherwise unassailable. With the courageous Gillespie, he added 66 from 15 overs, sufficient to conjure Australia

Alex Tudor, back in the England side after two years, fired their attack with five for 44 in Australia's first innings. But hopes that his potential was coming to fruition soon proved short-lived. By The Oval, he was *hors de combat* – back on the injury list. Not so Australian captain Steve Waugh. Three weeks after being carried off at Trent Bridge with a torn calf, he was carrying England's bowlers before him.

[*Patrick Eagar*

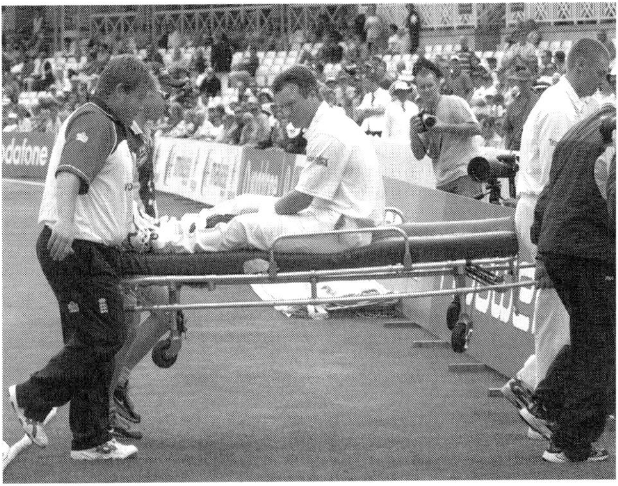

an undreamt-of first-innings lead. Tudor, who had been a doubtful starter because of a side strain, claimed five wickets in a Test innings for the first time, but England's bowling in general was spasmodic rather than systematic.

As the weather closed in after lunch, Atherton and Trescothick showed considerable composure in crafting their best opening stand of the series to date. For once, McGrath lacked penetration, and grew frustrated after Venkat declined an lbw appeal against Atherton when he was 12, the batsman playing no shot as at Lord's. The breakthrough, against the tide of play, came by freakish means. Trescothick's well-struck sweep rebounded from short leg Hayden's ankle and Gilchrist leapt forward to collect the catch. In fact, Trescothick was trebly unfortunate: television replays revealed that Warne had narrowly overstepped the front line, and immediately after his dismissal the players left the field because of rain.

The resumption brought a tense period of play, Lee touching his top speed in removing Butcher and hitting Atherton a glancing blow on the jaw at 91.8mph. But it was after a further break for bad light that Warne truly turned the Test on its head. Atherton may or may not have touched the ball he was judged to have edged to Gilchrist, but there was no doubt about the careless dismissals of Stewart and Ramprakash. The latter, in charging down the wicket with nine overs of the day remaining, squandered more than an hour and a half of painstaking application. White became Warne's fourth victim for 11 runs in 36 deliveries from the day's final ball, and the Australian advantage was consolidated when Gillespie claimed three for six from 14 deliveries on Saturday morning, including his 100th Test wicket (Caddick). Warne's six for 33 were then his best Test figures since November 1995, before the finger and shoulder operations that had imperilled his career.

Australia required 158, which they might have experienced some pangs about had Venkat upheld Gough's lbw shout against Hayden from his second ball. As it was, some punchy shots, judicious calling and a stream of boundaries to the untenanted third man set them on their way. The fifth and last fifty partnership of the match was the largest and fastest, an unbroken 69 in 11 overs as Mark Waugh and Martyn propelled Australia to victory. By then their captain had succumbed to a strained left calf – sustained while setting off for his first run – which was the only event to mar their visit. The scores were levelled by a stylish clip for four to mid-wicket by Mark Waugh, and the Ashes retained by a Caddick no-ball, an apt sequence of events for a series in which Australian style had been decisive but English ineptitude had played a part. – GIDEON HAIGH.

Man of the Match: S. K. Warne. *Attendance:* 59,040; *receipts* £1,323,113.

Close of play: First day, Australia 105-7 (Gilchrist 4*, Lee 3*); Second day, England 144-6 (Ward 13*).

England

*M. A. Atherton c M. E. Waugh b McGrath	0	– c Gilchrist b Warne	51
M. E. Trescothick c Gilchrist b Gillespie	69	– c Gilchrist b Warne	32
M. A. Butcher c Ponting b McGrath	13	– lbw b Lee	1
M. R. Ramprakash c Gilchrist b Gillespie	14	– st Gilchrist b Warne	26
†A. J. Stewart c M. E. Waugh b McGrath	46	– b Warne	0
I. J. Ward c Gilchrist b McGrath	6	– lbw b Gillespie	13
C. White c Hayden b McGrath	0	– c S. R. Waugh b Warne	7
A. J. Tudor lbw b Warne	3	– c Ponting b Warne	9
R. D. B. Croft c Ponting b Warne	3	– b Gillespie	0
A. R. Caddick b Lee	13	– c Gilchrist b Gillespie	4
D. Gough not out	0	– not out	5
B 1, l-b 9, w 1, n-b 7	18	B 4, l-b 3, n-b 7	14
1/0 (1) 2/30 (3) 3/63 (4) 4/117 (2) 5/142 (6) 6/147 (7) 7/158 (8) 8/168 (9) 9/180 (5) 10/185 (10)	185	1/57 (2) 2/59 (3) 3/115 (1) 4/115 (5) 5/126 (4) 6/144 (7) 7/144 (6) 8/146 (9) 9/156 (10) 10/162 (8)	162

Bowling: *First Innings*—McGrath 18–4–49–5; Lee 6.5–0–30–1; Gillespie 12–1–59–2; Warne 16–4–37–2. *Second Innings*—McGrath 11–3–31–0; Gillespie 20–8–61–3; Lee 8–1–30–1; Warne 18–5–33–6.

Australia

M. J. Slater b Gough	15	– (2) c Trescothick b Caddick	12
M. L. Hayden lbw b Tudor	33	– (1) lbw b Tudor	42
R. T. Ponting c Stewart b Gough	14	– c Stewart b Croft	17
M. E. Waugh c Atherton b Tudor	15	– not out	42
*S. R. Waugh c Atherton b Caddick	13	– retired hurt	1
D. R. Martyn c Stewart b Caddick	4	– not out	33
†A. C. Gilchrist c Atherton b Tudor	54		
S. K. Warne lbw b Caddick	0		
B. Lee c Butcher b Tudor	4		
J. N. Gillespie not out	27		
G. D. McGrath c Butcher b Tudor	2		
L-b 3, w 1, n-b 5	9	L-b 4, n-b 7	11
1/48 (2) 2/56 (1) 3/69 (3) 4/82 (5) 5/94 (4) 6/102 (6) 7/102 (8) 8/122 (9) 9/188 (7) 10/190 (11)	190	1/36 (2) 2/72 (3) 3/88 (1)	(3 wkts) 158

In the second innings S. R. Waugh retired hurt at 89.

Bowling: *First Innings*—Gough 15–3–63–2; Caddick 20–4–70–3; Tudor 15.5–5–44–5; White 2–1–8–0; Croft 2–0–2–0. *Second Innings*—Gough 9–1–38–0; Caddick 12.2–1–71–1; Tudor 7–0–37–1; Croft 1–0–8–1.

Umpires: S. Venkataraghavan (India) and J. H. Hampshire.
Third umpire: D. J. Constant. Referee: Talat Ali (Pakistan).

SUSSEX v AUSTRALIANS

At Hove, August 8, 9, 10. Australians won by eight wickets. Toss: Australians.

Superb batting illuminated the Australians' visit to Hove. True, there was an end-of-tour touch on the opening day, and the bowling was weakened when Noffke, treading on the ball as he aimed a kick at the stumps, damaged his ankle. But Sussex's opening stand of 202 was full of exhilarating strokeplay and excellent running. Goodwin hit his sixth hundred of the season, Montgomerie went on to his seventh, and Adams added an unbeaten half-century. Rain cut the second day to 13 overs, and third-day declarations left the Australians to get 337 in 68 overs. They did so ruthlessly. Gilchrist, dropped on 12, hit 19 fours and two sixes in his 102-ball 114; Ponting, no less belligerent, shared century stands with Gilchrist and Katich, and warmed up for Headingley with his own hundred. His 20th boundary produced the winning runs. Questions were raised about security after £1,200 worth of equipment was stolen from the visitors' dressing-room, including bats, gloves, sunglasses and copies of Warne's new autobiography.

Close of play: First day, Australians 19-2 (Slater 16*, Waugh 0*); Second day, Australians 86-2 (Slater 46*, Waugh 32*).

Sussex

M. W. Goodwin st Seccombe b Katich	105	– (7) not out	28
R. R. Montgomerie c Gilchrist b Fleming	157	– (6) lbw b Fleming	2
*C. J. Adams not out	66		
B. Zuiderent c Langer b Fleming	0	– (2) lbw b Fleming	6
M. H. Yardy run out	6	– (1) not out	21
U. B. A. Rashid not out	0	– (4) c Seccombe b Lee	7
†N. J. Wilton (did not bat)		– (3) c Waugh b Lee	1
M. J. G. Davis (did not bat)		– (5) c Seccombe b Fleming	1
L-b 4, n-b 17	21	N-b 1	1
1/202 2/328 3/330 4/355	(4 wkts dec.) 355	1/11 2/12 3/24 4/29 5/31	(5 wkts dec.) 67

J. D. Lewry, B. V. Taylor and M. A. Robinson did not bat.

Bowling: *First Innings*—Lee 23–2–117–0; Fleming 20–4–67–2; Noffke 8.3–1–29–0; Miller 24–8–78–0; Ponting 0.3–0–2–0; Katich 13–2–53–1; Langer 2–0–5–0. *Second Innings*—Lee 10–1–27–2; Fleming 8–2–20–3; Miller 2–0–20–0.

Australians

M. J. Slater not out	46		
J. L. Langer lbw b Taylor	2	– c Adams b Lewry	14
R. T. Ponting c Montgomerie b Taylor	0	– not out	147
M. E. Waugh not out	32		
*A. C. Gilchrist (did not bat)		– (1) st Wilton b Davis	114
S. M. Katich (did not bat)		– (4) not out	40
L-b 1, n-b 5	6	B 10, l-b 5, n-b 9	24
1/14 2/16	(2 wkts dec.) 86	1/57 2/208	(2 wkts) 339

†W. A. Seccombe, B. Lee, D. W. Fleming, A. A. Noffke and C. R. Miller did not bat.

Bowling: *First Innings*—Lewry 7–0–22–0; Taylor 10–1–39–2; Robinson 4–0–24–0. *Second Innings*—Lewry 11–2–52–1; Taylor 16.5–1–93–0; Robinson 13–1–71–0; Davis 12–1–56–1; Rashid 10–0–46–0; Montgomerie 1–0–6–0.

Umpires: G. I. Burgess and N. J. Llong.

†IRELAND v AUSTRALIANS

At Belfast, August 12. No result. Toss: Ireland.

Hayden had hit 52 from 74 balls when, to the disappointment of the 4,000-strong crowd, rain washed out Ormeau's farewell international. The ground, where an Australian touring team first played in 1880, had been sold to developers.

Australians

J. L. Langer c Joyce b Armstrong	22
M. L. Hayden not out	52
S. M. Katich not out	5
L-b 3, w 4	7
1/66 (1 wkt, 23.4 overs)	86

M. E. Waugh, *R. T. Ponting, D. R. Martyn, †W. A. Seccombe, S. K. Warne, B. Lee, C. R. Miller and G. D. McGrath did not bat.

Bowling: Mooney 7–0–35–0; McCoubrey 7–1–15–0; Heasley 5–0–12–0; Armstrong 4.4–0–21–1.

Ireland

J. A. M. Molins, A. R. White, P. J. Davy, D. Joyce, *W. K. McCallan, †A. D. Patterson, D. Heasley, P. J. K. Mooney, C. M. Armstrong, M. D. Dwyer and A. G. A. M. McCoubrey.

Umpires: E. Cooke and T. Henry.

ENGLAND v AUSTRALIA

Fourth npower Test

At Leeds, August 16, 17, 18, 19, 20. England won by six wickets. Toss: Australia. Test debut: S. M. Katich.

Few cricketers play a Test innings that will become an Ashes legend. Mark Butcher joined this elite when he struck an exhilarating 173 not out to ensure single-handedly that there would be no "greenwash", and show that, for a day at least, McGrath, Gillespie and Warne could be tamed. Butcher's score matched that of Don Bradman in 1948, when Australia made 404 for three here on the last day to win against the odds. But the immediate comparison was with Ian Botham's 149 not out in 1981, when his hitting transformed not only a match but a whole summer, and a whole sport. Butcher's knock was not as important as that. A fairer parallel would be the fabled 1902 innings of Gilbert Jessop, whose attacking shots and endless verve inspired a remarkable Test victory no one thought possible. As here, it was England's only win of the series.

Butcher's innings, entirely out of character with the rest of a one-sided Ashes contest, was Jessopian in vein: he cut anything short of a length with exquisite power and timing, stepped forward to drive McGrath through the covers, and clipped sweet boundaries off his legs when the bowlers erred in line. The Australians could not contain him and, though it was the only such day of the summer, his innings will never be forgotten.

Australia's stand-in captain, Gilchrist, had not thought anything like it possible when he closed his team's second innings on the fourth evening, with a lead of 314 runs and 110 overs still to play. Rain had seriously disrupted his game plan, taking maybe two sessions of Australian batting time. But Gilchrist's decision spoke volumes for the tourists' aura of invincibility, and their desire to win the series 5–0. Few in England gave the home side hope of victory either; only once, at Melbourne in 1928-29, had England scored as many in the fourth innings to win. Yet, by conventional cricketing logic, the target was attainable – even after bad light and further rain removed 17.3 overs that Sunday evening, revising England's task to 311 from 90 overs.

When openers Atherton and Trescothick fell cheaply on the fifth morning, it seemed that a routine humbling of the English batting would occur. Butcher's early overs were spent evading a wonderful spell from McGrath – but, at 60 for two, restored England captain Hussain hooked Gillespie out of the ground. Many thought this the turning-point, not for the bravura shot itself but for the fact that the ball was lost. Its replacement didn't help the bowlers as much and, on a pitch that was never the minefield predicted, batting became less of an ordeal.

Still, it needed a miraculous performance, and Butcher, whose technique had been modified the previous winter with help from his father, Alan, produced it. He was particularly severe in the overs just after lunch, when it dawned on the capacity crowd that they were witnessing an epic day of cricket. Butcher reached his hundred to a seemingly endless ovation, and when Hussain went, England's sole loss in a session

[*Graham Morris*

Headingley hammer blow to Australia's "greenwash": Mark Butcher's cavalier strokeplay left the Australian bowlers rocking and reeling, and had English cricket writers reaching for superlatives after a series of sackcloth and no Ashes. But one superlative doesn't make a summer, as the Australians proved a few days later.

worth 104, their partnership had added 181. McGrath and Warne had one last attempt to turn the screw, bowling with economy and menace, but, thanks to the generous declaration, Butcher could afford to be patient.

After tea, the outcome was not in doubt. Ramprakash succumbed within sight of the finishing line, leaving Butcher to complete the task. He carved Gillespie for a crackerjack six behind point in an over that brought 19 runs. Finally, he steered Warne away for three and England were home with 20 overs to spare. At their rate of scoring they could have chased 400 and still won, illustrating the extraordinary nature of Butcher's innings, and its entertainment value. He batted five and a quarter hours, faced 227 balls, and hit 23 fours as well as that six.

Gilchrist and all the Australian players shook the English hero's hand. Their sportsmanship was welcome, and genuine. Even though they had dominated the first four days and were superior in class and attitude, their smiles were not forced. On the first day, they had opted to bat after winning the toss and scorched to 288 for four. It may not sound much, but rain had delayed the start until 2.15 p.m. Hussain later lambasted his side's lackadaisical approach. Ponting batted with rare panache, his 144 from just 154 balls laced with three sixes and 20 fours, while Martyn had 18 fours when last out for 118 shortly after lunch next day. Simon Katich, Australia's first debutant specialist batsman for over three years, compiled a nervous 15, but a total of 447 looked a good score on a Headingley pitch with a worryingly dry top.

England responded with general competence, all the top-order batsmen starting well but failing to reach 50. Stewart, starting at No. 7 for the first time in 114 Tests, and unhappy at the demotion, responded with a bizarre innings of 76 not out, throwing the bat with daredevil irresponsibility. But his luck held, the follow-on was averted and, after a two-hour interruption either side of tea on Saturday, England reached 309, even making Australia take the second new ball for the first time in the series. McGrath's figures of seven for 76, which took him to 350 Test wickets, were those of a maestro and, in a normal Test, a match-winner. But this was no normal game.

When Ponting flew to 30 in 35 balls, before the light deteriorated, and increased his momentum with wonderful batting next morning, everything pointed to Australia taking the game beyond England's reach. Instead, the weather permitted only 30 runs between lunch and Gilchrist's declaration at 5.35 p.m., as well as limiting the day's play to just 25 overs. It was frustrating for the big crowd, but many would be back on Monday, little realising that Sunday's conditions had provided the stage on which Butcher would storm into Ashes history. – JIM HOLDEN.

Man of the Match: M. A. Butcher. *Attendance:* 71,256; *receipts* £1,283,508.

Close of play: First day, Australia 288-4 (Martyn 19*); Second day, England 155-2 (Butcher 47*, Hussain 45*); Third day, Australia 69-1 (Hayden 12*, Ponting 30*); Fourth day, England 4-0 (Atherton 4*, Trescothick 0*).

Australia

M. J. Slater lbw b Caddick	21	– (2) b Gough	16
M. L. Hayden lbw b Caddick	15	– (1) c Stewart b Mullally	35
R. T. Ponting c Stewart b Tudor	144	– lbw b Gough	72
M. E. Waugh c Ramprakash b Caddick	72	– not out	24
D. R. Martyn c Stewart b Gough	118	– lbw b Caddick	6
S. M. Katich b Gough	15	– not out	0
*†A. C. Gilchrist c Trescothick b Gough	19		
S. K. Warne c Stewart b Gough	0		
B. Lee c Ramprakash b Mullally	0		
J. N. Gillespie c Atherton b Gough	5		
G. D. McGrath not out	8		
B 5, l-b 15, w 1, n-b 9	30	B 5, l-b 7, n-b 11	23
1/39 (1) 2/42 (2) 3/263 (3) 4/288 (4) 5/355 (6) 6/396 (7) 7/412 (8) 8/422 (9) 9/438 (10) 10/447 (5)	447	1/25 (2) 2/129 (3) 3/141 (1) 4/171 (5) (4 wkts dec.)	176

Bowling: *First Innings*—Gough 25.1–4–103–5; Caddick 29–4–143–3; Mullally 23–8–65–1; Tudor 18–1–97–1; Butcher 1–0–7–0; Ramprakash 4–0–12–0. *Second Innings*—Gough 17–3–68–2; Caddick 11–2–45–1; Tudor 4–1–17–0; Mullally 7.3–2–34–1.

England

M. A. Atherton c Gilchrist b McGrath	22	– c Gilchrist b McGrath	8
M. E. Trescothick c Gilchrist b McGrath	37	– c Hayden b Gillespie	10
M. A. Butcher run out	47	– not out	173
*N. Hussain lbw b McGrath	46	– c Gilchrist b Gillespie	55
M. R. Ramprakash c Gilchrist b Lee	40	– c Waugh b Warne	32
U. Afzaal c Warne b McGrath	14	– not out	4
†A. J. Stewart not out	76		
A. J. Tudor c Gilchrist b McGrath	2		
A. R. Caddick c Gilchrist b Lee	5		
D. Gough c Slater b McGrath	8		
A. D. Mullally c Katich b McGrath	0		
B 2, l-b 3, n-b 7	12	B 14, l-b 16, n-b 3	33
1/50 (1) 2/67 (2) 3/158 (4) 4/158 (3) 5/174 (6) 6/252 (5) 7/267 (8) 8/289 (9) 9/299 (10) 10/309 (11)	309	1/8 (1) 2/33 (2) 3/214 (4) 4/289 (5)	(4 wkts) 315

Bowling: *First Innings*—McGrath 30.2–9–76–7; Gillespie 26–6–76–0; Lee 22–3–103–2; Warne 16–2–49–0. *Second Innings*—McGrath 16–3–61–1; Gillespie 22–4–94–2; Warne 18.2–3–58–1; Lee 16–4–65–0; Waugh 1–0–7–0.

Umpires: S. Venkataraghavan (India) and D. R. Shepherd.
Third umpire: N. A. Mallender. Referee: Talat Ali (Pakistan).

ENGLAND v AUSTRALIA

Fifth npower Test

At The Oval, August 23, 24, 25, 26, 27. Australia won by an innings and 25 runs. Toss: Australia. Test debut: J. Ormond.

Normally, the glow from a sensational Test match victory ought to last for weeks or months; in the case of Headingley '81 it has lasted 20 years. The last embers of English joy from Headingley '01 were snuffed out inside 72 hours, thanks to the first back-to-back Tests in England in 89 years, and a dramatic and total reversion to the familiar pattern of Australian mastery. This was only Australia's second win at The Oval since 1948, when Bradman led them to an innings victory despite a duck in his final Test. The other came in 1972 when the Chappell brothers both scored centuries; this time, the Waughs did the same.

[*Patrick Eagar*

Alec Stewart's bat may or may not have made contact with the ball – Stewart had no doubts – but the delivery and appeal were good enough to earn Shane Warne his 400th Test wicket.

Steve Waugh was not what anyone else would have called fit but, with awesome courage and determination, not to mention skill, he came back from injury to ensure that Australia returned to business as usual with astounding rapidity. He started by winning the toss, yet again, and England sensed what lay in front of them. Before the opening day was gone, the only question was, yet again, whether they might save the game.

But there was more discussion about the sub-plots: whether Mike Atherton really was going to retire (he was) and whether Gough and Stewart would be allowed to cherry-pick which parts of the winter tour they wanted to go on (they were not). Monday's hero, Butcher, who had increased his standing with one innings in a way reminiscent of Derek Randall at the 1977 Centenary Test, was loudly applauded to the crease twice by his home crowd – and back again, without achieving anything much.

Katich, as expected, had to make way for Steve Waugh, but Australia also dumped Slater. Being dropped by Australia is always a more fearful and sometimes final blow than being dropped by England, and in this case Slater's replacement, Langer, seized his opportunity on day one.

He was up against another makeshift England attack, with the retread Tufnell and debutant Jimmy Ormond replacing Mullally and Tudor, whose inability to stay fit remained a source of exasperation. Tufnell's triumph at The Oval four years earlier, however, seemed a lifetime away, and all the England bowlers had their hearts broken on the opening day. The pitch was benign, but the faster men might have been helped by a day of late-summer haze had even one of them struck up a rhythm. Instead, the new opening pair of Langer and Hayden put on 158 and, after a patchy start – understandable after batting so little on tour – Langer scored his eighth Test century in his familiar, understated style. Four overs later, he retired hurt, having been hit on the helmet trying to hook Caddick, but there seemed no other way to remove him.

It got worse for England. On Friday, the sun shone and, in four hours 35 minutes, Australia raced from 324 for two to 641 for four, their highest score on the ground since 1934, when double-centuries from Ponsford and Bradman propelled them to 701.

Mark Waugh's 20th Test century was a thing of beauty, as ever, and took him ahead of David Boon into fourth place on Australia's all-time run-list. But Steve's 27th – only Gavaskar (34) and Bradman (29) had scored more – showed that class is not the only determinant of quality. About 99 per cent of cricketers would not have dreamt of turning out in his condition: he winced his way to 157 not out.

England began their response in something of the same spirit, with Trescothick racing to a run-a-ball 55 before the close. But by then Warne had turned one massively on to Atherton's leg stump. And, next morning, Trescothick lasted only two balls and Butcher, having briefly displayed his new-found dominance, pushed a catch to short leg. The main business, thereafter, seemed to have more to do with fringe players establishing themselves than saving the follow-on. Ramprakash and Afzaal achieved their personal objectives without quite doing what the team required. Afzaal showed spirit in his 54, and something of the judgment the selectors had sensed when they picked him; Ramprakash survived until the fourth morning, scoring 133, his second Test century (on his new home ground). For the time being, it ended a decade of doubts about the gap between his ability and his temperament.

But no one ever truly mastered either McGrath or Warne, whose seven for 165, his best Test analysis overseas, made him the first Australian to reach 400 Test wickets. The landmark was not quite the moment of mellowness Warne deserved: Stewart was convinced he had not touched the ball on its way to Gilchrist, and made that clear enough to be fined 20 per cent of his match fee. Gilchrist concluded the innings with his own record, his 100th dismissal in his 22nd Test; previously, Mark Boucher was the quickest, in 23. England missed the follow-on target by ten.

They still had hopes of survival, even though Warne was getting ever more unplayable, because the Sunday was wet and only 21.3 overs were bowled. That was enough time for one last episode in the McGrath v Atherton saga, which ended in McGrath's 19th personal victory, a catch at first slip. Atherton, however, was determined to control what happened next: there would be no unseemly fuss, none of the showbizzy demonstrations that accompanied the farewells to Curtly Ambrose and Courtney Walsh here a year earlier. The only clue he gave that this really was goodbye was an extra wave of the bat. Thus ended the career of England's best batsman of the past decade. No flowers, please, by request. Cussed to the last, our Mike.

England as a whole were far less cussed. They lost four wickets to Warne and McGrath in the first hour on Monday, and the biggest stand of the innings was 58 for the ninth wicket between Ormond and Gough. It was over before teatime. Australia had won the series 4–1 and, in case anyone had taken Headingley too seriously, had reiterated that their reign goes on – ad infinitum, England fear. – MATTHEW ENGEL.

Man of the Match: S. K. Warne. *Attendance:* 84,752; *receipts* £1,900,199.

Men of the Series: England – M. A. Butcher; Australia – G. D. McGrath.

Close of play: First day, Australia 324-2 (M. E. Waugh 48*, S. R. Waugh 12*); Second day, England 80-1 (Trescothick 55*, Butcher 10*); Third day, England 409-8 (Ramprakash 124*, Gough 17*); Fourth day, England 40-1 (Trescothick 20*, Butcher 11*).

Australia

M. L. Hayden c Trescothick b Tufnell	68	D. R. Martyn not out	64
J. L. Langer retired hurt	102		
R. T. Ponting c Atherton b Ormond	62	B 10, l-b 13, w 1, n-b 19	43
M. E. Waugh b Gough	120		
*S. R. Waugh not out	157	1/158 (1) 2/292 (3)	(4 wkts dec.) 641
†A. C. Gilchrist c Ramprakash b Afzaal	25	3/489 (4) 4/534 (6)	

S. K. Warne, B. Lee, J. N. Gillespie and G. D. McGrath did not bat.

Langer retired hurt at 236.

Bowling: Gough 29–4–113–1; Caddick 36–9–146–0; Ormond 34–4–115–1; Tufnell 39–2–174–1; Butcher 1–0–2–0; Ramprakash 4–0–19–0; Afzaal 9–0–49–1.

England

M. A. Atherton b Warne	13	– c Warne b McGrath	9
M. E. Trescothick b Warne	55	– c and b McGrath	24
M. A. Butcher c Langer b Warne	25	– c S. R. Waugh b Warne	14
*N. Hussain b M. E. Waugh	52	– lbw b Warne	2
M. R. Ramprakash c Gilchrist b McGrath	133	– c Hayden b Warne	19
U. Afzaal c Gillespie b McGrath	54	– c Ponting b McGrath	5
†A. J. Stewart c Gilchrist b Warne	29	– b Warne	34
A. R. Caddick lbw b Warne	0	– b Lee	17
J. Ormond b Warne	18	– c Gilchrist b McGrath	17
D. Gough st Gilchrist b Warne	24	– not out	39
P. C. R. Tufnell not out	7	– c Warne b McGrath	0
B 3, l-b 13, w 1, n-b 5	22	L-b 2, n-b 2	4
1/58 (1) 2/85 (2) 3/104 (3) 4/166 (4) 5/255 (6) 6/313 (7) 7/313 (8) 8/350 (9) 9/424 (5) 10/432 (10)	432	1/17 (1) 2/46 (3) 3/48 (2) 4/50 (4) 5/55 (6) 6/95 (5) 7/126 (7) 8/126 (8) 9/184 (9) 10/184 (11)	184

Bowling: *First Innings*—McGrath 30–11–67–2; Gillespie 20–3–96–0; Warne 44.2–7–165–7; Lee 14–1–43–0; Ponting 2–0–5–0; M. E. Waugh 8–0–40–1. *Second Innings*—Lee 10–3–30–1; McGrath 15.3–6–43–5; Warne 28–8–64–4; Ponting 2–0–3–0; Gillespie 12–5–38–0; M. E. Waugh 1–0–4–0.

Umpires: R. E. Koertzen (South Africa) and P. Willey.
Third umpire: M. J. Kitchen. Referee: Talat Ali (Pakistan).

FICA/WCM PLACE IN HISTORY AWARD

The Federation of International Cricketers' Associations/*Wisden Cricket Monthly* International Place in History 2001 award went to Australia for their record 16 successive Test wins between October 1999 and March 2001. Steve Waugh accepted the award in July.

BRADMAN'S BEST

Sir Donald Bradman's team to beat all-comers appeared in the book *Bradman's Best*, published in August 2001. He had instructed the author, Roland Perry, that the selection should not appear in his lifetime. The team, in batting order, was: Barry Richards (South Africa), Arthur Morris (Australia), Don Bradman (Australia, *captain*), Sachin Tendulkar (India), Garry Sobers (West Indies), Don Tallon (Australia, *wicket-keeper*), Ray Lindwall (Australia), Dennis Lillee (Australia), Alec Bedser (England), Bill O'Reilly (Australia), Clarrie Grimmett (Australia) and Wally Hammond (England, *twelfth man*).

THE NATWEST SERIES, 2001

By MYLES HODGSON

The second NatWest Series, this time offering England the opportunity to test their capabilities against two of the best one-day sides in the world, ended as it began, with crowd trouble overshadowing a level of performance that the hosts never threatened to match. The beer can that thudded into Michael Bevan's cheek, as the Australians gathered on the Lord's Pavilion balcony to receive the NatWest Series Trophy, provided a symbolic signature to a tournament that disturbed as much as it entertained.

The cricket at times was breathtaking. Australia set a template for a new style of one-day cricket. Instead of frustrating the opposition with defensive bowling and field-settings, they played attacking cricket more akin to the opening session of a Test match, and Pakistan, led by a rejuvenated Waqar Younis, were almost as impressive. England, weakened by the loss of key players, were pedestrian in comparison and, after six successive defeats, opened an inquest into their long-term one-day strategy in the build-up to the 2003 World Cup.

Sadly, it was not the only inquiry to result from the tournament. Pakistan's frenzied supporters crossed the line between enthusiasm and unacceptable behaviour too often. They interrupted the opening day/night encounter against England in Birmingham, caused a steward to be taken to hospital with rib injuries at Headingley, and provoked Steve Waugh, the Australian captain, into leading his side off the field at Trent Bridge. Even after security had been tightened for the final at Lord's, the beer can thrown at the players during the presentation ceremony left Bevan with a mark on his cheek, and a sour taste overall.

Waugh, who had previous experience of crowd invasions during a tour of the West Indies shortly before the 1999 World Cup, repeatedly voiced his concern about security on English grounds. ECB chief executive Tim Lamb rejected Waugh's suggestion that the English authorities did not regard crowd invasions as a safety issue – and claimed after the Edgbaston match that the board were doing everything they could to ensure there was no repetition. Although it was thought at the time that the authorities were hindered by lack of legislation that would allow prosecution for encroachment of the playing field, the later inquiry into the disturbances concluded that existing laws were, in fact, strong enough, and ruled out introducing tougher ones.

Nor did England's fortunes on the pitch provide a much needed distraction. Already without captain Nasser Hussain and all-rounder Craig White through injury, they lost their most influential batsman, Graham Thorpe, with a calf strain in the warm-up for the opening match, leaving in disarray their plans to introduce new talent alongside senior players. Alec Stewart, as he had the previous year, accepted the opportunity to lead the side; Surrey team-mates Ben Hollioake and Ally Brown were recalled, and Owais Shah of Middlesex and Durham's Paul Collingwood given their first taste of international cricket.

The comprehensive opening defeat by Pakistan under Edgbaston's lights, once Waqar had personally appealed to the crowd to leave the field and allow the match to be completed, set the tone for England's performances. Unable to restrict the attacking strokeplay of Inzamam-ul-Haq, Saeed Anwar and Azhar Mahmood, they then struggled in reply against opponents vastly more experienced in these situations. Better displays against Australia and Pakistan in the next two games, resulting in last-over defeats, proved a false dawn; England's performances grew steadily worse while their opponents set ever-increasing standards of excellence. Only Marcus Trescothick and Nick Knight passed 200 runs for England in the tournament, while the bowling provided little penetration beyond the established trio of Darren Gough, Andrew Caddick and Alan Mullally.

Australia, by contrast, more than lived up to their status as world champions, growing stronger with every game and, after dismissing England for their lowest one-day total

[*Patrick Eagar*

The problem of the pitch invaders had the men in suits on the run during the NatWest Series; not even the sanctuary of Lord's was sacred from unruly crowd behaviour. Australia's Michael Bevan, gingerly feeling for damage, was struck on the cheek by the beer can under scrutiny from team-mate Mark Waugh.

[*Patrick Eagar*

of 86 at Old Trafford, went on to complete a comfortable final victory over Pakistan, as they had two years previously in the World Cup. Their attack was irrepressible. Jason Gillespie and Glenn McGrath's consistent accuracy enabled them to bowl to Test-match fields, while Brett Lee, working his way back to fitness following an elbow operation, demonstrated lightning-fast pace. The batsmen were equally impressive, with Steve Waugh and Ricky Ponting each averaging more than 90 and, later in the tournament, Adam Gilchrist displaying the destructive strokeplay that would soon light up the Ashes series.

For Pakistan, Waqar rose to the responsibilities of leading the side and finished as the tournament's leading wicket-taker with 17. Two days after claiming seven for 36 against England at Headingley, the second-best one-day international figures yet, he took six for 59 against Australia at Trent Bridge to inspire the world champions' only defeat of the competition.

Note: Matches in this section were not first-class.

ENGLAND v PAKISTAN

At Birmingham, June 7 (day/night). Pakistan won by 108 runs. Toss: Pakistan. International debut: P. D. Collingwood.

The late crowd invasion, which delayed Pakistan's inevitable victory, rightly dominated the headlines, but it also served to overshadow England's inadequacies and inexperience. None of their seven bowlers was able to restrict Pakistan's free-scoring batsmen. Saeed Anwar and Inzamam-ul-Haq propelled them to a challenging total with a 150-run partnership spanning 26 overs. Replying under the lights, England suffered in comparison as the regular fall of wickets forced Knight into an anchor role. Azhar Mahmood, having earlier hit an unbeaten 38 from 24 deliveries, exposed the lower middle order with the help of two wonderful diving catches in the covers.

Man of the Match: Saeed Anwar. *Attendance:* 19,223; *receipts* £421,961.

Pakistan

Saeed Anwar c Hollioake b Cork 77
Shahid Afridi c Ealham b Mullally 25
Abdur Razzaq run out. 9
Inzamam-ul-Haq c Trescothick b Cork . . 79
Yousuf Youhana run out. 12
Azhar Mahmood not out 38
Younis Khan c Stewart b Gough 9
Wasim Akram not out 4
B 4, l-b 5, w 9, n-b 2 20

1/34 (2) 2/55 (3) 3/205 (1) 4/210 (4) 5/236 (5) 6/265 (7) (6 wkts, 50 overs) 273

Score at 15 overs: 56-2

†Rashid Latif, *Waqar Younis and Saqlain Mushtaq did not bat.

Bowling: Gough 10–0–53–1; Mullally 10–1–44–1; Ealham 10–0–35–0; Cork 10–0–44–2; Vaughan 2–0–17–0; Collingwood 2–0–18–0; Hollioake 6–0–53–0.

England

M. E. Trescothick c Younis Khan b Waqar Younis . 28
A. D. Brown c Rashid Latif b Waqar Younis . 8
N. V. Knight not out 59
*†A. J. Stewart c sub (Shoaib Malik) b Azhar Mahmood . 10
M. P. Vaughan c Saeed Anwar b Azhar Mahmood . 5
P. D. Collingwood lbw b Abdur Razzaq . 2
B. C. Hollioake c and b Saqlain Mushtaq 6
D. G. Cork b Shahid Afridi 18
M. A. Ealham b Saqlain Mushtaq 4
D. Gough lbw b Shahid Afridi 1
A. D. Mullally c Rashid Latif b Shahid Afridi . 3
L-b 9, w 11, n-b 1. 21

1/28 (2) 2/47 (1) 3/69 (4) 4/86 (5) 5/92 (6) 6/108 (7) 7/135 (8) 8/144 (9) 9/147 (10) 10/165 (11) (47.2 overs) 165

Score at 15 overs: 61-2

Bowling: Wasim Akram 7–2–20–0; Waqar Younis 6–0–31–2; Azhar Mahmood 10–0–46–2; Abdur Razzaq 7–0–24–1; Saqlain Mushtaq 10–0–20–2; Shahid Afridi 7.2–2–15–3.

Umpires: B. Dudleston and J. H. Hampshire.
Third umpire: G. I. Burgess.

AUSTRALIA v PAKISTAN

At Cardiff, June 9. Australia won by seven wickets. Toss: Pakistan.

Australia's entry to the competition proved something of a culture shock both to their opponents and to hosts England, who witnessed one-day cricket of the highest calibre from the two sides. The world champions established their superiority from the start; an attack that included Lee, despite indications he would not feature until the Ashes tour, reduced Pakistan to 85 for six by the 23rd over. It took a world-record seventh-wicket partnership of 124 between Yousuf Youhana and Rashid Latif to get them to a respectable total. Australia lost Gilchrist early on, bowled for pace by Shoaib Akhtar, who later delivered a ball at 97mph, according to the speed gun. But speed alone was not enough against the Australians' formidable line-up. Mark Waugh and Ponting (68 balls, 12 fours) reversed the setback with a 92-run stand inside 15 overs, Bevan and Steve Waugh added 116 without being parted, and Australia triumphed with 4.2 overs remaining.

Man of the Match: R. T. Ponting. *Attendance:* 9,532; *receipts* £149,151.

Pakistan

Saeed Anwar c Warne b Harvey	35
Shahid Afridi c M. E. Waugh b Lee	11
Abdur Razzaq st Gilchrist b Warne	9
Inzamam-ul-Haq st Gilchrist b Warne	0
Yousuf Youhana not out	91
Younis Khan lbw b Harvey	13
Azhar Mahmood c Gilchrist b Warne	0
†Rashid Latif run out	66
*Waqar Younis c Warne b McGrath	14
Saqlain Mushtaq run out	2
Shoaib Akhtar c M. E. Waugh b McGrath	1
L-b 3, w 6, n-b 6	15
1/14 (2) 2/44 (3) 3/45 (4) 4/65 (1) 5/83 (6) 6/85 (7) 7/209 (8) 8/241 (9) 9/254 (10) 10/257 (11) (49.5 overs)	257

Score at 15 overs: 56-3

Bowling: McGrath 9.5–2–22–2; Lee 10–1–85–1; Harvey 10–2–39–2; Warne 10–0–52–3; Martyn 4–0–21–0; Symonds 4–0–23–0; Bevan 2–0–12–0.

Australia

M. E. Waugh c Younis Khan b Abdur Razzaq	47
†A. C. Gilchrist b Shoaib Akhtar	13
R. T. Ponting c Abdur Razzaq b Saqlain Mushtaq	70
M. G. Bevan not out	56
*S. R. Waugh not out	54
B 6, l-b 3, w 3, n-b 6	18
1/20 (2) 2/112 (1) 3/142 (3) (3 wkts, 45.4 overs)	258

Score at 15 overs: 95-1

A. Symonds, D. R. Martyn, I. J. Harvey, S. K. Warne, B. Lee and G. D. McGrath did not bat.

Bowling: Waqar Younis 7–0–41–0; Shoaib Akhtar 5–0–41–1; Azhar Mahmood 8–0–37–0; Abdur Razzaq 9–0–42–1; Saqlain Mushtaq 8.4–0–45–1; Shahid Afridi 8–0–43–0.

Umpires: A. G. T. Whitehead and P. Willey.
Third umpire: R. Julian.

ENGLAND v AUSTRALIA

At Bristol, June 10. Australia won by five wickets. Toss: England. International debut: O. A. Shah.

Another enforced change almost produced an exceptional England victory. Owais Shah, given his chance when Vaughan withdrew with a bruised finger, combined with the recalled Ben Hollioake to lift England to their highest total of the competition, and Australia needed all their expertise in pacing an innings to overhaul it with three balls to spare. Shah and Hollioake added a crucial

70 after Trescothick and Knight had provided a good foundation through solid half-centuries. Once again, though, Ponting delivered for Australia, this time completing a magnificent century, with two sixes and nine fours in 116 balls. As the game reached its climax, Harvey, on his county ground, eased the pressure with the day's 12th six – over extra cover off Hollioake – to leave Australia needing five from the final over. Steve Waugh, predictably, hit the winning runs. England's seventh successive defeat equalled their worst one-day sequence.

Man of the Match: R. T. Ponting. *Attendance:* 14,744; *receipts* £390,348.

England

M. E. Trescothick run out	69	B. C. Hollioake not out	37
A. D. Brown c Gilchrist b McGrath	12	L-b 10, w 2, n-b 1	13
N. V. Knight c Warne b Lee	84		—
*†A. J. Stewart lbw b Lee	25	1/13 (2) 2/137 (1) (4 wkts, 50 overs)	268
O. A. Shah not out	28	3/189 (3) 4/198 (4) Score at 15 overs: 66-1	

R. D. B. Croft, D. G. Cork, M. A. Ealham, D. Gough and A. D. Mullally did not bat.

Bowling: McGrath 10–1–45–1; Lee 10–1–55–2; Harvey 10–0–59–0; Warne 9–0–48–0; Symonds 3–0–24–0; M. E. Waugh 8–0–27–0.

Australia

†A. C. Gilchrist c Shah b Gough	4	I. J. Harvey not out	19
M. E. Waugh b Cork	46	B 1, l-b 4, w 1	6
R. T. Ponting run out	102		—
D. R. Martyn b Mullally	46	1/12 (1) 2/101 (2) (5 wkts, 49.3 overs)	272
A. Symonds b Gough	23	3/198 (4) 4/211 (3)	
*S. R. Waugh not out	26	5/230 (5) Score at 15 overs: 66-1	

M. L. Hayden, S. K. Warne, B. Lee and G. D. McGrath did not bat.

Bowling: Gough 10–2–44–2; Mullally 10–1–50–1; Ealham 8.3–0–60–0; Cork 10–0–39–1; Croft 7–0–46–0; Hollioake 4–0–28–0.

Umpires: J. H. Hampshire and R. Julian.
Third umpire: D. J. Constant.

ENGLAND v PAKISTAN

At Lord's, June 12. Pakistan won by two runs. Toss: England.

Another dramatic finish brought another England defeat, this time by the slimmest of margins. Trescothick's maiden one-day international hundred and record England fourth-wicket partnership of 170 with Shah should have ensured victory. Instead, in a manner similar to their Test victory at Old Trafford eight days before, Pakistan fought back by claiming seven wickets in the last ten overs. An eventful final over from Saqlain Mushtaq, with nine runs needed, included a collision in the deep between Shahid Afridi and Shoaib Malik as the former caught Trescothick for 137 from 142 balls (three sixes, 11 fours); it ended with Caddick being stumped, trying to hit over the top. Deprived of Saeed Anwar through injury, Pakistan owed their relatively modest total to another disciplined half-century from Yousuf Youhana, while Azhar Mahmood again weighed in with powerful strokeplay down the order.

Man of the Match: M. E. Trescothick. *Attendance:* 23,152; *receipts* £702,044.

Pakistan

Salim Elahi lbw b Gough	15	Shoaib Malik b Gough	9
Shahid Afridi c Trescothick b Caddick	30	*Waqar Younis not out	2
Yousuf Youhana c Shah b Mullally	81	L-b 2, w 3, n-b 6	11
Inzamam-ul-Haq b Caddick	0		—
Younis Khan c Knight b Cork	41	1/28 (1) 2/59 (2) (8 wkts, 50 overs)	242
†Rashid Latif b Ealham	23	3/60 (4) 4/140 (5)	
Abdur Razzaq c Gough b Mullally	3	5/190 (6) 6/195 (7)	
Azhar Mahmood not out	27	7/208 (3) 8/237 (9) Score at 15 overs: 60-3	

Saqlain Mushtaq did not bat.

Bowling: Caddick 10–1–37–2; Gough 10–1–38–2; Mullally 10–0–47–2; Cork 7–0–50–1; Ealham 7–0–32–1; Hollioake 6–0–36–0.

England

M. E. Trescothick c Shahid Afridi b Saqlain Mushtaq	137	D. Gough lbw b Abdur Razzaq	6
N. V. Knight run out	1	A. R. Caddick st Rashid Latif b Saqlain Mushtaq	10
*†A. J. Stewart c Younis Khan b Abdur Razzaq	4	A. D. Mullally not out	1
M. P. Vaughan c Azhar Mahmood b Waqar Younis	0	L-b 5, w 5, n-b 6	16
			—
O. A. Shah run out	62	1/6 (2) 2/19 (3) 3/26 (4) (50 overs)	240
B. C. Hollioake b Waqar Younis	0	4/196 (5) 5/197 (6) 6/201 (7)	
D. G. Cork run out	3	7/205 (8) 8/218 (9) 9/237 (1)	
M. A. Ealham lbw b Shahid Afridi	0	10/240 (10) Score at 15 overs: 36-3	

Bowling: Waqar Younis 10–2–20–2; Abdur Razzaq 10–0–41–2; Azhar Mahmood 10–0–50–0; Saqlain Mushtaq 9–0–50–2; Shoaib Malik 4–0–39–0; Shahid Afridi 7–0–35–1.

Umpires: N. A. Mallender and K. E. Palmer.
Third umpire: T. E. Jesty.

ENGLAND v AUSTRALIA

At Manchester, June 14 (day/night). Australia won by 125 runs (D/L method). Toss: Australia.

After coming so close to victory in their previous match, England were well and truly put in their place by a magnificent display of fast bowling from McGrath and Gillespie, returned from an ankle injury and playing his first game of the tournament. Given attacking Test-match fields and expertly utilising the damp atmosphere throughout nine-over spells, they reduced England to 40 for five as they chased a revised target of 212 from 44 overs. When rain ended Australia's innings two overs early, the target was initially 220 in 48. England's humiliating 86 all out was their lowest one-day score. Earlier they had celebrated Gough's equalling of Ian Botham's England record of 145 one-day international wickets, when he ended Waugh's determined innings of 64. That achievement, however, was quickly eclipsed by Australia's stirring response, and another defeat for England's increasingly dispirited squad.

Man of the Match: J. N. Gillespie. *Attendance:* 18,839; *receipts* £494,108.

Australia

M. L. Hayden c Gough b Caddick	0	S. K. Warne not out	14
†A. C. Gilchrist c Hollioake b Gough	5		
R. T. Ponting c Knight b Caddick	21	L-b 2, n-b 3	5
M. G. Bevan c Stewart b Mullally	37		—
*S. R. Waugh lbw b Gough	64	1/0 (1) 2/23 (2) (7 wkts, 48 overs)	208
D. R. Martyn not out	51	3/27 (3) 4/93 (4)	
A. Symonds c Vaughan b Mullally	11	5/161 (5) 6/188 (7)	
I. J. Harvey c Trescothick b Mullally	0	7/189 (8) Score at 15 overs: 61-3	

J. N. Gillespie and G. D. McGrath did not bat.

Bowling: Caddick 10–2–45–2; Gough 9–0–31–2; Cork 9–0–50–0; Mullally 10–1–50–3; Hollioake 10–0–30–0.

England

M. E. Trescothick b McGrath	15
N. V. Knight c Gilchrist b McGrath	12
*†A. J. Stewart c Bevan b Gillespie	0
M. P. Vaughan b Gillespie	0
O. A. Shah c Ponting b Gillespie	10
P. D. Collingwood c and b Symonds	9
B. C. Hollioake st Gilchrist b Warne	0
D. G. Cork c Hayden b Symonds	17
D. Gough lbw b Warne	2
A. R. Caddick not out	8
A. D. Mullally c Gilchrist b Harvey	6
L-b 1, w 5, n-b 1	7
1/25 (2) 2/26 (3) 3/26 (4) 4/40 (5) 5/40 (1) 6/40 (7) 7/65 (8) 8/69 (6) 9/69 (9) 10/86 (11) (32.4 overs)	86

Score at 13 overs: 32-3

Bowling: McGrath 9–3–19–2; Gillespie 9–5–20–3; Warne 7–2–16–2; Symonds 7–0–24–2; Harvey 0.4–0–6–1.

Umpires: J. W. Holder and J. W. Lloyds.
Third umpire: M. R. Benson.

AUSTRALIA v PAKISTAN

At Chester-le-Street, June 16. No result (abandoned).

ENGLAND v PAKISTAN

At Leeds, June 17. Pakistan won when England conceded the match. Toss: Pakistan.

One of the outstanding one-day international bowling performances was overshadowed by the ugliest scenes of the tournament. Another, more frightening, crowd invasion left a ground steward suffering broken ribs and prompted England captain Stewart to concede the match, an unprecedented occurrence at this level. Waqar Younis's magnificent swing and seam bowling earned him figures of seven for 36, the second-best return after Muralitharan's seven for 30 the previous October, and had England reeling at 58 for seven. They were saved from an even lower total than their 86 three days before by Hollioake, whose defiant half-century saw them into three figures. Pakistan were on the brink of victory at 153 for four, with more than ten overs remaining, when the crowd spilled on to the pitch and the steward, attempting to protect the stumps, was assaulted.

Man of the Match: Waqar Younis. *Attendance:* 12,818; *receipts* £340,422.

England

M. E. Trescothick b Waqar Younis	0
N. V. Knight c Shahid Afridi b Waqar Younis	9
*†A. J. Stewart c Abdur Razzaq b Waqar Younis	18
M. P. Vaughan c Younis Khan b Waqar Younis	2
O. A. Shah c Inzamam-ul-Haq b Waqar Younis	3
P. D. Collingwood c Younis Khan b Waqar Younis	0
B. C. Hollioake b Shahid Afridi	53
D. G. Cork c Rashid Latif b Waqar Younis	4
D. Gough not out	40
A. R. Caddick c Rashid Latif b Azhar Mahmood	6
A. D. Mullally run out	0
L-b 6, w 8, n-b 7	21
1/0 (1) 2/23 (2) 3/30 (4) 4/38 (5) 5/39 (6) 6/51 (3) 7/58 (8) 8/125 (7) 9/142 (10) 10/156 (11) (45.2 overs)	156

Score at 15 overs: 45-5

Bowling: Waqar Younis 10–0–36–7; Fazl-e-Akbar 10–2–29–0; Abdur Razzaq 7–2–24–0; Azhar Mahmood 7–1–25–1; Saqlain Mushtaq 7.2–0–17–0; Shahid Afridi 4–1–19–1.

Pakistan

Saeed Anwar c Stewart b Gough 24
Shahid Afridi c Stewart b Gough 2
Abdur Razzaq c Stewart b Cork 75
Yousuf Youhana c Stewart b Cork 24
Younis Khan not out 10
Azhar Mahmood not out 6
W 3, n-b 9 12

1/21 (2) 2/34 (1) 3/128 (4) 4/147 (3) (4 wkts, 39.5 overs) 153

Score at 15 overs: 44-2

Inzamam-ul-Haq, Fazl-e-Akbar, †Rashid Latif, *Waqar Younis and Saqlain Mushtaq did not bat.

Bowling: Gough 10–2–39–2; Caddick 10–1–28–0; Mullally 10–1–30–0; Cork 5.5–0–32–2; Hollioake 3–0–14–0; Collingwood 1–0–10–0.

Umpires: J. W. Holder and M. J. Kitchen.
Third umpire: J. W. Lloyds.

AUSTRALIA v PAKISTAN

At Nottingham, June 19 (day/night). Pakistan won by 36 runs. Toss: Pakistan.

Increased security in the aftermath of Edgbaston and Headingley did not prevent further trouble; when a firework exploded near Lee, Australian captain Waugh led his side off the field for 20 minutes. The incident inevitably detracted from another superlative display from Waqar Younis, who followed his seven wickets against England with a further six to provide the inspiration for Australia's only defeat of the series. He removed three early wickets in a line-up without three rested players before Gilchrist put his side back in contention with a hard-hitting 70 (44 balls, one six, 12 fours). Steve Waugh weighed in with a typically determined half-century, but Waqar's two wickets in six balls, after returning to the attack in the 32nd over, effectively decided the outcome. Earlier, Salim Elahi had taken his chance as opener to hit 79 from 91 balls and set Pakistan on their way to a mammoth total.

Man of the Match: Waqar Younis. *Attendance:* 13,874; *receipts* £247,511.

Pakistan

Saeed Anwar lbw b Lee 34
Salim Elahi lbw b Warne 79
Abdur Razzaq c Fleming b Lee 5
Yousuf Youhana st Gilchrist b Warne . . . 44
Younis Khan c Gillespie b Martyn 23
Faisal Iqbal run out 12
†Rashid Latif run out 26
Azhar Mahmood st Gilchrist b Symonds . 15
Wasim Akram not out 28
*Waqar Younis b Symonds 3
Saqlain Mushtaq not out 1
B 1, l-b 2, w 14, n-b 3 20

1/61 (1) 2/71 (3) 3/164 (4) 4/190 (2) 5/207 (5) 6/233 (6) 7/257 (8) 8/261 (7) 9/274 (10) (9 wkts, 50 overs) 290

Score at 15 overs: 75-2

Bowling: Fleming 10–2–38–0; Gillespie 10–0–58–0; Lee 10–1–41–2; Warne 9–1–60–2; Symonds 6–0–45–2; Martyn 5–0–45–1.

Australia

†A. C. Gilchrist b Saqlain Mushtaq 70
M. E. Waugh c Rashid Latif b Waqar Younis . 0
M. L. Hayden c Rashid Latif b Waqar Younis . 0
M. G. Bevan b Waqar Younis 5
*S. R. Waugh c Saqlain Mushtaq b Waqar Younis . 56
D. R. Martyn c Azhar Mahmood b Saqlain Mushtaq . 2
A. Symonds c sub (Imran Nazar) b Waqar Younis . 35
S. K. Warne c Wasim Akram b Azhar Mahmood . 14
B. Lee b Waqar Younis 10
D. W. Fleming not out 22
J. N. Gillespie b Abdur Razzaq 9
L-b 6, w 12, n-b 13 31

1/5 (2) 2/6 (3) 3/35 (4) 4/111 (1) 5/113 (6) 6/190 (5) 7/190 (7) 8/208 (9) 9/223 (8) 10/254 (11) (46.3 overs) 254

Score at 15 overs: 114-5

Bowling: Wasim Akram 10–0–68–0; Waqar Younis 8–0–59–6; Saqlain Mushtaq 10–0–50–2; Abdur Razzaq 8.3–1–16–1; Azhar Mahmood 10–0–55–1.

Umpires: N. A. Mallender and G. Sharp.
Third umpire: V. A. Holder.

ENGLAND v AUSTRALIA

At The Oval, June 21. Australia won by eight wickets. Toss: England.

A tournament that began badly and faded for England was completed with arguably their worst performance of the series, prompting an inquest into their one-day strategy following 11 successive defeats. Australia coasted to victory with nearly 20 overs to spare, despite resting Gillespie and Warne; even a change of signature tune from *The Great Escape* theme to the bizarrely appropriate "Always Look on the Bright Side of Life", from *Monty Python's Life of Brian*, could not change England's fortunes. Having slipped into trouble once again at 81 for five, they needed Hollioake, Croft and Caddick to save face. But for the eighth time in their last 11 innings England failed to pass 200. Once Gilchrist and Ponting joined forces, adding 124 in 137 balls, it was no contest.

Man of the Match: R. T. Ponting. *Attendance:* 18,136; *receipts* £558,565.

England

M. E. Trescothick b McGrath	0
*†A. J. Stewart c Bevan b Lee	22
N. V. Knight c Gilchrist b Fleming	48
O. A. Shah c Gilchrist b Harvey	1
A. D. Brown c Ponting b Lee	1
P. D. Collingwood c Harvey b McGrath	9
B. C. Hollioake run out	22
R. D. B. Croft c McGrath b Harvey	20
D. Gough b Lee	0
A. R. Caddick c Hayden b Bevan	36
A. D. Mullally not out	3
L-b 1, w 3, n-b 10	14
1/0 (1) 2/51 (2) 3/53 (4) 4/59 (5) 5/81 (6) 6/109 (3) 7/119 (7) 8/119 (9) 9/155 (8) 10/176 (10) (43.2 overs)	176

Score at 15 overs: 53-2

Bowling: McGrath 9–4–27–2; Fleming 10–1–37–1; Harvey 10–2–31–2; Lee 10–0–63–3; Symonds 3–0–13–0; Bevan 1.2–0–4–1.

Australia

†A. C. Gilchrist c and b Croft	80
M. L. Hayden c Mullally b Caddick	8
R. T. Ponting not out	70
M. G. Bevan not out	4
W 6, n-b 9	15
1/39 (2) 2/163 (1) (2 wkts, 30.1 overs)	177

Score at 15 overs: 101-1

M. E. Waugh, *S. R. Waugh, A. Symonds, I. J. Harvey, B. Lee, D. W. Fleming and G. D. McGrath did not bat.

Bowling: Gough 5–0–39–0; Caddick 8–0–51–1; Mullally 4–1–27–0; Croft 7–2–21–1; Hollioake 2–0–18–0; Collingwood 4.1–0–21–0.

Umpires: D. J. Constant and G. Sharp.
Third umpire: N. A. Mallender.

QUALIFYING TABLE

	Played	*Won*	*Lost*	*No result*	*Points*	*Net run-rate*
Australia	6	4	1	1	9	0.92
Pakistan	6	4	1	1	9	0.69
England	6	0	6	0	0	−1.32

Net run-rate is calculated by subtracting runs conceded per over from runs scored per over.

FINAL

AUSTRALIA v PAKISTAN

At Lord's, June 23. Australia won by nine wickets. Toss: Pakistan.

Australia took the NatWest Series Trophy with almost as much ease as they won the World Cup final against the same opponents on the same ground two years earlier. Contained by clinical, accurate bowling – even Lee, expensive earlier in the tournament, conceded only 20 runs from his eight overs – the frustrated Pakistan batsmen lost big wickets at key moments. When Abdur Razzaq mishooked Lee to short mid-wicket, just as he was beginning to accelerate midway through the innings, Pakistan were 92 for five and struggling. Once the Australian batting set to work, the one-sided nature of the game was fully evident; victory came with 23 overs to spare. Gilchrist continued his impressive finale to the tournament, smashing two sixes and eight fours in an unbeaten 76 from 93 balls, and fittingly hit the winning runs. Ponting's glorious cameo 35, containing five fours and a six in 23 balls, encapsulated the new heights to which Australia had taken one-day cricket.

Man of the Match: A. C. Gilchrist. *Attendance:* 25,484; *receipts* £821,913.
Man of the Series: Waqar Younis.

Pakistan

Saeed Anwar c Bevan b Harvey	27
Salim Elahi c Gilchrist b McGrath	10
Yousuf Youhana run out	11
Inzamam-ul-Haq lbw b Warne	23
Younis Khan c Warne b Lee	0
Abdur Razzaq c Warne b Lee	24
†Rashid Latif b Warne	23
Azhar Mahmood b Warne	1
Wasim Akram b Gillespie	17
*Waqar Younis lbw b Harvey	0
Saqlain Mushtaq not out	0
B 2, l-b 3, w 8, n-b 3	16
(42.3 overs)	152

1/28 (2) 2/47 (1) 3/60 (3) 4/60 (5) 5/92 (6) 6/102 (4) 7/110 (8) 8/151 (7) 9/152 (9) 10/152 (10) Score at 15 overs: 47-2

Bowling: McGrath 10–2–28–1; Gillespie 7–1–25–1; Harvey 7.3–0–18–2; Lee 8–1–20–2; Warne 10–0–56–3.

Australia

†A. C. Gilchrist not out	76
M. E. Waugh run out	36
R. T. Ponting not out	35
L-b 1, w 8	9
1/78 (2) (1 wkt, 26.3 overs)	156

Score at 15 overs: 66-0

M. G. Bevan, *S. R. Waugh, D. R. Martyn, I. J. Harvey, S. K. Warne, B. Lee, J. N. Gillespie and G. D. McGrath did not bat.

Bowling: Wasim Akram 7–0–15–0; Waqar Younis 5–0–32–0; Saqlain Mushtaq 8–0–50–0; Abdur Razzaq 5–0–40–0; Azhar Mahmood 1.3–0–18–0.

Umpires: D. R. Shepherd and P. Willey.
Third umpire: R. Palmer. Series referee: B. F. Hastings (New Zealand).

CRICINFO COUNTY CHAMPIONSHIP, 2001

David Byas

A strong Yorkshire, the adage goes, is a strong England, but modern-day cricket has turned that saw on its head. While Yorkshire were undeniably strong in 2001 – David Byas's hands were already on their first Championship for 33 years when August had a week to run – it was truer to say that a strong Australia meant a strong Yorkshire. Despite it being an Ashes summer, the world champions' depth in resources allowed Darren Lehmann, who would have strolled into any other international side, to return to Headingley. And to reinforce the point, Yorkshire were coached by Wayne Clark, who had guided Western Australia to both first-class and one-day honours. Other counties mined the same rich seam – 13 overseas players were émigrés from the Pura Cup – but none quite matched Yorkshire's success.

The competition itself was still in a state of flux: the two-division structure was only in its second year and, if the critics of the new format were not as vocal as in 2000, they had not disappeared. Some claimed that three-up, three-down, with a third of the 18 counties switching division from year to year, was too many; others that the system gave too few openings for younger players. A headache the ECB could cheerfully have done without was the search for a new sponsor after the departure of PPP healthcare. Two summers of lending their name to the Championship had met with moderate success in raising their lower-case profile, although their abandonment of the tournament, the ECB were at pains to point out, apparently reflected a change in the company's corporate strategy rather than dissatisfaction with the premier county competition. All the same, it did not look good. Nor did the delay in trumpeting a replacement backer until the Championship season had all but started.

The knight in shining, hi-tech armour was CricInfo, the cricket website, which had already agreed to support the women's Ashes series. The move smacked of desperation: CricInfo were known to be short of cash and could commit to no more than a single season, while the ECB would doubtless have preferred to sign up a prestigious household name from outside the game – another Vodafone or NatWest. For the bargain sum of £250,000 (with the women's Test series thrown in), CricInfo's blue and yellow logo was emblazoned on stumps and boundary boards up and down the country. The deal defrayed around two-thirds of the prize money.

It was further evidence of the unmarketability of domestic first-class cricket. In truth, despite the recent far-reaching changes carried out, at least in part, in the name of entertainment, the blue-chip businesses were unlikely to adopt the Championship. Yet the ECB could point to some encouraging signs. An express aim of the move to four-day cricket and to the weighting of bonus points away from bowling had been to improve the quality of batsmanship and of pitches. The 2001 Championship demonstrated that, given benign weather, those initiatives were perhaps beginning to

COUNTY CHAMPIONSHIP TABLE

Division One	*Matches*	*Won*	*Lost*	*Drawn*	*Bonus Points Batting*	*Bonus Points Bowling*	*Penalty*	*Points*
1 – Yorkshire (**3**)	16	9	3	4	50	45	0	219
2 – Somerset (**5**)	16	6	2	8	55	44	0	203
3 – Kent (**6**)	16	4	3	9	48	44	1	175
4 – Surrey (**1**)	16	3	1	12*	43	43	0.50	169.50
5 – Leicestershire (**4**)	16	5	6	5	38	47	0	165
6 – Lancashire (**2**)	16	4	5	7†	38	39	0	153
7 – Northamptonshire (*1*)	16	2	5	9	52	36	0	148
8 – Glamorgan (*3*)	16	2	5	9*	36	37	0	133
9 – Essex (*2*)	16	2	7	7	28	36	0	116

Division Two	*Matches*	*Won*	*Lost*	*Drawn*	*Bonus Points Batting*	*Bonus Points Bowling*	*Penalty*	*Points*
1 – Sussex (*9*)	16	9	3	4	42	42	0	208
2 – Hampshire (**7**)	16	7	2	7‡	34	44	0	192
3 – Warwickshire (*6*)	16	5	1	10	46	40	0.25	185.75
4 – Gloucestershire (*4*)	16	5	5	6	46	43	0	173
5 – Middlesex (*8*)	16	4	3	9	46	42	0	172
6 – Worcestershire (*5*)	16	4	5	7	35	41	0.25	151.75
7 – Nottinghamshire (*7*)	16	3	7	6	44	38	0.75	141.25
8 – Durham (**8**)	16	3	6	7	32	44	0	140
9 – Derbyshire (**9**)	16	1	9	6	20	37	0.75	92.25

2000 positions are shown in brackets: Division One in bold, Division Two in italic.

Win = 12 pts; draw = 4 pts.

* *Includes one abandoned match.* † *Includes two abandoned matches.* ‡ *Includes two points for levelling the scores in a drawn match.*

bear fruit. In 2000, five counties passed 40 batting points; in 2001, that figure had doubled, with three reaching 50. One player, Northamptonshire's Mike Hussey, stood out, becoming the first to make 2,000 Championship runs in a summer since Mark Ramprakash in 1995. Not that Hussey could prevent his side returning to the lower division. In fact, all three sides promoted for 2001 begin the new season back in unfashionable company. Intriguingly, 2001 was the third year in which the top six places had been filled by the same counties; only the order had changed. Those who foresaw a small cadre of counties forming an elite noted more grist in their mills.

Top of that elite pile for pretty much the entire season were Yorkshire. Once their fourth match, against Northamptonshire in late May, had brought a second win, they headed the table, never to be dislodged. A fortnight earlier, they had been well beaten by Somerset, but Yorkshire didn't lose again until Byas had the luxury of fielding young, inexperienced teams in September. The vagaries of nine per division meant that one team or more in each sat out every round, and ensured there were always fluctuations in position. Somerset and Kent, for example, in second and third, played box and cox in August while each missed a Championship game. Somerset finished the stronger, winning their last two games to end as runners-up for the first time; their total of 55 batting points was the highest since the divide. Kent too had a memorable batting year, transmuting 2000's base effort (they totalled 18) to a golden 48. David Fulton was alchemist-in-chief, with 1,729 Championship runs and eight hundreds.

With the title race effectively decided by early August, attention focused on the dogfight at the bottom. Defending champions Surrey remained hard to beat – their sole defeat came at home to Glamorgan – but the lack of incisive bowling support for the irrepressible Martin Bicknell meant they found it almost as hard to win. Just two victories before September meant relegation was a distinct possibility, as it was for Leicestershire and Lancashire. Leicestershire, spearheaded by the evergreen Devon Malcolm, stayed up in part because they claimed maximum bowling points in every game bar one, Lancashire because results when Muttiah Muralitharan was on board sustained them through the lean patch when he wasn't. A spirited late surge from Northamptonshire almost took them to sixth, and to safety, but in truth the bottom three had propped up the division all summer. Glamorgan occasionally turned in an impressive performance, but lacked consistency. The less said about Essex's season the better.

Life was cruel for Middlesex: their hopes were modest after a torrid time in 2000, but things began brightly for new coach John Emburey. As July ended, his charges had four wins under their belt and were leading Division Two; three losses and two draws then meant they slid to fifth. Sussex, who had finished bottom in 2000, enjoyed a season the mirror image of Middlesex's: an indifferent start saw them seventh as May gave way to June, but five wins in six games propelled them to first, a momentum they never lost. By contrast, Hampshire, relegated the previous autumn, remained in the top three from the end of their third match until the end of the season. As the final round began, four counties chased the last two promotion places and, since none was playing another, there were no dead games – just what the ECB had ordered. Warwickshire eventually finished third, helped by an easy ride against a dejected Derbyshire. For the second year running, Gloucestershire came fourth, their phenomenal late run of 90 points from five matches (including three victories by an innings and one by ten wickets) counting for naught when they stumbled at the last to Sussex. The two other sides to have tasted life in the first division, Durham and Derbyshire (who managed just one win) brought up the rear.

While it was commendable that no county was penalised for preparing a substandard pitch (though Hampshire, in their new headquarters, came close), the vexed business of points deductions had not gone away. In an innovation designed to discourage slow over-rates, six sides were docked a total of three and a half points. At first sight, the system, which applied to individual matches rather than the whole season, seemed to work: the previous year, as many as 13 counties had been fined. In 2001, the penalties made no difference to final standings, but controversy lies ahead when they determine promotion and relegation.

SUMMARY OF RESULTS, 2001

DIVISION ONE

	Essex	Glamorgan	Kent	Lancashire	Leicestershire	Northamptonshire	Somerset	Surrey	Yorkshire
Essex	–	L	L	D	D	D	L	D	D
Glamorgan	D	–	D	D	L	D	D	D	L
Kent	W	D	–	W	L	D	D	D	L
Lancashire	W	A	D	–	W	D	L	A	L
Leicestershire	L	W	L	W	–	W	D	D	L
Northamptonshire	W	D	D	L	W	–	D	D	D
Somerset	W	W	D	L	D	W	–	D	D
Surrey	D	L	D	D	D	W	W	–	W
Yorkshire	L	W	W	W	W	W	L	D	–

DIVISION TWO

	Derbyshire	Durham	Gloucestershire	Hampshire	Middlesex	Nottinghamshire	Sussex	Warwickshire	Worcestershrie
Derbyshire	–	D	D	L	D	D	L	L	L
Durham	L	–	D	L	D	W	L	D	D
Gloucestershire	W	D	–	D	L	W	W	D	L
Hampshire	W	W	D	–	W	W	D	D	W
Middlesex	W	W	L	D	–	D	D	D	D
Nottinghamshire	W	D	L	D	D	–	L	D	W
Sussex	W	L	W	W	W	W	–	L	W
Warwickshire	D	W	W	D	L	W	D	–	D
Worcestershire	D	L	W	W	D	L	D	D	–

Home teams listed on left, away teams across top; results are for home teams.

Leaders: *Division One* – from April 23 Lancashire; April 28 Essex; May 12 Somerset; May 28 Yorkshire. Yorkshire became champions on August 24.
Division Two – from April 23 Warwickshire; April 28 Durham and Middlesex; May 12 Middlesex; May 28 Hampshire; June 3 Middlesex; July 22 Sussex; July 30 Middlesex; August 6 Sussex. Sussex became champions on September 14.

Bottom place: *Division One* – from April 28 Leicestershire; May 12 Kent; May 19 Glamorgan; May 28 Leicestershire; June 3 Glamorgan; June 9 Northamptonshire; July 8 Essex.
Division Two – from April 28 Derbyshire.

Prize money

Division One
£105,000 for winners: YORKSHIRE.
£50,000 for runners-up: SOMERSET.

Division Two
£40,000 for winners: SUSSEX.
£25,000 for runners-up: HAMPSHIRE.

Winners of each match (both divisions): £2,000.

Scoring of Points

(*a*) For a win, 12 points plus any points scored in the first innings.

(*b*) In a tie, each side scores six points, plus any points scored in the first innings.

(*c*) In a drawn match, each side scores four points, plus any points scored in the first innings (see also paragraph (*f*)).

(*d*) If the scores are equal in a drawn match, the side batting in the fourth innings scores six points, plus any points scored in the first innings, and the opposing side scores four points plus any points scored in the first innings.

(*e*) First-innings points (awarded only for performances in the first 130 overs of each first innings and retained whatever the result of the match).

(i) A maximum of five batting points to be available: 200 to 249 runs – 1 point; 250 to 299 runs – 2 points; 300 to 349 runs – 3 points; 350 to 399 runs – 4 points; 400 runs or over – 5 points.

(ii) A maximum of three bowling points to be available: 3 to 5 wickets taken – 1 point; 6 to 8 wickets taken – 2 points; 9 to 10 wickets taken – 3 points.

(*f*) If play starts when less than eight hours' playing time remains and a one-innings match is played, no first-innings points shall be scored. The side winning on the one innings scores 12 points. In a tie, each side scores six points. In a drawn match, each side scores four points. If the scores are equal in a drawn match, the side batting in the second innings scores six points and the opposing side scores four points.

(*g*) If a match is abandoned without a ball being bowled, each side scores four points.

(*h*) The side which has the highest aggregate of points shall be the Champion County of their respective Division. Should any sides in the Championship table be equal on points, the following tie-breakers will be applied in the order stated: most wins, fewest losses, team achieving most points in head-to-head contests between teams level on points, most wickets taken, most runs scored. At the end of the season, the top three teams from the second division will be promoted and the bottom three teams from the first division will be relegated.

(*i*) The minimum over-rate to be achieved by counties will be 16 overs per hour. Overs will be calculated at the end of the match and penalties applied on a match-by-match basis. For each over (ignoring fractions) that a side has bowled short of the target number, 0.25 points will be deducted from their Championship total.

(*j*) A county which is adjudged to have prepared a pitch unfit for four-day first-class cricket will have 20 points deducted. A county adjudged to have prepared a poor pitch will have eight points deducted. This penalty will rise to 12 points if the county has prepared a poor or unfit pitch within the previous 12 months.

Under ECB playing conditions, two extras were scored for every no-ball and wide bowled whether scored off or not. Any runs scored off the bat were credited to the batsman, while byes and leg-byes were counted as no-balls or wides, as appropriate, in accordance with Law 24.13, in addition to the initial penalty.

CONSTITUTION OF COUNTY CHAMPIONSHIP

At least four possible dates have been given for the start of county cricket in England. The first, patchy, references began in 1825. The earliest mention in any cricket publication is in 1864 and eight counties have come to be regarded as first-class from that date, including Cambridgeshire, who dropped out after 1871. For many years, the County Championship was considered to have started in 1873, when regulations governing qualification first applied; indeed, a special commemorative stamp was issued by the Post Office in 1973. However, the Championship was not formally organised until 1890 and before then champions were proclaimed by the press; sometimes publications differed in their views and no definitive list of champions can start before that date. Eight teams contested the 1890 competition – Gloucestershire, Kent, Lancashire, Middlesex, Nottinghamshire, Surrey, Sussex and Yorkshire. Somerset joined in the following year, and in 1895 the Championship began to acquire something of its modern shape when Derbyshire, Essex, Hampshire, Leicestershire and Warwickshire were added. At that point MCC officially recognised the competition's existence. Worcestershire, Northamptonshire and Glamorgan were admitted to the Championship in 1899, 1905 and 1921 respectively and are regarded as first-class from these dates. An invitation in 1921 to Buckinghamshire to enter the Championship was declined, owing to the lack of necessary playing facilities, and an application by Devon in 1948 was unsuccessful. Durham were admitted to the Championship in 1992 and were granted first-class status prior to their pre-season tour of Zimbabwe.

In 2000, the Championship was split for the first time into two divisions, on the basis of counties' standings in the 1999 competition.

COUNTY CHAMPIONS

The title of champion county is unreliable before 1890. In 1963, *Wisden* formally accepted the list of champions "most generally selected" by contemporaries, as researched by the late Rowland Bowen (See *Wisden 1959*, pp 91–98). This appears to be the most accurate available list but has no official status. The county champions from 1864 to 1889 were, according to Bowen:

1864 Surrey; 1865 Nottinghamshire; 1866 Middlesex; 1867 Yorkshire; 1868 Nottinghamshire; 1869 Nottinghamshire and Yorkshire; 1870 Yorkshire; 1871 Nottinghamshire; 1872 Nottinghamshire; 1873 Gloucestershire and Nottinghamshire; 1874 Gloucestershire; 1875 Nottinghamshire; 1876 Gloucestershire; 1877 Gloucestershire; 1878 undecided; 1879 Lancashire and Nottinghamshire; 1880 Nottinghamshire; 1881 Lancashire; 1882 Lancashire and Nottinghamshire; 1883 Nottinghamshire; 1884 Nottinghamshire; 1885 Nottinghamshire; 1886 Nottinghamshire; 1887 Surrey; 1888 Surrey; 1889 Lancashire, Nottinghamshire and Surrey.

Official champions

1890	Surrey
1891	Surrey
1892	Surrey
1893	Yorkshire
1894	Surrey
1895	Surrey
1896	Yorkshire
1897	Lancashire
1898	Yorkshire
1899	Surrey
1900	Yorkshire
1901	Yorkshire
1902	Yorkshire
1903	Middlesex
1904	Lancashire
1905	Yorkshire
1906	Kent
1907	Nottinghamshire
1908	Yorkshire
1909	Kent
1910	Kent
1911	Warwickshire
1912	Yorkshire
1913	Kent
1914	Surrey
1919	Yorkshire
1920	Middlesex
1921	Middlesex
1922	Yorkshire
1923	Yorkshire
1924	Yorkshire
1925	Yorkshire
1926	Lancashire
1927	Lancashire
1928	Lancashire
1929	Nottinghamshire
1930	Lancashire
1931	Yorkshire
1932	Yorkshire
1933	Yorkshire
1934	Lancashire
1935	Yorkshire
1936	Derbyshire
1937	Yorkshire
1938	Yorkshire
1939	Yorkshire
1946	Yorkshire
1947	Middlesex
1948	Glamorgan
1949	Middlesex Yorkshire
1950	Lancashire Surrey
1951	Warwickshire
1952	Surrey
1953	Surrey
1954	Surrey
1955	Surrey
1956	Surrey
1957	Surrey
1958	Surrey
1959	Yorkshire
1960	Yorkshire
1961	Hampshire
1962	Yorkshire
1963	Yorkshire
1964	Worcestershire
1965	Worcestershire
1966	Yorkshire
1967	Yorkshire
1968	Yorkshire
1969	Glamorgan
1970	Kent
1971	Surrey
1972	Warwickshire
1973	Hampshire
1974	Worcestershire
1975	Leicestershire
1976	Middlesex
1977	Middlesex Kent
1978	Kent
1979	Essex
1980	Middlesex
1981	Nottinghamshire
1982	Middlesex
1983	Essex
1984	Essex
1985	Middlesex
1986	Essex
1987	Nottinghamshire
1988	Worcestershire
1989	Worcestershire
1990	Middlesex
1991	Essex
1992	Essex
1993	Middlesex
1994	Warwickshire
1995	Warwickshire
1996	Leicestershire
1997	Glamorgan
1998	Leicestershire
1999	Surrey
2000	Surrey
2001	Yorkshire

Notes: Since the Championship was constituted in 1890 it has been won outright as follows: Yorkshire 30 times, Surrey 17, Middlesex 10, Lancashire 7, Essex and Kent 6, Warwickshire and Worcestershire 5, Nottinghamshire 4, Glamorgan and Leicestershire 3, Hampshire 2, Derbyshire 1.

The title has been shared three times since 1890, involving Middlesex twice, Kent, Lancashire, Surrey and Yorkshire.

Wooden Spoons: since the major expansion of the Championship from nine teams to 14 in 1895, the counties have finished outright bottom as follows: Derbyshire 12; Northamptonshire and Somerset 11; Glamorgan 9; Nottinghamshire and Sussex 8; Gloucestershire and Leicestershire 7; Worcestershire 6; Hampshire 5; Durham and Warwickshire 3; Essex and Kent 2; Yorkshire 1. Lancashire, Middlesex and Surrey have never finished bottom. Leicestershire have also shared bottom place twice, once with Hampshire and once with Somerset.

From 1977 to 1983 the Championship was sponsored by Schweppes, from 1984 to 1998 by Britannic Assurance, from 1999 to 2000 by PPP healthcare and in 2001 by CricInfo.

COUNTY CHAMPIONSHIP – FINAL POSITIONS, 1890–2001

	Derbyshire	Essex	Glamorgan	Gloucestershire	Hampshire	Kent	Lancashire	Leicestershire	Middlesex	Northamptonshire	Nottinghamshire	Somerset	Surrey	Sussex	Warwickshire	Worcestershire	Yorkshire
1890	–	–	–	6	–	3	2	–	7	–	5	–	1	8	–	–	3
1891	–	–	–	9	–	5	2	–	3	–	4	5	1	7	–	–	8
1892	–	–	–	7	–	7	4	–	5	–	2	3	1	9	–	–	6
1893	–	–	–	9	–	4	2	–	3	–	6	8	5	7	–	–	1
1894	–	–	–	9	–	4	4	–	3	–	7	6	1	8	–	–	2
1895	5	9	–	4	10	14	2	12	6	–	12	8	1	11	6	–	3
1896	7	5	–	10	8	9	2	13	3	–	6	11	4	14	12	–	1
1897	14	3	–	5	9	12	1	13	8	–	10	11	2	6	7	–	4
1898	9	5	–	3	12	7	6	13	2	–	8	13	4	9	9	–	1
1899	15	6	–	9	10	8	4	13	2	–	10	13	1	5	7	12	3
1900	13	10	–	7	15	3	2	14	7	–	5	11	7	3	6	12	1
1901	15	10	–	14	7	7	3	12	2	–	9	12	6	4	5	11	1
1902	10	13	–	14	15	7	5	11	12	–	3	7	4	2	6	9	1
1903	12	8	–	13	14	8	4	14	1	–	5	10	11	2	7	6	3
1904	10	14	–	9	15	3	1	7	4	–	5	12	11	6	7	13	2
1905	14	12	–	8	16	6	2	5	11	13	10	15	4	3	7	8	1
1906	16	7	–	9	8	1	4	15	11	11	5	11	3	10	6	14	2
1907	16	7	–	10	12	8	6	11	5	15	1	14	4	13	9	2	2
1908	14	11	–	10	9	2	7	13	4	15	8	16	3	5	12	6	1
1909	15	14	–	16	8	1	2	13	6	7	10	11	5	4	12	8	3
1910	15	11	–	12	6	1	4	10	3	9	5	16	2	7	14	13	8
1911	14	6	–	12	11	2	4	15	3	10	8	16	5	13	1	9	7
1912	12	15	–	11	6	3	4	13	5	2	8	14	7	10	9	16	1
1913	13	15	–	9	10	1	8	14	6	4	5	16	3	7	11	12	2
1914	12	8	–	16	5	3	11	13	2	9	10	15	1	6	7	14	4
1919	9	14	–	8	7	2	5	9	13	12	3	5	4	11	15	–	1
1920	16	9	–	8	11	5	2	13	1	14	7	10	3	6	12	15	4
1921	12	15	17	7	6	4	5	11	1	13	8	10	2	9	16	14	3
1922	11	8	16	13	6	4	5	14	7	15	2	10	3	9	12	17	1
1923	10	13	16	11	7	5	3	14	8	17	2	9	4	6	12	15	1
1924	17	15	13	6	12	5	4	11	2	16	6	8	3	10	9	14	1
1925	14	7	17	10	9	5	3	12	6	11	4	15	2	13	8	16	1
1926	11	9	8	15	7	3	1	13	6	16	4	14	5	10	12	17	2
1927	5	8	15	12	13	4	1	7	9	16	2	14	6	10	11	17	3
1928	10	16	15	5	12	2	1	9	8	13	3	14	6	7	11	17	4
1929	7	12	17	4	11	8	2	9	6	13	1	15	10	4	14	16	2
1930	9	6	11	2	13	5	1	12	16	17	4	13	8	7	15	10	3
1931	7	10	15	2	12	3	6	16	11	17	5	13	8	4	9	14	1
1932	10	14	15	13	8	3	6	12	10	16	4	7	5	2	9	17	1
1933	6	4	16	10	14	3	5	17	12	13	8	11	9	2	7	15	1
1934	3	8	13	7	14	5	1	12	10	17	9	15	11	2	4	16	5
1935	2	9	13	15	16	10	4	6	3	17	5	14	11	7	8	12	1
1936	1	9	16	4	10	8	11	15	2	17	5	7	6	14	13	12	3
1937	3	6	7	4	14	12	9	16	2	17	10	13	8	5	11	15	1
1938	5	6	16	10	14	9	4	15	2	17	12	7	3	8	13	11	1
1939	9	4	13	3	15	5	6	17	2	16	12	14	8	10	11	7	1
1946	15	8	6	5	10	6	3	11	2	16	13	4	11	17	14	8	1
1947	5	11	9	2	16	4	3	14	1	17	11	11	6	9	15	7	7
1948	6	13	1	8	9	15	5	11	3	17	14	12	2	16	7	10	4
1949	15	9	8	7	16	13	11	17	1	6	11	9	5	13	4	3	1
1950	5	17	11	7	12	9	1	16	14	10	15	7	1	13	4	6	3

	Derbyshire	Durham	Essex	Glamorgan	Gloucestershire	Hampshire	Kent	Lancashire	Leicestershire	Middlesex	Northamptonshire	Nottinghamshire	Somerset	Surrey	Sussex	Warwickshire	Worcestershire	Yorkshire
1951	11	–	8	5	12	9	16	3	15	7	13	17	14	6	10	1	4	2
1952	4	–	10	7	9	12	15	3	6	5	8	16	17	1	13	10	14	2
1953	6	–	12	10	6	14	16	3	3	5	11	8	17	1	2	9	15	12
1954	3	–	15	4	13	14	11	10	16	7	7	5	17	1	9	6	11	2
1955	8	–	14	16	12	3	13	9	6	5	7	11	17	1	4	9	15	2
1956	12	–	11	13	3	6	16	2	17	5	4	8	15	1	9	14	9	7
1957	4	–	5	9	12	13	14	6	17	7	2	15	8	1	9	11	16	3
1958	5	–	6	15	14	2	8	7	12	10	4	17	3	1	13	16	9	11
1959	7	–	9	6	2	8	13	5	16	10	11	17	12	3	15	4	14	1
1960	5	–	6	11	8	12	10	2	17	3	9	16	14	7	4	15	13	1
1961	7	–	6	14	5	1	11	13	9	3	16	17	10	15	8	12	4	2
1962	7	–	9	14	4	10	11	16	17	13	8	15	6	5	12	3	2	1
1963	17	–	12	2	8	10	13	15	16	6	7	9	3	11	4	4	14	1
1964	12	–	10	11	17	12	7	14	16	6	3	15	8	4	9	2	1	5
1965	9	–	15	3	10	12	5	13	14	6	2	17	7	8	16	11	1	4
1966	9	–	16	14	15	11	4	12	8	12	5	17	3	7	10	6	2	1
1967	6	–	15	14	17	12	2	11	2	7	9	15	8	4	13	10	5	1
1968	8	–	14	3	16	5	2	6	9	10	13	4	12	15	17	11	7	1
1969	16	–	6	1	2	5	10	15	14	11	9	8	17	3	7	4	12	13
1970	7	–	12	2	17	10	1	3	15	16	14	11	13	5	9	7	6	4
1971	17	–	10	16	8	9	4	3	5	6	14	12	7	1	11	2	15	13
1972	17	–	5	13	3	9	2	15	6	8	4	14	11	12	16	1	7	10
1973	16	–	8	11	5	1	4	12	9	13	3	17	10	2	15	7	6	14
1974	17	–	12	16	14	2	10	8	4	6	3	15	5	7	13	9	1	11
1975	15	–	7	9	16	3	5	4	1	11	8	13	12	6	17	14	10	2
1976	15	–	6	17	3	12	14	16	4	1	2	13	7	9	10	5	11	8
1977	7	–	6	14	3	11	1	16	5	1	9	17	4	14	8	10	13	12
1978	14	–	2	13	10	8	1	12	6	3	17	7	5	16	9	11	15	4
1979	16	–	1	17	10	12	5	13	6	14	11	9	8	3	4	15	2	7
1980	9	–	8	13	7	17	16	15	10	1	12	3	5	2	4	14	11	6
1981	12	–	5	14	13	7	9	16	8	4	15	1	3	6	2	17	11	10
1982	11	–	7	16	15	3	13	12	2	1	9	4	6	5	8	17	14	10
1983	9	–	1	15	12	3	7	12	4	2	6	14	10	8	11	5	16	17
1984	12	–	1	13	17	15	5	16	4	3	11	2	7	8	6	9	10	14
1985	13	–	4	12	3	2	9	14	16	1	10	8	17	6	7	15	5	11
1986	11	–	1	17	2	6	8	15	7	12	9	4	16	3	14	12	5	10
1987	6	–	12	13	10	5	14	2	3	16	7	1	11	4	17	15	9	8
1988	14	–	3	17	10	15	2	9	8	7	12	5	11	4	16	6	1	13
1989	6	–	2	17	9	6	15	4	13	3	5	11	14	12	10	8	1	16
1990	12	–	2	8	13	3	16	6	7	1	11	13	15	9	17	5	4	10
1991	3	–	1	12	13	9	6	8	16	15	10	4	17	5	11	2	6	14
1992	5	18	1	14	10	15	2	12	8	11	3	4	9	13	7	6	17	16
1993	15	18	11	3	17	13	8	13	9	1	4	7	5	6	10	16	2	12
1994	17	16	6	18	12	13	9	10	2	4	5	3	11	7	8	1	15	13
1995	14	17	5	16	6	13	18	4	7	2	3	11	9	12	15	1	10	8
1996	2	18	5	10	13	14	4	15	1	9	16	17	11	3	12	8	7	6
1997	16	17	8	1	7	14	2	11	10	4	15	13	12	8	18	4	3	6
1998	10	14	18	12	4	6	11	2	1	17	15	16	9	5	7	8	13	3
1999	9	8	12	14	18	7	5	2	3	16	13	17	4	1	11	10	15	6
2000	**9**	**8**	*2*	*3*	*4*	**7**	**6**	**2**	**4**	*8*	*1*	*7*	**5**	**1**	*9*	*6*	*5*	**3**
2001	*9*	*8*	**9**	**8**	*4*	*2*	**3**	**6**	**5**	*5*	**7**	*7*	**2**	**4**	*1*	*3*	*6*	**1**

Note: For the 2000–2001 Championships, Division One placings are shown in bold, Division Two in italic.

MATCH RESULTS, 1864–2001

County	*Years of Play*	*Played*	*Won*	*Lost*	*Tied*	*Drawn*
Derbyshire	1871–87; 1895–2001	2,307	572	848	1	886
Durham.	1992–2001	172	28	94	0	50
Essex	1895–2001	2,269	653	665	5	946
Glamorgan	1921–2001	1,803	400	612	0	791
Gloucestershire . . .	1870–2001	2,543	756	941	2	844
Hampshire	1864–85; 1895–2001	2,378	621	818	4	935
Kent	1864–2001	2,667	961	800	5	901
Lancashire	1865–2001	2,742	1,020	573	3	1,146
Leicestershire	1895–2001	2,236	511	810	1	914
Middlesex	1864–2001	2,446	906	621	5	914
Northamptonshire .	1905–2001	2,004	493	697	3	811
Nottinghamshire . .	1864–2001	2,576	773	697	1	1,105
Somerset	1882–85; 1891–2001	2,277	542	905	3	827
Surrey.	1864–2001	2,823	1,120	623	4	1,076
Sussex.	1864–2001	2,716	759	939	6	1,012
Warwickshire	1895–2001	2,249	614	651	1	983
Worcestershire . . .	1899–2001	2,191	550	757	2	882
Yorkshire.	1864–2001	2,844	1,265	493	2	1,084
Cambridgeshire. . .	1864–69; 1871	19	8	8	0	3
		20,631	12,552	12,552	24	8,055

Notes: Matches abandoned without a ball bowled are wholly excluded.

Counties participated in the years shown, except that there were no matches in the years 1915–18 and 1940–45; Hampshire did not play inter-county matches in 1868–69, 1871–74 and 1879; Worcestershire did not take part in the Championship in 1919.

COUNTY CHAMPIONSHIP STATISTICS FOR 2001

	For			*Against*			
County	*Runs*	*Wickets*	*Avge*	*Runs*	*Wickets*	*Avge*	*RPF*
Derbyshire (*9*)	6,996	271	25.81	7,333	175	41.90	0.61
Durham (*8*)	7,385	269	27.45	7,579	243	31.18	0.88
Essex (**9**)	7,405	262	28.26	7,859	187	42.02	0.67
Glamorgan (**8**)	7,102	209	33.98	8,079	185	43.67	0.77
Gloucestershire (*4*) . .	7,783	229	33.98	7,336	241	30.43	1.11
Hampshire (*2*)	6,622	216	30.65	7,129	259	27.52	1.11
Kent (**3**)	7,832	209	37.47	6,799	224	30.35	1.23
Lancashire (**6**)	6,564	202	32.49	7,228	225	32.12	1.01
Leicestershire (**5**) . . .	8,294	249	33.30	7,970	259	30.77	1.08
Middlesex (*5*)	7,545	214	35.25	7,660	226	33.89	1.04
Northamptonshire (**7**)	8,984	242	37.12	9,308	216	43.09	0.86
Nottinghamshire (*7*) .	8,960	256	35.00	8,820	212	41.60	0.84
Somerset (**2**)	8,698	220	39.53	8,635	231	37.38	1.05
Surrey (**4**).	7,828	219	35.74	7,298	216	33.78	1.05
Sussex (*1*).	8,464	239	35.41	6,846	263	26.03	1.36
Warwickshire (*3*) . . .	6,738	173	38.94	7,691	234	32.86	1.18
Worcestershire (*6*). . .	6,979	223	31.29	7,078	237	29.86	1.04
Yorkshire (**1**)	7,853	211	37.21	7,384	280	26.37	1.41
	138,032	4,113	33.55	138,032	4,113	33.55	

2001 Championship positions are shown in brackets; Division One in bold, Division Two in italic.

Relative performance factor (RPF) is determined by dividing the average runs scored per wicket by the average runs conceded per wicket.

RUNS SCORED PER 100 BALLS IN THE COUNTY CHAMPIONSHIP, 2001

County	*Run-rate/ 100 balls*	*County*	*Run-rate/ 100 balls*
Derbyshire (*9*)	49.87	Middlesex (*5*)	49.97
Durham (*8*)	50.12	Northamptonshire (**7**)	55.36
Essex (**9**)	47.26	Nottinghamshire (*7*)	61.16
Glamorgan (**8**)	56.58	Somerset (**2**)	55.54
Gloucestershire (*4*)	54.83	Surrey (**4**)	57.31
Hampshire (*2*)	52.06	Sussex (*1*)	50.60
Kent (**3**)	54.70	Warwickshire (*3*)	54.38
Lancashire (**6**)	58.38	Worcestershire (*6*)	56.47
Leicestershire (**5**)	59.44	Yorkshire (**1**)	56.53
		2001 average rate	54.33

2001 Championship positions are shown in brackets: Division One in bold, Division Two in italic.

ECB PITCHES TABLE OF MERIT

First-Class Matches, Under-19 Tests and UCCE Matches

		Points	*Matches*	*Average in 2001*	*Average in 2000*
1	Somerset (2)	96	9	5.33	5.20
2	Lancashire (7=)	74	7	5.29	4.60
3	Northamptonshire (10=)	93	9	5.17	4.56
4	Surrey (1)	103	10	5.15	5.22
5	Kent (5)	89	9	4.94	4.72
6	Essex (6)	88	9	4.89	4.70
7	Leicestershire (15)	106	11	4.82	4.33
	Nottinghamshire (7=)	106	11	4.82	4.60
9	Gloucestershire (17=)	76	8	4.75	4.20
10	Middlesex (12)	94	10	4.70	4.55
	Sussex (16)	94	10	4.70	4.30
12	Durham (9)	93	10	4.65	4.56
	Glamorgan (19)	93	10	4.65	4.17
14	Warwickshire (10=)	83	9	4.61	4.56
15	Derbyshire (14)	91	10	4.55	4.39
16	Worcestershire (17=)	86	10	4.30	4.20
17	Yorkshire (20)	77	9	4.28	3.86
18	Hampshire (13)	76	9	4.22	4.40
	Cambridge UCCE	61	6	5.08	5.00
	Oxford UCCE	40	4	5.00	4.88
	Loughborough UCCE	10	1	5.00	–
	Bradford/Leeds UCCE	38	4	4.75	–
	Durham UCCE	28	3	4.67	–

ECB PITCHES TABLE OF MERIT

One-Day Matches

		Points	*Matches*	*Average in 2001*	*Average in 2000*
1	Somerset (3)	132	13	5.08	5.09
2 {	Essex (7)	130	13	5.00	4.75
	Northamptonshire (6)	110	11	5.00	4.77
4	Glamorgan (14)	126	13	4.85	4.38
5	Surrey (4)	124	13	4.77	4.91
6	Durham (9)	102	11	4.64	4.70
7	Leicestershire (17)	111	12	4.63	4.27
8	Nottinghamshire (5)	119	13	4.58	4.89
9	Kent (10)	98	11	4.45	4.59
10	Middlesex (12)	142	16	4.44	4.53
11	Hampshire (8)	96	11	4.36	4.72
12	Gloucestershire (15)	122	14	4.36	4.34
13	Warwickshire (13)	103	12	4.29	4.46
14	Sussex (2)	102	12	4.25	5.23
15	Yorkshire (11)	126	15	4.20	4.55
16	Derbyshire (19)	92	11	4.18	4.14
17	Lancashire (18)	108	13	4.15	4.27
18	Worcestershire (16)	103	13	3.96	4.32

In both tables 2000 positions are shown in brackets. Each umpire in a game marks the pitch on the following scale of merit: 6 – very good; 5 – good; 4 – above average; 3 – below average; 2 – poor; 1 – unfit.

The tables, provided by the ECB, cover major matches, including Tests, Under-19 internationals, women's internationals and UCCE games, played on grounds under the county or UCCE's jurisdiction. Middlesex pitches at Lord's are the responsibility of MCC.

The ECB point out that the tables of merit are not a direct assessment of the groundsmen's ability. Marks may be affected by many factors including weather, soil conditions and the resources available.

COUNTY BENEFITS AWARDED FOR 2002

Derbyshire	K. M. Krikken
Essex	M. C. Ilott
Glamorgan	A. Dale
Gloucestershire	M. C. J. Ball
Hampshire	S. D. Udal
Kent	M. J. McCague
Lancashire	P. J. Martin
Leicestershire	J. Birkenshaw/Academy
Middlesex	P. N. Weekes
Northamptonshire	A. L. Penberthy
Nottinghamshire	C. M. Tolley
Somerset	R. J. Turner
Surrey	A. D. Brown
Sussex	J. D. Lewry
Warwickshire	N. M. K. Smith
Yorkshire	C. White

No benefit was awarded by Durham or Worcestershire.

DERBYSHIRE

Michael Di Venuto

President: Sir Nigel Rudd
Chairman: G. T. Bowring
Chief Executive: J. T. Smedley
Chairman, Cricket Committee: L. C. Elliott
Captain: D. G. Cork
Cricket Manager: C. M. Wells
Head Groundsman: 2001 – B. Marsh
2002 – N. Godrich
Scorer: J. M. Brown

Derbyshire's inability to retain their best cricketers overtook and exposed them in a dreadful season. While more than a dozen of their former players were employed elsewhere, the county struggled along with an inadequate team that was barely competitive. Even before the final rounds of fixtures, they knew that bottom place in both second divisions was inevitable. Yet only five years earlier, Derbyshire had been second in the Championship under Dean Jones. Even as recently as 1999, when the competition was about to split, one more boundary in the final innings of the season would have lifted them to fourth. Such days seemed far distant as, in the Championship, they won only once, lost by an innings five times and were forced to follow on six times. The sum total of their one-day season amounted to five victories in 22 attempts.

The poor results threatened the position of cricket manager Colin Wells. He was reappointed for 2002, but one committee member resigned because he felt unable to accept the majority decision. Only after some delay did Dominic Cork confirm he would continue as captain, though he ended a personally disappointing summer with his optimism intact. Having returned early from Pakistan with a stress fracture of the back, Cork had had to establish his fitness before taking up an England contract. Derbyshire did not expect to see much of him, and were further frustrated when, having been omitted by England after the Lord's Test against Australia, he tore a hamstring at the end of July. With Tim Munton ruled out by an Achilles tendon injury at the same time, and Kevin Dean suffering further back problems in the first half of the season, they were unable to field a full-strength attack after the opening game.

Dean returned strongly for the last two months and added a different dimension to the bowling, but the standard of support was so poor that he and Graeme Welch were inevitably overused. Welch, engaged from Warwickshire, proved the most dedicated of cricketers. Essentially a change bowler, he had the new ball for most of the season and sent down twice as many overs as anybody else. He was deservedly capped, along with opening batsman Steve Stubbings, during the last game of the summer. Richard Illingworth, the other experienced newcomer, set off well, only to suffer from injuries and loss of confidence. He decided it was time to retire from the first-class game, having enjoyed a distinguished career with Worcestershire.

After fragile batting performances in 2000, it was strange that Derbyshire did not take firmer steps to strengthen that department. Chris Bassano, recruited with no previous first-class experience, made his debut against the Pakistanis and later enjoyed a unique first Championship appearance, scoring two centuries against Gloucestershire on one of many lifeless County Ground pitches. It was a remarkable display of concentration and unhurried tempo, but within a fortnight he had to return home to Tasmania because his father, cricket writer Brian Bassano, had suffered a stroke, from which he subsequently died.

The starts improved when, in July, Michael Di Venuto became Stubbings's opening partner. At one stage, Di Venuto had three centuries and three fifties in seven innings, form that persuaded Derbyshire to retain him as their overseas player and make him vice-captain for 2002. He and Stubbings both reached their 1,000 runs, in the defeat at Bristol, a target no Derbyshire player had achieved the year before.

Luke Sutton, who aims to make his way as a wicket-keeper/batsman if he can ever shift Karl Krikken, opened for the first half of the summer, and had his best moment after Di Venuto was injured while steering Derbyshire to their solitary victory over Durham. Restored as opener, Sutton carried his bat through the first innings against Sussex and was last out in the second. Rob Bailey and Mathew Dowman, expected to be sources of regular runs, had poor seasons. Bailey played two major innings in defeats, but became an uncertain starter, while Dowman, after a handsome century against the Pakistanis, reached 50 only once in the Championship and was in danger of becoming an unfulfilled talent.

There were flickers of promise from several younger players: Nathan Dumelow, Tom Lungley, Steve Selwood and, as a one-day bowler, Lian Wharton. The opportunity is there if they develop. Wasim Khan, who made no impact after being engaged on a sponsored basis, Trevor Smith and Steve Titchard were released. In the case of Smith, who set out so promisingly four years earlier, then lost control of line and length, it seemed premature to give up on a 24-year-old. Derbyshire hoped that Andrew Gait, from the Free State with English parentage, and Gloucestershire's Dominic Hewson would strengthen the batting, while Somerset's Jason Kerr was signed to add depth to the bowling.

Demolition of the County Ground's most notable feature, the grandstand, began soon after the end of the season. At one time there were plans to develop the structure, built in 1911 when Derby staged race meetings, but projected costs led to those being abandoned. The dome had already been removed and, with the interior no longer used, the stand itself became a target for vandals, some of whom assisted the destructive process during the final games. Work began on new and urgently needed outdoor practice facilities, and the aim was to finance a top-quality indoor school. Trevor Bowring, the chairman, irritated by articles suggesting first-class status was in jeopardy, pointed to the development as an indication of faith in the future, while remaining fully aware of the need to improve Derbyshire's performance on the field. – GERALD MORTIMER.

DERBYSHIRE 2001

[*Bill Smith*

Back row: L. J. Wharton, Z. M. Khan, T. Lungley, W. G. Khan, C. W. G. Bassano, R. M. Khan, N. R. C. Dumelow, A. J. Marsh. *Middle row:* J. M. Brown (*scorer*), C. M. Wells (*cricket manager*), G. Welch, R. K. Illingworth, S. P. Titchard, T. M. Smith, L. D. Sutton, C. Ranson (*physiotherapist*). *Front row:* L. C. Elliott (*chairman of cricket*), M. P. Dowman, P. Aldred, R. J. Bailey, D. G. Cork (*captain*), T. A. Munton, K. J. Dean, K. M. Krikken, M. J. Di Venuto, J. T. Smedley (*chief executive*). *Inset:* S. A. Selwood.

DERBYSHIRE RESULTS

All first-class matches – Played 17: Won 1, Lost 9, Drawn 7.

County Championship matches – Played 16: Won 1, Lost 9, Drawn 6.

CricInfo County Championship, 9th in Division 2; Cheltenham & Gloucester Trophy, 3rd round; Benson and Hedges Cup, 6th in North Group; Norwich Union League, 9th in Division 2.

COUNTY CHAMPIONSHIP AVERAGES

BATTING

Cap		*M*	*I*	*NO*	*R*	*HS*	*100s*	*50s*	*Avge*	*Ct/St*
	C. W. G. Bassano	7	12	2	493	186*	2	2	49.30	4
2000	M. J. Di Venuto§	14	25	1	1,082	165	4	5	45.08	15
1993	D. G. Cork‡	3	4	0	163	128	1	0	40.75	3
2001	S. D. Stubbings	16	29	0	1,024	127	3	6	35.31	4
	L. D. Sutton	14	25	3	628	140*	2	1	28.54	9
	N. R. C. Dumelow†	8	14	1	298	61	0	2	22.92	1
1992	K. M. Krikken	13	23	4	425	93*	0	3	22.36	33/1
2000	R. J. Bailey	14	25	1	515	136*	1	2	21.45	8
2001	G. Welch	16	29	2	511	64	0	1	18.92	3
	T. Lungley†	5	10	4	108	47	0	0	18.00	0
	R. K. Illingworth	5	8	1	125	61*	0	1	17.85	0
2000	M. P. Dowman	13	24	0	386	50	0	1	16.08	4
2000	T. A. Munton	9	13	1	145	50	0	1	12.08	2
1998	K. J. Dean†	8	12	2	117	23	0	0	11.70	2
	S. A. Selwood	2	4	0	43	18	0	0	10.75	1
1999	P. Aldred†	8	13	1	120	35	0	0	10.00	5
	T. M. Smith†	5	9	1	65	19	0	0	8.12	4
	L. J. Wharton†	10	17	9	29	13*	0	0	3.62	1

Also batted: A. D. Edwards (1 match) 4*, 23; R. M. Khan (1 match) 13, 5; W. G. Khan (1 match) 1; A. R. K. Pierson (1 match) 9, 1* (1 ct); S. P. Titchard (2 matches) 37, 39, 5.

* *Signifies not out.* † *Born in Derbyshire.* ‡ *ECB contract.* § *Overseas player.*

BOWLING

	O	*M*	*R*	*W*	*BB*	*5W/i*	*Avge*
K. J. Dean	250.5	58	888	34	6-73	2	26.11
R. K. Illingworth	126.4	39	316	10	4-37	0	31.60
T. A. Munton	242.1	61	659	19	5-85	1	34.68
G. Welch	502.3	108	1,631	44	6-30	3	37.06
P. Aldred	189.3	30	742	13	3-102	0	57.07
N. R. C. Dumelow	158.5	28	632	10	4-103	0	63.20

Also bowled: R. J. Bailey 76.3–17–245–7; C. W. G. Bassano 2–0–11–0; D. G. Cork 90.2–18–290–6; M. J. Di Venuto 30–2–124–1; M. P. Dowman 10–3–53–0; A. D. Edwards 13–3–40–0; K. M. Krikken 7–0–27–0; T. Lungley 97.1–12–449–9; A. R. K. Pierson 10–0–28–0; T. M. Smith 70.3–11–319–7; S. D. Stubbings 4–0–36–0; L. J. Wharton 206.3–56–600–8.

COUNTY RECORDS

Highest score for:	274	G. Davidson v Lancashire at Manchester	1896
Highest score against:	343*	P. A. Perrin (Essex) at Chesterfield	1904
Best bowling for:	10-40	W. Bestwick v Glamorgan at Cardiff	1921
Best bowling against:	10-45	R. L. Johnson (Middlesex) at Derby	1994
Highest total for:	645	v Hampshire at Derby	1898
Highest total against:	662	by Yorkshire at Chesterfield	1898
Lowest total for:	16	v Nottinghamshire at Nottingham	1879
Lowest total against:	23	by Hampshire at Burton upon Trent	1958

At Derby, April 16, 17, 18 (not first-class). Drawn. Toss: Derbyshire. Derbyshire 340 for nine dec. (L. D. Sutton 59, M. J. Di Venuto 127, K. M. Krikken 55, R. K. Illingworth 30 not out; S. J. Birtwisle three for 64) and 248 for three dec. (L. D. Sutton 102 not out, K. M. Krikken 86 retired hurt); Bradford/Leeds UCCE 180 (S. J. Birtwistle 64, J. W. Payn 33, C. J. Elstub 49; P. Aldred four for 42) and 69 for two (H. Marambe 32 not out).

County debuts: R. K. Illingworth, W. G. Khan.

DERBYSHIRE v MIDDLESEX

At Derby, April 25, 26, 27, 28. Drawn. Derbyshire 5 pts, Middlesex 7 pts. Toss: Derbyshire. County debut: G. Welch.

Rain washed out the first and last days – and when play was possible, conditions were uncomfortably cold. It was an important occasion for Cork, in action for the first time since returning early from England's tour of Pakistan with a back injury. An ECB contract was conditional on proof of his fitness, and David Graveney, chairman of selectors, came on the third day to monitor progress. Derbyshire's batsmen proceeded cautiously against bowling that was frugal – extras aside – and was backed up by excellent gully catches from Strauss and Shah. Illingworth, who had joined Derbyshire after 19 seasons with Worcestershire, took four of the five Middlesex wickets to fall, enjoying his best first-class return since 1997.

Close of play: First day, No play; Second day, Derbyshire 171-7 (Welch 28*, Illingworth 9*); Third day, Middlesex 146-5 (Nash 27*, Roseberry 21*).

Derbyshire

L. D. Sutton c Strauss b Cook	26
S. D. Stubbings lbw b Bloomfield	1
S. P. Titchard c Shah b Cook	37
M. J. Di Venuto c Hutton b Tufnell	3
R. J. Bailey c Nash b Tufnell	10
*D. G. Cork c Nash b Cook	12
G. Welch c Roseberry b Fraser	28
†K. M. Krikken c Nash b Bloomfield	10
R. K. Illingworth lbw b Tufnell	17
T. A. Munton c Hutton b Tufnell	12
K. J. Dean not out	1
B 2, l-b 8, w 4, n-b 27	41
1/8 2/49 3/54 4/76 5/106 6/109 7/157 8/171 9/195	198

Bonus points – Middlesex 3.

Bowling: Fraser 22–12–29–1; Bloomfield 17–3–47–2; Cook 20–4–59–3; Tufnell 29.4–10–42–4; Weekes 10–5–11–0.

Middlesex

A. J. Strauss c Krikken b Welch	38
B. L. Hutton b Illingworth	8
O. A. Shah c Krikken b Illingworth	24
S. P. Fleming lbw b Illingworth	3
P. N. Weekes lbw b Illingworth	15
†D. C. Nash not out	27
M. A. Roseberry not out	21
L-b 2, w 8	10
1/16 2/64 3/76 4/78 5/95	(5 wkts) 146

S. J. Cook, *A. R. C. Fraser, P. C. R. Tufnell and T. F. Bloomfield did not bat.

Bonus point – Derbyshire 1.

Bowling: Munton 16–6–35–0; Dean 9–3–24–0; Illingworth 20–7–37–4; Cork 9–4–15–0; Welch 14–5–33–1.

Umpires: M. J. Harris and B. Leadbeater.

At Derby, May 8, 9, 10. DERBYSHIRE drew with PAKISTANIS (see Pakistani tour section).

At Worcester, May 16, 17, 18, 19. DERBYSHIRE drew with WORCESTERSHIRE.

DERBYSHIRE v HAMPSHIRE

At Derby, May 25, 26, 27, 28. Hampshire won by nine wickets. Hampshire 20 pts, Derbyshire 5 pts. Toss: Derbyshire. Championship debuts: N. R. C. Dumelow, T. Lungley.

Hampshire made the most of Munton's unexpected decision to field on a bland pitch, and five of their top seven scored fifties, the best from Prittipaul. When Kendall was caught behind for a fluent 94, he gave off-spinner Nathan Dumelow his first Championship wicket – and Krikken his 500th first-class dismissal. Mullally helped Aymes add 80 for the last wicket – Hampshire's best against Derbyshire – and the value of that partnership became clear when Derbyshire failed by 18 to avoid the follow-on. Stubbings batted in assured fashion and Dumelow hit a promising fifty before Mullally took the last three wickets in four balls, all caught in the slips by Johnson, who made it five in a row when Derbyshire batted again. Di Venuto resisted for almost three hours until falling to a brilliant catch by Smith at short extra cover off Udal, whose controlled and varied off-spin brought him his best figures for nine years and left Hampshire ample time for victory.

Close of play: First day, Hampshire 344-6 (Aymes 32*, Mascarenhas 4*); Second day, Derbyshire 188-4 (Stubbings 84*, Illingworth 6*); Third day, Derbyshire 69-4 (Di Venuto 19*, Welch 1*).

Hampshire

D. A. Kenway c Krikken b Illingworth	57	– c Sutton b Lungley	11
G. W. White b Welch	3	– not out	29
W. S. Kendall c Krikken b Dumelow	94	– not out	6
*R. A. Smith c Di Venuto b Welch	2		
N. C. Johnson lbw b Munton	53		
L. R. Prittipaul c Di Venuto b Bailey	84		
†A. N. Aymes not out	83		
A. D. Mascarenhas run out	13		
S. D. Udal b Munton	12		
A. C. Morris c Dumelow b Munton	4		
A. D. Mullally lbw b Bailey	36		
B 5, l-b 12, w 2, n-b 4	23	L-b 1, w 2	3
1/3 2/134 3/141 4/207 5/257 6/338 7/356 8/380 9/384	464	1/23	(1 wkt) 49

Bonus points – Hampshire 5, Derbyshire 3 (Score at 130 overs: 430-9).

Bowling: *First Innings*—Welch 35–7–123–2; Munton 37–7–107–3; Lungley 21–6–72–0; Illingworth 31–12–71–1; Dumelow 12–1–57–1; Bailey 7.2–3–17–2. *Second Innings*—Welch 4–2–7–0; Munton 3–1–6–0; Lungley 4.1–0–13–1; Dumelow 4–0–22–0.

Derbyshire

S. D. Stubbings lbw b Morris	93	– (2) c Aymes b Mullally	29
L. D. Sutton c Aymes b Morris	9	– (1) c Johnson b Mullally	8
M. P. Dowman b Mascarenhas	3	– c Johnson b Udal	2
M. J. Di Venuto c Mascarenhas b Udal	22	– c Smith b Udal	52
R. J. Bailey lbw b Mullally	52	– lbw b Udal	0
R. K. Illingworth c Aymes b Udal	18	– (9) not out	61
G. Welch c Mascarenhas b Mullally	10	– (6) c Prittipaul b Udal	12
†K. M. Krikken c Johnson b Mullally	24	– (7) c White b Udal	0
N. R. C. Dumelow not out	50	– (8) c Smith b Udal	14
T. Lungley c Johnson b Mullally	0	– b Udal	9
*T. A. Munton c Johnson b Mullally	0	– b Mascarenhas	11
B 5, l-b 1, w 6, n-b 4	16	B 1, l-b 12, n-b 4	17
1/25 2/39 3/85 4/178 5/209 6/209 7/225 8/297 9/297	297	1/29 2/40 3/56 4/57 5/95 6/99 7/123 8/150 9/198	215

Bonus points – Derbyshire 2, Hampshire 3.

Bowling: *First Innings*—Morris 20–6–62–2; Mullally 26.4–10–52–5; Mascarenhas 21–3–85–1; Udal 33.5–13–90–2; White 1.1–0–2–0. *Second Innings*—Mullally 21–8–46–2; Morris 17–5–39–0; Mascarenhas 17.3–5–43–1; Udal 38–16–74–7.

Umpires: M. J. Kitchen and N. A. Mallender.

At Southgate, May 30, 31, June 1. DERBYSHIRE lost to MIDDLESEX by an innings and 185 runs.

DERBYSHIRE v DURHAM

At Derby, June 6, 7, 8, 9. Drawn. Derbyshire 10 pts, Durham 9 pts. Toss: Derbyshire.

Neither side managed to take a decisive grip on this game, played out on a docile pitch. Krikken, who for the first time scored twin half-centuries, gave Derbyshire valuable substance as Phillips's intelligent off-spin worked through the innings. By the end of the second day, Durham's batsmen were struggling, but sloppy bowling the following morning allowed them to limit the deficit to 58. Di Venuto then tipped the balance back towards Derbyshire with an admirably responsible 86 before he was caught by Speight, keeping wicket in place of the injured Pratt. Aware that, in their previous game, Durham had hit 318 for two to beat Nottinghamshire, Derbyshire batted on into the final day, eventually setting a target of 326 in 85 overs. Peng gave the visitors sight of victory, but when he was run out by a direct hit from substitute fielder Bassano at deep mid-wicket, they settled for the draw.

Close of play: First day, Derbyshire 239-6 (Krikken 45*, Dumelow 14*); Second day, Durham 201-7 (Hunter 13*, Phillips 2*); Third day, Derbyshire 214-6 (Krikken 52*, Dumelow 4*).

Derbyshire

S. D. Stubbings c Phillips b Harmison	29	– (2) lbw b Harmison	7
L. D. Sutton c Pratt b Hunter	15	– (1) b Phillips	13
M. P. Dowman b Phillips	45	– b Harmison	8
M. J. Di Venuto c Pratt b Phillips	19	– c Speight b Law	86
R. J. Bailey c Pratt b Harmison	26	– c sub b Gough	24
G. Welch c Love b Phillips	16	– b Hunter	9
†K. M. Krikken b Phillips	54	– b Phillips	75
N. R. C. Dumelow c Pratt b Hunter	25	– c Love b Phillips	8
R. K. Illingworth b Harmison	13	– c Phillips b Harmison	6
T. Lungley not out	8	– not out	6
*T. A. Munton c Pratt b Phillips	20	– c Lewis b Phillips	10
B 7, l-b 27, w 12, n-b 2	48	B 5, l-b 10	15
1/47 2/51 3/110 4/153 5/157 6/187 7/250 8/266 9/277	318	1/17 2/25 3/35 4/105 5/118 6/205 7/218 8/231 9/257	267

Bonus points – Derbyshire 3, Durham 3.

Bowling: *First Innings*—Brown 19–5–72–0; Harmison 28–3–83–3; Hunter 20–4–52–2; Phillips 36.3–13–64–5; Law 5–0–13–0. *Second Innings*—Harmison 20–5–65–3; Brown 9–2–23–0; Phillips 31–8–92–4; Gough 17–4–28–1; Hunter 7–1–29–1; Law 8–4–15–1.

Durham

*J. J. B. Lewis c Di Venuto b Welch	7	– c Krikken b Illingworth	28
M. A. Gough b Dumelow	42	– lbw b Munton	7
M. L. Love lbw b Illingworth	54	– c Krikken b Welch	40
M. P. Speight lbw b Welch	14	– run out	36
N. Peng c Bailey b Illingworth	34	– run out	90
D. R. Law c Welch b Lungley	10	– c Sutton b Bailey	37
†A. Pratt c Krikken b Munton	19	– c Krikken b Welch	5
I. D. Hunter c Krikken b Munton	18	– not out	15
N. C. Phillips c Munton b Illingworth	30	– not out	1
S. J. E. Brown c Krikken b Welch	22		
S. J. Harmison not out	0		
B 3, l-b 3, n-b 4	10	B 7, l-b 10, w 2, n-b 2	21
1/30 2/79 3/106 4/126 5/139 6/186 7/186 8/215 9/259	260	1/12 2/76 3/80 4/177 5/241 6/258 7/270	(7 wkts) 280

Bonus points – Durham 2, Derbyshire 3.

Bowling: *First Innings*—Welch 15.2–1–46–3; Munton 24–4–76–2; Dumelow 17–5–46–1; Lungley 14–4–40–1; Illingworth 21–8–46–3. *Second Innings*—Welch 25–8–65–2; Munton 23–6–57–1; Dumelow 11–2–36–0; Lungley 3–0–28–0; Illingworth 17.4–5–57–1; Di Venuto 1–0–1–0; Bailey 4–1–19–1.

Umpires: M. R. Benson and T. E. Jesty.

At Arundel, June 13, 14, 15. DERBYSHIRE lost to SUSSEX by an innings and 34 runs.

DERBYSHIRE v GLOUCESTERSHIRE

At Derby, June 20, 21, 22, 23. Drawn. Derbyshire 9 pts, Gloucestershire 10 pts. Toss: Gloucestershire. Championship debut: C. W. G. Bassano.

Chris Bassano's unparalleled achievement of two hundreds on Championship debut was the highlight of a game that reached an enthralling climax. Derbyshire ended nine runs from victory and Gloucestershire one wicket. In all, the match produced 1,466 runs and six centuries, with Alleyne hitting his second in consecutive matches and Snape the first of his career as Gloucestershire recorded their highest total against Derbyshire, and the best by a visiting side on the County Ground since Kent scored 615 in 1908. Russell marked his 500th innings for the county with a fifty. Derbyshire needed 411 to avoid the follow-on and, thanks to centuries from Stubbings and Bassano, whose 202 together was the county's first hundred partnership of the summer, they achieved it with ease. Bassano, who had played for Gloucestershire's Second Eleven in 2000, batted for 527 minutes and hit two sixes and 27 fours from 422 balls. Hewson was fed a maiden hundred to set Derbyshire 306 in 69 overs. Bassano went to his second century with 12 boundaries, but Alleyne produced a late six-over spell of three for 12 to set up the conclusion; Derbyshire's last pair had to keep out three balls.

Close of play: First day, Gloucestershire 374-4 (Alleyne 114*, Snape 52*); Second day, Derbyshire 142-1 (Stubbings 83*, Bassano 40*); Third day, Derbyshire 432-5 (Bassano 186*, Welch 13*).

Gloucestershire

D. R. Hewson b Munton	10	– not out	100
K. J. Barnett b Aldred	73	– not out	72
M. G. N. Windows c Bailey b Munton	11		
C. G. Taylor lbw b Aldred	83		
*M. W. Alleyne lbw b Munton	136		
J. N. Snape b Wharton	119		
†R. C. Russell b Aldred	53		
M. A. Hardinges lbw b Bailey	14		
M. C. J. Ball not out	12		
J. M. M. Averis not out	7		
B 15, l-b 10, w 9, n-b 8	42	L-b 1, w 2, n-b 2	5
1/21 2/69 3/124 4/271 5/414 6/502 7/536 8/542 (8 wkts dec.)	560	(no wkt dec.)	177

B. W. Gannon did not bat.

Bonus points – Gloucestershire 5, Derbyshire 1 (Score at 130 overs: 440-5).

Bowling: *First Innings*—Welch 29–4–102–0; Munton 28–6–90–3; Aldred 33–5–129–3; Wharton 37–12–98–1; Dumelow 23–4–82–0; Di Venuto 6–1–15–0; Bailey 7–1–19–1. *Second Innings*—Welch 6–0–33–0; Aldred 5–0–27–0; Wharton 3–0–17–0; Dumelow 3–0–25–0; Bailey 3–0–37–0; Bassano 2–0–11–0; Stubbings 2–0–11–0; Dowman 1–0–15–0.

Derbyshire

S. D. Stubbings b Alleyne	126	– lbw b Hardinges	9
†L. D. Sutton b Gannon	13	– (9) not out	3
C. W. G. Bassano not out	186	– c Windows b Alleyne	106
M. J. Di Venuto c Windows b Alleyne	2	– (2) c Hewson b Ball	43
R. J. Bailey c Ball b Alleyne	36	– (7) lbw b Ball	2
M. P. Dowman c Russell b Hardinges	25	– (4) c Windows b Ball	50
G. Welch not out	13	– (6) st Russell b Ball	45
N. R. C. Dumelow (did not bat)		– (5) lbw b Ball	21
P. Aldred (did not bat)		– (8) b Alleyne	0
*T. A. Munton (did not bat)		– b Alleyne	1
L. J. Wharton (did not bat)		– not out	1
L-b 8, w 13, n-b 10	31	B 1, l-b 7, w 2, n-b 6	16
1/36 2/238 3/240 4/350 5/388 (5 wkts dec.)	432	1/40 2/80 3/170 4/203 5/267 6/286 7/287 8/295 9/296 (9 wkts)	297

Bonus points – Derbyshire 4, Gloucestershire 1 (Score at 130 overs: 371-4).

Bowling: *First Innings*—Averis 25–5–89–0; Gannon 21–3–71–1; Hardinges 27–6–90–1; Ball 34–15–44–0; Alleyne 20–3–72–3; Snape 23–4–48–0; Hewson 3–1–7–0; Barnett 3–1–3–0. *Second Innings*—Averis 10–2–44–0; Gannon 7–1–23–0; Hardinges 9–1–36–1; Alleyne 17–2–57–3; Ball 23–2–100–5; Snape 3–0–29–0.

Umpires: R. Julian and R. A. White.

At Southampton, June 29, 30, July 1. DERBYSHIRE lost to HAMPSHIRE by ten wickets.

DERBYSHIRE v WORCESTERSHIRE

At Derby, July 5, 6, 7, 8. Worcestershire won by an innings and three runs. Worcestershire 20 pts, Derbyshire 2 pts. Toss: Worcestershire.

Cork, omitted by England for the First Test against Australia, joined the game 20 minutes after the start but could not prevent Hick and Solanki carrying Worcestershire to a commanding position with a partnership of 198 on a guileless pitch. Hick's third century in four Championship innings included 25 fours, while Solanki hit four sixes and 12 fours in his 109. Worcestershire's total was their highest in Derbyshire, beating 483 for three in 1901. Bassano withdrew after the first day to fly to Tasmania, where his father, cricket writer Brian Bassano, was seriously ill. But batting a man short could not excuse Derbyshire's collapse on the third morning, when eight wickets fell for 64. They followed on for the fifth time in seven matches. Bichel had sparked the first-innings slide with four for two in 13 balls, and when Derbyshire batted again Sheriyar took four for 12 in 24. Bailey's six-hour defiance, following a first-ball duck, merely delayed the inevitable.

Close of play: First day, Worcestershire 390-5 (Boulton 6*, Bichel 0*); Second day, Derbyshire 134-1 (Stubbings 63*, Titchard 37*); Third day, Derbyshire 185-5 (Bailey 56*, Welch 27*).

Worcestershire

W. P. C. Weston lbw b Cork	17	Kabir Ali c Dowman b Welch	13
A. Singh c Bassano b Cork	60	M. J. Rawnsley b Aldred	4
*G. A. Hick c Aldred b Bailey	171	A. Sheriyar c Cork b Aldred	14
V. S. Solanki c Wharton b Dumelow	109		
D. A. Leatherdale c Sutton b Welch	0	B 5, l-b 18, w 6, n-b 10	39
N. R. Boulton c Cork b Welch	7		
A. J. Bichel lbw b Aldred	25	1/56 2/149 3/347 4/349 5/390	496
†S. J. Rhodes not out	37	6/394 7/433 8/459 9/478	

Bonus points – Worcestershire 5, Derbyshire 2 (Score at 130 overs: 460-8).

Bowling: Welch 39–8–132–3; Aldred 31.3–3–102–3; Cork 27–5–84–2; Wharton 27–7–89–0; Dumelow 8–1–44–1; Bailey 6–0–22–1.

Derbyshire

S. D. Stubbings b Rawnsley	75	– (2) b Sheriyar	53
†L. D. Sutton c Rhodes b Ali	16	– (1) c Rhodes b Sheriyar	14
S. P. Titchard c Rhodes b Bichel	39	– c Rhodes b Sheriyar	5
M. P. Dowman c Hick b Bichel	2	– b Sheriyar	0
R. J. Bailey lbw b Bichel	0	– not out	136
*D. G. Cork c Leatherdale b Bichel	2	– c Rhodes b Bichel	21
G. Welch c Solanki b Hick	7	– lbw b Sheriyar	39
N. R. C. Dumelow b Rawnsley	33	– c Solanki b Rawnsley	7
P. Aldred c Solanki b Hick	0	– c Hick b Ali	2
L. J. Wharton not out	1	– lbw b Ali	0
C. W. G. Bassano absent		absent	
B 13, l-b 2, w 8	23	B 1, l-b 11, w 6	18
1/44 2/139 3/145 4/145 5/147 6/155 7/159 8/160 9/198	198	1/62 2/72 3/72 4/77 5/115 6/230 7/270 8/295 9/295	295

Bonus points – Worcestershire 3.

Bowling: *First Innings*—Bichel 17–2–53–4; Sheriyar 8–0–34–0; Ali 7–0–28–1; Rawnsley 18–7–60–2; Leatherdale 4–1–4–0; Hick 4–3–4–2. *Second Innings*—Bichel 21–4–57–1; Ali 20.4–5–51–2; Sheriyar 27–6–68–5; Rawnsley 27–5–74–1; Hick 5–1–16–0; Leatherdale 6–2–17–0.

Umpires: N. G. Cowley and B. Dudleston.

At Birmingham, July 18, 19, 20, 21. DERBYSHIRE drew with WARWICKSHIRE.

DERBYSHIRE v NOTTINGHAMSHIRE

At Derby, July 27, 28, 29, 30. Drawn. Derbyshire 12 pts, Nottinghamshire 11 pts. Toss: Nottinghamshire.

On the ground where he spent 14 seasons, Morris announced his intention to retire and, by hitting two centuries and sharing two partnerships over 300, promptly suggested his decision was premature. His first-innings 170 was a delight but, long before he and Pietersen had set a Nottinghamshire sixth-wicket record in the second with an unbroken stand of 372, the contest had drowned in a sea of runs. The gentlest of pitches had spawned 1,655 – the highest for a Derbyshire match – including six hundreds and a whopping 159 from Extras. On the opening day, the first two centurions, Morris (22 fours and three sixes) and Afzaal, put on 316 for the fourth wicket. Derbyshire then collected maximum batting points for the only time all season; Stubbings and Cork (who later tore a hamstring while bowling and missed the remainder of the summer) gave their innings substance. As the match meandered through a meaningless last day, Pietersen hit a first double-hundred, containing 23 fours and nine sixes, as Nottinghamshire, unwilling to set a target, batted on and on.

Close of play: First day, Nottinghamshire 478-6 (Read 12*, Logan 14*); Second day, Derbyshire 385-6 (Welch 17*, Krikken 2*); Third day, Nottinghamshire 131-2 (Blewett 39*, Randall 9*).

Nottinghamshire

*D. J. Bicknell c Krikken b Aldred	41	– lbw b Aldred	19
G. E. Welton lbw b Dean	19	– b Welch	50
G. S. Blewett c Bailey b Cork	31	– b Dean	52
U. Afzaal c Aldred b Bailey	138	– (5) c Cork b Dean	12
J. E. Morris run out	170	– (7) not out	136
K. P. Pietersen lbw b Bailey	0	– not out	218
†C. M. W. Read b Welch	23		
R. J. Logan lbw b Cork	14		
D. S. Lucas c Krikken b Cork	16		
S. J. Randall c Di Venuto b Cork	13	– (4) lbw b Dean	11
G. J. Smith not out	2		
B 2, l-b 17, w 4, n-b 36	59	B 3, l-b 18, w 14, n-b 24	59
1/54 2/99 3/125 4/441 5/447 6/456 7/478 8/498 9/522	526	1/45 2/116 3/147 4/148 5/185	(5 wkts) 557

Bonus points – Nottinghamshire 5, Derbyshire 3.

Bowling: *First Innings*—Cork 27.2–4–122–4; Dean 19–3–106–1; Welch 25–1–99–1; Aldred 14–2–64–1; Dumelow 15–1–71–0; Bailey 15–4–29–2; Di Venuto 3–0–16–0. *Second Innings*—Cork 27–5–69–0; Dean 23–5–100–3; Aldred 15–1–99–1; Welch 18–7–41–1; Dumelow 16–3–63–0; Bailey 11–0–53–0; Di Venuto 9–0–59–0; Stubbings 2–0–25–0; Krikken 7–0–27–0.

Derbyshire

S. D. Stubbings c Pietersen b Afzaal	127
M. J. Di Venuto c Morris b Smith	59
L. D. Sutton c Welton b Randall	0
R. J. Bailey lbw b Smith	3
M. P. Dowman b Randall	22
*D. G. Cork c Bicknell b Lucas	128
G. Welch b Logan	38
†K. M. Krikken not out	93
N. R. C. Dumelow b Lucas	23
P. Aldred c Blewett b Afzaal	35
K. J. Dean b Afzaal	3
B 3, l-b 10, w 12, n-b 16	41
1/124 2/125 3/138 4/185 5/305 6/381 7/425 8/470 9/562	572

Bonus points – Derbyshire 5, Nottinghamshire 2 (Score at 130 overs: 511-8).

Bowling: Smith 21–2–89–2; Logan 24–5–101–1; Lucas 25–3–99–2; Randall 36–7–132–2; Afzaal 29.1–5–88–3; Pietersen 13–1–49–0; Morris 1–0–1–0.

Umpires: M. R. Benson and K. E. Palmer.

At Chester-le-Street, August 8, 9, 10. DERBYSHIRE beat DURHAM by four wickets.

DERBYSHIRE v SUSSEX

At Derby, August 15, 16, 17, 18. Sussex won by 130 runs. Sussex 17 pts, Derbyshire 5 pts. Toss: Sussex.

Another Derbyshire collapse gave Sussex a victory that took them 24 points clear at the top of the second division. Over three innings, the match had been evenly contested, characterised by players on each side throwing away their wickets when apparently well set. There was one notable exception, however. Sutton, opening only because Di Venuto had picked up a groin injury in the win over Durham, became the first Derbyshire player to carry his bat since Adrian Rollins at Hove in 1996. Sutton spent six and a half hours at the crease for a career-best unbeaten 140, and was last out in Derbyshire's shorter second innings; he hit more than half their runs in the match. Needing 248, about par on this pitch, Derbyshire soon lost wickets to Lewry and Kirtley, who had earlier both reached 50 wickets for the season, and Robinson's accuracy finished them off.

Close of play: First day, Sussex 273-8 (Davis 51*, Kirtley 4*); Second day, Derbyshire 198-6 (Sutton 100*, Smith 6*); Third day, Sussex 224-8 (Davis 43*, Kirtley 7*).

Sussex

R. R. Montgomerie c Aldred b Smith	19	– (2) lbw b Dean	19
M. W. Goodwin c Bassano b Wharton	67	– (1) c Krikken b Welch	11
*C. J. Adams c Krikken b Aldred	17	– c Bailey b Wharton	59
B. Zuiderent c Krikken b Dean	21	– lbw b Dean	0
M. H. Yardy c Dowman b Smith	20	– c Krikken b Smith	30
R. S. C. Martin-Jenkins c Dowman b Smith	14	– c Krikken b Dean	22
†M. J. Prior c Krikken b Smith	31	– run out	15
M. J. G. Davis lbw b Dean	52	– c Stubbings b Welch	44
J. D. Lewry c Bassano b Dean	0	– c Smith b Welch	6
R. J. Kirtley c Krikken b Dean	5	– not out	9
M. A. Robinson not out	5	– c Krikken b Welch	3
B 11, l-b 6, w 4, n-b 8	29	L-b 4, w 2, n-b 6	12
1/56 2/106 3/118 4/154 5/157 6/174 7/236 8/243 9/275	280	1/18 2/30 3/30 4/85 5/146 6/146 7/172 8/186 9/225	230

Bonus points – Sussex 2, Derbyshire 3.

Bowling: *First Innings*—Welch 24–9–51–0; Dean 28.3–7–72–4; Smith 18–3–61–4; Aldred 17–5–43–1; Wharton 21–10–30–1; Bailey 4–2–6–0. *Second Innings*—Welch 22.2–4–58–4; Dean 23–5–70–3; Smith 12–1–41–1; Aldred 10–1–36–0; Wharton 17–9–21–1; Bailey 2–2–0–0.

Derbyshire

S. D. Stubbings b Lewry	0	– b Lewry	1
L. D. Sutton not out	140	– c Prior b Kirtley	54
*R. J. Bailey c Prior b Kirtley	8	– lbw b Lewry	3
C. W. G. Bassano c Prior b Lewry	18	– lbw b Kirtley	0
M. P. Dowman c Zuiderent b Robinson	10	– c sub b Robinson	8
†K. M. Krikken c Adams b Lewry	32	– c Adams b Robinson	4
G. Welch c Prior b Robinson	11	– b Robinson	6
T. M. Smith c sub b Martin-Jenkins	19	– lbw b Robinson	13
P. Aldred lbw b Martin-Jenkins	0	– c Martin-Jenkins b Lewry	6
K. J. Dean c Adams b Lewry	1	– lbw b Robinson	4
L. J. Wharton c Prior b Robinson	0	– not out	2
B 8, l-b 10, n-b 6	24	B 8, l-b 4, n-b 4	16
1/0 2/19 3/69 4/103 5/162 6/191 7/223 8/223 9/230	263	1/6 2/14 3/19 4/27 5/31 6/45 7/71 8/86 9/97	117

Bonus points – Derbyshire 2, Sussex 3.

Bowling: *First Innings*—Lewry 28–9–55–4; Kirtley 17–4–50–1; Martin-Jenkins 28–5–94–2; Robinson 15.5–4–30–3; Davis 9–1–16–0. *Second Innings*—Lewry 14–7–18–3; Kirtley 11–1–28–2; Robinson 15–3–38–5; Martin-Jenkins 5–1–21–0.

Umpires: J. H. Evans and R. Julian.

At Nottingham, August 22, 23, 24, 25. DERBYSHIRE lost to NOTTINGHAMSHIRE by seven wickets.

At Bristol, September 5, 6, 7. DERBYSHIRE lost to GLOUCESTERSHIRE by an innings and 20 runs.

DERBYSHIRE v WARWICKSHIRE

At Derby, September 12, 13, 14, 15. Warwickshire won by an innings and 100 runs. Warwickshire 20 pts, Derbyshire 1.25 pts. Toss: Warwickshire.

To win promotion, Warwickshire needed to collect four points more than Gloucestershire, and maintain their lead over Middlesex. Powell won an important toss but, although there was help for the bowlers, Derbyshire's batsmen were largely culpable as Dagnall, taking a career-best six for 50 in his second Championship game of the summer, and Brown swept them aside. From then on, Warwickshire were dominant, and the weather, which allowed just 62 overs on the first two days, was more of a threat than their opponents, already assured of the wooden spoon. On the third day, Knight and Bell scored uninhibited centuries, shared a partnership of 245 and steered Warwickshire to maximum batting points. Then Brown, who returned match figures of ten for 80, hustled Derbyshire to their fifth innings defeat. Lungley and Wharton, who began the game with eight runs from his previous 16 innings, delayed them with a 69-run last-wicket stand, broken moments before more rain arrived. As Warwickshire celebrated promotion, Derbyshire suffered further indignity when they were penalised three-quarters of a point for a slow over-rate.

Close of play: First day, Warwickshire 1-0 (Powell 1*, Knight 0*); Second day, Warwickshire 69-3 (Knight 26*, Bell 4*); Third day, Derbyshire 91-5 (Dumelow 3*, Dean 0*).

Derbyshire

S. D. Stubbings lbw b Dagnall	8	– lbw b Dagnall	13
*M. J. Di Venuto c Penney b Brown	36	– c Richardson b Brown	33
M. P. Dowman c Bell b Dagnall	8	– lbw b Brown	13
C. W. G. Bassano lbw b Brown	1	– b Dagnall	2
S. A. Selwood c Richardson b Dagnall	1	– lbw b Brown	9
N. R. C. Dumelow b Dagnall	0	– c Powell b Brown	8
†K. M. Krikken lbw b Dagnall	0	– (8) c Powell b Brown	0
G. Welch c Penney b Brown	3	– (9) b Dagnall	3
T. Lungley c Penney b Dagnall	13	– (10) b Betts	47
K. J. Dean b Brown	14	– (7) c Smith b Brown	23
L. J. Wharton not out	8	– not out	13
B 9, l-b 1, n-b 4	14	B 14, l-b 12, n-b 4	30
1/11 2/39 3/44 4/57 5/57 6/57 7/60 8/68 9/84	106	1/39 2/58 3/69 4/83 5/89 6/114 7/122 8/125 9/125	194

Bonus points – Warwickshire 3.

Bowling: *First Innings*—Betts 6–1–20–0; Dagnall 21–7–50–6; Richardson 1–0–6–0; Brown 14.2–8–20–4. *Second Innings*—Betts 7.4–1–30–1; Dagnall 23–4–78–3; Brown 19–2–60–6.

Warwickshire

*M. J. Powell c Dowman b Dean	1	†T. L. Penney c Krikken b Lungley	1
N. V. Knight c Krikken b Lungley	124	N. M. K. Smith not out	29
M. A. Wagh b Welch	30	B 1, l-b 9, n-b 14	24
D. L. Hemp lbw b Dean	3		—
I. R. Bell c Stubbings b Lungley	135	1/1 2/58 3/61 (6 wkts dec.)	400
D. R. Brown not out	53	4/306 5/319 6/327	

C. E. Dagnall, M. M. Betts and A. Richardson did not bat.

Bonus points – Warwickshire 5, Derbyshire 2.

Bowling: Welch 26–3–86–1; Dean 25–7–107–2; Lungley 15–0–89–3; Wharton 5–0–36–0; Dowman 2–0–18–0; Dumelow 12.4–3–54–0.

Umpires: K. E. Palmer and R. Palmer.

ONE HUNDRED YEARS AGO

From JOHN WISDEN'S CRICKETERS' ALMANACK for 1902

DERBYSHIRE IN 1901 – "Badly as Derbyshire did in 1899 and 1900, their record for 1901 was even poorer, disaster following disaster throughout the summer in the most depressing manner, with the result that out of 24 matches they were unable to place a victory of any sort to their credit… They went from bad to worse… even in drawn games the positions at the finish generally favoured their opponents… Unlike other counties, Derbyshire seldom seem able to gain any promising recruits… What is badly wanted is another bowler or two, and a strong captain to keep the eleven together."

THE LEADING COUNTIES IN 1901 – "Never has the struggle for the Championship been more one-sided than in 1901. The Yorkshiremen won all the way. They beat Lancashire – thought to be their most dangerous rivals – in… such style that when in July they suffered their sensational defeat at the hands of Somerset, they stood so far ahead of all opponents that the beating did not matter. They did not lose any other county match, and finished up with the wonderful record of twenty victories, one defeat, and six drawn games."

MR BOSANQUET'S TEAM v EIGHTEEN COLTS OF PHILADELPHIA AND A CAPTAIN – "Played at Philadelphia, on September 20, 21, 23. – With nineteen men in the field against them, the Englishmen started their tour very badly, being beaten by 186 runs."

NOTES BY THE EDITOR (Sydney H. Pardon) – "It is… becoming increasingly difficult in fine weather to play a game out… The use of the sort of liquid manure, of which some ground-keepers are now so fond, handicaps the bowler in two ways, first by taking nearly all the life out of the ground, and secondly by rendering the wicket almost impervious to natural wear… The mowing machine, the hose and the heavy roller have in combination made the task of the modern batsman sufficiently easy, and in the opinion of many good judges… he did not need the further help that has lately been accorded him."

THE LONDON COUNTY CLUB IN 1901 – "Interest usually centred in the doings of Mr. W. G. Grace. In his fielding the great cricketer showed more than ever the effect of advancing years, but he was in capital batting form, scoring 761 runs in twenty innings, with an average of 38. He would have made a good many more runs if he had been able to travel quicker between the wickets."

NOTES BY THE EDITOR (Sydney H. Pardon) – "[Of] the decision come to by the county captains in December, 1900 to debar certain bowlers from taking part in county matches… I felt perfectly certain that… nothing but benefit to the game of cricket would result from the action they had resolved on. Never within the last twenty years or more has there been so little unfair or doubtful bowling as in the season of 1901. Indeed the improvement was so marked as to make it clear that, if the captains stick to their guns, we shall soon be entirely free from an evil of which not very long ago it seemed impossible to get rid."

Paul Collingwood

DURHAM

President: J. D. Robson
Chairman: D. W. Midgley
Chief Executive: D. Harker
Chairman, Cricket Committee: R. Jackson
Director of Cricket: G. Cook
Captain: J. J. B. Lewis
Head Coach: M. D. Moxon
Head Groundsman: D. Measor
Scorer: B. Hunt

Winning National League promotion cushioned the blow of finishing next to bottom in the Championship, Durham's worst finish since 1997. Other than 18-year-old Nicky Peng making three glorious centuries, there were few obvious reasons why Durham had become a better one-day side; they also reached the quarter-finals of both cups. But it all pointed to good teamwork, and added up to a satisfactory first season for new coach Martyn Moxon. "Our one-day form has been very good, and very consistent," he said. "In the Championship, injuries haven't helped, coupled with a spate of lost tosses. But overall I'm delighted with the season. The attitude and application of the players have been fantastic and there has been a very good spirit. We have needed everybody, and in that sense the injuries have stood us in good stead, because we now know we have a squad of 20 players who can perform at this level."

Individually, the most significant factors were the continued emergence of Peng, who also made his maiden first-class hundred, the superb early-season form of Paul Collingwood, which earned him an England one-day place, and the brilliant wicket-keeping of Andrew Pratt, the members' Player of the Year. New all-rounder Danny Law overcame a slow start to reveal his true talent, thriving on the extra opportunities afforded by injuries to become the leading wicket-taker. He also hit an excellent maiden Championship hundred, against Hampshire.

Given that Durham's strength in recent seasons had been their seam attack, the departure of Melvyn Betts and John Wood, followed by injuries to Simon Brown and Neil Killeen, could have proved crippling. But with James Brinkley proving a good acquisition and Nicky Hatch emerging, they muddled through surprisingly well. Steve Harmison played 11 Championship matches, but continued the erratic form that plagued him in 2000, when he was included in England's Test squad, and Ian Hunter suffered similar problems after looking every inch a first-class cricketer early in the season. He became too wayward to risk, and was too prone to waste his batting talent by throwing his wicket away. Off-spinner Nicky Phillips showed signs of improvement, however, before he also was injured in mid-season. All this allowed Brinkley, signed as back-up, to become a successful fixture in the side when fit and available, while Hatch and 20-year-old left-arm spinner Graeme Bridge had the chance to prove they have a future in county cricket.

Although pitches were generally good, Durham's perennial problem of not enough batsmen averaging 30 continued. Only Queenslander Martin Love (50.51) and Collingwood (48.90) topped that mark in the Championship, which was a poorer record than any other county, and Durham never achieved maximum batting points. Love, signed when it became clear Simon Katich would be in Australia's Ashes squad, settled in quickly with two sixties in the opening match. But it set a trend. He reached 14 Championship half-centuries yet converted only one into a hundred – a disappointment from a classy and dedicated player who also proved his worth as a slip catcher. Although Michael Gough's off-spin bowling developed nicely, his batting remained more promising than productive, while Jimmy Daley was offered an 11th year on the staff despite his injury-hit season ending with only 300 Championship runs at 20.00.

Skipper Jon Lewis, third in the Championship batting, topped the one-day averages after his superb unbeaten 76 off 66 balls against Worcestershire clinched promotion in the final match. But he would look back on his run of nine lost tosses in the middle of the four-day programme as a big obstacle to progress. Every game tended to be similar, with Durham having to field first with a weakened attack and then finding themselves chasing the game. That was even the case in their first win. They trailed by 95 on first innings against visiting Nottinghamshire, who set a target of 315 in 102 overs. Love and Lewis put on 258 for the second wicket, 52 more than the previous best for any wicket by Durham in the Championship, and they won by eight wickets with an hour to spare. The only other Championship wins came at Kidderminster, where Law gave a fine all-round performance, and Hove, where Daley's gritty 89 helped to secure his future and Harmison produced his best new-ball bowling for two years.

While the Benson and Hedges Cup quarter-final defeat by holders Gloucestershire was a disappointment, Durham went back to Bristol in the fourth round of the Cheltenham & Gloucester Trophy and knocked them out in dramatic fashion. On his first senior one-day appearance, Bridge took three for 44 to claim the match award as Durham won by three runs. If the seven-wicket defeat by Lancashire in the quarter-finals was an anticlimax, there were still one-day dramas to come. Peng's hundred under the lights at Worcester was not enough to win a thrilling, high-scoring match, but the tables were turned when Worcestershire visited the Riverside for the League decider in September. Lewis gave Durham a competitive total, and Pratt's scintillating leg-side stumping of Graeme Hick proved a key moment in Durham's nine-run win.

Nick Speak and Martin Speight were released at the end of the season. Consequently, with four academy products awarded full-time contracts – all-rounders Gordon Muchall and Chris Mann, seamer Mark Davies, plus wicket-keeper Phil Mustard – only six players on the staff will not be from the North-East in 2002. One of those is another new recruit, Australian-born all-rounder Ashley Thorpe, 26, who has a residential qualification after living and playing club cricket in the region for seven years. – TIM WELLOCK.

DURHAM 2001

[*Ian Dobson Photography*

Standing: C. Sanctuary (*sports scientist*), N. A. Kent (*physiotherapist*), B. Hunt (*First Eleven scorer*), G. D. Bridge, M. J. Symington, I. D. Hunter, N. Peng, D. R. Law, N. G. Hatch, M. A. Gough, J. E. Brinkley, A. Pratt, N. C. Phillips, G. J. Pratt, A. Walker (*second-team coach*), D. Graham (*Second Eleven scorer*). *Seated:* J. A. Daley, P. D. Collingwood, M. P. Speight, M. L. Love, J. J. B. Lewis (*captain*), M. D. Moxon (*first-team coach*), S. J. E. Brown, N. J. Speak, N. Killeen, S. J. Harmison.

DURHAM RESULTS

All first-class matches – Played 17: Won 3, Lost 6, Drawn 8.

County Championship matches – Played 16: Won 3, Lost 6, Drawn 7.

CricInfo County Championship, 8th in Division 2; Cheltenham & Gloucester Trophy, q-f; Benson and Hedges Cup, q-f; Norwich Union League, 2nd in Division 2.

COUNTY CHAMPIONSHIP AVERAGES

BATTING

Cap		*M*	*I*	*NO*	*R*	*HS*	*100s*	*50s*	*Avge*	*Ct/St*
2001	M. L. Love§	15	29	2	1,364	149*	1	13	50.51	21
1998	P. D. Collingwood†	12	23	3	978	153	2	6	48.90	10
1998	J. J. B. Lewis	16	31	0	890	129	2	3	28.70	6
2001	N. Peng	12	22	2	551	101	1	3	27.55	6
2001	D. R. Law	15	26	1	586	103	1	1	23.44	10
1998	M. P. Speight	7	14	2	281	67*	0	1	23.41	1
1998	S. J. E. Brown†	4	5	2	64	29	0	0	21.33	1
1999	J. A. Daley†	8	15	0	300	89	0	1	20.00	1
2001	A. Pratt†	16	28	4	476	68*	0	3	19.83	49/7
	M. A. Gough†	12	22	0	428	79	0	1	19.45	8
	I. D. Hunter†	8	14	3	199	37	0	0	18.09	4
	N. G. Hatch†	9	16	8	129	24	0	0	16.12	1
	G. J. Pratt†	2	4	0	53	37	0	0	13.25	1
2001	N. C. Phillips	7	11	4	87	30	0	0	12.42	6
	G. D. Bridge†	7	13	2	125	39*	0	0	11.36	5
	J. E. Brinkley	9	13	2	111	65	0	1	10.09	4
1999	S. J. Harmison	11	14	4	97	27	0	0	9.70	0

Also batted: N. Killeen† (cap 1999) (3 matches) 5, 0, 1; G. M. Scott† (1 match) 8, 25 (1 ct); N. J. Speak (cap 1998) (2 matches) 41, 2, 7.

* *Signifies not out.* † *Born in Durham.* § *Overseas player.*

BOWLING

	O	*M*	*R*	*W*	*BB*	*5W/i*	*Avge*
J. E. Brinkley	207.1	49	629	30	6-14	2	20.96
G. D. Bridge	172	48	413	18	6-84	1	22.94
S. J. E. Brown	115	29	333	14	6-70	1	23.78
D. R. Law	339.1	69	1,070	40	6-53	3	26.75
N. G. Hatch	248.4	43	867	26	3-42	0	33.34
M. A. Gough	150	31	434	13	5-66	1	33.38
S. J. Harmison	397.5	76	1,228	34	6-111	2	36.11
N. C. Phillips	285.5	60	939	23	5-64	1	40.82
I. D. Hunter	181.3	27	700	16	4-55	0	43.75

Also bowled: P. D. Collingwood 154–41–463–7; N. Killeen 72–22–194–7; G. M. Scott 3–1–11–0.

COUNTY RECORDS

Highest score for:	210*	J. J. B. Lewis v Oxford University at Oxford	1997
Highest score against:	501*	B. C. Lara (Warwickshire) at Birmingham	1994
Best bowling for:	9-64	M. M. Betts v Northamptonshire at Northampton	1997
Best bowling against:	8-22	D. Follett (Middlesex) at Lord's	1996
Highest total for:	625-6 dec.	v Derbyshire at Chesterfield	1994
Highest total against:	810-4 dec.	by Warwickshire at Birmingham	1994
Lowest total for:	67	v Middlesex at Lord's	1996
Lowest total against:	67	by Durham UCCE at Chester-le-Street	2001

DURHAM v DURHAM UCCE

At Chester-le-Street, April 16, 17, 18. Drawn. Toss: Durham UCCE. First-class debuts: J. T. A. Bruce, R. S. Ferley, R. G. Gilbert, H. J. H. Loudon, J. G. C. Rowe, R. A. Stead. County debuts: J. E. Brinkley, D. R. Law.

Durham University Centre of Cricketing Excellence, making their first-class debut, quickly discovered the breadth of the gulf separating student and county cricket. Their opponents and neighbours were perhaps the Championship's least experienced side, but the newcomers were still dismissed for 67, the lowest total against Durham since they achieved first-class status in 1992. The students were hampered by a lack of outdoor practice, and only Will Jefferson, the towering 6ft 10in Essex opener, looked capable of putting bat to ball. The professionals owed most to Killeen, who claimed the first three wickets. Two of the three Durham century-makers retired, and the students, having removed Gough at 4.54 on the first afternoon, did not take another wicket until 4.58 on the second. Lewis hit 15 fours, Daley 16 and Collingwood 17 (as well as three sixes) before he was stumped. The university batsmen fared better on the final day when, between showers of rain, hail and snow, the fielders wore woolly hats.

Close of play: First day, Durham 134-1 (Lewis 61*, Daley 30*); Second day, Durham 485-4 (Speak 45*, Speight 23*).

Durham UCCE

M. J. Brown c Peng b Killeen	0	– lbw b Gough	31
W. I. Jefferson c Peng b Killeen	22	– lbw b Killeen	24
*M. J. Banes b Killeen	0	– not out	25
H. J. H. Loudon lbw b Brinkley	2	– not out	1
†J. S. Foster lbw b Collingwood	4		
J. G. C. Rowe b Collingwood	10		
T. J. Phillips run out	0		
R. A. Stead c Speight b Harmison	0		
R. S. Ferley c Speight b Law	3		
J. T. A. Bruce not out	14		
R. G. Gilbert b Law	0		
L-b 6, w 6	12	L-b 7, n-b 4	11
1/18 2/18 3/31 4/31 5/48 6/49 7/50 8/50 9/67	67	1/28 2/87	(2 wkts) 92

Bowling: *First Innings*—Harmison 12–8–9–1; Killeen 11–6–14–3; Brinkley 9–4–25–1; Law 6.5–1–11–2; Collingwood 10–8–2–2. *Second Innings*—Harmison 10–2–25–0; Killeen 6–1–14–1; Collingwood 1–1–0–0; Law 5–0–22–0; Brinkley 6–4–9–0; Gough 7.3–3–15–1.

Durham

*J. J. B. Lewis retired out	110	N. Peng st Foster b Phillips	0
M. A. Gough lbw b Ferley	22	†M. P. Speight not out	23
J. A. Daley retired hurt	128	B 3, l-b 6, w 2, n-b 16	27
P. D. Collingwood st Foster b Phillips	130		
N. J. Speak not out	45	1/50 2/232 3/439 4/447	(4 wkts dec.) 485

D. R. Law, J. E. Brinkley, N. Killeen and S. J. Harmison did not bat.

Daley retired hurt at 324.

Bowling: Bruce 23–4–67–0; Gilbert 18–5–54–0; Ferley 33–8–116–1; Stead 19–3–57–0; Phillips 45–11–122–2; Banes 18–5–60–0.

Umpires: I. J. Gould and N. A. Mallender.

DURHAM v GLOUCESTERSHIRE

At Chester-le-Street, April 20, 21, 22, 23. Drawn. Durham 8 pts, Gloucestershire 7 pts. Toss: Gloucestershire. Country debut: M. L. Love.

Innings of 61 and 67 confirmed Durham had signed a high-class performer in Queensland batsman Martin Love. Brinkley, also making his first Championship appearance for the county, took a career-best six for 32, seven years after taking six for 98 on his Championship debut for Worcestershire at The Oval. His spell of five for nine in 22 balls began with the demise of Barnett after a dashing 82 off 106 balls, and saw Gloucestershire plummet from 188 for four to 198 all out. Play on the third day did not start until 2.15, but Durham finished it 276 ahead with four wickets left. More rain severely disrupted the final day, denying Gloucestershire the chance to tilt at a target of 300 from 71 overs. A brief and otherwise pointless resumption in poor light at 4 p.m. helped Durham avoid a quarter-point penalty for a slow over-rate; they raced through two in three minutes.

Close of play: First day, Durham 237-8 (Pratt 26*, Brinkley 5*); Second day, Durham 104-2 (Love 63*, Daley 15*); Third day, Durham 232-6 (Collingwood 59*, Pratt 16*).

Durham

*J. J. B. Lewis c Cunliffe b Lewis	32	– b Lewis	1
M. A. Gough c Alleyne b Lewis	10	– lbw b Smith	24
M. L. Love lbw b Harvey	61	– c Windows b Harvey	67
J. A. Daley c Harvey b Snape	16	– c Alleyne b Lewis	28
P. D. Collingwood st Alleyne b Snape	22	– b Lewis	68
N. J. Speak b Averis	41	– c Cunliffe b Averis	2
D. R. Law c Taylor b Lewis	0	– c and b Smith	24
†A. Pratt not out	28	– not out	28
N. Killeen lbw b Snape	5		
J. E. Brinkley b Lewis	5		
S. J. Harmison lbw b Harvey	1		
B 1, l-b 4, w 2, n-b 14	21	B 1, l-b 6, n-b 6	13
1/13 2/102 3/110 4/146 5/161 6/166 7/203 8/216 9/239	242	1/4 2/58 3/124 4/124 5/132 6/182 7/255 (7 wkts dec.)	255

Bonus points – Durham 1, Gloucestershire 3.

Bowling: *First Innings*—Lewis 24–11–50–4; Smith 16–4–46–0; Harvey 25.3–10–54–2; Averis 17–5–47–1; Hancock 3–0–13–0; Snape 22–10–27–3. *Second Innings*—Lewis 22–7–56–3; Harvey 23–7–59–1; Averis 23–7–55–1; Smith 17–7–24–2; Snape 14–2–28–0; Barnett 11–2–26–0.

Gloucestershire

T. H. C. Hancock c Pratt b Brinkley	29	– (2) b Killeen	0
R. J. Cunliffe c Pratt b Killeen	0	– (1) not out	0
M. G. N. Windows c Pratt b Killeen	0	– not out	4
K. J. Barnett c Collingwood b Brinkley	82		
I. J. Harvey c Gough b Harmison	36		
*†M. W. Alleyne b Killeen	31		
C. G. Taylor lbw b Brinkley	0		
J. N. Snape b Brinkley	6		
J. M. M. Averis lbw b Brinkley	0		
J. Lewis not out	0		
A. M. Smith b Brinkley	4		
L-b 4, w 4, n-b 2	10	L-b 2	2
1/0 2/4 3/65 4/132 5/188 6/188 7/188 8/189 9/194	198	1/0 (1 wkt)	6

Bonus points – Durham 3.

Bowling: *First Innings*—Harmison 12–4–44–1; Killeen 17–7–35–3; Law 7–0–40–0; Brinkley 9.5–1–32–6; Collingwood 7–1–22–0; Gough 3–1–21–0. *Second Innings*—Harmison 2–2–0–0; Killeen 1–1–0–1; Collingwood 1–0–3–0; Gough 1–0–1–0.

Umpires: R. A. White and A. G. T. Whitehead.

At Nottingham, April 25, 26, 27, 28. DURHAM drew with NOTTINGHAMSHIRE.

At Birmingham, May 9, 10, 11, 12. DURHAM lost to WARWICKSHIRE by seven wickets.

DURHAM v MIDDLESEX

At Chester-le-Street, May 16, 17, 18, 19. Drawn. Durham 9 pts, Middlesex 11 pts. Toss: Middlesex.

Peng, aged 18, became Durham's youngest first-class century-maker, a year after scoring 98 on his debut. He showed commendable patience against the wiles of Tufnell and displayed a wide range of powerful strokes: his 101 contained 13 fours. He was upstaged, however, by Shah, who batted beautifully to make a career-best 190 in the first innings and 88 in the second. Then the highest Championship score at the Riverside, his 190 contained three sixes and 18 fours in seven hours 11 minutes, during which he shared a third-wicket stand of 248 with Fleming. Middlesex were 354 for three in the 118th over, but lost their remaining wickets in 11 overs in a scramble for maximum batting points, allowing off-spinner Gough to complete his first five-wicket haul. Shah, scoring at a run a ball second time round, soon extended Middlesex's first-innings lead of 112 and Durham were set 302 in 70 overs. When Peng and Collingwood were run out within five balls, they opted for a draw.

Close of play: First day, Middlesex 182-2 (Shah 86*, Fleming 63*); Second day, Durham 24-1 (Lewis 14*, Love 2*); Third day, Middlesex 83-1 (Roseberry 15*, Shah 62*).

Middlesex

A. J. Strauss run out	8	– c Pratt b Harmison	3
M. A. Roseberry c Pratt b Killeen	17	– b Phillips	46
O. A. Shah c Love b Gough	190	– run out	88
S. P. Fleming c Love b Phillips	114	– not out	31
B. L. Hutton st Pratt b Gough	15	– c Pratt b Harmison	14
P. N. Weekes c Law b Gough	1		
†D. C. Nash run out	19		
J. P. Hewitt c Lewis b Gough	3		
*A. R. C. Fraser b Phillips	0		
P. C. R. Tufnell c Law b Gough	0		
T. F. Bloomfield not out	0		
L-b 5, w 4, n-b 10	19	L-b 7	7
1/11 2/49 3/297 4/354 5/360 6/368 7/376 8/380 9/383	386	1/3 2/144 3/144 4/189 (4 wkts dec.)	189

Bonus points – Middlesex 4, Durham 3.

Bowling: *First Innings*—Harmison 22–5–43–0; Killeen 20–5–50–1; Hunter 19–1–73–0; Collingwood 10–6–16–0; Law 5–0–32–0; Phillips 31.2–4–101–2; Gough 21–2–66–5. *Second Innings*—Killeen 12–2–40–0; Harmison 12.3–3–47–2; Hunter 3–0–21–0; Phillips 8–0–36–1; Gough 8–0–38–0.

Durham

*J. J. B. Lewis b Hewitt	19	– b Bloomfield	5
M. A. Gough c Hutton b Tufnell	2	– lbw b Fraser	41
M. L. Love lbw b Fraser	13	– st Nash b Tufnell	31
P. D. Collingwood b Fraser	26	– run out	59
N. Peng c Shah b Weekes	101	– run out	28
D. R. Law c Strauss b Hewitt	20	– not out	36
†A. Pratt c Nash b Tufnell	8	– b Bloomfield	11
I. D. Hunter lbw b Weekes	31	– not out	7
N. Killeen b Bloomfield	1		
N. C. Phillips not out	10		
S. J. Harmison c Fleming b Tufnell	5		
B 3, l-b 12, w 2, n-b 16, p 5	38	L-b 2, n-b 6	8
1/22 2/33 3/73 4/74 5/140 6/165 7/239 8/244 9/262	274	1/7 2/56 3/118 4/169 5/173 6/205	(6 wkts) 226

Bonus points – Durham 2, Middlesex 3.

Bowling: *First Innings*—Bloomfield 10–0–42–1; Fraser 26–7–56–2; Tufnell 32.5–15–44–3; Shah 1–1–0–0; Weekes 15–3–54–2; Hewitt 11–1–58–2. *Second Innings*—Fraser 17–2–66–1; Bloomfield 16–4–45–2; Tufnell 26.3–4–74–1; Weekes 10–2–39–0.

Umpires: N. G. Cowley and M. J. Harris.

DURHAM v NOTTINGHAMSHIRE

At Chester-le-Street, May 30, 31, June 1, 2. Durham won by eight wickets. Durham 17 pts, Nottinghamshire 7 pts. Toss: Nottinghamshire.

Nottinghamshire dominated the match until the moment they declared – generously or condescendingly depending on the point of view. Thereafter, it was all Durham, who overhauled a target of 315 in 102 overs with an hour to spare. The bedrock of their victory was a second-wicket stand of 258 between Lewis and Love, a record for any Durham wicket in the Championship, beating the 206 by Wayne Larkins and Dean Jones at Cardiff in 1992 in Durham's maiden Championship win. Lewis scored strongly off the back foot between cover and third man, hitting 14 fours, while Love stroked 25 boundaries in his first hundred for the county. The match began with 31 of Nottinghamshire's first 54 coming in extras. Harmison contributed most, but he found his range on the second day to get rid of Afzaal and Johnson, who had shared an aggressive partnership of 172. Collingwood's unbeaten 91 saved Durham from following on, whereupon Blewett, opening because Bicknell had a side strain, set up the declaration with his second hundred of the season, each against Durham. On the rain-interrupted first day, Blewett had been distracted first by the bails coming off in the wind and fatally by three ducks waddling behind the umpire as Brinkley ran in.

Close of play: First day, Nottinghamshire 277-3 (Afzaal 88*, Johnson 89*); Second day, Durham 205-6 (Collingwood 49*, Hunter 0*); Third day, Durham 16-0 (Lewis 7*, Gough 3*).

Nottinghamshire

*D. J. Bicknell lbw b Harmison	45		
G. E. Welton c Hunter b Collingwood	16	– (1) b Harmison	4
G. S. Blewett lbw b Brinkley	3	– (2) not out	137
U. Afzaal b Harmison	89	– (3) c Law b Phillips	21
P. Johnson c Peng b Harmison	109	– (4) b Law	15
K. P. Pietersen b Hunter	38	– (5) st Pratt b Phillips	12
†C. M. W. Read c Brinkley b Harmison	4	– (6) c Hunter b Harmison	2
P. J. Franks not out	23	– (7) not out	20
A. J. Harris c Pratt b Harmison	2		
G. J. Smith c and b Hunter	1		
R. D. Stemp lbw b Hunter	2		
B 9, l-b 6, w 20, n-b 4	39	L-b 2, w 4, n-b 2	8
1/77 2/80 3/106 4/278 5/309 6/327 7/344 8/366 9/369	371	1/19 2/98 3/131 4/152 5/159 (5 wkts dec.)	219

Bonus points – Nottinghamshire 4, Durham 3.

Bowling: *First Innings*—Harmison 33–5–100–5; Hunter 16–2–52–3; Brinkley 13–4–71–1; Collingwood 11–4–26–1; Phillips 24–8–61–0; Law 4–0–20–0; Gough 6–0–26–0. *Second Innings*—Hunter 10–1–37–0; Harmison 17–2–39–2; Phillips 21–4–89–2; Brinkley 6–1–19–0; Law 6–0–28–1; Gough 1–0–5–0.

Durham

*J. J. B. Lewis c Read b Harris	21	– b Afzaal	112
M. A. Gough lbw b Stemp	35	– c Afzaal b Franks	18
M. L. Love c Read b Smith	16	– not out	149
P. D. Collingwood not out	91	– not out	0
N. Peng lbw b Harris	7		
D. R. Law c Pietersen b Franks	39		
†A. Pratt b Stemp	17		
I. D. Hunter c Afzaal b Smith	0		
J. E. Brinkley c Read b Smith	0		
N. C. Phillips lbw b Stemp	12		
S. J. Harmison c Read b Franks	9		
B 8, l-b 5, w 2, n-b 14	29	B 7, l-b 7, w 15, n-b 10	39
1/32 2/63 3/89 4/96 5/164 6/203 7/212 8/218 9/255	276	1/55 2/313 (2 wkts)	318

Bonus points – Durham 2, Nottinghamshire 3.

Bowling: *First Innings*—Smith 20–3–73–3; Franks 17.1–4–57–2; Harris 18–7–45–2; Stemp 28–5–88–3. *Second Innings*—Smith 9–1–41–0; Harris 15–4–55–0; Pietersen 21–4–69–0; Stemp 24–5–72–0; Franks 12–2–46–1; Afzaal 4.1–1–21–1.

Umpires: J. W. Holder and G. Sharp.

At Derby, June 6, 7, 8, 9. DURHAM drew with DERBYSHIRE.

At Gloucester, June 13, 14, 15, 16. DURHAM drew with GLOUCESTERSHIRE.

At Southampton, June 20, 21, 22. DURHAM lost to HAMPSHIRE by 47 runs.

DURHAM v WARWICKSHIRE

At Chester-le-Street, June 29, 30, July 1, 2. Drawn. Durham 8 pts, Warwickshire 10 pts. Toss: Warwickshire.

Ostler, whose century included 21 fours, was rarely troubled by a depleted Durham attack, which also lost Simon Brown with knee trouble after the first day. Warwickshire, too, lost a strike bowler to a knee injury, though Drakes, who sustained his playing football on the first evening, was able to bowl on the final day. On a pitch lacking in pace, progress in both teams' first innings was correspondingly slow. Warwickshire increased the tempo on the third day, when Wagh hit his second century of the season off Durham and Ostler was not far short of his second for the match as he helped add 185 in two stands. Wagh moved from 87 to 103 in one Phillips over that included two of his three sixes; he also struck 16 fours. Durham, set 404 from a minimum of 101 overs, were in trouble at 119 for four and 243 for seven, but Phillips survived 13 overs with Speight, who battled almost four hours for his highest score for nearly two years. Betts, back on home turf, again bowled with character and Drakes mounted a hostile attack on Peng, who, lbw first ball in the first innings, rode his luck – he was dropped twice and held off a no-ball – to hit a combative 70 in his century partnership with Speight.

Close of play: First day, Warwickshire 270-6 (Ostler 110*, Piper 30*); Second day, Durham 208-7 (Pratt 1*, Phillips 1*); Third day, Durham 12-0 (Lewis 7*, Gough 5*).

Warwickshire

*M. J. Powell c Pratt b Hatch	12	– b Hatch	1
N. V. Knight c Phillips b Law	75	– lbw b Law	25
M. A. Wagh c Pratt b Brown	6	– c Pratt b Gough	112
D. L. Hemp b Phillips	0	– b Law	14
D. P. Ostler b Law	121	– c sub b Collingwood	86
D. R. Brown c Pratt b Collingwood	21	– not out	67
N. M. K. Smith c Pratt b Brown	4	– lbw b Phillips	5
†K. J. Piper c Peng b Law	34	– not out	4
V. C. Drakes c Pratt b Law	11		
M. M. Betts not out	10		
A. Richardson run out	2		
B 4, l-b 6, w 4	14	B 5, l-b 1, w 4	10
1/44 2/86 3/95 4/117 5/163 6/181 7/282 8/293 9/304	310	1/2 2/46 3/97 4/196 5/282 6/295	(6 wkts dec.) 324

Bonus points – Warwickshire 3, Durham 3.

Bowling: *First Innings*—Brown 18–5–34–2; Hatch 23–5–60–1; Law 21.3–6–58–4; Collingwood 16–6–32–1; Phillips 26–5–79–1; Gough 13–3–37–0. *Second Innings*—Hatch 15–1–60–1; Law 15–2–48–2; Collingwood 16–3–62–1; Phillips 22–1–109–1; Gough 12–4–39–1.

Durham

*J. J. B. Lewis b Betts	15	– c Piper b Drakes	32
M. A. Gough c Knight b Brown	17	– b Betts	10
M. L. Love c Knight b Betts	66	– c Ostler b Smith	45
P. D. Collingwood b Smith	69	– c Ostler b Smith	21
N. Peng lbw b Betts	0	– b Brown	70
M. P. Speight b Richardson	21	– not out	67
D. R. Law c Brown b Smith	12	– b Brown	0
†A. Pratt b Betts	6	– c Piper b Betts	2
N. C. Phillips c Ostler b Smith	1	– c Hemp b Richardson	14
N. G. Hatch run out	12	– not out	0
S. J. E. Brown not out	2		
B 5, l-b 3, n-b 2	10	B 1, l-b 6, n-b 16	23
1/18 2/52 3/134 4/134 5/184 6/205 7/206 8/208 9/218	231	1/18 2/67 3/108 4/119 5/226 6/236 7/243 8/284	(8 wkts) 284

Bonus points – Durham 1, Warwickshire 3.

Bowling: *First Innings*—Betts 26–9–78–4; Richardson 29–8–55–1; Brown 29–7–74–1; Smith 13.2–6–16–3. *Second Innings*—Betts 20–7–36–2; Richardson 16–6–27–1; Smith 24–7–57–2; Drakes 24.5–4–106–1; Wagh 7–1–14–0; Brown 14–3–37–2.

Umpires: J. H. Hampshire and A. A. Jones.

DURHAM v SUSSEX

At Chester-le-Street, July 18, 19, 20, 21. Sussex won by 133 runs. Sussex 20 pts, Durham 5 pts. Toss: Sussex.

Sussex batted into the fourth afternoon before Adams set Durham an unlikely 336 from 61 overs. Desperate to make up ground in the table, Durham went for glory, and prospered until Robinson had Love and Peng lbw off successive balls. Left-arm spinner Rashid then took over, claiming four for nine to complete a successful game for him and his county. On the first two days, he had hit his second Championship hundred, sharing a century partnership with Montgomerie who, during his 156, came second – behind Kent's David Fulton – in the race to 1,000 runs. Two days later, Goodwin, his fellow-opener, came third. Montgomerie eventually fell to Harmison, who converted a first-day one for 80 to a career-best six for 111, as the last five Sussex wickets tumbled for eight. When Durham batted, Adams shaved a run off his best return to put the home side, who slumped from 222 for three to 245 for eight, at risk of following on. Pratt, supported by Harmison (prevented by a chest infection from batting on the last day) and Hatch, warded off that danger, but the respite was temporary. In Durham's first innings, it took three bowlers to deliver one over: Lewry was injured after two balls, Robinson was removed for running down the pitch and Adams completed it.

Close of play: First day, Sussex 338-4 (Montgomerie 134*, Rashid 56*); Second day, Durham 164-1 (Lewis 81*, Love 35*); Third day, Sussex 135-1 (Montgomerie 51*, Adams 33*).

Sussex

M. W. Goodwin lbw b Bridge	36	– (2) c Gough b Law	46
R. R. Montgomerie c Collingwood b Harmison	156	– (1) lbw b Bridge	71
*C. J. Adams c and b Law	53	– c Law b Bridge	90
B. Zuiderent c Pratt b Harmison	34	– b Law	0
M. H. Yardy c Pratt b Law	7	– b Bridge	5
U. B. A. Rashid c Pratt b Harmison	106	– c Pratt b Gough	19
†M. J. Prior c Gough b Harmison	17	– b Gough	5
M. J. G. Davis b Harmison	2	– not out	10
R. J. Kirtley c Pratt b Harmison	0	– c Lewis b Bridge	0
M. A. Robinson run out	1	– st Pratt b Gough	1
J. D. Lewry not out	4		
B 4, l-b 12, w 8, n-b 2	26	L-b 2, w 4	6
1/81 2/172 3/226 4/248 5/367 6/434 7/437 8/437 9/438	442	1/76 2/184 3/185 4/214 5/229 6/242 7/247 8/250 9/253	(9 wkts dec.) 253

Bonus points – Sussex 5, Durham 1 (Score at 130 overs: 428-5).

Bowling: *First Innings*—Harmison 35–4–111–6; Hatch 17–3–64–0; Law 32–4–101–2; Collingwood 10–3–40–0; Bridge 34.3–7–80–1; Gough 11–3–30–0. *Second Innings*—Harmison 5–0–37–0; Hatch 17–0–64–0; Law 18–3–49–2; Collingwood 16–4–35–0; Bridge 19–3–57–4; Gough 3–0–9–3.

Durham

*J. J. B. Lewis c Adams b Robinson	99	– b Kirtley	32
M. A. Gough c and b Kirtley	29	– lbw b Lewry	0
M. L. Love lbw b Kirtley	35	– lbw b Robinson	41
P. D. Collingwood c Kirtley b Adams	34	– b Rashid	34
N. Peng c and b Adams	2	– lbw b Robinson	0
M. P. Speight b Adams	6	– b Kirtley	31
D. R. Law st Prior b Adams	4	– b Rashid	11
†A. Pratt not out	51	– c Yardy b Rashid	22
G. D. Bridge lbw b Lewry	1	– c Prior b Rashid	0
S. J. Harmison b Kirtley	27	– absent ill	
N. G. Hatch lbw b Rashid	24	– (10) not out	8
B 8, l-b 18, w 2, n-b 20	48	L-b 7, w 4, n-b 12	23
1/77 2/176 3/192 4/222 5/231 6/231 7/240 8/245 9/307	360	1/15 2/66 3/94 4/94 5/145 6/167 7/177 8/177 9/202	202

Bonus points – Durham 4, Sussex 3.

Bowling: *First Innings*—Lewry 23.2–8–58–1; Kirtley 32–8–127–3; Robinson 26.2–6–69–1; Davis 18–4–46–0; Adams 11.2–2–28–4; Rashid 2–0–6–1. *Second Innings*—Lewry 10–1–51–1; Kirtley 15–2–71–2; Robinson 15–1–42–2; Davis 6–2–22–0; Rashid 9.1–5–9–4.

Umpires: G. I. Burgess and N. A. Mallender.

At Lord's, July 27, 28, 29. DURHAM lost to MIDDLESEX by an innings and 74 runs.

At Kidderminster, August 2, 3, 4, 5. DURHAM beat WORCESTERSHIRE by seven wickets.

DURHAM v DERBYSHIRE

At Chester-le-Street, August 8, 9, 10. Derbyshire won by four wickets. Derbyshire 15 pts, Durham 3 pts. Toss: Durham. First-class debut: G. M. Scott.

Lewis won Durham's first toss in ten Championship matches, chose to bat and watched a torrent of wickets as the ball swung extravagantly. He made a battling 41, but could not prevent Durham folding for 125. Derbyshire then fared even worse, conceding a 30-run advantage before reducing the hosts to 73 for four by the close. Of the 24 batsmen dismissed on the second day – the first was washed out – 17 fell in single figures. Next morning, pitch liaison officer Raman Subba Row saw 17-year-old debutant Gary Scott make a promising 25 which, with Pratt's career-best unbeaten 68, confirmed his view that the perils had been caused by the pitch sweating under covers for two days. As conditions eased, Di Venuto raced past a century before suffering a groin injury. Less than two days since the start, Bassano led Derbyshire to victory, the only one of their miserable summer. During the first-innings bedlam there were personal-best bowling figures for Welch and Brinkley, while Dean returned his best match figures for three years. Di Venuto equalled the Derbyshire records for catches in an innings (five) and match (six).

Close of play: First day, No play; Second day, Durham 73-4 (Speight 43*, Scott 0*).

Durham

*J. J. B. Lewis c Di Venuto b Welch	41	– lbw b Dean	4
J. A. Daley c Di Venuto b Welch	20	– c Krikken b Welch	3
M. L. Love b Dean	7	– b Dean	0
P. D. Collingwood c Di Venuto b Dean	0	– b Welch	19
M. P. Speight c Di Venuto b Welch	2	– c Dean b Aldred	43
G. M. Scott c Di Venuto b Welch	8	– c Di Venuto b Dean	25
†A. Pratt lbw b Dean	31	– not out	68
I. D. Hunter c Aldred b Welch	2	– c Bailey b Dean	4
G. D. Bridge lbw b Dean	5	– b Dean	1
J. E. Brinkley c Bailey b Welch	5	– b Dean	0
N. G. Hatch not out	0	– c and b Smith	17
L-b 2, w 2	4	L-b 7, n-b 2	9
1/34 2/43 3/43 4/50 5/62 6/108 7/114 8/114 9/125	125	1/5 2/5 3/11 4/72 5/74 6/137 7/141 8/147 9/147	193

Bonus points – Derbyshire 3.

Bowling: *First Innings*—Dean 14.2–4–32–4; Smith 7–0–45–0; Welch 15–5–30–6; Aldred 7–2–16–0. *Second Innings*—Welch 24–6–87–2; Dean 19–4–73–6; Aldred 8–2–22–1; Smith 1.1–0–4–1.

Derbyshire

S. D. Stubbings c Pratt b Hatch	5	– c Pratt b Brinkley	14
*M. J. Di Venuto c Scott b Brinkley	29	– retired hurt	111
L. D. Sutton c Pratt b Brinkley	14	– lbw b Hatch	4
C. W. G. Bassano b Hatch	6	– not out	70
R. J. Bailey c Love b Brinkley	5	– c Collingwood b Hatch	1
G. Welch lbw b Collingwood	1	– lbw b Hatch	10
†K. M. Krikken c Pratt b Brinkley	7	– run out	3
T. M. Smith c Lewis b Collingwood	16	– c Pratt b Hunter	1
P. Aldred c Love b Brinkley	3	– not out	7
K. J. Dean b Brinkley	0		
L. J. Wharton not out	0		
L-b 1, w 8	9	L-b 3	3
1/28 2/48 3/63 4/63 5/68 6/76 7/76 8/81 9/81	95	1/44 2/67 3/170 4/186 5/200 6/203	(6 wkts) 224

Bonus points – Durham 3.

In the second innings Di Venuto retired hurt at 159.

Bowling: *First Innings*—Hatch 8–0–32–2; Hunter 3–0–26–0; Brinkley 10–4–14–6; Collingwood 6–0–22–2. *Second Innings*—Hatch 17–4–56–3; Brinkley 19–4–71–1; Hunter 5.1–0–40–1; Bridge 11–1–35–0; Collingwood 3–0–8–0; Scott 3–1–11–0.

Umpires: N. G. Cowley and J. F. Steele.

DURHAM v HAMPSHIRE

At Chester-le-Street, August 17, 18, 19, 20. Hampshire won by seven wickets. Hampshire 18 pts, Durham 6 pts. Toss: Durham. Championship debut: J. E. K. Schofield.

By getting the better of a seesaw, rain-interrupted contest with Durham, Hampshire moved to second in Division Two. They began strongly, reducing Durham to 92 for five, effectively six, after Johnson had struck Peng on the helmet and sent him to hospital with concussion. The home side then rallied through a responsible maiden Championship hundred from Law and a career-best 65 from Brinkley; they put on 127 for the seventh wicket and steered Durham to a healthy 323. When they had their opponents 206 for seven, a substantial lead looked likely. However,

Mascarenhas and Morris did the rallying for Hampshire and, with Morris then exploiting a pitch with seam movement and bounce for a career-best five for 39, Durham could set a target of only 214. Given an ideal start by their openers, Hampshire won six balls before the scheduled close. Earlier, Bridge set personal-bests with bat and ball.

Close of play: First day, Hampshire 15-0 (White 4*, Laney 3*); Second day, Durham 9-0 (Lewis 4*, Daley 2*); Third day, Durham 87-4 (Love 43*, Law 26*).

Durham

*J. J. B. Lewis c Aymes b Mascarenhas	18	– c Aymes b Morris	8
J. A. Daley c Johnson b Morris	4	– c White b Morris	2
M. L. Love b Schofield	49	– lbw b Morris	52
P. D. Collingwood lbw b Mascarenhas	0	– c Aymes b Morris	3
N. Peng retired hurt	12	– c Johnson b Udal	0
D. R. Law b Morris	103	– lbw b Schofield	42
†A. Pratt c Johnson b Schofield	0	– lbw b Mascarenhas	14
G. D. Bridge lbw b Morris	31	– not out	39
J. E. Brinkley lbw b Mascarenhas	65	– lbw b Morris	6
S. J. Harmison c Kendall b Morris	14	– lbw b Udal	3
N. G. Hatch not out	8	– c Schofield b Udal	12
B 4, l-b 11, w 4	19	B 1, l-b 8, w 2, n-b 10	21
1/22 2/38 3/44 4/92 5/92 6/156 7/283 8/310 9/323	323	1/13 2/14 3/20 4/21 5/107 6/113 7/138 8/171 9/182	202

Bonus points – Durham 3, Hampshire 3.

In the first innings Peng retired hurt at 91.

Bowling: *First Innings*—Schofield 16–2–52–2; Morris 22–2–84–4; Mascarenhas 27–12–56–3; Tremlett 9–1–41–0; Johnson 10–0–29–0; Udal 12–2–46–0. *Second Innings*—Mascarenhas 14–3–46–1; Johnson 18–5–45–0; Udal 13.1–3–33–3; Morris 20–11–39–5; Schofield 12–5–28–1; White 1–0–2–0.

Hampshire

G. W. White c Pratt b Brinkley	31	– (2) b Bridge	74
J. S. Laney c Pratt b Brinkley	18	– (1) c Love b Bridge	60
W. S. Kendall c Collingwood b Brinkley	49	– lbw b Harmison	54
*R. A. Smith c Collingwood b Brinkley	2	– not out	9
N. C. Johnson c Collingwood b Bridge	27	– not out	2
A. D. Mascarenhas lbw b Bridge	76		
†A. N. Aymes c Love b Bridge	6		
S. D. Udal c Law b Bridge	0		
A. C. Morris c Pratt b Bridge	52		
C. T. Tremlett lbw b Bridge	12		
J. E. K. Schofield not out	21		
B 4, l-b 6, n-b 8	18	B 1, l-b 4, n-b 12	17
1/58 2/61 3/63 4/107 5/173 6/186 7/206 8/257 9/281	312	1/110 2/185 3/209	(3 wkts) 216

Bonus points – Hampshire 3, Durham 3.

Bowling: *First Innings*—Harmison 21–5–61–0; Law 14.3–1–48–0; Brinkley 19.3–2–67–4; Hatch 13–3–42–0; Bridge 35.1–12–84–6. *Second Innings*—Harmison 14–0–53–1; Law 6–1–29–0; Brinkley 8–0–40–0; Bridge 18–2–54–2; Hatch 6–0–35–0.

Umpires: A. Clarkson and B. Leadbeater.

At Hove, August 22, 23, 24, 25. DURHAM beat SUSSEX by 71 runs.

DURHAM v WORCESTERSHIRE

At Chester-le-Street, September 5, 6, 7, 8. Drawn. Durham 11 pts, Worcestershire 11 pts. Toss: Durham.

Hick equalled the highest score at the Riverside and became the first player to hit centuries at home and away against the other 17 counties; Walter Hammond (Gloucestershire) also had a full set before Durham's elevation. It was Hick's 117th hundred, equalling Sir Donald Bradman's total, though from twice as many innings. Dropped at deep mid-off on 88, Hick went to 200 off 238 balls with his only six; he also hit 26 fours in a stay of 336 minutes. He immediately declared, 13 behind Durham's highest Championship total all season, in which Lewis and Collingwood both hit hundreds. Collingwood's took him past 1,000 runs for the first time, while Lewis's second-innings 19 saw him reach the landmark for the third. Lewis declared shortly after lunch on the final day, setting Worcestershire 251 in what became 55 overs. Penetrating bowling reduced them to 63 for seven, but Rhodes and Liptrot – who faced 81 balls for a single – stonewalled for 28 overs.

Close of play: First day, Durham 215-2 (Lewis 97*, Collingwood 41*); Second day, Worcestershire 163-5 (Hick 68*, Bichel 11*); Third day, Durham 99-2 (Love 45*, Collingwood 26*).

Durham

*J. J. B. Lewis c Hick b Liptrot	129	– lbw b Bichel	19
G. J. Pratt lbw b Liptrot	37	– c Solanki b Bichel	8
M. L. Love c Rhodes b Leatherdale	26	– b Sheriyar	62
P. D. Collingwood c Rhodes b Liptrot	103	– c Solanki b Bichel	68
J. A. Daley c Hick b Bichel	5	– b Rawnsley	31
D. R. Law lbw b Leatherdale	20	– c Sheriyar b Rawnsley	21
†A. Pratt c Rhodes b Leatherdale	2	– c Weston b Liptrot	1
I. D. Hunter c Rawnsley b Sheriyar	12	– not out	18
G. D. Bridge b Leatherdale	11	– not out	3
S. J. Harmison c Pollard b Sheriyar	7		
N. G. Hatch not out	0		
B 1, l-b 6, w 2, n-b 8	17	B 2, l-b 2, w 2	6
1/85 2/138 3/276 4/308 5/314 6/324 7/337 8/358 9/363	369	1/11 2/38 3/141 4/164 5/210 6/213 7/216 (7 wkts dec.)	237

Bonus points – Durham 4, Worcestershire 3 (Score at 130 overs: 363-9).

Bowling: *First Innings*—Bichel 22–3–64–1; Sheriyar 31.3–14–55–2; Liptrot 23–5–85–3; Rawnsley 34–11–85–0; Leatherdale 20–6–70–4; Solanki 2–0–3–0. *Second Innings*—Bichel 14–2–48–3; Sheriyar 17–1–60–1; Liptrot 11–4–38–1; Leatherdale 3–0–10–0; Rawnsley 14.2–4–50–2; Solanki 7.4–1–27–0.

Worcestershire

W. P. C. Weston c Collingwood b Law	55	– c Law b Hatch	2
A. Singh b Hatch	9	– c Bridge b Harmison	0
*G. A. Hick not out	200	– c A. Pratt b Harmison	8
V. S. Solanki b Hunter	0	– (6) b Bridge	11
D. A. Leatherdale c A. Pratt b Hunter	7	– (4) c A. Pratt b Hunter	14
P. R. Pollard b Bridge	3	– (5) lbw b Law	6
A. J. Bichel c Love b Bridge	32	– lbw b Law	0
†S. J. Rhodes run out	9	– not out	21
C. G. Liptrot run out	0	– not out	1
M. J. Rawnsley run out	17		
A. Sheriyar not out	3		
B 2, l-b 13, w 2, n-b 4	21	B 7, l-b 1, w 10, n-b 4	22
1/20 2/84 3/85 4/93 5/131 6/201 7/227 8/227 9/326 (9 wkts dec.)	356	1/1 2/7 3/15 4/41 5/45 6/45 7/63 (7 wkts)	85

Bonus points – Worcestershire 4, Durham 3.

Bowling: *First Innings*—Harmison 23–3–91–0; Hatch 20–4–69–1; Hunter 16–2–77–2; Law 6–3–13–1; Bridge 23.2–5–72–2; Collingwood 5–0–19–0. *Second Innings*—Harmison 14–4–34–2; Hatch 9–3–16–1; Hunter 11–7–13–1; Law 8–5–10–2; Bridge 13–11–4–1.

Umpires: B. Dudleston and D. R. Shepherd.

YOUNG CRICKETER OF THE YEAR

(Elected by the Cricket Writers' Club)

1950	R. Tattersall	1977	I. T. Botham
1951	P. B. H. May	1978	D. I. Gower
1952	F. S. Trueman	1979	P. W. G. Parker
1953	M. C. Cowdrey	1980	G. R. Dilley
1954	P. J. Loader	1981	M. W. Gatting
1955	K. F. Barrington	1982	N. G. Cowans
1956	B. Taylor	1983	N. A. Foster
1957	M. J. Stewart	1984	R. J. Bailey
1958	A. C. D. Ingleby-Mackenzie	1985	D. V. Lawrence
1959	G. Pullar	1986	A. A. Metcalfe
1960	D. A. Allen		J. J. Whitaker
1961	P. H. Parfitt	1987	R. J. Blakey
1962	P. J. Sharpe	1988	M. P. Maynard
1963	G. Boycott	1989	N. Hussain
1964	J. M. Brearley	1990	M. A. Atherton
1965	A. P. E. Knott	1991	M. R. Ramprakash
1966	D. L. Underwood	1992	I. D. K. Salisbury
1967	A. W. Greig	1993	M. N. Lathwell
1968	R. M. H. Cottam	1994	J. P. Crawley
1969	A. Ward	1995	A. Symonds
1970	C. M. Old	1996	C. E. W. Silverwood
1971	J. Whitehouse	1997	B. C. Hollioake
1972	D. R. Owen-Thomas	1998	A. Flintoff
1973	M. Hendrick	1999	A. J. Tudor
1974	P. H. Edmonds	2000	P. J. Franks
1975	A. Kennedy	2001	O. A. Shah
1976	G. Miller		

An additional award, in memory of Norman Preston, Editor of *Wisden* from 1951 to 1980, was made to C. W. J. Athey in 1980.

Paul Grayson

ESSEX

President: D. J. Insole
Chairman: 2001 – D. L. Acfield/N. R. A. Hilliard
2002 – N. R. A. Hilliard
Chief Executive: D. E. East
Chairman, Cricket Committee: G. J. Saville
Club Captain: N. Hussain
Team Captain: R. C. Irani
First-Team Coach: 2001 – K. W. R. Fletcher
Head Coach: 2002 – G. A. Gooch
Head Groundsman: S. Kerrison
Scorer: D. J. Norris

It might be an exaggeration to describe 2001 as the most turbulent and disastrous season in Essex's history, but the team was certainly the worst this correspondent has seen in more than 30 years reporting on the club's fortunes. It lacked a collective spirit and quality; the inevitability of its plunge into the depths left members in despair. Two Championship victories explained why Essex occupied last place in Division One, 17 points behind Glamorgan, immediately above them. Third last in the Norwich Union League, and failure to make much progress in the Benson and Hedges Cup and Cheltenham & Gloucester Trophy, contributed further to the summer of discontent.

Off the field, the dressing-room was split asunder as Stuart Law accused team-mates and management of stabbing him in the back. It was no secret that he and some of his colleagues could hardly utter a civil word to each other. And within days of meeting a delegation of angry supporters, seeking answers to the sad decline, chairman David Acfield resigned, citing pressure of business – but that was fooling no one. He was simply fed up with all the flak, and no doubt relieved to hand over to Nigel Hilliard. A month or so later, Graham Gooch, perhaps Essex's favourite son and certainly their most successful player, gave up a blossoming media career to take over as head coach. He succeeded Keith Fletcher, who was to adopt a scouting role, while John Childs moved up from looking after the Second Eleven to become Gooch's assistant.

Predictably, following his verbal blast, Law was not offered a new contract – a sad conclusion to a six-year association, during which he thrilled spectators everywhere with his majestic strokes, while scoring 8,538 first-class runs at 58.88. He was replaced by Zimbabwe's prolific wicket-keeper/batsman, Andy Flower.

Also shown the door was Peter Such, whose 17 Championship wickets in 2001 had cost 65 each. However, his departure, after 12 seasons in which he took 573 first-class wickets for the county and won 11 Test caps, was softened by a substantial benefit cheque. In his place, Essex signed Yorkshire off-spinner James Middlebrook. Others to leave were spinners Tim Mason and Michael Davies, neither of whom was able to make an impact when given the opportunity, Ricky Anderson, Stephen Peters and Paul Prichard.

Prichard announced his impending departure midway through the season, declaring that he no longer felt part of the dressing-room and was not enjoying his cricket. After a playing career of 18 seasons that brought him nearly 17,000 first-class runs, along with the NatWest Trophy and Benson and Hedges Cup as captain, his was a sad severing of links. Law, at least, was included for the final match of the season at Chelmsford, and was able to savour a standing ovation from members. For Prichard to be denied a similar send-off showed a lack of feeling and sentiment when it came to team selection.

That Essex were asked to follow on eight times – Surrey spared them on another occasion – was evidence enough of their obvious failings with bat and ball. The best any of their bowlers could manage in the Championship was 32 wickets each by Ronnie Irani and Ashley Cowan; next best was Anderson, who took 29 before missing more than half the season because of shin splints. Mark Ilott was also out for much of the summer through injury. The arrival of Jon Dakin from Leicestershire should help to compensate for Anderson's departure to Northamptonshire.

Despite the inability to function as a coherent force, capable of winning on a regular basis, there was no shortage of praiseworthy individual batting. It came as no surprise that Law topped the list. In June, he made three centuries in as many days against Lancashire, in the Championship and then the League, though in neither could he save Essex from defeat. Old Trafford will see more of his mastery now he has moved there.

Paul Grayson and Darren Robinson also collected centuries in each innings of a match, Grayson at Northampton and Robinson against Leicestershire at Chelmsford. In addition, Grayson hit a career-best 189 against Glamorgan, one of six first-class centuries during a productive summer that brought him 1,275 runs at a shade under 50. The first was against Cambridge UCCE, when Prichard, Robinson and Graham Napier also reached three figures – the first time four players had hit hundreds in one innings for Essex. However, Law and Grayson were the only batsmen to record 1,000 first-class runs.

Peters, who contributed just one half-century in 14 Championship games, was a major disappointment, as was his decision to join Worcestershire. But one player whose career took off was James Foster. The young wicket-keeper replaced Barry Hyam after returning from Durham University and, by also proving himself a useful batsman, convinced the England selectors he should be taken on the tours of India and New Zealand. Not surprisingly, he was awarded his county cap. Justin Bishop was another youngster who could look back on the season with satisfaction. Although his figures did not always convey the fact, the left-arm seamer showed plenty of promise in difficult circumstances.

Finally, a fond farewell to George Clark, who for nearly two decades was the county's dressing-room attendant, a confidant and friend of the players and a character who commanded great respect. To journalists trying to gain access after matches, he often represented a formidable barrier; in short, a right awkward cuss at times, but lovely with it. – NIGEL FULLER.

ESSEX 2001

[*Bill Smith*

Standing: J. Davis (*physiotherapist*), T. J. Mason, M. L. Pettini, Z. K. Sharif, G. R. Napier, W. I. Jefferson, A. C. McGarry, M. K. Davies, J. E. Bishop, T. J. Phillips, J. S. Foster. *Seated:* R. S. G. Anderson, B. J. Hyam, A. P. Grayson, M. C. Ilott, P. M. Such, N. Hussain (*club captain*), R. C. Irani (*team captain*), S. G. Law, A. P. Cowan, D. D. J. Robinson, P. J. Prichard, S. D. Peters.

ESSEX RESULTS

All first-class matches – Played 18: Won 3, Lost 7, Drawn 8.

County Championship matches – Played 16: Won 2, Lost 7, Drawn 7.

CricInfo County Championship, 9th in Division 1; Cheltenham & Gloucester Trophy, 4th round; Benson and Hedges Cup, 5th in South Group; Norwich Union League, 7th in Division 2.

COUNTY CHAMPIONSHIP AVERAGES

BATTING

Cap		*M*	*I*	*NO*	*R*	*HS*	*100s*	*50s*	*Avge*	*Ct/St*
1996	S. G. Law§	13	23	3	1,311	153	4	8	65.55	18
1996	A. P. Grayson	14	27	3	1,148	189	5	1	47.83	6
1997	D. D. J. Robinson†	16	29	2	812	118*	2	4	30.07	10
1994	R. C. Irani	16	28	2	761	119	1	6	29.26	4
	G. R. Napier†	8	14	0	343	56	0	1	24.50	3
	R. S. Clinton	7	14	1	283	58*	0	1	21.76	2
	S. D. Peters†	14	25	3	464	56*	0	1	21.09	3
2001	J. S. Foster	11	19	0	388	79	0	2	20.42	20/4
1999	B. J. Hyam†	5	8	1	131	63	0	1	18.71	15
1993	M. C. Ilott	8	11	1	179	34	0	0	17.90	4
	T. J. Mason	2	4	1	46	41*	0	0	15.33	0
	R. S. G. Anderson	7	10	0	148	45	0	0	14.80	2
1997	A. P. Cowan	14	23	2	310	68	0	1	14.76	8
	T. J. Phillips	3	5	0	63	27	0	0	12.60	0
1991	P. M. Such	13	19	9	117	25	0	0	11.70	7
1986	P. J. Prichard†	6	10	0	90	34	0	0	9.00	1
	J. E. Bishop	7	11	2	74	18	0	0	8.22	0
	M. K. Davies	2	4	1	22	10*	0	0	7.33	0
	A. C. McGarry†	5	7	5	5	4*	0	0	2.50	1

Also batted: J. B. Grant (1 match) 1*; N. Hussain‡ (cap 1989) (1 match) 15, 34; W. I. Jefferson (1 match) 69; M. L. Pettini (1 match) 1, 41 (1 ct); Z. K. Sharif (1 match) 15, 2 (1 ct).

* *Signifies not out.* † *Born in Essex.* ‡ *ECB contract.* § *Overseas player.*

BOWLING

	O	*M*	*R*	*W*	*BB*	*5W/i*	*Avge*
R. S. G. Anderson	217.1	51	665	29	5-50	2	22.93
M. C. Ilott	229	47	728	23	5-85	1	31.65
R. C. Irani	346.5	94	1,029	32	6-79	3	32.15
J. E. Bishop	191	34	765	21	5-148	1	36.42
A. P. Cowan	442.5	97	1,475	32	3-64	0	46.09
P. M. Such	353	74	1,107	17	4-81	0	65.11

Also bowled: R. S. Clinton 1–1–0–0; M. K. Davies 38–4–141–3; J. B. Grant 19–0–101–3; A. P. Grayson 136–19–493–9; A. C. McGarry 118–17–430–9; T. J. Mason 14–5–40–0; G. R. Napier 88.1–14–390–8; T. J. Phillips 62–7–261–1; Z. K. Sharif 2–0–23–0.

COUNTY RECORDS

Highest score for:	343*	P. A. Perrin v Derbyshire at Chesterfield	1904
Highest score against:	332	W. H. Ashdown (Kent) at Brentwood	1934
Best bowling for:	10-32	H. Pickett v Leicestershire at Leyton	1895
Best bowling against:	10-40	E. G. Dennett (Gloucestershire) at Bristol	1906
Highest total for:	761-6 dec.	v Leicestershire at Chelmsford	1990
Highest total against:	803-4 dec.	by Kent at Brentwood	1934
Lowest total for:	30	v Yorkshire at Leyton	1901
Lowest total against:	14	by Surrey at Chelmsford	1983

At Leicester, April 20, 21, 22. ESSEX beat LEICESTERSHIRE by an innings and nine runs.

ESSEX v NORTHAMPTONSHIRE

At Chelmsford, April 25, 26, 27, 28. Drawn. Essex 8 pts, Northamptonshire 7 pts. Toss: Northamptonshire.

Rain, which had caused stoppages throughout the match, returned to frustrate Essex, eyeing a second Championship win in two starts, and to rescue Northamptonshire, who were seven down and 11 overs from safety. On the opening day, Robinson batted well for Essex in conditions made for seam and swing. Although Cousins prospered against his erstwhile colleagues, as he had the previous season when the sides jostled for promotion, he had to give second best to Irani's master-class on the third morning: the Essex captain's variation in pace brought him four for one from 41 deliveries as Northamptonshire lost their last six wickets for 14. Law struck nine boundaries in a fluent 58 when Essex went in again, and Peters's solid half-century enabled Irani to set a target of 314 from a day's play. Northamptonshire lost just three batsmen in reaching 152, thanks largely to a stand of 95 – the highest of the match – between Warren and Alec Swann. Once they were separated, Essex seized the initiative, only for the weather to snatch it away.

Close of play: First day, Essex 154-6 (Peters 2*, Anderson 1*); Second day, Northamptonshire 119-4 (Warren 29*, Penberthy 8*); Third day, Essex 257-8 (Peters 56*, Cowan 25*).

Essex

P. J. Prichard c Ripley b Cousins	8	– c Warren b Innes	22
N. Hussain b Cousins	15	– lbw b Innes	34
D. D. J. Robinson c A. J. Swann b G. P. Swann	61	– lbw b Innes	0
S. G. Law c Ripley b Taylor	26	– b G. P. Swann	58
*R. C. Irani c Hussey b Cousins	8	– c and b Innes	4
S. D. Peters c Warren b Penberthy	19	– not out	56
†B. J. Hyam run out	2	– lbw b G. P. Swann	22
R. S. G. Anderson c Ripley b Penberthy	2	– lbw b Penberthy	19
T. J. Mason c Hussey b Cousins	0	– c Ripley b Cousins	3
A. P. Cowan b Taylor	27	– not out	25
A. C. McGarry not out	0		
B 5, l-b 19, w 14	38	L-b 4, w 10	14
1/24 2/41 3/105 4/143 5/151 6/153 7/155 8/162 9/192	206	1/51 2/51 3/94 4/102 5/139 6/177 7/202 8/220 (8 wkts dec.)	257

Bonus points – Essex 1, Northamptonshire 3.

Bowling: *First Innings*—Cousins 28–8–62–4; Taylor 12.1–1–52–2; Penberthy 22–8–46–2; Innes 5–1–18–0; G. P. Swann 7–4–4–1. *Second Innings*—Cousins 20–2–71–1; Taylor 12.3–1–39–0; Penberthy 15–6–26–1; Innes 19–3–76–4; G. P. Swann 13–4–41–2.

Northamptonshire

M. E. K. Hussey c Hyam b Anderson	21	– lbw b Cowan	3
M. B. Loye lbw b Irani	13	– lbw b Anderson	26
J. W. Cook lbw b McGarry	20	– b McGarry	16
R. J. Warren lbw b Anderson	33	– c Law b McGarry	55
A. J. Swann c Robinson b Anderson	10	– lbw b Anderson	47
A. L. Penberthy c Hyam b Cowan	20	– c Cowan b Anderson	6
G. P. Swann c Hyam b Irani	3	– lbw b Cowan	29
*†D. Ripley c Robinson b Irani	6	– not out	4
K. J. Innes c Peters b Irani	0	– not out	0
J. P. Taylor not out	1		
D. M. Cousins b Irani	0		
L-b 5, w 10, n-b 8	23	L-b 3, n-b 10	13
1/42 2/46 3/84 4/105 5/136 6/139 7/147 8/147 9/149	150	1/10 2/47 3/57 4/152 5/164 6/168 7/199 (7 wkts)	199

Bonus points – Essex 3.

Bowling: *First Innings*—Cowan 16–3–34–1; Irani 24–11–43–5; Anderson 15–4–45–3; McGarry 7–0–23–1. *Second Innings*—Cowan 17–5–51–2; Irani 19–6–40–0; Anderson 21–3–56–3; Mason 8–4–11–0; McGarry 11–1–38–2.

Umpires: B. Dudleston and K. E. Palmer.

At Cambridge, May 9, 10, 11. ESSEX beat CAMBRIDGE UCCE by 335 runs.

ESSEX v YORKSHIRE

At Chelmsford, May 16, 17, 18, 19. Drawn. Essex 8 pts, Yorkshire 12 pts. Toss: Yorkshire. Championship debut: S. A. Richardson.

Once the first two days had been washed out, the teams' sole aim became the pursuit of bonus points, which Yorkshire achieved in full, despite six senior players being either injured or on international duty. Having slipped to 164 for six, they were bailed out by personal-bests from Middlebrook and Silverwood, whose 70 came in 74 balls. Helped along by some wayward bowling, notably from Cowan and Napier, they added 126 for the eighth wicket at better than five an over. Prichard went to the first ball of the Essex reply, but Law made 53 before he was the first of three wickets in 11 balls for Fellows's gentle medium-pace. The pitch was far from troublesome, but the home side, despite a solid unbeaten 49 from Peters, fell just short of a second batting point.

Close of play: First day, No play; Second day, No play; Third day, Yorkshire 376-9 (Fisher 11*, Hutchison 0*).

Yorkshire

S. A. Richardson c Law b Ilott	22
M. J. Wood c Ilott b Cowan	29
A. McGrath c Hyam b Cowan	13
D. S. Lehmann c Hyam b Ilott	7
*D. Byas lbw b Anderson	55
G. M. Fellows b Napier	20
†R. J. Blakey c Cowan b Napier	41
J. D. Middlebrook c Cowan b Irani	84
C. E. W. Silverwood c Hyam b Cowan	70
I. D. Fisher not out	28
P. M. Hutchison not out	9
L-b 7, w 6, n-b 12	25
1/33 2/73 3/73 4/91 5/130 6/164 7/238 8/364 9/366 (9 wkts dec.)	403

Bonus points – Yorkshire 5, Essex 3.

Bowling: Cowan 23–5–111–3; Ilott 23–5–57–2; Irani 23–6–70–1; Anderson 20–4–62–1; Napier 12.2–2–61–2; Grayson 13–3–35–0.

Essex

P. J. Prichard lbw b Silverwood	0
A. P. Grayson c sub b Middlebrook	17
D. D. J. Robinson b Middlebrook	16
S. G. Law c Blakey b Fellows	53
*R. C. Irani lbw b Fellows	34
S. D. Peters not out	49
G. R. Napier c Richardson b Fellows	0
†B. J. Hyam c Fellows b Middlebrook	17
R. S. G. Anderson b Fisher	21
A. P. Cowan c Blakey b Hutchison	0
M. C. Ilott c Byas b Lehmann	22
B 6, l-b 8, n-b 6	20
1/0 2/29 3/56 4/131 5/132 6/134 7/166 8/210 9/211	249

Bonus points – Essex 1, Yorkshire 3.

Bowling: Silverwood 18–1–67–1; Hutchison 16–3–59–1; Middlebrook 19–4–49–3; Fisher 13–3–32–1; Fellows 12–5–23–3; Lehmann 5–2–5–1.

Umpires: A. A. Jones and G. Sharp.

At The Oval, May 25, 26, 27, 28. ESSEX drew with SURREY.

At Tunbridge Wells, May 30, 31, June 1. ESSEX lost to KENT by an innings and 152 runs.

ESSEX v GLAMORGAN

At Chelmsford, June 6, 7, 8, 9. Glamorgan won by six wickets. Glamorgan 19 pts, Essex 3 pts. Toss: Glamorgan.

Challenged to score 364 from 84 overs on a featherbed, Glamorgan romped home with three overs to spare. James, whose 156 came from 246 balls, and Maynard, who struck 90 from 115, made the running with a partnership of 194 in 38 overs. On the first day, after the Essex bowlers had sunk their teeth into Glamorgan's top order, Thomas and Dale led a fine recovery, their seventh-wicket stand adding 163. Thomas hit 19 fours and a six in a maiden hundred; his 138 was the highest score by a Glamorgan No. 8, surpassing Malcolm Nash's 130 at The Oval in 1976. Next he took four wickets as Essex, for the fourth match in succession, failed to reach the follow-on mark. Grayson then underlined the pitch's friendliness with a career-best 189 that included 136 in boundaries. Fifties from Robinson, Law and Irani allowed Essex to declare during the first hour of the final day, setting Glamorgan a target they had achieved only once before to win – at Southampton in 1990, when they also hit 367.

Close of play: First day, Glamorgan 335-7 (Thomas 119*, Cosker 22*); Second day, Essex 136-1 (Grayson 56*, Robinson 59*); Third day, Essex 498-6 (Hyam 6*, Cowan 13*).

Glamorgan

*S. P. James lbw b Ilott	1	– c Law b Such	156
J. P. Maher b McGarry	21	– c Law b Such	38
M. P. Maynard b McGarry	9	– c Such b Grayson	90
M. J. Powell c Hyam b Irani	1	– c Law b Such	7
A. Dale c Hyam b McGarry	113	– not out	43
K. Newell c Robinson b Ilott	17	– not out	10
†A. D. Shaw c Cowan b Ilott	8		
S. D. Thomas c Grayson b Irani	138		
D. A. Cosker b Ilott	24		
S. L. Watkin not out	13		
O. T. Parkin lbw b Ilott	0		
L-b 11, w 6, n-b 8	25	L-b 7, w 10, n-b 6	23
1/5 2/38 3/39 4/57 5/108 6/128 7/291 8/343 9/367	370	1/84 2/278 3/299 4/350	(4 wkts) 367

Bonus points – Glamorgan 4, Essex 3.

Bowling: *First Innings*—Cowan 24–4–90–0; Ilott 26.5–6–85–5; Irani 22–6–55–2; McGarry 19–1–77–3; Such 12–4–21–0; Grayson 10–4–31–0. *Second Innings*—Ilott 17–2–66–0; Irani 12.5–2–66–0; Cowan 14–0–62–0; McGarry 7–0–33–0; Such 18–2–84–3; Grayson 12–0–49–1.

Essex

P. J. Prichard lbw b Watkin	6 – c Dale b Thomas	19
A. P. Grayson c and b Thomas	6 – c Cosker b Dale	189
D. D. J. Robinson c Shaw b Thomas	8 – c Shaw b Watkin	80
S. G. Law c and b Parkin	19 – c Powell b Parkin	67
*R. C. Irani c Maher b Thomas	22 – c Maher b Watkin	66
S. D. Peters c Cosker b Parkin	17 – lbw b Cosker	43
†B. J. Hyam b Cosker	63 – not out	23
A. P. Cowan c Powell b Thomas	22 – b Parkin	20
M. C. Ilott lbw b Cosker	4 – not out	18
P. M. Such c Watkin b Cosker	25	
A. C. McGarry not out	0	
L-b 1	1	B 1, l-b 9, w 5 15
1/7 2/16 3/23 4/41 5/67 6/99 7/127 8/148 9/186	193	1/34 2/192 3/339 4/368 5/479 6/481 7/511 (7 wkts dec.) 540

Bonus points – Glamorgan 3.

Bowling: *First Innings*—Thomas 15–2–54–4; Watkin 12–4–41–1; Parkin 13–2–45–2; Dale 3–0–23–0; Cosker 8.4–2–29–3. *Second Innings*—Thomas 27–4–122–1; Watkin 37–11–104–2; Parkin 31–2–131–2; Cosker 33–4–100–1; Newell 3–0–19–0; Dale 11–3–27–1; Maher 6–1–27–0.

Umpires: B. Leadbeater and N. A. Mallender.

ESSEX v SURREY

At Ilford, June 13, 14, 15, 16. Drawn. Essex 9 pts, Surrey 7 pts. Toss: Surrey. First-class debut: R. S. Clinton.

Essex were 56 runs from becoming the first county to defeat Surrey in the Championship for 12 months when rain halted play just before lunch, and washed out the final two sessions. Richard Clinton, 19-year-old son of Grahame, the former Kent and Surrey opener, marked his debut with a solid 36 in the first innings and, opening for the incapacitated Robinson, an unbeaten half-century in the second, sharing an unbroken stand of 118 with Law. On the first day, Hollioake batted well to rescue Surrey from 21 for three, then 47 for four, but the innings of the match was opposing captain Irani's century, to complement his earlier destruction of Surrey's lower order. He received fine support from the tail and established a lead of 98. When Surrey batted again, Anderson's five wickets took his first-class tally to 34, more than anyone in the country to date. Three middle-order fifties left the home side needing 209; Bicknell struck twice in an over, but the weather had the last word. The opening day had seen two miscreants entering Valentines Park: in one incident, a joyrider, after crashing a car near by, made his getaway through the park; in another, groundstaff discovered a man dangling from the railings, having tried to evade the admission fee.

Close of play: First day, Essex 145-7 (Irani 55*, Cowan 0*); Second day, Surrey 93-3 (Ramprakash 49*, Hollioake 0*); Third day, Essex 65-2 (Clinton 15*, Law 26*).

Surrey

M. A. Butcher c Clinton b Ilott	0	– c Hyam b Irani	2
I. J. Ward c Law b Cowan	5	– lbw b Ilott	22
M. R. Ramprakash lbw b Irani	8	– lbw b Ilott	61
N. Shahid c Such b Cowan	0	– c Irani b Anderson	14
*A. J. Hollioake c Hyam b Irani	77	– b Anderson	52
G. P. Butcher c Hyam b Cowan	36	– c Hyam b Anderson	56
†J. N. Batty c Such b Anderson	1	– c and b Anderson	0
M. P. Bicknell not out	26	– b Cowan	24
I. D. K. Salisbury b Irani	8	– c Hyam b Anderson	37
R. M. Amin lbw b Irani	1	– c Law b Irani	0
E. S. H. Giddins c Cowan b Irani	1	– not out	9
B 1, l-b 3, w 17, n-b 14	35	L-b 11, w 10, n-b 8	29
1/13 2/15 3/21 4/47 5/146 6/156 7/162 8/182 9/192	198	1/3 2/66 3/87 4/123 5/195 6/207 7/242 8/273 9/278	306

Bonus points – Essex 3.

Bowling: *First Innings*—Cowan 13–2–64–3; Ilott 6–1–34–1; Irani 17.5–3–58–5; Anderson 12–3–38–1; Clinton 1–1–0–0. *Second Innings*—Cowan 20–3–70–1; Irani 19–6–56–2; Anderson 27.5–7–79–5; Such 10–2–26–0; Ilott 18–2–64–2.

Essex

D. D. J. Robinson lbw b Bicknell	25		
A. P. Grayson c Batty b Bicknell	5	– c Batty b Bicknell	24
S. D. Peters c G. P. Butcher b M. A. Butcher	4	– lbw b Bicknell	0
S. G. Law c Ward b M. A. Butcher	1	– not out	66
*R. C. Irani c and b Amin	119		
R. S. Clinton lbw b Giddins	36	– (1) not out	58
†B. J. Hyam b Salisbury	0		
R. S. G. Anderson b Giddins	3		
A. P. Cowan c M. A. Butcher b Giddins	18		
M. C. Ilott c Ramprakash b Bicknell	29		
P. M. Such not out	21		
B 2, l-b 21, w 4, n-b 8	35	L-b 1, n-b 4	5
1/21 2/30 3/40 4/42 5/128 6/129 7/140 8/182 9/269	296	1/35 2/35	(2 wkts) 153

Bonus points – Essex 2, Surrey 3.

Bowling: *First Innings*—Bicknell 23.3–6–54–3; Giddins 29–6–94–3; M. A. Butcher 8–1–20–2; Salisbury 35–8–74–1; G. P. Butcher 3–1–11–0; Amin 7–3–18–1; Hollioake 1–0–2–0. *Second Innings*—Bicknell 16–1–60–2; Giddins 11–1–39–0; M. A. Butcher 4–1–10–0; Salisbury 3–2–14–0; G. P. Butcher 3–0–21–0; Hollioake 1–0–8–0.

Umpires: R. Julian and G. Sharp.

At Manchester, June 19, 20, 21, 22. ESSEX lost to LANCASHIRE by nine wickets.

At Chelmsford, June 29, 30, July 1. ESSEX drew with AUSTRALIANS (see Australian tour section).

At Taunton, July 4, 5, 6, 7. ESSEX lost to SOMERSET by an innings and 60 runs.

ESSEX v KENT

At Southend, July 18, 19, 20. Kent won by an innings and 132 runs. Kent 19 pts, Essex 2 pts. Toss: Essex.

Irani won the toss in a Championship game for the first time since the opening match of the season, but soon rued his decision to bat. The Essex top order – Law was absent with a broken finger – disintegrated in alarming fashion; Ealham, with seam and swing, took three for five after lunch and ended with five for 13. By the close, Kent were nine ahead without having lost a wicket. Although Fulton departed to Bishop's first ball next morning, Key's determined hundred, spread over more than six and a half hours and containing just nine boundaries, paved the way for a declaration. Essex, 246 in arrears, were soon in disarray once more. This time Saggers emerged with a bargain five-wicket return; only Grayson, last out for 54, offered any resistance. Kent's win was their second over Essex by an innings in seven weeks, and their seventh on the trot in all cricket; Essex's fifth defeat in six Championship games left them rooted to the bottom of Division One.

Close of play: First day, Kent 116-0 (Fulton 70*, Key 40*); Second day, Kent 253-4 (Key 100*, Ealham 10*).

Essex

R. S. Clinton b Patel	19	– c Nixon b Patel	13
A. P. Grayson c Symonds b Trott	0	– b Saggers	54
D. D. J. Robinson lbw b Ealham	24	– c Key b Saggers	2
S. D. Peters b Saggers	27	– b Saggers	7
*R. C. Irani c Nixon b Ealham	0	– c Fulton b Saggers	0
†J. S. Foster lbw b Ealham	18	– b Trott	8
T. J. Phillips b Ealham	0	– c Nixon b Fleming	11
A. P. Cowan b Ealham	2	– c Key b Trott	7
J. E. Bishop lbw b Trott	1	– c Symonds b Trott	0
P. M. Such not out	7	– b Saggers	0
A. C. McGarry lbw b Trott	0	– not out	0
L-b 7, w 2	9	B 6, l-b 6	12
1/2 2/31 3/45 4/45 5/75 6/77 7/85 8/90 9/106	107	1/28 2/31 3/43 4/43 5/60 6/89 7/103 8/103 9/113	114

Bonus points – Kent 3.

Bowling: *First Innings*—Saggers 14–5–24–1; Trott 13.5–4–27–3; Patel 11–4–22–1; Ealham 14–8–13–5; Symonds 1–0–3–0; Fleming 6–0–11–0. *Second Innings*—Saggers 11.1–4–24–5; Trott 11–1–32–3; Patel 16–5–24–1; Ealham 7–2–13–0; Fleming 2–0–9–1.

Kent

D. P. Fulton b Bishop	70
R. W. T. Key c Peters b Bishop	123
E. T. Smith c Robinson b Bishop	7
A. Symonds c Foster b Cowan	33
M. J. Walker c McGarry b Cowan	18
M. A. Ealham b Bishop	44
†P. A. Nixon b Cowan	3
*M. V. Fleming not out	14
M. M. Patel not out	17
B 1, l-b 5, w 6, n-b 12	24
1/116 2/124 3/171 4/229 5/299 6/312 7/316 (7 wkts dec.)	353

M. J. Saggers and B. J. Trott did not bat.

Bonus points – Kent 4, Essex 2.

Bowling: Cowan 34–10–78–3; Bishop 36–8–120–4; McGarry 20–4–70–0; Phillips 16–2–60–0; Such 10–2–19–0.

Umpires: B. Dudleston and R. Palmer.

At Northampton, July 27, 28, 29, 30. ESSEX lost to NORTHAMPTONSHIRE by ten wickets.

ESSEX v LEICESTERSHIRE

At Chelmsford, August 1, 2, 3, 4. Drawn. Essex 9 pts, Leicestershire 12 pts. Toss: Leicestershire.

Robinson became the third Essex batsman, after Law and Grayson, to hit two hundreds in a match in 2001. His second, an unbeaten 118, saw his side to safety after they were forced to follow on. On a slow pitch, Leicestershire's formidable total owed much to Sutcliffe's patient 165, which included 108 in fours and lasted more than seven hours, and to Habib's graceful 124; they added 233 in 66 overs. Sutcliffe survived a confident appeal for a catch behind shortly after passing 50; umpire Jeff Evans, shaven-headed and hatless, fainted at square leg next over, but quickly recovered. Bishop, left-arm fast-medium, claimed his first five-wicket return. When Essex eventually replied, Robinson completed his first Championship century for two years, while Law's 30th hundred for Essex, full of vintage drives and containing 22 fours, carried him beyond 1,000 for the season. Others, however, struggled against Shahid Afridi's wrist-spin – he finished with five for 84 – and Essex's 203-run deficit left Robinson with more work to do.

Close of play: First day, Leicestershire 342-2 (Sutcliffe 149*, Habib 101*); Second day, Leicestershire 559; Third day, Essex 329-7 (Phillips 22*, Cowan 25*).

Leicestershire

T. R. Ward c Such b Napier	25
I. J. Sutcliffe b Bishop	165
*B. F. Smith lbw b Bishop	37
A. Habib lbw b Bishop	124
D. L. Maddy c Foster b Bishop	55
Shahid Afridi c Such b Bishop	7
†N. D. Burns not out	50
P. A. J. DeFreitas c Napier b Cowan	31
J. M. Dakin c and b Napier	10
C. D. Crowe lbw b Irani	0
D. E. Malcolm b Napier	1
B 3, l-b 25, w 8, n-b 18	54
1/59 2/135 3/368 4/429 5/450 6/455 7/525 8/551 9/556	559

Bonus points – Leicestershire 5, Essex 1 (Score at 130 overs: 415-3).

Bowling: Cowan 40–10–102–1; Bishop 38–10–148–5; Irani 17–5–64–1; Napier 14.5–5–55–3; Such 27–6–86–0; Phillips 13–2–57–0; Grayson 4–0–19–0.

Essex

D. D. J. Robinson st Burns b Crowe	102	– (2) not out	118
S. D. Peters lbw b DeFreitas	0	– (1) b Shahid Afridi	19
S. G. Law c and b Shahid Afridi	115	– c Burns b Malcolm	23
*R. C. Irani c Burns b DeFreitas	2	– c Burns b Malcolm	3
†J. S. Foster lbw b Shahid Afridi	1	– c Sutcliffe b DeFreitas	21
G. R. Napier b Crowe	36	– c Shahid Afridi b Sutcliffe	44
A. P. Grayson c Smith b Shahid Afridi	9	– not out	2
T. J. Phillips c Burns b Malcolm	27		
A. P. Cowan lbw b Shahid Afridi	26		
J. E. Bishop b Shahid Afridi	16		
P. M. Such not out	4		
B 3, l-b 5, w 10	18	B 4, n-b 2	6
1/12 2/206 3/211 4/220 5/238 6/261 7/294 8/330 9/336	356	1/39 2/94 3/102 4/146 5/226	(5 wkts) 236

Bonus points – Essex 4, Leicestershire 3.

Bowling: *First Innings*—Malcolm 25–3–86–1; DeFreitas 26–6–72–2; Dakin 0.5–0–1–0; Maddy 8.1–1–31–0; Shahid Afridi 30.1–10–84–5; Crowe 27–8–74–2. *Second Innings*—Malcolm 17–5–49–2; DeFreitas 12–3–50–1; Shahid Afridi 20–7–45–1; Crowe 14–3–39–0; Sutcliffe 6–1–19–1; Maddy 6–1–30–0.

Umpires: A. Clarkson and J. H. Evans.

At Cardiff, August 15, 16, 17, 18. ESSEX drew with GLAMORGAN.

ESSEX v LANCASHIRE

At Colchester, August 22, 23, 24, 25. Drawn. Essex 7 pts, Lancashire 12 pts. Toss: Lancashire.

Essex had Grayson to thank for salvaging a draw. In sapping heat, he defied the Lancashire attack for almost eight and a quarter hours and finished unbeaten on 186, three short of a career-best, having faced 372 balls and struck 21 fours. His battling innings began as Essex followed on 187 behind. The lively Chapple had inflicted most damage, though in failing light late on the rain-interrupted second day there was also success for the gentle left-arm medium-pace of Fairbrother. He picked up only his seventh first-class wicket in 20 seasons when he had Irani lbw. On the opening day, Fairbrother displayed his more familiar skills as a batsman, compiling a stylish 132 – his fourth hundred of the summer, and his fifth in Essex – from 244 balls; he and the obdurate Chilton shared a third-wicket stand of 215. Schofield then hit a personal-best 80 not out, and Irani took six wickets for the first time.

Close of play: First day, Lancashire 316-6 (Haynes 4*, Schofield 11*); Second day, Essex 123-5 (Foster 5*, Napier 19*); Third day, Essex 110-3 (Grayson 38*, Irani 18*).

Lancashire

M. J. Chilton c Cowan b Such	98
*J. P. Crawley b Bishop	0
A. Flintoff c Foster b Irani	18
N. H. Fairbrother c Foster b Irani	132
J. C. Scuderi b Irani	14
G. D. Lloyd c and b Such	9
†J. J. Haynes lbw b Bishop	6
C. P. Schofield not out	80
G. Chapple b Irani	13
J. Wood c Grayson b Irani	15
G. Keedy c Foster b Irani	0
B 4, l-b 8, w 10, n-b 16	38
1/2 2/33 3/248 4/277 5/296 6/298 7/336 8/371 9/421	423

Bonus points – Lancashire 5, Essex 2 (Score at 130 overs: 408-8).

Bowling: Cowan 30–9–84–0; Bishop 21–3–71–2; Irani 28.3–5–79–6; Napier 18–2–77–0; Such 31–7–71–2; Mason 6–1–29–0.

Essex

D. D. J. Robinson lbw b Scuderi	13	– lbw b Chapple	0
A. P. Grayson b Chapple	26	– not out	186
S. D. Peters c Haynes b Chapple	26	– c Lloyd b Chapple	3
S. G. Law c Haynes b Scuderi	18	– c Scuderi b Flintoff	46
*R. C. Irani lbw b Fairbrother	9	– c Crawley b Scuderi	18
†J. S. Foster c Lloyd b Wood	32	– c Fairbrother b Flintoff	15
G. R. Napier b Chapple	23	– lbw b Chapple	11
A. P. Cowan c Fairbrother b Chapple	1	– b Flintoff	32
T. J. Mason not out	41	– lbw b Schofield	2
J. E. Bishop c Chapple b Wood	5	– not out	5
P. M. Such lbw b Schofield	21		
B 8, l-b 9, w 2, n-b 2	21	B 1, l-b 7, w 4, n-b 4	16
1/39 2/39 3/74 4/98 5/98 6/128 7/130 8/177 9/189	236	1/4 2/8 3/76 4/115 5/178 6/210 7/296 8/317	(8 wkts) 334

Bonus points – Essex 1, Lancashire 3.

Bowling: *First Innings*—Chapple 24–6–71–4; Wood 10–2–40–2; Scuderi 18–11–17–2; Fairbrother 5–1–18–1; Keedy 11–1–24–0; Flintoff 11–3–12–0; Schofield 18.1–5–37–1. *Second Innings*—Chapple 25–9–65–3; Wood 14–1–53–0; Scuderi 19–5–32–1; Schofield 28–7–73–1; Flintoff 19–5–48–3; Keedy 23–3–53–0; Crawley 1–0–2–0.

Umpires: N. G. Cowley and J. W. Holder.

ESSEX v SOMERSET

At Chelmsford, September 5, 6, 7. Somerset won by nine wickets. Somerset 19 pts, Essex 3 pts. Toss: Somerset.

Somerset won handsomely inside three days to make the £50,000 awarded to the Championship runners-up as good as theirs. Cox batted throughout the first day and struck 26 fours in the first hundred of his summer, sharing a sixth-wicket stand of 176 with Turner, who was hit on the forearm by Cowan and retired hurt. He resumed briefly in a vain attempt to secure maximum batting points. Robinson held the Essex reply together with a forceful 89, but could not prevent the follow-on: for the 13th time in 14 first-class games, they faced a first-innings deficit of 150 or more. This time it was Johnson and Dutch, Somerset's Middlesex recruits, who had benefited from reckless strokes on a blameless pitch. Law, after six highly productive seasons for Essex, then bowed out with an entertaining half-century in his final first-class appearance for them at their headquarters. Even so, they never looked capable of avoiding a seventh defeat. Somerset charged to their target in only 33 minutes, ensuring relegation was a certainty for Essex.

Close of play: First day, Somerset 304-5 (Cox 175*, Turner 65*); Second day, Essex 25-0 (Robinson 14*, Grayson 8*).

Somerset

*J. Cox c Robinson b Irani	186	– not out	33
M. J. Wood c Napier b Irani	8	– c Clinton b Cowan	20
M. Burns c Law b Bishop	7	– not out	3
P. D. Bowler b Cowan	18		
K. A. Parsons lbw b Napier	1		
I. D. Blackwell b Cowan	4		
†R. J. Turner c Foster b Bishop	70		
K. P. Dutch c Robinson b Cowan	0		
J. I. D. Kerr c Robinson b Bishop	36		
R. L. Johnson not out	35		
P. S. Jones lbw b Napier	0		
L-b 6, w 10, n-b 10	26	L-b 8	8
1/37 2/86 3/117 4/118 5/139 6/315 7/319 8/389 9/390	391	1/57	(1 wkt) 64

Bonus points – Somerset 4, Essex 3.

In the first innings Turner, when 69, retired hurt at 315-5 and resumed at 390.

Bowling: *First Innings*—Cowan 34–11–89–3; Bishop 23.2–4–94–3; Napier 12–2–56–2; Irani 21–6–80–2; Such 19–4–38–0; Davies 4–0–20–0; Grayson 5–1–8–0. *Second Innings*—Cowan 5–0–22–1; Bishop 4.1–0–34–0.

Essex

D. D. J. Robinson c Burns b Dutch	89	– lbw b Jones	35
A. P. Grayson c Burns b Johnson	6	– c Turner b Johnson	19
R. S. Clinton lbw b Johnson	0	– c and b Jones	21
S. G. Law c Cox b Jones	30	– c Parsons b Blackwell	66
*R. C. Irani b Dutch	6	– lbw b Johnson	32
†J. S. Foster b Johnson	7	– b Johnson	10
G. R. Napier c Dutch b Johnson	4	– c Jones b Blackwell	56
A. P. Cowan c Bowler b Dutch	14	– c Turner b Blackwell	2
J. E. Bishop c Bowler b Dutch	7	– c Turner b Dutch	18
M. K. Davies b Johnson	0	– not out	10
P. M. Such not out	0	– c Parsons b Dutch	4
B 2, l-b 5, n-b 2	9	L-b 5, w 2, n-b 2	9
1/29 2/31 3/83 4/128 5/143 6/143 7/147 8/166 9/166	172	1/53 2/80 3/87 4/175 5/191 6/191 7/203 8/267 9/274	282

Bonus points – Somerset 3.

Bowling: *First Innings*—Johnson 17–5–40–5; Jones 15–2–55–1; Kerr 9–4–33–0; Dutch 16.2–6–32–4; Parsons 2–0–5–0. *Second Innings*—Johnson 21–3–72–3; Jones 27–8–78–2; Burns 3–2–7–0; Dutch 16–3–49–2; Kerr 8–3–26–0; Blackwell 27–11–45–3.

Umpires: D. J. Constant and J. H. Hampshire.

At Scarborough, September 12, 13, 14, 15. ESSEX beat YORKSHIRE by 51 runs.

LORDS AND COMMONS RESULTS, 2001

Matches 12: Won 2, Lost 3, Drawn 7.

At Vincent Square, May 1. Drawn. Lords and Commons 70 for four v Westminster School.

At Stowell Park, Gloucestershire, June 17. Drawn. Gloucestershire Gypsies 227 for three dec.; Lords and Commons 157 for six.

At Bank of England Ground, Roehampton, June 21. Drawn. Parliamentary Staff 168 for six dec. (D. Harrison 41; M. Foster three for 35); Lords and Commons 112 for six (R. Spence three for 10).

At Utrecht, June 22. Dutch Parliament won by seven wickets. Lords and Commons 148 for six dec. (R. R. Kershaw 44); Dutch Parliament 149 for three (D. Kost 49; D. Dover three for 34).

At Bloemendaal, June 24. Dutch Parliament won by five wickets. Lords and Commons 142 for seven dec. (F. H. Meller 53); Dutch Parliament 143 for five (R. van Hessan 48).

At Highclere, July 8. Lords and Commons won by four wickets. Lord Carnarvon's XI 248 for four dec. (K. Storey 85, M. Ducis 51); Lords and Commons 249 for six (W. Rowe 125, F. H. Meller 62).

At Burton Court, July 12. Drawn. Baronets XI 244 for six dec. (K. Cornwall Leigh 71 not out, K. Storey 52; E. Brassey four for 83); Lords and Commons 188 for seven (R. R. Kershaw 70; M. Harford five for 30).

At Burton Court, July 18. Drawn. Lords and Commons 182 for seven (A. Rawlinson 41; R. Gouriet three for 24); Eton Ramblers 159 for four (E. Inkin 85 not out; A. Rawlinson three for 37).

At Old Emanuel CC, New Malden, July 24. Lords and Commons won by 21 runs. Lords and Commons 279 for four dec. (H. Robertson 112, C. Blunt 104 not out); Law Society 258 (Harbot 85; R. Heller three for 32).

At Harrow School, September 7. Harrow Wanderers won by eight wickets. Lords and Commons 123 (C. Blunt 42; J. Wilson four for 15); Harrow Wanderers 125 for two (S. Macdonald 55 not out, O. Bryant 52).

At Oporto, Portugal, September 14. Drawn. Law Society 132 for seven dec. (I. Dickinson 55; F. H. Meller five for 45); Lords and Commons 92 for five (S. Rogerson 33).

At Oporto, Portugal, September 16. Drawn. Oporto CC 170 for seven dec. (E. Chambers 92; R. Heller three for 36); Lords and Commons 149 for eight (A. Royce 40; B. Goodfellow three for 32).

At Civil Service Ground, Chiswick, September 11. Europhiles won by four wickets. Eurosceptics 183 for five (J. Collett 51); Europhiles 186 for six (H. Thurston 107, R. Thurston 43).

HONOURS' LIST, 2002

In 2002, the following were decorated for their services to cricket:

New Year's Honours, 2002: J. Dew (services to Horsham Cricket Club) MBE, N. Hussain (Essex and England; services to cricket) OBE, A. R. Lewis (Glamorgan and England; services to sport, broadcasting and Wales) CBE, C. H. Plomer (services to cricket in Angus) MBE.

Australia Day Honours, 2002: D. W. Rogers (former Australian Cricket Board chairman; services to cricket administration) AO, G. S. McKie (services to youth cricket and local cricket in Victoria) OAM.

Jimmy Maher

GLAMORGAN

President: A. R. Lewis
Chairman: G. Elias
Chief Executive: M. J. Fatkin
Chairman, Cricket Committee: P. J. E. Needham
Cricket Secretary: Mrs C. L. Watkin
Captain: S. P. James
First-Team Coach: 2001 – J. R. Hammond
2002 – J. Derrick
Head Groundsman: L. A. Smith
Scorer: 2001 – B. T. Denning
2002 – G. N. Lewis

At the start of the season, Glamorgan were confident that they had the resources not only to stay in Division One but also to challenge for a place in the top three. However, a combination of injuries, bad weather – 104 hours or 25 per cent of playing time was lost in the Championship – and ineffective bowling scuppered their hopes, with new captain Steve James admitting that the gap between first and second division clubs was now widening. There was consolation in the Norwich Union League, in which Glamorgan won Division Two on the day they were relegated in the Championship. After losing every group game in the Benson and Hedges Cup, they formulated a plan for one-day cricket that resulted in 11 League wins, including a 100 per cent home record. But they failed to proceed further than the fourth round in the Cheltenham & Gloucester Trophy.

James always knew he would have a difficult first year as captain, opening the batting and organising his benefit year in addition to leading the team. A pre-season knee operation prevented him from playing his first Championship innings until May 25, then a broken hand, inflicted by Andrew Caddick at Taunton in late July, restricted him to only nine Championship games in all. His contribution at the top of the order was sorely missed and, had he been fit throughout the summer, Glamorgan would surely have gained more than 36 batting points – the lowest in the division apart from bottom club Essex.

Only Jimmy Maher, the Queensland left-handed opener, and Adrian Dale passed 1,000 runs for the season. After adapting to the slower pitches, Maher proved an excellent overseas choice, making four Championship hundreds, including a double against Essex. But while he was popular with the players and members, the club hoped to sign an overseas bowler for 2002. At the same time, Australian coach Jeff Hammond ended his two-year association with Glamorgan, and also retired from cricket to concentrate on a new business venture in Sydney. He was succeeded by assistant coach John Derrick, who was first-team coach in 1998.

Dale, who led the side in James's absence, started the season with a double-century at Northampton. He played some important innings, but the middle order again performed below par. Michael Powell and Matthew Maynard scored 681 and 621 runs respectively, modest contributions from such talented batsmen, with Powell's aggregate and his average of 29.60 particularly disappointing for a young batsman whom many thought destined for international honours. Robert Croft played some useful innings, and was extremely effective in the League, scoring 570 runs, but he suffered an alarming run of low scores towards the end of the season, managing just one run in six Championship innings. Darren Thomas's previous role of seam bowler who could bat was reversed: his 562 runs included a maiden first-class hundred at Chelmsford.

The bowling, which garnered just 37 bonus points, was a major concern. In 15 Championship games – the Old Trafford fixture was washed out – Glamorgan bowled only two sides out twice: Surrey at The Oval, where they won for the first time since 1985, and Kent at Maidstone. They conceded three totals in excess of 550 – and Essex scored 540 for seven – before the last game, when Surrey threatened to post the highest score ever made against Glamorgan before declaring at 701 for nine.

Steve Watkin ended his first-class career on the final day of the season, his 37th birthday, but would not have been satisfied with his return of 43 victims, the lowest by Glamorgan's leading wicket-taker since 1978. One of the most dedicated bowlers in the club's history, he took 902 first-class wickets, and will remain with the county as the director of the Welsh Cricket Academy, based at Sophia Gardens. The absence of Alex Wharf, who played in only five Championship games owing to injury, allowed Simon Jones an extended run with the new ball. He again showed exceptional pace, even experimenting with a short run, but 17 Championship wickets at 52.17 were unacceptable. Glamorgan hoped a winter spent with the England Academy in Adelaide would help, as they needed someone to succeed Watkin as a strike bowler.

Thomas lost the previous few seasons' knack of taking wickets, but a bigger disappointment was his lack of control and ability to contain. Andrew Davies made an immediate impact when selected in mid-July for League games and, though playing only four times in the Championship, looked to have the potential to develop into a useful seamer. Had the England management released Croft when there was little chance of his playing in two Tests, he would have had a greater influence with the ball. As it was, he often had to be used as a stock bowler, and Dean Cosker's left-arm spin was more effective in one-day cricket than four.

Glamorgan used three wicket-keepers during the season. Adrian Shaw began well enough, but when he was taken ill, in mid-June, Mark Wallace immediately grabbed his chance, holding on to eight catches against Kent at Maidstone and rescuing his team with an undefeated 80, batting at No. 7. He later played two important innings at The Oval, retained his place for the remainder of the season, and joined Jones at the Academy. Meanwhile, the policy of handing the gloves to Maynard in one-day games was an unqualified success; not only did he keep wicket impeccably, but it gave Glamorgan the option of playing another batsman or bowler. Maynard captained and kept wicket for England in the Hong Kong Sixes Tournament in the autumn.

Many in Glamorgan and beyond were saddened to learn of the death in November of the county's scorer, Byron Denning. One of the circuit's much-loved characters, he had served the club since 1983. – EDWARD BEVAN.

GLAMORGAN 2001

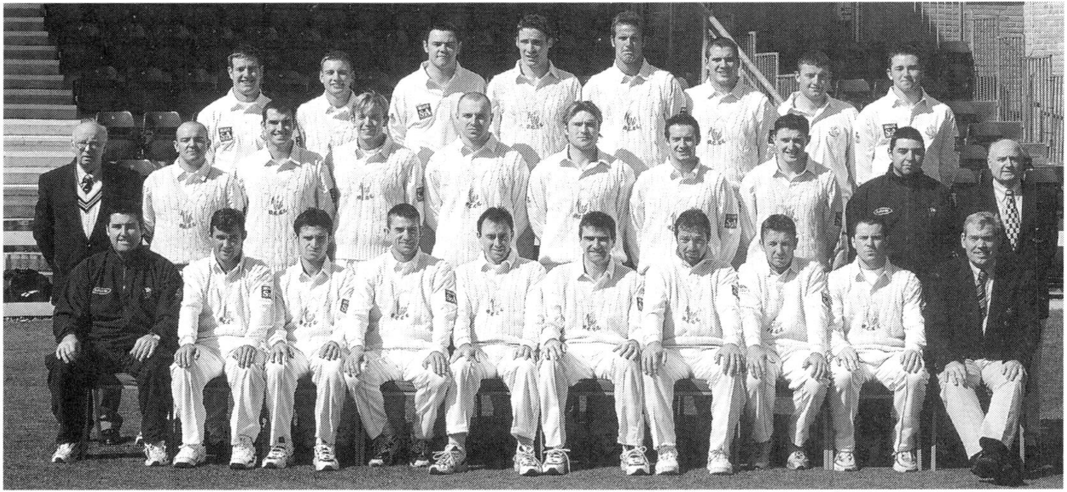

[*Huw John*

Back row: D. D. Cherry, M. A. Wallace, A. J. Davies, S. P. Jones, D. S. Harrison, I. J. Thomas, J. Hughes, R. Watkins. *Middle row:* B. T. Denning (*First Eleven scorer*), A. W. Evans, K. Newell, O. T. Parkin, A. G. Wharf, M. J. Powell, D. A. Cosker, A. P. Davies, E. Mustafa (*physiotherapist*), G. N. Lewis (*Second Eleven scorer*). *Front row:* J. Derrick (*assistant coach*), J. P. Maher, S. D. Thomas, S. L. Watkin, A. Dale, S. P. James (*captain*), M. P. Maynard, R. D. B. Croft, A. D. Shaw, J. R. Hammond (*coach*).

GLAMORGAN RESULTS

All first-class matches – Played 15: Won 2, Lost 5, Drawn 8. Abandoned 1.

County Championship matches – Played 15: Won 2, Lost 5, Drawn 8. Abandoned 1.

CricInfo County Championship, 8th in Division 1; Cheltenham & Gloucester Trophy, 4th round; Benson and Hedges Cup, 6th in Midlands/Wales/West Group; Norwich Union League, winners in Division 2.

COUNTY CHAMPIONSHIP AVERAGES

BATTING

Cap		*M*	*I*	*NO*	*R*	*HS*	*100s*	*50s*	*Avge*	*Ct/St*
2001	J. P. Maher§	14	23	2	1,133	217	4	3	53.95	13
1992	A. Dale	15	23	3	1,026	204	3	4	51.30	9
1992	S. P. James	9	15	3	568	156	1	4	47.33	5
	K. Newell	7	11	2	296	103	1	1	32.88	5
1992	R. D. B. Croft†	9	13	2	350	93	0	3	31.81	6
1987	M. P. Maynard	13	20	0	621	145	1	3	31.05	6
2000	M. J. Powell†	15	25	2	681	108	2	4	29.60	12
1997	S. D. Thomas†	15	21	2	562	138	1	4	29.57	5
1999	A. D. Shaw†	5	6	1	143	62	0	1	28.60	11
	M. A. Wallace†	10	16	3	290	80*	0	2	22.30	27/1
2000	A. G. Wharf	5	4	1	59	31	0	0	19.66	1
	I. J. Thomas†	6	11	1	194	59	0	1	19.40	2
1989	S. L. Watkin†	15	17	7	188	38	0	0	18.80	5
2000	D. A. Cosker	11	15	4	175	35	0	0	15.90	10
	A. P. Davies†	4	7	1	85	40	0	0	14.16	2
	S. P. Jones†	8	11	1	83	46	0	0	8.30	0

Also batted: A. W. Evans† (2 matches) 8, 5, 41 (1 ct); J. Hughes† (1 match) 38, 49; O. T. Parkin (1 match) 0 (1 ct).

* *Signifies not out.* † *Born in Wales.* § *Overseas player.*

BOWLING

	O	*M*	*R*	*W*	*BB*	*5W/i*	*Avge*
A. G. Wharf	127.4	19	448	14	5-63	1	32.00
S. L. Watkin	472.4	113	1,400	43	6-67	1	32.55
R. D. B. Croft	325.3	86	917	23	5-95	2	39.86
D. A. Cosker	423.5	84	1,390	33	4-48	0	42.12
S. D. Thomas	420.1	56	1,668	33	4-54	0	50.54
S. P. Jones	198.2	29	887	17	3-36	0	52.17

Also bowled: A. Dale 117–25–410–7; A. P. Davies 86–16–341–9; A. W. Evans 1–0–2–0; J. P. Maher 21–3–88–0; M. P. Maynard 1–1–0–0; K. Newell 13–0–48–0; O. T. Parkin 44–4–176–4; I. J. Thomas 3–1–2–0.

COUNTY RECORDS

Highest score for:	309*	S. P. James v Sussex at Colwyn Bay	2000
Highest score against:	322*	M. B. Loye (Northamptonshire) at Northampton	1998
Best bowling for:	10-51	J. Mercer v Worcestershire at Worcester	1936
Best bowling against:	10-18	G. Geary (Leicestershire) at Pontypridd	1929
Highest total for:	718-3 dec.	v Sussex at Colwyn Bay	2000
Highest total against:	712	by Northamptonshire at Northampton	1998
Lowest total for:	22	v Lancashire at Liverpool	1924
Lowest total against:	33	by Leicestershire at Ebbw Vale	1965

At Northampton, April 20, 21, 22, 23. GLAMORGAN drew with NORTHAMPTONSHIRE.

GLAMORGAN v SOMERSET

At Cardiff, April 25, 26, 27, 28. Drawn. Glamorgan 9 pts, Somerset 12 pts. Toss: Somerset.

With the first day – and the last two sessions of the final day – lost to rain, there was little chance of a result. In Glamorgan's innings, Powell and Dale continued their productive start to the season, while Shaw also hit a half-century. Dale, deputising for the injured James, declared once Glamorgan gained a fourth batting point. Trescothick and Holloway replied with 240, a record for Somerset's first wicket against Glamorgan, with Trescothick in imperious form. Dismissed just two balls after Holloway, he scored 147 to his partner's 78 and was especially strong on the off side, where he struck most of his 24 boundaries. Cox and Burns further profited from a perfect batting pitch to add 132 for the fourth wicket and gather maximum batting points. Cox was five runs short of his own century when a lunchtime downpour brought proceedings to a halt.

Close of play: First day, No play; Second day, Glamorgan 330-7 (Shaw 62*); Third day, Somerset 307-3 (Cox 42*, Burns 4*).

Glamorgan

A. W. Evans lbw b Jones	41	A. G. Wharf not out	14
J. P. Maher lbw b Rose	29	S. D. Thomas b Johnson	6
M. J. Powell b Johnson	64	S. L. Watkin not out	1
M. P. Maynard lbw b Johnson	21	L-b 7, w 10, n-b 8	25
*A. Dale b Dutch	64		
K. Newell lbw b Dutch	3	1/65 2/81 3/141 (9 wkts dec.)	353
†A. D. Shaw c Parsons b Johnson	62	4/182 5/189 6/270	
R. D. B. Croft b Johnson	23	7/330 8/331 9/343	

Bonus points – Glamorgan 4, Somerset 3.

Bowling: Johnson 28–1–106–5; Jones 24.2–2–83–1; Rose 19–8–36–1; Parsons 11–3–30–0; Dutch 20–4–56–2; Burns 5–1–35–0.

Somerset

P. C. L. Holloway run out	78	K. A. Parsons lbw b Wharf	0
M. E. Trescothick c Wharf b Thomas	147	B 16, l-b 7, w 4, n-b 2	29
P. D. Bowler c Shaw b Croft	16		
*J. Cox not out	95	1/240 2/244 3/302 (5 wkts)	435
M. Burns c and b Croft	70	4/434 5/435	

†R. J. Turner, G. D. Rose, K. P. Dutch, R. L. Johnson and P. S. Jones did not bat.

Bonus points – Somerset 5, Glamorgan 1 (Score at 130 overs: 428-3).

Bowling: Watkin 28–8–78–0; Wharf 19.4–2–102–1; Thomas 32–5–105–1; Croft 45–13–109–2; Maher 2–1–1–0; Dale 6–2–15–0; Evans 1–0–2–0.

Umpires: A. G. T. Whitehead and P. Willey.

At Manchester, May 16, 17, 18, 19. LANCASHIRE v GLAMORGAN. Abandoned.

GLAMORGAN v KENT

At Swansea, May 25, 26, 27, 28. Drawn. Glamorgan 8 pts, Kent 9 pts. Toss: Kent.

The first game of the Swansea festival was badly affected by the weather, with fewer than 17 overs possible on the third and fourth days. Had each captain not had his eye on another bonus point, the match might have been called off at lunch on the last day. As it happened, play was eventually resumed in gloomy light at 3.50 p.m. with Glamorgan 23 runs and Kent one wicket from their limited objectives. Both were realised, Saggers bowling Cosker for his fifth victim of the innings as Glamorgan homed in on a solitary batting point, and Thomas making sure that their 36 runs together were not in vain. On the first day, Kent had been rescued from 13 for three in the fifth over by Fulton and Walker, who added 149 for the fourth wicket. Walker's unbeaten 112 was his second Championship century of the season. Glamorgan were also in trouble at the start of their innings when Saggers removed the first four batsmen in a seven-over spell.

Close of play: First day, Glamorgan 42-4 (Dale 6*, Shaw 3*); Second day, Glamorgan 177-8 (Thomas 17*, Cosker 6*); Third day, No play.

Kent

D. P. Fulton lbw b Wharf	78	M. M. Patel b Cosker	0
R. W. T. Key b Watkin	1	M. J. Saggers c Shaw b Cosker	3
E. T. Smith c Cosker b Watkin	0	B. J. Trott lbw b Cosker	0
D. J. Cullinan c Maher b Wharf	2		
M. J. Walker not out	112	B 1, l-b 3, w 4, n-b 8	16
†P. A. Nixon b Wharf	0		——
M. A. Ealham b Cosker	15	1/6 2/6 3/13 4/162 5/170	252
*M. V. Fleming c Croft b Wharf	25	6/211 7/248 8/248 9/252	

Bonus points – Kent 2, Glamorgan 3.

Bowling: Wharf 18–2–66–4; Watkin 16–3–40–2; Dale 6–0–23–0; Thomas 16–3–56–0; Croft 7–1–15–0; Cosker 18.5–6–48–4.

Glamorgan

*S. P. James c Nixon b Saggers	1	S. D. Thomas c Key b Fleming	42
J. P. Maher c Nixon b Saggers	12	D. A. Cosker b Saggers	17
M. J. Powell c Patel b Saggers	0	S. L. Watkin not out	20
M. P. Maynard b Saggers	16		
A. Dale c Fulton b Patel	29	B 16, l-b 10, w 6	32
†A. D. Shaw c Fulton b Trott	18		——
R. D. B. Croft b Fleming	20	1/2 2/6 3/29 4/34 5/60	238
A. G. Wharf hit wkt b Patel	31	6/98 7/153 8/162 9/198	

Bonus points – Glamorgan 1, Kent 3.

Bowling: Saggers 22–6–70–5; Trott 18–1–65–1; Ealham 12–3–19–0; Patel 32–14–38–2; Fleming 8.2–2–20–2.

Umpires: J. W. Lloyds and K. E. Palmer.

GLAMORGAN v YORKSHIRE

At Swansea, May 30, 31, June 1. Yorkshire won by 328 runs. Yorkshire 17 pts, Glamorgan 3 pts. Toss: Yorkshire.

Midway through the third afternoon, Glamorgan suffered their heaviest defeat in terms of runs alone, two worse than the 326-run loss at Hove in 1925 but still a comfortable remove from the innings and 331 runs rout by Surrey at Cardiff Arms Park in 1936. Half-centuries from Lehmann and Byas enabled Yorkshire to reach a useful first-innings total on a pitch that favoured the seamers, while Wharf made a point to his original county by marginally improving his career-best figures. Silverwood then had Glamorgan in disarray at four for three. Maher and Dale added 56, but once they were out in successive overs to Hamilton, the innings soon folded. Surprisingly, given the mixed weather forecast, Byas did not enforce the follow-on and, having already put on 120 with Fellows, batted an hour into the third day, completing his first Championship hundred since 1998. Glamorgan, 453 in arrears, lost four wickets by lunch, two to Hamilton, who later took three in an over. The St Helen's Balconiers raised money to stage the game, but players and officials were critical of the facilities.

Close of play: First day, Glamorgan 0-0 (James 0*, Maher 0*); Second day, Yorkshire 208-6 (Byas 64*, Hamilton 12*).

Yorkshire

S. A. Richardson lbw b Watkin	0	– c Shaw b Watkin	5
M. J. Wood c Cosker b Wharf	1	– c Shaw b Wharf	0
C. White c Shaw b Wharf	39	– b Watkin	24
D. S. Lehmann lbw b Watkin	75	– c Watkin b Cosker	22
*D. Byas lbw b Cosker	63	– not out	105
G. M. Fellows c Maynard b Thomas	22	– c Shaw b Wharf	61
†R. J. Blakey c Maher b Wharf	23	– c James b Cosker	4
G. M. Hamilton c Shaw b Wharf	6	– c Maher b Wharf	13
J. D. Middlebrook c Maher b Watkin	35	– not out	25
C. E. W. Silverwood c Watkin b Wharf	2		
R. J. Sidebottom not out	1		
L-b 9, w 2, n-b 2	13	B 4, l-b 12, n-b 2	18
1/1 2/3 3/110 4/141 5/175 6/225 7/238 8/247 9/271	280	1/1 2/7 3/53 4/53 5/173 6/184 7/211 (7 wkts dec.)	277

Bonus points – Yorkshire 2, Glamorgan 3.

Bowling: *First Innings*—Wharf 25–6–63–5; Watkin 22.1–7–49–3; Thomas 23–3–81–1; Cosker 19–5–61–1; Dale 10–3–17–0. *Second Innings*—Wharf 18–2–57–3; Watkin 21–11–50–2; Thomas 12–2–51–0; Cosker 21–2–88–2; Dale 4–1–15–0.

Glamorgan

*S. P. James c Blakey b Silverwood	4	– b Hamilton	24
J. P. Maher lbw b Hamilton	35	– lbw b Sidebottom	8
M. J. Powell c Richardson b Silverwood	0	– c Blakey b Sidebottom	1
M. P. Maynard c Byas b Silverwood	0	– b Hamilton	10
A. Dale c White b Hamilton	20	– c Richardson b Sidebottom	4
K. Newell c Blakey b Silverwood	14	– c Blakey b Sidebottom	7
†A. D. Shaw c Richardson b Middlebrook	5	– c Richardson b Hamilton	17
A. G. Wharf c Middlebrook b Sidebottom	3	– c Blakey b Hamilton	11
S. D. Thomas c White b Sidebottom	12	– b Hamilton	0
D. A. Cosker lbw b Silverwood	0	– not out	9
S. L. Watkin not out	4	– c Silverwood b Lehmann	21
L-b 1, n-b 6	7	L-b 1, w 6, n-b 6	13
1/4 2/4 3/4 4/60 5/61 6/83 7/86 8/86 9/86	104	1/20 2/30 3/51 4/52 5/66 6/73 7/95 8/95 9/96	125

Bonus points – Yorkshire 3.

Bowling: *First Innings*—Silverwood 9–5–20–5; Sidebottom 10.3–3–37–2; Hamilton 8–3–15–2; Middlebrook 10–3–22–1; Fellows 2–0–5–0; Lehmann 2–1–4–0. *Second Innings*—Silverwood 10–4–25–0; Sidebottom 13–3–49–4; Hamilton 9–3–27–5; Middlebrook 5–1–23–0; Lehmann 0.4–0–0–1.

Umpires: D. J. Constant and M. J. Harris.

At Chelmsford, June 6, 7, 8, 9. GLAMORGAN beat ESSEX by six wickets.

At Maidstone, June 13, 14, 15, 16. GLAMORGAN drew with KENT.

At Cardiff, June 20, 21, 22 (not first-class). Glamorgan won by 140 runs. Toss: Cardiff UCCE. Glamorgan 373 for seven dec. (I. J. Thomas 38, A. W. Evans 137, M. J. Powell 104, D. D. Cherry 34 not out) and 170 for five dec. (D. S. Harrison 62 not out, A. W. Evans 44, M. J. Powell 33 not out; A. N. Bressington four for 38); Cardiff UCCE 236 (J. Cook 80, I. M. Bird 43; D. S. Harrison four for 62) and 167 (G. Hopkins 38, C. J. Yates 31; S. M. A. Bukhari three for 59, S. P. Jones five for 35).

GLAMORGAN v NORTHAMPTONSHIRE

At Cardiff, June 29, 30, July 1, 2. Drawn. Glamorgan 12 pts, Northamptonshire 8 pts. Toss: Glamorgan.

Glamorgan's first six batsmen each passed fifty – a feat the county had not achieved since 1951, when the Derbyshire bowlers were hit around the Arms Park. Maher led the way with 150, containing a six and 21 fours, and he was joined in century stands by James and Maynard as Glamorgan reached a commanding total. Hussey replied with his first Championship hundred, but the follow-on target of 407 proved beyond Northamptonshire. Batting again, Hussey put on 138 with Rollins for the first wicket, and there were sound contributions from Warren (surviving a stumping chance off Croft before he had scored) and Penberthy. Croft took four for 11 from 16 overs on the fourth morning and later finished with five wickets for the second time in the match, adding to his second-day 93. But there was little penetration from the other bowlers, and the visitors claimed the draw. On the first day, Glamorgan unveiled a set of gates in honour of Wilfred Wooller, their former captain, secretary and president, who died in 1997. Fifty years before the unveiling, he was one of the six who scored fifties against Derbyshire.

Close of play: First day, Glamorgan 370-3 (Powell 33*, Dale 42*); Second day, Northamptonshire 116-1 (Hussey 53*, Loye 53*); Third day, Northamptonshire 126-0 (Hussey 50*, Rollins 64*).

Glamorgan

*S. P. James c Taylor b Strong	62	S. D. Thomas not out	1
J. P. Maher c A. J. Swann b Penberthy	150		
M. P. Maynard c Hussey b Strong	69	B 7, l-b 8	15
M. J. Powell c Ripley b G. P. Swann	86		
A. Dale c Ripley b Cousins	54	1/114 2/265 3/290 (7 wkts dec.)	556
R. D. B. Croft c Loye b Taylor	93	4/389 5/459	
†M. A. Wallace run out	26	6/549 7/556	

A. G. Wharf, D. A. Cosker and S. L. Watkin did not bat.

Bonus points – Glamorgan 5, Northamptonshire 1 (Score at 130 overs: 464-5).

Bowling: Cousins 26–5–93–1; Taylor 27.2–3–112–1; Strong 31–3–125–2; Penberthy 28–5–77–1; G. P. Swann 41–7–131–1; A. J. Swann 2–1–3–0.

Northamptonshire

M. E. K. Hussey b Croft	159	– b Croft	68
A. S. Rollins lbw b Croft	5	– c Maher b Croft	65
M. B. Loye c James b Croft	73	– c James b Croft	8
R. J. Warren c Powell b Croft	0	– c Wallace b Croft	77
A. J. Swann lbw b Thomas	1	– c and b Croft	1
A. L. Penberthy c Maynard b Croft	21	– c Maher b Cosker	60
G. P. Swann b Thomas	47	– lbw b Dale	10
*†D. Ripley c Dale b Thomas	2	– not out	25
J. P. Taylor c Dale b Cosker	2	– not out	1
M. R. Strong b Cosker	12		
D. M. Cousins not out	2		
B 2, l-b 8, w 2, n-b 8	20	B 11, l-b 7, w 2, n-b 14	34
1/24 2/156 3/156 4/161 5/220 6/297 7/299 8/304 9/338	344	1/138 2/149 3/158 4/162 5/256 6/283 7/339	(7 wkts) 349

Bonus points – Northamptonshire 3, Glamorgan 3.

Bowling: *First Innings*—Wharf 10–2–26–0; Watkin 11–1–32–0; Croft 33.3–11–95–5; Thomas 16–2–72–3; Cosker 31–5–109–2; Dale 3–3–0–0. *Second Innings*—Wharf 17–4–42–0; Watkin 16–6–36–0; Croft 57–25–96–5; Thomas 15–2–56–0; Cosker 29–5–85–1; Maher 3–0–10–0; Maynard 1–1–0–0; Dale 3–0–6–1.

Umpires: B. Leadbeater and D. R. Shepherd.

GLAMORGAN v LEICESTERSHIRE

At Cardiff, July 18, 19, 20, 21. Leicestershire won by an innings and 90 runs. Leicestershire 20 pts, Glamorgan 3 pts. Toss: Leicestershire.

Leicestershire secured their fourth Championship win one ball into the final hour. They controlled this game throughout, and victory would have come sooner had weather not disrupted each day bar the second, by when they had amassed the highest total by an opposing team at Cardiff. Sutcliffe, hitting 26 of his 321 balls for four, batted six and three-quarter hours for a maiden double-hundred, putting on 198 with Ward from 41 overs, and 229 with Smith, who completed his third century in four games. Glamorgan batted poorly in response: careless shot selection, and a run-out when Powell declined Maynard's call for a safe fourth run, helped bring about a 377-run deficit. DeFreitas claimed six for 65, his best since rejoining Leicestershire in 2000. Following on, Glamorgan faltered against the speed and hostility of Malcolm, who removed James with his third ball and later became the first to 50 wickets for the summer. Dale and Croft (who supplied an aggressive 89 in the first innings) raised Welsh hopes with a stand of 98; Darren Thomas, dropped on 17, struck boldly, but Malcolm prevailed.

Close of play: First day, Leicestershire 210-1 (Sutcliffe 86*, Smith 7*); Second day, Glamorgan 52-1 (James 24*, Maynard 20*); Third day, Glamorgan 15-2 (Maynard 6*, Powell 5*).

Leicestershire

T. R. Ward c Dale b Watkin	109
I. J. Sutcliffe b Watkin	203
B. F. Smith lbw b Watkin	117
A. Habib not out	72
Shahid Afridi c James b Jones	2
D. L. Maddy c S. D. Thomas b Watkin	6
†N. D. Burns c Powell b Croft	24
*V. J. Wells c Watkin b S. D. Thomas	34
J. M. Dakin st Wallace b Croft	6
P. A. J. DeFreitas c Wallace b Croft	0
D. E. Malcolm b S. D. Thomas	0
B 8, l-b 5, w 2	15
1/198 2/427 3/454 4/463 5/482 6/521 7/580 8/587 9/587	588

Bonus points – Leicestershire 5, Glamorgan 2 (Score at 130 overs: 567-6).

Bowling: Jones 20–1–101–1; Watkin 31–6–126–4; Dale 6–1–18–0; S. D. Thomas 20.5–1–117–2; Croft 36–6–145–3; Cosker 19–2–68–0.

Glamorgan

*S. P. James c Burns b DeFreitas	24	– c Wells b Malcolm	0
I. J. Thomas c Smith b DeFreitas	5	– c Burns b Dakin	2
M. P. Maynard run out	31	– c Burns b Dakin	27
M. J. Powell c Sutcliffe b Malcolm	15	– c Burns b Malcolm	16
R. D. B. Croft c Smith b DeFreitas	89	– (6) c Burns b Malcolm	40
†M. A. Wallace c Burns b Malcolm	2	– (7) c Burns b Malcolm	7
A. Dale lbw b DeFreitas	20	– (5) c Shahid Afridi b Malcolm	89
S. D. Thomas c Sutcliffe b Dakin	4	– c Smith b Dakin	69
D. A. Cosker c Wells b DeFreitas	0	– c Smith b DeFreitas	13
S. L. Watkin c Ward b DeFreitas	7	– not out	0
S. P. Jones not out	6	– c Maddy b DeFreitas	4
B 2, l-b 4, n-b 2	8	B 4, l-b 8, w 6, n-b 2	20
1/8 2/57 3/65 4/106 5/110 6/181 7/192 8/198 9/204	211	1/0 2/6 3/39 4/74 5/172 6/189 7/192 8/281 9/281	287

Bonus points – Glamorgan 1, Leicestershire 3.

Bowling: *First Innings*—Malcolm 16–5–50–2; DeFreitas 23.3–5–65–6; Dakin 13–4–48–1; Afridi 13–3–22–0; Wells 6–2–20–0. *Second Innings*—Malcolm 23–1–98–5; DeFreitas 10.1–3–15–2; Dakin 19–1–83–3; Wells 4–1–14–0; Maddy 5–3–13–0; Shahid Afridi 20–8–52–0.

Umpires: T. E. Jesty and K. E. Palmer.

At Taunton, July 27, 28, 29. GLAMORGAN lost to SOMERSET by an innings and 67 runs.

GLAMORGAN v LANCASHIRE

At Colwyn Bay, August 1, 2, 3, 4. Drawn. Glamorgan 12 pts, Lancashire 11 pts. Toss: Glamorgan.

A downpour eight overs from the close denied this game a tense conclusion: having set Lancashire 298 from 49 overs, Glamorgan ended three wickets from victory. The visitors, after losing their seventh wicket shortly before the rain, 76 adrift, seemed already to have abandoned the chase. The Rhôs-on-Sea pitch, as it had for the past three years, favoured batsmen. Maynard struck 104 in boundaries in his first century of the season, and added 168 with Dale, who reached his third. At lunch on the second day, responding to 479, Lancashire were in trouble at nine for three, but Fairbrother revived their fortunes with a series of partnerships down the order, enabling Crawley to declare once the fifth batting point was gained. Glamorgan lurched to 135 for seven in their second innings, before Newell and Darren Thomas put on 85 and allowed Dale his own declaration. A stand of 118 between Chilton and Flintoff, who bashed 68 from 52 balls – his first Championship fifty of the season – briefly put Lancashire in contention.

Close of play: First day, Glamorgan 386-7 (Dale 92*, Cosker 5*); Second day, Lancashire 259-7 (Fairbrother 110*, Chapple 0*); Third day, Glamorgan 86-5 (Newell 9*, Cosker 1*).

Glamorgan

I. J. Thomas c Driver b Chapple	35	– c Fairbrother b Keedy	17
J. P. Maher st Hegg b Keedy	60	– c Hegg b Chapple	10
M. P. Maynard c Hegg b Martin	145	– lbw b Schofield	35
M. J. Powell c Hegg b Flintoff	5	– lbw b Keedy	3
*A. Dale c Hegg b Keedy	140	– c Hegg b Keedy	0
K. Newell b Chapple	13	– not out	73
†M. A. Wallace c Chilton b Keedy	6	– (8) lbw b Schofield	10
S. D. Thomas b Keedy	0	– (9) not out	44
D. A. Cosker c Hegg b Schofield	35	– (7) lbw b Chapple	8
S. L. Watkin not out	2		
S. P. Jones c Driver b Keedy	3		
B 6, l-b 13, w 2, n-b 14	35	B 1, l-b 9, n-b 10	20
1/84 2/116 3/167 4/335 5/358 6/374 7/374 8/469 9/475	479	1/19 2/41 3/59 4/59 5/85 6/103 7/135 (7 wkts dec.)	220

Bonus points – Glamorgan 5, Lancashire 2 (Score at 130 overs: 468-7).

Bowling: *First Innings*—Martin 26–5–93–1; Chapple 23–7–68–2; Flintoff 17–1–79–1; Keedy 35.2–7–98–5; Schofield 26–6–83–1; Scuderi 5–1–21–0; Driver 2–0–18–0. *Second Innings*—Chapple 13–4–30–2; Scuderi 5–0–15–0; Keedy 29–5–82–3; Flintoff 8–2–28–0; Schofield 16–3–55–2.

Lancashire

R. C. Driver c Powell b Cosker	9	– b Jones	2
M. J. Chilton c Maher b Jones	0	– c Cosker b Dale	83
*J. P. Crawley c Powell b Watkin	0	– b Cosker	10
A. Flintoff c Newell b Cosker	34	– b Jones	68
N. H. Fairbrother c Cosker b Dale	158	– c I. J. Thomas b Dale	23
J. C. Scuderi c Wallace b Jones	34	– c Newell b Dale	11
†W. K. Hegg c and b Cosker	13	– c Newell b Cosker	14
C. P. Schofield c Newell b Watkin	40	– not out	3
G. Chapple c Newell b Cosker	64	– not out	0
P. J. Martin not out	18		
G. Keedy not out	5		
B 16, l-b 3, w 8	27	B 4, l-b 1, w 6	11
1/4 2/5 3/9 4/88 5/144 6/176 7/257 8/361 9/381 (9 wkts dec.)	402	1/3 2/23 3/141 4/178 5/204 6/222 7/222 (7 wkts)	225

Bonus points – Lancashire 5, Glamorgan 3.

Bowling: *First Innings*—Watkin 23–5–74–2; Jones 18.4–3–104–2; Cosker 24–5–100–4; S. D. Thomas 14–0–80–0; Dale 7–2–22–1; Newell 3–0–3–0. *Second Innings*—Watkin 8–2–27–0; Jones 8–2–35–2; Cosker 12–3–72–2; S. D. Thomas 8–0–52–0; Dale 5–0–34–3.

Umpires: M. J. Harris and G. Sharp.

At The Oval, August 8, 9, 10, 11. GLAMORGAN beat SURREY by three wickets.

GLAMORGAN v ESSEX

At Cardiff, August 15, 16, 17, 18. Drawn. Glamorgan 12 pts, Essex 9 pts. Toss: Essex.

A career-best 217 from Maher improved by two Emrys Davies's record score for Glamorgan against Essex, made at Brentwood in 1948. Maher struck 32 fours from 324 balls, batted 385 minutes and with Powell added 284 for the third wicket, steering Glamorgan to a lead of 219 when the declaration came. On the first day, Law – aided by Foster – had rescued Essex from a precarious 55 for four; he seemed on course for a fifth century of the season before he was unluckily dismissed by an unintentional slower ball from Darren Thomas, who clipped the stumps with his hand in his delivery stride. Cowan and Ilott saw Essex to three batting points, while Watkin captured six wickets with a characteristic display of swing and seam. In 19 unthreatening overs on the third evening, Essex reduced the arrears to 155. A final-day washout prevented a positive outcome.

Close of play: First day, Essex 242-7 (Cowan 30*, Ilott 2*); Second day, Glamorgan 188-2 (Maher 102*, Powell 27*); Third day, Essex 64-0 (Robinson 38*, Grayson 21*).

Essex

D. D. J. Robinson c Wallace b Watkin	0	– not out	38
A. P. Grayson b Davies	13	– not out	21
S. D. Peters c Wallace b Watkin	14		
S. G. Law c Cosker b S. D. Thomas	91		
*R. C. Irani c Cosker b S. D. Thomas	9		
†J. S. Foster c Powell b Davies	57		
G. R. Napier c Wallace b Watkin	17		
A. P. Cowan b Watkin	68		
M. C. Ilott c Powell b Watkin	28		
J. E. Bishop c Wallace b Watkin	7		
P. M. Such not out	4		
L-b 7, w 8, n-b 4	19	L-b 5	5
1/0 2/16 3/34 4/55 5/174 6/199 7/224 8/310 9/322	327	(no wkt)	64

Bonus points – Essex 3, Glamorgan 3.

Bowling: *First Innings*—Watkin 26.4–7–67–6; Jones 17–3–66–0; S. D. Thomas 28–8–68–2; Davies 24–6–84–2; Dale 3–1–6–0; Cosker 12–2–29–0. *Second Innings*—Watkin 6–2–12–0; Jones 4–0–19–0; Davies 4–0–16–0; S. D. Thomas 5–2–12–0.

Glamorgan

I. J. Thomas c Law b Ilott	18
J. P. Maher c Grayson b Bishop	217
M. P. Maynard c Foster b Bishop	22
M. J. Powell b Irani	108
*A. Dale c Irani b Cowan	19
S. D. Thomas b Such	68
†M. A. Wallace c Foster b Irani	4
A. P. Davies lbw b Cowan	40
D. A. Cosker not out	8
B 5, l-b 8, w 6, n-b 23	42
1/63 2/94 3/378 4/418 5/418 6/434 7/532 8/546 (8 wkts dec.)	546

S. L. Watkin and S. P. Jones did not bat.

Bonus points – Glamorgan 5, Essex 2 (Score at 130 overs: 489-6).

Bowling: Cowan 31.5–7–112–2; Bishop 25–2–120–2; Ilott 8–0–34–1; Irani 20–2–69–2; Such 29–7–99–1; Napier 12–0–50–0; Grayson 12–2–49–0.

Umpires: J. W. Holder and R. Palmer.

At Scarborough, August 21, 22, 23, 24. GLAMORGAN lost to YORKSHIRE by an innings and 112 runs.

At Leicester, September 7, 8, 9. GLAMORGAN lost to LEICESTERSHIRE by ten wickets.

GLAMORGAN v SURREY

At Cardiff, September 12, 13, 14, 15. Drawn. Glamorgan 7 pts, Surrey 12 pts. Toss: Glamorgan. First-class debut: J. Hughes.

With Glamorgan relegated and Surrey unable to claim prize money, this was the sort of match a two-division Championship was supposed to avoid. Once Surrey had the four points which removed any theoretical danger of their own relegation, they treated the game with little seriousness. They still played better than Glamorgan, however, who by the first-day close had succumbed for 258, Croft supervising a recovery from 150 for seven. Surrey then batted on late into the last day. Against toothless bowling, they passed 700 for the fifth time and beat the record for an opposing team in Cardiff, set by Leicestershire in July. Butcher hit 24 of his 402 balls for four and batted seven and a half hours for his second double-hundred. Lowest score amongst the top five was Ward's 63. Surrey, 314 ahead when play began at one o'clock on the last day, still did not declare, eliciting an angry reaction from Gerard Elias, the Glamorgan chairman: "It was not in the spirit of the game, and extremely disappointing for spectators, not to mention sponsors, who paid a considerable amount of money to be here." Watkin received a rousing send-off on his final Championship appearance, while 20-year-old Jonathan Hughes, on his first, hit a quickfire 49.

Close of play: First day, Glamorgan 258; Second day, Surrey 140-1 (Carberry 44*, Butcher 30*); Third day, Surrey 572-3 (Butcher 215*, Brown 67*).

Glamorgan

*S. P. James c Ward b Bicknell	17		
J. P. Maher lbw b B. C. Hollioake	7		
I. J. Thomas lbw b B. C. Hollioake	0	– (1) not out	6
M. J. Powell c Bicknell b Giddins	56	– (3) not out	0
A. Dale c Stewart b Bicknell	13		
J. Hughes c B. C. Hollioake b Giddins	38	– (2) lbw b B. C. Hollioake	49
R. D. B. Croft not out	70		
†M. A. Wallace c Butcher b Giddins	0		
S. D. Thomas c A. J. Hollioake b Giddins	13		
D. A. Cosker lbw b Saqlain Mushtaq	24		
S. L. Watkin lbw b Salisbury	0		
L-b 4, w 4, n-b 12	20	B 4, l-b 2, w 4, n-b 4	14
1/30 2/30 3/30 4/62 5/143 6/150 7/150 8/170 9/247	258	1/67	(1 wkt) 69

Bonus points – Glamorgan 2, Surrey 3.

Bowling: *First Innings*—Bicknell 14–5–34–2; B. C. Hollioake 12–2–56–2; Butcher 6–1–22–0; Salisbury 17.4–4–44–1; Giddins 16–3–71–4; Saqlain Mushtaq 9–2–27–1. *Second Innings*—Bicknell 5–0–23–0; B. C. Hollioake 5–1–24–1; Giddins 4–0–16–0.

Surrey

I. J. Ward b Watkin	63
M. A. Carberry c Croft b Cosker	84
M. A. Butcher c Wallace b Watkin	230
*A. J. Hollioake lbw b S. D. Thomas	97
A. D. Brown c Wallace b Cosker	115
B. C. Hollioake lbw b Croft	27
M. P. Bicknell b Croft	6
I. D. K. Salisbury not out	23
Saqlain Mushtaq lbw b Cosker	1
E. S. H. Giddins b Cosker	0
B 15, l-b 21, w 6, n-b 8, p 5	55
1/89 2/224 3/423 4/595 5/640 6/652 7/686 8/701 9/701	(9 wkts dec.) 701

†A. J. Stewart did not bat.

Bonus points – Surrey 5, Glamorgan 1 (Score at 130 overs: 482-3).

Bowling: Watkin 32–3–110–2; S. D. Thomas 35–3–146–1; Dale 11–1–54–0; Croft 60–12–176–2; Cosker 48.3–6–159–4; Maher 2–0–13–0; I. J. Thomas 3–1–2–0.

Umpires: B. Dudleston and J. W. Holder.

GLOUCESTERSHIRE

Jeremy Snape

President: G. F. Collis
Chairman: 2001 – J. C. Higson
Chief Executive: T. E. M. Richardson
Chairman, Cricket Committee: A. S. Brown
Captain: M. W. Alleyne
Director of Cricket: J. G. Bracewell
Director of Development: A. W. Stovold
Head Groundsman: 2001 – D. Bridle
2002 – S. Williams
Scorer: K. T. Gerrish

Gloucestershire's Millennium summer, with its clean sweep of the three one-day trophies, was always going to be a hard act to follow. But, with just one final, relegation in the League and failure to win promotion in the Championship, the sense of anticlimax was very real. Problems began to emerge early on. The chief executive, Colin Sexstone, changed sports and departed for Bristol City FC; a slipped disc in February kept Jack Russell out until June; and Mike Smith disappeared with a groin and pelvic injury after the first match and was not seen again until the final two League games. Sexstone had been responsible for seeing through changes at Bristol and, more especially, had raised Gloucestershire's profile off the field.

While Russell had an able deputy behind the stumps in "Reggie" Williams, the zip and driving force he offers were missed by a team believing, perhaps, a little too much of the hype that came with winning five titles in two summers. Mark Alleyne's captaincy was as shrewd and sharp as ever, but he could not always rely on the right response. That super-alertness in the field, so carefully burnished by John Bracewell, was much less evident; after 30 catches had gone down, doors were locked and a long inquest held.

The county sailed through the Benson and Hedges, only to be outplayed by Surrey in the final before a half-full Lord's. Three days earlier, they had been sadly unfocused as Durham claimed a three-run win in the fourth round of the Cheltenham & Gloucester Trophy; in the same fortnight of July they lost matches in both the League and Championship. The Cheltenham Festival, where they had not won in the Championship since 1998, was ahead. This time they recorded some handsome wins, and the sun was shining on their season again, but it all imploded at the end, with unacceptable League results bringing relegation.

Yet more than half the side finished with better first-class figures than the year before. The evergreen Kim Barnett made his 1,000 runs, while Jeremy Snape and Chris Taylor would probably have joined him but for injuries. Bracewell declined to use a long injury list as an excuse, but a disturbing number of the mishaps occurred off the field of play. Tim Hancock, already out of form, broke a hand in fielding practice; Barnett damaged a calf while warming up; Snape, chasing a frisbee, went into plaster after colliding with an advertising hoarding; Taylor missed games after turning an ankle in training; and Mark Hardinges broke a foot in the nets. Has cricket gone too far in the quest for athleticism or was this, for Gloucestershire, simply a painful streak?

The injury that wrecked Smith's testimonial season was arguably the most decisive, because it cost the side his accuracy with the new ball and his left-armer's ability to straighten a delivery to win leg-before verdicts. His loss was compounded when a back injury brought Jon Lewis's season to an abrupt end – after 175 Championship overs and 21 wickets – just as Russell became fit. With the front-line attack gone, extra work was thrust on Ian Harvey and Jamie Averis, who had been developing as a first change. Always robust and forceful, Averis added economy to his action; he bowled 463 overs, which brought him 43 Championship wickets including a career-best return of five for 52 against Middlesex, setting up the first of three consecutive innings wins.

Harvey, who believes the English season is too long, was arguably the best overseas player in the county game, taking 70 wickets in all competitions and blasting the season's fastest first-class hundred – just 61 balls – off Derbyshire at Bristol. Concern that he would be drafted into the Australian Test squad sent Bracewell into the winter looking for a top-order batsman. He found fellow New Zealander Craig Spearman, a former Test player with a Welsh mother and thus an England qualification. A spinner was another priority for 2002, and he signed left-armer Ian Fisher from Yorkshire to link up with the ever-optimistic Martyn Ball, who had never had a Championship season to match 2001: 34 wickets, 21 slip catches and a batting average of 29, rewarded by a passage to India.

Vice-captain Hancock and Rob Cunliffe failed – Cunliffe to the point of asking for his release – while Matt Windows arrived at Cheltenham in uncertain form, especially in his first innings, where he had recorded five ducks and a top score of 11. Helped by the ball coming through quicker off Geoff Swift's excellent College square, Windows got his game back on track with 91 against Hampshire, and after the festival scored successive centuries against Middlesex and Nottinghamshire. Dominic Hewson made maturing progress with two centuries, one given, one earned, and both against Derbyshire, where he moved in the close season. Meanwhile, Williams finally decided to move on, after 12 years standing in for Russell.

The batting successes of the season were Chris Taylor and Jeremy Snape. Taylor, who strikes a clean shot through a wide arc, ended his second year with another three hundreds behind him, while Snape, regarded in the past as a "bit of both" player, made a startling improvement after a winter's work with the coach on his batting. Maiden centuries in both first-class and one-day cricket, and top spot in Gloucestershire's averages, led to an unexpected place in England's one-day squad during the winter. A century at Cheltenham gave him more satisfaction than anything; the previous summer, he couldn't get into the Championship side for the festival and must have wondered whether his move from Northampton had been the right one. A year later, there was no need for doubt. – GRAHAM RUSSELL.

GLOUCESTERSHIRE 2001

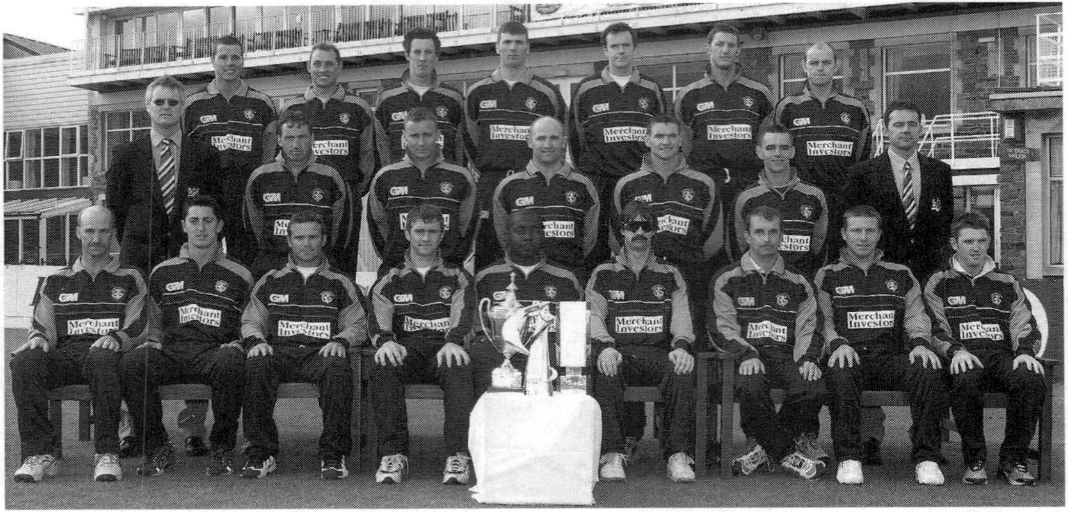

[*Getty Images*

Back row: M. A. Hardinges, J. M. M. Averis, T. P. Cotterell, D. J. Forder, M. J. Cawdron, B. W. Gannon, M. D. R. Sutliff. *Middle row:* J. G. Bracewell (*first-team coach*), R. C. J. Williams, D. R. Hewson, J. N. Snape, R. J. Cunliffe, C. G. Taylor, A. J. Wright (*second-team coach*). *Front row:* K. J. Barnett, J. Lewis, M. G. N. Windows, T. H. C. Hancock, M. W. Alleyne (*captain*), R. C. Russell, A. M. Smith, M. C. J. Ball, I. J. Harvey.

GLOUCESTERSHIRE RESULTS

All first-class matches – Played 16: Won 5, Lost 5, Drawn 6.

County Championship matches – Played 16: Won 5, Lost 5, Drawn 6.

CricInfo County Championship, 4th in Division 2; Cheltenham & Gloucester Trophy, 4th round; Benson and Hedges Cup, finalists; Norwich Union League, 7th in Division 1.

COUNTY CHAMPIONSHIP AVERAGES

BATTING

Cap		*M*	*I*	*NO*	*R*	*HS*	*100s*	*50s*	*Avge*	*Ct/St*
1999	J. N. Snape	14	21	3	868	131	3	5	48.22	10
2001	C. G. Taylor†	12	20	0	930	196	3	4	46.50	6
1999	K. J. Barnett	14	25	2	1,029	114	1	7	44.73	10
1998	J. Lewis	5	8	7	44	15*	0	0	44.00	0
1999	I. J. Harvey§	10	15	2	531	130*	2	1	40.84	8
1985	R. C. Russell†	10	12	2	373	91*	0	2	37.30	42/2
	D. R. Hewson†	14	25	2	816	168	2	4	35.47	6
1998	M. G. N. Windows†	16	27	3	840	174	3	3	35.00	6
1990	M. W. Alleyne	16	26	3	718	136	2	2	31.21	12/1
1996	M. C. J. Ball†	12	16	3	379	68	0	3	29.15	21
1998	T. H. C. Hancock	6	11	0	230	55	0	1	20.90	7
	R. J. Cunliffe	5	8	1	141	48	0	0	20.14	5
1996	R. C. J. Williams†	5	9	0	123	33	0	0	13.66	15/1
	A. N. Bressington†	5	5	2	40	17*	0	0	13.33	2
	M. J. Cawdron	6	9	2	82	29	0	0	11.71	1
	B. W. Gannon	5	6	4	12	10*	0	0	6.00	0
2001	J. M. M. Averis†	15	19	3	35	7*	0	0	2.18	3

Also batted: M. A. Hardinges† (4 matches) 22, 20, 14 (2 ct); R. J. Sillence (1 match) 0, 6; A. M. Smith (cap 1995) (1 match) 4 (1 ct).

* *Signifies not out.* † *Born in Gloucestershire.* § *Overseas player.*

BOWLING

	O	*M*	*R*	*W*	*BB*	*5W/i*	*Avge*
I. J. Harvey	288.4	92	773	41	5-33	2	18.85
J. Lewis	175.4	56	454	21	5-71	1	21.61
M. C. J. Ball	349.3	94	879	34	6-23	2	25.85
M. W. Alleyne	372.4	86	1,076	41	5-50	1	26.24
A. N. Bressington	120.4	31	397	11	3-42	0	36.09
J. M. M. Averis	463.2	100	1,621	43	5-52	1	37.69
M. J. Cawdron	168	50	498	12	4-79	0	41.50

Also bowled: K. J. Barnett 16–4–35–0; B. W. Gannon 97–12–380–8; T. H. C. Hancock 28–5–100–1; M. A. Hardinges 79–15–295–6; D. R. Hewson 3–1–7–0; R. J. Sillence 29.5–5–100–5; A. M. Smith 33–11–70–2; J. N. Snape 153–34–406–8.

COUNTY RECORDS

Highest score for:	318*	W. G. Grace v Yorkshire at Cheltenham	1876
Highest score against:	296	A. O. Jones (Nottinghamshire) at Nottingham	1903
Best bowling for:	10-40	E. G. Dennett v Essex at Bristol	1906
Best bowling against:	10-66	A. A. Mailey (Australians) at Cheltenham	1921
	10-66	K. Smales (Nottinghamshire) at Stroud	1956
Highest total for:	653-6 dec.	v Glamorgan at Bristol	1928
Highest total against:	774-7 dec.	by Australians at Bristol	1948
Lowest total for:	17	v Australians at Cheltenham	1896
Lowest total against:	12	by Northamptonshire at Gloucester	1907

At Chester-le-Street, April 20, 21, 22, 23. GLOUCESTERSHIRE drew with DURHAM.

At Abergavenny, April 25, 26, 27 (not first-class). CARDIFF UCCE v GLOUCESTERSHIRE. Cancelled.

GLOUCESTERSHIRE v MIDDLESEX

At Bristol, May 9, 10, 11, 12. Middlesex won by five wickets. Middlesex 16 pts, Gloucestershire 5 pts. Toss: Gloucestershire.

Middlesex exacted revenge for their double defeat at the hands of Gloucestershire the previous season. Defensive field-setting by Fraser and a lifeless pitch reduced Alleyne's room for manoeuvre as Gloucestershire spent much of the third day and some of the fourth constructing a target. Alleyne eventually plumped for 293 from a minimum of 82 overs, which, as the wicket dried on the last day and Fleming warmed to his task, proved inadequate. Fleming, with a calm, cultured approach that produced a first Championship hundred, paced the run-chase to perfection; Shah and Hutton helped out with elegant fifties. There were contrasting emotions for Gloucestershire's two top-scorers: disappointment for Barnett, who, after five and a half hours patiently waiting for anything outside off stump, was bowled trying to work to leg the run that would have raised three figures; relief for Windows, whose century ended a run of three ducks. Harvey took eight wickets in the match, but the Middlesex batsmen had the last laugh.

Close of play: First day, Gloucestershire 247-7 (Barnett 92*, Cawdron 17*); Second day, Middlesex 186-7 (Nash 19*, Fraser 1*); Third day, Gloucestershire 208-4 (Windows 88*, Alleyne 18*).

Gloucestershire

T. H. C. Hancock c Roseberry b Cook	29	– (2) c Fleming b Bloomfield	14
R. J. Cunliffe c Nash b Cook	24	– (1) c Fleming b Weekes	48
M. G. N. Windows c Fraser b Cook	0	– not out	106
K. J. Barnett b Tufnell	99	– c Weekes b Fraser	18
I. J. Harvey c Nash b Fraser	41	– c Hutton b Fraser	14
*M. W. Alleyne lbw b Bloomfield	0	– not out	49
J. N. Snape c Cook b Bloomfield	2		
†R. C. J. Williams c Nash b Weekes	15		
M. J. Cawdron b Bloomfield	29		
J. M. M. Averis b Fraser	1		
J. Lewis not out	5		
B 7, l-b 8, w 2, n-b 10	27	B 3, l-b 7, w 2, n-b 4	16
1/43 2/43 3/58 4/151 5/158 6/162 7/207 8/262 9/266	272	1/35 2/93 3/135 4/159 (4 wkts dec.)	265

Bonus points – Gloucestershire 2, Middlesex 3.

Bowling: *First Innings*—Bloomfield 33–7–97–3; Fraser 26.2–11–52–2; Cook 19–2–60–3; Tufnell 16–3–38–1; Weekes 6–4–10–1. *Second Innings*—Bloomfield 22–4–76–1; Cook 12–1–36–0; Tufnell 17–5–34–0; Fraser 24–4–75–2; Weekes 15–3–34–1.

Middlesex

A. J. Strauss c Hancock b Lewis	0	– b Harvey	7
M. A. Roseberry c Williams b Lewis	7	– c Barnett b Harvey	10
O. A. Shah lbw b Harvey	5	– c Williams b Alleyne	57
S. P. Fleming c and b Alleyne	52	– not out	121
B. L. Hutton c Williams b Averis	47	– c Averis b Harvey	59
P. N. Weekes b Alleyne	31	– (7) not out	9
†D. C. Nash not out	50		
S. J. Cook c Barnett b Harvey	4	– (6) lbw b Harvey	6
*A. R. C. Fraser c Snape b Harvey	25		
P. C. R. Tufnell c Williams b Lewis	0		
T. F. Bloomfield c Hancock b Harvey	0		
B 5, l-b 7, w 2, n-b 10	24	B 1, l-b 7, w 6, n-b 10	24
1/0 2/5 3/43 4/102 5/143 6/174 7/183 8/231 9/232	245	1/20 2/27 3/122 4/251 5/262	(5 wkts) 293

Bonus points – Middlesex 1, Gloucestershire 3.

Bowling: *First Innings*—Lewis 26–12–50–3; Harvey 31–5–96–4; Averis 15–5–39–1; Cawdron 18–10–28–0; Alleyne 13–6–14–2; Snape 7–4–6–0. *Second Innings*—Lewis 13–2–57–0; Harvey 22–1–83–4; Averis 15.5–2–50–0; Snape 6–0–28–0; Cawdron 9–4–22–0; Alleyne 14–4–45–1.

Umpires: A. A. Jones and N. A. Mallender.

At Southampton, May 16, 17, 18, 19. GLOUCESTERSHIRE drew with HAMPSHIRE.

GLOUCESTERSHIRE v WORCESTERSHIRE

At Bristol, May 25, 26, 27, 28. Worcestershire won by 252 runs. Worcestershire 18 pts, Gloucestershire 3 pts. Toss: Worcestershire.

Towards the end of the second day, Hick was contemplating a dilemma: a lead of 151 gave him the option of the follow-on, but he had to weigh a mixed forecast for the remaining days against doubts over the durability of the pitch. He chose to bat – a decision that raised many an eyebrow, but which ultimately delivered Worcestershire's first Championship win of the summer. Facing a target of 408, Gloucestershire caved in to the lift and movement of Bichel, who ended with a career-best six for 44. Top-scorer for Gloucestershire, as when they first batted, was Snape, who was alone in showing sufficient technique to survive. Worcestershire's healthy first-innings total was built around contrasting half-centuries: a patient, five-hour 83 from Weston, his best for two years, and an attractive 76 from Bichel, graced with 12 fours and a six. Lewis removed both on his way to five for 71. Lampitt then outdid him with five for 22, to give Hick his quandary.

Close of play: First day, Worcestershire 298-6 (Bichel 71*, Rhodes 10*); Second day, Worcestershire 21-2 (Weston 13*, Rawnsley 6*); Third day, Gloucestershire 35-3 (Barnett 13*, Taylor 1*).

Worcestershire

W. P. C. Weston c Barnett b Lewis	83	– c Williams b Lewis	58
A. Singh c Snape b Averis	15	– c Taylor b Lewis	0
*G. A. Hick c Williams b Averis	4	– lbw b Averis	2
V. S. Solanki c Williams b Lewis	30	– (5) c Williams b Cawdron	4
D. A. Leatherdale c Williams b Cawdron	45	– (6) c Hancock b Snape	41
Kadeer Ali lbw b Alleyne	4	– (7) c Williams b Lewis	1
A. J. Bichel c Alleyne b Lewis	76	– (8) c Barnett b Snape	37
†S. J. Rhodes b Lewis	21	– (9) not out	32
S. R. Lampitt b Lewis	0	– (10) not out	24
M. J. Rawnsley b Averis	8	– (4) b Alleyne	32
A. Sheriyar not out	0		
B 8, l-b 12, w 6, n-b 14	40	B 8, l-b 7, w 4, n-b 6	25
1/34 2/38 3/93 4/196 5/209 6/252 7/303 8/309 9/326	326	1/5 2/14 3/70 4/85 5/147 6/153 7/155 8/213 (8 wkts dec.)	256

Bonus points – Worcestershire 3, Gloucestershire 3.

Bowling: *First Innings*—Lewis 28.2–6–71–5; Averis 29–5–98–3; Alleyne 22–7–54–1; Cawdron 24–11–39–1; Snape 9–2–24–0; Hancock 7–1–20–0. *Second Innings*—Lewis 25–8–60–3; Averis 18–9–31–1; Cawdron 14–2–56–1; Alleyne 13–2–42–1; Snape 16–3–52–2.

Gloucestershire

T. H. C. Hancock lbw b Sheriyar	6	– (2) lbw b Bichel	9
D. R. Hewson c Rhodes b Sheriyar	35	– (1) c Bichel b Sheriyar	6
M. G. N. Windows b Lampitt	4	– c Rhodes b Bichel	4
K. J. Barnett c Solanki b Lampitt	6	– c Rhodes b Bichel	19
C. G. Taylor c Lampitt b Sheriyar	15	– c Rhodes b Sheriyar	1
*M. W. Alleyne c Rawnsley b Lampitt	1	– c Rhodes b Sheriyar	23
J. N. Snape b Lampitt	69	– c Weston b Bichel	42
†R. C. J. Williams c sub b Bichel	10	– c Hick b Bichel	28
M. J. Cawdron b Rawnsley	4	– not out	7
J. M. M. Averis lbw b Lampitt	1	– c Lampitt b Rawnsley	7
J. Lewis not out	9	– c Solanki b Bichel	2
L-b 9, n-b 6	15	B 1, w 2, n-b 4	7
1/11 2/48 3/56 4/64 5/67 6/103 7/116 8/165 9/166	175	1/7 2/18 3/23 4/38 5/52 6/76 7/127 8/146 9/153	155

Bonus points – Worcestershire 3.

Bowling: *First Innings*—Bichel 21–7–72–1; Sheriyar 21–7–46–3; Lampitt 12.5–4–22–5; Rawnsley 14–6–26–1; Hick 2–2–0–0. *Second Innings*—Bichel 21–6–44–6; Sheriyar 18–7–42–3; Lampitt 11–3–37–0; Rawnsley 11–2–25–1; Leatherdale 2–0–6–0.

Umpires: M. R. Benson and D. J. Constant.

At Birmingham, May 31, June 1, 2, 3. GLOUCESTERSHIRE lost to WARWICKSHIRE by ten wickets.

At Nottingham, June 6, 7, 8, 9. GLOUCESTERSHIRE beat NOTTINGHAMSHIRE by 187 runs.

GLOUCESTERSHIRE v DURHAM

At Gloucester, June 13, 14, 15, 16. Drawn. Gloucestershire 12 pts, Durham 9 pts. Toss: Gloucestershire.

The future of county cricket at Archdeacon Meadow, where short square boundaries counterbalance bowler-friendly wickets, is a matter for annual speculation. Having seen three Gloucestershire wickets fall to Brown in nine overs, Alleyne might have shared the doubts. Instead, he settled into his first county century for 13 months, scoring 88 of his 132 in boundaries before gloving Phillips's off-spin to slip. Durham, on their first visit to the ground, relied heavily on a productive second-wicket stand: Love, taking his third Championship fifty off Gloucestershire – he took a fourth two days later – added 124 with the vigilant Gough, who laboured three and three-quarter hours for 79. Rain, which had already curtailed the second and third days, washed away hopes of an interesting finish on the last. By the time play finally restarted at 3.30, Durham had only 40 overs in which to score 290. They could, however, take heart from Brown's first-innings performance – six for 70 in only his second Championship game of the summer.

Close of play: First day, Gloucestershire 359-7 (Russell 38*, Ball 16*); Second day, Durham 211-4 (Gough 73*, Law 11*); Third day, Gloucestershire 159-4 (Windows 60*, Snape 0*).

Gloucestershire

D. R. Hewson c Law b Brown	8	– c Gough b Hunter	29
K. J. Barnett c Phillips b Brown	14	– b Brown	15
M. G. N. Windows c Peng b Brown	0	– not out	60
C. G. Taylor lbw b Phillips	54	– c Brown b Law	13
*M. W. Alleyne c Love b Phillips	132	– c Peng b Phillips	30
J. N. Snape st Pratt b Phillips	53	– not out	0
†R. C. Russell lbw b Brown	48		
M. A. Hardinges b Harmison	20		
M. C. J. Ball not out	60		
M. J. Cawdron c Hunter b Brown	0		
J. M. M. Averis b Brown	0		
B 3, l-b 17, w 4, n-b 4	28	L-b 6, w 4, n-b 2	12
1/11 2/25 3/28 4/182 5/264 6/283 7/314 8/409 9/417	417	1/28 2/54 3/85 4/156 (4 wkts dec.)	159

Bonus points – Gloucestershire 5, Durham 3.

Bowling: *First Innings*—Harmison 25–6–78–1; Brown 22.4–5–70–6; Hunter 21–3–68–0; Law 14–1–56–0; Phillips 26–5–104–3; Gough 9–3–21–0. *Second Innings*—Harmison 10–3–25–0; Brown 14–4–41–1; Hunter 4–2–17–1; Law 7–1–18–1; Phillips 13–1–52–1.

Durham

*J. J. B. Lewis c Russell b Averis	11	– c Ball b Cawdron	14
M. A. Gough c Russell b Ball	79	– c Russell b Averis	10
M. L. Love c Russell b Alleyne	70	– not out	52
M. P. Speight c Hewson b Ball	1	– not out	26
N. Peng run out	21		
D. R. Law c Snape b Ball	24		
†A. Pratt c Alleyne b Averis	6		
I. D. Hunter c Taylor b Ball	24		
N. C. Phillips c Russell b Averis	3		
S. J. E. Brown not out	11		
S. J. Harmison c Russell b Averis	2		
L-b 12, w 4, n-b 19	35	L-b 2, n-b 12	14
1/36 2/160 3/161 4/199 5/227 6/240 7/254 8/264 9/276	287	1/19 2/48 (2 wkts)	116

Bonus points – Durham 2, Gloucestershire 3.

Bowling: *First Innings*—Averis 24.2–6–75–4; Cawdron 9–1–47–0; Hardinges 9–1–32–0; Alleyne 9–2–41–1; Ball 33–8–80–4. *Second Innings*—Averis 8–1–25–1; Ball 10–2–33–0; Cawdron 5–0–17–1; Snape 5–2–10–0; Hardinges 4–0–23–0; Barnett 2–1–6–0.

Umpires: J. H. Hampshire and B. Leadbeater.

At Derby, June 20, 21, 22, 23. GLOUCESTERSHIRE drew with DERBYSHIRE.

GLOUCESTERSHIRE v WARWICKSHIRE

At Bristol, July 4, 5, 6, 7. Drawn. Gloucestershire 7 pts, Warwickshire 8 pts. Toss: Gloucestershire.

After rain had prevented a start until 2.30, Gloucestershire skidded to 38 for five in humid conditions. Snape stabilised the innings with a half-century to get them through to the close, but the end came quickly next morning. Then it was Warwickshire's turn to struggle on a slow pitch, and their lead owed everything to Wagh: having dropped down the order because of an upset stomach, he battled for three and three-quarter hours before becoming Alleyne's fifth victim. Towards the end of a rain-affected third day, Gloucestershire were 41 ahead with five wickets down. Snape again came to the rescue, this time adding 136 with Russell for the sixth wicket. The battling Russell eventually ran out of partners, but by then Warwickshire had only 42 overs to score 239. Even so, spurred on by Knight and Wagh, they were almost halfway there when a thunderstorm intervened.

Close of play: First day, Gloucestershire 135-8 (Snape 53*); Second day, Warwickshire 204; Third day, Gloucestershire 157-5 (Snape 42*, Russell 15*).

Gloucestershire

D. R. Hewson c Piper b Richardson	26	– lbw b Richardson	11
K. J. Barnett c Hemp b Betts	0	– c Ostler b Brown	21
M. G. N. Windows c Ostler b Betts	0	– c Ostler b Smith	14
C. G. Taylor c Piper b Drakes	2	– c Piper b Richardson	33
*M. W. Alleyne c Piper b Brown	9	– c Wagh b Brown	10
J. N. Snape c Ostler b Richardson	61	– c and b Smith	89
†R. C. Russell b Richardson	12	– not out	91
M. C. J. Ball c Knight b Betts	13	– c Powell b Smith	0
M. J. Cawdron b Drakes	10	– c Brown b Drakes	4
J. M. M. Averis c Powell b Drakes	2	– c Knight b Betts	1
B. W. Gannon not out	0	– b Wagh	1
B 4, l-b 6	10	B 5, l-b 15, w 2	22
1/0 2/4 3/7 4/38 5/38 6/57 7/86 8/135 9/139	145	1/33 2/48 3/78 4/99 5/100 6/236 7/240 8/261 9/270	297

Bonus points – Warwickshire 3.

Bowling: *First Innings*—Drakes 19–8–38–3; Betts 11–5–28–3; Richardson 19.3–4–40–3; Brown 16–6–29–1. *Second Innings*—Drakes 31–8–97–1; Betts 10–3–21–1; Richardson 21–8–40–2; Brown 23–10–31–2; Smith 24–7–57–3; Wagh 11.4–2–31–1.

Warwickshire

*M. J. Powell c Russell b Averis	9	– c Snape b Gannon	16
N. V. Knight b Cawdron	13	– not out	47
†K. J. Piper c Ball b Averis	3		
D. L. Hemp lbw b Alleyne	24	– not out	5
D. P. Ostler c Hewson b Averis	3		
M. A. Wagh b Alleyne	89	– (3) c Alleyne b Ball	37
D. R. Brown c Barnett b Averis	6		
N. M. K. Smith b Alleyne	17		
V. C. Drakes b Alleyne	17		
M. M. Betts c Ball b Alleyne	1		
A. Richardson not out	2		
L-b 4, w 6, n-b 10	20	L-b 8	8
1/16 2/22 3/45 4/51 5/59 6/89 7/140 8/191 9/193	204	1/29 2/103	(2 wkts) 113

Bonus points – Warwickshire 1, Gloucestershire 3.

Bowling: *First Innings*—Averis 18–2–49–4; Gannon 13–2–45–0; Cawdron 20–6–45–1; Alleyne 20.1–5–50–5; Ball 5–2–11–0. *Second Innings*—Averis 8.5–1–42–0; Gannon 5–0–26–1; Cawdron 4–0–19–0; Ball 4–0–18–1.

Umpires: G. I. Burgess and M. J. Kitchen.

At Worcester, July 20, 21, 22, 23. GLOUCESTERSHIRE lost to WORCESTERSHIRE by seven wickets.

GLOUCESTERSHIRE v SUSSEX

At Cheltenham, July 27, 28, 29, 30. Gloucestershire won by ten wickets. Gloucestershire 20 pts, Sussex 2 pts. Toss: Sussex.

Adams, perhaps unaware that the team batting first on the College Ground had passed 500 three times in four matches, chose to bowl on another shirtfront. The high humidity brought early swing for the Sussex bowlers, but two dropped catches in the first session, and the loss of wicket-keeper Prior with an injured thumb, hardly helped rectify the misjudgment. After Barnett went for a fluent 79 – caught by Adams, who had taken the gloves – centuries from Snape and Chris Taylor swept Gloucestershire towards 500. Early on the third morning, after a supine batting performance, Sussex faced a deficit of 353. At last they knuckled down, Montgomerie reaching his sixth hundred of the summer before a sharp return catch to Ball ended his stand of 126 with Adams, who compiled a stylish and determined century that included 19 fours and three sixes. After tea, Harvey captured three wickets for four, ending next day with five for 33 – eight for 46 in the match – before Gloucestershire won their first Championship game at Cheltenham for three years.

Close of play: First day, Gloucestershire 415-5 (Snape 100*, Harvey 11*); Second day, Sussex 161-8 (Kirtley 3*, Taylor 0*); Third day, Sussex 315-6 (Adams 122*, Davis 32*).

Gloucestershire

D. R. Hewson b Kirtley	10	– not out	1
K. J. Barnett c Adams b Robinson	79	– not out	21
M. G. N. Windows c Prior b Adams	22		
C. G. Taylor c and b Davis	140		
*M. W. Alleyne c Zuiderent b Robinson	1		
J. N. Snape b Taylor	131		
I. J. Harvey c Adams b Taylor	11		
†R. C. Russell lbw b Adams	32		
M. C. J. Ball c Montgomerie b Adams	32		
J. M. M. Averis c Yardy b Kirtley	0		
B. W. Gannon not out	1		
B 16, l-b 13, w 6, n-b 26	61	L-b 1	1
1/16 2/79 3/175 4/193 5/397 6/415 7/456 8/509 9/510	520		(no wkt) 23

Bonus points – Gloucestershire 5, Sussex 2 (Score at 130 overs: 509-8).

Bowling: *First Innings*—Kirtley 34–8–127–2; Taylor 27–9–74–2; Robinson 24–9–91–2; Adams 10–1–31–3; Davis 24–6–90–1; Rashid 19–5–78–0. *Second Innings*—Kirtley 2–0–7–0; Taylor 1.3–0–15–0.

Sussex

R. R. Montgomerie c Barnett b Averis	33	– (2) c and b Ball	107
M. W. Goodwin c Russell b Alleyne	39	– (1) lbw b Alleyne	12
M. H. Yardy c Harvey b Ball	21	– (5) c Alleyne b Harvey	0
B. Zuiderent lbw b Harvey	11	– c Alleyne b Harvey	11
*C. J. Adams c Hewson b Ball	12	– (3) c Russell b Ball	123
U. B. A. Rashid run out	9	– c Russell b Averis	0
†M. J. Prior c Russell b Gannon	7	– c Snape b Harvey	1
M. J. G. Davis c Ball b Harvey	12	– c Russell b Averis	48
R. J. Kirtley c Snape b Harvey	8	– c Russell b Harvey	13
B. V. Taylor c Harvey b Ball	0	– not out	24
M. A. Robinson not out	0	– lbw b Harvey	0
L-b 5, w 2, n-b 8	15	B 8, l-b 4, w 6, n-b 18	36
1/52 2/86 3/112 4/112 5/135 6/138 7/151 8/160 9/167	167	1/49 2/175 3/214 4/214 5/241 6/244 7/319 8/333 9/375	375

Bonus points – Gloucestershire 3.

Bowling: *First Innings*—Averis 16–4–53–1; Gannon 11–1–46–1; Harvey 18.5–13–13–3; Alleyne 6–1–9–1; Ball 24–10–41–3. *Second Innings*—Averis 19–2–114–2; Gannon 10–1–61–0; Alleyne 22–5–59–1; Harvey 23–11–33–5; Snape 11–4–26–0; Ball 27–7–70–2.

Umpires: R. Palmer and P. Willey.

GLOUCESTERSHIRE v HAMPSHIRE

At Cheltenham, August 1, 2, 3, 4. Drawn. Gloucestershire 10 pts, Hampshire 8 pts. Toss: Gloucestershire.

Hampshire struggled to find 11 fit players for the start: Robin Smith dropped out late with sore ribs while Tremlett rushed off in search of emergency dental treatment. Kendall assumed the captaincy, but took the field with two substitutes – Stephen Cook, son of Hampshire coach Jimmy, and Mascarenhas, who had been sidelined with a hamstring injury. Laney eventually arrived from the Second Eleven game at Bristol for his first Championship game of the season. Windows was already cutting and driving with mounting confidence, and he added 137 for the third wicket with

Taylor. Udal captured four wickets on the first afternoon as the dry pitch took spin, though once the second day was lost to the rain, seam held sway. Johnson drove forcefully and Laney made the most of his chance, but Hampshire were bowled out in two sessions, young seamers Gannon and Bressington taking three each. Barnett helped set 350 from 65 overs; Hampshire were not interested, and the weather closed in at three o'clock.

Close of play: First day, Gloucestershire 334; Second day, No play; Third day, Gloucestershire 104-1 (Barnett 70*, Windows 16*).

Gloucestershire

D. R. Hewson c Aymes b Johnson	5	– c Laney b Tremlett	17
K. J. Barnett c Aymes b Johnson	41	– c Laney b Udal	93
M. G. N. Windows c Morris b Udal	91	– c Aymes b Mullally	21
C. G. Taylor c Kendall b Morris	56	– c Laney b Johnson	37
*M. W. Alleyne c White b Udal	12	– (6) not out	22
J. N. Snape c White b Udal	21	– (7) c Kendall b Udal	5
I. J. Harvey c Aymes b Johnson	11	– (5) c Laney b Udal	9
†R. C. Russell c Aymes b Udal	2	– not out	28
M. C. J. Ball c Johnson b Tremlett	40		
A. N. Bressington not out	17		
B. W. Gannon c Laney b Tremlett	0		
B 5, l-b 5, w 14, n-b 14	38	B 2, l-b 7, n-b 4	13
1/22 2/73 3/210 4/233 5/233 6/250 7/267 8/272 9/334	334	1/64 2/113 3/177 4/187 5/189 6/196 (6 wkts dec.)	245

Bonus points – Gloucestershire 3, Hampshire 3.

Bowling: *First Innings*—Mullally 14–5–43–0; Morris 20–1–82–1; Johnson 20–6–55–3; Tremlett 16.3–5–68–2; Udal 32–9–76–4. *Second Innings*—Mullally 14–4–26–1; Morris 13–2–52–0; Johnson 10.5–1–58–1; Udal 25–4–85–3; Tremlett 2–0–15–1.

Hampshire

D. A. Kenway c Russell b Bressington	20	– c Bressington b Harvey	17
G. W. White c Russell b Bressington	14	– not out	12
*W. S. Kendall b Gannon	19	– not out	11
L. R. Prittipaul lbw b Gannon	9		
N. C. Johnson c Taylor b Alleyne	72		
J. S. Laney not out	52		
†A. N. Aymes lbw b Alleyne	0		
S. D. Udal c Russell b Gannon	5		
A. C. Morris b Harvey	6		
C. T. Tremlett c Ball b Bressington	13		
A. D. Mullally c Taylor b Harvey	8		
B 4, l-b 8	12		
1/33 2/34 3/58 4/93 5/161 6/161 7/172 8/192 9/215	230	1/22 (1 wkt)	40

Bonus points – Hampshire 1, Gloucestershire 3.

Bowling: *First Innings*—Harvey 16–4–48–2; Bressington 14–4–56–3; Gannon 11–0–47–3; Ball 3–0–27–0; Alleyne 12–1–40–2. *Second Innings*—Harvey 6–1–19–1; Bressington 7–4–13–0; Ball 5–2–6–0; Gannon 4–3–2–0.

Umpires: M. R. Benson and R. Julian.

At Lord's, August 8, 9, 10, 11. GLOUCESTERSHIRE beat MIDDLESEX by an innings and 59 runs.

GLOUCESTERSHIRE v NOTTINGHAMSHIRE

At Bristol, August 15, 16, 17, 18. Gloucestershire won by an innings and 120 runs. Gloucestershire 20 pts, Nottinghamshire 4 pts. Toss: Gloucestershire.

Persistent drizzle on the final day threatened to come between Gloucestershire and the wicket that gave them the double over Nottinghamshire. A brief let-up in early afternoon allowed 21 balls but brought no breakthrough, and they had to wait until 5 p.m. for the weather to relent again. Averis finally finished matters when Randall fended a rising ball to short leg. Victory would have been far more comfortable but for Johnson's excellent hundred on a humid first day. Emerging from indifferent form, he batted for four hours, struck 96 in boundaries and was last out. His efforts, though, were eclipsed by three Gloucestershire centuries as they ploughed on to an unassailable total. The highlight was Windows and Taylor's stand of 306 – 30 short of the county record for the third wicket. Snape weighed in with a hundred off 96 balls, his second fifty coming from 34. Nottinghamshire clung on through the extra half-hour, but the last day's rain failed to reprieve them.

Close of play: First day, Gloucestershire 4-0 (Cunliffe 1*, Hewson 3*); Second day, Gloucestershire 305-2 (Windows 130*, Taylor 113*); Third day, Nottinghamshire 139-9 (Randall 16*, Malik 1*).

Nottinghamshire

*D. J. Bicknell c Russell b Alleyne	50	– c Russell b Bressington	0
G. E. Welton lbw b Averis	61	– b Alleyne	30
G. S. Blewett c Russell b Averis	0	– c Ball b Averis	0
P. Johnson c Cunliffe b Ball	149	– lbw b Averis	0
J. E. Morris c Taylor b Harvey	2	– (6) b Alleyne	54
K. P. Pietersen c Russell b Alleyne	1	– (5) c Russell b Bressington	13
†C. M. W. Read lbw b Alleyne	7	– c Russell b Ball	14
R. J. Logan lbw b Harvey	13	– c Snape b Alleyne	4
S. J. Randall b Harvey	5	– c Hewson b Averis	28
G. J. Smith c Windows b Averis	17	– run out	0
M. N. Malik not out	0	– not out	6
B 1, w 10, n-b 6	17	L-b 1, n-b 16	17
1/117 2/117 3/122 4/147 5/162 6/178 7/241 8/263 9/308	322	1/5 2/6 3/10 4/35 5/52 6/94 7/113 8/124 9/125	166

Bonus points – Nottinghamshire 3, Gloucestershire 3.

Bowling: *First Innings*—Averis 18–3–86–3; Bressington 20–6–51–0; Harvey 22–4–72–3; Alleyne 25–4–83–3; Ball 11.4–2–29–1. *Second Innings*—Averis 14.3–2–51–3; Bressington 11–0–38–2; Alleyne 17–4–45–3; Ball 12–1–31–1.

Gloucestershire

R. J. Cunliffe b Smith	28
D. R. Hewson c Pietersen b Logan	16
M. G. N. Windows c Blewett b Malik	174
C. G. Taylor b Randall	148
*M. W. Alleyne c Read b Smith	72
J. N. Snape not out	100
†R. C. Russell lbw b Randall	16
M. C. J. Ball c Morris b Logan	12
A. N. Bressington b Logan	4
I. J. Harvey not out	6
B 2, l-b 20, n-b 10	32
1/30 2/70 3/376 4/429 5/502 6/533 7/580 8/595 (8 wkts dec.)	608

J. M. M. Averis did not bat.

Bonus points – Gloucestershire 5, Nottinghamshire 1 (Score at 130 overs: 507-5).

Bowling: Smith 27–4–96–2; Malik 25–6–113–1; Logan 37–4–155–3; Randall 41–4–147–2; Pietersen 15–0–75–0; Johnson 1–1–0–0.

Umpires: D. J. Constant and A. A. Jones.

GLOUCESTERSHIRE v DERBYSHIRE

At Bristol, September 5, 6, 7. Gloucestershire won by an innings and 20 runs. Gloucestershire 20 pts, Derbyshire 4 pts. Toss: Gloucestershire. First-class debuts: R. M. Khan, S. A. Selwood.

Harvey's stunning century – the fastest of the season – swept aside Derbyshire's weak attack and diverted attention from a career-best 168 by Hewson who, driving freely on the off, produced the mature innings he had long promised. Dropped in the slips on nought, he hit 29 boundaries, dominating the first day until Harvey arrived in mid-afternoon. Harvey belted six sixes and a dozen fours, and acknowledged his hundred after 61 balls. Of the 115 runs scored while he was batting, he made 104; Barnett's contribution to a stand of 95 was three. As their openers put on 121, Derbyshire seemed unfazed; but then they collapsed to Ball's off-spin and followed on 298 behind. Stubbings, adding a fine hundred to his first-innings fifty, and, like Di Venuto, reaching 1,000 runs, rallied Derbyshire before Harvey again stole the show. First, his pace claimed five victims, including Dumelow, who had dared hook him for four sixes. Then, he held the catch that gave Gloucestershire their fourth win in five matches: 90 points from those games had lifted them five places to third.

Close of play: First day, Gloucestershire 418-5 (Alleyne 13*, Cunliffe 3*); Second day, Derbyshire 33-2 (Stubbings 13*, Khan 2*).

Gloucestershire

D. R. Hewson lbw b Wharton	168
T. H. C. Hancock c Krikken b Dean	49
M. G. N. Windows c Selwood b Lungley	30
K. J. Barnett b Dumelow	34
I. J. Harvey b Welch	104
*M. W. Alleyne b Welch	16
R. J. Cunliffe b Dean	3
†R. C. Russell c Welch b Dumelow	24
M. C. J. Ball b Dumelow	59
A. N. Bressington not out	2
J. M. M. Averis b Dean	0
B 1, l-b 4, w 2, n-b 12	19
1/120 2/207 3/290 4/385 5/405 6/419 7/421 8/506 9/507	508

Bonus points – Gloucestershire 5, Derbyshire 3.

Bowling: Welch 30–8–144–2; Dean 38–12–113–3; Dowman 7–3–20–0; Lungley 19–0–110–1; Wharton 24–4–87–1; Dumelow 12–4–29–3.

Derbyshire

S. D. Stubbings c Harvey b Ball	62	– c Hancock b Ball	120
*M. J. Di Venuto c Russell b Harvey	61	– lbw b Harvey	4
R. M. Khan c Cunliffe b Bressington	13	– (4) run out	5
M. P. Dowman lbw b Ball	3	– (5) c Russell b Ball	35
S. A. Selwood c Alleyne b Ball	18	– (6) c Russell b Harvey	15
N. R. C. Dumelow c Hancock b Bressington	0	– (7) c Ball b Harvey	48
†K. M. Krikken lbw b Ball	13	– (8) c Russell b Harvey	5
G. Welch c Hewson b Ball	18	– (3) c Barnett b Averis	5
T. Lungley not out	5	– not out	7
K. J. Dean c Harvey b Ball	0	– c Bressington b Harvey	15
L. J. Wharton c Russell b Bressington	2	– c Harvey b Ball	0
L-b 2, n-b 13	15	L-b 11, n-b 8	19
1/121 2/144 3/148 4/148 5/148 6/179 7/202 8/203 9/203	210	1/15 2/30 3/62 4/158 5/185 6/217 7/231 8/258 9/274	278

Bonus points – Derbyshire 1, Gloucestershire 3.

Bowling: *First Innings*—Averis 12–0–72–0; Bressington 11.4–4–42–3; Alleyne 14–4–24–0; Harvey 6–0–47–1; Ball 18–9–23–6. *Second Innings*—Harvey 28–5–89–5; Averis 13–1–57–1; Ball 33.1–10–67–3; Bressington 5–0–23–0; Alleyne 8–1–31–0.

Umpires: N. A. Mallender and A. G. T. Whitehead.

At Hove, September 12, 13, 14. GLOUCESTERSHIRE lost to SUSSEX by ten wickets.

Alex Morris

HAMPSHIRE

President: 2001 – W. J. Weld
2002 – A. C. D. Ingleby-Mackenzie
Chairman: R. G. Bransgrove
Chief Executive: 2001 – A. F. Baker
2002 – G. M. Walker
Chairman, Cricket Committee:
2001 – D. J. Robinson
Captain: R. A. Smith
First-Team Coach: S. J. Cook
Director of Cricket: T. M. Tremlett
Head Groundsman: N. Gray
Scorer: V. H Isaacs

Hampshire moved into their spacious new headquarters at the Rose Bowl to high expectations, but only after an acrimonious and difficult winter during which the club's survival came under threat more than once. The projected cost of the stadium, built on farmland at West End, rose beyond the budgeted £17 million to nearer £25 million, and the prospect of bankruptcy was staved off only by the timely intervention of Rod Bransgrove, a multi-millionaire entrepreneur. Bransgrove was elected chairman without opposition in March, after he had volunteered vital financial support, and his control was completed at an EGM two months later, when members voted to turn the club into a private limited company. Bransgrove himself underwrote the first £4 million of a share issue.

It was against this turbulent background that first-class cricket was staged for the first time in the still-uncompleted stadium, in front of woodland and fields and surrounded by a collection of Portakabins and temporary marquees. After nine months of uncompromising rain, groundsman Nigel Gray had performed miracles in fashioning a cricket square from mud, puddles and high grass, and delivered on time. His new pitches were a source of concern at times, with some lateral movement, swing and uneven bounce; four Championship matches failed to go beyond three days. Life could be hard for opening batsmen, but Hampshire were never docked points, and official criticism was levelled not at the pitches but those who batted on them. In December, the ECB announced that the Rose Bowl would stage one-day international cricket from 2004.

More modern facilities than those left behind at Northlands Road, combined with curiosity, meant spectator interest was higher than in recent years. Membership remained around 4,800 in spite of the replacement of Shane Warne as overseas player by the lower-profile Neil Johnson. But some members from Basingstoke and Portsmouth, both of which lost county cricket in the club's reorganisation, did not renew.

Although Johnson, the former Zimbabwean Test player, had been signed principally as a bowler, it was for his aggressive batting and sharp slip fielding that he will be best remembered in a season of contrasts for Hampshire. Early elimination from the cup competitions was countered by their successful campaign in Division Two of the Championship – they lost only two of their 16 fixtures, to finish second – and a narrow failure to match that with promotion in the Norwich Union League. Having been relegated in the Championship the previous year, Hampshire made new-home advantage count by winning five games and losing none at the Rose Bowl, where visiting teams often struggled to cope with alien conditions. Only some poor League results late in the season, notably at home to Lancashire and Middlesex, prevented a promotion double.

Hampshire's unreliable upper-order batting threatened at times to undermine their season and, particularly in the Championship, wicket-keeper Adrian Aymes, Shaun Udal and Alex Morris were obliged more than once to rectify the failures of those who had gone before. Hampshire moved to strengthen their batting by signing Nic Pothas, a 28-year-old wicket-keeper/batsman from Gauteng who had played three one-day internationals for South Africa. Under EU regulations, he qualified for county cricket by virtue of a Greek passport. While Derek Kenway maintained his promise, and gained a place at the ECB Academy, Giles White, Will Kendall and Robin Smith all struggled for consistency. Only Johnson reached 1,000 first-class runs. After two years without a hundred, Smith managed three, yet he still finished the season with less than 600 runs and an average of 24.91.

It was easier to praise the bowling. Alan Mullally's ability to swing and move the ball both ways was ideally suited to conditions at the Rose Bowl, and he earned his fleeting recall to the England team; his 64 first-class wickets at 18.50 made him the highest-placed front-line England-qualified bowler. Alex Morris and Udal also took 50 first-class wickets. Morris overcame his shin splint problems of recent years to win respect around the county circuit, while Udal's success owed something to Warne's advice the previous summer, about spinning upwards, and to his own maturity. He bowled better in 2001 than when selected for England in the mid-1990s. Dimitri Mascarenhas produced match-winning performances with his medium-pace against Derbyshire and Middlesex at the Rose Bowl, as well as rescuing his side on the first Championship day there with 104 against Worcestershire. Behind them was the 6ft 7in figure of Chris Tremlett who, 19 for most of the season, was at the forefront of a bright Hampshire future. His ability to get bounce and pace from unhelpful surfaces also resulted in a winter trip to Australia with the Academy.

Meanwhile, an array of young talent, under the guidance of the experienced John Stephenson, was winning the Second Eleven Championship. Some of these younger prospects, Iain Brunnschweiler, James Schofield and Lawrence Prittipaul, shared in the club's finest hour of the season, a two-wicket win over the Australians. They played in front of capacity 6,500 crowds on the first two days and a smaller but tense one on the last, which saw Brunnschweiler score the winning runs. Schofield had taken a wicket with his first ball in first-class cricket; at Worcester a month later, he began his League career in the same way.

Another large gathering witnessed Hampshire's first floodlit match, although the game itself, against Sussex, failed to live up to the occasion. But at the end of the season there was talk again of troubled finances. Stephenson, Zac Morris, Andrew Sexton and Simon Francis were released, while Tony Baker, whose contribution to the club's development over 15 years had not always been recognised or appreciated, stepped down as chief executive. – PAT SYMES.

HAMPSHIRE 2001

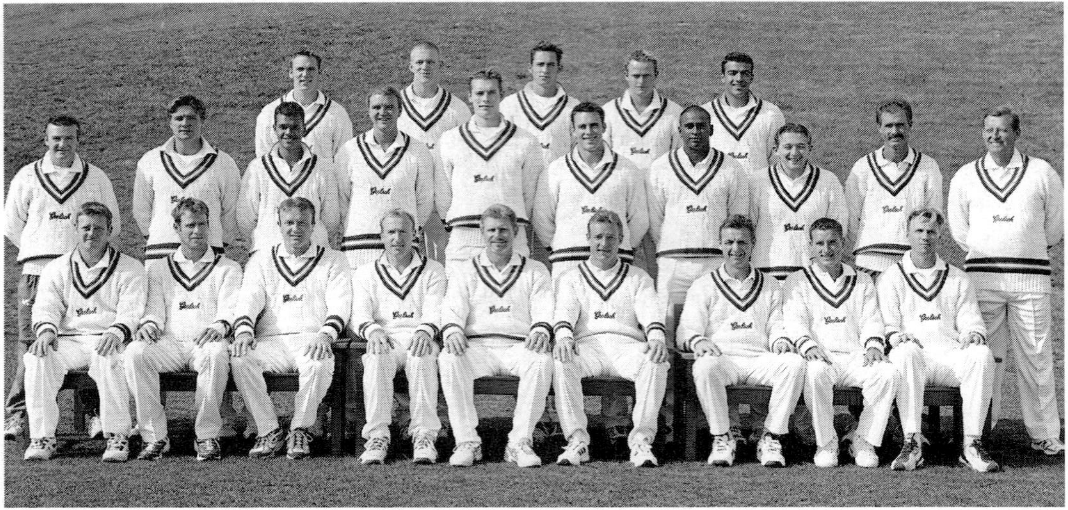

[*Bill Smith*

Back row: A. J. Sexton, J. H. K. Adams, I. Brunnschweiler, J. R. C. Hamblin, I. H. Shah. *Middle row:* T. C. Middleton (*second-team coach*), Z. C. Morris, L. R. Prittipaul, A. C. Morris, C. T. Tremlett, S. R. G. Francis, A. D. Mascarenhas, D. A. Kenway, S. J. Cook (*first-team coach*), T. M. Tremlett (*director of cricket*). *Front row:* J. S. Laney, N. C. Johnson, S. D. Udal, W. S. Kendall, R. A. Smith (*captain*), A. N. Aymes, J. P. Stephenson, G. W. White, A. D. Mullally.

HAMPSHIRE RESULTS

All first-class matches – Played 17: Won 8, Lost 2, Drawn 7. Abandoned 1.

County Championship matches – Played 16: Won 7, Lost 2, Drawn 7.

CricInfo County Championship, 2nd in Division 2; Cheltenham & Gloucester Trophy, 3rd round; Benson and Hedges Cup, 6th in South Group; Norwich Union League, 4th in Division 2.

COUNTY CHAMPIONSHIP AVERAGES

BATTING

Cap		*M*	*I*	*NO*	*R*	*HS*	*100s*	*50s*	*Avge*	*Ct/St*
	J. D. Francis	2	4	2	131	72*	0	1	65.50	1
2001	N. C. Johnson§	16	25	3	948	105*	2	7	43.09	24
1991	A. N. Aymes†	16	19	5	572	112*	1	4	40.85	43/2
1996	J. S. Laney†	4	5	1	137	60	0	2	34.25	8
2001	D. A. Kenway†	15	28	3	840	166	2	3	33.60	14
1998	G. W. White	16	30	4	731	141	2	1	28.11	16/2
1998	A. D. Mascarenhas	14	21	5	423	104	1	1	26.43	8
1995	J. P. Stephenson	3	6	1	128	51	0	1	25.60	1
1999	W. S. Kendall	16	28	3	629	94	0	3	25.16	11
2001	A. C. Morris	16	19	2	423	65	0	3	24.88	10
1992	S. D. Udal†	15	18	2	397	81	0	3	24.81	5
	L. R. Prittipaul†	6	7	0	155	84	0	1	22.14	4
1985	R. A. Smith	15	24	2	475	118	2	1	21.59	4
	C. T. Tremlett†	7	9	4	83	26	0	0	16.60	2
2000	A. D. Mullally	12	11	4	78	36	0	0	11.14	4

Also batted: J. R. C. Hamblin (1 match) 5; J. E. K. Schofield (2 matches) 21*, 1, 2 (1 ct).

* *Signifies not out.* † *Born in Hampshire.* § *Overseas player.*

BOWLING

	O	*M*	*R*	*W*	*BB*	*5W/i*	*Avge*
A. D. Mullally	427.3	135	1,047	57	8-90	5	18.36
C. T. Tremlett	131.2	37	401	20	4-34	0	20.05
A. D. Mascarenhas	389.4	110	990	39	6-26	2	25.38
A. C. Morris	472	106	1,428	51	5-39	2	28.00
S. D. Udal	518	133	1,455	49	7-74	1	29.69
N. C. Johnson	232.5	38	836	21	4-20	0	39.80

Also bowled: A. N. Aymes 12–0–107–2; J. D. Francis 6–0–34–1; J. R. C. Hamblin 18–1–88–1; W. S. Kendall 16–2–36–0; D. A. Kenway 8–0–66–1; L. R. Prittipaul 25–1–86–0; J. E. K. Schofield 55–12–154–8; J. P. Stephenson 17.4–3–60–4; G. W. White 19.1–0–71–1.

COUNTY RECORDS

Highest score for:	316	R. H. Moore v Warwickshire at Bournemouth	1937
Highest score against:	303*	G. A. Hick (Worcestershire) at Southampton	1997
Best bowling for:	9-25	R. M. H. Cottam v Lancashire at Manchester	1965
Best bowling against:	10-46	W. Hickton (Lancashire) at Manchester	1870
Highest total for:	672-7 dec.	v Somerset at Taunton	1899
Highest total against:	742	by Surrey at The Oval	1909
Lowest total for:	15	v Warwickshire at Birmingham	1922
Lowest total against:	23	by Yorkshire at Middlesbrough	1965

At Birmingham, April 20, 21, 22, 23. HAMPSHIRE drew with WARWICKSHIRE.

At Oxford, April 25, 26, 27. OXFORD UCCE v HAMPSHIRE. Abandoned.

HAMPSHIRE v WORCESTERSHIRE

At Southampton, May 9, 10, 11. Hampshire won by 124 runs. Hampshire 18 pts, Worcestershire 3.75 pts. Toss: Hampshire.

Hampshire celebrated the inaugural first-class match at their new headquarters with a confidence-boosting victory. Despite a three-day finish, the umpires praised the quality of Nigel Gray's pitch, blaming instead poor batting technique for the 20 wickets that fell on the last day. Sheriyar and Morris both took four in each innings to demonstrate the virtue of accuracy on such a surface. On the first day, Mascarenhas rescued Hampshire from 79 for six, hitting 18 fours in the second hundred of his county career. Hick, dropped by Stephenson when 21, responded in kind, making the Rose Bowl the 44th ground on which he had reached three figures. In the process, he overtook Allan Lamb's first-class aggregate of 32,502 to become the highest African-born run-scorer. Aymes dragged Hampshire out of trouble in their second innings, and Worcestershire's eventual target was 233. Hick's early demise precipitated a swift end in which the last five wickets tumbled for nine runs. Worcestershire became the first county to lose points for a slow over-rate, having fallen one short of the match minimum.

Close of play: First day, Hampshire 267-8 (Udal 14*, Morris 8*); Second day, Hampshire 16-0 (White 7*, Kenway 6*).

Hampshire

G. W. White c Rawnsley b Lampitt	26	– lbw b Sheriyar	9
D. A. Kenway c Rawnsley b Sheriyar	12	– c Rhodes b Liptrot	30
W. S. Kendall lbw b Sheriyar	10	– c Rhodes b Sheriyar	0
*R. A. Smith lbw b Sheriyar	4	– lbw b Bichel	3
N. C. Johnson c Rhodes b Lampitt	0	– c Rhodes b Lampitt	11
J. P. Stephenson c Singh b Bichel	51	– c Leatherdale b Liptrot	8
†A. N. Aymes run out	3	– not out	37
A. D. Mascarenhas lbw b Sheriyar	104	– lbw b Bichel	13
S. D. Udal c Rhodes b Bichel	23	– lbw b Sheriyar	1
A. C. Morris c Rhodes b Lampitt	32	– c Hick b Lampitt	20
A. D. Mullally not out	1	– c Hick b Sheriyar	1
L-b 9, w 12, n-b 22	43	L-b 7, w 7, n-b 12	26
1/20 2/42 3/48 4/49 5/66 6/79 7/221 8/251 9/304	309	1/21 2/21 3/30 4/50 5/73 6/76 7/107 8/114 9/155	159

Bonus points – Hampshire 3, Worcestershire 3.

Bowling: *First Innings*—Bichel 29.5–9–100–2; Sheriyar 32–12–85–4; Lampitt 15–3–45–3; Liptrot 16–4–43–0; Rawnsley 6–2–12–0; Leatherdale 2–0–15–0. *Second Innings*—Bichel 22–6–55–2; Sheriyar 14.5–2–30–4; Liptrot 8–3–26–2; Lampitt 10–3–27–2; Rawnsley 4–1–14–0.

Worcestershire

W. P. C. Weston b Mascarenhas	1	– lbw b Morris	4
A. Singh c Stephenson b Morris	7	– c Johnson b Morris	33
*G. A. Hick c Kendall b Morris	120	– c Aymes b Mullally	5
V. S. Solanki c Aymes b Mullally	10	– c White b Mullally	5
D. A. Leatherdale c Udal b Stephenson	34	– c and b Udal	4
A. J. Bichel b Udal	15	– (7) lbw b Morris	30
†S. J. Rhodes c Kenway b Udal	0	– (6) b Udal	14
S. R. Lampitt c Aymes b Mullally	5	– b Udal	0
M. J. Rawnsley b Morris	5	– c White b Udal	0
C. G. Liptrot c White b Morris	2	– c Aymes b Morris	5
A. Sheriyar not out	6	– not out	0
L-b 9, w 12, n-b 10	31	B 1, l-b 5, w 2	8
1/8 2/26 3/61 4/168 5/187 6/187 7/215 8/225 9/227	236	1/5 2/16 3/28 4/33 5/59 6/99 7/102 8/102 9/108	108

Bonus points – Worcestershire 1, Hampshire 3.

Bowling: *First Innings*—Mullally 28–9–66–2; Morris 17–3–39–4; Mascarenhas 17–7–26–1; Johnson 4–0–22–0; Udal 15–1–62–2; Stephenson 3–0–12–1. *Second Innings*—Mullally 13–5–23–2; Morris 10.5–2–27–4; Udal 16–6–32–4; Mascarenhas 5–0–20–0.

Umpires: B. Leadbeater and J. F. Steele.

HAMPSHIRE v GLOUCESTERSHIRE

At Southampton, May 16, 17, 18, 19. Drawn. Hampshire 13 pts, Gloucestershire 5 pts. Toss: Hampshire.

Hampshire lost out on six points when their batsmen panicked in a run-chase to score 56 from ten overs. They needed eight off the last over, then three from the last ball, but Mascarenhas could scamper only two and Hampshire had to settle for the six points awarded to the side batting fourth when the scores finish level, rather than the 12 for victory. Although much of the first two days was lost to rain, there was time for Kenway to compile a stylish century, containing 20 fours. Smith's hundred, with one boundary fewer, enabled him to declare on the third morning once the fourth batting point was gained. Mullally dismissed Hewson with his third ball and finished off the innings with four wickets in 31 deliveries as Gloucestershire lost their last seven for 42. When they followed on, 217 behind, Hewson led the resistance with a patient, career-best 89 over more than five hours, frequently frustrating the Hampshire bowlers in the sixth-wicket stand of 119 with Snape that helped set up the hectic finale.

Close of play: First day, Hampshire 122-2 (Kenway 55*, Smith 6*); Second day, Hampshire 244-2 (Kenway 124*, Smith 55*); Third day, Gloucestershire 36-2 (Hewson 19*, Taylor 8*).

Hampshire

D. A. Kenway c Alleyne b Lewis	131	– (2) lbw b Lewis	8
G. W. White c Cunliffe b Harvey	17	– (6) c Harvey b Lewis	0
W. S. Kendall c Williams b Alleyne	43	– run out	13
*R. A. Smith not out	102	– b Averis	1
N. C. Johnson lbw b Cawdron	23	– (1) c Cawdron b Averis	13
J. P. Stephenson not out	21	– (7) run out	2
A. D. Mascarenhas (did not bat)		– (5) not out	6
S. D. Udal (did not bat)		– not out	1
L-b 9, w 2, n-b 2	13	B 2, l-b 5, w 4	11
1/34 2/108 3/255 4/307	(4 wkts dec.) 350	1/19 2/35 3/38 4/43 5/48 6/52	(6 wkts) 55

†A. N. Aymes, A. C. Morris and A. D. Mullally did not bat.

Bonus points – Hampshire 4, Gloucestershire 1.

Bowling: *First Innings*—Lewis 27.2–7–82–1; Harvey 18–9–45–1; Averis 18–3–57–0; Cawdron 19–6–56–1; Alleyne 21–7–58–1; Snape 6–0–43–0. *Second Innings*—Lewis 5–0–22–2; Averis 5–0–26–2.

Gloucestershire

D. R. Hewson c Aymes b Mullally	0	– (2) b Mascarenhas	89
R. J. Cunliffe c Johnson b Udal	37	– (1) lbw b Morris	1
M. G. N. Windows run out	11	– c White b Morris	5
C. G. Taylor c Kenway b Johnson	26	– lbw b Morris	11
I. J. Harvey c White b Mullally	20	– c and b Morris	28
*M. W. Alleyne c White b Udal	0	– c Morris b Mullally	19
J. N. Snape lbw b Mullally	8	– lbw b Mascarenhas	73
†R. C. J. Williams c Aymes b Mullally	15	– c Aymes b Mullally	13
M. J. Cawdron c Aymes b Mullally	0	– c Aymes b Mullally	2
J. M. M. Averis st Aymes b Udal	0	– c Smith b Udal	4
J. Lewis not out	7	– not out	4
L-b 5, w 4	9	B 3, l-b 11, w 3, n-b 6	23
1/0 2/15 3/59 4/91 5/95 6/105 7/116 8/116 9/119	133	1/3 2/14 3/47 4/83 5/115 6/234 7/241 8/246 9/260	272

Bonus points – Hampshire 3.

Bowling: *First Innings*—Mullally 18.4–6–41–5; Morris 8–2–20–0; Mascarenhas 9–2–22–0; Johnson 8–4–15–1; Udal 9–2–30–3. *Second Innings*—Mullally 27.1–10–59–3; Morris 25–6–74–4; Udal 26–6–60–1; Johnson 7–2–31–0; Mascarenhas 17–5–34–2.

Umpires: G. I. Burgess and J. H. Evans.

At Derby, May 25, 26, 27, 28. HAMPSHIRE beat DERBYSHIRE by nine wickets.

HAMPSHIRE v SUSSEX

At Southampton, May 30, 31, June 1, 2. Drawn. Hampshire 8 pts, Sussex 10 pts. Toss: Sussex.

A match that saw 1,116 runs accumulated for 17 wickets contained just one period of tension. That came when Hampshire, needing 351 to avoid the follow-on, were 323 for eight, with Udal facing Martin-Jenkins on a hat-trick. The danger was averted, and Udal and Morris, who hit a career-best 65, added 95. White's century was his first in the Championship since 1998. Smith might have declared 108 behind at the end of the third day, but in extending the innings into a fourth he effectively ended the game as a contest. Goodwin, who had batted eight hours 41 minutes for a career-best 195 in Sussex's first innings, was an early casualty in their second when struck on the hand by Mascarenhas. However, Montgomerie and Yardy made the most of some optimistic bowling: Smith employed an arc of seven slips at one stage, but by the end had introduced wicket-keeper Aymes. Fewer than 50 spectators witnessed the meaningless last session, brought to a merciful end by Adams's declaration.

Close of play: First day, Sussex 290-4 (Goodwin 131*, Kirtley 1*); Second day, Hampshire 92-1 (White 45*, Kendall 9*); Third day, Hampshire 392-8 (Udal 26*, Morris 41*).

Sussex

R. R. Montgomerie b Udal	56	– not out	88
M. W. Goodwin lbw b White	195	– retired hurt	8
M. H. Yardy c Johnson b Mullally	8	– not out	75
B. Zuiderent run out	45		
*C. J. Adams lbw b Morris	25		
R. J. Kirtley c Aymes b Udal	33		
U. B. A. Rashid lbw b Mascarenhas	38		
R. S. C. Martin-Jenkins not out	56		
†M. J. Prior not out	15		
B 4, l-b 9, w 10, n-b 6	29	B 5, l-b 3	8
1/123 2/144 3/236 4/288 5/388 6/390 7/469 (7 wkts dec.)	500	(no wkt dec.)	179

M. J. G. Davis and J. D. Lewry did not bat.

Bonus points – Sussex 4, Hampshire 1 (Score at 130 overs: 365-4).

In the second innings Goodwin retired hurt at 17.

Bowling: *First Innings*—Mullally 28–10–71–1; Morris 33–14–73–1; Mascarenhas 31.3–6–104–1; Udal 55–8–167–2; Prittipaul 11–0–43–0; White 8–0–29–1. *Second Innings*—Mascarenhas 13–5–27–0; Morris 6–2–13–0; Udal 15–7–33–0; Prittipaul 14–1–43–0; Kendall 14–2–32–0; White 4–0–17–0; Aymes 1–0–6–0.

Hampshire

G. W. White c Prior b Lewry	141
D. A. Kenway lbw b Martin-Jenkins	35
W. S. Kendall c Montgomerie b Davis	32
*R. A. Smith c and b Davis	0
N. C. Johnson lbw b Martin-Jenkins	60
L. R. Prittipaul c Montgomerie b Davis	24
†A. N. Aymes c Goodwin b Martin-Jenkins	1
A. D. Mascarenhas c Adams b Martin-Jenkins	0
S. D. Udal c Goodwin b Kirtley	39
A. C. Morris b Kirtley	65
A. D. Mullally not out	3
B 2, l-b 21, w 2, n-b 12	37
1/59 2/142 3/142 4/276 5/301 6/313 7/317 8/323 9/418	437

Bonus points – Hampshire 3, Sussex 2 (Score at 130 overs: 334-8).

Bowling: Lewry 28–9–59–1; Kirtley 28.5–8–87–2; Martin-Jenkins 30–10–77–4; Davis 51–10–148–3; Rashid 17–6–38–0; Yardy 3–1–5–0.

Umpires: A. Clarkson and R. A. White.

At Southgate, June 13, 14, 15, 16. HAMPSHIRE drew with MIDDLESEX.

HAMPSHIRE v DURHAM

At Southampton, June 20, 21, 22. Hampshire won by 47 runs. Hampshire 16 pts, Durham 5 pts. Toss: Hampshire. First-class debut: N. G. Hatch.

A pitch of pace and erratic bounce helped bring about a three-day finish. Both sides played tall fast bowlers who relished the conditions. Durham's Nicky Hatch, standing at 6ft 8in, took five wickets on debut, while Hampshire's Tremlett, only an inch shorter, posed plenty of problems on his first home appearance in the Championship and finished with match figures of seven for 77. Durham were left to rue their inability to finish off their opponents' tail. In the first innings, Hampshire's last two wickets added 97; in the second, their last three contributed a vital 125, thanks to Johnson, who on what proved the final morning was dropped by wicket-keeper Pratt off a low but straightforward chance when 34. He went on to an unbeaten 86, the highest score of the game, which included 12 fours. Durham's task was always some 50 runs beyond them.

Close of play: First day, Durham 113-1 (Lewis 59*, Love 20*); Second day, Hampshire 134-7 (Johnson 31*, Udal 7*).

Hampshire

G. W. White c Pratt b Law	41	– (2) c Love b Phillips	44
D. A. Kenway b Hatch	15	– (1) b Brown	20
W. S. Kendall c Love b Hatch	2	– b Hatch	14
*R. A. Smith c Peng b Brown	13	– lbw b Hatch	1
N. C. Johnson lbw b Law	32	– not out	86
L. R. Prittipaul c Pratt b Law	6	– st Pratt b Phillips	4
A. D. Mascarenhas b Brown	7	– run out	6
†A. N. Aymes c Love b Law	41	– c Phillips b Law	1
S. D. Udal c Gough b Law	7	– b Brown	27
A. C. Morris c Hatch b Law	59	– lbw b Hatch	9
C. T. Tremlett not out	1	– lbw b Brown	1
L-b 6, w 16	22	B 6, l-b 5, w 6	17
1/32 2/34 3/55 4/115 5/125 6/132 7/138 8/149 9/241	246	1/24 2/64 3/76 4/88 5/96 6/104 7/105 8/189 9/215	230

Bonus points – Hampshire 1, Durham 3.

Bowling: *First Innings*—Brown 18–4–62–2; Hatch 12–2–55–2; Hunter 8–1–36–0; Law 16.3–4–53–6; Phillips 13–2–28–0; Gough 3–1–6–0. *Second Innings*—Brown 14.2–4–31–3; Hatch 13–3–42–3; Law 20–4–41–1; Hunter 10–1–35–0; Phillips 22–7–70–2.

Durham

*J. J. B. Lewis c Kenway b Tremlett	62	– c Prittipaul b Johnson	38
M. A. Gough b Mascarenhas	24	– c and b Morris	9
M. L. Love lbw b Udal	78	– c Johnson b Mascarenhas	9
M. P. Speight lbw b Tremlett	9	– b Johnson	21
N. Peng c Kendall b Johnson	15	– c White b Mascarenhas	49
D. R. Law c Aymes b Johnson	0	– c Kenway b Udal	7
†A. Pratt c and b Tremlett	17	– b Tremlett	7
I. D. Hunter c Johnson b Udal	0	– c and b Tremlett	0
N. C. Phillips c Prittipaul b Udal	1	– not out	11
S. J. E. Brown c Mascarenhas b Morris	29	– c Aymes b Tremlett	0
N. G. Hatch not out	16	– c Aymes b Tremlett	0
B 1, l-b 8, w 2, n-b 4	15	B 2, l-b 6, n-b 4	12
1/55 2/141 3/157 4/187 5/187 6/205 7/205 8/221 9/221	266	1/17 2/34 3/74 4/95 5/120 6/145 7/145 8/159 9/163	163

Bonus points – Durham 2, Hampshire 3.

Bowling: *First Innings*—Tremlett 21–8–43–3; Morris 16.2–2–53–1; Mascarenhas 15–1–41–1; Johnson 12–3–45–2; Udal 18–5–75–3. *Second Innings*—Morris 10–2–34–1; Tremlett 12–5–34–4; Mascarenhas 13–5–22–2; Udal 10–1–38–1; Johnson 6–1–27–2.

Umpires: J. W. Holder and K. E. Palmer.

HAMPSHIRE v DERBYSHIRE

At Southampton, June 29, 30, July 1. Hampshire won by ten wickets. Hampshire 19 pts, Derbyshire 3 pts. Toss: Hampshire.

Despite surviving only with discomfort between showers on the opening day, Hampshire inflicted a heavy defeat inside three which, when the current round of matches ended, narrowed the gap behind Division Two leaders Middlesex to two points. With six players unavailable, Derbyshire were in trouble even before they arrived. But they also failed to exploit the first-day conditions, when there was plenty of lateral movement. Although Johnson hit his fifth half-century in six innings, it needed Aymes and Udal to lift Hampshire with 130 for the eighth wicket. Mullally and Johnson, with four wickets apiece, met only fitful resistance and Derbyshire were following on, 243 behind, by the end of the second day. Bailey battled away for more than three hours for his 98, and Edwards offered him valiant support in a stand of 81 near the end. Both succumbed to the accuracy of Mascarenhas, who finished with a personal-best six for 60. Kenway struck Bailey's first ball for six to seal an emphatic victory that allowed Hampshire a day's glory on top of the table but left Derbyshire firmly rooted at the bottom.

Close of play: First day, Hampshire 207-7 (Aymes 17*); Second day, Derbyshire 10-0 (Sutton 0*, Stubbings 8*).

Hampshire

G. W. White b Munton	32	– not out	0
D. A. Kenway c Di Venuto b Welch	6	– not out	6
W. S. Kendall c Bailey b Aldred	26		
*R. A. Smith c Sutton b Wharton	38		
N. C. Johnson lbw b Munton	59		
L. R. Prittipaul b Munton	5		
A. D. Mascarenhas c Sutton b Welch	14		
†A. N. Aymes lbw b Aldred	73		
S. D. Udal c Bassano b Munton	81		
A. C. Morris c Stubbings b Munton	11		
A. D. Mullally not out	8		
L-b 14, w 10, n-b 6	30		
1/6 2/68 3/72 4/139 5/175 6/184 7/207 8/337 9/361	383	(no wkt)	6

Bonus points – Hampshire 4, Derbyshire 3.

Bowling: *First Innings*—Munton 32.1–8–85–5; Welch 26–8–87–2; Edwards 13–3–40–0; Aldred 26–5–104–2; Wharton 17–3–53–1. *Second Innings*—Wharton 1–1–0–0; Bailey 0.1–0–6–0.

Derbyshire

S. D. Stubbings lbw b Morris	13	– (2) c Johnson b Mullally	13
†L. D. Sutton c Aymes b Mullally	21	– (1) c Aymes b Mascarenhas	33
C. W. G. Bassano c Udal b Mullally	1	– run out	19
R. J. Bailey c Aymes b Mullally	8	– (5) c and b Mascarenhas	98
M. P. Dowman c Kendall b Udal	35	– (6) lbw b Mascarenhas	0
M. J. Di Venuto c and b Mullally	8	– (4) c Prittipaul b Udal	10
G. Welch b Johnson	22	– b Mascarenhas	0
P. Aldred c Aymes b Johnson	24	– c Smith b Udal	12
A. D. Edwards not out	4	– lbw b Mascarenhas	23
*T. A. Munton c White b Johnson	0	– c Johnson b Mascarenhas	23
L. J. Wharton c Kendall b Johnson	0	– not out	0
B 4	4	L-b 5, w 4, n-b 4	13
1/13 2/14 3/24 4/65 5/77 6/87 7/127 8/132 9/136	140	1/27 2/56 3/81 4/81 5/81 6/91 7/128 8/209 9/237	244

Bonus points – Hampshire 3.

Bowling: *First Innings*—Mullally 14–3–30–4; Morris 11–1–39–1; Mascarenhas 6–0–18–0; Udal 11–4–29–1; Johnson 6.3–1–20–4. *Second Innings*—Mullally 21–5–46–1; Morris 13–0–38–0; Mascarenhas 20.3–5–60–6; Johnson 11–2–30–0; Udal 25–4–65–2.

Umpires: D. J. Constant and G. Sharp.

At Hove, July 6, 7. HAMPSHIRE lost to SUSSEX by an innings and 113 runs.

HAMPSHIRE v NOTTINGHAMSHIRE

At Southampton, July 18, 19, 20, 21. Hampshire won by 338 runs. Hampshire 18 pts, Nottinghamshire 4 pts. Toss: Hampshire.

Hampshire's margin of victory was their largest, in terms of runs, in a home Championship match, surpassing their 315-run defeat of Gloucestershire at Bournemouth in 1913. In their defence, Nottinghamshire could point to the loss of Usman Afzaal, who was with the England party for the Lord's Test as emergency cover. Released next morning, he returned to Southampton only to find Nottinghamshire 74 for nine on a blameless pitch – and his place taken by the 17-year-old Shafayat. Read and Stemp, the latter improving his previous best by one run, saved the follow-on with a last-wicket stand of 135, a record between the counties. Kenway's 166 in five hours, with 26 fours and a six, enabled Hampshire to set an unlikely target of 491, but Nottinghamshire again capitulated. Mullally took five wickets, Tremlett three, and the match lasted just an hour into the final day. Aymes's typically obdurate century in the first innings was the eighth of his career.

Close of play: First day, Hampshire 292-8 (Aymes 86*, Tremlett 0*); Second day, Hampshire 85-3 (Kenway 50*, Johnson 15*); Third day, Nottinghamshire 113-7 (Logan 5*, Harris 6*).

Hampshire

D. A. Kenway c Read b Logan	25	– (2) c Read b Stemp	166
G. W. White b Logan	18	– (1) c Johnson b Logan	15
W. S. Kendall lbw b Smith	14	– b Logan	0
*R. A. Smith c Blewett b Pietersen	49	– c Blewett b Harris	1
N. C. Johnson c Read b Harris	16	– st Read b Stemp	49
A. D. Mascarenhas b Stemp	37	– b Stemp	36
†A. N. Aymes not out	112	– c Pietersen b Logan	39
S. D. Udal c Morris b Logan	20	– c Read b Logan	10
A. C. Morris c Pietersen b Smith	12	– not out	16
C. T. Tremlett c Read b Harris	26	– not out	1
A. D. Mullally c Blewett b Harris	0		
B 4, l-b 6, n-b 8	18	B 4, l-b 11, w 2, n-b 2	19
1/42 2/49 3/70 4/116 5/134 6/217 7/256 8/290 9/341	347	1/33 2/33 3/42 4/195 5/261 6/290 7/319 8/340 (8 wkts dec.)	352

Bonus points – Hampshire 3, Nottinghamshire 3.

Bowling: *First Innings*—Smith 24–2–62–2; Harris 26–6–79–3; Logan 19–2–75–3; Stemp 27–2–97–1; Pietersen 8–2–24–1. *Second Innings*—Smith 10–0–41–0; Logan 24–4–103–4; Harris 17–6–53–1; Stemp 28–8–86–3; Pietersen 15–1–54–0.

Nottinghamshire

*D. J. Bicknell lbw b Mullally	0	– b Morris	5
J. E. Morris c and b Morris	14	– c Kendall b Mullally	2
G. S. Blewett b Morris	13	– c Udal b Mullally	16
P. Johnson lbw b Tremlett	5	– c Morris b Mullally	0
K. P. Pietersen c Kenway b Morris	2	– c Kenway b Tremlett	8
†C. M. W. Read not out	76	– (7) c Aymes b Tremlett	38
R. J. Logan b Tremlett	1	– (8) c Kenway b Tremlett	28
B. M. Shafayat c Kenway b Mullally	4	– (6) b Mullally	14
A. J. Harris c Johnson b Tremlett	4	– c White b Mullally	10
G. J. Smith c Mullally b Mascarenhas	8	– (11) not out	0
R. D. Stemp c Kenway b Johnson	66	– (10) c Kenway b Johnson	10
B 2, l-b 8, w 4, n-b 2	16	L-b 3, w 8, n-b 10	21
1/0 2/27 3/28 4/30 5/37 6/47 7/54 8/65 9/74	209	1/7 2/9 3/9 4/37 5/39 6/95 7/99 8/124 9/148	152

Bonus points – Nottinghamshire 1, Hampshire 3.

Bowling: *First Innings*—Mullally 15–3–45–2; Morris 9–1–42–3; Mascarenhas 10–2–28–1; Tremlett 13–4–47–3; Udal 3–0–14–0; Johnson 5.3–0–23–1. *Second Innings*—Mullally 19–2–68–5; Morris 15–4–40–1; Udal 3–2–1–0; Tremlett 9.5–4–15–3; Johnson 3–1–13–1; Mascarenhas 4–0–11–0; White 1–0–1–0.

Umpires: M. J. Kitchen and D. R. Shepherd.

At Southampton, July 28, 29, 30. HAMPSHIRE beat AUSTRALIANS by two wickets (see Australian tour section).

At Cheltenham, August 1, 2, 3, 4. HAMPSHIRE drew with GLOUCESTERSHIRE.

HAMPSHIRE v WARWICKSHIRE

At Southampton, August 7, 8, 9, 10. Drawn. Hampshire 7 pts, Warwickshire 7 pts. Toss: Hampshire.

The only real winners to emerge from this soggy contest between sides chasing promotion were Hampshire's Mullally and Warwickshire's Bell. In Mullally's case, his eight for 90, ten days after his five for 18 against the Australians, helped earn him selection for the Fourth Test. Bell, meanwhile, came within a whisker of scoring Championship hundreds in consecutive matches. He hit 13 fours in a mature innings that belied his 19 years and, with Powell, put on 177 for the fourth wicket. When Mullally, extracting lift and movement from an otherwise docile strip, eventually removed Powell, Bell followed moments later. Brown and Piper added 73 before Mullally cut through the tail, Warwickshire's last five wickets falling for 17. A storm ended play before tea on the second day with the Hampshire reply still in its infancy; more rain washed out the third and, despite last-day sunshine, water – which had seeped under the covers – prevented cricket on the fourth.

Close of play: First day, Warwickshire 192-3 (Powell 67*, Bell 88*); Second day, Hampshire 26-1 (Kenway 18*, Kendall 4*); Third day, No play.

Warwickshire

*M. J. Powell lbw b Mullally	83
N. V. Knight c Morris b Mullally	4
M. A. Wagh c Aymes b Mullally	4
D. L. Hemp lbw b Tremlett	14
I. R. Bell lbw b Morris	98
D. R. Brown b Mullally	50
†K. J. Piper b Mullally	33
N. M. K. Smith c Aymes b Mullally	0
V. C. Drakes c Laney b Mullally	0
N. M. Carter c Kenway b Mullally	5
A. Richardson not out	0
L-b 5, w 6, n-b 6	17
1/13 2/23 3/41 4/218 5/218 6/291 7/291 8/291 9/306	308

Bonus points – Warwickshire 3, Hampshire 3.

Bowling: Mullally 32–10–90–8; Morris 25–8–60–1; Tremlett 15–3–46–1; Johnson 20–3–57–0; Udal 17–6–50–0.

Hampshire

D. A. Kenway not out	18
G. W. White c Powell b Carter	1
W. S. Kendall not out	4
B 1, w 2	3
1/22	(1 wkt) 26

*R. A. Smith, N. C. Johnson, J. S. Laney, †A. N. Aymes, C. T. Tremlett, S. D. Udal, A. C. Morris and A. D. Mullally did not bat.

Bowling: Drakes 3–1–2–0; Carter 5–0–18–1; Richardson 2.1–0–5–0.

Umpires: J. W. Holder and N. A. Mallender.

At Chester-le-Street, August 17, 18, 19, 20. HAMPSHIRE beat DURHAM by seven wickets.

At Worcester, August 22, 23, 24, 25. HAMPSHIRE lost to WORCESTERSHIRE by 112 runs.

HAMPSHIRE v MIDDLESEX

At Southampton, September 5, 6, 7. Hampshire won by five wickets. Hampshire 15 pts, Middlesex 3 pts. Toss: Middlesex. First-class debut: J. D. Francis.

For the fourth time in eight home Championship matches, Hampshire won inside three days. Pitch liaison officer Peter Walker was at the Rose Bowl on the first day when ten Middlesex and seven Hampshire wickets fell, but left early, satisfied that indifferent batting was as much the cause as the generous lateral movement extracted by both sides. No one was more adept at exploiting the conditions than Mascarenhas, who ended with a career-best six for 26. The turning point was an eighth-wicket stand of 102 between Aymes and Udal, which allowed Hampshire to convert 63 for seven into a comfortable lead. Twice Strauss batted with great patience, in the second innings carrying his bat after he and Fleming had added 127; both passed 1,000 runs for the season. On the third morning, however, Middlesex's last five wickets tumbled for 21, requiring Hampshire to make 164. Johnson assured victory, though another left-hander, John Francis, younger brother of Simon, hit the winning runs. Defeat left Middlesex fourth, having led the table a month earlier, while for Hampshire promotion was within their grasp.

Close of play: First day, Hampshire 99-7 (Aymes 22*, Udal 17*); Second day, Middlesex 232-5 (Strauss 100*, Nash 15*).

Middlesex

A. J. Strauss lbw b Mascarenhas	56	– not out	112
R. M. S. Weston c Aymes b Morris	6	– lbw b Mascarenhas	18
O. A. Shah lbw b Morris	2	– c and b Mascarenhas	1
S. P. Fleming c Morris b Mascarenhas	14	– lbw b Udal	74
E. C. Joyce lbw b Mullally	11	– lbw b Udal	0
P. N. Weekes st Aymes b Mascarenhas	1	– c Aymes b Udal	15
†D. C. Nash lbw b Mascarenhas	1	– lbw b Mullally	16
C. B. Keegan c Kenway b Mascarenhas	0	– lbw b Morris	0
*A. R. C. Fraser c White b Johnson	0	– c Aymes b Mascarenhas	5
T. F. Bloomfield not out	0	– b Mullally	0
P. C. R. Tufnell c Johnson b Mascarenhas	0	– c Udal b Mullally	2
B 4, w 2, n-b 4	10	B 5, l-b 1, w 2, n-b 2	10
1/6 2/8 3/50 4/71 5/78 6/84 7/94 8/101 9/101	101	1/56 2/58 3/185 4/185 5/205 6/233 7/236 8/244 9/249	253

Bonus points – Hampshire 3.

Bowling: *First Innings*—Mullally 18–9–23–1; Morris 9–0–33–2; Mascarenhas 16–5–26–6; Udal 4–1–4–0; Johnson 3–1–11–1. *Second Innings*—Mullally 24.3–7–70–3; Morris 22–5–56–1; Johnson 11–2–50–0; Mascarenhas 17–11–21–3; Udal 18–5–50–3.

Hampshire

G. W. White lbw b Bloomfield	6	– c Fleming b Bloomfield	2
D. A. Kenway b Fraser	13	– c Nash b Fraser	6
W. S. Kendall c Shah b Fraser	0	– c Fleming b Fraser	38
*R. A. Smith c Nash b Fraser	0	– c Joyce b Fraser	7
N. C. Johnson c Joyce b Keegan	16	– c Strauss b Weekes	74
J. D. Francis lbw b Keegan	15	– not out	29
A. D. Mascarenhas lbw b Keegan	9	– not out	0
†A. N. Aymes not out	57		
S. D. Udal c Fleming b Tufnell	62		
A. C. Morris b Bloomfield	0		
A. D. Mullally c Joyce b Keegan	4		
B 5, l-b 2, n-b 2	9	B 2, l-b 4, n-b 4	10
1/19 2/19 3/19 4/23 5/41 6/54 7/63 8/165 9/186	191	1/7 2/9 3/27 4/118 5/160	(5 wkts) 166

Bonus points – Middlesex 3.

Bowling: *First Innings*—Fraser 32–14–66–3; Bloomfield 15–4–37–2; Keegan 15.2–2–54–4; Tufnell 8–3–27–1. *Second Innings*—Fraser 14–2–46–3; Bloomfield 11.1–2–44–1; Keegan 3–0–12–0; Tufnell 12–1–40–0; Weekes 8–2–18–1.

Umpires: J. H. Evans and J. W. Lloyds.

At Nottingham, September 12, 13, 14, 15. HAMPSHIRE drew with NOTTINGHAMSHIRE.

I ZINGARI RESULTS, 2001

Matches 17: Won 4, Lost 8, Drawn 5. Abandoned 9.

April 26	Eton College	Abandoned
April 29	Charterhouse School	Abandoned
April 29	Hurlingham CC	Abandoned
May 3	Harrow School	Abandoned
May 6	Hampshire Hogs	Lost by five wickets
May 12	Eton Ramblers	Abandoned
May 13	Stragglers of Asia	Lost by 75 runs
May 26	Royal Armoured Corps	Lost by one wicket
June 3	Earl of Carnarvon's XI	Drawn
June 10	Sandhurst Wanderers	Abandoned
June 17	Bradfield Waifs	Abandoned
June 21	Winchester College	Lost by seven wickets
June 23	Guards CC	Won by 80 runs
June 24	Cormorants CC	Won by 174 runs
July 1	Hagley CC	Lost by five wickets
July 7	Green Jackets	Drawn
July 8	Old Wykehamists	Lost by four wickets
July 14	Lord Stafford's XI	Won by three wickets
July 15	Sir John Starkey's XI	Won by four wickets
July 22	Earl of Arundel's XI	Drawn
July 28	Willow Warblers	Lost by five wickets
July 29	Sir Paul Getty's XI	Lost by two wickets
August 5	Band of Brothers	Drawn
August 12	Lord Vestey's XI	Abandoned
August 19	South Wales Hunts	Abandoned
September 2	J. H. Pawle's XI	Drawn

David Fulton

KENT

President: 2001 – D. G. Ufton
2002 – The Rt Hon. Lord Kingsdown
Chairman: C. F. Openshaw
Chief Executive: P. E. Millman
Chairman, Cricket Committee: M. H. Denness
Captain: M. V. Fleming
Championship Captain: 2002 – D. P. Fulton
First-Team Coach: 2001 – R. J. Inverarity
Director of Cricket: 2002 – I. J. Brayshaw
Staff Coach: C. Stone
Head Groundsman: M. Grantham
Scorer: J. C. Foley

Kent, so often the "nearly men" of county cricket, enjoyed a successful season in 2001, culminating in winning the Norwich Union League, the county's first trophy for six years. Finishing third in the County Championship was another notable achievement for a team offered as rank outsiders, at the start of the summer, to win any major honours. They made less progress in the knockouts, but are now one of only three counties, Leicestershire and Yorkshire being the others, who have never experienced second-division cricket in either Championship or League.

The appointment of John Inverarity as "coaching adviser", succeeding John Wright, proved a shrewd move, even though he was available for only 14 weeks before returning to his teaching commitments in Western Australia. The question on everyone's lips was what would happen after that. As it turned out, the transition was seamless. When Inverarity went home to Perth, Second Eleven coach Chris Stone stepped up, leaving Alan Wells to skipper and coach the Seconds.

Inverarity had laid the necessary foundations for the summer, with everyone made aware of his responsibilities. Batsmen who had struggled for form and confidence in previous seasons blossomed, while Martin Saggers and Ben Trott both had excellent returns with the ball. Even the loss of overseas player Daryll Cullinan through a knee injury – the South African played only three first-class games before being ruled out – was overcome by recruiting Andrew Symonds, the county's import in 1999, who was already in England with the Australian one-day squad. He averaged 46.91 in the Championship, scored useful runs in the League and held some stunning catches.

The Championship season began with a high-scoring draw against Surrey at The Oval, followed by defeat against Yorkshire and rain-affected draws at Taunton and Swansea. An innings win over Essex at Tunbridge Wells, with a day to spare, was notable for Trott's match-winning 11 wickets as he improved his career-best figures twice in one day. But a second defeat by Yorkshire, at Headingley, and another draw against Glamorgan, at Maidstone, followed. After going down to Leicestershire, led by former Kent player Vince Wells, in one of the club's heaviest defeats in the modern era, Kent began July in the relegation zone. However, successive wins against Lancashire, Essex and Leicestershire gave them a real chance of collecting the runners-up prize money, only for rain to frustrate them in later games when they were in good positions.

The form of David Fulton was a revelation. He started the season with a hundred at Fenner's and ended it with a duck at Old Trafford; in between he hit eight hundreds in the Championship, including a career-best 208 not out as he scored two in one match, against Somerset at Canterbury. His 196 against Northamptonshire at Canterbury, on top of 197 at Northampton, equalled Arthur Fagg's run of nine centuries for Kent in 1938, one less than the county record of ten in a season, scored by Frank Woolley in 1928 and 1934. Fulton finished the summer as the leading English run-scorer – fifth in the national averages with 1,892 at 75.68 – but there was no Test or tour call-up as a reward. Being named PCA Player of the Year was some consolation.

Robert Key and Ed Smith also passed 1,000 first-class runs for the season, and were presented with their county caps by HRH the Duke of Kent, the club's patron, on the opening day of Festival Week, while Matthew Walker finished just 15 short. All told, Kent batsmen registered 23 first-class hundreds – compared with only one in the League – and the most popular was Mark Ealham's career-best 153 not out against Northamptonshire, his first century at Canterbury since 1997.

Saggers, another to be capped in 2001, took the bowling honours for the second successive season with 64 first-class wickets, seven better than the previous year although slightly more expensive at 24.23. He was well supported by Trott, who finished his first full season with 47, while Min Patel's 40 wickets included career-best match figures of 12 for 144 against Somerset at Canterbury.

The League season started with a washout against Warwickshire, followed by a win over Somerset, and a tie in the return fixture at Tunbridge Wells. Kent then took off with a five-match winning streak before back-to-back defeats by leaders Leicestershire, who opened up an eight-point lead, suggested the title's destination would be the Midlands. Not in Kent minds, though. Matthew Fleming's four direct hits helped beat Surrey, and eventually Leicestershire faltered. Fleming again starred with a one-day best 125 in the final home win, over Northamptonshire, taking the title race to the final weekend. Kent needed to beat Warwickshire, and Leicestershire to lose to Nottinghamshire, but the omens were bad until Symonds stepped up to return his best one-day figures for the county. Leicestershire had already lost, and Kent could celebrate the success that their team spirit had brought. Nobody was more pleased than captain Fleming himself. Scoring 345 runs, he was his side's second-highest contributor after James Hockley's 403; Saggers was again the leading wicket-taker, with 25.

Fleming handed over the captaincy of the Championship side to Fulton for 2002, when another Western Australian, Ian Brayshaw, became director of cricket. Wells announced his retirement from first-class cricket at the end of the season, when Kristian Adams, Paul Lazenbury and Ben Phillips were released. Middlesex seamer Jamie Hewitt, subject of an earlier illegal approach that earned Kent a rap over the knuckles, joined the staff for 2002, along with youngsters Alex Loudon and James Tredwell, and highly rated Robert Joseph has been given a development contract. – ANDREW GIDLEY.

KENT 2001

[*Terry Mahoney*

Back row: N. Reid (*second-team physiotherapist*), E. T. Smith, M. J. Banes, G. O. Jones, R. S. Ferley, P. S. Lazenbury, A. Khan, M. Sigley (*first-team physiotherapist*). *Middle row:* J. C. Foley (*scorer*), R. W. T. Key, M. J. Saggers, J. B. Hockley, D. D. Masters, B. J. Trott, J. M. Golding, C. Stone (*coach*), D. P. Fulton. *Front row:* M. J. Walker, P. A. Nixon, M. J. McCague, M. V. Fleming (*captain*), D. G. Ufton (*president*), M. A. Ealham, M. M. Patel, A. P. Wells. *Inset:* D. J. Cullinan.

KENT RESULTS

All first-class matches – Played 18: Won 4, Lost 3, Drawn 11.

County Championship matches – Played 16: Won 4, Lost 3, Drawn 9.

CricInfo County Championship, 3rd in Division 1; Cheltenham & Gloucester Trophy, q-f; Benson and Hedges Cup, 4th in South Group; Norwich Union League, winners in Division 1.

COUNTY CHAMPIONSHIP AVERAGES

BATTING

Cap		*M*	*I*	*NO*	*R*	*HS*	*100s*	*50s*	*Avge*	*Ct/St*
1998	D. P. Fulton	16	24	2	1,729	208*	8	3	78.59	26
1999	A. Symonds§	8	12	0	563	131	2	2	46.91	13
2000	M. J. Walker†	15	22	3	868	124	4	2	45.68	9
2001	R. W. T. Key	16	24	0	1,073	132	3	6	44.70	6
2001	E. T. Smith†	16	24	1	947	116	3	4	41.17	5
2000	P. A. Nixon	16	22	5	554	87*	0	3	32.58	42/3
1992	M. A. Ealham†	11	13	1	286	153*	1	0	23.83	8
1990	M. V. Fleming	16	21	4	381	59	0	1	22.41	6
1994	M. M. Patel	15	18	2	247	38	0	0	15.43	8
	J. B. Hockley†	5	9	0	132	29	0	0	14.66	6
2001	M. J. Saggers	16	20	5	185	61*	0	1	12.33	1
	J. M. Golding†	4	7	1	69	30	0	0	11.50	1
	B. J. Trott	13	13	3	57	13	0	0	5.70	3

Also batted: D. J. Cullinan§ (cap 2001) (3 matches) 57, 2, 63; G. O. Jones (1 match) 5 (1 ct); M. J. McCague (cap 1992) (1 match) 4; D. D. Masters† (3 matches) 2*, 6, 0* (1 ct); J. C. Tredwell† (1 match) 10.

* *Signifies not out.* † *Born in Kent.* § *Overseas player.*

BOWLING

	O	*M*	*R*	*W*	*BB*	*5W/i*	*Avge*
M. J. Saggers	492.3	112	1,520	63	6-92	3	24.12
M. A. Ealham	213	63	555	23	6-64	2	24.13
B. J. Trott	352.5	64	1,169	47	6-13	4	24.87
M. M. Patel	476.2	143	1,097	36	8-119	1	30.47
A. Symonds	106.2	23	333	10	3-28	0	33.30
M. V. Fleming	284	47	888	20	4-53	0	44.40

Also bowled: D. J. Cullinan 14–6–29–1; D. P. Fulton 1–0–2–0; J. M. Golding 82.3–15–298–6; J. B. Hockley 28–5–109–1; G. O. Jones 1–0–4–0; R. W. T. Key 1–0–5–0; M. J. McCague 18–3–64–2; D. D. Masters 73–10–258–5; J. C. Tredwell 26–5–123–2; M. J. Walker 20–3–69–2.

COUNTY RECORDS

Highest score for:	332	W. H. Ashdown v Essex at Brentwood	1934
Highest score against:	344	W. G. Grace (MCC) at Canterbury	1876
Best bowling for:	10-30	C. Blythe v Northamptonshire at Northampton	1907
Best bowling against:	10-48	C. H. G. Bland (Sussex) at Tonbridge	1899
Highest total for:	803-4 dec.	v Essex at Brentwood	1934
Highest total against:	676	by Australians at Canterbury	1921
Lowest total for:	18	v Sussex at Gravesend	1867
Lowest total against:	16	by Warwickshire at Tonbridge	1913

At Cambridge, April 16, 17, 18. KENT drew with CAMBRIDGE UCCE.

At The Oval, April 20, 21, 22, 23. KENT drew with SURREY.

KENT v YORKSHIRE

At Canterbury, April 25, 26, 27, 28. Yorkshire won by four wickets. Yorkshire 17 pts, Kent 3 pts. Toss: Kent. Championship debut: M. J. Lumb.

Yorkshire timed their chase to perfection to win their opening Championship game with two balls to spare. After dismissing Kent shortly before tea on the final day, they were left 38 overs to score 176. Lehmann's brisk 41 shored things up after a shaky start, and the final impetus came from uncapped all-rounder Fellows, who hit 43 from 50 balls. Kent, undone by Silverwood's opening-day five for 45, had trailed by 143 on first innings. Key fell just short of a second Championship hundred in successive matches as the home side made a better fist of batting second time. Smith, coming in at No. 7 after missing part of the third day with food poisoning, put on 91 in 48 overs with Patel, before Lumb, on his Championship debut, broke the partnership with his second delivery in first-class cricket; as an encore, he removed Saggers in his next over, but Masters stayed long enough to see Smith to his hundred.

Close of play: First day, Yorkshire 12-0 (Widdup 7*, Vaughan 4*); Second day, Yorkshire 208-4 (Byas 18*, Sidebottom 4*); Third day, Kent 192-5 (Key 97*, Smith 31*).

Kent

D. P. Fulton lbw b Hoggard	31	– c McGrath b Sidebottom	15
R. W. T. Key c Blakey b Sidebottom	17	– b Sidebottom	98
E. T. Smith lbw b Silverwood	19	– (7) not out	103
M. J. Walker c Fellows b Vaughan	12	– lbw b Fellows	33
†P. A. Nixon b Silverwood	10	– (3) lbw b Sidebottom	2
M. A. Ealham b Fellows	22	– (5) c Byas b Silverwood	0
J. B. Hockley c McGrath b Fellows	13	– (6) c Widdup b Silverwood	6
*M. V. Fleming c Widdup b Silverwood	4	– c Lehmann b Silverwood	1
M. M. Patel c Widdup b Silverwood	0	– c Widdup b Lumb	27
M. J. Saggers c Blakey b Silverwood	1	– b Lumb	4
D. D. Masters not out	2	– lbw b Sidebottom	6
B 2, l-b 1, w 2, n-b 6	11	B 1, l-b 14, w 6, n-b 2	23
1/23 2/63 3/71 4/90 5/100 6/130 7/139 8/139 9/139	142	1/30 2/40 3/121 4/134 5/144 6/195 7/204 8/295 9/299	318

Bonus points – Yorkshire 3.

Bowling: *First Innings*—Silverwood 18.1–3–45–5; Hoggard 12.1–3–32–1; Sidebottom 17–7–30–1; Vaughan 14.5–8–23–1; Fellows 8–3–9–2. *Second Innings*—Silverwood 32–6–96–3; Sidebottom 31.4–8–67–4; Fellows 26–6–69–1; Vaughan 19–2–48–0; Lehmann 12–4–13–0; Lumb 4–1–10–2.

Yorkshire

S. Widdup c Hockley b Saggers	14	– b Patel	27
M. P. Vaughan b Saggers	71	– c Ealham b Saggers	14
A. McGrath lbw b Saggers	29	– c Fulton b Ealham	2
D. S. Lehmann c Nixon b Fleming	68	– b Patel	41
*D. Byas c sub b Masters	27	– (6) lbw b Saggers	23
R. J. Sidebottom not out	40		
M. J. Lumb c Nixon b Masters	1	– run out	9
G. M. Fellows c Fulton b Ealham	18	– (5) not out	43
†R. J. Blakey lbw b Ealham	1	– (8) not out	6
C. E. W. Silverwood c Key b Ealham	0		
M. J. Hoggard c Nixon b Masters	2		
L-b 6, w 8	14	B 1, l-b 8, w 2	11
1/32 2/111 3/134 4/203 5/223 6/231 7/269 8/273 9/273	285	1/21 2/25 3/86 4/95 5/134 6/156	(6 wkts) 176

Bonus points – Yorkshire 2, Kent 3.

Bowling: *First Innings*—Saggers 33–11–64–3; Masters 26–6–52–3; Fleming 25–6–67–1; Patel 3–1–14–0; Ealham 25–7–72–3; Hockley 1–0–10–0. *Second Innings*—Saggers 10–0–37–2; Ealham 5–2–16–1; Masters 4–0–25–0; Fleming 9–0–43–0; Patel 9.4–0–46–2.

Umpires: R. Julian and M. J. Kitchen.

At Canterbury, May 12, 13, 14. KENT drew with PAKISTANIS (see Pakistani tour section).

At Taunton, May 16, 17, 18, 19. KENT drew with SOMERSET.

At Swansea, May 25, 26, 27, 28. KENT drew with GLAMORGAN.

KENT v ESSEX

At Tunbridge Wells, May 30, 31, June 1. Kent won by an innings and 152 runs. Kent 20 pts, Essex 3 pts. Toss: Kent.

Kent completed their first Championship win of the season in emphatic fashion, inside three days. Trott, released by Somerset in 1999 after just one Championship appearance, claimed 11 for 78 in his fourth for Kent. Twice in two and a half hours he set career-best returns, later putting his success down to advice from county coach John Inverarity, who at the close of the second day persuaded him to add two paces to his run-up. With his stride pattern and rhythm improved, Trott dismissed Essex captain Irani with the first ball of the third morning and finished with five for 65. He then ran through the Essex batting again when they followed on, taking three for four in 15 balls and ending with six for 13 as Essex plummeted to 68, the lowest Championship total of the summer. Fulton's fourth hundred of the season had occupied eight and a half hours, and he and Walker added 212 for the fourth wicket. Fleming declared one short of Kent's highest total at the Nevill Ground.

Close of play: First day, Kent 320-3 (Fulton 117*, Walker 37*); Second day, Essex 195-4 (Irani 64*, Peters 7*).

Kent

D. P. Fulton st Foster b Grayson	179	†P. A. Nixon not out	34
R. W. T. Key c Ilott b Anderson	48	B 6, l-b 11, w 12, n-b 29	58
E. T. Smith c Foster b Anderson	12		
D. J. Cullinan lbw b Grayson	63	1/93 2/126 3/236 (5 wkts dec.)	518
M. J. Walker c Irani b Such	124	4/448 5/518	

M. A. Ealham, *M. V. Fleming, M. M. Patel, M. J. Saggers and B. J. Trott did not bat.

Bonus points – Kent 5, Essex 1 (Score at 130 overs: 424-3).

Bowling: Ilott 24–4–78–0; McGarry 22–5–77–0; Anderson 28–9–68–2; Such 39.1–4–143–1; Irani 13–4–38–0; Grayson 23–3–97–2.

Essex

P. J. Prichard c Nixon b Trott	0	– run out	0
A. P. Grayson c Nixon b Trott	5	– b Trott	4
D. D. J. Robinson c Patel b Saggers	6	– c Nixon b Trott	3
S. G. Law b Patel	99	– lbw b Saggers	4
*R. C. Irani lbw b Trott	64	– c Ealham b Trott	2
S. D. Peters c Nixon b Trott	9	– c Fleming b Saggers	4
†J. S. Foster c Ealham b Patel	33	– b Trott	27
R. S. G. Anderson c Ealham b Cullinan	45	– c Nixon b Saggers	6
M. C. Ilott c Ealham b Trott	11	– c Ealham b Trott	11
P. M. Such c Nixon b Fleming	2	– lbw b Trott	0
A. C. McGarry not out	4	– not out	1
B 3, l-b 7, w 4, n-b 6	20	B 4, l-b 2	6
1/1 2/12 3/12 4/176 5/195 6/198 7/269 8/288 9/292	298	1/0 2/7 3/8 4/14 5/14 6/30 7/56 8/59 9/65	68

Bonus points – Essex 2, Kent 3.

Bowling: *First Innings*—Saggers 17–8–32–1; Trott 26–7–65–5; Ealham 18–6–46–0; Fleming 14.1–6–44–1; Patel 31–10–77–2; Cullinan 11–4–24–1. *Second Innings*—Trott 9.5–4–13–6; Ealham 4–2–3–0; Saggers 12–5–30–3; Fleming 2–1–5–0; Patel 13–7–11–0.

Umpires: V. A. Holder and P. Willey.

At Leeds, June 6, 7, 8, 9. KENT lost to YORKSHIRE by nine wickets.

KENT v GLAMORGAN

At Maidstone, June 13, 14, 15, 16. Drawn. Kent 10 pts, Glamorgan 9 pts. Toss: Kent.

Rain, which prevented play on the final day until 3.30 p.m., condemned to stalemate a game that, with Glamorgan requiring 377 from 104 overs, was intriguingly poised. In their previous Championship game, against Essex, Glamorgan had successfully chased 364, and, in what time remained on the final afternoon, the openers showed what might have been, by putting on an unbeaten 203. Maher, the Queensland left-hander, ended a lean start to his Glamorgan career with a first hundred for them. On the opening morning, Maynard kept wicket after Shaw withdrew ill and before Wallace, his 19-year-old understudy, arrived from a second-team game in Abergavenny. Wallace was worth the wait: he held eight catches – one short of Colin Metson's county record – and hit an impressive career-best 80 not out to guide Glamorgan out of trouble from 114 for six. A crisp partnership of 108 between Kent's Smith and Walker then helped set up what had the makings of a tense last day.

Close of play: First day, Glamorgan 7-1 (James 1*); Second day, Kent 47-1 (Fulton 11*, Saggers 4*); Third day, Glamorgan 36-0 (Maher 19*, James 17*).

Kent

D. P. Fulton c Maynard b Jones	4	– b Cosker	45
R. W. T. Key c Maher b Cosker	97	– lbw b Thomas	21
E. T. Smith c Watkin b Cosker	74	– (4) c Wallace b Cosker	116
M. J. Walker run out	5	– (5) lbw b Cosker	53
J. B. Hockley b Watkin	29	– (6) c Wallace b Thomas	0
†P. A. Nixon c Wallace b Thomas	16	– (7) c Wallace b Watkin	17
*M. V. Fleming c Wallace b Thomas	10	– (8) c Dale b Thomas	46
J. M. Golding c Wallace b Thomas	0	– (9) c Wallace b Jones	30
M. M. Patel c Maynard b Thomas	14	– (10) b Watkin	8
M. J. Saggers not out	27	– (3) c Wallace b Thomas	5
B. J. Trott b Watkin	13	– not out	1
B 12, l-b 3	15	B 4, l-b 8, n-b 4	16
1/8 2/129 3/139 4/197 5/229 6/239 7/239 8/262 9/263	304	1/43 2/55 3/97 4/205 5/206 6/268 7/270 8/341 9/356	358

Bonus points – Kent 3, Glamorgan 3.

Bowling: *First Innings*—Jones 18–3–72–1; Watkin 15–3–33–2; Thomas 23–2–67–4; Dale 11–4–27–0; Cosker 34–10–88–2; Newell 1–0–2–0. *Second Innings*—Jones 14.1–3–43–1; Watkin 28–5–88–2; Thomas 23–5–84–4; Cosker 35–11–93–3; Newell 6–0–24–0; Dale 2–0–14–0.

Glamorgan

*S. P. James c Nixon b Patel	27	– (2) not out	76
J. P. Maher lbw b Saggers	6	– (1) not out	123
M. P. Maynard c Fulton b Trott	0		
M. J. Powell c Patel b Saggers	16		
A. Dale b Hockley	41		
K. Newell c Hockley b Fleming	13		
†M. A. Wallace not out	80		
S. D. Thomas c Walker b Fleming	50		
D. A. Cosker b Patel	4		
S. L. Watkin c Key b Fleming	38		
S. P. Jones c Fulton b Golding	2		
B 6, l-b 1, w 2	9	B 1, l-b 1, n-b 2	4
1/7 2/8 3/49 4/51 5/99 6/114 7/190 8/210 9/283	286	(no wkt)	203

Bonus points – Glamorgan 2, Kent 3.

Bowling: *First Innings*—Saggers 16–2–60–2; Trott 16–1–61–1; Patel 34–10–72–2; Fleming 16–4–57–3; Hockley 13–5–21–1; Golding 2.3–0–8–1. *Second Innings*—Saggers 10–2–38–0; Trott 8–3–31–0; Patel 10–2–39–0; Hockley 7–0–48–0; Golding 5–0–28–0; Walker 4–1–17–0.

Umpires: T. E. Jesty and R. A. White.

KENT v LEICESTERSHIRE

At Canterbury, June 20, 21, 22. Leicestershire won by an innings and 149 runs. Leicestershire 20 pts, Kent 3 pts. Toss: Leicestershire.

On an excellent pitch, Kent suffered their heaviest defeat in Championship cricket since 1979, and their biggest at the St Lawrence Ground since the Australians' visit in 1953. Leicestershire's batting was a question of all or nothing: of the eight dismissed, two, including former Kent opener Ward, fell for ducks; the other six (plus DeFreitas, not out 59) all passed 50. Ben Smith hit his

HIGHEST TOTALS BY LEICESTERSHIRE

701-4 dec.	Leicestershire v Worcestershire at Worcester	1906
681-7 dec.	Leicestershire v Yorkshire at Bradford	1996
638-8 dec.	Leicestershire v Worcestershire at Leicester	1996
612-8 dec.	**Leicestershire v Kent at Canterbury**	**2001**
609-8 dec.	Leicestershire v Sussex at Leicester	1900
603	Leicestershire v Sir Julien Cahn's XI at West Bridgford	1935

first Championship hundred of the summer, sharing a second-wicket stand of 190 with Sutcliffe, while Wells, another ex-Kent player, enjoyed a magnificent all-round game. After a hundred of style and aggression – he smashed 21 fours and three sixes in his 122-ball 138 – he watched Malcolm and DeFreitas scatter the Kent first innings to the wind before joining in the slaughter with five for 36 to complete the three-day win. The only bright spot for Kent was Fulton's fifth hundred of the season, but his wicket sparked a collapse in which the last six wickets fell for seven runs.

Close of play: First day, Leicestershire 296-4 (Habib 29*); Second day, Kent 155-7 (Fleming 9*, Patel 10*).

Leicestershire

T. R. Ward c Nixon b Saggers	0
I. J. Sutcliffe run out	64
B. F. Smith c Walker b Saggers	110
D. J. Marsh c Nixon b Saggers	72
A. Habib c Smith b Golding	55
D. L. Maddy lbw b Trott	0
*V. J. Wells c Trott b Patel	138
†N. D. Burns c Golding b Saggers	51
P. A. J. DeFreitas not out	59
J. Ormond not out	34
B 1, l-b 18, w 10	29
1/0 2/190 3/199 4/296 5/303 6/373 7/457 8/551 (8 wkts dec.)	612

D. E. Malcolm did not bat.

Bonus points – Leicestershire 5, Kent 2 (Score at 130 overs: 403-6).

Bowling: Saggers 34–12–94–4; Trott 23–4–96–1; Fleming 23–1–101–0; Walker 5–2–14–0; Golding 23–3–118–1; Patel 47–8–140–1; Hockley 7–0–30–0.

Kent

D. P. Fulton c Burns b DeFreitas	19	– lbw b Ormond	107
R. W. T. Key c Burns b Malcolm	28	– (7) lbw b Wells	0
E. T. Smith c Burns b DeFreitas	5	– (2) lbw b Wells	33
M. J. Walker c Marsh b Malcolm	26	– (3) b DeFreitas	26
J. B. Hockley b Malcolm	26	– (4) c Habib b Malcolm	26
†P. A. Nixon run out	12	– (5) c Burns b Maddy	12
*M. V. Fleming c Smith b Malcolm	29	– (6) c Maddy b Wells	35
J. M. Golding lbw b Ormond	1	– not out	2
M. M. Patel c Habib b DeFreitas	34	– b Ormond	0
M. J. Saggers lbw b DeFreitas	1	– lbw b Wells	1
B. J. Trott not out	4	– lbw b Wells	0
B 5, l-b 4, w 8, n-b 8	25	L-b 7, w 2, n-b 2	11
1/55 2/55 3/72 4/110 5/131 6/144 7/145 8/195 9/206	210	1/63 2/110 3/163 4/182 5/246 6/246 7/250 8/252 9/253	253

Bonus points – Kent 1, Leicestershire 3.

Bowling: *First Innings*—Ormond 22–8–70–1; Malcolm 23–5–83–4; DeFreitas 12.2–2–43–4; Maddy 4–1–5–0. *Second Innings*—Malcolm 12–0–61–1; Ormond 18–2–65–2; Wells 13–5–36–5; DeFreitas 15–3–38–1; Maddy 10–2–29–1; Marsh 8–4–17–0.

Umpires: G. I. Burgess and J. H. Hampshire.

KENT v LANCASHIRE

At Canterbury, July 4, 5, 6. Kent won by 268 runs. Kent 17 pts (1 pt deducted for slow over-rate), Lancashire 4 pts. Toss: Lancashire.

Despite winning inside three days, Kent were docked a point for a slow over-rate; Fleming condemned the penalty as farcical and claimed "the law is an ass". On the first day, as Kent struggled to 205 for eight, Crawley's decision to bowl seemed vindicated. During his 65, Fulton had become the first to 1,000 runs for the season, but he received scant support. Saggers, however, teamed up with Nixon, helped him add 116, and celebrated his county cap with a career-best unbeaten 61. Although Ealham took six wickets for the first time in nearly two years, a team effort saw Lancashire past the follow-on target. Kent looked set to build a 400-plus lead, but lost their last five wickets for three runs as Muralitharan, before flying home to play for Sri Lanka, claimed three in four balls. At 11 for three, any hopes Lancashire entertained of making 375 had evaporated. Trott, with his third five-wicket return, and Ealham completed the rout; Scuderi, suffering from a back spasm, was unable to bat.

Close of play: First day, Kent 301-8 (Nixon 69*, Saggers 38*); Second day, Kent 77-1 (Key 28*, Smith 30*).

Kent

D. P. Fulton c Hegg b Muralitharan	65	– c Chilton b Scuderi	17
R. W. T. Key b Wood	13	– b Flintoff	83
E. T. Smith c Muralitharan b Flintoff	15	– lbw b Muralitharan	59
A. Symonds c Hegg b Wood	31	– c Haynes b Muralitharan	10
M. J. Walker c and b Muralitharan	11	– c Chilton b Keedy	7
M. A. Ealham c Hegg b Scuderi	10	– c Fairbrother b Muralitharan	3
†P. A. Nixon c Muralitharan b Wood	82	– not out	46
*M. V. Fleming c Hegg b Scuderi	23	– c Hegg b Flintoff	1
M. M. Patel c Flintoff b Muralitharan	3	– c Haynes b Muralitharan	1
M. J. Saggers not out	61	– lbw b Muralitharan	0
B. J. Trott c Hegg b Scuderi	10	– lbw b Muralitharan	0
B 4, l-b 3, w 2, n-b 10, p 5	24	B 4, l-b 7, n-b 2	13
1/25 2/61 3/119 4/147 5/150 6/166 7/202 8/205 9/321	348	1/29 2/133 3/147 4/156 5/163 6/237 7/239 8/240 9/240	240

Bonus points – Kent 3, Lancashire 3.

Bowling: *First Innings*—Wood 25–4–97–3; Smethurst 22–1–87–0; Flintoff 15–3–27–1; Scuderi 20.4–8–48–3; Muralitharan 30–11–69–3; Keedy 3–1–8–0. *Second Innings*—Wood 12–2–24–0; Smethurst 5–1–30–0; Scuderi 7–2–14–1; Flintoff 11–2–27–2; Chilton 1–0–5–0; Keedy 20–3–59–1; Muralitharan 28.5–5–70–6.

Lancashire

M. J. Chilton lbw b Trott	35	– (2) c Symonds b Trott	8
J. J. Haynes c Symonds b Ealham	7	– (1) c Patel b Saggers	0
*J. P. Crawley c Fulton b Ealham	13	– c Walker b Trott	3
A. Flintoff lbw b Ealham	12	– b Trott	23
N. H. Fairbrother not out	39	– b Ealham	33
J. C. Scuderi c Patel b Ealham	0	– absent hurt	
†W. K. Hegg c Fulton b Saggers	22	– (6) c Symonds b Trott	3
J. Wood c Smith b Symonds	25	– (7) b Ealham	8
G. Keedy c Nixon b Ealham	0	– (8) not out	7
M. P. Smethurst b Ealham	5	– (9) c Patel b Ealham	0
M. Muralitharan c Smith b Symonds	21	– (10) c Ealham b Trott	10
B 12, l-b 3, w 10, n-b 10	35	B 6, l-b 5	11
1/23 2/57 3/59 4/75 5/75 6/113 7/152 8/162 9/174	214	1/0 2/10 3/11 4/72 5/80 6/82 7/93 8/93 9/106	106

Bonus points – Lancashire 1, Kent 3.

Bowling: *First Innings*—Saggers 13–4–33–1; Trott 14–3–58–1; Ealham 16–2–64–6; Fleming 3–0–11–0; Symonds 7.2–0–33–2. *Second Innings*—Saggers 7–2–20–1; Trott 15–3–43–5; Ealham 8–3–20–3; Patel 4–1–12–0.

Umpires: D. J. Constant and N. A. Mallender.

At Southend, July 18, 19, 20. KENT beat ESSEX by an innings and 132 runs.

At Leicester, July 27, 28, 29, 30. KENT beat LEICESTERSHIRE by three wickets.

KENT v SOMERSET

At Canterbury, August 1, 2, 3, 4. Drawn. Kent 12 pts, Somerset 9 pts. Toss: Kent.

Fulton crowned a patch of purple form by scoring a double-hundred and a hundred in the same match. Although four others had done so for Kent, Fulton was alone in not being dismissed in either innings; he also took seven close catches, yet could not end on the winning side. His career-best 208 came in 430 minutes off 313 balls, with 25 fours and two sixes, and was the bedrock of Kent's substantial total. Somerset's attack was weakened at lunch on the first day, after Johnson had been summoned to Trent Bridge as emergency cover for the Ashes Test. Having missed the 11 balls rain allowed on the second day, he was back for the third, when he and Dutch bailed out Somerset, who had stumbled – despite several Kent fielding lapses – to 86 for five. Patel was the destroyer, claiming eight for 119 on his way to a career-best 12 for 144, though Somerset wriggled past the follow-on target. Fleming then opted for caution – setting 321 from a minimum of 41 overs – when Somerset's continuing inability to cope with spin suggested adventure might have achieved victory. On the opening day, Key and Smith were awarded their caps.

Close of play: First day, Kent 381-4 (Fulton 160*, Saggers 7*); Second day, Kent 388-4 (Fulton 167*, Saggers 7*); Third day, Somerset 300-9 (Dutch 55*, Bulbeck 8*).

Kent

D. P. Fulton not out	208	– not out	104
R. W. T. Key run out	50	– c Turner b Blackwell	20
E. T. Smith c Lathwell b Jones	8	– c and b Blackwell	19
A. Symonds lbw b Jones	56	– c Bulbeck b Burns	59
M. J. Walker c and b Dutch	81		
M. J. Saggers b Jones	16		
M. A. Ealham c Dutch b Jones	0		
†P. A. Nixon lbw b Jones	8		
*M. V. Fleming not out	3		
L-b 9, w 12	21	L-b 1, n-b 2	3
1/91 2/108 3/198 4/373 5/415 6/427 7/441	(7 wkts dec.) 451	1/68 2/128 3/205	(3 wkts dec.) 205

M. M. Patel and B. J. Trott did not bat.

Bonus points – Kent 5, Somerset 2.

Bowling: *First Innings*—Johnson 13.5–4–69–0; Bulbeck 25–0–114–0; Blackwell 22–6–56–0; Jones 31–4–115–5; Burns 12–3–39–0; Dutch 15–2–49–1. *Second Innings*—Johnson 8–0–31–0; Jones 7–1–25–0; Blackwell 11–0–63–2; Bulbeck 6–0–50–0; Burns 4.4–0–35–1.

Somerset

*J. Cox c Fulton b Patel	50	– (2) c Fleming b Patel	24
P. C. L. Holloway c Fulton b Saggers	20	– (1) c Nixon b Trott	3
M. Burns b Saggers	0	– c Fulton b Symonds	18
P. D. Bowler c Nixon b Patel	0	– c Fulton b Patel	26
M. N. Lathwell b Patel	63	– c Walker b Patel	9
I. D. Blackwell c Fulton b Patel	2	– c Fulton b Symonds	15
†R. J. Turner c Fleming b Patel	29	– c Fulton b Symonds	1
K. P. Dutch not out	75	– lbw b Patel	1
R. L. Johnson st Nixon b Patel	46	– not out	8
P. S. Jones lbw b Patel	10	– not out	3
M. P. L. Bulbeck c Symonds b Patel	18		
B 7, l-b 10, w 2, n-b 4	23	L-b 3, n-b 2	5
1/66 2/68 3/69 4/84 5/86 6/181 7/188 8/272 9/288	336	1/25 2/29 3/63 4/79 5/91 6/97 7/100 8/104	(8 wkts) 113

Bonus points – Somerset 3, Kent 3.

Bowling: *First Innings*—Saggers 26–6–72–2; Trott 11–0–46–0; Patel 43.2–12–119–8; Fleming 9–1–31–0; Ealham 14–2–38–0; Symonds 1–0–13–0. *Second Innings*—Saggers 5–0–24–0; Trott 8–1–33–1; Patel 22–13–25–4; Symonds 13–4–28–3.

Umpires: V. A. Holder and J. F. Steele.

At Northampton, August 8, 9, 10, 11. KENT drew with NORTHAMPTONSHIRE.

KENT v SURREY

At Canterbury, August 16, 17, 18, 19. Drawn. Kent 10 pts, Surrey 9 pts. Toss: Surrey.

Bicknell, abetted by the weather, which washed out the final day, frustrated Kent with bat and ball, denying them a fifth win. He arrived at 95 for six, after Saggers had cut through the top order – and claimed his 50th Championship wicket of the season when he removed Carberry. Immediately, Bicknell set about the recovery, added 64 with Batty and 74 with Salisbury, and guided Surrey to two unexpected batting points. He then removed Kent's prolific top four, three disappearing for a single as they veered from 153 for one to 154 for four. Nixon ensured a modest home lead, which in turn seemed to have ensured a home victory once Saggers (again) and Trott reduced Surrey to 44 for six, just one run to the good. Bicknell rescued them a second time, putting on 74 with Batty *en route* to a maiden first-class hundred in his 16th season. His exertions briefly made him both the country's leading wicket-taker (60) and Surrey's leading run-scorer in the Championship (660).

Close of play: First day, Kent 43-0 (Fulton 18*, Key 18*); Second day, Kent 301; Third day, Surrey 193-8 (Bicknell 110*, Saqlain Mushtaq 13*).

Surrey

I. J. Ward c Key b Symonds	47	– c Nixon b Saggers	1
M. A. Carberry c Fulton b Saggers	6	– lbw b Trott	15
N. Shahid b Saggers	0	– lbw b Saggers	0
*A. J. Hollioake c Fulton b Saggers	3	– b Trott	14
A. D. Brown lbw b Fleming	0	– c Fulton b Trott	8
B. C. Hollioake c Nixon b McCague	31	– c Nixon b Saggers	3
†J. N. Batty c Fulton b Patel	40	– c Nixon b McCague	18
M. P. Bicknell lbw b Symonds	78	– not out	110
I. D. K. Salisbury c Walker b Symonds	34	– c Nixon b Fleming	0
Saqlain Mushtaq b Saggers	13	– not out	13
E. S. H. Giddins not out	0		
L-b 4, w 2	6	B 3, l-b 6, w 2	11
1/31 2/31 3/39 4/42 5/83 6/95 7/159 8/233 9/250	258	1/16 2/16 3/22 4/39 5/42 6/44 7/118 8/129	(8 wkts) 193

Bonus points – Surrey 2, Kent 3.

Bowling: *First Innings*—Saggers 20.2–4–58–4; Trott 15–4–37–0; Fleming 11–1–46–1; McCague 10–1–36–1; Symonds 10–2–35–3; Patel 20–7–42–1. *Second Innings*—Saggers 15–3–37–3; Trott 16–2–48–3; Patel 9–2–30–0; Fleming 9–1–20–1; McCague 8–2–28–1; Symonds 7–1–21–0.

Kent

D. P. Fulton c A. J. Hollioake b Bicknell	25
R. W. T. Key lbw b Bicknell	79
E. T. Smith c Batty b Bicknell	37
A. Symonds c Batty b Bicknell	0
M. J. Walker c B. C. Hollioake b Saqlain Mushtaq	4
†P. A. Nixon not out	66
*M. V. Fleming b Saqlain Mushtaq	15
M. J. McCague lbw b Salisbury	4
M. M. Patel b B. C. Hollioake	38
M. J. Saggers b Salisbury	2
B. J. Trott c Batty b B. C. Hollioake	0
B 4, l-b 13, n-b 14	31
1/58 2/153 3/153 4/154 5/168 6/194 7/199 8/283 9/300	301

Bonus points – Kent 3, Surrey 3.

Bowling: Bicknell 25–7–47–4; Giddins 22–4–80–0; B. C. Hollioake 15.2–3–39–2; Saqlain Mushtaq 39–13–60–2; Salisbury 17–4–58–2.

Umpires: M. J. Harris and K. E. Palmer.

KENT v NORTHAMPTONSHIRE

At Canterbury, September 5, 6, 7, 8. Drawn. Kent 7 pts, Northamptonshire 11 pts. Toss: Kent. Championship debut: R. A. White.

Both sides needed a win – Kent for the £50,000 runners-up prize, Northamptonshire to escape relegation – but neither could force victory in this see-saw tussle. By lunch on the first day, after Fleming had chosen to bat, Blain had ripped apart the Kent innings with a career-best six for 42. Despite the early loss of Hussey, Northamptonshire were steered towards dominance by Warren and Penberthy, who added 167 before seven wickets fell for 49, Trott ending with five. A lead of 249 seemed conclusive, and might have been so, had Ripley not dropped Fulton, when 37. He went on to 196 – one run less than at Northampton a month earlier – his ninth hundred of the summer equalling Arthur Fagg's 1938 feat and just one short of Frank Woolley's county record. Fulton and Ealham, who ended a lean run with a personal-best 153 not out, added 219. Northamptonshire, set 328, were heading for defeat at 96 for seven, but Ripley stood firm for over two and a quarter hours. Although Strong fell to the first ball of the final over, the last pair survived the next five.

Close of play: First day, Northamptonshire 173-3 (Warren 27*, Penberthy 19*); Second day, Kent 158-3 (Fulton 80*, Walker 22*); Third day, Kent 463-6 (Ealham 109*, Fleming 15*).

Kent

D. P. Fulton c Ripley b Blain	9	– c G. P. Swann b Strong	196
R. W. T. Key b Taylor	4	– b Blain	1
E. T. Smith c Ripley b Blain	0	– c Ripley b Blain	40
A. Symonds c Warren b Taylor	23	– c and b Penberthy	4
M. J. Walker lbw b Blain	1	– b Blain	35
†P. A. Nixon c Ripley b Blain	4	– lbw b Strong	17
M. A. Ealham c Warren b Blain	2	– not out	153
*M. V. Fleming c G. P. Swann b Blain	0	– b G. P. Swann	33
M. M. Patel c Hussey b Penberthy	32	– c Hussey b Strong	30
M. J. Saggers b Taylor	0	– not out	16
B. J. Trott not out	11		
L-b 4, w 2, n-b 16	22	L-b 16, w 7, n-b 28	51
1/11 2/15 3/15 4/16 5/32 6/40 7/48 8/64 9/73	108	1/6 2/92 3/97 4/176 5/202 6/421 7/489 8/544	(8 wkts dec.) 576

Bonus points – Northamptonshire 3.

Bowling: *First Innings*—Taylor 12–0–58–3; Blain 10–3–42–6; Strong 2–0–2–0; Penberthy 1–0–2–1. *Second Innings*—Taylor 36–4–118–0; Blain 32–5–132–3; Penberthy 33–4–97–1; Strong 32–8–98–3; G. P. Swann 23–3–83–1; White 3–0–7–0; Cook 12–3–25–0.

Northamptonshire

M. E. K. Hussey lbw b Trott	7	– c Symonds b Trott	23
A. J. Swann lbw b Ealham	61	– c Fulton b Saggers	2
J. W. Cook c Nixon b Saggers	50	– c Symonds b Trott	0
R. J. Warren c Symonds b Trott	104	– c Fulton b Patel	28
A. L. Penberthy c Patel b Walker	73	– c Patel b Trott	12
G. P. Swann lbw b Trott	6	– c and b Saggers	26
R. A. White b Trott	4	– lbw b Saggers	2
*†D. Ripley b Saggers	16	– not out	62
J. P. Taylor c Walker b Trott	10	– lbw b Symonds	11
M. R. Strong c Symonds b Saggers	2	– st Nixon b Symonds	20
J. A. R. Blain not out	0	– not out	1
B 7, l-b 9, w 4, n-b 4	24	B 10, l-b 2	12
1/21 2/112 3/141 4/308 5/318 6/324 7/337 8/347 9/357	357	1/25 2/25 3/29 4/57 5/89 6/95 7/96 8/145 9/198	(9 wkts) 199

Bonus points – Northamptonshire 4, Kent 3.

Bowling: *First Innings*—Saggers 28–6–98–3; Trott 27.4–3–89–5; Ealham 17–4–35–1; Fleming 16–3–39–0; Patel 13–6–30–0; Symonds 11–2–38–0; Walker 3–0–12–1. *Second Innings*—Saggers 17–1–77–3; Trott 13.3–2–37–3; Patel 27–14–33–1; Symonds 15–5–36–2; Fleming 3.3–1–4–0.

Umpires: N. G. Cowley and G. Sharp.

At Manchester, September 12, 13, 14, 15. KENT drew with LANCASHIRE.

Warren Hegg

LANCASHIRE

President: J. F. Blackledge
Chairman: J. Simmons
Chief Executive: J. Cumbes
Chairman, Cricket Committee: G. Ogden
Cricket Secretary: 2001 – D. M. R. Edmundson
Captain: 2001 – J. P. Crawley
2002 – W. K. Hegg
First-Team Coach: 2001 – R. B. Simpson
Cricket Manager: 2002 – M. Watkinson
Head Groundsman: P. Marron
Scorer: A. West

A batsman had one of his better seasons, a seamer was converted into a valuable all-rounder, the wicket-keeper did so well that he earned an England recall and the No. 1 spinner claimed 50 wickets in seven matches – the basis, one might think, of a decent season. Yet, while Neil Fairbrother, Glen Chapple, Warren Hegg and Muttiah Muralitharan can look back with some degree of satisfaction, Lancashire as a whole will want to forget 2001. Relegation became a real possibility in the Championship and they plunged to near oblivion in two of the one-day competitions. If not, statistically, the worst season in the club's modern history, it was probably the most depressing, with poor performances on the field aggravated by a quarrelsome tone off it.

By early August, the recriminations were flying thick and fast, with a quickly widening rift between the Bob Simpson–John Crawley axis and an influential section of the Old Trafford establishment. Almost inevitably, Simpson left after two years as coach. Crawley lost the captaincy to Hegg; by the end of the year, he was threatening to sue the club if they would not release him from the remaining three years of his contract. Ian Austin retired with a verbal blast in Simpson's direction and Joe Scuderi, a controversial signing two years earlier, was sacked. The cricket secretary, Dave Edmundson, was also a casualty, while Mike Atherton packed in the game without a farewell appearance or a flicker of regret. Lancashire, looking to the future, handed ex-captain Mike Watkinson a three-year contract as cricket manager, and he began with the club at its lowest ebb for many years.

Where did it all go wrong? Team selection, left in the hands of the captain and coach, was an obvious bone of contention with club chairman Jack Simmons, particularly over the way Austin and Graham Lloyd were side-lined. Two Championship fixtures at the start of the season were wiped out because of a marshy patch on the Old Trafford outfield, and Muralitharan missed six weeks because of international duties. Going further back, Lancashire were suffering from a dearth of local talent and had failed to strengthen a side which, after the successes of the 1990s, was entering a transitional phase when Crawley took over in 1999.

Yet they had an encouraging start with a Championship win at Taunton, where Fairbrother launched his season with an unbeaten 179. Recently he and Hegg, who also batted well, had undergone laser operations to improve their eyesight. Wearing protective goggles, they rushed from the London clinic to Euston station – and found neither could read the departures board. While making enquiries, they lost sight of each other, had to make contact by mobile phone and missed the train. They missed little else all season.

Fairbrother, in his 20th season, topped the county's averages with 62.60 from 939 runs. Hegg, later called up for England's winter tours, was second with 48.87 – between them they contributed six centuries – and both accepted that their batting had benefited from Simpson's coaching. But no one managed 1,000 runs. Chapple, given more responsibility with the bat, responded with some top-class performances, notably his 155 against Somerset at Old Trafford, and also claimed 53 wickets. Otherwise, the team fell short of consistency with bat and ball. Crawley's best performances came too late, and Peter Martin struggled with injury.

Three wins on the trot in June pulled them into title contention, but a heavy defeat at Canterbury and Muralitharan's return to Sri Lanka in July signalled a dramatic slump. The writing was on the wall for Simpson after a seven-wicket Roses defeat at Headingley, and he took his fate into his own hands by announcing, during the next game at Colwyn Bay, that he would not be returning in 2002. The situation deteriorated over the following week, with an innings mauling by Yorkshire at Old Trafford and defeat in the Cheltenham & Gloucester Trophy semi-final at Grace Road, where Crawley was widely condemned for batting first in overcast conditions. One of his severest critics was Paul Allott, a Sky TV commentator and also a member of Lancashire's committee. A few days later, the two had a frank exchange of views over the phone.

Whatever the rights and wrongs, the outcome was that Simpson and Crawley felt more isolated, perceiving a lack of support from the committee. In turn, the club's power brokers believed that major changes were necessary, and a blueprint for the future was already under informal discussion, based on the role of "director of cricket". That evolved, some might say was downgraded, to "cricket manager". Meanwhile, avoiding relegation became the main concern. That was achieved by flying Muralitharan back for the last game, against Kent; fortunately, the weather was kind for long enough to allow him to claim five wickets and Lancashire to collect the bonus points they desperately needed. In his two seasons at Old Trafford, Muralitharan had taken 116 wickets in 14 Championship games. His only weakness was his frequent unavailability; for 2002, Lancashire looked to strengthen the batting by signing Australian Stuart Law, who had become disenchanted with Essex.

The season finished with a virtually meaningless League fixture which they lost to bottom-placed Derbyshire; Crawley further exasperated Simmons by omitting himself. Twenty-four hours later he walked out of an Old Trafford meeting believing he had been, or would be, sacked, although Lancashire refused to confirm that until the cricket committee's recommendation was rubber stamped a fortnight later by the general committee.

With Old Trafford booked for two rock concerts, Lancashire switched the bulk of their cup ties to outgrounds, three Benson and Hedges games going to Liverpool and the C&G quarter-final to Blackpool. The first concert fell through, but the second, featuring Robbie Williams, pulled in around 150,000 fans over three nights. It was the success of the season. – COLIN EVANS.

LANCASHIRE 2001

[*Bill Smith*

Back row: J. C. Scuderi, J. J. Haynes, J. M. Anderson, R. C. Driver, J. Wood, M. P. Smethurst, M. J. Chilton, K. W. Hogg, T. W. Roberts. *Middle row:* A. West (*First Eleven scorer*), R. B. Simpson (*head coach*), G. Keedy, R. J. Green, C. P. Schofield, M. Watkinson, L. G. Brown (*physiotherapist*), D. White (*Second Eleven scorer*). *Front row:* G. Yates, I. D. Austin, P. J. Martin, M. A. Atherton, J. P. Crawley (*captain*), W. K. Hegg, N. H. Fairbrother, G. D. Lloyd, A. Flintoff, G. Chapple. *Inset:* M. Muralitharan.

LANCASHIRE RESULTS

All first-class matches – Played 15: Won 4, Lost 5, Drawn 6. Abandoned 2.

County Championship matches – Played 14: Won 4, Lost 5, Drawn 5. Abandoned 2.

CricInfo County Championship, 6th in Division 1; Cheltenham & Gloucester Trophy, s-f; Benson and Hedges Cup, 5th in North Group; Norwich Union League, 6th in Division 2.

COUNTY CHAMPIONSHIP AVERAGES

BATTING

Cap		*M*	*I*	*NO*	*R*	*HS*	*100s*	*50s*	*Avge*	*Ct/St*
1985	N. H. Fairbrother† . .	12	19	4	939	179*	4	1	62.60	16
1989	W. K. Hegg†	13	20	4	782	133	2	5	48.87	35/3
1989	M. A. Atherton†‡ . .	4	8	1	330	160	1	0	47.14	4
1994	J. P. Crawley	14	24	2	898	280	2	5	40.81	4
1994	G. Chapple	13	19	3	497	155	1	2	31.06	3
	M. J. Chilton	13	23	1	668	104	1	4	30.36	10
	C. P. Schofield†	8	13	2	328	80*	0	3	29.81	7
	J. C. Scuderi	12	17	2	444	89	0	3	29.60	2
1998	A. Flintoff†	13	22	1	566	68	0	2	26.95	17
1994	P. J. Martin†	9	12	3	169	51*	0	1	18.77	2
	J. J. Haynes	4	7	0	103	57	0	1	14.71	6
2000	G. Keedy	12	14	8	81	20*	0	0	13.50	6
	J. Wood	7	9	0	112	35	0	0	12.44	0
	R. C. Driver	4	7	0	77	35	0	0	11.00	5
1999	M. Muralitharan§ . . .	7	8	1	70	21	0	0	10.00	4
	M. P. Smethurst† . . .	4	7	1	29	7	0	0	4.83	0
1992	G. D. Lloyd†	3	4	0	19	9	0	0	4.75	3

Also batted: T. W. Roberts (1 match) 3, 0; G. Yates† (cap 1994) (1 match) 8* (2 ct).

* *Signifies not out.* † *Born in Lancashire.* ‡ *ECB contract.* § *Overseas player.*

BOWLING

	O	*M*	*R*	*W*	*BB*	*5W/i*	*Avge*
M. Muralitharan	484.5	159	971	50	6-53	5	19.42
G. Chapple	379.2	87	1,174	53	6-46	4	22.15
P. J. Martin	322.3	86	969	33	5-52	1	29.36
A. Flintoff	236.3	44	713	19	3-36	0	37.52
G. Keedy	368.3	68	1,114	27	5-73	2	41.25
C. P. Schofield	234.1	49	704	11	2-50	0	64.00

Also bowled: M. J. Chilton 1–0–5–0; J. P. Crawley 1–0–2–0; R. C. Driver 4–0–33–0; N. H. Fairbrother 6–1–20–1; J. C. Scuderi 115.4–33–318–9; M. P. Smethurst 82–13–315–7; J. Wood 131.3–14–511–9; G. Yates 19.5–4–65–2.

COUNTY RECORDS

Highest score for:	424	A. C. MacLaren v Somerset at Taunton	1895
Highest score against:	315*	T. W. Hayward (Surrey) at The Oval	1898
Best bowling for:	10-46	W. Hickton v Hampshire at Manchester	1870
Best bowling against:	10-40	G. O. B. Allen (Middlesex) at Lord's	1929
Highest total for:	863	v Surrey at The Oval	1990
Highest total against:	707-9 dec.	by Surrey at The Oval	1990
Lowest total for:	25	v Derbyshire at Manchester	1871
Lowest total against:	22	by Glamorgan at Liverpool	1924

At Taunton, April 20, 21, 22, 23. LANCASHIRE beat SOMERSET by an innings and four runs.

LANCASHIRE v SURREY

At Manchester, April 25, 26, 27, 28. Abandoned. Lancashire 4 pts, Surrey 4 pts.

At Leicester, May 9, 10, 11. LANCASHIRE lost to LEICESTERSHIRE by six runs.

LANCASHIRE v GLAMORGAN

At Manchester, May 16, 17, 18, 19. Abandoned. Lancashire 4 pts, Glamorgan 4 pts.

At Northampton, May 30, 31, June 1, 2. LANCASHIRE beat NORTHAMPTONSHIRE by three wickets.

LANCASHIRE v LEICESTERSHIRE

At Manchester, June 6, 7, 8, 9. Lancashire won by six wickets. Lancashire 17 pts, Leicestershire 4 pts. Toss: Leicestershire.

The Manchester weather, which had forced the abandonment of both Lancashire's previous home Championship matches, relented at last. Though rain was never far away – it first intervened 13 balls after lunch on the opening day – Lancashire made the most of the opportunity, avenging their narrow defeat at Grace Road a month earlier, and going third in Division One. Their seamers worked diligently to dismiss Leicestershire for 202, though it needed Fairbrother, later joined by Hegg, both in fine form after pre-season eye surgery, to haul Lancashire round after Ormond had seized their first three wickets in an eight-ball spell. Muralitharan then nagged away at the visiting batsmen for 40 overs, interrupted on the fourth morning by more rain, to claim six for 74. As time began to look increasingly tight, a decisive third-wicket partnership between Crawley and Flintoff all but saw Lancashire home; moments after victory was achieved, the heavens opened.

Close of play: First day, Leicestershire 83-3 (Smith 31*, Maddy 11*); Second day, Lancashire 191-5 (Fairbrother 70*, Hegg 9*); Third day, Leicestershire 208-6 (Maddy 32*, Dakin 31*).

Leicestershire

T. R. Ward b Martin	3	– b Muralitharan	11
I. J. Sutcliffe c Atherton b Chapple	1	– lbw b Muralitharan	24
B. F. Smith b Martin	35	– lbw b Muralitharan	33
D. J. Marsh c Chilton b Chapple	28	– c Flintoff b Martin	38
D. L. Maddy not out	57	– c Atherton b Muralitharan	40
*V. J. Wells c Hegg b Chapple	12	– lbw b Martin	5
†N. D. Burns c Crawley b Flintoff	25	– c Hegg b Martin	2
J. M. Dakin c Chapple b Muralitharan	12	– b Martin	35
C. D. Crowe lbw b Flintoff	0	– c Atherton b Muralitharan	2
J. Ormond lbw b Flintoff	4	– b Muralitharan	20
D. E. Malcolm c Chilton b Martin	4	– not out	4
B 2, l-b 5, n-b 14	21	B 4, l-b 9, n-b 24	37
1/8 2/8 3/47 4/91 5/110 6/150 7/174 8/175 9/189	202	1/31 2/61 3/126 4/130 5/140 6/156 7/212 8/221 9/232	251

Bonus points – Leicestershire 1, Lancashire 3.

Bowling: *First Innings*—Martin 17.5–9–32–3; Chapple 18–2–49–3; Muralitharan 22–2–75–1; Flintoff 13–1–36–3; Keedy 3–1–3–0. *Second Innings*—Martin 27–9–64–4; Chapple 5–1–17–0; Muralitharan 40–17–74–6; Flintoff 8–1–45–0; Keedy 11–1–38–0.

Lancashire

M. A. Atherton b Malcolm	48	– c Burns b Marsh	39
M. J. Chilton lbw b Ormond	8	– b Ormond	13
*J. P. Crawley b Ormond	0	– c Burns b Marsh	50
A. Flintoff b Ormond	0	– c and b Crowe	43
N. H. Fairbrother b Dakin	101	– not out	9
J. C. Scuderi c Dakin b Marsh	46	– not out	4
†W. K. Hegg c Maddy b Dakin	51		
G. Chapple c Smith b Dakin	8		
P. J. Martin c Wells b Dakin	8		
G. Keedy not out	6		
M. Muralitharan c Maddy b Marsh	1		
L-b 7, w 6, n-b 2	15	B 3, l-b 1, w 2	6
1/43 2/51 3/53 4/68 5/179 6/264 7/269 8/278 9/289	292	1/37 2/81 3/146 4/154	(4 wkts) 164

Bonus points – Lancashire 2, Leicestershire 3.

Bowling: *First Innings*—Ormond 27–7–67–3; Malcolm 13–1–76–1; Wells 4–0–19–0; Dakin 16–2–53–4; Maddy 2–0–16–0; Crowe 2–0–17–0; Marsh 19.2–7–37–2. *Second Innings*—Ormond 7–2–28–1; Malcolm 11–2–39–0; Marsh 15–1–66–2; Dakin 4–2–6–0; Crowe 5.1–0–21–1.

Umpires: V. A. Holder and G. Sharp.

At Durham, June 13, 14, 15, 16. LANCASHIRE drew with DURHAM UCCE.

LANCASHIRE v ESSEX

At Manchester, June 19, 20, 21, 22. Lancashire won by nine wickets. Lancashire 19 pts, Essex 3 pts. Toss: Lancashire. County debut: M. K. Davies.

Law made an unbeaten century in each innings, the first visiting player to hit two hundreds in a county match at Old Trafford since Mike Smedley for Nottinghamshire in 1971. All told, he scored 239 runs, batted eight and a half hours, faced 512 balls and struck three sixes and 29 fours, without offering a chance, yet still finished on the losing side. That was testimony both to the skills of Law's overseas counterpart, Muralitharan, and to the weaknesses in the rest of the Essex batting. Murali had match figures of ten for 123 from 87 overs; Law apart, no Essex batsman reached 40. Atherton's painstaking 160 in almost seven hours, his 54th and last hundred before retiring, and Hegg's 133 – taking his tally from his last three Championship innings to 291 – were the mainstays of Lancashire's total. Pitch liaison officer Tony Brown, called in because the wicket, used for the previous week's one-day international, had bare patches at each end, decided no action was necessary. Lancashire moved up to second.

Close of play: First day, Lancashire 230-5 (Atherton 125*, Hegg 35*); Second day, Essex 101-4 (Law 47*, Peters 2*); Third day, Essex 160-4 (Law 60*, Peters 9*).

Lancashire

M. A. Atherton c Law b Davies	160	– not out	24
M. J. Chilton c Hyam b Anderson	9	– lbw b Irani	0
*J. P. Crawley b Cowan	1	– not out	21
A. Flintoff c Law b Such	18		
N. H. Fairbrother c Law b Such	19		
J. C. Scuderi lbw b Davies	11		
†W. K. Hegg c Hyam b Cowan	133		
G. Chapple c Grayson b Davies	12		
P. J. Martin c Cowan b Such	19		
G. Keedy not out	17		
M. Muralitharan b Cowan	14		
B 5, l-b 7, w 4, n-b 2	18	L-b 4, n-b 4	8
1/31 2/49 3/84 4/129 5/156 6/299 7/327 8/364 9/409	431	1/8	(1 wkt) 53

Bonus points – Lancashire 4, Essex 2 (Score at 130 overs: 355-7).

Bowling: *First Innings*—Cowan 25.4–4–65–3; Irani 21–8–42–0; Anderson 22–6–59–1; Such 45–12–124–3; Davies 34–4–121–3; Grayson 3–1–8–0. *Second Innings*—Cowan 3–0–14–0; Irani 5–1–25–1; Such 2.5–1–10–0.

Essex

R. S. Clinton c Fairbrother b Muralitharan	25	– c Flintoff b Chapple	38
A. P. Grayson b Martin	5	– c Hegg b Chapple	36
D. D. J. Robinson lbw b Muralitharan	2	– c Martin b Chapple	1
S. G. Law not out	116	– not out	123
*R. C. Irani c and b Keedy	7	– c Flintoff b Muralitharan	1
S. D. Peters b Keedy	5	– c Flintoff b Muralitharan	18
†B. J. Hyam c Fairbrother b Muralitharan	0	– b Muralitharan	4
R. S. G. Anderson c Fairbrother b Muralitharan	10	– lbw b Muralitharan	3
A. P. Cowan c Keedy b Muralitharan	10	– run out	0
M. K. Davies b Muralitharan	7	– b Martin	5
P. M. Such c Flintoff b Chapple	7	– c Keedy b Martin	9
B 26, l-b 6	32	B 13, l-b 4, n-b 2	19
1/13 2/22 3/76 4/95 5/107 6/108 7/146 8/182 9/207	226	1/81 2/86 3/89 4/116 5/190 6/211 7/223 8/224 9/237	257

Bonus points – Essex 1, Lancashire 3.

Bowling: *First Innings*—Martin 14–6–37–1; Chapple 10.5–1–27–1; Muralitharan 48–22–53–6; Keedy 38–13–72–2; Flintoff 3–1–5–0. *Second Innings*—Martin 11.5–4–35–2; Chapple 16–4–55–3; Muralitharan 39–14–70–4; Flintoff 10–0–24–0; Keedy 22–4–52–0; Scuderi 1–0–4–0.

Umpires: N. G. Cowley and A. A. Jones.

At The Oval, June 29, 30, July 1, 2. LANCASHIRE drew with SURREY.

At Canterbury, July 4, 5, 6. LANCASHIRE lost to KENT by 268 runs.

LANCASHIRE v SOMERSET

At Manchester, July 19, 20, 21. Somerset won by ten wickets. Somerset 19 pts, Lancashire 6 pts. Toss: Lancashire.

A career-best 155 in 164 balls from Chapple – his only previous hundred had come off Glamorgan's declaration bowling in 1993 – pulled Lancashire from 82 for six to 324, though ultimately it was to no avail. He shared stands of 84 with Schofield for the seventh wicket and 129 with Keedy for the tenth, hitting six sixes and 15 fours in a score that matched the highest by a No. 8 for Lancashire: Wasim Akram had also hit 155 at Nottingham in 1998. In all, 401 runs came on a helter-skelter first day, which began an hour late to allow the Lancashire players to recover from their floodlit exertions against Worcestershire the night before. On a pitch offering spinners encouragement, Lancashire sorely missed Muralitharan, now with Sri Lanka. Although Keedy tried hard, ending with a creditable five for 73, he could not prevent Somerset regaining the initiative. Turner chiselled out 72 off 202 balls and the forceful Blackwell hammered 64, gaining Somerset a useful lead. Lancashire, without Crawley, whose mother had died, promptly folded again; this time there were no lower-order heroics. On the second morning, Cox, after accompanying his wife to hospital, did not resume his innings until the fall of the third wicket.

Close of play: First day, Somerset 77-1 (Cox 29*, Burns 38*); Second day, Somerset 385-9 (Jones 13*, Bulbeck 13*).

Lancashire

J. J. Haynes c Turner b Johnson	13	– (2) lbw b Johnson	11
M. J. Chilton lbw b Johnson	9	– (1) c Turner b Jones	18
*J. P. Crawley lbw b Bulbeck	8	– absent	
A. Flintoff c Turner b Bulbeck	6	– (3) b Blackwell	45
N. H. Fairbrother c Burns b Jones	22	– (4) c Turner b Jones	0
†W. K. Hegg b Burns	8	– (5) c Bowler b Blackwell	9
C. P. Schofield b Dutch	58	– (6) b Johnson	23
G. Chapple b Blackwell	155	– (7) c Burns b Johnson	4
P. J. Martin c Turner b Jones	16	– (8) c Turner b Johnson	0
J. Wood c Bulbeck b Jones	3	– (9) c and b Blackwell	8
G. Keedy not out	20	– (10) not out	0
L-b 2, w 4	6	B 1, l-b 3, w 4	8
1/17 2/30 3/32 4/41 5/58 6/82 7/166 8/189 9/195	324	1/17 2/58 3/58 4/75 5/98 6/103 7/115 8/124 9/126	126

Bonus points – Lancashire 3, Somerset 3.

Bowling: *First Innings*—Johnson 22–4–77–2; Bulbeck 13–0–46–2; Jones 19–3–91–3; Burns 5–1–19–1; Dutch 11–0–62–1; Blackwell 6.2–1–27–1. *Second Innings*—Johnson 15.1–5–40–4; Bulbeck 7–1–13–0; Blackwell 15–4–47–3; Jones 7–2–22–2.

Somerset

P. C. L. Holloway c sub b Martin	2	– (2) not out	23
*J. Cox b Schofield	46	– (1) not out	39
M. Burns c and b Keedy	55		
P. D. Bowler c Schofield b Keedy	65		
M. N. Lathwell c Schofield b Keedy	7		
†R. J. Turner c Schofield b Keedy	72		
K. P. Dutch lbw b Chapple	31		
I. D. Blackwell b Wood	64		
R. L. Johnson run out	3		
P. S. Jones not out	13		
M. P. L. Bulbeck lbw b Keedy	13		
L-b 8, n-b 6	14	B 4	4
1/12 2/128 3/136 4/171 5/199 6/240 7/337 8/345 9/363	385		(no wkt) 66

Bonus points – Somerset 4, Lancashire 3.

In the first innings Cox, when 29, retired at 77 and resumed at 136.

Bowling: *First Innings*—Martin 21–7–77–1; Chapple 21–5–60–1; Flintoff 6–1–30–0; Wood 15–1–61–1; Schofield 29–5–76–1; Keedy 34.3–10–73–5. *Second Innings*—Martin 4–0–19–0; Chapple 4–0–12–0; Keedy 7–1–21–0; Schofield 3–1–10–0.

Umpires: B. Leadbeater and R. A. White.

At Leeds, July 27, 28, 29, 30. LANCASHIRE lost to YORKSHIRE by seven wickets.

At Colwyn Bay, August 1, 2, 3, 4. LANCASHIRE drew with GLAMORGAN.

LANCASHIRE v YORKSHIRE

At Manchester, August 7, 8, 9, 10. Yorkshire won by an innings and 37 runs. Yorkshire 20 pts, Lancashire 4 pts. Toss: Lancashire.

The first four sessions were lost to rain, but it made little odds: a bedraggled Lancashire capitulated in scarcely two days' playing time. Yorkshire scored at four and a half an over while White and Wood put on 309; only Holmes and Sutcliffe, with 323 at Sheffield in 1931, had crafted a bigger opening stand in Roses matches. Casting aside received wisdom about how these games should be played, White walloped a six in the third over, and eventually passed his previous best by five, having hit 24 fours and two further sixes. Lancashire, who had just learned that Bob Simpson would not return as coach in 2002, were in disarray. Twice they batted badly, with defeat – their fourth in five Championship games – coming in a hurry shortly after lunch on the last day. Their final five wickets crumbled for 15. In his *Daily Telegraph* report, Michael Henderson sniped: "So abject were Lancashire, so feeble in every aspect of the game, that there really ought to be an asterisk against this fixture in next year's *Wisden*, thus: *, team couldn't be bothered."

Close of play: First day, No play; Second day, Yorkshire 358-2 (White 179*, Lehmann 26*); Third day, Lancashire 74-1 (Chilton 21*, Flintoff 34*).

Yorkshire

C. White c Hegg b Chapple	186	R. K. J. Dawson lbw b Keedy	2
M. J. Wood lbw b Smethurst	115	C. E. W. Silverwood not out	34
A. McGrath lbw b Smethurst	5	P. M. Hutchison not out	11
D. S. Lehmann c Flintoff b Chapple	26	L-b 8, w 6, n-b 24	38
*D. Byas b Keedy	27		—
G. M. Fellows c Schofield b Flintoff	17	1/309 2/323 3/365 (9 wkts dec.)	467
G. M. Hamilton b Keedy	6	4/368 5/406 6/416	
†R. J. Blakey lbw b Keedy	0	7/416 8/420 9/430	

Bonus points – Yorkshire 5, Lancashire 3.

Bowling: Chapple 19–1–92–2; Wood 9–1–49–0; Smethurst 10–0–49–2; Flintoff 19–2–72–1; Keedy 23–5–110–4; Schofield 16–2–69–0; Scuderi 4–0–18–0.

Lancashire

M. J. Chilton c Blakey b Hamilton	10	– st Blakey b Dawson	74
*J. P. Crawley lbw b Silverwood	1	– c Dawson b Silverwood	8
A. Flintoff b Dawson	52	– b Hamilton	43
J. C. Scuderi run out	15	– lbw b Hamilton	0
G. D. Lloyd c Blakey b Hutchison	5	– c Fellows b Hamilton	2
†W. K. Hegg c McGrath b Silverwood	78	– c Byas b Dawson	26
C. P. Schofield c Lehmann b Hutchison	8	– c and b Lehmann	5
G. Chapple st Blakey b Lehmann	35	– st Blakey b Dawson	7
J. Wood lbw b Lehmann	3	– c White b Dawson	3
G. Keedy not out	1	– b White	1
M. P. Smethurst lbw b Lehmann	7	– not out	1
B 4, l-b 5, n-b 18	27	B 8, l-b 4, n-b 6	18
1/7 2/39 3/92 4/97 5/106 6/118 7/203 8/217 9/233	242	1/13 2/100 3/100 4/112 5/162 6/173 7/174 8/182 9/186	188

Bonus points – Lancashire 1, Yorkshire 3.

Bowling: *First Innings*—Silverwood 10–0–71–2; Hutchison 11–3–40–2; Hamilton 8–1–41–1; Dawson 13–0–49–1; White 4–0–19–0; Lehmann 7.3–2–13–3. *Second Innings*—Silverwood 4–1–12–1; Hutchison 14–1–51–0; Hamilton 13–3–33–3; Dawson 17–8–29–4; Lehmann 8–2–23–1; White 8.2–1–19–1; Fellows 2–0–9–0.

Umpires: M. R. Benson and A. G. T. Whitehead.

LANCASHIRE v NORTHAMPTONSHIRE

At Manchester, August 15, 16, 17, 18. Drawn. Lancashire 11 pts, Northamptonshire 10 pts. Toss: Lancashire.

On a beautiful batting pitch, Crawley hit a glorious 280 to put behind him a difficult few weeks both on and off the pitch. His fifth double-hundred lasted 503 minutes and 399 balls, and included 39 fours and a six, enabling Lancashire to reach 600, their second-highest total at Old Trafford. Fairbrother passed 20,000 first-class runs in his half-century. Needing 451 to avert the follow-on, Northamptonshire soon lost Loye when his little finger was cracked by Chapple, but the three Lancashire spinners – Muralitharan was on international duty – struggled to restrain the prolific Hussey. Once he had gone for an aggressive 93, Warren took control with a magnificent 194 that included 26 fours and a six; he shared century stands with Swann and Ripley. Crawley, unwilling to countenance defeat to a team more threatened by relegation than his own, declined Ripley's challenging declaration. After taking his personal contribution to 348, he let the Lancashire lead build until it reached the same figure. Only 140 minutes remained, and the forecast rain stole most of those.

Close of play: First day, Lancashire 444-3 (Crawley 208*, Scuderi 89*); Second day, Northamptonshire 218-3 (Warren 63*, Bailey 4*); Third day, Lancashire 64-0 (Chilton 23*, Crawley 41*).

Lancashire

M. J. Chilton c Ripley b Penberthy	46	– c Ripley b Brown	30
*J. P. Crawley c Rollins b Strong	280	– lbw b Brown	68
A. Flintoff b Brown	38	– c Ripley b Brown	0
N. H. Fairbrother lbw b Swann	51	– c Ripley b Swann	44
J. C. Scuderi b Taylor	89	– not out	61
†W. K. Hegg not out	75	– b Strong	8
C. P. Schofield b Strong	2	– b Swann	1
G. Chapple not out	2	– c and b Swann	11
G. Yates (did not bat)		– not out	8
B 3, l-b 8, w 2, n-b 4	17	B 4, l-b 2, w 6	12
1/85 2/161 3/264 4/446 5/593 6/598 (6 wkts dec.)	600	1/78 2/78 3/115 4/170 5/189 6/200 7/232 (7 wkts dec.)	243

J. Wood and G. Keedy did not bat.

Bonus points – Lancashire 5, Northamptonshire 1 (Score at 130 overs: 553-4).

Bowling: *First Innings*—Strong 21–1–106–2; Taylor 31–5–125–1; Penberthy 26.4–6–102–1; Brown 32–4–145–1; Hussey 3–0–15–0; Swann 22–3–96–1. *Second Innings*—Strong 19–2–51–1; Taylor 8–1–22–0; Brown 30–3–89–3; Swann 27–5–75–3; Hussey 1–1–0–0.

Northamptonshire

M. E. K. Hussey lbw b Schofield	93	– not out	10
A. S. Rollins b Keedy	21		
M. B. Loye retired hurt	10		
R. J. Warren b Schofield	194	– (3) not out	0
A. L. Penberthy c Flintoff b Keedy	17		
T. M. B. Bailey c Yates b Flintoff	11	– (2) c Yates b Wood	3
G. P. Swann c Hegg b Wood	54		
*†D. Ripley b Yates	43		
J. P. Taylor b Yates	17		
M. R. Strong not out	6		
L-b 11, w 2, n-b 16	29		
1/38 2/171 3/197 4/248 5/352 6/468 7/476 8/495 (8 wkts dec.)	495	1/13 (1 wkt)	13

J. F. Brown did not bat.

Bonus points – Northamptonshire 5, Lancashire 2.

In the first innings Loye retired hurt at 57.

Bowling: *First Innings*—Chapple 19–4–70–0; Scuderi 7–1–40–0; Keedy 33–2–134–2; Wood 13–1–45–1; Flintoff 16–4–58–1; Schofield 21–3–72–2; Yates 19.5–4–65–2. *Second Innings*—Chapple 2–0–7–0; Wood 3.3–0–6–1; Keedy 3–3–0–0.

Umpires: J. H. Hampshire and J. F. Steele.

At Colchester, August 22, 23, 24, 25. LANCASHIRE drew with ESSEX.

LANCASHIRE v KENT

At Manchester, September 12, 13, 14, 15. Drawn. Lancashire 7 pts, Kent 8 pts. Toss: Lancashire.

Lancashire began this game with relegation a real possibility, Kent with an outside chance of finishing second in the Championship. A notable absentee was Atherton, whose troublesome back ruled him out of what should have been his final first-class game before retiring. Better news for Lancashire, though an indication of how seriously they viewed their plight, was the reappearance of Muralitharan, flown back from Sri Lanka specially. He made the expense worth while, probing away for five for 130 and taking his tally from seven Championship games to 50. Kent's innings was remarkable for Fulton's only duck of a prodigious summer and for Key's career-best 132. Rain, which washed out much of the first day, all the second and all the last, wrecked the match, but the result from Taunton, where Northamptonshire were beaten, ensured Lancashire's first division survival.

Close of play: First day, Kent 117-3 (Key 42*, Walker 13*); Second day, No play; Third day, Lancashire 21-1 (Chilton 9*, Flintoff 9*).

Kent

D. P. Fulton lbw b Chapple	0
R. W. T. Key st Hegg b Schofield	132
E. T. Smith c Chilton b Chapple	7
A. Symonds c and b Muralitharan	43
M. J. Walker c Keedy b Muralitharan	40
†P. A. Nixon not out	87
M. A. Ealham lbw b Muralitharan	7
*M. V. Fleming c Schofield b Muralitharan	9
M. M. Patel b Muralitharan	5
M. J. Saggers c Fairbrother b Schofield	3
B. J. Trott c and b Keedy	5
B 9, l-b 20, w 2, n-b 8	39
1/0 2/12 3/89 4/160 5/263 6/276 7/306 8/320 9/335	377

Bonus points – Kent 4, Lancashire 3.

Bowling: Chapple 15–2–53–2; Wood 13–1–42–0; Muralitharan 38–6–130–5; Flintoff 11–3–40–0; Keedy 7.5–0–33–1; Schofield 19–2–50–2.

Lancashire

M. J. Chilton not out	9
*J. P. Crawley b Saggers	3
A. Flintoff not out	9
1/3	(1 wkt) 21

N. H. Fairbrother, J. C. Scuderi, †W. K. Hegg, C. P. Schofield, G. Chapple, J. Wood, M. Muralitharan and G. Keedy did not bat.

Bowling: Saggers 6.4–3–10–1; Trott 6–3–11–0.

Umpires: G. I. Burgess and M. J. Harris.

COUNTY CAPS AWARDED IN 2001

Derbyshire	S. D. Stubbings, G. Welch.
Durham	D. R. Law, M. L. Love, N. Peng, N. C. Phillips, A. Pratt.
Essex	J. S. Foster.
Glamorgan	J. P. Maher.
Gloucestershire	J. M. M. Averis, C. G. Taylor.
Hampshire	N. C. Johnson, D. A. Kenway, A. C. Morris.
Kent	D. J. Cullinan, R. W. T. Key, M. T. Saggers, E. T. Smith.
Leicestershire	N. D. Burns, D. E. Malcolm, D. J. Marsh, Shahid Afridi, T. R. Ward.
Middlesex	T. F. Bloomfield, S. P. Fleming, A. J. Strauss, R. M. S. Weston.
Northamptonshire	M. E. K. Hussey.
Nottinghamshire	G. S. Blewett, G. J. Smith.
Somerset	I. D. Blackwell, K. P. Dutch, R. L. Johnson, P. S. Jones, J. I. D. Kerr.
Surrey	J. N. Batty.
Sussex	M. W. Goodwin.
Warwickshire	I. R. Bell, M. M. Betts, V. C. Drakes.
Worcestershire	A. J. Bichel.
Yorkshire	M. J. Wood.

No caps were awarded by Lancashire.

Neil Burns

LEICESTERSHIRE

President: B. A. F. Smith
Chairman: 2001 – R. Goadby
2002 – B. G. Groves
Secretary/General Manager: J. J. Whitaker
Chairman, Cricket Committee: P. R. Haywood
Administrative Secretary: K. Hill
Captain: V. J. Wells
Cricket Manager: 2001 – J. Birkenshaw
Head Coach: 2002 – P. Whitticase
Head Groundsmen: A. Ward and A. Whiteman
Scorer: G. A. York

It is doubtful whether winning the Cheltenham & Gloucester Trophy and the Norwich Union League, rather than finishing runners-up in both, would have altered the course of events that followed Leicestershire's season. Well before they completed their summer of near misses by blowing the League title at Trent Bridge, there had been much soul-searching and planning for the future. A loss of £150,000 in 2000 had sharpened minds and focused attention on the difficult decisions that had to be taken if the county were to survive, let alone progress.

Although they had won the Championship as recently as 1996 and 1998, Leicestershire have never possessed the membership or financial clout of, say, Yorkshire, Lancashire or Surrey. Which is why James Whitaker, captain in those Championship-winning seasons and now secretary/general manager, found himself facing the task of putting Leicestershire's finances back on an even keel. The result was not simply a few cosmetic changes but a complete makeover.

"We couldn't continue with the way it was and survive," Whitaker said after some of the toughest months of his career. "We have to be more frugal and constrained; it's a case of getting the balance right. Naturally, people want success on the field, and I believe we still have a squad of players capable of achieving that. There has been streamlining in all areas and I am optimistic that what we have done will reap its reward. It has been an eye-opener for everyone, but we have come through it and I hope we'll be stronger for it."

Not everyone would totally agree. On paper, at least, Leicestershire appear weakened by the departure of three key players. Fast bowler James Ormond and batsman Ben Smith rejected new contracts and joined Surrey and Worcestershire respectively; Aftab Habib bought himself out of his contract. In addition, all-rounder Jon Dakin was released by mutual agreement and went to Essex, while Scott Boswell, Billy Stelling and Paul Griffiths were not offered new contracts. Charlie Dagnall from Warwickshire and Somerset's Jamie Grove were signed to boost what, on occasions in 2001, looked a limited attack.

Initially, there were fears that Darren Stevens, Iain Sutcliffe and wicket-keeper Neil Burns would also go, but they eventually agreed new deals, along with Darren Maddy and Ashley Wright. Even so, the leave-taking meant that only five players – Vince Wells, Aftab Habib, Carl Crowe, Maddy and Sutcliffe – remained from the Championship-winning squad of 1998. There was a major change to the backroom staff as well. Former wicket-keeper and Second Eleven coach Phil Whitticase was appointed head coach, and Jack Birkenshaw stepped down after ten years as cricket manager. He became coaching consultant, with the responsibility of establishing an ECB-accredited Leicestershire academy.

Birkenshaw would have liked to sign off with another trophy, and there should have been at least one. Without ever threatening the top three in the Championship, Leicestershire preserved their Division One status comfortably enough; but they looked to be running away with the League after winning their first nine matches, including consecutive victories over nearest challengers Kent. Then, at Taunton on August 14, Somerset beat them by one run. It proved to be the defining moment of Leicestershire's season; the West Countrymen beat them a fortnight later at Grace Road, by ten runs, and then, five days after that, completed the hat-trick by winning the C&G Trophy final at Lord's by 41 runs.

Leicestershire's nerve failed them on the day. The unfortunate Boswell sent down eight wides in his second over, Phil DeFreitas was hit for successive sixes off the last two balls of the innings, and a target of 272 required something special from Pakistani all-rounder Shahid Afridi if Leicestershire were to have a chance. For once, he was unable to provide it, falling for 20 in a disappointing innings.

Afridi had been far from disappointing on earlier occasions, though, producing some spectacular exhibitions of big hitting. At Northampton, in the Championship, he raced to 164 from 121 balls with six sixes and 22 fours, having reached three figures in 74 deliveries, and he blitzed the Worcestershire and Lancashire bowlers in the C&G quarter- and semi-finals. He had joined Leicestershire in mid-season as their overseas player after Daniel Marsh of Tasmania had fractured his cheekbone while fielding at slip against Surrey. By the end of the season, Marsh was still top of the Championship averages, having scored 600 runs at 46.15, and was in the frame for a second season until Leicestershire decided on Michael Bevan for 2002. One-day, rather than four-day, considerations tipped the balance in Bevan's favour.

Smith was the leading scorer in the Championship, with five hundreds in his 1,197 runs, and his departure was a serious loss. However, Trevor Ward, after a nightmare first season at Grace Road, enjoyed an upturn in fortune, hitting four Championship hundreds and totalling 872 runs. With the ball, 38-year-old Devon Malcolm showed he was by no means a spent force, his 68 wickets leaving younger bowlers some way behind. Eight for 63 against Surrey at Grace Road were his career-best figures in the Championship.

The player of the season, though, was Burns, who was outstanding with the gloves and the bat, scoring almost 1,400 runs in all cricket. In the final Championship match, against Glamorgan, he made his first hundred for the club and claimed his 100th victim of the summer in all matches. For Burns it was a splendid finale to what, a week later, went down as a "nearly" season for Leicestershire. Quite what 2002 holds, now that the winter's wind of change has blown across Grace Road, is anyone's guess. – NEVILLE FOULGER.

LEICESTERSHIRE 2001

[Bill Smith

Back row: S. J. Adshead, D. I. Stevens, S. A. J. Boswell, M. J. A. Whiley, C. P. Crowe, A. S. Wright, T. New. *Middle row:* H. Eaton (*physiotherapist*), P. Whitticase (*Second Eleven coach*), G. A. York (*First Eleven scorer*), C. D. Crowe, T. R. Ward, J. Ormond, W. F. Stelling, J. M. Dakin, P. Griffiths, I. J. Sutcliffe, N. D. Burns, C. Morley (*Second Eleven scorer*), C. Eaton (*physiotherapist*). *Front row:* A. Habib, D. E. Malcolm, B. F. Smith, R. Goadby (*chairman*), J. Birkenshaw (*cricket manager*), B. A. F. Smith (*president*), V. J. Wells (*captain*), J. J. Whitaker (*secretary/general manager*), D. L. Maddy, D. J. Marsh, P. A. J. DeFreitas.

LEICESTERSHIRE RESULTS

All first-class matches – Played 17: Won 5, Lost 7, Drawn 5.

County Championship matches – Played 16: Won 5, Lost 6, Drawn 5.

CricInfo County Championship, 5th in Division 1; Cheltenham & Gloucester Trophy, finalists; Benson and Hedges Cup, 4th in North Group; Norwich Union League, 2nd in Division 1.

COUNTY CHAMPIONSHIP AVERAGES

BATTING

Cap		*M*	*I*	*NO*	*R*	*HS*	*100s*	*50s*	*Avge*	*Ct/St*
2001	D. J. Marsh§	9	16	3	600	138*	1	5	46.15	13
1995	B. F. Smith	16	28	2	1,197	180*	5	2	46.03	19
2001	T. R. Ward	12	21	2	872	160*	4	2	45.89	7
2001	Shahid Afridi§	5	7	0	295	164	1	1	42.14	6
2001	N. D. Burns	16	26	6	834	111	1	6	41.70	64/3
1998	A. Habib	13	21	2	779	153	3	3	41.00	8
1997	I. J. Sutcliffe	16	29	1	911	203	2	4	32.53	5
1994	V. J. Wells	13	22	1	628	138	2	2	29.90	8
1986	P. A. J. DeFreitas . . .	8	12	1	255	97	0	2	23.18	0
	D. I. Stevens†	7	12	2	218	63	0	1	21.80	2
1996	D. L. Maddy†	16	27	1	521	111	1	2	20.03	15
1999	J. Ormond	11	16	5	216	42	0	0	19.63	2
2000	J. M. Dakin	7	11	0	211	69	0	1	19.18	1
	C. D. Crowe†	6	8	1	71	42	0	0	10.14	3
2001	D. E. Malcolm	16	21	7	126	50	0	1	9.00	1
	M. J. A. Whiley	3	5	1	2	1*	0	0	0.50	0

Also batted: S. A. J. Boswell (1 match) 16*; R. P. Davis (1 match) 51, 0 (2 ct).

* *Signifies not out.* † *Born in Leicestershire.* § *Overseas player.*

BOWLING

	O	*M*	*R*	*W*	*BB*	*5W/i*	*Avge*
J. M. Dakin	122.3	22	427	16	4-53	0	26.68
J. Ormond	452.4	109	1,306	48	5-71	2	27.20
V. J. Wells	181	47	498	18	5-36	1	27.66
P. A. J. DeFreitas	285	62	893	32	6-65	1	27.90
D. E. Malcolm	545.1	94	1,944	68	8-63	4	28.58
D. L. Maddy	224.3	41	777	26	5-67	1	29.88
Shahid Afridi	153.1	39	511	11	5-84	1	46.45

Also bowled: S. A. J. Boswell 17–2–74–3; C. D. Crowe 107.1–30–292–8; R. P. Davis 42–7–161–7; D. J. Marsh 152.2–43–410–9; D. I. Stevens 7–1–28–0; I. J. Sutcliffe 17–3–64–3; M. J. A. Whiley 53.1–14–188–2.

COUNTY RECORDS

Highest score for:	261	P. V. Simmons v Northamptonshire at Leicester . .	1994
Highest score against:	341	G. H. Hirst (Yorkshire) at Leicester	1905
Best bowling for:	10-18	G. Geary v Glamorgan at Pontypridd	1929
Best bowling against:	10-32	H. Pickett (Essex) at Leyton	1895
Highest total for:	701-4 dec.	v Worcestershire at Worcester	1906
Highest total against:	761-6 dec.	by Essex at Chelmsford	1990
Lowest total for:	25	v Kent at Leicester	1912
Lowest total against:	24	by Glamorgan at Leicester	1971
	24	by Oxford University at Oxford	1985

At Leicester, April 16, 17, 18 (not first-class). Leicestershire won by 249 runs. Toss: Leicestershire. Leicestershire 376 for nine dec. (V. J. Wells 73, D. L. Maddy 31, A. Habib 73, J. M. Dakin 54, Extras 34; D. F. Watts six for 103) and 198 for four dec. (I. J. Sutcliffe 67 retired out, B. F. Smith 85 retired out); Loughborough UCCE 252 for nine dec. (J. D. Francis 107) and 73 (D. J. Marsh four for seven).

County debuts: D. E. Malcolm, D. J. Marsh.

LEICESTERSHIRE v ESSEX

At Leicester, April 20, 21, 22. Essex won by an innings and nine runs. Essex 18 pts, Leicestershire 3 pts. Toss: Essex. County debut: M. J. A. Whiley. Championship debut: D. J. Marsh.

Newly promoted Essex had the better of Leicestershire throughout, completing an emphatic victory by 2.30 on the third afternoon. A patient maiden first-class fifty from Jefferson, who batted almost four hours, and a more belligerent 87 by Irani provided the foundations for a solid Essex innings, despite lively fast bowling from Ormond and new recruit Malcolm, aged 38. Between them they took eight wickets – the last six for 45 – only to be upstaged as Essex seamers Anderson, Ilott and Cowan hustled Leicestershire out for 104. Anderson impressed again when they followed on: finding enough swing to disconcert the batsmen, he took five for 50 to return match figures of nine for 71. Leicestershire could at least take encouragement from an excellent 61 by their new overseas player, all-rounder Daniel Marsh, son of Rod, the former Australian wicket-keeper. Habib, whose mother had died the previous day, did not bat in the second innings.

Close of play: First day, Essex 276-5 (Irani 87*, Foster 1*); Second day, Leicestershire 62-2 (Sutcliffe 21*, Burns 11*).

Essex

P. J. Prichard lbw b Dakin	1
W. I. Jefferson b Whiley	69
D. D. J. Robinson c Burns b Ormond	34
S. G. Law b Malcolm	20
*R. C. Irani c Burns b Ormond	87
S. D. Peters lbw b Ormond	38
†J. S. Foster b Malcolm	2
R. S. G. Anderson c Wells b Ormond	31
A. P. Cowan c Habib b Malcolm	6
M. C. Ilott b Ormond	2
P. M. Such not out	0
B 2, l-b 16, w 2, n-b 8	28
1/1 2/86 3/124 4/154 5/273 6/276 7/278 8/308 9/311	318

Bonus points – Essex 3, Leicestershire 3.

Bowling: Malcolm 27–7–54–3; Dakin 22–5–54–1; Wells 12–4–35–0; Whiley 17–4–54–1; Ormond 33.1–11–71–5; Maddy 5–2–9–0; Marsh 8–0–23–0.

Leicestershire

*V. J. Wells lbw b Ilott	19	– c Law b Ilott	2
†N. D. Burns c Law b Ilott	0	– (4) c Foster b Anderson	21
I. J. Sutcliffe b Cowan	21	– c Foster b Anderson	21
B. F. Smith c Foster b Anderson	15	– (5) lbw b Anderson	26
A. Habib b Cowan	5	– absent	
D. J. Marsh not out	13	– c Foster b Cowan	61
D. L. Maddy c Law b Anderson	1	– (2) lbw b Irani	23
J. M. Dakin c Law b Anderson	16	– (7) c Peters b Anderson	28
J. Ormond lbw b Anderson	0	– (8) c Such b Cowan	4
M. J. A. Whiley b Ilott	0	– (9) b Anderson	1
D. E. Malcolm b Ilott	1	– (10) not out	9
L-b 5, w 2, n-b 6	13	L-b 5, w 2, n-b 2	9
1/0 2/29 3/60 4/68 5/68 6/69 7/95 8/95 9/102	104	1/3 2/44 3/62 4/79 5/155 6/165 7/171 8/172 9/205	205

Bonus points – Essex 3.

Bowling: *First Innings*—Cowan 12–2–32–2; Ilott 16.2–6–27–4; Irani 8–3–19–0; Anderson 13–6–21–4. *Second Innings*—Cowan 23.1–4–87–2; Ilott 13.5–7–19–1; Irani 12–5–18–1; Anderson 20.2–7–50–5; Such 6–1–26–0.

Umpires: M. R. Benson and J. F. Steele.

LEICESTERSHIRE v LANCASHIRE

At Leicester, May 9, 10, 11. Leicestershire won by six runs. Leicestershire 16 pts, Lancashire 3 pts. Toss: Leicestershire.

For the second successive Championship match at Grace Road, the fourth day was redundant. But this one was a thriller, with Leicestershire snatching victory when Marsh capped an excellent all-round game by taking two spectacular catches, at mid-wicket and slip, just as Lancashire were inching to their target. His two half-centuries had been crucial, he held three earlier catches in Lancashire's first innings, and took two wickets as their second innings faltered. On the first day, Leicestershire wasted a good start, their last five wickets cascading for 26 in 14 overs while Chapple was claiming four for ten in a five-wicket return. Next day, however, Malcolm topped and tailed Lancashire with five of his own and Leicestershire took a lead of 41. It would prove priceless, even if this was not so obvious after Martin and Muralitharan, with nine wickets between them, had left Lancashire needing 211. At 113 for two, they looked on course; then three wickets fell for eight and they never quite regained the initiative, despite Chapple's gritty fight to the very end.

Close of play: First day, Lancashire 45-0 (Atherton 18*, Chilton 23*); Second day, Leicestershire 72-4 (Sutcliffe 29*, Marsh 5*).

Leicestershire

*V. J. Wells c Fairbrother b Chapple	34	– lbw b Martin	0
D. L. Maddy lbw b Smethurst	44	– b Muralitharan	20
I. J. Sutcliffe lbw b Martin	22	– c Hegg b Martin	29
B. F. Smith c Fairbrother b Muralitharan	1	– lbw b Martin	14
A. Habib c Crawley b Muralitharan	0	– lbw b Muralitharan	1
D. J. Marsh lbw b Smethurst	71	– not out	50
D. I. Stevens lbw b Chapple	28	– c Chilton b Muralitharan	7
J. M. Dakin b Chapple	10	– b Chapple	3
†N. D. Burns not out	9	– c Fairbrother b Martin	39
M. J. A. Whiley b Chapple	0	– b Martin	0
D. E. Malcolm c Martin b Chapple	1	– b Muralitharan	0
L-b 6, w 8, n-b 6	20	L-b 2, w 4	6
1/70 2/95 3/96 4/96 5/146 6/214 7/226 8/238 9/238	240	1/0 2/40 3/63 4/64 5/78 6/91 7/112 8/168 9/168	169

Bonus points – Leicestershire 1, Lancashire 3.

Bowling: *First Innings*—Martin 13–2–53–1; Chapple 16.3–4–40–5; Smethurst 15–3–60–2; Muralitharan 25–10–56–2; Scuderi 3–0–25–0. *Second Innings*—Martin 27–9–52–5; Chapple 15–4–38–1; Smethurst 4–0–21–0; Muralitharan 37.2–13–56–4.

Lancashire

M. A. Atherton c Burns b Malcolm	29	– c Burns b Dakin	12
M. J. Chilton c Burns b Malcolm	23	– lbw b Dakin	11
*J. P. Crawley b Malcolm	8	– c Burns b Malcolm	53
R. C. Driver c Marsh b Dakin	1	– c Sutcliffe b Marsh	35
N. H. Fairbrother c Stevens b Wells	45	– b Malcolm	1
J. C. Scuderi c Marsh b Wells	30	– lbw b Wells	15
†W. K. Hegg not out	35	– lbw b Marsh	7
G. Chapple b Dakin	0	– c Marsh b Dakin	44
P. J. Martin c Marsh b Malcolm	0	– lbw b Maddy	5
M. P. Smethurst c Wells b Dakin	3	– c Marsh b Maddy	6
M. Muralitharan b Malcolm	14	– not out	1
B 1, l-b 2, w 6, n-b 2	11	B 1, l-b 6, w 7	14
1/45 2/56 3/59 4/83 5/138 6/147 7/152 8/153 9/168	199	1/22 2/23 3/113 4/119 5/121 6/139 7/147 8/176 9/202	204

Bonus points – Leicestershire 3.

Bowling: *First Innings*—Malcolm 28–6–78–5; Whiley 13.1–6–20–0; Dakin 17.5–3–69–3; Wells 10–2–18–2; Marsh 7–4–6–0; Stevens 1–0–5–0. *Second Innings*—Malcolm 19–2–70–2; Dakin 10.5–1–40–3; Wells 12–4–26–1; Maddy 8–0–26–2; Marsh 11–2–35–2.

Umpires: B. Dudleston and M. J. Kitchen.

At The Oval, May 16, 17, 18, 19. LEICESTERSHIRE drew with SURREY.

At Leicester, May 23. LEICESTERSHIRE lost to PAKISTANIS by seven wickets (see Pakistani tour section).

At Leicester, May 24, 25. LEICESTERSHIRE lost to PAKISTANIS by an innings and 26 runs (see Pakistani tour section).

LEICESTERSHIRE v SOMERSET

At Leicester, May 30, 31, June 1, 2. Drawn. Leicestershire 11 pts, Somerset 11 pts. Toss: Leicestershire.

One of the best Grace Road pitches in a long time produced 1,419 runs for 35 wickets, and nobody enjoyed the conditions more than Ward, the former Kent opener. In his first season at Leicestershire he had managed 110 runs in ten innings. Now he made 93, his first Championship fifty for three years, and 119, his first hundred for four, which included 23 fours and came off 144 balls. There were also centuries for Marsh, with 23 boundaries, and Bowler, who struck a six and 21 fours, while wicket-keeper Burns established a Leicestershire record by holding seven catches in an innings. In a tough game for bowlers, Malcolm's commitment and enthusiasm stood out: he took four for 96 in Somerset's first innings, and his three late wickets in the second came close to winning the match. Somerset had been challenged to make 404 in a minimum of 88 overs; when bad light interrupted play with seven overs remaining, and Malcolm steaming in, there were just two wickets between Leicestershire and victory. Dutch and Bulbeck survived six more balls when the light improved.

Close of play: First day, Leicestershire 387; Second day, Somerset 324-6 (Bowler 103*, Kerr 3*); Third day, Leicestershire 348-6 (Stevens 8*, Burns 0*).

Leicestershire

T. R. Ward c Lathwell b Kerr	93	– c Bulbeck b Jones	119
I. J. Sutcliffe lbw b Bulbeck	21	– c Dutch b Kerr	58
B. F. Smith b Kerr	11	– c Bowler b Dutch	66
D. J. Marsh not out	138	– c Kerr b Dutch	2
D. L. Maddy c Dutch b Trego	15	– c Cox b Dutch	1
*V. J. Wells c Turner b Bulbeck	2	– c Turner b Jones	86
D. I. Stevens c Cox b Burns	63	– c Turner b Kerr	14
†N. D. Burns c Turner b Kerr	0	– not out	33
C. D. Crowe lbw b Burns	0	– not out	3
J. Ormond lbw b Burns	11		
D. E. Malcolm b Jones	0		
B 10, l-b 8, w 6, n-b 9	33	L-b 8	8
1/79 2/105 3/162 4/189 5/192 6/339 7/342 8/358 9/386	387	1/182 2/183 3/190 4/194 5/326 6/348 7/378	(7 wkts dec.) 390

Bonus points – Leicestershire 4, Somerset 3.

Bowling: *First Innings*—Jones 23–4–74–1; Bulbeck 17–2–70–2; Trego 15–3–71–1; Dutch 18–3–77–0; Kerr 17–3–51–3; Burns 9–2–26–3. *Second Innings*—Jones 19–1–100–2; Kerr 14–3–57–2; Dutch 34–6–118–3; Bulbeck 15–0–77–0; Trego 4–0–30–0.

Somerset

*J. Cox c Burns b Malcolm	21	– (2) c Burns b Ormond	13
P. C. L. Holloway c Burns b Malcolm	35	– (1) lbw b Sutcliffe	85
M. Burns c Burns b Maddy	60	– c Crowe b Wells	7
P. D. Bowler not out	138	– c Crowe b Ormond	2
M. N. Lathwell lbw b Crowe	19	– c Smith b Maddy	63
†R. J. Turner c Burns b Marsh	27	– c Burns b Malcolm	34
P. D. Trego c Burns b Malcolm	21	– b Malcolm	17
J. I. D. Kerr b Ormond	7	– c Marsh b Malcolm	4
K. P. Dutch c Marsh b Ormond	10	– not out	10
M. P. L. Bulbeck c Burns b Malcolm	0	– not out	2
P. S. Jones c Burns b Ormond	1		
B 8, l-b 13, w 10, n-b 4	35	B 12, l-b 11, w 6, n-b 2	31
1/41 2/124 3/146 4/196 5/262 6/313 7/334 8/366 9/367	374	1/39 2/56 3/59 4/165 5/202 6/244 7/247 8/260	(8 wkts) 268

Bonus points – Somerset 4, Leicestershire 3.

Bowling: *First Innings*—Ormond 30.2–3–94–3; Malcolm 26–2–96–4; Wells 14–4–28–0; Maddy 15–5–30–1; Marsh 17–4–45–1; Crowe 20–5–60–1. *Second Innings*—Ormond 27–5–83–2; Malcolm 22–5–73–3; Wells 7–2–19–1; Maddy 9–0–27–1; Crowe 9–3–13–0; Marsh 5–2–9–0; Sutcliffe 4–0–21–1.

Umpires: B. Dudleston and B. Leadbeater.

At Manchester, June 6, 7, 8, 9. LEICESTERSHIRE lost to LANCASHIRE by six wickets.

LEICESTERSHIRE v NORTHAMPTONSHIRE

At Leicester, June 13, 14, 15. Leicestershire won by nine wickets. Leicestershire 15 pts, Northamptonshire 3 pts. Toss: Northamptonshire. Championship debut: L. C. Weekes.

An awesome exhibition of strokeplay from Ward made light of Leicestershire's target of 232. He brought a low-scoring match – 20 wickets littered the first day – to a rousing conclusion, flaying the Northamptonshire bowling for an unbeaten 160 off 172 balls, 28 of which went for four and one for six. His last 60 came from 45 balls and included 46 in boundaries; three off successive balls from Innes ushered Leicestershire to victory less than an hour after lunch on the third day, and took his match aggregate to 210. Malcolm continued to enjoy his Indian summer, returning match figures of seven for 110, while former opener Maddy revelled in his new-found role of all-rounder. Swinging the ball at a brisk medium-pace, he wrecked Northamptonshire's first-innings middle order with three for 28 and followed that up with a career-best five for 67. On the second day, pitch inspector Tony Brown found nothing wrong with the wicket; Ward proved him right on the third, leaving Northamptonshire, the only Division One county without a win, propping up the table.

Close of play: First day, Leicestershire 185; Second day, Leicestershire 5-0 (Ward 4*, Sutcliffe 1*).

Northamptonshire

M. E. K. Hussey lbw b Malcolm	10	– c Burns b Maddy	45
M. B. Loye c Smith b DeFreitas	0	– b Maddy	31
J. W. Cook c Sutcliffe b DeFreitas	7	– c Marsh b Malcolm	21
R. J. Warren b Maddy	13	– b DeFreitas	55
A. J. Swann lbw b DeFreitas	25	– c Maddy b Malcolm	4
G. P. Swann c Smith b Maddy	0	– c Marsh b Maddy	20
K. J. Innes lbw b Maddy	0	– c Marsh b Maddy	26
*†D. Ripley c Burns b Malcolm	31	– lbw b DeFreitas	1
L. C. Weekes not out	44	– c Burns b Maddy	18
D. M. Cousins c Burns b Malcolm	4	– not out	15
J. F. Brown b Malcolm	0	– c Burns b Malcolm	5
B 5, l-b 6, w 10, n-b 4	25	L-b 8, w 6, n-b 2	16
1/4 2/14 3/22 4/47 5/53 6/57 7/79 8/139 9/153	159	1/79 2/86 3/113 4/129 5/167 6/210 7/214 8/233 9/238	257

Bonus points – Leicestershire 3.

Bowling: *First Innings*—Malcolm 16.4–3–64–4; DeFreitas 16–4–43–3; Wells 8–3–13–0; Maddy 8–0–28–3. *Second Innings*—Malcolm 16.2–6–46–3; DeFreitas 19–4–54–2; Wells 13–1–38–0; Maddy 21–4–67–5; Marsh 13–4–33–0; Crowe 11–6–11–0.

Leicestershire

T. R. Ward c Warren b Weekes	50	– not out	160
I. J. Sutcliffe c Cook b Cousins	1	– c Cook b Cousins	55
B. F. Smith lbw b Weekes	39	– not out	7
D. J. Marsh c Ripley b Innes	25		
D. L. Maddy c Hussey b Innes	9		
*V. J. Wells b Weekes	2		
D. I. Stevens c Ripley b Innes	6		
†N. D. Burns lbw b Cousins	10		
P. A. J. DeFreitas b Brown	15		
C. D. Crowe c G. P. Swann b Cousins	6		
D. E. Malcolm not out	4		
L-b 8, w 2, n-b 8	18	L-b 3, n-b 8	11
1/3 2/92 3/99 4/110 5/123 6/143 7/144 8/163 9/175	185	1/175	(1 wkt) 233

Bonus points – Northamptonshire 3.

Bowling: *First Innings*—Cousins 19–4–58–3; Weekes 15–4–51–3; Brown 10.3–4–17–1; Innes 8–0–51–3. *Second Innings*—Cousins 12–1–60–1; Weekes 11–1–56–0; Innes 8.3–2–42–0; G. P. Swann 9–2–26–0; Brown 13–2–46–0.

Umpires: D. J. Constant and K. E. Palmer.

At Canterbury, June 20, 21, 22. LEICESTERSHIRE beat KENT by an innings and 149 runs.

At Leeds, June 29, 30, July 1. LEICESTERSHIRE lost to YORKSHIRE by an innings and 227 runs.

LEICESTERSHIRE v SURREY

At Leicester, July 4, 5, 6, 7. Drawn. Leicestershire 7 pts, Surrey 7 pts. Toss: Leicestershire. First-class debut: M. A. Carberry.

By the end of the opening day, this game had ostensibly run more than half its course: despite a blameless pitch, 20 wickets had fallen and Leicestershire, 79 for none in their second innings, enjoyed a lead of 142. It had been quite a day for Malcolm, who, in a career spanning 18 seasons, had taken eight Championship wickets in an innings for the first time. Surrey, cock-a-hoop at dismissing Leicestershire for 165, were themselves routed for 102. Smith then compiled a solidly impressive 179 as Saqlain Mushtaq, bowling 47 overs unchanged, picked away at Leicestershire's second innings. Salisbury, nursing an injured toe, was unable to bowl. Eventually, Wells declared

HIGHEST FOURTH-INNINGS TOTALS IN THE COUNTY CHAMPIONSHIP SINCE 1900

(Unless otherwise indicated, the side making the runs won the match.)

502-6	Middlesex v Nottinghamshire at Nottingham	1925
493-6	Glamorgan (*set 495 to win*) v Worcestershire at Abergavenny	1990
478-9	**Surrey (*set 536 to win*) v Leicestershire at Leicester**	**2001**
467-9	Worcestershire (*set 517 to win*) v Derbyshire at Kidderminster	1995
463-8	Hampshire (*set 568 to win*) v Kent at Southampton	1911
461-3	**Nottinghamshire v Worcestershire at Worcester**	**2001**
455-8	Sussex v Gloucestershire at Hove	1999

Research: Gordon Vince

535 ahead, leaving Leicestershire more than two days to take ten wickets. Aided by the loss of 55 overs, as well as by curiously defensive fields, Surrey somehow extended their unbeaten run in the Championship to 18 games. At 190 for six on the third afternoon, that had seemed most unlikely. However, the lower order fought a dogged rearguard action, none more so than Salisbury, batting with a runner, and Bicknell. They survived almost two and a half hours in adding 109 for the tenth wicket, guiding Surrey to their highest fourth-innings total and safety. Leicestershire's spirits were dampened further by news that Marsh had broken his cheekbone while fielding, and would be out for the rest of the season.

Close of play: First day, Leicestershire 79-0 (Ward 42*, Sutcliffe 23*); Second day, Surrey 28-1 (Carberry 8*, Saqlain Mushtaq 2*); Third day, Surrey 281-6 (Butcher 26*, Tudor 45*).

Leicestershire

T. R. Ward c Shahid b Saqlain Mushtaq	46	– c A. J. Hollioake b Saqlain Mushtaq	42
I. J. Sutcliffe c Shahid b Bicknell	0	– b Bicknell	25
B. F. Smith c and b Bicknell	6	– c Brown b Butcher	179
D. J. Marsh c B. C. Hollioake b Bicknell	1	– st Batty b Saqlain Mushtaq	82
A. Habib c A. J. Hollioake b Saqlain Mushtaq	3	– c B. C. Hollioake b Saqlain Mushtaq	5
D. L. Maddy c B. C. Hollioake b Tudor	1	– c Shahid b Saqlain Mushtaq	0
*V. J. Wells lbw b Tudor	14	– c B. C. Hollioake b A. J. Hollioake	32
†N. D. Burns lbw b Saqlain Mushtaq	45	– not out	66
P. A. J. DeFreitas lbw b Saqlain Mushtaq	22	– c Batty b Saqlain Mushtaq	3
J. Ormond not out	14		
D. E. Malcolm c A. J. Hollioake b Bicknell	3		
L-b 6, n-b 4	10	B 8, l-b 3, n-b 22, p 5	38
1/3 2/23 3/25 4/60 5/61 6/63 7/88 8/135 9/154	165	1/79 2/93 3/260 4/268 5/268 6/347 7/455 8/472 (8 wkts dec.)	472

Bonus points – Surrey 3.

Bowling: *First Innings*—Bicknell 15–4–54–4; Tudor 11–4–45–2; Saqlain Mushtaq 17–4–60–4. *Second Innings*—Bicknell 23–6–69–1; Tudor 8–1–52–0; Saqlain Mushtaq 52.2–9–172–5; B. C. Hollioake 6–0–41–0; Butcher 13–3–53–1; A. J. Hollioake 8–0–51–1; Brown 3–0–18–0.

Surrey

N. Shahid c Smith b Malcolm	7	– c Ward b Malcolm	14
M. A. Carberry lbw b DeFreitas	23	– c Burns b DeFreitas	13
B. C. Hollioake b Malcolm	0	– (4) b Ormond	59
*A. J. Hollioake lbw b Malcolm	0	– (5) b Wells	64
A. D. Brown c Habib b Malcolm	15	– (6) c Burns b Ormond	5
G. P. Butcher lbw b DeFreitas	9	– (7) b Marsh	38
A. J. Tudor c Burns b Malcolm	13	– (8) b DeFreitas	86
†J. N. Batty c Habib b Malcolm	0	– (9) b Malcolm	12
M. P. Bicknell b Malcolm	12	– (10) not out	85
I. D. K. Salisbury c Marsh b Malcolm	15	– (11) not out	30
Saqlain Mushtaq not out	5	– (3) lbw b Marsh	4
L-b 1, n-b 2	3	B 23, l-b 31, w 10, n-b 4	68
1/11 2/11 3/11 4/31 5/56 6/61 7/62 8/78 9/87	102	1/20 2/35 3/55 4/158 5/170 6/190 7/318 8/343 9/369 (9 wkts)	478

Bonus points – Leicestershire 3.

Bowling: *First Innings*—Ormond 12–3–25–0; Malcolm 18–3–63–8; DeFreitas 7–4–13–2; Marsh 1–1–0–0. *Second Innings*—Malcolm 43–12–124–2; Ormond 30–8–72–2; Marsh 30–11–76–2; DeFreitas 23–6–71–2; Maddy 7–2–21–0; Wells 16–2–56–1; Sutcliffe 3–1–4–0.

Umpires: A. Clarkson and V. A. Holder.

At Cardiff, July 18, 19, 20, 21. LEICESTERSHIRE beat GLAMORGAN by an innings and 90 runs.

LEICESTERSHIRE v KENT

At Leicester, July 27, 28, 29, 30. Kent won by three wickets. Kent 19 pts, Leicestershire 8 pts. Toss: Leicestershire. First-class debut: J. C. Tredwell.

A match bulging with runs came to a stirring climax as Nixon, 11 years a Leicestershire player, steered Kent to a last-ball triumph. Wells had seemed over-cautious in delaying his declaration until 40 minutes into the final day, to set a daunting 401 in 84 overs, albeit on a benign pitch.

But hundreds from Ed Smith and Symonds, who shared a third-wicket stand of 235 in 47 overs, kept Kent in the hunt and, as Maddy began the last over, 14 were needed. Nixon hit each of the first four balls for two, then struck successive boundaries to seal victory. It was Kent's second-highest total to win a match – Frank Woolley had led them to 416 against Surrey at Blackheath in 1934 – and the second time in a month that Leicestershire had conceded more than 400 in the fourth innings at Grace Road. All told, this match contained 1,583 runs and seven centuries; Ben Smith's was his third in consecutive innings, while Ward – once of Kent – received his cap after hitting 110. Off-spinner James Tredwell, a last-minute replacement for the injured Patel, left the England Under-19 squad at Hove at 10 a.m. and, travelling by train, eventually arrived shortly before tea, managing one over before the break and a wicket soon after.

Close of play: First day, Leicestershire 378-7 (Burns 53*, Ormond 15*); Second day, Kent 358-8 (Walker 107*, Saggers 0*); Third day, Leicestershire 305-6 (Maddy 98*, Burns 30*).

Leicestershire

T. R. Ward c Symonds b Saggers	28	– c Trott b Saggers	110
I. J. Sutcliffe lbw b Saggers	4	– c Ealham b Trott	5
B. F. Smith c and b Walker	111	– c Walker b Saggers	5
A. Habib b Tredwell	153	– c Nixon b Saggers	5
D. L. Maddy c Fulton b Saggers	5	– lbw b Ealham	111
Shahid Afridi c Nixon b Trott	5	– c Symonds b Tredwell	42
*V. J. Wells c and b Trott	1	– lbw b Trott	0
†N. D. Burns c Smith b Saggers	60	– not out	64
J. Ormond b Saggers	42	– not out	10
D. E. Malcolm c Walker b Saggers	8		
M. J. A. Whiley not out	1		
B 6, l-b 1	7	B 4, l-b 3, w 2, n-b 4	13
1/10 2/47 3/198 4/242 5/267 6/271 7/343 8/396 9/411	425	1/34 2/44 3/54 4/183 5/236 6/238 7/336 (7 wkts dec.)	365

Bonus points – Leicestershire 5, Kent 3.

Bowling: *First Innings*—Trott 24–4–99–2; Saggers 28.1–5–92–6; Ealham 17–5–53–0; Fleming 18–2–66–0; Symonds 19–2–61–0; Walker 3–0–9–1; Tredwell 8–2–38–1. *Second Innings*—Saggers 19–3–85–3; Trott 17–0–64–2; Ealham 23–9–52–1; Tredwell 18–3–85–1; Fleming 11–1–39–0; Symonds 6–1–23–0; Walker 3–0–8–0; Fulton 1–0–2–0.

Kent

D. P. Fulton b Malcolm	21	– c Maddy b Ormond	22
R. W. T. Key c Burns b Ormond	5	– b Ormond	36
E. T. Smith c Shahid Afridi b Ormond	19	– run out	107
A. Symonds c Ormond b Shahid Afridi	48	– b Maddy	125
M. J. Walker not out	120	– c Burns b Ormond	12
M. A. Ealham c Smith b Wells	5	– (7) lbw b Maddy	14
†P. A. Nixon lbw b Whiley	31	– (8) not out	29
*M. V. Fleming b Maddy	59	– (6) c Shahid Afridi b Maddy	15
J. C. Tredwell lbw b Sutcliffe	10		
M. J. Saggers c Wells b Ormond	2	– (9) not out	3
B. J. Trott c and b Ormond	13		
B 8, l-b 14, w 8, n-b 22, p 5	57	B 21, l-b 9, w 6, n-b 4	40
1/18 2/42 3/80 4/126 5/153 6/243 7/334 8/357 9/362	390	1/62 2/71 3/306 4/329 5/336 6/357 7/380 (7 wkts)	403

Bonus points – Kent 4, Leicestershire 3.

Bowling: *First Innings*—Malcolm 27–6–82–1; Ormond 26.1–6–90–4; Shahid Afridi 10–2–48–1; Whiley 16–3–87–1; Wells 7–2–21–1; Maddy 13–3–28–1; Sutcliffe 2–0–7–1. *Second Innings*—Ormond 31–7–114–3; Malcolm 10–1–59–0; Wells 2–0–2–0; Whiley 7–1–27–0; Maddy 22–1–118–3; Shahid Afridi 12–1–53–0.

Umpires: J. W. Holder and A. A. Jones.

At Chelmsford, August 1, 2, 3, 4. LEICESTERSHIRE drew with ESSEX.

At Taunton, August 7, 8, 9, 10. LEICESTERSHIRE drew with SOMERSET.

LEICESTERSHIRE v YORKSHIRE

At Leicester, August 15, 16, 17, 18. Yorkshire won by 168 runs. Yorkshire 16 pts, Leicestershire 3 pts. Toss: Yorkshire.

Before this game, Yorkshire had the Championship in their sights; afterwards, 37 points ahead with three to play, they had it within their grasp. They completely outplayed Leicestershire, despite being dismissed on the first day for a modest 230. Yorkshire's total would have been much lower but for a polished 82 from Vaughan, returning after injury. In reply, however, Leicestershire were routed in 35 overs, a feeble effort that seemed to sap their confidence. Lehmann, out for a duck in the first innings, made 193 (with 23 fours and two sixes) before becoming wicket-keeper Burns's ninth victim. Byas also scored a century, and raised eyebrows by waiting until after lunch on the third day – when the lead was 538 – to declare. Inside 13 overs, Leicestershire were 53 for five, three wickets falling to Kirby, fired up against the county that had let him go a year earlier; at one stage, Wells complained to umpire White about the verbal barrage. Leicestershire fought back through Wells and DeFreitas, whose eighth-wicket partnership of 152 took the game into a fourth day, but victory was always Yorkshire's.

Close of play: First day, Leicestershire 23-3 (Burns 0*); Second day, Yorkshire 267-3 (Lehmann 141*, Byas 37*); Third day, Leicestershire 243-7 (Wells 122*, DeFreitas 46*).

Yorkshire

C. White c Burns b Ormond	3	– c Burns b Ormond	8
M. J. Wood b Wells	33	– c Smith b Ormond	11
M. P. Vaughan c Burns b DeFreitas	82	– c Burns b Maddy	47
D. S. Lehmann c Burns b Wells	0	– st Burns b Ormond	193
*D. Byas c Burns b Maddy	20	– c Ward b Ormond	100
G. M. Fellows c Burns b DeFreitas	3	– run out	0
G. M. Hamilton c Habib b Ormond	15	– b Ormond	34
†R. J. Blakey b Wells	15	– not out	6
R. K. J. Dawson c Burns b Maddy	16	– lbw b Maddy	3
S. P. Kirby lbw b Maddy	15		
P. M. Hutchison not out	2		
B 6, l-b 4, w 6, n-b 10	26	B 6, l-b 8, w 2, n-b 6, p 5	27
1/6 2/102 3/102 4/144 5/154 6/159 7/185 8/189 9/227	230	1/18 2/23 3/161 4/347 5/348 6/417 7/422 8/429 (8 wkts dec.)	429

Bonus points – Yorkshire 1, Leicestershire 3.

Bowling: *First Innings*—Ormond 33–8–66–2; Malcolm 8–2–33–0; DeFreitas 20–11–41–2; Maddy 16.5–3–43–3; Wells 18–5–37–3; Sutcliffe 1–1–0–0. *Second Innings*—Ormond 45–6–146–5; DeFreitas 27–2–92–0; Wells 6–1–21–0; Maddy 16.1–1–72–2; Malcolm 11–1–43–0; Stevens 6–1–23–0; Sutcliffe 1–0–13–0.

Leicestershire

T. R. Ward c Byas b Kirby	4	– c Byas b Hutchison	0
I. J. Sutcliffe b Kirby	9	– b Kirby	5
B. F. Smith b Hutchison	2	– c Vaughan b Hutchison	2
†N. D. Burns b Hutchison	25	– (8) c Blakey b White	0
A. Habib b Hamilton	7	– (4) b Kirby	12
D. L. Maddy c Blakey b White	27	– (5) c Vaughan b White	25
D. I. Stevens b Dawson	7	– (6) c Byas b Kirby	11
*V. J. Wells not out	15	– (7) b White	133
P. A. J. DeFreitas c Wood b Dawson	8	– c Kirby b Hamilton	97
J. Ormond c Blakey b White	1	– not out	39
D. E. Malcolm b White	1	– c Byas b Dawson	16
B 2, l-b 9, n-b 4	15	B 14, l-b 6, w 8, n-b 2	30
1/16 2/19 3/23 4/40 5/74 6/93 7/97 8/118 9/119	121	1/7 2/13 3/17 4/33 5/53 6/122 7/132 8/284 9/326	370

Bonus points – Yorkshire 3.

Bowling: *First Innings*—Kirby 8–1–20–2; Hutchison 9–1–33–2; Hamilton 6–1–23–1; Dawson 7–1–23–2; White 5–2–11–3. *Second Innings*—Kirby 20–3–82–3; Hutchison 10–3–41–2; Dawson 27–8–109–1; Hamilton 15–2–76–1; White 14–6–28–3; Lehmann 7–1–14–0.

Umpires: N. G. Cowley and R. A. White.

At Northampton, August 23, 24, 25, 26. LEICESTERSHIRE lost to NORTHAMPTONSHIRE by 202 runs.

LEICESTERSHIRE v GLAMORGAN

At Leicester, September 7, 8, 9. Leicestershire won by ten wickets. Leicestershire 19 pts, Glamorgan 3 pts. Toss: Leicestershire.

The fact that relegation – a near certainty for Glamorgan – remained a distinct possibility for Leicestershire focused their minds on their final game. As it turned out, Glamorgan offered little resistance. Burns proved the match-winner, his first hundred for Leicestershire coming at a crucial time: arriving at 157 for six – itself an improvement on 93 for five – he and his captain shared a century partnership, broken when Wells became Watkin's 900th first-class victim. Burns went on to make 111 off 131 balls, with 19 fours. He then held six catches as the Leicestershire seamers ripped through Glamorgan, only James resisting to carry his bat. Following on 226 behind, Glamorgan, thanks to Maher's 112-ball century, forced Leicestershire to bat again, time enough for Sutcliffe to pass 1,000 runs for the season at the last gasp. Leicestershire's fifth victory of a topsy-turvy season came with a day and a half to spare and guaranteed their survival in the first division.

Close of play: First day, Leicestershire 274-7 (Burns 66*, Ormond 3*); Second day, Glamorgan 126-2 (Maher 78*, Powell 17*).

Leicestershire

T. R. Ward c Maynard b Jones	5	– (2) not out	14
I. J. Sutcliffe lbw b Watkin	9	– (1) not out	6
B. F. Smith lbw b Croft	68		
A. Habib b Jones	4		
D. L. Maddy c Wallace b Davies	25		
D. I. Stevens c Davies b Thomas	8		
*V. J. Wells lbw b Watkin	67		
†N. D. Burns b Davies	111		
J. Ormond b Thomas	24		
C. D. Crowe c Dale b Thomas	18		
D. E. Malcolm not out	13		
B 11, l-b 7, w 2	20		
1/10 2/18 3/26 4/75 5/93 6/157 7/271 8/336 9/352	372	(no wkt)	20

Bonus points – Leicestershire 4, Glamorgan 3.

Bowling: *First Innings*—Jones 16–2–87–2; Watkin 25–3–82–2; Davies 12–1–68–2; Thomas 18.2–2–77–3; Croft 14–3–40–1. *Second Innings*—Watkin 2–0–6–0; Jones 1.3–0–14–0.

Glamorgan

*S. P. James not out	61	– c Smith b Wells	17
J. P. Maher lbw b Ormond	24	– c Burns b Malcolm	100
M. P. Maynard lbw b Ormond	0	– lbw b Ormond	0
M. J. Powell c Burns b Malcolm	4	– c Wells b Maddy	25
A. Dale c Burns b Wells	1	– not out	32
R. D. B. Croft b Wells	0	– lbw b Maddy	1
†M. A. Wallace c Burns b Ormond	13	– c Maddy b Malcolm	1
S. D. Thomas c Burns b Malcolm	7	– c Ward b Malcolm	13
A. P. Davies c Burns b Ormond	5	– c Maddy b Ormond	17
S. L. Watkin c Burns b Wells	21	– c Smith b Ormond	4
S. P. Jones c Ward b Malcolm	4	– c Habib b Maddy	10
B 2, l-b 2, n-b 2	6	B 4, l-b 15, w 4, n-b 2	25
1/39 2/41 3/46 4/57 5/57 6/85 7/98 8/103 9/141	146	1/61 2/62 3/159 4/163 5/168 6/171 7/189 8/218 9/228	245

Bonus points – Leicestershire 3.

Bowling: *First Innings*—Ormond 15–4–43–4; Malcolm 16.5–3–60–3; Wells 10–3–24–3; Maddy 8–3–15–0. *Second Innings*—Ormond 19–5–52–3; Malcolm 14–1–65–3; Maddy 12.3–4–47–3; Wells 14–4–52–1; Crowe 2–0–10–0.

Umpires: R. Julian and R. Palmer.

Philip Tufnell

MIDDLESEX

President: 2001 – R. Gerard
2002 – R. A. Gale

Chairman: P. H. Edmonds

Chairman, Cricket Committee: 2001 – A. J. T. Miller
2002 – D. Bennett

Secretary: V. J. Codrington

Captain: A. R. C. Fraser

Club Coach: J. E. Emburey

Scorer: M. J. Smith

Middlesex in 2001 amply illustrated how circumstances can alter expectations. The new county coach, John Emburey, said when he took over that his was not an easy task and members would have to be patient. Certainly any Middlesex supporter suggesting in April that the county would challenge for Championship promotion would have been greeted with derision. The departure of Mark Ramprakash and Justin Langer meant there was a need to find some 2,500 runs, while that of Richard Johnson weakened the seam-bowling resources. Moreover, with only four players on the staff who had been capped before 2000, there was an alarming lack of experience. Yet Middlesex were unbeaten until the beginning of August, when they had more bonus points than any county in either division, led the second division for most of two months, and remained in the top three until early September. Consequently, their eventual fifth place was seen as disappointing.

Three of the last five Championship matches were lost, and there was an alarming decline in confidence as the chance of promotion slipped away. Against Warwickshire at Lord's, for instance, four Middlesex players hit hundreds – only the third time in their history this had happened – in a first-innings total of 502 for seven. The visitors then replied with 631, Mark Wagh scoring a triple-century, but on the final day Middlesex's batting slumped to 157 for six before wicket-keeper David Nash and off-spinner Jamie Dalrymple, a promising newcomer, secured a draw.

Inconsistency was the principal reason for Middlesex's failure to sustain their promotion bid. Owais Shah, for example, scored 190 at the Riverside and 203 against Derbyshire at Southgate, followed by a call-up to the England one-day squad, to suggest this would be his breakthrough year. At that stage, he had scored 675 Championship runs at an average of 75; his next 14 innings, four of which were scoreless, produced only 280 more. In addition, the lack of experience and penetration in the bowling meant that captain Angus Fraser felt he had to compensate for others' failings. As a result, he bowled far too much, sometimes while less than fully fit, and eventually showed the strain.

The attack would have been stronger had Aaron Laraman stayed fit and Jamie Hewitt, a close-season departure to Kent, not suffered a loss of confidence. Chad Keegan was a discovery but, as Emburey said, "Injuries mean he is having to learn how to bowl in the first team when, ideally, he should have been able to do so in the Seconds." Tim Bloomfield and Simon Cook lacked the necessary pace to get much out of good pitches and, with Fraser tiring, wickets became increasingly hard to come by. Indeed, the inability to bowl sides out twice proved crucial in the end. Durham and Nottinghamshire both saved their home games, which Middlesex really should have won; an extra 16 points would have brought promotion. Spinners Philip Tufnell and Paul Weekes took 97 Championship wickets between them, but only 16 in the last five games, in August and September, when pitches improved and the shortcomings in the attack were cruelly exposed.

Nevertheless, there was much to be positive about. Ben Hutton, uncertain of his place in 2000, established himself as a vital member of the team, scoring important runs and taking many fine catches. Andrew Strauss, Middlesex's Player of the Year, topped 1,000 runs for the first time, and Robin Weston, when he forced his way into the side, contributed significantly. Ed Joyce scored two centuries when he became available for the last three matches – his presence throughout 2002 should be a bonus – while Nash continued to do a good job behind the stumps, as well as playing some useful innings. New Zealand captain Stephen Fleming, although never likely to excite like Langer, proved reliable, though strangely he seemed to find his best form away from home. Not until the last Lord's game, when he hit his fourth hundred, did he reach 50 either there or at Southgate.

His replacement as overseas player, Pakistan all-rounder Abdur Razzaq, should strengthen the bowling in 2002 and take much of the strain off Fraser. He should also improve the lower middle-order batting, a disappointing facet of Middlesex's cricket for far too long, just as Sven Koenig, an opening batsman with an excellent record in South Africa – and an Italian passport – is expected to boost the early batting. Strauss again had several opening partners, none of whom was an established opener, and there were too few good starts.

Success in the one-day game proved elusive once more. Middlesex surprised just about everyone by beating the Australians, for the first time, in a 50-over match, but poor performances at Hove and Chelmsford prevented progress beyond the Benson and Hedges group stage. An embarrassing loss to Herefordshire saw the county's interest in the Cheltenham & Gloucester Trophy end at the first hurdle and, to complete the sorry tale, there were only three wins in the Norwich Union League.

So what of 2002? It is always more difficult to live up to expectations than exceed them. But the young players have gained an additional year's experience and, with Razzaq's all-round expertise and a settled opening partnership in prospect, Middlesex had several reasons to look ahead with optimism. Whatever happened, though, Michael Roseberry would not be a part of it, for he had retired after a career spanning 16 years, 12 with Middlesex. – NORMAN de MESQUITA.

[*Bill Smith*

Back row: B. L. Hutton, C. B. Keegan, T. A. Hunt, J. K. Maunders. *Middle row:* S. G. M. Shepard (*physiotherapist*), J. E. Emburey (*head coach*), S. J. Cook, T. F. Bloomfield, A. W. Laraman, D. Alleyne, R. M. S. Weston, J. C. Pooley (*assistant coach*), A. Jones (*Second Eleven scorer*), C. Phillips (*fitness advisor*). *Front row:* D. C. Nash, J. P. Hewitt, M. A. Roseberry, P. C. R. Tufnell, A. R. C. Fraser (*captain*), S. P. Fleming, P. N. Weekes, O. A. Shah, A. J. Strauss.
Insets: E. C. Joyce, J. W. M. Dalrymple, N. R. D. Compton, M. J. Brown.

MIDDLESEX RESULTS

All first-class matches – Played 17: Won 4, Lost 3, Drawn 10.

County Championship matches – Played 16: Won 4, Lost 3, Drawn 9.

CricInfo County Championship, 5th in Division 2; Cheltenham & Gloucester Trophy, 3rd round; Benson and Hedges Cup, 3rd in South Group; Norwich Union League, 8th in Division 2.

COUNTY CHAMPIONSHIP AVERAGES

BATTING

Cap		*M*	*I*	*NO*	*R*	*HS*	*100s*	*50s*	*Avge*	*Ct/St*
2001	S. P. Fleming§	13	21	2	1,059	151	4	6	55.73	20
2001	A. J. Strauss	16	26	1	1,208	176	3	6	48.32	7
	E. C. Joyce	3	6	1	234	108*	2	0	46.80	5
2001	R. M. S. Weston	10	17	1	671	135*	3	1	41.93	5
2000	O. A. Shah	14	23	0	955	203	3	3	41.52	13
2000	D. C. Nash	14	18	5	456	103*	1	4	35.07	35/4
	B. L. Hutton	13	20	1	648	139	2	2	34.10	20
	S. J. Cook	9	10	3	226	93*	0	1	32.28	3
1993	P. N. Weekes	16	25	4	659	107	1	4	31.38	14
1990	M. A. Roseberry	10	15	2	328	63	0	1	25.23	8
	D. Alleyne	2	4	0	55	44	0	0	13.75	4
1988	A. R. C. Fraser	12	11	0	144	41	0	0	13.09	3
2001	T. F. Bloomfield	15	15	3	85	28	0	0	7.08	2
	C. B. Keegan	7	10	2	45	30*	0	0	5.62	1
	J. P. Hewitt	4	5	1	22	10*	0	0	5.50	1
1990	P. C. R. Tufnell	15	17	7	44	11*	0	0	4.40	0

Also batted: M. J. Brown (1 match) 0, 10; J. W. M. Dalrymple (1 match) 11, 0* (2 ct); A. W. Laraman (1 match) 29 (1 ct).

* *Signifies not out.* § *Overseas player.*

BOWLING

	O	*M*	*R*	*W*	*BB*	*5W/i*	*Avge*
P. C. R. Tufnell	626.3	155	1,510	57	6-44	3	26.49
P. N. Weekes	427.5	95	1,179	40	5-90	1	29.47
C. B. Keegan	170	38	588	18	4-54	0	32.66
T. F. Bloomfield	451.4	67	1,653	47	5-58	2	35.17
A. R. C. Fraser	448.4	129	1,176	31	3-46	0	37.93
J. P. Hewitt	83	8	386	10	3-72	0	38.60
S. J. Cook	196.1	36	663	14	3-59	0	47.35

Also bowled: J. W. M. Dalrymple 30–1–113–1; S. P. Fleming 2–0–19–0; B. L. Hutton 9–0–48–0; A. W. Laraman 4.5–1–20–2; O. A. Shah 5–1–38–0; A. J. Strauss 1–0–3–0.

COUNTY RECORDS

Highest score for:	331*	J. D. Robertson v Worcestershire at Worcester	1949
Highest score against:	316*	J. B. Hobbs (Surrey) at Lord's	1926
Best bowling for:	10-40	G. O. B. Allen v Lancashire at Lord's	1929
Best bowling against:	9-38	R. C. Robertson-Glasgow (Somerset) at Lord's	1924
Highest total for:	642-3 dec.	v Hampshire at Southampton	1923
Highest total against:	665	by West Indians at Lord's	1939
Lowest total for:	20	v MCC at Lord's	1864
Lowest total against:	31	by Gloucestershire at Bristol	1924
	31	by Glamorgan at Cardiff	1997

At Oxford, April 16, 17, 18. MIDDLESEX drew with OXFORD UCCE.

MIDDLESEX v WORCESTERSHIRE

At Lord's, April 20, 21, 22, 23. Drawn. Middlesex 9 pts, Worcestershire 8 pts. Toss: Worcestershire. County debuts: A. Bichel, A. Singh. Championship debut: S. P. Fleming.

Rain prevented any play after an early lunch on the first day and washed out the fourth. The one surprise of an Arctic second day was Hick's failure to reach three figures – he was caught at silly mid-off for 81. Leatherdale also fell within sight of a hundred and, once Worcestershire had gained a third batting point, Hick declared. Strauss replied with the second hundred of his career, hitting 21 fours, and Middlesex's overseas player, the New Zealand captain Fleming, made a good first impression. The early form of these two, as well as encouraging performances from Roseberry and Shah, suggested Middlesex's batting was not as threadbare as had been predicted.

Close of play: First day, Worcestershire 73-1 (Singh 22*, Hick 37*); Second day, Middlesex 62-0 (Strauss 25*, Roseberry 33*); Third day, Middlesex 302-5 (Weekes 0*, Nash 0*).

Worcestershire

W. P. C. Weston c Nash b Bloomfield	9
A. Singh c Nash b Fraser	36
*G. A. Hick c Hutton b Tufnell	81
V. S. Solanki c Weekes b Fraser	16
D. A. Leatherdale b Fraser	93
P. R. Pollard lbw b Weekes	3
†S. J. Rhodes run out	6
A. J. Bichel c Fleming b Bloomfield	33
S. R. Lampitt not out	8
M. J. Rawnsley not out	4
L-b 6, n-b 6	12
1/13 2/107 3/135 4/183 5/204 6/212 7/285 8/289 (8 wkts dec.)	301

C. G. Liptrot did not bat.

Bonus points – Worcestershire 3, Middlesex 2.

Bowling: Fraser 29.1–6–70–3; Bloomfield 15–2–61–2; Cook 20–5–65–0; Hutton 3–0–13–0; Weekes 19–5–42–1; Tufnell 24–10–44–1.

Middlesex

A. J. Strauss c Rhodes b Hick	125
M. A. Roseberry c Bichel b Liptrot	63
O. A. Shah c Rhodes b Liptrot	48
S. P. Fleming c Rhodes b Bichel	42
B. L. Hutton c Rhodes b Rawnsley	4
P. N. Weekes not out	0
†D. C. Nash not out	0
B 3, l-b 3, w 4, n-b 10	20
1/129 2/226 3/290 4/298 5/302 (5 wkts)	302

S. J. Cook, *A. R. C. Fraser, P. C. R. Tufnell and T. F. Bloomfield did not bat.

Bonus points – Middlesex 3, Worcestershire 1.

Bowling: Bichel 29–9–85–1; Liptrot 17–6–44–2; Lampitt 15–5–51–0; Rawnsley 32–9–61–1; Leatherdale 5–1–26–0; Hick 9–3–12–1; Solanki 5–0–17–0.

Umpires: V. A. Holder and R. Palmer.

At Derby, April 25, 26, 27, 28. MIDDLESEX drew with DERBYSHIRE.

At Bristol, May 9, 10, 11, 12. MIDDLESEX beat GLOUCESTERSHIRE by five wickets.

At Chester-le-Street, May 16, 17, 18, 19. MIDDLESEX drew with DURHAM.

MIDDLESEX v NOTTINGHAMSHIRE

At Lord's, May 25, 26, 27, 28. Drawn. Middlesex 11 pts, Nottinghamshire 12 pts. Toss: Nottinghamshire.

Nottinghamshire were 38 for two in the eighth over when Afzaal joined Bicknell, and together they started a recovery later completed by Pietersen and Franks, who added 199, a county record for the seventh wicket against Middlesex. Both hit personal bests, Pietersen's maiden hundred containing two sixes and 22 fours and lasting a minute over five hours. Middlesex faltered in reply, and at 99 for four seemed unlikely to avert the follow-on. However, with Shah passing 50 for the fourth consecutive Championship innings, and three more half-centuries from the middle order – including a career-best 93 not out from Cook – the arrears were kept to 97. Pietersen's unbeaten 65 from just 47 balls, including four sixes, helped Bicknell set a target of 350. After Middlesex lost two quick wickets, Strauss batted with great patience for 336 minutes to make the draw almost certain. The electronic scoreboard, which had shown signs of fallibility during the Pakistan Test earlier in the week, failed to work for the first 40 minutes on the opening morning, and then functioned inconsistently.

Close of play: First day, Nottinghamshire 409-8 (Pietersen 135*, Smith 9*); Second day, Middlesex 273-6 (Nash 35*, Cook 38*); Third day, Middlesex 9-0 (Strauss 7*, Weston 0*).

Nottinghamshire

*D. J. Bicknell c Fleming b Tufnell	38	– b Weekes	44
G. E. Welton c Shah b Hewitt	11	– c Nash b Cook	0
G. S. Blewett c Weston b Hewitt	12	– c Nash b Weekes	76
U. Afzaal c Weekes b Hewitt	43	– c Hutton b Tufnell	22
P. Johnson c Cook b Tufnell	22	– c Fleming b Tufnell	12
K. P. Pietersen not out	165	– not out	65
†C. M. W. Read c Fleming b Bloomfield	1	– c Fleming b Tufnell	0
P. J. Franks lbw b Bloomfield	85	– c Hutton b Tufnell	6
A. J. Harris lbw b Bloomfield	0	– c Hutton b Tufnell	0
G. J. Smith c Nash b Bloomfield	11	– not out	8
R. D. Stemp c Nash b Bloomfield	22		
L-b 23, w 6, n-b 28	57	B 5, l-b 10, n-b 4	19
1/20 2/38 3/106 4/134 5/178 6/191 7/390 8/390 9/418	467	1/2 2/93 3/148 4/152 5/200 6/202 7/222 8/222 (8 wkts dec.)	252

Bonus points – Nottinghamshire 5, Middlesex 3.

Bowling: *First Innings*—Bloomfield 33.5–3–133–5; Hewitt 16–2–95–3; Cook 21–3–73–0; Tufnell 31–5–83–2; Weekes 11–1–40–0; Hutton 3–0–20–0. *Second Innings*—Bloomfield 16–2–64–0; Cook 8–3–24–1; Hewitt 3–0–19–0; Tufnell 26–8–61–5; Weekes 16–5–69–2.

Middlesex

A. J. Strauss c Read b Smith	20	– b Pietersen	78
R. M. S. Weston c Read b Franks	29	– c Afzaal b Smith	1
O. A. Shah c Read b Franks	58	– c and b Franks	2
*S. P. Fleming c Welton b Stemp	14	– c Afzaal b Stemp	42
B. L. Hutton c Read b Smith	2	– c Read b Harris	0
P. N. Weekes c Pietersen b Stemp	50	– c Bicknell b Stemp	2
†D. C. Nash c Blewett b Harris	56	– c Welton b Harris	12
S. J. Cook not out	93	– c Johnson b Stemp	16
J. P. Hewitt c Pietersen b Franks	0	– not out	10
P. C. R. Tufnell c Read b Franks	9	– not out	0
T. F. Bloomfield c Pietersen b Smith	3		
B 6, l-b 8, w 12, n-b 10	36	B 11, l-b 7, w 6, n-b 10	34
1/47 2/57 3/84 4/99 5/170 6/206 7/320 8/345 9/367	370	1/17 2/20 3/130 4/130 5/135 6/158 7/179 8/185 (8 wkts)	197

Bonus points – Middlesex 4, Nottinghamshire 3.

Bowling: *First Innings*—Smith 21.1–8–61–3; Harris 26–4–87–1; Franks 30–9–65–4; Stemp 26–8–77–2; Pietersen 12–2–57–0; Afzaal 2–0–9–0. *Second Innings*—Franks 15–3–45–1; Stemp 27–11–39–3; Smith 14–7–20–1; Harris 21.5–12–43–2; Afzaal 15–7–19–0; Pietersen 12–7–13–1.

Umpires: G. I. Burgess and A. G. T. Whitehead.

MIDDLESEX v DERBYSHIRE

At Southgate, May 30, 31, June 1. Middlesex won by an innings and 185 runs. Middlesex 20 pts, Derbyshire 1 pt. Toss: Middlesex. Championship debut: A. W. Laraman.

Taking full advantage of ideal batting conditions, Middlesex amassed their highest total for almost six years. Shah maintained his magnificent form with a chanceless maiden double-hundred to follow his 190 against Durham two weeks earlier. He batted 461 minutes, faced 371 balls and struck 32 boundaries. On the first day, he and Hutton, who hit a first Championship century, shared a partnership of 292, a record for the fourth wicket in games between these counties. On a pitch now taking spin, Derbyshire never looked like avoiding the follow-on, let alone saving the match. Tufnell and Weekes were in their element against ineffectual batting, and the visitors started again 411 behind. Dumelow provided some late resistance this time, but Tufnell still ended with match figures of ten for 133. The victory, which came with a day to spare, was Middlesex's biggest over Derbyshire, and their first in the Championship at the Walker Ground since first-class cricket resumed here in 1998.

Close of play: First day, Middlesex 358-4 (Shah 141*, Cook 4*); Second day, Derbyshire 111-9 (Welch 15*, Munton 0*).

Middlesex

A. J. Strauss b Lungley	33
M. A. Roseberry c Krikken b Lungley	21
O. A. Shah c Welch b Dumelow	203
*S. P. Fleming c Krikken b Lungley	0
B. L. Hutton c Sutton b Munton	139
S. J. Cook lbw b Munton	30
P. N. Weekes c Krikken b Dumelow	40
†D. C. Nash c Sutton b Dumelow	5
A. W. Laraman b Dumelow	29
P. C. R. Tufnell c Munton b Illingworth	6
T. F. Bloomfield not out	1
B 10, l-b 20, n-b 6	36
1/55 2/62 3/62 4/354 5/417 6/466 7/486 8/518 9/537	543

Bonus points – Middlesex 5, Derbyshire 1 (Score at 130 overs: 452-5).

Bowling: Welch 31–5–91–0; Munton 34–12–91–2; Lungley 21–2–97–3; Illingworth 35–6–103–1; Dumelow 25.1–4–103–4; Bailey 8–3–11–0; Di Venuto 6–0–17–0.

Derbyshire

S. D. Stubbings b Tufnell	35	– (2) lbw b Bloomfield	3
L. D. Sutton c Nash b Tufnell	18	– (1) c Nash b Weekes	15
M. P. Dowman st Nash b Tufnell	7	– c Cook b Laraman	44
M. J. Di Venuto c Fleming b Weekes	1	– st Nash b Tufnell	2
R. J. Bailey c Laraman b Weekes	1	– c Nash b Laraman	21
G. Welch not out	18	– c Hutton b Weekes	25
†K. M. Krikken c Hutton b Weekes	9	– lbw b Tufnell	29
N. R. C. Dumelow c Roseberry b Tufnell	0	– c Hutton b Weekes	61
R. K. Illingworth c Roseberry b Tufnell	0	– c Fleming b Tufnell	4
T. Lungley lbw b Weekes	11	– b Tufnell	2
*T. A. Munton c Nash b Tufnell	11	– not out	3
B 7, l-b 10, n-b 4	21	B 1, l-b 8, n-b 8	17
1/47 2/54 3/55 4/63 5/71 6/80 7/80 8/94 9/105	132	1/3 2/42 3/47 4/84 5/99 6/126 7/212 8/220 9/222	226

Bonus points – Middlesex 3.

In the first innings Welch, when 9, retired hurt at 77 and resumed at 94.

Bowling: *First Innings*—Bloomfield 6–2–10–0; Cook 6–2–24–0; Tufnell 27.4–11–44–6; Weekes 24–11–37–4. *Second Innings*—Bloomfield 9–2–25–1; Cook 4–1–13–0; Tufnell 34.3–5–89–4; Weekes 29.1–8–70–3; Laraman 4.5–1–20–2.

Umpires: J. H. Evans and J. H. Hampshire.

At Lord's, June 5. MIDDLESEX beat AUSTRALIANS by six wickets (see Australian tour section).

MIDDLESEX v HAMPSHIRE

At Southgate, June 13, 14, 15, 16. Drawn. Middlesex 11 pts, Hampshire 10 pts. Toss: Hampshire. First-class debut: C. B. Keegan. Championship debut: C. T. Tremlett.

It took 21-year-old Chad Keegan, born in South Africa but ECB-qualified, just 21 deliveries to claim his first victim. But with Fraser lacking match practice – it was his first appearance after four weeks off with a shoulder injury – and the Middlesex spinners making less impression than the pitch suggested, five Hampshire batsmen passed 50. Even so, Weekes took his first five-wicket haul since 1996. At 124 for five, Middlesex were in danger of following on. However, Weston, playing because Shah had been called up to the England one-day squad, scored his first hundred since leaving Derbyshire at the end of the 1999 season. He batted six hours, hitting 14 fours and adding 157 for the sixth wicket with Nash and 56 for the ninth with Fraser. A downpour ruled out any play on the last day, but the draw consolidated Middlesex's position at the top of Division Two.

Close of play: First day, Hampshire 310-7 (Aymes 63*, Udal 36*); Second day, Middlesex 169-5 (Weston 51*, Nash 18*); Third day, Hampshire 61-0 (White 20*, Kenway 39*).

Hampshire

D. A. Kenway c Hutton b Tufnell	58	– (2) not out	39
G. W. White lbw b Keegan	3	– (1) not out	20
W. S. Kendall c Fleming b Cook	1		
*R. A. Smith c and b Weekes	64		
N. C. Johnson b Weekes	54		
L. R. Prittipaul b Fraser	23		
A. D. Mascarenhas c Nash b Weekes	0		
†A. N. Aymes lbw b Tufnell	69		
S. D. Udal c Weston b Weekes	59		
A. C. Morris b Weekes	43		
C. T. Tremlett not out	17		
L-b 6, w 3, n-b 4	13	W 2	2
1/22 2/37 3/120 4/134 5/177 6/178 7/225 8/339 9/361	404		(no wkt) 61

Bonus points – Hampshire 4, Middlesex 3 (Score at 130 overs: 379-9).

Bowling: *First Innings*—Fraser 29–10–89–1; Keegan 16–4–57–1; Cook 13–2–49–1; Tufnell 46–8–113–2; Weekes 31.1–4–90–5. *Second Innings*—Fraser 3–0–7–0; Keegan 6–3–5–0; Tufnell 7–1–20–0; Weekes 5–0–29–0.

Middlesex

A. J. Strauss b Mascarenhas	33	C. B. Keegan b Mascarenhas	0
M. A. Roseberry c Johnson b Udal	30	*A. R. C. Fraser b Tremlett	25
S. P. Fleming c Morris b Mascarenhas	5	P. C. R. Tufnell b Morris	1
R. M. S. Weston not out	135	B 7, l-b 18, w 8	33
B. L. Hutton c Johnson b Udal	6		
P. N. Weekes c Mascarenhas b Tremlett	13	1/74 2/74 3/82	380
†D. C. Nash lbw b Morris	77	4/103 5/124 6/281	
S. J. Cook c Kenway b Udal	22	7/315 8/315 9/371	

Bonus points – Middlesex 4, Hampshire 2 (Score at 130 overs: 366-8).

Bowling: Tremlett 26–6–64–2; Morris 22.5–4–62–2; Udal 49–10–117–3; Johnson 6–0–23–0; Mascarenhas 26–5–69–3; White 4–0–20–0.

Umpires: G. I. Burgess and P. Willey.

At Birmingham, June 20, 21, 22, 23. MIDDLESEX beat WARWICKSHIRE by 129 runs.

MIDDLESEX v SUSSEX

At Lord's, June 29, 30, July 1, 2. Drawn. Middlesex 10 pts, Sussex 10 pts. Toss: Sussex.

Middlesex and Sussex, first and third in the table, fought out a drab draw that highlighted a negative aspect of the two-tier Championship: both sides were happier to settle for four points each rather than risk their opponents gaining the 12 for victory. Only Adams, who went to his fifty off 49 balls, enlivened the first day, though there was some amusement when Zuiderent, unleashing a full-blooded cover drive, was flukily caught at the wicket after the ball rebounded off Roseberry, taking evasive action at silly point. Weston anchored the Middlesex response, and added 108 for the sixth wicket with Nash. In Sussex's second innings, Montgomerie shared century stands for the first two wickets, but hit just eight fours in five and three-quarter hours as safety remained the priority. Middlesex made no attempt on the target of 313 from 70 overs; while the game petered out, Montgomerie took his first first-class wicket with his very occasional off-spin.

Close of play: First day, Sussex 301-9 (Lewry 19*, Robinson 0*); Second day, Middlesex 263-5 (Weston 70*, Nash 44*); Third day, Sussex 217-1 (Montgomerie 90*, Zuiderent 51*).

Sussex

M. W. Goodwin b Weekes	69	– (2) b Tufnell	61
R. R. Montgomerie c Nash b Hewitt	22	– (1) b Weekes	116
*C. J. Adams c Weekes b Tufnell	59	– (4) c Shah b Weekes	21
B. Zuiderent c Nash b Tufnell	11	– (3) c Hewitt b Fraser	56
M. H. Yardy c Nash b Hewitt	46	– not out	25
U. B. A. Rashid c Shah b Weekes	0	– c Weston b Fraser	3
†M. J. Prior b Hewitt	28	– run out	10
M. J. G. Davis lbw b Bloomfield	29	– not out	3
R. J. Kirtley c Shah b Fraser	1		
J. D. Lewry b Fraser	40		
M. A. Robinson not out	1		
B 2, l-b 7, n-b 8	17	B 4, l-b 10, w 2, n-b 4	20
1/46 2/124 3/142 4/192 5/192 6/248 7/251 8/282 9/294	323	1/108 2/232 3/262 4/285 5/292 6/311 (6 wkts dec.)	315

Bonus points – Sussex 3, Middlesex 3.

Bowling: *First Innings*—Fraser 26.1–10–47–2; Bloomfield 18–2–82–1; Hewitt 20–2–72–3; Hutton 3–0–15–0; Weekes 17–2–42–2; Tufnell 22–5–56–2. *Second Innings*—Fraser 23–7–53–2; Bloomfield 12–0–59–0; Tufnell 20–4–29–1; Weekes 42–6–108–2; Hewitt 13–1–52–0.

Middlesex

A. J. Strauss c Yardy b Robinson	48	– c Zuiderent b Robinson	26
M. A. Roseberry c sub b Lewry	44	– lbw b Robinson	8
O. A. Shah lbw b Lewry	11	– c Adams b Kirtley	0
R. M. S. Weston c Prior b Kirtley	83	– lbw b Montgomerie	34
B. L. Hutton lbw b Robinson	6	– not out	36
P. N. Weekes c Montgomerie b Davis	7	– not out	0
†D. C. Nash c and b Kirtley	50		
J. P. Hewitt b Lewry	7		
*A. R. C. Fraser c Adams b Kirtley	14		
T. F. Bloomfield b Lewry	4		
P. C. R. Tufnell not out	11		
B 13, l-b 8, w 4, n-b 16	41	B 13, l-b 4, w 2, n-b 12	31
1/96 2/115 3/119 4/150 5/164 6/272 7/289 8/305 9/310	326	1/33 2/38 3/54 4/135	(4 wkts) 135

Bonus points – Middlesex 3, Sussex 3.

Bowling: *First Innings*—Lewry 33–7–103–4; Kirtley 30.2–7–79–3; Robinson 22–7–54–2; Rashid 6–0–23–0; Davis 18–4–43–1; Adams 4–1–3–0. *Second Innings*—Lewry 13–3–31–0; Kirtley 15–7–32–1; Robinson 12–5–15–2; Davis 8–0–20–0; Adams 2–0–7–0; Rashid 6–1–13–0; Goodwin 2–2–0–0; Montgomerie 1–1–0–1.

Umpires: N. G. Cowley and K. E. Palmer.

At Nottingham, July 4, 5, 6, 7. MIDDLESEX drew with NOTTINGHAMSHIRE.

MIDDLESEX v DURHAM

At Lord's, July 27, 28, 29. Middlesex won by an innings and 74 runs. Middlesex 20 pts, Durham 2 pts. Toss: Middlesex.

First use of a good pitch in ideal batting conditions allowed Middlesex to dictate terms throughout and return to the top of Division Two. Strauss and Hutton added 168 for the fourth wicket, with each completing a second Championship hundred of the season. Strauss batted almost six and a half hours and hit 21 fours in his career-best 176. A 95-run eighth-wicket partnership between Hutton and Fraser guided Middlesex past 400 and brought what had seemed an unlikely fifth batting point. Durham collapsed from 131 for two to 187 all out, followed on 237 behind and fared even worse second time round. Peng's classy 66 did no more than delay the inevitable, and the match ended with a day and a half to spare. Tufnell, flighting the ball well on a pitch offering slow turn, collected five wickets, including his 50th of the season and the 1,000th of his first-class career. Among current players, only Allan Donald, Phillip DeFreitas and Wasim Akram had more.

Close of play: First day, Middlesex 326-7 (Hutton 76*); Second day, Durham 186-9 (Brinkley 13*, Hatch 3*).

Middlesex

A. J. Strauss c Daley b Hatch	176
M. A. Roseberry c Love b Hatch	0
O. A. Shah lbw b Law	38
R. M. S. Weston lbw b Law	13
B. L. Hutton c Peng b Law	120
P. N. Weekes c Love b Law	2
†D. C. Nash c Pratt b Hatch	1
C. B. Keegan c Lewis b Gough	4
*A. R. C. Fraser st Pratt b Gough	41
T. F. Bloomfield c Pratt b Law	0
P. C. R. Tufnell not out	0
B 2, l-b 17, w 4, n-b 6	29
1/10 2/101 3/133 4/301 5/303 6/306 7/326 8/421 9/424	424

Bonus points – Middlesex 5, Durham 2 (Score at 130 overs: 419-7).

Bowling: Law 31.4–8–94–5; Hatch 25–6–82–3; Brinkley 29–4–92–0; Collingwood 19–6–54–0; Gough 30–8–83–2.

Durham

*J. J. B. Lewis lbw b Bloomfield	18	– c Fraser b Bloomfield	6
J. A. Daley lbw b Keegan	17	– lbw b Keegan	22
M. L. Love c Hutton b Weekes	64	– b Tufnell	19
P. D. Collingwood lbw b Weekes	45	– b Tufnell	4
N. Peng lbw b Bloomfield	4	– c Nash b Tufnell	66
M. A. Gough c Roseberry b Tufnell	0	– c and b Keegan	0
D. R. Law b Tufnell	2	– c and b Weekes	27
†A. Pratt c Hutton b Tufnell	13	– lbw b Weekes	9
G. D. Bridge c Shah b Weekes	1	– lbw b Tufnell	4
J. E. Brinkley not out	13	– not out	3
N. G. Hatch b Keegan	3	– c Shah b Tufnell	3
B 2, l-b 3, n-b 2	7		
1/33 2/39 3/131 4/140 5/152 6/152 7/166 8/169 9/169	187	1/7 2/43 3/47 4/51 5/51 6/137 7/145 8/157 9/157	163

Bonus points – Middlesex 3.

Bowling: *First Innings*—Fraser 9–3–21–0; Bloomfield 15–3–31–2; Keegan 10.5–1–44–2; Tufnell 19–5–41–3; Weekes 21–6–45–3. *Second Innings*—Fraser 11–1–33–0; Bloomfield 11–3–30–1; Keegan 7–4–13–2; Tufnell 16.2–4–46–5; Weekes 10–2–41–2.

Umpires: D. J. Constant and R. Julian.

At Hove, August 2, 3, 4, 5. MIDDLESEX lost to SUSSEX by 192 runs.

MIDDLESEX v GLOUCESTERSHIRE

At Lord's, August 8, 9, 10, 11. Gloucestershire won by an innings and 59 runs. Gloucestershire 20 pts, Middlesex 2 pts. Toss: Gloucestershire.

After rain truncated the first day and obliterated the second, Windows and Harvey made up for lost time in a third-wicket stand of 193. As soon as maximum batting points were realised, Gloucestershire declared. The pivotal moment for Middlesex came late in the day when Shah played an irresponsible shot and was well caught at mid-wicket. Once 131 for two became 141 for four overnight, the follow-on began to look inescapable. Averis confirmed this next day by wrapping up the innings with a career-best five for 52. Yet with 60 overs left, a draw should have been within Middlesex's reach. However, only Weston and David Alleyne made double figures in an abject second-innings display; all told, 16 Middlesex wickets tumbled on the final day. On the third morning, the players observed a minute's silence as a tribute to George Mann, who had died two days before; the MCC and Middlesex flags were flown at half-mast.

Close of play: First day, Gloucestershire 198-2 (Windows 52*, Harvey 14*); Second day, No play; Third day, Middlesex 141-4 (Hutton 29*).

Gloucestershire

D. R. Hewson run out	77	*M. W. Alleyne not out	12
K. J. Barnett c Weston b Bloomfield	38	L-b 4, n-b 16	20
M. G. N. Windows c Strauss b Fraser	123		
I. J. Harvey not out	130	1/88 2/170 3/363 (3 wkts dec.)	400

†R. C. Russell, J. N. Snape, M. A. Hardinges, M. C. J. Ball, A. N. Bressington and J. M. M. Averis did not bat.

Bonus points – Gloucestershire 5, Middlesex 1.

Bowling: Fraser 31–7–100–1; Bloomfield 17–1–95–1; Keegan 16–2–79–0; Tufnell 31–4–86–0; Weekes 16–3–36–0.

Middlesex

A. J. Strauss lbw b Ball	38	– c Snape b Bressington	1
R. M. S. Weston c Russell b Ball	17	– b Alleyne	40
O. A. Shah c Ball b Snape	37	– c Averis b Ball	1
B. L. Hutton c Russell b Alleyne	35	– (5) c Barnett b Alleyne	0
†D. Alleyne lbw b Alleyne	3	– (7) c Alleyne b Ball	44
S. P. Fleming c Russell b Averis	10	– (4) c Barnett b Harvey	4
P. N. Weekes c Russell b Averis	37	– (6) c Ball b Harvey	0
C. B. Keegan c Russell b Averis	0	– b Harvey	1
*A. R. C. Fraser c Hardinges b Averis	16	– run out	3
T. F. Bloomfield c Alleyne b Averis	5	– c Russell b Harvey	2
P. C. R. Tufnell not out	1	– not out	6
B 2, l-b 7, w 6, n-b 8	23	B 2, l-b 7, n-b 8	17
1/51 2/70 3/131 4/141 5/154 6/169 7/169 8/199 9/211	222	1/4 2/9 3/23 4/25 5/105 6/105 7/109 8/109 9/111	119

Bonus points – Middlesex 1, Gloucestershire 3.

In the second innings Hutton, when 0, retired hurt at 23-3 and resumed at 109-7.

Bowling: *First Innings*—Averis 16.3–2–52–5; Bressington 13–5–36–0; Ball 27–9–54–2; Snape 11–1–31–1; Hardinges 6–1–19–0; Alleyne 12–2–21–2. *Second Innings*—Bressington 9–3–18–1; Ball 10–4–20–2; Harvey 14.2–7–20–4; Averis 5–0–30–0; Alleyne 9–2–22–2.

Umpires: A. Clarkson and B. Dudleston.

MIDDLESEX v WARWICKSHIRE

At Lord's, August 22, 23, 24, 25. Drawn. Middlesex 10 pts, Warwickshire 10 pts. Toss: Middlesex. First-class debut: J. A. Spires. Championship debut: J. W. M. Dalrymple.

For only the third time in their history – and the first time since 1923 – Middlesex hit four centuries in an innings, yet the feat was eclipsed by the prodigious efforts of Mark Wagh. On the first day, though, it was the turn of Joyce to record his maiden hundred, the first in the Championship by a born-and-bred Irishman, and of Fleming, who hit his first century at Lord's for Middlesex. Next day, Weekes and Nash completed the set. Warwickshire lost two early wickets, but Wagh proved the pitch remained a batsman's paradise. Displaying monumental powers of concentration, he batted for 630 minutes and faced 449 balls, 36 of which went for four, one for six. His 315 was only the fourth triple-hundred at Lord's, Wagh's exalted company being Graham Gooch, Jack Hobbs and Percy Holmes. It was also the second-highest score for Warwickshire, after Brian Lara's world-record 501 not out. Warwickshire led by 129 and, with the wicket taking turn, Wagh was soon bowling his off-breaks. Left-arm spinner Jamie Spires, aged 21, claimed his first wickets, and the visitors fleetingly glimpsed victory before Middlesex's lower middle order secured the draw. For all the game's hundreds, it was perhaps a near miss from Bell, with two sixes and 14 fours, that impressed most. Middlesex remained third in the division; Warwickshire moved up one to fourth.

Close of play: First day, Middlesex 338-5 (Weekes 47*, Nash 28*); Second day, Warwickshire 157-2 (Wagh 81*, Bell 65*); Third day, Warwickshire 538-6 (Wagh 266*, Drakes 9*).

Middlesex

A. J. Strauss b Dagnall	14	– (2) b Spires	29
M. J. Brown b Drakes	0	– (1) c Piper b Drakes	10
O. A. Shah c Piper b Dagnall	17	– c Brown b Drakes	0
S. P. Fleming c Piper b Brown	102	– c Knight b Wagh	65
E. C. Joyce run out	104	– c Brown b Spires	7
P. N. Weekes c Knight b Richardson	107	– c Powell b Wagh	21
†D. C. Nash not out	103	– not out	17
J. W. M. Dalrymple lbw b Richardson	11	– not out	0
S. J. Cook not out	14		
B 8, l-b 6, w 2, n-b 14	30	B 1, l-b 3, w 4, n-b 10	18
1/0 2/32 3/33 4/252 5/268 6/457 7/481	(7 wkts dec.) 502	1/40 2/42 3/50 4/90 5/142 6/157	(6 wkts) 167

*A. R. C. Fraser and T. F. Bloomfield did not bat.

Bonus points – Middlesex 5, Warwickshire 1 (Score at 130 overs: 424-5).

Bowling: *First Innings*—Dagnall 21–4–73–2; Drakes 31–5–78–1; Brown 19–3–79–1; Richardson 26.5–5–83–2; Spires 23–2–82–0; Wagh 33–6–93–0. *Second Innings*—Drakes 10–1–35–2; Dagnall 4–0–13–0; Spires 27–6–73–2; Richardson 4–2–13–0; Wagh 18–8–29–2.

Warwickshire

*M. J. Powell lbw b Fraser	6
N. V. Knight b Bloomfield	0
M. A. Wagh c Dalrymple b Bloomfield	315
I. R. Bell c Weekes b Cook	98
D. R. Brown c Joyce b Dalrymple	53
†K. J. Piper b Weekes	40
D. L. Hemp c Fleming b Cook	36
V. C. Drakes c Shah b Weekes	41
C. E. Dagnall c Dalrymple b Bloomfield	1
A. Richardson not out	4
B 5, l-b 6, w 8, n-b 18	37
1/6 2/6 3/215 4/361 5/450 6/516 7/612 8/614 9/631	(9 wkts dec.) 631

J. A. Spires did not bat.

Bonus points – Warwickshire 5, Middlesex 1 (Score at 130 overs: 488-5).

Bowling: Fraser 37–8–109–1; Bloomfield 20.4–0–111–3; Cook 20–3–96–2; Weekes 58–6–163–2; Dalrymple 30–1–113–1; Shah 2–0–28–0.

Umpires: G. Sharp and R. A. White.

At Southampton, September 5, 6, 7. MIDDLESEX lost to HAMPSHIRE by five wickets.

At Worcester, September 12, 13, 14, 15. MIDDLESEX drew with WORCESTERSHIRE.

Mike Hussey

NORTHAMPTONSHIRE

President: L. A. Wilson
Chairman: S. G. Schanschieff
Chief Executive: S. P. Coverdale
Chairman, Cricket Committee: 2001 – R. T. Virgin
Captain: 2001 – D. Ripley
2002 – M. E. K. Hussey
Director of Cricket: R. M. Carter
Director of Excellence: D. J. Capel
Head Groundsman: D. Bates
Scorer: A. C. Kingston

Northamptonshire spent much of 2001, too much of it perhaps, waiting for history to repeat itself. The previous season, a poor start had been redeemed by their strong showing from mid-July onwards, which ensured Championship promotion and third place in the League. The 2001 campaign began in equally unpromising fashion, but this time the revival failed to materialise. The game plan that served them so well the year before, built around slow-bowling strength, proved less effective. The result was relegation in both Championship and League, without the consolation of a lengthy run in either cup competition. Even the opportunity to beat the Australians was wasted, their one-day game ending in a tie after Northamptonshire had needed three off the last over.

The statistics tell a large part of the story. For the first time since 1995, three Northamptonshire batsmen – Mike Hussey, Russell Warren and Mal Loye – passed 1,000 first-class runs. Hussey, a well-organised and highly motivated left-hander from Western Australia, signed to replace Matthew Hayden, scored 2,055. It was the county's highest aggregate since Dennis Brookes made 2,198 (in 50 innings, compared to Hussey's 30) in 1952 – and Hussey was the first to reach 2,000 in an English season since Mark Ramprakash in 1995. With Tony Penberthy also enjoying a productive summer, Northamptonshire's tally of 52 batting points was surpassed only by Somerset in either division. But on the other side of the coin, their 36 bowling points were exceeded by every side except Essex.

Of the three key bowlers in 2000, Darren Cousins missed half the season through injury – yet still finished as leading wicket-taker with 36 – while off-spinners Graeme Swann and Jason Brown, both England tourists the preceding winter, struggled for consistency and confidence. It was apparent early on that the seam attack lacked strength in depth, and this resulted in Cousins being heavily overbowled until stress fractures in both feet ruled him out for the last ten weeks. His efforts up to that point were little short of heroic, not least against Lancashire at Northampton, when he captured all seven wickets in their second innings. But not for the first or last time, he received negligible support. Lancashire rallied from 68 for five to score 305 to win the game, and went on to avoid relegation, at Northamptonshire's expense, by five points. In the final analysis, the shortage of wickets had proved fatal, a fact reflected in the decision to release the long-serving Paul Taylor and three other seamers – Michael Strong, Kevin Innes and Lesroy Weekes – and sign Essex's Ricky Anderson, along with Michael Cawdron from Gloucestershire, Carl Greenidge (Surrey), Ben Phillips (Kent) and Tom Baker (Yorkshire).

Brown and Swann managed just 58 Championship wickets between them at almost 48 runs apiece, against 98 at 25 the year before. Factors contributing to this disappointing return included a succession of Wantage Road pitches that deteriorated only slightly and slowly, and the greater resilience displayed by most first-division batting orders. Swann's all-round form showed signs of improvement in the latter part of the season, and he was named in the ECB Academy's inaugural intake, but Brown remained out of sorts and lost his place for the final two Championship games. Monty Panesar, a highly promising England Under-19 slow left-armer, claimed match figures of eight for 131 on his debut against Leicestershire, and much is hoped of him.

Loughborough University student Robert White, voted the county's Young Player of the Year, also earned a first Championship appearance, against Kent at Canterbury in September. A stylish batsman and fine fielder who has worked hard on developing his leg-spin, he was included to give captain David Ripley another slow-bowling option in a match Northamptonshire needed to win. That he sent down only three of the 171 overs in Kent's second innings was just one more puzzling decision in a season full of them.

If Ripley was left to reflect on an anticlimactic end to his distinguished career with Northamptonshire, encompassing 18 seasons and nearly 600 matches in all cricket, then Hussey's first summer on the county circuit was a personal triumph. The most remarkable of his many outstanding performances came against Essex at Northampton when he followed his 329 not out in the first innings, the highest individual score in Northamptonshire's history, with an unbeaten 70 in the second to clinch their long-awaited first Championship victory. He was on the field for every ball of the match. Hussey's healthy appetite for runs also brought him subsequent double-centuries against Leicestershire and Somerset, and his agreement to return again in 2002, despite predictable interest from other counties, came as a relief to everyone at Wantage Road. He also set a magnificent example in the field, all too frequently a solitary beacon of alertness and enthusiasm, and was a natural choice to follow Ripley as captain.

Ripley's likely successor behind the stumps, the talented Toby Bailey, should help Hussey inject some much needed sparkle, although Bailey may face a challenge from the newly signed Gerry Brophy, South African-born but qualified for county cricket through British citizenship. Hussey can also look forward to the return of David Sales, who missed the entire Championship programme owing to the knee injury he incurred in the West Indies with England A. Alec Swann, however, chose to pursue a career at Old Trafford.

Looking to the longer term, Northamptonshire's academy was granted a four-year licence by the ECB, and 17 youngsters aged between 13 and 21 were selected for 2002. With the trade in ready-made players of proven quality more competitive than ever, Northamptonshire will be anxious to see this "grow your own" policy bear fruit in the years ahead. – ANDREW RADD.

NORTHAMPTONSHIRE 2001

[*Bill Smith*

Back row: R. Smith (*director of academy*), M. R. Strong, M. S. Panesar, L. C. Weekes, M. E. Cassar, D. J. Capel (*director of excellence*). *Middle row:* R. M. Carter (*director of cricket*), T. M. B. Bailey, J. F. Brown, G. P. Swann, A. S. Rollins, J. W. Cook, A. J. Swann, D. M. Cousins, N. G. B. Cook (*Second Eleven coach*). *Front row:* D. J. Sales, R. J. Warren, A. L. Penberthy, D. Ripley (*captain*), J. P. Taylor, M. B. Loye, M. E. K. Hussey.

NORTHAMPTONSHIRE RESULTS

All first-class matches – Played 16: Won 2, Lost 5, Drawn 9.

County Championship matches – Played 16: Won 2, Lost 5, Drawn 9.

CricInfo County Championship, 7th in Division 1; Cheltenham & Gloucester Trophy, 4th round; Benson and Hedges Cup, 5th in Midlands/Wales/West Group; Norwich Union League, 9th in Division 1.

COUNTY CHAMPIONSHIP AVERAGES

BATTING

Cap		*M*	*I*	*NO*	*R*	*HS*	*100s*	*50s*	*Avge*	*Ct/St*
2001	M. E. K. Hussey§	16	30	4	2,055	329*	5	9	79.03	19
1994	M. B. Loye†	12	21	3	1,003	197	3	4	55.72	4
1995	R. J. Warren†	16	27	3	1,303	194	4	7	54.29	8
1994	A. L. Penberthy	15	24	1	942	132*	3	5	40.95	11
	J. W. Cook	9	16	1	391	88	0	4	26.06	5
1987	D. Ripley	15	25	6	481	95	0	2	25.31	45/3
	A. S. Rollins	6	10	1	214	65	0	1	23.77	3
	A. J. Swann†	13	22	0	479	113	1	2	21.77	9
1999	G. P. Swann†	15	25	0	543	61	0	3	21.72	9
1992	J. P. Taylor	12	17	3	273	53	0	1	19.50	3
	T. M. B. Bailey†	5	7	0	113	41	0	0	16.14	3
	K. J. Innes†	4	7	1	86	40	0	0	14.33	1
	J. A. R. Blain	5	9	4	66	34	0	0	13.20	0
2000	D. M. Cousins	8	10	3	87	27	0	0	12.42	0
	M. R. Strong	9	13	4	110	34	0	0	12.22	2
2000	J. F. Brown	11	12	5	56	35*	0	0	8.00	2

Also batted: M. E. Cassar (1 match) 9, 0 (2 ct); M. S. Panesar (2 matches) 10, 2*, 3*; L. C. Weekes (1 match) 44*, 18; R. A. White (1 match) 4, 2.

* *Signifies not out.* † *Born in Northamptonshire.* § *Overseas player.*

BOWLING

	O	*M*	*R*	*W*	*BB*	*5W/i*	*Avge*
M. S. Panesar	101.3	28	358	11	4-11	0	32.54
D. M. Cousins	333.4	54	1,176	36	8-102	2	32.66
J. A. R. Blain	153	16	673	17	6-42	1	39.58
A. L. Penberthy	339.2	70	1,019	25	4-39	0	40.76
G. P. Swann	422.3	87	1,365	30	5-34	1	45.50
J. P. Taylor	379.2	49	1,345	29	4-100	0	46.37
J. F. Brown	473.5	102	1,407	28	5-107	1	50.25
M. R. Strong	256.3	46	992	19	3-98	0	52.21

Also bowled: J. W. Cook 47–16–124–1; M. E. K. Hussey 18–2–78–2; K. J. Innes 83.5–15–331–9; A. J. Swann 16–4–50–1; R. J. Warren 1–1–0–0; L. C. Weekes 26–5–107–3; R. A. White 3–0–7–0.

COUNTY RECORDS

Highest score for:	329*	M. E. K. Hussey v Essex at Northampton	2001
Highest score against:	333	K. S. Duleepsinhji (Sussex) at Hove	1930
Best bowling for:	10-127	V. W. C. Jupp v Kent at Tunbridge Wells	1932
Best bowling against:	10-30	C. Blythe (Kent) at Northampton	1907
Highest total for:	781-7 dec.	v Nottinghamshire at Northampton	1995
Highest total against:	670-9 dec.	by Sussex at Hove	1921
Lowest total for:	12	v Gloucestershire at Gloucester	1907
Lowest total against:	33	by Lancashire at Northampton	1977

NORTHAMPTONSHIRE v GLAMORGAN

At Northampton, April 20, 21, 22, 23. Drawn. Northamptonshire 10 pts, Glamorgan 11 pts. Toss: Glamorgan. County debuts: M. E. K. Hussey; J. P. Maher.

To the delight of the batsmen from both newly promoted sides, groundsman David Bates had, despite appalling spring weather, produced a firm, true pitch – and a fast outfield to match it. Powell had 16 fours in the season's first Championship century, while acting-captain Dale, with whom he added 123, hit 31, and passed 10,000 first-class runs, as he progressed to its first double-hundred. In all, Dale batted 362 minutes and faced 276 balls, while his partnership of 248 with Newell (17 fours) secured maximum batting points and restricted the home bowlers to just one. Northamptonshire were sinking at 127 for five before Warren – dropped on 25 and 134 – and Penberthy came to the rescue with a 250-run stand. Warren's five-hour 175 featured 27 fours and a six, and Penberthy had 20 boundaries in his century when Ripley declared 102 behind in an effort to breathe life into the match. Rain cut short the third day's play, however, and washed out the fourth.

Close of play: First day, Glamorgan 339-4 (Dale 130*, Newell 36*); Second day, Northamptonshire 181-5 (Warren 72*, Penberthy 21*); Third day, Glamorgan 66-1 (Maher 34*, Powell 23*).

Glamorgan

A. W. Evans c A. J. Swann b Cousins	8	– (2) lbw b Taylor	5
J. P. Maher c Cook b Taylor	34	– (1) not out	34
M. J. Powell c Penberthy b G. P. Swann	106	– not out	23
M. P. Maynard c Penberthy b Taylor	15		
*A. Dale b Brown	204		
K. Newell run out	103		
†A. D. Shaw not out	33		
R. D. B. Croft not out	14		
B 2, l-b 11, w 16, n-b 2	31	B 2, w 2	4
1/20 2/73 3/101 4/224 5/472 6/522 (6 wkts dec.)	548	1/12 (1 wkt)	66

A. G. Wharf, S. D. Thomas and S. L. Watkin did not bat.

Bonus points – Glamorgan 5, Northamptonshire 1 (Score at 130 overs: 442-4).

Bowling: *First Innings*—Cousins 36–4–141–1; Taylor 31–4–99–2; Penberthy 36–4–129–0; Brown 29–7–73–1; G. P. Swann 20–3–70–1; Hussey 2–0–11–0; Cook 7–4–12–0. *Second Innings*—Cousins 8–1–38–0; Taylor 7–0–26–1.

Northamptonshire

M. E. K. Hussey c Evans b Wharf	18
M. B. Loye c Maher b Watkin	25
J. W. Cook c Shaw b Thomas	14
R. J. Warren c Shaw b Watkin	175
A. J. Swann b Croft	21
G. P. Swann c Thomas b Croft	7
A. L. Penberthy not out	132
*†D. Ripley b Watkin	0
J. P. Taylor not out	26
B 4, l-b 16, w 4, n-b 4	28
1/37 2/53 3/57 4/113 5/127 6/377 7/381 (7 wkts dec.)	446

D. M. Cousins and J. F. Brown did not bat.

Bonus points – Northamptonshire 5, Glamorgan 2.

Bowling: Watkin 24–4–94–3; Wharf 20–1–92–1; Thomas 24–3–78–1; Croft 32–8–84–2; Dale 10–1–45–0; Maher 7–1–33–0.

Umpires: A. A. Jones and M. J. Kitchen.

At Chelmsford, April 25, 26, 27, 28. NORTHAMPTONSHIRE drew with ESSEX.

NORTHAMPTONSHIRE v SURREY

At Northampton, May 9, 10, 11, 12. Drawn. Northamptonshire 11 pts, Surrey 11 pts. Toss: Northamptonshire.

Another flawless Wantage Road batting strip produced 1,387 runs for just 21 wickets; five bowlers went for more than a century each. Northamptonshire's two Australian-born left-handers, Hussey and Cook, laid the foundations for a formidable total by putting on 172, after which a fifth-wicket stand of 161 between Alec Swann and Penberthy kept the home side on course for full batting points. Surrey lost Butcher and Ramprakash in successive balls early on, but prospered on the third day through Thorpe – taking advantage of the perfect conditions to warm up for the opening Test against Pakistan – and Brown, who added 193 in 42 overs. Bailey, standing in for the injured Ripley, kept immaculately and conceded no byes in Surrey's 607. Northamptonshire trailed by 131 with more than two sessions left, but the pitch remained true, enabling Loye to reach his first Championship hundred for two years, from 110 balls with 14 fours and three sixes, and milk runs when the part-time bowlers took over. A power failure on the second morning blacked out both electronic scoreboards and left spectators reliant on periodic updates over the Tannoy.

Close of play: First day, Northamptonshire 320-4 (Swann 64*, Penberthy 62*); Second day, Surrey 126-2 (Ward 58*, Thorpe 34*); Third day, Surrey 547-8 (Bicknell 20*, Salisbury 10*).

Northamptonshire

M. E. K. Hussey b Salisbury	75	– c Hollioake b Butcher	67
M. B. Loye c Thorpe b Tudor	5	– not out	167
J. W. Cook b Bicknell	80	– not out	52
R. J. Warren lbw b Salisbury	0		
A. J. Swann c Stewart b Butcher	96		
*A. L. Penberthy b Salisbury	75		
K. J. Innes c Amin b Tudor	5		
†T. M. B. Bailey c Tudor b Salisbury	41		
J. A. R. Blain c Hollioake b Bicknell	34		
D. M. Cousins c Thorpe b Bicknell	12		
J. F. Brown not out	3		
B 10, l-b 8, w 6, n-b 26	50	B 5, l-b 9, w 2, n-b 2	18
1/8 2/180 3/181 4/186 5/347 6/363 7/395 8/437 9/473	476	1/189	(1 wkt) 304

Bonus points – Northamptonshire 5, Surrey 2 (Score at 130 overs: 419-7).

Bowling: *First Innings*—Bicknell 38.1–9–129–3; Tudor 30–6–89–2; Butcher 12–1–37–1; Hollioake 8–2–14–0; Salisbury 39–3–130–4; Amin 22–6–59–0. *Second Innings*—Bicknell 9–1–27–0; Tudor 5–0–33–0; Salisbury 8–1–45–0; Amin 18–3–65–0; Brown 11–1–52–0; Butcher 7–0–34–1; Ramprakash 12–3–23–0; Thorpe 1–0–11–0; Stewart 1–1–0–0.

Surrey

M. A. Butcher c and b Penberthy	28
I. J. Ward c Bailey b Brown	79
M. R. Ramprakash b Penberthy	0
G. P. Thorpe b Swann	148
A. D. Brown b Blain	122
†A. J. Stewart b Blain	32
*A. J. Hollioake c Loye b Brown	50
A. J. Tudor lbw b Innes	36
M. P. Bicknell b Penberthy	56
I. D. K. Salisbury c Loye b Penberthy	33
R. M. Amin not out	0
L-b 9, n-b 14	23
1/51 2/51 3/172 4/365 5/402 6/435 7/496 8/518 9/602	607

Bonus points – Surrey 5, Northamptonshire 2 (Score at 130 overs: 499-7).

Bowling: Cousins 33–2–127–0; Blain 27–3–125–2; Brown 52–8–172–2; Penberthy 20.5–2–66–4; Innes 20–4–77–1; Swann 9–2–31–1.

Umpires: J. H. Hampshire and V. A. Holder.

At Northampton, May 17, 18, 19 (not first-class). Northamptonshire won by an innings and 66 runs. Toss: Northamptonshire. Northamptonshire 311 for three dec. (A. S. Rollins 109 retired out, M. B. Loye 79, D. Ripley 85); Bradford/Leeds UCCE 119 and 126 (S. Noach 30; J. A. R. Blain three for 35, A. J. Swann five for 35).

There was no play on the first day.

At Leeds, May 25, 26, 27. NORTHAMPTONSHIRE lost to YORKSHIRE by four wickets.

NORTHAMPTONSHIRE v LANCASHIRE

At Northampton, May 30, 31, June 1, 2. Lancashire won by three wickets. Lancashire 16 pts, Northamptonshire 7 pts. Toss: Northamptonshire. Championship debut: T. W. Roberts.

Lancashire staged a remarkable comeback to secure their first Championship victory at Northampton since 1979. Needing 302, they lost Driver on the third evening and, next morning, collapsed to 68 for five in the face of hostile fast bowling from Cousins. A win looked no more likely when Chapple joined Hegg at 169 for seven, and survived a caught and bowled chance to Brown before he had scored. Yet these two powered to their target with more than 20 overs to spare, adding an unbroken 136 and each striking two sixes and nine fours. Hegg notched his sixth first-class hundred, his third against Northamptonshire, while Cousins took all seven wickets, but badly lacked support. Chapple's innings, following match figures of nine for 137, completed an outstanding all-round performance. The first day had gone Northamptonshire's way as Loye hit his third hundred against Lancashire in three consecutive Championship matches – and the ultimate victors avoided the follow-on only thanks to the dogged Chilton and the ubiquitous Chapple.

Close of play: First day, Northamptonshire 365-6 (G. P. Swann 31*, Ripley 1*); Second day, Lancashire 251-8 (Chilton 102*, Martin 0*); Third day, Lancashire 18-1 (Chilton 7*, Crawley 8*).

Northamptonshire

M. E. K. Hussey c Hegg b Muralitharan	70	– c Hegg b Muralitharan	82
M. B. Loye b Martin	177	– c Hegg b Martin	9
J. W. Cook c Hegg b Martin	23	– c Flintoff b Martin	0
R. J. Warren lbw b Martin	0	– c Flintoff b Muralitharan	12
A. J. Swann lbw b Muralitharan	1	– c Chilton b Chapple	4
A. L. Penberthy st Hegg b Schofield	31	– c Fairbrother b Chapple	24
G. P. Swann c Flintoff b Chapple	33	– lbw b Chapple	15
*†D. Ripley c Hegg b Chapple	4	– not out	13
J. A. R. Blain c Hegg b Chapple	16	– lbw b Chapple	1
D. M. Cousins c Flintoff b Chapple	6	– c Schofield b Muralitharan	3
J. F. Brown not out	2	– b Chapple	1
B 2, l-b 7, w 12, n-b 14	35	B 5, l-b 9, w 8, n-b 8	30
1/159 2/248 3/252 4/257 5/314 6/343 7/370 8/371 9/393	398	1/29 2/29 3/50 4/79 5/145 6/171 7/173 8/174 9/189	194

Bonus points – Northamptonshire 4, Lancashire 2 (Score at 130 overs: 385-8).

Bowling: *First Innings*—Martin 36–9–95–3; Chapple 23.1–6–77–4; Driver 2–0–15–0; Muralitharan 49–9–116–2; Schofield 26–6–86–1. *Second Innings*—Martin 15–3–60–2; Chapple 25–5–60–5; Muralitharan 33–15–49–3; Schofield 5–0–9–0; Fairbrother 1–0–2–0.

Lancashire

M. J. Chilton c Warren b Penberthy	104	– (2) lbw b Cousins	25
R. C. Driver lbw b Blain	9	– (1) b Cousins	2
*J. P. Crawley c Cook b Cousins	20	– b Cousins	24
A. Flintoff c A. J. Swann b Brown	17	– c Ripley b Cousins	14
N. H. Fairbrother c and b Brown	23	– c Ripley b Cousins	33
T. W. Roberts b Blain	3	– b Cousins	0
†W. K. Hegg lbw b Cousins	23	– not out	107
C. P. Schofield c Ripley b Penberthy	4	– c Hussey b Cousins	15
G. Chapple c Ripley b Penberthy	31	– not out	72
P. J. Martin not out	38		
M. Muralitharan c G. P. Swann b Penberthy	0		
L-b 5, w 2, n-b 12	19	B 8, l-b 1, n-b 4	13
1/28 2/73 3/96 4/134 5/143 6/179 7/191 8/250 9/289	291	1/10 2/39 3/61 4/68 5/68 6/135 7/169	(7 wkts) 305

Bonus points – Lancashire 2, Northamptonshire 3.

Bowling: *First Innings*—Cousins 23–4–79–2; Blain 21–2–71–2; Brown 18–3–64–2; Penberthy 20–3–39–4; G. P. Swann 8–0–33–0. *Second Innings*—Cousins 28–3–120–7; Blain 11–0–67–0; Penberthy 12–4–27–0; G. P. Swann 10.2–2–35–0; Brown 16–2–47–0.

Umpires: J. F. Steele and A. G. T. Whitehead.

At Northampton, June 7. NORTHAMPTONSHIRE tied with AUSTRALIANS (see Australian tour section).

At Leicester, June 13, 14, 15. NORTHAMPTONSHIRE lost to LEICESTERSHIRE by nine wickets.

NORTHAMPTONSHIRE v SOMERSET

At Northampton, June 20, 21, 22, 23. Drawn. Northamptonshire 12 pts, Somerset 8 pts. Toss: Somerset.

Blackwell became the 14th batsman to score two centuries in a match for Somerset, so helping deny Northamptonshire a first Championship win of the season. As the final day began, with Somerset trailing by 138 and with four wickets down, a home victory seemed inevitable. But Blackwell – who struck a six and 20 fours – and Wood, in only his second Championship appearance, rescued Somerset. On the first morning, Cousins and Taylor had reduced Somerset to 35 for six, only for Blackwell and Dutch to pull the innings round by adding 182 for the seventh wicket. Northamptonshire secured a commanding lead thanks largely to Loye, whose third hundred in four Championship innings at Wantage Road spanned seven hours and contained three sixes and 25 fours. Penberthy and Ripley then pressed home the advantage. Northamptonshire were awarded five penalty runs when Trego, on the field as substitute for Blackwell but without the umpires' permission, touched the ball in contravention of Law 2.6.

Close of play: First day, Northamptonshire 28-1 (Loye 11*, Taylor 0*); Second day, Northamptonshire 358-5 (Loye 194*, Penberthy 4*); Third day, Somerset 130-4 (Turner 1*, Wood 5*).

Somerset

P. C. L. Holloway lbw b Taylor	9	– (2) c Ripley b Taylor	30
P. D. Bowler c Ripley b Cousins	7	– (1) lbw b Cousins	60
*M. Burns b Cousins	0	– c Ripley b Cousins	20
M. J. Wood lbw b Cousins	9	– (6) b Brown	90
M. N. Lathwell c Ripley b Taylor	0	– (4) c Hussey b Taylor	2
†R. J. Turner b Penberthy	5	– (5) c Penberthy b Brown	33
I. D. Blackwell b Cook	103	– c Ripley b Hussey	122
K. P. Dutch lbw b Cousins	84	– c Penberthy b Cousins	23
J. I. D. Kerr c Ripley b Taylor	32	– not out	18
R. L. Johnson b G. P. Swann	20	– not out	0
P. S. Jones not out	11		
B 8, l-b 5, w 6	19	B 13, l-b 11, w 4, n-b 4	32
1/17 2/19 3/19 4/24 5/28 6/35 7/217 8/247 9/283	299	1/97 2/109 3/116 4/124 5/229 6/300 7/358 8/430	(8 wkts) 430

Bonus points – Somerset 2, Northamptonshire 3.

Bowling: *First Innings*—Cousins 26–5–100–4; Taylor 19.3–3–57–3; Penberthy 19–6–47–1; Brown 13–0–52–0; Cook 11–6–17–1; G. P. Swann 7–4–13–1. *Second Innings*—Cousins 31–8–102–3; Taylor 30–5–92–2; G. P. Swann 32–12–79–0; Penberthy 9–3–16–0; Brown 29–8–84–2; Cook 4–1–14–0; Hussey 3–0–14–1; A. J. Swann 1–0–5–0; Warren 1–1–0–0.

Northamptonshire

M. E. K. Hussey lbw b Johnson	12
M. B. Loye c Turner b Jones	197
J. P. Taylor c Lathwell b Jones	18
J. W. Cook b Jones	7
R. J. Warren b Jones	64
A. J. Swann c Johnson b Dutch	37
A. L. Penberthy c sub b Johnson	80
G. P. Swann c Wood b Johnson	0
*†D. Ripley b Johnson	95
D. M. Cousins lbw b Johnson	27
J. F. Brown not out	5
L-b 12, w 2, n-b 6, p 5	25
1/27 2/71 3/103 4/263 5/347 6/362 7/363 8/524 9/560	567

Bonus points – Northamptonshire 5, Somerset 2 (Score at 130 overs: 420-7).

Bowling: Johnson 40.1–2–127–5; Jones 36–5–121–4; Kerr 27–5–84–0; Dutch 31–6–98–1; Burns 15–4–48–0; Blackwell 13–1–72–0.

Umpires: B. Dudleston and T. E. Jesty.

At Cardiff, June 29, 30, July 1, 2. NORTHAMPTONSHIRE drew with GLAMORGAN.

NORTHAMPTONSHIRE v YORKSHIRE

At Northampton, July 4, 5, 6, 7. Drawn. Northamptonshire 9 pts, Yorkshire 10 pts. Toss: Northamptonshire. First-class debut: A. K. D. Gray.

A relatively inexperienced attack – Yorkshire were missing five senior players – allowed Northamptonshire to reach a prosperous 138 for one. Loye, whose spectacular 62-ball innings included three sixes in five deliveries, looked to unsettle Yorkshire's two young off-spinners, debutant Andy Gray and Dawson. Once he had gone, though, Northamptonshire squandered their healthy start. Byas bolstered a shaky Yorkshire reply, batting for nearly five hours and nosing his team ahead in a ninth-wicket stand of 78 with Sidebottom. Hussey then rescued Northamptonshire from the depths of 91 for five – only 35 ahead – with a chanceless 122 that occupied more than six hours and contained 19 fours. It was the 16th hundred in five Championship matches at Wantage Road. On a pitch taking increasing spin, Yorkshire's target of 243 left matters intriguingly poised, only for the weather to spoil everything by allowing just 35 minutes' play on the final day. Northamptonshire also learned that Cousins, their leading wicket-taker, would miss the remainder of the season with stress fractures in both feet.

Close of play: First day, Yorkshire 45-1 (Wood 31*, Lumb 8*); Second day, Northamptonshire 26-1 (Hussey 11*, Loye 9*); Third day, Northamptonshire 298.

Northamptonshire

M. E. K. Hussey c Byas b Lehmann	64	– lbw b Kirby	122
A. S. Rollins c Blakey b Sidebottom	24	– c Richardson b Sidebottom	1
M. B. Loye c Blakey b Sidebottom	50	– c Blakey b Hamilton	38
R. J. Warren c Byas b Dawson	27	– lbw b Gray	0
A. J. Swann c Blakey b Hamilton	2	– lbw b Hamilton	8
A. L. Penberthy run out	18	– c Blakey b Hamilton	0
G. P. Swann c Byas b Dawson	5	– c Hamilton b Dawson	55
*†D. Ripley not out	21	– c sub b Gray	17
J. P. Taylor b Kirby	18	– b Hamilton	21
M. R. Strong c Blakey b Kirby	2	– not out	14
J. F. Brown c Byas b Kirby	0	– b Kirby	0
B 6, l-b 10, n-b 6	22	B 5, l-b 5, w 4, n-b 8	22
1/50 2/138 3/156 4/158 5/198 6/203 7/206 8/243 9/253	253	1/4 2/73 3/77 4/91 5/91 6/176 7/195 8/265 9/294	298

Bonus points – Northamptonshire 2, Yorkshire 3.

Bowling: *First Innings*—Kirby 14.5–5–34–3; Sidebottom 16–6–33–2; Hamilton 13–5–40–1; Dawson 26–5–79–2; Gray 12–5–39–0; Lehmann 7–2–12–1. *Second Innings*—Kirby 18–5–50–2; Sidebottom 17–3–54–1; Hamilton 18–6–47–4; Dawson 26–10–74–1; Gray 20–4–63–2.

Yorkshire

S. A. Richardson b Strong	6	– not out	1
M. J. Wood c Warren b Strong	55	– lbw b Taylor	2
M. J. Lumb st Ripley b Brown	25	– not out	5
D. S. Lehmann run out	29		
*D. Byas not out	110		
†R. J. Blakey lbw b Brown	2		
G. M. Hamilton c and b Brown	14		
R. K. J. Dawson st Ripley b G. P. Swann	23		
A. K. D. Gray c Hussey b G. P. Swann	0		
R. J. Sidebottom c Ripley b Taylor	20		
S. P. Kirby lbw b Taylor	1		
B 5, l-b 3, w 12, n-b 4	24	W 2	2
1/14 2/86 3/86 4/148 5/155 6/183 7/225 8/225 9/303	309	1/2	(1 wkt) 10

Bonus points – Yorkshire 3, Northamptonshire 3.

Bowling: *First Innings*—Strong 24–7–66–2; Taylor 19–1–66–2; G. P. Swann 31–6–84–2; Brown 37–11–85–3. *Second Innings*—Strong 4–2–3–0; Taylor 3.4–1–7–1.

Umpires: M. R. Benson and R. A. White.

At Guildford, July 18, 19, 20. NORTHAMPTONSHIRE lost to SURREY by an innings and 55 runs.

NORTHAMPTONSHIRE v ESSEX

At Northampton, July 27, 28, 29, 30. Northamptonshire won by ten wickets. Northamptonshire 19 pts, Essex 6 pts. Toss: Northamptonshire.

A phenomenal performance from Hussey earned Northamptonshire their first Championship victory and sent Essex to a fourth consecutive defeat. On the field throughout the match, he became the sixth Australian to hit a triple-century in England, after Victor Trumper, Warwick Armstrong, Charles Macartney, Don Bradman (twice) and Bob Simpson. Hussey, who admitted embarrassment at such illustrious company, struck a six and 48 fours from 444 balls in a ten-and-a-quarter-hour innings; his unbeaten 329 supplanted Loye's 322, made three years earlier, as Northamptonshire's highest score. He enjoyed support from Penberthy, and together they put on 210 for the fourth wicket. Despite excellent resistance from Grayson, Essex were unable to save the follow-on. Yet they seemed to have saved the match when Grayson, on the final afternoon, neared his second 150 in two days, only for his departure to spark a headlong collapse: the last five wickets fell for 14 runs, the last four for two in 28 balls. Northamptonshire suddenly found themselves chasing 95 off 15 overs, a cakewalk for someone in Hussey's form. He swashbuckled his way to 70 from 33 deliveries, and Northamptonshire raced home with four overs in hand.

Close of play: First day, Northamptonshire 378-3 (Hussey 200*, Penberthy 29*); Second day, Essex 152-1 (Grayson 91*, Robinson 48*); Third day, Essex 30-1 (Grayson 7*, Robinson 22*).

Northamptonshire

M. E. K. Hussey not out	329	– not out	70
A. S. Rollins b Such	39		
M. B. Loye lbw b Irani	52	– (2) not out	21
R. J. Warren c Foster b Phillips	38		
A. L. Penberthy c and b Grayson	101		
T. M. B. Bailey c Foster b Such	25		
G. P. Swann b Such	1		
*†D. Ripley not out	19		
B 7, l-b 6, w 8, n-b 8	29	L-b 1, w 2, n-b 2	5
1/135 2/237 3/320 4/530 5/588 6/606	(6 wkts dec.) 633		(no wkt) 96

J. P. Taylor, M. R. Strong and J. F. Brown did not bat.

Bonus points – Northamptonshire 5, Essex 1 (Score at 130 overs: 509-3).

Bowling: *First Innings*—Cowan 26–3–105–0; Irani 15–3–45–1; Such 53–13–182–3; Phillips 33–3–144–1; Napier 14–2–59–0; Grayson 21–2–85–1. *Second Innings*—Irani 6–0–43–0; Cowan 4–0–36–0; Grayson 1–0–16–0.

Essex

R. S. Clinton lbw b Taylor	5	– c Ripley b Strong	1
A. P. Grayson c Hussey b Swann	173	– lbw b Taylor	149
D. D. J. Robinson c Ripley b Taylor	63	– c Ripley b Brown	31
S. G. Law c Ripley b Penberthy	12	– b Strong	48
*R. C. Irani c Hussey b Taylor	5	– c Hussey b Brown	14
S. D. Peters c Rollins b Swann	6	– c Bailey b Brown	13
†J. S. Foster c Ripley b Penberthy	79	– c Rollins b Swann	16
G. R. Napier c Ripley b Strong	35	– b Swann	9
T. J. Phillips lbw b Swann	25	– lbw b Brown	0
A. P. Cowan not out	15	– b Brown	1
P. M. Such lbw b Penberthy	0	– not out	0
B 4, l-b 4, n-b 4	12	B 9, l-b 6	15
1/11 2/208 3/245 4/253 5/260 6/279 7/347 8/411 9/419	430	1/4 2/66 3/178 4/209 5/235 6/283 7/295 8/296 9/296	297

Bonus points – Essex 5, Northamptonshire 2 (Score at 130 overs: 419-8).

Bowling: *First Innings*—Strong 24–7–66–1; Taylor 28–4–85–3; Brown 32–5–101–0; Penberthy 16–2–60–3; Swann 32–10–96–3; Hussey 2–0–14–0. *Second Innings*—Strong 13–3–57–2; Taylor 13–6–30–1; Penberthy 5–3–6–0; Brown 40.2–10–107–5; Swann 29–6–82–2.

Umpires: M. J. Harris and A. G. T. Whitehead.

NORTHAMPTONSHIRE v KENT

At Northampton, August 8, 9, 10, 11. Drawn. Northamptonshire 9 pts, Kent 12 pts. Toss: Northamptonshire.

The loss of almost two days to the weather killed off the possibility of a result, though with Fulton reaching 197, his third century in succession, Kent easily managed maximum batting points. Surviving a simple chance to short extra cover on 28, he hit a six and 27 fours in a confident five-hour innings. When he eventually fell to Hussey's occasional medium-pace, he had scored 509 between dismissals. He and Smith put on 237 for the second wicket, before Symonds meted out further punishment to a listless Northamptonshire attack; his robust 131 came at better than a run a ball. Earlier, the Northamptonshire innings had suffered a setback when Symonds athletically ran out Hussey, another batsman in blissful touch. Despite frequent rain interruptions, Warren and Penberthy's fourth-wicket partnership added 153. Graeme Swann and Ripley then lent support, but only Fulton and Symonds took full advantage of another Wantage Road shirtfront.

Close of play: First day, Northamptonshire 228-4 (Penberthy 77*, Bailey 2*); Second day, Northamptonshire 277-5 (Bailey 20*, G. P. Swann 28*); Third day, Kent 202-1 (Fulton 116*, Smith 59*).

Northamptonshire

M. E. K. Hussey run out	35	– not out	7
A. S. Rollins c Nixon b Saggers	1	– not out	6
A. J. Swann lbw b Saggers	5		
R. J. Warren c sub b Fleming	84		
A. L. Penberthy c Nixon b Trott	77		
T. M. B. Bailey lbw b Saggers	22		
G. P. Swann lbw b Patel	46		
*†D. Ripley c Symonds b Trott	39		
J. P. Taylor c Fleming b Patel	11		
M. R. Strong not out	1		
J. F. Brown b Trott	0		
B 12, l-b 10, w 6, n-b 6	34		
1/7 2/16 3/67 4/220 5/230 6/284 7/316 8/344 9/355	355		(no wkt) 13

Bonus points – Northamptonshire 4, Kent 3.

Bowling: *First Innings*—Saggers 22–3–76–3; Trott 23–4–94–3; Patel 15–3–36–2; Fleming 22–4–58–1; Ealham 9–3–31–0; Symonds 13–4–38–0. *Second Innings*—Symonds 3–2–4–0; Walker 2–0–9–0.

Kent

D. P. Fulton c Ripley b Hussey	197
R. W. T. Key lbw b Strong	20
E. T. Smith c Ripley b Taylor	91
A. Symonds c Ripley b Taylor	131
M. J. Walker not out	15
B 1, l-b 5, w 2, n-b 2	10
1/28 2/265 3/378 4/464 (4 wkts dec.)	464

*M. V. Fleming, †P. A. Nixon, M. A. Ealham, M. M. Patel, M. J. Saggers and B. J. Trott did not bat.

Bonus points – Kent 5, Northamptonshire 1.

Bowling: Taylor 20.1–1–93–2; Strong 24–3–130–1; G. P. Swann 16–0–99–0; Brown 35–8–95–0; Penberthy 5–2–21–0; Hussey 5–1–15–1; A. J. Swann 2–0–5–0.

Umpires: G. Sharp and P. Willey.

At Manchester, August 15, 16, 17, 18. NORTHAMPTONSHIRE drew with LANCASHIRE.

NORTHAMPTONSHIRE v LEICESTERSHIRE

At Northampton, August 23, 24, 25, 26. Northamptonshire won by 202 runs. Northamptonshire 19 pts, Leicestershire 8 pts. Toss: Northamptonshire. First-class debut: M. S. Panesar. County debut: R. P. Davis.

By fielding three specialist spinners, including England Under-19 slow left-armer Monty Panesar, Northamptonshire gambled on winning the toss and on the deterioration of the pitch – used a fortnight earlier for the high-scoring, rain-affected draw with Kent. Leicestershire got wind of their tactics and hurriedly added experienced left-arm spinner Richard Davis to their meagre spin resources. Davis, who had last appeared in Championship cricket in 1997 for Gloucestershire, after spells with Kent and Warwickshire – and had played limited-overs games for Sussex – became the first to represent five first-class counties. After Ripley won the toss, Hussey dominated the Northamptonshire innings, his 232 coming from 298 balls with 34 fours, though for bravado he was eclipsed by Leicestershire's Shahid Afridi, whose extraordinary second-day assault forced five fielders to the boundary by the ninth over of the innings. Reaching his century off 74 balls, Afridi crashed six sixes and 22 fours, altogether facing 121 deliveries for a career-best 164. Four other fifties – one from Davis at No. 10 – gave Leicestershire a lead of 15 by the third afternoon. Alec Swann then emerged from a run of six single-figure scores to pave the way for Ripley's declaration 20 minutes after lunch, setting a target of 288. Leicestershire, three wickets down, seemed safe at tea, but the home spinners, led by Graeme Swann, eventually found the predicted turn, the last seven wickets fell for 18 and Northamptonshire had the win they desperately needed.

Close of play: First day, Northamptonshire 266-5 (Hussey 150*, Ripley 31*); Second day, Leicestershire 278-3 (Smith 19*, Burns 23*); Third day, Northamptonshire 123-0 (Hussey 55*, A. J. Swann 63*).

Northamptonshire

M. E. K. Hussey b Malcolm	232	– c Malcolm b Davis	82
A. J. Swann c Burns b DeFreitas	4	– lbw b Shahid Afridi	113
M. E. Cassar b Malcolm	9	– (4) c Maddy b Davis	0
R. J. Warren c Davis b Malcolm	37	– (5) not out	52
A. L. Penberthy c Smith b Shahid Afridi	15	– (6) c Maddy b Davis	0
G. P. Swann c Maddy b Davis	9	– (3) c Maddy b Davis	22
*†D. Ripley run out	31	– b Davis	7
J. P. Taylor st Burns b DeFreitas	34	– c Maddy b Shahid Afridi	1
M. R. Strong b Malcolm	34	– c and b Davis	1
M. S. Panesar c Burns b Maddy	10	– not out	2
J. F. Brown not out	35		
B 16, l-b 1, w 2	19	B 12, l-b 4, w 2, n-b 4	22
1/20 2/37 3/141 4/187 5/204 6/267 7/357 8/416 9/433	469	1/164 2/199 3/199 4/247 5/252 6/278 7/279 8/287 (8 wkts dec.)	302

Bonus points – Northamptonshire 5, Leicestershire 3.

Bowling: *First Innings*—Malcolm 34–5–134–4; DeFreitas 34–4–121–2; Davis 19–3–88–1; Shahid Afridi 20–3–84–1; Maddy 6.5–1–25–1. *Second Innings*—Malcolm 8–1–27–0; DeFreitas 13–0–80–0; Shahid Afridi 20–3–92–2; Maddy 3–1–14–0; Davis 23–4–73–6.

Leicestershire

I. J. Sutcliffe c Hussey b G. P. Swann	64	– c G. P. Swann b Panesar	17
Shahid Afridi lbw b G. P. Swann	164	– c Cassar b G. P. Swann	6
T. R. Ward c A. J. Swann b Brown	2	– st Ripley b G. P. Swann	20
B. F. Smith c Penberthy b Brown	29	– lbw b G. P. Swann	10
†N. D. Burns b Panesar	69	– c A. J. Swann b Panesar	13
A. Habib not out	74	– lbw b Panesar	0
D. L. Maddy c Cassar b G. P. Swann	1	– c Hussey b G. P. Swann	10
*V. J. Wells c Hussey b Panesar	6	– b Brown	5
P. A. J. DeFreitas c G. P. Swann b Panesar	4	– c Penberthy b Panesar	2
R. P. Davis c Ripley b Panesar	51	– lbw b G. P. Swann	0
D. E. Malcolm b Brown	2	– not out	0
B 10, l-b 4, w 2, n-b 2	18	L-b 2	2
1/233 2/236 3/236 4/297 5/359 6/366 7/377 8/393 9/477	484	1/9 2/36 3/52 4/67 5/67 6/67 7/79 8/85 9/85	85

Bonus points – Leicestershire 5, Northamptonshire 2 (Score at 130 overs: 469-8).

Bowling: *First Innings*—Strong 14–2–71–0; Taylor 18–3–64–0; Brown 36–8–110–3; Panesar 35–5–120–4; G. P. Swann 32–5–101–3; Penberthy 3–2–4–0. *Second Innings*—Strong 1–0–2–0; Taylor 1–0–7–0; G. P. Swann 17.1–7–34–5; Brown 23–13–29–1; Panesar 20–16–11–4.

Umpires: G. I. Burgess and B. Leadbeater.

At Canterbury, September 5, 6, 7, 8. NORTHAMPTONSHIRE drew with KENT.

At Taunton, September 12, 13, 14, 15. NORTHAMPTONSHIRE lost to SOMERSET by four wickets.

Kevin Pietersen

NOTTINGHAMSHIRE

President: 2001 – J. R. Cope
2002 – The Rt Hon. K. Clarke
Chairman: A. Bocking
Chief Executive: D. G. Collier
Chairman, Cricket Committee: S. E. Foster
Cricket Operations Manager: M. Newell
Captain: J. E. R. Gallian
Director of Cricket: C. E. B. Rice
Head Groundsman: S. Birks
Scorer: G. Stringfellow

Hopes and ambitions kindled by an encouraging start were never realised as Nottinghamshire ultimately underperformed again in 2001. Many had installed Clive Rice's new-look team as promotion favourites in the Championship after seeing their impressive early-season form, particularly in the Benson and Hedges Cup. But a first semi-final appearance in 11 seasons in the major cup competitions would be the highlight of their summer. They managed only three Championship wins, one more than the previous year, but their ranking remained unchanged at seventh in Division Two, and they fared little better in the League. Had it not been for a winning performance on the final day of the season, to deny neighbours Leicestershire the Norwich Union title, they would have ended up in the second division of that as well.

Initially, Rice's ability to identify potential match-winners appeared highly astute, with his new signings making excellent first impressions. From his homeland, the South African had brought in Greg Smith, an experienced left-arm seamer, and Kevin Pietersen, a promising off-spinning all-rounder, both possessing British passports through an English parent. Richard Logan, a young fast bowler, had moved from Northamptonshire in search of regular first-team cricket and appeared keen to make up for lost time, while in Australian Greg Blewett, Rice had procured the services of a world-class run-scorer. Eyebrows were certainly raised when Nottinghamshire started so positively, winning seven of their first eight one-day games. But they could neither transfer their form to the four-day game nor maintain it in the limited-overs competitions.

A cursory glance at the statistics reveals all too clearly why these racing certainties for promotion ended up also-rans. At the start of the season, Rice predicted his team would be promoted if four players scored 1,000 runs and four bowlers took 50 wickets. The batsmen rose to the challenge. Darren Bicknell, Blewett and Pietersen all obliged, as did Usman Afzaal if his runs for England are included. With the ball, however, only Smith reached the 50 mark, and Logan, taking 43, was the one other bowler to get beyond 30. Smith shouldered a huge burden but was reliable and accurate, while it was easy to forget that the 21-year-old Logan, who looked a real threat in bursts, had played only eight first-class matches before moving to Trent Bridge.

Otherwise, spells of sustained line-and-length bowling were rarely seen, and the attack's lack of penetration was one clear reason why Nottinghamshire failed to deliver. It is hoped that Chris Cairns's return to Trent Bridge in 2002, for his fourth spell as overseas player, will put this right.

There were also major problems with injuries. John Morris, Andrew Harris and Richard Stemp missed half the season, and even bigger holes resulted from the troublesome knees of Paul Franks, David Millns and captain Jason Gallian. Franks, widely regarded as one of England's finest young cricketers, missed nearly four months of the season with tendonitis; Millns and Gallian managed just one first-class outing each after struggling to regain fitness following pre-season operations. While Millns chose to retire at the start of July, ending a 13-year career in which he claimed 553 first-class wickets, Gallian, who had predicted a comeback in May, took until August to make an appearance, only to break a knuckle in his first Championship innings.

The injuries did give members an encouraging glimpse of two players of the future. Introduced against Middlesex, Bilal Shafayat became the first 16-year-old in the club's history to play in the Championship and did not disappoint, fending off Angus Fraser, Phil Tufnell and a fair amount of sledging to make a half-century in his maiden first-class innings. His compact technique and "wristy" on-side flicks should soon become part of the Trent Bridge scene. The other teenager to impress was Nadeem Malik, a tall 18-year-old seamer whose high action, nagging accuracy and ability to swing the ball both ways had numerous batsmen in trouble. From the moment he bagged Worcestershire's Graeme Hick as his first first-class victim, he grew in stature, and looked to be Nottinghamshire's most dangerous bowler in the closing matches.

Gallian's injury led to Bicknell taking what he believed would be temporary charge, though in the event he retained the captaincy for virtually the entire term. However, with the captain's return always predicted to be imminent, the understudy appeared somewhat shackled when making decisions and was reluctant to attempt anything too radical. By contrast, his batting was restraint free, and he matched his 1,000 first-class runs with 1,000 more in one-day cricket – a double achieved elsewhere only by Yorkshire's Darren Lehmann, another left-hander.

Bicknell's performance was not the only one of note. After a lacklustre season with Yorkshire in 1999, Blewett silenced his doubters with 1,292 first-class runs, including five centuries. Chris Read kept well throughout the year, and recorded his highest run aggregate to date to average 30 for the first time, while Morris, in his farewell season, gave glimpses of his prodigious talent by totalling 640 runs from just eight matches.

However, the most impressive cricket came from Pietersen, who scored 1,275 Championship runs at a remarkable 82 per 100 balls. At times, the giant 21-year-old from KwaZulu-Natal was impossible to bowl to, and he impressed not only with the sheer power of his hitting but also with the way he played with a ram-rod straight bat. It may be 2005 before he meets the residency requirements to play for England but, if he can maintain his first season's form, the name of Pietersen should be pencilled in for future Test squads. – PAUL FEARN.

NOTTINGHAMSHIRE 2001

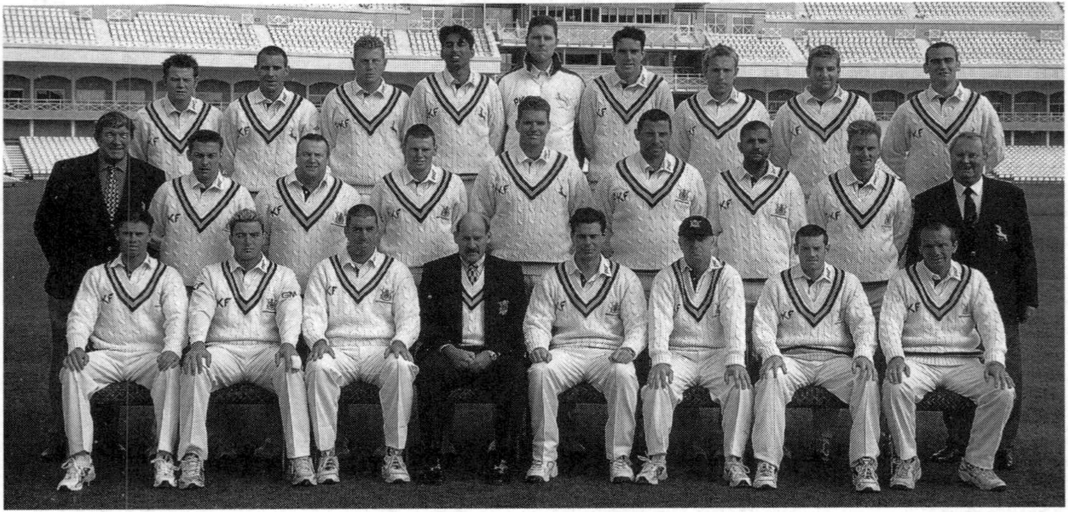

[*Getty Images*

Back row: S. J. Randall, G. D. Clough, D. S. Lucas, M. N. Malik, T. Leary (*physiotherapist*), K. P. Pietersen, G. E. Welton, R. J. Logan, C. J. Hewison. *Middle row:* B. Hewes (*second-team scorer*), W. M. Noon, J. E. Morris, A. J. Harris, G. J. Smith, D. J. Millns, U. Afzaal, R. D. Stemp, G. Stringfellow (*first-team scorer*). *Front row:* G. S. Blewett, P. J. Franks, D. J. Bicknell, C. E. B. Rice (*director of cricket*), J. E. R. Gallian (*captain*), P. Johnson, C. M. W. Read, M. Newell.

NOTTINGHAMSHIRE RESULTS

All first-class matches – Played 16: Won 3, Lost 7, Drawn 6.

County Championship matches – Played 16: Won 3, Lost 7, Drawn 6.

CricInfo County Championship, 7th in Division 2; Cheltenham & Gloucester Trophy, 4th round; Benson and Hedges Cup, s-f; Norwich Union League, 5th in Division 1.

COUNTY CHAMPIONSHIP AVERAGES

BATTING

Cap		*M*	*I*	*NO*	*R*	*HS*	*100s*	*50s*	*Avge*	*Ct/St*
	K. P. Pietersen.	15	26	4	1,275	218*	4	6	57.95	14
1999	P. J. Franks†	5	8	4	217	85	0	1	54.25	2
2001	G. S. Blewett§	16	30	3	1,292	137*	5	5	47.85	24
2000	J. E. Morris	8	16	2	640	170	2	4	45.71	3
2000	U. Afzaal	12	22	0	928	138	1	7	42.18	9
	B. M. Shafayat† . . .	3	6	0	231	75	0	2	38.50	0
2000	D. J. Bicknell	16	29	0	1,050	167	3	3	36.20	8
1986	P. Johnson†	13	24	2	684	149	2	2	31.09	7
1999	C. M. W. Read	16	27	5	666	78	0	5	30.27	43/1
	D. S. Lucas†.	5	8	0	145	41	0	0	18.12	0
2001	G. J. Smith.	15	20	9	195	44*	0	0	17.72	3
	G. E. Welton	12	22	0	337	61	0	2	15.31	5
2000	R. D. Stemp	5	7	0	105	66	0	1	15.00	1
	R. J. Logan.	10	15	2	162	37*	0	0	12.46	4
	S. J. Randall†	4	7	1	73	28	0	0	12.16	1
	M. N. Malik†	5	6	5	12	6*	0	0	12.00	0
2000	A. J. Harris	9	15	2	79	20*	0	0	6.07	0
	G. D. Clough	4	6	0	22	8	0	0	3.66	1

Also batted: J. E. R. Gallian (cap 1998) (1 match) 23*; D. J. Millns† (cap 2000) (1 match) 3*, 4 (1 ct). C. M. Tolley (cap 1997) (1 match) did not bat.

* *Signifies not out.* † *Born in Nottinghamshire.* § *Overseas player.*

BOWLING

	O	*M*	*R*	*W*	*BB*	*5W/i*	*Avge*
G. J. Smith	446.2	103	1,256	50	5-37	3	25.12
R. J. Logan	329.1	53	1,375	43	6-93	3	31.97
P. J. Franks	149.1	33	429	13	4-65	0	33.00
A. J. Harris	330.4	84	1,097	28	6-98	1	39.17
M. N. Malik	104	21	414	10	5-57	1	41.40
R. D. Stemp	244.4	51	707	16	3-39	0	44.18

Also bowled: U. Afzaal 149.2–29–530–9; G. S. Blewett 113–24–374–6; G. D. Clough 100–14–353–6; P. Johnson 1–1–0–0; D. S. Lucas 118–8–571–8; D. J. Millns 25.1–4–87–1; J. E. Morris 3.2–0–19–0; K. P. Pietersen 234–52–767–9; S. J. Randall 132.1–21–465–7; C. M. W. Read 3–0–25–0; G. E. Welton 1–0–4–0.

COUNTY RECORDS

Highest score for:	312*	W. W. Keeton v Middlesex at The Oval	1939
Highest score against:	345	C. G. Macartney (Australians) at Nottingham . . .	1921
Best bowling for:	10-66	K. Smales v Gloucestershire at Stroud	1956
Best bowling against:	10-10	H. Verity (Yorkshire) at Leeds.	1932
Highest total for:	739-7 dec.	v Leicestershire at Nottingham	1903
Highest total against:	781-7 dec.	by Northamptonshire at Northampton	1995
Lowest total for:	13	v Yorkshire at Nottingham	1901
Lowest total against:	16	by Derbyshire at Nottingham	1879
	16	by Surrey at The Oval	1880

At Nottingham, April 20, 21, 22 (not first-class). Nottinghamshire won by an innings and 131 runs. Toss: Loughborough UCCE. Loughborough UCCE 223 (J. D. Francis 80, R. A. White 38, Extras 55; G. J. Smith three for 20) and 172 (R. A. White 99; G. D. Clough three for 17, R. D. Stemp three for 21); Nottinghamshire 526 for seven dec. (G. E. Welton 150 retired hurt, U. Afzaal 30, K. P. Pietersen 122, C. M. W. Read 116, D. J. Millns 39 not out, Extras 46).

County debuts: G. S. Blewett, G. D. Clough, R. J. Logan, K. P. Pietersen, G. J. Smith.

NOTTINGHAMSHIRE v DURHAM

At Nottingham, April 25, 26, 27, 28. Drawn. Nottinghamshire 10 pts, Durham 8 pts. Toss: Durham.

Play began only after an estimated 12,000 gallons of rainwater had been removed from the extensive new Trent Bridge covers. In the 43 overs possible before the first-day close, Lewis revelled in the damp, hitting ten boundaries in his impressive half-century, but so did the Nottinghamshire seam attack with five wickets. Collingwood then coaxed 147 from the final five until, down to his last partner, he was caught on the boundary attempting to reach his century in the grand manner. Blewett, in county cricket because he was out of favour with the Australian selectors, plundered 21 fours in his five-hour 133 to become only the second player – after F. W. Stocks in 1946 – to hit a hundred on his Nottinghamshire Championship debut. Read and Franks helped take the lead to 60 but, after 120 overs had been lost on the first three days, the rain returned to wash out the fourth.

Close of play: First day, Durham 148-5 (Collingwood 15*, Speak 4*); Second day, Nottinghamshire 38-1 (Bicknell 6*, Blewett 24*); Third day, Nottinghamshire 344-6 (Read 39*, Franks 44*).

Durham

*J. J. B. Lewis c Read b Smith	56
M. A. Gough c Afzaal b Franks	34
M. L. Love lbw b Clough	23
J. A. Daley b Logan	4
P. D. Collingwood c Franks b Smith	95
N. Killeen c and b Logan	0
N. J. Speak c Blewett b Franks	7
†A. Pratt b Logan	12
D. R. Law b Franks	22
J. E. Brinkley c Blewett b Logan	4
S. J. Harmison not out	0
B 4, l-b 11, n-b 12	27
1/92 2/117 3/123 4/133 5/137 6/172 7/214 8/258 9/284	284

Bonus points – Durham 2, Nottinghamshire 3.

Bowling: Franks 25–4–74–3; Smith 19.4–1–61–2; Logan 16–2–69–4; Clough 19–3–52–1; Blewett 4–3–2–0; Afzaal 1–0–11–0.

Nottinghamshire

*D. J. Bicknell lbw b Law	34
G. E. Welton c Pratt b Killeen	0
G. S. Blewett st Pratt b Gough	133
U. Afzaal c Gough b Killeen	20
P. Johnson c Lewis b Law	30
K. P. Pietersen lbw b Brinkley	2
†C. M. W. Read not out	39
P. J. Franks not out	44
B 2, l-b 24, w 16	42
1/0 2/115 3/156 4/227 5/238 6/253	(6 wkts) 344

G. D. Clough, R. J. Logan and G. J. Smith did not bat.

Bonus points – Nottinghamshire 3, Durham 2.

Bowling: Harmison 25–6–81–0; Killeen 22–7–69–2; Brinkley 20–6–45–1; Law 18–4–65–2; Collingwood 8–0–34–0; Gough 12–2–24–1.

Umpires: T. E. Jesty and R. Palmer.

At Hove, May 9, 10, 11, 12. NOTTINGHAMSHIRE lost to SUSSEX by 162 runs.

NOTTINGHAMSHIRE v WARWICKSHIRE

At Nottingham, May 16, 17, 18, 19. Drawn. Nottinghamshire 9 pts, Warwickshire 6 pts. Toss: Warwickshire. First-class debut: M. N. Malik.

Persistent rain having permitted just 58 deliveries in three days, the game became a contest for bonus points on the last, when Nottinghamshire needed four an over to reach their target of 400. They achieved it with ease, thanks to a superbly paced innings from Bicknell and some toothless Warwickshire seam bowling. Bicknell, captain in place of the injured Gallian, added 173 for the second wicket with Blewett, who was unlucky to drag a ball on to his stumps one short of a century, and then 151 with Afzaal. By the time he eventually went for 167, including 21 fours and a six, Nottinghamshire were only ten away from their objective.

Close of play: First day, Nottinghamshire 41-1 (Bicknell 20*, Blewett 10*); Second day, No play; Third day, No play.

Nottinghamshire

*D. J. Bicknell c Ostler b Drakes	167
G. E. Welton c Piper b Betts	7
G. S. Blewett b Sheikh	99
U. Afzaal c Knight b Smith	61
P. Johnson c Powell b Smith	6
K. P. Pietersen c Betts b Smith	11
†C. M. W. Read not out	7
P. J. Franks not out	2
L-b 6, w 2, n-b 34	42
1/16 2/189 3/340 4/356 5/372 6/390 (6 wkts dec.)	402

C. M. Tolley, G. J. Smith and M. N. Malik did not bat.

Bonus points – Nottinghamshire 5, Warwickshire 2.

Bowling: Drakes 22–1–86–1; Betts 21–2–101–1; Sheikh 26.1–10–82–1; Richardson 11–1–51–0; Smith 22–3–74–3; Wagh 1–0–2–0.

Warwickshire

*M. J. Powell, N. V. Knight, M. A. Wagh, D. L. Hemp, D. P. Ostler, N. M. K. Smith, †K. J. Piper, M. A. Sheikh, V. C. Drakes, M. M. Betts and A. Richardson.

Umpires: K. E. Palmer and J. F. Steele.

At Lord's, May 25, 26, 27, 28. NOTTINGHAMSHIRE drew with MIDDLESEX.

At Chester-le-Street, May 30, 31, June 1, 2. NOTTINGHAMSHIRE lost to DURHAM by eight wickets.

NOTTINGHAMSHIRE v GLOUCESTERSHIRE

At Nottingham, June 6, 7, 8, 9. Gloucestershire won by 187 runs. Gloucestershire 20 points, Nottinghamshire 5 pts. Toss: Gloucestershire.

Gloucestershire, even though not at full strength, outplayed the home side from start to finish, gaining five batting points for the first time ever and taking full bonus points *en route* to their maiden Championship victory of the season. On a pitch offering bounce and movement, the

Nottinghamshire bowlers were hopelessly wayward. Barnett had 21 fours in his 58th first-class hundred and enjoyed a century stand with Taylor, who scored precisely 100 in the afternoon session, batted for almost six hours and hit 30 boundaries in his 196. His only other hundred had come on debut a year earlier. Nottinghamshire failed to take advantage of Gloucestershire's depleted attack, lost wickets to loose shots – only Afzaal provided real resistance – and were all out 57 shy of the follow-on target. Alleyne chose not to enforce it, and eventually set Nottinghamshire 472 from a minimum of 111 overs. Pietersen's defiant display of powerful hitting on the final afternoon – he clobbered 72 from 71 balls – was entertaining, if ultimately to no avail.

Close of play: First day, Gloucestershire 356-5 (Taylor 152*, Russell 17*); Second day, Nottinghamshire 207-7 (Afzaal 61*, Lucas 20*); Third day, Nottinghamshire 61-3 (Lucas 5*, Afzaal 9*).

Gloucestershire

D. R. Hewson lbw b Blewett	36	– c Welton b Blewett	51
K. J. Barnett c Blewett b Smith	114	– lbw b Clough	45
M. G. N. Windows lbw b Smith	0	– c Pietersen b Clough	73
C. G. Taylor c Read b Blewett	196	– c Bicknell b Blewett	19
*M. W. Alleyne c Bicknell b Harris	20	– c Pietersen b Clough	17
J. N. Snape c Blewett b Pietersen	1	– not out	21
†R. C. Russell c Read b Harris	29		
M. A. Hardinges b Clough	22		
M. C. J. Ball run out	7	– (7) not out	22
M. J. Cawdron not out	26		
J. M. M. Averis c Read b Smith	0		
L-b 14, w 4, n-b 4	22	B 1, l-b 14, n-b 2	17
1/91 2/108 3/219 4/287 5/300 6/382 7/439 8/441 9/463	473	1/81 2/110 3/144 4/196 5/235 (5 wkts dec.)	265

Bonus points – Gloucestershire 5, Nottinghamshire 3.

Bowling: *First Innings*—Smith 28–8–71–3; Harris 30–6–98–2; Lucas 15–0–95–0; Blewett 21–6–67–2; Clough 18–2–66–1; Pietersen 15–0–53–1; Afzaal 2–1–9–0. *Second Innings*—Smith 9–3–19–0; Harris 14–1–73–0; Clough 19–4–69–3; Lucas 9–0–35–0; Blewett 8–1–20–2; Pietersen 5–2–25–0; Afzaal 2–0–9–0.

Nottinghamshire

*D. J. Bicknell b Cawdron	21	– lbw b Cawdron	15
G. E. Welton c Ball b Cawdron	22	– c Snape b Averis	0
G. S. Blewett c Russell b Averis	22	– c Russell b Averis	23
U. Afzaal c Ball b Averis	88	– (5) lbw b Cawdron	9
P. Johnson c Russell b Cawdron	0	– (6) c Russell b Hardinges	35
K. P. Pietersen lbw b Hardinges	10	– (7) c Hardinges b Cawdron	72
†C. M. W. Read lbw b Cawdron	28	– (8) b Alleyne	15
G. D. Clough c Barnett b Averis	7	– (9) b Alleyne	3
D. S. Lucas b Alleyne	41	– (4) c Windows b Hardinges	28
A. J. Harris b Hardinges	2	– not out	20
G. J. Smith not out	0	– st Russell b Ball	27
B 1, l-b 9, n-b 16	26	B 4, l-b 7, w 4, n-b 22	37
1/36 2/65 3/69 4/69 5/80 6/141 7/158 8/247 9/266	267	1/3 2/39 3/43 4/61 5/120 6/129 7/177 8/185 9/239	284

Bonus points – Nottinghamshire 2, Gloucestershire 3.

Bowling: *First Innings*—Averis 19.2–8–52–3; Cawdron 24–5–79–4; Hardinges 15–3–59–2; Alleyne 14–3–49–1; Ball 4–1–18–0. *Second Innings*—Averis 22–3–104–2; Cawdron 22–5–90–3; Hardinges 9–3–36–2; Alleyne 8–4–26–2; Ball 4–1–17–1.

Umpires: M. J. Harris and R. Palmer.

NOTTINGHAMSHIRE v SUSSEX

At Nottingham, June 20, 21, 22, 23. Sussex won by 161 runs. Sussex 19 pts, Nottinghamshire 5 pts. Toss: Nottinghamshire.

Hundreds in each innings by Goodwin – the 14th to do so for Sussex, but only the third with a double – helped send Nottinghamshire to a third consecutive Championship defeat. Sussex, inserted by Bicknell, lost two cheap wickets before Goodwin, who hit 15 fours in his 115, put on 151 with Zuiderent. Harris took six for 98, his best since leaving Derbyshire. In reply, Nottinghamshire's top five all failed to convert starts into scores, leaving Morris to shackle his attacking instincts and ensure the follow-on was averted. The Sussex openers then batted through almost all day three to reach 372, the county's third-highest stand. Goodwin's maiden double-century contained 27 fours and two sixes, came from 289 balls and lasted 382 minutes, while Montgomerie, in his third Championship hundred against Nottinghamshire in four matches, struck 20 fours. Bicknell battled for six hours, including a stand of 141 with Read, but Robinson had the final say in the last hour. Play on the opening day had begun an hour late to assist the clearing-up after the previous evening's floodlit international.

Close of play: First day, Sussex 315-6 (Prior 24*, Davis 0*); Second day, Nottinghamshire 280; Third day, Nottinghamshire 16-1 (Bicknell 7*, Clough 4*).

HIGHEST PARTNERSHIPS FOR SUSSEX

490	for 1st	E. H. Bowley and J. G. Langridge v Middlesex at Hove	1933
385	for 2nd	E. H. Bowley and M. W. Tate v Northamptonshire at Hove	1921
372*	**for 1st**	**M. W. Goodwin and R. R. Montgomerie v Notts at Nottingham**	**2001**
368	for 1st	E. H. Bowley and J. H. Parks v Gloucestershire at Hove	1929
349	for 2nd	C. B. Fry and E. H. Killick v Yorkshire at Hove	1901
344	for 7th	K. S. Ranjitsinhji and W. Newham v Essex at Leyton	1902
326*	for 4th	James Langridge and G. Cox, jun. v Yorkshire at Leeds	1949
325	for 2nd	G. Brann and K. S. Ranjitsinhji v Surrey at The Oval	1899
313	for 2nd	J. W. Hall and C. M. Wells v Cambridge University at Hove	1993
307	for 2nd	J. G. Langridge and H. W. Parks v Kent at Tonbridge	1939
305	for 1st	H. W. Greenwood and J. G. Langridge v Essex at Hove	1935
303*	for 4th	A. P. Wells and C. M. Wells v Kent at Hove	1987
303	for 1st	F. W. Marlow and G. L. Wilson v Oxford University at Hove	1895

Sussex

R. R. Montgomerie c Johnson b Harris	13	– (2) not out	160
M. W. Goodwin c Stemp b Clough	115	– (1) not out	203
*C. J. Adams c Blewett b Harris	4		
B. Zuiderent b Stemp	73		
M. H. Yardy b Smith	50		
U. B. A. Rashid c Bicknell b Harris	16		
†M. J. Prior c Blewett b Harris	31		
M. J. G. Davis b Harris	16		
R. J. Kirtley c Blewett b Harris	1		
J. D. Lewry b Smith	12		
M. A. Robinson not out	1		
B 4, l-b 10, w 2, n-b 6	22	B 4, l-b 3, w 2	9
1/23 2/31 3/182 4/239 5/272 6/312 7/335 8/339 9/350	354	(no wkt dec.)	372

Bonus points – Sussex 4, Nottinghamshire 3.

Bowling: *First Innings*—Smith 26.4–9–58–2; Harris 34–10–98–6; Blewett 15–3–40–0; Clough 19–2–72–1; Stemp 23–4–68–1; Welton 1–0–4–0. *Second Innings*—Smith 14–1–43–0; Harris 16–1–56–0; Blewett 10–1–57–0; Stemp 31–3–97–0; Clough 18–2–71–0; Afzaal 8–1–41–0.

Nottinghamshire

*D. J. Bicknell lbw b Kirtley	29	– c Prior b Robinson	123
G. E. Welton c Adams b Robinson	15	– run out	0
G. S. Blewett run out	13	– (4) b Kirtley	0
U. Afzaal lbw b Lewry	40	– (5) c Prior b Lewry	7
P. Johnson c Lewry b Davis	25	– (6) c Zuiderent b Robinson	19
J. E. Morris c Adams b Kirtley	60	– (7) c Davis b Robinson	6
†C. M. W. Read c Adams b Davis	18	– (8) lbw b Kirtley	78
G. D. Clough c Adams b Robinson	2	– (3) b Kirtley	8
A. J. Harris lbw b Kirtley	6	– c Prior b Robinson	6
G. J. Smith not out	44	– not out	1
R. D. Stemp b Kirtley	0	– b Lewry	0
L-b 4, w 8, n-b 16	28	B 4, l-b 9, w 2, n-b 22	37
1/42 2/69 3/70 4/136 5/142 6/181 7/193 8/215 9/280	280	1/11 2/26 3/26 4/37 5/81 6/105 7/246 8/277 9/284	285

Bonus points – Nottinghamshire 2, Sussex 3.

Bowling: *First Innings*—Lewry 20–6–70–1; Kirtley 22–0–90–4; Robinson 19–2–71–2; Davis 25–9–45–2. *Second Innings*—Lewry 24–1–91–2; Kirtley 28–9–72–3; Robinson 21–4–70–4; Yardy 3–1–7–0; Rashid 8–2–27–0; Davis 6–4–5–0.

Umpires: J. H. Evans and M. J. Kitchen.

At Worcester, June 29, 30, July 1, 2. NOTTINGHAMSHIRE beat WORCESTERSHIRE by seven wickets.

NOTTINGHAMSHIRE v MIDDLESEX

At Nottingham, July 4, 5, 6, 7. Drawn. Nottinghamshire 9 pts, Middlesex 12 pts. Toss: Middlesex. First-class debut: B. M. Shafayat.

Twice on the final afternoon Middlesex players helped groundstaff remove the covers, but they could not stop the weather denying them probable victory. When there was play, they were frustrated by belated resistance from Nottinghamshire: at 139 for eight – still 74 from staving off an innings defeat – they had looked dead and buried, only for an unbroken ninth-wicket partnership of 76 between Read and Harris to save their side. On the opening day, perfect for batting, Fraser won an important toss, and Shah and Fleming completed stylish centuries. Next day, on the same flat pitch, Nottinghamshire's top order failed to respond in kind, the most encouraging contribution coming from Bilal Shafayat. The youngest player to represent Nottinghamshire in the Championship – he did not turn 17 for another five days – he showed huge determination during his three-and-a-half-hour fifty. Following on 213 behind, Nottinghamshire lurched to 98 for six just five overs after play restarted on the last afternoon. Bloomfield claimed five victims, but Read, Harris and the rain defied Middlesex, who nevertheless clung on to top spot in the division.

Close of play: First day, Middlesex 397-3 (Fleming 120*, Hutton 30*); Second day, Nottinghamshire 230-6 (Shafayat 54*, Lucas 2*); Third day, Nottinghamshire 93-3 (Bicknell 48*, Shafayat 21*).

Middlesex

A. J. Strauss b Harris	67
R. M. S. Weston c Read b Harris	7
O. A. Shah b Logan	144
S. P. Fleming c Read b Smith	151
B. L. Hutton b Smith	82
P. N. Weekes c Read b Logan	21
†D. C. Nash c Read b Lucas	6
J. P. Hewitt c Read b Logan	2
*A. R. C. Fraser c Read b Logan	3
T. F. Bloomfield lbw b Logan	0
P. C. R. Tufnell not out	0
B 8, l-b 16, w 10, n-b 10	44
1/22 2/131 3/337 4/448 5/483 6/490 7/511 8/527 9/527	527

Bonus points – Middlesex 5, Nottinghamshire 2 (Score at 130 overs: 515-7).

Bowling: Smith 27.1–9–84–2; Harris 29–11–101–2; Lucas 23–1–135–1; Logan 34–9–118–5; Blewett 21–7–53–0; Pietersen 4–2–12–0.

Nottinghamshire

*D. J. Bicknell c Nash b Bloomfield	27	– (2) c Weekes b Bloomfield	50
G. E. Welton b Bloomfield	0	– (1) c Nash b Bloomfield	10
G. S. Blewett c Fleming b Weekes	79	– b Bloomfield	3
K. P. Pietersen c Fleming b Tufnell	37	– c and b Bloomfield	2
B. M. Shafayat lbw b Tufnell	72	– c Nash b Bloomfield	24
P. Johnson c Fleming b Weekes	8	– c Weston b Tufnell	0
†C. M. W. Read c Nash b Bloomfield	12	– not out	76
D. S. Lucas c Shah b Hewitt	2	– c Nash b Fraser	11
R. J. Logan st Nash b Tufnell	19	– c Weekes b Hewitt	0
A. J. Harris c and b Weekes	11	– not out	14
G. J. Smith not out	32		
L-b 3, n-b 12	15	B 2, l-b 13, n-b 10	25
1/4 2/45 3/100 4/172 5/180 6/205 7/230 8/267 9/268	314	1/17 2/41 3/49 4/97 5/98 6/98 7/136 8/139	(8 wkts) 215

Bonus points – Nottinghamshire 3, Middlesex 3.

Bowling: *First Innings*—Fraser 16–4–52–0; Bloomfield 19–4–75–3; Tufnell 30–6–79–3; Hewitt 10–2–34–1; Weekes 22.4–5–71–3. *Second Innings*—Fraser 19.2–3–66–1; Bloomfield 23–6–58–5; Hewitt 10–0–56–1; Tufnell 11–2–20–1; Weekes 1–1–0–0.

Umpires: J. H. Hampshire and J. F. Steele.

At Southampton, July 18, 19, 20, 21. NOTTINGHAMSHIRE lost to HAMPSHIRE by 338 runs.

At Derby, July 27, 28, 29, 30. NOTTINGHAMSHIRE drew with DERBYSHIRE.

At Birmingham, August 3, 4, 5, 6. NOTTINGHAMSHIRE lost to WARWICKSHIRE by 139 runs.

NOTTINGHAMSHIRE v WORCESTERSHIRE

At Nottingham, August 8, 9, 10, 11. Nottinghamshire won by 61 runs. Nottinghamshire 15 pts, Worcestershire 5 pts. Toss: Worcestershire.

For the second time in six weeks, Nottinghamshire overcame Worcestershire despite conceding a useful first-innings lead. After a delayed start, all ten Nottinghamshire wickets fell between lunch and tea, with Sheriyar claiming four in 12 balls. Singh's 88 helped push Worcestershire ahead, and their advantage would have been greater but for Smith's aggressive left-arm seam bowling. In contrast to their first-innings fiasco, Nottinghamshire played superbly in their second: Blewett led the way, hitting 17 fours and reaching his century with a six; Pietersen smashed 86 off 100 balls to pass 1,000 runs in his first season in county cricket; and Read celebrated his 23rd birthday with a fifty. Asked to make 321, Worcestershire were dealt telling blows when Hick and Singh became the maiden first-class victims for the 18-year-old seamer, Malik. Although hope was renewed as Bichel blasted 42 from 37 balls, Nottinghamshire won with 12 overs to spare.

Close of play: First day, Worcestershire 130-3 (Singh 60*, Leatherdale 12*); Second day, Nottinghamshire 39-1 (Bicknell 13*, Blewett 10*); Third day, Worcestershire 9-0 (Weston 2*, Singh 7*).

Nottinghamshire

*D. J. Bicknell c Hick b Sheriyar	23	– lbw b Liptrot	38
J. E. Morris b Sheriyar	51	– b Sheriyar	6
G. S. Blewett b Leatherdale	31	– b Liptrot	108
U. Afzaal lbw b Sheriyar	0	– lbw b Liptrot	53
P. Johnson b Sheriyar	0	– c Rawnsley b Sheriyar	18
K. P. Pietersen lbw b Bichel	9	– run out	86
†C. M. W. Read b Bichel	2	– c Solanki b Sheriyar	65
R. J. Logan c Pollard b Liptrot	8	– lbw b Leatherdale	0
A. J. Harris c Bichel b Leatherdale	0	– c Rhodes b Bichel	3
G. J. Smith c Solanki b Leatherdale	10	– not out	2
M. N. Malik not out	0	– c Weston b Sheriyar	4
B 4, l-b 7, w 2, n-b 2	15	B 5, l-b 19, w 12, n-b 4	40
1/73 2/90 3/90 4/90 5/107 6/115 7/135 8/139 9/145	149	1/20 2/120 3/203 4/230 5/252 6/388 7/388 8/413 9/413	423

Bonus points – Worcestershire 3.

Bowling: *First Innings*—Bichel 15–7–27–2; Sheriyar 16–4–51–4; Leatherdale 9.3–2–31–3; Liptrot 11–2–29–1. *Second Innings*—Bichel 27–7–102–1; Sheriyar 25.1–8–80–4; Leatherdale 17–5–53–1; Liptrot 21–5–84–3; Rawnsley 14–2–72–0; Hick 3–0–8–0.

Worcestershire

W. P. C. Weston c Logan b Smith	19	– lbw b Smith	3
A. Singh b Logan	88	– c Afzaal b Malik	43
*G. A. Hick c Afzaal b Smith	17	– c Blewett b Malik	22
V. S. Solanki c Smith b Harris	14	– lbw b Smith	43
D. A. Leatherdale c Read b Harris	25	– c Read b Logan	9
P. R. Pollard lbw b Logan	0	– run out	22
A. J. Bichel c Blewett b Smith	53	– b Pietersen	42
†S. J. Rhodes run out	0	– not out	40
C. G. Liptrot b Smith	13	– c Blewett b Pietersen	6
M. J. Rawnsley b Smith	1	– b Logan	1
A. Sheriyar not out	0	– c and b Smith	1
L-b 6, n-b 16	22	B 2, l-b 4, w 2, n-b 19	27
1/36 2/64 3/92 4/156 5/157 6/200 7/210 8/243 9/249	252	1/18 2/62 3/91 4/120 5/134 6/199 7/223 8/235 9/244	259

Bonus points – Worcestershire 2, Nottinghamshire 3.

Bowling: *First Innings*—Smith 21.3–6–59–5; Harris 11–0–65–2; Logan 16–1–72–2; Malik 13–3–50–0; Pietersen 1–1–0–0. *Second Innings*—Smith 13.5–2–42–3; Malik 11–2–48–2; Logan 18–2–76–2; Harris 9–1–35–0; Pietersen 16–2–46–2; Afzaal 4–1–6–0.

Umpires: T. E. Jesty and R. Julian.

At Bristol, August 15, 16, 17, 18. NOTTINGHAMSHIRE lost to GLOUCESTERSHIRE by an innings and 120 runs.

NOTTINGHAMSHIRE v DERBYSHIRE

At Nottingham, August 22, 23, 24, 25. Nottinghamshire won by seven wickets. Nottinghamshire 17.5 pts, Derbyshire 6 pts. Toss: Derbyshire.

Pietersen's remarkable innings wrested the game from Derbyshire. He came in at 98 for four, the follow-on far likelier than the eventual modest lead, and promptly took control. Once Read departed for a brisk 44, Pietersen farmed the strike so adroitly that just 11 of the 115 added by Nottinghamshire's last four wickets came from his partners' bats; of the 75 added by their last two, he hit 73, the missing runs contributed by a no-ball. In all, he made 150 from 164 balls, with 19 fours and six sixes. Malik then claimed five wickets for the first time, and Logan added three to his earlier career-best six for 93 as Derbyshire were efficiently dismissed. Needing 220, Nottinghamshire soon lost both openers, but Blewett and Johnson shared a century stand, before Blewett's fifth Championship hundred of the summer ensured victory. Di Venuto supplied almost half Derbyshire's runs, principally a magnificent 165 on the first day, but defeat confirmed they would finish last. Nottinghamshire were docked half a point for a dilatory over-rate.

Close of play: First day, Derbyshire 320; Second day, Derbyshire 51-0 (Stubbings 19*, Di Venuto 30*); Third day, Nottinghamshire 172-3 (Blewett 76*, Morris 0*).

Derbyshire

S. D. Stubbings lbw b Logan	12	– b Smith	19
*M. J. Di Venuto lbw b Logan	165	– lbw b Logan	93
L. D. Sutton b Logan	10	– c Read b Malik	1
C. W. G. Bassano c and b Randall	56	– b Logan	28
R. J. Bailey run out	2	– b Malik	17
†K. M. Krikken b Logan	11	– b Malik	0
G. Welch b Logan	18	– b Logan	6
T. M. Smith lbw b Randall	0	– c Pietersen b Malik	5
P. Aldred b Logan	9	– b Malik	14
K. J. Dean b Smith	18	– not out	20
L. J. Wharton not out	0	– c Pietersen b Smith	1
B 1, l-b 8, n-b 10	19	B 7, w 4, n-b 6	17
1/59 2/85 3/209 4/212 5/236 6/262 7/263 8/286 9/320	320	1/51 2/65 3/149 4/164 5/165 6/176 7/178 8/182 9/199	221

Bonus points – Derbyshire 3, Nottinghamshire 3.

Bowling: *First Innings*—Smith 16–5–47–1; Malik 12–1–53–0; Logan 23.1–3–93–6; Blewett 3–1–6–0; Randall 26–7–64–2; Pietersen 21–6–48–0. *Second Innings*—Logan 24–3–89–3; Smith 12.2–4–25–2; Malik 18–3–57–5; Randall 8–0–35–0; Pietersen 1–0–8–0.

Nottinghamshire

*D. J. Bicknell c Krikken b Welch	21	– lbw b Welch	4
G. E. Welton st Krikken b Dean	42	– lbw b Dean	6
G. S. Blewett c Smith b Welch	27	– not out	106
P. Johnson c Aldred b Dean	0	– b Dean	65
J. E. Morris lbw b Aldred	9	– not out	20
K. P. Pietersen c Di Venuto b Smith	150		
†C. M. W. Read lbw b Dean	44		
R. J. Logan c Krikken b Wharton	4		
S. J. Randall c Krikken b Dean	7		
G. J. Smith lbw b Dean	0		
M. N. Malik not out	0		
L-b 4, w 2, n-b 12	18	B 4, l-b 2, w 2, n-b 14	22
1/44 2/74 3/74 4/98 5/122 6/207 7/220 8/247 9/265	322	1/4 2/44 3/172	(3 wkts) 223

Bonus points – Nottinghamshire 3, Derbyshire 3.

Bowling: *First Innings*—Welch 23–4–92–2; Dean 21–3–89–5; Smith 12.2–5–50–1; Aldred 9–3–42–1; Wharton 12–2–45–1. *Second Innings*—Welch 19–5–66–1; Dean 17–3–46–2; Smith 5–1–31–0; Aldred 3–0–25–0; Wharton 10.3–2–41–0; Bailey 4–1–8–0.

Umpires: M. J. Harris and V. A. Holder.

NOTTINGHAMSHIRE v HAMPSHIRE

At Nottingham, September 12, 13, 14, 15. Drawn. Nottinghamshire 6 pts, Hampshire 9 pts. Toss: Nottinghamshire.

To cement promotion, Hampshire needed three points; the third did not come until the second afternoon, the delay caused more by the weather than the Nottinghamshire batsmen. Afzaal proved most stubborn as Mullally and Morris – able because of the frequent interruptions to shoulder almost all the bowling – split the wickets evenly. Replying to a below-par 245, Hampshire prospered on the third day as Johnson, with a fine hundred, and Francis, with a maiden first-class fifty, saw them to the batting points which – thanks to results elsewhere – guaranteed the £25,000 runners-up cheque. Smith declared, 14 ahead, at tea on the third day, and had Nottinghamshire three down by the close. Next day, the game veered toward farce as wicket-keeper Aymes and his usual stand-in, Kenway, bowled in tandem, gifting Nottinghamshire 226 runs before Hampshire were set 301 in 63 overs. White and Kendall kept them up with the required rate until rain first interrupted and then ended play.

Close of play: First day, Nottinghamshire 164-5 (Afzaal 75*, Read 1*); Second day, Nottinghamshire 245; Third day, Nottinghamshire 88-3 (Bicknell 50*, Pietersen 24*).

Nottinghamshire

*D. J. Bicknell c Aymes b Morris	4	– lbw b Aymes	62
G. E. Welton lbw b Mullally	11	– c and b Mullally	0
G. S. Blewett b Morris	14	– b Morris	1
U. Afzaal b Morris	91	– c Aymes b Udal	12
K. P. Pietersen c Aymes b Mullally	14	– st White b Kenway	87
B. M. Shafayat c Aymes b Morris	42	– st White b Francis	75
†C. M. W. Read b Morris	17	– b Aymes	21
R. J. Logan b Mullally	29	– not out	37
S. J. Randall c Aymes b Mullally	1	– not out	8
G. J. Smith c Francis b Mullally	6		
M. N. Malik not out	2		
B 1, l-b 5, n-b 8	14	B 3, l-b 4, w 2, n-b 2	11
1/9 2/25 3/29 4/56 5/153 6/194 7/201 8/202 9/212	245	1/7 2/10 3/38 4/129 5/187 6/226 7/288 (7 wkts dec.)	314

Bonus points – Nottinghamshire 1, Hampshire 3.

Bowling: *First Innings*—Mullally 31.3–12–74–5; Morris 30–9–108–5; Mascarenhas 8–2–28–0; Johnson 4–0–19–0; Udal 3–1–10–0. *Second Innings*—Mullally 5–1–22–1; Morris 5–3–5–1; Mascarenhas 9–2–27–0; Udal 13–1–48–1; Kenway 8–0–66–1; Aymes 11–0–101–2; Francis 6–0–34–1; Kendall 2–0–4–0.

Hampshire

D. A. Kenway b Smith	9	– (2) lbw b Malik	5
G. W. White c Blewett b Malik	6	– (1) b Randall	112
W. S. Kendall lbw b Logan	27	– c Read b Logan	72
*R. A. Smith run out	24	– b Pietersen	0
N. C. Johnson not out	105	– c Read b Logan	8
J. D. Francis not out	72	– c Welton b Pietersen	15
A. D. Mascarenhas (did not bat)		– not out	20
L-b 8, w 2, n-b 6	16	L-b 11, n-b 2	13
1/16 2/16 3/73 4/76 (4 wkts dec.)	259	1/9 2/147 3/148 4/161 5/198 6/245 (6 wkts)	245

†A. N. Aymes, S. D. Udal, A. C. Morris and A. D. Mullally did not bat.

Bonus points – Hampshire 2, Nottinghamshire 1.

Bowling: *First Innings*—Smith 12–2–38–1; Malik 14–4–42–1; Logan 14–1–55–1; Randall 12–2–44–0; Pietersen 11–5–26–0; Afzaal 12–2–46–0. *Second Innings*—Malik 11–2–51–1; Smith 9–1–33–0; Randall 9.1–1–43–1; Logan 11–1–55–2; Pietersen 12–1–52–2.

Umpires: D. J. Constant and D. R. Shepherd.

Jamie Cox

SOMERSET

President: M. F. Hill
Chairman: R. Parsons
Chief Executive: P. W. Anderson
Chairman, Cricket Committee: V. J. Marks
Cricket Secretary: P. J. Robinson
Captain: J. Cox
First-Team Coach: K. J. Shine
Head Groundsman: P. Frost
Scorer: G. A. Stickley

By general agreement, certainly in every parish across the Mendips and the Quantocks, Somerset's season was the best in their variegated history. Perhaps there were more flash, pulsating days when players of mighty individual talent such as Botham, Richards and Garner were around; when, in 1979 for example, the county picked up two trophies. But 2001 was better, a more balanced triumph from lesser souls. Somerset finished runners-up in the Championship, higher than ever before – at one point, poised at the shoulders of Yorkshire, they actually looked capable of winning the pennant – and, amid much West Country elation, they vanquished Leicestershire in the Cheltenham & Gloucester final at Lord's.

Because of their central contracts, Marcus Trescothick played in just three Championship matches and Andrew Caddick two. They, in theory, represented the best of the batting and bowling, yet such deletions seemed to engender a rallying response from within the dressing-room. Players of more modest pedigree excelled in turn. Jamie Cox captained with quiet, popular authority, and if, by his own attractive off-driving terms, he was inclined to be tardy with big scores – he waited till September for his first hundred – he was still the only Somerset batsman to pass 1,000 first-class runs. The more pragmatic, less stylish Michael Burns, who constructed a double-century at Bath against Yorkshire, was 39 runs short.

Somerset have sometimes been criticised for a lack of resolve and fibre when it comes to the big occasions. Two years earlier, they had mismanaged their Lord's final against Gloucestershire, but their stature had visibly grown since then. This time round, they paraded a new-found self-confidence, as if they had learned to offset a natural and regional self-effacement. The team ethic served them heroically. Keith Parsons, an authentic Somerset lad from Taunton, unable to command a regular place in the Championship side, enjoyed a marvellous match. He figured in a significant stand with Rob Turner, rounded off the innings with two stunning sixes, took two important wickets and deservedly won the match award. It could be said he was an unlikely match-winner; yet that symbolised one of the county's virtues during the heady season.

Astute recruitment has been another factor in Somerset's successes. Ian Blackwell, boyish of features and comfortable of build, arrived from

Derbyshire in 2000 primarily as a slow bowler. But a year later he hit four Championship hundreds with well-judged, timely, beefy strokes to suggest he is a genuine all-rounder. After him came the Middlesex pair, Richard Johnson and Keith Dutch. They had moved west in 2001 at the persuasive behest of Kevin Shine, the accomplished coach who, probably to his surprise, had found himself succeeding Dermot Reeve. Shine knew them from his own Lord's days and reckoned they needed a career switch. Johnson proved an ideal replacement for Caddick, swinging the ball away and keeping the slips and wicket-keeper busy. He took 62 wickets at lively pace, came tantalisingly near a Test debut when summoned as an England stand-by, and went to India after Caddick cried off. Like Blackwell, on changing counties Dutch quickly demonstrated his value as an all-rounder. His off-breaks brought him 35 Championship wickets, and as a notable bonus he recorded his maiden century, against Essex.

Loyal Somerset supporters, too used to lapses and frustrations, were caught up in a new aura of positive play and overall reliability. The team lapses were still there; nothing was more disappointing, for instance, than the eight-wicket League defeat by Warwickshire two days after the Lord's final, when everyone wanted to cheer them. Yet over the summer, the signs were usually encouraging. Peter Bowler's solidarity and experience were steadying influences when most needed, and there were enough glimpses of vintage Mark Lathwell to illustrate that the affection and patience of his fans had not been in vain. Matthew Wood emerged with technical ability and the kind of calm temperament to suggest he could become an opener for the county. Unfortunately, injuries meant that Peter Trego and Matthew Bulbeck were seldom seen.

In the one-day competitions, Somerset fielded well and held their catches. They often went for quick early runs and appeared better equipped to adapt to the needs of the game, adding a measure of competitive zeal to tactical nous. There was an evident degree of sage pre-planning, as in the way they entrapped the impetuous Shahid Afridi at Lord's, though they still needed to survive some late-season scares to avoid relegation in the League.

Somerset have five times finished third in the Championship; at last, they have improved on that, but expectations may now be unrealistically high. They are better balanced than they have been for years, and are tougher in battle. They are not, however, the finished product. Even though Steffan Jones took 59 wickets and was capped, the seam support remains fragile. Should Johnson earn Test recognition, he would be seriously missed by a side which, for a number of seasons, has leant excessively on Caddick. Yet when Trescothick was rattling up three hundreds in the Benson and Hedges qualifiers, Somerset really did look like champions. His 121 against Glamorgan in the fourth round of the C&G Trophy was one of the wonders of the Taunton season. "My, that was the finest I've ever seen in a limited-overs match," his captain said.

There was much to savour: cricket that remained for the most part vigilant and entertaining (if we ignore a meandering finish against Yorkshire at Bath), Turner's return to top-class wicket-keeping form – he created a county catching record of seven in an innings against Northamptonshire, in a match where Somerset amassed the second-highest total in their history – and a dressing-room vibrant with achievement. – DAVID FOOT.

SOMERSET 2001

[*Alain Lockyer*

Back row: R. Dewar (*Second Eleven physiotherapist*), M. J. Wood, T. Webley, J. P. Tucker, P. S. Jones, J. I. D. Kerr, M. P. L. Bulbeck, I. Jones, C. M. Gazzard, C. A. Hunkin, A. Suppiah, D. Veness (*First Eleven physiotherapist*). *Middle row:* A. Hurry (*fitness instructor*), M. N. Lathwell, K. P. Dutch, K. A. Parsons, R. L. Johnson, I. D. Blackwell, A. R. Caddick, J. O. Grove, P. D. Trego, P. C. L. Holloway, J. G. Wyatt (*Second Eleven coach*). *Front row:* G. D. Rose, M. Burns, K. J. Shine (*First Eleven coach*), M. F. Hill (*president*), M. E. Trescothick, R. J. Turner, P. D. Bowler. *Inset:* J. Cox (*captain*).

SOMERSET RESULTS

All first-class matches – Played 17: Won 6, Lost 3, Drawn 8.

County Championship matches – Played 16: Won 6, Lost 2, Drawn 8.

CricInfo County Championship, 2nd in Division 1; Cheltenham & Gloucester Trophy, winners; Benson and Hedges Cup, q-f; Norwich Union League, 4th in Division 1.

COUNTY CHAMPIONSHIP AVERAGES

BATTING

Cap		*M*	*I*	*NO*	*R*	*HS*	*100s*	*50s*	*Avge*	*Ct*
1999	J. Cox§	15	25	3	1,264	186	1	9	57.45	6
1999	M. E. Trescothick†‡	3	4	0	216	147	1	0	54.00	3
2001	I. D. Blackwell	10	15	0	781	122	4	3	52.06	4
	M. J. Wood	6	10	0	439	122	1	3	43.90	2
1999	K. A. Parsons†	4	6	1	213	139	1	0	42.60	4
1995	P. D. Bowler	13	20	1	799	164	2	4	42.05	14
1999	M. Burns	16	26	1	893	221	1	6	35.72	13
1992	M. N. Lathwell	13	21	1	702	99	0	8	35.10	9
1994	R. J. Turner	16	24	3	710	115*	1	3	33.80	58
2001	R. L. Johnson	13	15	3	379	68	0	2	31.58	3
1997	P. C. L. Holloway	11	19	1	560	85	0	4	31.11	2
2001	J. I. D. Kerr	7	10	5	154	36	0	0	30.80	1
2001	K. P. Dutch	16	22	4	530	118	1	3	29.44	19
	P. D. Trego†	3	5	1	117	43	0	0	29.25	0
2001	P. S. Jones	16	16	5	180	29*	0	0	16.36	3
	M. P. L. Bulbeck†	5	7	2	50	18	0	0	10.00	3
1988	G. D. Rose	3	4	0	25	15	0	0	6.25	0

Also batted: A. R. Caddick‡ (cap 1992) (2 matches) 0, 10*, 5*; J. O. Grove (3 matches) 4*, 1, 19* (2 ct); J. P. Tucker† (1 match) 5*, 0*.

* *Signifies not out.* † *Born in Somerset.* ‡ *ECB contract.* § *Overseas player.*

BOWLING

	O	*M*	*R*	*W*	*BB*	*5W/i*	*Avge*
A. R. Caddick	88.4	17	319	18	5-81	3	17.72
R. L. Johnson	463.2	89	1,474	62	5-40	5	23.77
P. S. Jones	560	100	2,015	59	5-115	1	34.15
K. P. Dutch	367	64	1,268	35	4-32	0	36.22
M. Burns	127.5	21	510	12	6-54	1	42.50
I. D. Blackwell	259.4	69	783	18	5-122	1	43.50

Also bowled: P. D. Bowler 2–0–9–0; M. P. L. Bulbeck 110–6–501–4; J. O. Grove 58.2–7–316–5; P. C. L. Holloway 4–0–19–0; J. I. D. Kerr 150.4–33–504–8; M. N. Lathwell 7–0–37–0; K. A. Parsons 24–3–90–1; G. D. Rose 50–15–155–3; P. D. Trego 58–10–243–4; J. P. Tucker 17–2–82–0; R. J. Turner 10–3–29–0; M. J. Wood 7–1–30–0.

COUNTY RECORDS

Highest score for:	322	I. V. A. Richards v Warwickshire at Taunton	1985
Highest score against:	424	A. C. MacLaren (Lancashire) at Taunton	1895
Best bowling for:	10-49	E. J. Tyler v Surrey at Taunton	1895
Best bowling against:	10-35	A. Drake (Yorkshire) at Weston-super-Mare	1914
Highest total for:	675-9 dec.	v Hampshire at Bath	1924
Highest total against:	811	by Surrey at The Oval	1899
Lowest total for:	25	v Gloucestershire at Bristol	1947
Lowest total against:	22	by Gloucestershire at Bristol	1920

At Taunton, April 16, 17, 18 (not first-class). SOMERSET v CARDIFF UCCE. Cancelled.

SOMERSET v LANCASHIRE

At Taunton, April 20, 21, 22, 23. Lancashire won by an innings and four runs. Lancashire 19 pts, Somerset 4 pts. Toss: Lancashire. County debuts: K. P. Dutch, R. L. Johnson; R. C. Driver. Championship debut: J. P. Tucker.

This was a demoralising start to Somerset's season: their fielding was embarrassing, eight catches were dropped, and defeat was delayed until the last day only because rain washed out the third. Lancashire wore numbered shirts, a talking point that met with varying approval, but there was no need to identify Fairbrother, their experienced left-hander, on the second day. Showing minimal respect when the bowling wavered and parading his familiar one-day aggression, he dictated the pattern of the match with an unbeaten 179 from 201 balls that included a six and 27 fours. Useful support came from Keedy who, although in pain from a back injury and batting with a runner, stayed for more than an hour; his contribution to a last-wicket partnership of 98 was eight. Only Cox and Holloway displayed any real batting form for Somerset, who crumbled in the first innings as Chapple claimed six for 46. Johnson, signed from Middlesex, made an impressive Somerset debut with five wickets and forthright knocks at No. 9.

Close of play: First day, Lancashire 114-3 (Flintoff 18*); Second day, Somerset 106-6 (Holloway 52*, Dutch 12*); Third day, No play.

Somerset

*J. Cox c Flintoff b Martin	66	– (2) lbw b Chapple	0
P. C. L. Holloway run out	4	– (1) b Flintoff	74
M. Burns c Driver b Chapple	26	– c Hegg b Martin	1
P. D. Bowler c Driver b Flintoff	0	– c Fairbrother b Smethurst	8
K. A. Parsons b Chapple	35	– c Fairbrother b Smethurst	2
†R. J. Turner c Fairbrother b Chapple	7	– c Flintoff b Smethurst	0
G. D. Rose c Driver b Scuderi	4	– c Chilton b Scuderi	15
K. P. Dutch c Fairbrother b Chapple	6	– lbw b Martin	12
R. L. Johnson b Chapple	18	– c Hegg b Flintoff	37
P. S. Jones b Chapple	22	– b Martin	4
J. P. Tucker not out	5	– not out	0
L-b 7, w 4	11	B 4, l-b 7, w 4, n-b 2	17
1/22 2/79 3/88 4/120 5/140 6/149 7/149 8/158 9/181	204	1/6 2/7 3/26 4/28 5/40 6/83 7/106 8/161 9/170	170

Bonus points – Somerset 1, Lancashire 3.

Bowling: *First Innings*—Martin 16–3–57–1; Chapple 17.5–9–46–6; Smethurst 12–3–36–0; Scuderi 10–1–40–1; Flintoff 6–1–18–1. *Second Innings*—Martin 21–7–55–3; Chapple 17–4–41–1; Smethurst 14–5–32–3; Scuderi 11–3–24–1; Flintoff 5.1–2–7–2.

Lancashire

R. C. Driver c Burns b Johnson	19
M. J. Chilton lbw b Johnson	53
*J. P. Crawley lbw b Jones	14
A. Flintoff lbw b Jones	19
N. H. Fairbrother not out	179
J. C. Scuderi b Parsons	48
†W. K. Hegg c Turner b Johnson	6
G. Chapple b Jones	0
P. J. Martin c Turner b Johnson	3
M. P. Smethurst c Bowler b Johnson	7
G. Keedy c Turner b Rose	8
B 3, l-b 5, w 10, n-b 4	22
1/38 2/87 3/114 4/124 5/207 6/234 7/235 8/264 9/280	378

Bonus points – Lancashire 4, Somerset 3.

Bowling: Johnson 35–9–107–5; Tucker 17–2–82–0; Jones 28–6–86–3; Rose 17–4–73–1; Parsons 4–0–22–1.

Umpires: G. I. Burgess and D. R. Shepherd.

At Cardiff, April 25, 26, 27, 28. SOMERSET drew with GLAMORGAN.

At Leeds, May 9, 10, 11, 12. SOMERSET beat YORKSHIRE by 161 runs.

SOMERSET v KENT

At Taunton, May 16, 17, 18, 19. Drawn. Somerset 7 pts, Kent 10 pts. Toss: Kent. First-class debut: G. O. Jones. Championship debut: J. M. Golding.

Somerset's bowling may often have looked nondescript – they were without Caddick (like Trescothick on Test duty) and the injured Johnson and Rose – but Fulton's third hundred of the season should not be devalued. He gave reassurance to a Kent top order that had struggled for runs in 2000. Playing no shot, Key's downfall, was to prove contagious: debutant Geraint Jones (born in Papua New Guinea, raised in Australia) and Nixon went similarly. Cullinan looked on song, however, hitting a flurry of fours in his first Championship appearance for Kent. So, too, did Golding, who suffered a stress fracture of the back the previous season; he took three wickets in ten overs of accurate seam, helping ensure Somerset followed on 159 in arrears. They fared better second time round, led by Cox, Bowler and Lathwell. As the game petered out, Key bowled an over of imitation Shoaib Akhtar; to complete the verisimilitude, he was called by umpire Holder at square leg.

Close of play: First day, Kent 312-5 (Fulton 138*, Fleming 15*); Second day, Somerset 12-0 (Cox 4*, Holloway 7*); Third day, Somerset 109-2 (Cox 59*, Bowler 1*).

Kent

D. P. Fulton lbw b Trego	140
R. W. T. Key b Jones	0
E. T. Smith lbw b Grove	48
D. J. Cullinan c Grove b Kerr	57
G. O. Jones lbw b Dutch	5
†P. A. Nixon lbw b Jones	21
*M. V. Fleming c Turner b Dutch	16
J. M. Golding c Turner b Trego	21
M. M. Patel c Dutch b Jones	7
M. J. Saggers c Turner b Trego	0
D. D. Masters not out	0
B 1, l-b 7, w 18, n-b 2	28
1/1 2/120 3/198 4/226 5/283 6/314 7/318 8/343 9/343	343

Bonus points – Kent 3, Somerset 3.

Bowling: Jones 26.5–6–71–3; Grove 19–3–85–1; Trego 27–5–85–3; Kerr 17–1–63–1; Dutch 10–2–31–2.

Somerset

*J. Cox c Nixon b Fleming	11	– (2) c Nixon b Fleming	63
P. C. L. Holloway lbw b Masters	39	– (1) c Fleming b Masters	13
M. Burns c Fulton b Golding	21	– b Saggers	20
P. D. Bowler lbw b Saggers	42	– c Nixon b Golding	87
M. N. Lathwell b Patel	1	– lbw b Fleming	58
†R. J. Turner c Nixon b Golding	4	– b Fleming	0
K. P. Dutch c Nixon b Patel	0	– (8) not out	5
J. I. D. Kerr c Jones b Golding	3	– (9) not out	12
P. D. Trego c Nixon b Saggers	32	– (7) c Smith b Fleming	43
P. S. Jones c Nixon b Saggers	1		
J. O. Grove not out	4		
B 4, l-b 12, w 10	26	B 1, l-b 8, w 20, n-b 4	33
1/27 2/69 3/94 4/97 5/104 6/105 7/108 8/178 9/179	184	1/60 2/106 3/114 4/249 5/249 6/287 7/311	(7 wkts) 334

Bonus points – Kent 3.

Bowling: *First Innings*—Saggers 15.1–3–36–3; Masters 10–1–45–1; Fleming 16–4–35–1; Patel 19–4–29–2; Golding 10–1–23–3. *Second Innings*—Saggers 26–4–68–1; Fleming 23–3–74–4; Golding 28–8–70–1; Patel 32–8–67–0; Masters 11–2–32–1; Cullinan 3–2–5–0; Key 1–0–5–0; Jones 1–0–4–0.

Umpires: J. W. Holder and A. G. T. Whitehead.

At Leicester, May 30, 31, June 1, 2. SOMERSET drew with LEICESTERSHIRE.

At The Oval, June 6, 7, 8, 9. SOMERSET lost to SURREY by six wickets.

SOMERSET v YORKSHIRE

At Bath, June 13, 14, 15, 16. Drawn. Somerset 10 pts, Yorkshire 10 pts. Toss: Yorkshire. First-class debut: M. J. Wood (Somerset).

The benignest of pitches produced too many runs (1,142) and too few wickets (ten). By the rain-shortened fourth day, the cricket had become meaningless, with Somerset using ten bowlers including an extended spell from wicket-keeper Turner. It might have been 11 had Cox not fractured his thumb while fielding; Burns took over the captaincy. Byas, perhaps mindful of the caprices of the Recreation Ground track, put Somerset in, which proved a misjudgment. Revealing a variety of assertive strokes on both sides of the wicket, Burns assembled a maiden double-hundred, batting seven and three-quarter hours, facing 367 balls and hitting 28 fours and a six. His 221 was the highest by a Somerset player in more than 100 years of first-class cricket at Bath. Cox contributed 95 and later left Lathwell, out for 99 in the previous match, stranded on 98 when he declared at lunch on the second day. It was an auspicious game for players named Matthew James Wood: Somerset's – a 20-year-old Devonian making his debut – had every reason to be pleased with 71, while Yorkshire's hit his first century in over a year. At the end, Lehmann was 13 from converting his 50th first-class hundred into a double, chiding Somerset for dropping him on 49 and 93.

Close of play: First day, Somerset 371-2 (Burns 162*, Wood 60*); Second day, Yorkshire 119-0 (Richardson 56*, Wood 56*); Third day, Yorkshire 425-4 (Lehmann 105*, Fellows 61*).

Somerset

*J. Cox c Byas b Fellows	95	P. D. Trego not out	4
P. C. L. Holloway c Blakey b Hamilton	5		
M. Burns c Blakey b Middlebrook	221	B 7, l-b 8, w 10, n-b 30	55
M. J. Wood c Blakey b Kirby	71		
M. N. Lathwell not out	98	1/26 2/232 3/393 (5 wkts dec.)	553
†R. J. Turner c Blakey b Lehmann	4	4/525 5/542	

K. P. Dutch, J. I. D. Kerr, R. L. Johnson and P. S. Jones did not bat.

Bonus points – Somerset 5, Yorkshire 1 (Score at 130 overs: 488-3).

Bowling: Hoggard 26–5–82–0; Kirby 23–3–79–1; Hamilton 24–6–81–1; Middlebrook 24–2–116–1; White 19–2–59–0; Fellows 13–1–53–1; Lehmann 14–0–68–1.

Yorkshire

S. A. Richardson b Dutch	68	†R. J. Blakey not out	78
M. J. Wood b Johnson	124		
C. White c Lathwell b Dutch	16	B 4, l-b 9, w 2, n-b 18	33
D. S. Lehmann not out	187		
*D. Byas c Turner b Jones	20	1/179 2/217 3/228 (5 wkts)	589
G. M. Fellows c sub b Johnson	63	4/281 5/430	

G. M. Hamilton, J. D. Middlebrook, S. P. Kirby and M. J. Hoggard did not bat.

Bonus points – Yorkshire 5, Somerset 1 (Score at 130 overs: 459-5).

Bowling: Johnson 35–3–110–2; Jones 30–6–104–1; Trego 12–2–57–0; Kerr 22–6–66–0; Burns 13–0–60–0; Dutch 24–6–64–2; Wood 7–1–30–0; Lathwell 7–0–37–0; Holloway 4–0–19–0; Turner 10–3–29–0.

Umpires: N. G. Cowley and R. Palmer.

At Northampton, June 20, 21, 22, 23. SOMERSET drew with NORTHAMPTONSHIRE.

SOMERSET v ESSEX

At Taunton, July 4, 5, 6, 7. Somerset won by an innings and 60 runs. Somerset 20 pts, Essex 3 pts. Toss: Somerset. Championship debut: J. E. Bishop.

Dutch, recruited by Somerset primarily for his off-spin, revealed a golden touch that extended to every sphere of the game. Beginning with a maiden hundred, he followed up with three sharp catches at second slip (though he did drop Irani) and four second-innings wickets. Somerset were 158 for six when he joined Turner, and together they added 222, with Turner making his first hundred for nearly two years. Johnson and Jones then exploited the humidity to rattle the Essex top order, and Essex followed on 285 behind. Now it was the turn of Dutch the bowler. Cox claimed the extra half-hour on the third evening, was thwarted, but hadn't long to wait next morning. Irani batted bravely in both innings, but Essex, missing the injured Law, were quite simply outplayed. This fourth defeat in five games left them bottom of Division One; Somerset, meanwhile, moved up to second.

Close of play: First day, Somerset 291-6 (Turner 71*, Dutch 56*); Second day, Essex 34-3 (Clinton 11*, Irani 9*); Third day, Essex 189-8 (Ilott 16*, Bishop 5*).

Somerset

*J. Cox c Robinson b Irani	47
P. C. L. Holloway c Foster b Cowan	6
M. Burns c Foster b Irani	11
P. D. Bowler lbw b Bishop	39
M. N. Lathwell b Ilott	16
I. D. Blackwell c Robinson b Bishop	26
†R. J. Turner not out	115
K. P. Dutch c Foster b Ilott	118
R. L. Johnson b Ilott	9
P. S. Jones c and b Ilott	5
J. O. Grove b Cowan	1
B 4, l-b 6, w 6, n-b 6	22
1/28 2/67 3/70 4/101 5/151 6/158 7/380 8/408 9/414	415

Bonus points – Somerset 5, Essex 3.

Bowling: Ilott 38–7–116–4; Cowan 29.1–9–99–2; Bishop 25–4–91–2; Irani 23–10–38–2; Such 6–0–32–0; Grayson 8–0–29–0.

Essex

R. S. Clinton c Dutch b Jones	11	– c Turner b Jones 15
A. P. Grayson c Burns b Johnson	1	– c Turner b Johnson 9
D. D. J. Robinson lbw b Jones	1	– c Lathwell b Dutch 24
S. D. Peters lbw b Johnson	11	– c Bowler b Grove 31
*R. C. Irani c Dutch b Johnson	40	– c Bowler b Blackwell 57
†J. S. Foster b Johnson	2	– c Lathwell b Dutch 0
G. R. Napier c Dutch b Jones	38	– c Turner b Dutch 21
A. P. Cowan c Bowler b Grove	0	– c Bowler b Dutch 0
M. C. Ilott lbw b Burns	8	– b Jones 34
J. E. Bishop c Burns b Grove	4	– not out 11
P. M. Such not out	0	– c Grove b Jones 4
L-b 6, w 2, n-b 6	14	L-b 7, w 6, n-b 6 19
1/1 2/4 3/23 4/45 5/64 6/73 7/86 8/126 9/126	130	1/15 2/52 3/61 4/117 5/122 6/152 7/152 8/174 9/211 225

Bonus points – Somerset 3.

Bowling: *First Innings*—Johnson 17–6–43–4; Jones 17–5–34–3; Grove 4.2–0–46–2; Burns 4–3–1–1. *Second Innings*—Johnson 17–8–42–1; Jones 18.1–2–66–3; Grove 13–3–40–1; Burns 4–0–12–0; Dutch 27–6–57–4; Blackwell 10–9–1–1.

Umpires: J. W. Holder and D. R. Shepherd.

At Taunton, July 13, 14, 15, 16. SOMERSET lost to AUSTRALIANS by 176 runs (see Australian tour section).

At Manchester, July 19, 20, 21. SOMERSET beat LANCASHIRE by ten wickets.

SOMERSET v GLAMORGAN

At Taunton, July 27, 28, 29. Somerset won by an innings and 67 runs. Somerset 20 pts, Glamorgan 2 pts. Toss: Glamorgan.

Somerset's leisured win before tea on the third day left Glamorgan ruing the lost advantage of batting first, especially as their openers had 59 up inside even time. The reason lay in Caddick's fiery exploitation of a pitch blessed with pace and bounce. In his first Championship match since May, he finished with eight wickets, and Johnson, bowling a fuller length, played his part, too. Somerset, in reply, also set off at a lick, and after Watkin had sent back Cox and Trescothick in successive overs, Burns and Bowler added 135 in sparkling style. Bowler's six-hour stay included another big century stand, this time with Blackwell, whose 102 contained 15 fours and two sixes; later on, Dutch and Johnson sent Somerset racing towards 600 with 84 from ten overs. Batting was never easier, as James and Maher confirmed while bringing Somerset's lead down to 279 on Saturday evening. But Sunday was another story. James had a finger broken in Caddick's fifth over, and soon afterwards Maher and Powell edged him to slip. Maynard held out for three hours, always looking composed, but Cox, with three pace aces and a pair of spinning jacks, held the winning hand.

Close of play: First day, Somerset 246-3 (Bowler 63*, Lathwell 34*); Second day, Glamorgan 152-0 (James 63*, Maher 82*).

Glamorgan

*S. P. James c Cox b Johnson	21	– retired hurt	77
J. P. Maher c Turner b Caddick	62	– c Dutch b Caddick	98
M. P. Maynard c Turner b Caddick	6	– c Cox b Jones	80
M. J. Powell lbw b Caddick	21	– c Trescothick b Caddick	0
A. Dale c Trescothick b Caddick	0	– c Bowler b Johnson	16
R. D. B. Croft b Johnson	0	– c Turner b Johnson	0
†M. A. Wallace c Johnson b Jones	8	– c Lathwell b Blackwell	15
S. D. Thomas c Dutch b Caddick	8	– c Turner b Jones	21
D. A. Cosker not out	2	– not out	20
S. L. Watkin c Blackwell b Johnson	22	– c Dutch b Jones	11
S. P. Jones b Johnson	0	– b Caddick	0
L-b 7, n-b 12	19	B 4, l-b 16, w 2, n-b 4	26
1/59 2/87 3/102 4/116 5/117 6/125 7/133 8/141 9/169	169	1/191 2/197 3/247 4/247 5/302 6/324 7/337 8/359 9/364	364

Bonus points – Somerset 3.

In the second innings James retired hurt at 172.

Bowling: *First Innings*—Caddick 18–2–84–5; Johnson 12.1–3–33–4; Jones 17–6–45–1. *Second Innings*—Caddick 24.4–5–62–3; Johnson 20–3–93–2; Jones 20–4–83–3; Burns 3–0–15–0; Dutch 15–2–45–0; Blackwell 23–8–46–1.

Somerset

*J. Cox c Powell b Watkin	29	R. L. Johnson c Thomas b Croft	36
M. E. Trescothick b Watkin	26	A. R. Caddick not out	5
M. Burns lbw b Jones	81		
P. D. Bowler c James b Thomas	164	B 2, l-b 12, w 2, n-b 4	20
M. N. Lathwell lbw b Watkin	53		
I. D. Blackwell c Powell b Croft	102	1/53 2/58 3/193 (8 wkts dec.)	600
†R. J. Turner c Croft b Jones	15	4/265 5/428 6/457	
K. P. Dutch not out	69	7/505 8/589	

P. S. Jones did not bat.

Bonus points – Somerset 5, Glamorgan 2.

Bowling: Jones 26–2–123–2; Watkin 22–4–99–3; Thomas 23–2–99–1; Dale 6–0–35–0; Croft 32–4–137–2; Cosker 18–3–93–0.

Umpires: N. G. Cowley and J. H. Hampshire.

At Canterbury, August 1, 2, 3, 4. SOMERSET drew with KENT.

SOMERSET v LEICESTERSHIRE

At Taunton, August 7, 8, 9, 10. Drawn. Somerset 9 pts, Leicestershire 9 pts. Toss: Somerset.

A match rich in boundaries and entertainment, if noticeably short on technical proficiency, came to little once the third day was washed out. Smith and Habib reigned supreme for much of the final day in a stand of 300 that was 16 short of Leicestershire's third-wicket record. Rain had previously punctuated the opening day, allowing only 48 overs, but they were enough for Leicestershire to make a mess of things as Michael Burns, wobbling the ball effectively in the overcast, humid conditions, picked up his first five-wicket return. Shahid Afridi hit an unbeaten 62 in 51 balls, adding 69 in nine uninhibited overs with Stevens, but such batting suggested little appreciation of Leicestershire's situation. Still, it inspired Malcolm, who next morning smote his second fifty in 18 seasons as a professional No. 11. Somerset batted with similar midsummer madness until, from 54 for five, Turner took the innings in hand for three hours. Johnson, who helped him add 109, provided the mayhem content with a dozen fours and a six in a display of straight driving that took him to 68 in 70 balls, one short of his career-best.

Close of play: First day, Leicestershire 200-8 (Shahid Afridi 62*, Boswell 0*); Second day, Leicestershire 19-1 (Ward 5*); Third day, No play.

Leicestershire

T. R. Ward c Turner b Jones	20	– b Johnson	11
I. J. Sutcliffe c Turner b Johnson	9	– b Johnson	13
*B. F. Smith b Johnson	28	– not out	180
A. Habib lbw b Burns	24	– c Burns b Dutch	149
D. L. Maddy c Turner b Burns	15	– c Jones b Dutch	6
D. I. Stevens c Bowler b Burns	29	– not out	28
Shahid Afridi c Blackwell b Jones	69		
†N. D. Burns c Turner b Burns	1		
J. Ormond c Turner b Burns	5		
S. A. J. Boswell not out	16		
D. E. Malcolm b Burns	50		
L-b 9, n-b 2	11	B 3, l-b 6, w 2, n-b 2	13
1/21 2/43 3/68 4/99 5/100 6/169 7/175 8/189 9/208	277	1/19 2/38 3/338 4/352 (4 wkts)	400

Bonus points – Leicestershire 2, Somerset 3.

Bowling: *First Innings*—Johnson 23–2–69–2; Jones 24–3–101–2; Burns 16.1–2–54–6; Bulbeck 6–0–44–0. *Second Innings*—Johnson 12–0–52–2; Jones 18–4–57–0; Burns 10–1–66–0; Bulbeck 13–3–45–0; Dutch 25–3–103–2; Blackwell 17–3–59–0; Bowler 2–0–9–0.

Somerset

*J. Cox run out	0	R. L. Johnson c Ward b Ormond	68
M. J. Wood b Boswell	27	P. S. Jones run out	22
M. Burns c Burns b Ormond	5	M. P. L. Bulbeck not out	1
P. D. Bowler c Smith b Boswell	10	L-b 14, w 4, n-b 12	30
M. N. Lathwell c Ward b Ormond	1		
I. D. Blackwell c Shahid Afridi b Malcolm	16	1/5 2/38 3/38	298
†R. J. Turner c Maddy b Boswell	93	4/54 5/54 6/84	
K. P. Dutch c Burns b Shahid Afridi	25	7/141 8/250 9/296	

Bonus points – Somerset 2, Leicestershire 3.

Bowling: Ormond 24–8–71–3; Malcolm 10–1–47–1; Boswell 17–2–74–3; Maddy 11–0–61–0; Shahid Afridi 8–2–31–1.

Umpires: M. J. Harris and J. W. Lloyds.

SOMERSET v SURREY

At Taunton, August 23, 24, 25, 26. Drawn. Somerset 11 pts, Surrey 9 pts. Toss: Somerset. Championship debut: G. J. Batty.

As Johnson was not released by England until the morning of the match, and then held up in traffic driving back from The Oval, Somerset batted first when they would have preferred to bowl. Consequently, Bicknell employed the helpful conditions once play started, the morning having been lost to drizzle. Cox's diligent innings set his side a splendid example and, next day, Blackwell gained a fourth bonus point with his fourth Championship hundred of the season. Scoring all 57 runs to come off the bat after lunch, he put on 107 in 19 overs with Grove for the tenth wicket. At the close, each also had a wicket to his name, but Johnson did the real damage in a four-over spell of three for seven. By now, Somerset knew the Championship was in Yorkshire's hands; second place was the best they could hope for. Burns consolidated their lead with a steady 70, and another round of Blackwell (67 in 75 balls) allowed Cox to set Surrey 407 in 84 overs. Brown and the Hollioakes occasionally suggested a charge, but ultimately Somerset were the only side scenting victory. Johnson finished with nine wickets in the match – as did Surrey's Saqlain Mushtaq – while Turner held nine catches to equal Somerset's wicket-keeping record.

Close of play: First day, Somerset 207-6 (Blackwell 21*); Second day, Surrey 224-6 (B. C. Hollioake 51*, Bicknell 19*); Third day, Somerset 265-5 (Blackwell 36*, Turner 14*).

Somerset

*J. Cox c B. C. Hollioake b Bicknell	76	– b Saqlain Mushtaq	46
M. J. Wood b Bicknell	24	– lbw b Giddins	3
M. Burns c G. J. Batty b Saqlain Mushtaq	38	– b Saqlain Mushtaq	70
P. D. Bowler c Salisbury b Saqlain Mushtaq	0	– c A. J. Hollioake b Bicknell	34
M. N. Lathwell b Bicknell	1	– c Carberry b B. C. Hollioake	27
I. D. Blackwell c Salisbury b Saqlain Mushtaq	120	– c Carberry b Saqlain Mushtaq	67
†R. J. Turner lbw b Giddins	29	– not out	28
K. P. Dutch lbw b Saqlain Mushtaq	23		
R. L. Johnson b Saqlain Mushtaq	10		
P. S. Jones c G. J. Batty b Saqlain Mushtaq	6		
J. O. Grove not out	19		
B 4, l-b 4, w 8, n-b 11	27	B 10, l-b 18, w 2, n-b 6	36
1/49 2/142 3/152 4/154 5/159 6/207 7/246 8/256 9/266	373	1/12 2/87 3/164 4/200 5/233 6/311	(6 wkts dec.) 311

Bonus points – Somerset 4, Surrey 3.

Bowling: *First Innings*—Bicknell 27–5–84–3; Giddins 20–3–79–1; A. J. Hollioake 5–0–27–0; B. C. Hollioake 6–1–23–0; Saqlain Mushtaq 42.4–13–107–6; Salisbury 9–2–45–0. *Second Innings*—Bicknell 24–6–62–1; Giddins 12–2–25–1; Saqlain Mushtaq 41.4–10–114–3; Salisbury 6–0–27–0; B. C. Hollioake 10–0–52–1; Brown 2–0–3–0.

Surrey

I. J. Ward c Dutch b Grove	48	– lbw b Johnson	4
M. A. Carberry c Bowler b Blackwell	34	– run out	33
G. J. Batty c Turner b Johnson	25	– c Turner b Johnson	19
*A. J. Hollioake c Turner b Johnson	20	– c Turner b Jones	83
A. D. Brown c Turner b Johnson	7	– c Turner b Johnson	64
B. C. Hollioake c Turner b Johnson	56	– c Dutch b Johnson	56
†J. N. Batty c Dutch b Jones	9	– not out	8
M. P. Bicknell c Turner b Johnson	34	– not out	12
I. D. K. Salisbury c Turner b Jones	7		
Saqlain Mushtaq lbw b Jones	18		
E. S. H. Giddins not out	1		
L-b 12, w 2, n-b 5	19	B 5, l-b 6, w 2, n-b 2	15
1/65 2/94 3/133 4/134 5/155 6/187 7/246 8/249 9/265	278	1/4 2/24 3/90 4/185 5/259 6/274 (6 wkts)	294

Bonus points – Surrey 2, Somerset 3.

Bowling: *First Innings*—Johnson 26–8–62–5; Jones 20.2–1–98–3; Grove 10–1–55–1; Blackwell 5–2–14–1; Burns 8–0–36–0; Dutch 2–1–1–0. *Second Innings*—Johnson 28–8–90–4; Jones 19–4–70–1; Blackwell 22–11–29–0; Grove 12–0–90–0; Dutch 3–2–4–0.

Umpires: J. H. Evans and R. Julian.

At Chelmsford, September 5, 6, 7. SOMERSET beat ESSEX by nine wickets.

SOMERSET v NORTHAMPTONSHIRE

At Taunton, September 12, 13, 14, 15. Somerset won by four wickets. Somerset 20 pts, Northamptonshire 7 pts. Toss: Somerset.

What with a flat pitch, fast outfield, inviting straight boundaries and five hundreds – at least one each day – an aggregate of 1,795 runs, the second-highest for a first-class match in England, was hardly surprising. Once Somerset had secured the runners-up prize money on the third day, interest centred on whether Northamptonshire could achieve the win that would save them from relegation. They gave it a good shot. Ripley, in his farewell appearance for them, challenged Somerset to chase 246 at just under six an over. Cox and Wood rattled up 147 in 32 overs, whereupon Graeme Swann, whose 61 from 48 balls had helped set up the declaration, kept Northamptonshire in the frame with three wickets. Eventually, however, Somerset needed only seven from the last over, and Parsons's somewhat agricultural six saw to that. Earlier, Hussey's third double-hundred of the season – off 358 balls, with 30 fours, in 433 minutes – made him the first since Mark Ramprakash in 1995 to score 2,000 runs in a summer, while Turner's seven catches in the innings were a record by a Somerset keeper. The fast-emerging Wood hit his maiden hundred, from 181 balls with 17 fours and a six, as Somerset amassed their highest total at Taunton, but there was widespread disappointment when Lathwell again narrowly failed to reach three figures.

Close of play: First day, Northamptonshire 382-5 (Hussey 192*, Ripley 1*); Second day, Somerset 224-2 (Wood 102*, Lathwell 33*); Third day, Northamptonshire 89-1 (Hussey 29*, Cook 55*).

Northamptonshire

M. E. K. Hussey c Turner b Johnson	208	c Lathwell b Blackwell	48
A. J. Swann c Turner b Jones	0	c Dutch b Jones	0
J. W. Cook c Turner b Johnson	13	b Blackwell	88
R. J. Warren c Turner b Dutch	144	c Parsons b Blackwell	42
A. L. Penberthy c Turner b Jones	7	c Wood b Dutch	101
G. P. Swann lbw b Jones	16	c Burns b Blackwell	61
*†D. Ripley c Turner b Johnson	1	c Lathwell b Dutch	16
J. P. Taylor c Turner b Johnson	33	c Burns b Dutch	53
M. R. Strong b Jones	5	c sub b Blackwell	1
J. A. R. Blain not out	12	not out	0
M. S. Panesar not out	3		
B 4, l-b 15, n-b 2	21	B 8, l-b 8, w 6	22
1/0 2/31 3/318 4/337 5/375 6/383 7/416 8/437 9/443 (9 wkts dec.)	463	1/0 2/140 3/155 4/216 5/314 6/350 7/429 8/431 9/432 (9 wkts dec.)	432

Bonus points – Northamptonshire 5, Somerset 3 (Score at 130 overs: 443-9).

Bowling: *First Innings*—Johnson 37–10–90–4; Jones 35–8–111–4; Burns 10–2–33–0; Kerr 15–4–47–0; Dutch 21–0–83–1; Parsons 7–0–33–0; Blackwell 9–0–47–0. *Second Innings*—Johnson 6–2–13–0; Jones 10–1–74–1; Blackwell 39.2–6–122–5; Kerr 3–0–19–0; Dutch 31–2–188–3.

Somerset

*J. Cox c Ripley b Penberthy	82	c Warren b G. P. Swann	86
M. J. Wood c Strong b Taylor	122	c Hussey b G. P. Swann	65
M. Burns c Ripley b Penberthy	1	(4) run out	26
M. N. Lathwell c Taylor b Panesar	92	(5) b Panesar	14
K. A. Parsons b Taylor	139	(6) not out	36
I. D. Blackwell c Ripley b Strong	77	(3) c Ripley b G. P. Swann	0
†R. J. Turner c Strong b Taylor	36	(8) not out	6
K. P. Dutch b Panesar	12	(7) c A. J. Swann b G. P. Swann	2
J. I. D. Kerr not out	20		
R. L. Johnson b Taylor	17		
P. S. Jones c Ripley b Strong	29		
B 4, l-b 9, w 6, n-b 4	23	B 4, l-b 11	15
1/163 2/169 3/264 4/350 5/496 6/551 7/576 8/584 9/603	650	1/147 2/150 3/177 4/187 5/234 6/237 (6 wkts)	250

Bonus points – Somerset 5, Northamptonshire 2 (Score at 130 overs: 602-8).

Bowling: *First Innings*—Blain 20–0–121–0; Taylor 25–3–100–4; Strong 15.3–2–79–2; Panesar 28–5–120–2; Cook 13–2–56–0; Penberthy 24–4–104–2; G. P. Swann 12–0–57–0. *Second Innings*—Taylor 3–0–11–0; Strong 5–1–32–0; Panesar 18.3–2–107–1; G. P. Swann 16–0–85–4.

Umpires: M. R. Benson and A. Clarkson.

GROUNDSMEN OF THE YEAR, 2001

Phil Frost of Somerset was named the ECB's Groundsman of the Year for his work at Taunton, with the previous year's winner, Paul Brind of Surrey, runner-up for The Oval. Geoff Swift of Cheltenham won the award for county outgrounds from Colin Dick of Arundel. A new award for the best UCCE ground was won by John Moden of Fenner's, Cambridge, with Richard Sula of The Parks, Oxford, second.

Mark Butcher

SURREY

President: The Rt Hon. J. Major
Chairman: M. J. Soper
Chief Executive: P. C. J. Sheldon
Director of Cricket Development: M. J. Edwards
Cricket Secretary: A. Gibson
Captain: A. J. Hollioake
Cricket Manager: K. T. Medlycott
Head Groundsman: P. D. Brind
Scorer: K. R. Booth

Greatness, elusive at the best of times, comfortably sidestepped Surrey in 2001, after their successes of the previous two seasons. And the air of sadness around The Oval at losing their Championship title was heightened by the death in October of a Surrey legend, Alf Gover, at the age of 93. As a fast bowler and subsequently president, Gover had been associated with the county for more than 70 years, witnessing many of their triumphs including the most recent, the Benson and Hedges Cup victory in July.

Instead of the longed-for hat-trick of County Championships, Surrey for a few uncomfortable weeks found themselves flirting with relegation – and indeed did drop straight back into Division Two of the Norwich Union League. That they finished fourth in the Championship owed much to team spirit, self-belief and to individual players who contributed mightily to the collective cause. Unbeaten they might have been up to August, but a string of poor draws is not the way to win a title.

The weather prevented them getting off to a half-decent start. Then there was the absence of Saqlain Mushtaq while he was with the Pakistani tourists; by the time he returned to The Oval, he had missed seven matches. Although he began well, taking 16 wickets in his first two games, both were drawn. He did bowl Surrey to a somewhat empty victory over Yorkshire, who by then had taken their title, and pick up 43 Championship wickets in all at 22.13, but overall the spin wizard was short of match-winning spells.

The significant setback was England call-ups. It is all very well boasting a squad with as many internationals as a porcupine has quills, but strip it of those protective quills and it poses little threat. So it proved for Surrey. Even their midwinter signing of Mark Ramprakash, to shore up batting weakened by England calls, backfired. He fulfilled Surrey's expectations for the first half of the campaign, but his class shone through so brightly, in a couple of marvellous hundreds and a clutch of half-centuries, that the England selectors could no longer ignore him. Mark Butcher was another unexpectedly recalled to the colours; he made a magnificent Test comeback and scored 1,300 first-class runs at 56.52 for county and country. In addition, Alec Stewart and Graham Thorpe were contracted to the ECB and played only seven Championship matches between them. Four other Surrey players – Ian

Ward, Alex Tudor, Alistair Brown and Ben Hollioake (back in form after a disastrous 2000) – were required by England at various times.

It remained a mystery to Surrey fans that Martin Bicknell did not get a call as well, though it was a mercy for the county. His record the previous season had suggested he might be regarded as an all-rounder; this time it was fairly shouted from every street corner, and not only in South London. He topped Surrey's bowling averages, was the country's second-highest wicket-taker, and showed his batting colleagues a clean pair of heels until some established practitioners hauled him back at the finish. Bicknell's 748 runs at 46.75, coupled with 72 wickets at 21.36, reinforced the impression that he is not getting older, just better. According to reports, he was within 20 minutes of an England call for the fourth Ashes Test, but it was not to be. Just before Surrey colleague Butcher grabbed headlines for his heroics at Headingley, though, Bicknell hit his maiden first-class hundred, against Kent at Canterbury, having picked up four first-innings wickets.

But his was a lone furrow. Injuries, and an unfortunate lack of adequate stand-ins, also cost Surrey dearly. The recruitment of Ed Giddins to bolster the attack did not have quite the desired impact, his 30 Championship wickets costing 36 runs apiece, and those expected to challenge for regular first-team places were disappointing. Slow left-armer Rupesh Amin and fast bowlers Carl Greenidge and Ian Bishop were released, along with Gary Butcher, despite some handy performances in his three seasons at The Oval. There was little doubt that more personnel changes would be necessary, and Leicestershire's England seamer Jimmy Ormond was signed to reinforce the squad in that department.

Jason Ratcliffe, one of the unsung heroes of the consecutive Championship triumphs, missed the season through a long-term knee injury, while Tudor struggled for much of the time with a side strain, although it did not prevent him making his maiden first-class hundred. Thorpe, when not with England (which was not that often), was another to be found on the treatment table. Though Ian Salisbury did not miss a match, he was troubled by painful toe and finger problems that affected his technique and form, while, midway through the season, Brown broke his thumb while fielding against Northamptonshire at Guildford. It did not stop him scoring a fine hundred, but – such was Surrey's plight, he took no time off – his next half-dozen outings produced barely 50 runs.

An unbeaten century from Brown had been instrumental in helping Surrey through their Benson and Hedges quarter-final at Hove. In the semi-final, a total of 361, a competition record by one first-class county against another, saw off Nottinghamshire, led by former Surrey stalwart Darren Bicknell, to set up the Lord's showdown against holders Gloucestershire. A comfortable victory there meant Surrey had a trophy in the cabinet by mid-season, but they put up a flabby show in the Cheltenham & Gloucester Trophy and, ultimately, the one title they really wanted proved beyond them. – DAVID LLEWELLYN.

SURREY 2001

[*Bill Smith*

Back row: M. A. Carberry, G. J. Batty, T. J. Murtagh, P. J. Sampson, C. G. Greenidge, B. J. M. Scott. *Middle row:* K. R. Booth (*scorer*), D. Naylor (*physiotherapist*), G. P. Butcher, J. N. Batty, R. M. Amin, E. S. H. Giddins, I. E. Bishop, M. R. Ramprakash, K. T. Medlycott (*cricket manager*), A. R. Butcher (*Second Eleven coach*). *Front row:* I. J. Ward, A. J. Tudor, J. D. Ratcliffe, A. D. Brown, G. P. Thorpe, A. J. Hollioake (*captain*), A. J. Stewart (*honorary club captain*), M. P. Bicknell, M. A. Butcher, I. D. K. Salisbury, N. Shahid, B. C. Hollioake. *Inset:* Saqlain Mushtaq.

SURREY RESULTS

All first-class matches – Played 15: Won 3, Lost 1, Drawn 11. Abandoned 1.

County Championship matches – Played 15: Won 3, Lost 1, Drawn 11. Abandoned 1.

CricInfo County Championship, 4th in Division 1; Cheltenham & Gloucester Trophy, 4th round; Benson and Hedges Cup, winners; Norwich Union League, 8th in Division 1.

COUNTY CHAMPIONSHIP AVERAGES

BATTING

Cap		*M*	*I*	*NO*	*R*	*HS*	*100s*	*50s*	*Avge*	*Ct/St*
1996	M. A. Butcher†	10	15	1	844	230	2	5	60.28	11
	M. R. Ramprakash	9	14	0	776	146	3	4	55.42	4
1989	M. P. Bicknell†	15	22	6	748	110*	1	4	46.75	5
1999	A. J. Tudor	7	11	1	399	116	1	1	39.90	2
1995	A. J. Hollioake	13	20	1	758	97	0	7	39.89	15
1985	A. J. Stewart†‡	5	6	1	196	106	1	0	39.20	13/1
1994	A. D. Brown	13	20	0	630	122	3	2	31.50	3
2000	I. J. Ward	11	18	0	561	79	0	4	31.16	5
	M. A. Carberry†	6	10	0	311	84	0	1	31.10	6
1999	B. C. Hollioake	12	19	0	586	118	1	4	30.84	18
1998	I. D. K. Salisbury	15	21	4	440	54	0	1	25.88	9
	G. P. Butcher	4	8	1	175	56	0	1	25.00	1
1998	N. Shahid	7	12	0	208	65	0	1	17.33	8
2001	J. N. Batty	10	16	1	239	59	0	1	15.93	26/2
1998	Saqlain Mushtaq§	9	14	5	131	38	0	0	14.55	1
	E. S. H. Giddins	12	14	8	36	9*	0	0	6.00	2
	R. M. Amin	3	4	1	1	1	0	0	0.33	2

Also batted: G. J. Batty (1 match) 25, 19 (2 ct); T. J. Murtagh (1 match) 2; G. P. Thorpe†‡ (cap 1991) (2 matches) 148, 32 (2 ct).

* *Signifies not out.* † *Born in Surrey.* ‡ *ECB contract.* § *Overseas player.*

BOWLING

	O	*M*	*R*	*W*	*BB*	*5W/i*	*Avge*
M. P. Bicknell	541.5	132	1,538	72	7-60	3	21.36
Saqlain Mushtaq	411.2	109	952	43	7-58	4	22.13
E. S. H. Giddins	352.5	83	1,102	30	5-48	1	36.73
A. J. Tudor	206.2	46	732	19	5-54	1	38.52
I. D. K. Salisbury	396.2	72	1,151	27	5-95	1	42.62

Also bowled: R. M. Amin 102–28–272–5; A. D. Brown 23–1–97–0; G. P. Butcher 34.4–5–138–2; M. A. Butcher 45–5–162–4; A. J. Hollioake 54–11–165–3; B. C. Hollioake 133.2–21–530–9; T. J. Murtagh 11–5–28–1; M. R. Ramprakash 51–14–84–0; A. J. Stewart 1–1–0–0; G. P. Thorpe 1–0–11–0.

COUNTY RECORDS

Highest score for:	357*	R. Abel v Somerset at The Oval	1899
Highest score against:	366	N. H. Fairbrother (Lancashire) at The Oval	1990
Best bowling for:	10-43	T. Rushby v Somerset at Taunton	1921
Best bowling against:	10-28	W. P. Howell (Australians) at The Oval	1899
Highest total for:	811	v Somerset at The Oval	1899
Highest total against:	863	by Lancashire at The Oval	1990
Lowest total for:	14	v Essex at Chelmsford	1983
Lowest total against:	16	by MCC at Lord's	1872

SURREY v KENT

At The Oval, April 20, 21, 22, 23. Drawn. Surrey 11 pts, Kent 12 pts. Toss: Kent. County debuts: E. S. H. Giddins, M. R. Ramprakash.

Ramprakash, the former Middlesex captain, made the perfect entrance on his Surrey debut, looking relaxed and in total command as he put together the 52nd first-class hundred of his career. A model of timing and placement, it came off 231 balls with two sixes and 15 fours. But there was a less auspicious introduction for Giddins, new from Warwickshire, who along with Tudor conceded a century of runs while Kent's Fulton, Key and Walker became the 18th trio to score hundreds in a single Championship innings against Surrey. Surrey themselves had not achieved this feat since 1937, when Andy Sandham, Bob Gregory and Errol Holmes did so against Sussex at Hove. The century opening partnership between Fulton and Key was the first by any county against Surrey since Martyn Moxon and Ashley Metcalfe compiled 221 for Yorkshire at The Oval in 1992. Temperatures remained low throughout the match, which was called off an hour before the scheduled start of the final day after the outfield had become saturated.

Close of play: First day, Kent 176-0 (Fulton 86*, Key 88*); Second day, Surrey 86-1 (Ward 29*, Ramprakash 51*); Third day, Surrey 473.

Kent

D. P. Fulton c Salisbury b B. C. Hollioake	111
R. W. T. Key b Giddins	101
E. T. Smith c Batty b Giddins	2
M. J. Walker c Batty b Tudor	105
†P. A. Nixon c Ramprakash b A. J. Hollioake	22
M. A. Ealham lbw b Tudor	11
J. B. Hockley lbw b Salisbury	23
*M. V. Fleming not out	35
M. M. Patel b Salisbury	27
M. J. Saggers not out	7
B 1, l-b 11	12
1/198 2/204 3/253 4/294 5/316 6/379 7/385 8/425	(8 wkts dec.) 456

D. D. Masters did not bat.

Bonus points – Kent 5, Surrey 2 (Score at 130 overs: 401-7).

Bowling: Bicknell 20–1–76–0; Tudor 33–7–105–2; B. C. Hollioake 16–3–53–1; Giddins 32–7–103–2; Salisbury 24–4–72–2; Butcher 2–0–9–0; A. J. Hollioake 13–3–26–1.

Surrey

M. A. Butcher lbw b Saggers	0
I. J. Ward lbw b Ealham	70
M. R. Ramprakash b Patel	146
*A. J. Hollioake c Fulton b Saggers	49
A. D. Brown c Hockley b Patel	72
B. C. Hollioake run out	41
†J. N. Batty c Fleming b Patel	59
M. P. Bicknell c Masters b Ealham	19
A. J. Tudor c Hockley b Ealham	2
I. D. K. Salisbury c Fulton b Patel	0
E. S. H. Giddins not out	2
L-b 11, w 2	13
1/0 2/151 3/240 4/331 5/354 6/404 7/443 8/449 9/450	473

Bonus points – Surrey 5, Kent 3.

Bowling: Saggers 25–3–106–2; Masters 22–1–104–0; Ealham 24–5–80–3; Patel 38.3–7–117–4; Fleming 16–3–55–0.

Umpires: A. Clarkson and J. W. Lloyds.

At Manchester, April 25, 26, 27, 28. LANCASHIRE v SURREY. Abandoned.

At Northampton, May 9, 10, 11, 12. SURREY drew with NORTHAMPTONSHIRE.

SURREY v LEICESTERSHIRE

At The Oval, May 16, 17, 18, 19. Drawn. Surrey 7 pts, Leicestershire 8 pts. Toss: Leicestershire. Championship debut: T. J. Murtagh.

The loss of the first two days to the weather left both sides with little choice but to concentrate on salvaging bonus points. Leicestershire, indebted to Dakin's chunky half-century and to solid contributions from Burns and Crowe, fell four short of a second batting point. Dakin had pulled them round after Bicknell reduced his favourite opponents to a precarious 88 for six. In 2000, Bicknell had claimed 16 Leicestershire wickets at Guildford and another six at Oakham School. Now he added seven more, though in the first innings it was Giddins who ended with the better figures. Off-spinner Crowe, who gained some appreciable turn and took a career-best four for 47, and pace bowler Ormond, who also claimed four, denied the champions any batting points.

Close of play: First day, No play; Second day, No play; Third day, Surrey 46-0 (Butcher 21*, Shahid 19*).

Leicestershire

D. L. Maddy c Batty b Giddins	8	– c Batty b Bicknell	6
I. J. Sutcliffe lbw b Giddins	1	– c Batty b Bicknell	10
A. Habib c B. C. Hollioake b Bicknell	33	– c Batty b B. C. Hollioake	23
*B. F. Smith c Salisbury b Bicknell	28	– c Butcher b Bicknell	12
D. J. Marsh lbw b Bicknell	0	– c Batty b Murtagh	15
D. I. Stevens c B. C. Hollioake b Bicknell	0	– not out	17
†N. D. Burns c Brown b Salisbury	45	– not out	7
J. M. Dakin c Ramprakash b Giddins	69		
C. D. Crowe c B. C. Hollioake b Giddins	42		
J. Ormond c Batty b Giddins	5		
D. E. Malcolm not out	0		
B 4, l-b 9, n-b 2	15	L-b 2, w 2	4
1/6 2/15 3/70 4/75 5/75 6/88 7/147 8/239 9/242	246	1/6 2/25 3/37 4/70 5/74	(5 wkts dec.) 94

Bonus points – Leicestershire 1, Surrey 3.

Bowling: *First Innings*—Bicknell 21–5–61–4; Giddins 17.5–6–48–5; B. C. Hollioake 9–1–44–0; Murtagh 5–2–13–0; Butcher 2–0–15–0; Salisbury 15–1–42–1; A. J. Hollioake 9–4–10–0. *Second Innings*—Bicknell 7–0–25–3; Giddins 5–2–19–0; Murtagh 6–3–15–1; B. C. Hollioake 5–1–17–1; Brown 3–0–13–0; Ramprakash 2–0–3–0.

Surrey

M. A. Butcher run out	26
N. Shahid c Smith b Malcolm	19
M. R. Ramprakash lbw b Crowe	29
B. C. Hollioake b Crowe	30
A. D. Brown c Burns b Ormond	2
*A. J. Hollioake c Stevens b Crowe	5
†J. N. Batty b Ormond	9
M. P. Bicknell c Maddy b Ormond	16
I. D. K. Salisbury not out	36
T. J. Murtagh c Marsh b Crowe	2
E. S. H. Giddins b Ormond	5
B 5, l-b 4, w 2	11
1/46 2/63 3/108 4/113 5/115 6/121 7/132 8/153 9/158	190

Bonus points – Leicestershire 3.

Bowling: Ormond 25–10–55–4; Malcolm 18–3–61–1; Marsh 1–0–5–0; Dakin 2–0–13–0; Crowe 17–5–47–4.

Umpires: T. E. Jesty and D. R. Shepherd.

SURREY v ESSEX

At The Oval, May 25, 26, 27, 28. Drawn. Surrey 12 pts, Essex 10 pts. Toss: Surrey.

Tudor's maiden first-class hundred – he had come within a whisker two years earlier when, as night-watchman in the Edgbaston Test against New Zealand, he finished 99 not out – suggested he should be considered seriously as an all-rounder. In three and a half hours at the crease, he displayed patience as well as confident strokeplay, hitting one six and 16 fours. He and Stewart, with his first Championship century since 1997, added 206, a record seventh-wicket partnership for Surrey against Essex, exactly doubling the score. Essex owed more than half their total to Law, who batted over five and a half hours and hit 21 fours. Stewart, captain in place of the injured Adam Hollioake, raised eyebrows by not enforcing the follow-on and eventually set Essex 405 in four sessions. Helped by Saqlain Mushtaq's absence with the touring Pakistanis and three dropped catches, they hung on for a draw against Surrey's 11 England internationals, thanks to a six-hour hundred from Grayson and fifties by Law and Irani.

Close of play: First day, Surrey 393-6 (Stewart 97*, Tudor 96*); Second day, Essex 265-7 (Law 132*, Ilott 11*); Third day, Essex 73-0 (Prichard 32*, Grayson 30*).

Surrey

M. A. Butcher c Grayson b McGarry	52	– c Anderson b Such	72
I. J. Ward c Law b Anderson	43	– b McGarry	3
M. R. Ramprakash b Ilott	3	– st Foster b Such	52
G. P. Thorpe b Anderson	32		
A. D. Brown b Anderson	12	– st Foster b Such	33
*†A. J. Stewart b Anderson	106	– not out	24
B. C. Hollioake c Law b Ilott	31	– (4) c Foster b Such	0
A. J. Tudor c Prichard b Ilott	116	– (7) not out	18
I. D. K. Salisbury c Ilott b McGarry	26		
M. P. Bicknell b Irani	38		
E. S. H. Giddins not out	4		
B 4, l-b 11, n-b 20	35	L-b 2, w 2	4
1/76 2/85 3/129 4/151 5/160 6/206 7/412 8/434 9/472	498	1/20 2/120 3/120 4/141 5/176 (5 wkts dec.)	206

Bonus points – Surrey 5, Essex 3.

Bowling: *First Innings*—Ilott 33–7–127–3; Irani 13.4–2–47–1; Anderson 29–1–154–4; Such 24–4–65–0; McGarry 22–4–71–2; Grayson 7–1–19–0. *Second Innings*—Ilott 5–0–21–0; McGarry 10–2–41–1; Such 21–5–81–4; Anderson 9–1–33–0; Grayson 7–0–28–0.

Essex

P. J. Prichard c and b Bicknell	0	– c Stewart b Bicknell	34
A. P. Grayson c Ward b Giddins	37	– b Tudor	115
D. D. J. Robinson b Bicknell	7	– c Stewart b Bicknell	2
S. G. Law c and b Salisbury	153	– c Stewart b Salisbury	57
*R. C. Irani b Tudor	17	– not out	51
S. D. Peters lbw b Bicknell	23	– not out	22
†J. S. Foster b Giddins	4		
R. S. G. Anderson c Hollioake b Salisbury	8		
M. C. Ilott lbw b Bicknell	12		
P. M. Such not out	9		
A. C. McGarry c Hollioake b Salisbury	0		
B 8, l-b 6, w 6, n-b 10	30	B 3, l-b 12, w 4, n-b 12	31
1/8 2/22 3/74 4/105 5/152 6/196 7/229 8/277 9/300	300	1/78 2/80 3/183 4/256 (4 wkts)	312

Bonus points – Essex 3, Surrey 3.

Bowling: *First Innings*—Bicknell 29–8–65–4; Tudor 19–2–65–1; Giddins 25–7–69–2; Hollioake 7–1–39–0; Salisbury 12.4–1–46–3; Ramprakash 2–0–2–0. *Second Innings*—Bicknell 17–8–27–2; Tudor 19–5–53–1; Giddins 14–3–37–0; Ramprakash 35–11–56–0; Salisbury 38–10–106–1; Butcher 4–1–15–0; Brown 2–0–3–0.

Umpires: J. H. Evans and J. F. Steele.

At The Oval, May 30, 31, June 1 (not first-class). Surrey won by 231 runs. Toss: Surrey. Surrey 353 for seven dec. (M. A. Carberry 112, A. J. Hollioake 56, A. J. Tudor 41, J. N. Batty 40 not out, I. D. K. Salisbury 33; R. A. White three for 89) and 226 (M. A. Butcher 53, A. D. Brown 37, C. G. Greenidge 32; R. A. White five for 43); Loughborough UCCE 209 (J. D. Francis 33, C. P. Coleman 51; I. D. K. Salisbury five for 73) and 139 (R. A. White 38; C. G. Greenidge three for 37, A. J. Hollioake five for 29).

SURREY v SOMERSET

At The Oval, June 6, 7, 8, 9. Surrey won by six wickets. Surrey 20 pts, Somerset 7 pts. Toss: Somerset.

The brilliance of Ramprakash, who fell ten runs short of a second century in the match, dominated Surrey's first win in their title defence, a victory achieved despite the absence of Stewart, Thorpe, Brown and Ben Hollioake, with the England one-day squad. Ramprakash's first-innings 143 came from 247 balls with 18 fours, while his final-day 90 was a breathtaking display of strokeplay exemplified by a six and 14 fours in 99 balls. This was Ramprakash at his devastating and destructive best, the footwork flawless, the shot selection supreme. Spin accounted for 19 of the 34 wickets, and it was Dutch who lured Ramprakash into trying to repeat a straight six, only to be caught by Johnson at long-on – a dismissal reuniting three recent Middlesex colleagues. The opening day saw the continuing return to form of Lathwell, who was out in the penultimate over seeking a first hundred since missing all of the 1999 season with injury.

Close of play: First day, Somerset 260-6 (Blackwell 2*, Dutch 0*); Second day, Surrey 322-3 (Ramprakash 116*, Hollioake 19*); Third day, Somerset 190-8 (Johnson 17*, Jones 5*).

Somerset

*J. Cox c M. A. Butcher b Bicknell	26	– (2) lbw b Bicknell	15
P. C. L. Holloway c M. A. Butcher b Salisbury	15	– (1) c Bicknell b Giddins	11
M. Burns c Shahid b Hollioake	20	– lbw b Salisbury	42
P. D. Bowler b Amin	73	– c Batty b G. P. Butcher	10
M. N. Lathwell c M. A. Butcher b Amin	99	– c Shahid b Salisbury	13
†R. J. Turner b Amin	9	– c Ward b Salisbury	22
I. D. Blackwell b Bicknell	33	– c and b Salisbury	30
K. P. Dutch c Hollioake b Salisbury	10	– st Batty b Amin	2
R. L. Johnson b Bicknell	51	– c Batty b Bicknell	21
M. P. L. Bulbeck c Shahid b Bicknell	7	– (11) c and b Salisbury	9
P. S. Jones not out	15	– (10) not out	29
B 5, l-b 6, w 6, n-b 2	19	B 2, l-b 7, w 13, n-b 8	30
1/46 2/46 3/74 4/214 5/254 6/259 7/282 8/318 9/326	377	1/27 2/45 3/58 4/100 5/111 6/156 7/159 8/185 9/207	234

Bonus points – Somerset 4, Surrey 3 (Score at 130 overs: 377-9).

Bowling: *First Innings*—Bicknell 22.1–5–62–4; Giddins 20–3–82–0; Salisbury 45–9–115–2; G. P. Butcher 3–0–8–0; Hollioake 7–2–19–1; Amin 33–11–80–3. *Second Innings*—Bicknell 18–6–47–2; Giddins 8–3–25–1; Salisbury 35.2–7–95–5; G. P. Butcher 4–1–8–1; Amin 22–5–50–1.

Surrey

M. A. Butcher c Bowler b Dutch	76	– c Bowler b Dutch	24
I. J. Ward c Dutch b Jones	32	– c and b Dutch	24
M. R. Ramprakash b Jones	143	– c Johnson b Dutch	90
N. Shahid c Dutch b Johnson	65	– c Holloway b Blackwell	27
*A. J. Hollioake lbw b Jones	48	– not out	17
G. P. Butcher c Turner b Dutch	8	– not out	16
†J. N. Batty b Dutch	0		
M. P. Bicknell c Burns b Dutch	7		
I. D. K. Salisbury lbw b Johnson	6		
R. M. Amin lbw b Johnson	0		
E. S. H. Giddins not out	1		
L-b 13, w 2, n-b 2	17	B 4, l-b 4, w 4	12
1/76 2/155 3/274 4/365 5/382 6/386 7/388 8/399 9/399	403	1/41 2/106 3/166 4/182	(4 wkts) 210

Bonus points – Surrey 5, Somerset 3.

Bowling: *First Innings*—Bulbeck 8–0–42–0; Johnson 21–3–66–3; Jones 25–3–82–3; Blackwell 27–5–91–0; Dutch 29.1–5–96–4; Burns 4–0–13–0. *Second Innings*—Johnson 9–0–42–0; Jones 9–1–41–0; Dutch 18.3–5–55–3; Blackwell 13–2–64–1.

Umpires: A. A. Jones and J. W. Lloyds.

At Ilford, June 13, 14, 15, 16. SURREY drew with ESSEX.

SURREY v LANCASHIRE

At The Oval, June 29, 30, July 1, 2. Drawn. Surrey 8 pts, Lancashire 9 pts. Toss: Surrey.

Three nails protruding from the inside edge of Ramprakash's bat resulted in the ball being changed twice on the third day before the umpires took a closer interest. Two runs later he was out for 35, but the timing of his first-day half-century had already ensured an England recall for the first Ashes Test. Bicknell's three-hour 50 had been equally vital as Surrey struggled to combat Muralitharan. Not that Lancashire, Hegg excepted, fared much better against Saqlain Mushtaq, making his first Championship appearance of the season. Most observers reckoned the match would turn on which off-spinner prospered more; in fact, with the pitch becoming easier, neither did. Butcher batted with growing confidence to make his best score of the summer so far – only 86, but enough to get him an unexpected Test place at Edgbaston when Ramprakash and Vaughan were unfit. Surrey's decision to bat 17 overs into the final day, for just 35 runs, killed off Lancashire's interest in chasing a target. Crawley and Flintoff used up 41 overs while adding 81, and Crawley's defensive technique stood his side in good stead over four and a half hours.

Close of play: First day, Surrey 248; Second day, Surrey 0-0 (Butcher 0*, Ward 0*); Third day, Surrey 285-8 (Bicknell 11*, Salisbury 0*).

Surrey

M. A. Butcher c Lloyd b Martin	11	– c Hegg b Martin	86
I. J. Ward c Flintoff b Chapple	12	– c Hegg b Martin	18
M. R. Ramprakash b Martin	59	– c Scuderi b Keedy	35
*A. J. Hollioake lbw b Chapple	8	– b Muralitharan	73
A. D. Brown b Muralitharan	19	– c Haynes b Muralitharan	2
B. C. Hollioake lbw b Muralitharan	14	– c Hegg b Flintoff	10
†J. N. Batty c Haynes b Muralitharan	10	– run out	2
A. J. Tudor c Hegg b Flintoff	28	– c Crawley b Chapple	9
M. P. Bicknell b Muralitharan	50	– not out	26
I. D. K. Salisbury lbw b Muralitharan	23	– c Flintoff b Muralitharan	13
Saqlain Mushtaq not out	0	– not out	7
B 5, l-b 9	14	B 16, l-b 17, w 4, n-b 2	39
1/16 2/34 3/44 4/91 5/125 6/133 7/141 8/175 9/237	248	1/39 2/130 3/182 4/187 5/222 6/229 7/261 8/281 9/303 (9 wkts dec.)	320

Bonus points – Surrey 1, Lancashire 3.

Bowling: *First Innings*—Martin 19–3–56–2; Chapple 15–2–45–2; Muralitharan 39.4–12–81–5; Flintoff 15–2–31–1; Keedy 7–4–16–0; Scuderi 4–1–5–0. *Second Innings*—Martin 20.5–5–58–2; Chapple 9–0–45–1; Muralitharan 55–23–72–3; Flintoff 18–6–44–1; Keedy 19–0–68–1.

Lancashire

J. J. Haynes lbw b Saqlain Mushtaq	57	– c Butcher b Tudor	9
*J. P. Crawley lbw b Bicknell	43	– not out	84
A. Flintoff c Butcher b Tudor	40	– lbw b Saqlain Mushtaq	34
N. H. Fairbrother c Ramprakash b Saqlain Mushtaq	1	– not out	26
J. C. Scuderi c Butcher b Saqlain Mushtaq	3		
G. D. Lloyd c B. C. Hollioake b Tudor	3		
†W. K. Hegg not out	74		
G. Chapple c A. J. Hollioake b Saqlain Mushtaq	6		
P. J. Martin c A. J. Hollioake b Salisbury	11		
G. Keedy b Saqlain Mushtaq	0		
M. Muralitharan c Salisbury b Saqlain Mushtaq	9		
B 7, l-b 6, w 6, n-b 10	29	B 4, l-b 7, n-b 6	17
1/110 2/112 3/139 4/150 5/155 6/172 7/209 8/239 9/248	276	1/23 2/104 (2 wkts)	170

Bonus points – Lancashire 2, Surrey 3.

Bowling: *First Innings*—Bicknell 20–4–80–1; Tudor 15–6–36–2; B. C. Hollioake 6–2–17–0; Saqlain Mushtaq 36.3–7–89–6; Salisbury 18–3–41–1. *Second Innings*—Bicknell 13–4–23–0; Tudor 12–2–48–1; Saqlain Mushtaq 28–9–44–1; Salisbury 16–3–36–0; A. J. Hollioake 2–0–8–0.

Umpires: M. R. Benson and R. Palmer.

At Leicester, July 4, 5, 6, 7. SURREY drew with LEICESTERSHIRE.

SURREY v NORTHAMPTONSHIRE

At Guildford, July 18, 19, 20. Surrey won by an innings and 55 runs. Surrey 19 pts, Northamptonshire 3 pts. Toss: Northamptonshire.

This may have been only the second win in Surrey's defence of their Championship title, but it was certainly impressive. That's more than can be said for Northamptonshire's batting. True, the pitch provided steep bounce, which Tudor exploited well after lunch on the opening day: having conceded 51 runs, including three sixes, he then took five for three in 31 balls. But for Northamptonshire to lose seven wickets for five runs was a poor effort, and Surrey's Brown put it in context by making a gritty, responsible hundred despite a broken thumb – the legacy of an attempted slip catch. The Surrey lead was eventually 248, and Bicknell's five wickets before the close of the second day left Northamptonshire without an escape route. His line was immaculate, his length and movement probing and disconcerting; when, on the third morning, he took the next two wickets, he looked good for all ten. It wasn't to be, but 19 points and a day and a half off were satisfactory compensation.

Close of play: First day, Surrey 209-5 (Brown 55*); Second day, Northamptonshire 99-5 (Bailey 4*, Swann 6*).

Northamptonshire

M. E. K. Hussey c Batty b Giddins	15	– c Batty b Bicknell	41
A. S. Rollins c Giddins b Bicknell	38	– c Batty b Bicknell	14
M. B. Loye run out	21	– c Tudor b Bicknell	14
R. J. Warren c Carberry b Giddins	3	– c Carberry b Bicknell	0
A. L. Penberthy c Batty b Tudor	19	– c Batty b Bicknell	5
T. M. B. Bailey c B. C. Hollioake b Tudor	3	– c Batty b Bicknell	8
G. P. Swann c Shahid b Tudor	0	– c Carberry b Giddins	41
*†D. Ripley b Tudor	1	– c sub b Bicknell	11
J. P. Taylor c Bicknell b Giddins	0	– c Batty b B. C. Hollioake	16
M. R. Strong c Batty b Tudor	0	– not out	12
J. F. Brown not out	0	– b Tudor	5
B 1, l-b 9, n-b 10	20	B 5, l-b 8, w 5, n-b 8	26
1/62 2/70 3/80 4/115 5/115 6/116 7/119 8/120 9/120	120	1/21 2/80 3/80 4/87 5/92 6/115 7/147 8/151 9/176	193

Bonus points – Surrey 3.

Bowling: *First Innings*—Bicknell 11–2–23–1; Tudor 13–3–54–5; Giddins 17–9–18–3; Saqlain Mushtaq 3–0–15–0. *Second Innings*—Bicknell 21–6–60–7; Tudor 13.2–5–38–1; Giddins 15–3–44–1; Saqlain Mushtaq 5–2–8–0; Salisbury 1–0–7–0; B. C. Hollioake 6–1–23–1.

Surrey

†J. N. Batty lbw b Strong	39
M. A. Carberry c Ripley b Strong	46
N. Shahid c Penberthy b Strong	4
*A. J. Hollioake c Ripley b Taylor	47
A. D. Brown c Penberthy b Brown	103
B. C. Hollioake c Hussey b Brown	11
A. J. Tudor c Bailey b Brown	35
M. P. Bicknell c Taylor b Brown	18
I. D. K. Salisbury not out	42
Saqlain Mushtaq c Hussey b Penberthy	4
E. S. H. Giddins c and b Penberthy	8
L-b 7, w 4	11
1/78 2/86 3/97 4/178 5/209 6/269 7/297 8/319 9/352	368

Bonus points – Surrey 4, Northamptonshire 3.

Bowling: Taylor 22–3–82–1; Strong 27–5–104–3; Penberthy 19.5–0–75–2; Hussey 2–0–9–0; Brown 28–6–91–4.

Umpires: D. J. Constant and N. G. Cowley.

At Leeds, August 1, 2, 3, 4. SURREY drew with YORKSHIRE.

SURREY v GLAMORGAN

At The Oval, August 8, 9, 10, 11. Glamorgan won by three wickets. Glamorgan 16 pts, Surrey 4.5 pts. Toss: Surrey.

Other than Butcher carrying his bat, for the second time in four years, and Bicknell's eleven-wicket return, Surrey were poor value in their first defeat at The Oval since 1998. Some of their batting was careless beyond belief. Yet they looked to have the game in hand when Glamorgan were 83 for six early on the third day, the second having been washed out. Instead, Wallace had some luck and, through a dogged stand of 94 with Darren Thomas, kept the visitors in contention. Bicknell finished with six for 69, reaching 50 first-class wickets for the tenth time in 16 seasons, but Surrey's lead was only 58 and they soon threw that advantage away. Butcher, having survived 215 balls – and a catch to third slip on 79 – in his first-innings 145, was out to his sixth delivery second time round. With the ball still seaming about, 200 was never going to be a straightforward target for Glamorgan, particularly once Bicknell checked their advance with four middle-order wickets in seven balls. Once again, though, Wallace was equal to the crisis, and he found an equally unflustered ally in Davies. The last 35 runs came at almost a run a minute, leaving Surrey seven balls adrift of the required over-rate.

Close of play: First day, Glamorgan 64-2 (Maynard 28*, Powell 15*); Second day, No play; Third day, Surrey 129-7 (Bicknell 25*, Salisbury 19*).

Surrey

M. A. Butcher not out	145	– c Dale b Jones	2
I. J. Ward c S. D. Thomas b Watkin	3	– c Powell b S. D. Thomas	24
M. R. Ramprakash c Wallace b Davies	19	– c Wallace b Jones	0
B. C. Hollioake c Dale b S. D. Thomas	0	– c Wallace b Watkin	15
A. D. Brown lbw b S. D. Thomas	0	– c Davies b Watkin	1
†A. J. Stewart c and b Dale	26	– (7) c Wallace b Davies	8
A. J. Tudor c Wallace b Jones	27	– (6) c I. J. Thomas b Davies	29
*M. P. Bicknell b S. D. Thomas	11	– c Maynard b Watkin	29
I. D. K. Salisbury c Powell b Davies	17	– c Maher b Watkin	19
Saqlain Mushtaq c Wallace b Croft	10	– c Wallace b Jones	4
E. S. H. Giddins c Croft b Davies	1	– not out	2
B 4, l-b 8, w 8, n-b 2	22	B 5, l-b 3	8
1/19 2/65 3/66 4/70 5/115 6/178 7/210 8/245 9/275	281	1/3 2/7 3/42 4/48 5/48 6/74 7/95 8/134 9/139	141

Bonus points – Surrey 2, Glamorgan 3.

Bowling: *First Innings*—Watkin 17–4–53–1; Jones 16–2–52–1; S. D. Thomas 15–0–69–3; Davies 18–4–76–3; Dale 4–1–15–1; Croft 5–2–4–1. *Second Innings*—Watkin 17.5–6–28–4; Jones 16–6–36–3; S. D. Thomas 6–2–29–1; Davies 7–1–24–2; Croft 4–1–16–0.

Glamorgan

I. J. Thomas b Bicknell	13	– c Giddins b Saqlain Mushtaq	59
J. P. Maher c Hollioake b Bicknell	6	– lbw b Bicknell	2
M. P. Maynard lbw b Bicknell	31	– lbw b Giddins	14
M. J. Powell c Stewart b Tudor	24	– c Stewart b Bicknell	51
*A. Dale c Hollioake b Bicknell	5	– c Stewart b Bicknell	15
R. D. B. Croft c Stewart b Bicknell	0	– lbw b Bicknell	0
†M. A. Wallace not out	63	– not out	18
S. D. Thomas b Tudor	57	– c Hollioake b Bicknell	0
A. P. Davies c Stewart b Bicknell	0	– not out	16
S. L. Watkin lbw b Saqlain Mushtaq	8		
S. P. Jones b Saqlain Mushtaq	4		
B 3, l-b 5, w 2, n-b 2	12	B 2, l-b 8, n-b 16	26
1/21 2/22 3/69 4/79 5/79 6/83 7/177 8/188 9/207	223	1/5 2/52 3/101 4/163 5/163 6/166 7/166	(7 wkts) 201

Bonus points – Glamorgan 1, Surrey 3.

Bowling: *First Innings*—Bicknell 24–9–69–6; Tudor 20–4–74–2; Giddins 7–2–30–0; Saqlain Mushtaq 14.3–4–21–2; Salisbury 5–2–11–0; Hollioake 3–1–10–0. *Second Innings*—Bicknell 18–4–48–5; Tudor 8–1–40–0; Giddins 10–2–44–1; Saqlain Mushtaq 11.2–1–38–1; Salisbury 8–1–21–0.

Umpires: D. R. Shepherd and R. A. White.

At Canterbury, August 16, 17, 18, 19. SURREY drew with KENT.

At Taunton, August 23, 24, 25, 26. SURREY drew with SOMERSET.

SURREY v YORKSHIRE

At The Oval, September 5, 6, 7, 8. Surrey won by an innings and 46 runs. Surrey 20 pts, Yorkshire 3 pts. Toss: Yorkshire.

Satisfying as it was to beat their successors as champions, Surrey rejoiced more in the maximum points that diminished the prospect of relegation. Yorkshire, after all, had treated this game more as a trial, and fielded only four capped players. One of them, McGrath, batted almost five hours for his only century of the summer, albeit needing support from the tail to get there. Butcher and Ward then sent Surrey off in style with an even-time 164, and off-spinner Gray's three wickets in ten balls on the second evening held more long-term promise than immediate influence once Ben Hollioake and Ramprakash had embarked on a double-hundred partnership replete with quality, often elegant, strokeplay. Both hit centuries: Hollioake's, containing 16 fours and three sixes, was his first in his six seasons of Championship cricket. From the way Vaughan and McGrath saw Yorkshire to the third-day close with a century stand of their own, there was a chance Surrey would not have everything their own way. But they added only 24 next morning before Bicknell intervened, whereupon Saqlain Mushtaq put the young pretenders to flight by taking six of the last seven wickets in 49 balls.

Close of play: First day, Yorkshire 179-5 (McGrath 69*, Dawson 2*); Second day, Surrey 291-5 (Ramprakash 53*, B. C. Hollioake 43*); Third day, Yorkshire 171-2 (Vaughan 55*, McGrath 52*).

Yorkshire

C. R. Taylor lbw b Bicknell	7	– c A. J. Hollioake b Saqlain Mushtaq	18
M. J. Wood c Butcher b Bicknell	51	– b Bicknell	27
M. P. Vaughan c A. J. Hollioake b Giddins	11	– c B. C. Hollioake b Saqlain Mushtaq	61
A. McGrath not out	116	– c Stewart b Bicknell	73
V. J. Craven lbw b Bicknell	0	– c Stewart b Saqlain Mushtaq	7
*D. Byas b Salisbury	24	– c and b Saqlain Mushtaq	4
R. K. J. Dawson c Stewart b Salisbury	2	– c Butcher b Saqlain Mushtaq	1
A. K. D. Gray c Ward b Salisbury	3	– c Brown b Bicknell	1
†S. M. Guy c A. J. Hollioake b Saqlain Mushtaq	0	– not out	12
S. P. Kirby lbw b Saqlain Mushtaq	2	– b Saqlain Mushtaq	0
M. J. Hoggard lbw b Salisbury	0	– st Stewart b Saqlain Mushtaq	2
B 1, l-b 10, w 4, n-b 4	19	B 1, l-b 16, w 10, n-b 2	29
1/34 2/64 3/99 4/99 5/167 6/179 7/197 8/208 9/234	235	1/57 2/65 3/195 4/207 5/208 6/212 7/217 8/223 9/223	235

Bonus points – Yorkshire 1, Surrey 3.

Bowling: *First Innings*—Bicknell 16–2–43–3; Giddins 19–6–42–1; Saqlain Mushtaq 48–17–70–2; B. C. Hollioake 6–2–20–0; Salisbury 25.4–5–49–4. *Second Innings*—Bicknell 26–9–83–3; Giddins 6–0–21–0; B. C. Hollioake 2–0–4–0; Saqlain Mushtaq 25.4–8–58–7; Salisbury 10–1–52–0.

Surrey

M. A. Butcher c Byas b McGrath 90
I. J. Ward lbw b Hoggard. 63
M. R. Ramprakash b Gray 131
*A. J. Hollioake c Craven b Gray 18
A. D. Brown c and b Gray. 2
†A. J. Stewart b Gray 0
B. C. Hollioake b McGrath 118
M. P. Bicknell b Hoggard 36
I. D. K. Salisbury c and b Kirby 11
Saqlain Mushtaq not out 11

B 7, l-b 15, w 4, n-b 10. 36

1/164 2/171 3/208 4/222 5/222 6/437 7/494 8/498 9/516 (9 wkts dec.) 516

E. S. H. Giddins did not bat.

Bonus points – Surrey 5, Yorkshire 2 (Score at 130 overs: 514-8).

Bowling: Hoggard 30–5–99–2; Kirby 21.4–1–104–1; Dawson 22–7–94–0; Craven 10–1–47–0; Gray 39–7–128–4; McGrath 8–4–22–2.

Umpires: G. I. Burgess and T. E. Jesty.

At Cardiff, September 12, 13, 14, 15. SURREY drew with GLAMORGAN.

DATES OF FORMATION OF FIRST-CLASS COUNTIES

		Present Club		
County	*First known organisation*	*Original date*	*Reorganisation, if substantial*	*First-class status from*
Derbyshire	1870	1870	–	1871
Durham	1874	1882	1991	1992
Essex	By 1790	1876	–	1895
Glamorgan	1861	1888	–	1921
Gloucestershire	1863	1871	–	1870
Hampshire	1849	1863	1879	1864
Kent	1842	1859	1870	1864
Lancashire	1864	1864	–	1865
Leicestershire	By 1820	1879	–	1895
Middlesex	1863	1864	–	1864
Northamptonshire	1820†	1878	–	1905
Nottinghamshire	1841	1841	1866	1864
Somerset	1864	1875	–	1882
Surrey	1845	1845	–	1864
Sussex	1836	1839	1857	1864
Warwickshire	1826	1882	–	1895
Worcestershire	1844	1865	–	1899
Yorkshire	1861	1863	1891	1864

Note: Derbyshire lost first-class status from 1888 to 1894, Hampshire between 1886 and 1894 and Somerset between 1886 and 1890.

† *Town club.*

Richard Montgomerie

SUSSEX

President: 2001 – The Duke of Richmond & Gordon
2002 – The Rt Rev. Lord Sheppard

Chairman: D. G. Trangmar

Chief Executive: 2001 – D. R. Gilbert

Captain: C. J. Adams

Cricket Manager and Senior Coach: P. Moores

Head Groundsman: D. J. Traill

Scorer: 2001 – L. V. Chandler
2002 – J. Hartridge

The wheel turned full circle for Sussex in 2001. Twelve months after a two-day defeat by Gloucestershire condemned them to the Championship wooden spoon, they beat the same opponents in three days to secure the Division Two title. Fittingly, Murray Goodwin, one of the stars of an unforgettable summer at Hove, hit the runs that completed a ten-wicket win. If Sussex supporters were reluctant to drag themselves away on a sunny afternoon, it was entirely understandable. The county's five previous titles had come in one-day competitions; this success, while hardly ranking alongside Yorkshire's in Division One, deserved to be savoured.

No one enjoyed it more than Chris Adams. A year earlier, his future as captain was under scrutiny when Sussex capitulated in the closing weeks, having gone into August as second division leaders. They were similarly placed in 2001, but this time there was no loss of form or focus. What shone through was the tremendous team spirit and work ethic fostered by Adams and coach Peter Moores, evident even during the pre-season training in Grenada. These two knew their side was capable of success if the batsmen supported one of the best seam attacks around, and so it proved.

Goodwin, who had retired from Test cricket after Zimbabwe's tour of England in 2000, was an inspired choice as overseas player, scoring 2,465 runs in all cricket including eight centuries, a phenomenal performance by someone reluctantly agreeing to open in the absence of a specialist. Moreover, he brought out the best in opening partner Richard Montgomerie, whose 2,554 runs included 1,704 in first-class matches with eight hundreds. Among their six century partnerships was an unbroken 372 at Trent Bridge, the third-highest for any Sussex wicket, and it was hardly surprising that Goodwin was given a further two-year contract.

Adams, despite missing two Championship games early in the season, passed 1,000 runs for the second time in his four seasons with Sussex, and it certainly assisted the development of younger players that the top order established strong foundations on a regular basis. With Tony Cottey sidelined because of tennis elbow, Sussex had no alternative but to invest in youth. Matt Prior appeared to solve the problem of too few runs from the wicket-keeper, yet still found his place under threat from another talented teenager in Australian-born Tim Ambrose. Bas Zuiderent, without a Championship game in his first three years, and the hard-working left-hander, Michael Yardy, both made substantial contributions, while champagne corks were popping in the press box during the Championship-deciding game when Robin Martin-Jenkins made his maiden first-class hundred, to the obvious delight of his father, Christopher, *The Times's* cricket correspondent.

Victory over Worcestershire at Horsham proved to be the catalyst. It was the first of five Championship wins in six games and, although momentum was briefly lost by defeat at Cheltenham and later at home to Durham, promotion was secured at Edgbaston in the penultimate game. James Kirtley's match-winning performance against Gloucestershire, ten for 93 and an unbeaten half-century, helped guarantee the title and closed an outstanding personal season, capped by selection for England's one-day series in Zimbabwe. Doubts over his bowling action resurfaced there, but Kirtley, who had been cleared by the ECB in 2000, was confident he would be allowed to continue his international career. The country's leading first-class wicket-taker with 75, he claimed 102 in all cricket, the second time he had reached 100 wickets in a season.

He again had a useful foil in left-armer Jason Lewry, whose seven for 42 in a two-day win over Hampshire included his second hat-trick, and the first for 20 years by a Sussex bowler at Hove. But the unsung hero was undoubtedly Mark Robinson, who in his final season, before taking up a coaching appointment with the club, took 50 first-class wickets for only the second time, finishing with 56 at an impressive 19.33. Although pitches didn't offer them much assistance, spinners Mark Davis and Umer Rashid chipped in with a combined 35 wickets, as well as making useful lower-order runs; in Rashid's case, that included a century against Durham. Martin-Jenkins was restricted to nine first-class games by a side strain, though he took vital wickets on his return, and concern over the depth of their seam bowling led Sussex to sign left-armer Paul Hutchison from Yorkshire.

Martin-Jenkins's absence clearly affected the balance of the one-day side, even if the performances of Ambrose, Billy Taylor and all-rounder Carl Hopkinson bode well for the future. After winning their Benson and Hedges group, Sussex were outplayed by Surrey in the quarter-finals and, despite winning four of their last five League games, had to settle for fifth in Division Two.

After four years in which he helped transform the administrative and commercial side of the club, chief executive David Gilbert returned to Sydney to take up a similar appointment with New South Wales. Another departure, after 20 years' sterling service, was first-team scorer Len Chandler. The new chief executive's challenge will be to oversee the long-overdue redevelopment of facilities at Hove. Planning permission has been received for a new indoor school on the site of the old squash club, and this will also be the home of a youth academy, launched in November with Keith Greenfield as its first director. Redevelopment of the team, which began in 1997, has borne fruit, but Sussex are well aware they face an even more difficult task in establishing themselves as a first-division county. – ANDY ARLIDGE.

SUSSEX 2001

[*Roger Ockenden*

Back row: S. Osborne (*First Eleven physiotherapist*), J. Carmichael (*Second Eleven physiotherapist*), P. M. R. Havell, J. R. Carpenter, B. V. Taylor, B. Zuiderent, U. B. A. Rashid. *Middle row:* N. J. Wilton, M. J. G. Davis, M. J. Prior, T. R. Ambrose, W. J. House, D. A. Clapp, M. H. Yardy. *Front row:* J. D. Lewry, R. S. C. Martin-Jenkins, K. Greenfield (*Second Eleven coach*), R. J. Kirtley, P. Moores (*First Eleven coach*), C. J. Adams (*captain*), M. W. Goodwin, P. A. Cottey, R. R. Montgomerie, M. A. Robinson.

SUSSEX RESULTS

All first-class matches – Played 18: Won 9, Lost 4, Drawn 5.

County Championship matches – Played 16: Won 9, Lost 3, Drawn 4.

CricInfo County Championship, winners in Division 2;
Cheltenham & Gloucester Trophy, 4th round;
Benson and Hedges Cup, q-f; Norwich Union League, 5th in Division 2.

COUNTY CHAMPIONSHIP AVERAGES

BATTING

Cap		*M*	*I*	*NO*	*R*	*HS*	*100s*	*50s*	*Avge*	*Ct/St*
2001	M. W. Goodwin§.	16	30	4	1,521	203*	6	5	58.50	8
1999	R. R. Montgomerie . . .	16	30	3	1,461	160*	7	4	54.11	16
1998	C. J. Adams	14	22	1	1,020	192	3	6	48.57	27
2000	R. S. C. Martin-Jenkins	9	15	4	524	113	1	3	47.63	4
	M. H. Yardy.	15	26	4	741	87*	0	5	33.68	9
	M. J. G. Davis	14	21	4	438	52	0	1	25.76	5
	B. Zuiderent.	15	25	1	613	122	1	3	25.54	17
	W. J. House	2	4	0	80	46	0	0	20.00	1
	M. J. Prior.	15	24	2	433	66	0	1	19.68	39/2
	U. B. A. Rashid	12	19	0	360	106	1	0	18.94	0
1996	J. D. Lewry†	15	18	4	202	47	0	0	14.42	7
1998	R. J. Kirtley†	16	24	6	196	51*	0	1	10.88	8
1997	M. A. Robinson	12	15	7	32	10	0	0	4.00	1

Also batted: T. R. Ambrose (2 matches) 26, 52, 14 (3 ct); P. A. Cottey (cap 1999) (1 match) 46, 4* (1 ct); B. V. Taylor (2 matches) 11, 0, 24*.

* *Signifies not out.* † *Born in Sussex.* § *Overseas player.*

BOWLING

	O	*M*	*R*	*W*	*BB*	*5W/i*	*Avge*
C. J. Adams	40.2	6	111	10	4-28	0	11.10
M. A. Robinson	392.4	120	978	54	5-35	3	18.11
R. J. Kirtley	566.3	135	1,749	75	6-34	5	23.32
J. D. Lewry	489.1	123	1,465	57	7-42	3	25.70
R. S. C. Martin-Jenkins	248	63	764	24	4-18	0	31.83
U. B. A. Rashid	120.2	37	333	10	4-9	0	33.30
M. J. G. Davis	337.3	81	900	23	6-116	1	39.13

Also bowled: M. W. Goodwin 13–3–40–0; R. R. Montgomerie 5–1–11–1; B. V. Taylor 38.5–17–95–5; M. H. Yardy 21–6–53–1.

COUNTY RECORDS

Highest score for:	333	K. S. Duleepsinhji v Northamptonshire at Hove . .	1930
Highest score against:	322	E. Paynter (Lancashire) at Hove	1937
Best bowling for:	10-48	C. H. G. Bland v Kent at Tonbridge	1899
Best bowling against:	9-11	A. P. Freeman (Kent) at Hove.	1922
Highest total for:	705-8 dec.	v Surrey at Hastings	1902
Highest total against:	726	by Nottinghamshire at Nottingham	1895
Lowest total for:	19	v Surrey at Godalming	1830
	19	v Nottinghamshire at Hove	1873
Lowest total against:	18	by Kent at Gravesend	1867

At Worcester, April 25, 26, 27, 28. SUSSEX drew with WORCESTERSHIRE.

SUSSEX v NOTTINGHAMSHIRE

At Hove, May 9, 10, 11, 12. Sussex won by 162 runs. Sussex 19 pts, Nottinghamshire 5 pts. Toss: Sussex. Championship debut: M. J. G. Davis.

An inept second-innings display by Nottinghamshire on a blameless pitch gave Sussex their first home Championship win for almost a year. An hour into the final morning, Kirtley, captaining Sussex in place of the injured Adams, declared 370 ahead. And when he removed Blewett first ball after lunch to leave Nottinghamshire 45 for four, the result seemed beyond doubt. Johnson, however, held things together with customary cussedness before running out of partners; Lewry finished with match figures of nine for 160. On the opening day, Zuiderent picked Sussex up from 15 for two, sharing stands of 92 with Yardy, 102 with House and 74 with Martin-Jenkins. His maiden first-class hundred came two days after his first in one-day cricket, and included 18 boundaries. There were useful contributions throughout Nottinghamshire's reply, though no one could get the measure of Lewry, who consistently swung the ball off an attacking length. Yardy, with a maiden first-class fifty, and Montgomerie extended Sussex's lead with a century stand, but Smith, left-arm like Lewry and taking ten wickets in a match for the first time, made everyone work hard to set up the declaration.

Close of play: First day, Sussex 316-5 (Zuiderent 122*, Martin-Jenkins 38*); Second day, Nottinghamshire 214-4 (Johnson 35*, Pietersen 36*); Third day, Sussex 237-5 (Rashid 13*, Martin-Jenkins 22*).

Sussex

R. R. Montgomerie b Smith	0	– c Read b Smith	66
M. W. Goodwin lbw b Smith	9	– c Read b Smith	2
M. H. Yardy c Afzaal b Smith	36	– c Read b Blewett	68
B. Zuiderent c Blewett b Smith	122	– b Afzaal	22
W. J. House c Read b Afzaal	46	– b Smith	0
U. B. A. Rashid run out	19	– c Read b Smith	23
R. S. C. Martin-Jenkins c Millns b Franks	55	– c Clough b Afzaal	28
†M. J. Prior c Read b Franks	1	– c Blewett b Smith	11
M. J. G. Davis c Smith b Millns	42	– not out	14
*R. J. Kirtley c Pietersen b Smith	8	– not out	8
J. D. Lewry not out	0		
B 8, l-b 24, w 20, n-b 14	66	B 5, l-b 21, w 18, n-b 12	56
1/0 2/15 3/107 4/209 5/242 6/316 7/323 8/365 9/393	404	1/5 2/133 3/182 4/190 5/194 6/250 7/260 8/279 (8 wkts dec.)	298

Bonus points – Sussex 4, Nottinghamshire 2 (Score at 130 overs: 373-8).

Bowling: *First Innings*—Smith 36–13–64–5; Franks 36–8–95–2; Millns 22.1–3–69–1; Clough 7–1–23–0; Pietersen 24–7–52–0; Blewett 8–0–34–0; Afzaal 12–0–35–1. *Second Innings*—Smith 18–5–37–5; Franks 14–3–47–0; Millns 3–1–18–0; Pietersen 5–2–21–0; Afzaal 30–6–115–2; Blewett 8–0–34–1.

Nottinghamshire

*D. J. Bicknell c Zuiderent b Martin-Jenkins	14	– c Prior b Lewry	17
G. E. Welton c and b Lewry	30	– b Kirtley	3
G. S. Blewett c Prior b Kirtley	49	– c Prior b Kirtley	12
U. Afzaal c Montgomerie b Martin-Jenkins	29	– lbw b Kirtley	5
P. Johnson b Lewry	43	– not out	88
K. P. Pietersen c Goodwin b Davis	51	– c Prior b Lewry	13
†C. M. W. Read c Kirtley b Lewry	50	– lbw b Kirtley	4
P. J. Franks st Prior b Davis	13	– lbw b Martin-Jenkins	24
G. D. Clough b Lewry	2	– lbw b Martin-Jenkins	0
D. J. Millns not out	3	– lbw b Lewry	4
G. J. Smith c Prior b Lewry	3	– b Lewry	20
B 4, l-b 5, n-b 36	45	L-b 5, w 3, n-b 10	18
1/28 2/82 3/127 4/148 5/230 6/267 7/310 8/319 9/320	332	1/24 2/24 3/32 4/45 5/62 6/67 7/130 8/130 9/156	208

Bonus points – Nottinghamshire 3, Sussex 3.

Bowling: *First Innings*—Lewry 24.2–4–95–5; Kirtley 21–2–85–1; Martin-Jenkins 19–3–66–2; Davis 25–5–64–2; Rashid 2–0–13–0. *Second Innings*—Lewry 15.3–2–65–4; Kirtley 14–2–50–4; Martin-Jenkins 11–2–42–2; Rashid 10–2–23–0; Davis 2–0–23–0.

Umpires: J. W. Lloyds and G. Sharp.

At Cambridge, May 16, 17, 18. SUSSEX drew with CAMBRIDGE UCCE.

SUSSEX v WARWICKSHIRE

At Hove, May 25, 26, 27, 28. Warwickshire won by eight wickets. Warwickshire 19 pts, Sussex 3 pts. Toss: Warwickshire. County debut: N. M. Carter.

Warwickshire extended their Championship sequence at Hove to five wins, though they were lucky to have the best of the conditions, batting in warm sunshine then bowling once a sea fret had freshened the pitch. They were also aided by some poor Sussex out-cricket on the first day. Powell was dropped three times in the thirties before, timing his drives with increasing confidence, he put down the foundations on which Wagh and the belligerent Brown built. Sussex fought back well to deny Warwickshire a fifth bonus point and take the last seven wickets for 100, but their own batting collapsed even more feebly as the mists rolled in. Following on, they resisted into the fourth morning through Montgomerie's first century of the season and a promising contribution by Prior. Spin rather than seam was causing the problems now: Wagh, required to remodel his action in the close season, claimed three wickets, and Davis took a consolation two in three balls for Sussex as Warwickshire eased to victory with almost two sessions to spare.

Close of play: First day, Warwickshire 281-3 (Wagh 78*, Ostler 17*); Second day, Sussex 151-6 (Martin-Jenkins 17*, Kirtley 2*); Third day, Sussex 197-6 (Montgomerie 96*, Prior 9*).

Warwickshire

*M. J. Powell c Goodwin b Lewry	93	– c Kirtley b Davis	11
N. V. Knight lbw b Kirtley	46	– b Davis	26
M. A. Wagh c Prior b Lewry	90	– not out	20
D. L. Hemp c Prior b Martin-Jenkins	30	– not out	4
D. P. Ostler b Lewry	22		
D. R. Brown b Rashid	63		
N. M. K. Smith c Prior b Lewry	19		
†K. J. Piper b Rashid	2		
V. C. Drakes not out	3		
M. M. Betts c Zuiderent b Davis	2		
N. M. Carter c Yardy b Davis	2		
B 5, l-b 4, w 4, n-b 10	23	B 8, l-b 1	9
1/115 2/164 3/202 4/295 5/298 6/362 7/383 8/388 9/393	395	1/35 2/37	(2 wkts) 70

Bonus points – Warwickshire 4, Sussex 2 (Score at 130 overs: 362-6).

Bowling: *First Innings*—Lewry 32–10–101–4; Kirtley 33–13–82–1; Martin-Jenkins 29–7–89–1; Davis 35–11–66–2; Yardy 4–1–17–0; Rashid 13–6–20–2; Adams 2–0–11–0. *Second Innings*—Lewry 6–1–18–0; Kirtley 3–0–13–0; Davis 6.3–2–20–2; Rashid 4–1–10–0.

Sussex

R. R. Montgomerie c Piper b Brown	36	– (2) b Smith	116
M. W. Goodwin c Piper b Drakes	0	– (1) lbw b Betts	4
M. H. Yardy b Carter	39	– c Piper b Drakes	5
B. Zuiderent lbw b Betts	4	– c Wagh b Smith	33
*C. J. Adams c Ostler b Betts	4	– lbw b Smith	17
U. B. A. Rashid c Carter b Wagh	22	– c Piper b Drakes	13
R. S. C. Martin-Jenkins not out	42	– c Piper b Wagh	11
R. J. Kirtley c Ostler b Drakes	2	– (10) c Hemp b Wagh	5
†M. J. Prior c Piper b Drakes	0	– (8) lbw b Smith	35
M. J. G. Davis c Betts b Smith	6	– (9) c Ostler b Wagh	1
J. D. Lewry c Betts b Smith	7	– not out	2
L-b 12, n-b 34	46	B 3, n-b 8	11
1/1 2/81 3/100 4/104 5/124 6/133 7/163 8/165 9/194	208	1/15 2/24 3/107 4/135 5/154 6/182 7/226 8/239 9/249	253

Bonus points – Sussex 1, Warwickshire 3.

Bowling: *First Innings*—Drakes 14–4–45–3; Betts 20–8–35–2; Brown 22–10–33–1; Carter 6–0–50–1; Smith 17–5–29–2; Wagh 4–1–4–1. *Second Innings*—Drakes 27–6–55–2; Betts 18–6–47–1; Brown 10–2–25–0; Carter 4–1–18–0; Smith 34–6–76–4; Wagh 14–2–29–3.

Umpires: B. Leadbeater and R. Palmer.

At Southampton, May 30, 31, June 1, 2. SUSSEX drew with HAMPSHIRE.

SUSSEX v WORCESTERSHIRE

At Horsham, June 6, 7, 8, 9. Sussex won by 33 runs. Sussex 15 pts, Worcestershire 3 pts. Toss: Sussex.

For once, the Horsham Festival escaped the rain, and good crowds were treated to an absorbing tussle effectively decided by an opening stand of 212 between Montgomerie and Goodwin on the second day. Such riches had seemed unlikely on the first, when swing, injudicious strokes and questionable decisions resulted in 18 wickets. The umpires, however, were adamant that a pitch inspection was not needed. Rhodes's doggedness gave Worcestershire a lead of 46 before the Sussex openers put the conditions in perspective with some glorious strokeplay. Both made centuries and, though Sussex struggled after their departure, Worcestershire were left to chase 327 on a pitch increasingly taking spin. While Solanki was stroking a typically elegant 89, they had a chance, but he threw his wicket away before lunch. Davis, having worked steadily through the innings, finished with a Championship-best six for 116, and Kirtley's eighth wicket of the match gave him his second Championship win as stand-in captain.

Close of play: First day, Worcestershire 133-8 (Rhodes 23*, Rawnsley 1*); Second day, Sussex 242-4 (Montgomerie 108*, House 0*); Third day, Worcestershire 173-3 (Solanki 29*, Leatherdale 38*).

Sussex

R. R. Montgomerie lbw b Bichel	12	– (2) c Hick b Rawnsley	112
M. W. Goodwin lbw b Sheriyar	19	– (1) c Leatherdale b Sheriyar	109
M. H. Yardy lbw b Lampitt	4	– c Rhodes b Sheriyar	2
B. Zuiderent c Rhodes b Sheriyar	2	– lbw b Bichel	8
W. J. House b Lampitt	13	– (6) c and b Bichel	21
U. B. A. Rashid c Leatherdale b Rawnsley	1	– (7) c Rhodes b Sheriyar	38
†M. J. Prior c Rhodes b Sheriyar	40	– (8) c Rhodes b Sheriyar	5
M. J. G. Davis b Lampitt	23	– (9) not out	43
*R. J. Kirtley b Bichel	1	– (5) c Rhodes b Bichel	1
J. D. Lewry c Bichel b Sheriyar	14	– b Rawnsley	10
M. A. Robinson not out	0	– lbw b Rawnsley	1
L-b 2, n-b 6	8	B 5, l-b 7, w 4, n-b 6	22
1/20 2/37 3/39 4/52 5/52 6/54 7/98 8/109 9/130	137	1/212 2/214 3/236 4/242 5/250 6/286 7/295 8/333 9/366	372

Bonus points – Worcestershire 3.

Bowling: *First Innings*—Bichel 15–5–37–2; Sheriyar 14.3–5–53–4; Lampitt 16–8–22–3; Rawnsley 5–0–23–1. *Second Innings*—Bichel 30–8–88–3; Sheriyar 23–5–83–4; Lampitt 18–5–51–0; Rawnsley 39.5–13–72–3; Solanki 18–3–51–0; Hick 3–0–15–0.

Worcestershire

W. P. C. Weston c Prior b Kirtley	42	– lbw b Robinson	21
A. Singh lbw b Lewry	0	– c Lewry b Davis	43
*G. A. Hick b Kirtley	13	– c Prior b Davis	13
V. S. Solanki c Montgomerie b Robinson	26	– c Goodwin b Davis	89
D. A. Leatherdale lbw b Robinson	1	– c Prior b Kirtley	39
Kadeer Ali lbw b Robinson	0	– b Davis	1
A. J. Bichel c Prior b Kirtley	8	– b Kirtley	2
†S. J. Rhodes c Yardy b Kirtley	46	– not out	41
S. R. Lampitt c House b Rashid	0	– c Lewry b Davis	11
M. J. Rawnsley c Prior b Kirtley	24	– c Zuiderent b Davis	0
A. Sheriyar not out	4	– lbw b Kirtley	0
B 2, l-b 11, w 4, n-b 2	19	B 25, l-b 6, w 2	33
1/7 2/26 3/69 4/75 5/75 6/97 7/122 8/129 9/178	183	1/66 2/100 3/103 4/176 5/181 6/184 7/262 8/292 9/292	293

Bonus points – Sussex 3.

Bowling: *First Innings*—Lewry 16–5–43–1; Kirtley 23.4–4–60–5; Davis 11–1–35–0; Robinson 14–4–25–3; Rashid 4–2–7–1. *Second Innings*—Lewry 11–4–33–0; Kirtley 17.5–3–49–3; Robinson 20–8–43–1; Davis 36–6–116–6; Rashid 10–4–21–0.

Umpires: J. W. Holder and J. F. Steele.

SUSSEX v DERBYSHIRE

At Arundel, June 13, 14, 15. Sussex won by an innings and 34 runs. Sussex 18 pts, Derbyshire 3 pts. Toss: Sussex.

Shortly after lunch on the third day, Sussex brushed aside a demoralised Derbyshire to complete an innings victory. It had seemed unlikely on the first morning when both Sussex openers went for ducks, but Adams immediately began the fightback, reaching 50 off just 45 balls. He then settled down, eventually hitting 192, the highest first-class score at Arundel and his own highest since acrimoniously leaving Derbyshire in 1997. He cut and drove powerfully, faced 286 balls, struck 23 fours and shared partnerships of 141 with Zuiderent and 176 with Prior, who made a maiden half-century. For Derbyshire, Welch's whole-hearted contribution earned him a career-best six for 82, but, after a healthy start, their brittle batting was exposed by Robinson, whose five wickets rewarded his meticulous off-stump line. Having narrowly failed to save the follow-on, Derbyshire's batting was, if anything, even poorer second time round. The run-out of Di Venuto did not help. Kirtley polished them off, taking the last three wickets in four balls to inflict Derbyshire's sixth defeat in their last seven games in all competitions.

Close of play: First day, Sussex 349-8 (Kirtley 1*, Lewry 0*); Second day, Derbyshire 33-1 (Sutton 12*, Dowman 15*).

Sussex

R. R. Montgomerie c Sutton b Welch	0
M. W. Goodwin c Krikken b Munton	0
*C. J. Adams c Sutton b Welch	192
B. Zuiderent lbw b Welch	58
M. H. Yardy c Di Venuto b Wharton	2
U. B. A. Rashid c Krikken b Wharton	2
†M. J. Prior c Pierson b Di Venuto	66
M. J. G. Davis c Smith b Welch	16
R. J. Kirtley not out	1
J. D. Lewry c Di Venuto b Welch	0
M. A. Robinson b Welch	0
B 1, l-b 7, n-b 4	12
1/0 2/8 3/149 4/152 5/154 6/330 7/348 8/349 9/349	349

Bonus points – Sussex 3, Derbyshire 3.

Bowling: Welch 22.5–2–82–6; Munton 22–4–57–1; Smith 12–1–66–0; Wharton 28–6–74–2; Di Venuto 5–1–16–1; Pierson 10–0–28–0; Bailey 5–0–18–0.

Derbyshire

S. D. Stubbings lbw b Lewry	67	– (2) c Goodwin b Lewry	0
L. D. Sutton c Adams b Lewry	33	– (1) c Prior b Kirtley	14
M. P. Dowman c Adams b Robinson	2	– b Kirtley	17
M. J. Di Venuto lbw b Kirtley	8	– run out	9
R. J. Bailey c Adams b Robinson	4	– c Zuiderent b Kirtley	33
G. Welch c Prior b Yardy	32	– b Lewry	21
†K. M. Krikken not out	19	– lbw b Davis	3
T. M. Smith b Kirtley	4	– c Adams b Kirtley	2
A. R. K. Pierson b Robinson	9	– not out	1
*T. A. Munton c Prior b Robinson	0	– b Kirtley	4
L. J. Wharton c Zuiderent b Robinson	0	– lbw b Kirtley	0
B 5, l-b 6, w 6, n-b 2	19	B 4, l-b 8, w 2	14
1/82 2/103 3/105 4/117 5/117 6/167 7/174 8/193 9/197	197	1/1 2/35 3/46 4/62 5/104 6/107 7/113 8/114 9/118	118

Bonus points – Sussex 3.

Bowling: *First Innings*—Lewry 23–7–55–2; Kirtley 19–2–71–2; Robinson 17.5–6–35–5; Davis 8–4–12–0; Yardy 7–3–13–1. *Second Innings*—Lewry 16–7–28–2; Kirtley 15–3–45–6; Robinson 7–4–7–0; Yardy 4–0–11–0; Davis 8–2–15–1.

Umpires: B. Dudleston and V. A. Holder.

At Nottingham, June 20, 21, 22, 23. SUSSEX beat NOTTINGHAMSHIRE by 161 runs.

At Lord's, June 29, 30, July 1, 2. SUSSEX drew with MIDDLESEX.

SUSSEX v HAMPSHIRE

At Hove, July 6, 7. Sussex won by an innings and 113 runs. Sussex 18 pts, Hampshire 3 pts. Toss: Sussex.

Lewry exploited ideal conditions for swing bowling to hustle Hampshire to defeat in less than five sessions and earn himself career-best match figures of 13 for 79, including a hat-trick. Moving the ball late off an attacking length, the left-armer prised open Hampshire's second innings by dismissing Kenway, Kendall and Smith in his opening over. The hat-trick – his second, and the first by a Sussex bowler at Hove for 20 years – completed a sequence for Lewry of seven wickets in 13 balls spanning both innings, the best in the Championship since Surrey's Pat Pocock took seven in 11 against Sussex at Eastbourne in 1972. Lewry later claimed another three wickets in four balls. But the game wasn't just about his exploits. Conditions were no easier for Sussex, but they batted with more application. Adams struck a forceful 71 in 78 balls, and the left-handed Yardy coaxed 130 runs and all three bonus points from the tail before running out of partners within sight of a maiden century. Taylor played his part with bat and ball after being called from a Second Eleven game at The Oval on the first morning to replace the incapacitated Robinson.

Close of play: First day, Sussex 220-7 (Yardy 34*, Kirtley 3*).

Hampshire

G. W. White c Prior b Lewry	9	– b Kirtley	5
D. A. Kenway lbw b Lewry	18	– c Montgomerie b Lewry	0
W. S. Kendall lbw b Lewry	22	– lbw b Lewry	0
*R. A. Smith lbw b Taylor	7	– lbw b Lewry	0
N. C. Johnson c Adams b Taylor	0	– c Prior b Lewry	19
A. D. Mascarenhas c Yardy b Adams	8	– c Goodwin b Lewry	7
†A. N. Aymes b Lewry	6	– lbw b Lewry	8
S. D. Udal c Montgomerie b Lewry	2	– not out	40
A. C. Morris lbw b Kirtley	0	– b Lewry	0
C. T. Tremlett not out	2	– c Adams b Kirtley	10
A. D. Mullally lbw b Lewry	0	– c Kirtley b Taylor	17
L-b 1, w 2, n-b 4	7	L-b 2	2
1/28 2/29 3/42 4/42 5/68 6/76 7/78 8/79 9/81	81	1/1 2/1 3/1 4/9 5/32 6/41 7/42 8/42 9/89	108

Bonus points – Sussex 3.

Bowling: *First Innings*—Lewry 15.4–5–37–6; Kirtley 15–5–27–1; Taylor 10–8–5–2; Davis 2–0–5–0; Adams 2–0–6–1. *Second Innings*—Lewry 12–2–42–7; Kirtley 12–2–63–2; Taylor 0.2–0–1–1.

Sussex

R. R. Montgomerie b Morris	7
M. W. Goodwin lbw b Morris	9
*C. J. Adams b Mullally	71
B. Zuiderent c Kenway b Tremlett	20
M. H. Yardy not out	87
U. B. A. Rashid c Kendall b Mullally	15
†M. J. Prior lbw b Johnson	15
M. J. G. Davis c Aymes b Mascarenhas	19
R. J. Kirtley c Aymes b Mullally	4
J. D. Lewry c Mascarenhas b Morris	6
B. V. Taylor c Johnson b Mascarenhas	11
B 4, l-b 12, w 6, n-b 16	38
1/14 2/19 3/51 4/129 5/151 6/172 7/213 8/221 9/236	302

Bonus points – Sussex 3, Hampshire 3.

Bowling: Mullally 20–4–75–3; Morris 19–2–68–3; Mascarenhas 11.3–3–38–2; Tremlett 7–1–28–1; Udal 10–1–28–0; Johnson 15–0–49–1.

Umpires: R. Julian and P. Willey.

At Chester-le-Street, July 18, 19, 20, 21. SUSSEX beat DURHAM by 133 runs.

At Cheltenham, July 27, 28, 29, 30. SUSSEX lost to GLOUCESTERSHIRE by ten wickets.

SUSSEX v MIDDLESEX

At Hove, August 2, 3, 4, 5. Sussex won by 192 runs. Sussex 19 pts, Middlesex 3 pts. Toss: Middlesex. First-class debut: D. Alleyne.

Sussex returned to the top of Division Two, winning with almost an hour to spare after losing much of the first day to rain. But Middlesex, who headed the table going into this game, should really have been able to preserve their unbeaten record, despite not being at full strength. Set a notional 354 in 82 overs on an easy-paced pitch, they began well enough through Strauss and Roseberry, who passed 10,000 runs for Middlesex in what proved to be his last match. After Strauss, though, only acting-captain Weekes showed much stomach for the fight as Martin-Jenkins and Robinson imposed a stranglehold. The last five wickets fell for just 15 runs. Middlesex had been on the back foot from the moment Weekes, seduced by a green-tinged surface, put Sussex in. His bowlers extracted little from it, and Goodwin's first Championship century at Hove gave Sussex a strong platform. Only Weekes's vigilance and his partnerships with Bloomfield and Tufnell saw Middlesex avoid the follow-on. Sussex had their four front-line seamers in action for the first time since April, and their influence was pronounced.

Close of play: First day, Sussex 118-1 (Goodwin 73*, Adams 1*); Second day, Middlesex 48-2 (Weston 20*, Cook 0*); Third day, Sussex 140-2 (Adams 45*, Yardy 69*).

Sussex

M. W. Goodwin c Alleyne b Bloomfield	127	– (2) lbw b Keegan	0
R. R. Montgomerie c Alleyne b Bloomfield	39	– (1) c Roseberry b Bloomfield	6
*C. J. Adams lbw b Tufnell	16	– c Hutton b Tufnell	54
B. Zuiderent lbw b Tufnell	43	– (5) not out	25
M. H. Yardy lbw b Keegan	41	– (4) c Alleyne b Weekes	72
U. B. A. Rashid c Alleyne b Weekes	21	– c Hutton b Weekes	14
R. S. C. Martin-Jenkins not out	36	– c Strauss b Weekes	9
†M. J. Prior c Weekes b Cook	7	– c Strauss b Weekes	2
J. D. Lewry b Cook	5		
R. J. Kirtley not out	2		
B 1, l-b 1, n-b 12	14	B 11, l-b 7, n-b 10	28
1/116 2/149 3/234 4/234 5/285 6/306 7/336 8/344	(8 wkts dec.) 351	1/2 2/6 3/149 4/159 5/194 6/207 7/210	(7 wkts dec.) 210

M. A. Robinson did not bat.

Bonus points – Sussex 4, Middlesex 2.

Bowling: *First Innings*—Bloomfield 23–3–87–2; Keegan 16–1–63–1; Cook 25.1–6–57–2; Tufnell 33–7–96–2; Weekes 17–7–46–1. *Second Innings*—Bloomfield 18–2–56–1; Keegan 11–4–35–1; Tufnell 19–3–59–1; Cook 4–1–17–0; Weekes 5.5–0–25–4.

Middlesex

A. J. Strauss c Prior b Lewry	8	– c Yardy b Rashid	51
R. M. S. Weston c Kirtley b Lewry	25	– (4) c Zuiderent b Martin-Jenkins	4
O. A. Shah c Prior b Robinson	5	– c Zuiderent b Robinson	0
S. J. Cook b Lewry	4	– (8) c Prior b Martin-Jenkins	0
B. L. Hutton lbw b Kirtley	5	– c Martin-Jenkins b Kirtley	4
*P. N. Weekes c Adams b Robinson	64	– lbw b Robinson	41
M. A. Roseberry c Adams b Robinson	20	– (2) b Martin-Jenkins	11
†D. Alleyne c Yardy b Kirtley	0	– (7) c Montgomerie b Martin-Jenkins	8
C. B. Keegan lbw b Kirtley	2	– not out	4
T. F. Bloomfield b Lewry	28	– c Lewry b Robinson	4
P. C. R. Tufnell not out	7	– b Robinson	0
B 3, l-b 7, w 6, n-b 24	40	B 5, l-b 15, n-b 14	34
1/20 2/44 3/56 4/61 5/71 6/133 7/138 8/142 9/193	208	1/54 2/55 3/72 4/80 5/117 6/146 7/146 8/146 9/159	161

Bonus points – Middlesex 1, Sussex 3.

Bowling: *First Innings*—Lewry 21–4–64–4; Kirtley 24–10–63–3; Robinson 18–2–56–3; Martin-Jenkins 10–4–15–0. *Second Innings*—Lewry 13–3–30–0; Kirtley 11–1–36–1; Robinson 19.3–12–34–4; Martin-Jenkins 17–10–18–4; Rashid 7–3–20–1; Adams 1–0–3–0.

Umpires: D. R. Shepherd and A. G. T. Whitehead.

At Hove, August 8, 9, 10. SUSSEX lost to AUSTRALIANS by eight wickets (see Australian tour section).

At Derby, August 15, 16, 17, 18. SUSSEX beat DERBYSHIRE by 130 runs.

SUSSEX v DURHAM

At Hove, August 22, 23, 24, 25. Durham won by 71 runs. Durham 17 pts, Sussex 3 pts. Toss: Durham.

Sussex's title aspirations received a setback with their first defeat by Durham in the Championship. The key session came on the second morning when, under sullen skies with the ball swinging lavishly, they were bowled out for their lowest total of the season, having avoided the follow-on with the last pair at the crease. Harmison made the breakthrough with four of the first five wickets. Durham, choosing to bat first, had owed much to Daley's obdurate 89, which occupied five and three-quarter hours before he was Kirtley's fifth and final victim. Conditions were better when Durham began their second innings, and Lewis and Love increased the lead to 254 before cloud cover signalled Kirtley's return. He dismissed them both, Robinson picked up Daley and Peng, and next morning they cleaned out the last five for the addition of only 20 runs; Kirtley finished with ten in a match for the second time. A target of 337 looked within Sussex's compass when Goodwin and Montgomerie were putting on 84, but only 70 runs came between lunch and tea at a cost of five wickets. Although Martin-Jenkins batted valiantly for a career-best 94, Durham wrapped up the win an hour into the final morning.

Close of play: First day, Durham 254-9 (Daley 89*, Hatch 5*); Second day, Durham 179-5 (Law 27*, A. Pratt 12*); Third day, Sussex 238-7 (Martin-Jenkins 84*, Kirtley 2*).

Durham

*J. J. B. Lewis c Prior b Kirtley	10	– c Yardy b Kirtley	33
G. J. Pratt lbw b Kirtley	8	– lbw b Kirtley	0
M. L. Love c Montgomerie b Lewry	45	– lbw b Kirtley	82
J. A. Daley b Kirtley	89	– c Zuiderent b Robinson	16
N. Peng c Zuiderent b Robinson	0	– c Davis b Robinson	2
D. R. Law b Kirtley	2	– c Lewry b Kirtley	27
†A. Pratt lbw b Davis	26	– b Robinson	19
G. D. Bridge c and b Adams	22	– c Davis b Robinson	7
J. E. Brinkley c Lewry b Adams	0	– lbw b Robinson	2
S. J. Harmison c Prior b Kirtley	9	– not out	3
N. G. Hatch not out	5	– c Prior b Kirtley	0
B 5, l-b 9, w 2, n-b 22	38	B 2, l-b 2, n-b 4	8
1/20 2/23 3/99 4/100 5/112 6/169 7/211 8/211 9/229	254	1/0 2/117 3/128 4/137 5/146 6/180 7/188 8/193 9/196	199

Bonus points – Durham 2, Sussex 3.

Bowling: *First Innings*—Lewry 30–8–76–1; Kirtley 29–12–48–5; Robinson 18–7–42–1; Martin-Jenkins 12–2–36–0; Adams 7–2–17–2; Davis 9–2–21–1. *Second Innings*—Lewry 9–3–31–0; Kirtley 19.1–7–47–5; Martin-Jenkins 12–4–36–0; Robinson 24–7–59–5; Davis 6–2–17–0; Adams 1–0–5–0.

Sussex

R. R. Montgomerie c Law b Hatch	24	– (2) run out	25
M. W. Goodwin c Brinkley b Harmison	17	– (1) c A. Pratt b Hatch	65
*C. J. Adams c Bridge b Brinkley	0	– c Bridge b Hatch	5
B. Zuiderent c Bridge b Harmison	0	– c Love b Harmison	2
M. H. Yardy lbw b Harmison	0	– c G. J. Pratt b Bridge	13
R. S. C. Martin-Jenkins c Love b Harmison	3	– c A. Pratt b Law	94
†M. J. Prior run out	38	– lbw b Bridge	14
M. J. G. Davis c A. Pratt b Brinkley	7	– b Harmison	4
R. J. Kirtley c Law b Brinkley	1	– b Harmison	12
J. D. Lewry c A. Pratt b Hatch	23	– c Brinkley b Law	0
M. A. Robinson not out	3	– not out	5
L-b 1	1	B 5, l-b 11, w 8, n-b 2	26
1/33 2/34 3/35 4/35 5/43 6/49 7/58 8/70 9/101	117	1/84 2/105 3/110 4/114 5/149 6/189 7/229 8/251 9/251	265

Bonus points – Durham 3.

Bowling: *First Innings*—Harmison 15–2–52–4; Brinkley 12–5–27–3; Hatch 8.4–1–37–2. *Second Innings*—Harmison 32.2–6–86–3; Brinkley 16–7–33–0; Hatch 15–2–50–2; Law 21–6–58–2; Bridge 16–6–22–2.

Umpires: J. W. Lloyds and N. A. Mallender.

At Birmingham, September 7, 8, 9, 10. SUSSEX drew with WARWICKSHIRE.

SUSSEX v GLOUCESTERSHIRE

At Hove, September 12, 13, 14. Sussex won by ten wickets. Sussex 19 pts, Gloucestershire 4 pts. Toss: Gloucestershire. First-class debut: R. J. Sillence.

On a glorious late summer's day, in front of their biggest Championship crowd for some time, Sussex claimed the second-division title and dashed any chance a weakened Gloucestershire had of promotion. Such an emphatic victory had seemed unlikely when Sussex were 70 for five on the first day, but Yardy and Martin-Jenkins launched a thrilling counter-attack, with Martin-Jenkins reaching his maiden first-class hundred off 126 balls, with 17 fours and two sixes. The champagne his father Christopher, cricket correspondent of *The Times*, had been saving for just such an occasion was finally cracked open in the press box. Bad light ended play after 75 overs, but next day the lower order added a further 121; in all, the last five wickets put on 314. Seamer Roger Sillence marked his debut with five wickets. In Gloucestershire's response, only Harvey, ignoring a rib injury that prevented him bowling, and Barnett, who passed 1,000 runs for the 16th season, offered serious resistance against Kirtley and Robinson. Hewson, out first ball in the first innings, batted doggedly when Gloucestershire followed on but, with Kirtley waiting in the wings, there was a limit to their resistance. His five wickets, as the last six were skittled for 24, gave him ten for the second successive home match, and it was almost time for the celebrations to begin in earnest.

Close of play: First day, Sussex 263-6 (Martin-Jenkins 111*, Davis 43*); Second day, Gloucestershire 228.

Sussex

R. R. Montgomerie c Ball b Averis	11	– (2) not out	11
M. W. Goodwin c Hancock b Bressington	5	– (1) not out	7
*C. J. Adams c Williams b Sillence	11		
B. Zuiderent b Sillence	6		
M. H. Yardy lbw b Ball	42		
†T. R. Ambrose c Williams b Bressington	14		
R. S. C. Martin-Jenkins c Williams b Sillence	113		
M. J. G. Davis c sub b Sillence	44		
R. J. Kirtley not out	51		
J. D. Lewry run out	47		
M. A. Robinson c Ball b Sillence	10		
B 1, l-b 8, w 7, n-b 14	30		
1/16 2/24 3/37 4/44 5/70 6/164 7/264 8/269 9/351	384	(no wkt)	18

Bonus points – Sussex 4, Gloucestershire 3.

Bowling: *First Innings*—Averis 14–8–23–1; Bressington 28–5–105–2; Sillence 28.5–5–97–5; Alleyne 26–6–105–0; Ball 16–1–45–1. *Second Innings*—Bressington 2–0–15–0; Sillence 1–0–3–0.

Gloucestershire

D. R. Hewson lbw b Lewry	0	– (2) c Montgomerie b Robinson	79
T. H. C. Hancock c Zuiderent b Kirtley	14	– (1) c Ambrose b Kirtley	0
M. G. N. Windows c Zuiderent b Davis	41	– c Zuiderent b Robinson	27
K. J. Barnett c Ambrose b Robinson	37	– b Martin-Jenkins	10
I. J. Harvey b Kirtley	71	– c Kirtley b Martin-Jenkins	37
*M. W. Alleyne lbw b Robinson	33	– c Montgomerie b Kirtley	5
M. C. J. Ball b Kirtley	3	– c Montgomerie b Kirtley	0
†R. C. J. Williams c Zuiderent b Robinson	4	– c Goodwin b Kirtley	0
R. J. Sillence c Montgomerie b Kirtley	0	– c Montgomerie b Kirtley	6
A. N. Bressington c Montgomerie b Robinson	17	– b Kirtley	0
J. M. M. Averis not out	0	– not out	4
B 3, l-b 1, n-b 4	8	L-b 3, n-b 2	5
1/0 2/30 3/89 4/143 5/171 6/181 7/190 8/193 9/225	228	1/7 2/50 3/79 4/137 5/149 6/149 7/163 8/163 9/168	173

Bonus points – Gloucestershire 1, Sussex 3.

Bowling: *First Innings*—Lewry 6–0–33–1; Kirtley 18–3–59–4; Robinson 17.1–6–39–4; Martin-Jenkins 11–0–64–0; Davis 8–2–29–1. *Second Innings*—Lewry 9–0–42–0; Kirtley 14.1–3–34–6; Robinson 17–8–46–2; Martin-Jenkins 15–3–48–2.

Umpires: T. E. Jesty and J. F. Steele.

Mark Wagh

WARWICKSHIRE

President: The Rt Hon. The Lord Guernsey

Chairman: M. J. K. Smith

Chief Executive: D. L. Amiss

Chairman, Cricket Committee: T. A. Lloyd

Captain: M. J. Powell

Director of Coaching: R. A. Woolmer

Head Groundsman: S. J. Rouse

Scorer: D. Wainwright

The champagne celebrations that followed Warwickshire's last-day win at Derby may have appeared inappropriate for a side that had just finished 12th-best in the Championship, but promotion to Division One at least gave them cause for cautious optimism after another moderate season. Progress had undoubtedly been made in several areas: Warwickshire won three more Championship matches than in 2000 – they were beaten only once – and are one of five counties in both first divisions in 2002. Yet they scrambled into the final promotion place with a squad that, on paper at least, contained quality in depth but performed to its full potential only intermittently.

The batting was solid and dependable, with the emergence of Ian Bell and Mark Wagh – both were included in the first National Academy intake – giving particular cause for satisfaction. Both are Warwickshire-born and have emerged from the county's successful youth system under the shrewd tutelage of Neal Abberley and Steve Perryman. Bell had already won favourable notices with England Under-19 and England A, but Warwickshire made him wait as they backed their capped batsmen in the first half of the summer. When Nick Knight was called up by England and Dominic Ostler's season was ended in July by an elbow injury, 19-year-old Bell seized his chance with 836 runs from just 16 first-class innings. There were three centuries and two scores of 98, the result of a mature temperament and superb shot selection, and on the last day of the season Warwickshire made him their youngest capped player ever. Wagh's 1,277 runs included a marathon 315 against Middlesex; he was only the fourth player to score a triple-century at Lord's. He welded patience to destructive strokeplay, and ended speculation about his future by signing a new contract until the end of the 2004 season.

The improvement in the quality of Edgbaston's pitches was appreciated by the batsmen but not by the bowlers, who dismissed the opposition twice in only two matches there. Warwickshire hoped that the return of Shaun Pollock as their overseas player in 2002, after a five-season absence, would improve the penetration of an attack in which no bowler took 50 wickets for the first time since 1993. Dougie Brown and Vasbert Drakes were the leading wicket-takers, with 42 each, but Drakes's performances fell well short of expectation. He did help set up victory over Gloucestershire, with his only five-wicket haul, and averted defeat against Sussex with his solitary 50.

Otherwise, he looked innocuous, his performances affected by niggling injuries and the knowledge that Warwickshire had no intention of re-engaging him for a second season. Brown worked tirelessly, often in unfavourable conditions, provided 666 runs in a solid all-round contribution, and also prospered in one-day cricket with 531 runs and 46 wickets. But his consistency was rarely matched by his team-mates.

Warwickshire's one-day form fluctuated dramatically. They beat Somerset three times but, crucially, lost the Cheltenham & Gloucester Trophy semi-final against them, having twice squandered match-winning positions. They also choked in their Benson and Hedges Cup quarter-final at Trent Bridge, where they failed to build on a patient century from Knight, whose season began and ended with Championship hundreds but sagged in the middle. Third place in the Norwich Union League was respectable, and might have been better but for an ignominious collapse to 59 all out, their lowest score in the competition, at Headingley. Ostler's spectacular unbeaten 134 against Gloucestershire, equalling Warwickshire's highest individual League score, provided one of the highlights of the season. Vice-captain David Hemp was omitted for half the one-day matches so that Warwickshire could accommodate Trevor Penney, who was otherwise engaged as Second Eleven captain and assistant coach. Though continuing to score freely in the Championship, Hemp decided to rejoin Glamorgan after his request for a long-term contract was refused.

Michael Powell was the major batting disappointment. His form, no doubt affected by the captaincy, deserted him after a promising start; he reached 50 only once in his last 17 Championship innings. However, he proved to be a strong and popular captain even if, inevitably, he made mistakes in his first season in charge. Powell enjoyed a close working relationship with Bob Woolmer, the director of coaching, but their squad rotation system and policy of playing only one spinner met with limited success. There were times when the captain over-bowled his seamers and allowed the opposition to wriggle off the hook.

Rotating bowlers may have kept them fresh, but it meant a lack of regular cricket and caused some discontent. Charlie Dagnall, frustrated by a lack of Championship opportunities, was released at his own request and joined Leicestershire. A similar request from Alan Richardson, whose appearances were confined mostly to the Championship, was refused, but he declined the offer of a contract extension. As Ashley Giles was either injured or with England for most of the summer, the spin bowling was shared by Wagh, with his occasional off-breaks, Neil Smith and Jamie Spires, a left-armer and another home-grown player. Smith had a difficult first season back in the ranks after losing the captaincy, and he needed to contribute more with bat and ball to secure a new contract.

Woolmer's own contract was also due to expire at the end of 2002, and he had already indicated that he might not seek a renewal. He had yet to weave his magic on a squad very different in character from the one that won three trophies in 1994, during his first spell at Edgbaston. His ambition, when he returned in 2000, was to win the Championship again; he might now have only one season in which to achieve it. – PAUL BOLTON.

WARWICKSHIRE 2001

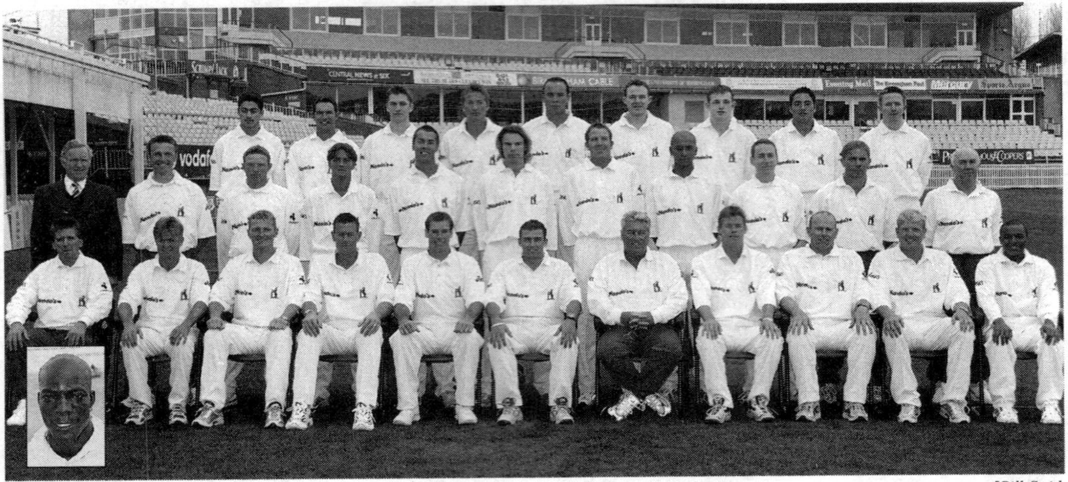

[*Bill Smith*

Back row: N. Tahir, R. E. Sierra, J. O. Troughton, J. A. Spires, N. M. Carter, G. D. Franklin, G. G. Wagg, N. A. Warren, E. J. Wilson. *Middle row:* D. L. Amiss (*chief executive*), S. J. Hollyhead (*fitness and conditioning coach*), I. R. Bell, M. M. Betts, M. A. Wagh, C. E. Dagnall, A. Richardson, M. A. Sheikh, T. Frost, G. Mostert (*physiotherapist*), R. N. Abberley (*head coach, indoor cricket centre*). *Front row:* S. P. Perryman (*Second Eleven coach*), T. L. Penney, D. R. Brown, A. F. Giles, D. L. Hemp, M. J. Powell (*captain*), R. A. Woolmer (*director of coaching*), N. V. Knight, N. M. K. Smith, D. P. Ostler, K. J. Piper. *Inset:* V. C. Drakes.

WARWICKSHIRE RESULTS

All first-class matches – Played 17: Won 5, Lost 1, Drawn 11.

County Championship matches – Played 16: Won 5, Lost 1, Drawn 10.

CricInfo County Championship, 3rd in Division 2; Cheltenham & Gloucester Trophy, s-f; Benson and Hedges Cup, q-f; Norwich Union League, 3rd in Division 1.

COUNTY CHAMPIONSHIP AVERAGES

BATTING

Cap		*M*	*I*	*NO*	*R*	*HS*	*100s*	*50s*	*Avge*	*Ct/St*
2001	I. R. Bell†	10	15	3	706	135	2	4	58.83	10
2000	M. A. Wagh†	15	22	2	1,170	315	3	5	58.50	4
1995	N. V. Knight	12	17	2	744	140	2	3	49.60	16
1991	D. P. Ostler†	10	12	1	520	121	2	2	47.27	22
1997	D. L. Hemp	16	23	4	852	186*	3	2	44.84	12
1995	D. R. Brown	15	18	3	629	104	1	6	41.93	15
1992	K. J. Piper	15	17	5	426	92*	0	2	35.50	39/1
1999	M. J. Powell	16	23	0	519	133	1	2	22.56	13
1993	N. M. K. Smith†	14	14	2	254	54	0	1	21.16	2
2001	V. C. Drakes§	14	13	3	209	50	0	1	20.90	1
2001	M. M. Betts	12	11	3	92	19	0	0	11.50	9
	A. Richardson	12	9	4	20	6*	0	0	4.00	6
	N. M. Carter	5	4	1	10	5	0	0	3.33	2

Also batted: C. E. Dagnall (2 matches) 1; A. F. Giles‡ (cap 1996) (2 matches) 0, 40*, 24 (4 ct); T. L. Penney (cap 1994) (1 match) 1 (3 ct); M. A. Sheikh† (3 matches) 19, 0, 14; J. O. Troughton (1 match) 27, 5*. J. A. Spires† (1 match) did not bat.

* *Signifies not out.* † *Born in Warwickshire.* ‡ *ECB contract.* § *Overseas player.*

BOWLING

	O	*M*	*R*	*W*	*BB*	*5W/i*	*Avge*
C. E. Dagnall	69	15	214	11	6-50	1	19.45
M. M. Betts	308.2	72	979	37	5-22	2	26.45
A. Richardson	369.5	102	918	32	5-89	1	28.68
D. R. Brown	465.1	123	1,264	42	6-60	1	30.09
N. M. K. Smith	314	75	813	25	4-76	0	32.52
N. M. Carter	95	8	362	11	5-78	1	32.90
M. A. Wagh	179	36	466	13	3-3	0	35.84
V. C. Drakes	505.2	107	1,537	42	5-37	1	36.59

Also bowled: I. R. Bell 17–4–40–1; A. F. Giles 89–22–241–5; D. L. Hemp 12–1–28–0; K. J. Piper 1–0–3–0; M. J. Powell 34–2–100–2; M. A. Sheikh 99.1–36–238–7; J. A. Spires 50–8–155–2; J. O. Troughton 2–0–17–0.

COUNTY RECORDS

Highest score for:	501*	B. C. Lara v Durham at Birmingham	1994
Highest score against:	322	I. V. A. Richards (Somerset) at Taunton	1985
Best bowling for:	10-41	J. D. Bannister v Combined Services at Birmingham	1959
Best bowling against:	10-36	H. Verity (Yorkshire) at Leeds	1931
Highest total for:	810-4 dec.	v Durham at Birmingham	1994
Highest total against:	887	by Yorkshire at Birmingham	1896
Lowest total for:	16	v Kent at Tonbridge	1913
Lowest total against:	15	by Hampshire at Birmingham	1922

WARWICKSHIRE v HAMPSHIRE

At Birmingham, April 20, 21, 22, 23. Drawn. Warwickshire 12 pts, Hampshire 6 pts. Toss: Hampshire. First-class debut: J. R. C. Hamblin. County debuts: V. C. Drakes; N. C. Johnson.

Knight's century increased Hampshire's discomfort on an opening day so cold that fielders and umpires wore an assortment of woolly hats. The pitch was damp at the City End where rain had leaked through the covers, but Hampshire's attack, with the exception of Mullally, failed to exploit it. Knight's fourth-wicket stand of 196 with Ostler was broken by Morris in the second over of the second day, whereupon Ostler gorged himself on some wayward bowling to complete his own century; Neil Smith helped himself to a fifty. Only White and Johnson applied themselves in Hampshire's first innings, which saw the first seven wickets go for 49 as Sheikh bowled unchanged for career-best figures of four for 36. Following on, Hampshire were in disarray at 114 for four when rain ended play 40 minutes after lunch on the third day. By the time Robin Smith and Stephenson resumed, the pitch had eased and they moved Hampshire closer to safety with 106 off 66 overs. When Smith departed after batting six hours for his first century since August 1998, having hit 16 fours and a six, Mascarenhas and Morris held out for the last hour.

Close of play: First day, Warwickshire 297-3 (Knight 140*, Ostler 75*); Second day, Hampshire 150-8 (Johnson 26*, Hamblin 2*); Third day, Hampshire 114-4 (Smith 41*, Stephenson 1*).

Warwickshire

*M. J. Powell c Johnson b Morris	0
N. V. Knight lbw b Morris	140
M. A. Wagh b Mullally	46
D. L. Hemp b Mullally	5
D. P. Ostler b Mascarenhas	119
D. R. Brown lbw b Mullally	2
N. M. K. Smith lbw b Stephenson	54
†K. J. Piper c Aymes b Hamblin	4
M. A. Sheikh lbw b Stephenson	19
V. C. Drakes not out	17
A. Richardson c Mullally b Stephenson	5
B 4, l-b 10, w 14, n-b 16	44
1/5 2/97 3/105 4/301 5/304 6/377 7/382 8/422 9/439	455

Bonus points – Warwickshire 5, Hampshire 2 (Score at 130 overs: 402-7).

Bowling: Mullally 37–12–77–3; Morris 28–6–72–2; Hamblin 18–1–88–1; Mascarenhas 27–9–56–1; Johnson 21–3–100–0; Stephenson 14.4–3–48–3.

Hampshire

D. A. Kenway b Sheikh	23	– c Ostler b Brown	52
G. W. White c Piper b Brown	44	– c Piper b Richardson	0
W. S. Kendall lbw b Brown	0	– c Ostler b Drakes	11
*R. A. Smith c Piper b Sheikh	4	– b Sheikh	118
N. C. Johnson c Ostler b Drakes	43	– c Ostler b Brown	0
J. P. Stephenson c Piper b Sheikh	7	– c Piper b Drakes	39
†A. N. Aymes b Brown	3	– c Piper b Richardson	4
A. D. Mascarenhas c Ostler b Sheikh	11	– not out	11
A. C. Morris b Richardson	20	– not out	25
J. R. C. Hamblin c Piper b Drakes	5		
A. D. Mullally not out	0		
L-b 2, n-b 8	10	L-b 3, w 6, n-b 16	25
1/62 2/69 3/78 4/82 5/93 6/96 7/111 8/148 9/159	170	1/0 2/38 3/113 4/113 5/219 6/247 7/247	(7 wkts) 285

Bonus points – Warwickshire 3.

Bowling: *First Innings*—Drakes 10.5–1–34–2; Richardson 18–3–55–1; Sheikh 20–7–36–4; Brown 14–4–42–3; Smith 2–1–1–0. *Second Innings*—Drakes 26–5–74–2; Richardson 22–10–32–2; Sheikh 34–15–67–1; Smith 18–5–40–0; Powell 2–0–13–0; Brown 23–10–44–2; Wagh 8.1–4–12–0.

Umpires: T. E. Jesty and G. Sharp.

WARWICKSHIRE v DURHAM

At Birmingham, May 9, 10, 11, 12. Warwickshire won by seven wickets. Warwickshire 16 pts, Durham 6 pts. Toss: Durham.

Betts set up Warwickshire's first Championship win at Edgbaston since September 1999 with five wickets on the third day against his former county. He exploited humid conditions and a pitch of variable bounce as Durham squandered a lead of 124. On the opening day, Collingwood, assisted by Pratt and Hunter, had rescued Durham from 58 for five, hitting 153 off 261 balls with 20 fours and a six. Warwickshire's early batting also faltered, although controversy surrounded the dismissal of Hemp, run out by Law's direct hit after colliding with Harmison, the bowler. The umpires consulted before ruling him out. Betts's three for eight in a ten-over opening spell, followed by his two wickets in four balls after lunch, changed the complexion of the match; Warwickshire suddenly found themselves needing 227 for victory with time immaterial. Wagh flayed Durham's inaccurate bowling, already depleted by the absence of Brown and Killeen and further weakened when Brinkley left to attend the birth of his daughter. He returned on the final day but was not allowed to bowl.

Close of play: First day, Durham 250-7 (Collingwood 105*, Brinkley 0*); Second day, Durham 0-0 (Lewis 0*, Gough 0*); Third day, Warwickshire 176-2 (Wagh 76*, Hemp 24*).

Durham

*J. J. B. Lewis c Brown b Drakes	8	– c Piper b Betts	5
M. A. Gough b Betts	13	– c Powell b Betts	8
M. P. Speight b Drakes	4	– c Knight b Drakes	0
P. D. Collingwood c and b Betts	153	– c Hemp b Betts	1
N. Peng c Piper b Drakes	4	– c Knight b Betts	22
D. R. Law c Piper b Richardson	9	– c Knight b Brown	23
†A. Pratt c Ostler b Richardson	52	– c and b Betts	0
I. D. Hunter b Richardson	31	– lbw b Brown	37
J. E. Brinkley c Knight b Drakes	3	– absent	
N. C. Phillips c Hemp b Richardson	4	– (9) not out	0
S. J. Harmison not out	17	– (10) c Powell b Brown	0
L-b 15, w 2, n-b 14	31	B 4, l-b 2	6
1/20 2/22 3/32 4/36 5/58 6/166 7/249 8/265 9/291	329	1/9 2/10 3/11 4/16 5/43 6/43 7/99 8/102 9/102	102

Bonus points – Durham 3, Warwickshire 3.

Bowling: *First Innings*—Drakes 27–2–83–4; Betts 16.2–2–57–2; Brown 25–4–81–0; Richardson 20–5–61–4; Smith 7–2–24–0; Powell 5–1–8–0. *Second Innings*—Betts 14–7–22–5; Drakes 16–8–19–1; Brown 8.2–3–16–3; Richardson 12–1–29–0; Smith 5–2–10–0.

Warwickshire

*M. J. Powell b Harmison	3	– c and b Collingwood	20
N. V. Knight lbw b Hunter	1	– lbw b Collingwood	22
M. A. Wagh b Brinkley	15	– c Phillips b Hunter	104
D. L. Hemp run out	10	– not out	38
D. P. Ostler run out	3	– not out	7
D. R. Brown lbw b Hunter	45		
N. M. K. Smith c Pratt b Phillips	47		
†K. J. Piper c Gough b Brinkley	37		
V. C. Drakes not out	12		
M. M. Betts b Hunter	2		
A. Richardson c Pratt b Hunter	1		
B 4, l-b 7, w 12, n-b 6	29	B 6, l-b 6, w 14, n-b 10	36
1/5 2/11 3/40 4/47 5/49 6/127 7/185 8/193 9/199	205	1/38 2/85 3/200	(3 wkts) 227

Bonus points – Warwickshire 1, Durham 3.

Bowling: *First Innings*—Hunter 14.3–1–55–4; Harmison 13–4–43–1; Brinkley 13–2–41–2; Collingwood 6–3–19–0; Law 5–2–14–0; Phillips 4–0–22–1. *Second Innings*—Harmison 19–4–55–0; Hunter 13.5–1–69–1; Collingwood 8–2–22–2; Law 7–0–37–0; Phillips 8–2–32–0.

Umpires: G. I. Burgess and D. J. Constant.

At Nottingham, May 16, 17, 18, 19. WARWICKSHIRE drew with NOTTINGHAMSHIRE.

At Hove, May 25, 26, 27, 28. WARWICKSHIRE beat SUSSEX by eight wickets.

WARWICKSHIRE v GLOUCESTERSHIRE

At Birmingham, May 31, June 1, 2, 3. Warwickshire won by ten wickets. Warwickshire 19 pts, Gloucestershire 6 pts. Toss: Gloucestershire.

Gloucestershire's abject batting on the final morning transformed a game that, over the preceding days, had looked set for a tame conclusion. They were undermined by quality fast bowling from Drakes, who became the first overseas player to be capped by three different counties (after Sussex in 1996 and Nottinghamshire in 1999). Only some late hitting by Hancock prevented an innings defeat. Gloucestershire's collapse was in sharp contrast to their determined performance on the first day, which Hancock and Ball augmented next morning by adding 80 in 15 overs. Bell, Warwickshire's highly regarded England A batsman, then gave evidence of his talent with a maiden first-class fifty, in only his second senior game for them, and Powell's first century at Edgbaston laid the foundations for what proved a match-winning total. Ostler's belligerent 92 and Piper's 55 made the lead certain. On the second day, the new "Brumbrella" pitch cover, which had been installed during the winter at a cost of £80,000, broke down and had to be shifted by 20 volunteers.

Close of play: First day, Gloucestershire 261-6 (Hancock 28*, Williams 33*); Second day, Warwickshire 186-2 (Powell 97*, Hemp 26*); Third day, Warwickshire 448-9 (Betts 10*, Carter 3*).

Gloucestershire

D. R. Hewson c Hemp b Drakes	30	– b Drakes	0
K. J. Barnett b Drakes	32	– c Piper b Betts	12
M. G. N. Windows lbw b Drakes	1	– lbw b Betts	1
C. G. Taylor lbw b Wagh	44	– lbw b Drakes	2
*M. W. Alleyne c Ostler b Smith	53	– c Bell b Brown	15
J. N. Snape c Powell b Smith	10	– c Bell b Drakes	17
T. H. C. Hancock b Betts	55	– b Betts	25
†R. C. J. Williams c Piper b Carter	33	– c Bell b Drakes	5
M. C. J. Ball c Betts b Brown	68	– b Brown	2
J. M. M. Averis lbw b Betts	0	– b Drakes	2
J. Lewis not out	2	– not out	15
L-b 8, w 6, n-b 18	32	N-b 10	10
1/80 2/81 3/84 4/182 5/188 6/201 7/270 8/350 9/350	360	1/1 2/2 3/17 4/17 5/52 6/54 7/66 8/69 9/72	106

Bonus points – Gloucestershire 4, Warwickshire 3 (Score at 130 overs: 350-9).

Bowling: *First Innings*—Drakes 30–9–83–3; Betts 26–3–81–2; Carter 27–5–76–1; Brown 12.4–5–23–1; Smith 21–7–59–2; Wagh 16–5–30–1. *Second Innings*—Betts 8.2–4–17–3; Drakes 19–3–37–5; Carter 4–0–16–0; Brown 14–7–29–2; Smith 5–2–7–0.

Warwickshire

*M. J. Powell c Ball b Hancock	133		
I. R. Bell c and b Ball	51	– not out	15
M. A. Wagh lbw b Averis	1		
D. L. Hemp c Williams b Alleyne	36		
D. P. Ostler st Williams b Snape	92		
D. R. Brown b Ball	1		
N. M. K. Smith c Ball b Alleyne	25		
†K. J. Piper c Hancock b Averis	55	– (1) not out	7
V. C. Drakes c sub b Snape	13		
M. M. Betts not out	10		
N. M. Carter not out	3		
B 9, l-b 3, w 2, n-b 14	28		
1/119 2/124 3/204 4/257 5/262 6/303 7/397 8/421 9/436 (9 wkts dec.)	448	(no wkt)	22

Bonus points – Warwickshire 4, Gloucestershire 2 (Score at 130 overs: 363-6).

Bowling: *First Innings*—Lewis 5–3–6–0; Averis 36–10–104–2; Alleyne 37–7–82–2; Hancock 18–4–67–1; Ball 44–8–131–2; Snape 18–2–46–2. *Second Innings*—Snape 2–0–8–0; Ball 1.4–0–14–0.

Umpires: N. L. Bainton and T. E. Jesty.

At Oxford, June 6, 7, 8. WARWICKSHIRE drew with OXFORD UCCE.

At Worcester, June 13, 14, 15, 16. WARWICKSHIRE drew with WORCESTERSHIRE.

WARWICKSHIRE v MIDDLESEX

At Birmingham, June 20, 21, 22, 23. Middlesex won by 129 runs. Middlesex 17 pts, Warwickshire 5 pts. Toss: Middlesex.

A compelling battle between the second division's top two tilted decisively Middlesex's way on the third day when Weston, making his second hundred in successive Championship matches, and Fleming extended their partnership to 181. That helped Fraser, despite a modest first-innings lead, time his declaration to perfection, asking Warwickshire to score 382 from a minimum 117 overs. Hemp followed up his first-innings hundred, which included 15 fours and a six, with a half-century, he and Wagh cracking 107 in 18 enthralling overs before both perished to Tufnell. When Warwickshire, now caught between attack and defence, were dismissed ten minutes after tea, it was their first Championship defeat by Middlesex since 1993. Victory took Middlesex 11 points clear at the top, while Warwickshire slipped to fourth; Betts's feisty five-wicket return on the first day had deserved better.

Close of play: First day, Warwickshire 33-3 (Wagh 10*, Hemp 9*); Second day, Middlesex 81-1 (Weston 32*, Fleming 1*); Third day, Warwickshire 30-0 (Powell 3*, Bell 20*).

Middlesex

A. J. Strauss c Giles b Betts	18	– c Ostler b Brown	44
M. A. Roseberry c Bell b Sheikh	20	– not out	10
R. M. S. Weston c Piper b Giles	19	– c and b Brown	100
S. P. Fleming b Brown	67	– c Wagh b Giles	92
B. L. Hutton c Giles b Betts	36	– run out	30
P. N. Weekes c Ostler b Betts	22	– c Giles b Brown	52
†D. C. Nash c Brown b Giles	6	– run out	9
C. B. Keegan not out	30		
*A. R. C. Fraser c Piper b Betts	12		
P. C. R. Tufnell c Bell b Betts	1		
T. F. Bloomfield b Drakes	11		
B 4, l-b 5, n-b 22	31	B 15, l-b 5, n-b 2	22
1/43 2/57 3/103 4/172 5/193 6/206 7/216 8/241 9/247	273	1/69 2/250 3/258 4/316 5/346 6/359 (6 wkts dec.)	359

Bonus points – Middlesex 2, Warwickshire 3.

In the second innings Roseberry, when 0, retired hurt at 17 and resumed at 346.

Bowling: *First Innings*—Drakes 19.3–3–64–1; Betts 22–2–88–5; Sheikh 12–4–25–1; Brown 12–4–33–1; Giles 24–7–54–2. *Second Innings*—Drakes 30–8–85–0; Betts 11–3–36–0; Brown 26.5–5–58–3; Sheikh 7–0–28–0; Giles 46–11–132–1.

Warwickshire

*M. J. Powell c Hutton b Bloomfield	4	– lbw b Fraser	11
I. R. Bell c Nash b Bloomfield	0	– lbw b Fraser	20
M. A. Wagh c Fleming b Fraser	10	– c Fraser b Tufnell	77
M. A. Sheikh c Weekes b Bloomfield	0	– (8) c Hutton b Tufnell	14
D. L. Hemp c Hutton b Tufnell	105	– (4) c Weekes b Tufnell	61
D. P. Ostler b Bloomfield	44	– (5) b Fraser	3
D. R. Brown run out	0	– (6) b Keegan	7
†K. J. Piper c Roseberry b Tufnell	15	– (10) not out	20
A. F. Giles not out	40	– (7) c Roseberry b Keegan	24
V. C. Drakes c Nash b Fraser	4	– (9) c Hutton b Tufnell	0
M. M. Betts c Nash b Fraser	14	– c Bloomfield b Keegan	0
B 5, l-b 2, n-b 8	15	B 4, l-b 9, n-b 2	15
1/0 2/11 3/13 4/41 5/111 6/112 7/153 8/204 9/219	251	1/33 2/42 3/149 4/170 5/184 6/216 7/217 8/220 9/251	252

Bonus points – Warwickshire 2, Middlesex 3.

Bowling: *First Innings*—Fraser 29.4–11–64–3; Bloomfield 22–3–89–4; Keegan 10–2–42–0; Tufnell 24–8–49–2. *Second Innings*—Fraser 24–7–75–3; Bloomfield 11–2–48–0; Keegan 16.5–7–52–3; Tufnell 26–10–57–4; Weekes 3–0–7–0.

Umpires: M. R. Benson and J. W. Lloyds.

At Chester-le-Street, June 29, 30, July 1, 2. WARWICKSHIRE drew with DURHAM.

At Bristol, July 4, 5, 6, 7. WARWICKSHIRE drew with GLOUCESTERSHIRE.

WARWICKSHIRE v DERBYSHIRE

At Birmingham, July 18, 19, 20, 21. Drawn. Warwickshire 8 pts, Derbyshire 7 pts. Toss: Derbyshire.

Former Warwickshire stalwarts Munton and Welch enjoyed their return to Edgbaston. When play eventually began after a blank first day, Derbyshire's batsmen failed, but acting-captain Munton delivered a defiant fifty, his fourth in first-class cricket although his first at Edgbaston, where he had spent 15 seasons. He and Welch then restricted Warwickshire to a slender lead, with Welch taking more wickets in the innings than in seven Championship games the previous summer. While batting, Ostler suffered a recurrence of an elbow injury, which ended his season. Stubbings and Di Venuto gave Derbyshire's fortunes a further boost by compiling their highest opening partnership in almost a year, Di Venuto's fluent century containing 18 fours. The match was nicely balanced, but more rain delayed the start on the last morning and the captains could not concoct an acceptable target. The sole beneficiary of the stalemate was Sutton, who completed a maiden hundred, albeit against part-time bowlers and to jeers from the sparse crowd.

Close of play: First day, No play; Second day, Warwickshire 88-2 (Knight 37*, Betts 0*); Third day, Derbyshire 204-2 (Sutton 13*, Bailey 8*).

Derbyshire

S. D. Stubbings c Brown b Richardson	27	– c Piper b Brown	62
M. J. Di Venuto lbw b Betts	9	– c Betts b Brown	109
L. D. Sutton c Bell b Betts	2	– not out	110
R. J. Bailey c Piper b Carter	6	– c Knight b Carter	8
M. P. Dowman c Richardson b Smith	14	– c Knight b Richardson	33
G. Welch c Ostler b Brown	2	– c and b Powell	64
†K. M. Krikken lbw b Richardson	18	– not out	8
P. Aldred c Piper b Carter	8		
*T. A. Munton c Hemp b Richardson	50		
K. J. Dean c Bell b Richardson	18		
L. J. Wharton not out	1		
B 5, l-b 3, n-b 2	10	B 9, l-b 20, w 12	41
1/15 2/17 3/32 4/56 5/60 6/71 7/85 8/101 9/156	165	1/170 2/183 3/204 4/251 5/394 (5 wkts dec.)	435

Bonus points – Warwickshire 3.

Bowling: *First Innings*—Betts 14–2–46–2; Carter 16–0–40–2; Richardson 19.3–9–28–4; Smith 8–2–22–1; Brown 9–2–21–1. *Second Innings*—Betts 9–2–19–0; Carter 14–0–66–1; Brown 21–4–77–2; Richardson 20–4–75–1; Smith 20–2–68–0; Powell 20–0–54–1; Bell 9–1–16–0; Hemp 12–1–28–0; Piper 1–0–3–0.

Warwickshire

*M. J. Powell b Welch	37
N. V. Knight c Krikken b Munton	47
I. R. Bell c Bailey b Welch	6
M. M. Betts c Stubbings b Welch	5
D. L. Hemp run out	38
D. P. Ostler run out	10
D. R. Brown c and b Dean	15
N. M. K. Smith c Di Venuto b Welch	11
†K. J. Piper not out	26
N. M. Carter lbw b Welch	0
A. Richardson lbw b Munton	0
L-b 3, w 4, n-b 2	9
1/65 2/85 3/99 4/111 5/151 6/176 7/185 8/193 9/199	204

Bonus points – Warwickshire 1, Derbyshire 3.

Ostler, when 10, retired hurt at 125 and resumed at 193.

Bowling: Dean 14–2–56–1; Munton 19–5–50–2; Welch 23–5–53–5; Aldred 11–1–33–0; Wharton 4–0–9–0.

Umpires: J. H. Hampshire and P. Willey.

WARWICKSHIRE v NOTTINGHAMSHIRE

At Birmingham, August 3, 4, 5, 6. Warwickshire won by 139 runs. Warwickshire 18 pts, Nottinghamshire 6.75 pts. Toss: Warwickshire.

Ian Bell, aged 19 years and 115 days, became the youngest Warwickshire player to make a Championship hundred, being 181 days younger than Richard Sale was when he hit his maiden century against Sussex in 1939. After two escapes in single figures, Bell batted five and three-quarter hours and hit 15 boundaries; he and Brown (18 fours) turned Warwickshire round with a stand of 176 in 46 overs. Blewett just missed a century for Nottinghamshire, but passed 1,000 runs for the season, and there were exhilarating strokes from Afzaal and Pietersen before Hemp rose to Bicknell's challenging declaration with a hundred from 101 balls; he hit 18 fours and two sixes. The loss of the last morning to the weather meant contrivance became necessary: though they used occasional bowlers to hasten the declaration, Nottinghamshire were still penalised for a slow over-rate. Chasing 281 from 62 overs, they subsided to 85 for five but were threatening to hold on for a draw until Wagh's off-breaks claimed three wickets in two overs. To cap a grim match for the visitors, their captain, Gallian, playing his first Championship match of the season after recovering from a knee injury, had his knuckle broken by Drakes in the first innings.

Close of play: First day, Warwickshire 270-5 (Bell 80*, Piper 0*); Second day, Nottinghamshire 164-1 (Blewett 89*, Afzaal 31*); Third day, Warwickshire 212-3 (Knight 74*, Bell 10*).

Warwickshire

*M. J. Powell c Read b Smith	15	– c Blewett b Smith	9
N. V. Knight c Read b Smith	0	– not out	98
M. A. Wagh b Smith	7	– c Read b Harris	0
D. L. Hemp c Bicknell b Blewett	52	– b Smith	105
I. R. Bell c Logan b Smith	103	– not out	29
D. R. Brown c Read b Pietersen	104		
†K. J. Piper c and b Logan	20		
N. M. K. Smith c Read b Logan	16		
V. C. Drakes c sub b Pietersen	13		
M. M. Betts not out	15		
A. Richardson c Blewett b Harris	0		
B 4, l-b 3, w 9, n-b 12	28	B 1, l-b 3, w 2, n-b 10	16
1/11 2/21 3/30 4/94 5/270 6/303 7/327 8/348 9/355	373	1/16 2/19 3/182 (3 wkts dec.)	257

Bonus points – Warwickshire 4, Nottinghamshire 3.

Bowling: *First Innings*—Smith 24–6–48–4; Logan 22–4–94–2; Harris 22–7–63–1; Lucas 8–1–49–0; Blewett 6–2–23–1; Afzaal 6–2–22–0; Pietersen 20–6–67–2. *Second Innings*—Smith 13–1–44–2; Harris 10–1–54–1; Logan 10–2–41–0; Pietersen 3–1–16–0; Afzaal 7–0–55–0; Read 3–0–25–0; Morris 2.2–0–18–0.

Nottinghamshire

D. J. Bicknell lbw b Betts	4	– c Richardson b Brown	45
*J. E. R. Gallian retired hurt	23	– absent hurt	
G. S. Blewett b Drakes	97	– c Powell b Drakes	1
U. Afzaal c Knight b Smith	86	– c Piper b Smith	14
J. E. Morris b Richardson	5	– (2) c Bell b Drakes	8
K. P. Pietersen c sub b Bell	71	– (5) c Brown b Wagh	35
†C. M. W. Read not out	19	– (6) c Brown b Smith	4
D. S. Lucas c Brown b Richardson	10	– (7) lbw b Smith	16
R. J. Logan not out	4	– (8) c Brown b Wagh	0
A. J. Harris (did not bat)		– (9) b Wagh	0
G. J. Smith (did not bat)		– (10) not out	3
B 6, l-b 9, w 2, n-b 14	31	B 1, l-b 8, w 6	15
1/7 2/201 3/222 4/279 5/327 6/341 (6 wkts dec.)	350	1/23 2/35 3/60 4/78 5/85 6/137 7/137 8/137 9/141	141

Bonus points – Nottinghamshire 4, Warwickshire 2.

In the first innings Gallian retired hurt at 92.

Bowling: *First Innings*—Drakes 26.5–4–116–1; Betts 2–0–5–1; Brown 24–5–70–0; Richardson 27–6–66–2; Smith 20–6–39–1; Wagh 2–0–15–0; Bell 8–3–24–1. *Second Innings*—Drakes 11–3–35–2; Richardson 9–6–13–0; Brown 12–1–39–1; Smith 16.4–4–42–3; Wagh 3–1–3–3.

Umpires: B. Dudleston and R. A. White.

At Southampton, August 7, 8, 9, 10. WARWICKSHIRE drew with HAMPSHIRE.

WARWICKSHIRE v WORCESTERSHIRE

At Birmingham, August 15, 16, 17, 18. Drawn. Warwickshire 12 pts, Worcestershire 11 pts. Toss: Worcestershire. First-class debut: J. O. Troughton.

Warwickshire's cautious approach and finally rain frustrated Worcestershire's push for victory. Hemp's career-best 186 not out, made in almost eight hours with 25 fours and two sixes, and built around century partnerships with Wagh and Brown, ensured that Warwickshire avoided the follow-on. But Powell's decision not to declare once they had maximum batting points was perplexing, given that his side needed wins to challenge for promotion. Instead, Warwickshire pottered around for a further 19 overs. Hick had dominated the opening day with his 116th first-class hundred, and first ball next morning he reached his 12th double with his 22nd four. He also hit three sixes and in all batted for six hours 44 minutes, facing 299 balls. His third-wicket stand with Solanki produced 217 in 48 overs. Carter's improved accuracy earned him his first five-wicket return for Warwickshire, but it was generally heavy going for bowlers until Bichel and Liptrot found some lift on the rain-cut last afternoon. Ahead of that, Weston had also helped himself to a hundred, and Hick completed 1,000 runs for the 16th time in an English season before giving Warwickshire 62 overs to get 311. Jim Troughton, a left-hander from Stratford and grandson of actor Patrick Troughton, of *Dr Who* fame, looked at ease on his Warwickshire debut.

Close of play: First day, Worcestershire 435-5 (Hick 196*, Bichel 39*); Second day, Warwickshire 223-4 (Hemp 89*, Brown 4*); Third day, Worcestershire 113-1 (Weston 57*, Solanki 29*).

Worcestershire

W. P. C. Weston c Piper b Carter	23	– not out	102
A. Singh c Piper b Carter	0	– c Piper b Smith	22
*G. A. Hick c Drakes b Carter	201	– (4) not out	41
V. S. Solanki st Piper b Wagh	112	– (3) c Richardson b Powell	56
N. R. Boulton c Hemp b Richardson	0		
D. A. Leatherdale c Piper b Brown	23		
A. J. Bichel c Brown b Carter	42		
†S. J. Rhodes not out	28		
C. G. Liptrot c and b Carter	15		
M. J. Rawnsley c Piper b Brown	19		
A. Sheriyar lbw b Wagh	9		
B 6, l-b 14, w 2, n-b 30	52	L-b 6, n-b 6	12
1/0 2/47 3/264 4/271 5/353 6/443 7/445 8/475 9/505	524	1/49 2/162 (2 wkts dec.)	233

Bonus points – Worcestershire 5, Warwickshire 3 (Score at 130 overs: 505-9).

Bowling: *First Innings*—Drakes 31–5–111–0; Carter 19–2–78–5; Richardson 21–5–56–1; Brown 30–3–133–2; Smith 5–0–28–0; Wagh 26.1–2–81–2; Troughton 2–0–17–0. *Second Innings*—Drakes 9.2–2–42–0; Richardson 9–4–17–0; Brown 6–3–8–0; Wagh 15–0–68–0; Smith 23–4–67–1; Powell 7–1–25–1.

Warwickshire

*M. J. Powell c Solanki b Sheriyar	5	– c Rhodes b Bichel	0
M. A. Wagh c Rhodes b Liptrot	83	– b Liptrot	29
I. R. Bell lbw b Liptrot	4	– c Rhodes b Liptrot	28
D. L. Hemp not out	186	– lbw b Liptrot	8
J. O. Troughton c Leatherdale b Sheriyar	27	– not out	5
D. R. Brown c Rhodes b Sheriyar	85	– not out	2
†K. J. Piper b Leatherdale	21		
N. M. K. Smith not out	11		
B 2, l-b 13, w 6, n-b 4	25	B 1, w 4	5
1/17 2/30 3/150 4/215 5/379 6/423 (6 wkts dec.)	447	1/4 2/46 3/66 4/75 (4 wkts)	77

N. M. Carter, V. C. Drakes and A. Richardson did not bat.

Bonus points – Warwickshire 5, Worcestershire 2 (Score at 130 overs: 432-6).

Bowling: *First Innings*—Bichel 22–6–91–0; Sheriyar 28–8–94–3; Liptrot 27–6–89–2; Leatherdale 11–1–41–1; Rawnsley 37–8–88–0; Hick 11–3–28–0; Boulton 1–0–1–0. *Second Innings*—Bichel 9–2–28–1; Sheriyar 7–2–28–0; Liptrot 8–3–12–3; Leatherdale 2.1–0–8–0.

Umpires: V. A. Holder and M. J. Kitchen.

At Lord's, August 22, 23, 24, 25. WARWICKSHIRE drew with MIDDLESEX.

WARWICKSHIRE v SUSSEX

At Birmingham, September 7, 8, 9, 10. Drawn. Warwickshire 8 pts, Sussex 10 pts. Toss: Sussex. First-class debut: T. R. Ambrose.

Sussex secured promotion with safety-first batting on the third day and final morning, while the draw also gave Warwickshire sufficient points to sustain their own promotion bid. After losing Montgomerie to the first ball of the match, Goodwin held Sussex together throughout the opening day with a painstaking 150, before pulling his 300th delivery to deep square leg, giving Richardson his fifth wicket. It was Goodwin's seventh century of the summer. Bell, batting for nigh on four hours, rescued Warwickshire from 21 for three, and added 85 for the sixth wicket with Drakes, who hit his only fifty of a lean season. As Sussex added 312 on the third day for the loss of only two wickets – and one of those was the night-watchman – Montgomerie hit his eighth first-class hundred of the summer and Adams his third, while also completing 1,000 runs. Tim Ambrose, 18, Australian-born but ECB-qualified, impressed with a maiden fifty before Adams eventually declared with 84 overs remaining and Warwickshire unlikely to chase 450.

Close of play: First day, Sussex 315-8 (Kirtley 13*, Lewry 12*); Second day, Sussex 12-1 (Montgomerie 8*, Kirtley 4*); Third day, Sussex 324-3 (Adams 132*, Ambrose 41*).

Sussex

R. R. Montgomerie c Bell b Drakes	0	– (2) c Wagh b Drakes	121
M. W. Goodwin c Betts b Richardson	150	– (1) b Richardson	0
*C. J. Adams b Brown	33	– (4) b Betts	139
M. H. Yardy c Powell b Richardson	21	– (6) not out	22
T. R. Ambrose c Hemp b Richardson	26	– c and b Richardson	52
R. S. C. Martin-Jenkins b Richardson	4	– (7) not out	11
†M. J. Prior c Knight b Brown	14		
M. J. G. Davis c Brown b Richardson	3		
R. J. Kirtley not out	17	– (3) c Hemp b Richardson	13
J. D. Lewry c Knight b Drakes	12		
M. A. Robinson c Hemp b Drakes	1		
B 10, l-b 6, w 4, n-b 20	40	B 4, l-b 10, n-b 4	18
1/0 2/68 3/131 4/202 5/214 6/239 7/256 8/293 9/319	321	1/1 2/47 3/246 4/334 5/364 (5 wkts dec.)	376

Bonus points – Sussex 3, Warwickshire 3.

Bowling: *First Innings*—Drakes 22.5–6–51–3; Betts 15–2–71–0; Richardson 31–8–89–5; Brown 25–8–50–2; Smith 12–2–44–0. *Second Innings*—Drakes 21–5–60–1; Richardson 30.5–7–77–3; Betts 18–1–71–1; Brown 19–2–71–0; Smith 13–2–28–0; Wagh 20–4–55–0.

Warwickshire

*M. J. Powell c Adams b Lewry	0	– c Adams b Robinson	27
N. V. Knight lbw b Martin-Jenkins	17	– b Robinson	59
M. A. Wagh b Kirtley	5	– not out	74
D. L. Hemp lbw b Kirtley	16	– c Robinson b Davis	45
I. R. Bell c Adams b Robinson	80	– not out	22
D. R. Brown c Adams b Lewry	23		
V. C. Drakes c Prior b Martin-Jenkins	50		
N. M. K. Smith c Ambrose b Martin-Jenkins	8		
†K. J. Piper c Prior b Martin-Jenkins	13		
M. M. Betts c Martin-Jenkins b Kirtley	14		
A. Richardson not out	6		
B 3, l-b 3, n-b 10	16	B 2, l-b 5, w 2, n-b 4	13
1/0 2/5 3/21 4/59 5/101 6/186 7/205 8/221 9/234	248	1/90 2/93 3/182 (3 wkts)	240

Bonus points – Warwickshire 1, Sussex 3.

Bowling: *First Innings*—Lewry 16–5–57–2; Kirtley 20.3–5–64–3; Martin-Jenkins 25–6–75–4; Robinson 25–7–46–1. *Second Innings*—Lewry 8–2–29–0; Kirtley 12–2–46–0; Robinson 16–6–32–2; Martin-Jenkins 12–3–33–0; Davis 16–4–42–1; Goodwin 11–1–40–0; Montgomerie 4–0–11–0.

Umpires: A. Clarkson and A. A. Jones.

At Derby, September 12, 13, 14, 15. WARWICKSHIRE beat DERBYSHIRE by an innings and 100 runs.

CRICKET SOCIETY AWARDS

Ian Bell of Warwickshire won the Cricket Society's Most Promising Young Cricketer Award, 2001. The A. A. Thomson Fielding Prize, for the best schoolboy fielder, went to Tom Smith of Parklands High School, Chorley. The Sir John Hobbs Jubilee Memorial Prize, for the outstanding Under-16 schoolboy, was won by Adam Harrison of West Monmouth Comprehensive School. Wetherell awards went to Martin Bicknell of Surrey, for the second year running, as the outstanding all-rounder in the first-class game, with the schools award going to Brendan McKerchar of Merchiston Castle School.

Andy Bichel

WORCESTERSHIRE

President: M. G. Jones
Chairman: J. W. Elliott
Chief Executive: M. Newton
Chairman, Cricket Committee: M. J. Horton
Captain: G. A. Hick
Director of Cricket: T. M. Moody
Head Groundsman: 2001 – R. McLaren
2002 – T. R. Packwood
Scorer: 2001 – S. S. Hale
2002 – W. Clarke

Worcestershire, after too many years of minimal success, took the first steps towards rebuilding under their new director of cricket, former captain Tom Moody. Brought back to New Road after the resignation of Bill Athey, and given a free hand in all cricketing matters, he set out the guidelines for a five-year plan aimed at restoring Worcestershire as a force to be reckoned with. Crucial to Moody's thinking was a revamped cricket academy, due to be launched in early 2002, after he had pinpointed the paucity of homegrown talent breaking into the senior side in the past decade. Admittedly, the break-up of the side that won six trophies in the late 1980s and early 1990s had been a tardy process; the county had rested on its laurels for too long instead of capitalising on the golden years of Ian Botham and Graham Dilley. But only Graeme Hick and Steve Rhodes from that era were likely to play a full part in 2002.

Worcestershire never threatened to mount a serious challenge for promotion in the Championship, and eventually finished sixth. However, there was reason for celebration after they secured the third promotion spot in the Norwich Union League on the final day of the season. It meant a return to the top flight at the first attempt, following their spectacular decline in fortunes in 2000, when they led Division One by eight points midway through the season.

Off the field, meanwhile, a different kind of revolution was taking place. Secretary Mike Vockins retired in June after 30 years' inestimable service to the club, making his farewells as the Australians played their traditional tour-opener at Worcester, and Mark Newton succeeded him with the new title of chief executive. One of Newton's first observations was the need to improve the standard of pitches at New Road, not only to make the cricket more attractive to tempt stay-away spectators, but also to persuade top batsmen to join the county. Within weeks of his arrival, Roy McLaren's 18 years as head groundsman had come to an end. It was common knowledge that he and Moody had often not seen eye to eye in Moody's days as captain, and his assistant, Tim Packwood, now took charge. In McLaren's defence, Worcester had just experienced its worst floods in more than 100 years. Much of the autumn work on the square was destroyed, and two early-season one-day matches had been switched to Kidderminster. Nor was he the only casualty: cricket development officer Mark Scott, Worcestershire Cricket

Board development officer Harshad Patel, first-team physio Jane Ross and first-team scorer Sam Hale were all replaced.

In terms of individual playing performances, the positives outweighed the negatives, even if it was rare in the Championship for all the good elements to come together at the same time. Phil Weston put two lean, injury-hit years behind him as his decision to be ultra-positive, in order to combat the uncertain New Road pitches, paid handsome dividends; he topped 1,000 runs and earned a new two-year contract. His new opening partner, Anurag Singh, recruited from Warwickshire, also showed great promise. Frustrated with being pigeonholed as a middle-order one-day batsman, he showed he had the application to move up the order without losing much fluency and reached four figures in a first-class season for the first time.

If Hick was disappointed at losing his England place after a below-par winter, it hardly showed as he scored 1,409 first-class runs with six centuries in his first full season as captain. But the middle-order batting did disappoint, with Vikram Solanki and David Leatherdale experiencing their least productive returns for years. Paul Pollard also failed to produce any consistency, and the acquisition of Ben Smith from Leicestershire and Stephen Peters from Essex on three-year contracts should stimulate much-needed competition for places. Rhodes, often dropping down to No. 8 in the order, had fewer chances to make an impression with the bat but, in his 17th season with Worcestershire, was as dependable as ever behind the stumps.

There was little to fault in the opening attack of Alamgir Sheriyar and Andy Bichel, who between them shared 137 first-class wickets. Sheriyar had asked to be released in 2000 after a fall-out with Athey and a dramatic slump in form, compared with the previous year when he was the country's leading wicket-taker. But he reconsidered his decision when Moody arrived, reverted to his longer run-up and responded with 65 Championship wickets. Bichel, who had the unenviable task of filling Glenn McGrath's shoes, none the less emulated his fellow-Australian by winning the county's Player of the Year award, having made telling contributions with bat and ball in both forms of the game.

The big plus for Worcestershire in the pace department was the advance made by the recent England Under-19 bowlers, Kabir Ali and Chris Liptrot. Ali showed great promise; he took a career-best five for 22 against Gloucestershire before a shoulder injury, suffered while fielding, ruled him out. Liptrot, thrust straight into the first team from the Northern League in 1999, established himself in the Championship side after a difficult second season and was arguably the best bowler in the last two months of the campaign. Their emergence meant Stuart Lampitt, a loyal and dependable stalwart, was expected to play primarily in one-day cricket in 2002. As for spin, much will depend on the way Packwood's pitches roll out. It could be an interesting year. – JOHN CURTIS.

WORCESTERSHIRE 2001

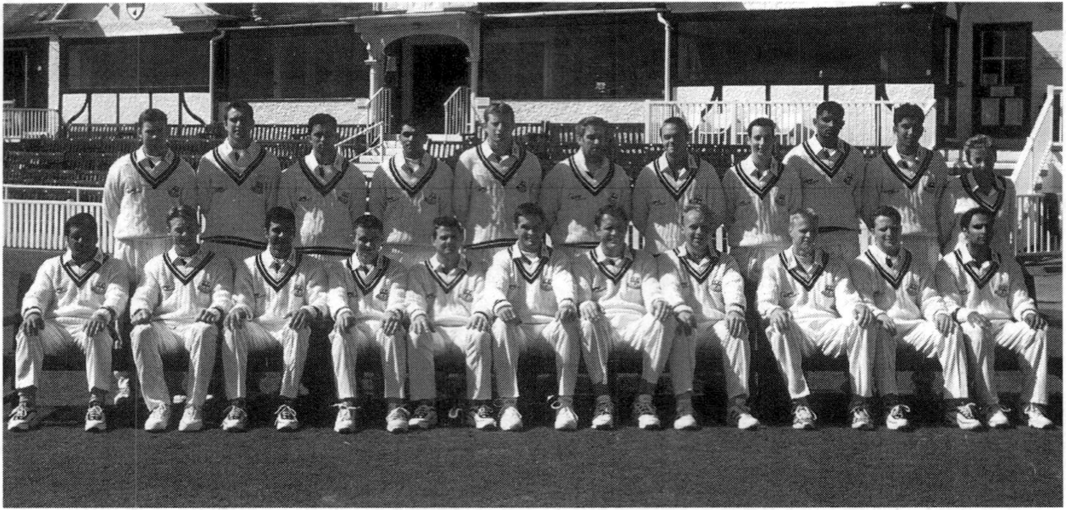

[*Mike Pollard*

Standing: N. R. Boulton, C. G. Liptrot, Kabir Ali, A. Singh, M. J. Rawnsley, P. R. Pollard, D. J. Pipe, D. N. Catterall, D. B. Patel, Kadeer Ali, J. Rees (*physiotherapist*). *Seated:* D. B. D'Oliveira (*assistant coach*), A. J. Bichel, V. S. Solanki, D. A. Leatherdale, S. J. Rhodes, G. A. Hick (*captain*), T. M. Moody (*director of cricket*), S. R. Lampitt, W. P. C. Weston, K. R. Spiring, A. Sheriyar.

WORCESTERSHIRE RESULTS

All first-class matches – Played 18: Won 4, Lost 6, Drawn 8.

County Championship matches – Played 16: Won 4, Lost 5, Drawn 7.

CricInfo County Championship, 6th in Division 2; Cheltenham & Gloucester Trophy, q-f; Benson and Hedges Cup, 4th in Midlands/Wales/West Group; Norwich Union League, 3rd in Division 2.

COUNTY CHAMPIONSHIP AVERAGES

BATTING

Cap		*M*	*I*	*NO*	*R*	*HS*	*100s*	*50s*	*Avge*	*Ct/St*
1986	G. A. Hick	16	26	3	1,390	201	6	3	60.43	19
1995	W. P. C. Weston	16	28	4	1,044	192	2	6	43.50	10
1986	S. J. Rhodes	15	20	7	442	52	0	1	34.00	51/1
	A. Singh	16	28	2	853	168	1	3	32.80	4
2001	A. J. Bichel§	16	24	0	627	78	0	3	26.12	5
1998	V. S. Solanki	16	26	0	678	112	2	2	26.07	16
1989	S. R. Lampitt	10	13	5	205	42*	0	0	25.62	4
1994	D. A. Leatherdale	16	25	3	476	93	0	1	21.63	5
	P. R. Pollard	9	11	0	178	45	0	0	16.18	5
	M. J. Rawnsley	13	18	4	186	39	0	0	13.28	7
	C. G. Liptrot	10	12	2	111	22	0	0	11.10	3
	Kadeer Ali	3	5	0	44	38	0	0	8.80	0
1997	A. Sheriyar	14	17	8	63	20	0	0	7.00	2
	N. R. Boulton	3	4	0	28	21	0	0	7.00	0

Also batted: Kabir Ali (2 matches) 13, 25; D. J. Pipe (1 match) 22, 0 (3 ct).

* *Signifies not out.* § *Overseas player.*

BOWLING

	O	*M*	*R*	*W*	*BB*	*5W/i*	*Avge*
Kabir Ali	56	16	143	10	5-22	1	14.30
A. Sheriyar	472.3	115	1,534	65	6-88	3	23.60
C. G. Liptrot	242.4	67	749	28	3-12	0	26.75
A. J. Bichel	555.5	137	1,804	66	6-44	4	27.33
S. R. Lampitt	203.2	49	669	24	5-22	1	27.87
D. A. Leatherdale	153	39	534	16	4-70	0	33.37
M. J. Rawnsley	337.2	88	922	18	3-72	0	51.22

Also bowled: Kadeer Ali 8–2–27–0; N. R. Boulton 4–1–15–0; G. A. Hick 105.4–30–287–7; V. S. Solanki 46.4–6–161–0; W. P. C. Weston 2.4–0–19–0.

COUNTY RECORDS

Highest score for:	405*	G. A. Hick v Somerset at Taunton	1988
Highest score against:	331*	J. D. Robertson (Middlesex) at Worcester	1949
Best bowling for:	9-23	C. F. Root v Lancashire at Worcester	1931
Best bowling against:	10-51	J. Mercer (Glamorgan) at Worcester	1936
Highest total for:	670-7 dec.	v Somerset at Worcester	1995
Highest total against:	701-4 dec.	by Leicestershire at Worcester	1906
Lowest total for:	24	v Yorkshire at Huddersfield	1903
Lowest total against:	30	by Hampshire at Worcester	1903

At Lord's, April 20, 21, 22, 23. WORCESTERSHIRE drew with MIDDLESEX.

WORCESTERSHIRE v SUSSEX

At Worcester, April 25, 26, 27, 28. Drawn. Worcestershire 6 pts, Sussex 6 pts. Toss: Worcestershire. First-class debuts: M. J. Prior, B. Zuiderent. County debut: M. W. Goodwin.

The 1,000th first-class fixture at New Road was wrecked by the weather, and even three final-day declarations failed to engineer a positive result. The ground had experienced its worst winter flooding for 50 years, yet the season would have begun on schedule had heavy downpours not washed out the opening two days. Play at last began on the third afternoon, when Goodwin, Sussex's new overseas player, scored a confident 94 off 116 balls before becoming one of four victims for Bichel, his Worcestershire counterpart, making his home debut. Adams had his thumb fractured by Sheriyar and was forced to retire. Hick resisted the temptation to go for batting points on the final day and declared in the seventh over; Sussex in return set Worcestershire a daunting 296 in 49 overs. Despite a solid innings from Weston providing a useful platform, the assault was called off as the asking-rate exceeded ten an over.

Close of play: First day, No play; Second day, No play; Third day, Sussex 192-5 (Martin-Jenkins 9*, Kirtley 0*).

Sussex

R. R. Montgomerie c Hick b Liptrot	15	– b Bichel	0
M. W. Goodwin b Bichel	94	– not out	42
*C. J. Adams retired hurt	15		
B. Zuiderent run out	0	– (3) b Lampitt	6
P. A. Cottey c Hick b Bichel	46	– (4) not out	4
U. B. A. Rashid b Bichel	1		
R. S. C. Martin-Jenkins c Rhodes b Bichel	26		
R. J. Kirtley c Solanki b Hick	0		
†M. J. Prior not out	25		
J. D. Lewry not out	14		
B 2, l-b 3, n-b 14	19	W 2	2
1/45 2/95 3/173 4/182 5/191 6/211 7/215	(7 wkts dec.) 255	1/0 2/33	(2 wkts dec.) 54

M. A. Robinson did not bat.

Bonus points – Sussex 2, Worcestershire 2.

In the first innings Adams retired hurt at 82.

Bowling: *First Innings*—Bichel 26–9–84–4; Sheriyar 11–1–43–0; Liptrot 13–2–43–1; Lampitt 4–0–37–0; Leatherdale 5–1–21–0; Hick 9.4–3–22–1. *Second Innings*—Bichel 2–1–5–1; Liptrot 1–0–7–0; Lampitt 6–2–14–1; Sheriyar 2–0–5–0; Hick 4–0–23–0.

Worcestershire

W. P. C. Weston c Prior b Lewry	6	– not out	78
A. Singh not out	8	– c and b Martin-Jenkins	20
*G. A. Hick (did not bat)		– c Cottey b Martin-Jenkins	31
A. J. Bichel (did not bat)		– b Martin-Jenkins	15
V. S. Solanki (did not bat)		– b Rashid	34
D. A. Leatherdale (did not bat)		– not out	0
		L-b 6, w 2, n-b 2	10
1/14	(1 wkt dec.) 14	1/43 2/99 3/132 4/188	(4 wkts) 188

P. R. Pollard, †S. J. Rhodes, S. R. Lampitt, A. Sheriyar and C. G. Liptrot did not bat.

Bowling: *First Innings*—Lewry 3.2–0–13–1; Kirtley 3–2–1–0. *Second Innings*—Lewry 9–0–37–0; Kirtley 7–0–36–0; Martin-Jenkins 12–3–50–3; Robinson 9–2–34–0; Rashid 3.1–0–25–1.

Umpires: J. H. Hampshire and D. R. Shepherd.

At Southampton, May 9, 10, 11. WORCESTERSHIRE lost to HAMPSHIRE by 124 runs.

WORCESTERSHIRE v DERBYSHIRE

At Worcester, May 16, 17, 18, 19. Drawn. Worcestershire 4 pts, Derbyshire 4 pts. Toss: Worcestershire.

A muddy outfield prevented any cricket on the opening three days, and a single-innings contest was possible only after the captains agreed to brave the wet conditions. Even then, the only act of significance, after Sheriyar had picked up two early wickets, was Di Venuto's first Championship hundred for Derbyshire, in his 27th innings. He hit 19 boundaries, twice striking Lampitt for three in an over, and with Sutton added 94 for the third wicket. Munton's meaningless declaration after tea notionally set Worcestershire a target of 223 in 25 overs, which ensured a tame draw and an early finish. It was a disappointing conclusion to the Rev. Mike Vockins's last home Championship match before retiring: his 30 seasons as Worcestershire secretary had made him county cricket's longest-serving senior administrator.

Close of play: First day, No play; Second day, No play; Third day, No play.

Derbyshire

L. D. Sutton c Rhodes b Bichel	42
S. D. Stubbings c Weston b Sheriyar	1
M. P. Dowman lbw b Sheriyar	0
M. J. Di Venuto c Rhodes b Lampitt	108
R. J. Bailey c Hick b Leatherdale	11
W. G. Khan b Liptrot	1
G. Welch lbw b Leatherdale	29
†K. M. Krikken not out	8
R. K. Illingworth b Leatherdale	6
T. M. Smith not out	5
B 1, l-b 4, n-b 6	11
1/10 2/10 3/104 4/163 5/164 6/188 7/203 8/213 (8 wkts dec.)	222

*T. A. Munton did not bat.

Bowling: Bichel 15–5–51–1; Sheriyar 14–3–51–2; Lampitt 15–3–55–1; Liptrot 13–2–31–1; Leatherdale 7–2–23–3; Solanki 5–2–6–0.

Worcestershire

W. P. C. Weston not out	17
A. Singh not out	26
L-b 1, w 8	9
(no wkt)	52

*G. A. Hick, V. S. Solanki, D. A. Leatherdale, P. R. Pollard, †S. J. Rhodes, A. J. Bichel, S. R. Lampitt, C. G. Liptrot and A. Sheriyar did not bat.

Bowling: Welch 6–1–23–0; Munton 4–2–5–0; Smith 3–0–21–0; Illingworth 2–1–2–0.

Umpires: J. W. Lloyds and R. A. White.

At Bristol, May 25, 26, 27, 28. WORCESTERSHIRE beat GLOUCESTERSHIRE by 252 runs.

At Worcester, June 1, 2, 3. WORCESTERSHIRE lost to AUSTRALIANS by 360 runs (see Australian tour section).

At Horsham, June 6, 7, 8, 9. WORCESTERSHIRE lost to SUSSEX by 33 runs.

WORCESTERSHIRE v WARWICKSHIRE

At Worcester, June 13, 14, 15, 16. Drawn. Worcestershire 10 pts, Warwickshire 7.75 pts. Toss: Warwickshire.

Losing the fourth day to rain not only denied Worcestershire the chance to press for victory after Hick's 124 had put them in a commanding position; it prevented Warwickshire from improving their over-rate and so cost them a quarter-point. On the first day, Sheriyar's three wickets in his 16th over reduced Warwickshire to 122 for seven. But Piper, dropped on four at third slip, masterminded a remarkable recovery on a pitch still full of pace and bounce, adding 136 for the last two wickets with Drakes and Betts before being stranded eight short of a deserved century. Hick, who had scored only 56 in the seven innings since his hundred at Southampton, bestrode the second day until bad light and rain ended play, hitting 17 fours and two sixes to reach 116 off 128 balls. Giles, in his first Championship match of the season, was struck for 19 off his first two overs, but he regained some composure next morning, when Hick was one of four wickets to fall to him and Drakes in 18 balls. However, the weather allowed only 24 overs all day, and Saturday became the sixth full day lost in the three Championship games at New Road.

Close of play: First day, Warwickshire 256-9 (Piper 79*, Betts 11*); Second day, Worcestershire 272-3 (Hick 116*, Leatherdale 4*); Third day, Worcestershire 347-7 (Rhodes 22*, Lampitt 17*).

Warwickshire

*M. J. Powell c Singh b Lampitt	23
I. R. Bell c Pollard b Sheriyar	17
M. A. Wagh lbw b Leatherdale	16
D. L. Hemp b Sheriyar	17
D. P. Ostler b Lampitt	10
D. R. Brown c Hick b Bichel	32
N. M. K. Smith c Rhodes b Sheriyar	8
A. F. Giles c Rhodes b Sheriyar	0
†K. J. Piper not out	92
V. C. Drakes c Rhodes b Bichel	28
M. M. Betts c Rhodes b Lampitt	19
B 6, l-b 7, n-b 2	15
1/30 2/62 3/62 4/80 5/114 6/122 7/122 8/141 9/216	277

Bonus points – Warwickshire 2, Worcestershire 3.

Bowling: Bichel 28–5–92–2; Sheriyar 33–12–76–4; Lampitt 23.3–5–58–3; Leatherdale 11–2–36–1; Rawnsley 3–1–2–0.

Worcestershire

W. P. C. Weston c Ostler b Drakes	74
A. Singh c Hemp b Betts	23
*G. A. Hick c Brown b Drakes	124
V. S. Solanki c Betts b Brown	29
D. A. Leatherdale b Drakes	18
P. R. Pollard c and b Giles	0
A. J. Bichel lbw b Giles	5
†S. J. Rhodes not out	22
S. R. Lampitt not out	17
B 3, l-b 12, w 6, n-b 14	35
1/66 2/181 3/262 4/294 5/295 6/295 7/301	(7 wkts) 347

A. Sheriyar and M. J. Rawnsley did not bat.

Bonus points – Worcestershire 3, Warwickshire 2.

Bowling: Drakes 23.1–5–101–3; Betts 13–2–70–1; Brown 17–2–81–1; Giles 19–4–55–2; Smith 4–0–25–0.

Umpires: M. J. Harris and N. A. Mallender.

WORCESTERSHIRE v DURHAM UCCE

At Worcester, June 20, 21, 22. Drawn. Toss: Durham UCCE.

Wicket-keeper Foster showed why he was being touted as an England prospect, hitting a determined maiden century off 289 balls, including 18 fours. But it was grim going as the students ground out their runs at barely two an over on a flat pitch with a short boundary. Worcestershire's batsmen further emphasised the class divide by hauling in the University's total in less than half their time, going on to amass the county's third-highest total. Singh registered his first hundred since his winter move from Warwickshire, Solanki, captaining Worcestershire for the first time, reached three figures off just 84 balls and, in what amounted to a glorified net practice, Pollard grafted 131 off 201 balls before crying off over lunch on the third day. Kabir Ali's unbeaten 50 from 24 deliveries stretched the lead to 347. Three and a half hours remained when Durham began their second innings, but openers Brown, who scored his second fifty of the match, and Rowe batted in untroubled fashion to earn a draw.

Close of play: First day, Durham UCCE 236-6 (Foster 100*, Stead 19*); Second day, Worcestershire 396-4 (Pollard 44*, Boulton 8*).

Durham UCCE

M. J. Brown c Kadeer Ali b Rawnsley	55	– not out	60
J. G. C. Rowe b Sheriyar	1	– not out	74
*M. J. Banes c Solanki b Sheriyar	10		
A. G. R. Loudon b Rawnsley	3		
†J. S. Foster lbw b Liptrot	103		
H. J. H. Loudon lbw b Liptrot	16		
T. J. Phillips lbw b Liptrot	15		
R. A. Stead b Rawnsley	28		
R. S. Ferley not out	17		
M. Thorburn c Boulton b Sheriyar	11		
J. T. A. Bruce c Liptrot b Sheriyar	1		
B 5, l-b 13, w 4, n-b 2	24	B 4, l-b 5, n-b 21	30
1/11 2/33 3/53 4/108 5/163 6/207 7/250 8/250 9/272	284	(no wkt)	164

Bowling: *First Innings*—Sheriyar 25.4–4–78–4; Kabir Ali 5–0–12–0; Liptrot 32–9–81–3; Rawnsley 47–23–55–3; Solanki 14–7–18–0; Boulton 4–1–12–0; Kadeer Ali 2–0–10–0. *Second Innings*—Sheriyar 6–2–19–0; Liptrot 6–1–25–0; Solanki 4–0–12–0; Rawnsley 15–4–36–0; Boulton 9–2–21–0; Kadeer Ali 7–3–20–0; Weston 5–0–22–0.

Worcestershire

W. P. C. Weston c Foster b A. G. R. Loudon	60
A. Singh c Brown b A. G. R. Loudon	128
*V. S. Solanki c Rowe b Phillips	106
Kadeer Ali lbw b Ferley	14
P. R. Pollard retired hurt	131
N. R. Boulton c Stead b A. G. R. Loudon	47
†D. J. Pipe c Foster b Thorburn	24
Kabir Ali not out	50
M. J. Rawnsley not out	15
B 13, l-b 15, w 4, n-b 24	56
1/211 2/215 3/254 4/365 5/486 6/558 (6 wkts dec.)	631

C. G. Liptrot and A. Sheriyar did not bat.

Pollard retired hurt at 558-5.

Bowling: Bruce 20–1–132–0; Thorburn 9–0–76–1; Phillips 22–4–119–1; Stead 16–2–50–0; Ferley 27–2–103–1; A. G. R. Loudon 20–5–86–3; Banes 10–0–37–0.

Umpires: N. L. Bainton and A. G. T. Whitehead.

WORCESTERSHIRE v NOTTINGHAMSHIRE

At Worcester, June 29, 30, July 1, 2. Nottinghamshire won by seven wickets. Nottinghamshire 15 pts, Worcestershire 4 pts. Toss: Worcestershire. Championship debut: N. R. Boulton.

A remarkable game in which 20 wickets fell on the first day culminated in Nottinghamshire achieving 461 for three, their highest fourth-innings total to win a Championship match: it surpassed their 419 for six against Leicestershire at Trent Bridge in 1926. Worcestershire had never conceded so many runs in the last innings to lose. Along with the tumbling wickets, there were spectacular first-day hundreds from Hick (123 off 151 balls) and Pietersen, whose 92-ball counter-attack revived Nottinghamshire after Bichel had reduced them to 30 for five. Worcestershire built on their lead of 88 through Weston's first century for almost two years, though they were in danger of squandering the advantage until Lampitt helped him add 120 for the eighth wicket. Reprieved on 32, Weston batted six and a half hours for his 192, hitting 31 boundaries in 309 balls. Nottinghamshire had almost two days in which to score 458 but, on a pitch now devoid of its earlier indifferent bounce, they wasted no time going about their task. Morris set the tone, reeling off 18 fours with gloriously flowing strokes while making 94 in a two-hour opening stand with Bicknell. Bicknell then added 102 with Blewett, who slept on 99 and woke to help Afzaal and Johnson plunder the last 94 runs in 65 minutes.

Close of play: First day, Nottinghamshire 160; Second day, Worcestershire 356-8 (Weston 185*, Liptrot 6*); Third day, Nottinghamshire 367-2 (Blewett 99*, Afzaal 63*).

Worcestershire

W. P. C. Weston c Pietersen b Lucas	5	– lbw b Harris	192
A. Singh c Blewett b Logan	17	– c Bicknell b Stemp	27
*G. A. Hick c Johnson b Logan	123	– b Stemp	17
V. S. Solanki b Lucas	5	– c Johnson b Afzaal	15
D. A. Leatherdale b Logan	12	– c Blewett b Lucas	9
N. R. Boulton lbw b Harris	0	– b Afzaal	21
A. J. Bichel c Johnson b Logan	2	– c Bicknell b Harris	17
†D. J. Pipe lbw b Logan	22	– b Harris	0
S. R. Lampitt c Afzaal b Lucas	24	– c Blewett b Lucas	40
C. G. Liptrot not out	19	– c Read b Harris	11
A. Sheriyar c Johnson b Stemp	0	– not out	0
L-b 7, w 8, n-b 4	19	B 4, l-b 12, w 4	20
1/11 2/71 3/80 4/115 5/116 6/119 7/153 8/198 9/244	248	1/96 2/130 3/158 4/171 5/196 6/225 7/225 8/345 9/368	369

Bonus points – Worcestershire 1, Nottinghamshire 3.

Bowling: *First Innings*—Harris 11–2–36–1; Lucas 17–1–80–3; Logan 20–4–96–5; Blewett 4–0–20–0; Stemp 3.4–0–9–1. *Second Innings*—Harris 20.5–5–56–4; Lucas 21–2–78–2; Logan 17–6–83–0; Blewett 5–0–18–0; Stemp 27–5–74–2; Afzaal 15–3–44–2.

Nottinghamshire

*D. J. Bicknell b Sheriyar	6	– c Pipe b Lampitt	104
J. E. Morris c Pipe b Bichel	3	– c Lampitt b Bichel	94
G. S. Blewett b Bichel	0	– not out	134
U. Afzaal c Pipe b Bichel	0	– lbw b Sheriyar	88
P. Johnson c Liptrot b Bichel	9	– not out	26
K. P. Pietersen not out	103		
†C. M. W. Read c and b Liptrot	2		
R. J. Logan c Weston b Liptrot	1		
D. S. Lucas b Lampitt	21		
A. J. Harris c Solanki b Lampitt	1		
R. D. Stemp c Singh b Bichel	5		
B 2, l-b 3, w 2, n-b 2	9	L-b 9, w 4, n-b 2	15
1/5 2/11 3/11 4/15 5/30 6/45 7/51 8/143 9/151	160	1/157 2/259 3/404	(3 wkts) 461

Bonus points – Worcestershire 3.

Bowling: *First Innings*—Bichel 14.4–4–45–5; Sheriyar 12–0–44–1; Liptrot 5–2–20–2; Lampitt 11–2–46–2. *Second Innings*—Bichel 24–2–127–1; Sheriyar 27–5–92–1; Lampitt 16–3–61–1; Liptrot 14–2–56–0; Hick 25–8–70–0; Solanki 4–0–18–0; Boulton 3–1–14–0; Weston 2.2–0–14–0.

Umpires: A. Clarkson and J. W. Holder.

At Derby, July 5, 6, 7, 8. WORCESTERSHIRE beat DERBYSHIRE by an innings and three runs.

WORCESTERSHIRE v GLOUCESTERSHIRE

At Worcester, July 20, 21, 22. Worcestershire won by seven wickets. Worcestershire 16 pts, Gloucestershire 4 pts. Toss: Gloucestershire.

Roy McLaren's last pitch after 18 years as head groundsman at New Road was a typical grassy seamer. When overcast skies and unpredictable bounce entered the equation on the second day, the bowlers were in their element: 20 wickets fell and the match was over an hour into the third morning. Bichel again exposed the brittle nature of Gloucestershire's batting, following his six for 44 at Bristol in May with his first ten-wicket match return for Worcestershire. He twice took two wickets in an over on the opening day, beginning crucially with Barnett, who along with Taylor and Ball demonstrated the tenacity to adapt to the conditions. Worcestershire openers Weston and Singh provided a rapid response on the first evening, but it was all change next day. Without Pollard's disciplined two-and-a-half-hour 45, the home side would have struggled to lead at all. In the event, the gain was not important: Kabir Ali, capturing five for the first time, and Bichel were virtually unplayable as Gloucestershire were bundled out in an hour and a half. Weston, using his height to get forward, saw Worcestershire to victory before Harvey could cause too much damage.

Close of play: First day, Worcestershire 84-0 (Weston 35*, Singh 34*); Second day, Worcestershire 14-0 (Weston 6*, Singh 4*).

Gloucestershire

D. R. Hewson c Rhodes b Ali	5	– b Ali	7
K. J. Barnett c Weston b Bichel	54	– c Singh b Ali	0
M. G. N. Windows lbw b Leatherdale	9	– c Lampitt b Bichel	8
C. G. Taylor c Rhodes b Ali	50	– lbw b Ali	0
*M. W. Alleyne c Rhodes b Bichel	0	– c Rhodes b Bichel	0
J. N. Snape c Rhodes b Bichel	15	– lbw b Ali	25
I. J. Harvey lbw b Lampitt	0	– c Solanki b Bichel	13
†R. C. Russell c Weston b Bichel	18	– lbw b Leatherdale	20
M. C. J. Ball c Hick b Bichel	45	– b Bichel	4
J. M. M. Averis b Bichel	0	– c Hick b Ali	6
B. W. Gannon not out	10	– not out	0
L-b 2, n-b 14	16	L-b 4	4
1/7 2/47 3/91 4/91 5/135 6/140 7/150 8/183 9/183	222	1/6 2/19 3/19 4/19 5/21 6/40 7/75 8/81 9/81	87

Bonus points – Gloucestershire 1, Worcestershire 3.

Bowling: *First Innings*—Bichel 20.3–7–54–6; Ali 18–6–42–2; Lampitt 16–0–76–1; Leatherdale 11–3–39–1; Rawnsley 3–0–9–0. *Second Innings*—Bichel 12–4–32–4; Ali 10.2–5–22–5; Leatherdale 6–2–29–1.

Worcestershire

W. P. C. Weston c Snape b Harvey	35	– not out	38
A. Singh b Averis	42	– c Averis b Harvey	15
*G. A. Hick c Ball b Harvey	10	– lbw b Harvey	0
V. S. Solanki c Harvey b Averis	6	– c Russell b Harvey	12
D. A. Leatherdale lbw b Alleyne	9	– not out	4
P. R. Pollard c Ball b Alleyne	45		
A. J. Bichel c Russell b Alleyne	13		
†S. J. Rhodes c Russell b Gannon	0		
S. R. Lampitt c Russell b Gannon	11		
Kabir Ali c Ball b Alleyne	25		
M. J. Rawnsley not out	0		
L-b 16, n-b 28	44	W 2, n-b 2	4
1/88 2/96 3/110 4/118 5/153 6/171 7/176 8/194 9/231	240	1/34 2/34 3/60	(3 wkts) 73

Bonus points – Worcestershire 1, Gloucestershire 3.

Bowling: *First Innings*—Averis 22–4–90–2; Harvey 28–14–59–2; Gannon 10–1–45–2; Alleyne 11.5–4–30–4. *Second Innings*—Harvey 7–1–36–3; Averis 1–0–6–0; Gannon 5–0–14–0; Alleyne 1.4–0–17–0.

Umpires: J. H. Evans and G. Sharp.

WORCESTERSHIRE v DURHAM

At Kidderminster, August 2, 3, 4, 5. Durham won by seven wickets. Durham 17 pts, Worcestershire 4 pts. Toss: Worcestershire.

Worcestershire, unbeaten in their first ten fixtures at Kidderminster after the resumption of first-class cricket there in 1987, now suffered a fifth successive defeat on Durham's first visit to Chester Road. With rain around, and humidity high, conditions were less batsman-friendly than usual and, for the first time since 1991, no one hit a hundred. Hick and Solanki both departed first ball to Hatch as Worcestershire lost three wickets in six deliveries, and it took a last-wicket stand of 54 between Lampitt and Sheriyar to get them past 200. Durham, quite brilliant in the field, found batting equally perilous after a promising start. Love raced to 50 off 38 balls, and Collingwood had guided them to 133 for three when Sheriyar blew the innings apart with five for 11 in 26 deliveries. Law, however, launched a furious counter-attack in a last-wicket partnership of 84 with Hatch and, on the third morning, inflicted irreversible damage when he had Hick and Solanki caught behind in three balls. More rain meant Durham had to wait another day to make 115 for victory. Although Lewis was out in the first over, Bichel's 50th wicket of the season, Love's second high-class fifty (58 in 61 balls this time), with good support from Daley, guaranteed that the visitors would enjoy their lunch.

Close of play: First day, Worcestershire 149-7 (Bichel 32*, Lampitt 0*); Second day, Durham 260; Third day, Worcestershire 147.

Worcestershire

W. P. C. Weston run out	5	– lbw b Law	2
A. Singh c Bridge b Brinkley	45	– c Love b Law	57
*G. A. Hick lbw b Hatch	0	– c Pratt b Law	12
V. S. Solanki c Collingwood b Hatch	0	– c Pratt b Law	0
D. A. Leatherdale c Pratt b Hatch	12	– c Gough b Brinkley	0
P. R. Pollard lbw b Law	45	– b Hatch	28
A. J. Bichel c Love b Law	37	– c Collingwood b Hatch	7
†S. J. Rhodes c Love b Law	1	– b Law	10
S. R. Lampitt not out	42	– not out	23
M. J. Rawnsley b Brinkley	6	– c Love b Brinkley	1
A. Sheriyar c Pratt b Brinkley	20	– c and b Brinkley	1
B 4, l-b 2, n-b 8	14	L-b 4, w 2	6
1/14 2/18 3/18 4/34 5/96 6/131 7/133 8/160 9/173	227	1/2 2/32 3/32 4/41 5/101 6/101 7/119 8/126 9/141	147

Bonus points – Worcestershire 1, Durham 3.

Bowling: *First Innings*—Law 22–2–78–3; Hatch 14–5–48–3; Brinkley 21.3–5–58–3; Collingwood 8–2–37–0. *Second Innings*—Law 21–8–52–5; Hatch 16–1–55–2; Brinkley 10.2–4–19–3; Collingwood 4–1–12–0; Bridge 2–1–5–0.

Durham

*J. J. B. Lewis b Bichel	7	– lbw b Bichel	0
J. A. Daley c Solanki b Sheriyar	5	– lbw b Rawnsley	38
M. L. Love lbw b Lampitt	50	– c Weston b Lampitt	58
P. D. Collingwood b Sheriyar	47	– not out	16
N. Peng c Rhodes b Bichel	22	– not out	2
M. A. Gough lbw b Sheriyar	16		
D. R. Law c Rhodes b Bichel	64		
†A. Pratt b Sheriyar	2		
G. D. Bridge b Sheriyar	0		
J. E. Brinkley lbw b Sheriyar	5		
N. G. Hatch not out	21		
B 4, l-b 5, w 2, n-b 10	21	W 2, n-b 2	4
1/15 2/25 3/87 4/133 5/157 6/158 7/164 8/164 9/176	260	1/2 2/90 3/104	(3 wkts) 118

Bonus points – Durham 2, Worcestershire 3.

Bowling: *First Innings*—Bichel 19–1–72–3; Lampitt 6–1–37–1; Sheriyar 18–5–88–6; Leatherdale 5–2–21–0; Rawnsley 13–3–33–0. *Second Innings*—Bichel 9–1–40–1; Sheriyar 9–2–38–0; Lampitt 8–2–30–1; Rawnsley 2–1–5–1; Weston 0.2–0–5–0.

Umpires: J. W. Lloyds and K. E. Palmer.

At Nottingham, August 8, 9, 10, 11. WORCESTERSHIRE lost to NOTTINGHAMSHIRE by 61 runs.

At Birmingham, August 15, 16, 17, 18. WORCESTERSHIRE drew with WARWICKSHIRE.

WORCESTERSHIRE v HAMPSHIRE

At Worcester, August 22, 23, 24, 25. Worcestershire won by 112 runs. Worcestershire 16 pts, Hampshire 4 pts. Toss: Worcestershire.

As the first-day scores indicate, batsmen were never wholly at ease on another New Road pitch bedevilled by unpredictable, frequently low, bounce. The exception was Johnson, who, having taken the first three Worcestershire wickets, next day bailed out Hampshire with his first Championship hundred for them, hitting 14 fours and two sixes in 195 balls. Kendall, Smith and Mascarenhas helped him add 194, but then four wickets fell for 15 to leave the scores level. At 106 for five, Worcestershire looked to have let the game slip away, even though Hick was still there. But first Bichel – in a partnership of 67 to which Hick contributed 17 – and then Rhodes, with his first Championship fifty of the season, put them on course for the highest total of the match. Rhodes and Rawnsley, with his best score to date, added 73 for the ninth wicket. Hampshire appeared to be heading for a three-day defeat when Hick claimed the extra half-hour. But Morris smashed two sixes and six fours in an entertaining riposte that delayed the inevitable until the morning. It then took Bichel 20 minutes to complete the win by collecting another five-wicket return.

Close of play: First day, Hampshire 46-4 (Kendall 12*, Johnson 3*); Second day, Worcestershire 88-3 (Hick 43*, Leatherdale 25*); Third day, Hampshire 186-8 (Aymes 22*, Morris 44*).

Worcestershire

W. P. C. Weston b Johnson	30	– c Mascarenhas b Schofield	16
A. Singh lbw b Johnson	32	– c Johnson b Schofield	0
*G. A. Hick b Johnson	9	– c White b Udal	76
V. S. Solanki c White b Udal	27	– c Laney b Morris	1
D. A. Leatherdale b Morris	7	– b Mascarenhas	25
P. R. Pollard lbw b Mascarenhas	26	– c Laney b Mascarenhas	0
A. J. Bichel c Kendall b Udal	35	– c Morris b Schofield	78
†S. J. Rhodes c Johnson b Udal	32	– c Aymes b Johnson	52
C. G. Liptrot c Kendall b Schofield	22	– b Schofield	0
M. J. Rawnsley not out	5	– b Mascarenhas	39
A. Sheriyar run out	2	– not out	0
B 5, l-b 11, w 4	20	B 10, l-b 5, w 4	19
1/60 2/76 3/89 4/119 5/119 6/166 7/201 8/233 9/241	247	1/7 2/20 3/25 4/98 5/106 6/173 7/221 8/227 9/300	306

Bonus points – Worcestershire 1, Hampshire 3.

Bowling: *First Innings*—Schofield 9–4–23–1; Morris 12–2–63–1; Mascarenhas 16–6–37–1; Johnson 18–3–58–3; Udal 26–10–50–3. *Second Innings*—Schofield 18–1–51–4; Morris 13–1–51–1; Johnson 13–0–56–1; Mascarenhas 18.4–6–45–3; Udal 18–5–88–1.

Hampshire

G. W. White b Bichel	17	– (2) lbw b Sheriyar	0
D. A. Kenway lbw b Sheriyar	0	– (1) c Rhodes b Rawnsley	40
W. S. Kendall c Solanki b Leatherdale	36	– lbw b Bichel	31
J. S. Laney b Liptrot	1	– c Hick b Bichel	6
S. D. Udal c Rawnsley b Sheriyar	4	– (9) b Sheriyar	4
N. C. Johnson c Pollard b Bichel	103	– (5) lbw b Liptrot	23
*R. A. Smith c and b Liptrot	26	– (6) c Sheriyar b Bichel	0
A. D. Mascarenhas not out	39	– (7) c Hick b Rawnsley	6
†A. N. Aymes c Pollard b Bichel	1	– (8) not out	28
A. C. Morris lbw b Liptrot	5	– c Rhodes b Bichel	44
J. E. K. Schofield c Hick b Rawnsley	1	– c Solanki b Bichel	2
B 4, l-b 4, w 2, n-b 4	14	L-b 8, w 2	10
1/4 2/24 3/33 4/38 5/105 6/181 7/232 8/234 9/244	247	1/10 2/49 3/55 4/95 5/104 6/108 7/111 8/124 9/190	194

Bonus points – Hampshire 1, Worcestershire 3.

Bowling: *First Innings*—Bichel 23–8–64–3; Sheriyar 15–3–47–2; Liptrot 22–8–43–3; Rawnsley 15.1–5–45–1; Leatherdale 8–3–10–1; Hick 14–5–30–0. *Second Innings*—Bichel 13.5–2–62–5; Sheriyar 12–1–50–2; Liptrot 10–7–10–1; Leatherdale 3–1–15–0; Rawnsley 11–3–29–2; Hick 2–0–20–0.

Umpires: B. Dudleston and J. H. Hampshire.

At Chester-le-Street, September 5, 6, 7, 8. WORCESTERSHIRE drew with DURHAM.

WORCESTERSHIRE v MIDDLESEX

At Worcester, September 12, 13, 14, 15. Drawn. Worcestershire 12 pts, Middlesex 10 pts. Toss: Middlesex.

Strauss's exhilarating strokeplay lit up a rain-interrupted first day, when his opening partner, Robin Weston, went on to his third century of the summer. However, Middlesex never capitalised fully on their efforts, even missing a fourth batting point by one run when Sheriyar took the last two wickets with successive deliveries. Singh and Philip Weston, older brother of Robin, responded with a first-wicket stand of 180 at almost five an over on another rain-shortened day, whereupon Singh took the game beyond Middlesex with a career-best 168. His first Championship hundred in the book, he reached his 1,000 runs for the season and batted in all for 236 balls, hitting 25 fours and a six. The visitors hustled to give themselves runs and overs to bowl Worcestershire out a second time: Strauss again led the way, and Joyce made a delightful 108 off 112 balls, with three sixes and 17 fours, before Worcestershire were set 284 at more than five an over. Long before Hick's unbeaten half-century put the game in stalemate, Middlesex knew promotion was a lost cause.

Close of play: First day, Middlesex 258-6 (Weekes 45*, Cook 1*); Second day, Worcestershire 182-1 (Singh 103*, Hick 1*); Third day, Middlesex 152-2 (Strauss 64*, Fleming 14*).

Middlesex

A. J. Strauss c Weston b Hick	92	– b Sheriyar	83
R. M. S. Weston c and b Hick	106	– st Rhodes b Rawnsley	34
O. A. Shah lbw b Sheriyar	0	– b Liptrot	24
S. P. Fleming b Sheriyar	1	– b Rawnsley	55
E. C. Joyce c Rawnsley b Liptrot	4	– not out	108
*P. N. Weekes b Liptrot	63	– not out	45
†D. C. Nash b Hick	1		
S. J. Cook not out	37		
C. B. Keegan b Sheriyar	4		
T. F. Bloomfield c Weston b Sheriyar	27		
P. C. R. Tufnell c Rhodes b Sheriyar	0		
L-b 4, w 4, n-b 6	14	B 4, l-b 3, w 12	19
1/143 2/147 3/149 4/158 5/253 6/257 7/290 8/299 9/349	349	1/66 2/125 3/193 4/231 (4 wkts dec.)	368

Bonus points – Middlesex 3, Worcestershire 3.

Bowling: *First Innings*—Bichel 22–5–73–0; Sheriyar 24.3–1–121–5; Liptrot 16–6–41–2; Leatherdale 10–2–44–0; Rawnsley 11–2–33–0; Hick 11–1–33–3. *Second Innings*—Bichel 12–0–52–0; Sheriyar 12–1–70–1; Rawnsley 23–3–104–2; Liptrot 6.4–0–48–1; Hick 3–1–6–0; Leatherdale 5.2–3–15–0; Ali 8–2–27–0; Solanki 5–0–39–0.

Worcestershire

W. P. C. Weston c Strauss b Tufnell	71	– c Nash b Keegan	36
A. Singh c Nash b Keegan	168	– c Nash b Keegan	17
*G. A. Hick lbw b Bloomfield	31	– (4) not out	59
V. S. Solanki b Bloomfield	0	– (5) b Tufnell	24
D. A. Leatherdale c and b Weekes	33	– (6) not out	12
Kadeer Ali c Shah b Cook	38		
A. J. Bichel c Joyce b Keegan	0	– (3) b Tufnell	23
†S. J. Rhodes lbw b Cook	30		
C. G. Liptrot c Shah b Bloomfield	17		
M. J. Rawnsley not out	20		
A. Sheriyar c Fleming b Bloomfield	3		
B 6, l-b 7, w 2, n-b 8	23	B 1, l-b 3, w 4	8
1/180 2/230 3/230 4/313 5/317 6/317 7/369 8/411 9/417	434	1/28 2/73 3/91 4/122 (4 wkts)	179

Bonus points – Worcestershire 5, Middlesex 3.

Bowling: *First Innings*—Bloomfield 30–2–111–4; Keegan 26–5–92–2; Cook 21–3–77–2; Tufnell 23–5–94–1; Weekes 13–3–47–1. *Second Innings*—Bloomfield 8–1–40–0; Keegan 16–3–40–2; Cook 3–0–13–0; Tufnell 14–3–45–2; Weekes 2–1–5–0; Shah 2–0–10–0; Fleming 2–0–19–0; Strauss 1–0–3–0.

Umpires: M. J. Kitchen and J. W. Lloyds.

Steve Kirby

YORKSHIRE

President: R. A. Smith
Chairman: K. H. Moss
Chief Executive: C. D. Hassell
Chairman, Cricket Committee: R. K. Platt
Captain: 2001 – D. Byas
2002 – D. S. Lehmann
First-Team Coach: W. M. Clark
Head Groundsman: A. W. Fogarty
Scorer: J. T. Potter

At 13 minutes past midday on August 24, and with two matches still to play, Yorkshire became county champions and ended 33 years of anguish. Fittingly, Brian Close and Vic Wilson, two of Yorkshire's previous Championship-winning captains, were on the pavilion balcony at Scarborough when David Byas crowned his own leadership by holding the catch that brought victory over Glamorgan by an innings and 112 runs. It was Yorkshire's ninth win of the season, out of 14 matches, and made them uncatchable.

The joy of the crowd that swarmed on to the field at North Marine Road was testimony to the sense of relief and satisfaction felt around the county at Yorkshire being on top of the pile again. For Byas, who had achieved his ambition just two days before his 38th birthday, and towards the end of his sixth season in charge, it was the stuff of dreams. Even better, the winning line was crossed on his home club ground, after he himself had contributed one of the three centuries that crushed Glamorgan's spirit. The tough farmer from Kilham was close to tears as he was showered with congratulations. It was the pinnacle of an outstanding career, in which Byas unflinchingly demanded the highest standards of those around him without ever compromising the game's Laws. And within ten days of the season's end, he announced his retirement, deciding not to linger on and risk the downward slope upon which so many senior county cricketers have stumbled. The subsequent appointment of Darren Lehmann, Yorkshire's Australian overseas player, would have been unthinkable a decade earlier, but now seemed the obvious choice.

If Byas was the old hand who guided Yorkshire to the top, then Wayne Clark was the new broom who so effectively swept the cobwebs out of the cupboard. The former Australian fast bowler, who in the previous six seasons as coach to Western Australia had taken them to the Sheffield Shield and Mercantile Mutual Cup, joined Yorkshire in March after Martyn Moxon had gone to Durham. Clark's changes were subtle rather than obvious, for he quickly realised how heavy lay the burden of trying to win trophies. He banned all talk of silverware, saying that if the team concentrated on each session of each day's play, and got the basics right, the titles would follow. It was down to earth and completely in tune with Byas's own way of thinking.

On the field, Lehmann's continued brilliance was the biggest single factor, his five hundreds and five half-centuries helping him to 1,416 Championship runs and an average of 83.29. His batting throughout the summer was a delight to watch, never more so than while he was compiling his 252 against Lancashire at Headingley, the highest innings in a Roses match, and he remained as well-balanced, irreverent and audacious as ever. No one who saw his 191 off 103 balls against Nottinghamshire at Scarborough, in the League, is likely to forget it.

Matthew Wood shrugged off two disappointing seasons to top 1,000 Championship runs for the first time and receive his county cap. Byas crafted four valuable centuries, and Michael Vaughan batted majestically whenever free from England calls or injury. Craig White, never really fit for Test cricket, found his real batting form once England discarded him, and his 186, opening the innings at Old Trafford, stunned Lancashire almost as much as Lehmann's monumental effort at Headingley.

Well though Yorkshire planned their campaign, they would not have triumphed without two pieces of good fortune. First, there was Byas's luck with the weather, which was almost always on his side. Rain often held off until all was done and dusted – as it did at Scarborough, where the skies opened the moment the Championship was won. Then there was the sensational arrival of Steve Kirby, formerly with Leicestershire Seconds, who was signed during the Kent match at Headingley so he could replace Matthew Hoggard, requisitioned by England after taking four first-innings wickets. The red-headed pace bowler, giving every indication of nerves as he fielded on the boundary, was quickly transformed from lamb to lion once introduced to the action. Genuinely hostile bowling, backed up by glares and stares at astonished batsmen, earned him figures of seven for 50, the joint second-best by a Yorkshire bowler on Championship debut. Kirby went on to become Yorkshire's leading wicket-taker, with 47 dismissals at 20.85 runs apiece.

The promotion of Richard Dawson above fellow-spinners James Middlebrook and Ian Fisher, both subsequently released, also paid off. His 30 wickets in the second half of the season not only contributed greatly to Yorkshire's success but earned him a surprise place on England's winter tours of India and New Zealand.

Yorkshire were much less sure of themselves in the one-day game and, on what was the blackest day of their season, were blown to pieces by Gloucestershire in the Benson and Hedges Cup semi-finals. After barely deserving to beat Bedfordshire in the third round of the Cheltenham & Gloucester Trophy, they saw off Surrey before caving in to Warwickshire in the quarter-finals, and they also blew hot and cold in the League. Without a match themselves, they had to wait nervously on the final Sunday before discovering they had avoided relegation, so preserving their record of never being outside either of the first divisions.

Away from the cricket, the club was embroiled in controversies about a frieze depicting Asians in the new Sir Leonard Hutton memorial gates at Headingley, and over an invitation to Surrey president John Major to open the new West Stand, which the former prime minister diplomatically declined. For once, however, it was a season in which actions on the field spoke far louder than words off it. – DAVID WARNER.

YORKSHIRE 2001

[*Bill Smith*

Back row: C. J. Elstub, T. M. Baker, G. A. Lambert, C. R. Taylor, S. A. Richardson, R. A. Stead. *Middle row:* M. Carrico (*first-team physiotherapist*), S. M. Guy, M. J. Wood, I. D. Fisher, V. J. Craven, M. J. Lumb, J. D. Middlebrook, G. M. Fellows, S. Widdup, A. Sidebottom (*second-team coach*), M. Seraj (*second-team physiotherapist*). *Front row:* W. M. Clark (*first-team coach*), M. J. Hoggard, A. McGrath, C. E. W. Silverwood, C. White, D. S. Lehmann, D. Byas (*captain*), M. P. Vaughan, D. Gough, R. J. Blakey, G. M. Hamilton, P. M. Hutchison, R. J. Sidebottom.

YORKSHIRE RESULTS

All first-class matches – Played 16: Won 9, Lost 3, Drawn 4.

County Championship matches – Played 16: Won 9, Lost 3, Drawn 4.

CricInfo County Championship, winners in Division 1; Cheltenham & Gloucester Trophy, q-f; Benson and Hedges Cup, s-f; Norwich Union League, 6th in Division 1.

COUNTY CHAMPIONSHIP AVERAGES

BATTING

Cap		*M*	*I*	*NO*	*R*	*HS*	*100s*	*50s*	*Avge*	*Ct/St*
1997	D. S. Lehmann§	13	19	2	1,416	252	5	5	83.29	6
1995	M. P. Vaughan‡	7	13	0	673	133	2	4	51.76	6
	J. D. Middlebrook†	4	4	1	145	84	0	1	48.33	1
2001	M. J. Wood†	14	23	1	1,060	124	4	6	48.18	10
1991	D. Byas†	16	24	5	853	110*	4	2	44.89	38
1993	C. White†‡	9	15	1	567	186	2	0	40.50	5
	M. J. Lumb	4	7	1	218	122	1	1	36.33	0
1999	A. McGrath†	9	15	2	417	116*	1	2	32.07	6
	G. M. Fellows†	12	17	1	455	63	0	3	28.43	4
1987	R. J. Blakey†	15	21	6	405	78*	0	3	27.00	49/5
	S. A. Richardson	7	11	2	215	69	0	2	23.88	6
1996	C. E. W. Silverwood†	8	9	1	167	70	0	1	20.87	2
2000	R. J. Sidebottom†	8	8	4	78	40*	0	0	19.50	3
1998	G. M. Hamilton	8	9	0	114	34	0	0	12.66	1
	S. Widdup†	2	4	0	44	27	0	0	11.00	5
	V. J. Craven†	2	4	1	33	23*	0	0	11.00	2
	C. R. Taylor†	3	6	0	60	18	0	0	10.00	1
	R. K. J. Dawson†	9	11	1	95	37	0	0	9.50	6
	S. P. Kirby	10	10	2	49	15*	0	0	6.12	5
2000	M. J. Hoggard†‡	7	6	1	11	4	0	0	2.20	0
	A. K. D. Gray	3	4	0	4	3	0	0	1.00	2

Also batted: I. D. Fisher† (1 match) 28*; D. Gough†‡ (cap 1993) (2 matches) 11*, 2, 96; S. M. Guy† (1 match) 0, 12*; P. M. Hutchison† (cap 1998) (3 matches) 9*, 11*, 2*.

* *Signifies not out.* † *Born in Yorkshire.* ‡ *ECB contract.* § *Overseas player.*

BOWLING

	O	*M*	*R*	*W*	*BB*	*5W/i*	*Avge*
C. E. W. Silverwood . .	209.1	42	644	33	5-20	3	19.51
S. P. Kirby	280.3	60	980	47	7-50	3	20.85
M. J. Hoggard	192	50	561	26	6-51	2	21.57
R. J. Sidebottom	258.2	73	646	27	4-49	0	23.92
C. White.	167.3	45	410	16	4-57	0	25.62
G. M. Hamilton	211.2	43	672	26	5-27	1	25.84
A. K. D. Gray	92	23	281	10	4-128	0	28.10
D. S. Lehmann.	139.1	33	368	12	3-13	0	30.66
G. M. Fellows	156	43	398	12	3-23	0	33.16
R. K. J. Dawson.	315.5	69	1,014	30	6-82	2	33.80

Also bowled: V. J. Craven 13–1–69–0; I. D. Fisher 13–3–32–1; D. Gough 88–18–275–8; P. M. Hutchison 60–11–224–7; M. J. Lumb 4–1–10–2; A. McGrath 17–4–53–3; J. D. Middlebrook 82–15–265–5; M. P. Vaughan 63.5–14–165–7.

COUNTY RECORDS

Highest score for:	341	G. H. Hirst v Leicestershire at Leicester	1905
Highest score against:	318*	W. G. Grace (Gloucestershire) at Cheltenham. . . .	1876
Best bowling for:	10-10	H. Verity v Nottinghamshire at Leeds	1932
Best bowling against:	10-37	C. V. Grimmett (Australians) at Sheffield	1930
Highest total for:	887	v Warwickshire at Birmingham	1896
Highest total against:	681-7 dec.	by Leicestershire at Bradford	1996
Lowest total for:	23	v Hampshire at Middlesbrough	1965
Lowest total against:	13	by Nottinghamshire at Nottingham	1901

At Canterbury, April 25, 26, 27, 28. YORKSHIRE beat KENT by four wickets.

YORKSHIRE v SOMERSET

At Leeds, May 9, 10, 11, 12. Somerset won by 161 runs. Somerset 17 pts, Yorkshire 4 pts. Toss: Yorkshire.

Somerset owed much to Caddick, who bowled aggressively throughout. Five wickets in each innings gave him a match return of ten for 173, while his England team-mates and Yorkshire adversaries, Gough and White, managed combined figures of four for 204. Put in on a difficult pitch, Somerset rallied from 114 for four through Lathwell and Turner, who added 111, but six wickets then tumbled for 32. Caddick soon had Yorkshire reeling in turn. However, Vaughan, another England colleague, batted with style for four and a half hours until he was eighth out. Fellows hit his maiden Championship fifty, Lehmann – resuming after being struck on the hand by Caddick – thrashed eight boundaries in 38 balls, and the deficit was limited to 26. As Somerset progressed steadily towards a declaration, Vaughan returned a Championship-best four for 47 before ceding centre stage to Caddick again. Only Lehmann, whose 77 came at a run a ball, showed much spirit in Yorkshire's approach to a target of 354. Caddick pointedly dug in a delivery to his last victim, Gough, who could only fend it into the hands of Cox at point.

Close of play: First day, Yorkshire 2-0 (Widdup 2*, Vaughan 0*); Second day, Somerset 101-1 (Holloway 58*, Cox 7*); Third day, Yorkshire 96-3 (Lehmann 53*, Byas 26*).

Somerset

P. C. L. Holloway c Blakey b Silverwood	23	– run out	85
M. E. Trescothick c and b Sidebottom	12	– c and b Lehmann	31
*J. Cox b Gough	35	– c Widdup b Gough	80
M. Burns c Byas b Sidebottom	20	– c and b Vaughan	50
M. N. Lathwell c Blakey b White	65	– run out	1
†R. J. Turner c Byas b Gough	38	– st Blakey b Vaughan	33
G. D. Rose run out	5	– c Sidebottom b Vaughan	1
K. P. Dutch lbw b Silverwood	7	– c and b Vaughan	5
J. I. D. Kerr not out	10	– not out	12
A. R. Caddick run out	0	– not out	10
P. S. Jones c McGrath b Silverwood	9		
L-b 5, w 12, n-b 16	33	B 4, l-b 9, n-b 6	19
1/34 2/64 3/114 4/114 5/225 6/225 7/235 8/242 9/242	257	1/63 2/165 3/220 4/222 5/282 6/290 7/302 8/305 (8 wkts dec.)	327

Bonus points – Somerset 2, Yorkshire 3.

Bowling: *First Innings*—Gough 22–10–47–2; Silverwood 18–3–57–3; Sidebottom 18–3–46–2; Fellows 16–8–19–0; White 15–2–51–1; Vaughan 6–0–22–0; Lehmann 4–1–10–0. *Second Innings*—Gough 22–3–67–1; Silverwood 11–1–47–0; Sidebottom 18–10–32–0; White 18–5–39–0; Lehmann 21–4–53–1; Fellows 10–2–29–0; Vaughan 15–1–47–4.

Yorkshire

S. Widdup b Caddick	2	– lbw b Jones	1
M. P. Vaughan c Burns b Caddick	79	– c Turner b Caddick	8
A. McGrath b Caddick	0	– c Trescothick b Caddick	5
D. S. Lehmann c Burns b Caddick	38	– c Turner b Caddick	77
*D. Byas c Turner b Caddick	3	– c Turner b Caddick	31
C. White lbw b Jones	4	– lbw b Jones	4
G. M. Fellows lbw b Rose	63	– b Jones	29
†R. J. Blakey c Turner b Kerr	0	– c Holloway b Jones	5
C. E. W. Silverwood c Turner b Jones	7	– c Turner b Kerr	22
D. Gough not out	11	– c Cox b Caddick	2
R. J. Sidebottom b Jones	0	– not out	3
L-b 6, w 4, n-b 14	24	L-b 1, n-b 4	5
1/2 2/2 3/16 4/35 5/160 6/208 7/209 8/209 9/229	231	1/9 2/9 3/30 4/116 5/123 6/147 7/158 8/165 9/188	192

Bonus points – Yorkshire 1, Somerset 3.

In the first innings Lehmann, when 4, retired hurt at 6 and resumed at 160.

Bowling: *First Innings*—Caddick 25–7–81–5; Jones 18.2–8–37–3; Rose 14–3–46–1; Kerr 14–3–50–1; Burns 2–0–11–0. *Second Innings*—Caddick 21–3–92–5; Jones 16–0–91–4; Kerr 4.4–1–8–1.

Umpires: J. H. Evans and K. E. Palmer.

At Chelmsford, May 16, 17, 18, 19. YORKSHIRE drew with ESSEX.

YORKSHIRE v NORTHAMPTONSHIRE

At Leeds, May 25, 26, 27. Yorkshire won by four wickets. Yorkshire 19 pts, Northamptonshire 3 pts. Toss: Northamptonshire.

Distracted perhaps by the forecast of rain, Yorkshire made heavy weather of reaching just 77 for the victory that put them top of the Championship. Until then they had dominated the game. But without the reassuring presence of Lehmann, absent with a stiff neck, they struggled late on the third afternoon as Blain picked up career-best figures of four for 34. After Ripley had surprisingly chosen to bowl on a good pitch, Vaughan relished his opportunity with some stunning shots. He pierced gaps in the covers with ease and pulled anything short, reaching his century with a hooked six; he also struck 18 fours in his 133. Although Cousins enjoyed no early success, his perseverance brought later reward and he claimed the last eight wickets for 34, becoming the first bowler to take eight for Northamptonshire since Jim Griffiths, against Glamorgan at Northampton in 1981. In Northamptonshire's reply, only Warren looked comfortable against Silverwood, whose pace brought five wickets, including his 300th for Yorkshire. When they followed on, Hoggard celebrated his Test call with a five-wicket return from three in six balls and two in three.

Close of play: First day, Yorkshire 300-5 (Lumb 42*, Fellows 26*); Second day, Northamptonshire 9-0 (Hussey 3*, Loye 6*).

Yorkshire

S. A. Richardson c G. P. Swann b Penberthy	12	– b Blain	0
M. P. Vaughan b Cousins	133	– c A. J. Swann b Cousins	4
M. J. Wood b Innes	44	– b Blain	5
C. White c Hussey b Cousins	20	– c G. P. Swann b Blain	7
*D. Byas b Cousins	5	– not out	26
M. J. Lumb c Ripley b Cousins	50	– lbw b Penberthy	6
G. M. Fellows c Loye b Cousins	30	– b Blain	0
†R. J. Blakey not out	42	– not out	2
C. E. W. Silverwood c A. J. Swann b Cousins	0		
R. J. Sidebottom lbw b Cousins	6		
M. J. Hoggard c Cook b Cousins	4		
L-b 18, w 10	28	L-b 4, w 16, n-b 7	27
1/38 2/181 3/221 4/227 5/230 6/307 7/334 8/334 9/354	374	1/5 2/15 3/35 4/43 5/73 6/75	(6 wkts) 77

Bonus points – Yorkshire 4, Northamptonshire 3.

Bowling: *First Innings*—Cousins 34.4–5–102–8; Blain 24–3–81–0; Penberthy 22–6–62–1; G. P. Swann 18–4–41–0; Innes 22–5–64–1; A. J. Swann 2–1–6–0. *Second Innings*—Cousins 9–2–23–1; Blain 8–0–34–4; Penberthy 2–0–13–1; Innes 1.2–0–3–0.

Northamptonshire

M. E. K. Hussey lbw b Silverwood	22	– c Blakey b Hoggard	17
M. B. Loye c Blakey b Hoggard	14	– c Byas b Vaughan	52
J. W. Cook b Silverwood	0	– c Blakey b Hoggard	0
R. J. Warren not out	65	– b Hoggard	1
A. J. Swann run out	16	– b Silverwood	21
A. L. Penberthy c Byas b Fellows	3	– c Wood b Vaughan	45
G. P. Swann c White b Silverwood	6	– c Wood b Fellows	31
*†D. Ripley c Vaughan b Silverwood	2	– b Hoggard	14
K. J. Innes c Blakey b Hoggard	15	– c and b Silverwood	40
J. A. R. Blain lbw b Sidebottom	2	– b Hoggard	0
D. M. Cousins c Blakey b Silverwood	11	– not out	7
B 9, l-b 2, w 8, n-b 20	39	B 11, l-b 8, w 2, n-b 6	27
1/38 2/40 3/40 4/81 5/90 6/105 7/115 8/149 9/166	195	1/56 2/56 3/62 4/98 5/110 6/175 7/196 8/230 9/232	255

Bonus points – Yorkshire 3.

Bowling: *First Innings*—Silverwood 21.4–5–58–5; Hoggard 22–8–46–2; Sidebottom 17–6–55–1; Fellows 14–5–25–1. *Second Innings*—Silverwood 17.4–4–37–2; Hoggard 24–7–82–5; Sidebottom 18–2–52–0; Fellows 12–3–40–1; Vaughan 9–3–25–2.

Umpires: J. W. Holder and R. Julian.

At Swansea, May 30, 31, June 1. YORKSHIRE beat GLAMORGAN by 328 runs.

YORKSHIRE v KENT

At Leeds, June 6, 7, 8, 9. Yorkshire won by nine wickets. Yorkshire 20 pts, Kent 4 pts. Toss: Yorkshire. First-class debut: S. P. Kirby.

The tale of 23-year-old Steve Kirby's performance on his first-class debut, and of the circumstances of his selection, stretched the bounds of belief. He had been released by Leicestershire after achieving little with their Second Eleven, other than a problematic back.

However, he persuaded Yorkshire to give him a trial, and shone brightly enough for them to intend to sign him before long. Hoggard's unexpected call-up by England – after he had taken four wickets on the first day – galvanised Yorkshire. Kirby dashed to Leeds from his Leicester home, was registered, and joined the team with sensational results. First, his unbeaten 11 helped secure a fifth batting point and enabled Blakey to reach his fifty. Then, 20 overs of hostile pace brought him seven for 50, the second-best figures by a Yorkshire bowler on Championship debut, equalling Paul Hutchison's return at Portsmouth in 1997 and bettered only by Wilfred Rhodes's seven for 24 at Bath in 1898. After Nixon and Saggers had dug in on the fourth morning, Kirby ripped out Kent's last five wickets for nine runs in 29 balls and was given a guard of honour as he left the field. Twice he had been on a hat-trick. Yorkshire's fifth consecutive Championship victory over Kent extended their lead to 24 points.

Close of play: First day, Yorkshire 5-0 (Richardson 2*, Wood 0*); Second day, Yorkshire 287-6 (Lehmann 66*, Blakey 1*); Third day, Kent 174-5 (Nixon 3*, Saggers 1*).

Kent

D. P. Fulton lbw b White	24	– lbw b Kirby	42
R. W. T. Key c Blakey b Hoggard	58	– b Kirby	38
E. T. Smith c Byas b Hoggard	84	– b Fellows	42
M. J. Walker lbw b Hoggard	9	– c Blakey b White	19
J. B. Hockley c Byas b Silverwood	0	– b Fellows	9
†P. A. Nixon b White	1	– lbw b Kirby	34
*M. V. Fleming lbw b Hamilton	3	– (8) not out	5
J. M. Golding c Middlebrook b Silverwood	15	– (9) c Blakey b Kirby	0
M. M. Patel not out	2	– (10) b Kirby	2
M. J. Saggers lbw b Silverwood	3	– (7) lbw b Kirby	30
B. J. Trott b Hoggard	0	– lbw b Kirby	0
L-b 9, n-b 4	13	B 9, l-b 2, w 4, n-b 14	29
1/39 2/96 3/128 4/129 5/136 6/165 7/207 8/207 9/211	212	1/93 2/94 3/135 4/170 5/171 6/237 7/244 8/244 9/250	250

Bonus points – Kent 1, Yorkshire 3.

Bowling: *First Innings*—Silverwood 16–4–38–3; Hoggard 19.2–5–48–4; White 9–4–19–2; Middlebrook 7–1–18–0; Hamilton 14–1–44–1; Fellows 5–2–24–0; Lehmann 3–0–12–0. *Second Innings*—Silverwood 7–3–18–0; Hamilton 26–6–62–0; White 25–11–34–1; Kirby 20–4–50–7; Middlebrook 17–4–37–0; Lehmann 11–6–7–0; Fellows 11–3–31–2.

Yorkshire

S. A. Richardson run out	69	– not out	29
M. J. Wood c Hockley b Patel	90	– c Nixon b Trott	10
C. White c Nixon b Fleming	26	– not out	5
D. S. Lehmann c Hockley b Patel	90		
*D. Byas lbw b Fleming	3		
G. M. Fellows lbw b Fleming	20		
J. D. Middlebrook c Nixon b Fleming	1		
†R. J. Blakey st Nixon b Patel	59		
G. M. Hamilton c Nixon b Saggers	0		
C. E. W. Silverwood c Nixon b Trott	25		
S. P. Kirby not out	11		
B 4, l-b 8, w 7	19	L-b 1, w 8	9
1/152 2/175 3/228 4/236 5/276 6/278 7/335 8/336 9/389	413	1/24	(1 wkt) 53

M. J. Hoggard did not bat.

Bonus points – Yorkshire 5, Kent 3.

Bowling: *First Innings*—Saggers 34–6–125–1; Trott 31–9–98–1; Golding 14–3–51–0; Fleming 21–3–53–4; Patel 26.5–5–74–3. *Second Innings*—Saggers 6–1–30–0; Trott 6–1–22–1.

Umpires: A. Clarkson and M. J. Kitchen.

At Bath, June 13, 14, 15, 16. YORKSHIRE drew with SOMERSET.

At Bradford, June 20, 21 (not first-class). YORKSHIRE beat BRADFORD/LEEDS UCCE by an innings and 186 runs (see Other UCCE Matches).

YORKSHIRE v LEICESTERSHIRE

At Leeds, June 29, 30, July 1. Yorkshire won by an innings and 227 runs. Yorkshire 20 pts, Leicestershire 2 pts. Toss: Yorkshire. First-class debut: R. K. J. Dawson.

Kirby's achievements in his second home match were as phenomenal as in his first. Six wickets in each innings against his former county gave him match figures of 12 for 72, the best at Headingley since Ron Aspinall's 13 for 100 against Somerset in 1949, and Yorkshire's best against Leicestershire since Fred Trueman took 12 for 58 at Sheffield in 1961. Jack Birkenshaw, Leicestershire's cricket manager and usually an astute judge of ability, conceded the club "had not been sharp enough" in failing to make Kirby an offer ahead of Yorkshire. Hundreds from Lumb (his first, with 20 fours), Wood and Lehmann gave Yorkshire three centurions in a Championship innings for the first time since 1975, when Lumb's father, Richard, Geoff Boycott and John Hampshire held court at Bristol. Lehmann killed a pigeon, pecking seed at backward point, with a fierce cut, and Kirby's blistering pace twice snuffed out Leicestershire, the match finishing before lunch on the third day.

Close of play: First day, Yorkshire 299-3 (Lehmann 35*, Byas 9*); Second day, Leicestershire 174.

Yorkshire

S. A. Richardson c Burns b Ormond	3
M. J. Wood b Dakin	102
M. J. Lumb c Burns b Malcolm	122
D. S. Lehmann c Smith b DeFreitas	104
*D. Byas lbw b Malcolm	30
G. M. Fellows c Habib b DeFreitas	34
†R. J. Blakey b Malcolm	15
C. E. W. Silverwood b DeFreitas	7
R. K. J. Dawson c Wells b Malcolm	37
S. P. Kirby lbw b Malcolm	0
M. J. Hoggard not out	1
B 8, l-b 21, w 14, n-b 2	45
1/12 2/239 3/270 4/380 5/405 6/446 7/448 8/464 9/473	500

Bonus points – Yorkshire 5, Leicestershire 2 (Score at 130 overs: 471-8).

Bowling: Ormond 28–6–94–1; Malcolm 32.2–2–123–5; DeFreitas 27–5–95–3; Dakin 17–4–60–1; Wells 5–2–19–0; Maddy 7–3–22–0; Marsh 17–3–58–0.

Leicestershire

I. J. Sutcliffe c Blakey b Kirby	40	– lbw b Kirby	9
D. L. Maddy c Blakey b Kirby	4	– c Blakey b Kirby	6
B. F. Smith lbw b Kirby	0	– b Hoggard	26
D. J. Marsh b Kirby	4	– c Blakey b Kirby	0
A. Habib c Kirby b Silverwood	25	– b Kirby	5
*V. J. Wells b Hoggard	17	– c Blakey b Silverwood	4
†N. D. Burns b Dawson	33	– lbw b Kirby	31
J. M. Dakin b Kirby	18	– b Hoggard	4
P. A. J. DeFreitas c Byas b Kirby	12	– c Wood b Hoggard	2
J. Ormond not out	2	– b Kirby	1
D. E. Malcolm b Silverwood	8	– not out	1
B 4, w 3, n-b 4	11	B 1, l-b 1, n-b 8	10
1/4 2/14 3/18 4/71 5/128 6/128 7/154 8/159 9/161	174	1/9 2/26 3/34 4/42 5/51 6/53 7/59 8/71 9/90	99

Bonus points – Yorkshire 3.

In the first innings Habib, when 23, retired hurt at 80 and resumed at 154.

Bowling: *First Innings*—Hoggard 14–6–43–1; Kirby 15–4–46–6; Dawson 10–2–44–1; Fellows 2–1–4–0; Silverwood 9.4–1–33–2. *Second Innings*—Hoggard 11–2–43–3; Kirby 9.2–1–26–6; Silverwood 7–1–20–1; Dawson 1–0–8–0.

Umpires: N. A. Mallender and P. Willey.

At Northampton, July 4, 5, 6, 7. YORKSHIRE drew with NORTHAMPTONSHIRE.

YORKSHIRE v LANCASHIRE

At Leeds, July 27, 28, 29, 30. Yorkshire won by seven wickets. Yorkshire 20 pts, Lancashire 7 pts. Toss: Lancashire.

Yorkshire's first Championship win over Lancashire in six years preserved their 14-point lead at the top of the table with a game in hand. It was achieved through a phenomenal innings by Lehmann, whose 252 was the highest in Roses history, beating Maurice Leyland's 211 not out in 1930 and Graham Lloyd's 225 in the 1997 non-Championship "friendly". In 365 minutes, facing 288 balls, he never offered a chance, and at times toyed with the bowling, periods of relative calm being followed by salvos of audacious shots fired off to all parts of the ground. The boundary toll was 35 fours and a six. Lehmann's brilliance overshadowed a commendable 86 from Wood, and even Gough's 96 could not keep the spotlight off the Australian. Lancashire faced a first-innings deficit of 158 but never gave up. Crawley, impressive enough on the first day, was outstanding in compiling a splendid century, his first of the season. And with Lancashire's tail wagging sufficiently, Yorkshire needed 157 to win. They got them by the final afternoon, thanks to a second fifty from Wood and another ferocious assault by Lehmann, who hammered 48 from 24 balls, with seven fours and two sixes. His 300 runs in the match took him past 1,000 for the season.

Close of play: First day, Lancashire 358-9 (Wood 1*, Keedy 8*); Second day, Yorkshire 376-5 (Lehmann 222*, Blakey 17*); Third day, Lancashire 280-8 (Martin 32*, Wood 28*).

Lancashire

M. A. Atherton c Wood b Kirby	17	– c Byas b Kirby	1
M. J. Chilton b Kirby	0	– lbw b Gough	2
*J. P. Crawley c and b Dawson	73	– c Blakey b White	113
A. Flintoff c Byas b Sidebottom	12	– c Byas b White	21
J. C. Scuderi c White b Gough	56	– c Blakey b Sidebottom	7
†W. K. Hegg c Dawson b Gough	76	– c and b Dawson	14
C. P. Schofield c Byas b Sidebottom	55	– c Lehmann b Kirby	34
G. Chapple c McGrath b Gough	33	– c Byas b White	0
P. J. Martin b Gough	0	– not out	51
J. Wood c Dawson b Kirby	12	– run out	35
G. Keedy not out	12	– c Blakey b White	4
B 4, l-b 5, n-b 18	27	L-b 10, w 6, n-b 16	32
1/4 2/35 3/63 4/138 5/173 6/288 7/348 8/348 9/349	373	1/3 2/3 3/66 4/100 5/149 6/203 7/203 8/233 9/301	314

Bonus points – Lancashire 4, Yorkshire 3.

Bowling: *First Innings*—Gough 24–4–65–4; Kirby 23.4–4–103–3; Sidebottom 16–5–45–2; White 15–2–43–0; Fellows 2–0–11–0; Dawson 18–3–62–1; Lehmann 9–1–35–0. *Second Innings*—Gough 20–1–96–1; Kirby 12–2–48–2; Sidebottom 15–5–31–1; White 17.1–3–57–4; Dawson 11–0–62–1; Lehmann 5–3–10–0.

Yorkshire

C. White c Hegg b Chapple	23	– b Keedy	19
M. J. Wood c Hegg b Wood	86	– c Flintoff b Keedy	51
A. McGrath c and b Chapple	0	– not out	21
D. S. Lehmann b Chapple	252	– b Keedy	48
*D. Byas c Schofield b Flintoff	7	– not out	14
G. M. Fellows c Hegg b Martin	5		
†R. J. Blakey c Chilton b Chapple	18		
R. K. J. Dawson c Atherton b Chapple	0		
D. Gough c Hegg b Flintoff	96		
R. J. Sidebottom c Hegg b Martin	0		
S. P. Kirby not out	15		
B 4, l-b 7, w 4, n-b 14	29	L-b 1, n-b 4	5
1/31 2/45 3/214 4/275 5/300 6/386 7/396 8/447 9/448	531	1/55 2/80 3/144	(3 wkts) 158

Bonus points – Yorkshire 5, Lancashire 3 (Score at 130 overs: 520-9).

Bowling: *First Innings*—Martin 28–4–113–2; Chapple 22–7–83–5; Wood 15–0–84–1; Flintoff 18.2–3–55–2; Keedy 28–3–103–0; Schofield 22–6–67–0; Scuderi 1–0–15–0. *Second Innings*—Martin 5–1–13–0; Chapple 4–0–23–0; Flintoff 7–1–27–0; Keedy 10.5–1–67–3; Wood 2–1–10–0; Schofield 5–3–17–0.

Umpires: B. Dudleston and J. W. Lloyds.

YORKSHIRE v SURREY

At Leeds, August 1, 2, 3, 4. Drawn. Yorkshire 8 pts, Surrey 9 pts. Toss: Surrey. First-class debut: C. R. Taylor.

It was in Yorkshire's truest traditions that, while they were trying to strengthen their lead at the top of the table against the current champions, the air was thick with talk about off-the-field controversies. Surrey president John Major, a former prime minister, turned down his invitation to open the new West Stand at Headingley after protests that the honour should have gone to a Yorkshireman, and the club were forced to apologise to Bob Appleyard for accusing him of "racist implications" when he queried the depiction of Asian women in one of the friezes of the new gates erected in memory of Sir Leonard Hutton. On the field, the loss of 22 overs on the final morning, when Yorkshire were 63 for two, appeared to have come to their rescue as they chased 356. But Wood and Lehmann batted so well on the resumption, extending their partnership to 190 and the total to 244, that they might have won but for the interruption. After Surrey's frenzied start – 127 for six by lunch – the game had settled down to a hard-fought tussle, with the visitors leading by 74 on first innings. On the rain-broken third day, the eve of his 21st birthday, Dawson claimed six for 98, the best Championship figures by a Yorkshire spinner on the ground since Phil Carrick's six for 70 against Warwickshire in 1989.

Close of play: First day, Yorkshire 61-2 (McGrath 11*, Lehmann 14*); Second day, Surrey 171-4 (Brown 42*, B. C. Hollioake 23*); Third day, Yorkshire 50-1 (Wood 16*, McGrath 11*).

Surrey

†J. N. Batty c Byas b Kirby	23	– lbw b Sidebottom	9
M. A. Carberry c Wood b Hamilton	11	– lbw b Dawson	46
N. Shahid lbw b Kirby	25	– c Lehmann b Dawson	33
*A. J. Hollioake c Byas b Kirby	33	– c and b Dawson	0
A. D. Brown b Fellows	4	– c McGrath b Dawson	44
B. C. Hollioake b Sidebottom	16	– c Blakey b Hamilton	68
G. P. Butcher c Blakey b Sidebottom	3	– c Byas b Hamilton	9
M. P. Bicknell c Fellows b Kirby	32	– not out	23
I. D. K. Salisbury c Blakey b Dawson	54	– b Hamilton	6
Saqlain Mushtaq c Sidebottom b Hamilton	38	– c Byas b Dawson	3
E. S. H. Giddins not out	2	– lbw b Dawson	0
B 1, l-b 10, w 4, n-b 22	37	B 14, l-b 8, n-b 18	40
1/35 2/47 3/105 4/112 5/114 6/127 7/152 8/189 9/261	278	1/25 2/90 3/92 4/129 5/182 6/223 7/252 8/270 9/281	281

Bonus points – Surrey 2, Yorkshire 3.

Bowling: *First Innings*—Kirby 20–2–90–4; Sidebottom 17–5–39–2; Hamilton 17.2–0–69–2; Fellows 10–1–26–1; Dawson 10–1–34–1; Lehmann 6–2–9–0. *Second Innings*—Kirby 16–5–54–0; Sidebottom 6–3–6–1; Hamilton 19–2–66–3; Fellows 11–3–21–0; Dawson 36.5–5–98–6; Lehmann 4–1–14–0.

Yorkshire

C. R. Taylor c Salisbury b Giddins	14	– lbw b Giddins	15
M. J. Wood c A. J. Hollioake b Giddins	7	– not out	85
A. McGrath lbw b Bicknell	11	– lbw b Bicknell	14
D. S. Lehmann b Saqlain Mushtaq	52	– not out	106
*D. Byas c Batty b Giddins	6		
G. M. Fellows c Batty b Giddins	27		
G. M. Hamilton c Carberry b Bicknell	25		
†R. J. Blakey c Shahid b Saqlain Mushtaq	12		
R. K. J. Dawson b Bicknell	2		
R. J. Sidebottom not out	8		
S. P. Kirby b Saqlain Mushtaq	5		
B 4, l-b 11, w 4, n-b 16	35	B 6, l-b 5, n-b 13	24
1/26 2/33 3/61 4/82 5/124 6/171 7/185 8/191 9/191	204	1/27 2/54	(2 wkts) 244

Bonus points – Yorkshire 1, Surrey 3.

Bowling: *First Innings*—Bicknell 21–4–67–3; Giddins 19–6–50–4; B. C. Hollioake 10–1–31–0; Saqlain Mushtaq 11.4–6–23–3; Butcher 4–0–18–0. *Second Innings*—Bicknell 18–5–36–1; Giddins 24–5–66–1; Saqlain Mushtaq 26–4–46–0; B. C. Hollioake 9–1–37–0; Salisbury 8–1–21–0; Brown 2–0–8–0; Butcher 4.4–0–19–0.

Umpires: J. W. Holder and B. Leadbeater.

At Manchester, August 7, 8, 9, 10. YORKSHIRE beat LANCASHIRE by an innings and 37 runs.

At Leicester, August 15, 16, 17, 18. YORKSHIRE beat LEICESTERSHIRE by 168 runs.

YORKSHIRE v GLAMORGAN

At Scarborough, August 21, 22, 23, 24. Yorkshire won by an innings and 112 runs. Yorkshire 20 pts, Glamorgan 3 pts. Toss: Glamorgan.

At 12.13 on the final day, Byas took the catch that returned the Championship title to Yorkshire after 33 years. He also contributed one of three centuries to his side's impregnable total, but – not for the first time in the season – he had refused to be hurried into his declaration by gloomy weather forecasts, preferring to go by his farmer's instincts. Even so, he cut it fine, for heavy rain was setting in as the jubilant winners left the field. Glamorgan, their injury problems exacerbated when Maynard twisted an ankle during a warm-up session, were picked open by Dawson, who bowled Maher round his legs in his first over and went on to a career-best return. Shortly before the first day's close, Wood retired hurt after ducking into a bouncer from Jones – his helmet grille cut into his cheek, requiring six stitches – but on resuming next morning he pulled his second ball from the same bowler for six: after that, he and fellow-opener White exercised complete control for 63 overs in a 243-run stand. Wood struck 18 fours and two sixes; White, who powered on to 183, hit 25 fours and two sixes. When Glamorgan were six down on the third evening, it was decided to fling open the gates on the final morning, although the 5,000 crowd had to watch a spectacular counter-attack by Jones before acclaiming the new champions. Tearing into Lehmann's bowling, he lashed 46 off 14 balls, hitting six sixes and two fours before slicing to backward point where Byas, having dashed from slip, held the catch that sent the champagne corks popping.

Close of play: First day, Yorkshire 33-0 (White 17*, Kirby 0*); Second day, Yorkshire 433-5 (McGrath 29*, Byas 31*); Third day, Glamorgan 142-6 (Dale 21*, Davies 0*).

Glamorgan

I. J. Thomas lbw b Dawson	18	– c Wood b Sidebottom	21
J. P. Maher b Dawson	36	– lbw b Hamilton	21
M. J. Powell b Dawson	28	– c Byas b Lehmann	21
K. Newell c Blakey b Sidebottom	13	– lbw b Dawson	30
*A. Dale c Byas b White	59	– not out	45
†M. A. Wallace c Byas b Dawson	31	– lbw b Kirby	6
S. D. Thomas c Wood b Dawson	9	– b Kirby	0
A. P. Davies lbw b Dawson	0	– c Blakey b Kirby	7
D. A. Cosker c Wood b Sidebottom	5	– c Byas b Kirby	6
S. L. Watkin not out	8	– c Blakey b Lehmann	8
S. P. Jones c Wood b Sidebottom	4	– c Byas b Lehmann	46
B 4, l-b 2, n-b 6	12	B 5, l-b 21, w 4, n-b 4	34
1/48 2/84 3/89 4/113 5/185 6/202 7/206 8/206 9/215	223	1/36 2/54 3/102 4/127 5/136 6/138 7/150 8/162 9/189	245

Bonus points – Glamorgan 1, Yorkshire 3.

Bowling: *First Innings*—Kirby 11–4–35–0; Sidebottom 16.1–3–34–3; Hamilton 11–2–27–0; White 14–4–27–1; Dawson 30–5–82–6; Lehmann 4–0–10–0; McGrath 2–0–2–0. *Second Innings*—Kirby 20–10–40–4; Sidebottom 12–1–36–1; Hamilton 10–2–21–1; White 4–3–4–0; Dawson 25–7–62–1; Lehmann 9–1–56–3.

Yorkshire

C. White b S. D. Thomas	183
M. J. Wood lbw b Cosker	124
S. P. Kirby c Wallace b Jones	0
M. P. Vaughan b Watkin	45
D. S. Lehmann c and b Cosker	1
A. McGrath lbw b Cosker	29
*D. Byas lbw b Jones	104
G. M. Hamilton c Wallace b Watkin	1
†R. J. Blakey c Maher b Cosker	54
R. K. J. Dawson not out	9
B 6, l-b 16, w 2, n-b 6	30
1/34 2/277 3/353 4/354 5/374 6/434 7/435 8/548 9/580	(9 wkts dec.) 580

R. J. Sidebottom did not bat.

Bonus points – Yorkshire 5, Glamorgan 2 (Score at 130 overs: 441-7).

Wood, when 15, retired hurt at 32 and resumed at 34.

Bowling: Watkin 32–8–71–2; Jones 23–2–135–2; Cosker 60.5–13–168–4; Davies 21–4–73–0; S. D. Thomas 21–3–93–1; Dale 6–2–14–0; Maher 1–0–4–0.

Umpires: A. Clarkson and D. J. Constant.

At The Oval, September 5, 6, 7, 8. YORKSHIRE lost to SURREY by an innings and 46 runs.

YORKSHIRE v ESSEX

At Scarborough, September 12, 13, 14, 15. Essex won by 51 runs. Essex 15 pts, Yorkshire 3 pts. Toss: Essex. First-class debuts: M. L. Pettini, Z. K. Sharif. County debut: J. B. Grant.

This match appeared to be going nowhere once rain set in at lunch on the first day – when Yorkshire received the Lord's Taverners Trophy as county champions – and prevented any further play until the third morning. Hoggard finished Essex off to earn career-best figures, but it was Yorkshire's declaration as soon as the follow-on was avoided that brought the game to life. Essex eventually declared in turn to leave Yorkshire a target of 319 from at least 65 overs. After both openers had gone without scoring, Vaughan and McGrath batted with such bravura that 204 came in 26 overs. Then, shortly before tea, Grayson had McGrath caught at long-on and beat Vaughan through the air. Vaughan's 113, from 89 deliveries, contained 16 fours and four sixes. If that was a setback, however, what happened after the interval suspended belief. Grayson's left-arm slows picked off another three batsmen, giving him a career-best five for 20, and 32-year-old debutant Joe Grant – recruited from Dunnington in the Yorkshire Senior League, but with 14 appearances for Jamaica in the early 1990s under his belt – banished the tail with his first three Championship wickets. Half the side had been swept away in little more than three overs for just nine runs – certainly not the finale the new champions' supporters expected.

Close of play: First day, Essex 99-3 (Clinton 33*, Irani 10*); Second day, No play; Third day, Essex 48-3 (Pettini 10*, Sharif 2*).

Essex

D. D. J. Robinson c Taylor b Dawson	27	– lbw b Hoggard	0
A. P. Grayson b Hoggard	4	– c Craven b Kirby	33
R. S. Clinton c Blakey b Hoggard	40	– c Gray b Kirby	1
M. L. Pettini c Byas b Dawson	1	– c Byas b Gray	41
*R. C. Irani lbw b Hoggard	33	– (6) not out	51
†J. S. Foster c Byas b Hoggard	41	– (8) c Vaughan b Gray	15
G. R. Napier lbw b McGrath	42	– st Blakey b Gray	7
Z. K. Sharif lbw b Hoggard	15	– (5) lbw b Kirby	2
A. P. Cowan c Kirby b Gray	5	– b Hoggard	9
J. E. Bishop lbw b Hoggard	0		
J. B. Grant not out	1		
B 1, l-b 6, w 2, n-b 32	41	B 1, l-b 2, n-b 10	13
1/16 2/77 3/83 4/134 5/135 6/210 7/231 8/240 9/241	250	1/0 2/9 3/45 4/53 5/105 6/129 7/147 8/172	(8 wkts dec.) 172

Bonus points – Essex 2, Yorkshire 3.

Bowling: *First Innings*—Kirby 15–3–81–0; Hoggard 23.3–6–51–6; Craven 3–0–22–0; Dawson 17–4–39–2; Gray 12–4–21–1; McGrath 7–0–29–1. *Second Innings*—Hoggard 10–3–35–2; Kirby 13–3–38–3; Dawson 19–3–66–0; Gray 9–3–30–3.

Yorkshire

C. R. Taylor c Cowan b Bishop	6	– lbw b Cowan	0
M. J. Wood c Irani b Bishop	8	– c Robinson b Bishop	0
M. P. Vaughan b Cowan	5	– b Grayson	113
A. McGrath lbw b Napier	29	– c Pettini b Grayson	70
V. J. Craven c Sharif b Cowan	3	– not out	23
*D. Byas not out	41	– st Foster b Grayson	5
†R. J. Blakey not out	3	– c Foster b Grayson	19
R. K. J. Dawson (did not bat)		– lbw b Grayson	0
A. K. D. Gray (did not bat)		– b Grant	0
S. P. Kirby (did not bat)		– lbw b Grant	0
M. J. Hoggard (did not bat)		– b Grant	2
L-b 3, n-b 6	9	L-b 3, n-b 32	35
1/14 2/21 3/23 4/37 5/81 (5 wkts dec.)	104	1/0 2/0 3/204 4/212 5/230 6/258 7/258 8/259 9/265	267

Bonus point – Essex 1.

Bowling: *First Innings*—Cowan 10–5–21–2; Bishop 10.3–3–30–2; Grant 6–0–20–0; Irani 4–0–15–0; Napier 3–1–15–1. *Second Innings*—Cowan 8–1–47–1; Bishop 8–0–57–1; Grant 13–0–81–3; Irani 2–0–19–0; Napier 2–0–17–0; Sharif 2–0–23–0; Grayson 10–2–20–5.

Umpires: V. A. Holder and N. A. Mallender.

DATES OF WINNING COUNTY CHAMPIONSHIP

The dates on which the County Championship has been settled since 1979 are as follows:

			Final margin
1979	Essex	August 21	77 pts
1980	Middlesex	September 2	13 pts
1981	Nottinghamshire	September 14	2 pts
1982	Middlesex	September 11	39 pts
1983	Essex	September 13	16 pts
1984	Essex	September 11	14 pts
1985	Middlesex	September 17	18 pts
1986	Essex	September 10	28 pts
1987	Nottinghamshire	September 14	4 pts
1988	Worcestershire	September 16	1 pt
1989	Worcestershire	August 31	6 pts
1990	Middlesex	September 20	31 pts
1991	Essex	September 19	13 pts
1992	Essex	September 3	41 pts
1993	Middlesex	August 30	36 pts
1994	Warwickshire	September 2	42 pts
1995	Warwickshire	September 16	32 pts
1996	Leicestershire	September 21	27 pts
1997	Glamorgan	September 20	4 pts
1998	Leicestershire	September 19	15 pts
1999	Surrey	September 2	56 pts
2000	Surrey	September 13	20 pts
2001	Yorkshire	August 24	16 pts

Note: The earliest date on which the Championship has been won since it was expanded in 1895 was August 12, 1910, by Kent.

CHELTENHAM & GLOUCESTER TROPHY, 2001

Shahid Afridi

The premier domestic limited-overs competition had new sponsors and new winners, though in neither case was the change far-reaching. Sponsorship remained on the High Street, transferring from one bank to another, while the trophy stayed in the West Country, shifting 50 miles down the M5 from Bristol to Taunton. Given the geographic allegiance of the new benefactors, Gloucestershire might have proved more tactful winners, but a third consecutive win was – as the Benson and Hedges Cup had been earlier in the summer – beyond them.

In fact, for the first time in six domestic finals, Gloucestershire were missing. They had stumbled in the fourth round to Durham, whose much improved one-day side inflicted one of the surprises of the tournament. The trophy holders' first defeat in 20 knockout games, stretching back to July 1998, had a demoralising effect: Gloucestershire lost the Benson and Hedges final three days later and, despite winning the National League the previous year, were relegated at the end of the season.

Leicestershire, the team many saw as the natural heirs to Gloucestershire's fallen crown, were in imperious form leading up to the C&G final. Their record in competitive limited-overs games since early May read: played 17, won 15, lost two. (Tellingly, both defeats came at the hands of Somerset, who made it a triumphant hat-trick when things really mattered.) Leicestershire's one-day resources had been boosted by Shahid Afridi, a replacement for their injured overseas player, Dan Marsh. In the quarter-final, Afridi mauled the Worcestershire bowling for a 44-ball 67; in the semi, he tore Lancashire apart with an even more ruthless 58-ball 95. In the final, he managed 20, but took his competition total to 205 from 136 balls, an average of 51.25 at a strike-rate of over 150. For good measure, Afridi also took seven wickets, more than any other Leicestershire player – and more than anyone with an ECB contract. Marcus Trescothick, who also missed out at Lord's, aggregated 186, thanks largely to a big hundred against Glamorgan. The biggest came from Leicestershire's Jon Dakin, who piled up 179 – the competition's fourth-best innings – against Wales. Highest aggregate in the inaugural C&G Trophy was 258 by Graeme Hick, who was alone in hitting two hundreds.

Just one bowler, Lancashire's experienced seamer, Peter Martin, managed ten wickets in the tournament, although Somerset had two – Keith Parsons and Richard Johnson – who took nine. It typified the all-round effort of Somerset who, in not relying on big names, were following Gloucestershire's path to success. A lesser-known name, David Pipe, Worcestershire's stand-in wicket-keeper, set a competition record when he caught eight Hertfordshire batsmen. (He was the only player, keeper or otherwise, to take more catches than Kent's David Fulton, who held seven, all in the field.) It was a bad day for Hertfordshire: Hick helped himself to 155 before they lost by 267 runs, the widest margin in 50-over cricket in England. Things went rather better in the third round for their near namesakes, Herefordshire. They bestowed a dose of romance on the competition by becoming the 11th minor team in its 39 seasons to claim a first-class scalp when they embarrassed Middlesex.

There were some minor housekeeping changes during the summer. The final, after being hoicked into a wet August Bank Holiday weekend in 2000, was allowed back into its more traditional September berth, though it sneaks into August again for 2002. And in order to counter early-season fixture congestion, the first two rounds of the 2002 Trophy were played late in 2001. These matches will be found in *Wisden 2003*.

Prize money

£53,000 for winners: SOMERSET.
£27,000 for runners-up: LEICESTERSHIRE.
£16,500 for each losing semi-finalist: LANCASHIRE, WARWICKSHIRE.
£11,500 for each losing quarter-finalist: DURHAM, KENT, WORCESTERSHIRE, YORKSHIRE.

Man of the Match award winners received £1,750 in the final, £550 in the semi-finals, £500 in the quarter-finals, £450 in the fourth round, £350 in the third round, £325 in the second round and £300 in the first round. The prize money was unchanged from the 2000 competition.

*In the following scores, * by the name of a team indicates that they won the toss.*

FIRST ROUND

At Luton, May 1. Bedfordshire won by three wickets. Nottinghamshire Board XI 210 for eight (50 overs) (C. M. Tolley 34, B. M. Shafayat 36, A. F. D. Jackman 73; W. E. Sneath three for 44); Bedfordshire* 212 for seven (49.4 overs) (D. R. Clarke 93, O. J. Clayson 56 not out, Extras 52; J. P. Hart three for 36).

Man of the Match: D. R. Clarke.

Clarke and Clayson put on 121 for Bedfordshire's fifth wicket. Nottinghamshire Board XI conceded 34 wides and 12 no-balls. At 15 years 360 days, their wicket-keeper, Aaron Thomas, was believed to have been the tournament's youngest player.

At Maidstone, May 1, 2. Kent Board XI beat Hampshire Board XI 3–1 in a bowling contest after rain stopped play on the first day. Hampshire Board XI 29 for two (10 overs) v Kent Board XI*.

At Nelson, May 1. Yorkshire Board XI won by 77 runs. Yorkshire Board XI 160 for six (50 overs) (Extras 33); Lancashire Board XI* 83 (42 overs) (P. J. Swanepoel three for nine).

Man of the Match: S. J. Foster.

For Yorkshire Board XI, N. S. Gill's figures were 7–2–8–2, Swanepoel's 8–2–9–3 and Foster's 10–5–11–2.

At Sleaford, May 1. Suffolk won by four wickets. Lincolnshire* 223 for six (50 overs) (J. C. Harrison 71, K. D. Mills 36, S. N. Warman 32, M. A. Fell 41); Suffolk 227 for six (49 overs) (I. D. Graham 48, C. W. J. Athey 71).

Man of the Match: I. D. Graham.

At Southgate, May 1, 2. Middlesex Board XI beat Northumberland 5–4 in a bowling contest after the match had been abandoned.

At Challow & Childrey, May 1. Huntingdonshire Board XI won by 77 runs. Huntingdonshire Board XI 252 for five (50 overs) (W. Larkins 73, M. A. E. Burton 34, D. E. Gillett 46 not out, C. J. Malton 37, Extras 44); Oxfordshire* 175 (46 overs) (B. J. Thompson 42, Extras 36).

Man of the Match: W. Larkins.

At Shrewsbury, May 1. Shropshire won by seven runs. Shropshire 196 for eight (50 overs) (J. B. R. Jones 30, G. J. Byram 56, Extras 33); Devon* 189 for seven (50 overs) (G. T. J. Townsend 60, S. C. B. Tomlinson 30, Extras 33).

Man of the Match: G. J. Byram.

At North Perrott, May 1, 2. Wales won by 20 runs. Wales 159 for eight (50 overs) (R. J. Pannell three for 21); Somerset Board XI* 139 (47.1 overs). *Close of play:* Wales 59-2 (22 overs).

Man of the Match: A. D. Towse (Wales).

Towse's figures were 10–5–13–2.

At Wolstanton, May 1. Worcestershire Board XI won by eight wickets. Staffordshire 78 (36.3 overs) (Extras 30; M. A. Hodgkiss three for 16, J. P. Wright five for 21); Worcestershire Board XI* 79 for two (15.4 overs) (M. A. Hodgkiss 48 not out).

Man of the Match: M. A. Hodgkiss.

For Staffordshire, only J. F. Jervis (19), R. P. Harvey (12) and Extras passed four runs. Worcestershire Board XI won with more than 34 overs to spare.

At Chippenham, May 1, 2. Derbyshire Board XI won by 49 runs. Derbyshire Board XI* 193 for five (50 overs) (A. J. Goodwin 38, J. R. Benstead 61, I. J. Darlington 39 not out; R. J. Bates three for 34); Wiltshire 144 (46.4 overs) (R. J. Rowe 40; I. C. Parkin five for 24). *Close of play:* Derbyshire Board XI 193-5 (35.2 overs).

Man of the Match: J. R. Benstead.

SECOND ROUND

At March, May 15. Cambridgeshire won by eight wickets. Derbyshire Board XI 146 (46.3 overs) (B. L. Spendlove 55; A. Akhtar three for 28, I. N. Blanchett three for 24); Cambridgeshire* 147 for two (35.1 overs) (N. Mohammed 54 not out, R. J. Rollins 40 not out).

Man of the Match: N. Mohammed.

At Camborne, May 15, 16. Cornwall won by three wickets. Cheshire* 256 for five (50 overs) (A. J. Hall 66, R. G. Hignett 61, N. D. Cross 33 not out, S. A. Stoneman 34 not out); Cornwall 258 for seven (49.1 overs) (S. C. Pope 38, T. G. Sharp 61, T. Edwards 53 not out). *Close of play:* Cornwall 66-2 (13 overs).

Man of the Match: T. Edwards.

At Bournemouth, May 15. Bedfordshire won by seven wickets. Dorset 197 for nine (50 overs) (M. Keech 73, S. W. D. Rintoul 41, Extras 35; S. Rashid three for 41); Bedfordshire* 199 for three (45 overs) (J. A. Knott 66 not out, S. Young 78 not out, Extras 30).

Man of the Match: S. Young.

Knott and Young added 157 unbroken for Bedfordshire's fourth wicket. Young also had figures of 10–4–17–1.

At Brockhampton, May 15. Herefordshire won by five wickets. Gloucestershire Board XI 169 for nine (50 overs) (J. W. Shaw three for 49); Herefordshire* 172 for five (38.3 overs) (N. W. Round 32, A. N. Edwards 34 not out, A. R. Adams 46).

Man of the Match: A. R. Adams.

Adams took two for 29, held two catches and with Edwards shared a partnership of 79 for Herefordshire's fifth wicket.

At Welwyn Garden City, May 15. Hertfordshire won by virtue of losing fewer wickets with the scores tied. Durham Board XI 172 (47.2 overs) (A. Worthy 74; M. E. Smith three for 43); Hertfordshire* 172 for eight (50 overs) (I. Fletcher 60, S. P. White 31 not out).

Man of the Match: I. Fletcher.

Hertfordshire, whose wicket-keeper S. J. Lowe held three catches and made one stumping, recovered from 47 for six.

At Maidstone, May 15. Kent Board XI won by five wickets. Buckinghamshire* 221 for seven (50 overs) (M. H. Richardson 62, R. P. Lane 55, D. R. Drepaul 47 not out); Kent Board XI 222 for five (49.5 overs) (J. D. P. Bowden 60, J. C. Tredwell 71, L. J. P. Jenkins 41).

Man of the Match: J. C. Tredwell.

At Richmond, May 15. Berkshire won by eight wickets. Middlesex Board XI 218 for seven (50 overs) (P. E. Wellings 60, S. K. Ranasinghe 48, A. G. J. Fraser 57 not out); Berkshire* 219 for two (43.1 overs) (L. H. Nurse 45, T. D. Fray 87 not out, J. R. Wood 53 not out, Extras 34).

Man of the Match: T. D. Fray.

Wellings and Ranasinghe added 101 for Middlesex Board XI's fourth wicket. In Berkshire's reply, Fray put on 105 for the first wicket with Nurse and 112 unbroken for the third with Wood. Middlesex Board XI used nine bowlers, who between them conceded 28 wides.

At Hellsdon, May 15. Wales won by 35 runs. Wales* 186 for eight (50 overs) (L. O. Jones 38, A. D. Towse 30 not out; C. J. Rogers three for 26); Norfolk 151 (46.3 overs) (C. J. Rogers 45).

Man of the Match: C. J. Rogers.

At Northampton, May 15. Northamptonshire Board XI won by 30 runs. Northamptonshire Board XI 225 for seven (50 overs) (T. E. Coleman 82, D. J. Capel 57); Yorkshire Board XI* 195 for nine (50 overs) (M. A. Gilliver 48, S. J. Foster 44, Extras 30; M. A. Wolstenholme five for 41).

Man of the Match: T. E. Coleman.

Coleman and Capel added 114 for Northamptonshire Board XI's fourth wicket.

At Mildenhall, May 15. Suffolk won by six wickets. Essex Board XI 134 (47.2 overs) (Extras 36; R. W. Pineo three for 38, I. D. Graham three for 26); Suffolk* 135 for four (43.1 overs) (D. J. Callaghan 32; D. J. Gandhi three for 19).

Man of the Match: D. J. Callaghan.

At Cheam, May 15. Surrey Board XI won by 59 runs. Surrey Board XI* 246 for eight (50 overs) (Z. de Bruyn 113 not out, Extras 31; L. R. Peacock three for 65); Huntingdonshire Board XI 187 (46.1 overs) (J. R. Woodward 30, Extras 36).

Man of the Match: Z. de Bruyn.

At Hastings, May 15. Sussex Board XI won by 36 runs. Sussex Board XI 307 for four (50 overs) (G. R. A. Campbell 141, P. J. P. Stevens 62, D. J. Hussey 46); Shropshire* 271 (46.5 overs) (J. B. R. Jones 39, J. T. Ralph 73, A. N. Johnson 62, Asif Din 60; H. F. G. Southwell three for 39, D. J. Hussey three for 56).

Man of the Match: G. R. A. Campbell.

There were three century stands in the match: for Sussex Board XI, Campbell and Stevens opened with 127; for Shropshire, Jones and Ralph put on 109 for the second wicket and Johnson and Asif Din 112 for the fourth. Shropshire lost their last seven wickets for 37.

At Coventry & North Warwicks, May 15. Warwickshire Board XI won by 67 runs. Warwickshire Board XI 181 (49.4 overs) (N. V. Humphrey 58; N. J. Pullen five for 41); Leicestershire Board XI* 114 (44 overs) (N. J. Pullen 32; D. A. T. Dalton three for 16).

Man of the Match: D. A. T. Dalton.

At Kidderminster, May 15, 16. Cumberland beat Worcestershire Board XI 3–2 in a bowling contest after rain stopped play. Cumberland 111 for six (38.4 overs) (Extras 35) v Worcestershire Board XI*.

There was no play on the first day.

THIRD ROUND

BEDFORDSHIRE v YORKSHIRE

At Luton, June 27. Yorkshire won by four wickets. Toss: Bedfordshire.

With Yorkshire 62 for four, 150 from averting embarrassment, Bedfordshire had cause for optimism. But Lehmann, the toughest of adopted Yorkshiremen, was at the crease – as he was until the requirement was nine and the issue beyond doubt. Under pressure, he hit a near-perfect 88 from 98 balls, gaining valuable support from the lower-middle order after medium-pacer Shaun Rashid had lopped the top off the Yorkshire reply. In truth, Yorkshire's plight was partly of their own making. They had bowled an undisciplined line, giving away 36 in wides and no-balls: Extras was easily the biggest contributor to the Bedfordshire total.

Man of the Match: D. S. Lehmann.

Bedfordshire

*A. R. Roberts b Sidebottom	24	J. G. Hughes b Sidebottom	9
N. A. Stanley c Blakey b Silverwood	0	S. Rashid not out	2
D. R. Clarke c Blakey b Sidebottom	15	W. E. Sneath not out	0
S. Young c Wood b Hamilton	20	L-b 3, w 24, n-b 12	39
O. J. Clayson st Blakey b Lehmann	34		—
D. J. M. Mercer c Byas b Lehmann	13	1/1 2/52 3/83 (9 wkts, 50 overs)	211
†J. A. Knott b Sidebottom	29	4/102 5/135 6/152	
A. J. Trott b Silverwood	26	7/200 8/200 9/211	

Bowling: Silverwood 10–0–39–2; Hamilton 5–0–36–1; Sidebottom 10–2–39–4; Dawson 10–0–39–0; Lehmann 9–0–39–2; Fellows 6–0–16–0.

Yorkshire

*D. Byas lbw b Rashid	15	G. M. Hamilton not out	30
M. J. Wood c and b Rashid	4	†R. J. Blakey not out	2
M. J. Lumb c Knott b Rashid	11	B 2, l-b 2, w 12, n-b 14	30
D. S. Lehmann b Rashid	88		—
G. M. Fellows st Knott b Roberts	6	1/20 2/36 3/41 (6 wkts, 46.3 overs)	212
V. J. Craven c Stanley b Sneath	26	4/62 5/124 6/203	

C. E. W. Silverwood, R. K. J. Dawson and R. J. Sidebottom did not bat.

Bowling: Young 10–0–30–0; Rashid 10–0–54–4; Roberts 7–1–30–1; Hughes 6–0–28–0; Sneath 8.3–0–33–1; Trott 5–0–33–0.

Umpires: P. D. Clubb and B. Dudleston.

BERKSHIRE v ESSEX

At Reading, June 27. Essex won by 69 runs. Toss: Essex.

Essex never found progress against a spirited Berkshire side straightforward. Chris Batt, once of Middlesex, removed Robinson with the first ball of the day and Hussain, desperate for some match practice after breaking his thumb in May, for just ten. Irani held the innings together with a steady fifty before Hyam coaxed runs from the tail. While Jon Moss and Julian Wood were adding a confident 74 for the third wicket, Berkshire hopes remained high. Once they were parted, though, it became an unequal struggle, Irani adding three wickets to his earlier runs.

Man of the Match: R. C. Irani.

Essex

D. D. J. Robinson c Patel b Batt	0	A. P. Cowan b Moss	14
N. Hussain lbw b Batt	10	J. E. Bishop st Harvey b Lambert	3
S. G. Law c Harvey b Moss	20	T. J. Mason not out	7
*R. C. Irani c Harvey b Davis	55	L-b 3, w 6, n-b 6	15
S. D. Peters b Davis	9		—
A. P. Grayson c Davis b Lambert	36	1/0 2/29 3/35 (9 wkts, 50 overs)	218
R. S. Clinton c Patel b Moss	13	4/73 5/139 6/145	
†B. J. Hyam not out	36	7/177 8/200 9/205	

Bowling: Batt 8–0–37–2; Moss 10–2–52–3; Gunter 4–0–25–0; Davis 10–1–27–2; Patel 10–0–43–0; Lambert 8–0–31–2.

Berkshire

L. H. Nurse lbw b Irani	16	†N. Harvey c Hussain b Bishop	7
T. D. Fray lbw b Cowan	0	N. E. L. Gunter run out	5
J. Moss st Hyam b Grayson	28	T. L. Lambert not out	1
*J. R. Wood b Bishop	54	L-b 7, w 6, n-b 2	15
S. A. Seymour c Cowan b Grayson	14		
R. P. Davis b Cowan	1	1/12 2/16 3/90 (47.4 overs)	149
S. S. Patel b Irani	1	4/109 5/114 6/122	
C. J. Batt b Irani	7	7/132 8/138 9/147	

Bowling: Irani 9–1–37–3; Cowan 9.4–3–26–2; Bishop 9–1–34–2; Grayson 10–1–28–2; Mason 10–3–17–0.

Umpires: A. R. Bundy and B. Leadbeater.

CAMBRIDGESHIRE v SOMERSET

At March, June 27. Somerset won by 50 runs. Toss: Cambridgeshire.

Somerset needed a slick, run-a-ball hundred from Lathwell to lift them out of trouble at 69 for four. He shared stands of 80 with Burns and 78 with Turner (who as a student had played for Cambridgeshire) to help set an exacting target. Grove, with four top-order scalps, stopped the Cambridgeshire reply in its tracks before a battling sixth-wicket partnership between Simon Kellett, a Yorkshire regular in the early 1990s, and Ajaz Akhtar added 121 in 21 overs. Kellett hit an immaculate 67, Akhtar a riskier 78 from 75 balls to complement his two wickets. As their stand ended, so did any chance of an upset.

Man of the Match: A. Akhtar.

Somerset

P. C. L. Holloway c Smith b Akhtar	12	J. I. D. Kerr c Rollins b Wilson	11
P. D. Bowler lbw b Smith	18	P. S. Jones not out	14
M. N. Lathwell c Blanchett b Akhtar	101		
I. D. Blackwell lbw b Mason	0	L-b 8, w 15, n-b 8	31
K. A. Parsons run out	1		
*M. Burns c Durant b Blanchett	36	1/42 2/57 3/62 (9 wkts, 50 overs)	271
†R. J. Turner c Mason b Wilson	46	4/69 5/149 6/227	
K. P. Dutch c Rollins b Blanchett	1	7/240 8/246 9/271	

J. O. Grove did not bat.

Bowling: Akhtar 10–1–50–2; Blanchett 10–1–39–2; Smith 10–2–39–1; Mason 6–2–32–1; Khan 10–0–68–0; Wilson 4–0–35–2.

Cambridgeshire

S. A. Kellett b Dutch	67	T. S. Smith b Kerr	0
N. T. Gadsby lbw b Jones	2	†C. D. Durant not out	12
A. Khan lbw b Grove	3	M. J. G. Mason lbw b Jones	0
R. J. Rollins c Parsons b Grove	7	L-b 11, w 15, n-b 2	28
D. G. Wilson c Dutch b Grove	0		
G. D. Freear c Dutch b Grove	4	1/14 2/22 3/48 (49.1 overs)	221
*A. Akhtar c Blackwell b Parsons	78	4/52 5/56 6/177	
I. N. Blanchett c Blackwell b Dutch	20	7/192 8/199 9/218	

Bowling: Jones 9.1–3–30–2; Grove 10–1–36–4; Kerr 8–0–49–1; Parsons 10–0–48–1; Blackwell 3–0–19–0; Dutch 9–1–28–2.

Umpires: T. R. Riley and R. A. White.

CORNWALL v SUSSEX

At Truro, June 27. Sussex won by 33 runs. Toss: Cornwall.

While Jon Kent and Tom Sharp were adding 62 for the fifth wicket, it briefly looked as though Sussex's long westward journey might end in ignominy. The professionals had never managed to dominate the Cornish attack, even the adventurous Adams scoring at a relatively sedate pace. Cornwall might have faced a more gettable target if Goodwin had not been dropped twice before reaching double figures. Five of Cornwall's top six made it to 25, but none hung around long enough to convert potential into success.

Man of the Match: C. J. Adams.

Sussex

R. R. Montgomerie c Hands b Shreck	33
M. W. Goodwin c Curnow b Munday	66
*C. J. Adams not out	89
B. Zuiderent lbw b Pope	16
W. J. House c Stephens b Pope	18
M. H. Yardy lbw b Hands	0
†M. J. Prior c G. D. Edwards b Stephens	8
M. J. G. Davis not out	11
B 1, l-b 5, w 4, n-b 2	12
1/45 2/139 3/180 4/208 5/210 6/226 (6 wkts, 50 overs)	253

J. D. Lewry, B. V. Taylor and M. A. Robinson did not bat.

Bowling: Shreck 10–3–42–1; Stephens 10–2–45–1; Pope 10–0–44–2; Kent 5–0–36–0; Hands 10–0–41–1; Munday 5–0–39–1.

Cornwall

S. C. Pope b Robinson	29
*G. M. Thomas lbw b Lewry	2
J. M. Hands c Zuiderent b Davis	33
N. S. Curnow c Prior b Yardy	25
J. P. Kent c Prior b Lewry	30
T. G. Sharp c Zuiderent b Davis	30
†G. D. Edwards not out	14
J. C. J. Stephens lbw b Lewry	6
T. Edwards c Prior b Taylor	14
C. E. Shreck not out	2
B 8, l-b 11, w 14, n-b 2	35
1/14 2/48 3/99 4/105 5/167 6/178 7/185 8/217 (8 wkts, 50 overs)	220

M. K. Munday did not bat.

Bowling: Lewry 10–1–43–3; Taylor 10–1–34–1; Robinson 10–0–33–1; House 4–0–24–0; Davis 10–0–37–2; Yardy 6–0–30–1.

Umpires: R. Palmer and A. G. T. Whitehead.

CUMBERLAND v KENT

At Barrow, June 27. Kent won by nine wickets. Toss: Kent.

Kent took just 62 balls – one more than the shortest innings in the competition's 39-year history – to put Cumberland out of their misery. Losing the toss was a significant blow for the Minor County, and Trott immediately exploited the muggy conditions. He finished with a one-day best five for 18, his new-ball partner Saggers three for 14 as they ran through the Cumberland batting with almost indecent ease. Hockley, hitting all but two of his 48 runs in boundaries, was apparently eager to start the long trek home, and play ended at 3.01 p.m. In all, spectators had less than 44 overs' entertainment.

Man of the Match: B. J. Trott.

Cumberland

S. T. Knox lbw b Trott	1	D. B. Pennett c Trott b Saggers	0
T. E. H. Prime c Nixon b Trott	0	M. A. Sharp not out	2
A. Williams lbw b Ealham	19	D. M. Wheatman c Fulton b Symonds	0
T. A. Hunte c Fulton b Trott	1	L-b 2, w 7, n-b 2	11
S. J. O'Shaughnessy lbw b Trott	0		
†S. M. Dutton c Walker b Trott	3	1/1 2/18 3/26 (33.3 overs)	72
*J. M. Lewis b Saggers	21	4/26 5/26 6/36	
J. M. Fielding c Nixon b Saggers	14	7/64 8/68 9/70	

Bowling: Saggers 10–3–14–3; Trott 10–3–18–5; Ealham 7–2–14–1; Golding 3–0–19–0; Symonds 3.3–1–5–1.

Kent

J. B. Hockley not out	48
D. P. Fulton c Pennett b Sharp	10
R. W. T. Key not out	12
N-b 4	4
1/43 (1 wkt, 10.2 overs)	74

M. J. Walker, A. Symonds, *M. A. Ealham, †P. A. Nixon, J. M. Golding, M. M. Patel, M. J. Saggers and B. J. Trott did not bat.

Bowling: Pennett 3–0–20–0; Sharp 4.2–1–24–1; Wheatman 2–0–23–0; Fielding 1–0–7–0.

Umpires: J. W. Holder and K. Shuttleworth.

DURHAM v HAMPSHIRE

At Chester-le-Street, June 27. Durham won by seven wickets. Toss: Hampshire.

Peng, aged 18, took the game from Hampshire with a magnificent, mature 119 off 128 balls. He reached his century with a swept six off Mascarenhas and built a platform from which Durham raced past Hampshire's 262 for five with almost ten overs to spare. Fifties from Love and Collingwood, off 46 and 49 balls respectively, helped negate the efforts of Johnson (113 not out), who hit top gear only as Hampshire plundered 48 off their last three overs; Collingwood's last 12 balls haemorrhaged 38 runs.

Man of the Match: N. Peng.

Hampshire

J. S. Laney b Law	23	A. D. Mascarenhas not out	35
N. C. Johnson not out	113		
†D. A. Kenway run out	26	L-b 6, w 10	16
*R. A. Smith c Pratt b Hatch	25		
W. S. Kendall c Pratt b Hatch	15	1/37 2/86 3/139 (5 wkts, 50 overs)	262
L. R. Prittipaul run out	9	4/157 5/172	

S. D. Udal, A. C. Morris, C. T. Tremlett and A. D. Mullally did not bat.

Bowling: Brown 8–1–22–0; Hatch 10–0–51–2; Law 10–0–55–1; Collingwood 8–0–64–0; Phillips 10–0–40–0; Gough 4–0–24–0.

Durham

N. Peng b Mullally	119	*J. J. B. Lewis not out	18
D. R. Law c Morris b Mullally	8	L-b 2, w 2, n-b 4	8
M. L. Love st Kenway b Udal	51		
P. D. Collingwood not out	59	1/12 2/132 3/240 (3 wkts, 40.2 overs)	263

M. A. Gough, M. P. Speight, †A. Pratt, N. C. Phillips, S. J. E. Brown and N. G. Hatch did not bat.

Bowling: Mullally 10–1–79–2; Mascarenhas 8–2–41–0; Tremlett 4–0–35–0; Morris 6–0–37–0; Johnson 3–0–27–0; Udal 9–0–41–1; Smith 0.2–0–1–0.

Umpires: J. H. Evans and A. A. Jones.

GLAMORGAN v DERBYSHIRE

At Cardiff, June 27. Glamorgan won by three wickets. Toss: Derbyshire.

Glamorgan, having listed from 75 for one to 164 for seven, were indebted to Wharf, whose run-a-ball 24 included 14 off Wharton's tenth over. The wobble was largely down to Cork, who took three for nine in 12 deliveries. Earlier, batting for Derbyshire for the first time in seven weeks, he had helped shore up their faltering innings with a precious fifty. Even so, just 113 came from the final 30 overs, and the last 20 runs cost five wickets. Cork, who had run out Bailey, suffered the same fate when Welch sent him back. Powell anchored the Glamorgan reply, scoring an unbeaten 39 in 30 overs, but Wharf's assault won the day.

Man of the Match: D. G. Cork.

Derbyshire

S. D. Stubbings c Watkin b Thomas	47	N. R. C. Dumelow c Maynard b Dale	0
M. J. Di Venuto c Maynard b Wharf	18	T. A. Munton c James b Dale	3
M. P. Dowman c Maher b Thomas	25	L. J. Wharton not out	0
R. J. Bailey run out	34	L-b 6, w 1, n-b 2	9
†L. D. Sutton c Maynard b Dale	2		
*D. G. Cork run out	50	1/38 2/77 3/105 (9 wkts, 50 overs)	195
W. G. Khan st Maynard b Cosker	1	4/112 5/175 6/184	
G. Welch not out	6	7/184 8/184 9/194	

Bowling: Watkin 6–0–39–0; Wharf 8–1–28–1; Thomas 9–0–27–2; Croft 10–1–43–0; Dale 7–1–15–3; Cosker 10–1–37–1.

Glamorgan

K. Newell run out	13	S. D. Thomas c Di Venuto b Cork	14
J. P. Maher c Di Venuto b Cork	30	A. G. Wharf not out	24
R. D. B. Croft c Di Venuto b Cork	21	B 4, l-b 14, w 7, n-b 4	29
*S. P. James lbw b Cork	0		
†M. P. Maynard c Cork b Munton	17	1/34 2/75 3/75 (7 wkts, 47.2 overs)	199
M. J. Powell not out	39	4/85 5/113	
A. Dale lbw b Wharton	12	6/131 7/164	

D. A. Cosker and S. L. Watkin did not bat.

Bowling: Munton 10–1–32–1; Welch 10–1–42–0; Cork 10–0–35–4; Wharton 10–0–41–1; Dumelow 7–0–27–0; Bailey 0.2–0–4–0.

Umpires: G. Sharp and D. R. Shepherd.

HEREFORDSHIRE v MIDDLESEX

At Kingsland, June 27. Herefordshire won by three wickets. Toss: Middlesex.

Victory did not arrive in the grand manner, but the scrambled leg-bye off the penultimate ball brought Herefordshire the proudest moment in their brief existence as a Minor County, having replaced Durham only in 1992. For Middlesex, the shudder of horror as they became the 11th first-class side to lose to a minor team was all too familiar. Four years earlier, they had played Goliath to Ireland's David in the Benson and Hedges Cup. Middlesex set a testing target, but the pitch was true and Herefordshire were given the ideal start. Harshad Patel, a cousin of New Zealand Test cricketer Dipak, and Nathan Round put on 129. This allowed quickfire contributions from Ismail Dawood and Nick Davies, each of whom faced 27 balls for aggressive thirties.

Man of the Match: H. V. Patel.

Middlesex

A. J. Strauss c Boroughs b Thomas	4	P. N. Weekes not out	19
B. L. Hutton c Round b Davies	14	A. W. Laraman not out	16
R. M. S. Weston c Farooque b Adams	47	B 2, l-b 7, w 16, n-b 8	33
O. A. Shah b Farooque	41		——
†D. C. Nash c Dawood b Thomas	58	1/4 2/42 3/99 (6 wkts, 50 overs)	278
M. A. Roseberry c Thomas b Adams	46	4/136 5/223 6/252	

*A. R. C. Fraser, J. P. Hewitt and P. C. R. Tufnell did not bat.

Bowling: Thomas 10–0–50–2; Davies 10–1–50–1; Cooper 10–0–48–0; Adams 10–1–69–2; Farooque 5–0–20–1; Edwards 2–0–18–0; Pearson 3–0–14–0.

Herefordshire

H. V. Patel c Laraman b Tufnell	68	K. Pearson run out	6
N. W. Round c Hutton b Fraser	66	A. Farooque not out	8
*C. W. Boroughs lbw b Shah	10	L-b 8, w 6, n-b 20	34
A. R. Adams c Shah b Hewitt	9		——
†I. Dawood lbw b Hutton	34	1/129 2/163 3/167 (7 wkts, 49.5 overs)	279
A. N. Edwards lbw b Hutton	5	4/191 5/211	
N. M. Davies not out	39	6/236 7/266	

K. E. Cooper and P. A. Thomas did not bat.

Bowling: Fraser 10–0–63–1; Hewitt 9–0–75–1; Hutton 6–1–42–2; Tufnell 10–4–15–1; Weekes 9.5–0–40–0; Shah 5–0–36–1.

Umpires: V. A. Holder and W. E. Smith.

HERTFORDSHIRE v WORCESTERSHIRE

At Hertford, June 27. Worcestershire won by 267 runs. Toss: Hertfordshire.

Softened up by a savage 155 from Hick, Hertfordshire traipsed like lambs to the slaughter; at 11 for four and 31 for six, they were in danger of being dismissed for the lowest total in the competition's history. They avoided that record, but handed another to Pipe, the Worcestershire wicket-keeper. Standing in for the injured Rhodes, he held eight catches, passing the seven taken by Alec Stewart for Surrey against Glamorgan in 1994. Hick faced 113 balls and hit 18 fours and five sixes before Ben Frazer, whose five previous deliveries he had thumped for 24, beat his flailing bat.

Man of the Match: G. A. Hick.

Worcestershire

W. P. C. Weston c S. J. Lowe b O'Reilly	2
A. Singh lbw b Frazer	79
*G. A. Hick b Frazer	155
D. A. Leatherdale c S. J. Lowe b White	0
N. R. Boulton c Cooper b O'Reilly	39
A. J. Bichel c Cooper b Ruskin	27
†D. J. Pipe run out	4
S. R. Lampitt not out	2
Kabir Ali c White b Ruskin	2
C. G. Liptrot not out	2
L-b 2, w 8, n-b 14	24
1/3 2/191 3/192 4/281 5/321 6/329 7/329 8/332 (8 wkts, 50 overs)	336

A. Sheriyar did not bat.

Bowling: O'Reilly 9–0–54–2; Ruskin 9–0–73–2; Cooper 6–0–44–0; White 10–0–54–1; Frazer 10–0–74–2; Smith 6–0–35–0.

Hertfordshire

*M. H. James c Pipe b Bichel	0
D. Lowe c Pipe b Bichel	3
†S. J. Lowe c Pipe b Sheriyar	0
S. G. Cordingley c Pipe b Ali	11
M. A. Everett c Pipe b Bichel	0
M. E. Smith c Pipe b Lampitt	18
S. P. White b Ali	0
B. J. Frazer c Lampitt b Liptrot	7
L. M. Cooper c Pipe b Liptrot	6
S. N. Ruskin c Pipe b Lampitt	6
P. J. O'Reilly not out	0
L-b 7, w 7, n-b 4	18
1/0 2/4 3/11 4/11 5/27 6/31 7/45 8/63 9/63 (25.5 overs)	69

Bowling: Bichel 6–2–9–3; Sheriyar 6–1–14–1; Ali 6–3–9–2; Liptrot 5–2–12–2; Lampitt 2.5–0–18–2.

Umpires: D. J. Constant and N. J. Llong.

KENT BOARD XI v WARWICKSHIRE

At Canterbury, June 27. Warwickshire won by seven wickets. Toss: Warwickshire.

Warwickshire won by a comfortable margin, though not before two young Kent batsmen, James Tredwell and Paul Lazenbury, had exposed the shortcomings of their attack. With the exception of Drakes, who conceded 17 from his ten overs, the Warwickshire bowlers exercised insufficient control. Tredwell, aged 19, hit a solid 57 off 117 balls while fellow left-hander Lazenbury, Herefordshire's centurion at Lord's ten months earlier in the 38-County Cup, cut loose at the death and ended unbeaten on 88 from 93. Kevin Masters initially stifled Warwickshire's reply, but Brown, Ostler and Powell saw them home by the 40th over.

Man of the Match: P. S. Lazenbury.

Kent Board XI

J. D. P. Bowden b Drakes	28
J. C. Tredwell c Ostler b Smith	57
P. S. Lazenbury not out	88
J. S. Hodgson not out	29
B 5, l-b 6, w 22, n-b 2	35
1/71 2/163 (2 wkts, 50 overs)	237

*H. Iqbal, L. J. P. Jenkins, †M. S. Alexander, J. E. G. Lincoln, A. Tutt, A. R. Bray and K. D. Masters did not bat.

Bowling: Brown 9–0–51–0; Betts 7–1–39–0; Sheikh 9–1–47–0; Drakes 10–3–17–1; Giles 9–1–45–0; Smith 6–0–27–1.

Warwickshire

N. V. Knight c Bowden b Masters	32	*M. J. Powell not out	33
N. M. K. Smith c Tutt b Bray	12	L-b 3, w 6	9
D. R. Brown lbw b Lazenbury	70		——
D. P. Ostler not out	82	1/28 2/72 3/172 (3 wkts, 39.3 overs)	238

T. L. Penney, A. F. Giles, †K. J. Piper, M. A. Sheikh, V. C. Drakes and M. M. Betts did not bat.

Bowling: Masters 10–1–26–1; Bray 9–0–53–1; Tutt 6.3–0–60–0; Tredwell 5–0–37–0; Lincoln 4–0–31–0; Lazenbury 5–0–28–1.

Umpires: P. Adams and T. E. Jesty.

LANCASHIRE v WARWICKSHIRE BOARD XI

At Blackpool, June 27. Lancashire won by seven wickets. Toss: Warwickshire Board XI.

An innings of the highest calibre by Gavin Shephard rescued the Warwickshire Board XI from imminent meltdown. He reached the crease at 22 for five, with Martin and Chapple in full cry. But he saw off both – and Muralitharan – to coax 141 from the last five partnerships. His ninth-wicket stand of 86 with Spencer Platt was only one short of the competition record, and he finished unbeaten on 73 from 107 balls, having hit ten fours and two sixes. Lancashire, however, had little difficulty collecting the required runs, with Haynes playing the anchor role to perfection.

Man of the Match: G. F. Shephard.

Warwickshire Board XI

D. A. T. Dalton c Flintoff b Martin	0	N. Sajjad b Muralitharan	0
D. J. Barr lbw b Chapple	0	†S. Platt lbw b Schofield	22
W. Mohammed lbw b Martin	2	T. Mees b Martin	0
N. V. Humphrey b Martin	7	B 1, l-b 12, w 16	29
*C. R. Howell c Haynes b Muralitharan	16		——
S. McDonald c Flintoff b Martin	2	1/2 2/2 3/10 (47 overs)	163
G. F. Shephard not out	73	4/18 5/22 6/62	
K. G. Bray b Muralitharan	12	7/76 8/76 9/162	

Bowling: Martin 9–2–16–5; Chapple 6–1–22–1; Smethurst 10–2–44–0; Flintoff 8–1–33–0; Muralitharan 10–3–21–3; Schofield 4–0–14–1.

Lancashire

J. J. Haynes not out	59	N. H. Fairbrother not out	16
G. Chapple b Sajjad	10	L-b 1, w 6	7
A. Flintoff b Dalton	40		——
*J. P. Crawley c and b Sajjad	33	1/16 2/72 3/124 (3 wkts, 34.5 overs)	165

G. D. Lloyd, †W. K. Hegg, C. P. Schofield, P. J. Martin, M. Muralitharan and M. P. Smethurst did not bat.

Bowling: Mees 8–1–47–0; Sajjad 10–2–25–2; Dalton 5–1–28–1; Bray 5.5–1–36–0; Mohammed 4–0–20–0; Shephard 2–0–8–0.

Umpires: R. Julian and K. J. Lyons.

NORTHAMPTONSHIRE BOARD XI v NORTHAMPTONSHIRE

At Northampton, June 27. Northamptonshire won by nine wickets. Toss: Northamptonshire Board XI.

A belter of a pitch produced 555 runs for the loss of seven wickets. Despite facing an apparently stiff target, the senior Northamptonshire side eased home with plenty to spare, Loye claiming the match award for an undefeated 124 from 122 balls. Hussey and Warren each hit rapid fifties. The parent club's task was made simpler because David Capel, who had injured his back the day before, was unable to bowl. Earlier, the Board XI's healthy total had relied on a powerful hundred from David Paynter, great-grandson of the England and Lancashire left-hander, Eddie. He sprinkled 17 fours in his 106-ball innings and received useful support from his opening partner, Tim Coleman; together they put on 159.

Man of the Match: M. B. Loye.

Northamptonshire Board XI

D. E. Paynter c Warren b Cousins	104
T. E. Coleman c Cousins b Hussey	68
*D. J. Capel c G. P. Swann b Penberthy	6
J. R. Wade run out	38
D. J. Roberts c Rollins b Brown	40
M. C. Dobson run out	1
B. C. Fourie not out	0
M. Steed not out	4
L-b 5, w 5, n-b 6	16
1/159 2/167 3/207 4/265 5/268 6/273 (6 wkts, 50 overs)	277

†T. O. Dann, M. A. Wolstenholme and T. Barratt did not bat.

Bowling: Cousins 10–0–39–1; Weekes 10–1–63–0; Penberthy 10–0–53–1; Brown 10–2–46–1; G. P. Swann 7–0–51–0; Hussey 3–0–20–1.

Northamptonshire

M. E. K. Hussey c Wolstenholme b Dobson	59
M. B. Loye not out	124
R. J. Warren not out	70
B 4, l-b 1, w 14, n-b 6	25
1/125 (1 wkt, 41.2 overs)	278

G. P. Swann, A. S. Rollins, A. J. Swann, A. L. Penberthy, *†D. Ripley, L. C. Weekes, D. M. Cousins and J. F. Brown did not bat.

Bowling: Barratt 5–0–40–0; Wolstenholme 8.2–0–43–0; Fourie 8–0–50–0; Dobson 8–0–58–1; Steed 6–0–36–0; Paynter 6–0–46–0.

Umpires: M. R. Benson and M. Dixon.

SUFFOLK v NOTTINGHAMSHIRE

At Mildenhall, June 27. Nottinghamshire won by nine wickets. Toss: Nottinghamshire.

Nottinghamshire inflicted a crushing defeat on Suffolk, putting behind them their humiliation at the hands of Surrey in the Benson and Hedges semi-final 48 hours earlier. The Minor County had sailed steadily to 42 for one when Logan had Bill Athey caught for 22. From then on, the innings became a procession as Logan, with a one-day best five for 24, and Smith shared nine wickets. Five Suffolk batsmen fell for ducks.

Man of the Match: R. J. Logan.

Suffolk

R. J. Catley lbw b Smith	17	R. W. Pineo not out	11
I. D. Graham b Smith	0	A. K. Poole b Logan	0
C. W. J. Athey c Pietersen b Logan	22	G. M. Kirk b Stemp	.0
D. J. Callaghan c Pietersen b Logan	11	L-b 7, w 14, n-b 2	23
*P. J. Caley c Read b Smith	0		
A. D. Brown c Read b Logan	0	1/2 2/42 3/54 (32.3 overs)	87
†C. J. Warn c Welton b Smith	2	4/55 5/56 6/63	
C. P. Seal lbw b Logan	1	7/66 8/70 9/70	

Bowling: Smith 8–0–25–4; Harris 6–3–7–0; Blewett 5–1–18–0; Logan 10–2–24–5; Stemp 3.3–2–6–1.

Nottinghamshire

*D. J. Bicknell not out	48
G. E. Welton c Warn b Poole	13
G. S. Blewett not out	3
L-b 1, w 12, n-b 12	25
1/64 (1 wkt, 21.5 overs)	89

U. Afzaal, P. Johnson, K. P. Pietersen, †C. M. W. Read, R. J. Logan, A. J. Harris, G. J. Smith and R. D. Stemp did not bat.

Bowling: Pineo 2–0–5–0; Kirk 8–2–16–0; Callaghan 6–1–27–0; Graham 2–0–19–0; Poole 2.5–0–13–1; Seal 1–0–8–0.

Umpires: I. J. Gould and K. E. Palmer.

SURREY BOARD XI v SURREY

At Guildford, June 27. Surrey won by ten wickets. Toss: Surrey.

Having scorned the romance of the occasion by barring two of their contracted players, Ian Bishop and Phil Sampson, from turning out against them, the senior Surrey side sauntered to an emphatic, if devalued, ten-wicket win. The Board XI began encouragingly, with openers Jon Wileman and Tim Hodgson putting on 46. Four wickets – two to the accurate Giddins – then fell for seven before the middle order pulled things round. Surrey cricket development officer Chris Bullen, who bowled off-spin for the county in the 1980s, top-scored, but 159 was no challenge for a side that had amassed 361 in their Benson and Hedges semi-final two days earlier.

Man of the Match: E. S. H. Giddins.

Surrey Board XI

J. R. Wileman c A. J. Hollioake b Bicknell	15	†E. P. Cruz run out	8
T. P. Hodgson run out	26	K. Marc b A. J. Hollioake	2
Z. de Bruyn c Batty b Giddins	2	R. B. Bowers not out	0
S. A. Newman lbw b A. J. Hollioake	27	L-b 1, w 9, n-b 8	18
S. J. W. Andrew lbw b Giddins	0		
*M. R. Bainbridge c Shahid b Tudor	22	1/46 2/48 3/52 (45.1 overs)	158
D. Gorrod c Tudor b Bicknell	2	4/53 5/98 6/102	
C. K. Bullen lbw b Saqlain Mushtaq	36	7/125 8/148 9/158	

Bowling: Bicknell 10–1–28–2; Tudor 10–2–45–1; Giddins 10–2–21–2; Saqlain Mushtaq 8–1–29–1; A. J. Hollioake 7.1–1–34–2.

Surrey

M. A. Butcher not out	73
I. J. Ward not out	70
L-b 4, w 7, n-b 6	17
(no wkt, 27.1 overs)	160

N. Shahid, A. D. Brown, *A. J. Hollioake, B. C. Hollioake, A. J. Tudor, †J. N. Batty, M. P. Bicknell, Saqlain Mushtaq and E. S. H. Giddins did not bat.

Bowling: Marc 3–0–25–0; Bullen 7.1–1–43–0; Gorrod 6–1–31–0; Bowers 5–1–30–0; Andrew 6–0–27–0.

Umpires: C. S. Kelly and P. Willey.

SUSSEX BOARD XI v GLOUCESTERSHIRE

At Horsham, June 27. Gloucestershire won by 95 runs. Toss: Sussex Board XI.

Given Gloucestershire's invincibility in knockout matches – unbeaten, except for a void game, since July 1998 – the Board XI could reflect on a creditable performance. Or at least their bowlers could: they harried the first-class side and made run-scoring a tricky business. Windows, dropped at slip on eight, compiled 82 from 123 balls, but no one else reached 30. Gloucestershire may have set a below-par target, but they wasted no time defending it: Averis blew a gaping hole in the Board reply by bowling two in the first over. Chris Mole and Carl Hopkinson added a useful 64 but, coming together at a calamitous 37 for five, they could do no more than ward off humiliation.

Man of the Match: M. G. N. Windows.

Gloucestershire

T. H. C. Hancock c Hussey b Ades	29
K. J. Barnett b Morgan	8
M. G. N. Windows run out	82
I. J. Harvey c Stevens b Ades	23
C. G. Taylor c Campbell b Hussey	25
*M. W. Alleyne c Stevens b Hussey	22
M. A. Hardinges c Stevens b Morgan	0
†R. C. Russell run out	0
M. C. J. Ball b Hussey	18
M. J. Cawdron not out	1
J. M. M. Averis not out	12
L-b 9, w 5, n-b 4	18
1/15 2/70 3/97 4/147 5/201 6/204 7/204 8/210 9/224 (9 wkts, 50 overs)	238

Bowling: Morgan 10–3–30–2; Alderman 10–3–23–0; Halsall 8–0–43–0; Ades 10–0–57–2; Hopkinson 5–0–28–0; Hussey 7–0–48–3.

Sussex Board XI

G. R. A. Campbell b Averis	0
P. J. P. Stevens c Russell b Cawdron	5
D. J. Hussey b Averis	0
R. N. Jackson c Taylor b Harvey	22
H. F. G. Southwell c Russell b Cawdron	0
†C. M. Mole lbw b Alleyne	41
C. D. Hopkinson c Russell b Hardinges	43
D. A. Alderman c Windows b Alleyne	8
*R. G. Halsall not out	13
S. R. Ades c Hardinges b Ball	1
J. R. Morgan c and b Ball	1
L-b 2, w 7	9
1/0 2/2 3/31 4/31 5/37 6/101 7/116 8/138 9/141 (39.2 overs)	143

Bowling: Averis 6–1–21–2; Harvey 6–2–22–1; Cawdron 8–2–24–2; Alleyne 8–1–37–2; Ball 8.2–0–26–2; Hardinges 3–0–11–1.

Umpires: J. H. Hampshire and M. J. Harris.

WALES v LEICESTERSHIRE

At Swansea, June 27. Leicestershire won by 133 runs. Toss: Leicestershire.

Leicestershire's Dakin pummelled his way to 179, the highest score since the competition became a 50-overs affair in 1999. Alvin Kallicharran (206), Vince Wells (201) and Tom Moody (180 not out) had hit more, but in 60-over innings. Feasting on a flimsy attack, Dakin totalled 120 in boundaries – 60 in sixes and 60 in fours – from 145 balls, and with Smith, who clobbered 64 from 47 balls, shared a fourth-wicket stand of 161. At 39 for three, Wales looked destined for ignominy, but Ryan Sylvester's sensible 73 ensured otherwise. For Phil Simmons, who captained Leicestershire to the Championship in 1998, it was an unhappy reunion: he cost more than seven an over and hit just four runs.

Man of the Match: J. M. Dakin.

Leicestershire

*V. J. Wells b Towse	19	D. L. Maddy not out	3
J. M. Dakin c J. P. J. Sylvester b Towse	179	L-b 14, w 3, n-b 6	23
A. Habib b Gage	19		
D. J. Marsh c Gage b Jones	25	1/50 2/95 (4 wkts, 50 overs)	332
B. F. Smith not out	64	3/160 4/321	

S. A. J. Boswell, D. I. Stevens, P. A. J. DeFreitas, †N. D. Burns and D. E. Malcolm did not bat.

Bowling: Towse 10–1–52–2; George 2.4–0–16–0; Simmons 9.2–0–66–0; Gage 10–1–60–1; Barwick 10–0–39–0; Jones 6–0–61–1; J. P. J. Sylvester 2–0–24–0.

Wales

J. P. J. Sylvester b Malcolm	11	N. A. Gage not out	8
M. J. Newbold c Burns b Boswell	9	S. R. Barwick not out	5
K. M. Bell run out	33		
*P. V. Simmons c Smith b DeFreitas	4	L-b 8, w 16, n-b 4	28
R. W. Sylvester c Malcolm b Stevens	73		
†R. I. Clitheroe c Dakin b Marsh	23	1/22 2/28 3/39 (8 wkts, 50 overs)	199
L. O. Jones c Smith b Dakin	0	4/75 5/143 6/149	
A. D. Towse c Habib b Stevens	5	7/179 8/183	

P. S. George did not bat.

Bowling: Malcolm 6–1–17–1; Boswell 8–2–12–1; DeFreitas 5–0–18–1; Wells 5–2–6–0; Marsh 10–1–50–1; Maddy 5–0–26–0; Dakin 3–0–15–1; Stevens 4–0–26–2; Smith 3–0–15–0; Habib 1–0–6–0.

Umpires: M. J. Kitchen and J. F. Steele.

FOURTH ROUND

GLOUCESTERSHIRE v DURHAM

At Bristol, July 11. Durham won by three runs. Toss: Gloucestershire.

Graeme Bridge, a 20-year-old playing his first senior one-day game, brought Gloucestershire's odyssey of 19 successive wins in knockout cricket to an end. Flighting his left-arm spin into the wind, he bowled Barnett off his pads and Snape sweeping, and had Russell well caught. Gloucestershire's familiar game plan of tight bowling and keen fielding had earlier restricted Durham to 232, Lewis contributing an unbeaten 65. Harvey's run-out was a telling blow for the trophy holders, but a solid half-century from Windows seemed to have settled the issue: 54 needed, seven wickets and more than ten overs in hand. Then Taylor holed out to the square-leg boundary, ending a stand of 74 with Windows, and the trouble started. A target of 33 from five overs came down to four off the last ball to level the scores and win with fewer wickets lost. Law kept it full – and Ball's desperate sweep brought only a single.

Man of the Match: G. D. Bridge.

Durham

N. Peng c and b Alleyne	18	G. D. Bridge b Averis	6
D. R. Law c Ball b Averis	19	A. M. Davies b Averis	0
M. L. Love c Windows b Cawdron	20	S. J. Harmison c Russell b Harvey	2
P. D. Collingwood c Russell b Averis	38	B 1, l-b 4, w 6, n-b 2	13
*J. J. B. Lewis not out	65		
M. A. Gough c Snape b Ball	26	1/37 2/43 3/77 (49.2 overs)	232
M. P. Speight lbw b Harvey	18	4/118 5/170 6/204	
†A. Pratt lbw b Cawdron	7	7/213 8/225 9/226	

Bowling: Harvey 9.2–0–40–2; Averis 10–0–42–4; Alleyne 10–0–43–1; Cawdron 9–0–43–2; Ball 7–0–34–1; Barnett 4–0–25–0.

Gloucestershire

D. R. Hewson lbw b Collingwood	35	M. C. J. Ball not out	14
K. J. Barnett b Bridge	32	M. J. Cawdron c Gough b Law	3
M. G. N. Windows c Love b Davies	56	J. M. M. Averis not out	0
I. J. Harvey run out	9	B 2, l-b 6, w 14	22
C. G. Taylor c Gough b Law	32		
J. N. Snape b Bridge	16	1/66 2/92 3/105 (9 wkts, 50 overs)	229
†R. C. Russell c Peng b Bridge	3	4/179 5/199 6/199	
*M. W. Alleyne c Pratt b Law	7	7/208 8/211 9/228	

Bowling: Law 10–0–51–3; Harmison 10–1–46–0; Collingwood 8–1–31–1; Davies 10–2–31–1; Bridge 10–0–44–3; Gough 2–0–18–0.

Umpires: A. Clarkson and A. G. T. Whitehead.

KENT v NORTHAMPTONSHIRE

At Canterbury, July 11. Kent won by six wickets. Toss: Kent.

The all-round skills of Symonds, Kent's locum overseas player, ushered them to a straightforward win. Bowling medium-pace rather than his more usual off-spin, he demolished the Northamptonshire innings with a burst of five for six in 26 balls as they collapsed from 73 for one to 92 for seven; then he joined stand-in captain Ealham in an unbroken partnership of 60, clinching victory with two overs to spare. The visitors' troubles had begun when Symonds bowled Loye for 29, and it needed a battling 57 from Taylor – more than twice his previous limited-overs best – for Northamptonshire to set a half-decent target. Playing his 200th one-day game in his 18th season, Taylor put on 93 with Ripley, but the Kent batsmen had few problems. Fulton led the way, as he did all summer, with a solid 63, his first fifty in the competition. His four catches equalled the tournament record.

Man of the Match: A. Symonds.

Northamptonshire

A. S. Rollins c Jones b Trott	25	J. P. Taylor c Fulton b Walker	57
M. B. Loye b Symonds	29	M. R. Strong b Ealham	8
R. J. Warren b Symonds	14	J. F. Brown not out	2
M. E. K. Hussey c Fulton b Symonds	8	L-b 6, w 10	16
A. L. Penberthy c Fulton b Symonds	0		
T. M. B. Bailey b Symonds	4	1/50 2/73 3/74 (49.1 overs)	200
G. P. Swann lbw b Ealham	2	4/77 5/87 6/92	
*†D. Ripley c Fulton b Trott	35	7/92 8/185 9/198	

Bowling: Saggers 10–1–45–0; Trott 9.1–1–45–2; Ealham 10–1–22–2; Symonds 10–2–21–5; Patel 5–0–27–0; Walker 5–0–34–1.

Kent

J. B. Hockley b Strong	12	*M. A. Ealham not out	27
D. P. Fulton lbw b Taylor	63	L-b 4, w 5	9
R. W. T. Key c Hussey b Brown	18		
M. J. Walker c Strong b Swann	36	1/16 2/67 (4 wkts, 47.5 overs)	204
A. Symonds not out	39	3/131 4/144	

†P. A. Nixon, G. O. Jones, M. M. Patel, M. J. Saggers and B. J. Trott did not bat.

Bowling: Strong 8.5–2–29–1; Taylor 10–2–38–1; Brown 10–2–33–1; Penberthy 10–1–57–0; Swann 7–0–33–1; Hussey 2–0–10–0.

Umpires: J. W. Holder and J. W. Lloyds.

LANCASHIRE v SUSSEX

At Manchester, July 11, 12. Lancashire won by seven wickets. Toss: Lancashire.

Flintoff, omitted from England's NatWest squad, hit prime one-day form to pilot Lancashire safely into the quarter-finals. Wood chipped in with bat and ball, putting Sussex on the back foot with two early wickets and then, as Lancashire's pinch-hitter, hammering 25 off 24 balls. However, this was Flintoff's match: he bowled ten frugal overs, claimed two wickets and, after rain forced the game into a second day, dominated a third-wicket stand of 75 with Crawley that effectively sealed the win. His unbeaten 65, including two sixes, was his first fifty of the season against county opposition. On the windswept first day, Atherton held three catches, all at slip.

Man of the Match: A. Flintoff.

Close of play: Sussex 119-7 (38 overs) (Davis 16*, Lewry 4*).

Sussex

M. W. Goodwin c Atherton b Flintoff	39	J. D. Lewry c Fairbrother b Martin	16
R. R. Montgomerie c Atherton b Wood	4	R. J. Kirtley lbw b Wood	0
M. H. Yardy b Wood	0	M. A. Robinson lbw b Smethurst	0
*C. J. Adams c Atherton b Martin	14	B 3, l-b 13, w 2, n-b 4	22
†M. J. Prior lbw b Muralitharan	12		
B. Zuiderent lbw b Flintoff	0	1/10 2/12 3/47 (45.1 overs)	151
J. R. Carpenter c Schofield b Smethurst	14	4/74 5/74 6/86	
M. J. G. Davis not out	30	7/115 8/140 9/143	

Bowling: Martin 10–2–29–2; Wood 10–0–43–3; Flintoff 10–1–19–2; Smethurst 5.1–0–20–2; Muralitharan 10–3–24–1.

Lancashire

M. A. Atherton c Prior b Robinson	18	N. H. Fairbrother not out	5
J. Wood b Lewry	25	B 1, l-b 2, w 2, n-b 6	11
A. Flintoff not out	65		
*J. P. Crawley b Davis	31	1/45 2/51 3/126 (3 wkts, 35.2 overs)	155

G. D. Lloyd, †W. K. Hegg, C. P. Schofield, P. J. Martin, M. P. Smethurst and M. Muralitharan did not bat.

Bowling: Lewry 10–2–43–1; Kirtley 4–0–37–0; Robinson 8–1–27–1; Davis 10–3–22–1; Adams 3–0–15–0; Yardy 0.2–0–8–0.

Umpires: V. A. Holder and K. E. Palmer.

NOTTINGHAMSHIRE v LEICESTERSHIRE

At Nottingham, July 11, 12. Leicestershire won by six wickets. Toss: Leicestershire. County debut: Shahid Afridi.

Nottinghamshire, in a calamitous 18-ball spell, threw away a sound start, lost their last five wickets for five runs and set Leicestershire an inadequate target. Heavy showers interrupted the Nottinghamshire innings seven times (and the match ten), perhaps giving Blewett and Johnson an excuse for their dismissals, since both departed soon after stoppages. But it was unfathomable why four team-mates should commit *hara-kiri* in running themselves out, leaving more than nine overs redundant. In response to such a meagre total, Wells decided all he need do to win was stay put, which was precisely what he did. He anchored Leicestershire to the overnight close with three wickets down and to victory with four. Shahid Afridi's debut as Marsh's overseas understudy brought two wickets and a run-a-ball 23.

Man of the Match: V. J. Wells.

Close of play: Leicestershire 125-3 (29.2 overs) (Wells 45*, Smith 24*).

Nottinghamshire

*D. J. Bicknell c Burns b Ormond	33
G. S. Blewett lbw b Dakin	25
U. Afzaal c Smith b Wells	49
P. Johnson lbw b Shahid Afridi	10
K. P. Pietersen c DeFreitas b Shahid Afridi	15
B. M. Shafayat run out	4
†C. M. W. Read run out	15
R. J. Logan lbw b DeFreitas	0
G. J. Smith run out	1
A. J. Harris run out	0
R. D. Stemp not out	0
B 1, l-b 7, w 14, n-b 2	24
1/57 2/91 3/110 4/136 5/143 6/171 7/173 8/174 9/174 (40.4 overs)	176

Bowling: Ormond 10–1–40–1; Boswell 5–0–25–0; Dakin 7–0–27–1; DeFreitas 10–1–36–1; Shahid Afridi 8–1–40–2; Wells 0.4–0–0–1.

Leicestershire

*V. J. Wells not out	54
J. M. Dakin c Logan b Smith	14
Shahid Afridi c Read b Smith	23
D. I. Stevens b Smith	0
B. F. Smith c Blewett b Logan	27
D. L. Maddy not out	34
L-b 5, w 12, n-b 10	27
1/36 2/71 3/80 4/128 (4 wkts, 42.1 overs)	179

A. Habib, †N. D. Burns, P. A. J. DeFreitas, J. Ormond and S. A. J. Boswell did not bat.

Bowling: Smith 10–0–36–3; Harris 10–0–61–0; Logan 10–1–29–1; Blewett 10–1–24–0; Stemp 1.1–0–11–0; Pietersen 1–0–13–0.

Umpires: N. G. Cowley and R. Julian.

SOMERSET v GLAMORGAN

At Taunton, July 11. Somerset won by seven wickets. Toss: Somerset.

Trescothick's hundred was described by his captain, Cox, as one of the best limited-overs innings he had seen. He had gone on the attack from the word go, though always with attractive, orthodox shots. His first 50 came off 23 balls with ten fours, and his 121 off 83 with 20. This was his seventh century of the season in all cricket, his third against Glamorgan. Speculation that Trescothick might be named England captain in place of the injured Hussain appeared not to perturb him one jot. Bowler was his reliable self, and Cox lofted three sixes off Cosker as Somerset won with 50 balls in hand. Glamorgan, put in to bat, had compiled a demanding total against some undemanding bowling. Maynard, close to a hundred at the end of the innings, had found willing partners in James and Powell, but Trescothick eclipsed them all.

Man of the Match: M. E. Trescothick.

Glamorgan

K. Newell b Johnson	26	A. Dale c Turner b Caddick	0
I. J. Thomas c Blackwell b Johnson	11	S. D. Thomas not out	19
R. D. B. Croft c Turner b Caddick	0	L-b 1, w 9, n-b 12	22
*S. P. James c Cox b Parsons	46		
†M. P. Maynard not out	93	1/44 2/44 3/44 (6 wkts, 50 overs)	269
M. J. Powell run out	52	4/137 5/230 6/233	

D. A. Cosker, O. T. Parkin and S. L. Watkin did not bat.

Bowling: Caddick 10–1–44–2; Johnson 10–0–64–2; Jones 10–0–54–0; Parsons 8–0–45–1; Dutch 8–0–36–0; Blackwell 4–0–25–0.

Somerset

M. E. Trescothick b Croft	121	K. A. Parsons not out	27
P. D. Bowler c I. J. Thomas b Croft	43	L-b 2, w 8	10
*J. Cox not out	63		
M. Burns c Cosker b Croft	6	1/143 2/173 3/205 (3 wkts, 41.4 overs)	270

†R. J. Turner, I. D. Blackwell, K. P. Dutch, R. L. Johnson, A. R. Caddick and P. S. Jones did not bat.

Bowling: Parkin 4–0–28–0; Watkin 6–0–45–0; S. D. Thomas 7–0–52–0; Croft 10–1–56–3; Cosker 8–0–51–0; Dale 6–0–28–0; Newell 0.4–0–8–0.

Umpires: G. I. Burgess and A. A. Jones.

WARWICKSHIRE v ESSEX

At Birmingham, July 11. Warwickshire won by five wickets. Toss: Warwickshire.

Carter, an ECB-qualified left-arm seamer recruited from Boland, enjoyed his first one-day appearance in England: after derailing Essex with four for 21, he revealed his all-round skills by pummelling 40 of Warwickshire's first 46 runs, off 43 balls. He had already taken three for 12 when Powell decided to keep his last two overs in reserve, allowing Irani and Foster to regroup and ensure Essex had at least a modest total to defend. In fact, with Grayson's accurate left-arm spin troubling Warwickshire – they had lurched to 93 for five – there was a danger Carter's flying start would count for naught. Then Brown, with a solid fifty, and Penney shared an unflustered stand of 68 to navigate Warwickshire home without further scare.

Man of the Match: N. M. Carter.

Essex

D. D. J. Robinson b Carter	30	T. J. Mason not out	18
S. D. Peters c Powell b Carter	5	J. E. Bishop lbw b Giles	0
S. G. Law c Ostler b Sheikh	4	A. J. Clarke c Penney b Carter	9
*R. C. Irani c Drakes b Brown	48	L-b 5, w 1, n-b 4	10
A. P. Grayson c Knight b Carter	1		
†J. S. Foster b Sheikh	33	1/30 2/39 3/41 (49.3 overs)	160
G. R. Napier st Piper b Giles	0	4/43 5/106 6/107	
A. P. Cowan run out	2	7/121 8/138 9/139	

Bowling: Brown 10–1–38–1; Carter 9.3–3–21–4; Sheikh 10–2–31–2; Drakes 10–1–42–0; Giles 10–0–23–2.

Warwickshire

N. M. Carter c Foster b Cowan	40	T. L. Penney not out	29
N. V. Knight c Irani b Clarke	5		
M. A. Wagh c Irani b Grayson	14	B 1, w 9	10
D. R. Brown not out	52		
D. P. Ostler b Mason	5	1/46 2/53 3/77 (5 wkts, 43.1 overs)	161
*M. J. Powell c Foster b Grayson	6	4/82 5/93	

A. F. Giles, †K. J. Piper, M. A. Sheikh and V. C. Drakes did not bat.

Bowling: Cowan 10–1–40–1; Irani 8–0–33–0; Clarke 7–1–19–1; Bishop 5.1–0–27–0; Grayson 10–0–27–2; Mason 3–0–14–1.

Umpires: T. E. Jesty and P. Willey.

WORCESTERSHIRE v HEREFORDSHIRE

At Worcester, July 11. Worcestershire won by seven wickets. Toss: Worcestershire.

Despite a century of great character from Ravi Nagra, whom Worcestershire had rejected after a trial in 1998, Herefordshire were soundly beaten. Nagra, a 22-year-old pharmacy student from the University of Sussex, was playing only because of an injury to New Zealand international Andre Adams. He made the most of his opportunity, hitting a belligerent 105 off 107 balls, two of which went for six and 12 for four. Nathan Round, one of the heroes of the Middlesex match, contributed 41, but no one else passed 16. A comfortable unbeaten hundred from Hick, backed up by forties from Singh and Solanki, ended the Herefordshire dream.

Man of the Match: R. Nagra.

Herefordshire

H. V. Patel lbw b Bichel	5	N. M. Davies c Ali b Lampitt	2
N. W. Round c Singh b Lampitt	41	K. E. Cooper not out	3
R. Nagra c Leatherdale b Lampitt	105	P. A. Thomas c Leatherdale b Bichel	6
*C. W. Boroughs c Singh b Sheriyar	13	L-b 5, w 4, n-b 2	11
†I. Dawood lbw b Bichel	0		
A. N. Edwards c Rhodes b Ali	16	1/23 2/78 3/125 (47 overs)	210
K. Pearson b Ali	4	4/125 5/179 6/191	
A. Farooque lbw b Ali	4	7/199 8/201 9/201	

Bowling: Bichel 9–0–36–3; Sheriyar 7–0–36–1; Lampitt 10–2–36–3; Ali 10–2–35–3; Rawnsley 9–1–44–0; Leatherdale 2–0–18–0.

Worcestershire

W. P. C. Weston run out	5	D. A. Leatherdale not out	14
A. Singh b Cooper	42	L-b 2, w 7, n-b 2	11
*G. A. Hick not out	101		
V. S. Solanki c Boroughs b Farooque	41	1/10 2/100 3/189 (3 wkts, 37.1 overs)	214

A. J. Bichel, †S. J. Rhodes, S. R. Lampitt, Kabir Ali, M. J. Rawnsley and A. Sheriyar did not bat.

Bowling: Thomas 6–1–37–0; Davies 8.1–1–49–0; Cooper 10–0–37–1; Nagra 5–0–31–0; Pearson 3–0–22–0; Farooque 5–0–36–1.

Umpires: J. H. Evans and R. A. White.

YORKSHIRE v SURREY

At Leeds, July 11, 12. Yorkshire won by six wickets. Toss: Yorkshire.

A stirring fightback by Fellows and White, who put on an unbroken 160 in 29 overs for the fifth wicket, took Yorkshire to victory when all had seemed lost. Coming together at 7.25 on a damp evening and with Yorkshire 84 for four, they added 47 before play was abandoned for the day. Next morning, Surrey's out-of-sorts attack could stop neither quick singles nor fours: Fellows's 80 was his best for Yorkshire in any cricket, and White's 73 his first fifty of the season. Surrey had looked in control on the first day as their batsmen thrashed Gough for 60 and White for 44 from just six overs, though the latter did grab three late wickets. Ramprakash, nearing recovery from the hamstring injury that ruled him out of the First Test against Australia, weighed in with a powerful fifty in support of Ward's meticulous 81.

Man of the Match: G. M. Fellows.

Close of play: Yorkshire 131-4 (29 overs) (Fellows 18*, White 29*).

Surrey

M. A. Butcher lbw b Silverwood	18	Saqlain Mushtaq c Silverwood b White	24
I. J. Ward b Sidebottom	81	T. J. Murtagh b White	2
M. R. Ramprakash c Blakey b Lehmann	51	E. S. H. Giddins not out	0
†A. J. Stewart run out	19		
A. D. Brown c Silverwood b Dawson	3	B 2, l-b 1, w 10, n-b 4	17
*A. J. Hollioake c Sidebottom b Silverwood	12	1/34 2/126 3/156 (50 overs)	243
B. C. Hollioake c Blakey b Silverwood	0	4/168 5/193 6/193	
M. P. Bicknell b White	16	7/212 8/228 9/243	

Bowling: Gough 10–0–60–0; Silverwood 10–0–44–3; White 6–0–44–3; Sidebottom 10–1–32–1; Dawson 7–0–32–1; Lehmann 7–0–28–1.

Yorkshire

*D. Byas lbw b Bicknell	12	C. White not out	73
M. J. Wood lbw b Bicknell	24	L-b 4, w 21	25
M. J. Lumb c Giddins b Murtagh	30		
D. S. Lehmann lbw b Bicknell	0	1/52 2/67 (4 wkts, 48.1 overs)	244
G. M. Fellows not out	80	3/73 4/84	

†R. J. Blakey, R. K. J. Dawson, C. E. W. Silverwood, R. J. Sidebottom and D. Gough did not bat.

Bowling: Bicknell 10–2–34–3; Giddins 10–1–41–0; Murtagh 10–0–46–1; Saqlain Mushtaq 8–0–48–0; A. J. Hollioake 3.1–0–29–0; Butcher 4–0–20–0; B. C. Hollioake 3–0–22–0.

Umpires: N. A. Mallender and J. F. Steele.

QUARTER-FINALS

WORCESTERSHIRE v LEICESTERSHIRE

At Worcester, July 24. Leicestershire won by 118 runs. Toss: Leicestershire.

Worcestershire maintained their recent dismal record against first-class opposition in this competition: a single win since lifting the trophy in 1994. Shahid Afridi was the inspiration for the Leicestershire victory, giving their innings a momentum which, despite the regular fall of wickets, was seldom lost. When he was third out in the 20th over for a 44-ball 67, including 25 in one over from Lampitt, Leicestershire had already reached 150. Some more violent hitting by DeFreitas down the order steered them to 297. In need of a confident start, Worcestershire stumbled, crucially losing Hick in single figures. When Rhodes came in at 72 for five, the match was beyond salvaging; instead, he saved face with a spirited fifty.

Man of the Match: Shahid Afridi.

Leicestershire

J. M. Dakin c Rhodes b Bichel	14
Shahid Afridi c Leatherdale b Sheriyar	67
T. R. Ward c Rhodes b Ali	35
*V. J. Wells st Rhodes b Leatherdale	34
B. F. Smith c Solanki b Rawnsley	18
D. L. Maddy c Sheriyar b Rawnsley	32
†N. D. Burns c Solanki b Bichel	16
A. Habib not out	22
P. A. J. DeFreitas c Hick b Sheriyar	35
J. Ormond run out	0
S. A. J. Boswell not out	0
L-b 10, w 12, n-b 2	24
1/28 2/80 3/150 (9 wkts, 50 overs)	297
4/178 5/208 6/234	
7/239 8/292 9/293	

Bowling: Bichel 10–0–57–2; Sheriyar 9–0–47–2; Ali 8–0–44–1; Lampitt 6–0–54–0; Rawnsley 10–0–49–2; Leatherdale 6–0–20–1; Hick 1–0–16–0.

Worcestershire

W. P. C. Weston b Dakin	40
A. Singh lbw b Boswell	2
*G. A. Hick c Burns b Ormond	2
V. S. Solanki c Burns b DeFreitas	23
D. A. Leatherdale lbw b DeFreitas	0
A. J. Bichel lbw b Dakin	3
†S. J. Rhodes not out	56
S. R. Lampitt b Wells	17
Kabir Ali b Shahid Afridi	5
M. J. Rawnsley c and b Wells	12
A. Sheriyar run out	4
L-b 7, w 4, n-b 4	15
1/15 2/23 3/69 (44.5 overs)	179
4/69 5/72 6/89	
7/128 8/135 9/152	

Bowling: Ormond 10–0–32–1; Boswell 8–0–43–1; DeFreitas 6–0–17–2; Dakin 6–0–23–2; Shahid Afridi 8–0–25–1; Wells 4–0–23–2; Maddy 2.5–0–9–0.

Umpires: M. J. Harris and P. Willey.

KENT v SOMERSET

At Canterbury, July 25. Somerset won by 52 runs. Toss: Somerset.

The pivotal moment came as early as the 12th over, when Trescothick, having limped to an unconvincing eight, edged Trott to Patel in the slips. Reprieved, he promptly hit three boundaries off the same over and, though he was out seven short of a fifty, the tone was set. Half-centuries from Burns – his 71 came from 83 deliveries – and Blackwell, at better than a run a ball, propelled Somerset to a challenging total. An exemplary new-ball spell from Caddick removed both Kent openers and ensured the home side struggled to gain any momentum. Key had a solitary boundary in his 58, and by the time Fleming completed a jaunty 40, Somerset were thinking ahead to the semi-finals.

Man of the Match: M. Burns.

Somerset

M. E. Trescothick b Ealham	43
P. D. Bowler c Fulton b Saggers	10
*J. Cox c Nixon b Saggers	13
M. Burns lbw b Ealham	71
K. A. Parsons c Nixon b Trott	16
I. D. Blackwell c Walker b Symonds	50
†R. J. Turner not out	30
R. L. Johnson b Symonds	0
K. P. Dutch run out	6
A. R. Caddick not out	0
B 1, l-b 10, w 13	24
1/19 2/38 3/84 (8 wkts, 50 overs)	263
4/151 5/206 6/251	
7/252 8/259	

P. S. Jones did not bat.

Bowling: Saggers 10–1–40–2; Trott 10–0–54–1; Ealham 10–1–38–2; Fleming 10–0–58–0; Symonds 6–0–34–2; Patel 4–0–28–0.

Kent

J. B. Hockley b Caddick	7	M. M. Patel not out	27
D. P. Fulton lbw b Caddick	31	M. J. Saggers b Jones	1
R. W. T. Key b Dutch	58	B. J. Trott run out	0
M. J. Walker c Cox b Johnson	6	L-b 4, w 10, n-b 4	18
A. Symonds c Trescothick b Parsons	4		
M. A. Ealham c Burns b Parsons	15	1/24 2/59 3/75 (46.2 overs)	211
†P. A. Nixon b Parsons	4	4/80 5/111 6/120	
*M. V. Fleming b Johnson	40	7/169 8/210 9/211	

Bowling: Caddick 10–1–35–2; Johnson 8–0–36–2; Jones 8.2–0–40–1; Parsons 10–0–38–3; Dutch 4–0–27–1; Burns 4–0–18–0; Trescothick 2–0–13–0.

Umpires: N. G. Cowley and T. E. Jesty.

LANCASHIRE v DURHAM

At Blackpool, July 25. Lancashire won by seven wickets. Toss: Lancashire.

To the dismay of some Lancashire members, cricket was elbowed out of Old Trafford by pop sensation Robbie Williams, whose three-day sell-out concert took precedence over the one-day visit of Durham, contesting their second quarter-final in the competition. As it turned out, Lancashire were quids in twice over. The Stanley Park ground was bursting at the seams, and the home side responded positively to the 5,000-plus crowd, none more than Flintoff, who hails from these parts. He dismissed Collingwood after a steady 60, then Gough, and later put together a laid-back 72 not out, allowing Fairbrother to take centre stage in their partnership of 136. Initially, Flintoff dealt exclusively in boundaries, including a six off Davies, but eased up. Lancashire's target had been made the more attainable by Yates's niggardly off-spin.

Man of the Match: A. Flintoff.

Durham

N. Peng lbw b Martin	12	G. D. Bridge run out	0
D. R. Law c Hegg b Wood	12	A. M. Davies not out	0
M. L. Love lbw b Yates	38		
P. D. Collingwood c Atherton b Flintoff	60	B 1, l-b 5, w 4, n-b 4	14
*J. J. B. Lewis c and b Schofield	9		
M. P. Speight b Yates	0	1/22 2/48 3/95 (8 wkts, 50 overs)	198
M. A. Gough c Scuderi b Flintoff	27	4/118 5/119 6/160	
†A. Pratt not out	26	7/181 8/197	

J. E. Brinkley did not bat.

Bowling: Martin 7–1–11–1; Chapple 9–0–47–0; Wood 6–0–25–1; Flintoff 8–0–46–2; Yates 10–0–23–2; Schofield 10–1–40–1.

Lancashire

M. A. Atherton lbw b Davies	14	G. D. Lloyd not out	6
G. Chapple st Pratt b Law	23	L-b 3, w 8	11
A. Flintoff not out	72		
N. H. Fairbrother c Speight b Bridge	73	1/34 2/46 3/182 (3 wkts, 38.4 overs)	199

*†W. K. Hegg, C. P. Schofield, J. C. Scuderi, G. Yates, J. Wood and P. J. Martin did not bat.

Bowling: Law 9.4–0–53–1; Davies 8–1–39–1; Bridge 9–0–45–1; Brinkley 5–0–14–0; Gough 5–0–22–0; Collingwood 2–0–23–0.

Umpires: G. I. Burgess and J. H. Hampshire.

YORKSHIRE v WARWICKSHIRE

At Leeds, July 25. Warwickshire won by four wickets. Toss: Warwickshire.

Two days earlier, Yorkshire had drubbed Warwickshire in a League match, and most expected a home win, especially with Gough and White back in the side. But the England bowlers claimed one wicket between them as Warwickshire, guided by Penney's defiant unbeaten fifty, passed their modest target with nearly six overs in hand. Even so, it was Yorkshire's batting, not their bowling, that stood accused: their last five wickets toppled for 15 in 25 balls, three to run-outs. The slide started at 173 for five, when McGrath's solid 82 was ended by Knight's brilliance at extra cover, first diving headlong to stop the ball, then managing a direct hit as he lay on the ground. The ensuing panic caused Yorkshire to squander 21 deliveries – described by coach Wayne Clark as "criminal".

Man of the Match: T. L. Penney.

Yorkshire

G. M. Hamilton b Sheikh	29
M. J. Wood c Piper b Carter	1
A. McGrath run out	82
D. S. Lehmann c Piper b Drakes	2
G. M. Fellows b Sheikh	11
C. White c Giles b Carter	11
*D. Byas run out	17
†R. J. Blakey c Piper b Brown	0
D. Gough not out	6
R. J. Sidebottom run out	6
S. P. Kirby c Piper b Drakes	0
L-b 10, w 7, n-b 6	23
1/2 2/65 3/83 4/120 5/143 6/173 7/173 8/178 9/188 (46.3 overs)	188

Bowling: Brown 10–4–24–1; Carter 8–0–35–2; Sheikh 10–1–37–2; Drakes 8.3–1–31–2; Giles 10–0–51–0.

Warwickshire

N. V. Knight c Blakey b Sidebottom	29
M. A. Wagh c Fellows b Hamilton	8
D. R. Brown c McGrath b Kirby	30
D. L. Hemp c Blakey b White	0
*M. J. Powell c Blakey b Sidebottom	0
T. L. Penney not out	58
†K. J. Piper b Sidebottom	17
A. F. Giles not out	19
L-b 10, w 10, n-b 8	28
1/32 2/61 3/62 4/63 5/100 6/130 (6 wkts, 44.1 overs)	189

N. M. Carter, V. C. Drakes and M. A. Sheikh did not bat.

Bowling: Gough 10–2–28–0; Kirby 10–1–53–1; Hamilton 2–0–11–1; White 9.1–0–36–1; Sidebottom 10–3–32–3; Fellows 3–0–19–0.

Umpires: A. Clarkson and N. A. Mallender.

SEMI-FINALS

SOMERSET v WARWICKSHIRE

At Taunton, August 11. Somerset won by four wickets. Toss: Somerset.

There were moments in this match when Warwickshire seemed on their way to Lord's: when, after being put in, they were 101 without loss and their openers in no apparent trouble; and again at the beginning of the Somerset reply, when they had their opponents six for three. Yet the game was ultimately taken from them by the assertive and unbeaten partnership of Turner and Dutch (hitting a one-day best), who added 100 off 86 balls to get Somerset into the final with four overs to spare. Warwickshire must have feared they had insufficient runs, despite Powell and Penney doing their best to boost the total after the middle order sagged. Their hopes resurfaced, though, as Trescothick, Bowler and Burns rapidly departed, then ebbed as Cox approached a half-century. All was in the melting pot at 130 for six, which was the cue for Turner and Dutch to make a stand.

Man of the Match: K. P. Dutch.

Warwickshire

N. V. Knight b Parsons	45	N. M. K. Smith c Dutch b Johnson	1
M. A. Wagh c and b Parsons	46	V. C. Drakes b Jones	7
D. R. Brown c Johnson b Burns	2	L-b 10, w 9, n-b 12	31
D. L. Hemp c Dutch b Burns	11		—
*M. J. Powell b Johnson	39	1/101 2/104 3/125 (8 wkts, 50 overs)	228
T. L. Penney c Burns b Johnson	39	4/129 5/199 6/214	
†K. J. Piper not out	7	7/219 8/228	

M. A. Sheikh and N. M. Carter did not bat.

Bowling: Caddick 10–0–40–0; Johnson 10–1–42–3; Jones 10–0–58–1; Burns 10–1–30–2; Parsons 10–0–48–2.

Somerset

M. E. Trescothick b Brown	4	†R. J. Turner not out	42
P. D. Bowler c Penney b Carter	0	K. P. Dutch not out	61
*J. Cox st Piper b Sheikh	47	B 1, l-b 5, w 7, n-b 2	15
M. Burns c Penney b Brown	0		—
K. A. Parsons lbw b Sheikh	31	1/4 2/4 3/6 (6 wkts, 46 overs)	230
I. D. Blackwell c and b Smith	30	4/62 5/102 6/130	

R. L. Johnson, A. R. Caddick and P. S. Jones did not bat.

Bowling: Brown 8–0–41–2; Carter 9–2–41–1; Sheikh 9–0–44–2; Drakes 10–0–55–0; Smith 10–0–43–1.

Umpires: M. J. Kitchen and B. Leadbeater.

LEICESTERSHIRE v LANCASHIRE

At Leicester, August 12, 13. Leicestershire won by seven wickets. Toss: Lancashire.

An extraordinary exhibition of uninhibited strokeplay from Shahid Afridi swept Leicestershire into the final. Equally extraordinary in some people's consideration was Crawley's decision to bat in damp, murky conditions that had delayed the start – and would interrupt play again before the close. Ormond and Boswell, who collected a competition-best four for 44, soon had Lancashire in disarray at 38 for five, then 60 for six. Next day, Hegg and Schofield engineered a recovery when they completed a resourceful stand of 102 that produced a moderate target, though far short of one that would have troubled Afridi. Not that everything went Leicestershire's way: they slipped to nine for two before Afridi cut loose. He struck Martin, who had hitherto looked unplayable, for 17 in an over that included two successive sixes, raced to 50 off 29 balls and reached 95 off 57, with eight fours and six sixes, before being caught on the rope. Wells's 64 went almost unnoticed as Leicestershire extended their winning sequence in competitive one-day games to 13.

Man of the Match: Shahid Afridi.

Close of play: Lancashire 84-6 (26 overs) (Hegg 24*, Schofield 10*).

Lancashire

M. A. Atherton c Stevens b Boswell	8	G. Yates c Smith b Shahid Afridi	9
G. Chapple c Burns b Ormond	3	J. Wood not out	4
A. Flintoff c Stevens b Boswell	5	P. J. Martin not out	11
*J. P. Crawley c Burns b Ormond	3	B 1, l-b 13, w 22, n-b 4	40
N. H. Fairbrother c Burns b Boswell	0		—
G. D. Lloyd c and b Boswell	5	1/18 2/18 3/29 (9 wkts, 50 overs)	190
†W. K. Hegg c Ward b DeFreitas	60	4/31 5/38 6/60	
C. P. Schofield c and b Wells	42	7/162 8/167 9/175	

Bowling: Ormond 10–3–16–2; Boswell 10–2–44–4; DeFreitas 10–1–31–1; Wells 10–1–39–1; Shahid Afridi 10–0–46–1.

Leicestershire

T. R. Ward c Schofield b Martin	0	B. F. Smith not out	11
Shahid Afridi c Flintoff b Chapple	95	B 4, l-b 10, w 7	21
D. I. Stevens c Atherton b Martin	3		
*V. J. Wells not out	64	1/0 2/9 3/161 (3 wkts, 29.5 overs)	194

D. L. Maddy, †N. D. Burns, A. Habib, P. A. J. DeFreitas, J. Ormond and S. A. J. Boswell did not bat.

Bowling: Martin 8–0–47–2; Chapple 8–0–42–1; Wood 3–0–26–0; Flintoff 7–0–28–0; Schofield 3.5–0–37–0.

Umpires: D. J. Constant and R. Palmer.

FINAL

LEICESTERSHIRE v SOMERSET

At Lord's, September 1. Somerset won by 41 runs. Toss: Somerset.

It took Somerset 18 years to carry off a one-day trophy at Lord's again. Unlike the late 1970s and early 1980s, when they won four, they triumphed with collective style and without reliance on stars. Parsons, a genuine local from Taunton, ten seasons with the county and never sure of a Championship place, symbolised the mode of West Country success. Revealing once more his facility for one-day disciplines, he hit three sixes, two of them thrillingly off Somerset's last two balls, bowled by DeFreitas. Parsons, the senior partner in a crucial, sensibly paced unbroken stand of 95 with Turner, then took two important wickets. It earned him the match award, his first.

A big – largely West Country – crowd and a heady, good-natured atmosphere added to the enjoyment of a well-balanced final. At times, it appeared to be tilting towards Leicestershire, but they suffered from unscheduled flaws. After Somerset had decided to bat, Boswell's temperament let him down on the big occasion. He might have taken four wickets in the semi-final, but now he bowled eight wides in his second over, five in succession. When at last the ordeal ended, Wells immediately withdrew him from the attack, forcing Leicestershire to revise their intentions.

Shahid Afridi, bowling his skiddy leg-breaks earlier than planned, responded with three wickets. That notable feat was offset by an air of what seemed flamboyant irresponsibility when he opened Leicestershire's batting. His recent reputation as an unorthodox, entertaining and effective slogger had lent a *frisson* to Lord's as he took guard. Immediately, as if eager to parade a showman's intrepid technique, he began swinging his bat at Somerset's canny opening bowlers. It was not a wise thing to do, and one could imagine his coach and team-mates in the pavilion hiding their eyes. He scored an unconvincing 20 off ten balls and then, unfamiliar with Johnson's pace and bounce, was out to a leading edge that shot up miles into the clouds, a hovering, swaying catch for which Turner did well to position himself.

Thanks in the main to their sixth-wicket pair, Somerset had earlier reached a challenging total, setting the highest target – in terms of run-rate – in the competition's history. Trescothick had gone to a mistimed pull after only 18 balls but Bowler and Cox, in their own time, grew in composure. The Somerset captain, maybe burdened by his determination, was not quite at his best. He was also perilously close to being lbw early on: compensation, perhaps, for his unlucky dismissal in the final two years before.

Leicestershire were all out in the 46th over. There was a good-looking half-century by Ward, while Maddy fell just short. These two gave fleeting hope to their side, but after they had gone to Parsons and Dutch there was precious little offered by the middle and late order. Caddick was miserly without taking a wicket; Jones took three as if to celebrate his selection, having been controversially overlooked for Somerset's previous final. – DAVID FOOT.

Man of the Match: K. A. Parsons. *Attendance:* 23,553; *receipts* £559,194.

Somerset

M. E. Trescothick c Shahid Afridi b Ormond	18	†R. J. Turner not out	37
P. D. Bowler b Shahid Afridi	42	L-b 19, w 15	34
*J. Cox b Shahid Afridi	44		—
I. D. Blackwell b Shahid Afridi	15	1/40 (1) 2/107 (2) (5 wkts, 50 overs)	271
M. Burns c Maddy b Wells	21	3/132 (4) 4/149 (3)	
K. A. Parsons not out	60	5/176 (5) Score at 15 overs: 60-1	

K. P. Dutch, R. L. Johnson, A. R. Caddick and P. S. Jones did not bat.

Bowling: Ormond 10–2–38–1; Boswell 2–0–23–0; DeFreitas 10–1–57–0; Wells 10–1–40–1; Maddy 8–0–47–0; Shahid Afridi 10–0–47–3.

Leicestershire

T. R. Ward b Parsons	54	J. Ormond not out	18
Shahid Afridi c Turner b Johnson	20	S. A. J. Boswell b Jones	2
D. L. Maddy c and b Dutch	49	L-b 3, w 2, n-b 6	11
*V. J. Wells c Turner b Parsons	3		—
B. F. Smith c Trescothick b Dutch	15	1/20 (2) 2/105 (1) (45.4 overs)	230
D. I. Stevens lbw b Jones	23	3/111 (4) 4/142 (5)	
†N. D. Burns c Turner b Jones	6	5/156 (3) 6/171 (7) 7/182 (6)	
A. Habib c Dutch b Blackwell	15	8/194 (8) 9/225 (9)	
P. A. J. DeFreitas b Johnson	14	10/230 (11) Score at 15 overs: 66-1	

Bowling: Caddick 10–2–33–0; Johnson 8–0–39–2; Jones 7.4–0–40–3; Parsons 6–0–40–2; Dutch 10–0–50–2; Blackwell 4–0–25–1.

Umpires: B. Dudleston and G. Sharp.
Third umpire: R. A. White.

CHELTENHAM & GLOUCESTER TROPHY RECORDS

(Including Gillette Cup, 1963–80, and NatWest Trophy, 1981–2000)

65-over games in 1963; 60-over games 1964–98; 50-over games 1999–2001.

Batting

Highest individual scores: 206, A. I. Kallicharran, Warwickshire v Oxfordshire, Birmingham, 1984; 201, V. J. Wells, Leicestershire v Berkshire, Leicester, 1996; 180*, T. M. Moody, Worcestershire v Surrey, The Oval, 1994; 179, J. M. Dakin, Leicestershire v Wales, Swansea, 2001; 177, C. G Greenidge, Hampshire v Glamorgan, Southampton, 1975; 177, A. J. Wright, Gloucestershire v Scotland, Bristol, 1997; 173*, M. J. Di Venuto, Derbyshire v Derbyshire Board XI, Derby, 2000; 172*, G. A. Hick, Worcestershire v Devon, Worcester, 1987; 165*, V. P. Terry, Hampshire v Berkshire, Southampton, 1985; 162*, C. J. Tavaré, Somerset v Devon, Torquay, 1990; 162*, I. V. A. Richards, Glamorgan v Oxfordshire, Swansea, 1993. *In the final:* 146, G. Boycott, Yorkshire v Surrey, 1965. (355 hundreds have been scored in the competition. The most hundreds in one season was 26 in 1996.)

Most runs: 2,547, G. A. Gooch; 2,334, R. A. Smith; 2,148, M. W. Gatting; 2,032, K. J. Barnett; 1,998, A. J. Lamb; 1,950, D. L. Amiss and G. A. Hick.

Fastest hundred: G. D. Rose off 36 balls, Somerset v Devon, Torquay, 1990.

Most hundreds: 8, R. A. Smith; 7, C. L. Smith; 6, G. A. Gooch and G. A. Hick; 5, D. I. Gower, I. V. A. Richards and G. M. Turner.

Highest totals: 413 for four, Somerset v Devon, Torquay, 1990; 406 for five, Leicestershire v Berkshire, Leicester, 1996; 404 for three, Worcestershire v Devon, Worcester, 1987; 392 for five, Warwickshire v Oxfordshire, Birmingham, 1984; 386 for five, Essex v Wiltshire, Chelmsford, 1988; 384 for six, Kent v Berkshire, Finchampstead, 1994; 384 for nine, Sussex v Ireland, Belfast, 1996; 381 for three, Lancashire v Hertfordshire, Radlett, 1999; 373 for seven, Glamorgan v Bedfordshire, Cardiff, 1998; 372 for five, Lancashire v Gloucestershire, Manchester, 1990; 371 for four, Hampshire v Glamorgan, Southampton, 1975. *In the final:* 322 for five, Warwickshire v Sussex, Lord's, 1993.

Highest total by a minor county: 323 for seven, Hertfordshire v Leicestershire Board XI, Radlett, 1999.

Highest total by a side batting first and losing: 327 for eight (60 overs), Derbyshire v Sussex, Derby, 1997. *In the final:* 321 for six (60 overs), Sussex v Warwickshire, 1993.

Highest totals by a side batting second: 350 (59.5 overs), Surrey lost to Worcestershire, The Oval, 1994; 339 for nine (60 overs), Somerset lost to Warwickshire, Birmingham, 1995; 329 for five (59.2 overs), Sussex beat Derbyshire, Derby, 1997; 326 for nine (60 overs), Hampshire lost to Leicestershire, Leicester, 1987; 322 for five (60 overs), Warwickshire beat Sussex, Lord's, 1993 (*in the final*); 319 for nine (59.5 overs), Essex beat Lancashire, Chelmsford, 1992.

Lowest completed totals: 39 (26.4 overs), Ireland v Sussex, Hove, 1985; 41 (20 overs), Cambridgeshire v Buckinghamshire, Cambridge, 1972; 41 (19.4 overs), Middlesex v Essex, Westcliff, 1972; 41 (36.1 overs), Shropshire v Essex, Wellington, 1974. *In the final:* 57 (27.2 overs), Essex v Lancashire, 1996.

Lowest total by a side batting first and winning: 98 (56.2 overs), Worcestershire v Durham, Chester-le-Street, 1968.

Shortest innings: 10.1 overs (60 for one), Worcestershire v Lancashire, Worcester, 1963.

Matches rearranged on a reduced number of overs are excluded from the above.

Record partnerships for each wicket

311	for 1st	A. J. Wright and N. J. Trainor, Gloucestershire v Scotland at Bristol . .	1997
286	for 2nd	I. S. Anderson and A. Hill, Derbyshire v Cornwall at Derby	1986
309*	for 3rd	T. S. Curtis and T. M. Moody, Worcestershire v Surrey at The Oval . . .	1994
234*	for 4th	D. Lloyd and C. H. Lloyd, Lancashire v Gloucestershire at Manchester .	1978
166	for 5th	M. A. Lynch and G. R. J. Roope, Surrey v Durham at The Oval	1982
226	for 6th	N. J. Llong and M. V. Fleming, Kent v Cheshire at Bowdon	1999
160*	for 7th	C. J. Richards and I. R. Payne, Surrey v Lincolnshire at Sleaford	1983
112	for 8th	A. L. Penberthy and J. E. Emburey, Northamptonshire v Lancashire at Manchester	1996
87	for 9th	M. A. Nash and A. E. Cordle, Glamorgan v Lincolnshire at Swansea . .	1974
81	for 10th	S. Turner and R. E. East, Essex v Yorkshire at Leeds	1982

Bowling

Most wickets: 87, A. A. Donald; 81, G. G. Arnold; 80, C. A. Connor; 79, J. Simmons.

Best bowling (12 overs unless stated): eight for 21 (10.1 overs), M. A. Holding, Derbyshire v Sussex, Hove, 1988; eight for 31 (11.1 overs), D. L. Underwood, Kent v Scotland, Edinburgh, 1987; seven for 15, A. L. Dixon, Kent v Surrey, The Oval, 1967; seven for 15 (9.3 overs), R. P. Lefebvre, Somerset v Devon, Torquay, 1990; seven for 19, N. V. Radford, Worcestershire v Bedfordshire, Bedford, 1991; seven for 27 (9.5 overs), D. Gough, Yorkshire v Ireland, Leeds, 1997; seven for 30, P. J. Sainsbury, Hampshire v Norfolk, Southampton, 1965; seven for 32, S. P. Davis, Durham v Lancashire, Chester-le-Street, 1983; seven for 33, R. D. Jackman, Surrey v Yorkshire, Harrogate, 1970; seven for 35 (10.1 overs), D. E. Malcolm, Derbyshire v Northamptonshire, Derby, 1997; seven for 37, N. A. Mallender, Northamptonshire v Worcestershire, Northampton, 1984. *In the final:* six for 18 (6.2 overs), G. Chapple, Lancashire v Essex, 1996.

Most economical analysis: 12–9–3–1, J. Simmons, Lancashire v Suffolk, Bury St Edmunds, 1985.

Most expensive analysis: 12–0–107–2, C. C. Lovell, Cornwall v Warwickshire, St Austell, 1996.

Hat-tricks (11): J. D. F. Larter, Northamptonshire v Sussex, Northampton, 1963; D. A. D. Sydenham, Surrey v Cheshire, Hoylake, 1964; R. N. S. Hobbs, Essex v Middlesex, Lord's, 1968; N. M. McVicker, Warwickshire v Lincolnshire, Birmingham, 1971; G. S. le Roux, Sussex v Ireland, Hove, 1985; M. Jean-Jacques, Derbyshire v Nottinghamshire, Derby, 1987; J. F. M. O'Brien, Cheshire v Derbyshire, Chester, 1988; R. A. Pick, Nottinghamshire v Scotland, Nottingham, 1995; J. E. Emburey, Northamptonshire v Cheshire, Northampton, 1996; A. R. Caddick, Somerset v Gloucestershire, Taunton, 1996; D. Gough, Yorkshire v Ireland, Leeds, 1997.

Four wickets in five balls: D. A. D. Sydenham, Surrey v Cheshire, Hoylake, 1964.

Wicket-keeping and Fielding

Most dismissals: 87 (74 ct, 13 st), R. C. Russell; 66 (57 ct, 9 st), S. J. Rhodes; 66 (58 ct, 8 st), R. W. Taylor; 65 (59 ct, 6 st), A. P. E. Knott.

Most dismissals in an innings: 8 (all ct), D. J. Pipe, Worcestershire v Hertfordshire, Hertford, 2001; 7 (all ct), A. J. Stewart, Surrey v Glamorgan, Swansea, 1994.

Most catches by a fielder: 27, J. Simmons; 26, M. W. Gatting and G. A. Gooch; 25, G. Cook; 24, P. J. Sharpe.

Most catches by a fielder in an innings: 4 – A. S. Brown, Gloucestershire v Middlesex, Bristol, 1963; G. Cook, Northamptonshire v Glamorgan, Northampton, 1972; C. G. Greenidge, Hampshire v Cheshire, Southampton, 1981; D. C. Jackson, Durham v Northamptonshire, Darlington, 1984; T. S. Smith, Hertfordshire v Somerset, St Albans, 1984; H. Morris, Glamorgan v Scotland, Edinburgh, 1988; C. C. Lewis, Nottinghamshire v Worcestershire, Nottingham, 1992; G. Yates, Lancashire v Essex, Manchester, 2000; D. P. Fulton, Kent v Northamptonshire, Canterbury, 2001.

Results

Largest victories in runs: Somerset by 346 runs v Devon, Torquay, 1990; Sussex by 304 runs v Ireland, Belfast, 1996; Worcestershire by 299 runs v Devon, Worcester, 1987; Essex by 291 runs v Wiltshire, Chelmsford, 1988; Worcestershire by 267 runs v Hertfordshire, Hertford, 2001; Sussex by 244 runs v Ireland, Hove, 1985; Lancashire by 241 runs v Gloucestershire, Manchester, 1990.

Victories by ten wickets (20): By Essex, Glamorgan, Hampshire (twice), Holland, Lancashire, Middlesex, Northamptonshire, Nottinghamshire, Somerset, Surrey (twice), Sussex (twice), Warwickshire (twice), Yorkshire (four times).

Earliest finishes: both at 2.20 p.m. Worcestershire beat Lancashire by nine wickets at Worcester, 1963; Essex beat Middlesex by eight wickets at Westcliff, 1972.

Scores level (11): Nottinghamshire 215, Somerset 215 for nine at Taunton, 1964; Surrey 196, Sussex 196 for eight at The Oval, 1970; Somerset 287 for six, Essex 287 at Taunton, 1978; Surrey 195 for seven, Essex 195 at Chelmsford, 1980; Essex 149, Derbyshire 149 for eight at Derby, 1981; Northamptonshire 235 for nine, Derbyshire 235 for six at Lord's, 1981 (*in the final*); Middlesex 222 for nine, Somerset 222 for eight at Lord's, 1983; Hampshire 224 for eight, Essex 224 for seven at Southampton, 1985; Essex 307 for six, Hampshire 307 for five at Chelmsford, 1990; Hampshire 204 for nine, Leicestershire 204 for nine at Leicester, 1995; Cheshire 204, Lincolnshire 204 for nine at Chester, 2000.

Under competition rules the side which lost fewer wickets won; at Leicester in 1995, Leicestershire won by virtue of their higher total after 30 overs.

Match Awards

Most awards: 9, G. A. Gooch and R. A. Smith; 8, C. H. Lloyd and C. L. Smith.

WINNERS 1963–2001

Gillette Cup

		Man of the Match
1963	SUSSEX* beat Worcestershire by 14 runs.	N. Gifford†
1964	SUSSEX beat Warwickshire* by eight wickets.	N. I. Thomson
1965	YORKSHIRE beat Surrey* by 175 runs.	G. Boycott
1966	WARWICKSHIRE* beat Worcestershire by five wickets.	R. W. Barber
1967	KENT* beat Somerset by 32 runs.	M. H. Denness
1968	WARWICKSHIRE beat Sussex* by four wickets.	A. C. Smith
1969	YORKSHIRE beat Derbyshire* by 69 runs.	B. Leadbeater
1970	LANCASHIRE* beat Sussex by six wickets.	H. Pilling
1971	LANCASHIRE* beat Kent by 24 runs.	Asif Iqbal†
1972	LANCASHIRE* beat Warwickshire by four wickets.	C. H. Lloyd
1973	GLOUCESTERSHIRE* beat Sussex by 40 runs.	A. S. Brown
1974	KENT* beat Lancashire by four wickets.	A. P. E. Knott
1975	LANCASHIRE* beat Middlesex by seven wickets.	C. H. Lloyd
1976	NORTHAMPTONSHIRE* beat Lancashire by four wickets.	P. Willey
1977	MIDDLESEX* beat Glamorgan by five wickets.	C. T. Radley
1978	SUSSEX* beat Somerset by five wickets.	P. W. G. Parker
1979	SOMERSET beat Northamptonshire* by 45 runs.	I. V. A. Richards
1980	MIDDLESEX* beat Surrey by seven wickets.	J. M. Brearley

NatWest Trophy

1981	DERBYSHIRE* beat Northamptonshire by losing fewer wickets with the scores level.	G. Cook†
1982	SURREY* beat Warwickshire by nine wickets.	D. J. Thomas
1983	SOMERSET beat Kent* by 24 runs.	V. J. Marks
1984	MIDDLESEX beat Kent* by four wickets.	C. T. Radley
1985	ESSEX beat Nottinghamshire* by one run.	B. R. Hardie
1986	SUSSEX* beat Lancashire by seven wickets.	D. A. Reeve
1987	NOTTINGHAMSHIRE* beat Northamptonshire by three wickets.	R. J. Hadlee
1988	MIDDLESEX* beat Worcestershire by three wickets.	M. R. Ramprakash
1989	WARWICKSHIRE beat Middlesex* by four wickets.	D. A. Reeve
1990	LANCASHIRE* beat Northamptonshire by seven wickets.	P. A. J. DeFreitas
1991	HAMPSHIRE* beat Surrey by four wickets.	R. A. Smith
1992	NORTHAMPTONSHIRE* beat Leicestershire by eight wickets.	A. Fordham
1993	WARWICKSHIRE* beat Sussex by five wickets.	Asif Din
1994	WORCESTERSHIRE* beat Warwickshire by eight wickets.	T. M. Moody
1995	WARWICKSHIRE beat Northamptonshire* by four wickets.	D. A. Reeve
1996	LANCASHIRE beat Essex* by 129 runs.	G. Chapple
1997	ESSEX* beat Warwickshire by nine wickets.	S. G. Law
1998	LANCASHIRE* beat Derbyshire by nine wickets.	I. D. Austin
1999	GLOUCESTERSHIRE beat Somerset* by 50 runs.	R. C. Russell
2000	GLOUCESTERSHIRE* beat Warwickshire by 22 runs (D/L method).	A. A. Donald†

Cheltenham & Gloucester Trophy

2001	SOMERSET* beat Leicestershire by 41 runs.	K. A. Parsons

* *Won toss.* † *On losing side.*

TEAM RECORDS 1963–2001

	Rounds reached				*Matches*		
	W	*F*	*SF*	*QF*	*P*	*W*	*L*
Derbyshire	1	3	4	13	80*	42	38
Durham	0	0	0	2	47	16	31
Essex	2	3	6	15	86	49	37
Glamorgan	0	1	4	16	84	45	39
Gloucestershire	3	3	7	16	87	50	37
Hampshire	1	1	10	22	99	61	38
Kent	2	5	7	16	90	53	37
Lancashire	7	10	17	23	114	82	32
Leicestershire	0	2	5	16	84	45	39
Middlesex	4	6	13	21	103	68	35
Northamptonshire	2	7	10	21	99	62	37
Nottinghamshire	1	2	3	13	81	43	38
Somerset	3	6	11	19	98	62	36
Surrey	1	4	11	23	100*	62	38
Sussex	4	8	13	19	99	64	35
Warwickshire	5	11	18	23	115	81	34
Worcestershire	1	4	10	15	88	50	38
Yorkshire	2	2	7	18	86	49	37

* Derbyshire and Surrey totals each include a bowling contest after their first-round matches were abandoned in 1991; Derbyshire lost to Hertfordshire and Surrey beat Oxfordshire.

MINOR COUNTY RECORDS

From 1964 to 1979 the previous season's top five Minor Counties were invited to take part in the competition. In 1980 these were joined by Ireland, and in 1983 the competition was expanded to embrace 13 Minor Counties, Ireland and Scotland. The number of Minor Counties dropped to 12 in 1992 when Durham attained first-class status, and 11 in 1995 when Holland were admitted to the competition.

Between 1964 and 1991 Durham qualified 21 times, including 15 years in succession from 1977–91. They reached the second round a record six times.

Up to the 1998 tournament, Staffordshire qualified most among the remaining Minor Counties, 20 times, followed by Devon, 19. Only Hertfordshire have ever reached the quarter-finals, in 1976.

From 1999, the competition was reformed and two preliminary rounds introduced, in which 42 teams compete for the right to join the first-class counties in the third round. They are all 20 Minor Counties (including Wales), plus Huntingdonshire Board XI, the first-class county Board XIs (excluding Glamorgan, who are covered by Wales) and the national teams of Denmark, Holland, Ireland and Scotland. These four national teams did not take part in the 2001 Trophy because of the forthcoming ICC Trophy.

Wins by a minor team over a first-class county (11)**:** Durham v Yorkshire (by five wickets), Harrogate, 1973; Lincolnshire v Glamorgan (by six wickets), Swansea, 1974; Hertfordshire v Essex (by 33 runs), 2nd round, Hitchin, 1976; Shropshire v Yorkshire (by 37 runs), Telford, 1984; Durham v Derbyshire (by seven wickets), Derby, 1985; Buckinghamshire v Somerset (by seven runs), High Wycombe, 1987; Cheshire v Northamptonshire (by one wicket), Chester, 1988; Hertfordshire v Derbyshire (2–1 in a bowling contest after the match was abandoned), Bishop's Stortford, 1991; Scotland v Worcestershire (by four runs), Edinburgh, 1998; Holland v Durham (by five wickets), Amstelveen, 1999; Herefordshire v Middlesex (by three wickets), Kingsland, 2001.

BENSON AND HEDGES CUP, 2001

SURREY
COUNTY CRICKET CLUB

Ben Hollioake

In pitting Surrey, the reigning county champions, against Gloucestershire, triple one-day champions of 2000, the Benson and Hedges Cup final could have been one of the summer's highlights. Instead, it drew the smallest crowd for a one-day final at Lord's. Some uncertain early-morning weather might have been a contributing factor, as might ticket prices ranging from £22 to £45, although the latter did not stop Gloucestershire's supporters taking up more than their initial allocation. Not even the offer of half-price entry for children and pensioners could hide the gaps around the ground, and not all the hospitality boxes were in use. The conclusion to be drawn was that the English season's new format, with a one-day international final at this venue only three weeks earlier and a Test match starting there later in the week, had relegated this domestic occasion to the second division in the cricketing public's consciousness.

Gloucestershire deserved better. Before them only Kent, from 1976 to 1978, had reached three consecutive Benson and Hedges finals, and this was their fifth Lord's appearance in succession; quite without precedent. They had qualified for the quarter-finals before their sole group defeat and won handsomely in the knockout rounds. But, for all their experience, they were handicapped by injuries to key players. Vice-captain Tim Hancock and beneficiary Mike Smith, who had played in the previous four Lord's finals, and Jon Lewis, with ten wickets up to and including the quarter-finals, were all unavailable. Moreover, just a few days earlier, Durham had avenged their quarter-final defeat by ending Gloucestershire's defence of their other knockout title at the first serious hurdle.

Surrey, too, had fallen in the fourth round of the Cheltenham & Gloucester Trophy. But they went into the club's fifth Benson and Hedges final able to select 11 internationals and still allow Graham Thorpe to rest his suspect calf muscle before the forthcoming Test against Australia. They had overwhelmed Nottinghamshire in the semi-finals; now they had the chance to close Gloucestershire's cycle of achievement, which began in 1999 when they beat Surrey by seven wickets in the opening round of the short-lived Benson and Hedges Super Cup. Sure enough, as the final unfolded, it became apparent that Gloucestershire's glorious reign had run its course. Just as pertinently, many were saying the same of the competition itself.

Ian Harvey's three wickets in the final took his 2001 Benson and Hedges tally to 16, putting him ahead of Warwickshire's Dougie Brown (13), whose interest in the competition ended at the quarter-finals. Nottinghamshire left-armer Greg Smith followed them with 12. Like Brown, leading run-scorer Marcus Trescothick progressed no further than the quarter-finals, but his weight of runs in Somerset's group games helped him to an aggregate of 385 at 77.00. Darren Bicknell, whose unbeaten century against Warwickshire put Nottinghamshire in the semi-finals, ran Trescothick close with 361 at 60.16, followed by Nick Knight of Warwickshire (340 at 68.00). Trescothick and Knight both hit three hundreds to match Darren Maddy's haul in 1998, when the Leicestershire opener set a competition record of 629 runs at 125.80.

Prize money

£52,000 for winners: SURREY.
£26,000 for runners-up: GLOUCESTERSHIRE.
£15,500 for each losing semi-finalist: NOTTINGHAMSHIRE, YORKSHIRE.
£10,500 for each losing quarter-finalist: DURHAM, SOMERSET, SUSSEX, WARWICKSHIRE.

Gold Award winners received £1,750 in the final, £550 in the semi-finals, £500 in the quarter-finals and £300 in the group matches; these figures were unchanged from the 2000 competition, and the total sponsorship also remained at £850,000.

FINAL GROUP TABLES

	Played	*Won*	*Lost*	*No result*	*Points*	*Net run-rate*
Midlands/Wales/West Group						
SOMERSET	5	4	1	0	8	0.74
GLOUCESTERSHIRE	5	4	1	0	8	–0.27
WARWICKSHIRE*	5	3	2	0	6	0.30
Worcestershire	5	2	3	0	4	0.17
Northamptonshire	5	2	3	0	4	–0.53
Glamorgan	5	0	5	0	0	–0.44
North Group						
NOTTINGHAMSHIRE	5	4	1	0	8	0.77
DURHAM	5	3	2	0	6	0.33
YORKSHIRE*	5	3	2	0	6	0.04
Leicestershire	5	3	2	0	6	–0.32
Lancashire	5	1	4	0	2	–0.27
Derbyshire	5	1	4	0	2	–0.43
South Group						
SUSSEX	5	3	0	2	8	0.88
SURREY	5	2	1	2	6	0.24
Middlesex	5	2	2	1	5	–0.59
Kent	5	2	2	1	5	–0.02
Essex	5	1	2	2	4	0.34
Hampshire	5	0	3	2	2	–0.72

* *Warwickshire and Yorkshire qualified as the most successful third-placed teams.*

Where two or more counties finished with an equal number of points, the positions were decided by (a) most wins (b) most points in head-to-head matches (c) net run-rate (runs scored per over minus runs conceded per over, revising figures in matches where the Duckworth/Lewis method was used and discounting those not achieving a result) (d) most wickets taken per balls bowled in matches achieving a result.

MIDLANDS/WALES/WEST GROUP

WORCESTERSHIRE v NORTHAMPTONSHIRE

At Kidderminster, April 30. Worcestershire won by 96 runs. Toss: Worcestershire.

With their soggy New Road headquarters out of commission, Worcestershire recorded a second victory in as many days at their temporary Kidderminster home. Fifties from Pollard and Leatherdale, boosted by a late 22-ball onslaught from Bichel, guided them to 227 on a sluggish pitch. Cousins, who finished with one-day best figures of four for 23, was the only Northamptonshire bowler to cause problems. His Worcestershire counterparts, however, proved more penetrative, and reduced the visitors to 68 for six. Swann then lofted Leatherdale for a couple of defiant sixes, but the result was already beyond doubt. Pollard's match award was his first in 13 seasons in the competition.

Gold Award: P. R. Pollard.

Worcestershire

P. R. Pollard c Warren b Innes 69
A. Singh b Cousins 6
*G. A. Hick lbw b Cousins 9
V. S. Solanki c Loye b Swann 28
D. A. Leatherdale c Warren b Cousins . . 58
A. J. Bichel c Hussey b Blain. 29
W. P. C. Weston not out. 11
†S. J. Rhodes c and b Cousins 0
S. R. Lampitt not out 7
L-b 4, w 2, n-b 4 10

1/15 2/42 3/99 (7 wkts, 50 overs) 227
4/144 5/204
6/213 7/214

M. J. Rawnsley and A. Sheriyar did not bat.

Bowling: Cousins 10–3–23–4; Blain 8–0–69–1; Innes 8–0–35–1; Penberthy 10–0–44–0; Brown 6–0–23–0; Swann 8–0–29–1.

Northamptonshire

M. E. K. Hussey c Rhodes b Bichel . . . 5
M. B. Loye c Solanki b Sheriyar. 1
J. W. Cook c Bichel b Lampitt 38
R. J. Warren c Solanki b Sheriyar 0
A. L. Penberthy run out. 8
G. P. Swann c Bichel b Leatherdale. . . . 37
K. J. Innes c Bichel b Lampitt 0
*†D. Ripley b Bichel 14
J. A. R. Blain c Weston b Rawnsley. . . . 11
D. M. Cousins lbw b Bichel. 3
J. F. Brown not out. 5
L-b 4, w 5. 9

1/6 2/17 3/17 (37.2 overs) 131
4/43 5/64 6/68
7/107 8/111 9/118

Bowling: Sheriyar 8–2–14–2; Bichel 10–2–38–3; Lampitt 7–1–18–2; Rawnsley 6.2–0–38–1; Leatherdale 6–1–19–1.

Umpires: A. Clarkson and J. H. Evans.

GLAMORGAN v SOMERSET

At Cardiff, May 1. Somerset won by six wickets. Toss: Glamorgan.

Trescothick struck his second century at Sophia Gardens in five days to make light of a testing target on a slow pitch. Captaining the side in the absence of Cox, out with an injured groin, he shared a partnership of 121 with Dutch, who marked his promotion to No. 3 with a maiden Benson and Hedges fifty. On 35, Trescothick offered a caught-and-bowled chance to Watkin, but otherwise he played immaculately, hitting ten of his 118 balls for boundaries before falling with just five needed for victory. Earlier, Glamorgan had relied on a half-century from the in-form Powell, but they lost three of their top five to run-outs.

Gold Award: M. E. Trescothick.

Glamorgan

*S. P. James run out. 33
J. P. Maher c Bowler b Jones 7
M. J. Powell c Lathwell b Johnson 67
A. Dale run out. 3
M. P. Maynard run out 36
K. Newell lbw b Kerr. 18
†A. D. Shaw not out. 24
S. D. Thomas not out 28
L-b 5, w 9, n-b 2 16

1/12 2/71 3/75 (6 wkts, 50 overs) 232
4/159 5/159 6/189

R. D. B. Croft, A. P. Davies and S. L. Watkin did not bat.

Bowling: Johnson 10–2–39–1; Jones 10–0–39–1; Kerr 8–0–50–1; Parsons 10–0–41–0; Dutch 5–0–22–0; Blackwell 7–0–36–0.

Somerset

*M. E. Trescothick c Powell b Thomas	113	K. A. Parsons not out	2
P. D. Bowler lbw b Watkin	21	L-b 5, w 4, n-b 2	11
K. P. Dutch c Powell b Maher	55		—
M. N. Lathwell run out	7	1/47 2/168 (4 wkts, 47 overs)	233
M. Burns not out	24	3/190 4/228	

I. D. Blackwell, †R. J. Turner, J. I. D. Kerr, R. L. Johnson and P. S. Jones did not bat.

Bowling: Watkin 10–1–39–1; Thomas 9–0–56–1; Davies 10–0–55–0; Dale 4–0–22–0; Croft 10–0–36–0; Maher 4–0–20–1.

Umpires: M. R. Benson and B. Dudleston.

WARWICKSHIRE v GLOUCESTERSHIRE

At Birmingham, May 1. Gloucestershire won by virtue of losing fewer wickets. Toss: Gloucestershire. County debut: M. M. Betts.

Taylor smashed the last ball through the covers and tied the scores, bringing the cup holders victory by dint of losing six wickets to Warwickshire's nine. Had Drakes kept his head for the previous delivery, Gloucestershire would have faced the last ball five behind. Instead, having pinned Williams in his crease with a yorker, Drakes turned and shied at the non-striker's stumps, conceding a scrambled single as the ball ricocheted away. Warwickshire's innings had been constructed around a stand of 136 between Ostler and Powell; no one else made it past 17 as Harvey's variation of pace claimed five wickets. In reply, Barnett, Cunliffe – with a measured half-century – and Windows all played their part, though four overs from the end the asking-rate had reached nine. Spectators might have guessed a tight finish was on the cards: the last time a side scored 213 in a 50-over game at Edgbaston was the tied 1999 World Cup semi-final.

Gold Award: I. J. Harvey.

Warwickshire

N. V. Knight lbw b Harvey	17	V. C. Drakes b Harvey	9
M. A. Wagh c Williams b Harvey	4	†K. J. Piper st Williams b Harvey	4
M. A. Sheikh c Williams b Lewis	7		
D. P. Ostler b Harvey	77	L-b 17	17
T. L. Penney c Williams b Lewis	4		—
*M. J. Powell c Windows b Alleyne	55	1/10 2/23 3/31 (9 wkts, 50 overs)	213
N. M. K. Smith c Harvey b Averis	8	4/39 5/175 6/182	
D. R. Brown not out	11	7/192 8/209 9/213	

M. M. Betts did not bat.

Bowling: Lewis 10–4–24–2; Harvey 10–1–32–5; Cawdron 10–0–55–0; Averis 8–0–40–1; Alleyne 10–1–35–1; Barnett 2–0–10–0.

Gloucestershire

T. H. C. Hancock c Piper b Betts	3	C. G. Taylor not out	6
K. J. Barnett c and b Sheikh	34	†R. C. J. Williams not out	1
R. J. Cunliffe b Brown	75	B 1, l-b 13, w 6, n-b 6	26
M. G. N. Windows c Powell b Betts	42		—
I. J. Harvey b Brown	0	1/6 2/83 3/171 (6 wkts, 50 overs)	213
*M. W. Alleyne b Drakes	26	4/171 5/202 6/208	

M. J. Cawdron, J. M. M. Averis and J. Lewis did not bat.

Bowling: Betts 10–0–49–2; Drakes 10–1–40–1; Brown 10–0–43–2; Sheikh 10–1–27–1; Smith 10–0–40–0.

Umpires: D. J. Constant and J. H. Evans.

GLAMORGAN v WORCESTERSHIRE

At Cardiff, May 2. Worcestershire won by five wickets. Toss: Glamorgan. County debut: N. R. Boulton.

A hundred from Bichel – his first in one-day cricket – guided Worcestershire from 46 for three towards a convincing victory. A surprise choice as No. 3 (though he had sometimes batted one lower for Queensland the previous winter), he took 82 balls for his first 50, just 34 for his second, and put on 106 with Solanki. Glamorgan had earlier made 228, though at 93 for one they would have expected more. James was then run out for 49 when Powell's drive was deflected on to the stumps and, despite Maynard's run-a-ball 63, the innings lost its way. A second defeat left Glamorgan, beaten finalists in 2000, facing an uphill struggle to progress beyond the group stage.

Gold Award: A. J. Bichel.

Glamorgan

*S. P. James run out	49	R. D. B. Croft run out	4
J. P. Maher lbw b Bichel	14	A. P. Davies not out	3
M. J. Powell b Rawnsley	24		
M. P. Maynard c Lampitt b Bichel	63	B 2, l-b 2, w 4, n-b 8	16
A. Dale c Rawnsley b Leatherdale	8		
K. Newell b Hick	36	1/33 2/93 3/94 (9 wkts, 50 overs)	228
†A. D. Shaw c Lampitt b Hick	6	4/121 5/179 6/207	
S. D. Thomas lbw b Hick	5	7/219 8/223 9/228	

S. L. Watkin did not bat.

Bowling: Bichel 10–2–34–2; Sheriyar 7–0–27–0; Lampitt 10–0–58–0; Leatherdale 8–0–36–1; Rawnsley 10–0–46–1; Hick 5–0–23–3.

Worcestershire

W. P. C. Weston lbw b Watkin	7	N. R. Boulton not out	22
A. Singh c Maynard b Watkin	0		
A. J. Bichel run out	100	L-b 7, w 2	9
*G. A. Hick c Maynard b Davies	12		
V. S. Solanki st Shaw b Croft	44	1/3 2/24 3/46 (5 wkts, 47.3 overs)	229
D. A. Leatherdale not out	35	4/152 5/179	

†S. J. Rhodes, S. R. Lampitt, M. J. Rawnsley and A. Sheriyar did not bat.

Bowling: Watkin 10–1–42–2; Thomas 8.3–2–35–0; Davies 10–1–40–1; Maher 3–0–18–0; Croft 10–0–46–1; Dale 6–0–41–0.

Umpires: V. A. Holder and R. Julian.

GLOUCESTERSHIRE v NORTHAMPTONSHIRE

At Bristol, May 2. Gloucestershire won by nine runs. Toss: Northamptonshire.

Both sides recovered from disastrous starts, Gloucestershire eventually prevailing because their collapse was the less precipitous. They were 80 for six when Williams, Jack Russell's long-term understudy, joined Windows, and together they added 86, during which Windows reached a circumspect 111-ball fifty. There was nothing circumspect about what followed, however: he hit three sixes, five fours and totalled 58 runs from his next 40 deliveries. The final over, bowled by Brown, went for 20 and included two sixes, the second bringing Windows a maiden limited-overs hundred. Northamptonshire had crumbled to 41 for six when Innes and Alec Swann began the repairs. Swann battled defiantly for a magnificent undefeated 83, but, needing 14 from the final over, from Harvey, Northamptonshire managed four.

Gold Award: M. G. N. Windows.

Gloucestershire

T. H. C. Hancock c G. P. Swann b Innes	29	†R. C. J. Williams c Hussey b Cousins	27
K. J. Barnett lbw b Penberthy	11	M. J. Cawdron not out	9
R. J. Cunliffe b Penberthy	0	L-b 2, w 1	3
M. G. N. Windows not out	108		
I. J. Harvey run out	1	1/23 2/25 3/57 (7 wkts, 50 overs)	202
*M. W. Alleyne c Penberthy b Cousins	14	4/59 5/80	
C. G. Taylor c Ripley b Cousins	0	6/80 7/166	

J. M. M. Averis and J. Lewis did not bat.

Bowling: Cousins 10–0–42–3; Penberthy 10–2–21–2; Innes 10–2–36–1; Cook 6–0–22–0; Brown 10–1–59–0; G. P. Swann 4–0–20–0.

Northamptonshire

M. E. K. Hussey b Harvey	4	*†D. Ripley b Averis	14
M. B. Loye c Taylor b Lewis	8	D. M. Cousins c Alleyne b Averis	6
J. W. Cook lbw b Harvey	0	J. F. Brown not out	5
R. J. Warren c Williams b Cawdron	19	B 3, l-b 6, w 4, n-b 2	15
G. P. Swann b Lewis	0		
A. L. Penberthy c Williams b Cawdron	2	1/7 2/7 3/19 (9 wkts, 50 overs)	193
A. J. Swann not out	83	4/23 5/26 6/41	
K. J. Innes c Williams b Lewis	37	7/96 8/141 9/159	

Bowling: Harvey 10–0–51–2; Lewis 10–1–13–3; Cawdron 10–2–26–2; Averis 10–3–42–2; Alleyne 8–0–44–0; Barnett 2–0–8–0.

Umpires: R. A. White and P. Willey.

SOMERSET v WARWICKSHIRE

At Taunton, May 2. Warwickshire won by four wickets. Toss: Warwickshire.

By the 24th over, Somerset, struggling at 64 for six, were in danger of being dismissed for double figures. Betts, a close-season arrival from Durham, had inflicted much of the damage, taking a one-day best return of four for 22 from his ten overs, bowled off the reel. Parsons, however, on his 28th birthday, struck a defiant 72, also a one-day best, to salvage some Somerset pride. And when Jones had Warwickshire 25 for three, it briefly looked as though 174 might prove enough. Then Penney and Powell settled to their task, and put the Somerset total into perspective.

Gold Award: M. M. Betts.

Somerset

*M. E. Trescothick c Ostler b Betts	23	J. I. D. Kerr lbw b Powell	11
P. D. Bowler lbw b Drakes	1	R. L. Johnson b Drakes	24
M. N. Lathwell b Betts	2	P. S. Jones not out	2
I. D. Blackwell b Betts	5	L-b 8, w 4, n-b 6	18
M. Burns b Betts	5		
K. A. Parsons c Sheikh b Drakes	72	1/11 2/28 3/29 (49.2 overs)	174
†R. J. Turner lbw b Brown	2	4/39 5/44 6/64	
K. P. Dutch c Piper b Brown	9	7/82 8/115 9/162	

Bowling: Drakes 9.2–2–35–3; Betts 10–3–22–4; Sheikh 10–1–26–0; Brown 10–2–33–2; Powell 8–0–39–1; Smith 2–0–11–0.

Warwickshire

N. V. Knight c Blackwell b Jones	12	N. M. K. Smith c Parsons b Trescothick	20
M. A. Wagh c Bowler b Jones	9	†K. J. Piper not out	2
D. R. Brown c Turner b Jones	3	L-b 3, w 7	10
D. P. Ostler b Kerr	18		
T. L. Penney not out	73	1/15 2/24 3/25 (6 wkts, 49.1 overs)	178
*M. J. Powell c Parsons b Johnson	31	4/71 5/141 6/169	

M. A. Sheikh, V. C. Drakes and M. M. Betts did not bat.

Bowling: Johnson 10–1–33–1; Jones 10–1–38–3; Kerr 10–1–23–1; Parsons 10–1–32–0; Burns 5–0–23–0; Dutch 2–0–7–0; Trescothick 2.1–0–19–1.

Umpires: A. Clarkson and J. F. Steele.

GLOUCESTERSHIRE v GLAMORGAN

At Bristol, May 4. Gloucestershire won by five wickets. Toss: Gloucestershire.

As they had in the final 11 months before, Glamorgan lost to Gloucestershire after over-reliance on a single batsman. At Lord's, Maynard had reached three figures; now Maher, their left-hander from Queensland, dominated the innings from start to finish, his undefeated 142, from 151 balls with 12 fours and a six, constituting more than 60 per cent of the total. James lent support until he bottom-edged an attempted pull on to his injury-prone knee and was forced to retire. No one else passed 15. In reply, Barnett became only the second player after Graham Gooch to reach 3,000 runs in this competition, but was out soon after; with Gloucestershire faltering at 66 for four, Glamorgan might yet have smelt revenge. However, Alleyne, first with Windows and latterly with Snape, calmly steered the home side to what became a comfortable win.

Gold Award: M. W. Alleyne.

Glamorgan

K. Newell c Williams b Harvey	10	R. D. B. Croft b Harvey	15
J. P. Maher not out	142	S. D. Thomas not out	12
*S. P. James retired hurt	30		
M. P. Maynard c Williams b Alleyne	12	L-b 2, w 4, n-b 2	8
M. J. Powell c Harvey b Averis	0		
A. Dale run out	6	1/11 2/102 3/103 (6 wkts, 50 overs)	236
†A. D. Shaw lbw b Alleyne	1	4/121 5/127 6/180	

A. P. Davies and S. L. Watkin did not bat.

James retired hurt at 85.

Bowling: Harvey 10–0–52–2; Lewis 10–0–41–0; Cawdron 6–0–35–0; Alleyne 10–1–36–2; Averis 8–0–43–1; Snape 6–0–27–0.

Gloucestershire

R. J. Cunliffe c Maher b Watkin	7	J. N. Snape not out	46
K. J. Barnett c Shaw b Thomas	22		
C. G. Taylor c Maher b Watkin	5	L-b 5, w 12	17
M. G. N. Windows c Maher b Croft	40		
I. J. Harvey run out	24	1/15 2/35 3/35 (5 wkts, 48.3 overs)	240
*M. W. Alleyne not out	79	4/66 5/143	

†R. C. J. Williams, M. J. Cawdron, J. M. M. Averis and J. Lewis did not bat.

Bowling: Watkin 10–2–34–2; Thomas 9–1–45–1; Davies 10–0–56–0; Dale 7.3–0–40–0; Maher 2–0–14–0; Croft 10–1–46–1.

Umpires: A. Clarkson and N. G. Cowley.

NORTHAMPTONSHIRE v WARWICKSHIRE

At Northampton, May 4. Northamptonshire won by seven wickets. Toss: Warwickshire. County debut: L. C. Weekes.

The combination of an excellent pitch and largely indifferent bowling made this a batsman's match. Knight was slow to start, taking 90 balls for his first fifty, but he needed only 30 more to reach his hundred. Montserrat-born Lesroy Weekes, released by Yorkshire at the end of the previous season, claimed two wickets on his Northamptonshire debut. Two other foreign-born players, Cook and Hussey – both left-handers from Australia, although Cook, like Weekes, is England-qualified – then took the game from Warwickshire. They added 110 for the second wicket at five an over before Graeme Swann administered the *coup de grâce* with a tempestuous 30-ball 51.

Gold Award: M. E. K. Hussey.

Warwickshire

N. V. Knight run out	101	†K. J. Piper c Cousins b Innes	1
M. A. Wagh c Cousins b G. P. Swann	39	V. C. Drakes not out	2
D. R. Brown run out	3	L-b 6, w 1, n-b 2	9
D. P. Ostler lbw b Cousins	39		
T. L. Penney b Weekes	6	1/71 2/77 3/130 (7 wkts, 50 overs)	263
N. M. K. Smith c Warren b Weekes	40	4/143 5/205	
*M. J. Powell not out	23	6/254 7/255	

M. A. Sheikh and M. M. Betts did not bat.

Bowling: Cousins 10–1–46–1; Penberthy 10–2–46–0; Weekes 10–0–47–2; Innes 10–1–54–1; G. P. Swann 8–0–43–1; Cook 2–0–21–0.

Northamptonshire

M. E. K. Hussey b Brown	93	R. J. Warren not out	0
M. B. Loye b Sheikh	24	L-b 6, w 4	10
J. W. Cook b Brown	86		
G. P. Swann not out	51	1/56 2/166 3/251 (3 wkts, 47.4 overs)	264

A. J. Swann, A. L. Penberthy, K. J. Innes, *†D. Ripley, L. C. Weekes and D. M. Cousins did not bat.

Bowling: Drakes 10–1–40–0; Betts 8.4–0–64–0; Sheikh 10–3–31–1; Smith 8–0–45–0; Brown 9–0–59–2; Powell 2–0–19–0.

Umpires: T. E. Jesty and A. A. Jones.

WORCESTERSHIRE v SOMERSET

At Worcester, May 4. Somerset won by 20 runs. Toss: Somerset.

Few batsmen could find the measure of a damp New Road pitch. Cox elected to bat, only to see his side career to 64 for five. He was sixth out at 106 for a dogged 39, though the real Somerset saviour was Blackwell, who hit a typically forceful 64 from 74 balls, with six fours and a six. Worcestershire made a calamitous start to their pursuit of 180, the Somerset seamers reducing them to 43 for four, then 79 for six. Bichel, fresh from a maiden century, and Leatherdale then added 52, but once they were parted, any faint hopes of a home win disappeared.

Gold Award: I. D. Blackwell.

Somerset

M. E. Trescothick c Rhodes b Sheriyar	16
P. D. Bowler c Rhodes b Bichel	6
*J. Cox c Rhodes b Hick	39
M. Burns b Bichel	1
K. A. Parsons lbw b Lampitt	10
†R. J. Turner b Rawnsley	0
I. D. Blackwell c Solanki b Sheriyar	64
K. P. Dutch run out	6
J. I. D. Kerr c Singh b Leatherdale	9
R. L. Johnson c Leatherdale b Bichel	11
P. S. Jones not out	4
B 2, l-b 2, w 9	13
1/25 2/29 3/30 4/53 5/64 6/106 7/122 8/136 9/164 (49.3 overs)	179

Bowling: Bichel 10–1–42–3; Sheriyar 9.3–1–31–2; Lampitt 8–3–20–1; Rawnsley 10–0–30–1; Hick 7–1–30–1; Leatherdale 5–0–22–1.

Worcestershire

W. P. C. Weston c Turner b Jones	4
A. Singh c Parsons b Kerr	7
*G. A. Hick c Turner b Jones	7
V. S. Solanki c Bowler b Kerr	13
D. A. Leatherdale c Blackwell b Johnson	55
N. R. Boulton c Turner b Dutch	4
†S. J. Rhodes c Parsons b Blackwell	4
A. J. Bichel c Bowler b Dutch	31
S. R. Lampitt not out	15
M. J. Rawnsley b Johnson	0
A. Sheriyar lbw b Kerr	0
B 5, l-b 4, w 5, p 5	19
1/9 2/17 3/32 4/43 5/68 6/79 7/131 8/152 9/157 (47.3 overs)	159

Bowling: Johnson 9–1–26–2; Jones 7–3–12–2; Kerr 9.3–1–30–3; Parsons 4–1–14–0; Blackwell 9–0–41–1; Dutch 9–2–22–2.

Umpires: G. I. Burgess and G. Sharp.

NORTHAMPTONSHIRE v SOMERSET

At Northampton, May 5. Somerset won by eight wickets. Toss: Northamptonshire.

Somerset's third win briefly raised them to the top of the group. Trescothick was again the hero, hitting an unbeaten 109 and adding 145 for the second wicket with Cox, whose 72 came at almost a run a ball. Trescothick needed 117 for his 109, complete with 15 fours, and Somerset won with more than ten overs to spare. The Northamptonshire innings had promised much at 43 without loss, only for five wickets to fall for 51. Although Penberthy and Alec Swann steadied the ship, a total of 219 proved wholly inadequate. Swann's brother, Graeme, injured his shoulder swinging his bat as he walked to the crease, was out first ball and played no further part in the game.

Gold Award: M. E. Trescothick.

Northamptonshire

M. E. K. Hussey c sub b Dutch	37
M. B. Loye lbw b Caddick	27
J. W. Cook run out	8
R. J. Warren c Lathwell b Kerr	3
G. P. Swann lbw b Kerr	0
A. L. Penberthy b Caddick	58
A. J. Swann not out	54
K. J. Innes not out	19
L-b 4, w 9	13
1/43 2/56 3/68 4/68 5/94 6/180 (6 wkts, 50 overs)	219

*†D. Ripley, L. C. Weekes and D. M. Cousins did not bat.

Bowling: Johnson 6–1–28–0; Caddick 10–2–42–2; Kerr 10–0–44–2; Parsons 4–0–17–0; Trescothick 6–0–30–0; Dutch 10–1–34–1; Blackwell 4–0–20–0.

Somerset

M. E. Trescothick not out	109
M. N. Lathwell c Hussey b Cousins	6
*J. Cox c Ripley b Hussey	72
K. P. Dutch not out	26
L-b 4, w 2, n-b 2	8
1/31 2/176 (2 wkts, 39.1 overs)	221

M. Burns, K. A. Parsons, †R. J. Turner, I. D. Blackwell, A. R. Caddick, J. I. D. Kerr and R. L. Johnson did not bat.

Bowling: Cousins 10–0–60–1; Penberthy 7–0–29–0; Innes 9.1–0–44–0; Weekes 7–0–49–0; A. J. Swann 3–0–20–0; Hussey 3–0–15–1.

Umpires: D. J. Constant and B. Leadbeater.

WARWICKSHIRE v GLAMORGAN

At Birmingham, May 5. Warwickshire won by 55 runs. Toss: Warwickshire.

Knight's second hundred in two days reminded the England selectors that there were other talented left-handed openers apart from Trescothick. Indeed, Knight was the sole batsman to master a pitch devoid of any pace. He and Wagh put on 91 for Warwickshire's first wicket before Newell induced a mini-collapse. Knight's partners came and went, but he saw out the 50 overs, ending unbeaten on 107 from 143 balls. Glamorgan, unable to reach the quarter-finals after three successive defeats, never looked settled. A partnership of 48 for the eighth wicket between Shaw and Thomas was the best they could muster.

Gold Award: N. V. Knight.

Warwickshire

N. V. Knight not out	107
M. A. Wagh b Newell	35
D. P. Ostler b Newell	7
T. L. Penney lbw b Cosker	4
*M. J. Powell c Maher b Croft	3
N. M. K. Smith c Croft b Newell	15
D. R. Brown c Powell b Croft	17
†K. J. Piper lbw b Wharf	22
M. A. Sheikh lbw b Wharf	1
B 3, l-b 7, w 6	16
1/91 2/103 3/114 4/122 5/145 6/178 7/221 8/227 (8 wkts, 50 overs)	227

V. C. Drakes and C. E. Dagnall did not bat.

Bowling: Thomas 1–0–8–0; Wharf 9–1–31–2; Dale 10–2–53–0; Croft 10–0–53–2; Cosker 10–1–35–1; Newell 10–0–37–3.

Glamorgan

K. Newell c Dagnall b Smith	27
J. P. Maher c Sheikh b Dagnall	18
M. J. Powell b Drakes	3
M. P. Maynard c Powell b Sheikh	34
*A. Dale b Sheikh	18
A. W. Evans lbw b Sheikh	0
†A. D. Shaw b Brown	39
R. D. B. Croft c Brown b Dagnall	0
S. D. Thomas b Brown	22
A. G. Wharf not out	4
D. A. Cosker b Brown	0
B 2, l-b 5	7
1/28 2/41 3/63 4/95 5/95 6/114 7/115 8/163 9/172 (45.5 overs)	172

Bowling: Drakes 8–3–11–1; Dagnall 9–0–58–2; Smith 10–0–33–1; Brown 8.5–0–36–3; Sheikh 10–2–27–3.

Umpires: G. I. Burgess and R. Palmer.

GLOUCESTERSHIRE v WORCESTERSHIRE

At Bristol, May 6. Gloucestershire won by 21 runs. Toss: Gloucestershire.

Gloucestershire's fourth win guaranteed the holders a quarter-final place with one to play. Their innings was built around two contrasting half-centuries. At 141 balls, Barnett's patient 85 lasted more than twice as long as Harvey's explosive 92, his best one-day score. He faced 64 balls, 11 of which flew for four and three for six. Sheriyar, finishing with four for 19 from ten overs, was fortunate in not bowling to Harvey. Weston and Singh, the Worcestershire openers, then established a solid base, reaching 150 after 36 overs, but once the breach was made, the middle order could not keep pace with the spiralling asking-rate. For good measure, Harvey took two for 35.

Gold Award: I. J. Harvey.

Gloucestershire

R. J. Cunliffe c Rhodes b Sheriyar 0
K. J. Barnett c Leatherdale b Sheriyar . . 85
C. G. Taylor c Hick b Rawnsley 23
M. G. N. Windows lbw b Lampitt 0
I. J. Harvey c Rhodes b Leatherdale . . . 92
J. N. Snape c Weston b Sheriyar 31
*M. W. Alleyne c Hick b Sheriyar 7
†R. C. J. Williams run out 5
M. C. J. Ball not out 7
L-b 4, w 5, n-b 4 13

1/0 2/49 3/50 4/176 5/242 6/245 7/255 8/263 (8 wkts, 50 overs) 263

J. M. M. Averis and J. Lewis did not bat.

Bowling: Sheriyar 10–3–19–4; Bichel 10–1–43–0; Lampitt 10–0–70–1; Rawnsley 10–0–65–1; Leatherdale 10–0–62–1.

Worcestershire

W. P. C. Weston c Taylor b Ball 65
A. Singh c Lewis b Averis 83
*G. A. Hick c Snape b Alleyne 19
V. S. Solanki c Taylor b Harvey 25
D. A. Leatherdale run out 22
A. J. Bichel c Taylor b Averis 5
N. R. Boulton not out 6
†S. J. Rhodes c Snape b Harvey 2
S. R. Lampitt not out 0
B 4, l-b 6, w 5 15

1/150 2/168 3/183 4/209 5/225 6/234 7/239 (7 wkts, 50 overs) 242

M. J. Rawnsley and A. Sheriyar did not bat.

Bowling: Lewis 10–1–44–0; Harvey 10–1–35–2; Averis 9–0–49–2; Alleyne 10–0–45–1; Snape 6–0–31–0; Ball 5–0–28–1.

Umpires: N. G. Cowley and K. E. Palmer.

GLAMORGAN v NORTHAMPTONSHIRE

At Cardiff, May 7. Northamptonshire won by eight wickets. Toss: Northamptonshire.

With neither side able to reach the knockout stage, proceedings might have followed a dull course. Northamptonshire ensured otherwise, first reducing Glamorgan to a parlous five for three and then – after Maynard and Dale, who hit an unruffled 98 not out, had breathed life back into the Glamorgan innings – setting a county-record first-wicket stand for the competition. Responding to 237, the Northamptonshire openers put on 158 before Loye fell for 77. Hussey had moved on to 114 from 140 balls when victory came with three overs unused. For the first time since 1986, Glamorgan had lost all their preliminary games.

Gold Award: M. E. K. Hussey.

Glamorgan

K. Newell c Penberthy b Blain	0	†A. D. Shaw run out	20
J. P. Maher c Ripley b Strong	1	R. D. B. Croft not out	28
*S. P. James b Strong	0	B 1, l-b 2, w 6, n-b 8	17
M. P. Maynard lbw b Innes	59		
M. J. Powell c Cook b Penberthy	14	1/3 2/3 3/5 (6 wkts, 50 overs)	237
A. Dale not out	98	4/50 5/131 6/183	

A. G. Wharf, D. A. Cosker and A. P. Davies did not bat.

Bowling: Strong 10–0–47–2; Blain 10–0–41–1; Penberthy 10–0–57–1; Innes 10–0–46–1; Brown 10–0–43–0.

Northamptonshire

M. E. K. Hussey not out	114
M. B. Loye c Dale b Cosker	77
J. W. Cook b Davies	28
R. J. Warren not out	9
L-b 5, w 3, n-b 2	10
1/158 2/204 (2 wkts, 47 overs)	238

A. J. Swann, A. L. Penberthy, K. J. Innes, *†D. Ripley, M. R. Strong, J. A. R. Blain and J. F. Brown did not bat.

Bowling: Wharf 8–1–40–0; Davies 8–0–38–1; Dale 8–1–24–0; Croft 9–0–61–0; Cosker 9–2–44–1; Newell 5–1–26–0.

Umpires: M. J. Kitchen and D. R. Shepherd.

SOMERSET v GLOUCESTERSHIRE

At Taunton, May 7. Somerset won by 108 runs. Toss: Somerset.

A crowd of around 5,000 watched Somerset, given another fine start by Trescothick, crush neighbours Gloucestershire. Trescothick's 112, from 99 balls and containing 12 fours and a six, was his third Benson and Hedges hundred in five outings, and took his aggregate for the 2001 competition to 373. With Bowler and Blackwell contributing useful support, Somerset looked set for 300. But the fielding side stuck to their task, and the last five overs produced 17 runs and five wickets. Already assured of a quarter-final place, an under-strength Gloucestershire reached 70 for one in the 14th over, only to lose seven wickets for 40, Trescothick the all-rounder finishing with three. In the end, each side achieved a home tie for the next round.

Gold Award: M. E. Trescothick.

Somerset

M. E. Trescothick b Snape	112	†R. J. Turner not out	6
P. D. Bowler c and b Ball	53	P. S. Jones c Windows b Lewis	3
I. D. Blackwell c Lewis b Snape	35	A. R. Caddick not out	2
*J. Cox b Cawdron	18	B 4, l-b 1, w 4	9
P. C. L. Holloway lbw b Snape	14		
M. Burns c Cunliffe b Snape	9	1/138 2/197 3/215 (9 wkts, 50 overs)	262
K. P. Dutch run out	0	4/234 5/249 6/249	
J. I. D. Kerr run out	1	7/249 8/250 9/255	

Bowling: Averis 7–0–41–0; Lewis 10–2–36–1; Cawdron 9–1–57–1; Ball 10–0–49–1; Barnett 3–0–21–0; Snape 8–0–32–4; Hancock 3–0–21–0.

Gloucestershire

*T. H. C. Hancock run out	30	M. J. Cawdron lbw b Trescothick	0
K. J. Barnett c Trescothick b Jones	19	J. M. M. Averis b Dutch	19
R. J. Cunliffe b Kerr	18	J. Lewis not out	6
M. G. N. Windows lbw b Kerr	0	L-b 6, w 3, n-b 4	13
C. G. Taylor lbw b Dutch	17		
J. N. Snape c Turner b Trescothick	4	1/35 2/70 3/70 (38.2 overs)	154
†R. C. J. Williams c Cox b Kerr	28	4/75 5/90 6/107	
M. C. J. Ball b Trescothick	0	7/108 8/110 9/138	

Bowling: Caddick 7–2–31–0; Jones 7–0–38–1; Kerr 6.2–1–14–3; Trescothick 10–0–30–3; Dutch 8–0–35–2.

Umpires: B. Leadbeater and G. Sharp.

WORCESTERSHIRE v WARWICKSHIRE

At Worcester, May 7. Warwickshire won by one wicket. Toss: Worcestershire.

Losing their ninth wicket at 105, still 33 behind, Warwickshire looked destined for defeat and subsequent elimination. But their inexperienced last pair, Sheikh and Dagnall, played with cool heads to see them through. Dagnall – a colourful character who, as Thelonious Phonq, sang in his brother's soul-funk band, Frisco Crabbe and the Atlantic Frantics – had earlier taken the wickets of Weston and Hick and conceded only 18. Crucially, however, he hit Leatherdale for the boundary that made him Warwickshire's top-scorer and ushered them into the quarter-finals. It was especially hard on Leatherdale, whose fifty had rescued Worcestershire from ten for three. All the seamers had enjoyed conditions that gave the ball the edge throughout.

Gold Award: C. E. Dagnall.

Worcestershire

W. P. C. Weston b Dagnall	4	M. J. Rawnsley b Brown	1
A. Singh b Drakes	1	C. G. Liptrot run out	3
*G. A. Hick b Dagnall	3	A. Sheriyar not out	1
V. S. Solanki c Piper b Sheikh	14	L-b 5, w 7	12
D. A. Leatherdale b Drakes	55		
A. J. Bichel c and b Powell	12	1/1 2/5 3/10 (9 wkts, 50 overs)	138
†S. J. Rhodes lbw b Brown	1	4/34 5/61 6/62	
S. R. Lampitt not out	31	7/120 8/123 9/134	

Bowling: Drakes 10–6–14–2; Dagnall 10–2–18–2; Sheikh 10–1–30–1; Brown 10–2–38–2; Powell 10–0–33–1.

Warwickshire

N. V. Knight c Hick b Bichel	0	M. A. Sheikh not out	19
M. A. Wagh c Solanki b Lampitt	14	V. C. Drakes c Liptrot b Hick	2
D. R. Brown c Bichel b Sheriyar	18	C. E. Dagnall not out	21
D. P. Ostler c Solanki b Lampitt	8	L-b 11, w 7, n-b 4	22
T. L. Penney b Lampitt	7		
*M. J. Powell c Rawnsley b Leatherdale	19	1/1 2/37 3/43 (9 wkts, 45.1 overs)	142
N. M. K. Smith c Hick b Leatherdale	12	4/56 5/62 6/92	
†K. J. Piper b Hick	0	7/97 8/99 9/105	

Bowling: Bichel 10–4–32–1; Sheriyar 6–0–24–1; Lampitt 10–2–25–3; Liptrot 4–1–11–0; Hick 8–1–13–2; Leatherdale 7.1–2–26–2.

Umpires: N. G. Cowley and P. Willey.

NORTH GROUP

NOTTINGHAMSHIRE v LEICESTERSHIRE

At Nottingham, April 30. Nottinghamshire won by eight wickets. Toss: Nottinghamshire.

Nottinghamshire, without a group win in 2000, sparkled in spring sunshine while cantering home with almost 20 overs to spare. Their seam bowlers had put sufficient pressure on the Leicestershire batsmen to encourage unnecessary errors. Ben Smith, around whom the middle order might have built a challenging total, was run out by bowler Logan when Maddy called for a quick single; Habib and Burns faced three balls between them. Bicknell, hitting three fours in one Malcolm over, and Welton, dropped at second slip when six, then asked questions of Leicestershire's bowlers. Welton's bravura 71 featured a six and eight fours, while Blewett provided composure and elegance with 59 in 52 balls.

Gold Award: G. E. Welton.

Leicestershire

*V. J. Wells b Clough	22
T. R. Ward c Blewett b Logan	0
B. F. Smith run out	51
D. J. Marsh c Bicknell b Smith	28
D. L. Maddy c Blewett b Smith	30
A. Habib b Logan	0
†N. D. Burns st Read b Pietersen	0
J. M. Dakin not out	11
W. F. Stelling c Welton b Clough	2
J. Ormond b Smith	5
D. E. Malcolm b Smith	0
L-b 11, w 8, n-b 2	21
1/2 2/44 3/95 4/117 5/118 6/119 7/158 8/161 9/170 (48.5 overs)	170

Bowling: Smith 9.5–0–34–4; Logan 10–0–19–2; Franks 9–1–39–0; Clough 10–1–36–2; Pietersen 10–0–31–1.

Nottinghamshire

*D. J. Bicknell b Ormond	27
G. E. Welton c Ormond b Malcolm	71
G. S. Blewett not out	59
U. Afzaal not out	13
W 4	4
1/57 2/135 (2 wkts, 30.3 overs)	174

P. Johnson, K. P. Pietersen, †C. M. W. Read, P. J. Franks, G. D. Clough, R. J. Logan and G. J. Smith did not bat.

Bowling: Ormond 8–0–39–1; Malcolm 6.3–0–41–1; Dakin 7–0–38–0; Stelling 5–0–30–0; Marsh 4–0–26–0.

Umpires: N. A. Mallender and R. A. White.

YORKSHIRE v DERBYSHIRE

At Leeds, April 30. Yorkshire won by five wickets. Toss: Yorkshire. First-team debut: T. M. Baker.

Lehmann's beautifully crafted 103 from 114 balls was too much for a tidy Derbyshire attack which, when Yorkshire were 36 for three in the 12th over, looked as if it might defend 200. Lehmann and Fellows added 118 in 25 overs, however, with the Australian left-hander hitting 13 fours – three in succession off Illingworth – and the six off Aldred that took him to 99. Derbyshire's batsmen had never mastered the slow pitch after being put in and were grateful for the 25 that Yorkshire's bowlers gifted in wides and no-balls. With injuries and England contracts depleting their bowling resources, Yorkshire gave a debut to 19-year-old Tom Baker, who had Stubbings lbw with his first legitimate delivery, having begun with a wide.

Gold Award: D. S. Lehmann.

Derbyshire

S. D. Stubbings lbw b Baker	12
R. J. Bailey c McGrath b Silverwood	28
M. P. Dowman c Blakey b Vaughan	40
M. J. Di Venuto c Lumb b Sidebottom	36
*D. G. Cork c Byas b Hamilton	21
L. D. Sutton c Vaughan b Hamilton	1
†K. M. Krikken c McGrath b Baker	0
R. K. Illingworth not out	10
P. Aldred b Hamilton	0
T. M. Smith not out	19
B 1, l-b 7, w 17, n-b 8	33
1/28 2/92 3/114 4/158 5/163 6/165 7/175 8/175 (8 wkts, 50 overs)	200

T. A. Munton did not bat.

Bowling: Silverwood 10–0–52–1; Sidebottom 10–1–30–1; Hamilton 10–2–56–3; Baker 5–1–13–2; Fellows 5–0–17–0; Vaughan 10–0–24–1.

Yorkshire

M. P. Vaughan b Cork	2
G. M. Hamilton c Di Venuto b Cork	14
A. McGrath c Sutton b Aldred	12
D. S. Lehmann c Sutton b Aldred	103
G. M. Fellows c Di Venuto b Smith	38
†R. J. Blakey not out	12
*D. Byas not out	0
B 1, l-b 8, w 11, n-b 2	22
1/2 2/25 3/36 4/154 5/199 (5 wkts, 44.2 overs)	203

M. J. Lumb, C. E. W. Silverwood, T. M. Baker and R. J. Sidebottom did not bat.

Bowling: Cork 10–2–23–2; Munton 10–1–34–0; Aldred 9–0–55–2; Smith 7.2–0–35–1; Illingworth 8–0–47–0.

Umpires: V. A. Holder and R. Palmer.

LANCASHIRE v DURHAM

At Liverpool, May 1. Durham won by 54 runs. Toss: Lancashire. County debut: J. Wood.

Competition-best performances by Daley and Killeen helped Durham record their first one-day victory over Lancashire since winning their opening exchange of the 1992 Sunday League. Muralitharan was magical, allowing just 11 runs from nine overs after his first cost eight, and normally an asking-rate of four an over should not have taxed Lancashire unduly. However, the warm, sunny conditions had extracted moisture from the slowish pitch and Killeen moved the ball off the seam to devastating effect. Love held three catches at slip, including a deflection by wicket-keeper Pratt, who took excellent catches of his own. Former Durham seamer Wood made his Lancashire debut after Martin dislocated a finger during fielding practice.

Gold Award: N. Killeen.

Durham

J. A. Daley lbw b Scuderi	70
M. A. Gough c Haynes b Wood	19
M. L. Love c Haynes b Muralitharan	16
P. D. Collingwood b Wood	6
*J. J. B. Lewis c Muralitharan b Scuderi	21
N. J. Speak c Crawley b Chapple	25
D. R. Law c Lloyd b Chapple	16
†A. Pratt not out	8
B 1, l-b 6, w 5	12
1/55 2/94 3/103 4/129 5/157 6/174 7/193 (7 wkts, 50 overs)	193

N. C. Phillips, N. Killeen and J. E. Brinkley did not bat.

Bowling: Chapple 10–1–38–2; Austin 10–1–45–0; Wood 10–1–39–2; Scuderi 10–0–45–2; Muralitharan 10–2–19–1.

Lancashire

M. A. Atherton c Love b Killeen	7	I. D. Austin c Killeen b Collingwood	14
*J. P. Crawley c Love b Killeen	4	J. Wood not out	15
J. C. Scuderi c Love b Killeen	11	M. Muralitharan c Killeen b Brinkley	0
A. Flintoff c Pratt b Killeen	8	B 1, l-b 4, w 9, n-b 2	16
N. H. Fairbrother c Pratt b Law	22		
G. D. Lloyd c Lewis b Law	13	1/12 2/13 3/24 (40.4 overs)	139
†J. J. Haynes st Pratt b Gough	29	4/39 5/58 6/77	
G. Chapple run out	0	7/86 8/122 9/138	

Bowling: Killeen 8–0–18–4; Brinkley 7.4–1–25–1; Collingwood 9–2–35–1; Law 7–2–22–2; Phillips 7–0–24–0; Gough 2–0–10–1.

Umpires: R. Palmer and D. R. Shepherd.

DERBYSHIRE v DURHAM

At Derby, May 2. Durham won by 29 runs. Toss: Durham.

Collingwood, in partnerships of 80 with Lewis and 70 with Speak, reversed the advantage Derbyshire derived from Munton's three for 18 in his first eight overs. He was dropped at 37 and 71 but, on an excruciatingly cold – and at times rainy – day, fielders were entitled to sympathy rather than censure. These were not conditions for cricket, and a very slow pitch made batting a grafter's game. Collingwood hit only four boundaries – no one else managed more than one for Durham – as did Bailey in reply. Bailey's 50 from 109 balls provided a solid foundation but Derbyshire could not build on it.

Gold Award: P. D. Collingwood.

Durham

J. A. Daley lbw b Munton	9	†A. Pratt not out	8
M. A. Gough c Illingworth b Munton	12	I. D. Hunter not out	1
M. L. Love b Munton	11	L-b 5, w 4	9
P. D. Collingwood c Pierson b Cork	89		
*J. J. B. Lewis c Aldred b Illingworth	30	1/19 2/26 3/36 (6 wkts, 50 overs)	204
N. J. Speak c Pierson b Cork	35	4/116 5/186 6/199	

N. C. Phillips, N. Killeen and J. E. Brinkley did not bat.

Bowling: Cork 10–1–58–2; Munton 10–2–28–3; Aldred 10–0–45–0; Pierson 10–0–37–0; Illingworth 10–0–31–1.

Derbyshire

S. D. Stubbings lbw b Collingwood	16	P. Aldred c and b Gough	7
R. J. Bailey st Pratt b Phillips	50	A. R. K. Pierson b Gough	7
M. P. Dowman st Pratt b Brinkley	15	T. A. Munton not out	2
M. J. Di Venuto b Brinkley	5	B 1, l-b 14, w 8	23
*D. G. Cork c Pratt b Hunter	20		
L. D. Sutton b Killeen	26	1/40 2/57 3/75 (47.2 overs)	175
†K. M. Krikken c and b Phillips	3	4/119 5/134 6/144	
R. K. Illingworth run out	1	7/147 8/157 9/171	

Bowling: Killeen 9–0–32–1; Hunter 9–1–41–1; Collingwood 6–0–23–1; Brinkley 8–1–17–2; Phillips 10–0–35–2; Gough 5.2–0–12–2.

Umpires: D. J. Constant and M. J. Kitchen.

LEICESTERSHIRE v LANCASHIRE

At Leicester, May 2. Leicestershire won by 27 runs (D/L method). Toss: Leicestershire.

Three hours of rain between innings turned this match on its head. Given a revised target of 118 in 21 overs, after their bowlers had contained Leicestershire most competently, Lancashire found themselves having to chase on a pitch that had picked up pace while under the covers. Malcolm had Crawley and Scuderi edging catches off successive balls in his opening over, and bowled Atherton in his third. When Ormond bowled Lloyd, having already undone Flintoff's ambitions, Lancashire were 25 for five. Fairbrother, batting with a runner, kept them in the game; when he and Chapple went in the 20th over, Lancashire faced their second defeat in two days.

Gold Award: D. E. Malcolm.

Leicestershire

*V. J. Wells c Scuderi b Austin	35
D. L. Maddy lbw b Flintoff	15
B. F. Smith b Muralitharan	24
D. J. Marsh b Austin	42
A. Habib b Chapple	10
D. I. Stevens b Martin	9
J. M. Dakin not out	31
†N. D. Burns c Hegg b Muralitharan	7
J. Ormond not out	7
L-b 9, n-b 4	13
1/47 2/61 3/94 4/121 5/140 6/150 7/175 (7 wkts, 50 overs)	193

D. E. Malcolm and S. A. J. Boswell did not bat.

Bowling: Martin 10–0–35–1; Chapple 10–0–45–1; Austin 10–2–34–2; Flintoff 10–0–30–1; Muralitharan 10–1–40–2.

Lancashire

M. A. Atherton b Malcolm	1
*J. P. Crawley c Burns b Malcolm	7
J. C. Scuderi c Marsh b Malcolm	0
A. Flintoff b Ormond	1
N. H. Fairbrother c Ormond b Wells	32
G. D. Lloyd b Ormond	2
†W. K. Hegg c Habib b Dakin	26
G. Chapple b Wells	8
I. D. Austin c Dakin b Maddy	2
M. Muralitharan c Malcolm b Maddy	0
P. J. Martin not out	0
B 1, l-b 6, w 4	11
1/8 2/8 3/11 4/17 5/25 6/71 7/88 8/89 9/90 (20.2 overs)	90

Bowling: Ormond 5–1–7–2; Malcolm 4–0–13–3; Wells 4–0–17–2; Dakin 4–0–19–1; Boswell 2–0–14–0; Maddy 1.2–0–13–2.

Umpires: J. H. Evans and A. G. T. Whitehead.

YORKSHIRE v NOTTINGHAMSHIRE

At Leeds, May 2. Nottinghamshire won by six wickets. Toss: Nottinghamshire.

This was another command performance by Nottinghamshire, and by the Australian Blewett in particular. Their bowlers skilfully exploited the bounce in a pitch being used for the second time in three days, and Read's leg-side stumping of McGrath and high leg-side catch to dismiss Lehmann characterised the new-look Nottinghamshire. The loss of three early wickets – Fellows's direct hit from cover ran out Welton – warned that victory would not be plain sailing. But Blewett, who spent a disastrous summer with Yorkshire in 1999, had a point to prove. He and Johnson added 150 in 24 overs and there was nothing Yorkshire's second-string attack could do about it.

Gold Award: G. S. Blewett.

Yorkshire

G. M. Hamilton c Read b Franks	27
M. P. Vaughan c Smith b Franks	19
A. McGrath st Read b Pietersen	14
D. S. Lehmann c Read b Logan	41
G. M. Fellows c Smith b Clough	6
†R. J. Blakey not out	32
*D. Byas c Pietersen b Logan	0
M. J. Lumb run out	8
C. E. W. Silverwood not out	13
L-b 15, w 17, n-b 2	34
1/38 2/61 3/95 4/112 5/143 6/145 7/158 (7 wkts, 50 overs)	194

T. M. Baker and R. J. Sidebottom did not bat.

Bowling: Smith 9–2–32–0; Logan 9–0–40–2; Franks 10–2–39–2; Clough 10–0–32–1; Pietersen 10–0–28–1; Afzaal 2–0–8–0.

Nottinghamshire

*D. J. Bicknell b Sidebottom	10
G. E. Welton run out	6
G. S. Blewett c Baker b Silverwood	84
U. Afzaal c Blakey b Hamilton	10
P. Johnson not out	71
K. P. Pietersen not out	8
B 1, l-b 6, w 2	9
1/16 2/19 3/39 4/189 (4 wkts, 39.4 overs)	198

†C. M. W. Read, P. J. Franks, R. J. Logan, G. D. Clough and G. J. Smith did not bat.

Bowling: Silverwood 10–1–51–1; Sidebottom 10–1–36–1; Hamilton 6.4–1–32–1; Baker 4–0–22–0; Vaughan 4–0–22–0; Lehmann 3–0–13–0; Fellows 2–0–15–0.

Umpires: N. A. Mallender and D. R. Shepherd.

LEICESTERSHIRE v YORKSHIRE

At Leicester, May 3. Leicestershire won by 14 runs. Toss: Yorkshire.

Yorkshire looked to be cruising to victory at 163 for two, with Vaughan 92 from 88 balls (15 fours) and Ormond out of the Leicestershire attack with a dodgy hamstring. Then Marsh, at backward point, spectacularly hung on to a square cut to end Vaughan's accomplished competition-best, and Ormond, his left thigh strapped, returned to take four for 19 in 38 balls. Wells chipped in with two wickets in quick succession, having earlier underscored Leicestershire's 224 with a chancy 76. He and Smith added 119 before Vaughan and Lehmann checked Leicestershire with accurate slow bowling.

Gold Award: J. Ormond.

Leicestershire

*V. J. Wells c McGrath b Silverwood	76
D. L. Maddy c Blakey b Baker	7
B. F. Smith c Blakey b Vaughan	50
D. J. Marsh lbw b Vaughan	17
J. M. Dakin c Lumb b Lehmann	2
D. I. Stevens c Baker b Vaughan	34
A. Habib c and b Lehmann	0
†N. D. Burns not out	23
J. Ormond c Sidebottom b Vaughan	0
S. A. J. Boswell not out	0
L-b 4, w 11	15
1/18 2/137 3/156 4/161 5/172 6/175 7/217 8/218 (8 wkts, 50 overs)	224

D. E. Malcolm did not bat.

Bowling: Silverwood 8–2–18–1; Baker 7–0–32–1; Sidebottom 8–0–40–0; Fellows 5–0–22–0; Middlebrook 4–0–22–0; Lehmann 9–0–40–2; Vaughan 9–0–46–4.

Yorkshire

*D. Byas c Burns b Dakin	7
M. P. Vaughan c Marsh b Malcolm	92
A. McGrath c Stevens b Ormond	46
D. S. Lehmann c Burns b Ormond	8
M. J. Lumb c Burns b Ormond	3
G. M. Fellows b Ormond	14
†R. J. Blakey run out	5
J. D. Middlebrook lbw b Wells	3
C. E. W. Silverwood c Maddy b Wells	4
T. M. Baker run out	3
R. J. Sidebottom not out	2
L-b 11, w 6, n-b 6	23
1/47 2/137 3/163 4/167 5/186 6/192 7/198 8/202 9/206 (48.3 overs)	210

Bowling: Ormond 9.4–1–25–4; Malcolm 9–0–55–1; Boswell 3.2–0–19–0; Dakin 7–1–24–1; Wells 4.3–0–19–2; Marsh 5–1–25–0; Maddy 10–0–32–0.

Umpires: M. R. Benson and M. J. Harris.

DURHAM v NOTTINGHAMSHIRE

At Chester-le-Street, May 4. Nottinghamshire won by five wickets. Toss: Durham. First-team debut: M. N. Malik.

Batsmen rather than bowlers appreciated the first-class conditions when the group's unbeaten teams met at Riverside. Both opening pairs provided century starts, with Bicknell and Welton getting Nottinghamshire off at a quicker rate. Only Blewett's mid-innings aberrations, running out Welton and then hitting a catch to mid-on, disturbed the inevitability of a Nottinghamshire victory. Daley had anchored Durham's innings by staying until the penultimate over.

Gold Award: G. E. Welton.

Durham

J. A. Daley b Smith	92
M. A. Gough c Clough b Afzaal	45
M. L. Love lbw b Clough	59
P. D. Collingwood not out	28
D. R. Law not out	7
L-b 6, w 11, n-b 4	21
1/116 2/194 3/241 (3 wkts, 50 overs)	252

*J. J. B. Lewis, N. J. Speak, †A. Pratt, N. Killeen, J. E. Brinkley and N. C. Phillips did not bat.

Bowling: Smith 10–1–38–1; Malik 3–0–20–0; Clough 10–1–53–1; Franks 10–0–55–0; Pietersen 10–0–50–0; Afzaal 7–0–30–1.

Nottinghamshire

*D. J. Bicknell b Phillips	62
G. E. Welton run out	75
G. S. Blewett c Law b Brinkley	21
U. Afzaal run out	5
P. Johnson c Killeen b Brinkley	24
K. P. Pietersen not out	35
†C. M. W. Read not out	14
L-b 9, w 8	17
1/131 2/156 3/173 4/175 5/229 (5 wkts, 49.1 overs)	253

P. J. Franks, M. N. Malik, G. D. Clough and G. J. Smith did not bat.

Bowling: Killeen 10–0–49–0; Brinkley 10–1–50–2; Collingwood 5.1–0–31–0; Law 4–0–24–0; Phillips 10–0–47–1; Gough 10–0–43–0.

Umpires: J. H. Hampshire and A. G. T. Whitehead.

LANCASHIRE v DERBYSHIRE

At Liverpool, May 4. Lancashire won by ten wickets. Toss: Derbyshire.

Derbyshire, managing just three scoring shots off Muralitharan, were comprehensively clobbered on a slow pitch more suited to seam bowling. The Sri Lankan spinner's return of 10–7–4–1 was one of the most economical in the competition, comparing with Chris Old's 11–9–3–1 for Yorkshire against Middlesex on a difficult pitch at Lord's in 1979, or John Childs's 11–9–4–1 for Gloucestershire against Nottinghamshire at Gloucester two years later. Dowman held out for 84 balls before becoming the first of Flintoff's three cheap wickets, but in general Derbyshire put on a poor display. Atherton, hitting 11 fours, and Chilton reinforced this impression by remaining unbeaten and winning the game with 16 overs in hand.

Gold Award: M. Muralitharan.

Derbyshire

R. J. Bailey c Hegg b Wood	8
M. J. Di Venuto b Martin	16
M. P. Dowman c Atherton b Flintoff	36
L. D. Sutton c Flintoff b Martin	0
W. G. Khan lbw b Austin	8
*D. G. Cork b Austin	4
†K. M. Krikken not out	23
R. K. Illingworth c Hegg b Flintoff	2
T. M. Smith c Flintoff b Muralitharan	3
A. R. K. Pierson run out	2
T. A. Munton lbw b Flintoff	4
L-b 7, w 4	11
1/14 2/27 3/30 4/61 5/65 6/81 7/85 8/98 9/111 (47.1 overs)	117

Bowling: Martin 10–1–30–2; Wood 9–1–38–1; Austin 10–4–18–2; Muralitharan 10–7–4–1; Scuderi 3–0–8–0; Flintoff 5.1–1–12–3.

Lancashire

M. A. Atherton not out	77
M. J. Chilton not out	42
W 2	2
(no wkt, 33.3 overs)	121

*J. P. Crawley, J. C. Scuderi, A. Flintoff, G. D. Lloyd, †W. K. Hegg, J. Wood, I. D. Austin, P. J. Martin and M. Muralitharan did not bat.

Bowling: Cork 5–2–12–0; Munton 9–0–20–0; Smith 6–0–42–0; Pierson 5.3–0–15–0; Illingworth 5–1–21–0; Khan 3–0–11–0.

Umpires: B. Dudleston and N. A. Mallender.

DURHAM v LEICESTERSHIRE

At Chester-le-Street, May 5. Durham won by seven wickets. Toss: Leicestershire.

From his first-ball slip catch that accounted for Leicestershire captain Wells until finishing the match unbeaten with 95 – having added 140 in 25 overs with his own captain, Lewis – Collingwood was rarely out of the action. Another slip catch and some tidy bowling, with the important wicket of Habib, also contributed to his second match award of the week. Leicestershire lost Stelling to a back injury after only two deliveries – Collingwood hit both for four. Earlier in the day, Durham's Killeen had damaged an ankle and Speak pulled a hamstring while fielding. They were also without Love, who cracked a finger when fielding the previous day.

Gold Award: P. D. Collingwood.

Leicestershire

*V. J. Wells c Collingwood b Killeen	0	†N. D. Burns not out	20
D. L. Maddy lbw b Brinkley	25	W. F. Stelling not out	12
B. F. Smith c Collingwood b Brinkley	22	L-b 9, w 7, n-b 2	18
D. J. Marsh b Phillips	38		—
A. Habib b Collingwood	6	1/0 2/51 3/59 (7 wkts, 50 overs)	200
D. I. Stevens c Pratt b Killeen	54	4/78 5/134	
J. M. Dakin c Hunter b Phillips	5	6/153 7/174	

S. A. J. Boswell and D. E. Malcolm did not bat.

Bowling: Killeen 8.3–3–13–2; Hunter 10–2–38–0; Brinkley 8–0–38–2; Collingwood 8.3–0–34–1; Phillips 10–1–41–2; Gough 5–0–27–0.

Durham

J. A. Daley c Burns b Boswell	7	*J. J. B. Lewis not out	59
M. A. Gough lbw b Malcolm	0	B 2, l-b 9, w 9, n-b 4	24
M. P. Speight b Wells	17		—
P. D. Collingwood not out	95	1/2 2/11 3/62 (3 wkts, 42.4 overs)	202

N. J. Speak, †A. Pratt, I. D. Hunter, J. E. Brinkley, N. Killeen and N. C. Phillips did not bat.

Bowling: Malcolm 9–1–39–1; Boswell 8–1–22–1; Stelling 0.2–0–8–0; Stevens 0.4–0–2–0; Maddy 7.4–0–48–0; Wells 6–0–27–1; Dakin 7–0–25–0; Marsh 4–0–20–0.

Umpires: J. H. Hampshire and J. W. Holder.

DERBYSHIRE v NOTTINGHAMSHIRE

At Derby, May 6. Derbyshire won by six wickets. Toss: Derbyshire.

Dowman, given his papers by Nottinghamshire in 1999, hit a six and four off the first balls of the last over to complete the surprise defeat of the group leaders. As Clive Rice, the Trent Bridge director of cricket, conceded afterwards, Nottinghamshire's total was "about 15 runs short of par" on a good batting pitch. Several players lost their wickets when apparently well set. None of which detracts from Derbyshire's determined reply, given a stylish start by Di Venuto, anchored by Bailey's 62, and seen to conclusion by Dowman's unbeaten 76.

Gold Award: M. P. Dowman.

Nottinghamshire

*D. J. Bicknell run out	41	†C. M. W. Read not out	8
G. E. Welton c Illingworth b Cork	17		
G. S. Blewett st Krikken b Illingworth	35	L-b 2, w 6	8
U. Afzaal c Sutton b Cork	50		—
P. Johnson st Krikken b Pierson	38	1/24 2/88 3/102 (5 wkts, 50 overs)	231
K. P. Pietersen not out	34	4/172 5/208	

P. J. Franks, G. D. Clough, G. J. Smith and R. D. Stemp did not bat.

Bowling: Cork 10–1–48–2; Munton 10–2–34–0; Illingworth 10–0–35–1; Smith 8–1–42–0; Pierson 10–0–58–1; Khan 2–0–12–0.

Derbyshire

R. J. Bailey c Welton b Afzaal	62	W. G. Khan not out	12
M. J. Di Venuto run out	44	B 2, l-b 7, w 9, n-b 8	26
M. P. Dowman not out	76		—
L. D. Sutton c Read b Franks	13	1/88 2/162 (4 wkts, 49.2 overs)	233
*D. G. Cork b Smith	0	3/193 4/194	

†K. M. Krikken, R. K. Illingworth, T. M. Smith, A. R. K. Pierson and T. A. Munton did not bat.

Bowling: Smith 10–1–43–1; Franks 10–0–49–1; Clough 7.2–0–45–0; Stemp 10–0–41–0; Pietersen 6–0–25–0; Afzaal 6–0–21–1.

Umpires: A. A. Jones and P. Willey.

LANCASHIRE v YORKSHIRE

At Liverpool, May 6. Yorkshire won by five wickets. Toss: Lancashire.

Lancashire didn't need names and numbers on their backs to identify the culprits. The Aigburth scoreboard told the sorry story of wasted opportunities: Atherton and Crawley had added 110 in 30 overs before Atherton mishit a full toss to long leg. Lehmann accepted the catch, and bowled Crawley next over. Byas and Vaughan began Yorkshire's reply with 40 in nine overs, and Byas and Lehmann, both left-handers, saw off the threat of Muralitharan. As if being denied a quarter-final place by their old enemy wasn't penance enough, Lancashire also lost Flintoff to a torn side muscle immediately after he dismissed Lehmann.

Gold Award: D. S. Lehmann.

Lancashire

M. A. Atherton c Lehmann b Fellows	60	J. Wood c and b Silverwood	2
M. J. Chilton c Blakey b Silverwood	2	P. J. Martin not out	3
*J. P. Crawley b Lehmann	52	M. Muralitharan not out	1
A. Flintoff c Silverwood b Sidebottom	15	B 1, l-b 5, w 3	9
J. C. Scuderi c Blakey b Fellows	6		—
G. D. Lloyd run out	17	1/8 2/118 3/121 (9 wkts, 50 overs)	170
†W. K. Hegg c Vaughan b Gough	3	4/136 5/147 6/157	
I. D. Austin c Byas b Silverwood	0	7/161 8/163 9/169	

Bowling: Gough 9–0–33–1; Silverwood 8–1–30–3; White 10–0–32–0; Sidebottom 9–1–23–1; Vaughan 3–0–18–0; Fellows 5–0–15–2; Lehmann 6–1–13–1.

Yorkshire

*D. Byas b Scuderi	55	G. M. Fellows not out	3
M. P. Vaughan b Martin	24		
A. McGrath c Muralitharan b Scuderi	13	B 2, l-b 5, w 8, n-b 2	17
D. S. Lehmann c Chilton b Flintoff	35		—
C. White b Wood	4	1/40 2/84 3/135 (5 wkts, 46.4 overs)	171
M. J. Lumb not out	20	4/137 5/157	

†R. J. Blakey, D. Gough, R. J. Sidebottom and C. E. W. Silverwood did not bat.

Bowling: Martin 10–0–45–1; Wood 8.4–1–32–1; Muralitharan 10–3–33–0; Austin 10–1–25–0; Flintoff 2.5–0–10–1; Scuderi 5–1–17–2; Chilton 0.1–0–2–0.

Umpires: T. E. Jesty and A. G. T. Whitehead.

LEICESTERSHIRE v DERBYSHIRE

At Leicester, May 7. Leicestershire won by 21 runs. Toss: Derbyshire. First-team debuts: C. W. G. Bassano, N. R. C. Dumelow.

As run-rate was going to determine who reached the quarter-finals, the last thing Leicestershire needed was Derbyshire's Di Venuto batting through the innings and delaying their victory until the 49th over. On a slow pitch, the strokeplay in the Australian left-hander's century set him in a class apart, while his eighth-wicket stand of 62 with Trevor Smith virtually shut the door on Leicestershire qualifying. The recurrence of Ormond's hamstring problem proved a severe blow to the home side after their batsmen had earlier displayed a lively appreciation of the situation. Wells and Dakin began with 84 in 11 overs, the exuberant Wells striking eight fours and two sixes in his 42-ball fifty. Maddy, in contrast, managed only two fours in his, though he kept the score moving, and a rapid 46 from Burns, batting with a runner, lifted Leicestershire to 267.

Gold Award: M. J. Di Venuto.

Leicestershire

*V. J. Wells c sub b Lungley	57
J. M. Dakin st Krikken b Lungley	39
D. I. Stevens c sub b Munton	2
D. L. Maddy c Krikken b Illingworth	56
B. F. Smith c Di Venuto b Dumelow	23
D. J. Marsh c Krikken b Smith	15
T. R. Ward st Krikken b Illingworth	9
†N. D. Burns c Bassano b Lungley	46
J. Ormond not out	13
D. E. Malcolm b Smith	4
S. A. J. Boswell b Smith	0
L-b 1, w 2	3
1/84 2/87 3/103 4/150 5/171 6/192 7/215 8/262 9/267 (49.5 overs)	267

Bowling: Smith 7.5–0–43–3; Munton 10–0–59–1; Khan 2–0–23–0; Lungley 10–0–55–3; Illingworth 10–1–40–2; Dumelow 10–0–46–1.

Derbyshire

L. D. Sutton b Malcolm	2
M. J. Di Venuto run out	108
M. P. Dowman c sub b Boswell	26
C. W. G. Bassano c Maddy b Dakin	9
W. G. Khan c Ward b Wells	18
†K. M. Krikken run out	0
N. R. C. Dumelow b Maddy	18
R. K. Illingworth lbw b Marsh	2
T. M. Smith c Smith b Wells	27
T. Lungley st Burns b Maddy	0
*T. A. Munton not out	17
B 1, l-b 6, w 12	19
1/16 2/62 3/81 4/117 5/117 6/150 7/153 8/215 9/225 (48.1 overs)	246

Bowling: Ormond 4–0–25–0; Malcolm 4–0–20–1; Boswell 6–2–17–1; Dakin 7.1–0–39–1; Marsh 10–0–44–1; Wells 7–0–51–2; Maddy 10–0–43–2.

Umpires: J. H. Evans and R. Palmer.

NOTTINGHAMSHIRE v LANCASHIRE

At Nottingham, May 7. Nottinghamshire won by seven wickets. Toss: Nottinghamshire.

Nottinghamshire's fourth win in five games left Lancashire contemplating their fourth defeat in five. They had both Lancashire openers back in the pavilion at 17, Crawley and Lloyd were never given a chance to create any momentum, and Scuderi's one-day best unbeaten 73 from 96 balls rarely threatened to break the bowlers' stranglehold. Nottinghamshire's batsmen suffered no such inhibitions. Acting-captain Bicknell and Blewett put on 85 in 18 overs, whereupon Afzaal's 56 not out in 63 balls gave further evidence of his early-season form and walked Nottinghamshire home with six overs to spare.

Gold Award: D. J. Bicknell.

Lancashire

M. A. Atherton b Franks	2	†W. K. Hegg b Smith	31
M. J. Chilton c Pietersen b Smith	10	G. Chapple not out	6
*J. P. Crawley b Clough	37	L-b 2, w 4, n-b 6	12
G. D. Lloyd b Pietersen	27		—
J. C. Scuderi not out	73	1/17 2/17 3/78 (6 wkts, 50 overs)	203
C. P. Schofield c Read b Malik	5	4/97 5/108 6/178	

I. D. Austin, M. Muralitharan and P. J. Martin did not bat.

Bowling: Smith 10–3–34–2; Franks 10–2–45–1; Malik 10–0–42–1; Clough 9–0–43–1; Pietersen 10–1–33–1; Blewett 1–0–4–0.

Nottinghamshire

*D. J. Bicknell b Scuderi	89	P. Johnson not out	10
G. E. Welton c Atherton b Martin	4	L-b 4, w 3, n-b 6	13
G. S. Blewett lbw b Schofield	35		—
U. Afzaal not out	56	1/13 2/98 3/179 (3 wkts, 43.4 overs)	207

K. P. Pietersen, †C. M. W. Read, P. J. Franks, G. D. Clough, G. J. Smith and M. N. Malik did not bat.

Bowling: Martin 8–1–25–1; Chapple 9–1–41–0; Austin 6–0–36–0; Muralitharan 8–0–33–0; Schofield 7–0–29–1; Scuderi 5.4–0–39–1.

Umpires: M. R. Benson and G. I. Burgess.

YORKSHIRE v DURHAM

At Leeds, May 7. Yorkshire won by 30 runs. Toss: Durham.

Durham's target to secure second place on run-rate was 193, and when Michael Gough and Collingwood went in quick succession, soon followed by Peng, they adjusted their sights to this rather than victory. Law, profiting from a near miss at deep mid-wicket when six, picked it off with a rumbustious 57 not out that contained eight fours and two sixes. Lehmann's 88 in 76 balls for Yorkshire, with 11 fours and two sixes, had set pulses racing earlier as he and McGrath added 114 in 19 overs. It proved the basis for Yorkshire's eventual victory, though they could not be sure of qualifying for the quarter-finals – as one of the two better-placed thirds – until Leicestershire's fate was decided on run-rate 100 miles down the M1.

Gold Award: D. S. Lehmann.

Yorkshire

*D. Byas b Hunter	39	†R. J. Blakey not out	1
M. P. Vaughan c Gough b Hunter	26	C. E. W. Silverwood not out	2
A. McGrath c Hunter b Harmison	43	B 1, l-b 4, w 5, n-b 6	16
D. S. Lehmann c Collingwood b Law	88		—
C. White c Pratt b Brinkley	14	1/71 2/78 3/192 (7 wkts, 50 overs)	257
M. J. Lumb b Hunter	20	4/217 5/238	
G. M. Fellows b Hunter	8	6/249 7/254	

D. Gough and R. J. Sidebottom did not bat.

Bowling: Harmison 10–1–50–1; Brinkley 10–1–45–1; Hunter 10–0–48–4; Law 10–0–58–1; Collingwood 7–0–27–0; Gough 3–0–24–0.

Durham

J. A. Daley retired hurt	14	D. R. Law not out	57
M. A. Gough c Fellows b Vaughan	58		
M. P. Speight c Blakey b White	7	B 3, l-b 6, w 3, n-b 4	16
P. D. Collingwood c and b Vaughan	27		
*J. J. B. Lewis not out	45	1/63 2/112 (4 wkts, 50 overs)	227
N. Peng st Blakey b Vaughan	3	3/114 4/126	

†A. Pratt, I. D. Hunter, J. E. Brinkley and S. J. Harmison did not bat.

Daley retired hurt at 44.

Bowling: Gough 10–0–51–0; Silverwood 10–1–39–0; Sidebottom 10–2–35–0; White 10–1–42–1; Vaughan 10–0–51–3.

Umpires: V. A. Holder and A. A. Jones.

SOUTH GROUP

KENT v HAMPSHIRE

At Canterbury, May 1. No result. Toss: Kent. First-team debut: A. Khan. County debut: D. J. Cullinan.

Rain prevented more than four overs' play – time enough for 20-year-old Danish international Amjad Khan to bowl his first overs in county cricket.

Hampshire

N. C. Johnson not out	13
*R. A. Smith not out	6
(no wkt, 4 overs)	19

D. A. Kenway, J. S. Laney, W. S. Kendall, J. P. Stephenson, A. D. Mascarenhas, S. D. Udal, A. C. Morris, †A. N. Aymes and A. D. Mullally did not bat.

Bowling: Ealham 2–0–7–0; Khan 2–0–12–0.

Kent

*M. V. Fleming, R. W. T. Key, D. J. Cullinan, M. J. Walker, M. A. Ealham, †P. A. Nixon, J. B. Hockley, M. J. McCague, J. M. Golding, A. Khan and D. D. Masters.

Umpires: J. H. Hampshire and G. Sharp.

SURREY v MIDDLESEX

At The Oval, May 1. No result. Toss: Middlesex. First-team debut: C. B. Keegan.

But for the rain's intervention, Middlesex might have rued giving Surrey, and especially Ward, first use of a good early-season pitch. With Ward untroubled in his progress to 71 not out from 97 balls, the home side were well placed to push on to a commanding total.

Surrey

M. A. Butcher c Nash b Cook	20
I. J. Ward not out	71
M. R. Ramprakash b Weekes	27
G. P. Thorpe not out	23
L-b 1, w 2, n-b 2	5
1/46 2/98 (2 wkts, 35 overs)	146

A. D. Brown, *A. J. Hollioake, B. C. Hollioake, †J. N. Batty, M. P. Bicknell, A. J. Tudor and E. S. H. Giddins did not bat.

Bowling: Fraser 8–1–29–0; Cook 6–0–26–1; Keegan 6–0–36–0; Weekes 7–0–25–1; Tufnell 7–0–24–0; Hutton 1–0–5–0.

Middlesex

A. J. Strauss, M. A. Roseberry, S. P. Fleming, O. A. Shah, P. N. Weekes, B. L. Hutton, †D. C. Nash, C. B. Keegan, S. J. Cook, *A. R. C. Fraser and P. C. R. Tufnell.

Umpires: J. W. Holder and T. E. Jesty.

SUSSEX v ESSEX

At Hove, May 1. No result (abandoned).

HAMPSHIRE v ESSEX

At Southampton, May 2. No result (abandoned).

This was to have been Hampshire's first match at their new Rose Bowl stadium at West End. But the waterlogged ground left umpires John Holder and Trevor Jesty, both former Hampshire players, with no alternative but to call it off an hour and a quarter before the start.

SURREY v SUSSEX

At The Oval, May 2. No result (abandoned).

MIDDLESEX v KENT

At Lord's, May 3. Middlesex won by one run. Toss: Kent.

Golding was run out off the last ball, beaten by Keegan's throw from fine leg as he went for a second run to level the scores and win the game for Kent on the "fewer wickets lost" rule. Excellent work by the groundstaff to dry the outfield had allowed a 31-overs-a-side match to start after lunch. Strauss, dropped by Matthew Fleming when eight, impressed while making 61 in 71 balls, and Shah, albeit on the slow side, showed a recently acquired discipline to accompany his natural talent. Fleming claimed three wickets in four balls late in the innings, as Weekes did for Middlesex just as Walker was threatening to see Kent to victory.

Gold Award: P. N. Weekes.

Middlesex

A. J. Strauss c Ealham b Golding	61
M. A. Roseberry c Walker b Khan	0
S. P. Fleming c Nixon b Masters	0
O. A. Shah c Key b Golding	48
P. N. Weekes c Nixon b Golding	1
B. L. Hutton c Nixon b McCague	4
†D. C. Nash b Fleming	18
C. B. Keegan b Fleming	1
S. J. Cook b Fleming	0
*A. R. C. Fraser not out	1
T. F. Bloomfield not out	0
B 2, l-b 4, w 2, n-b 4	12
1/11 2/21 3/95 4/102 5/109 6/141 7/143 8/143 9/144 (9 wkts, 31 overs)	146

Bowling: Masters 7–1–20–1; Khan 4–0–23–1; McCague 6–0–30–1; Fleming 6–0–25–3; Ealham 3–0–17–0; Golding 5–0–25–3.

Kent

*M. V. Fleming c Strauss b Bloomfield	24	J. M. Golding run out	7
R. W. T. Key c Fleming b Cook	27	A. Khan not out	0
D. J. Cullinan run out	2		
M. J. Walker b Weekes	36	L-b 7, w 7, n-b 2	16
M. A. Ealham st Nash b Weekes	13		—
†P. A. Nixon b Fraser	20	1/29 2/39 3/71 (9 wkts, 31 overs)	145
M. J. McCague c and b Weekes	0	4/102 5/133 6/133	
J. B. Hockley st Nash b Weekes	0	7/134 8/143 9/145	

D. D. Masters did not bat.

Bowling: Fraser 7–2–12–1; Bloomfield 6–0–33–1; Keegan 6–0–32–0; Cook 6–0–27–1; Hutton 2–0–17–0; Weekes 4–0–17–4.

Umpires: B. Leadbeater and K. E. Palmer.

ESSEX v KENT

At Chelmsford, May 4. Kent won by three wickets. Toss: Kent.

When Kent lost their fifth wicket at 102, still needing 154 from 23 overs, Essex were in line for a comfortable win. Walker had other ideas. Going on to 106 not out from 121 balls, yet hitting only six fours, he coaxed match-winning partnerships out of Hockley, McCague and finally Golding, who helped him add an unbroken 78 in ten overs. Before Walker's intervention, Essex had controlled the game. Hussain (118 balls) and Robinson (75 balls) opened with 129 in 30 overs, and it seemed of little consequence when Masters ran out Law at the non-striker's end with a deflection. In the event, it was just the luck Kent needed.

Gold Award: M. J. Walker.

Essex

N. Hussain lbw b Fleming	58	G. R. Napier not out	22
D. D. J. Robinson c and b Ealham	69	A. P. Cowan not out	4
S. G. Law run out	31	L-b 8, w 4	12
*R. C. Irani run out	33		—
S. D. Peters lbw b Golding	16	1/129 2/145 3/187 (6 wkts, 50 overs)	255
A. P. Grayson run out	10	4/217 5/219 6/243	

†B. J. Hyam, A. C. McGarry and R. S. G. Anderson did not bat.

Bowling: Masters 10–0–54–0; Ealham 10–1–28–1; McCague 4–0–25–0; Golding 9–0–54–1; Patel 8–0–45–0; Fleming 9–0–41–1.

Kent

*M. V. Fleming b Cowan	16	M. J. McCague c Anderson b Irani	11
R. W. T. Key lbw b Irani	0	J. M. Golding not out	33
D. J. Cullinan lbw b Irani	20	L-b 11, w 5, n-b 4	20
M. J. Walker not out	106		—
M. A. Ealham c Hussain b McGarry	19	1/5 2/38 3/41 (7 wkts, 49.1 overs)	257
†P. A. Nixon c Hussain b Anderson	5	4/91 5/102	
J. B. Hockley b Grayson	27	6/151 7/179	

D. D. Masters and M. M. Patel did not bat.

Bowling: Irani 10–1–48–3; Cowan 9.1–0–44–1; McGarry 8–0–35–1; Anderson 10–1–63–1; Grayson 10–0–41–1; Napier 2–0–15–0.

Umpires: J. W. Lloyds and J. F. Steele.

HAMPSHIRE v SURREY

At Southampton, May 4. Surrey won by 23 runs. Toss: Hampshire.

However great the desire to christen their new ground with a win, Hampshire were never likely to manage it against a Surrey side better equipped to cope with the slow, holding pitch. Their left-handed openers, Butcher and Ward, used the fielding restrictions profitably, while Brown capitalised on lives at nought and 19 to top-score with 33 from 39 balls. Hampshire lost Johnson in the first over, and later fell prey to the Hollioakes, with Ben making a welcome return after the disappointments of 2000.

Gold Award: B. C. Hollioake.

Surrey

M. A. Butcher lbw b Morris	28	A. J. Tudor run out	26
I. J. Ward c Morris b Johnson	30	M. P. Bicknell c Kendall b Mascarenhas	4
M. R. Ramprakash lbw b Udal	16	E. S. H. Giddins not out	0
G. P. Thorpe st Aymes b Udal	19	B 1, l-b 11, w 7	19
A. D. Brown b Morris	33		—
*A. J. Hollioake c Aymes b Mullally	1	1/55 2/68 3/96 (50 overs)	194
B. C. Hollioake c Aymes b Johnson	15	4/109 5/110 6/132	
†J. N. Batty b Johnson	3	7/141 8/178 9/192	

Bowling: Mascarenhas 10–2–42–1; Morris 10–1–33–2; Mullally 10–1–33–1; Udal 10–0–33–2; Johnson 10–0–41–3.

Hampshire

N. C. Johnson b Bicknell	0	A. C. Morris lbw b A. J. Hollioake	13
*R. A. Smith lbw b Giddins	10	†A. N. Aymes lbw b A. J. Hollioake	17
D. A. Kenway run out	30	A. D. Mullally not out	7
J. S. Laney b B. C. Hollioake	22	L-b 9, w 7, n-b 4	20
W. S. Kendall c B. C. Hollioake b Tudor	20		—
A. D. Mascarenhas lbw b B. C. Hollioake	6	1/1 2/35 3/54 (9 wkts, 50 overs)	171
J. P. Stephenson b B. C. Hollioake	2	4/92 5/102 6/105	
S. D. Udal not out	24	7/106 8/126 9/155	

Bowling: Bicknell 10–1–21–1; Tudor 10–2–28–1; Giddins 10–0–37–1; B. C. Hollioake 10–1–29–3; A. J. Hollioake 10–0–47–2.

Umpires: R. Julian and P. Willey.

SUSSEX v MIDDLESEX

At Hove, May 4. Sussex won by 62 runs. Toss: Middlesex.

Goodwin's 108 from 116 balls set up Sussex for a rare victory over Middlesex in this competition: the last was in 1973. He and the left-handed Yardy, hitting his first fifty for Sussex, added an attractive 104 in 17 overs, and the Middlesex bowlers did well in the closing stages to keep the target under 250. That became irrelevant once Martin-Jenkins and Kirtley rocked the visitors with three early wickets. By the time Fleming was stumped in the 24th over, overbalancing as he stretched forward, the asking-rate had climbed past six. Weekes and Hutton hung around, but a Sussex side brimming with new-season resolve never looked like conceding the initiative and leap-frogged to the top of the group.

Gold Award: M. W. Goodwin.

Sussex

R. R. Montgomerie b Fraser	18	†M. J. Prior c Weekes b Cook	6
M. W. Goodwin c Keegan b Tufnell	108	M. J. G. Davis not out	0
B. Zuiderent c Fleming b Cook	22	L-b 6, w 2, n-b 2	10
M. H. Yardy c Nash b Fraser	59		—
W. J. House lbw b Weekes	8	1/42 2/101 3/205 (7 wkts, 50 overs)	243
R. S. C. Martin-Jenkins c Cook b Fraser	0	4/221 5/225	
U. B. A. Rashid not out	12	6/225 7/242	

M. A. Robinson and *R. J. Kirtley did not bat.

Bowling: Fraser 10–0–30–3; Cook 9–0–63–2; Keegan 10–0–43–0; Tufnell 10–0–47–1; Weekes 10–0–40–1; Hutton 1–0–14–0.

Middlesex

A. J. Strauss lbw b Kirtley	5	S. J. Cook b Kirtley	1
M. A. Roseberry b Martin-Jenkins	0	*A. R. C. Fraser not out	2
S. P. Fleming st Prior b Davis	44		
O. A. Shah c Prior b Martin-Jenkins	2	L-b 7, w 4, n-b 2	13
P. N. Weekes c Goodwin b Kirtley	35		—
B. L. Hutton b Martin-Jenkins	52	1/5 2/7 3/15 (8 wkts, 50 overs)	181
†D. C. Nash b Robinson	27	4/72 5/107 6/170	
C. B. Keegan not out	0	7/177 8/178	

P. C. R. Tufnell did not bat.

Bowling: Martin-Jenkins 10–1–42–3; Kirtley 10–2–29–3; Yardy 2–0–7–0; Robinson 10–0–33–1; Davis 10–0–28–1; Rashid 8–0–35–0.

Umpires: M. J. Kitchen and K. E. Palmer.

SURREY v ESSEX

At The Oval, May 5. Surrey won by six wickets. Toss: Essex.

Essex began propitiously through Hussain and Law, who put on 109 in 24 overs, then handed the advantage to Salisbury and Adam Hollioake, losing five wickets for 55 in little more than 15 overs. Stewart and Ramprakash, disciplined and stylish, emphasised the extent of Essex's wasted opportunity while adding 151 in 35 generally untroubled overs. Mason's subsequent breakthrough was quickly countered by Brown's 19-ball 26 that prevented Ramprakash (116 balls) reaching his century.

Gold Award: M. R. Ramprakash.

Essex

N. Hussain c Stewart b Hollioake	63	†B. J. Hyam c Hollioake b Tudor	7
D. D. J. Robinson run out	0	T. J. Mason not out	0
S. G. Law c Brown b Salisbury	55		
*R. C. Irani run out	21	B 4, l-b 8, w 10, n-b 2	24
S. D. Peters c Brown b Hollioake	9		—
A. P. Grayson b Hollioake	23	1/5 2/114 3/147 (8 wkts, 50 overs)	222
G. R. Napier c Ramprakash b Hollioake	0	4/163 5/166 6/169	
A. P. Cowan not out	20	7/211 8/220	

A. C. McGarry did not bat.

Bowling: Tudor 7–0–34–1; Bicknell 10–2–38–0; Giddins 6–1–26–0; Butcher 7–0–42–0; Salisbury 10–1–34–1; Hollioake 10–0–36–4.

Surrey

I. J. Ward c Hyam b Irani	18	G. P. Butcher not out	1
†A. J. Stewart c Robinson b Mason	59	L-b 1, w 13	14
M. R. Ramprakash not out	97		—
G. P. Thorpe c Peters b Mason	8	1/20 2/171 (4 wkts, 47 overs)	223
A. D. Brown b McGarry	26	3/183 4/217	

*A. J. Hollioake, A. J. Tudor, M. P. Bicknell, E. S. H. Giddins and I. D. K. Salisbury did not bat.

Bowling: Cowan 8–1–46–0; Irani 8–0–31–1; McGarry 7–0–29–1; Napier 4–0–30–0; Grayson 10–2–35–0; Mason 10–0–51–2.

Umpires: M. J. Harris and M. J. Kitchen.

MIDDLESEX v HAMPSHIRE

At Lord's, May 6. Middlesex won by 25 runs. Toss: Middlesex.

Shah announced his presence with a second-ball six over mid-wicket off Morris, went to 99 by hitting the same bowler high into the Grand Stand and, having taken 66 balls to reach his fifty, finished with 118 not out from 109 balls. In all, he hit three sixes and nine fours; he and Weekes added 121 in 26 overs. Hampshire in reply needed a good start. Johnson showed intent but Smith was uncharacteristically slow out of the traps, scoring 11 in 39 balls and allowing the Middlesex seamers, supported by some enthusiastic fielding, time to settle into a rhythm.

Gold Award: O. A. Shah.

Middlesex

A. J. Strauss c Johnson b Udal	36	†D. C. Nash not out	6
M. A. Roseberry lbw b Mascarenhas	0		
S. P. Fleming lbw b Morris	4	B 2, l-b 3, w 2	7
O. A. Shah not out	118		—
P. N. Weekes b Mascarenhas	46	1/5 2/36 3/54 (5 wkts, 50 overs)	225
B. L. Hutton run out	8	4/175 5/208	

C. B. Keegan, S. J. Cook, *A. R. C. Fraser and T. F. Bloomfield did not bat.

Bowling: Mascarenhas 10–3–30–2; Mullally 10–0–47–0; Morris 10–1–49–1; Udal 10–0–36–1; Johnson 7–0–37–0; Stephenson 3–0–21–0.

Hampshire

N. C. Johnson c Strauss b Fraser	24	S. D. Udal run out	1
*R. A. Smith run out	11	†A. N. Aymes not out	17
D. A. Kenway c Fleming b Weekes	19		
J. S. Laney c Nash b Keegan	23	L-b 8, w 2, n-b 2	12
W. S. Kendall c Hutton b Keegan	12		—
J. P. Stephenson c Roseberry b Fraser	31	1/35 2/47 3/82 (8 wkts, 50 overs)	200
A. D. Mascarenhas c Hutton b Keegan	25	4/90 5/105 6/152	
A. C. Morris not out	25	7/155 8/158	

A. D. Mullally did not bat.

Bowling: Fraser 10–1–44–2; Bloomfield 10–1–30–0; Cook 10–2–38–0; Keegan 10–2–39–3; Weekes 10–0–41–1.

Umpires: D. J. Constant and J. W. Lloyds.

SUSSEX v KENT

At Hastings, May 6. Sussex won by five wickets. Toss: Sussex.

Horntye Park staged county cricket's return to Hastings 12 years after stumps were drawn at the old Central Ground. The home side adapted better to its slow pitch, no one better than Robinson, whose three wickets in eight balls prevented a late surge by Kent. Walker, with 52 from 78 balls, applied the patience necessary in such conditions; Cullinan, one, six, four and out, was over-ambitious. Montgomerie anchored Sussex's innings for 26 overs, after which Zuiderent and House added 61 in 13 overs. Martin-Jenkins won the match with a six.

Gold Award: M. A. Robinson.

Kent

*M. V. Fleming c Davis b Martin-Jenkins	21	J. M. Golding not out	10
R. W. T. Key c Prior b Rashid	25	M. M. Patel c Robinson b Kirtley	3
D. J. Cullinan b Robinson	11	D. D. Masters c Kirtley b Martin-Jenkins	6
M. J. Walker c Zuiderent b Robinson	52	L-b 7, w 4	11
M. A. Ealham run out	5		
†P. A. Nixon b Kirtley	21	1/43 2/59 3/59 (48.2 overs)	175
J. B. Hockley st Prior b Robinson	10	4/75 5/124 6/150	
M. J. McCague c Kirtley b Robinson	0	7/150 8/157 9/166	

Bowling: Kirtley 9–0–39–2; Martin-Jenkins 9.2–1–36–2; Robinson 10–3–29–4; Rashid 10–1–33–1; Davis 10–0–31–0.

Sussex

R. R. Montgomerie lbw b Patel	37	R. S. C. Martin-Jenkins not out	12
M. W. Goodwin c Patel b Walker	16		
B. Zuiderent run out	42	L-b 9, w 5	14
M. H. Yardy c Fleming b Patel	0		
W. J. House b Ealham	35	1/40 2/73 3/73 (5 wkts, 48.4 overs)	180
U. B. A. Rashid not out	24	4/134 5/146	

†M. J. Prior, M. J. G. Davis, *R. J. Kirtley and M. A. Robinson did not bat.

Bowling: Masters 6.4–1–31–0; Ealham 10–0–29–1; Fleming 10–2–24–0; Walker 4–0–16–1; Patel 10–3–34–2; Golding 3–0–13–0; McCague 5–0–24–0.

Umpires: A. Clarkson and M. J. Harris.

ESSEX v MIDDLESEX

At Chelmsford, May 7. Essex won by 71 runs. Toss: Essex.

Essex denied Middlesex the win they needed to go in the frame for a quarter-final place. In truth, they never looked like achieving it once they were three wickets down after nine overs. Fleming, seventh out, provided the only real threat, and even then the Essex bowlers made good use of a stopping pitch to restrict his strokeplay. His colleagues were unable to match the earlier consistent contribution by the Essex batsmen. After Hussain and Law had added 50 in nine overs, Peters gave the innings its focus and Cowan provided the damaging late impetus with 45 in 47 balls.

Gold Award: A. P. Grayson.

Essex

N. Hussain c Nash b Keegan	41	†B. J. Hyam c Shah b Weekes	0
D. D. J. Robinson c Nash b Fraser	0	T. J. Mason c Hutton b Keegan	12
S. G. Law b Fraser	24	A. C. McGarry not out	0
*R. C. Irani st Nash b Weekes	25	L-b 9, n-b 2	11
S. D. Peters lbw b Cook	48		
A. P. Grayson lbw b Hutton	22	1/5 2/55 3/86 (50 overs)	232
G. R. Napier c Nash b Bloomfield	4	4/103 5/149 6/154	
A. P. Cowan b Keegan	45	7/207 8/208 9/232	

Bowling: Fraser 10–2–37–2; Bloomfield 10–1–42–1; Cook 10–0–45–1; Keegan 10–0–51–3; Weekes 7–0–33–2; Hutton 3–0–15–1.

Middlesex

A. J. Strauss lbw b Irani	10	S. J. Cook c Irani b McGarry	11
R. M. S. Weston c Law b Irani	10	*A. R. C. Fraser c Irani b Mason	8
S. P. Fleming c and b Mason	73	T. F. Bloomfield not out	7
O. A. Shah b Cowan	0	L-b 1, w 5, n-b 5	11
P. N. Weekes st Hyam b Grayson	22		
†D. C. Nash b Grayson	4	1/11 2/38 3/44 (42 overs)	161
B. L. Hutton c Law b McGarry	2	4/99 5/118 6/122	
C. B. Keegan c Irani b Mason	3	7/135 8/136 9/154	

Bowling: Cowan 8–0–37–1; Irani 6–0–25–2; McGarry 10–1–34–2; Grayson 8–1–24–2; Mason 10–0–40–3.

Umpires: R. Julian and J. F. Steele.

HAMPSHIRE v SUSSEX

At Southampton, May 7. Sussex won by 60 runs. Toss: Sussex.

As Dutch treats go, Zuiderent's maiden county hundred was too costly for Hampshire, who were ultimately swept to defeat by Sussex acting-captain Kirtley's hat-trick. The victory left Sussex (whose first two games were abandoned) the only unbeaten side in the qualifying rounds. Initially foil to Goodwin, who steamed along at nearly a run a ball as they added 144 in 28 overs, Zuiderent exhibited his own attacking qualities while taking 18 runs off one Mascarenhas over to reach 99. His unbeaten 102, from 139 balls, contained 13 fours, as did Goodwin's 87. Smith kept the home side in with a chance, but 90 from ten overs proved much too demanding on another sluggish West End pitch.

Gold Award: B. Zuiderent.

Sussex

R. R. Montgomerie c Aymes b Mullally	2	R. S. C. Martin-Jenkins c Aymes b A. C. Morris	8
M. W. Goodwin c Z. C. Morris b A. C. Morris	87	†M. J. Prior run out	1
B. Zuiderent not out	102	L-b 10, w 9	19
M. H. Yardy st Aymes b Stephenson	8		
W. J. House b Mullally	26	1/7 2/151 3/165 (7 wkts, 50 overs)	255
U. B. A. Rashid b A. C. Morris	2	4/241 5/244 6/254 7/255	

M. J. G. Davis, *R. J. Kirtley and M. A. Robinson did not bat.

Bowling: Johnson 7–0–42–0; Mascarenhas 10–1–62–0; Mullally 10–1–25–2; Z. C. Morris 6–0–27–0; A. C. Morris 10–0–49–3; Stephenson 7–0–40–1.

Hampshire

N. C. Johnson c Kirtley b Rashid	40	Z. C. Morris b Kirtley	0
J. S. Laney run out	13	†A. N. Aymes lbw b Kirtley	0
D. A. Kenway c Rashid b Yardy	8	A. D. Mullally run out	0
*R. A. Smith not out	77	B 1, l-b 5, w 4	10
W. S. Kendall b Rashid	33		
A. D. Mascarenhas b Robinson	3	1/48 2/61 3/65 (46.2 overs)	195
J. P. Stephenson b Davis	3	4/158 5/166 6/169	
A. C. Morris b Kirtley	8	7/192 8/192 9/192	

Bowling: Kirtley 8–3–31–3; Martin-Jenkins 6–0–25–0; Robinson 10–1–34–1; Yardy 3–1–10–1; Rashid 10–0–44–2; Davis 9.2–0–45–1.

Umpires: B. Dudleston and M. J. Harris.

KENT v SURREY

At Canterbury, May 7. Kent won by one run. Toss: Kent.

Although their last-over victory had no bearing on the quarter-final places, Kent could be satisfied with the nature of their cricket. So could England's winter wicket-keepers, with Stewart hitting 15 fours in his 92 from 97 balls to provide the impetus to Surrey's reply. Ben Hollioake's 45-ball fifty looked to be winning the game for them, but Kent never gave an inch. Their own innings had been launched by a century stand in 22 overs from Key and Hockley, and boosted at the end by Nixon, who hit two sixes and six fours in his first one-day fifty for Kent.

Gold Award: P. A. Nixon.

Kent

*M. V. Fleming c Ramprakash b Tudor	8	M. J. McCague b A. J. Hollioake	1
R. W. T. Key c Ward b Salisbury	45	M. M. Patel run out	2
J. B. Hockley run out	55	M. J. Saggers not out	1
D. J. Cullinan c Stewart b Tudor	15	L-b 6, w 7, n-b 4	17
M. J. Walker b A. J. Hollioake	18		
†P. A. Nixon not out	65	1/13 2/115 3/123 (9 wkts, 50 overs)	265
M. A. Ealham c and b Salisbury	12	4/154 5/156 6/176	
J. M. Golding b A. J. Hollioake	26	7/242 8/246 9/251	

Bowling: Tudor 10–1–67–2; Bicknell 10–2–27–0; Giddins 10–0–44–0; B. C. Hollioake 3–0–27–0; Salisbury 10–0–45–2; A. J. Hollioake 7–0–49–3.

Surrey

I. J. Ward b McCague	1	M. P. Bicknell run out	24
†A. J. Stewart c Ealham b Golding	92	I. D. K. Salisbury lbw b Ealham	0
M. R. Ramprakash c Nixon b Ealham	32	E. S. H. Giddins lbw b Golding	2
G. P. Thorpe b Fleming	4	L-b 4, w 7	11
A. D. Brown b Fleming	0		
*A. J. Hollioake c sub b Saggers	20	1/6 2/65 3/86 (49.1 overs)	264
B. C. Hollioake not out	50	4/92 5/149 6/154	
A. J. Tudor c sub b Golding	28	7/201 8/240 9/244	

Bowling: Saggers 10–0–56–1; McCague 8–0–58–1; Fleming 7–1–20–2; Ealham 10–0–42–2; Golding 8.1–0–47–3; Patel 6–0–37–0.

Umpires: N. A. Mallender and R. A. White.

QUARTER-FINALS

GLOUCESTERSHIRE v DURHAM

At Bristol, May 22. Gloucestershire won by 66 runs. Toss: Gloucestershire.

While other batsmen were bogged down by the testiness of a typically slow Bristol pitch, Harvey smacked a crisp 43 from 37 balls. It was enough to sustain Gloucestershire through a lean mid-innings patch before Snape and Ball picked up the tempo to set a target of 200. At 103 for three, Durham must have had high hopes of becoming the first visiting side to win a knockout game at Nevil Road for almost three years. But Jon Lewis – the Gloucestershire one – undid the good work of Peng and Collingwood with a stint of accurate, penetrative seam bowling that brought him one-day best figures and kept his team's record intact.

Gold Award: J. Lewis.

Gloucestershire

R. J. Cunliffe b Killeen	0	M. C. J. Ball c Phillips b Gough	27
K. J. Barnett c Collingwood b Killeen	16	J. M. M. Averis c Law b Gough	3
I. J. Harvey c Phillips b Brinkley	43	J. Lewis not out	0
M. G. N. Windows c and b Collingwood	23	B 4, l-b 5, w 10	19
*M. W. Alleyne c and b Collingwood	25		—
C. G. Taylor b Gough	12	1/3 2/47 3/70 (49.5 overs)	199
J. N. Snape c Love b Killeen	24	4/119 5/126 6/147	
†R. C. J. Williams b Phillips	7	7/161 8/181 9/199	

Bowling: Killeen 10–0–32–3; Hunter 7–1–37–0; Phillips 10–0–31–1; Brinkley 7–2–15–1; Collingwood 8–1–39–2; Gough 7.5–0–36–3.

Durham

M. A. Gough c Williams b Lewis	2	N. Killeen lbw b Lewis	0
N. Peng c Ball b Lewis	32	J. E. Brinkley c Averis b Ball	2
M. L. Love c and b Ball	19	N. C. Phillips b Alleyne	0
P. D. Collingwood lbw b Averis	39	L-b 1, w 2	3
*J. J. B. Lewis c Windows b Averis	19		—
D. R. Law b Lewis	11	1/10 2/41 3/65 (42.3 overs)	133
I. D. Hunter b Alleyne	0	4/103 5/116 6/117	
†A. Pratt not out	6	7/129 8/129 9/133	

Bowling: Lewis 10–2–23–4; Harvey 7–0–25–0; Averis 7–0–26–2; Ball 8–1–19–2; Alleyne 8.3–0–26–2; Snape 2–0–13–0.

Umpires: V. A. Holder and D. R. Shepherd.

NOTTINGHAMSHIRE v WARWICKSHIRE

At Nottingham, May 23. Nottinghamshire won by six wickets. Toss: Nottinghamshire.

Greg Smith vindicated acting-captain Bicknell's decision to field in conditions that gave the bowlers early assistance. He quickly removed Wagh and Brown, would have had Ostler not long after had the ball stuck in Blewett's hands, and ended with exemplary figures of four for 18. The normally flamboyant Knight completed a solid century – his third in the competition in 2001 – but failed to increase the pace of his innings against some accurate bowling. With Knight's partners scoring slowly at the other end, some questioned an anchor-role mentality that saw him to 103 from 161 balls, with eight fours. Bicknell secured Nottinghamshire's victory simply by scoring his own century – 117 off 140 balls with 16 fours – at a faster rate.

Gold Award: D. J. Bicknell.

Warwickshire

N. V. Knight c Pietersen b Smith 103
M. A. Wagh c Blewett b Smith 0
D. R. Brown c Read b Smith 5
D. P. Ostler c Pietersen b Blewett 26
T. L. Penney st Read b Clough 30
*M. J. Powell c Bicknell b Clough 7
N. M. K. Smith not out 34
V. C. Drakes b Smith 0
†K. J. Piper not out 0
B 1, l-b 4, w 2 7

1/9 2/25 3/83 4/146 5/156 6/210 7/211 (7 wkts, 50 overs) 212

M. A. Sheikh and C. E. Dagnall did not bat.

Bowling: Smith 10–3–18–4; Franks 9–1–48–0; Clough 9–0–53–2; Blewett 8–0–38–1; Stemp 10–0–30–0; Pietersen 4–0–20–0.

Nottinghamshire

*D. J. Bicknell not out 117
G. E. Welton b Brown 9
G. S. Blewett lbw b Sheikh 21
P. Johnson c Piper b Brown 18
U. Afzaal c Piper b Smith 28
K. P. Pietersen not out 16
L-b 2, w 3 5

1/41 2/82 3/110 4/183 (4 wkts, 46.1 overs) 214

†C. M. W. Read, P. J. Franks, G. D. Clough, G. J. Smith and R. D. Stemp did not bat.

Bowling: Drakes 9–1–24–0; Dagnall 10–0–49–0; Brown 9.1–0–54–2; Sheikh 10–1–38–1; Smith 6–1–33–1; Powell 2–0–14–0.

Umpires: B. Dudleston and J. F. Steele.

SOMERSET v YORKSHIRE

At Taunton, May 23. Yorkshire won by eight wickets. Toss: Somerset.

Vaughan breezed Yorkshire into the semi-finals. His first one-day hundred, a fine innings that contained 18 fours and a six and occupied 128 balls, was achieved by brisk and attractive strokeplay. He and Lehmann took full advantage of some nondescript Somerset bowling, allowing Yorkshire to canter to victory with fewer than 37 overs gone. It turned into a one-sided match despite both counties having their internationals returned to them. Caddick proved more than three times as costly as Gough, who conceded only 18 runs and removed his England colleague, Trescothick, for a brief 12. But, while Bowler and Cox were adding 108, Taunton hopes were high. The innings petered out, however, and the total, on a good pitch, was never going to be defensible.

Gold Award: M. P. Vaughan.

Somerset

M. E. Trescothick c Lehmann b Gough . 12
P. D. Bowler c Vaughan b Sidebottom . . 62
*J. Cox c Lumb b Lehmann 62
I. D. Blackwell c Lehmann b Fellows . . . 12
M. Burns c Lehmann b Hoggard 24
K. A. Parsons c Middlebrook b Sidebottom . 8
†R. J. Turner not out 9
K. P. Dutch c Wood b Hoggard 0
J. I. D. Kerr not out 8
L-b 5, w 6, n-b 2 13

1/23 2/131 3/150 4/159 5/184 6/199 7/200 (7 wkts, 50 overs) 210

A. R. Caddick and P. S. Jones did not bat.

Bowling: Gough 10–1–18–1; Hoggard 10–0–54–2; Sidebottom 10–1–34–2; Fellows 5–0–28–1; Middlebrook 10–0–53–0; Lehmann 5–0–18–1.

Yorkshire

*D. Byas c Bowler b Caddick	13
M. P. Vaughan not out	125
M. J. Wood lbw b Kerr	7
D. S. Lehmann not out	51
L-b 2, w 5, n-b 10	17
1/34 2/73 (2 wkts, 36.4 overs)	213

M. J. Lumb, G. M. Fellows, †R. J. Blakey, J. D. Middlebrook, R. J. Sidebottom, D. Gough and M. J. Hoggard did not bat.

Bowling: Caddick 10–0–57–1; Jones 8–2–28–0; Kerr 6–0–36–1; Dutch 3–0–14–0; Trescothick 5–0–35–0; Blackwell 2–0–14–0; Burns 2.4–0–27–0.

Umpires: M. R. Benson and A. A. Jones.

SUSSEX v SURREY

At Hove, May 23. Surrey won by 53 runs. Toss: Surrey.

With two batsmen – Adams, in his first game after recovering from a broken thumb, and the in-form Montgomerie – going well, Sussex, needing 102 off 15 overs, were scenting victory over a strong Surrey side. But Tudor's dismissal of Adams ended the century third-wicket stand and sparked a dismal collapse, which saw eight wickets fall for 48. Brown had underpinned Surrey's total with a chanceless 147-ball century, adding 125 in 24 overs with Ramprakash. But even he was eventually bogged down (he hit no fours in his last 39 runs), as much by Sussex's improved bowling as the Readers ball, which had already been changed. "It was like trying to hit a grapefruit," Brown commented later.

Gold Award: A. D. Brown.

Surrey

A. D. Brown not out	108
†A. J. Stewart lbw b Martin-Jenkins	0
M. R. Ramprakash c House b Robinson	53
G. P. Thorpe c Zuiderent b Robinson	11
I. J. Ward run out	12
*A. J. Hollioake run out	4
B. C. Hollioake run out	18
A. J. Tudor b Kirtley	4
I. D. K. Salisbury not out	6
B 1, l-b 4, w 10, n-b 8	23
1/2 2/127 3/148 4/170 5/180 6/217 7/223 (7 wkts, 50 overs)	239

M. P. Bicknell and E. S. H. Giddins did not bat.

Bowling: Martin-Jenkins 10–0–48–1; Kirtley 10–0–47–1; Adams 7–0–27–0; Robinson 10–1–49–2; Rashid 3–0–22–0; Davis 10–0–41–0.

Sussex

R. R. Montgomerie c Giddins b B. C. Hollioake	83
M. W. Goodwin b Bicknell	11
B. Zuiderent lbw b Bicknell	1
*C. J. Adams b Tudor	37
W. J. House b Tudor	2
U. B. A. Rashid c Bicknell b B. C. Hollioake	3
R. S. C. Martin-Jenkins c Tudor b Giddins	7
†M. J. Prior run out	5
M. J. G. Davis not out	2
R. J. Kirtley b Giddins	8
M. A. Robinson b B. C. Hollioake	1
L-b 13, w 9, n-b 4	26
1/34 2/38 3/138 4/151 5/158 6/168 7/169 8/174 9/183 (47.2 overs)	186

Bowling: Bicknell 10–1–29–2; Tudor 10–0–37–2; Giddins 10–0–29–2; A. J. Hollioake 6–1–25–0; Ramprakash 4–0–23–0; Salisbury 3–0–17–0; B. C. Hollioake 4.2–0–13–3.

Umpires: J. W. Holder and R. A. White.

SEMI-FINALS

SURREY v NOTTINGHAMSHIRE

At The Oval, June 25. Surrey won by 174 runs. Toss: Surrey.

Nottinghamshire began their first semi-final in either knockout competition for 11 years in better one-day form than their opponents, who were contesting their sixth in six years. They ended it chastened and demoralised, having conceded more runs than any other first-class county in the history of the competition – admittedly on a strip made for batting – before crumpling in the face of Surrey's international seam attack. Had the last pair not put up spirited resistance, Nottinghamshire would also have suffered the heaviest defeat inflicted on a first-class county in the Benson and Hedges Cup. Butcher, brought in because Ramprakash was unfit, epitomised the ebullient Surrey strokeplay, hitting a magnificent 84 from 86 balls. Such was Surrey's untrammelled progress against ill-disciplined bowling, however, that he was the sole member of the top six to score at less than a run a ball as they romped to 361, the county's highest total in knockout cricket. Stewart's 67 made him the third batsman after Gooch and Barnett to pass 3,000 runs in the competition. Afzaal and Pietersen did their best to save face.

Gold Award: M. A. Butcher.

Surrey

M. A. Butcher c Bicknell b Harris	84
I. J. Ward st Read b Stemp	58
N. Shahid b Afzaal	32
†A. J. Stewart c Read b Afzaal	67
A. D. Brown c and b Afzaal	49
B. C. Hollioake not out	39
*A. J. Hollioake b Blewett	7
A. J. Tudor b Blewett	0
M. P. Bicknell c Morris b Blewett	3
Saqlain Mushtaq not out	2
B 4, l-b 6, w 10	20
1/112 2/160 3/206 4/304 5/307 6/332 7/332 8/345 (8 wkts, 50 overs)	361

E. S. H. Giddins did not bat.

Bowling: Smith 10–0–55–0; Harris 10–0–63–1; Clough 5–0–46–0; Stemp 9–0–58–1; Pietersen 5–0–37–0; Afzaal 5–0–51–3; Blewett 6–0–41–3.

Nottinghamshire

*D. J. Bicknell c Stewart b Bicknell	15
J. E. Morris run out	6
G. S. Blewett b Giddins	9
U. Afzaal b Tudor	37
P. Johnson lbw b Bicknell	1
K. P. Pietersen not out	78
†C. M. W. Read lbw b Giddins	2
G. D. Clough c Shahid b Tudor	0
A. J. Harris lbw b B. C. Hollioake	0
G. J. Smith c Bicknell b Tudor	2
R. D. Stemp c Giddins b Saqlain Mushtaq	29
L-b 3, w 5	8
1/19 2/23 3/44 4/47 5/115 6/120 7/137 8/137 9/143 (31.5 overs)	187

Bowling: Bicknell 7–1–43–2; Tudor 10–1–52–3; Giddins 10–0–57–2; B. C. Hollioake 4–0–29–1; Saqlain Mushtaq 0.5–0–3–1.

Umpires: J. W. Lloyds and A. G. T. Whitehead.

YORKSHIRE v GLOUCESTERSHIRE

At Leeds, June 25. Gloucestershire won by 97 runs. Toss: Gloucestershire.

Gloucestershire maintained their domination of the knockout competitions, their straightforward win rewarded with a fifth consecutive Lord's final. By contrast, Yorkshire's defeat meant that in seven years they had won one and lost six semi-finals. Everyone chipped in with useful runs in a typical Gloucestershire team effort, top score coming from Windows with a solid 54 from 93 balls. Requiring 240, Yorkshire were just recovering from the loss of Byas and Lumb when a moment's carelessness gifted Gloucestershire their most prized wicket: Lehmann played the ball to mid-off, where Taylor picked up and threw in to Russell, who instinctively flicked off the bails. Lehmann had not attempted a run, but television showed he had unwittingly wandered from his crease. Minutes later, a shell-shocked Yorkshire were 25 for five and the game was dead. White and Hamilton's sixth-wicket stand of 59, the highest of the match, was purely academic.

Gold Award: M. G. N. Windows.

Gloucestershire

T. H. C. Hancock run out	42	†R. C. Russell c and b White	7
K. J. Barnett c Blakey b Hamilton	31	M. C. J. Ball not out	11
M. G. N. Windows c Blakey b Silverwood	54	B 1, l-b 5, w 1, n-b 6	13
I. J. Harvey b Gough	12		
C. G. Taylor c Sidebottom b White	18	1/48 2/92 3/106 (7 wkts, 50 overs)	239
*M. W. Alleyne c Byas b Silverwood	26	4/138 5/181	
J. N. Snape not out	25	6/207 7/223	

J. M. M. Averis and M. J. Cawdron did not bat.

Bowling: Gough 10–1–47–1; Silverwood 9–0–52–2; Hamilton 4–2–15–1; Sidebottom 10–0–46–0; White 10–0–47–2; Lehmann 7–0–26–0.

Yorkshire

*D. Byas c Russell b Averis	1	C. E. W. Silverwood c Ball b Cawdron	5
M. P. Vaughan c Hancock b Harvey	13	D. Gough c Averis b Ball	13
M. J. Lumb c Alleyne b Harvey	1	R. J. Sidebottom run out	4
D. S. Lehmann run out	8	B 4, w 2	6
C. White b Alleyne	25		
G. M. Fellows lbw b Averis	0	1/6 2/7 3/24 (37.5 overs)	142
G. M. Hamilton lbw b Ball	31	4/25 5/25 6/84	
†R. J. Blakey not out	35	7/86 8/101 9/125	

Bowling: Averis 7–2–16–2; Harvey 6–3–10–2; Alleyne 8–0–30–1; Cawdron 8.5–0–51–1; Ball 8–0–31–2.

Umpires: A. A. Jones and R. Julian.

FINAL

GLOUCESTERSHIRE v SURREY

At Lord's, July 14. Surrey won by 47 runs. Toss: Surrey.

Gloucestershire's run of four successive Lord's victories ended with their fifth final in a row. There would be no record third consecutive Benson and Hedges title. Earlier in the week, moreover, they had been knocked out of the Cheltenham & Gloucester Trophy, successor to the NatWest, and there were early signs – after play began half an hour late under gun-metal skies – that this was a team on the down side of its wave. Nor had injuries helped. There were signs, too, that this was a competition that had seen better days. The ground looked half-full, the Pavilion even less, and there was none of the atmosphere associated with Gloucestershire's previous visits.

Butcher's dismissal in Harvey's second over proved a false augury for the cup-holders. The three overthrows that helped Ramprakash on his silky way with four runs, and the catch Harvey dropped at first slip when Ward was 16, provided a more accurate prognosis. Runs from Ward's reprieve took Surrey past 50 in the tenth over; before Ramprakash surprisingly pulled Alleyne's long-hop straight to Taylor at square leg, Surrey had raced to 71 in 12 overs.

Alleyne, whose opening over cost 13, helped pull the run-rate down with a spell of three for eight in 24 balls. When Ward was caught behind for 54 in 59 balls, Surrey were 118 for five at the halfway stage and Gloucestershire were looking more like their champion selves. But the Hollioake brothers regained the advantage. Ben was ebullient, rekindling memories of his Lord's batting against Australia and Kent in 1997 with flowing drives and two easy sixes into the Grand Stand in his

76-ball 73; Adam hit no boundaries but worked the gaps for ones and twos in a partnership of 84 that sapped Gloucestershire. By the time Bicknell pulled a six through Taylor's hands off Harvey, and was dropped by him again two balls later, Surrey had claimed the morale high ground.

Gloucestershire, not always happiest chasing, never took flight in pursuit of 245. Bicknell and Tudor's tight line cramped Russell and Barnett. It took the latter 19 balls to get his first run, and Giddins only three balls to dismiss him. But Giddins's vital strike was getting Harvey lbw in the 20th over. With Russell, opening in place of Hancock, and Alleyne together, there was the hint of a chance for Gloucestershire. It went when they were out in successive overs. Surrey were simply too efficient; they took their opponents' game from them as well as their cup.

Gold Award: B. C. Hollioake. *Attendance:* 16,952; *receipts* £407,845.

Surrey

M. A. Butcher lbw b Harvey	0
I. J. Ward c Russell b Hardinges	54
M. R. Ramprakash c Taylor b Alleyne	39
†A. J. Stewart c Snape b Alleyne	8
A. D. Brown c Harvey b Alleyne	3
*A. J. Hollioake lbw b Ball	39
B. C. Hollioake c Alleyne b Averis	73
A. J. Tudor lbw b Ball	1
M. P. Bicknell b Harvey	19
Saqlain Mushtaq not out	1
E. S. H. Giddins b Harvey	0
L-b 4, w 3	7
(49.5 overs)	244

1/7 (1) 2/71 (3) 3/89 (4) 4/97 (5) 5/118 (2) 6/202 (6) 7/204 (8) 8/242 (7) 9/244 (9) 10/244 (11)

Score at 15 overs: 88-2

Bowling: Harvey 9.5–2–43–3; Averis 10–1–65–1; Alleyne 10–1–51–3; Ball 10–0–39–2; Hardinges 7–0–31–1; Barnett 3–0–11–0.

Gloucestershire

†R. C. Russell c Stewart b Tudor	62
K. J. Barnett b Giddins	7
D. R. Hewson c Bicknell b Saqlain Mushtaq	11
I. J. Harvey lbw b Giddins	1
M. G. N. Windows b Giddins	10
*M. W. Alleyne c and b Saqlain Mushtaq	26
J. N. Snape c Stewart b Tudor	22
C. G. Taylor b Saqlain Mushtaq	12
M. A. Hardinges c Stewart b Bicknell	12
M. C. J. Ball not out	3
J. M. M. Averis b Tudor	1
L-b 16, w 14	30
(45.5 overs)	197

1/35 (2) 2/68 (3) 3/71 (4) 4/89 (5) 5/131 (1) 6/133 (6) 7/161 (8) 8/190 (7) 9/194 (9) 10/197 (11)

Score at 15 overs: 48-1

Bowling: Bicknell 10–1–38–1; Tudor 9.5–3–28–3; Giddins 8–1–31–3; Saqlain Mushtaq 8–0–37–3; B. C. Hollioake 10–0–47–0.

Umpires: J. H. Hampshire and K. E. Palmer.
Third umpire: B. Leadbeater.

BENSON AND HEDGES CUP RECORDS

55 overs available in all games 1972–95, 50 overs in 1996–2001.
Only eight teams took part in 1999.

Batting

Highest individual scores: 198*, G. A. Gooch, Essex v Sussex, Hove, 1982; 177, S. J. Cook, Somerset v Sussex, Hove, 1990; 173*, C. G. Greenidge, Hampshire v Minor Counties (South), Amersham, 1973; 167*, A. J. Stewart, Surrey v Somerset, The Oval, 1994; 160, A. J. Stewart, Surrey v Hampshire, The Oval, 1996; 158*, B. F. Davison, Leicestershire v Warwickshire, Coventry, 1972; 158, W. J. Cronje, Leicestershire v Lancashire, Manchester, 1995; 157*, M. G. Bevan, Sussex v Essex, Chelmsford, 2000; 155*, M. D. Crowe, Somerset v Hampshire, Southampton, 1987; 155*, R. A. Smith, Hampshire v Glamorgan, Southampton, 1989; 154*, M. J. Procter, Gloucestershire v Somerset, Taunton, 1972; 154*, C. L. Smith, Hampshire v Combined Universities, Southampton, 1990; 151*, M. P. Maynard, Glamorgan v Middlesex, Lord's, 1996; 151, D. L.

Maddy, Leicestershire v Minor Counties, Leicester, 1998. *In the final:* 132*, I. V. A. Richards, Somerset v Surrey, 1981. (339 hundreds have been scored in the competition. The most hundreds in one season was 26 in 1996.)

Most runs: 5,176, G. A. Gooch; 3,165, K. J. Barnett; 3,040, A. J. Stewart; 2,921, M. W. Gatting; 2,849, N. H. Fairbrother; 2,837, R. J. Bailey; 2,822, G. A. Hick; 2,761, C. J. Tavaré; 2,718, W. Larkins; 2,663, D. W. Randall; 2,636, A. J. Lamb; 2,567, R. T. Robinson; 2,551, C. W. J. Athey.

Fastest hundred: M. A. Nash in 62 minutes, Glamorgan v Hampshire at Swansea, 1976.

Most hundreds: 15, G. A. Gooch; 7, G. A. Hick and W. Larkins; 6, M. P. Maynard and N. R. Taylor; 5, C. G. Greenidge, A. J. Lamb and R. A. Smith.

Highest totals: 388 for seven, Essex v Scotland, Chelmsford, 1992; 382 for six, Leicestershire v Minor Counties, Leicester, 1998; 371 for six, Leicestershire v Scotland, Leicester, 1997; 369 for eight, Warwickshire v Minor Counties, Jesmond, 1996; 366 for four, Derbyshire v Combined Universities, Oxford, 1991; 361 for eight, Surrey v Nottinghamshire, The Oval, 2001; 359 for seven, Essex v Ireland, Chelmsford, 1998; 353 for seven, Lancashire v Nottinghamshire, Manchester, 1995; 350 for three, Essex v Oxford & Cambridge Univs, Chelmsford, 1979; 349 for seven, Somerset v Ireland, Taunton, 1997; 338 for six, Kent v Somerset, Maidstone, 1996; 333 for four, Essex v Oxford & Cambridge Univs, Chelmsford, 1985; 333 for six, Surrey v Hampshire, The Oval, 1996; 331 for five, Surrey v Hampshire, The Oval, 1990; 331 for five, Essex v British Univs, Chelmsford, 1996; 330 for four, Lancashire v Sussex, Manchester, 1991. *In the final:* 291 for nine, Gloucestershire v Yorkshire, 1999.

Highest total by a side batting second and winning: 318 for five (54.3 overs), Lancashire v Leicestershire (312 for five), Manchester, 1995. *In the final:* 244 for six (55 overs), Yorkshire v Northamptonshire (244 for seven), 1987; 244 for seven (55 overs), Nottinghamshire v Essex (243 for seven), 1989.

Highest total by a side batting second and losing: 303 for seven (55 overs), Derbyshire v Somerset (310 for three), Taunton, 1990. *In the final:* 255 (51.4 overs), Surrey v Essex (290 for six), 1979.

Highest match aggregates: 631 for 15 wickets, Kent (338 for six) v Somerset (293 for nine), Maidstone, 1996; 630 for ten wickets, Leicestershire (312 for five) v Lancashire (318 for five), Manchester, 1995; 629 for 14 wickets, Lancashire (353 for seven) v Nottinghamshire (276 for seven), Manchester, 1995; 628 for 15 wickets, Warwickshire (312 for six) v Lancashire (316 for nine), Manchester, 1996; 626 for ten wickets, British Univs (312 for eight) v Glamorgan (314 for two), Cambridge, 1996; 615 for 11 wickets, Gloucestershire (307 for four) v Surrey (308 for seven), The Oval, 1996; 613 for ten wickets, Somerset (310 for three) v Derbyshire (303 for seven), Taunton, 1990; 610 for eight wickets, Sussex (303 for six) v Kent (307 for two), Hove, 1995; 610 for 14 wickets, Warwickshire (304 for eight) v Kent (306 for six), Canterbury, 1997.

Lowest totals: 50 in 27.2 overs, Hampshire v Yorkshire, Leeds, 1991; 52 in 26.5 overs, Minor Counties v Lancashire, Lakenham, 1998; 56 in 26.2 overs, Leicestershire v Minor Counties, Wellington, 1982; 59 in 34 overs, Oxford & Cambridge Univs v Glamorgan, Cambridge, 1983; 60 in 26 overs, Sussex v Middlesex, Hove, 1978; 61 in 25.3 overs, Essex v Lancashire, Chelmsford, 1992; 62 in 26.5 overs, Gloucestershire v Hampshire, Bristol, 1975. *In the final:* 76 in 27.4 overs, Leicestershire v Essex, 1998.

Shortest completed innings: 21.4 overs (156), Surrey v Sussex, Hove, 1988.

Record partnership for each wicket

252	for 1st	V. P. Terry and C. L. Smith, Hampshire v Combined Universities at Southampton	1990
285*	for 2nd	C. G. Greenidge and D. R. Turner, Hampshire v Minor Counties (South) at Amersham	1973
271	for 3rd	C. J. Adams and M. G. Bevan, Sussex v Essex at Chelmsford	2000

207	for 4th	R. C. Russell and A. J. Wright, Gloucestershire v British Universities at Bristol	1998
160	for 5th	A. J. Lamb and D. J. Capel, Northamptonshire v Leicestershire at Northampton	1986
167*	for 6th	M. G. Bevan and R. J. Blakey, Yorkshire v Lancashire at Manchester	1996
149*	for 7th	J. D. Love and C. M. Old, Yorkshire v Scotland at Bradford	1981
109	for 8th	R. E. East and N. Smith, Essex v Northamptonshire at Chelmsford	1977
83	for 9th	P. G. Newman and M. A. Holding, Derbyshire v Nottinghamshire at Nottingham	1985
80*	for 10th	D. L. Bairstow and M. Johnson, Yorkshire v Derbyshire at Derby	1981

Bowling

Most wickets: 149, J. K. Lever; 132, I. T. Botham.

Best bowling: seven for 12, W. W. Daniel, Middlesex v Minor Counties (East), Ipswich, 1978; seven for 22, J. R. Thomson, Middlesex v Hampshire, Lord's, 1981; seven for 24, Mushtaq Ahmed, Somerset v Ireland, Taunton, 1997; seven for 32, R. G. D. Willis, Warwickshire v Yorkshire, Birmingham, 1981. *In the final:* five for 13, S. T. Jefferies, Hampshire v Derbyshire, 1988.

Hat-tricks (13)**:** G. D. McKenzie, Leicestershire v Worcestershire, Worcester, 1972; K. Higgs, Leicestershire v Surrey in the final, Lord's, 1974; A. A. Jones, Middlesex v Essex, Lord's, 1977; M. J. Procter, Gloucestershire v Hampshire, Southampton, 1977; W. Larkins, Northamptonshire v Oxford & Cambridge Univs, Northampton, 1980; E. A. Moseley, Glamorgan v Kent, Cardiff, 1981; G. C. Small, Warwickshire v Leicestershire, Leicester, 1984; N. A. Mallender, Somerset v Combined Universities, Taunton, 1987; W. K. M. Benjamin, Leicestershire v Nottinghamshire, Leicester, 1987; A. R. C. Fraser, Middlesex v Sussex, Lord's, 1988; S. M. Pollock (four in four balls), Warwickshire v Leicestershire, Birmingham, 1996; Saqlain Mushtaq, Surrey v Lancashire, The Oval, 1998; R. J. Kirtley, Sussex v Hampshire, Southampton, 2001.

Wicket-keeping and Fielding

Most dismissals: 122 (117 ct, 5 st), D. L. Bairstow; 106 (96 ct, 10 st), S. J. Rhodes; 102 (96 ct, 6 st), W. K. Hegg.

Most dismissals in an innings: 8 (all ct), D. J. S. Taylor, Somerset v Oxford & Cambridge Univs, Taunton, 1982.

Most catches by a fielder: 68, G. A. Gooch; 55, C. J. Tavaré; 53, I. T. Botham.

Most catches by a fielder in an innings: 5, V. J. Marks, Oxford & Cambridge Univs v Kent, Oxford, 1976.

Results

Largest victories in runs: Essex by 272 runs v Scotland, Chelmsford, 1992; Leicestershire by 256 runs v Minor Counties, Leicester, 1998; Somerset by 233 runs v Ireland, Eglinton, 1995; Somerset by 221 runs v Ireland, Taunton, 1997; Glamorgan by 217 runs v Combined Universities, Cardiff, 1995; Essex by 214 runs v Oxford & Cambridge Univs, Chelmsford, 1979; Derbyshire by 206 runs v Combined Universities, Oxford, 1991; Warwickshire by 195 runs v Minor Counties, Jesmond, 1996.

Victories by ten wickets (20)**:** By Derbyshire, Essex (twice), Glamorgan, Hampshire, Kent (twice), Lancashire (twice), Leicestershire (twice), Middlesex, Northamptonshire, Somerset, Warwickshire, Worcestershire (twice), Yorkshire (three times).

Gold Awards

Most awards: 22, G. A. Gooch; 11, K. J. Barnett, M. W. Gatting, G. A. Hick, T. E. Jesty and B. Wood.

WINNERS 1972–2001

		Gold Award
1972	LEICESTERSHIRE* beat Yorkshire by five wickets.	J. C. Balderstone
1973	KENT* beat Worcestershire by 39 runs.	Asif Iqbal
1974	SURREY* beat Leicestershire by 27 runs.	J. H. Edrich
1975	LEICESTERSHIRE beat Middlesex* by five wickets.	N. M. McVicker
1976	KENT* beat Worcestershire by 43 runs.	G. W. Johnson
1977	GLOUCESTERSHIRE* beat Kent by 64 runs.	A. W. Stovold
1978	KENT beat Derbyshire* by six wickets.	R. A. Woolmer
1979	ESSEX beat Surrey* by 35 runs.	G. A. Gooch
1980	NORTHAMPTONSHIRE* beat Essex by six runs.	A. J. Lamb
1981	SOMERSET* beat Surrey by seven wickets.	I. V. A. Richards
1982	SOMERSET* beat Nottinghamshire by nine wickets.	V. J. Marks
1983	MIDDLESEX beat Essex* by four runs.	C. T. Radley
1984	LANCASHIRE* beat Warwickshire by six wickets.	J. Abrahams
1985	LEICESTERSHIRE* beat Essex by five wickets.	P. Willey
1986	MIDDLESEX beat Kent* by two runs.	J. E. Emburey
1987	YORKSHIRE* beat Northamptonshire, having taken more wickets with the scores tied.	J. D. Love
1988	HAMPSHIRE* beat Derbyshire by seven wickets.	S. T. Jefferies
1989	NOTTINGHAMSHIRE beat Essex* by three wickets.	R. T. Robinson
1990	LANCASHIRE beat Worcestershire* by 69 runs.	M. Watkinson
1991	WORCESTERSHIRE beat Lancashire* by 65 runs.	G. A. Hick
1992	HAMPSHIRE beat Kent* by 41 runs.	R. A. Smith
1993	DERBYSHIRE beat Lancashire* by six runs.	D. G. Cork
1994	WARWICKSHIRE* beat Worcestershire by six wickets.	P. A. Smith
1995	LANCASHIRE beat Kent* by 35 runs.	P. A. de Silva†
1996	LANCASHIRE* beat Northamptonshire by 31 runs.	I. D. Austin
1997	SURREY beat Kent* by eight wickets.	B. C. Hollioake
1998	ESSEX beat Leicestershire* by 192 runs.	P. J. Prichard
1999‡	GLOUCESTERSHIRE* beat Yorkshire by 124 runs.	M. W. Alleyne
2000	GLOUCESTERSHIRE beat Glamorgan* by seven wickets.	M. P. Maynard†
2001	SURREY* beat Gloucestershire by 47 runs.	B. C. Hollioake

** Won toss. † On losing side. ‡ Super Cup.*

WINS BY NON-CHAMPIONSHIP TEAMS

1973	OXFORD beat Northamptonshire at Northampton by two wickets.
1975	OXFORD & CAMBRIDGE beat Worcestershire at Cambridge by 66 runs.
	OXFORD & CAMBRIDGE beat Northamptonshire at Oxford by three wickets.
1976	OXFORD & CAMBRIDGE beat Yorkshire at Barnsley by seven wickets.
1980	MINOR COUNTIES beat Gloucestershire at Chippenham by three runs.
1981	MINOR COUNTIES beat Hampshire at Southampton by three runs.
1982	MINOR COUNTIES beat Leicestershire at Wellington by 131 runs.
1984	OXFORD & CAMBRIDGE beat Gloucestershire at Bristol by 27 runs.
1986	SCOTLAND beat Lancashire at Perth by three runs.
1987	MINOR COUNTIES beat Glamorgan at Oxford (Christ Church) by seven wickets.
1989	COMBINED UNIVERSITIES beat Surrey at Cambridge by nine runs.
	COMBINED UNIVERSITIES beat Worcestershire at Worcester by five wickets.
1990	COMBINED UNIVERSITIES beat Yorkshire at Leeds by two wickets.
	SCOTLAND beat Northamptonshire at Northampton by two runs.
1992	MINOR COUNTIES beat Sussex at Marlow by 19 runs.
1995	MINOR COUNTIES beat Leicestershire at Leicester by 26 runs.
1997	IRELAND beat Middlesex at Dublin (Castle Avenue) by 46 runs.
	BRITISH UNIVERSITIES beat Sussex at Cambridge by 19 runs.
1998	BRITISH UNIVERSITIES beat Gloucestershire at Bristol by seven runs.

TEAM RECORDS 1972–2001

	Rounds reached				*Matches*			
	W	*F*	*SF*	*QF*	*P*	*W*	*L*	*NR*
Derbyshire	1	3	4	9	131	66	55	10
Durham	0	0	0	3	38	17	19	2
Essex	2	6	9	16	146	86	52	8
Glamorgan	0	1	2	9	127	54	66	7
Gloucestershire	3	4	5	10	135	70	59	6
Hampshire	2	2	5	14	137	64	64	9
Kent	3	8	13	19	155	96	51	8
Lancashire	4	6	11	19	153	95	51	7
Leicestershire	3	5	8	12	142	77	56	9
Middlesex	2	3	5	15	139	69	57	13
Northamptonshire	1	3	6	11	133	61	61	11
Nottinghamshire	1	2	6	14	137	76	53	8
Somerset	2	2	8	14	138	73	59	6
Surrey	3	5	11	16	148	84	55	9
Sussex	0	0	2	12	129	61	62	6
Warwickshire	1	2	8	16	142	77	55	10
Worcestershire	1	5	8	15	141	71	63	7
Yorkshire	1	3	9	15	140	77	55	8
Cambridge University	0	0	0	0	8	0	8	0
Oxford University	0	0	0	0	4	1	3	0
Oxford & Cambridge Universities	0	0	0	0	48	4	42	2
Combined/British Universities	0	0	0	1	47	5	41	1
Minor Counties	0	0	0	0	75	6	65	4
Minor Counties (North)	0	0	0	0	20	0	20	0
Minor Counties (South)	0	0	0	0	20	0	19	1
Minor Counties (East)	0	0	0	0	12	0	12	0
Minor Counties (West)	0	0	0	0	12	0	12	0
Scotland	0	0	0	0	70	2	64	4
Ireland	0	0	0	0	17	1	14	2

Middlesex beat Gloucestershire on the toss of a coin in their quarter-final in 1983. Derbyshire, Kent, Somerset and Warwickshire totals each include a bowling contest; Derbyshire beat Somerset and Warwickshire beat Kent when their quarter-finals, in 1993 and 1994 respectively, were abandoned. In 1999, only eight counties took part; from 2000, the competition was restricted to the 18 first-class counties.

NATIONAL CRICKET ACADEMY

The National Cricket Academy, under the directorship of former Australian Test wicket-keeper R. W. Marsh, opened in November 2001. It was initially based at the Commonwealth Bank Cricket Academy in Adelaide, and its inaugural intake comprised the following 15 players: I. R. Bell (Warwickshire), S. J. Harmison (Durham), S. P. Jones (Glamorgan), D. A. Kenway (Hampshire), R. W. T. Key (Kent), S. P. Kirby (Yorkshire), N. Peng (Durham), C. P. Schofield (Lancashire), A. J. Strauss (Middlesex), G. P. Swann (Northamptonshire), C. T. Tremlett (Hampshire), A. J. Tudor (Surrey), M. A. Wagh (Warwickshire), M. A. Wallace (Glamorgan), M. J. Wood (Yorkshire).

NORWICH UNION LEAGUE, 2001

Matthew Fleming

When Leicestershire beat Kent mid-season in consecutive games home and away, there was a groundswell of opinion that the Norwich Union League title was bound for Grace Road. It wasn't simply that Division One leaders Leicestershire had put two over their only previously unbeaten rivals; it was the confident way they went about it, a confidence born of solid teamwork and enhanced by the outrageous hitting of 21-year-old Shahid Afridi, their replacement overseas player. But Kent did not throw in the towel. They hung on tenaciously, brilliantly marshalled – sometimes salvaged – by their captain, Matthew Fleming, spurred by their own overseas substitute, Andrew Symonds, and cheered on by fervent supporters. More than 30 years after its inception, there is still a snooty tendency to write down the League's entertainment value. Kent were not alone in packing in large crowds in 2001.

Leicestershire's one-run defeat by Somerset nine days after their Kent double seemed to have more to say about their forthcoming meeting at Lord's, in the Cheltenham & Gloucester final, than the outcome of the League. What no one realised was that the West Countrymen had a hex on the Midlanders. They would see them off again in a fortnight (and at Lord's five days after that), triggering a meltdown in which Leicestershire's last four games realised just two points. Kent, meanwhile, held their nerve and took the title by beating third-placed Warwickshire on the last Sunday.

At the other end of the division, defending champions Gloucestershire and Surrey, the previous season's Division Two winners, were relegated along with Northamptonshire. Gloucestershire had finished their Cheltenham Festival, in early August, well positioned to challenge for a top-three place, but won only once more in five attempts. Their past two seasons' one-day glories were fast becoming a memory. Surrey never looked the part and were not helped by England's demands on their all-star batting line-up. Northamptonshire had no such excuse and spent the season adrift at eighth or ninth.

Three up, three down may be one team too many in the County Championship, but it certainly gives the League some cut and thrust. There was a touch of romance, too, when Durham emerged as Division Two's unlikely front-runner, and Paul Collingwood's value was recognised by elevation to England's one-day squad. As with the Division One pacemakers, no single batsman or bowler starred among the season's foremost run-makers or wicket-takers. Their campaign was essentially a team effort. Worcestershire, with Vikram Solanki and Andy Bichel among the runs and wickets respectively, headed Durham throughout July but it was they, rather than Durham, who slipped off the pace once steady Glamorgan kicked ahead with eight unbeaten games. Robert Croft's 570 runs for Glamorgan, mostly batting at No. 3, put him fourth among the League's run-scorers, while his economical bowling (3.54 an over) was as valuable to the second division champions as his 16 wickets.

Glamorgan, when they lost their penultimate game to Sussex, might still have been pipped by Worcestershire. But five games without a win had Worcestershire remembering 2000, when dreams of the League title turned into the nightmare of relegation. An immediate return to Division One, not prize money, became their goal, and that was not decided until they beat Essex on the final day of the season.

NORWICH UNION LEAGUE

Division One

	M	*W*	*L*	*T*	*NR*	*Pts*	*Net run-rate*
1 – Kent Spitfires (**5**)	16	11	2	1	2	50	4.26
2 – Leicestershire Foxes (**4**)	16	11	4	0	1	46	7.80
3 – Warwickshire Bears (*3*)	16	8	5	0	3	38	1.58
4 – Somerset Sabres (**6**)	16	7	7	1	1	32	−4.60
5 – Nottinghamshire Outlaws (*2*)	16	7	8	0	1	30	−8.01
6 – Yorkshire Phoenix (**2**)	16	7	9	0	0	28	9.65
7 – Gloucestershire Gladiators (**1**)	16	6	9	0	1	26	1.48
8 – Surrey Lions (*1*)	16	6	10	0	0	24	−5.05
9 – Northamptonshire Steelbacks (**3**)	16	3	12	0	1	14	−9.02

Division Two

	M	*W*	*L*	*T*	*NR*	*Pts*	*Net run-rate*
1 – Glamorgan Dragons (*6*)	16	11	3	0	2	48	15.20
2 – Durham Dynamos (*7*)	16	9	4	0	3	42	1.74
3 – Worcestershire Royals (**7**)	16	9	5	0	2	40	9.61
4 – Hampshire Hawks (*8*)	16	9	6	0	1	38	5.28
5 – Sussex Sharks (**9**)	16	8	7	0	1	34	−1.10
6 – Lancashire Lightning (**8**)	16	5	8	0	3	26	−3.70
7 – Essex Eagles (*5*)	16	5	9	1	1	24	−9.92
8 – Middlesex Crusaders (*4*)	16	3	9	1	3	20	−8.31
9 – Derbyshire Scorpions (*9*)	16	4	12	0	0	16	−7.20

2000 positions are shown in brackets: Division One in bold, Division Two in italic.

The bottom three teams in Division One are relegated for 2002, the top three teams in Division Two are promoted. The bottom four teams in Division Two play each other in the third round of the 2002 Cheltenham & Gloucester Trophy.

When two or more counties finished with an equal number of points, the positions were decided by a) most wins, b) higher net run-rate (runs scored per 100 balls minus runs conceded per 100 balls).

Prize money

Division One
£54,000 for winners: KENT.
£27,000 for runners-up: LEICESTERSHIRE.

Division Two
£20,000 for winners: GLAMORGAN.
£11,000 for runners-up: DURHAM.

Winners of each match (both divisions): £600.

Leading run-scorers: D. S. Lehmann 753, *R. R. Montgomerie* 673, D. J. Bicknell 592, *R. D. B. Croft* 570, A. D. Brown 565, P. D. Bowler 560, *M. P. Maynard* 527, M. E. K. Hussey 510, *V. S. Solanki* 502, G. S. Blewett 501.

Leading wicket-takers: D. R. Brown 29, J. M. M. Averis and *A. J. Bichel* 27, *C. B. Keegan* 26, M. J. Saggers 25, *S. R. Lampitt* and *C. P. Schofield* 23, *A. P. Cowan*, P. S. Jones, *A. Sheriyar* and *C. T. Tremlett* 22.

Most economical bowlers (runs per over, minimum 100 overs): *M. A. Robinson* 3.15, M. A. Sheikh 3.19, *A. D. Mascarenhas* 3.52, *R. D. B. Croft* 3.54, *A. J. Bichel* 3.70, M. W. Alleyne 3.76, *S. R. Lampitt* 3.86, J. Ormond 3.87, *S. D. Udal* 3.87, *G. Welch* 3.88.

Leading wicket-keepers: R. J. Blakey 24 (20 ct, 4 st) and *S. J. Rhodes* 24 (18 ct, 6 st), *K. M. Krikken* 22 (14 ct, 8 st), J. N. Batty 21 (19 ct, 2 st) and *A. Pratt* 21 (14 ct, 7 st), C. M. W. Read 20 (17 ct, 3 st).

Leading fielders: *N. C. Johnson* 15, M. C. J. Ball and D. Byas 11, D. P. Fulton 10, *J. P. Crawley, D. A. Leatherdale* and D. S. Lehmann 9.

Players who appeared in Division Two are shown in italics.

DIVISION ONE

GLOUCESTERSHIRE

At Leicester, April 29. GLOUCESTERSHIRE lost to LEICESTERSHIRE by two wickets.

At Northampton, May 13. GLOUCESTERSHIRE beat NORTHAMPTONSHIRE by 20 runs (D/L method).

GLOUCESTERSHIRE v YORKSHIRE

At Bristol, May 20. Gloucestershire won by five wickets. Toss: Yorkshire.

Windows and Cunliffe made the difference, adding 63 in 15 overs, as Gloucestershire chased a deceptively modest 159 on a slow wicket better suited to placement than power. Windows, reprieved on 31, was going for only the fourth boundary in his fifty when he was caught at long-on, leaving Alleyne to guide his side home with four balls to spare. Earlier, Alleyne's economical bowling had not only kept Yorkshire on a tight rein but also made him the fourth player – after Peter Willey, Trevor Jesty and Ian Botham – to take 200 wickets and score 4,000 runs in the League.

Yorkshire

*D. Byas c and b Ball	22	J. D. Middlebrook b Averis	7
M. J. Wood lbw b Lewis	7	I. D. Fisher run out	0
C. E. W. Silverwood b Lewis	11	M. J. Hoggard b Averis	2
C. White lbw b Alleyne	0	L-b 2, w 3	5
D. S. Lehmann c Williams b Barnett	56		—
M. J. Lumb c Williams b Alleyne	2	1/13 2/25 3/26 (44.5 overs)	158
G. M. Fellows lbw b Ball	30	4/48 5/53 6/126	
†R. J. Blakey not out	16	7/134 8/151 9/151	

Bowling: Lewis 9–3–23–2; Averis 8.5–0–33–2; Alleyne 9–0–17–2; Ball 9–0–39–2; Snape 5–0–24–0; Barnett 4–0–20–1.

Gloucestershire

T. H. C. Hancock c White b Silverwood . 28
K. J. Barnett run out 29
C. G. Taylor lbw b Fellows 0
M. G. N. Windows c Silverwood b Fellows . 51
R. J. Cunliffe lbw b Fellows 28
*M. W. Alleyne not out 11
J. N. Snape not out 2
B 1, l-b 7, w 4 12

1/43 2/44 3/77 4/140 5/149 (5 wkts, 44.2 overs) 161

M. C. J. Ball, †R. C. J. Williams, J. M. M. Averis and J. Lewis did not bat.

Bowling: Hoggard 7.2–2–29–0; Silverwood 6–1–16–1; Fellows 9–1–34–3; Fisher 8–0–33–0; Middlebrook 5–0–18–0; Lehmann 9–1–23–0.

Umpires: J. H. Hampshire and M. J. Kitchen.

At Birmingham, May 29 (day/night). GLOUCESTERSHIRE lost to WARWICKSHIRE by 39 runs.

At Nottingham, June 10. GLOUCESTERSHIRE lost to NOTTINGHAMSHIRE by six wickets (D/L method).

GLOUCESTERSHIRE v WARWICKSHIRE

At Gloucester, June 17. Warwickshire won by five wickets. Toss: Warwickshire.

Put in on a grassy pitch with plenty of movement, defending champions Gloucestershire were ten for four inside six overs and well on course for their fourth defeat in six games. Alleyne's defiant 68 off 115 balls, containing ten fours, and Cawdron's unbeaten 29 off 27 balls at the end lent honour to a sorry scorecard, but they could not save Gloucestershire's weakened attack from having to defend the indefensible. Brown, whose opening spell of three for eight in six overs had destroyed Gloucestershire, now settled into a third-wicket stand of 115 with Ostler. Both hit half-centuries, with Ostler getting Warwickshire home in the 43rd over.

Gloucestershire

T. H. C. Hancock b Brown 2
K. J. Barnett c Piper b Brown 1
M. G. N. Windows b Dagnall 2
C. G. Taylor lbw b Brown 1
*M. W. Alleyne c Sheikh b Giles 68
J. N. Snape c Penney b Sheikh 13
†R. C. Russell lbw b Sheikh 1
M. A. Hardinges b Giles 8
M. C. J. Ball b Sheikh 9
M. J. Cawdron not out 29
J. M. M. Averis not out 4
L-b 5, w 9 14

1/6 2/7 3/10 4/10 5/49 6/55 7/71 8/88 9/134 (9 wkts, 45 overs) 152

Bowling: Brown 9–1–34–3; Dagnall 9–2–22–1; Drakes 9–1–33–0; Sheikh 9–2–17–3; Giles 9–0–41–2.

Warwickshire

N. M. K. Smith b Averis 6
D. L. Hemp c Ball b Cawdron 1
D. R. Brown lbw b Ball 61
D. P. Ostler not out 70
*M. J. Powell c Hancock b Ball 7
T. L. Penney c Taylor b Ball 0
A. F. Giles not out 1
L-b 6, w 4 10

1/3 2/11 3/126 4/148 5/148 (5 wkts, 42.2 overs) 156

†K. J. Piper, V. C. Drakes, M. A. Sheikh and C. E. Dagnall did not bat.

Bowling: Averis 9–1–32–1; Cawdron 8.2–1–28–1; Alleyne 9–1–29–0; Hardinges 6–0–23–0; Barnett 5–0–23–0; Ball 5–1–15–3.

Umpires: J. H. Hampshire and B. Leadbeater.

At Taunton, July 1. GLOUCESTERSHIRE beat SOMERSET by eight runs.

At Canterbury, July 8. GLOUCESTERSHIRE lost to KENT by 31 runs (D/L method).

GLOUCESTERSHIRE v SOMERSET

At Bristol, July 17 (day/night). No result (abandoned).

GLOUCESTERSHIRE v NOTTINGHAMSHIRE

At Cheltenham, July 31. Gloucestershire won by 116 runs. Toss: Nottinghamshire.

Barnett's second one-day hundred of the season, the 16th of his career, launched Gloucestershire towards their highest League total to date, two more than they made against Leicestershire on the College Ground five years earlier. His first 50 came off 40 balls, his second off 71, and the opening stand of 124 with Hewson rattled along at six an over. Harvey added to Nottinghamshire's misery with a 36-ball cameo that produced two sixes and six fours before he was caught on the backward-square boundary. It was just not Nottinghamshire's day. They lost Bicknell to a twisted knee in the field and, in reply, their first four wickets went inside 21 overs. Blewett hit an enterprising 44 off 58 balls before becoming the first of three victims for Snape's off-spin.

Gloucestershire

D. R. Hewson c Logan b Randall	52
K. J. Barnett b Clough	100
I. J. Harvey c Shafayat b Randall	46
M. G. N. Windows c Shafayat b Logan	7
J. N. Snape c Harris b Randall	5
C. G. Taylor c Read b Clough	0
M. A. Hardinges b Logan	26
*M. W. Alleyne run out	5
M. C. J. Ball not out	17
†R. C. Russell not out	1
B 4, l-b 13, w 6, n-b 4	27
1/124 2/190 3/213 4/223 5/224 6/225 7/235 8/282 (8 wkts, 45 overs)	286

J. M. M. Averis did not bat.

Bowling: Logan 9–1–55–2; Harris 9–0–77–0; Clough 9–0–59–2; Pietersen 9–1–34–0; Randall 9–0–44–3.

Nottinghamshire

G. E. Welton c Russell b Averis	4
G. S. Blewett c Averis b Snape	44
P. Johnson c Snape b Averis	17
K. P. Pietersen c Hewson b Ball	19
B. M. Shafayat run out	24
†C. M. W. Read c Ball b Snape	2
G. D. Clough c and b Snape	9
R. J. Logan lbw b Hardinges	21
S. J. Randall not out	15
A. J. Harris c Alleyne b Ball	8
*D. J. Bicknell absent hurt	
L-b 2, w 1, n-b 4	7
1/13 2/51 3/86 4/86 5/89 6/104 7/137 8/147 9/170 (39 overs)	170

Bowling: Harvey 5–0–19–0; Averis 7–0–35–2; Alleyne 5–0–12–0; Ball 8–0–32–2; Snape 9–2–34–3; Hardinges 5–0–36–1.

Umpires: R. Palmer and P. Willey.

GLOUCESTERSHIRE v NORTHAMPTONSHIRE

At Cheltenham, August 5. Gloucestershire won by 83 runs. Toss: Northamptonshire.

This was Sunday cricket for the all-action enthusiast. Gloucestershire ran up 344 for six, the highest total since the League settled on a 45-over format and the third-highest in the competition's history. Harvey blasted 67 in 34 balls, with three sixes and eight fours, but Windows out-hit him with five sixes and ten fours as he scorched to 117 off 94 deliveries, his first League century. Chris Taylor, given his county cap before the start, partnered Windows in a fourth-wicket stand of 155 in 18 overs, but retired soon after with a cricked neck – sustained, it was suggested, through following too many balls in the sky. Strong's nine overs cost a competition-record 99. Five wickets for Averis ensured Northamptonshire were not going to cut loose.

Gloucestershire

D. R. Hewson c Strong b Penberthy	38
K. J. Barnett c Ripley b Strong	17
I. J. Harvey c Loye b Taylor	67
M. G. N. Windows c Taylor b Brown	117
C. G. Taylor retired hurt	63
J. N. Snape not out	15
M. A. Hardinges st Ripley b Swann	5
M. C. J. Ball c Ripley b Swann	0
*M. W. Alleyne not out	9
L-b 5, w 4, n-b 4	13
1/29 2/113 3/149 4/304 5/326 6/326 (6 wkts, 45 overs)	344

†R. C. Russell and J. M. M. Averis did not bat.

Taylor retired hurt at 315.

Bowling: Strong 9–0–99–1; Taylor 9–0–45–1; Brown 7–0–60–1; Penberthy 9–1–51–1; Swann 7–0–35–2; Weekes 4–0–49–0.

Northamptonshire

M. E. K. Hussey c Russell b Averis	4
M. B. Loye c Ball b Averis	28
G. P. Swann b Averis	26
R. J. Warren c sub b Ball	34
A. S. Rollins st Russell b Ball	29
A. L. Penberthy c Snape b Averis	52
L. C. Weekes c Averis b Snape	1
*†D. Ripley c Alleyne b Averis	35
J. P. Taylor c Hewson b Ball	19
M. R. Strong not out	6
J. F. Brown b Snape	1
L-b 5, w 11, n-b 10	26
1/6 2/60 3/63 4/115 5/135 6/140 7/225 8/236 9/258 (40.5 overs)	261

Bowling: Harvey 6–0–42–0; Averis 9–1–56–5; Alleyne 7–0–32–0; Ball 8–0–49–3; Snape 7.5–0–53–2; Barnett 3–0–24–0.

Umpires: M. R. Benson and R. Julian.

At The Oval, August 12. GLOUCESTERSHIRE lost to SURREY by two wickets.

GLOUCESTERSHIRE v KENT

At Bristol, August 27. Kent won by one run. Toss: Kent.

Kent captain Fleming kept their title hopes alive – six points behind Leicestershire with three games to go – but dumped Gloucestershire in the relegation zone. After winning the toss and deciding to open, he hit 58 off 75 balls, then later claimed a League-best five for 40. Ball was run out off Fleming's final delivery, trying to level the scores. Fleming's half-century was his first of the season in the League, but it did not look enough when Kent lost their last five wickets for 13 in five overs as Averis again claimed five. The large crowd, enjoying the Bank Holiday sunshine, expected a home win as Harvey took Gloucestershire to 97 for one, but he fell in Patel's first over. Patel and Ealham then constricted Hancock and Windows to 17 from ten overs, and Fleming squeezed that initiative into points.

Kent

*M. V. Fleming c and b Ball	58
D. P. Fulton c Ball b Averis	10
J. B. Hockley b Alleyne	39
A. Symonds lbw b Ball	21
M. J. Walker b Hardinges	8
†P. A. Nixon run out	20
R. W. T. Key b Averis	19
M. A. Ealham not out	4
M. J. McCague c Hewson b Averis	4
M. M. Patel b Averis	0
M. J. Saggers c Alleyne b Averis	0
B 1, l-b 4, w 8, n-b 4	17
1/21 2/110 3/120 4/136 5/147 6/187 7/188 8/196 9/200 (43.5 overs)	200

Bowling: Averis 8.5–1–40–5; Harvey 8–0–42–0; Hardinges 9–1–36–1; Alleyne 9–0–36–1; Ball 9–0–41–2.

Gloucestershire

T. H. C. Hancock lbw b Fleming	43
K. J. Barnett c Nixon b Saggers	15
I. J. Harvey b Patel	45
M. G. N. Windows c Ealham b Fleming	33
D. R. Hewson run out	15
C. G. Taylor c McCague b Fleming	7
*M. W. Alleyne lbw b Fleming	10
†R. C. Russell b Fleming	9
M. A. Hardinges not out	5
M. C. J. Ball run out	3
L-b 4, w 10	14
1/34 2/97 3/133 4/160 5/170 6/170 7/181 8/194 9/199 (9 wkts, 45 overs)	199

J. M. M. Averis did not bat.

Bowling: Saggers 6–1–27–1; Ealham 9–2–42–0; McCague 5–0–34–0; Fleming 7–1–40–5; Patel 9–3–19–1; Symonds 9–0–33–0.

Umpires: B. Dudleston and J. H. Evans.

GLOUCESTERSHIRE v LEICESTERSHIRE

At Bristol, September 3. Gloucestershire won by 28 runs (D/L method). Toss: Gloucestershire.

Having lost to Somerset two days earlier in the Cheltenham & Gloucester final, Leicestershire faltered again. This defeat left them only two points clear of Kent at the top of Division One. Hancock made good use of a batsman's pitch, 38 of his 68-ball 67 coming in boundaries, but it still needed Alleyne and Cunliffe to get the momentum going again, adding 53 in nine overs ahead of the incoming rain. Facing a revised target of 215 in 38 overs, Leicestershire lost half their wickets for 100. Smith and Stevens matched Gloucestershire's seventh-wicket run-rate with 48 in eight overs, but the visitors were heading for their third League loss in five games once Smith was run out, answering his partner's unwise call.

Gloucestershire

T. H. C. Hancock b Shahid Afridi	67
K. J. Barnett b Wells	23
I. J. Harvey b Malcolm	13
†R. C. Russell c Habib b Shahid Afridi	24
M. G. N. Windows c Stevens b Wells	19
D. R. Hewson c Smith b Ormond	9
*M. W. Alleyne b Maddy	25
R. J. Cunliffe not out	27
M. C. J. Ball not out	10
B 2, l-b 5, w 8	15
1/70 2/83 3/127 4/142 5/161 6/162 7/215 (7 wkts, 45 overs)	232

A. N. Bressington and J. M. M. Averis did not bat.

Bowling: Ormond 9–1–48–1; Malcolm 7–1–48–1; Wells 9–1–45–2; Maddy 9–0–39–1; Shahid Afridi 9–1–33–2; Dakin 2–0–12–0.

Leicestershire

T. R. Ward b Averis	10	†N. D. Burns c Cunliffe b Ball	6
Shahid Afridi c Barnett b Averis	17	J. Ormond c Harvey b Averis	4
D. L. Maddy c Barnett b Bressington	2	D. E. Malcolm c Ball b Harvey	0
J. M. Dakin c Bressington b Ball	23	L-b 2, w 2, n-b 2	6
A. Habib run out	17		—
B. F. Smith run out	53	1/25 2/31 3/33 (35.1 overs)	186
*V. J. Wells c Windows b Alleyne	2	4/57 5/100 6/106	
D. I. Stevens not out	46	7/154 8/173 9/182	

Bowling: Averis 7–1–40–3; Harvey 6.1–0–36–1; Bressington 7–0–31–1; Alleyne 8–0–27–1; Ball 7–0–50–2.

Umpires: T. E. Jesty and A. A. Jones.

At Scarborough, September 10. GLOUCESTERSHIRE lost to YORKSHIRE by 70 runs.

GLOUCESTERSHIRE v SURREY

At Bristol, September 16. Surrey won by 36 runs. Toss: Surrey.

Surrey, already relegated, took Gloucestershire down with them. The defending champions had to win to stay up, and losing three wickets to Murtagh in the 12th over was a serious setback to their pursuit of a moderate 158 on another slow Bristol pitch. Surrey's total was built around Gareth Batty's third successive half-century, after he survived a difficult chance to mid-off early on. Windows rallied Gloucestershire with a watchful 37, but Batty chipped in again with a second wicket and Hollioake wrapped up the innings with four for 19 as his second-string side won with three overs to spare. There were presentations to umpire Ray Julian, standing in his last match on the county circuit, and groundsman David Bridle, retiring after 34 years with Gloucestershire.

Surrey

S. A. Newman b Smith	10	†J. N. Batty run out	11
A. D. Brown c Bressington b Smith	12	T. J. Murtagh not out	2
G. J. Batty c Averis b Ball	54	B 1, l-b 4, w 2	7
M. A. Carberry run out	20		—
R. R. Clarke b Alleyne	7	1/19 2/36 3/90 (8 wkts, 45 overs)	157
I. J. Ward c Alleyne b Ball	20	4/103 5/110 6/135	
*A. J. Hollioake c Alleyne b Snape	14	7/153 8/157	

P. J. Sampson and E. S. H. Giddins did not bat.

Bowling: Averis 8–0–26–0; Smith 9–3–19–2; Bressington 7–0–30–0; Ball 9–0–36–2; Alleyne 9–0–25–1; Snape 3–0–16–1.

Gloucestershire

T. H. C. Hancock c Giddins b Murtagh	10	A. N. Bressington c Brown b Hollioake	15
K. J. Barnett b Sampson	8	J. M. M. Averis c G. J. Batty b Hollioake	5
D. R. Hewson c J. N. Batty b Murtagh	1	A. M. Smith b Hollioake	0
J. N. Snape lbw b Murtagh	0	B 1, l-b 10, w 6	17
M. G. N. Windows c Brown b G. J. Batty	37		—
*M. W. Alleyne b G. J. Batty	9	1/19 2/29 3/29 (42 overs)	121
†R. C. Russell b Hollioake	4	4/31 5/61 6/84	
M. C. J. Ball not out	15	7/85 8/111 9/120	

Bowling: Sampson 9–0–25–1; Murtagh 9–4–15–3; G. J. Batty 9–2–20–2; Giddins 7–1–31–0; Hollioake 8–2–19–4.

Umpires: R. Julian and A. G. T. Whitehead.

KENT

KENT v WARWICKSHIRE

At Canterbury, April 29. No result (abandoned).

At Taunton, May 20. KENT beat SOMERSET by 31 runs.

KENT v SOMERSET

At Tunbridge Wells, June 3. Tied. Toss: Kent.

Turner's improvisation earned him a deserved fifty and Somerset their first points of the season when he and Jones extracted 14 runs from the final over. With five needed from Fleming's last delivery, Turner scooped it over his head to the long-leg boundary. Having been treated to an unscheduled pre-match fly-past by the Red Arrows, the crowd of almost 4,000 at The Nevill could hardly complain about value for money. Hockley gave Kent a good start with 41 off 31 balls, but few of the others found scoring as easy. Somerset had looked out of contention at 92 for five, after Trott had bowled impressively against his former county, but 62 in 12 overs from Turner and Dutch made the dramatic finale possible.

Kent

J. B. Hockley b Jones	41
D. P. Fulton c Turner b Trego	12
E. T. Smith lbw b Jones	3
D. J. Cullinan b Kerr	30
M. J. Walker c and b Dutch	23
M. A. Ealham lbw b Dutch	19
†P. A. Nixon lbw b Grove	1
*M. V. Fleming b Jones	23
J. M. Golding lbw b Blackwell	9
M. M. Patel not out	11
B. J. Trott not out	2
L-b 3, w 2, n-b 2	7
1/49 2/55 3/57 4/107 5/125 6/126 7/142 8/162 9/178 (9 wkts, 45 overs)	181

Bowling: Jones 9–1–29–3; Kerr 6–1–36–1; Trego 6–0–40–1; Grove 8–1–27–1; Dutch 9–1–22–2; Blackwell 7–0–24–1.

Somerset

P. D. Bowler c Patel b Ealham	9
*J. Cox lbw b Trott	21
P. C. L. Holloway c Nixon b Trott	4
M. Burns c Fulton b Patel	32
I. D. Blackwell c Hockley b Patel	10
†R. J. Turner not out	56
K. P. Dutch st Nixon b Fleming	28
P. D. Trego st Nixon b Golding	4
J. I. D. Kerr b Golding	0
P. S. Jones not out	1
B 4, l-b 5, w 7	16
1/25 2/37 3/38 4/65 5/92 6/154 7/167 8/167 (8 wkts, 45 overs)	181

J. O. Grove did not bat.

Bowling: Trott 9–4–19–2; Golding 9–0–38–2; Ealham 9–1–34–1; Fleming 9–0–54–1; Patel 9–1–27–2.

Umpires: V. A. Holder and P. Willey.

At Leeds, June 10. KENT beat YORKSHIRE by four wickets.

KENT v NOTTINGHAMSHIRE

At Maidstone, June 17. Kent won by 60 runs (D/L method). Toss: Nottinghamshire.

Kent were 85 for three after 20 overs, but Nixon's assault on Stemp – he went for six, four, four, four, four leg-byes and six in the 23rd over – helped them add 103 off the next ten. A late start and subsequent stoppage had reduced the innings to 30 overs each. Hockley batted throughout Kent's for his highest one-day score. Chasing a target of 194, Nottinghamshire were never in the hunt after Walker ran out Blewett in the second over. Bicknell resisted with 59 off 63 balls; once he went, sixth out with the total 100, Kent were poised to overtake Nottinghamshire and join Leicestershire at the top of the first division.

Kent

J. B. Hockley not out	70	J. M. Golding c Johnson b Smith	15
D. P. Fulton c Read b Harris	10	R. W. T. Key not out	5
E. T. Smith c Pietersen b Harris	2	B 2, l-b 6, w 4	12
M. J. Walker c Read b Clough	34		——
†P. A. Nixon c Harris b Afzaal	29	1/17 2/19 3/83 (6 wkts, 30 overs)	188
*M. V. Fleming c sub b Blewett	11	4/129 5/140 6/168	

M. M. Patel, M. J. Saggers and B. J. Trott did not bat.

Bowling: Smith 6–0–23–1; Harris 6–1–34–2; Blewett 6–0–33–1; Clough 6–0–30–1; Stemp 4–0–41–0; Afzaal 2–0–19–1.

Nottinghamshire

*D. J. Bicknell c Key b Patel	59	A. J. Harris c Nixon b Walker	0
G. S. Blewett run out	0	G. J. Smith b Walker	8
P. Johnson c Nixon b Saggers	4	R. D. Stemp not out	1
U. Afzaal c Fulton b Saggers	4	L-b 2, w 2	4
†C. M. W. Read lbw b Trott	4		——
G. E. Welton c Patel b Golding	15	1/2 2/7 3/23 (28.1 overs)	133
K. P. Pietersen lbw b Fleming	11	4/36 5/77 6/100	
G. D. Clough c Patel b Golding	23	7/100 8/101 9/131	

Bowling: Saggers 6–0–21–2; Trott 6–0–30–1; Fleming 6–1–29–1; Golding 5–0–18–2; Patel 2–0–16–1; Walker 3.1–0–17–2.

Umpires: T. E. Jesty and R. A. White.

At The Oval, June 24. KENT beat SURREY by two wickets.

KENT v GLOUCESTERSHIRE

At Canterbury, July 8. Kent won by 31 runs (D/L method). Toss: Gloucestershire.

Kent preserved their unbeaten League record with a fourth successive win that seemed unlikely when they were dismissed for 114. Russell took his 200th catch in the competition, and Barnett needed only 20 balls to take four for 12 – his best figures in 313 League games – after the match had been cut to 33 overs a side. However, Gloucestershire were soon eight for three in pursuit of 118. When Snape and Barnett fell in successive overs, leaving them 32 for six, Harvey was the visitors' best bet. But his 39 in 40 balls, including three sixes off Golding, one of which smashed a picture in a vacant hospitality box, was not enough. Saggers's five wickets gave him one-day best figures, while Ealham conceded only five runs in seven overs.

Kent

J. B. Hockley c Ball b Averis	2	J. M. Golding not out	7
D. P. Fulton b Averis	23	M. J. Saggers lbw b Barnett	0
R. W. T. Key st Russell b Ball	21	B. J. Trott b Barnett	1
M. J. Walker b Barnett	8	L-b 4, w 3	7
A. Symonds c Russell b Ball	16		
*M. A. Ealham st Russell b Alleyne	16	1/5 2/45 3/61 (29.2 overs)	114
†P. A. Nixon c Alleyne b Barnett	13	4/63 5/88 6/99	
G. O. Jones lbw b Alleyne	0	7/99 8/111 9/111	

Bowling: Harvey 5–1–14–0; Averis 6–0–17–2; Hardinges 2–0–12–0; Ball 7–0–27–2; Barnett 3.2–0–12–4; Alleyne 6–1–28–2.

Gloucestershire

D. R. Hewson b Trott	5	M. A. Hardinges run out	2
K. J. Barnett c Fulton b Ealham	14	M. C. J. Ball not out	3
M. G. N. Windows c Hockley b Saggers	1	J. M. M. Averis b Saggers	3
C. G. Taylor lbw b Saggers	0	B 1, l-b 2, w 2, n-b 2	7
*M. W. Alleyne lbw b Saggers	5		
J. N. Snape c Nixon b Trott	4	1/7 2/8 3/8 (27 overs)	86
I. J. Harvey c Key b Saggers	39	4/18 5/30 6/32	
†R. C. Russell c Hockley b Ealham	3	7/64 8/75 9/81	

Bowling: Saggers 7–0–22–5; Trott 7–0–20–2; Ealham 7–3–5–2; Golding 3–0–24–0; Symonds 3–1–12–0.

Umpires: D. J. Constant and N. A. Mallender.

At Nottingham, July 15. KENT beat NOTTINGHAMSHIRE by one run.

At Leicester, July 22. KENT lost to LEICESTERSHIRE by five wickets.

KENT v LEICESTERSHIRE

At Canterbury, August 5. Leicestershire won by 14 runs. Toss: Leicestershire.

Leicestershire, unbeaten in the League, went eight points clear of Kent at the top of Division One with their ninth win. Shahid Afridi launched their innings with 24 off 11 balls (four fours, one six), and Stevens and captain Wells – released by Kent ten years earlier – later added 75 at almost a run a ball. Patel, Symonds and Ealham contained them after that, but Kent in reply made a poor start. Key took the anchor role in stands of 52 with Fulton and 79 with Nixon, whose 63-ball half-century, containing only one boundary, still left Kent needing 23 off the final over.

Leicestershire

I. J. Sutcliffe c Nixon b Trott	37	J. Ormond not out	1
Shahid Afridi c Walker b Fleming	24	S. A. J. Boswell lbw b Ealham	1
D. I. Stevens b Patel	51		
*V. J. Wells c Nixon b Symonds	39	L-b 2, w 2	4
B. F. Smith lbw b Patel	22		
D. L. Maddy lbw b Symonds	13	1/46 2/80 3/155 (9 wkts, 45 overs)	236
†N. D. Burns run out	34	4/155 5/179 6/201	
A. Habib c Fleming b Ealham	10	7/232 8/234 9/236	

D. E. Malcolm did not bat.

Bowling: Saggers 7–1–43–0; Trott 6–0–51–1; Fleming 7–0–35–1; Ealham 9–1–36–2; Patel 9–0–46–2; Symonds 7–0–23–2.

Kent

J. B. Hockley c Stevens b Boswell	1	M. M. Patel b Ormond	6
D. P. Fulton lbw b Wells	46	M. J. Saggers not out	4
A. Symonds c and b Boswell	5	B. J. Trott not out	0
M. J. Walker c Stevens b Malcolm	5	B 2, l-b 15, w 8	25
R. W. T. Key lbw b Maddy	59		—
†P. A. Nixon run out	55	1/5 2/20 3/32 (9 wkts, 45 overs)	222
M. A. Ealham b Shahid Afridi	1	4/84 5/163 6/168	
*M. V. Fleming b Maddy	15	7/207 8/215 9/215	

Bowling: Malcolm 8–0–37–1; Boswell 5–0–25–2; Ormond 9–1–31–1; Wells 7–1–28–1; Shahid Afridi 9–1–49–1; Maddy 7–0–35–2.

Umpires: V. A. Holder and J. F. Steele.

At Northampton, August 12. NORTHAMPTONSHIRE v KENT. No result (abandoned).

KENT v SURREY

At Canterbury, August 14 (day/night). Kent won by 43 runs. Toss: Kent.

Three run-outs by Fleming in the space of four balls, all with direct hits, earned Kent an unlikely victory as Surrey lost seven wickets for 17 runs. He had already triggered this astonishing collapse by running out Ward in the 31st over, also with a direct hit. Next over, Ben Hollioake was furious to be given out stumped when third umpire Trevor Jesty decided, following a lengthy review of the evidence, that he had momentarily lifted his back foot. Symonds's 74 off 68 balls was the cornerstone of Kent's innings, after Bicknell's three wickets had caused a faltering start; he fell to Gareth Batty, who went on to return a career-best four for 36.

Kent

*M. V. Fleming c Brown b Bicknell	2	M. M. Patel lbw b Saqlain Mushtaq	15
D. P. Fulton c Giddins b Bicknell	11	M. J. Saggers b G. J. Batty	2
J. B. Hockley b Bicknell	16	B. J. Trott not out	0
R. W. T. Key c Brown b Saqlain Mushtaq	26	L-b 1, w 17, n-b 4	22
A. Symonds lbw b G. J. Batty	74		—
M. J. Walker c Ward b B. C. Hollioake	15	1/3 2/32 3/34 (42 overs)	207
†P. A. Nixon c J. N. Batty b G. J. Batty	19	4/127 5/151 6/164	
M. J. McCague lbw b G. J. Batty	5	7/170 8/201 9/205	

Bowling: Bicknell 7–0–35–3; Giddins 5–0–39–0; Murtagh 5–0–29–0; Saqlain Mushtaq 8–1–36–2; B. C. Hollioake 9–1–31–1; G. J. Batty 8–0–36–4.

Surrey

I. J. Ward run out	51	Saqlain Mushtaq run out	0
A. D. Brown c Hockley b Saggers	27	T. J. Murtagh not out	4
G. J. Batty lbw b Saggers	0	E. S. H. Giddins b McCague	3
*A. J. Hollioake c Nixon b McCague	43	B 6, l-b 5, w 8	19
B. C. Hollioake st Nixon b Symonds	13		—
N. Shahid c Nixon b Symonds	1	1/42 2/42 3/116 (38.1 overs)	164
M. P. Bicknell run out	3	4/147 5/147 6/151	
†J. N. Batty run out	0	7/152 8/152 9/153	

Bowling: Saggers 8–1–36–2; Trott 9–0–39–0; Patel 4–0–22–0; Fleming 6–0–24–0; McCague 7.1–1–21–2; Symonds 4–0–11–2.

Umpires: B. Dudleston and K. E. Palmer.

At Bristol, August 27. KENT beat GLOUCESTERSHIRE by one run.

KENT v YORKSHIRE

At Canterbury, August 29. Kent won by eight runs. Toss: Kent.

Another three-wickets-in-four-balls finish had home fans smiling in disbelief, with Saggers producing the turnaround this time as Yorkshire looked to score 13 off the last over. Byas and Dawson were bowled by consecutive balls, and Blakey was caught at long-off from the penultimate one. In the previous over, Fulton had run out McGrath, whose solid maiden League hundred and 108-run stand in 21 overs with White had taken Yorkshire so close. Only Hockley and Symonds managed much of a partnership in a Kent total that looked below par, adding 86 in 14 overs. Its highlight was Symonds's straight-driven six off Sidebottom that cleared the pavilion. Yorkshire were clear favourites when they needed 27 from five overs, with seven wickets in hand, but skilful bowling by Fleming and Ealham set up the denouement for Saggers.

Kent

*M. V. Fleming b Elstub	17
D. P. Fulton b Elstub	17
J. B. Hockley b Lehmann	66
A. Symonds st Blakey b Dawson	37
M. J. Walker c Wood b Lehmann	15
†P. A. Nixon b White	14
R. W. T. Key c Byas b Lehmann	3
M. A. Ealham not out	23
M. M. Patel c Lehmann b Hoggard	4
M. J. Saggers not out	6
B 1, l-b 7, w 6	14
1/37 2/40 3/126 4/161 5/163 6/167 7/189 8/194 (8 wkts, 45 overs)	216

B. J. Trott did not bat.

Bowling: Hoggard 7–1–39–1; Elstub 9–1–30–2; White 9–0–34–1; Sidebottom 1–0–12–0; Dawson 9–1–46–1; Hamilton 2–0–16–0; Lehmann 8–0–31–3.

Yorkshire

M. J. Wood b Trott	5
G. M. Hamilton lbw b Ealham	20
A. McGrath run out	102
D. S. Lehmann c Ealham b Patel	24
C. White c Patel b Ealham	44
*D. Byas b Saggers	0
†R. J. Blakey c Symonds b Saggers	1
R. K. J. Dawson b Saggers	0
R. J. Sidebottom not out	3
C. J. Elstub not out	0
B 5, l-b 2, w 2	9
1/5 2/50 3/89 4/197 5/204 6/205 7/205 8/208 (8 wkts, 45 overs)	208

M. J. Hoggard did not bat.

Bowling: Saggers 9–1–46–3; Trott 8–2–31–1; Ealham 9–0–38–2; Patel 8–0–38–1; Symonds 4–0–15–0; Fleming 7–0–33–0.

Umpires: A. A. Jones and B. Leadbeater.

KENT v NORTHAMPTONSHIRE

At Canterbury, September 9. Kent won by 26 runs. Toss: Kent.

Kent captain Fleming turned in another inspirational all-round display to ensure their fourth successive win and keep the title race open to the last weekend of the season. His career-best one-day score of 125, off 107 balls including 15 fours, and good support down the order produced a demanding target for Northamptonshire, albeit on a true surface. Though already relegated, they accepted the challenge, with Graeme Swann (61 off 44 balls) and Cook (55 at a run a ball) leading the charge. However, Fleming's three for 28 was evidence enough, were evidence required, that the force was with him.

Kent

*M. V. Fleming run out	125	M. J. Walker not out	7
D. P. Fulton c Blain b Strong	39		
J. B. Hockley c Warren b Cook	32	B 4, l-b 6, w 1	11
A. Symonds c Taylor b G. P. Swann	31		
†P. A. Nixon c Hussey b Strong	7	1/98 2/169 3/225 (5 wkts, 45 overs)	284
M. A. Ealham not out	32	4/237 5/246	

R. W. T. Key, B. J. Trott, M. M. Patel and M. J. Saggers did not bat.

Bowling: Blain 4–0–40–0; Taylor 7–0–47–0; Strong 9–0–62–2; Cook 9–1–37–1; Brown 7–0–38–0; G. P. Swann 9–0–50–1.

Northamptonshire

*M. E. K. Hussey c Fulton b Fleming	19	M. R. Strong b Saggers	9
G. P. Swann b Fleming	61	J. A. R. Blain not out	3
R. J. Warren b Ealham	40	J. F. Brown not out	1
D. J. Sales lbw b Fleming	7	B 3, l-b 8, w 14, n-b 2	27
A. J. Swann b Patel	3		
J. W. Cook c Ealham b Trott	55	1/74 2/99 3/122 (9 wkts, 45 overs)	258
†T. M. B. Bailey c Hockley b Saggers	22	4/131 5/158 6/218	
J. P. Taylor c Fleming b Saggers	11	7/227 8/251 9/257	

Bowling: Saggers 8–0–52–3; Trott 6–0–49–1; Ealham 9–0–54–1; Fleming 9–2–28–3; Patel 9–0–41–1; Symonds 4–0–23–0.

Umpires: N. G. Cowley and G. Sharp.

At Birmingham, September 16. KENT beat WARWICKSHIRE by nine runs (D/L method).

LEICESTERSHIRE

LEICESTERSHIRE v GLOUCESTERSHIRE

At Leicester, April 29. Leicestershire won by two wickets. Toss: Leicestershire.

Leicestershire, requiring 16 off the last two overs from Alleyne and Averis, scrambled to victory with three balls to spare in a low-scoring match reduced to 41 overs a side after a delayed start. Malcolm put Gloucestershire on the back foot by taking the vital wickets of Barnett and Harvey as four wickets fell in 13 balls, and their total of 116 looked inadequate – until the home side slumped to 14 for five against Lewis and Harvey. They were 76 for eight in the 32nd over when Dakin and Ormond came to the rescue with an unbroken stand of 41.

Gloucestershire

T. H. C. Hancock c Burns b Ormond	17	M. J. Cawdron lbw b Stelling	0
K. J. Barnett c Burns b Malcolm	27	J. M. M. Averis c Smith b Wells	14
I. J. Harvey c Maddy b Malcolm	8	J. Lewis not out	2
R. J. Cunliffe run out	32	L-b 2, w 5	7
M. G. N. Windows c Burns b Malcolm	0		
*M. W. Alleyne run out	4	1/44 2/52 3/53 (38.4 overs)	116
J. N. Snape c Smith b Stelling	0	4/53 5/69 6/69	
†R. C. J. Williams run out	5	7/82 8/82 9/103	

Bowling: Ormond 9–1–29–1; Malcolm 8–0–34–3; Dakin 6–1–16–0; Stelling 8–1–20–2; Marsh 4.4–0–10–0; Wells 3–0–5–1.

Leicestershire

*V. J. Wells lbw b Lewis	4	W. F. Stelling b Averis	10
T. R. Ward c Williams b Harvey	0	J. Ormond not out	13
B. F. Smith b Lewis	1		
D. J. Marsh c Williams b Harvey	5	L-b 4, w 1	5
D. L. Maddy c Williams b Lewis	3		
A. Habib b Cawdron	20	1/4 2/4 3/10 (8 wkts, 40.3 overs)	117
†N. D. Burns b Alleyne	20	4/10 5/14 6/51	
J. M. Dakin not out	36	7/57 8/76	

D. E. Malcolm did not bat.

Bowling: Lewis 8–2–20–3; Harvey 9–4–7–2; Averis 7.3–0–31–1; Cawdron 8–2–16–1; Alleyne 8–0–39–1.

Umpires: J. W. Holder and G. Sharp.

At The Oval, May 20. LEICESTERSHIRE beat SURREY by four wickets.

LEICESTERSHIRE v NOTTINGHAMSHIRE

At Oakham School, June 3. Leicestershire won by six wickets. Toss: Leicestershire.

Dakin's belligerent opening batting and an excellent all-round game from Marsh, including a terrific one-handed diving catch at short cover, steered Leicestershire to the top of the League. Marsh's left-arm spin helped spark the collapse that saw Nottinghamshire's last five wickets fall for five runs in 12 balls, undoing the good work of Johnson's 75 in 74 balls. Chasing 205, Wells and Dakin had 70 up in nine overs, with the hard-hitting Dakin going on to 65 from 55 balls. Marsh's unbeaten 67 off 61 walked Leicestershire home with nine overs to spare.

Nottinghamshire

*D. J. Bicknell c Burns b Boswell	7	A. J. Harris st Burns b Marsh	1
G. E. Welton c Marsh b Ormond	38	R. D. Stemp c and b Marsh	0
G. S. Blewett c Smith b Boswell	0	G. J. Smith b Maddy	0
U. Afzaal c Ward b Marsh	43	L-b 3, w 4	7
P. Johnson c Burns b Maddy	75		
K. P. Pietersen c Maddy b Marsh	15	1/15 2/17 3/74 (43.2 overs)	204
†C. M. W. Read c Ward b Maddy	14	4/118 5/170 6/199	
P. J. Franks not out	4	7/200 8/203 9/203	

Bowling: Malcolm 6–0–25–0; Boswell 7–0–33–2; Ormond 7–0–38–1; Dakin 9–1–27–0; Marsh 9–0–44–4; Wells 1–0–14–0; Maddy 4.2–0–20–3.

Leicestershire

*V. J. Wells c Harris b Franks	21	D. L. Maddy not out	8
J. M. Dakin c Stemp b Pietersen	65	B 1, l-b 9, w 4, n-b 2	16
T. R. Ward c Pietersen b Franks	4		
D. J. Marsh not out	67	1/70 2/101 (4 wkts, 36 overs)	207
B. F. Smith c Read b Stemp	26	3/101 4/197	

D. I. Stevens, †N. D. Burns, J. Ormond, S. A. J. Boswell and D. E. Malcolm did not bat.

Bowling: Smith 4–0–32–0; Harris 4–0–35–0; Franks 7–1–26–2; Blewett 2–0–23–0; Pietersen 5–0–25–1; Stemp 8–2–32–1; Afzaal 6–1–24–0.

Umpires: B. Dudleston and B. Leadbeater.

LEICESTERSHIRE v NORTHAMPTONSHIRE

At Leicester, June 17. Leicestershire won by three wickets. Toss: Leicestershire.

An unbroken partnership of 116 in 21 overs between Burns and DeFreitas, an eighth-wicket record in the League, produced a dramatic victory that left vanquished Northamptonshire shell-shocked. Despite their own disappointing batting, the visitors seemed to be heading for their first points of the season when Leicestershire were 30 for six in the tenth over, and later 57 for seven. With the exception of Wells, none of the top six survived more than ten balls from Weekes and Cousins. However, a one-day best 90 (14 fours) off 96 balls by wicket-keeper Burns, ably supported by DeFreitas, turned the League leaders round and brought victory with seven overs in hand. Burns was awarded his county cap after the match.

Northamptonshire

M. E. K. Hussey lbw b Ormond	16
M. B. Loye c Burns b Boswell	10
R. J. Warren b Ormond	3
G. P. Swann lbw b Maddy	22
A. J. Swann c Dakin b Marsh	47
A. L. Penberthy run out	3
K. J. Innes c Burns b Dakin	19
*†D. Ripley c Wells b Dakin	12
L. C. Weekes not out	10
D. M. Cousins b Dakin	3
J. F. Brown not out	1
B 5, l-b 9, w 10, n-b 2	26
1/20 2/37 3/40 4/83 5/88 6/127 7/143 8/156 9/169 (9 wkts, 45 overs)	172

Bowling: Ormond 9–3–25–2; Boswell 9–1–27–1; DeFreitas 4–0–18–0; Maddy 6–0–19–1; Wells 5–1–18–0; Marsh 7–0–37–1; Dakin 5–0–14–3.

Leicestershire

*V. J. Wells lbw b Weekes	4
J. M. Dakin lbw b Cousins	17
T. R. Ward b Cousins	2
D. J. Marsh c Ripley b Weekes	1
B. F. Smith c Penberthy b Weekes	0
D. L. Maddy lbw b Cousins	3
D. I. Stevens b Innes	10
†N. D. Burns not out	90
P. A. J. DeFreitas not out	33
L-b 8, w 5	13
1/20 2/22 3/23 4/25 5/28 6/30 7/57 (7 wkts, 38 overs)	173

S. A. J. Boswell and J. Ormond did not bat.

Bowling: Cousins 8–1–34–3; Weekes 9–2–34–3; Penberthy 9–2–27–0; Innes 5–2–34–1; Brown 5–0–18–0; G. P. Swann 2–0–18–0.

Umpires: D. J. Constant and K. E. Palmer.

At Birmingham, June 24. LEICESTERSHIRE beat WARWICKSHIRE by five wickets.

LEICESTERSHIRE v SURREY

At Leicester, July 8. Leicestershire won by 128 runs. Toss: Surrey.

With Stewart, Thorpe, Mark Butcher, Ramprakash and Ward all missing, Surrey were simply overpowered as Leicestershire swept to victory on the back of their highest League score of the season to date. Stevens gave the innings early momentum with 63 from 71 balls, Sutcliffe helping him get 100 on the board in the 19th over, and Maddy and Habib later added 67 in six overs to reverse a middle-order hiccup. Surrey's reply was always behind the clock. They struggled to 83 for five in 25 overs and eventually capitulated to 112 all out, having hit only one boundary; Maddy claimed their last three wickets in four balls.

Leicestershire

J. M. Dakin c J. N. Batty b Giddins	10
I. J. Sutcliffe c Greenidge b Saqlain Mushtaq	36
D. I. Stevens c J. N. Batty b B. C. Hollioake	63
B. F. Smith c A. J. Hollioake b B. C. Hollioake	13
*V. J. Wells b G. J. Batty	12
D. L. Maddy b A. J. Hollioake	44
†N. D. Burns c A. J. Hollioake b B. C. Hollioake	6
P. A. J. DeFreitas lbw b G. J. Batty	3
A. Habib not out	26
J. Ormond c B. C. Hollioake b A. J. Hollioake	2
S. A. J. Boswell run out	0
B 4, l-b 13, w 8	25
1/28 2/101 3/135 4/155 5/159 6/166 7/171 8/238 9/240 (45 overs)	240

Bowling: Giddins 8–2–29–1; Greenidge 4–1–28–0; Butcher 3–0–20–0; Saqlain Mushtaq 9–0–45–1; A. J. Hollioake 6–0–25–2; B. C. Hollioake 8–0–44–3; G. J. Batty 7–1–32–2.

Surrey

N. Shahid lbw b Boswell	2
M. A. Carberry c Stevens b Ormond	5
G. J. Batty b DeFreitas	30
*A. J. Hollioake c Habib b DeFreitas	11
A. D. Brown c Burns b Dakin	10
B. C. Hollioake run out	13
G. P. Butcher b Dakin	16
†J. N. Batty not out	11
Saqlain Mushtaq b Maddy	5
C. G. Greenidge b Maddy	0
E. S. H. Giddins b Maddy	0
B 1, l-b 3, w 5	9
1/5 2/24 3/54 4/64 5/68 6/88 7/98 8/112 9/112 (35.4 overs)	112

Bowling: Ormond 9–2–24–1; Boswell 9–1–27–1; DeFreitas 7–0–29–2; Dakin 7–0–19–2; Wells 2–0–8–0; Maddy 1.4–0–1–3.

Umpires: A. Clarkson and V. A. Holder.

At Scarborough, July 15. LEICESTERSHIRE beat YORKSHIRE by 16 runs.

LEICESTERSHIRE v KENT

At Leicester, July 22. Leicestershire won by five wickets. Toss: Kent.

Grace Road's biggest crowd so far, attracted by this top-of-the-table clash between Division One's unbeaten sides, were treated to memorable batting by Shahid Afridi on his home debut for Leicestershire. The 21-year-old Pakistani, replacing the injured Marsh as overseas player, smashed a brilliant 70 off 32 balls, hitting six fours and five sixes as the home side reached 100 off 12 overs in response to Kent's dismal 144. Ormond had severely damaged the visitors' challenge early on with a spell of three for four in five overs. Afridi, however, was the talk of the town when Leicestershire stormed to their eighth successive win with 18 overs unused.

Kent

J. B. Hockley b Ormond	37
D. P. Fulton c Burns b Boswell	11
G. O. Jones st Burns b DeFreitas	6
A. Symonds b Ormond	1
M. J. Walker b Ormond	6
M. A. Ealham b Shahid Afridi	34
†P. A. Nixon c Wells b Dakin	19
*M. V. Fleming lbw b Dakin	4
M. M. Patel lbw b Maddy	9
M. J. Saggers run out	6
B. J. Trott not out	0
B 2, l-b 4, w 5	11
1/20 2/56 3/57 4/58 5/65 6/107 7/120 8/130 9/144 (43.3 overs)	144

Bowling: Ormond 9–2–16–3; Boswell 7–0–26–1; DeFreitas 9–0–35–1; Dakin 9–0–27–2; Shahid Afridi 9–0–33–1; Maddy 0.3–0–1–1.

Leicestershire

J. M. Dakin lbw b Ealham 23
Shahid Afridi c Trott b Patel 70
T. R. Ward b Ealham 1
*V. J. Wells b Ealham 3
†N. D. Burns b Patel 1
B. F. Smith not out 15
D. L. Maddy not out 25
L-b 4, w 3 7

1/58 2/60 3/82 4/100 5/102 (5 wkts, 27 overs) 145

A. Habib, S. A. J. Boswell, P. A. J. DeFreitas and J. Ormond did not bat.

Bowling: Saggers 5–0–31–0; Trott 6–2–38–0; Ealham 7–3–19–3; Patel 5–1–34–2; Fleming 2–0–4–0; Walker 2–0–15–0.

Umpires: A. A. Jones and R. Julian.

At Canterbury, August 5. LEICESTERSHIRE beat KENT by 14 runs.

At Taunton, August 14. LEICESTERSHIRE lost to SOMERSET by one run.

LEICESTERSHIRE v YORKSHIRE

At Leicester, August 19. Leicestershire won by one wicket (D/L method). Toss: Yorkshire.

A last-wicket stand of 36 between Ormond and Boswell snatched victory for Leicestershire with one ball to spare. Chasing a revised target of 178 in 42 overs, they had been on the brink of a second consecutive defeat at 142 for nine. With 19 needed off the last two overs, Boswell hit the first six of his career as Sidebottom conceded 11; White then went for eight. Wells, taking four for 30 in his nine overs, had restricted Yorkshire to 176 after they had chosen to bat first. An expectant crowd was disappointed when 16-year-old Bresnan had Shahid Afridi caught first ball, but Boswell provided sufficient consolation at the end.

Yorkshire

M. J. Wood b Wells 28
C. White run out 4
A. McGrath lbw b Wells 32
D. S. Lehmann c Burns b Wells 20
G. M. Fellows c Stevens b Shahid Afridi 3
*D. Byas c Ormond b Shahid Afridi . . . 23
†R. J. Blakey not out 28
T. T. Bresnan b Wells 7
R. K. J. Dawson b Maddy 0
R. J. Sidebottom not out 2
B 1, l-b 5, w 21, n-b 2 29

1/14 2/67 3/97 4/102 5/124 6/141 7/171 8/172 (8 wkts, 42 overs) 176

M. J. Hoggard did not bat.

Bowling: Ormond 7–0–35–0; Boswell 5–0–26–0; DeFreitas 9–1–31–0; Wells 9–0–30–4; Maddy 7–0–28–1; Shahid Afridi 5–0–20–2.

Leicestershire

I. J. Sutcliffe c Blakey b Sidebottom . . . 9
Shahid Afridi c Wood b Bresnan 0
D. I. Stevens c Blakey b Bresnan 20
*V. J. Wells c Blakey b Sidebottom 18
B. F. Smith st Blakey b Lehmann 21
D. L. Maddy c Byas b Fellows 26
†N. D. Burns b Sidebottom 29
A. Habib b Dawson 1
P. A. J. DeFreitas b Lehmann 5
J. Ormond not out 9
S. A. J. Boswell not out 23
B 1, l-b 9, w 5, n-b 2 17

1/4 2/28 3/56 4/57 5/104 6/110 7/111 8/142 9/142 (9 wkts, 41.5 overs) 178

Bowling: Hoggard 6–1–18–0; Bresnan 6–1–27–2; Sidebottom 9–2–38–3; White 6.5–1–30–0; Fellows 3–0–17–1; Lehmann 8–0–18–2; Dawson 3–1–20–1.

Umpires: N. G. Cowley and R. A. White.

At Northampton, August 22 (day/night). LEICESTERSHIRE beat NORTHAMPTONSHIRE by seven wickets.

LEICESTERSHIRE v SOMERSET

At Leicester, August 27. Somerset won by ten runs. Toss: Somerset.

Somerset, who 13 days earlier had become the first side to beat Leicestershire in the League, completed the double and dealt a psychological blow ahead of their Cheltenham & Gloucester final. A close match provided excellent entertainment for the bank holiday crowd. Bowler and Blackwell again put Leicestershire to the sword with an opening stand of 138 in 24 overs, and a bigger total than 250 looked likely. Leicestershire's start was even more explosive: 96 in nine overs from Ward and Shahid Afridi, the young Pakistani crashing six sixes and four fours in 58 off 25 balls. Then Leicestershire lost their way, until Neil Burns and Habib added 71 for the seventh wicket. They needed 24 from the last three overs, but Burns was run out and Grove took two quick wickets. Leicestershire, front-runners all season, now had to win two of their last three games to be sure of the title.

Somerset

P. D. Bowler c Habib b Maddy	77
I. D. Blackwell b Shahid Afridi	75
†R. J. Turner c Wells b Maddy	35
M. J. Wood c Stevens b Shahid Afridi	4
K. A. Parsons lbw b Maddy	30
*J. Cox b Shahid Afridi	6
M. Burns not out	10
K. P. Dutch not out	2
L-b 2, w 9	11
1/138 2/193 3/194 4/210 5/223 6/245 (6 wkts, 45 overs)	250

J. I. D. Kerr, P. S. Jones and J. O. Grove did not bat.

Bowling: Malcolm 4–1–33–0; Boswell 5–1–35–0; DeFreitas 9–0–47–0; Wells 9–0–48–0; Maddy 9–0–40–3; Shahid Afridi 9–0–45–3.

Leicestershire

T. R. Ward run out	43
Shahid Afridi b Jones	58
D. I. Stevens b Jones	6
*V. J. Wells b Grove	17
B. F. Smith lbw b Parsons	4
D. L. Maddy lbw b Burns	10
†N. D. Burns run out	55
A. Habib not out	28
P. A. J. DeFreitas b Grove	1
S. A. J. Boswell b Grove	0
D. E. Malcolm not out	2
B 4, l-b 7, w 5	16
1/96 2/104 3/121 4/129 5/134 6/157 7/228 8/230 9/235 (9 wkts, 45 overs)	240

Bowling: Jones 9–0–66–2; Kerr 7–0–53–0; Grove 7–0–24–3; Parsons 5–0–17–1; Dutch 9–0–34–0; Burns 7–0–32–1; Blackwell 1–0–3–0.

Umpires: J. H. Hampshire and A. G. T. Whitehead.

At Bristol, September 3. LEICESTERSHIRE lost to GLOUCESTERSHIRE by 28 runs (D/L method).

LEICESTERSHIRE v WARWICKSHIRE

At Leicester, September 5 (day/night). No result. Toss: Leicestershire.

Rain washed out Leicestershire's only floodlit home game of the season. Their two points meant they needed victory at Trent Bridge in 11 days' time to become League champions. Warwickshire, meanwhile, consolidated their hold on third place.

Leicestershire

T. R. Ward b Dagnall	1
Shahid Afridi c Piper b Brown	3
*V. J. Wells not out	3
B. F. Smith not out	0
W 2	2
1/4 2/6 (2 wkts, 3.5 overs)	9

D. I. Stevens, D. L. Maddy, †N. D. Burns, A. Habib, J. M. Dakin, J. Ormond and D. E. Malcolm did not bat.

Bowling: Brown 2–0–5–1; Dagnall 1.5–0–4–1.

Warwickshire

N. V. Knight, M. A. Wagh, D. R. Brown, D. L. Hemp, *M. J. Powell, T. L. Penney, N. M. K. Smith, M. A. Sheikh, †K. J. Piper, C. E. Dagnall and A. Richardson.

Umpires: J. W. Holder and P. Willey.

At Nottingham, September 16. LEICESTERSHIRE lost to NOTTINGHAMSHIRE by five wickets.

NORTHAMPTONSHIRE

NORTHAMPTONSHIRE v GLOUCESTERSHIRE

At Northampton, May 13. Gloucestershire won by 20 runs (D/L method). Toss: Northamptonshire.

A heavy thunderstorm ended play with Northamptonshire, having just lost the key wicket of Hussey, well adrift on the Duckworth/Lewis calculation. The day belonged to Barnett, who, hitting only five fours, anchored Gloucestershire's innings with 101 off 124 balls and, with his 100th run, passed Graham Gooch's League record of 8,573 runs. It was the 40-year-old Barnett's 307th League match, and his 295th innings, stretching back to his debut for Derbyshire against Essex in May 1979. Taylor, hitting 22 from 11 deliveries, provided the late acceleration that brought Gloucestershire 58 in the last five overs.

Gloucestershire

R. J. Cunliffe b Brown	23
K. J. Barnett c Bailey b Innes	101
I. J. Harvey st Bailey b Brown	0
M. G. N. Windows c Cook b Penberthy	34
*M. W. Alleyne lbw b Innes	21
C. G. Taylor not out	22
J. N. Snape not out	4
L-b 5, w 8, n-b 4	17
1/65 2/69 3/146 4/180 5/209 (5 wkts, 45 overs)	222

M. C. J. Ball, †R. C. J. Williams, M. J. Cawdron and J. M. M. Averis did not bat.

Bowling: Cousins 9–0–41–0; Weekes 9–0–40–0; Penberthy 8–0–40–1; Brown 9–0–32–2; Innes 8–0–48–2; Swann 2–0–16–0.

Northamptonshire

M. E. K. Hussey st Williams b Harvey	53	A. J. Swann not out	7
M. B. Loye st Williams b Ball	19	L-b 4	4
J. W. Cook b Snape	0		——
A. S. Rollins not out	25	1/58 2/59 3/96 (3 wkts, 31 overs)	108

*A. L. Penberthy, K. J. Innes, †T. M. B. Bailey, L. C. Weekes, D. M. Cousins and J. F. Brown did not bat.

Bowling: Harvey 7–1–23–1; Averis 7–1–21–0; Cawdron 6–1–23–0; Ball 8–0–30–1; Snape 3–0–7–1.

Umpires: J. H. Hampshire and V. A. Holder.

NORTHAMPTONSHIRE v SURREY

At Northampton, June 3. Surrey won by four wickets. Toss: Surrey.

Ramprakash guided Surrey to their first League win of the season with his unbeaten 85 from 100 balls, including eight fours. After a bright start courtesy of Mark Butcher – the first 50 were rattled up at seven an over – they had collapsed from 90 for one to 155 for six on a slow pitch that made fluent strokeplay difficult. With 59 runs needed from the last eight overs, Ramprakash, with help from Jonathan Batty, knocked them off in six. Put in, Northamptonshire had lost Loye in the second over but rallied through Hussey (121 balls, four fours) and Cook, who added 96 at four an over.

Northamptonshire

M. E. K. Hussey c Ramprakash b B. C. Hollioake	80	A. L. Penberthy b Giddins	17
M. B. Loye c J. N. Batty b Giddins	0	K. J. Innes not out	7
J. W. Cook c B. C. Hollioake b A. J. Hollioake	47	L. C. Weekes not out	1
G. P. Swann run out	12	L-b 13, w 8	21
A. J. Swann b B. C. Hollioake	28		——
		1/2 2/98 3/143 4/176 5/202 6/208 (6 wkts, 45 overs)	213

*†D. Ripley, D. M. Cousins and J. F. Brown did not bat.

Bowling: Bicknell 9–0–34–0; Giddins 9–3–22–2; G. P. Butcher 3–0–15–0; G. J. Batty 7–0–35–0; Ramprakash 3–0–17–0; A. J. Hollioake 9–0–42–1; B. C. Hollioake 5–0–35–2.

Surrey

M. A. Butcher c Ripley b Brown	55	G. P. Butcher c Loye b Penberthy	7
A. D. Brown b Cousins	15	†J. N. Batty not out	21
M. R. Ramprakash not out	85	L-b 5, w 4, n-b 6	15
N. Shahid st Ripley b Penberthy	6		——
*A. J. Hollioake c Cook b Penberthy	6	1/50 2/90 3/99 4/107 5/129 6/155 (6 wkts, 43 overs)	217
B. C. Hollioake run out	7		

G. J. Batty, M. P. Bicknell and E. S. H. Giddins did not bat.

Bowling: Cousins 8–0–55–1; Weekes 9–1–53–0; Brown 8–1–29–1; Penberthy 9–0–43–3; Innes 5–1–17–0; G. P. Swann 4–0–15–0.

Umpires: J. F. Steele and A. G. T. Whitehead.

NORTHAMPTONSHIRE v WARWICKSHIRE

At Northampton, June 10. Warwickshire won by five wickets. Toss: Northamptonshire.

Warwickshire captain Powell and Brown combined clever improvisation with urgent running between the wickets to get their side home with five balls to spare. Powell's 62-ball 78 contained a six and seven fours from some marvellous hitting, while Brown, less spectacular, helped him add 128 in 20 overs. It meant that Loye, who had taken the batting honours for Northamptonshire with 90, ended up on the losing side. He struck a dozen boundaries before becoming the first of Brown's two victims in an over, leaving Alec Swann to provide the late impetus with an unbeaten 37 from 21 balls as Warwickshire conceded 89 in the last ten overs.

Northamptonshire

M. E. K. Hussey c Penney b Giles	27
M. B. Loye c Piper b Brown	90
J. W. Cook c Penney b Giles	0
G. P. Swann b Brown	32
A. L. Penberthy not out	12
A. J. Swann not out	37
B 3, l-b 9, w 4, n-b 2	18
1/93 2/93 3/161 4/162 (4 wkts, 45 overs)	216

K. J. Innes, *†D. Ripley, L. C. Weekes, D. M. Cousins and J. F. Brown did not bat.

Bowling: Dagnall 5–1–20–0; Brown 8–1–42–2; Drakes 9–4–33–0; Sheikh 9–0–38–0; Giles 9–1–43–2; Smith 5–0–28–0.

Warwickshire

N. M. K. Smith b Innes	32
D. L. Hemp b Innes	9
D. R. Brown run out	73
D. P. Ostler st Ripley b Brown	13
*M. J. Powell st Ripley b G. P. Swann	78
T. L. Penney not out	4
A. F. Giles not out	0
L-b 2, w 2, n-b 6	10
1/40 2/58 3/82 4/210 5/215 (5 wkts, 44.1 overs)	219

†K. J. Piper, M. A. Sheikh, V. C. Drakes and C. E. Dagnall did not bat.

Bowling: Cousins 9–1–35–0; Weekes 9–0–39–0; Innes 9–0–52–2; Penberthy 9–0–34–0; Brown 6–0–42–1; G. P. Swann 2.1–0–15–1.

Umpires: G. I. Burgess and B. Dudleston.

At Leicester, June 17. NORTHAMPTONSHIRE lost to LEICESTERSHIRE by three wickets.

At Leeds, June 24. NORTHAMPTONSHIRE lost to YORKSHIRE by 16 runs.

NORTHAMPTONSHIRE v YORKSHIRE

At Northampton, July 8. Northamptonshire won by three wickets. Toss: Yorkshire.

Northamptonshire registered their first win – and their first points – of the season at the sixth attempt, seeing off Yorkshire with nearly four overs to spare in a largely uninspiring contest. Apart from Fellows and Wood, who added 83 for the third wicket, and Blakey's 41-ball 33 at the end, the Yorkshire batsmen failed to make headway on a slow pitch. The injured Lehmann was sorely missed, not just by Yorkshire but also by the crowd. Northamptonshire made hard work of the chase. But for Loye's level-headed approach throughout their reply, they might easily have fallen short after sliding from 77 for one to 120 for six in the space of 13 overs.

Yorkshire

*D. Byas c G. P. Swann b Strong	2	A. K. D. Gray b Strong	2
M. J. Wood c Hussey b Brown	35	R. J. Sidebottom not out	1
M. J. Lumb c Ripley b Strong	3		
G. M. Fellows c Warren b Strong	67	B 2, l-b 6, w 5	13
V. J. Craven run out	0		
G. M. Hamilton st Ripley b Penberthy	5	1/7 2/14 3/97 (8 wkts, 45 overs)	161
†R. J. Blakey not out	33	4/98 5/109 6/152	
R. K. J. Dawson c Brown b Taylor	0	7/152 8/160	

S. P. Kirby did not bat.

Bowling: Strong 9–1–28–4; Taylor 9–0–31–1; Penberthy 9–1–33–1; G. P. Swann 9–0–37–0; Brown 9–1–24–1.

Northamptonshire

M. E. K. Hussey c Fellows b Kirby	5	*†D. Ripley c Sidebottom b Dawson	23
M. B. Loye not out	65	J. P. Taylor not out	0
R. J. Warren b Fellows	30	L-b 4, w 6, n-b 10	20
J. W. Cook c Wood b Hamilton	1		
A. J. Swann c Byas b Hamilton	7	1/18 2/77 3/78 (7 wkts, 41.1 overs)	165
A. L. Penberthy c Lumb b Dawson	14	4/92 5/120	
G. P. Swann lbw b Dawson	0	6/120 7/160	

M. R. Strong and J. F. Brown did not bat.

Bowling: Kirby 9–0–37–1; Sidebottom 8–0–25–0; Hamilton 9–2–35–2; Fellows 6–0–32–1; Dawson 9–2–28–3; Gray 0.1–0–4–0.

Umpires: M. R. Benson and R. A. White.

At Birmingham, July 15. NORTHAMPTONSHIRE lost to WARWICKSHIRE by four wickets.

At Guildford, July 22. NORTHAMPTONSHIRE beat SURREY by eight wickets (D/L method).

At Cheltenham, August 5. NORTHAMPTONSHIRE lost to GLOUCESTERSHIRE by 83 runs.

NORTHAMPTONSHIRE v KENT

At Northampton, August 12. No result (abandoned).

At Nottingham, August 19. NORTHAMPTONSHIRE lost to NOTTINGHAMSHIRE by 81 runs (D/L method).

NORTHAMPTONSHIRE v LEICESTERSHIRE

At Northampton, August 22 (day/night). Leicestershire won by seven wickets. Toss: Northamptonshire.

Victory left Leicestershire ten points clear of Kent at the top of the table, with four matches to play. Dropped by Ward at short mid-wicket on one, Graeme Swann hit 83 from 70 balls and added 99 with Penberthy to lift the spirits of the 5,000 capacity crowd. But their optimism soon evaporated as Ward, making amends for his fielding lapse, and Shahid Afridi led off with 62 in only six overs. The Pakistani's hectic 36 came off 18 deliveries, and it was left to Stevens and Smith to see Leicestershire home with a minimum of fuss. Penberthy passed Peter Willey's record of 157 League wickets for Northamptonshire.

Northamptonshire

M. E. K. Hussey c Burns b Wells	26
M. E. Cassar b DeFreitas	29
R. J. Warren c and b DeFreitas	0
A. L. Penberthy b Wells	50
G. P. Swann c Ward b Wells	83
A. J. Swann run out	15
K. J. Innes run out	0
*†D. Ripley not out	9
J. P. Taylor run out	4
B 4, l-b 2, w 7, n-b 2	15
1/55 2/55 3/66 4/165 5/202 6/207 7/221 8/231 (8 wkts, 45 overs)	231

M. R. Strong and J. F. Brown did not bat.

Bowling: DeFreitas 9–2–43–2; Boswell 9–2–43–0; Wells 9–1–34–3; Maddy 9–0–47–0; Dakin 0.3–0–8–0; Stevens 0.3–0–1–0; Shahid Afridi 8–0–49–0.

Leicestershire

T. R. Ward c G. P. Swann b Penberthy	56
Shahid Afridi c Innes b Taylor	36
D. I. Stevens not out	68
*V. J. Wells lbw b Brown	21
B. F. Smith not out	44
L-b 3, w 2, n-b 2	7
1/62 2/112 3/159 (3 wkts, 40.3 overs)	232

D. L. Maddy, †N. D. Burns, A. Habib, P. A. J. DeFreitas, S. A. J. Boswell and J. M. Dakin did not bat.

Bowling: Strong 5–0–51–0; Penberthy 5–0–52–1; Taylor 8–1–24–1; G. P. Swann 7–0–41–0; Brown 9–1–24–1; Innes 5–0–26–0; Cassar 1.3–0–11–0.

Umpires: G. I. Burgess and B. Leadbeater.

NORTHAMPTONSHIRE v SOMERSET

At Northampton, August 30. Somerset won by 70 runs (D/L method). Toss: Northamptonshire.

Northamptonshire were condemned to relegation after failing to mount a serious challenge on a murky, autumnal afternoon. Only Warren, with a solid, competition-best 93 in 103 balls, and the more aggressive Graeme Swann contributed significantly. Somerset off-spinner Dutch captured six for 40, including three wickets in his final over. In reply, Cox and Trescothick picked off boundaries at will, the latter stroking 11 fours in his assured 65-ball 72, and Somerset were well ahead of the par score when heavy rain set in. Sales made his first appearance since recovering from the serious knee injury he incurred at the start of England A's winter tour to the Caribbean.

Northamptonshire

*M. E. K. Hussey c Trescothick b Caddick	24
M. E. Cassar lbw b Kerr	8
R. J. Warren c Grove b Dutch	93
D. J. Sales c Cox b Parsons	11
G. P. Swann b Blackwell	41
A. J. Swann c Cox b Dutch	1
K. J. Innes c Grove b Dutch	18
†T. M. B. Bailey b Dutch	2
J. P. Taylor b Dutch	7
J. A. R. Blain not out	0
J. F. Brown st Turner b Dutch	0
L-b 6, w 1, n-b 2	9
1/22 2/46 3/93 4/153 5/160 6/189 7/195 8/212 9/214 (45 overs)	214

Bowling: Caddick 9–2–21–1; Kerr 9–1–45–1; Parsons 4–0–29–1; Grove 6–0–31–0; Blackwell 9–1–42–1; Dutch 8–0–40–6.

Somerset

*J. Cox not out	76
M. E. Trescothick c Blain b Brown	72
L-b 5, n-b 2	7
1/155 (1 wkt, 24.4 overs)	155

M. Burns, I. D. Blackwell, M. J. Wood, †R. J. Turner, K. A. Parsons, K. P. Dutch, J. I. D. Kerr, A. R. Caddick and J. O. Grove did not bat.

Bowling: Taylor 5–1–35–0; Blain 5–0–37–0; Cassar 3–0–25–0; Innes 5–0–24–0; Brown 4.4–0–26–1; G. P. Swann 2–1–3–0.

Umpires: B. Dudleston and R. Julian.

NORTHAMPTONSHIRE v NOTTINGHAMSHIRE

At Northampton, September 2. Northamptonshire won by four wickets (D/L method). Toss: Northamptonshire.

Northamptonshire set aside their disappointing season to win Ripley's final home match. Blain and Taylor reduced Nottinghamshire to 44 for five inside a dozen overs – which included five fours in 20 balls from Blewett – and the 74-run stand between Pietersen and Noon could not repair the damage. Graeme Swann launched Northamptonshire's reply with 56 from 61 balls, and not even the loss of three wickets in as many overs could spoil Ripley's emotional farewell. He added 55 with Alec Swann and received a standing ovation when dismissed ten short of the revised target of 182 in 44 overs.

Nottinghamshire

*D. J. Bicknell b Blain	0
J. E. Morris b Taylor	3
G. S. Blewett b Taylor	23
U. Afzaal b Taylor	6
P. Johnson c A. J. Swann b Blain	7
K. P. Pietersen b G. P. Swann	58
†W. M. Noon run out	17
G. D. Clough b Innes	24
R. J. Logan c Cassar b Blain	24
G. J. Smith run out	1
M. N. Malik not out	3
L-b 6, w 6, n-b 4	16
1/0 2/21 3/31 4/42 5/44 6/118 7/120 8/169 9/171 (43.2 overs)	182

Bowling: Blain 9–0–45–3; Taylor 9–0–28–3; Innes 7.2–1–33–1; Cassar 2–0–16–0; Brown 7–0–28–0; G. P. Swann 9–0–26–1.

Northamptonshire

M. E. K. Hussey c Noon b Smith	16
G. P. Swann c Blewett b Pietersen	56
R. J. Warren c Noon b Logan	14
D. J. Sales c Johnson b Clough	26
M. E. Cassar st Noon b Pietersen	4
A. J. Swann not out	34
*†D. Ripley b Smith	24
K. J. Innes not out	8
L-b 1, w 2	3
1/32 2/69 3/106 4/116 5/117 6/172 (6 wkts, 37.1 overs)	185

J. P. Taylor, J. A. R. Blain and J. F. Brown did not bat.

Bowling: Smith 9–1–38–2; Malik 6–0–32–0; Logan 6–0–39–1; Clough 8.1–1–34–1; Pietersen 8–0–41–2.

Umpires: K. E. Palmer and A. G. T. Whitehead.

At Canterbury, September 9. NORTHAMPTONSHIRE lost to KENT by 26 runs.

At Taunton, September 16. NORTHAMPTONSHIRE lost to SOMERSET by 12 runs.

NOTTINGHAMSHIRE

At The Oval, May 13. NOTTINGHAMSHIRE beat SURREY by 17 runs.

NOTTINGHAMSHIRE v WARWICKSHIRE

At Nottingham, May 20. Nottinghamshire won by four wickets. Toss: Warwickshire.

Three days ahead of their Benson and Hedges Cup quarter-final, Nottinghamshire gained the psychological high ground over Warwickshire by sneaking a last-over victory in the dress rehearsal. It was achieved thanks largely to Afzaal, who refused to give up on a game that appeared to be slipping from the home team's grasp and hit a superb unbeaten 94 from 105 balls. Fine bowling by Smith and spinners Stemp and Pietersen had restricted Warwickshire's total on a pitch providing pace and bounce, but Nottinghamshire struggled themselves until Read and Afzaal put on 77 inside 11 overs to get them back up to the required rate. Read fell with 21 needed, but the left-handed Afzaal manipulated the strike expertly to see his team home and keep his name in the England selectors' thoughts.

Warwickshire

N. V. Knight c Pietersen b Franks	15
M. A. Wagh c Bicknell b Pietersen	50
D. R. Brown c and b Stemp	44
D. P. Ostler b Stemp	0
T. L. Penney c Stemp b Pietersen	30
N. M. K. Smith b Pietersen	3
*M. J. Powell run out	15
†K. J. Piper not out	12
M. A. Sheikh not out	0
B 7, l-b 14, w 10, n-b 2	33
1/29 2/110 3/110 4/162 5/164 6/172 7/201 (7 wkts, 45 overs)	202

V. C. Drakes and C. E. Dagnall did not bat.

Bowling: Smith 9–3–27–0; Franks 8–0–40–1; Clough 5–0–18–0; Blewett 5–0–29–0; Stemp 9–0–28–2; Pietersen 9–0–39–3.

Nottinghamshire

*D. J. Bicknell c Ostler b Dagnall	18
G. E. Welton c Ostler b Dagnall	5
G. S. Blewett c Piper b Smith	14
U. Afzaal not out	94
P. Johnson c Ostler b Brown	20
K. P. Pietersen b Brown	4
†C. M. W. Read b Brown	36
P. J. Franks not out	4
B 1, l-b 5, w 2	8
1/21 2/26 3/61 4/94 5/105 6/182 (6 wkts, 44.4 overs)	203

G. D. Clough, R. D. Stemp and G. J. Smith did not bat.

Bowling: Dagnall 9–1–35–2; Drakes 8.4–1–27–0; Sheikh 9–1–40–0; Smith 9–0–39–1; Brown 9–0–56–3.

Umpires: K. E. Palmer and J. F. Steele.

At Oakham School, June 3. NOTTINGHAMSHIRE lost to LEICESTERSHIRE by six wickets.

NOTTINGHAMSHIRE v GLOUCESTERSHIRE

At Nottingham, June 10. Nottinghamshire won by six wickets (D/L method). Toss: Nottinghamshire.

Snape and Hardinges turned Gloucestershire's innings round with 164, a record seventh-wicket partnership in English one-day cricket, but the visitors still fell short of preventing a Nottinghamshire victory. Invited to bat, they were 33 for five inside ten overs, whereupon Snape orchestrated a remarkable recovery, hitting an unbeaten century – his first in nine years of county cricket, with a six and ten fours in 119 balls. Nottinghamshire, their target adjusted to 228 after showers had interrupted Gloucestershire's innings, made a sound start through Bicknell and Johnson, yet still needed 96 from the final 12 overs. Pietersen accelerated the scoring with 57 from 40 balls before Johnson, reprieved on 72 by Snape off his own bowling, hit the winning run with four balls to spare.

Gloucestershire

T. H. C. Hancock c Read b Harris	0
K. J. Barnett c Read b Harris	5
M. G. N. Windows c Read b Harris	17
C. G. Taylor c Blewett b Smith	9
*M. W. Alleyne lbw b Smith	0
J. N. Snape not out	104
†R. C. Russell c Read b Clough	4
M. A. Hardinges st Read b Blewett	65
M. C. J. Ball c Blewett b Smith	4
M. J. Cawdron not out	3
B 5, l-b 3, w 7, n-b 2	17
1/0 2/15 3/32 4/32 5/33 6/52 7/216 8/223 (8 wkts, 44 overs)	228

J. M. M. Averis did not bat.

Bowling: Harris 9–2–34–3; Smith 9–2–25–3; Clough 9–0–27–1; Blewett 9–0–69–1; Stemp 6–0–37–0; Pietersen 2–0–28–0.

Nottinghamshire

*D. J. Bicknell b Hardinges	64
G. S. Blewett lbw b Cawdron	1
P. Johnson not out	88
U. Afzaal run out	7
K. P. Pietersen c Windows b Cawdron	57
†C. M. W. Read not out	0
B 4, l-b 2, w 3, n-b 2	11
1/7 2/125 3/142 4/226 (4 wkts, 43.2 overs)	228

G. E. Welton, A. J. Harris, G. D. Clough, R. D. Stemp and G. J. Smith did not bat.

Bowling: Cawdron 8–1–43–2; Averis 8.2–0–47–0; Alleyne 9–0–34–0; Ball 8–0–45–0; Hardinges 6–0–30–1; Snape 4–0–23–0.

Umpires: M. J. Harris and R. Palmer.

At Maidstone, June 17. NOTTINGHAMSHIRE lost to KENT by 60 runs (D/L method).

NOTTINGHAMSHIRE v SOMERSET

At Nottingham, June 24. Nottinghamshire won by six wickets. Toss: Somerset.

Somerset's tactics of all-out attack proved foolhardy and allowed Nottinghamshire to achieve a comfortable victory with five balls to spare. Bowler, Kerr, Trescothick and Lathwell all perished to attacking strokes, and Stemp applied further pressure with an exemplary spell of slow left-arm bowling to match his best one-day figures. Parsons, 58 not out from 47 balls, helped revive the innings, and 50 came from the last five overs. Nottinghamshire's Blewett and Afzaal emphasised the folly of Somerset's ways with a stand of 161 in 31 overs. Afzaal remained to finish the job, unbeaten on 94 from 104 balls – his first limited-overs century eluding him for the second time in just over a month.

Somerset

P. D. Bowler c Read b Harris	1	K. P. Dutch c Bicknell b Smith	15
M. E. Trescothick c Bicknell b Clough	27	R. L. Johnson run out	19
J. I. D. Kerr b Smith	7	P. S. Jones not out	0
I. D. Blackwell st Read b Stemp	59	B 3, l-b 2, w 4	9
M. N. Lathwell b Stemp	1		
*M. Burns b Stemp	36	1/2 2/22 3/57 (9 wkts, 45 overs)	232
K. A. Parsons not out	58	4/75 5/128 6/141	
†R. J. Turner b Stemp	0	7/141 8/182 9/223	

Bowling: Smith 9–1–63–2; Harris 9–1–48–1; Clough 5–0–23–1; Stemp 9–1–25–4; Blewett 3–0–20–0; Afzaal 6–0–35–0; Pietersen 4–0–13–0.

Nottinghamshire

*D. J. Bicknell c Turner b Jones	18	K. P. Pietersen not out	7
J. E. Morris b Johnson	5	L-b 5, w 4	9
G. S. Blewett c Turner b Dutch	89		
U. Afzaal not out	94	1/13 2/36 (4 wkts, 44.1 overs)	235
P. Johnson c Kerr b Blackwell	13	3/197 4/214	

†C. M. W. Read, A. J. Harris, G. J. Smith, G. D. Clough and R. D. Stemp did not bat.

Bowling: Johnson 9–3–22–1; Jones 9–0–53–1; Kerr 8–0–52–0; Dutch 9–0–42–1; Blackwell 7.1–0–48–1; Parsons 2–0–13–0.

Umpires: J. H. Evans and M. J. Kitchen.

At Taunton, July 8. NOTTINGHAMSHIRE beat SOMERSET by three wickets.

NOTTINGHAMSHIRE v KENT

At Nottingham, July 15. Kent won by one run. Toss: Kent.

Kent maintained their unbeaten record by the narrowest of margins, despite a heroic innings by Pietersen that took the game to the final ball. Nottinghamshire had bowled accurately to restrict the visitors, with top-scorer Fulton unable to profit from his solid start. But, for all the best efforts of Bicknell over two hours, their reply slipped behind the asking-rate against Kent's spinners. Pietersen and Read brought the target down from 45 off five overs to 21 from 16 balls but, when Read went, Pietersen (48 in 45 balls, with a six and two fours) was unable to keep enough strike. Attempting to reach the bowler's end for the second run that would tie the scores, he was beaten by Symonds's pin-point return from long-on.

Kent

J. B. Hockley lbw b Smith	0	M. M. Patel c Pietersen b Afzaal	3
D. P. Fulton c Read b Logan	39	M. J. Saggers not out	21
M. J. Walker c Stemp b Harris	23	B. J. Trott c Pietersen b Smith	2
A. Symonds c Stemp b Logan	29	B 1, l-b 6, w 7, n-b 2	16
M. A. Ealham c Logan b Pietersen	25		
†P. A. Nixon c Shafayat b Stemp	16	1/0 2/53 3/79 (44.5 overs)	196
G. O. Jones b Afzaal	14	4/98 5/122 6/152	
*M. V. Fleming b Smith	8	7/153 8/158 9/178	

Bowling: Smith 8.5–0–37–3; Harris 9–0–40–1; Logan 8–0–37–2; Stemp 9–0–36–1; Blewett 4–1–12–0; Pietersen 3–0–14–1; Afzaal 3–0–13–2.

Nottinghamshire

*D. J. Bicknell c Fulton b Ealham	64	R. J. Logan not out	5
G. S. Blewett b Trott	13		
U. Afzaal st Nixon b Patel	8	B 1, l-b 5, w 3, n-b 2	11
P. Johnson c Symonds b Patel	26		
K. P. Pietersen run out	48	1/44 2/69 3/116 (7 wkts, 45 overs)	195
B. M. Shafayat b Ealham	8	4/133 5/147	
†C. M. W. Read b Ealham	12	6/176 7/195	

G. J. Smith, A. J. Harris and R. D. Stemp did not bat.

Bowling: Saggers 9–2–43–0; Trott 9–2–31–1; Ealham 9–0–53–3; Patel 9–1–27–2; Symonds 9–1–35–0.

Umpires: A. Clarkson and T. E. Jesty.

At Cheltenham, July 31. NOTTINGHAMSHIRE lost to GLOUCESTERSHIRE by 116 runs.

At Birmingham, August 2 (day/night). WARWICKSHIRE v NOTTINGHAMSHIRE. No result.

NOTTINGHAMSHIRE v YORKSHIRE

At Nottingham, August 13 (day/night). Yorkshire won by three wickets. Toss: Nottinghamshire.

Yorkshire battled back after an inauspicious start to win with four balls to spare, thanks largely to a magnificent century stand in 20 overs between Lehmann and White. Taking first use of a good pitch, Nottinghamshire had made steady progress before Pietersen, setting about Hamilton and Fellows, picked up the tempo with his 45-ball 49. As if 245 wasn't an awkward enough target under lights, Yorkshire made it all the more difficult by losing their first four wickets to Smith and Malik for 31. Lehmann and White turned the game on its head, however, and then White and Byas saw Yorkshire to within 33 runs of victory. Blakey and Gray completed the job with some panache.

Nottinghamshire

*D. J. Bicknell b Bresnan	16	G. D. Clough not out	5
G. S. Blewett c and b Gray	43	R. J. Logan not out	3
U. Afzaal run out	53	B 8, l-b 6, w 7	21
P. Johnson c Vaughan b Bresnan	29		
K. P. Pietersen b White	49	1/29 2/87 3/134 (7 wkts, 45 overs)	244
†C. M. W. Read c Hamilton b Elstub	16	4/169 5/215	
B. M. Shafayat b White	9	6/235 7/239	

G. J. Smith and M. N. Malik did not bat.

Bowling: Elstub 8–0–36–1; Bresnan 9–1–31–2; White 9–0–44–2; Hamilton 4–0–28–0; Gray 9–0–45–1; Lehmann 4–0–18–0; Fellows 2–0–28–0.

Yorkshire

G. M. Hamilton c Afzaal b Smith	11	†R. J. Blakey not out	15
M. J. Wood lbw b Smith	0	A. K. D. Gray not out	19
M. P. Vaughan c Blewett b Malik	1	B 6, l-b 5, w 6, n-b 2	19
D. S. Lehmann b Blewett	71		
G. M. Fellows b Malik	2	1/1 2/10 3/28 (7 wkts, 44.2 overs)	246
C. White c Pietersen b Clough	73	4/31 5/144	
*D. Byas c Johnson b Clough	35	6/212 7/212	

T. T. Bresnan and C. J. Elstub did not bat.

Bowling: Smith 9–0–47–2; Malik 9–3–34–2; Logan 8.2–0–49–0; Clough 6–0–39–2; Pietersen 6–0–36–0; Blewett 6–0–30–1.

Umpires: J. H. Hampshire and R. Julian.

NOTTINGHAMSHIRE v NORTHAMPTONSHIRE

At Nottingham, August 19. Nottinghamshire won by 81 runs (D/L method). Toss: Nottinghamshire. County debut: M. E. Cassar.

Bicknell and Blewett, having added 166 in 26 overs, had batted struggling Northamptonshire out of the game long before Duckworth and Lewis put it beyond reach by setting a target of 281 from 42 overs, later revised to 267 from 37. Rain had fallen just as Nottinghamshire, after losing five for 28 in five overs, were preparing for a final onslaught. Even so, 267 was their season's best in the League to date. Bicknell hit his 115 in 120 balls, and Northamptonshire had no one to counter this once Hussey had edged to slip early on. Cassar, the former Derbyshire all-rounder, marked his debut for them with a solid half-century.

Nottinghamshire

*D. J. Bicknell b Innes	115	G. E. Welton not out	7
J. E. Morris b Taylor	37	G. D. Clough not out	4
G. S. Blewett c Hussey b Innes	71	B 4, l-b 3, w 7	14
K. P. Pietersen c Cassar b Penberthy	12		
P. Johnson c Taylor b Penberthy	5	1/63 2/229 3/242 (6 wkts, 42.2 overs)	267
†C. M. W. Read c and b Innes	2	4/249 5/255 6/257	

R. J. Logan, G. J. Smith and M. N. Malik did not bat.

Bowling: Taylor 8–0–42–1; Strong 7.2–0–40–0; Penberthy 9–1–49–2; Innes 9–1–60–3; Brown 6–0–40–0; G. P. Swann 3–0–29–0.

Northamptonshire

M. E. K. Hussey c Blewett b Smith	14	J. P. Taylor run out	1
M. E. Cassar b Logan	58	M. R. Strong c Smith b Clough	11
R. J. Warren c Read b Malik	4	J. F. Brown b Johnson	5
A. L. Penberthy c Read b Logan	12	L-b 3, w 4, n-b 4	11
G. P. Swann lbw b Malik	4		
A. J. Swann run out	16	1/16 2/33 3/59 (36.4 overs)	185
K. J. Innes b Pietersen	9	4/64 5/96 6/110	
*†D. Ripley not out	40	7/138 8/143 9/173	

Bowling: Smith 5–1–15–1; Malik 9–0–38–2; Logan 7–0–47–2; Pietersen 9–0–45–1; Clough 6–0–35–1; Johnson 0.4–0–2–1.

Umpires: J. H. Evans and J. W. Holder.

At Scarborough, August 26. NOTTINGHAMSHIRE lost to YORKSHIRE by 179 runs.

At Northampton, September 2. NOTTINGHAMSHIRE lost to NORTHAMPTONSHIRE by four wickets (D/L method).

NOTTINGHAMSHIRE v SURREY

At Nottingham, September 9. Surrey won by five wickets. Toss: Surrey. First-team debuts: R. R. Clarke, S. A. Newman.

Just when a win would have secured Nottinghamshire's first-division status with a game remaining, they were well beaten by a depleted Surrey team. Already relegated, the visitors omitted ten current or former Test players; not that it mattered. Brown, crucially dropped on 12, destroyed the Nottinghamshire bowling with a 65-ball century while adding 189 with Gareth Batty. Harris struck back with three quick wickets, but Brown carried on to 130, from 97 balls with 13 fours and five sixes, his 12th League hundred. A fifty partnership between captain Hollioake and Shahid saw Surrey home with two overs to spare. Morris had put the home side on course to improve again their highest League total of the season, hitting a run-a-ball hundred, and Pietersen's unbeaten 61 off 34 balls got them there. Johnson became Nottinghamshire's leading run-maker in the League when, in his 252nd game, he overtook Derek Randall's 7,062 from 257 games.

Nottinghamshire

*D. J. Bicknell c Carberry b Giddins	11	G. D. Clough c Brown b Hollioake	6
J. E. Morris c Clarke b G. J. Batty	102	R. J. Logan not out	0
G. S. Blewett b Murtagh	11	B 2, l-b 5, w 4	11
U. Afzaal st J. N. Batty b Brown	50		
K. P. Pietersen not out	61	1/33 2/50 3/179 (7 wkts, 45 overs)	277
P. Johnson run out	14	4/181 5/217	
†C. M. W. Read run out	11	6/261 7/274	

A. J. Harris and G. J. Smith did not bat.

Bowling: Giddins 9–1–44–1; Murtagh 9–1–54–1; Hollioake 9–0–54–1; G. J. Batty 9–0–57–1; Amin 3–0–21–0; Brown 6–0–40–1.

Surrey

S. A. Newman c Read b Smith	0	N. Shahid not out	20
A. D. Brown c Johnson b Harris	130		
G. J. Batty b Harris	63	L-b 5, w 13, n-b 2	20
M. A. Carberry c Read b Harris	3		
R. R. Clarke b Harris	0	1/0 2/189 3/194 (5 wkts, 43 overs)	279
*A. J. Hollioake not out	43	4/195 5/228	

†J. N. Batty, T. J. Murtagh, R. M. Amin and E. S. H. Giddins did not bat.

Bowling: Smith 9–0–55–1; Logan 9–0–64–0; Harris 9–0–42–4; Clough 9–0–47–0; Blewett 2–0–34–0; Pietersen 5–0–32–0.

Umpires: M. R. Benson and V. A. Holder.

NOTTINGHAMSHIRE v LEICESTERSHIRE

At Nottingham, September 16. Nottinghamshire won by five wickets. Toss: Nottinghamshire.

Both teams desperately needed to win – Nottinghamshire to avoid relegation and Leicestershire, with only two points from their last three games, to win the title race they had led since June. Excellent seam bowling by Smith and Malik restricted Leicestershire to just 22 runs in the first quarter, and Harris kept up the pressure by taking four for 24. In stark contrast, and easier batting conditions, Nottinghamshire's Morris, in his final professional game before retiring, made stroke-play look easy, scoring 57 from only 48 deliveries. Blewett just missed a half-century on his own farewell appearance at Trent Bridge, and Pietersen's typical run-a-ball cameo saw the home side win at a canter, leaving Leicestershire to reflect on a season in which two trophies were lost at the last. Poor Boswell, unable to control the ball at Lord's in the Cheltenham & Gloucester final, conceded 18 runs in his only over here before withdrawing with a calf injury.

Leicestershire

T. R. Ward b Harris	13	P. A. J. DeFreitas b Smith	6
J. M. Dakin b Malik	12	C. D. Crowe b Smith	5
*V. J. Wells c Afzaal b Harris	15	S. A. J. Boswell not out	1
B. F. Smith run out	1	L-b 3, w 5	8
D. I. Stevens c Morris b Clough	35		
†N. D. Burns c Morris b Harris	43	1/22 2/39 3/41 (9 wkts, 45 overs)	185
D. L. Maddy not out	46	4/51 5/110 6/142	
A. Habib c Read b Harris	0	7/143 8/168 9/184	

Bowling: Smith 9–4–25–2; Malik 9–0–36–1; Harris 8–0–24–4; Clough 7–0–33–1; Pietersen 4–0–27–0; Afzaal 8–0–37–0.

Nottinghamshire

*D. J. Bicknell c Habib b Crowe	35	†C. M. W. Read not out	8
J. E. Morris run out	57		
G. S. Blewett st Burns b Crowe	48	L-b 1, w 11	12
U. Afzaal st Burns b Crowe	1		
K. P. Pietersen not out	21	1/71 2/149 3/149 (5 wkts, 38.3 overs)	186
B. M. Shafayat c and b Crowe	4	4/152 5/170	

G. D. Clough, A. J. Harris, G. J. Smith and M. N. Malik did not bat.

Bowling: DeFreitas 9–2–23–0; Dakin 9–1–46–0; Boswell 1–0–18–0; Wells 5–1–35–0; Maddy 7–0–33–0; Crowe 7.3–0–30–4.

Umpires: D. J. Constant and D. R. Shepherd.

SOMERSET

At Leeds, May 13. SOMERSET lost to YORKSHIRE by five wickets.

SOMERSET v KENT

At Taunton, May 20. Kent won by 31 runs. Toss: Somerset.

Once Steffan Jones and Kerr had been awarded their county caps before the start of play, there was little else to celebrate from Somerset's viewpoint. The pitch was unreliable, making strokeplay difficult, although this did not excuse some of the technical shortcomings. Kent were 14 for three before Cullinan gave substance to their innings. Somerset had no one to rescue them from 15 for four after Trott, opening the visitors' bowling against the club that released him two years earlier, had struck early blows by sending back Holloway and Cox.

Kent

D. P. Fulton lbw b Jones	8	J. M. Golding b Jones	10
R. W. T. Key lbw b Kerr	1	M. M. Patel not out	10
J. B. Hockley b Jones	3	L-b 11, w 4, n-b 2	17
D. J. Cullinan c Jones b Blackwell	70		
M. J. Walker b Trego	14	1/2 2/5 3/14 (7 wkts, 45 overs)	180
†P. A. Nixon lbw b Grove	26	4/58 5/127	
*M. V. Fleming not out	21	6/134 7/157	

M. J. Saggers and B. J. Trott did not bat.

Bowling: Jones 8–2–34–3; Kerr 7–0–20–1; Burns 5–0–25–0; Trego 6–1–18–1; Dutch 5–0–27–0; Grove 9–0–24–1; Blackwell 5–0–21–1.

Somerset

P. D. Bowler run out	5	J. I. D. Kerr b Saggers	16
P. C. L. Holloway c Nixon b Trott	0	P. S. Jones not out	17
*J. Cox b Trott	3	J. O. Grove b Saggers	0
M. Burns b Saggers	5	L-b 6, w 3	9
I. D. Blackwell run out	32		
†R. J. Turner lbw b Fleming	28	1/4 2/8 3/15 (42.4 overs)	149
K. P. Dutch c Saggers b Patel	13	4/15 5/70 6/89	
P. D. Trego c Cullinan b Patel	21	7/101 8/122 9/149	

Bowling: Saggers 7.4–2–19–3; Trott 9–2–22–2; Golding 9–1–39–0; Fleming 8–0–25–1; Patel 9–0–38–2.

Umpires: J. W. Holder and A. G. T. Whitehead.

At Tunbridge Wells, June 3. SOMERSET tied with KENT.

At The Oval, June 10. SOMERSET beat SURREY by eight wickets.

SOMERSET v YORKSHIRE

At Bath, June 17. Somerset won by 15 runs. Toss: Yorkshire.

A festival crowd of more than 3,000 saw 500 runs scored on a benign track. Just back from law exams, Bowler batted with considerable aplomb for his 97. He added 112 in 15 overs with Blackwell, who built on his recent match-winning form with a pugnacious 76, off 54 balls, that featured five fours and four sixes. In the process, one or two usually capable bowlers, notably Hoggard, were savaged. In Yorkshire's reply, Byas never scored quite fast enough. Lehmann tried to recover lost ground, but the run-rate was always against him. Jones came up with four well-earned wickets, helped by Dutch's dazzlingly difficult catch to dismiss Fellows.

Somerset

P. D. Bowler c Hoggard b Hamilton	97
J. I. D. Kerr b Hutchison	5
P. C. L. Holloway c Byas b Hutchison	11
R. L. Johnson c Hamilton b Hutchison	1
M. N. Lathwell st Blakey b Fisher	27
I. D. Blackwell c and b White	76
*M. Burns not out	12
K. P. Dutch c Hutchison b Hoggard	1
†R. J. Turner not out	13
L-b 5, w 1, n-b 10	16
1/14 2/45 3/52 4/110 5/222 6/233 7/235 (7 wkts, 45 overs)	259

P. S. Jones and J. O. Grove did not bat.

Bowling: Hoggard 9–0–72–1; Hutchison 9–1–26–3; White 9–1–41–1; Hamilton 8–0–42–1; Fisher 7–0–53–1; Fellows 3–0–20–0.

Yorkshire

*D. Byas c Grove b Jones	81
M. J. Lumb c Bowler b Jones	9
C. White c Dutch b Kerr	39
D. S. Lehmann not out	75
G. M. Fellows c Dutch b Jones	6
†R. J. Blakey b Jones	1
V. J. Craven c Turner b Johnson	11
G. M. Hamilton not out	0
B 1, l-b 11, w 10	22
1/16 2/95 3/198 4/225 5/228 6/242 (6 wkts, 45 overs)	244

I. D. Fisher, M. J. Hoggard and P. M. Hutchison did not bat.

Bowling: Johnson 9–1–50–1; Jones 9–0–40–4; Grove 9–0–49–0; Kerr 9–1–56–1; Dutch 6–0–25–0; Blackwell 3–0–12–0.

Umpires: N. G. Cowley and R. Palmer.

At Nottingham, June 24. SOMERSET lost to NOTTINGHAMSHIRE by six wickets.

SOMERSET v GLOUCESTERSHIRE

At Taunton, July 1. Gloucestershire won by eight runs. Toss: Gloucestershire.

Barnett, approaching his 41st birthday and on the point of extending his contract with Gloucestershire, set up their win with a typically wily innings of 94 inside 44 overs. He had good support from Hancock and Windows early on, but little of note after that. Somerset's target looked accessible for a time. Johnson, going in first, provided early runs, and Bowler moved the innings along at a controlled tempo. Ultimately, however, Harvey's pace and movement dictated the closing play. He conceded only two runs off the final over as well as having Dutch stumped, for a fourth wicket.

Gloucestershire

T. H. C. Hancock c and b Parsons	43	M. A. Hardinges run out	0
K. J. Barnett lbw b Jones	94	M. C. J. Ball not out	5
J. N. Snape b Parsons	0	J. M. M. Averis not out	5
M. G. N. Windows c Turner b Grove	33	L-b 2, w 8	10
I. J. Harvey run out	4		
C. G. Taylor b Grove	9	1/77 2/77 3/163 (9 wkts, 45 overs)	219
*M. W. Alleyne c Dutch b Jones	1	4/167 5/178 6/180	
†R. C. Russell c Turner b Johnson	15	7/205 8/208 9/210	

Bowling: Johnson 8–0–36–1; Jones 9–0–48–2; Grove 8–0–40–2; Parsons 7–0–32–2; Dutch 6–0–31–0; Blackwell 7–0–30–0.

Somerset

P. D. Bowler c Snape b Ball	60	K. P. Dutch st Russell b Harvey	13
R. L. Johnson b Harvey	20	P. S. Jones not out	0
P. C. L. Holloway c Ball b Harvey	3		
M. N. Lathwell b Alleyne	30	L-b 4, w 1	5
I. D. Blackwell c Windows b Ball	8		
K. A. Parsons run out	28	1/27 2/31 3/77 (8 wkts, 45 overs)	211
*M. Burns not out	32	4/96 5/145 6/158	
†R. J. Turner c Barnett b Harvey	12	7/179 8/211	

J. O. Grove did not bat.

Bowling: Averis 9–1–35–0; Harvey 9–1–42–4; Alleyne 9–1–34–1; Hardinges 3–0–30–0; Ball 9–0–43–2; Barnett 6–0–23–0.

Umpires: G. I. Burgess and J. F. Steele.

SOMERSET v NOTTINGHAMSHIRE

At Taunton, July 8. Nottinghamshire won by three wickets. Toss: Somerset.

This was Somerset's fifth League defeat in eight matches. Their total was largely reliant on the in-form Bowler, whose 98 in 101 balls contained two sixes and ten fours. But the pitch was easy, and Nottinghamshire's Bicknell and Johnson took advantage of some wayward bowling as they rattled the score to 92 from the first 15 overs. Bicknell, with 79 from 70 balls, appeared less than pleased when adjudged run out by Peter Robinson – the home county's security officer and former chief coach – who was deputising at square leg for a limping David Shepherd. By then, though, the platform was in place for the middle order to complete the win.

Somerset

*J. Cox run out	13	R. L. Johnson not out	24
P. D. Bowler c Pietersen b Harris	98	J. I. D. Kerr not out	7
M. N. Lathwell c Bicknell b Logan	22		
M. Burns b Stemp	13	B 1, l-b 8, w 11	20
I. D. Blackwell st Read b Pietersen	15		
K. A. Parsons c Hewison b Stemp	19	1/21 2/72 3/96 (8 wkts, 45 overs)	248
K. P. Dutch run out	17	4/117 5/154 6/199	
†R. J. Turner lbw b Harris	0	7/209 8/223	

P. S. Jones did not bat.

Bowling: Smith 9–0–30–0; Harris 9–0–63–2; Logan 9–0–56–1; Stemp 9–0–45–2; Pietersen 9–0–45–1.

Nottinghamshire

*D. J. Bicknell run out	79	R. J. Logan b Johnson	0
K. P. Pietersen c Lathwell b Jones	11	G. J. Smith not out	5
G. S. Blewett c Turner b Johnson	6	L-b 2, w 1	3
P. Johnson c Parsons b Kerr	67		
B. M. Shafayat c Bowler b Johnson	31	1/18 2/35 3/146 (7 wkts, 44 overs)	252
†C. M. W. Read not out	30	4/196 5/199	
C. J. Hewison lbw b Kerr	20	6/235 7/245	

A. J. Harris and R. D. Stemp did not bat.

Bowling: Johnson 8–0–51–3; Jones 9–0–42–1; Kerr 9–0–55–2; Dutch 9–0–51–0; Parsons 6–0–27–0; Blackwell 3–0–24–0.

Umpires: J. W. Holder and D. R. Shepherd.

At Bristol, July 17 (day/night). GLOUCESTERSHIRE v SOMERSET. No result (abandoned).

SOMERSET v LEICESTERSHIRE

At Taunton, August 14. Somerset won by one run. Toss: Somerset.

Leaders Leicestershire, with one wicket left, required 16 off the last over to save their 100 per cent League record. Former Somerset wicket-keeper Neil Burns struck Kerr for four and, with ten needed off two balls, a six; but he could manage only two off the final delivery. It certainly whetted the appetite for the Cheltenham & Gloucester final, for which these counties had just qualified. Both sides were launched by major opening partnerships. Blackwell's 69-ball 86 spurred Somerset, and Bowler went on to his sixth one-day hundred; each hit 12 fours and a six. But the pyrotechnics came from Shahid Afridi as Leicestershire charged off at eight an over. Dropped twice, he smashed a ferocious 68 in 30 balls, hammering 66 in sixes and fours before being caught at deep mid-wicket. Even so, Leicestershire would not have gone so close but for a seventh-wicket stand of 69 between Habib and Burns.

Somerset

P. D. Bowler c Ward b Shahid Afridi	104	P. D. Trego lbw b Maddy	4
I. D. Blackwell c Burns b Ormond	86	J. I. D. Kerr not out	1
*J. Cox c Habib b Wells	26	B 1, l-b 6, w 6	13
K. P. Dutch c Wells b Shahid Afridi	9		
K. A. Parsons b Maddy	4	1/163 2/218 3/233 (7 wkts, 45 overs)	263
M. Burns b Maddy	5	4/241 5/241	
†R. J. Turner not out	11	6/250 7/262	

P. S. Jones and J. O. Grove did not bat.

Bowling: Ormond 9–0–42–1; Boswell 8.3–0–54–0; DeFreitas 4.3–0–34–0; Maddy 9–0–55–3; Shahid Afridi 7–0–37–2; Wells 7–0–34–1.

Leicestershire

T. R. Ward run out	19	P. A. J. DeFreitas c Dutch b Jones	9
Shahid Afridi c Burns b Kerr	68	J. Ormond b Jones	6
D. I. Stevens c Cox b Dutch	27	S. A. J. Boswell not out	1
*V. J. Wells c Blackwell b Kerr	1	B 2, l-b 2, w 5, n-b 2	11
B. F. Smith run out	13		
D. L. Maddy c Jones b Blackwell	4	1/82 2/94 3/97 (9 wkts, 45 overs)	262
A. Habib c Burns b Grove	44	4/130 5/131 6/145	
†N. D. Burns not out	59	7/214 8/235 9/248	

Bowling: Jones 9–0–59–2; Grove 9–0–65–1; Kerr 9–0–55–2; Dutch 9–0–40–1; Blackwell 9–0–39–1.

Umpires: J. H. Evans and M. J. Harris.

At Birmingham, August 19. SOMERSET lost to WARWICKSHIRE by ten wickets (D/L method).

SOMERSET v SURREY

At Taunton, August 21 (day/night). Somerset won by four wickets. Toss: Surrey.

To the relief of the massed Somerset supporters, Surrey failed to build on an ominously fluent stand of 155 between Brown and Adam Hollioake. Blackwell's three for 16, beginning with a fine return catch to deprive Brown of his century, applied the brake. Bowler and Burns produced the confident strokeplay in Somerset's reply; in the case of Burns – just recovered from chicken-pox – this tended to be more unorthodox, with some effective reverse sweeps. They added 87 in 12 overs, and by the time Bowler was caught at the wicket, like Brown in sight of his hundred, Somerset needed only nine more with overs to spare.

Surrey

I. J. Ward c Bowler b Jones	11
A. D. Brown c and b Blackwell	98
G. J. Batty c Turner b Jones	0
*A. J. Hollioake st Turner b Dutch	70
B. C. Hollioake c Dutch b Blackwell	18
G. P. Butcher b Blackwell	2
M. P. Bicknell not out	23
†J. N. Batty c Bowler b Johnson	3
Saqlain Mushtaq run out	1
T. J. Murtagh not out	2
L-b 5, w 3	8
1/27 2/27 3/182 4/185 5/191 6/212 7/218 8/220 (8 wkts, 45 overs)	236

E. S. H. Giddins did not bat.

Bowling: Johnson 9–0–58–1; Jones 7–1–22–2; Grove 9–1–53–0; Parsons 9–0–45–0; Dutch 5–0–37–1; Blackwell 6–2–16–3.

Somerset

P. D. Bowler c J. N. Batty b Giddins	86
I. D. Blackwell c J. N. Batty b Giddins	24
*J. Cox lbw b Giddins	16
M. J. Wood c J. N. Batty b Murtagh	13
M. Burns b B. C. Hollioake	53
K. A. Parsons c J. N. Batty b B. C. Hollioake	16
†R. J. Turner not out	3
K. P. Dutch not out	8
B 4, l-b 5, w 5, n-b 4	18
1/44 2/70 3/119 4/206 5/224 6/228 (6 wkts, 41 overs)	237

R. L. Johnson, P. S. Jones and J. O. Grove did not bat.

Bowling: Bicknell 9–0–48–0; Giddins 9–2–31–3; B. C. Hollioake 8–0–60–2; Saqlain Mushtaq 6–0–22–0; Murtagh 6–0–41–1; G. J. Batty 3–0–26–0.

Umpires: J. H. Evans and R. Palmer.

At Leicester, August 27. SOMERSET beat LEICESTERSHIRE by ten runs.

At Northampton, August 30. SOMERSET beat NORTHAMPTONSHIRE by 70 runs (D/L method).

SOMERSET v WARWICKSHIRE

At Taunton, September 3. Warwickshire won by eight wickets. Toss: Somerset.

With 14 overs remaining when Warwickshire passed their modest 190, this was very much an anticlimax for Somerset after their heady triumph in the Cheltenham & Gloucester final two days earlier. The warmest applause came with the award of county caps to Blackwell, Dutch and Richard Johnson. Only Lord's hero Parsons and Cox gave Somerset's batting any real substance, and their bowling looked decidedly ordinary; Grove conceded three sixes in one over and was particularly expensive. Knight remained unbeaten off 101 balls, while the promoted Drakes (35 balls) and Brown (44 balls) helped him reel in the target.

Somerset

P. D. Bowler c Hemp b Drakes	8	J. I. D. Kerr not out	8
I. D. Blackwell c Smith b Drakes	8	P. S. Jones not out	8
*J. Cox c Hemp b Sheikh	42		
M. Burns b Richardson	27	B 1, l-b 8, w 5	14
K. A. Parsons c Knight b Richardson	42		
†R. J. Turner c Powell b Sheikh	6	1/14 2/34 3/92 (8 wkts, 45 overs)	190
K. P. Dutch lbw b Smith	10	4/100 5/109 6/124	
M. J. Wood b Smith	17	7/173 8/177	

J. O. Grove did not bat.

Bowling: Brown 9–1–48–0; Drakes 9–0–40–2; Richardson 9–0–36–2; Sheikh 9–1–23–2; Smith 9–1–34–2.

Warwickshire

N. V. Knight not out	84
M. A. Wagh c Turner b Kerr	0
V. C. Drakes lbw b Parsons	43
D. R. Brown not out	59
B 2, l-b 1, w 2	5
1/0 2/80 (2 wkts, 30.4 overs)	191

D. L. Hemp, *M. J. Powell, T. L. Penney, †K. J. Piper, N. M. K. Smith, M. A. Sheikh and A. Richardson did not bat.

Bowling: Jones 6–1–22–0; Kerr 7–0–40–1; Grove 4–0–49–0; Parsons 6–1–28–1; Burns 3–0–13–0; Dutch 3–0–24–0; Blackwell 1.4–0–12–0.

Umpires: J. W. Holder and R. Palmer.

SOMERSET v NORTHAMPTONSHIRE

At Taunton, September 16. Somerset won by 12 runs. Toss: Northamptonshire.

Under threat of relegation if they lost, Somerset preserved their first-division status, despite spirited batting from Hussey and Warren. Relegated Northamptonshire were 159 for one before Hussey, so prolific here recently in the Championship, was stumped off Dutch when nine short of his hundred; he faced just 81 balls. Wicket-keeper Turner then caught Warren off Blackwell, and the middle order capitulated, leaving Alec Swann to revive the challenge with 31 not out from 29 balls. Kerr's tight spell at the end compensated for the 14 conceded in his first over. Burns had earlier hit an opportunistic hundred for Somerset, completed in 112 deliveries off the last ball of the innings. He and Turner put on an unbroken 129 after Cox, batting part of the time with a runner because of a strained hamstring, had established the innings.

Somerset

*J. Cox c Brown b Cook	68	†R. J. Turner not out	41
I. D. Blackwell b Taylor	4	B 2, l-b 11, w 2, n-b 2	17
M. J. Wood c Warren b Taylor	23		
M. Burns not out	101	1/6 2/56 (4 wkts, 45 overs)	255
K. A. Parsons c Bailey b Cook	1	3/121 4/126	

K. P. Dutch, R. L. Johnson, J. I. D. Kerr, P. S. Jones and M. P. L. Bulbeck did not bat.

Bowling: Weekes 4–0–33–0; Taylor 9–0–58–2; Penberthy 9–0–37–0; Cook 9–1–44–2; Brown 5–0–18–0; G. P. Swann 9–0–52–0.

Northamptonshire

*M. E. K. Hussey st Turner b Dutch	91	J. P. Taylor b Kerr	6
G. P. Swann b Johnson	11	L. C. Weekes b Kerr	7
R. J. Warren c Turner b Blackwell	59	J. F. Brown b Jones	1
D. J. Sales c Wood b Dutch	8	B 2, l-b 4, w 2	8
A. L. Penberthy b Blackwell	5		——
J. W. Cook c and b Dutch	3	1/46 2/159 3/171 (43.5 overs)	243
A. J. Swann not out	31	4/173 5/182 6/182	
†T. M. B. Bailey c Dutch b Blackwell	13	7/206 8/224 9/240	

Bowling: Johnson 9–0–44–1; Jones 8.5–1–55–1; Kerr 5–0–33–2; Bulbeck 2–0–22–0; Dutch 9–1–38–3; Blackwell 9–1–39–3; Parsons 1–0–6–0.

Umpires: M. R. Benson and A. Clarkson.

SURREY

SURREY v NOTTINGHAMSHIRE

At The Oval, May 13. Nottinghamshire won by 17 runs. Toss: Nottinghamshire.

Ben Hollioake's thrilling 70 off 66 balls gave Surrey hope, but in truth their target was always out of reach after top-order failures: 63 off the last five overs looked improbable and 23 from the last, after Hollioake had hit Franks for four successive boundaries in the penultimate over, proved impossible. Darren Bicknell, returning to his old stamping-ground as acting Nottinghamshire captain, had given the visitors a good start before being yorked by his younger brother, while Blewett provided substance and Afzaal acceleration to a total some observers still thought insufficient.

Nottinghamshire

*D. J. Bicknell b Bicknell	50	P. J. Franks not out	1
G. E. Welton lbw b G. P. Butcher	26	G. D. Clough b Giddins	0
G. S. Blewett b A. J. Hollioake	69	L-b 7, w 4	11
U. Afzaal c Bicknell b A. J. Hollioake	49		——
P. Johnson run out	17	1/52 2/110 3/181 (8 wkts, 45 overs)	233
K. P. Pietersen c Batty b A. J. Hollioake	1	4/216 5/218 6/232	
†C. M. W. Read run out	9	7/232 8/233	

G. J. Smith and R. D. Stemp did not bat.

Bowling: G. P. Butcher 7–0–36–1; Giddins 9–1–34–1; Bicknell 9–0–47–1; Salisbury 9–0–39–0; A. J. Hollioake 9–0–56–3; Brown 2–0–14–0.

Surrey

M. A. Butcher lbw b Clough	20	M. P. Bicknell run out	8
A. D. Brown c Bicknell b Smith	0	I. D. K. Salisbury b Smith	2
M. R. Ramprakash c Read b Clough	30		
N. Shahid c Bicknell b Stemp	43	L-b 5, w 9	14
*A. J. Hollioake run out	1		——
B. C. Hollioake not out	70	1/3 2/42 3/79 (9 wkts, 45 overs)	216
G. P. Butcher run out	13	4/86 5/117 6/152	
†J. N. Batty c Blewett b Smith	15	7/187 8/212 9/216	

E. S. H. Giddins did not bat.

Bowling: Smith 8–0–32–3; Franks 9–0–53–0; Clough 9–0–33–2; Blewett 4–0–22–0; Stemp 9–0–36–1; Pietersen 6–0–35–0.

Umpires: N. G. Cowley and A. G. T. Whitehead.

SURREY v LEICESTERSHIRE

At The Oval, May 20. Leicestershire won by four wickets. Toss: Surrey.

Leicestershire's Marsh masterminded a close but comfortable win that shaded Brown's typically bold unbeaten hundred for Surrey and his entertaining 127-run partnership with Ben Hollioake in the last 20 overs. Brown's 111, off 129 balls, contained a six and 11 fours; Hollioake's 64, his second successive unbeaten half-century in the League, came off 63. But Marsh, whose 102-ball innings included a six and nine fours, always had Surrey's measure. He first put Leicestershire on course by adding 56 with Ward, then he and Maddy sent them racing towards victory with a run-a-ball stand of 77.

Surrey

M. A. Butcher c Marsh b Boswell	4
A. D. Brown not out	111
M. R. Ramprakash c Crowe b Boswell	10
N. Shahid c Burns b Boswell	1
*A. J. Hollioake c Boswell b Marsh	27
B. C. Hollioake not out	64
B 3, l-b 2, w 8	13
1/5 2/23 3/40 4/103 (4 wkts, 45 overs)	230

G. P. Butcher, A. J. Tudor, †J. N. Batty, I. D. K. Salisbury and E. S. H. Giddins did not bat.

Bowling: Ormond 9–2–34–0; Boswell 9–2–32–3; Marsh 9–0–48–1; Wells 9–0–33–0; Maddy 5–0–54–0; Dakin 4–0–24–0.

Leicestershire

*V. J. Wells b Tudor	3
J. M. Dakin b Tudor	15
T. R. Ward lbw b G. P. Butcher	31
D. J. Marsh not out	97
B. F. Smith c A. J. Hollioake b Salisbury	14
D. L. Maddy lbw b A. J. Hollioake	46
D. I. Stevens b A. J. Hollioake	10
†N. D. Burns not out	2
L-b 4, w 9	13
1/18 2/19 3/75 4/117 5/194 6/227 (6 wkts, 44.3 overs)	231

J. Ormond, C. D. Crowe and S. A. J. Boswell did not bat.

Bowling: Tudor 9–2–35–2; Giddins 9–0–50–0; A. J. Hollioake 9–0–43–2; G. P. Butcher 3–0–23–1; Salisbury 9–0–42–1; B. C. Hollioake 5.3–0–34–0.

Umpires: T. E. Jesty and D. R. Shepherd.

At Northampton, June 3. SURREY beat NORTHAMPTONSHIRE by four wickets.

SURREY v SOMERSET

At The Oval, June 10. Somerset won by eight wickets. Toss: Surrey.

Rain, setting in after the captains had tossed, reduced the match to a ten-over thrash; Somerset fast bowler Ian Jones, who had arrived at the ground as a spectator, cut Surrey to the quick with three wickets in his two overs after being drafted into the Somerset side because Johnson had been taken ill. Surrey fell woefully short of setting a challenging target and Blackwell's 18-ball blitz for 33 made a nonsense of it as he drove Somerset to their first League win of the season.

Surrey

I. J. Ward b I. Jones 22
M. R. Ramprakash c Burns b Grove . . . 11
*A. J. Hollioake b Trego 2
M. A. Butcher b I. Jones 2
N. Shahid b I. Jones 19
G. P. Butcher not out 6
G. J. Batty not out 2
B 1, l-b 3 4

1/22 2/31 3/34 4/58 5/59 (5 wkts, 10 overs) 68

†J. N. Batty, M. P. Bicknell, C. G. Greenidge and E. S. H. Giddins did not bat.

Bowling: P. S. Jones 2–0–13–0; Kerr 2–0–10–0; Grove 2–0–18–1; Trego 2–0–9–1; I. Jones 2–0–14–3.

Somerset

*J. Cox b Greenidge 22
I. D. Blackwell not out 33
†M. Burns c Giddins b Greenidge 4
K. P. Dutch not out. 10

1/37 2/41 (2 wkts, 6.3 overs) 69

M. N. Lathwell, P. C. L. Holloway, P. D. Trego, J. I. D. Kerr, I. Jones, P. S. Jones and J. O. Grove did not bat.

Bowling: Bicknell 2–0–23–0; Giddins 1–0–14–0; Greenidge 2–0–17–2; Hollioake 1–0–9–0; Ramprakash 0.3–0–6–0.

Umpires: A. A. Jones and J. W. Lloyds.

SURREY v KENT

At The Oval, June 24. Kent won by two wickets. Toss: Surrey.

Saqlain Mushtaq, in his first game for Surrey since touring with Pakistan, made a duck, went wicketless and conceded most runs. It was not his weekend: the previous day, he had been on the losing side at Lord's in the NatWest Series final. The Hollioake brothers had pulled Surrey out of trouble at 23 for four, and after a tight spell from Bicknell and four wickets for Tudor they appeared to have turned the tables when Kent were 70 for six. Jones and Fleming then added 54 and, after Patel followed Jones second ball, Saggers helped Fleming preserve Kent's unbeaten record.

Surrey

M. A. Butcher b Saggers 8
I. J. Ward c Walker b Trott. 9
N. Shahid c Nixon b Saggers 3
A. D. Brown c Patel b Trott 0
*A. J. Hollioake st Nixon b Walker 36
B. C. Hollioake b Ealham 46
A. J. Tudor b Saggers 6
†J. N. Batty lbw b Ealham. 0
M. P. Bicknell not out. 19
I. D. K. Salisbury c and b Walker 13
Saqlain Mushtaq c Fulton b Walker 0
L-b 8, w 6. 14

1/14 2/22 3/22 4/23 5/108 6/114 7/115 8/124 9/154 (44.2 overs) 154

Bowling: Saggers 9–1–21–3; Trott 9–2–19–2; Ealham 9–0–41–2; Fleming 5–0–13–0; Patel 6–0–31–0; Walker 6.2–0–21–3.

Kent

J. B. Hockley c Batty b Bicknell. 0
D. P. Fulton lbw b Bicknell 20
E. T. Smith c A. J. Hollioake b Tudor . . 10
M. J. Walker c Salisbury b Tudor 4
M. A. Ealham c Brown b Tudor 13
†P. A. Nixon b Tudor 7
G. O. Jones c Batty b B. C. Hollioake . . 39
*M. V. Fleming not out 26
M. M. Patel lbw b A. J. Hollioake. 0
M. J. Saggers not out 15
B 4, w 16, n-b 4. 24

1/0 2/24 3/35 4/44 5/59 6/70 7/124 8/125 (8 wkts, 39.3 overs) 158

B. J. Trott did not bat.

Bowling: Bicknell 9–1–16–2; Tudor 9–0–36–4; Saqlain Mushtaq 9–1–42–0; Salisbury 2–0–22–0; B. C. Hollioake 7–2–22–1; A. J. Hollioake 3.3–0–16–1.

Umpires: B. Dudleston and J. H. Hampshire.

At Leicester, July 8. SURREY lost to LEICESTERSHIRE by 128 runs.

SURREY v NORTHAMPTONSHIRE

At Guildford, July 22. Northamptonshire won by eight wickets (D/L method). Toss: Northamptonshire. County debut: J. J. Porter.

Rain trimmed the match to 42 overs apiece, and its imminent return during Northamptonshire's reply was all the spur Hussey and Loye needed. Either side of the inevitable interruption, which resulted in a revised target of 176 off 37 overs, they hammered an unbroken 170 in 26 to achieve victory with almost seven overs to spare. Hussey made an impressive 96 off 88 balls, while Loye needed 76 for his 70. In the circumstances, Bicknell's figures of two for 16 in eight overs were exceptional. Adam Hollioake's 66 off 67 balls was also notable, but Surrey missed their England batsmen as well as Ben Hollioake and Brown, out through injury.

Surrey

N. Shahid b Weekes	20
M. A. Carberry lbw b Taylor	1
G. J. Batty c Ripley b Taylor	26
*A. J. Hollioake b Strong	66
G. P. Butcher c Weekes b Penberthy	17
J. J. Porter b Brown	23
A. J. Tudor c Brown b Weekes	21
M. P. Bicknell c Swann b Penberthy	6
†J. N. Batty b Strong	5
Saqlain Mushtaq b Strong	1
E. S. H. Giddins not out	0
L-b 2, w 5, n-b 2	9
1/10 2/46 3/54 4/91 5/134 6/174 7/185 8/193 9/195 (41.1 overs)	195

Bowling: Strong 8–0–52–3; Taylor 9–1–28–2; Weekes 9–0–55–2; Penberthy 7.1–1–28–2; Brown 8–0–30–1.

Northamptonshire

A. S. Rollins c Tudor b Bicknell	1
M. B. Loye not out	70
A. L. Penberthy lbw b Bicknell	1
M. E. K. Hussey not out	96
L-b 2, w 6	8
1/2 2/6 (2 wkts, 30.2 overs)	176

L. C. Weekes, G. P. Swann, T. M. B. Bailey, *†D. Ripley, J. P. Taylor, M. R. Strong and J. F. Brown did not bat.

Bowling: Bicknell 8–1–16–2; Tudor 7–1–41–0; Giddins 6–0–50–0; Saqlain Mushtaq 8–0–51–0; Hollioake 1–0–14–0; G. J. Batty 0.2–0–2–0.

Umpires: D. J. Constant and N. G. Cowley.

At Birmingham, July 29. SURREY lost to WARWICKSHIRE by three wickets.

At Leeds, August 5. SURREY lost to YORKSHIRE by 67 runs.

SURREY v GLOUCESTERSHIRE

At The Oval, August 12. Surrey won by two wickets. Toss: Gloucestershire.

Surrey's second League win in ten games, achieved with two balls to spare, was not enough to lift them from the foot of the table, where they had been since the beginning of July. It was the second time in the season they'd had the better of Gloucestershire, following their victory in the Benson and Hedges Cup final. Adam Hollioake returned from injury to share a critical partnership of 76 with his younger brother, but Snape's three late wickets set up a tense finish. Snape had earlier put on 109 in 22 overs with Windows; otherwise Gloucestershire's batting never got going.

Gloucestershire

D. R. Hewson lbw b Giddins	0
K. J. Barnett c and b Giddins	5
I. J. Harvey c Saqlain Mushtaq b Greenidge	4
M. G. N. Windows c J. N. Batty b B. C. Hollioake	70
*M. W. Alleyne b Greenidge	19
J. N. Snape c J. N. Batty b Murtagh	49
T. H. C. Hancock c J. N. Batty b B. C. Hollioake	4
†R. C. Russell c J. N. Batty b B. C. Hollioake	4
M. A. Hardinges not out	3
M. C. J. Ball st J. N. Batty b G. J. Batty	0
J. M. M. Averis c sub b G. J. Batty	1
B 2, l-b 9, w 6	17
1/0 2/10 3/11 4/48 5/157 6/164 7/167 8/170 9/171 (40.1 overs)	176

Bowling: Giddins 6–1–22–2; Greenidge 8–1–39–2; B. C. Hollioake 7–0–24–3; Murtagh 8–0–41–1; Saqlain Mushtaq 9–1–34–0; G. J. Batty 2.1–0–5–2.

Surrey

M. A. Carberry c Hardinges b Harvey	4
A. D. Brown b Averis	27
G. J. Batty c Russell b Alleyne	17
*A. J. Hollioake c Russell b Harvey	56
B. C. Hollioake c Windows b Averis	42
†J. N. Batty c Russell b Snape	7
N. Shahid c Hewson b Snape	9
Saqlain Mushtaq c Hewson b Snape	1
T. J. Murtagh not out	4
C. G. Greenidge not out	0
L-b 7, w 6	13
1/25 2/49 3/78 4/154 5/161 6/174 7/174 8/176 (8 wkts, 40.4 overs)	180

E. S. H. Giddins did not bat.

Bowling: Harvey 9–0–36–2; Averis 8–0–37–2; Ball 8–0–31–0; Alleyne 8–1–37–1; Snape 6.4–1–30–3; Hardinges 1–0–2–0.

Umpires: D. R. Shepherd and R. A. White.

At Canterbury, August 14 (day/night). SURREY lost to KENT by 43 runs.

At Taunton, August 21 (day/night). SURREY lost to SOMERSET by four wickets.

SURREY v WARWICKSHIRE

At Whitgift School, Croydon, August 30. Surrey won by 123 runs. Toss: Surrey.

Ally Brown's stunning 116 transcended the vagaries of a grassy pitch and enthralled the sizeable crowd at this delightful venue. Coming in at 15 for three, he hit four sixes and 14 fours in 108 balls. Warwickshire threatened briefly until Ward took a brilliant catch, leaping to his left in the covers, to dismiss Wagh. Knight followed 22 runs later, and the visitors lost their last eight wickets for 42 in just under 15 overs. However, the victory, only their third of the season, did little to improve Surrey's prospects of avoiding relegation.

Surrey

M. A. Butcher b Dagnall	5
I. J. Ward b Brown	9
†A. J. Stewart c Wagh b Richardson	19
*A. J. Hollioake b Brown	0
A. D. Brown lbw b Brown	116
B. C. Hollioake b Dagnall	31
G. J. Batty b Brown	37
M. P. Bicknell c Richardson b Smith	7
Saqlain Mushtaq not out	1
T. J. Murtagh b Smith	0
E. S. H. Giddins b Smith	0
B 1, w 5	6
1/12 2/15 3/15 4/92 5/156 6/212 7/225 8/231 9/231 (45 overs)	231

Bowling: Brown 9–1–56–4; Dagnall 9–3–27–2; Richardson 9–0–45–1; Sheikh 9–0–30–0; Smith 6–0–52–3; Powell 3–0–20–0.

Warwickshire

N. V. Knight c Stewart b B. C. Hollioake	34
M. A. Wagh c Ward b Giddins	16
D. R. Brown c A. J. Hollioake b Bicknell	0
D. L. Hemp b Murtagh	14
*M. J. Powell c Bicknell b B. C. Hollioake	9
T. L. Penney c Batty b Murtagh	24
†K. J. Piper b Murtagh	0
N. M. K. Smith c A. J. Hollioake b B. C. Hollioake	1
M. A. Sheikh run out	1
C. E. Dagnall b Murtagh	2
A. Richardson not out	0
L-b 1, w 2, n-b 4	7
1/44 2/45 3/66 4/66 5/84 6/85 7/88 8/95 9/108 (29.5 overs)	108

Bowling: Bicknell 7–0–30–1; Giddins 7–0–36–1; B. C. Hollioake 8–4–10–3; Murtagh 7.5–0–31–4.

Umpires: J. H. Hampshire and A. A. Jones.

SURREY v YORKSHIRE

At The Oval, September 3 (day/night). Surrey won by seven wickets (D/L method). Toss: Yorkshire.

A Yorkshireman's maiden fifty brought about the downfall of his native county, and had Byas and his men contemplating the drop to Division Two alongside Surrey. All-rounder Gareth Batty, a member of the Headingley staff in 1997, reached 50 off just 38 balls, sharing in a stand of 121 with Butcher, and finished unbeaten on 83 as Surrey achieved their revised target of 186 with four balls to spare. Once Yorkshire had lost Lehmann to a stinging return catch in Saqlain Mushtaq's first over, their innings lost its impetus.

Yorkshire

M. J. Wood c J. N. Batty b Giddins	25
M. P. Vaughan c J. N. Batty b Giddins	24
A. McGrath b B. C. Hollioake	15
D. S. Lehmann c and b Saqlain Mushtaq	47
*D. Byas lbw b Saqlain Mushtaq	22
G. M. Fellows run out	23
†R. J. Blakey c Murtagh b B. C. Hollioake	28
R. K. J. Dawson c and b Saqlain Mushtaq	9
D. Gough not out	16
C. J. Elstub not out	0
W 3, n-b 2	5
1/40 2/58 3/73 4/121 5/160 6/160 7/176 8/214 (8 wkts, 45 overs)	214

M. J. Hoggard did not bat.

Bowling: Bicknell 9–0–30–0; Giddins 7–1–33–2; B. C. Hollioake 7–0–31–2; Murtagh 8–0–51–0; Saqlain Mushtaq 9–0–44–3; G. J. Batty 5–1–25–0.

Surrey

M. A. Butcher c and b Dawson	50	*A. J. Hollioake not out	18
I. J. Ward c Byas b Elstub	6	B 2, l-b 3, w 5, n-b 2	12
G. J. Batty not out	83		
A. D. Brown b Gough	19	1/13 2/134 3/167 (3 wkts, 33.2 overs)	188

B. C. Hollioake, †J. N. Batty, M. P. Bicknell, Saqlain Mushtaq, T. J. Murtagh and E. S. H. Giddins did not bat.

Bowling: Hoggard 6.2–1–24–0; Elstub 4–0–32–1; Fellows 3–0–15–0; Gough 7–0–38–1; Dawson 7–0–41–1; Lehmann 6–0–33–0.

Umpires: J. W. Lloyds and G. Sharp.

At Nottingham, September 9. SURREY beat NOTTINGHAMSHIRE by five wickets.

At Bristol, September 16. SURREY beat GLOUCESTERSHIRE by 36 runs.

WARWICKSHIRE

At Canterbury, April 29. KENT v WARWICKSHIRE. No result (abandoned).

At Nottingham, May 20. WARWICKSHIRE lost to NOTTINGHAMSHIRE by four wickets.

WARWICKSHIRE v GLOUCESTERSHIRE

At Birmingham, May 29 (day/night). Warwickshire won by 39 runs. Toss: Warwickshire.

Ostler's maiden League hundred – his 134 not out equalled Nick Knight's county record for the competition – dominated the first floodlit game of the summer, played in perfect weather before a crowd of 7,000. After taking 70 balls to reach 50, he launched a blistering attack that brought his next 84 runs from just 44. He struck 12 fours and three sixes in all and received intelligent support from Penney, whose undefeated 30 in 17 balls contained five fours, in an unbroken stand of 113 in nine overs. Averis went for 23 in the last of them. Powell had earlier helped Ostler add 90 in 19 overs. Gloucestershire missed the improvisational skills of Harvey, who was 30 miles down the M5 with the Australians at Worcester, and they slipped quietly to defeat.

Warwickshire

M. A. Wagh c Ball b Lewis	7	T. L. Penney not out	30
D. L. Hemp c Ball b Cawdron	23	L-b 3, w 4	7
N. M. K. Smith run out	6		
D. P. Ostler not out	134	1/10 2/23 (4 wkts, 45 overs)	248
*M. J. Powell run out	41	3/45 4/135	

D. R. Brown, M. A. Sheikh, †K. J. Piper, V. C. Drakes and C. E. Dagnall did not bat.

Bowling: Averis 9–2–54–0; Lewis 9–2–31–1; Cawdron 9–1–58–1; Alleyne 9–1–45–0; Ball 7–0–44–0; Hancock 2–0–13–0.

Gloucestershire

T. H. C. Hancock b Brown	2
K. J. Barnett b Drakes	28
R. J. Cunliffe c Piper b Brown	6
M. G. N. Windows st Piper b Sheikh	37
*M. W. Alleyne st Piper b Sheikh	9
J. N. Snape run out	27
†R. C. J. Williams b Smith	28
M. C. J. Ball b Drakes	28
M. J. Cawdron lbw b Smith	4
J. M. M. Averis not out	17
J. Lewis c Ostler b Smith	12
B 3, l-b 7, w 1	11
1/5 2/29 3/51 4/79 5/100 6/132 7/158 8/170 9/180 (44.4 overs)	209

Bowling: Dagnall 9–1–30–0; Brown 9–2–35–2; Sheikh 9–0–32–2; Drakes 9–2–38–2; Smith 8.4–0–64–3.

Umpires: T. E. Jesty and N. A. Mallender.

At Northampton, June 10. WARWICKSHIRE beat NORTHAMPTONSHIRE by five wickets.

At Gloucester, June 17. WARWICKSHIRE beat GLOUCESTERSHIRE by five wickets.

WARWICKSHIRE v LEICESTERSHIRE

At Birmingham, June 24. Leicestershire won by five wickets. Toss: Warwickshire.

Smith and Maddy's resourceful, unbroken stand of 90 in 11 overs turned what looked like being Leicestershire's first League loss into a fifth consecutive win. Drakes and Ostler held spectacular catches as the Division One leaders limped to 135 for five, but the celebrations of home supporters in the 4,000 crowd proved premature as the sixth-wicket pair unsettled Warwickshire with their superb running and skilful dissection of Powell's field placings. Warwickshire's own batsmen had struggled to assess the pace of a slowish pitch, and Ormond's accuracy pegged them back in his unchanged opening spell. The innings was revived by the in-form Ostler and Powell, who added 107 for the fourth wicket.

Warwickshire

N. V. Knight c Sutcliffe b Ormond	12
N. M. K. Smith c Burns b Ormond	11
D. R. Brown c Sutcliffe b Boswell	1
D. P. Ostler b DeFreitas	54
*M. J. Powell c Wells b Maddy	48
T. L. Penney lbw b Wells	20
A. F. Giles b Maddy	23
M. A. Sheikh not out	12
V. C. Drakes not out	8
B 8, l-b 16, w 8	32
1/24 2/25 3/38 4/145 5/151 6/200 7/202 (7 wkts, 45 overs)	221

†T. Frost and C. E. Dagnall did not bat.

Bowling: Ormond 9–0–37–2; Boswell 8–1–28–1; DeFreitas 9–1–38–1; Dakin 3–0–12–0; Marsh 5–0–32–0; Maddy 9–0–39–2; Wells 2–0–11–1.

Leicestershire

*V. J. Wells c Drakes b Dagnall	16
J. M. Dakin c Giles b Brown	22
D. I. Stevens c Powell b Dagnall	7
I. J. Sutcliffe c Penney b Smith	36
D. J. Marsh c Ostler b Giles	36
B. F. Smith not out	65
D. L. Maddy not out	37
L-b 6	6
1/23 2/40 3/51 4/102 5/135 (5 wkts, 43 overs)	225

†N. D. Burns, P. A. J. DeFreitas, S. A. J. Boswell and J. Ormond did not bat.

Bowling: Brown 8–2–50–1; Dagnall 7–0–32–2; Sheikh 7–0–40–0; Drakes 8–1–30–0; Giles 9–0–41–1; Smith 4–0–26–1.

Umpires: M. R. Benson and J. W. Lloyds.

WARWICKSHIRE v NORTHAMPTONSHIRE

At Birmingham, July 15. Warwickshire won by four wickets. Toss: Northamptonshire.

Notwithstanding the loss of their first three wickets in eight balls to Strong, Warwickshire had little trouble pursuing Northamptonshire's modest total. A two-paced pitch restricted attacking strokeplay, and there were only ten boundaries in Northamptonshire's innings, eight by Warren, whose patient unbeaten 80 held things together. Carter marked his first League outing with three wickets, including both openers, though he was not such a hit opening Warwickshire's reply. Knight and Ostler regrouped successfully, however, with a fourth-wicket partnership of 76 in 20 overs, and Warwickshire were 13 short of victory when Ostler eventually went. Penney and Giles completed the formalities with 40 balls to spare.

Northamptonshire

M. E. K. Hussey c Powell b Carter	7	*†D. Ripley b Brown	6
M. B. Loye c Piper b Carter	2	M. R. Strong not out	1
R. J. Warren not out	80		
A. L. Penberthy b Giles	13	B 3, l-b 7, w 7, n-b 2	19
J. W. Cook c Sheikh b Brown	16		
G. P. Swann c Knight b Sheikh	0	1/8 2/17 3/58 (8 wkts, 45 overs)	158
T. M. B. Bailey c Ostler b Brown	12	4/109 5/109 6/130	
J. P. Taylor b Carter	2	7/134 8/146	

J. F. Brown did not bat.

Bowling: Dagnall 9–0–19–0; Carter 9–2–28–3; Brown 9–0–35–3; Giles 9–0–37–1; Sheikh 9–1–29–1.

Warwickshire

N. M. Carter c Ripley b Strong	13	T. L. Penney not out	10
N. V. Knight c Penberthy b Swann	47	A. F. Giles not out	3
M. A. Wagh c Cook b Strong	0	L-b 5, w 3	8
D. R. Brown c Cook b Strong	0		
D. P. Ostler c Ripley b Brown	49	1/18 2/18 3/18 (6 wkts, 38.2 overs)	159
*M. J. Powell c Warren b Strong	29	4/94 5/146 6/146	

†K. J. Piper, M. A. Sheikh and C. E. Dagnall did not bat.

Bowling: Strong 9–1–39–4; Taylor 8–1–33–0; Penberthy 7.2–0–27–0; Brown 9–0–27–1; Swann 5–1–28–1.

Umpires: V. A. Holder and J. W. Lloyds.

At Leeds, July 23 (day/night). WARWICKSHIRE lost to YORKSHIRE by 175 runs.

WARWICKSHIRE v SURREY

At Birmingham, July 29. Warwickshire won by three wickets. Toss: Warwickshire.

Ward, Butcher, Ramprakash, Stewart and Tudor had just been named for the Third Test, but could not prevent Surrey's seventh defeat in eight games. The five mustered only 41 runs between them on an unreliable surface, and Butcher required hospital treatment after Carter's bouncer cut his left ear. Ben Hollioake made a determined half-century, but only Saqlain Mushtaq lent substantial support. Giddins was out first ball in his first innings at Edgbaston since leaving Warwickshire. The home side stuttered to victory somewhat, but still had seven overs to spare after Brown had followed up his three wickets with a belligerent 63 containing ten fours.

Surrey

M. A. Butcher retired hurt	3	M. P. Bicknell b Sheikh	2
I. J. Ward c Piper b Carter	8	Saqlain Mushtaq b Brown	20
M. R. Ramprakash c Piper b Drakes	20	E. S. H. Giddins lbw b Brown	0
†A. J. Stewart lbw b Carter	0	L-b 4, w 3, n-b 4	11
*A. J. Hollioake c Piper b Brown	6		
B. C. Hollioake not out	52	1/16 2/16 3/35 (42.2 overs)	136
N. Shahid lbw b Drakes	4	4/43 5/49 6/74	
A. J. Tudor c Piper b Drakes	10	7/86 8/135 9/136	

Butcher retired hurt at 11.

Bowling: Brown 7.2–1–14–3; Carter 8–0–40–2; Drakes 9–2–35–3; Sheikh 9–2–19–1; Smith 9–0–24–0.

Warwickshire

N. V. Knight c Stewart b Tudor	1	N. M. K. Smith c sub b B. C. Hollioake	0
M. A. Wagh b Bicknell	0	V. C. Drakes not out	4
D. R. Brown c Giddins b A. J. Hollioake	63	L-b 5, w 7, n-b 2	14
D. L. Hemp c Stewart b Giddins	10		
*M. J. Powell b Giddins	9	1/2 2/4 3/31 (7 wkts, 37.3 overs)	137
T. L. Penney c sub b B. C. Hollioake	35	4/55 5/128	
†K. J. Piper not out	1	6/133 7/133	

N. M. Carter and M. A. Sheikh did not bat.

Bowling: Bicknell 6–3–11–1; Tudor 9–3–24–1; Giddins 8.5–1–30–2; Saqlain Mushtaq 4–0–28–0; B. C. Hollioake 8.3–0–39–2; A. J. Hollioake 1.1–1–0–1.

Umpires: M. J. Kitchen and G. Sharp.

WARWICKSHIRE v NOTTINGHAMSHIRE

At Birmingham, August 2 (day/night). No result. Toss: Nottinghamshire.

Gallian, making his first appearance of the season after recovering from knee surgery, was one of two early victims for Dagnall. However, Blewett and Afzaal repaired the damage with 82 in 14 overs before the weather closed in and prevented a result for the first time in 12 floodlit League fixtures at Edgbaston. The match had already been reduced to 30 overs a side.

Nottinghamshire

D. J. Bicknell c Piper b Dagnall	6	K. P. Pietersen not out	7
*J. E. R. Gallian c Piper b Dagnall	1	L-b 3, w 4	7
G. S. Blewett c Brown b Smith	44		
U. Afzaal not out	40	1/7 2/9 3/91 (3 wkts, 20.2 overs)	105

P. Johnson, †C. M. W. Read, R. J. Logan, G. J. Smith, D. S. Lucas and G. D. Clough did not bat.

Bowling: Carter 3–0–18–0; Dagnall 4–0–18–2; Sheikh 6–0–23–0; Brown 3.2–0–20–0; Smith 4–0–23–1.

Warwickshire

N. M. Carter, N. V. Knight, M. A. Wagh, D. R. Brown, D. L. Hemp, *M. J. Powell, T. L. Penney, N. M. K. Smith, †K. J. Piper, M. A. Sheikh and C. E. Dagnall.

Umpires: B. Dudleston and R. A. White.

WARWICKSHIRE v SOMERSET

At Birmingham, August 19. Warwickshire won by ten wickets (D/L method). Toss: Warwickshire.

Warwickshire emphatically avenged defeat by Somerset in their Cheltenham & Gloucester semi-final eight days earlier. Somerset never looked comfortable on a two-paced pitch that had just seen four days' Championship use, and the Warwickshire bowlers got away with 12 maidens. Richardson marked his first one-day game of the season with his best limited-overs return. Wagh made a mockery of Somerset's difficulties. There were 15 fours in his highest one-day innings, 70 from 64 balls, and he and Knight achieved Warwickshire's revised target of 119 in 73 minutes. A brief stoppage in Somerset's innings had reduced the match to 43 overs each.

Somerset

P. D. Bowler lbw b Richardson	15
I. D. Blackwell lbw b Brown	0
*J. Cox lbw b Brown	8
M. J. Wood c Penney b Smith	29
K. A. Parsons b Richardson	3
†R. J. Turner run out	2
R. L. Johnson c Brown b Smith	5
K. P. Dutch c Smith b Dagnall	12
P. D. Trego not out	15
P. S. Jones b Smith	9
J. O. Grove b Richardson	6
B 2, l-b 10, w 2, n-b 2	16
1/0 2/16 3/34 4/42 5/59 6/64 7/74 8/90 9/107 (42.4 overs)	120

Bowling: Dagnall 9–2–28–1; Brown 8–4–20–2; Richardson 7.4–3–17–3; Sheikh 9–2–24–0; Smith 9–1–19–3.

Warwickshire

N. V. Knight not out	40
M. A. Wagh not out	70
W 4, n-b 6	10
(no wkt, 17.5 overs)	120

D. R. Brown, D. L. Hemp, *M. J. Powell, T. L. Penney, †K. J. Piper, N. M. K. Smith, M. A. Sheikh, A. Richardson and C. E. Dagnall did not bat.

Bowling: Johnson 5–0–29–0; Jones 7.5–0–46–0; Grove 4–0–31–0; Trego 1–0–14–0.

Umpires: V. A. Holder and M. J. Kitchen.

WARWICKSHIRE v YORKSHIRE

At Birmingham, August 27. Warwickshire won by seven wickets. Toss: Warwickshire.

Yorkshire's batsmen failed to adjust from a run-laden pitch at Scarborough (where 24 hours earlier they had compiled their highest limited-overs total) to an awkward bowler-friendly one. In fact, Edgbaston might have been tailor-made for Sheikh, whose intelligent use of his skiddy seamers brought him four for 17, his best return in all cricket. McGrath tried to hold Yorkshire together, but he lacked support and they limped to their lowest one-day score in 2001. Although Warwickshire lost Wagh to Hoggard's second ball, Knight and Hemp eased them to an untroubled win with 64 in 14 overs. Knight's half-century, from 76 balls with eight fours, was his first of the season in the League.

Yorkshire

G. M. Hamilton c Piper b Dagnall	0	R. J. Sidebottom run out	8
M. J. Wood c Piper b Brown	5	S. P. Kirby not out	4
A. McGrath c Brown b Sheikh	38	M. J. Hoggard not out	5
D. S. Lehmann c Brown b Sheikh	14	L-b 7, w 4	11
C. White b Sheikh	21		
G. M. Fellows c Knight b Sheikh	9	1/0 2/18 3/56 (9 wkts, 45 overs)	137
*D. Byas b Brown	17	4/63 5/81 6/101	
†R. J. Blakey b Richardson	5	7/115 8/128 9/129	

Bowling: Dagnall 9–2–27–1; Brown 9–1–28–2; Richardson 9–0–20–1; Sheikh 9–4–17–4; Powell 9–0–38–0.

Warwickshire

N. V. Knight c Kirby b Lehmann	53	*M. J. Powell not out	11
M. A. Wagh b Hoggard	0	L-b 1, w 4, n-b 10	15
D. R. Brown c Hamilton b Sidebottom	16		
D. L. Hemp not out	43	1/2 2/43 3/107 (3 wkts, 26.5 overs)	138

T. L. Penney, N. M. K. Smith, M. A. Sheikh, †K. J. Piper, C. E. Dagnall and A. Richardson did not bat.

Bowling: Kirby 6–1–48–0; Hoggard 4–0–18–1; Sidebottom 4–2–21–1; Hamilton 3–0–18–0; White 5–0–14–0; Lehmann 4.5–0–18–1.

Umpires: M. J. Harris and D. R. Shepherd.

At Whitgift School, Croydon, August 30. WARWICKSHIRE lost to SURREY by 123 runs.

At Taunton, September 3. WARWICKSHIRE beat SOMERSET by eight wickets.

At Leicester, September 5 (day/night). LEICESTERSHIRE v WARWICKSHIRE. No result.

WARWICKSHIRE v KENT

At Birmingham, September 16. Kent won by nine runs (D/L method). Toss: Warwickshire.

Kent, ten points adrift of League leaders Leicestershire in late August, held their nerve here to capture the title for the fifth time. The architect of their win was Birmingham-born Symonds, who took five for 18 and also ran out Hemp off his own bowling, after Warwickshire had needed 60 from the last ten overs with seven wickets in hand. The decline began when Brown was stumped in Symonds's first over. Kent recovered from the loss of three early wickets, on a pitch that encouraged seamers, through Hockley's one-day best 90 (12 fours, one six) and Key's 35-ball half-century. Rain reduced the match to 40 overs a side, and Warwickshire's revised target was 218.

Kent

*M. V. Fleming c Brown b Dagnall	14	M. A. Ealham not out	10
D. P. Fulton c Powell b Brown	6	†P. A. Nixon not out	1
J. B. Hockley b Brown	90	B 4, l-b 11, w 1	16
A. Symonds b Sheikh	7		
M. J. Walker c Brown b Sheikh	22	1/17 2/69 3/80 (6 wkts, 40 overs)	216
R. W. T. Key b Brown	50	4/124 5/197 6/214	

B. J. Trott, M. M. Patel and M. J. Saggers did not bat.

Bowling: Brown 8–1–30–3; Dagnall 8–1–39–1; Richardson 5–0–49–0; Sheikh 8–0–23–2; Smith 8–0–34–0; Wagh 3–0–26–0.

Warwickshire

N. V. Knight c Hockley b Saggers	11	M. A. Sheikh b Symonds	4
M. A. Wagh c Fleming b Patel	58	C. E. Dagnall not out	3
I. R. Bell c Fulton b Fleming	48	A. Richardson not out	8
N. M. K. Smith c Patel b Symonds	38	L-b 7, w 7	14
D. R. Brown st Nixon b Symonds	2		
D. L. Hemp run out	21	1/18 2/107 3/153 (9 wkts, 40 overs)	208
*†M. J. Powell b Symonds	0	4/158 5/180 6/180	
T. L. Penney c Trott b Symonds	1	7/188 8/197 9/199	

Bowling: Trott 6–0–42–0; Saggers 7–1–32–1; Ealham 8–0–37–0; Fleming 8–0–34–1; Patel 5–0–38–1; Symonds 6–1–18–5.

Umpires: J. H. Evans and M. J. Harris.

YORKSHIRE

YORKSHIRE v SOMERSET

At Leeds, May 13. Yorkshire won by five wickets. Toss: Somerset.

Sidebottom's selection for the First Test against Pakistan prompted his withdrawal from this match. Yet in spite of their pace attack being weakened already by the absence of Gough and White for the same reason, and Hamilton being injured, Yorkshire felt able to rest Silverwood. Hutchison took his chance with three wickets in his first game of the season, and Hoggard returned from injury; spinners Lehmann and Middlebrook gave little away. Rose held Somerset together with a solid 58 on an uncertain pitch, and it was a blow for the visitors when he broke down with a knee strain at the start of Yorkshire's reply. McGrath and Byas put on 72 in 15 overs, with Byas overtaking Boycott (5,051 runs) as Yorkshire's highest scorer in the League, and they cantered to victory courtesy of Lumb's straight six off Blackwell.

Somerset

P. C. L. Holloway run out	1	J. I. D. Kerr c Blakey b Hutchison	9
*J. Cox c Byas b Baker	30	P. S. Jones c Blakey b Hoggard	6
M. Burns c McGrath b Hutchison	1	J. O. Grove not out	3
G. D. Rose c Baker b Middlebrook	58	B 4, l-b 4, w 7	15
M. N. Lathwell c and b Lehmann	5		
†R. J. Turner c Middlebrook b Lehmann	2	1/18 2/25 3/52 (44 overs)	154
I. D. Blackwell c Blakey b Middlebrook	3	4/73 5/79 6/86	
K. P. Dutch c Byas b Hutchison	21	7/127 8/130 9/144	

Bowling: Hoggard 8–2–14–1; Hutchison 8–1–40–3; Baker 5–1–22–1; Fellows 5–0–14–0; Lehmann 9–2–23–2; Middlebrook 9–0–33–2.

Yorkshire

*D. Byas c Cox b Dutch	48	†R. J. Blakey not out	4
M. J. Wood lbw b Jones	5		
A. McGrath b Blackwell	58	L-b 1, w 7	8
D. S. Lehmann lbw b Kerr	12		—
M. J. Lumb not out	23	1/21 2/93 3/118 (5 wkts, 35 overs)	158
G. M. Fellows lbw b Dutch	0	4/143 5/144	

J. D. Middlebrook, T. M. Baker, M. J. Hoggard and P. M. Hutchison did not bat.

Bowling: Jones 9–2–31–1; Rose 1–0–2–0; Kerr 7–0–38–1; Dutch 9–0–41–2; Grove 5–0–26–0; Blackwell 4–0–19–1.

Umpires: J. H. Evans and K. E. Palmer.

At Bristol, May 20. YORKSHIRE lost to GLOUCESTERSHIRE by five wickets.

YORKSHIRE v KENT

At Leeds, June 10. Kent won by four wickets. Toss: Kent. First-team debut: T. T. Bresnan.

Kent's Fulton transferred his first-class form – four centuries so far – to the one-day arena with his best limited-overs score, batting through the innings to the penultimate over for 82. Chasing 190, Kent might have been under greater pressure had Lehmann held a difficult return chance from Nixon at 106 for four. Instead, Nixon saw the score to 158. White, still working his way back to fitness, bowled economically, and there was a tidy four-over spell from Tim Bresnan, at 16 years and 102 days Yorkshire's second-youngest debutant behind Paul Jarvis (16 years 62 days). Earlier, their uncapped left-handers, Lumb and Craven, had hit maiden one-day half-centuries, adding 108 in 23 overs, but Walker's career-best four for 24 stifled the later batting as the overs ran out.

Yorkshire

*D. Byas b Saggers	7	J. D. Middlebrook not out	10
M. J. Lumb c Nixon b Trott	66	T. T. Bresnan not out	5
C. White c Nixon b Saggers	1		
D. S. Lehmann c Fulton b Trott	3	L-b 20, w 5	25
V. J. Craven c Patel b Walker	55		—
G. M. Fellows c Fulton b Walker	3	1/12 2/15 3/24 (8 wkts, 45 overs)	189
†R. J. Blakey c Fulton b Walker	8	4/132 5/136 6/158	
G. M. Hamilton b Walker	6	7/172 8/175	

P. M. Hutchison did not bat.

Bowling: Saggers 6–0–21–2; Trott 9–0–40–2; Golding 8–1–20–0; Fleming 9–0–35–0; Patel 5–0–29–0; Walker 8–0–24–4.

Kent

J. B. Hockley c Byas b Hamilton	6	*M. V. Fleming not out	21
D. P. Fulton lbw b Hutchison	82	J. M. Golding not out	1
E. T. Smith c Bresnan b Hamilton	5	L-b 2, w 4	6
M. J. Walker c Blakey b White	21		—
R. W. T. Key c and b Lehmann	17	1/7 2/14 3/68 (6 wkts, 44 overs)	191
†P. A. Nixon c Lehmann b Fellows	32	4/95 5/158 6/186	

M. J. Saggers, M. M. Patel and B. J. Trott did not bat.

Bowling: Hutchison 6–0–36–1; Hamilton 9–1–36–2; White 9–1–22–1; Middlebrook 5–0–27–0; Lehmann 6–0–28–1; Bresnan 4–0–15–0; Fellows 5–0–25–1.

Umpires: A. Clarkson and M. J. Kitchen.

At Bath, June 17. YORKSHIRE lost to SOMERSET by 15 runs.

YORKSHIRE v NORTHAMPTONSHIRE

At Leeds, June 24. Yorkshire won by 16 runs. Toss: Northamptonshire. County debut: R. K. J. Dawson.

Brown arrested Yorkshire's early progress by claiming their first three wickets in a nine-over spell costing just 25 runs. Byas held firm to reach his second successive half-century in the League before he was bowled, aiming to hit Penberthy over mid-wicket, but it needed 49 from Blakey and Silverwood (27 in 20 balls) to set a target over 200. Weekes, although expensive, took two wickets against the county that refused to sign him the previous year. By the time Northamptonshire's requirement was down to 40 from five overs, it looked as if Yorkshire would rue twice dropping Hussey. Then Silverwood struck twice in three balls. When Swann went in the penultimate over, Yorkshire were on track to end a run of three defeats, leaving Northamptonshire still searching for their first points after five games.

Yorkshire

*D. Byas b Penberthy	52
M. J. Lumb c Cousins b Brown	21
C. White c Weekes b Brown	11
D. S. Lehmann c Hussey b Brown	7
G. M. Fellows c Ripley b Weekes	27
G. M. Hamilton c Cook b Weekes	24
†R. J. Blakey not out	26
C. E. W. Silverwood not out	27
L-b 4, w 3, n-b 2	9
1/44 2/59 3/73 4/109 5/147 6/155 (6 wkts, 45 overs)	204

R. K. J. Dawson, M. J. Hoggard and R. J. Sidebottom did not bat.

Bowling: Cousins 9–0–61–0; Weekes 9–0–50–2; Brown 9–0–25–3; Taylor 9–1–32–0; Penberthy 9–1–32–1.

Northamptonshire

M. E. K. Hussey c Blakey b White	32
M. B. Loye c Blakey b Silverwood	0
R. J. Warren b Hoggard	54
J. W. Cook c Blakey b White	7
A. J. Swann c White b Hoggard	54
A. L. Penberthy c Lumb b Silverwood	11
L. C. Weekes c Blakey b Silverwood	0
*†D. Ripley c Lehmann b Sidebottom	4
J. P. Taylor c and b White	1
D. M. Cousins not out	5
J. F. Brown not out	3
L-b 8, w 7, n-b 2	17
1/11 2/63 3/77 4/132 5/170 6/171 7/176 8/177 9/182 (9 wkts, 45 overs)	188

Bowling: Silverwood 9–2–28–3; Hoggard 6–0–40–2; Sidebottom 9–0–36–1; White 9–2–30–3; Dawson 7–0–22–0; Lehmann 5–0–24–0.

Umpires: M. J. Harris and J. F. Steele.

At Northampton, July 8. YORKSHIRE lost to NORTHAMPTONSHIRE by three wickets.

YORKSHIRE v LEICESTERSHIRE

At Scarborough, July 15. Leicestershire won by 16 runs. Toss: Yorkshire.

Gough, "tired and jaded" according to Yorkshire coach Wayne Clark, was rested ahead of the Lord's Test. But with three wickets from his five one-day appearances for the county, at a cost of 209 runs, there was speculation whether they really wanted to give him his first League game of the season. The best individual performances were by Yorkshire, but leaders Leicestershire had so much depth that they had little trouble extending their unblemished record to seven consecutive wins. After striking ten fours, Lehmann went to his maiden League hundred with a six off Maddy, having faced 105 balls. Three balls later Wells had him lbw and Yorkshire's challenge was effectively over. Lumb was unable to bat after tearing knee ligaments while fielding.

Leicestershire

*V. J. Wells c Dawson b White	12
J. M. Dakin c Byas b Sidebottom	39
I. J. Sutcliffe c and b Lehmann	48
D. I. Stevens c Blakey b Sidebottom	0
B. F. Smith lbw b Lehmann	31
D. L. Maddy c Sidebottom b Kirby	12
†N. D. Burns c Lehmann b Sidebottom	31
A. Habib not out	37
P. A. J. DeFreitas c Wood b Kirby	11
J. Ormond b Silverwood	7
S. A. J. Boswell not out	1
B 4, l-b 9, w 1, n-b 4	18
1/52 2/74 3/75 4/136 5/151 6/153 7/198 8/221 9/246 (9 wkts, 45 overs)	247

Bowling: Silverwood 6–0–37–1; Kirby 7–0–38–2; Sidebottom 9–1–49–3; White 9–0–38–1; Dawson 5–0–32–0; Lehmann 9–0–40–2.

Yorkshire

*D. Byas c Wells b Boswell	3
M. J. Wood c Wells b Ormond	6
D. S. Lehmann lbw b Wells	103
G. M. Fellows c Boswell b Ormond	18
C. White run out	1
†R. J. Blakey b Wells	34
C. E. W. Silverwood not out	23
R. K. J. Dawson b Maddy	1
R. J. Sidebottom not out	17
L-b 1, w 24	25
1/5 2/22 3/70 4/71 5/162 6/199 7/205 (7 wkts, 45 overs)	231

M. J. Lumb and S. P. Kirby did not bat.

Bowling: Ormond 9–1–44–2; Boswell 7–1–24–1; DeFreitas 5–0–26–0; Dakin 6–0–32–0; Maddy 9–0–53–1; Wells 9–0–51–2.

Umpires: G. I. Burgess and G. Sharp.

YORKSHIRE v WARWICKSHIRE

At Leeds, July 23 (day/night). Yorkshire won by 175 runs. Toss: Yorkshire.

For the second year running, Headingley's one floodlit match of the season was over while the sun still lit the sky. Warwickshire were bowled out for their lowest one-day score – six below their 65 in the League at Maidstone in 1979 – after Silverwood and Kirby had them 12 for six. The final total would have been lower had Kirby not given away 14 from three free hits by no-balling. Wood top-scored for Yorkshire with a limited-overs best of 68, and Lehmann plundered 39 from 32 balls. But the most furious assault came from Fellows. He smashed 40 from 24 balls, including five fours and a six, and was particularly severe on Giles, whose nine overs cost 66.

Yorkshire

G. M. Hamilton b Carter	24
M. J. Wood c Knight b Drakes	68
A. McGrath st Piper b Giles	30
D. S. Lehmann c Sheikh b Drakes	39
G. M. Fellows c Brown b Carter	40
*D. Byas b Giles	0
†R. J. Blakey not out	18
C. E. W. Silverwood not out	2
B 3, l-b 5, w 5	13
1/28 2/96 3/159 4/174 5/183 6/230 (6 wkts, 45 overs)	234

S. P. Kirby, R. J. Sidebottom and R. K. J. Dawson did not bat.

Bowling: Carter 9–0–33–2; Brown 9–1–56–0; Sheikh 9–0–28–0; Drakes 9–0–43–2; Giles 9–0–66–2.

Warwickshire

N. M. Carter c Blakey b Silverwood	0	A. F. Giles b Silverwood	0
N. V. Knight c Blakey b Kirby	4	V. C. Drakes c and b Sidebottom	9
M. A. Wagh b Silverwood	0	M. A. Sheikh not out	0
D. R. Brown c Byas b Kirby	1	B 2, w 2, n-b 6	10
D. L. Hemp b Kirby	0		
*M. J. Powell b Silverwood	1	1/0 2/0 3/6 (15.2 overs)	59
T. L. Penney run out	17	4/7 5/8 6/12	
†K. J. Piper c Blakey b Sidebottom	17	7/45 8/48 9/54	

Bowling: Silverwood 8–1–21–4; Kirby 5–0–35–3; Sidebottom 2.2–1–1–2.

Umpires: G. I. Burgess and A. Clarkson.

YORKSHIRE v SURREY

At Leeds, August 5. Yorkshire won by 67 runs. Toss: Yorkshire.

Although Surrey had Ramprakash and Ward available following England's three-day defeat at Trent Bridge, Yorkshire were much too strong for them, even without their own Test pair, Gough and White. They were always in control after an opening stand of 94 between Hamilton and Wood, though Bicknell bowled well to pick up three for 20. Surrey in reply lost both openers to Elstub's first League wickets – he went on to finish with four for 25 – and only Ramprakash and Saqlain Mushtaq, late on, supplied any resistance. Hoggard bowled for the first time since his foot injury, but the problem flared up again and required further rest. The defeat was Surrey's eighth in nine matches.

Yorkshire

G. M. Hamilton lbw b Bicknell	57	R. K. J. Dawson not out	10
M. J. Wood c J. N. Batty b Greenidge	47	T. T. Bresnan not out	0
A. McGrath c Brown b Bicknell	31	B 4, l-b 6, w 7, n-b 2	19
D. S. Lehmann run out	22		
G. M. Fellows c Greenidge b Bicknell	11	1/94 2/149 3/158 (7 wkts, 45 overs)	230
*D. Byas b Hollioake	30	4/172 5/217	
†R. J. Blakey c Greenidge b Hollioake	3	6/217 7/224	

M. J. Hoggard and C. J. Elstub did not bat.

Bowling: Bicknell 9–3–20–3; Giddins 9–1–54–0; Hollioake 8–1–54–2; Greenidge 6–0–28–1; Saqlain Mushtaq 9–0–46–0; G. J. Batty 4–0–18–0.

Surrey

I. J. Ward lbw b Elstub	17	Saqlain Mushtaq not out	38
N. Shahid b Elstub	15	C. G. Greenidge c Fellows b Lehmann	1
M. R. Ramprakash c Bresnan b Lehmann	58	E. S. H. Giddins c Blakey b Elstub	1
A. D. Brown c Blakey b Hoggard	0	W 2, n-b 2	4
B. C. Hollioake b Elstub	12		
G. J. Batty run out	5	1/32 2/34 3/35 (40 overs)	163
†J. N. Batty c Blakey b Hamilton	10	4/62 5/77 6/94	
*M. P. Bicknell c and b Dawson	2	7/100 8/158 9/160	

Bowling: Hoggard 7–2–30–1; Bresnan 4–1–13–0; Elstub 8–1–25–4; Hamilton 7–0–32–1; Dawson 8–0–44–1; Lehmann 6–0–19–2.

Umpires: J. W. Holder and B. Leadbeater.

At Nottingham, August 13 (day/night). YORKSHIRE beat NOTTINGHAMSHIRE by three wickets.

At Leicester, August 19. YORKSHIRE lost to LEICESTERSHIRE by one wicket (D/L method).

YORKSHIRE v NOTTINGHAMSHIRE

At Scarborough, August 26. Yorkshire won by 179 runs. Toss: Nottinghamshire.

Lehmann's 191, the highest for Yorkshire in a one-day match, helped Yorkshire to their best limited-overs score. An astonishing array of shots produced his runs off 103 balls, with 20 fours and 11 sixes coming in a 116-minute stay that included an eight-minute stoppage while an ambulance drove on to the field to attend to a spectator. Lehmann's 50 came off 38 balls, his 100 off 67 and his 150 off 86; a full house saw the ball disappear out of the ground three times. Only Surrey's Alistair Brown, with 203 against Hampshire at Guildford in 1997, had hit a higher League score. Lehmann then held a catch and took two wickets as Nottinghamshire fell for 173.

Yorkshire

G. M. Hamilton c Read b Logan	24
M. J. Wood c Bicknell b Smith	23
A. McGrath c Johnson b Logan	38
D. S. Lehmann c Clough b Pietersen	191
C. White c Clough b Pietersen	25
G. M. Fellows not out	22
*D. Byas c Logan b Clough	5
†R. J. Blakey not out	8
B 1, l-b 8, w 7	16
1/46 2/52 3/224 4/304 5/326 6/334 (6 wkts, 45 overs)	352

M. J. Hoggard, R. K. J. Dawson and C. J. Elstub did not bat.

Bowling: Smith 9–1–46–1; Malik 7–0–65–0; Logan 9–0–73–2; Clough 7–0–51–1; Randall 4–0–42–0; Pietersen 9–0–66–2.

Nottinghamshire

*D. J. Bicknell c Blakey b Hamilton	50
G. E. Welton lbw b Elstub	20
G. S. Blewett b White	25
P. Johnson c Lehmann b Hamilton	2
K. P. Pietersen c Fellows b Hamilton	5
†C. M. W. Read c Wood b Lehmann	36
G. D. Clough c Byas b Dawson	2
R. J. Logan st Blakey b Lehmann	5
S. J. Randall not out	13
G. J. Smith b Dawson	5
M. N. Malik b McGrath	1
L-b 5, w 4	9
1/32 2/95 3/100 4/104 5/109 6/116 7/141 8/160 9/170 (43.3 overs)	173

Bowling: Hoggard 6–0–31–0; Elstub 7–1–23–1; White 7–0–28–1; Lehmann 9–0–38–2; Hamilton 5–0–14–3; Dawson 9–0–33–2; McGrath 0.3–0–1–1.

Umpires: A. Clarkson and D. J. Constant.

At Birmingham, August 27. YORKSHIRE lost to WARWICKSHIRE by seven wickets.

At Canterbury, August 29. YORKSHIRE lost to KENT by eight runs.

At The Oval, September 3 (day/night). YORKSHIRE lost to SURREY by seven wickets (D/L method).

YORKSHIRE v GLOUCESTERSHIRE

At Scarborough, September 10. Yorkshire won by 70 runs. Toss: Yorkshire. First-team debut: A. P. R. Gidman.

Two wickets apiece for Gough and Hoggard with Gloucestershire's score on 13 meant Yorkshire had no trouble defending their modest total in a game both sides needed to win to ease relegation fears. Lehmann had led the way for Yorkshire with 69, giving him 363 runs from the three League matches at North Marine Road and taking his season's aggregate to 753, a county record. Blakey's 52, meanwhile, put him alongside Boycott and Byas as the only Yorkshire batsmen to top 5,000 runs in the League. Smith, making his first League appearance of the summer, dismissed Wood and McGrath in his second over, and Averis grabbed the last four Yorkshire wickets to fall. Alleyne kept wicket because Russell had gone to hospital for stitches after a ball struck his face during the pre-match warm-up.

Yorkshire

M. J. Wood c Alleyne b Smith	2	D. Gough c Windows b Averis	13
M. P. Vaughan run out	5	R. J. Sidebottom not out	7
A. McGrath lbw b Smith	0	L-b 2, w 2, n-b 4	8
D. S. Lehmann c Alleyne b Averis	69		——
*D. Byas c Cunliffe b Barnett	0	1/2 2/2 3/23 (8 wkts, 45 overs)	161
†R. J. Blakey c Cunliffe b Averis	52	4/38 5/111 6/131	
R. K. J. Dawson c Cunliffe b Averis	5	7/150 8/161	

C. J. Elstub and M. J. Hoggard did not bat.

Bowling: Smith 9–3–18–2; Bressington 9–3–35–0; Barnett 9–2–28–1; Averis 9–0–42–4; Ball 9–1–36–0.

Gloucestershire

T. H. C. Hancock c Vaughan b Hoggard	7	A. N. Bressington b Lehmann	5
K. J. Barnett c Lehmann b Hoggard	6	J. M. M. Averis b Gough	2
D. R. Hewson b Gough	0	A. M. Smith not out	3
M. G. N. Windows lbw b Gough	0	L-b 2, w 2, n-b 2	6
*†M. W. Alleyne c Dawson b Sidebottom	15		——
R. J. Cunliffe c Blakey b Sidebottom	2	1/13 2/13 3/13 (36.5 overs)	91
A. P. R. Gidman c Hoggard b Elstub	7	4/13 5/20 6/33	
M. C. J. Ball run out	38	7/55 8/83 9/86	

Bowling: Gough 9–3–15–3; Hoggard 7.5–2–14–2; Sidebottom 9–1–22–2; Elstub 5–2–15–1; Lehmann 6–0–23–1.

Umpires: K. E. Palmer and D. R. Shepherd.

DIVISION TWO

DERBYSHIRE

DERBYSHIRE v GLAMORGAN

At Derby, April 29. Derbyshire won by four wickets. Toss: Glamorgan. County debut: A. R. K. Pierson.

Welch continued a promising start for his new county with five for 22, his best figures in limited-overs cricket, as only two Glamorgan players, Dale and Newell, reached double figures on a slow, seaming pitch. They added 63 for the fifth wicket before Dale set off for an ill-judged single to Bailey at mid-off. Newell was left high and dry by those who followed. Cork, timing the ball with a fluency that eluded his team-mates, dominated Derbyshire's response, which had been in trouble at five for three. His ninth four produced the winning runs and provided further evidence of fitness to take up his England contract.

Glamorgan

*S. P. James c Krikken b Munton	3	S. D. Thomas c Krikken b Aldred	4
J. P. Maher c Aldred b Welch	5	D. A. Cosker c Illingworth b Welch	5
M. J. Powell lbw b Welch	4	S. L. Watkin lbw b Welch	3
M. P. Maynard b Welch	3	L-b 4, w 11	15
A. Dale run out	37		—
K. Newell not out	47	1/7 2/13 3/13 (44.4 overs)	138
†A. D. Shaw st Krikken b Aldred	6	4/20 5/83 6/97	
R. D. B. Croft c Cork b Illingworth	6	7/112 8/121 9/132	

Bowling: Welch 8.4–0–22–5; Munton 9–4–18–1; Cork 9–2–22–0; Illingworth 9–0–36–1; Aldred 9–0–36–2.

Derbyshire

S. D. Stubbings b Thomas	0	†K. M. Krikken b Dale	0
R. J. Bailey lbw b Thomas	5	R. K. Illingworth not out	21
M. J. Di Venuto lbw b Watkin	0	B 6, l-b 5, w 9	20
*D. G. Cork not out	83		—
L. D. Sutton st Shaw b Cosker	11	1/4 2/5 3/5 (6 wkts, 41.4 overs)	140
G. Welch lbw b Cosker	0	4/68 5/68 6/85	

P. Aldred, A. R. K. Pierson and T. A. Munton did not bat.

Bowling: Thomas 7.4–3–32–2; Watkin 9–1–36–1; Dale 7–1–17–1; Croft 9–2–23–0; Cosker 9–2–21–2.

Umpires: M. J. Harris and B. Leadbeater.

DERBYSHIRE v ESSEX

At Derby, May 13. Derbyshire won by 67 runs. Toss: Essex.

Bailey survived a chance on 41 to bat throughout Derbyshire's innings, adding 95 in 23 overs with Sutton, and was bowled aiming for the last-ball six that would bring his hundred. Welch and Munton pinned Essex back from the start of their reply and, as later batsmen looked to improve the run-rate, Lungley had Cowan and Anderson lbw with successive balls. He finished with career-best figures while Derbyshire, after just two games, equalled their total of League wins in 2000.

Derbyshire

R. J. Bailey b Cowan	94	†K. M. Krikken not out	8
M. J. Di Venuto c McGarry b Cowan	4		
M. P. Dowman c Hyam b Irani	24	L-b 7, w 6, n-b 2	15
L. D. Sutton b Cowan	39		—
G. Welch b McGarry	0	1/9 2/46 3/141 (6 wkts, 45 overs)	198
W. G. Khan b Irani	14	4/145 5/186 6/198	

T. Lungley, R. K. Illingworth, *T. A. Munton and N. R. C. Dumelow did not bat.

Bowling: Cowan 9–0–46–3; Irani 9–3–37–2; McGarry 7–0–32–1; Anderson 8–0–30–0; Grayson 7–1–21–0; Mason 5–0–25–0.

Essex

D. D. J. Robinson lbw b Lungley	27	†B. J. Hyam not out	30
W. I. Jefferson lbw b Welch	2	T. J. Mason st Krikken b Khan	3
G. R. Napier c Khan b Welch	1	A. C. McGarry lbw b Illingworth	1
S. D. Peters st Krikken b Munton	9	L-b 5	5
*R. C. Irani b Illingworth	35		
A. P. Grayson b Lungley	16	1/3 2/5 3/31 (35.2 overs)	131
A. P. Cowan lbw b Lungley	2	4/44 5/74 6/82	
R. S. G. Anderson lbw b Lungley	0	7/82 8/115 9/124	

Bowling: Welch 7–0–17–2; Munton 7–2–13–1; Dumelow 9–0–48–0; Lungley 7–0–28–4; Illingworth 3.2–0–13–2; Khan 2–1–7–1.

Umpires: D. J. Constant and R. Julian.

At Worcester, May 20. DERBYSHIRE lost to WORCESTERSHIRE by three wickets.

At Southgate, June 3. DERBYSHIRE lost to MIDDLESEX by 16 runs.

DERBYSHIRE v DURHAM

At Derby, June 10. Durham won by four wickets. Toss: Derbyshire.

Aldred, back after injury, was hit in the ribs by Harmison while opening the batting and, unable to field, left Derbyshire a bowler light to defend a total owing much to Di Venuto's excellence on an awkward pitch. Di Venuto's was the third wicket to fall in six balls with the score on 114, but brisk batting by Krikken and Illingworth ensured that Durham's task was not straightforward. Even with solid contributions from the middle order, the outcome remained in the balance as Gough and Pratt whittled away at the 59 needed from the last ten overs. Pratt's highest one-day score kept Durham at the top of the division, while Derbyshire slipped from second to fourth.

Derbyshire

M. J. Di Venuto c Pratt b Gough	71	†K. M. Krikken not out	27
P. Aldred b Hunter	13	R. K. Illingworth not out	14
M. P. Dowman c Pratt b Hunter	0	L-b 7, w 4	11
R. J. Bailey b Law	24		
C. W. G. Bassano lbw b Law	0	1/34 2/38 3/114 (7 wkts, 45 overs)	179
G. Welch c and b Law	13	4/114 5/114	
S. D. Stubbings st Pratt b Gough	6	6/128 7/143	

T. Lungley and *T. A. Munton did not bat.

Bowling: Harmison 7–0–39–0; Hunter 7–1–19–2; Brinkley 7–1–27–0; Phillips 6–0–18–0; Law 9–1–33–3; Gough 9–2–36–2.

Durham

N. Peng c Bassano b Welch	0	†A. Pratt not out	42
D. R. Law c Lungley b Welch	4	I. D. Hunter not out	2
M. L. Love b Lungley	39	L-b 6, w 11	17
M. P. Speight c Dowman b Lungley	10		——
*J. J. B. Lewis c and b Illingworth	31	1/2 2/11 3/58 (6 wkts, 44.3 overs)	180
M. A. Gough b Munton	35	4/70 5/107 6/172	

N. C. Phillips, J. E. Brinkley and S. J. Harmison did not bat.

Bowling: Welch 9–2–31–2; Munton 9–4–19–1; Lungley 9–1–32–2; Bailey 4–0–25–0; Illingworth 8.3–0–37–1; Di Venuto 5–0–30–0.

Umpires: M. R. Benson and T. E. Jesty.

At Arundel, June 17. DERBYSHIRE lost to SUSSEX by eight runs.

DERBYSHIRE v MIDDLESEX

At Derby, June 24. Derbyshire won by 42 runs. Toss: Derbyshire. County debut: A. D. Edwards.

The absence of six senior bowlers – five injured and Cork withdrawn by England – was no obstacle to Derbyshire ending a run of ten games without a win since May 13. In the circumstances, they had registered seamer Alex Edwards, who was on the Middlesex staff in 2000. Bailey's third League fifty of the season – after Dowman had been Fraser's 200th League wicket – underpinned a total Derbyshire were able to defend, with acting-captain Di Venuto marshalling his bowling resources thoughtfully on a slow pitch. There was a fine spell of left-arm spin from Wharton; Sutton's wicket-keeping and the keen fielding helped maintain pressure; and off-spinner Dumelow chimed in with three wickets at the end. Fleming dislocated a finger while fielding and Middlesex missed his experience higher in the order.

Derbyshire

S. D. Stubbings run out	33	†L. D. Sutton not out	18
*M. J. Di Venuto lbw b Fraser	27	P. Aldred not out	12
M. P. Dowman lbw b Fraser	0	L-b 8, w 3, n-b 4	15
R. J. Bailey b Keegan	55		——
C. W. G. Bassano c Nash b Weekes	5	1/40 2/40 3/79 (7 wkts, 45 overs)	196
G. Welch c Keegan b Hewitt	11	4/92 5/131	
N. R. C. Dumelow b Keegan	20	6/165 7/168	

A. D. Edwards and L. J. Wharton did not bat.

Bowling: Fraser 9–1–27–2; Keegan 9–1–36–2; Hutton 9–1–28–0; Hewitt 9–0–49–1; Weekes 9–0–48–1.

Middlesex

A. J. Strauss lbw b Wharton	35	C. B. Keegan b Dumelow	1
B. L. Hutton st Sutton b Welch	3	J. P. Hewitt not out	11
R. M. S. Weston c Sutton b Aldred	16	*A. R. C. Fraser c Aldred b Dumelow	17
O. A. Shah c Sutton b Aldred	2	L-b 2, w 12, n-b 4	18
†D. C. Nash c Dowman b Edwards	6		——
M. A. Roseberry lbw b Wharton	6	1/7 2/40 3/60 (40.2 overs)	154
P. N. Weekes lbw b Dumelow	14	4/75 5/77 6/94	
S. P. Fleming c Bassano b Bailey	25	7/116 8/121 9/131	

Bowling: Welch 7–2–19–1; Aldred 7–1–41–2; Edwards 9–1–25–1; Wharton 9–1–23–2; Dumelow 5.2–0–32–3; Bailey 3–0–12–1.

Umpires: R. Julian and R. A. White.

DERBYSHIRE v WORCESTERSHIRE

At Derby, July 3 (day/night). Worcestershire won by 138 runs. Toss: Worcestershire.

Worcestershire's top-order batting put injury-struck Derbyshire to the sword and set up the win that took them to the top of Division Two. Weston hit his highest limited-overs score, also the highest individual innings against Derbyshire in the League, pummelling five sixes and 11 fours in his 134 from 141 balls. With Hick posting an inevitable fifty on the slow, flat pitch, and Solanki racing to 63 with five fours and two sixes in 38 balls, Worcestershire reached their highest League total for 26 years. As if Derbyshire didn't have enough problems, they then had to bat as the sun set on a pitch with an east–west axis, under floodlights of limited effectiveness. Not that their innings lasted far into the night.

Worcestershire

W. P. C. Weston c Bailey b Dumelow	134
A. Singh c Dowman b Welch	0
*G. A. Hick b Dumelow	53
V. S. Solanki b Aldred	63
D. A. Leatherdale b Edwards	1
A. J. Bichel b Aldred	6
†S. J. Rhodes not out	4
S. R. Lampitt not out	3
B 2, l-b 7, w 13, n-b 2	24
1/1 2/129 3/264 4/275 5/279 6/285 (6 wkts, 45 overs)	288

Kabir Ali, M. J. Rawnsley and A. Sheriyar did not bat.

Bowling: Welch 9–1–51–1; Aldred 9–0–55–2; Edwards 9–0–49–1; Wharton 9–0–46–0; Bailey 4–0–19–0; Dumelow 5–0–59–2.

Derbyshire

S. D. Stubbings c Rhodes b Bichel	11
†L. D. Sutton c Rhodes b Sheriyar	1
M. P. Dowman b Bichel	16
*R. J. Bailey b Ali	8
N. R. C. Dumelow b Lampitt	4
C. W. G. Bassano b Sheriyar	26
G. Welch c Bichel b Ali	3
W. G. Khan c Rhodes b Ali	8
P. Aldred c Bichel b Ali	37
A. D. Edwards b Sheriyar	17
L. J. Wharton not out	9
W 10	10
1/3 2/22 3/36 4/44 5/47 6/61 7/70 8/101 9/120 (38.4 overs)	150

Bowling: Bichel 9–0–35–2; Sheriyar 9–1–31–3; Ali 6.4–0–22–4; Lampitt 5–0–20–1; Rawnsley 9–0–42–0.

Umpires: N. G. Cowley and J. W. Lloyds.

At Southampton, July 15. DERBYSHIRE lost to HAMPSHIRE by 16 runs.

At Cardiff, July 22. DERBYSHIRE lost to GLAMORGAN by six wickets.

DERBYSHIRE v HAMPSHIRE

At Derby, August 5. Hampshire won by nine wickets. Toss: Derbyshire.

Udal restricted Derbyshire in a match trimmed to 44 overs each, conceding only 14 runs in his full allocation. Di Venuto took 79 balls to reach 42, and thereafter only Sutton and Krikken made much headway with a stand of 84 in the last 14 overs. Laney and Kenway, adding 144 in 24 overs, made short work of Hampshire's modest target, and they eased home with more than eight overs to spare. Kenway, who survived two stumping chances off Wharton, was particularly destructive in his unbeaten 93 from 87 balls, hitting ten fours and two sixes off some loose bowling.

Derbyshire

*M. J. Di Venuto lbw b Hamblin	42	†K. M. Krikken not out	42
R. J. Bailey c Kenway b Johnson	11		
S. D. Stubbings c Udal b Johnson	2	L-b 12, w 11, n-b 4	27
M. P. Dowman b Hamblin	10		
L. D. Sutton not out	42	1/49 2/57 3/75 (5 wkts, 44 overs)	184
G. Welch c Kenway b Mullally	8	4/76 5/100	

P. Aldred, A. D. Edwards, K. J. Dean and L. J. Wharton did not bat.

Bowling: Mullally 9–1–37–1; Mascarenhas 9–0–39–0; Johnson 9–0–43–2; Hamblin 8–1–39–2; Udal 9–3–14–0.

Hampshire

J. S. Laney not out	62
N. C. Johnson lbw b Aldred	23
†D. A. Kenway not out	93
B 1, l-b 3, w 4	8
1/42 (1 wkt, 35.3 overs)	186

L. R. Prittipaul, W. S. Kendall, A. D. Mascarenhas, *R. A. Smith, S. D. Udal, G. W. White, J. R. C. Hamblin and A. D. Mullally did not bat.

Bowling: Welch 7–3–21–0; Dean 7.3–0–46–0; Aldred 7–0–38–1; Edwards 4–0–29–0; Wharton 9–0–33–0; Bailey 1–0–15–0.

Umpires: T. E. Jesty and M. J. Kitchen.

At Chester-le-Street, August 12. DERBYSHIRE lost to DURHAM by 32 runs (D/L method).

DERBYSHIRE v SUSSEX

At Derby, August 27. Sussex won by seven wickets. Toss: Derbyshire. First-team debut: T. R. Ambrose.

Stubbings provided a sound foundation through his highest one-day score, but Derbyshire, with wickets in hand, should have made more of their position, given their limited bowling depth. Instead, after Stubbings's third-wicket stand of 106 with Bassano, they were unable to accelerate against a varied attack. Although Bailey's 39 came off 40 balls, during which he reached 7,000 runs in the competition, Derbyshire managed only 31 off the last five overs. The in-form Montgomerie always had the target comfortably in his sights, and Goodwin's 53 off 43 balls hurried Sussex to victory.

Derbyshire

S. D. Stubbings not out	96	*R. J. Bailey not out	39
L. D. Sutton lbw b Taylor	0	B 1, l-b 12, w 4	17
M. P. Dowman st Ambrose b Robinson	14		
C. W. G. Bassano st Ambrose b Davis	40	1/4 2/39 3/145 (3 wkts, 45 overs)	206

G. Welch, †K. M. Krikken, T. Lungley, A. D. Edwards, K. J. Dean and L. J. Wharton did not bat.

Bowling: Kirtley 9–0–49–0; Taylor 7–1–19–1; Robinson 9–0–25–1; Havell 4–0–20–0; Davis 7–1–42–1; House 2–0–11–0; Adams 7–0–27–0.

Sussex

R. R. Montgomerie c Sutton b Lungley	94	W. J. House not out	8
†T. R. Ambrose lbw b Lungley	21	L-b 3, w 8	11
*C. J. Adams c Krikken b Wharton	22		—
M. W. Goodwin not out	53	1/52 2/116 3/188 (3 wkts, 41 overs)	209

J. R. Carpenter, B. V. Taylor, M. J. G. Davis, R. J. Kirtley, P. M. R. Havell and M. A. Robinson did not bat.

Bowling: Welch 7–1–24–0; Dean 6–0–28–0; Lungley 7–1–35–2; Edwards 7–0–42–0; Wharton 9–0–51–1; Bailey 5–0–26–0.

Umpires: M. R. Benson and B. Leadbeater.

At Manchester, September 3 (day/night). DERBYSHIRE lost to LANCASHIRE by 60 runs.

At Chelmsford, September 9. DERBYSHIRE lost to ESSEX by five wickets.

DERBYSHIRE v LANCASHIRE

At Derby, September 16. Derbyshire won by six wickets. Toss: Lancashire. First-team debut: J. M. Anderson.

The rain that had threatened Warwickshire's resounding Championship win the previous day delayed the start and reduced this match to 25 overs each. Hegg, captaining Lancashire after Crawley chose not to play, went against convention in a shortened contest by batting first. But Roberts, with a maiden half-century off 47 balls, and Scuderi backed his decision by adding 84 in 14 overs. In reply, Di Venuto and Selwood gave Derbyshire a good start with 82 in 11 overs for the second wicket. This took the pressure off Bassano and Dumelow, who with four balls to spare ended the home side's sequence of eight League defeats.

Lancashire

R. C. Driver lbw b Aldred	9	C. P. Schofield not out	11
M. J. Chilton st Krikken b Dean	16		
G. D. Lloyd lbw b Dean	5	L-b 5, w 3	8
T. W. Roberts c Aldred b Dumelow	55		—
J. C. Scuderi not out	50	1/11 2/18 3/41 (5 wkts, 25 overs)	159
*†W. K. Hegg c Dumelow b Aldred	5	4/125 5/144	

G. Chapple, G. Yates, K. W. Hogg and J. M. Anderson did not bat.

Bowling: Dean 5–1–25–2; Aldred 5–0–30–2; Lungley 5–0–27–0; Wharton 5–0–19–0; Dowman 3–0–30–0; Dumelow 2–0–23–1.

Derbyshire

S. D. Stubbings lbw b Anderson	1	N. R. C. Dumelow not out	16
*M. J. Di Venuto b Schofield	56	B 2, l-b 7, w 16, n-b 4	29
S. A. Selwood c and b Schofield	33		—
C. W. G. Bassano not out	25	1/9 2/91 (4 wkts, 24.2 overs)	162
M. P. Dowman b Schofield	2	3/113 4/117	

†K. M. Krikken, P. Aldred, T. Lungley, K. J. Dean and L. J. Wharton did not bat.

Bowling: Anderson 4–0–33–1; Hogg 3–0–22–0; Chapple 4.2–0–35–0; Driver 3–0–23–0; Schofield 5–0–22–3; Yates 5–0–18–0.

Umpires: K. E. Palmer and R. Palmer.

DURHAM

At Lord's, April 29. MIDDLESEX v DURHAM. No result (abandoned).

DURHAM v MIDDLESEX

At Chester-le-Street, May 20. Durham won by two wickets. Toss: Middlesex.

Durham needed 19 off 16 balls when Law, on 20, was bowled by Keegan. However, there were not enough fielders in the circle and, as the ball flew off the stumps to the boundary, it counted as six no-balls instead. Durham got home with one ball to spare, and Law unbeaten on 31. Middlesex, having raced to 76 before losing their first wicket in the 14th over, were pegged back by Brinkley's medium-pace and Phillips's off-spin – only 19 runs came between the 20th and 30th overs – and their eventual 182 owed much to Hutton's one-day best 77.

Middlesex

A. J. Strauss lbw b Phillips	39
B. L. Hutton b Hunter	77
C. B. Keegan b Brinkley	5
*S. P. Fleming c Pratt b Phillips	0
O. A. Shah run out	8
R. M. S. Weston run out	0
P. N. Weekes b Killeen	22
†D. C. Nash not out	7
S. J. Cook b Hunter	0
J. P. Hewitt not out	5
B 2, l-b 3, w 14	19
1/76 2/83 3/84 4/96 5/99 6/162 7/167 8/172 (8 wkts, 45 overs)	182

T. F. Bloomfield did not bat.

Bowling: Killeen 8–0–37–1; Hunter 6–1–40–2; Phillips 9–0–31–2; Brinkley 9–2–18–1; Gough 9–0–32–0; Collingwood 4–0–19–0.

Durham

M. A. Gough b Hewitt	3
N. Peng b Cook	9
M. L. Love c Nash b Keegan	38
P. D. Collingwood run out	47
*J. J. B. Lewis lbw b Keegan	15
D. R. Law not out	31
I. D. Hunter run out	20
†A. Pratt c Hewitt b Keegan	0
J. E. Brinkley b Keegan	0
N. C. Phillips not out	4
L-b 5, w 2, n-b 12	19
1/9 2/36 3/80 4/110 5/130 6/163 7/164 8/171 (8 wkts, 44.5 overs)	186

N. Killeen did not bat.

Bowling: Bloomfield 9–0–27–0; Hewitt 3–0–16–1; Cook 9–1–32–1; Weekes 9–0–31–0; Keegan 8.5–1–43–4; Hutton 6–0–32–0.

Umpires: N. G. Cowley and M. J. Harris.

DURHAM v LANCASHIRE

At Chester-le-Street, May 27. Durham won by 24 runs. Toss: Durham. First-team debut: T. W. Roberts.

Whereas Pratt and Gough had plundered 48 from Durham's last five overs, taking them to 211, Lancashire fell well short when they needed 48 off five to win. Spin – from Gough and Phillips – played a crucial role after Lancashire had begun splendidly. Chapple's first one-day fifty came off 41 balls, with nine fours, but once both openers were stumped by Pratt, the game swung Durham's way. Phillips finished with four for 21. Durham, too, had made a good start through Law, opening for the first time, and Peng.

Durham

N. Peng c Atherton b Schofield	47	I. D. Hunter c Hegg b Chapple	4
D. R. Law b Muralitharan	45	†A. Pratt not out	25
M. L. Love run out	10		
P. D. Collingwood st Hegg b Muralitharan	23	L-b 3, w 9	12
*J. J. B. Lewis c Hegg b Wood	19	1/85 2/102 3/107 (6 wkts, 45 overs)	211
M. A. Gough not out	26	4/151 5/156 6/163	

N. C. Phillips, J. E. Brinkley and N. Killeen did not bat.

Bowling: Martin 8–0–47–0; Wood 9–2–45–1; Chapple 9–1–43–1; Muralitharan 9–2–24–2; Schofield 7–0–35–1; Roberts 3–0–14–0.

Lancashire

M. A. Atherton st Pratt b Gough	62	J. Wood c Phillips b Gough	0
G. Chapple st Pratt b Phillips	52	P. J. Martin not out	3
*J. P. Crawley c Pratt b Phillips	2		
A. Flintoff c Lewis b Phillips	0	B 1, l-b 2, w 5	8
T. W. Roberts b Phillips	1		
N. H. Fairbrother not out	39	1/83 2/93 3/95 (8 wkts, 45 overs)	187
C. P. Schofield c Love b Collingwood	18	4/103 5/144 6/173	
†W. K. Hegg run out	2	7/180 8/181	

M. Muralitharan did not bat.

Bowling: Killeen 9–0–36–0; Hunter 6–0–34–0; Brinkley 6–0–24–0; Phillips 9–2–21–4; Gough 7–0–27–2; Collingwood 8–0–42–1.

Umpires: J. H. Hampshire and R. A. White.

At Derby, June 10. DURHAM beat DERBYSHIRE by four wickets.

At Ilford, June 17. DURHAM beat ESSEX by 24 runs.

At Southampton, June 24. DURHAM lost to HAMPSHIRE by 64 runs.

DURHAM v GLAMORGAN

At Chester-le-Street, July 8. Durham won by two wickets. Toss: Durham.

Put in, Glamorgan were unhappy about a pitch that had sweated under the covers and offered lateral movement and uneven bounce. Yet after recovering from 15 for four to reach 145, they had the chance to win when Durham were 98 for seven – itself a recovery from ten for three. Croft, easily the game's top-scorer with 67, had taken two wickets, but he dropped a slip catch when Durham needed eight for victory. Lewis's unbeaten 46, alongside some resolute support from the tail, helped his side return to the top of the table. Collingwood hit three sixes in his 25 before, going for a fourth, he was caught by Parkin on the boundary.

Glamorgan

K. Newell c Peng b Harmison	0	S. D. Thomas c Collingwood b Law	13
J. P. Maher b Hatch	4	S. L. Watkin b Collingwood	2
R. D. B. Croft b Gough	67	O. T. Parkin not out	2
*S. P. James c Pratt b Hatch	0	B 1, l-b 3, w 12, n-b 4	20
†M. P. Maynard c Pratt b Hatch	3		—
M. J. Powell c Peng b Collingwood	26	1/9 2/10 3/11 (40.2 overs)	145
A. Dale st Pratt b Davies	4	4/15 5/108 6/115	
A. W. Evans lbw b Collingwood	4	7/122 8/130 9/140	

Bowling: Harmison 5–0–28–1; Hatch 7–1–26–3; Law 6.2–0–26–1; Davies 8–1–25–1; Collingwood 9–1–21–3; Gough 5–0–15–1.

Durham

N. Peng lbw b Watkin	4	A. M. Davies lbw b Thomas	10
D. R. Law b Parkin	1	S. J. Harmison not out	11
M. L. Love c Evans b Parkin	2		
P. D. Collingwood c Parkin b Thomas	25	B 1, l-b 3, w 8, n-b 2	14
*J. J. B. Lewis not out	46		—
M. A. Gough c Dale b Croft	17	1/4 2/9 3/10 (8 wkts, 43.3 overs)	146
M. P. Speight c Powell b Croft	9	4/42 5/79 6/89	
†A. Pratt lbw b Watkin	7	7/98 8/128	

N. G. Hatch did not bat.

Bowling: Watkin 9–3–26–2; Parkin 8–3–24–2; Thomas 9–0–37–2; Dale 5.3–0–17–0; Croft 9–0–27–2; Newell 3–0–11–0.

Umpires: B. Leadbeater and J. W. Lloyds.

At Manchester, July 15. LANCASHIRE v DURHAM. No result (abandoned).

DURHAM v SUSSEX

At Chester-le-Street, July 22. Durham won by seven wickets. Toss: Sussex.

Davies, Durham's 20-year-old seamer, claimed all the wickets as Sussex slumped to 24 for four on a greenish pitch after winning the toss. Moving the ball into the right-hander, he conceded only two singles off the bat in taking four for 13 in seven overs; his first two balls were wides, one of them going for four, and he bowled six in all (another cost two). Wicket-keeper Pratt equalled the Durham one-day record with five victims, and Sussex's total of 144 presented no problems. Love's unbeaten 75 carried Durham home with 11 overs to spare.

Sussex

M. W. Goodwin c Pratt b Davies	1	R. J. Kirtley c Pratt b Gough	3
R. R. Montgomerie c Bridge b Brinkley	47	B. V. Taylor run out	1
M. J. G. Davis c Collingwood b Davies	0	M. A. Robinson not out	1
*C. J. Adams c Pratt b Davies	10	W 19	19
U. B. A. Rashid c Pratt b Davies	0		—
B. Zuiderent st Pratt b Bridge	7	1/9 2/9 3/21 (44.3 overs)	144
W. J. House c Speight b Gough	30	4/24 5/47 6/105	
†M. J. Prior c Brinkley b Law	25	7/123 8/138 9/141	

Bowling: Law 7.3–2–22–1; Davies 7–2–13–4; Brinkley 8–0–31–1; Collingwood 5–0–11–0; Bridge 8–1–27–1; Gough 9–0–40–2.

Durham

N. Peng b Kirtley	6	M. P. Speight not out	1
D. R. Law c Prior b Taylor	19	L-b 3, w 5, n-b 2	10
M. L. Love not out	75		——
P. D. Collingwood c Goodwin b Rashid	34	1/11 2/37 3/140 (3 wkts, 34 overs)	145

*J. J. B. Lewis, M. A. Gough, †A. Pratt, A. M. Davies, G. D. Bridge and J. E. Brinkley did not bat.

Bowling: Taylor 9–1–24–1; Kirtley 5–0–24–1; Robinson 6–0–22–0; Rashid 8–0–45–1; Davis 6–1–27–0.

Umpires: G. I. Burgess and N. A. Mallender.

At Worcester, July 31 (day/night). DURHAM lost to WORCESTERSHIRE by seven wickets.

DURHAM v DERBYSHIRE

At Chester-le-Street, August 12. Durham won by 32 runs (D/L method). Toss: Durham.

Pratt's one-day best of 86 off 72 balls – and an opening partnership of 128 in less than 19 overs with Peng – meant Durham could afford to be tied down by the left-arm spin of Wharton and still reach 269. Any aspirations Derbyshire may have had were quickly quashed by Harmison, and they were out of the running at 134 for five when rain arrived. An hour later it was announced that play would resume at 7.10 p.m., with the visitors needing 56 off 13 balls under Duckworth/Lewis rules. Fortunately, after a few more spots of rain, common sense prevailed.

Durham

N. Peng c Stubbings b Aldred	50	A. M. Davies b Welch	0
†A. Pratt c Krikken b Wharton	86	J. E. Brinkley not out	1
M. L. Love lbw b Wharton	18		
P. D. Collingwood lbw b Wharton	9	L-b 8, w 11	19
*J. J. B. Lewis c Krikken b Edwards	21		——
J. A. Daley st Krikken b Welch	30	1/128 2/149 3/162 (8 wkts, 45 overs)	269
D. R. Law c Dowman b Welch	21	4/189 5/202 6/240	
G. D. Bridge not out	14	7/268 8/268	

S. J. Harmison did not bat.

Bowling: Welch 8–1–51–3; Dean 8–0–57–0; Aldred 6–0–43–1; Edwards 5–0–42–1; Wharton 9–2–23–3; Bailey 9–0–45–0.

Derbyshire

S. D. Stubbings c Love b Harmison	14	†K. M. Krikken c Bridge b Brinkley	35
L. D. Sutton b Harmison	3	L-b 1, w 6	7
M. P. Dowman c Brinkley b Harmison	12		——
C. W. G. Bassano b Davies	32	1/12 2/27 3/40 (5 wkts, 28.5 overs)	134
*R. J. Bailey not out	31	4/69 5/134	

G. Welch, P. Aldred, A. D. Edwards, K. J. Dean and L. J. Wharton did not bat.

Bowling: Harmison 7–1–31–3; Law 6–0–23–0; Brinkley 3.5–0–26–1; Davies 7–0–31–1; Bridge 5–0–22–0.

Umpires: K. Shuttleworth and J. F. Steele.

DURHAM v HAMPSHIRE

At Chester-le-Street, August 15 (day/night). Durham won by 17 runs (D/L method). Toss: Durham. First-team debut: J. D. Francis.

A third-wicket stand of 166 in 28 overs between Love and Collingwood set up Durham's third successive total of more than 250 in this competition. And for the first time in four floodlit games featuring Durham, the team batting second were unable to knock off the runs. Hampshire, after racing to 61 without loss in eight overs through Laney's 38 in 29 balls, were checked by a change of pace. Mascarenhas had 31 off 32 balls when rain ended play, but 72 from the last seven overs would have been a daunting challenge for the lower order under lights.

Durham

N. Peng c and b Mascarenhas	13
†A. Pratt c Francis b Johnson	1
M. L. Love c Hamblin b Mascarenhas	89
P. D. Collingwood c Johnson b Hamblin	84
D. R. Law c White b Hamblin	28
*J. J. B. Lewis c White b Johnson	22
J. A. Daley not out	8
G. D. Bridge not out	4
L-b 3, w 7	10
1/11 2/29 3/195 4/199 5/231 6/253 (6 wkts, 45 overs)	259

J. E. Brinkley, S. J. Harmison and N. G. Hatch did not bat.

Bowling: Johnson 9–0–62–2; Mascarenhas 9–1–31–2; Tremlett 6–0–44–0; Udal 9–0–41–0; Hamblin 9–0–60–2; Prittipaul 3–0–18–0.

Hampshire

J. S. Laney lbw b Hatch	38
G. W. White st Pratt b Bridge	50
N. C. Johnson c Pratt b Brinkley	5
L. R. Prittipaul c Bridge b Brinkley	3
*R. A. Smith b Collingwood	18
J. D. Francis c Peng b Bridge	21
A. D. Mascarenhas not out	31
†A. N. Aymes not out	9
L-b 1, w 10, n-b 2	13
1/64 2/77 3/85 4/119 5/133 6/160 (6 wkts, 38 overs)	188

S. D. Udal, C. T. Tremlett and J. R. C. Hamblin did not bat.

Bowling: Harmison 4–0–30–0; Law 4–0–31–0; Hatch 7–1–28–1; Brinkley 6–1–19–2; Collingwood 9–0–37–1; Bridge 8–0–42–2.

Umpires: A. Clarkson and G. Sharp.

At Hove, August 26. SUSSEX v DURHAM. No result (abandoned).

At Cardiff, August 27. DURHAM lost to GLAMORGAN by 24 runs.

DURHAM v ESSEX

At Chester-le-Street, September 2. Essex won by three wickets. Toss: Durham.

Durham's promotion campaign suffered a blow from their first League defeat at home. Grayson's well-flighted left-arm spin undermined them with three key wickets, and a total of 178 always looked under par on a slow pitch. Robinson's dashing 58-ball half-century had Essex on the way to a crushing win until careless strokes, and Phillips's floated off-breaks, sent them sliding from 125 for two to 141 for seven. Foster and Clinton restored sanity.

Durham

N. Peng b Irani	29	N. C. Phillips run out	5
†A. Pratt c Foster b Bishop	4	S. J. Harmison b Bishop	6
M. L. Love b Grayson	36	N. G. Hatch not out	8
P. D. Collingwood c Foster b Grayson	31	B 1, l-b 5, w 3	9
*J. J. B. Lewis b Clarke	4		—
J. A. Daley run out	35	1/19 2/66 3/81 (44.4 overs)	178
D. R. Law b Grayson	10	4/88 5/134 6/144	
G. D. Bridge b Cowan	1	7/145 8/150 9/165	

Bowling: Cowan 9–0–40–1; Bishop 8–0–34–2; Irani 8.4–0–32–1; Napier 5–0–25–0; Grayson 9–0–23–3; Clarke 5–0–18–1.

Essex

D. D. J. Robinson b Bridge	64	†J. S. Foster not out	20
G. R. Napier c Love b Law	14	R. S. Clinton not out	16
A. P. Cowan b Phillips	29	B 2, l-b 4, w 3	9
S. D. Peters b Phillips	20		—
S. G. Law c Collingwood b Phillips	0	1/23 2/103 3/125 (7 wkts, 41.5 overs)	179
*R. C. Irani c Peng b Collingwood	6	4/125 5/139	
A. P. Grayson c Collingwood b Phillips	1	6/141 7/141	

J. E. Bishop and A. J. Clarke did not bat.

Bowling: Harmison 8–0–38–0; Law 6–0–27–1; Hatch 2–0–17–0; Bridge 9–0–29–1; Phillips 9–0–36–4; Collingwood 5.5–0–19–1; Love 2–0–7–0.

Umpires: B. Leadbeater and P. Willey.

DURHAM v WORCESTERSHIRE

At Chester-le-Street, September 9. Durham won by nine runs (D/L method). Toss: Durham.

Durham won promotion courtesy of an unbeaten 76 off 66 balls by captain Lewis and an exceptional all-round performance by wicket-keeper Pratt. Having hit a run-a-ball half-century at the top of the order, Pratt later made a brilliant leg-side stumping off Law to remove Hick, held two catches also standing up to the seamers, and ran out Solanki with a spot-on kick. After one shower had reduced the match to 41 overs a side, a second left Worcestershire with a revised target of 208 from 39 overs. At 83 for none in the 13th over they were cruising, but Law changed ends and, with the wind behind him, reduced them to 89 for three. As the pressure mounted – a win would guarantee promotion for Worcestershire – they were always just off the pace.

Durham

N. Peng b Sheriyar	12	D. R. Law not out	0
†A. Pratt run out	56		
M. L. Love c Bichel b Rawnsley	43	W 6	6
P. D. Collingwood b Lampitt	0		—
*J. J. B. Lewis not out	76	1/36 2/91 3/93 (5 wkts, 41 overs)	212
J. A. Daley c Hick b Sheriyar	19	4/132 5/206	

I. D. Hunter, N. C. Phillips, G. D. Bridge and S. J. Harmison did not bat.

Bowling: Sheriyar 8–1–44–2; Bichel 9–0–51–0; Lampitt 7–0–27–1; Rawnsley 8–0–46–1; Leatherdale 8–0–36–0; Hick 1–0–8–0.

Worcestershire

W. P. C. Weston b Law	43	S. R. Lampitt b Hunter	0
A. Singh c Pratt b Collingwood	58	M. J. Rawnsley not out	3
P. R. Pollard c Pratt b Law	0		
*G. A. Hick st Pratt b Law	2	B 3, l-b 8, w 2	13
V. S. Solanki run out	9		
D. A. Leatherdale c Love b Collingwood	33	1/83 2/83 3/89 (8 wkts, 39 overs)	198
A. J. Bichel run out	19	4/103 5/136 6/163	
†S. J. Rhodes not out	18	7/183 8/189	

A. Sheriyar did not bat.

Bowling: Harmison 5–0–39–0; Law 8–2–28–3; Hunter 8–1–34–1; Phillips 8–0–47–0; Collingwood 7–0–30–2; Bridge 3–0–9–0.

Umpires: B. Dudleston and D. R. Shepherd.

ESSEX

At Derby, May 13. ESSEX lost to DERBYSHIRE by 67 runs.

ESSEX v SUSSEX

At Chelmsford, May 20. Sussex won by one run. Toss: Sussex.

Requiring nine from the final over, with two wickets remaining, Essex found the task just out of reach. Yet, as Peters and Law took them to 147 by the 27th over, they had looked to have the game under control. Then four wickets fell for 15 in five overs, leaving Grayson and Cowan to repair the damage with 48 in six overs. Montgomerie, with a League-best 91 from 116 deliveries, and Goodwin had laid the Sussex foundations with an opening stand of 106 in 24 overs, but 25 wides by the Essex bowlers were an over-generous contribution to the visitors' total.

Sussex

R. R. Montgomerie run out	91	R. S. C. Martin-Jenkins not out	5
M. W. Goodwin c Law b Anderson	42	†M. J. Prior not out	7
B. Zuiderent run out	8	L-b 8, w 25	33
M. H. Yardy c Cowan b Grayson	8		
W. J. House c and b Grayson	21	1/106 2/129 3/169 (6 wkts, 45 overs)	243
U. B. A. Rashid lbw b Cowan	28	4/194 5/205 6/236	

M. J. G. Davis, *R. J. Kirtley and M. A. Robinson did not bat.

Bowling: Ilott 9–0–60–0; Irani 9–0–48–0; Cowan 9–2–30–1; Anderson 9–0–41–1; Grayson 6–0–29–2; Mason 3–0–27–0.

Essex

D. D. J. Robinson c Goodwin b Robinson	26	R. S. G. Anderson b Martin-Jenkins	3
S. D. Peters b Davis	66	T. J. Mason b Kirtley	2
S. G. Law run out	40	M. C. Ilott not out	0
*R. C. Irani run out	1	B 1, l-b 6, w 17, n-b 2	26
A. P. Grayson not out	48		
G. R. Napier c Kirtley b Rashid	1	1/58 2/147 3/152 (9 wkts, 45 overs)	242
†B. J. Hyam c Martin-Jenkins b Davis	9	4/161 5/162 6/181	
A. P. Cowan c Prior b Kirtley	20	7/229 8/234 9/241	

Bowling: Martin-Jenkins 9–0–55–1; Kirtley 9–1–43–2; Robinson 9–1–37–1; Rashid 7–1–50–1; Davis 9–0–39–2; House 2–0–11–0.

Umpires: A. A. Jones and G. Sharp.

At Southampton, June 3. ESSEX beat HAMPSHIRE by eight runs.

ESSEX v GLAMORGAN

At Chelmsford, June 10. Glamorgan won by eight wickets (D/L method). Toss: Glamorgan.

A rain-interrupted match, reduced to 34 overs a side, produced totals that counties elsewhere could not match in 45. After his top order gave Essex a racing start, Irani plundered 108 not out from just 61 balls, hitting four sixes and 13 fours, including 28 in boundaries from a Watkin over. Glamorgan retaliated with 27 off an Ilott over, from which Newell smashed three sixes in an exhibition that made their revised target of 254 anything but daunting. His 97 in 53 balls contained another two sixes and ten fours; Maynard, with whom he added 100 in ten overs, became the first Glamorgan batsman to reach 6,000 League runs and finished with 87 from 77 balls as the visitors coasted to victory.

Essex

D. D. J. Robinson b Parkin	40
S. D. Peters c James b Dale	33
S. G. Law b Cosker	16
*R. C. Irani not out	108
A. P. Grayson c Maher b Dale	19
†J. S. Foster c Powell b Newell	13
A. P. Cowan b Thomas	2
M. C. Ilott not out	3
B 1, l-b 1, w 5, n-b 2	9
1/64 2/90 3/97 4/126 5/212 6/237 (6 wkts, 34 overs)	243

A. C. McGarry, J. E. Bishop and T. J. Mason did not bat.

Bowling: Parkin 7–0–46–1; Watkin 7–0–62–0; Thomas 5–0–47–1; Dale 7–0–42–2; Cosker 7–0–32–1; Newell 1–0–12–1.

Glamorgan

K. Newell c Ilott b Bishop	97
J. P. Maher b Irani	12
M. P. Maynard not out	87
M. J. Powell not out	36
L-b 4, w 18	22
1/59 2/159 (2 wkts, 31.5 overs)	254

*S. P. James, A. Dale, S. D. Thomas, †A. D. Shaw, D. A. Cosker, S. L. Watkin and O. T. Parkin did not bat.

Bowling: Irani 6–0–47–1; Cowan 5.5–0–33–0; McGarry 1–0–13–0; Ilott 5–0–59–0; Grayson 7–0–51–0; Bishop 7–0–47–1.

Umpires: B. Leadbeater and N. A. Mallender.

ESSEX v DURHAM

At Ilford, June 17. Durham won by 24 runs. Toss: Durham. First-team debut: N. G. Hatch.

Durham's Peng, dropped three times, the first when three, became at 18 years 272 days the youngest to make a League hundred; also his first senior one-day century, his 112 not out came from 116 balls, with a six and 13 fours. Former Essex players Danny Law and Lewis contributed substantially and quickly to a total that ensured unbeaten Durham would remain at the top of the division, and consign the home team to the bottom. Clinton's 56 from 57 balls was in keeping with the positive response of an Essex innings that ultimately subsided beneath the pressure of Durham's imposing total.

Durham

D. R. Law lbw b Bishop	47	*J. J. B. Lewis not out	63
M. L. Love c Law b Cowan	6	L-b 2, n-b 4	6
N. Peng not out	112		—
M. P. Speight c Foster b Grayson	30	1/12 2/84 3/136 (3 wkts, 45 overs)	264

M. A. Gough, †A. Pratt, I. D. Hunter, N. C. Phillips, J. E. Brinkley and N. G. Hatch did not bat.

Bowling: Irani 9–2–47–0; Cowan 9–1–61–1; Bishop 9–0–55–1; Anderson 9–0–52–0; Grayson 9–0–47–1.

Essex

D. D. J. Robinson b Hunter	6	R. S. G. Anderson c Phillips b Hunter	10
S. D. Peters run out	44	T. J. Mason not out	2
S. G. Law b Hatch	4	J. E. Bishop c Gough b Law	2
*R. C. Irani c Brinkley b Hunter	21	B 2, l-b 4, w 6, n-b 2	14
A. P. Grayson c Love b Brinkley	43		—
†J. S. Foster run out	19	1/14 2/23 3/66 (43 overs)	240
R. S. Clinton c Phillips b Law	56	4/123 5/133 6/170	
A. P. Cowan b Law	19	7/223 8/236 9/237	

Bowling: Hatch 9–0–52–1; Hunter 9–2–47–3; Phillips 9–1–50–0; Brinkley 6–0–29–1; Law 7–1–28–3; Gough 3–0–28–0.

Umpires: R. Julian and G. Sharp.

At Manchester, June 23 (day/night). ESSEX lost to LANCASHIRE by 37 runs.

At Southgate, July 8. ESSEX tied with MIDDLESEX.

At Hove, July 16 (day/night). ESSEX lost to SUSSEX by 27 runs.

ESSEX v HAMPSHIRE

At Southend, July 22. Hampshire won by 85 runs. Toss: Hampshire.

Johnson's first League century for Hampshire paved the way for his side's fifth successive win since losing at home to Essex seven weeks earlier. Batting throughout the innings, he shared a stand of 113 in 23 overs with Mascarenhas, and made his 105 from 121 balls. Essex, missing the injured Law, never mounted a serious challenge in reply. Grayson top-scored with 44, to add to his two wickets, but Essex's seventh defeat in nine League games seemed a foregone conclusion as they struggled to counter a varied, accurate attack.

Hampshire

J. S. Laney c Irani b Cowan	8	*R. A. Smith run out	17
N. C. Johnson not out	105		
†D. A. Kenway lbw b Irani	2	L-b 7, w 8	15
A. D. Mascarenhas run out	53		—
L. R. Prittipaul st Foster b Grayson	13	1/23 2/26 3/139 (6 wkts, 45 overs)	213
W. S. Kendall c and b Grayson	0	4/168 5/168 6/213	

S. D. Udal, C. T. Tremlett, J. R. C. Hamblin and A. D. Mullally did not bat.

Bowling: Cowan 9–0–27–1; Irani 9–1–41–1; Bishop 9–0–55–0; Clarke 4–0–22–0; Grayson 9–1–32–2; Mason 5–0–29–0.

Essex

D. D. J. Robinson c Kenway b Mullally	0	A. J. Clarke c Prittipaul b Udal	0
S. D. Peters c Johnson b Mascarenhas	5	T. J. Mason not out	4
G. R. Napier c Mascarenhas b Hamblin	22	J. E. Bishop c Smith b Tremlett	14
*R. C. Irani c Hamblin b Mascarenhas	2	L-b 5, w 4	9
A. P. Grayson c and b Udal	44		
†J. S. Foster c Johnson b Hamblin	4	1/5 2/12 3/14 (38.4 overs)	128
R. S. Clinton c Udal b Johnson	11	4/50 5/60 6/90	
A. P. Cowan c Kenway b Hamblin	13	7/105 8/109 9/109	

Bowling: Mullally 5–0–8–1; Mascarenhas 7–0–30–2; Tremlett 5.4–0–14–1; Hamblin 9–0–33–3; Udal 9–3–28–2; Johnson 3–0–10–1.

Umpires: B. Dudleston and R. Palmer.

ESSEX v WORCESTERSHIRE

At Chelmsford, August 12. Essex won by 33 runs. Toss: Essex.

Napier's one-man show stunned Division Two leaders Worcestershire and earned Essex their second League win of the summer. The 21-year-old carved a swashbuckling 73 from 60 balls, hitting four sixes in his ten boundaries, and then, with career-best figures, became the first Essex bowler since Don Topley in 1988 to take six wickets in a League match. Napier's remarkable performance trumped Bichel's hat-trick in his five-wicket return for the visitors. England captain Hussain, out of action for five weeks since breaking his finger at Edgbaston, and with the Headingley Test four days away, came in for his second League match of the season; he managed only four scoring shots in 24 balls.

Essex

D. D. J. Robinson lbw b Bichel	0	A. P. Cowan b Bichel	6
N. Hussain b Bichel	7	J. E. Bishop b Bichel	1
G. R. Napier c Catterall b Rawnsley	73	A. J. Clarke not out	0
S. G. Law b Lampitt	10	L-b 6, w 4, n-b 2	12
*R. C. Irani c Singh b Rawnsley	23		
A. P. Grayson c Hick b Leatherdale	28	1/0 2/51 3/64 (39.2 overs)	200
S. D. Peters c and b Leatherdale	27	4/119 5/129 6/176	
†J. S. Foster c Leatherdale b Bichel	13	7/179 8/195 9/200	

Bowling: Bichel 7.2–1–21–5; Sheriyar 5–0–45–0; Lampitt 8–0–39–1; Catterall 4–0–31–0; Rawnsley 8–0–37–2; Leatherdale 7–0–21–2.

Worcestershire

W. P. C. Weston c Napier b Bishop	11	D. N. Catterall c Foster b Clarke	0
A. Singh b Napier	61	M. J. Rawnsley not out	4
*G. A. Hick c Robinson b Bishop	19	A. Sheriyar b Napier	9
V. S. Solanki c Peters b Clarke	41	L-b 2, w 3	5
D. A. Leatherdale c Grayson b Napier	5		
A. J. Bichel b Napier	3	1/29 2/59 3/122 (38.2 overs)	167
†S. J. Rhodes c Irani b Napier	7	4/130 5/143 6/146	
S. R. Lampitt c Irani b Napier	2	7/150 8/154 9/154	

Bowling: Cowan 6–0–26–0; Bishop 6–0–33–2; Irani 6–1–15–0; Grayson 5–0–23–0; Clarke 8–0–39–2; Napier 7.2–0–29–6.

Umpires: G. I. Burgess and J. H. Evans.

At Cardiff, August 19. ESSEX lost to GLAMORGAN by 178 runs.

ESSEX v LANCASHIRE

At Colchester, August 26. No result. Toss: Lancashire.

Two points from this washed-out game were not enough to lift Essex from the bottom of the League. Before the rain came, Lancashire's batsmen had struggled to make progress against Irani and Cowan.

Lancashire

G. Chapple c Foster b Cowan	6
M. J. Chilton not out	17
A. Flintoff c Peters b Cowan	7
*J. P. Crawley not out	0
L-b 1, w 1	2
1/12 2/30 (2 wkts, 11 overs)	32

N. H. Fairbrother, G. D. Lloyd, J. C. Scuderi, †J. J. Haynes, C. P. Schofield, G. Yates and J. Wood did not bat.

Bowling: Irani 5–1–14–0; Cowan 5–2–15–2; Napier 1–0–2–0.

Essex

D. D. J. Robinson, S. D. Peters, G. R. Napier, S. G. Law, *R. C. Irani, A. P. Grayson, †J. S. Foster, R. S. Clinton, A. P. Cowan, A. J. Clarke and A. C. McGarry.

Umpires: P. Adams and J. W. Holder.

ESSEX v MIDDLESEX

At Colchester, August 28 (day/night). Essex won by four wickets. Toss: Middlesex.

Essex coasted to only their third League win of the season, in front of a crowd approaching 6,000, and moved two rungs up the Division Two ladder. At 53 for four, Irani joined Law with work to do and they added 70 in 79 balls. Law's 51 came from as many deliveries, while Irani stamped his authority with an unbeaten 56 off 72. Strauss had dominated the early Middlesex innings, scoring 59 out of 92 before Grayson bowled him. Useful thirties from Weekes and Dalrymple gave the Middlesex total a reasonable appearance, but it required something more substantial to test their opponents.

Middlesex

A. J. Strauss b Grayson	59
S. P. Fleming c Law b Irani	0
O. A. Shah c Foster b Irani	2
E. C. Joyce c Foster b Napier	6
†D. C. Nash run out	9
P. N. Weekes c Clarke b Cowan	36
J. W. M. Dalrymple not out	38
C. B. Keegan c Law b Grayson	16
S. J. Cook not out	3
L-b 1, w 3	4
1/5 2/25 3/40 4/70 5/92 6/140 7/159 (7 wkts, 45 overs)	173

*A. R. C. Fraser and T. F. Bloomfield did not bat.

Bowling: Irani 9–2–26–2; Cowan 9–1–39–1; Napier 9–0–44–1; Clarke 9–1–21–0; Grayson 9–0–42–2.

Essex

S. D. Peters c Weekes b Bloomfield	6	A. P. Grayson c Fraser b Cook	7
D. D. J. Robinson c Nash b Fraser	28	†J. S. Foster not out	9
A. P. Cowan c Nash b Keegan	13	L-b 1, w 2	3
G. R. Napier c Fleming b Keegan	1		
S. G. Law c Joyce b Keegan	51	1/27 2/43 3/48 (6 wkts, 38.3 overs)	174
*R. C. Irani not out	56	4/53 5/123 6/146	

R. S. Clinton, A. J. Clarke and A. C. McGarry did not bat.

Bowling: Fraser 9–2–28–1; Bloomfield 9–1–45–1; Keegan 9–1–28–3; Cook 6.3–0–42–1; Weekes 5–0–30–0.

Umpires: J. H. Hampshire and N. A. Mallender.

At Chester-le-Street, September 2. ESSEX beat DURHAM by three wickets.

ESSEX v DERBYSHIRE

At Chelmsford, September 9. Essex won by five wickets. Toss: Derbyshire. First-team debut: M. L. Pettini.

Law was given a standing ovation to and from the middle on what was to be his last appearance for Essex. But there was no final flourish; only nine runs before he was caught behind. Instead it was Napier's 47 from 24 balls and Irani's unbeaten 45 that condemned Derbyshire to their eighth successive League defeat, which left them eight points adrift at the bottom of Division Two. They had been plunged into dire straits early on when Cowan and Bishop removed half the side for 38. Their eventual 164 was too modest a total for their bowlers to defend, and Essex passed it with nearly 14 overs to spare.

Derbyshire

S. D. Stubbings c Foster b Bishop	0	T. Lungley c Foster b Cowan	45
*M. J. Di Venuto lbw b Cowan	10	K. J. Dean run out	7
M. P. Dowman c Grayson b Cowan	10	L. J. Wharton not out	3
J. P. Pyemont lbw b Bishop	2	B 2, l-b 6, w 5, n-b 4	17
S. A. Selwood c Foster b Clarke	37		
N. R. C. Dumelow c Robinson b Cowan	5	1/0 2/22 3/23 (44.2 overs)	164
†K. M. Krikken lbw b Irani	2	4/25 5/38 6/64	
G. Welch b Irani	26	7/78 8/139 9/148	

Bowling: Bishop 7–1–18–2; Cowan 8.2–0–22–4; Clarke 7–1–35–1; Irani 8–1–32–2; Grayson 9–0–23–0; Napier 5–0–26–0.

Essex

D. D. J. Robinson b Dean	31	†J. S. Foster not out	0
G. R. Napier b Dean	47		
A. P. Cowan b Lungley	20	L-b 5, w 2	7
S. G. Law c Krikken b Wharton	9		
*R. C. Irani not out	45	1/62 2/91 3/109 (5 wkts, 31.2 overs)	165
A. P. Grayson b Dumelow	6	4/121 5/150	

R. S. Clinton, M. L. Pettini, J. E. Bishop and A. J. Clarke did not bat.

Bowling: Welch 5–0–35–0; Dean 6–0–40–2; Lungley 6–0–43–1; Wharton 9–3–25–1; Dumelow 5–2–9–1; Selwood 0.2–0–8–0.

Umpires: G. I. Burgess and R. A. White.

At Worcester, September 16. ESSEX lost to WORCESTERSHIRE by 96 runs (D/L method).

GLAMORGAN

At Derby, April 29. GLAMORGAN lost to DERBYSHIRE by four wickets.

At Manchester, May 20. GLAMORGAN beat LANCASHIRE by four wickets.

GLAMORGAN v SUSSEX

At Swansea, June 3. Glamorgan won by six wickets. Toss: Sussex.

Maher's 71 from 82 balls fired Glamorgan after Sussex had failed to capitalise on their best first-wicket stand against them in limited-overs cricket. Montgomerie and Goodwin put on 92 in 22 overs but, while Adams kept the innings moving along with 61 not out from 56 balls, Dale restricted late acceleration with two wickets in his last four overs. A target of 225 was certainly attainable on a pitch giving the bowlers no margin for error. Maher and Croft, not wanted by England at Old Trafford, put on 69 for Glamorgan's second wicket, after which James, with his first fifty of the season, guided them to victory with three overs in hand.

Sussex

R. R. Montgomerie c Cosker b Croft	68	U. B. A. Rashid not out	0
M. W. Goodwin c Thomas b Croft	51	L-b 4, w 6	10
*C. J. Adams not out	61		
B. Zuiderent b Dale	24	1/92 2/149 (4 wkts, 45 overs)	224
W. J. House b Dale	10	3/208 4/224	

R. S. C. Martin-Jenkins, †M. J. Prior, R. J. Kirtley, M. J. G. Davis and M. A. Robinson did not bat.

Bowling: Watkin 9–0–41–0; Parkin 9–0–51–0; Thomas 4–0–17–0; Dale 6–0–29–2; Croft 9–1–31–2; Cosker 8–0–51–0.

Glamorgan

K. Newell c House b Robinson	25	M. J. Powell not out	14
J. P. Maher b Robinson	71	B 2, l-b 11, w 12	25
R. D. B. Croft c Kirtley b Rashid	35		
*S. P. James not out	52	1/41 2/110 (4 wkts, 42 overs)	228
†M. P. Maynard c and b Kirtley	6	3/162 4/173	

A. Dale, S. D. Thomas, O. T. Parkin, D. A. Cosker and S. L. Watkin did not bat.

Bowling: Martin-Jenkins 3–0–20–0; Kirtley 9–0–45–1; Robinson 9–0–39–2; Adams 3–0–20–0; Davis 9–0–38–0; Rashid 8–0–51–1; House 1–0–2–0.

Umpires: D. J. Constant and M. J. Harris.

At Chelmsford, June 10. GLAMORGAN beat ESSEX by eight wickets (D/L method).

GLAMORGAN v WORCESTERSHIRE

At Cardiff, June 24. Glamorgan won by 111 runs. Toss: Glamorgan.

Glamorgan raced to their highest League total on the back of a second-wicket partnership of 151 in 20 overs between Maher and Croft, dropped once and three times respectively. Just when it looked as if second-placed Worcestershire had reined in their Division Two rivals, Dale and Thomas snatched back the advantage with 51 from the last 4.3 overs. Maher also created a club one-day record by striking 18 fours in his 76-ball innings, beating Jacques Kallis's 17 against Surrey at Pontypridd in 1999. Needing to score at nearly seven runs an over, Worcestershire maintained the run-rate for the first 11 overs. When Croft dismissed Hick and Solanki in eight balls, however, their challenge fell away.

Glamorgan

K. Newell b Sheriyar	8
J. P. Maher lbw b Hick	94
R. D. B. Croft b Hick	59
†M. P. Maynard st Pipe b Hick	7
*S. P. James c Leatherdale b Lampitt	19
M. J. Powell c Singh b Bichel	29
A. Dale not out	52
S. D. Thomas not out	25
B 2, l-b 2, w 8	12
1/10 2/161 3/166 4/185 5/207 6/254 (6 wkts, 45 overs)	305

A. G. Wharf, D. A. Cosker and S. L. Watkin did not bat.

Bowling: Bichel 8–0–54–1; Sheriyar 8–0–55–1; Ali 5–0–59–0; Lampitt 7–0–41–1; Hick 9–0–41–3; Solanki 8–0–51–0.

Worcestershire

W. P. C. Weston c Powell b Watkin	14
A. Singh b Wharf	5
†D. J. Pipe c James b Wharf	26
*G. A. Hick c Maher b Croft	25
V. S. Solanki lbw b Croft	22
D. A. Leatherdale c Dale b Cosker	40
A. J. Bichel st Maynard b Croft	0
N. R. Boulton run out	20
S. R. Lampitt not out	3
Kabir Ali c Maynard b Thomas	4
A. Sheriyar b Thomas	0
B 4, l-b 8, w 15, n-b 8	35
1/7 2/45 3/68 4/111 5/122 6/122 7/176 8/190 9/194 (34.3 overs)	194

Bowling: Watkin 6–0–32–1; Wharf 7–0–53–2; Thomas 6.3–0–30–2; Croft 9–1–31–3; Cosker 6–0–36–1.

Umpires: D. J. Constant and A. G. T. Whitehead.

At Chester-le-Street, July 8. GLAMORGAN lost to DURHAM by two wickets.

GLAMORGAN v DERBYSHIRE

At Cardiff, July 22. Glamorgan won by six wickets. Toss: Derbyshire.

Glamorgan's fifth win in seven games was rarely in doubt once Ian Thomas and Newell had launched their reply with 91 in 14 overs. The left-handed Thomas, deputising for the injured Maher, gave the partnership its impetus with a 43-ball fifty – his first in one-day cricket – and, even when wickets fell, Glamorgan had Maynard to stroke them to victory. Derbyshire were themselves well placed at 154 for two, thanks to a 109-run stand between Stubbings and Dowman, but Cosker's three wickets in eight balls knocked them back. Davies, in his first League game of the season, had struck with his fourth ball, dismissing Bailey, and later accounted for Dowman.

Derbyshire

*M. J. Di Venuto c Maynard b Parkin	32	P. Aldred lbw b S. D. Thomas	0
R. J. Bailey c Powell b Davies	0	A. D. Edwards not out	1
S. D. Stubbings b Cosker	60		
M. P. Dowman b Davies	64	B 2, l-b 4	6
L. D. Sutton c and b Cosker	0		
G. Welch c and b Cosker	2	1/1 2/45 3/154 (8 wkts, 45 overs)	199
†K. M. Krikken not out	24	4/154 5/158 6/164	
N. R. C. Dumelow b S. D. Thomas	10	7/186 8/186	

L. J. Wharton did not bat.

Bowling: Davies 7–1–36–2; Parkin 8–0–32–1; S. D. Thomas 7–0–38–2; Dale 5–0–20–0; Cosker 9–0–40–3; Croft 9–0–27–0.

Glamorgan

K. Newell st Krikken b Bailey	59	M. J. Powell not out	1
I. J. Thomas c Edwards b Wharton	53	L-b 3, w 2	5
R. D. B. Croft c Bailey b Welch	20		
*S. P. James c Krikken b Aldred	22	1/91 2/131 (4 wkts, 40.4 overs)	200
†M. P. Maynard not out	40	3/139 4/178	

A. Dale, S. D. Thomas, O. T. Parkin, D. A. Cosker and A. P. Davies did not bat.

Bowling: Welch 9–1–36–1; Aldred 6–0–38–1; Wharton 9–1–39–1; Edwards 2–0–25–0; Dumelow 7.4–1–34–0; Bailey 7–0–25–1.

Umpires: T. E. Jesty and K. E. Palmer.

GLAMORGAN v LANCASHIRE

At Colwyn Bay, August 5. Glamorgan won by 46 runs. Toss: Lancashire.

Glamorgan's sixth win from eight matches kept them in contention near the top of Division Two, with games in hand. Put in, they raced to 100 by the 12th over, with Croft (who played in borrowed kit identifying him as Jones, after arriving from the Test match in Nottingham) top-scoring with 64. Yates's off-spin slowed Glamorgan's progress, but 266 was a useful total on a sluggish pitch used for the previous Championship match. Lancashire reached 50 by the seventh over but, apart from 93 between Chilton and Lloyd, they rarely threatened.

Glamorgan

K. Newell c Smethurst b Scuderi	40	A. P. Davies not out	10
I. J. Thomas c Hegg b Wood	35	D. A. Cosker b Flintoff	2
R. D. B. Croft st Hegg b Chapple	64	O. T. Parkin lbw b Flintoff	0
J. P. Maher st Hegg b Yates	24	B 12, l-b 7, w 1, n-b 8	28
†M. P. Maynard c Scuderi b Schofield	22		
M. J. Powell c Hegg b Schofield	1	1/55 2/100 3/147 (43.5 overs)	266
*A. Dale lbw b Chapple	22	4/200 5/208 6/228	
S. D. Thomas b Scuderi	18	7/249 8/263 9/266	

Bowling: Wood 4–0–45–1; Chapple 9–0–48–2; Smethurst 2–0–18–0; Flintoff 3.5–0–31–2; Scuderi 7–1–32–2; Yates 9–1–20–1; Schofield 9–0–53–2.

Lancashire

G. Chapple c Maher b S. D. Thomas	35	C. P. Schofield lbw b Cosker	0
J. Wood b Parkin	12	G. Yates c Parkin b Dale	16
A. Flintoff b Davies	20	M. P. Smethurst not out	1
M. J. Chilton c Newell b Croft	34	L-b 3, w 11, n-b 2	16
*J. P. Crawley c Maynard b Davies	0		
G. D. Lloyd c Powell b Cosker	51	1/22 2/68 3/73 (41.5 overs)	220
J. C. Scuderi c and b Cosker	9	4/73 5/166 6/167	
†W. K. Hegg c Davies b Dale	26	7/188 8/188 9/213	

Bowling: Parkin 4–0–40–1; Davies 9–0–36–2; S. D. Thomas 5–0–20–1; Cosker 9–0–58–3; Dale 5.5–0–26–2; Croft 9–0–37–1.

Umpires: M. J. Harris and G. Sharp.

At Southampton, August 12. GLAMORGAN beat HAMPSHIRE by six wickets.

GLAMORGAN v ESSEX

At Cardiff, August 19. Glamorgan won by 178 runs. Toss: Glamorgan.

Even though the match was limited to 41 overs each, Glamorgan recorded their largest winning margin in the competition. The boost to their net run-rate took on extra significance as they moved into the promotion zone. Croft's 92 from 83 balls was his best one-day innings yet. Essex, needing to score at seven an over, were never in contention once Davies had taken out five of their top six and enjoyed career-best figures. When the last wicket fell, 16 overs remained unbowled.

Glamorgan

K. Newell c Cowan b Irani	65	S. D. Thomas not out	12
J. P. Maher c Irani b Bishop	23	†A. D. Shaw not out	9
R. D. B. Croft b Clarke	92	L-b 10, w 5, n-b 2	17
M. P. Maynard c Foster b Clarke	7		
M. J. Powell lbw b Grayson	46	1/54 2/119 3/131 (6 wkts, 41 overs)	289
*A. Dale c Cowan b Grayson	18	4/232 5/259 6/268	

D. A. Cosker, A. P. Davies and O. T. Parkin did not bat.

Bowling: Bishop 6–0–48–1; Cowan 9–0–58–0; Irani 7–0–38–1; Clarke 8–0–79–2; Grayson 8–0–40–2; Napier 3–0–16–0.

Essex

D. D. J. Robinson st Shaw b Parkin	33	A. P. Cowan b Croft	7
R. S. Clinton c Maher b Davies	7	A. J. Clarke c Dale b Thomas	5
G. R. Napier b Davies	9	J. E. Bishop b Croft	1
S. G. Law b Davies	17	L-b 4, w 2	6
*R. C. Irani c Maynard b Davies	13		
A. P. Grayson c Powell b Davies	0	1/15 2/30 3/54 (24.2 overs)	111
S. D. Peters not out	13	4/76 5/76 6/85	
†J. S. Foster b Thomas	0	7/89 8/96 9/108	

Bowling: Davies 9–1–39–5; Parkin 6–1–40–1; Thomas 6–1–16–2; Croft 3.2–0–12–2.

Umpires: R. Julian and R. Palmer.

At Lord's, August 26. MIDDLESEX v GLAMORGAN. No result.

GLAMORGAN v DURHAM

At Cardiff, August 27. Glamorgan won by 24 runs. Toss: Glamorgan.

Glamorgan replaced their visitors at the top of Division Two after Durham lost their last five wickets for five runs in 13 balls. Peng's 92 from 103 balls established Durham's challenge but, once Davies split the 57-run partnership between Lewis and Daley, the lower order was unable to maintain the demanding run-rate. Newell and Ian Thomas had given Glamorgan a rapid send-off with 73 in ten overs and, although three wickets fell in quick succession, Maynard and Maher then added 71 to provide the basis of a defendable total.

Glamorgan

K. Newell c Collingwood b Brinkley	32	A. P. Davies not out	1
I. J. Thomas c Love b Harmison	27	D. A. Cosker run out	1
R. D. B. Croft c Love b Harmison	4		
J. P. Maher b Bridge	36	L-b 15, w 15, n-b 5	35
†M. P. Maynard c Pratt b Collingwood	54		
M. J. Powell c Harmison b Bridge	21	1/73 2/73 3/82 (9 wkts, 45 overs)	250
*A. Dale c Collingwood b Harmison	20	4/153 5/198 6/201	
S. D. Thomas b Harmison	19	7/246 8/247 9/250	

O. T. Parkin did not bat.

Bowling: Harmison 9–2–43–4; Law 7–0–43–0; Brinkley 3.2–1–11–1; Phillips 8.4–0–48–0; Bridge 9–0–50–2; Collingwood 8–0–40–1.

Durham

N. Peng c Maher b Cosker	92	N. C. Phillips c Croft b Parkin	1
†A. Pratt b Parkin	4	S. J. Harmison b Parkin	1
M. L. Love b S. D. Thomas	11	J. E. Brinkley not out	1
P. D. Collingwood b S. D. Thomas	6	B 1, l-b 3, w 6, n-b 4	14
*J. J. B. Lewis lbw b Davies	57		
J. A. Daley b Davies	32	1/8 2/57 3/81 (44 overs)	226
D. R. Law run out	7	4/149 5/206 6/221	
G. D. Bridge lbw b S. D. Thomas	0	7/222 8/222 9/223	

Bowling: Davies 9–0–60–2; Parkin 7–1–37–3; S. D. Thomas 8–1–27–3; Dale 2–0–10–0; Cosker 9–0–49–1; Croft 9–0–39–0.

Umpires: V. A. Holder and T. E. Jesty.

GLAMORGAN v HAMPSHIRE

At Cardiff, August 29 (day/night). Glamorgan won by 51 runs. Toss: Glamorgan.

Glamorgan virtually assured themselves of promotion in front of a near capacity crowd, increasing their lead to four points with a game in hand over second-placed Durham. Maynard's 14th one-day hundred, a club record, picked Glamorgan up from 55 for four, and his 12-over partnership of 92 with Dale helped set a challenging target. Still, Hampshire's openers rattled up 68 in ten overs as Hamblin – usually a tailender, with a previous highest score of five – played the pinch-hitter's role to the manner born. Croft's introduction initiated a collapse in which five wickets fell for 25. When he bowled Johnson, who hit 13 boundaries in his 66, Hampshire faded out of contention.

Glamorgan

K. Newell c Hamblin b Mullally	18	*A. Dale c Johnson b Tremlett	35
I. J. Thomas c Johnson b Mascarenhas	18	S. D. Thomas not out	6
R. D. B. Croft run out	8	B 5, l-b 12, w 1, n-b 2	20
J. P. Maher c Johnson b Mascarenhas	2		
†M. P. Maynard not out	116	1/34 2/51 3/54 (6 wkts, 45 overs)	244
M. J. Powell c Kenway b Johnson	21	4/55 5/123 6/215	

A. P. Davies, D. A. Cosker and O. T. Parkin did not bat.

Bowling: Mullally 9–1–47–1; Mascarenhas 9–1–37–2; Tremlett 9–1–27–1; Hamblin 4–0–24–0; Udal 9–0–57–0; Johnson 5–1–35–1.

Hampshire

J. R. C. Hamblin b Parkin	37	S. D. Udal c Cosker b S. D. Thomas	17
N. C. Johnson b Croft	66	C. T. Tremlett lbw b Davies	1
J. S. Laney c Powell b Croft	18	A. D. Mullally not out	1
†D. A. Kenway c Davies b Cosker	8	L-b 8, w 4	12
*R. A. Smith c Maynard b Croft	2		
J. D. Francis lbw b Croft	6	1/68 2/120 3/133 (40.2 overs)	193
G. W. White b S. D. Thomas	15	4/135 5/139 6/145	
A. D. Mascarenhas c Maher b Davies	10	7/170 8/176 9/191	

Bowling: Davies 8–0–50–2; Parkin 7–0–40–1; S. D. Thomas 7.2–0–37–2; Cosker 9–0–25–1; Croft 9–0–33–4.

Umpires: G. I. Burgess and J. W. Holder.

At Worcester, September 2. WORCESTERSHIRE v GLAMORGAN. No result.

At Hove, September 4 (day/night). GLAMORGAN lost to SUSSEX by 34 runs.

GLAMORGAN v MIDDLESEX

At Cardiff, September 16. Glamorgan won by 40 runs. Toss: Glamorgan. First-team debut: N. R. D. Compton.

Watkin, in his final game for the club, received an emotional farewell as Glamorgan, already confirmed as Division Two champions, ended the season with a 100 per cent home record. Croft achieved his first one-day century (111 balls, ten fours, three sixes), having missed out narrowly the previous month, and added 181 for the third wicket in 29 overs with James, whose 93 came off 94 balls. Middlesex were given a solid start by Shah and Maunders but, despite a 50-ball half-century from Cook, fell behind the run-rate against accurate bowling. Their young side included, for the first time, Nicholas Compton, grandson of Denis.

Glamorgan

K. Newell c Coleman b Keegan	15	S. D. Thomas not out	3
J. P. Maher c Maunders b Cook	26	L-b 11, w 1	12
R. D. B. Croft not out	114		
*S. P. James st Nash b Keegan	93	1/22 2/59 (4 wkts, 45 overs)	272
†M. P. Maynard b Keegan	9	3/240 4/254	

M. J. Powell, A. Dale, A. P. Davies, O. T. Parkin and S. L. Watkin did not bat.

Bowling: Bloomfield 7–0–39–0; Keegan 9–0–42–3; Cook 9–0–64–1; Coleman 4–0–23–0; Dalrymple 7–0–33–0; Weekes 9–0–60–0.

Middlesex

O. A. Shah c Maynard b Croft	34
J. K. Maunders lbw b Thomas	49
S. J. Cook c Thomas b Davies	50
E. C. Joyce lbw b Croft	6
J. W. M. Dalrymple c Powell b Dale	20
N. R. D. Compton b Davies	6
*P. N. Weekes not out	28
C. B. Keegan c Davies b Dale	3
†D. C. Nash c Maher b Davies	4
A. J. Coleman not out	11
L-b 9, w 10, n-b 2	21
1/87 2/94 3/104 4/164 5/179 6/181 7/188 8/210 (8 wkts, 45 overs)	232

T. F. Bloomfield did not bat.

Bowling: Davies 9–0–36–3; Parkin 5–0–20–0; Thomas 8–0–37–1; Watkin 8–0–50–0; Croft 9–0–47–2; Dale 6–0–33–2.

Umpires: B. Dudleston and J. W. Holder.

HAMPSHIRE

At Manchester, April 29. LANCASHIRE v HAMPSHIRE. No result (abandoned).

HAMPSHIRE v WORCESTERSHIRE

At Southampton, May 13. Hampshire won by three wickets. Toss: Worcestershire.

Zac Morris, the younger of the two Yorkshire-born brothers on Hampshire's staff, made a League debut worth remembering. Having switched from slow left-arm spin to seam in order to revive his career, he first enjoyed figures of three for 31, including the prized wicket of Hick, bowled between bat and pad. Solanki and Leatherdale, and finally Rhodes and Lampitt, almost did enough in half-century stands to perplex a Hampshire side seeking their first one-day victory of the season at the seventh attempt. But Kendall, with two run-outs and a catch to his credit, and Prittipaul added a vital 73 in 13 overs after Smith got Hampshire going. Three quick wickets in the closing stages then set the stage for Morris to win the game with a final-over four to long-off.

Worcestershire

W. P. C. Weston c Kendall b Morris	3
A. Singh run out	17
*G. A. Hick b Morris	13
V. S. Solanki c Kendall b Udal	38
D. A. Leatherdale c and b Udal	37
A. J. Bichel run out	20
N. R. Boulton c Kenway b Morris	1
†S. J. Rhodes not out	21
S. R. Lampitt not out	27
L-b 2, w 4	6
1/4 2/30 3/40 4/105 5/131 6/133 7/133 (7 wkts, 45 overs)	183

M. J. Rawnsley and A. Sheriyar did not bat.

Bowling: Mascarenhas 9–2–24–0; Morris 7–1–31–3; Mullally 9–1–24–0; Johnson 7–0–37–0; Udal 9–0–39–2; Hamblin 4–0–26–0.

Hampshire

N. C. Johnson c Rhodes b Bichel	13	S. D. Udal not out	4
J. S. Laney c Singh b Sheriyar	4	Z. C. Morris not out	7
†D. A. Kenway b Lampitt	15	B 3, l-b 1, w 3	7
*R. A. Smith c Leatherdale b Bichel	46		—
W. S. Kendall lbw b Lampitt	47	1/14 2/18 3/63 (7 wkts, 44.4 overs)	186
L. R. Prittipaul c Lampitt b Sheriyar	42	4/95 5/168	
A. D. Mascarenhas run out	1	6/175 7/177	

J. R. C. Hamblin and A. D. Mullally did not bat.

Bowling: Sheriyar 8.4–1–28–2; Bichel 9–1–40–2; Lampitt 9–1–21–2; Leatherdale 6–0–32–0; Rawnsley 9–0–42–0; Hick 3–0–19–0.

Umpires: B. Leadbeater and J. F. Steele.

HAMPSHIRE v ESSEX

At Southampton, June 3. Essex won by eight runs. Toss: Hampshire.

Hampshire, having needed 51 from ten overs, looked out of contention when three wickets fell for one run, leaving them 48 adrift with last man Tremlett joining Prittipaul. Yet they reached the final over needing nine to win before Irani bowled Prittipaul. Law's 45 and Foster's breezy stand of 83 in 14 overs with Cowan had bolstered the Essex innings. Johnson opened the reply with a run-a-ball 48, but after he went it needed a half-century stand between Prittipaul, playing shots of undeniable class, and Mascarenhas to get Hampshire's challenge back on track.

Essex

P. J. Prichard b Tremlett	13	A. P. Cowan run out	31
D. D. J. Robinson c Johnson b Mascarenhas	12	R. S. G. Anderson b Tremlett	0
S. G. Law b Hamblin	45	B 6, l-b 10, w 5	21
*R. C. Irani c Kendall b Udal	16		—
A. P. Grayson c Kendall b Tremlett	31	1/27 2/30 3/81 (7 wkts, 45 overs)	216
†J. S. Foster not out	47	4/113 5/133	
		6/216 7/216	

A. C. McGarry, T. J. Mason and M. C. Ilott did not bat.

Bowling: Mascarenhas 9–0–44–1; Morris 9–0–44–0; Tremlett 9–0–39–3; Hamblin 9–0–49–1; Udal 9–1–24–1.

Hampshire

N. C. Johnson c Law b McGarry	48	Z. C. Morris b Ilott	0
J. S. Laney b Irani	5	J. R. C. Hamblin b Ilott	0
†D. A. Kenway lbw b Anderson	18	C. T. Tremlett not out	15
*R. A. Smith run out	16	L-b 12, w 13, n-b 2	27
W. S. Kendall c Foster b Ilott	4		—
L. R. Prittipaul b Irani	45	1/6 2/71 3/85 (44.1 overs)	208
A. D. Mascarenhas c Irani b Grayson	23	4/98 5/99 6/153	
S. D. Udal b Grayson	7	7/168 8/169 9/169	

Bowling: Cowan 9–1–46–0; Irani 7.1–1–46–2; McGarry 4–0–26–1; Anderson 3.4–1–5–1; Mason 5.2–0–21–0; Ilott 6–0–20–3; Grayson 9–1–32–2.

Umpires: A. Clarkson and K. E. Palmer.

At Southgate, June 17. HAMPSHIRE beat MIDDLESEX by 17 runs.

HAMPSHIRE v DURHAM

At Southampton, June 24. Hampshire won by 64 runs. Toss: Hampshire.

Durham's target had an unattainable look once they lost openers Peng, second ball to Mullally, and Law, with 14 on the board. Mullally then accounted for Collingwood with a spectacular one-handed catch, running back 25 yards from mid-on, and when Hamblin removed Love and Lewis in his first over, unbeaten Durham were a terminal 55 for five. Kenway, capped along with Johnson and Alex Morris before the start, had hit a bright 46 from 41 balls as Hampshire built a total that was always going to be testing on a pitch with uneven bounce.

Hampshire

J. S. Laney b Collingwood	41
N. C. Johnson c Love b Hatch	10
A. D. Mascarenhas b Hatch	5
†D. A. Kenway lbw b Phillips	46
W. S. Kendall lbw b Collingwood	3
L. R. Prittipaul b Phillips	35
*R. A. Smith c Hunter b Phillips	34
S. D. Udal not out	18
C. T. Tremlett not out	8
L-b 9, w 11, n-b 2	22
1/48 2/56 3/92 4/108 5/127 6/185 7/200 (7 wkts, 45 overs)	222

J. R. C. Hamblin and A. D. Mullally did not bat.

Bowling: Hunter 2–0–12–0; Hatch 8–1–21–2; Davies 5–1–23–0; Collingwood 7–0–39–2; Law 9–0–39–0; Phillips 9–0–46–3; Gough 5–0–33–0.

Durham

N. Peng b Mullally	0
D. R. Law c Smith b Mascarenhas	1
M. L. Love lbw b Hamblin	39
P. D. Collingwood c Mullally b Mascarenhas	4
*J. J. B. Lewis b Hamblin	5
M. A. Gough c Udal b Johnson	28
†A. Pratt c Kenway b Johnson	26
I. D. Hunter b Tremlett	21
N. C. Phillips not out	13
A. M. Davies c Kenway b Mullally	4
N. G. Hatch b Tremlett	5
B 1, l-b 4, w 5, n-b 2	12
1/0 2/14 3/26 4/53 5/55 6/106 7/123 8/138 9/147 (39.1 overs)	158

Bowling: Mullally 8–0–29–2; Mascarenhas 7–1–27–2; Tremlett 8.1–2–23–2; Hamblin 5–1–24–2; Udal 7–0–37–0; Johnson 4–0–13–2.

Umpires: V. A. Holder and K. E. Palmer.

HAMPSHIRE v SUSSEX

At Southampton, July 4 (day/night). Hampshire won by 79 runs. Toss: Hampshire.

Floodlit cricket came to the Rose Bowl for the first time and a crowd of more than 5,000 grossed in the region of £100,000 for Hampshire's beleaguered coffers. That the cricket ultimately failed to match the vibrant occasion reflected the control Hampshire had on the game by the time the lights came into play – and the problems associated with batting second. Sussex never overcame the loss of the prolific Goodwin to Mullally's second ball; within the hour, three more wickets had fallen to leave Sussex facing the gloom at 38 for four. Johnson at slip was involved in three of the dismissals. It was all a considerable contrast to Hampshire's batting in bright sunshine. Kenway anchored the innings with seven fours in his 76; Laney and Smith provided the impetus at either end.

Hampshire

J. S. Laney run out	43	S. D. Udal b Adams	6
N. C. Johnson lbw b Taylor	13	C. T. Tremlett not out	13
†D. A. Kenway run out	76	B 2, l-b 10, w 5	17
A. D. Mascarenhas c Prior b Robinson	0		
W. S. Kendall run out	10	1/14 2/88 3/88 (7 wkts, 45 overs)	231
L. R. Prittipaul b Adams	15	4/119 5/153	
*R. A. Smith not out	38	6/191 7/204	

J. R. C. Hamblin and A. D. Mullally did not bat.

Bowling: Kirtley 9–2–31–0; Taylor 7–0–43–1; Robinson 9–0–35–1; Yardy 5–0–25–0; Davis 8–0–36–0; Adams 7–0–49–2.

Sussex

M. W. Goodwin c Johnson b Mullally	0	R. J. Kirtley not out	10
R. R. Montgomerie c Kenway b Tremlett	18	B. V. Taylor c Mullally b Udal	4
*C. J. Adams c Johnson b Mascarenhas	18	M. A. Robinson b Tremlett	4
B. Zuiderent c Kendall b Udal	19	B 2, l-b 5, w 1	8
M. H. Yardy c Johnson b Mascarenhas	0		
W. J. House run out	39	1/0 2/34 3/38 (43.2 overs)	152
†M. J. Prior hit wkt b Udal	5	4/38 5/71 6/83	
M. J. G. Davis b Tremlett	27	7/129 8/135 9/145	

Bowling: Mullally 8–2–16–1; Mascarenhas 9–1–42–2; Tremlett 8.2–1–22–3; Udal 9–2–23–3; Hamblin 6–0–31–0; Johnson 3–0–11–0.

Umpires: R. Julian and R. Palmer.

HAMPSHIRE v DERBYSHIRE

At Southampton, July 15. Hampshire won by 16 runs. Toss: Hampshire.

Sorry Derbyshire lost their last five wickets for 11 runs after falling behind the rate required to overhaul Hampshire's lowest League total of the season yet. The pitch did not help either team; uneven bounce and lateral movement, along with later cloud cover, made batting difficult from the first ball of the match, which had Laney well caught by keeper Krikken. It took the experienced Bailey 29 overs for his 40, top score of the match – his and Dowman's 65 for Derbyshire's fourth wicket was also the day's best stand – but controlled bowling by Mullally and Tremlett left his diligence unrewarded.

Hampshire

J. S. Laney c Krikken b Cork	0	C. T. Tremlett b Wharton	10
N. C. Johnson lbw b Cork	6	J. R. C. Hamblin c Cork b Wharton	0
†D. A. Kenway c Stubbings b Aldred	29	A. D. Mullally not out	5
A. D. Mascarenhas c Di Venuto b Aldred	6	L-b 4, w 10	14
W. S. Kendall lbw b Cork	22		
L. R. Prittipaul c Cork b Aldred	28	1/0 2/21 3/40 (9 wkts, 45 overs)	155
*R. A. Smith c Krikken b Welch	7	4/48 5/88 6/99	
S. D. Udal not out	28	7/111 8/139 9/139	

Bowling: Cork 9–0–38–3; Welch 9–1–22–1; Aldred 9–3–17–3; Edwards 9–0–30–0; Wharton 8–0–37–2; Bailey 1–0–7–0.

Derbyshire

M. J. Di Venuto c Kenway b Tremlett	24	P. Aldred b Mullally	1
G. Welch b Mascarenhas	0	A. D. Edwards c Mascarenhas b Mullally	0
S. D. Stubbings b Mascarenhas	2	L. J. Wharton not out	1
R. J. Bailey c Tremlett b Udal	40	L-b 10, w 6	16
M. P. Dowman c Tremlett b Mullally	35		
*D. G. Cork b Tremlett	4	1/4 2/25 3/33 (44.2 overs)	139
J. P. Pyemont b Johnson	7	4/98 5/113 6/128	
†K. M. Krikken b Tremlett	9	7/132 8/138 9/138	

Bowling: Mullally 9–3–19–3; Mascarenhas 9–3–21–2; Tremlett 8.2–2–15–3; Johnson 7–0–30–1; Udal 9–0–28–1; Hamblin 2–0–16–0.

Umpires: M. J. Harris and A. G. T. Whitehead.

At Southend, July 22. HAMPSHIRE beat ESSEX by 85 runs.

At Derby, August 5. HAMPSHIRE beat DERBYSHIRE by nine wickets.

HAMPSHIRE v GLAMORGAN

At Southampton, August 12. Glamorgan won by six wickets. Toss: Hampshire.

With six successive wins behind them, Hampshire would have gone top had they won a seventh here. But they were trounced by a Glamorgan side building their own case for promotion and slipped back to third, albeit with a game in hand. Smith's decision to bat first was difficult to defend once the ball began to move around alarmingly and at different heights, conditions that Davies, returning his best figures to date, Dale, Parkin and the unrewarded Watkin could not have used more skilfully. Extras equalled Smith's top score of 26 not out. Glamorgan won with more than 17 overs to spare after Maher and Maynard's fourth-wicket stand of 61.

Hampshire

J. S. Laney lbw b Davies	2	C. T. Tremlett lbw b Dale	4
N. C. Johnson lbw b Parkin	16	J. R. C. Hamblin b Parkin	5
†D. A. Kenway c I. J. Thomas b Dale	22	A. D. Mullally c S. D. Thomas b Parkin	0
L. R. Prittipaul c Croft b Davies	10	L-b 6, w 20	26
W. S. Kendall b Davies	0		
A. D. Mascarenhas b Davies	6	1/26 2/26 3/45 (38.5 overs)	120
*R. A. Smith not out	26	4/45 5/61 6/87	
S. D. Udal lbw b Dale	3	7/93 8/100 9/111	

Bowling: Davies 9–2–18–4; Parkin 8.5–1–39–3; Watkin 9–2–16–0; Dale 8–0–22–3; S. D. Thomas 4–0–19–0.

Glamorgan

K. Newell c Laney b Mullally	0	M. J. Powell not out	4
I. J. Thomas c Udal b Tremlett	22	W 4, n-b 2	6
R. D. B. Croft c Kendall b Mullally	12		
J. P. Maher c Kendall b Tremlett	36	1/0 2/23 (4 wkts, 27.5 overs)	121
†M. P. Maynard not out	41	3/54 4/115	

*A. Dale, S. D. Thomas, A. P. Davies, S. L. Watkin and O. T. Parkin did not bat.

Bowling: Mullally 9–1–31–2; Mascarenhas 5–0–30–0; Tremlett 7–0–39–2; Hamblin 3–1–9–0; Udal 3.5–0–12–0.

Umpires: J. W. Holder and N. A. Mallender.

At Chester-le-Street, August 15 (day/night). HAMPSHIRE lost to DURHAM by 17 runs (D/L method).

At Worcester, August 26. HAMPSHIRE beat WORCESTERSHIRE by two wickets (D/L method).

HAMPSHIRE v LANCASHIRE

At Southampton, August 27. Lancashire won by 43 runs. Toss: Hampshire.

Hampshire lost their last six wickets in as many overs for 31, surrendering a potentially winning position of 138 for four and a return to the top three. Lancashire recovered from a hesitant start after being put in, with Flintoff's big boundary-hitting providing great entertainment as he and Crawley added 151 in 28 overs. Hampshire's reply rested on Johnson and Smith after Chapple, and some uneven bounce, had sent back Laney and Kenway with successive deliveries. They added 71 before Smith was run out by Chilton; when Johnson was bowled by one that kept low, the collapse was under way.

Lancashire

M. J. Chilton c Kenway b Mascarenhas	6	G. D. Lloyd c Udal b Tremlett	6
G. Chapple c Laney b Mullally	5	B 4, l-b 10, w 4	18
A. Flintoff c Prittipaul b Mascarenhas	78		
*J. P. Crawley not out	84	1/10 2/12 3/163 (5 wkts, 45 overs)	212
N. H. Fairbrother c Prittipaul b Tremlett	15	4/197 5/212	

J. C. Scuderi, †J. J. Haynes, C. P. Schofield, G. Yates and J. Wood did not bat.

Bowling: Mascarenhas 9–1–33–2; Mullally 9–4–26–1; Tremlett 9–0–45–2; Johnson 9–0–57–0; Udal 9–1–37–0.

Hampshire

J. S. Laney c Haynes b Chapple	6	S. D. Udal c Yates b Wood	0
N. C. Johnson b Scuderi	67	C. T. Tremlett run out	7
†D. A. Kenway lbw b Chapple	0	A. D. Mullally run out	2
*R. A. Smith run out	29	L-b 5, w 6	11
J. D. Francis c Wood b Chapple	16		
G. W. White c Crawley b Yates	15	1/10 2/10 3/81 (41 overs)	169
A. D. Mascarenhas lbw b Scuderi	10	4/118 5/138 6/148	
L. R. Prittipaul not out	6	7/152 8/153 9/164	

Bowling: Chapple 7–1–19–3; Wood 7–0–28–1; Flintoff 9–0–32–0; Scuderi 9–1–39–2; Yates 9–0–46–1.

Umpires: R. Julian and K. E. Palmer.

At Cardiff, August 29 (day/night). HAMPSHIRE lost to GLAMORGAN by 51 runs.

HAMPSHIRE v MIDDLESEX

At Southampton, September 9. Middlesex won by four wickets. Toss: Hampshire.

Cook and Dalrymple hit 65 in six overs to transform a match Hampshire were winning easily, and put promotion beyond the home side's control. Impressive half-centuries from White and Francis had underpinned Hampshire's innings, while in reply Shah and Joyce added 98 inside an hour to put the visitors on track. Even so, the asking-rate had risen above ten an over before Cook's late assault carried him to 46 off 36 balls, and Middlesex to victory. Mullally's last full over, the 43rd, cost 19 runs, an experience he later described as the worst five minutes of his career.

Hampshire

J. R. C. Hamblin c Dalrymple b Cook	23	S. D. Udal b Weekes	22
N. C. Johnson c and b Bloomfield	20	C. T. Tremlett b Weekes	1
†D. A. Kenway c Joyce b Cook	2		
G. W. White run out	59	B 4, l-b 5, w 7	16
J. D. Francis not out	57		
W. S. Kendall lbw b Dalrymple	10	1/31 2/38 3/66 (9 wkts, 45 overs)	220
A. D. Mascarenhas c Nash b Keegan	1	4/134 5/155 6/161	
*R. A. Smith b Weekes	9	7/188 8/216 9/220	

A. D. Mullally did not bat.

Bowling: Bloomfield 9–0–38–1; Cook 9–0–48–2; Keegan 7–0–35–1; Coleman 7–0–31–0; Weekes 8–0–37–3; Dalrymple 5–0–22–1.

Middlesex

A. J. Strauss c Smith b Mascarenhas	5	J. W. M. Dalrymple b Tremlett	23
J. K. Maunders run out	6	†D. C. Nash not out	0
O. A. Shah c Hamblin b Johnson	69	B 11, l-b 8, w 13	32
E. C. Joyce c and b Udal	38		
S. J. Cook not out	46	1/7 2/30 3/128 (6 wkts, 44.1 overs)	224
*P. N. Weekes c Tremlett b Udal	5	4/143 5/151 6/216	

C. B. Keegan, A. J. Coleman and T. F. Bloomfield did not bat.

Bowling: Mullally 8.1–0–44–0; Mascarenhas 9–2–26–1; Tremlett 9–1–39–1; Udal 9–1–46–2; Hamblin 7–0–37–0; Johnson 2–0–13–1.

Umpires: J. H. Evans and J. W. Lloyds.

At Hove, September 16. HAMPSHIRE beat SUSSEX by seven wickets.

LANCASHIRE

LANCASHIRE v HAMPSHIRE

At Manchester, April 29. No result (abandoned).

LANCASHIRE v GLAMORGAN

At Manchester, May 20. Glamorgan won by four wickets. Toss: Lancashire.

After the first nine scheduled days of cricket at Old Trafford had been lost to rain, this was a disappointing way for Lancashire to raise the curtain. Fairbrother, hit on the helmet by Wharf, showed no ill-effects in scoring 62 off 107 balls, but spinners Croft, bowling round the wicket, and Cosker conceded little. Crawley must have wondered about his decision to bat first as he watched Wharf use the humid conditions to take three for 23. Muralitharan gave even less away than his Glamorgan counterparts, but Lancashire also needed wickets. Flintoff, back from injury, didn't bowl and Maynard made sure Glamorgan cruised to their first one-day win in seven attempts.

Lancashire

R. C. Driver b Wharf	0	†W. K. Hegg not out	11
*J. P. Crawley run out	32	J. Wood not out	2
A. Flintoff c Maynard b Wharf	2	L-b 8, w 4	12
N. H. Fairbrother run out	62		—
G. D. Lloyd st Maynard b Cosker	11	1/3 2/9 3/62 (6 wkts, 45 overs)	147
C. P. Schofield c Croft b Wharf	15	4/93 5/132 6/139	

I. D. Austin, P. J. Martin and M. Muralitharan did not bat.

Bowling: Watkin 9–2–26–0; Wharf 9–1–23–3; Thomas 6–0–31–0; Dale 3–0–16–0; Croft 9–1–21–0; Cosker 9–3–22–1.

Glamorgan

K. Newell c Flintoff b Wood	29	A. Dale b Martin	4
J. P. Maher c Crawley b Martin	19	S. D. Thomas not out	3
R. D. B. Croft c Fairbrother b Austin	7	B 2, l-b 2, w 5	9
*S. P. James b Wood	16		—
†M. P. Maynard not out	39	1/25 2/48 3/74 (6 wkts, 40.5 overs)	148
M. J. Powell c and b Schofield	22	4/77 5/125 6/137	

A. G. Wharf, D. A. Cosker and S. L. Watkin did not bat.

Bowling: Martin 9–0–46–2; Wood 9–0–29–2; Austin 6.5–1–32–1; Muralitharan 9–1–14–0; Schofield 7–0–23–1.

Umpires: A. Clarkson and R. Julian.

At Chester-le-Street, May 27. LANCASHIRE lost to DURHAM by 24 runs.

LANCASHIRE v MIDDLESEX

At Manchester, June 10. Lancashire won by seven wickets. Toss: Middlesex.

Atherton cracked a second-ball six over extra cover to spark a lightning-fast chase and, with Chapple, the pinch-hitter, hitting 56 from 50 deliveries, Lancashire raced to 100 at almost eight an over. Middlesex, too, had started confidently. Strauss and Hutton put on 60 in the first ten overs but, with Muralitharan in niggardly form, only 24 came from the next ten. Three wickets each for Flintoff and Chapple were later complemented by their robust hitting.

Middlesex

A. J. Strauss c Crawley b Flintoff	34	C. B. Keegan not out	11
B. L. Hutton b Schofield	44	J. P. Hewitt c Atherton b Chapple	5
*S. P. Fleming c Crawley b Muralitharan	3	P. C. R. Tufnell not out	0
R. M. S. Weston c Fairbrother b Schofield	8	B 8, l-b 4, w 8, n-b 2	22
†D. C. Nash b Flintoff	14		—
M. A. Roseberry c Hegg b Chapple	9	1/64 2/72 3/100 (9 wkts, 45 overs)	184
P. N. Weekes c Atherton b Chapple	28	4/101 5/116 6/142	
S. J. Cook b Flintoff	6	7/156 8/174 9/181	

Bowling: Martin 8–0–34–0; Wood 3–0–27–0; Chapple 9–0–29–3; Flintoff 9–0–27–3; Muralitharan 9–3–18–1; Schofield 7–0–37–2.

Lancashire

M. A. Atherton b Hewitt	25	N. H. Fairbrother not out	14
G. Chapple c Hutton b Weekes	56	B 6, l-b 3, w 1, n-b 4	14
A. Flintoff st Nash b Tufnell	40		—
*J. P. Crawley not out	36	1/37 2/118 3/140 (3 wkts, 29.2 overs)	185

M. J. Chilton, C. P. Schofield, †W. K. Hegg, J. Wood, P. J. Martin and M. Muralitharan did not bat.

Bowling: Keegan 6–0–49–0; Hewitt 5–1–28–1; Cook 1–0–14–0; Weekes 9–2–36–1; Tufnell 8.2–1–49–1.

Umpires: V. A. Holder and G. Sharp.

At Worcester, June 17. LANCASHIRE lost to WORCESTERSHIRE by ten runs.

LANCASHIRE v ESSEX

At Manchester, June 23 (day/night). Lancashire won by 37 runs. Toss: Lancashire.

Having hit two centuries in the Championship game that ended the previous day, Law made it three on the trot and took his tally from the visit to 347 for once out, brilliantly caught by Lloyd at mid-wicket. But again he finished on the losing side, this time through Fairbrother's fifth League hundred, achieved off 87 balls, and deft work by Hegg and Schofield as Essex collapsed from 191 for four to 217 all out. Crawley, who added 151 with Fairbrother, went past 2,500 League runs, and Hussain returned after breaking his thumb in the Lord's Test against Pakistan.

Lancashire

M. A. Atherton lbw b Irani	18	†W. K. Hegg not out	9
G. Chapple c Grayson b Irani	0	C. P. Schofield not out	7
A. Flintoff c Foster b Bishop	24	L-b 6, w 11	17
*J. P. Crawley c Grayson b Bishop	63		—
N. H. Fairbrother c Bishop b Irani	101	1/21 2/27 3/57 (6 wkts, 45 overs)	254
G. D. Lloyd c Bishop b Cowan	15	4/208 5/225 6/242	

P. J. Martin, M. Muralitharan and M. P. Smethurst did not bat.

Bowling: Cowan 9–1–31–1; Irani 9–0–51–3; Bishop 9–0–40–2; Ilott 8–0–50–0; Grayson 7–0–51–0; Clinton 3–0–25–0.

Essex

D. D. J. Robinson lbw b Martin	4	A. P. Cowan st Hegg b Schofield	9
N. Hussain lbw b Chapple	21	M. C. Ilott st Hegg b Schofield	2
S. G. Law c Lloyd b Muralitharan	108	J. E. Bishop not out	0
*R. C. Irani c Atherton b Martin	37	B 1, l-b 10	11
S. D. Peters c Hegg b Schofield	3		—
A. P. Grayson b Muralitharan	13	1/12 2/50 3/133 (41.4 overs)	217
†J. S. Foster c Hegg b Schofield	0	4/160 5/191 6/191	
R. S. Clinton run out	9	7/191 8/210 9/215	

Bowling: Martin 8–1–37–2; Chapple 7–0–34–1; Smethurst 2–0–24–0; Muralitharan 9–1–34–2; Flintoff 7–0–36–0; Schofield 8.4–1–41–4.

Umpires: N. G. Cowley and A. A. Jones.

LANCASHIRE v DURHAM

At Manchester, July 15. No result (abandoned).

LANCASHIRE v WORCESTERSHIRE

At Manchester, July 18 (day/night). Worcestershire won by 109 runs. Toss: Worcestershire.

Muralitharan had returned to Sri Lanka for a spell of international cricket, but Lancashire stuck with their policy of two spinners and saw Schofield and Keedy clattered for 76 off just nine overs. Singh did most of the damage. Kabir Ali rocked Lancashire by trapping Flintoff and Crawley lbw with successive balls in his first over and, although Fairbrother survived the hat-trick, Lancashire were soon 63 for five with the floodlights still not needed. Their one consolation was that Chapple again underlined his effectiveness at the top of the order.

Worcestershire

W. P. C. Weston lbw b Martin	18	†S. J. Rhodes not out	3
A. Singh st Hegg b Schofield	80		
*G. A. Hick run out	18	B 1, l-b 6, w 5	12
V. S. Solanki c Crawley b Keedy	45		
D. A. Leatherdale c and b Chapple	24	1/24 2/58 3/129 (5 wkts, 45 overs)	236
A. J. Bichel not out	36	4/167 5/216	

S. R. Lampitt, Kabir Ali, M. J. Rawnsley and A. Sheriyar did not bat.

Bowling: Martin 9–2–28–1; Wood 9–1–31–0; Flintoff 9–1–54–0; Chapple 9–0–40–1; Schofield 5–0–39–1; Keedy 4–0–37–1.

Lancashire

M. J. Chilton c Rhodes b Bichel	2	P. J. Martin st Rhodes b Leatherdale	6
G. Chapple lbw b Ali	34	J. Wood not out	19
A. Flintoff lbw b Ali	9	G. Keedy b Leatherdale	2
*J. P. Crawley lbw b Ali	0	B 1, l-b 2, w 5, n-b 6	14
N. H. Fairbrother b Lampitt	5		
G. D. Lloyd c Rhodes b Sheriyar	23	1/7 2/36 3/36 (35.4 overs)	127
†W. K. Hegg run out	6	4/53 5/63 6/82	
C. P. Schofield c Lampitt b Leatherdale	7	7/99 8/102 9/123	

Bowling: Bichel 6–2–16–1; Sheriyar 6.2–1–31–1; Ali 9–0–37–3; Lampitt 7–1–20–1; Leatherdale 4.4–0–11–3; Hick 0.4–0–2–0; Rawnsley 2–0–7–0.

Umpires: B. Leadbeater and R. A. White.

At Colwyn Bay, August 5. LANCASHIRE lost to GLAMORGAN by 46 runs.

At Lord's, August 14. LANCASHIRE lost to MIDDLESEX by three wickets.

LANCASHIRE v SUSSEX

At Manchester, August 20 (day/night). Lancashire won by 22 runs. Toss: Lancashire.

Crawley steered his side out of early trouble and Lloyd's run-a-ball 56 provided acceleration, as well as one of the few highlights of his testimonial season after he had been dropped from the Championship side. Lancashire's seamers bowled tightly, while Chapple's direct run-out of Goodwin from long leg epitomised the keen support in the field. Montgomerie, ninth out, kept Sussex's hopes alive until he lost House after a 74-run stand. Yates and Schofield went for six an over from ten between them, but Schofield compensated by wrapping up the tail.

Lancashire

M. J. Chilton c House b Taylor	1	C. P. Schofield not out	11
G. Chapple c Robinson b Martin-Jenkins	0	†J. J. Haynes b Kirtley	11
A. Flintoff b Robinson	18	G. Yates not out	5
*J. P. Crawley st Prior b Martin-Jenkins	54	L-b 4, w 10	14
N. H. Fairbrother c Martin-Jenkins b Davis	26	1/1 2/1 3/38 (8 wkts, 45 overs)	200
G. D. Lloyd b Taylor	56	4/75 5/154 6/169	
J. C. Scuderi c Taylor b Kirtley	4	7/172 8/194	

J. Wood did not bat.

Bowling: Martin-Jenkins 9–2–35–2; Taylor 9–1–37–2; Robinson 9–2–25–1; Kirtley 9–0–52–2; Davis 9–0–47–1.

Sussex

†M. J. Prior c Haynes b Wood	3	B. V. Taylor c Crawley b Schofield	6
R. R. Montgomerie b Flintoff	76	*R. J. Kirtley c Chilton b Schofield	11
M. J. G. Davis lbw b Chapple	12	M. A. Robinson not out	0
M. W. Goodwin run out	1	B 4, l-b 10, w 7	21
B. Zuiderent c Fairbrother b Scuderi	5		
W. J. House c Crawley b Wood	35	1/5 2/18 3/22 (44.1 overs)	178
R. S. C. Martin-Jenkins lbw b Flintoff	3	4/41 5/115 6/123	
M. H. Yardy st Haynes b Schofield	5	7/136 8/151 9/178	

Bowling: Chapple 7–1–13–1; Wood 9–3–20–2; Flintoff 9–1–38–2; Scuderi 9–0–32–1; Yates 5–0–31–0; Schofield 5.1–0–30–3.

Umpires: J. F. Steele and P. Willey.

At Colchester, August 26. ESSEX v LANCASHIRE. No result.

At Southampton, August 27. LANCASHIRE beat HAMPSHIRE by 43 runs.

At Hove, August 30 (day/night). LANCASHIRE lost to SUSSEX by 138 runs.

LANCASHIRE v DERBYSHIRE

At Manchester, September 3 (day/night). Lancashire won by 60 runs. Toss: Lancashire. First-team debut: S. A. Selwood.

Fairbrother, promoted to opener, responded by taking 32 balls to score four, then picked up the pace with a flurry of boundaries and finished with 78 from 98 balls. Lloyd and Hegg also entertained, with a mixture of reverse sweeps, big hitting and quick running. After Hogg had marked his one-day debut for Lancashire with a wicket, a combination of run-outs and quality spin left Derbyshire well short. Yates had Dowman caught behind with his first ball and Schofield achieved a one-day best of five for 31.

Lancashire

*J. P. Crawley b Lungley	28	C. P. Schofield c Krikken b Lungley	0
N. H. Fairbrother c Krikken b Dumelow	78		
A. Flintoff run out	23	L-b 4, w 8	12
G. D. Lloyd not out	36		
J. C. Scuderi b Dumelow	4	1/80 2/134 3/143 (6 wkts, 45 overs)	210
†W. K. Hegg c Bailey b Lungley	29	4/149 5/205 6/210	

G. Chapple, M. P. Smethurst, G. Yates and K. W. Hogg did not bat.

Bowling: Welch 9–1–28–0; Dean 8–3–36–0; Lungley 9–0–43–3; Dowman 1–0–8–0; Wharton 9–0–41–0; Dumelow 9–0–50–2.

Derbyshire

S. D. Stubbings lbw b Hogg	17	G. Welch c and b Schofield	3
M. P. Dowman c Hegg b Yates	41	K. J. Dean b Schofield	2
C. W. G. Bassano run out	7	L. J. Wharton not out	5
S. A. Selwood run out	5	B 4, l-b 9, w 8	21
*R. J. Bailey c Crawley b Schofield	6		
N. R. C. Dumelow lbw b Yates	33	1/49 2/60 3/73 (39.2 overs)	150
T. Lungley b Schofield	2	4/79 5/108 6/116	
†K. M. Krikken c Hogg b Schofield	8	7/130 8/138 9/144	

Bowling: Chapple 5–0–31–0; Smethurst 7–2–23–0; Hogg 6–1–14–1; Scuderi 5–1–17–0; Yates 9–1–21–2; Schofield 7.2–0–31–5.

Umpires: D. R. Shepherd and J. F. Steele.

At Derby, September 16. LANCASHIRE lost to DERBYSHIRE by six wickets.

MIDDLESEX

MIDDLESEX v DURHAM

At Lord's, April 29. No result (abandoned).

At Chester-le-Street, May 20. MIDDLESEX lost to DURHAM by two wickets.

MIDDLESEX v DERBYSHIRE

At Southgate, June 3. Middlesex won by 16 runs. Toss: Middlesex.

Lungley's three wickets offset Strauss's half-century, and Middlesex needed the unbroken partnership of 124 in 20 overs between Weston and Nash to set a reasonable challenge. Both achieved one-day bests but had to run hard – Nash hit only two fours. As long as Bailey was at the crease, Derbyshire were in with a chance, but five wickets for Hutton – another one-day best – broke their reply. Tufnell was playing his first League game since August 1999.

Middlesex

A. J. Strauss st Krikken b Illingworth	55	P. N. Weekes b Illingworth	8
B. L. Hutton run out	4	†D. C. Nash not out	57
*S. P. Fleming c Khan b Lungley	18	L-b 8, w 2	10
O. A. Shah c Krikken b Lungley	1		
M. A. Roseberry b Lungley	0	1/18 2/64 3/72 (6 wkts, 45 overs)	233
R. M. S. Weston not out	80	4/72 5/94 6/109	

S. J. Cook, C. B. Keegan and P. C. R. Tufnell did not bat.

Bowling: Welch 9–1–55–0; Munton 9–2–53–0; Lungley 8–1–38–3; Illingworth 9–0–29–2; Dumelow 6–0–25–0; Bailey 4–0–25–0.

Derbyshire

R. J. Bailey c Shah b Hutton	71	R. K. Illingworth not out	10
M. J. Di Venuto run out	25	*T. A. Munton st Nash b Weekes	3
M. P. Dowman c Hutton b Tufnell	33	T. Lungley not out	8
G. Welch c Fleming b Hutton	4	B 1, l-b 10, w 6	17
W. G. Khan c Roseberry b Hutton	6		
L. D. Sutton c Keegan b Hutton	7	1/39 2/93 3/116 (9 wkts, 45 overs)	217
†K. M. Krikken c Weekes b Hutton	2	4/137 5/160 6/162	
N. R. C. Dumelow c Weekes b Keegan	31	7/170 8/205 9/209	

Bowling: Cook 9–1–35–0; Keegan 9–1–37–1; Tufnell 9–0–36–1; Weekes 9–0–53–1; Hutton 9–1–45–5.

Umpires: J. H. Evans and J. H. Hampshire.

At Manchester, June 10. MIDDLESEX lost to LANCASHIRE by seven wickets.

MIDDLESEX v HAMPSHIRE

At Southgate, June 17. Hampshire won by 17 runs. Toss: Hampshire.

Keegan's three wickets in four balls in the penultimate over – giving him figures of five for 17 – kept the Hampshire total within bounds, but Kenway's half-century ultimately proved more decisive. Middlesex in reply were making steady progress until Tremlett and Hamblin each took wickets in their first overs. Although Roseberry and Weekes chipped away at the target, Middlesex arrived at the last over still needing 26. Hamblin, in his third League match, and 19-year-old Tremlett shared seven wickets.

Hampshire

J. S. Laney b Hutton	32	C. T. Tremlett b Keegan	0
N. C. Johnson b Keegan	17	Z. C. Morris b Keegan	0
A. D. Mascarenhas lbw b Keegan	0	J. R. C. Hamblin not out	3
†D. A. Kenway c Weston b Weekes	65	L-b 9, w 2	11
L. R. Prittipaul b Weekes	3		
W. S. Kendall c Roseberry b Hutton	12	1/29 2/30 3/96 (9 wkts, 45 overs)	171
*R. A. Smith not out	18	4/103 5/126 6/139	
S. D. Udal b Keegan	10	7/164 8/164 9/164	

Bowling: Fraser 9–1–23–0; Keegan 8–2–17–5; Cook 5–0–31–0; Hewitt 5–1–15–0; Hutton 9–0–45–2; Weekes 9–1–31–2.

Middlesex

A. J. Strauss c Prittipaul b Tremlett	12	C. B. Keegan not out	7
B. L. Hutton lbw b Hamblin	25	J. P. Hewitt b Tremlett	3
S. P. Fleming c Kenway b Mascarenhas	10		
R. M. S. Weston c Johnson b Hamblin	13	B 6, l-b 5, w 5	16
M. A. Roseberry c Prittipaul b Hamblin	22		
S. J. Cook c Kendall b Hamblin	1	1/29 2/51 3/59 (9 wkts, 45 overs)	154
P. N. Weekes b Tremlett	29	4/88 5/89 6/109	
†D. C. Nash run out	16	7/141 8/143 9/154	

*A. R. C. Fraser did not bat.

Bowling: Mascarenhas 9–1–28–1; Morris 9–1–27–0; Tremlett 9–2–28–3; Hamblin 9–0–29–4; Udal 9–1–31–0.

Umpires: G. I. Burgess and P. Willey.

At Derby, June 24. MIDDLESEX lost to DERBYSHIRE by 42 runs.

MIDDLESEX v ESSEX

At Southgate, July 8. Tied. Toss: Essex. First-team debut: A. J. Clarke.

A fast, straight delivery by Bishop was too much for Bloomfield, leaving Middlesex, who looked as if they had retrieved a lost cause, to settle for a tie. Although Law was absent with a damaged finger, his claims of a bust-up in the Essex dressing-room hung over a low-scoring match in which he might have made the difference. Instead, Shah's obdurate 52 almost won it for the home team after Cowan had taken five for 14 – his best one-day analysis. Dalrymple made an encouraging reappearance for Middlesex after his first summer at Oxford, taking four for 14 with his off-breaks as Essex struggled on a difficult pitch.

Essex

D. D. J. Robinson b Fraser	9	T. J. Mason c Nash b Dalrymple	12
S. D. Peters b Keegan	27	T. J. Phillips c and b Dalrymple	2
G. R. Napier c Weston b Fraser	0	J. E. Bishop not out	10
*R. C. Irani c Bloomfield b Fraser	6	B 1, l-b 5, w 5	11
A. P. Grayson c Nash b Keegan	6		
†J. S. Foster lbw b Hutton	23	1/22 2/22 3/32 (42.5 overs)	120
A. P. Cowan lbw b Dalrymple	10	4/50 5/63 6/87	
A. J. Clarke c Weekes b Dalrymple	4	7/89 8/100 9/104	

Bowling: Bloomfield 8–2–17–0; Fraser 8–1–29–3; Weekes 9–1–21–0; Keegan 7–0–26–2; Dalrymple 7.5–1–14–4; Hutton 3–0–7–1.

Middlesex

A. J. Strauss lbw b Cowan	5	J. W. M. Dalrymple b Cowan	0
B. L. Hutton lbw b Cowan	0	*A. R. C. Fraser c Bishop b Grayson	2
C. B. Keegan c Foster b Cowan	0	T. F. Bloomfield b Bishop	2
S. P. Fleming b Irani	21	L-b 1, w 8	9
O. A. Shah not out	52		
†D. C. Nash c Foster b Grayson	2	1/1 2/3 3/18 (43 overs)	120
R. M. S. Weston b Grayson	15	4/31 5/42 6/62	
P. N. Weekes lbw b Cowan	12	7/94 8/94 9/101	

Bowling: Cowan 9–2–14–5; Irani 9–1–24–1; Bishop 3–1–6–1; Grayson 9–0–29–3; Mason 8–0–34–0; Phillips 5–1–12–0.

Umpires: M. J. Harris and A. A. Jones.

At Worcester, July 15. MIDDLESEX lost to WORCESTERSHIRE by five wickets.

At Hove, August 1 (day/night). MIDDLESEX lost to SUSSEX by seven runs.

MIDDLESEX v LANCASHIRE

At Lord's, August 14. Middlesex won by three wickets. Toss: Middlesex.

Middlesex's first League win in more than two months looked anything but likely when they needed 16 off the last over, with the inexperienced Dalrymple and Keegan together. But Dalrymple swung Chapple's first ball for six, edged his next for four, and Keegan swept the fourth for four. A single chanced against Fairbrother's arm brought victory with a ball to spare. Lancashire had shown their mettle several times, first to recover from 85 for five and then to bowl themselves into a strong position after Strauss, then Shah and Weekes with a stand of 69, had established Middlesex's position.

Lancashire

M. J. Chilton b Fraser	4
G. Chapple c Shah b Fraser	5
A. Flintoff c Shah b Keegan	45
*J. P. Crawley c Alleyne b Keegan	25
N. H. Fairbrother c Alleyne b Cook	2
G. D. Lloyd b Dalrymple	46
J. C. Scuderi c Joyce b Fraser	42
†W. K. Hegg b Bloomfield	16
C. P. Schofield not out	6
G. Yates not out	7
B 1, l-b 4, w 2	7
1/8 2/9 3/72 4/79 5/85 6/157 7/190 8/191 (8 wkts, 45 overs)	205

J. Wood did not bat.

Bowling: Fraser 9–1–24–3; Bloomfield 9–1–48–1; Cook 9–2–31–1; Keegan 8–0–43–2; Weekes 6–1–28–0; Dalrymple 4–0–26–1.

Middlesex

A. J. Strauss c Hegg b Scuderi	54
†D. Alleyne c Crawley b Chapple	8
S. P. Fleming lbw b Scuderi	28
O. A. Shah c Fairbrother b Flintoff	49
E. C. Joyce lbw b Scuderi	2
P. N. Weekes lbw b Chapple	28
J. W. M. Dalrymple not out	15
S. J. Cook b Flintoff	0
C. B. Keegan not out	8
L-b 5, w 9	14
1/30 2/84 3/105 4/112 5/181 6/183 7/184 (7 wkts, 44.5 overs)	206

*A. R. C. Fraser and T. F. Bloomfield did not bat.

Bowling: Chapple 8.5–1–38–2; Wood 8–1–47–0; Scuderi 9–1–28–3; Flintoff 8–0–37–2; Yates 9–1–37–0; Schofield 2–0–14–0.

Umpires: G. I. Burgess and A. Clarkson.

MIDDLESEX v WORCESTERSHIRE

At Lord's, August 19. No result (abandoned).

MIDDLESEX v GLAMORGAN

At Lord's, August 26. No result. Toss: Middlesex.

It was so dark when the first over was bowled that it was surprising the match ever started. The teams left the field at the end of it and, though they returned 45 minutes later, the weather had the last word.

Glamorgan

K. Newell b Fraser	6	*M. P. Maynard not out	19
I. J. Thomas lbw b Fraser	15	B 2, l-b 9, w 1	12
R. D. B. Croft c Shah b Fraser	13		——
J. P. Maher not out	35	1/14 2/40 3/47 (3 wkts, 21 overs)	100

M. J. Powell, A. Dale, †A. D. Shaw, A. P. Davies, S. D. Thomas and O. T. Parkin did not bat.

Bowling: Fraser 8–3–15–3; Bloomfield 6–0–34–0; Keegan 4–0–23–0; Cook 3–0–17–0.

Middlesex

A. J. Strauss, P. N. Weekes, S. P. Fleming, O. A. Shah, E. C. Joyce, †D. C. Nash, J. W. M. Dalrymple, S. J. Cook, C. B. Keegan, *A. R. C. Fraser and T. F. Bloomfield.

Umpires: G. Sharp and R. A. White.

At Colchester, August 28 (day/night). MIDDLESEX lost to ESSEX by four wickets.

MIDDLESEX v SUSSEX

At Richmond, September 2. Sussex won by eight wickets. Toss: Sussex. First-team debut: A. J. Coleman.

In a season of poor batting performances, this was probably Middlesex's worst, even if the Old Deer Park pitch was far from being a batsman's paradise. Shah, their only player to make more than 13, took 73 balls for his 23, and Middlesex would not have reached three figures without Extras top-scoring. Davis was the pick of the bowlers, with his best limited-overs figures. Chasing 110, the Sussex batsmen found putting bat to ball much less of a trial.

Middlesex

P. N. Weekes b Kirtley	0	S. J. Cook run out	5
A. J. Strauss b Martin-Jenkins	12	A. J. Coleman not out	4
O. A. Shah c Taylor b Davis	23	T. F. Bloomfield b Davis	1
E. C. Joyce c Carpenter b Robinson	11		
J. W. M. Dalrymple c Martin-Jenkins b Robinson	3	B 5, l-b 21, w 6	32
			——
C. B. Keegan b Davis	13	1/2 2/27 3/62 (37.1 overs)	109
*S. P. Fleming c Taylor b Davis	2	4/72 5/83 6/92	
†D. C. Nash b Kirtley	3	7/92 8/102 9/108	

Bowling: Kirtley 6–1–8–2; Martin-Jenkins 9–0–28–1; Taylor 6–3–7–0; Robinson 9–2–16–2; Davis 7.1–2–24–4.

Sussex

R. R. Montgomerie not out	34
J. R. Carpenter c Shah b Bloomfield	18
M. J. G. Davis lbw b Bloomfield	16
M. W. Goodwin not out	20
B 6, l-b 8, w 6, n-b 2	22
	——
1/46 2/67 (2 wkts, 28.1 overs)	110

*C. J. Adams, W. J. House, R. S. C. Martin-Jenkins, †M. J. Prior, R. J. Kirtley, B. V. Taylor and M. A. Robinson did not bat.

Bowling: Keegan 7–1–14–0; Cook 3–0–19–0; Bloomfield 7–1–16–2; Weekes 5–0–28–0; Dalrymple 4–1–12–0; Coleman 2.1–1–7–0.

Umpires: N. G. Cowley and M. J. Kitchen.

At Southampton, September 9. MIDDLESEX beat HAMPSHIRE by four wickets.

At Cardiff, September 16. MIDDLESEX lost to GLAMORGAN by 40 runs.

SUSSEX

At Kidderminster, April 29. SUSSEX lost to WORCESTERSHIRE by five wickets.

At Chelmsford, May 20. SUSSEX beat ESSEX by one run.

At Swansea, June 3. SUSSEX lost to GLAMORGAN by six wickets.

SUSSEX v WORCESTERSHIRE

At Horsham, June 10. Worcestershire won by 70 runs. Toss: Sussex.

Cricket week ended with some ignominious Sussex batting; five wickets fell for six runs in 35 balls to Lampitt and Rawnsley, and later the last four went for 15. Only Montgomerie, Adams and House got to grips with the slow pitch. Earlier, Sussex had let the game slip away after their bowlers, Robinson in particular, restricted Worcestershire to two an over for half the innings. Hick and Solanki, dropped when six, upped the tempo with 65 in 12 overs, and Bichel and Leatherdale added quick runs.

Worcestershire

P. R. Pollard run out	25
A. Singh b Robinson	4
*G. A. Hick lbw b Kirtley	50
V. S. Solanki c Davis b Kirtley	63
D. A. Leatherdale b Adams	25
A. J. Bichel c Zuiderent b Lewry	20
†S. J. Rhodes not out	2
S. R. Lampitt not out	0
B 6, l-b 5, w 10	21
1/18 2/52 3/117 4/164 5/204 6/209 (6 wkts, 45 overs)	210

Kabir Ali, M. J. Rawnsley and A. Sheriyar did not bat.

Bowling: Lewry 9–0–41–1; Robinson 9–1–17–1; Kirtley 9–0–41–2; Davis 9–1–44–0; Rashid 7–0–44–0; Adams 2–0–12–1.

Sussex

R. R. Montgomerie lbw b Lampitt	42
M. W. Goodwin b Sheriyar	1
*C. J. Adams c Leatherdale b Rawnsley	33
B. Zuiderent b Lampitt	0
W. J. House c Bichel b Ali	34
U. B. A. Rashid c Singh b Lampitt	1
†M. J. Prior c Solanki b Rawnsley	0
M. J. G. Davis c Bichel b Hick	18
J. D. Lewry c Rhodes b Hick	0
R. J. Kirtley not out	3
M. A. Robinson lbw b Ali	1
L-b 3, w 4	7
1/10 2/73 3/77 4/77 5/79 6/79 7/125 8/126 9/137 (40.1 overs)	140

Bowling: Sheriyar 9–1–38–1; Bichel 5–0–12–0; Ali 5.1–1–22–2; Lampitt 9–2–25–3; Rawnsley 9–1–32–2; Hick 3–0–8–2.

Umpires: J. W. Holder and J. F. Steele.

SUSSEX v DERBYSHIRE

At Arundel, June 17. Sussex won by eight runs. Toss: Sussex.

Sussex hauled themselves off the bottom of Division Two by inflicting a fourth consecutive League defeat on Derbyshire. A stand of 120 between Goodwin and Zuiderent should have laid the foundations for a more competitive total, but Derbyshire's bowlers conceded only 66 more in the next 14 overs. Their batsmen were well in the hunt until Yardy picked up two wickets in successive overs. Bassano and Krikken revived hopes by adding 67 in 12 overs, but when Krikken was run out by Adams, and Bassano bowled eight runs later, 24 from the last two overs proved too much for the tail. Krikken's innings took him to a League double of 1,000 runs and 100 dismissals.

Sussex

M. W. Goodwin c Krikken b Illingworth	63	R. J. Kirtley lbw b Munton	10
R. R. Montgomerie lbw b Munton	1	B. V. Taylor not out	3
*C. J. Adams c Bailey b Munton	13	M. A. Robinson not out	1
B. Zuiderent lbw b Bailey	65	L-b 1, w 8	9
W. J. House run out	12		
M. H. Yardy c Stubbings b Illingworth	19	1/3 2/23 3/143 (9 wkts, 45 overs)	209
†M. J. Prior b Illingworth	8	4/151 5/164 6/184	
M. J. G. Davis c Di Venuto b Bailey	5	7/193 8/196 9/205	

Bowling: Welch 9–1–28–0; Munton 8–0–32–3; Smith 4–0–37–0; Dumelow 7–0–31–0; Illingworth 9–0–52–3; Bailey 8–0–28–2.

Derbyshire

G. Welch b Kirtley	2	T. M. Smith not out	6
M. J. Di Venuto c Taylor b Yardy	24	*T. A. Munton not out	1
M. P. Dowman c Taylor b Robinson	45		
R. J. Bailey c Prior b Yardy	1	B 4, l-b 4, w 8, n-b 6	22
C. W. G. Bassano b Taylor	45		
S. D. Stubbings b Davis	12	1/8 2/64 3/66 (8 wkts, 45 overs)	201
†K. M. Krikken run out	33	4/92 5/111 6/178	
N. R. C. Dumelow b Kirtley	10	7/186 8/194	

R. K. Illingworth did not bat.

Bowling: Kirtley 9–1–29–2; Taylor 9–1–49–1; Robinson 9–2–32–1; Yardy 9–0–34–2; Davis 8–0–44–1; Adams 1–0–5–0.

Umpires: B. Dudleston and V. A. Holder.

At Southampton, July 4 (day/night). SUSSEX lost to HAMPSHIRE by 79 runs.

SUSSEX v ESSEX

At Hove, July 16 (day/night). Sussex won by 27 runs. Toss: Sussex.

Montgomerie's first League hundred set up a comfortable win for Sussex in Hove's first floodlit game of the summer. His stand with Goodwin of 176 in 34 overs was a county first-wicket record in the League. Essex's reply never really recovered after they slumped to 44 for four in the 14th over. Foster and Grayson made composed half-centuries and added 85 for the fifth wicket, but it was too little too late and Essex remained bottom of the table.

Sussex

R. R. Montgomerie run out 108	U. B. A. Rashid not out. 1
M. W. Goodwin c Peters b Mason 87	L-b 1, w 11, n-b 2. 14
*C. J. Adams c Peters b Cowan 25	
W. J. House not out 6	1/176 2/231 3/235 (3 wkts, 45 overs) 241

B. Zuiderent, J. D. Lewry, †M. J. Prior, M. J. G. Davis, R. J. Kirtley and M. A. Robinson did not bat.

Bowling: Cowan 9–0–51–1; Bishop 9–0–42–0; Anderson 4–0–31–0; Clarke 6–0–36–0; Grayson 8–0–33–0; Mason 9–0–47–1.

Essex

D. D. J. Robinson c Montgomerie b Robinson . 18	R. S. G. Anderson run out 22
S. D. Peters run out 0	T. J. Mason not out. 10
G. R. Napier c Prior b Lewry. 5	B 2, l-b 9, w 11, n-b 4. 26
*R. C. Irani c House b Adams 18	
A. P. Grayson b Kirtley 52	1/3 2/8 3/44 (7 wkts, 45 overs) 214
†J. S. Foster not out 56	4/44 5/129
A. P. Cowan run out 7	6/137 7/188

J. E. Bishop and A. J. Clarke did not bat.

Bowling: Lewry 9–2–37–1; Kirtley 9–2–32–1; Adams 2–0–12–1; Robinson 9–0–37–1; Davis 9–0–57–0; Rashid 7–0–28–0.

Umpires: D. J. Constant and J. W. Holder.

At Chester-le-Street, July 22. SUSSEX lost to DURHAM by seven wickets.

SUSSEX v MIDDLESEX

At Hove, August 1 (day/night). Sussex won by seven runs. Toss: Sussex.

Sussex conceded six extra runs for not starting the last over on time, the first instance of this penalty since its introduction at the beginning of the season. But the reduced target of 15 off the over was still beyond Middlesex. Goodwin's patient 68 on a desperately slow pitch proved crucial in a Sussex innings that provided only seven boundaries – scant fare for a good house. Martin-Jenkins, returning after two months away through injury, took three early Middlesex wickets and later ran out Hutton just as he and Weekes were threatening to turn the tide with their 25-over partnership of 88.

Sussex

R. R. Montgomerie c Cook b Keegan . . 16	†M. J. Prior c and b Weekes 1
M. W. Goodwin c Strauss b Cook 68	B. V. Taylor not out 1
*C. J. Adams c Weston b Weekes 6	B 4, l-b 10, w 6 20
B. Zuiderent c Weekes b Cook 21	
W. J. House b Weekes. 7	1/40 2/60 3/119 (7 wkts, 45 overs) 161
U. B. A. Rashid st Nash b Dalrymple. . . 11	4/121 5/140
R. S. C. Martin-Jenkins not out 10	6/154 7/157

R. J. Kirtley and M. A. Robinson did not bat.

Bowling: Bloomfield 9–3–12–0; Keegan 7–0–28–1; Cook 9–0–33–2; Weekes 9–0–28–3; Hutton 4–0–16–0; Dalrymple 7–1–30–1.

Middlesex

A. J. Strauss c Goodwin b Martin-Jenkins	16
M. A. Roseberry c Prior b Taylor	13
O. A. Shah lbw b Martin-Jenkins	2
R. M. S. Weston b Taylor	2
†D. C. Nash c Adams b Martin-Jenkins	0
B. L. Hutton run out	26
*P. N. Weekes c Adams b Kirtley	55
J. W. M. Dalrymple not out	3
S. J. Cook run out	0
C. B. Keegan b Taylor	8
T. F. Bloomfield not out	1
B 1, l-b 6, w 8, n-b 7, p 6	28
1/20 2/29 3/37 4/38 5/38 6/126 7/129 8/129 9/152 (9 wkts, 45 overs)	154

Bowling: Martin-Jenkins 9–1–20–3; Kirtley 9–0–30–1; Taylor 9–1–29–3; Robinson 9–0–28–0; Rashid 5–0–16–0; Adams 4–0–18–0.

Umpires: D. R. Shepherd and A. G. T. Whitehead.

At Manchester, August 20 (day/night). SUSSEX lost to LANCASHIRE by 22 runs.

SUSSEX v DURHAM

At Hove, August 26. No result (abandoned).

At Derby, August 27. SUSSEX beat DERBYSHIRE by seven wickets.

SUSSEX v LANCASHIRE

At Hove, August 30 (day/night). Sussex won by 138 runs. Toss: Sussex. First-team debut: C. D. Hopkinson.

Ambrose was the star of Sussex's crushing win. On his Hove debut, the 18-year-old ECB-qualified wicket-keeper/batsman from New South Wales made 87, and then took two catches and pulled off a smart leg-side stumping. Montgomerie and Adams shared stands of 99 and 54 with him, and finally House hit 28 off 17 balls as Sussex raced to 229. Lancashire started and finished badly, losing their last six wickets for 29, five of them in the space of four overs. Only Fairbrother, not out at the end, emerged with any credit in the face of tight bowling from Robinson and Taylor, who shared nine maidens in 17 overs. Carl Hopkinson, 19, took a wicket with the third ball of his debut.

Sussex

R. R. Montgomerie c Chapple b Smethurst	53
†T. R. Ambrose run out	87
*C. J. Adams c Wood b Schofield	21
M. W. Goodwin c Yates b Wood	20
W. J. House not out	28
J. R. Carpenter c Schofield b Chapple	3
C. D. Hopkinson not out	10
L-b 5, w 2	7
1/99 2/153 3/181 4/195 5/199 (5 wkts, 45 overs)	229

M. J. G. Davis, B. V. Taylor, R. J. Kirtley and M. A. Robinson did not bat.

Bowling: Wood 8–1–47–1; Chapple 9–1–32–1; Scuderi 7–0–48–0; Smethurst 5–0–32–1; Yates 7–0–28–0; Schofield 9–0–37–1.

Lancashire

G. Chapple c Adams b Kirtley	0
T. W. Roberts st Ambrose b Robinson	12
A. Flintoff c Ambrose b Taylor	1
*J. P. Crawley c Hopkinson b Taylor	15
N. H. Fairbrother not out	37
J. C. Scuderi run out	13
C. P. Schofield b Robinson	1
†J. J. Haynes run out	0
G. Yates b Robinson	0
J. Wood c Ambrose b Hopkinson	0
M. P. Smethurst b Kirtley	1
L-b 5, w 4, n-b 2	11
1/1 2/3 3/34 4/38 5/62 6/72 7/74 8/76 9/77 (31.3 overs)	91

Bowling: Taylor 8–5–16–2; Kirtley 6.3–0–22–2; Robinson 9–4–17–3; House 4–0–15–0; Davis 1–0–10–0; Adams 1–0–4–0; Hopkinson 2–0–2–1.

Umpires: J. H. Evans and T. E. Jesty.

At Richmond, September 2. SUSSEX beat MIDDLESEX by eight wickets.

SUSSEX v GLAMORGAN

At Hove, September 4 (day/night). Sussex won by 34 runs. Toss: Sussex.

Glamorgan's title celebrations were put on hold after Sussex eased to their fourth League win in nine days. Adams hit his first one-day hundred for 14 months, batting through the innings after Montgomerie was out to its first ball. Ambrose impressed again as they put on 80, and Goodwin then helped Adams add 145 at better than a run a ball. Glamorgan's reply never recovered from 54 for four, but Hopkinson starred in the field for Sussex with four catches and a direct-hit run-out. By taking 18 points from their last five games, Sussex had given themselves a chance of promotion should results go their way in the final rounds.

Sussex

R. R. Montgomerie lbw b Davies	0
†T. R. Ambrose c and b Cosker	46
*C. J. Adams not out	100
M. W. Goodwin not out	67
B 4, l-b 2, w 6	12
1/0 2/80 (2 wkts, 45 overs)	225

J. R. Carpenter, W. J. House, C. D. Hopkinson, M. J. G. Davis, R. J. Kirtley, B. V. Taylor and M. A. Robinson did not bat.

Bowling: Davies 9–1–26–1; Parkin 9–1–49–0; Thomas 5–0–30–0; Dale 4–0–22–0; Cosker 9–0–57–1; Croft 9–0–35–0.

Glamorgan

K. Newell c Hopkinson b Taylor	13
J. P. Maher c Hopkinson b Kirtley	54
R. D. B. Croft c Hopkinson b Taylor	8
*S. P. James lbw b House	5
†M. P. Maynard b Robinson	3
M. J. Powell lbw b Robinson	26
A. Dale c Hopkinson b House	29
S. D. Thomas run out	3
A. P. Davies b Taylor	24
D. A. Cosker not out	14
O. T. Parkin c Ambrose b Kirtley	0
L-b 3, w 9	12
1/24 2/34 3/41 4/54 5/103 6/118 7/126 8/156 9/190 (42.5 overs)	191

Bowling: Kirtley 7.5–0–31–2; Taylor 8–0–43–3; House 9–0–50–2; Robinson 9–1–32–2; Davis 9–0–32–0.

Umpires: M. R. Benson and A. A. Jones.

SUSSEX v HAMPSHIRE

At Hove, September 16. Hampshire won by seven wickets. Toss: Sussex.

Although Hampshire completed a League double over their old rivals, third-placed Worcestershire's promotion-clinching win against Essex meant it was something of a hollow victory. Only Martin-Jenkins came to terms with the seaming pitch as frail Sussex were bundled out for 142, and Hampshire went on to win with 22 overs unused. Hamblin, who had taken three wickets, made a mockery of Sussex's hopes of promotion. In a thrilling onslaught he smashed 61 off 42 balls (ten fours, one six), having reached his maiden fifty off only 28, and Johnson hit 41 off 37 as they put on 103.

Sussex

R. R. Montgomerie c Hamblin b Mascarenhas	10
†T. R. Ambrose c Kenway b Mullally	10
*C. J. Adams c Johnson b Tremlett	13
M. W. Goodwin b Mascarenhas	1
W. J. House c Mascarenhas b Udal	8
J. R. Carpenter b Udal	7
R. S. C. Martin-Jenkins c Prittipaul b Hamblin	38
M. J. G. Davis b Mullally	7
B. V. Taylor c Johnson b Hamblin	19
R. J. Kirtley not out	9
M. A. Robinson lbw b Hamblin	1
L-b 1, w 14, n-b 4	19
1/20 2/26 3/35 4/45 5/58 6/63 7/84 8/128 9/128 (37 overs)	142

Bowling: Mullally 7–0–30–2; Mascarenhas 9–1–18–2; Tremlett 7–2–29–1; Udal 8–0–32–2; Hamblin 5–0–23–3; Johnson 1–0–9–0.

Hampshire

J. R. C. Hamblin c Martin-Jenkins b Davis	61
N. C. Johnson b Robinson	41
†D. A. Kenway not out	24
L. R. Prittipaul lbw b Robinson	1
J. D. Francis not out	11
L-b 1, n-b 4	5
1/103 2/107 3/108 (3 wkts, 22.5 overs)	143

W. S. Kendall, *R. A. Smith, A. D. Mascarenhas, S. D. Udal, C. T. Tremlett and A. D. Mullally did not bat.

Bowling: Taylor 3–0–15–0; Martin-Jenkins 3–0–27–0; Robinson 8.5–3–30–2; Kirtley 2–0–26–0; Davis 6–0–44–1.

Umpires: T. E. Jesty and J. F. Steele.

WORCESTERSHIRE

WORCESTERSHIRE v SUSSEX

At Kidderminster, April 29. Worcestershire won by five wickets. Toss: Sussex. County debut: M. J. G. Davis.

The soggy state of New Road, plus an unfavourable forecast, prompted a switch at 48 hours' notice to Kidderminster. On a slow, seaming surface – in sharp contrast to the batting conditions associated with Championship fixtures here in August – Sussex needed Zuiderent's resourceful half-century to set any sort of challenge after Lampitt's first four overs brought four wickets, including his 200th in the League. Worcestershire, too, had problems, but from 73 for five the game was settled by an unbroken stand of 82 in 13 overs between Hick and Rhodes. It was Worcestershire's first win in ten League matches, after the dramatic about-turn that led to relegation the previous season.

Sussex

R. R. Montgomerie b Lampitt	15	M. J. G. Davis not out	2
M. W. Goodwin b Lampitt	9	*R. J. Kirtley b Bichel	2
B. Zuiderent c and b Bichel	53	M. A. Robinson not out	0
P. A. Cottey lbw b Lampitt	0		
W. J. House c Rhodes b Lampitt	2	L-b 3, w 17	20
R. S. C. Martin-Jenkins st Rhodes b Rawnsley	26	1/22 2/31 3/31 (9 wkts, 45 overs)	154
†M. J. Prior run out	1	4/37 5/92 6/98	
M. H. Yardy c Rhodes b Rawnsley	24	7/142 8/149 9/154	

Bowling: Bichel 9–3–28–2; Sheriyar 9–2–20–0; Lampitt 9–1–37–4; Leatherdale 4–0–9–0; Rawnsley 9–0–32–2; Hick 5–1–25–0.

Worcestershire

P. R. Pollard c House b Davis	24	†S. J. Rhodes not out	39
A. Singh c and b Martin-Jenkins	1		
*G. A. Hick not out	61	L-b 3, w 5	8
V. S. Solanki run out	0		
D. A. Leatherdale c Goodwin b Davis	17	1/6 2/42 3/43 (5 wkts, 40.4 overs)	155
W. P. C. Weston c Cottey b Robinson	5	4/68 5/73	

A. J. Bichel, S. R. Lampitt, M. J. Rawnsley and A. Sheriyar did not bat.

Bowling: Kirtley 7.4–2–30–0; Martin-Jenkins 7–1–17–1; Yardy 5–0–19–0; Robinson 9–0–24–1; Davis 8–1–39–2; House 4–0–23–0.

Umpires: J. H. Hampshire and D. R. Shepherd.

At Southampton, May 13. WORCESTERSHIRE lost to HAMPSHIRE by three wickets.

WORCESTERSHIRE v DERBYSHIRE

At Worcester, May 20. Worcestershire won by three wickets. Toss: Derbyshire.

The ball swung on an unreliable pitch and Derbyshire flattered to deceive as Bailey and Di Venuto put on 61. Khan's 30 was their top score, although Extras were only three behind after some wayward bowling by Sheriyar. Worcestershire had their own difficulties, facing Munton in particular, and were 40 for three before Solanki and Leatherdale added 84. Solanki's half-century was his first in one-day cricket since the previous June. The loss of four wickets for 17 put the game back in the balance at 141 for seven, but Worcestershire had seasoned campaigners in Rhodes and Lampitt to get them to their first League win at New Road for 11 months.

Derbyshire

R. J. Bailey lbw b Sheriyar	17	†K. M. Krikken b Sheriyar	13
M. J. Di Venuto lbw b Lampitt	27	N. R. C. Dumelow not out	16
M. P. Dowman c Rhodes b Leatherdale	3	B 4, l-b 7, w 16	27
L. D. Sutton c Solanki b Rawnsley	18		
G. Welch c Leatherdale b Rawnsley	17	1/61 2/63 3/73 (6 wkts, 45 overs)	168
W. G. Khan not out	30	4/99 5/114 6/137	

R. K. Illingworth, T. Lungley and *T. A. Munton did not bat.

Bowling: Sheriyar 9–0–42–2; Bichel 9–2–19–0; Lampitt 9–1–25–1; Leatherdale 9–1–36–1; Rawnsley 9–0–35–2.

Worcestershire

P. R. Pollard c Sutton b Munton	18	†S. J. Rhodes not out	26
A. Singh c Sutton b Munton	2	S. R. Lampitt not out	6
*G. A. Hick b Munton	2	L-b 13, w 10	23
V. S. Solanki c Krikken b Dumelow	52		
D. A. Leatherdale lbw b Munton	38	1/3 2/20 3/40 (7 wkts, 44.2 overs)	172
A. J. Bichel lbw b Lungley	4	4/124 5/133	
N. R. Boulton st Krikken b Dumelow	1	6/136 7/141	

M. J. Rawnsley and A. Sheriyar did not bat.

Bowling: Munton 9–0–31–4; Welch 9–2–33–0; Lungley 9–3–19–1; Illingworth 8.2–0–42–0; Dumelow 9–0–34–2.

Umpires: J. W. Lloyds and R. A. White.

At Horsham, June 10. WORCESTERSHIRE beat SUSSEX by 70 runs.

WORCESTERSHIRE v LANCASHIRE

At Worcester, June 17. Worcestershire won by ten runs. Toss: Worcestershire.

Dismissed for just 99, Worcestershire still managed victory on a bowler-friendly pitch. Yet there had been little indication of the mayhem to follow as openers Singh and Pollard put on 40 in eight overs. Any thoughts that Lancashire might have a comfortable path to their modest target were quickly dispelled when Bichel removed Atherton and Flintoff cheaply. Schofield's late flurry, while not enough to save the visitors, certainly strained the nerves of the Worcestershire players and supporters. Their reaction at the end was more akin to that associated with winning a trophy.

Worcestershire

P. R. Pollard c Atherton b Flintoff	24	Kabir Ali run out	6
A. Singh b Chapple	30	M. J. Rawnsley c Hegg b Martin	1
*G. A. Hick b Chapple	2	A. Sheriyar c Flintoff b Martin	0
V. S. Solanki c Atherton b Smethurst	10	B 5, l-b 2, w 1	8
D. A. Leatherdale c Hegg b Flintoff	2		
A. J. Bichel c Chilton b Flintoff	6	1/40 2/42 3/59 (34.5 overs)	99
†S. J. Rhodes run out	6	4/66 5/72 6/86	
S. R. Lampitt not out	4	7/86 8/97 9/99	

Bowling: Martin 6.5–1–24–2; Chapple 9–0–41–2; Smethurst 9–4–9–1; Flintoff 6–2–16–3; Muralitharan 4–3–2–0.

Lancashire

M. A. Atherton c Lampitt b Bichel	2	P. J. Martin c Rhodes b Sheriyar	5
G. Chapple b Sheriyar	11	M. Muralitharan c Lampitt b Bichel	1
A. Flintoff c Pollard b Bichel	2	M. P. Smethurst not out	2
*J. P. Crawley c Hick b Lampitt	18	L-b 3, w 3, n-b 6	12
N. H. Fairbrother lbw b Ali	11		
M. J. Chilton c Rhodes b Lampitt	4	1/14 2/22 3/22 (29.2 overs)	89
†W. K. Hegg c Lampitt b Ali	1	4/53 5/53 6/55	
C. P. Schofield b Sheriyar	20	7/67 8/81 9/82	

Bowling: Bichel 8–3–23–3; Sheriyar 5.2–0–23–3; Ali 9–4–22–2; Lampitt 7–0–18–2.

Umpires: M. J. Harris and N. A. Mallender.

At Cardiff, June 24. WORCESTERSHIRE lost to GLAMORGAN by 111 runs.

At Derby, July 3 (day/night). WORCESTERSHIRE beat DERBYSHIRE by 138 runs.

WORCESTERSHIRE v MIDDLESEX

At Worcester, July 15. Worcestershire won by five wickets. Toss: Middlesex.

Worcestershire went back to the top of Division Two by winning another low-scoring home match dominated by seam bowlers. Middlesex were immediately on the back foot at 22 for four. However, the fifth-wicket stand of 55 between Nash and Roseberry looked to have been a lifeline when Fraser, bowling unchanged for figures of three for 13, had Worcestershire struggling in turn at 49 for four; Solanki was bowled by his final delivery. Leatherdale steadied the innings – Bichel lent support in a decisive half-century stand – and his unbeaten 55 from 65 balls saw them home with seven overs in hand.

Middlesex

A. J. Strauss c Solanki b Bichel	0
B. L. Hutton b Lampitt	8
O. A. Shah c Rhodes b Bichel	2
R. M. S. Weston c Rhodes b Sheriyar	1
†D. C. Nash st Rhodes b Ali	43
M. A. Roseberry b Rawnsley	35
P. N. Weekes c Leatherdale b Rawnsley	8
J. W. M. Dalrymple lbw b Ali	12
C. B. Keegan lbw b Leatherdale	0
*A. R. C. Fraser not out	10
T. F. Bloomfield b Leatherdale	2
L-b 2, w 5	7
1/4 2/6 3/7 4/22 5/77 6/91 7/112 8/113 9/122 (43.1 overs)	128

Bowling: Bichel 8–4–11–2; Sheriyar 7–3–17–1; Lampitt 9–3–24–1; Ali 8–1–31–2; Rawnsley 8–0–34–2; Leatherdale 3.1–0–9–2.

Worcestershire

W. P. C. Weston c Weekes b Fraser	14
A. Singh lbw b Fraser	6
*G. A. Hick c Weekes b Keegan	20
V. S. Solanki b Fraser	0
D. A. Leatherdale not out	55
A. J. Bichel c Hutton b Keegan	23
†S. J. Rhodes not out	8
B 1, l-b 2	3
1/13 2/42 3/42 4/49 5/99 (5 wkts, 37.4 overs)	129

S. R. Lampitt, Kabir Ali, M. J. Rawnsley and A. Sheriyar did not bat.

Bowling: Fraser 9–3–13–3; Bloomfield 8–3–19–0; Keegan 8–0–40–2; Weekes 6–0–19–0; Hutton 4–0–15–0; Dalrymple 2.4–0–20–0.

Umpires: A. A. Jones and R. Palmer.

At Manchester, July 18 (day/night). WORCESTERSHIRE beat LANCASHIRE by 109 runs.

WORCESTERSHIRE v DURHAM

At Worcester, July 31 (day/night). Worcestershire won by seven wickets. Toss: Durham.

Worcestershire made a nonsense of the accepted difficulty of batting second under lights by achieving, with 16 balls to spare, the highest target in a League day/night fixture. Durham's opening partnership of 102 in 16 overs between Peng and Pratt laid the foundations for a commanding total, and Peng's superb strokeplay, producing 19 fours and a six, took him to his limited-overs best of 121 from 113 balls. Kabir Ali dislocated a shoulder trying to stop one of his boundaries. Worcestershire in reply were given a similarly explosive start. Pollard raced to 62 off 44 balls, providing a momentum that Hick and Solanki maintained in a third-wicket stand of 160 in 27 overs. Solanki, reaching 91 off 104 deliveries, stayed to complete a memorable win.

Durham

N. Peng c Rawnsley b Bichel	121	M. A. Gough not out	6
†A. Pratt c Rhodes b Hick	36	G. D. Bridge not out	1
M. L. Love c Hick b Bichel	25	B 2, l-b 5, w 3, n-b 2	12
P. D. Collingwood c Hick b Sheriyar	31		—
D. R. Law c Leatherdale b Sheriyar	19	1/102 2/171 3/196 (7 wkts, 45 overs)	274
*J. J. B. Lewis lbw b Bichel	14	4/238 5/240	
M. P. Speight c Bichel b Sheriyar	9	6/256 7/273	

A. M. Davies and J. E. Brinkley did not bat.

Bowling: Bichel 9–1–51–3; Sheriyar 7–0–48–3; Lampitt 9–1–45–0; Ali 3–0–17–0; Hick 3–0–19–1; Rawnsley 5–0–47–0; Leatherdale 9–0–40–0.

Worcestershire

P. R. Pollard c Speight b Brinkley	62	D. A. Leatherdale not out	5
A. Singh b Davies	14	B 4, l-b 2, w 10	16
*G. A. Hick b Law	87		—
V. S. Solanki not out	91	1/40 2/101 3/261 (3 wkts, 42.2 overs)	275

A. J. Bichel, †S. J. Rhodes, S. R. Lampitt, Kabir Ali, M. J. Rawnsley and A. Sheriyar did not bat.

Bowling: Law 8–0–68–1; Davies 7–1–42–1; Brinkley 7.2–0–49–1; Bridge 9–0–39–0; Gough 6–1–36–0; Collingwood 5–0–35–0.

Umpires: A. A. Jones and K. E. Palmer.

At Chelmsford, August 12. WORCESTERSHIRE lost to ESSEX by 33 runs.

At Lord's, August 19. MIDDLESEX v WORCESTERSHIRE. No result (abandoned).

WORCESTERSHIRE v HAMPSHIRE

At Worcester, August 26. Hampshire won by two wickets (D/L method). Toss: Worcestershire.

Hampshire, who won when the sides met in May, now inflicted Worcestershire's first home defeat of their League campaign. From 18 for three, Worcestershire were staging a recovery when rain intervened for two hours, and Solanki's unbeaten 65 off 69 balls gave their shortened innings a late thrust. Schofield took a wicket with his first delivery in the League, having begun his first-class career with a first-ball wicket against the Australians the previous month. Hampshire's revised target of 166 in 32 overs looked formidable – more so when they, too, lost three early wickets – but Johnson and Loughborough University's Francis picked them up with 58 in 11 overs. Francis went on to make 78 from 81 balls, showing great composure as the tension built. He survived Singh's run-out attempt from mid-on to scramble the winning single off the last ball.

Worcestershire

W. P. C. Weston c Johnson b Mascarenhas	3	A. J. Bichel b Udal	9
A. Singh c Kenway b Schofield	0	†S. J. Rhodes not out	5
*G. A. Hick c Johnson b Mascarenhas	8	B 3, l-b 1, w 15	19
V. S. Solanki not out	65		—
D. A. Leatherdale b Udal	32	1/2 2/14 3/18 (5 wkts, 32 overs)	141
		4/83 5/103	

S. R. Lampitt, C. G. Liptrot, M. J. Rawnsley and A. Sheriyar did not bat.

Bowling: Mascarenhas 7–3–11–2; Schofield 6–0–22–1; Hamblin 6–0–31–0; Johnson 7–0–42–0; Udal 6–0–31–2.

Hampshire

J. S. Laney b Bichel	0	S. D. Udal run out	2
N. C. Johnson c Weston b Lampitt	31	J. R. C. Hamblin not out	0
†D. A. Kenway c Rhodes b Bichel	4		
L. R. Prittipaul b Sheriyar	0	L-b 3, w 6	9
J. D. Francis not out	78		—
G. W. White c Solanki b Hick	21	1/0 2/10 3/17 (8 wkts, 32 overs)	166
A. D. Mascarenhas c Rhodes b Bichel	21	4/75 5/110 6/152	
*R. A. Smith st Rhodes b Rawnsley	0	7/153 8/165	

J. E. K. Schofield did not bat.

Bowling: Bichel 7–2–36–3; Sheriyar 5–0–20–1; Lampitt 6–0–28–1; Liptrot 3–0–18–0; Leatherdale 3–0–15–0; Rawnsley 5–0–23–1; Hick 3–0–23–1.

Umpires: J. H. Hampshire and C. S. Kelly.

WORCESTERSHIRE v GLAMORGAN

At Worcester, September 2. No result. Toss: Glamorgan.

Glamorgan clinched promotion from their two points here. Their weather-interrupted innings was built around a fourth-wicket stand of 111 in 21 overs between Maynard and Croft, whose 61 in 65 balls contained seven fours. Powell and Darren Thomas plundered 47 from the last five overs. Worcestershire were given a target of 264 in 43 overs, but the heavens opened before they could start their reply. Had the minimum ten overs been possible, they would have been chasing 90 – entirely within their capability.

Glamorgan

K. Newell c Liptrot b Sheriyar	22	S. D. Thomas lbw b Bichel	25
I. J. Thomas st Rhodes b Lampitt	24		
R. D. B. Croft b Leatherdale	61	B 4, l-b 5, w 6, n-b 4	19
J. P. Maher b Liptrot	12		—
†M. P. Maynard c Hick b Lampitt	71	1/41 2/56 3/77 (6 wkts, 43 overs)	254
M. J. Powell not out	20	4/188 5/207 6/254	

*A. Dale, D. A. Cosker, A. P. Davies and O. T. Parkin did not bat.

Bowling: Bichel 8–1–28–1; Sheriyar 8–0–51–1; Lampitt 9–0–51–2; Liptrot 7–0–41–1; Rawnsley 6–0–41–0; Leatherdale 5–0–33–1.

Worcestershire

W. P. C. Weston, S. R. Lampitt, *G. A. Hick, V. S. Solanki, D. A. Leatherdale, P. R. Pollard, A. J. Bichel, †S. J. Rhodes, C. G. Liptrot, M. J. Rawnsley and A. Sheriyar.

Umpires: R. Julian and N. A. Mallender.

At Chester-le-Street, September 9. WORCESTERSHIRE lost to DURHAM by nine runs (D/L method).

WORCESTERSHIRE v ESSEX

At Worcester, September 16. Worcestershire won by 96 runs (D/L method). Toss: Worcestershire.

Worcestershire's win guaranteed third place and their immediate return to Division One – tangible reward from Tom Moody's first season as director of cricket. There were five interruptions for rain during their innings, but Weston's 68 off 86 balls ensured that Essex would receive a demanding target. Once it had been calculated at 194 in 30 overs, they were never in the hunt; 97 all out was a sorry summary of their miserable season. Bichel claimed the final wicket on the day he received all three of Worcestershire's annual awards and was confirmed as their overseas player for 2002.

Worcestershire

W. P. C. Weston c Pettini b Grayson	68	P. R. Pollard not out	1
A. Singh c Foster b Clarke	21		
*G. A. Hick c Cowan b Bishop	46	L-b 7, w 3, n-b 10	20
V. S. Solanki c Foster b Bishop	3		
D. A. Leatherdale b Cowan	1	1/55 2/129 3/145 (6 wkts, 30 overs)	166
A. J. Bichel b Bishop	6	4/148 5/155 6/166	

†S. J. Rhodes, S. R. Lampitt, M. J. Rawnsley and A. Sheriyar did not bat.

Bowling: Cowan 5–0–29–1; Bishop 6–0–33–3; Irani 5–0–29–0; Clarke 7–1–34–1; Grayson 5–0–25–1; Napier 2–0–9–0.

Essex

D. D. J. Robinson c Hick b Sheriyar	6	B. J. Hyam run out	1
G. R. Napier lbw b Bichel	1	A. J. Clarke c Hick b Leatherdale	1
A. P. Cowan b Lampitt	16	J. E. Bishop c Leatherdale b Bichel	0
*R. C. Irani b Rawnsley	15	B 4, n-b 4	8
A. P. Grayson c Solanki b Rawnsley	6		
†J. S. Foster c Rhodes b Lampitt	3	1/7 2/7 3/40 (24.2 overs)	97
R. S. Clinton not out	26	4/40 5/47 6/51	
M. L. Pettini st Rhodes b Rawnsley	14	7/78 8/80 9/95	

Bowling: Bichel 4.2–2–3–2; Sheriyar 4–1–14–1; Leatherdale 4–1–21–1; Lampitt 6–1–27–2; Rawnsley 6–0–28–3.

Umpires: V. A. Holder and M. J. Kitchen.

NORWICH UNION LEAGUE RECORDS

40 overs available in all games up to 1998, except for 1993, when teams played 50 overs; 45 overs 1999–2001.

Batting

Highest individual scores: 203, A. D. Brown, Surrey v Hampshire, Guildford, 1997; 191, D. S. Lehmann, Yorkshire v Nottinghamshire, Scarborough, 2001; 176, G. A. Gooch, Essex v Glamorgan, Southend, 1983; 175*, I. T. Botham, Somerset v Northamptonshire, Wellingborough School, 1986.

Most runs: 8,920, K. J. Barnett; 8,573, G. A. Gooch; 7,589, G. A. Hick; 7,526, C. W. J. Athey; 7,499, W. Larkins; 7,074, P. Johnson; 7,062, D. W. Randall; 7,040, D. L. Amiss; 7,031, R. J. Bailey; 6,961, N. H. Fairbrother; 6,695, R. T. Robinson; 6,673, M. W. Gatting; 6,650, C. T. Radley. **In a season:** 917, T. M. Moody, Worcestershire, 1991.

Most hundreds: 14, W. Larkins; 12, A. D. Brown and G. A. Gooch; 11, C. G. Greenidge and G. A. Hick; 10, T. M. Moody and R. A. Smith; 9, K. S. McEwan and B. A. Richards. 657 hundreds have been scored in the League. The most in one season is 40 in 1990.

Most sixes in an innings: 13, I. T. Botham, Somerset v Northamptonshire, Wellingborough School, 1986. **By a team in an innings:** 18, Derbyshire v Worcestershire, Knypersley, 1985, and Surrey v Yorkshire, Scarborough, 1994. **In a season:** 26, I. V. A. Richards, Somerset, 1977.

Highest total: 375 for four, Surrey v Yorkshire, Scarborough, 1994. **By a side batting second:** 317 for six, Surrey v Nottinghamshire, The Oval, 1993 (50-overs match).

Highest match aggregate: 631 for 13 wickets, Nottinghamshire (314 for seven) v Surrey (317 for six), The Oval, 1993 (50-overs match).

Lowest total: 23 (19.4 overs), Middlesex v Yorkshire, Leeds, 1974.

Shortest completed innings: 16 overs (59), Northamptonshire v Middlesex, Tring, 1974.

Record partnerships for each wicket

239	for 1st	G. A. Gooch and B. R. Hardie, Essex v Nottinghamshire at Nottingham .	1985
273	for 2nd	G. A. Gooch and K. S. McEwan, Essex v Nottinghamshire at Nottingham	1983
223	for 3rd	S. J. Cook and G. D. Rose, Somerset v Glamorgan at Neath	1990
219	for 4th	C. G. Greenidge and C. L. Smith, Hampshire v Surrey at Southampton .	1987
220*	for 5th	C. C. Lewis and P. A. Nixon, Leicestershire v Kent, Canterbury	1999
137	for 6th	M. P. Speight and I. D. K. Salisbury, Sussex v Surrey at Guildford	1996
164	for 7th	J. N. Snape and M. A. Hardinges, Gloucestershire v Notts at Nottingham	2001
116*	for 8th	N. D. Burns and P. A. J. DeFreitas, Leicestershire v Northants at Leicester .	2001
105	for 9th	D. G. Moir and R. W. Taylor, Derbyshire v Kent at Derby	1984
82	for 10th	G. Chapple and P. J. Martin, Lancashire v Worcestershire at Manchester .	1996

Bowling

Most wickets: 386, J. K. Lever; 368, J. E. Emburey; 346, D. L. Underwood; 307, J. Simmons; 303, S. Turner; 284, N. Gifford; 281, E. E. Hemmings; 273, R. K. Illingworth; 267, J. N. Shepherd; 261, G. C. Small; 260, A. C. S. Pigott; 256, I. T. Botham. **In a season:** 39, A. J. Hollioake, Surrey, 1996.

Best bowling: eight for 26, K. D. Boyce, Essex v Lancashire, Manchester, 1971; seven for 15, R. A. Hutton, Yorkshire v Worcestershire, Leeds, 1969; seven for 16, S. D. Thomas, Glamorgan v Surrey, Swansea, 1998; seven for 30, M. P. Bicknell, Surrey v Glamorgan, The Oval, 1999; seven for 39, A. Hodgson, Northamptonshire v Somerset, Northampton, 1976; seven for 41, A. N. Jones, Sussex v Nottinghamshire, Nottingham, 1986; six for six, R. W. Hooker, Middlesex v Surrey, Lord's, 1969; six for seven, M. Hendrick, Derbyshire v Nottinghamshire, Nottingham, 1972; six for nine, N. G. Cowans, Middlesex v Lancashire, Lord's, 1991.

Most economical analysis: 8–8–0–0, B. A. Langford, Somerset v Essex, Yeovil, 1969.

Most expensive analyses: 9–0–99–1, M. R. Strong, Northamptonshire v Gloucestershire, Cheltenham, 2001; 8–0–96–1, D. G. Cork, Derbyshire v Nottinghamshire, Nottingham, 1993; 8–0–94–2, P. N. Weekes, Middlesex v Leicestershire, Leicester, 1994; 7.5–0–89–3, G. Miller, Derbyshire v Gloucestershire, Gloucester, 1984; 8–0–88–1, E. E. Hemmings, Nottinghamshire v Somerset, Nottingham, 1983.

Hat-tricks: There have been 32 hat-tricks, four of them for Glamorgan.

Four wickets in four balls: A. Ward, Derbyshire v Sussex, Derby, 1970; V. C. Drakes, Nottinghamshire v Derbyshire, Nottingham, 1999.

Wicket-keeping and Fielding

Most dismissals: 360 (277 ct, 83 st), S. J. Rhodes; 257 (234 ct, 23 st), D. L. Bairstow; 254 (205 ct, 49 st), R. C. Russell; 253 (215 ct, 38 st), W. K. Hegg; 240 (201 ct, 39 st), R. J. Blakey; 236 (187 ct, 49 st), R. W. Taylor; 223 (184 ct, 39 st), E. W. Jones; 220 (197 ct, 23 st), S. A. Marsh. **In a season:** 32 (26 ct, 6 st), R. J. Blakey, Yorkshire, 1999. **In an innings:** 7 (6 ct, 1 st), R. W. Taylor, Derbyshire v Lancashire, Manchester, 1975.

Most catches in an innings: 6, K. Goodwin, Lancashire v Worcestershire, Worcester, 1969; R. W. Taylor, Derbyshire v Lancashire, Manchester, 1975; K. M. Krikken, Derbyshire v Hampshire, Southampton, 1994; and P. A. Nixon, Leicestershire v Essex, Leicester, 1994.

Most stumpings in an innings: 4, S. J. Rhodes, Worcestershire v Warwickshire, Birmingham, 1986 and N. D. Burns, Somerset v Kent, Taunton, 1991.

Most catches by a fielder: 103, K. J. Barnett and V. P. Terry; 101, J. F. Steele; 100, G. A. Gooch; 97, D. P. Hughes; 95, C. W. J. Athey†; 94, G. Cook and P. W. G. Parker. **In a season:** 16, J. M. Rice, Hampshire, 1978. **In an innings:** 5, J. M. Rice, Hampshire v Warwickshire, Southampton, 1978.

† C. W. J. Athey also took two catches as a wicket-keeper.

Results

Largest victory in runs: Somerset by 220 runs v Glamorgan, Neath, 1990.

Victories by ten wickets (34): By Derbyshire, Durham, Essex (four times), Glamorgan (twice), Hampshire (twice), Kent, Lancashire, Leicestershire (twice), Middlesex (twice), Northamptonshire, Nottinghamshire, Somerset (twice), Surrey (three times), Warwickshire (twice), Worcestershire (six times) and Yorkshire (three times).

This does not include those matches in which the side batting second was set a reduced target but does include matches where both sides faced a reduced number of overs.

Ties: There have been 57 tied matches. Worcestershire have tied 11 times.

Shortest match: 1 hr 53 min (26.3 overs), Surrey v Leicestershire, The Oval, 1996.

WINNERS 1969–2001

John Player's County League

1969 Lancashire

John Player League

1970 Lancashire
1971 Worcestershire
1972 Kent
1973 Kent
1974 Leicestershire
1975 Hampshire
1976 Kent
1977 Leicestershire
1978 Hampshire
1979 Somerset
1980 Warwickshire
1981 Essex
1982 Sussex
1983 Yorkshire

John Player Special League

1984 Essex
1985 Essex
1986 Hampshire

Refuge Assurance League

1987 Worcestershire
1988 Worcestershire
1989 Lancashire
1990 Derbyshire
1991 Nottinghamshire

Sunday League

1992 Middlesex

AXA Equity & Law League

1993 Glamorgan
1994 Warwickshire
1995 Kent
1996 Surrey

AXA Life League

1997 Warwickshire

AXA League

1998 Lancashire

CGU National League

1999 Lancashire

Norwich Union National League

2000 Gloucestershire

Norwich Union League

2001 Kent

MATCH RESULTS 1969–2001

	Matches					League positions		
	P	*W*	*L*	*T*	*NR*	*1st*	*2nd*	*3rd*
Derbyshire	535	214	262	5	54	1	0	1
Durham	167	50	94	3	20	0	0	0
Essex	535	267	213	10	45	3	5*	4
Glamorgan	535	199	273	7	56	1	0	0
Gloucestershire	535	191	277	4	63	1	1	1
Hampshire	535	250	234	7	44	3	1	3
Kent	535	290	186	7	52	5	4	5
Lancashire	535	273	191	10	61	5	2	3
Leicestershire	535	235	230	5	65	2	3*	2
Middlesex	535	233	235	10	57	1	1	3
Northamptonshire	535	211	263	6	55	0	0	2
Nottinghamshire	535	230	253	4	48	1	3	1
Somerset	535	255	225	4	51	1	6*	0
Surrey	535	237	237	5	56	1	0	1
Sussex	535	230	243	6	56	1	2*	1
Warwickshire	535	235	236	7	57	3	2	2
Worcestershire	535	262	211	11	51	3	4	2
Yorkshire	535	242	241	3	49	1	2	1

* *Includes one shared 2nd place in 1976.*

COUNTY MEMBERSHIP

	1991	*2000*	*2001*	*Variation*
Derbyshire	1,894	2,525	1,877*	−648
Durham	–	8,901	5,678	−3,223
Essex	8,475	6,173	6,181	+8
Glamorgan	2,787	8,280	7,680	−600
Gloucestershire	4,245	6,382	5,800	−582
Hampshire	5,097	4,757	4,839	+82
Kent	4,667	8,051	7,259	−792
Lancashire	13,928	12,979	11,674	−1,305
Leicestershire	2,833	4,775	4,619	−156
Middlesex	8,982	8,585	8,533	−52
Northamptonshire	2,095	3,295	3,822	+527
Nottinghamshire	4,500	6,191	6,759	+568
Somerset	5,083	6,741	6,605	−136
Surrey	5,157	8,541	8,777	+236
Sussex	4,317	5,720	5,409	−311
Warwickshire	10,044	12,378	12,106	−272
Worcestershire	5,044	4,954	5,285	+331
Yorkshire	7,825	16,695	15,331	−1,364
MCC	18,983	19,825	20,187	+362
	115,956	155,748	148,421	−7,327

Note: All the first-class counties now quote their membership in terms of the total number of individuals affiliated to their clubs. Until 2000, Derbyshire, Kent and Yorkshire registered corporate or joint membership as representing one person.

* *Includes 16 dogs.*

CAREER FIGURES

Players not expected to appear in county cricket in 2002.

BATTING

	M	*I*	*NO*	*R*	*HS*	*100s*	*Avge*	*1,000r/ season*
K. Adams	1	0	–	–	–	–	–	–
M. A. Atherton	336	584	47	21,929	268*	54	40.83	7
I. D. Austin	124	172	37	3,778	115*	2	27.98	0
I. E. Bishop	7	10	4	25	12	0	4.16	0
S. A. J. Boswell	22	30	10	249	35	0	12.45	0
N. R. Boulton	5	7	0	90	47	0	12.85	0
G. P. Butcher	53	78	12	1,841	101*	1	27.89	0
D. Byas	268	449	42	14,398	213	28	35.37	5
T. P. Cotterell	9	11	4	7	5*	0	1.00	0
M. K. Davies	33	48	14	338	32*	0	9.94	0
A. D. Edwards	16	25	3	183	23	0	8.31	0
R. J. Green	31	32	12	324	51	0	16.20	0
P. Griffiths	1	2	1	5	4*	0	5.00	0
D. W. Headley	139	187	44	2,373	91	0	16.59	0
C. J. Hewison	1	2	0	30	24	0	15.00	0
R. K. Illingworth	376	435	122	7,027	120*	4	22.45	0
K. J. Innes	21	32	6	522	63	0	20.07	0
I. Jones	3	4	1	78	35	0	26.00	0
W. G. Khan	58	102	8	2,835	181	5	30.15	0
Z. M. Khan	1	0	–	–	–	–	–	–
G. A. Lambert	2	3	2	6	3*	0	6.00	0
T. J. Mason	20	25	5	311	52*	0	15.55	0
D. J. Millns	171	203	63	3,082	121	3	22.01	0
J. E. Morris	362	612	35	21,539	229	52	37.32	11
Z. C. Morris	2	4	0	11	10	0	2.75	0
P. J. Prichard	330	540	49	16,834	245	32	34.28	8
D. Ripley	307	410	104	8,693	209	9	28.40	0
M. A. Roseberry	236	401	43	11,950	185	21	33.37	4
J. C. Scuderi	82	130	18	3,372	125*	3	30.10	0
A. J. Sexton	4	7	0	71	36	0	10.14	0
T. M. Smith	32	42	11	377	53*	0	12.16	0
N. J. Speak	177	307	34	9,692	232	15	35.50	3
M. P. Speight	193	323	31	9,225	184	13	31.59	3
K. R. Spiring	45	78	10	2,237	150	4	32.89	1
W. F. Stelling	18	28	2	475	53	0	18.26	0
R. D. Stemp	165	196	63	1,649	66	0	12.39	0
J. P. Stephenson	281	474	45	13,847	202*	24	32.27	5
M. R. Strong	15	23	8	235	35*	0	15.66	0
P. M. Such	306	327	125	1,645	54	0	8.14	0
J. P. Taylor	183	213	65	2,253	86	0	15.22	0
S. P. Titchard	107	186	14	5,319	163	6	30.92	0
S. L. Watkin	266	297	109	2,037	51	0	10.83	0
L. C. Weekes	24	36	6	535	46	0	17.83	0
A. P. Wells	376	628	81	21,099	253*	46	38.57	11
S. J. Widdup	11	18	1	245	44	0	14.41	0
R. C. J. Williams	44	59	9	911	90	0	18.22	0
N. J. Wilton	17	26	4	353	55	0	16.04	0

* *Signifies not out.*

BOWLING AND FIELDING

	R	W	BB	Avge	5W/i	10W/m	Ct/St
K. Adams	58	2	2-58	29.00	–	–	0
M. A. Atherton	4,733	108	6-78	43.82	3	0	268
I. D. Austin	7,954	262	6-43	30.35	6	1	35
I. E. Bishop	376	7	2-45	53.71	–	–	4
S. A. J. Boswell	1,665	42	5-94	39.64	1	0	6
N. R. Boulton	48	0	–	–	–	–	1
G. P. Butcher	2,390	63	7-77	37.93	2	0	19
D. Byas	727	12	3-55	60.58	–	–	351
T. P. Cotterell	663	11	3-69	60.27	–	–	2
M. K. Davies	2,566	96	6-49	26.72	5	0	8
A. D. Edwards	1,109	26	5-34	42.65	1	0	11
R. J. Green	2,297	55	6-41	41.76	1	0	7
P. Griffiths	51	2	2-51	25.50	–	–	0
D. W. Headley	13,293	466	8-98	28.52	25	2	60
R. K. Illingworth	26,213	831	7-50	31.54	27	6	161
K. J. Innes	1,117	38	4-61	29.39	–	–	10
I. Jones	341	6	3-81	56.83	–	–	0
W. G. Khan	62	0	–	–	–	–	36
Z. M. Khan	45	1	1-32	45.00	–	–	0
G. A. Lambert	133	4	2-62	33.25	–	–	1
T. J. Mason	1,252	30	5-40	41.73	1	0	8
D. J. Millns	15,129	553	9-37	27.35	23	4	76
J. E. Morris	958	8	1-6	119.75	–	–	156
Z. C. Morris	99	0	–	–	–	–	0
P. J. Prichard	497	2	1-28	248.50	–	–	202
D. Ripley	103	2	2-89	51.50	–	–	678/85
M. A. Roseberry	406	4	1-1	101.50	–	–	165
J. C. Scuderi	6,073	179	7-79	33.92	8	1	26
T. M. Smith	2,135	73	6-32	29.24	5	1	11
N. J. Speak	191	2	1-0	95.50	–	–	108
M. P. Speight	32	2	1-2	16.00	–	–	292/5
K. R. Spiring	10	0	–	–	–	–	22
W. F. Stelling	1,029	33	5-49	31.18	1	0	8
R. D. Stemp	13,495	384	6-37	35.14	14	1	68
J. P. Stephenson	11,253	332	7-51	33.89	10	0	174
M. R. Strong	1,426	31	4-46	46.00	–	–	4
P. M. Such	25,936	849	8-93	30.54	48	9	119
J. P. Taylor	16,618	559	7-23	29.72	18	4	61
S. P. Titchard	195	4	1-11	48.75	–	–	54
S. L. Watkin	25,191	902	8-59	27.92	31	4	71
L. C. Weekes	1,871	69	6-56	27.11	2	0	17
A. P. Wells	820	10	3-67	82.00	–	–	227
S. J. Widdup	22	1	1-22	22.00	–	–	11

Note: The following players did not bowl but made fielding or wicket-keeping dismissals: C. J. Hewison 5 ct; A. J. Sexton 3 ct; R. C. J. Williams 123 ct, 17 st; N. J. Wilton 37 ct, 3 st.

THE UNIVERSITIES, 2001

The 2001 season saw university cricket take on a new shape, under the aegis of the England and Wales Cricket Board, in partnership with the British Universities Sports Association. The top layer would no longer be the exclusive preserve of Oxford and Cambridge, who became two of six University Centres of Cricketing Excellence. Each of these six UCCEs was granted three three-day matches against the first-class counties. In addition, they held their own competition of two-day fixtures, played under "grade" rules, and competed in the long-standing British Universities Championship.

There were still distinctions within the UCCE group. Three – Oxford University, combined with neighbours Oxford Brookes University, Cambridge University with neighbours Anglia Polytechnic University, and, for the first time, Durham – were given first-class status in their county matches. The other three – Loughborough University/Loughborough College, Cardiff University/UWIC/University of Glamorgan, and Bradford University/Bradford College/Leeds University/Leeds Metropolitan University – were not. But in both the Inter-UCCE competition and the British Universities Championship, it was first-class Durham and non-first-class Loughborough who took the final spoils, with Loughborough coming out on top every time.

The ECB's initiative was a bold one that deserved to succeed, although the success should not be bought at the expense of students' academic needs. Confronted by so many pressures on their time and talent – three different forms of the game and, simultaneously, demanding examinations – the students responded well, despite their performances against the counties showing the size of the gulf between university cricketers and county professionals – GRENVILLE HOLLAND.

OXFORD

President: A. C. Smith (Brasenose)
Chairman: Dr S. R. Porter (St Cross College)

Oxford UCCE Captain: J. J. Porter (St John's, Leatherhead and Oxford Brookes)
Oxford University Captain: N. Millar (Fettes and Christ Church)
Captain for 2002: J. W. M. Dalrymple (Radley and St Peters)

This was the second season in which the universities of Oxford and Oxford Brookes combined forces, but the first in which they played under the title of Oxford University Centre of Cricketing Excellence as part of the ECB's reorganisation of top-level university cricket. The mix between the two institutions generally appeared to be working well, with no perceptible divisions in the side. The number of Brookes players rose in 2001; five played in each of the UCCE's county games, and Joe Porter, from Brookes, led the combined team.

Clearly there were more promising players to hand, although with a mere two county matches (a third was a total washout), it was difficult to assess the true value of the new system. There remained an immense gulf between professional county teams and the enthusiastic potential of the students. Nevertheless, the UCCE threatened to embarrass Middlesex on the opening day of the first-class season, reducing them to 15 for three and eventually dismissing them for 269, which relied heavily on two substantial partnerships. Normal service was resumed in the second innings, when the bowling lost its penetration. Next time the students took the field against a county, in June, Warwickshire set the pace from the outset, and a frenetic pace it proved to be.

Oxford had more success against Cambridge, whom they played three times during the season. They took first-innings points when they drew in the newly established championship for the six UCCEs. At the end of June, in the two games restricted to players from the traditional universities, Oxford won both the Lord's fixture, now a one-day game, and the first-class match, banished to Fenner's. The spinners helped them to their first victory in the first-class Varsity Match since 1995. The combined team finished fourth in the UCCE Championship, and reached the semi-finals of the British Universities competition, where they crashed by ten wickets to eventual winners Loughborough.

Porter failed to score the runs his talent suggested, but was not the first to find that the cares of captaincy can detract from statistical contributions. Another Brookes player, Tom Mees, grabbed three Middlesex wickets in his opening spell in first-class cricket, showing the benefit of two seasons with Warwickshire Second Eleven, and hinted at a bright future. His fellow-seamer, Toby Sharpe, improved as the season progressed, but the leading wicket-taker, again, was off-spinner Tom Hicks.

The leading first-class run-scorer was Jamie Dalrymple, the England Under-19 all-rounder, who later made his Championship debut for Middlesex. He took time to find his feet, both as an off-spinner and batsman, but it was encouraging to see him battle to justify early expectations. He was named captain – of both teams – for 2002. University medical student Charlie Warren was a solid presence as an opener, but the find of the season could be a precocious 17-year-old batsman, Pranay Sanklecha. He had left his home village in India for Brighton College, with the financial assistance of Brighton Rotary Club, and now arrived at Oxford University, where an exciting range of wristy strokes marked him down as an exceptional prospect. It remained to be seen whether he could add the maturity needed to fulfil his potential.

Whether the new system will secure a first-class future for university cricket is not yet clear; but there is no reason why it should not continue to play a valuable part in the development of young cricketers. – RALPH DELLOR.

OXFORD UCCE/UNIVERSITY RESULTS

First-class matches – Played 3: Won 1, Drawn 2. Abandoned 1.

FIRST-CLASS AVERAGES

BATTING AND FIELDING

	M	*I*	*NO*	*R*	*HS*	*100s*	*50s*	*Avge*	*Ct*
M. K. Floyd	3	6	1	174	128*	1	0	34.80	0
J. W. M. Dalrymple	3	6	0	189	70	0	1	31.50	4
H. R. Jones	2	4	1	90	57	0	1	30.00	2
J. J. Porter	2	4	1	78	46	0	0	26.00	2
T. C. Hicks	3	4	0	103	58	0	1	25.75	7
N. Millar	3	5	1	87	36	0	0	21.75	0
C. C. M. Warren	3	6	1	96	40*	0	0	19.20	4

Also batted: A. S. Bones (1 match) 3 (2 ct); G. R. Butcher (1 match) 10, 6; T. J. Daniels (1 match) 0 (1 ct, 2 st); A. F. Gofton (1 match) 4, 4*; S. J. Hawinkels (1 match) 26, 2; T. Mees (2 matches) 4, 4 (1 ct); Salman Khan (2 matches) 1, 6 (1 ct); P. Sanklecha (1 match) 8, 15* (1 ct); T. J. Sharpe (2 matches) 0*, 0*; R. G. Smalley (1 match) 2, 67 (3 ct, 1 st); T. H. Wortley (1 match) 0 (1 ct).

* *Signifies not out.*

BOWLING

	O	M	R	W	BB	5W/i	Avge
T. H. Wortley	20	6	50	3	2-17	0	16.66
J. J. Porter	22.2	1	84	4	3-50	0	21.00
T. C. Hicks	143	30	394	13	5-77	1	30.30
T. Mees	67.3	9	222	7	6-64	1	31.71
Salman Khan	72	20	162	4	2-53	0	40.50
J. W. M. Dalrymple	164.3	44	434	9	4-86	0	48.22

Also bowled: A. F. Gofton 8–1–36–0; N. Millar 35–4–122–2; S. J. Hawinkels 4–3–3–0; T. J. Sharpe 41–10–150–1.

Note: Matches in this section which were not first-class are signified by a dagger.

†At Oxford, April 12. Oxford UCCE won by 40 runs. Toss: Oxford UCCE. Oxford UCCE 215 for eight (50 overs) (J. W. M. Dalrymple 48, C. C. M. Warren 52); Worcestershire Second Eleven 175 for eight (50 overs) (N. R. Boulton 89; T. Mees three for 16, J. W. M. Dalrymple three for 29).

†At Bournemouth, April 13. Dorset v Oxford UCCE. Abandoned.

†At Oxford, April 14. Oxfordshire won by three wickets. Toss: Oxford UCCE. Oxford UCCE 172 (49.2 overs) (J. W. M. Dalrymple 47, A. S. Bones 40; M. R. Bellhouse three for 42); Oxfordshire 173 for seven (48.2 overs) (C. A. Haupt 47, R. J. Williams 32).

OXFORD UCCE v MIDDLESEX

At Oxford, April 16, 17, 18. Drawn. Toss: Oxford UCCE. First-class debuts: J. W. M. Dalrymple, M. K. Floyd, H. R. Jones, T. Mees, T. J. Sharpe. County debut: S. P. Fleming.

Three wickets by Tom Mees in his first four overs, including New Zealand captain Fleming, raised the students' hopes – only for them to be dashed by the left-handed Hutton's maiden hundred, the first first-class century of the season. He hit 20 fours and a six, providing the bulk of partnerships of 82 with Shah and 112 with Weekes, and kept the cover fielders on their toes with quality drives. He, too, and finally Weekes fell to Mees, who used his height and accuracy advantageously in the conditions, moving the ball disconcertingly at a bit above medium pace, to earn figures of six for 64. In reply, Oxford kept Middlesex in the field for nearly 94 overs, but Extras was top-scorer. The final afternoon featured the traditional halt for a snow flurry before Fraser set Oxford an improbable target of 289, the delayed declaration probably owing more to the county's reluctance to field in freezing conditions than any thought of a result.

Close of play: First day, Oxford UCCE 32-0 (Warren 7*, Floyd 14*); Second day, Middlesex 56-1 (Roseberry 29*, Fleming 19*).

Middlesex

A. J. Strauss b Mees	0	– lbw b Salman Khan	3
M. A. Roseberry b Mees	5	– b Sharpe	87
S. P. Fleming lbw b Mees	2	– c Warren b Mees	30
O. A. Shah c Porter b Hicks	29	– c and b Hicks	56
B. L. Hutton c Bones b Mees	133	– not out	5
P. N. Weekes c Bones b Mees	55	– not out	5
†D. C. Nash c Dalrymple b Mees	2		
S. J. Cook b Dalrymple	10		
*A. R. C. Fraser c Jones b Hicks	5		
P. C. R. Tufnell c Jones b Hicks	1		
T. F. Bloomfield not out	0		
B 3, l-b 6, w 4, n-b 14	27	B 9, l-b 3, n-b 12	24
1/0 2/4 3/15 4/97 5/209 6/217 7/249 8/260 9/265	269	1/5 2/72 3/177 4/201 (4 wkts dec.)	210

Bowling: *First Innings*—Mees 22.3–2–64–6; Salman Khan 15–3–49–0; Sharpe 9–2–39–0; Millar 5–2–15–0; Dalrymple 20–7–44–1; Hicks 21–5–49–3. *Second Innings*—Mees 22–4–67–1; Salman Khan 17–5–34–1; Hicks 5–0–16–1; Sharpe 13–3–49–1; Dalrymple 13–1–32–0.

Oxford UCCE

C. C. M. Warren c Fleming b Cook	15	– c Nash b Cook	7
M. K. Floyd c Weekes b Bloomfield	28	– c Nash b Cook	0
J. W. M. Dalrymple c Nash b Bloomfield	32	– b Cook	1
*J. J. Porter c Shah b Fraser	15	– not out	17
H. R. Jones c Nash b Tufnell	22	– not out	11
†A. S. Bones b Bloomfield	3		
N. Millar c Fraser b Hutton	9		
T. C. Hicks c Roseberry b Tufnell	23		
Salman Khan c Fleming b Cook	1		
T. Mees lbw b Cook	4		
T. J. Sharpe not out	0		
B 6, l-b 11, n-b 22	39	L-b 3, w 4, n-b 2	9
1/49 2/70 3/114 4/125 5/141 6/155 7/168 8/169 9/185	191	1/4 2/8 3/21	(3 wkts) 45

Bowling: *First Innings*—Bloomfield 21–8–49–3; Fraser 16–9–23–1; Tufnell 21.3–7–36–2; Cook 13–5–23–3; Weekes 12–5–19–0; Hutton 10–2–24–1. *Second Innings*—Bloomfield 7–4–7–0; Cook 9–6–10–3; Fraser 5–2–5–0; Hutton 5–2–19–0; Tufnell 3–2–1–0.

Umpires: K. E. Palmer and K. Shuttleworth.

†At Oxford, April 19, 20, 21. Drawn. Toss: Oxford UCCE. Oxford UCCE 239 for nine dec. (S. J. Lowe 80, H. R. Jones 57; A. Parker three for 35, R. J. Nicol four for 63) and 243 for eight (N. Millar 30, A. S. Bones 82, J. J. Porter 40, H. R. Jones 57 not out); MCC Young Cricketers 401 (M. Wilkie 54, A. A. Duncan 41, A. P. R. Gidman 45, Bazid Khan 145, M. J. W. Wright 34; T. C. Hicks four for 117, N. Millar three for 55).

†At Oxford, April 23. Oxford UCCE v Wiltshire. Abandoned.

OXFORD UCCE v HAMPSHIRE

At Oxford, April 25, 26, 27. Abandoned.

†At Oxford, May 4. Buckinghamshire won by 32 runs. Toss: Buckinghamshire. Buckinghamshire 257 for seven (50 overs) (M. H. Richardson 32, G. D. T. Paskins 101, D. R. Drepaul 30; T. C. Hicks three for 41); Oxford UCCE 225 for nine (50 overs) (G. R. Butcher 38, H. R. Jones 62; A. R. Clarke three for 36).

†At Arundel, May 15. Drawn. Toss: Oxford University. Oxford University 212 for six dec. (M. K. Floyd 69, G. R. Butcher 39, P. Sanklecha 42, Salman Khan 32 not out; Iqbal Sikandar six for 39); Earl of Arundel's XI 37 for two.

†At Oxford, May 21, 22, 23. MCC won by 104 runs. Toss: MCC. MCC 336 for eight dec. (H. T. Pedrola 38, J. B. R. Jones 128, Sohail Mohammed 74, J. P. B. Barnes 35 not out; T. C. Hicks three for 76, S. J. Hawinkels three for 61) and 148 for eight dec. (H. T. Pedrola 37, G. Morgan 54; T. C. Hicks five for 30); Oxford University 233 (G. R. Butcher 112, S. J. Hawinkels 38; H. T. Pedrola three for 72, Iqbal Sikandar five for 74) and 147 (M. K. Floyd 40; Iqbal Sikandar three for 31, H. T. Pedrola three for 25).

†At Oxford, May 24. Tied. Toss: Midlands CCC. Midlands CCC 254 for three (50 overs) (N. Davies 61, K. Pearson 57, D. Banks 56 not out, M. Davies 46 not out); Oxford UCCE 254 for seven (50 overs) (T. J. Daniels 55, G. R. Butcher 99, J. W. M. Dalrymple 49; G. Bulpitt four for 58).

†At Shenley Park, May 27. Sir Paul Getty's XI won by 43 runs. Toss: Oxford UCCE. Sir Paul Getty's XI 149 (T. J. G. O'Gorman 58; T. Mees four for 29); Oxford UCCE 106 (A. R. Whittall four for 32).

†At Oxford, June 1. Oxford University won by 21 runs. Toss: Oxford University. Oxford University 274 for three dec. (J. W. M. Dalrymple 56, T. C. Hicks 78 not out, P. Sanklecha 117 not out); Harlequins 253 (J. A. Claughton 76, B. W. Byrne 52, M. P. W. Jeh 40 not out; T. C. Hicks six for 59).

†At Christ Church, Oxford, June 4. Lashings won by 94 runs. Toss: Oxford UCCE. Lashings 229 for six (40 overs) (M. J. Day 49, R. B. Richardson 85; T. Mees four for 40); Oxford UCCE 135 (36.2 overs) (T. Mees 36; R. B. Richardson three for 35).

OXFORD UCCE v WARWICKSHIRE

At Oxford, June 6, 7, 8. Drawn. Toss: Warwickshire. First-class debuts: T. J. Daniels, P. Sanklecha.

A fine pitch produced 504 runs on the first day. Warwickshire rattled along at nearly five an over after the first wicket saw captain Powell, with his first double-hundred, and Bell, with a maiden century, put on 343. Powell's eventual 236 took a mere 251 minutes and 230 balls – he hit 33 fours and four sixes – while Bell, at 19 years 56 days, became the county's youngest first-class centurion. The previous youngest, Paul Smith, had also made his first hundred against Oxford, in 1983. Oxford, by contrast, were three down at the close. Dalrymple played with great application next day for his first first-class fifty, adding 94 with Millar, and Porter impressed with 46. Giles claimed five wickets on his return to first-class cricket after damaging his Achilles tendon over the winter. Warwickshire did not enforce the follow-on; instead, former Oxford captain Wagh went close to a century, and Hemp did reach three figures on the last morning. When Powell then declared, Warwickshire were 525 ahead. Jones's half-century, and more good batting by Dalrymple and Millar, helped Oxford achieve the draw.

Close of play: First day, Oxford UCCE 47-3 (Dalrymple 14*, Millar 14*); Second day, Warwickshire 177-2 (Hemp 42*, Brown 0*).

Warwickshire

*M. J. Powell st Daniels b Millar	236		
I. R. Bell c Mees b Porter	130		
D. L. Hemp c Daniels b Porter	35	– not out	100
M. A. Wagh c Sanklecha b Millar	14	– (2) st Daniels b Porter	93
D. R. Brown c Warren b Hicks	14	– (4) c and b Dalrymple	23
A. F. Giles c Hicks b Porter	1	– not out	0
†T. Frost not out	0	– (5) run out	17
M. A. Sheikh (did not bat)		– (1) c Porter b Hicks	33
B 15, l-b 8, n-b 4	27	B 8, l-b 4	12
1/343 2/394 3/414 4/443 5/456 6/457	(6 wkts dec.) 457	1/84 2/177 3/241 4/277	(4 wkts dec.) 278

N. M. Carter, C. E. Dagnall and A. Richardson did not bat.

Bowling: *First Innings*—Mees 17–2–64–0; Sharpe 14–3–50–0; Millar 15–0–50–2; Dalrymple 13–0–98–0; Hicks 27–1–122–1; Porter 8.2–0–50–3. *Second Innings*—Mees 6–1–27–0; Sharpe 5–2–12–0; Millar 5–0–18–0; Hicks 26–5–64–1; Dalrymple 35.3–3–111–1; Porter 14–1–34–1.

Oxford UCCE

M. K. Floyd c Frost b Richardson	10	– b Richardson	0
C. C. M. Warren c Frost b Carter	0	– c Frost b Giles	4
J. W. M. Dalrymple c Brown b Giles	70	– c Frost b Sheikh	41
H. R. Jones lbw b Carter	0	– (5) c Powell b Carter	57
N. Millar c Bell b Giles	36	– (6) not out	32
*J. J. Porter st Frost b Giles	46	– (4) lbw b Dagnall	0
P. Sanklecha lbw b Richardson	8	– not out	15
T. C. Hicks st Frost b Giles	0		
†T. J. Daniels c Frost b Richardson	0		
T. Mees lbw b Giles	4		
T. J. Sharpe not out	0		
B 13, l-b 3, w 6, n-b 14	36	B 8, l-b 11, w 2, n-b 12	33
1/12 2/12 3/16 4/110 5/147 6/166 7/177 8/180 9/191	210	1/0 2/34 3/35 4/89 5/165 (5 wkts)	182

Bowling: *First Innings*—Richardson 19–4–56–3; Carter 11–2–31–2; Giles 18.5–8–46–5; Sheikh 6–2–11–0; Dagnall 7–1–29–0; Wagh 4–1–6–0; Hemp 2–0–9–0; Brown 2–0–6–0. *Second Innings*—Richardson 7–5–9–1; Carter 14–2–63–1; Giles 22–11–34–1; Dagnall 7–0–36–1; Sheikh 4–2–6–1; Brown 5–0–14–0; Wagh 1–0–1–0.

Umpires: N. L. Bainton and P. Willey.

†At Oxford, June 20, 21, 22. Drawn. Toss: Oxford University. Oxford University 253 (M. K. Floyd 36, C. C. M. Warren 55, N. Millar 80; Lt Cdr C. A. Slocombe four for 48) and 286 for six dec. (S. J. Hawinkels 54, R. G. Smalley 91, A. F. Gofton 54 not out, P. Sanklecha 53); Combined Services 327 for nine dec. (Lt T. Osman 117, Lt J. Mathews 31, Sgt N. Palmer 64, Mne B. S. Phelps 34; T. C. Hicks seven for 109) and 145 for six (Sgt S. Hole 43; T. C. Hicks five for 78).

†At Oxford, June 25. Sussex Board XI won by five wickets. Toss: Oxford University. Oxford University 157 (45.1 overs) (C. C. M. Warren 38, A. F. Gofton 32 not out; A. Cornford three for 27, M. A. Hazleton three for 26); Sussex Board XI 158 for five (40 overs) (G. R. A. Campbell 100 not out).

At Lord's, June 28. OXFORD UNIVERSITY beat CAMBRIDGE UNIVERSITY by eight wickets (see One-Day University Match, 2001).

At Cambridge, June 30, July 1, 2, 3. OXFORD UNIVERSITY beat CAMBRIDGE UNIVERSITY by three wickets.

CAMBRIDGE

President: Professor A. D. Buckingham (Pembroke)

Captain: B. J. Collins (St Albans School and Girton)
Captain for 2002: J. W. R. Parker (Tonbridge and St Catharine's)

The 2001 season was a difficult one for Cambridge, as a new era in university cricket opened with a dearth of talent at Fenner's. As part of the reforms introduced by the ECB, Cambridge University joined forces with Anglia Polytechnic University to form the Cambridge University Centre of Cricketing Excellence, which would play first-class matches against the counties, as well as competing in inter-university cricket. But in 2001, Anglia formed half of the UCCE in name only. They had no cricketing tradition before the merger and, although they made great strides, had not yet attracted cricketers able to compete at first-class level. In the inaugural season, they provided no first-class players and had only a token presence in the squad, an imbalance they were working hard to correct.

The over-reliance on players from the older University was exacerbated come examination time. Previously, the University tried to avoid scheduling significant fixtures at the same time as exams; this year, there were games when two-thirds of the squad were unavailable. Moreover, a broken finger kept James Pyemont, their best player and the only contracted cricketer in the side (on Derbyshire's books), out of some key inter-university games.

Although Cambridge were confident they could field a stronger side in 2002, the uneven spread of talent needed to be addressed by all parties involved in the Centres of Excellence concept. It will not be best served if all the top players go to one or two universities; there is no point in one centre recruiting 17 with county connections when they can play only 11 at a time.

Cambridge's most critical shortage was of slow bowlers – they were galled to find, when they played Durham, that their opponents could call on four left-armers. The lack of spin proved fatal in the Varsity Match, which was staged at Fenner's, the Lord's fixture having been reduced to 50 overs a side. One benefit of the change was that the first-class game could be played over four days. Cambridge more than held their own for the first two days, but without a proper slow bowler failed to force home their advantage. Oxford's two off-spinners, meanwhile, claimed seven wickets each.

That was, officially, Cambridge University's only first-class outing; they played their three fixtures against the counties as Cambridge UCCE. Two matches were rain-affected draws; the other they lost by 335 runs to Essex. Cambridge were no more successful in inter-university cricket, finishing fifth of six in the Inter-UCCE Championship, and fourth of six in their league of the British Universities Championship; they also lost the one-day game to Oxford.

The players available to coach Chris Scott, the former Nottinghamshire and Durham keeper, worked hard. Pyemont, apart from being Cambridge's best batsman, was forced to bear the brunt of the bowling, sending down 146 first-class overs, far more than anyone else, despite being little more than an occasional off-spinner. Vikram Kumar was the leading first-class run-scorer, with 199 runs, Adam Clarke made some useful contributions and headed the bowling averages, and there was a bonus in June when Jamie Parker, son of former Cambridge, Sussex and Durham batsman Paul Parker, made himself available. He had spent his first year at university concentrating on his studies and hockey, and now, after staking a claim with some impressive innings, made his first-class debut in the Varsity Match, scoring 44 and 83. He was elected captain for 2002. – DAVID HALLETT.

CAMBRIDGE UCCE/UNIVERSITY RESULTS

First-class matches – Played 4: Lost 2, Drawn 2.

FIRST-CLASS AVERAGES

BATTING AND FIELDING

	M	*I*	*NO*	*R*	*HS*	*100s*	*50s*	*Avge*	*Ct*
V. H. Kumar	4	7	1	199	86*	0	1	33.16	2
J. P. Pyemont	4	7	1	145	70	0	1	24.16	4
S. A. A. Block	4	7	1	139	56*	0	1	23.16	1
A. H. V. Johnson	4	5	1	72	55*	0	1	18.00	5
B. J. Collins	4	6	1	79	28*	0	0	15.80	0
A. D. Simcox	3	5	1	56	19	0	0	14.00	3
C. A. Sayers	4	6	1	42	23	0	0	8.40	3

	M	I	NO	R	HS	100s	50s	Avge	Ct
J. B. Scott	4	5	1	27	14	0	0	6.75	0
G. J. Dill	4	6	1	27	8	0	0	5.40	3
T. R. Hughes	3	5	0	12	7	0	0	2.40	0
J. A. Cliffe	3	3	0	2	2	0	0	0.66	0

Also batted: A. C. S. Clarke (2 matches) 44, 0; J. W. R. Parker (1 match) 44, 83.

* *Signifies not out.*

BOWLING

	O	M	R	W	BB	5W/i	Avge
A. C. S. Clarke	37.2	7	102	6	3-44	0	17.00
T. R. Hughes	89	18	277	7	2-38	0	39.57
J. P. Pyemont	146	31	512	10	4-101	0	51.20
G. J. Dill	81	17	301	5	2-54	0	60.20
J. B. Scott	86.2	16	320	4	1-33	0	80.00

Also bowled: J. A. Cliffe 52.4–7–190–2; J. W. R. Parker 1–0–8–0.

Note: Matches in this section which were not first-class are signified by a dagger.

CAMBRIDGE UCCE v KENT

At Cambridge, April 16, 17, 18. Drawn. Toss: Cambridge UCCE. First-class debuts: J. A. Cliffe, G. J. Dill, A. H. V. Johnson, V. H. Kumar, J. B. Scott, A. D. Simcox.

In their first match as a Centre of Excellence, Cambridge fielded six debutants against a county near full strength. James Scott removed Key in his opening over, which included seven no-balls, but after that the students struggled as Kent's batsmen took the opportunity for some early-season acclimatisation until hail ended play for the day. Fulton launched what was to be a prosperous season with a solid century, and next day Block became the first to carry his bat for Cambridge since Mike Atherton in 1987. In four and a half hours, he made almost half his side's runs off the bat, with only two team-mates reaching double figures. Waiving the follow-on, Kent batted to lunch on the final day, but bad weather in the afternoon ruled out anything other than an early finish.

Close of play: First day, Kent 299-7 (Nixon 55*, Patel 0*); Second day, Kent 87-0 (Smith 36*, Key 40*).

Kent

D. P. Fulton c and b Dill	120		
R. W. T. Key c Symcox b Scott	1	– lbw b Hughes	67
E. T. Smith c and b Dill	42	– (1) c Symcox b Scott	48
M. J. Walker c Sayers b Pyemont	15	– (3) c Block b Hughes	4
†P. A. Nixon not out	55		
M. A. Ealham c and b Pyemont	13	– not out	0
J. B. Hockley lbw b Pyemont	17	– (4) c Dill b Pyemont	11
*M. V. Fleming run out	1	– (5) not out	11
M. M. Patel not out	0		
B 2, l-b 3, w 4, n-b 26	35	B 5, l-b 5, w 6, n-b 10	26
1/22 2/108 3/157 4/227 5/249 6/281 7/286 (7 wkts dec.)	299	1/117 2/134 3/145 4/163 (4 wkts dec.)	167

D. D. Masters and M. J. Saggers did not bat.

Bowling: *First Innings*—Hughes 22–8–36–0; Scott 12–3–57–1; Cliffe 13.4–1–56–0; Pyemont 27–3–91–3; Dill 23–7–54–2. *Second Innings*—Hughes 12–2–61–2; Scott 9.4–5–33–1; Pyemont 19–4–41–1; Dill 2–0–5–0; Cliffe 6–2–17–0.

Cambridge UCCE

S. A. A. Block not out	56	– c Fulton b Patel	19
A. D. Simcox lbw b Saggers	4	– not out	18
V. H. Kumar c Nixon b Ealham	8	– lbw b Fleming	4
J. P. Pyemont c Nixon b Masters	19	– not out	10
*B. J. Collins c Patel b Masters	0		
C. A. Sayers c Masters b Hockley	10		
G. J. Dill lbw b Ealham	6		
†A. H. V. Johnson st Nixon b Patel	9		
J. B. Scott b Patel	3		
T. R. Hughes c Key b Patel	0		
J. A. Cliffe b Fleming	2		
B 1, l-b 9, n-b 2	12	L-b 2	2
1/5 2/32 3/60 4/60 5/81 6/89 7/110 8/116 9/116	129	1/31 2/40 (2 wkts)	53

Bowling: *First Innings*—Saggers 13–4–17–1; Masters 11–4–14–2; Ealham 11–5–12–2; Patel 23–11–34–3; Hockley 9–1–25–1; Fleming 10.4–6–17–1. *Second Innings*—Saggers 7–2–14–0; Masters 4–2–7–0; Patel 11–4–14–1; Fleming 8–6–5–1; Ealham 2.5–0–7–0; Hockley 2–1–4–0.

Umpires: N. L. Bainton and B. Leadbeater.

†At Arundel, May 8. Earl of Arundel's XI won by 97 runs. Toss: Cambridge University. Earl of Arundel's XI 230 for eight dec. (G. W. Jones 44, C. Walsh 58, D. P. Waugh 57 not out; J. A. Cliffe five for 65); Cambridge University 133 (C. A. Sayers 42; E. Howe three for 25, C. Charlton four for 14).

CAMBRIDGE UCCE v ESSEX

At Cambridge, May 9, 10, 11. Essex won by 335 runs. Toss: Essex.

Cambridge were simply overwhelmed. Essex openers Prichard and Grayson rustled up 200 before lunch, with Grayson reaching his hundred in 79 balls; Prichard completed his after the interval, whereupon Robinson and Napier added a couple more. It was Napier's maiden first-class hundred – he batted 82 balls for his 104, getting there just before the close – and the first time four Essex batsmen had scored centuries in the same innings. Next day, in contrast, the students eked out 128 from 74 overs. Anderson finished them off with three wickets in four balls, and then he and his fellow-bowlers batted out the day. There was never any prospect of Cambridge chasing 502, but Kumar's aggressive 86 not out, with 13 fours, prevented the innings being entirely one-way traffic. Napier, removing his last two partners with successive deliveries, robbed the former Dulwich College batsman of a deserved first hundred, while off-spinner Mason enjoyed a career-best five for 40.

Close of play: First day, Essex 533-5 (Hyam 19*); Second day, Essex 96-1 (Cowan 50*, Mason 39*).

Essex

P. J. Prichard c Kumar b Cliffe	111		
A. P. Grayson c Sayers b Hughes	127		
*D. D. J. Robinson b Cliffe	109		
S. D. Peters c Johnson b Pyemont	44		
G. R. Napier c Johnson b Scott	104		
†B. J. Hyam not out	19		
R. S. G. Anderson (did not bat)		– (1) c Sayers b Dill	6
A. P. Cowan (did not bat)		– (2) not out	50
T. J. Mason (did not bat)		– (3) not out	39
B 4, l-b 5, w 4, n-b 6	19	L-b 1	1
1/238 2/265 3/365 4/455 5/533 (5 wkts dec.)	533	1/13 (1 wkt dec.)	96

M. C. Ilott and P. M. Such did not bat.

Bowling: *First Innings*—Hughes 18–1–71–1; Scott 20.4–1–95–1; Cliffe 20–4–71–2; Pyemont 29–0–174–1; Dill 19–0–113–0. *Second Innings*—Scott 6–1–22–0; Cliffe 7–0–23–0; Dill 9–1–34–1; Pyemont 3–0–16–0.

Cambridge UCCE

S. A. A. Block c Hyam b Napier	5	– lbw b Anderson	10
A. D. Simcox lbw b Anderson	19	– c Hyam b Cowan	8
V. H. Kumar lbw b Mason	32	– not out	86
J. P. Pyemont c Robinson b Anderson	6	– c Hyam b Mason	21
*B. J. Collins not out	28	– c Peters b Mason	11
C. A. Sayers lbw b Ilott	0	– c Peters b Mason	0
G. J. Dill lbw b Such	4	– lbw b Ilott	3
†A. H. V. Johnson lbw b Napier	0	– st Hyam b Mason	2
J. B. Scott c Hyam b Anderson	14	– c Peters b Mason	4
T. R. Hughes b Anderson	0	– c Hyam b Napier	5
J. A. Cliffe b Anderson	0	– b Napier	0
L-b 4, w 2, n-b 14	20	B 1, l-b 5, w 6, n-b 4	16
1/21 2/65 3/75 4/78 5/79 6/84 7/91 8/128 9/128	128	1/22 2/46 3/83 4/95 5/95 6/98 7/113 8/129 9/166	166

Bowling: *First Innings*—Ilott 14–8–25–1; Cowan 13–5–18–0; Napier 10–1–24–2; Anderson 9–3–21–5; Such 13–10–5–1; Mason 10–5–18–1; Grayson 5–1–13–0. *Second Innings*—Ilott 12–4–23–1; Cowan 6–1–25–1; Mason 15–3–40–5; Anderson 5–0–13–1; Such 5–0–20–0; Napier 6–0–39–2.

Umpires: M. J. Harris and K. Shuttleworth.

†At Shenley Park, May 13. Sir Paul Getty's XI won by four wickets. Toss: Cambridge University. Cambridge University 240 for four dec. (J. P. Pyemont 93, B. J. Collins 57 not out, A. D. Simcox 34 not out); Sir Paul Getty's XI 241 for six (Bazid Khan 79, D. M. Ward 63, J. D. Ricketts 35 not out).

CAMBRIDGE UCCE v SUSSEX

At Cambridge, May 16, 17, 18. Drawn. Toss: Cambridge UCCE. First-class debuts: A. C. S. Clarke; P. M. R. Havell.

Rain prevented any play until the final two sessions of the match, when the teams agreed to split the remaining time between them. Cambridge declared at 94 for five, with 31 coming from no-balls, and Montgomerie almost matched their total off his own bat.

Close of play: First day, No play; Second day, No play.

Cambridge UCCE

S. A. A. Block lbw b Lewry	4	G. J. Dill not out		2
A. D. Simcox lbw b Taylor	7			
V. H. Kumar c Zuiderent b Robinson	27	L-b 1, n-b 31		32
J. P. Pyemont c and b Rashid	13			
*B. J. Collins lbw b Robinson	0	1/8 2/65 3/65	(5 wkts dec.)	94
C. A. Sayers not out	9	4/65 5/85		

†A. H. V. Johnson, J. B. Scott, A. C. S. Clarke and J. A. Cliffe did not bat.

Bowling: Lewry 5–1–9–1; Havell 7–3–16–0; Taylor 7–1–31–1; Robinson 6–4–10–2; Rashid 4–1–19–1; Yardy 2–0–8–0.

Sussex

*R. R. Montgomerie not out		84
P. A. Cottey c Simcox b Clarke		20
M. H. Yardy not out		28
L-b 1, w 2, n-b 12		15
1/55	(1 wkt)	147

B. Zuiderent, W. J. House, U. B. A. Rashid, †M. J. Prior, J. D. Lewry, P. M. R. Havell, B. V. Taylor and M. A. Robinson did not bat.

Bowling: Scott 7–0–35–0; Cliffe 6–0–23–0; Clarke 5–1–20–1; Dill 6–1–41–0; Pyemont 4–0–27–0.

Umpires: M. Dixon and V. A. Holder.

†At Cambridge, June 10. Cambridge University won by 14 runs. Toss: Cambridge University. Cambridge University 179 for nine dec. (J. W. R. Parker 55, C. A. Sayers 35; R. O. Jones six for 26); Free Foresters 165 for five (G. Jones 52, R. O. Jones 63).

†At Cambridge, June 11. Lashings won by 109 runs. Toss: Lashings. Lashings 219 for nine (45 overs) (S. C. Williams 46, J. R. Murray 38, J. C. Adams 31, R. B. Richardson 39; E. Howe three for 37, T. R. Hughes three for 42); Cambridge University 110 (38.5 overs) (R. O. Jones 41, J. Allen 28; M. Wooderson three for 32).

†At Cambridge, June 20, 21, 22. Cambridge University won by three wickets. Toss: MCC. MCC 281 for six dec. (J. P. Arscott 38, C. M. Gupte 58, P. D. Atkins 57, B. W. Byrne 58 not out; B. J. Collins three for 49) and 156 for three dec. (S. T. Crawley 58 not out, J. H. Louw 31); Cambridge University 188 for seven dec. (J. W. R. Parker 38, G. J. Dill 33; R. J. Pack three for 49) and 250 for seven (C. A. Sayers 49, G. J. Dill 70, J. W. R. Parker 47 not out, B. J. Collins 44; J. H. Louw four for 54).

†At Cambridge, June 24. Quidnuncs won by five wickets. Toss: Cambridge University. Cambridge University 213 for eight dec. (B. J. Collins 59); Quidnuncs 217 for five (I. Mohammed 45, A. R. Danson 62 not out, K. D. M. Walker 52 not out).

†At Cambridge, June 25. MCC Young Cricketers won by six wickets. Toss: Cambridge University. Cambridge University 197 for seven (50 overs) (V. H. Kumar 74, A. D. Simcox 35 not out; N. E. L. Gunter three for 37); MCC Young Cricketers 198 for four (42 overs) (R. M. Wilkinson 54, M. J. Eyles 32).

ONE-DAY UNIVERSITY MATCH, 2001

OXFORD UNIVERSITY v CAMBRIDGE UNIVERSITY

At Lord's, June 28. Oxford University won by eight wickets. Toss: Oxford University.

With Oxford and Cambridge's traditional first-class match moved to Fenner's, the recently established one-day equivalent took its place at Lord's. Oxford won with more than 11 overs to spare, pulling back their deficit in the fixture to 3–4. Cambridge were in immediate trouble; Gofton reduced them to 11 for three by the sixth over. Collins and Block halted the collapse, and Block was eventually able to cut loose with a couple of sixes. But Oxford's target was only 178, and Smalley and Hawinkels cruised home with an unbroken stand of 92 in 20 overs. The Oxbridge women's teams played their own Varsity Match simultaneously on the adjacent Nursery Ground: Cambridge won that by six wickets, thanks to a century from Jill Andrews. Jodie Collins, sister of men's captain Ben, was their twelfth man.

Cambridge University

J. P. Pyemont (*Tonbridge and Trinity Hall*) c Smalley b Millar . 17
C. A. Sayers (*Millfield and Trinity Hall*) c Smalley b Gofton . 1
†V. H. Kumar (*Dulwich and St John's*) c Dalrymple b Gofton . 1
J. W. R. Parker (*Tonbridge and St Catharine's*) c Hicks b Gofton . 0
*B. J. Collins (*St Albans and Girton*) c Millar b Hicks . 37
S. A. A. Block (*Cheltenham and Downing*) b Millar . 65
G. J. Dill (*St Albans, Swansea U. and Homerton*) b Dalrymple . 9
J. L. Hartley (*Sir J. Williamson's MS and Emmanuel*) c Smalley b Dalrymple . 0
A. C. S. Clarke (*Kimberley CS and Downing*) not out . 25
T. R. Hughes (*Oldbury Wells and Homerton*) not out . 4
B 1, l-b 5, w 12 18

1/9 2/11 3/11 4/24 5/95 6/117 7/117 8/170 (8 wkts, 50 overs) 177

J. A. Cliffe (*St Birinus and Gonville & Caius*) did not bat.

Bowling: Salman Khan 10–2–48–0; Gofton 10–2–26–3; Millar 8–0–30–2; Dalrymple 10–0–30–2; Hicks 9–2–26–1; Stearn 3–0–11–0.

Oxford University

J. W. M. Dalrymple (*Radley and St Peter's*) b Clarke . 16
†R. G. Smalley (*RGS Newcastle and Keble*) not out . 75
*N. Millar (*Fettes and Christ Church*) lbw b Pyemont . 16
S. J. Hawinkels (*St Stithians, Island School Hong Kong and University*) not out . 50
L-b 6, w 14, n-b 1. 21

1/21 2/86 (2 wkts, 38.3 overs) 178

C. P. Stearn (*Bedford and Worcester*), P. Sanklecha (*Innisfree House Bangalore, Brighton and Lincoln*), G. R. Butcher (*Wallington County GS and Oriel*), C. C. M. Warren (*Sherborne and Worcester*), A. F. Gofton (*Tapton and Wadham*), T. C. Hicks (*Lord Wandsworth and St Catherine's*) and Salman Khan (*Islamabad GS, UCL and Wadham*) did not bat.

Bowling: Hughes 8–0–32–0; Clarke 9–0–34–1; Cliffe 4.3–0–38–0; Dill 6–1–18–0; Pyemont 7–0–33–1; Parker 4–0–17–0.

Umpires: G. I. Burgess and N. G. Cowley.

THE UNIVERSITY MATCH, 2001

CAMBRIDGE UNIVERSITY v OXFORD UNIVERSITY

At Cambridge, June 30, July 1, 2, 3. Oxford University won by three wickets. Toss: Cambridge University. First-class debuts: J. W. R. Parker; G. R. Butcher, S. J. Hawinkels, T. H. Wortley.

This was the first first-class Varsity Match not played at Lord's since 1850, when Oxford won by 127 runs at the Magdalen College Ground, Oxford. It was also the first staged over four days, increasing the likelihood of a result. For much of the game, that result looked likely to go Cambridge's way. They had started smartly, Pyemont leading them to 137 for two, and, after a mid-innings wobble, Johnson and Clarke added 83 for the eighth wicket. It was another eighth-wicket stand, however, that pulled Oxford back into the game. They were 203 for seven, 93 behind, early on the third day, before Floyd and Hicks put on 109, and they eventually led by 29. Floyd carried his bat for a maiden century, occupying nearly eight hours at the crease, while seven of his team-mates were lbw. Jamie Parker, on first-class debut, hit 11 fours in a 97-ball 83 in the Cambridge second innings, but off-spinners Hicks and Dalrymple quickly gathered the remaining wickets on the final morning. Chasing 205 in 69 overs, Oxford slipped to 47 for three, before Smalley's 67 led the recovery and Warren, with 40 in 35 balls, completed a thrilling win.

Close of play: First day, Cambridge University 252-7 (Johnson 27*, Clarke 38*); Second day, Oxford University 194-5 (Floyd 82*, Warren 30*); Third day, Cambridge University 184-4 (Collins 23*, Sayers 8*).

Cambridge University

S. A. A. Block (*Cheltenham and Downing*) c and b Hicks	28	–	c Salman Khan b Dalrymple	17
J. P. Pyemont (*Tonbridge and Trinity Hall*) c Smalley b Hicks	70	–	c and b Hicks	6
V. H. Kumar (*Dulwich and St John's*) c Dalrymple b Wortley	12	–	lbw b Wortley	30
J. W. R. Parker (*Tonbridge and St Catharine's*) b Salman Khan	44	–	st Smalley b Hicks	83
*B. J. Collins (*St Albans and Girton*) lbw b Dalrymple	13	–	c Dalrymple b Salman Khan	27
C. A. Sayers (*Millfield and Trinity Hall*) c Warren b Dalrymple	0	–	c Warren b Hicks	23
G. J. Dill (*St Albans, Swansea U. and Homerton*) c Hicks b Dalrymple	4	–	b Dalrymple	8
†A. H. V. Johnson (*Tapton and Jesus*) not out	55	–	c Smalley b Hicks	6
A. C. S. Clarke (*Kimberley CS and Downing*) c Smalley b Salman Khan	44	–	b Dalrymple	0
J. B. Scott (*Radley and Downing*) c Hicks b Dalrymple	0	–	not out	6
T. R. Hughes (*Oldbury Wells and Homerton*) c and b Wortley	7	–	c and b Hicks	0
B 7, l-b 6, w 2, n-b 4	19		B 10, l-b 7, n-b 10	27
1/70 2/107 3/137 4/162 5/162 6/180 7/180 8/263 9/268	296		1/20 2/32 3/108 4/155 5/193 6/208 7/216 8/221 9/231	233

Bowling: *First Innings*—Salman Khan 30–11–53–2; Gofton 8–1–36–0; Millar 7–2–22–0; Hicks 35–14–66–2; Dalrymple 47–16–86–4; Wortley 11–6–17–2; Hawinkels 4–3–3–0. *Second Innings*—Salman Khan 10–1–26–1; Hicks 29–5–77–5; Dalrymple 36–17–63–3; Wortley 9–0–33–1; Millar 3–0–17–0.

Oxford University

M. K. Floyd (*University CS and Keble*)	not out	128	– c Johnson b Clarke	8
G. R. Butcher (*Wallington County GS and Oriel*)	c Pyemont b Hughes	10	– c Kumar b Pyemont	6
J. W. M. Dalrymple (*Radley and St Peter's*)	c Johnson b Scott	19	– c Pyemont b Clarke	26
S. J. Hawinkels (*St Stithians, Island School Hong Kong and University*)	lbw b Dill	26	– b Hughes	2
†R. G. Smalley (*RGS Newcastle and Keble*)	lbw b Pyemont	2	– b Dill	67
*N. Millar (*Fettes and Christ Church*)	lbw b Pyemont	1	– b Hughes	9
C. C. M. Warren (*Sherborne and Worcester*)	lbw b Pyemont	30	– (8) not out	40
A. F. Gofton (*Tapton and Wadham*)	lbw b Hughes	4	– (9) not out	4
T. C. Hicks (*Lord Wandsworth and St Catherine's*)	lbw b Pyemont	58	– (7) c Johnson b Clarke	22
Salman Khan (*Islamabad GS, UCL and Wadham*)	lbw b Clarke	6		
T. H. Wortley (*Sutton GS and Jesus*)	c Pyemont b Clarke	0		
	B 8, l-b 17, w 10, n-b 6	41	B 3, l-b 10, w 6, n-b 4	23
1/25 2/52 3/97 4/110 5/116 6/194 7/203 8/312 9/325		325	1/20 2/40 3/47 4/80 5/120 6/151 7/190	(7 wkts) 207

Bowling: *First Innings*—Hughes 24–6–71–2; Clarke 16.5–2–38–2; Pyemont 43–18–101–4; Scott 22–4–49–1; Dill 19–8–41–1. *Second Innings*—Hughes 13–1–38–2; Pyemont 21–6–62–1; Clarke 15.3–4–44–3; Scott 9–2–29–0; Dill 3–0–13–1; Parker 1–0–8–0.

Umpires: B. Dudleston and A. G. T. Whitehead.

OXFORD v CAMBRIDGE, NOTES

The University Match dates back to 1827. Altogether there have been 156 official matches, Cambridge winning 56 and Oxford 49, with 51 drawn. Since the war Cambridge have won ten times (1949, 1953, 1957, 1958, 1972, 1979, 1982, 1986, 1992 and 1998) and Oxford ten (1946, 1948, 1951, 1959, 1966, 1976, 1984, 1993, 1995 and 2001). All other matches have been drawn; the 1988 fixture was abandoned without a ball being bowled. The first-class fixture was moved from its traditional venue at Lord's in 2001, to be staged alternately at Cambridge and Oxford, and a one-day game was played instead at Lord's.

One hundred and eight three-figure innings have been played in the University matches, 51 for Oxford and 57 for Cambridge. For the fullest lists see the 1940 and 1993 *Wisdens*. There have been three double-centuries for Cambridge (211 by G. Goonesena in 1957, 201 by A. Ratcliffe in 1931 and 200 by Majid Khan in 1970) and two for Oxford (238* by Nawab of Pataudi, sen. in 1931 and 201* by M. J. K. Smith in 1954). Ratcliffe's score was a record for the match for only one day, before being beaten by Pataudi's. M. J. K. Smith and R. J. Boyd-Moss (Cambridge) are the only players to score three hundreds.

The highest totals in the fixture are 513 for six in 1996, 503 in 1900, 457 in 1947, 453 for eight in 1931 and 453 for nine in 1994, all by Oxford. Cambridge's highest is 432 for nine in 1936. The lowest totals are 32 by Oxford in 1878 and 39 by Cambridge in 1858.

F. C. Cobden, in the Oxford v Cambridge match in 1870, performed the hat-trick by taking the last three wickets and won an extraordinary game for Cambridge by two runs. Other hat-tricks, all for Cambridge, have been achieved by A. G. Steel (1879), P. H. Morton (1880), J. F. Ireland (1911) and R. G. H. Lowe (1926). S. E. Butler, in the 1871 match, took all ten wickets in the Cambridge first innings.

D. W. Jarrett (Oxford 1975, Cambridge 1976), S. M. Wookey (Cambridge 1975-76, Oxford 1978) and G. Pathmanathan (Oxford 1975-78, Cambridge 1983) gained Blues for both Universities.

A full list of Blues from 1837 may be found in Wisdens *published between 1923 and 1939. The lists thereafter were curtailed, covering more recent years only, and dropped after 1992.*

DURHAM

President: Dr J. G. Holland (Collingwood College)
Hon. Treasurer: B. R. Lander (Hatfield College)

Captain: M. J. Banes (Tonbridge and Collingwood College)

Durham University's first first-class match in April 2001 marked the beginning of a new era, and a turning-point in a journey that began in 1843. In June that year, the University met Sunderland in a low-scoring encounter at the Racecourse Ground. The students managed only 46 and 34, and lost by an innings and four runs. A week later, they put on an even less distinguished performance, against Durham City: 28 and 12, to lose by an innings and 27 runs.

The founding fathers of Durham University Cricket Club were Joseph Waite, who became Master of University College, and Charles Henry Ford, the Rector of Sedgefield. From the start, the University played at the Racecourse Ground, which in 1843 belonged to the Bishop of Chester, a canon of the Cathedral. In 1844, the Bishop leased it to Durham City; although the lease soon passed to the University, the two clubs shared its use until 1887, when the City moved upstream. Meanwhile, to deter student gambling, the University authorities halted horse-racing on the site. The following year, the University club took full possession of the Racecourse Ground and began a programme of regular fixtures that has continued to the present day.

In the early 20th century, the University played only friendly fixtures against local clubs. But in 1927, the national Universities Athletic Union Championship was founded. Durham won their first UAU title in 1938, retained it in 1939, but had to wait for their next until 1953. There was no doubt about the leading player that season: Frank Tyson intimidated not just students but the Australians a year later. His old team, however, disappeared back into the doldrums until 1972, when Steve Walford led them to a memorable victory over Loughborough in the semi-finals, then beat Exeter to regain the title. The University won the championship five more times during the next 15 years, during which their teams included future Test players in Paul Allott, Graeme Fowler, Tim Curtis, John Stephenson and Nasser Hussain. Hussain played the first of his three finals in 1987, aged 19, on a sodden Second Eleven pitch at Birmingham University after rain had forced a transfer from Southampton; he scored 15 in support of Stephenson's unbeaten fifty to help defeat Exeter.

The golden era, in which Durham seemed virtually invincible, began in 1990, when a balanced, well-organised and exceptionally happy team, led by Sean Morris, won the first of four successive titles. South African pace bowler Rob Macdonald took six wickets and Pakistan Test all-rounder Wasim Raja scored 57 not out in the final, once more against Exeter. In 1991, Durham brushed aside Southampton, and in 1992 their total of 308 was far too much for Kent. They soared to even greater heights in 1993, their 150th anniversary year. Under the cavalier leadership of Simon Ecclestone, the UAU Championship was a mere formality, with Manchester overwhelmed by 210 runs in the final, while the indoor squad claimed the UAU and National Cricket Association titles. In 1994, the last UAU final, Durham lost to Swansea, but they bounced back to win the first BUSA final the following year, when Matt Windows and Toby Peirce shared a second-wicket stand of 275 to set up a massive 239-run win over Exeter.

In 1996 they failed to reach the final for the first time in 13 years, losing the semi-final to Loughborough, who were becoming their greatest rivals. These two teams were to contest four of the next five BUSA finals, the only interruption coming in 1999, when they met in the semis, and Durham's final victory came at the expense of UWIC, a recent newcomer at this level. Durham defeated Loughborough in 1997, shared the title with them in 1998, because of miserable weather, but lost to them by a single wicket in 2000, and more heavily in 2001.

The 1999 title was Durham's 17th (including the joint one the previous year), ten of them in 14 years, and they have missed only one final since 1984. This unmatched record has attracted many able students to Durham, and the club has more than 200 members, fields 16 teams, and has a successful women's section. It also played an active role in helping Durham County Cricket Club achieve first-class status in 1992, and hosted the county's first home match, against Lancashire, at the Racecourse Ground. But the first steps towards the University acquiring first-class status in its own right came in 1995, when it applied to the ECB for recognition as a University Centre of Cricketing Excellence. A pilot scheme began in the autumn of 1996, with Graeme Fowler as senior coach, and the model was adopted four years later at five other university centres selected by the ECB.

In their first first-class season, the University struggled to raise their standards. For all its obvious qualities at university level, the batting was insufficiently robust for the requirements of the county circuit, while the bowling lacked penetration. Time and again, despite strenuous efforts in the field, the opposition compiled insurmountable totals. Even so, helped indubitably by some awful weather, Durham were unbeaten in their three county games. Their opening encounter against Durham County, staged in a snowstorm at the Riverside with players wearing balaclavas, was a rude awakening. Electing to bat on an initially gruesome pitch, to the delighted surprise of the county bowlers, they were demolished for 67, then conceded 485 for four as conditions eased. Back at the Racecourse, they held their own better against Lancashire, and the third draw, against Worcestershire, saw James Foster, the Essex wicket-keeper/batsman, score their first first-class century. This match proved little, however, other than the fact that the pitch was excellent and that Worcestershire, who scored 631 for six, needed to get runs off someone.

Of the University batsmen, the tall and elegant Will Jefferson, another Essex player, stood out as an excellent prospect until a back injury curtailed his season. Foster had already played for England A in the West Indies, and his abilities received further recognition when he was picked for the full England parties to Zimbabwe and India, where he made his Test debut. Captain Matt Banes, contracted to Kent, led by example and confronted the pressures of the first-class game well. Michael Brown, from Middlesex, consolidated his position with two fifties against Worcestershire, and Alex Loudon, England Under-19's captain for the 1999-2000 World Cup and now on Kent's books, was the most promising freshman.

Durham flourished in the new UCCE competition, in which the six Centres of Excellence played each other in a round-robin league of two-day games before a one-day final at Lord's. They were the only side to win any outright victories in the league, with innings wins over Cambridge and Bradford/Leeds, but Loughborough still edged them out of first place on the table – and then went on to beat them by 22 runs in the One-Day Challenge at Lord's. Loughborough had already defeated them in the final of the British Universities Championship; they had taken the top two places in the Northern Premier League and won their respective semi-finals. Meanwhile, Durham's Second Eleven won their own title, beating Brunel West London in the final of the British Universities Championship First Eleven Shield, and the Combined Colleges team, effectively the Third Eleven, took the Second Eleven title against Exeter. The Ladies also reached their British Universities final but, like their male counterparts, fell victim to Loughborough. Durham greatly missed the services of the talented Caroline Atkins, away on Test duty with England against Australia, as they subsided for 171 in reply to Loughborough's 210. – GRENVILLE HOLLAND.

DURHAM UCCE RESULTS

First-class matches – Played 3: Drawn 3.

FIRST-CLASS AVERAGES

BATTING AND FIELDING

	M	*I*	*NO*	*R*	*HS*	*100s*	*50s*	*Avge*	*Ct/St*
J. S. Foster	3	3	0	185	103	1	1	61.66	4/2
M. J. Brown	3	5	1	168	60*	0	2	42.00	2
J. G. C. Rowe	3	4	1	113	74*	0	1	37.66	1
M. J. Banes	3	4	1	41	25*	0	0	13.66	1
R. S. Ferley	3	3	1	26	17*	0	0	13.00	1
J. T. A. Bruce	3	3	1	19	14*	0	0	9.50	0
H. J. H. Loudon	3	4	1	26	16	0	0	8.66	1
T. J. Phillips	3	3	0	17	15	0	0	5.66	0

Also batted: R. G. Gilbert (1 match) 0; W. I. Jefferson (1 match) 22, 24; A. G. R. Loudon (2 matches) 39, 3 (1 ct); R. A. Stead (2 matches) 0, 28 (1 ct); M. Thorburn (2 matches) 8*, 11; C. G. van der Gucht (1 match) 38.

* *Signifies not out.*

BOWLING

	O	*M*	*R*	*W*	*BB*	*5W/i*	*Avge*
A. G. R. Loudon	20	5	86	3	3-86	0	28.66
M. J. Banes	46	8	162	3	3-65	0	54.00
R. S. Ferley	82	19	271	5	3-52	0	54.20
T. J. Phillips	82	17	321	5	2-80	0	64.20

Also bowled: J. T. A. Bruce 48–6–211–0; R. G. Gilbert 18–5–54–0; R. A. Stead 35–5–107–0; M. Thorburn 34–5–159–2; C. G. van der Gucht 12–1–63–1.

At Chester-le-Street, April 16, 17, 18. DURHAM UCCE drew with DURHAM.

DURHAM UCCE v LANCASHIRE

At Durham, June 13, 14, 15. Drawn. Toss: Lancashire. First-class debuts: A. G. R. Loudon, M. Thorburn; K. W. Hogg.

The University performed far better on their home first-class debut than they had up the road against Durham County two months earlier. Lancashire fielded no fewer than three former Durham University batsmen – Driver, Chilton and Roberts – though none reached 20 on his return to the Racecourse Ground. The first day was enlivened by a sparkling 78 from Foster, who struck 11 fours in nearly four hours before succumbing to debutant Kyle Hogg, the grandson of Sonny Ramadhin and son of the former Lancashire and Warwickshire fast bowler, Willie Hogg. The second day, however, belonged to Flintoff. Leading Lancashire for the first time, he added a measure of responsibility to his usual belligerence, although this did not prevent him from bludgeoning a high percentage of his 22 fours. Fifties from Schofield and Yates provided the back-up, but the University managed to keep Lancashire's lead to 121 and a sepulchral third day saved them from any likelihood of defeat.

Close of play: First day, Lancashire 18-0 (Driver 11*, Chilton 2*); Second day, Lancashire 372.

Durham UCCE

M. J. Brown c Haynes b Hogg	22	– not out	6
J. G. C. Rowe c Schofield b Yates	28	– not out	15
*M. J. Banes lbw b Yates	6		
A. G. R. Loudon b Keedy	39		
†J. S. Foster c Roberts b Hogg	78		
H. J. H. Loudon lbw b Schofield	7		
T. J. Phillips b Schofield	2		
R. S. Ferley lbw b Schofield	6		
C. G. van der Gucht run out	38		
M. Thorburn not out	8		
J. T. A. Bruce b Hogg	4		
B 1, l-b 8, w 1, n-b 3	13		
1/51 2/61 3/64 4/116 5/133 6/135 7/145 8/234 9/243	251		(no wkt) 21

Bowling: *First Innings*—Smethurst 18–4–48–0; Wood 8.2–2–29–0; Hogg 9–3–17–3; Flintoff 9–4–23–0; Yates 19–6–23–2; Keedy 18.4–8–36–1; Schofield 18–3–53–3; Chilton 4–0–13–0. *Second Innings*—Smethurst 3–0–8–0; Hogg 3–0–13–0.

Lancashire

R. C. Driver b Phillips	16
M. J. Chilton c Foster b Thorburn	16
†J. J. Haynes c A. G. R. Loudon b Banes	30
*A. Flintoff b Phillips	120
T. W. Roberts c Foster b van der Gucht	17
C. P. Schofield b Banes	62
G. Yates c H. J. H. Loudon b Banes	57
K. W. Hogg c and b Ferley	19
J. Wood not out	15
G. Keedy c Brown b Ferley	0
M. P. Smethurst c Banes b Ferley	0
B 1, l-b 16, w 2, n-b 1	20
1/28 2/45 3/110 4/165 5/241 6/296 7/347 8/364 9/372	372

Bowling: Bruce 5–1–12–0; Thorburn 25–5–83–1; Phillips 15–2–80–2; Ferley 22–9–52–3; Banes 18–3–65–3; van der Gucht 12–1–63–1.

Umpires: J. H. Evans and D. R. Shepherd.

At Worcester, June 20, 21, 22. DURHAM UCCE drew with WORCESTERSHIRE.

OTHER UCCES, 2001

By GRENVILLE HOLLAND

The disparity between the six Centres of Excellence and the first-class counties was made very clear from the outset. Whether professional superiority was converted into victory often depended on the intentions of the counties, some of whom regarded the games simply as useful practice in the middle, some as contests to be won. Another reason for the number of draws was the inclement weather, which claimed so many hours of play.

Loughborough, who swept the board in the Inter-UCCE and BUSA inter-university competitions, lost all three of their county games. They began the season at Grace Road, where an unforgiving Leicestershire crushed them by 249 runs; Loughborough's John Francis scored a century in the first innings, but they were rolled over for 73 in the second. Against Nottinghamshire a few days later, they conceded 526 and went down by an innings and 131 runs. Several weeks after that, a trip to The Oval saw Surrey beat them by 231 runs.

One way to measure the relative performance of the students and the counties is to compare runs per wicket for and against the university teams. Overall, Loughborough compiled 1,068 runs for the loss of 59 wickets, an average of 18.10 runs per wicket; their county opponents accumulated 1,679 runs for 37, an average of 45.37. Dividing Loughborough's average by their opponents' produces a relative performance factor of 0.39 – if they had been on level terms, this RPF would have been around 1.00.

Of the three UCCEs who, unlike Loughborough, were granted first-class status, Durham drew all three county games and had an RPF of 0.37; Oxford drew two matches, with the third washed out, and had an RPF of 0.44; while Cambridge's statistics were lost one, drew two, RPF 0.22. Of the remaining non-first-class UCCEs, Cardiff were victims of atrocious weather; their first two games, against Somerset and Gloucestershire, never saw a ball bowled. When they finally made it on to the field, against Glamorgan in June, they lost by 140 runs, which gave them an RPF of 0.44. Bradford/Leeds lost to Northamptonshire and Yorkshire by an innings, after drawing their opening match with Derbyshire, and finished with an RPF of just 0.20, the lowest of all.

Allowing for local conditions and the whims of county captains, these relative statistics were reflected to some extent in the inter-UCCE competition, where Cambridge and Bradford/Leeds languished at the bottom of the table, well behind the other four. But the fact that even the stronger teams were still well short of 0.50 of the professionals' performance illustrated how far the UCCEs had to go.

Notes: Matches in this section were not first-class. UCCE away games may be found in the county sections.

At Derby, April 16, 17, 18. BRADFORD/LEEDS UCCE drew with DERBYSHIRE.

At Leicester, April 16, 17, 18. LOUGHBOROUGH UCCE lost to LEICESTERSHIRE by 249 runs.

At Taunton, April 16, 17, 18. SOMERSET v CARDIFF UCCE. Cancelled.

At Nottingham, April 20, 21, 22. LOUGHBOROUGH UCCE lost to NOTTINGHAMSHIRE by an innings and 131 runs.

At Abergavenny, April 25, 26, 27. CARDIFF UCCE v GLOUCESTERSHIRE. Cancelled.

At Northampton, May 17, 18, 19. BRADFORD/LEEDS UCCE lost to NORTHAMPTONSHIRE by an innings and 66 runs.

At The Oval, May 30, 31, June 1. LOUGHBOROUGH UCCE lost to SURREY by 231 runs.

At Bradford, June 20, 21. Yorkshire won by an innings and 186 runs. Toss: Bradford/Leeds UCCE. Bradford/Leeds UCCE 129 (S. J. Birtwisle 38; P. M. Hutchison three for 39, G. M. Hamilton three for 35) and 74 (P. M. Hutchison three for 14); Yorkshire 389 for five dec. (M. J. Wood 48, M. J. Lumb 107, G. M. Hamilton 67, D. H. Wigley 32, V. J. Craven 80 not out; C. J. Elstub three for 79).

Yorkshire won with a day to spare. County debuts: A. K. D. Gray, D. H. Wigley.

At Cardiff, June 20, 21, 22. CARDIFF UCCE lost to GLAMORGAN by 140 runs.

INTER-UCCE CRICKET, 2001

By GRENVILLE HOLLAND

In addition to their three-day games against the counties, and taking part in the long-established inter-university BUSA competition, the six UCCEs played their own tournament. The Inter-UCCE Championship consisted of a league played under two-day "grade" rules on the Australian model, similar to those the Minor Counties tried in 1998 and 1999, followed by a One-Day Challenge for the top two teams. Loughborough won both the Championship Shield, for heading the table, and the Challenge, defeating Durham at Lord's.

To produce an outright result, two-day cricket frequently relies on three declarations plus a fourth-innings run-chase. However, with ten points offered for a first-innings win – the same as for an outright win (though that could be raised to 15 if combined with a first-innings lead) – and bonus points available in both innings, most teams were happy to concentrate on securing a first-innings win and as many bonus points as possible. The matches were scheduled for a minimum of 204 overs. A typical contest, between Bradford/Leeds and Oxford at Bradford Park Avenue in June, illustrates the strategy. Oxford took 106.1 overs to score 229; in reply, Bradford/Leeds managed 219 in 93.2 overs. Oxford were awarded 16 points (ten for the first-innings lead, two for batting and four for bowling), Bradford/Leeds received six (two batting, four bowling). Despite the dreary run-rate, both sides were satisfied that this was an excellent game with a fair outcome, which helps explain why, out of 15 UCCE fixtures, only two ended with an outright result.

Both were won by Durham – innings victories over Cambridge and Bradford/Leeds at the Racecourse Ground in May – and bore the strong imprint of academic commitments. Durham's players, with home advantage, could sit their examinations at dawn, whereas those with exams at the visiting university had to forego the fixture. Bad weather prevented Durham from reaching even a first-innings result in their other three games, and so they finished behind Loughborough, who never won a match outright but had four first-innings wins and more bonus points than anyone else. These two were well ahead of the field, and so advanced to the 50-over Challenge match at Lord's, where Loughborough beat Durham for the third time in 2001.

INTER-UCCE CHAMPIONSHIP, 2001

					1st-inns	*Bonus points*		
	Played	*Won*	*Lost*	*Drawn*	*points*	*Batting*	*Bowling*	*Points*
Loughborough	5	0	0	5	43	13	24	80
Durham	5	2	0	3	9	10	22	71
Cardiff	5	0	0	5	33	11	15	58*
Oxford	5	0	0	5	23	11	18	52
Cambridge	5	0	1	4	10	11	15	36
Bradford/Leeds	5	0	1	4	0	9	16	25

Outright win = 10 pts; 1st-innings lead in a match reaching an outright result = 5 pts; 1st-innings win in a drawn match = 10 pts; no result on 1st innings = 3 pts.
Up to four bonus points for batting and bowling were available in each innings, though in the first innings batting points were available only for the first 102 overs (or 50 per cent of the total overs in a shortened match). The first innings of the side batting first could not use more than 60 per cent of the total overs available in the match.

* *1 pt deducted for slow over-rate.*

Note: Matches in this section were not first-class.

At Bradford, May 1, 2. Drawn. Cambridge won by 35 runs on first innings. Bradford/Leeds 190 (C. J. Elstub 57 not out, S. Noach 30; T. R. Hughes three for 38) and 78 for two; Cambridge 225 (B. J. Collins 55, V. H. Kumar 51; N. P. Murrills four for 32). *Bradford/Leeds 5 pts, Cambridge 16 pts.*

At Loughborough, May 1, 2. Drawn. Loughborough won by 50 runs on first innings. Cardiff 150 (M. A. Tournier five for 30) and 103 for seven; Loughborough 200 for nine. *Loughborough 19 pts, Cardiff 6 pts.*

At Oxford, May 1, 2. Drawn (no result). Durham 203 for nine (M. J. Banes 36, H. J. H. Loudon 42; T. Mees four for 51, J. W. M. Dalrymple three for 57) v Oxford. *Oxford 7 pts, Durham 5 pts.*

At Cardiff, May 9, 10. Drawn. Cardiff won by three wickets on first innings. Bradford/Leeds 251 for eight dec. (H. Marambe 82, J. W. M. Lucas 57); Cardiff 253 for seven (A. N. Bressington 48, J. Cook 42). *Cardiff 16 pts, Bradford/Leeds 6 pts.*

At Oxford, May 9, 10. Drawn. Loughborough won by two wickets on first innings. Oxford 334 for nine (M. K. Floyd 33, A. S. Bones 84, N. Millar 32, T. C. Hicks 67 not out; M. A. Tournier five for 81, A. M. Dobson three for 71); Loughborough 335 for eight (S. A. Selwood 128, M. T. Byrne 30, J. D. Francis 71, M. J. Powell 47; J. W. M. Dalrymple four for 117). *Oxford 6 pts, Loughborough 18 pts.*

At Abergavenny, May 15, 16. Drawn. Cardiff won by 45 runs on first innings. Oxford 206 (J. W. M. Dalrymple 37, J. J. Porter 38, H. R. Jones 46; C. Yates three for 43) and 49 for one (C. C. M. Warren 34 not out); Cardiff 251 for six dec. (A. N. French 82, A. N. Bressington 105; T. J. Sharpe four for 40). *Cardiff 17 pts, Oxford 4 pts.*

At Durham, May 15, 16. Drawn (no result). Loughborough 217 (S. A. Selwood 82; T. J. Phillips four for 90, R. S. Ferley three for 73) v Durham. *Durham 7 pts, Loughborough 5 pts.*

At Bradford, May 22, 23. Drawn. Loughborough won by 67 runs on first innings. Bradford/Leeds 120 (G. I. Maiden four for 33) and 201 for eight (A. P. Siddall 66); Loughborough 187 (S. A. Selwood 64; T. D. Durance three for ten). *Bradford/Leeds 7 pts, Loughborough 18 pts.*

Appearing for Bradford/Leeds, England international Kathryn Leng became the first woman to play in an otherwise male match at this level.

At Durham, May 22, 23. Durham won by an innings and 33 runs. Cambridge 118 (J. P. Pyemont 39; R. S. Ferley three for 24) and 163 (J. A. Heath 39, A. H. V. Johnson 31; R. S. Ferley three for 19); Durham 314 for seven dec. (A. G. R. Loudon 85, T. J. Phillips 40, R. A. Stead 76 not out, R. S. Ferley 34 not out). *Durham 27 pts, Cambridge 5 pts.*

At Cambridge, May 29, 30. Drawn. Oxford won by 164 runs on first innings. Oxford 309 for eight dec. (M. K. Floyd 84, J. J. Porter 118, N. Millar 45; T. R. Hughes three for 63); Cambridge 145 (G. J. Dill 40; J. W. M. Dalrymple four for 69, T. C. Hicks three for 36) and 108 for three (V. H. Kumar 38, G. J. Dill 36 not out; T. C. Hicks three for 39). *Cambridge 4 pts, Oxford 19 pts.*

At Durham, May 29, 30. Durham won by an innings and 124 runs. Durham 300 for four dec. (A. G. R. Loudon 131 not out); Bradford/Leeds 90 (C. G. van der Gucht five for 33) and 86 (R. G. Gilbert four for 22, R. S. Ferley three for nine). *Durham 27 pts, Bradford/Leeds 1 pt.*

At Durham, June 6, 7. Drawn (no result). Cardiff 143 for six (A. N. French 49, J. Cook 33; T. J. Phillips four for 30) v Durham. *Durham 5 pts, Cardiff 3 pts.*

At Loughborough, June 6, 7. Drawn. Loughborough won by 174 runs on first innings. Cambridge 128 (V. H. Kumar 52; M. A. Tournier three for 30, A. M. Dobson four for 37) and 327 for six (J. P. Pyemont 136, J. L. Hartley 64); Loughborough 302 for three dec. (S. A. Selwood 126, N. C. Stovold 115). *Loughborough 20 pts, Cambridge 5 pts.*

At Bradford, June 13, 14. Drawn. Oxford won by ten runs on first innings. Oxford 229 (A. S. Bones 39, S. J. Hawinkels 50; R. A. McLean three for 44); Bradford/Leeds 219 (J. W. M. Lucas

41, S. J. Birtwisle 57; T. J. Sharpe three for 60, T. C. Hicks four for 55). *Bradford/Leeds 6 pts, Oxford 16 pts.*

At Cambridge, June 13, 14. Drawn. Cardiff won by 12 runs on first innings. Cardiff 235 (G. McCulloch 35, E. Brown 30; T. R. Hughes three for 64, J. P. Pyemont five for 63) and 103 for one (A. N. French 38 not out, J. Cook 38); Cambridge 223 (V. H. Kumar 53, C. A. Sayers 54; A. N. French six for 53). *Cambridge 6 pts, Cardiff 16 pts.*

ONE-DAY UCCE CHALLENGE

DURHAM v LOUGHBOROUGH

At Lord's, June 27. Loughborough won by 22 runs. Toss: Durham.

Having met three times already in the season, the players were not surprisingly tired of the sight of each other. Moreover, with the academic term ended, many were looking ahead to playing for their counties, and this seemed more like an exhibition match than the earlier British Universities final at Fenner's. Still, given the rivalry between the sides, Loughborough welcomed another triumph over their first-class opponents. Despite a 52-ball 40 from Nick Stovold, they had looked in trouble when Alex Stead reduced them to 82 for four. But Durham could not capitalise on this advantage; former team-mate Rob White scored a thoughtful 58, ably supported by Matthew Byrne, and the target ended up being a challenging 215. A steady 44 from Michael Brown gave Durham a much better start than in the British Universities final, and they were up with the asking-rate at 123 for four. However, three run-outs changed the complexion of the chase, and Mark Tournier, Durham's tormentor at Fenner's, wrapped it up with 21 balls to spare.

Man of the Match: R. A. White.

Loughborough

S. A. Selwood b Thorburn	21
N. C. Stovold c Ferley b Stead	40
J. D. Francis b Stead	4
*M. J. Powell c Loudon b Stead	4
R. A. White c Stead b Phillips	58
M. T. Byrne c Foster b Phillips	31
D. W. Furnivall st Foster b Banes	1
†C. P. Coleman not out	18
G. R. Johnson c Foster b Phillips	0
M. A. Tournier not out	17
L-b 2, w 8, n-b 10	20
1/41 2/71 3/76 4/82 5/167 6/168 7/178 8/178 (8 wkts, 50 overs)	214

A. M. Dobson did not bat.

Bowling: Bruce 10–2–43–0; Thorburn 5–0–30–1; Stead 10–0–37–3; Ferley 10–1–42–0; van der Gucht 7–1–23–0; Phillips 7–0–33–3; Banes 1–0–4–1.

Durham

M. J. Brown c Stovold b Powell	44
J. G. C. Rowe c Francis b Tournier	4
*M. J. Banes c Coleman b Dobson	18
A. G. R. Loudon lbw b Powell	6
†J. S. Foster c Powell b White	32
T. J. Phillips run out	13
R. A. Stead c Powell b Tournier	29
R. S. Ferley run out	17
C. G. van der Gucht run out	1
M. Thorburn b Tournier	4
J. T. A. Bruce not out	1
L-b 5, w 14, n-b 4	23
1/10 2/57 3/89 4/94 5/123 6/150 7/177 8/179 9/191 (46.3 overs)	192

Bowling: Tournier 8.3–1–22–3; Dobson 10–1–27–1; Johnson 2–0–27–0; Powell 6–1–19–2; White 10–0–48–1; Francis 10–0–44–0.

Umpires: G. I. Burgess and N. G. Cowley.

THE HALIFAX BRITISH UNIVERSITIES CHAMPIONSHIP, 2001

By GRENVILLE HOLLAND

Durham and Loughborough continued their domination of the inter-university championship. Loughborough retained the Premier title, crushing Durham in the final at Cambridge, but Durham had the distinction of reaching four British Universities finals. Their Ladies team also lost to Loughborough, but the men's Second Eleven claimed the First Eleven Shield, winning their final against Brunel West London, and their Combined Colleges side beat Exeter in the Second Eleven Championship. Derby won the First Eleven Plate, defeating South Bank.

Since 2000, the Premier League had been reduced from 18 teams to 12, divided into two regional leagues, rather than three. Half of the places were taken by the six University Centres of Cricketing Excellence established by the ECB.

Exeter topped the Southern league, winning all but one of their five matches – a six-wicket defeat by St Mary's University College, Twickenham, who were unlucky not to reach the semi-finals in their first season at this level. St Mary's won three matches, all chasing a target, but were squeezed out on net run-rate by Oxford UCCE, with whom they tied on points. Oxford were the only other team to threaten Exeter's dominance, losing to them by a single run, and their 98-run victory over St Mary's eventually proved enough to nose them ahead in the table.

In the Northern league, Loughborough easily won all five of their games, the tightest being the five-wicket victory over Cambridge UCCE. They beat a lacklustre Durham by nine wickets, though Durham had no difficulty qualifying in their wake. Apart from a washout against Bradford/Leeds UCCE, they won their three remaining matches by large margins, and quite destroyed Nottingham, who were all out for 100 in reply to 447 for three.

In the semi-finals, Durham defeated Southern leaders Exeter, despite having to field first without a full eleven when some of their players were late arriving at The Parks. Alex Loudon, whose older brother Hugh was also in the side, hit an unbeaten fifty to guide them home by six wickets. Meanwhile, at Dean Park, Bournemouth, Loughborough were thrashing Oxford by ten wickets; Mark Tournier and Mark Powell bowled them out for 153, and a century from left-hander Steve Selwood saw Loughborough complete victory in less than half their allotted 50 overs. Durham provided a little more resistance, but no serious problems, in the final.

BRITISH UNIVERSITIES PREMIER LEAGUES

Southern	*Played*	*Won*	*Lost*	*No result*	*Points*
EXETER	5	4	1	0	12
OXFORD UCCE	5	3	1	1	10
St Mary's	5	3	1	1	10
Bristol	5	2	2	1	7
Cardiff UCCE	5	1	3	1	4
Reading	5	0	5	0	0

Northern	Played	Won	Lost	No result	Points
LOUGHBOROUGH UCCE	5	5	0	0	15
DURHAM UCCE	5	3	1	1	10
Bradford/Leeds UCCE	5	2	2	1	7
Cambridge UCCE	5	1	3	1	4
Nottingham	5	1	3	1	4
Liverpool	5	1	4	0	3

Where two or more teams finished level on points, the positions were decided by net run-rate.

Liverpool beat Reading in a relegation play-off; Reading were replaced by Brunel West London, the runners-up in the First Eleven Shield, because Shield winners Durham already had a team in the Premier League.

SEMI-FINALS

At Oxford, June 11. Durham won by six wickets. Toss: Exeter. Exeter 231 for seven (50 overs) (C. Coulson 91, R. Marshall 63); Durham 232 for four (48.3 overs) (A. G. R. Loudon 55 not out).

At Bournemouth, June 11. Loughborough won by ten wickets. Toss: Oxford. Oxford 153 (44.5 overs) (J. W. M. Dalrymple 36, A. S. Bones 30; M. A. Tournier three for 27, M. J. Powell three for 35); Loughborough 157 for no wkt (24 overs) (S. A. Selwood 100 not out, N. C. Stovold 49 not out).

FINAL

DURHAM v LOUGHBOROUGH

At Cambridge, June 18. Loughborough won by 78 runs. Toss: Durham.

Loughborough emerged comfortable winners of a low-scoring match. Invited to bat on a slow pitch, they made steady but not spectacular headway against a moderate attack. John Francis and Rob White, both former Durham students, held the innings together, and Scotland international Greg Maiden contributed a late flourish as Charlie van der Gucht's left-arm spin chipped away at the other end. Durham made the worst possible start when Mark Tournier, a 30-year-old Australian and Loughborough's perennial postgraduate, removed three men for ducks with his ambling out-swingers in his first two overs. Only James Foster, with a sweet taste of the talent that was attracting England's selectors, picked up the challenge, scoring the game's sole fifty and helping Durham recover from 11 for four to 92 without further loss. From there, however, Loughborough's off-spinners, captain Mark Powell and Maiden, nipped out Durham's remaining six wickets for 27.

Loughborough

S. A. Selwood b Bruce	18
N. C. Stovold c and b Ferley	26
J. D. Francis run out	35
*M. J. Powell lbw b Phillips	8
R. A. White c Rowe b van der Gucht	38
D. W. Furnivall lbw b van der Gucht	0
G. I. Maiden not out	33
D. F. Watts st Foster b van der Gucht	6
†C. P. Coleman lbw b van der Gucht	0
M. A. Tournier not out	3
B 6, l-b 7, w 3, n-b 14	30
1/36 2/88 3/103 4/121 5/122 6/178 7/186 8/186 (8 wkts, 50 overs)	197

A. M. Dobson did not bat.

Bowling: Bruce 10–1–47–1; Thorburn 10–1–43–0; Ferley 10–2–26–1; Phillips 10–0–32–1; van der Gucht 10–1–36–4.

Durham

M. J. Brown c Coleman b Tournier	0	C. G. van der Gucht b Powell	2
J. G. C. Rowe c Maiden b Tournier	0	M. Thorburn not out	8
*M. J. Banes c Powell b Dobson	7	J. T. A. Bruce lbw b Maiden	5
A. G. R. Loudon b Tournier	0		
†J. S. Foster c Maiden b Powell	53	B 1, l-b 7, w 4	12
H. J. H. Loudon c Coleman b Powell	27		
T. J. Phillips st Coleman b Maiden	5	1/0 2/7 3/7 4/11 5/92 (40.5 overs)	119
R. S. Ferley c Coleman b Maiden	0	6/103 7/103 8/105 9/105	

Bowling: Tournier 6–1–17–3; Dobson 10–0–29–1; Watts 5–0–16–0; Powell 10–1–21–3; Maiden 9.5–0–28–3.

Umpires: K. Hopley and R. McLeod.

WINNERS 1927–2001

The UAU Championship was replaced by the British Universities Championship from 1995.

1927 Manchester
1928 Manchester
1929 Nottingham
1930 Sheffield
1931 Liverpool
1932 Manchester
1933 Manchester
1934 Leeds
1935 Sheffield
1936 Sheffield
1937 Nottingham
1938 Durham
1939 Durham
1946 Not completed
1947 Sheffield
1948 Leeds
1949 Leeds
1950 Manchester
1951 Manchester
1952 Loughborough Colls.
1953 Durham
1954 Manchester
1955 Birmingham
1956 Null and void
1957 Loughborough Colls.
1958 Null and void
1959 Liverpool
1960 Loughborough Colls.
1961 Loughborough Colls.
1962 Manchester
1963 Loughborough Colls.
1964 Loughborough Colls.
1965 Hull
1966 {Newcastle / Southampton}
1967 Manchester
1968 Southampton
1969 Southampton
1970 Southampton
1971 Loughborough Colls.
1972 Durham
1973 {Leicester / Loughborough Colls.}
1974 Durham
1975 Loughborough Colls.
1976 Loughborough
1977 Durham
1978 Manchester
1979 Manchester
1980 Exeter
1981 Durham
1982 Exeter
1983 Exeter
1984 Bristol
1985 Birmingham
1986 Durham
1987 Durham
1988 Swansea
1989 Loughborough
1990 Durham
1991 Durham
1992 Durham
1993 Durham
1994 Swansea
1995 Durham
1996 Loughborough
1997 Durham
1998 {Durham / Loughborough}
1999 Durham
2000 Loughborough
2001 Loughborough

MCC MATCHES, 2001

By STEVEN LYNCH

Once again MCC arranged more than 400 matches against schools, clubs and representative bodies. In an indifferent summer, not quite that many took place – 49 matches were abandoned without a ball bowled, and 11 cancelled, most because of the ramifications of foot-and-mouth disease. Of the games that were played, MCC won almost twice as many as they lost – 158 to 82. A further 111 were drawn, 27 with significant interference from the weather, and the match against St Bartholomew's School ended in a tie.

The only first-class match was played not at Lord's or, as in recent years, at Shenley Park, but in the beautiful surroundings of Arundel Castle. Although MCC fielded a strong multinational side, captained by West Indian Jimmy Adams, the Australian tourists won by 280 runs, with Simon Katich making a stroke-filled 168 in their first innings.

In all, 77 centuries were scored for MCC in 2001. Heath Pedrola, a Queenslander, and Phil Wise made three each, as did Tim O'Gorman, the ex-Derbyshire batsman. O'Gorman's undefeated 107 against Eastbourne College was followed by seven for 64 from his father, Brian. Jeffrey Clarke hit 130 and 151 not out against Woodbridge School and Framlingham College on successive days, while Stephen Benjamin, Jamie Butler, Stephen Cook (son of the former South African opener, Jimmy), Matthew Dallaway, Russell Evans, Edward Fowler and Mike Hood also reached two centuries during the season. Butler's 159 not out – he scored the third fifty from only 15 balls – in a match to celebrate the centenary of the I'Anson League in Surrey, was the highest individual score for MCC in 2001. However, schoolboy Joe Hill trumped it with 165 not out for Wells Cathedral School, who made light of a testing target to beat MCC by six wickets.

Despite what the manager described as the "banquet interval", 553 runs were scored in a day at Bath, where MCC (275 for five) narrowly lost to Lansdown CC (278 for seven). Even that aggregate was topped when the Warwickshire Pilgrims (299 for eight) progressed past MCC's 298. The best bowling analysis of the year was seven for 20 by Pakistan leg-spinner Iqbal Sikandar against Arnold School. Sikandar also returned match figures of ten for 66 to secure victory over Durham University.

The MCC women's team continued to expand their programme. In 2001, 13 matches were arranged; three were won, two lost, six drawn (in three of which the opposition had nine wickets down) and two abandoned. For the first time, MCC sent a women's team on tour, to The Netherlands, where they won two matches against the Dutch national side and lost one. In the first game, Enid Bakewell, the England all-rounder of the 1960s and 1970s, scored 54 at the age of 60.

MCC's male teams made several overseas trips, visiting Bermuda, Germany, Hong Kong, Namibia, Portugal, South America – where Middlesex's Chad Keegan clubbed 142 not out against Chile – Sri Lanka, and Thailand and Singapore. MCC Young Cricketers won 18 of their 38 matches, including victories over the Second Elevens of Durham, Essex, Kent, Somerset and Sussex. Bazid Khan topped the averages with 795 runs at 61.15, including 145 against Oxford UCCE. His father, Majid, caned Oxford for 200 in the 1970 Varsity Match.

Cross Arrows, the club that plays on the Nursery Ground at Lord's every September, celebrated a record innings of 226 not out by their secretary, Kevin Sedgbeer, against the Adastrians. Clive Radley, the former England batsman who is now MCC's head coach, scored three centuries and a 91. Of the Cross Arrows' 16 matches, three were won, two lost, six drawn and five abandoned.

Note: Matches in this section were not first-class except for the game v Australians.

At Sidmouth, April 29. Devon won by eight wickets. Toss: Devon. MCC 123 for eight (40 overs) (J. F. M. Nicolson 34; P. M. Warren three for 19); Devon 124 for two (32.1 overs) (D. F. Lye 53, N. A. Folland 37 not out).

At Lord's, May 4. MCC Young Cricketers won by four wickets. Toss: MCC. MCC 185 for six dec. (R. A. Kettleborough 53, G. S. Katz 40; A. A. Duncan five for 54); MCC Young Cricketers 186 for six (R. J. Nicol 34, Bazid Khan 53, M. J. W. Wright 31 not out; I. J. Curtis three for 32).

At Walsall, May 9. England Board XI won by 36 runs. Toss: MCC. England Board XI 262 for four (50 overs) (P. R. J. Bryson 65, J. R. Wood 77, S. Chapman 47 not out); MCC 226 (48.3 overs) (D. R. Clarke 70, A. Saleem 38; P. E. Wellings three for 33).

At Oxford, May 21, 22, 23. MCC beat OXFORD UNIVERSITY by 104 runs (see The Universities section).

At Shenley Park, May 29. MCC won by 101 runs. Toss: Ireland. MCC 291 for four (50 overs) (M. H. Richardson 117, J. D. Bean 72, Z. de Bruyn 47 not out); Ireland 190 (38.5 overs) (A. R. White 69, P. J. K. Mooney 34; G. T. Prince three for 31).

At Wimbledon, May 30. MCC won by two wickets. Toss: Club Cricket Conference. Club Cricket Conference 170 for seven (55 overs) (G. Martin 51, A. Richards 55; J. R. Wileman four for 18); MCC 173 for eight (52.3 overs) (D. R. Thomas 43 not out; M. Stear three for 37, R. Ellison three for 45).

At Shenley Park, May 30. MCC won by nine wickets. Toss: Ireland. Ireland 164 (48 overs) (W. K. McCallan 41; Z. de Bruyn three for 18, M. P. W. Jeh three for 24); MCC 168 for one (31.4 overs) (M. H. Richardson 77, J. D. Bean 60 not out).

At Shenley Park, May 31. Ireland won by four wickets. Toss: MCC. MCC 167 for nine (50 overs) (J. D. Robinson 55); Ireland 170 for six (42.4 overs) (J. D. Curry 57 not out).

At Lord's, June 14. Drawn. Toss: Wales. MCC 223 for nine dec. (R. J. Boon 34, M. W. Gatting 36, G. R. E. Martin 61); Wales 103 for one (M. J. Newbold 63 not out, R. I. Clitheroe 36 not out).

At Cambridge, June 20, 21, 22. MCC lost to CAMBRIDGE UNIVERSITY by three wickets (see The Universities section).

At Arundel, June 25, 26, 27. MCC lost to AUSTRALIANS by 280 runs (see Australian tour section).

At Durham, June 25, 26, 27. MCC won by 210 runs. Toss: MCC. MCC 315 for nine dec. (J. D. Bean 33, M. R. Bradshaw 33, H. T. Pedrola 110, P. E. Wellings 45; S. L. J. M. Hawk three for 63) and 176 for four dec. (Iqbal Sikandar 74, M. R. Bradshaw 34 not out, J. D. Gray 36; R. G. Gilbert three for 32); Durham University 85 (W. A. Kirby 52; R. Kotkamp five for 18, Iqbal Sikandar four for 13) and 196 (W. A. Kirby 70, A. Hollingsworth 32, M. F. Thomson 34; Iqbal Sikandar six for 53).

At Arundel, July 1. Earl of Arundel's XI won by 127 runs. Toss: Earl of Arundel's XI. Earl of Arundel's XI 259 for five dec. (G. Morgan 59, D. Penfold 40 not out, C. J. Hollins 100 not out); MCC 132 (A. J. Murphy 34; D. P. Mather six for 31, R. O. Jones three for 55).

At Castleford, July 4. MCC won by seven wickets. Toss: University of New South Wales. University of New South Wales 164 (50 overs) (D. Christian 49; Iqbal Sikandar four for 24); MCC 165 for three (41.1 overs) (J. S. Booth 53 not out, M. I. Mortimer 63).

At Wormsley, July 11. Sir Paul Getty's XI won by seven wickets. Toss: MCC. MCC 184 for nine dec. (N. R. Gaywood 70, G. J. Kruis 44 not out; D. R. Doshi three for 53); Sir Paul Getty's XI 185 for three (R. J. Bailey 132 not out).

At Lord's, July 24. MCC won by 23 runs. Toss: MCC. MCC 217 for eight (50 overs) (M. W. Cowell 59, W. S. Kendall 43, A. I. C. Dodemaide 46; H. Lane three for 34); Melbourne CC 194 (47.1 overs) (B. J. Hodge 36, L. J. R. McRae 42, C. Sutherland 32 not out; G. J. Kruis three for 26, J. M. Attfield three for 52).

At Exmouth, August 2. Minor Counties won by seven wickets. Toss: Minor Counties. MCC 138 (29.4 overs) (A. Lewin 32, K. G. Sedgbeer 38; S. Rashid four for 40, A. Akhtar three for 16); Minor Counties 141 for three (32.5 overs) (P. R. J. Bryson 32 not out, A. J. Hall 47).

At Scarborough, August 20. MCC won by seven wickets. Toss: Combined Services. Combined Services 163 for nine (50 overs) (S/Off. T. Adcock 43); MCC 165 for three (48.3 overs) (D. F. Watts 34, J. R. Goldthorp 37, A. E. McKenna 41).

At Scarborough, August 22. MCC won by 30 runs. Toss: MCC. MCC 234 for five (50 overs) (H. T. Pedrola 100 not out, R. A. Kettleborough 40); Scotland 204 for nine (50 overs) (C. M. Wright 53; M. P. W. Jeh three for 36).

At Scarborough, August 23, 24. Drawn. Toss: Scotland. Scotland 88 (G. T. Prince four for 34, R. Kotkamp five for 33) and 185 for eight (S. D. Gilmour 37, C. J. O. Smith 63; Iqbal Sikandar five for 53); MCC 155 (R. A. Kettleborough 46 not out, R. Kotkamp 48; C. M. Wright four for 44, D. F. Watts four for 35).

PRESIDENTS OF MCC SINCE 1946

1946	General Sir Ronald Adam, Bart
1947	Captain Lord Cornwallis
1948	Brig.-Gen. The Earl of Gowrie
1949	HRH The Duke of Edinburgh
1950	Sir Pelham Warner
1951-52	W. Findlay
1952-53	The Duke of Beaufort
1953-54	The Earl of Rosebery
1954-55	Viscount Cobham
1955-56	Field Marshal Earl Alexander of Tunis
1956-57	Viscount Monckton of Brenchley
1957-58	The Duke of Norfolk
1958-59	Marshal of the RAF Viscount Portal of Hungerford
1959-60	H. S. Altham
1960-61	Sir Hubert Ashton
1961-62	Col. Sir William Worsley, Bart
1962-63	Lt-Col. Lord Nugent
1963-64	G. O. B. Allen
1964-65	R. H. Twining
1965-66	Lt-Gen. Sir Oliver Leese, Bart
1966-67	Sir Alec Douglas-Home
1967-68	A. E. R. Gilligan
1968-69	R. Aird
1969-70	M. J. C. Allom
1970-71	Sir Cyril Hawker
1971-72	F. R. Brown
1972-73	A. M. Crawley
1973-74	Lord Caccia
1974-75	HRH The Duke of Edinburgh
1975-76	C. G. A. Paris
1976-77	W. H. Webster
1977-78	D. G. Clark
1978-79	C. H. Palmer
1979-80	S. C. Griffith
1980-81	P. B. H. May
1981-82	G. H. G. Doggart
1982-83	Sir Anthony Tuke
1983-84	A. H. A. Dibbs
1984-85	F. G. Mann
1985-86	J. G. W. Davies
1986-87	M. C. Cowdrey
1987-88	J. J. Warr
1988-89	Field Marshal The Lord Bramall
1989-90	The Hon. Sir Denys Roberts
1990-91	The Rt Hon. The Lord Griffiths
1991-92	M. E. L. Melluish
1992-94	D. R. W. Silk
1994-96	The Hon. Sir Oliver Popplewell
1996-98	A. C. D. Ingleby-Mackenzie
1998-2000	A. R. Lewis
2000-01	Lord Alexander of Weedon
2001-02	E. R. Dexter

Since 1951, Presidents of MCC have taken office on October 1. Previously they took office immediately after the annual general meeting at the start of the season. From 1992 to 2000, Presidents were eligible for two consecutive years of office; since then the period has reverted to one year.

OTHER MATCHES, 2001

Note: Matches in this section were not first-class.

At Nottingham, June 30. Sir Richard Hadlee Invitation XI won by seven wickets. Toss: Sir Garfield Sobers Invitation XI. Sir Garfield Sobers Invitation XI 166 for six (45 overs) (P. A. de Silva 32, J. C. Adams 47 not out); Sir Richard Hadlee Invitation XI 167 for three (28.5 overs) (G. Kirsten 74 not out).

This match, and the one the next day, raised funds for developing Trent Bridge pavilion.

At Nottingham, July 1. England Masters XII won by 33 runs. Toss: Australia Masters XII. England Masters XII 248 for eight (45 overs) (R. T. Robinson 38, D. W. Randall 54, A. P. Wells 30, D. A. Reeve 35, C. C. Lewis 41; D. M. Jones three for 41); Australia Masters XII 215 (44.1 overs) (D. C. Boon 44, D. M. Jones 65, A. I. C. Dodemaide 40; D. A. Reeve five for 26).

THE TRIPLE CROWN

At Arundel, August 14. England Board XI won by 32 runs. Toss: England Board XI. England Board XI 214 (49.2 overs) (P. R. J. Bryson 66, R. W. J. Howitt 54, S. Chapman 56; P. Hoffman five for 34); Scotland 182 (45.5 overs) (B. M. W. Patterson 39, C. J. O. Smith 42; I. C. Parkin three for 60).

At Horsham, August 14. Wales won by two wickets. Toss: Ireland. Ireland 149 (44.5 overs) (A. D. Patterson 39; P. E. Jenkins three for 24, K. M. Bell three for 29); Wales 150 for eight (43 overs) (A. J. Jones 45).

At Stirlands, August 15. England Board XI won by six wickets. Toss: Ireland. Ireland 109 (37.4 overs) (D. Joyce 43; C. J. Batt three for 14, M. A. Sharp three for 15); England Board XI 111 for four (24.5 overs) (S. Chapman 33 not out).

At Worthing, August 15. Scotland won by six wickets. Toss: Wales. Wales 120 (49.3 overs); Scotland 121 for four (28 overs) (C. J. O. Smith 35).

At Brighton College, August 16. England Board XI won by 102 runs. Toss: England Board XI. England Board XI 213 for six (50 overs) (C. Amos 65, P. R. J. Bryson 50, S. J. Foster 38); Wales 111 (35.5 overs) (M. A. Sharp three for 15, I. C. Parkin three for 19, S. Chapman three for 18).

England Board XI, who finished bottom of the table in 2000, completed their third straight win to claim the Triple Crown.

At East Grinstead, August 16. Scotland won by three wickets. Toss: Scotland. Ireland 211 (50 overs) (A. D. Patterson 36, P. J. Davy 53, P. G. Gillespie 32; C. M. Wright three for 35); Scotland 214 for seven (48.3 overs) (C. M. Wright 45 not out, G. I. Maiden 79 not out).

Scotland were 88 for seven before Wright and Maiden added 126 for the eighth wicket.

Final table

	Played	*Won*	*Lost*	*Points*
England Board XI	3	3	0	6
Scotland	3	2	1	4
Wales	3	1	2	2
Ireland	3	0	3	0

THE MINOR COUNTIES, 2001

The Minor Counties Championship was shared for the first time since 1900. On that earlier occasion Glamorgan, Durham and Northamptonshire were declared joint-winners, amidst a dispute over whether matches involving Staffordshire and Yorkshire Second Eleven should be included. In 2001, Cheshire and Lincolnshire shared the title after drawing their Championship final, on an unusually flat Grantham pitch. Cheshire were runaway winners of the Western Division, but Lincolnshire had been runners-up in the Eastern Division until the leaders, Cambridgeshire, were found to have unwittingly fielded an ineligible player and had 53 points deducted.

The new Championship format, with each county playing six three-day games, was set to continue for an experimental three-year period, by which time each county would have played all the others in their group on a home and away basis. It was not, however, without its critics. The three-day format may have advantages in that it truly challenges sides, but it poses problems for amateurs with commitments to family and work – especially as companies become less accommodating in allowing employees time off to play cricket. Many counties suffered from not being able to field a regular team. There were discussions, but no decision, concerning the introduction of a different format of three divisions of seven counties, with relegation and promotion, and possibly including as the 21st side the Channel Islands, who were newcomers in 2001 to the ECB 38-County Cup. Norfolk, who won nine of their ten one-day games, were third-time winners of the knockout competition after trouncing Devon in the final.

MINOR COUNTIES CHAMPIONSHIP, 2001

					Bonus Points		*Total*
Eastern Division	*P*	*W*	*L*	*D*	*Batting*	*Bowling*	*Points*
Lincolnshire	6	3	1	2	13	23	92
Staffordshire	6	2	0	4	14	24	86
Northumberland	6	2	0	4	12	22	82
Hertfordshire	6	2	1	3	13	20	77
Cumberland	6	2	2	2	10	23	73
Norfolk	6	1	1	4	10	16	58
Cambridgeshire	6	4	0	2	9	24	52*
Buckinghamshire	6	0	2	4	7	16	39
Suffolk	6	0	4	2	6	17	31
Bedfordshire	6	0	5	1	6	19	29

					Bonus Points		*Total*
Western Division	*P*	*W*	*L*	*D*	*Batting*	*Bowling*	*Points*
Cheshire	6	4	0	2	15	21	108
Shropshire	6	3	0	3	10	23	93
Devon	6	3	1	2	14	22	92
Herefordshire	6	3	2	1	12	23	87
Berkshire	6	3	3	0	8	22	78
Wales	6	1	2	3	14	20	62
Cornwall	6	1	2	3	4	23	53†
Oxfordshire	6	1	3	2	5	17	46
Wiltshire	6	1	3	2	2	19	45
Dorset	6	0	4	2	11	20	39

Final: Lincolnshire drew with Cheshire.

Win = 16 points; draw = 4 points.
** 53 points deducted for fielding an ineligible player.*
† 2 points deducted for slow over-rate.

BEDFORDSHIRE

With many players unavailable for three-day fixtures, Bedfordshire's season was a disappointing one with no wins, despite their twice being in a strong position. In his first year as captain, former Northamptonshire leg-spinner Andy Roberts led by example, scoring the most runs and taking nearly twice as many wickets as anyone else. Newcomers James Knott and Tony Bristow both batted well, and Knott, son of former England keeper Alan, also kept wicket to a high standard. But the opening attack proved expensive and the bowlers generally lacked penetration.

Batting	*M*	*I*	*NO*	*R*	*HS*	*100s*	*50s*	*Avge*
J. A. Knott	4	8	2	360	75*	0	2	60.00
A. R. Roberts	6	11	0	484	113	1	4	44.00
A. R. Bristow	4	8	1	304	114*	1	0	43.42
N. A. Stanley	3	5	0	141	101	1	0	28.20
O. J. Clayson	5	10	0	199	50	0	1	19.90
D. J. M. Mercer	6	12	0	179	34	0	0	14.91
J. G. Hughes	5	9	0	134	41	0	0	14.88

Six matches: S. Rashid 50 runs, W. E. Sneath 39 runs. *Three matches:* N. Coles 61 runs, D. A. Dass 34 runs, R. J. Pack 10 runs, K. Patel 76 runs. *Two matches:* A. A. Shankar 63 runs, M. Stedman 15 runs. *One match:* D. M. Salt 0 runs, W. R. Smith 39 runs, J. Sneath 1 run, C. P. Stern 0 runs, S. J. Watts 4 runs.

Bowling	*O*	*M*	*R*	*W*	*BB*	*5W/i*	*Avge*
A. R. Roberts	181.5	42	541	23	5-70	2	23.52
W. E. Sneath	143.3	40	410	12	5-64	1	34.16
S. Rashid	138	31	524	12	5-72	1	43.66

Other wicket-takers: 9 – R. J. Pack; 6 – J. G. Hughes; 5 – N. A. Stanley; 2 – D. M. Salt.

BERKSHIRE

Julian Wood took over as captain of the young side from Gary Loveday, whose retirement, and that of Simon Myles, left the batting looking frail at times. Even so, a satisfactory mid-table position was achieved with three good victories, all ironically enough within two days. Wales, dismissed for 47 in 28 overs thanks to a return of seven for 26 by pace bowler Nick Denning, and Cornwall were both vanquished by an innings; Dorset were beaten in the last match. Left-arm spinner Richard Davis replaced John Emburey as player-coach and made a big impact, his 36 wickets including nine in each of the last two victories.

Batting	*M*	*I*	*NO*	*R*	*HS*	*100s*	*50s*	*Avge*
J. R. Wood	6	10	0	341	65	0	3	34.10
P. R. Carter	4	7	1	169	64	0	1	28.16
J. R. Perkins	4	7	0	195	76	0	1	27.85
T. L. Lambert	4	6	0	161	86	0	1	26.83
M. G. Lane	5	9	2	187	82	0	1	26.71
L. H. Nurse	5	8	0	180	48	0	0	22.50
S. Wyatt	4	7	0	130	51	0	1	18.57
T. D. Fray	6	10	0	167	51	0	1	16.70
R. P. Davis	6	8	0	100	24	0	0	12.50

Four matches: N. A. Denning 5 runs, S. S. Patel 80 runs. *Three matches:* N. E. L. Gunter 64 runs, J. E. Theunisson 4 runs. *Two matches:* S. A. Seymour 56 runs. *One match:* C. J. Batt 28 runs, T. Burrows 12 runs, G. I. Edwards 10 runs, M. J. O'Sullivan 5 runs, T. Perkins 35 runs, D. M. Williams 8 runs.

Bowling	*O*	*M*	*R*	*W*	*BB*	*5W/i*	*Avge*
S. S. Patel.	43.5	9	142	11	4-11	0	12.90
R. P. Davis	219.2	63	576	36	7-95	4	16.00
N. A. Denning	61.2	18	186	11	7-26	1	16.90

Other wicket-takers: 8 – P. R. Carter, J. E. Theunisson; 7 – N. E. L. Gunter; 6 – T. L. Lambert; 3 – C. J. Batt; 1 – M. J. O'Sullivan.

BUCKINGHAMSHIRE

The three-day format caused problems of availability for Buckinghamshire, who called on 23 players for their six matches, giving debuts to a number of younger players. Experienced leg-spinner Andy Clarke, back in the side after a year with Norfolk, headed the bowling, but without Jamie Bovill, who had moved abroad, the attack lacked a cutting edge. Buckinghamshire finished with fewer bowling points than anyone except Norfolk, who also had 16. Wicket-keeper/batsman Danny Drepaul topped the batting averages in his first season, and shared a second-wicket stand of 229 against Cumberland with Graeme Paskins; both hit hundreds. A low-key season with no Championship wins finished on a high note with qualification for the third round of the 2002 Cheltenham & Gloucester Trophy.

Batting	*M*	*I*	*NO*	*R*	*HS*	*100s*	*50s*	*Avge*
D. R. Drepaul	5	8	2	288	135	1	0	48.00
R. P. Lane.	4	7	0	293	87	0	3	41.85
G. D. T. Paskins.	5	10	0	417	122	1	2	41.70
P. D. Atkins.	6	10	2	302	95*	0	3	37.75
S. P. Naylor.	6	10	2	232	65*	0	1	29.00
A. E. Pusey.	4	6	0	105	64	0	1	17.50

Five matches: A. R. Clarke 39 runs. *Three matches:* S. J. Brandon 24 runs, N. D. Doshi 65 runs, S. F. Stanway 2 runs, A. W. Thomas 41 runs, N. W. Tilley 78 runs, P. J. Woodroffe 20 runs. *Two matches:* J. D. Batty 42 runs, K. J. Locke 42 runs, G. R. Steptoe 85 runs. *One match:* N. Baig 2 runs, S. Bird 18 runs, M. Goldsmith 17 runs, R. A. Jones 4 runs, S. G. Lynch 11 runs, Z. A. Sher 26 runs; T. A. Brooks did not bat.

Bowling	*O*	*M*	*R*	*W*	*BB*	*5W/i*	*Avge*
A. R. Clarke	166.5	40	502	19	6-117	2	26.42
N. D. Doshi	76.4	11	285	10	5-86	1	28.50

Other wicket-takers: 9 – S. P. Naylor; 5 – A. W. Thomas, P. J. Woodroffe; 4 – R. P. Lane; 3 – J. D. Batty, S. J. Brandon; 2 – S. F. Stanway; 1 – S. Bird, M. Goldsmith, N. W. Tilley.

CAMBRIDGESHIRE

Although Cambridgeshire's playing season was a great success, with four wins and more bowling points than any side except Staffordshire, it ended disastrously when they were stripped of the Eastern Division crown after being docked 53 points for fielding an ineligible player. Fast bowler Joe Grant had given inaccurate information regarding his last appearance for Jamaica, in 1995-96, and was found after all to be ineligible in 2001 under Minor Counties qualification rules – despite being able, under first-class county regulations, to make his Championship debut for Essex later in the season. The 53 points were those earned in the three games Grant played, taking 21 wickets against Norfolk, Bedfordshire and Cumberland. Robert Rollins was second-highest run-scorer in the Championship, in which his 204 against Hertfordshire at March was one of only two double-centuries. The season had begun sadly with the death of the president, Maurice Crouch, an outstanding captain and player between 1936 and 1964. He had the second-highest aggregate for Cambridgeshire (8,474) and still held the fifth- and sixth-wicket records.

Batting	*M*	*I*	*NO*	*R*	*HS*	*100s*	*50s*	*Avge*
R. J. Rollins	6	12	1	597	204*	1	4	54.27
D. G. Wilson	6	12	4	393	82	0	3	49.12
S. A. Kellett	5	10	1	312	100*	1	2	34.66
C. Jones	4	8	1	203	75	0	1	29.00
N. T. Gadsby	2	4	0	112	58	0	1	28.00
A. Akhtar	6	9	1	155	46	0	0	19.37
S. Shipp	4	8	1	114	47	0	0	16.28

Six matches: I. N. Blanchett 96 runs, C. D. Durant 35 runs. *Four matches:* R. P. W. Daynes 14 runs. *Three matches:* J. B. Grant 6 runs, A. Khan 84 runs. *Two matches:* J. S. G. Norman 51 runs, B. J. Potter 94 runs, T. D. Smith 0 runs. *One match:* N. J. Adams 31 runs, G. D. Freear 2 runs, T. B. Huggins 18 runs, R. D. Powell 20 runs, R. Pryor 16 runs.

Bowling	*O*	*M*	*R*	*W*	*BB*	*5W/i*	*Avge*
J. B. Grant	104.3	25	260	21	6-34	2	12.38
T. D. Smith	82.5	33	213	12	6-81	1	17.75
A. Akhtar	235.3	79	551	27	4-38	0	20.40
I. N. Blanchett	154	44	411	18	4-28	0	22.83

Other wicket-takers: 9 – D. G. Wilson; 5 – R. P. W. Daynes, A. Khan; 3 – S. A. Kellett, B. J. Potter; 2 – N. T. Gadsby; 1 – J. S. G. Norman.

CHESHIRE

Unbeaten, and with victories over Oxfordshire, Wiltshire, Dorset and Berkshire, Cheshire won the Western Division, going on to share the Championship title with Lincolnshire when the final ended in a draw. Traditionally strong in batting, they also boasted in 2001 an attack that bowled out the opposition twice in five of their six matches. Former Hampshire seamer Simon Renshaw was one of four bowlers to pass 20 wickets. Of the five batsmen making hundreds, Mark Currie and Ian Cockbain did so in the first innings against Dorset. Cockbain, a stalwart of the county for 18 years and captain for the last 11, announced his retirement, having moved to second place behind James Sutton in Cheshire's list of Championship run-scorers, with 8,496 at an average of almost 42, including 16 centuries.

Batting	*M*	*I*	*NO*	*R*	*HS*	*100s*	*50s*	*Avge*
N. T. Wood	1	2	0	140	83	0	2	70.00
A. J. Hall	5	8	2	338	120	1	2	56.33
M. R. Currie	5	10	2	383	121	1	1	47.87
P. R. J. Bryson	4	8	1	318	113	1	3	45.42
I. Cockbain	7	12	2	331	110	1	1	33.10
R. G. Hignett	7	12	1	340	110	1	1	30.90
S. J. Renshaw	5	8	0	196	70	0	1	24.50
N. D. Cross	6	10	2	167	35	0	0	20.87

Six matches: S. Ogilby 45 runs. *Five matches:* C. C. Finegan 44 runs, C. S. Lamb 61 runs. *Four matches:* R. W. Fisher 3 runs, S. J. Marshall 62 runs, J. P. Whittaker 76 runs. *Two matches:* J. Abbas 34 runs, S. M. Eaton 23 runs, R. J. Shenton 90 runs. *One match:* S. Bramhall 19 runs, Z. R. Feather 12 runs; M. W. Hillaby did not bat.

Bowling	*O*	*M*	*R*	*W*	*BB*	*5W/i*	*Avge*
N. D. Cross	116.4	40	293	21	7-40	2	13.95
S. J. Renshaw	164.2	34	534	25	5-57	3	21.36
R. W. Fisher	172.3	44	459	21	7-73	1	21.85
C. S. Lamb	187.4	56	483	22	7-49	1	21.95

Other wicket-takers: 9 – S. J. Marshall, J. P. Whittaker; 7 – C. C. Finegan; 3 – R. G. Hignett; 2 – S. M. Eaton, M. W. Hillaby; 1 – R. J. Shenton.

CORNWALL

A highlight in a mixed season was the performance of opening bowlers Justin Stephens and Charlie Shreck, who took 59 wickets between them – including six in each innings against Wiltshire by Stephens in Cornwall's only win. Less satisfying was the innings defeat at Penzance, where they were dismissed for 78 and 85 by Berkshire, the last county to bowl them out twice for under 100, back in 1969. Work commitments prevented Stephen Williams, Cornwall's fourth-highest run-scorer, from playing, but former captain Godfrey Furse returned at the age of 40 after a season's absence. The Cheltenham & Gloucester Trophy provided consolation for the Championship results. Victory over Cheshire at Camborne in May brought a third-round tie against Sussex at Truro, and September's first-ever win on Cheshire soil was rewarded by a home tie against Worcestershire in 2002.

Batting	*M*	*I*	*NO*	*R*	*HS*	*100s*	*50s*	*Avge*
J. M. Hands	2	4	0	113	80	0	1	28.25
T. G. Sharp	6	11	0	298	90	0	2	27.09
N. A. Stoddard	3	6	1	128	54	0	1	25.60
N. S. Curnow	5	9	0	210	46	0	0	23.33
G. M. Thomas	5	9	0	198	42	0	0	22.00
J. P. Kent	3	6	1	110	58	0	1	22.00
A. M. Pearce	5	9	0	127	61	0	1	14.11

Six matches: C. E. Shreck 48 runs, J. C. J. Stephens 96 runs. *Five matches:* G. D. Edwards 80 runs, G. R. Furse 99 runs, M. K. Munday 17 runs. *Three matches:* A. P. Birkett 83 runs. *Two matches:* P. J. Davey 5 runs, N. T. P. George 15 runs. *One match:* M. K. Burley 7 runs, S. P. Pollard 1 run, B. P. Price 2 runs.

Bowling	*O*	*M*	*R*	*W*	*BB*	*5W/i*	*Avge*
J. C. J. Stephens	194.1	59	462	32	6-32	3	14.43
C. E. Shreck	238.2	59	809	27	4-47	0	29.96

Other wicket-takers: 7 – N. T. P. George, M. K. Munday; 4 – G. R. Furse; 2 – J. M. Hands, J. P. Kent.

CUMBERLAND

Martin Lewis took over as captain in a transitional season, following the retirement of five key players. Cumberland called on 28, and did well to finish in the middle of the table. In line with a decision to play more home-bred cricketers, ten from the Under-17 and Under-19 squads made their debuts. David Pennett's 24 wickets included a hat-trick in match figures of 11 for 110 when Suffolk were beaten at Carlisle, but the only other win was against Lincolnshire at the end of the season. The match against Norfolk at Barrow was abandoned after two days when fierce overnight winds moved the covers and rain rendered the pitch unplayable. For 2002, former Lancashire all-rounder Ian Austin was expected to join Ashley Metcalfe to help bring on the younger players.

Batting	*M*	*I*	*NO*	*R*	*HS*	*100s*	*50s*	*Avge*
A. Williams	2	4	1	181	105	1	1	60.33
A. A. Metcalfe	3	5	1	161	81	0	2	40.25
S. T. Knox	6	11	1	245	115	1	0	24.50
J. M. Lewis	5	7	0	151	113	1	0	21.57
T. A. Hunte	3	5	0	103	63	0	1	20.60

Five matches: S. W. Horne 16 runs, M. A. Sharp 44 runs. *Four matches:* D. B. Pennett 50 runs. *Three matches:* G. R. Armstrong 43 runs, P. J. Lawson 29 runs, R. W. Mason 42 runs, D. M. Wheatman 14 runs, D. R. Williams 25 runs. *Two matches:* P. A. Bayman 25 runs, S. M. Dutton 73 runs, R. C. Faulkner 48 runs. *One match:* D. E. Barnes 34 runs, R. M. Bell 42 runs, J. Bruce 6 runs, G. N. Dawson 1 run, J. M. Fielding 88 runs, M. R. Hadwin 5 runs, J. Mason 56 runs, J. R. Moyes 11 runs, S. J. O'Shaughnessy 39 runs, T. E. H. Prime 1 run, R. Smith 17 runs, G. E. White 38 runs.

Bowling	O	M	R	W	BB	5W/i	Avge
M. A. Sharp	185.2	77	354	21	4-31	0	16.85
D. B. Pennett	142.4	37	441	24	7-65	2	18.37
D. M. Wheatman	76.4	19	221	12	3-39	0	18.41
P. J. Lawson	69.3	16	275	10	4-72	0	27.50

Other wicket-takers: 8 – P. A. Bayman; 7 – J. M. Fielding, J. M. Lewis; 5 – S. W. Horne; 3 – R. W. Mason; 2 – S. J. O'Shaughnessy; 1 – R. Smith.

DEVON

In his last season, following his appointment as headmaster of St Aubyn's School, Tiverton, Nick Folland became the first Devon player to pass 10,000 Championship runs. He closed his 19 seasons with the county on 10,132 at 51.69, while other Devon records included 20 centuries, a highest score of 249 not out, and partnerships for the second and seventh wickets. He also finished with the record for any player in Minor Counties cup cricket – 1,827 runs at 67.66. Bobby Dawson, who headed the batting in his second season since returning from Gloucestershire, scored a match-winning 221 against Oxfordshire – the highest by anyone in the Championship in 2001 – while match figures of 12 for 64 by Ian Bishop, back with Devon after two seasons at Surrey, were instrumental in the ten-wicket defeat of Cornwall. Wiltshire were the other side beaten. However, the season ended in disappointment at Lord's when, in pursuit of a record fourth one-day title, Devon were outplayed by Norfolk in the final of the ECB 38-County Cup.

Batting	M	I	NO	R	HS	100s	50s	Avge
R. I. Dawson	6	10	1	559	221	1	4	62.11
P. M. Roebuck	5	7	3	225	98	0	2	56.25
N. A. Folland	3	4	0	201	97	0	2	50.25
G. T. J. Townsend	4	6	1	199	110	1	0	39.80
A. J. Pugh	5	6	0	147	67	0	1	24.50
D. F. Lye	6	9	0	202	63	0	1	22.44
A. J. Procter	6	8	0	146	76	0	1	18.25

Five matches: I. E. Bishop 31 runs, J. Rhodes 61 runs. *Four matches:* P. M. Warren 42 runs, T. A. Wright 72 runs. *Three matches:* S. M. Eustace 51 runs, A. K. Hele 13 runs. *Two matches:* N. Davey 42 runs, M. P. Hunt 4 runs. *One match:* I. A. Bond 80 runs, D. J. Burke 0 runs, A. W. Paddison 9 runs.

Bowling	O	M	R	W	BB	5W/i	Avge
I. E. Bishop	169.2	49	377	31	6-20	3	12.16
P. M. Warren	72.1	19	190	14	5-16	1	13.57
J. Rhodes	100.5	24	289	16	4-32	0	18.06
P. M. Roebuck	149.4	47	303	13	4-29	0	23.30
A. J. Procter	170	47	418	12	2-18	0	34.83

Other wicket-takers: 7 – T. A. Wright; 1 – I. A. Bond, R. I. Dawson.

DORSET

Champions in 2000, and Western Division leaders since 1998, Dorset were without a win in 2001 and plummeted to the bottom of the table. Failure to come to terms with the requirements of three-day cricket, the unavailability of key players, frequent mid-order collapses and rain affecting half their games all contributed to their decline. The mainstays of the batting were Matt Swarbrick, the left-handed Darren Cowley, and Glyn Treagus, who recorded his maiden Championship century. Leg-spinner Vyv Pike and left-arm opener David Kidner headed the bowling, but Pike was one of those who found three-day cricket too great a demand on his time, and he decided to retire at the end of the season.

Batting	M	I	NO	R	HS	100s	50s	Avge
M. Swarbrick	6	11	0	437	149	1	2	39.72
D. J. Cowley	5	9	0	355	114	1	2	39.44
G. R. Treagus	6	11	0	352	115	1	0	32.00
C. Park	3	5	1	111	50*	0	1	27.75
D. A. Kidner	5	8	1	150	73*	0	1	21.42
T. C. Z. Lamb	5	9	1	143	98*	0	1	17.87
S. W. D. Rintoul	6	11	1	169	61	0	1	16.90
P. J. Deakin	5	9	1	101	24*	0	0	12.62

Six matches: V. J. Pike 99 runs. *Four matches:* N. G. Thurgood 76 runs. *Three matches:* T. C. Hicks 35 runs, T. J. Sharpe 1 run. *Two matches:* J. Eliot-Square 64 runs, S. R. Walbridge 9 runs, K. J. Wilson 14 runs. *One match:* N. M. Johnson 11 runs, B. J. Lawes 25 runs, M. G. Miller 52 runs.

Bowling	O	M	R	W	BB	5W/i	Avge
D. A. Kidner	144.3	38	418	16	6-14	1	26.12
V. J. Pike	251.2	57	739	28	5-104	1	26.39

Other wicket-takers: 9 – T. J. Sharpe; 6 – T. C. Hicks; 5 – G. R. Treagus; 3 – D. J. Cowley, S. R. Walbridge; 2 – J. Eliot-Square, K. J. Wilson; 1 – N. M. Johnson.

HEREFORDSHIRE

Herefordshire, cup-winners at Lord's in 2000, regained their one-day form to become the first Minor County for ten years to upset a first-class county when they beat Middlesex at Kingsland in the third round of the Cheltenham & Gloucester Trophy. But this was the high point: early reversals in the ECB 38-County Cup had put paid to another trip to Lord's and, in late summer, Suffolk ended their interest in the 2002 C&G competition. In the Championship, there were victories over Dorset, Berkshire and Devon, along with some outstanding bowling by Kevin Cooper. His 31 wickets from just three games included five-wicket returns in all six innings, earning him the only single-figure average by a Minor Counties bowler taking ten wickets, and the Frank Edwards bowling award. His opening partner, Paul Humphries, became only the second bowler, after Cooper, to pass 100 wickets for the county.

Batting	M	I	NO	R	HS	100s	50s	Avge
A. N. Edwards	3	4	1	166	82*	0	1	55.33
N. W. Round	3	5	1	182	130	1	0	45.50
C. W. Boroughs	6	10	0	420	124	2	1	42.00
R. Nagra	3	5	0	178	85	0	2	35.61
I. Dawood	5	9	0	286	68	0	2	31.77
H. V. Patel	4	7	0	195	78	0	2	27.85
K. Pearson	5	9	2	193	60	0	1	27.57
N. M. Davies	6	10	1	173	54*	0	1	19.22
R. D. Hughes	4	8	0	126	42	0	0	15.75

Five matches: P. J. Humphries 3 runs. *Three matches:* K. E. Cooper 9 runs, P. A. Thomas 35 runs. *Two matches:* M. Horrocks 11 runs, A. N. Mason 39 runs, N. V. Prabhu 71 runs, G. M. Roberts 91 runs, J. W. Shaw 33 runs. *One match:* J. F. Cotterell 4 runs, A. Farooque 13 runs, R. J. Hall 26 runs, S. Pathan 96 runs, S. T. Swaffield 23 runs, T. N. Wolfendale 20 runs.

Bowling	O	M	R	W	BB	5W/i	Avge
K. E. Cooper	141.1	46	285	31	6-57	6	9.19
P. J. Humphries	171.2	45	507	22	5-55	1	23.04
P. A. Thomas	80.2	15	273	11	3-27	0	24.81
N. M. Davies	114	15	481	13	4-42	0	37.00

Other wicket-takers: 7 – J. W. Shaw; 5 – A. N. Edwards, M. Horrocks; 4 – K. Pearson; 3 – R. Nagra, G. M. Roberts; 1 – A. N. Mason.

HERTFORDSHIRE

Hertfordshire moved up to fourth place in the Eastern Division, thanks to an improved performance and wins against Buckinghamshire and Bedfordshire in their last two matches. In accordance with their youth policy, more than half the players selected were 22 or under. Brothers Richard and Stephen Cordingley made their debuts in the match against Cambridgeshire, while in the encounter with Staffordshire the Lowe brothers, David and Stephen, took the honours with a century apiece in a county record second-wicket stand of 224. By far the most prolific batsman, though, was David Ward, the only player to pass 600 runs in the Championship in 2001 and winner of the Wilfred Rhodes Trophy.

Batting	*M*	*I*	*NO*	*R*	*HS*	*100s*	*50s*	*Avge*
S. G. Cordingley	1	2	1	116	84*	0	1	116.00
D. M. Ward	5	10	2	636	172	2	3	79.50
D. Lowe	4	8	1	323	142*	2	0	46.14
S. J. Lowe	6	12	0	500	116	2	2	41.66
B. J. Frazer	5	9	2	201	44	0	0	28.71
M. H. James	6	11	0	275	70	0	2	25.00
I. Fletcher	4	8	0	178	38	0	0	22.25
S. P. White	5	9	2	134	48	0	0	19.14
M. A. Everett	4	8	1	124	70*	0	1	17.71

Five matches: L. M. Cooper 80 runs, P. J. O'Reilly 5 runs. *Four matches:* M. E. Smith 73 runs. *Three matches:* C. J. Box 40 runs. *Two matches:* S. D. Fan 77 runs, N. Gladwin 47 runs, K. G. Smith 34 runs. *One match:* R. J. Cordingley 5 runs, S. N. Ruskin 17 runs, E. R. Tucker 12 runs.

Bowling	*O*	*M*	*R*	*W*	*BB*	*5W/i*	*Avge*
P. J. O'Reilly	127	25	327	17	4-23	0	19.23
L. M. Cooper	107.5	22	378	13	3-20	0	29.07
B. J. Frazer	139.1	34	428	11	3-37	0	38.90

Other wicket-takers: 9 – S. P. White; 8 – M. E. Smith; 7 – C. J. Box; 6 – K. G. Smith; 4 – E. R. Tucker; 2 – R. J. Cordingley.

LINCOLNSHIRE

Having originally finished second in the Eastern Division, with wins over Bedfordshire, Suffolk and Norfolk, Lincolnshire shared the Championship title with Cheshire – thanks in the first place to the deduction of points from Cambridgeshire, at whose expense they moved to the top of the table. They were able to field a relatively settled side, using just 15 in all and regularly playing at least seven under the age of 22. The one-day game remained a problem, although they did qualify for the third round of the 2002 Cheltenham & Gloucester Trophy. Steve Plumb's century in the Championship final was his 21st, taking him to a new overall record, and at 47 he became only the second player, after Oxfordshire's Mike Nurton, to pass 12,000 runs in the competition. Other highlights were a match haul of ten wickets for David Pipes against Bedfordshire, and the wicket-keeping of 21-year-old Oliver Burford, whose 21 dismissals were the second best in the Championship. Mark Fell said he would relinquish the captaincy after the 2002 season.

Batting	M	I	NO	R	HS	100s	50s	Avge
J. Trower	5	8	2	393	149	1	3	65.50
M. A. Fell	7	11	4	416	69	0	3	59.42
J. C. Harrison	6	12	2	549	117	2	3	54.90
S. G. Plumb	6	12	2	333	103*	1	0	33.30
S. N. Warman	7	13	3	277	50*	0	1	27.70
R. W. J. Howitt	7	13	2	287	75*	0	3	26.09
J. Clarke	6	12	1	239	88*	0	2	21.72
O. E. Burford	7	9	1	165	68	0	2	20.62
R. J. Chapman	7	9	2	141	53*	0	1	20.14
D. J. Pipes	7	8	2	102	61	0	1	17.00

Five matches: S. Oakes 42 runs. *Four matches:* J. R. Davies 16 runs. *One match:* J. Davies 24 runs, D. Heath 9 runs; D. A. Christmas did not bat.

Bowling	O	M	R	W	BB	5W/i	Avge
J. R. Davies	83.1	18	282	12	3-18	0	23.50
S. G. Plumb	198.2	55	551	22	4-42	0	25.04
D. J. Pipes	184.3	38	585	23	6-51	1	25.43
R. J. Chapman	152.1	27	542	21	5-55	1	25.80
S. Oakes	131.5	37	401	15	3-26	0	26.73

Other wicket-takers: 6 – M. A. Fell; 5 – J. Davies; 2 – D. A. Christmas, R. W. J. Howitt; 1 – J. Clarke, J. Trower.

NORFOLK

Victory at Lord's in the final of the ECB 38-County Cup, and the defeat of ICC Trophy champions Holland in the first round of the 2002 Cheltenham & Gloucester Trophy gave Norfolk a season to remember. They soon adapted to their new surroundings at Manor Park, especially in the one-day competitions, in which the two Carls, Rogers and Amos, hit hundreds, while Paul Bradshaw and off-spinner Chris Brown, formerly with Cheshire, were regularly among the wickets. The introduction of three-day cricket was largely seen as a success, although two matches were extended until late on the second day (8.26 p.m. against Wales and 7.24 p.m. against Buckinghamshire, in their only victory) to save players from incurring overnight expenses and taking another day off work. There was a pleasing return to all-round form by Steve Goldsmith, with Championship hundreds from him, Amos and Rogers.

Batting	M	I	NO	R	HS	100s	50s	Avge
C. Amos	6	10	0	405	138	1	3	40.50
S. C. Goldsmith	6	9	1	320	109	1	2	40.00
C. S. Carey	5	8	4	132	72*	0	1	33.00
J. R. Walker	5	8	0	239	65	0	2	29.87
C. J. Rogers	6	10	0	244	118	1	0	24.40
C. Brown	6	6	1	121	40*	0	0	24.20
C. R. Borrett	5	8	1	104	35	0	0	14.85

Six matches: P. J. Bradshaw 95 runs, P. G. Newman 37 runs. *Four matches:* L. T. S. Newton 20 runs, D. A. Whitney 98 runs. *Two matches:* P. J. Free 58 runs, J. P. Garner 97 runs. *One match:* R. J. Austin 7 runs, S. J. Cooper 27 runs, S. J. B. Livermore 36 runs.

Bowling	O	M	R	W	BB	5W/i	Avge
C. Brown	189	46	577	22	6-111	1	26.22
S. C. Goldsmith	137.5	30	401	15	5-61	1	26.73
P. J. Bradshaw	91.2	18	308	11	3-57	0	28.00

Other wicket-takers: 9 – P. G. Newman; 5 – C. J. Rogers; 2 – R. J. Austin, C. R. Borrett, C. S. Carey; 1 – C. Amos.

NORTHUMBERLAND

Northumberland remained unbeaten all season in the Eastern Division, and – with victories over Bedfordshire and Suffolk – moved up a place to third after Cambridgeshire's demotion.

Batting

	M	*I*	*NO*	*R*	*HS*	*100s*	*50s*	*Avge*
J. B. Windows	4	7	2	246	93	0	3	49.20
P. J. Nicholson	6	6	1	214	64	0	3	42.80
G. Hallam	4	7	1	253	85*	0	3	42.16
G. Angus	5	4	1	120	66	0	1	40.00
S. Chapman	5	9	2	240	92	0	2	34.28
B. Parker	6	11	2	307	81	0	2	34.11
J. A. Graham	5	8	0	241	85	0	2	30.12
A. T. Heather	6	11	1	282	75	0	2	28.20
R. J. Sellers	5	5	0	124	74	0	1	24.80

Five matches: M. L. Pollard 23 runs, D. J. Rutherford 68 runs. *Three matches:* J. N. Miller 30 runs. *One match:* C. I. Beever 3 runs, S. J. Birtwisle 46 runs, A. D. Brown 0 runs, L. J. Crozier 27 runs, I. Smart 0 runs, B. Stewart 8 runs, N. Tomlinson 4 runs.

Bowling

	O	*M*	*R*	*W*	*BB*	*5W/i*	*Avge*
S. Chapman	154.3	47	337	24	5-63	1	14.04
G. Angus	158.1	41	441	21	3-31	0	21.00
M. L. Pollard	117.1	31	309	11	3-47	0	28.09
D. J. Rutherford	145	38	379	13	4-39	0	29.15

Other wicket-takers: 9 – J. B. Windows; 4 – J. A. Graham; 2 – L. J. Crozier; 1 – A. D. Brown, I. Smart, B. Stewart.

OXFORDSHIRE

There was early-season optimism inspired by improved results in 2000, the challenge of the three-day format, and the appointment of the county's first full-time coach – Jack Potter, formerly head of the Australian Cricket Academy and Oxford University coach. In the event, unavailability and injuries frequently prevented Oxfordshire from fielding their strongest side. In all, 29 players were called on in both competitions, including some promising colts. Although results were disappointing, with Herefordshire providing the only Championship win, the spirit in the side was always good. The mainstay of the bowling remained the veteran Keith Arnold, albeit not fully fit after a riding accident. Adam Cook, a left-hander who scored the most runs, had the look of a genuine all-rounder as he bowled his off-breaks with increasing confidence.

Batting

	M	*I*	*NO*	*R*	*HS*	*100s*	*50s*	*Avge*
K. R. Mustow	3	6	0	236	110	1	0	39.33
A. P. Cook	6	11	3	311	70*	0	3	38.87
B. J. Thompson	4	8	1	271	121*	1	1	38.71
R. Hawkins	3	6	0	188	62	0	1	31.33
S. V. Laudat	3	6	0	147	40	0	0	24.50
C. S. Knightley	4	8	1	166	54	0	1	23.71
R. Eason	4	8	1	120	33	0	0	17.14
R. J. Williams	4	7	0	105	40	0	0	15.00

Six matches: I. A. Hawtin 86 runs. *Four matches:* I. Adams 8 runs, K. A. Arnold 54 runs. *Three matches:* I. Evans 36 runs, P. A. Jeacock 28 runs, G. S. Peddy 10 runs. *Two matches:* S. J. Ali 44 runs, P. J. Evans 4 runs, S. Miller 49 runs. *One match:* M. R. Bellhouse 7 runs, P. M. Jobson 11 runs, J. Phillips 13 runs, T. S. Smith 42 runs, P. A. White 0 runs, D. C. Woods 45 runs.

Bowling	*O*	*M*	*R*	*W*	*BB*	*5W/i*	*Avge*
S. V. Laudat	82.3	20	229	11	6-54	1	20.81
K. A. Arnold	134	38	354	17	6-81	1	20.82
A. P. Cook	86.1	12	341	14	4-48	0	24.35

Other wicket-takers: 7 – B. J. Thompson; 6 – I. Adams, P. A. Jeacock, G. S. Peddy; 4 – S. Miller, P. A. White; 1 – I. Evans.

SHROPSHIRE

A successful Championship season, with good wins over Oxfordshire, Berkshire and Dorset, saw Shropshire finish a best-ever second in the Western Division; had rain not disrupted their last two games, things might have been even better. The Oxfordshire match was memorable for the side's only Championship century – 141 not out by leading batsman Marcus Marvell – and a hat-trick by David Boden. Dominic Williamson made his mark in the Dorset match, recording the season's best innings return by any bowler, eight for 56, as well as scoring 92 in the second innings. Other highlights were match figures of ten for 54 off 46 overs by Kevin Evans against Cheshire, and a superb performance behind the stumps by 19-year-old Gareth Mumford, who made 18 catches and one stumping in his first full season. Shropshire won their group in the one-day competition, but lost heavily at home to Devon in the quarter-finals. The season was overshadowed by the deaths of the club's president, Vesey Holt, and of Dick Hamar, treasurer for 40 years.

Batting	*M*	*I*	*NO*	*R*	*HS*	*100s*	*50s*	*Avge*
Asif Din	3	6	2	199	67*	0	1	49.75
G. J. Byram	4	8	3	238	74*	0	2	47.60
M. J. Marvell	6	12	2	437	141*	1	2	43.70
D. Williamson	3	5	0	177	92	0	1	35.40
R. P. L. Burton	3	6	0	206	90	0	2	34.33
G. L. Home	4	7	2	161	51*	0	1	32.20
J. B. R. Jones	6	11	1	213	71	0	1	21.30
D. J. P. Boden	5	8	3	101	33	0	0	20.20
J. T. Ralph	4	8	0	159	28	0	0	19.87

Six matches: G. J. Mumford 42 runs. *Five matches:* K. P. Evans 99 runs. *Four matches:* A. B. Byram 95 runs. *Three matches:* M. Downes 62 runs. *Two matches:* A. J. Shantry 5 runs; A. M. Shimmons did not bat. *One match:* D. J. Bowett 45 runs, R. de Silva 16 runs, E. L. Home 16 runs, A. N. Johnson 15 runs, A. P. O'Connor 0 runs; C. C. Lewis did not bat.

Bowling	*O*	*M*	*R*	*W*	*BB*	*5W/i*	*Avge*
A. M. Shimmons	65.4	21	161	13	5-39	1	12.38
A. B. Byram	93.2	30	220	16	5-42	1	13.75
D. Williamson	85.1	21	264	17	8-56	1	15.52
K. P. Evans	173.4	59	321	19	5-15	2	16.89
D. J. P. Boden	157.5	52	441	20	6-32	2	22.05

Other wicket-takers: 7 – A. N. Johnson; 6 – Asif Din; 4 – M. Downes, A. J. Shantry; 3 – G. J. Byram, A. P. O'Connor; 2 – C. C. Lewis.

STAFFORDSHIRE

Staffordshire moved back up the table to finish runners-up in the Eastern Division. The batting was headed by the left-handed Paul Shaw, while Steve Dean extended his career aggregate to 9,388, overtaking David Hancock's record for the county. David Follett returned to the side to make a spectacular contribution in the defeat of Bedfordshire, with figures of seven for 27 and seven for 29, including nine bowled. Another impressive bowling performance was Laurie Potter's second-innings analysis of 26–22–4–4 as Cumberland were beaten. Mark Humphries completed an unbroken run of 100 Championship matches and, with 24 catches and one stumping, effected more dismissals than any other wicket-keeper in 2001. Despite an early exit from the 2001 Cheltenham & Gloucester Trophy, the side earned a third-round draw against neighbouring Warwickshire for 2002.

Batting

	M	I	NO	R	HS	100s	50s	Avge
L. Potter	2	4	1	165	158*	1	0	55.00
P. F. Shaw	6	10	0	480	131	1	2	48.00
M. I. Humphries	6	8	3	201	62	0	1	40.20
G. F. Archer	6	10	0	363	108	1	2	36.30
S. J. Dean	6	10	0	337	127	1	1	33.70
D. R. Womble	6	10	2	182	58*	0	1	22.75
R. P. Harvey	6	8	1	135	53*	0	1	19.28
M. Longmore	5	8	0	139	53	0	1	17.37

Six matches: G. Bulpitt 8 runs, R. A. Cooper 55 runs. *Five matches:* D. Follett 34 runs. *Three matches:* A. J. Jones 39 runs. *One match:* D. J. Edwards 1 run, P. S. J. Goodwin 10 runs, A. M. Reynolds 52 runs.

Bowling

	O	M	R	W	BB	5W/i	Avge
D. Follett	163.2	35	436	23	7-27	2	18.95
D. R. Womble	140.3	24	494	26	5-41	1	19.00
G. Bulpitt	148.1	44	328	13	3-47	0	25.23
R. A. Cooper	174.5	43	516	20	4-36	0	25.80

Other wicket-takers: 6 – L. Potter; 4 – A. J. Jones; 2 – R. P. Harvey; 1 – A. M. Reynolds.

SUFFOLK

Suffolk, without a win, dropped to ninth in the Eastern Division. Derek Randall, who retired at the end of 2000, was replaced as professional by Test batsman Bill Athey, formerly of Yorkshire, Gloucestershire and Sussex, while Andy Brown joined as player-coach from Derbyshire. In his 20th season, Phil Caley headed the batting and took his career tally to 7,701, passing Tony Warrington's 7,623 to line up in second place for the county behind Simon Clements (9,219).

Batting

	M	I	NO	R	HS	100s	50s	Avge
P. J. Caley	6	10	2	393	95	0	4	49.12
I. D. Graham	5	9	1	231	52	0	2	28.87
R. J. Catley	5	9	1	216	100*	1	1	27.00
C. W. J. Athey	6	11	1	205	87	0	1	20.50
A. M. Brown	6	11	0	219	56	0	2	19.90

Six matches: D. F. Cross 43 runs, C. J. Warn 59 runs. *Five matches:* C. P. Seal 78 runs. *Four matches:* P. D. King 41 runs, C. A. Swallow 62 runs. *Three matches:* M. D. Jones 45 runs, G. M. Kirk 4 runs, R. W. Pineo 72 runs. *One match:* M. D. Catley 5 runs, T. M. Catley 7 runs, J. P. East 43 runs, A. K. Poole 8 runs.

Bowling

	O	M	R	W	BB	5W/i	Avge
G. M. Kirk	130.4	43	314	21	5-46	2	14.95
I. D. Graham	140.1	32	477	21	5-79	1	22.71
C. P. Seal	105	25	324	13	4-45	0	24.92

Other wicket-takers: 8 – D. F. Cross; 5 – R. W. Pineo; 4 – C. W. J. Athey; 3 – P. J. Caley, P. D. King; 2 – A. K. Poole; 1 – R. J. Catley, J. P. East, C. A. Swallow.

WALES

Wales enjoyed their best season for four years, climbing from last in the Western Division to sixth. They won their first five matches in all competitions, which included their solitary Championship victory, against Herefordshire, when the Sylvester brothers, Jamie and Ryan, scored respectively 116 and 124 not out (a maiden Championship century). Against Oxfordshire, David Lovell set new county records with his 150 not out and fifth-wicket stand of 161 with 19-year-old Owen Dawkins, who contributed 75. Less welcome was a new lowest total, 47, in the game against Berkshire. Pace bowler Nathan Gage took 16 wickets in his debut season.

Batting	M	I	NO	R	HS	100s	50s	Avge
D. J. Lovell	2	3	1	204	150*	1	0	102.00
J. P. J. Sylvester	4	7	0	395	116	1	3	56.42
O. C. Dawkins	4	7	2	272	75	0	3	54.40
A. J. Jones	3	6	0	296	92	0	3	49.33
R. W. Sylvester	5	9	2	308	124*	1	1	44.00
S. Morris	4	6	0	201	61	0	2	33.50
L. O. Jones	4	6	1	137	47	0	0	27.40
N. A. Gage	6	9	4	104	36	0	0	20.80
M. J. Newbold	4	7	0	109	43	0	0	15.57

Five matches: C. P. Metson 51 runs. *Four matches:* A. J. L. Barr 84 runs. *Three matches:* O. C. Hopkins 17 runs. *Two matches:* K. M. Bell 9 runs, I. M. Bird 65 runs, J. Davies 4 runs. *One match:* C. J. Barnsley 0 runs, R. I. Clitheroe 3 runs, O. A. Dawkins 11 runs, D. A. Fury 4 runs, M. Hembrow 14 runs, K. Khanna 4 runs, J. H. Langworth 54 runs, R. J. Skone 0 runs, A. C. Smith 16 runs, I. J. Thomas 41 runs, M. A. Wallace 12 runs, R. Williams 1 run.

Bowling	O	M	R	W	BB	5W/i	Avge
L. O. Jones	84.2	22	247	10	3-36	0	24.70
R. W. Sylvester	59	5	269	10	4-62	0	26.90
N. A. Gage	176.1	51	437	16	5-54	1	27.31

Other wicket-takers: 8 – J. Davies; 5 – A. J. L. Barr, A. C. Smith; 4 – O. C. Dawkins; 3 – K. M. Bell; 2 – R. J. Skone, J. P. J. Sylvester; 1 – O. A. Dawkins, M. Hembrow, I. J. Thomas, R. Williams.

WILTSHIRE

Wiltshire were another county who struggled to field a settled side for the three-day games and called on 24 players. Inconsistent first-innings batting was reflected in only two bonus points – fewer than any other county. However, seamer Richard Bedbrook, in his first full season, was the highest wicket-taker in both divisions, his 37 including 12 against Herefordshire and 11 in Wiltshire's only victory, against Wales. Russell Rowe had five fifties in his 471 runs and carried his bat for 89 in the first innings against Cheshire; captain Steve Perrin struck 190 in 141 balls against Herefordshire, with seven sixes and 25 fours; and Mark Coxon made 144 against Shropshire.

Batting	M	I	NO	R	HS	100s	50s	Avge
S. M. Perrin	3	5	0	219	190	1	0	43.80
R. J. Rowe	6	12	1	471	89*	0	5	42.81
M. D. Coxon	5	10	1	284	144	1	1	31.55
R. J. Bates	4	7	0	214	64	0	1	30.57
T. N. Shardlow	5	10	2	232	80	0	2	29.00
P. R. Draper	2	4	0	100	62	0	1	25.00
D. A. Winter	4	7	0	161	59	0	2	23.00

Six matches: R. D. Bedbrook 62 runs. *Four matches:* D. P. Moore 20 runs, C. J. Rogers 96 runs. *Three matches:* P. R. Bates 91 runs, T. Caines 16 runs, C. R. Gibbens 15 runs. *Two matches:* C. C. Chaplin 1 run, M. E. Scully 80 runs, J. L. Taylor 55 runs. *One match:* P. R. Clifford 60 runs, D. A. Goldstraw 4 runs, J. R. Goode 17 runs, L. A. Leach 0 runs, K. J. Nash 0 runs, C. C. Steedon 3 runs, S. A. Whatling 1 run, S. M. Woodhouse 42 runs.

Bowling	O	M	R	W	BB	5W/i	Avge
C. R. Gibbens	82.2	19	253	11	6-80	1	23.00
D. P. Moore	113.4	30	349	15	4-57	0	23.26
R. D. Bedbrook	231.4	47	861	37	7-97	4	23.27
R. J. Bates	141.3	33	418	14	3-22	0	29.85

Other wicket-takers: 4 – P. R. Draper; 3 – K. J. Nash; 2 – P. R. Clifford.

CHAMPIONSHIP FINAL

LINCOLNSHIRE v CHESHIRE

At Grantham, September 9, 10, 11. Drawn. Toss: Lincolnshire.

The Championship was shared for the first time since 1900, after a game featuring four centuries and 1,039 runs on a placid pitch had petered out in a draw. Harrison set the tone during a chanceless 110 off 204 balls, with 16 fours, putting on 173 for Lincolnshire's second wicket with the left-handed Howitt. However, Fisher's left-arm spin inspired a collapse of seven for 44, and Cheshire were able to secure a 41-run lead in their allotted 70 overs. Hall kept the innings moving with 120 off 159 balls (one six, 16 fours), adding 110 with Currie but twisting his ankle soon after reaching his century; his runner, Fisher, was thrown out by Warman. By the end of the second day, Lincolnshire's Trower had reached a maiden hundred, which he extended next day to 149 off 294 balls, with 19 boundaries, as he and Plumb put on 151. Plumb's unbeaten 103, off 239 balls with 15 fours, was his 21st in the Championship and gave him the record he had shared with Jack Mendl of Oxfordshire and Devon's Neil Folland. Fell did not declare until Plumb had reached his landmark in the early afternoon, and, with Cheshire facing a target of 351 off 50 overs, there was little hope of victory for either side. As it was, bad light put an early end to proceedings.

Man of the Match: A. J. Hall.

Close of play: First day, Cheshire 84-1 (Currie 39*, Hall 23*); Second day, Lincolnshire 214-3 (Trower 108*, Plumb 35*).

Lincolnshire

J. C. Harrison c Hignett b Marshall	110	– c Ogilby b Lamb	8
J. Trower b Renshaw	0	– b Whittaker	149
R. W. J. Howitt c Whittaker b Fisher	74	– lbw b Lamb	4
R. J. Chapman c Currie b Fisher	11		
J. Clarke c Whittaker b Fisher	6	– (4) b Marshall	53
S. G. Plumb c Bryson b Fisher	17	– (5) not out	103
*M. A. Fell run out	4	– (6) c Currie b Fisher	30
S. N. Warman c Renshaw b Marshall	4	– (7) not out	13
†O. E. Burford run out	0		
D. J. Pipes not out	4		
S. Oakes not out	10		
B 1, l-b 11, n-b 2	14	B 7, l-b 4, n-b 20	31
1/1 2/174 3/194 4/207 5/214 6/223 7/227 8/233 9/238 (9 wkts, 70 overs)	254	1/21 2/27 3/136 4/287 5/344 (5 wkts dec.)	391

Bowling: *First Innings*—Renshaw 14–4–37–1; Lamb 12–3–47–0; Whittaker 5–1–19–0; Fisher 23–3–84–4; Marshall 16–1–55–2. *Second Innings*—Renshaw 23–5–76–0; Lamb 31–5–101–2; Whittaker 12–2–52–1; Fisher 32–6–109–1; Marshall 5–0–34–1; Hignett 1–0–8–0.

Cheshire

P. R. J. Bryson c Burford b Oakes	21	– c Clarke b Pipes	50
M. R. Currie c Clarke b Plumb	70	– not out	39
A. J. Hall run out	120		
R. G. Hignett lbw b Pipes	15		
S. J. Renshaw b Plumb	23		
*I. Cockbain not out	26		
C. S. Lamb run out	15		
J. P. Whittaker (did not bat)		– (3) b Plumb	5
S. J. Marshall (did not bat)		– (4) not out	1
L-b 5	5	L-b 2, w 2	4
1/50 2/160 3/177 4/230 5/280 6/295 (6 wkts, 70 overs)	295	1/62 2/88 (2 wkts)	99

†S. Ogilby and R. W. Fisher did not bat.

Bowling: *First Innings*—Chapman 11–2–34–0; Oakes 17–3–63–1; Pipes 15–3–56–1; Plumb 18–4–94–2; Fell 9–0–43–0. *Second Innings*—Chapman 6–0–35–0; Oakes 14–4–43–0; Pipes 5–1–14–1; Plumb 3–1–5–1.

Umpires: W. E. Smith and J. M. Tythcott.

THE MINOR COUNTIES CHAMPIONS

1895	Norfolk; Durham; Worcestershire
1896	Worcestershire
1897	Worcestershire
1898	Worcestershire
1899	Northamptonshire; Buckinghamshire
1900	Glamorgan; Durham; Northamptonshire
1901	Durham
1902	Wiltshire
1903	Northamptonshire
1904	Northamptonshire
1905	Norfolk
1906	Staffordshire
1907	Lancashire II
1908	Staffordshire
1909	Wiltshire
1910	Norfolk
1911	Staffordshire
1912	In abeyance
1913	Norfolk
1914	Staffordshire†
1920	Staffordshire
1921	Staffordshire
1922	Buckinghamshire
1923	Buckinghamshire
1924	Berkshire
1925	Buckinghamshire
1926	Durham
1927	Staffordshire
1928	Berkshire
1929	Oxfordshire
1930	Durham
1931	Leicestershire II
1932	Buckinghamshire
1933	Undecided
1934	Lancashire II
1935	Middlesex II
1936	Hertfordshire
1937	Lancashire II
1938	Buckinghamshire
1939	Surrey II
1946	Suffolk
1947	Yorkshire II
1948	Lancashire II
1949	Lancashire II
1950	Surrey II
1951	Kent II
1952	Buckinghamshire
1953	Berkshire
1954	Surrey II
1955	Surrey II
1956	Kent II
1957	Yorkshire II
1958	Yorkshire II
1959	Warwickshire II
1960	Lancashire II
1961	Somerset II
1962	Warwickshire II
1963	Cambridgeshire
1964	Lancashire II
1965	Somerset II
1966	Lincolnshire
1967	Cheshire
1968	Yorkshire II
1969	Buckinghamshire
1970	Bedfordshire
1971	Yorkshire II
1972	Bedfordshire
1973	Shropshire
1974	Oxfordshire
1975	Hertfordshire
1976	Durham
1977	Suffolk
1978	Devon
1979	Suffolk
1980	Durham
1981	Durham
1982	Oxfordshire
1983	Hertfordshire
1984	Durham
1985	Cheshire
1986	Cumberland
1987	Buckinghamshire
1988	Cheshire
1989	Oxfordshire
1990	Hertfordshire
1991	Staffordshire
1992	Staffordshire
1993	Staffordshire
1994	Devon
1995	Devon
1996	Devon
1997	Devon
1998	Staffordshire
1999	Cumberland
2000	Dorset
2001	Cheshire; Lincolnshire

† *Disputed. Most sources claim the Championship was never decided.*

THE ECB 38-COUNTY CUP FINAL

DEVON v NORFOLK

At Lord's, September 4. Norfolk won by 114 runs. Toss: Devon.

Norfolk, winners in 1986 and 1997, won the knockout trophy for a third time after demolishing Devon, who had come to Lord's for the fifth time in 11 seasons, looking to win a record fourth one-day trophy. Instead they ended the day in disarray after being bowled out for the lowest total by any side in the final and losing by the biggest margin in runs. As when they last won the trophy, Rogers was Norfolk's mainstay with a patient half-century, while Borrett made a robust contribution and the captain, Newman, took them past 200 with consecutive fours off the last two balls. Just nine balls into their reply, Devon were seven for two, and looked beyond redemption at 51 for five. Off-spinner Brown, who had been on the losing side with Cheshire in the previous year's final, finished them off with four for 15.

Norfolk

C. Amos lbw b Rhodes	12	C. Brown not out	8
C. J. Rogers lbw b Roebuck	54	P. J. Bradshaw b Warren	1
J. R. Walker st Hele b Procter	23	*P. G. Newman not out	8
S. C. Goldsmith run out	1	B 1, l-b 9, w 21, n-b 2	33
S. J. B. Livermore lbw b Rhodes	20		
†J. P. Garner c Roebuck b Rhodes	7	1/32 2/76 3/79 (9 wkts, 50 overs)	202
C. R. Borrett c Procter b Bishop	33	4/128 5/137 6/166	
P. J. Free run out	2	7/176 8/188 9/194	

Bowling: Bishop 10–0–39–1; Procter 10–2–23–1; Warren 8–1–44–1; Rhodes 10–0–43–3; Roebuck 10–0–30–1; Pugh 2–0–13–0.

Devon

G. T. J. Townsend lbw b Bradshaw	1	I. E. Bishop lbw b Brown	0
R. I. Dawson b Bradshaw	6	P. M. Warren not out	8
*P. M. Roebuck b Newman	0	J. Rhodes b Bradshaw	1
D. F. Lye c Rogers b Goldsmith	18		
R. J. Baggs b Borrett	15	L-b 12, w 2	14
A. J. Pugh lbw b Brown	15		
A. J. Procter c Newman b Brown	6	1/2 2/7 3/25 4/35 5/51 (28.1 overs)	88
†A. K. Hele c Borrett b Brown	4	6/58 7/73 8/73 9/83	

Bowling: Bradshaw 7.1–2–10–3; Newman 4–0–22–1; Goldsmith 3–0–10–1; Borrett 7–1–19–1; Brown 7–2–15–4.

Umpires: K. Coburn and M. Dixon.

WINNERS 1983–2001

1983	Cheshire	1990	Buckinghamshire	1997	Norfolk
1984	Hertfordshire	1991	Staffordshire	1998	Devon
1985	Durham	1992	Devon	1999	Bedfordshire
1986	Norfolk	1993	Staffordshire	2000	Herefordshire
1987	Cheshire	1994	Devon	2001	Norfolk
1988	Dorset	1995	Cambridgeshire		
1989	Cumberland	1996	Cheshire		

UMPIRES FOR 2002

FIRST-CLASS UMPIRES

M. R. Benson, G. I. Burgess, A. Clarkson, D. J. Constant, N. G. Cowley, B. Dudleston, J. H. Evans, I. J. Gould, J. H. Hampshire, M. J. Harris, J. W. Holder, V. A. Holder, T. E. Jesty, A. A. Jones, M. J. Kitchen, B. Leadbeater, N. J. Llong, J. W. Lloyds, N. A. Mallender, K. E. Palmer, R. Palmer, G. Sharp, D. R. Shepherd, J. F. Steele, A. G. T. Whitehead, P. Willey. *Reserves:* P. Adams, N. L. Bainton, M. Dixon, P. J. Hartley, A. Hill, C. S. Kelly, R. A. Kettleborough, K. J. Lyons, R. T. Robinson, K. Shuttleworth.

MINOR COUNTIES UMPIRES

P. Adams, N. L. Bainton, S. F. Bishopp, P. Brown, A. R. Bundy, D. L. Burden, P. D. Clubb, K. Coburn, M. Dixon, R. G. Eagleton, A. J. Hardy, J. Ilott, J. H. James, J. S. Johnson, P. W. Joy, P. W. Kingston-Davey, S. W. Kuhlmann, C. L. McNamee, C. Megennis, M. P. Moran, W. Morgan, A. P. Price, C. T. Puckett, G. P. Randall-Johnson, J. G. Reed, G. Ripley, K. S. Shenton, W. E. Smith, R. M. Sutton, D. G. Tate, J. M. Tythcott, G. Watkins, J. Wilkinson, T. G. Wilson, R. Wood. *Reserves:* S. Boulton, R. Dowd, H. Evans, S. Z. Marszal, J. Mitchell, D. Moseby, C. G. Pocock, P. L. Ratcliffe, D. J. Todd, M. C. White.

SECOND ELEVEN CHAMPIONSHIP, 2001

Since the Second Eleven Championship was introduced in 1959, *Wisden* has provided averages for each county, as well as a brief report. From this edition, the section will give only the averages of the leading performers. This reflects the changing nature of the competition. Players move freely between counties for trials, while older, contracted players, unable to get first-team cricket, serve out their time with counties that cannot always afford large staffs; first-team players use Second Eleven Championship matches to regain form in the middle. The result is that the Championship has become a competition more suited to the ambitions, or otherwise, of individuals, rather than a genuine team event.

Initially, it was designed to provide regular cricket of a higher standard than club cricket for younger players and those in the process of qualifying by residence. Today, residency is not so much the issue: instead, there has been an influx, predominantly but not exclusively from South Africa, of players with access to a European Union passport. Employment law means the holder has *carte blanche* to ply his trade in county cricket. The effects are most pronounced in the Second Eleven Championship, which has become something of a free-for-all, and not always to the advantage of the home-grown player. Of the 44 cricketers used by Middlesex in 2001, for example, 15 were born outside the United Kingdom; the ratio was similar at Worcestershire, where a third of their 33 Second Eleven players were not UK-born. Even allowing for players born overseas but who subsequently grew up in England, the high proportion playing county cricket under flags of convenience should concern the ECB.

Hampshire, captained by John Stephenson in his last year with the club, won the Championship for the fifth time, providing the county with good reason for optimism as they return to Division One of the County Championship in 2002. Third-placed Nottinghamshire won more games but, like second-placed Yorkshire, had also played more than Hampshire. In a change from the previous season, each county had to play

SECOND ELEVEN CHAMPIONSHIP, 2001

	P	*W*	*L*	*D*	*Bonus points* *Batting*	*Bowling*	*Points*	*Avge*
1 – Hampshire (11)	11	8	0	3	28	33	171*	15.54
2 – Yorkshire (5)	13	8	2	3	35	34	177	13.61
3 – Nottinghamshire (4)	15	9	3	3	35	37	192	12.80
4 – Gloucestershire (9)	13	7	3	3	45	25	166	12.76
5 – Northamptonshire (14)	14	5	4	5	40	42	162	11.57
6 – Kent (2)	11	5	4	2	20	31	119	10.81
7 – Surrey (8)	12	4	4	4	28	36	128	10.66
8 – Warwickshire (3)	12	3	3	6	22	32	116*	9.66
9 – Lancashire (7)	11	3	4	4	19	29	100	9.09
10 – Durham (12)	11	1	3	7	22	36	98	8.90
11 – Middlesex (1)	13	2	5	6	28	38	114	8.76
12 – Leicestershire (15)	12	2	4	6	30	27	105	8.75
13 – Worcestershire (17)	11	1	4	6	31	29	96	8.72
14 – Essex (10)	10	2	4	4	16	31	87	8.70
15 – Somerset (16)	10	2	4	4	25	22	87	8.70
16 – Glamorgan (13)	11	3	5	3	16	30	94	8.54
17 – Sussex (6)	10	2	6	2	20	23	75	7.50
18 – Derbyshire (18)	12	1	6	5	14	31	77	6.41

2000 positions are shown in brackets.

Win = 12 pts; draw = 4 pts.
** Includes 2 pts for draw in which scores were level.*

Essex finished above Somerset by virtue of taking one more wicket.

a minimum of ten Championship games, as opposed to 12 in 2000, and at least four of them had to be four-day fixtures. Counties were then free to organise additional three- or four-day games, which counted towards the Championship.

Surrey won the Second Eleven Trophy for the third time in ten seasons, after Gary Butcher hit 131 off 115 balls against Somerset in the final. In their semi-final against Middlesex, he had made 97 not out from 96 balls. Whether these blazing innings were sufficient to secure his future in county cricket was another matter, for he was not retained by Surrey. It says something about English cricket in general, rather than Second Eleven cricket in particular, when the right man for an occasion is not necessarily the man for a season.

LEADING AVERAGES, 2001

BATTING

(Qualification: 300 runs, average 30.00)

	M	*I*	*NO*	*R*	*HS*	*100s*	*50s*	*Avge*	*Ct/St*
R. J. Cunliffe (*Glos*)	7	10	3	779	198*	3	3	111.28	10
T. M. B. Bailey (*Northants*)	5	9	2	568	168*	2	3	81.14	12/4
J. A. Daley (*Durham*)	3	6	1	378	88	0	4	75.60	1
W. A. Deacon (*Warwicks*)	6	7	2	375	108	2	1	75.00	6
T. H. C. Hancock (*Glos*)	5	9	1	594	211	2	2	74.25	4
C. R. Taylor (*Yorks*)	9	15	4	756	148*	3	3	68.72	12
A. J. Swann (*Northants*)	5	9	1	537	105	1	4	67.12	3
M. J. Brown (*Middx*)	6	11	3	528	160*	3	1	66.00	5
L. R. Prittipaul (*Hants*)	4	6	1	325	175*	1	1	65.00	2
R. A. White (*Northants*)	6	10	2	494	122	1	4	61.75	5
N. Shahid (*Surrey*)	5	10	1	554	170	2	2	61.55	2
A. D. Shaw (*Glam*)	5	8	1	419	193*	2	0	59.85	12/2
G. J. Muchall (*Durham*)	5	8	1	407	101*	1	3	58.14	0
A. S. Rollins (*Northants*)	6	12	2	575	212*	2	1	57.50	7
C. W. G. Bassano (*Derbys*)	5	9	2	399	112*	1	1	57.00	3
R. C. Driver (*Lancs*)	9	15	1	781	222	3	1	55.78	5
S. A. Newman (*Surrey*)	7	13	0	719	122	2	5	55.30	4
J. A. Knott (*Somerset*)	9	12	2	525	126*	1	3	52.50	19/1
G. D. Rose (*Somerset*)	6	9	2	365	134*	2	1	52.14	5
J. W. Cook (*Northants*)	6	10	1	461	131	3	0	51.22	10
V. J. Craven (*Yorks*)	10	16	2	715	144*	1	3	51.07	4
J. O. Troughton (*Warwicks*)	10	15	2	628	103	1	5	48.30	4
M. Gooch (*Essex*)	6	11	1	470	109	1	2	47.00	7
M. D. R. Sutliff (*Kent & Glos*)	12	18	3	692	167*	2	3	46.13	6/1
S. M. Guy (*Yorks*)	11	14	5	410	108	1	2	45.55	34/3
W. J. Durston (*Somerset*)	8	12	2	453	142	1	2	45.30	7
N. R. Boulton (*Worcs*)	8	16	1	679	110	1	5	45.26	9
A. S. Wright (*Leics*)	11	19	1	812	105	2	5	45.11	3
S. J. Adshead (*Leics*)	10	18	1	755	119	1	6	44.41	20/3
C. D. Crowe (*Leics*)	4	7	0	310	93	0	2	44.28	3
S. C. Moore (*Sussex & Worcs*)	6	10	1	391	140	1	2	43.44	3
D. A. T. Dalton (*Warwicks*)	5	9	0	379	189	1	2	42.11	1
J. D. Francis (*Hants*)	7	12	0	504	143	1	3	42.00	5
G. S. Kandola (*Worcs*)	9	16	2	582	152*	2	2	41.57	4
G. E. Welton (*Notts*)	5	8	0	328	124	1	2	41.00	3
G. J. Batty (*Surrey*)	8	14	2	485	123	1	4	40.41	7
J. L. Sadler (*Yorks*)	9	13	1	481	104*	1	2	40.08	11
D. Alleyne (*Middx*)	9	14	2	476	127	1	2	39.66	25/5
D. J. Pipe (*Worcs*)	11	20	1	750	114	3	3	39.47	26/1
J. Hughes (*Glam*)	10	18	1	666	105	1	4	39.17	8

	M	*I*	*NO*	*R*	*HS*	*100s*	*50s*	*Avge*	*Ct/St*
N. R. D. Compton (*Middx*)	5	8	0	310	97	0	3	38.75	2
J. K. Maunders (*Middx*)	11	19	3	614	113	2	2	38.37	8
G. L. Brophy (*Northants & Notts*)	8	16	1	575	112	1	4	38.33	9/2
D. D. Cherry (*Glam*)	6	11	1	380	145	1	1	38.00	4
J. S. Laney (*Hants*)	9	16	1	566	88	0	5	37.73	9
G. D. Clough (*Notts*)	7	12	3	338	78	0	3	37.55	2
W. J. House (*Sussex*)	6	10	0	373	80	0	4	37.30	5
S. A. Richardson (*Yorks*)	6	11	1	355	103	1	2	35.50	11
A. G. R. Loudon (*Kent*)	6	10	1	319	132	1	2	35.44	4
L. C. Weekes (*Northants*)	6	10	1	318	138	1	2	35.33	3
I. Brunnschweiler (*Hants*)	11	17	6	388	58*	0	2	35.27	39/1
R. S. Clinton (*Essex & Northants*)	8	15	1	493	112	1	3	35.21	7
B. J. Hyam (*Essex*)	7	10	0	352	96	0	3	35.20	13/4
I. N. Flanagan (*Glos, Kent, Notts & Somerset*)	12	22	0	769	89	0	5	34.95	8
M. Coles (*Somerset*)	6	10	0	348	74	0	3	34.80	6
C. Mann (*Durham*)	6	12	0	413	113	1	2	34.41	1
G. P. Butcher (*Surrey*)	8	14	1	441	167	1	0	33.92	4
N. J. Wilton (*Sussex*)	10	18	1	574	130	1	2	33.76	25/1
B. J. Phillips (*Kent*)	8	12	3	302	82	0	1	33.55	5
D. N. Catterall (*Worcs*)	9	15	2	431	103	1	2	33.15	2
R. E. Sierra (*Warwicks*)	11	16	1	470	116	1	3	31.33	8
V. Atri (*Notts*)	9	16	1	467	63	0	2	31.13	7
A. J. Sexton (*Hants*)	11	17	0	526	116	1	4	30.94	11
D. G. Brandy (*Leics*)	10	16	2	433	113	1	2	30.92	3
G. O. Jones (*Kent*)	10	19	2	513	136	1	2	30.17	32/1
S. P. Titchard (*Derbys*)	10	19	3	481	139*	1	1	30.06	2

BOWLING

(Qualification: 10 wickets, average 25.00)

	O	*M*	*R*	*W*	*BB*	*5W/i*	*Avge*
S. P. Kirby (*Yorks*)	57.1	20	137	12	5-24	1	11.41
J. A. Voros (*Sussex*)	112	31	297	21	8-33	2	14.14
M. C. Ilott (*Essex*)	81	29	157	11	4-31	0	14.27
A. G. R. Loudon (*Kent*)	51.1	12	144	10	7-27	1	14.40
S. R. G. Francis (*Hants*)	92.5	23	247	17	5-44	1	14.52
J. E. K. Schofield (*Hants & Worcs*)	245.4	73	649	43	6-49	1	15.09
P. J. McMahon (*Notts*)	80.5	34	168	11	6-55	1	15.27
P. Aldred (*Derbys*)	60	16	172	11	5-47	1	15.63
A. Richardson (*Warwicks*)	142.3	45	288	18	4-24	0	16.00
A. J. Harris (*Notts*)	118.1	29	325	20	6-40	3	16.25
J. P. Stephenson (*Hants*)	109.1	31	260	16	5-41	1	16.25
A. W. Evans (*Glam*)	94	20	277	17	5-37	1	16.29
R. S. Ferley (*Kent*)	133.2	52	284	17	6-55	1	16.70
C. E. Dagnall (*Warwicks*)	118.5	35	337	20	8-57	1	16.85
M. P. L. Bulbeck (*Somerset*)	103	25	292	17	5-33	1	17.17
I. D. Hunter (*Durham*)	181	45	501	27	5-34	2	18.55
P. M. Hutchison (*Yorks*)	240	45	847	45	7-37	5	18.82
J. M. Anderson (*Lancs*)	163.1	40	435	23	6-63	2	18.91
A. Khan (*Kent*)	137.1	29	449	22	5-55	2	20.40
J. F. Brown (*Northants*)	92	28	205	10	4-39	0	20.50
J. R. C. Hamblin (*Hants*)	331.3	89	904	44	6-42	2	20.54
S. A. J. Boswell (*Leics*)	131	39	331	16	3-24	0	20.68
G. A. Lambert (*Derbys, Essex & Kent*)	147.2	32	509	24	8-59	1	21.20

	O	M	R	W	BB	5W/i	Avge
S. J. Cook (*Middx*)	90	22	255	12	5-58	1	21.25
O. T. Parkin (*Glam*)	150.1	40	426	20	4-47	0	21.30
J. E. Bishop (*Essex*)	50.4	10	219	10	4-80	0	21.90
G. Keedy (*Lancs*)	208.1	65	469	21	5-59	1	22.33
G. W. Walker (*Leics*)	92.1	21	251	11	3-68	0	22.81
A. P. R. Gidman (*Glos*)	94.2	11	349	15	4-56	0	23.26
J. W. M. Dalrymple (*Middx*)	163.1	34	469	20	5-46	2	23.45
G. D. Clough (*Notts*)	198.3	48	615	26	4-98	0	23.65
J. P. Taylor (*Northants*)	96.1	22	285	12	6-62	1	23.75
L. J. Irish (*Leics*)	127.3	21	428	18	3-25	0	23.77
P. D. Trego (*Somerset*)	77.2	16	311	13	4-21	0	23.92
I. H. Shah (*Hants*)	207.2	51	625	26	6-69	1	24.03
A. K. D. Gray (*Worcs & Yorks*)	231.2	68	557	23	5-42	2	24.21
Z. C. Morris (*Hants*)	114.2	35	341	14	3-13	0	24.35
N. C. Phillips (*Durham*)	126.2	42	268	11	3-20	0	24.36
N. G. Hatch (*Durham*)	116.3	29	317	13	5-41	1	24.38
B. J. Phillips (*Kent*)	183.2	51	439	18	6-49	1	24.38
J. P. Hewitt (*Middx*)	231.1	57	783	32	6-37	3	24.46
P. Griffiths (*Leics*)	109.1	25	344	14	5-61	1	24.57
G. J. Batty (*Surrey*)	280.5	74	792	32	8-56	2	24.75

SECOND ELEVEN CHAMPIONS 1959–2001

1959	Gloucestershire	1974	Middlesex	1988	Surrey
1960	Northamptonshire	1975	Surrey	1989	Middlesex
1961	Kent	1976	Kent	1990	Sussex
1962	Worcestershire	1977	Yorkshire	1991	Yorkshire
1963	Worcestershire	1978	Sussex	1992	Surrey
1964	Lancashire	1979	Warwickshire	1993	Middlesex
1965	Glamorgan	1980	Glamorgan	1994	Somerset
1966	Surrey	1981	Hampshire	1995	Hampshire
1967	Hampshire	1982	Worcestershire	1996	Warwickshire
1968	Surrey	1983	Leicestershire	1997	Lancashire
1969	Kent	1984	Yorkshire	1998	Northamptonshire
1970	Kent	1985	Nottinghamshire	1999	Middlesex
1971	Hampshire	1986	Lancashire	2000	Middlesex
1972	Nottinghamshire	1987	Kent / Yorkshire	2001	Hampshire
1973	Essex				

SECOND ELEVEN TROPHY, 2001

A Zone

	Played	Won	Lost	No result	Points
Yorkshire	8	7	1	0	14
Lancashire	8	6	2	0	12
Nottinghamshire	8	4	4	0	8
Durham	8	3	5	0	6
Derbyshire	8	0	8	0	0

B Zone

	Played	Won	Lost	No result	Points
Middlesex	8	6	1	1	13
Warwickshire	8	5	1	2	12
Northamptonshire	8	3	4	1	7
Leicestershire	8	3	4	1	7
Minor Counties	8	0	7	1	1

C Zone

	Played	Won	Lost	No result	Points
Somerset	8	6	1	1	13
Hampshire	8	6	2	0	12
Glamorgan	8	2	4	2	6
Worcestershire	8	2	5	1	5
Gloucestershire	8	1	5	2	4

D Zone

	Played	Won	Lost	No result	Points
Surrey	8	7	1	0	14
Kent	8	5	3	0	10
Essex	8	3	5	0	6
MCC Young Cricketers	8	3	5	0	6
Sussex	8	2	6	0	4

Semi-finals

At The Oval, August 6. Surrey won by seven wickets. Toss: Surrey. Middlesex 235 for eight (50 overs) (J. K. Maunders 44, J. W. M. Dalrymple 48, A. W. Laraman 42; C. G. Greenidge three for 45, P. J. Sampson three for 52); Surrey 239 for three (40.3 overs) (G. J. Batty 101, G. P. Butcher 97 not out).

At Scarborough, August 6, 7. Somerset won by 50 runs. Toss: Somerset. Somerset 190 (48 overs) (P. D. Trego 31, C. A. Hunkin 37, K. A. Parsons 44; T. T. Bresnan three for 37, I. D. Fisher four for 34); Yorkshire 140 (38.4 overs) (G. D. Rose three for 29).

Close of play: Yorkshire 72-4 (19 overs).

Final

At Taunton, September 10. Surrey won by six wickets. Toss: Surrey. Somerset 256 for six (50 overs) (P. D. Trego 32, M. J. Wood 39, A. V. Suppiah 49, J. I. D. Kerr 31, M. P. L. Bulbeck 33); Surrey 260 for four (40.3 overs) (S. A. Newman 53, G. P. Butcher 131).

WINNERS 1986–2001

1986 Northamptonshire
1987 Derbyshire
1988 Yorkshire
1989 Middlesex
1990 Lancashire
1991 Nottinghamshire
1992 Surrey
1993 Leicestershire
1994 Yorkshire
1995 Leicestershire
1996 Leicestershire
1997 Surrey
1998 Northamptonshire
1999 Kent
2000 Leicestershire
2001 Surrey

LEAGUE CRICKET IN ENGLAND AND WALES, 2001

By GEOFFREY DEAN

In their quest to spread premier league cricket across England and Wales, the ECB increased the number of accredited leagues from 20 in 2000 to 24 in 2001. Cornwall, North Staffordshire & South Cheshire, North Wales and South Wales were the four new additions to the premier family. Their ranks appeared unlikely to swell any further in 2002, however, and there was even a possibility that they might be reduced. The status of both the Northern and Yorkshire Leagues came under question in the winter; the ECB wanted more visible links to lower divisions, preferably in the form of promotion and relegation.

Only Leicestershire, with whom discussions were at an early stage during the winter, possessed a slim chance of gaining accreditation for the 2002 season. Two prominent leagues, the Lancashire and the Central Lancashire, remained outside the premier fold, where a match must last 110 overs unless it is concluded inside the distance. The board's preferred quota of 120 overs was implemented in only seven leagues: Surrey, Sussex, Essex, Middlesex, East Anglia, Home Counties and North East. The East Anglian League satisfied the board's requirements for movement between divisions by awarding promotion to the winner of play-offs between the three champions of lower leagues. Only two wanted to take part at the end of 2001, which simplified the issue.

With premier status came a much valued handout from the board of £2,500 per club, or £3,000 in some regional leagues to cover higher travel costs. The Kent Cricket League, which had been receiving £4,000 per club per annum for taking part in the board's three-year pilot scheme of two-day matches over successive Saturdays, was due to have its grant reduced to the standard £2,500 in 2002. The trial had been successful enough for the participating clubs to vote 6–4 in favour of keeping two-day cricket in 2002, and it will now take a two-thirds majority (effectively 7–3) for Kent to return to one-day matches. They remained the only league to play over two days, however.

Folkestone, the Kent champions, secured their first title for 12 years in their final match, winning six of their nine games on first innings and gaining an outright victory over Dartford. Lordswood and Orpington were promoted to the top flight, with Ashford and Beckenham relegated. Not far away, in Sussex, where Horsham completed a league and cup double, Worthing's Australian, Ben Cameron, set a league record of 1,052 runs. In Hampshire, where the Southern League play half a season of limited-overs and half of "time" cricket, BAT Sports pipped Havant for the title thanks to a 100 per cent record in time games.

One of the closest finishes in any of the premier leagues saw Guildford snatch the Surrey Championship from Banstead by two points. When the final round began, Banstead needed only a winning draw (reckoned on superior run-rate) against Weybridge to become champions. But having allowed their opponents to recover from 130 for eight to 280, Banstead slipped from 100 without loss to 238 all out. Guildford's match against Sunbury was heading for a draw when the final hour began, with Sunbury only three wickets down. Then came a collapse as spinners Noel Brett and Sri Lankan Carman Mapatuna, who shared 91 victims during the summer, whittled through the batting until Sunbury's last wicket fell with six minutes remaining.

An incident in May, when Banstead visited Guildford, made their narrow miss all the more galling. The home groundsman, Bill Clutterbuck, achieved national notoriety – and a six-point penalty for his club – when he parked his heavy roller on the edge of the square, locked it and disappeared for the day with the keys. After heavy rain the day before, when the square was not covered, Clutterbuck argued that irreparable damage might be inflicted, affecting Surrey's Championship match on the ground in July. The Banstead players felt that a late start might have been possible, and the local borough council, who own the ground and employ Clutterbuck, were not amused that the Guildford club's interests had been put second to the county's so far ahead of the annual festival. After long deliberation, the league penalised Guildford, but did not award the game to Banstead. Had they done so, Banstead would have become champions.

Ealing won the Middlesex League a year after being promoted, while Pentyrch secured the South Wales League at their first attempt. Stratford were first-time winners of the Birmingham League, which they led for most of the season, thanks in large part to seamer Mike Palmer, who claimed 57 wickets. In the Devon League, Pakistani off-spinner Aqeel Ahmed took 66 for Paignton at an average of just 8.83, but failed to prevent newly promoted Sandford from becoming champions. Almost as impressive was Tim Smith's tally of 65 victims at 9.91 for Essex League winners Saffron Walden. In the Northamptonshire Championship, won for a third successive time by Finedon Dolben, Peterborough's Ajaz Akhtar became the first bowler to reach 100 wickets in a season. He started the last game against Northampton Saints five short of the mark and did not take his fifth until the final ball of the 55-over innings.

Another new milestone was set in the Yorkshire League, which was won by Sheffield Collegiate for the seventh time since 1990. Mathew Sinclair, the New Zealand Test batsman, passed 1,000 runs for Cleethorpes before the end of June, and appeared certain to break David Byas's league record of 1,394, set in 1984. But after missing a total of nine games, largely through international commitments, Sinclair finished the season with 1,195 runs at an average of nearly 92.

Early in the season, tragedy struck Birmingham League club Coventry & North Warwicks, when their overseas all-rounder, Mark Lavine, died of a heart attack. The 28-year-old Lavine, a cousin of Gordon Greenidge, had made his debut for his native Barbados in 1992-93, but later settled in South Africa, where he played for North West. After making a hundred in Coventry's home match against Barnt Green, he opened the bowling, but collapsed soon afterwards. Despite first aid, he died before an ambulance arrived. The match was immediately abandoned.

ECB PREMIER LEAGUE TABLES, 2001

Birmingham and District Premier Cricket League

	P	*W*	*L*	*Pts*
Stratford	22	11	4	289
Halesowen	22	10	8	264
Old Hill	22	8	5	259
Knowle & Dorridge	22	8	5	251
Walsall	22	7	7	239
Wolverhampton	22	7	7	233
Barnt Green	22	6	5	228
Cannock	22	6	5	222
Aston Unity	22	5	7	215
Coventry & N. Warwicks	22	3	7	186
W. Bromwich Dartmouth	22	2	8	167
Kidderminster	22	3	8	161

Cheshire County Cricket League

	P	*W*	*L*	*T*	*Pts*
Didsbury	22	13	2	0	367
Bowdon	22	9	2	0	321
Neston	22	11	6	0	315
Oulton Park	22	8	3	0	308
Alderley Edge	22	6	6	0	281
Chester Boughton Hall	22	7	8	2	276
Hyde	22	5	6	0	271
Nantwich	22	7	8	2	259
Macclesfield	22	3	6	0	238
Cheadle Hulme	22	4	11	0	225
Toft	22	2	10	1	214
Oxton	22	3	10	0	201

The ties do not come to an even number, because a team batting last and levelling the scores was awarded a tie while the other team was awarded a draw.

Cornwall Premier League

	P	W	L	Pts
Truro	18	11	0	282
St Buryan	18	9	1	234
Camborne	18	8	6	211
Callington	18	6	4	204
St Just	18	5	6	187
Grampound Road	18	4	6	179
Troon	18	4	5	179
Falmouth	18	4	6	179
Penzance	18	5	7	175
Helston	18	0	15	72

Derbyshire Premier League

	P	W	L	Pts
Alvaston & Boulton	22	8	1	342
Dunstall	22	7	2	323
Ockbrook & Borrowash	22	7	2	321
Sandiacre Town	22	7	3	315
Stainsby Hall	22	8	7	285
Chesterfield	22	5	4	264
Quarndon	22	4	4	259
Heanor Town	22	5	5	243
Ilkeston Rutland	22	3	4	234
Denby	22	1	6	228
Langley Mill United	22	2	7	167
Shipley Hall	22	1	13	126

Devon Cricket League

	P	W	L	Pts	Avge
Sandford	18	7	3	226	14.13
Torquay	18	8	3	228	13.41
Bovey Tracey	18	5	5	214	13.38
Paignton	18	5	3	198	12.38
Barton	18	8	7	206	12.12
Exeter	18	5	5	199	11.71
Exmouth	18	5	6	191	11.24
Plympton	18	6	7	175	10.94
Sidmouth	18	3	7	166	10.38
Cornwood	18	2	8	163	10.19

East Anglian Premier Cricket League

	P	W	L	Pts	Avge
Norwich	18	7	0	209	16.08
Swardeston	18	8	2	228	15.20
Cambridge & Godmanchester	18	4	3	177	11.80
Cambridge Granta	18	4	5	146	11.23
Mildenhall	18	4	4	152	10.86
Bury St Edmunds	18	4	3	158	10.53
Clacton	18	2	3	134	9.57
Vauxhall Mallards	18	1	3	85	8.50
Maldon	18	1	4	98	7.54
Halstead	18	1	9	72	5.14

Essex Premier League

	P	W	L	Pts
Saffron Walden	18	11	2	258
Wanstead	18	6	2	202
Fives & Heronians	18	5	3	183
Gidea Park & Romford	18	5	3	181
Colchester & East Essex	18	5	4	179
Hainault & Clayhall	18	5	3	176
Loughton	18	3	4	158
Shenfield	18	3	6	149
Hadleigh & Thundersley	18	4	7	146
Horndon on the Hill	18	0	13	52

Home Counties Premier Cricket League

	P	W	L	Pts
Finchampstead	18	11	1	333
Banbury	18	7	3	272
High Wycombe	18	7	4	259
Basingstoke & N. Hants	18	5	4	224
Slough	18	4	3	212
Reading	18	3	3	205
Beaconsfield	18	3	3	194
Bicester & N. Oxford	18	2	5	181
Radlett	18	2	8	152
Luton Town	18	0	10	105

Kent Cricket League

	P	W	L	Pts
Folkestone	9	7	0	289
The Mote	9	6	1	274
St Lawrence	9	6	2	257
Sevenoaks Vine	9	5	4	219
Bromley	9	4	5	214
Dartford	9	4	5	197
Bexley	9	5	3	196
Tunbridge Wells	9	3	6	156
Beckenham	9	1	8	114
Ashford	9	1	8	104

Lincolnshire Cricket Board Premier League

	P	W	L	Pts	%
Bourne	16	8	3	235	73.44
Market Deeping	16	11	3	234	73.13
Grantham	14	9	2	204	72.86
Messingham	14	7	4	176	62.86
Market Rasen	16	8	7	169	52.81
Caistor	15	7	6	149	49.67
Grimsby Town	15	4	9	129	43.00
Sleaford	16	3	8	137	42.81
Lindum	16	4	10	98	30.62
Long Sutton	14	2	11	74	26.43

Liverpool and District Cricket Competition

	P	W	L	Pts
Ormskirk	22	14	3	349
Bootle	22	13	4	327
Wallasey	22	12	7	320
Leigh	22	9	8	265
New Brighton	22	9	7	260
Northop Hall	22	10	6	253
Lytham	22	9	11	233
Wigan	22	7	6	215
Northern	22	6	13	188
Sefton Park	22	5	11	177
Colwyn Bay	22	4	12	148
Huyton	22	4	14	141

Middlesex County Cricket League

	P	W	L	Pts
Ealing	18	8	0	102
Brondesbury	18	6	3	84
Winchmore Hill	18	5	3	75
Teddington	18	5	3	72
Wembley	18	5	5	58
Eastcote	18	3	5	49
Finchley	18	2	2	46
Richmond	18	1	3	45
Brentham	18	3	5	43
Uxbridge	18	1	10	20

Northamptonshire Cricket Championship

	P	W	L	Pts
Finedon Dolben	22	16	2	206
Wellingborough Town	22	11	7	162
County Colts	22	10	2	152
Old Northamptonians	22	11	7	148
Bedford Town	22	10	4	135
Peterborough Town	22	9	11	127
Rothwell Town	22	7	6	112
Northampton Saints	22	6	6	105
Brixworth	22	6	10	92
Horton House	22	2	12	66
Old Wellingburians	22	2	13	50
Irthlingborough Town	22	2	12	49

North East Premier Cricket League

	P	W	L	Pts
Chester-le-Street	20	9	1	341
Benwell Hill	20	8	3	311
Blaydon	20	8	4	288
Newcastle	20	8	4	278
Durham Cricket Academy	20	6	5	262
Sunderland	20	7	6	251
Stockton	20	5	7	223
South Northumberland	20	5	7	215
Norton	20	3	5	199
Tynemouth	20	3	8	188
Gateshead Fell	20	0	12	102

Northern Cricket League

	P	W	L	Pts
Netherfield	22	13	2	200
Chorley	22	7	4	168
Blackpool	22	9	5	166
Kendal	22	11	7	163
Darwen	22	7	4	161
St Annes	22	7	4	155
Morecambe	22	5	2	147
Preston	22	6	8	137
Leyland	22	5	9	112
Fleetwood	22	4	12	91
Leyland Motors	22	3	12	91
Lancaster	22	1	9	81

North Staffs & South Cheshire League

	P	W	L	Pts
Leek	22	13	1	321
Longton	22	10	2	317
Betley	22	10	4	301
Porthill Park	22	10	4	284
Crewe	22	8	10	245
Caverswall	22	4	8	200
Moddershall	22	4	8	199
Knypersley	22	4	6	193
Checkley	22	4	8	189
Audley	22	4	7	176
Cheadle	22	4	9	164
Little Stoke	22	2	10	144

North Wales Premier League

	P	W	L	T	Pts
Bangor	22	17	0	0	395
Hawarden Park	22	9	5	0	287
Mold	22	10	7	0	287
Brymbo	22	9	7	1	263
Northop	22	8	5	0	249
Halkyn	22	6	6	1	225
Pontblyddin	22	5	7	0	215
Llandudno	22	4	6	0	211
Connah's Quay	22	6	12	0	199
Marchweil & Wrexham	22	3	5	0	192
Mochdre	22	4	12	0	176
Bethesda	22	1	10	0	105

Nottinghamshire Cricket Board Premier League

	P	W	L	Pts
West Indian Cavaliers	22	14	3	338
Kimberley	22	11	5	319
Caythorpe	22	12	5	303
Bracebridge	22	8	6	264
Welbeck	22	4	5	250
Bridon	22	8	8	225
Clifton	22	6	6	220
Wollaton	22	7	9	218
Blidworth	22	6	8	211
Notts Unity	22	6	7	205
Radcliffe	22	1	11	155
Balderton	22	2	12	127

Southern Premier Cricket League

	P	W	L	Pts	Avge
BAT Sports	18	14	2	303	18.94
Havant	17	11	1	269	17.93
Bashley Rydal I	17	9	6	221	13.81
Calmore Sports	15	7	5	182	13.00
Bournemouth	16	6	5	190	12.67
South Wiltshire	16	4	7	153	10.93
Burridge	17	5	7	165	10.31
Andover	17	4	9	131	8.19
Liphook & Ripsley	18	4	12	131	7.71
Hungerford	17	2	12	87	5.80

South Wales Cricket League

	P	W	L	Pts	Avge
Pentyrch	18	7	1	201	16.75
Cardiff	18	6	1	187	15.58
Sudbrook	18	5	2	175	14.58
Newport	18	5	5	139	11.58
Usk	18	5	6	150	11.54
Abergavenny	18	5	7	159	11.36
St Fagans	18	4	5	122	11.09
Pontypridd	18	3	6	112	10.18
Chepstow	18	3	6	113	9.42
Panteg	18	3	7	112	8.62

Surrey Championship

	P	W	L	Pts
Guildford	18	9	3	123
Banstead	18	9	4	121
Weybridge	18	8	5	112
Esher	18	7	5	103
Reigate Priory	18	6	7	92
Sunbury	18	5	6	84
Sutton	18	6	7	82
Wimbledon	18	5	5	82
Malden Wanderers	18	3	8	55
Farnham	18	2	10	32

Sussex Cricket League

	P	W	L	Pts
Horsham	18	12	1	388
Hastings	18	11	3	368
Crowborough	18	7	5	296
Brighton & Hove	18	7	6	294
Worthing	18	5	4	259
Eastbourne	18	6	7	253
Three Bridges	18	5	6	253
Chichester	18	3	7	197
Haywards Heath	18	2	10	180
East Grinstead	18	2	11	146

West of England Premier League

	P	W	L	Pts	Avge
Taunton St Andrews	14	10	2	215	15.36
Optimists & Clifton	14	9	2	188	13.43
Bath	14	8	3	186	13.29
Cheltenham	13	7	3	147	11.31
Thornbury	13	7	4	142	10.92
Bristol West Indians	13	5	7	96	7.38
Keynsham	14	3	8	83	5.93
Knowle	13	3	9	70	5.38
Chippenham	15	3	10	66	4.40
Downend	13	2	9	50	3.85

Yorkshire ECB County Premier League

	P	W	L	T	Pts
Sheffield Collegiate	26	18	4	1	139
Scarborough	26	17	6	0	138
Sheffield United	26	14	6	0	124
Yorkshire Academy	26	14	7	0	121
Harrogate	26	15	9	0	118
Cleethorpes	26	13	10	0	108
Doncaster	26	11	11	1	89
Appleby Frodingham	26	9	11	2	87
York	26	11	12	0	83
Castleford	26	9	16	0	74
Rotherham	26	9	15	0	71
Hull	26	7	16	0	62
Driffield	26	5	16	0	56
Barnsley	26	5	18	0	51

OTHER LEAGUE WINNERS, 2001

Airedale & Wharfedale	Bilton
Bassetlaw	Retford
Bolton Association	Walshaw
Bolton League	Walkden
Bradford	Pudsey Congs
Cambs & Hunts	Ramsey
Central Yorkshire	Townville
Durham County	Kimblesworth
Durham Senior	Horden
Hertfordshire	Hertford
Huddersfield	Scholes
Lancashire County	Dukinfield
Leicestershire County	Kibworth
Merseyside Competition	Birkenhead St Mary's
Norfolk Alliance	Fakenham
North Lancashire	Cleator
Northumberland & Tyneside Senior	Ashington
North Yorks & South Durham	Guisborough
Pembrokeshire	Lamphey
Ribblesdale	Cherry Tree
Saddleworth	Moorside
Shropshire	Wroxeter
Somerset	Winscombe
South Wales Association	Swansea
Thames Valley	Farnham Royal
Two Counties	Exning
West Wales Association	Bayswater
York Senior	Dunnington

THE LANCASHIRE LEAGUES, 2001

By CHRIS ASPIN

In what was a high-scoring season, Bacup owed their Lancashire League title to one of the most fruitful bowling partnerships since the league's formation. Australian Shaun Young collected 94 wickets at 11.76, and David Ormerod 79 at 16.87; they bowled out Accrington for only 22, and on seven further occasions dismissed the opposition in double figures. With 1,004 runs, Young narrowly missed the double. Even so, East Lancashire's strong challenge meant that Bacup had to wait until the last day of the season to celebrate their second successive championship after a 40-year drought. They also reached the Worsley Cup final, but lost by six wickets to Ramsbottom.

For Rawtenstall, Matthew Mott of Victoria scored an unbeaten 161 against Lowerhouse, and totalled 1,391 runs, both club records. He was the league's leading run-scorer, 50 ahead of South African Martin van Jaarsveld at Enfield. Another Victorian, Brad Hodge, hit 1,246 for Ramsbottom, including five centuries. Peter Sleep, the former Australian Test player now captaining Rishton, led the amateurs with 918 at 54.00, while Chris Bleazard of Lowerhouse scored 812 at 54.13.

Asif Mujtaba performed the best afternoon's work in league history, for Lowerhouse. Against Todmorden, he took nine for 41, then scored 103 out of 168 in a six-wicket win. Mujtaba, the professional at Norden in the Central Lancashire League, was one of several professionals called in after Lowerhouse lost Jon Kent early on; South African Claude Henderson did almost as well, securing victory over Haslingden with 86 runs followed by nine for 89, including a hat-trick. Another stand-in, Lancashire batsman Graham Lloyd, conceded 84 in 12 overs as Clinton Perren and Russell Whalley added 225 for the second wicket in Rishton's 340 for six; the total was a league record in limited-overs cricket, as was their 222-run win. Uniquely, Lowerhouse conceded 300 for a second time in the season, this time against Rawtenstall, despite borrowing Mike Rindel, whose 107-ball 165 lifted them to 298 for eight. Mott's 161 helped Rawtenstall scramble home in the final over.

Other outstanding performances came from Church openers James Bryant and Craig Fergusson, who put on 225, a club record, against Todmorden; Lancashire all-rounder Ian Austin, who returned to his old club Haslingden and combined 84 runs with seven for eight against Rishton; Western Australian Marcus North, who struck ten sixes and 19 fours in an unbeaten 172, a Colne record, against Haslingden; and Todmorden keeper David Whitehead, who dismissed six Accrington batsmen.

In the Central Lancashire League, Rochdale regained the championship – their 26th – after a year's gap. South African Dirk de Vos scored 980 runs at 98.00, and added 61 wickets at 12.16, receiving strong support from amateurs Peter Wilcock, with 852 runs at 40.57, and Neil Avery, whose 80 wickets cost only 12.41 each. Middleton ran them close, thanks to Sri Lankan Ruwin Peiris, the league's leading scorer with 1,577, Mark Gardener, with 865 at 39.31, and Lee Wolstenholme, the most successful amateur wicket-taker with 88 at 15.96.

Another South African, Brandon Nash of Oldham, became the first player to hit two double-centuries in this league. In 2000, he scored 245 not out against Ashton; now it was Crompton who wilted before an unbeaten 222, containing eight sixes and 18 fours, out of 349 for three. His countryman Peter Koortzen also completed a double-hundred, seeing Walsden to victory over Stand with 210, including 13 sixes, a league record, and 16 fours. Nash hammered six more centuries and finished the season with 1,563 runs, just behind Peiris. The averages were headed, however, by Littleborough pro Lee Carseldine, who scored 722 at 180.50 before being injured. The highest aggregate by an amateur was Mark Wakefield's 899 at 39.08 for Milnrow. His team-mate, West Indian Goldwyn Prince, was the season's leading bowler, with 97 at 15.85, while Asif Mujtaba topped the averages with 92 at 11.07 for Norden.

After a 24-year wait, Middleton won the Lees Wood Cup, with Peiris hitting a century in the final against Radcliffe. Lancashire League sides dominated the Inter-League Cup knockout, though CLL club Littleborough did reach the final, only to lose to Rishton.

LANCASHIRE LEAGUE

	P	*W*	*L*	*NR*	*Bonus Pts*	*Pts*	*Professional*	*Runs*	*Avge*	*Wkts*	*Avge*
Bacup	26	21	3	2	28	244	S. Young	1,004	55.77	94	11.76
East Lancs	26	20	2	4	30	240†	‡B. E. Young	434	33.38	57	14.05
Rishton	26	13	9	4	29	171	C. T. Perren	858	45.15	39	18.64
Burnley	26	12	10	4	32	163†	D. M. Benkenstein	832	39.61	52	17.86
Rawtenstall	26	11	10	5	37	162	M. P. Mott	1,391	81.82	38	16.05
Enfield	26	12	12	2	20	146	M. van Jaarsveld	1,341	78.88	65	17.27
Lowerhouse	26	12	11	3	19	146†	‡J. C. Kent	68	17.00	6	28.16
Haslingden	26	10	11	5	29	144	I. D. Austin	853	40.61	51	14.01
Todmorden	26	10	15	1	38	140†	M. J. Nicholson	484	26.88	72	20.06
Ramsbottom	26	10	10	6	19	137	B. J. Hodge	1,246	77.87	38	16.05
Colne	26	11	13	2	21	137	M. J. North	1,134	66.70	34	29.35
Church	26	6	15	5	32	106†	J. D. C. Bryant	941	49.52	1	97.00
Nelson	26	5	17	4	41	103	W. R. Wingfield	676	45.06	26	26.69
Accrington	26	4	19	3	45	94	T. K. Canning	908	39.47	53	19.24

Notes: Ten points awarded for a win; seven for a tie; two points for dismissing opposition and three for an uncompleted game. A maximum of five bonus points available to losing sides for batting and bowling.

† *Points deducted for slow over-rates.* ‡ *Did not play the whole season.*

CENTRAL LANCASHIRE LEAGUE

	P	*OW*	*LW*	*L*	*D*	*Losing Pts*	*Pts*	*Professional*	*Runs*	*Avge*	*Wkts*	*Avge*
Rochdale	28	16	4	2	6	0	108	D. J. J. de Vos	980	98.00	61	12.16
Middleton	28	14	5	5	4	1	99	G. R. P. Peiris	1,577	83.00	14	23.14
Norden	28	11	4	4	9	0	89	Asif Mujtaba	1,149	88.38	92	11.07
Radcliffe	28	11	3	4	10	1	88	S. E. Dearden	701	35.05	59	17.81
Littleborough	28	10	5	6	7	1	85	‡L. Carseldine	722	180.50	27	17.92
Milnrow	28	13	2	10	3	5	84	G. T. Prince	418	18.17	97	15.85
Werneth	28	8	4	10	6	1	69	S. Fernando	770	33.47	80	16.31
Heywood	28	8	3	11	6	4	68	J. Louw	1,026	42.75	75	19.30
Oldham	28	4	7	9	8	1	65	B. A. Nash	1,563	86.83	42	18.16
Walsden	28	5	2	14	7	5	52	P. P. J. Koortzen	1,108	69.25	19	23.31
Unsworth	28	6	0	13	9	2	50	W. M. P. N. Wanasinghe	952	45.33	89	17.49
Royton	28	2	4	16	6	3	41	S. S. Bhave	1,372	68.60	42	21.59
Ashton	28	2	1	18	7	8	36	M. Conroy	309	12.87	24	25.29
Stand	28	3	0	19	6	7	34	B. Flegg	916	36.64	23	28.60
Crompton	28	1	2	19	6	2	27	Zafar Iqbal	775	32.29	42	28.28

Notes: Five points awarded for an outright win; four points for a limited win; two points for a draw. A team achieves an outright win by bowling out the opposition. One losing point is awarded if a team batting second and losing achieves at least 75 per cent of the first team's total, or if the team bowling second and losing takes seven or more wickets. CLL averages include cup games.

‡ *Did not play the whole season.*

NATIONAL CLUB CHAMPIONSHIP, 2001

Bramhall, whose unbeaten league campaign in 2001 won them promotion to the Cheshire County Premier League, added the National Club Championship to their season's achievements when they beat favourites Bath on September 6. This was the day their middle-order batsman, Snehal Lapsia, had picked for his wedding; instead, the ceremony was brought forward a day so he could play at Lord's. The final proved a tense one, with Bramhall's victory, by four runs, uncertain until the last ball. But it was by no means their closest result. In the first round, they had beaten Longridge by a single run, and in their quarter-final against 1999 champions Wolverhampton the scores finished level at 230; Bramhall went through by virtue of losing six wickets to Wolverhampton's ten. Their next opponents, Scottish club Ayr, had played a quarter-final almost as tight, beating Wickersley Old Village by two runs. When Ayr and Bramhall met in the semi-finals, however, a century from former Lancashire batsman Paddy McKeown helped take the English club to Lord's.

Six of Bath's players had appeared there in 1998, when they lost the National Club final to Doncaster Town. They earned their return by defeating High Wycombe, who had overwhelmed Finchley by 102 runs in the quarter-finals. Bath captain Stuart Priscott's remarkable analysis of 7–1–11–3 helped restrict High Wycombe to 117, but in reply his team slumped to 67 for six. Gregg Brown saved the day with an unbeaten 27, and they lost only one more wicket before winning with four overs to spare.

Sponsorship by website play-cricket.com provided prize money for the first time in this competition, which in 2001 attracted 379 entrants. Bramhall finished £6,000 richer, Bath could console themselves with £3,000, and there was £1,500 each for the losing semi-finalists.

FINAL

BATH v BRAMHALL

At Lord's, September 6. Bramhall won by four runs. Toss: Bath.

Bath needed 22 from the final two overs, then 11 from one; they managed six before Charlie Lamb bowled No. 11 Ian Shrubsole with the last ball of the match. Grant Sheppard had very nearly retrieved the game for Bath after their collapse from 103 for three, by the 31st over, to 128 for eight. Earlier in the day, Bramhall were invited to bat and Andy Hall, who was to play for Cheshire in the Minor Counties Championship final against Lincolnshire three days later, responded with 53, the game's top score. Their eventual total of 175, however, owed much to Mike Bolger and Lamb, who between them helped Bramhall add 40 in the last four overs.

Man of the Match: A. J. Hall.

Bramhall

P. C. McKeown st Griffiths b Swinney	35	C. S. Lamb not out	19
†T. S. Gane c Griffiths b Barnes	6	*J. Mellor not out	3
A. J. Hall lbw b Shrubsole	53	L-b 4, w 7, n-b 2	13
S. K. Lapsia st Griffiths b Swinney	12		
E. McCray b Sheppard	11	1/20 2/70 3/100 (6 wkts, 45 overs)	175
M. Bolger b Shrubsole	23	4/123 5/128 6/159	

N. Thompson, I. Bailey and A. Birley did not bat.

Bowling: Barnes 9–3–39–1; Shrubsole 9–0–33–2; Sheppard 7–0–35–1; Sage 2–0–15–0; Swinney 9–0–21–2; Priscott 9–1–28–0.

Bath

*S. M. Priscott c Gane b Lamb	0	†S. P. Griffiths b Thompson	14
D. N. Pippett run out	41	G. Sheppard not out	22
G. R. Swinney b Thompson	20	I. P. Shrubsole b Lamb	8
B. R. F. Staunton lbw b Thompson	12	L-b 11, w 17, n-b 1	29
M. P. Sage c Gane b Lamb	9		
G. Brown st Gane b McKeown	8	1/1 2/33 3/79	(45 overs) 171
M. J. Rowe b McCray	8	4/103 5/103 6/115	
S. N. Barnes lbw b McCray	0	7/116 8/128 9/149	

Bowling: Lamb 9–2–23–3; Bailey 6–1–16–0; Birley 9–0–51–0; Thompson 8–2–22–3; McCray 9–0–37–2; McKeown 4–1–11–1.

Umpires: S. W. Kuhlmann and T. G. Wilson.

WINNERS 1969–2001

1969	Hampstead	1980	Moseley	1991	Teddington
1970	Cheltenham	1981	Scarborough	1992	Optimists
1971	Blackheath	1982	Scarborough	1993	Old Hill
1972	Scarborough	1983	Shrewsbury	1994	Chorley
1973	Wolverhampton	1984	Old Hill	1995	Chorley
1974	Sunbury	1985	Old Hill	1996	Walsall
1975	York	1986	Stourbridge	1997	Eastbourne
1976	Scarborough	1987	Old Hill	1998	Doncaster Town
1977	Southgate	1988	Enfield	1999	Wolverhampton
1978	Cheltenham	1989	Teddington	2000	Sheffield Collegiate
1979	Scarborough	1990	Blackpool	2001	Bramhall

NATIONAL VILLAGE CHAMPIONSHIP, 2001

Ynystawe, a village near Swansea that had never advanced further than the quarter-finals, defeated title-holders Elvaston by 99 runs to win the last Village Championship sponsored by brewers Wadworth. Paul Discombe, a 23-year-old seamer from the DVLA in Swansea, grabbed six wickets to provide the first Welsh triumph since St Fagans' third win in 1991. In the semi-finals he had claimed three victims, and 48-year-old David Llewellyn four, against St Margaretsbury, inexperienced winners of the Bedfordshire/Hertfordshire group. St Margaretsbury, who could field three brothers Tilbury and three Ansteads, fell 11 runs short of reaching Lord's, scoring 156 in reply to Ynystawe's 166 for seven.

Elvaston, champions in 1994 and 2000, also had a close semi-final. Travelling to Wolviston, near Middlesbrough, they lost eight wickets before overtaking a total of 109. Until then, Elvaston had looked invincible. They won the Derbyshire group final for the sixth time in seven years after Lee Archer and Richard Johnson shared an unbroken opening partnership of 283 against Walton-on-Trent, and in their Midlands quarter-final they demolished Colwall for 37, including seven ducks, with Peter Birch taking three for four and Andy Barrett three for eight.

Highlights of earlier rounds included an even more precipitate collapse in Northamptonshire: Yelvertoft managed 19 in response to Weekley and Warkton's 333. In Gloucestershire, Alastair Watkins scored an unbeaten 199 as Redmarley beat Sheepscombe by 200 runs. Sparsholt and Hambledon both reached 300 in the Hampshire group semi-final; Hambledon won by 17 as they shared an aggregate of 617 runs for 13 wickets, beating the previous season's record of 608 for eight.

Many clubs had difficulty staging games because of the foot-and-mouth epidemic. In North Yorkshire, Ingleby Greenhow settled their fixture with Middleton Tyas at darts. Translating their darts scores into runs and wickets, Ingleby recorded an innings win, but they could not reproduce this form on the field. Sessay bowled them out for 77 in the next round.

FINAL

ELVASTON v YNYSTAWE

At Lord's, September 9. Ynystawe won by 99 runs. Toss: Ynystawe.

Paul Discombe crushed Elvaston with six for 18, the best analysis in 30 finals. His first three wickets reduced the defending champions to 33 for five; later, he ended Robert Torry's one-man counter-attack, having him caught on the boundary, and swiftly bowled two tailenders to clinch victory. Elvaston were not even halfway to a target of 191. They could not have expected to chase so many runs when Ynystawe were 94 for two in 30 overs. Glamorgan Under-19 batsman Jonathan Hubschmid did not score until the ninth over, but eventually completed the match's only fifty, from 91 balls. With wickets in hand, however, Ynystawe were well placed to make a vigorous final assault. Their last ten overs more than doubled the score, with Andrew Beasley (48 in 47 balls) and Gareth Bishop adding 67 in six.

Man of the Match: P. A. Discombe.

Ynystawe

M. Hayden lbw b Hall	19
J. Hubschmid run out	51
R. Evans c Bodill b Birch	11
A. Beasley b Hall	48
G. Bishop c Bodill b Barrett	24
C. Keen not out	0
†G. Jones not out	10
L-b 16, w 8, n-b 3	27
1/27 2/69 3/107 4/174 5/176 (5 wkts, 40 overs)	190

*D. Llewellyn, B. Northey, P. Crane and P. A. Discombe did not bat.

Bowling: Barrett 9–2–28–1; Hall 9–1–39–2; Murray 6–0–33–0; Thompson 9–0–31–0; Birch 6–1–26–1; Kettlewell 1–0–17–0.

Elvaston

†L. D. Archer b Discombe	2
*R. D. Johnson c Llewellyn b Discombe	17
P. E. Birch c Evans b Northey	1
A. Brear lbw b Northey	1
S. Thompson c Jones b Discombe	1
R. A. Torry c Hubschmid b Discombe	45
R. Kettlewell run out	7
J. R. Bodill st Jones b Llewellyn	0
S. R. Murray b Discombe	3
I. Hall not out	0
A. R. Barrett b Discombe	0
B 2, l-b 3, w 2, n-b 7	14
1/10 2/25 3/29 4/33 5/33 6/60 7/82 8/86 9/91 (26.5 overs)	91

Bowling: Discombe 8.5–4–18–6; Northey 7–1–20–2; Hubschmid 5–1–29–0; Evans 4–0–18–0; Llewellyn 2–1–1–1.

Umpires: R. L. Johnson and J. Townsend.

WINNERS 1972–2001

1972	Troon (Cornwall)
1973	Troon (Cornwall)
1974	Bomarsund (Northumberland)
1975	Gowerton (Glamorgan)
1976	Troon (Cornwall)
1977	Cookley (Worcestershire)
1978	Linton Park (Kent)
1979	East Bierley (Yorkshire)
1980	Marchwiel (Clwyd)
1981	St Fagans (Glamorgan)
1982	St Fagans (Glamorgan)
1983	Quarndon (Derbyshire)
1984	Marchwiel (Clwyd)
1985	Freuchie (Fife)
1986	Forge Valley (Yorkshire)
1987	Longparish (Hampshire)
1988	Goatacre (Wiltshire)
1989	Toft (Cheshire)
1990	Goatacre (Wiltshire)
1991	St Fagans (Glamorgan)
1992	Hursley Park (Hampshire)
1993	Kington (Herefordshire)
1994	Elvaston (Derbyshire)
1995	Woodhouse Grange (Yorkshire)
1996	Caldy (Cheshire)
1997	Caldy (Cheshire)
1998	Methley (Yorkshire)
1999	Linton Park (Kent)
2000	Elvaston (Derbyshire)
2001	Ynystawe (Glamorgan)

IRISH CRICKET, 2001

By DEREK SCOTT

Ireland had a disappointing season. They hoped to qualify for the 2003 World Cup by finishing third or higher in July's ICC Trophy but, after getting through the preliminaries, they propped up the Super League of eight. Five Irish batsmen averaged 39 or more, and Ed Joyce headed the tournament averages with 359 runs at 71.80; it was the bowling that let them down. Ireland also came last in the Triple Crown, held in Sussex, losing all three games, as in 1999; in the year between, rain restricted them to bowl-outs. All told, they played 19 matches in 2001, all limited-overs, and won only seven. The first-class fixture with Scotland was dropped in a crowded programme, which concluded in September with the preliminary rounds of the 2002 Cheltenham & Gloucester Trophy. In these, Jason Molins led Ireland to victory, having succeeded Kyle McCallan as captain.

Ed Joyce was Ireland's foremost batsman, but was available only in Toronto; after that he returned to Middlesex and became the first player born and wholly educated in Ireland to score a first-class century in county cricket. Meanwhile, his younger brother, Dominick, was the find of the season and scored the most runs, 455 at 28.43 – well ahead of Molins, with 365, and Peter Davy, 364. The leading wicket-taker was young fast bowler Adrian McCoubrey, who collected 20 at 17.40, while Paul Mooney took 18 at 24.38. Another promising newcomer was Jordan McGonigle, aged 19, a slow left-armer with a nice high action. He could fill the gap left by 42-year-old Matt Dwyer, who had taken 62 wickets for Ireland at 25.87 prior to retiring after the fixture with the touring Australians, unfortunately rained off.

The men's and women's cricket unions amalgamated for the 2001 season, and the women commemorated the occasion more successfully than the men, winning the European Championship at Reading with five straight victories. A hat-trick by Saibh Young set up their final win, over England Under-19, who fielded some full internationals. The men's youth teams had an excellent year, with the Under-17, Under-15 and Under-13 teams winning European tournaments.

In domestic cricket, Cork won the Munster League for the seventh year running, and the Munster Cup for the sixth in nine. By contrast, Merrion headed the Dublin Senior League for the first time since 1958; Brad Spanner and Chris Torrisi added 280 against The Hills, an all-wicket league record. YMCA won the Cup, while being demoted in the League for the first time since relegation was introduced in 1993. (Their women's team retained the Cup, but their League title passed to Malahide.) Aided by South African Andre Botha, newly promoted North County became only the second Leinster side to win the Royal Liver Irish Senior Cup in its 20 years, after Phoenix in 1986.

North Down completed their first Northern Union double since 1936. In the Cup final against NICC, Ryan Haire made an unbeaten century in their first innings, and his father Robin contributed 54 in the second. In the North-West, Limavady's League-winning streak ended at seven, two short of Donemana's record. Brigade claimed the title in a play-off against Donemana. These two also met in the final of the third Ulster Cup, for teams from the Northern and North-West Unions; Donemana were losing finalists for the third year running, though they did win the North-West Cup.

Winners of Irish Leagues and Cups

Royal Liver Irish Senior Cup: North County. **Ulster Cup:** Brigade. **Dublin Senior League:** Merrion. **Dublin Senior Cup:** YMCA. **Munster League:** Cork County. **Munster Cup:** Cork County. **Northern Union:** North Down. **Northern Union Cup:** North Down. **North-West League:** Brigade. **North-West Cup:** Donemana.

SCOTTISH CRICKET, 2001

By NEIL LEITCH

On the face of it, Scotland's national side had their most successful season ever, winning 11 of their 15 senior matches. But the overwhelming reaction was one of great disappointment. Qualification for the next World Cup was the primary objective for 2001, and for that Scotland had to finish in the top three at the ICC Trophy in Toronto. They finished fourth, losing a play-off to hosts Canada.

Scotland arrived in Toronto at the end of June as top seeds – they were third in the 1997 Trophy, whose finalists, Bangladesh and Kenya, were now automatic World Cup entrants. They opened their campaign by bowling Fiji out for 41. Sterner challenges were to come, but they finished second in their preliminary group, losing only to Holland, and won their first three matches in the Super League. The last league game, against Namibia, could have put them in the final. Some had been surprised by the Africans' rapid progress, but not the Scots, who had discovered their quality in a pre-season tour. Namibia rattled up 256 for six, but Colin Smith, Scotland's best batsman, replied with a superb 88. With 34 deliveries remaining, they required just 32 runs, with six wickets in hand. Those six wickets fell for 22 in 26 balls; team confidence sank, and the play-off against Canada, whom Scotland had beaten in a group game, ended in anticlimactic defeat.

Scotland faced further disappointment when losing to the England Board XI on the opening day of the Triple Crown tournament ultimately prevented them retaining that title. Consolation came in September with victories over the Middlesex Board XI and Dorset in the Cheltenham & Gloucester Trophy. Because of the ICC Trophy, Scotland had missed this tournament in 2001; these games were the preliminary rounds of the 2002 competition. Moreover, their exposure south of the border was set to increase. In December, it was announced that they would take part in the Norwich Union League on a three-year trial starting in 2003. Scotland also hosted the European Under-19 tournament, and won it to qualify for the World Cup in New Zealand in January 2002.

On the club front, Grange retained their title as premier division champions of the Scottish National Cricket League. However, Greenock could claim to be the team of the season: they easily won the first division, and beat Grange in the Scottish Cup final. It was a dramatic turnaround from 2000, when Greenock's alleged approaches to players at other clubs led to their being fined 75 points and thus relegated from the premier division. Penicuik and Edinburgh Academicals were both elevated to the National League after winning the play-offs between the champions of the four feeder leagues. But Glasgow Academicals and Dundee HSFP dropped down again after only one season.

There were significant changes in Scotland's administration, with the setting up of Scottish Cricket plc, which took over nearly all the duties of the Scottish Cricket Union. Zimbabwean Gwynne Jones was appointed its chief executive. Meanwhile, Jim Love resigned as director of cricket after ten years; Australian Tony Judd took over coaching duties on a part-time basis in the winter. Long-serving captain George Salmond announced his retirement from international cricket after scoring 3,307 runs, the fourth-highest aggregate for Scotland, in a record 146 appearances.

Winners of Scottish Leagues and Cups
Scottish National Cricket League: *Premier Division* – Grange; *First Division* – Greenock; *Second Division* – Dunfermline. **Scottish Cup:** Greenock. **SCU Trophy:** Penicuik. **Small Clubs' Cup:** Fauldhouse Victoria. **Border League:** Penicuik. **East of Scotland League:** Edinburgh Academicals. **Strathmore Union:** Meigle. **Western Union:** Weirs. **North of Scotland League:** Buckie. **Perthshire League:** Rossie Priory. **West League Cup:** Greenock. **Rowan Cup:** West of Scotland. **Masterton Trophy:** Carlton.

WEST INDIES UNDER-19 IN ENGLAND, 2001

By GARETH A. DAVIES

While West Indies' seniors attempted to fight their way out of a crisis, their Under-19 players shone in England. They had a strong squad – 12 of the 16 had already played first-class cricket – which performed consistently to get the better of England Under-19. On West Indies' last Under-19 tour of England, in 1993, they had lost both Test and one-day international series. This time, they took the limited-overs series 2–1, and went on to win the Tests, thanks to their victory in the first match, at Leicester. The remaining two Tests were rain-affected and drawn. The tourists lost only two games throughout the trip – the opening fixture against an England Board XI, and the second one-day international, by 13 runs.

Their outstanding player was Devon Smith, a left-handed opening batsman from Grenada, whose aggressive methods and fast scoring gave the West Indians the upper hand in most matches. He scored 243 at 121.50 in the one-day internationals, 374 at 62.33 in the Tests, and 882 at 67.84 in all matches, including three centuries. "He has all the signs of a batsman who will go on to full Test cricket," said tour manager Jeff Broomes. Smith was well supported by captain and fellow-opener Brenton Parchment, along with Narsingh Deonarine, who turned 18 during the trip, and Tonito Willett in the middle order. The other player to make a crucial contribution was Kenroy Peters, a steady, fast-medium left-armer from St Vincent. His admirable temperament and nagging accuracy brought him 16 wickets at 12.68 in four Test innings, and seven at 8.85 in the one-day internationals. He sealed the key victory in the First Test with 11 for 88, including a hat-trick.

England suffered badly from county interference in their selections, and their assistant coach, Neil Foster, conceded that the frequent changes of personnel affected the team's performance. It would not be unfair, either, to say that the ECB underestimated the tourists. Although it had been agreed that the Under-19 side should have first claim on county players, the ECB had promised "flexibility" in individual cases, and, as ever, the counties were swift to exploit the concession. Hampshire seamer Chris Tremlett was available only for the one-day series. Ian Bell of Warwickshire led the team in the one-day games, then disappeared until the final Test. Nicky Peng deputised in the First Test and, when he was recalled by Durham, Kent off-spinner James Tredwell took over for the Second.

That match, at Trent Bridge, saw England's high point of the series, however. After conceding 400 runs to Smith and his team-mates on the opening day, the home team hit back by piling up their highest-ever total – 620 for nine declared – with big hundreds from Gary Pratt of Durham and Worcestershire's Kadeer Ali. The game also featured the home international debut of Kyle Hogg, of Lancashire. His grandfather, West Indies spinner Sonny Ramadhin, had returned figures of 81.2–25–135–5 against England at Nottingham 51 years earlier; the grandson, playing for England on the same ground, began with five for 88, including three wickets in four balls. Though he played only two Tests, Hogg was his team's leading wicket-taker, with ten at 24.70. Pratt, who like Smith scored a hundred in a one-day international as well as the Tests, was named England's Man of the Series.

WEST INDIES UNDER-19 TOURING PARTY

B. A. Parchment (Jamaica) (*captain*), C. C. Alexander (Windward Islands), V. Arjune (Guyana), R. A. Austin (Barbados), O. A. C. Banks (Leeward Islands), C. Baugh (Jamaica), P. A. Browne (Barbados), N. Deonarine (Guyana), H. Garbarran (Guyana), J. J. C. Lawson (Jamaica), R. S. Matthews (Guyana), K. K. Peters (Windward Islands), A. P. Richardson (Jamaica), D. S. Smith (Windward Islands), R. Thomas (Guyana), T. A. Willett (Leeward Islands).

Manager: J. Broomes. *Coach:* A. L. Logie. *Physiotherapist:* D. Cumberbatch.

WEST INDIES UNDER-19 TOUR RESULTS

Matches – Played 13: Won 6, Lost 2, Drawn 5.

Note: Matches in this section were not first-class.

At Hastings, July 22. England Board XI won by 61 runs. Toss: England Board XI. England Board XI 196 for seven (50 overs) (I. Dawood 34, C. M. Mole 34 not out, A. J. Procter 33 not out); West Indies Under-19 135 (39.3 overs) (D. S. Smith 38; A. J. Pugh four for 21).

At Brighton College, July 23. West Indies Under-19 won by eight wickets. Toss: ECB Schools. ECB Schools 85 for nine (50 overs) (S. Marshall 33 not out; J. J. C. Lawson three for 21, A. P. Richardson three for 16); West Indies Under-19 86 for two (23.5 overs).

After the early finish, the teams played a 20-over match, which West Indies Under-19 won by 22 runs.

At Brighton College, July 24. West Indies Under-19 won by one run. Toss: West Indies Under-19. West Indies Under-19 141 (47.1 overs) (M. Todd three for 38); ECB Schools 140 (49.5 overs) (N. R. D. Compton 74).

At Hove, July 27 (day/night). First one-day international: West Indies Under-19 won by two wickets. Toss: England Under-19. England Under-19 142 for nine (50 overs) (J. L. Sadler 35; N. Deonarine three for 13); West Indies Under-19 143 for eight (49.5 overs) (D. S. Smith 75; C. T. Tremlett three for 21).

England Under-19 collapsed from 100 for four to 110 for nine in four overs. For West Indies, Kenroy Peters returned figures of 10–5–10–1.

At Chelmsford, July 29. Second one-day international: England Under-19 won by 13 runs. Toss: England Under-19. England Under-19 241 (49.5 overs) (G. J. Pratt 100, I. R. Bell 59; K. K. Peters three for 30, O. A. C. Banks three for 36); West Indies Under-19 228 (47.3 overs) (D. S. Smith 66, T. A. Willett 30, C. Baugh 47 not out, Extras 30; J. E. Bishop seven for 41).

Pratt scored 100 in 113 balls, with 13 fours, and added 138 for England Under-19's second wicket with Bell.

At Chelmsford, July 30. Third one-day international: West Indies Under-19 won by seven wickets. Toss: England Under-19. England Under-19 182 (47.5 overs) (Kadeer Ali 57, C. T. Tremlett 37; K. K. Peters three for 22, R. Thomas three for 41); West Indies Under-19 183 for three (38 overs) (D. S. Smith 102 not out).

Smith scored 102 in 107 balls, with 12 fours and two sixes. West Indies Under-19 won the one-day series 2–1.

At Arundel, August 1, 2, 3. Drawn. Toss: Development of Excellence (South) XI. Development of Excellence (South) XI 193 (A. V. Suppiah 77, C. D. Nash 30; R. Thomas three for 12) and 48 for one; West Indies Under-19 379 for six dec. (P. A. Browne 39, T. A. Willett 30, N. Deonarine 100, V. Arjune 103 not out, C. C. Alexander 51 not out, Extras 36).

ENGLAND v WEST INDIES

First Under-19 Test

At Leicester, August 6, 7, 8, 9. West Indies Under-19 won by 75 runs. Toss: England Under-19.

Smith and Parchment quickly made up for lost time after a rain-delayed start. They opened with 107 in 15 overs: Smith scored a 48-ball 54, with 11 fours, before falling to Tredwell's first delivery. Next day, Deonarine batted more sedately to be unbeaten after nearly three hours. Left-armer Peters then ripped out the home side's middle order with only the second hat-trick in England's 99 Under-19 Tests, after Richard Illingworth's against West Indies at Northampton in 1982. A resilient 53-run stand between Shafayat and Prior launched a recovery, and the tail wagged on the third morning to limit West Indies' lead to 35. Smith soon built on that with 90 runs, including

13 fours and a six over long-on. West Indies lost four for 11 in a hectic half-hour on the final morning, and England were set 301 in 87 overs. Kadeer Ali and Prior contributed half-centuries, but England subsided with seven overs to spare, Peters claiming match figures of 11 for 88.

Close of play: First day, West Indies Under-19 188-5 (Deonarine 13*, Banks 0*); Second day, England Under-19 207-7 (Prior 56*, Bishop 1*); Third day, West Indies Under-19 254-5 (Deonarine 15*).

West Indies Under-19

D. S. Smith c McGarry b Tredwell	54	– c Bishop b McGarry	90
*B. A. Parchment lbw b Bishop	62	– c Prior b Anderson	19
P. A. Browne b Muchall	25	– run out	20
T. A. Willett c Tredwell b McGarry	12	– c Prior b Anderson	75
N. Deonarine not out	67	– c Peng b McGarry	20
V. Arjune c Peng b Anderson	7	– (7) c Prior b Anderson	1
O. A. C. Banks c Tredwell b Anderson	3	– (8) b Anderson	0
†C. Baugh c and b Tredwell	15	– (6) lbw b Anderson	19
K. K. Peters c Kadeer Ali b Tredwell	0	– c Prior b McGarry	4
A. P. Richardson c Prior b Bishop	3	– not out	0
J. J. C. Lawson run out	9		
L-b 6, w 2, n-b 13	21	B 2, l-b 10, n-b 5	17
1/107 2/137 3/151 4/170 5/182 6/192 7/233 8/235 9/248	278	1/52 2/100 3/201 4/226 5/254 6/260 7/260 8/261 9/265 (9 wkts dec.)	265

Bowling: *First Innings*—Bishop 21–6–82–2; Anderson 18.2–5–60–2; McGarry 16–4–65–1; Tredwell 21–5–51–3; Muchall 4–1–14–1. *Second Innings*—Bishop 9–0–57–0; Anderson 20–5–45–5; Tredwell 30–10–82–0; McGarry 19.3–4–48–3; Muchall 4–1–21–0.

England Under-19

G. J. Pratt c Peters b Lawson	15	– c Deonarine b Lawson	4
J. J. Sayers lbw b Peters	25	– lbw b Lawson	7
Kadeer Ali c Baugh b Peters	7	– c Baugh b Peters	67
*N. Peng c Parchment b Richardson	8	– c Banks b Peters	22
G. J. Muchall lbw b Peters	0	– c Parchment b Arjune	37
B. M. Shafayat c Smith b Banks	33	– run out	5
†M. J. Prior c Smith b Peters	57	– c Baugh b Peters	51
J. C. Tredwell b Peters	33	– c Baugh b Peters	8
J. E. Bishop b Lawson	1	– not out	1
A. C. McGarry not out	18	– c Banks b Richardson	2
J. M. Anderson b Peters	16	– lbw b Peters	3
L-b 12, w 4, n-b 14	30	B 4, l-b 5, w 5, n-b 4	18
1/31 2/58 3/64 4/64 5/78 6/131 7/204 8/207 9/211	243	1/4 2/48 3/103 4/104 5/123 6/204 7/216 8/217 9/221	225

Bowling: *First Innings*—Richardson 11–2–57–1; Lawson 16–3–72–2; Peters 25.4–9–50–6; Willett 3–0–9–0; Banks 8–0–26–1; Deonarine 6–0–17–0. *Second Innings*—Lawson 21–4–83–2; Peters 28.1–15–38–5; Richardson 17–3–66–1; Banks 8–3–20–0; Arjune 6–1–9–1.

Umpires: A. A. Jones and M. J. Kitchen.

At Oakham School, August 11, 12, 13. Drawn. Toss: Development of Excellence (Midlands) XI. Development of Excellence (Midlands) XI 246 (A. J. Maiden 42, T. B. Huggins 60, Extras 38; R. A. Austin four for 42, C. C. Alexander four for 63) and 129 for six dec. (D. G. Brandy 42, G. Wagg 40 not out; R. A. Austin three for 61); West Indies Under-19 143 (N. Deonarine 32; G. Wagg five for 57, D. G. Brandy four for 38) and 101 for one (B. A. Parchment 43 not out, H. Garbarran 49).

ENGLAND v WEST INDIES

Second Under-19 Test

At Nottingham, August 15, 16, 17, 18. Drawn. Toss: West Indies Under-19.

The Trent Bridge pitch proved full of runs, as England trumped West Indies' 416 with 620 for nine, their highest total in Under-19 Tests. Smith set the tone with 169, including 27 fours and two sixes – his sixth consecutive score over 50 against England on this tour. He shrugged off a blow to his forearm in the very first over to raise a speedy 87 in 16 overs with Parchment, followed by 147 in 28 with Arjune. West Indies declared next morning, after Hogg seized three wickets in four balls. Pratt then took centre stage, striking 28 fours and a six in his 188 and sharing century partnerships with Sayers and Ali, who went on to bat more than seven hours, scoring 155 and adding another 154 with Sadler. England's eventual lead was 204; their hopes of levelling the series rose when Hogg trapped Smith cheaply. But the tourists batted solidly on the final day and were 60 ahead when the match was called off at tea because of bad weather.

Close of play: First day, West Indies Under-19 400-6 (Deonarine 40*, Alexander 23*); Second day, England Under-19 313-3 (Kadeer Ali 56*, Sadler 0*); Third day, West Indies Under-19 45-1 (Parchment 18*, Arjune 10*).

West Indies Under-19

D. S. Smith c Pope b Shafayat	169	– lbw b Hogg	15
*B. A. Parchment c Anderson b Tredwell	42	– b Tredwell	57
V. Arjune c Sayers b Hogg	79	– lbw b Anderson	47
T. A. Willett c Muchall b Anderson	10	– not out	87
N. Deonarine b Hogg	53		
O. A. C. Banks c Tredwell b Hogg	19	– (5) not out	50
†C. Baugh lbw b Muchall	1		
C. C. Alexander c Pope b Hogg	24		
K. K. Peters not out	1		
A. P. Richardson lbw b Hogg	0		
B 1, l-b 10, w 3, n-b 4	18	B 2, l-b 4, w 1, n-b 1	8
1/87 2/234 3/267 4/331 5/365 6/370 7/415 8/416 9/416 (9 wkts dec.)	416	1/29 2/102 3/130 (3 wkts)	264

J. J. C. Lawson did not bat.

Bowling: *First Innings*—Anderson 15–2–71–1; McGarry 18–4–72–0; Hogg 24–6–88–5; Tredwell 30–11–81–1; Muchall 16–3–56–1; Shafayat 11–0–37–1. *Second Innings*—Anderson 16–4–68–1; Hogg 18–4–59–1; Tredwell 25–9–49–1; McGarry 10–1–37–0; Muchall 8–2–30–0; Shafayat 3–1–5–0; Pratt 5–1–10–0.

England Under-19

G. J. Pratt c Baugh b Lawson	188
J. J. Sayers c Alexander b Lawson	45
Kadeer Ali c Banks b Willett	155
K. W. Hogg b Lawson	8
J. L. Sadler c Willett b Lawson	64
G. J. Muchall st Baugh b Willett	17
B. M. Shafayat st Baugh b Banks	32
*J. C. Tredwell c Lawson b Alexander	49
†S. P. Pope not out	14
J. M. Anderson c sub b Alexander	2
A. C. McGarry not out	7
B 14, l-b 8, w 4, n-b 13	39
1/116 2/305 3/313 4/467 5/502 6/511 7/592 8/597 9/600 (9 wkts dec.)	620

Bowling: Lawson 33–3–125–4; Peters 37–15–74–0; Banks 37–6–135–1; Richardson 22–2–101–0; Alexander 28–2–110–2; Arjune 18–3–44–0; Willett 5–1–9–2.

Umpires: M. R. Benson and P. Willey.

At Sleaford, August 20, 21, 22. West Indies Under-19 won by eight wickets. Toss: Development of Excellence (North) XI. Development of Excellence (North) XI 300 (A. Gail 33, R. Khan 54, D. Brown 31, T. Rees 86, Extras 35; R. A. Austin three for 66) and 96 (R. A. Austin five for 61); West Indies Under-19 288 (D. S. Smith 55, V. Arjune 99, C. C. Alexander 34 not out; R. Hodgkinson three for 46) and 109 for two (B. A. Parchment 60 not out).

At Durham University, August 24, 25, 26. Drawn. Toss: England Under-18. England Under-18 264 (M. L. Pettini 115, N. R. D. Compton 42, P. Mustard 34; O. A. C. Banks three for 37, R. S. Matthews five for 64) and 254 for five dec. (K. Bell 43, P. Mustard 62, W. R. Smith 46, A. Roberts 43, Extras 33); West Indies Under-19 194 (D. S. Smith 54, T. A. Willett 33, C. Baugh 30; C. Brice four for 44) and 202 for three (D. S. Smith 102 not out, T. A. Willett 48).

ENGLAND v WEST INDIES

Third Under-19 Test

At Chester-le-Street, August 28, 29, 30, 31. Drawn. Toss: West Indies Under-19.

Rain wiped out much of the third day and all the fourth to keep West Indies' winning margin to 1–0. England's hopes of pulling level had evaporated after they squandered an excellent start. Hogg began an incisive spell by extracting Smith, who edged the first ball of the match, and soon after lunch West Indies were 63 for five. Only Deonarine's patient 54 redeemed them. England, however, were unravelled by the steady accuracy of Peters. He claimed two wickets by the close, including captain Bell, and next day England's last eight fell for 59 – a 29-run deficit. Smith quickly made up for his first-innings failure with a run-a-ball 46, hustling West Indies to 76 in 14 overs. On the third day, Willett completed a century before, like Smith, he fell to Tredwell's spin. He had added 170 with Deonarine, who missed the opportunity to convert his fourth fifty of the series into a hundred when the final day was abandoned.

Close of play: First day, England Under-19 54-2 (Sayers 15*, Peng 15*); Second day, West Indies Under-19 193-3 (Willett 54*, Deonarine 18*); Third day, West Indies Under-19 322-4 (Deonarine 89*, Banks 3*).

West Indies Under-19

D. S. Smith c Prior b Hogg	0	– b Tredwell	46
*B. A. Parchment b Hogg	23	– c Bell b Panesar	59
V. Arjune lbw b Bishop	7	– lbw b Bishop	1
T. A. Willett c Sayers b Hogg	7	– c Peng b Tredwell	103
N. Deonarine b Panesar	54	– not out	89
O. A. C. Banks lbw b Bishop	0	– not out	3
†C. Baugh b Tredwell	28		
R. S. Matthews run out	5		
K. K. Peters c Pratt b Hogg	22		
R. A. Austin not out	0		
J. J. C. Lawson c and b Panesar	3		
B 5, l-b 4, w 1, n-b 7	17	B 3, l-b 8, w 3, n-b 7	21
1/0 2/35 3/40 4/57 5/63 6/112 7/131 8/149 9/163	166	1/76 2/82 3/146 4/316 (4 wkts)	322

Bowling: *First Innings*—Hogg 18–6–31–4; Anderson 14–3–34–0; Bishop 15–3–43–2; Panesar 20.5–9–35–2; Tredwell 11–5–14–1. *Second Innings*—Hogg 21–3–69–0; Anderson 13.2–3–50–0; Bishop 18–2–70–1; Panesar 19–4–74–1; Tredwell 28–12–48–2.

England Under-19

G. J. Pratt b Peters	22
J. J. Sayers c Baugh b Lawson	24
*I. R. Bell c Baugh b Peters	1
N. Peng c Arjune b Lawson	31
Kadeer Ali c Smith b Peters	7
J. C. Tredwell c Smith b Austin	25
†M. J. Prior c Baugh b Austin	4
K. W. Hogg lbw b Peters	7
J. E. Bishop not out	0
J. M. Anderson b Peters	0
M. S. Panesar c Deonarine b Austin	5
B 4, l-b 3, n-b 4	11
1/29 2/33 3/78 4/84 5/98 6/105 7/127 8/127 9/132	137

Bowling: Lawson 14–4–35–2; Peters 27–12–41–5; Austin 29.5–16–45–3; Matthews 4–0–9–0.

Umpires: D. J. Constant and J. F. Steele.

SCHOOLS CRICKET, 2001

The pre-season talk in PE departments around the country centred on the introduction of new public exams for lower-sixth students and the impact this additional academic burden would have on the organisation of cricket. The majority of masters in charge had their worst fears confirmed, reporting unavailability or reluctance from boys to make a commitment to the team, with the resulting cancellation of many games. Dartford GS, who called off six of their ten matches, were not alone in finding exam dates clashing with long-arranged fixtures. Lord Williams's played just five of 13, although four unplayed games fell victim to the weather, which again restricted the season for many schools. Langley Park and Ryde suffered such disruption to their programmes that they had "nothing of any significance left to report".

Even schools that managed to maintain their usual number of fixtures spoke somewhat despondently about the future. Oundle argued that, unless the balance between academic and extra-curricular activities can be redressed, the more protracted sports and arts would quickly disappear from school life. Brighton thought that standards were slipping because "fewer schools than ever take the game seriously; they feel it is too time-consuming and expensive".

However, it was generally agreed that if there is no major shift in exam timetables, the best way to stimulate enthusiasm for the game is for coaches to put even greater stress on playing positive, attacking cricket. This was reflected in many reports. Dulwich have devised a different plan to alleviate congestion in the summer term, engaging former Worcestershire coach Bill Athey for the whole school year and organising practice accordingly. The successful launch of two limited-overs leagues, among schools who had traditionally contested declaration matches, was another pointer to the motivation of hard-pressed but keen students. In one league Tonbridge were the appropriate winners of the Colin Cowdrey Cup, while Kingswood were undefeated in the Bath and District competition.

A wet May proved a further stumbling-block, especially for run-scoring, and Tom Huggins of Kimbolton was alone in passing 1,000 runs. His 1,069 at 106.90 included five centuries from 17 innings and, with 36 wickets at 15.30 as well, he was the leading all-rounder. Next among the runs were Mali Richards of Cheltenham with 958 at 56.35, Krishana Singh of Hurstpierpoint, who got 955 at 59.68, and Dominic Chambers from St Edmund's, Canterbury, with 927 at 92.70. No one else made 900.

Bedford Modern's Richard King was in commanding form, hitting the two highest individual innings of the term – 200 not out against The Perse and 186 not out against Wellingborough. The

The season's top scorers: Tom Huggins of Kimbolton (*left*) made 1,069 runs and, by claiming 36 wickets, was also the principal all-rounder. Next in line came Cheltenham's Mali Richards with 958.

next best was 172 from James Toms of Plymouth College. Of those passing 500 runs, three-figure averages were achieved by David Bowyer of Wolverhampton GS, with 554 at the season's best of 110.80, followed by 652 at 108.66, from Brendan McKerchar of Merchiston Castle, and Huggins's 106.90.

Leg-spinner Nick Dale-Lace of King's, Worcester, headed the bowlers, his 55 wickets at 11.01 being ten more than the best recorded in 2000. Close behind came Richard Harland of Bradford GS with 54 at 13.18, while Cheltenham's James Hayes took 48 at an impressive 9.97. Others with 30 wickets at single-figure averages were Toby Martin of Lord Wandsworth (40 at 6.25), Andrew Parkin-Coates of Worksop (42 at 8.07) and Tom Hunt of Alleyn's (33) and Ryan Bell of Bangor GS (32), both at 9.90.

The outstanding analysis came from Matthew Coult of Bromsgrove, who took eight for 25 against Bablake, with eight in an innings also recorded by Phil Martin of Manchester GS, and Ellesmere's Aishwarya Pandey. Other notable returns were seven for three from Alastair Mitchell of Simon Langton GS and seven for four by William Evered of Wellington College. Five hat-tricks were reported, with Charlie Foster of King's College School, Wimbledon, taking four in four balls. Marlborough's Edward Carpenter was the most industrious bowler, sending down 284 overs for his 42 wickets.

In a fair season for all-rounders, the leading exponents, after Huggins, were Parkin-Coates, who scored 504 runs at 45.81 in addition to his 42 wickets, and John Mason of Sedbergh with 566 at 51.45 and 37 at 12.29. Richards took 37 wickets at 14.72 to set beside his 958 runs, and Singh dismissed 33 at a cost of 17.96 to add to his 955 runs.

There were eight unbeaten sides, with pride of place going to Simon Langton GS, who had a 100 per cent record. The others were Eastbourne, Kingswood, Reading, Wells Cathedral School and Wrekin – all of whom won at least half their matches – plus Ashville and Colfe's, with a preponderance of draws. Others with excellent records included Campbell College, who were successful in 15 out of 18, and Berkhamsted, with ten wins in 12 games.

While the weather made its accustomed inroads into the fixtures early in the season, the foot and mouth crisis made matters worse for many: Giggleswick, for example, were forced to cancel six matches.

The five British schools that participated in the 15th Sir Garfield Sobers Schools Cricket Festival, held in Barbados in July, were Bedford, Gresham's, The Perse, Trent, and Trinity, Croydon. They found themselves outgunned by the other competitors and ended the tournament occupying five of the last six places in the qualifying table. The competition winners were Presentation College from Trinidad.

Details of records broken, other outstanding performances and interesting features of the season may be found in the returns from the schools that follow.

ECB SCHOOLS EAST v ECB SCHOOLS WEST

At Todmorden, July 10, 11. Drawn. Toss: ECB Schools West.

Poor weather prevented play before lunch on either day, though there was time enough for several batsmen to shine. The West looked as if they might squander their steady start when Nolan's medium-pace had both openers lbw. However, Hudson and Brown rebuilt the innings with a patient stand of 92, Brown hitting an attractive 37. Hudson, 80 not out overnight, went to a fine century next morning as the West gathered quick runs: 66 came from nine overs. His declaration left the East a minimum of 48 overs to bat. They too began promisingly, Maiden, with a sound fifty, and Jarvis putting on 87 for the first wicket before spinners Carpenter and Arfan Akram slowed the run-rate and claimed four wickets. In the end, though, despite the heroic efforts of the groundstaff, too many overs had been lost for either side to force a result.

ECB Schools West

W. T. Faulkner (*Lord Wandsworth College*)	lbw b Nolan	26
P. S. Coverdale (*Wellingborough*)	lbw b Nolan	13
*J. Hudson (*King's College, Taunton*)	not out	103
D. Brown (*Queen Elizabeth GS, Blackburn*)	c Savill b Roberts	37
V. Atri (*Bilborough College*)	c Symington b Savill	15
L. Smith (*Millfield*)	not out	17
	B 5, l-b 7, w 1, n-b 12	25
1/54 2/63 3/155 4/189	(4 wkts dec.)	236

Arfan Akram (*Leyton Sixth Form College*), J. Outar (*Oundle*), T. Seward (*Millfield*), †S. R. Anderson (*Woodhouse Grove*), E. J. Carpenter (*Marlborough College*) and A. Shantry (*Shrewsbury Sixth Form College*) did not bat.

Bowling: Savill 15–2–58–1; Palladino 12–1–42–0; Nolan 11–2–47–2; Buckham 13–3–33–0; Trevor 6–0–30–0; Roberts 6–2–14–1.

ECB Schools East

*A. J. Maiden (*King Edward VI College, Stourbridge*) run out	62
A. T. Jarvis (*Wellington College*) lbw b Carpenter	27
E. J. Crowther (*Repton*) b Carpenter	13
Adnam Akram (*Leyton Sixth Form College*) c Outar b Arfan Akram	10
†M. Barnes (*Bohunt School*) lbw b Arfan Akram	3
C. Symington (*Bede College*) not out	21
M. Trevor (*The Robert Smyth School*) not out	1
B 5, l-b 13, w 3, n-b 5	26
1/87 2/114 3/121 4/136 5/150 (5 wkts)	163

C. Buckham (*Homewood School and Sixth Form College*), B. P. F. Nolan (*The Cricket School, Christchurch*), A. Palladino (*Cardinal Pole Sixth Form College*), C. Roberts (*Gorseinon College*) and T. Savill (*Bilborough School*) did not bat.

Bowling: Shantry 7–3–8–0; Seward 7–1–21–0; Outar 6–0–23–0; Coverdale 5–0–19–0; Smith 5–0–10–0; Carpenter 8–0–29–2; Arfan Akram 7–1–25–2; Hudson 3.3–0–10–0.

Umpires: H. Evans and K. Shenton.

ETON v HARROW

At Lord's, June 16. Abandoned.

For the first time in ten years, the long-standing schools fixture returned to a Saturday. But the bad weather which had begun to dog the game on weekdays continued, and the umpires called it off after an inspection at one o'clock. It was only the third complete washout in the match's history, all of them in the past five years. The following teams were selected:

Eton

A. C. H. Rudd, A. W. England, T. P. McCall, B. R. Thompson, R. C. Wallace, H. W. A. Clarke, E. C. J. Fielding, H. E. F. Smith, *S. W. F. Collins, †J. H. Mathias and F. P. P. McN. Boyd.

Harrow

*N. R. D. Compton, S. W. MacDonald, S. R. L. Maydon, P. R. Dunbar, A. W. Stileman, J. M. Kostoris, R. V. G. Harmsworth, N. E. Defty, †A. B. Mitchum, H. A. Fleming and P. D. Moseley.

Of the 163 matches played between the two schools since 1805, Eton have won 52, Harrow 45 and 66 have been drawn. Matches during the two world wars are excluded from the reckoning. The fixture was reduced from a two-day, two-innings-a-side match to one day in 1982, and became a limited-overs fixture from 1999. Forty-nine centuries have been scored, the highest being 183 by D. C. Boles of Eton in 1904; M. C. Bird of Harrow is the only batsman to have made two hundreds in a match, in 1907. The highest score since the First World War is 161 not out by M. K. Fosh of Harrow in 1975, Harrow's last victory before 2000. Since then Eton have won in 1977, 1985, 1990 and 1991, Harrow in 2000. The 1997, 1999 and 2001 matches were abandoned and all other games have been drawn. A full list of centuries since 1918 and results from 1950 can be found in Wisdens *prior to 1994.*

REPORTS AND AVERAGES

(Qualification: Batting 150 runs; Bowling 10 wickets)

* *On name indicates captain.* * *On figures indicates not out.*

Note: The line for batting reads Innings–Not Outs–Runs–Highest Score–100s–Average; that for bowling reads Overs–Maidens–Runs–Wickets–Best Bowling–Average.

ABINGDON SCHOOL *Played 12: W 2, L 7, D 2, T 1*

Master i/c: S. Hibberd Professional: R. Davidson

In an exciting tied match at the Abingdon Festival, the home side looked to be well beaten by St Francis Xavier, Liverpool, who needed just five from 30 balls with three wickets in hand. But in the next over two wickets fell for the addition of three wides and a single before the last batsman was stumped off yet another wide.

Batting—I. R. Downie 7–1–236–100–1–39.33; R. W. Balch 11–3–263–64*–0–32.87; D. Desai 11–0–255–54–0–23.18; J. A. D. Watkins 10–0–225–80–0–22.50; M. T. Armitage 12–0–229–53–0–19.08.

Bowling—B. J. L. Garner 96.5–13–390–15–5/43–26.00.

ALDENHAM SCHOOL *Played 11: W 2, L 7, D 2. A 3*

Master i/c: A. P. Stephenson Professional: D. Goodchild

Batting—S. F. Gray 6–1–160–59–0–32.00; B. Hunter 10–1–250–59*–0–27.77; *M. S. Tennant 8–1–152–47–0–21.71.

Bowling—R. Brant 70–13–207–18–6/18–11.50; M. S. Tennant 60–15–174–14–4/20–12.42.

ALLEYN'S SCHOOL *Played 13: W 8, L 2, D 3. A 1*

Master i/c: R. Ody Professional: P. H. Edwards

Batting—D. Ellis 13–5–455–108*–2–56.87; E. Postma 10–2–263–62–0–32.87; *N. Dasandi 11–5–157–46*–0–26.16.

Bowling—A. Fuller 23.5–0–91–10–5/28–9.10; T. Hunt 116–23–327–33–5/60–9.90; N. Dasandi 96–13–248–21–3/14–11.80; T. Matthews 86.1–9–321–19–5/14–16.89; P. Baker 92.1–16–286–12–3/12–23.83; E. Postma 84–9–296–12–5/28–24.66.

AMPLEFORTH COLLEGE *Played 12: W 3, L 2, D 7. A 3*

Master i/c: G. D. Thurman Professional: D. Wilson

Batting—B. Fitzherbert 12–4–559–109–1–69.87; *P. Gretton 13–2–622–103*–1–56.54; T. Stanley 13–2–523–95–0–47.54; J. Smith 12–1–215–51–0–19.54.

Bowling—S. Mosey 145–30–476–25–5/17–19.04; A. Woodhead 118.4–27–315–13–4/22–24.23; T. Stanley 56–6–315–10–4/82–31.50; N. Brennan 157–20–548–17–5/41–32.23.

ARDINGLY COLLEGE *Played 14: W 6, L 6, D 2*

Master i/c: G. W. Hart Professional: T. Cruikshank

Batting—N. Patterson 12–1–499–111*–1–45.36; A. Beer 11–0–317–90–0–28.81; D. Anderson 8–1–188–59–0–26.85; F. Hussain 11–1–267–85*–0–26.70; D. Brooker 13–0–288–86–0–22.15; B. Cockell 11–2–151–48–0–16.77.

Bowling—N. Patterson 118–22–410–24–4/17–17.08; S. Turner 101.1–14–352–18–4/8–19.55; J. Eastoe 52.1–6–265–12–5/35–22.08; A. Beer 105.1–5–486–14–5/56–34.71.

ARNOLD SCHOOL *Played 11: W 3, L 6, D 2*

Master i/c: G. J. Marshall Professional: B. Denning

Batting—*S. Whiteside 11–0–620–122–2–56.36; C. Day 9–3–166–60–0–27.66; D. Atkinson 11–4–180–39–0–25.71; A. Wall 8–0–180–62–0–22.50.

Bowling—D. Atkinson 117–12–372–24–5/25–15.50; S. Laycock 38–2–206–10–3/22–20.60; S. Whiteside 95–6–390–14–5/45–27.85.

ASHVILLE COLLEGE *Played 14: W 5, L 0, D 9. A 1*

Master i/c: I. Walker

Batting—J. Manby 12–6–359–101*–1–59.83; A. Crystal 12–4–314–65–0–39.25; J. Chervak 11–1–390–98*–0–39.00; *J. Brecknock 14–1–306–92–0–23.53; D. Garfit 12–1–233–69–0–21.18; D. Chervak 11–0–217–60–0–19.72.

Bowling—G. Randle 132–28–411–21–4/22–19.57; B. Woolman 118–19–502–24–5/65–20.91; A. Crystal 87.3–12–367–17–4/37–21.58; J. Manby 127.4–16–542–19–4/31–28.52.

BANCROFT'S SCHOOL *Played 19: W 6, L 9, D 4*

Master i/c: J. K. Lever

After a poor start, results improved after the mid-season break for exams, when some promising colts were introduced. The batting relied heavily on Joe Johnson and Chris Leech, supported by the robust hitting of Stephen Gevertz. Seamers Jon Pittal and David Ossack offered, respectively, pace and nagging accuracy, and the balance of the attack was enhanced by the late-season inclusion of David Samuel's off-breaks.

Batting—J. C. F. Johnson 18–1–585–119*–2–34.41; C. F. Leech 18–0–484–110–1–26.88; *S. Gevertz 18–3–398–82*–0–26.53; S. C. Miller 15–1–296–51–0–21.14; J. H. T. Curran 12–4–159–43–0–19.87; O. N. Rodwell 13–1–159–47–0–13.25.

Bowling—D. Ossack 105–9–474–20–4/45–23.70; D. Samuel 59–5–293–12–4/34–24.41; J. Pittal 144–19–559–22–5/34–25.40.

BANGOR GRAMMAR SCHOOL *Played 16: W 10, L 3, D 3. A 2*

Master i/c: D. J. Napier Professional: C. C. J. Harte

A potent attack usually made amends for some disappointing batting, a highlight being the dismissal for 48 of Strabane GS, the holders, in the final of the Ulster Schools' Cup. Of the four bowlers who recorded single-figure averages, Ryan Bell, Andrew Gowdy and Paul McKenzie were rewarded with Ulster and Irish Schools selection, along with batsman Chris Kane.

Batting—C. J. R. Kane 12–3–253–74*–0–28.11; P. D. McKenzie 13–0–276–103–1–21.23.

Bowling—P. D. McKenzie 62.3–14–139–24–4/1–5.79; A. W. Gowdy 89.1–23–225–27–4/3–8.33; C. Anderson 64.1–15–170–19–7/13–8.94; R. M. Bell 100.4–13–317–32–4/15–9.90; A. G. Andrews 27–5–131–10–5/31–13.10.

BARNARD CASTLE SCHOOL *Played 9: W 4, L 2, D 3*

Master i/c: B. C. Usher

Matthew Brown and Edward Williamson formed the backbone of an inexperienced but improving side.

Batting—M. Brown 9–1–310–90*–0–38.75; E. Williamson 9–2–170–60–0–24.28; T. Henniker-Major 9–1–168–57–0–21.00; R. Wood 9–0–180–58–0–20.00; P. Obank 9–1–151–33*–0–18.87.

Bowling—E. Williamson 82–9–281–18–4/13–15.61; C. Damson 50–13–176–11–3/25–16.00; M. Brown 73–10–277–16–5/22–17.31; R. Wood 70–10–238–13–5/17–18.30.

BEDFORD SCHOOL *Played 15: W 7, L 3, D 5. A 1*

Master i/c: J. J. Farrell Professional: D. W. Randall

Alastair Cook led a solid batting line-up by contributing four hundreds – three unbeaten – and with James Stedman set a school record first-wicket partnership of 242 undefeated in the two-day match against Tonbridge.

Batting—A. Cook 15–3–876–117*–4–73.00; W. Smith 12–2–517–125*–1–51.70; J. Stedman 16–2–639–130*–2–45.64; R. Wycherley 13–2–414–101*–1–37.63; S. Edgington 11–2–166–69*–0–18.44.

Bowling—T. Coleman 65–10–179–11–2/27–16.27; P. Heady 149–22–438–24–3/23–18.25; W. Smith 101.5–20–303–15–6/27–20.20; M. Perera 116.3–12–440–21–3/35–20.95; A. Cook 77.2–16–291–11–3/4–26.45; J. Stedman 155–24–523–18–4/42–29.05; R. Ward 130.2–20–440–13–2/20–33.84.

BEDFORD MODERN SCHOOL *Played 14: W 7, L 4, D 3. A 1*

Master i/c: N. J. Chinneck

Richard King's innings of 200 not out against The Perse and 186 not out against Wellingborough were the two highest reported by schools in 2001.

Batting—R. E. King 13–3–785–200*–2–78.50; N. K. P. Choudhury 7–0–226–85–0–32.28; N. Parsooth 9–3–186–43–0–31.00; *O. J. Chinneck 10–2–224–54–0–28.00; N. Lockwood 13–2–288–90–0–26.18; D. N. G. Myers 14–0–364–59–0–26.00; A. L. Chinneck 9–2–164–63–0–23.42; B. N. Campbell 9–1–154–53–0–19.25.

Bowling—N. Lockwood 170–34–553–26–5/37–21.26; R. E. King 105–22–282–13–2/17–21.69; N. Parsooth 160–32–580–26–6/68–22.30; B. N. Campbell 97–17–335–10–2/12–33.50; E. Billson 84–10–337–10–2/24–33.70.

BERKHAMSTED COLLEGIATE SCHOOL *Played 12: W 10, L 1, D 1. A 4*

Master i/c: S. J. Dight Professionals: M. R. Herring and A. Fraser

A rewarding season was rounded off at the Castle Festival, hosted by Framlingham, with victory in all three matches. The captain, Ian Bartholomew, was joined in the side by his brother Richard.

Batting—T. C. Warren 8–4–227–90*–0–56.75; O. J. Terry 9–4–266–56*–0–53.20; *I. D. Bartholomew 12–3–418–100*–2–46.44; M. R. Herring 9–3–166–67*–0–27.66.

Bowling—C. G. Bailey 95.3–24–240–23–4/6–10.43; M. R. Herring 119.3–28–320–22–6/39–14.54; T. C. Warren 107–18–308–17–3/11–18.11; C. Jeffryes 72–15–208–11–3/26–18.90.

Richard King (*left*) enjoyed a rich vein of runs for Bedford Modern, while Richard Harland of Bradford GS snared 54 opponents with left-arm spin.

BETHANY SCHOOL *Played 8: W 1, L 6, D 1. A 5*

Master i/c: S. Brown

In a season delayed by the weather until the first week of June, the team played better than results suggest, finally achieving victory in their last match when Bilal Raja took five for eight against the Strollers.

Batting—C. Harding 7–1–317–103*–1–52.83; N. Khalid 7–1–216–68–0–36.00.

Bowling—B. Raja 47–8–251–16–5/8–15.68; N. Khalid 60–10–312–11–3/17–28.36.

BIRKENHEAD SCHOOL *Played 15: W 7, L 3, D 5*

Master i/c: M. H. Bowyer Professional: H. L. Alleyne

Simon Marshall was the linchpin of the team. He scored his runs quickly and was a constant source of encouragement to the younger members of the side, going on to play for Cheshire and England Under-18. Of the younger players, Simon Stokes and Ashley Dale-Jones made telling contributions, as did 14-year-old all-rounder Warren Goodwin.

Batting—*S. Marshall 8–1–428–118*–1–61.14; A. Dale-Jones 9–4–213–86–0–42.60; S. Stokes 10–1–219–63–0–24.33; W. Goodwin 15–5–230–33–0–23.00; E. Berstock 14–1–157–44–0–12.07.

Bowling—W. Goodwin 74–15–193–18–5/10–10.72; D. Milligan 114–25–276–19–3/20–14.52; S. Marshall 99–32–218–14–5/18–15.57.

BLOXHAM SCHOOL *Played 15: W 4, L 8, D 3*

Master i/c: N. C. W. Furley

Batting—I. Baig 14–1–539–118–1–41.46; R. Foxon 15–0–335–66–0–22.33; D. Taylor 15–0–306–51–0–20.40; R. Crofts 15–1–199–37–0–14.21; S. Whatman 15–2–170–35–0–13.07.

Bowling—R. Foxon 108–12–390–20–5/18–19.50; *H. Palmer 114.3–21–349–14–3/4–24.92; J. Barrett 80.3–11–289–11–5/41–26.27; I. Baig 81–9–375–13–3/23–28.84.

BLUNDELL'S SCHOOL *Played 17: W 9, L 7, D 1. A 1*

Master i/c: N. A. Folland

Inconsistent batting prevented the side from building on a heartening start to the season. Tom Wright dominated with bat and ball, topping the bowling averages for a fifth consecutive year and going on to play for Devon. His brother, Simon, showed promise as a batsman and leg-spinner.

Batting—*T. A. Wright 15–3–402–119*–1–33.50; J. C. Dark 12–1–336–70–0–30.54; J. H. K. White 16–0–334–60–0–20.87; S. B. Wright 15–1–260–61–0–18.57; A. M. O. Berry 15–3–216–67*–0–18.00; E. N. Buckland 12–3–151–43*–0–16.77.

Bowling—T. A. Wright 158–47–433–29–4/14–14.93; O. R. Bishop 64.5–7–260–17–5/20–15.29; S. B. Wright 136–27–388–20–3/23–19.40; E. N. Buckland 116.1–13–456–22–3/14–20.72.

BRADFIELD COLLEGE *Played 14: W 6, L 6, D 2. A 1*

Master i/c: C. C. Ellison Professional: J. F. Harvey

A successful tour to South Africa at Easter paid dividends when the side later defeated both Eton and Radley. William Edes, restricted by injury to eight innings, scored his 377 runs at an impressive 53.85.

Batting—W. M. H. Edes 8–1–377–108–1–53.85; S. P. J. Brain 10–4–249–77*–0–41.50; D. R. W. Irens 14–2–404–91*–0–33.66; A. S. G. Tod 13–0–329–52–0–25.30; J. C. Morris 12–1–216–46*–0–19.63; *C. P. Hose 13–1–214–74–0–17.83; D. J. Anderson 11–1–160–42–0–16.00.

Bowling—G. O. Pakeman 83.5–24–244–15–4/26–16.26; A. W. McCracken 97–8–299–15–4/30–19.93; C. P. Hose 113–15–416–12–4/23–34.66.

BRADFORD GRAMMAR SCHOOL *Played 16: W 5, L 6, D 5. A 5*

Master i/c: A. G. Smith

Richard Harland took 54 wickets with his slow left-arm bowling and guided a young side through an encouraging season. Thirteen-year-old Uzair Mahomed hit the season's top score, 93, while all-rounders Ajmal Shahzad and Sarfaraaz Mahomed made significant progress.

Batting—A. Shahzad 16–4–434–91*–0–36.16; S. Mahomed 14–5–296–85*–0–32.88; J. A. S. Benzafar 14–1–374–88–0–28.76; U. Mahomed 13–2–303–93–0–27.54; T. D. Ambepitiya 14–1–251–56–0–19.30.

Bowling—*R. M. Harland 213.5–56–712–54–7/20–13.18; S. Mahomed 86.4–27–309–19–4/27–16.26; J. N. MacDougall 99–12–404–15–3/87–26.93; A. Aziz 119–24–451–16–4/67–28.18.

BRENTWOOD SCHOOL *Played 12: W 4, L 3, D 5. A 5*

Master i/c: B. R. Hardie

Batting—*E. J. Bowler 11–2–635–109*–2–70.55; M. E. Westwood 11–1–469–100*–1–46.90; P. R. Gray 11–1–243–76–0–24.30; D. E. Johnson 10–1–210–83–0–23.33; J. G. Redwood 11–1–223–54–0–22.30; C. J. Westwood 9–2–150–39–0–21.42.

Bowling—F. N. Crosby 65.2–13–205–12–5/31–17.08; D. P. Selby 126.2–33–416–19–6/52–21.89; E. J. Bowler 154.1–11–734–25–5/110–29.36.

BRIGHTON COLLEGE *Played 23: W 14, L 5, D 4. A 2*

Master i/c: J. Spencer Professional: R. Halsall

Positive batting, challenging declarations and the use of three wrist-spinners resulted in attractive cricket – and brought 14 victories. A good team spirit had been developed on a worthwhile pre-season tour of the Caribbean.

Batting—M. N. Waller 23–8–819–117–1–54.60; C. M. Grammer 23–5–742–102–1–41.22; M. Gardner 18–0–683–107–1–37.94; M. J. Brackpool 19–0–602–88–0–31.68; T. R. Burton 17–1–505–80–0–31.56; M. B. Stevenson 14–3–224–45–0–20.36.

Bowling—N. A. Epstein 139–18–493–37–7/51–13.32; T. R. Burton 190–18–693–34–5/12–20.38; S. Murphy 130–18–463–22–3/8–21.04; M. N. Waller 257.4–51–894–37–6/55–24.16; M. J. Wood 147–33–459–15–3/35–30.60.

BRISTOL GRAMMAR SCHOOL *Played 15: W 5, L 9, D 1*

Master i/c: G. Clark Professional: L. Malloch-Brown

Batting—*P. W. Morris 13–0–402–104–1–30.92; J. R. A. Smith 9–0–256–78–0–28.44; P. J. Dacombe 14–0–337–88–0–24.07; R. A. Peattie 11–1–213–63*–0–21.30; S. J. Scott 11–0–152–46–0–13.81.

Bowling—T. D. Westray 66.2–4–275–14–3/50–19.64; J. R. A. Smith 80–8–332–11–4/39–30.18.

BROMSGROVE SCHOOL *Played 9: W 2, L 3, D 4. A 6*

Master i/c: P. Mullan Professional: P. Greetham

Miserable weather deprived the side of their first six games and they struggled to gain real momentum. Left-armer Matthew Coult recorded the season's best analysis with eight for 25 against Bablake and was selected for Cornwall Under-18.

Batting—M. J. Mullan 6–2–153–45*–0–38.25.

Bowling—M. L. Coult 125–23–349–19–8/25–18.36.

BRYANSTON SCHOOL *Played 13: W 7, L 2, D 4. A 3*

Master i/c: T. J. Hill

The most aggressive batsman in a capable line-up was Nick Brunner, who slammed an unbeaten 152 in 80 balls against Portsmouth GS and followed it with 99 in 52 against Exeter. Richard Turney led by example with outstanding performances in the field. The season had started bizarrely when the newly appointed coach from KwaZulu-Natal, Bryanston's first, disappeared from the premises after just two hours, leaving the school and his club, South Wilts, without a word of explanation.

Batting—N. J. P. Brunner 8–2–345–152*–1–57.50; B. C. Edgell 10–2–398–122–1–49.75; L. J. W. Publicover 8–2–279–100*–1–46.50; M. W. Pritchard 8–0–252–112–1–31.50; J. R. Denning 11–0–289–65–0–26.27; S. R. Martin 8–1–181–38*–0–25.85.

Bowling—G. M. Evans 55–12–157–16–5/11–9.81; B. R. Hornby 44–5–153–14–4/15–10.92; S. R. Martin 33–4–135–11–6/15–12.27; B. C. Edgell 76–13–245–13–3/12–18.84; *R. W. Turney 74.4–12–274–10–3/8–27.40.

CAMPBELL COLLEGE *Played 18: W 15, L 3, D 0*

Masters i/c: G. Fry and B. Robinson

Batting—M. McComish 14–3–606–88–0–55.09; S. Foster 11–2–336–122–1–37.33; J. Anderson 9–2–167–56–0–23.85; A. Clements 8–0–153–44–0–19.12.

Bowling—A. Coulter 81–19–183–16–6/4–11.43; M. McComish 88–11–341–28–6/15–12.17; J. Anderson 75–12–225–17–3/12–13.23; N. Wallace 76–8–380–19–4/31–20.00.

Influential skippers: Alex Gordon-Martin of Charterhouse (*left*) and Cheltenham's James Hayes successfully combined the roles of captain and all-rounder.

CANFORD SCHOOL *Played 12: W 9, L 3, D 0. A 1*

Master i/c: A. Copp Professionals: V. P. Terry and J. H. Shackleton

Batting—C. Martin 3–1–161–69*–0–80.50; A. Harms 12–4–266–76–0–33.25; J. Martin 7–1–186–88*–0–31.00; T. Norris 12–0–338–72–0–28.16; *M. Baxter 12–1–245–51–0–22.27; S. Stringer 10–1–183–55*–0–20.33; J. Holt 10–1–155–36–0–17.22.

Bowling—J. Haworth 99.5–20–281–18–6/26–15.61; E. Howat 78–7–263–16–4/48–16.43.

CHARTERHOUSE *Played 17: W 10, L 2, D 4, T 1. A 3*

Master i/c: P. J. Deakin Professional: R. V. Lewis

A trio of all-rounders saw the side through a highly encouraging season, including the first win against Eton for 16 years and a tie with Harrow. Alex Gordon-Martin led by example, with sound support from Will Young and Simon Hollingsworth, who went on to play for Surrey Second Eleven. Others to make an impression included James Assersohn, with 27 wickets in his debut term, and Andrew Gloak, who took a hat-trick against Free Foresters.

Batting—S. C. Hollingsworth 15–3–378–79*–0–31.50; L. P. Bernhard 12–4–238–58*–0–29.75; *A. G. Gordon-Martin 17–1–387–89–0–24.18; W. J. S. Clark 12–1–245–51–0–22.27; W. H. Young 15–1–272–46–0–19.42; J. A. Gilbert 13–2–212–58–0–19.27.

Bowling—J. W. Assersohn 140.3–27–404–27–4/32–14.96; A. G. Gordon-Martin 91.2–19–304–19–4/16–16.00; W. H. Young 155.2–30–484–28–4/37–17.28; S. C. Hollingsworth 112.1–15–345–17–3/18–20.29; A. J. Gloak 92.5–19–259–12–4/30–21.58.

CHELTENHAM COLLEGE *Played 21: W 10, L 5, D 6. A 3*

Master i/c: M. W. Stovold Professional: M. P. Briers

Vastly improved results were inspired by major contributions with bat and ball from Mali Richards, son of Sir Vivian, and James Hayes. They dispatched 85 opponents between them and, by making 958 runs, Richards had the second-highest aggregate in the country.

Batting—M. A. Richards 21–4–958–144*–2–56.35; *J. A. Hayes 14–5–306–51–0–34.00; J. P. Goodale 20–1–544–72–0–28.63; C. P. Davies 18–6–329–57–0–27.41; W. H. Marshall 13–3–193–35*–0–19.30; P. B. Geddes 21–0–370–65–0–17.61.

Bowling—J. A. Hayes 186.3–38–479–48–6/17–9.97; M. A. Richards 181–31–545–37–4/18–14.72; L. M. I. Bowles 107.4–17–389–26–4/9–14.96; W. H. Marshall 72–13–237–13–5/18–18.23; T. M. B. Brierley 119.1–23–353–14–3/15–25.21; G. W. McEwan 101–10–406–12–3/12–33.83.

CHIGWELL SCHOOL *Played 10: W 6, L 2, D 2. A 5*

Master i/c: D. N. Morrison Professional: F. A. Griffiths

Batting—R. W. Gull 10–1–265–78–0–29.44; C. S. Benn 10–0–273–46–0–27.30; *O. M. Compton 9–1–214–98*–0–26.75; R. Bhome 9–0–230–65–0–25.55; M. C. Woda 10–2–178–51–0–22.25; H. Ditta 8–0–174–52–0–21.75.

Bowling—M. C. Woda 48–5–207–15–7/57–13.80; R. W. Gull 96–18–251–15–5/46–16.73; R. Bhome 96–15–294–15–6/17–19.60.

CHRIST COLLEGE, BRECON *Played 13: W 6, L 6, D 1. A 1*

Masters i/c: J. R. Williams and N. C. Blackburn Professional: B. Murphy

A side with a blend of youth and experience enjoyed a season of very close finishes. Richard Cox and Phil Dyer formed a potent opening attack and set the tone for wins against Hereford Cathedral School, Wellington School and, most decisively, Llandovery, who were bowled out for 25.

Batting—W. J. Hitch 10–0–273–61–0–27.30; R. M. Wells 10–1–215–73–0–23.88; C. S. D. James 10–1–204–75–0–22.66; *I. T. Logan 10–2–169–86–0–21.12.

Bowling—R. G. Cox 89–21–298–19–6/49–15.68; P. L. Dyer 103–17–329–16–4/18–20.56; R. J. Price 86–11–324–15–3/32–21.60.

CHRIST'S COLLEGE, FINCHLEY *Played 9: W 2, L 4, D 3. A 4*

Master i/c: S. S. Goldsmith

Batting—C. Depala 8–2–188–50–0–31.33; A. Afzal 9–1–150–42*–0–18.75.

Bowling—*A. Rehman 54–3–193–11–4/7–17.54.

CHRIST'S HOSPITAL *Played 13: W 7, L 3, D 3. A 2*

Master i/c: H. P. Holdsworth Professional: L. J. Lenham

Batting—*N. J. Green 6–2–202–63*–0–50.50; S. Curtin 11–3–331–56*–0–41.37; A. M. Kruger 13–0–316–78–0–24.30; A. E. Woodbridge 10–1–174–57–0–19.33; J. W. S. Sheppard-Burgess 10–2–154–70*–0–19.25.

Bowling—A. E. Woodbridge 116.4–25–367–22–4/8–16.68; B. J. Walker 110–15–392–17–4/22–23.05; J. W. S. Sheppard-Burgess 119.4–14–436–17–3/19–25.64; A. M. Kruger 89–13–317–11–4/27–28.81.

CLAYESMORE SCHOOL *Played 15: W 6, L 8, D 1. A 1*

Master i/c: D. Rimmer Professional: P. Warren

Batting—T. Lack 13–2–739–122*–3–67.18; *C. Haniff 14–3–252–51–0–22.90; E. Calver 14–0–196–40–0–14.00.

Bowling—C. Haniff 94–12–334–20–5/12–16.70; E. Calver 83–5–351–14–2/13–25.07; T. Lack 124–19–481–18–4/35–26.72.

CLIFTON COLLEGE *Played 14: W 7, L 3, D 4. A 1*

Master i/c: D. C. Henderson Professional: P. W. Romaines

Openers Matthew Houcke and Hugh de Winton steadied an inexperienced batting line-up and guided the side to better results than anticipated. In the match with Prior Park they put on 219, a school record. Will Rudge, who played for Gloucestershire Second Eleven, was the mainstay of a strong and experienced attack, well marshalled by skipper David Romain.

Batting—M. Houcke 13–3–553–100*–1–55.30; H. W. de Winton 13–0–460–115–1–35.38; W. D. Rudge 11–2–251–100*–1–27.88; *D. B. Romain 14–2–273–74–0–22.75.

Bowling—R. A. Yates 74–17–241–17–5/22–14.17; J. F. A. Davies 78–12–256–18–6/26–14.22; W. A. Innes 93.1–17–322–15–4/35–21.46; W. D. Rudge 146–33–400–18–3/28–22.22; H. W. de Winton 101.5–15–349–12–2/10–29.08.

COLFE'S SCHOOL *Played 13: W 6, L 0, D 7. A 2*

Master i/c: G. S. Clinton

Batting—P. Clinton 8–3–279–82–0–55.80; *B. Khan 9–1–379–91*–0–47.37; M. Brown 7–1–214–79–0–35.66; T. Rowe 5–0–150–88–0–30.00.

Bowling—S. Cullum 41–7–70–14–7/18–5.00; P. Clinton 72.5–24–109–15–5/24–7.26; B. Khan 125–34–302–30–5/44–10.06.

CRANBROOK SCHOOL *Played 16: W 10, L 3, D 3*

Master i/c: A. J. Presnell

Batting—*J. Spencer 15–3–369–75–0–30.75; C. Sorensen 16–0–459–84–0–28.68; J. Thompson 12–1–262–54–0–23.81; R. Pickerill 13–2–195–77–0–17.72; C. Page 15–1–240–55–0–17.14.

Bowling—P. Towner 90–21–210–26–6/9–8.07; J. Spencer 126–20–408–36–5/10–11.33; M. Jones 61–6–191–12–3/27–15.91; R. Pickerill 134–25–379–22–6/17–17.22.

CRANLEIGH SCHOOL *Played 13: W 6, L 4, D 3. A 1*

Master i/c: D. C. Williams Professional: S. MacDonald

After early disruption from the weather, the side improved markedly under the captaincy of Andrew Houston, who set a fine example in all aspects of the game. All-round assistance came from wicket-keeper/batsman Ed McGregor (25 victims and 431 runs) and Sam Worthy, who hit powerfully and purveyed tidy off-spin.

Batting—R. H. Jones 6–3–198–61–0–66.00; E. G. McGregor 14–2–431–90–0–35.91; D. Hill 12–4–202–52*–0–25.25; S. C. Worthy 14–1–301–86–0–23.15; *A. R. Houston 13–4–187–33*–0–20.77; J. R. Gates 13–1–209–52–0–17.41.

Bowling—S. C. Worthy 155.1–27–433–24–5/55–18.04; A. R. Houston 150.1–21–562–23–5/59–24.43; L. H. P. Clark 107.1–17–391–16–5/17–24.43.

CULFORD SCHOOL *Played 12: W 4, L 7, D 1. A 3*

Master i/c: R. Shepperson Professional: D. Gibson

Batting—T. E. B. Beaney 12–3–263–51–0–29.22; *T. D. Hide 10–1–237–61–0–26.33; I. Beeby 11–0–262–71–0–23.81; N. K. Khagram 9–0–204–59–0–22.66; L. E. J. Cousins 10–0–206–61–0–20.60; N. M. Mackenzie 11–0–222–69–0–20.18.

Bowling—I. Beeby 96–17–327–12–3/41–27.25; N. K. Khagram 95–8–482–13–4/47–37.07.

Nick Anderson, the Dean Close captain (*left*), led his team from the front, while Chris Van Vliet gave a cutting edge to the Elizabeth College attack.

DARTFORD GRAMMAR SCHOOL *Played 4: W 0, L 3, D 1*

Master i/c: A. Futter

A fixture card of ten matches was reduced to just four games, as long-arranged fixture dates clashed with public examinations.

Batting—No batsman scored 150 runs. The leading batsman was A. Pinnock 4–0–96–55–0–24.00.

Bowling—No bowler took 10 wickets. The leading bowler was T. Warwick 20–2–53–4–2/13–13.25.

DAUNTSEY'S SCHOOL *Played 13: W 6, L 5, D 2. A 1*

Master i/c: A. J. Palmer Professional: R. Chaudhuri

A young side performed creditably to record good wins over Colston's, MCC and King's, Bruton. Oliver Smith found form at the end of June with 419 runs in five matches during one week.

Batting—E. Poulding 9–5–210–51*–0–52.50; *O. J. Smith 13–1–565–118*–1–47.08; J. W. Carter 12–1–217–56–0–19.72; N. J. Warde 13–1–225–82*–0–18.75; A. R. Bond 13–1–179–37–0–14.91.

Bowling—J. W. Carter 46–4–182–10–4/19–18.20; C. M. Holmes 51–3–234–12–4/34–19.50; N. J. Warde 85–11–338–16–3/6–21.12.

DEAN CLOSE SCHOOL *Played 17: W 10, L 4, D 3. A 3*

Master i/c: C. J. Townsend Professional: L. Lowrey

A powerful side recorded ten wins, including two by more than 100 runs – against Bloxham and King's, Gloucester – and two by ten wickets against Bromsgrove and Malvern. Gavin Curry put on a school record 195 for the first wicket with Mark Whitney in the Malvern match, and added 184 for the third with Nick Anderson against Free Foresters. Anderson was also the outstanding bowler, but it was Rob Kinder who provided the highlight with seven for eight, including a hat-trick, against Pate's. Fourteen-year-old Alex Carlisle took six for 15 against Prince Alfred College, Australia.

Batting—G. B. T. Curry 12–6–570–104*–1–95.00; M. Whitney 11–5–393–81*–0–65.50; *N. Anderson 10–4–328–101*–1–54.66; A. Fateh 11–2–450–115*–1–50.00; J. Jenkins 7–2–153–54–0–30.60; T. A. Judge 13–2–279–47–0–25.36; N. Mucadam 11–1–193–60–0–19.30.

Bowling—N. Anderson 124.5–24–398–30–3/6–13.26; T. P. Chamberlain 126.3–24–385–22–3/11–17.50; R. H. M. Kinder 84–14–327–18–7/8–18.16; N. P. Jones 73–14–298–14–5/41–21.28; T. A. Judge 82.4–9–317–14–3/30–22.64.

DENSTONE COLLEGE *Played 9: W 1, L 6, D 2. A 5*

Master i/c: A. N. James

Batting—M. A. Gouldstone 8–0–179–76–0–22.37; *B. J. Young 9–0–186–48–0–20.66.

Bowling—C. J. Whateley 45–4–228–12–3/15–19.00; M. A. Gouldstone 52–6–231–10–4/39–23.10; D. G. G. Soar 63–12–286–12–4/34–23.83; B. J. Young 87–9–337–13–3/45–25.92.

DOLLAR ACADEMY *Played 15: W 8, L 6, D 1*

Master i/c: J. G. Frost Professional: L. Spendlove

Batting—E. Wilson 11–2–284–68–0–31.55; *M. Forde 14–3–312–97–0–28.36; G. Wilson 12–1–294–60–0–26.72.

Bowling—G. Wilson 74–9–222–17–3/33–13.05; M. Forde 117–36–260–19–4/35–13.68; J. Barber Fleming 35–0–161–10–4/20–16.10; E. Wilson 112–30–254–15–4/9–16.93; J. McIntosh 54–3–255–12–4/27–21.25; V. Baxter 67–8–261–10–2/4–26.10.

DOVER COLLEGE *Played 8: W 1, L 7, D 0. A 3*

Master i/c: D. C. Butler

A wet spring and a new tier of examinations restricted the side to only eight matches – the smallest number in 25 years – all but two of which were played in a hectic cricket week at the end of term.

Batting—*J. Brasier 8–0–157–45–0–19.62.

Bowling—J. Brasier 60–11–176–13–5/22–13.53; A. Korobkin 82–17–225–14–4/22–16.07.

DOWNSIDE SCHOOL *Played 9: W 4, L 4, D 1*

Master i/c: B. Thomas

The admirable all-round effort of Neil Dexter, Scott Dixon and Michael Jackson could not prevent a series of uneven performances.

Batting—N. Dexter 9–3–306–102–1–51.00; S. Dixon 9–1–270–82–0–33.75; M. Jackson 9–1–236–76–0–29.50.

Bowling—M. Jackson 63–4–289–27–5/35–10.70; S. Dixon 63–4–350–25–4/52–14.00; N. Dexter 63–5–360–18–3/59–20.00.

DUKE OF YORK'S ROYAL MILITARY SCHOOL *Played 11: W 4, L 3, D 4. A 4*

Master i/c: S. Salisbury Professional: N. J. Llong

Batting—T. Gilbert 11–0–290–100–1–26.36; O. Donovan 11–2–217–77*–0–24.11; P. Jefferson 11–1–222–76–0–22.20.

Bowling—P. Jefferson 108–10–364–20–4/24–18.20.

DULWICH COLLEGE *Played 13: W 7, L 3, D 3. A 3*

Master i/c: D. J. Cooper Professional: A. Ranson

A lack of variation among the bowlers prevented a good campaign from becoming a vintage one. None the less, runs came steadily, with Mark Easter making three hundreds and Tom Askew, in his debut season, averaging 71.25. The most pleasing performance was an eight-wicket win against St Paul's.

Batting—M. J. Easter 11–3–583–106–3–72.87; T. T. Askew 6–2–285–103*–1–71.25; *I. Nasser 10–2–334–104*–1–41.75; P. R. J. Hazell 10–2–193–53–0–24.12.

Bowling—S. Sen 54.2–15–181–10–6/13–18.10; T. J. Bevan 108–11–363–17–3/22–21.35; D. S. Kularatnam 94.1–14–334–15–3/21–22.26; P. R. J. Hazell 95.5–24–306–13–3/43–23.53; M. J. Easter 82–16–289–12–4/18–24.08.

DURHAM SCHOOL *Played 14: W 6, L 7, D 1*

Master i/c: M. Hirsch

With senior players often unavailable, a relatively inexperienced side struggled to find their feet, but three defeats were followed by five wins. There was some fine batting from Tim Stonock, and the Muchall brothers, Gordon and Paul. Gordon, the elder, who played most of his cricket for Durham Second Eleven and Academy sides, closed his school career with an outstanding 167 against a touring Australian side. His enthusiasm and willingness to help the younger players will be missed.

Batting—G. J. Muchall 8–1–404–167–1–57.71; J. McCredie 12–3–337–62–0–37.44; T. Stonock 14–2–407–93*–0–33.91; P. Muchall 8–1–234–68–0–33.42; *N. Hooper 7–0–151–57–0–21.57.

Bowling—G. J. Muchall 106–23–215–16–5/36–13.43; J. Beattie 68–10–160–11–3/16–14.54; N. Harper 227–16–554–17–4/47–32.58; T. Stonock 128–10–427–13–2/28–32.84.

EASTBOURNE COLLEGE *Played 14: W 9, L 0, D 5. A 1*

Master i/c: N. L. Wheeler Professional: D. Kotze

The first unbeaten season since 1968 included victory over Brighton College in the final of the Langdale Cup. Run-scoring was never a problem, with five batsmen averaging over 30.

Batting—*L. J. A. Burgess 12–3–309–70*–0–34.33; E. H. Stafford 12–2–334–102*–1–33.40; J. C. Farley 11–2–289–56*–0–32.11; T. A. Eyre 12–1–339–60*–0–30.81; S. D. Cane-Hardy 14–3–336–65–0–30.54; O. L. Gale 11–0–177–61–0–16.09.

Bowling—N. J. Reid 48–17–135–14–4/10–9.64; J. C. Farley 122.2–32–311–24–4/29–12.95; M. D. Firth 105–23–290–21–4/18–13.80; S. D. Cane-Hardy 71.5–9–234–14–4/55–16.71; E. S. Pigott 122.5–24–369–19–3/12–19.42; T. A. Eyre 85.5–18–259–11–2/21–23.54.

THE EDINBURGH ACADEMY *Played 11: W 4, L 6, D 1. A 2*

Master i/c: M. Allingham

Batting—A. Moffat 9–4–293–69*–0–58.60; *C. Hillyard 13–3–404–82*–0–40.40; E. Mitchell 13–1–156–37–0–13.00.

Bowling—C. Hillyard 84.4–16–251–18–4/5–13.94; C. J. Osazuwa 78.5–18–262–16–5/43–16.37; R. Callicott 81–12–308–15–6/43–20.53.

ELIZABETH COLLEGE, GUERNSEY *Played 14: W 5, L 5, D 4*

Master i/c: M. E. Kinder

In a season of fluctuating fortunes, a one-wicket defeat by Victoria College and a match of 511 runs against the Old Elizabethans were the most thrilling games. Chris Van Vliet bowled fast and aggressively throughout and received staunch support from all-rounder Matthew Watson. Particularly pleasing was the return from serious injury of Michael Greenfield, who chipped in with 374 runs.

Batting—*M. C. Greenfield 11–0–374–95–0–34.00; M. J. Watson 14–1–378–91–0–29.07; R. P. Sherwell 14–0–277–42–0–19.78; S. R. Geall 14–2–226–87–0–18.83; C. A. Van Vliet 13–2–158–25–0–14.36; A. S. Harbour 13–0–165–46–0–12.69.

Bowling—C. A. Van Vliet 127.1–20–396–32–5/31–12.37; L. J. Gallienne 113.1–18–406–23–4/26–17.65; M. J. Watson 141.2–23–537–28–5/24–19.17; N. J. Cooper 51–3–294–10–5/49–29.40.

ELLESMERE COLLEGE *Played 10: W 3, L 6, D 1. A 2*

Master i/c: P. J. Hayes Professional: R. Mapp

Benn Camber, coming to the crease at 75 for five, bludgeoned an unbeaten 105 in 68 minutes against Liverpool College. His hundred came from 54 balls and he contributed all but 14 to the total scored while he was at the wicket. Another to enjoy a memorable match was Aishwarya Pandey, who took eight for 49 in a festival game with Hurstpierpoint.

Batting—B. R. Camber 4–1–194–105*–1–64.66; H. D. Thomas 10–1–294–116–1–32.66; E. J. Rowe 9–1–176–83*–0–22.00; *R. M. Mulvihill 10–1–169–76*–0–18.77.

Bowling—A. Pandey 84.2–17–228–17–8/49–13.41; P. F. McCarthy 94–23–290–18–5/45–16.11; R. M. Mulvihill 83–12–273–11–3/24–24.81.

ELTHAM COLLEGE *Played 15: W 8, L 2, D 5. A 2*

Masters i/c: I. Latham and B. M. Withecombe Professional: R. R. Hills

Batting—R. J. Malcolm-Hansen 10–1–345–71–0–38.33; J. P. Whitehead 11–3–290–68–0–36.25; P. J. Selvey-Clinton 14–0–495–71–0–35.35; R. P. Unwin 12–2–206–54–0–20.60; O. J. Willis 13–0–220–56–0–16.92.

Bowling—R. J. Malcolm-Hansen 102–12–314–22–5/34–14.27; M. L. Dransfield 86–12–344–16–5/39–21.50; A. J. Ring 125.4–24–376–17–3/20–22.11; P. J. Selvey-Clinton 113–14–472–17–4/36–27.76.

ENFIELD GRAMMAR SCHOOL *Played 9: W 0, L 6, D 3. A 4*

Master i/c: M. Alder

Batting—*E. Barber 9–0–233–75–0–25.88; B. Watts 8–0–176–55–0–22.00.

Bowling—T. Miller 92–17–284–19–3/29–14.94; T. Ansari 59–13–194–10–3/35–19.40.

EPSOM COLLEGE *Played 15: W 7, L 4, D 4. A 1*

Master i/c: P. J. Williams Professional: S. Cloete

Batting—R. D. Lammiman 13–4–352–81–0–39.11; A. J. Howard 15–2–409–96*–0–31.46; A. R. Vernon 15–0–361–69–0–24.06; A. A. J. Robinson 14–0–336–50–0–24.00; A. J. Cama 15–0–329–94–0–21.93; *J. P. A. Gale 16–1–240–40–0–16.00; G. Charles 16–0–235–58–0–14.68.

Bowling—N. Tanna 143–31–464–28–5/47–16.57; J. P. A. Gale 132–12–482–26–6/13–18.53; B. J. Sears 133–14–514–21–5/34–24.47; S. T. Moss 78–0–341–12–3/39–28.41; A. J. Cama 121–6–467–10–3/55–46.70.

ETON COLLEGE *Played 17: W 7, L 10, D 0. A 3*

Master i/c: R. D. Oliphant-Callum Professional: J. M. Rice

Batting—H. W. A. Clarke 14–7–316–62*–0–45.14; B. R. Thompson 17–3–500–104*–1–35.71; T. P. McCall 17–1–509–99*–0–31.81; A. C. H. Rudd 15–0–406–91–0–27.06; A. W. England 7–0–175–74–0–25.00; A. M. Goldberg 14–1–302–102–1–23.23; E. C. J. Fielding 13–1–219–49–0–18.25.

Bowling—T. P. McCall 205.1–45–668–29–5/58–23.03; A. M. Goldberg 129.1–14–470–18–3/41–26.11; *S. W. F. Collins 163–34–547–19–4/36–28.78; B. R. Thompson 100.5–3–442–15–2/26–29.46.

EXETER SCHOOL *Played 14: W 6, L 4, D 4*

Master i/c: W. Hughes

Batting—G. Turnbull 13–2–416–106*–1–37.81; A. Milton 14–0–291–64–0–20.78; R. Lovell 14–2–228–57*–0–19.00; D. Saunders 12–0–192–35–0–16.00.

Bowling—T. Duggan 62.5–14–163–18–3/7–9.05; R. Berryman 85–19–296–16–2/19–18.50; D. Saunders 43.4–8–189–10–5/11–18.90; T. Giles 99–23–296–15–4/17–19.73; G. Turnbull 100–19–399–18–5/16–22.16.

FELSTED SCHOOL *Played 14: W 5, L 6, D 2, T 1*

Master i/c: M. E. Allbrook Professionals: D. H. J. Griggs and N. J. Lockhart

Batting—B. D. H. Floyd 13–0–424–84–0–32.61; R. F. B. Staples 13–5–246–62*–0–30.75; T. Peacock 13–1–323–84–0–26.91; *N. J. Phillips 14–0–346–51–0–24.71; A. L. Stothard 14–0–302–65–0–21.57; E. T. Thorogood 11–1–168–58–0–16.80.

Bowling—W. D. C. Wright 42–10–152–15–5/20–10.13; E. T. Thorogood 109–12–426–23–4/20–18.52; A. L. Stothard 104–11–359–19–4/28–18.89; R. F. B. Staples 78–4–318–12–3/29–26.50; N. E. J. Porter 104–15–388–10–3/16–38.80.

FETTES COLLEGE *Played 10: W 5, L 3, D 2. A 3*

Master i/c: C. Thomson Professional: B. Russell

Batting—R. J. Mathew 13–2–475–83–0–43.18; A. W. Rathie 13–3–422–101–1–42.20; *A. Millar 12–4–191–34*–0–23.87; R. F. Jackson 9–1–183–51–0–22.87; J. F. Jackson 13–1–253–61–0–21.08.

Bowling—R. J. Mathew 110.1–26–114–17–5/17–6.70; A. Millar 90.2–25–241–20–5/13–12.05; R. F. Jackson 130–37–364–24–6/11–15.16.

FOREST SCHOOL *Played 14: W 8, L 4, D 2. A 5*

Master i/c: S. Turner

Batting—E. Buxton 13–4–553–105*–1–61.44; *D. Stevens 12–0–358–69–0–29.83; K. Paul 12–0–355–80–0–29.58; N. Rotsey 12–1–321–72*–0–29.18; T. Tidyman 9–1–161–107–1–20.12; M. De Claiterosse 13–0–260–46–0–20.00.

Bowling—T. Watkins 60–12–181–13–6/18–13.92; D. Stevens 104.1–14–378–24–6/19–15.75; R. Turner 51–14–162–10–2/14–16.20; J. Kay 142–39–397–24–4/15–16.54; E. Buxton 90–15–364–15–4/12–24.26.

FOYLE AND LONDONDERRY COLLEGE *Played 19: W 11, L 4, D 4*

Master i/c: G. R. McCarter

Batting—N. Cooke 15–4–510–77*–0–46.36; A. R. Duddy 17–3–537–86*–0–38.35; R. A. A. Cooke 12–4–185–52*–0–23.12; *D. J. Fleming 16–0–332–52–0–20.75; D. R. Robb 16–3–264–49–0–20.30.

Bowling—A. R. Duddy 28–3–88–11–3/15–8.00; R. A. A. Cooke 37.3–1–172–14–3/11–12.28; C. V. Appleby 52.3–8–158–12–2/1–13.16; S. A. Qureshi 150–30–423–31–4/25–13.64; N. Cooke 109.2–17–320–23–4/21–13.91; D. R. Robb 72–16–270–17–4/27–15.88; H. Shubber 51.3–6–254–13–5/17–19.53; R. A. Philson 73–11–300–14–3/4–21.42.

FRAMLINGHAM COLLEGE *Played 9: W 2, L 2, D 5*

Master i/c: R. Curtis

Batting—S. Veevers-Chorlton 9–4–401–92*–0–80.20; W. Gallagher 8–1–279–69–0–39.85.

Bowling—W. Gallagher 71–9–263–13–5/87–20.23; P. Grieves 81–10–282–11–4/25–25.63.

GIGGLESWICK SCHOOL *Played 8: W 4, L 3, D 1. A 6*

Master i/c: N. A. Gemmell Professional: P. Ridgeway

The fixture list was reduced by almost a half when six games were cancelled owing to the foot and mouth crisis.

Batting—*J. Hird 8–3–376–117*–1–75.20; T. Canaway 8–1–370–111*–1–52.85.

Bowling—S. Christian 76–14–229–20–4/22–11.45.

GLASGOW ACADEMY *Played 7: W 3, L 4, D 0. A 2*

Master i/c: A. Lyall Professional: V. Hariharan

Batting—No batsman scored 150 runs. The leading batsman was S. Ker 7–2–85–50*–0–17.00.

Bowling—*R. Andrew 67–7–203–12–4/32–16.91.

GLENALMOND *Played 11: W 1, L 6, D 4*

Master i/c: S. D. Hill

The best fielding for a number of years could not make up for a shortage of runs. However, excellent team spirit under the captaincy of Andrew Peters kept the side competitive, and there was some fine bowling from Freddie Weld Forester, who took six for 25 against Gordonstoun.

Batting—A. C. Weld Forester 9–0–161–32–0–17.88.

Bowling—A. C. Weld Forrester 77–22–222–20–6/25–11.10; J. Brunton 81–19–258–17–5/24–15.17.

GORDONSTOUN SCHOOL *Played 29: W 14, L 9, D 6. A 1*

Master i/c: G. Broad Professional: S. Humphries

A side which included students of five different nationalities played more matches than ever before, including a successful tour of the Caribbean.

Batting—S. Thompson 23–3–790–93–0–39.50; J. Slater 22–4–559–89*–0–31.05; *A. Morbey 23–2–566–71–0–26.95; E. Paterson 15–2–306–60*–0–23.53; G. Crow 17–1–251–47–0–15.68; J. Frankland 14–3–156–50*–0–14.18.

Bowling—J. Slater 140.4–20–467–37–6/15–12.62; J. McBeath 163.4–24–571–38–3/7–15.02; M. Mansell 89.1–9–400–24–5/15–16.66; S. Thompson 66.2–12–322–17–1/2–18.94; O. Valliani 76–15–263–13–3/17–20.23; R. Pyper 166.5–37–543–26–3/2–20.88.

GRESHAM'S SCHOOL *Played 14: W 8, L 4, D 2. A 3*

Master i/c: A. M. Ponder

The outstanding performance was Marcus Hedley's 120 in 73 balls against The Leys.

Batting—M. C. C. Hedley 13–2–409–120–1–37.18; R. A. J. Lintott 12–2–325–108–1–32.50; R. M. K. Steward 12–1–304–108–1–27.63; M. J. Pickett 14–0–352–90–0–25.14; J. A. C. Pearse 13–0–284–83–0–21.84; J. R. A. Pearse 9–1–171–50–0–21.37; *P. O. Dudman 11–3–167–63–0–20.87.

Bowling—P. O. Dudman 172.3–49–513–27–4/26–19.00; R. A. J. Lintott 100.4–12–366–18–3/18–20.33; C. D. Morrison 88.4–18–325–13–4/27–25.00.

HABERDASHERS' ASKE'S SCHOOL *Played 18: W 4, L 6, D 8. A 6*

Master i/c: S. D. Charlwood

Highlights in a mixed season were a successful run-chase against Old Haberdashers', when a target of 264 was reached with five balls to spare, and Nathan McGarry's six sixes off consecutive balls in a tour match against Branscombe CC.

Batting—R. Siva-Kumar 17–1–368–110*–1–23.00; A. M. Theivendra 15–2–289–82–0–22.23; K. Sethi 16–2–301–60*–0–21.50; *P. B. Duffy 16–2–294–66–0–21.00; J. S. T. Williams 11–2–162–34–0–18.00; V. Vaithianathan 11–2–153–27–0–17.00.

Bowling—P. B. Duffy 180.2–42–623–35–4/25–17.80; A. M. Theivendra 116.1–17–435–24–5/27–18.12; N. J. McGarry 121.2–12–487–23–4/45–21.17; P. Arumugam 70.2–24–221–10–3/29–22.10; V. Vaithianathan 103–13–389–14–3/31–27.78.

HAILEYBURY COLLEGE *Played 13: W 5, L 3, D 5. A 3*

Master i/c: T. P. Newman Professional: G. P. Howarth

The coaching of Geoff Howarth had a marked impact on the side. The batting was led by Nick Walker, who passed 500 runs, and five players made 275 or more; Darren Gerard also captured 25 wickets.

Batting—C. Wyles 12–5–313–93*–0–44.71; N. Walker 13–1–503–92–0–41.91; *D. Stewart 13–3–302–96–0–30.20; D. Gerard 14–3–307–57–0–27.90; Y. Qureshi 11–1–244–61–0–24.40; C. Scott 14–0–275–75–0–19.64.

Bowling—D. Gerard 153–35–420–25–5/38–16.80; N. Walker 154–29–562–24–4/48–23.41; P. Lundie 149.3–31–551–16–3/42–34.43; C. Wyles 112–20–534–11–2/40–48.54.

HAMPTON SCHOOL *Played 11: W 5, L 4, D 2. A 6*

Master i/c: E. M. Wesson

Batting—N. Khanna 10–0–466–97–0–46.60; N. E. Baker 10–2–336–77–0–42.00; J. M. Chapple 10–2–286–94–0–35.75; O. G. K. Roland-Jones 11–1–289–66*–0–28.90; *J. D. Irons 9–1–186–34–0–23.25.

Bowling—J. M. Chapple 93.2–18–341–23–5/46–14.82; N. E. Baker 59.4–6–209–13–4/33–16.07; J. D. Irons 126.2–38–417–20–6/96–20.85.

HARROW SCHOOL *Played 14: W 9, L 3, D 1, T 1*

Master i/c: S. J. Halliday Professional: R. K. Sethi

Harrow's most successful season for a number of years included wins at Wellington College and Bedford. Nick Compton achieved a notable double with a century and hat-trick against St Edward's, Oxford, going on to make his first-team debut for Middlesex.

Batting—P. R. Dunbar 10–3–352–100*–1–50.28; *N. R. D. Compton 14–0–685–113–3–48.92; S. R. L. Maydon 13–2–506–126*–2–46.00; A. W. Stileman 7–1–203–58–0–33.83; J. M. Kostoris 11–5–189–51*–0–31.50; S. W. MacDonald 10–1–225–101–1–25.00.

Bowling—P. D. Moseley 114.3–33–293–19–5/11–15.42; P. R. Dunbar 58–9–263–13–6/17–20.23; H. A. Fleming 93–18–281–13–4/27–21.61; R. V. G. Harmsworth 61.2–3–228–10–3/56–22.80; J. M. Kostoris 120–23–321–11–3/18–29.18.

HARVEY GRAMMAR SCHOOL *Played 14: W 8, L 4, D 2. A 3*

Master i/c: P. J. Harding

The season eventually ended in the second week of September, with a win in the final of the Lemon Cup, postponed from the summer term. With Hayes School closing on victory – needing six to win with four wickets in hand – Harvey's skipper, Samuel Hagger, captured all four in two overs, seeing his side home by three runs.

Batting—R. Hall 10–0–442–116–1–44.20; J. W. Flavell 14–3–294–65–0–26.72; *S. J. Hagger 14–1–338–77–0–26.00; M. Gamlyn 14–2–151–49–0–12.58.

Bowling—H. Large 82–15–221–18–4/13–12.27; S. J. Hagger 70–13–203–16–5/12–12.68; D. Mitchell 47.4–11–131–10–4/9–13.10; P. Goddard 80–27–204–15–5/43–13.60; S. Bentley 101–17–362–13–4/52–27.84.

HEREFORD CATHEDRAL SCHOOL *Played 15: W 5, L 7, D 3. A 1*

Master i/c: A. Connop

Batting—*A. J. Hewlett 15–0–520–112–1–34.66; A. M. Nahorniak 15–2–436–87*–0–33.53; M. A. Lowden 15–2–360–88–0–27.69; T. A. Harper 15–0–290–84–0–19.33; C. C. F. Powell 13–1–158–54–0–13.16.

Bowling—M. N. N. Desouza 99–26–326–19–3/11–17.15; C. C. F. Powell 149–22–661–24–4/50–27.54; C. J. Ball 79–12–341–11–3/0–31.00.

HIGHGATE SCHOOL *Played 7: W 1, L 4, D 2*

Master i/c: J. Hegan Professional: R. E. Jones

Batting—A. Varma 7–0–169–43–0–24.14.

Bowling—S. Whiteside-McFadden 60–9–167–14–5/43–11.92.

Hurstpierpoint's Krishana Singh (*left*) was the college's foremost batsman for the fourth consecutive year. Nick Dale-Lace, the season's leading wicket-taker, grabbed 55 at 11.01 for King's, Worcester.

HURSTPIERPOINT COLLEGE *Played 19: W 6, L 4, D 8, T 1*

Master i/c: C. W. Gray Professional: D. J. Semmence

Krishana Singh amassed 955 runs to take his career total to 3,100, passing the previous record held by Martin Speight, of Sussex and Durham. Opening the innings in a match against Sussex Martlets, he scored 144 not out in a total of 187, and later played for Sussex Second Eleven.

Batting—*K. R. Singh 19–3–955–144*–4–59.68; J. C. Andrews 15–3–314–82–0–26.16; K. D. Singh 13–1–291–64–0–24.25; J. R. Bayly 17–5–263–53*–0–21.91; J. G. Harrison 9–1–171–88–0–21.37; A. S. Godhania 17–0–352–105–1–20.70; D. W. Jones 9–1–157–74–0–19.62; J. F. C. Fitt 15–2–223–73–0–17.15; T. M. Price 12–1–167–44–0–15.18.

Bowling—J. R. Bayly 179–45–515–30–4/13–17.16; K. R. Singh 158.4–16–593–33–6/27–17.96; V. Singhania 97.4–14–426–18–4/38–23.66; A. J. A. Sinclair 88.2–10–395–13–2/16–30.38; J. F. C. Fitt 157.5–19–584–17–3/14–34.35.

IPSWICH SCHOOL *Played 14: W 6, L 2, D 6. A 2*

Master i/c: A. K. Golding Professional: R. E. East

Batting—M. Elliot 14–2–657–120*–3–54.75; T. Hembry 14–4–532–100*–1–53.20; R. Mann 14–2–628–136*–2–52.33; W. Burnell 14–5–355–84*–0–39.44; J. Southgate 8–1–203–65–0–29.00; T. Rash 9–2–186–36*–0–26.57.

Bowling—C. Flather 61.1–6–167–12–5/8–13.91; T. Caston 105–15–414–25–6/21–16.56; W. Burnell 105.4–17–269–16–4/17–16.81; T. Rash 139–23–440–20–3/25–22.00; I. Swallow 86.4–5–371–13–4/60–28.53.

THE JOHN LYON SCHOOL *Played 12: W 4, L 2, D 6*

Master i/c: I. R. Parker

Batting—R. T. James 12–6–342–71–0–57.00; N. Packianathan 6–2–153–42–0–38.25; C. S. Singh 12–4–152–47*–0–19.00.

Bowling—R. T. James 70.5–11–275–18–4/37–15.27; A. R. Pankhania 40–6–171–11–4/9–15.54; C. S. Singh 88–12–358–16–5/16–22.37.

KELLY COLLEGE *Played 9: W 2, L 1, D 6*

Master i/c: T. Ryder

Batting—A. Brown 6–2–311–107*–1–77.75; W. Grainger 6–1–162–102*–1–32.40.

Bowling—A. Brown 73–16–213–13–3/24–16.38; *J. T. Legodi 88.2–13–310–18–5/18–17.22.

KIMBOLTON SCHOOL *Played 17: W 10, L 4, D 3. A 3*

Master i/c: A. G. Tapp

Ten victories marked an outstanding season, in which Tom Huggins set three school records: an aggregate of 1,069 runs, 700 of which came in one week for once out; an average of 106.90; and five centuries. With 36 wickets as well, he was the country's top run-scorer and all-rounder, going on to play for Leicestershire Second Eleven, Cambridgeshire and an ECB Under-19 eleven. Also in the spotlight was Alex Lacey, whose off-spin foxed 42 opponents.

Batting—*T. B. Huggins 17–7–1,069–150*–5–106.90; E. Longmate 17–2–427–95–0–28.46; L. Bailey 17–0–405–64–0–23.82; A. Lacey 15–2–307–35–0–23.61; C. McCarthy 10–2–163–62–0–20.37.

Bowling—A. Lacey 146–32–511–42–6/27–12.16; T. B. Huggins 147–25–551–36–4/36–15.30; L. Bailey 111–25–383–21–3/23–18.19; M. Ellerbeck 86–13–337–16–4/13–21.06; C. McCarthy 104–16–410–18–3/9–22.77.

KING EDWARD VI COLLEGE, STOURBRIDGE *Played 9: W 4, L 2, D 3. A 2*

Masters i/c: M. L. Ryan and R. A. Williams

The batting was dominated by Mark Fisher and Alastair Maiden, whose unbeaten 144 against Bishop Vesey's came off 115 deliveries. Part way through the season Fisher switched from keeping wicket to pace bowling – and headed the averages.

Batting—*A. J. Maiden 7–1–453–144*–1–75.50; M. S. Fisher 7–2–251–80*–0–50.20.

Bowling—M. S. Fisher 30–2–82–10–4/34–8.20; G. Russon 46–3–162–11–4/5–14.72.

KING EDWARD VI SCHOOL, SOUTHAMPTON *Played 19: W 14, L 3, D 2. A 3*

Master i/c: R. J. Putt

Powerful batting down the order was the key to a successful season, in which targets of 220 or more were frequently overhauled. Memorable results included wins against Brighton College, Hampton, Charterhouse and MCC.

Batting—I. A. Strother 16–3–775–123*–3–59.61; W. E. Naylor 13–5–338–97*–0–42.25; J. P. Richardson 14–5–332–83*–0–36.88; T. C. Moore 15–1–500–87–0–35.71; G. H. Noble 9–0–313–116–1–34.77; *J. P. Dixon 11–1–313–141*–1–31.30; A. M. Paul 13–3–168–42–0–16.80.

Bowling—A. R. N. Warrick 71–16–257–18–4/21–14.27; N. H. Ellerby 82–17–275–15–4/9–18.33; R. M. Noble 101.2–15–373–16–2/15–23.31; A. M. Paul 151.2–41–407–17–3/22–23.94.

KING EDWARD VII & QUEEN MARY SCHOOL, LYTHAM

Played 20: W 12, L 5, D 2, T 1. A 3

Master i/c: A. M. Weston Professionals: D. J. Callaghan and P. Fulton

Jack Kelliher topped both averages and captained England Under-15. On a six-match tour to Sri Lanka in July, Ben Hall hit an unbeaten 146 in the win against Mahinda College, Matara.

Batting—J. Kelliher 13–1–475–100*–1–39.58; S. Holliday 18–10–246–29*–0–30.75; B. Hall 22–2–508–146*–1–25.40; T. Eastham 23–0–569–72–0–24.73; B. James 17–0–350–52–0–20.58; L. Blackett 17–2–297–53*–0–19.80; C. Roberts 19–2–335–47*–0–19.70; R. Cragg 16–3–229–38–0–17.61.

Bowling—J. Kelliher 91.1–16–293–18–6/32–16.27; S. Holliday 167.1–28–475–27–4/27–17.59; M. Ardern 83.2–8–335–17–3/27–19.70; C. Pickles 95.4–6–468–20–4/23–23.40; S. Pitman 129–12–505–20–4/8–25.25; L. Smith 117.5–12–520–20–4/26–26.00; L. Blackett 177.1–36–730–27–4/3–27.03.

KING EDWARD'S SCHOOL, BIRMINGHAM *Played 17: W 7, L 8, D 2. A 5*

Master i/c: M. D. Stead Professional: D. Collins

The side started slowly, peaked in June, then faded when key players were unavailable. Daniel Shilvock provided the backbone, scoring 417 runs and taking 40 wickets.

Batting—A. Singh 15–0–423–83–0–28.20; D. J. F. Shilvock 16–1–417–71–0–27.80; A. P. S. Holmes 15–1–364–93–0–26.00; B. N. Patel 15–2–311–61*–0–23.92; R. D. Tiwari 14–4–217–53–0–21.70; S. P. G. Chase 13–3–216–81*–0–21.60; *G. J. E. Brandrick 11–2–163–59–0–18.11.

Bowling—D. J. F. Shilvock 171.5–22–593–40–6/72–14.82; V. Banerjee 122.3–23–365–21–4/45–17.38; A. P. S. Thind 97.5–21–305–15–3/2–20.33; A. P. S. Holmes 105–15–354–12–4/38–29.50; R. D. Tiwari 112–21–349–11–2/24–31.72.

KING EDWARD'S SCHOOL, WITLEY *Played 13: W 3, L 7, D 3. A 4*

Master i/c: D. H. Messenger Professional: R. D. Jacobs

Rhythm and cohesion proved elusive on damp, slow pitches, but results improved with the weather after half-term. Craig Acquaye scored most runs and led the side well, while Marcus Amberton excelled with the ball.

Batting—T. P. L. Hodgson 10–1–348–110–1–38.66; R. C. Ledger 12–1–358–88–0–32.54; *W. C. Acquaye 13–1–366–85*–0–30.50; J. E. Crowne 9–1–157–37*–0–19.62.

Bowling—A. B. Fitzgerald 86–13–302–13–3/23–23.23; A. M. W. Manley 73–10–265–11–2/9–24.09; M. R. K. Amberton 121.5–15–483–19–6/73–25.42; W. Carruthers 102.2–20–388–15–5/74–25.86.

KING HENRY VIII SCHOOL, COVENTRY *Played 13: W 6, L 3, D 4*

Master i/c: A. M. Parker

Batting—*J. Whittingham 12–2–367–100*–1–36.70; A. Humphrey 13–2–335–100*–1–30.45; A. Jones 13–1–303–71–0–25.25; P. Adcock 9–0–166–64–0–18.44; P. Whittingham 13–2–201–39–0–18.27.

Bowling—R. Panchal 40–8–143–11–3/7–13.00; T. Leach 82.5–15–306–23–5/11–13.30; P. Whittingham 50.4–8–160–11–3/10–14.54.

KING WILLIAM'S COLLEGE *Played 8: W 2, L 3, D 3. A 3*

Masters i/c: M. J. Leaver and G. A. Garratt

Batting—D. Killa 9–1–360–111–1–45.00; *C. Byrne 8–0–290–156–1–36.25; G. Barratt 9–1–188–78–0–23.50.

Bowling—J. Howarth 75–8–233–10–3/37–23.30.

KING'S COLLEGE, TAUNTON *Played 11: W 7, L 4, D 0. A 2*

Master i/c: H. R. J. Trump Professional: D. J. Breakwell

Batting—J. Hudson 5–1–329–91–0–82.25; T. Webley 10–0–348–69–0–34.80; T. Beer 8–3–173–50*–0–34.60; W. Stafford 8–0–186–65–0–23.25.

Bowling—R. Excell 85.4–14–272–18–4/48–15.11; J. Baker 65–5–254–10–4/35–25.40; T. Webley 91–12–289–10–3/27–28.90.

KING'S COLLEGE SCHOOL, WIMBLEDON *Played 13: W 4, L 6, D 3. A 3*

Master i/c: G. C. McGinn Professional: M. Church

After a strong start, culminating in an exciting victory over local rivals St Paul's, the side's form ebbed away in the absence of some leading players. Pace bowler Charlie Foster had a match to remember against the Old Boys, when he captured four wickets in four balls.

Batting—H. F. Jones 11–0–427–90–0–38.81; D. E. Hitchman 13–1–316–54*–0–26.33; O. M. Fernie 11–0–250–85–0–22.72; O. H. Bretton 12–0–260–66–0–21.66; *P. J. Elks 13–0–213–40–0–16.38.

Bowling—C. T. Foster 96.2–15–265–20–5/16–13.25; N. A. Crosthwaite 70.5–5–238–15–7/34–15.86; P. J. Elks 55.3–9–203–10–3/36–20.30; S. M. O. Lewis 83.4–6–294–14–4/6–21.00; M. E. C. Jones 120.5–21–411–15–4/41–27.40.

KING'S SCHOOL, BRUTON *Played 17: W 2, L 13, D 2. A 1*

Master i/c: J. D. Roebuck Professional: A. P. Davis

Batting—A. J. Grazette 16–1–310–74–0–20.66; J. A. B. Edwards 8–0–156–37–0–19.50; C. M. Coward 13–0–251–55–0–19.30; J. F. Lee 12–2–156–32–0–15.60; *R. A. R. Tulloch 16–0–241–62–0–15.06; A. Lund 14–1–151–60*–0–11.61.

Bowling—A. Lund 137–34–469–25–4/13–18.76; J. Rutland 133–16–598–15–3/63–39.86.

THE KING'S SCHOOL, CANTERBURY *Played 17: W 5, L 1, D 11. A 1*

Master i/c: M. Afzal Professional: A. G. E. Ealham

Tom Bruce led by example in collecting most runs and wickets. He gained admirable support from John Stubbs with the bat, while Simon Darroch and Tom Morey formed an accurate and, at times, hostile opening attack.

Batting—J. D. E. Stubbs 16–4–479–104*–1–39.91; *T. O. Bruce 17–1–535–95–0–33.43; M. J. R. Page 13–2–223–43–0–20.27; J. A. Ellis 9–1–153–43–0–19.12; P. R. Archer 13–2–172–62–0–15.63; G. H. B. Brooke 13–2–163–27–0–14.81.

Bowling—T. J. L. Humphrey 77–22–201–13–4/16–15.46; T. O. Bruce 193–33–701–44–5/66–15.93; S. A. F. Darroch 155–21–470–22–4/40–21.36; G. H. B. Brooke 78–8–282–12–5/38–23.50; T. W. Morey 180–33–563–22–4/51–25.59.

THE KING'S SCHOOL, CHESTER *Played 12: W 9, L 3, D 0. A 4*

Master i/c: S. Neal

For their success the side owed much to their senior batsmen and spinners.

Batting—R. D. G. Brown 12–0–392–85–0–32.66; T. M. Simkin 10–3–228–47–0–32.57; *T. D. Bonser 12–1–332–84–0–30.18; D. J. Newham 7–0–153–74–0–21.85.

Bowling—M. J. Lister 62.4–6–292–20–4/27–14.60; T. D. Bonser 65.4–8–218–14–3/6–15.57; E. L. Owen 80.3–16–241–12–3/23–20.08.

THE KING'S SCHOOL, ELY *Played 11: W 1, L 8, D 2. A 5*

Masters i/c: H. G. Ingham and W. J. Marshall

Batting—*T. M. F. Sale 10–1–228–58–0–25.33; S. P. Blake 10–0–209–55–0–20.90; D. J. R. Cannie 11–0–155–31–0–14.09.

Bowling—D. G. J. Shepherd 75–3–404–14–4/61–28.85.

THE KING'S SCHOOL, MACCLESFIELD *Played 17: W 9, L 3, D 5. A 1*

Master i/c: S. Moores

Batting—A. M. Day 16–1–543–115*–1–36.20; T. M. Isherwood 15–3–346–46–0–28.83; J. P. Keep 15–4–290–70–0–26.36; *J. A. O. Duffy 17–1–412–62–0–25.75; O. D. Kenyon 17–2–297–87*–0–19.80.

Bowling—T. M. Isherwood 158.3–35–428–27–4/29–15.85; O. D. Kenyon 57.2–8–242–13–4/36–18.61; B. J. Coulbeck 51–6–234–11–5/53–21.27; H. M. Wheetman 82.1–11–324–14–4/16–23.14; T. A. Davenport 170.2–39–506–21–4/26–24.09; J. M. Arnfield 145–32–468–17–3/40–27.52; A. M. Day 124.4–31–394–13–3/14–30.30.

KING'S SCHOOL, ROCHESTER *Played 17: W 5, L 6, D 6. A 4*

Master i/c: G. R. Williams

Batting—*R. W. Hughes 15–2–438–105–1–33.69; S. G. Wakeman 16–1–454–94–0–30.26; B. A. Smith 11–2–260–54–0–28.88; J. N. Butler 16–2–402–102–1–28.71; J. M. Shakespeare 10–1–177–36*–0–19.66.

Bowling—R. W. Hughes 145.2–38–517–31–4/13–16.67; R. H. Barrett 57.5–7–266–11–3/17–24.18; B. A. Smith 61–11–269–10–3/24–26.90; J. M. Shakespeare 73.2–6–377–14–3/25–26.92; R. Lakhera 97–12–370–10–2/32–37.00.

KING'S SCHOOL, TYNEMOUTH *Played 12: W 2, L 9, D 1. A 1*

Masters i/c: W. Ryan and P. J. Nicholson

Batting—No batsman scored 150 runs. The leading batsman was *R. J. Gardham 8–1–143–51–0–20.42.

Bowling—No bowler took 10 wickets. The leading bowler was F. W. Bell 26–1–108–9–4/28–12.00.

KING'S SCHOOL, WORCESTER *Played 22: W 9, L 7, D 6. A 1*

Master i/c: D. P. Iddon — Professional: A. A. D. Gillgrass

Although the batting boasted strength in depth, the seam bowling was inconsistent, and it was leg-spinner Nick Dale-Lace, with a school-record 55 wickets, who was the mainstay. The season finished with a six-match tour of Barbados.

Batting—N. O. S. Major 16–3–553–101–1–42.53; R. J. Hallett 11–4–196–37*–0–28.00; J. R. Gwynne 15–3–324–82–0–27.00; P. A. Burdon 13–1–291–68–0–24.25; *N. J. D. Dale-Lace 15–1–304–45–0–21.71; J. W. Robinson 15–0–322–52–0–21.46.

Bowling—B. S. Pitts 27–2–130–12–4/33–10.83; N. J. D. Dale-Lace 198.1–47–606–55–7/45–11.01; J. W. Robinson 103–8–388–21–3/23–18.47; S. J. Daly 114–22–355–16–3/11–22.18.

KINGSTON GRAMMAR SCHOOL *Played 9: W 1, L 7, D 1*

Master i/c: D. E. C. Wethey Professional: C. S. Knightley

Batting—No batsman scored 150 runs. The leading batsman was R. Trivedi 7–2–127–52*–0–25.40.

Bowling—A. Crane 32–0–152–10–4/38–15.20.

KINGSWOOD SCHOOL *Played 9: W 8, L 0, D 1*

Master i/c: G. Opie

Top place in the Peak Sports Bath and District League, in its inaugural year, was a highlight in an unbeaten term. Jack Seddon, who averaged 75.00, won an award as the League's outstanding batsman and shared the bulk of the run-scoring with Sam Kelly, who headed the bowling.

Batting—J. A. Seddon 8–3–375–96*–0–75.00; *S. R. Kelly 7–0–219–55–0–31.28; M. N. Raisbeck 7–1–167–108–1–27.83; J. E. G. Thorne 8–1–169–62–0–24.14.

Bowling—S. R. Kelly 56–10–137–16–3/18–8.56; D. G. Gerrish 45.5–10–139–16–4/21–8.68; H. F. Seddon 55–9–183–12–4/35–15.25.

LANCING COLLEGE *Played 15: W 5, L 8, D 2*

Master i/c: M. P. Bentley Professional: R. J. Davies

Batting—R. H. Wakeford 14–0–689–154–2–49.21; J. A. G. Green 13–1–373–94*–0–31.08; *Y. M. Salameh 12–1–235–45–0–21.36; A. G. Dodsworth 13–0–178–50–0–13.69.

Bowling—N. J. Murray-Willis 87.3–14–309–24–6/17–12.87; P. J. Newman 56.1–7–191–11–2/24–17.36; R. H. Wakeford 72.2–13–264–14–6/25–18.85; J. A. G. Green 101–16–377–12–3/18–31.41.

LEEDS GRAMMAR SCHOOL *Played 11: W 3, L 3, D 5. A 4*

Master i/c: R. Hill

Batting—A. M. Rogowski 9–2–265–68*–0–37.85; A. J. Blakeborough 10–0–333–61–0–33.30; *A. D. Coyne 11–2–287–106–1–31.88; C. J. Smith 11–0–211–59–0–19.18; G. O. E. James 11–1–161–37–0–16.10.

Bowling—B. D. Jacklin 50.2–19–100–15–5/27–6.66; B. A. J. Tompkins 48–14–172–12–3/25–14.33; A. D. Coyne 143.3–54–308–20–4/20–15.40; B. R. Maude 107.2–22–330–16–4/17–20.62.

THE LEYS SCHOOL *Played 13: W 6, L 3, D 4*

Master i/c: A. Batterham Professional: C. Bradfield

Batting—S. O'Shea 5–3–290–115*–1–145.00; G. Houghton 8–4–276–57*–0–69.00; J. Waters 9–1–246–55*–0–30.75; J. Wyatt 9–0–223–70–0–24.77; *J. Houlder 10–1–187–80*–0–20.77.

Bowling—J. Wyatt 68–11–220–15–2/4–14.66; K. Coetzee 122–23–303–15–3/68–20.20; R. Barnett 37–3–203–10–2/14–20.30; G. Houghton 130–32–436– 21–4/72–20.76.

LIVERPOOL COLLEGE *Played 12: W 1, L 9, D 2. A 2*

Master i/c: A. Fox Professional: B. Mukherjee

Batting—J. Howarth 11–2–273–65–0–30.33.

Bowling—M. Melia 96–14–410–19–5/41–21.57.

Smiling assassins: left-arm spinners Toby Martin (*left*) and Edward Carpenter took 40 wickets apiece for Lord Wandsworth and Marlborough colleges respectively.

LLANDOVERY COLLEGE *Played 6: W 1, L 4, D 1. A 1*

Master i/c: T. Marks

Batting—R. J. Coles 4–1–150–101*–1–50.00.

Bowling—D. Rodman 49.3–5–204–10–3/24–20.40.

LORD WANDSWORTH COLLEGE *Played 18: W 11, L 3, D 4. A 4*

Master i/c: M. C. Russell Professional: S. A. Kent

The relatively inexperienced side equalled the college record of 11 wins. Left-arm spinner Toby Martin was outstanding with 40 wickets at 6.25 from 111 overs, and Charlie Pidgeon's return of six for 15 against Abbotholme was the best for six years.

Batting—J. D. E. Irving 14–1–491–112*–1–37.76; P. K. Knight 12–3–312–83*–0–34.66; J. A. D. Colvin 16–3–350–118–1–26.92; *J. J. Ablett 16–2–375–90*–0–26.78; M. J. Horn 12–2–222–53–0–22.20; L. A. Houghton 16–1–286–54*–0–19.06.

Bowling—T. H. Martin 111.1–39–250–40–6/28–6.25; J. B. Woodcock 118.4–20–286–19–3/27–15.05; C. W. Pidgeon 96.4–13–405–24–6/15–16.87; J. C. McCardle 95.1–9–439–23–4/14–19.08; P. K. Knight 73.1–9–289–10–3/22–28.90.

LORD WILLIAMS'S SCHOOL *Played 5: W 2, L 1, D 2. A 4*

Master i/c: J. E. Fulkes

Batting—J. Evans 4–0–157–115–1–39.25.

Bowling—P. Evans 39–10–114–11–3/24–10.36.

LOUGHBOROUGH GRAMMAR SCHOOL *Played 14: W 4, L 6, D 4. A 3*

Master i/c: H. T. Tunnicliffe Professional: J. Cameron

Batting—D. Howgate 14–1–375–79–0–28.84; R. Worrall 10–0–275–75–0–27.50; E. Barney 11–2–238–59*–0–26.44; P. Broster 14–0–312–53–0–22.28.

Bowling—P. Tilley 97–15–285–18–6/55–15.83; V. Mody 84–15–274–12–3/19–22.83; F. Baker 162–19–584–21–5/48–27.80.

MAGDALEN COLLEGE SCHOOL *Played 13: W 4, L 9, D 0*

Master i/c: S. J. Curwood

Batting—J. Kandola 14–1–326–52–0–25.07; N. Cook 15–0–286–44–0–19.06; *R. Craig 16–1–259–38–0–17.26; L. Phipps 13–0–212–68–0–16.30; M. Neilson 15–0–186–72–0–12.40.

Bowling—S. Wright 49–3–240–12–4/29–20.00; T. Phipps 105–13–457–22–7/9–20.77; R. Soddy 57–7–264–10–2/6–26.40; D. King 85–9–377–14–4/46–26.92; R. Craig 118–18–403–14–5/7–28.78; M. Neilson 83–15–392–12–4/15–32.66.

MALVERN COLLEGE *Played 15: W 6, L 6, D 3. A 3*

Master i/c: A. J. Murtagh Professional: R. W. Tolchard

Batting—H. D. Bailey 10–5–170–43–0–34.00; C. Wood 14–2–401–79*–0–33.41; B. W. Edkins 13–2–295–58–0–26.81; W. M. Gifford 14–3–281–121*–1–25.54; *J. J. C. Lewis 12–2–247–50*–0–24.70; J. E. P. Cartwright 12–4–190–37*–0–23.75; W. A. Murtagh 15–1–281–70–0–20.07; C. W. Tolchard 16–0–244–45–0–15.25.

Bowling—G. P. Vaughan 115.3–21–380–19–4/11–20.00; J. J. C. Lewis 183.4–5–309–14–3/19–22.07; B. W. Edkins 116.4–4–443–18–4/33–24.61; E. C. Latter 99–18–338–11–3/11–30.72.

MANCHESTER GRAMMAR SCHOOL *Played 14: W 7, L 1, D 6. A 3*

Master i/c: D. Moss

Astutely captained by John Whitaker, the side were beaten only by Stockport GS early in the season. Whitaker and Rana Malook were again the key fast bowlers, while contrasting slow left-armers Phil Martin and Daniel Woods took 50 wickets between them. Martin's eight for 33 against Arnold was the best for 25 years. Wicket-keeper/batsman Alastair Buchan proved an excellent focus in the field as well as scoring two centuries.

Batting—R. A. Buchan 12–4–408–110–2–51.00; D. R. Leech 13–1–442–69*–0–36.83; D. Ekstein 12–0–322–82–0–26.83; M. R. A. Tufft 14–0–285–57–0–20.35; P. C. Martin 12–4–162–34–0–20.25.

Bowling—R. J. Malook 127.4–39–267–23–4/11–11.60; P. C. Martin 105.3–25–290–23–8/33–12.60; *J. K. H. Whitaker 158.5–46–369–28–6/22–13.17; J. N. Clowes 61–10–207–12–5/41–17.25; D. A. Woods 180.4–39–490–27–6/28–18.14; R. A. Partington 80.5–14–239–12–5/33–19.91.

MARLBOROUGH COLLEGE *Played 12: W 3, L 2, D 7*

Master i/c: N. E. Briers Professional: R. M. Ratcliffe

Left-arm spinner Edward Carpenter, whose 42 wickets took his tally for the eleven to 115, played for ECB Schools West.

Batting—J. M. L. Bucknall 12–2–299–88–0–29.90; E. A. G. Nicholson 12–0–348–99–0–29.00; *H. G. Ingham 12–1–257–68–0–23.36; H. R. S. Adair 12–1–253–70*–0–23.00.

Bowling—E. J. Carpenter 284.2–99–607–42–7/30–14.45; T. G. Montagu-Pollock 145–32–352–14–4/19–25.14; A. R. G. Armstrong 158.4–32–464–18–3/38–25.77.

MERCHANT TAYLORS' SCHOOL, CROSBY *Played 18: W 8, L 4, D 6*

Master i/c: Rev. D. A. Smith Professional: A. Kuruvilla

Batting—J. F. Wildman 15–1–574–88–0–41.00; J. Cole 14–5–333–61–0–37.00; R. H. G. Byrom 15–1–292–71–0–20.85; A. D. Fraser 16–4–208–31–0–17.33; A. M. O'Leary 12–3–155–48*–0–17.22.

Bowling—*P. K. Battersby 74–22–163–12–3/0–13.58; D. M. Trapp 144–30–432–30–4/17–14.40; D. P. Guy 51–6–226–13–5/6–17.38; G. A. Barry 114–23–322–16–5/45–20.12; R. H. G. Byrom 44–3–241–11–3/19–21.90; J. F. Wildman 117–19–451–17–4/64–26.52.

MERCHANT TAYLORS' SCHOOL, NORTHWOOD *Played 15: W 5, L 3, D 7*

Master i/c: C. R. Evans-Evans Professional: H. C. Latchman

Steffan James led the inexperienced side well and headed the batting, in which the only hundred came from Stuart Simons, who also opened the bowling effectively. A highlight was Richard Booth's return of five for five against Loretto.

Batting—*S. G. James 13–0–434–76–0–33.38; S. M. Simons 12–1–332–110–1–30.18; A. P. Raja 12–2–235–62–0–23.50; S. Woolf 12–3–206–75*–0–22.88; R. J. M. Booth 13–1–164–71–0–13.66.

Bowling—S. M. Simons 163–33–527–32–4/15–16.46; S. N. K. Dave 74–14–215–10–3/13–21.50; S. G. James 150.5–30–386–17–3/38–22.70; R. J. M. Booth 108.4–14–386–14–5/5–27.57.

MERCHISTON CASTLE SCHOOL *Played 11: W 5, L 3, D 3. A 2*

Master i/c: C. W. Swan Professional: C. English

Brendan McKerchar was again in impressive all-round form, averaging 108.66 with the bat, as well as heading the bowling. He was selected for both the Scotland A and Under-19 sides.

Batting—B. T. McKerchar 10–4–652–150*–2–108.66; O. D. Abram 7–2–236–74–0–47.20; J. W. Welch 11–1–363–133–1–36.30; J. W. A. Duminy 10–0–233–54–0–23.30.

Bowling—B. T. McKerchar 118–35–273–26–4/21–10.50; A. W. Sharpe 106–26–295–26–5/44–11.34; *P. A. Swan 69–15–237–15–3/9–15.80; H. C. Dernie 59–14–189–11–3/3–17.18.

MILLFIELD SCHOOL *Played 17: W 11, L 4, D 2. A 1*

Master i/c: R. M. Ellison Professional: M. R. Davis

Batting—I. Haley 6–4–262–55*–0–131.00; L. Stokes 18–3–678–157–1–45.20; A. Suppiah 17–5–492–87–0–41.00; L. Smith 13–3–296–94–0–29.60; *N. Goodman 13–1–240–59–0–20.00; J. Hildreth 13–0–186–54–0–14.30.

Bowling—J. Hildreth 61–20–137–12–4/2–11.41; A. Suppiah 173.2–56–348–29–4/12–12.00; N. Goodman 95.3–27–235–17–3/19–13.82; L. Smith 111.1–25–319–15–4/10–21.26; T. Seward 127.1–15–370–17–5/22–21.76; J. Elliott-Square 105.3–21–320–14–2/12–22.85.

MILL HILL SCHOOL *Played 11: W 4, L 3, D 4. A 5*

Master i/c: P. H. Edwards Professional: I. J. F. Hutchinson

Batting—M. Hirsch 11–3–356–115*–1–44.50; M. Stein 10–2–174–34–0–21.75; *S. Da Re 11–0–233–47–0–21.18; J. Hutcheson 10–1–158–36–0–17.55.

Bowling—S. Da Re 68–11–269–22–5/40–12.22; M. Khan 48–14–160–12–3/22–13.33; S. Kochlar 43–9–172–11–5/29–15.63.

MILTON ABBEY SCHOOL *Played 10: W 3, L 6, D 1. A 3*

Master i/c: P. W. Wood

Batting—No batsman scored 150 runs. The leading batsman was *H. Dawes 9–1–148–49*–0–18.50.

Bowling—No bowler took 10 wickets. The leading bowler was H. Dawes 46–6–207–9–4/26–23.00.

MONKTON COMBE SCHOOL *Played 15: W 6, L 9, D 0. A 2*

Masters i/c: P. R. Wickens and N. D. Botton

A young and improving side bowled and fielded consistently, but the batting lacked depth.

Batting—M. A. Lynch 15–1–300–69*–0–21.42; T. Moore 10–2–171–46*–0–21.37; M. E. Lynch 14–2–172–37*–0–14.33; J. Darling 13–1–157–37–0–13.08.

Bowling—T. Quayle 60–17–137–17–5/5–8.05; M. E. Lynch 97–16–339–12–3/11–28.25.

MONMOUTH SCHOOL *Played 16: W 12, L 3, D 1. A 2*

Master i/c: A. J. Jones Professional: G. I. Burgess

The willingness of captain Kunnal Khanna to risk defeat resulted in an exciting and successful campaign, with 12 wins setting a new standard for the school.

Batting—J. Wyatt 16–3–732–128*–3–56.30; I. A. Clayton 16–3–658–110–1–50.61; *K. Khanna 15–0–476–101–1–31.73; J. Richards 13–0–313–60–0–24.07; T. Grubb 11–2–207–50–0–23.00.

Bowling—K. Khanna 155–31–442–33–6/62–13.39; B. Pike 128.4–25–387–26–4/19–14.88; J. Harrison 115–25–371–20–5/35–18.55; T. Robinson 117.1–25–338–11–4/25–30.72.

NEWCASTLE-UNDER-LYME SCHOOL *Played 10: W 6, L 3, D 1. A 4*

Master i/c: S. A. Robson Professional: O. D. Gibson

The batting skill of John James was largely responsible for greatly improved results. His 128 against Rydal Penrhos was the highest individual score for the school, while his century against King's, Tynemouth, contributed to a total of 403 for five and a winning margin of 311 runs – both records.

Batting—*J. W. James 10–2–554–128–2–69.25; S. J. P. Howland 7–0–234–82–0–33.42; D. J. Moss 10–2–185–60*–0–23.12; J. S. Legg 10–0–152–101–1–15.20.

Bowling—V. Kumar 46–12–150–12–4/5–12.50; J. W. James 66–14–224–12–3/7–18.66.

NORWICH SCHOOL *Played 12: W 5, L 5, D 2. A 2*

Master i/c: T. J. W. Day Professionals: R. A. Bunting and S. C. Goldsmith

A summer of team building, in preparation for a tour to Antigua in 2002, yielded encouraging results, including George Walker's selection for Leicestershire Second Eleven.

Batting—E. J. Foster 9–1–447–97*–0–55.87; *G. W. Walker 9–2–178–62*–0–25.42; E. D. Hopkins 11–1–248–72–0–24.80; C. J. M. Webster 10–1–208–49–0–23.11.

Bowling—A. J. Robinson 98–15–301–21–4/31–14.33; G. W. Walker 109.4–33–294–19–3/12–15.47; C. J. M. Webster 56.1–8–265–11–3/41–24.09.

NOTTINGHAM HIGH SCHOOL *Played 9: W 5, L 3, D 0, T 1. A 4*

Master i/c: J. Lamb Professional: K. E. Cooper

Batting—*R. J. M. Wild 9–2–237–64–0–33.85; T. R. Chalkley 9–0–276–70–0–30.66; C. P. Saxton 9–0–269–93–0–29.88; J. L. Hall 8–0–166–62–0–20.75.

Bowling—R. J. Tonkin 51–7–172–11–5/11–15.63; R. J. M. Wild 85–11–307–12–4/57–25.58.

OAKHAM SCHOOL *Played 20: W 14, L 2, D 4*

Master i/c: F. C. Hayes Professional: D. S. Steele

Purposeful batting provided the basis for a record 14 wins. Of the four batsmen to average over 50, David Jackson and Nick Ferraby went on to play for Leicestershire Second Eleven. Leg-spinner James Hamilton-Kennaway headed a competent and varied attack.

Batting—R. W. Cook 14–7–420–65–0–60.00; N. J. Ferraby 13–5–443–108*–2–55.37; *D. N. Jackson 13–3–544–105*–1–54.40; M. J. Matthews 8–1–377–76–0–53.85; W. F. Wright 13–3–447–85–0–44.70; G. R. Firmin 13–1–445–120–1–37.08; M. A. G. Boyce 13–4–265–41–0–29.44.

Bowling—J. E. B. A. Hamilton-Kennaway 159–25–625–29–4/13–21.55; P. G. Cook 150–27–525–23–4/11–22.82; M. S. Pilling 130–23–403–17–3/23–23.70; S. P. Gadher 224.3–67–586–24–4/21–24.41; N. J. Ferraby 126.5–20–477–16–5/17–29.81.

THE ORATORY SCHOOL *Played 14: W 8, L 3, D 3*

Master i/c: P. L. Tomlinson Professional: J. B. K. Howell

Batting—M. R. Bruce 11–2–318–54–0–35.33; N. J. Lo 11–0–372–68–0–33.81; T. T. Bailey 10–0–284–63–0–28.40; M. W. Housego 11–0–190–44–0–17.27; A. J. Wight 13–3–158–71–0–15.80.

Bowling—R. E. Greenland 79–15–224–15–5/43–14.93; L. W. Roycroft 81–21–230–15–3/17–15.33; M. J. Farmar 120.4–20–333–15–3/31–22.20.

OSWESTRY SCHOOL *Played 11: W 3, L 7, D 1. A 3*

Master i/c: P. S. Jones

Batting—C. Boyle 9–2–214–48–0–30.57.

Bowling—M. J. Nicholson 98–10–322–13–3/39–24.76; C. Boyle 80–5–320–12–4/13–26.66.

OUNDLE SCHOOL *Played 19: W 9, L 3, D 7. A 3*

Master i/c: J. R. Wake Professional: T. Howorth

The eleven continued to play positive, attacking cricket. Jonathan Outar led by example with bat and ball (chinamen), and was selected for ECB Schools West. He was well supported in both departments by the England Under-17 representative, leg-spinner Cameron Wake.

Batting—R. M. Fahrenheim 9–2–220–87*–0–31.42; *J. Outar 19–0–547–111–1–28.78; C. J. Wake 18–5–359–39–0–27.61; B. Redmond 15–2–334–76–0–25.69; J. A. R. Wilson 16–7–212–44*–0–23.55; D. Outar 17–2–265–75–0–17.66; M. J. Phythian 16–3–219–40*–0–16.84; T. J. Elliott 16–0–260–66–0–16.25.

Bowling—W. N. A. Kendall 63–20–148–11–3/18–13.45; J. Outar 192.4–41–537–28–3/23–19.17; J. A. R. Wilson 137.1–22–500–25–4/33–20.00; C. J. Wake 139–16–467–16–3/30–29.18; J. I. Hay 112.1–22–363–12–3/28–30.25.

PANGBOURNE COLLEGE *Played 6: W 1, L 5, D 0. A 8*

Masters i/c: R. H. A. Brodhurst and D. J. Tooze

Batting—*C. J. Sutton 6–0–177–102–1–29.50.

Bowling—J. Lewis 56–12–163–12–4/18–13.58; C. J. Frost 48–12–162–11–4/29–14.72.

THE PERSE SCHOOL *Played 10: W 3, L 2, D 5. A 1*

Master i/c: M. A. Judson Professional: D. C. Coward

Batting—T. Wilkins 9–0–281–90–0–31.22; O. R. Gregory 9–1–210–115*–1–26.25; *S. F. G. Smith 9–1–182–71–0–22.75.

Bowling—D. P. M. Hawkins 84–10–370–16–6/64–23.12; J. A. M. Crawford 111.3–18–380–15–5/29–25.33; T. Wilkins 101–26–300–11–5/47–27.27.

PLYMOUTH COLLEGE *Played 14: W 5, L 3, D 6*

Masters i/c: G. C. Roderick and G. Lane

James Toms set a college record with an innings of 172 against Plymouth Corporate Officers, and went on to play for Devon Under-17.

Batting—J. Toms 12–2–513–172–1–51.30; *A. Gould 8–0–198–68–0–24.75; M. Hanton 11–1–194–120–1–19.40; D. Vince 13–1–192–57*–0–16.00.

Bowling—J. Toms 82–23–253–21–5/28–12.04; P. Thorpe 65–9–270–13–3/21–20.76; J. Bowden 87–9–331–14–4/59–23.64; A. Lampe 62.5–5–298–11–4/36–27.09.

POCKLINGTON SCHOOL *Played 11: W 3, L 6, D 2. A 3*

Master i/c: R. Smith

Batting—T. P. Nettleton 8–2–155–42–0–25.83; *D. P. C. Izzard 10–2–202–76*–0–25.25; E. G. H. Smith 9–0–224–93–0–24.88; R. G. Booth 9–1–155–68–0–19.37.

Bowling—R. G. Booth 104–18–267–19–4/22–14.05; R. J. G. Owen 90–21–267–13–3/11–20.53; A. G. Almond 72–13–206–10–4/37–20.60; C. A. Pottage 89–13–252–12–3/4–21.00.

PORTSMOUTH GRAMMAR SCHOOL *Played 12: W 2, L 7, D 3*

Master i/c: G. D. Payne Professional: R. A. Parks

Brothers Matthew and Benjamin Morgan both made significant contributions with bat and ball.

Batting—B. R. W. Morgan 11–2–426–79*–0–47.33; A. T. Robinson 8–1–204–68*–0–29.14; *M. J. M. Morgan 10–1–212–51–0–23.55; S. G. Larbey 9–0–173–57–0–19.22; M. P. M. Saunders 9–1–151–67–0–18.87.

Bowling—Y. Y. Chung 88–18–439–22–4/34–19.95; B. R. W. Morgan 96–15–396–18–4/42–22.00; M. J. M. Morgan 82.1–15–378–16–3/37–23.62; C. J. Tebb 76.2–8–432–13–3/21–33.23.

PRIOR PARK COLLEGE *Played 12: W 2, L 7, D 3. A 1*

Master i/c: D. R. Holland Professional: M. D. Browning

Batting—R. Maunder 9–2–334–102*–1–47.71; H. Kidd 12–0–343–100–1–28.58; T. Grimshaw 12–1–230–61–0–20.90.

Bowling—S. Williams 93–10–398–15–4/15–26.53; H. Kidd 84–14–332–10–2/16–33.20.

QUEEN ELIZABETH GS, WAKEFIELD *Played 13: W 5, L 5, D 3*

Master i/c: T. Barker Professional: C. Jackson

Batting—*G. Fearns 10–0–288–78–0–28.80; D. Wood 12–0–235–70–0–19.58.

Bowling—J. Barkley 66.2–14–180–17–5/4–10.58; N. Bucknell 121–35–309–21–4/9–14.71; D. Wood 54.1–15–169–10–2/2–16.90; R. Wainwright 95–16–350–17–3/23–20.58.

QUEEN ELIZABETH'S HOSPITAL, BRISTOL *Played 12: W 5, L 4, D 3*

Master i/c: P. E. Joslin

Batting—H. J. Hanchet 10–2–278–62–0–34.75; *M. Beale 12–1–349–74*–0–31.72; A. J. Bamber 12–1–255–64*–0–23.18.

Bowling—A. J. Bamber 30–3–97–12–5/28–8.08; A. T. Hamid 82–17–226–14–2/18–16.14; M. Beale 66–4–273–16–2/9–17.06; H. J. Hanchet 55–7–233–11–4/44–21.18; D. J. Lee 68–9–288–10–2/18–28.80.

QUEEN'S COLLEGE, TAUNTON *Played 15: W 4, L 8, D 3. A 2*

Master i/c: A. S. Free

Victory over MCC was the high point of a season resurrected from a disastrous start. Lee Denslow made sound progress with his leg-spinners to top the bowling.

Batting—*J. R. Loder 13–4–349–84–0–38.77; A. G. Needs 10–4–195–63*–0–32.50; J. E. Trundley 15–1–432–91*–0–30.85; L. K. Denslow 10–1–237–66*–0–26.33; L. M. Evans 15–1–163–50–0–11.64.

Bowling—L. K. Denslow 109.3–21–373–25–7/47–14.92; A. G. Needs 83–5–360–15–3/33–24.00; J. R. Loder 110–26–245–10–3/21–24.50; J. J. Beadon 68–3–325–13–3/22–25.00.

RADLEY COLLEGE *Played 12: W 4, L 2, D 6*

Master i/c: W. J. Wesson Professionals: A. R. Wagner and A. G. Robinson

Batting—O. D. B. Powell 7–5–191–64*–0–95.50; S. M. Butler 12–0–561–102–1–46.75; S. H. Dalrymple 11–2–325–114*–1–36.11; I. Singh 8–1–153–63*–0–21.85; M. J. A. Yorke-Long 11–0–230–49–0–20.90.

Bowling—G. H. R. Holloway 114–22–281–19–6/34–14.78; *C. R. Langton 158–30–487–29–6/40–16.79; L. D. McLaren 101–17–298–11–3/41–27.09.

RATCLIFFE COLLEGE *Played 13: W 7, L 6, D 0. A 4*

Master i/c: R. M. Hughes Professional: M. Deane

Luke Wright's impressive form with the bat earned him selection for Leicestershire Second Eleven after his brother, Ashley, made his first-class debut for the county against the Pakistanis in May. Ratcliffe won the Emeriti Trophy for the third time in its five-year history, beating Downside in the final.

Batting—L. J. Wright 7–2–435–89–0–87.00; K. Jogia 13–0–415–95–0–31.92; T. L. Cabrelli 13–0–232–60–0–17.84.

Bowling—X. Schaaf 37.2–15–83–11–5/18–7.54; K. Jogia 73.1–10–242–20–4/8–12.10; L. J. Wright 41.2–8–135–10–3/16–13.50; S. J. Lansdowne 73.4–10–208–13–2/11–16.00; A. J. Smith 59.3–4–272–15–5/10–18.13; J. A. Sutliff 59.5–4–224–11–3/10–20.36.

READING SCHOOL *Played 10: W 5, L 0, D 5. A 2*

Masters i/c: R. F. Perkins and J. E. Bonneywell

A well-balanced young side were undefeated. Prominent amongst the batsmen were Martin Bushell, who scored an unbeaten 154 against Abingdon, and Tom Burrows, who at 16 years and 42 days is believed to be the youngest cricketer to play for Berkshire. The highlight of an end-of-season tour of Grenada was a match played in the new national stadium.

Batting—T. G. Burrows 7–4–202–76*–0–67.33; M. Bushell 6–1–315–154*–1–63.00; M. J. Orford 8–0–252–78–0–31.50.

Bowling—M. R. Jubb 63–13–176–15–4/13–11.73; E. J. McNeill 52.5–13–190–16–5/17–11.87; T. J. H. Jacob 68.2–13–238–14–4/8–17.00; M. Ahmed 53–7–196–11–5/30–17.81.

REED'S SCHOOL *Played 11: W 4, L 2, D 5. A 4*

Master i/c: M. R. Dunn

The game with the XL Club saw two school records broken as James Morrison made 154 not out and put on 220 for the second wicket with David Coates.

Batting—*D. B. Coates 9–3–479–102*–1–79.83; J. I. Morrison 8–1–424–154*–1–60.57; S. J. Day 11–2–326–101*–1–36.22; S. C. Waller 8–1–242–103–1–34.57.

Bowling—D. B. Coates 83.2–14–271–13–3/17–20.84; C. J. Durling 87.1–13–428–14–3/24–30.57.

REIGATE GRAMMAR SCHOOL *Played 16: W 2, L 8, D 6. A 1*

Master i/c: A. Reid Professional: J. Barnes

Batting—S. Mills 10–3–422–103*–1–60.28; *N. Bezodis 15–0–561–136–2–37.40; A. Diggles 15–1–407–66–0–29.07; J. Bailey 14–3–315–68*–0–28.63; D. Fell 7–0–163–60–0–23.28.

Bowling—A. Diggles 116–17–403–18–5/30–22.38; N. Bezodis 193–52–654–25–5/56–26.16; D. Hughan 49–1–304–11–6/32–27.63; M. Reid 123–20–457–15–3/28–30.46.

REPTON SCHOOL *Played 13: W 6, L 5, D 2. A 4*

Master i/c: F. P. Watson Professional: M. K. Kettle

Batting—E. J. Crowther 11–3–564–116*–2–70.50; *R. T. Alsop 13–1–367–86–0–30.58; S. R. Pearson 10–2–168–52–0–21.00; M. R. Rippon 13–0–271–60–0–20.84; M. O'Halloran 11–3–160–43*–0–20.00.

Bowling—D. H. Rippon 132.3–21–478–22–5/27–21.72; B. D. E. Dewhirst 150–24–532–22–4/47–24.18; S. K. Chilman 155.1–34–483–19–5/56–25.42.

ROSSALL SCHOOL *Played 16: W 5, L 7, D 4*

Master i/c: A. D. Todd

Batting—P. J. Heald 8–3–150–37–0–30.00; J. E. Bruck 15–0–241–51–0–16.06; R. J. Dingle 16–1–217–35–0–14.46; M. D. Allen 15–0–200–47–0–13.33.

Bowling—*J. R. Ferguson 157–36–487–27–5/34–18.03; M. D. Allen 97–19–339–16–4/10–21.18; R. J. Dingle 90–15–374–17–4/15–22.00; R. Cooke 104–19–386–12–2/13–32.16.

THE ROYAL GRAMMAR SCHOOL, COLCHESTER

Played 17: W 3, L 10, D 4. A 5

Master i/c: R. L. Bayes

Disrupted by a series of injuries, illness and the abandonment of the first four fixtures, the team never got into its stride. The batting failed to gel and seldom made defensible totals, yet the captain, Adrian Cook, maintained excellent team spirit.

Batting—T. W. R. George 18–1–363–67–0–21.35; *A. E. Cook 15–0–289–76–0–19.26; L. Cunnah 17–2–287–107*–1–19.13; M. Tyler 15–1–205–58–0–14.64; J. Warner 16–0–208–46–0–13.00.

Bowling—A. E. Cook 187.3–29–681–32–5/45–21.28; M. Tyler 233–43–793–36–5/24–22.02; P. C. Smith 144–20–555–22–3/20–25.22; N. S. Coles 64.4–7–329–13–3/19–25.30; T. G. Brook 95–11–416–16–3/20–26.00.

THE ROYAL GRAMMAR SCHOOL, GUILDFORD

Played 15: W 12, L 2, D 1. A 4

Master i/c: S. B. R. Shore — Professional: M. A. Lynch

The high points of a successful campaign were victories over MCC (chasing 210) and a strong Royal GS, Worcester side at the RGS festival, hosted by Guildford.

Batting—S. P. Barnsley 12–2–396–108*–1–39.60; S. P. Peel 8–1–231–94*–0–33.00; T. G. Markham 11–1–305–62–0–30.50; T. R. Barford 6–0–183–76–0–30.50; P. J. Hosier 9–1–192–70–0–24.00; *A. Tucker 14–4–190–50–0–19.00.

Bowling—S. P. Peel 31.5–3–120–12–5/14–10.00; T. A. Dickson 80.3–15–269–17–2/16–15.82; D. T. Jones 92–20–261–16–3/21–16.31; A. Tucker 101.5–16–344–15–2/8–22.93; M. P. Wycherley 81.1–12–273–10–2/11–27.30.

ROYAL GRAMMAR SCHOOL, HIGH WYCOMBE

Played 13: W 10, L 2, D 1

Master i/c: P. R. Miles

Batting—J. Allfrey 7–3–204–108–1–51.00; *C. Allfrey 13–1–378–78–0–31.50; N. Robinson 11–4–200–57–0–28.57; R. Bowry 12–1–238–54–0–21.63; J. Nelson 8–0–160–55–0–20.00; J. Anderson 11–2–164–47–0–18.22.

Bowling—J. Mahood 85–18–200–22–5/7–9.09; R. Bowry 121.4–32–318–28–7/39–11.35.

ROYAL GRAMMAR SCHOOL, LANCASTER

Played 14: W 9, L 1, D 4. A 1

Master i/c: I. D. Whitehouse — Professional: D. H. Cameron

Batting—D. J. Hagen 12–2–616–139*–2–61.60; T. D. Battarbee 14–3–412–100*–1–37.45; *B. P. Hughes 12–0–269–69–0–22.41.

Bowling—W. Quinn 89.4–24–214–22–6/64–9.72; D. Roberts 63–15–181–16–3/8–11.31; M. A. Bateson 86.2–23–199–17–5/10–11.70; C. R. Glover 130.2–21–298–25–4/29–11.92; D. M. Kidd 131.3–34–293–16–4/30–18.31.

ROYAL GRAMMAR SCHOOL, NEWCASTLE

Played 15: W 3, L 10, D 2. A 2

Master i/c: O. L. Edwards

Batting—*A. J. Nairn 15–1–368–82–0–26.28; P. T. Burton 10–0–226–56–0–22.60; M. M. Gray 14–0–314–79–0–22.42; D. A. D'Netto 13–0–168–40–0–12.92.

Bowling—C. W. Robson 88–23–227–15–3/47–15.13; M. C. Phillips 34–3–177–10–3/28–17.70; R. P. Malcolm 98.4–16–360–14–3/41–25.71; P. M. Avery 89.4–15–297–11–3/31–27.00.

ROYAL GRAMMAR SCHOOL, WORCESTER *Played 22: W 15, L 5, D 2, A 2*

Master i/c: B. M. Rees Professional: P. J. Newport

Sam Smith guided the team to 15 wins as well as hitting two sparkling centuries. Others to make their mark were opening batsman James Watkins, leg-spinner Jared Stone and medium-pacers Tim Darch and David Taylor.

Batting—J. R. Watkins 23–7–770–96*–0–48.12; *J. S. Smith 22–4–663–133–2–36.83; T. F. Jarvie 18–1–491–149–1–28.88; C. J. Edwards 19–2–486–107–1–28.58; D. C. Taylor 16–3–307–111*–1–23.61; T. S. Denyer 14–4–171–24*–0–17.10; T. G. Payton 15–1–194–60–0–13.85; A. J. Millington 16–1–184–40–0–12.26.

Bowling—J. A. D. Stone 138.3–14–548–31–3/6–17.67; T. R. Darch 153.5–21–533–28–4/24–19.03; D. C. Taylor 158.3–25–502–26–3/18–19.30; A. J. Millington 120–21–408–20–3/15–20.40; T. S. Denyer 166.2–29–556–26–4/13–21.38; J. S. Smith 135.4–19–418–16–3/32–26.12.

RUGBY SCHOOL *Played 15: W 1, L 6, D 8*

Master i/c: P. J. Rosser Professional: L. Tennant

In an otherwise undistinguished season, the Noble brothers, David and Jamie, played consistently well and comfortably headed the averages.

Batting—*D. J. Noble 14–0–441–83–0–31.50; J. F. Noble 14–1–378–79–0–29.07; A. H. Lennox 14–6–150–46–0–18.75; O. Benzie 13–1–214–37*–0–17.83; W. H. C. Thomas 15–0–266–57–0–17.73; H. T. Hawkesfield 13–0–228–65–0–17.53; P. Sinclair 12–1–175–51*–0–15.90; R. L. H. Crawford 13–0–155–55–0–11.92.

Bowling—J. F. Noble 170.3–33–507–23–5/65–22.04; D. J. Noble 145.3–25–520–23–4/45–22.60; O. Benzie 138.2–16–525–17–4/72–30.88.

RYDAL PENRHOS *Played 9: W 4, L 5, D 0*

Master i/c: M. T. Leach

David Watkins marshalled limited resources to good effect, backed up by Craig Stock and Patrick Leach.

Batting—*D. M. Watkins 9–0–306–70–0–34.00; C. D. R. Stock 7–1–191–66–0–31.83; P. J. H. Leach 9–2–168–54–0–24.00.

Bowling—P. J. H. Leach 62.4–8–259–16–4/25–16.18; S. J. Wilson 54.5–9–191–11–5/21–17.36; D. M. Watkins 55–10–210–10–3/22–21.00.

ST ALBANS SCHOOL *Played 15: W 7, L 2, D 6*

Master i/c: C. C. Hudson Professional: N. Dodd

The bowlers dominated a rewarding season; in five of the first six matches they disposed of the opposition for less than 80. Fifteen-year-old Nick Lamb, son of ECB chief executive Tim Lamb, hit the top score of the season, and at the end of term was elected captain – the youngest since 1903.

Batting—N. Lamb 12–3–269–82*–0–29.88; M. Searle 13–3–258–63*–0–25.80; J. Agnew 13–3–188–42*–0–18.80; E. Charlesworth 13–1–183–40*–0–15.25.

Bowling—J. Bateman 151.1–41–364–35–5/5–10.40; B. Cuppello 59–11–240–16–4/11–15.00; M. McCaskill 51.4–8–221–14–3/19–15.78; M. Pettit 90–18–367–16–3/14–22.93; T. Perry 99.5–14–317–13–3/18–24.38.

ST DUNSTAN'S COLLEGE *Played 13: W 1, L 6, D 6. A 1*

Master i/c: N. R. Taylor

Batting—*S. Giddins 11–0–574–101–1–52.18; A. Darroch 13–3–349–120*–2–34.90; A. Mahey 10–2–198–68–0–24.75; R. Bensted 12–1–175–30–0–15.90.

Bowling—K. Tuccaroglu 30.2–3–152–10–4/25–15.20; A. Mahey 78.3–2–447–16–5/63–27.93; P. Roscoe 108.5–16–461–11–3/73–41.90.

ST EDMUND'S COLLEGE, WARE *Played 5: W 0, L 5, D 0*

Master i/c: J. D. Faithfull

Batting—No batsman scored 150 runs. The leading batsman was T. Culunan 3–0–34–18–0–11.33.

Bowling—No bowler took 10 wickets. The leading bowler was *T. O. Marks 24–3–134–5–3/42–26.80.

ST EDMUND'S SCHOOL, CANTERBURY *Played 14: W 6, L 4, D 4*

Master i/c: M. C. Dobson Professional: R. P. Davis

In a strong batting line-up Dominic Chambers was outstanding with 927 runs, including three hundreds and two nineties. Slow left-armer Ashley Gerrard, who varied his pace and flight skilfully, typified improved consistency from the bowlers.

Batting—D. Chambers 14–4–927–142*–3–92.70; *S. Bokhari 12–1–351–67*–0–31.90; J. Logan 11–3–199–50*–0–24.87; A. Gerrard 14–2–278–90–0–23.16; T. Berry 14–0–292–47–0–20.85.

Bowling—A. Gerrard 156–22–555–33–7/55–16.81; S. Bokhari 126–26–453–20–5/36–22.65; W. Hilary 89–19–311–11–5/15–28.27.

ST EDWARD'S SCHOOL, OXFORD *Played 10: W 3, L 4, D 3. A 2*

Master i/c: J. Mills

Outstanding captaincy from William Conibear was important in a season of development.

Batting—T. H. Newell 11–2–297–67–0–33.00; J. B. Barrett 9–1–261–77*–0–32.62; C. M. Sutton 11–1–174–107*–1–17.40; W. M. Allen 10–0–168–66–0–16.80.

Bowling—J. Honey 83–16–328–16–6/28–20.50.

ST GEORGE'S COLLEGE, WEYBRIDGE *Played 13: W 4, L 4, D 5. A 3*

Master i/c: R. Ambrose Professional: D. Ottley

Batting—*T. J. S. Frost 12–0–469–93–0–39.08; J. R. Tindall 12–0–454–103–1–37.83; M. J. Arnot 9–2–220–92*–0–31.42; A. J. Fraser 12–4–250–75*–0–31.25; S. J. Daly 10–3–218–73–0–31.14; C. J. J. Caswell 9–2–199–52–0–28.42; A. D. R. Stanier 9–0–253–94–0–28.11; M. Cussans 12–0–244–70–0–20.33.

Bowling—T. J. S. Frost 124.3–17–477–26–4/8–18.34; A. A. S. Holman 124.1–23–476–21–4/20–22.66; A. J. Fraser 134–22–545–15–4/41–36.33.

ST JOHN'S SCHOOL, LEATHERHEAD *Played 14: W 8, L 4, D 2. A 1*

Master i/c: A. B. Gale Professional: I. Trott

Batting—*D. M. Eaton 13–4–283–66*–0–31.44; A. D. Garside 13–0–397–77–0–30.53; P. C. F. Scott 14–2–365–80–0–30.41; S. R. S. Bennett 12–1–320–76–0–29.09; D. J. Balcombe 12–1–252–56*–0–22.90.

Bowling—O. R. Graham 93.3–14–293–16–4/24–18.31; L. E. Hudson 110–11–401–18–3/21–22.28; J. T. E. Balcombe 122–20–426–17–4/28–25.05.

ST PAUL'S SCHOOL *Played 13: W 6, L 3, D 4. A 3*

Master i/c: G. Hughes Professional: M. Heath

St Paul's played all but three of their fixtures in the second half of term, finishing with a flurry of six in eight days and victory in all three matches at the Fettes College Festival. Ben Duncan was in commanding form with the bat and Roland Archdall closed his school career with another outstanding season behind the stumps.

Batting—B. J. Duncan 11–2–592–101*–1–65.77; F. W. H. Abrahams 9–2–308–85*–0–44.00; *R. M. Archdall 11–2–312–77–0–34.66; A. S. Charkham 10–1–245–98*–0–27.22.

Bowling—M. A. R. Morgan 46.2–9–177–10–3/22–17.70; A. T. L. Lee 86.1–9–313–14–7/40–22.35; A. S. Charkham 137.3–28–452–19–4/22–23.78; B. J. Duncan 81–12–276–10–3/27–27.60; A. R. Mason 104–17–357–10–3/54–35.70.

ST PETER'S SCHOOL, YORK *Played 20: W 8, L 4, D 8. A 2*

Master i/c: D. Kirby Professional: K. F. Mohan

A young side developed into an effective unit under the captaincy of all-rounder Trevor Smith. Significant progress was made by opener Tom Bartrum and left-arm spinner Tom Woolsey.

Batting—*T. C. Smith 21–4–581–112*–1–34.17; M. W. Spilman 19–3–531–90–0–33.18; R. N. R. Gibbon 16–5–249–53–0–22.63; J. E. Taylor 19–0–408–81–0–21.47; T. S. Bartram 16–0–335–47–0–20.93; T. Main 11–2–154–34–0–17.11; A. J. Chalmers 16–1–243–57*–0–16.20.

Bowling—M. S. Hodsdon 109.4–20–432–19–3/3–22.73; T. C. Smith 170.5–35–580–25–4/15–23.20; T. J. Woolsey 196.3–53–650–27–6/79–24.07; T. Main 82–21–291–11–3/17–26.45; R. F. Greetham 175–38–548–19–4/31–28.84; T. S. Bartram 80–15–318–11–2/9–28.90.

SEDBERGH SCHOOL *Played 18: W 10, L 4, D 4. A 1*

Master i/c: J. C. Bobby Professional: Kabir Khan

Batting—J. B. Mason 18–7–566–103*–1–51.45; M. W. E. Lofthouse 10–1–333–103–1–37.00; *R. W. G. Ross 19–2–613–89–0–36.05; T. E. B. Nickell-Lean 19–0–531–79–0–27.94; R. C. Owen 16–2–302–73–0–21.57; C. P. Howard 11–1–176–37–0–17.60; T. R. Laidler 16–1–175–29–0–11.66.

Bowling—R. W. S. Taylor 63.4–17–155–17–4/25–9.11; J. B. Mason 185–62–455–37–5/16–12.29; P. J. Howell 134.1–28–385–28–5/19–13.75; G. A. Mosey 84–39–175–12–4/15–14.58; C. P. Howard 173.3–66–446–27–4/2–16.51; R. W. G. Ross 151–53–376–22–4/32–17.09.

SEVENOAKS SCHOOL *Played 12: W 1, L 5, D 6. A 3*

Master i/c: C. J. Tavaré

Batting—S. Sharma 9–1–250–59–0–31.25; B. P. Spokes 7–0–209–74–0–29.85; O. T. R. Jones 10–0–233–92–0–23.30; *B. E. Sergeant 9–0–159–53–0–17.66.

Bowling—O. T. R. Jones 36–3–190–15–5/23–12.66; S. Sharma 65–7–236–11–3/42–21.45; S. J. G. Wilkin 81–19–215–10–4/17–21.50.

SHEBBEAR COLLEGE *Played 11: W 5, L 5, D 1*

Master i/c: A. Bryan

Batting—O. Wickett 9–0–242–59–0–26.88; E. Jones 11–0–259–63–0–23.54.

Bowling—O. Wickett 59.5–13–141–14–5/15–10.07; J. Vickerstaff 68–12–272–15–3/2–18.13.

SHERBORNE SCHOOL *Played 15: W 4, L 8, D 3*

Master i/c: M. D. Nurton Professional: A. Willows

Batting—P. Langly-Smith 15–1–352–86–0–25.14; L. Lewis 13–2–183–33*–0–16.63; W. Fegen 11–1–154–56–0–15.40; G. Bramble 15–1–168–48–0–12.00.

Bowling—W. Fegen 81–22–246–16–4/43–15.37; A. Westwood 84–11–267–17–3/19–15.70; W. Dawson 93–11–199–12–3/35–16.58; P. Langly-Smith 71–14–242–11–3/54–22.00; W. Hayler 106–16–341–13–3/11–26.23.

SHREWSBURY SCHOOL *Played 15: W 6, L 4, D 5. A 2*

Master i/c: M. J. Lascelles Professional: A. P. Pridgeon

Batting—A. M. McKeever 16–6–266–57–0–26.60; H. P. D. Clive 13–4–212–43–0–23.55; L. Briggs 17–2–321–71–0–21.40; I. R. Massey 14–1–274–46–0–21.07; C. J. G. Owen 16–0–324–68–0–20.25; R. J. Collinson 15–0–288–63–0–19.20; *T. W. E. Chapman 17–3–258–39*–0–18.42.

Bowling—C. J. G. Owen 140–33–379–24–4/20–15.79; A. M. McKeever 140–24–370–17–3/12–21.76; N. J. Bevan 190–36–575–26–3/49–22.11; T. W. Graham 207–30–665–28–4/28–23.75; P. M. Edmonds 163–36–497–19–4/20–26.15.

SIMON LANGTON GRAMMAR SCHOOL *Played 7: W 7, L 0, D 0*

Master i/c: R. H. Green

In a season limited to seven matches, the eleven won them all and secured the title in the Kent Schools' Under-19 League.

Batting—*O. Janaway 4–2–166–122–1–83.00.

Bowling—S. Cusden 42.3–14–74–15–6/12–4.93; A. Mitchell 21–7–62–11–7/3–5.63; R. Walker 49–11–141–11–2/11–12.81.

SIR ROGER MANWOOD'S SCHOOL *Played 6: W 2, L 4, D 0*

Master i/c: J. F. Willmott

Batting—No batsman scored 150 runs. The leading batsman was *S. Morris 6–0–148–54–0–24.66.

Bowling—No bowler took 10 wickets. The leading bowler was S. Morris 60–14–190–8–3/30–23.75.

SOLIHULL SCHOOL *Played 15: W 2, L 12, D 1*

Master i/c: S. A. Morgan Professional: C. Borroughs

Batting—J. Hemming 13–1–345–73*–0–28.75; T. Kirtland 10–1–197–43–0–21.88; D. Birch 8–0–158–40–0–19.75; A. Blasdale 14–2–221–55*–0–18.41; C. Bartley 13–1–220–105*–1–18.33; J. Pooley 14–2–215–51*–0–17.91; *J. Robinson 15–0–150–29–0–10.00.

Bowling—D. White 83–9–197–14–4/25–14.07; T. Kirtland 114–7–305–21–4/18–14.52; B. Watson 98–15–267–15–3/42–17.80; J. Pooley 73–6–298–11–4/10–27.09.

SOUTH CRAVEN SCHOOL *Played 9: W 4, L 5, D 0. A 1*

Master i/c: D. M. Birks

The Walker brothers vied with each other for the title of leading all-rounder: Matthew headed both averages while Chris scored most runs and took most wickets. A highlight was a first-ever win against Queen Elizabeth GS, Wakefield, in which Tom Hodgson took six for 13.

Batting—M. D. Walker 9–2–185–65–0–26.42; *C. P. Walker 9–0–197–78–0–21.88.

Bowling—M. D. Walker 19–3–79–10–5/43–7.90; P. M. Hardwick 27–1–97–10–6/54–9.70; T. E. Hodgson 47–8–170–10–6/13–17.00; C. P. Walker 84.2–9–328–11–3/56–29.81.

STAMFORD SCHOOL *Played 13: W 4, L 9, D 0. A 3*

Master i/c: A. N. Pike Professional: G. F. Archer

Batting—J. D. Barker 11–1–405–93–0–40.50; T. E. Lloyd 11–0–354–59–0–32.18; *M. P. Williams 12–0–293–81–0–24.41.

Bowling—T. J. Burwell 53.2–12–186–10–3/36–18.60; M. P. Williams 119–17–498–19–4/69–26.21; N. P. Wells 99–14–398–12–3/18–33.16.

STOCKPORT GRAMMAR SCHOOL *Played 11: W 7, L 2, D 2*

Master i/c: A. Brett Professional: D. J. Makinson

On an enjoyable end-of-term tour to Malta, the eleven won four of five matches played on matting wickets against club sides Marsa and Melita.

Batting—*C. Longden 9–3–240–79–0–40.00; E. Daber 8–0–296–93–0–37.00; J. Woodsmith 9–1–176–57–0–22.00.

Bowling—C. Longden 123–25–378–29–6/45–13.03.

STOWE SCHOOL *Played 11: W 2, L 5, D 4. A 1*

Master i/c: G. A. Cottrell Professional: H. J. Rhodes

Batting—B. J. Maclennan 8–1–235–77*–0–33.57; N. A. Oldridge 11–0–369–74–0–33.54; *A. G. Pearson 11–0–258–57–0–23.45.

Bowling—E. J. Clark 97–17–354–16–5/31–22.12; G. G. White 109–18–403–14–3/17–28.78.

STRATHALLAN SCHOOL *Played 14: W 5, L 6, D 3. A 1*

Master i/c: R. H. Fitzsimmons Professional: I. L. Philip

Batting—L. V. Court 12–3–322–93*–0–35.77; M. Ford 13–2–278–63–0–25.27; W. Bowry 12–0–198–60–0–16.50; N. J. McIlwraith 13–0–213–45–0–16.38; *J. A. Phillips 13–1–179–48–0–14.91.

Bowling—M. Ford 115.2–37–311–21–7/13–14.80; N. J. McIlwraith 152.3–40–367–22–4/14–16.68; I. Robb 71.1–12–217–11–4/30–19.72; D. Stewart 81–9–400–11–5/16–36.36.

SUTTON VALENCE SCHOOL *Played 11: W 5, L 3, D 3. A 3*

Masters i/c: A. P. Igglesden and W. D. Buck

Eight Under-14s made their debut and worked hard to overcome the absence of key players, one of whom – Robbie Joseph – was invited to bowl in England's pre-Ashes nets.

Batting—R. Joseph 8–1–256–53–0–36.57; A. Watson 9–0–321–93–0–35.66; P. Stileman 10–0–272–92–0–27.20.

Bowling—R. Joseph 46–7–156–15–5/39–10.40; P. Stileman 95.5–16–471–23–6/27–20.47.

TAUNTON SCHOOL *Played 11: W 7, L 2, D 2*

Master i/c: S. T. Hogg

Batting—P. Reid 7–4–273–109*–1–91.00; M. Collins 9–3–223–65–0–37.16; *T. Frith 11–4–223–50*–0–31.85.

Bowling—M. Collins 64.2–11–158–13–3/38–12.15; L. Fishlock 69–18–167–13–4/7–12.84; J. Kennedy 63–8–208–14–4/10–14.85.

TIFFIN SCHOOL *Played 17: W 7, L 2, D 8. A 6*

Master i/c: M. J. Williams

Going from strength to strength, the eleven won six of their last ten matches. The attack was well served by two orthodox left-arm spinners, newcomers Rathulan Gnanendran and Simon Crampton, who dismissed 61 opponents between them. Twins Dyan and Delon Sellayah were among seven batsmen who averaged over 25.

Batting—A. Harinath 10–1–317–57–0–35.22; *C. N. Weerasinghe 15–0–509–73–0–33.93; Dyan Sellayah 13–0–379–118–1–29.15; Delon Sellayah 13–3–284–73–0–28.40; R. Uthayashanker 15–0–404–66–0–26.93; S. Subesinghe 13–6–188–42–0–26.85; S. G. D. Crampton 13–1–316–65–0–26.33; D. W. Bates 15–1–206–45*–0–14.71.

Bowling—R. Gnanendran 157–27–686–39–7/81–17.58; S. G. D. Crampton 131.3–26–443–22–3/11–20.13; G. J. Nutt 107.1–11–465–23–5/21–20.21; A. Subesinghe 124.5–27–389–18–2/12–21.61; Delon Sellayah 98–17–348–15–4/18–23.20.

TONBRIDGE SCHOOL *Played 16: W 9, L 4, D 3*

Master i/c: N. Leamon Professional: D. Chadwick

Particularly pleasing were wins against Eton, Charterhouse and Harrow, which secured the Colin Cowdrey Cup in its inaugural year. Run-scoring was the strength, led by Greg Adams, who took his career aggregate past 2,000.

Batting—*G. Adams 17–5–699–101*–1–58.25; C. Atkinson 10–4–254–66–0–42.33; D. Norman 10–1–353–92*–0–39.22; W. Montgomery 12–2–383–80–0–38.30; F. Chillcott 12–2–316–78–0–31.60; M. Cooke 15–1–386–114*–1–27.57; R. Evans 15–1–350–120*–1–25.00; W. White 10–0–165–70–0–16.50.

Bowling—J. Burman 64–11–183–12–5/25–15.25; C. Young 97–10–304–12–4/24–25.33; T. Fordham 175–22–616–19–4/38–32.42; C. Haire 152–16–606–14–3/88–43.28; W. Murday 164–15–729–14–3/15–52.07.

TRENT COLLEGE *Played 11: W 4, L 5, D 1, T 1. A 1*

Master i/c: J. T. Jordison Professional: J. A. Afford

Batting—J. Siddall 9–1–308–84–0–38.50; F. O'Neill 11–1–348–108–1–34.80; C. Newman 11–1–342–75–0–34.20

Bowling—T. Baxter 76–16–222–15–3/17–14.80; C. Wood 87.2–15–273–12–4/34–22.75.

TRINITY SCHOOL, CROYDON *Played 11: W 1, L 3, D 7. A 5*

Master i/c: C. R. Burke

Batting—B. T. Shorten 10–0–273–97–0–27.30; J. A. Sargent 10–2–202–54–0–25.25; *R. J. Piggin 10–0–249–88–0–24.90.

Bowling—H. G. Proctor 47–8–174–11–4/24–15.81; R. J. Piggin 69–6–245–12–3/45–20.41; A. J. Humm 74–10–265–12–3/13–22.08; J. B. Bowes 82–9–273–10–4/42–27.30.

TRURO SCHOOL *Played 9: W 1, L 4, D 4. A 4*

Master i/c: D. M. Phillips

Batting—A. M. Wardle 6–2–175–73–0–43.75; D. W. Miller 5–0–207–78–0–41.40; D. J. Pollard 9–1–278–109*–1–34.75; *O. J. Turnbull 5–0–162–57–0–32.40.

Bowling—M. K. Munday 53.2–5–248–10–3/27–24.80; D. J. Pollard 64–4–325–10–3/17–32.50.

UNIVERSITY COLLEGE SCHOOL *Played 12: W 4, L 7, D 1. A 2*

Masters i/c: S. M. Bloomfield and C. P. Mahon Professional: W. G. Jones

Leading batsman James Floyd is the brother of Matthew Floyd, who scored a hundred for Oxford in the Varsity match in June.

Batting—J. Floyd 12–0–420–98–0–35.00; *J. Nissan 8–0–198–73–0–24.75; A. Cohen 12–0–193–65–0–16.08; T. Banks 10–0–154–82–0–15.40.

Bowling—J. Nissan 88–16–279–16–4/54–17.43; J. Floyd 86.2–9–345–16–4/15–21.56; E. Fisher 57–6–270–11–2/23–24.54.

UPPINGHAM SCHOOL *Played 17: W 8, L 4, D 5. A 4*

Master i/c: C. C. Stevens Professional: B. T. P. Donelan

Oliver Williams led the team with distinction and, in his final innings, took his career aggregate past 2,000 runs, beating the record previously held by James Whitaker, the Leicestershire secretary/general manager.

Batting—*O. C. W. Williams 18–2–741–91*–0–46.31; D. C. Wood 14–5–238–54*–0–26.44; H. M. C. Judd 12–1–279–67–0–25.36; B. J. Branson 12–1–238–54–0–21.63; H. J. L. Swayne 15–2–239–66–0–18.38; A. S. H. Ward 11–2–161–32–0–17.88; J. T. Branson 17–2–261–63–0–17.40; W. G. Hodson 14–3–176–62*–0–16.00; N. P. S. Charlwood 11–0–173–70–0–15.72.

Bowling—D. C. Wood 217.4–42–565–37–5/33–15.27; W. E. Crowder 207.3–30–651–38–5/19–17.13; W. G. Hodson 161.5–37–449–21–4/10–21.38; B. J. Branson 165.3–32–509–16–5/34–31.81.

VICTORIA COLLEGE, JERSEY *Played 18: W 11, L 3, D 4*

Master i/c: D. A. R. Ferguson

Batting—*T. J. Perchard 12–1–582–110–1–52.90; P. W. Gough 18–4–610–77*–0–43.57; O. M. Hughes 14–6–256–75–0–32.00; J. M. Gough 18–0–496–103–1–27.55; A. S. J. Dewhurst 18–3–347–95*–0–23.13; A. H. M. Crowther 9–2–156–37*–0–22.28; P. C. Gales 13–3–190–65–0–19.00.

Bowling—A. S. J. Dewhurst 140–26–481–38–5/16–12.65; J. M. Gough 171–28–593–33–6/78–17.96; O. M. Hughes 44–6–212–11–3/21–19.27; P. W. Gough 69–10–275–11–2/6–25.00; T. E. Minty 105–12–402–15–4/36–26.80.

WARWICK SCHOOL *Played 11: W 5, L 5, D 1. A 6*

Master i/c: G. A. Tedstone

Batting—C. M. Wilson 11–0–277–92–0–25.18; *J. P. Montanaro 11–1–245–76*–0–24.50; D. G. Roots 9–2–163–48–0–23.28; O. C. Higgens 11–0–245–66–0–22.27.

Bowling—R. E. Rees 84.1–8–333–14–4/10–23.78; T. W. Bravington 73–9–249–10–2/20–24.90.

WATFORD GRAMMAR SCHOOL *Played 8: W 1, L 5, D 2*

Master i/c: A. McGinty

Batting—No batsman scored 150 runs. The leading batsman was R. Snafe 8–0–137–40–0–17.12.

Bowling—J. Herbert 53.5–9–160–15–4/47–10.66.

WELLINGBOROUGH SCHOOL *Played 18: W 5, L 6, D 7. A 2*

Master i/c: M. H. Askham Professional: J. C. J. Dye

Batting—A. Tailor 17–7–364–53–0–36.40; A. Daniels 18–0–606–79–0–33.66; P. S. Coverdale 15–1–373–91–0–26.64; M. Carter 18–4–371–50–0–26.50; W. Tooley 16–0–184–52–0–11.50.

Bowling—P. S. Coverdale 136.2–37–394–28–5/21–14.07; A. Daniels 109.3–16–432–22–7/30–19.63.

WELLINGTON COLLEGE *Played 16: W 6, L 4, D 6. A 2*

Masters i/c: C. M. Oliphant-Callum and R. I. H. B. Dyer Professional: P. J. Lewington

Wellington enjoyed their first win against Radley since 1987 – their first defeat for five years – and a second successive victory over Eton. Adrian Jarvis was in stunning form, hitting three consecutive hundreds – 116 v Marlborough, 102 v Whitgift and 119 v Eton – a feat thought to be a college record. Whitgift also suffered at the hands of William Evered, who returned the sensational figures of 7–5–4–7.

Batting—E. A. Bostock 14–7–283–84–0–40.42; A. T. Jarvis 18–0–704–119–3–39.11; M. E. T. Briers 10–2–285–76–0–35.62; T. M. Williams 9–3–195–70*–0–32.50; H. R. Streatfeild 17–3–362–64*–0–25.85; H. T. Y. Shephard 14–2–294–66–0–24.50; J. A. F. Robertson 11–3–153–37–0–19.12.

Bowling—*W. H. Evered 126.3–32–267–24–7/4–11.12; J. A. F. Robertson 76–9–236–14–4/27–16.85; H. T. Y. Shephard 76–13–234–13–3/9–18.00; E. A. Bostock 88.2–21–292–14–2/7–20.85; T. M. Williams 124–15–390–17–5/44–22.94.

WELLINGTON SCHOOL *Played 14: W 5, L 8, D 1. A 1*

Master i/c: M. H. Richards

Batting—*J. T. House 14–3–629–109*–1–57.18; P. E. Short 11–0–195–52–0–17.72; G. R. Sheppard 14–1–224–51–0–17.23; A. M. Short 12–2–153–30–0–15.30.

Bowling—P. E. Short 122.2–13–394–25–5/14–15.76; J. T. House 105.5–10–460–23–4/16–20.00; P. J. Nicholls 85.3–8–356–15–3/50–23.73; T. R. M. Collins 68–5–347–12–4/36–28.91.

WELLS CATHEDRAL SCHOOL *Played 11: W 8, L 0, D 3. A 2*

Master i/c: M. Stringer

The most notable feature of an undefeated season – the first for at least 20 years – was Joe Hill's 165 not out against MCC.

Batting—J. Hill 11–2–597–165*–1–66.33; G. Oram 10–5–300–80–0–60.00; A. Mufti 11–3–222–52*–0–27.75.

Bowling—J. Hill 65.2–9–223–19–4/11–11.73; G. Oram 72–16–256–18–4/16–14.22; A. Mufti 114–17–360–25–5/26–14.40; A. Cowley 91–19–312–16–3/55–19.50.

WEST BUCKLAND SCHOOL *Played 11: W 4, L 4, D 3*

Master i/c: L. Whittal-Williams Professional: M. T. Brimson

Batting—*G. E. T. Cornish 9–2–320–76–0–45.71; C. M. Welch 10–0–312–71–0–31.20; G. J. Medland 9–0–215–54–0–23.88; J. K. Fowler 8–1–159–40–0–22.71; J. D. Wallace 9–1–154–52–0–19.25.

Bowling—G. E. T. Cornish 91.5–17–243–18–3/11–13.50; B. J. Wallace 78–14–294–14–3/29–21.00; C. M. Welch 63.4–11–257–11–4/41–23.36; J. D. Wallace 65–10–410–10–2/9–41.00.

WESTMINSTER SCHOOL *Played 10: W 4, L 5, D 1. A 2*

Master i/c: M. H. Feltham Professional: S. Massey

Excellent performances in the field were a hallmark of the season. The wicket-keeping and batting of David Stranger-Jones caught the eye, together with the bowling of Debashish Biswas and James Japhet.

Batting—*D. M. H. Stranger-Jones 9–3–277–80*–0–46.16.

Bowling—D. Biswas 73.3–16–185–16–6/22–11.56; J. N. Japhet 111.5–25–376–22–6/53–17.09.

WHITGIFT SCHOOL *Played 7: W 2, L 3, D 2. A 2*

Master i/c: D. M. Ward Professional: N. M. Kendrick

Batting—*D. Watson 8–0–285–88–0–35.62; S. Woodward 8–2–175–59*–0–29.16; J. Pearce 8–0–188–94–0–23.50.

Bowling—D. Watson 65.2–7–252–10–3/54–25.20.

WICKERSLEY COMPREHENSIVE SCHOOL *Played 8: W 2, L 2, D 4. A 2*

Masters i/c: P. Harper and R. D. Powell

Mark Cummins and Danny Kemp regularly launched the innings in style, and the team competed creditably throughout. However, the support batting, with the exception of Liam Heathcote, remained fragile.

Batting—M. Cummins 6–1–425–143–1–85.00; L. Heathcote 9–4–242–60–0–48.40; D. Kemp 8–0–321–100–1–40.12.

Bowling—J. Farmer 20–2–84–10–4/9–8.40.

WILSON'S SCHOOL *Played 11: W 6, L 3, D 2*

Master i/c: J. Molyneux

Batting—J. Didlick 9–1–255–102*–1–31.87.

Bowling—*A. Parkinson 61–11–118–10–4/18–11.80; U. Chaudry 54–12–124–10–3/5–12.40; J. Didlick 81–11–235–18–4/28–13.05; N. Ansari 66–7–292–10–3/24–29.20.

WINCHESTER COLLEGE *Played 14: W 5, L 5, D 4. A 1*

Master i/c: C. J. Good Professional: J. R. Ayling

Batting—J. Walters 14–1–454–79*–0–34.92; A. Walters 13–1–382–104–1–31.83; J. Merriott 10–2–179–46–0–22.37; T. White 10–1–187–36–0–20.77; J. Mortimer 13–1–243–50*–0–20.25; C. Walters 13–2–190–44–0–17.27.

Bowling—R. Birchell 48–5–147–11–4/20–13.36; J. Pringle 126–21–409–21–3/6–19.47; E. Foster 120–14–469–21–3/19–22.33; P. Glenday 123–13–482–19–5/44–25.36; J. Walters 107–14–367–11–3/35–33.36; T. White 119–11–458–13–4/25–35.23.

Rhodri Jones (*left*) established a career run-scoring record for Woodhouse Grove, while Andrew Parkin-Coates was a mainstay for Worksop with bat and ball.

WOLVERHAMPTON GRAMMAR SCHOOL

Played 11: W 4, L 3, D 4. A 4

Master i/c: N. H. Crust

Professional: T. King

In nine innings David Bowyer made two hundreds and three fifties, finishing with an average of 110.80.

Batting—D. Bowyer 9–4–554–118*–2–110.80; *N. Gray 7–1–204–70–0–34.00; W. MacFarlane 10–1–172–59*–0–19.11; M. Young 8–0–152–40–0–19.00.

Bowling—N. Gray 65–11–198–15–4/11–13.20; M. Young 89–19–211–15–3/6–14.06.

WOODBRIDGE SCHOOL

Played 15: W 5, L 8, D 2. A 3

Master i/c: C. Seal

Batting— M. Fernley 3–1–198–155*–1–99.00; P. Nicholls 15–2–407–76–0–31.30; *P. Steen 15–1–382–95–0–27.28; M. Lincoln 14–1–242–92–0–18.61.

Bowling—T. Johnson 45–6–174–12–4/12–14.50; P. Steen 156–41–453–31–5/35–14.61; P. Nicholls 140–23–441–27–5/20–16.33; J. Ayris 52–4–241–10–4/18–24.10; M. Lincoln 67–8–327–10–2/22–32.70.

WOODHOUSE GROVE SCHOOL

Played 15: W 7, L 2, D 6. A 2

Master i/c: R. I. Frost

Professional: G. R. J. Roope

The team toured Barbados in March and, on their return, remained unbeaten by schools. Rhodri Jones, who took his career total to a record 1,909 runs, was one of four students to represent Yorkshire Senior Schools, with further honours going to wicket-keeper Sam Anderson, who played for ECB Schools West.

Batting—*R. W. Jones 15–3–501–71–0–41.75; S. R. Anderson 9–1–296–69–0–37.00; M. A. Bray 13–3–319–64–0–31.90; M. S. Bottomley 12–3–213–99*–0–23.66; R. W. Verity 12–2–233–82–0–23.30; S. A. B. King 15–2–201–47–0–15.46.

Bowling—A. M. Pearce 69–13–211–18–5/19–11.72; T. R. Rawlins 30.3–2–121–10–3/2–12.10; M. A. Bray 121–28–288–22–6/21–13.09; R. W. Verity 80–21–238–16–6/17–14.87; K. V. Claxton 115–22–317–21–4/6–15.09; M. S. Bottomley 120–23–359–12–3/22–29.91.

WORKSOP COLLEGE *Played 15: W 11, L 2, D 2. A 2*

Master i/c: N. R. Gaywood Professional: A. Kettleborough

Andrew Parkin-Coates delivered miserly away-swing to defeat 42 opponents and, by adding 504 useful runs, was the second-most accomplished all-rounder in the country.

Batting—*S. Clark 15–5–531–112–2–53.10; A. W. Parkin-Coates 15–4–504–102*–1–45.81; S. Patel 13–1–402–102–1–33.50; L. Ambrose 12–5–156–48–0–22.28.

Bowling—A. W. Parkin-Coates 152–49–339–42–6/22–8.07; S. Patel 198–76–353–39–5/13–9.05; S. Clark 149–38–358–26–4/10–13.76; L. Ambrose 70–15–214–13–3/23–16.46.

WREKIN COLLEGE *Played 8: W 4, L 0, D 4. A 4*

Master i/c: M. de Weymarn Professional: J. P. Dawson

The all-round skills and astute captaincy of Charlie Catling helped steer the side through the term without defeat.

Batting—*C. Catling 6–0–324–133–1–54.00; J. Pee 8–3–185–54*–0–37.00; S. Blount 8–0–203–52–0–25.37.

Bowling—D. Darvel 51–13–145–11–3/18–13.18; C. Catling 55.5–15–195–13–5/28–15.00; S. Blount 74–18–200–10–4/28–20.00.

WYGGESTON & QUEEN ELIZABETH I COLLEGE *Played 8: W 4, L 3, D 1. A 3*

Master i/c: J. P. Murphy

A short term featured pleasing victories over Leicester GS, King Edward's, Stourbridge, and a top performance from batsman Mohssen Khan in the semi-final of the Leicestershire Under-18 Cup.

Batting—*M. G. Bobat 6–1–153–75*–0–30.60; M. Khan 8–0–215–91–0–26.87.

Bowling—K. Patel 52–10–159–12–3/12–13.25.

YOUTH CRICKET WINNERS, 2001

ECB Under-19 County Championship:	Warwickshire
ECB Under-17 County Championship:	Yorkshire
Under-15 County Championship:	Lancashire
Under-13 County Championship:	Middlesex
Sun Bank Under-15 Club Championship:	Wanstead CC (Essex)
ECB Under-13 National Club Championship:	Bessborough CC (Middlesex)

TEST MATCH SPECIAL UNDER-15 YOUNG CRICKETER OF THE YEAR

Adam Harrison of West Monmouth Comprehensive School and Glamorgan won the second BBC *Test Match Special* Under-15 Young Cricketer of the Year Award. During the summer of 2001, he opened the bowling for England Under-15 against the Denmark and Ireland Under-17 sides. The award was given to him by a panel of ECB national judges. The previous year's winner was Samit Patel of Nottinghamshire.

WOMEN'S CRICKET, 2001

By CAROL SALMON

AUSTRALIAN WOMEN IN ENGLAND, 2001

Australia used this tour to prove that their defeat by New Zealand in December's World Cup final was merely a blip: they won every one of their 11 fixtures. Meanwhile, England were in limbo. John Harmer, who coached Australia to new heights during his six years in charge, had accepted a contract, initially for two years, to attempt the same with England. But although Harmer had already relinquished his duties with Australia, he was not due to take over England until after the Ashes series. If he had any thoughts that his new charges were perhaps better than the sum of their recent parts, these were dispelled by five heavy defeats. England never reached 150 in the three one-day internationals, and Australia won both Tests by huge margins: an innings and 140 runs at Shenley Park and nine wickets at Headingley.

It was unfortunate that the appointment of Harmer was so protracted. Paul Farbrace was always going to step aside as coach after the World Cup in New Zealand. Former Test player Jane Powell, the best-qualified female coach in England, took responsibility for the winter coaching programme, and was asked to look after the side for the Australian series, even though her application for the permanent position had already been rejected.

Consequently, England prepared in a vacuum, and for the most part played the same way. As usual, Australia knew just who their best bats and bowlers were and stuck with their winning formula, whereas England chopped and changed, often looking as if they could not wait for the series to end. Charlotte Edwards, still England's most accomplished bat despite a poor World Cup, damaged cruciate ligaments in her knee playing hockey, and never appeared. Two debutantes, 19-year-old Arran Thompson and Caroline Atkins, just 20, were asked to open the innings against the world's best bowling attack. One of the few experienced players, Jane Cassar, who had played in England's last real triumph, the 1993 World Cup, started the series at No. 3 and ended it out of the side. The only saving grace in the batting department came from Claire Taylor, whose spunky 137 in the Second Test and unbeaten 50 in the third one-day international were easily the two highest scores for England. Captain Clare Connor, who took five for 65 at Shenley, was dignified throughout, earning the Australians' respect. But, despite the promise of some young players, Harmer will need something of a magic wand to mount a meaningful campaign for the 2005 World Cup in South Africa.

Australia's hard-hitting left-hander, South Australian Karen Rolton, was in fine fettle, except at Shenley, where the enigmatic Nicki Shaw produced something out of the bag to bowl her for a duck. Rolton received the Peden-Archdale Medal as the series' outstanding player, scoring two fifties in the one-day internationals and a superb 209 not out at Headingley. This was the fourth and highest double-hundred in women's Test cricket; all of them have been made against England. Michelle Goszko had already equalled the previous record of 204, at Shenley. Cathryn Fitzpatrick, aged 33, gathered 17 Test wickets at 10.23 each, and looked as if she would still be able to rattle a few stumps in South Africa during that 2005 World Cup. But her opening bowling partner, 30-year-old Charmaine Mason, announced her retirement as the tour ended with another 3–0 victory in Ireland, where she coached during the northern hemisphere summer.

AUSTRALIAN TOURING PARTY

B. J. Clark (New South Wales) (*captain*), K. L. Rolton (South Australia) (*vice-captain*), L. C. Broadfoot (Victoria), S. A. Cooper (Queensland), A. J. Fahey (Western Australia), C. L. Fitzpatrick (Victoria), M. A. J. Goszko (New South Wales), J. Hayes (New South Wales), L. M. Keightley (New South Wales), T. A. McGregor (New South Wales), O. J. Magno (South Australia), C. L. Mason (Victoria), J. C. Price (Queensland), L. C. Sthalekar (New South Wales).

Manager: J. Stainer. *Coach:* S. Jenkin. *Assistant coach:* C. Matthews.

Physiotherapist: L. Ross. *Physical conditioning co-ordinator:* S. Bailey.

AUSTRALIAN TOUR RESULTS

Matches – Played 11: Won 11.

Note: Matches in this section were not first-class.

At Southgate, June 18. Australians won by 142 runs. Toss: Australians. Australians 251 for nine (50 overs) (L. C. Broadfoot 51 retired out, M. A. J. Goszko 35, J. C. Price 51 retired out, O. J. Magno 34 retired out); MCC Women's Invitation XI 109 (44.4 overs) (H. M. Tiffen 34; O. J. Magno six for 34).

At Southgate, June 19. Australians won by 170 runs. Toss: ECB Development Women's XI. Australians 257 for eight (50 overs) (B. J. Clark 34, K. L. Rolton 56 retired out, L. M. Keightley 36, C. L. Mason 30 not out); ECB Development Women's XI 87 (48.4 overs) (J. Hayes three for 11, C. L. Mason four for 22).

At Radlett, June 21. Australians won by 88 runs. Toss: Australians. Australians 255 for eight (50 overs) (L. M. Keightley 40, B. J. Clark 67 retired out, K. L. Rolton 69 retired out); ECB Development Women's XI 167 for nine (50 overs) (S. L. Clarke 43; C. L. Fitzpatrick three for 39).

ENGLAND v AUSTRALIA

First Test Match

At Shenley Park, June 24, 25, 26. Australia won by an innings and 140 runs. Toss: England. Test debuts: C. M. G. Atkins, L. J. Harper, D. Holden, K. Lowe, N. J. Shaw, A. Thompson; L. C. Broadfoot, M. A. J. Goszko, T. A. McGregor.

Australia's first Test since they visited England in 1998 ended in a massive victory with a day and a half to spare. It was dominated by Michelle Goszko, whose 204 on debut equalled the then Test record of New Zealander Kirsty Flavell, at Scarborough in 1996. Goszko batted for 395 minutes, faced 345 balls and hit 24 fours, scoring 59 per cent of Australia's total. The next highest contribution was 36 from Lisa Keightley, one of five victims for Clare Connor. Electing to bat, England had managed a mere 1.24 runs per over, only Kate Lowe reaching 20. Though they dismissed Belinda Clark and Karen Rolton cheaply on the first evening, the next day belonged to Goszko. After she was last out, leg-spinner Olivia Magno took the new ball and trapped Caroline Atkins before the close. England batted no better on the final day, and Cathryn Fitzpatrick finished with eight wickets in the match.

Players of the Match: M. A. J. Goszko and C. J. Connor.

Close of play: First day, Australia 60-2 (Keightley 19*, Goszko 21*); Second day, England 8-1 (Thompson 4*, C. E. Taylor 0*).

England

C. M. G. Atkins lbw b Fitzpatrick	10	– lbw b Magno	0
A. Thompson c Broadfoot b Fitzpatrick	1	– c McGregor b Fahey	18
†J. Cassar b Fitzpatrick	1	– (4) lbw b Mason	1
*C. J. Connor lbw b McGregor	8	– (5) b McGregor	16
K. Lowe b Fitzpatrick	23	– (6) c Broadfoot b Fitzpatrick	18
S. C. Taylor run out	18	– (7) lbw b McGregor	0
L. J. Harper c Magno b McGregor	19	– (8) b Fitzpatrick	20
N. J. Shaw c Keightley b Magno	0	– (9) c Keightley b Magno	8
D. Holden b Fitzpatrick	7	– (10) not out	4
C. E. Taylor c Price b Magno	5	– (3) b Fitzpatrick	6
L. C. Pearson not out	0	– lbw b Magno	0
B 4, l-b 7	11	B 4, l-b 6	10
1/7 2/9 3/17 4/41 5/50 6/90 7/90 8/90 9/103	103	1/0 2/15 3/16 4/45 5/45 6/45 7/82 8/91 9/101	101

Bowling: *First Innings*—Fitzpatrick 18.1–6–29–5; Mason 18–12–15–0; McGregor 15–10–13–2; Magno 17–11–13–2; Fahey 14–6–22–0; Rolton 1–1–0–0. *Second Innings*—Magno 13–7–16–3; Fitzpatrick 19–6–33–3; Mason 10–6–17–1; McGregor 7–5–7–2; Fahey 12–6–18–1.

Australia

*B. J. Clark lbw b Pearson	9
L. M. Keightley c Thompson b Connor	36
K. L. Rolton b Shaw	0
M. A. J. Goszko lbw b C. E. Taylor	204
L. C. Broadfoot c Pearson b Connor	24
†J. C. Price c Cassar b Connor	0
O. J. Magno c Atkins b Holden	4
T. A. McGregor c Harper b Connor	23
C. L. Fitzpatrick c Connor b Holden	10
A. J. Fahey lbw b Connor	11
C. L. Mason not out	0
B 9, l-b 8, w 4, n-b 2	23
1/14 2/21 3/128 4/178 5/178 6/216 7/282 8/319 9/338	344

Bowling: Shaw 11–0–60–1; Pearson 24–5–56–1; C. E. Taylor 17.1–4–31–1; Holden 21–4–62–2; Harper 14–1–53–0; Connor 28–6–65–5.

Umpires: L. Elgar and N. A. Mallender.

At Derby, June 29. First one-day international: Australia won by 99 runs. Toss: England. Australia 238 for seven (50 overs) (L. M. Keightley 75, K. L. Rolton 79, M. A. J. Goszko 35); England 139 (47.5 overs) (S. C. Taylor 39; T. A. McGregor four for 15).

Rolton reached fifty with her fifth consecutive four off Sarah Collyer.

At Northampton, July 2. Second one-day international: Australia won by 118 runs. Toss: Australia. Australia 227 for nine (50 overs) (B. J. Clark 69, L. M. Keightley 34, K. L. Rolton 61; D. Holden three for 48); England 109 (47.3 overs) (K. L. Rolton three for 14).

At Lord's, July 3. Third one-day international: Australia won by 66 runs. Toss: Australia. Australia 206 for seven (50 overs) (L. M. Keightley 54, B. J. Clark 49, K. L. Rolton 36); England 140 for eight (50 overs) (S. C. Taylor 50 not out).

Australia won the series 3–0.

ENGLAND v AUSTRALIA

Second Test Match

At Leeds, July 6, 7, 8. Australia won by nine wickets. Toss: Australia. Test debut: J. Hayes.

Australia completed another three-day win, though this time a maiden century from Claire Taylor made them bat twice. Otherwise, it was a familiar script; Cathryn Fitzpatrick took nine wickets, and Karen Rolton raised the Test record to 209 not out. It was her second Test century against

England, and occupied six hours and one minute; she struck 29 fours and a six in 313 balls, and added 253 with Louise Broadfoot, a fourth-wicket Test record. Australia declared 239 ahead, having dismissed England for 144 – a recovery from 85 for six – on the opening day. When England collapsed again, to 80 for five, another innings defeat loomed. But Taylor, who had kept wicket for most of the previous day, and Laura Harper doubled the score, while Dawn Holden helped Taylor reach her century during an eighth-wicket stand of 51. When Taylor was last out, Australia needed seven to win; her namesake Clare bowled Lisa Keightley before Rolton hit the winning boundary.

Players of the Match: K. L. Rolton and S. C. Taylor.

Close of play: First day, Australia 68-1 (Keightley 29*, Rolton 26*); Second day, England 10-0 (Atkins 3*, Thompson 6*).

England

C. M. G. Atkins c Price b Fitzpatrick	8	– lbw b Mason	8
A. Thompson c Keightley b Fitzpatrick	4	– c Rolton b Fitzpatrick	6
S. V. Collyer c Rolton b McGregor	37	– c and b McGregor	23
†S. C. Taylor c Price b Mason	4	– b Mason	137
*C. J. Connor b Fitzpatrick	16	– b McGregor	0
K. Lowe c Clark b McGregor	11	– lbw b Fitzpatrick	8
L. J. Harper c Keightley b Fahey	31	– c Hayes b Fitzpatrick	30
N. J. Shaw c Price b Hayes	0	– c Price b Fitzpatrick	0
D. Holden b Fitzpatrick	24	– c Hayes b Mason	5
C. E. Taylor not out	1	– c Price b Mason	9
L. C. Pearson c Hayes b Fitzpatrick	0	– not out	0
B 6, l-b 1, w 1	8	B 7, l-b 10, w 2	19
1/11 2/12 3/17 4/53 5/78 6/85 7/103 8/131 9/144	144	1/12 2/37 3/55 4/55 5/80 6/161 7/161 8/212 9/236	245

Bowling: *First Innings*—Fitzpatrick 22.5–10–31–5; Mason 20–8–41–1; Hayes 13–5–28–1; McGregor 15–6–25–2; Fahey 7–2–12–1; Rolton 3–3–0–0. *Second Innings*—Fitzpatrick 36–14–81–4; Mason 34–9–66–4; McGregor 17–8–32–2; Fahey 12–6–24–0; Hayes 9–3–20–0; Rolton 4–1–5–0.

Australia

*B. J. Clark c Holden b C. E. Taylor	6	– (2) not out	0
L. M. Keightley run out	40	– (1) b C. E. Taylor	0
K. L. Rolton not out	209	– not out	9
M. A. J. Goszko b C. E. Taylor	0		
L. C. Broadfoot c Connor b Collyer	71		
†J. C. Price not out	9		
B 7, l-b 34, w 6, n-b 1	48		
1/16 2/93 3/105 4/358 (4 wkts dec.)	383	1/0 (1 wkt)	9

T. A. McGregor, C. L. Fitzpatrick, J. Hayes, A. J. Fahey and C. L. Mason did not bat.

Bowling: *First Innings*—Pearson 21–4–79–0; C. E. Taylor 29–7–87–2; Shaw 13–3–46–0; Collyer 19–6–50–1; Harper 7–0–27–0; Connor 19–8–36–0; Holden 4–0–17–0. *Second Innings*—C. E. Taylor 2–1–5–1; Pearson 1.1–1–4–0.

Umpires: A. Roberts and A. G. T. Whitehead.

At Rathmines, Dublin, July 12. First one-day international: Australia won by five wickets, their target having been revised to 117 in 46 overs. Toss: Ireland. Ireland 132 (49.1 overs) (C. M. O'Leary 42, C. M. Beggs 45; T. A. McGregor three for 21); Australia 119 for five (36.4 overs) (M. A. J. Goszko 36 not out).

At Trinity College, Dublin, July 14. Second one-day international: Australia won by nine wickets. Toss: Ireland. Ireland 119 for seven (50 overs) (C. M. O'Leary 30, M. E. Grealey 57; C. L. Fitzpatrick five for 14); Australia 120 for one (27.4 overs) (L. M. Keightley 51 not out, K. L. Rolton 51 not out).

At Trinity College, Dublin, July 15. Third one-day international: Australia won by 201 runs. Toss: Australia. Australia 247 for nine (50 overs) (B. J. Clark 80, S. A. Cooper 85; C. J. Metcalfe three for 43); Ireland 46 (23 overs) (T. A. McGregor four for eight, C. L. Fitzpatrick three for 20).

McGregor's full analysis was 6–3–8–4. Australia won the series 3–0.

EUROPEAN CHAMPIONSHIP, 2001

Ireland finally broke England's stranglehold on the European Championship when they beat the England Under-19 Development Squad in their final game. The full England team had won the first four European competitions, and England A claimed the title in Denmark in 1999. The Under-19s representing England at Reading in August 2001 included some of the players who had just appeared for the senior side against Australia, as well as 16-year-old fast bowler Isa Guha, who was named player of the tournament. But Ireland's blend of youth and experience – Anne Linehan had first appeared in the inaugural European Cup, in Denmark in 1989, when she was 15 – paid off.

Both Ireland and England entered the last round unbeaten, effectively making their game the final. Rain reduced the match to 35 overs, and a target of 117 should have been in England's range. But a stunning hat-trick from spinner Saibh Young rolled them over for just 60, leaving the Irish to celebrate. The other teams taking part were Holland and Scotland. The latter were making their international debut at this level, replacing Denmark, who had played in all the previous tournaments and hosted two of them, but were unable to travel to England this time.

Note: Matches in this section were not first-class.

At Bradfield College, Reading, August 10. England Under-19 won by 238 runs. Toss: Scotland. England Under-19 262 for seven (50 overs) (L. J. Harper 41, L. Spragg 33, S. L. Clarke 66 not out, Extras 38); Scotland 24 (21.3 overs) (L. J. Harper four for five).

Harper's full analysis was 5.3–2–5–4.

At Bradfield College, Reading, August 10. Ireland won by seven wickets. Toss: Ireland. Holland 99 for nine (50 overs) (C. F. Oudolf 32; I. M. Joyce three for ten); Ireland 100 for three (30 overs) (C. M. O'Leary 43, C. M. Beggs 39 not out).

At Bradfield College, Reading, August 11. England Under-19 won by nine wickets. Toss: England Under-19. Holland 74 (43.2 overs) (P. te Beest 35; I. Guha three for five, L. Spragg three for eight); England Under-19 76 for one (18.2 overs) (A. Thompson 38 not out).

Guha's full analysis was 8.2–6–5–3.

At Bradfield College, Reading, August 11. Ireland won by six wickets. Toss: Ireland. Scotland 88 (48.4 overs) (B. M. McDonald three for three, I. M. Joyce four for 20); Ireland 91 for four (25.1 overs).

At Bradfield College, Reading, August 12. Ireland won by 56 runs. Toss: England Under-19. Ireland 116 (34.1 overs) (C. M. Beggs 35; S. L. Clarke four for 15); England Under-19 60 (27 overs) (S. A. Young three for five).

Young took a hat-trick in England's innings.

At Bradfield College, Reading, August 12. Holland won by four wickets. Toss: Holland. Scotland 123 for six (40 overs); Holland 124 for six (36.2 overs) (P. te Beest 43 not out).

Ireland 6 pts, England Under-19 4 pts, Holland 2 pts, Scotland 0 pts.

EUROPEAN CUP WINNERS

1989	England	1991	England	1999	England A
1990	England	1995	England	2001	Ireland

ENGLISH WOMEN'S CRICKET, 2001

The format of the County Championship may have changed, with the Second Elevens removed in order to include more counties, but it made little difference to Yorkshire. For all that the England selectors had picked only one of their players, Clare Taylor, to face Australia in June, they comfortably retained the national title at the end of July, winning all five of their matches. The opening game, against Berkshire, was the closest; after beating them by 33 runs, Yorkshire proceeded inexorably to their ninth title in ten years.

Berkshire shook up the old pecking order by finishing second in Division One; the previous season's runners-up, Nottinghamshire (formerly known as East Midlands), won as many games, but slid down the rankings on points to finish fourth. Kent badly missed their injured international opener, Charlotte Edwards, lost all five matches and were relegated. They were replaced by Division Two champions Sussex, whose 100 per cent record owed much to two centuries from Haidee Tiffen, one of New Zealand's World Cup winners, who played for Brighton and Hove during the domestic season. Division Three winners Middlesex also benefited from an overseas player, Indian opener Chanda Kaul.

Essex, Warwickshire and Wiltshire, who had entered the Championship after the Second Elevens were excluded, took the bottom three places in Division Three. There was no relegation, however, as Northumberland had dropped out since 2000. Durham, who won the Emerging Counties tournament, contested also by Cumbria and Northamptonshire, were promoted to make up the numbers.

Yorkshire representative sides also reached the finals of all three age-group competitions. They won the Under-15 title, beating Essex by 11 runs; lost to Kent by 134 runs in the Under-17 final; and defeated Sussex by eight wickets to claim the Under-19 championship. It was Sussex's second Under-19 final of the year; the previous season's game had been held over because of the fuel crisis and, when it was eventually staged, Sussex beat Staffordshire by 89 runs.

Two Yorkshire clubs featured in the ECB national finals, North Riding in the League and Wakefield in the Knockout Cup. Kathryn Leng's fifty helped Wakefield to a narrow win over Brighton and Hove, though the previous week Middlesex club Gunnersbury had struck a blow for the South by beating North Riding. Kent newcomers Hayes beat Dukesmead by five wickets in the National Plate final.

In an attempt to improve domestic standards further, the ECB announced a Super Fours competition to be staged in 2002, with the country's top 48 players invited to play over successive weekends in May and June.

Note: Matches in this section were not first-class.

COUNTY CHAMPIONSHIP, 2001

Division One	*Played*	*Won*	*Lost*	*Points*
Yorkshire	5	5	0	100.5
Berkshire	5	3	2	75.5
Staffordshire	5	3	2	71
Nottinghamshire	5	3	2	69.25
Surrey	5	1	4	39.5
Kent	5	0	5	26

Division Two

	Played	Won	Lost	Points
Sussex	5	5	0	105
Lancashire	5	3	2	73
Somerset	5	3	2	72
Derbyshire	5	2	3	56
Hertfordshire	5	1	4	46
Cheshire	5	1	4	39

Division Three

	Played	Won	Lost	Points
Middlesex	4	4	0	89.5
Hampshire	4	3	1	70.75
Essex	4	2	2	59
Warwickshire	4	1	3	35.5
Wiltshire	4	0	4	20

Kent and Cheshire were relegated from their respective divisions; Sussex and Middlesex were promoted, with Durham entering Division Three.

ECB NATIONAL LEAGUE FINAL, 2001

At Milton Keynes, September 1. Gunnersbury won by 28 runs. Toss: North Riding. Gunnersbury 166 for six (50 overs) (D. Stock 58); North Riding 138 for nine (50 overs) (L. Spragg 32, M. A. Reynard 30; C. Mowat three for 38).

ECB NATIONAL KNOCKOUT FINAL, 2001

At Milton Keynes, September 8. Wakefield won by eight runs. Toss: Brighton and Hove. Wakefield 133 for nine (40 overs) (K. M. Leng 52); Brighton and Hove 125 (39 overs) (C. J. Connor 40).

PART FIVE: OVERSEAS CRICKET IN 2000-01 AND 2001

FEATURES OF 2000-01 AND 2001

Double-Hundreds (46)

394	Naved Latif	Sargodha v Gujranwala at Gujranwala.
308*‡	D. Mongia	Punjab v Jammu and Kashmir at Jullundur.
306	M. H. Richardson	New Zealanders v Zimbabwe A at Kwekwe.
300*	G. K. Khoda	Central Zone v South Zone at Panaji.
281‡	V. V. S. Laxman	India v Australia (Second Test) at Kolkata.
264	A. Pathak	Andhra v Goa at Margao.
260*	G. S. Blewett	South Australia v Queensland at Brisbane.
259*‡	C. H. Gayle	West Indians v ZCU President's XI at Harare.
233	R. T. Ponting	Tasmania v Queensland at Albion.
232*	A. Flower	Zimbabwe v India (Second Test) at Nagpur.
231	B. C. Lara	West Indians v Australia A at Hobart.
228*	S. M. Katich	Western Australia v South Australia at Perth.
224	Habibul Bashar	Biman Bangladesh Airlines v Khulna at Jessore.
224	S. Sharath	Tamil Nadu v Delhi at Chennai.
222	A. Chopra	Delhi v Himachal Pradesh at Delhi.
222	A. V. Kale	Maharashtra v Baroda at Baroda.
221*	Y. Gowda	Railways v Maharashtra at Pune.
221	Younis Khan	Peshawar v Lahore City Whites at Lahore.
220	R. R. Parida	Orissa v Jammu and Kashmir at Cuttack.
217‡	V. V. S. Laxman	South Zone v West Zone at Surat.
216‡	Imran Farhat	Biman Bangladesh Airlines v Chittagong at Savar.
212*	D. P. Kelly	Central Districts v Canterbury at Blenheim.
211	Farhan Adil	Karachi Blues v Gujranwala at Gujranwala.
208*†‡	C. H. Gayle	Jamaica v West Indies B at Montego Bay.
208‡	D. Mongia	North Zone v Central Zone at Delhi.
207*	Parender Sharma	Haryana v Himachal Pradesh at Mandi.
206*	D. J. Gandhi	Bengal v Tripura at Kolkata.
205	Mohammad Ramzan	Faisalabad v Sargodha at Faisalabad.
204*	M. S. Sinclair	New Zealand v Pakistan (Second Test) at Christchurch.
204*	A. S. Srivastava	Madhya Pradesh v Vidarbha at Indore.
203*	V. G. Kambli	Mumbai v Gujarat at Mumbai.
203	M. L. Hayden	Australia v India (Third Test) at Chennai.
203	V. Rathore	Punjab v Himachal Pradesh at Una.
203	Yousuf Youhana	Pakistan v New Zealand (Second Test) at Christchurch.
203	Zahoor Elahi	Lahore City Whites v Sheikhupura at Lahore.
202*	Asif Mujtaba	Karachi Whites v Sheikhupura at Karachi.
202	G. F. J. Liebenberg	Free State v Northerns at Centurion.
201*	M. S. Atapattu	Sri Lanka v England (First Test) at Galle.
201*	S. R. Tendulkar	India v Zimbabwe (Second Test) at Nagpur.
201	L. D. Ferreira	Western Province v North West at Potchefstroom.
201‡	D. Mongia	North Zone v South Zone at Vijayawada.
200*	R. Dravid	India v Zimbabwe (First Test) at Delhi.
200*†	L. V. Garrick	Jamaica v West Indies B at Montego Bay.
200*	R. P. Hewage	Nondescripts v Panadura at Colombo.
200	Faisal Iqbal	Karachi Blues v Sargodha at Karachi.
200‡	Imran Farhat	Lahore City Blues v Bahawalpur at Lahore.

† *Gayle and Garrick scored their double-hundreds in one innings.*
‡ *Mongia scored three double-hundreds, and Gayle, Imran Farhat and Laxman two each.*

Hundred on First-Class Debut

101	A. Basu	Bengal v Tripura at Kolkata.
101	C. Hemanth Kumar	Tamil Nadu v Kerala at Kochi.
	Hemanth Kumar scored 121 and 87 in his next two innings, against Delhi at Chennai.	
125*	K. Seth	Madhya Pradesh v Vidarbha at Indore.

Three Hundreds in Successive Innings

B. J. Hodge (Victoria)	101* v Queensland at Albion;
	134* v West Indians at Melbourne;
	104 v South Australia at Melbourne.

Hundred in Each Innings of a Match

Ali Naqvi	108	119	Islamabad v Gujranwala at Rawalpindi.
A. Chopra	110	125*	North Zone v South Zone at Vijayawada.
J. Cox	106	128*	Tasmania v New South Wales at Hobart.
A. V. Deshpande	128	156*	Vidarbha v Rajasthan at Nagpur.
A. R. Khurasiya	105	118*	Madhya Pradesh v Railways at Delhi.
Mohammad Ramzan	205	102*	Faisalabad v Sargodha at Faisalabad.
M. H. Parmar	115	107*	Gujarat v Maharashtra at Karad.
G. R. P. Peiris	134	114	Tamil Union v Antonians at Colombo.
R. T. Ponting	102	102*	Australians v Board President's XI at Delhi.
C. M. Spearman	100	115	New Zealanders v North West at Potchefstroom.
S. C. Williams	160	114	Leeward Islands v Trinidad & Tobago at Pointe-à-Pierre.

Eight Fifties in Successive Innings

A. Flower (Zimbabwe)	119*, 94, 183*, 70, 55, 232*, 79, 69*.

Carrying Bat through Completed Innings

C. C. Bradfield	64*	Eastern Province (149) v Northerns at Port Elizabeth.
M. I. Gidley	73*	Griqualand West (160) v Gauteng at Johannesburg.
Imran Abbas	105*	Gujranwala (302) v Faisalabad at Faisalabad.
Javed Omar	85*	Bangladesh (168) v Zimbabwe (First Test) at Bulawayo. *One batsman was absent hurt.*
D. P. Kelly	212*	Central Districts (538) v Canterbury at Blenheim.
Rafatullah Mohmand	91*	WAPDA (208) v Allied Bank at Lahore.
R. D. Shah	37*	Kenyans (68) v Sri Lanka A at Nairobi.

Hundred before Lunch

A. C. Gilchrist	101*	Western Australia v South Australia at Adelaide (2nd day).
S. M. Katich	6* to 109*	Western Australia v New South Wales at North Sydney (2nd day).

Long Innings

Mins		
780	Naved Latif (394)	Sargodha v Gujranwala at Gujranwala.
741	M. H. Richardson (306)	New Zealanders v Zimbabwe A at Kwekwe.
681	M. S. Atapattu (201*)	Sri Lanka v England (First Test) at Galle.

An Hour without Scoring a Run

S. L. Campbell (119)	87 mins on 20	West Indians v Western Australia at Perth.
H. J. H. Marshall (40*)	61 mins on 0	New Zealand v South Africa (Third Test) at Johannesburg.

Unusual Dismissal – Handled the Ball

S. R. Waugh . . . . 47 Australia v India (Third Test) at Chennai.

First-Wicket Partnership of 100 in Each Innings

117 140. . . . . P. K. Das/S. B. Saikia, Assam v Bengal at Guwahati.

Highest Partnerships

First Wicket

425*† L. V. Garrick/C. H. Gayle, Jamaica v West Indies B at Montego Bay.
380 L. N. P. Reddy/A. Pathak, Andhra v Goa at Margao.
296 N. L. Haldipur/A. A. Lahiri, Bengal v Bihar at Kolkata.
277 R. S. Ricky/V. Rathore, Punjab v Himachal Pradesh at Una.
254 J. M. Arthur/M. I. Gidley, Griqualand West v Gauteng at Johannesburg.

Second Wicket

313 S. S. Bhave/H. H. Kanitkar, Maharashtra v Saurashtra at Rajkot.
261 J. A. Rudolph/M. van Jaarsveld, Northerns v Boland at Centurion.

Third Wicket

409 V. V. S. Laxman/R. Dravid, South Zone v West Zone at Surat.
275 J. P. Maher/S. G. Law, Queensland v Western Australia at Perth.

Fourth Wicket

388 P. Dharmani/D. Mongia, Punjab v Jammu and Kashmir at Jullundur.
358 R. R. Parida/P. M. Mullick, Orissa v Jammu and Kashmir at Cuttack.
274 R. A. Jones/S. R. Mather, Wellington v Otago at Wellington.
261 M. L. Love/A. Symonds, Queensland v Tasmania at Albion.
259 Inzamam-ul-Haq/Yousuf Youhana, Pakistan v England (Third Test) at Karachi.

Fifth Wicket

376 V. V. S. Laxman/R. Dravid, India v Australia (Second Test) at Kolkata.
361*† Asif Mujtaba/Mohammad Masroor, Karachi Whites v Sheikhupura at Karachi.
324 Y. Gowda/Abhay Sharma, Railways v Maharashtra at Pune.
316 D. Mongia/R. S. Sodhi, North Zone v Central Zone at Delhi.
295† Habibul Bashar/Hasanuzzaman, Biman Bangladesh Airlines v Khulna at Jessore.
267 M. L. Nkala/H. H. Streak, Matabeleland v CFX Academy at Bulawayo.
264 M. A. Higgs/S. Lee, New South Wales v Queensland at Sydney.
260 Fareed Butt/Humayun Farhat, Lahore City Blues v Sargodha at Sargodha.

Sixth Wicket

365† B. C. Lara/R. D. Jacobs, West Indians v Australia A at Hobart.
240 C. N. Liyanage/W. N. M. Soysa, Police v Galle at Colombo.
227 R. Dravid/S. S. Dighe, Indians v Zimbabwe A at Mutare.

Seventh Wicket

248 Yousuf Youhana/Saqlain Mushtaq, Pakistan v New Zealand (Second Test) at Christchurch.
194*† H. P. Tillekeratne/T. T. Samaraweera, Sri Lanka v India (Third Test) at Colombo.
154 H. H. Streak/A. M. Blignaut, Zimbabwe v West Indies (Second Test) at Harare.

Eighth Wicket
204* A. N. Kudva/M. Suresh Kumar, Kerala v Andhra at Vijayawada.
204 M. Strydom/A. C. Thomas, North West v Western Province at Potchefstroom.
185 D. J. Nash/K. D. Mills, Auckland v Wellington at Wellington.
155 J. N. Gillespie/M. S. Kasprowicz, Australians v India A at Nagpur.
153 J. S. K. Peiris/G. A. S. Perera, Panadura v Singha at Panadura.
150 N. D. McKenzie/S. M. Pollock, South Africa v Sri Lanka (Third Test) at Centurion.

Ninth Wicket
249*† A. S. Srivastava/K. Seth, Madhya Pradesh v Vidarbha at Indore.
276 were added in all for this wicket, N. D. Hirwani replacing Srivastava (retired hurt).*

Tenth Wicket
174† A. C. Thomas/G. A. Roe, North West v Griqualand West at Kimberley.
158 M. R. Srinivas/S. Vidyuth, Tamil Nadu v Delhi at Chennai.
153 Faisal Afridi/Saeed Ajmal, KRL v National Bank at Karachi.
110 J. P. Das/A. Barik, Orissa v Bengal at Kolkata.

† National record. Lara and Jacobs set a sixth-wicket record for any team on Australian soil, though Australian and West Indian teams had both surpassed it elsewhere. Thomas and Roe equalled the South African tenth-wicket record.

Eight Wickets in an Innings (15)

10-46	D. S. Mohanty	East Zone v South Zone at Agartala.
9-68	R. O. Hinds	Barbados v Leeward Islands at Charlestown.
9-70	M. Kartik	Rest of India v Mumbai at Mumbai.
8-24	M. M. D. N. R. G. Perera	Sebastianites v Nondescripts at Colombo.
8-76	Ahsanullah Hasan	Barisal v Dhaka Metropolis at Barisal.
8-76	K. G. A. S. Kalum	Matara v Bloomfield at Colombo.
8-79	I. O. Jackson	Windward Islands v West Indies B at St Vincent.
8-80	Jai P. Yadav	Madhya Pradesh v Vidarbha at Indore.
8-84	Harbhajan Singh	India v Australia (Third Test) at Chennai.
8-85	S. Chandana	Antonians v Navy at Colombo.
8-87	M. Muralitharan	Sri Lanka v India (Third Test) at Colombo.
8-93	A. W. Ekanayake	Kurunegala Youth v Sebastianites at Katunayake.
8-101	C. A. Copeland	Griqualand West v Bangladeshis at Kimberley.
8-109	P. A. Strang	Zimbabwe v New Zealand (First Test) at Bulawayo.
8-164	Saqlain Mushtaq	Pakistan v England (First Test) at Lahore *(of eight in innings)*.

Twelve Wickets in a Match (11)

15-102	R. O. Hinds	Barbados v Leeward Islands at Charlestown.
15-111	Jai P. Yadav	Madhya Pradesh v Vidarbha at Indore.
15-217	Harbhajan Singh	India v Australia (Third Test) at Chennai.
14-91	D. S. Mohanty	East Zone v South Zone at Agartala.
13-143	M. Kartik	Rest of India v Mumbai at Mumbai.
13-196	Harbhajan Singh	India v Australia (Second Test) at Kolkata.
12-74	Mohammad Sharif	Biman Bangladesh Airlines v Dhaka Division at Faridpur.
12-89	Ali Gauhar	PIA v Habib Bank at Peshawar.
12-138	I. O. Jackson	Windward Islands v West Indies B at St Vincent.
12-212	S. Weerakoon	Burgher v Tamil Union at Panadura.
12-213	C. A. Copeland	Griqualand West v Bangladeshis at Kimberley.

Hat-Tricks (7)

S. V. Bahutule	West Zone v East Zone at Pune.
Harbhajan Singh	India v Australia (Second Test) at Kolkata.
G. J-P. Kruger	Eastern Province v Sri Lankans at Port Elizabeth.
G. J. Kruis	Griqualand West v KwaZulu-Natal at Durban.
G. D. McGrath	Australia v West Indies (Second Test) at Perth.
Mohammad Javed	Karachi Blues v Sheikhupura at Sheikhupura.
Mohammad Zahid, jun.	PIA v National Bank at Peshawar.

Wicket with First Ball in First-Class Cricket

R. A. Jones	Wellington v Northern Districts at Wellington.
D. Mohammed	Trinidad & Tobago v West Indies B at Roxborough.

Most Overs Bowled in an Innings

74–20–164–8	Saqlain Mushtaq	Pakistan v England (First Test) at Lahore.

Six Wicket-Keeping Dismissals in an Innings

7 ct, 1 st . . .	Y. S. S. Mendis	Bloomfield v Kurunegala Youth at Colombo.
7 ct.	R. D. Jacobs	West Indies v Australia (Fourth Test) at Melbourne.
6 ct.	Humayun Farhat	Lahore City Blues v Islamabad at Islamabad.
5 ct, 1 st . . .	Humayun Farhat	Lahore City Blues v Lahore City Whites at Lahore.
5 ct, 1 st . . .	Inam-ul-Haq Rashid	Bahawalpur v Lahore City Blues at Lahore.
5 ct, 1 st . . .	R. D. Jacobs	West Indians v ZCU President's XI at Harare.
6 ct.	D. Jennings	Easterns v KwaZulu-Natal at Benoni.
6 ct.	W. A. Seccombe	Queensland v Western Australia at Perth.
6 ct.	W. A. Seccombe	Queensland v Victoria at Albion.
5 ct, 1 st . . .	W. A. Seccombe	Queensland v New South Wales at Brisbane.
6 ct.	M. J. Walsh	Western Australia v South Australia at Perth.

M. Klinger and D. S. Berry shared six dismissals for Victoria v Queensland at Albion.

Nine Wicket-Keeping Dismissals in a Match

8 ct, 2 st . .	Y. S. S. Mendis	Bloomfield v Kurunegala Youth at Colombo.
10 ct.	M. N. van Wyk	Free State v Border at Bloemfontein.
8 ct, 1 st . .	Humayun Farhat	Lahore City Blues v Islamabad at Islamabad.
7 ct, 2 st . .	Inam-ul-Haq Rashid	Bahawalpur v Rawalpindi at Bahawalpur.
8 ct, 1 st . .	R. D. Jacobs	West Indies v Australia (Fourth Test) at Melbourne.
8 ct, 1 st . .	R. D. Jacobs	West Indians v ZCU President's XI at Harare.
9 ct.	E. G. Poole	North West v Easterns at Benoni.
8 ct, 1 st . .	W. A. Seccombe	Queensland v New South Wales at Brisbane.
9 ct.	M. J. Walsh	Western Australia v South Australia at Perth.

Five Catches in an Innings in the Field

Younis Khan.	Habib Bank v Pakistan Customs at Karachi.

Six Catches in a Match in the Field

S. B. Bangar.	Railways v Vidarbha at Delhi.
M. E. Waugh	Australia v India (Third Test) at Chennai.
Younis Khan.	Habib Bank v Pakistan Customs at Karachi.

No Byes Conceded in Total of 500 or More

A. C. Bhagat	Goa v Andhra (514-5 dec.) at Margao.
S. S. Dighe	India v Sri Lanka (610-6 dec.) (Third Test) at Colombo.
A. Flower.	Zimbabwe v India (609-6 dec.) (Second Test) at Nagpur.
N. R. Mongia	West Zone v South Zone (595-4 dec.) at Surat.
K. Sangakkara . . .	Sri Lanka v South Africa (504-7 dec.) (Second Test) at Cape Town.

Highest Innings Totals

721	Sargodha v Gujranwala at Gujranwala.
708-8 dec.	North Zone v South Zone at Vijayawada.
690-8 dec.	North Zone v Central Zone at Delhi.
677-7 dec.	New Zealanders v Zimbabwe A at Kwekwe.
657-7 dec.	India v Australia (Second Test) at Kolkata.
656-7 dec.	West Zone v East Zone at Pune.
656-5	Railways v Maharashtra at Pune.
610-6 dec.	Sri Lanka v India (Third Test) at Colombo.
609-6 dec.	India v Zimbabwe (Second Test) at Nagpur.
608-5 dec.	Bengal v Bihar at Kolkata.
605-8 dec.	Uttar Pradesh v Vidarbha at Nagpur.

Lowest Innings Totals

19	Matabeleland v Mashonaland at Harare.
51	Karachi Whites v Peshawar at Peshawar.
53	Navy v Tamil Union at Colombo.
59	Singha v Tamil Union at Colombo.
65	Northerns v Western Province at Centurion.
67	Peshawar v Bahawalpur at Bahawalpur.
67	Navy v Sinhalese at Colombo.
68	Kenyans v Sri Lanka A at Nairobi.
73	Faisalabad v Peshawar at Peshawar.
73	Border v New Zealanders at East London.
74	Kurunegala Youth v Galle at Colombo.

Highest Fourth-Innings Total

452-4	Dhaka Metropolis v Biman Bangladesh Airlines at Dhaka (set 451).

Match Aggregate of 1,500 Runs

1,621 for 29	Tamil Nadu (592 and 515-8 dec.) v Delhi (365 and 149-1) at Chennai.
1,530 for 31	Biman Bangladesh Airlines (354 and 410-7 dec.) v Dhaka Metropolis (314 and 452-4) at Dhaka.
1,511 for 20	South Zone (477) v North Zone (708-8 dec. and 326-3) at Vijayawada. *One batsman retired hurt in South Zone's innings.*

Victory after Following On

India (171 and 657-7 dec.) beat Australia (445 and 212) by 171 runs (Second Test) at Kolkata.

Most Extras in an Innings

	b	*l-b*	*w*	*n-b*	
86	42	7	1	36	Lahore City Blues (532-9) v Sargodha at Sargodha.
61	7	7	1	46	Peshawar (598) v Lahore City Whites at Lahore.
61	11	14	8	28	Pakistan Customs (375) v WAPDA at Faisalabad.

There were eight further instances of 50 extras in an innings.

Career Aggregate Milestones

20,000 runs	S. R. Waugh.
500 wickets	Saqlain Mushtaq.
500 dismissals	D. S. Berry.

ENGLAND IN PAKISTAN, 2000-01

By JOHN ETHERIDGE

The sun had dipped beneath the horizon and night was fast approaching when England turned a tour of significant progress into one of historic success. It was 5.52 p.m. – around 45 minutes after play would normally have been suspended for bad light – when an inside edge by Graham Thorpe gave England victory by six wickets in the deciding Third Test and a 1–0 triumph in the series. England's first tour of Pakistan for 13 years – since Mike Gatting, Shakoor Rana and all that – was always likely to be notable, but their win, and the manner in which it was achieved, was epoch-making. England had not won a Test match in Pakistan since their first full tour in 1961-62 under Ted Dexter's captaincy.

Nasser Hussain's presence at the wicket when the winning runs were scampered was entirely appropriate. Hussain's year-long struggle for runs continued, and as a batsman he made scant contribution. Yet the England captain was a towering figure. He was tactically sharp, refused to allow the frustrations and restrictions peculiar to touring Pakistan to affect his squad, motivated them superbly and, not least, displayed commendable restraint at being given out incorrectly at least three times on the tour, twice in the Second Test alone.

The technically enhanced television pictures and photographers' stills gave little indication of the darkness at the moment of victory. When Hussain lifted the trophy for winning the series, just 15 minutes later, it could have been midnight. There was hardly time or opportunity for an evening of celebration, but beer and wine were provided, courtesy of the British Embassy, before the players headed for the airport, intoxicated by their unexpected triumph.

Apart from Hussain, the major contributors were Mike Atherton and Thorpe, with Ashley Giles, Darren Gough and Craig White not far behind. Atherton batted for hours and hours – almost 23 in total – and made significant runs in all three Tests. After years of dodging and ducking the world's fastest bowlers, he now provided a series of masterclasses in the art of batting against spin. He played the ball late, his concentration was unbreakable, his footwork decisive and his hands were so soft he might have been holding a feather duster, not a stick of willow.

Similarly, the left-handed Thorpe's judgment of line and length was expert, his one lapse coming in the Second Test when he was bowled offering no shot. He also showed limitless patience, and his Lahore century included just two boundaries. The calm way he refused to be disturbed by the fading light or Pakistan's delaying tactics in Karachi was an outstanding demonstration of mental strength. He had controversially missed the previous winter's tour of South Africa to spend more time with his family but, with his batting here, his rehabilitation as an international cricketer was complete.

Having taken one for 106 in his only previous Test, Giles quickly emerged as England's foremost spinner, and his 17 wickets were a record for an England bowler in a series in Pakistan, surpassing the 14 taken by another left-arm spinner, Nick Cook, in 1983-84. Giles never looked like being a world-beater, but he showed control, patience and unflappability. His success was in marked contrast to the hapless Ian Salisbury who, recalled to the England team after more than two years, managed just one for 193 in three Tests. He lacked control and, with Hussain using him only reluctantly, his self-belief drained. Salisbury was subsequently dropped for England's tour of Sri Lanka in early 2001, having originally been selected; it was a public and humiliating rebuff.

White, at the age of 30, continued his emergence in 2000 as a genuine international all-rounder, more than six years after his Test debut. He was England's most aggressive batsman and, at times, their fastest bowler. White's game was all about confidence and feeling wanted. Gough, on the other hand, had never lacked confidence and, after a wicketless First Test, he overcame the moribund pitches with his indomitable spirit and willingness to experiment. Variety was particularly necessary because he failed to achieve his expected reverse swing.

The portents for the tour were not encouraging. England arrived in Pakistan after a fortnight in Nairobi, where they beat Bangladesh but then produced a thoroughly inept performance to be thrashed by South Africa in the ICC Knockout tournament. Within a further two months, however, coach Duncan Fletcher and Hussain had completed a highly successful year, during which England won Test series against Zimbabwe, West Indies and Pakistan.

The pitches, believed to be Pakistan's greatest aid, ultimately contributed to their downfall. After England successfully chased more than 300 in the first one-day international, Pakistan won the final two on sharply turning surfaces. So the instruction went out to groundsmen to prepare cracked, turning pitches for the Tests. To increase home advantage, England played their warm-up games on seaming strips more akin to Lord's than Lahore. In the event, the Test pitches were too slow. There was turn, but batsmen could adjust their shots. England spent hours practising in the nets against local spinners, and the results were instantly apparent as they batted into the third day in the First Test. Saqlain Mushtaq took all eight wickets in England's first innings, but he was never as potent again. Pakistan altogether used six spin bowlers.

At times during the tour, there was evidence of divisions in Pakistan's camp. Before the one-day series, a number of senior players expressed dissatisfaction with coach Javed Miandad over the distribution of the prize money for reaching the semi-finals in Nairobi, and they were said to be unhappy also with his degree of control over the team. Later, Wasim Akram did not play in Karachi, in what would have been his 101st Test. The official explanation was that he had strained his back while warming up, but many suspected he had been dropped. Moin Khan kept his job as captain but had to face an inquest from Lt-General Tauqir Zia, chairman of the board. Apart from Yousuf Youhana, who scored 342 runs in four innings, and Inzamam-ul-Haq, with 303 in five, Pakistan's batting lacked consistency.

For much of the time, the cricket was slow and attritional. But there was no shortage of incident on and off the field. Andrew Flintoff, for example, endured an amazing few weeks. Five days after being told he must go home before the Test leg of the tour, because his chronic back condition prevented him fulfilling his role as an all-rounder, he helped England to victory in the first one-day international with a swashbuckling 84. Flintoff was replaced by Alex Tudor but, when both Hussain and Michael Vaughan sustained injuries, he was recalled from Lancashire as a specialist batsman. Within hours of his return – to discover no bedroom was available when his flight arrived in the early hours – he had his nose broken while batting at his first practice session; in his only subsequent innings, he was out first ball.

Alec Stewart's naming in the Indian Central Bureau of Investigation's report into match-fixing – bookmaker M. K. Gupta claimed he paid him £5,000 in 1992-93 for pitch and team information – cast a shadow over his trip. Stewart was visibly shattered by the allegation and eventually decided to defend his reputation at a news conference. Although the reverberations diminished by the end of the tour, Stewart's contribution with the bat was minimal.

There had been controversy as England first flew in, after ECB chairman Lord MacLaurin was quoted as saying that the Pakistanis under suspicion for match-fixing following the Qayyum Report – in other words, several of their senior players – should be suspended until such time as their names were cleared. This caused outrage in Pakistan, and gave rise to accusations of double standards when MacLaurin endorsed Stewart's continued participation in the series.

England's players encountered dew, flies and tear-gas during matches, as well as the normal ration of controversial umpiring decisions. But they were able to choose the same eleven for three successive Tests for the first time since their tour of India in 1984-85. Marcus Trescothick attempted to be positive, but tailed off after scoring 71 in the First Test. Graeme Hick made an important contribution on the final day of the tour but, after reckless shot selection and static footwork in the first two Tests, would not have been playing but for Vaughan's calf injury. Andrew Caddick, disheartened by the flat pitches and some umpiring decisions, managed only three Test wickets. Of those who did not play in the Tests, Matthew Hoggard took 17 wickets in his two first-class matches, reserve wicket-keeper Paul Nixon was popular and worked hard in the gym on his first tour, and Tudor played just once. Dominic Cork went home early with a back injury.

ENGLAND TOURING PARTY

N. Hussain (Essex) (*captain*), M. W. Alleyne (Gloucestershire), M. A. Atherton (Lancashire), A. R. Caddick (Somerset), D. G. Cork (Derbyshire), M. A. Ealham (Kent), A. Flintoff (Lancashire), A. F. Giles (Warwickshire), D. Gough (Yorkshire), A. P. Grayson (Essex), G. A. Hick (Worcestershire), M. J. Hoggard (Yorkshire), P. A. Nixon (Kent), I. D. K. Salisbury (Surrey), V. S. Solanki (Worcestershire), A. J. Stewart (Surrey), G. P. Thorpe (Surrey), M. E. Trescothick (Somerset), M. P. Vaughan (Yorkshire), C. White (Yorkshire).

N. V. Knight (Warwickshire) and A. D. Mullally (Hampshire) were unfit and replaced before the tour by Solanki and Hoggard. Alleyne, Ealham, Grayson and Solanki returned home after the one-day series and were replaced by Atherton, Cork, Nixon, Salisbury and Vaughan for the first-class programme. A. J. Tudor (Surrey) replaced Flintoff, who was unfit to bowl, but was later recalled, as cover for the injured Vaughan. Cork returned home with a back injury.

Manager: P. A. Neale. *Coach:* D. A. G. Fletcher. *Assistant coaches:* R. M. H. Cottam and M. D. Moxon. *Scorer:* M. N. Ashton. *Physiotherapist:* D. O. Conway. *Physiologist:* N. P. Stockill. *Media relations managers:* D. A. Clarke and A. J. Walpole.

ENGLAND TOUR RESULTS

Test matches – Played 3: Won 1, Drawn 2.
First-class matches – Played 6: Won 3, Drawn 3.
Wins – Pakistan, PCB Patron's XI, North-West Frontier Province Governor's XI.
Draws – Pakistan (2), Pakistan Cricket Board XI.
One-day internationals – Played 3: Won 1, Lost 2.
Other non-first-class matches – Played 2: Won 2. *Wins* – Sind Governor's XI, Pakistan A.

TEST MATCH AVERAGES

PAKISTAN – BATTING

	T	*I*	*NO*	*R*	*HS*	*100s*	*50s*	*Avge*	*Ct/St*
Yousuf Youhana	3	4	0	342	124	2	1	85.50	8
Inzamam-ul-Haq	3	5	0	303	142	1	2	60.60	2
Salim Elahi	3	5	0	222	72	0	1	44.40	1
Abdur Razzaq	3	5	1	141	100*	1	0	35.25	2
Saeed Anwar	3	4	0	122	53	0	1	30.50	1
Saqlain Mushtaq	3	4	1	86	34	0	0	28.66	1
Moin Khan	3	4	0	109	65	0	1	27.25	5/2
Shahid Afridi	3	5	1	97	52	0	1	24.25	2
Danish Kaneria	2	3	2	8	8*	0	0	8.00	0
Wasim Akram	2	3	1	6	4*	0	0	3.00	1

Played in one Test: Arshad Khan 2; Imran Nazir 20, 4 (1 ct); Mushtaq Ahmed 0; Qaiser Abbas 2; Waqar Younis 17, 0.

* *Signifies not out.*

BOWLING

	O	*M*	*R*	*W*	*BB*	*5W/i*	*Avge*
Arshad Khan	38	16	60	3	2-31	0	20.00
Waqar Younis	42	5	115	5	4-88	0	23.00
Saqlain Mushtaq	203.2	52	431	18	8-164	1	23.94
Shahid Afridi	59.1	13	136	4	2-21	0	34.00
Danish Kaneria	91	26	217	4	2-80	0	54.25
Abdur Razzaq	82	14	231	4	3-74	0	57.75

Also bowled: Mushtaq Ahmed 52–6–164–1; Qaiser Abbas 16–3–35–0; Wasim Akram 59–20–123–2.

ENGLAND – BATTING

	T	*I*	*NO*	*R*	*HS*	*100s*	*50s*	*Avge*	*Ct/St*
M. A. Atherton	3	6	1	341	125	1	2	68.20	2
C. White	3	4	1	178	93	0	1	59.33	1
G. P. Thorpe	3	6	1	284	118	1	2	56.80	6
I. D. K. Salisbury	3	3	1	84	33	0	0	42.00	0
A. F. Giles	3	3	1	56	37*	0	0	28.00	3
M. E. Trescothick	3	6	0	149	71	0	1	24.83	2
N. Hussain	3	6	2	92	51	0	1	23.00	3
A. J. Stewart	3	6	1	99	29	0	0	19.80	4/1
G. A. Hick	3	6	0	99	40	0	0	16.50	3
A. R. Caddick	3	3	1	13	5*	0	0	6.50	0

Played in three Tests: D. Gough 19*, 18 (1 ct).

* *Signifies not out.*

BOWLING

	O	*M*	*R*	*W*	*BB*	*5W/i*	*Avge*
A. F. Giles	182	55	410	17	5-75	1	24.11
D. Gough	91.1	18	268	10	3-30	0	26.80
C. White	102.3	21	274	9	4-54	0	30.44
A. R. Caddick	95	11	282	3	1-40	0	94.00

Also bowled: G. A. Hick 8–0–42–1; I. D. K. Salisbury 69–8–193–1; M. E. Trescothick 14–1–34–1.

ENGLAND TOUR AVERAGES – FIRST-CLASS MATCHES

BATTING

	M	*I*	*NO*	*R*	*HS*	*100s*	*50s*	*Avge*	*Ct/St*
C. White	5	6	1	320	120	1	1	64.00	3
G. P. Thorpe	5	8	1	420	118	1	3	60.00	10
M. A. Atherton	5	9	1	399	125	1	2	49.87	3
I. D. K. Salisbury	6	5	2	105	33	0	0	35.00	1
M. E. Trescothick	6	10	1	311	93	0	3	34.55	6
A. F. Giles	6	6	1	147	39	0	0	29.40	5
A. J. Stewart	5	8	1	205	59	0	1	29.28	9/3
N. Hussain	5	9	3	153	51	0	1	25.50	3
G. A. Hick	5	8	0	185	81	0	1	23.12	9
M. P. Vaughan	3	4	1	46	20	0	0	15.33	3
A. R. Caddick	4	4	1	14	5*	0	0	4.66	1

Played in four matches: D. Gough 19*, 18, 1* (1 ct). Played in two matches: M. J. Hoggard 0; P. A. Nixon 31, 47* (11 ct). Played in one match: D. G. Cork 0; A. Flintoff 0 (1 ct); A. J. Tudor 4.

* *Signifies not out.*

BOWLING

	O	*M*	*R*	*W*	*BB*	*5W/i*	*Avge*
M. J. Hoggard	67.3	24	132	17	5-62	1	7.76
M. E. Trescothick	32.1	5	74	5	2-10	0	14.80
A. F. Giles	244.3	74	553	25	5-75	1	22.12
D. Gough	129.1	25	373	16	3-30	0	23.31
C. White	140.2	27	393	13	4-54	0	30.23
A. R. Caddick	129	21	357	7	2-24	0	51.00
I. D. K. Salisbury	135.5	15	395	5	2-30	0	79.00

Also bowled: D. G. Cork 24–7–66–2; G. A. Hick 8–0–42–1; G. P. Thorpe 1–0–4–0; A. J. Tudor 20–5–64–4; M. P. Vaughan 3–1–5–0.

Note: Matches in this section which were not first-class are signified by a dagger.

†At Karachi, October 20 (day/night). England XI won by 81 runs. Toss: England XI. England XI 323 for seven (50 overs) (M. E. Trescothick 102, N. Hussain 44, G. A. Hick 82; Shoaib Malik three for 59); Sind Governor's XI 242 (46.4 overs) (Asim Kamal 43, Salim Elahi 120; D. Gough five for 32).

†At Karachi, October 22 (day/night). England XI won by ten wickets. Toss: England XI. Pakistan A 169 for seven (50 overs) (Yasir Hameed 31, Naumanullah 64; A. R. Caddick three for 15, A. F. Giles three for 34); England XI 170 for no wkt (29.4 overs) (M. E. Trescothick 59 retired hurt, A. J. Stewart 50 retired hurt, N. Hussain 31 not out).

†PAKISTAN v ENGLAND

First One-Day International

At Karachi, October 24 (day/night). England won by five wickets. Toss: Pakistan.

England successfully chased 300 for the first time in a limited-overs international and, sweeping to victory with 16 balls to spare, recorded the fourth-highest winning total by a team batting second. Flintoff applied the brutal finale with 84 runs from 60 deliveries, and his partnership with Thorpe produced 138 in 17 overs. Flintoff's innings came five days after learning that his inability to bowl (he was still suffering from a long-term back problem) would prevent him from playing in the Tests. England's reply started controversially when umpire Riazuddin waited seven seconds before raising his finger to despatch Stewart. However, Hussain anchored the run-chase, Hick (56 from 51 balls) gave it momentum and Thorpe scampered while Flintoff savaged. On a flat pitch in searing heat, Abdur Razzaq had taken Pakistan beyond 300 with an unbeaten 75 from 40 balls as they added 106 from the final ten overs. But Pakistan's bowlers found the conditions much less to their liking. The evening dew made the ball so slippery that the next two matches were rescheduled to start at noon rather than 2.30 p.m.

Man of the Match: A. Flintoff.

Pakistan

Saeed Anwar c Stewart b White	24
Imran Nazir b Caddick	30
Salim Elahi c Stewart b Ealham	28
Inzamam-ul-Haq c Flintoff b Ealham	71
Yousuf Youhana c Stewart b Gough	35
Abdur Razzaq not out	75
*†Moin Khan c sub (V. S. Solanki) b White	18
Wasim Akram run out	0
Waqar Younis run out	1
Saqlain Mushtaq b Gough	3
Mushtaq Ahmed not out	2
L-b 7, w 4, n-b 6	17
1/39 (1) 2/87 (3) 3/97 (2) 4/197 (5) 5/219 (4) 6/267 (7) 7/271 (8) 8/277 (9) 9/302 (10) (9 wkts, 50 overs)	304

Score at 15 overs: 92-2

Bowling: Caddick 10–1–53–1; Gough 10–0–71–2; White 9–0–69–2; Ealham 10–0–49–2; Giles 8–0–37–0; Trescothick 3–0–18–0.

England

M. E. Trescothick c Mushtaq Ahmed b Waqar Younis	11
†A. J. Stewart c Moin Khan b Wasim Akram	0
*N. Hussain st Moin Khan b Mushtaq Ahmed	73
G. A. Hick c Moin Khan b Abdur Razzaq	56
G. P. Thorpe not out	64
A. Flintoff c Moin Khan b Abdur Razzaq	84
C. White not out	0
L-b 4, w 5, n-b 9	18
1/2 (2) 2/13 (1) 3/127 (4) 4/164 (3) 5/302 (6) (5 wkts, 47.2 overs)	306

Score at 15 overs: 89-2

M. A. Ealham, A. F. Giles, D. Gough and A. R. Caddick did not bat.

Bowling: Wasim Akram 8–0–59–1; Waqar Younis 10–0–66–1; Abdur Razzaq 10–0–71–2; Saqlain Mushtaq 9.2–0–54–0; Mushtaq Ahmed 10–0–52–1.

Umpires: Riazuddin and Salim Badar.
Third umpire: Feroze Butt.

†PAKISTAN v ENGLAND

Second One-Day International

At Lahore, October 27 (day/night). Pakistan won by eight wickets. Toss: Pakistan.

Pakistan triumphed on a turning pitch – amazingly for a one-day match, no wickets fell to seam bowlers. Shahid Afridi's skidding quicker delivery caused serious problems and he collected five wickets, the best return for Pakistan against England, although it later emerged that he was reported to the ICC by referee Barry Jarman for a suspect action. England, after reaching 171 for three in the 39th over, subsided alarmingly, their plan against the spinning ball amounting to little more than repeated sweep shots. Pakistan eased towards their target – Afridi contributing 61 in 69 balls – as swarms of flies, attracted by the humidity and floodlights, descended on the ground. England's fielders complained of midges in their mouths, eyes and noses; bowlers wore sunglasses and White even bowled in a cap. Afterwards, Pakistan captain Moin Khan said England's weakness had been exposed and that spin would be his trump card for the remainder of the tour.

Man of the Match: Shahid Afridi.

England

M. E. Trescothick c sub (Imran Nazir) b Shahid Afridi	65
†A. J. Stewart st Moin Khan b Mushtaq Ahmed	22
*N. Hussain st Moin Khan b Shahid Afridi	54
G. A. Hick run out	1
G. P. Thorpe b Shahid Afridi	20
A. Flintoff b Saqlain Mushtaq	17
C. White st Moin Khan b Shahid Afridi	0
M. A. Ealham b Saqlain Mushtaq	3
A. F. Giles b Shahid Afridi	3
D. Gough not out	6
A. R. Caddick not out	6
B 2, l-b 6, w 6	14
1/66 (2) 2/116 (1) 3/122 (4) 4/171 (5) 5/178 (3) 6/178 (7) 7/185 (8) 8/194 (9) 9/198 (6) (9 wkts, 50 overs)	211

Score at 15 overs: 76-1

Bowling: Wasim Akram 6–0–30–0; Abdur Razzaq 10–1–38–0; Azhar Mahmood 4–0–27–0; Mushtaq Ahmed 10–1–34–1; Saqlain Mushtaq 10–0–34–2; Shahid Afridi 10–1–40–5.

Pakistan

Saeed Anwar c Thorpe b Giles	41
Shahid Afridi c Thorpe b Giles	61
Salim Elahi not out	58
Yousuf Youhana not out	39
L-b 1, w 6, n-b 8	15
1/76 (1) 2/123 (2) (2 wkts, 44.2 overs)	214

Score at 15 overs: 66-0

Inzamam-ul-Haq, Abdur Razzaq, *†Moin Khan, Wasim Akram, Azhar Mahmood, Saqlain Mushtaq and Mushtaq Ahmed did not bat.

Bowling: Caddick 10–1–37–0; Gough 10–0–51–0; White 8.2–0–43–0; Giles 10–1–45–2; Ealham 4–0–23–0; Hick 2–0–14–0.

Umpires: Aleem Dar and Mohammad Nazir.
Third umpire: Afzaal Ahmed.

†PAKISTAN v ENGLAND

Third One-Day International

At Rawalpindi, October 30 (day/night). Pakistan won by six wickets. Toss: Pakistan.

The third game followed a similar plot to the second. This time, though, it was Saqlain Mushtaq who took five wickets, even more cheaply, in helpful conditions, while the England players swallowed tear-gas rather than flies. The noxious fumes twice drifted across the ground during their innings as police outside attempted to disperse spectators without tickets. Some of the batsmen, as well as the Pakistan fielders, suffered streaming eyes and choking throats. Several tossed away their wickets with loose shots or poor technique as England were dismissed inside 43 overs. Hussain was unlucky, given out lbw by umpire Mian Aslam even though the ball pitched well outside leg stump. He kept his emotions intact on the field, but smashed the glass door of the dressing-room fridge with his bat. Although the redoubtable Inzamam-ul-Haq guided Pakistan home with few problems, England produced a spirited fielding performance in which Hussain was magnificent. Pakistan's series victory was only their second in bilateral one-day tournaments with England, and their first since 1974.

Man of the Match: Saqlain Mushtaq.

England

M. E. Trescothick b Saqlain Mushtaq . . .	36
†A. J. Stewart c Moin Khan b Abdur Razzaq .	18
*N. Hussain lbw b Wasim Akram	1
G. A. Hick b Saqlain Mushtaq	3
G. P. Thorpe run out	39
A. Flintoff c Azhar Mahmood b Shahid Afridi .	10
C. White c Mushtaq Ahmed b Saqlain Mushtaq .	0
M. A. Ealham b Abdur Razzaq	23
A. F. Giles lbw b Saqlain Mushtaq	11
D. Gough b Saqlain Mushtaq	0
A. R. Caddick not out	1
L-b 5, w 4, n-b 7	16
1/36 (2) 2/38 (3) 3/63 (4) 4/64 (1) 5/85 (6) 6/86 (7) 7/133 (8) 8/156 (9) 9/156 (10) 10/158 (5) (42.5 overs)	158

Score at 15 overs: 63-2

Bowling: Wasim Akram 7–0–27–1; Abdur Razzaq 10–0–40–2; Azhar Mahmood 1–0–3–0; Mushtaq Ahmed 10–0–42–0; Saqlain Mushtaq 8–0–20–5; Shahid Afridi 6.5–1–21–1.

Pakistan

Imran Nazir c Hick b Caddick	0
Shahid Afridi c Hussain b Caddick	9
Salim Elahi c Hussain b Giles	23
Inzamam-ul-Haq not out	60
Yousuf Youhana b White	31
Abdur Razzaq not out	17
L-b 6, w 12, n-b 3.	21
1/0 (1) 2/9 (2) 3/51 (3) 4/128 (5) (4 wkts, 43.3 overs)	161

Score at 15 overs: 51-3

*†Moin Khan, Wasim Akram, Azhar Mahmood, Saqlain Mushtaq and Mushtaq Ahmed did not bat.

Bowling: Caddick 9–1–46–2; Gough 8–2–25–0; White 9.3–2–30–1; Giles 10–0–36–1; Ealham 5–0–9–0; Hick 2–0–9–0.

Umpires: Mian Aslam and Z. I. Pasha.
Third umpire: Aleem Dar. Series referee: B. N. Jarman (Australia).

PCB PATRON'S XI v ENGLAND XI

At Rawalpindi, November 1, 2, 3, 4. England XI won by an innings and 27 runs. Toss: PCB Patron's XI.

England's opening first-class match was overshadowed by the release of the Indian CBI's report into match-fixing, in which bookmaker M. K. Gupta claimed he paid Stewart £5,000 for information in 1992-93. While England were winning comfortably, Stewart was back at the hotel, first avoiding the press then emerging to protest his innocence. He had been rested from the game before the controversy erupted. England thrived on a switch to red balls after four weeks of playing and practising with white. Hoggard, who finished with nine wickets, displayed good pace in seamer-friendly conditions, totally unlike those in the one-day international on an adjacent pitch two days earlier, and there were six dismissals for Nixon in his first senior game for England. In between, Thorpe and Hick added 144 in 148 minutes, but White's first century for an England side was the highlight: he batted with a confidence and freedom he had rarely shown for his country.

Close of play: First day, PCB Patron's XI 188-5 (Qaiser Abbas 71*, Javed Qadir 2*); Second day, England XI 212-4 (Hick 77*, White 6*); Third day, PCB Patron's XI 49-1 (Naved Ashraf 23*, Kamran Ali 12*).

PCB Patron's XI

Naved Ashraf c Nixon b Trescothick	29	– c Nixon b Hoggard	44
Imran Abbas c Hick b Hoggard	10	– c Nixon b Salisbury	12
Kamran Ali c Thorpe b Hoggard	15	– run out	18
*Mohammad Wasim c Hick b Giles	29	– lbw b Hoggard	12
Qaiser Abbas lbw b Hoggard	71	– c Salisbury b Giles	44
Salman Shah c White b Hoggard	17	– c Nixon b Giles	7
†Javed Qadir b Hoggard	2	– lbw b Salisbury	0
Munir Ansari c Atherton b Trescothick	8	– (9) c Nixon b Hoggard	0
Shafiq Ahmed c Trescothick b Cork	32	– (8) c Nixon b Hoggard	26
Mohammad Akram c Thorpe b Cork	2	– c Trescothick b Giles	0
Mohammad Sami not out	6	– not out	0
B 4, l-b 5, n-b 7	16	B 1, l-b 5	6
1/35 2/44 3/85 4/95 5/162 6/188 7/189 8/225 9/229	237	1/26 2/59 3/86 4/97 5/111 6/126 7/165 8/169 9/169	169

Bowling: *First Innings*—Hoggard 27–11–62–5; Cork 15–4–42–2; Trescothick 8.1–2–12–2; White 16–3–46–0; Salisbury 14–4–32–0; Giles 18–6–25–1; Vaughan 3–1–5–0; Thorpe 1–0–4–0. *Second Innings*—Hoggard 18–2–40–4; Cork 9–3–24–0; Giles 16.3–5–38–3; Salisbury 19–0–51–2; Trescothick 3–1–10–0.

England XI

M. A. Atherton c Shafiq Ahmed b Mohammad Sami	22
M. E. Trescothick c Imran Abbas b Mohammad Akram	8
M. P. Vaughan c Javed Qadir b Mohammad Akram	3
*G. P. Thorpe c Mohammad Wasim b Qaiser Abbas	88
G. A. Hick c Naved Ashraf b Mohammad Sami	81
C. White c Javed Qadir b Mohammad Akram	120
†P. A. Nixon b Shafiq Ahmed	31
D. G. Cork b Shafiq Ahmed	0
A. F. Giles lbw b Qaiser Abbas	39
I. D. K. Salisbury not out	17
M. J. Hoggard b Mohammad Akram	0
L-b 10, n-b 14	24
1/21 2/33 3/52 4/196 5/223 6/306 7/306 8/389 9/433	433

Bowling: Mohammad Akram 23.5–3–105–4; Mohammad Sami 15–2–69–2; Shafiq Ahmed 37–10–99–2; Salman Shah 3–1–12–0; Munir Ansari 22–2–90–0; Qaiser Abbas 19–5–34–2; Naved Ashraf 1–0–14–0.

Umpires: Kamal Merchant and Z. I. Pasha.

NORTH-WEST FRONTIER PROVINCE GOVERNOR'S XI v ENGLAND XI

At Peshawar, November 8, 9, 10, 11. England XI won by eight wickets. Toss: England XI.

England completed their preparations for the First Test with a second successive win. Gough broke Wajahatullah Wasti's left thumb during a hostile, if wayward, opening spell on a pitch that again bore little resemblance to what they could expect in the Test series. Trescothick went within seven runs of his maiden first-class century for an England team, while Stewart, after a week defending his integrity, began his rehabilitation with a half-century. The Governor's XI offered only moderate resistance but, during their second innings, umpire Sajjad Asghar accused Caddick of saying "things about my country" after an appeal for a catch behind was rejected. It was the sort of diplomatic incident England were desperate to avoid on their first tour of Pakistan for 13 years. Asghar did not make an official complaint but, despite Caddick admitting in his newspaper column that he did make insulting comments, neither an apology nor a reprimand was forthcoming.

Close of play: First day, North-West Frontier Province Governor's XI 173-5 (Yasir Hameed 56*, Mohammad Hussain 34*); Second day, England XI 241-5 (Thorpe 27*); Third day, North-West Frontier Province Governor's XI 115-4 (Akhtar Sarfraz 53*, Sajid Shah 0*).

North-West Frontier Province Governor's XI

Wajahatullah Wasti retired hurt	0	– absent hurt	
Imran Farhat c Stewart b White	42	– (1) c Stewart b Caddick	0
Taufiq Umar c Stewart b Caddick	15	– (2) b Gough	1
Yasir Hameed c Vaughan b Caddick	57	– (3) lbw b Gough	5
Naumanullah c Vaughan b Giles	11	– (4) c Thorpe b Gough	50
Akhtar Sarfraz c White b Giles	0	– (5) c Stewart b Caddick	53
*†Rashid Latif c Trescothick b Gough	6	– (8) st Stewart b Salisbury	3
Mohammad Hussain c Caddick b Gough	65	– (7) c Thorpe b White	7
Sajid Shah b Gough	5	– (6) c Stewart b White	18
Kabir Khan b White	11	– (9) not out	22
Kashif Raza not out	2	– (10) st Stewart b Salisbury	4
L-b 2, n-b 8	10	B 4, l-b 2, n-b 1	7
1/58 2/60 3/101 4/101 5/113 6/179 7/206 8/211 9/224	224	1/1 2/1 3/13 4/115 5/115 6/139 7/142 8/150 9/170	170

In the first innings Wajahatullah Wasti retired hurt at 21.

Bowling: *First Innings*—Gough 23–4–54–3; Caddick 17–2–51–2; White 11.5–2–46–2; Trescothick 2–0–8–0; Salisbury 9–1–30–0; Giles 10–4–33–2. *Second Innings*—Gough 15–3–51–3; Caddick 17–8–24–2; White 10–1–27–2; Giles 9–2–32–0; Salisbury 9.5–2–30–2.

England XI

M. A. Atherton c sub (Taimur Khan) b Kashif Raza	22	– c Taufiq Umar b Kashif Raza	14
M. E. Trescothick b Mohammad Hussain	93	– c Rashid Latif b Kashif Raza	11
*N. Hussain lbw b Kabir Khan	15	– not out	23
M. P. Vaughan st Rashid Latif b Mohammad Hussain	20	– not out	19
†A. J. Stewart c Rashid Latif b Sajid Shah	59		
G. P. Thorpe c sub (Taimur Khan) b Sajid Shah	48		
C. White c Sajid Shah b Kabir Khan	22		
A. F. Giles c Akhtar Sarfraz b Kabir Khan	24		
I. D. K. Salisbury lbw b Kashif Raza	4		
A. R. Caddick c Taufiq Umar b Kashif Raza	1		
D. Gough not out	1		
B 1, l-b 1, n-b 4	6	L-b 6, n-b 7	13
1/35 2/75 3/112 4/177 5/241 6/282 7/289 8/297 9/305	315	1/35 2/37	(2 wkts) 80

Bowling: *First Innings*—Sajid Shah 22–5–66–2; Kabir Khan 28.5–5–82–3; Mohammad Hussain 28–7–68–2; Kashif Raza 21–7–66–3; Imran Farhat 7–0–26–0; Naumanullah 1–0–5–0. *Second Innings*—Kashif Raza 9–0–38–2; Sajid Shah 8.2–0–36–0.

Umpires: Iqbal Butt and Sajjad Asghar.

PAKISTAN v ENGLAND

First Test Match

At Lahore, November 15, 16, 17, 18, 19. Drawn. Toss: England. Test debut: Qaiser Abbas.

England's first Test in Pakistan since December 1987 was bound to attract its share of hype, and much of it centred on a pitch that was dry and cracked. Suspicions that the cracks would widen were strengthened when Pakistan included four spinners, leaving all-rounder Abdur Razzaq to share the new ball with Wasim Akram. But local knowledge held that the pitch would last five days and that any turn would be slow. So it proved,

[*Graham Morris*

Like all the Englishmen dismissed in the first innings at Lahore, Craig White lost his wicket to Saqlain Mushtaq (*right*). But, seven short of his first Test hundred, he had by then confirmed England's ascendancy over Pakistan's threatened spin supremacy.

from the moment Saqlain Mushtaq bowled the 11th over. Patient, at times attritional, batting dictated the course of the match.

Atherton and Trescothick established the pattern on the first day, building their second century opening stand in successive Tests. They had almost made it to tea when Trescothick, a little needlessly, tried to sweep Saqlain's leg-break and top-edged to backward square leg. Atherton, 55 at the time, went on to become the sixth Englishman to score 7,000 Test runs before he was similarly deceived by Saqlain; trying to check his stroke, he managed only to lap a catch behind square leg. When the Pakistani spinner also removed Stewart, awkward against the turning ball, and Hussain, who skied to cover attempting to repeat an earlier straight drive, England in six overs had slipped from 169 for one to 183 for four.

The balance would have tipped well and truly in Pakistan's favour had debutant Qaiser Abbas at slip caught Thorpe off Saqlain when he was two. Thorpe, who had come in unexpectedly at No. 3 because of concern over Hussain's back, gave another chance when 20. But next day, initially with Hick and then with White, he secured England's position. Saqlain apart, Pakistan's attack rarely threatened. White batted with great self-assurance, adding 166 with Thorpe, a sixth-wicket record for England–Pakistan Tests, in four hours 17 minutes. He drove Saqlain for four early on, sweep-pulled Mushtaq Ahmed and hit sixes off Shahid Afridi and Saqlain. Thorpe, however, hit what is believed to be the first Test hundred to contain only one boundary; in his 118, made from 301 balls in seven hours ten minutes, he hit just two.

White, 89 not out at the close, deserved a maiden Test hundred, but early on the third morning Saqlain obtained a fraction more bounce and short leg snapped up the chance. Saqlain, who had narrowly failed to take difficult caught-and-bowled chances when White was 22 and 69, now had all seven England wickets, varying his attack skilfully and conceding little more than two an over. After Salisbury and Giles had added 70, he picked up an eighth to finish with Test-best figures, and might have taken all ten had Hussain not declared at lunch.

Saeed Anwar and Afridi then rattled up 63 in 88 minutes, making England's innings look pedestrian. But when Anwar was lbw on the stroke of tea, padding up to Hick, and Afridi fell victim to his own impetuousness, well caught at long-off by Gough, the bowlers had a chance to settle as Salim Elahi and Inzamam-ul-Haq set about consolidating the innings. Even so, nothing suggested that, at tea on the fourth day, Pakistan would be eight wickets down and still needing five runs to avoid the follow-on.

White, with pace, and Giles, flighting the ball cleverly, made the breakthrough with three for 11 in eight overs before lunch. Caddick chipped in by removing Moin Khan, after which White's reverse swing and his low catch at mid-wicket accounted for Razzaq and Wasim. That, however, was England's high point. The elegant Yousuf Youhana, 37 not out at the fall of the eighth wicket, and Saqlain shut the door on them with a century stand. Youhana batted six and a quarter hours for his 124, hitting eight fours and a six; Saqlain faced 167 balls for his unbeaten 32 in four hours. England had to settle for a first-innings lead of 79 and an afternoon's batting.

That their second innings cost no more than four cheap wickets was fortunate. Wasim, bowling with real pace and bounce, quickly sent Trescothick packing and greeted Hussain with two consecutive bouncers. The third in as many balls struck the England captain on the wrist as he went to hook and forced his retirement. By the time Hick played all over a leg-break from Afridi, 10.5 overs remained and England were pleased to call it a day. They had shown their mettle and, more importantly, had proved to themselves that they had the technique and temperament to deal with Pakistan. In Giles and White, moreover, they possessed bowlers who could steer them into match-winning positions. – GRAEME WRIGHT.

Man of the Match: Saqlain Mushtaq.

Close of play: First day, England 195-4 (Thorpe 22*, Hick 6*); Second day, England 393-6 (White 89*, Salisbury 0*); Third day, Pakistan 119-2 (Salim Elahi 15*, Inzamam-ul-Haq 11*); Fourth day, Pakistan 333-8 (Yousuf Youhana 77*, Saqlain Mushtaq 14*).

England

M. A. Atherton c Yousuf Youhana b Saqlain Mushtaq	73	lbw b Mushtaq Ahmed	20
M. E. Trescothick c Salim Elahi b Saqlain Mushtaq	71	lbw b Wasim Akram	1
G. P. Thorpe c and b Saqlain Mushtaq	118	(4) c Abdur Razzaq b Saqlain Mushtaq	5
†A. J. Stewart lbw b Saqlain Mushtaq	3	(5) not out	27
*N. Hussain c Wasim Akram b Saqlain Mushtaq	7	(3) retired hurt	0
G. A. Hick lbw b Saqlain Mushtaq	16	b Shahid Afridi	14
C. White c Yousuf Youhana b Saqlain Mushtaq	93		
I. D. K. Salisbury lbw b Saqlain Mushtaq	31		
A. F. Giles not out	37		
A. R. Caddick not out	5		
B 3, l-b 13, n-b 10	26	L-b 7, n-b 3	10
1/134 (2) 2/169 (1) 3/173 (4) 4/183 (5) 5/225 (6) 6/391 (3) 7/398 (7) 8/468 (8)	(8 wkts dec.) 480	1/4 (2) 2/29 (4) 3/39 (1) 4/77 (6)	(4 wkts dec.) 77

D. Gough did not bat.

In the second innings N. Hussain retired hurt at 13.

Bowling: *First Innings*—Wasim Akram 22–8–40–0; Abdur Razzaq 22–6–55–0; Saqlain Mushtaq 74–20–164–8; Mushtaq Ahmed 44–6–132–0; Shahid Afridi 18–6–38–0; Qaiser Abbas 16–3–35–0. *Second Innings*—Wasim Akram 6–5–1–1; Abdur Razzaq 7–0–21–0; Saqlain Mushtaq 10–2–14–1; Mushtaq Ahmed 8–0–32–1; Shahid Afridi 1.1–0–2–1.

Pakistan

Saeed Anwar lbw b Hick	40
Shahid Afridi c Gough b Giles	52
Salim Elahi b White	44
Inzamam-ul-Haq b Giles	63
Yousuf Youhana c Stewart b Giles	124
Qaiser Abbas c Hick b White	2
*†Moin Khan lbw b Caddick	17
Abdur Razzaq lbw b White	10
Wasim Akram c White b Giles	1
Saqlain Mushtaq not out	32
Mushtaq Ahmed lbw b White	0
B 2, l-b 6, n-b 8	16
1/63 (1) 2/101 (2) 3/199 (3) 4/203 (4) 5/210 (6) 6/236 (7) 7/272 (8) 8/273 (9) 9/400 (5) 10/401 (11)	401

Bowling: Gough 17–6–45–0; Caddick 24–4–68–1; Giles 59–20–113–4; Salisbury 31–5–71–0; Hick 8–0–42–1; White 24.3–5–54–4.

Umpires: D. B. Hair (Australia) and Riazuddin.
Third umpire: Salim Badar. Referee: R. S. Madugalle (Sri Lanka).

PAKISTAN CRICKET BOARD XI v ENGLAND XI

At Bagh-i-Jinnah, Lahore, November 23, 24, 25. Drawn. Toss: England XI.

A three-day match, with the second day washed out, on a damp pitch in a picturesque, tree-lined park was no sort of practice for five-day Test cricket on cracked, parched surfaces in concrete bowls. But at least England were again dominant and would doubtless have won but for the weather: the home side were still 49 behind with six second-innings wickets down at the finish. Hoggard had match figures of eight for 30 and intimidated the PCB batsmen with his pace and movement, while Tudor enjoyed his only game since joining the tour as Flintoff's replacement. Flintoff, by now back with the squad, was out first ball, and Vaughan, testing the calf he strained while fielding in Peshawar, did not prove his fitness for the Second Test. Hussain failed after promoting himself to open, and his highest first-class score for the year 2000 remained 33.

Close of play: First day, England XI 76-2 (Trescothick 28*, Stewart 12*); Second day, No play.

Pakistan Cricket Board XI

Mohammad Ramzan c Nixon b Hoggard	0	(2) c Nixon b Tudor	0
Salman Butt c Flintoff b Tudor	16	(1) c Giles b Hoggard	9
Bazid Khan c Nixon b Giles	10	(5) c Hick b Hoggard	0
Hasan Raza c Nixon b Trescothick	14	(3) c Trescothick b Tudor	6
Faisal Iqbal b Tudor	18	(4) not out	27
Faisal Naved c Hick b Trescothick	1	c Hick b Hoggard	15
*Shoaib Malik c Hick b Hoggard	27	c Nixon b Hoggard	0
†Kamran Akmal not out	20	not out	10
Fazl-e-Akbar c and b Giles	0		
Stephen John lbw b Hoggard	0		
Shafiq Ahmed c Vaughan b Hoggard	0		
B 1, l-b 7, w 1, n-b 2	11	L-b 2, n-b 2	4
1/12 2/16 3/44 4/44 5/55 6/80 7/103 8/110 9/113	117	1/6 2/15 3/17 4/18 5/56 6/56	(6 wkts) 71

Bowling: *First Innings*—Hoggard 11.3–7–13–4; Tudor 11–2–44–2; Giles 8–2–13–2; Trescothick 5–1–10–2; Salisbury 7–0–29–0. *Second Innings*—Hoggard 11–4–17–4; Tudor 9–3–20–2; Salisbury 8–0–30–0; Giles 1–0–2–0.

England XI

*N. Hussain c Kamran Akmal b Fazl-e-Akbar	23
M. E. Trescothick retired hurt	50
G. A. Hick c Kamran Akmal b Stephen John	5
A. J. Stewart c Bazid Khan b Stephen John	47
M. P. Vaughan c and b Shoaib Malik	4
A. Flintoff c Mohammad Ramzan b Stephen John	0
†P. A. Nixon not out	47
A. J. Tudor c Faisal Iqbal b Stephen John	4
A. F. Giles b Fazl-e-Akbar	28
B 4, l-b 2, w 6, n-b 17	29
1/38 2/47 3/137 4/137 5/153 6/158 7/237 (7 wkts dec.)	237

I. D. K. Salisbury and M. J. Hoggard did not bat.

M. E. Trescothick retired hurt at 135.

Bowling: Fazl-e-Akbar 21.4–4–91–2; Stephen John 21–4–73–4; Shafiq Ahmed 2–0–8–0; Shoaib Malik 17–2–59–1.

Umpires: Asad Rauf and Ehtsham-ul-Haq.

PAKISTAN v ENGLAND

Second Test Match

At Faisalabad, November 29, 30, December 1, 2, 3. Drawn. Toss: Pakistan. Test debut: Danish Kaneria.

England, who competed resolutely for more than three days and gained a first-innings lead after losing an important toss, ended up needing a watchful, technically superb vigil from Atherton to ensure defeat was avoided. When Hick, his feet apparently frozen, was bowled on the final evening, England were 110 for five with a possible 13 overs remaining. But Atherton, in liaison with White, avoided further mishap.

The likelihood of a draw was increased by the loss of so much playing time. Days were scheduled to be only five and a half hours long, but the prescribed minimum of 83 overs was never completed because of rapidly fading light. Only 382 overs were bowled in a match unaffected by rain – more than two sessions short of the normal Test match allocation of 450. Nobody satisfactorily explained why play could not have started at 9.30 a.m. instead of 10.

There had been reports of two, perhaps even three, different pitches being prepared, from which Pakistan would apparently choose. But when England visited the ground two days before the match, this was exposed as a ruse. There was only one strip and, as in Lahore, the Test would be played on rolled mud. It offered encouragement to the spinners from the start, but again turn was slow and batsmen were able to remain uncommitted to their strokes until the last moment. Conversely, the lack of pace meant some painful moments against quicker bowlers. Saeed Anwar, Shahid Afridi, Trescothick, Atherton and Hussain were all struck, usually because they attempted to hook too early. England were unchanged, but Pakistan shuffled their spinners. Mushtaq Ahmed and Qaiser Abbas were replaced with Danish Kaneria, 19, a leg-spinner making his debut, and off-spinner Arshad Khan. Wasim Akram played his 100th Test match.

England's return to the venue of the bitterest dispute of their 1987-88 tour, where Mike Gatting's row with umpire Shakoor Rana caused a day's play to be lost, was not without further controversy involving the England captain and match officials. Hussain was given out lbw by Steve Bucknor when the television replay clearly showed a thick edge. In the second innings, he was adjudged caught behind off his pad by Mian Aslam, the same umpire who wrongly despatched him in the third one-day international. Hussain's response was stoic. He betrayed barely a flicker of anger or disbelief as he departed but, privately, he was distraught. He later admitted to being in a state of

[Laurence Griffiths, Getty Images

Abdur Razzaq repaid his promotion to No. 3 in Pakistan's second innings at Faisalabad with a maiden Test hundred resplendent with sumptuous off-driving.

"complete bewilderment" at his sequence of poor decisions, which also increased calls for the third umpire to be used for verdicts such as lbw and catches.

After Pakistan elected to bat, Anwar made a run-a-ball fifty before chipping to mid-wicket and becoming the first of five wickets for Giles. The left-arm spinner received some assistance – Inzamam-ul-Haq was bowled when the ball ricocheted off his leg, and Salim Elahi stepped back and slashed recklessly to point – but showed admirable control and patience. When Pakistan were half out for 151, England were making significant inroads. A sixth-wicket stand of 120 between Yousuf Youhana and Moin Khan shifted the advantage, but England were content enough to restrict Pakistan to 316.

Most of England's batsmen became established, yet only Thorpe reached a half-century. His 79 took 323 minutes and he found an ally in Salisbury who, although again wayward with the ball, applied himself for three and a half hours as night-watchman. Hick received universal criticism for pulling a catch to deep square leg the very next ball after Thorpe's departure. A string of powerful blows by White, who twice cleared the boundary, gave England an advantage of 26. They would have been behind but for 32 no-balls.

Pakistan were forced to adjust their second-innings batting order because Anwar was absent with an upset stomach. But, after the excitable Afridi again lost his personal battle with Gough, Elahi, Abdur Razzaq and Inzamam set about establishing a potentially match-winning lead. Elahi was the most aggressive before he fell to a diving catch by Stewart when an attempted sweep bounced off the batsman's gloves. Razzaq, relishing his promotion to No. 3 on his 21st birthday, registered his first Test century, an accomplished innings during which he accelerated only near the end. Inzamam holed out to long-off shortly before Moin's declaration. Salisbury celebrated his first wicket of the series – and only his second for England in more than four years – by ostentatiously kissing the ground.

England were set a nominal target of 244 in 62 overs, but a draw was their only realistic objective. Trescothick was bowled through the gate by Saqlain Mushtaq's "mystery" ball as he drove, whereupon Hussain received his second unfortunate decision of the match. When Thorpe offered no shot to a straight ball, England faced their first mini-emergency. Stewart stayed with Atherton for 23 overs but, after he and Hick departed in rapid succession, there were further flutters. In truth, though, England were always likely to survive while Atherton remained. – JOHN ETHERIDGE.

Man of the Match: Abdur Razzaq.

Close of play: First day, Pakistan 243-5 (Yousuf Youhana 61*, Moin Khan 57*); Second day, England 110-3 (Salisbury 1*, Thorpe 2*); Third day, England 282-8 (White 6*, Caddick 2*); Fourth day, Pakistan 186-2 (Abdur Razzaq 60*, Inzamam-ul-Haq 33*).

Pakistan

Saeed Anwar c Thorpe b Giles	53		
Shahid Afridi c Thorpe b Gough	10	– c Giles b Gough	10
Salim Elahi c Atherton b Giles	41	– (1) c Stewart b Giles	72
Inzamam-ul-Haq b Giles	0	– c Hick b Salisbury	71
Yousuf Youhana c Thorpe b Gough	77		
Abdur Razzaq b White	9	– (3) not out	100
*†Moin Khan c Hussain b Giles	65		
Wasim Akram st Stewart b Giles	1	– (5) not out	4
Saqlain Mushtaq c Trescothick b Gough	34		
Arshad Khan c Thorpe b White	2		
Danish Kaneria not out	8		
B 1, l-b 12, n-b 3	16	B 6, l-b 5, n-b 1	12
1/33 (2) 2/96 (1) 3/96 (4) 4/130 (3) 5/151 (6) 6/271 (5) 7/271 (7) 8/276 (8) 9/283 (10) 10/316 (9)	316	1/13 (2) 2/111 (1) 3/259 (4) (3 wkts dec.)	269

Bowling: *First Innings*—Gough 23.1–2–79–3; Caddick 15–3–49–0; White 25–6–71–2; Giles 35–13–75–5; Salisbury 10–0–29–0. *Second Innings*—Gough 10.2–1–32–1; Caddick 18–1–49–0; Giles 26–3–90–1; White 19–3–55–0; Salisbury 7–0–32–1.

England

M. A. Atherton c Yousuf Youhana b Saqlain Mushtaq	32	– not out	65
M. E. Trescothick st Moin Khan b Danish Kaneria	30	– b Saqlain Mushtaq	10
*N. Hussain lbw b Saqlain Mushtaq	23	– c Moin Khan b Arshad Khan	5
I. D. K. Salisbury c Yousuf Youhana b Arshad Khan	33		
G. P. Thorpe lbw b Wasim Akram	79	– (4) b Arshad Khan	0
†A. J. Stewart c Abdur Razzaq b Danish Kaneria	13	– (5) c Yousuf Youhana b Shahid Afridi	22
G. A. Hick c Yousuf Youhana b Abdur Razzaq	17	– (6) b Shahid Afridi	0
C. White b Saqlain Mushtaq	41	– (7) not out	9
A. F. Giles c Shahid Afridi b Abdur Razzaq	0		
A. R. Caddick c Moin Khan b Abdur Razzaq	5		
D. Gough not out	19		
B 4, l-b 14, n-b 32	50	L-b 4, n-b 10	14
1/49 (2) 2/105 (1) 3/106 (3) 4/203 (4) 5/235 (6) 6/274 (5) 7/274 (7) 8/275 (9) 9/295 (10) 10/342 (8)	342	1/44 (2) 2/57 (3) 3/57 (4) 4/108 (5) 5/110 (6) (5 wkts)	125

Bowling: *First Innings*—Wasim Akram 26–6–69–1; Abdur Razzaq 20–0–74–3; Danish Kaneria 34–9–89–2; Saqlain Mushtaq 30.4–8–62–3; Arshad Khan 25–12–29–1; Shahid Afridi 1–0–1–0. *Second Innings*—Wasim Akram 5–1–13–0; Abdur Razzaq 1–1–0–0; Saqlain Mushtaq 19–4–26–1; Danish Kaneria 7–0–30–0; Arshad Khan 13–4–31–2; Shahid Afridi 12–3–21–2.

Umpires: S. A. Bucknor (West Indies) and Mian Aslam.
Third umpire: Shakeel Khan. Referee: R. S. Madugalle (Sri Lanka).

PAKISTAN v ENGLAND

Third Test Match

At Karachi, December 7, 8, 9, 10, 11. England won by six wickets. Toss: Pakistan.

The pre-tour scripts proved wrong. The predictions went awry and the critics ate their words when, in near darkness, England achieved an extraordinary victory in a compelling climax to the tour. The win gave them their first Test triumph in Pakistan in 39 years and ended their five-series drought against Pakistan (their last series victory was at home in 1982). For Pakistan, it was their maiden defeat at the National Stadium in 35 Tests, after 17 wins and 17 draws. But it was also their fourth successive home series defeat in three seasons.

With failing light always going to be a factor, Pakistan captain Moin Khan adopted desperate delaying tactics, for which he was fiercely criticised, after his side were bundled out for 158 on the final afternoon, leaving England a target of 176 in a minimum of 44 overs. His bowlers took 40 minutes to send down the first seven of these before tea, and almost three and a half hours to bowl a total of 41.3 intense, nail-biting overs. Moin, who was warned for his go-slow strategy by referee Ranjan Madugalle during the tea interval, made three unsuccessful appeals for bad light to umpire Steve Bucknor as Thorpe and Hussain resolutely stood their ground. With victory in sight, but little else, Thorpe edged the winning runs. Some of the Pakistani players thought he had been bowled, until the ball was spotted by a searching fielder.

"The fielders in the deep just couldn't pick the ball. I have never played in such poor conditions," said Moin later, though in truth it was his defensive ploys and limited ideas that allowed England to claw their way back, after losing Atherton, Trescothick and Stewart in the space of 27 runs, with 111 still required from a minimum of 27 overs. "Another five minutes and it would have been complete darkness," said Hussain, who praised Hick and Thorpe for their decisive fourth-wicket stand of 91. Hick, who had failed dismally in his five previous innings, finally played a Test-winning hand with 40. Thorpe remained undefeated on 64, demonstrating to the end the patience and mental toughness that characterised his series.

The two of them had pushed the ball for ones and twos in the big gaps that were freely available. When Waqar Younis, playing his first match of the series, was brought back into the attack in the 37th over, Hick greeted him with a four before being bowled. Waqar had come into the side only 15 minutes before the toss after Wasim Akram mysteriously withdrew with a reported back spasm.

Pakistan's failure to capitalise on the turning pitches was England's gain, especially for left-arm spinner Giles who, on his first senior tour, finished with 17 wickets. His seven here included the key scalp of Inzamam-ul-Haq eight minutes before stumps on the penultimate evening. The ball spun across the batsman out of the bowlers' rough and clipped his off stump. It would prove to be the delivery of the series.

Still, starting the final day with a lead of 88, Pakistan appeared in no immediate danger, although night-watchman Saqlain Mushtaq was soon deceived by Gough's slower ball. Salim Elahi and Yousuf Youhana proceeded to add 50 before both perished in successive overs. Youhana went to hook but gloved White's bouncer to Stewart, and then Elahi was caught at silly point off pad and glove as he pushed forward to Giles. At lunch, six wickets were down and the draw remained the likeliest outcome. But

[*Graham Morris*

England captain Nasser Hussain relishes England's dramatic victory in Karachi's dying moments of daylight.

after the interval, Abdur Razzaq was caught in the gully when the ball bounced off his boot (television replays cast some doubt on whether it had also touched the bat), and, next, Moin hit a full toss to his opposing captain at mid-off. When Waqar was run out after a mix-up and Danish Kaneria fell to Gough's in-swinging yorker, Pakistan's last six wickets had fallen for 30 runs, setting the scene for the final drama.

Yet an England victory had looked a distant prospect on the first two days as Inzamam and Youhana punished the bowlers with flawless, stroke-filled centuries and a fourth-wicket stand of 259. They helped Pakistan post a decent 405, despite a collapse which saw their last seven wickets fall for 82. Inzamam, who when 79 was the first batsman to complete 1,000 Test runs in the calendar year, caned 22 boundaries in his six-hour 142, while Youhana's 117 – his second Test century in three innings – was spiced with 14 fours and a six in 311 minutes.

England's hopes of staying in the match rested on the shoulders of Atherton, who duly obliged with a marathon century. He defied the heat and the bowlers for nine hours 38 minutes to score 125, the cornerstone of his team's 388. In the First Test, he

---

SOME YOU WIN, SOME YOU LOSE

"But really for almost a whole day his [Atherton's] batting made for insufferable viewing. In 9hrs 38mins, in which time one could hear the whole of *Götterdämmerung* twice and still nip out to the pub for last orders, he failed to score off no fewer than 350 balls. It was, in its own way, admirable. It was also stultifying and, one could argue, counter-productive."

Michael Henderson, Daily Telegraph, *December 11, 2000*

had overtaken Hutton (6,971 Test runs); now, he passed Hammond (7,249) to become England's fifth-leading run-maker after Gooch, Gower, Boycott and Cowdrey. Hussain's valuable contribution, 51 in nearly four and a half hours, was his first half-century in 18 Test and 27 first-class innings in 2000. It could not have been more fitting that he was also there at the end to lead his team to glory. – SAMIUL HASAN.

Man of the Match: M. A. Atherton. *Man of the Series:* Yousuf Youhana.

Close of play: First day, Pakistan 292-3 (Inzamam-ul-Haq 123*, Yousuf Youhana 104*); Second day, England 79-1 (Atherton 43*, Hussain 13*); Third day, England 277-4 (Atherton 117*, Hick 12*); Fourth day, Pakistan 71-3 (Salim Elahi 14*, Saqlain Mushtaq 0*).

Pakistan

Saeed Anwar lbw b Gough	8	– c Thorpe b Caddick	21
Imran Nazir c Giles b Trescothick	20	– c Stewart b Gough	4
Salim Elahi b Caddick	28	– c Thorpe b Giles	37
Inzamam-ul-Haq c Trescothick b White	142	– b Giles	27
Yousuf Youhana c and b Giles	117	– (6) c Stewart b White	24
Abdur Razzaq c Hussain b Giles	21	– (7) c Atherton b Giles	1
*†Moin Khan c Hick b Giles	13	– (8) c Hussain b White	14
Shahid Afridi b Giles	10	– (9) not out	15
Saqlain Mushtaq b Gough	16	– (5) lbw b Gough	4
Waqar Younis b Gough	17	– run out	0
Danish Kaneria not out	0	– lbw b Gough	0
B 3, l-b 3, n-b 7	13	B 3, l-b 5, n-b 3	11
1/8 (1) 2/44 (2) 3/64 (3) 4/323 (5) 5/325 (4) 6/340 (7) 7/359 (8) 8/374 (6) 9/402 (9) 10/405 (10)	405	1/24 (2) 2/26 (1) 3/71 (4) 4/78 (5) 5/128 (6) 6/128 (3) 7/139 (7) 8/143 (8) 9/149 (10) 10/158 (11)	158

Bowling: *First Innings*—Gough 27.4–5–82–3; Caddick 23–1–76–1; Trescothick 14–1–34–1; White 22–3–64–1; Salisbury 18–3–49–0; Giles 35–7–94–4. *Second Innings*—Gough 13–4–30–3; Caddick 15–2–40–1; Giles 27–12–38–3; Salisbury 3–0–12–0; White 12–4–30–2.

England

M. A. Atherton c Moin Khan b Abdur Razzaq	125	– c Saeed Anwar b Saqlain Mushtaq	26
M. E. Trescothick c Imran Nazir b Waqar Younis	13	– c Inzamam-ul-Haq b Saqlain Mushtaq	24
*N. Hussain c Inzamam-ul-Haq b Shahid Afridi	51	– (6) not out	6
G. P. Thorpe lbw b Waqar Younis	18	– not out	64
†A. J. Stewart c Yousuf Youhana b Saqlain Mushtaq	29	– (3) c Moin Khan b Saqlain Mushtaq	5
G. A. Hick c Shahid Afridi b Waqar Younis	12	– (5) b Waqar Younis	40
C. White st Moin Khan b Danish Kaneria	35		
A. F. Giles b Waqar Younis	19		
I. D. K. Salisbury not out	20		
A. R. Caddick c Moin Khan b Danish Kaneria	3		
D. Gough c Yousuf Youhana b Saqlain Mushtaq	18		
B 12, l-b 9, n-b 24	45	B 8, l-b 2, w 1	11
1/29 (2) 2/163 (3) 3/195 (4) 4/256 (5) 5/278 (6) 6/309 (1) 7/339 (8) 8/345 (7) 9/349 (10) 10/388 (11)	388	1/38 (1) 2/51 (2) 3/65 (3) 4/156 (5)	(4 wkts) 176

Bowling: *First Innings*—Waqar Younis 36–5–88–4; Abdur Razzaq 28–7–64–1; Shahid Afridi 16–3–34–1; Saqlain Mushtaq 52.1–17–101–2; Danish Kaneria 47–17–80–2. *Second Innings*—Waqar Younis 6–0–27–1; Abdur Razzaq 4–0–17–0; Saqlain Mushtaq 17.3–1–64–3; Danish Kaneria 3–0–18–0; Shahid Afridi 11–1–40–0.

Umpires: S. A. Bucknor (West Indies) and Mohammad Nazir.
Third umpire: Feroze Butt. Referee: R. S. Madugalle (Sri Lanka).

ENGLAND IN SRI LANKA, 2000-01

By HUGH CHEVALLIER

On their first full tour of Sri Lanka, England confirmed their status as the most improved team in Test cricket. While Australia, undisputed masters of the international game, were stumbling to defeat after leading their three-Test series in India, England were striding to success after going behind. It was a clear demonstration of what leadership, conviction and mettle, plus a fair bit of ability, could achieve. By ensuring English heads never bowed, even after their rout at Galle, coach Duncan Fletcher and captain Nasser Hussain could take credit for a fourth consecutive series win. It was almost 22 years since Mike Brearley had led England to a similar run of success. Not that everything went their way after the First Test. At Kandy, dismal umpiring soured the sweet taste of victory, and in the one-day games that ended the trip, Sri Lanka won with embarrassing ease.

Before the tour, observers were unanimous that, on dry, dusty wickets, spin would settle the outcome – and, more specifically, one spinner, Muttiah Muralitharan. The last time these sides had met in a Test, on a dry, dusty wicket at The Oval in 1998, Murali had taken 16 for 220. But now he proved, if not ineffectual, then a shadow of his former destructive self. His strike-rate in home Tests had previously been one victim every 59 balls: in this series it was one every 101. Both Sanath Jayasuriya and Chaminda Vaas took more wickets at roughly half the cost. Murali did not bowl badly, but, after Galle, his colleagues did not provide the weight of runs to bowl against and, as importantly, the tourists developed a strategy to negate his wiles.

As Hussain explained, their method was to "pad him or hit him". Wisely, they did more of the former, the right-handers stepping down the wicket and allowing themselves to be struck outside off stump. There were dangers: if the umpires believed the batsman was making no genuine attempt to play the ball, he risked being lbw. So English bats stayed close behind English pads, and some sort of shot was judged to have been played. There was a chance of the ball brushing bat or glove after the pad, but umpires – even television replays – could rarely be sure, and Murali was thwarted time and again. The Sri Lankans never perfected the stratagem: at Colombo, Russel Arnold took a large pace forward, shouldered arms to Giles and, though hit outside the line, was given out leg-before by umpire Orchard. Matters were simpler still for the English left-handers, since Murali's stock ball pitched outside leg. Some of the Sri Lankan media cried foul at this blunting of the home side's most potent weapon, though the ploy elicited more grudging admiration than accusations of cheating.

Such accusations were apparently traded on the field during the Second Test, when team relations reached their nadir. Their mutual antipathy – traceable to a foul-tempered one-day match at Adelaide in 1998-99 – had been quick to resurface. In the tour opener at Moratuwa, Darren Gough was reported to the Sri Lankan board for abusive language and, at Matara, Ruchira Perera supposedly directed racist invective at Craig White, though some claimed it was simply a misunderstanding deriving from his surname. In the

[*Patrick Eagar*

England players cool off as temperatures rise in Sri Lanka.

First Test, Andrew Caddick and Aravinda de Silva were both warned to mind their behaviour, and, at Kurunegala, Gough tangled with an opposing batsman and wagged his finger at an umpire. So it was no surprise when a string of atrocious decisions in the Second Test sparked further confrontation. Mike Atherton, Jayasuriya and Kumar Sangakkara were reprimanded by referee Hanumant Singh.

Cricket arguably suffered greater damage from the umpires than the players. The umpiring at Galle had been poor, but had no bearing on the result. Kandy was different. The scale of the blunders – in the delicate match situation – might just have affected the result. It proved that the ICC's plan for an elite group of umpires to stand in all Tests could not come soon enough. Neither official had a good game, but local umpire B. C. Cooray had a shocker. Most errors favoured England, and banners appeared telling Cooray his British visa was ready at the High Commission. After England's nail-biting win, there were exaggerated reports of Cooray leaving the ground under armed guard and a mob ransacking his house.

Before the final Test at Colombo, Jayasuriya and Hussain met in an attempt to improve relations. But more important was the performance of the umpires: Dave Orchard enjoyed a satisfactory match, while Asoka de Silva, a former international leg-spinner standing in only his second Test, had an exemplary one. The issue of discipline simply did not arise. Even on the phenomenal third day – when 22 wickets fell for 229 and England triumphed – fuses were never blown.

For England, that heady day – Hussain said, "If it was good in Pakistan, it was twice as good here" – proved the high point of a triumphant winter. Though they must have been aching to leave the enervating heat and humidity (even the local press talked of a heatwave), most had first to negotiate the one-day series. Graham Thorpe took over as captain when Hussain returned home with an injured thigh, and the one-day specialists flew in. Andrew Flintoff briefly looked as if he might be sent back when he arrived with a suspect ankle, which his county, Lancashire, had chosen not to mention; he stayed, but was a marginal figure. In truth, none of the English one-day players had much influence. Sri Lanka greeted three resounding victories as compensation – if not quite revenge – for the Tests.

Thorpe's appointment as one-day captain was apparently a reward for his outstanding achievement during the Tests. He and Marcus Trescothick, England's two left-handers, totalled 517 runs – 39 more than the next four most successful batsmen combined. Only once in six innings did anyone else make England's top score. Not that they fired together. Trescothick averted English humiliation in the First Test with a hundred and a half-century, but did little thereafter, while Thorpe hit his stride only during the second game, when he was instrumental in seeing England home. At Colombo, the strength of his nerve was crucial: on the third and final day, he remained firm as 12 England wickets fell around him for 148.

The left-handers aside, England's batting only fitfully assumed an air of permanence. Ironically, their best opening stands – 83 and 101 – came in the innings defeat at Galle, even if Atherton never properly settled. To the list of his illustrious nemeses, Curtly Ambrose and Glenn McGrath to the fore, was added Vaas. Atherton seemed unable to pick the correct line, and on five occasions out of six Vaas had him leg-before or caught behind. Since his magnificent Pakistan tour, Atherton's footwork had become hesitant, and he ended the series without a fifty. Alec Stewart – rarely at home against spin – did manage one, but his keeping sometimes fell below his usual standards. At Kandy, Hussain finally threw off the shackles of wretched form – his last 12 Tests had brought 244 runs at 13.55 – and to his evident delight hit a century.

England made just one, reluctant, change in three Tests: Fletcher and Hussain had stuck by Graeme Hick through thick and thin, but after Kandy, where he drowned in a sea of self-doubt, the lean patch had become too thin. In came Michael Vaughan, eight years his junior, for the decider. His inclusion looked to the future of English cricket, and he gave Thorpe valuable support. Craig White, having enjoyed a 2000 as glorious as Hussain's was gruesome, continued to prosper as all-rounder; although he did not shine with quite his earlier brilliance, his cool head saw England home in the Second Test.

In Pakistan, the unexpected success of slow-left armer Ashley Giles had masked the inadequacy of Ian Salisbury's leg-spin. In Sri Lanka, however, as Giles lost rhythm and luck – until Colombo – Hussain could confidently turn to his second spinner. The previous summer, Robert Croft, whingeing about his omission from the Tests, had been a peripheral figure, but the celebrated inclusivity of Fletcher and Hussain's man-management claimed another success. Restored to the fold, Croft bowled with control and guile, and his resolute batting bolstered the lower order. He collected nine Test wickets to Giles's seven. But star billing went to Gough. Deservedly named Man of the Series, he consistently found enough pace to discomfit batsmen on largely unhelpful pitches, and in the two victories he claimed 13 wickets at 13.76, averaging a breakthrough every 26 balls. Caddick rediscovered his wicket-taking form with nine at 25.

Running Gough a close second for the series award was Vaas, effectively a one-man Sri Lankan pace attack. In six innings, his fellow-seamers – Dilhara Fernando in two games and Nuwan Zoysa in one – bowled a total of 25 overs for one for 104. Vaas, whose career-best six for 73 at Colombo gave him 16 for the series, became the first Sri Lankan to 100 wickets and 1,000 runs in Tests. Jayasuriya also managed 16 wickets, benefiting from batsmen dropping their guard against a spinner they considered less dangerous than Muralitharan, but he undeniably performed well. As did Murali himself, working tirelessly and without complaint, even when Cooray denied him a clutch of dismissals. But 14 wickets at 30.07 was a disappointing yield for a bowler of his class.

Just as the wickets came from three players, so the runs came from four. Marvan Atapattu began with a majestic undefeated double-hundred, but could barely strike the ball thereafter. It was a cruel turn of the wheel of fortune, though his lot was on the up by the end of the one-day series, when he captained Sri Lanka to their first ten-wicket victory in such games. De Silva also kicked off with a century before hitting more indifferent form. Two of the younger stars in the Sri Lankan firmament proved more consistent. Mahela Jayawardene played beautiful innings in all three Tests, while Sangakkara's 95 at Kandy was all the better for coming in adversity.

Throughout the tour, England spectators matched home supporters in numbers and in volume – and far exceeded them in spending power. There had been significant refurbishment of hotels beforehand, and newspapers frequently mentioned the boost to the Sri Lankan economy from the visitors – estimated at 10,000. Given England's past churlishness in granting Sri Lanka only occasional one-off Tests, it was fitting that the hosts should also benefit from the long-overdue tour.

ENGLAND TOURING PARTY

N. Hussain (Essex) (*captain*), M. A. Atherton (Lancashire), J. F. Brown (Northamptonshire), A. R. Caddick (Somerset), R. D. B. Croft (Glamorgan), A. F. Giles (Warwickshire), D. Gough (Yorkshire), G. A. Hick (Worcestershire), M. J. Hoggard (Yorkshire), P. A. Nixon (Kent), A. J. Stewart (Surrey), G. P. Thorpe (Surrey), M. E. Trescothick (Somerset), M. P. Vaughan (Yorkshire), C. White (Yorkshire).

Hussain flew home injured after the Tests, along with Atherton, Brown, Hoggard and Nixon. The squad for the one-day series was reinforced by M. W. Alleyne (Gloucestershire), M. A. Ealham (Kent), A. Flintoff (Lancashire), N. V. Knight (Warwickshire) and A. D. Mullally (Hampshire). Thorpe was appointed captain of the one-day team.

Manager: P. A. Neale. *Coach:* D. A. G. Fletcher. *Assistant coaches:* R. M. H. Cottam and M. D. Moxon. *Scorer:* M. N. Ashton. *Physiotherapist:* D. O. Conway. *Physiologist:* N. P. Stockill. *Media relations managers:* A. J. Walpole and M. C. K. Hodgson.

ENGLAND TOUR RESULTS

Test matches – Played 3: Won 2, Lost 1.
First-class matches – Played 5: Won 3, Lost 1, Drawn 1.
Wins – Sri Lanka (2), Sri Lankan Board President's XI.
Loss – Sri Lanka.
Draw – Sri Lankan Board President's XI.
One-day internationals – Played 3: Lost 3.
Other non-first-class matches – Played 3: Won 2, Drawn 1. *Wins* – Sri Lankan Colts XI, Sri Lankan Board President's XI. *Draw* – Sri Lankan Colts XI.

TEST MATCH AVERAGES

SRI LANKA – BATTING

	T	*I*	*NO*	*R*	*HS*	*100s*	*50s*	*Avge*	*Ct/St*
M. S. Atapattu	3	5	1	219	201*	1	0	54.75	0
D. P. M. D. Jayawardene	3	5	0	262	101	1	2	52.40	6
K. Sangakkara	3	5	0	215	95	0	2	43.00	12/1
P. A. de Silva	3	5	0	197	106	1	0	39.40	0
R. P. Arnold	3	5	1	88	65	0	1	22.00	2
S. T. Jayasuriya	3	5	0	91	45	0	0	18.20	2
W. P. U. J. C. Vaas	3	5	1	71	36	0	0	17.75	0
T. M. Dilshan	3	4	0	51	36	0	0	12.75	5
M. Muralitharan	3	4	2	18	10*	0	0	9.00	0

Played in two Tests: H. D. P. K. Dharmasena 1, 54; C. R. D. Fernando 2, 5 (1 ct). Played in one Test: D. Hettiarachchi 0, 0*; D. N. T. Zoysa 0, 0.

* *Signifies not out.*

BOWLING

	O	*M*	*R*	*W*	*BB*	*5W/i*	*Avge*
S. T. Jayasuriya	126.4	38	236	16	4-24	0	14.75
W. P. U. J. C. Vaas	110.5	30	244	16	6-73	1	15.25
M. Muralitharan	236	66	421	14	4-66	0	30.07
H. D. P. K. Dharmasena	73	16	171	3	1-21	0	57.00

Also bowled: R. P. Arnold 1–0–2–0; P. A. de Silva 6–3–7–0; C. R. D. Fernando 13–0–53–1; D. Hettiarachchi 27–7–41–2; D. N. T. Zoysa 12–2–51–0.

ENGLAND – BATTING

	T	*I*	*NO*	*R*	*HS*	*100s*	*50s*	*Avge*	*Ct/St*
G. P. Thorpe	3	6	2	269	113*	1	1	67.25	5
M. E. Trescothick	3	6	0	248	122	1	1	41.33	2
A. J. Stewart	3	6	1	117	54	0	1	23.40	4/1
N. Hussain	3	6	0	136	109	1	0	22.66	1
M. A. Atherton	3	6	0	129	44	0	0	21.50	2
R. D. B. Croft	3	5	1	77	33*	0	0	19.25	2
C. White	3	6	1	96	39	0	0	19.20	7
D. Gough	3	4	1	24	14	0	0	8.00	0
G. A. Hick	2	4	0	27	16	0	0	6.75	3
A. F. Giles	3	6	2	15	5	0	0	3.75	2
A. R. Caddick	3	4	0	8	7	0	0	2.00	0

Played in one Test: M. P. Vaughan 26, 8 (2 ct).

* *Signifies not out.*

BOWLING

	O	*M*	*R*	*W*	*BB*	*5W/i*	*Avge*
D. Gough	82	16	274	14	4-50	0	19.57
A. R. Caddick	87.1	24	225	9	4-55	0	25.00
R. D. B. Croft	111	28	258	9	4-56	0	28.66
A. F. Giles	121.1	30	309	7	4-11	0	44.14
C. White	69.1	13	237	4	2-42	0	59.25

Also bowled: G. A. Hick 4–0–8–0.

ENGLAND TOUR AVERAGES – FIRST-CLASS MATCHES

BATTING

	M	*I*	*NO*	*R*	*HS*	*100s*	*50s*	*Avge*	*Ct/St*
G. P. Thorpe	5	9	2	366	113*	1	2	52.28	9
M. E. Trescothick	4	7	0	286	122	1	1	40.85	3
C. White	5	9	2	283	85*	0	2	40.42	8
M. A. Atherton	5	9	0	283	85	0	1	31.44	4
N. Hussain	5	9	0	226	109	1	1	25.11	3
R. D. B. Croft	5	8	3	123	33*	0	0	24.60	4
A. J. Stewart	5	9	1	191	54	0	1	23.87	9/2
M. P. Vaughan	3	5	0	103	57	0	1	20.60	7
G. A. Hick	3	6	0	117	75	0	1	19.50	3
D. Gough	4	6	2	52	22	0	0	13.00	0
A. F. Giles	5	9	2	57	17	0	0	8.14	2
A. R. Caddick	5	6	1	38	26*	0	0	7.60	2

Played in one match: M. J. Hoggard did not bat (1 ct).

* *Signifies not out.*

BOWLING

	O	*M*	*R*	*W*	*BB*	*5W/i*	*Avge*
M. P. Vaughan	20.4	4	57	7	3-25	0	8.14
D. Gough	113	23	360	20	4-47	0	18.00
R. D. B. Croft	177.4	38	473	17	4-56	0	27.82
A. R. Caddick	140.1	38	338	12	4-55	0	28.16
A. F. Giles	184.1	41	521	13	4-11	0	40.07
C. White	106.1	23	356	8	2-32	0	44.50

Also bowled: G. A. Hick 4–0–8–0; M. J. Hoggard 28–9–53–3; M. E. Trescothick 2–0–14–0.

Note: Matches in this section which were not first-class are signified by a dagger.

†At Moratuwa, February 5, 6. Drawn. Toss: Sri Lankan Colts XI. England XI 252 (M. E. Trescothick 100 retired hurt, N. Hussain 38, G. P. Thorpe 32; D. G. R. Dhammika three for 59, K. S. Lokuarachchi three for 39) and 24 for two; Sri Lankan Colts XI 232 for eight dec. (W. M. S. M. Perera 50, J. S. K. Peiris 46, M. Pushpakumara 54; A. R. Caddick three for 33).

SRI LANKAN BOARD PRESIDENT'S XI v ENGLAND XI

At P. Saravanamuttu Stadium, Colombo, February 8, 9, 10, 11. England XI won by 165 runs. Toss: England XI.

Pleased as Hussain would have been at the result, his first-innings 81 – his highest score in any cricket since December 1999 – must have been even more welcome. All the same, England's batting, with only Trescothick missing from the Test line-up, looked fragile. A stand of 113 between Vaughan and White, backed up by a combative last-wicket 46, dragged them to a respectable total. Dilshan then made a persuasive case for Test selection by hitting a gleaming hundred, standing almost alone. Hick was the sole England batsman to pass 50 in the second innings, though Atherton and Thorpe made forties. Left-arm spinner Hettiarachchi had removed all three by the time Hussain declared to leave a target of 326. Gough ripped out three wickets in three overs before Dilshan and Tillekeratne effected a recovery. Giles snuffed it out to hasten a confidence-boosting win.

Close of play: First day, England XI 307-9 (Caddick 21*, Gough 6*); Second day, Sri Lankan Board President's XI 265; Third day, Sri Lankan Board President's XI 20-3 (Dilshan 5*, Tillekeratne 3*).

England XI

M. A. Atherton b de Silva	22	– c Jayawardene b Hettiarachchi	47
*N. Hussain c Jayawardene b Samaraweera	81	– c Jayawardene b Pushpakumara	2
G. P. Thorpe c Jayawardene b de Silva	0	– lbw b Hettiarachchi	40
†A. J. Stewart st Jayawardene b Hettiarachchi	23	– st Jayawardene b Samaraweera	11
G. A. Hick c Mubarak b Samaraweera	15	– c Mendis b Hettiarachchi	75
M. P. Vaughan c Jayawardene b Pushpakumara	57	– c sub (S. Weerakoon) b Samaraweera	0
C. White c Hettiarachchi b Pushpakumara	63	– c de Silva b Samaraweera	39
A. F. Giles c Samaraweera b Pushpakumara	9	– lbw b Hettiarachchi	16
R. D. B. Croft lbw b de Silva	1	– not out	15
A. R. Caddick not out	26	– b Hettiarachchi	4
D. Gough c Mubarak b Hettiarachchi	22	– not out	6
L-b 1, n-b 9	10	B 1, l-b 4, n-b 1	6
1/53 2/53 3/96 4/132 5/153 6/266 7/274 8/279 9/283	329	1/19 2/79 3/102 4/112 5/119 6/182 7/236 8/237 9/250 (9 wkts dec.)	261

Bowling: *First Innings*—Pushpakumara 21–3–88–3; de Silva 19–3–73–3; Hettiarachchi 30.1–8–83–2; Samaraweera 21–1–75–2; Mubarak 2–0–8–0; Tillekeratne 1–0–1–0. *Second Innings*—Pushpakumara 8.1–0–24–1; de Silva 9.5–1–44–0; Hettiarachchi 30–4–84–5; Samaraweera 25.3–6–91–3; Tillekeratne 1–0–9–0; Dilshan 2–1–4–0.

Sri Lankan Board President's XI

J. Mubarak c Caddick b Giles	24	– lbw b Gough	1
*C. Mendis c Stewart b Gough	7	– c Croft b Gough	2
M. G. van Dort c Vaughan b Croft	27	– b Gough	4
T. M. Dilshan c Stewart b Gough	122	– c Atherton b Giles	45
H. P. Tillekeratne c Vaughan b White	9	– c Hussain b Giles	43
L. P. C. Silva lbw b Croft	30	– c Caddick b Giles	0
†H. A. P. W. Jayawardene lbw b Croft	0	– c Atherton b Gough	14
T. T. Samaraweera c Croft b White	21	– b Vaughan	25
K. R. Pushpakumara b Vaughan	7	– c sub (M. E. Trescothick) b Giles	0
W. R. S. de Silva b Vaughan	0	– b Vaughan	10
D. Hettiarachchi not out	0	– not out	1
B 1, l-b 8, n-b 9	18	B 5, l-b 5, n-b 5	15
1/25 2/56 3/89 4/98 5/143 6/143 7/236 8/260 9/265	265	1/1 2/6 3/14 4/72 5/78 6/119 7/128 8/140 9/155	160

Bowling: *First Innings*—Gough 14–2–39–2; Caddick 12–4–30–0; Giles 20–3–69–1; White 13–4–32–2; Croft 19–2–78–3; Vaughan 3.2–1–8–2. *Second Innings*—Caddick 11–2–20–0; Gough 17–5–47–4; Croft 15–4–28–0; Giles 19–8–37–4; White 9–4–15–0; Vaughan 3.2–2–3–2.

Umpires: D. N. Pathirana and G. Silva.

SRI LANKAN BOARD PRESIDENT'S XI v ENGLAND XI

At Matara, February 15, 16, 17, 18. Drawn. Toss: England XI.

Despite a couple of injury scares, England negotiated their way through their final warm-up. Hick withdrew with a calf strain, giving Vaughan another chance to press for a recall. Giles, however, provided the major fright, limping out of the attack on the first day with a sore Achilles tendon. Hoggard had exploited propitious conditions to help reduce the Board President's XI to 24 for four, but the middle order turned the innings round thanks to three half-centuries. Atherton, Thorpe, Stewart and White – whose four innings on tour now totalled 204 – all managed scores, but crucially not Vaughan. He did better as a bowler on the last day, when Dilshan hit his second hundred against the tourists. Had more than two sessions not been lost to the weather, the England spinners, with Giles now restored, should have forced a win.

Close of play: First day, England XI 17-0 (Atherton 4*, Trescothick 11*); Second day, England XI 174-2 (Atherton 74*, Thorpe 34*); Third day, England XI 418-7 (White 85*, Croft 30*).

Sri Lankan Board President's XI

G. R. P. Peiris b Hoggard	6	– c Hussain b Croft	41
D. A. Gunawardene c Thorpe b Caddick	1	– c Trescothick b Caddick	10
*†T. M. Dilshan c Stewart b White	9	– not out	115
J. S. K. Peiris c Stewart b Hoggard	2	– c Vaughan b Croft	18
H. P. Tillekeratne c White b Hoggard	26	– c Stewart b Vaughan	12
H. G. J. M. Kulatunga c Thorpe b Caddick	54	– st Stewart b Giles	0
M. Pushpakumara c Thorpe b Croft	52	– b Vaughan	6
M. R. C. N. Bandaratilleke c Hoggard b Croft	73	– c Thorpe b Vaughan	0
K. A. D. M. Fernando c Vaughan b White	8	– not out	11
C. M. Bandara not out	4		
P. D. R. L. Perera c Vaughan b Croft	0		
B 5, l-b 5, n-b 8	18	B 10, l-b 4, n-b 7	21
1/3 2/20 3/24 4/24 5/84 6/122 7/214 8/247 9/249	253	1/38 2/76 3/139 4/169 5/174 6/190 7/190	(7 wkts) 234

Bowling: *First Innings*—Caddick 19–4–37–2; Hoggard 17–6–28–3; White 14–2–57–2; Giles 5–0–23–0; Croft 16.4–2–63–3; Vaughan 4–1–21–0; Trescothick 2–0–14–0. *Second Innings*—Caddick 11–4–26–1; Hoggard 11–3–25–0; Giles 19–0–83–1; Croft 16–2–46–2; White 1–0–15–0; Vaughan 10–0–25–3.

England XI

M. A. Atherton b Fernando	85
M. E. Trescothick c Pushpakumara b Bandaratilleke	38
*N. Hussain c Fernando b Pushpakumara	7
G. P. Thorpe c and b Bandaratilleke	57
†A. J. Stewart b Bandara	40
M. P. Vaughan c Tillekeratne b Pushpakumara	12
C. White not out	85
A. F. Giles c Bandaratilleke b Bandara	17
R. D. B. Croft not out	30
B 11, l-b 10, n-b 26	47
1/68 2/93 3/191 4/226 5/247 6/310 7/342	(7 wkts dec.) 418

A. R. Caddick and M. J. Hoggard did not bat.

Bowling: Perera 17–1–76–0; Fernando 14–1–59–1; Bandaratilleke 51–11–117–2; Pushpakumara 31–7–69–2; Bandara 47–21–76–2.

Umpires: L. V. Jayasundera and T. H. Wijewardene.

SRI LANKA v ENGLAND

First Test Match

At Galle, February 22, 23, 24, 25, 26. Sri Lanka won by an innings and 28 runs. Toss: Sri Lanka.

In a steaming cauldron of bad temper, Sri Lanka winkled out a browbeaten England to win by an innings soon after lunch on the final day. The game will be remembered for the *nonhomie* between the teams, incompetent umpiring and a broken window in the English dressing-room; referee Hanumant Singh handed down penalties to five players afterwards. It was a sad reflection on a match that coincided with the death of Sir Donald Bradman. Sad too because, between the lines, lurked achievement from Trescothick, dogged persistence from Atapattu, perseverance from England's seam attack and eight wickets for Jayasuriya.

England were fresh(ish) from their series-winning victory ten weeks earlier at Karachi, but Hussain was realistic. "We're a mediocre side that's improved over the last year," he deadpanned, but his luck remained mediocre come the toss: he lost for the eighth time in nine Tests. On the widely predicted dustbowl, there was only one decision for Jayasuriya, especially as Muralitharan, who had strained his groin in New Zealand, was passed fit. England made a single change from Karachi, with Croft coming in for the abandoned Salisbury.

The initial danger seemed to come from Jayasuriya, who blasted off with three peerless fours in 20 minutes. But after he fell, suckered by Gough and nimbly caught by White at gully, the real enemy revealed her hand. The clouds lifted and the heat kicked in, intense, sticky, wearing heat which only intensified. By the end of the day, the bowlers – despite wearing cravats impregnated with ice – had each lost more than three kilograms. Atapattu didn't make it any easier: with judicious stroke after judicious

[*Patrick Eagar*

Marcus Trescothick's first Test hundred, followed by his second-innings half-century, gave England's supporters something to be cheerful about in the heavy defeat at Galle.

stroke he ground England down. The entertainment came largely from 23-year-old batsman/keeper Sangakkara and from de Silva, who sparkled at the other end.

Atapattu soldiered on through the second morning and afternoon, first adding 230 with de Silva, then 111 with the energetic Jayawardene. White and Gough, drained but resourceful, resorted to off-cutters. Eventually, Atapattu became the ninth batsman to hit four Test double-hundreds, completing 200 in 674 minutes, the third-slowest double-century in Tests after fellow-Sri Lankan Brendon Kuruppu (777 minutes against New Zealand in 1986-87) and Gary Kirsten (741 minutes for South Africa against England in 1999-2000); only Kuruppu had taken more balls to reach the landmark, with 548 to Atapattu's 529. His entire vigil lasted 11 hours 21 minutes and 534 balls, including 18 fours. Shortly afterwards, Atherton and Trescothick trekked out to face the new ball, taken by an irrepressibly grinning Muralitharan and watched by a bevy of close fielders.

MOST DOUBLE-HUNDREDS IN TEST CRICKET

	Total	*v E*	*A*	*SA*	*WI*	*NZ*	*I*	*P*	*SL*	*Z*
D. G. Bradman (A) . . .	12	8	–	2	1	–	1	–	–	–
W. R. Hammond (E) . .	7	–	4	0	0	2	1	–	–	–
Javed Miandad (P) . . .	6	1	1	–	0	2	1	–	1	0
M. S. Atapattu (SL) . .	**4**	**1**	**0**	**0**	**0**	**0**	**0**	**1**	**–**	**2**
G. S. Chappell (A) . . .	4	0	–	–	0	1	1	2	0	–
S. M. Gavaskar (I) . . .	4	1	0	–	3	0	–	0	0	–
C. G. Greenidge (WI) .	4	2	1	–	–	1	0	0	–	–
L. Hutton (E).	4	–	1	0	2	1	0	0	–	–
Zaheer Abbas (P)	4	2	0	–	0	0	2	–	0	–

Note: In September 2001, Atapattu made a fifth double-hundred, against Bangladesh at Colombo (SSC). On the same ground, two months later, B. C. Lara (WI) made a fourth double-hundred, against Sri Lanka.

It was only Trescothick's seventh Test, but he played with the ease of a man with deep reservoirs of confidence. He was beaten by Murali more than once, but he just carried on, sweeping him when he could – he was the one English batsman to hit him over the boundary – and, to the admiration of the Sri Lankans, getting right forward to smother the spin. His first Test century was only his eighth in first-class cricket, and his opening partner, Atherton, said "he made the rest of us look like fools". England's five other specialist batsmen managed just 67, though Stewart, lbw to a ball that pitched outside leg stump, and Hick, caught by Sangakkara off one he never hit, were unlucky. The visibly disgruntled Hick later received a suspended one-match ban. Trescothick fell in the second over of the fourth day, and was back at the crease barely 45 minutes later after England had lost five for 47, disorientated by sharp Sri Lankan fielding, bowling and squawking.

The heavy roller looked as if it might have made batting a little easier as Atherton and Trescothick fought their way to a century opening stand – England's first against Sri Lanka. But Trescothick's concentration lapsed at last after tea and, 18 minutes later, Hussain's unerring ability to attract controversial decisions condemned him to another single-figure score. When Atherton was out early on the final day, to a catch that even in slow-motion replay was dubious, England seemed to lose confidence in themselves and faith in the umpires. Only Thorpe and Stewart made it into double figures as Murali and Jayasuriya spun an intricate web; this time England lost eight for 68. One down, with two to play, they needed to find ways both to play spin and to stop Sri Lanka getting under their skin.

The umpires must have been as glad to slink away as the England players. Men of inexperience – eight Tests apiece – they wilted under pressure, but 150 coachloads of baying English fans, egged on by televisions in the stands, cannot have helped. England were convinced that at least seven decisions went against them – hence the damage to the dressing-room window – but Sri Lanka could also point to the number of lbw shouts turned down. Muralitharan, Jayawardene, Arnold and Sangakkara were each fined 25 per cent of their match fees for rushing at the umpires.

Another aggrieved team was the one from BBC radio. They were banned from the ground on the second morning after a quarrel over media rights, and forced to broadcast, shaded by vast golfing umbrellas, from the ramparts of the 17th-century Dutch fort overlooking the stadium. An agreement let them back into the grounds for the remainder of the tour. – TANYA ALDRED.

Man of the Match: M. S. Atapattu.

Close of play: First day, Sri Lanka 221-2 (Atapattu 85*, de Silva 56*); Second day, England 27-0 (Atherton 12*, Trescothick 11*); Third day, England 202-4 (Trescothick 119*, Croft 0*); Fourth day, England 118-2 (Atherton 44*, Thorpe 2*).

Sri Lanka

M. S. Atapattu not out	201
*S. T. Jayasuriya c White b Gough	14
†K. Sangakkara c White b Croft	58
P. A. de Silva run out	106
D. P. M. D. Jayawardene run out	61
W. P. U. J. C. Vaas c White b Giles	8
R. P. Arnold not out	1
B 9, l-b 2, n-b 10	21
1/18 (2) 2/110 (3) 3/340 (4) 4/451 (5) 5/468 (6) (5 wkts dec.)	470

T. M. Dilshan, H. D. P. K. Dharmasena, C. R. D. Fernando and M. Muralitharan did not bat.

Bowling: Gough 26–3–95–1; Caddick 30–13–46–0; White 30–6–80–0; Giles 48–8–134–1; Croft 32–6–96–1; Hick 4–0–8–0.

England

M. A. Atherton lbw b Vaas	33	– c Sangakkara b Vaas	44
M. E. Trescothick c Sangakkara b Vaas	122	– c Sangakkara b Jayasuriya	57
*N. Hussain lbw b Muralitharan	3	– lbw b Muralitharan	1
G. P. Thorpe c Dilshan b Muralitharan	7	– lbw b Dharmasena	12
†A. J. Stewart lbw b Jayasuriya	19	– not out	34
R. D. B. Croft c Jayawardene b Jayasuriya	9	– (10) lbw b Jayasuriya	2
G. A. Hick c Sangakkara b Vaas	5	– (6) c Jayawardene b Jayasuriya	6
C. White c Sangakkara b Jayasuriya	25	– (7) lbw b Muralitharan	3
A. F. Giles c Dilshan b Muralitharan	4	– lbw b Muralitharan	1
A. R. Caddick c Jayawardene b Jayasuriya	0	– (8) b Jayasuriya	1
D. Gough not out	0	– b Muralitharan	0
B 2, l-b 3, n-b 21	26	B 11, l-b 6, n-b 11	28
1/83 (1) 2/93 (3) 3/117 (4) 4/197 (5) 5/206 (2) 6/217 (7) 7/239 (6) 8/253 (8) 9/253 (10) 10/253 (9)	253	1/101 (2) 2/105 (3) 3/121 (1) 4/145 (4) 5/167 (6) 6/176 (7) 7/182 (8) 8/183 (9) 9/188 (10) 10/189 (11)	189

Bowling: *First Innings*—Vaas 24–7–53–3; Muralitharan 54.3–14–79–3; Dharmasena 22–6–51–0; Fernando 2–0–10–0; Jayasuriya 27–7–50–4; de Silva 3–2–5–0. *Second Innings*—Vaas 15–6–29–1; Fernando 4–0–10–0; Jayasuriya 32–13–44–4; Dharmasena 16–6–21–1; Muralitharan 42.3–14–66–4; Arnold 1–0–2–0.

Umpires: A. V. Jayaprakash (India) and P. T. Manuel.
Third umpire: E. A. R. de Silva. Referee: Hanumant Singh (India).

†At Kurunegala, March 3. England XI won by eight wickets. Toss: England XI. Sri Lankan Colts XI 249 for seven (50 overs) (R. S. Kaluwitharana 37, S. K. L. de Silva 49, S. I. de Saram 62; C. White four for 37); England XI 250 for two (43.4 overs) (M. E. Trescothick 85, N. Hussain 73, G. A. Hick 38 not out, G. P. Thorpe 32 not out).

The game was changed from a three-day fixture at the request of the England management because of the travelling involved. Trescothick scored 85 in 68 balls, with 13 fours.

SRI LANKA v ENGLAND

Second Test Match

At Kandy, March 7, 8, 9, 10, 11. England won by three wickets. Toss: Sri Lanka.

This was a bruising, bar-room brawl of a Test, the type that, pre-Fletcher, England would not have won. But with a now-habitual steel, win it they did, squaring the series. In several respects, Kandy was a classic. Thanks to an exemplary pitch that encouraged strokeplay, rewarded seam and took spin – yet never broke up as predicted – the initiative was batted back and forth like a ping-pong ball. And the drama unfolded against a backdrop of hazy blue mountains, fringed with palm and flame trees.

Undermining it all, however, was more lamentable umpiring. By some counts there were 15 errors, and tempers inevitably boiled over, coming to a head on the explosive third day – ironically a *poya* day, or "day of peace" for the predominantly Buddhist population. Referee Hanumant Singh issued severe reprimands to Atherton and Sangakkara, as well as fining Jayasuriya 60 per cent of his match fee for dissent and adding a suspended ban of two Tests and two one-day internationals. Both umpires had dreadful games, and most errors favoured England. Home official B. C. Cooray was especially vilified: "BC Bats for England" ran one local headline.

On the first morning, Sri Lanka sped to 69 for two in 16 overs, de Silva and Sangakkara repairing early damage. Then White's third delivery induced two errors: first Sangakkara took his eye off the ball and deflected it, via his elbow, to gully, whereupon Koertzen gave him out. Ostentatious rubbing of his forearm earned Sangakkara his first reproof. Soon afterwards, White removed de Silva, and a precarious 80 for four would have become a teetering 80 for five had Trescothick, at gully, not dropped Arnold.

Sri Lanka lunched at 93 for four but took tea 123 sparkling runs on, the innings turned round by Jayawardene. Soon afterwards he completed a chanceless fifth Test century, bristling with confident pulls and cuts, then was out, mishooking Caddick. Arnold, let off by umpiring errors on 41 and 44, and Dilshan added another 56 before Gough and Caddick took the new ball. Its effect was devastating and immediate: the last five wickets clattered for 20 runs.

England spirits took a dent next morning, though, with both openers gone by 37. Fourteen months earlier, Cooray had started a nightmare run of form for Hussain when he interpreted an edged four as lbw. Now he helped to end it. Hussain and Thorpe played superbly, adding 167 (an all-wicket England record against Sri Lanka), but there was little doubt that Muralitharan twice had Hussain caught off pad and bat, on 53 and 62. Not so, ruled Cooray, provoking the fielders to fury. Hussain exploited his fortune to hit a courageous, morale-boosting hundred. By the close, though, he and Thorpe had gone, together with the feckless Hick. Twice reprieved by Cooray in 11 balls, Hick seemed determined to make a duck and did.

The third day began in familiar fashion: Stewart, not given out when he should have been, was later given out when he shouldn't. He, White and the tail steered the lead to 90. And then the match ignited, fuelled by a volatile mixture of execrable umpiring, irritating tail-end resistance and inspired new-ball bowling. Atapattu had already gone in Gough's first over when Caddick steamed in from the Buddhist Research Institute end, Jayasuriya flashed and Thorpe held a phenomenal airborne catch at third slip. Trouble was the batsman, unseen by Cooray, had hit the ball hard into the ground. The injustice of two for two was too much for Jayasuriya, who dashed his helmet to the ground as he left the field. Moments later, de Silva gloved to gully: 13 balls, three runs, three wickets. As the crowd struggled to catch breath, Atherton and Sangakkara clashed, Atherton wagging his finger first at the batsman, then seemingly at Koertzen. Order was somehow restored, but not to Sri Lanka's innings, which became a frenzy of coruscating boundaries and tumbling wickets. By the close, Croft, with his best Test

[*Patrick Eagar*

Darren Gough, England's Kandy man, strikes again, dismissing Galle double-centurion Marvan Atapattu for the second time in the match.

spell in years, helped ensure Sri Lanka were effectively eight for six. The match, surely, would be England's next morning.

But one player transmuted anger into gold. Leading a magnificent fightback, Sangakkara, aided by Dharmasena, punished anything loose. Though he should have been stumped the previous evening when 34, he played quite beautifully. Just before lunch, a precious maiden Test hundred was in sight. The lead was 91, and an unlikely home victory was beginning to take shape. Croft and Hussain, however, saw their chance. The captain pushed back the fielder at mid-on; the bowler tossed the ball up; Sangakkara went for glory and the initiative was back with England. Even so, the recovery continued into the afternoon before the new ball worked its magic again. Gough finished with eight wickets in the match.

England needed a tricky 161. In his fourth over, Vaas removed Atherton (for the fourth time) and Trescothick, before Hussain and Thorpe put on a nerve-steadying 61. Yet both were gone by stumps, leaving the last day exquisitely poised: 70 runs or six wickets for victory.

England probably had the edge if the tail was not exposed to Murali too soon. Stewart went early, handing Hick perhaps a final chance to rekindle the dying embers of a tortured Test career. The flame flickered briefly as a couple of balls sped to the boundary, then quietly, sadly went out. Wickets and runs came at perfect intervals to keep both teams' hopes alive, but Croft, White and then Giles kept admirably cool heads to weather the final storm.

Man of the Match: D. Gough.

Close of play: First day, England 1-0 (Atherton 0*, Trescothick 1*); Second day, England 249-5 (Stewart 16*, White 6*); Third day, Sri Lanka 98-6 (Sangakkara 47*, Dharmasena 1*); Fourth day, England 91-4 (Stewart 2*, Croft 1*).

Sri Lanka

M. S. Atapattu b Gough	16	– c Stewart b Gough	2
*S. T. Jayasuriya c Giles b Caddick	9	– c Thorpe b Caddick	0
†K. Sangakkara c Trescothick b White	17	– st Stewart b Croft	95
P. A. de Silva c and b White	29	– c White b Gough	1
D. P. M. D. Jayawardene c Thorpe b Caddick	101	– b White	18
R. P. Arnold c White b Gough	65	– lbw b Croft	22
T. M. Dilshan c Atherton b Gough	36	– c Hick b Croft	0
H. D. P. K. Dharmasena c Thorpe b Gough	1	– c Hick b Gough	54
W. P. U. J. C. Vaas c Thorpe b Caddick	2	– c Croft b White	36
D. N. T. Zoysa c Stewart b Caddick	0	– c Hick b Gough	0
M. Muralitharan not out	10	– not out	6
B 1, l-b 3, n-b 7	11	B 2, l-b 3, n-b 11	16
1/21 (1) 2/29 (2) 3/69 (3) 4/80 (4) 5/221 (5) 6/277 (6) 7/279 (8) 8/282 (9) 9/286 (7) 10/297 (10)	297	1/2 (1) 2/2 (2) 3/3 (4) 4/42 (5) 5/81 (6) 6/88 (7) 7/181 (3) 8/234 (8) 9/242 (10) 10/250 (9)	250

Bowling: *First Innings*—Gough 14–1–73–4; Caddick 20–3–55–4; Giles 15–2–47–0; White 17–3–70–2; Croft 20–2–48–0. *Second Innings*—Gough 22–6–50–4; Caddick 18–5–55–1; White 12.1–3–42–2; Croft 22–11–40–3; Giles 15–3–58–0.

England

M. A. Atherton lbw b Vaas	7	– c Sangakkara b Vaas	11
M. E. Trescothick c Sangakkara b Dharmasena	23	– lbw b Vaas	13
*N. Hussain b Muralitharan	109	– c Sangakkara b Vaas	15
G. P. Thorpe c Dilshan b Jayasuriya	59	– c Sangakkara b Muralitharan	46
†A. J. Stewart c Dilshan b Jayasuriya	54	– lbw b Vaas	7
G. A. Hick lbw b Muralitharan	0	– (7) b Jayasuriya	16
C. White st Sangakkara b Jayasuriya	39	– (8) not out	21
A. F. Giles b Muralitharan	5	– (9) not out	4
R. D. B. Croft not out	33	– (6) lbw b Dharmasena	17
A. R. Caddick b Muralitharan	7		
D. Gough lbw b Vaas	10		
B 16, l-b 20, w 1, n-b 4	41	B 1, l-b 8, n-b 2	11
1/16 (1) 2/37 (2) 3/204 (4) 4/232 (3) 5/236 (6) 6/323 (7) 7/330 (5) 8/336 (8) 9/346 (10) 10/387 (11)	387	1/24 (1) 2/25 (2) 3/86 (4) 4/89 (3) 5/97 (5) 6/122 (7) 7/142 (6)	(7 wkts) 161

Bowling: *First Innings*—Vaas 23–7–39–2; Zoysa 10–2–35–0; Muralitharan 63–21–127–4; Dharmasena 27–4–74–1; Jayasuriya 34–11–76–3. *Second Innings*—Vaas 18–4–39–4; Zoysa 2–0–16–0; Dharmasena 8–0–25–1; Muralitharan 27–7–50–1; Jayasuriya 16.1–6–22–1.

Umpires: R. E. Koertzen (South Africa) and B. C. Cooray.
Third umpire: P. T. Manuel. Referee: Hanumant Singh (India).

SRI LANKA v ENGLAND

Third Test Match

At Sinhalese Sports Club, Colombo, March 15, 16, 17. England won by four wickets. Toss: Sri Lanka. Test debut: D. Hettiarachchi.

Hard on the heels of Kandy's five-day classic came a three-day thriller at Colombo. On an astounding third day, 22 wickets fell for 229 runs – including ten Sri Lankans for 81 – to give England the series 2–1. True, they made a meal of hitting the required

74, but after losing the First Test by an innings it was a magnificent recovery. It wasn't just the Sri Lankans they overcame; the sun beat down remorselessly, and Thorpe said he had never played in such draining conditions. To widespread relief, the umpiring was of a high standard, and local official Asoka de Silva drew universal praise. With better umpiring came better behaviour, and the referee was invisible.

The case for Hick's replacement by Vaughan was now irresistible. Sri Lanka, meanwhile, recalled Fernando for Zoysa, and dropped Dharmasena, who had batted memorably but bowled forgettably. In came debutant Dinuka Hettiarachchi, whose left-arm spin had troubled England early on the tour. For the third time running – and the 17th in 21 Tests as captain – Jayasuriya won the toss. With the ball inevitably turning more as the game wore on, it made England's achievement the more outstanding.

In the second over, Caddick removed Atapattu with a beauty that pitched on leg and hit middle and off – Sri Lanka's sole setback of the morning, as Sangakkara played pace and spin with assured technique. Immediately after lunch, Gough struck him with a bouncer, then had him recoiling from a vicious, rising delivery; unnerved, Sangakkara spooned the next to cover. Jayasuriya quickly followed, but steady batting from de Silva and Jayawardene raised 200 halfway through the evening session.

Umpire Orchard may have erred in giving de Silva out – replays could not determine whether the ball brushed bat *en route* to silly mid-off – but here such controversies were the exception. The subsequent flurry of wickets renewed English hearts after a sweltering day in the field. By the close, Arnold had exited, offering no shot to Giles, and Croft had removed Dilshan and Jayawardene, whose elegant 71 featured several sweet shots off his legs. Next morning, Croft claimed a fourth victim before the new ball accounted for the tail, Caddick collecting his 150th Test wicket. Sri Lanka lost their last seven for 36.

Atherton walloped three fours in Vaas's second over, but the lbw Vaas later won was more typical of their contest in this series: six innings, five dismissals. Trescothick then provided Hettiarachchi's first Test wicket in bizarre circumstances. As he cracked

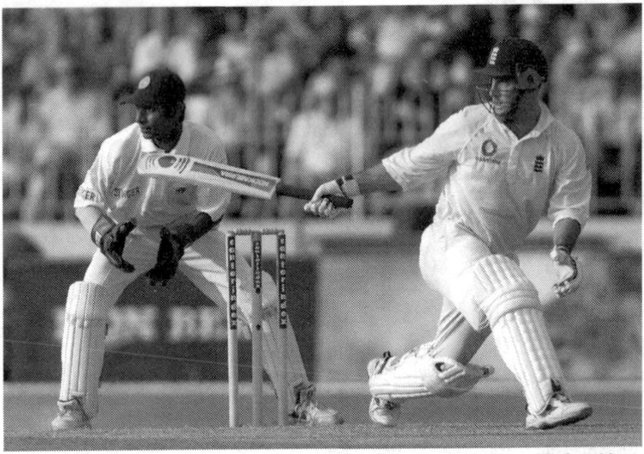

[*Graham Morris*

With scores of 113 and 32, both not out, Man of the Match Graham Thorpe held England's batting together virtually single-handed in the decisive Colombo Test.

a ball to leg, everyone followed the trajectory toward the boundary, only to discover it had lodged in the billowing material of Arnold's loose-fitting shirt at short leg. Hussain's was a brief, unhappy innings. After exacerbating a thigh injury he had picked up fielding – it ruled him out of the one-day series – he became Hettiarachchi's second victim, and England were 66 for three.

In the final session, Thorpe and Vaughan, playing his first innings for a month, advanced to 175 – 66 behind with six wickets intact – displaying stamina, patience and concentration, especially against Muralitharan's extravagant turn. A wet patch on the wicket caused a half-hour delay next morning, and in the chatter that whiled away the time, some considered a draw the likely outcome. No one thought the game would finish that evening.

Vaas quickly set the tone for the day, cajoling Vaughan and White to nibble at successive wide deliveries. Giles just averted the hat-trick, but went in near-identical fashion, giving Vaas three for one from 16 balls; he ended with a career-best six for 73. England's poor morning would have turned calamitous had Orchard noticed Thorpe

11 DUCKS IN A TEST MATCH

Australia (4) v England (7) at Melbourne	1903-04
South Africa (5*) v England (6) at Johannesburg	1913-14
India (6*) v Australia (5) at Madras	1964-65
West Indies (6) v England (5*) at Georgetown	1997-98
West Indies (6*) v Australia (5) at Port-of-Spain	1998-99
West Indies (4*) v Zimbabwe (7*) at Port-of-Spain	1999-2000
Sri Lanka (6*) v England (5) at Colombo (SSC)	**2000-01**

* *One batsman was also 0 not out.*

Research: Gordon Vince

edge Murali to silly point via his pad. Thorpe also ran out Croft for a solid 16 but, those errors aside, his eighth Test hundred was an innings of great maturity. It confirmed his arrival as a world-class batsman, as prepared to counter-attack as dig in, composed against spin or pace.

England's day had begun as it would end: with 74 runs for six wickets. They led by eight but, with the pitch offering increasing spin and bounce, Sri Lanka were better placed. Or so it seemed. Fortunes were about to change in startling fashion. Bowling with guile and aggression, Gough and Caddick made quick, deep cuts. Atapattu began the series with a double-hundred; he finished with a double duck. Sangakkara and Jayasuriya soon followed. De Silva, having pulled Caddick for two fours off three deliveries, went for a third, was deceived by his rare slower ball and caught at square leg. The middle order caved in and, shortly after tea, Muralitharan, declining to take guard, was lbw attempting an audacious reverse sweep. In just 28.1 overs, Sri Lanka were out for 81, their second-lowest Test total. England, who had not dismissed a team for less than 100 in 20 years, had now done so four times in ten months. Giles had rediscovered his Pakistan form, while Croft confounded critics with an extended spell of flighted, varied off-spin. Their combined match figures were 11 for 144.

Still the third day had more to offer. On a wearing pitch, England got into a muddle chasing 74. Atherton finally survived Vaas, only to succumb to Fernando. At 43 for four, Sri Lanka had prised open an escape hatch. Thorpe slammed it shut with an undefeated 32, but not before Hussain, batting at No. 7 with a runner, became the final victim of the St Patrick's Day massacre. He was the eighth and last duck of the day, a record-equalling 11th for the match. "Bring on the Aussies!" sang the Barmy Army.

Man of the Match: G. P. Thorpe. *Man of the Series:* D. Gough.

Close of play: First day, Sri Lanka 221-7 (Vaas 2*, Fernando 0*); Second day, England 175-4 (Thorpe 71*, Vaughan 26*).

Sri Lanka

M. S. Atapattu b Caddick	0	– c Croft b Gough	0
*S. T. Jayasuriya c White b Croft	45	– lbw b Gough	23
†K. Sangakkara c Vaughan b Gough	45	– c Stewart b Caddick	0
P. A. de Silva c Vaughan b Giles	38	– c Thorpe b Caddick	23
D. P. M. D. Jayawardene c Stewart b Croft	71	– lbw b Giles	11
R. P. Arnold lbw b Giles	0	– c Hussain b Croft	0
T. M. Dilshan lbw b Croft	5	– b Giles	10
W. P. U. J. C. Vaas not out	19	– c Atherton b Giles	6
C. R. D. Fernando c Trescothick b Croft	2	– c Giles b Gough	5
D. Hettiarachchi b Gough	0	– not out	0
M. Muralitharan b Caddick	1	– lbw b Giles	1
B 4, l-b 4, w 1, n-b 6	15	N-b 2	2
1/2 (1) 2/88 (3) 3/108 (2) 4/205 (4) 5/209 (6) 6/216 (7) 7/219 (5) 8/225 (9) 9/240 (10) 10/241 (11)	241	1/21 (1) 2/24 (3) 3/24 (2) 4/57 (4) 5/59 (6) 6/59 (5) 7/69 (8) 8/76 (7) 9/80 (9) 10/81 (11)	81

Bowling: *First Innings*—Gough 14–5–33–2; Caddick 11.1–1–40–2; White 10–1–45–0; Giles 34–13–59–2; Croft 32–9–56–4. *Second Innings*—Gough 6–1–23–3; Caddick 8–2–29–2; Giles 9.1–4–11–4; Croft 5–0–18–1.

England

M. A. Atherton lbw b Vaas	21	– c and b Fernando	13
M. E. Trescothick c Arnold b Hettiarachchi	23	– c Sangakkara b Jayasuriya	10
*N. Hussain c Jayasuriya b Hettiarachchi	8	– (7) c Arnold b Jayasuriya	0
G. P. Thorpe not out	113	– not out	32
†A. J. Stewart b Muralitharan	3	– c Dilshan b Jayasuriya	0
M. P. Vaughan c Sangakkara b Vaas	26	– (3) b Muralitharan	8
C. White c Sangakkara b Vaas	0	– (6) c Jayawardene b Jayasuriya	8
A. F. Giles c Jayawardene b Vaas	0	– not out	1
R. D. B. Croft run out	16		
A. R. Caddick c Jayasuriya b Vaas	0		
D. Gough c Jayawardene b Vaas	14		
B 10, l-b 9, n-b 6	25	L-b 1, n-b 1	2
1/45 (1) 2/55 (2) 3/66 (3) 4/91 (5) 5/177 (6) 6/177 (7) 7/181 (8) 8/209 (9) 9/223 (10) 10/249 (11)	249	1/23 (1) 2/24 (2) 3/42 (3) 4/43 (5) 5/63 (6) 6/71 (7)	(6 wkts) 74

Bowling: *First Innings*—Vaas 27.5–6–73–6; Fernando 5–0–26–0; de Silva 3–1–2–0; Muralitharan 41–9–73–1; Hettiarachchi 24–6–36–2; Jayasuriya 9–1–20–0. *Second Innings*—Vaas 3–0–11–0; Hettiarachchi 3–1–5–0; Muralitharan 8–1–26–1; Fernando 2–0–7–1; Jayasuriya 8.3–0–24–4.

Umpires: D. L. Orchard (South Africa) and E. A. R. de Silva.
Third umpire: B. C. Cooray. Referee: Hanumant Singh (India).

†At Maitland Crescent (CCC), Colombo, March 21. England XI won by 51 runs. Toss: England XI. England XI 279 (47.4 overs) (M. P. Vaughan 97, G. A. Hick 100 retired out; W. C. A. Ganegama four for 33); Sri Lankan Board President's XI 228 for nine (50 overs) (S. I. de Saram 32, R. P. Arnold 62, T. T. Samaraweera 51 not out, Extras 36; A. R. Caddick five for 31).

Caddick took a hat-trick, all bowled.

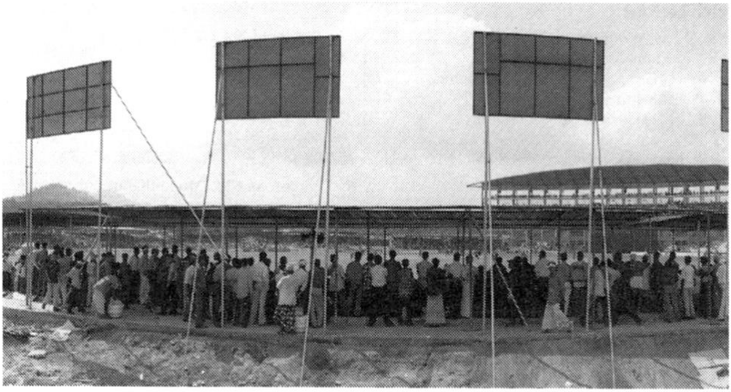

Phenomenal achievement or recipe for disaster? Dambulla's Rangiri stadium may not have been up to the mark for the many who came to watch the town's first one-day international – but six months earlier it was nothing more than a plot and an ambition.

†SRI LANKA v ENGLAND

First One-Day International

At Dambulla, March 23. Sri Lanka won by five wickets. Toss: England.

Six months earlier, the small town of Dambulla had no stadium; four weeks before the game, an army of women were planting grass seedlings by hand. There was plenty wrong with the Rangiri stadium – sheer drops had inadequate or non-existent barriers, hastily constructed stands were already crumbling, plate glass was secured with sticky tape – and it was hardly ready for thousands of spectators, many admitted free to enliven the occasion. Opinion differed as to whether bringing international cricket here, to exploit Dambulla's dry climate, was a phenomenal achievement or unmitigated folly. The vistas of lakes and mountains were glorious; the same could not be said of the inaugural match. A dour affair on a painfully slow pitch was leavened by Muralitharan's high-class off-spin and Jayasuriya's lightning 35-ball 39. Thorpe, maintaining the form that earned him the England captaincy after Hussain's injury, batted with a determination alien to his colleagues and ended undefeated on 62. The openers were the only others in double figures in a weary, end-of-tour display. In reply, Jayasuriya had just seen 50 up in the tenth over when he was – perhaps harshly – given lbw. Sri Lanka lost momentum, stumbling to 58 for four, but Atapattu and Arnold put them back on course.

Man of the Match: M. Muralitharan.

England

M. E. Trescothick b Arnold	26
†A. J. Stewart b Zoysa	21
G. A. Hick c Dharmasena b Zoysa	2
*G. P. Thorpe not out	62
M. P. Vaughan st Kaluwitharana b Muralitharan	9
A. Flintoff st Kaluwitharana b Muralitharan	2
C. White c de Saram b Muralitharan	0
A. F. Giles run out	7
A. R. Caddick c Muralitharan b Jayasuriya	0
D. Gough c Kaluwitharana b Vaas	4
A. D. Mullally lbw b Muralitharan	0
L-b 4, w 4, n-b 2	10
1/31 (2) 2/35 (3) 3/75 (1) 4/92 (5) 5/97 (6) 6/97 (7) 7/113 (8) 8/118 (9) 9/131 (10) 10/143 (11) (48.5 overs)	143

Score at 15 overs: 52-2

Bowling: Vaas 9–1–26–1; Zoysa 7–0–22–2; Dharmasena 9–1–18–0; Arnold 7–0–21–1; Muralitharan 9.5–1–29–4; Jayasuriya 7–0–23–1.

Sri Lanka

*S. T. Jayasuriya lbw b Mullally	39	R. P. Arnold not out	39
†R. S. Kaluwitharana c Stewart b Caddick	2	S. I. de Saram not out	6
M. S. Atapattu lbw b White	40	L-b 8, w 1, n-b 5	14
D. P. M. D. Jayawardene c Stewart b Gough	3	1/31 (2) 2/50 (1) 3/54 (4) 4/58 (5) 5/128 (3)	(5 wkts, 40.5 overs) 144
K. Sangakkara c Stewart b Caddick	1		Score at 15 overs: 58-3

H. D. P. K. Dharmasena, W. P. U. J. C. Vaas, D. N. T. Zoysa and M. Muralitharan did not bat.

Bowling: Caddick 8–1–42–2; Gough 10–2–24–1; Mullally 8–1–23–1; White 8–2–17–1; Giles 5–0–21–0; Vaughan 1–0–3–0; Hick 0.5–0–6–0.

Umpires: E. A. R. de Silva and L. V. Jayasundera.
Third umpire: T. H. Wijewardene.

†SRI LANKA v ENGLAND

Second One-Day International

At R. Premadasa Stadium, Colombo, March 25 (day/night). Sri Lanka won by 66 runs. Toss: Sri Lanka.

England's away form in floodlit matches was atrocious – they had won just three of their last 18 – and few believed a jaded side would improve that record in sauna-like conditions. Yet they began brightly, Gough inducing Jayasuriya to drag the second ball on to his stumps, and Mullally deceiving Kaluwitharana with a slower delivery. By the time the third wicket fell, however, Atapattu and Jayawardene had added 86. Although Jayawardene needed a runner after injuring his leg five overs from the end – those five overs yielded 46 – he reached a chanceless hundred off the final ball. England's batting never found any rhythm: Trescothick's poor run continued and, when four wickets – including the in-form Thorpe – had gone for 88, everything rested on Stewart. He compiled a steady fifty, but could not reduce the asking-rate.

Man of the Match: D. P. M. D. Jayawardene.

Sri Lanka

*S. T. Jayasuriya b Gough	0	H. D. P. K. Dharmasena not out	18
†R. S. Kaluwitharana c Hick b Mullally	18		
M. S. Atapattu c Caddick b Croft	57	L-b 5, w 3, n-b 4	12
D. P. M. D. Jayawardene not out	101		
K. Sangakkara c and b Croft	6	1/0 (1) 2/33 (2)	(6 wkts, 50 overs) 226
S. I. de Saram b Caddick	14	3/119 (3) 4/129 (5)	
R. P. Arnold c Stewart b Mullally	0	5/173 (6) 6/174 (7)	Score at 15 overs: 52-2

W. P. U. J. C. Vaas, D. N. T. Zoysa and M. Muralitharan did not bat.

Bowling: Gough 10–0–52–1; Caddick 10–2–37–1; White 10–0–55–0; Mullally 10–1–37–2; Croft 10–1–40–2.

England

M. E. Trescothick c Kaluwitharana b Zoysa	6	R. D. B. Croft b Muralitharan	11
†A. J. Stewart c Jayawardene b Muralitharan	55	A. R. Caddick b Dharmasena	8
A. Flintoff c Muralitharan b Vaas	10	D. Gough not out	3
G. A. Hick st Kaluwitharana b Jayasuriya	11	A. D. Mullally run out	1
*G. P. Thorpe c Jayawardene b Dharmasena	12	L-b 11, w 6	17
M. P. Vaughan c Arnold b Muralitharan	26	1/14 (1) 2/35 (3) 3/63 (4) 4/88 (5) 5/119 (2) 6/119 (7) 7/145 (6) 8/147 (8) 9/157 (9) 10/160 (11)	(45 overs) 160
C. White run out	0		Score at 15 overs: 50-2

Bowling: Vaas 8–2–22–1; Zoysa 7–0–30–1; Dharmasena 8–0–31–2; Muralitharan 9–2–11–3; Jayasuriya 8–0–36–1; Arnold 5–0–19–0.

Umpires: B. C. Cooray and D. N. Pathirana.
Third umpire: E. A. R. de Silva.

†SRI LANKA v ENGLAND

Third One-Day International

At Sinhalese Sports Club, Colombo, March 27. Sri Lanka won by ten wickets. Toss: Sri Lanka.

England's largely triumphant tour ended in embarrassment: for the first time, they lost a limited-overs international by ten wickets. Vaas bowled an exemplary opening spell of 7–5–5–2, and the four off-spinners kept things tight throughout. Sangakkara's breathtaking catch at cover point to dismiss Thorpe typified Sri Lanka's flawless fielding. England's belated decision to play one-day specialists Knight and Ealham gave some sense to their flight from Britain. Knight, like the openers, dragged a wide ball on to his stumps, but Ealham did support an off-colour Hick, who in searing heat battled cramp to reach 46 from 114 balls. Kaluwitharana and Atapattu, captain in place of the injured Jayasuriya, were 81 after 15 overs, almost halfway to their target, and with Kaluwitharana cutting and pulling his way to 102 from 116 balls, including 20 fours, the end came with almost indecent haste.

Man of the Match: R. S. Kaluwitharana. *Man of the Series:* M. S. Atapattu.

England

M. E. Trescothick b Vaas	16
†A. J. Stewart b Vaas	14
N. V. Knight b Zoysa	7
G. A. Hick c de Saram b Dharmasena	46
*G. P. Thorpe c Sangakkara b Zoysa	0
A. Flintoff c Dharmasena b Samaraweera	24
C. White b Arnold	4
M. A. Ealham c sub (T. M. Dilshan) b Dharmasena	28
R. D. B. Croft c Jayawardene b Vaas	4
D. Gough not out	0
A. D. Mullally not out	8
L-b 4, w 10	14
1/21 (2) 2/36 (1) 3/39 (3) 4/39 (5) 5/88 (6) 6/105 (7) 7/152 (4) 8/156 (8) 9/157 (9)	(9 wkts, 50 overs) 165

Score at 15 overs: 50-4

Bowling: Vaas 8–5–13–3; Zoysa 7–1–39–2; Dharmasena 10–0–35–2; Muralitharan 10–0–29–0; Samaraweera 7–0–26–1; Arnold 8–1–19–1.

Sri Lanka

*M. S. Atapattu not out	53
†R. S. Kaluwitharana not out	102
L-b 2, w 3, n-b 6	11
(no wkt, 33.5 overs)	166

Score at 15 overs: 81-0

D. P. M. D. Jayawardene, K. Sangakkara, S. I. de Saram, R. P. Arnold, T. T. Samaraweera, H. D. P. K. Dharmasena, W. P. U. J. C. Vaas, D. N. T. Zoysa and M. Muralitharan did not bat.

Bowling: Gough 7–0–30–0; Mullally 8–0–51–0; White 4–0–18–0; Croft 8–0–39–0; Ealham 6.5–1–26–0.

Umpires: G. Silva and T. H. Wijewardene.
Third umpire: D. N. Pathirana. Series referee: Hanumant Singh (India).

ENGLAND A IN THE WEST INDIES, 2000-01

By GEOFFREY DEAN

After 43 first-class matches unbeaten, England A's long and impressive run finally came to an end in Guyana in the last game of what was expected to be their last tour. Not since Natal in January 1994 had they suffered a first-class defeat; in the meantime they had recorded 22 wins and 21 draws, with one match abandoned. They certainly could have achieved a 22nd draw at Georgetown in their semi-final of the Busta International Shield, but, behind on first innings, England A had to win to progress to the final. They therefore threw the bat on the final morning, in the faint hope of giving themselves enough time to bowl Guyana out on a flat Bourda pitch. The gamble predictably failed and the tour ended in bitter disappointment.

ENGLAND A'S FIRST-CLASS RECORD OVERSEAS

Season	*Captain*	*Venue*	*P*	*W*	*L*	*D*	*Test series*
1989-90	M. C. J. Nicholas	Zimbabwe	3	1	0	2	1–0
1990-91	H. Morris	Pakistan	1	0	0	1	
		Sri Lanka	4	1	0	3	0–0
1991-92	H. Morris†	West Indies	5	0	2	3	0–2
1992-93	M. D. Moxon	Australia	4	0	2	2	
1993-94	H. Morris	South Africa	8	4	1	3	0–0
1994-95	A. P. Wells	India	5	4	0	1	3–0
1995-96	N. Hussain	Pakistan	6	3	0	3	1–0
1996-97	A. J. Hollioake	Australia	3	2	0	1	
1997-98	N. V. Knight	Kenya	1	0	0	1	
		Sri Lanka	5	3	0	2	2–0
1998-99	M. P. Vaughan	Zimbabwe	3*	1	0	2	1–0
		South Africa	2	2	0	0	
1999-2000	M. W. Alleyne	Bangladesh	2	0	0	2	
		New Zealand	5	3	0	2	1–0
2000-01	M. W. Alleyne	West Indies	8	3	1	4	
			65*	27	6	32	

† *The official captain, M. D. Moxon, was injured and never played.*
* *Excludes one match abandoned.*
All Test series consisted of three matches except for South Africa in 1993-94 (one match), Zimbabwe in 1998-99 and New Zealand in 1999-2000 (two each).

For much of the preceding Busta Cup tournament, played in a round-robin league format, England A appeared to be the best side in the competition, although their slow scoring-rate often left them with insufficient time to dismiss opponents twice. Invited by the West Indies Cricket Board to take part in their domestic season, in an initiative to help counter falling standards in the Caribbean, England A were top of the table going into the final round of matches. They could not win the Busta Cup itself: the board had decreed that only a West Indian territory could do so. But had they finished in the top two, they would have had the advantage of a "home" semi-final in Grenada, their base camp, for the ensuing knockout tournament for the Busta International Shield. By losing on first innings in a draw against the Leeward Islands, England A slipped to third. That meant an away semi in Guyana, now at full strength with their internationals home from touring Australia or recovered from injury.

Several England A players made their mark on the tour, while others did not match expectations. Ian Ward showed remarkable levels of concentration, batting for more than 36 hours in all to amass 769 runs including three hundreds and four fifties. At no stage did he ever dominate, but none of his team-mates came close to emulating his productivity on pitches that were all low and slow, apart from Jamaica and Anguilla. The next most successful batsmen, captain Mark Alleyne and his deputy, John Crawley, scored the only other centuries but managed less than half Ward's aggregate.

Of the pace bowlers, Yorkshiremen Chris Silverwood and Ryan Sidebottom were the pick; each took 16 wickets in five matches. Alex Tudor claimed 19, including a five-wicket haul in the first match, against West Indies B, but was troubled by a side strain and tended to bowl too short. Paul Franks and Jon Lewis both struggled to make an impression on pitches that did not suit them. Alleyne's medium-pace was equally ineffectual, but his captaincy commanded respect, even if, at times, he was over-defensive. Jason Brown bowled his off-spin with variation, guile and control in the three matches he played at the start of the tour before joining the senior England party to Sri Lanka. He was replaced by county colleague Graeme Swann, whose 18 wickets included nine against the Windwards. Not until the final Busta Cup match in Anguilla did leg-spinner Chris Schofield produce his best form; then, 14 wickets in two games made him the tour's leading wicket-taker, with 22. The two wicket-keepers were hard to separate in terms of their glovework, but James Foster showed himself a better batsman than Chris Read.

Injuries to batsmen proved costly. David Sales seriously damaged cruciate ligaments in his knee while playing beach volleyball in Grenada before the first match and flew home. Michael Powell of Warwickshire joined the party in Trinidad as his replacement. When a shoulder problem forced Aftab Habib out, Powell's young Warwickshire colleague, Ian Bell, was called up, fresh from leading England Under-19 in India. Vikram Solanki, an outstanding slip fieldsman who held 22 catches, damaged a finger in St Lucia and missed the vital Busta Cup game against the Leewards.

ENGLAND A TOURING PARTY

M. W. Alleyne (Gloucestershire) (*captain*), J. P. Crawley (Lancashire) (*vice-captain*), U. Afzaal (Nottinghamshire), J. F. Brown (Northamptonshire), J. S. Foster (Essex), P. J. Franks (Nottinghamshire), A. Habib (Leicestershire), J. Lewis (Gloucestershire), C. M. W. Read (Nottinghamshire), D. J. Sales (Northamptonshire), C. P. Schofield (Lancashire), R. J. Sidebottom (Yorkshire), C. E. W. Silverwood (Yorkshire), V. Solanki (Worcestershire), A. J. Tudor (Surrey), I. J. Ward (Surrey).

Lewis replaced S. J. Harmison (Durham), who withdrew injured before the tour. M. J. Powell and I. R. Bell (both Warwickshire) later replaced the injured Sales and Habib. G. P. Swann (Northamptonshire) replaced Brown when he was promoted to the senior tour of Sri Lanka.

Manager: J. J. Whitaker (Leicestershire). *Coach:* P. Moores (Sussex). *Physiotherapist:* A. E. Brentnall (Derbyshire). *Fitness consultant:* R. Smith.

ENGLAND A TOUR RESULTS

First-class matches – Played 8: Won 3, Lost 1, Drawn 4.
Wins – West Indies B, Jamaica, Windward Islands.
Loss – Guyana.
Draws – Trinidad & Tobago, Guyana, Barbados, Leeward Islands.

ENGLAND A AVERAGES – FIRST-CLASS MATCHES

BATTING

	M	*I*	*NO*	*R*	*HS*	*100s*	*50s*	*Avge*	*Ct/St*
A. Habib	3	4	2	169	87*	0	2	84.50	2
I. J. Ward	8	14	2	769	135	3	4	64.08	5
M. W. Alleyne	7	10	1	370	139	1	1	41.11	5
J. S. Foster	3	4	1	122	53	0	1	40.66	9/1
V. S. Solanki	7	10	2	281	89	0	1	35.12	22
C. P. Schofield	5	7	1	208	66	0	2	34.66	2
M. J. Powell	6	10	0	340	96	0	3	34.00	7
J. P. Crawley	8	14	2	373	104*	1	2	31.08	3
A. J. Tudor	5	7	1	144	32	0	0	24.00	5
U. Afzaal	6	9	1	188	39	0	0	23.50	3
C. M. W. Read	5	6	1	90	29*	0	0	18.00	12
G. P. Swann	4	6	0	95	49	0	0	15.83	3
C. E. W. Silverwood	5	5	1	44	16	0	0	11.00	0
R. J. Sidebottom	5	6	1	38	26	0	0	7.60	1
J. Lewis	4	4	1	22	10	0	0	7.33	2

Played in three matches: J. F. Brown 0, 1*, 1*; P. J. Franks 18, 5, 48 (4 ct). Played in one match: I. R. Bell 31, 19.

* *Signifies not out.*

BOWLING

	O	*M*	*R*	*W*	*BB*	*5W/i*	*Avge*
R. J. Sidebottom	109.5	31	269	16	5-31	1	16.81
G. P. Swann	144.3	48	362	18	5-27	1	20.11
U. Afzaal	97	32	168	8	3-9	0	21.00
P. J. Franks	66.4	12	193	9	3-44	0	21.44
C. E. W. Silverwood	161.4	42	382	16	4-45	0	23.87
A. J. Tudor	146	33	454	19	5-37	1	23.89
C. P. Schofield	195.2	43	578	22	4-72	0	26.27
J. F. Brown	119	32	263	10	4-85	0	26.30
J. Lewis	101	20	318	9	3-51	0	35.33

Also bowled: M. W. Alleyne 65–13–180–2; M. J. Powell 4–2–9–0; V. S. Solanki 18.1–10–20–1.

The Busta Cup table and details of matches not involving England A may be found in Cricket in the West Indies.

ENGLAND A v WEST INDIES B

At St George's (Grenada), January 5, 6, 7, 8. England A won by 224 runs. England A 12 pts. Toss: England A. First-class debuts: D. E. Bernard, J. J. C. Lawson, T. A. Willett.

It suited England A to begin their tour against one of the competition's weakest teams, West Indies B, mostly consisting of Under-23s not selected for the territorial squads. Some poor first-morning bowling was picked off by Ward and Crawley, who shared a century stand in 35 overs, but England's middle order, the disciplined Habib excepted, failed to exploit a docile pitch. Habib batted for 284 minutes and hit ten fours in his unbeaten 87. Alexander, a young leg-spinner from Grenada, impressed without much reward. The West Indians' reply was undermined by Brown, and they trailed by 102. Fine strokeplay took Solanki to 89 in 119 balls, and allowed Alleyne a third-evening declaration that set a target of 329. Tudor removed the top four with a fiery new-ball burst, and when Afzaal picked up three wickets in successive overs, England A had the match all but won before lunch on the final day.

Man of the Match: I. J. Ward.

Close of play: First day, England A 249-6 (Habib 41*, Tudor 15*); Second day, West Indies B 176-6 (Alexander 32*, Peters 17*); Third day, West Indies B 35-2 (Gonsalves 7*).

England A

I. J. Ward b Peters	49	– run out	69
J. P. Crawley b Lawson	65	– c Willett b Alexander	13
V. S. Solanki b Lawson	26	– c Phillip b Bernard	89
U. Afzaal lbw b Peters	19	– c Bernard b Alexander	19
A. Habib not out	87	– not out	21
*M. W. Alleyne c Phillip b Peters	7	– not out	7
†C. M. W. Read lbw b Lawson	19		
A. J. Tudor b Lawson	20		
C. E. W. Silverwood c Alexander b Sooklal	4		
R. J. Sidebottom c Gonsalves b Alexander	26		
J. F. Brown lbw b Richardson	0		
B 5, l-b 6	11	B 4, n-b 4	8
1/103 2/140 3/143 4/166 5/182 6/231 7/256 8/263 9/332	333	1/23 2/148 3/179 4/212 (4 wkts dec.)	226

Bowling: *First Innings*—Lawson 32–8–79–4; Peters 27–7–74–3; Wilkinson 6–2–8–0; Alexander 25–5–62–1; Sooklal 37–6–90–1; Richardson 2.5–0–9–1. *Second Innings*—Lawson 10–2–27–0; Wilkinson 16–2–52–0; Alexander 12–2–69–2; Sooklal 13–1–40–0; Willett 5–0–24–0; Bernard 2–0–10–1.

West Indies B

A. Gonsalves c Read b Tudor	6	– c Crawley b Tudor	8
D. E. Bernard b Silverwood	7	– lbw b Tudor	0
K. J. Wilkinson b Brown	28	– b Tudor	26
Z. R. Ali c Solanki b Brown	13	– c Solanki b Tudor	0
T. A. Willett c Solanki b Afzaal	41	– c Habib b Brown	11
†W. Phillip b Brown	15	– lbw b Afzaal	8
C. C. Alexander c Habib b Brown	40	– c Solanki b Afzaal	8
K. Peters c Solanki b Silverwood	17	– c Tudor b Afzaal	0
*R. B. Richardson run out	12	– absent hurt	
R. I. Sooklal not out	8	– (9) c Ward b Tudor	18
J. J. C. Lawson c Ward b Tudor	25	– (10) not out	14
B 1, l-b 13, n-b 5	19	B 1, l-b 1, n-b 9	11
1/13 2/30 3/52 4/65 5/96 6/151 7/177 8/196 9/198	231	1/0 2/35 3/35 4/47 5/56 6/65 7/65 8/70 9/104	104

Bowling: *First Innings*—Silverwood 17–3–46–2; Tudor 13.3–0–53–2; Alleyne 10–2–22–0; Brown 30–7–85–4; Afzaal 6–1–11–1. *Second Innings*—Silverwood 11–4–31–0; Tudor 10–1–37–5; Brown 17–7–25–1; Afzaal 11–7–9–3.

Umpires: B. R. Doctrove and G. A. Johnson.

TRINIDAD & TOBAGO v ENGLAND A

At Port-of-Spain, January 11, 12, 13, 14. Drawn. Trinidad & Tobago 6 pts, England A 3 pts. Toss: Trinidad & Tobago. First-class debuts: A. Jackson, G. Mahabir, T. Modeste.

England A paid dearly for dropping Roberts on 21: on a painfully slow surface, he alone timed his attacking strokes to reach 62 in 88 balls. The more dogged Mason supported him well, then skilfully shepherded the tail. Silverwood deserved a five-wicket haul, and might have had one had chances offered by Rampersad and Brown been held. England never came to terms with the wrist-spin of Ramnarine and Dhanraj but, with Ward batting throughout their eight-hour innings, still came within eight runs of a first-innings lead. Without once coming down the pitch to the spinners, Ward hit 47 singles and six fours before playing on. England had an outside chance of victory after reducing their hosts to 83 for six on the final afternoon, but wicket-keeper Mason and Brown rescued the innings in a two-hour stand of 74. Mason, dropped by Afzaal off his own bowling when 42, resisted for 196 minutes in all and struck 11 fours in his second half-century of the game.

Man of the Match: K. Mason.

Close of play: First day, Trinidad & Tobago 211-6 (Mason 32*, Brown 13*); Second day, England A 83-2 (Crawley 44*, Afzaal 22*); Third day, Trinidad & Tobago 25-1 (Jan 7*, Rampersad 6*).

Trinidad & Tobago

I. H. Jan lbw b Silverwood	24	– c Solanki b Brown	10
A. Jackson lbw b Silverwood	16	– c Read b Tudor	11
D. Rampersad c Read b Franks	39	– c Read b Tudor	6
*R. A. M. Smith c Solanki b Silverwood	2	– b Brown	11
G. Mahabir c Solanki b Tudor	11	– c Solanki b Brown	23
L. A. Roberts lbw b Franks	62	– c Alleyne b Afzaal	10
†K. Mason c Franks b Tudor	50	– c Franks b Solanki	82
D. Brown run out	13	– b Franks	18
D. Ramnarine lbw b Silverwood	6	– c Solanki b Franks	2
R. Dhanraj not out	10	– not out	2
T. Modeste c Solanki b Franks	1		
L-b 7, n-b 8	15	B 1, l-b 2, w 1, n-b 8	12
1/18 2/73 3/75 4/94 5/108 6/175 7/213 8/238 9/238	249	1/16 2/27 3/38 4/41 5/58 6/83 7/157 8/181 9/187	(9 wkts dec.) 187

Bowling: *First Innings*—Silverwood 32–12–45–4; Tudor 27–9–61–2; Franks 19.4–6–44–3; Brown 19–5–40–0; Alleyne 11–0–46–0; Afzaal 3–1–6–0. *Second Innings*—Silverwood 12–4–18–0; Tudor 12–5–21–2; Brown 27–10–43–3; Franks 13–1–43–2; Afzaal 13–3–32–1; Solanki 4.1–2–4–1; Alleyne 7–0–23–0.

England A

I. J. Ward b Ramnarine	109	– not out	13
J. P. Crawley lbw b Brown	0	– not out	9
V. S. Solanki b Ramnarine	11		
U. Afzaal lbw b Ramnarine	29		
A. Habib lbw b Dhanraj	8		
*M. W. Alleyne c Mason b Modeste	2		
†C. M. W. Read c Mason b Dhanraj	5		
A. J. Tudor b Ramnarine	32		
P. J. Franks lbw b Ramnarine	18		
C. E. W. Silverwood run out	9		
J. F. Brown not out	1		
B 1, l-b 5, w 2, n-b 10	18	N-b 3	3
1/7 2/33 3/96 4/109 5/112 6/123 7/180 8/228 9/238	242		(no wkt) 25

Bowling: *First Innings*—Modeste 11–1–44–1; Brown 25–4–50–1; Ramnarine 38.4–10–71–5; Dhanraj 31–14–44–2; Rampersad 10–2–17–0; Jan 3–1–10–0. *Second Innings*—Modeste 5–0–18–0; Brown 3–1–7–0; Dhanraj 2–2–0–0.

Umpires: C. Duncan and Z. Macuum.

ENGLAND A v GUYANA

At St George's (Grenada), January 19, 20, 21, 22. Drawn. England A 6 pts, Guyana 3 pts. Toss: England A.

Although another low, slow pitch at the National Stadium made a result unlikely, England's refusal to set a target on the final day was disappointing. Wary of Hooper's flashing bat, acting-captain Crawley – Alleyne had stood down – opted to bat on for a meaningless five-hour hundred. Ward grafted away unbeaten for six hours, to follow his seven-and-a-half-hour century in the first innings; his second in successive games, it contained just five fours. Powell, who dominated their opening stand of 134 in 48 overs, hit 12 fours in three hours, and without him the scoring-rate grew ever slower as England ground out 413 runs in 180 overs, 127 of them bowled by Guyana's four spinners. The match's best innings came from Sarwan, whose elegant 122 from 231 balls contained 19 fours; unlike Ward, he used his feet well to spin. Schofield wound up Guyana's reply with three wickets in an over.

Man of the Match: I. J. Ward.

Close of play: First day, England A 237-3 (Ward 87*, Habib 40*); Second day, Guyana 28-1 (Haniff 9*, Semple 10*); Third day, England A 20-0 (Powell 13*, Ward 5*).

England A

M. J. Powell c Haniff b Hooper	75	– c Nagamootoo b Darlington	24
I. J. Ward b Matthews	118	– not out	86
*J. P. Crawley lbw b Darlington	10	– not out	104
V. S. Solanki lbw b Darlington	9		
A. Habib c Katchay b Hooper	53		
†J. S. Foster b Sarwan	53		
C. P. Schofield st Nagamootoo b McGarrell	66		
P. J. Franks c Cush b McGarrell	5		
R. J. Sidebottom b McGarrell	0		
J. Lewis lbw b Sarwan	5		
J. F. Brown not out	1		
B 12, l-b 5, n-b 1	18	B 2, l-b 1, w 2, n-b 3	8
1/134 2/157 3/179 4/267 5/293 6/366 7/379 8/379 9/398	413	1/42	(1 wkt) 222

Bowling: *First Innings*—Darlington 28–7–67–2; Katchay 25–4–80–0; McGarrell 52.2–19–95–3; Matthews 20–7–44–1; Hooper 40–11–68–2; Sarwan 15–2–42–2. *Second Innings*—Darlington 24–6–70–1; Katchay 5.1–2–12–0; Hooper 27–10–50–0; McGarrell 18–2–42–0; Sarwan 17–2–45–0.

Guyana

N. A. De Groot c Solanki b Lewis	1
A. Haniff c Powell b Franks	23
K. F. Semple c Foster b Lewis	15
R. R. Sarwan c Foster b Franks	122
*C. L. Hooper c Foster b Sidebottom	39
L. J. Cush c Schofield b Brown	9
N. C. McGarrell c Powell b Brown	0
†V. Nagamootoo c Solanki b Schofield	46
R. S. Matthews not out	5
E. Katchay c Solanki b Schofield	0
K. G. Darlington c Powell b Schofield	0
B 4, l-b 1, n-b 23	28
1/10 2/38 3/65 4/159 5/174 6/192 7/264 8/288 9/288	288

Bowling: Lewis 21–4–63–2; Sidebottom 18–6–45–1; Franks 13–2–51–2; Brown 26–3–70–2; Schofield 20–6–54–3; Powell 2–2–0–0.

Umpires: I. Lord and B. E. W. Morgan.

BARBADOS v ENGLAND A

At Bridgetown, January 26, 27, 28, 29. Drawn. Barbados 3 pts, England A 6 pts. Toss: England A.

Another flat pitch gave Ward the opportunity to score his third century in as many matches; he and Powell shared England A's highest opening stand ever, 224, before Powell was lbw trying to reach his own hundred with a reverse sweep. The later batsmen raised the total to 444 against some undisciplined bowling, and the first first-class victory over Barbados by an England representative team since 1953-54 was in prospect when keen bowling by the tourists reduced the home side to 158 for eight. The last two wickets, however, held England up for 37 overs while adding 92: Bradshaw, dropped on 71, hit 15 fours in his maiden first-class hundred and Austin resisted 88 balls for six runs. Barbados still followed on, but Silverwood and Tudor were tiring, and Griffiths was badly dropped by Ward at 63 for two. He went on to bat through 82 overs and, as the final day wore on, Barbados looked less and less likely to be bowled out.

Man of the Match: I. D. R. Bradshaw.

Close of play: First day, England A 266-1 (Ward 131*, Solanki 25*); Second day, Barbados 71-3 (Hinds 12*, Holder 7*); Third day, Barbados 27-1 (Griffith 9*, Armstrong 14*).

England A

M. J. Powell lbw b Austin	96
I. J. Ward c Browne b Collymore	135
V. S. Solanki c Marshall b Bryan	41
J. P. Crawley c Griffith b Bradshaw	8
U. Afzaal b Collymore	7
*M. W. Alleyne c Griffith b Bradshaw	40
†J. S. Foster lbw b Bryan	17
C. P. Schofield c Browne b Bradshaw	42
A. J. Tudor c Hinds b Bryan	23
J. Lewis c Armstrong b Bryan	6
C. E. W. Silverwood not out	1
B 2, l-b 1, n-b 25	28
1/224 2/273 3/292 4/306 5/306 6/330 7/412 8/413 9/443	444

Bowling: Collymore 22–4–57–2; Bradshaw 16–1–90–3; Austin 39–7–122–1; Bryan 30–7–57–4; Hinds 11–2–28–0; Marshall 33–3–87–0.

Barbados

A. F. G. Griffith c Foster b Lewis	22	– c Solanki b Tudor	84
P. A. Wallace c Crawley b Silverwood	8	– c and b Lewis	0
S. H. Armstrong run out	15	– c Powell b Afzaal	17
R. O. Hinds lbw b Tudor	23	– lbw b Afzaal	30
R. I. C. Holder c Foster b Lewis	22	– lbw b Lewis	1
†C. O. Browne c Solanki b Schofield	19	– run out	29
*I. D. R. Bradshaw not out	109	– not out	18
D. K. Marshall lbw b Schofield	0	– not out	23
H. R. Bryan c Crawley b Tudor	5		
R. A. Austin b Tudor	6		
C. D. Collymore c Foster b Lewis	3		
B 2, l-b 2, n-b 14	18	B 14, l-b 5, n-b 8	27
1/15 2/40 3/58 4/93 5/104 6/146 7/146 8/158 9/215	250	1/1 2/32 3/116 4/117 5/177 6/179	(6 wkts dec.) 229

Bowling: *First Innings*—Silverwood 19–4–37–1; Tudor 19–5–59–3; Lewis 19–3–51–3; Schofield 28–9–89–2; Afzaal 8–4–10–0; Alleyne 2–2–0–0. *Second Innings*—Lewis 13–5–22–2; Tudor 8–2–15–1; Alleyne 2–0–6–0; Solanki 14–8–16–0; Schofield 26–4–82–0; Silverwood 12–3–23–0; Afzaal 30–10–37–2; Powell 2–0–9–0.

Umpires: B. R. Doctrove and H. Moore.

JAMAICA v ENGLAND A

At Kingston, February 2, 3, 4, 5. England A won by seven wickets. England A 12 pts. Toss: Jamaica. First-class debut: O. Baker.

Excellent seam bowling by Silverwood and Sidebottom, on a quickish pitch showing occasional unevenness, set up victory over tournament leaders Jamaica. Silverwood deserved a better reward than his three wickets on the first day, when Sidebottom mopped up the tail with four for three in 25 balls. Gayle, playing some superb off-side shots in his two-hour fifty, had given Jamaica a good start, but their last five wickets crashed in eight overs. England A managed only a 14-run lead, however, losing six wickets to spin, and, batting again, Jamaica looked well placed at 147 for four. Then Swann, in his first match of the tour, obtained some sharp turn and four wickets fell in five overs. England A had already benefited from the home side's inclusion of only two seamers, and their pursuit of 183 was further aided when Walsh broke down. Jamaica also paid for dropping Ward on 11; he hit another half-century, and next morning his team-mates needed only an hour to complete a good win.

Man of the Match: R. J. Sidebottom.

Close of play: First day, England A 44-2 (Crawley 23*, Solanki 12*); Second day, Jamaica 70-2 (Gayle 39*, Cunningham 0*); Third day, England A 133-2 (Crawley 37*, Solanki 6*).

Jamaica

L. V. Garrick c Read b Silverwood	8	– c Solanki b Sidebottom	31
C. H. Gayle c Solanki b Swann	56	– c Read b Sidebottom	39
†K. H. Hibbert b Silverwood	21	– lbw b Swann	0
W. E. Cuff c Ward b Sidebottom	46	– (5) c Solanki b Swann	46
*R. G. Samuels c Alleyne b Silverwood	1	– (6) c Lewis b Afzaal	30
G. R. Breese c Read b Sidebottom	10	– (7) not out	18
O. Baker c Powell b Sidebottom	5	– (8) lbw b Swann	0
N. O. Perry b Alleyne	8	– (9) b Swann	4
F. A. Rose not out	3	– (10) lbw b Silverwood	21
C. A. Walsh c Read b Sidebottom	0	– (11) c Powell b Silverwood	0
R. O. Cunningham b Sidebottom	0	– (4) c Solanki b Sidebottom	0
L-b 9, w 3, n-b 4	16	B 4, l-b 3	7
1/25 2/83 3/97 4/113 5/139 6/160 7/163 8/171 9/174	174	1/61 2/64 3/70 4/75 5/147 6/147 7/150 8/158 9/196	196

Bowling: *First Innings*—Silverwood 19–5–52–3; Lewis 10–1–47–0; Sidebottom 17.5–4–31–5; Swann 16–6–27–1; Alleyne 3–0–8–1. *Second Innings*—Silverwood 10–2–38–2; Lewis 5–0–22–0; Swann 23–6–79–4; Sidebottom 16–5–34–3; Afzaal 5–1–16–1.

England A

M. J. Powell c Hibbert b Walsh	5	– c Hibbert b Walsh	14
I. J. Ward c Cuff b Rose	2	– b Gayle	62
J. P. Crawley c Cuff b Walsh	25	– c Hibbert b Perry	41
V. S. Solanki c Hibbert b Cunningham	38	– not out	34
U. Afzaal st Hibbert b Breese	39	– not out	17
*M. W. Alleyne c Rose b Walsh	37		
G. P. Swann b Breese	0		
†C. M. W. Read c Perry b Breese	5		
C. E. W. Silverwood c Samuels b Perry	16		
J. Lewis st Hibbert b Cunningham	10		
R. J. Sidebottom not out	2		
B 2, l-b 3, n-b 4	9	B 3, l-b 12	15
1/9 2/15 3/50 4/91 5/141 6/143 7/157 8/161 9/180	188	1/27 2/123 3/145	(3 wkts) 183

Bowling: *First Innings*—Rose 14–0–51–1; Walsh 22–9–34–3; Perry 15–3–35–1; Breese 20–4–42–3; Cunningham 10.2–4–17–2; Gayle 4–1–4–0. *Second Innings*—Rose 13–4–35–0; Walsh 9.2–2–16–1; Cunningham 15–5–37–0; Breese 7.4–1–25–0; Perry 19–4–40–1; Gayle 5.2–1–15–1.

Umpires: C. Duncan and T. Wilson.

WINDWARD ISLANDS v ENGLAND A

At Castries (St Lucia), February 9, 10, 11. England A won by an innings and 17 runs. England A 12 pts. Toss: England A.

After a rain-delayed start, England A took advantage of a damp pitch and some slipshod batting to reduce the Windwards – still seeking their first points of the tournament – to 89 for seven. Sidebottom, making the ball move both ways, continually threatened, and there was some grip for Swann's off-breaks. England A also struggled on the uneven surface, slipping to 113 for five, but captain Alleyne batted 56 overs for a determined 64. He put on 83 with Swann, whose aggressive 49 contained two sixes, and at the end Franks also played positively, adding 33 with Solanki, who came in at No. 11 because of a finger injury. He had needed seven stitches after trying to catch a fast-travelling edge off a Franks full toss on the opening day. The Windwards quickly folded again on a turning pitch; only Smith, a 19-year-old left-hander, provided much resistance, hitting three successive fours off Franks before becoming one of Swann's nine wickets in the match. This three-day win by an innings put England A on top of the Busta Cup table.

Man of the Match: G. P. Swann.

Close of play: First day, Windward Islands 124-7 (Butler 18*, Jackson 17*); Second day, England A 208-6 (Alleyne 57*, Read 6*).

Windward Islands

D. S. Smith lbw b Sidebottom	30	– c sub (J. S. Foster) b Swann	42
R. K. Currency c Alleyne b Franks	9	– c Afzaal b Sidebottom	2
K. N. Casimir c Read b Sidebottom	4	– c Afzaal b Sidebottom	14
†J. R. Murray b Sidebottom	1	– lbw b Franks	7
J. Eugene c Franks b Swann	7	– (7) b Schofield	23
S. G. Wilson lbw b Swann	13	– c Alleyne b Schofield	15
*R. N. Lewis b Sidebottom	10	– (5) lbw b Swann	8
D. K. Butler c Ward b Swann	18	– c Read b Swann	9
I. O. Jackson c Franks b Swann	19	– c Read b Schofield	7
S. Shillingford lbw b Swann	1	– b Swann	4
F. Thomas not out	0	– not out	0
B 2, l-b 5, w 1, n-b 9	17	B 4, l-b 2, n-b 5	11
1/19 2/25 3/27 4/42 5/71 6/81 7/89 8/127 9/128	129	1/12 2/31 3/38 4/76 5/85 6/98 7/127 8/131 9/140	142

Bowling: *First Innings*—Franks 13–2–26–1; Sidebottom 18–6–34–4; Swann 19.3–8–27–5; Alleyne 6–2–18–0; Schofield 4–0–17–0. *Second Innings*—Franks 8–1–29–1; Sidebottom 8–0–27–2; Swann 17–6–35–4; Schofield 16.5–5–45–3.

England A

M. J. Powell c Murray b Thomas	6
I. J. Ward b Shillingford	25
J. P. Crawley c Murray b Thomas	23
U. Afzaal run out	11
*M. W. Alleyne c and b Shillingford	64
C. P. Schofield b Butler	16
G. P. Swann lbw b Jackson	49
†C. M. W. Read run out	8
P. J. Franks b Shillingford	48
R. J. Sidebottom c Murray b Thomas	7
V. S. Solanki not out	10
B 8, l-b 4, w 2, n-b 7	21
1/8 2/56 3/61 4/69 5/113 6/196 7/216 8/229 9/255	288

Bowling: Thomas 19.4–7–52–3; Butler 19–5–51–1; Shillingford 28.2–5–82–3; Jackson 20.2–6–46–1; Lewis 16–3–45–0.

Umpires: B. E. W. Morgan and L. Thomas
(D. Martial deputised for Morgan from the 2nd day).

LEEWARD ISLANDS v ENGLAND A

At The Valley (Anguilla), February 16, 17, 18, 19. Drawn. Leeward Islands 6 pts, England A 3 pts. Toss: Leeward Islands.

England A bowled inconsistently on the quickest pitch of the tour and allowed the Leewards to rebuild from 181 for five through positive strokeplay from Jacobs, scoring 100 on his return from the Australian tour, and Tuckett. Between them they hit 28 fours while adding 146. In reply, Alleyne made a businesslike 139, initially supported by Bell, who days after arriving in the Caribbean survived a barrage of short-pitched bowling to stay for 192 minutes. When Alleyne was last out, however, his side still trailed by 71. Despite starting the final day 178 ahead, the Leewards, who had to win to qualify for the Busta Shield, were unaccountably negative, taking 41 overs to add 91 before declaring 25 minutes after lunch. England A lost their top three within four balls; when they slumped to 89 for six, 23 overs still remained. Foster ensured their qualification for the Shield semi-finals by resisting for 134 minutes, and Tudor held out for three-quarters of an hour.

Man of the Match: R. D. Jacobs.

Close of play: First day, Leeward Islands 299-5 (Jacobs 87*, Tuckett 43*); Second day, England A 119-3 (Bell 16*, Alleyne 11*); Third day, Leeward Islands 107-2 (Mitchum 41*).

Leeward Islands

J. A. Mitchum c Tudor b Silverwood	4	– b Schofield	65
*S. C. Williams c Swann b Tudor	37		
F. A. Adams lbw b Lewis	75	– (2) c Alleyne b Silverwood	2
S. C. Joseph b Tudor	0	– (3) lbw b Schofield	61
W. W. Cornwall c Swann b Tudor	45	– (4) c Foster b Schofield	9
†R. D. Jacobs lbw b Lewis	100	– (7) not out	19
C. M. Tuckett c Foster b Schofield	84	– (6) lbw b Silverwood	23
O. A. C. Banks lbw b Schofield	31	– (5) b Schofield	9
K. C. B. Jeremy not out	5	– (8) b Silverwood	2
G. T. Prince st Foster b Schofield	0		
R. J. Christopher c Foster b Schofield	3		
B 5, l-b 6, n-b 7	18	B 3, l-b 4, w 1	8
1/16 2/73 3/73 4/142 5/181 6/327 7/387 8/389 9/391	402	1/3 2/107 3/121 4/151 5/152 6/196 7/198 (7 wkts dec.)	198

Bowling: *First Innings*—Silverwood 20–4–64–1; Tudor 23–3–94–3; Lewis 25–5–88–2; Swann 14–5–46–0; Schofield 29.2–8–79–4; Alleyne 9–4–20–0. *Second Innings*—Silverwood 9.4–1–28–3; Tudor 6–0–23–0; Schofield 31–6–72–4; Lewis 8–2–25–0; Swann 19–3–43–0.

England A

M. J. Powell c Adams b Cornwall	17	– lbw b Prince	9
I. J. Ward c Adams b Prince	16	– c Jacobs b Christopher	5
J. P. Crawley lbw b Prince	51	– lbw b Prince	0
I. R. Bell c Mitchum b Cornwall	31	– c Cornwall b Jeremy	19
*M. W. Alleyne c sub (D. Williams) b Tuckett	139	– b Jeremy	40
†J. S. Foster c Adams b Jeremy	10	– not out	42
C. P. Schofield c Jacobs b Christopher	14	– lbw b Jeremy	0
G. P. Swann c Jacobs b Christopher	13	– c Williams b Banks	21
A. J. Tudor c Jacobs b Christopher	2	– not out	18
C. E. W. Silverwood c Cornwall b Tuckett	14		
J. Lewis not out	1		
B 4, l-b 8, n-b 11	23	L-b 1, w 1, n-b 4	6
1/21 2/66 3/103 4/187 5/229 6/257 7/281 8/288 9/320	331	1/14 2/14 3/14 4/50 5/89 6/89 7/127 (7 wkts)	160

Bowling: *First Innings*—Prince 22–3–60–2; Christopher 23–3–68–3; Cornwall 18–3–80–2; Jeremy 21–3–59–1; Banks 11–2–20–0; Tuckett 10.2–2–32–2. *Second Innings*—Prince 15–1–66–2; Christopher 10–3–31–1; Jeremy 11–3–33–3; Cornwall 4–1–11–0; Banks 4–1–16–1; Adams 2–1–2–0; Mitchum 1–1–0–0.

Umpires: Z. Macuum and W. Mitchum.

SEMI-FINAL

GUYANA v ENGLAND A

At Georgetown, February 24, 25, 26, 27. Guyana won by seven wickets. Toss: Guyana.

England A fell to pieces at the last, losing their seven-year unbeaten record in a desperate attempt to steal a place in the Busta Shield final. Their last hope was to set a target and bowl Guyana out. Powell and Ward made an encouraging start, with 124 in 30 overs, but on the final morning seven wickets tumbled in 90 minutes, leaving Guyana plenty of time to chase 205. After a century partnership between Haniff and Dowlin, Chanderpaul saw them home. Put in, England A had been on the back foot for much of the game. Several batsmen made a start, but only Schofield reached 50 – and his half-century stands with tailenders Read and Tudor both ended in run-outs. Their best session came on the second afternoon, when Guyana were 33 for four in the 17th over. However, Hooper counter-attacked for three hours and added 157 with Sarwan, who next day not only advanced to his second hundred against the tourists but also achieved the crucial first-innings lead in an eighth-wicket stand of 104 with McGarrell. The deeply disappointed England fielders thought they had both of them out. The eventual difference was 43, and England's last gamble bankrupted them.

Man of the Match: C. L. Hooper.

Close of play: First day, England A 218-7 (Schofield 28*, Read 20*); Second day, Guyana 191-5 (Sarwan 60*, Stuart 0*); Third day, England A 165-3 (Solanki 20*, Afzaal 6*).

England A

M. J. Powell lbw b McGarrell	35	– lbw b King	59
I. J. Ward c Dowlin b M. V. Nagamootoo	24	– c Hooper b King	56
J. P. Crawley c Haniff b Hooper	24	– lbw b King	0
V. S. Solanki lbw b McGarrell	2	– c Dowlin b King	21
U. Afzaal c M. V. Nagamootoo b Hooper	33	– b Hooper	14
*M. W. Alleyne c V. Nagamootoo b Hooper	24	– c Haniff b King	10
C. P. Schofield not out	64	– b Hooper	6
G. P. Swann b Hooper	8	– c Dowlin b King	4
†C. M. W. Read run out	24	– not out	29
A. J. Tudor run out	32	– c Haniff b M. V. Nagamootoo	17
R. J. Sidebottom lbw b Hooper	1	– c Dowlin b King	2
B 3, l-b 10, w 1, n-b 8	22	B 5, l-b 10, w 2, n-b 12	29
1/34 2/88 3/96 4/97 5/149 6/156 7/164 8/223 9/277	293	1/124 2/124 3/158 4/169 5/180 6/189 7/194 8/205 9/240	247

Bowling: *First Innings*—King 18–4–59–0; Stuart 20–4–61–0; M. V. Nagamootoo 31–8–69–1; McGarrell 26–9–42–2; Hooper 26.4–8–49–5. *Second Innings*—King 21–1–89–7; Stuart 6–0–27–0; M. V. Nagamootoo 9–0–48–1; Hooper 21–1–68–2.

Guyana

A. Haniff c Afzaal b Sidebottom	10	– c sub (J. Lewis) b Alleyne	62
S. Chattergoon c and b Swann	15	– c Tudor b Schofield	25
T. M. Dowlin c Powell b Swann	0	– c Solanki b Schofield	57
R. R. Sarwan c Ward b Swann	110	– (5) not out	2
S. Chanderpaul c Read b Tudor	2	– (4) not out	49
*C. L. Hooper c Solanki b Schofield	91		
C. E. L. Stuart c and b Schofield	3		
M. V. Nagamootoo c Sidebottom b Schofield	7		
N. C. McGarrell c Tudor b Swann	56		
†V. Nagamootoo c Tudor b Schofield	13		
R. D. King not out	1		
B 6, l-b 9, w 1, n-b 12	28	B 8, l-b 3, w 1, n-b 1	13
1/27 2/27 3/27 4/33 5/190 6/196 7/211 8/315 9/329	336	1/40 2/142 3/168 (3 wkts)	208

Bowling: *First Innings*—Tudor 18–5–44–1; Sidebottom 23–8–60–1; Swann 24–7–84–4; Schofield 26.1–2–86–4; Afzaal 9–2–16–0; Alleyne 11–2–31–0. *Second Innings*—Tudor 9.3–3–47–0; Sidebottom 9–2–38–0; Schofield 14–3–54–2; Swann 12–7–21–0; Afzaal 12–3–31–0; Alleyne 4–1–6–1.

Umpires: G. E. Greaves and E. A. Nicholls.

INTERNATIONAL UMPIRES' PANEL

On December 21, 1993, the International Cricket Council announced the formation of an international umpires' panel. Each full member of ICC was to nominate two officials – apart from England, who named four, because of their large number of professional umpires. A third-country member of the panel was to stand with a "home" umpire, not necessarily from the panel, in every Test staged from February 1994. Teams would have no right of objection to appointments.

In April 2002, however, the ICC were to set up two panels of umpires: an elite group of eight full-time umpires (contracted to the ICC), and a supporting panel of 20 umpires, two from each Test nation. Two independent umpires were to stand in all Tests from this date, and one in every one-day international.

The new panels had not been announced when *Wisden* went to press, but the following umpires were on the panel from September 2001 to March 2002: S. A. Bucknor (West Indies), D. B. Cowie (New Zealand), E. A. R. de Silva (Sri Lanka), R. S. Dunne (New Zealand), D. B. Hair (Australia), J. H. Hampshire (England), D. J. Harper (Australia), A. V. Jayaprakash (India), R. E. Koertzen (South Africa), P. Manuel (Sri Lanka), Mian Aslam (Pakistan), E. A. Nicholls (West Indies), D. L. Orchard (South Africa), Riazuddin (Pakistan), I. D. Robinson (Zimbabwe), G. Sharp (England), D. R. Shepherd (England), R. B. Tiffin (Zimbabwe), S. Venkataraghavan (India), P. Willey (England). Compared with the 2000-01 list, E. A. R. de Silva had replaced B. C. Cooray of Sri Lanka.

THE NEW ZEALANDERS IN ZIMBABWE AND SOUTH AFRICA, 2000-01

New Zealand began their tour of southern Africa in September able to field a side rich in experience but, after injuries had taken their toll, returned home in December with captain Stephen Fleming talking of "raw talent" and of the tour creating "a bigger playing base of players who are able to step up to Test cricket". Between contrasting Test series in Zimbabwe and South Africa, however, they had taken the cricket world by surprise by winning their first major one-day tournament, beating India by four wickets in the final of the ICC Knockout in Nairobi.

But Kenya was as good as it got. The New Zealanders lost 5–0 to South Africa in the one-day series that followed and, shorn of their first-string attack by injuries to Chris Cairns, Dion Nash and Daniel Vettori, were overwhelmed 2–0 in the three Tests. At the tour's start they had won both Test matches in Zimbabwe but, with Cairns resting his suspect knee in readiness for the ICC Knockout and 21-year-old Vettori already returned home for diagnosis of yet another back problem, they went down 2–1 in the one-day series.

Just how threadbare their attack was in South Africa can be gauged by the combined experience of their seam bowling in the opening Test at Bloemfontein. Shayne O'Connor, Daryl Tuffey and debutant Chris Martin totalled just 15 Tests between them, of which O'Connor had played 14; he was the only one with Test wickets (44). South Africa's Allan Donald, meanwhile, was looking for his 300th Test wicket before his home crowd. Vettori's replacement, leg-spinner Brooke Walker, was also making his debut after off-spinner Paul Wiseman had sprained his ankle playing frisbee before the first-class game against Boland. Scott Styris, initially bracketed with Cairns for the all-rounder's role, was another pre-Test casualty, having injured his knee in training.

Wiseman's injury resulted in a second dash to Africa for off-spinner Glen Sulzberger, who had been New Zealand A's leading first-class wicket-taker in England a few months earlier. His first call-up, to replace Vettori in the one-day squad for Zimbabwe and Kenya, had found him at Sydney airport on the way to watch his fiancée play hockey for New Zealand in the Olympics. Just as bizarre was Andrew Penn's round trip. Named originally among the pace bowlers for the first-class itinerary of the South African tour, he injured his back playing club cricket in Wellington and his place was taken by Chris Martin, another New Zealand A graduate. Styris's misfortune brought Penn another chance, only for him to aggravate his injury, after promisingly taking five wickets in an innings against Border, and have to return home.

Not that the injuries were confined to the bowlers. Fleming went into the Second Test against South Africa with stitches after damaging a finger on his left hand in fielding practice. And Matthew Horne's tour ended early when he broke his hand in the First Test against Zimbabwe, having already set New Zealand on their way with a century. While that left the tourists without an experienced opener, it did give Mark Richardson, a 29-year-old left-hander who had averaged 71 for New Zealand A in England, the chance to establish his credentials as a Test batsman. Having got his tour going with a triple-hundred against Zimbabwe A, he made 99 in the Second Test there and was New Zealand's highest run-maker in the South African Tests. In all first-class matches in both countries, he averaged 71.07 from 995 runs. Patient, an astute judge of line and with improving shot selection, he was with medium-fast bowler Martin the tour's success.

Replacement opener Craig Spearman, a hard-hitting one-day batsman, never tarnished his reputation for inconsistency in the Tests or fulfilled the expectations raised by his twin hundreds in the game against North West. Promoting Adam Parore to partner Richardson in the Third Test against South Africa proved no more successful but did give 21-year-old Hamish Marshall an opportunity at the top level. While his technique underwent severe examination, his concentration stood him in good stead.

Like Richardson, Martin blossomed in the big time, impressing with his line and showing stamina in useful spells. He was leading wicket-taker in the Test series and in all first-class matches in South Africa, finishing with 19 at 20.63. O'Connor's left-arm pace was capable of surprising South Africa's best, and his willingness to carry a heavy workload was essential to New Zealand's Second Test victory over Zimbabwe.

In contrast to the Zimbabweans, whose best was seen in all-too-familiar back-to-the-wall situations, Shaun Pollock's South Africans proved formidable opponents. Jonty Rhodes's decision to quit the Test scene and concentrate on one-day cricket, in South Africa's build-up to the World Cup there in 2003, allowed Neil McKenzie to slot comfortably into the middle order after his unhappy experience as opener in Sri Lanka in July and August. And when Donald was unfit for the Johannesburg Test, there was a ready-made lightning-fast replacement in Eastern Province's Mfuneko Ngam, a product like Makhaya Ntini of the black development programme. It was the first time two black South Africans had played Test cricket together and, with his three wickets at the Wanderers, Ntini emerged with 13 all told against New Zealand and the Man of the Series award.

NEW ZEALAND TOURING PARTY

S. P. Fleming (Wellington) (*captain*), N. J. Astle (Canterbury), C. L. Cairns (Canterbury), M. J. Horne (Otago), C. D. McMillan (Canterbury), D. J. Nash (Auckland), S. B. O'Connor (Otago), A. C. Parore (Auckland), M. H. Richardson (Otago), M. S. Sinclair (Central Districts), C. M. Spearman (Central Districts), S. B. Styris (Northern Districts), D. R. Tuffey (Northern Districts), D. J. Vettori (Northern Districts), P. J. Wiseman (Otago).

G. I. Allott (Canterbury), C. Z. Harris (Canterbury), C. J. Nevin (Wellington), G. P. Sulzberger (Central Districts) and R. G. Twose (Wellington) joined the party for the one-day internationals in Zimbabwe, Kenya and South Africa; Harris flew out early when Horne and Vettori were injured in the First Test in Zimbabwe; both subsequently returned home. Richardson and Sinclair also returned to New Zealand during the one-day programme, but returned to South Africa for the first-class fixtures. H. J. H. Marshall (Northern Districts), C. S. Martin (Canterbury) and K. P. Walmsley (Otago) also joined the party at this point, replacing Horne, Nash, injured at the end of the Zimbabwean tour, and Cairns, unfit after the South African one-day internationals. B. G. K. Walker (Auckland) replaced the injured Vettori in South Africa; Sulzberger returned to South Africa as cover for Wiseman, while A. J. Penn (Wellington) replaced Styris, until he himself was injured.

Manager: J. J. Crowe. *Coach:* D. G. Trist.

NEW ZEALAND TOUR RESULTS

Test matches – Played 5: Won 2, Lost 2, Drawn 1.
First-class matches – Played 10: Won 4, Lost 2, Drawn 4.
Wins – Zimbabwe (2), North West, Border.
Losses – South Africa (2).
Draws – South Africa, ZCU President's XI, Zimbabwe A, Boland.
One-day internationals – Played 9: Won 1, Lost 7, No result 1. *Win* – Zimbabwe. *Losses* – Zimbabwe (2), South Africa (5). *No result* – South Africa.
Other non-first-class matches – Played 3: Won 3. *Wins* – CFX Academy, Gauteng, Border.

TEST MATCH AVERAGES – SOUTH AFRICA v NEW ZEALAND

SOUTH AFRICA – BATTING

	T	*I*	*NO*	*R*	*HS*	*100s*	*50s*	*Avge*	*Ct*
N. D. McKenzie	3	4	2	195	120	1	1	97.50	2
J. H. Kallis	3	5	1	287	160	1	1	71.75	4
M. V. Boucher	3	3	1	98	76	0	1	49.00	8
N. Boje	3	3	0	116	51	0	1	38.66	0
G. Kirsten	3	5	1	138	49	0	0	34.50	5
H. H. Dippenaar	3	5	0	162	100	1	0	32.40	0
D. J. Cullinan	3	5	1	126	33	0	0	31.50	4
L. Klusener	3	3	0	19	9	0	0	6.33	4

Played in three Tests: M. Ntini 0* (1 ct); S. M. Pollock 25, 33 (1 ct). Played in two Tests: A. A. Donald 21*, 9. Played in one Test: M. Ngam did not bat.

* *Signifies not out.*

BOWLING

	O	*M*	*R*	*W*	*BB*	*5W/i*	*Avge*
M. Ntini	101.4	38	226	13	6-66	1	17.38
A. A. Donald	82.3	21	197	11	4-69	0	17.90
S. M. Pollock	120	49	233	12	4-37	0	19.41
L. Klusener	40.3	14	86	4	3-8	0	21.50
J. H. Kallis	79.5	23	205	5	2-26	0	41.00
N. Boje	93	25	187	3	2-30	0	62.33

Also bowled: M. Ngam 19–8–34–2.

NEW ZEALAND – BATTING

	T	*I*	*NO*	*R*	*HS*	*100s*	*50s*	*Avge*	*Ct*
M. H. Richardson	3	5	0	232	77	0	2	46.40	1
M. S. Sinclair	3	5	0	212	150	1	0	42.40	2
S. P. Fleming	3	5	0	192	99	0	2	38.40	0
C. D. McMillan	3	5	0	137	78	0	1	27.40	1
B. G. K. Walker	3	5	1	76	27*	0	0	19.00	0
N. J. Astle	3	5	0	77	37	0	0	15.40	2
C. M. Spearman	2	4	0	54	23	0	0	13.50	2
S. B. O'Connor	3	5	0	52	20	0	0	10.40	1
A. C. Parore	3	5	0	40	12	0	0	8.00	7
C. S. Martin	3	5	3	12	7	0	0	6.00	0
D. R. Tuffey	2	3	0	14	8	0	0	4.66	1

Played in one Test: H. J. H. Marshall 40*; K. P. Walmsley 5, 0.

* *Signifies not out.*

BOWLING

	O	*M*	*R*	*W*	*BB*	*5W/i*	*Avge*
C. S. Martin	83.1	22	286	11	4-104	0	26.00
S. B. O'Connor	86.4	21	244	8	3-87	0	30.50
D. R. Tuffey	53	11	194	3	3-38	0	64.66
B. G. K. Walker	63.4	12	204	3	2-92	0	68.00

Also bowled: N. J. Astle 88–38–142–2; C. D. McMillan 47–13–110–1; H. J. H. Marshall 1–0–4–0; M. S. Sinclair 4–0–13–0; K. P. Walmsley 18–4–47–2.

Note: Matches in this section which were not first-class are signified by a dagger.

At Mutare, September 1, 2, 3. Drawn. Toss: New Zealanders. New Zealanders 339 for nine dec. (M. S. Sinclair 42, S. P. Fleming 30, N. J. Astle 57, A. C. Parore 103 not out, D. L. Vettori 43; M. L. Nkala four for 71) and 263 for three dec. (M. H. Richardson 47, M. S. Sinclair 100 not out, C. D. McMillan 57 not out); ZCU President's XI 205 (S. V. Carlisle 92; D. R. Tuffey four for 48) and 96 for three (G. J. Rennie 37).

At Kwekwe, September 7, 8, 9. Drawn. Toss: New Zealanders. New Zealanders 677 for seven dec. (M. H. Richardson 306, M. J. Horne 63, M. S. Sinclair 86, C. D. McMillan 79, A. C. Parore 61 not out, Extras 34; P. A. Strang three for 77) and 137 for three dec. (M. J. Horne 48 not out); Zimbabwe A 168 (G. W. Flower 46, T. N. Madondo 36; D. L. Vettori six for 43) and 72 for three (M. A. Vermeulen 43 not out).

Richardson's career-best 306, in 741 minutes from 669 balls with 43 fours, was the second-highest score for a New Zealand XI and the sixth-highest by a New Zealander. The previous four New Zealanders to hit triple-hundreds had been, like Richardson, Otago players at the time. His innings was the longest by a New Zealander, while the team total was the highest by a New Zealand XI, the third-highest by any New Zealand first-class side, and the highest first-class total in a match involving a Zimbabwean side.

ZIMBABWE v NEW ZEALAND

First Test Match

At Bulawayo, September 12, 13, 14, 15, 16. New Zealand won by seven wickets. Toss: Zimbabwe. Test debuts: D. T. Mutendera; M. H. Richardson.

When New Zealand's first innings was still struggling for parity at lunch on the fourth day, a draw looked inevitable. But that afternoon their bowlers swung the match with five wickets; next morning, Cairns sent back Campbell and Nkala in the third over and swept aside the tailenders to finish with his tenth five-wicket return in Tests. On the opening day, his 161st Test wicket (Andy Flower) had moved him ahead of Danny Morrison as New Zealand's second-highest wicket-taker. Sir Richard Hadlee's total of 431 looked unthreatened. But just as important as Cairns's pace were Wiseman's off-breaks, which claimed five wickets in Zimbabwe's long first innings and another three in their second. With two and a half sessions to score 132, New Zealand's batsmen put their side ahead in the series.

A slow pitch and cautious batting produced dull entertainment on the first three days. Campbell took 307 balls over his 88, his first fifty in 17 Tests since making 56 in Zimbabwe's last series against New Zealand, in February 1998. Horne batted a similar time for New Zealand, just over five and a half hours, though needing 30 fewer balls to score 110, his second hundred against Zimbabwe. Once again, however, New Zealand owed their eventual position, just 12 in arrears, to their lower order, after earlier tentative batting against leg-spinner Paul Strang. Out of Test cricket with a wrist injury since March 1998, Strang kept the visitors on a tight rein with five for 67 on the third day. His final return, eight for 109, bettered Streak's six for 87 – against England at Lord's in May – as Zimbabwe's best Test figures. By then, however, New Zealand's last four wickets had added 158. Their fighting spirit was typified by Vettori, who batted for two hours, with a runner, in spite of the back injury that ended his tour.

For all its *longueurs*, the match was not devoid of drama. Even before it began, controversy surrounded Zimbabwe's selection of the young fast bowler, David Mutendera, who had attended the MRF Pace Foundation in Chennai. Guy Whittall, claiming Mutendera's inclusion was politically motivated and at the expense of Wishart, withdrew from the side – whereupon Wishart was brought in. On the final day, as New Zealand were settling into their victory chase, Grant Flower was no-balled for throwing his slow left-arm deliveries and taken off. Umpire Hair at square leg called the second, fourth and sixth deliveries of his second over, the eighth of the innings, and Rennie completed the over.

Man of the Match: P. J. Wiseman.

Close of play: First day, Zimbabwe 185-4 (Campbell 37*, Wishart 10*); Second day, New Zealand 62-2 (Horne 40*, Wiseman 1*); Third day, New Zealand 252-7 (Cairns 33*); Fourth day, Zimbabwe 100-5 (Campbell 45*, Streak 9*).

Zimbabwe

G. W. Flower c Parore b Vettori	24	– c Parore b O'Connor	3
G. J. Rennie c McMillan b Wiseman	36	– b Cairns	2
S. V. Carlisle c Horne b Wiseman	38	– b Wiseman	15
A. D. R. Campbell lbw b Astle	88	– lbw b Cairns	45
†A. Flower c Astle b Cairns	29	– lbw b Astle	22
C. B. Wishart c Richardson b Wiseman	17	– c Richardson b Wiseman	1
*H. H. Streak c Parore b Wiseman	51	– c McMillan b Wiseman	15
P. A. Strang c Richardson b Wiseman	0	– (9) not out	8
M. L. Nkala not out	30	– (8) c Sinclair b Cairns	0
B. C. Strang c Parore b O'Connor	10	– b Cairns	5
D. T. Mutendera b Cairns	10	– c Parore b Cairns	0
B 5, l-b 4, n-b 8	17	L-b 1, w 1, n-b 1	3
1/40 (1) 2/91 (2) 3/120 (3) 4/157 (5) 5/206 (6) 6/282 (4) 7/291 (8) 8/300 (7) 9/323 (10) 10/350 (11)	350	1/6 (2) 2/23 (3) 3/23 (1) 4/75 (5) 5/86 (6) 6/100 (4) 7/100 (8) 8/110 (7) 9/119 (10) 10/119 (11)	119

Bowling: *First Innings*—Cairns 28.2–9–77–2; O'Connor 30–7–63–1; McMillan 9–3–23–0; Vettori 52–23–79–1; Astle 11–6–9–1; Wiseman 45–16–90–5. *Second Innings*—Cairns 14.5–5–31–5; O'Connor 9–5–8–1; Wiseman 25–8–54–3; Richardson 1–0–1–0; Astle 18–10–24–1.

New Zealand

M. H. Richardson c Carlisle b Streak	6	– lbw b Rennie	13
M. J. Horne lbw b P. A. Strang	110		
M. S. Sinclair lbw b P. A. Strang	12	– (2) not out	43
P. J. Wiseman lbw b P. A. Strang	14		
*S. P. Fleming c Rennie b P. A. Strang	11	– (3) lbw b P. A. Strang	12
N. J. Astle c A. Flower b P. A. Strang	0	– (4) c Nkala b P. A. Strang	27
C. D. McMillan c A. Flower b P. A. Strang	58	– (5) not out	31
C. L. Cairns b Streak	33		
†A. C. Parore not out	32		
D. L. Vettori c and b P. A. Strang	49		
S. B. O'Connor c Campbell b P. A. Strang	4		
L-b 1, n-b 8	9	L-b 2, w 1, n-b 3	6
1/15 (1) 2/52 (3) 3/109 (4) 4/139 (5) 5/139 (6) 6/180 (2) 7/252 (7) 8/252 (8) 9/330 (10) 10/338 (11)	338	1/27 (1) 2/43 (3) 3/93 (4)	(3 wkts) 132

Bowling: *First Innings*—Streak 26–9–67–2; Nkala 21–7–43–0; P. A. Strang 51.5–12–109–8; B. C. Strang 25–7–63–0; Mutendera 14–4–29–0; G. W. Flower 16–4–26–0. *Second Innings*—Streak 5–0–21–0; Nkala 2–1–2–0; P. A. Strang 20.4–3–49–2; G. W. Flower 1.3–0–5–0; Rennie 13.3–0–40–1; Campbell 1–0–3–0; B. C. Strang 2–0–10–0.

Umpires: D. B. Hair (Australia) and R. B. Tiffin.
Third umpire: M. A. Esat. Referee: C. W. Smith (West Indies).

ZIMBABWE v NEW ZEALAND

Second Test Match

At Harare, September 19, 20, 21, 22, 23. New Zealand won by eight wickets. Toss: New Zealand.

Whittall, restored to the Zimbabwe side along with seam bowlers Olonga and Mbangwa, batted almost eight hours over the last two days in a valiant attempt to prevent New Zealand winning the series 2–0. His, and the team's, resistance was in total contrast to their first innings, in which the last six wickets fell for 20 runs in 13 overs, starting with the loss of Whittall immediately before tea on the third afternoon. Faced with a deficit of 299, there was no question of them not following on and, at 48 for four next day, they were looking down the barrel of a heavy innings defeat.

Century partnerships of 135 between Richardson and Astle and of 144 between Cairns and Nash – beating New Zealand's record for the eighth wicket, which Nash previously shared with Vettori for their 137 against India in 1998-99 – were the framework for 465, the highest total in Tests between these sides. Nash had come in for the injured Vettori, while at the top of the order Spearman replaced Horne, who damaged his hand fielding in the First Test. A slow opening day ended with the dismissal of Richardson for 99, and there were already signs that the game was getting away from Zimbabwe. Olonga's pace and bounce, backed up by sharp catching behind the bat, had helped them share the first two sessions, but they let the New Zealanders add 95 between tea and the close. Cairns dominated the second day with his fourth Test hundred, hitting three sixes and 13 fours in 124 from 174 balls. He finally fell to Strang, one ball after Nash, when he was stumped by a rebound from Andy Flower's gloves. A few minutes later, brother Grant wrapped up the innings, having bowled nearly 21 overs without exciting either umpire in the way he had Darrell Hair at Bulawayo.

Cairns soon had Rennie caught at third slip, but next morning Grant Flower and Carlisle batted through to lunch and there was no suggestion of the collapse that would follow. The New Zealanders were keeping their cricket tight, however, and eventually the pressure told. Not until Andy Flower and Whittall joined forces to add 131 in Zimbabwe's second innings was the visitors' thrust frustrated. Flower, when 59, became the first Zimbabwean to reach 3,000 runs in Tests. The new ball and a stunning catch by Sinclair at backward point broke the stand, but Streak, Flower's successor as captain, saw Whittall reach his third Test hundred with a four, two and straight six off consecutive balls from Astle. Next day, they extended their partnership to 151 before the third new ball broke Zimbabwe's resistance, claiming four wickets in eight overs. Although Mbangwa held on at the end for ten overs, his run-out two balls after the delayed tea interval – leaving Whittall unbeaten with 188 (two sixes, 27 fours) from 429 balls – gave New Zealand 18 overs for the 72 runs that would make Fleming his country's most successful Test captain, with 12 wins in 29 Tests. The previous record was Geoff Howarth's 11 in 30. Cairns's dramatic one-handed six over long-leg summed up the match even more emphatically than the margin.

Man of the Match: C. L. Cairns.

Close of play: First day, New Zealand 226-4 (Astle 64*); Second day, Zimbabwe 31-1 (G. W. Flower 11*, Carlisle 15*); Third day, Zimbabwe 6-1 (G. W. Flower 0*, Carlisle 5*); Fourth day, Zimbabwe 228-5 (Whittall 105*, Streak 10*).

New Zealand

M. H. Richardson lbw b Nkala	99		
C. M. Spearman c A. Flower b Olonga	2	– (1) c Rennie b Streak	2
M. S. Sinclair c Carlisle b Olonga	44	– not out	35
*S. P. Fleming c Campbell b Mbangwa	9		
N. J. Astle run out	86		
C. D. McMillan lbw b Mbangwa	15		
C. L. Cairns st A. Flower b Strang	124	– (4) not out	19
†A. C. Parore c A. Flower b Olonga	4	– (2) c Carlisle b Streak	13
D. J. Nash c G. W. Flower b Strang	62		
P. J. Wiseman not out	1		
S. B. O'Connor c Whittall b G. W. Flower	2		
L-b 3, w 2, n-b 12	17	L-b 2, w 1, n-b 2	5
1/5 (2) 2/69 (3) 3/91 (4) 4/226 (1) 5/256 (5) 6/302 (6) 7/318 (8) 8/462 (9) 9/462 (7) 10/465 (11)	465	1/4 (1) 2/42 (2)	(2 wkts) 74

Bowling: *First Innings*—Olonga 27–5–115–3; Streak 29–6–74–0; Nkala 15–0–60–1; Mbangwa 28–10–58–2; Strang 38–11–80–2; G. W. Flower 20.3–6–59–1; Rennie 3–0–16–0. *Second Innings*—Streak 8–2–33–2; Nkala 3–0–17–0; Mbangwa 4.2–0–22–0.

Zimbabwe

G. W. Flower c Parore b Astle	49	– run out	10
G. J. Rennie c Spearman b Cairns	4	– c Spearman b O'Connor	1
S. V. Carlisle c Sinclair b Cairns	31	– c Fleming b Astle	20
A. D. R. Campbell c Fleming b O'Connor	0	– run out	10
†A. Flower lbw b McMillan	48	– c Sinclair b O'Connor	65
G. J. Whittall c Parore b Astle	9	– not out	188
*H. H. Streak c Wiseman b O'Connor	8	– lbw b Cairns	54
M. L. Nkala c Parore b McMillan	0	– lbw b O'Connor	0
P. A. Strang c Parore b O'Connor	5	– b Cairns	8
H. K. Olonga c Parore b Nash	4	– lbw b O'Connor	0
M. Mbangwa not out	0	– run out	5
B 3, l-b 3, w 1, n-b 1	8	B 4, l-b 4, n-b 1	9
1/5 (2) 2/76 (3) 3/77 (4) 4/118 (1) 5/146 (6) 6/151 (5) 7/151 (8) 8/157 (7) 9/164 (10) 10/166 (9)	166	1/1 (2) 2/27 (1) 3/39 (4) 4/48 (3) 5/179 (5) 6/330 (7) 7/335 (8) 8/348 (9) 9/349 (10) 10/370 (11)	370

Bowling: *First Innings*—Cairns 17.1–7–33–2; O'Connor 28–9–43–3; Nash 17–11–25–1; McMillan 12.5–2–29–2; Astle 14–9–22–2; Wiseman 3–0–8–0. *Second Innings*—O'Connor 45–17–73–4; Nash 17.3–8–28–0; McMillan 20–4–53–0; Astle 36–16–73–1; Cairns 33–7–80–2; Wiseman 27–11–55–0.

Umpires: D. R. Shepherd (England) and I. D. Robinson.
Third umpire: K. C. Barbour. Referee: C. W. Smith (West Indies).

†At Country Club, Harare, September 25. New Zealanders won by 68 runs. New Zealanders batted first by mutual agreement. New Zealanders 282 for eight (50 overs) (S. P. Fleming 41, R. G. Twose 30, C. M. Spearman 58, C. Z. Harris 53, Extras 38; T. J. Friend three for 49); CFX Academy 214 (48 overs) (D. A. Marillier 117).

†ZIMBABWE v NEW ZEALAND

First One-Day International

At Harare, September 27. New Zealand won by seven wickets. Toss: New Zealand. International debut: G. P. Sulzberger.

Campbell and Wishart got Zimbabwe off to a promising start, but the loss of both to O'Connor in the ninth over put the shackles on the innings. Though Carlisle and Andy Flower shared a fifty partnership, the New Zealanders, as in the recent Test, strained the batsmen's patience with accurate bowling supported by attacking fielding. Only Paul Strang, at the end, scored at a useful rate. In reply, the tourists' batsmen could afford to take their time. Spearman hit three sixes and six fours in his 86, Twose eight fours in his unbeaten 70, as they added 152 in 30 overs. It was all very efficient.

Man of the Match: N. J. Astle.

Zimbabwe

A. D. R. Campbell c Twose b O'Connor	19	P. A. Strang not out	29
C. B. Wishart c Fleming b O'Connor	7	B. C. Strang not out	6
S. V. Carlisle c Nevin b Astle	31		
†A. Flower st Nevin b Sulzberger	34	B 3, l-b 9, w 9, n-b 2	23
G. W. Flower c McMillan b Astle	3		
G. J. Whittall hit wkt b Astle	10	1/34 2/34 3/91 (8 wkts, 50 overs)	183
*H. H. Streak lbw b Harris	21	4/95 5/118 6/128	
D. P. Viljoen run out	0	7/128 8/150	

M. Mbangwa did not bat.

Bowling: O'Connor 7–2–18–2; Tuffey 6–1–24–0; Styris 8–0–39–0; Harris 10–1–30–1; Astle 10–2–24–3; Sulzberger 9–0–36–1.

New Zealand

†C. J. Nevin c P. A. Strang b B. C. Strang	1	R. G. Twose not out	70
N. J. Astle run out	10	C. D. McMillan not out	7
C. M. Spearman c G. W. Flower b P. A. Strang	86	B 4, l-b 3, w 3	10
		1/3 2/14 3/166 (3 wkts, 40.5 overs)	184

*S. P. Fleming, C. Z. Harris, S. B. Styris, G. P. Sulzberger, D. R. Tuffey and S. B. O'Connor did not bat.

Bowling: Streak 8–0–38–0; B. C. Strang 7–2–15–1; Mbangwa 5–0–32–0; Viljoen 5–0–28–0; P. A. Strang 8–0–33–1; G. W. Flower 7.5–0–31–0.

Umpires: K. C. Barbour and G. R. Evans.
Third umpire: Q. J. Goosen.

†ZIMBABWE v NEW ZEALAND

Second One-Day International

At Bulawayo, September 30. Zimbabwe won by 21 runs. Toss: New Zealand. International debuts: T. J. Friend, D. A. Marillier.

An excellent pitch, a fast outfield and an off-the-boil display in the field cost New Zealand their unbeaten record on this tour. Injury and illness kept Nevin and Harris out. Even so, at 189 for three in the 39th over, the New Zealanders were on a par with Zimbabwe – 193 for three at the same stage. Then Twose and McMillan, who had put on 77, went in three balls and, with 80 needed off the last ten overs, Parore ran out of support. The 11 wides and seven no-balls conceded by their bowlers told against New Zealand as much as Streak's last-over attack on Astle, which yielded two successive sixes towards his 11-ball 21. Again put in, Zimbabwe had made a flying start, with Campbell and newcomer Doug Marillier rattling up 83 by the 16th over. Campbell struck 96 from 108 balls.

Man of the Match: H. H. Streak.

Zimbabwe

A. D. R. Campbell b Allott	96	*H. H. Streak not out	21
D. A. Marillier c Fleming b Sulzberger	27		
S. V. Carlisle c Nash b McMillan	25	B 1, l-b 2, w 11, n-b 7	21
†A. Flower c Spearman b Tuffey	19		
G. W. Flower not out	45	1/83 2/139 3/176 (5 wkts, 50 overs)	273
G. J. Whittall b McMillan	19	4/193 5/236	

D. P. Viljoen, P. A. Strang, M. L. Nkala and T. J. Friend did not bat.

Bowling: Allott 10–0–44–1; Tuffey 6–0–48–1; Styris 7–0–47–0; Astle 10–1–52–0; Sulzberger 7–0–38–1; McMillan 10–1–41–2.

New Zealand

*S. P. Fleming c A. Flower b Streak	0	G. P. Sulzberger run out	3
N. J. Astle c Campbell b Streak	12	D. R. Tuffey b Streak	2
C. M. Spearman c Whittall b Viljoen	62	G. I. Allott not out	1
R. G. Twose c and b Strang	64		
C. D. McMillan run out	32	B 1, l-b 7, w 13, n-b 2	23
†A. C. Parore c sub (C. B. Wishart) b Nkala	28	1/1 2/56 3/112 (48.5 overs)	252
D. J. Nash b Viljoen	19	4/189 5/189 6/217	
S. B. Styris st A. Flower b Viljoen	6	7/229 8/237 9/241	

Bowling: Streak 9–0–50–3; Friend 7–0–29–0; Nkala 4.5–0–39–1; Viljoen 10–0–46–3; Strang 10–1–36–1; G. W. Flower 8–0–44–0.

Umpires: C. K. Coventry and R. B. Tiffin.
Third umpire: J. F. Fenwick.

†ZIMBABWE v NEW ZEALAND

Third One-Day International

At Bulawayo, October 1. Zimbabwe won by six wickets. Toss: New Zealand.

Campbell's unbeaten 99 guided Zimbabwe to their first one-day series success against a Test side since early 1997. He and Marillier had 97 on the board inside 20 overs; by the time O'Connor ripped out the Flowers with consecutive deliveries, Zimbabwe required 39 off 37 balls. Whittall's 28 off 14 made that a formality, with two overs in hand – though his big hitting meant Campbell went without a hundred for the second day running. Twose, whose four sixes included three in succession off Viljoen, and McMillan were again the engine-room of New Zealand's batting, putting on 92 in 14 overs. McMillan and Parore then added 68 in 13, but Zimbabwe's fielders – Twose and Parore went to spectacular diving catches – backed up their bowlers brilliantly in near-perfect one-day batting conditions.

Man of the Match: A. D. R. Campbell.

New Zealand

*S. P. Fleming c A. Flower b Streak	11	G. P. Sulzberger not out	6
N. J. Astle c Campbell b P. A. Strang	35	D. R. Tuffey not out	0
C. M. Spearman b B. C. Strang	11		
R. G. Twose c G. W. Flower b Campbell	63	L-b 8, w 11, n-b 1	20
C. D. McMillan lbw b Nkala	78		
†A. C. Parore c Whittall b B. C. Strang	30	1/35 2/54 3/78 (8 wkts, 50 overs)	264
C. Z. Harris c Viljoen b Streak	8	4/170 5/238 6/250	
S. B. Styris c Carlisle b Nkala	2	7/252 8/263	

S. B. O'Connor did not bat.

Bowling: Streak 10–0–30–2; B. C. Strang 10–1–56–2; Nkala 5–0–20–2; Viljoen 9–0–63–0; P. A. Strang 10–0–53–1; G. W. Flower 4–0–24–0; Campbell 2–0–10–1.

Zimbabwe

A. D. R. Campbell not out	99	G. J. Whittall not out	28
D. A. Marillier c Tuffey b Sulzberger	46	B 7, l-b 2, w 7, n-b 3	19
S. V. Carlisle c Spearman b McMillan	30		
†A. Flower b O'Connor	46	1/97 2/148 (4 wkts, 47.5 overs)	268
G. W. Flower b O'Connor	0	3/226 4/226	

*H. H. Streak, D. P. Viljoen, P. A. Strang, B. C. Strang and M. L. Nkala did not bat.

Bowling: O'Connor 8.5–0–56–2; Tuffey 5–0–40–0; Styris 9–0–41–0; Harris 9–0–50–0; Sulzberger 6–0–28–1; Astle 7–1–28–0; McMillan 3–0–16–1.

Umpires: J. F. Fenwick and I. D. Robinson.
Third umpire: C. K. Coventry. Series referee: C. W. Smith (West Indies).

†At Soweto, October 18. New Zealanders won by 79 runs. Toss: New Zealanders. New Zealanders 296 for five (50 overs) (N. J. Astle 137, S. P. Fleming 82, Extras 36; Z. de Bruyn three for 63); Gauteng 217 for six (50 overs) (A. M. Bacher 54, A. J. Hall 44, A. J. Seymore 48 not out; B. G. K. Walker four for 32).

†SOUTH AFRICA v NEW ZEALAND

First One-Day International

At Potchefstroom, October 20 (day/night). No result. Toss: New Zealand.

Torrential rain put paid to Potchefstroom's first one-day international – there had already been an 80-minute stoppage after 33 overs – but not before Boje completed his maiden hundred at this level. Some of his hitting matched the threatening storm clouds for dramatic effect as he thundered to 105 not out from 93 balls, with 12 fours. Dippenaar, with whom he added 129 in 25 overs, was much more sedate, taking 104 balls for his 57.

South Africa

H. H. Dippenaar c O'Connor b Harris . .	57
G. Kirsten c Cairns b O'Connor	13
N. Boje not out	105
J. H. Kallis not out.	8
L-b 3, w 2, n-b 3	8
1/33 2/162 (2 wkts, 38 overs)	191

D. J. Cullinan, J. N. Rhodes, L. Klusener, †M. V. Boucher, *S. M. Pollock, A. A. Donald and M. Ntini did not bat.

Bowling: Allott 7–1–33–0; O'Connor 8–0–41–1; Cairns 8–1–34–0; Styris 3–0–21–0; Harris 7–1–32–1; Astle 5–0–27–0.

New Zealand

C. J. Nevin, N. J. Astle, *S. P. Fleming, R. G. Twose, C. L. Cairns, C. D. McMillan, C. Z. Harris, †A. C. Parore, S. B. Styris, S. B. O'Connor and G. I. Allott.

Umpires: R. E. Koertzen and D. L. Orchard.
Third umpire: D. F. Becker.

†SOUTH AFRICA v NEW ZEALAND

Second One-Day International

At Benoni, October 22. South Africa won by six wickets. Toss: New Zealand. International debut: B. G. K. Walker.

New Zealand's batsmen never overcame a slow pitch producing disconcertingly low bounce from the start. Moreover, the decision to play two slow bowlers – leg-spinner Brooke Walker making his debut alongside Wiseman – meant that they lacked the wherewithal to exploit its vagaries when South Africa batted. Astle took 39 overs for his 58 and no one threatened the South African seamers' supremacy. Telemachus, having missed the opening game through suspension after a misdemeanour in Nairobi, conceded only ten runs in his first spell of six overs. A stand of 111 in 23 overs between Kirsten and Boje established the home team's reply, with Boje again a revelation in the No. 3 spot.

Man of the Match: N. Boje.

New Zealand

C. J. Nevin lbw b Telemachus	5	S. B. Styris not out	10
N. J. Astle b Donald	58	B. G. K. Walker not out	5
*S. P. Fleming b Donald	5		
R. G. Twose b Kallis	16	B 1, l-b 10, w 13, n-b 2	26
C. L. Cairns b Klusener	26		
C. Z. Harris c Kallis b Pollock	19	1/10 2/38 3/65 (8 wkts, 50 overs)	194
C. D. McMillan lbw b Pollock	13	4/118 5/134 6/162	
†A. C. Parore c Rhodes b Kallis	11	7/165 8/183	

P. J. Wiseman did not bat.

Bowling: Pollock 10–1–32–2; Telemachus 10–5–16–1; Kallis 7–1–34–2; Donald 10–1–51–2; Klusener 8–0–32–1; Boje 5–1–18–0.

South Africa

G. Kirsten b Styris	57	J. N. Rhodes not out	17
H. H. Dippenaar c Styris b Cairns	9	L-b 3, w 7, n-b 1	11
N. Boje c Twose b Harris	64		
J. H. Kallis not out	39	1/25 2/136 (4 wkts, 46.4 overs)	197
D. J. Cullinan c Cairns b Harris	0	3/158 4/159	

L. Klusener, †M. V. Boucher, *S. M. Pollock, R. Telemachus and A. A. Donald did not bat.

Bowling: Cairns 8–0–38–1; Styris 10–1–24–1; Astle 3–0–19–0; McMillan 3–0–20–0; Harris 10–0–39–2; Wiseman 4.4–0–24–0; Walker 8–2–30–0.

Umpires: D. F. Becker and R. E. Koertzen.
Third umpire: S. B. Lambson.

†SOUTH AFRICA v NEW ZEALAND

Third One-Day International

At Centurion, October 25 (day/night). South Africa won by 115 runs (D/L method). Toss: New Zealand.

For the third time in three games, Boje gave New Zealand the run-around, hitting a six and 13 fours in 129 from 114 balls. On a superb batting strip, he and Kirsten established a one-day South African second-wicket record, with 160 in 27 overs, and provided the platform for their second-highest one-day total, and best against a Test side (they scored 328 for three against Holland in the 1995-96 World Cup). Boje and Kallis then added 79 at seven an over. Rain in New Zealand's fifth over prompted a revised target of 305 from 43 overs. Astle and Fleming put on 56 in seven, after which 72 in 12 by Astle and Twose kept the Kiwis in the hunt. Then Telemachus, who had removed Nevin with his first ball (caught Boje at square leg), nipped out Twose and Cairns with successive deliveries. When Boje ran out McMillan and had Astle caught at mid-wicket, the result was as clear-cut as the match award.

Man of the Match: N. Boje.

South Africa

D. J. Cullinan b Cairns	22	J. N. Rhodes not out	0
G. Kirsten c Parore b Cairns	94	L-b 5, w 4, n-b 8	17
N. Boje c Cairns b Allott	129		
J. H. Kallis c Twose b Styris	45	1/44 2/204 (4 wkts, 50 overs)	324
L. Klusener not out	17	3/283 4/322	

H. H. Dippenaar, †M. V. Boucher, *S. M. Pollock, R. Telemachus and A. A. Donald did not bat.

Bowling: O'Connor 6–0–46–0; Allott 10–0–69–1; Cairns 8–0–62–2; Styris 10–0–56–1; Harris 10–0–55–0; Astle 6–0–31–0.

New Zealand

C. J. Nevin c Boje b Telemachus	7	S. B. Styris c Boucher b Donald	1
N. J. Astle c Dippenaar b Boje	46	S. B. O'Connor c Boucher b Pollock	1
*S. P. Fleming c Kirsten b Pollock	35	G. I. Allott c Boucher b Pollock	0
R. G. Twose b Telemachus	40	B 5, l-b 5, w 1, n-b 1	12
C. L. Cairns b Telemachus	0		
C. D. McMillan run out	13	1/7 2/63 3/135 (33.4 overs)	189
C. Z. Harris c Cullinan b Donald	17	4/135 5/149 6/151	
†A. C. Parore not out	17	7/185 8/187 9/189	

Bowling: Pollock 7.4–1–37–3; Telemachus 6–1–45–3; Donald 7–1–27–2; Kallis 7–0–39–0; Klusener 5–0–29–0; Boje 1–0–2–1.

Umpires: S. B. Lambson and D. L. Orchard.
Third umpire: B. G. Jerling.

†SOUTH AFRICA v NEW ZEALAND

Fourth One-Day International

At Kimberley, October 28. South Africa won by five wickets. Toss: South Africa.

Cairns, big-hitting hero of New Zealand's ICC Knockout success, was on the receiving end of a breathtaking finish that gave South Africa the series with two to play. They needed 16 off the last two overs: in just five balls, Boucher hit Cairns over long-on for six and Boje struck a straight six and four off him. Brisk batting by Nevin and Twose in support of Fleming had produced New Zealand's best total of the series, though Twose might have gone for nought had a power failure in an outside broadcast unit not prevented the third umpire from ruling on a close run-out call. Kirsten, hitting his tenth one-day international hundred, and Kallis kept South Africa in contention by adding 172 in just under 33 overs. It was the second time in four days that Kirsten had broken his country's second-wicket record.

Man of the Match: G. Kirsten.

New Zealand

C. J. Nevin b Boje	68	C. Z. Harris not out	11
N. J. Astle c Boucher b Telemachus	5	†A. C. Parore not out	0
*S. P. Fleming run out	85	B 2, l-b 2, w 2, n-b 1	7
R. G. Twose c Pollock b Kallis	89		
C. L. Cairns c Pollock b Kallis	21	1/20 2/113 3/223 (6 wkts, 50 overs)	287
C. D. McMillan c Kirsten b Pollock	1	4/272 5/275 6/283	

S. B. Styris, B. G. K. Walker and S. B. O'Connor did not bat.

Bowling: Pollock 10–0–40–1; Telemachus 9–0–60–1; Donald 5–0–46–0; Kallis 8–0–46–2; Boje 10–0–42–1; Klusener 8–0–49–0.

South Africa

D. J. Cullinan c Astle b Cairns	17	†M. V. Boucher not out	18
G. Kirsten c Parore b Cairns	101		
J. H. Kallis c Walker b Styris	93	L-b 2, w 3, n-b 1	6
J. N. Rhodes b Harris	25		
L. Klusener c Fleming b Styris	9	1/43 2/215 3/221 (5 wkts, 48.5 overs)	289
N. Boje not out	20	4/247 5/255	

H. H. Dippenaar, *S. M. Pollock, R. Telemachus and A. A. Donald did not bat.

Bowling: Cairns 9.5–2–67–2; O'Connor 8–0–46–0; Styris 10–0–56–2; Harris 10–0–58–1; Walker 7–0–41–0; Astle 4–0–19–0.

Umpires: B. G. Jerling and R. E. Koertzen.
Third umpire: W. A. Diedricks.

†SOUTH AFRICA v NEW ZEALAND

Fifth One-Day International

At Durban, November 1 (day/night). South Africa won by six wickets (D/L method). Toss: South Africa.

New Zealand were still coming to terms with an awkward pitch, along with the loss of Twose and Fleming in successive overs, when the rain that delayed the start returned to interrupt and then end their innings. South Africa's revised target was 153 from 32 overs. Kallis, whose earlier dismissal of Twose was his 100th one-day international wicket, anchored their reply with an unbeaten 50 from 81 balls. But it was Klusener, in front of his home crowd, who dashed New Zealand's hope of victory by hitting 41 in 18 balls, including 26 from his last six (4424 off Allott, two sixes off O'Connor).

Man of the Match: J. H. Kallis.

New Zealand

C. J. Nevin c Kallis b Pollock	0
N. J. Astle c Kallis b Donald	3
*S. P. Fleming lbw b Ntini	21
R. G. Twose b Kallis	38
C. L. Cairns not out	25
C. D. McMillan c Boucher b Ntini	3
C. Z. Harris not out	9
L-b 14, w 1	15
1/2 2/8 3/71 4/73 5/81 (5 wkts, 32.4 overs)	114

†A. C. Parore, S. B. Styris, S. B. O'Connor and G. I. Allott did not bat.

Bowling: Pollock 6–2–22–1; Donald 6–3–11–1; Ntini 8–2–21–2; Kallis 6–1–14–1; Klusener 4–0–26–0; Hall 2.4–1–6–0.

South Africa

D. J. Cullinan lbw b Allott	7
G. Kirsten c Parore b Cairns	3
J. H. Kallis not out	50
N. Boje c Harris b Astle	29
J. N. Rhodes b Astle	19
L. Klusener not out	41
L-b 1, w 7, n-b 1	9
1/11 2/11 3/76 4/100 (4 wkts, 30.3 overs)	158

†M. V. Boucher, *S. M. Pollock, A. J. Hall, A. A. Donald and M. Ntini did not bat.

Bowling: Allott 6–1–38–1; Cairns 7–0–29–1; O'Connor 5.3–1–22–0; Styris 6–0–27–0; Astle 5–0–32–2; McMillan 1–0–9–0.

Umpires: W. A. Diedricks and D. L. Orchard.
Third umpire: I. L. Howell.

†SOUTH AFRICA v NEW ZEALAND

Sixth One-Day International

At Cape Town, November 4. South Africa won by three wickets. Toss: South Africa. International debut: S. Abrahams.

Newlands' short straight boundaries brought out the best from Cairns (four sixes, seven fours) and Klusener (four sixes, two fours). And it was those two fours by Klusener off O'Connor, when South Africa needed seven from two balls, that consigned the Black Caps to a virtual whitewash. Cairns's partnership of 150 in 23 overs with Twose could have been the basis for a winning total had New Zealand's later batsmen not let South Africa back in the game. O'Connor reclaimed lost ground with three wickets in his first four overs, but Rhodes and Boucher rebuilt the home reply with a century stand at five an over. When three wickets fell in six overs, newcomer Shafiek Abrahams sensibly left the heroics to Klusener, whose 59 not out came from 42 balls.

Man of the Match: L. Klusener. *Man of the Series:* N. Boje.

New Zealand

C. J. Nevin c Abrahams b Telemachus	12
N. J. Astle c Boje b Pollock	8
*S. P. Fleming c Rhodes b Donald	8
R. G. Twose c Kallis b Boje	103
C. L. Cairns c Pollock b Telemachus	84
C. D. McMillan lbw b Pollock	7
C. Z. Harris c Pollock b Telemachus	6
†A. C. Parore run out	1
S. B. Styris run out	8
B. G. K. Walker not out	2
S. B. O'Connor not out	1
L-b 7, w 7, n-b 2	16
1/23 2/24 3/39 4/189 5/218 6/238 7/239 8/249 9/253 (9 wkts, 50 overs)	256

Bowling: Pollock 10–1–44–2; Telemachus 10–1–30–3; Donald 10–0–47–1; Kallis 5–0–52–0; Abrahams 10–0–40–0; Klusener 2–0–27–0; Boje 3–0–9–1.

South Africa

D. J. Cullinan b O'Connor	10
G. Kirsten c and b Harris	25
J. H. Kallis lbw b O'Connor	0
N. Boje c Parore b O'Connor	8
J. N. Rhodes st Parore b Walker	69
†M. V. Boucher b Harris	46
L. Klusener not out	59
*S. M. Pollock c sub (D. R. Tuffey) b Walker	8
S. Abrahams not out	16
L-b 9, w 5, n-b 3	17
1/16 2/16 3/30 4/65 5/171 6/173 7/189 (7 wkts, 50 overs)	258

R. Telemachus and A. A. Donald did not bat.

Bowling: Cairns 10–0–45–0; O'Connor 9–1–55–3; Styris 9–0–47–0; Harris 10–0–45–2; Walker 9–1–43–2; Astle 3–0–14–0.

Umpires: I. L. Howell and R. E. Koertzen.
Third umpire: W. A. Diedricks. Series referee: Talat Ali (Pakistan).

At Paarl, November 7, 8, 9. Drawn. Toss: New Zealanders. New Zealanders 403 for five dec. (M. H. Richardson 173 not out, M. S. Sinclair 86, H. J. H. Marshall 38, S. B. Styris 73 not out) and 142 for three dec. (M. S. Sinclair 51, C. D. McMillan 52 not out); Boland 189 (J. M. Henderson 61, J. L. Ontong 56; C. S. Martin three for 45, S. B. Styris three for 25) and 53 for two (I. J. L. Trott 30).

At Potchefstroom, November 11, 12, 13. New Zealanders won by 265 runs. Toss: New Zealanders. New Zealanders 280 for six dec. (C. M. Spearman 100, M. S. Sinclair 37, N. J. Astle 63, A. C. Parore 32 not out; F. van der Merwe three for 74) and 242 for two dec. (M. H. Richardson 39, C. M. Spearman 115 retired out, S. P. Fleming 52 not out); North West 100 (E. G. Poole 35; S. B. O'Connor three for 14, D. R. Tuffey three for 23, C. S. Martin three for 27) and 157 (M. Strydom 39; D. R. Tuffey three for 58, S. B. O'Connor five for 51).

Spearman, after scoring his second hundred of the match, was the first New Zealander to retire out in a first-class game.

SOUTH AFRICA v NEW ZEALAND

First Test Match

At Bloemfontein, November 17, 18, 19, 20, 21. South Africa won by five wickets. Toss: South Africa. Test debuts: C. S. Martin, B. G. K. Walker.

New Zealand's injury-inflicted predicament was amply illustrated by the record of the respective pace attacks. Chris Martin was making his debut and Tuffey playing in his second Test; only O'Connor had taken wickets in a Test match. Donald and Pollock, on the other hand, had 483 between them, with Donald in his 63rd Test needing three to become the first South African to 300 Test wickets.

It was not the time for the tourists to discover Kallis at the top of his form. Having Dippenaar caught at second slip off the second ball of the match lost all significance as Kallis blunted then battered bowlers who betrayed their inexperience by ignoring the basic disciplines. His seventh Test hundred, a Test-highest 160 from 289 balls, contained 26 fours and, particularly on the opening day, he was given too much width. McKenzie reached a maiden Test fifty after aiding Kallis in a century partnership. Although New Zealand broke through next morning, Boucher and Boje consolidated South Africa's position by adding 79 in 68 minutes.

New Zealand began the third day needing another 218 to avoid the follow-on, with eight wickets in hand. Fleming organised the resistance with a solid fifty, but from his dismissal, undone by Boje's sharp turn, his side lost their last seven wickets for 78. Walker and O'Connor held firm for 22 overs before Donald, who had captured his 299th wicket just before lunch when McMillan was caught behind, took the new ball and, with his sixth delivery, had O'Connor lbw. An appreciative home-town crowd and a three-gun salute from an armoured car near the boundary greeted the 300th wicket.

With the pitch playing slower and lower, New Zealand made a better fist of their second innings. Richardson's good technique and excellent judgment launched the fight for survival; he batted 63 overs for his 77. Fleming reached 50 for the 28th time in Tests, only to fall one short of a third Test hundred. When 98, with an hour's play remaining and New Zealand ahead for the first time in the match, he accepted the offer of bad light. But play resumed 23 minutes later, and Fleming had added just one run when Donald produced an explosive delivery he could only fend to gully. Next morning, Kallis's slower ball ended McMillan's 67-over stay, and straight after lunch Ntini took three wickets in three overs to complete Test-best figures of six for 66 – deserved reward for unstinting fast bowling in thankless conditions.

South Africa needed 101 for victory, with time no object. It should have been a formality; it could have been an embarrassment. They somehow contrived to lose five wickets by the final session before Boucher, sweeping three successive balls from leg-spinner Brooke Walker for four, completed South Africa's win.

Men of the Match: J. H. Kallis and M. Ntini.

Close of play: First day, South Africa 270-3 (Kallis 153*, McKenzie 42*); Second day, New Zealand 54-2 (Spearman 14*, Fleming 10*); Third day, New Zealand 82-1 (Richardson 50*, Sinclair 11*); Fourth day, New Zealand 260-5 (McMillan 25*, Walker 5*).

South Africa

H. H. Dippenaar c Astle b O'Connor	0	– c Parore b Tuffey	27
G. Kirsten c Astle b Martin	31	– lbw b O'Connor	1
J. H. Kallis c Parore b O'Connor	160	– lbw b Martin	13
D. J. Cullinan b Walker	29	– lbw b Tuffey	22
N. D. McKenzie c Parore b Martin	55	– not out	13
†M. V. Boucher lbw b Walker	76	– (7) not out	22
L. Klusener b O'Connor	9	– (6) c McMillan b Tuffey	4
N. Boje c Tuffey b Astle	43		
*S. M. Pollock c Sinclair b Martin	25		
A. A. Donald not out	21		
B 5, l-b 7, n-b 10	22	N-b 1	1
1/0 (1) 2/97 (2) 3/164 (4) 4/279 (3) 5/304 (5) 6/330 (7) 7/409 (8) 8/429 (6) 9/471 (9)	(9 wkts dec.) 471	1/3 (2) 2/16 (3) 3/55 (1) 4/69 (4) 5/75 (6)	(5 wkts) 103

M. Ntini did not bat.

Bowling: *First Innings*—O'Connor 30–4–87–3; Tuffey 26–6–96–0; Martin 22.1–4–89–3; Walker 27–4–92–2; Astle 24–5–57–1; McMillan 13–2–38–0. *Second Innings*—O'Connor 7–0–28–1; Martin 5–3–18–1; Tuffey 8–1–38–3; Walker 6.3–2–19–0.

New Zealand

M. H. Richardson b Donald	23	– lbw b Donald	77
C. M. Spearman c Klusener b Pollock	23	– c McKenzie b Ntini	15
M. S. Sinclair c Cullinan b Pollock	1	– c Klusener b Donald	20
*S. P. Fleming b Boje	57	– c Kirsten b Donald	99
N. J. Astle c Kallis b Ntini	37	– b Ntini	8
C. D. McMillan c Boucher b Donald	16	– c Kirsten b Kallis	78
†A. C. Parore lbw b Pollock	11	– (8) c Kallis b Ntini	12
B. G. K. Walker not out	27	– (7) c Boucher b Ntini	10
D. R. Tuffey b Pollock	0	– b Ntini	6
S. B. O'Connor lbw b Donald	15	– b Ntini	0
C. S. Martin c Boucher b Kallis	7	– not out	0
B 1, l-b 7, w 2, n-b 2	12	B 2, l-b 10, w 1, n-b 4	17
1/28 (1) 2/29 (3) 3/72 (2) 4/151 (4) 5/153 (5) 6/176 (6) 7/183 (7) 8/185 (9) 9/213 (10) 10/229 (11)	229	1/33 (2) 2/93 (3) 3/145 (1) 4/175 (5) 5/247 (4) 6/285 (7) 7/325 (6) 8/340 (9) 9/341 (8) 10/342 (10)	342

Bowling: *First Innings*—Donald 21–4–69–3; Pollock 22–10–37–4; Ntini 14–4–48–1; Kallis 13–5–30–1; Boje 16–4–35–1; Klusener 3–2–2–0. *Second Innings*—Donald 28–14–43–3; Pollock 25–11–47–0; Ntini 31.4–12–66–6; Kallis 23–4–88–1; Boje 40–14–61–0; Klusener 10–3–25–0.

Umpires: A. V. Jayaprakash (India) and D. L. Orchard.
Third umpire: R. E. Koertzen. Referee: Naushad Ali (Pakistan).

†At Alice, November 24. New Zealanders won by two wickets. Toss: New Zealanders. Border 226 for eight (50 overs) (L. L. Gamiet 84, C. B. Sugden 36, Extras 37; N. J. Astle four for 25); New Zealanders 227 for eight (49 overs) (M. H. Richardson 43, C. M. Spearman 31, C. D. McMillan 55, D. R. Tuffey 38 not out; S. C. Pope four for 38).

Astle (11–2–25–4) bowled one over too many.

At East London, November 25, 26, 27. New Zealanders won by 211 runs. Toss: New Zealanders. New Zealanders 311 for four dec. (M. H. Richardson 45, C. M. Spearman 56, N. J. Astle 69 not out, C. D. McMillan 76 not out) and 185 for no wkt dec. (A. C. Parore 101 not out, C. M. Spearman 57 retired hurt); Border 73 (A. J. Penn five for 38, B. G. K. Walker three for 13) and 212 (S. C. Pope 33, W. Wiblin 46, P. C. Strydom 32; D. R. Tuffey five for 69).

Penn returned to New Zealand after incurring a side strain in this match.

SOUTH AFRICA v NEW ZEALAND

Second Test Match

At Port Elizabeth, November 30, December 1, 2, 3, 4. South Africa won by seven wickets. Toss: South Africa.

"Poor batsmanship and poor option-taking," was how New Zealand captain Fleming explained the disastrous session that determined this match on the fourth day. Between lunch and tea, his side lost five second-innings wickets for 69; when Klusener subsequently took the last three wickets in ten balls, South Africa needed just 86 runs for their fourth successive series win at home since drawing with Pakistan in 1997-98

Until then, the cricket had been grudging and evenly contested on a pitch that offered bowlers fewer favours than Pollock expected when he inserted the New Zealanders. Donald's absence on the first afternoon with a bruised heel may have dampened South Africa's powder, but Pollock and Ntini gave the batsmen little respite with accurate bowling that produced regular breakthroughs. Ntini supported his captain further when he ran in from fine leg and dived forward to hold McMillan's top-edged hook.

By the end of the second day, New Zealand had clawed their way back through Sinclair's 150, his eighth-wicket stand of 73 with O'Connor, and tight, combative bowling after South Africa's openers had put on 81. The slip catches that Klusener missed when O'Connor was five and Sinclair 121 had taken on an important aspect. Watchful, and patiently waiting to play to his off-side strength, especially off the back foot, Sinclair batted six and a half hours for his second Test century – his first was 214 on debut against West Indies a year earlier – hitting a six and 23 fours in 321 balls. It was the highest for New Zealand against South Africa, beating John Reid's 142 at Johannesburg in 1961-62.

McKenzie's maiden Test hundred, a stylish four-and-a-half-hour 120 graced by 20 fours, regained the initiative for South Africa on the third afternoon. With the new ball claiming Pollock, Boucher and Klusener either side of lunch, leaving South Africa 209 for seven, New Zealand were in a good position to establish a handy lead. Then McKenzie and Boje – something of a scourge with the bat for these tourists – added 136, a South African eighth-wicket record against New Zealand, and at the close South Africa were 63 ahead.

Nor was Boje finished with the New Zealanders. Last out in the third over next morning, he trapped Sinclair lbw almost on the stroke of lunch and had new batsman Fleming caught at slip two overs later. New Zealand had just cleared the arrears. When Pollock removed Richardson and McMillan with successive balls, and Astle was caught behind off Ntini five balls later, South Africa finally gained the upper hand. Only Donald's incapacity with a stomach muscle strain, making him doubtful for the final game, cast a shadow over Pollock's first Test series win as captain.

Man of the Match: N. D. McKenzie.

Close of play: First day, New Zealand 206-7 (Sinclair 88*, O'Connor 3*); Second day, South Africa 123-3 (Cullinan 13*, Pollock 5*); Third day, South Africa 361-8 (Boje 51*, Donald 9*); Fourth day, South Africa 29-1 (Kirsten 22*, Kallis 6*).

New Zealand

M. H. Richardson b Ntini	26	– c Boucher b Pollock	60
C. M. Spearman c Kirsten b Donald	16	– lbw b Donald	0
M. S. Sinclair c Kirsten b Donald	150	– lbw b Boje	17
*S. P. Fleming c and b Pollock	14	– c Cullinan b Boje	8
N. J. Astle lbw b Pollock	2	– c Boucher b Ntini	18
C. D. McMillan c Ntini b Pollock	39	– lbw b Pollock	0
†A. C. Parore c Boucher b Donald	2	– c Kirsten b Ntini	5
B. G. K. Walker c Cullinan b Pollock	3	– lbw b Klusener	19
S. B. O'Connor b Kallis	20	– b Klusener	8
K. P. Walmsley c Cullinan b Donald	5	– lbw b Klusener	0
C. S. Martin not out	5	– not out	0
B 4, l-b 5, w 2, n-b 5	16	B 6, l-b 3, n-b 4	13
1/43 (2) 2/55 (1) 3/95 (4) 4/101 (5) 5/172 (6) 6/194 (7) 7/203 (8) 8/276 (9) 9/291 (3) 10/298 (10)	298	1/4 (2) 2/54 (3) 3/64 (4) 4/111 (1) 5/111 (6) 6/115 (5) 7/122 (7) 8/147 (9) 9/147 (10) 10/148 (8)	148

Bowling: *First Innings*—Donald 26.3–2–69–4; Pollock 32–15–64–4; Kallis 21–8–44–1; Ntini 22–7–59–1; Klusener 6–2–8–0; Boje 19–5–45–0. *Second Innings*—Donald 7–1–16–1; Pollock 15–4–44–2; Ntini 16–6–24–2; Boje 15–2–30–2; Kallis 7–2–17–0; Klusener 9.3–5–8–3.

South Africa

H. H. Dippenaar lbw b Martin	35	– lbw b O'Connor	0
G. Kirsten c Parore b Walmsley	49	– not out	47
J. H. Kallis c Parore b Astle	12	– c O'Connor b Martin	23
D. J. Cullinan b Walker	33	– b Walmsley	11
*S. M. Pollock c Spearman b Martin	33		
N. D. McKenzie c Spearman b McMillan	120	– (5) not out	7
†M. V. Boucher b O'Connor	0		
L. Klusener c Parore b Martin	6		
N. Boje c Parore b O'Connor	51		
A. A. Donald lbw b Martin	9		
M. Ntini not out	0		
B 7, l-b 4, w 2	13	L-b 1	1
1/81 (1) 2/96 (3) 3/114 (2) 4/151 (4) 5/181 (5) 6/184 (7) 7/209 (8) 8/345 (6) 9/361 (10) 10/361 (9)	361	1/4 (1) 2/53 (3) 3/71 (4)	(3 wkts) 89

Bowling: *First Innings*—O'Connor 26.4–8–68–2; Martin 29–8–104–4; Walmsley 13–2–40–1; Walker 23–5–61–1; Astle 36–18–46–1; McMillan 17–6–31–1. *Second Innings*—O'Connor 8–4–9–1; Martin 12–3–32–1; Astle 2–0–8–0; Walker 7.1–1–32–0; Walmsley 5–2–7–1.

Umpires: I. D. Robinson (Zimbabwe) and R. E. Koertzen.
Third umpire: D. L. Orchard. Referee: Naushad Ali (Pakistan).

SOUTH AFRICA v NEW ZEALAND

Third Test Match

At Johannesburg, December 8, 9, 10, 11, 12. Drawn. Toss: South Africa. Test debuts: M. Ngam; H. J. H. Marshall.

Rain and then a waterlogged outfield prevented any play on the first, third and fourth days; on the other two, South Africa confirmed their supremacy. In the absence of the injured Donald, they gave a debut to Mfuneko Ngam, while New Zealand made two changes, introducing Hamish Marshall and bringing back the inconsistent Tuffey for Walmsley, who had replaced him at Port Elizabeth for his third Test in almost six years.

Ngam should have had a wicket in his first over. Cullinan, at slip, dropped makeshift opener Parore, and in Ngam's third over did it again. Dippenaar, at short leg, also gave each opener a life – Richardson when 18 – and New Zealand could count their good fortune when they lunched at 83 for one. They were unable to capitalise on it. Five wickets fell for 38 runs in the second session, starting with the dismissals of Richardson – Ngam's first victim, at last – and Sinclair immediately after the resumption. The increasingly impressive Ntini had Fleming and Astle in successive overs and only newcomer Marshall survived the middle-order débâcle, if not without alarms. He was an hour and 38 balls over opening his Test account and was struck on the helmet more than once, but without his three-hour struggle New Zealand could not have reached 200.

South Africa lost Kirsten, caught at short leg, two balls before bad light sent the players off. When play resumed three days later, however, there were no easy pickings for the New Zealand bowlers. With Herschelle Gibbs's rehabilitation imminent, Dippenaar took advantage of the "dead" day to try to establish a Test place, putting together his maiden Test hundred from 192 balls with 21 fours. As if the pointlessness of the proceedings needed accentuating, Kallis hung around after their century partnership to finish 79 not out from 211 balls; Cullinan faced 112 for his unbeaten 31. In the circumstances, it was not surprising that the match award cheque went, not to a player, but to Wanderers groundsman Chris Scott and his staff.

Men of the Match: C. Scott and groundstaff. *Man of the Series:* M. Ntini.

Close of play: First day, No play; Second day, South Africa 18-1 (Dippenaar 5*, Boje 0*); Third day, No play; Fourth day, No play.

New Zealand

M. H. Richardson c Boucher b Ngam	46	S. B. O'Connor c Kallis b Pollock	9
†A. C. Parore c McKenzie b Ntini	10	C. S. Martin b Kallis	0
M. S. Sinclair c Klusener b Pollock	24		
*S. P. Fleming b Ntini	14	B 2, l-b 9, w 1, n-b 4	16
N. J. Astle c Kallis b Ntini	12		
C. D. McMillan c Klusener b Kallis	4	1/37 (2) 2/83 (1) 3/83 (3)	200
H. J. H. Marshall not out	40	4/112 (4) 5/113 (5) 6/117 (6)	
B. G. K. Walker lbw b Klusener	17	7/148 (8) 8/174 (9)	
D. R. Tuffey c Boucher b Ngam	8	9/199 (10) 10/200 (11)	

Bowling: Pollock 26–9–41–2; Ngam 19–8–34–2; Kallis 15.5–4–26–2; Ntini 18–9–29–3; Klusener 12–2–43–1; Boje 3–0–16–0.

South Africa

H. H. Dippenaar b O'Connor	100	D. J. Cullinan not out	31
G. Kirsten c Richardson b Martin	10	L-b 17, w 2	19
N. Boje c Sinclair b Martin	22		
J. H. Kallis not out	79	1/18 (2) 2/87 (3) 3/187 (1) (3 wkts dec.)	261

N. D. McKenzie, †M. V. Boucher, L. Klusener, *S. M. Pollock, M. Ntini and M. Ngam did not bat.

Bowling: O'Connor 15–5–52–1; Martin 15–4–43–2; Tuffey 19–4–60–0; Astle 26–15–31–0; McMillan 17–5–41–0; Marshall 1–0–4–0; Sinclair 4–0–13–0.

Umpires: G. Sharp (England) and D. L. Orchard.
Third umpire: R. E. Koertzen. Referee: Naushad Ali (Pakistan).

TEST RESULTS, 2000-01 AND 2001

	P	*W*	*L*	*D*	*% W*
Australia	13	10	3	0	76.92
South Africa	11	6	1	4	54.54
India	11	6	4	1	54.54
England	13	5	6	2	38.46
New Zealand	9	3	3	3	33.33
Sri Lanka	9	3	5	1	33.33
Zimbabwe	11	3	5	3	27.27
Pakistan	8	2	3	3	25.00
West Indies	12	2	7	3	16.66
Bangladesh	3	0	3	0	0.00

The table does not include Pakistan's victory over Bangladesh (August 29–31) in the 2001-02 Asian Test Championship.

THE BANGLADESHIS IN SOUTH AFRICA, 2000-01

Bangladesh made a short tour of South Africa after their early exit from the ICC Knockout Trophy in Nairobi, before returning home to play their inaugural Test against India in November. They lost all four fixtures, one first-class and three one-day.

BANGLADESHI TOURING PARTY

Naimur Rahman (Dhaka Metropolis) (*captain*), Akram Khan (Chittagong), Al-Shahriar Rokon (Dhaka Metropolis), Aminul Islam (Biman), Bikash Ranjan Das (Dhaka Division), Ehsanul Haque (Chittagong), Enamul Haque (Chittagong), Habibul Bashar (Biman), Hasibul Hussain (Sylhet), Javed Omar (Biman), Khaled Masud (Rajshahi), Manjurul Islam (Khulna), Mohammad Rafiq (Sylhet), Mushfiqur Rehman (Rajshahi).

Shahriar Hossain (Dhaka Division) withdrew after being injured and was replaced by Ehsanul Haque.

Manager: Mahmudul Huq Manu. *Coaches:* E. J. Barlow and Sarwar Imran.

BANGLADESHI TOUR RESULTS

First-class match – Lost v Griqualand West.
Non-first-class matches – Played 3: Lost 3. *Losses* – South African President's XI (3).

Note: Matches in this section which were not first-class are signified by a dagger.

At Kimberley, October 12, 13, 14, 15. Griqualand West won by 82 runs. Toss: Griqualand West. Griqualand West 324 (J. M. Arthur 47, G. D. Elliott 44, P. P. J. Koortzen 127, A. K. Kruger 48; Naimur Rahman three for 60, Mohammad Rafiq three for 46) and 339 for eight dec. (G. D. Elliott 125, W. M. Dry 41, G. J. Kruis 59, W. Bossenger 36; Naimur Rahman three for 116); Bangladeshis 333 (Al-Shahriar Rokon 47, Akram Khan 129 not out, Mohammad Rafiq 51, Extras 33; G. J. Kruis five for 80, C. A. Copeland four for 112) and 248 (Javed Omar 41, Al-Shahriar Rokon 70, Akram Khan 51 not out; C. A. Copeland eight for 101).

Scorer Piet Hourani died while preparing for the second day's play.

†At Bloemfontein, October 18. South African President's XI won by seven wickets. Toss: Bangladeshis. Bangladeshis 178 (45.4 overs) (Al-Shahriar Rokon 38, Naimur Rahman 52; A. Nel three for 36); South African President's XI 181 for three (49.1 overs) (M. L. Bruyns 55, D. J. Watson 39, D. M. Benkenstein 44 not out).

†At Pietermaritzburg, October 22. South African President's XI won by ten wickets. Toss: South African President's XI. Bangladeshis 51 (18.3 overs) (C. K. Langeveldt five for seven); South African President's XI 53 for no wkt (14.1 overs).

†At Durban, October 23 (day/night). South African President's XI won by 202 runs. Toss: Bangladeshis. South African President's XI 259 for five (50 overs) (G. C. Smith 56, A. M. Amla 68, J. A. Rudolph 48, M. van Jaarsveld 62; Naimur Rahman three for 45); Bangladeshis 57 (27.2 overs) (C. M. Willoughby three for nine, M. Ngam four for 20).

Extras (15) were the highest score in the Bangladeshis' innings here, as they had been the previous day at Pietermaritzburg (with 12).

THE WEST INDIANS IN AUSTRALIA, 2000-01

By GREG BAUM

Before their landmark triumph in the Caribbean in 1994-95, Australia had beaten West Indies only six times in 17 years in Test matches, mostly in dead rubbers. Now they beat them five times in six weeks to register the first clean sweep in series between these countries, though Greg Chappell's Australians won a six-Test series 5–1 in 1975-76, just before the long drought.

Surprisingly, there was little smirking in Australia, and no gloating. The crowds came to celebrate the home team's comprehensive and irresistible brilliance. There was no sense of vengeance, just sadness and emptiness because, in truth, the series was so one-sided as to be dull. Australia won all 15 internationals – Test and one-day – during the summer, making it 31 out of 34 home internationals since November 1999. These five Test wins were part of a run of 16 successive victories, far eclipsing West Indies' previous world record of 11.

It did not matter that Australia were without Shane Warne for the entire series, and Brett Lee and Jason Gillespie for parts of it. Corporate spirit, rather than individual brilliance or singular achievements, was the team's distinguishing quality. Cricket may famously be described as an individual sport played by teams, but Steve Waugh's Australians had made it a team sport played by individuals, none of whom was either above the team or indispensable to it. This applied even to the leadership: when injury forced out Waugh for a match, Adam Gilchrist, in only his 12th Test, stepped in as captain and the streak continued. Australia were to win all of Gilchrist's first 15 Tests, such was their time of plenty.

The West Indians, in contrast, were at a wretchedly low ebb. By summer's end, they had lost their sixth away series in a row, in which sequence they had won three and lost 21 Tests. They had also lost ten of their last 11 first-class matches, encompassing not only seven Test defeats, but heavy losses against Somerset, Western Australia and a half-strength Victoria. Jimmy Adams, for whom the captaincy was the most poisonous of chalices, remained dignified and gentlemanly throughout, but could provide no inspiration in word or deed. It was scarcely a surprise when he was sacked as leader and player after the tour, and vice-captain Sherwin Campbell went with him. As for the rest, some Caribbean commentators thought that they were on rather better terms with themselves than their achievements warranted.

Not for the first time, Brian Lara carried the batting; not for the first time, he buckled under the weight. He managed just one scoring shot in his first three Test innings, falling each time to Glenn McGrath's perfectly aimed cutters, and a mood was immediately set for the series. Lara, trying too hard to impose himself, played recklessly, making three Test ducks and three more in the one-day series. When he did come off, with 231 against Australia A in Hobart followed by 182 in the Third Test at Adelaide, the West Indians had their best two results for the summer – a draw and a mere five-wicket defeat. It was a measure of West Indies' standing that Lara was considered to have failed and yet was easily his team's highest scorer both in the Tests, with 321, and the Carlton Series, with 372. More than half his Test runs came in that one innings at Adelaide, however; in the other nine he made 139. He also had to contend with a silly debate in the press about the presence on tour of his English girlfriend; as the West Indian management noted, all the Australians brought partners along with no apparent adverse effect.

The most consistent batting came from Ridley Jacobs, 33, and Marlon Samuels, 19; between them lay the West Indians' lost generation. Jacobs fought rearguard actions with pride, character and not a little derring-do; Samuels, summoned late to the tour, showed impressive cool, not to mention a way forward. Adams and Campbell averaged less than 19 apiece, the loss of Shivnarine Chanderpaul after one Test was keenly felt, and poor Ramnaresh Sarwan, having prepared with five weeks at the Australian Academy, totalled three runs in six successive innings – against Victoria and in the first two Tests – and was not seen again until the final Test. In all, West Indies made 28 ducks in the series, breaking the previous record by two, and reached 200 just once in the first four Tests.

Adams insisted that his team's failings were not technical, but it was impossible to agree. Their general method was to stand flat-footed at the crease for a time, sometimes a long time, then fan a catch into the cordon. Mostly, the West Indians did not so much collapse in minutes as sink over hours, but the effect was the same. Only when all was lost was caution thrown to the winds, new blood introduced and some hope for the future kindled.

With Curtly Ambrose's retirement, Courtney Walsh had to sustain the bowling on his own. Though willing as ever, and still his team's best, he could not disguise his aging and finished with 11 wickets at 43.72. Marlon Black bowled some hostile early spells until injury cut his tour short, and Merv Dillon improved throughout to finish with 16 wickets at 29.93. All bowled well in bursts, but could not maintain pressure. They were so intent on keeping the ball away from Mark Waugh's pads, for example, that they gave him more to cut than he had had for seasons. There was so little spinning strength that, upon his arrival, Samuels was pressed immediately into the front line with his nascent off-spinners, and immediately took good wickets, too.

The West Indians spent the summer being battered and bowled. Their tour began with a blow on the jaw for tailender Kerry Jeremy in the opening first-class match, after which he was scarcely seen. It finished, just after they lost the one-day finals, with a vicious assault on Black, outside a Melbourne nightclub, which put him in hospital.

Australia were unremitting and unrelenting, but not without flair. The series was lacklustre because there was no sense of contest, not because it was short of skilful, elegant and entertaining cricket. In Brisbane, McGrath took ten for 27; in Perth, he rolled up his 300th wicket, Lara's, into a hat-trick; in Melbourne, his opening seven overs cost just one run, a no-ball – identical to Ambrose's opening spell on the same ground eight years previously, except that Ambrose conceded a wide. But McGrath was not alone. There were eight bags of five wickets or more for the Australians, including two in the Adelaide Test for Colin Miller. No West Indian took more than four in an innings.

Australia's batting was solid rather than indomitable. They reached 400 only twice, though less than 400 in the first two Tests was enough for innings victories. Only Mark Slater passed 350 for the series; the Waugh twins made Australia's only centuries. Mark began the summer under an injunction to make runs or make way, and spent it surrounded by opprobrium after the release of the CBI report in India. Such close attention from selectors and sleuths appeared to concentrate his mind, often apt to wander, until he was playing as in his silky heyday. Nor did Steve betray any sign of decline. At No. 3, Langer had a poor series, and Ponting made fewer than he would have liked. However, wicket-keeper Gilchrist provided attractive, timely runs and Martyn, replacing the injured Steve Waugh in Adelaide, played two composed and unbeaten innings when they were especially needed.

Only in etiquette did Australia let themselves down. It is difficult to know which was more risible: Stuart MacGill charging Sarwan with his shoulder at Adelaide, or referee A. C. Smith's declaration that all had been put right by MacGill's apology. Yet even the intemperate moments were instructive – a reminder that the players were only flesh and blood, that they did feel pressures, and that the game takes much conquering, physically and mentally. In the apparent simplicity of another victory, this was too easily overlooked.

One-sidedness notwithstanding, attendances were good all summer and easily surpassed the Australian Cricket Board's conservative budget. The allure of a champion team ought never to be underestimated. Before the First Test in Brisbane, a reunion of the teams of 1960-61 prompted glorious memories of that series, highlighted by the first tied Test, and the way it had lifted cricket from the doldrums. It was as if cricket were silently crying out for a reprise as the match-fixing scandal continued to deepen. It was fanciful, of course. What this series demonstrated above all else was the extent to which times and the game had changed.

WEST INDIAN TOURING PARTY

J. C. Adams (Jamaica) (*captain*), S. L. Campbell (Barbados) (*vice-captain*), M. I. Black (Trinidad & Tobago), C. O. Browne (Barbados), S. Chanderpaul (Guyana), M. Dillon (Trinidad & Tobago), D. Ganga (Trinidad & Tobago), W. W. Hinds (Jamaica), R. D. Jacobs (Leeward Islands), K. C. B. Jeremy (Leeward Islands), B. C. Lara (Trinidad & Tobago), N. A. M. McLean (Windward Islands), M. V. Nagamootoo (Guyana), R. R. Sarwan (Guyana), C. E. L. Stuart (Guyana), C. A. Walsh (Jamaica).

M. N. Samuels (Jamaica) replaced the injured Chanderpaul. S. C. Joseph (Leeward Islands), R. L. Powell (Jamaica) and L. R. Williams (Jamaica) replaced Browne, Jeremy, Sarwan and Walsh for the one-day Carlton Series, with C. E. Cuffy (Windward Islands) also added to the one-day squad when Dillon was injured.

Manager: R. O. Skerritt. *Coach:* R. A. Harper. *Assistant coach:* P. J. L. Dujon.

WEST INDIAN TOUR RESULTS

Test matches – Played 5: Lost 5.
First-class matches – Played 8: Lost 7, Drawn 1.
Losses – Australia (5), Western Australia, Victoria.
Draw – Australia A.
One-day internationals – Played 10: Won 3, Lost 7. *Wins* – Zimbabwe (3). *Losses* – Australia (6), Zimbabwe.
Other non-first-class matches – Played 4: Won 2, Lost 1, No result 1. *Wins* – Northern Territory Invitation XII, Australia A. *Loss* – Prime Minister's XI. *No result* – ACB Chairman's XII.

TEST MATCH AVERAGES

AUSTRALIA – BATTING

	T	*I*	*NO*	*R*	*HS*	*100s*	*50s*	*Avge*	*Ct/St*
S. R. Waugh	4	6	1	349	121*	2	0	69.80	0
M. J. Slater	5	8	1	373	96	0	4	53.28	3
M. E. Waugh	5	8	1	339	119	1	2	48.42	11
A. C. Gilchrist	5	6	1	241	87	0	2	48.20	19/2
R. T. Ponting	5	8	2	242	92	0	2	40.33	5
M. L. Hayden	5	8	0	236	69	0	2	29.50	8
C. R. Miller	3	4	1	78	37*	0	0	26.00	0
J. L. Langer	5	8	0	203	80	0	1	25.37	5
S. C. G. MacGill	4	4	1	44	19	0	0	14.66	3
J. N. Gillespie	4	4	0	48	23	0	0	12.00	2
G. D. McGrath	5	4	0	25	13	0	0	6.25	1

Played in two Tests: A. J. Bichel 8, 3 (1 ct); B. Lee 62*, 41*. Played in one Test: D. R. Martyn 46*, 34* (2 ct).

* *Signifies not out.*

BOWLING

	O	*M*	*R*	*W*	*BB*	*5W/i*	*Avge*
B. Lee	59.1	21	177	11	5-61	1	16.09
G. D. McGrath	183.5	69	359	21	6-17	1	17.09
A. J. Bichel	43.3	9	124	7	5-60	1	17.71
C. R. Miller	143.2	37	365	20	5-32	2	18.25
J. N. Gillespie	141	40	368	20	6-40	2	18.40
S. C. G. MacGill	156	39	501	16	7-104	1	31.31

Also bowled: M. L. Hayden 2–0–9–0; R. T. Ponting 1–1–0–0; M. E. Waugh 11–4–15–1.

WEST INDIES – BATTING

	T	*I*	*NO*	*R*	*HS*	*100s*	*50s*	*Avge*	*Ct/St*
M. N. Samuels	3	6	1	172	60*	0	1	34.40	1
B. C. Lara	5	10	0	321	182	1	0	32.10	5
R. D. Jacobs	5	10	1	288	96*	0	2	32.00	20/1
W. W. Hinds	4	8	0	247	70	0	2	30.87	3
J. C. Adams	5	10	2	151	49	0	0	18.87	3
S. L. Campbell	5	10	0	187	79	0	2	18.70	6
D. Ganga	4	8	0	107	32	0	0	13.37	1
M. Dillon	4	8	0	73	27	0	0	9.12	1
R. R. Sarwan	3	6	0	54	51	0	1	9.00	1
C. E. L. Stuart	2	4	1	21	12*	0	0	7.00	0
N. A. M. McLean	5	10	0	64	17	0	0	6.40	1
C. A. Walsh	5	10	2	19	9	0	0	2.37	0
M. I. Black	3	6	2	6	3*	0	0	1.50	0

Played in one Test: S. Chanderpaul 18, 62*; M. V. Nagamootoo 12, 68.

* *Signifies not out.*

BOWLING

	O	*M*	*R*	*W*	*BB*	*5W/i*	*Avge*
M. Dillon	128.4	20	479	16	4-76	0	29.93
C. E. L. Stuart	60	10	239	6	2-52	0	39.83
M. I. Black	67	8	257	6	4-83	0	42.83
C. A. Walsh	199.4	46	481	11	2-39	0	43.72
N. A. M. McLean	137	19	476	9	2-69	0	52.88

Also bowled: J. C. Adams 67.4–17–181–2; M. V. Nagamootoo 44–4–147–3; M. N. Samuels 60.5–12–185–3.

Note: Matches in this section which were not first-class are signified by a dagger.

†At Lilac Hill, Perth, November 7. No result. Toss: ACB Chairman's XII. West Indians 276 for two (50 overs) (S. L. Campbell 111 not out, D. Ganga 43, B. C. Lara 108) v ACB Chairman's XII.

Each side fielded 12 players, of whom 11 could bat and 11 field. Lara scored 108 in 105 balls, with 11 fours and three sixes; he added 162 with Campbell.

At Perth, November 9, 10, 11, 12. Western Australia won by seven wickets. Toss: Western Australia. West Indians 132 (M. J. Nicholson three for 32, G. G. Swan three for 31) and 293 (S. L. Campbell 119, S. Chanderpaul 43, J. C. Adams 44; T. M. Moody four for 14); Western Australia 358 (M. E. K. Hussey 41, J. L. Langer 45, M. J. Nicholson 54, S. M. Katich 73, T. M. Moody 36, G. B. Hogg 35 not out, B. P. Julian 32; M. I. Black four for 100, C. E. L. Stuart three for 84) and 70 for three.

The tourists' first innings ended when a ball from Nicholson broke Kerry Jeremy's jaw. In their second innings, Campbell batted for 422 minutes, having spent 87 minutes on 20.

†At Alice Springs, December 14. West Indians won by 57 runs. Toss: Northern Territory Invitation XII. West Indians 259 for six (50 overs) (D. Ganga 53, B. C. Lara 106, S. Chanderpaul 31 not out; C. R. Miller three for 40); Northern Territory Invitation XII 202 for nine (50 overs) (M. J. Di Venuto 52, S. Williams 40, K. E. Vowles 31; J. C. Adams three for 32).

Each side fielded 12 players, of whom 11 could bat and 11 field. Lara scored 106 in 113 balls. Courtney Walsh bowled 6–3–4–0.

At Melbourne, November 17, 18, 19. Victoria won by an innings and 63 runs. Toss: Victoria. West Indians 167 (M. V. Nagamootoo 48; M. W. H. Inness six for 26) and 114 (M. W. H. Inness three for 47, C. R. Miller three for 26); Victoria 344 for seven dec. (J. L. Arnberger 99, B. J. Hodge 134 retired hurt, M. Klinger 43; C. A. Walsh four for 66).

AUSTRALIA v WEST INDIES

First Test Match

At Brisbane, November 23, 24, 25. Australia won by an innings and 126 runs. Toss: Australia. Test debut: M. I. Black.

This Test may be summed up in the figures of its central player, McGrath, who bowled 33 overs to take ten for 27 and ensure that Australia would equal the West Indians' record of 11 consecutive Test wins. The pitch – put in place at the end of the Olympic soccer tournament and so providing the first instance of a drop-in pitch in Test cricket – was seamy but slow. On it, West Indies did not so much explode as erode, scoring at 1.9 an over in their innings of 82 (their third total in double figures since June) and 124. Australia also laboured to make 332 at 2.9 an over, but that was more than enough for a resounding innings win. Proceeding at once at a crawl and a rush, the match was over by its scheduled mid-point.

FEWEST RUNS CONCEDED FOR TEN WICKETS OR MORE IN A TEST

11-24 (5-6, 6-18)	H. Ironmonger	Australia v South Africa at Melbourne	1931-32
10-27 (6-17, 4-10)	**G. D. McGrath**	**Australia v West Indies at Brisbane**	**2000-01**
15-28 (7-17, 8-11)	J. Briggs	England v South Africa at Cape Town	1888-89
11-31 (5-2, 6-29)	E. R. H. Toshack	Australia v India at Brisbane	1947-48
15-45 (7-38, 8-7)	G. A. Lohmann	England v South Africa at Port Elizabeth	1895-96
11-48 (5-28, 6-20)	G. A. R. Lock	England v West Indies at The Oval	1957
10-49 (5-29, 5-20)	F. E. Woolley	England v Australia at The Oval	1912

Research: Gordon Vince

Australia preferred MacGill to Miller as substitute for Warne, and brought in Bichel at a couple of days' notice when Gillespie's hamstring twanged. West Indies kept faith with Sarwan, despite his pair against Victoria, and gave a debut to the burly fast bowler, Marlon Black. Sent in, the visitors lasted an hour without losing a wicket, and it took the unlikely agency of MacGill's leg-spin to launch the procession back to the dressing-room. McGrath, brought back after Lara's arrival, needed just one ball, an away-cutter, to execute his contract and begin his demolition of the innings. Wicket to wicket, he took six for eight in 68 balls, overtaking Craig McDermott (291) to become Australia's third-highest wicket-taker, and after three and a half tortuous hours West Indies were out for 82. The lowest point of ineptitude came when Sarwan, seeking a second leg-bye, ran himself out by half the length of the pitch for his third duck in a row.

Australia were in front that night, the openers raising three figures before Slater ran out Hayden when he was well set. Debutant Black besieged them next morning, taking three wickets in his first four overs of the day and cornering Mark Waugh for two and a half hours while he made 24. But Steve Waugh, Ponting and the dashing Gilchrist strained at and finally broke the tethers. Lee crashed his maiden first-class half-century, adorning it with a straight six, and Australia led by 250. Walsh took only the last wicket.

The game was basically decided that night when the leaden-footed Campbell fell to McGrath in the first over and Lara, having swished him to square leg for four, essayed a hook again and skied a catch to the running keeper. On the third day the last rites took three hours, the always obdurate Chanderpaul batting through for an unbeaten 62. McGrath remained miserly, Lee bowled a lightning spell to shoot out Adams and Sarwan in one over, and MacGill bowled with impressive control. West Indies, insisting that their problems were temperamental and not technical, called in psychologist Rudi Webster.

Man of the Match: G. D. McGrath. *Attendance:* 48,441.

Close of play: First day, Australia 107-1 (Slater 54*, Bichel 4*); Second day, West Indies 25-2 (Ganga 8*, Chanderpaul 7*).

West Indies

S. L. Campbell c M. E. Waugh b MacGill	10	– c Gilchrist b McGrath	0
D. Ganga c Ponting b Bichel	20	– st Gilchrist b MacGill	8
B. C. Lara c Gilchrist b McGrath	0	– c Gilchrist b McGrath	4
S. Chanderpaul c Gilchrist b McGrath	18	– not out	62
*J. C. Adams not out	16	– c Gilchrist b Lee	16
R. R. Sarwan run out	0	– b Lee	0
†R. D. Jacobs c M. E. Waugh b McGrath	2	– c M. E. Waugh b Bichel	4
N. A. M. McLean lbw b McGrath	0	– lbw b Lee	13
M. Dillon c Gilchrist b McGrath	0	– b McGrath	0
M. I. Black c MacGill b McGrath	0	– c Gilchrist b McGrath	2
C. A. Walsh c Langer b Lee	9	– c McGrath b MacGill	0
L-b 6, n-b 1	7	B 8, l-b 3, n-b 4	15
1/21 (1) 2/25 (3) 3/53 (4) 4/59 (2) 5/60 (6) 6/63 (7) 7/63 (8) 8/67 (9) 9/67 (10) 10/82 (11)	82	1/0 (1) 2/10 (3) 3/29 (2) 4/62 (5) 5/66 (6) 6/81 (7) 7/98 (8) 8/117 (9) 9/119 (10) 10/124 (11)	124

Bowling: *First Innings*—McGrath 20–12–17–6; Lee 11.1–5–24–1; MacGill 5–1–10–1; Bichel 13–3–25–1. *Second Innings*—McGrath 13–9–10–4; Lee 18–9–40–3; MacGill 16–5–42–2; Bichel 11–4–21–1.

Australia

M. J. Slater c Campbell b Black	54	S. C. G. MacGill run out	19
M. L. Hayden run out	44	G. D. McGrath b Walsh	0
A. J. Bichel c Jacobs b Black	8		
J. L. Langer c Jacobs b Black	3	L-b 5, n-b 4	9
M. E. Waugh c and b Dillon	24		
*S. R. Waugh c Campbell b Dillon	41	1/101 (2) 2/111 (1) 3/112 (3)	332
R. T. Ponting c Jacobs b Black	20	4/117 (4) 5/179 (5) 6/186 (6)	
†A. C. Gilchrist c Jacobs b Dillon	48	7/220 (7) 8/281 (8)	
B. Lee not out	62	9/331 (10) 10/332 (11)	

Bowling: Walsh 31.4–7–78–1; Black 28–5–83–4; Dillon 25–8–79–3; McLean 25–5–79–0; Adams 5–2–8–0.

Umpires: D. B. Cowie (New Zealand) and D. J. Harper.
Third umpire: P. D. Parker. Referee: A. C. Smith (England).

AUSTRALIA v WEST INDIES

Second Test Match

At Perth, December 1, 2, 3. Australia won by an innings and 27 runs. Toss: Australia.

Within an hour of the start McGrath had taken a hat-trick, Lara had made a duck and West Indies had lost five wickets. At times they played redoubtably in their efforts to mount a recovery, but their cause was always hopeless and they were spent before the end of the third day. It was their fourth defeat inside three days in their last six Tests, while Australia's victory broke the West Indians' world record of 11 successive Test wins between March and December 1984. Indeed, such was the Australians' mastery that McGrath was required to take only one other wicket in the match. The sole setback was the torn buttock muscle that put captain Steve Waugh out of the next Test.

West Indies' woes began even before the match: Sarwan, dropped for Hinds, had to be hastily recalled when Chanderpaul withdrew at the eleventh hour because of stress fractures; he would not play again on tour. Australia regained Gillespie, won the toss again and, on a typically pacy WACA pitch, were soon wreaking havoc. Ganga's lbw was unlucky, but it scarcely mattered when, from successive McGrath balls, Campbell and Lara snicked away-cutters to first and fourth slip respectively, and a mesmerised Adams popped a catch to short leg. Thus McGrath joined Merv Hughes, Damien Fleming and Shane Warne among the latter-day Australians with hat-tricks. Lara's wicket was also his 300th in 64 Tests; it panned out just as he had hoped in an interview before the match.

Sarwan followed as a matter of formality, but Ponting, the unaccustomed first slip in Warne's absence, dropped two catches and Gilchrist another. Hinds made bold with seven fours in 50, then lashed once too often at MacGill, and Jacobs showed courage, discretion and a good eye in batting out the last three hours and 40 minutes of the innings. He looked set for his maiden Test hundred until Gillespie's three-wicket burst abbreviated West Indies to 196 and left him stranded four short.

For almost three and a quarter hours, Hayden founded Australia's reply with only his second half-century in seven itinerant years of Test cricket. West Indies fought back well, and at 208 for six Australia led by just 12. However, Gilchrist's counter-attack, some lusty hitting by Lee and MacGill, and a masterly 18th Test century from Mark Waugh, in which he combined classic batsmanship with limited-overs imagination, regained the initiative. At 200 in front, Steve Waugh declared.

[*David Pillinger, Getty Images*

Brian Lara, caught at fourth slip by Stuart MacGill, becomes Glenn McGrath's 300th Test victim and the centre-point of the tenth hat-trick by an Australian in Tests.

Campbell, lost for footwork, again went quickly, and before nightfall the night-watchman had gone, too. Lara began the third day full of good intentions. He survived McGrath's barrage, but after almost an hour he shaped a horribly inappropriate pull shot at MacGill and was bowled. Hinds, Adams and Jacobs put up more than six hours of stout-hearted resistance between them, raising a cheer of genuine appreciation from the crowd and causing Australia to experiment with bowling casuals. When Jacobs was foolishly run out, Lee fired out the last three in one over to help himself to a five-wicket return and summarily finish the match. The West Indians had won all their five previous Tests on this ground, and one of the stalwarts from those better times, Sir Viv Richards, was among the early visitors to the Australians' rooms to congratulate them on their record 12th straight win.

Man of the Match: M. E. Waugh. *Attendance:* 44,044.

Close of play: First day, Australia 72-2 (Hayden 46*, Gillespie 1*); Second day, West Indies 16-2 (Ganga 9*).

West Indies

S. L. Campbell c Ponting b McGrath	3	– c Gillespie b Lee	4
D. Ganga lbw b Lee	0	– c Hayden b Gillespie	20
W. W. Hinds c M. E. Waugh b MacGill	50	– (4) b MacGill	41
B. C. Lara c MacGill b McGrath	0	– (5) b MacGill	17
*J. C. Adams c Langer b McGrath	0	– (6) not out	40
R. R. Sarwan c Slater b Lee	2	– (7) c Gilchrist b Lee	1
†R. D. Jacobs not out	96	– (8) run out	24
N. A. M. McLean b MacGill	7	– (9) b Lee	11
M. Dillon c Hayden b Gillespie	27	– (3) c Gilchrist b McGrath	3
M. I. Black c Hayden b Gillespie	0	– b Lee	0
C. A. Walsh c Gilchrist b Gillespie	1	– lbw b Lee	0
L-b 3, n-b 7	10	B 1, l-b 8, n-b 3	12
1/1 (2) 2/19 (1) 3/19 (4) 4/19 (5) 5/22 (6) 6/97 (3) 7/117 (8) 8/172 (9) 9/178 (10) 10/196 (11)	196	1/7 (1) 2/16 (3) 3/42 (2) 4/78 (5) 5/95 (4) 6/96 (7) 7/150 (8) 8/173 (9) 9/173 (10) 10/173 (11)	173

Bowling: *First Innings*—McGrath 19–2–48–3; Lee 15–5–52–2; Gillespie 12–2–46–3; MacGill 15–2–47–2. *Second Innings*—McGrath 18–7–26–1; Lee 15–2–61–5; MacGill 17–6–37–2; Gillespie 12–4–26–1; Hayden 2–0–9–0; M. E. Waugh 2–1–5–0.

Australia

M. L. Hayden b Black	69
M. J. Slater c Campbell b Dillon	19
J. L. Langer c Sarwan b McLean	5
J. N. Gillespie c Lara b McLean	23
M. E. Waugh c Adams b Dillon	119
*S. R. Waugh c Campbell b Walsh	26
R. T. Ponting b Black	5
†A. C. Gilchrist c McLean b Walsh	50
B. Lee not out	41
S. C. G. MacGill not out	18
B 2, l-b 10, w 2, n-b 7	21
1/52 (2) 2/62 (3) 3/111 (1) 4/123 (4) 5/188 (6) 6/208 (7) 7/303 (8) 8/348 (5) (8 wkts dec.)	396

G. D. McGrath did not bat.

Bowling: Walsh 31–10–74–2; Black 18–2–87–2; Dillon 29–4–130–2; McLean 22–3–78–2; Adams 8–3–15–0.

Umpires: J. H. Hampshire (England) and P. D. Parker.
Third umpire: R. J. Woolridge. Referee: A. C. Smith (England).

†At Canberra, December 7. Prime Minister's XI won by four wickets. Toss: West Indians. West Indians 230 for three (50 overs) (D. Ganga 97, J. C. Adams 59 not out); Prime Minister's XI 233 for six (48.3 overs) (A. C. Gilchrist 31, M. L. Love 56, A. D. McQuire 57, M. A. Higgs 49 not out).

Test wicket-keeper Gilchrist led the Prime Minister's XI and bowled 2.1–0–14–0.

At Hobart, December 9, 10, 11, 12. Drawn. Toss: West Indians. Australia A 439 for nine dec. (J. P. Maher 150, M. L. Love 76, D. R. Martyn 37, S. M. Katich 46, B. J. Haddin 37, D. A. Nash 30; C. E. L. Stuart three for 110, M. N. Samuels three for 100) and 210 for three (J. P. Maher 46, J. Cox 94, D. R. Martyn 58 not out); West Indians 492 (W. W. Hinds 40, R. D. Jacobs 131, B. C. Lara 231; D. A. Nash three for 81, B. J. Hodge four for 17).

Lara's 231 lasted 342 minutes and 265 balls and included 40 fours, a five and two sixes. He struck six fours in an over from Andy Bichel. After coming in at 80 for five because of a knee injury, Lara added 365 with Jacobs, a record for any team's sixth wicket on Australian soil, beating 346 by J. H. W. Fingleton and D. G. Bradman in the Third Test against England in 1936-37.

AUSTRALIA v WEST INDIES

Third Test Match

At Adelaide, December 15, 16, 17, 18, 19. Australia won by five wickets. Toss: West Indies. Test debut: M. N. Samuels.

The scales were as near balanced as they would ever be when Adams won his first toss of the series. Australia had lost Steve Waugh and Brett Lee to injuries, leaving the captaincy to a nervous Gilchrist in only his 12th Test. Lara had run into form at Hobart, and the pitch was a traditional Adelaide Oval belter. Yet these circumstances were enough only to cause the tide to slacken slightly, not to turn it back. Eight overs into the fifth day, Australia reaffirmed their hold on the Frank Worrell Trophy.

Lara had just played an astonishing innings of 231 against Australia A. Now, he raged across the first day and into the second to make 182, with 29 fours and a six. He was of a mood, latterly all too rare, when he seemed to know the speed, shape and movement of every ball long before it came to him, able to put it away on either side of the wicket at will. Even a blow to the helmet from McGrath did not faze him. His tormentor was tamed and it was Gillespie, by picking away steadily at the other end, who took the first five wickets. Adams kept him waiting almost three hours as he contributed 49 to a fourth-wicket stand of 183. Sarwan's replacement, Marlon Samuels, 19 years old and in just his eighth first-class game, played with impressive cool, but when Lara fell to a combination of extra bounce from Miller and Mark Waugh's genius at slip, the West Indians lost five for 37, all to the subtlety of Miller.

Australia's openers went breezily to 156 before Slater again ran out Hayden, whereupon Samuels's fledgling off-spinners quickly conjured up two more wickets to give West Indies an edge for the first time in the series. Crucially, fatally, they then bowled to contain rather than attack, and Australia, through the consistent Waugh and a flighty 92 from Ponting, recovered. But this match was a capricious affair: from six out and five behind, they also collapsed, losing four for 17. Only Martyn, in his first home Test for nearly seven years, kept his head. MacGill was so upset to be given out that he shoulder-charged twelfth man Sarwan on his way to the dressing-room; under a more stringent referee he could have faced suspension.

With only 12 runs separating the sides, the match now took on a madcap pace. Lara threatened mayhem again, reaching 39 at more than a run a ball before turning Miller's arm ball from around the wicket into short leg's hands. It was a more artful piece of cricket than it seemed, and by the simple virtue of bowling at the stumps Miller now took his second five-wicket haul of the match. From the fall of Lara, West Indies lost eight for 54 to be all out for 141.

Australia's target was 130, and old phobias about small targets were soon revived when they found themselves 48 for four. Walsh and Dillon proved more than disconcerting now that the bounce of the pitch was variable. Langer, without any great authority, made his first meaningful contribution of the series and, when he was out at 111 on the last morning, Martyn calmly gathered in the remaining runs. Characterising the depth in Australian cricket, Martyn scored 80 unbeaten in this match, all in the bemusing knowledge that none would matter when it came to selection for the next. Gilchrist was at the crease for the winning run, and to savour an improbable personal record: in little more than a year as a Test player, he had known nothing except victory, and now he was a winning Test captain.

[*Hamish Blair, Getty Images*

Jason Gillespie (*left*) and Colin Miller had every reason to be cheerful: their five-wicket returns accounted for 15 West Indian wickets at Adelaide.

After the match, a retrospective ruling awarded the first penalty runs in a Test under the newly introduced 2000 Code of the Laws of Cricket. On the opening morning, a ball from Gillespie passed both Ganga and Gilchrist and struck a fieldsman's helmet; though originally signalled as five byes, the runs were officially amended to penalties under Law 41.3.

Man of the Match: C. R. Miller. *Attendance:* 61,486.

Close of play: First day, West Indies 274-4 (Lara 136*, Dillon 3*); Second day, Australia 180-3 (Waugh 10*, Gillespie 2*); Third day, Australia 403-9 (Martyn 46*, McGrath 1*); Fourth day, Australia 98-4 (Langer 43*, Martyn 18*).

West Indies

S. L. Campbell lbw b Gillespie	18	– c Gilchrist b McGrath	8
D. Ganga b Gillespie	23	– lbw b Miller	32
W. W. Hinds c Ponting b Gillespie	27	– c Martyn b MacGill	9
B. C. Lara c Waugh b Miller	182	– c Langer b Miller	39
*J. C. Adams c Gilchrist b Gillespie	49	– c Martyn b Miller	15
M. Dillon c Waugh b Gillespie	9	– (9) lbw b McGrath	19
M. N. Samuels lbw b Miller	35	– (6) c Hayden b MacGill	3
†R. D. Jacobs c Langer b Miller	21	– (7) c Ponting b Miller	2
N. A. M. McLean lbw b Miller	0	– (8) c Hayden b Miller	0
M. I. Black not out	1	– not out	3
C. A. Walsh lbw b Miller	0	– c Gilchrist b McGrath	0
B 3, l-b 12, n-b 6, p 5	26	B 6, l-b 3, w 1, n-b 1	11
1/45 (2) 2/52 (1) 3/86 (3) 4/269 (5) 5/280 (6) 6/354 (4) 7/376 (7) 8/382 (9) 9/391 (8) 10/391 (11)	391	1/26 (1) 2/36 (3) 3/87 (4) 4/96 (2) 5/109 (6) 6/109 (5) 7/109 (8) 8/116 (7) 9/137 (9) 10/141 (11)	141

Bowling: *First Innings*—McGrath 36–14–83–0; Gillespie 32–9–89–5; Miller 35.5–13–81–5; MacGill 24–5–118–0; Ponting 1–1–0–0. *Second Innings*—McGrath 9.5–1–27–3; Gillespie 13–5–18–0; MacGill 12–2–55–2; Miller 17–6–32–5.

Australia

M. J. Slater c sub (R. R. Sarwan) b Samuels	83	– (2) c Jacobs b Dillon	1
M. L. Hayden run out	58	– (1) c Jacobs b Walsh	14
J. L. Langer c Lara b Samuels	6	– c Jacobs b Dillon	48
M. E. Waugh lbw b Dillon	63	– c Jacobs b Dillon	5
J. N. Gillespie lbw b Walsh	4		
R. T. Ponting c Jacobs b Walsh	92	– (5) lbw b Walsh	11
D. R. Martyn not out	46	– (6) not out	34
*†A. C. Gilchrist c Jacobs b McLean	9	– (7) not out	10
S. C. G. MacGill c Jacobs b Dillon	6		
C. R. Miller c Campbell b McLean	1		
G. D. McGrath b Dillon	1		
B 5, l-b 13, w 5, n-b 11	34	B 3, l-b 1, n-b 3	7
1/156 (2) 2/160 (1) 3/169 (3) 4/187 (5) 5/310 (4) 6/369 (6) 7/386 (8) 8/397 (9) 9/398 (10) 10/403 (11)	403	1/8 (2) 2/22 (1) 3/27 (4) 4/48 (5) 5/111 (3)	(5 wkts) 130

Bowling: *First Innings*—Walsh 32–7–73–2; Black 18–1–75–0; Dillon 24.4–2–84–3; McLean 21–1–69–2; Adams 13–2–35–0; Samuels 19–6–49–2. *Second Innings*—Walsh 14–4–39–2; Dillon 12–3–42–3; Samuels 6–1–17–0; McLean 5–1–9–0; Adams 3–0–7–0; Black 3–0–12–0.

Umpires: S. Venkataraghavan (India) and S. J. Davis.
Third umpire: D. J. Harper. Referee: A. C. Smith (England).

AUSTRALIA v WEST INDIES

Fourth Test Match

At Melbourne, December 26, 27, 28, 29. Australia won by 352 runs. Toss: West Indies. Test debut: C. E. L. Stuart.

The march of history would not be halted, or even slowed, at the MCG. Off the field, a controversial proposal was announced to bulldoze the storied members' pavilion in a massive redevelopment. On the ground, the wrecking of the once mighty West Indies continued. Only a wild Walsh slog, which saved the follow-on and compelled Australia to take a gratuitous second innings, stretched this match into a fourth day.

Australia regained Steve Waugh and replaced MacGill with Bichel, while West Indies introduced Colin Stuart in place of the tiring Black. Put in on an easy-paced pitch, the Australians played a little too casually on Boxing Day, four falling to pull shots, and at 149 for five mediocrity was upon them. Not, however, on the captain. He would not be lulled, nor tempted when another two from the last ball of the day would have raised his hundred. He was content to wait until next morning, when he rallied the tail to lift Australia to 364. His unbeaten century sped him past Viv Richards (8,540) to fifth on the list of Test cricket's highest run-scorers. Psychologically cowed, West Indies made no effort to press their early advantage, leaving too much of the bowling to newcomer Stuart and part-timer Samuels. Jacobs took seven catches, equalling the Test record, but his feat was scarcely acknowledged by his despondent team-mates.

McGrath began with a spell of eight overs for two runs, and Gillespie was scarcely more philanthropic. West Indies did not manage a run off the bat until the eighth over. Inevitably, there was a clatter of wickets, including Lara's to a needless flash at Bichel, and, after little more than an hour and a half, they were 28 for five. At length the bowlers tired, the ball was made squelchy by rain, and the siege was relaxed. Samuels and Jacobs, who together hit 12 from a Miller over, put on 75, McLean lashed Bichel for six and Walsh flailed twice, the first time to break his duck and the second to save the follow-on. This milestone so excited him that he ran himself out seeking a third run off the same ball. Samuels remained defiantly unbeaten with a maiden fifty. Having claimed only four wickets in his previous four Tests, Bichel took five in an afternoon.

Australia spent the first five and a half hours of day three extending their lead to the length of a piece of string. Some perished in the haste, but Langer swatted his first half-century of the series, Mark Waugh continued his rich run of form, and Steve Waugh played two pull shots, confirming that this was indeed a leap year. Australia sent in Miller at No. 6, for the gain of one long six. West Indies could do no more than limit the damage, Adams bowling himself in a long spell at and outside leg stump.

At the declaration, the West Indians needed 462. It was always academic. By stumps half an hour later, they were ten for three, with opener Campbell still to score. Early next morning, they were 23 for six, all of them to Gillespie: his prize had been Lara, who allowed a fast, breaking ball to bowl him for his third duck of the series. Adams fell first ball for a pair, putting West Indies comfortably on target to break the record of 26 ducks in a series. Against batsmen whose feet were stuck so fast, it was too easy for Australia: the straight balls either bowled them or trapped them lbw; the wider balls were caught in the cordon. It was left to Samuels and Jacobs, again, to rescue respectability, and the formalities ended when teenager Samuels was caught at long-on, aiming for his second half-century of the match. For the first time in 58 Tests, McGrath did not take a wicket in either innings.

Man of the Match: S. R. Waugh. *Attendance:* 133,299.

Close of play: First day, Australia 295-7 (S. R. Waugh 98*, Gillespie 14*); Second day, West Indies 165; Third day, West Indies 10-3 (Campbell 0*, Stuart 3*).

Australia

M. J. Slater c Jacobs b McLean	30	– (2) c Lara b Dillon	4
M. L. Hayden c Jacobs b Walsh	13	– (1) c Hinds b McLean	30
J. L. Langer c Jacobs b Stuart	31	– c Ganga b Adams	80
M. E. Waugh c Adams b Dillon	25	– not out	78
*S. R. Waugh not out	121	– c Jacobs b Stuart	20
R. T. Ponting c Hinds b McLean	23	– (7) not out	26
†A. C. Gilchrist c Campbell b Stuart	37		
A. J. Bichel c Jacobs b Dillon	3		
J. N. Gillespie c Jacobs b Walsh	19		
C. R. Miller c Jacobs b Dillon	29	– (6) st Jacobs b Adams	11
G. D. McGrath c Jacobs b Dillon	11		
L-b 4, w 1, n-b 17	22	B 5, l-b 4, w 1, n-b 3	13
1/41 (2) 2/47 (1) 3/101 (3) 4/105 (4) 5/149 (6) 6/210 (7) 7/225 (8) 8/306 (9) 9/347 (10) 10/364 (11)	364	1/8 (2) 2/49 (1) 3/165 (3) 4/212 (5) 5/228 (6)	(5 wkts dec.) 262

Bowling: *First Innings*—Walsh 33–6–62–2; Dillon 21–2–76–4; McLean 27–5–95–2; Stuart 15–4–52–2; Samuels 14–0–56–0; Adams 4–0–19–0. *Second Innings*—Walsh 18–3–46–0; Dillon 17–1–68–1; McLean 9–1–30–1; Stuart 15–2–66–1; Adams 18–8–43–2.

West Indies

S. L. Campbell c Hayden b Miller	5	– c Ponting b Gillespie	6
D. Ganga c Gilchrist b Gillespie	4	– lbw b Gillespie	0
W. W. Hinds c Slater b Gillespie	0	– c Bichel b Gillespie	4
B. C. Lara c M. E. Waugh b Bichel	16	– b Gillespie	0
*J. C. Adams c Gilchrist b Bichel	0	– (6) c M. E. Waugh b Gillespie	0
M. N. Samuels not out	60	– (7) c Gillespie b Miller	46
†R. D. Jacobs c M. E. Waugh b Bichel	42	– (8) c Gilchrist b Miller	23
N. A. M. McLean b Bichel	17	– (9) run out	1
M. Dillon b Gillespie	0	– (10) b Miller	15
C. E. L. Stuart b Bichel	1	– (5) lbw b Gillespie	4
C. A. Walsh run out	4	– not out	0
L-b 5, n-b 11	16	L-b 1, n-b 9	10
1/5 (2) 2/6 (3) 3/28 (4) 4/28 (1) 5/28 (5) 6/103 (7) 7/144 (8) 8/150 (9) 9/157 (10) 10/165 (11)	165	1/1 (2) 2/6 (3) 3/7 (4) 4/17 (1) 5/17 (6) 6/23 (5) 7/77 (8) 8/78 (9) 9/108 (10) 10/109 (7)	109

Bowling: *First Innings*—McGrath 13–7–15–0; Gillespie 18–6–48–3; Bichel 13.3–2–60–5; Miller 13–5–37–1. *Second Innings*—McGrath 12–6–10–0; Gillespie 17–5–40–6; Miller 14.3–2–40–3; Bichel 6–0–18–0.

Umpires: S. Venkataraghavan (India) and S. J. A. Taufel.
Third umpire: R. G. Patterson. Referee: A. C. Smith (England).

AUSTRALIA v WEST INDIES

Fifth Test Match

At Sydney, January 2, 3, 4, 5, 6. Australia won by six wickets. Toss: West Indies.

Australia duly completed their clean sweep, the first in series between these countries, and extended their record to 15 successive Test wins. At least this time West Indies attacked in a manner more befitting their heritage and Australia were made to sweat for their gains. The signal moment was when the blue dye in Miller's hair, applied overnight in honour of Australia's Centenary of Federation, began to trickle down his shirt on day one. But the margin was still wide.

Australia again swapped Bichel for MacGill, tailoring team to pitch. West Indies lost Ganga and Dillon because of injury, brought in Nagamootoo and reinstated Sarwan. They chose to bat first and Campbell, shotless in Melbourne, signalled a new outlook by hooking at McGrath in the first over. Hinds, a cavalier opening in place of Ganga, took up the theme, and the pair not only made it boldly to lunch but also crashed 74 in the first hour afterwards. However, their departure in successive MacGill overs detonated a collapse from 147 without loss to 272 all out. A combination of MacGill's persistence, West Indies' looseness and poor decisions against Samuels and McLean sped the leg-spinner to a seven-wicket haul. Lara was again like a flare, brief and brilliant, but the wretched Sarwan made his third duck in five Test innings.

Australia spent the second day pushing into the lead, and most of the third augmenting it. Without a spinner of any repute, West Indies were helpless to prevent them after early successes: Hayden provided Lara with his 100th Test catch, the 15th fielder to reach this landmark. Slater's innings was typically feverish, including 13 boundaries, culpability in the run-out of Mark Waugh and, at 96, his own demise when he took one liberty too many with Nagamootoo. His ninth 90-something in Tests equalled Steve Waugh's record. Waugh, however, had long since outgrown his frailties and rushes of blood. This was his 132nd Test, passing Kapil Dev's mark – only Allan Border, with 156, had played more – and he batted with characteristic resolution to his 24th century at this level. Ponting made only his second half-century of the series, sharing a stand of 132 with Waugh, after which Gilchrist, dropped first ball by Adams, struck a thrilling 87 out of 119 added while he was at the wicket. At length, Australia led by 180.

Hinds and Campbell gave West Indies another bountiful start, notwithstanding Waugh's ploy of opening the bowling with Miller. But the dismissal of Hinds by McGrath in the last over of the third day, and the loss of three for nought in five balls next morning, including Samuels first ball, raised the spectre of another rout. Lara belted three consecutive fours, then was dropped by Miller, all in one MacGill over, but Miller soon had him caught behind, another innings of wasteful extravagance. However, enterprising half-centuries from the beleaguered Sarwan, the dependable Jacobs and Nagamootoo drew from the Australians an old and unbecoming tetchiness, as well as bringing nearly 200 from the last five wickets. Even Walsh, given a guard of honour as he came to the crease, managed not to get out. Miller took the final three, but the marauding McGrath and Gillespie were Australia's mainstays.

Set 173, Australia were 46 for three early on the last day, prey to their own psychosis about small targets, a dying pitch and a fierce last hurrah from Walsh, who defied a bad ankle to take his Test aggregate to 494 wickets. But Slater, in his effervescent way, put on 102 at a run a minute with Steve Waugh, their partnership all but completing the task. The West Indians' lack of a wrist-spinner – Nagamootoo bowled as much with his fingers as his wrist – was again telling. Walsh received a generous farewell, but otherwise the West Indians filed off meekly into the footnotes of history.

Man of the Match: M. J. Slater. *Attendance:* 126,874.

Man of the Series: G. D. McGrath.

Close of play: First day, West Indies 256-9 (Stuart 0*, Walsh 0*); Second day, Australia 284-4 (S. R. Waugh 82*, Ponting 51*); Third day, West Indies 98-1 (Campbell 45*); Fourth day, Australia 44-2 (Slater 18*, M. E. Waugh 3*).

West Indies

S. L. Campbell c and b MacGill	79	– c Gilchrist b Gillespie	54
W. W. Hinds b MacGill	70	– b McGrath	46
*J. C. Adams lbw b McGrath	10	– lbw b McGrath	5
B. C. Lara c M. E. Waugh b MacGill	35	– c Gilchrist b Miller	28
M. N. Samuels c Langer b MacGill	28	– lbw b Gillespie	0
R. R. Sarwan lbw b MacGill	0	– c Gilchrist b McGrath	51
†R. D. Jacobs st Gilchrist b MacGill	12	– lbw b M. E. Waugh	62
M. V. Nagamootoo c Slater b Miller	12	– c Hayden b Miller	68
N. A. M. McLean lbw b MacGill	0	– c M. E. Waugh b Miller	15
C. E. L. Stuart not out	12	– lbw b Miller	4
C. A. Walsh c Hayden b Miller	4	– not out	1
B 4, l-b 4, n-b 2	10	B 5, l-b 10, n-b 3	18
1/147 (1) 2/152 (2) 3/174 (3) 4/210 (4) 5/210 (6) 6/235 (5) 7/240 (7) 8/240 (9) 9/252 (8) 10/272 (11)	272	1/98 (2) 2/112 (3) 3/112 (1) 4/112 (5) 5/154 (4) 6/239 (6) 7/317 (7) 8/347 (8) 9/351 (9) 10/352 (10)	352

Bowling: *First Innings*—McGrath 19–7–43–1; Gillespie 16–4–44–0; MacGill 37–11–104–7; Miller 30.1–8–73–2. *Second Innings*—McGrath 24–4–80–3; Miller 32.5–3–102–4; MacGill 30–7–88–0; Gillespie 21–5–57–2; M. E. Waugh 9–3–10–1.

Australia

M. J. Slater c Samuels b Nagamootoo	96	– (2) not out	86
M. L. Hayden c Lara b Walsh	3	– (1) lbw b Stuart	5
J. L. Langer c Jacobs b McLean	20	– lbw b Walsh	10
M. E. Waugh run out	22	– c Adams b McLean	3
*S. R. Waugh b Nagamootoo	103	– lbw b Samuels	38
R. T. Ponting lbw b Stuart	51	– not out	14
†A. C. Gilchrist c Lara b Stuart	87		
J. N. Gillespie c Hinds b Nagamootoo	2		
C. R. Miller not out	37		
S. C. G. MacGill run out	1		
G. D. McGrath run out	13		
B 1, l-b 5, n-b 11	17	B 3, l-b 7, w 1, n-b 7	18
1/17 (2) 2/55 (3) 3/109 (4) 4/157 (1) 5/289 (6) 6/360 (5) 7/374 (8) 8/408 (7) 9/410 (10) 10/452 (11)	452	1/5 (1) 2/38 (3) 3/46 (4) 4/148 (5)	(4 wkts) 174

Bowling: *First Innings*—Walsh 25–4–74–1; Stuart 23–4–81–2; Nagamootoo 35–3–119–3; McLean 20–2–81–1; Adams 16.4–2–54–0; Samuels 16–5–37–0. *Second Innings*—Walsh 15–5–35–1; Stuart 7–0–40–1; McLean 8–1–35–1; Nagamootoo 9–1–28–0; Samuels 5.5–0–26–1.

Umpires: R. E. Koertzen (South Africa) and D. B. Hair.
Third umpire: S. J. A. Taufel. Referee: A. C. Smith (England).

†At Adelaide, January 9 (day/night). West Indians won by four wickets. Toss: Australia A. Australia A 145 (42.3 overs) (S. Lee 30, A. J. Bichel 30; M. V. Nagamootoo three for 28); West Indians 146 for six (41.5 overs) (M. N. Samuels 45; D. W. Fleming three for 18).

West Indies' matches v Australia and Zimbabwe in the Carlton Series (January 11–February 9) may be found in that section.

THE INDIANS IN BANGLADESH, 2000-01

By RICHARD HOBSON

Saber Chowdhury, the president of the Bangladesh Cricket Board, described his country's elevation to Test status as the third most historic event in their national life, behind independence and the adoption of a United Nations mother-tongue day commemorating the suppression of the Bengali language under Pakistani rule. Certainly, the five days of celebrations leading up to the inaugural Test against India reflected its perceived importance to the national well-being. Events included a ceremonial dinner, a vivid firework display, school activities and the recording of a song written by a local journalist. Among the gestures of goodwill from the existing Test nations was the donation of ten corneas from the Board of Control for Cricket in Sri Lanka to help visually impaired Bangladeshis. Two of them were fitted in time for the beneficiaries to see the game.

A near-capacity crowd of around 40,000 watched the first day's play, which began after a simple but poignant opening ceremony in which parachutists carried flags from each of the ten Test-playing countries into the Bangabandhu Stadium. During the tea interval, Naimur Rahman, the Bangladesh captain, and Yuvraj Singh, a member of the Indian squad, gave four children a polio vaccine to promote a new immunisation programme. The Bangladesh team delighted supporters as they advanced to 400 over the first two days. Their performance then gradually dropped off; so did attendances, as the later stages coincided with the Muslim festival of Shab-e-Barat, during which Allah is said to write the destiny of all men. Bangladesh's destiny, on this occasion, was defeat.

INDIAN TOURING PARTY

S. C. Ganguly (Bengal) (*captain*), R. Dravid (Karnataka) (*vice-captain*), A. B. Agarkar (Mumbai), S. S. Das (Orissa), S. B. Joshi (Karnataka), S. S. Karim (Bengal), M. Kartik (Railways), V. V. S. Laxman (Hyderabad), B. K. V. Prasad (Karnataka), S. Ramesh (Tamil Nadu), J. Srinath (Karnataka), S. R. Tendulkar (Mumbai), Yuvraj Singh (Punjab), Zaheer Khan (Baroda).

Team manager: B. N. Singh. *Coach:* A. D. Gaekwad.

BANGLADESH v INDIA

Inaugural Test Match

At Dhaka, November 10, 11, 12, 13. India won by nine wickets. Toss: Bangladesh. Test debuts: Bangladesh (all); S. S. Das, S. S. Karim, Zaheer Khan.

For at least two-thirds of this contest, Bangladesh surpassed all expectations by matching their neighbours, and at times even enjoying the upper hand. Ultimately, they lacked the stamina, experience and, possibly, the self-belief to overcome an Indian side well short of their best. Even so, India ended a run of 22 away Tests without success since beating Sri Lanka at Colombo in August 1993. Australia, who beat England in 1876-77, and Zimbabwe, who drew with India in 1992-93, remained the only countries to avoid defeat on Test debut.

The quiet pessimism of those who felt Bangladesh would struggle to make India bat twice seemed well founded. They had failed to win any of their previous ten first-class matches, and had just completed a chastening tour of South Africa. Furthermore, their selection process was exposed as chaotic when two of the most experienced players, Enamul Haque and Habibul Bashar, were reinstated in the squad at the personal behest of board president Chowdhury, to the governing body's embarrassment. It was a reflection of how successfully they began that the expected defeat was eventually greeted with widespread disappointment, and heavy newspaper criticism for their second-innings collapse. If the players learned anything, it was that supporters have short memories.

Expectations were raised largely through the performance of Aminul Islam, a familiar figure on English club grounds. His 145 represented the third century for a country playing their inaugural Test, and the highest since Australian Charles Bannerman retired hurt on 165 in 1876-77. Only Dave Houghton of Zimbabwe had achieved the feat in between. Aminul demonstrated great patience, underpinning Bangladesh's first innings for 535 minutes of solid graft, hitting 17 fours from his 380 balls. Before the end of the game, he was a taka millionaire on donations alone, although an exchange rate of 80 taka to the pound meant this was not quite the fortune it appeared. He added 66 for the third wicket with Habibul Bashar, who lived up to his name with some beefy strikes against an attack badly missing Anil Kumble. Indian wicket-keeper Saba Karim suffered a torrid induction, and Srinath seemed rusty on his return from injury. Only Joshi, the left-arm spinner, exerted both control and menace, returning five for 142, the best figures of his punctuated Test career.

Almost as important as the 400 runs they scored, Bangladesh occupied the crease for more than ten hours on a pitch showing signs of variable bounce. When Tendulkar fell to a catch at short leg to leave India 190 for five, the possibility grew of a result that could, without exaggeration, have been described as sensational. However, Ganguly, captaining his country for the first time in Tests, and Joshi added 121 for the seventh wicket late on the third day to bring India closer to parity. A missed opportunity to run out Joshi just after tea proved crucial; only 12 at the time, he scored a Test-best 92 lasting four hours.

Captain Naimur Rahman returned six for 132, bettered only by Bannerman's colleague Tom Kendall (seven for 55) for a side in its first Test. But the fact that India's last three wickets saw them through to lunch on the fourth day clearly had a dispiriting effect on Bangladesh. Morale depreciated further when Srinath forced Shahriar Hossain to retire hurt after a short ball struck him on the head. The discipline they had shown first time around deserted them, with Mehrab Hossain, driving loosely, and Habibul, hooking compulsively, particularly at fault. Bangladesh's first-innings 400 had been the second-highest total on Test debut, after Zimbabwe's 456 against India; now 91 was the second-lowest, after South Africa's 84 against England in 1888-89. Dravid and Das saw India home comfortably under floodlights, switched on as the light started to fade.

Man of the Match: S. B. Joshi.

Close of play: First day, Bangladesh 239-6 (Aminul Islam 70*, Khaled Masud 3*); Second day, India 81-1 (Ramesh 40*, Kartik 7*); Third day, India 366-7 (Joshi 71*, Agarkar 5*).

Bangladesh

Shahriar Hossain c Ganguly b Joshi	12	– lbw b Joshi	7
Mehrab Hossain c Karim b Zaheer Khan	4	– c Kartik b Zaheer Khan	2
Habibul Bashar c Ganguly b Zaheer Khan	71	– c Zaheer Khan b Agarkar	30
Aminul Islam c Srinath b Agarkar	145	– lbw b Agarkar	6
Akram Khan c Dravid b Joshi	35	– (6) c Das b Joshi	2
Al-Shahriar Rokon lbw b Agarkar	12	– (5) c and b Joshi	6
*Naimur Rahman c Das b Joshi	15	– (8) c Ganguly b Srinath	3
†Khaled Masud c Das b Joshi	32	– (7) not out	21
Mohammad Rafiq c Das b Tendulkar	22	– c Ganguly b Srinath	4
Hasibul Hussain not out	28	– lbw b Srinath	0
Bikash Ranjan Das c Ganguly b Joshi	2	– c Das b Kartik	0
B 13, l-b 6, n-b 3	22	B 7, l-b 1, n-b 2	10
1/10 (2) 2/44 (1) 3/110 (3) 4/175 (5) 5/196 (6) 6/231 (7) 7/324 (8) 8/354 (9) 9/385 (4) 10/400 (11)	400	1/11 (2) 2/32 (4) 3/43 (5) 4/53 (3) 5/53 (6) 6/69 (8) 7/76 (1) 8/81 (9) 9/81 (10) 10/91 (11)	91

In the second innings Shahriar Hossain, when 3, retired hurt at 5 and resumed at 69.

Bowling: *First Innings*—Srinath 22–9–47–0; Zaheer Khan 21–6–49–2; Agarkar 31–13–68–2; Joshi 45.3–8–142–5; Kartik 24–9–41–0; Tendulkar 10–2–34–1. *Second Innings*—Srinath 11–3–19–3; Zaheer Khan 5–0–20–1; Agarkar 11–4–16–2; Joshi 18–5–27–3; Kartik 1.3–0–1–1.

India

S. S. Das b Naimur Rahman	29	– not out	22
S. Ramesh b Bikash Ranjan Das	58	– b Hasibul Hussain	1
M. Kartik c sub (Rajin Salah) b Naimur Rahman	43		
R. Dravid c Al-Shahriar Rokon b Mohammad Rafiq	28	– (3) not out	41
S. R. Tendulkar c sub (Rajin Salah) b Naimur Rahman	18		
*S. C. Ganguly c Al-Shahriar Rokon b Naimur Rahman	84		
†S. S. Karim st Shahriar Hossain b Naimur Rahman	15		
S. B. Joshi c Al-Shahriar Rokon b Mohammad Rafiq	92		
A. B. Agarkar c Bikash Ranjan Das b Naimur Rahman	34		
J. Srinath c and b Mohammad Rafiq	2		
Zaheer Khan not out	7		
B 13, l-b 4, w 2	19		
1/66 (1) 2/104 (2) 3/155 (4) 4/175 (3) 5/190 (5) 6/236 (7) 7/357 (6) 8/413 (8) 9/421 (10) 10/429 (9)	429	1/11 (2)	(1 wkt) 64

Bowling: *First Innings*—Hasibul Hussain 19–2–60–0; Bikash Ranjan Das 19–3–64–1; Naimur Rahman 44.3–9–132–6; Mohammad Rafiq 51–12–117–3; Habibul Bashar 8–0–39–0. *Second Innings*—Hasibul Hussain 6–0–31–1; Bikash Ranjan Das 3–0–8–0; Naimur Rahman 4–0–22–0; Mohammad Rafiq 2–0–3–0.

Umpires: S. A. Bucknor (West Indies) and D. R. Shepherd (England).
Third umpire: Mahbubur Rahman. Referee: R. Subba Row (England).

THE ZIMBABWEANS IN INDIA, 2000-01

By ANIRBAN SIRCAR

A Zimbabwean team in transition landed in India three hours behind schedule, and without their baggage, leg-spinner Brian Murphy or captain Heath Streak. Though all of these eventually caught up (Streak after completing dental treatment in Harare), the chaotic start epitomised Zimbabwean cricket's most turbulent phase since they celebrated the granting of Test status in 1992. Against a political backdrop growing ever more volatile with the continuing occupation of white-owned farms, Zimbabwe's shattered economy held no promise for some of its underpaid cricketers. Two of their most valuable players, Murray Goodwin and Neil Johnson, had walked out after an encouraging tour of England, to seek more prosperous lives in Australia and South Africa respectively. Without them, Zimbabwe had lost two home Tests to New Zealand in September. Now, on only their second Test tour of India, they confronted an ominous task in the difficult conditions of the subcontinent.

For the home side, the new management team of captain Sourav Ganguly and coach John Wright of New Zealand was on a mission. India had their own share of turbulence; during the tour, their board banned several players, including former captain Mohammad Azharuddin and all-rounder Ajay Jadeja, for their part in the match-fixing scandal. Meanwhile, master leg-spinner Anil Kumble was absent, handicapped by lingering shoulder pain. In March, India had lost a 13-year unbeaten record in home Test series, to South Africa; in October, they had reached two one-day finals, in Nairobi and Sharjah, only to be caught off-guard, first by New Zealand, then by Sri Lanka.

A tour by the depleted Zimbabweans looked like an opportunity to regain some self-belief, but the Indians had reason to be wary. The last time the two sides met in a Test, at Harare in 1998-99, they had committed *hara-kiri* chasing an achievable target of 235, and folded 62 runs short. A recharged India avenged that humiliation with victory at Delhi, which was to give them the Test series 1–0, and then took the one-day series 4–1. But the Zimbabweans looked resolute wherever they went on the 40-day tour, and earned their hosts' admiration for their fightback after following on at Nagpur. Though their blend of experience and youth failed to produce results, their determination no longer to be treated as the whipping boys of world cricket took another small but firm step forward.

Wicket-keeper/batsman Andy Flower emerged with great distinction. He stamped his class against spin bowling in particular, amassing 540 runs in the two Tests, where his lowest score was 55 and his highest 232 not out, and following up with two fifties in the limited-overs games. Another former captain, Alistair Campbell, finally scored a maiden hundred in his 47th Test. In the one-day series, new guns Trevor Madondo and Mluleki Nkala oozed confidence. Disappointingly, 19-year-old pace bowler Travis Friend, who had troubled the Indians at Sharjah in October and was expected to provide much-needed new-ball support to Streak, missed the Tests through a nagging injury to his left ankle. Though he took the field in all but one of the five one-day matches, he was a shadow of his best.

For India, the stylish Rahul Dravid finished the Test series with an astounding average of 432.00 – one of three batsmen with a three-figure average, alongside Flower and Sachin Tendulkar. Javagal Srinath enjoyed a fine return to form, grabbing 12 wickets, twice as many as any other bowler, at 22.91 apiece. Two new boys, opener Shiv Sunder Das and off-spinner Sarandeep Singh, made their mark in the Tests, while India found a limited-overs match-winner in left-hander Hemang Badani. Ganguly consolidated his position as the leading one-day international run-scorer in the year 2000 by mustering 264 at 88.00 in four matches, taking his tally for the year to 1,579. He missed the fifth and final match through a disciplinary ban.

ZIMBABWEAN TOURING PARTY

H. H. Streak (Matabeleland) (*captain*), G. J. Whittall (Manicaland) (*vice-captain*), A. D. R. Campbell (Mashonaland), S. V. Carlisle (Mashonaland A), A. Flower (Mashonaland), G. W. Flower (Mashonaland), T. J. Friend (Midlands), T. N. Madondo (Mashonaland), D. A. Marillier (Midlands), B. A. Murphy (Mashonaland A), M. L. Nkala (Matabeleland), H. K. Olonga (Matabeleland), G. J. Rennie (Mashonaland), B. C. Strang (Mashonaland), P. A. Strang (Mashonaland).

D. P. Viljoen (Mashonaland A) joined the party to replace the injured P. A. Strang.

Manager: M. A. Meman. *Coach:* C. G. Rackemann.

ZIMBABWEAN TOUR RESULTS

Test matches – Played 2: Lost 1, Drawn 1.
First-class matches – Played 4: Won 1, Lost 1, Drawn 2.
Win – Board President's XI.
Loss – India.
Draws – India, National Cricket Academy.
One-day internationals – Played 5: Won 1, Lost 4.

Note: Matches in this section which were not first-class are signified by a dagger.

At Indore, November 8, 9, 10. Drawn. Toss: Zimbabweans. Zimbabweans 322 for six dec. (D. A. Marillier 30, S. V. Carlisle 61, A. D. R. Campbell 114 not out, G. J. Whittall 30; R. B. Patel three for 69) and 320 for five dec. (T. N. Madondo 65, A. Flower 119 retired hurt, S. V. Carlisle 39, G. J. Whittall 36 not out); National Cricket Academy 323 for six dec. (S. Sriram 97, N. K. Patel 87, R. S. Sodhi 55 not out; P. A. Strang three for 82) and 42 for one.

At Faridabad, November 13, 14, 15. Zimbabweans won by four wickets. Toss: Board President's XI. Board President's XI 314 for five dec. (V. Dahiya 50, H. K. Badani 35, H. H. Kanitkar 118 not out, V. Sehwag 60; P. A. Strang three for 59) and 183 for two dec. (R. S. Ricky 44, H. H. Kanitkar 33 not out, V. Sehwag 58 not out); Zimbabweans 236 for five dec. (G. W. Flower 49, G. J. Rennie 79, G. J. Whittall 30 not out, Extras 34) and 262 for six (G. J. Rennie 71, A. Flower 94; R. L. Sanghvi three for 93).

INDIA v ZIMBABWE

First Test Match

At Delhi, November 18, 19, 20, 21, 22. India won by seven wickets. Toss: Zimbabwe. Test debut: V. Dahiya.

India took the honours in an engrossing opening act. For most of the Test, the pitch was a batsman's paradise; the first two innings raised 880 runs for 13 wickets and featured three centuries. But the game was turned by the fiery bowling of Srinath, who demolished Zimbabwe's second innings and returned match figures of nine for 141.

The Zimbabweans had shown healthy promise in their warm-up fixtures, and confidently took first strike. Srinath's pace extracted both openers cheaply, but some shoddy catching around the bat negated the initiative of Ganguly, who employed six bowlers on the first morning. The road to recovery was laid in a 119-run stand between Carlisle and Campbell, who became the third Zimbabwean after the Flower brothers to reach 2,000 Test runs. But when they went, swiftly followed by Whittall for a duck, the innings again threatened to fall apart. Andy Flower averted the crisis, carrying his side to a respectable 232 without further casualties by the close.

On a cold and hazy second morning, Srinath took the new ball and removed Streak with his opening delivery. But Flower ensured that the last four wickets added 190, including a Zimbabwean tenth-wicket Test record of 97 undefeated runs with Olonga, who survived 158 minutes for 11. Flower himself batted 466 minutes and 351 balls, hitting 24 fours and two sixes and revelling in the ideal conditions to reach an unbeaten 183, his eighth and highest Test hundred, and his second at Delhi after his 115 in 1992-93. Streak declared on the second evening at a handsome 422 for nine.

Next day, the Indians confronted Zimbabwe's fire with their own brimstone. They purchased 266 runs from a full day's shopping, which cost them only the openers. Dravid accompanied first Das and then the mercurial Tendulkar in two successive century stands; he passed 3,000 Test runs just before the end of play. India still trailed by 147, however, and a draw seemed most likely. But the fourth day saw them at their aggressive best. Dravid and Tendulkar extended their third-wicket partnership to 213, with Tendulkar cruising to his 23rd Test century and batting in all for four and three-quarter hours. Dravid remained to complete a flawless double-hundred, his first in 39 Tests, from a 541-minute stay that occupied 350 balls and was punctuated by 27 fours. At once, Ganguly made a bold declaration, shortly before tea, with a slim lead of 36.

The onus now shifted to the home bowlers to maintain the basics on a pitch showing little wear and tear. Ganguly's wishes were answered: Srinath dismissed both openers without scoring in his first three overs. The Zimbabweans began the final day a shaky 119 for five, with Andy Flower, 41 not out, their best hope. The Indians came at him with all guns blazing and, while he top-scored again with 70, he was unable to inspire another recovery. Zimbabwe fizzled out for 225, with Srinath grabbing his seventh five-wicket haul in 48 Tests. That left India to chase 190 in 47 overs; they rushed past the target in the 38th, riding high on unbeaten half-centuries from Dravid and Ganguly.

Man of the Match: J. Srinath.

Close of play: First day, Zimbabwe 232-5 (A. Flower 55*, Streak 25*); Second day, India 9-0 (Das 4*, Ramesh 3*); Third day, India 275-2 (Dravid 118*, Tendulkar 70*); Fourth day, Zimbabwe 119-5 (A. Flower 41*, Murphy 0*).

Zimbabwe

G. W. Flower b Srinath	0	– c Dahiya b Srinath	0
G. J. Rennie c Dahiya b Srinath	13	– c Ganguly b Srinath	0
S. V. Carlisle c Joshi b Tendulkar	58	– c Ganguly b Joshi	32
A. D. R. Campbell c Laxman b Srinath	70	– c Dravid b Srinath	8
†A. Flower not out	183	– lbw b Agarkar	70
G. J. Whittall c Dravid b Joshi	0	– c Ramesh b Kartik	29
*H. H. Streak c Dravid b Srinath	25	– (8) lbw b Kartik	26
P. A. Strang c Ganguly b Joshi	19	– (9) not out	14
B. A. Murphy run out	13	– (7) c Dahiya b Srinath	6
B. C. Strang lbw b Agarkar	6	– c Tendulkar b Joshi	15
H. K. Olonga not out	11	– lbw b Srinath	10
B 8, l-b 10, w 4, n-b 2	24	B 4, l-b 9, w 1, n-b 1	15
1/0 (1) 2/15 (2) 3/134 (3) 4/154 (4) 5/155 (6) 6/232 (7) 7/266 (8) 8/312 (9) 9/325 (10)	(9 wkts dec.) 422	1/0 (1) 2/15 (2) 3/25 (4) 4/47 (3) 5/109 (6) 6/144 (7) 7/171 (5) 8/181 (8) 9/213 (10) 10/225 (11)	225

Bowling: *First Innings*—Srinath 35–9–81–4; Agarkar 35–13–89–1; Ganguly 8–1–26–0; Joshi 46–11–116–2; Tendulkar 19–5–51–1; Kartik 24–7–40–0; Laxman 1–0–1–0. *Second Innings*—Srinath 24.1–6–60–5; Agarkar 16–4–48–1; Joshi 25–7–68–2; Tendulkar 4–1–10–0; Kartik 11–2–26–2.

India

S. S. Das lbw b Olonga	58	– run out	4
S. Ramesh lbw b Streak	13	– c P. A. Strang b Streak	0
R. Dravid not out	200	– not out	70
S. R. Tendulkar c P. A. Strang b Murphy	122	– c Murphy b P. A. Strang	39
*S. C. Ganguly c A. Flower b Olonga	27	– not out	65
V. V. S. Laxman not out	18		
B 2, l-b 10, w 2, n-b 6	20	B 9, l-b 1, w 1, n-b 1	12
1/27 (2) 2/134 (1) 3/347 (4) 4/430 (5) (4 wkts dec.)	458	1/3 (2) 2/15 (1) 3/80 (4) (3 wkts)	190

A. B. Agarkar, S. B. Joshi, †V. Dahiya, M. Kartik and J. Srinath did not bat.

Bowling: *First Innings*—Streak 30–9–78–1; B. C. Strang 28–9–95–0; Murphy 36–5–90–1; Olonga 20–3–79–2; P. A. Strang 15–1–52–0; G. W. Flower 13.4–3–52–0. *Second Innings*—Streak 5–2–18–1; B. C. Strang 3–0–20–0; Olonga 6–0–26–0; Murphy 11–0–56–0; P. A. Strang 4.2–0–26–1; G. W. Flower 1.4–0–10–0; Rennie 3.3–0–19–0; Campbell 3–1–5–0.

Umpires: J. H. Hampshire (England) and S. Venkataraghavan.
Third umpire: V. Chopra. Referee: B. N. Jarman (Australia).

INDIA v ZIMBABWE

Second Test Match

At Nagpur, November 25, 26, 27, 28, 29. Drawn. Toss: India. Test debut: Sarandeep Singh.

The bandwagon moved southwards to the orange groves of Nagpur, hosting its first Test in three years. The match was poorly attended, with headlines dominated by local political demands for autonomy, the Indian board's hearings into match-fixing, and gossip about captain Ganguly's fling with voluptuous actress Nagma. On the field, however, there was a feast of runs. Six batsmen ran up centuries, culminating in Andy Flower's undefeated 232, the highest Test score by a wicket-keeper, which foiled India's expectations of a series whitewash. Forced to follow on, Flower and his team-mates displayed great grit and poise as they camped at the crease to erase an unnecessarily tall home total of 609, a ground record. For nearly two days, the Indians laboured on a placid track.

Having claimed first use of the pitch, India might have driven the last nail in Zimbabwe's coffin had they not delayed their declaration until ten overs after tea on the second day, waiting for Tendulkar to complete his second double-century in Tests. Over-cautious batting had slowed them down when aggression was the need of the hour. Tendulkar's innings lasted 392 minutes and 281 balls, included 27 fours, and was the highlight of India's mammoth total, which was set on its way by opener Das's maiden century, in his third Test. In between, Dravid took his series aggregate to 432 before he was finally dismissed; he added 155 with Das and 249 with Tendulkar, their second double-century stand of the series and an Indian all-wicket record against Zimbabwe.

The visitors had rethought their batting order, after Rennie and Grant Flower's last five opening partnerships had totalled 12 runs. Flower dropped to No. 6, and Whittall moved up to weather the new ball for only the second time in his Test career. The switch did wonders for both; Whittall notched up a strokeful 84, while Flower followed his king pair at Delhi with a hard-hitting hundred. Zimbabwe began the fourth day on 359 for six, hoping to avoid the follow-on, but the later order lasted just 12 overs – time enough for Flower to complete his century, but leaving them 28 short of making India bat again.

The home side were counting down to victory shortly after lunch, when 21-year-old off-spinner Sarandeep Singh, a newcomer from Punjab, reduced Zimbabwe's second innings to 61 for three, still 166 behind. But the indomitable Andy Flower showed awe-inspiring skill and physical fortitude, remaining unconquered for 544 minutes and 444 balls, to build a career-best 232 laced with 30 fours and two sixes. It was his ninth Test century, and first double. The previous best by a Test wicket-keeper was 210 not out by Taslim Arif for Pakistan against Australia at Faisalabad in 1979-80. Surprisingly, Campbell, who like Flower had played in all Zimbabwe's 47 Tests, had never previously passed 99, but he put that right now as they added 209 to push their side into the lead. Viljoen, a last-minute fly-in for the injured Paul Strang, then helped Flower put on 113 for the sixth wicket to ensure safety.

Although the result meant the Indians took the series 1–0, Zimbabwe's fighting draw represented a moral victory. Ganguly, who could have become the first Indian captain to win his first three Tests in charge, complained that the Nagpur pitch was fit enough at the conclusion for another five-day match. He had craved turning tracks for the Test matches; instead, his bowlers were committed to grafting on flat batting surfaces.

Man of the Match: A. Flower. *Man of the Series:* A. Flower.

Close of play: First day, India 306-2 (Dravid 93*, Tendulkar 49*); Second day, Zimbabwe 59-1 (Whittall 34*, Carlisle 4*); Third day, Zimbabwe 359-6 (G. W. Flower 91*, Streak 16*); Fourth day, Zimbabwe 238-3 (Campbell 83*, A. Flower 88*).

India

S. S. Das c Campbell b Murphy	110
S. Ramesh run out	48
R. Dravid c A. Flower b Streak	162
S. R. Tendulkar not out	201
*S. C. Ganguly c Streak b G. W. Flower	30
A. B. Agarkar c Streak b Murphy	12
S. B. Joshi c Murphy b G. W. Flower	27
†V. Dahiya not out	2
L-b 11, w 4, n-b 2	17
1/72 (2) 2/227 (1) 3/476 (3) 4/535 (5) 5/564 (6) 6/601 (7)	(6 wkts dec.) 609

J. Srinath, Zaheer Khan and Sarandeep Singh did not bat.

Bowling: Streak 31–7–87–1; Olonga 24–4–98–0; Nkala 22–2–86–0; Murphy 40.5–2–175–2; Viljoen 14–2–51–0; G. W. Flower 24–0–101–2.

Zimbabwe

G. J. Whittall c Dravid b Sarandeep Singh	84	– c Tendulkar b Sarandeep Singh	11
G. J. Rennie run out	19	– c Ganguly b Sarandeep Singh	37
S. V. Carlisle c and b Agarkar	51	– c Tendulkar b Sarandeep Singh	8
A. D. R. Campbell c Ramesh b Sarandeep Singh	4	– c Joshi b Zaheer Khan	102
†A. Flower c Dahiya b Agarkar	55	– not out	232
G. W. Flower not out	106	– c Ganguly b Joshi	16
D. P. Viljoen c Dahiya b Zaheer Khan	19	– c Ganguly b Sarandeep Singh	38
*H. H. Streak lbw b Srinath	16	– not out	29
M. L. Nkala c Dahiya b Srinath	6		
B. A. Murphy c Das b Joshi	0		
H. K. Olonga b Srinath	0		
B 6, l-b 12, w 1, n-b 3	22	B 12, l-b 14, n-b 4	30
1/43 (2) 2/144 (3) 3/165 (4) 4/166 (1) 5/262 (5) 6/324 (7) 7/359 (8) 8/371 (9) 9/372 (10) 10/382 (11)	382	1/24 (1) 2/60 (3) 3/61 (2) 4/270 (4) 5/292 (6) 6/405 (7)	(6 wkts) 503

Bowling: *First Innings*—Srinath 28.1–7–81–3; Zaheer Khan 21–3–78–1; Joshi 25–7–69–1; Agarkar 23–7–59–2; Sarandeep Singh 22–7–70–2; Tendulkar 1–0–7–0. *Second Innings*—Zaheer Khan 17–5–48–1; Agarkar 14–3–29–0; Sarandeep Singh 49–10–136–4; Joshi 41–5–153–1; Tendulkar 11–3–19–0; Srinath 15–5–53–0; Ramesh 3–0–14–0; Dravid 7–0–15–0; Ganguly 1–0–3–0; Das 3–0–7–0.

Umpires: R. S. Dunne (New Zealand) and A. V. Jayaprakash.
Third umpire: K. S. Giridharan. Referee: B. N. Jarman (Australia).

†INDIA v ZIMBABWE

First One-Day International

At Cuttack, December 2. India won by three wickets. Toss: Zimbabwe. International debut: R. S. Sodhi.

The one-day series opener witnessed the emergence of the Tamil Nadu left-hander, Badani, who scored a decisive 58 in 69 balls. Batting first on a newly laid pitch, Zimbabwe benefited from half a dozen dropped catches, while an unbeaten 91 from Carlisle, who added 115 with Campbell, led them to a respectable 253. India were penalised one over for a slow over-rate, but Ganguly and Tendulkar set out in clinical fashion to keep them up with the run-rate, amassing 102 in 20 overs. And when a familiar middle-order collapse followed their departure, leaving India desperate at 144 for five, Badani inspired a rare late-order revival. He added 60 in ten overs with Dahiya and 50 in six with Agarkar to bring victory with ten balls to spare.

Man of the Match: H. K. Badani.

Zimbabwe

A. D. R. Campbell c Badani b Agarkar	68
D. A. Marillier c Tendulkar b Zaheer Khan	8
S. V. Carlisle not out	91
†A. Flower st Dahiya b Tendulkar	11
G. W. Flower c Yuvraj Singh b Agarkar	25
G. J. Whittall c Agarkar b Prasad	20
*H. H. Streak b Prasad	5
D. P. Viljoen run out	2
T. J. Friend not out	0
L-b 8, w 7, n-b 8	23
1/27 2/142 3/168 4/206 5/231 6/245 7/248 (7 wkts, 50 overs)	253

B. A. Murphy and H. K. Olonga did not bat.

Bowling: Zaheer Khan 10–1–46–1; Prasad 10–0–29–2; Agarkar 10–0–74–2; Joshi 8–0–43–0; Sodhi 8–0–31–0; Tendulkar 4–0–22–1.

India

*S. C. Ganguly c Campbell b Viljoen	44
S. R. Tendulkar c Streak b Viljoen	44
R. Dravid run out	9
Yuvraj Singh lbw b Murphy	11
H. K. Badani not out	58
R. S. Sodhi run out	9
†V. Dahiya c and b Murphy	35
S. B. Joshi lbw b Streak	0
A. B. Agarkar not out	19
L-b 9, w 11, n-b 6	26
1/102 2/109 3/122 4/129 5/144 6/204 7/205 (7 wkts, 47.2 overs)	255

B. K. V. Prasad and Zaheer Khan did not bat.

Bowling: Friend 7–0–36–0; Olonga 10–0–56–0; Streak 9.2–0–38–1; Murphy 6–0–45–2; Viljoen 9–0–46–2; G. W. Flower 6–0–25–0.

Umpires: Jasbir Singh and A. V. Jayaprakash.
Third umpire: S. C. Gupta.

†INDIA v ZIMBABWE

Second One-Day International

At Ahmedabad, December 5. India won by 61 runs. Toss: India.

Ganguly overcame a bothersome back spasm to notch up his seventh one-day international century of the calendar year and the 16th of his career. His majestic 144 runs in 152 balls featured six sixes and eight fours. Dravid assisted him in adding 175 for the second wicket, and later led India in the field when Ganguly's back pains forced him off. Zimbabwe's massive target of 307 was far too high a mountain for such a spin-wary side to scale. Fifties by the in-form Andy Flower and Streak provided some bite to the run-chase, but never threatened to alarm the home camp.

Man of the Match: S. C. Ganguly.

India

S. R. Tendulkar c A. Flower b Friend . . . 8
*S. C. Ganguly c Marillier b Viljoen . . . 144
R. Dravid run out 62
Yuvraj Singh c Streak b Murphy 17
S. B. Joshi c Campbell b Olonga 22
H. K. Badani not out 17
R. S. Sodhi not out 4
B 5, l-b 8, w 16, n-b 3 32

1/22 2/197 3/242 4/255 5/295 (5 wkts, 50 overs) 306

S. Sriram, †V. Dahiya, B. K. V. Prasad and Zaheer Khan did not bat.

Bowling: Olonga 10–0–59–1; Friend 10–1–37–1; Streak 10–0–63–0; Murphy 8–1–51–1; Viljoen 7–0–39–1; Marillier 5–0–44–0.

Zimbabwe

A. D. R. Campbell c Dravid b Tendulkar 32
D. A. Marillier b Prasad 2
S. V. Carlisle b Zaheer Khan 1
†A. Flower c and b Sriram 51
G. W. Flower c Yuvraj Singh b Joshi . . . 8
G. J. Whittall c Prasad b Sriram 26
D. P. Viljoen c sub (S. S. Das) b Joshi . . 26
*H. H. Streak not out 51
T. J. Friend c Zaheer Khan b Sriram . . . 8
B. A. Murphy not out 4
B 5, l-b 11, w 18, n-b 2 36

1/21 2/35 3/55 4/96 5/141 6/147 7/205 8/220 (8 wkts, 50 overs) 245

H. K. Olonga did not bat.

Bowling: Zaheer Khan 6–0–24–1; Prasad 6–0–15–1; Tendulkar 10–0–53–1; Sodhi 8–1–31–0; Joshi 8–0–30–2; Sriram 8–0–47–3; Badani 2–0–15–0; Yuvraj Singh 2–0–14–0.

Umpires: K. Hariharan and S. Venkataraghavan.
Third umpire: S. N. Bandekar.

†INDIA v ZIMBABWE

Third One-Day International

At Jodhpur, December 8. Zimbabwe won by one wicket. Toss: India.

The Barkatullah Khan Stadium's first one-day international was a cliffhanger, with Zimbabwe snatching victory to keep the series alive. India looked set to wrap it up after compiling an eminently defensible 283 and then reducing Zimbabwe to 52 for three. Tendulkar hit a brilliant 146 in 153 balls, with 15 fours and two sixes, his 27th century in one-day internationals, and the final over cost 27 runs as Zaheer Khan smashed four sixes off Olonga, reaching 32 in 11 balls. The Flower brothers, however, fought back with 158 in 30 overs, then a Zimbabwean fourth-wicket record. Later, Nkala hit 36 in 27 balls and, when he was run out in the final over, last man Olonga scrambled the winning single with one ball to spare.

Man of the Match: G. W. Flower.

India

*S. C. Ganguly b Strang 5
S. R. Tendulkar c Nkala b Streak 146
R. Dravid c Rennie b G. W. Flower 30
Yuvraj Singh c and b G. W. Flower 5
H. K. Badani run out 1
R. S. Sodhi c G. W. Flower b Strang . . . 4
S. B. Joshi st A. Flower b G. W. Flower . 25
†V. Dahiya b Streak 3
A. B. Agarkar not out 13
Zaheer Khan not out 32
B 1, l-b 8, w 10 19

1/22 2/136 3/148 4/149 5/163 6/220 7/227 8/235 (8 wkts, 50 overs) 283

B. K. V. Prasad did not bat.

Bowling: Friend 7–1–34–0; Strang 10–0–40–2; Olonga 4–0–52–0; Streak 8–0–51–2; Nkala 10–0–43–0; G. W. Flower 10–0–43–3; Rennie 1–0–11–0.

Zimbabwe

A. D. R. Campbell c Dahiya b Zaheer Khan	24
G. J. Whittall c Badani b Prasad	6
S. V. Carlisle c Dahiya b Prasad	12
†A. Flower c Dahiya b Tendulkar	77
G. W. Flower c Yuvraj Singh b Prasad	70
G. J. Rennie run out	0
*H. H. Streak c Yuvraj Singh b Joshi	23
M. L. Nkala run out	36
B. C. Strang not out	5
T. J. Friend b Agarkar	0
H. K. Olonga not out	1
B 5, l-b 7, w 15, n-b 3	30
1/28 2/32 3/52 4/210 5/211 6/214 7/258 8/283 9/283 (9 wkts, 49.5 overs)	284

Bowling: Zaheer Khan 10–1–46–1; Prasad 10–1–61–3; Agarkar 9.5–1–44–1; Joshi 10–0–58–1; Sodhi 2–0–11–0; Tendulkar 6–0–35–1; Ganguly 2–0–17–0.

Umpires: S. K. Bansal and C. R. Mohite.
Third umpire: S. Banerjee.

†INDIA v ZIMBABWE

Fourth One-Day International

At Kanpur, December 11. India won by nine wickets. Toss: Zimbabwe.

Ganguly dominated proceedings from start to finish. He took five wickets, top-scored with an unbeaten 71, hit the winning runs with 25 overs to spare to secure the series 3–1 – and received a one-match ban for excessive appealing and dissent. Dahiya was also given a suspended one-match ban. Zimbabwe's preparation had been hindered by the late arrival of their kit, but Campbell and Madondo showed no ill-effects from this setback as they opened with 60. Once Agarkar removed them, however, Ganguly ran through the order, beginning with the dangerous Andy Flower, and Zimbabwe subsided to 165 all out. Ganguly then clobbered their hapless bowlers for 71 runs in 68 balls. Accumulating 157, he and Tendulkar almost completed the victory unaided through their 12th century opening partnership in one-day internationals and their second of the series.

Man of the Match: S. C. Ganguly.

Zimbabwe

A. D. R. Campbell b Agarkar	32
T. N. Madondo lbw b Agarkar	32
†A. Flower c Agarkar b Ganguly	19
S. V. Carlisle b Ganguly	20
G. W. Flower b Ganguly	6
G. J. Whittall run out	13
*H. H. Streak c Dahiya b Ganguly	3
M. L. Nkala b Agarkar	4
T. J. Friend lbw b Ganguly	6
B. C. Strang not out	0
H. K. Olonga c and b Agarkar	2
B 2, l-b 8, w 16, n-b 2	28
1/60 2/71 3/91 4/106 5/134 6/141 7/142 8/159 9/159 (45.4 overs)	165

Bowling: Zaheer Khan 8–0–19–0; Prasad 8–0–32–0; Agarkar 9.4–0–25–4; Kapoor 7–0–28–0; Ganguly 10–1–34–5; Sriram 3–0–17–0.

India

*S. C. Ganguly not out	71
S. R. Tendulkar lbw b Friend	62
S. Sriram not out	1
B 9, l-b 9, w 9, n-b 5	32
1/157 (1 wkt, 25 overs)	166

H. K. Badani, R. Dravid, †V. Dahiya, A. B. Agarkar, A. R. Kapoor, Zaheer Khan, B. K. V. Prasad and V. Shewag did not bat.

Bowling: Friend 5–0–40–1; Strang 10–2–29–0; Streak 3–0–26–0; Olonga 5–0–41–0; Nkala 2–0–12–0.

Umpires: C. K. Sathe and D. D. Sharma.
Third umpire: G. A. Pratap Kumar.

†INDIA v ZIMBABWE

Fifth One-Day International

At Rajkot, December 14. India won by 39 runs. Toss: Zimbabwe.

Agarkar smashed the fastest fifty by an Indian in one-day internationals, a 21-ball blitz that beat Kapil Dev's 22 balls against West Indies at Berbice in 1982-83. He concluded the innings with two sixes off Campbell; in all, he struck four sixes and seven fours in his 25-ball 67. India's top order had failed in Ganguly's absence, but they were rescued from 114 for five by a 102-run partnership between Badani and Sodhi, a 20-year-old Sikh whose maiden international fifty was overwhelmed by Agarkar's run-riot as they added 85 in 39 balls. Yet Zimbabwe were not daunted by a target of 302. Madondo impressed with a defiant run-a-ball 71, and Marillier hit a brisk 38 before falling leg-before to India's man of the moment, Agarkar.

Man of the Match: A. B. Agarkar. *Man of the Series:* S. C. Ganguly.

India

S. Sriram c A. Flower b Streak	2	R. S. Sodhi not out	53
S. R. Tendulkar b Nkala	27	A. B. Agarkar not out	67
*R. Dravid c Streak b Strang	6	L-b 8, w 13	21
H. K. Badani c Rennie b Murphy	77		
Yuvraj Singh lbw b Murphy	29	1/10 2/23 3/42 (6 wkts, 50 overs)	301
V. Shewag c A. Flower b Murphy	19	4/84 5/114 6/216	

†V. Dahiya, A. R. Kapoor and B. K. V. Prasad did not bat.

Bowling: Streak 10–1–45–1; Strang 10–0–61–1; Nkala 9–0–62–1; G. W. Flower 10–0–41–0; Murphy 10–0–63–3; Campbell 1–0–21–0.

Zimbabwe

A. D. R. Campbell c Dahiya b Sodhi	23	M. L. Nkala not out	18
T. N. Madondo b Sriram	71	B. C. Strang c Yuvraj Singh b Prasad	18
G. J. Rennie c Badani b Sodhi	10	B. A. Murphy b Agarkar	1
†A. Flower c Sodhi b Agarkar	19	L-b 8, w 5, n-b 4	17
G. W. Flower lbw b Shewag	20		
G. J. Whittall c Agarkar b Shewag	10	1/35 2/68 3/103 (47.4 overs)	262
D. A. Marillier lbw b Agarkar	38	4/152 5/156 6/180	
*H. H. Streak c Dravid b Sriram	17	7/210 8/235 9/260	

Bowling: Prasad 9–0–61–1; Sodhi 6–1–43–2; Agarkar 8.4–1–26–3; Kapoor 7–0–37–0; Sriram 9–0–50–2; Shewag 8–0–37–2.

Umpires: V. N. Kulkarni and A. M. Saheba.
Third umpire: K. Murali. Series referee: B. N. Jarman (Australia).

FICA/PWC AWARDS

The Federation of International Cricketers' Associations/PricewaterhouseCoopers International Player of the Year Award was won in July 2001 by Andy Flower of Zimbabwe. The previous winner, Glenn McGrath, also made the shortlist, as did Shaun Pollock, Inzamam-ul-Haq, Darren Gough, Sachin Tendulkar and Muttiah Muralitharan. Abdur Razzaq of Pakistan was named Young International Player of the Year. Steve Waugh won the *Wisden Cricket Monthly* International Place in History award for leading Australia to 16 consecutive Test victories, and the Australian Test team were the Hub International Team of the Year.

THE SRI LANKANS IN SOUTH AFRICA, 2000-01

By NEIL MANTHORP

Five months earlier, Sri Lanka had played host to South Africa in a tense, even and consistently entertaining series – drawn with one victory each – so the prospect of a rematch made the taste buds tingle. Much had been said between the players regarding the state of Sri Lankan pitches, and how different things would be in South Africa. The return leg was promoted as a battle between the home side's fast bowlers and visiting batsmen reputed to be brittle on quick, seaming pitches against hostile pace.

Disappointingly, the Sri Lankans never adapted to the conditions, and were hammered. Inappropriate slashes and a tendency to push at deliveries wide of off stump were the constant undoing of their top-order batsmen, whose collective fate was epitomised by their captain, Sanath Jayasuriya, in the Third Test – caught at third man, upper-cutting, in the ninth over of the innings. Kumar Sangakkara, a batsman only recently retreaded as a wicket-keeper, marked himself as a player for the future, however. In a couple of lengthy innings, he displayed the willingness and the ability to move behind the line of a rising delivery before deciding whether to play or leave it. Mahela Jayawardene, too, counter-attacked impressively, though injudiciously, but in effect Jayasuriya and his vice-captain and opening partner, Marvan Atapattu, led from the front in proving that few Asian batsmen can prosper in the conditions they encountered. Both endured thoroughly miserable series, with aggregates of 66 and 41 runs respectively. Even the late call-up of Aravinda de Silva, after leg-spinning all-rounder Upul Chandana broke a finger, failed to stop the clatter of wickets.

Spin master Muttiah Muralitharan was a charm, however. Arriving in South Africa with 291 wickets in just 57 Tests, he expressed his great desire to reach 300 during the series, but acknowledged that there would be little to assist him in the pitches. He promptly reached the milestone in the First Test, with a match haul of 11 for 161, and was presented with a huge commemorative plaque to celebrate the occasion. South Africa were spared Murali in the Third Test – he withdrew on the morning of the match with a hamstring strain – but by then the momentum was so powerfully behind the home team that there would have been little he could have done.

Rain undoubtedly saved the tourists during the First Test at Durban, with the whole of the fourth day washed out. But there was no respite in Cape Town, where they were rattled by a fiery Mfuneko Ngam and then skittled for 95 by home captain Shaun Pollock, who took six for 30. The Third Test, too, was miserably one-sided; Pollock turned destroyer-with-bat, carving a maiden Test century at No. 9, before masterminding a second successive innings defeat. So complete was South Africa's demolition that, at first glance, there was not even a crumb of success from which Sri Lanka could draw comfort. They were walloped 5–1 in the one-day series, too.

On their departure, however, observers could not fail to be impressed with the Sri Lankans' dignity and togetherness in defeat. With the direst tour requiring just a dash of acrimony and a pinch of back-stabbing for total implosion, there was none. For that, at least, Jayasuriya could be grateful. It also demonstrated the regard his players had for him. Only after Sri Lanka reached New Zealand for another one-day series did news of a personal tragedy surface: during the final Test, Jayasuriya's wife had suffered a miscarriage at home in Sri Lanka. Given the personal trauma and the hopelessness of a tour gone badly wrong, it was a remarkable effort for him to bat at all.

SRI LANKAN TOURING PARTY

S. T. Jayasuriya (Bloomfield) (*captain*), M. S. Atapattu (Sinhalese) (*vice-captain*), R. P. Arnold (Nondescripts), U. D. U. Chandana (Tamil Union), T. M. Dilshan (Bloomfield), C. R. D. Fernando (Sinhalese), D. A. Gunawardene (Sinhalese), D. P. M. D. Jayawardene (Sinhalese), R. S. Kaluwitharana (Colts), M. Muralitharan (Tamil Union), M. Pushpakumara (Colts), K. Sangakkara (Nondescripts), W. P. U. J. C. Vaas (Colts), K. Weeraratne (Colts), G. P. Wickremasinghe (Sinhalese), D. N. T. Zoysa (Sinhalese).

P. A. de Silva (Nondescripts) joined the party to replace the injured Chandana, and P. D. R. L. Perera (Sinhalese) as cover for Vaas.

Manager: Air Commodore A. Jayasekara. *Coach:* D. F. Whatmore.

SRI LANKAN TOUR RESULTS

Test matches – Played 3: Lost 2, Drawn 1.
First-class matches – Played 5: Won 1, Lost 2, Drawn 2.
Win – Eastern Province.
Losses – South Africa (2).
Draws – South Africa, KwaZulu-Natal.
One-day internationals – Played 6: Won 1, Lost 5.
Other non-first-class matches – Played 3: Won 1, Tied 1, Drawn 1. *Win* – KwaZulu-Natal. *Tie* – Eastern Province. *Draw* – N. F. Oppenheimer's XI.

TEST MATCH AVERAGES

SOUTH AFRICA – BATTING

	T	*I*	*NO*	*R*	*HS*	*100s*	*50s*	*Avge*	*Ct/St*
G. Kirsten	2	3	0	266	180	1	1	88.66	2
L. Klusener	2	3	1	158	97	0	2	79.00	1
D. J. Cullinan	3	4	1	221	112	1	1	73.66	3
N. D. McKenzie	3	4	0	172	103	1	0	43.00	2
S. M. Pollock	3	3	0	124	111	1	0	41.33	6
M. V. Boucher	3	4	0	157	92	0	1	39.25	14/1
N. Boje	3	4	1	77	32	0	0	25.66	2
J. H. Kallis	3	4	0	92	49	0	0	23.00	5
H. H. Dippenaar	2	3	0	53	22	0	0	17.66	2

Played in three Tests: M. Ntini 8, 10 (1 ct). Played in two Tests: H. H. Gibbs 0, 1 (3 ct); M. Ngam 0* (1 ct). Played in one Test: A. A. Donald 10*; J. M. Kemp 2 (1 ct).

* *Signifies not out.*

BOWLING

	O	*M*	*R*	*W*	*BB*	*5W/i*	*Avge*
J. M. Kemp	17.5	3	52	5	3-33	0	10.40
S. M. Pollock	83.2	29	192	13	6-30	1	14.76
N. Boje	64	21	147	9	4-28	0	16.33
M. Ngam	46.2	7	155	9	3-26	0	17.22
M. Ntini	73.3	23	216	10	4-39	0	21.60
A. A. Donald	16	2	67	3	2-28	0	22.33
J. H. Kallis	47	9	133	4	2-39	0	33.25

Also bowled: L. Klusener 16–6–27–1.

SRI LANKA – BATTING

	T	*I*	*NO*	*R*	*HS*	*100s*	*50s*	*Avge*	*Ct*
K. Sangakkara	3	6	0	235	98	0	2	39.16	4
D. P. M. D. Jayawardene	3	6	0	190	98	0	1	31.66	2
R. P. Arnold	3	6	0	143	71	0	1	23.83	4
T. M. Dilshan	2	4	1	56	28*	0	0	18.66	3
W. P. U. J. C. Vaas	2	4	1	50	38	0	0	16.66	1
R. S. Kaluwitharana	2	4	0	59	32	0	0	14.75	8
S. T. Jayasuriya	3	6	0	66	26	0	0	11.00	2
M. S. Atapattu	3	6	0	41	20	0	0	6.83	1
C. R. D. Fernando	3	5	2	11	5*	0	0	3.66	0
D. N. T. Zoysa	3	5	0	16	10	0	0	3.20	0
M. Muralitharan	2	3	1	1	1*	0	0	0.50	1

Played in one Test: P. A. de Silva 5, 22; D. A. Gunawardene 24, 13; P. D. R. L. Perera 1*, 0*; G. P. Wickremasinghe 21, 1 (1 ct).

* *Signifies not out.*

BOWLING

	O	*M*	*R*	*W*	*BB*	*5W/i*	*Avge*
M. Muralitharan	111.3	28	260	12	6-39	2	21.66
R. P. Arnold	52.2	9	165	4	3-76	0	41.25
C. R. D. Fernando	85	7	358	8	5-98	1	44.75
D. N. T. Zoysa	73	17	239	4	4-76	0	59.75

Also bowled: P. A. de Silva 2–1–5–0; S. T. Jayasuriya 13–4–38–0; D. P. M. D. Jayawardene 1–0–2–0; P. D. R. L. Perera 19–3–73–1; W. P. U. J. C. Vaas 67–8–218–1; G. P. Wickremasinghe 12.3–3–51–2.

Note: Matches in this section which were not first-class are signified by a dagger.

†At Randjesfontein, December 7. Drawn. Toss: Sri Lankans. Sri Lankans 296 for six dec. (M. S. Atapattu 52, S. T. Jayasuriya 66, D. P. M. D. Jayawardene 70, R. P. Arnold 54 retired out); N. F. Oppenheimer's XI 80 for no wkt (A. J. Hall 61 not out).

At Port Elizabeth, December 9, 10. Sri Lankans won by eight wickets. Toss: Sri Lankans. Eastern Province 92 (J. D. C. Bryant 37; C. R. D. Fernando four for 27) and 214 (C. C. Bradfield 30, J. D. C. Bryant 50, M. W. Creed 40 not out, D. W. Murray 32; C. R. D. Fernando three for 76, M. Muralitharan four for 41); Sri Lankans 266 (S. T. Jayasuriya 38, M. S. Atapattu 42, K. Sangakkara 37, D. P. M. D. Jayawardene 87; J. M. Kemp four for 59, G. J-P. Kruger four for 76) and 41 for two.

Kruger took a hat-trick in the Sri Lankans' first innings, but the tourists won with a day to spare.

†At PPC Oval, Port Elizabeth, December 13. Tied. Toss: Eastern Province. Eastern Province 220 for seven (50 overs) (C. C. Bradfield 82, J. M. Kemp 93; W. P. U. J. C. Vaas four for 30); Sri Lankans 220 (50 overs) (S. T. Jayasuriya 69, K. Sangakkara 31; G. J-P. Kruger three for 23).

Kemp and Bradfield added 175 for the fourth wicket in 35 overs.

†SOUTH AFRICA v SRI LANKA

First One-Day International

At Port Elizabeth, December 15 (day/night). South Africa won by four wickets. Toss: Sri Lanka.

Kaluwitharana dominated the early scoring with a bullish 55, as Sri Lanka's top order wobbled until Sangakkara joined him. Sangakkara's skilfully paced 84, including a fifty partnership with Vaas, helped the visitors recover to a competitive 221 on a tricky pitch for strokeplayers. The contest looked to be shaping well when South Africa were scrambling to 91 for four in 19 overs; in effect, there was little more excitement after that as Kirsten shored up one end while Rhodes chased runs. Two further wickets shifted the balance slightly back towards Sri Lanka, but an unbroken stand of 80 between Rhodes and Klusener, marked by splendid running between the wickets, ensured a comfortable win.

Man of the Match: J. N. Rhodes.

Sri Lanka

*S. T. Jayasuriya b Pollock	3
†R. S. Kaluwitharana b Kallis	55
M. S. Atapattu c and b Telemachus	2
D. P. M. D. Jayawardene c Boucher b Ntini	13
K. Sangakkara b Pollock	84
R. P. Arnold c Boucher b Klusener	5
T. M. Dilshan run out	18
W. P. U. J. C. Vaas b Pollock	18
D. N. T. Zoysa c Pollock b Kallis	1
M. Muralitharan not out	2
G. P. Wickremasinghe b Pollock	1
L-b 5, w 7, n-b 7	19
1/16 2/21 3/63 4/91 5/112 6/159 7/211 8/214 9/219 (49.5 overs)	221

Bowling: Pollock 9.5–1–36–4; Telemachus 10–1–46–1; Kallis 9–1–34–2; Ntini 5–0–44–1; Klusener 10–0–26–1; Boje 6–0–30–0.

South Africa

G. Kirsten st Kaluwitharana b Muralitharan	58
A. J. Hall c Kaluwitharana b Zoysa	18
N. Boje run out	6
J. H. Kallis c and b Zoysa	0
H. H. Dippenaar c Kaluwitharana b Vaas	19
J. N. Rhodes not out	61
†M. V. Boucher run out	9
L. Klusener not out	39
L-b 8, w 4, n-b 1	13
1/49 2/56 3/57 4/91 5/126 6/143 (6 wkts, 47.2 overs)	223

*S. M. Pollock, R. Telemachus and M. Ntini did not bat.

Bowling: Vaas 9–1–50–1; Zoysa 9–0–35–2; Wickremasinghe 7.2–0–44–0; Muralitharan 10–1–39–1; Jayasuriya 7–0–31–0; Arnold 5–1–16–0.

Umpires: W. A. Diedricks and R. E. Koertzen.
Third umpire: I. L. Howell.

†SOUTH AFRICA v SRI LANKA

Second One-Day International

At East London, December 17. South Africa won by 95 runs. Toss: South Africa.

McKenzie's maiden one-day international century appeared to knock all belief in victory out of the tourists. Reprieved on 35, sweeping at Muralitharan, he scored 120 in 135 balls, with 13 fours and a six, relishing anything short but also showing unaccustomed skill against spin with a series of lapped sweep shots and late cuts. He shared rollicking stands with Rhodes and Boucher, who delighted his home crowd with 55 in just 48 balls. Only Muralitharan conceded less than five an over as South Africa ran up 302 for seven. When Pollock struck twice in his first three overs, the match was as good as over, which Jayawardene appeared to confirm during his leisurely 59 from 84 balls.

Man of the Match: N. D. McKenzie.

South Africa

G. Kirsten c Jayawardene b Zoysa	6
A. J. Hall lbw b Vaas	0
J. H. Kallis c Arnold b Wickremasinghe	35
N. D. McKenzie not out	120
J. N. Rhodes c Muralitharan b Jayasuriya	50
†M. V. Boucher c Wickremasinghe b Muralitharan	55
L. Klusener c Chandana b Zoysa	6
N. Boje run out	7
L-b 12, w 5, n-b 6	23
1/1 2/24 3/69 4/157 5/257 6/279 7/302 (7 wkts, 50 overs)	302

*S. M. Pollock, R. Telemachus and M. Ntini did not bat.

Bowling: Vaas 10–0–54–1; Zoysa 10–0–68–2; Wickremasinghe 7–0–39–1; Muralitharan 10–0–47–1; Chandana 7–0–43–0; Arnold 1–0–10–0; Jayasuriya 5–0–29–1.

Sri Lanka

*S. T. Jayasuriya b Pollock	7
†R. S. Kaluwitharana lbw b Pollock	2
M. S. Atapattu c Boucher b Ntini	36
D. P. M. D. Jayawardene c and b Boje	59
K. Sangakkara c Hall b Ntini	11
R. P. Arnold not out	39
U. D. U. Chandana lbw b Klusener	2
W. P. U. J. C. Vaas not out	34
L-b 3, w 7, n-b 7	17
1/8 2/17 3/80 4/106 5/141 6/147 (6 wkts, 50 overs)	207

D. N. T. Zoysa, M. Muralitharan and G. P. Wickremasinghe did not bat.

Bowling: Pollock 10–0–34–2; Telemachus 9–1–44–0; Ntini 10–0–38–2; Kallis 8–0–30–0; Klusener 9–2–32–1; Boje 3–0–21–1; McKenzie 1–0–5–0.

Umpires: I. L. Howell and D. L. Orchard.
Third umpire: W. A. Diedricks.

†At Chatsworth, December 19. Sri Lankans won by 55 runs. Toss: KwaZulu-Natal. Sri Lankans 266 for eight (50 overs) (D. P. M. D. Jayawardene 85, W. P. U. J. C. Vaas 52 not out, Extras 30; G. M. Gilder four for 43); KwaZulu-Natal 211 (44.4 overs) (D. J. Watson 42, G. H. Bodi 53; K. Weeraratne three for 37).

At Pietermaritzburg, December 21, 22, 23. Drawn. Toss: Sri Lankans. Sri Lankans 257 for eight dec. (D. P. M. D. Jayawardene 87, T. M. Dilshan 54, R. S. Kaluwitharana 40; G. M. Gilder three for 55); KwaZulu-Natal 299 for five dec. (M. L. Bruyns 89, D. J. Watson 81, A. Mall 34, E. L. R. Stewart 39 not out, W. R. Wingfield 39 not out).

SOUTH AFRICA v SRI LANKA

First Test Match

At Durban, December 26, 27, 28, 29, 30. Drawn. Toss: South Africa.

The loss of the entire fourth day helped Sri Lanka save the game, and meant that it would be remembered above all for the achievements of Muralitharan, who took 11 wickets including his 300th in Tests. Winning the toss, Pollock had resisted any temptation to bowl first, despite Sri Lanka's weather-hampered preparations and the allure of the country's bounciest pitch. Instead, he gave Kirsten first use, and the veteran opener cashed in with an unbeaten 112 before worsening conditions (staved off a while by floodlights) ended play with South Africa an imposing 230 for three. What the scorecard did not reflect was the number of times the top-order batsmen were beaten in the first three hours, particularly by the pace of Fernando, playing his second Test.

Next day, Muralitharan gained his reward for a marathon 58.3 overs by claiming five for 122. Fernando collected the other five and was no less deserving, having maintained a wonderful line to the right-handers, swinging the ball just enough. He it was who eventually accounted for Kirsten, caught behind, with his score at 180 from 461 balls in 574 minutes. Kirsten's graft could be measured by a final tally of 20 fours, after he had hit eight in his first 50.

Sri Lanka's reply began disastrously. With Atapattu too keen to scamper a single and Jayasuriya lashing a resoundingly fast bouncer from Ngam to cover, they were two for two in the fourth over. Sangakkara and Jayawardene added a defiant 168, a Sri Lankan third-wicket record against South Africa, before Sangakkara's classy 74 ended with a sharp catch by Kirsten, standing deep at extra cover. Jayawardene was robbed of a century when Klusener's away-swinger clipped the bat's edge. As soon as they were parted, the crashing resumed; their stand would provide a remarkable 78 per cent of the eventual total. When Pollock claimed the final three wickets in five balls, becoming the second South African (after Allan Donald) to reach 200 Test wickets, the last eight wickets had fallen in 20 overs. Zoysa provided the milestone by pulling him to Ngam.

Rather than enforce the follow-on in failing light, South Africa batted again. With an hour plus two days remaining, time hardly seemed a problem, but next day it rained without pause. On the final morning, Pollock promoted himself to No. 4 – and was praised for his initiative in seeking to accelerate the lead before declaring. The reality was that some batsmen were reluctant to risk their wickets chasing quick runs; the result was that the less selfish players appeared, and soon disappeared. For as South Africa attempted all-out attack on a fifth-day pitch, Muralitharan had the run of the candy store. When he tempted Pollock to drive too early at a cunningly looped delivery, he became the 17th player to reach 300 Test wickets, and easily the first Sri Lankan – Vaas was his nearest rival on 127. There was no mistaking his delight. Only Dennis Lillee had done it in fewer Tests, taking 56 to Murali's 58.

Sri Lanka's theoretical target was 345 in around 70 overs, sufficiently unappealing to suggest that Pollock remembered his mauling by Jayasuriya in Galle five months earlier. In fact, Jayasuriya and Atapattu managed 41, which would remain their highest opening stand of the series by 29 runs. Then, suddenly, the Sri Lankans were 80 for four in the 34th over, with defeat a strong possibility. Arnold and Dilshan now formed an alliance that yielded 52 runs and, more importantly, spanned 30 overs. Although Pollock grabbed a pair of wickets late in the day, the danger had passed.

Man of the Match: G. Kirsten.

Close of play: First day, South Africa 230-3 (Kirsten 112*, McKenzie 5*); Second day, Sri Lanka 62-2 (Sangakkara 25*, Jayawardene 31*); Third day, South Africa 47-1 (Kirsten 20*, Kallis 1*); Fourth day, No play.

South Africa

H. H. Dippenaar c Kaluwitharana b Fernando	11	– lbw b Muralitharan	22
G. Kirsten c Kaluwitharana b Fernando	180	– c Arnold b Muralitharan	34
J. H. Kallis c Muralitharan b Fernando	21	– b Muralitharan	15
D. J. Cullinan c Atapattu b Muralitharan	59	– (9) not out	2
N. D. McKenzie c Dilshan b Muralitharan	9	– (7) lbw b Muralitharan	13
†M. V. Boucher c Arnold b Muralitharan	17	– c Vaas b Muralitharan	10
L. Klusener c Sangakkara b Muralitharan	50	– (8) not out	11
N. Boje b Muralitharan	32	– (5) c Sangakkara b Fernando	8
*S. M. Pollock c Kaluwitharana b Fernando	2	– (4) c Dilshan b Muralitharan	11
M. Ntini b Fernando	8		
M. Ngam not out	0		
B 5, l-b 10, w 1, n-b 15	31	B 4, l-b 3, n-b 7	14
1/31 (1) 2/86 (3) 3/194 (4) 4/238 (5) 5/269 (6) 6/358 (7) 7/401 (2) 8/410 (9) 9/420 (10) 10/420 (8)	420	1/46 (1) 2/75 (3) 3/91 (2) 4/92 (4) 5/108 (6) 6/114 (5) 7/132 (7) (7 wkts dec.)	140

Bowling: *First Innings*—Vaas 26–1–84–0; Zoysa 20–3–62–0; Fernando 34–4–98–5; Muralitharan 58.3–16–122–5; Arnold 14–3–39–0. *Second Innings*—Vaas 9–1–25–0; Zoysa 5–0–21–0; Fernando 10–0–48–1; Muralitharan 10–1–39–6.

Sri Lanka

M. S. Atapattu run out	0	– c Boucher b Boje	20
*S. T. Jayasuriya c McKenzie b Ngam	0	– c Cullinan b Ngam	26
K. Sangakkara c Kirsten b Boje	74	– st Boucher b Boje	17
D. P. M. D. Jayawardene c Boucher b Klusener	98	– c Boucher b Ntini	7
R. P. Arnold b Boje	3	– c Dippenaar b Pollock	30
T. M. Dilshan b Ngam	6	– not out	28
†R. S. Kaluwitharana c Boucher b Ntini	16	– c Boje b Pollock	1
W. P. U. J. C. Vaas c Boucher b Pollock	2	– not out	3
D. N. T. Zoysa c Ngam b Pollock	3		
C. R. D. Fernando not out	5		
M. Muralitharan c Boucher b Pollock	0		
N-b 9	9	B 4, l-b 7, n-b 6	17
1/0 (1) 2/2 (2) 3/170 (3) 4/184 (4) 5/184 (5) 6/201 (7) 7/208 (6) 8/208 (8) 9/215 (9) 10/216 (11)	216	1/41 (2) 2/69 (3) 3/80 (1) 4/80 (4) 5/132 (5) 6/140 (7)	(6 wkts) 149

Bowling: *First Innings*—Pollock 20.4–7–40–3; Ngam 12–0–59–2; Ntini 16–5–36–1; Kallis 9–3–17–0; Boje 19–4–44–2; Klusener 11–5–20–1. *Second Innings*—Pollock 16–5–35–2; Ngam 13–3–34–1; Ntini 10–4–18–1; Kallis 6–1–14–0; Boje 24–12–30–2; Klusener 5–1–7–0.

Umpires: Riazuddin (Pakistan) and D. L. Orchard.
Third umpire: I. L. Howell. Referee: R. Subba Row (England).

SOUTH AFRICA v SRI LANKA

Second Test Match

At Cape Town, January 2, 3, 4. South Africa won by an innings and 229 runs. Toss: Sri Lanka.

Sri Lanka's escape at Durban was followed by their annihilation at Cape Town. Electing to bat on a pitch offering good bounce and helpful seam movement, the tourists dissolved for a pitiful 95. Pollock despatched four shell-shocked top-order batsmen for 13; then Ngam obliterated the back-up forces with aggression to match his new nickname – "Black Thunder", as successor to "White Lightning", Allan Donald. He had to wait until the sixth wicket before getting his name in the scorebook, but it belonged to the top-scorer, Sangakkara, who dealt with the pace onslaught in a manner his team-mates could only dream about.

Eight batsmen were caught between slip and gully or at short leg, before tailenders Zoysa and Muralitharan offered tame catches to the bowler and mid-off respectively. It was a perfect exhibition, albeit a sorry one, of how not to play quick bowling. Pollock's six for 30 was the best return by a South African captain, though he quickly pointed out: "Not many of our captains have been bowlers."

Unable to counter fire with fire, the tourists could offer little more than a lukewarm tea-towel. Cullinan led the charge with his 12th Test century, a South African record and his fifth against Sri Lanka. It was as measured as a Major-winning round of golf, shot after shot finishing just where he intended without apparent effort. But after four and three-quarter hours, he failed to make enough effort to complete a second run, and left the field with a dozen fours, three sixes and a contented smile.

South Africa's reply had begun in surreal style. Gibbs received a standing ovation from his home crowd as he walked out for his first international innings after a six-month suspension for involvement in Hansie Cronje's match-fixing schemes. The applause had hardly died down when he edged his second delivery to Sangakkara, who had taken the gloves from Kaluwitharana to accommodate an extra batsman. To some, Gibbs's fall was poetic justice after the unseemly haste of his recall, 24 hours after the suspension expired and at the expense of Boeta Dippenaar, who had scored a maiden Test century three weeks before against New Zealand.

Two more local boys settled the crowd. Kirsten, equalling Cronje's South African record of 68 Test caps, nudged a gravelly fifty, yet still outscored the grimly determined Kallis, who finally edged a perfect away-swinger from Fernando after a somnambulant 49. They had built a solid platform for Cullinan, however. By the time Nos 6 and 7 arrived at the crease, the bowlers were completely demoralised; Boucher and Klusener clubbed them repeatedly to the boundary until both perished carelessly to occasional spinner Arnold in sight of their centuries. Boucher top-edged a sweep to deep backward square leg, while Klusener smashed a long-hop to square leg, where Jayasuriya held a catch that should have done him an injury.

Having recorded their lowest total and conceded their highest against South Africa, Sri Lanka batted again facing a deficit of 409. Once Ngam had made a double breakthrough in his first four overs – Jayasuriya fended his second ball to gully – they went rapidly downhill. Unexpectedly, the middle order was dismissed by left-arm spinner Boje, whose ability they appeared to underestimate. Jayawardene batted pleasantly for 45, and Vaas belted an entertaining 38 from 26 balls, hitting six fours and two sixes. But this late flourish could not avert a three-day defeat. An innings and 229 runs represented South Africa's largest victory, Sri Lanka's heaviest defeat, and the ninth most decisive Test result ever.

Man of the Match: S. M. Pollock.

Close of play: First day, South Africa 130-2 (Kallis 49*, Cullinan 17*); Second day, South Africa 426-6 (Klusener 44*, Boje 7*).

Sri Lanka

M. S. Atapattu c Kallis b Pollock	5	– lbw b Pollock	13
*S. T. Jayasuriya c Boucher b Pollock	8	– c Pollock b Ngam	0
†K. Sangakkara c Cullinan b Ngam	32	– c Boucher b Ngam	11
D. P. M. D. Jayawardene c Kallis b Pollock	0	– lbw b Boje	45
R. P. Arnold c Kirsten b Pollock	0	– c Gibbs b Boje	26
T. M. Dilshan c Pollock b Kallis	5	– c Boucher b Boje	17
D. A. Gunawardene c Kallis b Ngam	24	– b Ntini	13
W. P. U. J. C. Vaas c Pollock b Ngam	7	– c and b Boje	38
D. N. T. Zoysa c and b Pollock	10	– c Klusener b Ntini	0
C. R. D. Fernando not out	0	– c Boucher b Ngam	5
M. Muralitharan c Ntini b Pollock	0	– not out	1
W 1, n-b 3	4	L-b 6, w 1, n-b 4	11
1/12 (1) 2/13 (2) 3/13 (4) 4/13 (5) 5/33 (6) 6/66 (3) 7/84 (7) 8/95 (8) 9/95 (9) 10/95 (11)	95	1/4 (2) 2/18 (3) 3/53 (1) 4/99 (4) 5/112 (5) 6/119 (6) 7/131 (7) 8/135 (9) 9/172 (8) 10/180 (10)	180

Bowling: *First Innings*—Pollock 13.4–6–30–6; Ngam 13–3–26–3; Kallis 6–2–19–1; Ntini 6–2–20–0. *Second Innings*—Pollock 9–3–29–1; Ngam 8.2–1–36–3; Kallis 7–1–29–0; Ntini 11–2–52–2; Boje 10–3–28–4.

South Africa

G. Kirsten c Dilshan b Muralitharan	52
H. H. Gibbs c Sangakkara b Vaas	0
J. H. Kallis c Jayawardene b Fernando	49
D. J. Cullinan run out	112
N. D. McKenzie c and b Arnold	47
†M. V. Boucher c Jayawardene b Arnold	92
L. Klusener c Jayasuriya b Arnold	97
N. Boje not out	31
L-b 5, w 1, n-b 18	24
1/1 (2) 2/97 (1) 3/130 (3) 4/231 (5) 5/317 (4) 6/411 (6) 7/504 (7)	(7 wkts dec.) 504

*S. M. Pollock, M. Ntini and M. Ngam did not bat.

Bowling: Vaas 32–6–109–1; Zoysa 26–6–80–0; Fernando 25–2–105–1; Muralitharan 43–11–99–1; Jayasuriya 7–1–28–0; Arnold 24.2–4–76–3; Jayawardene 1–0–2–0.

Umpires: E. A. Nicholls (West Indies) and I. L. Howell.
Third umpire: W. A. Diedricks. Referee: R. Subba Row (England).

†SOUTH AFRICA v SRI LANKA

Third One-Day International

At Paarl, January 9 (day/night). South Africa won by eight wickets. Toss: Sri Lanka.

Although Sri Lanka's old World Cup opening partnership, Jayasuriya and Kaluwitharana, ran up 110, and Atapattu contributed an unbeaten 51, Sri Lanka's final total was not nearly enough. The openers' usual blazing style was tempered as they felt their way towards respectability, and the later batsmen could not accelerate; Pollock conceded just 33 in ten overs. As in the Cape Town Test, Gibbs lasted only two balls. But Dippenaar, restored to the one-day side for the injured Kirsten, avoided further alarms, and Kallis switched between attack and defence with such apparent randomness that he seemed to be toying with the bowlers. His greatest problem was keeping up with the running of Rhodes. Kallis thumped the penultimate ball of the 49th over, his 139th, to the cover boundary to win the match and complete his sixth one-day international century.

Man of the Match: J. H. Kallis.

Sri Lanka

*S. T. Jayasuriya lbw b Boje	66
†R. S. Kaluwitharana b Pollock	83
M. S. Atapattu not out	51
D. P. M. D. Jayawardene b Boje	22
W. P. U. J. C. Vaas c Gibbs b Kallis	3
K. Sangakkara not out	16
B 1, l-b 4, w 1	6
1/110 2/184 3/217 4/225 (4 wkts, 50 overs)	247

R. P. Arnold, K. Weeraratne, D. N. T. Zoysa, C. R. D. Fernando and M. Muralitharan did not bat.

Bowling: Pollock 10–0–33–1; Dawson 9–0–58–0; Ntini 8–0–40–0; Kallis 8–0–40–1; Klusener 5–0–32–0; Boje 10–0–39–2.

South Africa

H. H. Dippenaar c Muralitharan b Weeraratne	65
H. H. Gibbs lbw b Vaas	1
J. H. Kallis not out	100
J. N. Rhodes not out	75
W 2, n-b 7	9
1/5 2/116 (2 wkts, 48.5 overs)	250

N. D. McKenzie, †M. V. Boucher, L. Klusener, N. Boje, A. C. Dawson, *S. M. Pollock and M. Ntini did not bat.

Bowling: Vaas 9.5–1–37–1; Zoysa 10–0–48–0; Fernando 7–0–54–0; Muralitharan 10–0–39–0; Weeraratne 6–0–30–1; Jayasuriya 5–0–31–0; Arnold 1–0–11–0.

Umpires: W. A. Diedricks and D. L. Orchard.
Third umpire: S. B. Lambson.

†SOUTH AFRICA v SRI LANKA

Fourth One-Day International

At Cape Town, January 11 (day/night). South Africa won by 99 runs. Toss: South Africa.

South Africa secured the series 4–0 from a match which, as a contest, was over before the halfway point. Dippenaar square cut and drove well for his second successive half-century, and Rhodes later notched up his fifth: one against New Zealand and four in this series. Meanwhile, Kallis followed his century two days earlier with a mighty 82 from 79 balls – four sixes but no fours – that took him past 4,000 runs in one-day internationals. Vaas emerged with credit and three for 44 from ten overs, but otherwise the hosts trampled their way to 290 for seven, a ground record. Kaluwitharana prevented complete embarrassment with a defiant 74, but lost partners throughout. Ntini's hostile accuracy claimed five wickets.

Man of the Match: M. Ntini.

South Africa

H. H. Dippenaar c Sangakkara b Muralitharan	77	†M. V. Boucher not out	5
H. H. Gibbs c Weeraratne b Vaas	13	*S. M. Pollock not out	1
N. Boje b Jayasuriya	32		
J. H. Kallis c Muralitharan b Zoysa	82	L-b 3, w 1, n-b 3	7
J. N. Rhodes c Kaluwitharana b Vaas	53	1/53 2/120 3/133 (7 wkts, 50 overs)	290
L. Klusener c Jayasuriya b Vaas	2	4/217 5/219	
N. D. McKenzie c Wickremasinghe b Zoysa	18	6/283 7/284	

R. Telemachus and M. Ntini did not bat.

Bowling: Vaas 10–0–44–3; Zoysa 7–0–52–2; Wickremasinghe 5–0–31–0; Weeraratne 2–0–24–0; Muralitharan 10–0–53–1; Jayasuriya 10–0–50–1; Arnold 6–0–33–0.

Sri Lanka

*S. T. Jayasuriya c Gibbs b Telemachus	12	D. N. T. Zoysa not out	3
†R. S. Kaluwitharana b Ntini	74	G. P. Wickremasinghe c Boucher b Ntini	2
K. Weeraratne b Ntini	13	M. Muralitharan c Boucher b Ntini	0
M. S. Atapattu c Pollock b Kallis	10		
K. Sangakkara c Boucher b Ntini	1	L-b 6, w 10, n-b 1	17
D. P. M. D. Jayawardene c Pollock b Telemachus	37	1/25 2/63 3/98 (42.2 overs)	191
R. P. Arnold c Ntini b Kallis	21	4/101 5/150 6/174	
W. P. U. J. C. Vaas run out	1	7/178 8/187 9/191	

Bowling: Pollock 8–0–29–0; Telemachus 8–0–44–2; Kallis 8–0–31–2; Ntini 8.2–0–37–5; Klusener 0.3–0–0–0; McKenzie 2.3–0–6–0; Boje 7–0–38–0.

Umpires: R. E. Koertzen and S. B. Lambson.
Third umpire: B. G. Jerling.

†SOUTH AFRICA v SRI LANKA

Fifth One-Day International

At Bloemfontein, January 14. South Africa won by five wickets. Toss: South Africa. International debut: J. M. Kemp.

Sri Lanka's batting recalled their international youth: six scores in the twenties and thirties but nothing substantial enough to provide a challenging target. Pollock collected his tenth wicket of the series before tailender Wickremasinghe had the audacity to belt him to the boundary on his way to a 40-ball 32. With only 207 needed to win, Gibbs played with obvious restraint for 79 in 112 deliveries, his first significant innings after three failures since his return from suspension. Boje once again relished batting up the order, his 40 coming from just 31 balls, and South Africa coasted to another victory.

Man of the Match: H. H. Gibbs.

Sri Lanka

*S. T. Jayasuriya c Boucher b Pollock	23	G. P. Wickremasinghe c Boucher b Boje	32
†R. S. Kaluwitharana c Boje b Pollock	9	C. R. D. Fernando not out	12
M. S. Atapattu b Ntini	20	M. Muralitharan run out	6
P. A. de Silva c and b Kallis	20		
D. P. M. D. Jayawardene c Boucher b Kallis	1	L-b 1, w 9, n-b 1	11
R. P. Arnold c Pollock b Boje	32	1/24 2/35 3/67 (49.2 overs)	206
K. Sangakkara c Dippenaar b Pollock	33	4/78 5/80 6/142	
W. P. U. J. C. Vaas c Kallis b Donald	7	7/152 8/160 9/194	

Bowling: Pollock 10–2–44–3; Donald 7–0–42–1; Kallis 8–0–33–2; Ntini 10–1–38–1; Kemp 5–0–15–0; Boje 9.2–0–33–2.

South Africa

H. H. Dippenaar c Arnold b Wickremasinghe . 28
H. H. Gibbs run out 79
N. Boje lbw b Muralitharan 40
J. H. Kallis lbw b Vaas 31
N. D. McKenzie c sub (T. M. Dilshan) b de Silva . 0
J. N. Rhodes not out 11
†M. V. Boucher not out 8

L-b 1, w 2, n-b 7 10

1/51 2/112 3/177 4/180 5/192 (5 wkts, 42 overs) 207

J. M. Kemp, *S. M. Pollock, A. A. Donald and M. Ntini did not bat.

Bowling: Vaas 8–2–30–1; Fernando 4–0–38–0; de Silva 6–0–32–1; Wickremasinghe 3–0–23–1; Muralitharan 10–1–31–1; Jayasuriya 9–1–34–0; Arnold 2–0–18–0.

Umpires: B. G. Jerling and R. E. Koertzen.
Third umpire: D. F. Becker.

†SOUTH AFRICA v SRI LANKA

Sixth One-Day International

At Johannesburg, January 17 (day/night). Sri Lanka won by four runs (D/L method). Toss: South Africa.

Chasing a South African record of 11 straight victories, Pollock held his destiny in his own hands: he had to hit the last two balls of the match for six to capture a slice of history. He managed one, straight back over the bowler's head, but Jayasuriya fired the final delivery into the blockhole to end Sri Lanka's miserable losing sequence with a four-run victory. Earlier, Arnold's audacious 65 from 56 balls had boosted the tourists' total from 85 for four to 214 for six. Rain after nine overs had reduced the match to 42 overs and South Africa's target to 209; they seemed well on their way until an over-confident stroke from Boje triggered a collapse.

Man of the Match: R. P. Arnold. *Man of the Series:* J. H. Kallis.

Sri Lanka

*S. T. Jayasuriya c Boucher b Telemachus 6
†R. S. Kaluwitharana lbw b Telemachus . 4
M. S. Atapattu c Kallis b Kemp 55
P. A. de Silva c Dippenaar b Telemachus 7
D. P. M. D. Jayawardene c Boucher b Kemp . 25
R. P. Arnold not out 65
K. Sangakkara run out 22
W. P. U. J. C. Vaas not out 13

L-b 6, w 11 17

1/7 2/12 3/20 4/85 5/124 6/174 (6 wkts, 42 overs) 214

D. N. T. Zoysa, C. R. D. Fernando and M. Muralitharan did not bat.

Bowling: Pollock 9–1–37–0; Telemachus 8–1–25–3; Donald 6–0–31–0; Kallis 9–0–53–0; Kemp 7–0–34–2; Boje 3–0–28–0.

South Africa

H. H. Dippenaar lbw b Fernando. 18
H. H. Gibbs c Sangakkara b Vaas 3
J. H. Kallis b Vaas 18
N. Boje c Kaluwitharana b Jayasuriya . . 46
N. D. McKenzie b Jayasuriya 47
J. N. Rhodes b Muralitharan. 23
†M. V. Boucher c and b de Silva. 7
J. M. Kemp c Arnold b de Silva 0
*S. M. Pollock not out 21
R. Telemachus b Muralitharan. 1
A. A. Donald run out 1

L-b 3, w 14, n-b 2. 19

1/7 2/38 3/55 4/131 5/169 6/179 7/179 8/181 9/182 (42 overs) 204

Bowling: Vaas 4.5–0–27–2; Zoysa 7–0–19–0; Jayawardene 0.1–0–4–0; Fernando 7–0–56–1; Muralitharan 9–2–25–2; de Silva 6–0–31–2; Jayasuriya 8–0–39–2.

Umpires: D. F. Becker and D. L. Orchard.
Third umpire: W. A. Diedricks.
Series referees: Naushad Ali (Pakistan) and R. Subba Row (England).

SOUTH AFRICA v SRI LANKA

Third Test Match

At Centurion, January 20, 21, 22. South Africa won by an innings and seven runs. Toss: Sri Lanka. Test debut: J. M. Kemp.

Sri Lanka surrendered 2–0 with a second three-day innings defeat, though at the last there were moments of the bullish counter-attack they had promised from the outset. Having chosen to bowl on a spicy yet not unpalatable track, Jayasuriya would have been looking forward to batting himself, in ever-improving conditions, when South Africa were an immature 204 for seven at tea – and this with Muralitharan unfit to play. Then Pollock transformed everything with a maiden Test century of such velocity, as well as class, that few believed his innings could have lasted 23 minutes, let alone 123. Deliveries that had reared to hit the splice of other bats hit nothing but the middle of Pollock's; everything he touched turned to gold, or four or six. While his power was well known, it was the timing of the extra-cover drives, played mostly on the up, that gave Pollock's hundred its signature.

TEST HUNDREDS BY BATSMEN AT No. 9

173	I. D. S. Smith	New Zealand v India at Auckland	1989-90
160	C. Hill	Australia v England at Adelaide	1907-08
146	Asif Iqbal	Pakistan v England at The Oval	1967
122	G. O. B. Allen	England v New Zealand at Lord's	1931
112	J. T. Murray	England v West Indies at The Oval	1966
111	**S. M. Pollock**	**South Africa v Sri Lanka at Centurion**	**2000-01**
106*	**S. M. Pollock**	**South Africa v West Indies at Bridgetown**	**2000-01**
102*	L. Klusener	South Africa v India at Cape Town	1996-97
100	J. M. Gregory	Australia v England at Melbourne	1920-21
100	R. R. Lindwall	Australia v England at Melbourne	1946-47

Research: Gordon Vince

Had he realised how close he was to Kapil Dev's Test record of fifty in 30 balls, against Pakistan in 1982-83, or Hansie Cronje's in 31 balls, also against Sri Lanka at Centurion in 1997-98, he would surely have attempted to beat them. But Pollock had no idea how many, or how few, balls he had faced; he treated several with unexplained respect before completing 50 in 35, with his tenth four. Six more flew from his bat, as well as a trio of sixes that cleared the boundary with a dozen rows to spare. His century arrived from 95 balls, equalling Jonty Rhodes's South African record, also at Centurion, against West Indies in 1998-99. Perhaps he was making up for lost time – no one had waited as long as his 51 Tests to score a maiden Test hundred (Ian Healy of Australia took 48). But he was only the ninth player to score a century from No. 9 – a feat he repeated at Bridgetown two months later.

In the circumstances, McKenzie's second Test century went virtually unnoticed. Despite a 66-run lead on Pollock, he reached 100 only two overs earlier, having played with volumes of composure and complete selflessness; out of 150 for the eighth wicket, he contributed 37. "It was just a pleasure being out there to watch," he said.

South Africa made 375 for nine on the first day and added three next morning. When a demoralised Sri Lanka replied, Gibbs's speed at extra cover ran out Atapattu early on, and Donald needed only five overs to announce his return after injury: the impressive Ngam had himself been sidelined by a stress fracture of the right femur. Within three balls, Jayasuriya fell to a smartly conceived, stunningly executed but blatantly obvious trap, carving a wide, short delivery straight to third man, and Sangakkara was bowled by a beauty. De Silva, a recent reinforcement (but less recent than Perera, who flew in the night before the match), chopped Kallis to cover, where Gibbs dived to hold a difficult catch; Ntini, fast, accurate and bouncy, shredded the middle order to such effect that Kaluwitharana's boisterous 32 in 30 balls was irrelevant.

When Sri Lanka followed on 259 behind, Sangakkara was promoted to open (partly, it later emerged, because Jayasuriya had just learned of his wife's miscarriage) and responded by batting throughout for a fine, defiant 98. While he and Arnold, who scored an aggressive 82-ball 71, were adding 113, South Africans had a glimpse of Sri Lankan batting at its best. But then Boje changed his line, turned one just enough to discover the outside edge and had Arnold caught at slip; debutant Justin Kemp, replacing the injured Klusener, again mopped up the tail with clever pace changes and late swing. Finally, after five and three-quarter hours, when it looked as if South Africa might have to bat again, Sangakkara was trapped by a skidder. A maiden century was the least he deserved – but his wicket was just reward for Ntini, who had applied claustrophobic pressure.

Man of the Match: S. M. Pollock. *Man of the Series:* S. M. Pollock.

Close of play: First day, South Africa 375-9 (Donald 10*, Ntini 8*); Second day, Sri Lanka 184-3 (Sangakkara 64*, de Silva 21*).

South Africa

H. H. Dippenaar c Kaluwitharana b Perera	20
H. H. Gibbs c Kaluwitharana b Zoysa	1
J. H. Kallis c Arnold b Fernando	7
D. J. Cullinan c Kaluwitharana b Wickremasinghe	48
N. D. McKenzie c Wickremasinghe b Zoysa	103
†M. V. Boucher c Kaluwitharana b Zoysa	38
N. Boje c Jayasuriya b Arnold	6
J. M. Kemp run out	2
*S. M. Pollock c Sangakkara b Zoysa	111
A. A. Donald not out	10
M. Ntini c Kaluwitharana b Wickremasinghe	10
B 4, l-b 2, w 1, n-b 15	22
	378

1/17 (2) 2/31 (1) 3/54 (3) 4/115 (4) 5/168 (6) 6/185 (7) 7/204 (8) 8/354 (5) 9/359 (9) 10/378 (11)

Bowling: Zoysa 22–8–76–4; Perera 19–3–73–1; Fernando 16–1–107–1; Wickremasinghe 12.3–3–51–2; Arnold 14–2–50–1; Jayasuriya 6–3–10–0; de Silva 2–1–5–0.

Sri Lanka

M. S. Atapattu run out	3	– c Cullinan b Pollock	0
*S. T. Jayasuriya c McKenzie b Donald	16	– (6) b Donald	16
K. Sangakkara b Donald	3	– (2) lbw b Ntini	98
P. A. de Silva c Gibbs b Kallis	5	– (5) c Pollock b Kallis	22
D. P. M. D. Jayawardene c Boucher b Ntini	17	– (3) c Dippenaar b Kallis	23
R. P. Arnold b Ntini	13	– (4) c Pollock b Boje	71
†R. S. Kaluwitharana c Boucher b Ntini	32	– c Boucher b Kemp	10
D. N. T. Zoysa c Kallis b Ntini	1	– c and b Kemp	2
G. P. Wickremasinghe c Gibbs b Kemp	21	– c Boucher b Ntini	1
C. R. D. Fernando lbw b Kemp	0	– c Kallis b Kemp	1
P. D. R. L. Perera not out	1	– not out	0
L-b 3, w 3, n-b 1	7	L-b 2, w 2, n-b 4	8
1/6 (1) 2/24 (2) 3/25 (3) 4/40 (4) 5/54 (5) 6/71 (6) 7/76 (8) 8/97 (7) 9/98 (10) 10/119 (9)	119	1/9 (1) 2/43 (3) 3/156 (4) 4/187 (5) 5/212 (6) 6/234 (7) 7/242 (8) 8/243 (9) 9/248 (10) 10/252 (2)	252

Bowling: *First Innings*—Donald 9–2–28–2; Pollock 7–3–15–0; Kallis 5–1–15–1; Ntini 11–5–39–4; Kemp 4.5–1–19–2. *Second Innings*—Pollock 17–5–43–1; Kallis 14–1–39–2; Donald 7–0–39–1; Kemp 13–2–33–3; Ntini 19.3–5–51–2; Boje 11–2–45–1.

Umpires: P. Willey (England) and R. E. Koertzen.
Third umpire: D. L. Orchard. Referee: R. Subba Row (England).

THE ZIMBABWEANS IN NEW ZEALAND AND AUSTRALIA, 2000-01

By DON CAMERON

New Zealand felt they had some accounts to square when Zimbabwe arrived from India for a short tour, which contained one Test. The Kiwis were determined to win it, and confirm their ascendancy of the two Tests in Africa in September; but they also wanted revenge after losing their one-day series in Zimbabwe 1–2. In the end, the home authorities ruined the Test by producing an impossibly slow pitch, useless for attacking batsmen or bowlers but pandering to batsmen prepared not to take risks. Then Zimbabwe, much to New Zealand's surprise, repeated their one-day triumph after the batting pyrotechnics of their captain, Heath Streak, turned round an apparently lost cause.

So Zimbabwe had an honourable draw in the Test, their first overseas one-day series win against another Test nation, and broad smiles on their honest faces when they flew off for another limited-overs tournament in Australia. The faces of the New Zealand players and officials looked mostly puzzled, as if success had been stolen from them. But it was they who had eagerly insisted that the Test pitch at Wellington's Basin Reserve should be a grassless wasteland. They intended to switch their bowling thrust away from their weakened pace attack – Chris Cairns, Geoff Allott, Dion Nash and Simon Doull were all unavailable – and provide a helpful surface for off-spinner Paul Wiseman and Brooke Walker, a leg-spinning tyro. The experienced Daniel Vettori was also unfit. As it turned out, the pitch was so dead that it would have infuriated a world-class slow bowler, let alone two still learning their craft. The only beneficiaries were batsmen Nathan Astle and Craig McMillan, whose places had been under threat until they scored big hundreds.

Fortunately, there were sufficient batsmen of skill on both sides to make the limited-overs games competitive, whatever the type of pitch. Andy Flower, who had just touched second place in the PricewaterhouseCoopers Test Ratings, gave a virtuoso display of one-day batting artistry and inventiveness as he led Zimbabwe to victory in the first match. New Zealand countered with blistering batting from Astle, Mathew Sinclair and Scott Styris for a clear-cut win in the second. Then came the thrilling denouement, in which Flower, Dirk Viljoen and the heroic Streak thrillingly stormed an apparently unassailable home position. Those marvellous days will be treasured for years in the folklore of Zimbabwe cricket.

ZIMBABWEAN TOURING PARTY

H. H. Streak (Matabeleland) (*captain*), G. J. Whittall (Manicaland) (*vice-captain*), A. D. R. Campbell (Mashonaland), S. V. Carlisle (Mashonaland A), A. Flower (Mashonaland), G. W. Flower (Mashonaland), T. J. Friend (Midlands), A. J. Mackay (Mashonaland), T. N. Madondo (Mashonaland), D. A. Marillier (Midlands), B. A. Murphy (Mashonaland A), M. L. Nkala (Matabeleland), H. K. Olonga (Matabeleland), G. J. Rennie (Mashonaland), B. C. Strang (Mashonaland), D. P. Viljoen (Mashonaland A).

Manager: M. A. Meman. *Coach:* C. G. Rackemann.

ZIMBABWEAN TOUR RESULTS

Test match – Played 1: Drawn 1.
First-class matches – Played 2: Drawn 2.
Draws – New Zealand, Canterbury.
One-day internationals – Played 11: Won 3, Lost 8. *Wins* – New Zealand (2), West Indies. *Losses* – New Zealand, West Indies (3), Australia (4).
Other non-first-class matches – Played 3: Won 1, Lost 2. *Win* – Canterbury. *Losses* – Australia A, Australian Country XII.

Note: Matches in this section which were not first-class are signified by a dagger.

†At Christchurch, December 19 (day/night). Zimbabweans won by four wickets. Toss: Zimbabweans. Canterbury 236 for nine (50 overs) (M. A. Hastings 31, G. R. Stead 56, C. L. Cairns 38, C. Z. Harris 39 not out); Zimbabweans 239 for six (49.3 overs) (A. D. R. Campbell 72, T. N. Madondo 52, G. J. Whittall 35 not out; C. Z. Harris three for 25).

At Christchurch, December 21, 22, 23. Drawn. Toss: Zimbabweans. Canterbury 330 for five dec. (R. M. Frew 44, H. T. G. James 30, H. D. Barton 48, G. R. Stead 100 not out, G. J. Hopkins 50 not out; H. K. Olonga three for 78) and 122 for no wkt dec. (R. M. Frew 53 not out, H. T. G. James 65 not out); Zimbabweans 150 (D. A. Marillier 73; S. E. Bond five for 51, W. A. Cornelius three for 31) and 38 for two.

Tourists Grant Flower and Dirk Viljoen both broke fingers in the field and were ruled out of the Test.

NEW ZEALAND v ZIMBABWE

Test Match

At Basin Reserve, Wellington, December 26, 27, 28, 29, 30. Drawn. Toss: New Zealand. Test debut: D. A. Marillier.

All New Zealand's spadework before this one-off Test seemed to have given the home side a decisive advantage when Fleming won the toss. They had picked two spinners, Wiseman, orthodox off-spin, and leg-spinner Walker, who they hoped would take control as the bare pitch became worn over the fourth and fifth days. In fact, only three wickets fell to spin in the match – and two of those were to Zimbabwe's leg-spinner, Murphy.

It was not immediately apparent that it would have required some literal spadework to extract a result from this constipated surface, though it was obviously suffering from over-preparation. New Zealand lost three wickets in the first 30 overs, before Richardson and the out-of-form pair, Astle and McMillan, slowly put the innings back on an even keel. Slowly was the word: three two-hour sessions saw the hosts score 63, 66 and 61 runs for the loss of only one more wicket.

Astle and McMillan jogged along until tea on the second day. Their stand of 222 was a fifth-wicket record for New Zealand, beating 183 between Mark Burgess and Robert Anderson against Pakistan at Lahore in 1976-77. Astle, so far out of form that critics had asserted this could be his last Test, defied everyone, almost including Father Time, by grinding out his highest Test score, 141 in 549 minutes. He faced 408 balls and allowed himself the luxury of 16 fours and two sixes. McMillan's 142, equalling his previous best, was also unusually circumspect by his standards, though he batted only 311 minutes, with 18 fours and two sixes from 209 balls. By stumps, New Zealand were 475 for six, and the game was effectively beyond Zimbabwe's reach.

Rain and bad light allowed only 29 overs on the third day, time for New Zealand to declare at 487 for seven and for Martin to snatch the wickets of Whittall and Carlisle in an opening spell of 8–6–15–2. Zimbabwe had two days to negotiate. Campbell went early next morning, but Rennie almost reached a maiden Test century, and Flower hit his sixth consecutive Test fifty, which carried him past 1,000 runs in nine Tests in the calendar year. With the pitch so slow and tedious, and the home spinners toothless, Zimbabwe avoided the follow-on when they reached 288 just before the close.

There were brave comments from both camps that final-day declarations could bring about a positive result. But Streak let Zimbabwe's innings go on to 340 for six – five of them to Martin's seam – with Madondo providing a cultured 74 not out. The draw was now certain, and Fleming's second declaration left the tourists a notional 43 overs to score 301. In the 16th over after tea, Wiseman finally claimed his first wicket; the game ended by mutual consent shortly after.

Man of the Match: C. D. McMillan.

Close of play: First day, New Zealand 190-4 (Astle 56*, McMillan 20*); Second day, New Zealand 475-6 (Parore 44*, Walker 21*); Third day, Zimbabwe 48-2 (Rennie 20*, Campbell 15*); Fourth day, Zimbabwe 288-5 (Madondo 44*, Marillier 26*).

New Zealand

M. H. Richardson run out	75		
M. J. Horne c Flower b Streak	1	(1) c Flower b Streak	0
M. S. Sinclair lbw b Strang	9	(2) c Flower b Murphy	18
*S. P. Fleming run out	22	(3) run out	55
N. J. Astle c Carlisle b Strang	141	(4) not out	51
C. D. McMillan b Murphy	142	(5) c Madondo b Strang	10
†A. C. Parore not out	50	(6) not out	3
B. G. K. Walker c Olonga b Strang	27		
P. J. Wiseman not out	0		
B 1, l-b 8, w 5, n-b 6	20	B 5, l-b 5, n-b 6	16
1/5 (2) 2/22 (3) 3/67 (4) 4/145 (1) 5/367 (6) 6/426 (5) 7/487 (8)	(7 wkts dec.) 487	1/4 (1) 2/44 (2) 3/103 (3) 4/126 (5)	(4 wkts dec.) 153

S. B. O'Connor and C. S. Martin did not bat.

Bowling: *First Innings*—Streak 37–10–74–1; Strang 46–16–116–3; Olonga 30–2–105–0; Murphy 46–9–128–1; Whittall 22–6–55–0. *Second Innings*—Streak 5–1–18–1; Strang 11–2–25–1; Murphy 18–0–86–1; Olonga 2–0–12–0; Whittall 4–3–2–0.

Zimbabwe

G. J. Whittall b Martin	9	c Parore b O'Connor	6
G. J. Rennie c Parore b McMillan	93	c Parore b Wiseman	37
S. V. Carlisle c Horne b Martin	0	not out	16
A. D. R. Campbell lbw b Martin	24	not out	0
†A. Flower c Parore b Martin	79		
T. N. Madondo not out	74		
D. A. Marillier c Parore b Martin	28		
*H. H. Streak not out	19		
B 3, l-b 9, n-b 2	14	L-b 1	1
1/21 (1) 2/23 (3) 3/66 (4) 4/196 (5) 5/237 (2) 6/295 (7)	(6 wkts dec.) 340	1/26 (1) 2/57 (2)	(2 wkts) 60

B. A. Murphy, B. C. Strang and H. K. Olonga did not bat.

Bowling: *First Innings*—Martin 32.5–11–71–5; O'Connor 16–7–29–0; Wiseman 54–13–131–0; Walker 22–1–68–0; McMillan 9–4–22–1; Astle 5–2–7–0. *Second Innings*—Martin 5–2–6–0; O'Connor 8–4–8–1; Wiseman 6–2–15–1; Walker 11–1–30–0.

Umpires: B. C. Cooray (Sri Lanka) and R. S. Dunne.
Third umpire: A. L. Hill. Referee: G. R. Viswanath (India).

†NEW ZEALAND v ZIMBABWE

First One-Day International

At Taupo, January 2 (day/night). Zimbabwe won by 70 runs (D/L method). Toss: New Zealand. International debut: J. E. C. Franklin.

The New Zealanders regarded this match as an opportunity to re-enter their one-day winning mode. But they were comprehensively outplayed by Zimbabwe, in particular by the batsmanship of Andy Flower, the game's top-scorer with 80 from 88 balls. The home bowling lost its cutting edge when Cairns, returning to international duty after a two-month lay-off, managed only three overs before succumbing to his leg injury. After Flower and Carlisle had put on 154 for the third wicket, the Zimbabweans raced away, raising 300 for seven. A shower revised the New Zealand target to 281 from 43 overs; once Fleming was sixth out at 151, the Zimbabwean bowlers had the game under control.

Man of the Match: A. Flower.

Zimbabwe

A. D. R. Campbell c Sinclair b Franklin	28	*H. H. Streak not out	30
T. N. Madondo c Twose b Styris	12	T. J. Friend not out	7
S. V. Carlisle c Fleming b McMillan	75	B 2, l-b 12, w 3, n-b 2	19
†A. Flower run out	80		
G. J. Rennie run out	23	1/47 2/48 3/202 (7 wkts, 50 overs)	300
G. J. Whittall lbw b McMillan	2	4/210 5/216	
D. A. Marillier c Martin b Franklin	24	6/262 7/264	

B. C. Strang and B. A. Murphy did not bat.

Bowling: Cairns 3–0–24–0; Martin 7–0–53–0; Styris 10–0–60–1; Franklin 5–0–28–2; Harris 5–0–41–0; Astle 10–2–39–0; McMillan 10–0–41–2.

New Zealand

M. S. Sinclair c Campbell b Streak	1	S. B. Styris c Strang b Marillier	8
N. J. Astle lbw b Streak	10	J. E. C. Franklin not out	25
*S. P. Fleming c Madondo b Murphy	64	C. S. Martin c Whittall b Marillier	3
R. G. Twose c Strang b Friend	27	L-b 3, w 4, n-b 1	8
C. L. Cairns b Whittall	5		
C. D. McMillan c Marillier b Whittall	18	1/2 2/24 3/72 (40 overs)	210
C. Z. Harris c Carlisle b Murphy	37	4/88 5/118 6/151	
†A. C. Parore c Murphy b Marillier	4	7/164 8/180 9/182	

Bowling: Streak 6–1–26–2; Strang 6–0–37–0; Friend 8–0–62–1; Whittall 7–0–27–2; Murphy 9–0–32–2; Marillier 4–0–23–3.

Umpires: D. M. Quested and E. A. Watkin.
Third umpire: A. L. Hill.

†NEW ZEALAND v ZIMBABWE

Second One-Day International

At WestpacTrust Stadium, Wellington, January 4 (day/night). New Zealand won by eight wickets. Toss: Zimbabwe. International debuts: J. D. P. Oram; A. J. Mackay.

Zimbabwe were given a brilliant start by Campbell, who made light of a sluggish pitch and outfield at Wellington's modern stadium. Unfortunately, he could not find a steady partner as Zimbabwe lost four middle-order wickets for 24. Campbell finally fell for 111, including nine fours and a six in 133 balls. Needing 237, New Zealand showed rare enterprise when Sinclair and Astle opened with 153 in 35 overs. When Sinclair was run out for 85, having struck nine fours and a six, pinch-hitter Styris weighed in with a 33-ball 48. Astle remained to the end, hitting the boundary that completed New Zealand's first one-day win since their ICC Knockout triumph in October. It was his seventh four, in addition to two sixes.

Man of the Match: M. S. Sinclair.

Zimbabwe

A. D. R. Campbell c Fleming b Styris	111	*H. H. Streak c Walker b Franklin	17
T. N. Madondo c Twose b Franklin	9		
S. V. Carlisle b Harris	32	L-b 4, w 1	5
†A. Flower c and b Astle	15		
D. A. Marillier lbw b McMillan	1	1/27 2/118 3/139 (7 wkts, 50 overs)	236
G. J. Whittall c Astle b McMillan	0	4/142 5/142	
G. J. Rennie not out	46	6/194 7/236	

A. J. Mackay, B. C. Strang and B. A. Murphy did not bat.

Bowling: Franklin 10–0–46–2; Styris 10–0–45–1; Oram 4–0–17–0; Harris 8–0–45–1; Walker 2–0–14–0; Astle 8–0–35–1; McMillan 8–1–30–2.

New Zealand

M. S. Sinclair run out	85
N. J. Astle not out	89
S. B. Styris b Murphy	48
*S. P. Fleming not out	8
B 1, l-b 4, w 1, n-b 1	7
1/153 2/209 (2 wkts, 45.2 overs)	237

R. G. Twose, C. D. McMillan, C. Z. Harris, †A. C. Parore, J. D. P. Oram, B. G. K. Walker and J. E. C. Franklin did not bat.

Bowling: Streak 8–0–34–0; Strang 9–1–48–0; Mackay 8–0–56–0; Whittall 10–0–52–0; Murphy 10–0–38–1; Marillier 0.2–0–4–0.

Umpires: R. S. Dunne and A. L. Hill.
Third umpire: D. M. Quested.

†NEW ZEALAND v ZIMBABWE

Third One-Day International

At Auckland, January 7. Zimbabwe won by one wicket. Toss: Zimbabwe.

Streak led a brilliant comeback, dramatically claiming both match and series by hitting McMillan for six over extra cover. It was Zimbabwe's first one-day series win overseas against another Test nation. Though Streak had sent New Zealand in and removed Sinclair early, most of the home batsmen scored solidly on a flat pitch. A blistering 75 from McMillan – 53 balls, including seven fours and three sixes – lifted them to an imposing 273, with 90 coming in the last ten overs. That looked impregnable when Zimbabwe were 64 for five in the 16th over. But Flower and Viljoen built a steady stand of 82, and then Streak played his amazing innings of 79 in 67 balls. Victory still seemed out of the question when McMillan struck twice in the 47th over, leaving Zimbabwe 19 short with one wicket left. But Streak's fifth six snatched the series from the stunned New Zealanders with eight balls to spare.

Man of the Match: H. H. Streak.

New Zealand

M. S. Sinclair c Murphy b Streak	7
N. J. Astle b Murphy	48
*S. P. Fleming c and b Murphy	44
R. G. Twose c Flower b Whittall	30
J. D. P. Oram c Streak b Murphy	21
C. D. McMillan not out	75
C. Z. Harris run out	8
†A. C. Parore run out	7
S. B. Styris c Madondo b Strang	9
J. E. C. Franklin b Streak	1
P. J. Wiseman not out	7
L-b 7, w 8, n-b 1	16
1/30 2/88 3/135 4/163 5/166 6/179 7/202 8/260 9/266 (9 wkts, 50 overs)	273

Bowling: Streak 8–1–34–2; Friend 6–0–31–0; Strang 6–0–50–1; Murphy 10–0–43–3; Viljoen 10–0–57–0; Whittall 10–0–51–1.

Zimbabwe

A. D. R. Campbell b Styris	2
T. N. Madondo run out	0
S. V. Carlisle b Franklin	13
†A. Flower c Franklin b Astle	81
G. J. Rennie c Fleming b Styris	0
G. J. Whittall b Styris	14
D. P. Viljoen st Parore b Harris	39
*H. H. Streak not out	79
T. J. Friend c Parore b McMillan	19
B. C. Strang b McMillan	0
B. A. Murphy not out	0
B 2, l-b 10, w 14, n-b 1	27
1/0 2/14 3/49 4/50 5/64 6/146 7/180 8/249 9/255 (9 wkts, 48.4 overs)	274

Bowling: Franklin 9–1–52–1; Styris 9–1–36–3; Oram 5–0–21–0; McMillan 6.4–0–49–2; Astle 10–0–47–1; Wiseman 2–0–21–0; Harris 7–0–36–1.

Umpires: B. F. Bowden and D. B. Cowie.
Third umpire: A. L. Hill. Series referee: G. R. Viswanath (India).

†At Brisbane, January 12. Australia A won by 216 runs. Toss: Zimbabweans. Australia A 321 for four (50 overs) (G. S. Blewett 131, S. M. Katich 80, M. J. Slater 52); Zimbabweans 105 (30 overs) (A. D. R. Campbell 31; A. C. Dale four for 31, S. C. G. MacGill three for seven).

Blewett scored his 131 off 122 balls, with nine fours and six sixes.

Zimbabwe's matches v West Indies and Australia in the Carlton Series (January 13–February 4) may be found in that section.

†At Bowral, January 19. Australian Country XII won by 51 runs. Toss: Zimbabweans. Australian Country XII 197 (49.1 overs) (C. Brown 54, A. D. McQuire 42, D. A. Todd 53; D. P. Viljoen four for 15, A. J. Mackay three for 39); Zimbabweans 146 (39.1 overs) (G. J. Whittall 37; A. J. Starr five for 37).

Each team contained 12 players, of whom 11 could bat and 11 field.

ICC REFEREES' PANEL

On July 10, 1991, the International Cricket Council agreed to form a panel of referees to enforce the new Code of Conduct for Tests and one-day internationals, to impose penalties for slow over-rates, breaches of the Code and other ICC regulations, and to support the umpires in upholding the conduct of the game. ICC referees began to supervise Tests and one-day internationals under a pilot scheme in the 1991-92 season.

In April 2002, however, when the system of international umpires was due to be reformed, the ICC were to appoint two panels of referees: an elite group of five full-time officials, supported by a part-time panel.

The new panels had not been announced when *Wisden* went to press, but the following referees were on the panel from September 2001 to March 2002: D. B. Arnott (Zimbabwe), M. H. Denness (England), R. L. Dias (Sri Lanka), G. T. Dowling (New Zealand), A. Ebrahim (Zimbabwe), Hanumant Singh (India), B. F. Hastings (New Zealand), J. L. Hendriks (West Indies), B. N. Jarman (Australia), D. T. Lindsay (South Africa), R. S. Madugalle (Sri Lanka), C. J. Mitchley (South Africa), Naushad Ali (Pakistan), J. R. Reid (New Zealand), A. C. Smith (England), C. W. Smith (West Indies), R. Subba Row (England), Talat Ali (Pakistan), G. R. Viswanath (India). Compared with the 2000-01 list, C. J. Mitchley had replaced M. R. Wilson of South Africa; R. L. Dias had replaced B. Warnapura of Sri Lanka; D. B. Arnott had replaced H. Gardiner of Zimbabwe; P. J. Burge of Australia had died.

THE SRI LANKANS IN NEW ZEALAND, 2000-01

By DON CAMERON

Both sides had points to prove when they began a series of five one-day internationals in New Zealand at the end of January. Since a rare one-day peak, when they won the ICC Knockout Trophy in October, the New Zealanders had been mauled 5–0 in South Africa and, worse still, pipped 1–2 on home soil by Zimbabwe. Sri Lanka had also just finished a tour of South Africa, in which they were outplayed in the Test and one-day series.

It was Sri Lanka who enjoyed the turnaround. Sanath Jayasuriya struck what was probably the decisive blow of the series when he won the toss and batted first at Napier, on a pitch he correctly judged would help the slow bowlers later. His star off-spinner, Muttiah Muralitharan, swept through the closing stages, taking five for 30. The New Zealand players seemed shattered, and some shrill radio commentators, who should have known better, revived the notion that Muralitharan's action was suspect. Safe in the knowledge that it had been exhaustively checked and cleared by the International Cricket Council, Jayasuriya probably sensed New Zealand were at his mercy. He himself secured a winning 3–0 lead with a neutron bomb of a century at Auckland.

To their credit, the New Zealanders fought back, and might have won the fourth match at Hamilton, where their own captain, Stephen Fleming, rediscovered his form. But bad light and Duckworth/Lewis worked in Sri Lanka's favour just as their challenge was faltering. The home side finally pulled one back in the last match, where they scored 282 on a typical batsman's pitch at Christchurch.

The Sri Lankans were gracious winners, and their victories at Napier and Auckland suggested their one-day form was regaining its old edge. Jayasuriya still looked a master, and while he was the only player on either side to reach 200 runs, both Russel Arnold and Marvan Atapattu averaged over 56 each. Kumar Sangakkara showed great promise as a wicket-keeper/batsman. The return of Muralitharan and the tall pace bowler, Nuwan Zoysa, to fitness paid dividends – ten and eight cheap wickets respectively. They were among four Sri Lankan bowlers who conceded four runs or less per over during the series; for New Zealand, only the experienced Chris Harris, with 4.01, and Daniel Vettori, 4.27, came close. The statistics highlighted the home team's major problem – the inability of their bowlers to develop a tight, economical attack.

SRI LANKAN TOURING PARTY

S. T. Jayasuriya (Bloomfield) (*captain*), R. P. Arnold (Nondescripts), M. S. Atapattu (Sinhalese), P. A. de Silva (Nondescripts), H. D. P. K. Dharmasena (Bloomfield), C. R. D. Fernando (Sinhalese), I. S. Gallage (Colombo), D. A. Gunawardene (Sinhalese), D. P. M. D. Jayawardene (Sinhalese), R. S. Kaluwitharana (Colts), M. Muralitharan (Tamil Union), P. D. R. L. Perera (Sinhalese), K. Sangakkara (Nondescripts), K. E. A. Upashantha (Colts), W. P. U. J. C. Vaas (Colts), K. Weeraratne (Colts), D. N. T. Zoysa (Sinhalese).

Manager: Air Commodore A. Jayasekara. *Coach:* D. F. Whatmore.

SRI LANKAN TOUR RESULTS

One-day internationals: Played 5: Won 4, Lost 1.
Other non first-class match: Lost v North Island Selection XI.

Note: Matches in this section were not first-class.

At New Plymouth, January 28. North Island Selection XI won by 28 runs. Toss: North Island Selection XI. North Island Selection XI 276 for eight (50 overs) (D. J. Nash 45, A. R. Adams 90 not out; P. D. R. L. Perera three for 64); Sri Lankans 248 (46.4 overs) (R. S. Kaluwitharana 42, K. Sangakkara 65, K. E. A. Upashantha 52; D. R. Tuffey three for 48).

NEW ZEALAND v SRI LANKA

First One-Day International

At Napier, January 31 (day/night). Sri Lanka won by 61 runs. Toss: Sri Lanka.

New Zealand welcomed back slow left-armer Vettori, but it was Muralitharan's off-spin which settled the result. Risking first use of a pitch of unknown quality, Sri Lanka were helped to a quick start when Penn, perhaps suffering stage-fright, sprayed four wides in his second over, which cost 19. But the scoring-rate slowed in mid-innings against Harris and Vettori, with the latter conceding a mere 21 and removing three top-order wickets. Only a 65-ball fifty from Arnold lifted Sri Lanka to 213. Upashantha then claimed New Zealand's first four wickets by the 14th over. Harris played a stoic hand, unbeaten for two hours, but Muralitharan completely mystified the lower order. He took five of the remaining six wickets – the other was a run-out – to wrap up the innings.

Man of the Match: M. Muralitharan.

Sri Lanka

*S. T. Jayasuriya c Parore b Martin	4
M. S. Atapattu c Parore b Vettori	29
†K. Sangakkara c Astle b Franklin	12
D. P. M. D. Jayawardene lbw b Vettori	32
P. A. de Silva lbw b Vettori	17
R. P. Arnold run out	50
H. D. P. K. Dharmasena c Harris b Astle	32
K. E. A. Upashantha c Parore b Martin	1
D. N. T. Zoysa not out	11
M. Muralitharan not out	1
B 1, l-b 5, w 16, n-b 2	24
1/9 2/43 3/90 4/95 5/116 6/177 7/180 8/212 (8 wkts, 50 overs)	213

C. R. D. Fernando did not bat.

Bowling: Martin 10–1–56–2; Penn 4–1–29–0; Franklin 10–0–39–1; Harris 10–0–33–0; Vettori 10–0–21–3; Astle 5–0–22–1; McMillan 1–0–7–0.

New Zealand

M. S. Sinclair c Muralitharan b Upashantha	25
N. J. Astle c Sangakkara b Upashantha	1
*S. P. Fleming lbw b Upashantha	0
R. G. Twose lbw b Muralitharan	23
C. D. McMillan c Jayasuriya b Upashantha	0
C. Z. Harris not out	39
†A. C. Parore c Fernando b Muralitharan	2
D. L. Vettori lbw b Muralitharan	11
J. E. C. Franklin run out	13
A. J. Penn b Muralitharan	15
C. S. Martin b Muralitharan	0
B 2, l-b 7, w 12, n-b 2	23
1/16 2/16 3/35 4/40 5/66 6/72 7/93 8/122 9/147 (42.5 overs)	152

Bowling: Zoysa 7–0–14–0; Upashantha 8–2–37–4; Dharmasena 8–1–19–0; Fernando 8–0–36–0; Muralitharan 7.5–0–30–5; de Silva 4–0–7–0.

Umpires: B. F. Bowden and A. L. Hill.
Third umpire: D. B. Cowie.

NEW ZEALAND v SRI LANKA

Second One-Day International

At WestpacTrust Stadium, Wellington, February 3 (day/night). Sri Lanka won by three wickets. Toss: New Zealand.

Assuming the pitch would become slower and the bounce lower, New Zealand batted first, but again lost early wickets. They were 48 for three in the 15th over, and then lost the in-form Twose when he damaged his hand, colliding with McMillan. The middle order reorganised around Harris until Zoysa and Fernando claimed four wickets in the last three overs. Chasing 206 from 49 overs (one was deducted for a slow over-rate), Sri Lanka were a modest 82 for four by the 24th. However, crafty batting by de Silva, determined work by Arnold and Zoysa's boundary saw them home with three balls to spare. Arnold made 78 not out in 90 balls, the slow pitch restricting him to four fours and a six.

Man of the Match: R. P. Arnold.

New Zealand

M. S. Sinclair c Sangakkara b Dharmasena	20
N. J. Astle c de Silva b Zoysa	17
*S. P. Fleming c Sangakkara b Zoysa	0
R. G. Twose retired hurt	11
C. D. McMillan c and b Jayasuriya	37
C. Z. Harris b Zoysa	56
†A. C. Parore c Atapattu b Fernando	34
J. D. P. Oram b Fernando	2
D. L. Vettori not out	6
J. E. C. Franklin b Zoysa	1
L-b 3, w 9, n-b 9	21
1/34 2/41 3/48 4/125 5/184 6/193 7/195 8/205 (8 wkts, 50 overs)	205

C. S. Martin did not bat.

Twose retired hurt at 62.

Bowling: Zoysa 9–2–28–4; Upashantha 5–0–30–0; Muralitharan 10–1–40–0; Dharmasena 8–0–25–1; Fernando 6–0–33–2; de Silva 3–0–14–0; Jayasuriya 9–0–32–1.

Sri Lanka

*S. T. Jayasuriya c Parore b Oram	38
M. S. Atapattu c Parore b Martin	5
†K. Sangakkara c Astle b Oram	13
D. P. M. D. Jayawardene run out	7
P. A. de Silva lbw b Vettori	37
R. P. Arnold not out	78
H. D. P. K. Dharmasena run out	4
K. E. A. Upashantha run out	4
D. N. T. Zoysa not out	9
L-b 10, w 1, n-b 3	14
1/23 2/56 3/63 4/82 5/145 6/164 7/191 (7 wkts, 48.3 overs)	209

M. Muralitharan and C. R. D. Fernando did not bat.

Bowling: Martin 7–0–35–1; Franklin 8–1–36–0; Oram 5–0–20–2; Vettori 10–1–30–1; Harris 10–0–38–0; Astle 2–0–10–0; McMillan 6.3–0–30–0.

Umpires: R. S. Dunne and D. M. Quested.
Third umpire: A. L. Hill.

NEW ZEALAND v SRI LANKA

Third One-Day International

At Auckland, February 6. Sri Lanka won by nine wickets. Toss: Sri Lanka. International debut: L. Vincent.

Sri Lanka clinched the series with their third straight win, thanks to the control of their bowlers and a magical century from Jayasuriya. Rain reduced the match to 47 overs a side, and New Zealand staggered to 22 for two in the 11th over. McMillan provided some body, with 61, but the Sri Lankan bowlers' all-round strength kept the creaky home batting to a modest 181. Any thoughts that the New Zealanders might stage a counter-attack on the slightly erratic pitch disappeared as Jayasuriya captivated the 22,000 crowd with 108 minutes of magnificent, classical batting. He simply slaughtered the bowling, hitting ten fours and six sixes in 83 balls. Atapattu collected crumbs at the other end to finish with 59, from the same number of balls as Jayasuriya, and see Sri Lanka home with 17 overs in hand.

Man of the Match: S. T. Jayasuriya.

New Zealand

M. S. Sinclair b Zoysa	5
N. J. Astle c Sangakkara b Muralitharan	33
*S. P. Fleming c Muralitharan b Vaas	9
C. D. McMillan b Dharmasena	61
L. Vincent c Jayasuriya b Dharmasena	17
J. D. P. Oram c and b Muralitharan	11
C. Z. Harris run out	8
†A. C. Parore c Sangakkara b Vaas	2
D. L. Vettori not out	17
J. E. C. Franklin b Dharmasena	4
C. S. Martin b Fernando	1
L-b 4, w 4, n-b 5	13
1/7 2/22 3/74 4/106 5/127 6/151 7/154 8/159 9/165 (45.4 overs)	181

Bowling: Vaas 8–2–32–2; Zoysa 7–1–13–1; Fernando 5.4–0–33–1; Muralitharan 10–2–41–2; Jayasuriya 5–0–25–0; Dharmasena 10–1–33–3.

Sri Lanka

*S. T. Jayasuriya c Oram b Harris	103
M. S. Atapattu not out	59
†K. Sangakkara not out	13
W 7	7
1/158 (1 wkt, 29.5 overs)	182

D. P. M. D. Jayawardene, P. A. de Silva, R. P. Arnold, H. D. P. K. Dharmasena, W. P. U. J. C. Vaas, D. N. T. Zoysa, M. Muralitharan and C. R. D. Fernando did not bat.

Bowling: Martin 6–0–26–0; Franklin 4–0–38–0; Oram 3–0–16–0; Vettori 7–0–44–0; McMillan 4–1–25–0; Harris 5.5–0–33–1.

Umpires: D. B. Cowie and E. A. Watkin.
Third umpire: B. F. Bowden.

NEW ZEALAND v SRI LANKA

Fourth One-Day International

At Hamilton, February 8. Sri Lanka won by three runs (D/L method). Toss: Sri Lanka.

The New Zealanders stiffened their resistance, but the weather turned against them. Rain had already cut the match to 35 overs, and when bad light ended play just after 8 p.m., with four overs remaining, Sri Lanka were 28 short, tight fielding having almost throttled their scoring-rate. On Duckworth/Lewis rules, however, they were still three ahead of par and so emerged the winners. Fleming had led his team's revival. After nine runs in three innings, he hit himself out of trouble, with five fours and a six in a 75-ball 67. Three sixes from Oram helped New Zealand to a competitive 182. A breezy start from Jayasuriya and Kaluwitharana raised 96 before Astle removed them both in the 14th over, and the New Zealanders' keen outcricket was pinning the Sri Lankans down as the light failed.

Man of the Match: S. T. Jayasuriya.

New Zealand

†A. C. Parore c Kaluwitharana b Zoysa	0	D. L. Vettori c sub (M. S. Atapattu) b Zoysa	13
N. J. Astle c Dharmasena b Gallage	7	D. R. Tuffey not out	0
*S. P. Fleming c Zoysa b de Silva	67	C. S. Martin not out	1
R. G. Twose st Kaluwitharana b Muralitharan	20	L-b 8, w 6, n-b 4	18
C. D. McMillan st Kaluwitharana b Muralitharan	19		
L. Vincent lbw b de Silva	0	1/6 2/42 3/85 (9 wkts, 35 overs)	182
C. Z. Harris lbw b Zoysa	13	4/127 5/128	
J. D. P. Oram c Muralitharan b Dharmasena	24	6/133 7/166 8/181 9/181	

Bowling: Zoysa 5–2–27–3; Gallage 7–0–37–1; Dharmasena 7–0–21–1; Muralitharan 7–0–23–2; Fernando 4–0–28–0; de Silva 4–0–35–2; Jayasuriya 1–0–3–0.

Sri Lanka

*S. T. Jayasuriya c Martin b Astle	52	H. D. P. K. Dharmasena not out	5
†R. S. Kaluwitharana lbw b Astle	34		
K. Sangakkara c Parore b Martin	20	L-b 7, w 8, n-b 2	17
D. P. M. D. Jayawardene not out	17		
P. A. de Silva c Oram b Tuffey	10	1/96 2/97 3/128 (5 wkts, 31 overs)	155
R. P. Arnold c Parore b Tuffey	0	4/144 5/144	

D. N. T. Zoysa, M. Muralitharan, C. R. D. Fernando and I. S. Gallage did not bat.

Bowling: Martin 7–1–33–1; Tuffey 7–0–36–2; Oram 2–0–19–0; Astle 5–0–22–2; Vettori 7–1–30–0; McMillan 2–0–6–0; Harris 1–0–2–0.

Umpires: R. S. Dunne and E. A. Watkin.
Third umpire: D. M. Quested.

NEW ZEALAND v SRI LANKA

Fifth One-Day International

At Christchurch, February 11. New Zealand won by 13 runs. Toss: Sri Lanka.

New Zealand regained some ground at Christchurch, their favourite venue in recent years, showing unusual authority from the start. This time, the experiment of opening with Parore worked: he stiffened the innings with 49, anchoring blitzes from Fleming and Oram, who hit four sixes and three fours in 57 balls. Harris and Vincent added the trimmings in an unbroken seventh-wicket stand of 85 in 10.3 overs. Sri Lanka needed a strong start, but lost three wickets by the seventh over. Atapattu and Jayawardene hit back, with 99 in 17 overs, and Arnold produced another half-century. But Sri Lanka were always competing against the clock. They needed 24 from 16 balls when McMillan removed Arnold, and he claimed two more as they ran out of batsmen.

Man of the Match: J. D. P. Oram.

New Zealand

†A. C. Parore b Gallage	49	C. Z. Harris not out	52
C. M. Spearman c Jayasuriya b Gallage	5	L. Vincent not out	31
*S. P. Fleming c Sangakkara b Fernando	40	B 1, l-b 11, w 5, n-b 5	22
R. G. Twose c Sangakkara b Fernando	1		
J. D. P. Oram c Atapattu b Muralitharan	59	1/18 2/85 3/87 (6 wkts, 50 overs)	282
C. D. McMillan run out	23	4/144 5/191 6/197	

D. L. Vettori, D. R. Tuffey and J. E. C. Franklin did not bat.

Bowling: Zoysa 9–0–46–0; Gallage 9–0–42–2; Dharmasena 9–0–58–0; Fernando 10–0–65–2; Muralitharan 10–0–44–1; Jayasuriya 3–0–15–0.

Sri Lanka

*S. T. Jayasuriya c Vincent b Franklin	3	C. R. D. Fernando b McMillan	0
M. S. Atapattu run out	76	M. Muralitharan b McMillan	4
P. A. de Silva c Fleming b Franklin	5	I. S. Gallage not out	3
†K. Sangakkara lbw b Tuffey	1		
D. P. M. D. Jayawardene b Harris	46	L-b 6, w 4, n-b 8	18
R. P. Arnold c Twose b McMillan	51		
H. D. P. K. Dharmasena c Harris b Franklin	30	1/9 2/19 3/21 4/120 5/150 6/209 7/259 8/260 9/263	(49.2 overs) 269
D. N. T. Zoysa c Vettori b Tuffey	32		

Bowling: Tuffey 10–1–51–2; Franklin 9–0–44–3; Oram 3–0–23–0; Vettori 9–0–59–0; Harris 10–0–42–1; McMillan 8.2–0–44–3.

Umpires: D. B. Cowie and D. M. Quested.
Third umpire: R. S. Dunne. Series referee: P. J. Burge (Australia).

PWC ONE-DAY INTERNATIONAL RATINGS

The PricewaterhouseCoopers (PwC) One-Day International Ratings, introduced in August 1998, follow similar principles to the Test Ratings (see page 1224).

The leading 20 batsmen and bowlers in the One-Day International Ratings after the series between Kenya and West Indies in Nairobi which ended on August 19 were:

	Batsmen	*Rating*		*Bowlers*	*Rating*
1	S. R. Tendulkar (*India*)	808	1	S. M. Pollock (*South Africa*)	910
2	M. G. Bevan (*Australia*)	804	2	M. Muralitharan (*Sri Lanka*)	902
3	R. T. Ponting (*Australia*)	776	3	G. D. McGrath (*Australia*)	896
4	S. T. Jayasuriya (*Sri Lanka*)	771	4	S. K. Warne (*Australia*)	736
5	J. H. Kallis (*South Africa*)	768	5	A. D. Mullally (*England*)	734
6	A. C. Gilchrist (*Australia*)	753	6	D. Gough (*England*)	728
7	Saeed Anwar (*Pakistan*)	750	7	W. P. U. J. C. Vaas (*Sri Lanka*)	717
8	Inzamam-ul-Haq (*Pakistan*)	734	8	A. R. Caddick (*England*)	699
9	M. E. Waugh (*Australia*)	731	9	D. W. Fleming (*Australia*)	697
10	N. J. Astle (*New Zealand*)	714	10	Abdur Razzaq (*Pakistan*)	686
11	S. C. Ganguly (*India*)	712	11	Saqlain Mushtaq (*Pakistan*)	685
12	B. C. Lara (*West Indies*)	709	12	C. Z. Harris (*New Zealand*)	679
13	S. R. Waugh (*Australia*)	699	13	B. Lee (*Australia*)	676
14	G. Kirsten (*South Africa*)	685	14	Waqar Younis (*Pakistan*)	675
15	R. P. Arnold (*Sri Lanka*)	662	15	R. D. King (*West Indies*)	672
16	M. S. Atapattu (*Sri Lanka*)	659	16	A. A. Donald (*South Africa*)	671
16	D. R. Martyn (*Australia*)	659	17	Wasim Akram (*Pakistan*)	670
18	L. Klusener (*South Africa*)	657	18	J. H. Kallis (*South Africa*)	669
19	R. Dravid (*India*)	645	19	I. J. Harvey (*Australia*)	667
19	Yousuf Youhana (*Pakistan*)	645	19	H. H. Streak (*Zimbabwe*)	667

THE PAKISTANIS IN NEW ZEALAND, 2000-01

By KIP BROOK

No cricket tour to New Zealand in recent years had attracted as much controversy as that of Moin Khan's Pakistanis. From the start it was overshadowed by allegations that Shoaib Akhtar, their mercurial fast bowler, was throwing; it ended with the sacking of their coach, Javed Miandad, who was then reported as saying the one-day series had been fixed. It was later announced that Miandad had in fact demanded an inquiry into the team's poor results "for purely cricketing reasons".

Pakistan's performances oscillated wildly from game to game; they possessed many fine players but, as a team, showed a predilection for the unexpected. New Zealand came from behind to take the one-day series 3–2. They were then crushed by 299 runs – their heaviest defeat by runs – in the First Test, only to square the series by recording their biggest win, by an innings and 185 runs, in the Third.

Moin missed that match through injury, which gave the Pakistan board an excuse to install Waqar Younis as captain for the ensuing one-day tournament in Sharjah; by the time Moin had recovered, he had been dropped from the tour of England. New Zealand's unflappable captain, Stephen Fleming, could be more confident about the future, although he too would be working with a new coach, the steady David Trist having already announced he would step down in June. Their often criticised side ended a trying, injury-plagued season with a record of three wins, three losses and three draws from nine Tests. An appalling run of injuries – which at various times deprived them of Chris Cairns, Dion Nash and Daniel Vettori, among others – put pressure on their remaining mainstays, Fleming, Craig McMillan and Nathan Astle, to perform.

Pakistan were also ravaged by injury, and might still have won the one-day series and the Tests had Wasim Akram and Shoaib been available for every game. Shoaib blew New Zealand's lower order away in the first one-day international in Auckland, taking five for 19 to set up a six-wicket win. He then injured his right thigh in the next match, and in the series decider reached speeds of 151kph (93mph) before limping off again. Meanwhile, his action was questioned in the official report of umpires Steve Dunne and Doug Cowie. As Shoaib returned home to attempt to prove that it was legal, Pakistan officials said that his lack of fitness would have ended his tour anyway. Wasim also left after the one-day games, with a side strain; the experienced opening batsman, Saeed Anwar, injured an ankle and missed the Tests; and all-rounders Abdur Razzaq and Azhar Mahmood also cut short their tours. Star spinner Saqlain Mushtaq was reported to be on the verge of being sent home after one awful spell in the fourth one-day international but remained on the insistence of Miandad and Moin.

Saqlain was still the tourists' most successful bowler in the Tests, with 11 wickets, combining with debutant pace bowler Mohammad Sami to trigger a collapse of eight wickets for ten runs at Auckland. But they lagged some way behind the New Zealand fast bowler, Daryl Tuffey, who took 16 including seven in a match twice. Mathew Sinclair was the series' leading scorer, with 325 at 108.33, thanks to his second Test double-hundred, while the patient Mark Richardson demonstrated that he was a Test batsman of quality, forming a highly successful partnership with Matthew Bell; they averaged 88.80 over five opening stands. Yousuf Youhana also compiled a double-century, and the gifted Younis Khan, added to the party for the Tests, rescued Pakistan from disaster time after time. Collectively, however, their team's erratic form made it too easy for a now suspicious world to ask questions.

PAKISTANI TOURING PARTY

Moin Khan (Karachi Whites) (*captain*), Inzamam-ul-Haq (Faisalabad) (*vice-captain*), Abdur Razzaq (Lahore Blues), Arshad Khan (Peshawar/Allied Bank), Azhar Mahmood (PIA), Humayun Farhat (Lahore Blues/Allied Bank), Imran Farhat (Lahore Blues), Imran Nazir (Sheikhupura/National Bank), Mohammad Sami (Karachi Whites), Mushtaq Ahmed (Lahore Blues), Saeed Anwar (Lahore Blues), Salim Elahi (Lahore Whites), Saqlain Mushtaq (PIA), Shahid Afridi (Karachi Whites/Habib Bank), Shoaib Akhtar (KRL), Waqar Younis (Lahore Blues), Wasim Akram (Lahore Blues), Younis Khan (Peshawar/Habib Bank), Yousuf Youhana (Lahore Blues).

Imran Nazir, Shahid Afridi and Shoaib Akhtar returned home after the one-day series and were replaced by Arshad Khan, Humayun Farhat and Younis Khan for the first-class programme. Faisal Iqbal (Karachi Blues/PIA), Fazl-e-Akbar (Peshawar/PIA) and Misbah-ul-Haq (Sargodha/KRL) also arrived before the Tests, when Azhar Mahmood, Saeed Anwar and Wasim Akram departed injured; Ijaz Ahmed, sen. (Habib Bank) also reinforced the party, and Mohammad Akram (Rawalpindi/Allied Bank) replaced Abdur Razzaq, who was suffering from food poisoning.

Manager: Fakir Aizazuddin. *Coach:* Javed Miandad.

PAKISTANI TOUR RESULTS

Test matches – Played 3: Won 1, Lost 1, Drawn 1.
First-class matches – Played 5: Won 1, Lost 2, Drawn 2.
Win – New Zealand.
Losses – New Zealand, New Zealand A.
Draws – New Zealand, Wellington.
One-day internationals – Played 5: Won 2, Lost 3.

TEST MATCH AVERAGES

NEW ZEALAND – BATTING

	T	*I*	*NO*	*R*	*HS*	*100s*	*50s*	*Avge*	*Ct*
M. S. Sinclair	3	5	2	325	204*	1	1	108.33	1
A. C. Parore	3	3	2	78	46	0	0	78.00	16
M. H. Richardson	3	5	1	285	106	1	2	71.25	2
S. P. Fleming	3	4	1	174	86	0	2	58.00	5
M. D. Bell	3	5	0	248	105	1	1	49.60	1
C. D. McMillan	3	4	0	172	98	0	2	43.00	2
D. R. Tuffey	3	3	0	15	13	0	0	5.00	1
N. J. Astle	3	3	0	7	6	0	0	2.33	3
C. S. Martin	3	3	0	0	0	0	0	0.00	2

Played in two Tests: G. E. Bradburn 0 (2 ct); J. E. C. Franklin 0, 0 (1 ct). Played in one Test: C. J. Drum 4 (1 ct); P. J. Wiseman 9, 8 (2 ct).

* *Signifies not out.*

BOWLING

	O	*M*	*R*	*W*	*BB*	*5W/i*	*Avge*
J. E. C. Franklin	54.5	13	150	7	4-26	0	21.42
D. R. Tuffey	129.5	36	368	16	4-39	0	23.00
C. S. Martin	100	17	424	12	4-52	0	35.33
C. D. McMillan	57	21	110	3	1-2	0	36.66

Also bowled: N. J. Astle 52–21–83–0; G. E. Bradburn 42–10–124–1; C. J. Drum 8–1–21–1; M. H. Richardson 9–0–16–1; P. J. Wiseman 43–6–142–1.

PAKISTAN – BATTING

	T	*I*	*NO*	*R*	*HS*	*100s*	*50s*	*Avge*	*Ct*
Younis Khan	3	5	1	280	149*	1	1	70.00	2
Yousuf Youhana	3	5	0	312	203	1	1	62.40	1
Inzamam-ul-Haq	2	3	0	155	130	1	0	51.66	0
Faisal Iqbal	3	5	1	162	63	0	2	40.50	1
Saqlain Mushtaq	3	5	1	119	101*	1	0	29.75	1
Imran Farhat	3	5	0	115	63	0	1	23.00	4
Ijaz Ahmed, sen.	2	3	0	33	17	0	0	11.00	0
Waqar Younis	3	4	0	20	12	0	0	5.00	2
Fazl-e-Akbar	2	3	2	0	0*	0	0	0.00	0

Played in two Tests: Mohammad Sami 0*; Moin Khan 47, 28 (3 ct). Played in one Test: Humayun Farhat 28, 26; Misbah-ul-Haq 28, 10; Mohammad Akram 1*, 4; Mushtaq Ahmed 19; Salim Elahi 24, 7.

* *Signifies not out.*

BOWLING

	O	*M*	*R*	*W*	*BB*	*5W/i*	*Avge*
Saqlain Mushtaq	148.4	37	332	11	4-24	0	30.18
Mohammad Sami	93.4	22	245	8	5-36	1	30.62
Fazl-e-Akbar	66.2	12	198	6	3-85	0	33.00
Waqar Younis	106	19	305	6	3-114	0	50.83

Also bowled: Faisal Iqbal 1–0–7–0; Mohammad Akram 22–1–106–0; Mushtaq Ahmed 31–10–83–1; Younis Khan 28–7–88–1; Yousuf Youhana 1–0–3–0.

Note: Matches in this section which were not first-class are signified by a dagger.

†NEW ZEALAND v PAKISTAN

First One-Day International

At Auckland, February 18. Pakistan won by six wickets. Toss: Pakistan. International debut: Imran Farhat.

Originally scheduled as a day/night match on Saturday, the game was delayed by rain until Sunday, when bye-laws prevented the use of floodlights. Shoaib Akhtar was a magnificent and threatening sight as he carved through the later batting, bagging five for 19 (four bowled), his best return at this level. Because of injury, it was his first international since the previous April. Put in, New Zealand had made a rocky start: Parore was bowled by the first ball. They fought back twice, reaching 142 by the 32nd over before Shoaib demolished them with five for two in 11 balls. Pakistan's own batsmen made slow progress, especially against Vettori, and were only 85 for three in the 30th over. But once Inzamam-ul-Haq and Yousuf Youhana raised the pace, a target of 150 was never enough. Waqar Younis became the seventh Pakistani to play in 200 one-day internationals.

Man of the Match: Shoaib Akhtar.

New Zealand

†A. C. Parore b Wasim Akram	0	D. L. Vettori b Shoaib Akhtar	0
N. J. Astle c Moin Khan b Waqar Younis	20	J. E. C. Franklin b Shoaib Akhtar	0
*S. P. Fleming b Saqlain Mushtaq	18	D. R. Tuffey lbw b Shoaib Akhtar	0
R. G. Twose c Shahid Afridi b Wasim Akram	0	L-b 13, w 10, n-b 1	24
C. D. McMillan run out	35		
J. D. P. Oram b Shoaib Akhtar	16	1/0 2/25 3/26 (35.3 overs)	149
L. Vincent b Shoaib Akhtar	31	4/88 5/89 6/142	
C. Z. Harris not out	5	7/147 8/147 9/149	

Bowling: Wasim Akram 6–1–20–2; Waqar Younis 6–0–24–1; Abdur Razzaq 7–1–38–0; Shoaib Akhtar 6.3–0–19–5; Saqlain Mushtaq 7–0–23–1; Shahid Afridi 3–0–12–0.

Pakistan

Saeed Anwar b Vettori	48	Shahid Afridi not out	4
Imran Farhat c McMillan b Tuffey	5	L-b 7, w 2, n-b 3	12
Abdur Razzaq c Oram b Vettori	19		
Inzamam-ul-Haq b Harris	32	1/16 2/78 (4 wkts, 45 overs)	150
Yousuf Youhana not out	30	3/85 4/143	

*†Moin Khan, Wasim Akram, Saqlain Mushtaq, Waqar Younis and Shoaib Akhtar did not bat.

Bowling: Tuffey 7–1–21–1; Franklin 10–1–36–0; Vettori 10–2–21–2; Harris 6–1–21–1; Astle 4–0–14–0; McMillan 8–0–30–0.

Umpires: B. F. Bowden and A. L. Hill.
Third umpire: D. B. Cowie.

†NEW ZEALAND v PAKISTAN

Second One-Day International

At Napier, February 20 (day/night). New Zealand won by six wickets. Toss: New Zealand.

The tables were turned from the moment that Saeed Anwar – like Parore two days earlier – was bowled by the match's first ball. Pakistan just lasted 50 overs, but 135 was their lowest completed one-day total against New Zealand, who beat it with nearly 20 overs in hand. Tuffey won the match award for a career-best four for 24, seizing the opportunity offered by Chris Cairns's injury. But just as important was Harris, whose figures of 10–2–12–1 reveal the respect with which the Pakistanis treated his tantalising slow-medium swing bowling; they equalled the fourth most economical performance for New Zealand at this level. Shahid Afridi provided him with his 159th wicket in one-day internationals, overtaking Richard Hadlee's New Zealand record (Hadlee played 115 games to Harris's 175). Once Shoaib Akhtar hobbled off after conceding 16 in 11 deliveries – including two no-balls – the Kiwis never looked back.

Man of the Match: D. R. Tuffey.

Pakistan

Saeed Anwar b Tuffey	0	Saqlain Mushtaq run out	10
Imran Farhat c and b Tuffey	4	Waqar Younis not out	22
Abdur Razzaq c Harris b Martin	50	Shoaib Akhtar b Tuffey	3
Inzamam-ul-Haq run out	6	L-b 6, w 3, n-b 3	12
Yousuf Youhana c Fleming b Vettori	9		
Shahid Afridi c Astle b Harris	10	1/0 2/14 3/21 (50 overs)	135
*†Moin Khan c Fleming b Tuffey	1	4/47 5/60 6/63	
Wasim Akram c Franklin b Vettori	8	7/79 8/96 9/121	

Bowling: Tuffey 10–0–24–4; Martin 10–1–37–1; Franklin 10–1–27–0; Vettori 10–1–29–2; Harris 10–2–12–1.

New Zealand

†A. C. Parore c Imran Farhat b Wasim Akram	0
N. J. Astle c Inzamam-ul-Haq b Wasim Akram	20
*S. P. Fleming c Yousuf Youhana b Waqar Younis	28
R. G. Twose c Moin Khan b Abdur Razzaq	5
C. D. McMillan not out	31
L. Vincent not out	33
L-b 7, w 3, n-b 9	19
1/1 2/51 3/59 4/74 (4 wkts, 30.3 overs)	136

C. Z. Harris, D. L. Vettori, J. E. C. Franklin, D. R. Tuffey and C. S. Martin did not bat.

Bowling: Wasim Akram 9–0–24–2; Waqar Younis 7–0–27–1; Shoaib Akhtar 1.3–0–16–0; Abdur Razzaq 6.3–1–27–1; Saqlain Mushtaq 5–0–23–0; Imran Farhat 1.3–0–12–0.

Umpires: B. F. Bowden and E. A. Watkin.
Third umpire: R. S. Dunne.

†NEW ZEALAND v PAKISTAN

Third One-Day International

At WestpacTrust Stadium, Wellington, February 22 (day/night). Pakistan won by 28 runs. Toss: New Zealand.

Though Shoaib Akhtar was still unfit, Pakistan staged a remarkable reversal of form against a scratchy home effort. They were anchored by a solid 57 from Saeed Anwar, while Yousuf Youhana, with a run-a-ball 47, helped boost the total by 80 runs in the last ten overs. New Zealand then staggered to 18 for three: Fleming's promotion to opener, with Parore dropping down the order after two ducks, failed to pay off. As in Napier, Vincent, showing the confidence of one who had learned much of his game in Australia, proved a useful ally for McMillan and together they added 100 in 20 overs. Once Saqlain Mushtaq separated them, through a stumping confirmed by the third umpire, the Pakistanis ripped through the rest of a shaky line-up. They were later fined 25 per cent of their match fees for a dismally slow over-rate.

Man of the Match: Saqlain Mushtaq.

Pakistan

Saeed Anwar run out	57
Imran Nazir c Fleming b Tuffey	32
Salim Elahi c and b Harris	30
Inzamam-ul-Haq c Twose b Harris	12
Yousuf Youhana c Astle b Franklin	47
Abdur Razzaq c Vincent b Franklin	8
*†Moin Khan c Astle b Tuffey	15
Wasim Akram c Vettori b Franklin	9
Azhar Mahmood b Tuffey	17
Waqar Younis not out	5
Saqlain Mushtaq not out	1
L-b 2, w 6, n-b 2	10
1/45 2/105 3/132 4/152 5/172 6/202 7/217 8/229 9/242 (9 wkts, 50 overs)	243

Bowling: Tuffey 9–0–52–3; Martin 7–1–30–0; Franklin 8–0–61–3; Vettori 10–1–43–0; Harris 10–0–31–2; Astle 6–0–24–0.

New Zealand

*S. P. Fleming lbw b Wasim Akram	1
N. J. Astle lbw b Wasim Akram	10
R. G. Twose c Moin Khan b Waqar Younis	1
C. D. McMillan c Yousuf Youhana b Abdur Razzaq	64
L. Vincent st Moin Khan b Saqlain Mushtaq	34
C. Z. Harris lbw b Abdur Razzaq	11
†A. C. Parore not out	34
D. L. Vettori b Azhar Mahmood	7
J. E. C. Franklin b Saqlain Mushtaq	8
D. R. Tuffey c Salim Elahi b Saqlain Mushtaq	3
C. S. Martin b Wasim Akram	1
B 3, l-b 25, w 6, n-b 7	41
1/12 2/16 3/18 4/118 5/152 6/152 7/161 8/187 9/207 (48.2 overs)	215

Bowling: Wasim Akram 9.2–0–41–3; Waqar Younis 10–1–43–1; Azhar Mahmood 10–0–33–1; Abdur Razzaq 10–0–44–2; Saqlain Mushtaq 9–1–26–3.

Umpires: R. S. Dunne and D. M. Quested.
Third umpire: E. A. Watkin.

†NEW ZEALAND v PAKISTAN

Fourth One-Day International

At Christchurch, February 25. New Zealand won by 138 runs. Toss: Pakistan.

The home team squared the series through their biggest one-day win over Pakistan after McMillan had hit a maiden one-day international century from 75 balls, equalling Chris Cairns's New Zealand record. With the electronic scoreboard blank throughout their innings, McMillan was not sure how many runs he had – he acknowledged the crowd once, only to find they were cheering his century partnership with Harris – and was still 97 when Saqlain Mushtaq came in to bowl the last ball. Two no-balls and two singles later, McMillan belted the real final delivery over the fence. It was his third six of the over, and fifth in all, to go with six fours. Astle and Twose had earlier shared a century stand to set up a total of 284. Pakistan's reply stalled when they lost a wicket in each of their first three overs. Inzamam-ul-Haq could not bat until No. 7, a groin injury having kept him off the field, and by then his side were 36 for five. He was one of three victims in four balls for Astle as the innings subsided barely halfway to the target.

Man of the Match: C. D. McMillan.

New Zealand

*S. P. Fleming b Waqar Younis	0
N. J. Astle c Moin Khan b Abdur Razzaq	71
R. G. Twose b Azhar Mahmood	42
J. D. P. Oram c Moin Khan b Abdur Razzaq	1
C. D. McMillan not out	104
L. Vincent lbw b Abdur Razzaq	4
C. Z. Harris not out	39
L-b 6, w 14, n-b 3	23
1/11 2/112 3/113 4/166 5/172 (5 wkts, 50 overs)	284

†A. C. Parore, D. L. Vettori, J. E. C. Franklin and D. R. Tuffey did not bat.

Bowling: Wasim Akram 10–0–62–0; Waqar Younis 10–0–59–1; Azhar Mahmood 10–0–53–1; Abdur Razzaq 10–0–41–3; Saqlain Mushtaq 10–0–63–0.

Pakistan

Saeed Anwar c Astle b Tuffey	2
Imran Nazir c Twose b Franklin	0
Azhar Mahmood c Parore b Tuffey	0
Salim Elahi c Harris b Oram	13
Yousuf Youhana run out	6
Abdur Razzaq c Tuffey b Harris	31
Inzamam-ul-Haq c Vincent b Astle	37
*†Moin Khan c Harris b Astle	50
Wasim Akram c Twose b Astle	0
Saqlain Mushtaq not out	1
Waqar Younis lbw b Tuffey	1
L-b 3, n-b 2	5
1/2 2/2 3/5 4/15 5/36 6/71 7/144 8/144 9/144 (47 overs)	146

Bowling: Tuffey 9–1–30–3; Franklin 8–1–21–1; Oram 7–1–21–1; Vettori 10–0–33–0; Harris 10–0–31–1; Astle 3–0–7–3.

Umpires: D. B. Cowie and A. L. Hill.
Third umpire: D. M. Quested.

†NEW ZEALAND v PAKISTAN

Fifth One-Day International

At Dunedin, February 28 (day/night). New Zealand won by four wickets. Toss: Pakistan.

Pakistani minds seemed to be anywhere but in the middle as they surrendered the series 3–2. Their batsmen were heading for more than 300 until the last four fell in nine balls. Astle and Fleming then plundered an opening stand of 193 in 33 overs, an all-wicket limited-overs record for New Zealand. Astle struck a belligerent ninth one-day century, hitting 21 fours in 116 balls, and Fleming finally flourished as an opener. Wayward fielding allowed them three lives, two from straightforward chances to Shoaib Akhtar, whose return to the side after injury had very mixed results. Clocked at 151kph (93mph), he limped off soon afterwards, only to come back in the closing stages, bowl off a shortened run-up and take two wickets in two balls as New Zealand's charge stumbled. Oram, however, hit him for the winning six. Shoaib flew home, citing injury, but the umpires were already reporting his controversial bowling action to the ICC.

Man of the Match: N. J. Astle.

Pakistan

Saeed Anwar c Parore b Franklin	12
Shahid Afridi c Parore b Harris	65
Abdur Razzaq c Parore b Tuffey	41
Yousuf Youhana lbw b McMillan	68
Imran Farhat c Vettori b McMillan	33
Salim Elahi c Astle b Tuffey	14
*†Moin Khan c Astle b Oram	36
Wasim Akram b McMillan	6
Azhar Mahmood c Tuffey b Oram	0
Waqar Younis run out	2
Shoaib Akhtar not out	0
L-b 2, w 1, n-b 5	8
1/43 2/91 3/157 4/225 5/226 6/259 7/281 8/282 9/285 (49.3 overs)	285

Bowling: Tuffey 9–0–71–2; Franklin 8–0–54–1; Oram 9–0–49–2; Harris 10–0–32–1; Vettori 10–0–57–0; McMillan 3.3–0–20–3.

New Zealand

*S. P. Fleming b Waqar Younis	60
N. J. Astle c Salim Elahi b Waqar Younis	119
R. G. Twose c Shahid Afridi b Wasim Akram	17
C. D. McMillan c Salim Elahi b Waqar Younis	13
L. Vincent c Shahid Afridi b Shoaib Akhtar	12
C. Z. Harris not out	14
†A. C. Parore b Shoaib Akhtar	0
J. D. P. Oram not out	16
B 1, l-b 8, w 25, n-b 5	39
1/193 2/213 3/234 4/251 5/252 6/252 (6 wkts, 48.1 overs)	290

D. L. Vettori, J. E. C. Franklin and D. R. Tuffey did not bat.

Bowling: Wasim Akram 10–0–44–1; Waqar Younis 10–1–66–3; Azhar Mahmood 10–0–63–0; Shoaib Akhtar 9.1–0–67–2; Abdur Razzaq 7–0–26–0; Shahid Afridi 2–0–15–0.

Umpires: D. B. Cowie and R. S. Dunne.
Third umpire: B. F. Bowden. Series referee: R. S. Madugalle (Sri Lanka).

At Bert Sutcliffe Oval, Lincoln, March 3, 4, 5. New Zealand A won by an innings and 54 runs. Toss: New Zealand A. Pakistanis 100 (C. J. Drum four for 42, A. J. Penn three for 25) and 124 (Imran Farhat 51; C. J. Drum four for 42, A. J. Penn four for 44); New Zealand A 278 (L. Vincent 57, J. D. P. Oram 88, Extras 32; Saqlain Mushtaq four for 45).

NEW ZEALAND v PAKISTAN

First Test Match

At Auckland, March 8, 9, 10, 11, 12. Pakistan won by 299 runs. Toss: New Zealand. Test debuts: J. E. C. Franklin; Faisal Iqbal, Imran Farhat, Misbah-ul-Haq, Mohammad Sami.

Mohammad Sami's Test career had a dream start when he captured five wickets for six runs in a seven-over spell of speed and reverse swing as New Zealand capitulated on the final morning. They began the day needing 326 more to win, but, with nine wickets in hand and Richardson unbeaten on 59, were confident they could secure the draw. The opener lasted only four more balls, however, before Saqlain Mushtaq's off-spin made the first breakthrough. Another ten overs passed without incident, then Sami entered the attack and bowled night-watchman Wiseman. Within 13 overs, and lunch still half an hour away, the game had finished. The final eight wickets had fallen for only ten runs – with the last five batsmen failing to score – recalling New Zealand's nightmare collapse of eight for five against Australia at Wellington in 1945-46. It was their heaviest defeat chasing a total, just beating 297 runs against Australia, also at Eden Park, in 1973-74. Sir Richard Hadlee, the chairman of selectors, made four changes to the squad for the Second Test.

This was Pakistan's ninth victory over New Zealand in their last 11 Tests, and a devastating show of bowling firepower, especially given that two of their big guns, Wasim Akram and Shoaib Akhtar, were unavailable. Sami, who was 20 in February, was comfortably the fastest bowler in evidence, regularly topping 140kph (87mph). "I just bowled line and length today," he explained, as he picked up the match award in his first Test.

This was also the first Test played on a drop-in pitch in New Zealand, an innovation partly prompted by the amount of rugby played at Eden Park. It was criticised for having no life – at least until New Zealand's final collapse. Fleming gambled on inserting Pakistan, who had just lost by an innings to New Zealand A. But the home attack was soon blunted, in particular by Younis Khan, who was dropped twice off McMillan's bowling and went on to score 91 in nearly three hours. He added 132 with the newly arrived Faisal Iqbal, 19-year-old nephew of coach Javed Miandad, before Tuffey dismissed both in his first three balls of a rain-affected second day. After a couple of lengthy breaks, the innings was wound up in the afternoon, whereupon New Zealand lost both openers by their second over. Fleming, supported by McMillan, fought back for six hours until he became the first of Saqlain's eight wickets in the match. Pakistan led by 94 on first innings; Younis and Faisal shared their second century stand of the match, an unbroken 147 for the sixth wicket, before Moin Khan declared at tea. Younis compiled his 149 not out in four and a quarter hours, with 14 fours and four sixes; his last three Test innings, going back to Galle in June, had brought him 356 runs for two dismissals.

New Zealand were given a target of 431 in 138 overs, and this time their opening batsmen rose to the challenge. Richardson and Bell put on 91 in 30 overs before Pakistan managed to break their partnership, and it took a run-out, by Saqlain, to achieve that. He was to claim four wickets plus a catch next morning, but it was Sami's magical spell that stole the headlines in the sensational conclusion.

Man of the Match: Mohammad Sami.

Close of play: First day, Pakistan 270-4 (Younis Khan 91*, Faisal Iqbal 42*); Second day, New Zealand 65-2 (Sinclair 28*, Fleming 32*); Third day, Pakistan 98-3 (Yousuf Youhana 17*, Saqlain Mushtaq 0*); Fourth day, New Zealand 105-1 (Richardson 59*, Wiseman 2*).

Pakistan

Imran Farhat c Parore b Martin	23	– c and b Wiseman	63
Salim Elahi c Parore b Tuffey	24	– c Wiseman b Tuffey	7
Misbah-ul-Haq c Sinclair b McMillan	28	– c Parore b Tuffey	10
Yousuf Youhana c Parore b Martin	51	– c Astle b Franklin	42
Younis Khan c McMillan b Tuffey	91	– (6) not out	149
Faisal Iqbal c Fleming b Tuffey	42	– (7) not out	52
*†Moin Khan c Parore b Tuffey	47		
Saqlain Mushtaq c Fleming b Martin	2	– (5) c Parore b Tuffey	2
Waqar Younis lbw b Martin	4		
Mushtaq Ahmed c Parore b Franklin	19		
Mohammad Sami not out	0		
B 2, l-b 7, n-b 6	15	B 4, l-b 6, n-b 1	11
1/46 (2) 2/52 (1) 3/130 (4) 4/138 (3) 5/270 (5) 6/271 (6) 7/286 (8) 8/294 (9) 9/346 (7) 10/346 (10)	346	1/21 (2) 2/59 (3) 3/97 (1) 4/110 (5) 5/189 (4)	(5 wkts dec.) 336

Bowling: *First Innings*—Tuffey 34–13–96–4; Martin 22–1–106–4; Franklin 21–6–55–1; Wiseman 7–0–35–0; McMillan 14–5–34–1; Astle 8–3–11–0. *Second Innings*—Tuffey 17–3–43–3; Martin 12–2–65–0; Franklin 18–2–59–1; Wiseman 36–6–107–1; McMillan 7–0–27–0; Astle 13–6–25–0.

New Zealand

M. H. Richardson b Mohammad Sami	1	– c Imran Farhat b Saqlain Mushtaq	59
M. D. Bell c Moin Khan b Waqar Younis	0	– run out	28
M. S. Sinclair c Imran Farhat b Mohammad Sami	34	– (4) c Yousuf Youhana b Mohammad Sami	10
*S. P. Fleming b Saqlain Mushtaq	86	– (5) lbw b Saqlain Mushtaq	5
N. J. Astle b Mushtaq Ahmed	0	– (6) b Saqlain Mushtaq	1
C. D. McMillan c Younis Khan b Waqar Younis	54	– (7) c Saqlain Mushtaq b Mohammad Sami	0
†A. C. Parore not out	32	– (8) not out	0
J. E. C. Franklin lbw b Saqlain Mushtaq	0	– (9) b Mohammad Sami	0
P. J. Wiseman lbw b Saqlain Mushtaq	9	– (3) b Mohammad Sami	8
D. R. Tuffey b Saqlain Mushtaq	2	– b Mohammad Sami	0
C. S. Martin b Mohammad Sami	0	– b Saqlain Mushtaq	0
B 8, l-b 20, n-b 6	34	B 12, l-b 7, n-b 1	20
1/1 (2) 2/1 (1) 3/82 (3) 4/83 (5) 5/194 (6) 6/217 (4) 7/217 (8) 8/237 (9) 9/251 (10) 10/252 (11)	252	1/91 (2) 2/105 (1) 3/121 (3) 4/126 (4) 5/127 (6) 6/130 (5) 7/130 (7) 8/130 (9) 9/130 (10) 10/131 (11)	131

Bowling: *First Innings*—Waqar Younis 22–8–44–2; Mohammad Sami 31.4–11–70–3; Saqlain Mushtaq 20–3–48–4; Mushtaq Ahmed 23–8–62–1. *Second Innings*—Waqar Younis 11–2–31–0; Mohammad Sami 15–4–36–5; Saqlain Mushtaq 25.4–12–24–4; Mushtaq Ahmed 8–2–21–0.

Umpires: R. B. Tiffin (Zimbabwe) and D. B. Cowie.
Third umpire: B. F. Bowden. Referee: R. S. Madugalle (Sri Lanka).

NEW ZEALAND v PAKISTAN

Second Test Match

At Christchurch, March 15, 16, 17, 18, 19. Drawn. Toss: Pakistan. Test debut: C. J. Drum.

The First Test may have had a dramatic climax, but the Second was a forgettable fizzler, fading to a dawdling draw, in a stadium that was mostly empty throughout. It was the first draw between these countries since a run-fest at Auckland in 1988-89, when 1,118 runs were scored for 18 wickets. This match, played like the First Test on a placid portable pitch that offered precious little to seam or spin bowlers, produced 1,243 runs for 19. At least it gave the New Zealand batsmen a chance to rediscover some form. They had survived the Eden Park disaster unscathed – off-spinner Bradburn and seamer Chris Drum replaced their equivalents, Wiseman and Franklin, in the bowling line-up. Bradburn was returning to Test cricket after a gap of more than eight years. Pakistan strengthened their batting by bringing in Inzamam-ul-Haq and Ijaz Ahmed. Mushtaq Ahmed's leg-spin gave way to the pace of Fazl-e-Akbar.

Put in, Richardson and Bell completed the century stand they narrowly missed the previous Sunday. Then Sinclair took centre-stage, and rekindled expectations often disappointed since his 214 on debut against West Indies 15 months earlier. He made a gritty 204 in 520 minutes and 348 balls, striking 27 fours and reaching his double-hundred with a second six just before losing his final partner seven overs after tea on the second day. Previously, only Glenn Turner had scored two double-centuries for New Zealand. Sinclair's was their highest score against Pakistan, beating Martin Crowe's 174 at Wellington in 1988-89.

Pakistan gave no indication of forcing the pace. They defended their series lead by batting New Zealand out of the game, establishing a 95-run lead after 14 hours of occupation. Inzamam, back from injury, accepted a life on ten to run up 130, while Yousuf Youhana compiled a maiden first-class double-hundred and, finally, Saqlain Mushtaq reached his first century. Youhana batted a little longer than Sinclair – 528 minutes – but had considerably more of the strike, with 429 balls, from which he hit 27 fours and three sixes. He and Saqlain put on 248 in 95 overs for the seventh wicket; Saqlain batted throughout the fourth day to progress from 20 overnight to 98 not out.

The final day meandered aimlessly like a silent brook. Saqlain took nearly 30 minutes to complete his century – he batted seven hours ten minutes in all – whereupon Pakistan finally declared. New Zealand never looked like repeating their collapse of the First Test and batted out 73 overs to reach 196 for one, with unbeaten fifties for Richardson and Sinclair. The final session, when Moin Khan had left the field with a bad knee, leaving Inzamam in charge, brought some frivolity with the introduction of occasional bowlers Youhana and Faisal Iqbal, along with the even more occasional off-spin of Waqar Younis. Both sides agreed to come off 40 minutes early.

Man of the Match: M. S. Sinclair.

Close of play: First day, New Zealand 284-5 (Sinclair 100*, McMillan 1*); Second day, Pakistan 65-2 (Faisal Iqbal 22*, Inzamam-ul-Haq 26*); Third day, Pakistan 341-6 (Yousuf Youhana 73*, Saqlain Mushtaq 20*); Fourth day, Pakistan 561-7 (Saqlain Mushtaq 98*, Waqar Younis 5*).

New Zealand

M. H. Richardson b Saqlain Mushtaq	46	– not out	73
M. D. Bell c Faisal Iqbal b Saqlain Mushtaq	75	– lbw b Younis Khan	40
M. S. Sinclair not out	204	– not out	50
*S. P. Fleming run out	32		
N. J. Astle c Moin Khan b Waqar Younis	6		
G. E. Bradburn c Imran Farhat b Fazl-e-Akbar	0		
C. D. McMillan c Younis Khan b Fazl-e-Akbar	20		
†A. C. Parore lbw b Saqlain Mushtaq	46		
D. R. Tuffey lbw b Fazl-e-Akbar	13		
C. J. Drum c Moin Khan b Waqar Younis	4		
C. S. Martin b Waqar Younis	0		
B 2, l-b 17, w 1, n-b 10	30	B 15, l-b 4, n-b 14	33
1/102 (1) 2/163 (2) 3/248 (4) 4/276 (5) 5/282 (6) 6/327 (7) 7/428 (8) 8/449 (9) 9/468 (10) 10/476 (11)	476	1/69 (2) (1 wkt dec.)	196

Bowling: *First Innings*—Waqar Younis 34–6–114–3; Mohammad Sami 36–4–107–0; Fazl-e-Akbar 32–6–87–3; Saqlain Mushtaq 48–11–134–3; Younis Khan 6–1–15–0. *Second Innings*—Waqar Younis 8–1–18–0; Mohammad Sami 11–3–32–0; Fazl-e-Akbar 7–0–26–0; Saqlain Mushtaq 24–5–44–0; Younis Khan 21–6–47–1; Yousuf Youhana 1–0–3–0; Faisal Iqbal 1–0–7–0.

Pakistan

Imran Farhat c Drum b Martin	4
Ijaz Ahmed, sen. hit wkt b Drum	11
Faisal Iqbal c Fleming b McMillan	63
Inzamam-ul-Haq c Fleming b Martin	130
Yousuf Youhana c and b Richardson	203
Younis Khan c Parore b Tuffey	0
*†Moin Khan c Martin b Bradburn	28
Saqlain Mushtaq not out	101
Waqar Younis c Parore b Tuffey	12
Fazl-e-Akbar not out	0
B 5, l-b 8, n-b 6	19
1/5 (1) 2/25 (2) 3/157 (3) 4/259 (4) 5/260 (6) 6/304 (7) 7/552 (5) 8/569 (9) (8 wkts dec.)	571

Mohammad Sami did not bat.

Bowling: Tuffey 49–13–152–2; Martin 41–9–153–2; Drum 8–1–21–1; Bradburn 42–10–124–1; McMillan 31–13–47–1; Astle 30–12–45–0; Richardson 9–0–16–1.

Umpires: D. J. Harper (Australia) and D. M. Quested.
Third umpire: A. L. Hill. Referee: R. S. Madugalle (Sri Lanka).

At Basin Reserve, Wellington, March 22, 23, 24. Drawn. Toss: Pakistanis. Pakistanis 175 (Younis Khan 73; M. D. J. Walker five for 29) and 340 for seven (Imran Farhat 34, Humayun Farhat 74, Faisal Iqbal 82, Misbah-ul-Haq 51; M. R. Jefferson four for 84); Wellington 343 for eight dec. (S. J. Blackmore 74, R. A. Jones 40, G. T. Donaldson 60, H. R. Morgan 35, C. J. Nevin 67; Fazl-e-Akbar three for 75).

NEW ZEALAND v PAKISTAN

Third Test Match

At Hamilton, March 27, 28, 29, 30. New Zealand won by an innings and 185 runs. Toss: New Zealand. Test debut: Humayun Farhat.

New Zealand achieved their largest Test victory to level the series, while the unpredictable Pakistanis went down to their heaviest defeat. On the fourth day, McMillan inspired his team-mates by thumping a single over for 26 runs, a Test record, after which the young Kiwi pace attack cleaned Pakistan out. With the second day, and half the third, washed out, the entire match lasted less than 190 overs, barely two days' play.

This was New Zealand's tenth win by an innings, and their 47th in all, in their 288 Tests. Their previous best was by an innings and 132 runs against England at Christchurch in 1983-84, whereas Pakistan's worst had come when West Indies beat them by an innings and 174 at Kingston in 1957-58. It was Fleming's 13th win in 36 Tests in charge, ending a run of six Tests without victory, but a disastrous start for novice captain Inzamam-ul-Haq, deputising for the injured Moin Khan. Wicket-keeper Humayun Farhat made his debut, while Mohammad Akram was a late replacement when Mohammad Sami was declared unfit. Franklin returned for New Zealand in place of the injured Drum.

For the first time in the series, the teams played on a traditional, well-grassed pitch, and Fleming made the most of winning the toss in overcast conditions. Even so, Pakistan batted recklessly. Their openers hit 28 in the first five overs; the next six saw half the side go for ten runs, and then Younis Khan and Humayun added 51 in nine. Younis did at least see Pakistan past their previous lowest total against New Zealand, 102 at Faisalabad in 1990-91, before he was last out in the second over after lunch. Tuffey and Martin claimed four wickets apiece.

MOST RUNS BY A BATSMAN IN A TEST OVER

26 (444464)	**C. D. McMillan (NZ) off Younis Khan (P) at Wellington**	**2000-01**
24 (462660*)	A. M. E. Roberts (WI) off I. T. Botham (E) at Port-of-Spain	1980-81
24 (444*0444)	S. M. Patil (I) off R. G. D. Willis (E) at Manchester	1982
24 (464604)	I. T. Botham (E) off D. A. Stirling (NZ) at The Oval	1986
24 (244266)	I. D. S. Smith (NZ) off A. S. Wassan (I) at Auckland	1989-90
24 (006666)	Kapil Dev (I) off E. E. Hemmings (E) at Lord's	1990

* *Roberts ran a leg-bye off Botham's final ball. Patil's third four off Willis came from a no-ball.*

Richardson and Bell, their opening partnership going from strength to strength, overtook the Pakistani total in 30 overs. By the time bad light brought an early close to the opening day, they had passed the previous New Zealand first-wicket record against Pakistan, 159 by Rodney Redmond and Glenn Turner at Auckland in 1972-73. When the weather finally relented and play resumed on the third afternoon, they took their stand to 181, and both recorded maiden Test hundreds: Richardson took seven hours to Bell's four and a half.

Richardson fell to the third delivery of the fourth day, clearing the way for McMillan's scorching 98 off 97 balls. He hit Younis Khan's single over for 444464 – three of the fours from reverse sweeps and the six a hefty off-drive out of the ground. McMillan went on to a record seventh consecutive boundary when he hit his next ball, from Saqlain Mushtaq, for another six, his third. Having taken 80 deliveries for his fifty, he advanced to 98 off another 16 before, trying to reach three figures, he was caught at deep third man. Fleming, who had helped him add 147, a New Zealand fourth-wicket record against Pakistan, promptly declared with a first-innings lead of 303.

Tuffey, Martin and Franklin, who returned a Test-best four for 26, now tore through the tourists' second innings inside 50 overs. A total of 118 would have been Pakistan's worst in New Zealand, had they not already lowered that landmark to 104 three days earlier. Despite McMillan's pyrotechnics, Tuffey took the match award for overall figures of seven for 77. To add to their discomfiture, the Pakistanis were later fined 75 per cent of their match fees for their slow over-rate.

Man of the Match: D. R. Tuffey.

Close of play: First day, New Zealand 160-0 (Richardson 64*, Bell 89*); Second day, No play; Third day, New Zealand 260-2 (Richardson 106*, McMillan 7*).

Pakistan

Imran Farhat c Astle b Martin	24	– c McMillan b Tuffey	1
Ijaz Ahmed, sen. c Parore b Martin	5	– c Parore b Franklin	17
Faisal Iqbal c Bell b Martin	0	– c Bradburn b Tuffey	5
*Inzamam-ul-Haq lbw b Martin	5	– c Tuffey b Franklin	20
Yousuf Youhana c Parore b Tuffey	0	– c Parore b Martin	16
Younis Khan c Richardson b Tuffey	36	– c Astle b Tuffey	4
†Humayun Farhat c Parore b Tuffey	28	– c Bradburn b Martin	26
Saqlain Mushtaq run out	0	– c Martin b Franklin	14
Waqar Younis c Fleming b Franklin	0	– c Parore b McMillan	4
Fazl-e-Akbar c Parore b Tuffey	0	– not out	0
Mohammad Akram not out	1	– c and b Franklin	4
L-b 3, n-b 2	5	L-b 2, n-b 5	7
1/28 (2) 2/28 (3) 3/29 (1) 4/34 (4) 5/38 (5) 6/89 (7) 7/89 (8) 8/91 (9) 9/103 (10) 10/104 (6)	104	1/10 (1) 2/20 (3) 3/43 (2) 4/54 (4) 5/69 (5) 6/71 (6) 7/97 (7) 8/114 (9) 9/114 (8) 10/118 (11)	118

Bowling: *First Innings*—Tuffey 10.5–2–39–4; Martin 10–3–52–4; Franklin 6–2–10–1. *Second Innings*—Tuffey 19–5–38–3; Martin 15–2–48–2; Franklin 9.5–3–26–4; McMillan 5–3–2–1; Astle 1–0–2–0.

New Zealand

M. H. Richardson c Imran Farhat b Fazl-e-Akbar	106
M. D. Bell lbw b Waqar Younis	105
M. S. Sinclair c Waqar Younis b Fazl-e-Akbar	27
C. D. McMillan c Waqar Younis b Fazl-e-Akbar	98
*S. P. Fleming not out	51
L-b 10, n-b 10	20
1/181 (2) 2/239 (3) 3/260 (1) 4/407 (4) (4 wkts dec.)	407

N. J. Astle, †A. C. Parore, G. E. Bradburn, J. E. C. Franklin, D. R. Tuffey and C. S. Martin did not bat.

Bowling: Waqar Younis 31–2–98–1; Fazl-e-Akbar 27.2–6–85–3; Mohammad Akram 22–1–106–0; Saqlain Mushtaq 31–6–82–0; Younis Khan 1–0–26–0.

Umpires: D. J. Harper (Australia) and R. S. Dunne.
Third umpire: E. A. Watkin. Referee: R. S. Madugalle (Sri Lanka).

THE AUSTRALIANS IN INDIA, 2000-01

By DICKY RUTNAGUR

Although the Australians began the tour with the awesome achievement of 15 consecutive Test wins, they deemed victory in the series against India as absolutely essential if they were to stand comparison with the greatest teams Australia had fielded. Winning in India was, in their eyes, a conquest of the "final frontier", not least because 31 years and four tours had passed since Australia last left there triumphant.

Steve Waugh's team seemed to be on the point of emulating Bill Lawry's when they won the First Test at Mumbai, by ten wickets in three days, and then made India follow on 274 behind in the Second at Kolkata (formerly Calcutta). However, India not only denied them a winning 2–0 lead there, but rallied strongly enough to achieve one of the most remarkable victories in the history of Test cricket. They went on to win the deciding Test in a gripping finish.

The chief architects of the epic win at Eden Gardens were V. V. S. Laxman and Rahul Dravid, whose partnership of 376, one of several records in this match, was the basis of the recovery, and the 20-year-old Sikh off-spinner, Harbhajan Singh. His hat-trick in the first innings – the first for India in Tests – was only the precursor to taking 13 wickets in the match. In the next Test, he topped that with 15. Harbhajan's and Laxman's glory was the greater for the fact that neither was hitherto established in the side.

Notwithstanding Australia's overwhelming superiority over India in the home series a year earlier, their win in the First Test was something of a surprise – the draw was the favourite – and highly creditable; they went into the match looking as if two warm-up games were inadequate preparation. Moreover, Mark Waugh, his hand injured, played without having had a single innings on the tour, and with very little net practice. The match started two days after Sir Donald Bradman's death, and Steve Waugh promised that his team would play it as the great man would have liked them to.

The spirit of that dedication was exemplified by the manner in which Australia's bowlers – Glenn McGrath especially – vindicated their captain's decision to put India in, and again by the daring and panache with which Matthew Hayden and Adam Gilchrist revived Australia's innings from the rubble of 99 for five. Both hit hundreds, Gilchrist making his in an unforgettable exhibition of unbridled aggression that boosted his career average to 58.35 in 15 Tests, all of which Australia had won. But he was soon to be reminded what a cruel game cricket can be. He bagged a pair in the Second Test, managed only a brace of singles in the Third – and his average fell back to 47.33.

Meanwhile, fellow left-hander Hayden, whose first eight Test appearances had been scattered over seven seasons, raised his average from 24.36 to 40.18. He had not found a regular place until the series against West Indies that preceded this tour, but now he was by far the Australians' main provider of runs. His *tour de force* was 203 out of a total of 391 in the Third Test. The big Queenslander was originally on the list of players to be replaced for the subsequent limited-overs internationals. But his 549 runs at 109.80 in the Tests were scored at such a high strike-rate – 66 per 100 balls – that he was retained for the one-day games, a move rewarded with innings of 99, 57, 111 and 36. Hayden's presence accounted in no small measure for Australia winning the one-day series 3–2.

The rest of Australia's batting in the Test series was uneven. Steve Waugh looked in excellent form, and completely on terms with the Indian spinners, yet he managed only one score above 50, a gallant century that had its roots in a crisis in the Second Test. His twin, Mark, waited until the last Test to sparkle with a delightful half-century in each innings. Furthermore, the phenomenal catch he took on the last day to dismiss Laxman could well have won Australia both Test and series at the last gasp. Michael Slater and Justin Langer had moderate series and Ricky Ponting a disastrous one, although Ponting's memorable catch, to dismiss a well-set Tendulkar, made a significant contribution to the First Test victory. A century towards the end of the one-day series redeemed his tour.

Among the bowlers, McGrath and Jason Gillespie distinguished themselves by taking 30 wickets between them. Their success set in focus the disadvantage to which Australia were put by the unavailability of Brett Lee. Shane Warne, his level of fitness criticised by coach John Buchanan after the defeat at Eden Gardens, could provide only the odd good spell. The Indians played him with such comfort, and sometimes even disdain, that Waugh did not dare use him during the tight finish of the final Test.

Australia were not alone in being handicapped by the absence of a key bowler. India were without Anil Kumble for the whole series and Javagal Srinath for the last two Tests. The bonus that went with victory was the maturity achieved by Laxman and Harbhajan. A batsman of stately style, Laxman scored 503 runs at 83.83 in the Tests and should be an adornment to the game for many a year. It took much strength of character for Harbhajan to retain his poise and confidence after the ferocious battering he took from Gilchrist and Hayden in the First Test, but he went on to claim 32 wickets in the series at an average of 17.03. Only three bowlers – George Lohmann, Sydney Barnes and Richard Hadlee – had collected more in a three-Test series; Harbhajan was the first spinner to take so many.

AUSTRALIAN TOURING PARTY

S. R. Waugh (New South Wales) (*captain*), A. C. Gilchrist (Western Australia) (*vice-captain*), D. W. Fleming (Victoria), J. N. Gillespie (South Australia), M. L. Hayden (Queensland), M. S. Kasprowicz (Queensland), J. L. Langer (Western Australia), G. D. McGrath (New South Wales), D. R. Martyn (Western Australia), C. R. Miller (Victoria), R. T. Ponting (Tasmania), M. J. Slater (New South Wales), S. K. Warne (Victoria), M. E. Waugh (New South Wales).

B. J. Haddin (New South Wales) joined the party as cover for Gilchrist. Gillespie, Kasprowicz, Langer, Miller and Slater returned home at the end of the first-class programme and were replaced for the one-day international series by M. G. Bevan (New South Wales), N. W. Bracken (New South Wales), I. J. Harvey (Victoria), S. Lee (New South Wales), D. S. Lehmann (South Australia) and A. Symonds (Queensland). M. E. Waugh flew home injured during the one-day series.

Manager: S. R. Bernard. *Coach:* J. M. Buchanan.

AUSTRALIAN TOUR RESULTS

Test matches – Played 3: Won 1, Lost 2.
First-class matches – Played 6: Won 1, Lost 2, Drawn 3.
Win – India.
Losses – India (2).
Draws – India A, Mumbai, Board President's XI.
One-day internationals – Played 5: Won 3, Lost 2.

TEST MATCH AVERAGES

INDIA – BATTING

	T	*I*	*NO*	*R*	*HS*	*100s*	*50s*	*Avge*	*Ct/St*
V. V. S. Laxman	3	6	0	503	281	1	3	83.83	3
R. Dravid	3	6	0	338	180	1	1	56.33	6
S. R. Tendulkar	3	6	0	304	126	1	2	50.66	1
S. S. Das	3	6	0	173	84	0	1	28.83	5
S. Ramesh	3	6	0	162	61	0	1	27.00	3
N. R. Mongia	2	4	1	60	28	0	0	20.00	5/1
S. C. Ganguly	3	6	0	106	48	0	0	17.66	4
Harbhajan Singh	3	6	3	34	17*	0	0	11.33	0
Zaheer Khan	2	4	1	30	23*	0	0	10.00	1

Played in one Test: A. B. Agarkar 0, 0; S. V. Bahutule 21*, 0 (1 ct); S. S. Dighe 4, 22* (1 st); N. M. Kulkarni 4; B. K. V. Prasad 7*; S. L. V. Raju 4; R. L. Sanghvi 2, 0; J. Srinath 12, 0 (1 ct).

* *Signifies not out.*

BOWLING

	O	*M*	*R*	*W*	*BB*	*5W/i*	*Avge*
Harbhajan Singh	178.3	44	545	32	8-84	4	17.03
S. R. Tendulkar	48	5	151	3	3-31	0	50.33
Zaheer Khan	55.4	15	189	3	2-89	0	63.00

Also bowled: A. B. Agarkar 13–1–58–2; S. V. Bahutule 30–3–102–2; S. C. Ganguly 17.2–4–65–1; N. M. Kulkarni 53–16–137–1; B. K. V. Prasad 33–6–102–0; S. L. V. Raju 35–5–116–1; R. L. Sanghvi 12.2–3–78–2; J. Srinath 18–3–77–2.

AUSTRALIA – BATTING

	T	*I*	*NO*	*R*	*HS*	*100s*	*50s*	*Avge*	*Ct*
M. L. Hayden	3	6	1	549	203	2	2	109.80	3
S. R. Waugh	3	5	0	243	110	1	0	48.60	4
G. D. McGrath	3	5	4	47	21*	0	0	47.00	1
M. J. Slater	3	6	1	166	48	0	0	33.20	0
J. L. Langer	3	5	0	161	58	0	1	32.20	0
M. E. Waugh	3	5	0	149	70	0	2	29.80	8
A. C. Gilchrist	3	5	0	124	122	1	0	24.80	13
J. N. Gillespie	3	5	0	54	46	0	0	10.80	0
S. K. Warne	3	5	0	50	39	0	0	10.00	2
R. T. Ponting	3	5	0	17	11	0	0	3.40	7

Played in one Test: D. W. Fleming 6; M. S. Kasprowicz 7, 13*; C. R. Miller 0, 2 (1 ct).

* *Signifies not out.*

BOWLING

	O	*M*	*R*	*W*	*BB*	*5W/i*	*Avge*
G. D. McGrath.	136.2	60	261	17	4-18	0	15.35
J. N. Gillespie	126.3	31	394	13	3-45	0	30.30
C. R. Miller.	55	7	201	6	3-41	0	33.50
M. E. Waugh	36	6	106	3	3-40	0	35.33
S. K. Warne.	152.1	31	505	10	4-47	0	50.50

Also bowled: D. W. Fleming 30–4–99–1; M. L. Hayden 7–0–31–0; M. S. Kasprowicz 48–8–178–2; J. L. Langer 1–0–3–0; R. T. Ponting 14–2–43–0; M. J. Slater 2–1–4–0.

Note: Matches in this section which were not first-class are signified by a dagger.

At Nagpur, February 17, 18, 19. Drawn. Toss: Australians. Australians 291 (M. L. Hayden 49, R. T. Ponting 56, J. N. Gillespie 57, M. S. Kasprowicz 92; A. Nehra three for 78, R. L. Sanghvi five for 40) and 365 for nine (M. L. Hayden 37, J. L. Langer 115, R. T. Ponting 68, D. R. Martyn 53; Harbhajan Singh three for 81, W. D. Balaji Rao three for 100); India A 368 (S. Ramesh 101, V. V. S. Laxman 94, N. R. Mongia 71 not out, Extras 39; C. R. Miller six for 90).

The venue was changed from Baroda in the aftermath of the Gujarat earthquake. In the first innings, Gillespie and Kasprowicz added 155 for the Australians' eighth wicket. Langer passed 15,000 first-class runs.

At Brabourne Stadium, Mumbai, February 22, 23, 24. Drawn. Toss: Mumbai. Mumbai (Ranji Trophy champions) 328 for nine dec. (S. S. Dighe 84, S. V. Bahutule 51, R. R. Powar 65 not out, Extras 30; G. D. McGrath three for 46) and 191 for eight dec. (V. R. Mane 57, Wasim Jaffer 52, J. V. Paranjpe 35; S. K. Warne seven for 56); Australians 203 (S. R. Waugh 106 not out; P. L. Mhambrey four for 59, N. M. Kulkarni four for 39) and 141 for six (M. J. Slater 32, S. R. Waugh 34 not out; S. V. Bahutule four for 38).

On the first day, Mumbai recovered from 82 for five. Mark Waugh injured his finger in the field and did not bat. The highest score in the Australians' first innings after Steve Waugh's 106 not out (ten fours, three sixes) was 25 from Langer.

INDIA v AUSTRALIA

First Test Match

At Mumbai, February 27, 28, March 1. Australia won by ten wickets. Toss: Australia. Test debut: R. L. Sanghvi.

Although Australia completed their 16th win in consecutive Tests in three days and by a vast margin, it was not as straightforward as it might appear: in their first innings, they lost five wickets before reaching three figures. Moreover, Steve Waugh's decision to put India in had been a major gamble, given the doubts about the durability of the pitch, even though the Wankhede Stadium invariably offers encouragement for seam bowlers on the first morning. Happily for him, his bowlers met his immediate expectations and later, by dismissing India cheaply a second time, left Australia needing only 47 in the final innings.

McGrath was outstanding, conceding a run an over, and Warne most guileful. But the Indians contributed to their plight through poor technique or misjudgment. True, the pitch was not of the desired quality, with spin accompanying bounce from day one, but they did bat first while it was at its best. Only Dravid and Ganguly were genuinely beaten, and even Tendulkar, meticulous and solid for 139 minutes, eventually succumbed driving on the up at a widish ball. He batted responsibly, but not without flair, as indicated by his 13 fours.

Australia, who had 16 overs of batting before the close of play, were 99 for five when the second day was little over an hour old, with the ball turning consistently and quite menacingly. Off-spinner Harbhajan Singh took three quick wickets – Langer and Mark Waugh, brilliantly caught, from successive balls – and Rahul Sanghvi, the left-arm orthodox spinner making his debut, had Steve Waugh held at slip. Despite this shocking start, however, the tourists were in a commanding position less than three hours later.

Not for the first time in his 16-month Test career, Gilchrist brought about a sudden and dramatic change in Australia's fortunes. His 122 off 112 balls, with 15 fours and four sixes, was almost a replica of his celebrated maiden century against Pakistan at Hobart in November 1999. The spinners could not find the line or length to shackle his sweeping, pulling and pull-driving. He went from 50 to 100 in only 29 balls and, having given a chance at 44 – Badani, a substitute, running back at mid-wicket, was not athletic enough to complete the catch off a top edge – immediately survived an overhead chance to slip.

Hayden, who had batted stolidly throughout the early collapse, heartily joined in the assault, using much the same methods, and the two left-handers added 197, a record for Australia's sixth wicket against India, in 32 overs. He reached his century one over after Gilchrist, despite a 30-over start, and his eventual 119, in 172 balls, included 18 fours and a six. Ganguly's options for stemming the tide of runs, or breaking the partnership, had been reduced while Srinath was off the field for treatment to an injured finger, but no sooner was he available again than he had Hayden caught behind.

India's second innings was another shambles. Ramesh was flattered by a score of 44, and just after he was out, night-watchman Mongia was struck on the finger by Gillespie and retired. Next day, Dravid and Tendulkar resisted hostile first spells by McGrath and Gillespie to bat through the morning and frustrate the Australians. But once Tendulkar, who again batted in masterly fashion, was out to a sensational catch by Ponting, the decline was rapid. India lost their last eight wickets for 65, including Agarkar's seventh duck in consecutive Test innings against Australia. Tendulkar, pulling, had struck Langer at short leg on the shoulder, and the impact kept the ball in the air long enough for Ponting to sprint and dive for it.

Australia's openers required only seven overs to win the match on the third evening, with Slater's unbeaten 19 taking him past 5,000 Test runs. He was later fined half his match fee and given a one-match ban, suspended for six months, for discussing in a radio interview his on-field altercation with umpire Venkat and batsman Dravid following a disallowed catch in India's second innings.

Man of the Match: A. C. Gilchrist.

Close of play: First day, Australia 49-1 (Hayden 25*, Langer 10*); Second day, India 58-2 (Dravid 6*, Tendulkar 0*).

India

S. S. Das c Hayden b Gillespie	14	– c S. R. Waugh b Gillespie	7
S. Ramesh c Gilchrist b McGrath	2	– c Ponting b McGrath	44
R. Dravid c Gilchrist b Fleming	9	– b Warne	39
S. R. Tendulkar c Gilchrist b McGrath	76	– (5) c Ponting b M. E. Waugh	65
*S. C. Ganguly c Hayden b Warne	8	– (6) run out	1
V. V. S. Laxman c Ponting b McGrath	20	– (7) c Gilchrist b M. E. Waugh	12
†N. R. Mongia not out	26	– (4) c Gilchrist b Gillespie	28
A. B. Agarkar c and b Warne	0	– b M. E. Waugh	0
J. Srinath c M. E. Waugh b Warne	12	– (11) b McGrath	0
Harbhajan Singh c S. R. Waugh b Warne	0	– (9) not out	17
R. L. Sanghvi c Gilchrist b Gillespie	2	– (10) b Gillespie	0
B 4, l-b 1, w 1, n-b 1	7	B 5, n-b 1	6
1/7 (2) 2/25 (3) 3/31 (1) 4/55 (5) 5/130 (6) 6/139 (4) 7/140 (8) 8/165 (9) 9/166 (10) 10/176 (11)	176	1/33 (1) 2/57 (2) 3/154 (5) 4/156 (6) 5/174 (7) 6/174 (3) 7/193 (8) 8/210 (4) 9/216 (10) 10/219 (11)	219

In the second innings Mongia, when 0, retired hurt at 58 and resumed at 174-5.

Bowling: *First Innings*—McGrath 19–13–19–3; Fleming 15–3–55–1; Gillespie 15.3–4–50–2; Warne 22–7–47–4. *Second Innings*—McGrath 17.1–9–25–2; Fleming 15–1–44–0; Warne 28–11–60–1; Gillespie 19–8–45–3; M. E. Waugh 15–5–40–3.

Australia

M. J. Slater b Agarkar	10	– (2) not out 19
M. L. Hayden c Mongia b Srinath	119	– (1) not out 28
J. L. Langer c Dravid b Harbhajan Singh	19	
M. E. Waugh c Ganguly b Harbhajan Singh	0	
*S. R. Waugh c Dravid b Sanghvi	15	
R. T. Ponting c Das b Harbhajan Singh	0	
†A. C. Gilchrist st Mongia b Harbhajan Singh	122	
S. K. Warne c Tendulkar b Sanghvi	39	
J. N. Gillespie c Mongia b Srinath	0	
D. W. Fleming c Srinath b Agarkar	6	
G. D. McGrath not out	0	
B 13, l-b 3, n-b 3	19	
1/21 (1) 2/71 (3) 3/71 (4) 4/98 (5) 5/99 (6) 6/296 (2) 7/326 (7) 8/327 (9) 9/349 (10) 10/349 (8)	349	(no wkt) 47

Bowling: *First Innings*—Srinath 16–3–60–2; Agarkar 12–1–50–2; Harbhajan Singh 28–3–121–4; Sanghvi 10.2–2–67–2; Tendulkar 7–1–35–0. *Second Innings*—Srinath 2–0–17–0; Agarkar 1–0–8–0; Harbhajan Singh 2–0–11–0; Sanghvi 2–1–11–0.

Umpires: D. R. Shepherd (England) and S. Venkataraghavan.
Third umpire: N. N. Menon. Referee: C. W. Smith (West Indies).

At Delhi, March 6, 7, 8. Drawn. Toss: Australians. Australians 451 (M. L. Hayden 31, M. E. Waugh 62, S. R. Waugh 109, R. T. Ponting 102, M. S. Kasprowicz 35; N. D. Hirwani three for 120, Sarandeep Singh five for 114) and 461 for seven (M. E. Waugh 164, D. R. Martyn 54, R. T. Ponting 102 not out, M. S. Kasprowicz 32 not out, Extras 33; N. D. Hirwani five for 168); Board President's XI 221 (M. Kaif 33, S. C. Ganguly 40, D. Mongia 66; M. S. Kasprowicz three for 68).

Ponting, 102 in each innings, shared fifth-wicket partnerships of 171 with Steve Waugh and 113 with Mark Waugh, who struck 17 fours and seven sixes in 181 balls.

INDIA v AUSTRALIA

Second Test Match

At Kolkata, March 11, 12, 13, 14, 15. India won by 171 runs. Toss: Australia.

An astonishing Indian recovery provided several records and culminated in only the third victory in Test history for a side who had followed on. Australia were the victims in the previous instances also, losing to England at Sydney in 1894-95 and Leeds in 1981. Laxman amassed 281, the highest Test score for India, while his partnership of 376 with Dravid was an Indian fifth-wicket record. Their feats almost overshadowed the outstanding performance of off-spinner Harbhajan Singh, who claimed India's first Test hat-trick while capturing a career-best seven wickets in the first innings, and followed up with a match-winning six in the second.

Fortune had already swayed quite vigorously before Australia achieved their formidable first-innings total of 445. Their early prosperity was based on large partnerships for the first two wickets, with Hayden the common factor. He made a robust four-hour 97, hitting 14 fours and three sixes, although India could have had him out at 67 from a sliced drive off Zaheer Khan. He was dismissed immediately after tea, and the decline that followed was expedited by Harbhajan's hat-trick, which claimed Ponting and Gilchrist lbw, both playing back, before Warne glanced a full toss to short leg. When Kasprowicz soon followed, Australia had lost seven wickets in the space of 26 overs and 76 runs, and were 269 for eight. But India were kept in the field until an hour after lunch on the second day as Steve Waugh batted more than five hours to orchestrate the revival. Tailenders Gillespie, who shared a stand of 133, an Australian ninth-wicket record against India, and McGrath lent noble support until Waugh was last out for 110. It was his 25th Test century, during which he passed 20,000 first-class runs.

The fact that Australia's last two batted for 222 minutes between them was proof enough that the pitch was playing easily. Yet India somehow contrived to get themselves in a terrible mess.

[*Hamish Blair, Getty Images*

Record-breakers V. V. S. Laxman (*left*) and Rahul Dravid, with a triple-hundred partnership in the scorebook, take their leave of Eden Gardens after batting throughout the fourth day.

All four bowlers succeeded but, predictably, McGrath dominated with four for 18 in 14 overs. If there was a silver lining to the débâcle, it was that Laxman's swashbuckling 59 from 83 balls prompted his promotion from No. 6 to No. 3 when India followed on 274 behind. The tall, elegant, Hyderabad batsman responded to the responsibility with a flawless display that stretched over ten hours 31 minutes, during which he faced 452 balls, picked up 44 fours with a wide range of exciting shots, and comfortably surpassed India's previous best, 236 not out by Sunil Gavaskar against West Indies at Madras in 1983-84. India lost four wickets before the first-innings deficit was cleared, but as Dravid's batting recovered its sparkle in Laxman's company, the game was transformed.

They batted together for 104 overs, including the whole of the fourth day, when they added 335 in 90 overs. Their stand of 376 overtook India's fifth-wicket record, a mere 214 between Mohammad Azharuddin and Ravi Shastri against England on this ground in 1984-85, and then India's all-wicket record against Australia, an unbroken 298 for the sixth wicket between Dilip Vengsarkar and Shastri at Bombay in 1986-87. By the time Laxman was out, it was the second-highest partnership for any Indian wicket, behind the opening stand of 413 between Vinoo Mankad and Pankaj Roy against New Zealand at Madras in 1955-56, and the third best by any country for the fifth wicket. Their efforts had not only dispelled India's troubles, but opened up an avenue to a momentous victory. Dravid was eventually run out for a chanceless 180 from 353 balls in seven hours 24 minutes, with 21 fours.

When Ganguly declared with a lead of 383, India had equalled the second-highest Test total by a side batting second, 657 for eight by Pakistan at Bridgetown in 1957-58; only New Zealand, with 671 for four against Sri Lanka at Wellington in 1990-91, had scored more. It meant Australia had to bat out 75 overs for a draw, on a pitch affording turn without being devilish. Their prospects looked good when Hayden, given an early life, and Slater stayed together for 23 overs. But once they were separated, wickets fell at regular intervals. The only pause in the collapse was provided by a fourth-wicket partnership of 50 between Hayden and Steve Waugh. Otherwise, the turning ball proved too disconcerting for the Australians. Harbhajan again did the major damage, and Tendulkar, bowling leg-spin, took three wickets, including the crucial ones of Hayden and Gilchrist – for a king pair. Australia were all out in the 69th over and their record run of Test wins had come to an abrupt and spectacular halt.

Man of the Match: V. V. S. Laxman.

Close of play: First day, Australia 291-8 (S. R. Waugh 29*, Gillespie 6*); Second day, India 128-8 (Laxman 26*, Raju 3*); Third day, India 254-4 (Laxman 109*, Dravid 7*); Fourth day, India 589-4 (Laxman 275*, Dravid 155*).

Australia

M. J. Slater c Mongia b Zaheer Khan	42	– (2) c Ganguly b Harbhajan Singh	43
M. L. Hayden c sub (H. K. Badani) b Harbhajan Singh	97	– (1) lbw b Tendulkar	67
J. L. Langer c Mongia b Zaheer Khan	58	– c Ramesh b Harbhajan Singh	28
M. E. Waugh c Mongia b Harbhajan Singh	22	– lbw b Raju	0
*S. R. Waugh lbw b Harbhajan Singh	110	– c sub (H. K. Badani) b Harbhajan Singh	24
R. T. Ponting lbw b Harbhajan Singh	6	– c Das b Harbhajan Singh	0
†A. C. Gilchrist lbw b Harbhajan Singh	0	– lbw b Tendulkar	0
S. K. Warne c Ramesh b Harbhajan Singh	0	– (9) lbw b Tendulkar	0
M. S. Kasprowicz lbw b Ganguly	7	– (10) not out	13
J. N. Gillespie c Ramesh b Harbhajan Singh	46	– (8) c Das b Harbhajan Singh	6
G. D. McGrath not out	21	– lbw b Harbhajan Singh	12
B 19, l-b 10, n-b 7	36	B 6, n-b 8, p 5	19
1/103 (1) 2/193 (2) 3/214 (3) 4/236 (4) 5/252 (6) 6/252 (7) 7/252 (8) 8/269 (9) 9/402 (10) 10/445 (5)	445	1/74 (2) 2/106 (3) 3/116 (4) 4/166 (5) 5/166 (6) 6/167 (7) 7/173 (1) 8/174 (9) 9/191 (8) 10/212 (11)	212

Bowling: *First Innings*—Zaheer Khan 28.4–6–89–2; Prasad 30–5–95–0; Ganguly 13.2–3–44–1; Raju 20–2–58–0; Harbhajan Singh 37.5–7–123–7; Tendulkar 2–0–7–0. *Second Innings*—Zaheer Khan 8–4–30–0; Prasad 3–1–7–0; Harbhajan Singh 30.3–8–73–6; Raju 15–3–58–1; Tendulkar 11–3–31–3; Ganguly 1–0–2–0.

India

S. S. Das c Gilchrist b McGrath	20	– hit wkt b Gillespie	39
S. Ramesh c Ponting b Gillespie	0	– c M. E. Waugh b Warne	30
R. Dravid b Warne	25	– (6) run out	180
S. R. Tendulkar lbw b McGrath	10	– c Gilchrist b Gillespie	10
*S. C. Ganguly c S. R. Waugh b Kasprowicz	23	– c Gilchrist b McGrath	48
V. V. S. Laxman c Hayden b Warne	59	– (3) c Ponting b McGrath	281
†N. R. Mongia c Gilchrist b Kasprowicz	2	– b McGrath	4
Harbhajan Singh c Ponting b Gillespie	4	– (9) not out	8
Zaheer Khan b McGrath	3	– (8) not out	23
S. L. V. Raju lbw b McGrath	4		
B. K. V. Prasad not out	7		
L-b 2, n-b 12	14	B 6, l-b 12, w 2, n-b 14	34
1/0 (2) 2/34 (1) 3/48 (4) 4/88 (3) 5/88 (5) 6/92 (7) 7/97 (8) 8/113 (9) 9/129 (10) 10/171 (6)	171	1/52 (2) 2/97 (1) 3/115 (4) 4/232 (5) 5/608 (3) 6/624 (7) 7/629 (6) (7 wkts dec.)	657

Bowling: *First Innings*—McGrath 14–8–18–4; Gillespie 11–0–47–2; Kasprowicz 13–2–39–2; Warne 20.1–3–65–2. *Second Innings*—McGrath 39–12–103–3; Gillespie 31–6–115–2; Warne 34–3–152–1; M. E. Waugh 18–1–58–0; Kasprowicz 35–6–139–0; Ponting 12–1–41–0; Hayden 6–0–24–0; Slater 2–1–4–0; Langer 1–0–3–0.

Umpires: P. Willey (England) and S. K. Bansal.
Third umpire: S. N. Bandekar. Referee: C. W. Smith (West Indies).

INDIA v AUSTRALIA

Third Test Match

At Chennai, March 18, 19, 20, 21, 22. India won by two wickets. Toss: Australia. Test debuts: S. V. Bahutule, S. S. Dighe.

Appropriately, the deciding Test of an enthralling series, marked by dramatic shifts of fortune, produced a grandstand finish. India, requiring 155 in the final innings, seemed to be heading for a comfortable win, only to encounter a brave, if unavailing, challenge from the Australian bowlers.

[*Hamish Blair, Getty Images*

Steve Waugh can only stand and watch as umpire Jayaprakash sends Ricky Pointing on his way and Harbhajan Singh celebrates the 11th of his 15 wickets in the match.

The bare pitch prompted both sides to alter the balance of their attacks towards spin. Australia picked Miller as a second spinner for the first time in the series; India included leg-spinner Sairaj Bahutule to back up Harbhajan Singh and the slow left-armer, Kulkarni. While all three shared the workload, the concentrated threat to Australia's batsmen was again posed by Harbhajan, who took 15 wickets, his second successive Test match return of ten or more wickets. Only leg-spinner Narendra Hirwani, with 16 against West Indies at Madras in 1987-88, had claimed more wickets in a Test for India.

That Australia took any advantage from their continued luck with the toss was all down to opener Hayden, who was last out for 203 made in 474 minutes off 320 balls. Fifteen fours and six sixes – the most sixes by an Australian in a Test innings – testified to his form and his positive approach regardless of the situation. But support was confined to Langer and the Waugh twins. He added 150 with Mark Waugh, who passed 7,000 Test runs, and 123 with Steve, whose dismissal in circumstances both unfortunate and bizarre triggered his side's collapse. Australia's captain became only the sixth batsman in Test history to be given out handled the ball. While Waugh's attention was fixed on the umpire after an lbw appeal, following a missed sweep at Harbhajan, the ball came to ground outside the popping crease and spun back vigorously towards the stumps at bail height. Alerted to the danger by Hayden from the other end, Waugh fatally intercepted the ball with the palm of his hand. Harbhajan now collected the remaining six wickets for 26 in 9.4 overs; Hayden's mastery was emphasised by the fact that he scored all but four runs of the 51 added in that time. Warne made his 23rd duck in Tests, an Australian record.

India's reply, launched by Das and Ramesh with a century partnership, also tapered away after the fall of the fifth wicket. The difference was that their collapse started with the total already at 453, which included four fifties and Tendulkar's superb century. He reached it with his second six off Miller, and also hit 15 fours in his 126. Helped by Tendulkar's 169-run partnership with Dravid, the eventual lead was 110. Hayden and Slater quickly chipped away at this, raising 82 in 18 overs before a diving catch by Zaheer Khan at deep mid-wicket dismissed Hayden. Mark Waugh then added 100 with Langer and Steve Waugh, and the latter, composed and assured, remained unbeaten at the end of the fourth day. Harbhajan had him caught next morning in the eighth over, and this time India's off-spinner took the last six wickets for 15 in 17.1 overs to finish with a career-best eight for 84.

Australia seemed beaten as India reached the hundred mark with only two wickets down. Laxman and Tendulkar were in such firm control that victory looked a formality. However, Gillespie's dismissal of Tendulkar, caught by Mark Waugh at second slip off a ball of lethal speed and aim, was the signal for two more wickets in the next three overs. Laxman was still scoring freely, but after tea, with 20 runs wanted, Mark Waugh removed him with an amazing mid-wicket catch that left the match wide open once more. When the seventh wicket fell at the same score, the balance was tipping Australia's way. Stand-in wicket-keeper Sameer Dighe and Zaheer tilted it back again and, with India nine short, McGrath – suffering from a stomach disorder and having to be sparingly used – was called on to make a final effort. Aided by Mark Waugh's fourth catch of the innings he prised out Zaheer, but it proved to be Australia's last throw. The target was now just four runs. Dighe and Harbhajan picked up a single each and then, fittingly, Harbhajan, voted Man of the Series, nonchalantly pushed a McGrath half-volley square of the wicket for the winning runs. The two-wicket margin matched India's narrowest Test win, also against Australia, at Bombay in 1964-65.

Men of the Match: Harbhajan Singh and M. L. Hayden.

Man of the Series: Harbhajan Singh.

Close of play: First day, Australia 326-3 (Hayden 147*, S. R. Waugh 43*); Second day, India 211-1 (Das 84*, Laxman 59*); Third day, India 480-9 (Bahutule 4*, Kulkarni 0*); Fourth day, Australia 241-7 (S. R. Waugh 43*).

Australia

M. J. Slater c Laxman b Zaheer Khan	4	– (2) c Laxman b Harbhajan Singh	48
M. L. Hayden c Ganguly b Harbhajan Singh	203	– (1) c Zaheer Khan b Kulkarni	35
J. L. Langer c Dravid b Harbhajan Singh	35	– (4) c Laxman b Bahutule	21
M. E. Waugh c sub (H. K. Badani) b Bahutule	70	– (5) c Dravid b Harbhajan Singh	57
*S. R. Waugh handled the ball	47	– (6) c Das b Harbhajan Singh	47
R. T. Ponting st Dighe b Harbhajan Singh	0	– (7) c Dravid b Harbhajan Singh	11
†A. C. Gilchrist lbw b Harbhajan Singh	1	– (3) lbw b Harbhajan Singh	1
S. K. Warne c Das b Harbhajan Singh	0	– lbw b Harbhajan Singh	11
J. N. Gillespie c Ganguly b Harbhajan Singh	0	– c Dravid b Harbhajan Singh	2
C. R. Miller c Bahutule b Harbhajan Singh	0	– lbw b Harbhajan Singh	2
G. D. McGrath not out	3	– not out	11
B 8, l-b 10, n-b 10	28	B 8, l-b 6, n-b 4	18
1/4 (1) 2/67 (3) 3/217 (4) 4/340 (5) 5/340 (6) 6/344 (7) 7/374 (8) 8/376 (9) 9/385 (10) 10/391 (2)	391	1/82 (1) 2/84 (3) 3/93 (2) 4/141 (4) 5/193 (5) 6/211 (7) 7/241 (8) 8/246 (6) 9/251 (9) 10/264 (10)	264

Bowling: *First Innings*—Zaheer Khan 15–5–57–1; Ganguly 2–1–11–0; Harbhajan Singh 38.2–6–133–7; Kulkarni 23–5–67–0; Bahutule 21–3–70–1; Tendulkar 16–1–35–0. *Second Innings*—Zaheer Khan 4–0–13–0; Ganguly 1–0–8–0; Harbhajan Singh 41.5–20–84–8; Kulkarni 30–11–70–1; Tendulkar 12–0–43–0; Bahutule 9–0–32–1.

India

S. S. Das lbw b McGrath	84	– c and b McGrath	9
S. Ramesh c Ponting b Warne	61	– run out	25
V. V. S. Laxman c M. E. Waugh b McGrath	65	– c M. E. Waugh b Miller	66
S. R. Tendulkar c Gilchrist b Gillespie	126	– c M. E. Waugh b Gillespie	17
*S. C. Ganguly c Gilchrist b McGrath	22	– c M. E. Waugh b Gillespie	4
R. Dravid c Gilchrist b Gillespie	81	– c S. R. Waugh b Miller	4
†S. S. Dighe lbw b Warne	4	– not out	22
S. V. Bahutule not out	21	– c Warne b Miller	0
Zaheer Khan c and b Miller	4	– c M. E. Waugh b McGrath	0
Harbhajan Singh c M. E. Waugh b Miller	2	– not out	3
N. M. Kulkarni lbw b Miller	4		
B 19, l-b 2, w 1, n-b 5	27	L-b 3, n-b 2	5
1/123 (2) 2/211 (1) 3/237 (3) 4/284 (5) 5/453 (6) 6/468 (4) 7/470 (7) 8/475 (9) 9/477 (10) 10/501 (11)	501	1/18 (1) 2/76 (2) 3/101 (4) 4/117 (5) 5/122 (6) 6/135 (3) 7/135 (8) 8/151 (9)	(8 wkts) 155

Bowling: *First Innings*—McGrath 36–15–75–3; Gillespie 35–11–88–2; Miller 46–6–160–3; Warne 42–7–140–2; Ponting 2–1–2–0; M. E. Waugh 3–0–8–0; Hayden 1–0–7–0. *Second Innings*—McGrath 11.1–3–21–2; Gillespie 15–2–49–2; Miller 9–1–41–3; Warne 6–0–41–0.

Umpires: R. E. Koertzen (South Africa) and A. V. Jayaprakash.
Third umpire: C. R. Vijayaraghavan. Referee: C. W. Smith (West Indies).

†INDIA v AUSTRALIA

First One-Day International

At Bangalore, March 25 (day/night). India won by 60 runs. Toss: India.

Having ended Australia's 16-Test winning streak, India now halted a run of ten one-day victories. Tendulkar set them off with a furious onslaught; Australia were fortunate that a run-out spared them further punishment after he hit six fours and a six in 26 balls. Laxman and local hero Dravid, whose 84-ball 80 lasted into the 44th over, reproduced their Test form, and there were rapid half-centuries from all-rounder Sehwag, who later bowled his off-spin to winning advantage, and wicket-keeper Dahiya. Even so, India's 315 was not overwhelming, given a good pitch and a quick outfield. Australia's hopes were raised by a partnership of 110 spanning 17.3 overs between Hayden, who scored 99 off 90 balls with seven fours and a six, and Bevan. Once Bevan went, however, pulling at a short ball, the challenge petered out.

Man of the Match: V. Sehwag.

India

*S. C. Ganguly c M. E. Waugh b Fleming	6
S. R. Tendulkar run out	35
V. V. S. Laxman c Martyn b Harvey	45
R. Dravid c Harvey b Martyn	80
H. K. Badani c M. E. Waugh b Warne	11
V. Sehwag b Fleming	58
†V. Dahiya run out	51
A. B. Agarkar c and b McGrath	13
Harbhajan Singh c Ponting b Harvey	0
Zaheer Khan not out	1
J. Srinath c Martyn b McGrath	2
W 7, n-b 6	13
1/16 2/52 3/102 4/122 5/222 6/283 7/306 8/311 9/312 (49.5 overs)	315

Bowling: McGrath 9.5–0–60–2; Fleming 10–0–62–2; Harvey 10–0–68–2; Warne 10–0–58–1; M. E. Waugh 6–0–42–0; Martyn 4–0–25–1.

Australia

M. L. Hayden lbw b Sehwag	99
M. E. Waugh b Srinath	5
R. T. Ponting c Dravid b Zaheer Khan	9
M. G. Bevan c sub (R. R. Singh) b Ganguly	49
*S. R. Waugh lbw b Sehwag	18
D. R. Martyn c Dahiya b Sehwag	1
†A. C. Gilchrist b Zaheer Khan	27
I. J. Harvey c Ganguly b Agarkar	17
S. K. Warne b Srinath	13
D. W. Fleming not out	0
G. D. McGrath lbw b Srinath	0
L-b 3, w 8, n-b 6	17
1/16 2/44 3/154 4/174 5/179 6/212 7/230 8/252 9/254 (43.3 overs)	255

Bowling: Srinath 7.3–0–49–3; Zaheer Khan 8–0–34–2; Agarkar 8–0–54–1; Harbhajan Singh 8–0–41–0; Sehwag 9–0–59–3; Ganguly 3–0–15–1.

Umpires: D. D. Sharma and S. K. Sharma.
Third umpire: K. G. Lakshminarayan.

†INDIA v AUSTRALIA

Second One-Day International

At Pune, March 28. Australia won by eight wickets. Toss: India. International debut: D. Mongia.

With the pitch expected to become unreliable in bounce, losing the toss boded ill for Australia. They had already picked only three specialist bowlers in order to reinforce their batting. But they levelled the series with most of the reinforcements still in the dressing-room. A vintage 133 not out from Mark Waugh, off 138 balls with 15 fours and a six, gave them a smooth passage. The consistent Hayden supported him in a stand of 143 in 26 overs, well above the asking-rate. Waugh's stickiest moment came a few overs later, when there was confusion about whether he or Lehmann had been run out. Eventually the umpires rejected India's contention that the batsmen had crossed, but while Waugh saw Australia to victory, another finger injury during this innings ended his tour. In the morning, India's innings had featured an attractive maiden hundred by left-hander Badani, made off 98 balls with ten fours and two sixes. It had not been helped, though, by the self-inflicted damage of three successive middle-order run-outs.

Man of the Match: M. E. Waugh.

India

*S. C. Ganguly b McGrath	4	Zaheer Khan b McGrath	15
S. R. Tendulkar c Lehmann b Fleming	32	Harbhajan Singh not out	1
V. V. S. Laxman run out	51	J. Srinath not out	3
R. Dravid run out	13	L-b 2, w 4	6
H. K. Badani c Lehmann b Bracken	100		
D. Mongia run out	2	1/29 2/37 3/60 (9 wkts, 50 overs)	248
†V. Dahiya c Bracken b Fleming	2	4/153 5/157 6/162	
S. B. Joshi c M. E. Waugh b Bracken	19	7/221 8/239 9/244	

Bowling: McGrath 10–1–49–2; Fleming 10–1–39–2; Bracken 10–1–54–2; Martyn 7–0–41–0; Symonds 10–0–41–0; M. E. Waugh 3–0–22–0.

Australia

M. E. Waugh not out	133
M. L. Hayden c Ganguly b Zaheer Khan	57
D. S. Lehmann run out	1
M. G. Bevan not out	33
B 4, l-b 10, w 7, n-b 4	25
1/143 2/163 (2 wkts, 45.1 overs)	249

A. Symonds, *S. R. Waugh, D. R. Martyn, †A. C. Gilchrist, N. W. Bracken, D. W. Fleming and G. D. McGrath did not bat.

Bowling: Srinath 7–0–33–0; Zaheer Khan 6–0–26–1; Harbhajan Singh 10–0–46–0; Joshi 9.1–0–54–0; Ganguly 3–0–17–0; Tendulkar 10–0–59–0.

Umpires: S. C. Gupta and I. Shivaram.
Third umpire: C. R. Mohite.

†INDIA v AUSTRALIA

Third One-Day International

At Indore, March 31. India won by 118 runs. Toss: Australia.

India's total, which proved well out of Australia's range on a pitch that lost pace and bounce, was based on Tendulkar's 28th century in one-day internationals. It made him the first batsman to pass 10,000 runs at this level, in his 266th game. Curbing his excesses for a change, Tendulkar took 66 balls over his first 50, then blazed through to his hundred from another 28. His 139 in 125 balls, including 19 fours, spanned all but 28 balls of India's allotment. Laxman, who helped add 199 in 30 overs, was the only other batsman with the scope to build an innings. Although Australia started their reply at the required momentum, there was little substance to their batting apart from a belligerent 70-ball 63 from Gilchrist. In one over from Zaheer Khan, he plundered 22 runs, with five boundary hits. Referee Cammie Smith was called on to adjudicate when the captains failed to agree who had won the toss.

Man of the Match: S. R. Tendulkar.

India

R. Dravid c Gilchrist b Fleming 15
S. R. Tendulkar c Fleming b McGrath . . 139
V. V. S. Laxman run out 83
*S. C. Ganguly c Bevan b Fleming 0
H. K. Badani run out 23
D. Mongia c and b McGrath 4
A. B. Agarkar lbw b Harvey 1
†V. Dahiya b McGrath 0
Zaheer Khan not out 7
Harbhajan Singh not out 9

L-b 7, w 7, n-b 4 18

1/32 2/231 3/231 (8 wkts, 50 overs) 299
4/268 5/279 6/282
7/283 8/284

J. Srinath did not bat.

Bowling: McGrath 10–0–52–3; Fleming 10–1–34–2; Harvey 10–0–48–1; Warne 10–0–64–0; Martyn 4–0–34–0; Symonds 4–0–37–0; Bevan 2–0–23–0.

Australia

†A. C. Gilchrist c Ganguly
b Harbhajan Singh . 63
D. R. Martyn c Dahiya b Srinath 19
R. T. Ponting c and b Agarkar 23
M. G. Bevan b Harbhajan Singh 6
*S. R. Waugh c Tendulkar b Ganguly. . . 23
A. Symonds c Dahiya b Agarkar. 5
D. S. Lehmann c Badani b Agarkar 1
I. J. Harvey c and b Harbhajan Singh. . . 1
S. K. Warne run out 18
D. W. Fleming c Dahiya b Srinath 9
G. D. McGrath not out 0

L-b 4, w 6, n-b 3 13

1/46 2/102 3/111 (35.5 overs) 181
4/122 5/127 6/129
7/136 8/171 9/172

Bowling: Srinath 8.5–1–34–2; Zaheer Khan 6–0–51–0; Agarkar 8–0–38–3; Harbhajan Singh 9–0–37–3; Ganguly 4–0–17–1.

Umpires: V. Chopra and K. Hariharan.
Third umpire: S. J. Phadkar.

†INDIA v AUSTRALIA

Fourth One-Day International

At Vishakhapatnam, April 3. Australia won by 93 runs. Toss: Australia.

Apart from another routine mauling by Hayden, who struck a maiden one-day international hundred, India had to contend with Ponting belatedly running into his best form. Both scored at high speed – Hayden hit 111 in 112 balls, Ponting 101 in 110 – while adding 219 in 35 overs. When that stand was breached, Bevan, Steve Waugh and Lee smashed 92 off the last ten overs, taking Australia to 338, the largest total of the series. If India had any remaining hopes of securing the series here, they were removed by the dismissal of Tendulkar in the 16th over. His 62 runs out of 85 came from only 38 balls and included 11 fours, three off consecutive balls from McGrath. Warne then had Laxman stumped to reach 250 wickets in limited-overs internationals, and it needed a late flurry from Harbhajan Singh to keep the margin down to double figures.

Man of the Match: M. L. Hayden.

Australia

†A. C. Gilchrist c Dahiya b Srinath. . . . 6
M. L. Hayden st Dahiya
b Harbhajan Singh . 111
R. T. Ponting c Tendulkar b Agarkar . . . 101
M. G. Bevan not out. 43
*S. R. Waugh c Srinath b Zaheer Khan . 35
S. Lee not out 25

L-b 7, w 7, n-b 3 17

1/6 2/225 (4 wkts, 50 overs) 338
3/246 4/304

D. R. Martyn, S. K. Warne, D. W. Fleming, N. W. Bracken and G. D. McGrath did not bat.

Bowling: Srinath 10–0–61–1; Zaheer Khan 10–0–71–1; Agarkar 9–0–63–1; Harbhajan Singh 10–0–58–1; R. R. Singh 6–0–37–0; Ganguly 4–0–29–0; Tendulkar 1–0–12–0.

India

*S. C. Ganguly c Warne b Bracken	9	Zaheer Khan c Waugh b McGrath	29
S. R. Tendulkar c Waugh b Bracken	62	Harbhajan Singh c Lee b McGrath	46
V. V. S. Laxman st Gilchrist b Warne	11	J. Srinath not out	7
R. Dravid c and b Warne	7	L-b 2, w 12, n-b 3	17
H. K. Badani c Warne b Waugh	25		——
R. R. Singh c Gilchrist b Waugh	16	1/47 2/85 3/87 (45 overs)	245
†V. Dahiya c Hayden b Warne	7	4/102 5/135 6/144	
A. B. Agarkar lbw b Waugh	9	7/149 8/169 9/228	

Bowling: McGrath 8–0–62–2; Fleming 8–1–53–0; Bracken 7–1–21–2; Warne 10–0–38–3; Lee 3–0–11–0; Waugh 6–0–29–3; Bevan 3–0–29–0.

Umpires: G. A. Pratap Kumar and S. K. Tarapore.
Third umpire: A. Bhattacharjee.

†INDIA v AUSTRALIA

Fifth One-Day International

At Margao, April 6. Australia won by four wickets. Toss: India.

Australia's convincing win gave them the series 3–2. Bevan kept a steady hand on the tiller to prevent their drifting off course after Hayden and Gilchrist had opened with 70 in ten overs. Gilchrist was rampant in scoring 76 off only 60 balls, including ten fours and a six. As when India batted, runs became difficult to come by when the white ball softened, and efforts to sustain the momentum resulted in casualties. Three wickets went down for 15 runs, including that of Waugh, Tendulkar's 100th victim in limited-overs internationals. That left Bevan and Harvey to get 64, which they did inside nine overs; Bevan finished unbeaten with 87 from 113 balls. Ganguly's only major score of the series, 74 off 83 balls, and Laxman's first one-day international century (101 in 107 balls) should have led to a bigger Indian total than 265. But the Australian bowlers limited them to 48 runs from their last ten overs. Earlier in the day, bogus ticket-holders had gained admission to the ground at the expense of many with genuine tickets. Subsequent police investigations resulted in the arrest of high-ranking officials at the Goan Cricket Association.

Man of the Match: M. G. Bevan. *Man of the Series:* M. L. Hayden.

India

*S. C. Ganguly c Ponting b McGrath	74	†V. Dahiya not out	15
S. R. Tendulkar c Gilchrist b Bracken	12	Zaheer Khan not out	0
V. V. S. Laxman c Gilchrist b Harvey	101	L-b 3, w 3	6
R. Dravid c Waugh b Symonds	31		——
H. K. Badani b Harvey	7	1/16 2/121 3/218 (6 wkts, 50 overs)	265
Yuvraj Singh run out	19	4/230 5/230 6/262	

A. B. Agarkar, Harbhajan Singh and J. Srinath did not bat.

Bowling: McGrath 8–0–37–1; Bracken 10–1–37–1; Harvey 10–1–49–2; Warne 8–0–62–0; Symonds 8–0–40–1; Lehmann 6–0–37–0.

Australia

M. L. Hayden c Ganguly b Srinath	36	A. Symonds c Badani b Srinath	7
†A. C. Gilchrist b Tendulkar	76	I. J. Harvey not out	25
R. T. Ponting c Dahiya b Srinath	4		
M. G. Bevan not out	87	B 4, l-b 9, w 1, n-b 2	16
*S. R. Waugh c Agarkar b Tendulkar	17		——
D. S. Lehmann c Yuvraj Singh b Tendulkar	1	1/70 2/74 3/142 (6 wkts, 48 overs)	269
		4/187 5/195 6/202	

S. K. Warne, N. W. Bracken and G. D. McGrath did not bat.

Bowling: Srinath 10–1–62–3; Zaheer Khan 9–0–43–0; Agarkar 6–0–45–0; Harbhajan Singh 10–0–55–0; Tendulkar 10–0–35–3; Yuvraj Singh 3–0–16–0.

Umpires: F. Gomes and S. K. Porel.
Third umpire: K. Murali. Series referee: C. W. Smith (West Indies).

THE SOUTH AFRICANS IN THE WEST INDIES, 2000-01

By TONY COZIER

On their first full tour of the West Indies, nine years after a fleeting visit for their inaugural, unsuccessful post-apartheid Test in April 1992, South Africa became the first team to triumph in twin Test and one-day international series in the Caribbean. They won the Second and Fourth Tests and drew the First and Third before the West Indians gained a consolation victory in the Fifth. Their superiority was even more pronounced in the shorter game, where they won 5–2 after a last-ball setback in the opening match.

Even though West Indies had lost only one Test series at home in 28 years, to the Australians in 1994-95, South Africa's success was not unexpected. Since their 5–0 whitewash of West Indies at home in 1998-99, they had won 12 of their 21 Tests, and lost only two. They had not lost a series since 1998 in England. Their record in limited-overs cricket was similarly impressive. If the embarrassment of Hansie Cronje's dealings with bookmakers lingered, it had no effect, either on or off the field.

In contrast, the West Indians were sinking into confusion and failure. They went into the Test series a month after returning from a disastrous tour of Australia, where they lost all five Tests and all six one-day matches against the powerful home team. Their board were so undecided over the captaincy that it was only a week before the First Test when Carl Hooper, back home almost two years after his sudden retirement from international cricket before the 1999 World Cup, was proclaimed the team's fifth leader in five years. Jimmy Adams, who had replaced Brian Lara a year earlier, was dropped after successive reversals in England and Australia, as was his deputy, opening batsman Sherwin Campbell.

Hooper's appointment created heated debate among the passionate public. Michael Holding, the outstanding fast bowler of an earlier generation and now a much respected analyst, felt so strongly that Hooper should not be elevated to lead the team immediately on returning to it that he turned down his job as television commentator for the series. However, chairman of selectors Mike Findlay reflected the majority opinion when he said that Hooper, a seasoned campaigner who made his international debut in 1987, was "the only logical choice"; and in the circumstances he handled the assignment creditably. West Indies were not overwhelmed in the Tests, which all went into the fifth day, although their deficiencies in the special demands of the one-day game were starkly exposed by their opponents' competence.

The South Africans' strengths were all-round depth, athletic fielding and obvious self-confidence. Their captain, Shaun Pollock, set a fine example. His unbeaten 106 at Bridgetown – his second Test hundred – was one of only five centuries on either side in the Tests, he headed the batting averages with 302 at 75.50, took 20 inexpensive Test wickets, and was the most economical bowler in the one-day internationals. Not only did he collect both Cable & Wireless series trophies, he also won the individual award for the outstanding player of the Tests and limited-overs games.

If wicket-keeper Mark Boucher and Lance Klusener, two of South Africa's more consistent performers, were well below their usual standard, there was not a player who did not contribute at some stage. What Jacques Kallis lacked in a Test batting average of 29.66, he made up for with fast, incisive bowling that brought him 20 wickets at 19.75, and most runs plus most wickets in the one-day series. When injury restricted Allan Donald in the Third Test and kept him out of the Fourth, Kallis filled the breach more than capably.

Slow, featureless pitches contributed to slow, low scoring in the Tests; the two sides averaged little more than two runs an over between them. South Africa's 454 in Bridgetown was the only total over 400 – and that was due to a ninth-wicket partnership of 132 between Pollock and Donald. In addition to Pollock, South Africa's Test centurions were Daryll Cullinan, who compiled two in successive matches at Port-of-Spain and Bridgetown, and Gary Kirsten, whose marathon 150 in Georgetown was followed by such a sudden decline in form that he managed only 100 more runs in nine innings.

It was an important tour for Herschelle Gibbs, only recently back after his suspension for involvement in the Cronje scandal. He secured his place as opener with a Test average of 51.55, followed by two hundreds in the shorter game. In addition, his out-fielding was dazzling, complemented for the limited-overs matches by the effervescent Jonty Rhodes. But, if his cricket reputation was enhanced, Gibbs again found himself in trouble when he and five others – Paul Adams, Justin Kemp, Andre Nel, Roger Telemachus and physiotherapist Craig Smith – were fined 10,000 rand each by the tour party's internal disciplinary committee for smoking marijuana at the team hotel in Antigua following the series-clinching victory in the Fourth Test. Nel denied the charge, saying he and Kemp were innocent bystanders, but for Gibbs it was another example of how his propensity for rashness off the field, rather than on it, remained the main threat to his career.

West Indies were again undermined by their batting's tendency to collapse under pressure. Needing 232, the lowest total of the match, to win the Second Test, they raised only 162. They were hurtling to defeat at 82 for seven in the final session of the Third Test, before the eighth-wicket pair resorted to demeaning, time-wasting methods. And their slump to 140 all out in the first innings of the Fourth inevitably led to the loss of the series, which gave South Africa the new Sir Vivian Richards Trophy. West Indies' highest total in seven one-day internationals was 220 for eight and they were dismissed for less than 200 three times.

The leading batsmen, Lara and Hooper, occasionally produced innings of note, but the solitary hundred in either form of the game was wicket-keeper Ridley Jacobs's 113 not out at Bridgetown, his first for West Indies. It was an overdue reward for a wholehearted cricketer who had run out of partners in the previous Test when seven short of the landmark. West Indies could take some comfort from the batting of 21-year-old Chris Gayle, the tall, left-handed opener, and Ramnaresh Sarwan and Marlon Samuels, two stylish young right-handers, both 20. Their inconsistency could be attributed to their inexperience.

The bowling was unusually, and beneficially, balanced by the inclusion of leg-spinner Dinanath Ramnarine for all five Tests, and the addition of left-arm spinner Neil McGarrell for the Fourth, when West Indies fielded only two fast bowlers for the first time since Kerry Packer hired the best for his World Series Cricket in 1977-78. Ramnarine, with only three previous Tests to his name, took 20 wickets and lent a variety long lacking.

Even so, Courtney Walsh was again the spearhead in what was his farewell series. As tireless and uncomplaining as always, the 38-year-old sent down an average of 53 overs a Test, conceded only 1.86 runs an over and took 25 wickets at 19.68, carrying his final record to 519 from 132 Tests. His 45 overs in the first innings at Bridgetown were the most he had bowled in a single innings. It was proper that he should have been on the winning side in his final Test, on his home ground of Sabina Park. West Indies will naturally suffer from Walsh's absence, but Merv Dillon showed continuing signs of eventually becoming a worthy replacement, claiming 20 wickets.

Large, enthusiastic crowds for the Tests and one-day internationals once more dispelled the notion that the game was losing popularity in the West Indies in the face of competition from televised American sports. But public patience was being tested by the continuing sequence of defeats.

SOUTH AFRICAN TOURING PARTY

S. M. Pollock (KwaZulu-Natal) (*captain*), M. V. Boucher (Border) (*vice-captain*), P. R. Adams (Western Province), N. Boje (Free State), D. J. Cullinan (Gauteng), H. H. Dippenaar (Free State), A. A. Donald (Free State), H. H. Gibbs (Western Province), J. H. Kallis (Western Province), J. M. Kemp (Eastern Province), G. Kirsten (Western Province), L. Klusener (KwaZulu-Natal), N. D. McKenzie (Northerns), A. Nel (Easterns), M. Ntini (Border).

R. Telemachus (Western Province) joined the squad after completing his provincial commitments, and J. L. Ontong (Boland) and J. N. Rhodes (KwaZulu-Natal) arrived for the one-day series. Adams, originally due to leave after the Tests, along with Cullinan, stayed on to replace the injured Boje when his initial replacement, G. H. Bodi (KwaZulu-Natal), was injured before setting out.

Manager: Goolam Rajah. *Coach:* G. X. Ford.

SOUTH AFRICAN TOUR RESULTS

Test matches – Played 5: Won 2, Lost 1, Drawn 2.
First-class matches – Played 7: Won 2, Lost 1, Drawn 4.
Wins – West Indies (2).
Loss – West Indies.
Draws – West Indies (2), Busta Cup XI, WICB President's XI.
One-day internationals – Played 7: Won 5, Lost 2.
Other non-first-class matches – Played 3: Won 2, Drawn 1. *Wins* – University of the West Indies Vice-Chancellor's XI, Jamaica. *Draw* – Jamaica.

TEST MATCH AVERAGES

WEST INDIES – BATTING

	T	*I*	*NO*	*R*	*HS*	*100s*	*50s*	*Avge*	*Ct*
R. D. Jacobs	5	10	4	317	113*	1	2	52.83	21
B. C. Lara	5	10	0	400	91	0	3	40.00	5
C. L. Hooper	5	10	1	358	74	0	4	39.77	6
C. H. Gayle	5	10	0	326	81	0	1	32.60	7
R. R. Sarwan	4	8	0	238	91	0	1	29.75	3
M. N. Samuels	4	8	0	206	59	0	2	25.75	2
S. Chanderpaul	2	4	0	70	40	0	0	17.50	0
W. W. Hinds	4	8	0	133	56	0	1	16.62	4
D. Ramnarine	5	9	2	79	35*	0	0	11.28	2
M. Dillon	5	9	1	84	24	0	0	10.50	5
C. A. Walsh	5	8	2	21	4*	0	0	3.50	1
N. A. M. McLean	2	4	0	11	6	0	0	2.75	1

Played in two Tests: C. E. Cuffy 4, 3, 13* (1 ct). Played in one Test: L. V. Garrick 0, 27 (2 ct); N. C. McGarrell 0, 6.

* *Signifies not out.*

BOWLING

	O	*M*	*R*	*W*	*BB*	*5W/i*	*Avge*
C. A. Walsh	263.4	87	492	25	6-61	1	19.68
N. C. McGarrell	58	22	113	5	4-72	0	22.60
M. Dillon	168	31	512	20	4-32	0	25.60
D. Ramnarine	290.3	93	617	20	5-78	1	30.85
N. A. M. McLean	66.5	6	236	6	3-60	0	39.33
C. L. Hooper	158	47	283	5	2-49	0	56.60

Also bowled: C. E. Cuffy 67–20–170–4; C. H. Gayle 1–0–3–0; W. W. Hinds 18.3–5–50–3; M. N. Samuels 7–1–15–0; R. R. Sarwan 1–0–4–0.

SOUTH AFRICA – BATTING

	T	*I*	*NO*	*R*	*HS*	*100s*	*50s*	*Avge*	*Ct*
S. M. Pollock	5	9	5	302	106*	1	0	75.50	4
H. H. Gibbs	5	10	1	464	87	0	4	51.55	2
D. J. Cullinan	5	10	1	459	134	2	2	51.00	10
N. D. McKenzie	5	9	0	301	72	0	2	33.44	7
J. H. Kallis	5	10	1	267	53	0	3	29.66	4
G. Kirsten	5	10	0	250	150	1	0	25.00	6
N. Boje	4	7	1	106	36	0	0	17.66	4
M. V. Boucher	5	9	0	126	52	0	1	14.00	18
L. Klusener	5	9	1	75	31*	0	0	9.37	2
A. A. Donald	4	7	1	51	37	0	0	8.50	1
M. Ntini	4	5	1	23	11	0	0	5.75	1

Played in two Tests: J. M. Kemp 16, 0, 0 (2 ct). Played in one Test: P. R. Adams 3, 4 (1 ct).

* *Signifies not out.*

BOWLING

	O	*M*	*R*	*W*	*BB*	*5W/i*	*Avge*
J. H. Kallis	189.4	67	395	20	6-67	1	19.75
S. M. Pollock	228.1	77	464	20	5-28	1	23.20
A. A. Donald	147	47	355	14	4-54	0	25.35
L. Klusener	118	49	219	8	3-15	0	27.37
N. Boje	176.5	51	442	15	4-17	0	29.46
M. Ntini	98	24	296	7	2-56	0	42.28

Also bowled: P. R. Adams 32.5–8–97–2; J. M. Kemp 48–17–99–3.

Note: Matches in this section which were not first-class are signified by a dagger.

At Everest CC, Georgetown, March 4, 5, 6. Drawn. Toss: South Africans. South Africans 271 for nine dec. (H. H. Gibbs 36, J. H. Kallis 45, M. V. Boucher 56; R. O. Hinds three for 48) and 289 for seven dec. (G. Kirsten 55, M. V. Boucher 48, L. Klusener 60, N. Boje 30 not out; S. J. Benn four for 111); Busta Cup XI 196 (D. Ganga 80, S. L. Campbell 55; M. Ntini four for 31) and 155 for four (D. Ganga 35, S. L. Campbell 86).

WEST INDIES v SOUTH AFRICA

First Test Match

At Georgetown, March 9, 10, 11, 12, 13. Drawn. Toss: West Indies.

Neither team could make enough headway on a slow, true pitch to claim an advantage. South Africa gained a first-innings lead of 28, thanks to Kirsten's 150, but there was encouragement for the home crowd when Hooper, in his first Test as captain, and Sarwan, both Guyanese, accelerated in a partnership of 89 to set up West Indies' declaration on the last morning. It offered South Africa a target of 306 and the West Indian bowlers 76 overs to press for victory. Neither was a genuine possibility. South Africa batted through without anxiety, losing only two wickets as Gibbs regained form and confidence; West Indies ended a run of seven Test defeats.

Hooper, whose contentious appointment was made only a week earlier, received a rapturous reception on the ground where he had played since he was a teenager, one of many banners proclaiming him "His Royal Majesty, the Captain". After he chose to bat, Gayle, in his first Test for nine months, and Samuels, promoted to No. 3 in his fourth Test, established a promising foundation. Gayle struck the ball with fierce power, especially through the off side, and had 14 fours in his 81 when he slashed at Kallis to give Boucher his 150th dismissal in his 38th Test, beating Rod Marsh's record of 39.

West Indies passed 200 with only three wickets down. But Lara's wild slog at Klusener's off-cutter sent a steepling catch to mid-off and triggered a collapse of four for 22 in the final session. Hooper was the one remaining batsman, and next morning he found a dogged partner in Dillon, who stayed with him for almost two hours as they added 62. The captain was last out for 69, a responsible three-and-a-half-hour innings that enhanced his position.

When South Africa replied, Gibbs was out early, but a stand of 146 between Kirsten and Kallis established a strong base. They were separated an hour and a half into the third day, Kallis unluckily ruled lbw to a ball from McLean that clipped his bat's inside edge. Either side of lunch, Ramnarine, in his first Test since recovering from a shoulder operation a year earlier, tilted the balance by dismissing Cullinan and McKenzie. He might also have had Boucher, who when two lobbed a leg-break between extra cover and mid-off. Disregarding that alarm, Boucher helped add 76 before Kirsten finally fell to a tired shot just ahead of tea, top-edging his attempted cut off Walsh to the keeper. His 12th Test hundred had brought him level with Cullinan again as South Africa's most prolific centurions; he was typically sound and purposeful for nearly seven and a half hours, striking a six over long-on off Ramnarine and 13 fours.

With Kirsten gone, the last five wickets managed only 58 more, whereupon Gayle and Hinds quickly erased the lead while hammering nine fours in 50 off 15 overs on the third evening. However, West Indies' progress was so slow next day that the 28 overs before lunch raised only 44 for the loss of both openers. Samuels and Lara avoided a middle-order collapse, but it was not until Hooper and Sarwan got going in the final session that a declaration came into the reckoning. Hooper survived a close lbw call to Kallis first ball and, after a cautious start, put on 62 with Sarwan in the last 11 overs of the day. Both fell next morning in the push for more quick runs, with Sarwan unwisely testing Gibbs at square leg to be run out nine short of a classy maiden hundred.

West Indies might have caused South Africa a few anxious moments had Hooper not missed a regulation catch at second slip, off Gibbs, from Dillon's fifth ball. Gibbs took full advantage to put together his highest score for South Africa since he was suspended for his part in the match-fixing affair.

Man of the Match: G. Kirsten.

Close of play: First day, West Indies 232-7 (Hooper 12*, Ramnarine 4*); Second day, South Africa 130-1 (Kirsten 80*, Kallis 39*); Third day, West Indies 50-0 (Hinds 13*, Gayle 26*); Fourth day, West Indies 286-4 (Sarwan 71*, Hooper 31*).

West Indies

W. W. Hinds c Boje b Pollock	13	– c Boucher b Donald	14
C. H. Gayle c Boucher b Kallis	81	– c Boucher b Boje	44
M. N. Samuels b Boje	40	– b Kallis	51
B. C. Lara c Donald b Klusener	47	– c Pollock b Ntini	45
R. R. Sarwan b Donald	7	– run out	91
*C. L. Hooper c Klusener b Boje	69	– c Cullinan b Boje	35
†R. D. Jacobs lbw b Donald	0	– not out	18
N. A. M. McLean b Klusener	6	– lbw b Boje	0
D. Ramnarine run out	5		
M. Dillon c Cullinan b Ntini	9		
C. A. Walsh not out	2		
B 2, l-b 12, w 2, n-b 9	25	B 10, l-b 10, w 2, n-b 8, p 5	35
1/43 (1) 2/131 (3) 3/165 (2) 4/206 (4) 5/221 (5) 6/221 (7) 7/228 (8) 8/238 (9) 9/300 (10) 10/304 (6)	304	1/51 (1) 2/78 (2) 3/147 (4) 4/210 (3) 5/299 (6) 6/333 (5) 7/333 (8)	(7 wkts dec.) 333

Bowling: *First Innings*—Donald 23–9–43–2; Pollock 18–2–54–1; Ntini 12–2–48–1; Kallis 17–2–33–1; Klusener 35–14–56–2; Boje 19.1–6–56–2. *Second Innings*—Donald 20–8–51–1; Pollock 17–4–51–0; Kallis 15–2–36–1; Boje 37–13–93–3; Ntini 20–5–50–1; Klusener 8–1–27–0.

South Africa

G. Kirsten c Jacobs b Walsh	150	– c Hinds b Ramnarine	24
H. H. Gibbs b Dillon	8	– not out	83
J. H. Kallis lbw b McLean	50	– lbw b McLean	30
D. J. Cullinan c Jacobs b Ramnarine	7	– not out	4
N. D. McKenzie b Ramnarine	4		
†M. V. Boucher lbw b Walsh	52		
L. Klusener lbw b McLean	5		
N. Boje c Hinds b Dillon	15		
*S. M. Pollock not out	17		
A. A. Donald c Lara b Ramnarine	2		
M. Ntini c Jacobs b Dillon	11		
B 4, l-b 5, n-b 2	11	B 1	1
1/25 (2) 2/171 (3) 3/186 (4) 4/198 (5) 5/274 (1) 6/285 (7) 7/287 (6) 8/310 (8) 9/315 (10) 10/332 (11)	332	1/66 (1) 2/134 (3)	(2 wkts) 142

Bowling: *First Innings*—Walsh 28–7–56–2; Dillon 27–5–64–3; McLean 22–0–75–2; Ramnarine 41–9–105–3; Hooper 8–0–21–0; Samuels 1–0–2–0. *Second Innings*—Walsh 10–3–19–0; Dillon 5–1–21–0; Ramnarine 27.3–14–46–1; McLean 10–3–25–1; Hooper 14–8–23–0; Sarwan 1–0–4–0; Samuels 2–0–3–0.

Umpires: J. H. Hampshire (England) and E. A. Nicholls.
Third umpire: C. Alfred. Referee: M. H. Denness (England).

WEST INDIES v SOUTH AFRICA

Second Test Match

At Port-of-Spain, March 17, 18, 19, 20, 21. South Africa won by 69 runs. Toss: South Africa.

The promise of a home victory attracted a last-day crowd of 12,000. West Indies started at 32 for one, requiring another 200 to go one up in the series, but lost four for 19 at the start and five for 19 either side of tea to fall well short. In between, Hooper and Sarwan had raised local hopes with a sixth-wicket partnership of 92, but the captain was eventually left stranded and forlorn. For West Indians, and Trinidadians in particular, it was a disappointing finale to what was billed as the Golden Test; Queen's Park Oval was staging its 50th Test, the eighth ground – and first outside England and Australia – to reach its half-century.

The match itself had a golden moment, midway through, when Walsh became the first player to take 500 Test wickets. There were immediate and emotional celebrations. His team-mates formed a guard of honour as they filed off at tea, when the first man to greet him was Donald, his South African counterpart, who also paid tribute after play as the West Indies Cricket Board presented Walsh with a trophy.

A slow, if true, pitch did not encourage free strokeplay. It was at its liveliest on the opening morning – Kirsten and Gibbs did well to survive, only to perish immediately after lunch – but in the afternoon session Kallis and Cullinan, with deliberate aggression, put on 99 in better than even time. To counter the assault, Hooper turned to Hinds to trundle his medium-pace for the first time in Tests. His third legitimate delivery did the trick, Kallis punching back a drive that Hinds held inches from the pitch. He also removed Boucher and, although Cullinan advanced to his 13th Test hundred, pulling ahead of Kirsten again, the innings never regained momentum. Cullinan, eighth out, had hit 14 fours by the time he top-edged a sweep off Ramnarine to mid-on; the last five wickets tumbled for 30.

On the second day, West Indies often appeared to be gaining the ascendancy, only for Donald to intervene. He removed Samuels and Hinds, after they had added 70 for the second wicket, then Sarwan and Hooper, who put on 75 for the fifth. Ntini accounted for Lara – an edged drive to slip – and West Indies began the third day 36 in arrears with only Jacobs and three bowlers remaining. A ninth-wicket stand of 71 between the doughty keeper and Dillon gave them a first-innings lead for the first time in the eight Tests between the countries. But Jacobs's maiden hundred again proved elusive; he was seven short, after nearly four chanceless hours, when Walsh was run out attempting to give him the strike.

Walsh was not long exacting retribution, striking twice in three balls in his historic seventh over. Kirsten became his 499th victim and a dubious lbw decision made Kallis his 500th. But any further advance was halted by a 149-run partnership between Gibbs and Cullinan, who stayed together until 20 minutes before lunch on the fourth day, when Cullinan skied Ramnarine to cover. Gibbs quickly followed and, after McKenzie and Boucher had put on 49, the new ball saw off the remaining five wickets for 34. Walsh picked off the last three to finish with six for 61 – his first return of five or more in an innings in his 14th and final Test at Queen's Park.

West Indies needed 232 to win, the lowest total of the match. But Ntini struck a vital blow on the final morning when he had Lara lbw for his first Test duck on his home ground, leaving them 51 for five. Hooper and Sarwan kept the contest alive with composed batting until Sarwan was lured into hooking Kallis's third bouncer of the penultimate over before tea, straight to square leg. Jacobs was run out by Gibbs's direct hit soon afterwards, and there was nothing Hooper could do to halt the slide as South Africa hurried to victory.

Man of the Match: D. J. Cullinan.

Close of play: First day, West Indies 2-0 (Hinds 0*, Gayle 0*); Second day, West Indies 250-7 (Jacobs 26*, Ramnarine 2*); Third day, South Africa 130-2 (Gibbs 57*, Cullinan 41*); Fourth day, West Indies 32-1 (Gayle 18*, Ramnarine 11*).

South Africa

H. H. Gibbs b Walsh	34	– c sub (S. Chanderpaul) b Walsh	87
G. Kirsten c Hooper b McLean	23	– c Jacobs b Walsh	22
J. H. Kallis c and b Hinds	53	– lbw b Walsh	0
D. J. Cullinan c Dillon b Ramnarine	103	– c Lara b Ramnarine	73
N. D. McKenzie c Gayle b Walsh	9	– c Jacobs b Dillon	25
†M. V. Boucher c Hooper b Hinds	16	– (7) b Dillon	38
L. Klusener c Jacobs b Ramnarine	15	– (6) c Gayle b Dillon	5
N. Boje c Jacobs b Ramnarine	3	– c Jacobs b Walsh	9
*S. M. Pollock not out	15	– b Walsh	8
A. A. Donald c Jacobs b McLean	0	– lbw b Walsh	1
M. Ntini c and b McLean	7	– not out	5
N-b 8	8	B 1, l-b 4, n-b 9	14
1/62 (2) 2/62 (1) 3/161 (3) 4/189 (5) 5/221 (6) 6/256 (7) 7/264 (8) 8/265 (4) 9/266 (10) 10/286 (11)	286	1/38 (2) 2/38 (3) 3/187 (4) 4/198 (1) 5/204 (6) 6/253 (5) 7/264 (7) 8/276 (8) 9/278 (10) 10/287 (9)	287

Bowling: *First Innings*—Walsh 21–5–47–2; Dillon 17–2–74–0; McLean 16.5–2–60–3; Ramnarine 18–6–57–3; Hooper 9–1–25–0; Hinds 5–0–23–2. *Second Innings*—Walsh 36.4–13–61–6; McLean 18–1–76–0; Dillon 28–8–58–3; Ramnarine 35–8–64–1; Hooper 13–4–23–0.

West Indies

W. W. Hinds c Boucher b Donald	56	– lbw b Kallis	2
C. H. Gayle lbw b Pollock	10	– c Boucher b Pollock	23
M. N. Samuels c Klusener b Donald	35	– (4) c Kallis b Donald	9
B. C. Lara c Kallis b Ntini	12	– (5) lbw b Ntini	0
R. R. Sarwan c Cullinan b Donald	34	– (6) c Boje b Kallis	39
*C. L. Hooper lbw b Donald	53	– (7) not out	54
†R. D. Jacobs not out	93	– (8) run out	4
N. A. M. McLean c Ntini b Pollock	3	– (9) c Boucher b Kallis	2
D. Ramnarine b Pollock	2	– (3) c Kallis b Donald	11
M. Dillon b Ntini	21	– lbw b Kallis	0
C. A. Walsh run out	0	– b Pollock	0
B 9, l-b 4, w 3, n-b 7	23	B 7, l-b 4, n-b 7	18
1/24 (2) 2/94 (3) 3/118 (1) 4/123 (4) 5/198 (5) 6/235 (6) 7/242 (8) 8/250 (9) 9/321 (10) 10/342 (11)	342	1/20 (1) 2/35 (3) 3/50 (4) 4/50 (2) 5/51 (5) 6/143 (6) 7/150 (8) 8/159 (9) 9/159 (10) 10/162 (11)	162

Bowling: *First Innings*—Donald 30–6–91–4; Pollock 28–11–55–3; Ntini 16–4–56–2; Kallis 21–10–44–0; Boje 19–2–65–0; Klusener 11–5–18–0. *Second Innings*—Donald 15–4–32–2; Pollock 23.1–8–35–2; Kallis 16–6–40–4; Ntini 16–4–22–1; Klusener 10–5–22–0.

Umpires: D. B. Hair (Australia) and B. R. Doctrove.
Third umpire: C. E. Cumberbatch. Referee: M. H. Denness (England).

At Bridgetown, March 24, 25, 26. Drawn. Toss: South Africans. South Africans 270 (N. D. McKenzie 58, S. M. Pollock 79, Extras 34; C. E. Cuffy three for 38, C. E. L. Stuart four for 57) and 143 for two dec. (H. H. Gibbs 55, H. H. Dippenaar 38 not out); WICB President's XI 186 (D. Ganga 43, R. L. Powell 47; A. Nel three for 53, N. Boje three for 11) and 84 for one (D. Ganga 33 not out).

WEST INDIES v SOUTH AFRICA

Third Test Match

At Bridgetown, March 29, 30, 31, April 1, 2. Drawn. Toss: West Indies.

As the prospect of defeat unexpectedly crept up on West Indies in the last session of the match, Dillon and Ramnarine resorted to blatant time-wasting. With seven wickets down and only Cuffy and Walsh to come, they stretched out the last five overs from Boje and Klusener for 25 minutes. Ramnarine called for on-field physiotherapy for a supposed hamstring strain, Dillon changed his boots, and there were other delays that brought a warning from umpire Bucknor.

Referee Mike Denness took no action after meeting the two players and team officials. But Pollock revealed that some senior West Indians had apologised to him. South African board president Percy Sonn called the tactics "a disgrace", and the West Indian board later issued a statement condemning them. It was an unsatisfactory end to a fluctuating contest featuring vital late-order hundreds from Pollock and Jacobs.

Sent in, South Africa lost Kirsten third ball and were 70 for three at lunch. Cullinan, who reached his 14th hundred – his second in successive Tests – before the close, and McKenzie stabilised the innings with a partnership of 149 in three hours, benefiting at times from inept West Indian fielding. Eventually Hooper called on Hinds, his stand-breaker of the Second Test, and again he obliged: in his second over, McKenzie pulled a long hop into square leg's hands. Boucher went cheaply, but Cullinan and Boje batted through to the close and next morning carried their stand to 76. Cullinan was badly dropped by Lara at deep mid-wicket off Hooper at 122, but not long after gave a low return catch to Dillon. He had hit 15 fours, one all-run, in just over six hours. Boje followed one run later and South Africa were faltering at 315 for eight when Klusener failed again.

Pollock and Donald restored their advantage with a partnership of 132, doubling South Africa's ninth-wicket record against West Indies. Pollock, missed at slip off Walsh when 46, gave the lead, while Donald lent sensible support for three and a half hours, compiling his highest Test score. When Donald finally edged Walsh to second slip, Pollock was 99; he completed his hundred next ball with a single off Ramnarine and remained unbeaten after four hours, with 13 fours. Having gone 50 Tests before scoring his first hundred, he now had two in four matches.

[*Touchline Photo/Getty Images*

Nothing more than a watching brief for Ridley Jacobs as Daryll Cullinan on-drives Dinanath Ramnarine on his way to his 14th Test hundred.

To the noisy delight of a packed Saturday crowd, Lara and Hooper gave the West Indian reply substance after an uncertain start, stroking 17 fours between them as they added 116. Kallis shifted the balance once more by removing both, with Lara miscuing a pull to mid-on late in the day and Hooper caught behind next morning – at the end of an opening over interrupted for half an hour while the bowlers' footholes were repaired. Now, with West Indies still 202 runs behind, Jacobs emulated Pollock's role for South Africa. Reprieved by Cullinan at first slip, on 25 and 56, he was assisted by Dillon and Ramnarine in successive stands yielding 101, to which they contributed 20. He was 89 when Ramnarine was out but went to his maiden Test hundred – and West Indies' first against South Africa – with a top-edged hook off Ntini, his fourth six. Jacobs also struck 11 fours and remained unbeaten when Kallis ended the innings with his sixth wicket.

West Indies' deficit was 67, but they had given themselves the chance of an unlikely victory when they reduced South Africa to 97 for six on the final morning. Once again, Cullinan and Pollock dashed their hopes by adding 70 over an hour and three-quarters. By the time Ramnarine removed Cullinan and Donald with successive balls, for his first five-wicket return in a Test innings, Pollock could declare with a lead of 264 and a minimum 36 overs remaining. Gayle lashed 11 fours in a 39-ball 48, but no one else reached double figures. As Boje and Klusener found turn on the worn pitch, the West Indians' slapdash approach to batting almost cost them the match. As it was, survival was guaranteed by gamesmanship at the expense of sportsmanship.

Man of the Match: D. J. Cullinan.

Close of play: First day, South Africa 244-5 (Cullinan 108*, Boje 3*); Second day, West Indies 7-0 (Hinds 0*, Gayle 5*); Third day, West Indies 252-5 (Hooper 74*, Jacobs 14*); Fourth day, South Africa 52-3 (Cullinan 12*, Kallis 5*).

South Africa

G. Kirsten c Gayle b Walsh	0	(2) c Samuels b Cuffy	0
H. H. Gibbs c Hooper b Dillon	34	(1) c Sarwan b Hooper	19
J. H. Kallis c Jacobs b Dillon	11	(5) c Sarwan b Hooper	20
D. J. Cullinan c and b Dillon	134	c Lara b Ramnarine	82
N. D. McKenzie c Dillon b Hinds	72	(3) c Jacobs b Ramnarine	12
†M. V. Boucher c Jacobs b Cuffy	3	(7) c Jacobs b Ramnarine	0
N. Boje c Ramnarine b Dillon	34	(9) not out	9
L. Klusener b Walsh	1	(6) c Cuffy b Ramnarine	4
*S. M. Pollock not out	106	(8) c Hooper b Walsh	40
A. A. Donald c Hooper b Walsh	37	lbw b Ramnarine	0
M. Ntini c and b Ramnarine	0		
B 6, l-b 4, w 2, n-b 10	22	L-b 3, n-b 8	11
1/0 (1) 2/53 (2) 3/58 (3) 4/207 (5) 5/230 (6) 6/306 (4) 7/307 (7) 8/315 (8) 9/447 (10) 10/454 (11)	454	1/2 (2) 2/31 (1) 3/36 (3) 4/80 (5) 5/95 (6) 6/97 (7) 7/167 (8) 8/197 (4) 9/197 (10)	(9 wkts dec.) 197

Bowling: *First Innings*—Walsh 45–15–87–3; Dillon 34–1–147–4; Cuffy 30–7–71–1; Ramnarine 33.1–6–86–1; Hooper 18–5–31–0; Hinds 10–5–13–1; Samuels 2–0–6–0; Gayle 1–0–3–0. *Second Innings*—Walsh 14–3–28–1; Cuffy 10–4–28–1; Hooper 34–12–49–2; Dillon 4–2–7–0; Ramnarine 31.5–10–78–5; Samuels 2–1–4–0.

West Indies

W. W. Hinds c Boucher b Kallis	2	(2) c Cullinan b Boje	8
C. H. Gayle c Cullinan b Ntini	40	(1) c Boucher b Kallis	48
M. N. Samuels c McKenzie b Kallis	6	c Cullinan b Boje	3
B. C. Lara c Boje b Kallis	83	b Klusener	8
R. R. Sarwan c Gibbs b Ntini	16	b Kallis	0
*C. L. Hooper c Boucher b Kallis	74	c Boucher b Boje	5
†R. D. Jacobs not out	113	c McKenzie b Boje	1
M. Dillon b Boje	14	not out	2
D. Ramnarine lbw b Boje	6	not out	0
C. E. Cuffy lbw b Kallis	4		
C. A. Walsh b Kallis	4		
B 4, l-b 9, n-b 12	25	B 8, l-b 1, n-b 4	13
1/37 (1) 2/49 (2) 3/57 (3) 4/102 (5) 5/218 (4) 6/252 (6) 7/316 (8) 8/353 (9) 9/381 (10) 10/387 (11)	387	1/34 (2) 2/59 (3) 3/64 (1) 4/64 (5) 5/72 (6) 6/82 (7) 7/82 (4)	(7 wkts) 88

Bowling: *First Innings*—Donald 14–7–30–0; Pollock 35–11–84–0; Kallis 36–17–67–6; Ntini 28–7–93–2; Boje 28–7–67–2; Klusener 10–3–33–0. *Second Innings*—Pollock 5–0–25–0; Kallis 8–1–34–2; Boje 16.4–10–17–4; Klusener 9–7–3–1.

Umpires: D. B. Hair (Australia) and S. A. Bucknor.
Third umpire: H. Moore. Referee: M. H. Denness (England).

WEST INDIES v SOUTH AFRICA

Fourth Test Match

At St John's, April 6, 7, 8, 9, 10. South Africa won by 82 runs. Toss: West Indies. Test debut: N. C. McGarrell.

South Africa claimed the series and the new Sir Vivian Richards Trophy just before tea on the last day. Whereas the victors had fought back from difficult positions in both innings, only Lara could respond for West Indies, and his blazing second-innings 91 was too little, too late.

The assertion of the chief groundsman, Keith Frederick, that "as a true West Indian" he had prepared a spinners' pitch indicated a change of priorities. Once, such a statement would have been seditious; now, it prompted the introduction of Neil McGarrell, the 28-year-old Guyanese slow left-armer, alongside leg-spinner Ramnarine. That reduced the attack to two fast bowlers for the first time since the Packer schism of 1977-78. The selectors also replaced Samuels with the experienced Chanderpaul, while South Africa made one enforced change, Kemp replacing the injured Donald.

Hooper's decision to bowl first – rather than offering his spinners the chance of a fourth-innings pitch – seemed to defy logic, but was no longer questioned when South Africa were 152 for seven at tea, six of the wickets falling to spin. McGarrell claimed four, including a spell of three for seven in 23 balls. Only Gibbs, whose 85 included two sixes and 12 fours, had batted with conviction, and when he was seventh out, to Jacobs's tumbling catch from a gloved sweep off Hooper, West Indies held the initiative. However, the consistent Pollock and Boje regrouped, adding 75 before Walsh gained an lbw decision against Boje next morning. The value of their stand, and of Pollock's unbeaten innings after four hours of defiance, was clear when West Indies collapsed for 140 against South Africa's varied attack. Their last four wickets went for ten runs in 13.1 overs on the third morning, and their troubles worsened when they took the field again. Dillon went off after bowling three balls, having sprained his right thumb in a collision with Lara.

Kirsten failed again, but Gibbs and McKenzie put on 78 for the second wicket as West Indies, 107 behind on first innings, were reduced to defensive tactics. By the close, South Africa had extended their lead to 229 with seven wickets remaining, a strong position on a dry, unpredictable pitch. The West Indians came back into contention by taking four for 34 in the first 17 overs on the fourth morning, with the indomitable Walsh claiming three. He would have had another if Gayle had held Kallis, then two, at slip. It proved a crucial miss: Kallis and Pollock carefully restored the balance with an unbroken partnership of 59 that allowed Pollock to declare, giving his bowlers a minimum of 131 overs while challenging the West Indians to score 323 to level the series.

With Boje and Klusener coaxing sharp turn from the dry pitch in their contrasting styles, batting was difficult. By the close, West Indies were already four down. Lara and Sarwan kept the South Africans at bay for most of the final morning, but Pollock's decision to take over from Klusener virtually settled the issue. He dismissed Sarwan and Jacobs in the third over of his spell and, after lunch, McGarrell in the ninth. That sparked a thrilling onslaught of 61 in 84 balls from Lara, who hoisted four leg-side sixes off Boje – visibly furious when a top-edged sweep was dropped by Ntini. Lara had repeatedly shown that, in such a mood, nothing was beyond him. But this time his threat was ended by the new ball; he mistimed a drive off Kallis and was caught at extra cover. Eleven balls later, Ramnarine sliced Kallis to gully, and South Africa had become only the second team in 28 years, after Australia in 1994-95, to win a Test series in the Caribbean.

Man of the Match: S. M. Pollock.

Close of play: First day, South Africa 210-7 (Pollock 36*, Boje 28*); Second day, West Indies 130-6 (Hooper 16*, Jacobs 1*); Third day, South Africa 122-3 (McKenzie 44*, Cullinan 17*); Fourth day, West Indies 101-4 (Lara 5*, Sarwan 4*).

South Africa

G. Kirsten c Dillon b McGarrell	8	– (2) c Sarwan b Walsh	9
H. H. Gibbs c Jacobs b Hooper	85	– (1) c Gayle b Ramnarine	45
J. H. Kallis b Dillon	5	– (6) not out	30
D. J. Cullinan c Lara b Ramnarine	4	– (5) c Gayle b McGarrell	28
N. D. McKenzie c Jacobs b McGarrell	35	– (3) b Walsh	44
L. Klusener lbw b McGarrell	0	– (7) c Hinds b Walsh	1
†M. V. Boucher c Gayle b McGarrell	1	– (8) c Jacobs b Walsh	3
*S. M. Pollock not out	48	– (9) not out	41
N. Boje lbw b Walsh	36	– (4) c sub (S. C. Joseph) b Hooper	0
J. M. Kemp b Dillon	16		
M. Ntini b Dillon	0		
B 2, l-b 5, n-b 2	9	B 6, l-b 3, w 4, n-b 1	14
1/29 (1) 2/35 (3) 3/53 (4) 4/120 (5) 5/126 (6) 6/136 (7) 7/148 (2) 8/223 (9) 9/247 (10) 10/247 (11)	247	1/17 (2) 2/95 (1) 3/96 (4) 4/123 (3) 5/135 (5) 6/146 (7) 7/156 (8) (7 wkts dec.)	215

Bowling: *First Innings*—Walsh 31–14–45–1; Dillon 18.2–4–47–3; McGarrell 43–19–72–4; Ramnarine 20–6–45–1; Hooper 10–2–31–1. *Second Innings*—Walsh 38–13–56–4; Dillon 0.3–0–3–0; Hinds 3.3–0–14–0; McGarrell 15–3–41–1; Hooper 24–7–37–1; Ramnarine 42–24–55–1.

West Indies

C. H. Gayle c Pollock b Kallis	11	– c McKenzie b Boje	12
W. W. Hinds c Boucher b Pollock	9	– c Kirsten b Boje	29
S. Chanderpaul c Cullinan b Kemp	40	– lbw b Boje	16
B. C. Lara c McKenzie b Kemp	19	– (5) c McKenzie b Kallis	91
R. R. Sarwan c Boje b Kallis	25	– (6) c Boucher b Pollock	26
*C. L. Hooper c Kirsten b Klusener	17	– (4) c McKenzie b Klusener	21
M. Dillon b Klusener	0	– (9) c Cullinan b Boje	1
†R. D. Jacobs not out	3	– (7) c Kirsten b Pollock	0
N. C. McGarrell lbw b Klusener	0	– (8) c Kemp b Pollock	6
D. Ramnarine run out	2	– c Kirsten b Kallis	9
C. A. Walsh lbw b Pollock	4	– not out	4
B 3, l-b 3, n-b 4	10	B 18, l-b 3, n-b 4	25
1/13 (1) 2/21 (2) 3/50 (4) 4/88 (5) 5/126 (3) 6/127 (7) 7/132 (6) 8/134 (9) 9/136 (10) 10/140 (11)	140	1/36 (1) 2/56 (2) 3/86 (4) 4/89 (3) 5/138 (6) 6/138 (7) 7/155 (8) 8/176 (9) 9/229 (5) 10/240 (10)	240

Bowling: *First Innings*—Pollock 22.1–11–25–2; Kallis 17–8–24–2; Ntini 6–2–27–0; Kemp 8–2–17–2; Boje 12–4–26–0; Klusener 11–4–15–3. *Second Innings*—Pollock 19–5–41–3; Kallis 15.4–6–23–2; Boje 45–9–118–4; Kemp 6–3–7–0; Klusener 14–6–30–1.

Umpires: S. Venkataraghavan (India) and E. A. Nicholls.
Third umpire: P. C. Whyte. Referee: M. H. Denness (England).

†At Montserrat, April 12. South Africans won by four wickets. Toss: South Africans. University of the West Indies Vice-Chancellor's XI 218 (47.5 overs) (D. Ganga 45, S. Chanderpaul 70, Extras 38; J. M. Kemp three for 35); South Africans 222 for six (48 overs) (G. Kirsten 39, H. H. Dippenaar 52, L. Klusener 41, S. M. Pollock 37 not out).

Curtly Ambrose came out of retirement to bowl 6–1–17–0 for the Vice-Chancellor's XI.

†At Montego Bay, April 15, 16. Drawn. Toss: South Africans. South Africans 199 for nine dec. (J. H. Kallis 30, L. Klusener 41; A. A. Sanson three for 28); Jamaica 380 for six (L. V. Garrick 174 not out, M. N. Samuels 84, N. O. Perry 66 not out).

WEST INDIES v SOUTH AFRICA

Fifth Test Match

At Kingston, April 19, 20, 21, 22, 23. West Indies won by 130 runs. Toss: West Indies. Test debut: L. V. Garrick.

For West Indies, a welcome, deserved and hard-fought win was their first in 14 Tests since Birmingham the previous June. For South Africa, it was their first loss in 13 Tests since Galle in July. Victory was a fitting gift for Walsh in his last Test, and his six wickets carried his series total to 25, more than anyone else on either side. They also lifted his Test record to 519.

[*Duif du Toit, Touchline Photo/Getty Images*

South African captain and fellow fast bowler Shaun Pollock congratulates Courtney Walsh after he ended his Test career on a fitting note, having taken six wickets in West Indies' victory at his home ground, Sabina Park.

In spite of a pitch Pollock rated the best of the series, with "bounce and carry" similar to those in South Africa, the scoring was again slow and low. There were no centuries and only six batsmen reached 50. West Indies coach Roger Harper said that, for the first time, his team had come very close to playing to their full capacity over all five days. Yet they started badly. Leon Garrick, rushed into the squad on the eve of the Test to replace Hinds, on the basis of an unbeaten 174 for Jamaica against the tourists, took the first ball – and cut it straight to gully. He thus became the second debutant, after Jimmy Cook, for South Africa against India at Durban in 1992-93, to fall to the opening delivery of a Test.

After that, only Lara of the top order batted with authority against the persistent pace attack. In three and three-quarter hours, he struck 12 fours, mainly on the off side. When he diverted an intended pull off Pollock to slip, West Indies were a shaky 167 for seven, and it needed some bold batting by Dillon and Ramnarine, who hit a Test-best 35 not out, to push the total past 200. Pollock finished with five for 28.

Walsh, Cuffy and Dillon followed the example of the South African fast bowlers, never let the opposition get going, and had them 97 for six. McKenzie carried the fight to the West Indians for just under three hours, until he was lbw sweeping Ramnarine, but no one else stayed more than an hour and a half. Pollock became the first South African to complete the Test double of 2,000 runs and 200 wickets, but his side were dismissed for 141, their lowest total in the 11 Tests between these countries.

West Indies led by 84, but they made heavy work of building on it. The usually quick-scoring Gayle spent four and a quarter hours over 32; when he was yorked by Pollock, and Hooper fended Kallis's steep bouncer to third slip, West Indies were 126 for five. The reliable Jacobs ensured their advantage was not wasted. He added 58 with Samuels, returning for the injured Sarwan, and 45 with Dillon to stretch the lead to 339 on the third evening. He was nearing another hundred when his mistimed hook off Klusener next morning found McKenzie at deep square leg.

As Walsh emerged for his last Test innings, the South Africans formed a guard of honour. Inevitably, he did not last long, but it was long enough to receive a painful blow on the foot which temporarily forced him off after an opening burst of nine overs. His work was not yet done, however, for there was still a rare victory to be fought for; on his return, he had the dangerous Cullinan lbw with his third ball. Earlier, Dillon had removed Kirsten cheaply, and Gibbs spoiled an impressive 51 with a wild sweep at Hooper.

South Africa began the last day on 140 for three, still 246 short of their goal, and they kept the West Indians waiting until seven overs before lunch for their next wicket. Three quick strikes either side of the interval by Ramnarine eased the tension. McKenzie was the first to go, well taken at silly point, and, in the first over on resumption, Kallis played on and Boucher was caught at the wicket. Klusener and Pollock lasted half an hour before Hooper claimed the new ball, whereupon Dillon and Walsh swiftly disposed of further resistance with two more wickets apiece. Walsh's 519th and last victim was his opposite number, Donald.

Man of the Match: R. D. Jacobs.

Close of play: First day, West Indies 214-9 (Ramnarine 28*, Walsh 0*); Second day, West Indies 34-0 (Garrick 21*, Gayle 10*); Third day, West Indies 255-7 (Jacobs 67*, Ramnarine 9*); Fourth day, South Africa 140-3 (McKenzie 40*, Kallis 5*).

COURTNEY WALSH'S BOWLING RECORD IN TESTS

	T	*O*	*M*	*R*	*W*	*BB*	*5W/i*	*10W/m*	*Avge*	*S/R*
v England.	36	1,469.4	358	3,683	145	6-74	5	1	25.40	60.81
v Australia	38	1,426.4	286	3,872	135	6-54	4	0	28.68	63.40
v South Africa. .	10	471.3	140	1,010	51	6-61	2	0	19.80	55.47
v New Zealand .	10	375.2	84	943	43	7-37	3	1	21.93	52.37
v India.	15	520.4	122	1,316	65	6-62	4	1	20.24	48.06
v Pakistan	18	561.4	111	1,452	63	5-22	4	0	23.04	53.49
v Sri Lanka . . .	3	97.1	15	278	8	4-73	0	0	34.75	72.87
v Zimbabwe . . .	2	80.3	29	134	9	3-21	0	0	14.88	53.66
Totals	**132**	**5,003.1**	**1,145**	**12,688**	**519**	**7-37**	**22**	**3**	**24.44**	**57.84**

West Indies

L. V. Garrick c Pollock b Donald	0	– c Boucher b Donald	27
C. H. Gayle c Kemp b Donald	25	– b Pollock	32
S. Chanderpaul c Boucher b Kallis	7	– c Cullinan b Kemp	7
B. C. Lara c Kallis b Pollock	81	– b Adams	14
M. N. Samuels c Boucher b Donald	3	– b Pollock	59
*C. L. Hooper c Kirsten b Pollock	25	– c Pollock b Kallis	5
†R. D. Jacobs c Boucher b Pollock	0	– c McKenzie b Klusener	85
M. Dillon c Boucher b Donald	24	– c Gibbs b Pollock	13
D. Ramnarine not out	35	– c Cullinan b Pollock	9
C. E. Cuffy c Boucher b Pollock	3	– not out	13
C. A. Walsh c Adams b Pollock	4	– c Kirsten b Adams	3
B 4, l-b 12, w 2	18	B 14, l-b 13, w 4, n-b 3 . .	34
1/0 (1) 2/21 (3) 3/50 (2) 4/54 (5) 5/107 (6) 6/113 (7) 7/167 (4) 8/188 (8) 9/203 (10) 10/225 (11)	225	1/47 (1) 2/55 (3) 3/77 (4) 4/103 (2) 5/126 (6) 6/184 (5) 7/229 (8) 8/255 (9) 9/287 (7) 10/301 (11)	301

Bowling: *First Innings*—Donald 25–5–54–4; Pollock 26.5–17–28–5; Kallis 16–5–38–1; Kemp 16–3–45–0; Adams 11–1–43–0; Klusener 2–1–1–0. *Second Innings*—Donald 20–8–54–1; Pollock 34–8–66–4; Kallis 28–10–56–1; Adams 21.5–7–54–2; Kemp 18–9–30–1; Klusener 8–3–14–1.

South Africa

H. H. Gibbs c Jacobs b Cuffy	18	– (2) b Hooper	51
G. Kirsten c Gayle b Walsh	0	– (1) c Jacobs b Dillon	14
J. H. Kallis c and b Dillon	17	– (5) b Ramnarine	51
D. J. Cullinan c Lara b Cuffy	6	– lbw b Walsh	18
N. D. McKenzie lbw b Ramnarine	45	– (3) c Garrick b Ramnarine	55
L. Klusener b Walsh	13	– not out	31
†M. V. Boucher c Garrick b Walsh	13	– c Jacobs b Ramnarine	0
*S. M. Pollock c Jacobs b Dillon	24	– c Jacobs b Dillon	3
J. M. Kemp c Walsh b Dillon	0	– lbw b Walsh	0
A. A. Donald not out	1	– b Walsh	10
P. R. Adams c Hooper b Dillon	3	– c Samuels b Dillon	4
W 1	1	B 4, l-b 13, n-b 1	18
1/9 (2) 2/24 (1) 3/35 (4) 4/51 (3) 5/77 (6) 6/97 (7) 7/137 (8) 8/137 (5) 9/137 (9) 10/141 (11)	141	1/37 (1) 2/102 (2) 3/124 (4) 4/190 (3) 5/209 (5) 6/209 (7) 7/235 (8) 8/236 (9) 9/250 (10) 10/255 (11)	255

Bowling: *First Innings*—Walsh 18–8–31–3; Cuffy 17–6–58–2; Dillon 15.1–5–32–4; Ramnarine 11–4–20–1. *Second Innings*—Walsh 22–6–62–3; Cuffy 10–3–13–0; Dillon 19–3–59–3; Ramnarine 31–6–61–3; Hooper 28–8–43–1.

Umpires: S. Venkataraghavan (India) and S. A. Bucknor.
Third umpire: T. Wilson. Referee: M. H. Denness (England).

†At Kingston, April 25. South Africans won by six wickets. Toss: South Africans. Jamaica 185 (46.4 overs) (D. E. Bernard 59, R. L. Powell 52; L. Klusener five for 23); South Africans 189 for four (45.4 overs) (H. H. Gibbs 54, J. N. Rhodes 49, L. Klusener 42 not out).

†WEST INDIES v SOUTH AFRICA

First One-Day International

At Kingston, April 28. West Indies won by three wickets. Toss: West Indies. International debut: J. L. Ontong.

Jacobs steered the last ball, a full toss from Donald, to the boundary to set off wild celebrations in a capacity 15,000 crowd. Put in, South Africa had been kept in check by West Indies' spinners, and only Kirsten and Rhodes got going. The last six wickets fell for 51, leaving Pollock stranded with overs unused. After West Indies' top three went in the first 16 overs, a stand of 89 between Lara and Hooper set them on course for victory. Then Rhodes removed Lara with a brilliant low catch at point off Donald, repeating their dismissal of Gayle. When Hooper, troubled by cramp, was caught in the deep, the match was wide open again. With 16 needed from ten balls, McGarrell hoisted Kallis for a straight six, but the result still hung on the final ball.

Man of the Match: N. C. McGarrell.

South Africa

G. Kirsten b Hooper	38
H. H. Gibbs run out	8
J. H. Kallis c Cuffy b McGarrell	23
J. N. Rhodes lbw b McGarrell	36
N. D. McKenzie c Jacobs b Cuffy	21
†M. V. Boucher c and b Samuels	14
L. Klusener b McGarrell	0
*S. M. Pollock not out	26
J. L. Ontong c Powell b Hooper	11
R. Telemachus c and b Samuels	3
A. A. Donald b Dillon	3
B 1, l-b 4, w 9, n-b 3	17
1/11 2/75 3/87 4/131 5/149 6/149 7/159 8/179 9/184 (47.4 overs)	200

Bowling: Dillon 6.4–1–33–1; Cuffy 10–2–37–1; Jeremy 5–0–30–0; Hooper 10–1–45–2; McGarrell 10–0–32–3; Samuels 6–0–18–2.

West Indies

L. V. Garrick c Boucher b Pollock	7
C. H. Gayle c Rhodes b Donald	27
M. N. Samuels c Boucher b Kallis	17
B. C. Lara c Rhodes b Donald	54
*C. L. Hooper c Kirsten b Telemachus	43
R. L. Powell run out	6
†R. D. Jacobs not out	17
N. C. McGarrell c and b Kallis	14
M. Dillon not out	2
B 1, l-b 5, w 6, n-b 3	15
1/14 2/51 3/60 4/149 5/162 6/177 7/193 (7 wkts, 50 overs)	202

K. C. B. Jeremy and C. E. Cuffy did not bat.

Bowling: Pollock 10–1–31–1; Telemachus 9–0–38–1; Donald 10–0–40–2; Kallis 10–1–34–2; Klusener 6–1–30–0; Ontong 5–0–23–0.

Umpires: S. A. Bucknor and B. E. W. Morgan.
Third umpire: J. R. Gayle.

†WEST INDIES v SOUTH AFRICA

Second One-Day International

At St John's, May 2. South Africa won by eight wickets. Toss: South Africa.

A partnership of 179 between Gibbs and Kallis beat South Africa's second-wicket record and ensured a comfortable victory. Gibbs scored 104 from 141 balls, hitting three sixes and eight fours in his fourth hundred in one-day internationals. Kallis joined him after Cuffy bowled Kirsten with the seventh ball of an eight-over spell yielding just 17 runs. For West Indies, Gayle's fifty had laid a solid foundation, but there was little for Lara to celebrate on his 32nd birthday. Although Chanderpaul and Hooper added 86 in 78 balls, their efforts to increase the scoring-rate led to Chanderpaul's run-out just when he looked most threatening; his 60 from 54 balls contained three sixes and two fours. The remaining wickets managed only 30, leaving South Africa a target that Gibbs and Kallis found trifling.

Man of the Match: H. H. Gibbs.

West Indies

L. V. Garrick run out	16
C. H. Gayle c Pollock b Klusener	50
B. C. Lara c Pollock b Klusener	13
S. Chanderpaul run out	60
*C. L. Hooper c Ontong b Pollock	48
†R. D. Jacobs not out	13
M. N. Samuels run out	3
N. C. McGarrell b Kallis	3
N. A. M. McLean c Gibbs b Kallis	0
M. Dillon not out	1
B 1, l-b 4, w 5, n-b 3	13
1/63 2/80 3/104 4/190 5/208 6/214 7/218 8/218 (8 wkts, 50 overs)	220

C. E. Cuffy did not bat.

Bowling: Pollock 10–1–34–1; Telemachus 9–0–50–0; Donald 10–1–40–0; Kallis 10–1–38–2; Klusener 5–0–28–2; Ontong 6–0–25–0.

South Africa

H. H. Gibbs st Jacobs b McGarrell	104
G. Kirsten b Cuffy	5
J. H. Kallis not out	78
J. N. Rhodes not out	21
L-b 2, w 2, n-b 9	13
1/11 2/190 (2 wkts, 45.5 overs)	221

H. H. Dippenaar, L. Klusener, †M. V. Boucher, *S. M. Pollock, J. L. Ontong, R. Telemachus and A. A. Donald did not bat.

Bowling: Dillon 6.5–0–39–0; Cuffy 10–1–27–1; McLean 4–0–40–0; McGarrell 10–0–34–1; Hooper 10–1–42–0; Samuels 3–0–22–0; Gayle 2–0–15–0.

Umpires: C. E. Mack and B. E. W. Morgan.
Third umpire: P. C. Whyte.

†WEST INDIES v SOUTH AFRICA

Third One-Day International

At St George's, May 5. South Africa won by 132 runs. Toss: West Indies.

This was South Africa's most comprehensive victory in 21 limited-overs internationals against West Indies, who were in such confusion over selection that Hooper was quarter of an hour late for the toss. He then offered his opponents first use of an ideal pitch and fast outfield, on which they amassed 287 for four, their second-best one-day total against West Indies. Kirsten, who passed Cronje's South African record of 5,565 limited-overs runs, and Gibbs built a platform of 88 in 15 overs; Kallis built on it in stands of 90 with Rhodes and 67 with Klusener. His second six took him to his seventh one-day international hundred, in the penultimate over, and he finished with 107 off 108 balls. West Indies lost Gayle to the fourth ball of the innings, and in 39 overs never mastered South Africa's tight bowling and sharp fielding.

Man of the Match: J. H. Kallis.

South Africa

G. Kirsten run out	50	*S. M. Pollock not out	1
H. H. Gibbs c Powell b McGarrell	46	L-b 5, w 4, n-b 2	11
J. H. Kallis c and b Gayle	107		
J. N. Rhodes b Hooper	47	1/88 2/129 (4 wkts, 50 overs)	287
L. Klusener not out	25	3/219 4/286	

H. H. Dippenaar, †M. V. Boucher, J. L. Ontong, A. A. Donald and M. Ntini did not bat.

Bowling: Dillon 6–0–43–0; Cuffy 10–0–54–0; McGarrell 10–0–60–1; Hooper 10–1–32–1; Samuels 9–0–61–0; Gayle 5–0–32–1.

West Indies

C. H. Gayle c Kirsten b Pollock	1	N. C. McGarrell c and b Ontong	8
R. L. Powell c Ntini b Pollock	15	M. Dillon b Ntini	4
S. Chanderpaul c Dippenaar b Pollock	16	C. E. Cuffy not out	1
B. C. Lara b Ntini	31	L-b 2, w 5, n-b 2	9
*C. L. Hooper run out	29		
M. N. Samuels lbw b Klusener	20	1/2 2/24 3/48 (39 overs)	155
†R. D. Jacobs run out	10	4/87 5/119 6/126	
W. W. Hinds c Ntini b Ontong	11	7/133 8/146 9/153	

Bowling: Pollock 6–0–23–3; Kallis 6–0–35–0; Donald 6–0–26–0; Ntini 7–1–27–2; Klusener 7–0–30–1; Ontong 7–1–12–2.

Umpires: B. E. W. Morgan and E. A. Nicholls.
Third umpire: E. Jones.

†WEST INDIES v SOUTH AFRICA

Fourth One-Day International

At St George's, May 6. South Africa won by eight wickets. Toss: South Africa.

A capacity crowd again left disappointed as South Africa reeled off their second resounding victory in back-to-back weekend matches in Grenada. Batting first this time, West Indies mustered only 73 for four by the halfway point. Samuels played with stylish authority for 65 in 71 balls, striking eight fours and adding 67 with Hooper, but he found no other support as Donald worked his way through the line-up. Lara's 25 made him the second West Indian, after Desmond Haynes, to pass 7,000 one-day international runs. Kirsten and Dippenaar, in his first international innings of the tour, effectively determined the result with a second-wicket stand of 96; when Kirsten was out for 72, Rhodes rounded the match off with a flourish.

Man of the Match: A. A. Donald.

West Indies

C. H. Gayle c Rhodes b Kemp	9
R. L. Powell c Ntini b Kemp	7
S. Chanderpaul c Kemp b Ntini	10
B. C. Lara c Boucher b Donald	25
*C. L. Hooper c Kemp b Donald	46
M. N. Samuels lbw b Pollock	65
†R. D. Jacobs c Pollock b Ntini	8
N. C. McGarrell c Donald b Kemp	2
N. A. M. McLean c Gibbs b Donald	7
K. C. B. Jeremy not out	8
C. E. Cuffy c Boucher b Donald	3
L-b 3, w 6, n-b 1	10
1/11 2/22 3/49 4/61 5/128 6/174 7/177 8/185 9/189 (49.3 overs)	200

Bowling: Pollock 10–3–16–1; Kemp 8.5–0–54–3; Donald 9.3–1–38–4; Ntini 10–1–26–2; Klusener 6.1–0–32–0; Ontong 5–0–31–0.

South Africa

H. H. Gibbs c Chanderpaul b Jeremy	27
G. Kirsten c Powell b Hooper	72
H. H. Dippenaar not out	62
J. N. Rhodes not out	30
L-b 4, w 2, n-b 4	10
1/58 2/154 (2 wkts, 46.1 overs)	201

L. Klusener, †M. V. Boucher, J. M. Kemp, *S. M. Pollock, J. L. Ontong, A. A. Donald and M. Ntini did not bat.

Bowling: Cuffy 8–2–36–0; McLean 6–0–34–0; Jeremy 4–1–18–1; McGarrell 4.1–0–21–0; Hooper 10–1–29–1; Gayle 10–0–38–0; Samuels 4–0–21–0.

Umpires: G. A. Johnson and E. A. Nicholls.
Third umpire: E. Jones.

†WEST INDIES v SOUTH AFRICA

Fifth One-Day International

At Bridgetown, May 9. South Africa won by seven wickets. Toss: South Africa.

More inept West Indian batting allowed South Africa to clinch the series. Even though Lara hit his highest score of the season, 92 from 125 balls with nine fours, West Indies still could not raise a challenging total. Kallis took four wickets, but Pollock's economy – his ten overs cost just 23 – and Gibbs's fielding – a direct hit to run out Chanderpaul and a stunning low, right-handed catch at cover to account for Jacobs – were just as influential. Gibbs then compiled his second hundred of the series, reaching 2,000 one-day international runs in the process; three sixes and 12 fours helped him to 107 off 132 balls. As in the previous match, Dippenaar hit the winning runs, this time with more than eight overs to spare.

Man of the Match: H. H. Gibbs.

West Indies

D. Ganga c and b Kallis	15
C. H. Gayle c Boucher b Kallis	6
B. C. Lara b Kallis	92
*C. L. Hooper b Ntini	21
M. N. Samuels c Boucher b Donald	1
S. Chanderpaul run out	24
†R. D. Jacobs c Gibbs b Ntini	21
M. Dillon c Boucher b Donald	0
D. Ramnarine c Rhodes b Donald	2
K. C. B. Jeremy c Ntini b Kallis	5
C. E. Cuffy not out	0
L-b 4, w 6, n-b 2	12
1/20 2/24 3/68 4/73 5/116 6/177 7/180 8/187 9/199 (49.2 overs)	199

Bowling: Pollock 10–2–23–0; Kallis 6.2–1–22–4; Ntini 10–1–47–2; Donald 10–0–41–3; Ontong 8–0–38–0; Kemp 5–0–24–0.

South Africa

G. Kirsten c Lara b Samuels	18
H. H. Gibbs c Hooper b Ramnarine	107
J. H. Kallis run out	18
H. H. Dippenaar not out	42
J. N. Rhodes not out	10
L-b 1, w 4, n-b 2	7
1/54 2/103 3/182 (3 wkts, 41.4 overs)	202

†M. V. Boucher, J. M. Kemp, *S. M. Pollock, J. L. Ontong, A. A. Donald and M. Ntini did not bat.

Bowling: Cuffy 7.4–1–44–0; Dillon 3–0–18–0; Hooper 8–0–35–0; Samuels 10–1–37–1; Ramnarine 10–0–48–1; Gayle 3–0–19–0.

Umpires: B. R. Doctrove and E. A. Nicholls.
Third umpire: H. Moore.

†WEST INDIES v SOUTH AFRICA

Sixth One-Day International

At Port-of-Spain, May 12. South Africa won by 53 runs. Toss: West Indies. International debut: A. Nel.

The home bowlers earned West Indies the chance to pull one back, dismissing South Africa for 190 in the final over. But runs were hard to come by on a two-paced pitch, and a sell-out crowd of 25,000 had their hopes dashed as West Indies' last eight wickets tumbled for 40 inside 15 overs. McKenzie and Kemp provided the backbone of South Africa's innings with a stand of 92 that began during Cuffy's mean ten-over spell of two for 26. Lara held the key to the West Indian reply. Once he was run out by Rhodes's direct hit from mid-wicket, and Chanderpaul, without a boundary in 84 balls, was stumped after losing patience, the effort folded. The previous day, the South African board had announced that five players were fined for smoking marijuana; pointedly, all five played here, with Andre Nel taking three wickets on international debut.

Man of the Match: N. D. McKenzie.

South Africa

H. H. Dippenaar lbw b Cuffy	7
H. H. Gibbs b Cuffy	1
N. D. McKenzie c Jacobs b Collymore	73
J. M. Kemp lbw b Hooper	46
J. H. Kallis b Hooper	3
J. N. Rhodes c Lara b Collymore	25
*S. M. Pollock c and b Samuels	5
†M. V. Boucher b Jeremy	3
R. Telemachus b Jeremy	2
P. R. Adams b Samuels	6
A. Nel not out	3
B 2, l-b 9, w 4, n-b 1	16
1/2 2/31 3/123 4/131 5/152 6/157 7/170 8/177 9/184 (49.5 overs)	190

Bowling: Cuffy 10–2–26–2; Collymore 8.5–1–29–2; Jeremy 9–0–42–2; Hooper 10–0–27–2; Ramnarine 7–0–41–0; Samuels 5–1–14–2.

West Indies

D. Ganga c Kemp b Nel	11	K. C. B. Jeremy b Telemachus	0
S. Chanderpaul st Boucher b Adams	27	C. E. Cuffy not out	3
B. C. Lara run out	41	C. D. Collymore lbw b Pollock	1
M. N. Samuels b Telemachus	29	W 4, n-b 5	9
*C. L. Hooper c Boucher b Nel	8		
R. L. Powell c Boucher b Nel	0	1/18 2/71 3/97 (47 overs)	137
†R. D. Jacobs c Adams b Kallis	7	4/108 5/108 6/126	
D. Ramnarine c Boucher b Kemp	1	7/131 8/132 9/135	

Bowling: Pollock 9–3–15–1; Nel 8.1–2–20–3; Telemachus 9–0–26–2; Kallis 8–0–25–1; Adams 6–0–24–1; Kemp 6.5–0–27–1.

Umpires: S. A. Bucknor and C. Duncan.
Third umpire: C. E. Cumberbatch.

†WEST INDIES v SOUTH AFRICA

Seventh One-Day International

At St Vincent, May 16. West Indies won by six wickets. Toss: South Africa.

Cuffy's ten economical overs off the reel, bringing him three for 24, helped West Indies to a consolation victory in his first international appearance on his home island. In spite of Kallis's fighting 69, sharp catching and keen ground fielding restricted South Africa to 163 for seven, their third-lowest completed one-day total against West Indies. The loss of Lara and Hooper, both caught by Gibbs at short extra cover off Kemp, caused some flutterings, but Samuels and Chanderpaul put on 62 to see their team home, delighting a crowd that swelled beyond its 8,000 capacity during the day. The winning run came off Rhodes, bowling for the first time in one-day internationals on his 200th appearance (a South African record). Pollock received the Cable & Wireless "Bowled Over" Trophy for his team and the Man of the Series award for himself, rewarding his all-round performances in both Tests and one-day internationals.

Man of the Match: C. E. Cuffy.

Man of the Series (Tests and one-day internationals): S. M. Pollock.

South Africa

H. H. Gibbs c Collymore b Cuffy	1	J. M. Kemp not out	12
G. Kirsten c Ganga b Collymore	6	*S. M. Pollock not out	7
N. D. McKenzie c Ganga b Cuffy	13	L-b 6, w 3, n-b 3	12
J. L. Ontong c Gayle b Cuffy	2		
J. H. Kallis c Lara b Samuels	69	1/2 2/9 3/14 (7 wkts, 50 overs)	163
J. N. Rhodes b McGarrell	16	4/40 5/79	
†M. V. Boucher c McGarrell b Samuels	25	6/132 7/150	

R. Telemachus and M. Ntini did not bat.

Bowling: Cuffy 10–3–24–3; Collymore 9–0–37–1; Jeremy 6–0–19–0; McGarrell 10–0–26–1; Hooper 10–0–37–0; Samuels 5–0–14–2.

West Indies

D. Ganga run out	15	S. Chanderpaul not out	31
C. H. Gayle b Kallis	28	L-b 5, w 4, n-b 4	13
B. C. Lara c Gibbs b Kemp	18		
M. N. Samuels not out	54	1/40 2/56 (4 wkts, 44.2 overs)	164
*C. L. Hooper c Gibbs b Kemp	5	3/92 4/102	

†R. D. Jacobs, N. C. McGarrell, K. C. B. Jeremy, C. E. Cuffy and C. D. Collymore did not bat.

Bowling: Pollock 8–3–17–0; Telemachus 7–0–35–0; Ntini 6–0–29–0; Kallis 8–0–29–1; Kemp 6–1–16–2; Ontong 8–0–30–0; Rhodes 1.2–0–3–0.

Umpires: S. A. Bucknor and B. R. Doctrove.
Third umpire: G. T. Brown. Series referee: J. R. Reid (New Zealand).

THE BANGLADESHIS IN ZIMBABWE, 2000-01

By JOHN WARD

Bangladesh, the tenth and youngest Test-playing nation, visited Zimbabwe, the ninth, for their first Test tour in April 2001. They themselves admitted that they did not expect to win but saw the trip as a chance to learn. In that regard they succeeded, improving steadily, without ever posing a real threat to their hosts. Though Zimbabwe were still ranked ninth in the World Test Championship, the difference in experience between the sides was insurmountable. But Bangladesh did show, as in their inaugural Test against India, that they had talented players; with a population of 130 million to draw from, they also had the potential to develop rapidly.

For once, the pressure was on Zimbabwe and, in the unaccustomed position of favourites, they failed to play to their highest standard. Their batsmen did not always exploit weak bowling, missing out on the high scores that might have been theirs for the taking; the attack was disappointing. In the two Tests, the Zimbabweans ran up nine fifties, but only Guy Whittall, coming out of a lean patch, went on to a century. He was the leading batsman on either side, with 238 runs at 79.33. The omission of left-arm swing bowler Bryan Strang from the Tests left captain Heath Streak supported by promising but newly blooded bowlers who had not learned to step up the pressure. Streak himself was well below his best form, despite flattering figures.

More experienced batsmen would have taken advantage, but Bangladesh could not yet do so. Opener Javed Omar was the batting find of the tour, showing a sound defence and impressive powers of concentration; his colleagues, however, were inconsistent, unsurprisingly finding it difficult to build an innings at Test level. Aminul Islam, a centurion in the inaugural Test against India, began with a good 84, but Zimbabwe discovered his weakness against the rising ball. Captain Naimur Rahman achieved little with bat or ball.

Bangladesh's best bowler was left-arm pace man Manjurul Islam, who took six wickets at Bulawayo, but none at Harare, where the batsmen had worked him out. In the one-day matches, his opening partner Mohammad Sharif, officially just 15 years old, took some good wickets, but the side was surprisingly weak in spin. In the field, Bangladesh worked hard. They were fallible in the slips, however, the inevitable result of a diet of one-day cricket, and they suffered a serious blow when Khaled Masud, who had kept wicket impressively, was injured and returned home.

Easy wins to the home side in all five international matches further emphasised the gulf between the Test-playing countries and the Associates, whose ranks Bangladesh had just left. Inexperience in the longer game was their main weakness, and the International Cricket Council would do well to consider how they prepare prospective Full Members for Test status. With more foresight, Bangladesh could have entered Test cricket much better equipped. That said, these Bangladeshis were fine ambassadors for their country, enthusiastic and cheerful, and sporting on the field of play. One wondered how long this would last in the often cynical world of modern Test cricket.

BANGLADESHI TOURING PARTY

Naimur Rahman (Dhaka Metropolis) (*captain*), Khaled Masud (Rajshahi) (*vice-captain*), Akram Khan (Chittagong), Al-Shahriar Rokon (Dhaka Metropolis), Aminul Islam (Biman), Enamul Haque (Chittagong), Habibul Bashar (Biman), Hasibul Hussain (Sylhet), Javed Omar (Biman), Manjurul Islam (Khulna), Mehrab Hossain (Dhaka Metropolis), Mohammad Ashraful (Dhaka Metropolis), Mohammad Rafiq (Sylhet), Mohammad Sharif (Biman), Mushfiqur Rehman (Rajshahi).

Manager: Mahbubul Anam. *Coach:* T. M. Chappell. *Physiotherapist:* J. Gloster.

BANGLADESHI TOUR RESULTS

Test matches – Played 2: Lost 2.
First-class matches – Played 3: Lost 2, Drawn 1.
Losses – Zimbabwe (2).
Draw – Zimbabwe A.
One-day internationals – Played 3: Lost 3.
Other non-first-class match – Won v CFX Academy.

Note: Matches in this section which were not first-class are signified by a dagger.

†At Alexandra Sports Club, Harare, April 4. Bangladeshis won by seven wickets. Toss: CFX Academy. CFX Academy 183 (48.5 overs) (T. Duffin 55, B. G. Rogers 46, S. M. Ervine 31; Mohammad Sharif five for 30, Naimur Rahman three for 45); Bangladeshis 184 for three (32.2 overs) (Javed Omar 35, Habibul Bashar 79).

†ZIMBABWE v BANGLADESH

First One-Day International

At Harare, April 7. Zimbabwe won by seven wickets. Toss: Bangladesh. International debuts: D. D. Ebrahim; Mohammad Sharif.

Bangladesh inadvertently signed their own death warrant and showed their inexperience by electing to bat on a grassy Harare Sports Club pitch, traditionally helpful to the bowlers in the first hour or so. When Strang and Streak reduced them to 15 for four, the contest was as good as over. But from 49 for six, Akram Khan and Mushfiqur Rehman added 64, a record for Bangladesh's seventh wicket, and further contributions of worth from the lower order took the total past 150. Zimbabwe were never challenged, but a heavy outfield and some rather laboured batting provided little entertainment for a moderate crowd.

Man of the Match: B. C. Strang.

Bangladesh

Javed Omar c Streak b Strang	3
Al-Shahriar Rokon c A. Flower b Streak	7
Habibul Bashar run out	0
Aminul Islam c G. W. Flower b Strang	2
Akram Khan b Blignaut	35
*Naimur Rahman c Whittall b Mutendera	19
†Khaled Masud b Mutendera	0
Mushfiqur Rehman c Streak b Blignaut	31
Mohammad Rafiq not out	22
Mohammad Sharif not out	13
L-b 3, w 14, n-b 2	19
1/6 2/7 3/14 4/15 5/47 6/49 7/113 8/114 (8 wkts, 50 overs)	151

Manjurul Islam did not bat.

Bowling: Streak 10–1–27–1; Strang 10–3–25–2; Blignaut 10–1–24–2; Mutendera 10–1–45–2; Viljoen 5–0–12–0; G. W. Flower 5–0–15–0.

Zimbabwe

A. D. R. Campbell b Mohammad Sharif . 5
G. J. Whittall c Javed Omar b Mushfiqur Rehman . 26
S. V. Carlisle c Khaled Masud b Mohammad Rafiq . 40
†A. Flower not out 40
G. W. Flower not out 32
L-b 7, w 4, n-b 1 12

1/15 2/73 3/89 (3 wkts, 43.1 overs) 155

D. D. Ebrahim, A. M. Blignaut, *H. H. Streak, D. P. Viljoen, D. T. Mutendera and B. C. Strang did not bat.

Bowling: Manjurul Islam 10–1–33–0; Mohammad Sharif 10–1–31–1; Mushfiqur Rehman 10–2–20–1; Mohammad Rafiq 8–1–24–1; Naimur Rahman 5–0–36–0; Habibul Bashar 0.1–0–4–0.

Umpires: K. C. Barbour and G. R. Evans.
Third umpire: M. A. Esat.

†ZIMBABWE v BANGLADESH

Second One-Day International

At Harare, April 8. Zimbabwe won by 127 runs. Toss: Bangladesh.

A more closely cut pitch ensured better batting conditions, although the outfield remained slow. Bangladesh had learned their lesson and put Zimbabwe in, but the home batsmen weathered the first hour. Campbell advanced to his seventh one-day century for Zimbabwe, a record. He batted for 44 overs, striking eight fours and a six in 145 balls, and added 133 with Carlisle. It was clear a target of 231 was beyond Bangladesh's reach. After two early wickets, Javed Omar dropped anchor to carry his bat, but his team-mates, apart from the aggressive Naimur Rahman, had no answer to Zimbabwe's seamers and were dismissed with 19 overs remaining. During the brief ninth-wicket stand, the batsmen's names on the scoreboard read "Omar" and "Sharif".

Man of the Match: A. D. R. Campbell.

Zimbabwe

A. D. R. Campbell c Al-Shahriar Rokon b Manjurul Islam . 103
G. J. Whittall c Manjurul Islam b Mohammad Sharif . 16
S. V. Carlisle c Khaled Masud b Manjurul Islam . 56
A. M. Blignaut c Mohammad Rafiq b Manjurul Islam . 13
*H. H. Streak c Mehrab Hossain b Mohammad Sharif . 15
†A. Flower c Javed Omar b Mohammad Sharif . 6
G. W. Flower run out 0
D. D. Ebrahim not out. 5
D. P. Viljoen not out 0
L-b 10, w 5, n-b 1. 16

1/49 2/182 3/188 4/211 5/218 6/220 7/229 (7 wkts, 50 overs) 230

D. T. Mutendera and B. C. Strang did not bat.

Bowling: Manjurul Islam 10–0–37–3; Mohammad Sharif 10–1–48–3; Mushfiqur Rehman 10–2–29–0; Mehrab Hossain 2–0–18–0; Mohammad Rafiq 10–0–44–0; Naimur Rahman 8–0–44–0.

Bangladesh

Javed Omar not out	33
Al-Shahriar Rokon lbw b Streak	0
Habibul Bashar c A. Flower b Streak	5
Mehrab Hossain c A. Flower b Blignaut	11
Akram Khan c Campbell b Strang	1
*Naimur Rahman b Viljoen	25
†Khaled Masud c Streak b Blignaut	3
Mushfiqur Rehman b Viljoen	1
Mohammad Rafiq c Strang b Mutendera	8
Mohammad Sharif c A. Flower b Mutendera	0
Manjurul Islam c Carlisle b Mutendera	1
L-b 1, w 13, n-b 1	15
1/1 2/9 3/38 4/41 5/75 6/78 7/82 8/98 9/99 (30.4 overs)	103

Bowling: Streak 5–0–20–2; Strang 7–1–17–1; Blignaut 8–0–28–2; Mutendera 5.4–1–23–3; Viljoen 5–1–14–2.

Umpires: M. A. Esat and I. D. Robinson.
Third umpire: K. C. Barbour.

†ZIMBABWE v BANGLADESH

Third One-Day International

At Bulawayo, April 11. Zimbabwe won by 36 runs. Toss: Zimbabwe. International debut: Mohammad Ashraful.

Queens Sports Club offered a more appropriate pitch and outfield, and thus a more entertaining contest. Bangladesh never threatened, but lost with dignity in scoring 272, their highest one-day international total yet. They had started by dismissing Zimbabwe's top three for 39, but then the Flower brothers added 148. Grant went on to 142, equalling Dave Houghton's one-day record for Zimbabwe, against New Zealand at Hyderabad in the 1987-88 World Cup. He faced 128 balls, hitting ten fours and two sixes, and put on another 121 with Carlisle in the final 12 overs. Javed Omar and Habibul Bashar shared a stand of 84 at five an over, but once they were parted the later batsmen could not continue the momentum. Blignaut, near the wide mid-wicket boundary, took a sensational one-handed leaping catch to dismiss Khaled Masud.

Man of the Match: G. W. Flower. *Man of the Series:* G. W. Flower.

Zimbabwe

A. D. R. Campbell c Khaled Masud b Manjurul Islam	0
G. J. Whittall b Mushfiqur Rehman	26
D. D. Ebrahim c Akram Khan b Manjurul Islam	5
†A. Flower c Mohammad Sharif b Mohammad Ashraful	81
G. W. Flower not out	142
S. V. Carlisle not out	42
L-b 4, w 7, n-b 1	12
1/0 2/21 3/39 4/187 (4 wkts, 50 overs)	308

A. M. Blignaut, *H. H. Streak, D. P. Viljoen, D. T. Mutendera and B. C. Strang did not bat.

Bowling: Manjurul Islam 10–1–50–2; Mohammad Sharif 10–0–77–0; Mushfiqur Rehman 8–0–48–1; Mohammad Rafiq 8–0–45–0; Naimur Rahman 10–0–59–0; Mohammad Ashraful 4–0–25–1.

Bangladesh

Javed Omar run out	69	†Khaled Masud c Blignaut b Mutendera	8
Mehrab Hossain b Blignaut	13	Mushfiqur Rehman not out	17
Mohammad Ashraful c Ebrahim b Strang	9	Mohammad Sharif not out	9
Habibul Bashar c A. Flower b Strang	74	B 1, l-b 6, w 11, n-b 3	21
Akram Khan c Campbell b Blignaut	25		
*Naimur Rahman run out	25	1/46 2/55 3/139 (8 wkts, 50 overs)	272
Mohammad Rafiq c G. W. Flower b Strang	2	4/205 5/205 6/213 7/235 8/242	

Manjurul Islam did not bat.

Bowling: Streak 9–0–58–0; Strang 10–0–56–3; Blignaut 10–0–41–2; Mutendera 8–0–44–1; Viljoen 7–0–39–0; G. W. Flower 6–0–27–0.

Umpires: C. K. Coventry and R. B. Tiffin.
Third umpire: J. F. Fenwick. Series referee: B. Warnapura (Sri Lanka).

At Bulawayo Athletic Club, Bulawayo, April 13, 14, 15. Drawn. Toss: Zimbabwe A. Bangladeshis 333 (Mehrab Hossain 76, Habibul Bashar 66, Akram Khan 55, Khaled Masud 82; B. T. Watambwa four for 81) and 166 (Akram Khan 32, Naimur Rahman 32; M. L. Nkala four for 46, H. K. Olonga three for 25); Zimbabwe A 222 for eight dec. (H. Masakadza 62, C. B. Wishart 30) and 205 for three (G. J. Rennie 79 not out, D. A. Marillier 77).

ZIMBABWE v BANGLADESH

First Test Match

At Bulawayo, April 19, 20, 21, 22. Zimbabwe won by an innings and 32 runs. Toss: Zimbabwe. Test debuts: A. M. Blignaut, D. D. Ebrahim, B. T. Watambwa; Javed Omar, Manjurul Islam, Mohammad Sharif, Mushfiqur Rehman.

Bangladesh's inaugural overseas Test, like their first at home, ended in defeat as they were outclassed by the vastly more experienced Zimbabweans. But the home side were often unimpressive and below their best. Indeed, some players felt – as they had in the last home series in September – that their strongest team had not been selected. Gavin Rennie, who scored 93 and 37 when he opened at Wellington in Zimbabwe's previous Test, was dropped in favour of 20-year-old Dion Ebrahim, while Bryan Strang, a pillar of strength in the bowling for several seasons, gave way to newcomers Andy Blignaut and Brighton Watambwa.

This meant that, apart from Streak, four home bowlers began the match with 11 Tests and 20 wickets between them. Blignaut, however, rose to the occasion with some fine new-ball bowling, becoming the first Zimbabwean to take five wickets in an innings on Test debut. (John Traicos took five in Zimbabwe's inaugural Test back in 1992-93, but he had already played three Tests for South Africa.) Streak had put Bangladesh in on a pitch that had more grass than usual at this venue, but lacked pace. Against mostly mediocre bowling, Bangladesh reached 194 for four after tea on the first day, with Aminul Islam threatening to become the first man to score centuries in both of his country's first two Tests. But he fell to the second new ball for 84 as Zimbabwe fought back with five wickets in the last 20 overs.

SEVEN CONSECUTIVE TEST FIFTIES

E. D. Weekes (West Indies)

141	v England at Kingston	1947-48
128	v India at Delhi	1948-49
194	v India at Bombay	1948-49
162, 101	v India at Calcutta	1948-49
90	v India at Madras	1948-49
56	v India at Bombay	1948-49

A. Flower (Zimbabwe)

65	v New Zealand at Harare	2000-01
183*, 70	v India at Delhi	2000-01
55, 232*	v India at Nagpur	2000-01
79	v New Zealand at Wellington	2000-01
73	v Bangladesh at Bulawayo	2000-01

After that, they never really released their grip, although Manjurul Islam was on a hat-trick after dismissing Ebrahim with the final ball of his second over and Carlisle with the first of his third. Some of Zimbabwe's early batting was too cavalier, but Whittall put his head down, batting four and a quarter hours for 119, his fourth Test century, all scored at home, while Andy Flower equalled Everton Weekes's 1940s record with his seventh consecutive Test score of fifty or more. When both were out with Zimbabwe still behind, Grant Flower and Streak, grimly at first, added 120 to put their team well ahead. Manjurul went one better than Blignaut, claiming six in an innings on debut, and Zimbabwean coach Carl Rackemann later named him the best bowler of the match. However, Bangladesh were now without wicket-keeper Khaled Masud, who broke his ankle during the lethal pre-play warm-ups on the third day. This put him out of the tour; Mehrab Hossain took over behind the stumps.

On the fourth day, Bangladesh's second innings was virtually a procession from one end while Javed Omar repeated his feat in the second one-day international by carrying his bat. He was only the third batsman, and the first for more than 100 years, to do so on Test debut, following Jack Barrett for Australia at Lord's in 1890 and Pelham Warner for England at Johannesburg in 1898-99. Omar might well have emulated Warner by reaching a century, too, had the tail given him even moderate support. But his achievement was enough to earn him the match award, a rare honour for a player whose team had lost by an innings. He dedicated it to his brother Asif, who had inspired his cricketing career until his early death in 1995.

Man of the Match: Javed Omar.

Close of play: First day, Bangladesh 256-9 (Mohammad Sharif 0*); Second day, Zimbabwe 287-5 (G. W. Flower 30*, Streak 25*); Third day, Bangladesh 91-2 (Javed Omar 47*, Aminul Islam 10*).

Bangladesh

Javed Omar c Ebrahim b Murphy	62	– not out	85
Mehrab Hossain c Whittall b Blignaut	16	– b Streak	0
Habibul Bashar c Murphy b Blignaut	0	– c Murphy b Watambwa	24
Aminul Islam c A. Flower b Blignaut	84	– c Ebrahim b Streak	11
Akram Khan run out	21	– c Ebrahim b Blignaut	8
*Naimur Rahman c Blignaut b Watambwa	22	– c and b Nkala	6
†Khaled Masud c A. Flower b Streak	30	– absent hurt	
Mushfiqur Rehman c Streak b Blignaut	4	– (7) c Nkala b Watambwa	2
Hasibul Hussain lbw b Streak	1	– (8) c G. W. Flower b Streak	6
Mohammad Sharif c Campbell b Blignaut	0	– (9) c Whittall b Blignaut	8
Manjurul Islam not out	1	– (10) c and b Blignaut	6
L-b 1, w 6, n-b 9	16	L-b 2, w 6, n-b 4	12
1/26 (2) 2/30 (3) 3/114 (1) 4/149 (5) 5/194 (6) 6/226 (4) 7/253 (7) 8/256 (9) 9/256 (8) 10/257 (10)	257	1/6 (2) 2/61 (3) 3/105 (4) 4/116 (5) 5/129 (6) 6/138 (7) 7/149 (8) 8/160 (9) 9/168 (10)	168

Bowling: *First Innings*—Streak 21–7–47–2; Blignaut 23.3–5–73–5; Watambwa 17–4–38–1; Nkala 13–2–45–0; Murphy 17–2–53–1. *Second Innings*—Streak 19–5–42–3; Blignaut 13.3–4–37–3; Nkala 9–0–34–1; Watambwa 13–3–44–2; Murphy 4–1–9–0.

Zimbabwe

G. J. Whittall c Mohammad Sharif b Hasibul Hussain	119
D. D. Ebrahim c Khaled Masud b Manjurul Islam	2
S. V. Carlisle b Manjurul Islam	3
A. D. R. Campbell c Khaled Masud b Mohammad Sharif	19
†A. Flower c Naimur Rahman b Manjurul Islam	73
G. W. Flower c Mohammad Sharif b Hasibul Hussain	68
*H. H. Streak c sub (Mohammad Rafiq) b Manjurul Islam	67
A. M. Blignaut c and b Manjurul Islam	0
M. L. Nkala c Mehrab Hossain b Manjurul Islam	47
B. A. Murphy c Habibul Bashar b Naimur Rahman	30
B. T. Watambwa not out	4
B 2, l-b 10, w 1, n-b 12	25
1/18 (2) 2/27 (3) 3/66 (4) 4/215 (5) 5/233 (1) 6/353 (7) 7/353 (8) 8/389 (6) 9/445 (9) 10/457 (10)	457

Bowling: Hasibul Hussain 30–7–125–2; Manjurul Islam 35–12–81–6; Mohammad Sharif 29–3–112–1; Mushfiqur Rehman 20–5–53–0; Naimur Rahman 24.4–7–74–1.

Umpires: R. E. Koertzen (South Africa) and K. C. Barbour.
Third umpire: C. K. Coventry. Referee: B. Warnapura (Sri Lanka).

ZIMBABWE v BANGLADESH

Second Test Match

At Harare, April 26, 27, 28, 29, 30. Zimbabwe won by eight wickets. Toss: Zimbabwe. Test debut: Enamul Haque.

Another convincing victory gave Zimbabwe their first proper home series win (they beat India in a one-off Test at Harare in 1998-99), but Bangladesh did take the match into the final day and avoided the innings defeat to confirm their steady improvement. This was Zimbabwe's 50th Test match, a landmark that went almost unnoticed locally; Andy Flower and Alistair Campbell had played in all of them, a unique achievement for any country, and Campbell set another record by becoming the first Zimbabwean fielder to take 50 Test catches.

Bangladesh brought in Al-Shahriar Rokon for the injured Khaled Masud and slow left-armer Enamul Haque for seamer Hasibul Hussain, while Zimbabwe also added a left-arm spinner, replacing Murphy with Price. Streak again put Bangladesh in, but although there was some movement it was a much better batting pitch than Harare had tended to offer recently. Zimbabwe's bowling was again disappointing – Price was much the best, flighting the ball impressively – yet Bangladesh were still unable to take full advantage. There were useful fifties, however: Mehrab Hossain anchored the innings for more than five hours, adding 114 with Habibul Bashar for the fourth wicket, and on the second day Akram Khan helped to hold off the home attack until after lunch. Then they lost their last three wickets in 11 balls.

Zimbabwe batted solidly. After a sound opening partnership of 90, Campbell began the third day with fours off each of the first four deliveries, from Manjurul Islam, the first three all pulls to mid-wicket off short balls. There was much interest in whether Andy Flower would beat Everton Weekes by hitting a record eighth consecutive Test fifty, but on 23 he was sent back by Campbell when attempting a risky single, and a fine throw from Javed Omar resulted in only his second run-out in 88 Test innings.

As in Bulawayo, Zimbabwe lost five wickets before taking the lead, whereupon a determined stand between Grant Flower and Streak took a grip on the match; this time they added 133. Streak recorded his fourth fifty in seven matches since becoming captain; before then, he had only two in 31 Tests. He had a century in his sights when he slashed at a wide ball from Mohammad Sharif, walked to a catch to the keeper, and immediately declared.

Needing 167 to avoid an innings defeat, Bangladesh were helped by a resolute second-wicket stand between Omar and Al-Shahriar after losing Mehrab. Another good partnership followed, between Habibul and Akram, but once this was broken, it was only a matter of time. The tail collapsed again, the last four wickets falling for two runs, leaving Zimbabwe exactly 100 to win. Though Bangladesh bowled with great spirit, Whittall, with another positive half-century, was not to be denied. He fell with victory in sight, and two powerful leg-side hits by Carlisle off Naimur Rahman settled the issue.

The tour had gone according to script throughout, Zimbabwe winning all the internationals and gaining valued experience in how to win Tests, even if they did not do so in polished fashion. But Bangladesh also showed that they were learning quickly. This series did good to both teams.

Man of the Match: G. J. Whittall. *Man of the Series:* H. H. Streak.

Close of play: First day, Bangladesh 198-6 (Akram Khan 15*, Mushfiqur Rehman 0*); Second day, Zimbabwe 144-2 (Carlisle 21*, Campbell 22*); Third day, Zimbabwe 377-6 (Streak 65*); Fourth day, Bangladesh 219-5 (Habibul Bashar 66*, Naimur Rahman 7*).

Bangladesh

Javed Omar c Blignaut b Streak	1	– c G. W. Flower b Price	43
†Mehrab Hossain c Carlisle b Price	71	– c Blignaut b Watambwa	0
Al-Shahriar Rokon c G. W. Flower b Streak	11	– c Streak b Watambwa	68
Aminul Islam c Campbell b Price	12	– lbw b Price	2
Habibul Bashar st A. Flower b Price	64	– c A. Flower b Streak	76
Akram Khan c Campbell b Streak	44	– c Campbell b Price	31
*Naimur Rahman lbw b Price	16	– run out	36
Mushfiqur Rehman c A. Flower b Streak	2	– (9) not out	2
Enamul Haque not out	20	– (8) c A. Flower b Watambwa	3
Mohammad Sharif c Carlisle b Watambwa	0	– c Carlisle b Streak	0
Manjurul Islam c Campbell b Watambwa	0	– c A. Flower b Watambwa	0
L-b 8, w 3, n-b 2	13	L-b 2, w 1, n-b 2	5
1/1 (1) 2/23 (3) 3/48 (4) 4/162 (5) 5/171 (2) 6/196 (7) 7/207 (8) 8/253 (6) 9/254 (10) 10/254 (11)	254	1/2 (2) 2/97 (1) 3/99 (4) 4/127 (3) 5/203 (6) 6/246 (5) 7/264 (7) 8/264 (8) 9/265 (10) 10/266 (11)	266

Bowling: *First Innings*—Blignaut 27–6–67–0; Streak 30–12–38–4; Watambwa 14.5–3–48–2; Nkala 19–11–22–0; Price 30–9–71–4. *Second Innings*—Streak 21–7–47–2; Watambwa 22–5–64–4; Blignaut 15–6–27–0; Price 30–9–94–3; G. W. Flower 6–0–13–0; Nkala 6–0–19–0.

Zimbabwe

G. J. Whittall run out	59	– b Enamul Haque	60
D. D. Ebrahim c Akram Khan b Naimur Rahman	39	– run out	10
S. V. Carlisle c Habibul Bashar b Mohammad Sharif	21	– not out	29
A. D. R. Campbell c Mushfiqur Rehman b Naimur Rahman	73	– not out	0
†A. Flower run out	23		
G. W. Flower c Mohammad Sharif b Enamul Haque	84		
*H. H. Streak c Mehrab Hossain b Mohammad Sharif	87		
A. M. Blignaut run out	15		
M. L. Nkala c Mushfiqur Rehman b Enamul Haque	7		
R. W. Price not out	0		
B 7, l-b 6	13	L-b 1	1
1/90 (1) 2/104 (2) 3/164 (3) 4/210 (5) 5/244 (4) 6/377 (6) 7/397 (8) 8/419 (9) 9/421 (7)	(9 wkts dec.) 421	1/35 (2) 2/92 (1)	(2 wkts) 100

B. T. Watambwa did not bat.

Bowling: *First Innings*—Manjurul Islam 34–9–113–0; Mohammad Sharif 28.4–6–108–2; Enamul Haque 46–15–94–2; Mushfiqur Rehman 11–1–33–0; Naimur Rahman 28–12–60–2. *Second Innings*—Manjurul Islam 8–2–21–0; Mohammad Sharif 6–0–36–0; Enamul Haque 3–0–8–1; Mushfiqur Rehman 6–1–26–0; Naimur Rahman 0.3–0–8–0.

Umpires: D. B. Cowie (New Zealand) and R. B. Tiffin.
Third umpire: G. R. Evans. Referee: B. Warnapura (Sri Lanka).

THE INDIANS IN ZIMBABWE, 2001

By JOHN WARD

India arrived in Zimbabwe determined to win their first Test series outside Asia since they beat England in 1986. They had recently overcome the might of Australia at home and, with a middle order comprising the record-breaking V. V. S. Laxman, Sachin Tendulkar, captain Sourav Ganguly and Rahul Dravid, were confident they could avenge the embarrassment of the inaugural Test in Zimbabwe in 1992-93, when they had to fight to avoid following on, and their surprise defeat in the one-off Test of 1998-99. In the event, they not only failed to take the series – Zimbabwe fought back from one down to level it – but also unexpectedly lost the final of the ensuing one-day triangular tournament to West Indies, after cruising through the qualifiers. The bare results, however, hide the fact that India played much good cricket.

The batting, expected to be their strength, proved their weakest link; the Indian batsmen never fully adjusted to the Zimbabwean pitches' extra bounce, and their only international century came from Tendulkar in the one-day tournament. Laxman, full of splendid strokes, was perhaps too aggressive for his own good in foreign conditions, while Ganguly had a dismal time with the bat for most of the tour. Dravid provided the backbone, and it was his second-innings dismissal that proved to be the turning-point of the Harare Test. But India's most impressive batsman of the Tests was the determined Shiv Sunder Das, whom some Indian critics began to rate as their best opener since Sunil Gavaskar, a television commentator on this tour. Das scored 239 runs at 79.66 and was named Man of the Series – though he was not retained for the triangular tournament.

The bowlers did a good job, although Australia's destroyer, off-spinner Harbhajan Singh, could not dominate on Zimbabwean soil as in India. The local batsmen had clearly done their homework on how to play him. More interesting was the progress made by the quickish left-armer, Ashish Nehra, who had played one previous Test. His accuracy and movement, especially when the ball swung early on the winter mornings, forced his opponents to play him with great respect and prompted the Indians to keep him on, contrary to original plans, after the Tests. He had good seam support, and the only time the Indian attack was mastered was in the one-day final. The tourists' fielding was a revelation, and a credit to their new coach, John Wright. Ground fielding and close catching alike were the best seen from India for some time, with Laxman, Dravid and Das in particular taking numerous brilliant close catches.

Zimbabwe did well to level the series after letting themselves down badly on the first day in Bulawayo. As usual, the batting owed much to the Flower brothers in the middle order, while captain Heath Streak was again the bulwark of the bowling. He had a hostile new opening partner in Brighton Watambwa, and it was a remarkable effort to force a home victory in Harare after Watambwa had been injured on the first morning. Crowds for the Tests were much larger than usual, owing to the new policy of busing in schoolchildren from the development areas in the townships. On most days, more than 1,000 were present, which greatly added to the atmosphere. If there was one jarring note, it was the pathetic over-rate by both teams: play ran between 25 and 50 minutes late every day, highlighting the failure of the ICC to tackle this problem effectively.

INDIAN TOURING PARTY

S. C. Ganguly (Bengal) (*captain*), R. Dravid (Karnataka) (*vice-captain*), A. B. Agarkar (Mumbai), H. K. Badani (Tamil Nadu), S. V. Bahutule (Mumbai), S. S. Das (Orissa), S. S. Dighe (Mumbai), Harbhajan Singh (Punjab), V. V. S. Laxman (Hyderabad), D. S. Mohanty (Orissa), A. Nehra (Delhi), S. Ramesh (Tamil Nadu), J. Srinath (Karnataka), S. R. Tendulkar (Mumbai), Zaheer Khan (Baroda).

Harvinder Singh (Railways), D. Mongia (Punjab), V. Sehwag (Delhi) and R. S. Sodhi (Punjab) replaced Bahutule, Das, Ramesh and Srinath for the one-day triangular tournament.

Team manager: C. P. S. Chauhan. *Coach:* J. G. Wright.

INDIAN TOUR RESULTS

Test matches – Played 2: Won 1, Lost 1.
First-class matches – Played 4: Won 2, Lost 1, Drawn 1.
Wins – Zimbabwe, CFX Academy XI.
Loss – Zimbabwe.
Draw – Zimbabwe A.
One-day internationals – Played 5: Won 4, Lost 1. *Wins* – Zimbabwe (2), West Indies (2). *Loss* – West Indies.
Other non-first-class match – Won v Zimbabwe A.

Note: Matches in this section which were not first-class are signified by a dagger.

At Mutare, May 28, 29, 30. Drawn. Toss: Indians. Indians 336 for nine dec. (R. Dravid 137, S. S. Dighe 87; D. T. Mutendera three for 69, B. A. Murphy three for 77) and 150 for seven (V. V. S. Laxman 33, S. R. Tendulkar 33; T. J. Friend three for 30); Zimbabwe A 175 (D. D. Ebrahim 46, C. B. Wishart 68; Zaheer Khan three for 41, A. Nehra three for 43, Harbhajan Singh three for 24).

In the Indians' first innings, Dravid and Dighe added 227 for the sixth wicket.

At Harare Country Club, Harare, June 2, 3, 4. Indians won by 226 runs. Toss: CFX Academy XI. Indians 447 for four dec. (S. S. Das 110 retired out, S. Ramesh 42, V. V. S. Laxman 100 retired out, H. K. Badani 112 not out, S. C. Ganguly 53 retired out) and 128 for five dec. (H. K. Badani 35 retired out, S. Ramesh 52 retired out); CFX Academy XI 192 (G. B. Brent 72 not out; Harbhajan Singh four for 43) and 157 (B. G. Rogers 65 not out, M. L. Nkala 59; J. Srinath three for nine, Harbhajan Singh six for 37).

ZIMBABWE v INDIA

First Test Match

At Bulawayo, June 7, 8, 9, 10. India won by eight wickets. Toss: Zimbabwe.

Zimbabwe sealed their own fate with an inept batting performance on the opening day; from then on, they were engaged in a vain battle for survival in their country's first winter Test. Choosing to bat, they had struggled against some early life and movement, but this was no excuse for the poor strokes that cost most of them their wickets. Andy Flower, as so often, made the top score, but his 51 off 45 balls comprised an uncharacteristic array of daring strokes never suggesting permanence. A total of 173 was Zimbabwe's lowest against India.

Their bowlers struck back in the closing session with three wickets, and next morning, despite lacking the accuracy needed to put pressure on the batsmen, they reduced the tourists to 98 for five. Tendulkar and Dravid checked that advance and had taken India into the lead before Tendulkar was brilliantly caught by Carlisle at second slip, having batted responsibly over three hours for 74. When Dravid followed 30 runs later, there was a good chance Zimbabwe might keep the lead down to 50, but not for the first time an opponent's eighth wicket wrested the match away. In 1999-2000, Zimbabwe had conceded three eighth-wicket century stands; this time, the damage was 72. Harbhajan Singh hit out with merry abandon for a maiden Test fifty as the last three partnerships added 110 and stretched the lead to 145. By now, a strained hamstring had robbed the attack of Olonga, himself a last-minute replacement for the injured all-rounder Travis Friend, who had been earmarked to make his debut.

The home side ended the second day still 66 behind, with seven wickets left. But the third day belonged to them, and particularly to the Flower brothers, the heart of Zimbabwe's batting throughout their nine-year Test history. Only four wickets were lost during the day for 224 runs, and both Flowers made fighting fifties – Andy's was his ninth in ten Test innings – but no one produced the monumental score required to turn the tables. India's best bowler, Nehra, was ordered out of the attack by umpire Harper after two warnings from umpire Tiffin for running on the pitch. His fellow left-arm seamer, Zaheer Khan, was also warned twice, arousing suspicions that this was a deliberate policy by the Indians to rough up the pitch for Harbhajan's off-spin. In fact, Zimbabwe played Harbhajan with great determination and never let him gain control.

When Grant Flower ran himself out in the third over of the fourth day, the end was in sight. The pitch was too good to give India many misgivings as they contemplated a target of 184, especially as the home attack was further handicapped by Streak's bad knee preventing him from bowling. But there was bitter disappointment for the Zimbabweans when an appeal for a leg-side catch against Das, off the second ball of the innings, was rejected. Das also survived on 18 when Blignaut missed a low return catch, and was dropped on 49 by Murphy before guiding his side to victory with a sound, unbeaten innings of 82. The opportunity was there for a century, but the free strokeplay of Laxman and Tendulkar made it increasingly unlikely. This was India's first win in any Test outside Asia for 15 years.

Man of the Match: S. S. Das.

Close of play: First day, India 83-3 (Tendulkar 16*, Srinath 1*); Second day, Zimbabwe 79-3 (Carlisle 27*, Murphy 10*); Third day, Zimbabwe 303-7 (G. W. Flower 67*, Blignaut 11*).

Zimbabwe

G. J. Whittall b Nehra	6	– c Ramesh b Srinath	20
D. D. Ebrahim run out	12	– c Dravid b Srinath	0
S. V. Carlisle c Laxman b Zaheer Khan	29	– c Laxman b Nehra	52
A. D. R. Campbell c Dighe b Harbhajan Singh	21	– c Das b Harbhajan Singh	16
†A. Flower c Das b Nehra	51	– (6) c Ramesh b Nehra	83
G. W. Flower c Dighe b Srinath	5	– (7) run out	71
*H. H. Streak run out	16	– (8) lbw b Zaheer Khan	14
A. M. Blignaut lbw b Nehra	0	– (9) not out	32
B. A. Murphy c Dravid b Zaheer Khan	7	– (5) c Das b Zaheer Khan	10
H. K. Olonga c Dighe b Harbhajan Singh	16	– b Srinath	0
B. T. Watambwa not out	0	– run out	0
L-b 4, n-b 6	10	B 1, l-b 17, w 2, n-b 10	30
1/9 (1) 2/46 (2) 3/65 (3) 4/89 (4) 5/97 (6) 6/137 (5) 7/139 (8) 8/154 (7) 9/165 (9) 10/173 (10)	173	1/14 (2) 2/34 (1) 3/63 (4) 4/86 (5) 5/134 (3) 6/235 (6) 7/273 (8) 8/308 (7) 9/312 (10) 10/328 (11)	328

Bowling: *First Innings*—Srinath 15–5–47–1; Nehra 12–1–23–3; Zaheer Khan 11–1–54–2; Harbhajan Singh 20.5–6–45–2. *Second Innings*—Srinath 32.2–11–71–3; Nehra 26.4–4–77–2; Harbhajan Singh 37.5–8–92–1; Zaheer Khan 22–6–44–2; Tendulkar 6–0–23–0; Ganguly 1–0–3–0.

India

S. S. Das c Ebrahim b Murphy	30	– not out	82
S. Ramesh b Watambwa	2	– c Carlisle b Blignaut	17
V. V. S. Laxman c Whittall b Olonga	28	– c and b G. W. Flower	38
S. R. Tendulkar c Carlisle b Blignaut	74	– not out	36
J. Srinath c Whittall b Watambwa	1		
*S. C. Ganguly c A. Flower b Streak	5		
R. Dravid c A. Flower b Blignaut	44		
†S. S. Dighe c A. Flower b Streak	47		
Harbhajan Singh c Whittall b Watambwa	66		
Zaheer Khan b Streak	0		
A. Nehra not out	9		
L-b 4, w 1, n-b 7	12	B 4, w 1, n-b 6	11
1/2 (2) 2/54 (3) 3/81 (1) 4/83 (5) 5/98 (6) 6/178 (4) 7/208 (7) 8/280 (8) 9/280 (10) 10/318 (9)	318	1/71 (2) 2/132 (3)	(2 wkts) 184

Bowling: *First Innings*—Streak 24–7–63–3; Watambwa 25.5–6–94–3; Blignaut 16–2–68–2; Olonga 8–1–35–1; Murphy 16–3–54–1. *Second Innings*—Watambwa 15–4–54–0; Blignaut 12–3–25–1; Murphy 18.4–1–78–0; G. W. Flower 8–0–23–1.

Umpires: D. J. Harper (Australia) and R. B. Tiffin.
Third umpire: J. F. Fenwick. Referee: D. T. Lindsay (South Africa).

ZIMBABWE v INDIA

Second Test Match

At Harare, June 15, 16, 17, 18. Zimbabwe won by four wickets. Toss: India. Test debuts: T. J. Friend; H. K. Badani.

India lost their chance of a rare overseas series win when they emulated Zimbabwe's mistake in the previous Test: they threw away the advantage of the toss, and eventually the match itself, by a poor first innings. Conditions looked better for batting first than they had for some time at Harare Sports Club, but the Indian batsmen failed to exploit them, wasting their opportunity with too many undisciplined strokes. Ultimately, their team paid the penalty in a thrilling match of constant fluctuations.

Das and Dravid stood out amid the ruins against a Zimbabwe attack that was weakened when Watambwa limped off with a hamstring injury in the seventh over of the match. Streak's persistence was rewarded as the Indian middle order imploded after lunch, when five wickets fell for 87 runs before Dravid and Harbhajan Singh staged a rally with 56 for the eighth wicket. Nehra's three quick wickets in the 11 overs to the close left India marginally ahead on points, but Zimbabwe's remaining batsmen recovered admirably on the second day, despite the tendency to lose their wickets when on the verge of greater things. Grant Flower, in his 50th Test, was the only batsman to reach fifty, brother Andy for once falling five short, against spirited bowling and fielding from India. When Grant was last out on the third morning, the home lead was only 78.

India then appeared to be fighting their way out of trouble against bowlers assuming a defensive line outside off stump. Das reached his third consecutive fifty and Tendulkar made amends for the first innings with a composed 69 while they added 118 for the third wicket. The turning-point came when Zimbabwe took the new ball one over before the close and Blignaut had Dravid caught at the wicket. They followed up next morning by grabbing the next four wickets for ten runs in six overs. The inexperienced Badani, making his debut, held out for 82 minutes but was unable to galvanise runs from the tail. Blignaut's fifth wicket left Zimbabwe needing 157 to win.

It was no simple task: only once before had they successfully chased a target in a Test against a more senior team, when they scored 162 for three to beat Pakistan at Peshawar in 1998-99. To make it more difficult, Andy Flower had sustained a serious thumb injury keeping wicket that morning, which was to put him out for two months. In the circumstances, Carlisle played one of the finest and most valuable innings of Zimbabwe's Test history, batting virtually without flaw for more than three hours to hold the innings together with an unbeaten 62, his highest Test score. None of his partners could exceed 20. Finally, Andy Flower came in and hit two fours to snatch the series from India and bring Zimbabwe their sixth Test victory in 52 matches.

The match had commenced with a minute's silence in memory of Zimbabwe's recent Test batsman, Trevor Madondo, who had died of cerebral malaria only four days beforehand. The Zimbabwean team played in black armbands and, at the post-match ceremony, Streak dedicated his team's victory to Madondo.

Man of the Match: A. M. Blignaut. *Man of the Series:* S. S. Das.

Close of play: First day, Zimbabwe 31-3 (Ebrahim 13*, A. Flower 5*); Second day, Zimbabwe 301-8 (G. W. Flower 80*, Murphy 17*); Third day, India 197-4 (Das 68*).

India

S. S. Das c A. Flower b Blignaut	57	– lbw b Streak	70
H. K. Badani lbw b Watambwa	2	– (7) not out	16
V. V. S. Laxman c Blignaut b Streak	15	– c Murphy b Friend	20
S. R. Tendulkar b Streak	20	– c G. W. Flower b Streak	69
*S. C. Ganguly c Blignaut b Streak	9	– (6) lbw b Blignaut	0
R. Dravid not out	68	– (5) c A. Flower b Blignaut	26
†S. S. Dighe c G. W. Flower b Friend	20	– (2) c A. Flower b Blignaut	4
A. B. Agarkar c Blignaut b Friend	6	– c A. Flower b Streak	0
Harbhajan Singh b Murphy	31	– c Ebrahim b Blignaut	5
J. Srinath run out	0	– c A. Flower b Streak	3
A. Nehra c sub (P. A. Strang) b Murphy	0	– b Blignaut	0
L-b 2, w 6, n-b 1	9	L-b 9, w 12	21
1/7 (2) 2/45 (3) 3/90 (4) 4/103 (1) 5/122 (5) 6/165 (7) 7/172 (8) 8/228 (9) 9/237 (10) 10/237 (11)	237	1/8 (2) 2/32 (3) 3/150 (4) 4/197 (5) 5/199 (6) 6/202 (1) 7/202 (8) 8/207 (9) 9/226 (10) 10/234 (11)	234

Bowling: *First Innings*—Watambwa 3.4–0–14–1; Streak 20–4–69–3; Friend 20.2–4–48–2; Blignaut 20–1–84–1; Murphy 9.2–3–17–2; G. W. Flower 1–0–3–0. *Second Innings*—Streak 27–12–46–4; Blignaut 31.5–14–74–5; Friend 22–4–47–1; Whittall 7–4–15–0; Murphy 10–1–42–0; G. W. Flower 1–0–1–0.

Zimbabwe

G. J. Whittall c Dravid b Nehra	0	– c Dravid b Srinath	10
D. D. Ebrahim lbw b Harbhajan Singh	49	– c Badani b Harbhajan Singh	20
S. V. Carlisle c Badani b Nehra	3	– not out	62
A. D. R. Campbell b Nehra	8	– lbw b Nehra	13
†A. Flower c Das b Harbhajan Singh	45	– (8) not out	8
G. W. Flower c Laxman b Srinath	86	– (5) c Laxman b Agarkar	3
*H. H. Streak b Tendulkar	40	– (6) c Dighe b Srinath	8
A. M. Blignaut st Dighe b Harbhajan Singh	35	– (7) b Nehra	16
T. J. Friend b Nehra	15		
B. A. Murphy b Harbhajan Singh	17		
B. T. Watambwa not out	2		
B 4, l-b 5, w 2, n-b 4	15	B 1, l-b 11, n-b 5	17
1/5 (1) 2/9 (3) 3/18 (4) 4/105 (5) 5/110 (2) 6/175 (7) 7/242 (8) 8/271 (9) 9/301 (10) 10/315 (6)	315	1/25 (1) 2/45 (2) 3/71 (4) 4/89 (5) 5/119 (6) 6/144 (7)	(6 wkts) 157

Bowling: *First Innings*—Srinath 29.3–7–82–1; Nehra 24–6–72–4; Agarkar 24–7–62–0; Harbhajan Singh 26–5–71–4; Tendulkar 4–0–19–1. *Second Innings*—Nehra 13–0–45–2; Srinath 13–1–46–2; Harbhajan Singh 19–6–25–1; Agarkar 8–3–22–1; Tendulkar 1–0–7–0.

Umpires: E. A. R. de Silva (Sri Lanka) and I. D. Robinson.
Third umpire: G. R. Evans. Referee: D. T. Lindsay (South Africa).

†At Sunrise Sports Club, Harare, June 22. Indians won by ten wickets. Toss: Zimbabwe A. Zimbabwe A 103 (32.4 overs) (S. Matsikenyeri 38); Indians 108 for no wkt (17 overs) (S. C. Ganguly 31 not out, V. Sehwag 75 not out).

India's matches v Zimbabwe and West Indies in the Coca-Cola Cup (June 24–July 7) may be found in that section.

THE WEST INDIANS IN ZIMBABWE AND KENYA, 2001

By TONY COZIER

West Indies broke new ground with their tour of Zimbabwe and Kenya. Though they had sent A-teams in the 1980s before Zimbabwe gained Test status, the senior side's visit, for a triangular tournament involving India, followed by two Tests, was long overdue. They found excellent facilities and conditions – the rain during the Second Test was an unexpected interruption in Zimbabwe's mild, dry winter – and, while Zimbabwe were clearly weaker than the countries who had handed West Indies 18 defeats in their previous 20 overseas Tests, they could take justifiable satisfaction from their successes.

They defeated India to win the limited-overs Coca-Cola Cup, and overwhelmed Zimbabwe in the First Test. Even though their bowlers conceded Zimbabwe's highest ever total in the Second Test, when their cricket descended into familiar mediocrity, they drew it with a little help from the weather. In Kenya, against talented opponents thirsting for competition, they triumphed in all three one-day internationals.

The West Indians were dogged by injuries. Brian Lara withdrew after one innings in a warm-up match, complaining of a persistent hamstring strain. Three fast bowlers, Kerry Jeremy (back strain), Cameron Cuffy (stress fracture of the left instep) and Merv Dillon (torn knee ligaments), returned home before the Tests, along with leg-spinner Dinanath Ramnarine (back strain). One of the replacements, Pedro Collins, played one Test, then succumbed to a groin strain. West Indies were further handicapped when Ridley Jacobs was suspended for the Second Test because of an incident in the one-day series.

Meanwhile, Zimbabwe's leading batsman and wicket-keeper, Andy Flower, was missing after playing in every one of Zimbabwe's first 52 Tests, plus 172 one-day internationals; he had torn tendons in his right thumb during the Second Test against India. Fast bowlers Henry Olonga and the impressive newcomer, Brighton Watambwa, were also injured, and Stuart Carlisle broke a finger in the First Test. These problems were compounded by open discord between the players and the Zimbabwe Cricket Union, leading to Heath Streak's brief surrender of the captaincy, and by an emotional debate over the proposal of racial quotas for the national team.

This rendered timely and significant the performances of two young black players, batsman Hamilton Masakadza and the dynamic little wicket-keeper, Tatenda Taibu. Eleven days short of his 18th birthday, Masakadza became the youngest player to score a hundred on Test debut, inspiring a remarkable Zimbabwean recovery. Three months older, Taibu stood in for Andy Flower with natural poise. Both last-year students at Churchill High School, they could be vital role models for cricketers of their race and background.

The tourists were also seeking new heroes. This was their first Test series since 1984 without Courtney Walsh, who had followed Curtly Ambrose into retirement. Their only remaining world-class player, Lara, seemed to have lost his drive. But under Carl Hooper, clearly in control on his first overseas assignment as captain, some gifted young batsmen seemed to be emerging. Chris Gayle, a powerful 21-year-old left-hander, scored 839 first-class runs at 139.83, and made maiden Test and one-day international hundreds. He shared six century opening stands in all matches with Daren Ganga, plus one with Leon Garrick, a heartening development after the years spent searching for a reliable top pair. Ramnaresh Sarwan, 21, missed his maiden Test hundred through a silly run-out at Harare, but he and Marlon Samuels, 20, were stylish and assured, while Hooper and Shivnarine Chanderpaul provided experience.

Walsh's retirement and the various injuries meant that the bowling had to be entirely rejigged from the recent home series against South Africa. Colin Stuart, the fastest and most direct of the bowlers, restaked his claims, while left-arm spinner Neil McGarrell capably deputised for Ramnarine.

Until Masakadza replaced the injured Carlisle, Zimbabwe relied on their tried and trusted. Alistair Campbell – now the only man who had played in all of Zimbabwe's Tests – was promoted to open and registered his second Test hundred. But until Zimbabwe put together their record 563 for nine, in the second innings at Harare, the batting was prone to collapse. The bowling, still heavily dependent on Streak, lacked penetration without Olonga and Watambwa.

Kenya, too, relied on their experienced players. Five of those involved in the famous victory over West Indies in the 1996 World Cup appeared in the one-day series, whereas Chanderpaul was the only West Indian survivor. Captain Maurice Odumbe noted that the young players coming through Kenya's development programmes needed more exposure against the best teams.

WEST INDIAN TOURING PARTY

C. L. Hooper (Guyana) (*captain*), R. D. Jacobs (Leeward Islands) (*vice-captain*), S. Chanderpaul (Guyana), C. D. Collymore (Barbados), C. E. Cuffy (Windward Islands), M. Dillon (Trinidad & Tobago), D. Ganga (Trinidad & Tobago), C. H. Gayle (Jamaica), K. C. B. Jeremy (Leeward Islands), R. D. King (Guyana), B. C. Lara (Trinidad & Tobago), N. C. McGarrell (Guyana), M. V. Nagamootoo (Guyana), D. Ramnarine (Trinidad & Tobago), M. N. Samuels (Jamaica), R. R. Sarwan (Guyana), C. E. L. Stuart (Guyana).

L. V. Garrick and W. W. Hinds (both of Jamaica) replaced the injured Lara, M. I. Black (Trinidad & Tobago) and P. T. Collins (Barbados) replaced the injured Cuffy, Dillon and Jeremy, and D. Mohammed (Trinidad & Tobago) replaced the injured Ramnarine. C. O. Browne (Barbados) joined the party early when Jacobs was suspended for the Second Test.

Manager: R. O. Skerritt. *Coach:* R. A. Harper.

WEST INDIAN TOUR RESULTS

Test matches – Played 2: Won 1, Drawn 1.
First-class matches – Played 6: Won 3, Drawn 3.
Wins – Zimbabwe, ZCU President's XI, Kenyans.
Draws – Zimbabwe, Zimbabwe A, Kenyans.
One-day internationals – Played 8: Won 6, Lost 2. *Wins* – Zimbabwe (2), India, Kenya (3). *Losses* – India (2).
Other non-first-class matches – Played 3: Won 2, Lost 1. *Wins* – CFX Academy, Zimbabwe A. *Loss* – Zimbabwe Country Districts.

Note: Matches in this section which were not first-class are signified by a dagger.

†At Country Club, Harare, June 17. West Indians won by six runs. Toss: West Indians. West Indians 211 for three (45 overs) (D. Ganga 101, C. H. Gayle 76); CFX Academy 205 for five (45 overs) (A. J. C. Neethling 54, G. M. Croxford 86, Extras 31; M. N. Samuels three for 29).

†At Harare South Country Club, Harare, June 20. Zimbabwe Country Districts won by seven wickets. Toss: West Indians. West Indians 206 for nine (50 overs) (C. L. Hooper 34, S. Chanderpaul 84; A. J. Mackay three for 22, B. G. Rogers three for 36); Zimbabwe Country Districts 210 for three (48 overs) (G. J. Rennie 72, A. C. Waller 124).

Rennie and Waller opened with 201, and were separated only six short of victory.

West Indies' matches v Zimbabwe and India in the Coca-Cola Cup (June 23–July 7) may be found in that section.

†At Harare Sports Club, Harare, June 26. West Indians won by 153 runs. Toss: Zimbabwe A. West Indians 277 for six (50 overs) (W. W. Hinds 55, R. R. Sarwan 94, M. V. Nagamootoo 43); Zimbabwe A 124 (34 overs) (G. B. Brent 36; M. V. Nagamootoo four for 44).

At Country Club, Harare, July 9, 10, 11. West Indians won by 214 runs. Toss: ZCU President's XI. West Indians 191 (N. C. McGarrell 47; D. T. Mutendera three for 41) and 457 for five dec. (C. H. Gayle 259 not out, S. Chanderpaul 52, R. R. Sarwan 76); ZCU President's XI 128 for nine dec. (H. Masakadza 35; R. D. King three for 22, D. Ramnarine three for 28) and 306 (H. Masakadza 38, G. J. Whittall 45, D. P. Viljoen 50, P. A. Strang 81 not out, D. T. Mutendera 34; R. D. King three for 42, C. E. L. Stuart three for 49, D. Ramnarine three for 98).

Gayle's 259 not out lasted 410 minutes and 297 balls and included 40 fours. In the President's XI's second innings, Strang and Mutendera added 114 for the ninth wicket in 81 minutes.

At Kwekwe, July 14, 15, 16. Drawn. Toss: Zimbabwe A. West Indians 374 (D. Ganga 79, C. H. Gayle 164, C. L. Hooper 49, M. N. Samuels 50; R. W. Price five for 121) and 395 (C. H. Gayle 99, R. R. Sarwan 43, M. N. Samuels 84, C. L. Hooper 95); Zimbabwe A 345 (A. D. R. Campbell 140, H. Masakadza 33, G. J. Rennie 32, B. C. Strang 50 not out; M. I. Black three for 109, C. E. L. Stuart five for 58) and 55 for no wkt (G. M. Croxford 41 not out).

ZIMBABWE v WEST INDIES

First Test Match

At Bulawayo, July 19, 20, 21, 22. West Indies won by an innings and 176 runs. Toss: Zimbabwe. Test debut: T. Taibu.

For all but the four hours Ebrahim and Campbell occupied during a record opening stand of 164, the West Indians were wholly dominant, completing their massive victory ten balls after tea on the fourth day. On an excellent pitch, even in pace and bounce and unaffected by the layer of ice that formed nightly on the covers, they started the match by routing Zimbabwe in just over two sessions. Their batsmen then made best use of the conditions to amass what was briefly the highest total in any Test in Zimbabwe, 559 for six declared, with hundreds from Gayle and Hooper. Once they separated Zimbabwe's openers in the second innings, West Indies hurried to victory by claiming all nine wickets for 64 runs in 38 overs. The home side were one man short, Carlisle having broken his finger in the field.

Injuries had already weakened both teams, and to reinforce their ravaged pace attack West Indies had flown in Collins, the Barbadian left-arm fast bowler, who had not played a first-class match for more than a year. Picked purely on his performance in the nets, he started Zimbabwe's first-innings woes with two wickets in his opening seven-over spell (though his second spell saw him break down in mid-over). King and Stuart capitalised on some loose batting, and only Whittall resisted long.

Ganga and Gayle had 100 in the bank by the end of the first day. They carried on to 214 before Ganga, handicapped by a blow to the calf from a stray throw-in, fell to Price's left-arm spin for 89, his highest Test score. Gayle had already reached his maiden international hundred, though he was lucky umpire Riazuddin didn't detect an edge off Streak when 96. Otherwise, it was an impressive display. Thumping his strokes with a fierce power that brought him 34 fours from 255 balls, he had plundered 175 in six and a half hours when he spooned a catch to mid-on. Not that there was any respite for the beleaguered Zimbabweans. Hooper smoothly advanced to his tenth Test hundred, and first as captain, adding 131 with Sarwan and 100 with Samuels. His only error came in the third over of the third day, when he was dropped by Streak at short extra cover off Strang. Hooper struck a six and 18 fours in all directions before providing wicket-keeper Tatenda Taibu, the 18-year-old schoolboy debutant, with his first catch; 40 minutes later, he declared with an advantage of 404.

Ebrahim, in his fifth Test, and Campbell, who had been promoted to open for the first time in his 53rd, were undaunted. By the close, they had reduced the deficit by 112, and they proceeded to erase Zimbabwe's first-wicket record of 156, between Grant Flower and Gavin Rennie against New Zealand in 1997-98. But when the pacy Stuart, consistently clocked in the high 80s, claimed three lbw decisions to remove Ebrahim, Taibu, promoted above his station, and Wishart, the fight went out of Zimbabwe. Campbell escaped when caught at 97 off a Stuart no-ball and reached his second Test hundred, only to misread the line from McGarrell and be lbw offering no stroke. It was a rare misjudgment in almost five hours' batting, during which he struck ten fours. Once he had gone, the last five wickets added only 35.

Man of the Match: C. H. Gayle.

Close of play: First day, West Indies 100-0 (Ganga 44*, Gayle 52*); Second day, West Indies 393-3 (Sarwan 47*, Hooper 66*); Third day, Zimbabwe 112-0 (Ebrahim 51*, Campbell 58*).

Zimbabwe

D. D. Ebrahim lbw b Collins	0	– lbw b Stuart	71
A. D. R. Campbell c Jacobs b King	21	– lbw b McGarrell	103
S. V. Carlisle c Hooper b Collins	10	– absent hurt	
C. B. Wishart c Chanderpaul b Stuart	36	– lbw b Stuart	4
G. J. Whittall c Gayle b Stuart	42	– not out	10
G. W. Flower c Jacobs b King	6	– c Gayle b McGarrell	2
*H. H. Streak c Chanderpaul b McGarrell	5	– c Sarwan b McGarrell	2
A. M. Blignaut c Gayle b King	21	– c and b McGarrell	9
†T. Taibu c Sarwan b Stuart	6	– (3) lbw b Stuart	4
B. C. Strang not out	0	– (9) c sub (L. V. Garrick) b King	7
R. W. Price lbw b King	0	– (10) c sub (L. V. Garrick) b King	4
L-b 3, n-b 5	8	L-b 8, n-b 4	12
1/1 (1) 2/31 (3) 3/31 (2) 4/80 (4) 5/105 (6) 6/119 (7) 7/139 (5) 8/155 (9) 9/155 (8) 10/155 (11)	155	1/164 (1) 2/170 (3) 3/187 (4) 4/193 (2) 5/195 (6) 6/197 (7) 7/211 (8) 8/218 (9) 9/228 (10)	228

Bowling: *First Innings*—King 17–4–51–4; Collins 13.3–4–29–2; Stuart 15.3–3–45–3; McGarrell 12–5–22–1; Hooper 1–0–5–0. *Second Innings*—King 23.4–9–47–2; Collins 13–1–47–0; McGarrell 24–9–38–4; Stuart 19–5–45–3; Hooper 21–6–38–0; Samuels 1–0–5–0.

West Indies

D. Ganga c and b Price	89
C. H. Gayle c Price b Streak	175
S. Chanderpaul c Whittall b Streak	7
R. R. Sarwan c Blignaut b Strang	58
*C. L. Hooper c Taibu b Strang	149
M. N. Samuels b Price	42
†R. D. Jacobs not out	19
N. C. McGarrell not out	8
B 1, l-b 10, n-b 1	12
1/214 (1) 2/261 (3) 3/289 (2) 4/420 (4) 5/520 (6) 6/538 (5) (6 wkts dec.)	559

C. E. L. Stuart, P. T. Collins and R. D. King did not bat.

Bowling: Streak 35–8–110–2; Blignaut 30–6–116–0; Strang 45–15–111–2; Price 44–6–157–2; Flower 13–1–52–0; Whittall 1–0–2–0.

Umpires: Riazuddin (Pakistan) and I. D. Robinson.
Third umpire: C. K. Coventry. Referee: D. T. Lindsay (South Africa).

ZIMBABWE v WEST INDIES

Second Test Match

At Harare, July 27, 28, 29, 30, 31. Drawn. Toss: West Indies. Test debut: H. Masakadza.

Eleven days short of his 18th birthday, schoolboy Hamilton Masakadza became the youngest batsman to score a hundred on Test debut, inspiring a remarkable Zimbabwean recovery from a first-innings deficit of 216. It was ironic that their bid for an extraordinary victory should have been spoiled by the first significant rain of the season. Streak's second-innings declaration at 563 for nine, Zimbabwe's highest Test score, left his bowlers a theoretical 114 overs to dismiss West Indies, chasing a target of 348. The weather allowed only 46.2 overs, 31 of them on a damp, grey, frigid final day before the match was abandoned as a draw with only one West Indian wicket down.

The performance of Masakadza, the ninth black cricketer to represent his country in Tests, carried significance even beyond its statistical merit. He was cheered on by hundreds of schoolchildren, bused there in an effort to spread the cricketing gospel to the majority black population.

Until Masakadza made history on the third day, helped by Campbell and Wishart, West Indies held a firm grip. Zimbabwe folded on the first day, for even less than in Bulawayo, through inept batting against a varied attack in which Black replaced the injured Collins. McGarrell took four for one in 18 balls immediately after lunch, and the collapse was only briefly halted by Whittall.

Although Gayle failed for once, Ganga and Chanderpaul added 100 at a run a minute to carry West Indies to within five of the lead by the close. Chanderpaul was undone by Streak with the sixth ball next morning but the middle order effortlessly pushed the lead past 200. The stylish Sarwan shared half-century stands with Hooper, Samuels and McGarrell but, for the second time in his brief career, was run out in sight of a maiden Test hundred. He fell for 91 against South Africa in March; now he was 14 away when Masakadza's direct hit from mid-off found him short of his ground. He hit 13 fours in five hours.

The last thing Zimbabwe needed was to lose Ebrahim to a dubious decision off the last ball of the day. But their revival followed over the next two as West Indies dropped their guard. Masakadza, tall, upright and strong on the leg side, benefited from chances at 28 and 101, yet was never unsettled. He put on 91 with Campbell and 169 with Wishart to take Zimbabwe into the lead. Wishart was carelessly run out seven short of his own maiden hundred as his young partner closed in on the landmark. When Masakadza finally went early on the fourth morning, after just under six and a half hours and 316 balls, from which he hit 12 fours, and was soon followed by Flower, Zimbabwe's position was slipping. But Streak and Blignaut restored the balance with a no-nonsense, run-a-minute stand of 154, a Zimbabwean seventh-wicket record that exposed the worst of their shattered opponents. Dropped twice, Blignaut hit three sixes and 12 fours in a 118-ball 92 before missing a wild swing at Stuart. Streak was unbeaten at the declaration with 83, including a six and ten fours, and was soon back out to remove Ganga. Then the weather that spoiled the last day began to set in. There was time only for Gayle to maintain his prolific form with another half-century.

Man of the Match: H. Masakadza. *Man of the Series:* C. H. Gayle.

Close of play: First day, West Indies 126-2 (Chanderpaul 74*, Sarwan 2*); Second day, Zimbabwe 27-1 (Campbell 9*); Third day, Zimbabwe 324-4 (Masakadza 115*); Fourth day, West Indies 42-1 (Gayle 17*, Sarwan 11*).

Zimbabwe

D. D. Ebrahim c Browne b King	19	– c Browne b Stuart	12
A. D. R. Campbell lbw b Stuart	13	– c Gayle b Hooper	65
H. Masakadza b Stuart	9	– c Hooper b McGarrell	119
C. B. Wishart lbw b McGarrell	8	– run out	93
G. J. Whittall c Ganga b Black	43	– lbw b McGarrell	12
G. W. Flower c Browne b McGarrell	0	– c Chanderpaul b King	15
*H. H. Streak lbw b McGarrell	6	– not out	83
A. M. Blignaut c Browne b McGarrell	0	– b Stuart	92
†T. Taibu c King b Stuart	9	– b Stuart	10
B. C. Strang c Sarwan b Black	20	– c Gayle b McGarrell	13
R. W. Price not out	0		
L-b 1, w 2, n-b 1	4	B 11, l-b 21, n-b 17	49
1/20 (1) 2/42 (2) 3/43 (3) 4/62 (4) 5/62 (6) 6/68 (7) 7/72 (8) 8/95 (9) 9/116 (5) 10/131 (10)	131	1/27 (1) 2/118 (2) 3/287 (4) 4/324 (5) 5/333 (3) 6/367 (6) 7/521 (8) 8/535 (9) 9/563 (10)	(9 wkts dec.) 563

Bowling: *First Innings*—King 16–6–39–1; Black 11.1–2–35–2; Stuart 13–2–33–3; McGarrell 17–7–23–4. *Second Innings*—King 27–7–80–1; Black 17–1–93–0; McGarrell 60–19–162–3; Stuart 32–9–99–3; Hooper 28–7–86–1; Samuels 3–0–11–0.

West Indies

D. Ganga c Taibu b Blignaut	43	– c Strang b Streak	5
C. H. Gayle lbw b Strang	6	– not out	52
S. Chanderpaul c Taibu b Streak	74		
R. R. Sarwan run out	86	– (3) not out	31
*C. L. Hooper c Streak b Strang	39		
M. N. Samuels c Campbell b Price	39		
†C. O. Browne c Taibu b Blignaut	13		
N. C. McGarrell c sub (T. J. Friend) b Strang	33		
C. E. L. Stuart lbw b Strang	1		
M. I. Black b Price	6		
R. D. King not out	2		
L-b 2, w 2, n-b 1	5	B 4, l-b 5, w 1	10
1/14 (2) 2/114 (1) 3/126 (3) 4/180 (5) 5/259 (6) 6/283 (7) 7/333 (4) 8/338 (9) 9/345 (8) 10/347 (10)	347	1/25 (1)	(1 wkt) 98

Bowling: *First Innings*—Streak 22–6–75–1; Strang 32–13–83–4; Blignaut 16–2–92–2; Price 35.2–13–81–2; Flower 6–3–14–0. *Second Innings*—Streak 15.2–4–34–1; Blignaut 8–3–24–0; Strang 14–8–19–0; Price 8–3–9–0; Masakadza 1–0–3–0.

Umpires: A. V. Jayaprakash (India) and K. C. Barbour.
Third umpire: Q. J. Goosen. Referee: D. T. Lindsay (South Africa).

At Ruaraka Sports Club, Nairobi, August 4, 5, 6. West Indians won by an innings and 47 runs. Toss: West Indians. Kenyans 233 (S. O. Tikolo 59, M. A. Suji 37, C. O. Otieno 47; P. T. Collins three for 43) and 134 (M. I. Black six for 35, C. D. Collymore three for 27); West Indians 414 for seven dec. (L. V. Garrick 71, W. W. Hinds 83, R. R. Sarwan 108, S. Chanderpaul 46, C. O. Browne 52 not out; M. O. Odumbe three for 58).

At Mombasa, August 9, 10, 11, 12. Drawn. Toss: West Indians. Kenyans 290 (S. O. Tikolo 75, H. S. Modi 36, T. M. Odoyo 33, M. A. Suji 47 not out; R. D. King three for 42); West Indians 403 for seven (D. Ganga 105, C. H. Gayle 84, W. W. Hinds 50, C. O. Browne 56, N. C. McGarrell 54 not out; M. O. Odumbe three for 71).

†KENYA v WEST INDIES

First One-Day International

At Simba Union, Nairobi, August 15. West Indies won by 106 runs. Toss: Kenya. International debuts: C. O. Obuya, D. O. Obuya.

Gayle converted his maiden one-day international hundred into 152 off 150 balls, and his opening partnership of 174 with Ganga in 34 overs virtually settled the outcome. Gayle struck three sixes and 17 fours in a chanceless display of powerful strokes; Ganga was less assured, offering two early catches plus a stumping. His dismissal was quickly followed by the run-outs of Hinds and Hooper, but Chanderpaul and Sarwan finished with a flourish: 55 off the last 25 balls. From 63 for six against West Indies' pace, Odoyo's run-a-ball 40 and enterprising lower-order batting brought the Kenyan reply some respectability. Stuart claimed five wickets in his third one-day international.

Man of the Match: C. H. Gayle.

West Indies

C. H. Gayle b Odoyo	152	R. R. Sarwan not out	32
D. Ganga lbw b Tikolo	68	B 1, l-b 5, w 3, n-b 2	11
W. W. Hinds run out	6		
*C. L. Hooper run out	4	1/174 2/185 (4 wkts, 50 overs)	311
S. Chanderpaul not out	38	3/196 4/256	

†C. O. Browne, N. C. McGarrell, C. E. L. Stuart, C. D. Collymore and R. D. King did not bat.

Bowling: M. A. Suji 10–2–49–0; Odoyo 9–1–51–1; T. O. Suji 3–0–27–0; Odumbe 9–0–59–0; Ababu 6–0–34–0; C. O. Obuya 5–0–25–0; Tikolo 7–0–45–1; Kamande 1–0–15–0.

Kenya

R. D. Shah c Browne b Stuart	10	C. O. Obuya c Gayle b Stuart	27
†D. O. Obuya c Hooper b Collymore	7	J. K. Kamande not out	28
S. O. Tikolo lbw b Collymore	0	J. S. Ababu c Stuart b Gayle	17
H. S. Modi c Gayle b Stuart	4	B 4, l-b 8, w 18, n-b 1	31
*M. O. Odumbe c McGarrell b King	13		
T. M. Odoyo c McGarrell b Collymore	40	1/18 2/18 3/27 (49.3 overs)	205
M. A. Suji c Browne b Stuart	1	4/47 5/60 6/63	
T. O. Suji c Hooper b Stuart	27	7/105 8/152 9/161	

Bowling: King 10–2–31–1; Collymore 9–2–26–3; Stuart 10–1–44–5; McGarrell 10–1–46–0; Gayle 7.3–2–23–1; Sarwan 3–0–23–0.

Umpires: D. L. Orchard (South Africa) and S. R. Modi.
Third umpire: N. N. Dave.

†KENYA v WEST INDIES

Second One-Day International

At Gymkhana, Nairobi, August 18. West Indies won by six wickets. Toss: Kenya.

There was a hint that Kenya might repeat their stunning victory of the 1996 World Cup when their last three wickets added 108 and the lively Martin Suji reduced West Indies to 17 for three in nine overs. But Chanderpaul struck an unbeaten 87 from 95 balls, with a six and ten fours, to

---

HIGHEST TENTH-WICKET PARTNERSHIPS IN ONE-DAY INTERNATIONALS

106*	I. V. A. Richards (189*) and M. A. Holding (12*), West Indies v England at Manchester	1984
72	Abdur Razzaq (46*) and Waqar Younis (33), Pakistan v South Africa at Durban	1997-98
71	A. M. E. Roberts (37*) and J. Garner (37), West Indies v India at Manchester	1983
66	**J. K. Kamande (32*) and P. Ochieng (36), Kenya v West Indies at Nairobi**	**2001**
65	M. C. Snedden (40) and E. J. Chatfield (19*), New Zealand v Sri Lanka at Derby	1983

Research: Gordon Vince

---

guarantee another straightforward victory. He added 91 with Samuels and 85 unbroken with Hooper. Kenya had looked unlikely to raise even 100 when Martin Suji was seventh out at 84. Then the tail exploited West Indian complacency; the last-wicket stand of 66 between Kamande and Ochieng was the fourth-highest in all one-day internationals.

Man of the Match: S. Chanderpaul.

Kenya

†D. O. Obuya c Hooper b King	11
R. D. Shah b Collymore	5
S. O. Tikolo c Browne b Stuart	14
H. S. Modi c Browne b King	1
*M. O. Odumbe c Browne b King	28
T. M. Odoyo c Hinds b Stuart	5
M. A. Suji c Hinds b McGarrell	2
T. O. Suji c Browne b King	9
C. O. Obuya c Gayle b Samuels	25
J. K. Kamande not out	32
P. Ochieng b Gayle	36
L-b 5, w 19	24
1/18 2/22 3/24 4/58 5/71 6/80 7/84 8/101 9/126 (49.1 overs)	192

Bowling: King 10–2–32–4; Collymore 10–0–36–1; Stuart 10–1–37–2; McGarrell 10–0–35–1; Samuels 6–0–38–1; Gayle 3.1–1–9–1.

West Indies

D. Ganga c Odoyo b M. A. Suji	4
C. H. Gayle c Odoyo b M. A. Suji	10
W. W. Hinds lbw b M. A. Suji	0
M. N. Samuels b C. O. Obuya	46
S. Chanderpaul not out	87
*C. L. Hooper not out	33
L-b 5, w 2, n-b 6	13
1/14 2/14 3/17 4/108 (4 wkts, 45.5 overs)	193

†C. O. Browne, N. C. McGarrell, C. E. L. Stuart, C. D. Collymore and R. D. King did not bat.

Bowling: M. A. Suji 8–1–23–3; Ochieng 9–1–26–0; Odoyo 6–0–34–0; Tikolo 3–0–14–0; C. O. Obuya 8–0–41–1; Odumbe 5–0–25–0; T. O. Suji 4–0–16–0; Kamande 2.5–0–9–0.

Umpires: D. L. Orchard (South Africa) and N. N. Dave.
Third umpire: L. K. Bhudia.

†KENYA v WEST INDIES

Third One-Day International

At Gymkhana, Nairobi, August 19. West Indies won by seven wickets. Toss: Kenya. International debut: B. J. Patel.

Kenya raised their highest total of the series but were unable to prevent West Indies completing a clean sweep with plenty in reserve. Odumbe called for more commitment from his top order – and his was the only single-figure score from the first six. David Obuya and Shah opened with a solid 74 and, after McGarrell had removed both plus Odumbe in 15 balls, Tikolo showed his class with a 65-ball 71; he hit three sixes and five fours, and shared fifty stands with Odoyo and Modi. The tail, however, could not reproduce their earlier contributions. Garrick replaced Ganga as Gayle's opening partner and, after a shaky start, helped him run up 116. Gayle completed his prolific African tour with a run-a-ball 70.

Man of the Match: S. O. Tikolo. *Man of the Series:* C. H. Gayle.

Kenya

†D. O. Obuya b McGarrell	34
R. D. Shah c Browne b McGarrell	29
S. O. Tikolo lbw b Stuart	71
*M. O. Odumbe c Browne b McGarrell	2
T. M. Odoyo c Hooper b Collymore	31
H. S. Modi not out	29
T. O. Suji st Browne b Gayle	3
P. Ochieng b Gayle	1
C. O. Obuya not out	7
L-b 12, w 8, n-b 5	25
1/74 2/87 3/97 4/158 5/208 6/220 7/222 (7 wkts, 50 overs)	232

J. K. Kamande and B. J. Patel did not bat.

Bowling: Collymore 10–1–37–1; Collins 10–1–40–0; Stuart 10–1–33–1; McGarrell 10–0–44–3; Gayle 9–0–58–2; Hooper 1–0–8–0.

West Indies

L. V. Garrick b Tikolo	76	S. Chanderpaul not out	4
C. H. Gayle c D. O. Obuya b Tikolo	70		
W. W. Hinds not out	44	L-b 2, w 8	10
M. N. Samuels st D. O. Obuya b Kamande	30	1/116 2/188 3/226 (3 wkts, 47.1 overs)	234

*C. L. Hooper, †C. O. Browne, N. C. McGarrell, C. E. L. Stuart, C. D. Collymore and P. T. Collins did not bat.

Bowling: Odoyo 7–1–24–0; Ochieng 5–0–40–0; Suji 5–1–20–0; C. O. Obuya 7–0–43–0; Odumbe 10–0–42–0; Tikolo 10–0–43–2; Kamande 3–0–16–1; Modi 0.1–0–4–0.

Umpires: D. L. Orchard (South Africa) and R. D'Mello.
Third umpire: S. R. Modi. Series referee: G. R. Viswanath.

PWC TEST RATINGS

Introduced in 1987, the PricewaterhouseCoopers (PwC) Ratings (originally the Deloitte Ratings, and later the Coopers & Lybrand Ratings) rank Test cricketers on a scale up to 1,000 according to their performances in Test matches. The ratings take into account playing conditions, the quality of the opposition and the result of the matches. In August 1998, a similar set of ratings for one-day internationals was added (see page 1156).

The leading 20 batsmen and bowlers in the Test ratings after the 2001 Test series between Sri Lanka and India which ended on September 2 were:

	Batsmen	*Rating*		*Bowlers*	*Rating*
1	S. R. Waugh (*Australia*)	876	1	G. D. McGrath (*Australia*)	919
2	S. R. Tendulkar (*India*)	866	2	S. M. Pollock (*South Africa*)	896
3	A. Flower (*Zimbabwe*)	830	3	M. Muralitharan (*Sri Lanka*)	824
4	Inzamam-ul-Haq (*Pakistan*)	818	4	A. A. Donald (*South Africa*)	817
5	R. Dravid (*India*)	798	5	D. Gough (*England*)	746
6	A. C. Gilchrist (*Australia*)	790	6	S. K. Warne (*Australia*)	736
7	D. P. M. D. Jayawardene (*Sri Lanka*)	786	7	H. H. Streak (*Zimbabwe*)	706
8	B. C. Lara (*West Indies*)	768	8	Waqar Younis (*Pakistan*)	686
9	D. J. Cullinan (*South Africa*)	746	9	Saqlain Mushtaq (*Pakistan*)	678
10	M. E. Waugh (*Australia*)	743	10	C. L. Cairns (*New Zealand*)	663
11	Saeed Anwar (*Pakistan*)	694	11	J. N. Gillespie (*Australia*)	661
12	C. D. McMillan (*New Zealand*)	688	12	J. H. Kallis (*South Africa*)	646
13	G. P. Thorpe (*England*)	686	13	Harbhajan Singh (*India*)	640
14	Yousuf Youhana (*Pakistan*)	668	14	C. R. Miller (*Australia*)	621
15	R. T. Ponting (*Australia*)	667	15	Wasim Akram (*Pakistan*)	615
16	M. H. Richardson (*New Zealand*)	666	16	J. Srinath (*India*)	614
17	A. J. Stewart (*England*)	665	17	A. R. Caddick (*England*)	606
18	D. R. Martyn (*Australia*)	659	18	D. J. Nash (*New Zealand*)	604
19	C. L. Cairns (*New Zealand*)	657	19	D. W. Fleming (*Australia*)	580
19	J. L. Langer (*Australia*)	657	20	S. C. G. MacGill (*Australia*)	563

The following players have topped the ratings since they were launched on June 17, 1987. The date shown is that on which they first went top; those marked by an asterisk have done so more than once.

Batting: D. B. Vengsarkar, June 17, 1987; Javed Miandad*, February 28, 1989; R. B. Richardson*, November 20, 1989; M. A. Taylor, October 23, 1990; G. A. Gooch*, June 10, 1991; D. L. Haynes, May 6, 1993; B. C. Lara*, April 21, 1994; S. R. Tendulkar*, December 5, 1994; J. C. Adams, December 14, 1994; S. R. Waugh*, May 3, 1995; Inzamam-ul-Haq, December 3, 1997.

Bowling: R. J. Hadlee*, June 17, 1987; M. D. Marshall*, June 21, 1988; Waqar Younis*, December 17, 1991; C. E. L. Ambrose*, July 26, 1992; S. K. Warne*, November 29, 1994; G. D. McGrath*, December 3, 1996; A. A. Donald*, March 30, 1998; S. M. Pollock*, November 1, 1999.

THE INDIANS IN SRI LANKA, 2001

By SA'ADI THAWFEEQ

Sri Lanka recorded only their second Test series win against India when they beat them 2–1 at home. Their one previous Test match win over their neighbours had come in 1985-86, when Duleep Mendis led them to victory in the Second Test at Colombo and took the series 1–0. They had lost the next home series, in 1993-94, and drew both matches on India's last full tour, in August 1997. That was best remembered for a run glut, with Sri Lanka amassing the highest total in Test cricket, 952 for six declared, including 340 to Sanath Jayasuriya.

For Jayasuriya, now captain, and his team, this current success was even greater cause for celebration because it was their first in four home series. Since beating Australia in September 1999, they had lost to Pakistan, drawn with South Africa and lost to England. In the last two series, Sri Lanka had begun on a winning note at Galle, only to squander the lead by losing at Kandy. Against India, history repeated itself. But this time, Sri Lanka broke the unlucky sequence in the final Test at Colombo, coming up with a compelling performance to triumph by an innings and 77 runs. It was Indian captain Sourav Ganguly's first Test series loss since taking charge the previous year.

The difference between the two sides lay in the home batting and the off-spin of Muttiah Muralitharan. In the First Test, Jayasuriya set the tone for a ten-wicket victory with an aggressive century; in the Third, four batsmen made hundreds in a total of 610 for six declared, after Muralitharan had spun out India on the opening day with figures of eight for 87. The champion spinner was in his element and finished the series with 23 wickets, more than the next two most successful bowlers put together. This was in marked contrast to his fellow off-spinner, Harbhajan Singh, who came to Sri Lanka with a huge reputation after destroying world champions Australia in India with a rich haul of 32 wickets. He was expected to flourish on Sri Lankan pitches, but the home batsmen tackled him so well – as the Zimbabweans had two months earlier – that he returned a meagre four wickets at 73.00 each.

Sandwiched between Sri Lanka's victories was their defeat at Kandy, where a sense of complacency crept in and the batsmen failed to apply themselves. They took first-innings lead, but effectively lost the Test on the third morning, when four top-order wickets tumbled for 64. Kandy was the only Test in which the Indian batting clicked, with Ganguly and his deputy, Rahul Dravid, leading the run-chase to victory. In the absence of the injured Sachin Tendulkar and V. V. S. Laxman, the tourists relied heavily on the experience of these two. Ganguly came the closest to three figures, with an unbeaten 98 at Kandy, while Dravid led the averages with 235 runs at 47.00. Against this, four Sri Lankans averaged more than 50, and six scored centuries. Mahela Jayawardene was the leading batsman, with 296 at 74.00, including two hundreds.

Overall, the Sri Lankans had their game plan well organised and they capitalised fully on India's mistakes. But, in their defence, the tourists were severely depleted. Anil Kumble had missed most of the season through injury, Tendulkar was forced to withdraw before setting out – ending a sequence of 84 consecutive Tests – Laxman and Ashish Nehra joined the injury list during the preceding one-day tournament, and Javagal Srinath returned home after fracturing a finger in the First Test. Although this gave some of the younger Indian players an opportunity to press their claims, they showed far less ability to adapt to Test cricket than the Sri Lankan youngsters.

The series was played in a friendly atmosphere, the only black mark being Ganguly's one-match suspension for dissent and a later fine for bringing the game into disrepute during the triangular one-day tournament. In this, India recovered from a poor start, only to lose to Sri Lanka at the last. It confirmed India's reputation for choking in finals, just as the Tests confirmed their dismal record overseas; it was 15 years since they won a full Test series on foreign soil.

INDIAN TOURING PARTY

S. C. Ganguly (Bengal) (*captain*), R. Dravid (Karnataka) (*vice-captain*), A. B. Agarkar (Mumbai), H. K. Badani (Tamil Nadu), S. V. Bahutule (Mumbai), S. S. Das (Orissa), S. S. Dighe (Mumbai), Harbhajan Singh (Punjab), Harvinder Singh (Railways), M. Kaif (Uttar Pradesh), A. R. Khurasiya (Madhya Pradesh), V. V. S. Laxman (Hyderabad), J. J. Martin (Baroda), D. S. Mohanty (Orissa), D. Mongia (Punjab), A. Nehra (Delhi), B. K. V. Prasad (Karnataka), S. Ramesh (Tamil Nadu), R. L. Sanghvi (Delhi), V. Sehwag (Delhi), R. S. Sodhi (Punjab), J. Srinath (Karnataka), Yuvraj Singh (Punjab), Zaheer Khan (Baroda).

Bahutule, Das, Harvinder Singh, Kaif, Mongia, Prasad, Ramesh and Srinath joined the party for the Test leg of the tour, while Agarkar, Khurasiya, Laxman, Mohanty, Nehra, Sehwag, Sodhi and Yuvraj Singh left after the one-day internationals. S. R. Tendulkar (Mumbai), who was also scheduled to arrive then, withdrew injured and was replaced by Martin.

Team manager: A. N. Mate. *Coach:* J. G. Wright.

INDIAN TOUR RESULTS

Test matches – Played 3: Won 1, Lost 2.
First-class matches – Played 4: Won 1, Lost 2, Drawn 1.
Win – Sri Lanka.
Losses – Sri Lanka (2).
Draw – Sri Lankan Board XI.
One-day internationals – Played 7: Won 3, Lost 4. *Wins* – Sri Lanka (2), New Zealand. *Losses* – New Zealand (2), Sri Lanka (2).

TEST MATCH AVERAGES

SRI LANKA – BATTING

	T	*I*	*NO*	*R*	*HS*	*100s*	*50s*	*Avge*	*Ct/St*
D. P. M. D. Jayawardene	3	4	0	296	139	2	0	74.00	3
K. Sangakkara	3	4	1	196	105*	1	0	65.33	6/1
H. P. Tillekeratne	3	4	1	173	136*	1	0	57.66	6
M. S. Atapattu	3	5	1	225	108	1	0	56.25	3
S. T. Jayasuriya	3	5	1	156	111	1	0	39.00	3
M. Muralitharan	3	3	0	80	67	0	1	26.66	1
W. P. U. J. C. Vaas	3	3	0	59	42	0	0	19.66	0
R. P. Arnold	3	4	0	60	31	0	0	15.00	4
A. S. A. Perera	2	3	0	34	18	0	0	11.33	1
P. D. R. L. Perera	2	3	2	6	6*	0	0	6.00	0
C. R. D. Fernando	3	3	0	11	4	0	0	3.66	1

Played in one Test: D. K. Liyanage 3; T. T. Samaraweera 103*.

* *Signifies not out.*

BOWLING

	O	*M*	*R*	*W*	*BB*	*5W/i*	*Avge*
M. Muralitharan	177.3	51	444	23	8-87	2	19.30
P. D. R. L. Perera	36	9	95	4	2-21	0	23.75
C. R. D. Fernando	101	24	304	9	5-42	1	33.77
W. P. U. J. C. Vaas	130.4	40	312	9	4-65	0	34.66

Also bowled: R. P. Arnold 2–0–7–0; S. T. Jayasuriya 31–13–56–2; D. K. Liyanage 14–2–44–0; A. S. A. Perera 17–0–54–0; T. T. Samaraweera 10–4–22–1.

INDIA – BATTING

	T	*I*	*NO*	*R*	*HS*	*100s*	*50s*	*Avge*	*Ct*
R. Dravid	3	6	1	235	75	0	2	47.00	2
S. Ramesh	3	6	0	223	55	0	1	37.16	4
S. S. Das	3	6	0	217	68	0	2	36.16	1
S. C. Ganguly	3	6	1	166	98*	0	1	33.20	0
M. Kaif	3	6	1	106	37	0	0	21.20	1
B. K. V. Prasad	3	5	3	35	20	0	0	17.50	0
Harbhajan Singh	3	5	0	79	44	0	0	15.80	0
H. K. Badani	3	5	0	76	38	0	0	15.20	4
Zaheer Khan	3	5	1	48	45	0	0	12.00	0
S. S. Dighe	3	5	0	44	28	0	0	8.80	8

Played in one Test: S. V. Bahutule 18, 0; Harvinder Singh 6; J. Srinath 0* (1 ct).

* *Signifies not out.*

BOWLING

	O	*M*	*R*	*W*	*BB*	*5W/i*	*Avge*
J. Srinath	25.5	6	114	5	5-114	1	22.80
B. K. V. Prasad	97	23	308	11	5-72	1	28.00
Zaheer Khan	98.5	16	367	10	4-76	0	36.70
Harbhajan Singh	98	21	292	4	2-185	0	73.00

Also bowled: H. K. Badani 8–2–17–0; S. V. Bahutule 31–5–101–1; S. C. Ganguly 39.3–12–134–2; Harvinder Singh 22.3–2–87–2; S. Ramesh 5–0–24–0.

India's matches v New Zealand and Sri Lanka in the Coca-Cola Cup (July 20–August 5) may be found in that section.

At P. Saravanamuttu Stadium, Colombo, August 8, 9, 10. Drawn. Toss: Sri Lankan Board XI. Sri Lankan Board XI 326 (M. G. van Dort 116, T. T. Samaraweera 76; J. Srinath three for 68, R. L. Sanghvi three for 143); Indians 281 for five dec. (S. S. Das 72, S. Ramesh 63, S. C. Ganguly 74 not out).

The match was moved from Matara on security grounds. On the third day, the Indians declared after one over because of a dangerous pitch; attempts to restore it to a fit state failed and play was abandoned.

SRI LANKA v INDIA

First Test Match

At Galle, August 14, 15, 16, 17. Sri Lanka won by ten wickets. Toss: Sri Lanka.

The series began, like the two preceding ones in Sri Lanka, with a home win at Galle. India's only consolation was that a defiant half-century from Dravid ensured that, unlike South Africa and England, they did not suffer the ignominy of an innings defeat. Even so, Jayasuriya needed only two scoring shots to complete a ten-wicket victory on the fourth morning, having already played a major role in his team's first win over India for 15 years by contributing a stroke-filled century to their first-innings total of 362. India, who had gone into a Test without Tendulkar for the first time since April 1989, recorded their lowest total against Sri Lanka in the first innings, then did even worse in the second.

Sri Lanka had never before fielded four seamers in a home Test. This shift of emphasis derived from a policy of producing pitches with grass and bounce in the run-up to the 2003 World Cup, and Jayasuriya, winning the toss for the 18th time in 22 Tests, put India in on a strip that looked green but was dry underneath. Initially, as the openers ground their way to 79 without loss in three hours, his decision looked mistaken. But the complexion of the innings, as well as the match, changed when 22-year-old fast bowler Fernando took the second new ball at 155 for three and snatched two wickets just before the close. Next morning he completed a fiery spell of five for 18 in seven overs to record his best Test figures. He also struck the little finger of Srinath's left hand, which eventually forced him out of the series.

India had surrendered their last six wickets for 32 runs, and Jayasuriya promptly capitalised by seizing the initiative. He blazed away, cutting and pulling, unleashing a stunning square cut for six over point off Srinath as well as hitting 16 fours in his 111, made off 138 balls. Harbhajan Singh dismissed Atapattu after a two-hour century opening stand, and would have added Sangakkara, whose place was under pressure, for eight had Dravid not missed the chance at slip. It was a costly mistake; the spunky Sangakkara batted for six hours, almost twice as long as Jayasuriya, to hold the innings together while wickets fell at the other end to the Indian pace men. Tillekeratne, recalled for his first Test since March 1999, made little impression.

Earlier in the year, Sangakkara had twice narrowly missed his maiden Test hundred, against South Africa and England, and he was 93 here when last man Muralitharan came in. Murali saw him to his century – the 100th by a wicket-keeper in Tests, going back to Englishman Harry Wood's unbeaten 134 against South Africa at Cape Town in 1891-92 – and was out three balls later, a fifth wicket for Srinath, who had bravely sent down 25 overs.

Trailing by 175, India were soon under more pressure, slumping to 81 for six against pace and spin. They were all at sea against Muralitharan's guile, which some of them were encountering for the first time, and he picked up his 25th five-wicket haul in Tests. Dravid alone held out, for 219 minutes, getting India into the fourth day and making sure Sri Lanka had to bat again, even if their target was merely six. Of more concern to the Sri Lankans was their fourth seamer, Suresh Perera, who bowled just 12 overs in the match without a wicket and was reported to referee Cammie Smith by umpire Steve Bucknor over his action.

Man of the Match: S. T. Jayasuriya.

Close of play: First day, India 163-5 (Ganguly 10*, Dighe 2*); Second day, Sri Lanka 264-3 (Sangakkara 54*, Arnold 19*); Third day, India 130-8 (Dravid 37*, Prasad 5*).

India

S. S. Das c Jayasuriya b Vaas	40	– c A. S. A. Perera b P. D. R. L. Perera	23
S. Ramesh c Jayasuriya b Muralitharan	42	– b P. D. R. L. Perera	2
M. Kaif b Fernando	37	– c Tillekeratne b Muralitharan	14
R. Dravid c Arnold b Muralitharan	12	– not out	61
*S. C. Ganguly c Sangakkara b Fernando	15	– b Fernando	4
H. K. Badani c Sangakkara b Fernando	6	– c Sangakkara b Muralitharan	5
†S. S. Dighe c Sangakkara b Fernando	9	– c Arnold b Muralitharan	3
J. Srinath retired hurt	0	– absent hurt	
Harbhajan Singh b Fernando	4	– (8) c and b Muralitharan	12
Zaheer Khan not out	0	– (9) c Arnold b Jayasuriya	3
B. K. V. Prasad b Muralitharan	0	– (10) lbw b Muralitharan	20
B 4, l-b 3, w 2, n-b 13	22	B 12, l-b 8, n-b 13	33
1/79 (2) 2/105 (1) 3/124 (4) 4/155 (3) 5/161 (6) 6/176 (5) 7/181 (9) 8/185 (7) 9/187 (11)	187	1/15 (2) 2/37 (1) 3/53 (3) 4/64 (5) 5/73 (6) 6/81 (7) 7/104 (8) 8/120 (9) 9/180 (10)	180

In the first innings Srinath retired hurt at 177.

Bowling: *First Innings*—Vaas 22–10–38–1; Fernando 25–9–42–5; P. D. R. L. Perera 12–4–25–0; Muralitharan 24.3–8–41–3; A. S. A. Perera 12–0–34–0. *Second Innings*—Vaas 16–2–45–0; Fernando 17–4–35–1; P. D. R. L. Perera 8–1–21–2; Muralitharan 26.5–10–49–5; Jayasuriya 7–3–10–1.

Sri Lanka

M. S. Atapattu c Badani b Harbhajan Singh	33	– not out	0
*S. T. Jayasuriya c Dravid b Zaheer Khan	111	– not out	6
†K. Sangakkara not out	105		
D. P. M. D. Jayawardene c Dighe b Srinath	28		
R. P. Arnold c Ramesh b Prasad	20		
H. P. Tillekeratne lbw b Srinath	11		
A. S. A. Perera lbw b Srinath	1		
W. P. U. J. C. Vaas c Ramesh b Zaheer Khan	13		
C. R. D. Fernando c Srinath b Zaheer Khan	3		
P. D. R. L. Perera c Dighe b Srinath	0		
M. Muralitharan c Kaif b Srinath	8		
B 1, l-b 6, w 8, n-b 14	29		
1/101 (1) 2/171 (2) 3/211 (4) 4/274 (5) 5/292 (6) 6/296 (7) 7/316 (8) 8/340 (9) 9/342 (10) 10/362 (11)	362	(no wkt)	6

Bowling: *First Innings*—Srinath 24.5–5–114–5; Prasad 24–4–83–1; Zaheer Khan 26–3–89–3; Harbhajan Singh 33–12–69–1. *Second Innings*—Srinath 1–1–0–0; Zaheer Khan 0.5–0–6–0.

Umpires: S. A. Bucknor (West Indies) and E. A. R. de Silva.
Third umpire: P. T. Manuel. Referee: C. W. Smith (West Indies).

SRI LANKA v INDIA

Second Test Match

At Kandy, August 22, 23, 24, 25. India won by seven wickets. Toss: India.

The curse of Kandy struck again as Sri Lanka let slip a golden opportunity to go 2–0 up. An uncharacteristic collapse on the third morning, when their top order threw away the advantage of a useful 42-run first-innings lead, allowed India back into the series. Only a 64-run partnership between Muralitharan and Ruchira Perera, a Sri Lankan last-wicket record against India, raised the target to 264, and India had more than two days to chase that. Dravid was once again in the thick of things as they did so, winning the duel with Muralitharan through some audacious back-foot play square of the wicket and oozing class as he scored 75 vital runs. Meanwhile the left-handed Ganguly, without a half-century in his last 13 Test innings, made a timely return to form and, for the first time in the series, the Indian batting looked dominant. Ganguly, dismantling the bowling with his scorching drives, was a man transformed as he led his country to victory with an unbeaten 98, including 15 fours. "We were determined to stay positive," he said after the dust had settled.

For once, Jayasuriya lost the toss, and then gave India a huge psychological boost when he needlessly ran himself out, going for a second in the fifth over. But Sri Lanka rode through the day on a century from Jayawardene, who scored 104, with 17 fours and a five, out of 154 runs in almost four hours at the crease. The next best score was 42 from Vaas, who followed up with a penetrative spell of left-arm seam bowling to claim four for 65. India's eventual 232 owed everything to a face-saving 64-run stand for the seventh wicket between Dighe and Harbhajan Singh. Harbhajan's cameo 44 off 32 balls included nine fours, four off successive deliveries from Fernando.

With the game still only in its second day, Sri Lanka's priority should have been to consolidate the first-innings lead earned by their bowlers. Instead, the top order succumbed to excellent seam bowling from the left/right combination of Zaheer Khan and Prasad. Jayasuriya went cheaply again, bowled by Zaheer, who first thing on the third morning had Sangakkara caught behind with his third ball, one of four wickets to fall before lunch. Tillekeratne was the only recognised batsman to survive into the afternoon, becoming the fourth Sri Lankan to score 3,000 Test runs on the way, and when the ninth wicket fell, the overall lead was just 199.

Muralitharan, taking a leaf out of Harbhajan's book, unexpectedly opened up a prospect for Sri Lanka's bowlers to win the game. To the delight of his home crowd, he smashed an astonishing maiden Test fifty, picking everything from off to leg and reaching 67 off 65 balls with three sixes and five fours; Perera contributed just six to their heroic stand of 64. Ganguly ran out of ideas to separate them. He kept his fast bowlers on too long and set defensive fields with eight men on the line. Finally he turned to Harbhajan, who had Murali caught going for another six. Next day, it was the turn of Dravid and Ganguly to lay on the heroics, and for India to celebrate a four-day win.

Man of the Match: S. C. Ganguly.

Close of play: First day, Sri Lanka 274-9 (Vaas 42*, P. D. R. L. Perera 0*); Second day, Sri Lanka 52-1 (Atapattu 30*, Sangakkara 13*); Third day, India 55-1 (Ramesh 15*, Dravid 11*).

Sri Lanka

M. S. Atapattu b Zaheer Khan	39	– c Dighe b Prasad	45
*S. T. Jayasuriya run out	3	– b Zaheer Khan	6
†K. Sangakkara c Ramesh b Ganguly	31	– c Dighe b Zaheer Khan	13
D. P. M. D. Jayawardene c Dighe b Prasad	104	– c Badani b Zaheer Khan	25
R. P. Arnold c Dravid b Zaheer Khan	5	– (6) lbw b Zaheer Khan	4
H. P. Tillekeratne c Dighe b Prasad	10	– (5) lbw b Prasad	16
A. S. A. Perera lbw b Ganguly	18	– c Badani b Prasad	15
W. P. U. J. C. Vaas b Harvinder Singh	42	– lbw b Prasad	4
M. Muralitharan b Harvinder Singh	5	– c Ramesh b Harbhajan Singh	67
C. R. D. Fernando c Dighe b Zaheer Khan	4	– b Prasad	4
P. D. R. L. Perera not out	0	– not out	6
L-b 7, w 1, n-b 5	13	B 4, l-b 7, n-b 5	16
1/18 (2) 2/78 (3) 3/82 (1) 4/101 (5) 5/138 (6) 6/189 (7) 7/232 (4) 8/245 (9) 9/274 (10) 10/274 (8)	274	1/20 (2) 2/52 (3) 3/84 (1) 4/108 (4) 5/116 (6) 6/137 (7) 7/140 (5) 8/153 (8) 9/157 (10) 10/221 (9)	221

Bowling: *First Innings*—Zaheer Khan 22–6–62–3; Harvinder Singh 14.3–1–62–2; Prasad 18–4–52–2; Ganguly 17–5–69–2; Harbhajan Singh 7–1–22–0. *Second Innings*—Zaheer Khan 23–4–76–4; Harvinder Singh 8–1–25–0; Prasad 21–7–72–5; Ganguly 10–4–21–0; Harbhajan Singh 4.3–2–16–1.

India

S. S. Das lbw b Vaas	8	– b Muralitharan	19
S. Ramesh c Sangakkara b Fernando	47	– c Jayasuriya b Fernando	31
R. Dravid lbw b Vaas	15	– c Arnold b Muralitharan	75
*S. C. Ganguly c Tillekeratne b P. D. R. L. Perera	18	– not out	98
M. Kaif c Atapattu b Fernando	17	– not out	19
H. K. Badani c Fernando b P. D. R. L. Perera	16		
†S. S. Dighe lbw b Vaas	28		
Harbhajan Singh b Vaas	44		
Zaheer Khan c Tillekeratne b Muralitharan	0		
B. K. V. Prasad not out	1		
Harvinder Singh b Muralitharan	6		
L-b 7, w 2, n-b 23	32	B 4, l-b 2, n-b 16	22
1/11 (1) 2/36 (3) 3/68 (4) 4/120 (5) 5/123 (2) 6/154 (6) 7/218 (7) 8/223 (9) 9/223 (8) 10/232 (11)	232	1/42 (1) 2/103 (2) 3/194 (3)	(3 wkts) 264

Bowling: *First Innings*—Vaas 21–3–65–4; Fernando 14–2–66–2; P. D. R. L. Perera 7–2–23–2; Muralitharan 20.1–5–62–2; A. S. A. Perera 2–0–9–0. *Second Innings*—Vaas 20.4–9–42–0; Fernando 16–4–64–1; P. D. R. L. Perera 9–2–26–0; Muralitharan 25–2–96–2; Jayasuriya 3–0–12–0; A. S. A. Perera 3–0–11–0; Arnold 2–0–7–0.

Umpires: S. A. Bucknor (West Indies) and T. H. Wijewardene.
Third umpire: G. Silva. Referee: C. W. Smith (West Indies).

SRI LANKA v INDIA

Third Test Match

At Sinhalese Sports Club, Colombo, August 29, 30, 31, September 1, 2. Sri Lanka won by an innings and 77 runs. Toss: India. Test debut: T. T. Samaraweera.

Sri Lanka took the series by equalling their biggest winning margin in Tests, against Zimbabwe nearly five years before. They had abandoned their four-seamer strategy, dropping the two Pereras to strengthen the batting with all-rounders Liyanage, recalled for his first Test for seven years, and Thilan Samaraweera, who was making his debut on his club ground. The policy paid off splendidly. After Muralitharan had claimed eight wickets, a phenomenal achievement by any spinner on a first-day pitch, Sri Lanka batted India out of the game. Four batsmen scored hundreds in one awesome innings – an unprecedented feat for Sri Lanka – as they ran up 610 for six, their second highest total in Test cricket.

Yet until the fourth over of the first afternoon, it was India who seemed on course for a large total. Ganguly had not hesitated to bat on a pitch full of runs, and Das and Ramesh opened with 97. By the evening, the entire Indian line-up was back in the pavilion for 234, spun out by an exotic bag of tricks from Muralitharan, who exploited slight bounce in the wicket to return eight for 87 in a single spell of 34.1 overs. It was his second-best Test analysis, after nine for 65 against England in 1998, and the best by a Sri Lankan at home. The two wickets that eluded him went to Vaas, who in his 51st match became only the second bowler after Murali to take 150 Test wickets for Sri Lanka.

On the second day, the home batsmen began their feast, fed by the Indians' failure to bowl a consistent line on one side of the wicket. Atapattu provided the *hors d'oeuvre*, striking 11 fours in his 108; Jayawardene joined him in a 133-run third-wicket partnership, and next day proceeded to 139, which included one six, a five and 14 fours. But the stand that finally knocked India out was from Tillekeratne and Samaraweera. After three failures, Tillekeratne finally came good; like Atapattu and Jayawardene, he registered his seventh Test century, and advanced to a Test-best 136 not out, with 16 fours. Samaraweera became only the third Sri Lankan to make a hundred on Test debut. Though needing a runner in the later stages because of cramp, he reached an undefeated 103 off 175 balls with his tenth four, whereupon Jayasuriya immediately called them in. They had added an unbroken 194 in 201 minutes, Sri Lanka's best for the seventh wicket against any country, beating 144 by Aravinda de Silva and Ravi Ratnayeke against Australia in 1989-90.

With more than two days to go, India faced a massive deficit of 376. Once again the openers started well, this time completing their century partnership; once again Muralitharan removed them both. He had Das caught at silly point just before lunch on the fourth day, and an hour later he bowled Ramesh with a ball that pitched outside the left-hander's leg stump and whipped across him to clip the off bail – a lethal delivery to rank with Australian leg-spinner Shane Warne's "Ball of the Century" that bowled Mike Gatting at Old Trafford in 1993.

Dravid and Ganguly thwarted the home attack by taking India to a promising 186 for two that evening. Then two brilliant run-outs swung the scales back in Sri Lanka's favour. Dravid, who had completed 4,000 runs in his 48th Test and looked well set, was beaten by Atapattu's direct throw from mid-on; ten runs later, Kaif failed to make his ground after being refused a run by Ganguly. On the final day, it took Sri Lanka barely an hour to clean up. No. 10 Zaheer Khan struck five fours and two sixes in a Test-best 45 off 40 balls before Muralitharan snapped him up for final match figures of 11 for 196.

Man of the Match: M. Muralitharan. *Man of the Series:* M. Muralitharan.

Close of play: First day, Sri Lanka 13-0 (Atapattu 2*, Jayasuriya 10*); Second day, Sri Lanka 323-5 (Jayawardene 95*, Tillekeratne 0*); Third day, India 28-0 (Das 22*, Ramesh 4*); Fourth day, India 217-6 (Badani 8*, Dighe 4*).

India

S. S. Das b Muralitharan	59 – c Tillekeratne b Muralitharan	68
S. Ramesh c Jayawardene b Muralitharan	46 – b Muralitharan	55
R. Dravid c Tillekeratne b Muralitharan	36 – run out	36
*S. C. Ganguly lbw b Muralitharan	1 – c Jayawardene b Samaraweera	30
M. Kaif c Sangakkara b Vaas	14 – run out	5
H. K. Badani c Tillekeratne b Muralitharan	38 – lbw b Vaas	11
†S. S. Dighe lbw b Muralitharan	0 – (8) run out	4
S. V. Bahutule st Sangakkara b Muralitharan	18 – (7) b Jayasuriya	0
Harbhajan Singh lbw b Vaas	2 – c Atapattu b Vaas	17
Zaheer Khan c Jayawardene b Muralitharan	0 – c Atapattu b Muralitharan	45
B. K. V. Prasad not out	10 – not out	4
B 2, l-b 3, w 2, n-b 3	10 B 8, l-b 5, w 2, n-b 9	24
1/97 (1) 2/115 (2) 3/119 (4) 4/146 (5) 5/192 (3) 6/192 (7) 7/207 (6) 8/210 (9) 9/213 (10) 10/234 (8)	234 1/107 (1) 2/147 (2) 3/186 (3) 4/196 (5) 5/210 (4) 6/211 (7) 7/221 (6) 8/221 (8) 9/269 (9) 10/299 (10)	299

Bowling: *First Innings*—Vaas 24–7–60–2; Liyanage 9–2–32–0; Fernando 12–2–38–0; Muralitharan 34.1–9–87–8; Samaraweera 2–0–12–0. *Second Innings*—Vaas 27–9–62–2; Fernando 17–3–59–0; Muralitharan 46.5–17–109–3; Jayasuriya 21–10–34–1; Liyanage 5–0–12–0; Samaraweera 8–4–10–1.

Sri Lanka

M. S. Atapattu c Das b Harbhajan Singh	108
*S. T. Jayasuriya b Prasad	30
†K. Sangakkara c Badani b Prasad	47
D. P. M. D. Jayawardene lbw b Bahutule	139
R. P. Arnold b Prasad	31
D. K. Liyanage c Dighe b Harbhajan Singh	3
H. P. Tillekeratne not out	136
T. T. Samaraweera not out	103
L-b 4, w 4, n-b 5	13
1/48 (2) 2/119 (3) 3/252 (1) 4/310 (5) 5/321 (6) 6/416 (4)	(6 wkts dec.) 610

W. P. U. J. C. Vaas, M. Muralitharan and C. R. D. Fernando did not bat.

Bowling: Zaheer Khan 27–3–134–0; Prasad 34–8–101–3; Harbhajan Singh 53.3–6–185–2; Ganguly 12.3–3–44–0; Bahutule 31–5–101–1; Badani 8–2–17–0; Ramesh 5–0–24–0.

Umpires: D. L. Orchard (South Africa) and E. A. R. de Silva.
Third umpire: T. H. Wijewardene. Referee: C. W. Smith (West Indies).

CEAT CRICKETER OF THE YEAR

The sixth CEAT International Cricketer of the Year was Muttiah Muralitharan of Sri Lanka. The CEAT formula awarded him 111 points for his performances in Tests and limited-overs internationals to April 30, 2001; his team-mates Marvan Atapattu and Sanath Jayasuriya were second and third, with 95 and 93 respectively. Previous winners were Brian Lara (West Indies), Venkatesh Prasad (India), Jayasuriya (Sri Lanka), Jacques Kallis (South Africa) and Sourav Ganguly (India). South Africa won the team award.

GODREJ SINGAPORE CHALLENGE, 2000-01

By ANIRBAN SIRCAR

Cricket's global bandwagon camped on the Equator as the garden city state of Singapore hosted its third one-day international tournament in five years. India were due to return for the third time but withdrew at the last minute, stating that participation would be inappropriate during the match-fixing crisis. Pakistan, who had played in the first Singapore tournament in April 1996, agreed to step in, while South Africa and New Zealand made their first appearances at the spruced-up Kallang Ground.

South Africa flew in from Melbourne, where they had just completed an indoor one-day series with Australia. They had been travelling since July, when they began their tour of Sri Lanka, but even without star pace bowler Allan Donald, who was playing for Warwickshire, Jonty Rhodes, who had returned home, and injured wicket-keeper Mark Boucher, they romped to victory over Pakistan in the final. Evident throughout was their commitment to prove that they remained a major force in world cricket, despite the eruption of "Hansiegate". Gary Kirsten was easily the player of the tournament, with 191 runs at 95.50; Pakistan's Ijaz Ahmed was the only other batsman to reach three figures. In complete contrast to South Africa, New Zealand had not played since early April and, barely emerged from their winter hibernation, lost both their fixtures.

Pakistan's squad was much depleted. Injury forced out their captain and wicket-keeper, Moin Khan, as well as vice-captain Inzamam-ul-Haq and the explosive fast bowler, Shoaib Akhtar. Off-spinner Saqlain Mushtaq, like Donald, was committed to his English county, while Wasim Akram was taking time out from one-day cricket. They were, moreover, pursued by controversy on and off the field. A day before they boarded their flight to Singapore, Shahid Afridi, Hasan Raza and Atiq-uz-Zaman were reported to have invited girls into their hotel rooms in Lahore. Later, stand-in captain Waqar Younis was accused of tampering with the ball during the league match against South Africa, but the ICC referee, Justice Ahmed Ebrahim of Zimbabwe, dismissed the evidence as insufficient for disciplinary action.

Note: Matches in this section were not first-class.

NEW ZEALAND v PAKISTAN

At Kallang Ground, Singapore, August 20. Pakistan won by 12 runs. Toss: New Zealand.

New Zealand lost this rain-truncated encounter, but not before making Pakistan sweat on a pleasant tropical afternoon. Invited to bat, the Pakistanis engaged in frantic hitting, reaching 76 by the 11th over – but losing three wickets. The steady Yousuf Youhana and flamboyant Ijaz Ahmed then provided rigour to their assault, adding 89 in a sparkling 12-over stand. Ijaz, in his first international since March, hit a whirlwind 49 in 37 balls, with five fours and a six. New Zealand started their run-chase boldly. All-rounder Cairns, promoted to open, struck two sixes and a four in a brief onslaught lasting 16 balls. But his team-mates could not sustain the pace, and although Harris plundered 40 runs off 30 balls, it was in a losing cause.

Man of the Match: Ijaz Ahmed.

Pakistan

Imran Nazir b Allott	12	Azhar Mahmood c Styris b Allott	0
Shahid Afridi c McMillan b Vettori	33	†Atiq-uz-Zaman not out	7
Saeed Anwar c Twose b Vettori	22	L-b 3, w 2, n-b 5	10
Yousuf Youhana c O'Connor b Allott	46		—
Ijaz Ahmed, sen. c Astle b Cairns	49	1/26 2/66 3/76 (6 wkts, 25 overs)	191
Abdur Razzaq not out	12	4/165 5/175 6/175	

*Waqar Younis, Arshad Khan and Kabir Khan did not bat.

Bowling: Allott 5–0–33–3; Cairns 5–0–48–1; O'Connor 1–0–11–0; Styris 1–0–12–0; Vettori 4–0–23–2; Astle 4–0–28–0; Harris 5–0–33–0.

New Zealand

C. L. Cairns c Shahid Afridi b Waqar Younis	21	†A. C. Parore c sub (Younis Khan) b Abdur Razzaq	9
N. J. Astle b Kabir Khan	15	D. L. Vettori b Arshad Khan	6
R. G. Twose lbw b Arshad Khan	35	S. B. Styris b Waqar Younis	16
*S. P. Fleming c Azhar Mahmood b Kabir Khan	15	S. B. O'Connor b Abdur Razzaq	0
C. Z. Harris c Yousuf Youhana b Azhar Mahmood	40	G. I. Allott not out	1
C. D. McMillan st Atiq-uz-Zaman b Arshad Khan	5	L-b 7, w 7, n-b 2	16
			—
		1/34 2/39 3/70 4/135 5/139 (24.4 overs) 6/148 7/157 8/177 9/177	179

Bowling: Waqar Younis 3.4–0–22–2; Kabir Khan 5–0–27–2; Abdur Razzaq 5–0–32–2; Azhar Mahmood 5–0–36–1; Shahid Afridi 1–0–10–0; Arshad Khan 5–0–45–3.

Umpires: S. K. Bansal and V. K. Ramaswamy.
Third umpire: G. Silva.

PAKISTAN v SOUTH AFRICA

At Kallang Ground, Singapore, August 23. Pakistan won by 28 runs. Toss: Pakistan. International debut: N. Pothas.

The talented Abdur Razzaq ensured Pakistan a hard-fought win and a place in the final. After a positive start on a slow pitch from Imran Nazir and Shahid Afridi, Pakistan were found wanting at 81 for four in the 19th over. Ijaz Ahmed rallied them again, scoring 56 of a 104-run stand with Razzaq. The South Africans were on track at 123 for three, then Razzaq bowled the ominous-looking Klusener, and Cullinan followed in the next over. All was not lost while McKenzie was adding 63 in 14 overs with wicket-keeper Nic Pothas, who was deputising for the injured Boucher after a 27-hour flight from Barbados, where he had just arrived with South Africa A. But the last five wickets fell for seven runs. Pothas scored 24, having earlier made three dismissals.

Man of the Match: Abdur Razzaq.

Pakistan

Imran Nazir run out	36	*Waqar Younis not out	4
Shahid Afridi c Kirsten b Telemachus	25	Arshad Khan run out	0
Younis Khan c Pothas b Kallis	1	Kabir Khan not out	3
Yousuf Youhana c Pothas b Kallis	7	B 4, l-b 2, w 15, n-b 7	28
Abdur Razzaq run out	47		—
Ijaz Ahmed, sen. st Pothas b Boje	56	1/56 2/61 3/74 (9 wkts, 50 overs)	227
Azhar Mahmood c Ntini b Boje	11	4/81 5/185 6/198	
†Atiq-uz-Zaman c Kirsten b Pollock	9	7/210 8/218 9/218	

Bowling: Pollock 9–0–32–1; Telemachus 9–0–53–1; Kallis 6–0–19–2; Ntini 6–0–27–0; Boje 10–0–37–2; Klusener 8–0–44–0; Hall 2–0–9–0.

South Africa

G. Kirsten run out 54
A. J. Hall c Atiq-uz-Zaman b Azhar Mahmood . 26
J. H. Kallis c Atiq-uz-Zaman b Azhar Mahmood . 5
D. J. Cullinan c Younis Khan b Kabir Khan . 12
L. Klusener b Abdur Razzaq 12
N. D. McKenzie b Abdur Razzaq 41
†N. Pothas c sub (Hasan Raza) b Azhar Mahmood . 24
*S. M. Pollock b Abdur Razzaq 0
N. Boje run out 1
R. Telemachus c Atiq-uz-Zaman b Waqar Younis . 1
M. Ntini not out. 1
B 4, l-b 5, w 1, n-b 12. 22

1/61 2/90 3/97 4/123 5/129 6/192 7/194 8/195 9/196 (48.4 overs) 199

Bowling: Waqar Younis 9–1–39–1; Kabir Khan 10–0–46–1; Azhar Mahmood 10–1–37–3; Arshad Khan 10–0–29–0; Abdur Razzaq 9.4–0–39–3.

Umpires: V. K. Ramaswamy and G. Silva.
Third umpire: S. K. Bansal.

NEW ZEALAND v SOUTH AFRICA

At Kallang Ground, Singapore, August 25. South Africa won by eight wickets. Toss: New Zealand.

South Africa sailed into the final with a crushing triumph over New Zealand, whose batsmen failed to exploit a surprisingly dry and bouncy track. Losing their top five for 55 runs by the 15th over, with experimental opener Vettori lasting only three balls, they never put together any partnership of substance. Only Harris thrived, scoring 42, and there was some deplorable shot selection as the side folded for 158. Kirsten and Hall launched South Africa's chase in style, putting on 94 in 18 overs, and Kirsten was still there, unbeaten on 75, when the Proteas breezed home with 16 overs to spare. He became the second South African after Hansie Cronje to reach 5,000 one-day international runs, in his 137th game.

Man of the Match: S. M. Pollock.

New Zealand

D. L. Vettori c Kallis b Pollock. 0
N. J. Astle b Pollock. 5
C. L. Cairns c Pollock b Kallis. 27
*S. P. Fleming run out 12
R. G. Twose b Kallis. 8
C. D. McMillan c Kallis b Klusener . . . 1
C. Z. Harris c Pothas b Telemachus 42
†A. C. Parore c Pothas b Hall 5
S. B. Styris lbw b Pollock 23
P. J. Wiseman not out 12
G. I. Allott b Hall 1
L-b 13, w 6, n-b 3. 22

1/1 2/10 3/39 4/54 5/55 6/72 7/94 8/129 9/157 (47.4 overs) 158

Bowling: Pollock 9–1–24–3; Telemachus 10–1–36–1; Kallis 5–1–15–2; Klusener 9–1–23–1; Boje 10–0–33–0; Hall 4.4–0–14–2.

South Africa

G. Kirsten not out 75
A. J. Hall c Cairns b Wiseman 46
J. H. Kallis c and b Styris 22
D. J. Cullinan not out 8
L-b 1, w 3, n-b 4 8

1/94 2/141 (2 wkts, 34 overs) 159

L. Klusener, N. D. McKenzie, H. H. Dippenaar, *S. M. Pollock, †N. Pothas, N. Boje and R. Telemachus did not bat.

Bowling: Allott 4–0–24–0; Cairns 4–0–18–0; Vettori 7–0–40–0; Wiseman 6–0–30–1; Harris 6–1–23–0; Styris 7–1–23–1.

Umpires: S. K. Bansal and G. Silva.
Third umpire: V. K. Ramaswamy.

QUALIFYING TABLE

	Played	*Won*	*Lost*	*Points*	*Net run-rate*
Pakistan	2	2	0	4	0.53
South Africa	2	1	1	2	0.41
New Zealand	2	0	2	0	–1.43

Net run-rate is calculated by subtracting runs conceded per over from runs scored per over.

FINAL

PAKISTAN v SOUTH AFRICA

At Kallang Ground, Singapore, August 27. South Africa won by 93 runs (D/L method). Toss: South Africa.

A near-capacity Sunday crowd thronged the Kallang expecting a dogfight, but South Africa won toss, match and title with consummate ease. Interrupted by a lengthy rain-break, they ran up 197 in 35 overs thanks to a classy 97-run partnership in 14 overs between left-handers Kirsten and Boje. Both made fifties: Kirsten's was his third in succession, Boje's his first in one-day internationals. Pakistan's target was set at 215 in 35 overs and, after three early blows, they were clawing their way back into contention at 74 for three in the 17th over. Then Kirsten's accurate throw from the deep ended the 24-run cameo by an unfit but spirited Saeed Anwar. The next two wickets fell in 11 balls, and the last-gasp aggression of Ijaz Ahmed and Atiq-uz-Zaman could not revive Pakistan's challenge.

Man of the Match: N. Boje. *Man of the Series:* G. Kirsten.

South Africa

G. Kirsten b Azhar Mahmood. 62
A. J. Hall c Ijaz Ahmed b Kabir Khan . . 5
J. H. Kallis b Kabir Khan 1
N. Boje c Salim Elahi b Arshad Khan . . 54
L. Klusener c Arshad Khan b Abdur Razzaq . 12
D. J. Cullinan not out 31
N. D. McKenzie b Abdur Razzaq 3
H. H. Dippenaar c sub (Younis Khan) b Waqar Younis . 17
*S. M. Pollock not out 2
L-b 6, w 1, n-b 3 10

1/7 2/29 3/126 4/138 5/143 6/152 7/188 (7 wkts, 35 overs) 197

†N. Pothas and R. Telemachus did not bat.

Bowling: Waqar Younis 7–1–28–1; Kabir Khan 7–0–33–2; Abdur Razzaq 7–0–54–2; Azhar Mahmood 7–0–48–1; Arshad Khan 7–1–28–1.

Pakistan

Imran Nazir c Kirsten b Telemachus . . . 1
Salim Elahi lbw b Telemachus 26
Yousuf Youhana c Boje b Pollock 8
Saeed Anwar run out 24
Ijaz Ahmed, sen. lbw b Klusener. 31
Abdur Razzaq c and b Klusener 0
Azhar Mahmood lbw b Boje 0
†Atiq-uz-Zaman c Pollock b Hall 18
*Waqar Younis c Cullinan b Pollock . . . 11
Arshad Khan run out 0
Kabir Khan not out. 0
L-b 1, n-b 1 2

1/7 2/33 3/35 4/74 5/75 6/76 7/102 8/119 9/119 (28.1 overs) 121

Bowling: Pollock 6.1–0–26–2; Telemachus 6–1–20–2; Kallis 4–1–9–0; Klusener 7–0–35–2; Boje 4–0–24–1; Hall 1–0–6–1.

Umpires: S. K. Bansal and V. K. Ramaswamy.
Third umpire: G. Silva. Series referee: A. M. Ebrahim.

ICC KNOCKOUT, 2000-01

By SIMON BRIGGS

In most respects, the second ICC Knockout, staged in Kenya, was a tremendous success. Like the 1996 World Cup, it threw up a parade of cavalier strokeplay, and a champion drawn from the ranks of cricket's underdogs. "New Zealand's never got to a final before, let alone won it," enthused a jubilant Chris Cairns, who overcame a knee injury to play the decisive innings – a majestic 102 not out – in the final. Yet the Black Caps' achievement was no breakthrough to a new era: their next 13 one-dayers produced 11 defeats and just one win.

In fact, the biggest strides were arguably made by India, the eventual runners-up, who defeated Australia and South Africa, the two favourites. Their captain, Sourav Ganguly, had an extraordinary tournament, scoring 348 runs at 116.00 and clearing the boundary 12 times. But it was the emergence of three dynamic debutants, Yuvraj Singh, Zaheer Khan and Vijay Dahiya, that really made India's fortnight.

Since the previous ICC Knockout – the mini World Cup played by the then nine Test nations in Dhaka two years earlier – Bangladesh and Kenya had joined the roll of entrants. They were knocked out in the first round, along with the fading West Indians. Sri Lanka's triumph over West Indies was short-lived, however, and they succumbed to Pakistan, who later lost their semi-final to New Zealand despite a second successive century from Saeed Anwar. Zimbabwe had just won a one-day series at home to New Zealand, but could not match them in the quarter-finals; England hiccuped after their successful summer, conceding 232 to Bangladesh and then scoring only 182 against South Africa.

If there had been a prize for the man of the tournament, Andy Atkinson, the former Warwickshire groundsman, would have deserved to win it. His stewardship transformed the Gymkhana Club's pitches, once notorious for their sluggishness, into strips of sprung steel. Their pace and bounce, coupled with Nairobi's thin air and short boundaries, helped produce some ballistic batting displays – especially from Ganguly, whose monumental straight hitting belied his slim shoulders.

The only sadness was the lack of local interest, and the suggestions of match-fixing that subsequently surfaced in the Anti-Corruption Unit's report to the ICC. While India's matches attracted decent numbers of ex-pats, indigenous Kenyans were noticeable by their absence throughout. Critics blamed high ticket prices (up to £20) and excessive bureaucracy. One thing was certain: the tournament ought to have done more to promote cricket in East Africa. It will take a fat slice of the $US13 million profit to make up for that.

Note: Matches in this section were not first-class.

FIRST ROUND

KENYA v INDIA

At Gymkhana, Nairobi, October 3. India won by eight wickets. Toss: India. International debuts: V. Dahiya, Yuvraj Singh, Zaheer Khan.

The hosts hoped to repeat their upset of India in the Coca-Cola Cup in May 1998; instead, they were peremptorily evicted from their own party. After losing early wickets to Kumble, Kenya regrouped through an 81-run stand between Odumbe and Shah, who swatted one superb six over extra cover off Prasad. His attempt to replicate the shot, however, started another slide, of five for 29, despite a run-a-ball innings from Odoyo. India's batsmen took a measured approach to a target of 209 until Kambli, carving an unbeaten 39 from 33 balls, lifted the run-rate from four to six an over. A disappointing turn-out left the redeveloped Gymkhana Club stadium half-empty, suggesting that cricket had yet to catch the country's imagination.

Man of the Match: A. Kumble.

Kenya

†K. O. Otieno c Ganguly b Agarkar	6	T. O. Suji c Dahiya b Agarkar	2
R. D. Shah c Dahiya b Prasad	60	M. A. Suji c Ganguly b Zaheer Khan	14
J. K. Kamande c Dravid b Kumble	18	L. N. Onyango not out	0
S. O. Tikolo lbw b Kumble	5	L-b 10, w 4, n-b 3	17
*M. O. Odumbe lbw b Prasad	51		
T. M. Odoyo not out	35	1/16 2/54 3/64 (9 wkts, 50 overs)	208
Mohammad Sheikh b Zaheer Khan	0	4/145 5/158 6/159	
H. S. Modi b Zaheer Khan	0	7/159 8/174 9/206	

Bowling: Zaheer Khan 10–0–48–3; Agarkar 10–1–40–2; Prasad 10–0–47–2; Kumble 10–1–22–2; Tendulkar 6–0–25–0; Yuvraj Singh 4–1–16–0.

India

*S. C. Ganguly st Otieno b Odumbe	66
S. R. Tendulkar lbw b T. O. Suji	25
R. Dravid not out	68
V. G. Kambli not out	39
B 1, l-b 2, w 7, n-b 1	11
1/47 2/135 (2 wkts, 42.3 overs)	209

Yuvraj Singh, R. R. Singh, †V. Dahiya, A. B. Agarkar, A. Kumble, Zaheer Khan and B. K. V. Prasad did not bat.

Bowling: M. A. Suji 10–2–30–0; Odoyo 6–1–18–0; T. O. Suji 10–0–56–1; Onyango 4.3–0–34–0; Mohammad Sheikh 4–0–27–0; Tikolo 2–0–13–0; Odumbe 4–0–18–1; Shah 2–0–10–0.

Umpires: S. A. Bucknor and D. L. Orchard.
Third umpire: D. B. Hair. Referee: R. S. Madugalle.

SRI LANKA v WEST INDIES

At Gymkhana, Nairobi, October 4. Sri Lanka won by 108 runs. Toss: West Indies. International debuts: K. C. B. Jeremy, M. N. Samuels.

West Indies suffered the most humbling defeat of the three "qualifying finals". After the travails of their England tour, here at least they could point to an inexperienced side. Four up-and-coming batsmen had been sent to the Australian Academy instead, and Jimmy Adams had injured his rib. Stand-in captain Campbell's enjoyment of the post must have lasted about as long as the opening spells of McLean and Dillon, who claimed two wickets in the fifth over to leave Sri Lanka ten for two. From there, Gunawardene and Jayawardene revelled in some hapless fielding and support bowling to add 160. Gunawardene, a bulky 23-year-old left-hander, was dropped twice and caught off a no-ball on his way to 132, his first international century. The West Indians soon abandoned hope when Lara was caught behind off Zoysa, who snapped up three top-order wickets. Muralitharan's ten overs cost just nine runs.

Man of the Match: D. A. Gunawardene.

Sri Lanka

*S. T. Jayasuriya c Browne b Dillon . . . 2	†R. S. Kaluwitharana not out 16
D. A. Gunawardene b McLean 132	W. P. U. J. C. Vaas not out 7
M. S. Atapattu b Dillon 2	
D. P. M. D. Jayawardene c Browne b Jeremy . 72	L-b 4, w 8, n-b 1 13
K. Sangakkara run out 2	1/8 2/10 3/170 (6 wkts, 50 overs) 287
R. P. Arnold b McLean 41	4/177 5/250 6/274

D. N. T. Zoysa, G. P. Wickremasinghe and M. Muralitharan did not bat.

Bowling: Dillon 10–2–46–2; McLean 10–0–56–2; Jeremy 8–0–54–1; Williams 10–0–59–0; Samuels 6–0–30–0; Nagamootoo 6–0–38–0.

West Indies

*S. L. Campbell run out 20	M. V. Nagamootoo run out 33
†C. O. Browne c Kaluwitharana b Zoysa 15	N. A. M. McLean b Arnold 8
B. C. Lara c Kaluwitharana b Zoysa . . . 5	M. Dillon c Vaas b Jayasuriya 6
W. W. Hinds c Jayawardene b Wickremasinghe . 20	K. C. B. Jeremy not out 4
S. C. Joseph c Kaluwitharana b Zoysa . . 0	L-b 4, w 2, n-b 2 8
M. N. Samuels c and b Wickremasinghe. 19	1/34 2/37 3/41 (46.4 overs) 179
L. R. Williams c Wickremasinghe b Jayasuriya . 41	4/41 5/76 6/85
	7/159 8/160 9/170

Bowling: Vaas 8–1–36–0; Zoysa 7–0–34–3; Wickremasinghe 6–0–37–2; Muralitharan 10–4–9–0; Jayasuriya 10–1–30–2; Arnold 5.4–0–29–1.

Umpires: S. Venkataraghavan and P. Willey.
Third umpire: D. R. Shepherd. Referee: R. Subba Row.

BANGLADESH v ENGLAND

At Gymkhana, Nairobi, October 5. England won by eight wickets. Toss: Bangladesh.

Initially disappointed to have conceded 232 to these international novices, England were reassured when Hussain, their captain, put in some much-needed batting practice. Coming into the game with 162 runs from his last 18 England innings, Hussain scored a one-day international best 95, striking five sixes and nine fours, before chipping a simple catch back to Mohammad Rafiq. He put on 175 with Stewart, whose unbeaten 87 won him his third match award in four games. Earlier, England had put down six chances to let Bangladesh escape from 96 for four. Opener Javed Omar, who had retired hurt when Caddick hit him on the right index finger, was patched up and returned to bat out the overs, completing his second international half-century. Eddie Barlow, Bangladesh coach until his stroke in April, watched from a wheelchair.

Man of the Match: A. J. Stewart.

Bangladesh

Javed Omar not out 63	Enamul Haque c Hussain b White 2
Al-Shahriar Rokon c Alleyne b Caddick . 13	Hasibul Hussain not out 16
Habibul Bashar run out 18	
Aminul Islam c Caddick b Ealham 30	L-b 5, w 7, n-b 4 16
Akram Khan b Ealham 6	
*Naimur Rahman c Hussain b Caddick . 46	1/33 2/70 3/83 (8 wkts, 50 overs) 232
†Khaled Masud c Hick b Ealham 17	4/96 5/160 6/184
Mohammad Rafiq c Trescothick b White 5	7/203 8/206

Mushfiqur Rehman did not bat.

Javed Omar, when 14, retired hurt at 36 and resumed at 96.

Bowling: Caddick 10–1–35–2; Gough 10–1–38–0; White 10–0–45–2; Ealham 10–0–48–3; Hick 7–0–35–0; Alleyne 3–0–26–0.

England

M. E. Trescothick c Khaled Masud b Hasibul Hussain	15	G. A. Hick not out	23
†A. J. Stewart not out	87	B 1, l-b 3, w 3, n-b 9	16
*N. Hussain c and b Mohammad Rafiq	95		
		1/33 2/208 (2 wkts, 43.5 overs)	236

G. P. Thorpe, A. Flintoff, C. White, M. A. Ealham, M. W. Alleyne, A. R. Caddick and D. Gough did not bat.

Bowling: Hasibul Hussain 10–0–60–1; Mushfiqur Rehman 7.5–0–43–0; Mohammad Rafiq 10–1–43–1; Enamul Haque 10–0–46–0; Naimur Rahman 6–0–40–0.

Umpires: D. B. Hair and D. L. Orchard.
Third umpire: S. A. Bucknor. Referee: C. W. Smith.

QUARTER-FINALS

AUSTRALIA v INDIA

At Gymkhana, Nairobi, October 7. India won by 20 runs. Toss: Australia.

India shaded a classic match through the deeds of their two youngest players. In his first international innings, 18-year-old Yuvraj Singh displayed astonishing poise, thrashing Australia's star-studded attack for 84 from 80 balls. No other batsman reached 40, though Tendulkar's violent assault on McGrath's new-ball spell gave India much of their momentum. Australia's innings – deducted two overs for a slow over-rate – revealed another budding hero in Zaheer Khan, on his 22nd birthday. Bowling left-arm over at some pace, Zaheer castled Steve Waugh in the 43rd over to curtail a dangerous partnership with Brett Lee, and effectively decide the match. Yuvraj, whose father Yograj played one Test for India, was in the thick of things again, taking a marvellous catch off Harvey and running out Bevan with a direct hit.

Man of the Match: Yuvraj Singh.

India

*S. C. Ganguly c Gilchrist b Gillespie	24	A. Kumble run out	12
S. R. Tendulkar c Martyn b B. Lee	38	Zaheer Khan not out	13
R. Dravid c S. Lee b Gillespie	9	B. K. V. Prasad not out	6
V. G. Kambli c Gilchrist b S. R. Waugh	29	B 1, l-b 12, w 8, n-b 2	23
Yuvraj Singh c and b S. Lee	84		
R. R. Singh b Harvey	19	1/66 2/76 3/90 (9 wkts, 50 overs)	265
†V. Dahiya c M. E. Waugh b B. Lee	5	4/130 5/194 6/215	
A. B. Agarkar c McGrath b S. Lee	3	7/222 8/239 9/258	

Bowling: McGrath 9–0–61–0; B. Lee 10–0–39–2; Gillespie 8–0–39–2; Harvey 9–1–54–1; S. Lee 10–0–31–2; S. R. Waugh 4–0–28–1.

Australia

M. E. Waugh c Kumble b Agarkar	7	B. Lee c Ganguly b Agarkar	31
†A. C. Gilchrist c Ganguly b Zaheer Khan	33	J. N. Gillespie c R. R. Singh b Prasad	14
I. J. Harvey c Yuvraj Singh b Prasad	25	G. D. McGrath not out	6
R. T. Ponting c R. R. Singh b Tendulkar	46	L-b 4, w 7, n-b 2	13
M. G. Bevan run out	42		
*S. R. Waugh b Zaheer Khan	23	1/43 2/51 3/86 (46.4 overs)	245
D. R. Martyn b R. R. Singh	1	4/159 5/163 6/169	
S. Lee run out	4	7/189 8/224 9/226	

Bowling: Zaheer Khan 10–0–40–2; Agarkar 8–1–59–2; Prasad 7.4–0–43–2; Kumble 8–0–42–0; Tendulkar 7–0–31–1; R. R. Singh 6–0–26–1.

Umpires: S. A. Bucknor and D. R. Shepherd.
Third umpire: P. Willey. Referee: R. S. Madugalle.

PAKISTAN v SRI LANKA

At Gymkhana, Nairobi, October 8. Pakistan won by nine wickets. Toss: Sri Lanka.

A potentially intriguing fixture declined into a Pakistan cakewalk. For Sri Lanka, dismissed 26 balls inside the distance, only Jayasuriya threatened to set up any kind of score as he bludgeoned 39 from 41 balls, including two square-cut sixes off Wasim Akram and another pulled off Azhar Mahmood. Arnold's 38, by contrast, was one of the slowest innings of this free-scoring competition. On the small Gymkhhana Club ground, Sri Lanka's total of 194 was indefensible, and only one Pakistan batsman fell in the chase. Saeed Anwar's match-winning six brought up his 18th one-day hundred, and surely one of his easiest.

Man of the Match: Saeed Anwar.

Sri Lanka

*S. T. Jayasuriya c Moin Khan b Wasim Akram	39
D. A. Gunawardene b Wasim Akram	5
M. S. Atapattu c Moin Khan b Azhar Mahmood	0
D. P. M. D. Jayawardene run out	11
K. Sangakkara b Abdur Razzaq	19
R. P. Arnold c Moin Khan b Azhar Mahmood	38
†R. S. Kaluwitharana lbw b Azhar Mahmood	27
W. P. U. J. C. Vaas c Imran Nazir b Saqlain Mushtaq	11
U. D. U. Chandana not out	13
D. N. T. Zoysa b Saqlain Mushtaq	10
M. Muralitharan b Wasim Akram	0
L-b 7, w 9, n-b 5	21
1/7 2/8 3/63 4/76 5/100 6/156 7/159 8/179 9/191 (45.4 overs)	194

Bowling: Wasim Akram 7.4–2–40–3; Azhar Mahmood 10–0–52–3; Abdur Razzaq 10–1–30–1; Saqlain Mushtaq 8–0–30–2; Arshad Khan 10–1–35–0.

Pakistan

Saeed Anwar not out	105
Imran Nazir run out	40
Yousuf Youhana not out	42
L-b 1, w 2, n-b 5	8
1/90 (1 wkt, 43.2 overs)	195

Inzamam-ul-Haq, Ijaz Ahmed, sen., *†Moin Khan, Abdur Razzaq, Wasim Akram, Azhar Mahmood, Saqlain Mushtaq and Arshad Khan did not bat.

Bowling: Vaas 10–0–42–0; Zoysa 7–0–44–0; Arnold 5–0–19–0; Muralitharan 10–1–39–0; Chandana 8.2–1–34–0; Jayasuriya 3–0–16–0.

Umpires: D. L. Orchard and P. Willey.
Third umpire: S. Venkataraghavan. Referee: R. Subba Row.

NEW ZEALAND v ZIMBABWE

At Gymkhana, Nairobi, October 9. New Zealand won by 64 runs. Toss: Zimbabwe.

New Zealand's first match set the pattern for their tournament: canny bowling, light-fingered fielding, and plenty of runs from Twose. A fifth-wicket stand of 95 between Twose and McMillan set them on the way to 265 for seven, but Zimbabwe were very much in the game at 88 for one. Then came the turning-point. Campbell, on 47, was ruled lbw as he swept at Harris, even though the ball seemed to hit him outside off stump. Campbell's apoplectic reaction earned him a one-match suspension from referee Cammie Smith. Carlisle hung around for 67, but seven of his team-mates failed to reach double figures and the match ended with 7.4 overs to spare as Wiseman collected his fourth wicket.

Man of the Match: R. G. Twose.

New Zealand

C. M. Spearman c Streak b Olonga	20	†A. C. Parore not out	20
N. J. Astle c G. W. Flower b Olonga	0	P. J. Wiseman not out	0
*S. P. Fleming run out	34	L-b 12, w 12, n-b 1	25
R. G. Twose c Olonga b Viljoen	85		
C. L. Cairns c Viljoen b Strang	13	1/4 2/57 3/69 (7 wkts, 50 overs)	265
C. D. McMillan c Olonga b Viljoen	52	4/120 5/215	
C. Z. Harris c G. W. Flower b Olonga	16	6/234 7/259	

S. B. O'Connor and G. I. Allott did not bat.

Bowling: Streak 10–1–48–0; Olonga 9–0–58–3; Nkala 10–1–44–0; Strang 7–0–40–1; Viljoen 10–0–40–2; G. W. Flower 4–0–23–0.

Zimbabwe

A. D. R. Campbell lbw b Harris	47	P. A. Strang lbw b Astle	3
C. B. Wishart c Twose b Allott	5	M. L. Nkala b Wiseman	2
S. V. Carlisle c Parore b Wiseman	67	H. K. Olonga not out	2
†A. Flower c and b Wiseman	1	B 1, l-b 8, w 4, n-b 1	14
G. W. Flower b Wiseman	5		
G. J. Whittall run out	26	1/24 2/88 3/91 (42.2 overs)	201
*H. H. Streak c and b Astle	20	4/108 5/154 6/168	
D. P. Viljoen run out	9	7/190 8/196 9/199	

Bowling: Allott 8–0–45–1; O'Connor 7–0–20–0; Astle 7–1–39–2; Cairns 1–0–6–0; Harris 10–0–37–1; Wiseman 9.2–0–45–4.

Umpires: S. A. Bucknor and D. R. Shepherd.
Third umpire: D. L. Orchard. Referee: C. W. Smith.

ENGLAND v SOUTH AFRICA

At Gymkhana, Nairobi, October 10. South Africa won by eight wickets. Toss: England. International debut: A. P. Grayson.

England's batsmen failed to cope with the strategy that Bob Woolmer, South Africa's former coach, used to call "aggressive containment". After choosing to bat, they found runs elusive, collecting just five from their first eight overs. Telemachus, Pollock's new-ball partner, registered 92.2mph on the speed-gun. Starved of scoring opportunities, five of England's top six perished to catches around the on-side boundary, and the only noteworthy stand, 65 between Hick and Flintoff, was achieved while the four main seamers were resting. South Africa's pursuit of 183, the lowest target of the tournament, was hardly ruffled by Gough's early dismissal of Hall. Kallis (two sixes, nine fours) and Dippenaar put on an unbroken 132 to carry them through.

Man of the Match: J. H. Kallis.

England

M. E. Trescothick c Donald b Pollock	26	A. P. Grayson c Pollock b Kallis	0
†A. J. Stewart c Dippenaar b Donald	18	A. R. Caddick run out	0
*N. Hussain c Boucher b Donald	5	D. Gough not out	6
G. A. Hick c Hall b Kallis	65	L-b 2, w 5, n-b 3	10
G. P. Thorpe c Hall b Boje	14		
A. Flintoff c Klusener b Pollock	25	1/33 2/50 3/55 (44.1 overs)	182
C. White run out	3	4/89 5/154 6/160	
M. A. Ealham c Boucher b Pollock	10	7/167 8/168 9/174	

Bowling: Pollock 9.1–2–27–3; Telemachus 9–2–45–0; Donald 8–1–25–2; Kallis 8–0–26–2; Boje 5–0–24–1; Klusener 5–0–33–0.

South Africa

A. J. Hall c Hick b Gough	1
G. Kirsten c Hick b White	32
J. H. Kallis not out	78
H. H. Dippenaar not out	65
W 2, n-b 6	8
1/19 2/52 (2 wkts, 39.1 overs)	184

J. N. Rhodes, L. Klusener, †M. V. Boucher, *S. M. Pollock, N. Boje, R. Telemachus and A. A. Donald did not bat.

Bowling: Caddick 7–1–40–0; Gough 9–2–43–1; White 8.1–0–40–1; Ealham 10–1–41–0; Grayson 5–0–20–0.

Umpires: D. B. Hair and S. Venkataraghavan.
Third umpire: S. A. Bucknor. Referee: R. S. Madugalle.

SEMI-FINALS

NEW ZEALAND v PAKISTAN

At Gymkhana, Nairobi, October 11. New Zealand won by four wickets. Toss: Pakistan.

New Zealand's draw threw up a familiar prospect: a semi-final against Pakistan, who had denied them a place in both the 1992 and 1999 World Cup finals. In Nairobi, though, the Black Caps avenged those defeats by pulling off a thrilling run-chase. Styris, a replacement for the injured Cairns, rounded off a seventh-wicket stand of 68 with McMillan by hitting the winning boundary. But New Zealand's innings was a collective effort: there were also star turns from Astle and Twose. Pakistan should have made more of a sublime hundred from Saeed Anwar, his second in four days. Their middle order imploded, then a promising tail-end revival was swept away by O'Connor's five wickets, the best haul of the tournament. Still, no chasing side had yet reached 250 in this competition. New Zealand got there with some help from substitute fielder Faisal Iqbal, who fluffed a crucial run-out chance against Styris.

Man of the Match: S. B. O'Connor.

Pakistan

Saeed Anwar c Parore b Allott	104
Imran Nazir c Spearman b O'Connor	21
Yousuf Youhana c Fleming b Astle	24
Inzamam-ul-Haq st Parore b Astle	1
Ijaz Ahmed, sen. c and b Harris	3
*†Moin Khan run out	2
Abdur Razzaq c Astle b O'Connor	48
Wasim Akram c Fleming b O'Connor	34
Azhar Mahmood c Styris b O'Connor	4
Saqlain Mushtaq c and b O'Connor	2
Arshad Khan not out	2
L-b 3, w 2, n-b 2	7
1/59 2/111 3/120 4/133 5/143 6/178 7/237 8/243 9/249 (49.2 overs)	252

Bowling: Allott 10–0–57–1; O'Connor 9.2–0–46–5; Styris 10–1–41–0; Astle 10–0–50–2; Harris 7–0–36–1; Wiseman 3–0–19–0.

New Zealand

C. M. Spearman b Azhar Mahmood	1
N. J. Astle c Moin Khan b Azhar Mahmood	49
*S. P. Fleming c Inzamam-ul-Haq b Azhar Mahmood	12
R. G. Twose c Wasim Akram b Saqlain Mushtaq	87
C. D. McMillan not out	51
†A. C. Parore b Azhar Mahmood	10
C. Z. Harris run out	0
S. B. Styris not out	28
B 4, l-b 3, w 5, n-b 5	17
1/3 2/15 3/150 4/169 5/187 6/187 (6 wkts, 49 overs)	255

P. J. Wiseman, S. B. O'Connor and G. I. Allott did not bat.

Bowling: Wasim Akram 10–0–47–0; Azhar Mahmood 10–0–65–4; Abdur Razzaq 10–0–41–0; Saqlain Mushtaq 10–0–40–1; Arshad Khan 9–0–55–0.

Umpires: D. L. Orchard and D. R. Shepherd.
Third umpire: S. Venkataraghavan. Referee: R. Subba Row.

INDIA v SOUTH AFRICA

At Gymkhana, Nairobi, October 13. India won by 95 runs. Toss: India.

The favourites ran into a breathtaking innings from Ganguly, who creamed an unbeaten 141 from 142 balls, his 14th hundred in one-day internationals. India were heading for 300 until he lost the strike in the last over, bowled by Donald, which yielded three wickets and just two runs. Ganguly had started temperately, but went airborne when left-arm spinner Boje came on at the halfway stage. Three of his six sixes came during Boje's two overs, which cost 26 runs and opened the floodgates for some rousing strokeplay. Ganguly had one lucky break, on 75, when he guided a Klusener no-ball to backward point. Under pressure to score quickly, South Africa lost their top four inside eight overs. Ganguly then continued his masterclass by dismissing Boucher, their top-scorer, for 60, but his exertions finally caught up with him: fielding at slip, he dropped Boje twice in two balls. Telemachus was later suspended for one game for barging into Dravid.

Man of the Match: S. C. Ganguly.

India

*S. C. Ganguly not out	141
S. R. Tendulkar c Klusener b Kallis	39
R. Dravid c Boucher b Klusener	58
Yuvraj Singh c Rhodes b Kallis	41
R. R. Singh run out	0
V. G. Kambli lbw b Donald	0
†V. Dahiya c Hall b Donald	1
B 1, l-b 6, w 5, n-b 3	15
1/66 2/211 3/293 4/293 5/293 6/295 (6 wkts, 50 overs)	295

A. B. Agarkar, A. Kumble, Zaheer Khan and B. K. V. Prasad did not bat.

Bowling: Pollock 10–1–43–0; Telemachus 9–0–62–0; Donald 10–1–34–2; Kallis 10–0–71–2; Klusener 6–0–29–1; Boje 2–0–26–0; Hall 3–0–23–0.

South Africa

G. Kirsten run out	12
A. J. Hall b Zaheer Khan	1
J. H. Kallis c Ganguly b Prasad	15
H. H. Dippenaar c Dahiya b Zaheer Khan	5
J. N. Rhodes c Prasad b Yuvraj Singh	32
†M. V. Boucher c Tendulkar b Ganguly	60
L. Klusener c Dahiya b Kumble	29
*S. M. Pollock st Dahiya b Kumble	4
N. Boje b Tendulkar	10
R. Telemachus c Prasad b Tendulkar	13
A. A. Donald not out	1
B 3, l-b 4, w 7, n-b 4	18
1/13 2/23 3/28 4/50 5/106 6/161 7/171 8/179 9/199 (41 overs)	200

Bowling: Zaheer Khan 5–0–27–2; Prasad 8–0–54–1; Kumble 9–1–28–2; Agarkar 7–1–21–0; Yuvraj Singh 4–1–15–1; Tendulkar 5–0–32–2; R. R. Singh 2–0–11–0; Ganguly 1–0–5–1.

Umpires: S. A. Bucknor and P. Willey.
Third umpire: D. R. Shepherd. Referee: C. W. Smith.

FINAL

INDIA v NEW ZEALAND

At Gymkhana, Nairobi, October 15. New Zealand won by four wickets. Toss: New Zealand.

Cairns, returning bravely from a knee injury, won the match with an inspirational century that resuscitated a failing run-chase and carried New Zealand to one of their proudest moments. They certainly had to win this one the hard way, after Ganguly and Tendulkar had opened with 141 in just 26.3 overs, their tenth century first-wicket stand in one-day internationals. However, Tendulkar was stranded by a bad call and, while Ganguly carried on to his second successive hundred, 123 from the remaining overs represented diminishing returns. Trusting in their deep batting order, New Zealand were aggressive from the start. But when Twose fell 19 runs short of a sixth consecutive half-century, and McMillan followed, the score was an unconvincing 132 for five. It was now that Harris joined Cairns for a cool-headed partnership of 122. Though the required run-rate continued to climb, Cairns refused to be fazed. He hit two sixes, one a glorious straight drive off Kumble into the red clay of the car park in the 47th over, and ultimately the winning run with just two balls remaining.

Man of the Match: C. L. Cairns.

India

*S. C. Ganguly c Harris b Astle	117
S. R. Tendulkar run out	69
R. Dravid run out	22
Yuvraj Singh c Twose b Styris	18
V. G. Kambli c O'Connor b Styris	1
R. R. Singh c Spearman b Allott	13
A. B. Agarkar not out	15
†V. Dahiya not out	1
L-b 2, w 4, n-b 2	8
1/141 2/202 3/220 4/229 5/237 6/256 (6 wkts, 50 overs)	264

A. Kumble, Zaheer Khan and B. K. V. Prasad did not bat.

Bowling: Allott 10–0–54–1; O'Connor 5–0–37–0; Cairns 10–2–40–0; Styris 10–0–53–2; Astle 10–0–46–1; Harris 5–0–32–0.

New Zealand

C. M. Spearman c Yuvraj Singh b Prasad	3
N. J. Astle c R. R. Singh b Kumble	37
*S. P. Fleming lbw b Prasad	5
R. G. Twose st Dahiya b Kumble	31
C. L. Cairns not out	102
C. D. McMillan c Ganguly b Tendulkar	15
C. Z. Harris c Singh b Prasad	46
†A. C. Parore not out	3
L-b 15, w 1, n-b 7	23
1/6 2/37 3/82 4/109 5/132 6/254 (6 wkts, 49.4 overs)	265

S. B. Styris, S. B. O'Connor and G. I. Allott did not bat.

Bowling: Zaheer Khan 7–0–54–0; Prasad 7–0–27–3; Agarkar 6.4–0–44–0; Kumble 9–0–55–2; Tendulkar 10–1–38–1; Yuvraj Singh 10–0–32–0.

Umpires: S. A. Bucknor and D. R. Shepherd.
Third umpire: D. B. Hair. Referee: R. S. Madugalle.

COCA-COLA CHAMPIONS' TROPHY, 2000-01

Sri Lanka won their third title at Sharjah, and easily their most convincing, with an unbeaten record that culminated with a record-shattering performance in the final. They demolished India by 245 runs, the biggest winning margin in any one-day international; India were all out for a miserable 54. Sri Lankan captain Sanath Jayasuriya symbolised his team's dominance, winning the match award in the final for an innings of 189, five short of the one-day record. He also collected the series award – he had an overall aggregate of 413 runs at 82.60 – and picked up individual prizes for best batsman and best fielder. Muttiah Muralitharan shared the limelight with 15 wickets at 9.06, including a world one-day international record of seven for 30 in the last qualifying game.

Five days before the tournament, India had lost a far more closely contested final, to New Zealand, in the ICC Knockout at Nairobi, so they arrived with high hopes of continuing their Kenyan form. But despite individual successes – another hundred for Sachin Tendulkar, 85 for Rahul Dravid, further encouraging signs from the left-arm seamer, Zaheer Khan – they managed only two narrow wins over Zimbabwe. Assorted injuries and an apparent dispute between captain Sourav Ganguly and coach Anshuman Gaekwad about whether Ganguly should open the batting (he preferred to drop down the order) did not help. Zimbabwe lost all four games, though they were seriously embarrassed only once, in a 123-run defeat by Sri Lanka. There were centuries for Andy Flower and Alistair Campbell, while Travis Friend, a 19-year-old pace bowler, claimed nine wickets, a return bettered only by the Sri Lankans, Muralitharan and Chaminda Vaas.

With all matches starting in the afternoon and finishing under floodlights, the evening dew made it difficult for bowlers to grip the ball. After the first round of qualifiers was completed, tournament officials agreed to amend the regulations so that the ball could be changed more frequently.

Note: Matches in this section were not first-class.

INDIA v SRI LANKA

At Sharjah, October 20 (day/night). Sri Lanka won by five wickets. Toss: India.

Tendulkar's 26th hundred in one-day internationals was not enough to set up an Indian victory. Only Robin Singh offered him significant support – they shared a century stand for the fifth wicket – and the loss of four wickets in the last four overs squandered the possibility of a more challenging total. Gunawardene finally made up for dropping Tendulkar on 26 by breaking his stumps with a direct hit, one of four run-outs in the innings. Jayasuriya negotiated Sri Lanka out of a shaky start, hitting seven fours in 53 balls, and later Sangakkara and Arnold added 95 as the Indian bowlers struggled to control the wet ball in the evening dew.

Man of the Match: S. R. Tendulkar.

India

*S. C. Ganguly c Gunawardene b Vaas	17
S. R. Tendulkar run out	101
R. Dravid run out	16
V. G. Kambli run out	12
Yuvraj Singh b Muralitharan	7
R. R. Singh c Atapattu b Muralitharan	35
A. Kumble b Vaas	11
A. B. Agarkar not out	7
†V. Dahiya run out	0
Zaheer Khan not out	1
L-b 6, w 5, n-b 6	17
1/33 2/64 3/87 4/102 5/202 6/205 7/222 8/222 (8 wkts, 50 overs)	224

B. K. V. Prasad did not bat.

Bowling: Vaas 9–0–40–2; Zoysa 10–1–48–0; Weeraratne 8–0–41–0; Muralitharan 10–0–36–2; Jayasuriya 9–0–36–0; Arnold 4–0–17–0.

Sri Lanka

*S. T. Jayasuriya c Yuvraj Singh b Agarkar	48
D. A. Gunawardene c Dahiya b Prasad	9
M. S. Atapattu c Dahiya b Prasad	0
D. P. M. D. Jayawardene b Kumble	38
K. Sangakkara not out	40
R. P. Arnold c Dahiya b Agarkar	59
†R. S. Kaluwitharana not out	9
B 4, l-b 2, w 11, n-b 5	22
1/17 2/21 3/94 4/113 5/208 (5 wkts, 43.5 overs)	225

W. P. U. J. C. Vaas, K. Weeraratne, D. N. T. Zoysa and M. Muralitharan did not bat.

Bowling: Zaheer Khan 8.5–1–36–0; Prasad 8–1–48–2; Agarkar 8–0–39–2; Kumble 10–1–50–1; Tendulkar 5–0–22–0; Ganguly 1–0–13–0; R. R. Singh 3–0–11–0.

Umpires: R. S. Dunne and G. Sharp.
Third umpire: D. J. Harper.

SRI LANKA v ZIMBABWE

At Sharjah, October 21 (day/night). Sri Lanka won by seven wickets. Toss: Sri Lanka. International debut: M. A. Vermeulen.

Sri Lanka turned in another winning performance, playing to almost the same script as the previous night: another century from the opposition, a target only one run higher, and an equally comfortable win. Even so, Flower deservedly claimed the match award for his unbeaten 120, turning his side round in a 153-run partnership with Viljoen, who hit three sixes. They had joined forces after 24 overs, at a discouraging 72 for four (Campbell was unavailable, suspended for one game after the ICC Knockout). Jayasuriya and Atapattu shaded Flower and Viljoen by adding 157 for Sri Lanka's second wicket, after Streak had bowled Gunawardene in the first over of their reply. Sangakkara again hit the winning boundary to complete the sense of *déjà vu*.

Man of the Match: A. Flower.

Zimbabwe

D. A. Marillier c Kaluwitharana b Zoysa	7
M. A. Vermeulen c Jayasuriya b Weeraratne	22
S. V. Carlisle run out	0
†A. Flower not out	120
G. J. Whittall c and b Muralitharan	8
D. P. Viljoen not out	63
B 1, l-b 1, w 3	5
1/12 2/13 3/56 4/72 (4 wkts, 50 overs)	225

*H. H. Streak, P. A. Strang, B. C. Strang, T. J. Friend and M. L. Nkala did not bat.

Bowling: Vaas 8–0–40–0; Zoysa 10–1–30–1; Weeraratne 8–0–33–1; Muralitharan 9–0–45–1; Jayasuriya 6–0–31–0; Arnold 9–0–44–0.

Sri Lanka

*S. T. Jayasuriya c Carlisle b P. A. Strang	78
D. A. Gunawardene b Streak	0
M. S. Atapattu run out	90
D. P. M. D. Jayawardene not out	25
K. Sangakkara not out	15
L-b 7, w 14	21
1/2 2/159 3/203 (3 wkts, 47 overs)	229

R. P. Arnold, †R. S. Kaluwitharana, W. P. U. J. C. Vaas, K. Weeraratne, D. N. T. Zoysa and M. Muralitharan did not bat.

Bowling: Streak 10–0–47–1; B. C. Strang 10–1–37–0; Friend 8–0–50–0; Nkala 5–0–25–0; P. A. Strang 4–0–26–1; Viljoen 10–0–37–0.

Umpires: D. J. Harper and G. Sharp.
Third umpire: R. S. Dunne.

INDIA v ZIMBABWE

At Sharjah, October 22 (day/night). India won by 13 runs. Toss: Zimbabwe.

India earned their first points through a narrow win. Both teams were 184 for four after 40 overs, but India's later order, especially Dahiya, made better use of the final ten, plundering 81 runs, including 50 from the last four. Dravid batted into the closing stages for 85, after being promoted to open with Tendulkar in Ganguly's place. However, the switch became a one-off when Dravid cracked a finger attempting to catch Campbell off the bowling of Zaheer Khan. Zaheer soon bowled Campbell anyway, along with fellow-opener Marillier, before a 118-run stand between Carlisle and Andy Flower put Zimbabwe in good stead. Earlier, Friend had taken four wickets, including one curious dismissal when umpire Harper called wide – only for his colleague to notice that the ball had dislodged Yuvraj Singh's bail.

Man of the Match: Zaheer Khan.

India

R. Dravid c G. W. Flower b Viljoen	85
S. R. Tendulkar c A. Flower b Streak	8
V. G. Kambli c Viljoen b Friend	18
*S. C. Ganguly c A. Flower b Friend	18
Yuvraj Singh b Friend	34
R. R. Singh run out	22
†V. Dahiya c Marillier b Friend	32
S. B. Joshi b Streak	19
A. B. Agarkar not out	12
Zaheer Khan not out	4
L-b 5, w 5, n-b 3	13
1/21 2/51 3/93 4/147 5/189 6/206 7/234 8/252 (8 wkts, 50 overs)	265

B. K. V. Prasad did not bat.

Bowling: Streak 10–1–63–2; Strang 10–1–32–0; Friend 10–0–55–4; Mbangwa 9–0–40–0; Viljoen 7–0–40–1; G. W. Flower 2–0–19–0; Campbell 2–0–11–0.

Zimbabwe

A. D. R. Campbell b Zaheer Khan	28
D. A. Marillier b Zaheer Khan	2
S. V. Carlisle b Joshi	60
†A. Flower c Joshi b Tendulkar	63
G. W. Flower c Ganguly b Agarkar	22
G. J. Whittall not out	36
D. P. Viljoen c Dahiya b Zaheer Khan	12
*H. H. Streak not out	11
B 7, l-b 10, n-b 1	18
1/21 2/32 3/150 4/165 5/214 6/235 (6 wkts, 50 overs)	252

B. C. Strang, T. J. Friend and M. Mbangwa did not bat.

Bowling: Zaheer Khan 10–0–37–3; Prasad 7–0–25–0; Agarkar 9–0–43–1; Joshi 10–0–44–1; Yuvraj Singh 3–0–14–0; R. R. Singh 5–0–26–0; Tendulkar 6–0–46–1.

Umpires: R. S. Dunne and D. J. Harper.
Third umpire: G. Sharp.

SRI LANKA v ZIMBABWE

At Sharjah, October 25 (day/night). Sri Lanka won by 123 runs. Toss: Zimbabwe.

Sri Lanka swept into the final in ever more dominant form. The tone was set by Jayasuriya, whose renewed opening partnership with Kaluwitharana piled up 110 by the 16th over. Jayasuriya was eventually bowled for 87 in 66 balls, including 22 in one over from Bryan Strang; in all, he struck 12 fours and two sixes. His team-mates could not maintain the pace, though Vaas hit three sixes in five deliveries late on. Zimbabwe's ambitions did not outlive the opening salvos from Vaas and Zoysa, and they crashed to 46 for six in 18 overs. A half-century from Viljoen kept them afloat almost to the end of the innings, but their hopes of remaining in the competition now depended on overwhelming India next day.

Man of the Match: S. T. Jayasuriya.

Sri Lanka

*S. T. Jayasuriya b Friend	87
†R. S. Kaluwitharana run out	25
M. S. Atapattu run out	58
D. P. M. D. Jayawardene run out	5
K. Sangakkara b Viljoen	4
R. P. Arnold c Carlisle b G. W. Flower	18
T. M. Dilshan c Friend b G. W. Flower	16
W. P. U. J. C. Vaas c Carlisle b Friend	23
K. Weeraratne not out	14
D. N. T. Zoysa b Streak	4
M. Muralitharan not out	1
L-b 10, w 9, n-b 2	21
1/110 2/132 3/143 4/155 5/195 6/228 7/234 8/259 9/265 (9 wkts, 50 overs)	276

Bowling: Streak 8–0–59–1; Strang 10–0–52–0; Mbangwa 4–0–36–0; Friend 10–0–52–2; Viljoen 10–0–38–1; G. W. Flower 8–0–29–2.

Zimbabwe

A. D. R. Campbell c Jayawardene b Zoysa	20
D. A. Marillier c Jayawardene b Vaas	11
S. V. Carlisle lbw b Vaas	0
†A. Flower c Kaluwitharana b Zoysa	0
G. W. Flower lbw b Muralitharan	10
G. J. Whittall b Muralitharan	1
D. P. Viljoen c Jayawardene b Zoysa	60
*H. H. Streak run out	25
B. C. Strang b Arnold	0
T. J. Friend not out	12
M. Mbangwa c sub (U. D. U. Chandana) b Jayawardene	4
B 4, l-b 2, w 4	10
1/24 2/24 3/25 4/35 5/43 6/46 7/108 8/109 9/143 (48.3 overs)	153

Bowling: Vaas 10–3–27–2; Zoysa 9–3–16–3; Weeraratne 10–0–51–0; Muralitharan 10–3–19–2; Jayasuriya 4–0–18–0; Arnold 4–0–12–1; Jayawardene 1.3–1–4–1.

Umpires: R. S. Dunne and G. Sharp.
Third umpire: D. J. Harper.

INDIA v ZIMBABWE

At Sharjah, October 26 (day/night). India won by three wickets. Toss: India.

India overtook a modest target with nine balls to spare and knocked Zimbabwe out of the tournament. Friend had struck twice in his third over before Ganguly, returning to the top of the order, shared a century stand with Kambli and passed 6,000 one-day international runs. A further flurry of wickets kept the Indians on edge almost until the end. Zimbabwe might have set a stiffer task if Campbell had been able to find a similar long-term ally. He batted throughout their innings to finish unbeaten on 105, with six fours and a six. Zaheer Khan added another four wickets to his tournament haul as he efficiently curtailed the closing stages of Zimbabwe's innings.

Man of the Match: A. D. R. Campbell.

Zimbabwe

A. D. R. Campbell not out	105
G. W. Flower c R. R. Singh b Prasad	10
P. A. Strang c Zaheer Khan b Joshi	17
S. V. Carlisle run out	20
†A. Flower c Kambli b Zaheer Khan	7
G. J. Whittall run out	26
D. P. Viljoen b Prasad	9
*H. H. Streak b Zaheer Khan	12
T. J. Friend b Zaheer Khan	4
B. C. Strang b Zaheer Khan	0
M. Mbangwa not out	0
L-b 3, w 2, n-b 3	8
1/24 2/61 3/111 4/124 5/174 6/187 7/207 8/215 9/218 (9 wkts, 50 overs)	218

Bowling: Zaheer Khan 10–0–42–4; Prasad 10–0–38–2; Agarkar 10–0–37–0; Joshi 7–0–35–1; Sriram 2–0–9–0; Tendulkar 3–0–16–0; R. R. Singh 8–1–38–0.

India

S. R. Tendulkar c P. A. Strang b Friend	4	S. B. Joshi not out	25
*S. C. Ganguly c sub (D. A. Marillier) b Friend	66	A. B. Agarkar not out	16
S. Sriram c Mbangwa b Friend	0	B 1, l-b 6, w 9, n-b 1	17
V. G. Kambli c Streak b G. W. Flower	60		
Yuvraj Singh c P. A. Strang b Mbangwa	4	1/18 2/18 3/124 (7 wkts, 48.3 overs)	219
R. R. Singh run out	7	4/133 5/153	
†V. Dahiya c A. Flower b Streak	20	6/158 7/200	

Zaheer Khan and B. K. V. Prasad did not bat.

Bowling: Friend 10–0–39–3; B. C. Strang 10–0–36–0; Streak 8–0–38–1; Mbangwa 7–0–29–1; P. A. Strang 3–0–20–0; Viljoen 7.3–0–42–0; G. W. Flower 3–1–8–1.

Umpires: R. S. Dunne and D. J. Harper.
Third umpire: G. Sharp.

INDIA v SRI LANKA

At Sharjah, October 27 (day/night). Sri Lanka won by 68 runs. Toss: India.

Muralitharan returned the best analysis in the history of one-day internationals, seven for 30, in this dress rehearsal for the final. The previous record was seven for 37 by Aqib Javed of Pakistan, also against India at Sharjah, nine years and two days earlier. Murali's first victim, Robin Singh, was his 200th in limited-overs games for Sri Lanka. When Sri Lanka were put in to bat, Jayasuriya's first failure of the week hardly mattered as Atapattu and Jayawardene ran up 226 in 36 overs, a Sri Lankan third-wicket record, on what seemed a batsman's pitch. Jayawardene scored 128 in 123 balls, with 15 fours, while Atapattu was comparatively staid, hitting just five fours in 111 balls. Vaas then made two early breakthroughs before Muralitharan began his opening spell of four for 21 in seven overs, including Tendulkar for a 54-ball 61. While he rested, Badani and Dahiya rallied India's reply, but his second spell, culminating in a double-wicket maiden, reduced them to 211 for nine, leaving Jayasuriya to complete the victory.

Man of the Match: M. Muralitharan.

Sri Lanka

*S. T. Jayasuriya c Zaheer Khan b Agarkar	11	R. P. Arnold run out	28
†R. S. Kaluwitharana lbw b Agarkar	8	W. P. U. J. C. Vaas run out	1
M. S. Atapattu not out	102	B 1, l-b 9, w 4, n-b 2	16
D. P. M. D. Jayawardene c Zaheer Khan b Agarkar	128	1/22 2/25 3/251 (5 wkts, 50 overs)	294
		4/290 5/294	

K. Sangakkara, T. M. Dilshan, K. E. A. Upashantha, D. N. T. Zoysa and M. Muralitharan did not bat.

Bowling: Zaheer Khan 10–0–54–0; Agarkar 10–0–48–3; Joshi 10–1–46–0; Ganguly 5–0–34–0; Sriram 7–0–35–0; Yuvraj Singh 1–0–10–0; R. R. Singh 4–0–36–0; Tendulkar 3–0–21–0.

India

*S. C. Ganguly c Sangakkara b Vaas	1	S. B. Joshi c Kaluwitharana b Muralitharan	3
S. R. Tendulkar c Vaas b Muralitharan	61	A. B. Agarkar not out	5
S. Sriram c Dilshan b Vaas	6	Zaheer Khan b Jayasuriya	6
R. R. Singh c sub (U. D. U. Chandana) b Muralitharan	31	L-b 4, w 4, n-b 6	14
V. G. Kambli c and b Muralitharan	10		
Yuvraj Singh c Dilshan b Muralitharan	7	1/2 2/24 3/99 (48.5 overs)	226
H. K. Badani c Jayasuriya b Muralitharan	42	4/109 5/120 6/129	
†V. Dahiya c Arnold b Muralitharan	40	7/206 8/211 9/211	

Bowling: Vaas 6–0–36–2; Zoysa 8–1–37–0; Upashantha 5–0–41–0; Muralitharan 10–1–30–7; Arnold 8–1–26–0; Jayawardene 4–0–26–0; Jayasuriya 7.5–0–26–1.

Umpires: R. S. Dunne and G. Sharp.
Third umpire: P. Mishra.

QUALIFYING TABLE

	Played	*Won*	*Lost*	*Points*	*Net run-rate*
Sri Lanka	4	4	0	8	1.22
India	4	2	2	4	−0.39
Zimbabwe	4	0	4	0	−0.81

Net run-rate is calculated by subtracting runs conceded per over from runs scored per over.

FINAL

INDIA v SRI LANKA

At Sharjah, October 29 (day/night). Sri Lanka won by 245 runs. Toss: Sri Lanka.

Sri Lanka completed the most crushing victory in any one-day international after bowling out India in 26.3 overs. Their 245-run margin beat the record of 233 set in June by Pakistan against Bangladesh, just before their elevation to Test status. India's 54 was the third-lowest total in limited-overs internationals; only Pakistan, with 43 against West Indies at Cape Town in 1992-93, and Canada, 45 against England in the 1979 World Cup, had done worse. Their own previous low was 63, against Australia 20 years earlier. Robin Singh was the only batsman to reach double figures as Vaas collected a career-best five for 14 and Muralitharan three for six in six overs. With conditions less humid than before, Jayasuriya was the first captain to choose to bat since Ganguly in the opening game. He backed his judgment with the third-highest score in one-day internationals: 189 from 161 balls, with 21 fours and four sixes, five runs fewer than Saeed Anwar's 194 against India in 1996-97, and level with Viv Richards's unbeaten 189 at Manchester in 1984. Jayasuriya's last 89 runs came off only 43 balls, and took him past 6,000 one-day runs for Sri Lanka. Arnold helped him add 166 in 20 overs, a Sri Lankan fifth-wicket record, which helped transform 116 for four into 299 for five, the highest total of the tournament.

Man of the Match: S. T. Jayasuriya. *Man of the Series:* S. T. Jayasuriya.

Sri Lanka

*S. T. Jayasuriya st Dahiya b Ganguly	189
†R. S. Kaluwitharana b Zaheer Khan	15
M. S. Atapattu run out	9
D. P. M. D. Jayawardene c Yuvraj Singh b Joshi	3
K. Sangakkara b Tendulkar	8
R. P. Arnold not out	52
W. P. U. J. C. Vaas not out	1
B 4, l-b 7, w 5, n-b 6	22
1/44 2/90 3/98 4/116 5/282 (5 wkts, 50 overs)	299

T. M. Dilshan, K. Weeraratne, D. N. T. Zoysa and M. Muralitharan did not bat.

Bowling: Zaheer Khan 10–1–53–1; Agarkar 10–1–67–0; Prasad 7–0–73–0; Joshi 9–2–33–1; Tendulkar 10–0–28–1; Yuvraj Singh 1–0–6–0; R. R. Singh 2–0–13–0; Ganguly 1–0–15–1.

India

*S. C. Ganguly c Jayasuriya b Vaas	3	A. B. Agarkar b Muralitharan	2
S. R. Tendulkar c and b Vaas	5	Zaheer Khan c Kaluwitharana b Vaas	1
Yuvraj Singh c Sangakkara b Vaas	3	B. K. V. Prasad not out	3
V. G. Kambli c Jayasuriya b Vaas	3	L-b 2, w 2, n-b 2	6
H. K. Badani c Arnold b Zoysa	9		
R. R. Singh b Muralitharan	11	1/8 2/10 3/15 (26.3 overs)	54
†V. Dahiya b Muralitharan	4	4/19 5/30 6/39	
S. B. Joshi run out	4	7/44 8/49 9/50	

Bowling: Vaas 9.3–1–14–5; Zoysa 7–0–21–1; Weeraratne 4–0–11–0; Muralitharan 6–3–6–3.

Umpires: D. J. Harper and G. Sharp.
Third umpire: R. S. Dunne. Series referee: D. T. Lindsay.

ONE-DAY INTERNATIONAL COMPETITIONS, 2000-01

Competition	*Winners*	*Runners-up*	*Others*
Godrej Singapore Challenge	**South Africa**	Pakistan	New Zealand
ICC Knockout	**New Zealand**	India	All Full Members and Kenya
Coca-Cola Champions' Trophy	**Sri Lanka**	India	Zimbabwe
Carlton Series	**Australia**	West Indies	Zimbabwe
ARY Gold Cup	**Sri Lanka**	Pakistan	New Zealand
NatWest Series	**Australia**	Pakistan	England
Coca-Cola Cup (Zimbabwe)	**West Indies**	India	Zimbabwe
Coca-Cola Cup (Sri Lanka)	**Sri Lanka**	India	New Zealand

Note: Only competitions held during 2000-01 and 2001 seasons involving three or more teams are included.

CARLTON SERIES, 2000-01

Australia followed their 5–0 whitewash of West Indies in the Tests with ten straight wins in the limited-overs Carlton Series. It was the first time any team had achieved a 100 per cent record in this competition, going back to its original incarnation as the World Series Cup in 1979-80. Only once were they in any danger: in a dead group game when Zimbabwe, who could no longer qualify, finished one short of Australia's 302.

The hosts' only problems occurred off the field. Midway through the tournament, Mark Waugh was threatened with suspension when his lawyers announced that he "presently declined" to meet investigators from the Australian Cricket Board and the International Cricket Council. They wished to interview him about Indian bookmaker M. K. Gupta's claim that Waugh had accepted $US20,000 for information on matches. The board told him to agree to the interview by 4 p.m. on January 25, or miss playing West Indies the following evening; Waugh quickly changed his mind, explaining that he had been waiting for full details of the current allegation. In fact, he met Greg Melick, for the Australian board, and Sir Paul Condon, from the ICC's Anti-Corruption Unit, the day after the second, decisive, final against West Indies on February 9, in which he made 173, the highest one-day score for Australia.

That concluded a remarkable performance from Waugh on the field. In seven innings, he aggregated 542 runs at 108.40, including three hundreds. No other batsmen reached 400 runs, though two had even higher averages. Darren Lehmann scored 197 for one dismissal – but had dropped out of the team by the finals. Damien Martyn averaged 149, thanks to four not-outs. Shane Warne, who had missed the Tests with a broken finger, was easily the leading wicket-taker of the tournament, with 18; more controversially, he was rebuked by the police for kicking tennis balls into the crowd, and there was further embarrassment when a stump microphone recorded him swearing after a rejected appeal in Hobart. As in the Test series, captain Steve Waugh dropped out briefly through injury, and again Adam Gilchrist deputised without any disruption to Australia's inexorable progress.

Meanwhile, the West Indians showed few signs of halting an inexorable decline. This was not their worst showing in this tournament's history; on three of their previous ten appearances, they had failed to reach the finals. But, having qualified, they had come away empty-handed only once, in 1996-97 against Pakistan. They had won all five final series played against Australia. West Indies did enjoy three wins against Zimbabwe – improving on their record in England a few months earlier – but lost one after being bowled out for 91. They were helpless against Australia, the closest margin being 28 runs in a rain-affected game when a virtuoso hundred from Brian Lara almost single-handedly turned them round. Lara was named Man of the Series, for 372 runs at 46.50, an award which seemed to surprise him as much as the Melbourne crowd. Marlon Samuels enhanced his reputation with 282 runs and 14 wickets, and fellow-Jamaican Ricardo Powell contributed some explosive innings.

Zimbabwe managed only that one victory, when Heath Streak and his seamers laid West Indies low at Sydney. But coming so close to beating the Australians in their last game boosted morale. Alistair Campbell, at Hobart, and Stuart Carlisle, in Perth, scored centuries against Australia, though it seemed inevitable that both would be in a losing cause. Nothing ever seriously looked like stopping the home bandwagon.

Note: Matches in this section were not first-class.

AUSTRALIA v WEST INDIES

At Melbourne, January 11 (day/night). Australia won by 74 runs. Toss: Australia. International debut: N. W. Bracken.

Australia were irresistible from the moment that Steve Waugh – the third player to appear in 300 one-day internationals, after Mohammad Azharuddin and Wasim Akram – won the toss. His brother, Mark, and Ponting batted fluently, adding 111 at five an over as temperatures topped 40 degrees Centigrade. In West Indies' reply, McGrath conceded a miserly seven in his six overs, and debutant left-armer Nathan Bracken removed Campbell with his 16th ball. Samuels hit his maiden fifty in limited-overs internationals, then was one of three wickets seized by Symonds in one over, two caught and bowled. Adams halted the slide, but never threatened the distant target. Warne's return after injury was notable only for a police warning when he kicked some tennis balls back into a rowdy crowd. He was told this could incite the spectators further; as it was, there were 34 arrests.

Man of the Match: R. T. Ponting. *Attendance:* 56,732.

Australia

M. E. Waugh c Hinds b Williams	51
†A. C. Gilchrist c McLean b Cuffy	7
R. T. Ponting c Powell b Cuffy	73
M. G. Bevan c Lara b Williams	17
*S. R. Waugh c Nagamootoo b Samuels	29
D. R. Martyn run out	42
A. Symonds not out	38
L-b 6, w 4	10
1/7 2/118 3/144 4/174 5/193 6/267 (6 wkts, 50 overs)	267

I. J. Harvey, S. K. Warne, N. W. Bracken and G. D. McGrath did not bat.

Bowling: Cuffy 9–1–45–2; McLean 10–1–54–0; Williams 8–0–39–2; Nagamootoo 10–0–50–0; Adams 3–0–19–0; Samuels 10–0–54–1.

West Indies

S. L. Campbell c Bevan b Bracken	4
W. W. Hinds c Ponting b McGrath	1
B. C. Lara c Gilchrist b Harvey	28
M. N. Samuels c and b Symonds	57
R. L. Powell c S. R. Waugh b Symonds	12
†R. D. Jacobs c and b Symonds	24
M. V. Nagamootoo lbw b Symonds	3
*J. C. Adams not out	25
L. R. Williams not out	26
L-b 9, w 4	13
1/3 2/9 3/57 4/84 5/132 6/139 7/139 (7 wkts, 50 overs)	193

N. A. M. McLean and C. E. Cuffy did not bat.

Bowling: McGrath 6–2–7–1; Bracken 9–3–30–1; Harvey 9–0–55–1; Martyn 6–1–19–0; Warne 10–1–38–0; Symonds 10–1–35–4.

Umpires: D. J. Harper and S. J. A. Taufel.
Third umpire: R. G. Patterson.

WEST INDIES v ZIMBABWE

At Brisbane, January 13 (day/night). West Indies won by one wicket. Toss: Zimbabwe.

Zimbabwe looked to be on the verge of their fourth successive one-day win against West Indies when they had them 183 for seven in 38 overs, still needing 58. But Powell, already scoring freely, contributed 43 of those as the tail held out long enough to complete victory with eight balls and one wicket to spare. Powell finished unbeaten with 83 from 90 balls, having hit nine fours and a six. Zimbabwe's 240 owed almost everything to Alistair Campbell, whose 81, with four fours and a six, incorporated half-century stands with Carlisle and Flower. Streak's 34 from 28 balls at the end was almost enough to give his side a winning start.

Man of the Match: R. L. Powell. *Attendance:* 12,034.

Zimbabwe

A. D. R. Campbell c and b Samuels	81
T. N. Madondo c Campbell b McLean	6
S. V. Carlisle c Jacobs b Williams	29
†A. Flower c Jacobs b Samuels	33
G. J. Rennie b McLean	29
G. J. Whittall b Nagamootoo	1
D. P. Viljoen run out	2
*H. H. Streak not out	34
M. L. Nkala c Hinds b Cuffy	9
T. J. Friend b McLean	0
B. A. Murphy not out	1
L-b 3, w 9, n-b 3	15
1/14 2/68 3/154 4/161 5/167 6/174 7/214 8/231 9/231 (9 wkts, 50 overs)	240

Bowling: Cuffy 9–0–52–1; McLean 10–1–48–3; Williams 8–1–38–1; Nagamootoo 10–0–45–1; Samuels 10–0–41–2; Adams 3–0–13–0.

West Indies

S. L. Campbell c Flower b Whittall	42
W. W. Hinds b Friend	0
B. C. Lara c Viljoen b Nkala	21
M. N. Samuels b Viljoen	34
*J. C. Adams c Flower b Nkala	24
R. L. Powell not out	83
†R. D. Jacobs hit wkt b Murphy	4
L. R. Williams b Friend	9
M. V. Nagamootoo c Flower b Streak	8
N. A. M. McLean c Flower b Whittall	1
C. E. Cuffy not out	1
L-b 6, w 7, n-b 1	14
1/6 2/52 3/72 4/119 5/137 6/155 7/183 8/229 9/239 (9 wkts, 48.4 overs)	241

Bowling: Streak 10–1–41–1; Friend 10–1–37–2; Nkala 7–0–50–2; Whittall 3.4–0–16–2; Murphy 10–0–52–1; Viljoen 8–0–39–1.

Umpires: P. D. Parker and S. J. A. Taufel.
Third umpire: S. J. Davis.

AUSTRALIA v WEST INDIES

At Brisbane, January 14 (day/night). Australia won by nine wickets. Toss: West Indies.

Acting-captain Gilchrist and Mark Waugh took Australia most of the way home with an opening stand of 206 in 39 overs. Only Geoff Marsh and David Boon, with 212 against India at Jaipur in 1986-87, had put on more for Australia's first wicket in a one-day game. Waugh advanced to his 15th hundred at this level, hitting seven fours in 128 balls as they won with more than six overs in hand. Gilchrist, leading his country for the second time in the summer, because Steve Waugh had a groin strain, made his 150th dismissal in one-day internationals when he caught Campbell in the first over of the match. He himself could have gone in the first over of Australia's reply, but Hinds, West Indies' top-scorer with 54 (two sixes, four fours), dropped the chance at mid-on.

Man of the Match: M. E. Waugh. *Attendance:* 35,168.

West Indies

S. L. Campbell c Gilchrist b McGrath	0
W. W. Hinds c and b Warne	54
B. C. Lara c Gilchrist b Ponting	19
M. N. Samuels c Waugh b Warne	20
*J. C. Adams c Martyn b Lee	44
R. L. Powell c Waugh b Warne	19
†R. D. Jacobs not out	44
L. R. Williams run out	15
M. V. Nagamootoo c Symonds b Bracken	0
N. A. M. McLean not out	6
L-b 1, w 5, n-b 7	13
1/0 2/36 3/86 4/103 5/145 6/174 7/203 8/207 (8 wkts, 50 overs)	234

M. I. Black did not bat.

Bowling: McGrath 10–2–42–1; Lee 7–0–40–1; Bracken 8–0–46–1; Ponting 5–0–28–1; Warne 10–0–41–3; Symonds 10–0–36–0.

Australia

*†A. C. Gilchrist c Williams b Powell	98
M. E. Waugh not out	112
R. T. Ponting not out	10
B 4, l-b 2, w 3, n-b 7	16
1/206 (1 wkt, 43.4 overs)	236

M. G. Bevan, D. S. Lehmann, D. R. Martyn, A. Symonds, S. K. Warne, B. Lee, N. W. Bracken and G. D. McGrath did not bat.

Bowling: McLean 9.4–0–38–0; Black 10–0–55–0; Williams 5–0–22–0; Samuels 5–0–38–0; Nagamootoo 8–0–43–0; Adams 3–0–19–0; Powell 3–1–15–1.

Umpires: S. J. Davis and D. B. Hair.
Third umpire: P. D. Parker.

AUSTRALIA v WEST INDIES

At Sydney, January 17 (day/night). Australia won by 28 runs (D/L method). Toss: West Indies.

Rain cut short a *tour de force* from Lara, but he would have needed a near-miracle to change the result. West Indies' rejigged batting stumbled to 94 for five before Powell offered Lara some support; then three more wickets fell in eight balls, leaving West Indies 111 behind in the 37th over, and 67 below par on Duckworth/Lewis calculations. Lara was 74 at the time; he scored his next 42 runs from 25 balls, while one-day debutant Stuart contributed three, and his unbeaten 116, his 14th century at this level, had come from 106 balls with ten fours and two sixes. The Duckworth/Lewis deficit was now down to 28. Earlier, Waugh and Gilchrist had narrowly missed their second successive hundred opening partnership, after which Ponting, dropped twice, hit 93 in 74 balls.

Man of the Match: B. C. Lara. *Attendance:* 39,540.

Australia

M. E. Waugh c Powell b Samuels	58
*†A. C. Gilchrist c Powell b Williams	40
R. T. Ponting c Adams b McLean	93
M. G. Bevan c Campbell b McLean	31
D. R. Martyn not out	21
D. S. Lehmann not out	19
L-b 9, w 5, n-b 1	15
1/98 2/109 3/187 4/246 (4 wkts, 50 overs)	277

A. Symonds, I. J. Harvey, S. K. Warne, N. W. Bracken and G. D. McGrath did not bat.

Bowling: McLean 10–0–45–2; Black 8–0–49–0; Stuart 8–0–57–0; Williams 10–0–43–1; Samuels 10–1–39–1; Powell 2–0–22–0; Adams 2–0–13–0.

West Indies

W. W. Hinds c Warne b Bracken	1
†R. D. Jacobs c Warne b Bracken	21
S. L. Campbell c Martyn b Harvey	23
B. C. Lara not out	116
M. N. Samuels c Gilchrist b Harvey	1
*J. C. Adams b Warne	9
R. L. Powell c Bracken b Warne	28
L. R. Williams st Gilchrist b Warne	1
N. A. M. McLean lbw b Symonds	0
C. E. L. Stuart not out	3
B 2, l-b 1, w 3, n-b 2	8
1/3 2/31 3/67 4/69 5/94 6/161 7/164 8/166 (8 wkts, 42.4 overs)	211

M. I. Black did not bat.

Bowling: McGrath 7.4–1–37–0; Bracken 7–1–21–2; Harvey 7–1–16–2; Symonds 9–0–55–1; Warne 10–0–62–3; Martyn 2–0–17–0.

Umpires: D. B. Hair and S. J. A. Taufel.
Third umpire: S. J. Davis.

AUSTRALIA v ZIMBABWE

At Melbourne, January 21 (day/night). Australia won by eight wickets. Toss: Zimbabwe. International debut: S. M. Katich.

Australia's first meeting with Zimbabwe in this tournament was a virtual walkover, for they won with 13 overs in hand. The Zimbabwean openers did make a bold start, plundering Lee for 35 as they raised 50 in eight overs, but Harvey broke through with his first delivery and went on to claim three more wickets. For Australia, Gilchrist charged to 39 in 29 balls, while Lehmann, promoted to open as Mark Waugh was rested, seized his chance and hit an unbeaten 92 from 104 balls. He added 144 in 25 overs with Ponting, and new cap Simon Katich never had a chance to bat.

Man of the Match: D. S. Lehmann. *Attendance:* 43,033.

Zimbabwe

A. D. R. Campbell c Bevan b Harvey	30
G. J. Whittall c Gilchrist b Harvey	25
S. V. Carlisle c Harvey b Warne	12
†A. Flower c Lehmann b Symonds	23
G. W. Flower c and b Warne	51
G. J. Rennie st Gilchrist b Symonds	13
D. P. Viljoen c and b Lehmann	7
*H. H. Streak c Lehmann b Harvey	23
M. L. Nkala b Harvey	16
T. J. Friend not out	0
L-b 7, w 9, n-b 7	23
1/50 2/67 3/78 4/117 5/145 6/160 7/187 8/219 9/223 (9 wkts, 50 overs)	223

B. A. Murphy did not bat.

Bowling: Lee 8–0–70–0; Bracken 6–0–23–0; Harvey 9–0–28–4; Warne 10–2–21–2; Symonds 10–2–38–2; Lehmann 7–0–36–1.

Australia

*†A. C. Gilchrist c Murphy b Friend	39
D. S. Lehmann not out	92
R. T. Ponting run out	68
M. G. Bevan not out	14
B 1, l-b 5, w 6, n-b 1	13
1/54 2/198 (2 wkts, 36.5 overs)	226

S. M. Katich, D. R. Martyn, A. Symonds, I. J. Harvey, S. K. Warne, B. Lee and N. W. Bracken did not bat.

Bowling: Streak 5–1–37–0; Friend 6.5–0–52–1; Murphy 10–0–47–0; Nkala 7–0–30–0; Viljoen 6–0–37–0; Whittall 2–0–17–0.

Umpires: S. J. Davis and P. D. Parker.
Third umpire: R. G. Patterson.

WEST INDIES v ZIMBABWE

At Sydney, January 23 (day/night). Zimbabwe won by 47 runs. Toss: West Indies.

Zimbabwe secured their first win after an extraordinary collapse by West Indies. Needing only 139, they were 31 for eight by the 17th over, 12 short of the lowest total in one-day internationals (they themselves dismissed Pakistan for 43 at Cape Town in 1992-93). But McLean struck 40 from 32 balls and, with Adams's help, steered West Indies past their own worst score, 87 against Australia on this same ground, also in 1992-93. He remained unbeaten when the innings ended at 91 in the 32nd over. Zimbabwean captain Streak, backed to the hilt by his fellow-seamers, had triggered the slide with four wickets, and he conceded only eight runs in eight overs. Zimbabwe's batsmen, too, had been mown down, by Cuffy in particular, and were 66 for six when Streak came to the crease. He saw another 72 added – helped by five penalty runs, the first awarded in a one-day international, when Jacobs, attempting a world record-equalling sixth catch, lost his hat and it fell on the ball.

Man of the Match: H. H. Streak. *Attendance:* 8,474.

Zimbabwe

A. D. R. Campbell c Jacobs b Cuffy	4
G. J. Whittall c Campbell b Cuffy	11
S. V. Carlisle c Powell b Williams	29
†A. Flower c Jacobs b Cuffy	3
G. W. Flower c Jacobs b Cuffy	7
G. J. Rennie c Powell b Williams	14
D. P. Viljoen c Jacobs b McLean	2
*H. H. Streak c sub (S. C. Joseph) b Samuels	45
M. L. Nkala c Lara b Williams	0
B. C. Strang c Jacobs b Samuels	1
B. A. Murphy not out	7
L-b 5, w 4, n-b 1, p 5	15
1/9 2/30 3/45 4/62 5/62 6/66 7/88 8/88 9/104 (47.2 overs)	138

Bowling: McLean 9–1–28–1; Cuffy 10–1–24–4; Williams 10–1–24–3; Samuels 8.2–0–28–2; Nagamootoo 8–0–19–0; Adams 2–0–5–0.

West Indies

W. W. Hinds c Campbell b Streak	8
†R. D. Jacobs lbw b Streak	6
S. L. Campbell c Campbell b Strang	0
B. C. Lara lbw b Strang	0
M. N. Samuels c Carlisle b Strang	1
*J. C. Adams c and b Nkala	22
R. L. Powell lbw b Streak	0
L. R. Williams c Carlisle b Streak	0
M. V. Nagamootoo c Viljoen b Nkala	3
N. A. M. McLean not out	40
C. E. Cuffy c Carlisle b Nkala	0
L-b 7, w 3, n-b 1	11
1/16 2/22 3/22 4/22 5/24 6/25 7/25 8/31 9/91 (31.5 overs)	91

Bowling: Streak 8–4–8–4; Strang 8–4–15–3; Nkala 5.5–1–12–3; Whittall 7–0–42–0; Murphy 3–1–7–0.

Umpires: P. D. Parker and S. J. A. Taufel.
Third umpire: D. B. Hair.

WEST INDIES v ZIMBABWE

At Adelaide, January 25 (day/night). West Indies won by 77 runs (D/L method). Toss: West Indies.

West Indies recovered swiftly from their humiliation at Sydney. After their third opening pair in six games had failed, Samuels struck 68, his highest international score yet, and Lara 70 as they put on 133 for the third wicket. They benefited from three lives between them. The innings was in full flow when rain deprived the later batsmen of the last three overs, and Zimbabwe's target was raised to 253. This looked possible while the Flower brothers were adding 90, but then Andy Flower, having just become the first to score 5,000 one-day international runs for Zimbabwe, was dismissed quite spectacularly. Nagamootoo leapt high to his left to catch him off his own bowling, and claimed three more wickets in eight balls as Zimbabwe's challenge disintegrated.

Man of the Match: M. N. Samuels. *Attendance:* 6,878.

West Indies

S. L. Campbell c Campbell b Streak	5
D. Ganga run out	6
M. N. Samuels c A. Flower b Viljoen	68
B. C. Lara c Campbell b Streak	70
R. L. Powell b Streak	33
†R. D. Jacobs run out	7
*J. C. Adams not out	13
M. V. Nagamootoo not out	22
L-b 3, w 5, n-b 3	11
1/11 2/16 3/149 4/183 5/199 6/203 (6 wkts, 47 overs)	235

N. A. M. McLean, C. E. Cuffy and M. I. Black did not bat.

Bowling: Streak 8–1–27–3; Strang 10–1–44–0; Whittall 3–0–16–0; Nkala 8–0–43–0; Murphy 5–0–33–0; Viljoen 10–0–47–1; G. W. Flower 3–0–22–0.

Zimbabwe

A. D. R. Campbell c Powell b McLean	20
G. J. Whittall c Samuels b McLean	17
S. V. Carlisle b Cuffy	4
†A. Flower c and b Nagamootoo	50
G. W. Flower c Ganga b Samuels	41
G. J. Rennie not out	17
*H. H. Streak lbw b Nagamootoo	3
D. P. Viljoen c Adams b Nagamootoo	7
M. L. Nkala b Nagamootoo	0
B. C. Strang run out	0
B. A. Murphy run out	1
L-b 7, w 5, n-b 3	15
1/38 2/45 3/47 4/137 5/149 6/157 7/167 8/169 9/170 (40.2 overs)	175

Bowling: McLean 8–1–31–2; Cuffy 10–1–37–1; Black 7–0–30–0; Samuels 8–0–38–1; Nagamootoo 7.2–0–32–4.

Umpires: D. B. Hair and P. D. Parker.
Third umpire: S. J. Davis.

AUSTRALIA v WEST INDIES

At Adelaide, January 26 (day/night). Australia won by ten wickets. Toss: West Indies.

On Australia Day, Steve Waugh returned from injury to lead his country to their first ten-wicket victory in 30 years of one-day internationals. For the second time in a week, West Indies' lowest limited-overs total was under threat, despite easier batting conditions than at Sydney. From six overs they were ten for four after Lee and Fleming had scythed through the top order (Lara went first ball); from 26, they were 82 for nine, still five short of their all-time low. McLean, once more, and Cuffy salvaged some honour with a last-wicket stand of 41 – as much as the first six wickets managed between them. Lehmann and his new opening partner, Martyn, won the game before the floodlights were switched on. The winning boundary lifted Lehmann's aggregate in this tournament to 161 runs in three unbeaten innings.

Man of the Match: B. Lee. *Attendance:* 27,640.

West Indies

†R. D. Jacobs b Lee	2
D. Ganga c Warne b Fleming	0
M. N. Samuels c Gilchrist b Fleming	4
B. C. Lara lbw b Lee	0
*J. C. Adams lbw b Lee	4
R. L. Powell b Harvey	16
S. C. Joseph lbw b Warne	11
M. V. Nagamootoo c Gilchrist b Lee	20
N. A. M. McLean not out	24
M. I. Black lbw b Fleming	4
C. E. Cuffy lbw b Harvey	13
B 2, l-b 9, w 8, n-b 6	25
1/0 2/6 3/6 4/10 5/32 6/41 7/65 8/75 9/82 (35.1 overs)	123

Bowling: Lee 10–3–33–4; Fleming 10–2–32–3; Harvey 7.1–3–11–2; Warne 8–1–36–1.

Australia

D. S. Lehmann not out	50
D. R. Martyn not out	69
B 1, w 3, n-b 1	5
(no wkt, 22.5 overs)	124

M. E. Waugh, M. G. Bevan, *S. R. Waugh, †A. C. Gilchrist, A. Symonds, I. J. Harvey, S. K. Warne, B. Lee and D. W. Fleming did not bat.

Bowling: McLean 5–0–31–0; Cuffy 7–0–35–0; Black 4–0–19–0; Samuels 2–0–9–0; Nagamootoo 4.5–0–29–0.

Umpires: S. J. Davis and S. J. A. Taufel.
Third umpire: P. D. Parker.

AUSTRALIA v ZIMBABWE

At Sydney, January 28 (day/night). Australia won by 86 runs. Toss: Australia.

Having missed out in Adelaide, the rest of the Australian batting had a chance to shine here. Gilchrist and Mark Waugh, reunited as openers, put together their second successive opening stand of 98, but it was the middle order who stepped up the pace, amassing 291, the tournament's biggest total to date. Their final assault brought a round 100 from ten overs. Bevan top-scored, accumulating an unbeaten 74 in 70 balls, and later he ended the Zimbabweans' best stand, 92 between Carlisle and Andy Flower. Carlisle struck two sixes off Warne, but was eventually trapped by him. There had never been much chance that Zimbabwe could prevent Australia's sixth straight win.

Man of the Match: M. G. Bevan. *Attendance:* 33,748.

Australia

†A. C. Gilchrist c Campbell b Strang	63
M. E. Waugh run out	36
*S. R. Waugh c A. Flower b Viljoen	36
M. G. Bevan not out	74
R. T. Ponting c Whittall b Viljoen	15
A. Symonds b Viljoen	22
D. S. Lehmann b Streak	36
L-b 4, w 1, n-b 4	9
1/98 2/111 3/159 4/187 5/241 6/291 (6 wkts, 50 overs)	291

S. K. Warne, D. W. Fleming, N. W. Bracken and G. D. McGrath did not bat.

Bowling: Streak 10–0–56–1; Strang 10–0–50–1; Nkala 8–0–56–0; Whittall 4–0–25–0; Murphy 8–0–38–0; Viljoen 10–0–62–3.

Zimbabwe

A. D. R. Campbell lbw b Fleming	3
G. J. Whittall c Warne b McGrath	10
S. V. Carlisle lbw b Warne	44
†A. Flower c Symonds b Bevan	39
G. W. Flower st Gilchrist b Symonds	30
G. J. Rennie st Gilchrist b Symonds	11
D. P. Viljoen b Warne	31
*H. H. Streak c Bevan b Ponting	9
M. L. Nkala c Gilchrist b Fleming	4
B. C. Strang run out	2
B. A. Murphy not out	2
B 3, l-b 6, w 5, n-b 6	20
1/13 2/13 3/105 4/119 5/143 6/159 7/190 8/200 9/200 (47.5 overs)	205

Bowling: McGrath 6.5–1–26–1; Fleming 6–1–21–2; Warne 10–0–52–2; Bracken 5–0–25–0; Bevan 7–0–25–1; Symonds 8–0–35–2; Ponting 5–0–12–1.

Umpires: D. B. Hair and P. D. Parker.
Third umpire: S. J. A. Taufel.

AUSTRALIA v ZIMBABWE

At Hobart, January 30. Australia won by six wickets. Toss: Australia. International debut: B. J. Haddin.

Zimbabwe's batsmen flourished in a rare daylight game, but their bowlers failed to defend a target of 280. Campbell scored 124, a Hobart record, with ten fours and a six, and added 101 with Andy Flower before Warne removed them both in one over. Stumping Campbell off a wide gave Brad Haddin his first international dismissal, though he had already contributed to the run-out of Whittall. Zimbabwe were convinced that Symonds, opening in place of the resting Gilchrist, was caught behind first ball – Campbell was later fined for his comments – and could only smart as he smashed 60 (47 balls, 12 fours) out of 89 in 13 overs. Mark Waugh, playing a comparatively restrained hand, then put on 120 with his twin, Steve, who joined him as only the second player to score 7,000 one-day runs for Australia. Mark continued until victory was achieved with six overs to spare, finishing on 102 not out.

Man of the Match: A. D. R. Campbell. *Attendance:* 11,115.

Zimbabwe

A. D. R. Campbell st Haddin b Warne	124	D. P. Viljoen b McGrath	1
G. J. Whittall run out	36		
S. V. Carlisle c Symonds b Martyn	36	L-b 6, w 8, n-b 4	18
†A. Flower c Martyn b Warne	51		
*H. H. Streak not out	10	1/94 2/164 3/265 (6 wkts, 50 overs)	279
G. W. Flower b McGrath	3	4/266 5/269 6/279	

M. L. Nkala, A. J. Mackay, B. C. Strang and B. A. Murphy did not bat.

Bowling: McGrath 10–1–43–2; Fleming 10–0–46–0; Harvey 10–1–54–0; Warne 9–0–51–2; Symonds 7–0–51–0; Martyn 4–0–28–1.

Australia

A. Symonds c Viljoen b Murphy	60	I. J. Harvey not out	13
M. E. Waugh not out	102	B 3, l-b 1, w 3, n-b 2	9
R. T. Ponting c Mackay b Nkala	6		
*S. R. Waugh lbw b Murphy	79	1/89 2/114 (4 wkts, 44 overs)	282
†B. J. Haddin c Whittall b Murphy	13	3/234 4/258	

D. R. Martyn, D. S. Lehmann, S. K. Warne, D. W. Fleming and G. D. McGrath did not bat.

Bowling: Streak 10–0–49–0; Strang 6–0–42–0; Nkala 5–0–33–1; Mackay 4–0–33–0; Murphy 10–0–52–3; Viljoen 4–0–28–0; Whittall 5–0–41–0.

Umpires: S. J. Davis and S. J. A. Taufel.
Third umpire: J. H. Smeaton.

WEST INDIES v ZIMBABWE

At Perth, February 2 (day/night). West Indies won by 44 runs. Toss: West Indies.

Victory secured West Indies a place in the finals although, apart from Lara, left stranded on 83 from 98 balls, their batsmen still inspired little confidence. No one else, on either side for that matter, reached 40. Five West Indians were run out, equalling the one-day international record, with Sherwin Campbell unfortunate to go after colliding with the bowler, Streak. He stopped dead in mid-pitch while the bails were removed, but the third umpire ruled that the Zimbabwean captain had not deliberately obstructed him. Zimbabwe needed only 179 to keep their ambitions alive, but McLean grabbed their first three wickets for 12 runs in his first 21 balls, and they were a feeble 64 for six by the halfway mark. Although Viljoen and Streak fought back, Samuels and his off-spin had the final say. The match was Trevor Madondo's last international before his tragic death in June.

Man of the Match: B. C. Lara. *Attendance:* 8,000.

West Indies

D. Ganga run out	22	M. V. Nagamootoo c A. Flower b Viljoen	4
S. L. Campbell run out	0	N. A. M. McLean c Viljoen b Nkala	0
M. N. Samuels c Campbell b Nkala	10	C. E. Cuffy lbw b Viljoen	1
B. C. Lara not out	83	L-b 2, w 2	4
R. L. Powell c Campbell b Murphy	37		
*J. C. Adams run out	8	1/4 2/24 3/43 (47.2 overs)	178
†R. D. Jacobs run out	9	4/105 5/130 6/154	
L. R. Williams run out	0	7/160 8/171 9/172	

Bowling: Streak 9–3–20–0; Strang 10–1–30–0; Nkala 8–0–34–2; Murphy 10–0–35–1; Viljoen 6.2–0–31–2; Whittall 4–0–26–0.

Zimbabwe

A. D. R. Campbell c Jacobs b McLean	1	M. L. Nkala c McLean b Samuels	7
G. J. Whittall lbw b Nagamootoo	33	B. C. Strang run out	4
S. V. Carlisle c Campbell b McLean	5	B. A. Murphy c Williams b Samuels	2
†A. Flower c Jacobs b McLean	4	L-b 2, w 3	5
G. W. Flower c Powell b Cuffy	1		
T. N. Madondo c Campbell b Williams	10	1/2 2/14 3/20 (42.3 overs)	134
D. P. Viljoen c Jacobs b Samuels	29	4/25 5/42 6/64	
*H. H. Streak not out	33	7/104 8/125 9/129	

Bowling: McLean 9–2–21–3; Cuffy 8–4–17–1; Williams 7–0–31–1; Nagamootoo 10–2–31–1; Samuels 7.3–1–25–3; Adams 1–0–7–0.

Umpires: D. B. Hair and S. J. A. Taufel.
Third umpire: R. J. Woolridge.

AUSTRALIA v ZIMBABWE

At Perth, February 4. Australia won by one run. Toss: Australia.

A dead fixture turned into a thriller when Zimbabwe almost overhauled Australia's 302. With 15 needed from McGrath's final over, Marillier hit 11 off the first four balls; after a single from Viljoen, however, he managed only one run off the last. Had it not been for a short run during Carlisle's stand of 187 with Grant Flower – an all-wicket limited-overs record for Zimbabwe – the match could have been tied. Carlisle, dropped by Steve Waugh in the gully when one, hit 11 fours and a six, finally going for 119 in the 48th over. Earlier, Martyn had batted through Australia's innings for 144 from 149 balls, including 12 fours, while Harvey hit 24 (66624) in one over from Viljoen before being caught in the deep off the sixth ball. Streak became the first to take 150 one-day wickets for Zimbabwe when he bowled Lee; he could have had little idea at the time how close his team would come to stealing victory.

Man of the Match: D. R. Martyn. *Attendance:* 20,143.

Australia

†A. C. Gilchrist c A. Flower b Streak	30	D. W. Fleming not out	6
D. R. Martyn not out	144		
R. T. Ponting run out	32	L-b 6, w 1	7
M. G. Bevan lbw b Murphy	44		
I. J. Harvey c Carlisle b Viljoen	37	1/66 2/110 3/204 (5 wkts, 50 overs)	302
B. Lee b Streak	2	4/273 5/282	

M. E. Waugh, *S. R. Waugh, N. W. Bracken and G. D. McGrath did not bat.

Bowling: Streak 10–0–63–2; Mackay 10–0–48–0; Nkala 8–0–45–0; Murphy 9–0–50–1; Viljoen 8–0–63–1; G. W. Flower 5–0–27–0.

Zimbabwe

A. D. R. Campbell c Gilchrist b Lee	27	D. A. Marillier not out	12
G. J. Rennie c M. E. Waugh b McGrath	0	D. P. Viljoen not out	1
S. V. Carlisle c M. E. Waugh b McGrath	119	L-b 5, n-b 19	24
†A. Flower c Gilchrist b Bracken	24		
G. W. Flower run out	85	1/1 2/54 3/91 (6 wkts, 50 overs)	301
*H. H. Streak c and b Harvey	9	4/278 5/288 6/288	

M. L. Nkala, A. J. Mackay and B. A. Murphy did not bat.

Bowling: McGrath 10–1–46–2; Fleming 9–1–53–0; Bracken 9–1–46–1; Lee 8–0–72–1; Harvey 9–0–49–1; Bevan 5–0–30–0.

Umpires: S. J. Davis and D. J. Harper.
Third umpire: D. B. Hair.

QUALIFYING TABLE

	Played	*Won*	*Lost*	*Points*	*Net run-rate*
Australia	8	8	0	16	1.36
West Indies	8	3	5	6	−0.72
Zimbabwe	8	1	7	2	−0.54

Net run-rate is calculated by subtracting runs conceded per over from runs scored per over.

AUSTRALIA v WEST INDIES

First Final Match

At Sydney, February 7 (day/night). Australia won by 134 runs. Toss: West Indies.

Australia went one up with another crushing win – despite scoring their lowest total batting first in this series. Put in, they were a disappointing 179 for six before Harvey entered for the last ten overs and recaptured his Perth form: his career-best 47 not out from 33 balls, with two fours and two sixes, lifted the total to 253. West Indies' chances of beating that plummeted when they lost both openers without a run on the board, although Ganga was unfortunate to be given lbw when replays suggested the ball came off an inside edge. Lara made 35 in 38 balls, but his colleagues offered little more once he was out. Harvey complemented his flamboyant batting with parsimonious bowling, conceding only five runs in six overs for the wickets of Adams and Powell.

Man of the Match: I. J. Harvey. *Attendance:* 35,797.

Australia

M. E. Waugh c Lara b Cuffy	10
†A. C. Gilchrist run out	44
R. T. Ponting c Joseph b Nagamootoo	33
M. G. Bevan c Jacobs b Williams	23
*S. R. Waugh c Jacobs b Williams	38
D. R. Martyn run out	18
A. Symonds c Jacobs b McLean	8
I. J. Harvey not out	47
S. K. Warne c Jacobs b Cuffy	7
D. W. Fleming c Nagamootoo b Samuels	14
G. D. McGrath not out	1
L-b 5, w 5	10
1/28 2/72 3/111 4/137 5/168 6/179 7/199 8/219 9/242 (9 wkts, 50 overs)	253

Bowling: McLean 10–0–47–1; Cuffy 10–1–45–2; Williams 10–0–55–2; Nagamootoo 10–0–55–1; Samuels 10–0–46–1.

West Indies

D. Ganga lbw b McGrath	0
†R. D. Jacobs c Gilchrist b Fleming	0
M. N. Samuels run out	24
B. C. Lara c Gilchrist b Fleming	35
*J. C. Adams c Gilchrist b Harvey	9
R. L. Powell lbw b Harvey	3
S. C. Joseph c and b Warne	18
L. R. Williams c Ponting b McGrath	1
M. V. Nagamootoo c Warne b Symonds	8
N. A. M. McLean c Martyn b Symonds	0
C. E. Cuffy not out	0
B 5, l-b 4, w 11, n-b 1	21
1/0 2/0 3/58 4/74 5/74 6/77 7/81 8/103 9/103 (37.2 overs)	119

Bowling: McGrath 10–4–25–2; Fleming 7–2–34–2; Warne 9.2–1–28–1; Harvey 6–2–5–2; Symonds 5–0–18–2.

Umpires: D. J. Harper and S. J. A. Taufel.
Third umpire: D. B. Hair.

AUSTRALIA v WEST INDIES

Second Final Match

At Melbourne, February 9 (day/night). Australia won by 39 runs. Toss: West Indies.

Australia secured the trophy with their tenth straight limited-overs win. Mark Waugh's 173, his 17th hundred and the ninth-highest innings in one-day internationals, was a record for Australia, beating Gilchrist's 154 against Sri Lanka in 1998-99; he also became the first Australian to reach 8,000 runs at this level. Waugh shared century partnerships with Ponting and Bevan, and struck 16 fours and three sixes in 148 balls before he was eventually caught off Samuels in the 49th over. Australia's 338 for six was their second-highest total and the highest in any one-day international on Australian soil, beating their 337 for seven in the previous year's final against Pakistan. For once, the West Indians were not overwhelmed and responded with 299, easily their best of the series. Though Lara made a duck in Warne's opening over, there were fifties for Hinds, Samuels and Jacobs. To no one's surprise, Waugh won the match award, but there were boos from the crowd when the series award went to Lara. He shared their astonishment: "I agree," he said, "one of the Australians should have got this." It was just about all they failed to get throughout the summer.

Man of the Match: M. E. Waugh. *Attendance:* 31,915.
Man of the Series: B. C. Lara.

Australia

†A. C. Gilchrist c Hinds b McLean	5
M. E. Waugh c Lara b Samuels	173
R. T. Ponting c Hinds b Nagamootoo	63
A. Symonds c Nagamootoo b Cuffy	7
M. G. Bevan c Williams b Samuels	58
I. J. Harvey c McLean b Samuels	2
*S. R. Waugh not out	10
D. R. Martyn not out	4
B 2, l-b 2, w 12	16
1/12 2/137 3/155 4/291 5/311 6/328 (6 wkts, 50 overs)	338

S. K. Warne, D. W. Fleming and G. D. McGrath did not bat.

Bowling: McLean 10–1–58–1; Cuffy 10–0–53–1; Nagamootoo 10–0–54–1; Williams 8–0–72–0; Samuels 10–0–71–3; Adams 2–0–26–0.

West Indies

W. W. Hinds c Ponting b Symonds	60
R. L. Powell lbw b Warne	21
B. C. Lara c Martyn b Warne	0
M. N. Samuels c Martyn b Warne	63
*J. C. Adams c and b Fleming	18
†R. D. Jacobs c S. R. Waugh b McGrath	59
M. V. Nagamootoo b Fleming	5
N. A. M. McLean c S. R. Waugh b Bevan	16
D. Ganga b McGrath	18
L. R. Williams not out	10
C. E. Cuffy c Martyn b Warne	6
B 2, l-b 8, w 8, n-b 5	23
1/54 2/56 3/128 4/159 5/201 6/218 7/237 8/279 9/288 (49.3 overs)	299

Bowling: McGrath 10–1–48–2; Fleming 8–0–49–2; Warne 8.3–0–48–4; Harvey 10–0–59–0; Symonds 8–0–55–1; Martyn 2–0–10–0; Bevan 3–0–20–1.

Umpires: S. J. Davis and D. B. Hair.
Third umpire: D. J. Harper. Series referee: D. T. Lindsay (South Africa).

ARY GOLD CUP, 2000-01

Victory over Pakistan gave Sri Lanka their second Sharjah trophy in six months, though they never approached their dominance of the October tournament, when they won all five games and crushed India by a record 245 runs. This time it was Pakistan who coasted through the qualifiers undefeated, despite missing several key players, while Sri Lanka won only one match and squeezed into the final on net run-rate.

The third team should have been India, but they pulled out a week before the start after their government announced that, in the aftermath of match-fixing allegations, "The Indian team should not participate in tournaments at non-regular venues such as Sharjah, Singapore, Toronto etc, for at least three years." Former Pakistan captain Asif Iqbal, one of the Sharjah tournament's principal organisers, resigned, citing the problems caused by such political interventions. Still, plans had been laid in case of a withdrawal, and New Zealand accepted an invitation at very short notice. They were well below strength, partly through injuries, partly because their board used the opportunity to give experience to newer players. Craig McMillan led the side, as Stephen Fleming was about to join Middlesex for the English season. He won only one victory, against Sri Lanka, but the series was a triumph for opening batsman Mathew Sinclair, who scored 304 runs, including two centuries, at 101.33.

Pakistan also had a new captain, officially because Moin Khan had been injured during the New Zealand Tests, and Waqar Younis did well enough to be reappointed for the subsequent tour of England. He also took eight wickets, a total exceeded only by team-mate Saqlain Mushtaq and Sri Lanka's Muttiah Muralitharan, the world's leading off-spinners, who claimed nine each. Saeed Anwar was the highest run-scorer, with 329, and Inzamam-ul-Haq was named Man of the Series for his 290 at 96.66. Sri Lankan captain Sanath Jayasuriya could not quite recapture his October form, but he and Mahela Jayawardene scored centuries in their first game against New Zealand, when Jayasuriya broke his own record for runs in an international over, hitting Chris Harris for 30.

Another consequence of India's late withdrawal was the loss of sponsors Coca-Cola. Their place was filled by ARY, a gold and jewellery business with television interests, who donated a gold trophy weighing one kilo.

Note: Matches in this section were not first-class.

PAKISTAN v SRI LANKA

At Sharjah, April 8 (day/night). Pakistan won by 16 runs. Toss: Pakistan. International debut: W. C. A. Ganegama.

Pakistan made a winning start when Saqlain Mushtaq removed the last two Sri Lankans with successive deliveries, ending their run-chase 17 short with nine balls remaining. Sri Lanka's hopes were high after 43 overs, at 201 for five, but Waqar Younis then brought himself back on and bowled three men in his first 11 balls. He had earlier trapped Jayasuriya in the first over of the innings. However, the match award went to Saeed Anwar, who had opened with 90, striking eight fours and adding 88 with Inzamam-ul-Haq. Sri Lanka's reply also featured an 88-run stand, between Kaluwitharana and Atapattu.

Man of the Match: Saeed Anwar.

Pakistan

Saeed Anwar c Arnold b Muralitharan	90	*Waqar Younis not out	7
Shahid Afridi c Arnold b Ganegama	21	Saqlain Mushtaq c Kaluwitharana b Vaas	4
Imran Farhat lbw b Ganegama	6	Mohammad Sami not out	1
Inzamam-ul-Haq c Muralitharan b Arnold	44	L-b 1, w 8	9
Younis Khan c Vaas b Muralitharan	37		
Abdur Razzaq b Jayasuriya	9	1/49 2/61 3/149 (9 wkts, 50 overs)	255
Shoaib Malik c Jayasuriya b Zoysa	24	4/197 5/204 6/220	
†Humayun Farhat run out	3	7/237 8/245 9/251	

Bowling: Vaas 10–0–47–1; Zoysa 8–0–48–1; Ganegama 4–0–27–2; Muralitharan 10–0–52–2; Jayasuriya 10–1–43–1; Arnold 8–0–37–1.

Sri Lanka

*S. T. Jayasuriya lbw b Waqar Younis	0	M. Muralitharan b Waqar Younis	7
†R. S. Kaluwitharana b Shoaib Malik	63	W. P. U. J. C. Vaas not out	16
M. S. Atapattu st Humayun Farhat b Shoaib Malik	28	D. N. T. Zoysa lbw b Saqlain Mushtaq	6
D. P. M. D. Jayawardene lbw b Shahid Afridi	27	W. C. A. Ganegama st Humayun Farhat b Saqlain Mushtaq	0
K. Sangakkara c Imran Farhat b Shahid Afridi	11	B 1, l-b 7, w 7, n-b 3	18
R. P. Arnold b Waqar Younis	25	1/0 2/88 3/101 (48.3 overs)	239
S. I. de Saram b Waqar Younis	38	4/135 5/151 6/201	
		7/209 8/222 9/239	

Bowling: Waqar Younis 8–0–49–4; Mohammad Sami 6–0–24–0; Abdur Razzaq 8–2–37–0; Saqlain Mushtaq 9.3–0–46–2; Shoaib Malik 10–0–42–2; Shahid Afridi 7–0–33–2.

Umpires: D. B. Cowie and D. L. Orchard.
Third umpire: J. H. Hampshire.

NEW ZEALAND v SRI LANKA

At Sharjah, April 10 (day/night). Sri Lanka won by 106 runs. Toss: Sri Lanka. International debut: A. R. Adams.

Jayasuriya broke his own one-day international record of 29 runs off a single over when he smashed Harris for four sixes, a four and a two. Harris shared the record for the most expensive over at this level with Jayasuriya's earlier victim, Aamir Sohail of Pakistan, whose total of 30 conceded at Singapore in 1996 included a wide. The fourth six of the over took Jayasuriya to his hundred; in all, he hit 107 in 116 balls, with three fours and six sixes, and added 184 in 37 overs with Jayawardene after Tuffey had extracted Atapattu and Sangakkara (promoted because Kaluwitharana had flown home when his mother died) in the first over of the match. Jayawardene scored 116 in 129 balls, hitting 13 fours. New Zealand's reply followed an opposite course. Openers Nevin and Sinclair hurried to 82 before Muralitharan separated them in the 16th over, but the last nine wickets mustered only 81 as the spinners took control.

Man of the Match: D. P. M. D. Jayawardene.

Sri Lanka

M. S. Atapattu lbw b Tuffey	0	W. P. U. J. C. Vaas run out	6
*S. T. Jayasuriya c Bell b Adams	107	M. Muralitharan b Oram	5
†K. Sangakkara c Nevin b Tuffey	0	D. N. T. Zoysa not out	3
D. P. M. D. Jayawardene c Vincent b Tuffey	116	W 4, n-b 2	6
R. P. Arnold c and b Oram	1	1/0 2/1 3/185 (9 wkts, 50 overs)	269
S. I. de Saram run out	21	4/188 5/236 6/240	
H. D. P. K. Dharmasena lbw b Oram	4	7/250 8/264 9/269	

W. C. A. Ganegama did not bat.

Bowling: Tuffey 8–0–49–3; Franklin 6–0–20–0; Adams 7–0–39–1; Walker 6–0–30–0; Harris 10–0–66–0; McMillan 4–0–25–0; Oram 9–0–40–3.

New Zealand

†C. J. Nevin lbw b Muralitharan	48	J. E. C. Franklin run out	1
M. S. Sinclair lbw b Arnold	60	B. G. K. Walker lbw b Dharmasena	3
A. R. Adams c de Saram b Muralitharan	1	D. R. Tuffey not out	7
*C. D. McMillan c and b Arnold	11		
L. Vincent b Jayasuriya	2	B 4, l-b 1, w 4, n-b 1	10
J. D. P. Oram b Jayasuriya	4		
C. Z. Harris c Jayawardene b Muralitharan	14	1/82 2/85 3/110 4/116 5/128 6/134 7/137 8/139 9/146	(42.1 overs) 163
M. D. Bell c and b Dharmasena	2		

Bowling: Vaas 5–0–32–0; Zoysa 5–0–24–0; Dharmasena 10–1–31–2; Muralitharan 7.1–1–12–3; Jayasuriya 8–0–37–2; Arnold 7–0–22–2.

Umpires: J. H. Hampshire and D. L. Orchard.
Third umpire: D. B. Cowie.

MOST RUNS BY A BATSMAN IN A ONE-DAY INTERNATIONAL OVER

30 (666642)	**S. T. Jayasuriya (SL) off C. Z. Harris (NZ) at Sharjah**	**2000-01**
29 (*4066661)	S. T. Jayasuriya (SL) off Aamir Sohail (P) at Singapore	1995-96
28 (662644)	Shahid Afridi (P) off S. T. Jayasuriya (SL) at Nairobi	1996-97
26 (64646W)	R. W. Marsh (A) off B. L. Cairns (NZ) at Adelaide	1980-81
26 (464660)	B. L. Cairns (NZ) off V. B. John (SL) at Colombo (PSS)	1983-84
26 (442466)	I. T. Botham (E) off S. P. Davis (A) at Perth	1986-87
26 (204266*6)	A. P. Kuiper (SA) off C. J. McDermott (A) at Centurion	1993-94
26 (226664)	Saeed Anwar (P) off A. Kumble (I) at Chennai	1996-97
26 (66446)	S. T. Jayasuriya (SL) off Akram Khan (B) at Colombo (SSC)	1997-98
26 (64646)	**Shahid Afridi (P) off G. E. Bradburn (NZ) at Sharjah**	**2000-01**

* *Aamir Sohail's first ball to Jayasuriya was a wide and his 2nd a no-ball, which he hit for four. Kuiper struck his second six off McDermott off a no-ball. Some players did not face an entire over.*

NEW ZEALAND v PAKISTAN

At Sharjah, April 12 (day/night). Pakistan won by eight wickets. Toss: New Zealand.

Shahid Afridi might have threatened Jayasuriya's two-day-old record of 30 runs in an over, but had to be satisfied with 26 off five balls (64646) from Bradburn, Imran Nazir having taken a single off the first delivery. Afridi hit his next ball, from Oram, for another four, which lifted Pakistan to 83 in the eighth over. The introduction of Adams checked the flow a little, and eventually he had Afridi caught at mid-on for 70 off 43 balls, with seven fours and six sixes. Nazir, with whom Afridi put on 113 in 15 overs, was out four balls later, but old hands Saeed Anwar and Inzamam-ul-Haq completed a comfortable win with a comparatively sedate partnership of 157 in 27 overs. Earlier, Sinclair had scored his maiden century in one-day internationals, batting for all but seven balls of the innings and striking six fours in 144 balls.

Man of the Match: Shahid Afridi.

New Zealand

†C. J. Nevin c Inzamam-ul-Haq b Mohammad Sami . 15
M. S. Sinclair c Shoaib Malik b Abdur Razzaq . 117
M. D. Bell b Abdur Razzaq 5
*C. D. McMillan b Shahid Afridi 46
L. Vincent lbw b Shahid Afridi. 15
C. Z. Harris c sub (Imran Farhat) b Waqar Younis . 29
J. D. P. Oram b Waqar Younis. 10
A. R. Adams not out. 4
G. E. Bradburn not out 0

L-b 13, w 8, n-b 4. 25

1/45 2/71 3/151 4/186 5/251 6/262 7/263 (7 wkts, 50 overs) 266

B. G. K. Walker and J. E. C. Franklin did not bat.

Bowling: Waqar Younis 8–1–37–2; Mohammad Sami 6–0–42–1; Abdur Razzaq 7–0–31–2; Saqlain Mushtaq 9–0–46–0; Shoaib Malik 10–0–48–0; Shahid Afridi 10–0–49–2.

Pakistan

Imran Nazir lbw b Walker 35
Shahid Afridi c Franklin b Adams 70
Saeed Anwar not out. 81
Inzamam-ul-Haq not out 71
L-b 7, w 5, n-b 1 13

1/113 2/113 (2 wkts, 42.1 overs) 270

Younis Khan, Abdur Razzaq, Shoaib Malik, †Humayun Farhat, *Waqar Younis, Saqlain Mushtaq and Mohammad Sami did not bat.

Bowling: Franklin 2–0–23–0; Oram 6–0–24–0; Bradburn 7.1–0–61–0; Adams 8–0–38–1; Walker 9–0–63–1; Harris 4–0–23–0; McMillan 6–1–31–0.

Umpires: D. B. Cowie and J. H. Hampshire.
Third umpire: D. L. Orchard.

PAKISTAN v SRI LANKA

At Sharjah, April 13 (day/night). Pakistan won by 28 runs. Toss: Pakistan. International debut: Kashif Raza.

Pakistan's third successive victory secured their place in the final. Shahid Afridi and Imran Nazir were quickly brought down to earth, both falling in the fourth over. But Saeed Anwar and Inzamam-ul-Haq carried on with their second successive century stand. They became the first two batsmen to score 2,000 runs at Sharjah, and Anwar went on to 8,000 in his 221 one-day internationals at all venues. Despite three late wickets from Fernando, Pakistan reached 278, the highest total of the tournament to date. Most of the Sri Lankan batsmen made a start, but Afridi pinned back their reply with three mid-innings wickets. Although Vaas retorted with an unbeaten 59-ball fifty, he could not quite achieve the required rate.

Man of the Match: Saeed Anwar.

Pakistan

Imran Nazir c Arnold b Zoysa 2
Shahid Afridi run out 13
Saeed Anwar lbw b Vaas 88
Inzamam-ul-Haq c Jayasuriya b Muralitharan . 87
Younis Khan c de Saram b Fernando . . . 29
Shoaib Malik c de Saram b Fernando. . . 0
†Humayun Farhat run out 18
Yasir Arafat c Muralitharan b Fernando . 4
*Waqar Younis run out 14
Saqlain Mushtaq not out 6
Kashif Raza not out 2

L-b 2, w 4, n-b 9 15

1/17 2/18 3/190 4/208 5/209 6/244 7/254 8/260 9/273 (9 wkts, 50 overs) 278

Bowling: Vaas 9–1–47–1; Zoysa 8–0–45–1; Fernando 9–0–52–3; Muralitharan 10–0–57–1; Jayasuriya 4–0–26–0; Dharmasena 5–0–29–0; Arnold 5–0–20–0.

Sri Lanka

*S. T. Jayasuriya b Waqar Younis	20
†R. S. Kaluwitharana b Kashif Raza	25
M. S. Atapattu c and b Shahid Afridi	36
D. P. M. D. Jayawardene c Humayun Farhat b Yasir Arafat	31
R. P. Arnold c Humayun Farhat b Shahid Afridi	19
H. D. P. K. Dharmasena c Humayun Farhat b Shoaib Malik	5
S. I. de Saram c and b Shahid Afridi	8
W. P. U. J. C. Vaas not out	50
D. N. T. Zoysa run out	16
M. Muralitharan not out	13
B 8, l-b 5, w 13, n-b 1	27
1/48 2/49 3/103 4/140 5/147 6/149 7/171 8/205 (8 wkts, 50 overs)	250

C. R. D. Fernando did not bat.

Bowling: Waqar Younis 8–0–39–1; Kashif Raza 5–0–36–1; Yasir Arafat 7–0–37–1; Saqlain Mushtaq 10–0–49–0; Shahid Afridi 10–0–44–3; Shoaib Malik 10–0–32–1.

Umpires: D. B. Cowie and D. L. Orchard.
Third umpire: J. H. Hampshire.

NEW ZEALAND v PAKISTAN

At Sharjah, April 15 (day/night). Pakistan won by seven wickets. Toss: New Zealand. International debut: K. D. Mills.

Pakistan completed the qualifiers with a 100 per cent record. They crushed New Zealand in a curious match lasting barely half its scheduled length; only four of the 16 who batted reached double figures. Nevin was the first, hitting a dashing fifty from 40 balls, but became Abdur Razzaq's third victim in the 12th over. New Zealand never recovered, and Saqlain Mushtaq wrapped up the innings with four wickets. Pakistan also made a shaky start, losing their top three even more cheaply. But by then Inzamam-ul-Haq was at the crease. He struck two sixes off the spinners and, with 12 fours as well in his 85 from 67 balls, saw Pakistan home in their 26th over.

Man of the Match: Saqlain Mushtaq.

New Zealand

†C. J. Nevin c Mohammad Sami b Abdur Razzaq	50
M. S. Sinclair b Abdur Razzaq	9
M. D. Bell b Abdur Razzaq	5
*C. D. McMillan run out	16
L. Vincent c Humayun Farhat b Saqlain Mushtaq	9
J. D. P. Oram c and b Mohammad Sami	6
C. Z. Harris b Mohammad Sami	5
K. D. Mills lbw b Saqlain Mushtaq	4
G. E. Bradburn lbw b Saqlain Mushtaq	1
B. G. K. Walker not out	3
D. R. Tuffey b Saqlain Mushtaq	6
L-b 7, w 3, n-b 3	13
1/38 2/44 3/79 4/89 5/106 6/112 7/113 8/117 9/120 (31.3 overs)	127

Bowling: Waqar Younis 5–0–32–0; Mohammad Sami 10–1–41–2; Abdur Razzaq 6–1–22–3; Saqlain Mushtaq 7.3–1–17–4; Shoaib Malik 3–0–8–0.

Pakistan

Saeed Anwar run out	8
Imran Nazir c Walker b Mills	7
Younis Khan lbw b Oram	8
Inzamam-ul-Haq not out	85
Faisal Iqbal not out	17
L-b 3, w 2, n-b 1	6
1/13 2/17 3/67 (3 wkts, 25.2 overs)	131

Abdur Razzaq, †Humayun Farhat, Shoaib Malik, *Waqar Younis, Saqlain Mushtaq and Mohammad Sami did not bat.

Bowling: Tuffey 5–1–16–0; Mills 7.2–0–33–1; Walker 2–0–28–0; Oram 5–0–23–1; Bradburn 6–1–28–0.

Umpires: J. H. Hampshire and D. L. Orchard.
Third umpire: D. B. Cowie.

NEW ZEALAND v SRI LANKA

At Sharjah, April 17 (day/night). New Zealand won by 79 runs. Toss: Sri Lanka.

New Zealand broke their duck, but could not improve their net run-rate sufficiently to reach the final. Jayasuriya became the only captain to field first in this tournament, and won a swift reward when Nevin was caught behind first ball. But with Sinclair and Bell adding 141, it was nearly 30 overs before the next breakthrough. Sinclair advanced to his second century of the week, with five fours and two sixes, and was unbeaten at the end. He had to share the match award, though, with team-mate Kyle Mills, who in his second international claimed Sri Lanka's first three wickets and also took a leaping catch. Even Jayawardene could not raise his team's momentum and they limped to 169 for eight.

Men of the Match: K. D. Mills and M. S. Sinclair.

New Zealand

†C. J. Nevin c Kaluwitharana b Vaas	0
M. S. Sinclair not out	118
M. D. Bell st Kaluwitharana b Arnold	66
*C. D. McMillan c Samaraweera b Jayasuriya	17
J. D. P. Oram c Samaraweera b Muralitharan	2
C. Z. Harris c and b Jayasuriya	16
L. Vincent c Jayawardene b Zoysa	8
A. R. Adams not out	13
L-b 2, w 3, n-b 3	8
1/0 2/141 3/167 4/176 5/200 6/227 (6 wkts, 50 overs)	248

G. E. Bradburn, K. D. Mills and D. R. Tuffey did not bat.

Bowling: Vaas 9–1–57–1; Zoysa 8–0–42–1; Muralitharan 10–0–38–1; Samaraweera 8–0–37–0; Jayasuriya 10–0–47–2; Arnold 5–0–25–1.

Sri Lanka

*S. T. Jayasuriya c sub (B. G. K. Walker) b Mills	25
†R. S. Kaluwitharana b Mills	0
M. S. Atapattu c Nevin b Mills	5
D. P. M. D. Jayawardene c and b Bradburn	41
S. I. de Saram c Mills b Bradburn	11
K. Sangakkara lbw b Harris	6
R. P. Arnold run out	1
W. P. U. J. C. Vaas not out	24
T. T. Samaraweera run out	27
D. N. T. Zoysa not out	19
L-b 3, w 4, n-b 3	10
1/14 2/23 3/37 4/78 5/87 6/91 7/97 8/138 (8 wkts, 50 overs)	169

M. Muralitharan did not bat.

Bowling: Tuffey 8–0–25–0; Mills 10–2–30–3; Oram 5–0–20–0; Bradburn 10–1–22–2; Harris 10–0–27–1; Adams 3–0–12–0; McMillan 4–0–30–0.

Umpires: D. B. Cowie and J. H. Hampshire.
Third umpire: D. L. Orchard.

QUALIFYING TABLE

	Played	*Won*	*Lost*	*Points*	*Net run-rate*
Pakistan	4	4	0	8	1.16
Sri Lanka	4	1	3	2	–0.08
New Zealand	4	1	3	2	–0.98

Net run-rate is calculated by subtracting runs conceded per over from runs scored per over.

FINAL

PAKISTAN v SRI LANKA

At Sharjah, April 20 (day/night). Sri Lanka won by 77 runs. Toss: Sri Lanka.

Sri Lanka astonished a sell-out crowd by overwhelming in-form Pakistan. If less comprehensive than when they beat India by 245 runs in their previous Sharjah final, in October, it was nevertheless a convincing victory. Their 297, the tournament's highest total, was anchored by Atapattu, who shared hundred stands with Jayasuriya and Jayawardene, each of whom hit three sixes. All benefited from dropped catches, while Pakistan were also profligate with wides. The last ten overs brought 100 runs, and in addition saw Saqlain Mushtaq claim three wickets to reach 250 in only 138 one-day internationals, fewer than anyone else had needed. Pakistan's reply suffered two early blows, Zoysa dismissing both openers in his first over. Humayun Farhat and Saeed Anwar fought back, adding 69 in eight overs, and Pakistan were well ahead of the asking-rate after 15, with 108. By then, however, they had only four wickets left. Shoaib Malik and Waqar Younis saw them past 200, but once Muralitharan removed them, the innings subsided with eight overs to spare.

Man of the Match: M. S. Atapattu. *Man of the Series:* Inzamam-ul-Haq.

Sri Lanka

*S. T. Jayasuriya c Inzamam-ul-Haq b Shoaib Malik	70
†R. S. Kaluwitharana run out	7
M. S. Atapattu run out	89
D. P. M. D. Jayawardene c and b Saqlain Mushtaq	67
S. I. de Saram st Humayun Farhat b Saqlain Mushtaq	12
W. P. U. J. C. Vaas c Inzamam-ul-Haq b Saqlain Mushtaq	4
R. P. Arnold b Waqar Younis	2
T. M. Dilshan not out	3
D. N. T. Zoysa not out	11
L-b 6, w 20, n-b 6	32
1/8 2/122 3/233 4/263 5/267 6/275 7/277 (7 wkts, 50 overs)	297

C. R. D. Fernando and M. Muralitharan did not bat.

Bowling: Waqar Younis 10–1–55–1; Abdur Razzaq 9–0–53–0; Mohammad Sami 7–1–30–0; Saqlain Mushtaq 9–0–54–3; Shoaib Malik 8–0–56–1; Shahid Afridi 7–0–43–0.

Pakistan

Imran Nazir c Kaluwitharana b Zoysa	5
Shahid Afridi c Vaas b Zoysa	10
†Humayun Farhat c Muralitharan b Vaas	39
Saeed Anwar c and b Jayasuriya	62
Inzamam-ul-Haq c Arnold b Vaas	3
Younis Khan c Jayawardene b Vaas	4
Abdur Razzaq c and b Fernando	5
Shoaib Malik b Muralitharan	44
*Waqar Younis c Zoysa b Muralitharan	20
Saqlain Mushtaq c Dilshan b Fernando	7
Mohammad Sami not out	4
L-b 3, w 6, n-b 8	17
1/13 2/17 3/86 4/95 5/103 6/108 7/159 8/205 9/207 (41.4 overs)	220

Bowling: Vaas 6–0–36–3; Zoysa 6–0–51–2; Fernando 9.4–1–49–2; Muralitharan 10–1–29–2; Arnold 6–0–30–0; Jayasuriya 4–0–22–1.

Umpires: D. B. Cowie and D. L. Orchard.
Third umpire: J. H. Hampshire. Series referee: A. M. Ebrahim.

COCA-COLA CUP (ZIMBABWE), 2001

By JOHN WARD

The first international triangular one-day competition in Zimbabwe proved a disaster for the home side, a disappointment for India and a triumph for West Indies, who surprised many by turning in a superb batting performance to win the final. It was their first victory in a one-day tournament since September 1999 in Singapore. India had been favourites, thanks to an efficient seam attack, Sachin Tendulkar's 282 runs and a 100 per cent record in the preliminaries. Much was made in the Indian press about their failure to win finals, but in this case the match was torn from their grasp by inspired batting from the West Indian openers, Daren Ganga and Chris Gayle.

Before then, India's bowlers had kept a tight rein on the opposing batsmen, as indeed had West Indies' Cameron Cuffy: before a foot injury ruled him out, his 30 overs cost just 2.33 runs apiece. Ashish Nehra and Zaheer Khan formed an impressive and consistent opening pair, and Zimbabwe's 234 for six in Bulawayo was the highest total India conceded in the qualifying games. It was little short of astonishing to see how Ganga and Gayle subsequently seized the initiative so decisively after West Indies had been asked to bat first in the final.

The series enjoyed the expected dry weather and was well supported by the public. Winter play meant an early start, and generally for the first ten overs or so the ball moved about considerably in the dewy atmosphere. This gave the team winning the toss, and without fail inserting the opposition, a strong advantage; Sourav Ganguly won all five tosses for India, and only in the final did it fail him. The one other match lost by the team winning the toss was the first, when Zimbabwe, a side in crisis, relinquished their advantage with poor bowling against West Indies. They went on to lose all four matches.

It certainly didn't help that they played those games under three different captains. Heath Streak dramatically drew attention to his disagreements with the administrators over selection policy by resigning the captaincy before the opening match. When vice-captain Guy Whittall refused to take his place, Grant Flower stepped in. The dispute was resolved when Streak and coach Carl Rackemann were added to the selectors' panel, which already numbered six. Streak resumed the captaincy for the second match, but missed the third through injury, when Whittall did take over. Zimbabwe were already without Andy Flower, injured in the Second Test against India; while 18-year-old Tatenda Taibu was impressive behind the stumps, nobody could replace Flower's runs and experience.

There was further controversy when referee Denis Lindsay suspended West Indies' wicket-keeper, Ridley Jacobs, after an incident in the final qualifier. Jacobs had "stumped" Virender Sehwag with his right hand while the ball was in his left, and although the keeper, a cricketer of good reputation, did not claim the stumping, nor did he call Sehwag back when his colleagues' appeal was upheld. Originally, Jacobs was to be banned for three one-day internationals in Kenya. When Lindsay discovered that he had not been picked for the Kenyan leg of the tour, the suspension was changed to the Second Test against Zimbabwe.

Note: Matches in this section were not first-class.

ZIMBABWE v WEST INDIES

At Harare, June 23. West Indies won by 27 runs. Toss: Zimbabwe. International debut: T. Taibu.

Streak resigned as Zimbabwe's captain before the match, claiming that the administrators and selectors persistently ignored his views. Vice-captain Whittall was unwilling to take over in these circumstances, so Grant Flower went out to toss at a moment's notice. In understandable disarray, Zimbabwe failed to use the advantageous bowling conditions properly, and the West Indian openers put on 113 without undue trouble. Chanderpaul backed them up with 51 in 46 balls. Zimbabwe never looked like making 267, even though the pitch had eased; the final margin was deceptive. Campbell played a solid anchor role but he needed a partner to share a major stand. Cuffy won the match award for his single spell of ten overs for 20 runs, despite not taking a wicket.

Man of the Match: C. E. Cuffy.

West Indies

D. Ganga st Taibu b Murphy	66
C. H. Gayle c Friend b Murphy	53
W. W. Hinds run out	37
S. Chanderpaul c Friend b Blignaut	51
*C. L. Hooper c Flower b Streak	29
M. N. Samuels not out	7
†R. D. Jacobs not out	0
B 4, l-b 3, w 13, n-b 3	23
1/113 2/168 3/180 4/242 5/264 (5 wkts, 50 overs)	266

M. V. Nagamootoo, M. Dillon, C. E. Cuffy and R. D. King did not bat.

Bowling: Blignaut 10–0–53–1; Streak 10–0–35–1; Friend 7–0–56–0; Nkala 4–0–34–0; Murphy 9–0–43–2; Flower 10–0–38–0.

Zimbabwe

A. D. R. Campbell c sub (R. R. Sarwan) b Dillon	68
D. D. Ebrahim c Jacobs b King	11
S. V. Carlisle c Hooper b Dillon	17
*G. W. Flower c Jacobs b Nagamootoo	29
A. M. Blignaut run out	25
G. J. Whittall c Hinds b Samuels	32
H. H. Streak b Samuels	16
M. L. Nkala c Jacobs b Dillon	0
T. J. Friend b Samuels	17
†T. Taibu not out	1
B. A. Murphy not out	15
B 2, l-b 4, w 1, n-b 1	8
1/18 2/44 3/99 4/137 5/187 6/188 7/190 8/221 9/224 (9 wkts, 50 overs)	239

Bowling: Cuffy 10–2–20–0; King 9–0–57–1; Dillon 10–2–48–3; Hooper 6–0–29–0; Nagamootoo 10–0–51–1; Samuels 5–0–28–3.

Umpires: K. C. Barbour and R. B. Tiffin.
Third umpire: Q. J. Goosen.

ZIMBABWE v INDIA

At Harare, June 24. India won by nine wickets. Toss: India.

Streak returned to lead Zimbabwe, having won a seat on the selectors' panel, and the most immediate result was the recall of left-arm seamer Bryan Strang, the players' choice. Here the good news for Zimbabwe ended. The pitch, watered too liberally after being used the previous day, was still damp, which exaggerated the advantage of winning the toss. Inevitably, Zimbabwe lost it. When five wickets tumbled in the first 13 overs to the delighted Indian seamers, the contest was as good as over. Ganguly continued his run of poor form from the Tests, but Badani, promoted after Laxman injured a finger in the field, added 135 with Tendulkar, who looked at ease from beginning to end. That came with 23 overs to spare.

Man of the Match: S. R. Tendulkar.

Zimbabwe

A. D. R. Campbell c Dighe b Nehra . . . 0
D. D. Ebrahim c Laxman b Agarkar. . . . 32
S. V. Carlisle c Laxman b Zaheer Khan . 6
G. W. Flower b Zaheer Khan 4
G. J. Whittall c Dravid b Agarkar 7
D. P. Viljoen c Ganguly b Nehra 1
*H. H. Streak run out 16
A. M. Blignaut c Harbhajan Singh b Ganguly . 13
T. J. Friend c Sehwag b Ganguly. 11
†T. Taibu not out 19
B. C. Strang b Agarkar 4
B 4, l-b 4, w 7, n-b 5 20

1/0 2/15 3/20 4/35 5/39 6/77 7/82 8/102 9/104 (41.5 overs) 133

Bowling: Nehra 10–2–33–2; Zaheer Khan 7–1–18–2; Agarkar 9.5–1–26–3; Harbhajan Singh 9–1–28–0; Ganguly 6–1–20–2.

India

*S. C. Ganguly c Taibu b Streak 2
S. R. Tendulkar not out 70
H. K. Badani not out 52
L-b 2, w 9, n-b 2 13

1/2 (1 wkt, 26.2 overs) 137

V. V. S. Laxman, R. Dravid, V. Sehwag, †S. S. Dighe, A. B. Agarkar, Harbhajan Singh, Zaheer Khan and A. Nehra did not bat.

Bowling: Streak 6–0–28–1; Strang 6.2–0–30–0; Friend 8–2–41–0; Blignaut 6–0–36–0.

Umpires: G. R. Evans and I. D. Robinson.
Third umpire: K. C. Barbour.

ZIMBABWE v INDIA

At Bulawayo, June 27. India won by four wickets. Toss: India.

With Streak sidelined by a leg injury, Whittall became Zimbabwe's third captain in three matches. And after he failed to win another important toss, they lost two wickets in the second over as India's opening bowlers enjoyed appreciable early swing. A most creditable partnership of 87 between 20-year-old Ebrahim and Wishart gave the innings substance, and allowed Flower and Whittall, the latter playing a typically improvised innings at the death, to concentrate on the scoring-rate once conditions improved. India's reply saw Ganguly rediscover his form at last, while Dravid's superb 72 not out, featuring some classical strokeplay, eased India home after Flower's left-arm spin claimed four for 12 in 19 balls. Strang, another left-armer, justified his place with immaculate seam bowling, but the loss of two world-class players in Streak and Andy Flower was too great a handicap for Zimbabwe.

Man of the Match: R. Dravid.

Zimbabwe

D. D. Ebrahim lbw b Zaheer Khan 42
A. D. R. Campbell c Ganguly b Zaheer Khan . 2
S. V. Carlisle lbw b Zaheer Khan 0
C. B. Wishart c Agarkar b Ganguly 46
G. W. Flower c Sehwag b Zaheer Khan . 45
*G. J. Whittall not out 58
A. M. Blignaut c Harbhajan Singh b Agarkar . 11
†T. Taibu not out 2
L-b 7, w 9, n-b 12. 28

1/5 2/7 3/94 4/122 5/184 6/215 (6 wkts, 50 overs) 234

T. J. Friend, B. C. Strang and D. T. Mutendera did not bat.

Bowling: Nehra 10–0–31–0; Zaheer Khan 10–0–42–4; Agarkar 10–0–55–1; Harbhajan Singh 9–0–42–0; Ganguly 7–0–38–1; Sehwag 4–0–19–0.

India

*S. C. Ganguly c Campbell b Flower	85	†S. S. Dighe c and b Flower	9
S. R. Tendulkar c Flower b Strang	9	A. B. Agarkar not out	13
D. Mongia c Whittall b Mutendera	37	L-b 1, w 7, n-b 2	10
R. Dravid not out	72		—
H. K. Badani b Flower	0	1/22 2/91 3/184 (6 wkts, 49.2 overs)	237
V. Sehwag c Ebrahim b Flower	2	4/187 5/193 6/210	

Harbhajan Singh, Zaheer Khan and A. Nehra did not bat.

Bowling: Blignaut 10–0–41–0; Strang 10–2–26–1; Friend 9–0–45–0; Mutendera 8.2–0–52–1; Whittall 4–0–28–0; Flower 8–0–44–4.

Umpires: M. A. Esat and J. F. Fenwick.
Third umpire: C. K. Coventry.

INDIA v WEST INDIES

At Bulawayo, June 30. India won by six wickets. Toss: India.

Their place in the final virtually assured, India rested Nehra. But their new opening pair, Mohanty and Harvinder Singh, enjoyed the early swing just as much. By the halfway mark, West Indies were five down with only 47 on the board, less than two an over. Samuels and Jacobs led a recovery, adding 72 in 15 overs, but the accurate Indian bowling allowed few liberties and a target of 170 was a weak challenge for their in-form batsmen. Yet they too started slowly. Cuffy bowled his now-familiar single miserly spell and by the 21st over India were 63 for three. Tendulkar, playing well within himself, took 47 balls over his first 19 runs, but once he opened up, scoring his next 62 from 63, victory was never in doubt. When it arrived, India still had six overs in hand.

Man of the Match: S. R. Tendulkar.

West Indies

D. Ganga c Sodhi b Mohanty	2	†R. D. Jacobs not out	53
C. H. Gayle lbw b Harvinder Singh	0	M. V. Nagamootoo c and b Zaheer Khan	17
W. W. Hinds c Sodhi b Mohanty	9	M. Dillon not out	5
S. Chanderpaul c Dighe b Harvinder Singh	10	L-b 8, w 3, n-b 4	15
*C. L. Hooper c Ganguly b Zaheer Khan	14	1/2 2/2 3/18 (7 wkts, 50 overs)	169
M. N. Samuels c Harvinder Singh b Mohanty	44	4/26 5/47 6/119 7/156	

C. E. Cuffy and R. D. King did not bat.

Bowling: Mohanty 10–1–18–3; Harvinder Singh 10–3–25–2; Zaheer Khan 10–2–27–2; Sodhi 10–0–38–0; Sehwag 8–0–39–0; Tendulkar 2–0–14–0.

India

*S. C. Ganguly c Jacobs b Cuffy	20	V. Sehwag not out	11
S. R. Tendulkar not out	81	L-b 6, w 12, n-b 1	19
D. Mongia c Jacobs b Hinds	8		—
R. Dravid st Jacobs b Nagamootoo	4	1/31 2/58 (4 wkts, 43.5 overs)	170
H. K. Badani c and b Dillon	27	3/63 4/137	

R. S. Sodhi, †S. S. Dighe, Harvinder Singh, Zaheer Khan and D. S. Mohanty did not bat.

Bowling: Cuffy 10–3–20–1; King 7.5–1–39–0; Dillon 10–1–28–1; Hinds 4–0–12–1; Nagamootoo 9–0–48–1; Hooper 3–0–17–0.

Umpires: C. K. Coventry and Q. J. Goosen.
Third umpire: J. F. Fenwick.

ZIMBABWE v WEST INDIES

At Bulawayo, July 1. West Indies won by five wickets. Toss: West Indies.

Needing to win and vastly improve their run-rate to stay in the tournament, Zimbabwe took the match to the penultimate ball – despite losing their third successive toss and three cheap wickets. Again Wishart launched the rescue, this time with Flower helping him add 126 in 22 overs. Flower produced some superb strokes, hitting two sixes and five fours; with Whittall and Blignaut chipping in, Zimbabwe's last ten overs brought 82 runs on a pitch getting ever better. West Indies started well against some inaccurate bowling – Murphy was out of the attack after injuring his ankle – and with wickets in hand they could afford to drop behind the asking-rate later on. Chanderpaul's unlucky dismissal – he lost hold of his bat, sweeping, and it crashed into the stumps – left them needing 79 from ten overs. In Jacobs, however, they had the ideal man for such a situation.

Man of the Match: G. W. Flower.

Zimbabwe

A. D. R. Campbell c Gayle b Cuffy	17	A. M. Blignaut not out	12
D. D. Ebrahim c Jacobs b Cuffy	1		
S. V. Carlisle c Gayle b Collymore	4	B 4, l-b 5, w 6, n-b 2	17
C. B. Wishart c Collymore b Dillon	71		—
G. W. Flower c Nagamootoo b Dillon	94	1/4 2/9 3/27 (5 wkts, 50 overs)	255
G. J. Whittall not out	39	4/153 5/234	

*H. H. Streak, †T. Taibu, B. C. Strang and B. A. Murphy did not bat.

Bowling: Cuffy 10–2–30–2; Collymore 10–0–42–1; Dillon 10–0–47–2; Hooper 9–0–48–0; Nagamootoo 5–0–32–0; Samuels 5–0–36–0; Hinds 1–0–11–0.

West Indies

D. Ganga run out	34	M. N. Samuels not out	6
C. H. Gayle c Blignaut b Flower	76		
W. W. Hinds c Taibu b Streak	54	L-b 9, w 9, n-b 1	19
S. Chanderpaul hit wkt b Campbell	23		—
*C. L. Hooper c Carlisle b Flower	24	1/93 2/137 3/177 (5 wkts, 49.5 overs)	258
†R. D. Jacobs not out	22	4/206 5/237	

M. V. Nagamootoo, M. Dillon, C. E. Cuffy and C. D. Collymore did not bat.

Bowling: Streak 8.5–0–52–1; Strang 10–0–40–0; Blignaut 10–1–50–0; Flower 10–0–46–2; Campbell 9–0–48–1; Whittall 2–0–13–0.

Umpires: J. F. Fenwick and Q. J. Goosen.
Third umpire: M. A. Esat.

INDIA v WEST INDIES

At Harare, July 4. India won by six wickets. Toss: India.

This dead match offered a useful lesson to West Indies. Wary of early life in the pitch, their top order played with caution, insuring against a collapse but failing to set an adequate target. In the final, they would attack, superbly and successfully. With Cuffy forced out by a fractured foot, Dillon took the new ball and bowled just as economically, his ten overs yielding just 22. But Ganguly and Tendulkar, opening with 133 in 26 overs, had little trouble with the others. Tendulkar piled up his 29th one-day international century, hitting 12 fours and a six in his 131-ball 122, to claim his third match award in four games. Earlier, Sehwag had been controversially given out stumped when Jacobs broke the wicket with his right hand, while holding the ball in his left. Referee Denis Lindsay acknowledged that Jacobs had not joined his team-mates' appeal, but said he should have recalled Sehwag. He was suspended, initially for three one-day internationals, later revised to one Test, for sharp practice and bringing the game into disrepute.

Man of the Match: S. R. Tendulkar.

West Indies

D. Ganga run out	55	†R. D. Jacobs not out	27
C. H. Gayle c Sodhi b Harbhajan Singh	23	R. R. Sarwan not out	12
W. W. Hinds c and b Harvinder Singh	66	W 2, n-b 3	5
S. Chanderpaul c Ganguly b Mohanty	17		——
*C. L. Hooper c Dravid b Harvinder Singh	24	1/47 2/118 3/162 4/170 5/201 (5 wkts, 50 overs)	229

N. C. McGarrell, M. Dillon, R. D. King and C. E. L. Stuart did not bat.

Bowling: Mohanty 10–1–39–1; Nehra 9–1–33–0; Harvinder Singh 10–0–65–2; Harbhajan Singh 10–1–33–1; Sehwag 5–0–30–0; Tendulkar 2–0–11–0; Sodhi 4–1–18–0.

India

*S. C. Ganguly c Ganga b Dillon	62	R. S. Sodhi not out	16
S. R. Tendulkar not out	122	L-b 1, w 5, n-b 1	7
V. Sehwag st Jacobs b Hooper	4		——
H. K. Badani b Hooper	4	1/133 2/138 3/152 4/207 (4 wkts, 48.1 overs)	230
R. Dravid b Gayle	15		

†S. S. Dighe, Harbhajan Singh, Harvinder Singh, D. S. Mohanty and A. Nehra did not bat.

Bowling: King 7.1–0–49–0; Dillon 10–4–22–1; Stuart 5–0–34–0; McGarrell 10–1–55–0; Hooper 10–1–39–2; Gayle 6–0–30–1.

Umpires: K. C. Barbour and G. R. Evans.
Third umpire: Q. J. Goosen.

QUALIFYING TABLE

	Played	*Won*	*Lost*	*Points*	*Net run-rate*
India	4	4	0	8	0.79
West Indies	4	2	2	4	–0.04
Zimbabwe	4	0	4	0	–0.81

Net run-rate is calculated by subtracting runs conceded per over from runs scored per over.

FINAL

INDIA v WEST INDIES

At Harare, July 7. West Indies won by 16 runs. Toss: India.

Again asked to bat in difficult conditions, West Indies concluded that attack was their only hope of success. Ganga and Gayle went for it with no half-measures, driving superbly in a daring stand of 86 at more than six an over. The astonished Indians had no answer. Ganga raced to 71 in 62 balls, and the later batsmen kept up the momentum, Hooper and Chanderpaul adding 108 in 19 overs. India's target of 291 looked well beyond reach once Tendulkar, who had a stomach upset, lofted his fourth ball to Ganga at mid-wicket. When the top five were dismissed for 80, three of them by the excellent Collymore, they seemed dead and buried. But they refused to lie down. Sodhi and Dighe launched a fierce assault that resulted in India reaching the final over with 25 needed. West Indies had taken their chances magnificently, but India lost with honour.

Man of the Match: C. D. Collymore. *Man of the Series:* S. R. Tendulkar.

West Indies

D. Ganga c Laxman b Sodhi 71
C. H. Gayle c sub (Harvinder Singh) b Harbhajan Singh . 43
W. W. Hinds c and b Sodhi 10
*C. L. Hooper c Harbhajan Singh b Zaheer Khan . 66
S. Chanderpaul b Nehra 50
†R. D. Jacobs not out 26
R. R. Sarwan b Nehra 16
M. N. Samuels not out 3
L-b 2, w 2, n-b 1 5

1/86 2/120 3/130 4/238 5/252 6/285 (6 wkts, 50 overs) 290

M. Dillon, R. D. King and C. D. Collymore did not bat.

Bowling: Mohanty 5–0–43–0; Nehra 10–1–60–2; Zaheer Khan 10–0–63–1; Harbhajan Singh 10–2–35–1; Sehwag 7–0–48–0; Sodhi 7–0–31–2; Ganguly 1–0–8–0.

India

*S. C. Ganguly lbw b Collymore 28
S. R. Tendulkar c Ganga b Collymore . . 0
V. V. S. Laxman c sub (L. V. Garrick) b Collymore . 18
R. Dravid b King 30
V. Sehwag c sub (L. V. Garrick) b Dillon 2
R. S. Sodhi c Dillon b Collymore 67
†S. S. Dighe not out 94
Harbhajan Singh b Gayle 12
Zaheer Khan b Gayle 0
D. S. Mohanty not out 18
L-b 4, w 1 5

1/9 2/35 3/58 4/74 5/80 6/181 7/209 8/209 (8 wkts, 50 overs) 274

A. Nehra did not bat.

Bowling: Collymore 10–1–49–4; Dillon 8–1–31–1; King 10–1–47–1; Hooper 10–1–63–0; Samuels 3–0–26–0; Gayle 9–0–54–2.

Umpires: I. D. Robinson and R. B. Tiffin.
Third umpire: G. R. Evans. Series referee: D. T. Lindsay (South Africa).

ONE-DAY INTERNATIONAL RESULTS, 2000-01

	P	*W*	*L*	*NR*	*% W (excl. NR)*
Australia	22	18	4	0	81.81
South Africa	24	18	5	1	78.26
Sri Lanka	33	21	12	0	63.63
Pakistan	24	15	9	0	62.50
India	31	18	13	0	58.06
West Indies	26	11	15	0	42.30
New Zealand	37	12	24	1	33.33
Zimbabwe	31	9	22	0	29.03
England	14	2	12	0	14.28
Bangladesh	4	0	4	0	0.00
Kenya	4	0	4	0	0.00

COCA-COLA CUP (SRI LANKA), 2001

By SA'ADI THAWFEEQ

As they had at Sharjah in April, Sri Lanka proved themselves capable of winning when it mattered most, outclassing India in the floodlit final of the Coca-Cola Cup in early August. The third team in the competition were New Zealand, whose reluctance to play a Test series in Sri Lanka beforehand resulted in an extra round of matches being added to the round-robin stage, to compensate for potential gate losses from the Tests. As a result, the tournament dragged on somewhat. At the halfway stage, the remaining league games seemed meaningless, with India on the verge of elimination after three defeats. But they staged a remarkable comeback to win their last three qualifying matches and reach the final ahead of the luckless Kiwis. Moreover, India's sudden revival gave the tournament a new dimension; after poor attendances earlier on, the R. Premadasa Stadium was almost packed for the final. That match, however, turned out totally one-sided, with India offering no sort of challenge to Sri Lanka's imposing 295 and suffering their eighth consecutive defeat in a one-day final since they beat Zimbabwe at Sharjah in November 1998.

Sri Lankan captain Sanath Jayasuriya was named Man of the Series after scoring 305 runs at 43.57. The next best aggregate was 290 by New Zealand opener Nathan Astle, who reeled off two centuries but rarely found sufficient support for his team to put up totals big enough for their bowlers to defend. Even when they did, scoring 264 for seven in the last, decisive league game, they were upstaged by Virender Sehwag, whose 69-ball century helped India coast home with more than four overs to spare.

The R. Premadasa Stadium had to host an additional three matches when the Sri Lankan board were forced to shift them from the controversial Rangiri Dambulla International Stadium, following a legal dispute over the ownership of the land. Meanwhile, the home team lost their manager in mid-tournament, when Air Commodore Ajit Jayasekara was temporarily recalled by the Sri Lankan Air Force after the Tamil Tigers attacked the SLAF base at Katunayake. Former Test bowler Rumesh Ratnayake took charge in his absence, and saw them to their final victory.

Note: Matches in this section were not first-class.

SRI LANKA v NEW ZEALAND

At R. Premadasa Stadium, Colombo, July 18 (day/night). Sri Lanka won by 16 runs. Toss: Sri Lanka.

Jayasuriya set the tone for the tournament with a superlative 108-ball 80, including eight fours. New Zealand did well to restrict Sri Lanka to 220, after they had elected to bat and reached a healthy 150 for four in the 34th over. Once Vettori removed Jayasuriya, the rest fell away. New Zealand lost both openers in the first seven balls of their reply and, uncomfortable against the extra pace of Fernando, were 61 for four after 12 overs. A 57-run partnership between Harris and Parore turned the innings round, but New Zealand still finished 17 short, having been docked one over for a slow over-rate.

Man of the Match: S. T. Jayasuriya.

Sri Lanka

*S. T. Jayasuriya c Oram b Vettori	80
D. A. Gunawardene c Vettori b Tuffey	13
M. S. Atapattu c Harris b Vettori	22
D. P. M. D. Jayawardene c McMillan b Harris	14
R. P. Arnold lbw b Harris	9
†R. S. Kaluwitharana run out	14
H. D. P. K. Dharmasena run out	9
A. S. A. Perera c Sinclair b McMillan	19
W. P. U. J. C. Vaas c Fleming b Mills	4
M. Muralitharan c Vincent b Oram	6
C. R. D. Fernando not out	1
B 1, l-b 7, w 9, n-b 12	29
1/39 2/95 3/124 4/145 5/170 6/187 7/187 8/197 9/217 (48.5 overs)	220

Bowling: Tuffey 8–1–40–1; Mills 10–1–41–1; Oram 9–0–41–1; Vettori 10–0–42–2; Harris 10–0–42–2; Astle 1–0–4–0; McMillan 0.5–0–2–1.

New Zealand

M. S. Sinclair lbw b Perera	1
N. J. Astle b Vaas	2
*S. P. Fleming c Perera b Fernando	21
C. D. McMillan c Kaluwitharana b Fernando	20
L. Vincent b Muralitharan	25
C. Z. Harris c Perera b Jayasuriya	48
†A. C. Parore not out	51
J. D. P. Oram run out	6
D. L. Vettori c Kaluwitharana b Muralitharan	3
K. D. Mills b Dharmasena	2
D. R. Tuffey not out	6
L-b 10, w 6, n-b 3	19
1/3 2/3 3/43 4/61 5/100 6/157 7/170 8/174 9/186 (9 wkts, 49 overs)	204

Bowling: Vaas 7–0–37–1; Perera 3–1–18–1; Fernando 6–0–28–2; Muralitharan 10–1–36–2; Dharmasena 10–1–29–1; Jayasuriya 10–0–32–1; Arnold 3–0–14–0.

Umpires: L. V. Jayasundera and D. N. Pathirana.
Third umpire: P. T. Manuel.

INDIA v NEW ZEALAND

At R. Premadasa Stadium, Colombo, July 20 (day/night). New Zealand won by 84 runs. Toss: New Zealand.

The Kiwis bounced back, securing an impressive victory with nearly nine overs to spare on a pitch that was never easy. Sinclair fell to the very first ball, and Astle had an amazing escape in the next over when a ball from Nehra rolled on to his stumps without disturbing the bails. He made the most of his good fortune, hitting a tenth one-day hundred and batting into the final over. His 117, with one six and nine fours, constituted more than half a moderate total of 211. In turn, Laxman contributed nearly half of India's feeble 127, after Nash had reduced them to 50 for five.

Man of the Match: N. J. Astle.

New Zealand

M. S. Sinclair lbw b Zaheer Khan	0
N. J. Astle run out	117
*S. P. Fleming c Sehwag b Harbhajan Singh	25
C. D. McMillan st Dighe b Yuvraj Singh	17
L. Vincent c Yuvraj Singh b Harbhajan Singh	16
C. Z. Harris run out	1
†A. C. Parore st Dighe b Badani	9
D. J. Nash b Zaheer Khan	5
D. L. Vettori not out	5
K. D. Mills not out	1
L-b 4, w 9, n-b 2	15
1/0 2/70 3/106 4/158 5/163 6/190 7/198 8/208 (8 wkts, 50 overs)	211

D. R. Tuffey did not bat.

Bowling: Zaheer Khan 9–1–41–2; Nehra 7–0–35–0; Sodhi 1–0–7–0; Harbhajan Singh 10–1–25–2; Sehwag 8–1–31–0; Yuvraj Singh 10–0–43–1; Badani 5–0–25–1.

India

Yuvraj Singh lbw b Mills	6	Harbhajan Singh c and b Harris	0
*S. C. Ganguly c Harris b Tuffey	5	Zaheer Khan c McMillan b Vettori	2
V. V. S. Laxman c Harris b Vettori	60	A. Nehra not out	2
R. Dravid c Sinclair b Nash	15	B 2, l-b 3, w 2, n-b 1	8
H. K. Badani c Parore b Nash	2		
V. Sehwag c Harris b Nash	0	1/13 2/13 3/41 (41.1 overs)	127
R. S. Sodhi b Harris	18	4/50 5/50 6/88	
†S. S. Dighe c Nash b Harris	9	7/118 8/123 9/125	

Bowling: Tuffey 7–2–7–1; Mills 7–1–24–1; Nash 6–0–13–3; Vettori 8.1–0–39–2; Harris 8–1–23–3; Astle 5–0–16–0.

Umpires: D. N. Pathirana and G. Silva.
Third umpire: E. A. R. de Silva.

SRI LANKA v INDIA

At R. Premadasa Stadium, Colombo, July 22 (day/night). Sri Lanka won by six runs. Toss: Sri Lanka.

India, chasing 222, were on course for victory at 151 for four, with Ganguly in full cry, having struck a six and seven fours in his 69 and added 80 with Dravid. Then Arnold had him caught, sweeping, in his second over. Jayasuriya's introduction of the part-time off-spinner had been seen as a final throw of the dice; it couldn't have been better timed. Dravid, for all his experience and ability, failed to hit a single boundary in an unbeaten 49, and India, needing 12 runs off the final over, managed only five. Earlier, Gunawardene had been dropped twice in a scrappy 63, but Perera hit 28 off 31 balls to give Sri Lanka something to bowl at. He then cemented his place for the tournament by taking India's first two wickets.

Man of the Match: A. S. A. Perera.

Sri Lanka

*S. T. Jayasuriya st Dighe b Harbhajan Singh	34	W. P. U. J. C. Vaas lbw b Harbhajan Singh	1
D. A. Gunawardene b Sehwag	63	A. S. A. Perera c Ganguly b Yuvraj Singh	28
M. S. Atapattu c Khurasiya b Harbhajan Singh	5	M. Muralitharan not out	6
D. P. M. D. Jayawardene c Dighe b Sodhi	0	C. R. D. Fernando not out	5
†R. S. Kaluwitharana c Dighe b Yuvraj Singh	36	B 3, l-b 4, w 6, n-b 3	16
R. P. Arnold run out	1	1/48 2/60 3/61 (9 wkts, 50 overs)	221
H. D. P. K. Dharmasena c Ganguly b Zaheer Khan	26	4/144 5/147 6/149	
		7/154 8/203 9/210	

Bowling: Zaheer Khan 9–0–42–1; Mohanty 5–0–27–0; Harbhajan Singh 10–1–29–3; Sodhi 9–0–42–1; Sehwag 7–0–33–1; Yuvraj Singh 10–1–41–2.

India

A. R. Khurasiya lbw b Perera	12	V. Sehwag c Perera b Muralitharan	12
Yuvraj Singh c Muralitharan b Perera	12	†S. S. Dighe not out	11
V. V. S. Laxman c Kaluwitharana b Fernando	17	L-b 1, w 6, n-b 6	13
Harbhajan Singh c Jayasuriya b Vaas	1		
*S. C. Ganguly c Jayasuriya b Arnold	69	1/26 2/29 3/30 (7 wkts, 50 overs)	215
R. Dravid not out	49	4/71 5/151	
R. S. Sodhi b Muralitharan	19	6/178 7/200	

Zaheer Khan and D. S. Mohanty did not bat.

Bowling: Vaas 7–1–22–1; Perera 6–0–26–2; Fernando 7–0–29–1; Muralitharan 10–1–35–2; Dharmasena 10–0–46–0; Jayasuriya 7–0–44–0; Arnold 3–0–12–1.

Umpires: P. T. Manuel and T. H. Wijewardene.
Third umpire: G. Silva.

SRI LANKA v NEW ZEALAND

At R. Premadasa Stadium, Colombo, July 25. Sri Lanka won by five wickets. Toss: New Zealand.

Sri Lanka staged a great comeback after New Zealand creamed off their top order by grabbing four for 27 in the first nine overs. Arnold inspired the recovery and saw them home with nine balls to spare. Although lacking the natural gifts of some of his team-mates, he tenaciously carved out 91 in 116 balls, sharing century partnerships with Atapattu and Perera. Perera, requiring a runner after straining his thigh, lashed an entertaining maiden international fifty, with six fours in 51 balls. Astle and Sinclair had given New Zealand their first decent start of the tournament, with Astle scoring another fifty, but Fleming's absence because of a stomach upset hindered their attempts to set a significant challenge.

Man of the Match: R. P. Arnold.

New Zealand

M. S. Sinclair c Jayasuriya b Fernando	21
N. J. Astle b Arnold	54
J. D. P. Oram c Jayawardene b Dharmasena	11
*C. D. McMillan b Muralitharan	38
L. Vincent c Gunawardene b Arnold	30
C. Z. Harris c Gunawardene b Dharmasena	13
†A. C. Parore not out	37
D. L. Vettori c Atapattu b Jayasuriya	3
K. D. Mills c and b Dharmasena	0
G. E. Bradburn not out	2
L-b 15, w 8, n-b 4	27
1/70 2/98 3/120 4/164 5/184 6/210 7/217 8/217 (8 wkts, 50 overs)	236

D. R. Tuffey did not bat.

Bowling: Vaas 6–0–24–0; Perera 5–0–23–0; Fernando 3–1–18–1; Dharmasena 10–0–52–3; Muralitharan 10–0–31–1; Jayasuriya 10–0–51–1; Arnold 6–1–22–2.

Sri Lanka

*S. T. Jayasuriya lbw b Mills	5
D. A. Gunawardene c Harris b Tuffey	5
†R. S. Kaluwitharana c Parore b Mills	0
M. S. Atapattu run out	66
D. P. M. D. Jayawardene run out	0
R. P. Arnold not out	91
A. S. A. Perera not out	56
B 1, l-b 4, w 10, n-b 2	17
1/5 2/5 3/27 4/27 5/137 (5 wkts, 48.3 overs)	240

H. D. P. K. Dharmasena, W. P. U. J. C. Vaas, M. Muralitharan and C. R. D. Fernando did not bat.

Bowling: Tuffey 6–1–19–1; Mills 8–0–32–2; Oram 7–0–38–0; Vettori 10–1–38–0; Harris 10–0–49–0; Bradburn 2–0–12–0; McMillan 3.3–0–35–0; Astle 2–0–12–0.

Umpires: E. A. R. de Silva and L. V. Jayasundera.
Third umpire: P. T. Manuel.

INDIA v NEW ZEALAND

At R. Premadasa Stadium, Colombo, July 26. New Zealand won by 67 runs. Toss: India.

India crumpled like a house of cards to their third consecutive defeat. The match was already down to 48 overs a side because of a moist pitch, and they lost another for their slow over-rate; even so, 201 in 47 did not look daunting. In the event, they were bundled out inside 40 overs for 133, only Sehwag reaching 30. Their downfall owed more to their inability to build partnerships than to anything outstanding in the New Zealand attack – though Harris conceded only nine runs in seven overs. New Zealand simply got the basics right. Top-scorer Nash's eighth-wicket stand of 43 in 44 balls with Vettori could have been vital; in fact, it merely increased the winning margin. Adding to India's gloom, Ganguly was suspended for one match by referee Cammie Smith for pointing at his bat when adjudged lbw.

Man of the Match: D. J. Nash.

New Zealand

M. S. Sinclair c Dravid b Ganguly	36	D. L. Vettori lbw b Sehwag	19
N. J. Astle c Dighe b Nehra	5	K. D. Mills c and b Zaheer Khan	2
J. D. P. Oram c Dravid b Harbhajan Singh	40	D. R. Tuffey not out	2
*C. D. McMillan c Badani b Ganguly	17	L-b 1, w 5, n-b 3	9
L. Vincent c Laxman b Ganguly	16		
C. Z. Harris c Badani b Yuvraj Singh	12	1/21 2/85 3/99 (46.4 overs)	200
†A. C. Parore b Yuvraj Singh	0	4/108 5/125 6/126	
D. J. Nash c Ganguly b Sehwag	42	7/143 8/186 9/198	

Bowling: Zaheer Khan 8–0–44–1; Nehra 7–0–36–1; Harbhajan Singh 8–1–42–1; Ganguly 9–1–32–3; Yuvraj Singh 10–0–24–2; Sehwag 4.4–0–21–2.

India

*S. C. Ganguly lbw b Mills	4	Harbhajan Singh b Harris	6
V. Sehwag run out	33	Zaheer Khan not out	11
V. V. S. Laxman b Tuffey	1	A. Nehra b Nash	2
R. Dravid b Oram	27	W 2, n-b 4	6
H. K. Badani c McMillan b Vettori	6		
Yuvraj Singh c Parore b Harris	28	1/5 2/9 3/59 (39.4 overs)	133
R. S. Sodhi run out	9	4/66 5/99 6/111	
†S. S. Dighe run out	0	7/112 8/114 9/122	

Bowling: Tuffey 4–0–15–1; Mills 4–0–20–1; Nash 7.4–0–25–1; Oram 4–0–18–1; Vettori 10–0–33–1; Astle 3–0–13–0; Harris 7–3–9–2.

Umpires: P. T. Manuel and G. Silva.
Third umpire: L. V. Jayasundera.

SRI LANKA v INDIA

At R. Premadasa Stadium, Colombo, July 28. India won by seven wickets. Toss: Sri Lanka.

Without their captain, Ganguly, and with three players carrying injuries, India raised their game convincingly to claim their first win. After Jayasuriya and Kaluwitharana had opened with 103, Sri Lanka began the 36th over at 143 for two – then lost eight for 40 in the next 12. Prominent in causing the collapse were left-arm seamers Zaheer Khan, who had a painful shin, and Nehra, nursing a sore groin. Next it was Laxman's turn. Visibly in pain from a damaged knee cartilage, he showed much courage as he steered India home with an unbeaten 87, including ten fours. Acting-captain Dravid, who became Vaas's 200th one-day international victim when he edged a catch behind, helped him add 84.

Man of the Match: V. V. S. Laxman.

Sri Lanka

*S. T. Jayasuriya c Khurasiya b Harbhajan Singh	57
†R. S. Kaluwitharana c Sodhi b Yuvraj Singh	46
M. S. Atapattu c Sodhi b Sehwag	34
D. P. M. D. Jayawardene c Dighe b Badani	5
W. P. U. J. C. Vaas c Laxman b Harbhajan Singh	5
R. P. Arnold c Yuvraj Singh b Nehra	11
A. S. A. Perera b Zaheer Khan	4
K. Sangakkara run out	2
H. D. P. K. Dharmasena c Dighe b Zaheer Khan	1
M. Muralitharan b Nehra	2
C. R. D. Fernando not out	1
L-b 10, n-b 5	15
1/103 2/128 3/143 4/160 5/166 6/177 7/177 8/178 9/181 (46.5 overs)	183

Bowling: Zaheer Khan 8–0–30–2; Nehra 7.5–0–31–2; Harbhajan Singh 10–1–32–2; Sodhi 3–0–13–0; Sehwag 10–0–40–1; Yuvraj Singh 6–1–20–1; Badani 2–0–7–1.

India

A. R. Khurasiya b Vaas	0
V. Sehwag c Sangakkara b Dharmasena	27
V. V. S. Laxman not out	87
*R. Dravid c Kaluwitharana b Vaas	43
H. K. Badani not out	11
L-b 5, w 9, n-b 2	16
1/1 2/67 3/151 (3 wkts, 45.4 overs)	184

Yuvraj Singh, R. S. Sodhi, †S. S. Dighe, Harbhajan Singh, Zaheer Khan and A. Nehra did not bat.

Bowling: Vaas 10–1–47–2; Perera 2–0–12–0; Fernando 6–1–25–0; Muralitharan 10–3–28–0; Dharmasena 10–0–36–1; Jayasuriya 5–0–22–0; Arnold 2.4–0–9–0.

Umpires: E. A. R. de Silva and P. T. Manuel.
Third umpire: G. Silva.

SRI LANKA v NEW ZEALAND

At Sinhalese Sports Club, Colombo, July 31. Sri Lanka won by 106 runs. Toss: New Zealand.

Sri Lanka secured a place in the final through an awesome display of batting, running up 221 for six in a match reduced to 36 overs each after persistent rain. All the top order chipped in with useful scores, while Jayawardene's breathtaking half-century provided the impetus. Under some pressure to deliver after a string of poor scores, he raced to a stylish 46-ball 58 with two sixes and four fours. Clearly rattled by this onslaught, New Zealand found themselves in deep water by the eighth over; Vaas and Fernando had them 18 for four on a pitch affording bounce and movement. When three more wickets fell at 57, the contest was as good as over.

Man of the Match: W. P. U. J. C. Vaas.

Sri Lanka

*S. T. Jayasuriya c Tuffey b Mills	20
D. A. Gunawardene c Sinclair b Harris	38
†R. S. Kaluwitharana run out	25
M. S. Atapattu st Parore b Vettori	34
D. P. M. D. Jayawardene c Nash b McMillan	58
R. P. Arnold not out	22
A. S. A. Perera b McMillan	1
W. P. U. J. C. Vaas not out	4
L-b 10, w 7, n-b 2	19
1/32 2/89 3/109 4/165 5/208 6/211 (6 wkts, 36 overs)	221

H. D. P. K. Dharmasena, M. Muralitharan and C. R. D. Fernando did not bat.

Bowling: Tuffey 3–0–18–0; Mills 4–0–22–1; Nash 6–0–36–0; Oram 6–0–41–0; Harris 7–0–39–1; Vettori 8–1–38–1; McMillan 2–0–17–2.

New Zealand

M. S. Sinclair lbw b Vaas	1	D. L. Vettori lbw b Dharmasena	0
N. J. Astle c Gunawardene b Fernando	4	K. D. Mills not out	18
J. D. P. Oram c Arnold b Vaas	0	D. R. Tuffey not out	20
*S. P. Fleming c Gunawardene b Vaas	6	B 6, l-b 5, w 13, n-b 1	25
C. D. McMillan run out	0		
D. J. Nash run out	23	1/3 2/3 3/16 (9 wkts, 36 overs)	115
C. Z. Harris lbw b Fernando	18	4/18 5/18 6/57	
†A. C. Parore c and b Dharmasena	0	7/57 8/57 9/83	

Bowling: Vaas 7–1–20–3; Fernando 7–2–19–2; Perera 4–0–24–0; Muralitharan 8–1–21–0; Dharmasena 7–1–16–2; Jayasuriya 2–1–2–0; Arnold 1–0–2–0

Umpires: D. N. Pathirana and T. H. Wijewardene.
Third umpire: E. A. R. de Silva.

SRI LANKA v INDIA

At Sinhalese Sports Club, Colombo, August 1. India won by 46 runs. Toss: Sri Lanka.

India's revival continued, as Yuvraj Singh played a dazzling innings to rescue them from 38 for four. He scored an unbeaten 98 off 110 balls, with one six and six fours, added 102 in 22 overs with Dravid and, despite straining a hamstring, saw India to a total of 227. Sri Lanka were always struggling after losing their first two wickets by the third over. Their batting never clicked as India bowled a disciplined line and built up the pressure. Ganguly was again in trouble with the referee, who fined him 75 per cent of his match fee and severely reprimanded him for bringing the game into disrepute by his outburst after trapping Arnold lbw.

Man of the Match: Yuvraj Singh.

India

V. Sehwag lbw b Vaas	0	Harbhajan Singh b Muralitharan	4
*S. C. Ganguly c Sangakkara b Vaas	0	Zaheer Khan not out	3
V. V. S. Laxman c Jayasuriya b Fernando	10		
R. Dravid st Kaluwitharana b Jayasuriya	47	B 2, l-b 7, w 15, n-b 6	30
H. K. Badani c Jayawardene b Fernando	2		
Yuvraj Singh not out	98	1/0 2/7 3/31 (8 wkts, 50 overs)	227
R. S. Sodhi b Muralitharan	30	4/38 5/140 6/197	
†S. S. Dighe c Kaluwitharana b Fernando	3	7/200 8/213	

A. Nehra did not bat.

Bowling: Vaas 9–1–35–2; Fernando 9–1–47–3; Perera 3–0–20–0; Muralitharan 10–2–29–2; Dharmasena 8–0–39–0; Jayasuriya 7–0–28–1; Arnold 4–0–20–0.

Sri Lanka

*S. T. Jayasuriya c Dravid b Nehra	10	W. P. U. J. C. Vaas c Harbhajan Singh b Nehra	13
†R. S. Kaluwitharana run out	0	M. Muralitharan c sub (A. B. Agarkar) b Zaheer Khan	11
M. S. Atapattu c Dighe b Zaheer Khan	1	C. R. D. Fernando not out	2
D. P. M. D. Jayawardene b Ganguly	34	L-b 8, w 3, n-b 8	19
R. P. Arnold lbw b Ganguly	21		
K. Sangakkara b Nehra	18	1/6 2/7 3/24 4/67 5/93 (45.5 overs)	181
A. S. A. Perera c Zaheer Khan b Harbhajan Singh	30	6/109 7/151 8/157 9/178	
H. D. P. K. Dharmasena run out	22		

Bowling: Zaheer Khan 8–1–24–2; Nehra 8.5–0–35–3; Harbhajan Singh 10–0–30–1; Ganguly 10–1–31–2; Sehwag 3–0–19–0; Sodhi 6–0–34–0.

Umpires: E. A. R. de Silva and G. Silva.
Third umpire: T. H. Wijewardene.

INDIA v NEW ZEALAND

At Sinhalese Sports Club, Colombo, August 2. India won by seven wickets. Toss: New Zealand.

With a place in the final at stake, this match developed as the best of the tournament. New Zealand must have thought they were there when they ran up 264 for seven. Astle hit his second century of the tournament, with nine fours in a solid 108, and his partnership of 138 in 173 balls with Fleming provided an ideal base for the late assault that brought 82 from the last ten overs. India struck back thrillingly with an opening stand of 143 in 23 overs between Ganguly and Sehwag, of which Sehwag scored exactly 100, hitting one six and 19 fours before playing on to his 70th delivery. His maiden century for India, it was also, coming in 69 balls, the seventh-fastest one-day international hundred. A stand of 88 in 13 overs between Dravid and Badani carried India into the final with four overs to spare.

Man of the Match: V. Sehwag.

New Zealand

M. S. Sinclair c Badani b Zaheer Khan	3
N. J. Astle c Sehwag b Nehra	108
*S. P. Fleming st Dighe b Yuvraj Singh	66
C. D. McMillan c Sodhi b Yuvraj Singh	4
L. Vincent b Nehra	45
D. J. Nash c Nehra b Zaheer Khan	0
C. Z. Harris not out	1
†A. C. Parore lbw b Nehra	0
D. L. Vettori not out	2
L-b 16, w 18, n-b 1	35
1/28 2/166 3/182 4/247 5/259 6/262 7/262 (7 wkts, 50 overs)	264

K. D. Mills and D. R. Tuffey did not bat.

Bowling: Zaheer Khan 9–0–59–2; Nehra 9–1–30–3; Harbhajan Singh 10–1–46–0; Sehwag 3–0–26–0; Ganguly 6–0–23–0; Sodhi 4–0–27–0; Yuvraj Singh 9–0–37–2.

India

*S. C. Ganguly c Fleming b Harris	64
V. Sehwag b McMillan	100
V. V. S. Laxman b McMillan	0
R. Dravid not out	57
H. K. Badani not out	35
B 4, l-b 1, w 4, n-b 2	11
1/143 2/146 3/179 (3 wkts, 45.4 overs)	267

Yuvraj Singh, R. S. Sodhi, †S. S. Dighe, Harbhajan Singh, Zaheer Khan and A. Nehra did not bat.

Bowling: Tuffey 6–1–37–0; Mills 3–0–26–0; Nash 4–0–29–0; Vettori 10–0–56–0; Harris 8–0–39–1; Astle 6–0–26–0; McMillan 8.4–1–49–2.

Umpires: L. V. Jayasundera and T. H. Wijewardene.
Third umpire: D. N. Pathirana.

QUALIFYING TABLE

	Played	*Won*	*Lost*	*Points*	*Net run-rate*
Sri Lanka	6	4	2	8	0.24
India	6	3	3	6	−0.22
New Zealand	6	2	4	4	−0.01

Net run-rate is calculated by subtracting runs conceded per over from runs scored per over.

FINAL

SRI LANKA v INDIA

At R. Premadasa Stadium, Colombo, August 5 (day/night). Sri Lanka won by 121 runs. Toss: Sri Lanka.

A near full house witnessed a meek surrender. Losing a crucial toss had condemned India to chase under lights, and they were already looking out of sorts as Sri Lanka built their commanding 295 for five. Jayasuriya had led the charge with a power-packed 99, off 102 balls with 11 fours, though late in his innings he was afflicted by cramp. He and Gunawardene opened with 71 in 11 overs, but the heart of Sri Lanka's total was his liaison of 104 in 20 with Jayawardene. Arnold provided the final flourish, cutting loose in a 45-ball 52 and adding 77 in the last 11 overs with Kaluwitharana. India needed a repeat of their start three days earlier; instead, they lost Ganguly and Sehwag by the second over. Things did not improve, with 56 from Laxman and Dravid the only partnership of note. Arnold followed his bravura batting with the wicket of Yuvraj Singh, two catches and two run-outs; India subsided for a disappointing 174.

Man of the Match: R. P. Arnold. *Man of the Series:* S. T. Jayasuriya.

Sri Lanka

*S. T. Jayasuriya c Ganguly b Sehwag	99
D. A. Gunawardene lbw b Harbhajan Singh	34
M. S. Atapattu c Ganguly b Sehwag	5
D. P. M. D. Jayawardene lbw b Harbhajan Singh	57
R. P. Arnold c Ganguly b Zaheer Khan	52
†R. S. Kaluwitharana not out	31
L-b 8, w 8, n-b 1	17
1/71 2/100 3/204 4/218 5/295 (5 wkts, 50 overs)	295

A. S. A. Perera, H. D. P. K. Dharmasena, W. P. U. J. C. Vaas, M. Muralitharan and C. R. D. Fernando did not bat.

Bowling: Zaheer Khan 8–0–58–1; Nehra 9–0–65–0; Harbhajan Singh 10–0–29–2; Sehwag 9–0–58–2; Ganguly 4–0–20–0; Yuvraj Singh 10–0–57–0.

India

*S. C. Ganguly c Arnold b Fernando	1
V. Sehwag run out	4
V. V. S. Laxman c Jayawardene b Dharmasena	37
R. Dravid b Fernando	21
H. K. Badani run out	22
Yuvraj Singh b Arnold	6
R. S. Sodhi b Muralitharan	7
†S. S. Dighe c Kaluwitharana b Vaas	23
Harbhajan Singh c Arnold b Muralitharan	15
Zaheer Khan b Vaas	16
A. Nehra not out	2
L-b 6, w 7, n-b 7	20
1/5 2/5 3/61 4/91 5/100 6/100 7/114 8/136 9/169 (47.2 overs)	174

Bowling: Vaas 9.2–2–41–2; Fernando 10–2–32–2; Dharmasena 8–0–33–1; Jayasuriya 3–0–9–0; Arnold 7–1–21–1; Muralitharan 10–1–32–2.

Umpires: E. A. R. de Silva and T. H. Wijewardene.
Third umpire: P. T. Manuel. Series referee: C. W. Smith (West Indies).

OTHER A-TEAM TOURS

SRI LANKA A IN KENYA, 2000-01

Sri Lanka A toured Kenya in January 2001, with two first-class matches and four one-day games scheduled against the Kenyans. Both first-class matches were drawn; Sri Lanka A won the one-day series 2–0, with the last two games abandoned.

The squad of 16 for the tour was: H. D. P. K. Dharmasena (Bloomfield) (*captain*), C. Mendis (Colts) (*vice-captain*), M. R. C. N. Bandaratilleke (Tamil Union), S. K. L. de Silva (Colombo), W. R. S. de Silva (Sebastianites), U. A. Fernando (Sinhalese), I. S. Gallage (Colombo), D. Hettiarachchi (Colts), H. A. P. W. Jayawardene (Sinhalese), J. Mubarak (Colombo), G. R. P. Peiris (Tamil Union), P. D. R. L. Perera (Sinhalese), K. R. Pushpakumara (Nondescripts), L. P. C. Silva (Panadura), M. G. van Dort (Colombo), W. M. P. N. Wanasinghe (Galle). *Manager:* E. R. Fernando. *Coach:* H. H. Devapriya. S. I. de Saram (Tamil Union) was originally named, but was replaced by Peiris.

At Mombasa, January 16, 17, 18. Drawn. Toss: Sri Lanka A. Sri Lanka A 345 for nine dec. (C. Mendis 90, L. P. C. Silva 46, H. D. P. K. Dharmasena 68, W. M. P. N. Wanasinghe 43; C. O. Obuya three for 53) and 179 for four dec. (L. P. C. Silva 87 not out, U. A. Fernando 51; T. M. Odoyo three for 39); Kenyans 200 (S. O. Tikolo 85, T. M. Odoyo 44, M. O. Odumbe 32; H. D. P. K. Dharmasena four for 47) and 135 for three (R. D. Shah 32, S. O. Tikolo 71 not out).

The venue was changed to Mombasa because of heavy rain in Nairobi.

At Nairobi, January 23, 24, 25. Drawn. Toss: Sri Lanka A. Kenyans 68 (R. D. Shah 37 not out; I. S. Gallage five for 14, W. R. S. de Silva three for 25) and 90 for four (T. M. Odoyo 36, K. O. Otieno 33 not out; M. R. C. N. Bandaratilleke three for 29); Sri Lanka A 151 for five dec. (J. Mubarak 69 not out; T. M. Odoyo three for 28).

Shah carried his bat through the 28 overs of the Kenyans' first innings, in which the next highest score was Extras 10.

PAKISTAN A IN SRI LANKA, 2001

Pakistan A toured Sri Lanka in June and July 2001, playing three Tests and three one-day games against Sri Lanka A. They won the Test series 1–0 by taking the third Test after the first two were drawn, and shared the one-day series 1–1, the third game not reaching a result because of rain.

The squad of 15 for the tour was: Hasan Raza (Karachi/Habib Bank) (*captain*), Imran Farhat (Lahore City) (*vice-captain*), Azam Hussain (Karachi), Danish Kaneria (Karachi/Habib Bank), Faisal Naved (ADBP), Humayun Farhat (Lahore City/Allied Bank), Irfan Fazil (Lahore City/Habib Bank), Kashif Raza (Sheikhupura/WAPDA), Misbah-ul-Haq (Sargodha/KRL), Najaf Shah (Rawalpindi/PIA), Qaiser Abbas (Sheikhupura/National Bank), Salman Butt (Lahore City), Shabbir Ahmed (National Bank), Taufeeq Umar (Lahore City/Habib Bank), Yasir Arafat (Rawalpindi/KRL). *Manager/coach:* Mudassar Nazar.

At Dambulla, June 13, 14, 15, 16. First A-team Test: Drawn. Toss: Pakistan A. Sri Lanka A 220 (L. P. C. Silva 52; Yasir Arafat three for 46, Danish Kaneria three for 69) and 216 (M. G. van Dort 84, K. Sangakkara 54; Irfan Fazil three for 63, Yasir Arafat three for 35, Danish Kaneria four for 64); Pakistan A 223 (Hasan Raza 107, Misbah-ul-Haq 40; T. T. Samaraweera four for 47, S. Weerakoon three for 64) and 185 for nine (Misbah-ul-Haq 91; T. T. Samaraweera six for 55).

At Nondescripts Cricket Club, Colombo, June 19, 20, 21, 22. Second A-team Test: Drawn. Toss: Sri Lanka A. Pakistan A 229 (Taufeeq Umar 69, Misbah-ul-Haq 34; W. C. A. Ganegama three for 57, A. S. A. Perera three for 33) and 312 for eight dec. (Imran Farhat 45, Faisal Naved 80, Taufeeq Umar 30, Hasan Raza 58, Misbah-ul-Haq 41 not out, Yasir Arafat 32; T. T. Samaraweera five for 80); Sri Lanka A 252 (D. A. Gunawardene 132, A. S. A. Perera 45; Danish Kaneria six for 83) and 129 for three (M. G. van Dort 55 not out).

At Galle, June 25, 26, 27. Third A-team Test: Pakistan A won by five wickets. Toss: Sri Lanka A. Sri Lanka A 141 (D. A. Gunawardene 53; Irfan Fazil six for 38) and 174 (D. A. Gunawardene 52, M. G. van Dort 35; Danish Kaneria six for 38); Pakistan A 179 (Hasan Raza 100 not out; T. T. Samaraweera four for 37) and 137 for five (Faisal Naved 42 not out).

ICC TROPHY, 2001

By CLIVE ELLIS

The International Cricket Council needed a charismatic focus for their ambitious development programme; Namibia supplied it at the seventh ICC Trophy, at Toronto in July 2001. Previously disregarded, the highly motivated Africans marched through the Associate Members' tournament unbeaten before succumbing to human frailty in the final against Holland. An undistinguished game gained belated drama as the Dutch scampered to a two-wicket victory, running three off the last ball. Two days later, Canada overwhelmed top seeds Scotland in the third-place play-off, to enter the World Cup for the first time since 1979.

World Cup organisers swiftly announced that all three qualifiers had been invited to a six-team tournament in the Namibian capital, Windhoek, in April 2002. It was a welcome indicator of the ICC's determination to give these emerging countries a chance to perform respectably in the 2003 World Cup in South Africa. From the $US13 million raised at the senior nations' Knockout in Nairobi, in October 2000, $US1 million was set aside to aid the preparations of Holland, Namibia and Canada, as well as Kenya, automatic qualifiers through their one-day international status.

Although this was the first time they had won, Holland had appeared in every ICC Trophy since it began in 1979. They were losing finalists twice in the days when only the winners qualified for the World Cup but, when the senior competition expanded, third place was enough to send them to India and Pakistan in 1996. Consequently, there was no surprise in their success or their cricket. Built in the dependable all-round mould of 38-year-old captain Roland Lefebvre, in his fifth ICC Trophy, the Dutch team compensated for a lack of flair with discipline in the field; Ireland were the only team to reach 200 against them, and still lost. But Lefebvre, whose 20 wickets made him the tournament's joint leading wicket-taker with Denmark's Søren Vestergaard, admitted that cricket was still a long way from becoming part of Holland's cultural make-up. The point was underlined when Bas Zuiderent withdrew from their squad to concentrate on preserving his newly won place in the Sussex side.

Namibia first appeared in the 1994 competition, and in 1997 finished a mere 15th out of 22 at Kuala Lumpur. Though Bangladesh and Kenya were no longer competing, that still put them in Division Two under the Trophy's new format, which aimed to reduce the number of one-sided matches through seeding based on the 1997 rankings. Each division was subdivided into two groups; the Division Two group winners played the fourth-placed teams from Division One for the right to join the top six in the Super League. Namibia had a little luck when Italy and West Africa dropped out of their group within the division – Italy in protest at the ICC's stringent eligibility regulations, West Africa when their visa applications were rejected *en masse* (the United Arab Emirates and Nepal were forced to replace some players denied visas). Namibia easily won their remaining three games to head the group. They then had to negotiate a play-off against Bermuda. Controversially, victory meant that they inherited Bermuda's Division One record, so entered the Super League four points adrift of leaders Holland.

After their failure at Kuala Lumpur, the resourceful Namibians had worked tirelessly on their fielding. They benefited enormously from playing in the UCB Bowl, South Africa's Second Eleven championship. Despite a precarious base of about 500 cricketers, they had also begun to develop young talent. The average age of the side was 23, and they blooded two promising 19-year-olds, pace bowler Burton van Rooi, who returned the best analysis of the tournament with six for 43 against Scotland, and batsman Stefan Swanepoel. Their captain, opener Daniel Keulder, was the tournament's highest run-scorer, with 366 at 45.75, and a disciplined bowling attack included double international Rudi van Vuuren, who played fly-half for Namibia in the rugby union World Cup of 1999. South Africa's Ali Bacher, executive director for the 2003 World Cup, pointed out that the longer-term challenge was to appeal to Namibia's majority black population, whose sporting horizons have tended to begin and end with soccer; he also stressed the importance of free-access television coverage in underwriting that crusade.

For all Scotland's misery at leaving Toronto empty-handed after winning seven of their first eight matches, it was hard to begrudge Canada their success in securing the third and last place in the World Cup. The host association had lurched from crisis to crisis in the build-up to the tournament. Their finances were on a rocky footing after the cancellation of the lucrative Sahara Cup games between India and Pakistan in Toronto, and Canada's climate of extremes made the laying of pitches chancy. In the event, the pitches played well, for the most part, and the weather co-operated so fully that every game produced a result. Toronto relishes its cosmopolitan reputation, and the Canadian team reflected the same appealing mix. Their captain, Joseph Harris, was a flamboyant Madras-born strokeplayer who had appeared for Barbados in 1988-89, and they fielded four more players with first-class experience from across the world: off-spinner John Davison (Victoria), and batsmen Nicholas De Groot (Guyana), Ian Billcliff (Auckland, Otago and Wellington) and Muneeb Diwan (Essex).

Though claims that a quarter of Greater Toronto's population of four million had an active interest in cricket may have been slightly exaggerated, the game is a very real part of the city's sporting fabric. The local association has four divisions, 62 clubs and over 1,000 registered players, as well as 25 grounds, seven of which were used for the tournament. With the exception of the versatile headquarters at Toronto Cricket, Skating and Curling Club, they had the relaxed air of rural clubs.

There was no official protest, but the Scottish camp certainly felt that third place in the Super League should have been enough for a World Cup place. Instead, they had to play off against Canada, who were four points below them. In Kuala Lumpur, Scotland had won their play-off against Ireland; this time, they perished. Defeat was hard enough on the players, still traumatised by throwing away their last match, against Namibia, but it was doubly depressing for coach Mike Hendrick, who had been in charge of the Irish team last time round. Scottish wicket-keeper/batsman Colin Smith was outstanding, with 326 runs and 19 dismissals.

Scotland were let down as much by nerves as want of ability in the final stages, but Ireland's failure was a more drawn-out affair. For all the batting flair of brothers Ed and Dominick Joyce – Ed scored 359 runs at 71.80 – they performed erratically, failing to defend a total of 283 against the United Arab Emirates in the tournament's highest-scoring match, and finished bottom of the Super League. Morale was not helped when Decker Curry was sent home early, after an argument with coach Ken Rutherford about his place in the batting order.

The other sides who reached the Super League were all let down by brittle temperament. Denmark, having won their group, proved panicky in the run-chase and lost all four League games. The United Arab Emirates, who claimed the Trophy in 1994, won three League games, but an earlier defeat by Canada, at the group stage, edged them out of the third-place play-off. The USA, coached by Indian bowler Abid Ali, had the tournament's only Test player in former West Indian opener Faoud Bacchus; at the age of 47, he was still a victim for bowlers to savour, but he could hardly be expected to win matches.

Uganda, who had previously played under the umbrella of East and Central Africa, made their independent debut (alongside France, Germany and Nepal), and were an instant success. Like Namibia, they won their Division Two group with a 100 per cent record, but they failed to get past the free-scoring United Arab Emirates in the play-off. The Ugandans brought to the tournament an innocent pleasure and, in 20-year-old Kenneth Kamyuka, the most exciting raw talent. Primarily a bowler, with the potential for genuine pace, Kamyuka played the most spectacular innings in the competition, coming in at No. 10 to hit an unbeaten 100 off 54 balls against Malaysia. Argentina were runners-up to Uganda in their group, and exceeded expectations by winning four of their five matches.

The ICC promised to review the eligibility regulations in the light of Italy's objections, forcefully voiced by Simone Gambino, president of the Italian federation. Four of their players – including the Lancashire and former South Australian all-rounder, Joe Scuderi, and Michael Di Venuto's brother, Peter – were rejected by the ICC although recognised as citizens by Italian law. It was probably right to put principle before pragmatism, but a determination to encourage indigenous talent meant the rules applied were more stringent than those at Test level. The ICC also came away from Toronto knowing that, for all the smooth running of the tournament, it was no longer practical both to expand the number of Associate countries and to stage an event in which all could take part. The challenge now is to provide more frequent competition for the leading Associates, while sustaining the interest, loyalty and ambition of the second-string nations.

Division One

Group A	*Played*	*Won*	*Lost*	*Points*
Holland	5	5	0	10
Scotland	5	4	1	8
Canada	5	3	2	6
United Arab Emirates	5	2	3	4
Fiji	5	1	4	2
Singapore	5	0	5	0

Group B	*Played*	*Won*	*Lost*	*Points*
Denmark	5	4	1	8
USA	5	3	2	6
Ireland	5	3	2	6
Bermuda	5	3	2	6
Hong Kong	5	1	4	2
Papua New Guinea	5	1	4	2

Teams with equal points were separated on the results of their head-to-head games. The top three teams from each group advanced directly to the Super League; the fourth-placed teams went into the play-offs.

Division Two

Group A	*Played*	*Won*	*Lost*	*No result*	*Points*
Namibia	5	5	0	0	10
Nepal	5	4	1	0	8
Germany	5	3	2	0	6
Gibraltar	5	2	3	0	4
Italy	5*	0	4	1	0
West Africa	5*	0	4	1	0

Group B	*Played*	*Won*	*Lost*	*Points*
Uganda	5	5	0	10
Argentina	5	4	1	8
Malaysia	5	3	2	6
East and Central Africa	5	2	3	4
France	5	1	4	2
Israel	5	0	5	0

The two group-winners advanced to the play-offs.

* *Italy and West Africa withdrew from the tournament, but other teams in Group A were awarded wins for their unplayed matches.*

Play-offs

Namibia beat Bermuda by 75 runs; United Arab Emirates beat Uganda by five wickets.

Super League

	Played	Won	Lost	Points
Holland	7	6	1	12
Namibia	7	5	2	10*
Scotland	7	5	2	10
Canada	7	3	4	6
United Arab Emirates	7	3	4	6
Denmark	7	2	5	4
USA	7	2	5	4
Ireland	7	2	5	4

Teams carried forward results and points gained against fellow-qualifiers in Division One group games, but not those against the teams eliminated. Teams with equal points were separated on the results of their head-to-head games.

* *Namibia, having qualified from Division Two by beating Bermuda, inherited Bermuda's points, rather than carrying forward their own.*

Final

Holland beat Namibia by two wickets.

Third-place play-off

Canada beat Scotland by five wickets.

Note: Matches in this section were not first-class.

Division One

Group A

At Toronto Cricket, Skating and Curling Club, June 28. Canada won by nine wickets. Toss: Singapore. Singapore 169 (49.3 overs) (J. Dearing 77); Canada 171 for one (34.2 overs) (N. A. De Groot 82 not out, I. Maraj 58).

At Maple Leaf Ground, June 28. Scotland won by six wickets. Toss: Scotland. Fiji 41 (20.4 overs) (Asim Butt five for 11, C. M. Wright three for 16); Scotland 45 for four (13.3 overs).

At Sunnybrook Park, June 29. Holland won by 90 runs. Toss: United Arab Emirates. Holland 144 (48.2 overs) (K. J. J. van Noortwijk 38; Khuram Khan four for 18); United Arab Emirates 54 (30.2 overs) (R. P. Lefebvre five for 16).

At Maple Leaf Ground, June 30. Scotland won by 12 runs. Toss: Canada. Scotland 201 for eight (50 overs) (D. R. Lockhart 46, B. M. W. Patterson 40, R. A. Parsons 42); Canada 189 (49 overs) (M. Diwan 36; J. G. Williamson three for 22).

At Maple Leaf Ground, June 30. United Arab Emirates won by five wickets. Toss: United Arab Emirates. Singapore 191 for nine (50 overs) (Z. Schroff 34, K. M. Deshpande 35); United Arab Emirates 192 for five (39.2 overs) (Ahmed Nadeem 63, Khuram Khan 57 not out).

At Ajax Cricket Club, July 1. Holland won by seven wickets. Toss: Holland. Fiji 127 (44.2 overs) (L. P. van Troost three for 20); Holland 130 for three (36.5 overs) (R. F. van Oosterom 52, J. F. Kloppenburg 40).

At G. Ross Lord Park, July 2. Holland won by six wickets. Toss: Holland. Canada 95 (32 overs) (J. M. Davison 32; T. B. M. de Leede four for 23, J-J. Esmeijer four for 26); Holland 98 for four (34.4 overs).

At Malton Cricket Club, July 2. Fiji won by 86 runs. Toss: Fiji. Fiji 189 for eight (50 overs) (T. Batina 39, Extras 36; S. Mani three for 39); Singapore 103 (34.3 overs) (J. Dearing 30; N. D. Maxwell five for ten).

At Sunnybrook Park, July 2. Scotland won by five wickets. Toss: United Arab Emirates. United Arab Emirates 119 (43.2 overs) (Babar Malik 30; J. E. Brinkley three for 25, G. I. Maiden four for eight); Scotland 122 for five (35.1 overs) (Asim Butt 37).

At Toronto Cricket, Skating and Curling Club, July 3. Canada won by two wickets. Toss: Canada. United Arab Emirates 228 for seven (50 overs) (Asim Saeed 55, Khuram Khan 47, Ahmed Nadeem 62 not out); Canada 229 for eight (49.4 overs) (M. Diwan 47, I. S. Billcliff 63; Mohammad Tauqeer three for 38).

At Malton Cricket Club, July 3. Scotland won by ten wickets. Toss: Scotland. Singapore 114 (47.1 overs) (K. L. P. Sheridan four for 13); Scotland 115 for no wkt (27 overs) (D. R. Lockhart 47 not out, C. M. Wright 58 not out).

At Ajax Cricket Club, July 5. Canada won by 179 runs. Toss: Fiji. Canada 315 for four (50 overs) (I. Maraj 60, D. Chumney 58, I. S. Billcliff 40, J. V. Harris 76 not out, Extras 35); Fiji 136 (42.4 overs) (J. Bulabalavu 31; S. Thuraisingham three for 20).

At Toronto Cricket, Skating and Curling Club, July 5. Holland won by 38 runs. Toss: Scotland. Holland 206 for eight (50 overs) (J. F. Kloppenburg 30, K. J. J. van Noortwijk 41, T. B. M. de Leede 37); Scotland 168 (46.2 overs) (J. A. R. Blain 30; T. B. M. de Leede three for 30).

At Maple Leaf Ground, July 6. United Arab Emirates won by seven wickets. Toss: Fiji. Fiji 194 for nine (50 overs) (J. Sorovakatini 43 not out, N. D. Maxwell 54; Khuram Khan four for 25); United Arab Emirates 195 for three (38.5 overs) (Arshad Ali 78 not out, Ahmed Nadeem 49 not out).

At Maple Leaf Ground, July 6. Holland won by nine wickets. Toss: Singapore. Singapore 47 (26.2 overs) (S. F. Gokke three for 15, L. P. van Troost three for seven); Holland 48 for one (13.5 overs).

Division One

Group B

At G. Ross Lord Park, June 28. Bermuda won by two runs. Toss: Denmark. Bermuda 200 for nine (50 overs) (A. B. Steede 49, C. M. Marshall 69; T. M. Hansen three for 11, S. Vestergaard three for 23); Denmark 198 for nine (50 overs) (M. Lund 35, M. H. Andersen 55, T. M. Hansen 32, Extras 33).

At Maple Leaf Ground, June 29. Denmark won by 181 runs. Toss: Hong Kong. Denmark 284 for six (50 overs) (C. R. Pedersen 103, A. Khan 73, S. Vestergaard 47); Hong Kong 103 (29.1 overs) (S. J. Brew 41; A. Khan three for 11).

At Toronto Cricket, Skating and Curling Club, June 29. USA won by six wickets. Toss: Ireland. Ireland 209 (49.2 overs) (A. R. White 43, E. C. Joyce 80; Nasir Islam four for 32); USA 210 for four (37.5 overs) (M. Johnson 54, R. W. Staple 46 not out, S. F. A. F. Bacchus 44).

At Ajax Cricket Club, June 30. Ireland won by eight wickets. Toss: Hong Kong. Hong Kong 193 for nine (50 overs) (D. Chaudhuri 53, R. Sharma 42); Ireland 197 for two (46.4 overs) (J. A. M. Molins 81 not out, D. Joyce 46, E. C. Joyce 51 not out).

At G. Ross Lord Park, June 30. Papua New Guinea won by eight runs. Toss: Papua New Guinea. Papua New Guinea 216 for nine (50 overs) (N. Maha 42, Extras 38); USA 208 (49.2 overs) (D. Wallace 62, Extras 31; N. Maha four for 42).

At G. Ross Lord Park, July 1. Bermuda won by nine wickets. Toss: Bermuda. Papua New Guinea 131 (39 overs) (H. Bascombe four for 23); Bermuda 132 for one (31.3 overs) (A. B. Steede 43 not out, C. J. Smith 60 not out).

At Maple Leaf Ground, July 2. Ireland won by eight wickets. Toss: Ireland. Bermuda 115 (46 overs) (P. J. K. Mooney four for 17, A. G. A. M. McCoubrey three for 28); Ireland 118 for two (29.3 overs) (J. A. M. Molins 30, P. J. Davy 44).

At G. Ross Lord Park, July 2. Denmark won by 101 runs. Toss: Denmark. Denmark 181 for seven (50 overs) (Aftab Ahmed 35, M. Lund 43 not out, L. H. Andersen 32 not out; D. Blake three for 30); USA 80 (24.4 overs) (S. Vestergaard three for 11, L. Slepsager three for 22).

Vestergaard took a hat-trick.

At Sunnybrook Park, July 3. Denmark won by six wickets. Toss: Denmark. Papua New Guinea 92 (32.5 overs) (L. H. Andersen five for 24); Denmark 97 for four (26.2 overs) (Aftab Ahmed 39 not out; T. Raka three for 21).

At Maple Leaf Ground, July 3. USA won by 49 runs. Toss: Hong Kong. USA 254 for eight (50 overs) (R. Alexander 110 not out, D. Wallace 68; Tabarak Dar four for 34); Hong Kong 205 for eight (50 overs) (Saleem Malik 37, R. Sharma 37, S. J. Brew 31, Extras 33; Javid Nasir four for 46).

Alexander and Wallace opened with 153 in 33 overs for USA's first wicket.

At Toronto Cricket, Skating and Curling Club, July 4. Hong Kong won by 104 runs (D/L method). Toss: Hong Kong. Hong Kong 216 for five (36 overs) (R. Sharma 98, M. I. N. Eames 45); Papua New Guinea 136 (25.1 overs) (A. Uda 35, J. Brazier 53; S. J. Brew three for 34, Jawaid Iqbal three for 29).

Papua New Guinea's target was revised to 241 from 36 overs.

At G. Ross Lord Park, July 5. USA won by 57 runs. Toss: USA. USA 200 (49.3 overs) (S. F. A. F. Bacchus 38, D. Hoillet 43; R. Basden three for 38, D. Leverock three for 18); Bermuda 143 (46.1 overs) (C. M. Marshall 62; Javid Nasir five for 23).

At Maple Leaf Ground, July 5. Denmark won by 12 runs. Toss: Denmark. Denmark 231 for six (46 overs) (S. Vestergaard 39, Aftab Ahmed 86 not out, Extras 32); Ireland 219 (45.5 overs) (D. Joyce 50, E. C. Joyce 40, D. Heasley 40; A. Khan three for 39).

At Malton Cricket Club, July 6. Bermuda won by 104 runs. Toss: Bermuda. Bermuda 206 for nine (50 overs) (C. J. Smith 91, J. J. Tucker 42; Mohammad Zubair three for 40); Hong Kong 102 (40 overs) (Saleem Malik 34; D. Leverock four for 15).

At G. Ross Lord Park, July 6. Ireland won by nine wickets. Toss: Papua New Guinea. Papua New Guinea 146 (45 overs) (A. Uda 43; D. Heasley five for 25); Ireland 149 for one (32.3 overs) (D. J. Curry 95 not out, D. Joyce 38 not out).

Division Two

Group A

At G. Ross Lord Park, June 28. Germany v West Africa. Cancelled. Germany awarded walkover.

At Eglinton Flats Ground, June 29. Gibraltar v West Africa. Cancelled. Gibraltar awarded walkover.

At G. Ross Lord Park, June 29. Italy v Nepal. Cancelled. Nepal awarded walkover.

At Malton Cricket Club, June 30. Namibia won by nine wickets. Toss: Germany. Germany 105 (45.5 overs) (M. Brodersen 30); Namibia 106 for one (21.1 overs) (D. Keulder 52 not out, A. J. Burger 38 not out).

At Malton Cricket Club, July 1. Nepal won by three wickets. Toss: Gibraltar. Gibraltar 133 for six (43 overs) (C. Rocca 54); Nepal 134 for seven (39.5 overs) (P. Luniya 36; D. J. Johnson four for 23).

At Eglinton Flats Ground, July 1. Italy v Namibia. Cancelled. Namibia awarded walkover.

At Eglinton Flats Ground, July 2. Germany won by three wickets. Toss: Gibraltar. Gibraltar 243 for eight (50 overs) (C. Rocca 76, T. Buzaglo 89); Germany 247 for seven (46.5 overs) (T. Rathore 37, G. Müller 110 not out; T. Buzaglo three for 40).

At Ajax Cricket Club, July 2. Italy v West Africa. Cancelled. No points awarded.

At Eglinton Flats Ground, July 2. Namibia won by eight wickets. Toss: Nepal. Nepal 131 for seven (50 overs) (J. P. Sarraf 47 not out; B. L. Kotze four for 37); Namibia 136 for two (32.4 overs) (R. Walters 61 not out, B. G. Murgatroyd 51 not out).

At Eglinton Flats Ground, July 3. Nepal v West Africa. Cancelled. Nepal awarded walkover.

At Eglinton Flats Ground, July 4. Germany v Italy. Cancelled. Germany awarded walkover.

At G. Ross Lord Park, July 4. Namibia won by 179 runs (D/L method). Toss: Gibraltar. Namibia 258 for three (40 overs) (D. Keulder 82, S. Swanepoel 64, D. B. Kotze 65, B. G. Murgatroyd 31 not out); Gibraltar 100 (33.2 overs) (C. Rocca 41).

Gibraltar's target was revised to 280 from 40 overs.

At Maple Leaf Ground, July 5. Nepal won by two runs. Toss: Nepal. Nepal 175 for nine (48 overs) (D. Chaudhary 52; Abdul Hamid Bhatti five for 31); Germany 173 (47.3 overs) (T. Rathore 35, Shamasuddin Khan 68; P. Luniya four for 23, J. P. Sarraf three for 22).

At Malton Cricket Club, July 5. Gibraltar v Italy. Cancelled. Gibraltar awarded walkover.

At Sunnybrook Park, July 5. Namibia v West Africa. Cancelled. Namibia awarded walkover.

Division Two

Group B

At Eglinton Flats Ground, June 28. Argentina won by four wickets. Toss: Israel. Israel 190 for eight (50 overs) (D. Silver 58, A. Vard 38 not out; C. J. Tunon four for 41); Argentina 194 for six (49.2 overs) (G. F. Arizaga 57, P. Ferguson 38 not out, M. E. Cortabarria 36).

At Ajax Cricket Club, June 28. Malaysia won by 166 runs. Toss: France. Malaysia 321 for eight (50 overs) (S. Retinam 118, R. Madhavan 39, M. A. Muniandy 31 not out, Extras 45; L. Brumant four for 48); France 155 for nine (50 overs) (L. Brumant 30, Extras 39; S. Navaratnam three for 14, N. M. Krishnamurthi three for 15).

Retinam scored 118 in 112 balls to help Malaysia reach 321 for eight, the highest individual innings and team total of the tournament.

At Eglinton Flats Ground, June 29. Uganda won by 64 runs. Toss: Uganda. Uganda 223 for eight (50 overs) (K. Kamyuka 100 not out, Extras 42; R. V. Suppiah four for 24, S. Vickneswaran three for 41); Malaysia 159 (42.3 overs) (S. Navaratnam 46).

Kamyuka, coming in at No. 10, scored a 54-ball 100, including eight sixes, out of a ninth-wicket stand of 124.

At G. Ross Lord Park, June 30. Argentina won by four wickets. Toss: East and Central Africa. East and Central Africa 212 for nine (50 overs) (A. Ebrahim 39, Y. S. Patel 38; A. R. Perez Rivero three for 33); Argentina 213 for six (49.1 overs) (M. J. Paterlini 33, D. Forrester 65, P. Ferguson 51, G. P. Kirschbaum 44).

At Eglinton Flats Ground, June 30. France won by three wickets. Toss: Israel. Israel 187 (48.2 overs) (Y. Nagavkar 47, Extras 37); France 188 for seven (49 overs) (G. Edwards 43, S. Hewitt 52; I. Massil three for 33).

At Maple Leaf Ground, July 1. Argentina won by six runs. Toss: France. Argentina 220 for five (40 overs) (M. J. Paterlini 57, D. Forrester 35); France 214 for eight (40 overs) (G. James 46, S. Hussain 86, S. Hewitt 38; H. P. Pereyra three for 34).

At Eglinton Flats Ground, July 1. Uganda won by six wickets (D/L method). Toss: East and Central Africa. East and Central Africa 170 (40.3 overs) (V. Kamania 55, Extras 40; J. Kwebiha five for 22, F. Nsubuga three for 29); Uganda 173 for four (37.4 overs) (C. Lwanga 48, J. Olweny 59, J. Kwebiha 39 not out).

Uganda's target was revised to 171 from 44 overs.

At Sunnybrook Park, July 1. Malaysia won by six wickets. Toss: Malaysia. Israel 117 for nine (44 overs) (S. Vickneswaran three for 17); Malaysia 118 for four (25 overs) (R. Madhavan 41).

At Maple Leaf Ground, July 3. Uganda won by 187 runs. Toss: Argentina. Uganda 303 for five (50 overs) (C. Lwanga 58, J. Kwebiha 109 not out, K. Kamyuka 36, J. Lubia 35 not out); Argentina 116 (35.4 overs) (G. P. Kirschbaum 31).

At G. Ross Lord Park, July 3. Malaysia won by four wickets. Toss: East and Central Africa. East and Central Africa 140 (48.2 overs) (Extras 36; R. V. Suppiah three for 20); Malaysia 143 for six (43.5 overs) (R. M. Selvaratnam 48 not out, S. Navaratnam 34).

At Eglinton Flats Ground, July 4. Argentina won by five wickets (D/L method). Toss: Malaysia. Malaysia 240 for six (41 overs) (R. Madhavan 105 not out, Suresh Singh 51, Yazid Imran 42); Argentina 258 for five (40.1 overs) (M. J. Paterlini 66, P. Ferguson 67, M. K. van Steeden 42, G. P. Kirschbaum 34 not out, Extras 31).

Argentina's target was revised to 255 from 41 overs.

At Ajax Cricket Club, July 4. East and Central Africa won by 65 runs (D/L method). Toss: Israel. East and Central Africa 160 for nine (47.3 overs) (A. A. Dudhia 44, V. Kamania 45 not out; I. Massil three for 35, B. Kehimkar three for 22); Israel 91 (31.2 overs) (C. M. Gomm four for 17, A. Ebrahim four for 15).

Israel's target was revised to 157 from 42 overs.

At Sunnybrook Park, July 4. Uganda won by 86 runs (D/L method). Toss: Uganda. Uganda 166 (39 overs) (B. Musoke 49; S. Hewawalandanage four for 42, P. A. Linton four for 32); France 75 for nine (42 overs) (J. Kwebiha three for 14).

France's target was revised to 162 from 42 overs.

At Eglinton Flats Ground, July 6. East and Central Africa won by 98 runs. Toss: East and Central Africa. East and Central Africa 218 for nine (50 overs) (A. Ebrahim 34, K. Cummings 51, Y. S. Patel 31; V. Brumant three for 44); France 120 (41.1 overs).

At Ajax Cricket Club, July 6. Uganda won by seven wickets. Toss: Israel. Israel 153 for nine (50 overs) (I. Massil 55 not out, Extras 30; F. Nsubuga three for 23); Uganda 154 for three (30.4 overs) (C. Lwanga 47, F. Nsubuga 33).

Play-offs

At Maple Leaf Ground, July 7. Namibia won by 75 runs. Toss: Bermuda. Namibia 221 (49.1 overs) (R. Walters 59, D. B. Kotze 51, M. Karg 52, Extras 33; H. Bascombe three for 52); Bermuda 146 (45.4 overs) (A. B. Steede 56; D. B. Kotze three for 27).

At Maple Leaf Ground, July 7. United Arab Emirates won by five wickets. Toss: Uganda. Uganda 154 (46.3 overs) (J. Lubia 76 not out; Asim Saeed three for 18); United Arab Emirates 155 for five (41.5 overs) (Asim Saeed 31, Ahmed Nadeem 67).

Super League

At Toronto Cricket, Skating and Curling Club, July 9. Namibia won by two wickets. Toss: Namibia. Canada 189 (48 overs) (I. S. Billcliff 54; R. J. van Vuuren four for 33); Namibia 190 for eight (49.3 overs) (R. Walters 44, M. van Schoor 68 not out).

At Ajax Cricket Club, July 9. Holland won by 41 runs. Toss: Holland. Holland 174 (48.5 overs) (J. F. Kloppenburg 36; S. Vestergaard three for 26); Denmark 133 (45.4 overs) (S. Vestergaard 39, Aftab Ahmed 35; R. P. Lefebvre three for 14, A. K. Raja three for 28).

At Malton Cricket Club, July 9. Scotland won by seven wickets. Toss: Ireland. Ireland 174 for eight (50 overs) (D. Joyce 36, E. C. Joyce 33); Scotland 175 for three (42 overs) (D. R. Lockhart 64, C. J. O. Smith 68 not out).

At Maple Leaf Ground, July 9. United Arab Emirates won by seven wickets. Toss: United Arab Emirates. USA 153 for eight (50 overs) (S. F. A. F. Bacchus 47, D. Hoillet 30); United Arab Emirates 155 for three (37.1 overs) (Asim Saeed 52 not out, Ahmed Nadeem 47 not out).

At Maple Leaf Ground, July 10. Canada won by 25 runs. Toss: Canada. Canada 161 (47 overs) (M. Diwan 44, J. M. Davison 35; A. Khan three for 34, S. Vestergaard three for 31); Denmark 136 (47.4 overs) (L. H. Andersen 31; J. M. Davison three for 15).

At G. Ross Lord Park, July 10. Namibia won by 73 runs. Toss: Holland. Namibia 181 for eight (50 overs) (R. Walters 30, B. G. Murgatroyd 47, L. Burger 41 not out); Holland 108 (44 overs) (B. O. van Rooi three for 24, J. Louw three for 13, D. B. Kotze three for 23).

At Toronto Cricket, Skating and Curling Club, July 10. United Arab Emirates won by four wickets. Toss: Ireland. Ireland 283 for seven (50 overs) (J. A. M. Molins 37, A. D. Patterson 35, E. C. Joyce 87, D. Joyce 62); United Arab Emirates 285 for six (46.4 overs) (Babar Malik 35, Arshad Ali 102, Mahmood Pir Baksh 43, Asim Saeed 40, Khuram Khan 35 not out).

At G. Ross Lord Park, July 10. Scotland won by five wickets. Toss: Scotland. USA 159 (47.5 overs) (R. Alexander 41, R. W. Staple 37, M. Johnson 30; K. L. P. Sheridan four for 23); Scotland 161 for five (45.5 overs) (G. Salmond 38, C. J. O. Smith 64 not out; J. J. Zinto three for 34).

At Toronto Cricket, Skating and Curling Club, July 12. Canada won by 121 runs. Toss: USA. Canada 265 (50 overs) (J. V. Harris 79, N. A. De Groot 47; M. Springer three for 29, Nasir Islam five for 41); USA 144 (38.4 overs) (R. W. Staple 30, S. F. A. F. Bacchus 36; J. M. Davison three for 30).

At Malton Cricket Club, July 12. Scotland won by 29 runs. Toss: Scotland. Scotland 194 for eight (50 overs) (C. J. O. Smith 45, J. G. Williamson 31, G. I. Maiden 40 not out); Denmark 165 (46.5 overs) (Aftab Ahmed 33, L. H. Andersen 38; J. A. R. Blain three for 42, G. I. Maiden three for 29).

At Maple Leaf Ground, July 12. Holland won by two runs. Toss: Ireland. Holland 217 (48.2 overs) (Zulfiqar Ahmed 87; W. K. McCallan three for 34); Ireland 215 (49.5 overs) (J. A. M. Molins 93, W. K. McCallan 41, P. J. Davy 30).

Journalist James Fitzgerald, by his own admission an average-to-poor club player from Dublin, and in Toronto to report on Ireland's progress, fielded as substitute in this match, and Ireland's next, against Canada, after injuries and disciplinary action had reduced the Irish squad to 11 fit players.

At Ajax Cricket Club, July 12. Namibia won by 62 runs. Toss: United Arab Emirates. Namibia 179 for seven (50 overs) (D. Keulder 84, L. Burger 40 not out; Ahmed Nadeem three for 22); United Arab Emirates 117 (34.3 overs) (Babar Malik 32; L. Burger four for 25, B. O. van Rooi four for 18).

At G. Ross Lord Park, July 13. Ireland won by seven wickets. Toss: Canada. Canada 217 (49.5 overs) (J. V. Harris 73, A. Bagai 56; A. G. A. M. McCoubrey four for 35, A. R. White three for 39); Ireland 218 for three (44.4 overs) (P. J. Davy 104 not out, E. C. Joyce 51 not out).

Davy and Joyce added an unbroken 138 in 27 overs for Ireland's fourth wicket.

At G. Ross Lord Park, July 13. United Arab Emirates won by five wickets. Toss: Denmark. Denmark 167 (47.5 overs) (F. Klokker 36; Arshad Ali four for 25); United Arab Emirates 168 for five (37.3 overs) (Arshad Ali 37, Mahmood Pir Baksh 33, Khuram Khan 43 not out).

At Maple Leaf Ground, July 13. Holland won by 33 runs. Toss: USA. Holland 203 for eight (50 overs) (R. F. van Oosterom 34, K. J. J. van Noortwijk 43; Ajaz Ali three for 23, J. J. Zinto three for 32); USA 170 (47.5 overs) (S. F. Gokke five for 43).

At Toronto Cricket, Skating and Curling Club, July 13. Namibia won by nine runs. Toss: Namibia. Namibia 256 for six (50 overs) (R. Walters 43, D. Keulder 104, A. J. Burger 30, B. G. Murgatroyd 35, M. van Schoor 32 not out); Scotland 247 (48.4 overs) (J. G. Williamson 33, C. J. O. Smith 88, R. A. Parsons 53; B. O. van Rooi six for 43).

FINAL

HOLLAND v NAMIBIA

At Toronto Cricket, Skating and Curling Club, July 15. Holland won by two wickets. Toss: Namibia.

Holland needed ten off the final over, from Bjorn Kotze. Jacob-Jan Esmeijer and Asim Khan whittled that down to three off the last ball, and got them thanks to a fumble by Riaan Walters at short fine leg. Namibia, who had earlier inflicted Holland's only defeat, struggled to dominate the Dutch attack, but 50 from Bryan Murgatroyd helped to set a target of 196. The Dutch began poorly, and seemed out of the game at 98 for five in the 33rd over. Even after Esmeijer, dropped in the deep on 15 as Namibia's previously brilliant fielding faltered, and Roland Lefebvre had added 52, Holland still needed 38 in four overs. However, Esmeijer held his nerve as the tension increased and saw his side to victory. His unbeaten 58 from 51 balls included two leg-side sixes.

Man of the Match: J-J. Esmeijer. *Player of the Tournament:* R. P. Lefebvre.

Namibia

R. Walters b Khan	6	B. O. van Rooi c Bradley b de Leede	5
*D. Keulder run out	24	B. L. Kotze not out	0
A. J. Burger lbw b Lefebvre	38		
B. G. Murgatroyd c Khan b Lefebvre	50	W 6	6
D. B. Kotze c Lefebvre b van Troost	28		
†M. van Schoor run out	25	1/7 2/61 3/79 (9 wkts, 50 overs)	195
L. Burger st Scholte b de Leede	3	4/139 5/157 6/167	
J. Louw lbw b de Leede	10	7/182 8/194 9/195	

R. J. van Vuuren did not bat.

Bowling: Khan 10–2–47–1; Gokke 5–1–12–0; van Troost 10–0–29–1; Lefebvre 10–1–42–2; de Leede 10–2–47–3; Esmeijer 5–1–18–0.

Holland

R. F. van Oosterom run out	13	J-J. Esmeijer not out	58
Zulfiqar Ahmed c Murgatroyd b van Vuuren	6	*R. P. Lefebvre c Keulder b van Vuuren	19
R. R. A. F. Bradley lbw b van Vuuren	0	†R. H. Scholte run out	6
K. J. J. van Noortwijk b B. L. Kotze	50	Asim Khan not out	3
T. B. M. de Leede c L. Burger b van Rooi	16	B 2, l-b 9, w 4	15
L. P. van Troost c van Schoor b D. B. Kotze	10	1/12 2/12 3/32 (8 wkts, 50 overs)	196
		4/59 5/98 6/106	
		7/158 8/182	

S. F. Gokke did not bat.

Bowling: B. L. Kotze 10–2–36–1; van Vuuren 10–1–35–3; van Rooi 10–0–38–1; Louw 8–1–28–0; D. B. Kotze 10–0–36–1; L. Burger 2–0–12–0.

Umpires: R. E. Koertzen (South Africa) and E. A. Nicholls (West Indies).
Third umpire: D. B. Hair (Australia). Referee: J. R. Reid (New Zealand).

THIRD-PLACE PLAY-OFF

CANADA v SCOTLAND

At Toronto Cricket, Skating and Curling Club, July 17. Canada won by five wickets. Toss: Scotland.

Canada secured a convincing victory with more than ten overs to spare. Surprisingly, Scotland chose to bat after a rain-delayed start, and faulty shot selection against the pace of Sri Lankan-born Sanjayan Thuraisingham had them in deep trouble at 24 for three. Drew Parsons and George Salmond rebuilt sensibly in a stand of 101, but the innings subsequently stalled. In easier batting conditions, Canadian opener Ishwar Maraj gave his side a sound foundation with a patient 77-ball 50. Missing the injured Asim Butt, their steadiest bowler, the Scots were powerless to prevent Canada surging to victory – and a World Cup place – in front of an increasingly animated crowd of around 3,000.

Man of the Match: S. Thuraisingham.

Scotland

D. R. Lockhart c Davison b Thuraisingham	8
J. G. Williamson c Diwan b Thuraisingham	5
†C. J. O. Smith c De Groot b Thuraisingham	6
R. A. Parsons lbw b Harris	48
*G. Salmond c Billcliff b Davison	43
C. M. Wright b Thuraisingham	25
G. I. Maiden b Harris	0
J. A. R. Blain b Thuraisingham	14
J. E. Brinkley run out	0
K. L. P. Sheridan not out	0
B 2, l-b 17, w 7, n-b 1	27
1/7 2/24 3/24 4/125 5/129 6/133 7/173 8/174 9/176 (9 wkts, 50 overs)	176

D. J. Cox did not bat.

Bowling: Joseph 8–1–24–0; Thuraisingham 8–2–25–5; Davison 10–0–34–1; De Groot 6–0–24–0; Seebaran 10–1–22–0; Harris 8–0–28–2.

Canada

J. M. Davison c Smith b Blain	0
I. Maraj c Salmond b Blain	50
D. Chumney c Salmond b Sheridan	36
I. S. Billcliff run out	23
*J. V. Harris b Cox	35
N. A. De Groot not out	19
M. Diwan not out	1
B 2, l-b 1, w 5, n-b 5	13
1/1 2/57 3/111 4/122 5/175 (5 wkts, 39.5 overs)	177

†A. Bagai, S. Thuraisingham, D. Joseph and B. B. Seebaran did not bat.

Bowling: Blain 8–0–34–2; Cox 8–0–40–1; Brinkley 8.5–1–27–0; Sheridan 7–0–38–1; Maiden 6–0–24–0; Parsons 2–0–11–0.

Umpires: D. B. Hair (Australia) and R. E. Koertzen (South Africa).
Third umpire: E. A. Nicholls (West Indies). Referee: J. L. Hendriks (West Indies).

ICC TROPHY FINALS

1979	SRI LANKA beat Canada by 60 runs at Worcester.
1982	ZIMBABWE beat Bermuda by five wickets at Leicester.
1986	ZIMBABWE beat Holland by 25 runs at Lord's.
1990	ZIMBABWE beat Holland by six wickets at The Hague.
1993-94	UNITED ARAB EMIRATES beat Kenya by two wickets at Nairobi.
1996-97	BANGLADESH beat Kenya by two wickets (D/L method) at Kuala Lumpur.
2001	HOLLAND beat Namibia by two wickets at Toronto.

ENGLAND UNDER-19 IN INDIA, 2000-01

By JOHN STERN

Possessing the more mature, streetwise and, in most cases, talented cricketers, India Under-19 held sway over their English counterparts in early 2001, winning their Test series 1–0 and the one-day internationals 2–1. It was the first time England had lost an Under-19 Test series overseas since 1994-95 in the West Indies. In fact, they won only two out of nine matches on the six-week visit, both one-day fixtures.

A family bereavement meant that manager Tim Tremlett and his son Chris, the Hampshire all-rounder, missed the first fortnight of the tour; Graham Saville deputised as manager. Later, an earthquake in Gujarat made it necessary to move the one-day series, originally assigned to that state, southwards. There was local controversy, too, about the ages of some Indians after a furore in the domestic Under-19 final, when six Haryana and five Madhya Pradesh players were sent for medical checks. (On the fourth day, Madhya Pradesh managed only nine fielders, and when the seventh Haryana wicket fell soon after tea, with no one left to bat, the umpires and captains decided to call off the match. Haryana were declared winners on first innings.) The board tested their entire squad's bone development, yet rumour and innuendo persisted.

On benign pitches offering slow turn, Essex seamers Andrew McGarry and Justin Bishop bowled with heart and no little skill. They helped force a first-innings lead in the First Test and the follow-on in the Second. But containing the Indians in both innings, once the new ball had lost its sheen and hardness, proved beyond them. Openers Vinayak Mane, a Tendulkar clone from Mumbai, and Gautam Gambhir, a flashy left-hander from Delhi, revelled in a constant display of one-upmanship, which peaked as they ran up 391 in the Second Test follow-on. Mane was comfortably the leading batsman in the Tests, with 461 runs at 92.20. Their captain, Ajay Ratra, the sole survivor from India's Under-19 World Cup-winning side in Sri Lanka a year earlier, batted valuably; his second-innings 94 turned the First Test.

England's lack of depth in spin was exposed. They took only two specialists, both left-armers: Monty Panesar, the slender Sikh from Northamptonshire, looked out of his depth and was an embarrassment in the field; Rob Ferley of Kent possessed a combative attitude, and swung the second one-day international, but he showed little penetration in the Tests. India used four spinners, the most successful being Sivaramakrishnan Vidyuth, of Tamil Nadu. A tall, rather tubby left-armer, with an unpleasant line in sledging, he took 17 Test wickets at 23.17. His spell of seven for six in the First Test effectively settled the series.

England's real successes were three batsmen: captain Ian Bell and two Durham players, Nicky Peng and Gary Pratt. Bell, who had burst on to the junior international scene in New Zealand in 1998-99, aged 16, acknowledged a technical weakness early on and, by remaining more still at the crease, became England's leading batsman in Tests (332 runs at 55.33) and one-day internationals (169 at 56.33). Like him, Peng learned quickly to deal with the constant diet of spin, and was bold enough to leave the crease and attack; his Test record was 286 at 47.66, while the left-handed Pratt scored 278 at 55.60, passing 500 in all matches.

ENGLAND UNDER-19 TOURING PARTY

I. R. Bell (Warwickshire) (*captain*), Kadeer Ali (Worcestershire), J. E. Bishop (Essex), R. S. Ferley (Kent), K. W. Hogg (Lancashire), A. C. McGarry (Essex), M. N. Malik (Nottinghamshire), G. J. Muchall (Durham), M. S. Panesar (Northamptonshire), I. Pattison (Durham), N. Peng (Durham), G. J. Pratt (Durham), J. L. Sadler (Yorkshire), C. T. Tremlett (Hampshire), M. A. Wallace (Glamorgan).

Malik replaced A. V. Suppiah (Somerset), who withdrew injured before the start of the tour.
Manager: T. M. Tremlett (Hampshire). *Acting-manager:* G. J. Saville (Essex). *Coach:* T. J. Boon (Leicestershire). *Physiotherapist:* K. A. Russell (Northamptonshire). *Physiologist:* M. Simpson.

ENGLAND UNDER-19 TOUR RESULTS

Matches – Played 9: Won 2, Lost 4, Drawn 3. Abandoned 1

Note: Matches in this section were not first-class.

At Nehru Stadium, Pune, December 31, January 1, 2. West Zone Under-19 v England Under-19. Abandoned.

At Nehru Stadium, Pune, January 2. England Under-19 won by 58 runs. Toss: West Zone Under-19. England Under-19 223 (50 overs) (J. L. Sadler 33, G. J. Pratt 59, I. R. Bell 40; U. N. Karkera three for 43); West Zone Under-19 165 (39.3 overs) (K. R. Khadkikar 39; R. S. Ferley three for 31).

At Middle Income Group Sports Club Ground, Bandra, Mumbai, January 4, 5, 6. Rest of India Under-19 won by ten wickets. Toss: England Under-19. England Under-19 210 (G. J. Pratt 78, I. Pattison 39; M. Dharmichand five for 65) and 155 (R. S. Ferley 33; M. Dharmichand seven for 65, K. R. Khadkikar three for 35); Rest of India Under-19 321 for seven dec. (Gaganinder Singh 62, K. R. Khadkikar 36, Y. Gnaneswara Rao 123 not out, Extras 41; R. S. Ferley four for 71) and 46 for no wkt.

INDIA v ENGLAND

First Under-19 Test

At Wankhede Stadium, Mumbai, January 9, 10, 11, 12. India Under-19 won by 167 runs. Toss: India Under-19.

England capitulated on the final afternoon to the left-arm spin of Vidyuth, whose final spell was 18.3–15–6–7. They were 160 for one when Bell was lbw to a sharply spun off-break from Dharmichand, straight after a drinks break; that sparked a collapse of nine for 23, with the last four falling for three runs in 12 overs. Wallace was left high and dry on five not out, after an hour and a half, as India won with only five minutes to spare. England had led by 28 on first innings through Bell's second century in his tenth Under-19 Test; he was bowled offering no stroke to Aggarwal. But the game turned India's way on the third afternoon. After Mane had been dropped twice on his way to a 99-ball 93, Ratra, hitting 94 in 92 balls, and Khadkikar added 141 in 25 overs.

Close of play: First day, England Under-19 24-0 (Pratt 4*, Peng 18*); Second day, England Under-19 281-9 (Bishop 13*, Panesar 1*); Third day, England Under-19 3-0 (Pratt 3*, Peng 0*).

India Under-19

V. R. Mane c Bell b Hogg	20	– (2) c Hogg b Pattison	93
G. Gambhir b Bishop	2	– (1) lbw b Hogg	29
I. Ganda c Peng b Hogg	27	– c Peng b Pattison	19
Y. Gnaneswara Rao lbw b Bishop	16	– c and b Pattison	2
A. S. Naidu b Panesar	83	– c Bell b Hogg	30
K. R. Khadkikar c Wallace b Bishop	1	– c and b Ferley	65
*†A. Ratra c Panesar b McGarry	43	– c Wallace b McGarry	94
S. Vidyuth c Wallace b McGarry	18	– c Kadeer Ali b Ferley	2
M. Dharmichand not out	8	– c Bell b McGarry	26
S. K. Trivedi b Panesar	18	– c Pattison b Ferley	7
N. Aggarwal b Hogg	0	– not out	2
L-b 6, w 3, n-b 12	21	L-b 7, n-b 2	9
1/10 2/30 3/64 4/87 5/102 6/208 7/229 8/229 9/252	257	1/58 2/128 3/144 4/153 5/186 6/327 7/329 8/344 9/372	378

Bowling: *First Innings*—McGarry 14–1–39–2; Bishop 15–5–24–3; Hogg 11.5–3–33–3; Pattison 12–3–50–0; Ferley 7–1–37–0; Panesar 16–3–63–2; Bell 3–0–5–0. *Second Innings*—McGarry 11–3–49–2; Bishop 11–1–53–0; Hogg 14–1–56–2; Pattison 10–1–32–3; Ferley 19.2–1–93–3; Panesar 15–0–71–0; Bell 3–0–17–0.

England Under-19

G. J. Pratt c and b Vidyuth	28	– c Gambhir b Vidyuth	66
N. Peng run out	30	– c Ganda b Vidyuth	28
*I. R. Bell b Aggarwal	109	– lbw b Dharmichand	48
Kadeer Ali c Naidu b Dharmichand	11	– c Ratra b Vidyuth	2
I. Pattison b Vidyuth	1	– c Mane b Dharmichand	3
†M. A. Wallace c Naidu b Vidyuth	13	– not out	5
R. S. Ferley lbw b Khadkikar	29	– lbw b Vidyuth	1
K. W. Hogg run out	23	– lbw b Vidyuth	5
J. E. Bishop not out	15	– c Khadkikar b Vidyuth	0
A. C. McGarry b Aggarwal	4	– c Gambhir b Vidyuth	0
M. S. Panesar c Mane b Vidyuth	3	– lbw b Vidyuth	0
B 3, l-b 2, n-b 14	19	B 1, l-b 7, w 9, n-b 8	25
1/43 2/107 3/122 4/134 5/175 6/214 7/259 8/260 9/274	285	1/58 2/160 3/166 4/169 5/171 6/172 7/180 8/180 9/183	183

Bowling: *First Innings*—Trivedi 11–3–30–0; Aggarwal 19–3–58–2; Dharmichand 29–9–75–1; Vidyuth 30.3–5–84–4; Khadkikar 11–2–16–1; Ganda 9–2–17–0. *Second Innings*—Vidyuth 34.3–20–38–8; Aggarwal 6–0–34–0; Trivedi 14–2–37–0; Dharmichand 30–16–46–2; Gnaneswara Rao 2–0–9–0; Khadkikar 11–7–10–0; Ganda 1–0–1–0.

Umpires: S. N. Bandekar and S. K. Sharma.

At Guru Nanak College Ground, Chennai, January 15, 16, 17. Drawn. Toss: South Zone Under-19. South Zone Under-19 275 for eight dec. (T. S. Suman 42, D. A. Chougule 97, V. S. Suri 44) and 201 for four dec. (T. S. Suman 53, N. A. Yadav 101 not out; M. S. Panesar three for 40); England Under-19 183 (J. L. Sadler 32, C. T. Tremlett 49; L. Balaji four for 54, M. Faiq four for 40) and 110 for four (J. L. Sadler 32, G. J. Muchall 48 not out).

INDIA v ENGLAND

Second Under-19 Test

At M. A. Chidambaram Stadium, Chennai, January 20, 21, 22, 23. Drawn. Toss: England Under-19.

Solid batting and then impressive pace bowling by McGarry allowed England to enforce the follow-on, only for India to fight back with a staggering first-wicket stand of 391 in 312 minutes that put the match beyond the tourists' reach. On the opening day, Peng hit five sixes and 11 fours to reach 132, his second Under-19 hundred in his fifth Test, and next day Muchall and Tremlett were quick to make their mark on the series with solid batting. India were bowled out 168 behind, McGarry claiming four wickets, but their second innings was a different story. Gambhir and Mane flogged a tiring attack for more than five runs an over as both made double-hundreds. Gambhir, dropped on 89 and 90, hit 25 fours and two sixes in his 242 balls, while Mane, who gave a leg-side chance to Wallace before scoring, hit 23 fours and two sixes from 239. Of the 94 overs England sent down, only four were maidens.

Close of play: First day, England Under-19 286-3 (Pratt 39*, Muchall 14*); Second day, India Under-19 122-4 (Ganda 44*, Khadkikar 9*); Third day, India Under-19 241-0 (Gambhir 121*, Mane 115*).

England Under-19

J. L. Sadler run out	22	– not out	31
N. Peng c Ganda b Vidyuth	132	– c Ratra b Aggarwal	0
*I. R. Bell c Dharmichand b Ganda	61	– b Vidyuth	7
G. J. Pratt c Ratra b Aggarwal	40	– not out	19
G. J. Muchall run out	49		
I. Pattison b Trivedi	7		
†M. A. Wallace c Ratra b Dharmichand	6		
C. T. Tremlett c Khadkikar b Dharmichand	61		
J. E. Bishop run out	0		
A. C. McGarry lbw b Aggarwal	0		
M. S. Panesar not out	2		
B 1, l-b 1, w 5, n-b 12	19	B 1, w 5, n-b 1	7
1/57 2/199 3/251 4/290 5/301 6/313 7/354 8/354 9/354	399	1/17 2/41	(2 wkts) 64

Bowling: *First Innings*—Trivedi 16–4–56–1; Aggarwal 19–6–46–2; Vidyuth 45–13–102–1; Dharmichand 39.2–8–126–2; Khadkikar 12–2–21–0; Ganda 12–1–44–1; Gambhir 1–0–2–0. *Second Innings*—Trivedi 5–2–12–0; Aggarwal 9–2–18–1; Vidyuth 11–5–13–1; Dharmichand 6–2–9–0; Ganda 2–1–10–0; Khadkikar 1–0–1–0.

India Under-19

G. Gambhir c Sadler b Tremlett	23	– run out	212
V. R. Mane b McGarry	12	– c Bell b Muchall	201
I. Ganda c Wallace b Tremlett	67		
Y. Gnaneswara Rao lbw b McGarry	30	– (3) c Sadler b Muchall	3
A. S. Naidu c Wallace b McGarry	0	– (4) c Muchall b Panesar	35
K. R. Khadkikar c Wallace b Bishop	30	– (5) not out	19
*†A. Ratra c Bishop b Panesar	28		
S. Vidyuth c Pattison b McGarry	11	– (6) not out	7
M. Dharmichand c Sadler b Pattison	5		
S. K. Trivedi c Wallace b Pattison	12		
N. Aggarwal not out	5		
L-b 3, w 2, n-b 3	8	B 2, l-b 1, w 7, n-b 5	15
1/33 2/39 3/103 4/103 5/156 6/171 7/195 8/212 9/216	231	1/391 2/397 3/431 4/481	(4 wkts dec.) 492

Bowling: *First Innings*—McGarry 17–3–44–4; Bishop 15–6–52–1; Tremlett 11–4–31–2; Panesar 21–5–64–1; Pattison 15.4–5–37–2. *Second Innings*—McGarry 13–1–64–0; Pattison 12–0–56–0; Bishop 11–0–56–0; Tremlett 13–0–67–0; Panesar 24–3–122–1; Muchall 16–0–80–2; Bell 1–0–10–0; Sadler 4–0–34–0.

Umpires: G. A. Pratap Kumar and C. R. Vijayaraghavan.

INDIA v ENGLAND

Third Under-19 Test

At Lal Bahadur Shastri Stadium, Hyderabad, January 27, 28, 29, 30. Drawn. Toss: England Under-19.

Leg-spinner Mishra entered the series and made an immediate impact when Sadler was caught in his second over by Ratra, running round to take the ball after Mane had juggled it at short leg. Mishra soon claimed Peng as well, but Pratt batted four and a half hours, surviving three chances, to reach 114 by the close. He was bowled third ball next morning, and England's remaining wickets added only 60. Gambhir and Mane then continued the party they had begun at Chennai, rattling up 112 in 23 overs until Gambhir lifted Hogg to cover. Mane went on to 135 in 187 balls before Pratt ran him out from extra cover, and Ratra made 141 before he was last out. England trailed by 176. Sadler and Peng responded with their own century stand, but when the middle order fell away, defeat looked a real possibility. Ferley and Bishop held out for 17 overs to make the game safe.

Close of play: First day, England Under-19 256-4 (Pratt 114*, Bishop 1*); Second day, India Under-19 220-3 (Mane 114*, Naidu 4*); Third day, England Under-19 58-0 (Sadler 17*, Peng 37*).

England Under-19

J. L. Sadler c Ratra b Mishra	22	– st Ratra b Vidyuth	27
N. Peng c Ganda b Mishra	24	– c Naidu b Mishra	72
*I. R. Bell lbw b Dharmichand	46	– c Ratra b Vidyuth	61
G. J. Pratt b Aggarwal	114	– c Maninder Singh b Mishra	11
G. J. Muchall c Ganda b Aggarwal	36	– c Ratra b Ganda	3
J. E. Bishop lbw b Aggarwal	2	– (10) not out	21
C. T. Tremlett lbw b Vidyuth	9	– (6) c Naidu b Ganda	1
†M. A. Wallace b Mishra	10	– (7) lbw b Aggarwal	22
R. S. Ferley not out	29	– (8) not out	37
K. W. Hogg c Gnaneswara Rao b Mishra	0	– (9) c Ratra b Aggarwal	2
A. C. McGarry lbw b Aggarwal	8		
L-b 6, n-b 10	16	B 3, l-b 3, n-b 16	22
1/41 2/66 3/168 4/249 5/256 6/263 7/276 8/293 9/297	316	1/104 2/108 3/120 4/158 5/174 6/199 7/220 8/226	(8 wkts) 279

Bowling: *First Innings*—Maninder Singh 17–10–20–0; Aggarwal 17.3–6–50–4; Vidyuth 42–11–102–1; Mishra 36–8–96–4; Dharmichand 18–8–36–1; Ganda 2–1–6–0. *Second Innings*—Maninder Singh 7–2–14–0; Aggarwal 15–5–36–2; Mishra 29–6–81–2; Dharmichand 24–10–44–0; Vidyuth 35–10–55–2; Ganda 13–3–28–2; Gambhir 3–0–11–0; Gnaneswara Rao 1–0–4–0.

India Under-19

G. Gambhir c Pratt b Hogg	65	S. Vidyuth c Wallace b McGarry	38
V. R. Mane run out	135	M. Dharmichand b Bishop	33
I. Ganda c Pratt b Ferley	18	N. Aggarwal not out	4
Y. Gnaneswara Rao c Wallace b Bishop	13		
A. S. Naidu c Wallace b Bishop	19	B 5, l-b 15	20
*†A. Ratra c Bell b Bishop	141		—
Maninder Singh c Peng b Ferley	6	1/112 2/189 3/215 4/248 5/266	492
A. Mishra c Wallace b Bishop	0	6/322 7/335 8/406 9/473	

Bowling: McGarry 18–3–70–1; Bishop 20.3–4–64–5; Hogg 20–3–92–1; Tremlett 14–2–65–0; Ferley 33–3–139–2; Muchall 11–1–42–0.

Umpires: O. Krishna and V. K. Ramaswamy.

At Lal Bahadur Shastri Stadium, Hyderabad, February 2. First one-day international: India Under-19 won by three wickets. Toss: England Under-19. England Under-19 127 (46 overs) (S. Vidyuth three for 26, N. A. Yadav three for 20); India Under-19 130 for seven (26.1 overs) (C. T. Tremlett three for 31).

At Indira Gandhi Stadium, Vijayawada, February 4. Second one-day international: England Under-19 won by 31 runs. Toss: England Under-19. England Under-19 248 for nine (50 overs) (N. Peng 60, I. R. Bell 91; S. K. Trivedi four for 26); India Under-19 217 (47.2 overs) (M. Bisla 93, N. A. Yadav 35, Maninder Singh 31 not out; M. N. Malik three for 33, R. S. Ferley four for 32).

Ferley, celebrating his 19th birthday, took three wickets in nine balls.

At Lal Bahadur Shastri Stadium, Hyderabad, February 6. Third one-day international: India Under-19 won by 28 runs. Toss: India Under-19. India Under-19 277 for nine (50 overs) (G. Gambhir 81, A. Das 33, A. Ratra 45, S. K. Trivedi 37 not out; C. T. Tremlett three for 47); England Under-19 249 (45.2 overs) (G. J. Pratt 71, I. R. Bell 51, G. J. Muchall 42; S. Vidyuth four for 50).

England Under-19's reply was restricted to 47 overs because of their slow over-rate. India Under-19 won the one-day series 2–1.

CRICINFO WOMEN'S WORLD CUP, 2000-01

By STEVE WHITING

Two days before Christmas, hosts New Zealand made it third time lucky in a World Cup final, beating the holders by four runs after finishing runners-up to England in 1993 and Australia in 1997-98. Nor was there any concealing local delight as hundreds poured on to the ground to acclaim the "White Ferns", captained by Emily Drumm. It was no more than the country deserved for staging a successful tournament. After a storm on the eve of the first round-robin match, all 31 games were played over four weeks in clement conditions. The pitches, at Lincoln University just outside Christchurch and at Hagley Park in the city, had few vices, while the hospitality accorded the seven visiting countries was... well, this was New Zealand.

To avoid as many one-sided matches as occurred in the previous World Cup, in India, the International Women's Cricket Council had limited the participants here to the 1997-98 quarter-finalists: Australia, England, Holland, India, Ireland, New Zealand, South Africa and Sri Lanka. And whereas, four years earlier, the 11 countries were divided into two groups, this time the eight played in a round robin, with the top four going into the semi-finals. Australia and New Zealand headed the table, and were joined in the knockout round by India and South Africa. As expected after their showing in 1997-98, their first World Cup, the South Africans had come on impressively, as they illustrated in beating England by five wickets in the first week.

When England lost to India two days later, they found themselves having to play catch-up cricket for a semi-final place, hoping that India or South Africa would falter. There certainly seemed little likelihood of them shaping their own destiny by recovering points against Australia or New Zealand. After their disastrous tour "Down Under" the previous year, the tournament provided another indication of England's slide down the international ladder, despite generous sponsorship, the financial support of Sport England, and a full-time ECB back-up team. Winners in 1993, after losing successive finals to Australia in 1981-82 and 1988-89, and semi-finalists in 1997-98, they now failed to progress beyond the qualifying stage.

What let England down most was their batting. Against South Africa, for example, five of the top six managed just 22 runs in 23 overs. Only Claire Taylor featured among the tournament's top ten batsmen, finishing sixth equal with 267 runs at 66.75 – half of those coming from her unbeaten 137 against Sri Lanka when she and Jane Cassar shared a world-record fifth-wicket stand of 188 unbroken. Apart from Taylor, Charlotte Edwards (157) and Barbara Daniels (155), no England player totalled 100 runs. However, England's other Taylor, bowler Clare, emerged from the group matches as leading wicket-taker, with 14 at 10.85, and finished second for the tournament behind Australia's Charmaine Mason (17 at 10.76), who picked up five in the semi-final and final.

By the end of the round robin, Australia's Karen Rolton was out on her own as leading run-scorer with 390, which included sparkling centuries against Sri Lanka and South Africa. The first of these saw her race to three figures off 85 balls, with 12 fours, but that was simply limbering up for the South African bowlers and the fastest international hundred by a woman – achieved in 57 balls with 17 fours. Next time Rolton met the South Africans, in their semi-final, Belinda Clark and Lisa Keightley opened with 170 and she had time only to make two not out. In the final, she was run out for one after Keightley had been caught behind without scoring.

Some consolation came Keightley's way from winning the Player of the Tournament trophy, awarded on points given by the umpires after every game. Also in close contention were Rolton and the New Zealand opener, Anna O'Leary, whose final aggregate of 308 runs came just behind Drumm's 339, though the New Zealand captain played one game fewer. In fact, Drumm missed two early games after the middle finger on her right hand was broken by Australia's Cathryn Fitzpatrick in the opening match.

She never let on publicly, however, played with her finger in a splint, and subsequently revealed that she had been unable to use her fingers for catching or fielding, having to use her palm instead to stop the ball. But for someone whose World Cup memories had been blighted by her duck and two dropped catches at Lord's in the 1993 final, the pain was worth it.

For another New Zealander, 38-year-old Debbie Hockley, a winners' medal in her fifth World Cup crowned an illustrious career that had seen her become the leading run-scorer in the women's game and the first to play 100 one-day internationals. Four years earlier, she had edged ahead of England's Janette Brittin as leading run-scorer in World Cups; now she moved ahead of her to top the list of World Cup appearances with 45, in addition to extending her World Cup aggregate to 1,501 at 42.88.

Bizarrely, the tournament was threatened with disruption at one stage by allegations of throwing against at least four bowlers, made by, of all people, the sponsors. Slow-motion replays can reveal abnormalities in almost any action if you choose to look closely enough, but the attention drawn to the actions of India's Purnima Rau and Renu Margreat, Kiwi Erin McDonald and Caroline Salomons of Holland smacked of sensation seeking. Rau, a bespectacled, 33-year-old from Hyderabad, was so upset that she nearly went home.

So it was good to see Australia's coach, John Harmer, the man from Fern Tree Gully, Victoria, take over the post-final press conference and declare that television, with all its paraphernalia, was in danger of robbing cricket of the one thing that separated it from many other sports – sportsmanship. "I would do away with all the third-umpire decisions," he said, "even for run-outs and stumpings. That's what the umpire is there for, and if he makes a mistake, so be it. Batsmen and bowlers make mistakes, so why not umpires? The cameras may take the errors out of the game, but they are also taking out the sportsmanship, and that is what cricket cannot do without."

Note: Matches in this section were not first-class.

*In the following scores, * by the name of a team indicates that they won the toss.*

At BIL Oval, Lincoln, November 29. Australia won by six wickets. New Zealand 166 for nine (50 overs) (E. C. Drumm 74, K. A. Ramel 32; T. A. McGregor four for 18); Australia* 167 for four (47.3 overs) (L. M. Keightley 44, K. L. Rolton 51 not out, C. Bambury 38).

At BIL Oval, Lincoln, November 30. England won by 140 runs. England* 256 for three (50 overs) (C. M. Edwards 139 not out, B. A. Daniels 79); Holland 116 for nine (50 overs) (S. V. Collyer five for 32).

Edwards and Daniels added 184 for the second wicket. Clare Taylor's ten overs cost just 11 runs.

At Hagley Oval, Christchurch, November 30. India won by eight wickets. South Africa 128 for eight (50 overs) (Y. van der Merwe 42 not out; P. Rau three for 12); India* 129 for two (39.4 overs) (M. Raj 69 not out).

Kim Price (19 not out) and van der Merwe put on 66 for the ninth wicket.

At Hagley Oval, Christchurch, December 1. Australia won by 200 runs. Australia* 282 for three (50 overs) (L. M. Keightley 56, K. L. Rolton 154 not out, O. J. Magno 38); Sri Lanka 82 (39 overs) (A. J. Fahey three for 11).

Rolton, who faced 118 balls and hit 19 boundaries, put on 117 for the second wicket with Keightley and 129 for the third with Magno.

At BIL Oval, Lincoln, December 1. New Zealand won by eight wickets. Ireland* 99 (49.4 overs) (C. M. Beggs 31); New Zealand 102 for two (24.5 overs) (P. B. Flannery 49 not out).

At BIL Oval, Lincoln, December 2. South Africa won by five wickets. England 143 (47.5 overs) (K. M. Leng 46; Y. van der Merwe three for 25); South Africa* 144 for five (46.5 overs) (M. Terblanche 41, S. Viljoen 54 not out).

At Lincoln Green, December 2. India won by 154 runs. India 275 for four (50 overs) (A. Jain 32, A. Chopra 69, M. Raj 51, H. Kala 56, C. K. Kaul 39 not out); Holland* 121 for six (50 overs) (P. te Beest 33, C. M. S. Verheul 46 not out).

Chopra and Raj put on 101 for the second wicket before Kala and Kaul came together to add 99 for the fourth. When Holland batted, Smitha Harikrishna took two for ten in ten overs.

At Hagley Park, Christchurch, December 3. Australia won by ten wickets. Ireland* 90 (49.3 overs) (Z. J. Goss four for ten); Australia 91 for no wkt (20.3 overs) (L. M. Keightley 49 not out, B. J. Clark 40 not out).

At Lincoln Green, December 3. New Zealand won by 122 runs. New Zealand* 210 for four (50 overs) (A. M. O'Leary 91 not out, H. M. Tiffen 58); Sri Lanka 88 (49.3 overs) (A. D. H. Abeysinghe 30).

O'Leary put on 137 for the third wicket with Tiffen, who also took two wickets and was involved in three of four run-outs in Sri Lanka's innings.

At Lincoln Green, December 4. India won by eight runs. India* 155 for seven (50 overs) (M. Raj 32, C. K. Kaul 45); England 147 (49.2 overs) (S. C. Taylor 60; R. Shastri three for 25).

At Hagley Park, Christchurch, December 4. South Africa won by four wickets. Holland* 92 (37.1 overs) (M. A. Koster 36; L. P. Lewis four for 20); South Africa 93 for six (26.2 overs) (M. Terblanche 37 not out, S. Viljoen 32; C. F. F. Oudolf three for 31).

At Lincoln Green, December 5. Sri Lanka won by ten runs. Sri Lanka 129 (47.3 overs) (A. D. H. Abeysinghe 52); Ireland* 119 (49.5 overs) (K. N. Young 30; C. R. Seneviratne three for 18).

At BIL Oval, Lincoln, December 6. Australia won by 51 runs. Australia* 223 for five (50 overs) (L. M. Keightley 74, K. L. Rolton 61); India 172 for eight (50 overs) (A. Jain 36, A. Chopra 47; T. A. McGregor three for 38).

Keightley and Rolton put on 110 for the second wicket.

At Hagley Park, Christchurch, December 6. New Zealand won by eight wickets. Holland* 80 (48 overs) (H. M. Watson three for 28); New Zealand 81 for two (16.3 overs) (P. B. Flannery 36 not out).

Catherine Campbell returned figures of 10–7–3–0 for New Zealand.

At BIL Oval, Lincoln, December 7. England won by eight wickets. Ireland* 103 (44.2 overs) (C. E. Taylor four for 25); England 105 for two (29.3 overs) (A. Thompson 44 not out, B. A. Daniels 31).

At Lincoln Green, December 8. South Africa won by six wickets. Sri Lanka 134 for nine (50 overs); South Africa* 135 for four (45.3 overs) (M. Terblanche 53 not out).

At BIL Oval, Lincoln, December 9. New Zealand won by 74 runs. New Zealand* 224 for five (50 overs) (A. M. O'Leary 89, D. A. Hockley 53, H. M. Tiffen 50 not out); India 150 for seven (50 overs) (C. K. Kaul 59 not out).

At Lincoln Green, December 10. Australia won by 54 runs. Australia* 190 for seven (50 overs) (Z. J. Goss 49, O. J. Magno 32; C. E. Taylor three for 30); England 136 (47.3 overs) (S. C. Taylor 45; C. L. Fitzpatrick three for 22, C. L. Mason three for 20, A. J. Fahey three for 23).

At Hagley Park, Christchurch, December 10. Sri Lanka won by 26 runs. Sri Lanka 139 (47.1 overs) (S. A. R. C. Silva 53, Extras 37; T. van der Gun three for 18); Holland* 113 (39.4 overs) (H. W. Rambaldo 38; S. A. R. C. Silva three for 24, C. R. Seneviratne four for 23, K. J. Indika three for 14).

At Hagley Park, Christchurch, December 11. India won by 30 runs. India 199 for nine (50 overs) (A. Chopra 70, H. Kala 40, S. Harikrishna 34; C. O'Neill three for 33); Ireland* 169 (47.2 overs).

At Lincoln Green, December 11. New Zealand won by 158 runs. New Zealand 265 for five (50 overs) (A. M. O'Leary 32, R. J. Rolls 44, E. C. Drumm 108 not out, H. M. Tiffen 35 not out); South Africa* 107 (35.4 overs) (C. E. Eksteen 47 not out; H. M. Watson three for 14).

At BIL Oval, Lincoln, December 12. England won by 105 runs. England* 242 for four (50 overs) (S. C. Taylor 137 not out, J. Cassar 63 not out); Sri Lanka 137 for nine (50 overs) (A. D. H. Abeysinghe 57; M. A. Reynard three for 27, K. M. Leng three for 16).

Taylor and Cassar added 188 unbroken, a world record for the fifth wicket. Laura Harper's figures were 10–5–10–0.

At BIL Oval, Lincoln, December 13. Australia won by nine wickets. South Africa* 169 for eight (50 overs) (L. Olivier 34, A. A. Burger 44, C. E. Eksteen 46; C. L. Mason three for 29); Australia 171 for one (25 overs) (B. J. Clark 49 not out, K. L. Rolton 107 not out).

Rolton, who featured in an unbroken second-wicket stand of 151 with Clark, faced 67 balls and hit 18 fours.

At BIL Oval, Lincoln, December 14. New Zealand won by 93 runs. New Zealand 238 for eight (50 overs) (R. J. Rolls 65, E. C. Drumm 53); England* 145 (47.3 overs) (K. M. Keenan three for 16).

At Hagley Park, Christchurch, December 14. Ireland won by 41 runs. Ireland 232 for six (50 overs) (A. Linehan 54, C. M. Beggs 66 not out, M. E. Grealey 32, Extras 45); Holland* 191 for eight (50 overs) (R. C. Milburn 71, T. van der Gun 43).

At Lincoln Green, December 15. India won by 141 runs. India* 230 for four (50 overs) (S. Harikrishna 32, A. Chopra 68 not out, C. K. Kaul 80); Sri Lanka 89 (49.2 overs).

Chopra and Kaul put on 151 for the third wicket.

At Lincoln Green, December 16. Australia won by ten wickets. Holland* 107 for seven (50 overs) (P. te Beest 42; A. J. Fahey three for 19); Australia 109 for no wkt (24 overs) (L. M. Keightley 51 not out, B. J. Clark 48 not out).

At Hagley Park, Christchurch, December 16. South Africa won by nine wickets. Ireland 176 for nine (50 overs) (A. Linehan 40, M. E. Grealey 30; H. Strydom three for 33, S. Viljoen three for 27); South Africa* 177 for one (36.2 overs) (L. Olivier 101 not out, H. Strydom 46).

Olivier and Strydom opened with 117.

QUALIFYING TABLE

	Played	*Won*	*Lost*	*Points*	*Net run-rate*
Australia	7	7	0	14	1.98
New Zealand	7	6	1	12	2.00
India	7	5	2	10	0.71
South Africa	7	4	3	8	−0.40
England	7	3	4	6	0.44
Sri Lanka	7	2	5	4	−1.57
Ireland	7	1	6	2	−0.98
Holland	7	0	7	0	−2.09

Net run-rate is calculated by subtracting runs conceded per over from runs scored per over.

Semi-finals

At BIL Oval, Lincoln, December 18. Australia won by nine wickets. South Africa 180 for eight (50 overs) (L. Olivier 41; C. L. Mason three for 39); Australia* 181 for one (31.2 overs) (B. J. Clark 75, L. M. Keightley 91 not out).

Clark and Keightley put on 170 for the first wicket.

At BIL Oval, Lincoln, December 20. New Zealand won by nine wickets. India* 117 (45.2 overs) (P. Rau 67 not out); New Zealand 121 for one (26.5 overs) (A. M. O'Leary 50 not out, E. C. Drumm 47 not out).

Opener Rau carried her bat.

FINAL

NEW ZEALAND v AUSTRALIA

At BIL Oval, Lincoln, December 23. New Zealand won by four runs. Toss: New Zealand.

Australia reached the final over needing five runs from their last-wicket pair; tension enough, without New Zealand captain Drumm in a quandary over who should bowl it. Tiffen looked the candidate, but only because Drumm thought off-spinner Nicholson had completed her quota. She hadn't, took the ball and, with her first delivery, had Mason caught behind, attempting to cut. It was the signal for jubilant fans to swarm on to the field to acclaim a victory that, earlier in the day, had seemed unlikely. "When we went to lunch after scoring only 184, I thought, 'Oh God, here we go again,'" Drumm admitted. She need not have worried. Defending a total thought to be at least 20 runs under par, New Zealand rocked the Australians by removing the tournament's leading scorers in the first three overs. Keightley was caught fourth ball by wicket-keeper Rolls, diving to her right, and Rolton was run out at the non-striker's end by Watson's direct hit from square leg. New Zealand had included Watson only after dithering over selecting a batsman or bowler. They went instead for a specialist fielder and she came up trumps again with another direct hit – side on from square leg – to remove McGregor just when the Australians were looking to build on captain Clark's 91 from 102 balls. Clark had taken them to 150 for seven by the 42nd over, then Nicholson bowled her on the sweep. It was the big wicket – but Nicholson's crowning moment still awaited her.

Player of the Match: B. J. Clark. *Player of the Tournament:* L. M. Keightley.

New Zealand

A. M. O'Leary b McGregor	1
†R. J. Rolls c McGregor b Mason	34
*E. C. Drumm c Price b McGregor	21
D. A. Hockley lbw b Fahey	24
H. M. Tiffen c Bambury b Goss	14
K. A. Ramel c Clark b Fitzpatrick	41
H. M. Watson b Fitzpatrick	11
C. M. Nicholson b Mason	11
R. J. Pullar not out	9
K. M. Keenan b Fitzpatrick	0
C. A. Campbell run out	0
L-b 9, w 8, n-b 1	18
1/17 2/60 3/60 4/92 5/121 6/136 7/172 8/175 9/184 (48.4 overs)	184

Bowling: Fitzpatrick 9.4–2–52–3; McGregor 10–5–26–2; Mason 9–2–30–2; Magno 6–0–22–0; Goss 4–0–14–1; Rolton 6–0–12–0; Fahey 4–0–19–1.

Australia

L. M. Keightley c Rolls b Keenan	0
*B. J. Clark b Nicholson	91
K. L. Rolton run out	1
C. Bambury c Hockley b Pullar	14
Z. J. Goss b Campbell	1
O. J. Magno b Keenan	4
†J. C. Price b Pullar	10
T. A. McGregor run out	19
C. L. Fitzpatrick b Ramel	6
C. L. Mason c Rolls b Nicholson	11
A. J. Fahey not out	3
B 1, l-b 6, w 12, n-b 1	20
1/0 2/2 3/85 4/88 5/95 6/115 7/150 8/159 9/175 (49.1 overs)	180

Bowling: Keenan 10–3–19–2; Pullar 10–0–35–2; Tiffen 5–1–27–0; Ramel 5–0–26–1; Campbell 10–2–28–1; Nicholson 9.1–1–38–2.

Umpires: P. D. Parker (Australia) and D. M. Quested.
Third umpire: B. G. Jerling (South Africa).

WORLD CUP WINNERS

1973	England
1977-78	Australia
1981-82	Australia
1988-89	Australia
1993	England
1997-98	Australia
2000-01	New Zealand

ENGLAND WOMEN IN NEW ZEALAND, 2000-01

Before their unsuccessful World Cup campaign began at the end of November, England's women played a short one-day international series against the hosts, New Zealand. The tone was set by home captain Emily Drumm, who hit a century in the opening game and went on to lead her side to a 3–0 whitewash. This brought England's losing streak in one-day internationals against New Zealand to 12; their last victory came in the 1993 World Cup final.

ENGLAND TOURING PARTY

C. J. Connor (Sussex) (*captain*), M. A. Reynard (Yorkshire) (*vice-captain*), J. Cassar (Nottinghamshire), S. V. Collyer (Cheshire), B. A. Daniels (Staffordshire), C. M. Edwards (Kent), L. J. Harper (Somerset), D. Holden (Nottinghamshire), K. M. Leng (Yorkshire), L. C. Pearson (Staffordshire), N. J. Shaw (Nottinghamshire), C. E. Taylor (Yorkshire), S. C. Taylor (Berkshire), A. Thompson (Lancashire).

Manager/coach: P. Farbrace. *Assistant coach:* G. R. Dilley.

ENGLAND TOUR RESULTS

Matches – Played 4: Won 1, Lost 3.

Note: Matches in this section were not first-class.

At Christchurch College, Christchurch, November 17. England XII won by eight wickets. Toss: Canterbury XII. Canterbury XII 179 for eight (50 overs) (L. M. Astle 59); England XII 180 for two (34.5 overs) (S. C. Taylor 97 not out, A. Thompson 49 not out).

At Oamaru, November 19. First one-day international: New Zealand won by 165 runs. Toss: New Zealand. New Zealand 275 for five (50 overs) (R. J. Rolls 31, E. C. Drumm 116, D. A. Hockley 67); England 110 for seven (50 overs) (J. Cassar 33 not out).

Drumm scored 116 in 152 balls, with 11 fours.

At Timaru, November 21. Second one-day international: New Zealand won by two wickets. Toss: England. England 134 (50 overs) (J. Cassar 48 not out); New Zealand 135 for eight (45.2 overs) (R. J. Rolls 34; S. V. Collyer three for 20).

At Timaru, November 22. Third one-day international: New Zealand won by eight wickets. Toss: England. England 109 (41 overs) (N. J. Shaw 35; K. M. Keenan three for 15); New Zealand 110 for two (30.2 overs) (A. M. O'Leary 40, E. C. Drumm 43 not out).

CRICKET IN AUSTRALIA, 2000-01

By JOHN MacKINNON

Joe Dawes

The Pura Milk Cup, which ousted the Sheffield Shield as Australia's premier domestic trophy in 1999-2000, gave way within a season to the Pura Cup. The outcome was the same, however: Queensland headed the table from Victoria, and this time won the five-day final outright to secure a second successive title, their fourth in seven seasons.

Six outright wins in the preliminaries, four of them at home, left Queensland comfortably topping the league for the third year running. All-round strength and team stability fuelled this superiority. Such was their depth in batting that they were dismissed twice in only one match, rather surprisingly in Sydney after New South Wales had made 499 for six. It was their one outright defeat. Matthew Hayden played just three matches, having at last found his feet in the Test side, but was barely missed as Jimmy Maher, Martin Love and Stuart Law restated their own claims to international recognition. Maher thrived at the top of the order, scoring 1,142 first-class runs, including 150 for Australia A against the West Indians. Love also had the thousand mark in his sights, until a hand injury kept him out of two late games, while Law's combative captaincy augmented his value as an aggressive and prolific No. 4. Then there was Andrew Symonds, the ever-unpredictable excitement machine. A single hundred may seem a small return for one of his ability, but coming when it did, with Queensland chasing 373 to beat Tasmania, it created not only an unlikely victory but also a winning momentum that never faltered.

In bowling, as ever, pace was Queensland's forte, and in Andy Bichel, Joe Dawes and Adam Dale they possessed the tournament's three leading wicket-takers. Dawes, at 30, was due to make his mark after some years on the fringe, and did so with 49 wickets in nine matches. Bichel, two days his senior but with a far more successful track record, missed four games while on Test duty but still claimed 40 Pura Cup wickets, and tied on 49 with Dawes in all first-class cricket. Though Dale's reputation has been for containment rather than strike power, 46 wickets rewarded his extraordinary accuracy and patience in wearing down batsmen. Ashley Noffke, aged 23, showed promise and, with the Queensland selectors unimpressed by their spin options, was recalled for the final: he responded with seven wickets and the match award to attract the attention of the Australian selectors. He was awarded an ACB contract in May and subsequently called up as a replacement for Nathan Bracken on the tour of England. Some past stalwarts were less fortunate. A shoulder operation kept Michael Kasprowicz on the sidelines, and he managed only one appearance before flying to India in February. Scott Muller, a Test player one year, was never sighted the next. But Wade Seccombe established himself in Queensland's great tradition of wicket-keepers; along with Maher, Law and Dale, he played in all 11 games, made 58 dismissals, and was taken to England as back-up for Adam Gilchrist.

Victoria did well to reach their second successive final. Two opening defeats suggested Matthew Elliott's unavailability through injury for four matches might be critical. But thereafter the Victorians won points from every game. Melbourne's drop-in pitches made run-scoring hard work, and the achievement of Brad Hodge, for so long an unrealised talent, and Jason Arnberger in reaching 1,000 first-class runs was all the more praiseworthy. Elliott, on his return, never quite got going – a seven-and-a-half-hour 98 in the final was his best score – while Matthew Mott at No. 3 usually guarded his wicket zealously. With the team exceeding 400 only once, at Sydney in March, much was needed from the bowlers, led by captain Paul Reiffel. In consecutive weeks, Mathew Inness destroyed the West Indian and the South Australian batting, taking six for 26 on both occasions. With the national selectors looking for a left-arm quick, 23-year-old Inness led the field, but Bracken of New South Wales won the call. Inness finished with 43 first-class wickets. Michael Lewis and Ian Harvey had their moments, though Lewis's best return, five for 57 in Queensland's first innings of the final, was followed by a loss of control in the second which cost Victoria dearly. For Reiffel, Australia's most phlegmatic cricketer, the season ended with a $A200 fine after he disputed an umpiring decision on the last day.

Three wins from their last three matches not only lifted Tasmania from bottom place to third; they also camouflaged some serious shortcomings. Jamie Cox was a shining beacon. He scored 1,070 runs for the state, more than twice any colleague's total, and was deservedly voted Pura Cup Player of the Year by the umpires. Cox overtook David Boon as Tasmania's leading run-scorer, finishing on 9,932, and took a hundred in each innings off New South Wales – for the third time. He also shared a less desirable record when he and fellow-opener Dene Hills both made pairs against Victoria, a unique instance in Australian state cricket. Test batsman Ricky Ponting played just the first two games but amassed 484 runs, including a masterly 233 against Queensland followed by 187 not out against New South Wales. Other batsmen made sporadic contributions; 19-year-old Shane Watson looked a decent prospect and, as an expat Queenslander, survived some hefty sledging from his former compatriots. Colin Miller having defected to Victoria, David Saker travelled the other way and was the leading wicket-taker in an attack that struggled on Bellerive's benign surface. Shaun Young, of more gentle pace, passed Miller's record of 218 wickets for Tasmania, reaching 225.

With Steve Rixon returning as coach after his stint running New Zealand, and Shane Lee becoming captain in Steve Waugh's absence, New South Wales looked for some improvement on a dreadful 1999-2000, when they lost eight games. They rose from last to fourth. At full strength for three matches, they took eight points from the first two – a win at Richmond and a draw in Hobart – but missed out against South Australia when their game at Bankstown Oval was washed out. (New South Wales did not return to the resurfaced SCG until February.) They also won twice when the side was below strength, recovering from a 187-run deficit to beat Western Australia and then inflicting Queensland's only defeat. The victors were vanquished in both return fixtures, however, with their old batting frailties horribly exposed. In the search for talent, 26 players were called up, far more than for any other state. The batting relied heavily on Michael Bevan, who, by his own standards, underachieved. There were two big hundreds, from Mark Higgs and Greg Mail, but precious little else. The brightest stars were Brad Haddin, at 23 a promising wicket-keeper/batsman, and 23-year-old Bracken, who like many left-armers needed a decent in-swinger to complement his line and pace. Bracken was named Bradman Young Cricketer of the Year. Stuart MacGill bowled nearly 300 overs, but lacked the support to be more than an occasional threat. With Shane Warne unfit for the Test series, MacGill rather missed the chance to press his claims; his form was spasmodic and his best return, seven for 104 in the Sydney Test, owed as much to West Indies' profligacy as to his own prowess.

The big plus of Western Australia's season was the batting of Simon Katich. However, the loss of four senior officials, including coach Wayne Clark and captain Tom Moody, suggested problems in other areas. Restored to health after a virus the previous year, and buoyed by a successful season in England with Durham, Katich was the country's leading scorer, plundering 1,282 first-class runs, with six hundreds – one off each state and two off Queensland; he also assumed the captaincy for the last two games after Moody retired. Moody decided that, at 35, it was time to move on, in fact back to Worcestershire as director of cricket. His last match was the 300th of a wonderful playing career in which he scored 21,001 first-class runs (with 64 hundreds) at 46.25 and took 361 wickets at 30.70. Moody represented his country in eight Tests and 76 one-day internationals, while his 145 matches and 9,520 runs for Western Australia were easily state records. The back problems that kept him out the previous season were always lurking, yet a return of five for 26 against New South Wales underlined his continued value and spirit. Nevertheless, two wins represented a paltry return on Western Australia's talent. Apart from Katich, runs were at a premium: the Mike Hussey–Ryan Campbell opening partnership faltered and was abandoned, while international commitments meant there were limited opportunities for Gilchrist and Damien Martyn. Jo Angel and Brendon Julian, both over 30, carried the bowling, and Matthew Nicholson showed glimpses of his ability, but the previous season's star turn, Brad Williams, was out injured until March. Shaun Marsh, a left-handed all-rounder who bowled both seam and spin, and is the son of former Test player and coach Geoff, made his debut aged 17.

South Australia took the wooden spoon, beginning and ending the season with runs of three pointless games and finishing two points shy of their western neighbours. It was as well for them that Greg Blewett had lost his Test place. After a poor start, he took off in December with 260 not out in Brisbane and never looked back; his 1,162 runs were the most in the tournament. Darren Lehmann's only hundred came off some ordinary New South Wales bowling in Adelaide, though in February he was named State Player of the Year for his form over the previous 12 months. Shane Deitz, a left-hander from Bankstown in Sydney, who came into the side late the previous season, battled out two gritty hundreds, but in general the newer players made little impression: South Australia blooded four in the last three games. The bowlers were able to dismiss the opposition twice in only two matches. They lost slow left-armer Brad Young to a knee injury, playing handball in Sydney as the players waited for the rain to stop, while Paul Wilson missed half the programme after an ankle operation and Brett Swain managed only six games. Mark Harrity and the genial leg-spinner, Peter McIntyre, toiled away but at considerable expense. With the Australian board determined to spare their fast bowlers the unnecessary rigours of domestic cricket, Jason Gillespie made one fleeting appearance for his beleaguered state. South Australia need him or his ilk if they are to have any future impact on this competition.

The limited-overs Mercantile Mutual Cup was extended to include home and away rounds for the first time, but Australian Capital Territory were dropped from the tournament after a three-year trial. Western Australia, the defending champions and unbeaten in Perth, hosted the final against New South Wales and were hot favourites. The only possible stumbling block was Bevan, whose apparent fallibility against pace they expected to test fully at the WACA. As it happened, he batted faultlessly for 135 not out, and New South Wales won comfortably.

FIRST-CLASS AVERAGES, 2000-01

BATTING

(Qualification: 500 runs)

	M	*I*	*NO*	*R*	*HS*	*100s*	*Avge*
R. T. Ponting (*Tasmania*)	7	12	3	726	233	2	80.66
M. L. Love (*Queensland*)	10	15	3	910	172*	3	75.83
S. M. Katich (*Western Australia*)	12	23	5	1,282	228*	6	71.22
G. S. Blewett (*South Australia*)	9	18	1	1,162	260*	3	68.35
D. R. Martyn (*Western Australia*)	8	15	4	746	122	2	67.81
J. Cox (*Tasmania*)	11	21	3	1,170	160	5	65.00
J. P. Maher (*Queensland*)	12	21	3	1,142	175	4	63.44
S. G. Law (*Queensland*)	11	15	2	814	161	2	62.61
M. E. Waugh (*New South Wales*)	7	11	1	590	152	2	59.00
A. C. Gilchrist (*Western Australia*)	8	11	2	531	109*	2	59.00
B. J. Hodge (*Victoria*)	13	23	3	1,129	134*	5	56.45
M. G. Bevan (*New South Wales*)	8	13	2	557	119	2	50.63
J. L. Arnberger (*Victoria*)	12	22	1	1,006	173	2	47.90
A. Symonds (*Queensland*)	9	13	1	558	133	1	46.50
D. S. Lehmann (*South Australia*)	8	16	2	645	146	1	46.07
M. L. Hayden (*Queensland*)	8	13	1	537	118*	1	44.75
M. T. G. Elliott (*Victoria*)	7	14	1	524	98	0	40.30
D. J. Marsh (*Tasmania*)	9	16	3	514	110	1	39.53
S. A. Deitz (*South Australia*)	9	18	0	608	114	2	33.77
M. P. Mott (*Victoria*)	12	22	1	695	154	1	33.09
M. E. K. Hussey (*Western Australia*)	11	21	1	605	137	1	30.25

* *Signifies not out.*

BOWLING

(Qualification: 20 wickets)

	O	*M*	*R*	*W*	*BB*	*5W/i*	*Avge*
G. D. McGrath (*New South Wales*)	207.5	77	425	23	6-17	1	18.47
J. H. Dawes (*Queensland*)	358.3	101	1,003	49	7-98	3	20.46
B. Lee (*New South Wales*)	133	40	411	20	5-42	2	20.55
J. N. Gillespie (*South Australia*)	175	51	463	22	6-40	2	21.04
T. M. Moody (*Western Australia*)	189	61	455	20	5-26	1	22.75
A. J. Bichel (*Queensland*)	400.3	99	1,144	49	5-60	3	23.34
A. C. Dale (*Queensland*)	570.3	226	1,076	46	5-37	2	23.39
J. Angel (*Western Australia*)	333.3	109	867	37	5-78	1	23.43
N. W. Bracken (*New South Wales*)	240.1	65	688	29	5-22	2	23.72
C. R. Miller (*Victoria*)	377.1	104	998	40	5-32	2	24.95
M. W. H. Inness (*Victoria*)	403.2	126	1,077	43	6-26	2	25.04
S. Young (*Tasmania*)	203.3	63	532	21	4-33	0	25.33
D. G. Wright (*Tasmania*)	192.1	42	593	22	4-54	0	26.95
P. R. Reiffel (*Victoria*)	325.1	84	824	30	4-50	0	27.46
B. P. Julian (*Western Australia*)	266.2	46	935	32	4-87	0	29.21
S. C. G. MacGill (*New South Wales*)	453.4	98	1,390	46	7-104	3	30.21
M. J. Nicholson (*Western Australia*)	289	86	773	25	4-119	0	30.92
M. A. Harrity (*South Australia*)	243.3	62	728	23	4-55	0	31.65
P. E. McIntyre (*South Australia*)	322.2	67	927	28	5-102	1	33.10
M. L. Lewis (*Victoria*)	246.2	52	772	23	5-57	1	33.56
D. A. Nash (*New South Wales*)	243.2	56	730	20	4-57	0	36.50
D. J. Saker (*Tasmania*)	350	66	1,080	26	5-98	1	41.53

PURA CUP, 2000-01

	Played	Won	Lost	Drawn	1st-inns Points	Points	Quotient
Queensland	10	6	1	3	4	40	1.375
Victoria	10	4	3	3	8	32	1.032
Tasmania.	10	3	4	3	4	22	1.011
New South Wales . . .	10	3	3	4	4	22	0.837
Western Australia . . .	10	2	4	4	4	16	0.967
South Australia.	10	2	5	3	2	14	0.824

Final: Queensland beat Victoria by four wickets.

Outright win = 6 pts; lead on first innings in a drawn or lost game = 2 pts.
Quotient = runs per wicket scored divided by runs per wicket conceded.

Full scores, match reports and statistics of the 2000-01 Australian season can be found in *Wisden Cricketers' Almanack Australia* 2001-02.

*In the following scores, * by the name of a team indicates that they won the toss.*

At Perth, October 13, 14, 15, 16. Drawn. Queensland 442 (M. L. Hayden 47, J. P. Maher 175, S. G. Law 128; M. J. Nicholson four for 119, S. M. Katich three for 46); Western Australia* 195 (M. E. K. Hussey 41, A. C. Gilchrist 59, M. J. Nicholson 35; A. C. Dale five for 41, A. A. Noffke three for 51) and 349 for five (D. R. Martyn 78, S. M. Katich 105 not out, A. C. Gilchrist 109 not out; A. J. Bichel four for 54). *Queensland 2 pts.*

Maher and Law added 275 for the third wicket in five and a quarter hours. Wicket-keeper Wade Seccombe took six catches in Western Australia's first innings. They were 43 for three following on, but only two wickets fell on the final day. Katich's 105 took 477 minutes and 392 balls; he reached 100 in 460 minutes (379 balls), the slowest century for Western Australia.

At Richmond, October 25, 26, 27, 28. New South Wales won by 117 runs. New South Wales 250 (C. J. Richards 30, M. E. Waugh 53, M. G. Bevan 39, S. Lee 53; P. R. Reiffel three for 34, C. R. Miller four for 71) and 210 for six dec. (M. E. Waugh 46, B. J. Haddin 40, D. A. Nash 46); Victoria* 194 for six dec. (B. J. Hodge 85 not out, P. R. Reiffel 63 not out; S. C. G. MacGill three for 54) and 149 (B. J. Hodge 32; B. Lee five for 42, S. C. G. MacGill three for 50). *New South Wales 6 pts.*

The first four sessions were rained off. Reiffel took his 300th first-class wicket for Victoria, whose first innings stood at 62 for six before Hodge and Reiffel added an unbroken 132. Shane Warne cracked a finger catching Waugh in the first innings and was ruled out of the West Indian Test series.

At Albion, October 26, 27, 28, 29. Queensland won by four wickets. Tasmania* 403 (R. T. Ponting 233, D. J. Marsh 61; A. J. Bichel five for 126) and 258 for seven dec. (J. Cox 44, R. T. Ponting 61, J. A. Dykes 32, D. J. Marsh 58 not out; A. J. Bichel four for 105); Queensland 289 (M. L. Hayden 41, J. P. Maher 47, M. L. Love 35, A. Symonds 49, A. J. Bichel 48; D. G. Wright three for 61, D. J. Marsh three for 50) and 373 for six (M. L. Love 161 not out, A. Symonds 133, W. A. Seccombe 31 not out). *Queensland 6 pts, Tasmania 2 pts.*

This match and the one starting on November 5 were played at the Allan Border Field because the Gabba pitch was being relaid after the Olympic football tournament. Ponting's career-best 233 lasted 388 minutes and 326 balls and included 37 fours and four sixes. Queensland needed 373, their highest winning fourth-innings total, in 72 overs; Love and Symonds added 261 in 156 minutes for the fourth wicket to help them win with an over to spare.

At Adelaide, October 26, 27, 28, 29. Drawn. Western Australia* 480 for eight dec. (M. E. K. Hussey 48, R. J. Campbell 34, J. L. Langer 60, D. R. Martyn 122, T. M. Moody 57, A. C. Gilchrist 102; P. Wilson three for 99, P. E. McIntyre three for 130); South Australia 282 (S. A. Deitz 60, D. S. Lehmann 38, J. N. Gillespie 51, B. A. Johnson 67; M. J. Nicholson three for 73, G. G. Swan three for 51) and 358 for five (S. A. Deitz 31, D. S. Lehmann 67, J. M. Vaughan 131 not out, B. E. Young 71 not out). *Western Australia 2 pts.*

Gilchrist scored 101 before lunch on the second day.

At Albion, November 5, 6, 7, 8. Queensland won by ten wickets. Victoria* 249 (J. L. Arnberger 64, M. P. Mott 31, M. Klinger 38, I. J. Harvey 35; A. J. Bichel four for 69, A. C. Dale three for 50) and 326 (S. A. J. Craig 35, B. J. Hodge 101 not out, I. J. Harvey 100; A. C. Dale three for 87, J. H. Dawes six for 98); Queensland 347 (M. L. Hayden 81, M. L. Love 51, A. Symonds 49, W. A. Seccombe 35; P. R. Reiffel three for 33, M. L. Lewis four for 74) and 229 for no wkt (M. L. Hayden 118 not out, J. P. Maher 103 not out). *Queensland 6 pts.*

Seccombe took six catches in Victoria's first innings; his first in the second took him to 300 first-class dismissals. Stuart Law overtook Allan Border (7,661) as Queensland's second leading run-scorer. Hayden and Maher achieved the target of 229 in 59 overs in 44.4.

At Hobart, November 7, 8, 9, 10. Drawn. Tasmania 362 (J. Cox 106, R. T. Ponting 187 not out; B. Lee three for 94, N. W. Bracken three for 102) and 315 for three (J. Cox 128 not out, M. J. Di Venuto 86, D. J. Marsh 60 not out); New South Wales* 464 (M. J. Slater 100, C. J. Richards 69, M. E. Waugh 152, D. A. Nash 32, N. W. Bracken 30; D. J. Marsh four for 80). *New South Wales 2 pts.*

Cox hit a hundred in each innings for the fourth time, three of them against New South Wales. In the first innings, when five Tasmanians made ducks, he added 242 with Ponting and passed 8,000 Shield/Pura runs; in the second, he added 195 with Di Venuto and passed David Boon's Tasmanian record of 9,096 runs.

At Bankstown, November 15, 16, 17, 18. New South Wales v South Australia. Abandoned.

This was only the third wholly abandoned match in Australian first-class interstate cricket since a time limit was introduced for the Sheffield Shield in 1927-28.

At Hobart, November 19, 20, 21, 22. Drawn. Tasmania 446 for nine dec. (J. Cox 87, D. J. Marsh 110, S. Young 43, S. P. Kremerskothen 81, S. G. Clingeleffer 50; B. P. Julian three for 94, B. J. Oldroyd four for 90) and 238 for nine dec. (J. Cox 87, M. J. Di Venuto 51, S. Young 48; B. J. Oldroyd three for 87, T. M. Moody three for 23); Western Australia* 298 for seven dec. (M. E. K. Hussey 35, S. M. Katich 38, D. R. Martyn 122, M. J. Walsh 50; S. Young three for 37) and 373 for nine (S. M. Katich 152, D. R. Martyn 90, B. P. Julian 39; D. J. Saker five for 98, S. P. Kremerskothen three for 64). *Tasmania 2 pts.*

Moody took his 350th first-class wicket.

At Melbourne, November 23, 24, 25, 26. Victoria won by 108 runs. Victoria 231 (S. A. J. Craig 30, B. J. Hodge 104, I. J. Harvey 31; B. A. Swain three for 33, P. Wilson four for 49) and 259 (J. L. Arnberger 56, M. P. Mott 88; P. Wilson three for 43, B. A. Swain three for 66); South Australia* 96 (S. A. Deitz 32; M. W. H. Inness six for 26) and 286 (G. S. Blewett 49, S. A. Deitz 114, D. S. Lehmann 43; C. R. Miller three for 90). *Victoria 6 pts.*

The match was played on a drop-in pitch. Hodge scored his third century in successive first-class innings (including one against the West Indians) and Inness claimed six for 26 for the second time in a week. Deitz's 114 took 461 minutes and 360 balls; he reached his maiden hundred in 438 minutes (338 balls), the slowest century for South Australia. Peter McIntyre, nursing a knee injury, was allowed to sit out between overs when bowling in Victoria's second innings.

At Melbourne, November 29, 30, December 1, 2. Drawn. Victoria* 384 for nine dec. (J. L. Arnberger 100, B. J. Hodge 111, I. J. Harvey 93; A. C. Dale three for 71, S. J. O'Leary four for 105); Queensland 184 (M. L. Love 30; P. R. Reiffel four for 50) and 380 for six (J. P. Maher 98, M. L. Love 126, S. G. Law 74 not out, A. Symonds 39). *Victoria 2 pts.*

Hodge hit his fourth hundred in five innings and four matches.

At North Sydney, December 1, 2, 3, 4. New South Wales won by 51 runs. New South Wales* 226 (M. A. Higgs 34, B. J. Haddin 87; J. Angel three for 53, B. P. Julian three for 70, B. J. Oldroyd three for 45) and 327 (G. J. Mail 92, M. G. Bevan 57, C. J. Richards 66, D. A. Nash 32; J. Angel three for 64, B. P. Julian three for 73); Western Australia 413 (R. J. Campbell 35, S. M. Katich 117, D. R. Martyn 92, B. P. Julian 76, J. Angel 37; N. W. Bracken three for 121) and 89 (B. P. Julian 32; D. A. Nash three for 31, N. W. Bracken five for 22). *New South Wales 6 pts, Western Australia 2 pts.*

Floodlights were used on the first afternoon. Katich scored 103 before lunch on the second day.

At Adelaide, December 1, 2, 3, 4. South Australia won by 161 runs. South Australia* 316 (G. S. Blewett 70, J. M. Vaughan 63, B. A. Johnson 68, G. A. Manou 53; B. S. Targett five for 62) and

179 (G. S. Blewett 43, J. M. Vaughan 85 not out; D. J. Saker four for 49, D. J. Marsh three for 53); Tasmania 159 for nine dec. (S. Young 50 not out) and 175 (S. P. Kremerskothen 37, D. J. Saker 34 not out; M. A. Harrity three for 51, P. E. McIntyre four for 63). *South Australia 6 pts.*

At Melbourne, December 14, 15, 16, 17. Victoria won by 179 runs. Victoria 322 (M. T. G. Elliott 79, M. P. Mott 78, B. J. Hodge 30, J. M. Davison 33; D. J. Saker four for 102, S. Young three for 21) and 192 for five dec. (J. L. Arnberger 67 not out, B. J. Hodge 81); Tasmania* 162 (M. J. Di Venuto 66, S. P. Kremerskothen 41; M. W. H. Inness three for 26, M. L. Lewis three for 39) and 173 (S. P. Kremerskothen 41, S. G. Clingeleffer 38; P. R. Reiffel three for 32, I. J. Harvey three for 17). *Victoria 6 pts.*

Reiffel became Victoria's second-leading wicket-taker, with 317. Team-mate Darren Berry made his 500th first-class dismissal. Tasmanian openers Dene Hills and Jamie Cox both made pairs – the first instance in an Australian first-class match.

At Brisbane, December 15, 16, 17, 18. Drawn. Queensland 378 (J. P. Maher 62, M. L. Love 59, S. G. Law 87, A. Symonds 85, Extras 31; B. A. Swain four for 96); South Australia* 126 (D. S. Lehmann 57; A. C. Dale four for 42, J. H. Dawes three for 41, B. N. Creevey three for 42) and 493 for five dec. (S. A. Deitz 106, G. S. Blewett 260 not out, B. A. Johnson 45, D. S. Lehmann 47 not out). *Queensland 2 pts.*

Lehmann passed 15,000 runs in first-class cricket. Blewett's 260 not out lasted 629 minutes and 524 balls, and included 30 fours and two sixes; he and Deitz added 230 for South Australia's second wicket.

At Perth, December 15, 16, 17. Western Australia won by nine wickets. New South Wales 131 (J. Angel three for 39, G. G. Swan three for 34, B. P. Julian three for 28) and 130 (M. G. Bevan 36; T. M. Moody five for 26); Western Australia* 189 (S. M. Katich 40, M. J. North 47; D. A. Nash four for 57, S. Lee four for 43) and 73 for one. *Western Australia 6 pts.*

Mike Hussey passed 5,000 first-class runs.

At Hobart, January 3, 4, 5. Queensland won by an innings and 144 runs. Tasmania 112 (M. S. Kasprowicz five for 29, J. H. Dawes four for 47) and 212 (J. Cox 32, S. Young 34; M. S. Kasprowicz three for 81, J. H. Dawes three for 39, S. J. O'Leary three for 62); Queensland* 468 for four dec. (J. L. Cassell 136, J. P. Maher 48, M. L. Love 172 not out, S. G. Law 49, A. Symonds 47). *Queensland 6 pts.*

Cassell, making his maiden hundred, and Love added 203 in four hours for Queensland's second wicket.

At Adelaide, January 4, 5, 6, 7. South Australia won by 168 runs. South Australia* 428 for nine dec. (D. A. Fitzgerald 107, G. S. Blewett 80, D. S. Lehmann 146; D. A. Nash three for 63, N. W. Bracken three for 66) and 237 for five dec. (D. A. Fitzgerald 51, G. S. Blewett 69, D. S. Lehmann 45 not out); New South Wales 265 (M. A. Higgs 33, B. J. Haddin 93, S. D. Bradstreet 36 not out; P. E. McIntyre five for 102, M. A. Harrity three for 31) and 232 (M. G. Bevan 37, M. A. Higgs 31, S. D. Bradstreet 60; P. Wilson four for 23). *South Australia 6 pts.*

Corey Richards of New South Wales made his second successive pair.

At Perth, January 4, 5, 6. Victoria won by 77 runs. Victoria* 254 (J. L. Arnberger 45, M. P. Mott 42, I. J. Harvey 41; B. P. Julian four for 87) and 239 (J. L. Arnberger 63, M. T. G. Elliott 30, C. J. Peake 33, D. S. Berry 33; J. Angel four for 60, S. J. Karppinen three for 34); Western Australia 235 (M. E. K. Hussey 35, M. W. Goodwin 59, M. J. North 54, Extras 40; S. K. Warne four for 53) and 181 (M. E. K. Hussey 42, S. M. Katich 72; S. K. Warne five for 49). *Victoria 6 pts.*

At Sydney, February 14, 15, 16, 17. Drawn. Tasmania* 369 (J. Cox 160, S. Young 67; N. W. Bracken four for 78, S. C. G. MacGill three for 117) and 306 (J. Cox 81, S. P. Kremerskothen 64, S. B. Tubb 42; S. C. G. MacGill five for 125); New South Wales 530 (G. J. Mail 176, M. G. Bevan 119, M. J. Clarke 41, B. J. Haddin 56; S. J. Jurgensen four for 113) and 18 for one. *New South Wales 2 pts.*

At Brisbane, February 18, 19, 20. Queensland won by eight wickets. Western Australia* 78 (J. H. Dawes six for 19) and 274 (S. M. Katich 101, M. W. Goodwin 31, T. M. Moody 32, M. J. Walsh

35; A. J. Bichel five for 74, A. C. Dale three for 56); Queensland 218 (M. L. Love 71, A. J. Bichel 38; T. M. Moody four for 38, B. P. Julian three for 59) and 135 for two (J. P. Maher 59, A. Symonds 39 not out). *Queensland 6 pts.*

At Adelaide, February 19, 20, 21, 22. Victoria won by five wickets. South Australia* 340 (D. A. Fitzgerald 50, G. S. Blewett 117, C. J. Davies 52 retired hurt; J. M. Davison four for 90) and 186 (G. S. Blewett 95, D. S. Lehmann 42; I. J. Harvey four for 19); Victoria 336 (M. T. G. Elliott 59, M. P. Mott 62, B. J. Hodge 46, I. J. Harvey 87, P. R. Reiffel 34; M. A. Harrity four for 55) and 191 for five (M. P. Mott 40, B. J. Hodge 36, M. Klinger 66 not out; P. E. McIntyre four for 62). *Victoria 6 pts, South Australia 2 pts.*

Lehmann became the second batsman to score 10,000 Shield/Pura runs, after Jamie Siddons; both played for Victoria and South Australia. South Australia's second innings collapsed from 164 for three to 186 all out. McIntyre took his 300th first-class wicket.

At Sydney, March 2, 3, 4, 5. New South Wales won by eight wickets. New South Wales* 499 for six dec. (G. J. Mail 71, M. G. Bevan 111, M. A. Higgs 181 not out, S. Lee 114; A. C. Dale three for 81) and 25 for two; Queensland 276 (J. L. Cassell 68, M. L. Love 46, A. Symonds 54; N. W. Bracken four for 44, S. C. G. MacGill three for 126) and 247 (J. L. Cassell 31, S. G. Law 98, B. P. Nash 44; S. C. G. MacGill three for 79, S. Lee three for ten). *New South Wales 6 pts.*

Higgs, making his maiden hundred, and Lee added 264 for New South Wales's fifth wicket. Law broke Allan Border's record of 115 catches for Queensland and later passed 16,000 first-class runs; when out, he demolished his stumps, without penalty. New South Wales wicket-keeper Brad Haddin was summoned by the Australian team in India after the third day; Graeme Rummans replaced him, batting on the final day after Mail had kept wicket.

At Hobart, March 2, 3, 4, 5. Tasmania won by six wickets. Victoria 393 for five dec. (M. T. G. Elliott 54, J. L. Arnberger 173, M. Klinger 99 not out; A. G. Downton four for 95) and 216 (J. L. Arnberger 33, M. T. G. Elliott 55, P. R. Reiffel 70; A. G. Downton four for 51); Tasmania* 324 for four dec. (D. F. Hills 120, J. Cox 41, M. J. Di Venuto 63, S. R. Watson 60) and 286 for four (J. Cox 139 not out, M. J. Di Venuto 60, D. J. Marsh 35). *Tasmania 6 pts, Victoria 2 pts.*

Reiffel declared with Klinger one short of a maiden hundred. Hills scored his 20th century. Elliott passed 10,000 first-class runs. Cox passed 1,000 first-class runs for the season.

At Perth, March 2, 3, 4, 5. Western Australia won by 36 runs. Western Australia* 474 for seven dec. (M. J. North 35, S. M. Katich 228 not out, T. M. Moody 55, B. P. Julian 78, M. J. Nicholson 32 not out; M. A. Harrity three for 115) and 160 for six dec. (M. E. K. Hussey 35, M. J. North 38); South Australia 256 (G. S. Blewett 138; J. Angel four for 41) and 342 (S. A. Deitz 66, G. S. Blewett 77, D. S. Lehmann 51, B. H. Higgins 59; M. J. Nicholson three for 80). *Western Australia 6 pts.*

Katich's career-best 228 not out lasted 458 minutes and 331 balls, included 42 fours, and took him past 1,000 first-class runs for the season. Moody reached 21,001 first-class runs in his 300th and, he said, final first-class match. Blewett hit his 30th first-class hundred and also passed 1,000 runs for the season. Western Australia wicket-keeper Mark Walsh took nine catches in the match.

At Sydney, March 9, 10, 11, 12. Drawn. Victoria* 409 (J. L. Arnberger 90, B. J. Hodge 125, M. Klinger 67, J. Moss 32; N. W. Bracken five for 68) and 21 for one; New South Wales 371 (M. G. Bevan 62, M. J. Clarke 106, S. Lee 94; J. M. Davison three for 101, C. L. White four for 65). *Victoria 2 pts.*

At Adelaide, March 9, 10, 11, 12. Queensland won by ten wickets. South Australia* 215 (S. A. Deitz 45, G. S. Blewett 88; A. J. Bichel three for 59, J. H. Dawes three for 43) and 280 (S. A. Deitz 32, M. J. Smith 76, D. S. Lehmann 45, N. T. Adcock 48; J. H. Dawes seven for 98); Queensland 475 for nine dec. (J. P. Maher 47, C. T. Perren 112, S. G. Law 161, A. J. Bichel 61, A. C. Dale 45 not out; P. E. McIntyre three for 139) and 24 for no wkt. *Queensland 6 pts.*

At Perth, March 9, 10, 11. Tasmania won by nine wickets. Western Australia 229 (M. E. K. Hussey 90, S. E. Marsh 46; D. G. Wright four for 65) and 139 (S. W. Meuleman 46; D. J. Saker three for 38); Tasmania* 280 (D. F. Hills 69, S. R. Watson 54, D. J. Marsh 34, S. P. Kremerskothen 37; J. Angel five for 78) and 89 for one (J. Cox 30 not out, M. J. Di Venuto 48 not out). *Tasmania 6 pts.*

Angel took his 400th first-class wicket.

At Brisbane, March 15, 16, 17. Queensland won by nine wickets. New South Wales 140 (M. J. Phelps 40, P. A. Jaques 40; A. C. Dale five for 37, J. H. Dawes four for 37) and 267 (M. J. Phelps 30, M. A. Higgs 37, G. C. Rummans 46, D. A. Nash 35; A. C. Dale four for 78, A. A. Noffke three for 61); Queensland* 344 (J. P. Maher 113, S. G. Law 63, W. A. Seccombe 52; S. C. G. MacGill five for 78) and 64 for one (J. P. Maher 39 not out). *Queensland 6 pts.*

Shane Lee withdrew with a virus and debutant Philip Jaques was summoned to replace him, arriving at 70 for eight; he opened in the second innings. Maher passed 1,000 first-class runs for the season. Seccombe made six dismissals in New South Wales's second innings and nine in the match, passing 50 for the season. In New South Wales's first innings, five penalty runs were awarded when the ball hit a towel on the field.

At Hobart, March 15, 16, 17, 18. Tasmania won by an innings and 41 runs. Tasmania 413 for five dec. (D. F. Hills 50, J. Cox 102, S. R. Watson 105, S. Young 83 not out, S. P. Kremerskothen 46 not out; M. J. Smith four for 81); South Australia* 185 (B. H. Higgins 52, G. A. Manou 38; D. G. Wright three for 42, S. Young three for 24) and 187 (B. H. Higgins 65, N. T. Adcock 32; D. G. Wright four for 54, S. Young four for 33). *Tasmania 6 pts.*

Cox's 40th first-class hundred took him past 1,000 Pura runs for the season. Young became Tasmania's leading first-class wicket-taker, passing Colin Miller's 218. Tasmania's Michael Di Venuto took his 100th first-class catch.

At Melbourne, March 15, 16, 17, 18. Drawn. Western Australia* 215 (S. M. Katich 78, M. J. North 51, M. J. Nicholson 48; M. W. H. Inness three for 46, B. J. Hodge three for 21) and 295 for four dec. (M. E. K. Hussey 137, S. M. Katich 102, M. J. North 30); Victoria 219 for seven dec. (B. J. Hodge 81, P. J. Roach 51 not out; B. A. Williams three for 31) and 287 for seven (M. T. G. Elliott 40, M. P. Mott 154, J. Moss 62; J. Angel three for 62). *Victoria 2 pts.*

Hodge passed 1,000 first-class runs for the season. Victoria were only five short of victory.

FINAL

QUEENSLAND v VICTORIA

At Brisbane, March 23, 24, 25, 26, 27. Queensland won by four wickets. Toss: Victoria.

Queensland retained the state title in style, winning shortly after lunch on the last day. Victoria needed their first victory at Brisbane for 17 years to win the Cup, and their prospects sank when they were bowled out in five hours, having chosen to bat. Queensland's four-man pace attack was irresistible; Noffke took five in an innings for the first time, helped by a 17-ball spell of three for nought. Next day, he added a career-best 43, batting over four hours as night-watchman. However, Lewis's spirited seam bowling, supported by Hodge's deceptive spin, restricted Queensland's lead to 66. Victoria had regained a foothold, but their batsmen made slow headway against defensive fields. Arnberger just had time to pass 1,000 for the season; Elliott took six and three-quarter hours to reach 98, then was becalmed for another 45 minutes before driving to cover. His 73-run partnership with Mott had occupied 46 overs and three hours – failing to impress a Sunday crowd of nearly 5,000. Berry offered more entertainment on Monday, hitting nine fours, and Queensland were finally left to make 224. Apart from Lewis, who became erratic, the Victorians gave little away. Early on the last morning, however, Law survived a disputed catch in the gully off his first ball, the television footage proving inconclusive. Reiffel was fined $A200 for expressing his disappointment. Law was later caught off a no-ball, and dropped twice, but went on to hit the winning boundary.

Man of the Match: A. A. Noffke.

Close of play: First day, Queensland 37-1 (Maher 22*, Noffke 4*); Second day, Victoria 2-0 (Arnberger 2*, Elliott 0*); Third day, Victoria 172-4 (Elliott 88*, Moss 5*); Fourth day, Queensland 137-2 (Love 50*, Perren 25*).

Victoria

M. T. G. Elliott c Maher b Bichel	3	– (2) c Cassell b Bichel	98
J. L. Arnberger c Seccombe b Dawes	63	– (1) c Seccombe b Dale	33
M. P. Mott c Seccombe b Bichel	4	– b Dale	19
B. J. Hodge c Seccombe b Noffke	47	– c Perren b Bichel	3
M. Klinger c Seccombe b Noffke	0	– lbw b Dawes	9
J. Moss b Noffke	0	– c Seccombe b Noffke	19
†D. S. Berry c Law b Bichel	2	– c Dawes b Bichel	61
*P. R. Reiffel b Noffke	23	– run out	18
J. M. Davison c Perren b Dawes	10	– c Perren b Noffke	10
M. L. Lewis c Dale b Noffke	11	– not out	2
M. W. H. Inness not out	1	– c Seccombe b Bichel	0
L-b 6, n-b 6	12	L-b 1, w 1, n-b 15	17
1/4 2/16 3/89 4/89 5/89 6/112 7/149 8/153 9/175	176	1/49 2/122 3/140 4/149 5/198 6/215 7/260 8/287 9/289	289

Bowling: *First Innings*—Bichel 17–4–42–3; Dale 23–10–34–0; Dawes 17.4–4–53–2; Noffke 18–7–41–5. *Second Innings*—Bichel 30.4–12–44–4; Dawes 28–11–55–1; Noffke 28–7–79–2; Dale 39–14–73–2; Law 7–0–37–0.

Queensland

J. L. Cassell c Elliott b Lewis	9	– lbw b Inness	15
J. P. Maher c Berry b Lewis	25	– c Berry b Inness	37
A. A. Noffke c Elliott b Hodge	43		
M. L. Love c Berry b Lewis	24	– (3) c Mott b Reiffel	52
C. T. Perren c Mott b Lewis	56	– (4) run out	41
*S. G. Law lbw b Hodge	0	– (5) not out	47
B. P. Nash b Reiffel	10	– (6) c Berry b Moss	0
†W. A. Seccombe not out	33	– (7) c Hodge b Inness	12
A. J. Bichel c Hodge b Moss	28	– (8) not out	6
A. C. Dale lbw b Hodge	4		
J. H. Dawes b Lewis	0		
L-b 2, n-b 8	10	B 4, l-b 4, n-b 6	14
1/22 2/41 3/88 4/152 5/152 6/174 7/174 8/224 9/239	242	1/27 2/76 3/139 4/169 5/169 6/197	(6 wkts) 224

Bowling: *First Innings*—Reiffel 17–4–45–1; Inness 22–9–51–0; Lewis 23–9–57–5; Davison 12–4–29–0; Moss 9–1–24–1; Hodge 12–7–19–3; Mott 4–1–15–0. *Second Innings*—Lewis 18.3–1–82–0; Inness 25–8–48–3; Hodge 5–0–16–0; Reiffel 16–4–34–1; Davison 8–3–19–0; Moss 8–3–17–1.

Umpires: S. J. Davis and S. J. A. Taufel.
Third umpire: P. D. Parker. Referee: P. J. Burge.

CHAMPIONS

Sheffield Shield

1892-93	Victoria
1893-94	South Australia
1894-95	Victoria
1895-96	New South Wales
1896-97	New South Wales
1897-98	Victoria
1898-99	Victoria
1899-1900	New South Wales
1900-01	Victoria
1901-02	New South Wales
1902-03	New South Wales
1903-04	New South Wales
1904-05	New South Wales
1905-06	New South Wales
1906-07	New South Wales
1907-08	Victoria
1908-09	New South Wales
1909-10	South Australia
1910-11	New South Wales
1911-12	New South Wales
1912-13	South Australia

1913-14	New South Wales
1914-15	Victoria
1915-19	No competition
1919-20	New South Wales
1920-21	New South Wales
1921-22	Victoria
1922-23	New South Wales
1923-24	Victoria
1924-25	Victoria
1925-26	New South Wales
1926-27	South Australia
1927-28	Victoria
1928-29	New South Wales
1929-30	Victoria
1930-31	Victoria
1931-32	New South Wales
1932-33	New South Wales
1933-34	Victoria
1934-35	Victoria
1935-36	South Australia
1936-37	Victoria
1937-38	New South Wales
1938-39	South Australia
1939-40	New South Wales
1940-46	No competition
1946-47	Victoria
1947-48	Western Australia
1948-49	New South Wales
1949-50	New South Wales
1950-51	Victoria
1951-52	New South Wales
1952-53	South Australia
1953-54	New South Wales
1954-55	New South Wales
1955-56	New South Wales
1956-57	New South Wales
1957-58	New South Wales
1958-59	New South Wales
1959-60	New South Wales
1960-61	New South Wales
1961-62	New South Wales
1962-63	Victoria
1963-64	South Australia
1964-65	New South Wales
1965-66	New South Wales
1966-67	Victoria
1967-68	Western Australia
1968-69	South Australia
1969-70	Victoria
1970-71	South Australia
1971-72	Western Australia
1972-73	Western Australia
1973-74	Victoria
1974-75	Western Australia
1975-76	South Australia
1976-77	Western Australia
1977-78	Western Australia
1978-79	Victoria
1979-80	Victoria
1980-81	Western Australia
1981-82	South Australia
1982-83	New South Wales
1983-84	Western Australia
1984-85	New South Wales
1985-86	New South Wales
1986-87	Western Australia
1987-88	Western Australia
1988-89	Western Australia
1989-90	New South Wales
1990-91	Victoria
1991-92	Western Australia
1992-93	New South Wales
1993-94	New South Wales
1994-95	Queensland
1995-96	South Australia
1996-97	Queensland
1997-98	Western Australia
1998-99	Western Australia

Pura Milk Cup

1999-2000 Queensland

Pura Cup

2000-01 Queensland

New South Wales have won the title 42 times, Victoria 25, Western Australia 15, South Australia 13, Queensland 4, Tasmania 0.

MERCANTILE MUTUAL CUP, 2000-01

Note: Matches in this section were not first-class.

	Played	*Won*	*Lost*	*No Result*	*Bonus points*	*Points*	*Net run-rate*
Western Australia . . .	10	6	3	1	3	29	0.18
New South Wales . . .	10	6	4	0	2	26	0.24
South Australia.	10	6	4	0	1	25	−0.08
Queensland	10	4	5	1	2	20	−0.14
Tasmania.	10	4	6	0	3	19	0.14
Victoria.	10	3	7	0	2	14	−0.29

Final

At Perth, February 25. New South Wales won by six wickets. Western Australia* 272 for seven (50 overs) (T. M. Moody 78, M. W. Goodwin 38, M. E. K. Hussey 84 not out); New South Wales 276 for four (48.2 overs) (M. J. Clarke 57, M. G. Bevan 135 not out, G. C. Rummans 30 not out).

PURA CUP PLAYER OF THE YEAR

The Pura Cup Player of the Year award for 2000-01 was won by Jamie Cox of Tasmania, who was one point ahead of Western Australia's Simon Katich. The award, instituted in 1975-76, was adjudicated by the umpires over the course of the season. The umpires standing in each of the 30 Pura Cup matches (excluding the final) each allocated marks of 3, 2 and 1 to the three players who most impressed them during the game. The Mercantile Mutual Player of the Year award was shared by Darren Lehmann of South Australia and Shaun Young of Tasmania.

SHEFFIELD SHIELD/PURA CUP FINALS

1982-83	NEW SOUTH WALES* beat Western Australia by 54 runs.
1983-84	WESTERN AUSTRALIA beat Queensland by four wickets.
1984-85	NEW SOUTH WALES beat Queensland by one wicket.
1985-86	NEW SOUTH WALES drew with Queensland.
1986-87	WESTERN AUSTRALIA drew with Victoria.
1987-88	WESTERN AUSTRALIA beat Queensland by five wickets.
1988-89	WESTERN AUSTRALIA drew with South Australia.
1989-90	NEW SOUTH WALES beat Queensland by 345 runs.
1990-91	VICTORIA beat New South Wales by eight wickets.
1991-92	WESTERN AUSTRALIA beat New South Wales by 44 runs.
1992-93	NEW SOUTH WALES beat Queensland by eight wickets.
1993-94	NEW SOUTH WALES beat Tasmania by an innings and 61 runs.
1994-95	QUEENSLAND beat South Australia by an innings and 101 runs.
1995-96	SOUTH AUSTRALIA drew with Western Australia.
1996-97	QUEENSLAND* beat Western Australia by 160 runs.
1997-98	WESTERN AUSTRALIA beat Tasmania by seven wickets.
1998-99	WESTERN AUSTRALIA* beat Queensland by an innings and 31 runs.
1999-2000	QUEENSLAND drew with Victoria.
2000-01	QUEENSLAND beat Victoria by four wickets.

Note: The team that finished top of the table had home advantage over the runners-up. In a drawn final, the home team won the title.

* *Denotes victory for the away team.*

ALLAN BORDER MEDAL

Australian captain Steve Waugh won the Allan Border Medal in February 2001 by one vote from his twin, Mark. Team-mates, umpires and journalists voted for the best Australian international player of the past 12 months. The previous winner was Glenn McGrath, who was named One-day International Player of the Year this time. Colin Miller was Test Player of the Year after a tie-breaker separated him from Steve Waugh and Michael Slater. Darren Lehmann of South Australia was State Player of the Year for the second time running, and Nathan Bracken of New South Wales won the Sir Donald Bradman Young Player of the Year award.

CRICKET IN SOUTH AFRICA, 2000-01

By COLIN BRYDEN and ANDREW SAMSON

Graeme Smith

At first glance, it might have looked as though the traditional powers of South African cricket held sway in 2000-01, with Western Province winning the first-class SuperSport Series and KwaZulu-Natal the limited-overs Standard Bank Cup. In truth, though, it was a strange season, albeit a happier one overall as the national side recovered from the shock of the Cronje affair to win series against New Zealand, Sri Lanka and West Indies. Western Province were worthy winners of the four-day tournament, but neither KwaZulu-Natal nor defending champions Gauteng qualified for the Super Eight stage. Even more astonishingly, these two giants were bottom of the three-team Shield Series, very much a consolation tournament, which was won by Griqualand West.

For Gauteng, formerly the mighty Transvaal and now marketed as the Highveld Strikers, it was a disastrous campaign. Having won the SuperSport Series in 1999-2000, they plummeted down the lists to be ranked 11th of the 11 provinces. The steady player exodus of recent years continued, and off-field rumblings culminated in the resignation of chief executive Ziggy Wadvalla.

Western Province were at the opposite end of the seesaw. Champions in 1998-99, they had sunk to eighth the following year, when their poor showing led to a full-scale inquiry. They had strengthened their playing staff with three good recruits: former Zimbabwe all-rounder Neil Johnson, left-arm opening bowler Charl Willoughby (from Boland) and the highly promising 19-year-old left-hand batsman, Graeme Smith (from Gauteng). Under new leadership, with Hylton "H.D." Ackerman as captain and respected former international Eric Simons joining Vincent Barnes as joint-coach, Western Province won seven of their nine matches – including the final against Border by an innings and 26 runs.

It seemed not to matter whether Western Province's international stars were available. The batting was so sound that only once did they fail to top 300 in the first innings. Ackerman thrived on responsibility, having his best season since 1997-98, when he scored 1,373 first-class runs, a South African record, and won four Test caps. He was named "Cavalier of the Season". Smith and another tall left-hander, Andrew Puttick, showed a maturity and an appetite for runs that could take them both to higher honours, while the experienced Lloyd Ferreira, who was selected only for the last four matches, made a double-century in his first turn at bat and headed the domestic averages. The bowling was well balanced, despite the long-term finger injury that restricted Johnson to occasional off-spin. Claude Henderson, the orthodox slow left-armer who joined from Boland two years earlier, overshadowed the unorthodox Test wrist-spinner, Paul Adams, with 36 wickets at 22.25 in seven matches; Adams, who played only five before flying to the West Indies, had to be satisfied with 18 at 32.33. Another promising young left-armer, Paul Harris, made his debut in March.

One of the requirements of the United Cricket Board's transformation policy was that all provincial teams should include at least two "players of colour". This was never a problem for Western Province, who had as many as five in their side, entirely on merit. Other teams had more difficulty. Northerns went into the closing stages of the Standard Bank Cup with two black players who neither batted nor bowled in the best-of-three semi-finals (which they won) or the final (which they lost). For 2001-02, the quota was to be lifted to three, adding to the market value of capable non-white cricketers, and there were several off-season transfers. Northerns signed Eastern Province off-spinner Shafiek Abrahams, who played a one-day international in November, and fast bowler Mulligan George, originally from Western Province, who had just spent a season at Gauteng.

Border reached the SuperSport final for the third year running, but lost yet again. It was a disappointing end to a campaign during which they won all four of their Super Eight matches by convincing margins. Barbadian Vasbert Drakes led the tournament's wicket-takers for the third successive season, although 41 was well short of his record haul of 60 the previous year. Border, however, lacked strength in depth, especially with their Test players, Mark Boucher and Makhaya Ntini, available for only two matches each. The batting was carried by captain Pieter Strydom and the much-improved Steven Pope, but injuries meant that their seam-based attack relied too much on Drakes. There was further disappointment for Border when they finished second on the Standard Bank Cup log but were knocked out in the semi-finals by Northerns.

The surprise packet of the season was the Easterns team, representing the East Rand gold-mining and industrial area, and long regarded as minnows in comparison with neighbouring Gauteng and Northerns. They bought shrewdly, attracting international all-rounder Derek Crookes, Kenny Benjamin, the former West Indies fast bowler, and, in mid-season, batsman Andre Seymore, all from Gauteng, while 37-year-old Mike Rindel joined from Northerns. The experience of the imports, blended with some talented local youngsters, proved a potent mix, well managed by coach Ray Jennings; Easterns finished third in the Super Eight.

Andre Nel, a raw-boned fast bowler, played himself on to the West Indian tour with some fiery performances, having made headlines when he felled Allan Donald, a boyhood hero, with a bouncer during a match against Free State at Benoni. Free State alleged that Jennings had offered his bowlers money to hit Donald and, after the United Cricket Board held an inquiry, Jennings was summoned to a disciplinary hearing, charged with bringing the game into disrepute. It was cancelled, however, when Jennings stated that an offer made in jest "was perhaps taken seriously by certain of the younger players", and he regretted any such "misinterpretation".

Notwithstanding problems with the quota system, Northerns finished fourth in the Super Eight, as well as reaching the limited-overs final. With Neil McKenzie becoming a regular member of the national team, Gerald Dros proved a capable captain – and scored a maiden hundred in his eighth season. In Jacques Rudolph and Johan Myburgh, moreover, they had two of the most exciting young batsmen in the country. Rudolph scored 638 first-class runs, and they formed a thrilling opening combination in limited-overs matches. Seamers Greg Smith and Steve Elworthy claimed 30 wickets each, though Smith's decision to claim a British passport in order to play for Nottinghamshire meant that he officially became a foreign player.

Another left-armer, Neil Carter of Boland, also decided to seek a career as an England-qualified county cricketer. He and Henry Williams had led Boland's attack, with 54 SuperSport wickets between them. Justin Ontong began to fulfil his exciting potential, making an overdue maiden first-class century, and joined the national one-day team in the West Indies; Henry Davids also showed promise as a batsman. But Boland failed to match their achievements of the previous season, when they won the Standard Bank Cup and were third in the SuperSport Series.

Free State were inconsistent, and welcomed Donald's decision to make himself available on a regular basis in 2001-02. They appointed a young captain in 24-year-old Gerard Brophy, who did a fair job with a team in which lack of experience was a problem. Three of the senior players – batsmen Louis Wilkinson and Gerry Liebenberg, and all-rounder Kosie Venter – made substantial contributions, while two young fast bowlers, Victor Mpitsang and Dewald Pretorius, collected 33 and 37 wickets respectively.

North West achieved their modest ambition of reaching the Super Eight, but were plagued by unreliable top-order batting. Mark Lavine, the former Barbados all-rounder who had become a naturalised South African citizen, had an excellent season, with 477 runs and 30 wickets. It was a major shock when the province heard in May that he had collapsed and died in England – aged 28 – after scoring a century in a club match. Seamer Garth Roe gave Lavine much-needed support, taking 40 wickets. Alfonso Thomas scored 531 first-class runs, a seasonal record for North West, and averaged 46.55 in the SuperSport Series, though he was never promoted above No. 8. Thomas and Roe equalled the South African tenth-wicket record when they added 174 against Griqualand West.

Eastern Province won only one first-class match, against North West, but reached the one-day semi-finals. Their bowling, potentially strong, was stricken by injuries and loss of form, while the batting was inconsistent despite some significant efforts from captain Carl Bradfield. Justin Kemp was the province's shining light: a tall all-rounder, he forced his way into the South African Test and one-day teams. During a career-best 188, he hit the first five balls of an over from North West off-spinner Morne Strydom for six.

Griqualand West had the dubious honour of winning the three-team SuperSport Shield, played home and away over three days each. All but one of the Shield games were drawn; Griquas beat Gauteng by a single wicket. They had several disruptions, with Mickey Arthur deciding to retire after three games to concentrate on his duties as coach, and Martyn Gidley giving up the captaincy in a (successful) attempt to regain batting form. Wicket-keeper Wendell Bossenger took over and was able to inject new spirit into the side. Pieter Koortzen had a fine season, especially in the limited-overs game, in which he scored two centuries and two 99s. Deon Kruis took 46 first-class wickets, more than anyone else in the country.

KwaZulu-Natal failed to win a first-class match, but their one-day form was excellent. While bowling was their main weakness, much of the batting was disappointing as well. Jon Kent headed the batting averages, and was also their leading seam bowler; unorthodox slow left-armer Goolam Bodi took most wickets. In limited-overs cricket, however, they won the four-team SuperSport Challenge at the start of the season, and their victory in the Standard Bank Cup took them to Perth in Australia for a tournament between the limited-overs champions of Australia, South Africa, India and New Zealand. Doug Watson and Ashraf Mall batted solidly, and there were valuable all-round efforts from Kent, Bodi, Wade Wingfield and Eldine Baptiste. Former West Indies Test player Baptiste retired in March after a career spanning more than two decades, which brought him 8,070 runs and 723 wickets. He was appointed coach.

Gauteng's woes continued, as they finished bottom of their pool – not helped by the washout of their match at Paarl – and then the Shield Series. A capable team could be fielded from players who have left the Wanderers in recent years; the trend was set to continue with Sven Koenig, the country's leading run-scorer in 2000-01 with 789 at 60.69, deciding to try his luck in England. Alan Kourie, the tough former Transvaal all-rounder, was appointed coach for 2001-02, a move which Gauteng hoped would be a first step towards reviving their champion form of two years before.

With the 2003 World Cup drawing nearer, every one of the 11 unions hosted a limited-overs international during the season, with only Cape Town getting two. It was the first time South Africa had played internationals at Potchefstroom, Benoni, Kimberley or Paarl, and with some grounds needing to be upgraded before the World Cup, 35 million rands were set aside for this purpose. – C.B.

FIRST-CLASS AVERAGES, 2000-01

BATTING

(Qualification: 6 innings, average 40.00)

	M	*I*	*NO*	*R*	*HS*	*100s*	*Avge*
L. D. Ferreira (*W. Province*)	4	6	0	397	201	1	66.16
N. D. McKenzie (*Northerns*)	9	14	3	672	123	3	61.09
S. G. Koenig (*Gauteng*)	7	13	0	789	155	3	60.69
J. H. Kallis (*W. Province*)	8	13	1	671	160	1	55.91
G. Kirsten (*W. Province*)	6	10	1	496	180	1	55.11
A. G. Prince (*W. Province*)	8	14	4	539	120*	1	53.90
P. R. Adams (*W. Province*)	5	7	4	159	61*	0	53.00
N. Boje (*Free State*)	7	9	1	375	105	1	46.87
H. D. Ackerman (*W. Province*)	9	16	3	606	128	3	46.61
D. J. J. de Vos (*Northerns*)	3	6	1	233	97	0	46.60
G. F. J. Liebenberg (*Free State*)	8	13	0	595	202	1	45.76
D. N. Crookes (*Easterns*)	8	16	1	671	117	1	44.73
J. C. Kent (*KwaZulu-Natal*)	7	13	3	435	178*	1	43.50
L. J. Wilkinson (*Free State*)	9	15	0	642	169	1	42.80
M. V. Boucher (*Border*)	8	11	3	341	92	0	42.62
G. C. Smith (*W. Province*)	9	16	0	676	183	2	42.25
J. L. Ontong (*Boland*)	9	15	2	546	131*	1	42.00
J. M. Henderson (*Boland*)	8	15	1	584	98	0	41.71
J. M. Kemp (*E. Province*)	7	11	0	455	188	1	41.36
A. C. Thomas (*North West*)	10	18	5	531	106*	1	40.84
A. G. Puttick (*W. Province*)	7	12	1	441	153*	1	40.09

* *Signifies not out.*

BOWLING

(Qualification: 25 wickets)

	O	*M*	*R*	*W*	*BB*	*5W/i*	*Avge*
G. A. Roe (*North West*)	291.1	92	631	40	7-47	3	15.77
K. C. G. Benjamin (*Easterns*)	190.4	45	549	29	6-73	1	18.93
J. M. Kemp (*E. Province*)	241.3	69	552	29	6-56	2	19.03
S. M. Pollock (*KwaZulu-Natal*)	253.2	98	515	27	6-30	1	19.07
M. Ntini (*Border*)	268.2	89	688	36	6-59	2	19.11
A. C. Dawson (*W. Province*)	238.2	74	583	27	5-51	1	21.59
H. S. Williams (*Boland*)	245.2	70	629	29	6-40	4	21.68
C. M. Willoughby (*W. Province*)	298.5	107	683	31	5-26	1	22.03
P. V. Mpitsang (*Free State*)	268.1	62	733	33	5-24	3	22.21
C. W. Henderson (*W. Province*)	400.3	138	801	36	5-6	3	22.25
G. J. Kruis (*Griqualand W.*)	433	118	1,083	46	5-50	2	23.54
S. Elworthy (*Northerns*)	243.2	65	711	30	5-41	2	23.70
V. C. Drakes (*Border*)	368	100	975	41	5-80	1	23.78
D. Pretorius (*Free State*)	276.3	57	881	37	4-51	0	23.81
G. H. Bodi (*KwaZulu-Natal*)	239.3	46	750	29	6-63	1	25.86
D. H. Townsend (*Northerns*)	239.2	63	761	29	5-49	1	26.24
J. F. Venter (*Free State*)	289.2	66	858	31	6-90	2	27.67
A. C. Thomas (*North West*)	292	84	788	28	6-26	1	28.14
Z. A. Abrahim (*Griqualand W.*)	273.1	58	790	28	5-22	1	28.21
G. J. Smith (*Northerns*)	330.4	87	869	30	5-25	1	28.96
N. M. Carter (*Boland*)	255.4	53	839	28	6-63	2	29.96
M. J. Lavine (*North West*)	323	80	995	30	6-53	3	33.16
G. T. Love (*Border*)	372	99	979	28	7-116	1	34.96

SUPERSPORT SERIES, 2000-01

First Round

Pool A	Played	Won	Lost	Drawn	Bonus Points Batting	Bonus Points Bowling	Points
Northerns	5	3	0	2	13	17	60
Free State	5	2	1	2	16	15	51
Boland	5	2	1	2*	8	16	44
North West	5	1	3	1	10	19	39
Griqualand West	5	0	3	2	11	18	29
Gauteng	5	1	1	3*	7	8	25

* *Includes one abandoned match.*

Pool B	Played	Won	Lost	Drawn	Bonus Points Batting	Bonus Points Bowling	Points
Western Province	4	3	0	1	14	14	58
Easterns	4	2	2	0	7	14	41
Border	4	1	1	2	10	13	33
Eastern Province	4	0	2	2	12	16	28
KwaZulu-Natal	4	0	1	3	7	14	21

The top four teams from each pool advanced to the Super Eight; the remaining three contested the Shield Series.

Super Eight	Played	Won	Lost	Drawn	Bonus Points Batting	Bonus Points Bowling	Points
Western Province	7	6	0	1	30	21	111
Border	7	5	1	1	16	26	92
Easterns	7	4	3	0	14	23	77
Northerns	7	2	3	2	18	23	61
Boland	7	2	3	2	13	26	59
Free State	7	2	4	1	12	26	58
North West	7	1	5	1	16	26	52
Eastern Province	7	1	4	2	14	24	48

Super Eight teams carried forward results and points gained against fellow-qualifiers in the first round, but not those gained against the teams eliminated.

Final

Western Province beat Border by an innings and 26 runs.

Shield Series	Played	Won	Lost	Drawn	Bonus Points Batting	Bonus Points Bowling	Points
Griqualand West	4	1	0	3	11	15	41.80
KwaZulu-Natal	4	0	0	4	13	14	32.25
Gauteng	4	0	1	3	13	12	30.00

* *Teams carried forward their average points gained per match in the first round.*

Outright win = 10 pts.
Bonus points awarded for the first 100 overs of each team's first innings. One batting point was awarded for the first 150 runs and for every subsequent 50. One bowling point was awarded for the third wicket taken and for every subsequent two.

*In the following scores, * by the name of a team indicates that they won the toss.*

Pool A

At Johannesburg, October 20, 21, 22, 23. Drawn. Griqualand West* 427 for four dec. (J. M. Arthur 165, M. I. Gidley 86, P. P. J. Koortzen 82 not out, W. Bossenger 72 not out); Gauteng 184 (S. G. Koenig 94; G. J. Kruis four for 43, C. A. Copeland five for 52) and 384 for nine dec. (A. M. Bacher 35, S. G. Koenig 108, G. Toyana 42, S. S. Ndima 38, M. F. George 33 not out). *Gauteng 2 pts, Griqualand West 7 pts.*

Arthur and Gidley opened with 254, a first-wicket record for Griqualand West, surpassing 221 by J. P. McNally and A. Dunn v Eastern Province, Kimberley, 1947-48.

At Paarl, October 27, 28, 29. Boland won by ten wickets. Free State 102 (M. N. van Wyk 39; C. K. Langeveldt five for 19, B. T. Player three for 11) and 249 (L. J. Wilkinson 89, J. F. Venter 40; B. T. Player five for 26, A. A. W. Pringle three for 55); Boland* 330 (J. M. Henderson 76, P. H. Barnard 120, L. J. Koen 41; J. F. Venter six for 90) and 23 for no wkt. *Boland 18 pts, Free State 2 pts.*

In his 15th season, Wilkinson became Free State's leading first-class run-scorer, passing Neil Rosendorff's record of 4,914 between 1962-63 and 1978-79.

At Potchefstroom, October 27, 28, 29, 30. Gauteng won by 121 runs. Gauteng 224 (N. Pothas 93, O. D. Gibson 52; M. J. Lavine six for 55) and 322 (S. G. Koenig 80, A. J. Seymore 58, C. E. Eksteen 50, M. F. George 58; G. A. Roe three for 58, A. C. Thomas four for 84); North West* 277 (H. M. de Vos 35, M. C. Venter 35, M. J. Lavine 85; D. J. Terbrugge three for 53, W. B. Masimula three for 44) and 148 (G. M. Hewitt 38; O. D. Gibson three for 36, D. J. Terbrugge five for 39). *Gauteng 16 pts, North West 7 pts.*

At Bloemfontein, November 3, 4, 5, 6. Drawn. Gauteng* 368 (A. M. Bacher 58, S. G. Koenig 116, A. J. Seymore 50, Z. de Bruyn 35; H. C. Bakkes six for 108) and 204 for five (S. G. Koenig 36, A. M. Bacher 38, Z. de Bruyn 59 not out; D. Pretorius three for 23); Free State 525 for seven dec. (G. F. J. Liebenberg 67, L. J. Wilkinson 99, W. J. Smit 88, M. N. van Wyk 49, J. F. Venter 112 not out). *Free State 6 pts, Gauteng 4 pts.*

Wilkinson played his 95th first-class match for Free State, passing Robbie East's record.

At Centurion, November 3, 4, 5, 6. Northerns won by 153 runs. Northerns 321 (J. A. Rudolph 33, M. van Jaarsveld 70, N. D. McKenzie 70, G. Dros 40, A. Paleker 36; Z. A. Abrahim four for 73, J. Louw three for 75) and 289 for two dec. (P. J. R. Steyn 188 not out, N. D. McKenzie 75 not out); Griqualand West* 210 (M. I. Gidley 62, G. D. Elliott 34, W. Bossenger 54; N. G. Brouwers three for 43) and 247 (Z. A. Abrahim 42, G. D. Elliott 41, J. Brooker 43; G. J. Smith three for 55, G. Dros three for 35). *Northerns 17 pts, Griqualand West 4 pts.*

At Johannesburg, November 10, 11, 12, 13. Northerns won by 139 runs. Northerns* 356 (M. van Jaarsveld 59, N. D. McKenzie 123, G. Dros 49, S. Elworthy 75 not out; A. J. Hall five for 93) and 248 for four dec. (J. A. Rudolph 65, M. van Jaarsveld 58, G. Dros 100 not out); Gauteng 184 (A. M. Bacher 61; S. Elworthy four for 34, D. H. Townsend three for 48) and 281 (A. M. Bacher 54, Z. de Bruyn 66, A. J. Hall 30, N. Pothas 60; S. Elworthy five for 81, G. Dros three for 37). *Northerns 18 pts, Gauteng 3 pts.*

Dros scored his maiden first-class century in his 48th match and 82nd innings.

At Kimberley, November 10, 11, 12, 13. Free State won by 54 runs. Free State* 352 (L. J. Wilkinson 169, N. Boje 77, G. L. Brophy 40; Z. A. Abrahim four for 68) and 280 for five dec. (G. F. J. Liebenberg 31, W. J. Smit 94, N. Boje 105); Griqualand West 277 (M. I. Gidley 42, W. M. Dry 80, J. Brooker 71; N. Boje five for 67, D. Pretorius four for 51) and 301 (P. P. J. Koortzen 78, J. Brooker 77, G. J. Kruis 34; D. Pretorius four for 63, J. F. Venter four for 105). *Free State 18 pts, Griqualand West 7 pts.*

Boje became the second player after Bruce Mitchell (Transvaal v Natal, Durban, 1937-38) to score a century and a fifty and to take five wickets in an innings in the Currie Cup/SuperSport Series.

At Paarl, November 17, 18, 19, 20. Boland v Gauteng. Abandoned.

At Kimberley, November 17, 18, 19, 20. North West won by 65 runs. North West* 313 (G. M. Hewitt 30, M. Strydom 43, A. C. Thomas 106 not out, G. A. Roe 66; Z. A. Abrahim three for 56, E. W. Kidwell three for 38) and 215 (A. G. Lawson 52, G. M. Hewitt 39; G. J. Kruis four for 53, C. R. Tatton five for 80); Griqualand West 284 (G. D. Elliott 36, L. L. Bosman 115 not out, Z. A. Abrahim 57; M. J. Lavine five for 97, G. A. Roe three for 70) and 179 (W. M. Dry 31, M. I. Gidley 36, G. D. Elliott 59; M. Strydom six for 23). *North West 16 pts, Griqualand West 7 pts.*

In North West's first innings, Thomas (who scored his century at No. 10) and Roe added 174 for the last wicket, equalling the South African record of "Tiger" Lance and Don Mackay-Coghill for Transvaal v Natal, Johannesburg, 1965-66. Hendrik de Vos became the first player to score 2,000 first-class runs for North West.

At Centurion, November 17, 18, 19, 20. Drawn. Northerns 291 (P. J. R Steyn 66, G. Dros 34, C. F. K. van Wyk 59, N. G. Brouwers 59; P. V. Mpitsang five for 64) and 140 for seven (P. J. R. Steyn 30, G. Dros 31 not out, C. F. K. van Wyk 36; P. V. Mpitsang four for 43, D. Pretorius three for 56); Free State* 417 for eight dec. (G. F. J. Liebenberg 202, A. I. Gait 64, H. C. Bakkes 54 not out, Extras 44; G. Dros three for 32). *Northerns 5 pts, Free State 7 pts.*

Liebenberg's 202 lasted 478 minutes and 375 balls and included 30 fours and three sixes.

At Paarl, November 24, 25, 26, 27. Boland won by one wicket. North West* 216 (M. C. Venter 44 retired hurt, G. M. Hewitt 34, C. Light 31, A. C. Thomas 33; C. K. Langeveldt four for 48, N. M. Carter three for 50) and 225 (C. Light 101, A. C. Thomas 43; C. K. Langeveldt three for 51); Boland 224 (J. M. Henderson 86, S. J. Palframan 31, B. T. Player 31; M. J. Lavine six for 53, G. A. Roe three for 57) and 218 for nine (L. J. Koen 77, J. L. Ontong 68 not out; M. J. Lavine four for 71, G. A. Roe three for 37). *Boland 16 pts, North West 6 pts.*

Lavine became the second bowler to take ten wickets in a first-class match for North West, after David Pryke, 11 for 81 v Western Province B, Potchefstroom, 1997-98.

At Bloemfontein, December 1, 2, 3. Free State won by an innings and 53 runs. Free State 302 (G. F. J. Liebenberg 60, L. J. Wilkinson 32, M. N. van Wyk 38, J. F. Venter 57, G. L. Brophy 33, H. C. Bakkes 34, Extras 35; G. A. Roe seven for 47); North West* 126 (A. Jacobs 33, M. J. Lavine 31; P. V. Mpitsang four for 33, D. Pretorius three for 44) and 123 (P. V. Mpitsang five for 24). *Free State 18 pts, North West 4 pts.*

At Centurion, December 1, 2, 3, 4. Northerns won by 53 runs. Northerns 211 (M. van Jaarsveld 91, Q. R. Still 34, C. F. K. van Wyk 48; H. S. Williams five for 43, C. K. Langeveldt three for 53) and 343 for four dec. (J. A. Rudolph 141, M. van Jaarsveld 132, S. Elworthy 31 not out); Boland* 132 (B. T. Player 37 not out; S. Elworthy five for 41, D. H. Townsend four for 35) and 369 (H. Davids 124, L. J. Koen 97, S. J. Palframan 46; G. J. Smith three for 99, D. H. Townsend four for 116). *Northerns 16 pts, Boland 4 pts.*

In Northerns' second innings, Rudolph and van Jaarsveld added 261 for the second wicket. Henry Davids scored 124 on SuperSport debut, after one first-class match against the New Zealanders.

At Kimberley, December 8, 9, 10, 11. Drawn. Griqualand West 137 (L. L. Bosman 53 not out; H. S. Williams six for 40, C. K. Langeveldt three for 20) and 205 (M. I. Gidley 31, L. L. Bosman 33, W. Bossenger 30, G. J. Kruis 46; N. M. Carter six for 63); Boland* 230 (H. Davids 51, J. L. Ontong 68, Extras 31; G. J. Kruis four for 61, C. R. Tatton three for 35) and 31 for no wkt. *Griqualand West 4 pts, Boland 6 pts.*

At Potchefstroom, December 8, 9, 10, 11. Drawn. North West 327 (R. Niewoudt 35, C. Light 47, M. J. Lavine 49, M. Strydom 89 not out, A. C. Thomas 31; G. J. Smith four for 84); Northerns* 175 for seven (P. J. R. Steyn 45). *North West 6 pts, Northerns 4 pts.*

Pool B

At Port Elizabeth, October 27, 28, 29, 30. Western Province won by 127 runs. Western Province 362 (H. H. Gibbs 61, G. C. Smith 35, H. D. Ackerman 128, N. C. Johnson 30, A. G. Prince 47; M. Ngam four for 78) and 212 for eight dec. (G. C. Smith 80, A. C. Dawson 53 not out; M. Ngam three for 59); Eastern Province* 282 (D. J. Callaghan 129, J. M. Kemp 44) and 165 (J. D. C. Bryant 40; C. W. Henderson five for 40). *Western Province 18 pts, Eastern Province 7 pts.*

At Benoni, October 27, 28, 29, 30. Easterns won by 108 runs. Easterns 245 (B. M. White 33, P. de Bruyn 83; J. C. Kent six for 77) and 284 for eight dec. (D. Jordaan 75, G. E. Flusk 31 not out, K. C. G. Benjamin 48 not out, Extras 32; J. C. Kent three for 75); KwaZulu-Natal* 123 (M. L. Bruyns 32; K. C. G. Benjamin three for 23, G. E. Flusk three for 31) and 298 (R. E. Veenstra 38, G. H. Bodi 104, Extras 30; K. C. G. Benjamin four for 79, A. Nel five for 64). *Easterns 16 pts, KwaZulu-Natal 4 pts.*

This was Easterns' first win in a SuperSport Series match. Batting at No. 9, Bodi hit 104 off 94 balls with 11 fours and six sixes, reaching his maiden century in 81 balls. Easterns wicket-keeper Dylan Jennings took six catches in KwaZulu-Natal's first innings.

At East London, November 3, 4, 5, 6. Western Province won by 77 runs. Western Province 350 for nine dec. (H. H. Gibbs 91, A. G. Puttick 66, H. D. Ackerman 42, N. C. Johnson 31, A. G. Prince 46 not out; L. Graham three for 69) and 222 for four dec. (H. H. Gibbs 46, A. G. Puttick 30, H. D. Ackerman 68, N. C. Johnson 53 not out); Border* 252 (W. Wiblin 51, P. C. Strydom 30, I. Mitchell 61, G. T. Love 30; C. M. Willoughby three for 52, C. W. Henderson three for 79, P. R. Adams three for 33) and 243 (L. L. Gamiet 30, I. Mitchell 46 not out; C. M. Willoughby three for 57). *Western Province 17 pts, Border 4 pts.*

At Benoni, November 3, 4, 5, 6. Easterns won by five wickets. Eastern Province* 256 (C. C. Bradfield 46, R. J. Peterson 96 not out; K. C. G. Benjamin three for 66) and 191 (D. W. Murray 58 not out; K. C. G. Benjamin four for 35); Easterns 172 (B. M. White 31, D. Jordaan 47; D. M. Senekal three for 42, D. J. Callaghan five for 24) and 276 for five (D. N. Crookes 117, P. de Bruyn 71 not out). *Easterns 15 pts, Eastern Province 7 pts.*

Peterson was stranded on 96 not out from 77 balls, with 13 fours and three sixes.

At Port Elizabeth, November 10, 11, 12, 13. Drawn. Eastern Province* 177 (C. C. Bradfield 35, D. W. Murray 39; M. Ntini six for 59) and 332 (C. C. Bradfield 91, J. M. Kemp 81, M. W. Creed 31, S. Abrahams 35, R. J. Peterson 36; V. C. Drakes five for 80, M. Ntini three for 112); Border 231 (S. C. Pope 55, L. L. Gamiet 37, V. C. Drakes 39; J. M. Kemp six for 56) and 215 for six (I. Mitchell 37, W. Wiblin 64 not out, M. V. Boucher 33 not out; R. J. Peterson five for 87). *Eastern Province 5 pts, Border 6 pts.*

At Cape Town, November 10, 11, 12, 13. Drawn. Western Province* 352 (H. H. Gibbs 43, G. Kirsten 38, J. H. Kallis 99, P. R. Adams 42 not out; L. Klusener four for 111, J. C. Kent three for 70) and 221 for five dec. (G. Kirsten 54, J. H. Kallis 84, H. D. Ackerman 33, N. C. Johnson 36 not out); KwaZulu-Natal 293 (A. C. Hudson 38, D. M. Benkenstein 37, J. C. Kent 74 not out; A. C. Dawson four for 69) and 134 for five (D. J. Watson 60 not out). *Western Province 6 pts, KwaZulu-Natal 4 pts.*

At East London, November 17, 18, 19, 20. Border won by 56 runs. Border* 244 (S. C. Pope 92, P. C. Strydom 63; K. C. G. Benjamin six for 73, A. G. Botha three for 23) and 202 for nine dec. (C. B. Sugden 54, W. Wiblin 39, L. L. Gamiet 39; G. E. Flusk five for 55); Easterns 212 (M. J. R. Rindel 64, P. de Bruyn 53, A. G. Botha 34 not out; V. C. Drakes four for 48, G. T. Love three for 63) and 178 (M. J. R. Rindel 49, D. N. Crookes 33; V. C. Drakes four for 47, G. T. Love three for 55). *Border 16 pts, Easterns 6 pts.*

At Cape Town, November 24, 25, 26, 27. Western Province won by 194 runs. Western Province* 332 for eight dec. (G. C. Smith 57, A. G. Puttick 153 not out, H. D. Ackerman 50; K. C. G. Benjamin three for 59) and 285 for six dec. (T. L. Tsolekile 95, A. G. Puttick 39, N. C. Johnson 50, A. G. Prince 40 not out); Easterns 228 (M. J. R. Rindel 91, D. N. Crookes 79; A. C. Dawson five for 51, P. R. Adams three for 61) and 195 (D. Jennings 53, D. N. Crookes 87 not out; R. Telemachus three for 20, A. C. Dawson three for 32). *Western Province 17 pts, Easterns 4 pts.*

At Durban, December 1, 2, 3, 4. Drawn. Eastern Province 421 (M. R. Benfield 93, D. J. Callaghan 42, J. M. Kemp 65, M. W. Creed 32, D. W. Murray 48) and 47 for three; KwaZulu-Natal* 245 (M. L. Bruyns 43, A. Mall 30, E. L. R. Stewart 41 not out, Extras 32; M. Hayward three for 70, R. J. Peterson four for 65) and 382 (J. C. Kent 178 not out, J. N. Rhodes 42; J. M. Kemp five for 69). *KwaZulu-Natal 6 pts, Eastern Province 9 pts.*

At Durban, December 8, 9, 10, 11. Drawn. KwaZulu-Natal 253 for seven dec. (A. Mall 36, D. M. Benkenstein 86) and 117 for five (D. M. Benkenstein 56 not out; V. C. Drakes three for 20); Border* 321 (C. B. Sugden 34, P. J. Botha 39, P. C. Strydom 80, I. Mitchell 31, Extras 33; G. H. Bodi four for 37). *KwaZulu-Natal 7 pts, Border 7 pts.*

Super Eight

At East London, February 1, 2, 3. Border won by seven wickets. Northerns* 190 (G. Dros 35, C. F. K. van Wyk 30; M. Ntini three for 32, P. J. Botha three for 16, G. T. Love three for 58) and 150 (J. A. Rudolph 39; V. C. Drakes four for 35, P. C. Strydom three for 29); Border 236 (C. B. Sugden 30, P. C. Strydom 86, V. C. Drakes 35; D. H. Townsend five for 49) and 108 for three (S. C. Pope 33). *Border 16 pts, Northerns 5 pts.*

At Port Elizabeth, February 1, 2, 3, 4. Eastern Province won by nine wickets. North West* 341 (R. Niewoudt 98, A. G. Lawson 61, Extras 40; S. Abrahams five for 37) and 227 (A. C. Thomas 41 not out, J. N. Dreyer 40; G. J-P. Kruger four for 70, R. J. Peterson three for 74); Eastern Province 448 (J. D. C. Bryant 70, D. J. Callaghan 38, J. M. Kemp 188, M. W. Creed 33, D. W. Murray 32; F. van der Merwe five for 62) and 123 for one (M. R. Benfield 66 not out, U. Abrahams 30). *Eastern Province 16 pts, North West 6 pts.*

In Eastern Province's first innings, Kemp hit 31 runs off an over from Morne Strydom, including five consecutive sixes.

At Benoni, February 1, 2, 3, 4. Easterns won by 109 runs. Easterns 224 (M. J. R. Rindel 69, A. G. Botha 59; A. A. Donald three for 46, J. F. Venter three for 54) and 309 (D. Jennings 37, M. J. R. Rindel 78, D. N. Crookes 95, A. Nel 44; P. V. Mpitsang three for 38, D. Pretorius three for 58); Free State* 195 (G. F. J. Liebenberg 54, W. J. Smit 49; J. A. Morkel four for 36, A. G. Botha three for 50) and 229 (G. F. J. Liebenberg 73, L. J. Wilkinson 36, M. R. Lewis 49 not out; A. Nel five for 43). *Easterns 16 pts, Free State 5 pts.*

At Cape Town, February 1, 2, 3, 4. Drawn. Boland* 398 (J. M. Henderson 42, J. G. Strydom 34, J. L. Ontong 84, I. J. L. Trott 93, H. Davids 42; J. H. Kallis three for 77) and 255 (J. G. Strydom 73, L. J. Koen 46, S. J. Palframan 30; R. Telemachus six for 54); Western Province 394 (G. C. Smith 126, J. H. Kallis 69, N. C. Johnson 75; N. M. Carter six for 122) and 205 for five (G. C. Smith 52, J. H. Kallis 40, P. R. Adams 61 not out). *Western Province 6 pts, Boland 7 pts.*

At Paarl, March 1, 2, 3, 4. Drawn. Boland* 236 (L. J. Koen 50, I. J. L. Trott 74; G. J-P. Kruger four for 49) and 360 for nine dec. (J. G. Strydom 41, J. L. Ontong 131 not out, I. J. L. Trott 65, Extras 47; G. J-P. Kruger three for 66, M. Hayward three for 69); Eastern Province 328 (C. C. Bradfield 35, J. D. C. Bryant 44, M. W. Creed 47, S. Abrahams 85, Extras 36; J. L. Ontong three for 71) and 266 for five (C. C. Bradfield 85, U. Abrahams 51, J. D. C. Bryant 44, D. J. Callaghan 42 not out; N. M. Carter three for 63). *Boland 5 pts, Eastern Province 7 pts.*

At Bloemfontein, March 1, 2, 3, 4. Border won by 162 runs. Border 308 (P. J. Botha 42, P. C. Strydom 42, I. Mitchell 58, V. C. Drakes 30; D. Pretorius four for 66) and 298 (C. B. Sugden 50, W. Wiblin 88, P. C. Strydom 50, I. Mitchell 30; J. F. Venter three for 60); Free State* 225 (A. I. Gait 112, L. J. Wilkinson 43; P. C. Strydom three for 37, P. J. Botha three for 35) and 219 (J. A. Beukes 64, L. J. Wilkinson 56, G. F. J. Liebenberg 34; T. Henderson six for 56). *Border 18 pts, Free State 6 pts.*

Wilkinson became the first player to appear in 100 first-class matches for Free State, and Strydom the first to score 4,000 runs for Border. Free State wicket-keeper Morne van Wyk took ten catches.

At Centurion, March 1, 2, 3, 4. Easterns won by four wickets. Northerns* 415 (J. A. Rudolph 144, P. J. R. Steyn 31, D. J. J. de Vos 97; P. de Bruyn three for 78) and 192 (A. Paleker 38 not out, D. H. Townsend 45; A. G. Botha three for 34); Easterns 380 (A. J. Seymore 174, D. N. Crookes 59, P. de Bruyn 36, A. G. Botha 33; S. Elworthy three for 70, G. J. Smith three for 62) and 229 for six (A. J. Seymore 69, D. Brand 39, M. J. R. Rindel 45, P. de Bruyn 32 not out; S. Elworthy four for 53). *Easterns 16 pts, Northerns 7 pts.*

Elworthy took his 400th first-class wicket.

At Potchefstroom, March 1, 2, 3. Western Province won by an innings and seven runs. North West* 330 (M. J. Lavine 39, M. Strydom 124, A. C. Thomas 95 not out, Extras 38; C. M. Willoughby three for 64, A. C. Dawson four for 11) and 126 (B. C. de Wett 30, M. Strydom 33 not out; C. M. Willoughby three for 34, C. W. Henderson three for 25); Western Province 463 (L. D. Ferreira 201, A. G. Prince 39, N. C. Johnson 76, T. L. Tsolekile 78, Extras 32; M. J. Lavine four for 144, G. A. Roe five for 79). *Western Province 20 pts, North West 7 pts.*

In the first innings, Strydom and Thomas added 204 for the eighth wicket, a North West all-wicket record. Ferreira's 201 lasted 402 minutes and 290 balls and included 26 fours and a six.

At East London, March 8, 9, 10, 11. Border won by 164 runs. Border 192 (P. C. Strydom 55; H. S. Williams five for 38, A. A. W. Pringle four for 49) and 354 (C. B. Sugden 43, S. C. Pope 125, P. C. Strydom 63, L. L. Gamiet 31; J. L. Ontong four for 120); Boland* 153 (J. L. Ontong 33, H. S. Williams 33; P. J. Botha three for 38, G. T. Love four for 26) and 229 (J. M. Henderson 98, L. J. Koen 62; V. C. Drakes four for 42, P. J. Botha four for 48). *Border 15 pts, Boland 5 pts.*

Williams became the second bowler after Claude Henderson to take 200 first-class wickets for Boland.

At Port Elizabeth, March 8, 9, 10. Northerns won by 368 runs. Northerns* 451 for nine dec. (J. G. Myburgh 68, J. A. Rudolph 36, M. van Jaarsveld 94, P. J. R. Steyn 59, D. J. J. de Vos 48, F. C. Brooker 31, P. Joubert 72 not out; M. Hayward three for 128) and 174 for six dec. (J. A. Rudolph 35, P. J. R. Steyn 35, D. J. J. de Vos 60 not out; M. W. Pringle four for 32); Eastern Province 108 (G. J. Smith five for 25, P. Joubert five for ten) and 149 (C. C. Bradfield 64 not out; R. E. Bryson five for 33). *Northerns 17 pts, Eastern Province 1 pt.*

Northerns recorded the second-highest margin of victory by runs in South African provincial cricket; Transvaal beat Griqualand West by 386 at Johannesburg, 1929-30. Bradfield carried his bat through Eastern Province's second innings.

At Benoni, March 8, 9, 10, 11. North West won by ten wickets. Easterns 106 (A. J. Seymore 32; A. C. Thomas six for 26) and 299 (M. J. R. Rindel 42, P. de Bruyn 33, J. A. Morkel 117; G. A. Roe six for 31); North West* 336 (R. Niewoudt 44, A. G. Lawson 64, M. Strydom 37, A. C. Thomas 32, E. G. Poole 50; J. A. Morkel three for 77) and 70 for no wkt (R. Niewoudt 43 not out). *North West 17 pts, Easterns 3 pts.*

Roe passed Corrie Jordaan's 1998-99 record of 30 first-class wickets in a season for North West. Poole took nine catches in the match, becoming the first wicket-keeper to reach 100 first-class dismissals for North West.

At Cape Town, March 8, 9, 10, 11. Western Province won by 127 runs. Western Province* 265 (G. C. Smith 41, A. G. Prince 43, N. C. Johnson 38, R. Munnik 45, T. L. Tsolekile 31; J. J. van der Wath three for 46, D. Pretorius four for 78) and 299 for eight dec. (A. G. Puttick 60, L. D. Ferreira 34, H. D. Ackerman 100 not out, R. Munnik 35; J. F. Venter five for 103); Free State 291 (A. I. Gait 34, J. F. Venter 86, J. J. van der Wath 49, G. L. Brophy 36; C. W. Henderson four for 71) and 146 (J. F. Venter 42; C. M. Willoughby five for 26, P. L. Harris three for 56). *Western Province 15 pts, Free State 6 pts.*

At Paarl, March 15, 16, 17, 18. Easterns won by 139 runs. Easterns* 340 (A. M. van den Berg 59, D. N. Crookes 95, A. G. Botha 49 not out; H. S. Williams five for 66) and 278 for eight dec. (A. J. Seymore 67, D. Brand 31, P. de Bruyn 67; W. J. du Toit seven for 82); Boland 169 (J. M. Henderson 86, L. J. Koen 31; B. L. Reddy three for 39, G. E. Flusk three for 55, P. de Bruyn four for 34) and 310 (J. M. Henderson 38, J. G. Strydom 40, L. J. Koen 66, B. T. Player 73, W. J. du Toit 32; A. G. Botha six for 106). *Easterns 17 pts, Boland 4 pts.*

Williams played his 62nd first-class match for Boland, passing Claude Henderson's record. Easterns wicket-keeper Dylan Jennings ended the season with 39 dismissals (37 ct, 2 st), well ahead of Bruce McBride's 1994-95 record of 27 for the province.

At Bloemfontein, March 15, 16, 17. Free State won by four wickets. Eastern Province 180 (C. C. Bradfield 35, M. W. Creed 32; H. C. Bakkes three for 31, P. V. Mpitsang five for 70) and 187 (C. C. Bradfield 38, J. Botha 43; H. C. Bakkes three for 45, J. J. van der Wath five for 59); Free State* 110 (M. W. Pringle three for 27, D. J. Callaghan five for 31) and 258 for six (J. F. Venter 79, A. I. Gait 74, M. N. van Wyk 32; D. J. Callaghan five for 80). *Free State 14 pts, Eastern Province 5 pts.*

Louis Wilkinson became the first fielder to take 100 first-class catches for Free State.

At Centurion, March 15, 16, 17, 18. Western Province won by 298 runs. Western Province* 316 for nine dec. (L. D. Ferreira 62, A. G. Prince 79, N. C. Johnson 84, T. L. Tsolekile 49; R. E. Bryson four for 65) and 314 for three dec. (A. G. Puttick 31, H. D. Ackerman 109 not out, A. G. Prince 120 not out); Northerns 267 for nine dec. (J. A. Rudolph 71, A. N. Petersen 30, P. J. R. Steyn 35, P. Joubert 35 not out; R. Munnik four for 58) and 65 (C. W. Henderson five for six). *Western Province 18 pts, Northerns 7 pts.*

Johnson set a new record for catches by a fielder in a South African season, overtaking 21 by Mike Procter (1972-73), Alan Kourie (1984-85), Louis Koen and Gerry Liebenberg (both 1999-2000). Northerns' second-innings 65 was believed to be the lowest first-class total to include a fifty partnership (52 for the fourth wicket between Finley Brooker and Dirkie de Vos). Henderson took his 300th first-class wicket.

At Potchefstroom, March 15, 16, 17, 18. Border won by 90 runs. Border* 274 (P. C. Strydom 54, I. Mitchell 83, V. C. Drakes 53; G. A. Roe three for 70, A. C. Thomas three for 46) and 283 (P. J. Botha 50, S. C. Pope 100, L. L. Gamiet 39; A. C. Thomas four for 76, F. van der Merwe five for 84); North West 248 (G. M. Hewitt 62, M. J. Lavine 113; T. Henderson four for 53, P. J. Botha three for 54) and 219 (G. M. Hewitt 48, M. J. Lavine 34, A. C. Thomas 57; V. C. Drakes three for 56, P. C. Strydom three for 55). *Border 17 pts, North West 6 pts.*

Drakes became the second bowler after Ian Howell to take 200 first-class wickets for Border. Thomas passed Andre van Deventer's record of 502 first-class runs in a season for North West. North West wicket-keeper Ezra Poole finished with 37 dismissals, all caught, easily breaking his own provincial record of 21 in the previous two seasons.

FINAL

WESTERN PROVINCE v BORDER

At Cape Town, March 21, 22, 23, 24. Western Province won by an innings and 26 runs. Toss: Western Province.

A ten-hour innings by 20-year-old Smith helped Western Province win with a day to spare, and without the scares of their previous final against Border in 1998-99. On the first day, Johnson raised his record for catches in a South African season to 24, taking Mitchell in a juggling effort after a rebound off the wicket-keeper. Pope's cautious fifty was followed by Border's best stand, 77 in 20 overs between Makalima and Drakes, but Western Province wrapped up the innings in 11 balls next morning. They then settled in to bat Border out of the match. Smith shared century partnerships with Ferreira and Prince on his way to 183, including 18 fours. Tsolekile and the tail extended the lead to 217 before off-spinner Love completed a career-best seven for 116. Gamiet, promoted to open Border's second innings, fought bravely with a maiden fifty, batting four hours before Claude Henderson's left-arm spin claimed him in a spell of four for two in 11 balls that swept Border to an innings defeat. Henderson's namesake, Tyron, averted a hat-trick but succumbed soon afterwards.

Man of the Match: G. C. Smith.

Close of play: First day, Border 247-7 (Makalima 40*, Drakes 46*); Second day, Western Province 229-2 (Smith 120*, Ackerman 4*); Third day, Western Province 446-7 (Dawson 11*, Henderson 18*).

Border

C. B. Sugden c Willoughby b Telemachus	1	– (6) lbw b Telemachus	11
P. J. Botha c Ferreira b Telemachus	10	– (1) lbw b Willoughby	1
S. C. Pope b Dawson	58	– c Tsolekile b Dawson	26
W. Wiblin c Puttick b Henderson	24	– c Prince b Willoughby	0
*P. C. Strydom c Johnson b Dawson	28	– c Tsolekile b Henderson	22
L. L. Gamiet c Tsolekile b Johnson	24	– (2) c Puttick b Henderson	80
†I. Mitchell c Johnson b Henderson	3	– c Tsolekile b Henderson	12
D L. Makalima not out	42	– b Henderson	0
V. C. Drakes c Smith b Telemachus	46	– c Puttick b Henderson	2
G. T. Love c Tsolekile b Telemachus	2	– not out	7
T. Henderson c Ackerman b Willoughby	1	– b Dawson	12
L-b 7, w 1, n-b 5	13	L-b 2, n-b 16	18
1/14 2/15 3/48 4/104 5/147 6/150 7/172 8/249 9/251	252	1/7 2/59 3/72 4/121 5/143 6/165 7/170 8/172 9/172	191

Bowling: *First Innings*—Telemachus 13–2–47–4; Willoughby 19.3–7–56–1; Dawson 17–5–58–2; Henderson 31–11–62–2; Johnson 13–6–22–1. *Second Innings*—Telemachus 12–0–47–1; Willoughby 13–4–38–2; Dawson 15.2–6–29–2; Henderson 19–4–62–5; Johnson 6–1–13–0.

Western Province

G. C. Smith c Mitchell b Love	183
A. G. Puttick c Mitchell b Drakes	12
L. D. Ferreira c Mitchell b Drakes	81
*H. D. Ackerman c Sugden b Love	17
A. G. Prince lbw b Drakes	53
N. C. Johnson lbw b Love	2
†T. L. Tsolekile c Sugden b Love	53
A. C. Dawson c Sugden b Love	19
C. W. Henderson not out	28
R. Telemachus lbw b Love	2
C. M. Willoughby b Love	0
B 3, l-b 1, w 2, n-b 13	19
1/49 2/215 3/257 4/357 5/359 6/378 7/425 8/454 9/464	469

Bowling: Drakes 42–11–127–3; Botha 23–6–49–0; Henderson 32–12–60–0; Love 56.2–21–116–7; Strydom 32–12–75–0; Pope 7–1–20–0; Wiblin 5–1–18–0.

Umpires: I. L. Howell and B. G. Jerling.
Third umpire: A. G. O'Connor.

CHAMPIONS

Currie Cup

1889-90	Transvaal
1890-91	Kimberley
1892-93	Western Province
1893-94	Western Province
1894-95	Transvaal
1896-97	Western Province
1897-98	Western Province
1902-03	Transvaal
1903-04	Transvaal
1904-05	Transvaal
1906-07	Transvaal
1908-09	Western Province
1910-11	Natal
1912-13	Natal
1920-21	Western Province
1921-22	Transvaal/Natal/W. Prov. (Tied)
1923-24	Transvaal
1925-26	Transvaal
1926-27	Transvaal
1929-30	Transvaal
1931-32	Western Province
1933-34	Natal
1934-35	Transvaal
1936-37	Natal
1937-38	Natal/Transvaal (Tied)
1946-47	Natal
1947-48	Natal
1950-51	Transvaal
1951-52	Natal
1952-53	Western Province
1954-55	Natal
1955-56	Western Province
1958-59	Transvaal

1959-60	Natal
1960-61	Natal
1962-63	Natal
1963-64	Natal
1965-66	Natal/Transvaal (Tied)
1966-67	Natal
1967-68	Natal
1968-69	Transvaal
1969-70	Transvaal/W. Province (Tied)
1970-71	Transvaal
1971-72	Transvaal
1972-73	Transvaal
1973-74	Natal
1974-75	Western Province
1975-76	Natal
1976-77	Natal
1977-78	Western Province
1978-79	Transvaal
1979-80	Transvaal
1980-81	Natal
1981-82	Western Province
1982-83	Transvaal
1983-84	Transvaal
1984-85	Transvaal
1985-86	Western Province
1986-87	Transvaal
1987-88	Transvaal
1988-89	Eastern Province
1989-90	E. Province/W. Province (Shared)

Castle Cup

1990-91	Western Province
1991-92	Eastern Province
1992-93	Orange Free State
1993-94	Orange Free State
1994-95	Natal
1995-96	Western Province

SuperSport Series

1996-97	Natal
1997-98	Free State
1998-99	Western Province
1999-2000	Gauteng
2000-01	Western Province

Transvaal/Gauteng have won the title outright 25 times, Natal 20, Western Province 17, Orange Free State/Free State 3, Eastern Province 2, Kimberley 1. The title has been shared five times as follows: Transvaal 4, Natal and Western Province 3, Eastern Province 1.

Shield Series

At Durban, January 12, 13, 14. Drawn. Griqualand West 279 (M. I. Gidley 60, L. L. Bosman 71, P. P. J. Koortzen 32, W. Bossenger 45; J. E. Bastow four for 46, G. H. Bodi three for 60) and 222 (B. H. Tucker 47, J. Louw 50; G. H. Bodi four for 88, J. C. Kent three for 34); KwaZulu-Natal* 241 (M. L. Bruyns 52, D. J. Watson 51, J. C. Kent 58; G. J. Kruis four for 57, E. W. Kidwell four for 71) and 198 for four (D. J. Watson 33, A. M. Amla 69, D. M. Benkenstein 42 not out). *KwaZulu-Natal 6 pts, Griqualand West 7 pts.*

Kruis took a hat-trick in KwaZulu-Natal's first innings.

At Johannesburg, January 26, 27, 28. Drawn. KwaZulu-Natal* 303 (M. L. Bruyns 53, D. J. Watson 33, A. M. Amla 50, J. C. Kent 34, E. L. R. Stewart 30, E. A. E. Baptiste 57; O. D. Gibson six for 53) and 252 for six (D. J. Watson 36, J. C. Kent 33, G. H. Bodi 70 not out, E. L. R. Stewart 38 not out); Gauteng 333 for six dec. (A. M. Bacher 190, S. G. Koenig 78). *Gauteng 8 pts, KwaZulu-Natal 6 pts.*

At Kimberley, February 2, 3, 4. Drawn. Gauteng* 350 for seven dec. (S. G. Koenig 155, N. Pothas 83, Z. de Bruyn 66) and 273 for nine (J. M. Otto 88, A. J. Hall 92; G. J. Kruis three for 77, E. W. Kidwell three for 43); Griqualand West 406 (B. H. Tucker 35, M. I. Gidley 151, G. D. Elliott 34, P. P. J. Koortzen 102; N. A. Fusedale five for 170). *Griqualand West 7 pts, Gauteng 6 pts.*

At Johannesburg, March 2, 3, 4. Griqualand West won by one wicket. Gauteng 172 (S. C. Cook 43, Z. de Bruyn 41, J. M. Otto 59; G. J. Kruis three for 64, Z. A. Abrahim five for 22) and 176 (N. Pothas 60; G. J. Kruis three for 55, J. Louw three for 25); Griqualand West* 160 (M. I. Gidley 73 not out, Z. A. Abrahim 42; J. T. Mafa six for 62) and 190 for nine (G. D. Elliott 52, W. Bossenger 33, Z. A. Abrahim 43 not out; N. A. Fusedale four for 83). *Griqualand West 15 pts, Gauteng 5 pts.*

Gidley carried his bat through Griqualand West's first innings.

At Durban, March 9, 10, 11. Drawn. KwaZulu-Natal* 360 (M. L. Bruyns 31, A. Mall 64, J. N. Rhodes 76, W. R. Wingfield 89 not out, R. B. MacQueen 31; N. A. Fusedale four for 78) and 170 for no wkt dec. (M. L. Bruyns 102 not out, D. J. Watson 64 not out); Gauteng 261 (S. G. Koenig 76, S. C. Cook 55, F. Herbst 35 not out; G. H. Bodi six for 63) and 57 for one. *KwaZulu-Natal 8 pts, Gauteng 6 pts.*

At Kimberley, March 16, 17, 18. Drawn. KwaZulu-Natal* 258 (A. Mall 40, E. L. R. Stewart 79, R. B. MacQueen 42; G. J. Kruis five for 50) and 292 for nine (M. L. Bruyns 41, D. J. Watson 58, E. L. R. Stewart 53, G. H. Bodi 74 not out; E. W. Kidwell three for 70, Z. A. Abrahim three for 56); Griqualand West 280 (G. D. Elliott 83, W. Bossenger 74 not out; A. N. W. Tweedie four for 65). *Griqualand West 7 pts, KwaZulu-Natal 7 pts.*

Bossenger became the first wicket-keeper to make 150 first-class dismissals for Griqualand West and equalled his own provincial record of 39 in a season (38 ct, 1 st).

STANDARD BANK CUP, 2000-01

Note: Matches in this section were not first-class.

	Played	*Won*	*Lost*	*Tied*	*Bonus Points*	*Points*	*Net run-rate*
KwaZulu-Natal	10	7	3	0	5	33	0.52
Border	10	6	4	0	6	30	0.47
Northerns	10	7	3	0	1	29	−0.07
Eastern Province	10	6	3	1	2	28	0.10
Western Province	10	5	5	0	6	26	0.48
Easterns	10	4	5	1	7	25	0.28
Free State	10	6	4	0	0	24	−0.20
Boland	10	4	6	0	4	20	0.07
Griqualand West	10	4	6	0	4	20	−0.12
Gauteng	10	3	7	0	4	16	−0.44
North West	10	2	8	0	2	10	−1.14

Semi-finals

In the best-of-three semi-finals, KwaZulu-Natal beat Eastern Province 2–1 (after one no-result) and Northerns beat Border 2–1.

Final

At Durban, February 21. KwaZulu-Natal won by three wickets. Northerns 214 for four (45 overs) (J. A. Rudolph 33, M. van Jaarsveld 36, G. Dros 34 not out, C. F. K. van Wyk 50 not out); KwaZulu-Natal* 217 for seven (44 overs) (A. Mall 40, W. R. Wingfield 61).

CRICKET IN THE WEST INDIES, 2000-01

By TONY COZIER

Carl Hooper

Struggling with failures on the field and problems within the administration, West Indies cricket experienced far-reaching changes in the first half of 2001. After another disastrous overseas tour, to Australia where the team lost all five Tests, captain Jimmy Adams paid the price for their defeat and his own decline in form. In March, Carl Hooper was controversially appointed West Indies' fifth captain in five years. He had abruptly retired from international cricket nearly two years earlier, just before the 1999 World Cup, and moved to Australia. But he returned to Guyana in October for the one-day domestic tournament, and then performed so emphatically in the first-class Busta Cup that he claimed not only a Test place but the highest position.

His reign started with defeats in the Test and one-day series against the visiting South Africans, to which West Indies Cricket Board president Pat Rousseau and vice-president Clarvis Joseph responded by dismissing team manager Ricky Skerritt. When, a week later, their decision was overturned by the board's directors, both resigned, ending five turbulent years under Rousseau, a Jamaican attorney who had risen through the marketing committee. In a reversion to the practice of eminent former cricketers heading the board, Wes Hall, the dynamic fast bowler of the 1960s, one-time team manager and selector, former Barbados government minister and now an ordained minister of the Christian Pentecostal Church, became president.

Some saw it as a hopeful sign that Hall's unopposed election coincided with victories in Zimbabwe and Kenya. West Indies beat Zimbabwe to end five straight losses in overseas Test series, defeated India in the final of a triangular limited-overs tournament, and won all three one-day internationals in Kenya, easing painful memories of their 1996 World Cup defeat. Hooper, whose level-headed leadership gradually dispelled doubts over his suitability, kept these successes in perspective, just as the Under-19s' manager cautioned against overestimating that team's winning campaign in England. Yet West Indian cricket had passed through such troubled times that any good news was welcome.

The opening of the Shell Cricket Academy at St George's University in Grenada, while overdue, was another cause for optimism. Under Rudi Webster, who had recently acted as psychologist to the Test team, and in the 1960s was a fast bowler for Warwickshire and Otago, it aimed to prepare promising youngsters for the modern international game. Specialist coaches from the Caribbean and Australia took charge of 24 of the best Under-23 cricketers.

Amid these hopeful developments, however, the WICB faced a financial crisis. Within days of leaving office, Rousseau revealed that they had lost "a substantial amount" after investing $US3 million on the US equities market, and alleged that chief financial officer Richard Jodhan and secretary Andrew Sealy had acted behind the board's back. An investigating committee found "absolutely no evidence of any falsification of board resolutions by Jodhan and Sealy", but the board admitted to losing $US525,000 – a crippling amount for an organisation with an operating loss of $US5.4 million for the previous year.

One of Rousseau's last innovations had been to introduce an overseas team into the domestic first-class competition in an attempt to raise standards. To counter fears of a foreign champion, the tournament ran in two stages. Only the six West Indian territories were eligible to win the Busta Cup, decided on a round-robin league format. Points earned by the first overseas guests, England A, and a new team, the Under-23s competing as West Indies B, counted only towards determining the semi-finalists for the subsequent Busta International Shield, which any team could win. The format proved successful, and Kenya and Bangladesh were invited for 2001-02.

Barbados and Guyana led the table with 57 points each; Barbados were awarded the Busta Cup for winning four outright victories to Guyana's three. England A and Jamaica joined them in the Shield semi-finals, where Guyana inflicted England A's first first-class defeat in seven overseas tours since 1994-95. The previous year's champions, Jamaica, qualified in fourth position, only three points ahead of the Leeward Islands; they had lost heavily to England A, and their tardy declarations allowed Barbados and Leewards to hold on for draws. But strengthened by the return of their internationals from Australia, they overwhelmed Barbados in the semi-final, then secured the Shield by claiming a comfortable first-innings lead over Guyana in the final at Kingston. Guyana, who already felt they should have shared the Busta Cup with Barbados, had objected when the WICB awarded Jamaica home advantage on account of their superior net run-rate, arguing that their second place should have meant a Georgetown final. A former High Court judge disagreed, though the hearing delayed the match by a day.

Jamaica's outstanding players were their openers, tall left-hander Chris Gayle and little right-hander Leon Garrick, and off-spinners Nehemiah Perry and Gareth Breese. Gayle had been the leading run-scorer of the 1999-2000 Busta Cup, but lost his international place after a disappointing tour of England. He regained it by piling up 945 Busta runs at 63.00. Only Hooper, who set a tournament record of 954 at 95.40, scored more. Gayle hit three hundreds, and shared a West Indian first-wicket record of 425 against West Indies B with Garrick; both made double-hundreds. Perry, in his 15th season, and Breese epitomised spin's continuing dominance in domestic cricket. Breese claimed 36 wickets through flight and control, Perry 31 through turn and bounce, although both were well short of leg-spinner Dinanath Ramnarine's 41 for Trinidad & Tobago.

Guyana finished the season unbeaten. Hooper was their guiding light; he compiled four hundreds, and fell only 46 runs short of 1,000, which would have won him a $US50,000 prize. His off-spin and sharp slip catching added to his value, but not nearly as much as his leadership of a young team. Back from a dreadful Test series in Australia, Ramnaresh Sarwan regained confidence, hitting stylish hundreds in both matches against England A and averaging 67.33. The well-organised Travis Dowlin strengthened the middle order with 422 at 52.75. Guyana's bowling, too, centred on spin. Neil McGarrell bowled 448.2 overs, far more than anyone else in the Busta series, for 32 wickets, Hooper had 25, and leg-spinners Mahendra Nagamootoo and teenager Ron Matthews 17 and 15 respectively. It made fast bowler Kevin Darlington's 26 wickets at 19.11 all the more impressive – and his omission from the last three games, for Test players Reon King and Colin Stuart, all the more inexplicable.

Outplayed in drawn matches by Jamaica and England A, who made them follow on, Barbados were unconvincing regional champions. They stuck to aging, established players, four of whom – Philo Wallace, Sherwin Campbell, Floyd Reifer and Roland Holder – built a winning total of 281 for four against Trinidad & Tobago in the last, decisive league match. But their general lack of fitness showed in substandard fielding, and they proved no match for the full-strength Jamaica in the semi-finals. Still, they could take heart for the future from 20-year-old all-rounder Ryan Hinds, one of only two Barbados batsmen to average above 30, whose accurate left-arm spin earned 27 Busta wickets, including 15 for 102 against Leewards. His first-innings nine for 68 was a competition record, and only the fourth nine-wicket return in the regional tournament's 35 seasons.

England A looked what they were, a competent, professional outfit. Surrey left-hander Ian Ward was in compelling form early on, with hundreds in three successive matches, but, like his team, ran out of steam. England A struggled to a draw against the Leewards in their last qualifying match; by conceding first-innings lead, they finished third, so had to play their semi-final against Guyana in Georgetown, rather than Grenada, their home base. "A bit of fatigue set in, and that shouldn't really happen because we play a lot of four-day cricket back home," said a disappointed captain, Mark Alleyne, after their semi-final loss.

No team was more inconsistent than the Leeward Islands. One match they were overpowering Trinidad & Tobago by 183 runs, the next their last pair was just holding on for a draw against Guyana. An outright victory over England A would have put them in the semi-finals, but they could only draw. Although captain Stuart Williams began with twin hundreds against Trinidad & Tobago, there were no more centuries until Ridley Jacobs returned from Australia to hit 100 against England A. Ricky Christopher and Kerry Jeremy, two 21-year-old seamers, took 26 wickets each, and 18-year-old Omari Banks showed all-round promise.

Trinidad & Tobago suffered so badly from international calls that former Test players Phil Simmons, Rajindra Dhanraj and Suruj Ragoonath were brought out of retirement. None lasted the distance. Test opener Daren Ganga scored a hundred against Barbados in his single match, but there was only one other century – a match-winning 102 not out by Lincoln Roberts against the Windwards – and one total of 300 in seven matches. The batting failures cancelled out Ramnarine's 41 wickets at 18.58 each. A shoulder operation had removed none of his skill and, recalled to play South Africa, he added another 20 in five Tests. Ramnarine's team-mate, 21-year-old left-arm wrist-spinner Dave Mohammed, claimed a wicket with his first ball in first-class cricket and so impressed the selectors that he was fast-tracked into the Test squad; when Ramnarine was injured, he was sent to Zimbabwe as a replacement.

The West Indies B team served its purpose of giving Under-23 players not selected for their territories early exposure to first-class cricket. Apart from Richie Richardson, the former Test captain who returned to lead them three years after retiring, only four had played at this level. Yet they were not disgraced, beating the Windwards in three days and taking a first-innings lead over Jamaica. There was obvious talent in batsmen Kurt Wilkinson and Tonito Willett, 18-year-old son of former Test spinner Elquemedo Willett, and the tall, slim, slow left-armer, Sulieman Benn.

The only team among the traditional territories never to win the first-class championship, the Windward Islands started 2000-01 on a high. The Under-19 team had won their annual tournament in August, and in October the senior side took the limited-overs Red Stripe Bowl. But their Busta Cup expectations were conclusively dashed – they lost all seven matches outright – leaving their one-day triumph, their first title since 1988-89, a rare high point. Junior Murray, named Man of the Series, Nixon McLean, Cameron Cuffy and 18-year-old opener Romel Currency figured prominently as they won five out of six games, including the final against Leewards.

The real upset of the Bowl tournament came when Barbados, the most successful of all West Indian teams, were humbled by the United States, who won by two wickets after bowling them out for 129 in 38 overs. It was the first such victory for the USA, whose team comprised mainly aging West Indian expatriates. They were one of three ICC Associates, along with Bermuda and Canada, invited for the Bowl; the addition of the Cayman Islands, an ICC Affiliate, made this ten-team tournament the largest staged by the WICB. Grandiose plans for 20 teams in 2000-01, with the islands of the Leewards and Windwards competing separately, were scrapped for financial reasons. All the invited teams dropped out, and numbers fell to eight, with the Windwards split into two teams, north and south, and Antigua – the 2001 Leeward champions – gaining independent entry.

FIRST-CLASS AVERAGES, 2000-01

BATTING

(Qualification: 250 runs, average 30.00)

	M	*I*	*NO*	*R*	*HS*	*100s*	*Avge*
C. L. Hooper (*Guyana*)	14	22	3	1,312	159	4	69.05
I. J. Ward (*England A*)	8	14	2	769	135	3	64.08
D. Ganga (*T & T*)	3	6	1	312	105	1	62.40
R. D. Jacobs (*Leeward I.*)	6	12	5	436	113*	2	62.28
S. C. Williams (*Leeward I.*)	6	9	0	522	160	2	58.00
S. L. Campbell (*Barbados*)	3	6	0	319	86	0	53.16
C. H. Gayle (*Jamaica*)	14	27	2	1,271	208*	3	50.84
R. R. Sarwan (*Guyana*)	12	20	3	844	122	2	49.64
T. M. Dowlin (*Guyana*)	8	11	2	438	116*	1	48.66
L. V. Garrick (*Jamaica*)	11	21	1	861	200*	2	43.05
M. W. Alleyne (*England A*)	7	10	1	370	139	1	41.11
C. M. Tuckett (*Leeward I.*)	6	10	2	326	84	0	40.75
B. C. Lara (*West Indies*)	5	10	0	400	91	0	40.00
L. A. Roberts (*T & T*)	7	14	1	465	102*	1	35.76
V. S. Solanki (*England A*)	7	10	2	281	89	0	35.12
M. J. Powell (*England A*)	6	10	0	340	96	0	34.00
W. W. Hinds (*Jamaica*)	7	12	0	394	101	2	32.83
R. O. Hinds (*Barbados*)	8	14	3	351	87	0	31.90
J. R. Murray (*Windward I.*)	7	14	1	405	97*	0	31.15
J. P. Crawley (*England A*)	8	14	2	373	104*	1	31.08
J. A. Mitchum (*Leeward I.*)	7	14	2	364	81	0	30.33

* *Signifies not out.*

BOWLING

(Qualification: 20 wickets)

	O	*M*	*R*	*W*	*BB*	*5W/i*	*Avge*
G. R. Breese (*Jamaica*)	328.4	131	544	36	7-60	3	15.11
R. O. Hinds (*Barbados*)	230.2	63	518	32	9-68	2	16.18
C. A. Walsh (*Jamaica*)	379	132	691	37	6-61	1	18.67
K. G. Darlington (*Guyana*)	183.4	48	497	26	6-25	2	19.11
N. O. Perry (*Jamaica*)	339.2	106	648	31	4-39	0	20.90
O. A. C. Banks (*Leeward I.*)	216	62	443	21	7-70	1	21.09
K. C. B. Jeremy (*Leeward I.*)	234	51	621	28	6-46	1	22.17
R. O. Cunningham (*Jamaica*)	274.4	101	489	22	4-62	0	22.22
D. Ramnarine (*T & T*)	655.3	208	1,379	61	6-54	6	22.60
R. J. Christopher (*Leeward I.*)	235.5	51	671	29	5-32	2	23.13

	O	*M*	*R*	*W*	*BB*	*5W/i*	*Avge*
C. D. Collymore (*Barbados*)	244	57	612	26	6-109	2	23.53
S. J. Benn (*West Indies B*)	297.5	57	836	32	5-51	1	26.12
C. P. Schofield (*England A*)	195.2	43	578	22	4-72	0	26.27
H. R. Bryan (*Barbados*)	282.3	64	736	27	4-57	0	27.25
I. O. Jackson (*Windward I.*)	254	60	683	25	8-79	1	27.32
M. Dillon (*T & T*)	198	42	577	21	4-32	0	27.47
S. Shillingford (*Windward I.*)	193.1	27	552	20	7-66	1	27.60
N. C. McGarrell (*Guyana*)	506.2	168	1,035	37	5-82	1	27.97
C. L. Hooper (*Guyana*)	465.3	122	918	30	5-49	1	30.60

BUSTA CUP, 2000-01

	Played	*Won*	*Lost*	*Drawn*	*1st-inns Points*	*Points*
Barbados	7	4	0	3	0	57
Guyana	7	3	0	4	9	57
England A	7	3	0	4	6	54
Jamaica	7	3	1	3	6	51
Leeward Islands	7	3	1	3	3	48
Trinidad & Tobago	7	2	4	1	11	38
West Indies B	7	1	6	0	8	20
Windward Islands	7	0	7	0	0	0

Win = 12 pts; draw = 3 pts; 1st-innings lead in a drawn match = 3 pts;1st-innings lead in a lost match = 4 pts.

Barbados won the Busta Cup and became regional champions by virtue of winning more games than Guyana. Matches involving England A and West Indies B counted for points, but neither of these teams could win the Busta Cup. The top four teams qualified for the Busta International Shield.

*In the following scores, * by the name of a team indicates that they won the toss.*

At Guaracara Park, Pointe-à-Pierre, January 4, 5, 6, 7. Leeward Islands won by 183 runs. Leeward Islands 371 (S. C. Williams 160, W. W. Cornwall 84, C. M. Tuckett 38; D. Ramnarine five for 107) and 220 (S. C. Williams 114, F. A. Adams 31; R. Dhanraj six for 57); Trinidad & Tobago* 156 (R. A. M. Smith 42; R. J. Christopher five for 61) and 252 (I. H. Jan 33, D. Rampersad 46, R. A. M. Smith 38, L. A. Roberts 42, D. Ramnarine 30 not out; G. T. Prince four for 75, R. J. Christopher four for 49). *Leeward Islands 12 pts.*

Williams hit a hundred in each innings.

At Kensington Oval, Bridgetown, January 5, 6, 7, 8. Drawn. Barbados 422 (A. F. G. Griffith 77, P. A. Wallace 39, S. H. Armstrong 33, R. O. Hinds 60, R. I. C. Holder 117, I. D. R. Bradshaw 30; N. C. McGarrell three for 145, C. L. Hooper four for 88, R. S. Matthews three for 82) and 116 for five (A. F. G. Griffith 34, P. A. Wallace 32); Guyana* 436 (N. A. De Groot 49, A. Haniff 32, K. F. Semple 40, C. L. Hooper 159, Extras 42; C. D. Collymore six for 109). *Barbados 3 pts, Guyana 6 pts.*

At Queen's Park, St George's (Grenada), January 5, 6, 7, 8. ENGLAND A beat WEST INDIES B by 224 runs (see England A tour section). *England A 12 pts.*

At Sabina Park, Kingston, January 5, 6, 7, 8. Jamaica won by three wickets. Windward Islands 168 (D. S. Smith 34, J. R. Murray 39, R. N. Lewis 45 not out; G. R. Breese five for 40, R. O. Cunningham three for 29) and 189 (R. N. Lewis 35; N. O. Perry four for 39); Jamaica* 175 (L. V. Garrick 51, C. H. Gayle 55; S. Shillingford seven for 66, I. O. Jackson three for 46) and 183 for seven (R. G. Samuels 69 not out, N. O. Perry 59; F. Thomas five for 53). *Jamaica 12 pts.*

At Queen's Park Oval, Port-of-Spain, January 11, 12, 13, 14. TRINIDAD & TOBAGO drew with ENGLAND A (see England A tour section). *Trinidad & Tobago 6 pts, England A 3 pts.*

At Kensington Oval, Bridgetown, January 12, 13, 14, 15. Drawn. Jamaica 274 (W. E. Cuff 65, K. H. Hibbert 45, N. O. Perry 37; H. R. Bryan three for 55, D. K. Marshall five for 91) and 255 for six dec. (C. H. Gayle 131 not out, W. E. Cuff 39; H. R. Bryan four for 71); Barbados* 213 (A. F. G. Griffith 44, S. H. Armstrong 48, R. I. C. Holder 38; G. R. Breese six for 47, N. O. Perry three for 64) and 138 for eight (F. L. Reifer 56, C. O. Browne 45; G. R. Breese three for 46, R. O. Cunningham three for 33). *Barbados 3 pts, Jamaica 6 pts.*

At Recreation Ground, St John's, January 12, 13, 14, 15. Drawn. Guyana 353 (K. F. Semple 35, R. R. Sarwan 52, L. J. Cush 90, Extras 33; R. J. Christopher four for 112) and 192 (C. L. Hooper 66; G. T. Prince three for 53, K. C. B. Jeremy six for 46); Leeward Islands* 277 (S. C. Williams 45, R. S. Morton 64, F. A. Adams 44, C. D. Cannonier 36, W. W. Cornwall 43; K. G. Darlington three for 40, C. L. Hooper three for 57) and 244 for nine (J. A. Mitchum 34, R. S. Morton 65, C. D. Cannonier 32, W. W. Cornwall 30, C. M. Tuckett 34 not out; R. R. Sarwan six for 62). *Leeward Islands 3 pts, Guyana 6 pts.*

At Arnos Vale, St Vincent, January 12, 13, 14. West Indies B won by 162 runs. West Indies B 213 (D. E. Bernard 34, T. A. Willett 81; M. J. Morgan three for 38, I. O. Jackson four for 59) and 204 (A. Gonsalves 43, D. E. Bernard 30, T. A. Willett 48 not out, S. J. Benn 47; I. O. Jackson eight for 79); Windward Islands* 110 (J. Eugene 31; S. J. Benn four for 36, N. Deonarine four for 35) and 145 (S. J. Benn five for 51, C. C. Alexander four for 66). *West Indies B 12 pts.*

Jackson's eight for 79 represented the best bowling in an innings for Windwards in the regional competition.

At Wilson Road Recreation Ground, Peñal (Trinidad), January 18, 19, 20, 21. Barbados won by ten wickets. West Indies B 177 (K. J. Wilkinson 32, T. A. Willett 54; D. K. Marshall four for 31) and 143 (A. Gonsalves 30, N. Deonarine 40, R. B. Richardson 40; R. A. Austin four for 39, H. R. Bryan three for 35); Barbados* 291 for seven dec. (P. A. Wallace 43, S. H. Armstrong 71, S. M. Clarke 65 not out, C. O. Browne 65; S. J. Benn four for 75) and 30 for no wkt. *Barbados 12 pts.*

At Queen's Park, St George's (Grenada), January 19, 20, 21, 22. ENGLAND A drew with GUYANA (see England A tour section). *England A 6 pts, Guyana 3 pts.*

At Edgar Gilbert Sporting Complex, Molyneux (St Kitts), January 19, 20, 21, 22. Drawn. Jamaica 238 (L. V. Garrick 66, C. H. Gayle 48, K. H. Hibbert 44; O. A. C. Banks seven for 70) and 257 for seven dec. (L. V. Garrick 55, R. G. Samuels 40, G. R. Breese 54 not out, N. O. Perry 31 not out; O. A. C. Banks three for 78); Leeward Islands* 235 (D. A. Williams 48, J. M. Simmonds 52, O. A. C. Banks 43; R. O. Cunningham four for 62, N. O. Perry three for 29) and 106 for eight (R. O. Cunningham three for 11). *Leeward Islands 3 pts, Jamaica 6 pts.*

At Arnos Vale, St Vincent, January 19, 20, 21, 22. Trinidad & Tobago won by five wickets. Windward Islands* 257 (J. Eugene 30, R. N. Lewis 66, D. K. Butler 54 not out, Extras 33; D. Ramnarine six for 54) and 219 (J. R. Murray 97 not out; M. Persad four for 50, R. Dhanraj five for 68); Trinidad & Tobago 261 (S. Ragoonath 59, I. H. Jan 30, R. A. M. Smith 73; S. Shillingford three for 71, I. O. Jackson three for 86) and 216 for five (D. Rampersad 51, L. A. Roberts 102 not out). *Trinidad & Tobago 12 pts.*

At Queen's Park Oval, Port-of-Spain, January 25, 26, 27. Guyana won by an innings and 24 runs. West Indies B* 191 (K. J. Wilkinson 45, T. A. Willett 89; K. G. Darlington five for 53) and 196

(A. Gonsalves 58, K. J. Wilkinson 51, D. E. Bernard 33; K. G. Darlington four for 39, N. C. McGarrell four for 36); Guyana 411 for nine dec. (K. F. Semple 30, R. R. Sarwan 90, T. M. Dowlin 116 not out, C. L. Hooper 98). *Guyana 12 pts.*

At Queen's Park, St George's (Grenada), January 25, 26, 27, 28. Leeward Islands won by nine wickets. Leeward Islands* 308 (J. A. Mitchum 30, C. M. Tuckett 48, J. M. Simmonds 54, K. C. B. Jeremy 70 not out; D. K. Butler four for 63) and 42 for one; Windward Islands 128 (J. R. Murray 34; K. C. B. Jeremy three for 37) and 219 (R. K. Currency 48, K. N. Casimir 63, I. O. Jackson 31; K. C. B. Jeremy four for 49, C. M. Tuckett three for 12). *Leeward Islands 12 pts.*

Umpire Bucknor called Windwards off-spinner Shane Shillingford for throwing on the first day.

At Kensington Oval, Bridgetown, January 26, 27, 28, 29. BARBADOS drew with ENGLAND A (see England A tour section). *Barbados 3 pts, England A 6 pts.*

At Chedwin Park, Spanish Town (Jamaica), January 26, 27, 28, 29. Jamaica won by two wickets. Trinidad & Tobago* 177 (L. A. Roberts 52, R. A. M. Smith 44; N. O. Perry three for 30) and 144 (R. A. M. Smith 49; N. O. Perry three for 49); Jamaica 158 (C. H. Gayle 32, G. R. Breese 46 not out, N. O. Perry 30; M. Persad four for 36, D. Ramnarine four for 49) and 164 for eight (C. H. Gayle 67; D. Ramnarine five for 54, M. Persad three for 44). *Jamaica 12 pts, Trinidad & Tobago 4 pts.*

At Guaracara Park, Pointe-à-Pierre, February 1, 2, 3. Leeward Islands won by ten wickets. West Indies B 140 (D. E. Bernard 33; R. J. Christopher five for 32, C. M. Tuckett three for 36) and 215 (K. J. Wilkinson 38, N. Deonarine 73, S. J. Benn 31; W. W. Cornwall three for 65, R. S. Morton three for 17); Leeward Islands* 338 (S. C. Williams 39, J. A. Mitchum 81, F. A. Adams 56, C. M. Tuckett 70 not out; J. J. C. Lawson four for 102, S. J. Benn three for 112, R. I. Sooklal three for 60) and 20 for no wkt. *Leeward Islands 12 pts.*

At Kensington Oval, Bridgetown, February 2, 3, 4, 5. Barbados won by 111 runs. Barbados* 267 (R. O. Hinds 87, C. O. Browne 72, I. D. R. Bradshaw 37; F. Thomas three for 60, D. K. Butler three for 44) and 192 for five dec. (P. A. Wallace 78, S. H. Armstrong 53; D. K. Butler three for 71); Windward Islands 125 (H. R. Bryan three for 31, D. K. Marshall three for 44) and 223 (J. R. Murray 39, S. G. Wilson 52 not out; C. D. Collymore three for 40, R. A. Austin four for 64, R. O. Hinds three for 27). *Barbados 12 pts.*

At Enmore, Demerara, February 2, 3, 4, 5. Guyana won by seven wickets. Trinidad & Tobago 106 (D. Brown 47; K. G. Darlington six for 25) and 307 (L. A. Roberts 58, R. A. M. Smith 96; N. C. McGarrell three for 81, R. S. Matthews three for 64); Guyana* 357 for nine dec. (R. R. Sarwan 75, T. M. Dowlin 58, C. L. Hooper 142; D. Brown four for 80, L. A. Roberts three for 45) and 57 for three. *Guyana 12 pts.*

At Sabina Park, Kingston, February 2, 3, 4, 5. JAMAICA lost to ENGLAND A by seven wickets (see England A tour section). *England A 12 pts.*

At Roxborough, Tobago, February 8, 9, 10, 11. Trinidad & Tobago won by 79 runs. Trinidad & Tobago* 143 (A. Jackson 51, K. Mason 31; S. J. Benn four for 74, R. I. Sooklal three for 28) and 258 (A. Jackson 33, I. H. Jan 32, D. Mohammed 42, L. A. Roberts 33, K. Mason 54; S. J. Benn three for 66); West Indies B 154 (R. B. Richardson 49 not out; D. Ramnarine four for 48, D. Mohammed four for 36) and 168 (D. E. Bernard 43, Z. R. Ali 40; D. Ramnarine six for 81, D. Mohammed four for 24). *Trinidad & Tobago 12 pts, West Indies B 4 pts.*

Mohammed on debut took a wicket with his first ball in first-class cricket and eight for 60 in the match.

At Albion, Berbice, February 9, 10, 11, 12. Drawn. Guyana 334 (T. M. Dowlin 77, C. L. Hooper 128; D. B. Powell four for 46, N. O. Perry three for 68) and 130 for four (A. Haniff 50); Jamaica* 256 (L. V. Garrick 60, W. E. Cuff 36, R. G. Samuels 39, K. H. Hibbert 52; N. C. McGarrell five for 82, R. S. Matthews three for 68). *Guyana 6 pts, Jamaica 3 pts.*

At Grove Park, Charlestown (Nevis), February 9, 10, 11, 12. Barbados won by six wickets. Leeward Islands* 236 (S. C. Williams 88, J. A. Mitchum 58; R. O. Hinds nine for 68) and 115 (D. A. Williams 31; R. O. Hinds six for 34); Barbados 253 (P. A. Wallace 76, A. F. G. Griffith 39; K. C. B. Jeremy three for 53, O. A. C. Banks three for 62) and 99 for four. *Barbados 12 pts.*

Hinds's nine for 68 was the best innings return in the history of the West Indian regional first-class competition, beating Derek Parry's nine for 76 for Combined Islands against Jamaica in 1979-80; his 15 for 102 was the second-best match return after Parry's 15 for 101 on the same occasion.

At Mindoo Phillip Park, Castries (St Lucia), February 9, 10, 11. WINDWARD ISLANDS lost to ENGLAND A by an innings and 17 runs (see England A tour section). *England A 12 pts.*

At Kensington Oval, Bridgetown, February 16, 17, 18, 19. Barbados won by six wickets. Trinidad & Tobago 254 (D. Ganga 105, L. A. Roberts 45; C. D. Collymore five for 66) and 204 (A. Jackson 48, L. A. Roberts 32, D. Mohammed 34; I. D. R. Bradshaw four for 46, H. R. Bryan three for 37); Barbados* 180 (S. L. Campbell 40, R. O. Hinds 36; D. Ramnarine three for 54, D. Mohammed three for 30) and 281 for four (P. A. Wallace 45, S. L. Campbell 55, F. L. Reifer 64 not out, R. I. C. Holder 73, Extras 31). *Barbados 12 pts, Trinidad & Tobago 4 pts.*

At Bourda, Georgetown, February 16, 17, 18, 19. Guyana won by seven wickets. Windward Islands* 350 (R. K. Currency 33, J. Eugene 139, R. N. Lewis 74; M. V. Nagamootoo six for 92) and 199 (J. R. Murray 56, J. Eugene 46, R. N. Lewis 31; N. C. McGarrell three for 40, M. V. Nagamootoo three for 73, C. L. Hooper three for 31); Guyana 425 for nine dec. (S. Chattergoon 56, R. R. Sarwan 73, T. M. Dowlin 67, C. L. Hooper 128, N. C. McGarrell 47 not out; S. Shillingford three for 123, I. O. Jackson three for 111) and 128 for three (R. R. Sarwan 39 not out). *Guyana 12 pts.*

At Jarrett Park, Montego Bay, February 16, 17, 18, 19. Jamaica won by 166 runs. Jamaica* 129 (L. V. Garrick 40; K. J. Wilkinson three for eight) and 425 for no wkt dec. (L. V. Garrick 200 not out, C. H. Gayle 208 not out); West Indies B 184 (K. J. Wilkinson 86; R. O. Cunningham three for 36, W. W. Hinds three for nine) and 204 (W. Phillip 40, S. J. Benn 33; A. A. Sanson five for 56). *Jamaica 12 pts, West Indies B 4 pts.*

In Jamaica's first innings, Wilkinson's figures were 6.5–3–8–3; Hinds responded in West Indies B's first innings with 6–3–9–3. In Jamaica's second innings, Garrick's 200 not out lasted 502 minutes and 386 balls and included 21 fours; Gayle's 208 not out lasted the same time, but he faced 336 balls and hit 19 fours. Together, they put on 425 in 117.3 overs, a record for any first wicket in the West Indies, beating 390 by G. L. Wight and G. L. Gibbs for British Guiana against Barbados in 1951-52.

At Ronald Webster Park, The Valley (Anguilla), February 16, 17, 18, 19. LEEWARD ISLANDS drew with ENGLAND A (see England A tour section). *Leeward Islands 6 pts, England A 3 pts.*

BUSTA INTERNATIONAL SHIELD, 2000-01

Semi-finals

At Kensington Oval, Bridgetown, February 23, 24, 25, 26. Jamaica won by 234 runs. Jamaica* 496 (L. V. Garrick 172, W. W. Hinds 101, M. N. Samuels 37, J. C. Adams 56 not out; I. D. R. Bradshaw three for 97) and 91 for three dec. (W. W. Hinds 50; R. O. Hinds three for 12); Barbados 171 (S. L. Campbell 36, A. F. G. Griffith 47; G. R. Breese three for 36, N. O. Perry three for 39) and 182 (S. L. Campbell 47, H. R. Bryan 36, R. A. Austin 35; G. R. Breese seven for 60).

At Bourda, Georgetown, February 24, 25, 26, 27. GUYANA beat ENGLAND A by seven wickets (see England A tour section).

FINAL

JAMAICA v GUYANA

At Sabina Park, Kingston, March 3, 4, 5, 6. Drawn. Toss: Jamaica.

The final began contentiously – Guyana had delayed the start a day by arguing it should be held in Georgetown, and Hooper was booed after supplanting Jamaica's Adams as West Indies captain. Gayle dismissed such negative thoughts by batting nearly five hours for his century, hitting 12 fours and adding 147 with Hinds. Next morning, Hinds completed his second hundred in two matches, and immediately presented Mahendra Nagamootoo with a fourth wicket. Breese, however, helped to steer Jamaica to an imposing 375, while on the third day his off-spin had Guyana 105 for five. Hooper fought back, aided by Nagamootoo, until controversially given lbw. McGarrell and Stuart put on 89 for the ninth wicket but, with their dismissals on the last morning, Guyana conceded a first-innings lead of 85. That was enough to secure Jamaica the Shield. Gayle scored another fifty in the remaining play but fell just nine runs short of Hooper's record-aggregate 954 in the competition.

Man of the Match: C. H. Gayle.

Close of play: First day, Jamaica 277-4 (Hinds 94*, Breese 4*); Second day, Guyana 81-2 (Haniff 39*, Sarwan 5*); Third day, Guyana 258-8 (McGarrell 40*, Stuart 15*).

Jamaica

L. V. Garrick c McGarrell b Hooper	25	– c Haniff b Stuart	11
C. H. Gayle c McGarrell b M. V. Nagamootoo	125	– c Chattergoon b M. V. Nagamootoo	51
W. W. Hinds c and b M. V. Nagamootoo	100		
M. N. Samuels c Chanderpaul b M. V. Nagamootoo	18	– (3) c McGarrell b M. V. Nagamootoo	21
*J. C. Adams c Dowlin b M. V. Nagamootoo	0	– not out	28
G. R. Breese run out	43		
L. R. Williams b Stuart	21		
†K. H. Hibbert c V. Nagamootoo b King	9	– (4) c Sarwan b Chanderpaul	44
N. O. Perry c V. Nagamootoo b King	4		
F. A. Rose not out	12		
C. A. Walsh lbw b King	0		
B 2, l-b 3, n-b 13	18	B 1, l-b 1, n-b 4	6
1/82 2/229 3/275 4/275 5/292 6/339 7/352 8/361 9/375	375	1/14 2/74 3/93 4/161 (4 wkts)	161

Bowling: *First Innings*—King 22–3–67–3; Stuart 17–2–70–1; M. V. Nagamootoo 45–7–126–4; Hooper 32–11–54–1; McGarrell 24–5–53–0. *Second Innings*—King 8–5–18–0; Stuart 7–1–29–1; McGarrell 24–11–46–0; M. V. Nagamootoo 23–9–50–2; Chattergoon 2–0–5–0; Chanderpaul 2–0–7–1; Haniff 1–0–4–0.

Guyana

A. Haniff c Gayle b Breese	39
S. Chattergoon c Gayle b Perry	20
T. M. Dowlin c Garrick b Adams	11
R. R. Sarwan lbw b Walsh	9
S. Chanderpaul c Samuels b Breese	8
*C. L. Hooper lbw b Walsh	65
M. V. Nagamootoo c Hibbert b Rose	33
N. C. McGarrell lbw b Breese	52
†V. Nagamootoo c Hibbert b Rose	4
C. E. L. Stuart c Rose b Perry	33
R. D. King not out	0
L-b 3, n-b 13	16
1/58 2/71 3/85 4/85 5/105 6/197 7/197 8/201 9/290	290

Bowling: Rose 27–7–70–2; Williams 18–3–44–0; Walsh 30–12–51–2; Breese 38–21–47–3; Perry 30.2–9–49–2; Adams 9–4–16–1; Samuels 4–2–2–0; Gayle 4–0–8–0.

Umpires: S. A. Bucknor and B. R. Doctrove.
Third umpire: T. Wilson.

REGIONAL CHAMPIONS

Shell Shield		*Red Stripe Cup*	
1965-66	Barbados	1987-88	Jamaica
1966-67	Barbados	1988-89	Jamaica
1967-68	No competition	1989-90	Leeward Islands
1968-69	Jamaica	1990-91	Barbados
1969-70	Trinidad	1991-92	Jamaica
1970-71	Trinidad	1992-93	Guyana
1971-72	Barbados	1993-94	Leeward Islands
1972-73	Guyana	1994-95	Barbados
1973-74	Barbados	1995-96	Leeward Islands
1974-75	Guyana	1996-97	Barbados
1975-76	{ Trinidad / Barbados		
1976-77	Barbados	*President's Cup*	
1977-78	Barbados	1997-98	{ Leeward Islands / Guyana
1978-79	Barbados		
1979-80	Barbados		
1980-81	Combined Islands		
1981-82	Barbados	*Busta Cup*	
1982-83	Guyana	1998-99	Barbados
1983-84	Barbados	1999-2000	Jamaica
1984-85	Trinidad & Tobago	2000-01	Barbados
1985-86	Barbados		
1986-87	Guyana		

Barbados have won the title outright 16 times, Guyana and Jamaica 5, Leeward Islands and Trinidad/Trinidad & Tobago 3, Combined Islands 1. Barbados, Guyana, Leeward Islands and Trinidad have also shared the title.

RED STRIPE BOWL, 2000-01

Note: Matches in this section were not first-class.

	Played	*Won*	*Lost*	*Points*	*Net run-rate*
Zone A (in Jamaica)					
Barbados	4	3	1	6	0.88
Jamaica	4	3	1	6	1.22
Trinidad & Tobago	4	2	2	4	0.28
Canada	4	1	3	2	−0.62
USA	4	1	3	2	−2.10
Zone B (in Leeward Islands)					
Windward Islands	4	3	1	6	1.02
Leeward Islands	4	3	1	6	0.93
Guyana	4	3	1	6	0.48
Bermuda	4	1	3	2	−0.27
Cayman Islands	4	0	4	0	−3.30

Barbados finished ahead of Jamaica, and Canada ahead of USA, by virtue of winning their head-to-head matches. Windwards, Leewards and Guyana were separated on net run-rate, all three having won one of their head-to-head matches. Net run-rate was calculated by subtracting runs conceded per over from runs scored per over.

Semi-finals

At Sabina Park, Kingston, October 20. Leeward Islands won by 13 runs. Leeward Islands 169 (49.5 overs) (R. D. Jacobs 44, C. M. Tuckett 39; H. R. Bryan three for 25); Barbados* 156 (48.4 overs) (D. M. Richards 31, R. O. Hinds 44; W. W. Cornwall three for 25).

At Sabina Park, Kingston, October 21. Windward Islands won by four wickets. Jamaica* 187 for nine (50 overs) (M. N. Samuels 52, Extras 31; N. A. M. McLean four for 28); Windward Islands 191 for six (48.2 overs) (R. K. Currency 30, J. R. Murray 42, J. Eugene 44 not out).

Final

At Sabina Park, Kingston, October 22. Windward Islands won by five wickets. Leeward Islands* 163 for eight (50 overs) (W. W. Cornwall 53; R. N. Lewis three for 31); Windward Islands 164 for five (42.5 overs) (J. R. Murray 30, R. A. Marshall 36 not out; A. J. A. Lake three for 23).

THE DUCKWORTH/LEWIS METHOD

In 1997, the ECB's limited-overs competitions adopted a new method to revise targets in interrupted games, devised by Frank Duckworth of the Royal Statistical Society and Tony Lewis of the University of the West of England. The method was gradually taken up by other countries and, in 1999, ICC decided to incorporate it into the standard playing conditions for limited-overs internationals for an experimental period of two years to August 2001, now extended to August 2004.

The system aims to preserve any advantage that one team has established before the interruption. It uses the idea that teams have two resources from which they make runs – an allocated number of overs and ten wickets. It also takes into account when the interruption occurs, because of the different scoring-rates typical of different stages of an innings. Traditional run-rate calculations relied only on the overs available, and ignored wickets lost.

After modifications, the system now uses one table with 50 rows, covering matches of any length up to 50 overs, and ten columns, from nought to nine wickets down. Each figure in the table gives the percentage of the total runs in an innings that would, on average, be scored with a certain number of overs left and wickets lost.

If overs are lost, the table is used to calculate the percentage of runs the team would be expected to score in those missing overs. This is obtained by reading off the figure for the number of overs left and wickets down when play stops and subtracting from it the corresponding figure for the number of overs remaining when it resumes.

If the first innings is complete and the second innings is interrupted, the target to be beaten is reduced by the percentage of the innings lost. If the suspension occurs between innings, as in the ICC Trophy final between Bangladesh and Kenya at Kuala Lumpur in April 1997, only one figure is required: the percentage of the innings remaining for the reduced number of overs with no wicket lost. Kenya scored 241 from 50 overs, but rain restricted Bangladesh to 25 overs. On the traditional average run-rate, losing half their overs would have halved the target to 121. But they had all ten wickets, so had more than half their run-scoring resources. The table showed that, on average, 25 overs should yield 68.7 per cent of a 50-over total. Bangladesh's target was set at 166 (68.7 per cent of 241 = 165.56), which they reached off the final ball.

The system also covers interruptions to the first innings, multiple interruptions and innings terminated by rain.

If penalty runs are awarded against a team batting second, these runs are added to their target; no other recalculation is made. In all other circumstances, penalty runs are added to the opposition's total as normal.

CRICKET IN NEW ZEALAND, 2000-01

By DON CAMERON and FRANCIS PAYNE

Mark Richardson

From August 2000 to August 2001, no fewer than 33 New Zealand cricketers waged campaigns from Singapore to Zimbabwe, Kenya to South Africa, Sharjah to Sri Lanka – and hosted visits by Zimbabwe, Sri Lanka and Pakistan. They played nine Tests (three won, three lost, three drawn) and 37 one-day internationals (12 won, 24 lost, one washed out). Lifting New Zealand's first international trophy at the ICC Knockout in Nairobi in October provided an early high, from which they immediately plummeted back to earth in South Africa. Subsequent results were mixed – although the home season concluded with an encouraging recovery against Pakistan – but, after one of the most exhaustive examinations undertaken by a New Zealand squad, no one could really say whether the national team were better, worse or the same as when they began.

Their variable form drew comments both waspish and admiring; the more charitable noted another exasperating injury list that shredded a potentially match-winning attack. In Africa, Chris Cairns often looked like the world's leading all-rounder; but after missing the South African Tests he was barely seen again before his knee went under the surgeon's knife. Daniel Vettori succumbed to another back problem and, when he returned, his left-arm spin lacked its former bite and rhythm. Geoff Allott's back eventually forced him into retirement, and Dion Nash's kept him out of the New Zealand side for most of the season. Shayne O'Connor developed into a clever, aggressive new-ball bowler in South Africa, then he too was injured. Meanwhile the injury-prone Simon Doull battled along for Northern Districts, only to find that the national selectors would not risk him.

In their place came a succession of newcomers. Chris Martin and Daryl Tuffey, a bonny Maori with the size and zest that All Black flankers once displayed, offered a pleasing contrast of new-ball styles. Martin's spindly frame generated remarkable nip and bounce, while the muscular, aggressive Tuffey left the right-hander's bat testingly. Tuffey may also have offered the insight of the season after taking four wickets in a surprising one-day win over Pakistan. Asked if some secret accounted for his sudden success, the beaming Tuffey replied: "Not really, I tossed aside a lot of the things I'd been advised to do, and just ran in and bowled as fast as I could."

Quite a few observers reckoned that Sir Richard Hadlee, the new chairman of selectors and an instant dartboard for the critics, David Trist, who stepped down as national coach in June, and the fellow-travelling "co-ordinators" and "performance analysts" tended towards over-elaborate preparation and planning. Near the end of the summer, there was a subtle change. After the abject surrender of the First Test to

Pakistan, when the last eight wickets fell for ten runs, the *New Zealand Herald* trumpeted that captain Stephen Fleming would have to go. But New Zealand Cricket's top brass told Fleming he was the man they wanted, and it was intimated that he might do better if, in fact, he did captain the team, rather than appearing as just one of a committee of managers and selectors. As Fleming's confidence was restored, New Zealand smashed Pakistan at Hamilton by an innings and 185 runs, their biggest victory and Pakistan's widest loss.

In contrast to the parade of ailing bowlers, only one batsman, opener Matt Horne, was unfit. Even so, it took months to sort out the order, and especially to find an efficient opening pair. Then in March the selectors paired Mark Richardson, the find of the season, with Matthew Bell, tossed aside the previous year but recalled after an outstanding run for Wellington. This combination started the upward spiral of success against Pakistan. They began the First Test with a single run between them, but put on 91 in the second innings (a rich overture to the shocking collapse), 102 and 69 in the Second Test, and 181 (with maiden Test centuries for both) in the Third.

Richardson enjoyed an astonishing season, ending it as New Zealand's Cricketer of the Year. Some ten years before, he was a promising slow left-armer in Auckland, but his form was fitful and he left for Otago, where his bowling ambitions were halted by an attack of the "yips"; at times, it seemed, his fingers would not let the ball go. He reinvented himself as a batsman, scoring 103 against the West Indians in 1994-95, but remained in the background as a flood of supposedly promising youngsters flowed through New Zealand's academy. In June 2000, aged 29, he toured England with New Zealand A, scored 212 not out against Sussex, and was taken to Africa. There, he warmed up with 306 against Zimbabwe A, and was by far the most consistent batsman in the South African Tests (flashier players were preferred for the limited-overs games). Richardson's century against Pakistan ended a startling ten months in which he amassed 2,672 first-class runs at 66.80. In the home season, his 1,035 were exceeded only by Bell.

Now 24, Bell had been a prolific teenager, but lost confidence after his early, uncertain international exposure. Former Test left-hander Bruce Edgar persuaded him that, once he established his survival in the middle, runs would come. So they did: he scored 844, including five centuries, a Wellington record, in ten matches, captained the province to the Shell Trophy, and earned a Test recall. His hundred against Pakistan lifted him to 1,092 first-class runs, the fourth-highest aggregate in a New Zealand season.

Wellington's title was their 19th – the most by any province – but their first since 1989-90, a heartening turnaround after they finished fifth of six the previous two seasons. Since then, the four-day competition's format had been revised; the number of matches was doubled, with home and away rounds, though the final was dropped. In the last round, Wellington faced second-placed Northern Districts, the reigning champions and the only team to have beaten them in the 2000-01 competition. But Northern had to win again, without conceding any points, to pull level. In the event, the match was drawn, and Wellington secured the title just before lunch on the third day when they gained two points for a first-innings lead. Having advanced to 508, they relaxed in the closing stages. All 11 Wellingtonians would have bowled if the tenth, Richard Jones, had not ended play a few minutes early with his first ball in first-class cricket, a rank full toss that Grant Bradburn hit to square leg to be caught by off-duty wicket-keeper Chris Nevin.

Jones, who had moved from Auckland, blossomed as a batsman, passing 800 runs. Another crucial player in Wellington's success was Iain O'Brien, a 24-year-old seamer whose background included softball rather than the academy's elaborate talent-scouting system. Tall, lean, but surprisingly durable, O'Brien was the Shell Trophy's leading wicket-taker with 41 at 17.87 in his debut season.

Northern Districts, like Wellington, won four matches, but a lack of consistent runs meant they fell behind on first-innings points. Their strength lay in their bowling. Off-spinner Bradburn, now 34, overtook Andy Roberts's record of 104 first-class matches for Northern, was named domestic cricket's outstanding player, and regained his Test place after an eight-year gap. Joseph Yovich's medium-pace claimed 34 wickets; Tuffey, available for only three matches, grabbed 18.

Auckland possessed the first-class season's leading wicket-taker in seamer Chris Drum, with 48. The last of these arrived on his Test debut against Pakistan – whereupon he joined the injured. Drum's promising medium-fast colleague, Kyle Mills, provided the surprise of the season, striking such a rich vein of middle-order runs that he scored 606 at 101.00 in the Trophy, and made his international debut at Sharjah.

Otago had a share of Richardson's bountiful form – he scored 675 in seven matches for them – but it was not enough to mount a serious challenge in the Shell Trophy. David Sewell and Craig Pryor took 29 wickets each, and Nathan McCullum looked like a wicket-keeper/batsman of high promise.

Former New Zealand all-rounder Dipak Patel made his mark on the coaching front when his Central Districts side won the one-day Shell Cup, coming from behind to beat Canterbury 2–1 in the finals. In the Trophy, though, they won only two matches, despite having the competition's heaviest scorer in Leicestershire's Ben Smith, with 939 runs at 58.68. Jacob Oram, a Cairns-type medium-fast bowler and stalwart batsman, earned an international call, while opener Craig Spearman, dropped by New Zealand, made 611 runs at 50.91. David Kelly's 212 not out against Canterbury was the highest individual score of the season.

Jarrod Englefield continued to make progress, scoring 724 runs for Canterbury, while captain Gary Stead hit 875 in all first-class cricket. However, the usual exodus of their international stars took its toll again and Canterbury finished bottom of the Trophy for the third year running, losing half their matches and winning none. Their worst moment came on a dreadful morning against Central Districts at Christchurch in January, when they lost five wickets in eight balls while the score remained stuck on eight.

The weeks before Christmas saw New Zealand host the women's World Cup, and for the third tournament running the "White Ferns" reached the final. This time they won, with Emily Drumm's team edging out a powerful Australian side by four runs. It was a remarkable achievement, which attracted high television ratings, but sadly the women's triumph slipped into the background as the troughs and peaks of the men's team claimed the New Year headlines.

Christopher Doig left after five years as New Zealand Cricket's chief executive. Coming from an operatic background, he had made a dramatic start, sacking national coach Glenn Turner and head-hunting Australian Steve Rixon, and he soon took a prominent role in New Zealand and world cricket. Doig doubled NZC's turnover to $NZ20 million, and attracted not only sponsorship and television rights but also wealthy patrons. One of these was Michael Watt, a multimillionaire with an abiding love for Canterbury and New Zealand cricket, who contributed $NZ3–4 million, mostly to develop the academy and high-performance centre at Lincoln University. Doig will, as the cliché goes, be missed. – D.C.

FIRST-CLASS AVERAGES, 2000-01

BATTING

(Qualification: 5 completed innings, average 40.00)

	M	*I*	*NO*	*R*	*HS*	*100s*	*Avge*
K. D. Mills (*Auckland*)	8	13	6	606	117*	1	86.57
M. S. Sinclair (*C. Districts*)	8	13	3	724	204*	2	72.40
M. H. Richardson (*Otago*)	11	19	2	1,035	166	2	60.88
R. G. Twose (*Wellington*)	4	6	1	298	108	1	59.60

	M	*I*	*NO*	*R*	*HS*	*100s*	*Avge*
B. F. Smith (*C. Districts*)	10	17	1	939	168	2	58.68
C. D. McMillan (*Canterbury*)	4	6	0	324	142	1	54.00
M. D. Bell (*Wellington*)	13	21	0	1,092	134	6	52.00
C. M. Spearman (*C. Districts*)	7	12	0	611	130	1	50.91
S. P. Fleming (*Wellington*)	4	6	1	251	86	0	50.20
G. R. Stead (*Canterbury*)	12	20	2	875	121*	3	48.61
G. P. Sulzberger (*C. Districts*)	8	12	1	525	103	1	47.72
R. A. Jones (*Wellington*)	12	19	0	860	188	3	45.26
C. D. Cumming (*Otago*)	10	19	5	626	125*	2	44.71
N. J. Astle (*Canterbury*)	5	6	1	216	141	1	43.20
G. J. Hopkins (*Canterbury*)	11	19	7	517	100*	1	43.08
C. J. Nevin (*Wellington*)	12	17	4	554	99	0	42.61
M. W. Douglas (*C. Districts*)	10	16	2	583	134	2	41.64

* *Signifies not out.*

BOWLING

(Qualification: 15 wickets)

	O	*M*	*R*	*W*	*BB*	*5W/i*	*Avge*
B. E. Hefford (*C. Districts*)	202.5	74	438	24	5-50	1	18.25
C. J. Drum (*Auckland*)	342.5	99	889	48	5-65	1	18.52
D. R. Tuffey (*N. Districts*)	238.5	78	630	34	7-12	2	18.52
I. E. O'Brien (*Wellington*)	319.1	81	807	41	6-55	3	19.68
J. E. C. Franklin (*Wellington*)	204.5	40	622	31	5-39	1	20.06
A. M. Schwass (*C. Districts*)	169	45	457	22	5-53	2	20.77
M. D. J. Walker (*Wellington*)	193.4	69	387	18	5-29	1	21.50
T. K. Canning (*Auckland*)	243.5	75	585	27	4-36	0	21.66
W. C. McSkimming (*Otago*)	226.5	75	585	26	6-39	1	22.50
C. R. Pryor (*Otago*)	255.1	65	684	29	5-28	2	23.58
A. R. Adams (*Auckland*)	216.4	53	626	26	4-12	0	24.07
A. J. Penn (*Wellington*)	291.5	79	794	32	4-28	0	24.81
D. G. Sewell (*Otago*)	283.4	82	799	29	6-70	1	27.55
J. A. F. Yovich (*N. Districts*)	332.4	95	938	34	7-64	1	27.58
K. D. Mills (*Auckland*)	169	36	442	16	4-57	0	27.62
M. R. Jefferson (*Wellington*)	192.1	49	498	18	4-84	0	27.66
S. E. Bond (*Canterbury*)	187.4	52	536	19	5-51	1	28.21
S. J. Cunis (*Canterbury*)	214.4	37	658	22	4-83	0	29.90
G. E. Bradburn (*N. Districts*)	342.1	107	781	25	5-114	1	31.24

SHELL TROPHY, 2000-01

	Played	*Won*	*Lost*	*Drawn*	*1st-inns Points*	*Points*	*Net avge runs per wkt*
Wellington	10	4	1	5	10	34	8.75
Northern Districts	10	4	2	4	2	26	–4.54
Auckland	10	4	3	3	0	24	4.32
Otago	10	3	2	5	6	24	2.69
Central Districts	10	2	4	4	8	20	–0.18
Canterbury	10	0	5	5	6	6	–15.43

Outright win = 6 pts; lead on first innings in a drawn or lost game = 2 pts.
Auckland finished third by virtue of having more wins than Otago.
Net average runs per wicket is calculated by subtracting average runs conceded per wicket from average runs scored per wicket.

*In the following scores, * by the name of a team indicates that they won the toss.*

At Basin Reserve, Wellington, November 27, 28, 29, 30. Drawn. Wellington 331 for four dec. (M. D. Bell 134, R. A. Jones 67, J. D. Wells 65, R. G. Twose 37 not out) and forfeited innings; Canterbury* forfeited innings and 267 for five (G. R. Stead 88, C. Z. Harris 69 not out, A. J. Redmond 33; M. R. Jefferson three for 79). *Wellington 2 pts.*

There was no play on the second and third days, after which both sides forfeited an innings, the first such instance in New Zealand first-class cricket.

At Victoria Park, Wanganui, November 29, 30, December 1. Central Districts won by nine wickets. Otago 175 (M. G. Croy 78; E. P. Thompson three for 52) and 139 (M. J. Horne 73; M. J. Mason five for 44, G. L. West three for 46); Central Districts* 280 (D. P. Kelly 70, B. F. Smith 124, M. W. Douglas 34; D. G. Sewell six for 70) and 35 for one. *Central Districts 6 pts.*

At Seddon Park, Hamilton, November 29, 30, December 1, 2. Northern Districts won by two wickets. Auckland 146 (J. A. F. Yovich three for 51, G. W. Aldridge five for 50) and 204 (B. A. Pocock 32, R. T. King 36, A. C. Barnes 45; S. B. Doull three for 25, G. W. Aldridge four for 41); Northern Districts* 178 (B. P. Martin 51; R. G. Morgan five for 44) and 173 for eight (M. D. Bailey 76; C. J. Drum three for 33). *Northern Districts 6 pts.*

At Queen Elizabeth II Park, Christchurch, December 6, 7, 8, 9. Drawn. Canterbury 477 (G. R. Stead 100, C. Z. Harris 145, M. H. W. Papps 35, G. J. Hopkins 48, W. A. Wisneski 58 not out, Extras 39; R. G. Morgan three for 61, A. R. Adams three for 109) and 141 for five (M. H. W. Papps 40, C. J. Anderson 45 not out; A. R. Adams four for 28); Auckland* 435 (T. G. McIntosh 182, L. Vincent 78, T. K. Canning 35, B. A. Pocock 48; W. A. Wisneski seven for 151). *Canterbury 2 pts.*

McIntosh scored his maiden first-class century, batting 559 minutes in all for 182, with 22 fours and a six.

At Owen Delany Park, Taupo, December 6, 7, 8, 9. Northern Districts won by eight wickets. Central Districts* 289 (B. F. Smith 92, M. W. Douglas 130) and 182 (D. P. Kelly 31, B. F. Smith 48, J. D. P. Oram 34; J. A. F. Yovich three for 50, G. E. Bradburn three for 56); Northern Districts 372 (M. E. Parlane 46, N. R. Parlane 89, G. E. Bradburn 57, Extras 31; E. P. Thompson four for 83) and 100 for two (M. D. Bailey 48 not out, N. R. Parlane 42 not out). *Northern Districts 6 pts.*

In Central's first innings, Smith and Douglas put on 210 in 163 minutes for the third wicket.

At Carisbrook, Dunedin, December 6, 7, 8. Wellington won by seven wickets. Otago* 135 (B. B. McCullum 45; J. E. C. Franklin three for 54, M. R. Gillespie four for 34) and 268 (M. J. Horne 35, C. B. Gaffaney 51, C. R. Pryor 61, N. L. McCullum 38; J. E. C. Franklin three for 60, I. E. O'Brien five for 39); Wellington 297 (M. D. Bell 70, R. A. Jones 38, J. S. Patel 58 not out, C. E. Bulfin 47; W. C. McSkimming four for 72, K. R. O'Dowda three for 67) and 110 for three (R. G. Twose 84). *Wellington 6 pts.*

Iain O'Brien took five wickets in an innings on his first-class debut. Twose scored his 84 from just 38 balls, with 18 fours and a six; his fifty came off 22 balls in 32 minutes.

At Eden Park Outer Oval, Auckland, December 13, 14, 15. Otago won by six wickets. Auckland 157 (R. T. King 34, D. J. Nash 32, Extras 30; C. R. Pryor four for 44) and 201 (R. T. King 49, D. J. Nash 49; D. G. Sewell three for 22, P. J. Wiseman three for 41); Otago* 274 (C. B. Gaffaney 99, P. J. Wiseman 75; C. J. Drum three for 65, T. K. Canning three for 79) and 85 for four (M. J. Horne 50 not out). *Otago 6 pts.*

This was the 100th first-class match between these provinces since 1873-74 and Otago's 22nd victory (Auckland had won 53 with 25 drawn).

At Dudley Park, Rangiora, December 13, 14, 15, 16. Drawn. Canterbury* 344 (G. R. Stead 80, R. M. Frew 53, C. Z. Harris 46, M. H. W. Papps 35, G. J. Hopkins 43, A. J. Redmond 41; J. A. F. Yovich three for 73, B. P. Martin five for 104) and 192 for five (C. Z. Harris 79, C. J. Anderson 46; J. A. F. Yovich three for 39); Northern Districts 330 (M. E. Parlane 45, N. R. Parlane 35, M. N. Hart 72 not out, S. B. Doull 54; C. J. Anderson three for 37, S. J. Cunis five for 74). *Canterbury 2 pts.*

Grant Bradburn became the eighth player, and second from Northern, to appear in 100 first-class games for his province.

At Basin Reserve, Wellington, December 13, 14, 15, 16. Wellington won by an innings and 69 runs. Central Districts 111 (J. E. C. Franklin five for 39) and 189 (B. F. Smith 78, M. W. Douglas 45, J. D. P. Oram 34; J. E. C. Franklin four for 75); Wellington* 369 for seven dec. (M. D. Bell 109, R. G. Twose 57, S. J. Blackmore 41, C. J. Nevin 82 not out; J. D. P. Oram three for 73). *Wellington 6 pts.*

At Eden Park Outer Oval, Auckland, January 2, 3, 4, 5. Auckland won by an innings and 275 runs. Auckland* 547 for eight dec. (B. A. Pocock 123, J. M. Aiken 85, R. T. King 68, L. Vincent 49, T. K. Canning 48, A. R. Adams 54, K. D. Mills 34 not out, C. J. Drum 60 not out; D. R. Tuffey five for 113); Northern Districts 195 (G. E. Bradburn 63, M. N. Hart 80; C. J. Drum three for 50, A. R. Adams four for 42) and 77 (T. K. Canning three for 21, A. R. Adams four for 12). *Auckland 6 pts.*

Pocock hit his tenth first-class hundred after being dropped off the second ball of the match, and Drum, batting at No. 10, made his maiden fifty. Auckland equalled their second-biggest winning margin.

At McLean Park, Napier, January 2, 3, 4, 5. Drawn. Wellington 415 (M. D. Bell 117, R. A. Jones 68, S. J. Blackmore 38, G. T. Donaldson 66, A. J. Penn 43, C. E. Bulfin 32; T. P. Robin three for 84, G. P. Sulzberger four for 79) and 228 for four dec. (M. D. Bell 31, S. J. Blackmore 86 not out, G. T. Donaldson 33); Central Districts* 266 (B. F. Smith 55, G. P. Sulzberger 44, E. P. Thompson 30 not out; J. S. Patel five for 48) and 295 for five (C. M. Spearman 130, G. P. Sulzberger 52, M. W. Douglas 30 not out, M. A. Sigley 34 not out). *Wellington 2 pts.*

Jacob Oram of Central was called up for a one-day international against Zimbabwe after the match began, and replaced by Greg Todd.

At Molyneux Park, Alexandra, January 2, 3, 4, 5. Otago won by seven wickets. Canterbury 201 (A. J. Redmond 44 not out, W. A. Wisneski 36, S. J. Cunis 33; S. B. O'Connor three for 56, W. C. McSkimming four for 39) and 224 (R. M. Frew 38, J. I. Englefield 66, G. J. Hopkins 51 not out; S. B. O'Connor three for 51); Otago* 279 (M. J. Horne 100, C. D. Cumming 50, C. B. Gaffaney 44; S. E. Bond three for 52, S. J. Cunis five for 59) and 147 for three (M. J. Horne 50, C. B. Gaffaney 32 not out, A. J. Hore 30 not out). *Otago 6 pts.*

Paul Wiseman of Otago was called up for a one-day international against Zimbabwe after the match began, and replaced by Nathan McCullum.

At Queen Elizabeth II Park, Christchurch, January 8, 9, 10, 11. Drawn. Canterbury* 220 (G. R. Stead 92, C. J. Anderson 63; M. J. Mason five for 71, G. L. West four for 62) and 362 for eight (R. M. Frew 61, A. J. Redmond 80, G. J. Hopkins 100 not out, W. A. Wisneski 41; G. L. West three for 59); Central Districts 465 (M. S. Sinclair 69, B. F. Smith 168, G. P. Sulzberger 61, M. A. Sigley 71 not out; C. S. Martin three for 120, S. J. Cunis three for 82, C. J. Anderson three for 81). *Central Districts 2 pts.*

On the first morning, Canterbury lost five wickets in eight balls while the score was eight. They were 52 for seven before Stead and Anderson added 136 for the eighth wicket.

At Carisbrook, Dunedin, January 8, 9, 10, 11. Drawn. Northern Districts 232 (J. A. F. Yovich 42, S. B. Doull 38, Extras 32; K. P. Walmsley three for 42, C. R. Pryor three for 68, C. D. Cumming three for 31) and 285 for six dec. (H. J. H. Marshall 83, N. R. Parlane 56, B. P. Martin 48, G. E. Bradburn 41 not out; M. H. Richardson three for 136); Otago* 236 for three dec. (M. H. Richardson 76, A. J. Hore 54, C. D. Cumming 89 not out; G. E. Bradburn three for 36) and 200 for five (C. D. Cumming 43, C. B. Gaffaney 67). *Otago 2 pts.*

At the start of the final day, two Otago bowlers were injured in warm-ups, prompting Otago to declare at their overnight score and donate 285 runs in 76 minutes of declaration bowling to set up a target of 282 in 88 overs.

At Basin Reserve, Wellington, January 8, 9, 10, 11. Drawn. Auckland 255 (T. G. McIntosh 61, L. Vincent 65, A. R. Adams 35; I. E. O'Brien four for 67) and 347 for nine dec. (D. J. Nash 100, K. D. Mills 117 not out, Extras 35; J. E. C. Franklin three for 64); Wellington* 301 (M. D. Bell 104, R. G. Twose 108; K. D. Mills four for 57, T. K. Canning three for 52) and 161 for five (R. A. Jones 42, S. J. Blackmore 45). *Wellington 2 pts.*

In Auckland's second innings, Mills joined Nash at 109 for seven; they added 185 for the eighth wicket, with Mills going to his maiden first-class hundred.

At Queen Elizabeth II Park, Christchurch, February 1, 2, 3, 4. Otago won by 55 runs. Otago* 329 (M. J. Horne 71, A. J. Hore 100, P. J. Wiseman 30; R. D. Burson four for 78, S. J. Cunis three for 57) and 255 for six dec. (C. D. Cumming 39, C. B. Gaffaney 63 retired hurt, A. J. Hore 77, M. G. Croy 32 not out); Canterbury 207 (J. I. Englefield 46, M. N. McKenzie 39, G. J. Hopkins 39; W. C. McSkimming six for 39) and 322 (R. M. Frew 111, M. H. W. Papps 68, A. J. Redmond 36, C. J. Anderson 52, Extras 32; W. C. McSkimming three for 55, C. R. Pryor five for 70). *Otago 6 pts.*

At Fitzherbert Park, Palmerston North, February 1, 2. Auckland won by eight wickets. Central Districts* 132 (M. W. Douglas 40; C. J. Drum three for 40, K. D. Mills three for 26) and 108 (C. M. Spearman 37; C. J. Drum three for 45, D. J. Nash three for 16); Auckland 223 (D. J. Nash 64, K. D. Mills 67; B. E. Hefford four for 57, T. R. Anderson six for 37) and 18 for two. *Auckland 6 pts.*

John Aiken made a pair for Auckland; in each innings, he faced a wide from Hefford before being dismissed by the first legitimate ball.

At Seddon Park, Hamilton, February 1, 2. Northern Districts won by an innings and 46 runs. Northern Districts 283 (M. E. Parlane 60, M. D. Bailey 47, M. N. Hart 31, S. B. Doull 46, Extras 34; M. R. Gillespie three for 87, I. E. O'Brien four for 64, M. Y. Pasupati three for 51); Wellington* 78 (M. R. Gillespie 33 not out; D. R. Tuffey seven for 12) and 159 (G. T. Donaldson 56; D. R. Tuffey four for 54, J. A. F. Yovich four for 43). *Northern Districts 6 pts.*

At Queen Elizabeth II Park, Christchurch, February 6, 7, 8, 9. Wellington won by 38 runs. Wellington* 493 for eight dec. (M. D. Bell 112, R. A. Jones 145, M. D. J. Walker 98, C. J. Nevin 30, A. J. Penn 53 not out; R. D. Burson three for 144, A. J. Redmond four for 114) and 149 for one dec. (C. J. Nevin 80 not out, R. A. Jones 53); Canterbury 232 (M. N. McKenzie 61, C. J. Anderson 55; A. J. Penn three for 67, I. E. O'Brien six for 55) and 372 (R. M. Frew 88, J. I. Englefield 83, M. N. McKenzie 76, S. J. Cunis 39; M. R. Gillespie three for 48). *Wellington 6 pts.*

At McLean Park, Napier, February 6, 7, 8, 9. Central Districts won by six wickets. Northern Districts* 216 (M. D. Bailey 47, H. J. H. Marshall 41, J. A. F. Yovich 31; B. E. Hefford five for 50) and 225 (M. N. Hart 69, S. B. Doull 59; A. M. Schwass five for 53); Central Districts 151 (D. P. Kelly 40, G. P. Sulzberger 42; J. A. F. Yovich seven for 64) and 291 for four (D. P. Kelly 72, B. F. Smith 43, G. P. Sulzberger 63 not out, C. M. Spearman 90). *Central Districts 6 pts, Northern Districts 2 pts.*

In Central's second innings, Spearman scored his 90 in 81 balls with ten fours and five sixes.

At Carisbrook, Dunedin, February 6, 7, 8, 9. Drawn. Auckland 277 (K. D. Mills 63, B. G. K. Walker 69 not out, A. R. Adams 40; D. G. Sewell three for 67, B. E. Scott six for 48) and 338 for eight dec. (J. M. Aiken 46, B. A. Pocock 41, K. D. Mills 89 not out, T. K. Canning 72, A. R. Adams 42; P. J. Wiseman four for 115); Otago* 339 (M. H. Richardson 95, M. J. Horne 41, C. B. Gaffaney 54, A. J. Hore 30; C. J. Drum three for 69, B. G. K. Walker three for 64) and 72 for one (M. J. Horne 30 not out). *Otago 2 pts.*

Left-arm seamer Bradley Scott took six for 48 on his first day of first-class cricket.

At Eden Park Outer Oval, Auckland, February 12, 13, 14, 15. Auckland won by four wickets. Central Districts 397 for six dec. (C. M. Spearman 96, M. S. Sinclair 145, B. F. Smith 57, G. P. Sulzberger 34) and 192 for one dec. (D. P. Kelly 85 not out, C. M. Spearman 61, M. S. Sinclair 32 not out); Auckland* 224 for eight dec. (R. A. Young 101 not out, C. J. Drum 39 not out; A. M. Schwass five for 53) and 368 for six (T. G. McIntosh 53, R. T. King 98, D. J. Nash 40, K. D. Mills 90 not out, A. R. Adams 62). *Auckland 6 pts, Central Districts 2 pts.*

No play was possible on the first day; on the second, shortened when a motorised roller broke down and had to be dismantled rather than moved, Central scored 397 for six off 82 overs. Next morning, Auckland lost their first three wickets for one run, and were 65 for seven before wicket-keeper Young hit a maiden hundred, adding 104 for the ninth wicket with Drum. On the last day, they successfully chased 366 to win.

At Cobham Oval, Whangarei, February 12, 13, 14, 15. Northern Districts won by five wickets. Canterbury 244 for nine dec. (G. R. Stead 121 not out; G. E. Bradburn four for 76) and 143 for seven dec. (R. M. Frew 32, G. R. Stead 63; A. R. Tait four for 38); Northern Districts* 114 for five dec. (G. E. Bradburn 36 not out) and 275 for five (M. E. Parlane 105, H. J. H. Marshall 31, G. E. Bradburn 59 not out). *Northern Districts 6 pts, Canterbury 2 pts.*

Bradburn played his 105th first-class game for Northern Districts, breaking Andy Roberts's record.

At Basin Reserve, Wellington, February 12, 13, 14, 15. Drawn. Wellington 272 (S. R. Mather 33, C. J. Nevin 99, M. R. Gillespie 81 not out; K. R. O'Dowda four for 67) and 407 for seven dec. (R. A. Jones 188, S. R. Mather 107); Otago* 192 (C. B. Gaffaney 62; A. J. Penn four for 66, I. E. O'Brien three for 26) and 241 for one (M. H. Richardson 94 not out, M. J. Horne 110). *Wellington 2 pts.*

In Wellington's second innings, Jones and Mather added 274 for the fourth wicket.

At Horton Park, Blenheim, February 17, 18, 19, 20. Drawn. Canterbury* 268 (J. I. Englefield 172; B. E. Hefford three for 73, A. M. Schwass four for 52) and 422 for eight (J. I. Englefield 90, M. H. W. Papps 41, G. R. Stead 79, A. J. Redmond 35, C. J. Anderson 65, S. E. Bond 66 not out; T. R. Anderson four for 150); Central Districts 538 (D. P. Kelly 212 not out, B. F. Smith 59, G. P. Sulzberger 72, M. W. Douglas 55, W. A. S. Silva 43; C. J. Anderson four for 97). *Central Districts 2 pts.*

Englefield scored his maiden hundred, batting 386 minutes in all for 172, with 25 fours and three sixes; he was ninth out. Kelly's 212 not out, his maiden double-hundred, lasted 570 minutes and 420 balls and included 28 fours and one six. He carried his bat and was on the field throughout the match apart from 20 minutes of Canterbury's second innings.

At Seddon Park, Hamilton, February 17, 18, 19, 20. Drawn. Northern Districts 155 (S. B. Doull 41 not out; D. G. Sewell three for 36, C. R. Pryor five for 28) and 149 for five (M. N. Hart 31 not out, J. A. F. Yovich 30 not out); Otago* 238 for two dec. (M. H. Richardson 97, C. D. Cumming 125 not out). *Otago 2 pts.*

At Cornwall Park, Auckland, February 18, 19, 20. Wellington won by 127 runs. Wellington* 247 (M. D. Bell 42, S. J. Blackmore 65, G. T. Donaldson 33, M. D. J. Walker 43; C. J. Drum five for 65, M. J. Haslam three for 29) and 137 (S. R. Mather 43; B. G. K. Walker four for 30); Auckland 182 (K. D. Mills 50; M. D. J. Walker three for 21) and 75 (A. J. Penn four for 28, I. E. O'Brien five for 27). *Wellington 6 pts.*

This was Auckland's first interprovincial first-class match at Cornwall Park, which staged two matches against New Zealand Under-23s in the 1970s.

At Eden Park Outer Oval, Auckland, February 23, 24, 25, 26. Auckland won by 112 runs. Auckland* 361 for four dec. (T. G. McIntosh 167, R. T. King 45, D. J. Nash 68 not out, K. D. Mills 54 not out; S. E. Bond three for 70) and 149 for six dec. (R. T. King 70, B. A. Pocock 58; J. S. Ward three for 71); Canterbury 137 (G. R. Stead 39; T. K. Canning four for 36, C. J. Drum three for 27) and 261 (J. I. Englefield 125, G. J. Hopkins 58 not out; C. J. Drum three for 47, B. G. K. Walker five for 71). *Auckland 6 pts.*

At Molyneux Park, Alexandra, February 23, 24, 25, 26. Drawn. Central Districts* 359 (C. M. Spearman 78, B. F. Smith 74, M. W. Douglas 134; W. C. McSkimming three for 42, P. J. Wiseman four for 102) and 392 for six dec. (C. M. Spearman 65, M. S. Sinclair 97, B. F. Smith 76, G. P. Sulzberger 103); Otago 316 (M. H. Richardson 166, C. D. Cumming 41, M. G. Croy 42, C. R. Pryor 33; B. E. Hefford four for 48, A. M. Schwass four for 85) and 236 for four (M. H. Richardson 72, C. D. Cumming 122 not out; B. E. Hefford three for 21). *Central Districts 2 pts.*

At Basin Reserve, Wellington, February 23, 24, 25, 26. Drawn. Northern Districts* 315 (M. E. Parlane 33, G. E. Bradburn 35, M. N. Hart 55, J. A. F. Yovich 43, S. B. Doull 32, G. W. Aldridge 37; A. J. Penn three for 99) and 247 for six (H. J. H. Marshall 46, G. E. Bradburn 104); Wellington 508 (M. D. Bell 64, R. A. Jones 147, G. T. Donaldson 56, M. D. J. Walker 57, M. R. Jefferson 71 not out, J. S. Patel 42; J. A. F. Yovich three for 99, G. E. Bradburn five for 114). *Wellington 2 pts.*

Wellington secured the Shell Trophy on gaining a first-innings lead just before lunch on the third day. Yovich bowled the first ball after the break with a red apple, an event recorded on the official scoresheet. In Northern's second innings, ten Wellington players bowled, four for the first time in first-class cricket. One of them, Jones, dismissed Bradburn with his first (and only) ball.

CHAMPIONS

Plunket Shield		1951-52	Canterbury	1976-77	Otago
1921-22	Auckland	1952-53	Otago	1977-78	Auckland
1922-23	Canterbury	1953-54	Central Districts	1978-79	Otago
1923-24	Wellington	1954-55	Wellington	1979-80	Northern Districts
1924-25	Otago	1955-56	Canterbury	1980-81	Auckland
1925-26	Wellington	1956-57	Wellington	1981-82	Wellington
1926-27	Auckland	1957-58	Otago	1982-83	Wellington
1927-28	Wellington	1958-59	Auckland	1983-84	Canterbury
1928-29	Auckland	1959-60	Canterbury	1984-85	Wellington
1929-30	Wellington	1960-61	Wellington	1985-86	Otago
1930-31	Canterbury	1961-62	Wellington	1986-87	Central Districts
1931-32	Wellington	1962-63	Northern Districts	1987-88	Otago
1932-33	Otago	1963-64	Auckland	1988-89	Auckland
1933-34	Auckland	1964-65	Canterbury	1989-90	Wellington
1934-35	Canterbury	1965-66	Wellington	1990-91	Auckland
1935-36	Wellington	1966-67	Central Districts	1991-92	Central Districts / Northern Districts
1936-37	Auckland	1967-68	Central Districts		
1937-38	Auckland	1968-69	Auckland	1992-93	Northern Districts
1938-39	Auckland	1969-70	Otago	1993-94	Canterbury
1939-40	Auckland	1970-71	Central Districts	1994-95	Auckland
1940-45	No competition	1971-72	Otago	1995-96	Auckland
1945-46	Canterbury	1972-73	Wellington	1996-97	Canterbury
1946-47	Auckland	1973-74	Wellington	1997-98	Canterbury
1947-48	Otago	1974-75	Otago	1998-99	Central Districts
1948-49	Canterbury			1999-2000	Northern Districts
1949-50	Wellington	*Shell Trophy*		2000-01	Wellington
1950-51	Otago	1975-76	Canterbury		

Wellington have won the title outright 19 times, Auckland 18, Canterbury 14, Otago 13, Central Districts 6, Northern Districts 4. Central Districts and Northern Districts also shared the title once.

SHELL CUP, 2000-01

Note: Matches in this section were not first-class.

	Played	*Won*	*Lost*	*No result*	*Points*	*Net run-rate*
Canterbury	10	5	3	2	12	0.23
Central Districts	10	4	2	4	12	0.89
Northern Districts	10	5	4	1	11	−0.49
Auckland	10	4	4	2	10	−0.02
Wellington	10	4	6	0	8	0.14
Otago	10	3	6	1	7	−0.48

Play-off

At McLean Park, Napier, January 21. Central Districts won by three wickets. Northern Districts 227 for six (50 overs) (D. L. Vettori 75, H. J. H. Marshall 44, G. E. Bradburn 39 not out); Central Districts* 229 for seven (47.2 overs) (C. M. Spearman 68, M. W. Douglas 89 not out; D. L. Vettori three for 50).

Finals

At McLean Park, Napier, January 24. Canterbury won by 13 runs. Canterbury* 174 for eight (50 overs) (C. Z. Harris 51, C. J. Anderson 39); Central Districts 161 (48.4 overs) (J. D. P. Oram 65; C. S. Martin four for 35).

At Lancaster Park, Christchurch, January 27 (day/night). Central Districts won by 45 runs. Central Districts* 173 (48.2 overs) (B. F. Smith 35, G. P. Sulzberger 43; S. J. Cunis three for 26); Canterbury 128 (43.1 overs) (B. J. K. Doody 40; B. E. Hefford three for 13, G. P. Sulzberger three for 18).

At Lancaster Park, Christchurch, January 28. Central Districts won by eight wickets. Canterbury* 176 for eight (50 overs) (N. J. Astle 45, C. D. McMillan 45, C. Z. Harris 47 not out; G. P. Sulzberger three for 27); Central Districts 178 for two (38 overs) (M. S. Sinclair 54, C. M. Spearman 71 not out, B. F. Smith 44 not out).

Central Districts won the best-of-three final 2–1.

FIFTY YEARS AGO

From WISDEN CRICKETERS' ALMANACK 1952

NOTES BY THE EDITOR (Norman Preston) – "The summer of 1951 will go down into cricket history as one that did not set a high standard of play. After the breezy exhibitions of batting by the West Indies the previous year the stolid defence of the South African batsmen provided a big contrast and the same dourness pervaded most of our county batsmen… Attendances fell to an alarming degree… Another drawback is the constant day-to-day fixture list… Many players are cricket-weary and travel-tired before August arrives. We should prune the competitive programme or players should be rested in turn as they are when on tour."

WARWICKSHIRE IN 1951 – "Warwickshire, by winning the County Championship after a lapse of forty years and for only the second time since they entered the competition in 1895, reaped the reward for a good deal of foresight and enterprise since the war. Back in 1911, Warwickshire set something like a precedent when they elected a 22-year-old captain, F. R. Foster, who led them to victory. Last season Warwickshire established other precedents in English cricket. They were the first county to win the title with a professional captain and an all-professional team."

NOTTINGHAMSHIRE IN 1951 – "Their steady decline of the post-war years reached a climax in 1951 when Nottinghamshire, for so long among the most powerful of cricket counties, found themselves at the foot of the table for the first time in their long history. How poor was their record can be gauged from the fact that they gained only 40 points from 28 Championship matches – 20 less than any other county… Never has lack of balance in the side been more apparent, with the batting adequate but the bowling far below the necessary standard."

MCC TEAM IN AUSTRALIA, 1950–1951, by R. J. Hayter – "On Wednesday, February 28, 1951, at Melbourne, Australia's record of twenty-six post-war Tests without defeat came to an end. That was a day for F. R. Brown and his England colleagues to rejoice. Australia had not been beaten since the Kennington Oval Test of 1938, and rightly the victory was acclaimed as a fillip to English cricket. In a match played under equal conditions to both, the better side triumphed and Australia, as a whole, applauded the victors generously. Most Australians, in fact, were as delighted at England's success as were the players."

FIVE CRICKETERS OF THE YEAR, R. APPLEYARD, by W. E. Bowes – "In a younger man the magnificent performance of Robert Appleyard of taking 200 wickets in his first full season of county cricket would have provided the perfect fairy story. Nevertheless, it was amazing that a 27-year-old bowler, comparatively unknown, should begin a first-class cricket career with such unprecedented success. Appleyard bowled Yorkshire to second position in the championship table. With his last ball of the season he took his 200th wicket at an average cost of only 14.14 runs each."

CRICKET IN INDIA, 2000-01

By R. MOHAN and MOHANDAS MENON

Debasis Mohanty

India's national team played like giant-killers in March 2001, when they ended Australia's run of 16 consecutive Test victories in a thrilling turnaround at Kolkata, and then took the series 2–1 at Chennai. Meanwhile the closing stages of the Ranji Trophy, which ran alongside the Australian tour, proved that India's own domestic giants could no longer rule the land unchallenged.

Cricket is known to have existed in India since 1721, when British sailors played on a beach on the western coast. But for much of the past 280 years, the game has been an elitist pursuit, generally confined to the major cities, such as Calcutta, Bombay, Madras (now known as Kolkata, Mumbai and Chennai) and Delhi. It also took root, however, in the princely states of the hinterland, such as Holkar and Patiala, whose royal house commissioned the handsome Ranji Trophy for the winners of the national championship in 1934. In the glory days of the Raj, cricket thrived in the palace grounds of Baroda, and continued to do so in the decade after independence. Baroda won the Ranji Trophy four times between 1942-43 and 1957-58; even now, only Mumbai (34 times), Delhi and Karnataka (six times each) have more titles. But they had to wait 43 years to add to their roll of honour.

There could have been no greater confirmation that the game has permeated the length and breadth of India than the semi-finals of the 2000-01 Ranji Trophy, in which Baroda and the Indian Railways overcame Orissa and Punjab respectively. Punjab, the modern heirs of Patiala, had won the title in 1992-93, and now reached the semi-finals having won all seven of their Ranji matches, five by an innings. But Orissa, a state more often in the news for bearing the brunt of natural calamities, were playing in the semi-finals for the first time; after conceding a 288-run first-innings lead to Baroda, they progressed no further.

Railways, in the final for only the second time, had first joined the Ranji tournament in 1958-59, with Lala Amarnath, towards the end of his playing career, at the helm. They were a product of government patronage in the early days of independent India, when national institutions were asked to take on the Maharajas' role in sponsoring sport. Their greatest success previously had been reaching the final in 1987-88, when Tamil Nadu trounced them by an innings and 144 runs. This time, Railways had a fine chance of winning the championship after building a first-innings lead of 151. The chance was blown in a nervous fourth innings, in which as much dust rose from the fifth-day pitch as controversy raged over umpiring decisions, and so Baroda celebrated a fifth Ranji title.

The desperation with which both teams sought to win brought the contest an intensity quite different from that of a clash between the traditional giants of Indian cricket. They had won through to the final despite the huge imbalance in resources between the haves and have-nots of Indian cricket. The facilities at the Gujarat State Fertiliser Corporation ground in Baroda were far removed from what Steve Waugh's Australians found at the major Test venues, and the success of the have-nots should have sent a message to the selectors.

After four years, the Ranji Trophy's secondary Super League stage was dismantled, reverting to a straight knockout after the preliminary zonal leagues. This should have eliminated a lot of meaningless cricket, in which batsmen piled up runs on dry pitches as the sun moved towards its equatorial perch. But at the same time, the Duleep Trophy was restored to a league format after four years as a knockout, and was scheduled between the Ranji league and knockout stages. In theory, the Duleep Trophy should be domestic first-class cricket's highest form; instead, too many of its matches were of dubious quality. The Zone teams, loosely knit sides of individuals looking for national selection, hardly make combative units.

North Zone retained their Duleep title and provided the competition's leading run-scorer in Dinesh Mongia, whose 532 in four games included two double-hundreds – to follow his unbeaten 308 for Punjab in November. After him came V. V. S. Laxman, who gathered 478 for South, continuing an extraordinary run of form that dated back to 1999-2000 and found its apotheosis in a match-winning 281 against Australia at Kolkata. He passed 1,400 first-class runs for the second season running – well over 300 more than anyone else – but this time 521 of them were in Test cricket; he appeared only once for Hyderabad. All of the eight most prolific scorers in the Ranji Trophy came from the four semi-finalists. No one reached 1,000 this time – Yere Gowda of Railways topped the tournament's list with 901 runs at 75.08, while Rashmi Parida of Orissa averaged 110.62 from his 885.

The season's bowling highlight was in the Duleep Trophy, when Debasis Mohanty claimed ten for 46 in an innings for East Zone against South. Even though the winter conditions favoured swing, it was a remarkable performance. Mohanty also took 35 wickets for Orissa, giving him 58 at 16.27 in all first-class cricket. But, as ever, there was little evidence in domestic cricket of the type of performances Indian bowlers can string together in Tests. None of the six leading Ranji bowlers donned Indian colours: pace bowler Dodda Ganesh of Karnataka, forgotten by the Test side since his four matches in 1996-97, took most wickets, with 37 at 21.67. Harbhajan Singh was the most successful of the current internationals, with 28, and his amazing Test performances against Australia made him easily the leading first-class wicket-taker with 70.

Although a board directive supposedly ruled that India's stars must play domestic cricket when they had no international engagements, these players generally continued to turn their back on any obligations to their teams or zones. The BCCI, however, were too busy handling the aftermath of the Delhi police's match-fixing exposé to take action. Ajay Jadeja, who had moved from Haryana to lead Jammu and Kashmir, played only one innings, in which he scored 120, before a five-year ban for match-fixing activities appeared to have ended his career; despite losing him, Jammu and Kashmir qualified for the Ranji knockout for the first time.

The season had opened with the Rest of India beating reigning Ranji champions Mumbai by ten wickets. Runs continued to flow from Laxman's bat, with a fine innings of 167 for the Rest, while their spinners routed Mumbai. Left-armer Murali Kartik took 13 wickets, including nine for 70 in the second innings, and off-spinner Sarandeep Singh had five – both earned brief Test call-ups. In limited-overs cricket, Central and South Zones shared the Deodhar Trophy after both scored 298 in what was believed to be the first tie in any national one-day final. Before the Australian tour, the Challenger limited-overs series provided some excitement: the Seniors won again and a few prominent performers made the Indian team. The selectors who took credit for India's Test series win should appreciate that the spread of the game throughout India has given them more options. The establishment of regional academies, which will send their cream to the National Cricket Academy in Bangalore, also testified to a growing awareness that cricket is essentially egalitarian, and that it is possible to derive quality from quantity. – R.M.

FIRST-CLASS AVERAGES, 2000-01

BATTING

(Qualification: 600 runs, average 40.00)

	M	*I*	*NO*	*R*	*HS*	*100s*	*Avge*
R. Dravid (*Karnataka*)	7	12	2	1,024	200*	4	102.40
V. V. S. Laxman (*Hyderabad*)	11	17	2	1,420	281	5	94.66
S. R. Tendulkar (*Mumbai*)	7	12	1	978	201*	5	88.90
Y. Gowda (*Railways*)	10	16	3	1,093	221*	3	84.07
H. H. Kanitkar (*Maharashtra*)	11	14	2	912	190	3	76.00
D. Mongia (*Punjab*)	12	16	2	1,041	308*	3	74.35
P. Dharmani (*Punjab*)	9	12	1	812	176	3	73.81
A. Chopra (*Delhi*)	9	16	3	915	222	4	70.38
R. R. Parida (*Orissa*)	11	18	3	1,026	220	2	68.40
A. V. Kale (*Maharashtra*)	9	13	2	674	222	2	61.27
G. K. Khoda (*Rajasthan*)	8	12	1	661	300*	2	60.09
V. Sehwag (*Delhi*)	10	15	2	757	162*	3	58.23
S. S. Parab (*Baroda*)	8	14	0	809	141	4	57.78
J. J. Martin (*Baroda*)	14	21	2	1,030	121	3	54.21
R. S. Gavaskar (*Bengal*)	9	14	2	630	146	4	52.50
S. Sriram (*Tamil Nadu*)	11	16	0	820	150	2	51.25
R. S. Sodhi (*Punjab*)	11	16	2	715	137	2	51.07
A. R. Khurasiya (*Madhya Pradesh*)	10	15	1	711	118*	3	50.78
Jai P. Yadav (*Madhya Pradesh*)	10	15	0	737	177	1	49.13
V. Rathore (*Punjab*)	12	18	0	881	203	2	48.94
Wasim Jaffer (*Mumbai*)	11	18	3	702	97	0	46.80
N. R. Mongia (*Baroda*)	13	21	5	737	181	1	46.06
C. C. Williams (*Baroda*)	11	20	1	835	116	1	43.94
A. A. Pagnis (*Railways*)	11	18	1	736	143	1	43.29
S. S. Raul (*Orissa*)	11	18	1	702	134	3	41.29

* *Signifies not out.*

BOWLING

(Qualification: 25 wickets)

	O	*M*	*R*	*W*	*BB*	*5W/i*	*Avge*
D. S. Mohanty (*Orissa*)	375.5	109	944	58	10-46	5	16.27
A. Nehra (*Delhi*)	298.1	62	931	54	7-14	5	17.24
Gagandeep Singh (*Punjab*)	248.1	73	580	32	6-14	2	18.12
Harbhajan Singh (*Punjab*)	457.4	106	1,275	70	8-84	6	18.21
Sukhbinder Singh (*Assam*)	236.1	63	675	36	6-57	3	18.75
A. Qayoom (*Jammu and Kashmir*)	188.2	48	574	27	5-42	2	21.25
J. Srinath (*Karnataka*)	192	40	594	26	6-32	2	22.84
R. S. Sodhi (*Punjab*)	250.5	73	608	26	5-40	1	23.38
S. V. Bahutule (*Mumbai*)	352.5	72	1,019	41	6-49	3	24.85
T. P. Singh (*Railways*)	263.2	53	701	28	6-95	2	25.03
Sarandeep Singh (*Punjab*)	271.3	62	789	30	6-38	2	26.30
Jai P. Yadav (*Madhya Pradesh*)	337	67	960	36	8-80	2	26.66
D. Ganesh (*Karnataka*)	378.2	86	1,213	44	6-87	3	27.56
R. B. Patel (*Baroda*)	345.4	58	1,188	43	6-37	2	27.62
S. V. Ghag (*Services*)	233.1	47	710	25	7-122	2	28.40
R. L. Sanghvi (*Delhi*)	335.3	91	914	32	6-71	2	28.56

	O	M	R	W	BB	5W/i	Avge
K. S. Parida (*Railways*)	384.3	113	914	32	5-33	1	28.56
S. K. Satpathy (*Orissa*)	251	65	736	25	4-25	0	29.44
S. J. Srivastava (*Uttar Pradesh*)	311.2	65	931	31	4-62	0	30.03
V. N. Buch (*Baroda*)	361.4	78	1,188	38	6-54	1	31.26
Zaheer Khan (*Baroda*)	317.3	74	942	30	5-43	1	31.40
Surendra Singh (*Jammu and Kashmir*)	302.3	76	979	30	5-115	1	32.63
Iqbal Siddiqui (*Maharashtra*)	341.5	72	1,073	32	5-116	1	33.53
N. D. Hirwani (*Madhya Pradesh*)	308.4	58	984	25	6-90	2	39.36
S. L. V. Raju (*Hyderabad*)	373.2	90	1,043	26	5-16	1	40.11
A. R. Kapoor (*Tamil Nadu*)	332.1	61	1,047	26	7-59	1	40.26
S. B. Joshi (*Karnataka*)	367.2	80	1,133	27	4-38	0	41.96

*In the following scores, * by the name of a team signifies that they won the toss.*

IRANI CUP, 2000-01

Ranji Trophy Champions (Mumbai) v Rest of India

At Wankhede Stadium, Mumbai, October 13, 14, 15, 16. Rest of India won by ten wickets. Mumbai* 260 (Wasim Jaffer 56, R. R. Powar 40; M. Kartik four for 73, Sarandeep Singh four for 55) and 184 (V. R. Mane 37, Wasim Jaffer 50, A. A. Muzumdar 37; M. Kartik nine for 70); Rest of India 389 (V. V. S. Laxman 167, M. Kaif 75, J. J. Martin 51; S. R. Saxena three for 72, N. M. Kulkarni three for 121) and 58 for no wkt (S. S. Das 34 not out).

Kartik's nine for 70 was an Irani Cup record, bettering nine for 101 by Ravi Shastri for Bombay at Indore in 1981-82. His match figures of 13 for 143 were the second-best in the competition.

RANJI TROPHY, 2000-01

Central Zone

At Karnail Singh Stadium, Delhi, October 30, 31, November 1, 2. Drawn. Railways* 525 (A. A. Pagnis 143, S. B. Bangar 41, Abhay Sharma 76, Raja Ali 40, Y. Gowda 56, P. S. Rawat 67, S. K. Sahu 45 not out, Extras 36; H. S. Sodhi three for 95); Madhya Pradesh 283 (A. R. Khurasiya 105, S. Abbas Ali 105; M. Kartik three for 82, K. S. Parida three for 39) and 189 for one (H. S. Sodhi 50 not out, A. R. Khurasiya 118 not out). *Railways 5 pts, Madhya Pradesh 3 pts.*

Khurasiya scored a century in each innings.

At K. L. Saini Stadium, Jaipur, October 30, 31, November 1, 2. Rajasthan won by six wickets. Uttar Pradesh* 270 (Jyoti P. Yadav 34, G. K. Pandey 40, M. Saif 67, A. W. Zaidi 53; Shamsher Singh three for 19, R. J. Kanwat three for 52) and 161 (Rizwan Shamshad 31; M. Aslam four for 52, Sanjeev Sharma three for 22); Rajasthan 296 (P. K. Krishnakumar 41, S. Bhatia 79, Sanjeev Sharma 85; A. W. Zaidi five for 84, S. J. Srivastava four for 98) and 137 for four (R. J. Kanwat 59 not out, G. K. Khoda 40). *Rajasthan 8 pts.*

At Captain Roop Singh Stadium, Gwalior, November 6, 7, 8, 9. Drawn. Madhya Pradesh* 408 (Jai P. Yadav 70, A. R. Khurasiya 59, N. A. Patwardhan 77, H. S. Sodhi 70 not out, S. S. Lahore 33) and 24 for no wkt; Rajasthan 449 (V. Saxena 93, R. J. Kanwat 81, G. K. Khoda 112, P. K. Krishnakumar 56, Extras 59; N. D. Hirwani six for 90). *Madhya Pradesh 3 pts, Rajasthan 5 pts.*

At Karnail Singh Stadium, Delhi, November 6, 7, 8, 9. Railways won by an innings and 28 runs. Vidarbha* 89 (T. P. Singh five for 37) and 339 (A. V. Deshpande 88, V. C. Naidu 44, A. S. Naidu 68, A. S. Manohar 72; T. P. Singh six for 95); Railways 456 for six dec. (A. A. Pagnis 53, S. B. Bangar 46, Abhay Sharma 49, Y. Gowda 96, Raja Ali 112, S. K. Sahu 52 not out). *Railways 8 pts.*

Bangar took six catches in the match.

At Nehru Stadium, Indore, November 13, 14, 15. Madhya Pradesh won by an innings and 176 runs. Madhya Pradesh 552 for eight dec. (Jai P. Yadav 36, D. S. Bundela 83, C. S. Pandit 31, A. S. Srivastava 204 retired hurt, K. Seth 125 not out, Extras 43; U. I. Patil three for 102); Vidarbha* 157 (V. C. Naidu 39; Jai P. Yadav seven for 31) and 219 (S. U. Harbade 36, S. A. Khare 44, A. M. Piprode 32; Jai P. Yadav eight for 80). *Madhya Pradesh 8 pts.*

No. 8 Srivastava's 204 lasted 341 minutes and 237 balls and included 30 fours and one six, while No. 10 Kapil Seth scored 125 not out on first-class debut. They put on 249 runs, an Indian ninth-wicket record, before Srivastava retired hurt; in all, this wicket added 276 runs unbeaten. Opening batsman Jai P. Yadav then claimed 15 for 111, including eight for 80 in Vidarbha's second innings – the best match and innings figures of the Ranji season.

At Sports Stadium, Meerut, November 13, 14, 15, 16. Drawn. Railways* 234 (Y. Gowda 125 not out; A. W. Zaidi four for 45) and 248 for nine dec. (T. P. Singh 32, Raja Ali 34, A. A. Pagnis 62 not out, Harvinder Singh 37, Extras 32; S. J. Srivastava three for 49); Uttar Pradesh 157 (G. K. Pandey 56 not out; K. S. Parida five for 33) and 48 for two (M. S. Mudgal 33). *Uttar Pradesh 3 pts, Railways 5 pts.*

At K. L. Saini Stadium, Jaipur, November 29, 30, December 1, 2. Drawn. Railways 271 (A. A. Pagnis 86, Y. Gowda 37; D. P. Singh four for 25) and 325 for six (Y. Gowda 38, Raja Ali 124 not out, S. K. Sahu 95); Rajasthan* 459 for nine dec. (N. S. Doru 121, R. J. Kanwat 61, G. K. Khoda 50, P. K. Krishnakumar 104, R. B. Jhalani 41, Extras 46). *Rajasthan 5 pts, Railways 3 pts.*

At VCA Ground, Nagpur, December 28, 29, 30, 31. Uttar Pradesh won by an innings and 175 runs. Uttar Pradesh* 605 for eight dec. (N. Ali 58, Jyoti P. Yadav 109, M. Kaif 95, G. K. Pandey 69, Rizwan Shamshad 37, M. Saif 124 not out, M. B. Tripathi 49, Extras 34; S. A. Khare four for 156); Vidarbha 208 (A. V. Deshpande 39, D. Sharma 30; A. Sharma three for 51) and 222 (D. Sharma 30, H. V. Shitoot 44, P. V. Gandhe 31; S. J. Srivastava four for 90, G. K. Pandey five for 49). *Uttar Pradesh 8 pts.*

On the third day, play was delayed for 20 minutes by a mad dog on the field.

At Green Park, Kanpur, January 18, 19, 20, 21. Drawn. Uttar Pradesh 143 (Jyoti P. Yadav 33; Jai P. Yadav four for 41, D. S. Bundela six for 37) and 375 for nine dec. (Jyoti P. Yadav 35, Rizwan Shamshad 153, M. S. Mudgal 55, Extras 39; D. S. Bundela five for 102); Madhya Pradesh* 283 (A. R. Khurasiya 65, D. S. Bundela 39, H. S. Sodhi 57, N. A. Patwardhan 45; S. J. Srivastava three for 84, A. W. Zaidi four for 89) and 158 for seven (Jai P. Yadav 36, C. S. Pandit 47 not out; A. W. Zaidi three for 38). *Uttar Pradesh 3 pts, Madhya Pradesh 5 pts.*

At VCA Ground, Nagpur, January 18, 19, 20, 21. Drawn. Rajasthan* 380 (V. Saxena 117, A. Jain 37, G. K. Khoda 32, P. K. Krishnakumar 36, Sanjeev Sharma 33, R. B. Jhalani 63, Extras 33; C. E. Atram three for 157, P. V. Gandhe four for 58) and 234 for seven dec. (N. S. Doru 71, R. J. Kanwat 34, A. Jain 38; A. M. Piprode three for 65, P. V. Gandhe three for 85); Vidarbha 306 (A. V. Deshpande 128, A. S. Manohar 30, R. S. Paradkar 56; A. M. Dave three for 75, L. Jain three for 36) and 220 for two (A. V. Deshpande 156 not out, S. U. Harbade 42). *Vidarbha 3 pts, Rajasthan 5 pts.*

Deshpande scored a century in each innings.

Rajasthan 23 pts, Railways 21 pts, Madhya Pradesh 19 pts, Uttar Pradesh 14 pts, Vidarbha 3 pts. Rajasthan, Railways and Madhya Pradesh qualified for the knockout stage.

East Zone

At Eden Gardens, Kolkata, November 19, 20, 21, 22. Bengal won by an innings and 134 runs. Tripura 170 (M. Gupta 49, Extras 31; U. Chatterjee three for 23) and 154 (G. H. Banik 51; W. Majumder three for 30); Bengal* 458 for four dec. (A. Basu 101, A. Banerjee 48, D. J. Gandhi 206 not out, Extras 43). *Bengal 8 pts.*

Basu scored 101 on first-class debut. Gandhi's 206 not out lasted 389 minutes and 285 balls and included 27 fours and three sixes.

At Keenan Stadium, Jamshedpur, November 19, 20, 21, 22. Drawn. Bihar 292 (N. Ranjan 53, Sunil Kumar 77, M. S. Dhoni 39; D. S. Mohanty three for 41, A. Barik three for 97) and 214 for seven (Rajiv Kumar 33, Sunil Kumar 46, A. Hashmi 49); Orissa* 478 for seven dec. (P. K. Das 88, S. S. Raul 98, R. R. Parida 90, P. Jayachandra 101 not out). *Bihar 3 pts, Orissa 5 pts.*

At North-East Frontier Railway Stadium, Maligaon, Guwahati, November 26, 27, 28, 29. Drawn. Assam* 291 (P. K. Das 68, S. B. Saikia 34, R. Borah 55, S. Ganesh Kumar 33, Extras 32; U. Chatterjee three for 56, S. S. Lahiri four for 63) and 292 for five (P. K. Das 118, S. B. Saikia 52, S. Z. Zuffri 82); Bengal 383 (D. J. Gandhi 54, S. J. Kalyani 75, R. S. Gavaskar 114, S. S. Karim 44, Extras 31; S. Subramaniam five for 59). *Assam 3 pts, Bengal 5 pts.*

Das and Saikia opened with 117 in Assam's first innings and 140 in the second.

At Keenan Stadium, Jamshedpur, November 26, 27, 28, 29. Drawn. Tripura 236 (S. Dasgupta 30, M. Gupta 61, B. Prajapati 38, R. Dutta 40 not out; Dhiraj Kumar three for 62, M. Diwakar three for 61) and 333 for seven (S. Dasgupta 62, S. Chowdhury 47, M. Gupta 99, C. Sachdev 37, G. H. Banik 32); Bihar* 450 for six dec. (N. Ranjan 110, M. S. Dhoni 39, Tariq-ur-Rehman 83, Rajiv Kumar 80, Sunil Kumar 87, Extras 35; C. Sachdev three for 118). *Bihar 5 pts, Tripura 3 pts.*

At Maharaja Bir Bikram College Stadium, Agartala, December 14, 15, 16. Assam won by an innings and 92 runs. Tripura 116 (S. Dasgupta 42; G. Dutta three for 30, Sukhbinder Singh five for 15) and 179 (R. Chowdhury 32, M. Gupta 39; Sukhbinder Singh five for 30, S. Subramaniam five for 36); Assam* 387 for eight dec. (S. B. Saikia 38, S. Z. Zuffri 50, R. Borah 77, S. Ganesh Kumar 47, Sukhbinder Singh 68 not out; S. Roy four for 84, S. Dasgupta three for 104). *Assam 8 pts.*

At Tinsukia District Sports Association Ground, Guwahati, December 22, 23, 24. Assam won by an innings and ten runs. Bihar* 85 (G. Dutta three for 33, Javed Zaman four for 39, Sukhbinder Singh three for ten) and 146 (Tariq-ur-Rehman 62; G. Dutta five for 42, Sukhbinder Singh four for 45); Assam 241 (R. Borah 33, S. Ganesh Kumar 32, Sukhbinder Singh 47; M. Diwakar three for 73). *Assam 8 pts.*

At Maharaja Bir Bikram College Stadium, Agartala, December 22, 23, 24. Orissa won by an innings and 156 runs. Tripura 114 (S. K. Satpathy four for 25, J. P. Das three for 36) and 108 (C. Sachdev 56; D. S. Mohanty three for 28, J. P. Das four for 28); Orissa* 378 for four dec. (S. S. Das 178, S. S. Raul 134). *Orissa 8 pts.*

Das and Raul put on 233 runs in 233 minutes for Orissa's third wicket.

At Eden Gardens, Kolkata, December 28, 29, 30, 31. Orissa won by 129 runs. Orissa* 256 (S. S. Raul 118, R. R. Parida 71; S. S. Paul three for 64, S. C. Ganguly six for 46) and 249 (P. Jayachandra 54, J. P. Das 44, A. Barik 50 not out; S. C. Ganguly three for 71, U. Chatterjee three for 57); Bengal 117 (S. J. Kalyani 39; D. S. Mohanty six for 48, A. Barik three for 48) and 259 (A. Basu 32, S. C. Ganguly 39, D. Dasgupta 39, U. Chatterjee 53 not out; D. S. Mohanty five for 45, P. Jayachandra three for 27). *Orissa 8 pts.*

This was Orissa's first victory over Bengal in the Ranji Trophy. In their second innings, Das and Barik added 110 for the last wicket.

At Eden Gardens, Kolkata, January 3, 4, 5, 6. Drawn. Bengal* 608 for five dec. (N. L. Haldipur 153, A. A. Lahiri 130, D. J. Gandhi 71, R. S. Gavaskar 121 not out, D. Dasgupta 89, Extras 34); Bihar 323 (N. Ranjan 31, Tariq-ur-Rehman 59, M. S. Dhoni 114 not out; U. Chatterjee five for 60, S. S. Lahiri three for 45) and 302 for three (N. Ranjan 126 not out, Rajiv Kumar 82, Tariq-ur-Rehman 32, Sunil Kumar 56 not out). *Bengal 5 pts, Bihar 3 pts.*

Haldipur and Lahiri opened with 296.

At Tinsukia District Sports Association Ground, Guwahati, January 4, 5, 6. Orissa won by nine wickets. Assam* 167 (S. B. Saikia 31, S. Z. Zuffri 66; S. K. Satpathy three for 41) and 188 (P. K. Das 45, S. Z. Zuffri 46, S. Ghosh 36; D. S. Mohanty five for 39, S. S. Raul three for 48); Orissa 341 (S. S. Das 54, R. R. Parida 75, S. K. Satpathy 41, S. S. Raul 45, G. Gopal 85 not out; S. Ganesh Kumar five for 67) and 18 for one. *Orissa 8 pts.*

Orissa 29 pts, Assam 19 pts, Bengal 18 pts, Bihar 11 pts, Tripura 3 pts. Orissa, Assam and Bengal qualified for the knockout stage.

North Zone

At Feroz Shah Kotla Ground, Delhi, October 30, 31, November 1, 2. Delhi won by 168 runs. Delhi 256 (M. Manhas 136 not out; Arun Sharma four for 45) and 235 (A. Chopra 46, P. Chawla 69, Devendra Sharma 38; M. V. Rao three for 67, S. V. Ghag three for 61, Arun Sharma three for 41); Services* 224 (H. Bhaskar 46, S. V. Ghag 62; R. Singh five for 61) and 99 (S. Verma 39 not out; A. Nehra six for 31). *Delhi 8 pts.*

At Indira Gandhi Stadium, Una, October 30, 31, November 1, 2. Punjab won by an innings and 235 runs. Punjab* 526 for seven dec. (R. S. Ricky 113, V. Rathore 203, R. S. Sodhi 125 not out); Himachal Pradesh 130 (R. Nayyar 44, Amit Sharma 46; R. S. Sodhi three for 40, Harbhajan Singh three for 29, Sarandeep Singh three for 17) and 161 (Virender Sharma 39; Navdeep Singh three for 15, Harbhajan Singh three for 39). *Punjab 8 pts.*

Rathore's 203 lasted 445 minutes and 333 balls and included 25 fours; he put on 277 for Punjab's first wicket with Ricky and 108 for the second with Sodhi.

At Maulana Azad Stadium, Jammu, October 30, 31, November 1, 2. Jammu and Kashmir won by nine wickets. Haryana 174 (Parender Sharma 44; A. Qayoom four for 36, Vijay Sharma three for 44) and 212 (A. Ratra 77; Surendra Singh three for 22, A. Qayoom five for 55); Jammu and Kashmir* 364 (V. Bhaskar 62, Kavaljit Singh 93, A. Jadeja 120, Extras 39; A. Mishra five for 99) and 23 for one. *Jammu and Kashmir 8 pts.*

This was Jadeja's only appearance for Jammu and Kashmir before he received a five-year ban for match-fixing.

At Tata Energy Research Institute, Gurgaon, November 5, 6, 7, 8. Drawn. Delhi 349 (A. Chopra 51, A. Dani 40, V. Sehwag 44, A. Bhandari 72; F. Ghayas three for 63, P. Thakur five for 107) and 147 for two (A. Chopra 65 not out, A. Dani 54); Haryana* 339 (P. S. Sehrawat 30, Jasvir Singh 68, Parender Sharma 73, I. Ganda 62, A. Mishra 34; A. Nehra four for 93, R. L. Sanghvi three for 61). *Haryana 3 pts, Delhi 5 pts.*

At Burlton Park, Jullundur, November 5, 6, 7, 8. Punjab won by an innings and 193 runs. Jammu and Kashmir* 168 (Kavaljit Singh 54, I. Gundroo 43; S. K. Sanwal four for 39) and 226 (Kavaljit Singh 31, A. Gupta 37, D. M. Gupta 65; Harbhajan Singh five for 88, S. K. Sanwal five for 82); Punjab 587 for five dec. (P. Dharmani 176, D. Mongia 308 not out, S. K. Sanwal 50 not out; Surendra Singh four for 97). *Punjab 8 pts.*

Mongia's 308 not out lasted 499 minutes and 409 balls, and included 15 fours and five sixes; he added 388 for Punjab's fourth wicket with Dharmani.

At Air Force Complex, Palam, New Delhi, November 5, 6, 7, 8. Drawn. Services* 276 (A. A. Nadkarni 84, Sarabjit Singh 79, J. Pandey 30; J. Rai four for 57) and 339 for six (H. Bhaskar 82, A. A. Nadkarni 65, J. Pandey 50 not out, S. Javed 52 not out; Amit Sharma three for 98); Himachal Pradesh 459 for eight dec. (N. Gaur 68, R. Nayyar 121, Amit Sharma 120, Virender Sharma 52 not out, Extras 34; Arun Sharma three for 119). *Services 3 pts, Himachal Pradesh 5 pts.*

At Harbax Singh Stadium, Delhi, November 11, 12, 13, 14. Delhi won by an innings and 54 runs. Delhi* 417 for eight dec. (A. Chopra 222, A. Dani 31, M. Manhas 79); Himachal Pradesh 225 (A. Verma 37, R. Nayyar 75, R. Kapoor 37, Sangram Singh 33; A. Bhandari three for 72, A. Nehra five for 74) and 138 (Virender Sharma 42; A. Nehra five for 44). *Delhi 8 pts.*

Chopra's 222 lasted 502 minutes and 380 balls and included 27 fours and two sixes.

At Maulana Azad Stadium, Jammu, November 11, 12, 13. Jammu and Kashmir won by seven wickets. Services* 162 (H. Bhaskar 61; A. Qayoom five for 42, A. Gupta three for 22) and 121 (S. V. Ghag 31; A. Qayoom four for 19); Jammu and Kashmir 176 (A. Gupta 56 not out, D. M. Gupta 35; M. V. Rao three for 65, S. V. Ghag six for 56) and 108 for three (V. Bhaskar 30). *Jammu and Kashmir 8 pts.*

At Gandhi Ground, Amritsar, November 11, 12, 13, 14. Punjab won by an innings and 123 runs. Punjab* 486 (Manish Sharma 131, A. Kakkar 52, P. Dharmani 89, Harbhajan Singh 84, B. Bhushan 30 not out; V. Jain three for 111, P. Thakur three for 138); Haryana 281 (P. S. Sehrawat 88, I. Ganda 67; Gagandeep Singh three for 55, Harbhajan Singh four for 77) and 82 (R. Puri 33; Gagandeep Singh six for 14). *Punjab 8 pts.*

Reetinder Sodhi of Punjab and wicket-keeper Ajay Ratra of Haryana had travelled back from Indore, where they had been playing the Zimbabwean tourists the previous day. Haryana fielded with ten men until Ratra arrived on the first afternoon, reclaimed the gloves from Jasvir Singh and took a catch within two overs.

At Paddal Stadium, Mandi, November 17, 18, 19, 20. Drawn. Haryana* 457 for five dec. (P. S. Sehrawat 79, Parender Sharma 207 not out, R. Puri 55, S. Dalal 61; R. Thakur three for 103) and 62 for no wkt (A. Ratra 36 not out); Himachal Pradesh 366 (A. Verma 37, N. Gaur 64, Amit Sharma 82, Virender Sharma 45, R. Kapoor 32, Sangram Singh 50 not out; A. Mishra six for 138). *Himachal Pradesh 3 pts, Haryana 5 pts.*

Parender Sharma's 207 not out lasted 494 minutes and 381 balls and included 23 fours and one six.

At Maulana Azad Stadium, Jammu, November 17, 18, 19. Delhi won by ten wickets. Jammu and Kashmir* 198 (Kavaljit Singh 53, A. Gupta 32, Vijay Sharma 30 not out; A. Nehra four for 39) and 269 (D. M. Gupta 55, Kavaljit Singh 117 not out; R. L. Sanghvi six for 71); Delhi 466 for five dec. (A. Chopra 133, A. Dani 48, G. Gambhir 114, M. Manhas 31, V. Sehwag 91) and five for no wkt. *Delhi 8 pts.*

At Air Force Complex, Palam, New Delhi, November 17, 18, 19. Punjab won by an innings and 166 runs. Services* 87 (B. Bhushan seven for 51) and 177 (D. Sehrawar 56; S. K. Sanwal four for 41, Harbhajan Singh five for 40); Punjab 430 (V. Rathore 83, P. Dharmani 128, R. S. Sodhi 35, Harbhajan Singh 52, S. K. Sanwal 41 not out, Extras 30; S. V. Ghag three for 102, S. Javed three for 112). *Punjab 8 pts.*

At Harbax Singh Stadium, Delhi, November 23, 24, 25. Punjab won by 199 runs. Punjab 187 (R. S. Sodhi 78; A. Nehra four for 53) and 196 (P. Dharmani 31, D. Mongia 34, Harbhajan Singh 37; A. Nehra six for 59, R. Singh three for 20); Delhi* 104 (Gagandeep Singh six for 34) and 80 (Gagandeep Singh three for 29, Harbhajan Singh four for 17). *Punjab 8 pts.*

Punjab completed the zonal league with a 100 per cent record – five wins, four of them by an innings. Delhi's second-innings total of 80 in 35.4 overs was the lowest of the season.

At Maulana Azad Stadium, Jammu, November 23, 24, 25, 26. Jammu and Kashmir won by four wickets. Himachal Pradesh* 316 for nine dec. (N. Gaur 101, R. Nayyar 45, Virender Sharma 44, R. Panta 46 not out; A. Qayoom three for 72, Surendra Singh four for 71) and 110 for six dec. (R. Panta 66; Vijay Sharma three for 38); Jammu and Kashmir 176 (Vijay Sharma 33, Sanjay Sharma 32; R. Thakur three for 65) and 251 for six (R. Bali 138, A. Gupta 43). *Jammu and Kashmir 8 pts.*

At Air Force Complex, Palam, New Delhi, November 23, 24, 25, 26. Drawn. Haryana 392 (P. S. Sehrawat 43, I. Ganda 122, Parender Sharma 39, R. Puri 89, Extras 33; S. V. Ghag seven for 122, Arun Sharma three for 89) and 176 for eight dec. (Parender Sharma 103 not out); Services* 327 (S. Verma 116, K. K. Dixit 57, P. Maitreya 40, S. Javed 36; F. Ghayas five for 63, A. Mishra three for 86) and 152 for seven (H. Bhaskar 30, Sarabjit Singh 51; A. Mishra three for 69). *Services 3 pts, Haryana 5 pts.*

Punjab 40 pts, Delhi 29 pts, Jammu and Kashmir 24 pts, Haryana 13 pts, Himachal Pradesh 8 pts, Services 6 pts. Punjab, Delhi and, for the first time, Jammu and Kashmir qualified for the knockout stage.

South Zone

At Indira Gandhi Stadium, Vijayawada, November 1, 2, 3, 4. Drawn. Andhra* 244 (A. Pathak 58, R. V. C. Prasad 95, K. S. T. Sai 35; T. Yohannan five for 78) and 228 for three (L. N. P. Reddy 43, A. Pathak 101, Y. Gnaneswara Rao 56 not out); Kerala 461 for seven dec. (V. Girilal 84, M. P. Sorab 32, A. N. Kudva 158 not out, B. Ramprakash 38, M. Suresh Kumar 101 not out; N. Madhukar three for 116, H. H. Watekar three for 115). *Andhra 3 pts, Kerala 5 pts.*

Kudva and Suresh Kumar shared an unbroken stand of 204 for Kerala's eighth wicket.

At Dr Rajendra Prasad Stadium, Margao, November 1, 2, 3, 4. Tamil Nadu won by 203 runs. Tamil Nadu* 204 (S. Sriram 71, R. Paul 37, T. Kumaran 47 not out; A. I. Aware three for 58, N. S. Kalekar five for 39) and 311 for six dec. (S. Sriram 45, S. Ramesh 79, R. Bhatia 69 not out, R. Paul 46; R. P. Rane three for 31); Goa 201 (P. K. Amre 66, Extras 35; S. Mahesh five for 57, W. D. Balaji Rao three for 29) and 111 (V. V. Kolambkar 48; R. Bhatia three for 24, S. Sriram three for six). *Tamil Nadu 8 pts.*

At M. Chinnaswamy Stadium, Bangalore, November 1, 2, 3, 4. Drawn. Karnataka* 545 for nine dec. (M. R. Beerala 73, B. M. Rowland 70, S. Somasunder 43, R. V. Bharadwaj 50, V. S. T. Naidu 122, S. B. Joshi 92; S. L. V. Raju four for 118); Hyderabad 291 (D. S. Manohar 73, V. V. S. Laxman 60, D. Vinay Kumar 68; J. Srinath four for 86) and 233 for two (D. S. Manohar 49, A. Nandakishore 43, V. V. S. Laxman 100 not out). *Karnataka 5 pts, Hyderabad 3 pts.*

At Nuclear Fuel Complex Ground, Hyderabad, November 8, 9, 10, 11. Hyderabad won by an innings and 46 runs. Hyderabad* 489 for nine dec. (D. S. Manohar 30, A. Nandakishore 53, Anirudh Singh 47, V. Pratap 128, D. Vinay Kumar 71, P. R. Satwalkar 55, M. F. Ahmed 49 not out, Extras 41; T. Yohannan six for 117); Kerala 165 (R. Menon 50; N. P. Singh four for 70, S. L. V. Raju four for 49) and 278 (V. Girilal 31, R. Menon 49, A. N. Kudva 61, S. C. Oasis 43; P. R. Satwalkar three for 64, N. P. Singh five for 39). *Hyderabad 8 pts.*

At Indian Institute of Technology Chemplast Ground, Chennai, November 8, 9, 10, 11. Drawn. Tamil Nadu* 477 (S. Badrinath 100, H. K. Badani 76, S. Sharath 43, R. R. Singh 106, S. Mahesh 36, A. R. Kapoor 62; D. Ganesh five for 113) and 114 for four (R. Bhatia 34, S. Badrinath 48; M. A. Khan three for 30); Karnataka 254 (M. R. Beerala 46, B. M. Rowland 54; T. Kumaran three for 57, W. D. Balaji Rao three for 55). *Tamil Nadu 5 pts, Karnataka 3 pts.*

At Dr Rajendra Prasad Stadium, Margao, November 9, 10, 11, 12. Andhra won by an innings and 20 runs. Goa* 163 (P. K. Amre 40, A. I. Aware 33 not out; H. H. Watekar three for 22) and 331 (T. Jabbar 94, A. C. Bhagwat 41, A. I. Aware 35 not out; Y. S. Ranganath four for 59); Andhra 514 for five dec. (L. N. P. Reddy 138, A. Pathak 264, Y. Venugopala Rao 30). *Andhra 8 pts.*

Pathak's 264 lasted 454 minutes and 295 balls and included 35 fours; he and Reddy put on 380 for Andhra's first wicket in 401 minutes.

At Nuclear Fuel Complex Ground, Hyderabad, November 15, 16, 17, 18. Drawn. Tamil Nadu* 566 (S. Sriram 98, R. Bhatia 134, S. Sharath 122, R. R. Singh 33, S. Mahesh 68; D. S. Manohar four for 72) and 205 for five (S. Mahesh 41, S. Badrinath 34, S. Vidyuth 82; N. P. Singh three for 26); Hyderabad 380 (D. S. Manohar 66, A. Nandakishore 128, Anirudh Singh 90, M. Srinivas 36; S. Vidyuth four for 79, S. Sriram three for 51). *Hyderabad 3 pts, Tamil Nadu 5 pts.*

At Union Gymkhana Ground, Belgaum, November 15, 16, 17. Karnataka won by five wickets. Andhra* 195 (L. N. P. Reddy 31, Y. Venugopala Rao 42, K. S. Sahabuddin 33: M. A. Khan three for 48, S. K. Vadiaraj three for 41) and 206 (L. N. P. Reddy 55, Y. Venugopala Rao 82; D. Ganesh five for 69, S. K. Vadiaraj three for 52); Karnataka 139 (K. S. Sahabuddin six for 63) and 265 for five (J. Arun Kumar 82, S. Somasunder 36, V. S. T. Naidu 71 not out, D. Ganesh 30 not out; Y. S. Ranganath three for 63). *Karnataka 8 pts.*

At Nehru Stadium, Kochi, November 15, 16, 17, 18. Drawn. Kerala 370 (M. P. Sorab 38, S. C. Oasis 47, S. R. Nair 88, K. N. A. Padmanabhan 63, Extras 40; A. I. Aware three for 90, S. H. A. Khalid five for 63); Goa* 180 (Y. C. Barde 41, S. Medappa 34; K. N. A. Padmanabhan three for 49) and 321 (V. V. Kolambkar 32, S. Medappa 116, R. P. Rane 75; B. Ramprakash three for 53, K. N. A. Padmanabhan four for 79). *Kerala 5 pts, Goa 3 pts.*

At Nuclear Fuel Complex, Hyderabad, November 22, 23, 24, 25. Hyderabad won by 153 runs. Hyderabad* 315 (A. Nandakishore 33, Anirudh Singh 86, J. S. Yadav 39; A. I. Aware five for 92, R. P. Rane three for 56) and 239 for eight dec. (D. S. Manohar 82, V. Pratap 77 not out; S. H. A. Khalid four for 51); Goa 175 (Y. C. Barde 30, S. Medappa 36, R. P. Rane 31; M. Ghouse three for 38, S. L. V. Raju five for 16) and 226 (V. V. Kolambkar 40, D. S. Rao 54; N. P. Singh four for 81, M. Ghouse three for 43). *Hyderabad 8 pts.*

At Nehru Stadium, Kochi, November 22, 23, 24, 25. Kerala won by ten wickets. Karnataka* 236 (J. Arun Kumar 69, B. Akhil 45, D. Ganesh 41; T. Yohannan three for 61) and 133 (R. V. Bharadwaj 32, A. R. Mahesh 31; S. R. Nair three for 20, M. Suresh Kumar three for 22); Kerala 365 for nine dec. (C. P. Menon 63, S. C. Oasis 120; S. K. Vadiaraj four for 88) and five for no wkt. *Kerala 8 pts.*

At Guru Nanak College Ground, Chennai, November 22, 23, 24, 25. Drawn. Tamil Nadu* 353 for five dec. (S. Sriram 119, H. K. Badani 51, S. Badrinath 31, S. Mahesh 77 not out, R. Paul 38); Andhra 228 for nine (L. N. P. Reddy 36, A. Pathak 30, Y. Venugopala Rao 59, Fayaz Ahmed 51; W. D. Balaji Rao three for 54). *Tamil Nadu 3 pts, Andhra 3 pts.*

At Kurnool Stadium, Kurnool, November 29, 30, December 1, 2. Drawn. Andhra* 386 (L. N. P. Reddy 37, A. Pathak 64, G. N. Srinivas Rao 106, Y. Venugopala Rao 59, I. G. Srinivas 45; N. P. Singh four for 108) and 193 for nine (G. N. Srinivas Rao 88, N. M. Khan 32; J. S. Yadav seven for 70); Hyderabad 349 (D. S. Manohar 56, A. Nandakishore 53, D. Vinay Kumar 97, Extras 39; K. S. Sahabuddin five for 106). *Andhra 5 pts, Hyderabad 3 pts.*

At Dr Rajendra Prasad Stadium, Margao, November 29, 30, December 1, 2. Karnataka won by nine wickets. Goa* 303 (V. V. Kolambkar 46, T. Jabbar 116, P. K. Amre 33, R. P. Rane 44 not out; D. Ganesh six for 87, M. A. Khan three for 65) and 136 (T. Jabbar 40, A. C. Bhagwat 51; D. Ganesh four for 52, M. A. Khan four for 24); Karnataka 321 (M. R. Beerala 36, B. M. Rowland 80, B. Akhil 79, D. Ganesh 36; S. H. A. Khalid four for 108, N. S. Kalekar four for 85) and 119 for one (J. Arun Kumar 55, M. R. Beerala 38 not out). *Karnataka 8 pts.*

At Nehru Stadium, Kochi, November 29, 30, December 1, 2. Drawn. Kerala* 206 (C. P. Menon 49, V. Kamaruddin 42; S. Mahesh three for 22, W. D. Balaji Rao three for 55) and 167 for six (M. P. Sorab 61, A. N. Kudva 46; W. D. Balaji Rao four for 60); Tamil Nadu 251 for nine dec. (C. Hemanth Kumar 101, J. R. Madanagopal 84; S. R. Nair three for 47, C. P. Menon four for 44). *Kerala 3 pts, Tamil Nadu 5 pts.*

Hemanth Kumar scored 101 on first-class debut.

Tamil Nadu 26 pts, Hyderabad 25 pts, Karnataka 24 pts, Kerala 21 pts, Andhra 19 pts, Goa 3 pts. Tamil Nadu, Hyderabad and Karnataka qualified for the knockout stage.

West Zone

At GSFC Ground, Baroda, November 25, 26, 27, 28. Baroda won by an innings and 94 runs. Baroda 481 (C. C. Williams 51, H. R. Jadhav 165, T. B. Arothe 78, S. S. Parab 32, M. P. Mewada 31; S. Mehta three for 96, H. J. Parsana three for 77); Saurashtra* 197 (R. V. Dhruv 44, P. J. Bhatt 63; I. S. Pathan five for 55, V. N. Buch three for 26) and 190 (S. H. Kotak 51, R. V. Dhruv 65; R. B. Patel six for 37). *Baroda 8 pts.*

At Shri Shivaji Stadium, Karad, November 25, 26, 27, 28. Drawn. Maharashtra 476 (S. S. Bhave 71, H. H. Kanitkar 94, A. V. Kale 35, K. D. Aphale 115, M. V. Sane 32, S. M. Kondhalkar 33, Extras 46; H. A. Majmudar three for 84, L. A. Patel five for 73); Gujarat* 212 (M. H. Parmar 115; Iqbal Siddiqui four for 47, S. A. Shaikh three for 63) and 324 for five (N. K. Patel 58, T. N. Varsania 64, M. H. Parmar 107 not out, P. H. Patel 52 not out). *Maharashtra 5 pts, Gujarat 3 pts.*

Parmar hit a hundred in each innings for the fourth time – a record in the Ranji Trophy.

At Wankhede Stadium, Mumbai, December 2, 3, 4, 5. Mumbai won by nine wickets. Mumbai 521 for five dec. (V. R. Mane 57, Wasim Jaffer 97, V. G. Kambli 203 not out, S. S. Dighe 87) and five for one; Gujarat* 274 (N. K. Patel 54, M. H. Parmar 61, T. N. Varsania 41, B. N. Mehta 50 not out; R. R. Powar five for 77) and 250 (N. D. Modi 90, V. H. Gandhi 54, M. H. Parmar 43; R. R. Powar three for 77, S. V. Bahutule five for 58). *Mumbai 8 pts.*

Kambli's 203 not out lasted 338 minutes and 241 balls and included 23 fours and five sixes; he added 234 in 220 minutes with Dighe for the fifth wicket.

At Municipal Ground, Rajkot, December 2, 3, 4, 5. Drawn. Maharashtra* 539 for six dec. (S. S. Bhave 149, H. H. Kanitkar 190, A. V. Kale 55, S. A. Shah 45 not out); Saurashtra 314 (S. S. Tanna 48, P. P. Joshi 107, S. H. Kotak 61; Iqbal Siddiqui three for 76, S. V. Aradhye four for 75) and 204 for three (P. P. Joshi 78, S. H. Kotak 75, P. J. Bhatt 35 not out). *Saurashtra 3 pts, Maharashtra 5 pts.*

Bhave and Kanitkar added 313 runs for Maharashtra's second wicket.

At IPCL Ground, Baroda, December 8, 9, 10, 11. Drawn. Baroda* 273 (C. C. Williams 36, S. S. Parab 51, T. B. Arothe 61, A. P. Bhoite 62; Iqbal Siddiqui four for 83) and 431 for five (C. C.

Williams 116, S. S. Parab 140, J. J. Martin 101 not out, N. R. Mongia 55 not out; M. V. Sane three for 99); Maharashtra 407 (H. H. Kanitkar 55, A. V. Kale 222, M. V. Sane 45; R. B. Patel three for 128, I. S. Pathan three for 68, V. N. Buch four for 113). *Baroda 3 pts, Maharashtra 5 pts.*

Kale's 222 lasted 393 minutes and 272 balls and included 25 fours.

At Indian Farmers' Fertilisers Co-operative Udyognagar Stadium, Gandhidham, December 8, 9, 10, 11. Drawn. Saurashtra* 354 (P. P. Joshi 113, S. H. Kotak 38, B. M. Pathak 47, R. V. Dhruv 30, Extras 47; S. V. Bahutule six for 104) and 179 for nine (P. P. Joshi 45, B. M. Pathak 44 not out; P. L. Mhambrey three for 30); Mumbai 377 for eight dec. (V. R. Mane 84, Wasim Jaffer 77, A. A. Muzumdar 67, V. G. Kambli 90; N. R. Odedra five for 78). *Saurashtra 3 pts, Mumbai 5 pts.*

At Lalabhai Contractor Stadium, Surat, December 23, 24, 25, 26. Gujarat won by six wickets. Saurashtra 222 (S. H. Kotak 68, H. J. Parsana 65; H. A. Majmudar three for 57, L. A. Patel five for 72) and 265 (P. J. Bhatt 30, H. J. Parsana 53, M. M. Parmar 65; H. A. Majmudar six for 74, L. A. Patel four for 77); Gujarat* 276 (N. D. Modi 104, M. H. Parmar 33, T. N. Varsania 63; N. R. Odedra three for 49, H. J. Parsana four for 56) and 212 for four (N. D. Modi 43, M. H. Parmar 126 not out). *Gujarat 8 pts.*

At Middle Income Group Sports Club Ground, Bandra, Mumbai, December 23, 24, 25, 26. Drawn. Mumbai 410 (S. R. Tendulkar 108, V. G. Kambli 42, S. V. Bahutule 67, A. B. Agarkar 75, P. L. Mhambrey 42; Zaheer Khan three for 75, R. B. Patel three for 99) and 255 (A. A. Muzumdar 81, S. S. Dighe 52, R. R. Powar 36 not out; R. B. Patel five for 84); Baroda* 202 (C. C. Williams 39, J. J. Martin 30, R. B. Patel 36; R. F. Morris four for 27) and 360 for nine (C. C. Williams 87, S. S. Parab 33, H. R. Jadhav 41, T. B. Arothe 59, N. R. Mongia 41 not out, Extras 31; A. B. Agarkar three for 66, R. F. Morris four for 64). *Mumbai 5 pts, Baroda 3 pts.*

At Sardar Patel (Gujarat) Stadium, Motera, Ahmedabad, December 29, 30, 31, January 1. Drawn. Gujarat* 298 (N. D. Modi 43, N. K. Patel 40, M. H. Parmar 54, K. A. Damani 90; Zaheer Khan four for 63, R. B. Patel three for 84) and 114 for four; Baroda 488 for eight dec. (C. C. Williams 57, S. S. Parab 109, H. R. Jadhav 31, J. J. Martin 78, N. R. Mongia 80, U. C. Patel 57 not out). *Gujarat 3 pts, Baroda 5 pts.*

At Shivaji Stadium, Kolhapur, December 29, 30, 31, January 1. Drawn. Maharashtra* 445 (D. S. Jadhav 31, H. H. Kanitkar 61, A. V. Kale 165, K. D. Aphale 69, S. A. Shah 49, Extras 35; S. Hazare four for 75, R. R. Powar four for 98) and 213 (S. M. Kondhalkar 30 not out; N. M. Kulkarni four for 54, S. V. Bahutule three for 40); Mumbai 433 (V. R. Mane 63, S. Sawant 56, S. S. Dighe 98, S. V. Bahutule 63, P. L. Mhambrey 34, Extras 34; S. V. Aradhye three for 92, Iqbal Siddiqui four for 124). *Maharashtra 5 pts, Mumbai 3 pts.*

Mumbai 21 pts, Maharashtra 20 pts, Baroda 19 pts, Gujarat 14 pts, Saurashtra 6 pts. Mumbai, Maharashtra and Baroda qualified for the knockout stage; Mumbai advanced directly to the quarter-finals as holders of the Ranji Trophy.

Pre-quarter-finals

At Nehru Stadium, Guwahati, March 10, 11, 12. Karnataka won by seven wickets. Assam* 321 (P. K. Das 95, S. B. Saikia 49, S. Z. Zuffri 62, V. R. Samant 55; D. Ganesh four for 93, A. R. Yalvigi three for 92) and 134 (S. Ganesh Kumar 50; D. Ganesh four for 46, S. B. Joshi four for 38); Karnataka 312 (J. Arun Kumar 64, B. M. Rowland 66, V. S. T. Naidu 50, S. B. Joshi 33, A. R. Yalvigi 38 not out, Extras 31; G. Dutta three for 64, Javed Zaman four for 68) and 144 for three (R. V. Bharadwaj 41, B. Akhil 51 not out).

At GSFC Ground, Baroda, March 10, 11, 12, 13, 14. Baroda won by 222 runs. Baroda 467 (C. C. Williams 86, J. J. Martin 103, T. B. Arothe 57, A. P. Bhoite 54, M. P. Mewada 62, Extras 32; L. R. Shukla four for 119, U. Chatterjee three for 88) and 355 (S. S. Parab 56, C. C. Williams 32, J. J. Martin 54, A. P. Bhoite 50, R. B. Patel 33, V. N. Buch 50 not out; L. R. Shukla three for 94, A. K. Das three for 47); Bengal* 247 (S. J. Kalyani 48, R. S. Gavaskar 61, A. K. Das 32, U. Chatterjee 52 not out; I. S. Pathan four for 59, I. K. Pathan three for 40) and 353 (R. S. Gavaskar 125 not out, D. Dasgupta 40, D. J. Gandhi 62; A. P. Bhoite five for 22).

At Daly College Ground, Indore, March 10, 11, 12, 13, 14. Drawn. Madhya Pradesh were declared winners by virtue of their first-innings lead. Madhya Pradesh* 489 (H. S. Sodhi 87, N. V. Ojha 41, A. R. Khurasiya 30, D. S. Bundela 144, S. Abbas Ali 57, Jai P. Yadav 44, Extras 36; Kanwaljit Singh four for 95, J. S. Yadav four for 114) and 291 (H. S. Sodhi 36, N. V. Ojha 40, A. R. Khurasiya 35, Jai P. Yadav 48, C. S. Pandit 69 not out; Kanwaljit Singh five for 100, M. Ghouse five for 97); Hyderabad 382 (D. S. Manohar 55, M. Srinivas 107, Anirudh Singh 42, V. Pratap 48; Jai P. Yadav three for 88, R. K. Chauhan three for 84) and 50 for two.

At Poona Club, Pune, March 10, 11, 12, 13, 14. Drawn. Railways were declared winners by virtue of their first-innings lead. Railways* 431 (A. A. Pagnis 96, T. P. Singh 77, Y. Gowda 49, Abhay Sharma 59, S. N. Khanolkar 76, K. S. Parida 32; M. S. Kulkarni three for 114, Iqbal Siddiqui three for 90) and 656 for five (S. B. Bangar 80, T. P. Singh 42, K. S. Parida 84, Y. Gowda 221 not out, Abhay Sharma 188); Maharashtra 308 (J. S. Narse 40, H. H. Kanitkar 124, K. D. Aphale 37, Iqbal Siddiqui 38; Harvinder Singh five for 95, S. B. Bangar three for 58).

Gowda's 221 not out lasted 532 minutes and 400 balls and included 21 fours and two sixes; he and Abhay Sharma added 324 for Railways' fifth wicket to help them to their highest total.

At PCA Stadium, Mohali, March 10, 11, 12. Punjab won by an innings and 12 runs. Rajasthan* 111 (Vineet Kumar four for 25, R. S. Sodhi five for 40) and 306 (G. K. Khoda 40, R. J. Kanwat 88, S. Bhatia 53, Sanjeev Sharma 37; S. K. Sanwal three for 127, Babloo Kumar five for 48); Punjab 429 (R. S. Ricky 40, V. Rathore 39, P. Dharmani 101, D. Mongia 75, R. S. Sodhi 55, S. K. Sanwal 36; Sanjeev Sharma five for 84, M. Aslam three for 52).

At Indian Institute of Technology Chemplast Ground, Chennai, March 10, 11, 12, 13, 14. Drawn. Tamil Nadu were declared winners by virtue of their first-innings lead. Tamil Nadu* 592 (S. Badrinath 32, S. Sriram 38, C. Hemanth Kumar 121, S. Sharath 58, J. R. Madanagopal 54, R. R. Singh 63, R. Paul 35, M. R. Srinivas 42 not out, S. Vidyuth 115; R. Singh three for 96, A. K. Suman three for 93) and 515 for eight dec. (C. Hemanth Kumar 87, S. Sharath 224, S. Mahesh 71, S. Vidyuth 42); Delhi 365 (R. L. Sanghvi 31, M. Manhas 58, V. Sehwag 106, P. Chawla 30, H. Chowdhury 60; S. Mahesh three for 102, M. R. Srinivas four for 111) and 149 for one (A. Chopra 61, G. Gambhir 69 not out).

In Tamil Nadu's first innings, No. 11 Vidyuth made 115 out of 158 with Srinivas for the last wicket. In the second, Sharath's 224 lasted 404 minutes and 352 balls and included 29 fours and three sixes. The match featured 1,621 runs for 29 wickets; Tamil Nadu scored 1,107 runs for 18. Hemanth Kumar added 121 and 87 to his debut century against Kerala, narrowly missing Joe Solomon's record of hundreds in each of his first three first-class innings, for British Guiana in 1956-57 and 1957-58.

At Barabati Stadium, Cuttack, March 11, 12, 13, 14. Orissa won by 420 runs. Orissa 501 (R. R. Parida 220, P. M. Mullick 191; A. Qayoom three for 79, Vijay Sharma five for 98) and 299 for four dec. (Suresh Kumar 55, S. S. Raul 113 not out, P. Jayachandra 41, D. S. Mohanty 50 not out; Jagtar Singh three for 65); Jammu and Kashmir* 151 (Kavaljit Singh 57; S. K. Satpathy four for 39, J. P. Das three for 15) and 229 (Kavaljit Singh 67, V. Taggar 33, D. M. Gupta 32, Shashi Kumar 39; D. S. Mohanty three for 21, S. K. Satpathy four for 51).

Parida's 220 lasted 341 minutes and 326 balls and included 35 fours; he and Mullick put on 358 for Orissa's fourth wicket.

Quarter-finals

At Wankhede Stadium, Mumbai, March 20, 21, 22, 23, 24. Punjab won by 207 runs. Punjab 383 (A. Kakkar 46, P. Dharmani 68, Yuvraj Singh 135, R. S. Sodhi 46, Extras 30; P. L. Mhambrey five for 77, R. V. Pawar three for 115) and 322 (R. S. Ricky 55, Manish Sharma 93, P. Dharmani 73 not out, Yuvraj Singh 33; R. V. Pawar six for 109); Mumbai* 285 (V. R. Mane 97, J. V. Paranjpe 68, A. A. Muzumdar 48; Gagandeep Singh three for 51, R. S. Sodhi three for 63) and 213 (V. R. Mane 56, Wasim Jaffer 51, J. V. Paranjpe 59; Sarandeep Singh six for 38).

At GSFC Ground, Baroda, March 22, 23, 24, 25. Baroda won by 160 runs. Baroda* 324 (S. S. Parab 110, J. J. Martin 34, A. P. Bhoite 78; M. R. Srinivas four for 80, A. R. Kapoor four for 64) and 184 (C. C. Williams 47, N. R. Mongia 61 not out, R. B. Patel 39; A. R. Kapoor seven for 59); Tamil Nadu 186 (S. Sriram 51, S. Badrinath 38; V. N. Buch six for 54) and 162 (C. Hemanth Kumar 56, J. R. Madanagopal 45; R. B. Patel four for 47, A. P. Bhoite three for 35, V. N. Buch three for 38).

At Captain Roop Singh Stadium, Gwalior, March 22, 23, 24, 25, 26. Orissa won by seven wickets. Madhya Pradesh 437 (H. S. Sodhi 57, D. S. Bundela 78, Jai P. Yadav 64, R. K. Chauhan 36, Y. Golwalkar 41 not out, Extras 41; P. M. Mullick three for 45) and 233 (S. Abbas Ali 37, Jai P. Yadav 46, C. S. Pandit 50; P. M. Mullick three for 63); Orissa* 479 (Suresh Kumar 35, R. R. Parida 162, S. S. Raul 40, P. M. Mullick 51, P. Jayachandra 40, G. Gopal 63 not out, Extras 48; Jai P. Yadav three for 112, N. D. Hirwani three for 121) and 192 for three (R. R. Parida 64 not out, P. M. Mullick 74 not out).

Play was held up for 38 minutes on the fourth day after journalists invaded the pitch to demand an apology from Hirwani and Yadav who, they claimed, had manhandled one of their colleagues.

At Karnail Singh Stadium, Delhi, March 22, 23, 24, 25, 26. Drawn. Railways were declared winners by virtue of their first-innings lead. Railways* 451 (S. B. Bangar 46, T. P. Singh 80, S. N. Khanolkar 64, S. K. Sahu 122, K. S. Parida 48; S. K. Vadiaraj four for 94, R. V. Bharadwaj three for 44) and 418 for nine dec. (A. A. Pagnis 68, S. B. Bangar 59, Y. Gowda 92, S. N. Khanolkar 90, Extras 33; D. Ganesh three for 63, R. V. Bharadwaj three for 77); Karnataka 237 (J. Arun Kumar 55, B. M. Rowland 35, V. S. T. Naidu 46, Extras 34; T. P. Singh four for 64, K. S. Parida four for 62) and 279 for four (M. R. Beerala 35, B. M. Rowland 100 not out, R. V. Bharadwaj 43, V. S. T. Naidu 46).

Semi-finals

At GSFC Ground, Baroda, April 5, 6, 7, 8, 9. Drawn. Baroda were declared winners by virtue of their first-innings lead. Baroda* 568 (C. C. Williams 35, S. S. Parab 60, N. R. Mongia 181, J. J. Martin 86, T. B. Arothe 86, I. K. Pathan 40 not out; D. S. Mohanty three for 110, S. S. Raul three for 76) and 409 (S. S. Parab 56, H. R. Jadhav 78, J. J. Martin 33, T. B. Arothe 62, N. R. Mongia 53, A. P. Bhoite 45; S. S. Raul three for 70); Orissa 280 (S. S. Das 54, R. R. Parida 94, P. Jayachandra 48, S. K. Satpathy 30; V. N. Buch four for 96, A. P. Bhoite three for 32) and 361 for five (R. R. Parida 71, S. S. Raul 36, P. M. Mullick 131 not out, P. Jayachandra 82).

At PCA Stadium, Mohali, April 5, 6, 7, 8 9. Railways won by five wickets. Punjab 249 (R. S. Ricky 33, V. Rathore 44, A. Kakkar 53; Harvinder Singh five for 66) and 356 (R. S. Ricky 54, Manish Sharma 61, V. Rathore 31, P. Dharmani 77, R. S. Sodhi 89, Extras 30; T. P. Singh three for 132, K. S. Parida three for 72); Railways* 407 (S. B. Bangar 89, Abhay Sharma 53, S. N. Khanolkar 48, K. S. Parida 36 not out, Zakir Hussain 30; Babloo Kumar three for 48) and 199 for five (S. B. Bangar 47, T. P. Singh 34, Raja Ali 32 not out).

FINAL

BARODA v RAILWAYS

At GSFC Ground, Baroda, April 19, 20, 21, 22, 23. Baroda won by 21 runs. Toss: Baroda.

Just when Railways could see a first title in prospect, Baroda's dramatic fightback turned the tables. Railways led by 151 on first innings, but Parab's fourth century of the season revived their opponents, and Zaheer Khan's left-arm pace cut them down in the run-chase. Four days earlier, after Baroda chose to bat, the match's very first delivery had removed Parab, and his side were three down in 11 overs. Though Baroda recovered ground, seamers Harvinder Singh and Bangar dismissed them for 243. Railways captain and wicket-keeper, Abhay Sharma, needed treatment after being struck in the face and, when he returned, Wankhede kept the gloves for the remainder of the innings. Next day, Railways reached 196 for two before losing six for 50, which left them only three ahead. But with Patel sidelined by injury, Kartik and Parida added 113, and last man Harvinder helped stretch the lead. Second time round, Parab batted six and a half hours; century partnerships with Williams and Martin cleared the arrears, and by the time Martin was stranded on 87 Railways needed 223. They started the final day on 91 for four, which Zaheer swiftly made 107 for six. Wankhede and Sahu rallied against the spinners, adding 83 to reduce the target to 33. Then Zaheer returned, and the last four wickets fell in four overs. Baroda celebrated their fifth Ranji title in the company of Dattajirao Gaekwad, who had led them to their fourth in 1957-58.

Man of the Match: Zaheer Khan.

Close of play: First day, Railways 91-1 (Bangar 21*, T. P. Singh 60*); Second day, Railways 318-8 (Kartik 46*, Parida 24*); Third day, Baroda 183-2 (Parab 98*, Martin 9*); Fourth day, Railways 91-4 (Gowda 17*, Wankhede 11*).

Baroda

S. S. Parab c Abhay Sharma b Harvinder Singh	0	– (2) st Abhay Sharma b T. P. Singh	141
C. C. Williams c Gowda b Parida	65	– (1) c Bangar b T. P. Singh	41
†N. R. Mongia c Khanolkar b Bangar	4	– c Harvinder Singh b Kartik	15
*J. J. Martin c Abhay Sharma b Harvinder Singh	0	– not out	87
T. B. Arothe c Khanolkar b Harvinder Singh	52	– c Bangar b T. P. Singh	21
H. R. Jadhav lbw b Parida	10	– c Abhay Sharma b Bangar	1
A. P. Bhoite b Bangar	57	– c Abhay Sharma b Bangar	14
R. B. Patel c Kartik b Bangar	16	– (11) c Gowda b Kartik	0
V. N. Buch not out	10	– (8) c Kartik b Harvinder Singh	0
Zaheer Khan c Wankhede b Harvinder Singh	5	– c Abhay Sharma b T. P. Singh	19
I. K. Pathan run out	0	– (9) c Abhay Sharma b Bangar	6
B 3, n-b 21	24	B 9, l-b 3, w 2, n-b 14	28
1/0 2/20 3/30 4/107 5/149 6/150 7/219 8/238 9/243	243	1/102 2/143 3/259 4/299 5/302 6/324 7/325 8/342 9/370	373

Bowling: *First Innings*—Harvinder Singh 20–5–59–4; Bangar 12.1–2–55–3; Kartik 12–2–70–0; Parida 16–5–36–2; T. P. Singh 4–0–20–0. *Second Innings*—Harvinder Singh 25–3–83–1; Bangar 34–10–94–3; Kartik 36–7–82–2; T. P. Singh 27–0–82–4; Khanolkar 2–0–20–0.

Railways

A. A. Pagnis b Patel	7	– c and b Bhoite	31
S. B. Bangar c Jadhav b Zaheer Khan	62	– b Buch	7
T. P. Singh lbw b Bhoite	67	– c Zaheer Khan b Bhoite	5
Y. Gowda c Martin b Buch	65	– c Mongia b Zaheer Khan	20
*†Abhay Sharma lbw b Zaheer Khan	8	– c Williams b Buch	17
S. N. Khanolkar c Bhoite b Patel	4	– (7) lbw b Zaheer Khan	3
S. K. Sahu lbw b Buch	0	– (8) c Martin b Zaheer Khan	42
S. V. Wankhede lbw b Zaheer Khan	14	– (6) b Zaheer Khan	58
M. Kartik st Mongia b Bhoite	79	– c Mongia b Bhoite	2
K. S. Parida c Pathan b Buch	47	– c Buch b Zaheer Khan	0
Harvinder Singh not out	17	– not out	2
L-b 11, n-b 13	24	B 4, l-b 7, w 1, n-b 2	14
1/17 2/108 3/196 4/206 5/216 6/221 7/240 8/246 9/359	394	1/40 2/44 3/48 4/69 5/101 6/107 7/190 8/193 9/194	201

Bowling: *First Innings*—Zaheer Khan 37–10–92–3; Patel 25.2–9–49–2; Pathan 15.4–1–85–0; Buch 39–15–86–3; Bhoite 16–1–64–2; Arothe 2–0–7–0. *Second Innings*—Zaheer Khan 18.2–1–43–5; Pathan 2–0–13–0; Buch 26–7–75–2; Bhoite 18–1–59–3.

Umpires: Jasbir Singh and S. K. Tarapore.
Referee: R. C. Shukla.

RANJI TROPHY WINNERS

1934-35	Bombay	1942-43	Baroda	1950-51	Holkar
1935-36	Bombay	1943-44	Western India	1951-52	Bombay
1936-37	Nawanagar	1944-45	Bombay	1952-53	Holkar
1937-38	Hyderabad	1945-46	Holkar	1953-54	Bombay
1938-39	Bengal	1946-47	Baroda	1954-55	Madras
1939-40	Maharashtra	1947-48	Holkar	1955-56	Bombay
1940-41	Maharashtra	1948-49	Bombay	1956-57	Bombay
1941-42	Bombay	1949-50	Baroda	1957-58	Baroda

1958-59	Bombay	1973-74	Karnataka	1988-89	Delhi
1959-60	Bombay	1974-75	Bombay	1989-90	Bengal
1960-61	Bombay	1975-76	Bombay	1990-91	Haryana
1961-62	Bombay	1976-77	Bombay	1991-92	Delhi
1962-63	Bombay	1977-78	Karnataka	1992-93	Punjab
1963-64	Bombay	1978-79	Delhi	1993-94	Bombay
1964-65	Bombay	1979-80	Delhi	1994-95	Bombay
1965-66	Bombay	1980-81	Bombay	1995-96	Karnataka
1966-67	Bombay	1981-82	Delhi	1996-97	Mumbai
1967-68	Bombay	1982-83	Karnataka	1997-98	Karnataka
1968-69	Bombay	1983-84	Bombay	1998-99	Karnataka
1969-70	Bombay	1984-85	Bombay	1999-2000	Mumbai
1970-71	Bombay	1985-86	Delhi	2000-01	Baroda
1971-72	Bombay	1986-87	Hyderabad		
1972-73	Bombay	1987-88	Tamil Nadu		

Bombay/Mumbai have won the Ranji Trophy 34 times, Delhi and Karnataka 6, Baroda 5, Holkar 4, Bengal, Hyderabad, Madras/Tamil Nadu and Maharashtra 2, Haryana, Nawanagar, Punjab and Western India 1.

DULEEP TROPHY, 2000-01

	Played	*Won*	*Lost*	*Drawn*	*1st-innings Points*	*Points*
North Zone	4	1	0	3	6	23
Central Zone . . .	4	1	0	3	2	19
West Zone	4	1	0	3	0	17
East Zone	4	1	2	1	2	13
South Zone . . .	4	0	2	2	2	8

Outright win = 8 pts; draw = 3 pts; lead on first innings in drawn match = 2 pts.

At VCA Ground, Nagpur, January 4, 5, 6, 7. Drawn. Central Zone* 536 (Jai P. Yadav 177, A. A. Pagnis 62, M. Kaif 119 not out, Raja Ali 58, Abhay Sharma 45; S. V. Bahutule three for 94) and 156 for eight dec. (G. K. Khoda 31, Raja Ali 55; V. N. Buch three for 49, S. V. Bahutule four for 26); West Zone 421 (Wasim Jaffer 94, J. J. Martin 121, A. V. Kale 49, N. K. Patel 62, S. V. Bahutule 39; S. J. Srivastava four for 62, R. J. Kanwat three for 104, K. S. Parida three for 127) and 44 for no wkt. *Central Zone 5 pts, West Zone 3 pts.*

At Indira Gandhi Stadium, Vijayawada, January 4, 5, 6, 7. Drawn. North Zone* 708 for eight dec. (A. Chopra 110, V. Rathore 143, D. Mongia 201, V. Sehwag 108, Harbhajan Singh 41, R. L. Sanghvi 33 not out; S. B. Joshi three for 167) and 326 for three (A. Chopra 125 not out, V. Rathore 69, Harbhajan Singh 38, Yuvraj Singh 80 not out); South Zone 477 (T. Kumaran 106, V. V. S. Laxman 179, H. K. Badani 44, R. R. Singh 67; Surendra Singh five for 115). *South Zone 3 pts, North Zone 5 pts.*

Mongia's 201 lasted 364 minutes and 266 balls and included 30 fours and a six. Chopra hit a hundred in each innings. Night-watchman Kumaran scored his maiden first-class hundred.

At Green Park, Kanpur, January 11, 12, 13, 14. Drawn. Central Zone 421 (Jai P. Yadav 95, A. R. Khurasiya 110, M. Kaif 83, Abhay Sharma 31, M. Kartik 45; Javed Zaman five for 99, Sukhbinder Singh three for 89); East Zone* 484 (S. S. Das 40, N. L. Haldipur 34, R. R. Parida 53, R. S. Gavaskar 146, D. Dasgupta 72, Extras 52; K. S. Parida four for 126). *Central Zone 3 pts, East Zone 5 pts.*

At PCA Stadium, Mohali, January 11, 12, 13, 14. Drawn. West Zone 284 (Wasim Jaffer 39, H. H. Kanitkar 61, S. V. Bahutule 42, Extras 32; A. Nehra four for 103, Surendra Singh four for 80) and 50 for one; North Zone* 331 (A. Chopra 54, V. Sehwag 162 not out; Iqbal Siddiqui five for 116, S. R. Saxena three for 74). *North Zone 5 pts, West Zone 3 pts.*

At North-East Frontier Railway Stadium, Maligaon, Guwahati, January 18, 19, 20. North Zone won by 237 runs. North Zone* 206 (D. Mongia 72; D. S. Mohanty six for 58) and 268 (V. Rathore 35, Yuvraj Singh 77, V. Dahiya 70, Sarandeep Singh 42 not out; Sukhbinder Singh three for 60, S. S. Raul three for 24); East Zone 81 (A. Nehra seven for 14) and 156 (A. Nehra three for 76, R. L. Sanghvi four for 17). *North Zone 8 pts.*

At Lalabhai Contractor Stadium, Surat, January 18, 19, 20, 21. Drawn. West Zone* 376 (Wasim Jaffer 49, H. H. Kanitkar 95, J. J. Martin 89, V. G. Kambli 56; D. Ganesh four for 81, S. B. Joshi three for 78) and 330 for six (C. C. Williams 43, N. R. Mongia 60, J. J. Martin 47, V. G. Kambli 66, A. V. Kale 52; S. B. Joshi three for 62); South Zone 595 for four dec. (S. Sriram 38, S. Ramesh 99, V. V. S. Laxman 217, R. Dravid 188). *West Zone 3 pts, South Zone 5 pts.*

Laxman's 217 lasted 404 minutes and 286 balls and included 25 fours and two sixes; he and Dravid added 409 for South Zone's third wicket, an all-wicket Duleep Trophy record.

At Maharaja Bir Bikram College Stadium, Agartala, January 25, 26, 27. East Zone won by four wickets. South Zone* 113 (S. B. Joshi 32; D. S. Mohanty ten for 46) and 177 (V. V. S. Laxman 40, R. Dravid 66; D. S. Mohanty four for 45, Sukhbinder Singh six for 57); East Zone 124 (S. Z. Zuffri 30, Sukhbinder Singh 31; J. Srinath six for 32) and 170 for six (S. S. Das 79, D. Dasgupta 32 not out; B. K. V. Prasad three for 44). *East Zone 8 pts.*

Mohanty became the sixth bowler to take all ten wickets in a first-class innings in India. His figures of 19–5–46–10 were the second most economical after P. M. Chatterjee, who returned 19–11–20–10 for Bengal against Assam at Jorhat in 1956-57. The previous best analysis in a Duleep Trophy match was nine for 55 by leg-spinner Baloo Gupte for West Zone against South Zone at Calcutta in 1962-63.

At Feroz Shah Kotla Ground, Delhi, January 25, 26, 27, 28. Drawn. North Zone 690 for eight dec. (V. Dahiya 81, V. Rathore 94, Yuvraj Singh 34, D. Mongia 208, V. Sehwag 43, R. S. Sodhi 137, Harbhajan Singh 42, Extras 39; D. S. Bundela three for 108, R. J. Kanwat three for 122) and 233 for eight (Yuvraj Singh 130; S. J. Srivastava three for 50); Central Zone* 439 (Jai P. Yadav 78, A. R. Khurasiya 51, M. Kaif 61, Y. Gowda 107 not out, Extras 31; Harbhajan Singh three for 126, R. L. Sanghvi four for 77). *North Zone 5 pts, Central Zone 3 pts.*

Mongia's 208, his second double-hundred in three weeks and his third of the season, following his 308 not out for Punjab in November, lasted 433 minutes and 319 balls and included 27 fours and two sixes; he added 316 for the fifth wicket with Sodhi.

At Bhausaheb Bandodkar (Gymkhana) Stadium, Panaji, February 1, 2, 3, 4. Central Zone won by an innings and 14 runs. South Zone* 141 (R. V. Bharadwaj 50; D. S. Bundela four for 58, Jai P. Yadav three for 46) and 395 (S. Sriram 150, R. V. Bharadwaj 40, S. B. Joshi 45, J. Srinath 30, H. K. Badani 48, Extras 32; N. D. Hirwani three for 115); Central Zone 550 for seven dec. (G. K. Khoda 300 not out, A. R. Khurasiya 51, M. Kaif 69, Y. Gowda 85; S. L. V. Raju three for 133). *Central Zone 8 pts.*

Khoda's 300 not out lasted 610 minutes and 467 balls and included 33 fours and six sixes. He was only the second batsman to score a triple-hundred in the Duleep Trophy, after Raman Lamba, who made 320 for North Zone v West Zone at Bhilai in 1987-88.

At Nehru Stadium, Pune, February 1, 2, 3. West Zone won by an innings and 363 runs. West Zone* 656 for seven dec. (H. H. Kanitkar 42, S. R. Tendulkar 199, V. G. Kambli 117, J. J. Martin 39, S. V. Bahutule 62, R. R. Powar 113 not out, A. B. Agarkar 32 not out, Extras 45); East Zone 132 (S. S. Das 38; A. B. Agarkar five for 22) and 161 (R. R. Parida 41; S. V. Bahutule six for 49). *West Zone 8 pts.*

Tendulkar, whose 199 in his only Duleep match took 299 minutes and 214 balls and included 30 fours and four sixes, and Kambli put on 225 for West Zone's fourth wicket. Bahutule took a hat-trick in East Zone's second innings.

DULEEP TROPHY WINNERS

1961-62	West Zone
1962-63	West Zone
1963-64	West Zone
1964-65	West Zone
1965-66	South Zone
1966-67	South Zone
1967-68	South Zone
1968-69	West Zone
1969-70	West Zone
1970-71	South Zone
1971-72	Central Zone
1972-73	West Zone
1973-74	North Zone
1974-75	South Zone
1975-76	South Zone
1976-77	West Zone
1977-78	West Zone
1978-79	North Zone
1979-80	North Zone
1980-81	West Zone
1981-82	West Zone
1982-83	North Zone
1983-84	North Zone
1984-85	South Zone
1985-86	West Zone
1986-87	South Zone
1987-88	North Zone
1988-89	North Zone West Zone
1989-90	South Zone
1990-91	North Zone
1991-92	North Zone
1992-93	North Zone
1993-94	North Zone
1994-95	North Zone
1995-96	South Zone
1996-97	Central Zone
1997-98	Central Zone West Zone
1998-99	Central Zone
1999-2000	North Zone
2000-01	North Zone

SOUTH AFRICA A IN INDIA, 2001

South Africa A were due to tour India in September 2001, but the trip was cancelled in June, with concerns over the monsoon weather at the time of year scheduled. The squad of 14 named for the tour was: H. D. Ackerman (Western Province) (*captain*), J. L. Ontong (Boland) (*vice-captain*), G. H. Bodi (KwaZulu-Natal), C. W. Henderson (Western Province), J. C. Kent (KwaZulu-Natal), G. J-P. Kruger (Eastern Province), C. K. Langeveldt (Boland), P. V. Mpitsang (Free State), A. Nel (Easterns), A. G. Prince (Western Province), J. A. Rudolph (Northerns), G. C. Smith (Western Province), T. L. Tsolekile (Western Province), M. van Jaarsveld (Northerns).

CRICKET IN PAKISTAN, 2000-01

By ABID ALI KAZI

Naved Latif

Pakistan played less international cricket in 2000-01 than in the last few seasons. From Singapore in August to England in June, they played eight Tests and 24 one-day internationals, against 12 and 41 the previous year. They performed below their potential – winning only two Tests – and sometimes lacked application. There was no lack of controversy, however. In April, Javed Miandad, who had just lost his job as coach, was reported to have accused the team of fixing matches during the recent tour of New Zealand. He later denied having said anything of the sort.

That tour, in which New Zealand came from behind to win the one-day series and square the Tests, also saw the end of Moin Khan's tenure as captain. His stock had already fallen after he lost the home Test series against England in December, when the visitors won their first Test victory on Pakistani soil since 1961-62. Moin was injured in New Zealand, so Waqar Younis was named stand-in captain at Sharjah in April – as he had been for the Singapore one-day tournament the previous August. He was swiftly confirmed as captain in his own right for the ensuing trip to England, with South African Richard Pybus, sacked the year before, returning as coach. Moin also lost his place as wicket-keeper to Rashid Latif, who had withdrawn from international cricket a few years earlier after making his own match-fixing allegations. Under Waqar, Pakistan levelled the Test series in England after losing heavily at Lord's, where they later lost the final of the following triangular series to Australia.

The Pakistan Cricket Board regained some stability after the politically inspired changes of recent years, and the domestic season reverted to two first-class tournaments, for regional and commercial departmental sides. The deposed chairman, Mujeeb-ur-Rehman, had integrated both types of teams into the 1999-2000 Quaid-e-Azam Trophy, making the Patron's Trophy non-first-class. Now the PCB decided that departmental teams should be gradually phased out of first-class competitions, and restricted to one-day tournaments. First-class cricket should be reserved for city, divisional or district representative sides. A host of new districts and divisions were admitted to the Quaid-e-Azam's non-first-class Grade II, but in 2000-01, as in the past, the regional and departmental sides formed the first-class grades of the Quaid-e-Azam and Patron's Trophies respectively.

The Quaid-e-Azam was contested by 12 teams in a single league, with Sheikhupura promoted to first-class status. Karachi Whites led the table by 24 points from Lahore City Blues, but lost the January final when Lahore scraped home by one wicket with two days remaining. It was only the fourth time a Lahore team had lifted the trophy, but the third in eight years. The cancellation of a proposed tour by India meant both finalists could call on their internationals. For Lahore Blues, Wasim Akram and Abdur Razzaq took 19 wickets between them; Karachi's stars included Shahid Afridi, who scored a dazzling first-day century. The Grade II title went to Sialkot. They were promoted, with fellow-finalists Hyderabad, for 2001-02 at the expense of Sheikhupura and Karachi Blues, who finished at the opposite end of the table from Karachi Whites.

The Patron's Trophy, originally scheduled to begin immediately after the Quaid-e-Azam final, was postponed for a few weeks in favour of practice matches for the New Zealand tour probables. It was contested by eight departmental teams and produced a first-time champion in Pakistan Customs, who squeezed through to the final ahead of Habib Bank on run-rate. There, they beat table leaders National Bank. KRL were relegated and replaced by Grade II winners PWD. Sadly, Pakistan Railways, an integral part of the nation's cricket history, were disbanded, citing lack of funds. They had made their first-class debut in the original Quaid-e-Azam Trophy, in 1953-54, were highly successful in the early 1970s, but were relegated from the top level in 1995-96 – to be replaced by Customs.

The PCB introduced separate departmental and regional one-day tournaments. Habib Bank were the departmental champions, with National Bank losing another final. The regional tournament was divided into two pools, headed by Sheikhupura, with a 100 per cent record, and Karachi Whites; both won their respective semis before Karachi Whites triumphed in the final. Karachi won the National Under-19 Grade I, with Sheikhupura taking Grade II.

The season's leading run-scorer was Naved Latif of Sargodha and Customs, whose 1,352 at 46.62 included 394 against Gujranwala, the tenth-highest individual score in all first-class cricket. Only Hanif Mohammad and Aftab Baloch had compiled higher innings in Pakistan. But Naved was brought swiftly back to earth when Gujranwala's Khalid Mahmood hit him for 32 in an over on the final day, reaching 56 in 17 balls. One other player reached four figures, Zahoor Elahi (Lahore City Whites and ADBP) scoring 1,225 runs at 49.00, including four centuries. The leading wicket-taker was Naved-ul-Hasan, with 91 at 22.93 apiece, for Sheikhupura and Customs. Wicket-keeper Atiq-uz-Zaman of Karachi Whites and Habib Bank created a national record with 76 dismissals (70 caught, six stumped), beating Wasim Yousufi's 74 in 1998-99, while Aamer Bashir of Customs, who held 20 catches in just eight matches, headed the fielders' list.

FIRST-CLASS AVERAGES, 2000-01

BATTING

(Qualification: 600 runs)

	M	*I*	*NO*	*R*	*HS*	*100s*	*Avge*
Mohammad Ramzan (*Faisalabad*)	9	17	4	719	205	3	55.30
Ali Naqvi (*Islamabad/Pakistan Customs*)	8	15	3	628	119	2	52.33
Humayun Farhat (*Lahore City Blues/Allied Bank*)	11	20	1	977	188	3	51.42
Imran Farhat (*Lahore City Blues*)	9	17	1	816	200	2	51.00
Misbah-ul-Haq (*Sargodha/KRL*)	12	20	1	953	142	4	50.15
Asif Mujtaba (*Karachi Whites/PIA*)	17	25	5	987	202*	2	49.35
Zahoor Elahi (*Lahore City Whites/ADBP*)	18	29	4	1,225	203	4	49.00
Naved Latif (*Sargodha/Pakistan Customs*)	18	29	0	1,352	394	2	46.62
Mohammad Masroor (*Karachi Whites*)	11	19	5	606	171*	1	43.28
Akhtar Sarfraz (*Peshawar/National Bank*)	15	25	4	903	142	2	43.00
Farhan Adil (*Karachi Blues/Habib Bank*)	14	24	1	952	211	1	41.39
Wajahatullah Wasti (*Peshawar/Allied Bank*)	12	20	4	626	162*	2	39.12

	M	*I*	*NO*	*R*	*HS*	*100s*	*Avge*
Usman Tariq (*Bahawalpur/Allied Bank*)	15	24	3	819	106*	1	39.00
Hammad Tariq (*Bahawalpur*)	11	17	1	606	134	1	37.87
Mohammad Wasim (*Rawalpindi/KRL*)	15	26	0	972	147	3	37.38
Ijaz Ahmed, jun. (*Faisalabad/Allied Bank*)	13	22	1	760	138	2	36.19
Taufeeq Umar (*Lahore City Whites/Habib Bank*)	14	27	2	897	120	1	35.88
Hasan Raza (*Karachi Whites/Habib Bank*)	19	33	5	974	100*	2	34.78
Qaiser Abbas (*Sheikhupura/National Bank*)	16	26	1	808	84	0	32.32
Kamran Akmal (*Lahore City Whites/ National Bank*)	16	26	6	640	174	1	32.00
Yasir Hameed (*Peshawar/PIA*)	15	25	0	766	103	1	30.64
Naumanullah (*Karachi Blues/National Bank*)	18	28	1	802	91	0	29.70
Pervez Aziz (*Rawalpindi/KRL*)	13	23	2	617	154	1	29.38
Imran Abbas (*Gujranwala/ADBP*)	14	24	2	628	108	2	28.54
Naseer Ahmed (*Rawalpindi/KRL*)	16	30	2	771	126	1	27.53
Mujahid Jamshed (*Sheikhupura/Habib Bank*)	14	24	0	659	104	1	27.45
Shahid Anwar (*Lahore City Blues/National Bank*)	16	31	3	720	104*	2	25.71
Yasir Arafat (*Rawalpindi/KRL*)	17	30	6	612	76*	0	25.50
Rafatullah Mohmand (*Peshawar/WAPDA*)	15	27	2	600	91*	0	24.00
Naved-ul-Hasan (*Sheikhupura/Pakistan Customs*)	19	30	4	608	70	0	23.38

* *Signifies not out.*

BOWLING

(Qualification: 30 wickets)

	O	*M*	*R*	*W*	*BB*	*5W/i*	*Avge*
Aleem Moosa (*National Bank*)	138.2	28	415	37	7-39	3	11.21
Shakeel Ahmed (*Rawalpindi/KRL*)	308.2	114	621	39	6-33	3	15.92
Mohammad Sami (*Karachi Whites*)	233.5	49	746	45	6-72	4	16.57
Waqar Ahmed (*Peshawar/Pakistan Customs*)	225.3	45	717	42	7-86	2	17.07
Arshad Khan (*Peshawar/Allied Bank*)	272	75	646	37	7-66	2	17.45
Kashif Raza (*Sheikhupura/WAPDA*)	351	72	1,089	59	6-59	6	18.45
Sajid Shah (*Peshawar/Habib Bank*)	313.3	60	971	52	6-34	1	18.67
Naeem Akhtar (*Rawalpindi/KRL*)	370	114	803	43	6-18	2	18.67
Mohammad Akram (*Rawalpindi/Allied Bank*)	208.1	38	659	33	4-18	0	19.96
Shabbir Ahmed (*National Bank*)	286.4	56	847	42	6-51	3	20.16
Nadeem Iqbal (*Pakistan Customs*)	342.3	85	876	43	7-53	5	20.37
Mohammad Hussain (*Lahore City Blues*)	303.1	100	809	39	5-54	3	20.74
Iftikhar Anjum (*Islamabad/ADBP*)	490.1	103	1,532	73	6-82	7	20.98
Aqeel Ahmed (*Faisalabad/WAPDA*)	401.4	78	1,206	54	7-115	5	22.33
Mohammad Zahid (*Bahawalpur/Allied Bank*)	458.5	109	1,097	49	6-58	3	22.38
Danish Kaneria (*Karachi Whites/Habib Bank*)	527.3	141	1,354	60	7-39	3	22.56
Stephen John (*Islamabad/Pakistan Customs*)	435.1	67	1,352	59	6-32	3	22.91
Naved-ul-Hasan (*Sheikhupura/Pakistan Customs*)	658.2	130	2,087	91	7-86	5	22.93
Mohammad Zahid, jun. (*Karachi Whites/PIA*)	216.2	34	721	31	7-71	2	23.25
Ali Gauhar (*PIA*)	222.3	53	700	30	7-41	2	23.33
Shahid Nazir (*Faisalabad/Habib Bank*)	362	73	1,168	48	6-58	2	24.33
Jaffer Nazir (*Sheikhupura/KRL*)	491.2	90	1,570	64	7-46	2	24.53
Yasir Arafat (*Rawalpindi/KRL*)	531	88	1,798	73	6-9	2	24.63
Fazl-e-Akbar (*Peshawar/PIA*)	264.1	50	944	38	5-25	3	24.84
Kamran Hussain (*Bahawalpur/WAPDA*)	471.2	85	1,577	63	6-53	3	25.03
Mohammad Sarfraz (*Sargodha/KRL*)	261.5	40	844	33	5-43	2	25.57
Waqas Ahmed (*Lahore City Blues/WAPDA*)	443	84	1,428	55	7-45	2	25.96
Irfan Fazil (*Lahore City Whites/Habib Bank*)	422.3	59	1,620	57	6-100	5	28.42
Mubashir Nazir (*Gujranwala/ADBP*)	474.1	88	1,546	54	6-56	3	28.62
Tanvir Ahmed (*Karachi Blues/Allied Bank*)	259.4	37	988	31	6-81	2	31.87

QUAID-E-AZAM TROPHY, 2000-01

	Played	Won	Lost	Drawn	1st-inns Points	Points
Karachi Whites	11	7	2	2	24	87
Lahore City Blues	10	6	1	3	9	63
Peshawar	10	5	2	3	15	60
Faisalabad	10	4	3	3	12	48
Rawalpindi	11	3	1	7	21	48
Bahawalpur	11	3	2	6	15	42
Gujranwala	11	3	2	6	15	42
Lahore City Whites	11	3	3	5	6	33
Sargodha	10	1	3	6	15	24
Islamabad	11	1	6	4	9	18
Sheikhupura	11	1	7	3	9	18
Karachi Blues	11	1	6	4	6	15

Note: The matches between Lahore City Blues and Faisalabad, and Sargodha and Peshawar, were abandoned.

Outright win = 9 pts; lead on first innings in a won or drawn game = 3 pts.

Final: Lahore City Blues beat Karachi Whites by one wicket.

*In the following scores, * by the name of a team indicates that they won the toss.*

At Bohranwala Ground, Faisalabad, October 11, 12, 13, 14. Faisalabad won by ten wickets. Gujranwala 302 (Imran Abbas 105 not out, Rizwan Malik 38, Rana Qayyum 30, Zahid Fazal 39, Sarfraz Ahmed 30, Extras 46; Aqeel Ahmed seven for 115) and 102 (Aqeel Ahmed three for 50, Farooq Iqbal five for 16); Faisalabad* 287 (Fida Hussain 116 not out, Farooq Iqbal 53; Mubashir Nazir three for 49, Abdur Rehman four for 113) and 119 for no wkt (Mohammad Ramzan 38 not out, Ijaz Mahmood 79 not out). *Faisalabad 9 pts.*

Imran Abbas carried his bat through Gujranwala's first innings.

At Shalimar (Margalla) Cricket Ground, Islamabad, October 11, 12, 13, 14. Drawn. Islamabad 436 for nine dec. (Mohammad Shahbaz 49, Bilal Asad 86, Zaheer Abbasi 127, Bilal Rana 50, Extras 59) and 104 (Bilal Rana 48 not out; Imran Adil five for 36, Kamran Hussain three for 29); Bahawalpur* 309 (Hammad Tariq 134, Usman Tariq 37, Kamran Hussain 53, Extras 32; Aamir Nazir five for 88) and 19 for no wkt. *Islamabad 3 pts.*

At KCCA Ground, Karachi, October 11, 12, 13, 14. Karachi Whites won by 80 runs. Karachi Whites* 315 for three dec. (Shadab Kabir 37, Shahid Afridi 46, Zeeshan Pervez 115, Hasan Raza 100 not out) and 244 for three dec. (Shadab Kabir 35, Shahid Afridi 56, Zeeshan Pervez 36, Hasan Raza 55 not out, Mohammad Masroor 50 not out); Karachi Blues 312 (Naumanullah 48, Afsar Nawaz 165; Mohammad Sami four for 73, Danish Kaneria three for 82) and 167 (Naumanullah 78, Saeed Azad 30; Danish Kaneria four for 58, Adnan Malik five for 47). *Karachi Whites 12 pts.*

At LCCA Ground, Lahore, October 11, 12, 13, 14. Lahore City Blues won by 143 runs. Lahore City Blues 471 (Shahid Anwar 100, Imran Farhat 66, Bazid Khan 39, Intikhab Alam 77, Imran Yousuf 47, Humayun Farhat 47 not out, Extras 56; Maqsood Rana three for 88, Taufeeq Umar three for 33) and 187 for eight dec. (Mohammad Hussain 42); Lahore City Whites* 325 for seven dec. (Taufeeq Umar 120, Ali Hussain 92, Kamran Akmal 40 not out; Mohammad Hussain four for 113) and 190 (Taufeeq Umar 57, Kamran Akmal 51; Mohammad Hussain five for 77, Imran Farhat three for 25). *Lahore City Blues 12 pts.*

Lahore City Blues wicket-keeper Humayun Farhat held five catches and made one stumping in Lahore City Whites' second innings.

At Arbab Niaz Stadium, Peshawar, October 11, 12, 13, 14. Drawn. Peshawar 282 (Abdus Salam 43, Taimur Khan 33, Rafatullah Mohmand 30, Extras 51; Naeem Akhtar four for 79, Yasir Arafat three for 58) and 270 for nine (Rafatullah Mohmand 49, Wajahatullah Wasti 33, Younis Khan 74, Extras 33; Yasir Arafat six for 66); Rawalpindi* 234 (Naved Ashraf 46, Pervez Aziz 57; Fazl-e-Akbar five for 80). *Peshawar 3 pts.*

At Sheikhupura Stadium, Sheikhupura, October 11, 12, 13, 14. Sargodha won by 126 runs. Sargodha 212 (Naved Latif 64, Misbah-ul-Haq 33, Haroon Malik 36; Jaffer Nazir six for 62) and 254 (Naved Latif 35, Misbah-ul-Haq 102; Kashif Raza five for 52); Sheikhupura* 209 (Qaiser Abbas 46, Naved-ul-Hasan 48, Extras 31; Ahmed Hayat three for 66, Mohammad Sarfraz four for 58) and 131 (Majid Majeed 46; Ahmed Hayat five for 62). *Sargodha 12 pts.*

At Bahawal Stadium, Bahawalpur, October 17, 18, 19, 20. Bahawalpur won by four wickets. Karachi Blues* 226 (Saeed Azad 34, Iqbal Imam 44, Farhan Adil 80; Maqbool Hussain three for 42, Mohammad Zahid four for 73) and 280 (Iqbal Imam 43, Farhan Adil 76, Iqbal Sheikh 30, Extras 31; Mohammad Altaf three for 48, Mohammad Zahid three for 83); Bahawalpur 266 (Bilal Moin 36, Aamir Sohail 42, Usman Tariq 63, Kamran Hussain 44; Riaz Sheikh four for 27) and 242 for six (Hammad Tariq 82, Usman Tariq 33 not out, Aamir Sohail 32; Tabish Nawab four for 95). *Bahawalpur 12 pts.*

At Bohranwala Ground, Faisalabad, October 17, 18, 19, 20. Drawn. Faisalabad 468 for seven dec. (Mohammad Ramzan 205, Mohammad Nawaz 60, Fida Hussain 42, Wasim Haider 71, Extras 44) and 128 for one (Mohammad Ramzan 102 not out); Sargodha* 363 (Mohammad Hafeez 54, Naved Latif 79, Misbah-ul-Haq 83, Haroon Malik 68, Extras 41; Aqeel Ahmed four for 110, Farooq Iqbal four for 46). *Faisalabad 3 pts.*

Mohammad Ramzan hit a hundred in each innings. His first-innings 205 lasted 544 minutes and 415 balls and included 22 fours.

At Shalimar (Margalla) Cricket Ground, Islamabad, October 17, 18, 19, 20. Drawn. Rawalpindi 336 (Saeed Anwar 53, Naeem Akhtar 52, Nadeem Abbasi 90 not out; Stephen John four for 60) and 312 for eight dec. (Naved Ashraf 32, Saeed Anwar 66, Naseer Ahmed 31, Pervez Aziz 96, Naeem Akhtar 38; Aamir Nazir three for 66); Islamabad* 308 (Asif Ali 126, Zaheer Abbasi 54; Naeem Akhtar four for 93, Pervez Iqbal four for 59). *Rawalpindi 3 pts.*

At UBL Sports Complex, Karachi, October 17, 18, 19, 20. Karachi Whites won by an innings and 46 runs. Karachi Whites* 435 for nine dec. (Zeeshan Pervez 91, Asif Mujtaba 168, Adnan Malik 44, Aamer Hanif 31, Extras 33); Lahore City Whites 270 (Mustaqeem Ahmed 51, Zahoor Elahi 103, Ghaffar Kazmi 47; Mohammad Sami six for 72, Danish Kaneria three for 101) and 119 (Imran Tahir 32, Zahoor Elahi 30; Mohammad Sami three for one, Danish Kaneria five for 20). *Karachi Whites 12 pts.*

At LCCA Ground, Lahore, October 17, 18, 19, 20. Gujranwala won by three wickets. Lahore City Blues* 179 (Imran Yousuf 35, Fareed Butt 39; Sarfraz Ahmed three for 66, Abdur Rehman four for 54) and 212 (Fareed Butt 73, Hafeez Qureshi 34; Sarfraz Ahmed five for 36, Abdur Rehman three for 75); Gujranwala 217 (Imran Abbas 37, Rizwan Malik 43, Rana Qayyum 46; Mohammad Hussain five for 54, Farhan Rasheed four for 66) and 177 for seven (Atiq-ur-Rehman 36, Asim Munir 30 not out; Waqas Ahmed three for 43, Mohammad Hussain three for 76). *Gujranwala 12 pts.*

At Arbab Niaz Stadium, Peshawar, October 17, 18, 19, 20. Peshawar won by 78 runs. Peshawar 259 (Akhtar Sarfraz 78, Wasim Yousufi 55; Naved-ul-Hasan four for 52, Jaffer Nazir four for 72) and 158 (Taimur Khan 30; Kashif Raza three for 53, Jaffer Nazir three for 38); Sheikhupura* 263 (Qaiser Abbas 84, Yasir Bashir 49, Extras 58; Waqar Ahmed seven for 86) and 76 (Waqar Ahmed four for 37, Taimur Khan three for 20). *Peshawar 9 pts.*

At Jinnah Stadium, Gujranwala, October 23, 24, 25. Gujranwala won by four wickets. Sheikhupura 146 (Qaiser Abbas 67, Mujahid Jamshed 35; Mubashir Nazir three for 46, Sarfraz Ahmed five for 43) and 194 (Zahid Javed 59, Mujahid Jamshed 32, Yasir Bashir 40 not out, Naved-ul-Hasan 39; Mubashir Nazir six for 56); Gujranwala* 198 (Abdur Rehman 41, Khalid Mahmood 42; Jaffer Nazir three for 32, Naved-ul-Hasan six for 80) and 145 for six (Majid Saeed 94 not out; Naved-ul-Hasan three for 39). *Gujranwala 12 pts.*

At Shalimar (Margalla) Cricket Ground, Islamabad, October 23, 24, 25, 26. Lahore City Blues won by 167 runs. Lahore City Blues 199 (Imran Farhat 43, Mohammad Hussain 48; Stephen John five for 82, Rauf Akbar four for 36) and 357 for nine dec. (Imran Farhat 77, Intikhab Alam 43, Mohammad Hussain 65, Extras 38; Stephen John five for 128); Islamabad* 209 (Khalid Zafar 38, Zaheer Abbasi 45, Extras 38; Hasnain Kazim six for 58, Waqas Ahmed four for 57) and 180 (Asif Ali 63; Hasnain Kazim three for 57, Waqas Ahmed four for 81). *Lahore City Blues 9 pts.*

Lahore City Blues wicket-keeper Humayun Farhat took six catches in Islamabad's first innings. In all he made nine dismissals in the match.

At UBL Sports Complex, Karachi, October 23, 24, 25, 26. Drawn. Karachi Whites* 485 for eight dec. (Shadab Kabir 49, Mohammad Masroor 97, Hasan Raza 81, Asif Mujtaba 81, Atiq-uz-Zaman 62, Extras 43; Usman Tariq five for 113) and 267 for four (Shadab Kabir 116, Zeeshan Pervez 96; Mohammad Zahid three for 36); Bahawalpur 367 (Bilal Moin 43, Usman Tariq 62, Kamran Hussain 84, Tariq Hafeez 33, Mohammad Zahid 40; Danish Kaneria three for 131). *Karachi Whites 3 pts.*

At LCCA Ground, Lahore, October 23, 24, 25. Lahore City Whites won by ten wickets. Karachi Blues 259 (Afsar Nawaz 114, Farhan Adil 48; Maqsood Rana three for 45, Imran Tahir five for 57) and 192 (Iqbal Imam 37; Irfan Fazil six for 100); Lahore City Whites* 428 (Zahoor Elahi 63, Taufeeq Umar 58, Tariq Mahmood 46, Kamran Akmal 174; Rizwan Saeed five for 116, Faheem Ahmed three for 87) and 26 for no wkt. *Lahore City Whites 12 pts.*

At Arbab Niaz Stadium, Peshawar, October 23, 24, 25. Peshawar won by 108 runs. Peshawar 174 (Aftab Khan 39, Taimur Khan 41; Shahid Nazir three for 55, Nadeem Afzal three for 38, Saadat Gul three for 34) and 177 (Shahid Nazir six for 58); Faisalabad* 73 (Nauman Habib five for 11) and 170 (Asif Hussain 36; Fazl-e-Akbar four for 66, Waqar Ahmed four for 32). *Peshawar 12 pts.*

At KRL Cricket Ground, Rawalpindi, October 23, 24, 25. Rawalpindi won by an innings and 58 runs. Sargodha 106 (Mohammad Akram four for 18, Yasir Arafat three for 55) and 219 (Misbah-ul-Haq 73; Mohammad Akram four for 50, Yasir Arafat three for 97); Rawalpindi* 383 for nine dec. (Salman Ahmed 31, Pervez Aziz 154, Naeem Akhtar 64, Nadeem Abbasi 30, Yasir Arafat 35 not out; Faisal Afridi three for 84, Ahmed Hayat four for 131). *Rawalpindi 12 pts.*

At Bahawal Stadium, Bahawalpur, October 29, 30, 31, November 1. Bahawalpur won by an innings and 42 runs. Bahawalpur* 377 (Hammad Tariq 31, Azhar Shafiq 122, Bilal Moin 31, Usman Tariq 58, Kamran Hussain 41; Ashraf Bashir four for 71, Mohammad Hafeez three for 83); Sargodha 112 (Mohammad Altaf three for 19, Mohammad Zahid three for 25, Maqbool Hussain four for 26) and 223 (Mohammad Hafeez 59, Misbah-ul-Haq 71; Mohammad Zahid five for 64). *Bahawalpur 12 pts.*

At Gujranwala Cricket Academy Ground, Gujranwala, October 29, 30, 31, November 1. Drawn. Karachi Blues 463 (Farhan Adil 211, Asim Kamal 86, Ahmed Zeeshan 57, Extras 39; Abdur Rehman five for 144) and nought for no wkt; Gujranwala* 557 (Atiq-ur-Rehman 71, Rizwan Malik 156, Asim Munir 73, Majid Saeed 125, Khalid Mahmood 36, Mubashir Nazir 38; Tanvir Ahmed three for 131). *Gujranwala 3 pts.*

Farhan Adil's 211 lasted 482 minutes and 357 balls and included 26 fours and two sixes.

At Shalimar (Margalla) Cricket Ground, Islamabad, October 29, 30, 31. Peshawar won by nine wickets. Islamabad 226 (Bilal Asad 64, Zaheer Abbasi 53, Extras 35; Arshad Khan seven for 66) and 115 (Zaheer Abbasi 32; Sajid Shah six for 34); Peshawar* 297 (Yasir Hameed 89, Taimur Khan 42, Zulfiqar Jan 56, Arshad Khan 46, Extras 37; Iftikhar Anjum five for 55) and 45 for one (Rafatullah Mohmand 33 not out). *Peshawar 12 pts.*

At UBL Sports Complex, Karachi, October 29, 30, 31. Karachi Whites won by ten wickets. Faisalabad* 212 (Mohammad Ramzan 40, Ijaz Ahmed, jun. 45, Wasim Haider 51; Danish Kaneria four for 83, Adnan Malik three for 47) and 113 (Saadat Gul 40; Danish Kaneria five for 32, Tahir Khan three for 31); Karachi Whites 265 (Hasan Raza 94, Atiq-uz-Zaman 54, Kashif Ibrahim 34; Aqeel Ahmed five for 116) and 61 for no wkt (Shadab Kabir 36 not out). *Karachi Whites 12 pts.*

At LCCA Ground, Lahore, October 29, 30, 31, November 1. Lahore City Whites won by nine wickets. Sheikhupura* 258 (Majid Majeed 116, Zahid Javed 30, Mohammad Islam 37; Imran

Tahir three for 82) and 246 (Mujahid Jamshed 86, Saleem Mughal 31, Jaffer Nazir 32; Imran Tahir three for 84, Kashif Shafi four for 68); Lahore City Whites 434 for nine dec. (Zahoor Elahi 203, Ghaffar Kazmi 69, Imran Tahir 39; Kashif Raza three for 58) and 73 for one (Tariq Mahmood 66 not out). *Lahore City Whites 12 pts.*

Zahoor Elahi's 203 lasted 368 minutes and 287 balls and included 28 fours and two sixes.

At KRL Cricket Ground, Rawalpindi, October 29, 30, 31. Lahore City Blues won by 122 runs. Lahore City Blues 168 (Shahid Anwar 47; Yasir Arafat three for 57, Shakeel Ahmed four for seven) and 288 (Bazid Khan 104, Shabbir Khan 30, Humayun Farhat 57; Mohammad Ghufran three for 77, Shakeel Ahmed five for 54); Rawalpindi* 179 (Naseer Ahmed 57; Waqas Ahmed three for 44) and 155 (Nadeem Abbasi 58; Hasnain Kazim three for 59, Waqas Ahmed four for 58). *Lahore City Blues 9 pts.*

At Bahawal Stadium, Bahawalpur, November 4, 5, 6, 7. Faisalabad won by one wicket. Bahawalpur* 121 (Kamran Hussain 39; Aqeel Ahmed three for 39) and 256 (Rehan Rafiq 48, Kamran Hussain 31, Aamir Sohail 36, Inam-ul-Haq Rashid 44; Aqeel Ahmed five for 114); Faisalabad 150 (Ijaz Ahmed, jun. 52; Mohammad Zahid four for 56, Usman Tariq four for 27) and 231 for nine (Fida Hussain 63, Wasim Haider 88 not out; Kamran Hussain three for 27, Mohammad Altaf three for 53). *Faisalabad 12 pts.*

At KCCA Ground, Karachi, November 4, 5, 6, 7. Karachi Whites won by 208 runs. Karachi Whites* 169 (Shadab Kabir 52; Mubashir Nazir three for 32, Abdur Rehman three for 39) and 292 for five dec. (Khalid Saleem 40, Zeeshan Pervez 35, Hasan Raza 100 not out, Asif Mujtaba 50, Mohammad Masroor 51 not out); Gujranwala 92 (Atiq-ur-Rehman 42; Danish Kaneria seven for 39) and 161 (Zahid Fazal 74; Tahir Khan four for 44). *Karachi Whites 12 pts.*

At LCCA Ground, Lahore, November 4, 5, 6, 7. Drawn. Rawalpindi 225 (Naseer Ahmed 91, Extras 48; Irfan Fazil five for 80, Sajid Ali three for 51) and 221 (Saeed Anwar 31, Ahmed Said 30, Mujahid Hameed 58 not out, Yasir Arafat 31, Extras 34; Sajid Ali three for 54); Lahore City Whites* 196 (Tariq Aziz 31, Tariq Mahmood 52; Naeem Akhtar four for 42, Yasir Arafat three for 94) and 202 for eight (Zahoor Elahi 41, Kashif Siddiq 64, Tariq Aziz 45; Yasir Arafat three for 73). *Rawalpindi 3 pts.*

At Gymkhana Club Ground, Peshawar, November 4, 5. Lahore City Blues won by seven wickets. Peshawar 108 (Taimur Khan 37 not out; Hasnain Kazim six for 46) and 103 (Yasir Hameed 66; Hasnain Kazim three for 48, Waqas Ahmed seven for 45); Lahore City Blues* 161 (Bazid Khan 48, Humayun Farhat 58; Fazl-e-Akbar three for 53, Waqar Ahmed five for 50) and 51 for three. *Lahore City Blues 12 pts.*

At Sports Stadium, Sargodha, November 4, 5, 6, 7. Drawn. Sargodha* 283 (Mohammad Hafeez 52, Misbah-ul-Haq 120, Saboor Ahmed 34; Iftikhar Anjum three for 73, Stephen John three for 67, Bilal Rana three for 57) and 165 (Mohammad Hafeez 58; Bilal Rana five for 32); Islamabad 159 (Bilal Rana 58; Akram Raza three for 40, Saboor Ahmed four for 58) and 228 for eight (Ashar Zaidi 56, Naved Ahmed 33, Imran Qadir 41, Bilal Asad 56 not out; Akram Raza three for 86, Saboor Ahmed four for 61). *Sargodha 3 pts.*

At Sheikhupura Stadium, Sheikhupura, November 4, 5, 6, 7. Sheikhupura won by seven wickets. Karachi Blues 314 (Naumanullah 50, Iqbal Imam 51, Ahmed Zeeshan 38, Tanvir Ahmed 41, Extras 37; Jaffer Nazir four for 116, Naved-ul-Hasan five for 102) and 181 for six dec. (Afsar Nawaz 45, Farhan Adil 33 not out, Extras 38; Jaffer Nazir three for 63); Sheikhupura* 243 (Mohammad Javed 58, Waqar Khan 69, Extras 42; Tanvir Ahmed three for 73, Mohammad Javed six for 50) and 253 for three (Majid Majeed 33, Mohammad Javed 69 not out, Mujahid Jamshed 104, Extras 31). *Sheikhupura 9 pts.*

Mohammad Javed took a hat-trick in Sheikhupura's first innings.

At Bahawal Stadium, Bahawalpur, November 10, 11, 12, 13. Drawn. Rawalpindi 174 (Shakeel Ahmed 34, Mujahid Hameed 32, Naeem Akhtar 49; Mohammad Altaf three for 28, Mohammad Zahid three for 54) and 349 (Naved Ashraf 39, Saeed Anwar 33, Mohammad Wasim 147, Naeem Akhtar 32; Mohammad Altaf three for 85, Mohammad Zahid five for 109); Bahawalpur* 260 (Hammad Tariq 65, Kamran Hussain 62; Shakeel Ahmed three for 58, Yasir Arafat four for 50) and 194 for eight (Hammad Tariq 32, Aamir Sohail 72 not out; Jawad Hameed four for 59). *Bahawalpur 3 pts.*

Bahawalpur wicket-keeper Inam-ul-Haq Rashid took seven catches and made two stumpings in the match.

At Iqbal Stadium, Faisalabad, November 10, 11, 12, 13. Faisalabad won by eight wickets. Faisalabad 357 (Mohammad Ramzan 94, Ijaz Ahmed, jun. 91, Fida Hussain 79 not out; Mohammad Javed three for 53, Faheem Ahmed three for 116) and 98 for two (Ijaz Mahmood 30, Mohammad Ramzan 33 not out); Karachi Blues* 174 (Asim Kamal 49, Afsar Nawaz 48, Mohammad Javed 38; Aqeel Ahmed six for 61) and 277 (Asim Kamal 66, Farhan Adil 34, Afsar Nawaz 78, Ahmed Zeeshan 46; Sarfraz Butt three for 62, Wasim Haider four for 14). *Faisalabad 12 pts.*

At Jinnah Stadium, Gujranwala, November 10, 11, 12, 13. Drawn. Gujranwala 445 (Imran Abbas 90, Zahid Fazal 121, Majid Saeed 38, Bilal Hussain 45, Khalid Mahmood 73, Extras 38; Waqar Ahmed three for 102, Jannisar Khan four for 102) and 187 for four (Atiq-ur-Rehman 45, Bilal Hussain 69 not out; Ibrar Ahmed three for 46); Peshawar* 312 (Rafatullah Mohmand 41, Abdul Nasir 31, Shoaib Khan 81, Fakhar-e-Alam 77, Saleem Khan 30; Sarfraz Ahmed three for 72). *Gujranwala 3 pts.*

At UBL Sports Complex, Karachi, November 10, 11, 12, 13. Karachi Whites won by an innings and 13 runs. Sheikhupura 312 (Majid Majeed 88, Tahir Usman 98, Waqar Khan 32; Tahir Khan four for 93) and 218 (Mohammad Javed 50, Usman Akram 38, Asif Raza 35; Athar Laeeq three for 28, Tahir Khan three for 67, Adnan Malik three for 63); Karachi Whites* 543 for four dec. (Mohammad Ghazan 63, Hasan Raza 87, Asif Mujtaba 202 not out, Mohammad Masroor 171 not out). *Karachi Whites 12 pts.*

Asif Mujtaba's 202 not out lasted 297 minutes and 210 balls and included 25 fours and one six. He added an unbroken 361, a Pakistani fifth-wicket record, with Mohammad Masroor.

At LCCA Ground, Lahore, November 10, 11, 12, 13. Lahore City Whites won by 57 runs. Lahore City Whites 247 (Tariq Aziz 46, Naeem Ashraf 106; Iftikhar Anjum five for 70, Bilal Rana three for 91) and 312 for two dec. (Zahoor Elahi 161 not out, Tariq Mahmood 32, Ghaffar Kazmi 78 not out); Islamabad* 266 (Naved Ahmed 41, Imran Qadir 69, Asif Ali 51, Extras 30; Irfan Fazil five for 85, Kashif Shafi three for 73) and 236 (Bilal Asad 68, Mohammad Shahbaz 50 not out, Fahad Khan 37; Irfan Fazil four for 67, Imran Tahir three for 65). *Lahore City Whites 9 pts.*

At Sports Stadium, Sargodha, November 10, 11, 12, 13. Drawn. Lahore City Blues 247 (Faisal Ashraf 30, Bazid Khan 40, Humayun Farhat 37, Extras 46; Mohammad Sarfraz five for 43) and 532 for nine (Fareed Butt 166 not out, Shahid Anwar 38, Humayun Farhat 188, Extras 86); Sargodha* 418 (Mohammad Hafeez 82, Naved Latif 52, Misbah-ul-Haq 142, Tanvir Hussain 32, Extras 44; Shahid Anwar three for 42). *Sargodha 3 pts.*

In Lahore City Blues' second innings, Fareed Butt and Humayun Farhat added 260 for the fifth wicket.

At Bahawal Stadium, Bahawalpur, November 16, 17, 18, 19. Drawn. Lahore City Whites 323 (Salman Butt 60, Taufeeq Umar 66, Naeem Khan 62, Irfan Fazil 30; Kamran Hussain three for 43, Mohammad Zahid three for 114) and 217 (Zahoor Elahi 57, Salman Butt 32, Imran Tahir 35; Mohammad Zahid six for 58); Bahawalpur* 333 (Hammad Tariq 52, Usman Tariq 63, Aamir Sohail 53, Kamran Hussain 31; Irfan Fazil five for 69) and 203 for nine (Azhar Shafiq 63, Hammad Tariq 50; Kashif Shafi four for 80, Imran Tahir three for 23). *Bahawalpur 3 pts.*

At Bohranwala Ground, Faisalabad, November 16, 17, 18, 19. Faisalabad won by 145 runs. Faisalabad* 213 (Ijaz Ahmed, jun. 104, Farooq Iqbal 32; Stephen John four for 51, Hakim Butt four for 42) and 328 for five dec. (Bilal Haider 57, Ijaz Ahmed, jun. 37, Mohammad Ramzan 100 not out, Wasim Haider 51, Farooq Iqbal 33 not out); Islamabad 228 (Hakim Butt 43, Ali Raza 75, Extras 30; Aqeel Ahmed five for 84) and 168 (Hakim Butt 33, Bilal Asad 41; Aqeel Ahmed four for 73, Farooq Iqbal three for 10). *Faisalabad 9 pts.*

At Jinnah Stadium, Gujranwala, November 16, 17, 18, 19. Drawn. Gujranwala 261 (Faisal Butt 32, Rana Qayyum 117, Majid Saeed 37; Ahmed Hayat four for 94, Mohammad Sarfraz four for 55) and 60 for one (Khalid Mahmood 56); Sargodha* 721 (Mohammad Hafeez 57, Naved Latif

394, Misbah-ul-Haq 93, Tanvir Hussain 57, Mohammad Shafiq 32; Ghulam Murtaza four for 149). *Sargodha 3 pts.*

Naved Latif's 394 lasted 780 minutes and 595 balls and included 52 fours and five sixes. It was the tenth-highest first-class score of all time, and the third-highest in Pakistan after Hanif Mohammad's 499 for Karachi against Bahawalpur in 1958-59 and Aftab Baloch's 428 for Sind against Baluchistan in 1973-74. In Gujranwala's second innings, he bowled a single over which cost 32 (666662) as Khalid Mahmood went to 56 in 17 balls and 15 minutes (four fours and six sixes).

At UBL Sports Complex, Karachi, November 16, 17, 18, 19. Drawn. Karachi Blues* 362 (Asim Kamal 32, Faisal Iqbal 71, Farhan Adil 53, Iqbal Imam 50, Faheem Ahmed 48, Extras 30; Arshad Khan four for 117, Mohammad Aslam five for 78) and 237 for five (Naumanullah 52, Farhan Adil 33, Iqbal Imam 55 not out, Maisam Hasnain 53 not out; Arshad Khan five for 85); Peshawar 437 (Rafatullah Mohmand 55, Yasir Hameed 103, Akhtar Sarfraz 142, Shoaib Khan 101 not out; Faheem Ahmed six for 127, Tabish Nawab three for 134). *Peshawar 3 pts.*

At LCCA Ground, Lahore, November 16, 17, 18, 19. Lahore City Blues won by 58 runs. Lahore City Blues 291 (Shahid Anwar 41, Humayun Farhat 106, Waqas Ahmed 35; Kashif Ibrahim three for 47, Mohammad Zahid, jun. three for 104, Asif Mujtaba three for 37) and 170 (Bazid Khan 50; Mohammad Zahid, jun. five for 77); Karachi Whites* 222 (Ghulam Ali 57, Asif Mujtaba 82 not out; Asim Iqbal six for 90) and 181 (Mohammad Ghazan 73, Tahir Khan 37; Adnan Naeem four for 29). *Lahore City Blues 12 pts.*

At Sheikhupura Stadium, Sheikhupura, November 16, 17, 18. Rawalpindi won by seven wickets. Sheikhupura* 200 (Mohammad Shafiq 31, Saleem Mughal 45, Waqar Khan 48; Mohammad Akram four for 67, Shakeel Ahmed four for 35) and 117 (Shakeel Ahmed five for 42); Rawalpindi 130 (Yasir Arafat 37; Jaffer Nazir three for 41, Naved-ul-Hasan four for 47) and 188 for three (Mujahid Hameed 73, Naseer Ahmed 73 not out). *Rawalpindi 9 pts.*

At Bahawal Stadium, Bahawalpur, November 22, 23, 24. Bahawalpur won by an innings and 35 runs. Bahawalpur 248 (Ahsan Raza 37, Hasnain Raza 46 not out, Inam-ul-Haq Rashid 30, Extras 37; Arshad Khan four for 81); Peshawar* 67 (Kamran Hussain five for 34, Azhar Shafiq four for 19) and 146 (Akhtar Sarfraz 64, Sajid Shah 33; Mohammad Altaf four for 17, Mohammad Zahid four for 43). *Bahawalpur 12 pts.*

At Bohranwala Ground, Faisalabad, November 22, 23, 24, 25. Drawn. Faisalabad 268 (Ijaz Mahmood 45, Ijaz Ahmed, jun. 138, Extras 38; Irfan Fazil six for 105) and 267 for eight dec. (Asif Hussain 100, Fida Hussain 79; Ghaffar Kazmi three for 34); Lahore City Whites* 252 (Zahoor Elahi 50, Taufeeq Umar 42, Kashif Siddiq 41, Ali Raza 49; Aqeel Ahmed four for 96, Ijaz Ahmed, jun. three for 37) and 165 for one (Kamran Sajid 82, Zahoor Elahi 71 not out). *Faisalabad 3 pts.*

At UBL Sports Complex, Karachi, November 22, 23, 24, 25. Lahore City Blues won by three wickets. Karachi Blues* 286 (Suleman Huda 91, Farhan Adil 31, Mohammad Javed 78, Ahmed Zeeshan 31 not out; Mohammad Hussain three for 120, Mohammad Asif five for 74) and 197 for seven dec. (Maisam Hasnain 66, Suleman Huda 34, Farhan Adil 30; Mohammad Hussain five for 65); Lahore City Blues 149 (Salman Fazal three for 33, Tabish Nawab seven for 64) and 335 for seven (Humayun Farhat 87, Shahid Anwar 41, Tariq Sheikh 47, Intikhab Alam 33, Mohammad Hussain 50, Waqas Ahmed 32 not out; Salman Fazal three for 106). *Lahore City Blues 9 pts.*

At Pindi Cricket Stadium, Rawalpindi, November 22, 23, 24, 25. Drawn. Rawalpindi 341 (Naseer Ahmed 32, Mohammad Wasim 112, Nadeem Abbasi 102, Extras 30; Adnan Farooq three for 88, Adnan Butt three for 90) and 274 for four (Asif Mahmood 94, Naseer Ahmed 126); Gujranwala* 303 (Ataullah Butt 34, Atiq-ur-Rehman 62, Basit Murtaza 56, Khalid Mahmood 38, Adnan Farooq 38; Yasir Arafat four for 97, Iftikhar Mahmood three for 49). *Rawalpindi 3 pts.*

At Sports Stadium, Sargodha, November 22, 23, 24, 25. Karachi Whites won by six wickets. Sargodha 178 (Tanvir Hussain 65; Mohammad Sami five for 52) and 102 (Mohammad Sami three for 53, Mohammad Zahid, jun. four for 23, Mohammad Hasnain three for 12); Karachi Whites* 227 for eight dec. (Saeed Bin Nasir 35, Asif Mujtaba 49, Atiq-uz-Zaman 36, Extras 33; Faisal Afridi four for 45) and 57 for four. *Karachi Whites 12 pts.*

At Sheikhupura Stadium, Sheikhupura, November 22, 23, 24, 25. Islamabad won by 178 runs. Islamabad 167 (Ashar Zaidi 52; Jaffer Nazir four for 49, Naved-ul-Hasan five for 66) and 237 (Ashar Zaidi 45, Iftikhar Hussain 44, Extras 36; Jaffer Nazir four for 82, Waqas Chugtai three for 27); Sheikhupura* 96 (Mohammad Azam 31; Iftikhar Anjum three for 57, Rauf Akbar seven for 27) and 130 (Naved-ul-Hasan 39; Iftikhar Anjum three for 45, Rauf Akbar three for 44, Hakim Butt three for eight). *Islamabad 12 pts.*

At Jinnah Stadium, Gujranwala, January 2, 3, 4, 5. Drawn. Gujranwala 59 for five (Maqsood Rana four for 23) v Lahore City Whites*.

At KCCA Ground, Karachi, January 2, 3, 4, 5. Karachi Blues won by an innings and 14 runs. Karachi Blues 370 (Maisam Hasnain 67, Faisal Iqbal 60, Asim Kamal 53, Mohammad Javed 90, Ahmed Zeeshan 47; Stephen John four for 73, Anwaar-ul-Haq four for 98); Islamabad* 143 (Tabish Nawab three for 36, Salman Fazal six for 45) and 213 (Zaheer Abbasi 53, Aqeel Mukhtar 32, Asif Ali 72; Mohammad Javed five for 43, Salman Fazal three for 64). *Karachi Blues 12 pts.*

At LCCA Ground, Lahore, January 2, 3, 4, 5. Lahore City Blues v Faisalabad. Abandoned.

At Pindi Cricket Stadium, Rawalpindi, January 2, 3, 4, 5. Drawn. Rawalpindi 199 (Naved Ashraf 37, Naseer Ahmed 53, Extras 30; Mohammad Sami four for 87) and 267 (Asif Mahmood 43, Shahid Javed 76, Pervez Aziz 33; Danish Kaneria four for 90); Karachi Whites* 173 (Zeeshan Pervez 56, Kashif Ibrahim 35; Naeem Akhtar four for 46, Yasir Arafat three for 38) and 146 for five (Hasan Raza 58 not out; Mohammad Akram three for 38). *Rawalpindi 3 pts.*

At Sports Stadium, Sargodha, January 2, 3, 4, 5. Sargodha v Peshawar. Abandoned.

At Sheikhupura Stadium, Sheikhupura, January 2, 3, 4, 5. Drawn. Sheikhupura 313 (Majid Majeed 51, Tahir Usman 33, Mujahid Jamshed 50, Naved-ul-Hasan 32, Mohammad Haroon 34, Extras 49; Kamran Hussain three for 68, Amjad Jam four for 76); Bahawalpur* 209 (Usman Tariq 82, Hasnain Raza 52, Extras 37; Jaffer Nazir seven for 46). *Sheikhupura 3 pts.*

At Jinnah Stadium, Gujranwala, January 8, 9, 10. Gujranwala won by ten wickets. Bahawalpur* 231 (Hammad Tariq 35, Usman Tariq 106 not out, Hasnain Raza 35; Mubashir Nazir four for 61, Abdur Rehman three for 78) and 78 (Mubashir Nazir five for 32); Gujranwala 296 (Faisal Butt 84, Imran Abbas 54, Rana Qayyum 35, Extras 39; Kamran Hussain four for 71, Usman Tariq four for 63) and 14 for no wkt. *Gujranwala 12 pts.*

At KRL Cricket Ground, Rawalpindi, January 8, 9, 10, 11. Karachi Whites won by an innings and 11 runs. Islamabad 207 (Mohammad Altaf 36, Iftikhar Hussain 51, Mohammad Shahbaz 43; Shahid Iqbal four for 50) and 190 (Iftikhar Anjum 50; Shahid Afridi three for 50, Ali Raza four for 68); Karachi Whites* 408 for eight dec. (Shadab Kabir 105, Shahid Afridi 88, Hasan Raza 75, Saeed Bin Nasir 54; Iftikhar Anjum three for 112). *Karachi Whites 12 pts.*

At UBL Sports Complex, Karachi, January 8, 9, 10, 11. Drawn. Sargodha* 180 (Ashraf Bashir 39, Faisal Afridi 31, Tariq Munir 44; Imranullah three for 26, Salman Fazal three for 74) and 270 for five (Naved Latif 38, Misbah-ul-Haq 134 not out, Haroon Malik 51 not out; Tabish Nawab four for 120); Karachi Blues 445 (Maisam Hasnain 44, Faisal Iqbal 200, Rashid Latif 67, Extras 44; Umair Hasan five for 94). *Karachi Blues 3 pts.*

Faisal Iqbal's 200 lasted 532 minutes and 410 balls and included 14 fours.

At LCCA Ground, Lahore, January 8, 9, 10, 11. Peshawar won by an innings and 146 runs. Peshawar 598 (Wajahatullah Wasti 34, Rafatullah Mohmand 31, Yasir Hameed 36, Younis Khan 221, Taimur Khan 50, Zulfiqar Jan 37, Arshad Khan 57, Sajid Shah 36 not out, Extras 61); Lahore City Whites* 282 (Aamir Sohail 110, Naeem Ashraf 86, Extras 34; Sajid Shah three for 37, Arshad Khan three for 52) and 170 (Arshad Khan four for 63). *Peshawar 12 pts.*

Younis Khan's 221 lasted 377 minutes and 290 balls and included 31 fours and three sixes.

At Pindi Cricket Stadium, Rawalpindi, January 8, 9, 10, 11. Rawalpindi won by 94 runs. Rawalpindi 234 (Shahid Javed 60, Extras 52; Shahid Nazir five for 109, Wasim Haider three for 31) and 221 (Mohammad Wasim 96, Mohammad Zubair 31; Nadeem Afzal five for 85, Moazzam Ali three for 31); Faisalabad* 154 (Shahid Nazir 52; Naeem Akhtar six for 18, Yasir Arafat three for 29) and 207 (Mohammad Ramzan 48, Wasim Haider 33, Extras 44; Mohammad Akram four for 87, Yasir Arafat four for 48). *Rawalpindi 12 pts.*

At Sheikhupura Stadium, Sheikhupura, January 8, 9, 10, 11. Drawn. Lahore City Blues 294 (Imran Farhat 170, Tariq Sheikh 32; Kashif Raza five for 76) and 58 for four; Sheikhupura* 295 (Imran Nazir 54, Saleem Mughal 57, Tahir Usman 41, Extras 38; Abdur Razzaq four for 83, Mohammad Hussain three for 55). *Sheikhupura 3 pts.*

At Iqbal Stadium, Faisalabad, January 14, 15, 16, 17. Drawn. Sheikhupura 247 (Imran Nazir 30, Qaiser Abbas 31, Naved-ul-Hasan 62; Wasim Haider four for 39); Faisalabad* 233 (Mohammad Salman 36, Wasim Haider 56, Ijaz Ahmed, jun. 60; Naved-ul-Hasan seven for 86). *Sheikhupura 3 pts.*

At KRL Cricket Ground, Rawalpindi, January 14, 15, 16, 17. Drawn. Islamabad* 293 (Ali Naqvi 108, Irfan Bhatti 32, Mohammad Shahbaz 32; Imran Amin three for 48) and 388 for six dec. (Ali Naqvi 119, Mohammad Shahbaz 108, Bilal Asad 112; Mubashir Nazir three for 56); Gujranwala 229 (Mudassar Mushtaq 57, Asim Munir 114; Iftikhar Anjum five for 58) and 276 for three (Faisal Butt 132 not out, Imran Abbas 108). *Islamabad 3 pts.*

Ali Naqvi hit a hundred in each innings.

At UBL Sports Complex, Karachi, January 14, 15, 16, 17. Drawn. Rawalpindi* 360 (Arif Butt 36, Asif Mahmood 84, Shahid Javed 82, Mohammad Wasim 42, Yasir Arafat 36, Extras 31; Tanvir Ahmed three for 84, Tabish Nawab three for 84) and 397 (Arif Butt 38, Shahid Javed 32, Mohammad Wasim 110, Yasir Arafat 69, Wasim Ahmed 82; Salman Fazal three for 126, Zafar Jadoon four for 34); Karachi Blues 233 (Maisam Hasnain 41, Farhan Adil 60; Yasir Arafat three for 72) and 56 for two (Zafar Jadoon 31). *Rawalpindi 3 pts.*

At LCCA Ground, Lahore, January 14, 15, 16, 17. Drawn. Lahore City Blues* 567 (Irfan Munawwar 41, Imran Farhat 200, Shahid Anwar 39, Mohammad Hussain 69, Humayun Farhat 105, Extras 32; Zeeshan Khalid five for 139); Bahawalpur 118 for three (Asif Iqbal 40 not out, Usman Tariq 63 not out; Waqar Younis three for 53).

Imran Farhat's 200 lasted 322 minutes and 228 balls and included 26 fours and one six. Bahawalpur keeper Inam-ul-Haq Rashid took five catches and effected one stumping in Lahore City Blues' innings.

At Arbab Niaz Stadium, Peshawar, January 14, 15, 16. Peshawar won by 94 runs. Peshawar 228 (Javed Iqbal 47, Younis Khan 64, Arshad Khan 45; Mohammad Sami three for 67, Shahid Iqbal four for 44) and 198 (Javed Iqbal 38, Taimur Khan 51 not out; Mohammad Sami five for 65); Karachi Whites* 281 (Shahid Afridi 108, Hasan Raza 32, Mohammad Masroor 46, Extras 38) and 51 (Fazl-e-Akbar five for 25, Sajid Shah three for 21). *Peshawar 9 pts.*

At Sports Stadium, Sargodha, January 14, 15, 16, 17. Drawn. Lahore City Whites 140 (Irfan Fazil 36; Faisal Afridi three for 33, Ahmed Hayat three for 56, Umair Hasan three for 34); Sargodha* 141 for six (Naved Latif 71). *Sargodha 3 pts.*

FINAL

KARACHI WHITES v LAHORE CITY BLUES

At National Stadium, Karachi, January 20, 21, 22. Lahore City Blues won by one wicket. Toss: Lahore City Blues.

Lahore City Blues secured the title through their last pair, on the third evening of the five-day final. They had inserted Karachi Whites on a greenish pitch, only to see Shahid Afridi hit a brilliant 102 from 107 balls – forcing Wasim Akram to bowl with a single slip. His dismissal began a collapse of four for 24, though Karachi recovered to reach 297, enough for a 79-run lead: next day, only Imran Farhat and Abdur Razzaq stood out as Lahore's reply crumbled. On the third day, however, Wasim and Razzaq seized control, skittling Karachi for 104; Razzaq finished with ten wickets for the match and Wasim nine (the other was a run-out). Afridi, having retired hurt early on, could do little to save the innings on returning at 48 for five, but he was by no means done with the game, reducing Lahore to a desperate 66 for six as they chased 184. However, Humayun Farhat added 63 in eight overs with Mohammad Hussain, and his 53-ball 63 had seen his side to the brink of victory when he was ninth out at 179.

Close of play: First day, Karachi Whites 286-6 (Aamer Hanif 43*, Mohammad Masroor 57*); Second day, Karachi Whites 14-0 (Shahid Afridi 12*, Shadab Kabir 0*).

Karachi Whites

Shadab Kabir c Humayun Farhat b Abdur Razzaq	0	– (2) c Humayun Farhat b Wasim Akram	0
Shahid Afridi c Humayun Farhat b Abdur Razzaq	102	– (1) c Mohammad Hussain b Wasim Akram	14
Zeeshan Pervez c Fareed Butt b Wasim Akram	19	– lbw b Wasim Akram	12
*Asif Mujtaba c Shahid Anwar b Abdur Razzaq	39	– c Bazid Khan b Abdur Razzaq	1
Hasan Raza c Humayun Farhat b Abdur Razzaq	0	– b Abdur Razzaq	14
Aamer Hanif c Tariq Sheikh b Wasim Akram	44	– c Bazid Khan b Wasim Akram	18
†Moin Khan c Humayun Farhat b Wasim Akram	7	– (8) lbw b Wasim Akram	18
Mohammad Masroor run out	57	– (7) b Abdur Razzaq	0
Shahid Iqbal b Abdur Razzaq	4	– b Abdur Razzaq	6
Mohammad Sami not out	4	– not out	2
Danish Kaneria c Wasim Akram b Abdur Razzaq	0	– b Wasim Akram	0
B 1, l-b 4, w 2, n-b 14	21	B 1, l-b 3, w 1, n-b 14	19
1/1 2/29 3/166 4/169 5/178 6/190 7/287 8/290 9/297	297	1/18 2/31 3/33 4/48 5/48 6/62 7/76 8/88 9/104	104

In the second innings Shahid Afridi, when 12, retired hurt at 15 and resumed at 48-5.

Bowling: *First Innings*—Wasim Akram 27–8–67–3; Abdur Razzaq 26.4–4–79–6; Waqas Ahmed 14–2–57–0; Mohammad Hussain 5–1–22–0; Adnan Naeem 10.1–0–49–0; Shahid Anwar 7.5–0–18–0. *Second Innings*—Wasim Akram 17.5–6–36–6; Abdur Razzaq 21–5–54–4; Waqas Ahmed 4–1–10–0.

Lahore City Blues

*Shahid Anwar c Moin Khan b Shahid Iqbal	21	– b Mohammad Sami	17
Imran Farhat c and b Shahid Afridi	67	– c Mohammad Sami b Shahid Iqbal	10
Fareed Butt b Mohammad Sami	8	– c Shahid Afridi b Shahid Iqbal	1
Bazid Khan c Aamer Hanif b Mohammad Sami	10	– (5) c and b Shahid Afridi	7
Tariq Sheikh c Aamer Hanif b Asif Mujtaba	9	– (4) b Shahid Afridi	18
Abdur Razzaq b Mohammad Sami	51	– c Asif Mujtaba b Shahid Afridi	3
Mohammad Hussain c Mohammad Masroor b Shahid Afridi	9	– (8) c Shadab Kabir b Shahid Afridi	29
Wasim Akram b Mohammad Sami	6	– (9) run out	23
†Humayun Farhat c Danish Kaneria b Shahid Afridi	4	– (7) c Danish Kaneria b Mohammad Sami	63
Waqas Ahmed c Moin Khan b Mohammad Sami	7	– not out	4
Adnan Naeem not out	1	– not out	1
L-b 7, w 13, n-b 5	25	B 4, l-b 2, n-b 3	9
1/35 2/111 3/123 4/124 5/154 6/167 7/182 8/188 9/199	218	1/20 2/22 3/42 4/49 5/57 6/66 7/129 8/178 9/179	(9 wkts) 185

Bowling: *First Innings*—Mohammad Sami 24.2–7–64–5; Shahid Iqbal 17–4–45–1; Shahid Afridi 21–4–75–3; Danish Kaneria 1–0–21–0; Asif Mujtaba 3–0–6–1. *Second Innings*—Mohammad Sami 19–5–87–2; Shahid Iqbal 13.3–5–34–2; Shahid Afridi 10–0–58–4.

Umpires: Aleem Dar and Mohammad Nazir, jun.
Referee: Ehteshamuddin.

QUAID-E-AZAM TROPHY WINNERS

1953-54	Bahawalpur	1973-74	Railways	1988-89	ADBP
1954-55	Karachi	1974-75	Punjab A	1989-90	PIA
1956-57	Punjab	1975-76	National Bank	1990-91	Karachi Whites
1957-58	Bahawalpur	1976-77	United Bank	1991-92	Karachi Whites
1958-59	Karachi	1977-78	Habib Bank	1992-93	Karachi Whites
1959-60	Karachi	1978-79	National Bank	1993-94	Lahore City
1961-62	Karachi Blues	1979-80	PIA	1994-95	Karachi Blues
1962-63	Karachi A	1980-81	United Bank	1995-96	Karachi Blues
1963-64	Karachi Blues	1981-82	National Bank	1996-97	Lahore City
1964-65	Karachi Blues	1982-83	United Bank	1997-98	Karachi Blues
1966-67	Karachi	1983-84	National Bank	1998-99	Peshawar
1968-69	Lahore	1984-85	United Bank	1999-2000	PIA
1969-70	PIA	1985-86	Karachi	2000-01	Lahore City Blues
1970-71	Karachi Blues	1986-87	National Bank		
1972-73	Railways	1987-88	PIA		

PCB PATRON'S TROPHY, 2000-01

	Played	*Won*	*Lost*	*Drawn*	*1st-inns Points*	*Points*
National Bank	7	4	1	2	9	45
Pakistan Customs	7	3	2	2	12	37*
Habib Bank	7	3	2	2	12	37*
WAPDA	7	3	2	2	9	34*
ADBP	7	2	3	2	9	25*
Allied Bank	7	1	3	3	6	15
PIA	7	1	1	5	6	13*
KRL	7	1	4	2	6	13*

Outright win = 9 pts; lead on first innings in a won or drawn game = 3 pts.

* *Two points deducted from Pakistan Customs, Habib Bank, WAPDA, ADBP, PIA and KRL, each of whom failed to submit captains' reports on umpires in two matches.*

Final: Pakistan Customs beat National Bank by four wickets.

*In the following scores, * by the name of a team indicates that they won the toss.*

At Iqbal Stadium, Faisalabad, February 20, 21, 22. ADBP won by four wickets. PIA 192 (Faisal Iqbal 37; Fahad Masood three for 71, Iftikhar Anjum three for 50) and 136 (Yasir Hameed 57, Faisal Iqbal 32; Fahad Masood four for 47, Iftikhar Anjum four for 18); ADBP* 119 (Fazl-e-Akbar five for 54, Ali Gauhar four for 29) and 215 for six (Mohammad Nadeem 45, Mansoor Rana 39, Ijaz Mahmood 40 not out; Ali Gauhar three for 60). *ADBP 9 pts.*

At Gaddafi Stadium, Lahore, February 20, 21, 22. WAPDA won by four wickets. Allied Bank 132 (Aamir Sohail 31, Humayun Farhat 52; Kashif Raza three for 23, Kamran Hussain six for 53) and 179 (Humayun Farhat 48, Arshad Khan 32; Kashif Raza five for 84, Kamran Hussain three for 65); WAPDA* 208 (Rafatullah Mohmand 91 not out, Sarfraz Ahmed 33; Ata-ur-Rehman three for 53, Arshad Khan three for 55) and 105 for six (Ata-ur-Rehman four for 38). *WAPDA 12 pts.*
Rafatullah Mohmand carried his bat through WAPDA's first innings.

At National Stadium, Karachi, February 20, 21, 22, 23. Habib Bank won by 23 runs. Habib Bank 278 (Moin-ul-Atiq 40, Taufeeq Umar 46, Younis Khan 66, Hasan Raza 67; Waqar Ahmed three for 51, Naved-ul-Hasan three for 82) and 188 (Taufeeq Umar 62, Hasan Raza 40 not out, Extras 32; Waqar Ahmed three for 54); Pakistan Customs* 188 (Ali Naqvi 34, Naved Latif 36, Extras

31; Sajid Shah three for 60) and 255 (Ali Naqvi 32, Aamer Bashir 41, Iqbal Imam 62; Sajid Shah three for 76, Akram Raza three for 61). *Habib Bank 12 pts.*

Younis Khan took five catches in the field in Customs' second innings.

At UBL Sports Complex, Karachi, February 20, 21, 22, 23. National Bank won by eight wickets. KRL 274 (Pervez Aziz 34, Faisal Afridi 95, Saeed Ajmal 50 not out; Shabbir Ahmed six for 87) and 155 (Saeed Anwar 38; Zahid Saeed four for 68, Qaiser Abbas four for 16); National Bank* 197 (Tariq Mohammad 38, Shahid Anwar 37, Naumanullah 33; Shakeel Ahmed six for 33) and 233 for two (Shahid Anwar 104 not out, Qaiser Abbas 49, Akhtar Sarfraz 54 not out). *National Bank 9 pts.*

In KRL's first innings, Faisal Afridi and Saeed Ajmal added 153 for the last wicket.

At Pindi Cricket Stadium, Rawalpindi, February 26, 27, 28, March 1. Drawn. Allied Bank 356 (Mohammad Nawaz 41, Ijaz Ahmed, jun. 54, Manzoor Akhtar 92, Wajahatullah Wasti 44, Ata-ur-Rehman 31; Mubashir Nazir three for 81, Fahad Masood three for 85) and 332 for four (Mohammad Nawaz 61, Wajahatullah Wasti 162 not out, Rashid Latif 55 not out, Extras 31); ADBP* 438 (Zahoor Elahi 44, Faisal Naved 121, Mansoor Rana 59, Ijaz Mahmood 49, Mohammad Nadeem 33, Fahad Khan 50, Mubashir Nazir 31, Extras 34; Ata-ur-Rehman three for 118, Aamir Nazir three for 114). *ADBP 3 pts.*

At UBL Sports Complex, Karachi, February 26, 27, 28, March 1. Drawn. Habib Bank* 303 (Asadullah Butt 49, Farhan Adil 90, Atiq-uz-Zaman 48; Shabbir Ahmed three for 74, Mohammad Javed three for 61) and 264 (Taufeeq Umar 52, Mujahid Jamshed 94, Akram Raza 39; Shabbir Ahmed six for 51, Qaiser Abbas four for 72); National Bank 254 (Qaiser Abbas 67, Naumanullah 51, Kamran Akmal 47, Extras 31; Irfan Fazil three for 71) and 182 for six (Qaiser Abbas 62). *Habib Bank 3 pts.*

At National Stadium, Karachi, February 26, 27, 28, March 1. KRL won by three wickets. Pakistan Customs 300 (Aamer Bashir 92, Naved Latif 78, Azam Khan 63, Extras 33; Saeed Anwar four for 25) and 183 (Ali Naqvi 42, Extras 34; Jaffer Nazir four for 55, Mohammad Sarfraz five for 52); KRL* 323 (Naseer Ahmed 39, Intikhab Alam 74, Yasir Arafat 76 not out, Naeem Akhtar 35, Extras 50; Nadeem Iqbal six for 81) and 162 for seven (Iftikhar Hussain 33, Pervez Aziz 53 not out). *KRL 12 pts.*

At Iqbal Stadium, Faisalabad, February 26, 27, 28, March 1. Drawn. PIA 283 (Yasir Hameed 38, Asif Mujtaba 69, Sohail Jaffer 38, Shoaib Malik 83; Kashif Raza five for 65) and 309 for eight dec. (Yasir Hameed 31, Faisal Iqbal 68, Shoaib Malik 130 not out); WAPDA* 212 (Bilal Moin 46, Extras 31; Shoaib Malik seven for 81) and 251 for eight (Tariq Aziz 52, Adil Nisar 93, Hasan Adnan 50 not out). *PIA 3 pts.*

Shoaib Malik scored a century and took seven wickets in an innings.

At KRL Cricket Ground, Rawalpindi, March 10, 11, 12. ADBP won by seven wickets. WAPDA 228 (Rafatullah Mohmand 82, Hasan Adnan 62; Iftikhar Anjum six for 86) and 130 (Waqas Ahmed 40; Iftikhar Anjum five for 58, Fahad Masood three for 63); ADBP* 293 (Inam-ul-Haq 62, Mansoor Rana 117, Extras 35; Kamran Hussain three for 98, Waqas Ahmed six for 87) and 67 for three. *ADBP 12 pts.*

At Pindi Cricket Stadium, Rawalpindi, March 10, 11, 12, 13. Drawn. Allied Bank 304 (Wajahatullah Wasti 36, Aaley Haider 66, Rashid Latif 72, Extras 40; Najaf Shah three for 57, Ali Gauhar three for 92) and 247 for five dec. (Wajahatullah Wasti 105 not out, Rashid Latif 52 not out); PIA* 192 (Asif Mujtaba 90 not out; Mohammad Akram three for 31, Tanvir Ahmed three for 55). *Allied Bank 3 pts.*

At Iqbal Stadium, Faisalabad, March 10, 11, 12. Habib Bank won by 46 runs. Habib Bank 222 (Sajid Shah 78 not out, Extras 39; Jaffer Nazir four for 49, Mohammad Sarfraz three for 70) and 114 (Taufeeq Umar 42; Yasir Arafat six for nine); KRL* 147 (Intikhab Alam 49; Sajid Shah three for ten) and 143 (Saeed Anwar 39; Shahid Nazir three for 47, Sajid Shah three for 33). *Habib Bank 12 pts.*

At Sheikhupura Stadium, Sheikhupura, March 10, 11, 12. Pakistan Customs won by nine wickets. National Bank 209 (Qaiser Abbas 32, Naumanullah 60, Extras 36; Naved-ul-Hasan three for 40) and 116 (Naved-ul-Hasan three for 50, Nadeem Iqbal seven for 53); Pakistan Customs* 281 (Naved Latif 95, Aamer Iqbal 32, Extras 50; Athar Laeeq three for 49, Zahid Saeed four for 84) and 45 for one. *Pakistan Customs 12 pts.*

At KRL Cricket Ground, Rawalpindi, March 16, 17, 18. Habib Bank won by seven wickets. ADBP 322 (Faisal Naved 115, Zahoor Elahi 79; Shahid Nazir four for 88, Sajid Shah four for 74) and 102 (Shahid Nazir three for 35, Kabir Khan five for 56); Habib Bank* 285 (Taufeeq Umar 38, Asadullah Butt 33, Mujahid Jamshed 34, Akram Raza 46, Shahid Nazir 47 not out; Mubashir Nazir five for 84) and 140 for three (Taufeeq Umar 55 not out; Fahad Masood three for 33). *Habib Bank 9 pts.*

At Sheikhupura Stadium, Sheikhupura, March 16, 17, 18, 19. Allied Bank won by 186 runs. Allied Bank 358 (Mohammad Nawaz 109, Usman Tariq 81, Manzoor Akhtar 70, Extras 33; Naeem Akhtar three for 73, Yasir Arafat three for 93, Saeed Anwar three for 20) and 257 for four dec. (Aaley Haider 62, Taimur Khan 69 not out, Rashid Latif 65 not out); KRL* 264 (Mohammad Wasim 77, Saeed Bin Nasir 50, Yasir Arafat 45 not out; Aamir Nazir three for 89, Tanvir Ahmed three for 82) and 165 (Naseer Ahmed 42 not out; Aamir Nazir four for 66). *Allied Bank 12 pts.*

At Iqbal Stadium, Faisalabad, March 16, 17, 18. National Bank won by ten wickets. National Bank 271 (Imran Nazir 111, Sajid Ali 32, Akhtar Sarfraz 42, Extras 36; Kashif Raza six for 61) and 50 for no wkt (Imran Nazir 33 not out); WAPDA* 80 (Adil Nisar 30; Shabbir Ahmed five for 25, Aleem Moosa four for 23) and 239 (Maqsood Akbar 59, Tariq Aziz 93, Hasan Adnan 37; Aleem Moosa seven for 39). *National Bank 12 pts.*

At Pindi Cricket Stadium, Rawalpindi, March 16, 17, 18, 19. Drawn. PIA 258 (Shoaib Mohammad 30, Yasir Hameed 52, Sohail Jaffer 81; Nadeem Iqbal five for 60) and 229 (Ghulam Ali 98, Yasir Hameed 51, Extras 41; Naved-ul-Hasan six for 30, Azhar Shafiq four for 30); Pakistan Customs* 261 (Ali Naqvi 76, Aamer Iqbal 56, Naved-ul-Hasan 31; Shoaib Malik three for 82) and 119 for four (Ali Naqvi 55 not out). *Pakistan Customs 3 pts.*

At Iqbal Stadium, Faisalabad, March 21, 22, 23. Pakistan Customs won by 63 runs. Pakistan Customs 149 (Iqbal Imam 36; Iftikhar Anjum five for 53, Fahad Masood four for 54) and 232 (Nasim Khan 34, Naved Latif 88; Iftikhar Anjum six for 82); ADBP* 175 (Mansoor Rana 35; Nadeem Iqbal five for 68, Stephen John three for 43) and 143 (Zahoor Elahi 33; Stephen John six for 32, Ali Naqvi three for 19). *Pakistan Customs 9 pts.*

At Sheikhupura Stadium, Sheikhupura, March 21, 22, 23. National Bank won by ten wickets. Allied Bank 188 (Usman Tariq 71; Shabbir Ahmed four for 83, Aleem Moosa four for 62) and 197 (Mohammad Nawaz 30, Wajahatullah Wasti 61 not out; Aleem Moosa seven for 81, Zahid Saeed three for 96); National Bank* 376 (Sajid Ali 35, Qaiser Abbas 66, Akhtar Sarfraz 71, Naumanullah 71, Shabbir Ahmed 50, Extras 35; Aqib Javed four for 44, Ata-ur-Rehman four for 89) and 13 for no wkt. *National Bank 12 pts.*

At Arbab Niaz Stadium, Peshawar, March 21, 22, 23. PIA won by seven wickets. Habib Bank* 106 (Extras 30; Ali Gauhar seven for 41) and 142 (Nadeem Afzal three for 46, Ali Gauhar five for 48); PIA 220 (Ghulam Ali 60, Mahmood Hamid 38; Sajid Shah three for 42, Kabir Khan five for 42) and 31 for three. *PIA 12 pts.*

At KRL Cricket Ground, Rawalpindi, March 21, 22, 23. WAPDA won by seven wickets. KRL* 130 (Mohammad Wasim 64; Kashif Raza six for 59) and 148 (Mohammad Wasim 33; Waqas Ahmed four for 27); WAPDA 182 (Tariq Aziz 64, Bilal Moin 35; Naeem Akhtar five for 33) and 100 for three (Adil Nisar 45 not out). *WAPDA 12 pts.*

At Pindi Cricket Stadium, Rawalpindi, March 26, 27, 28, 29. Drawn. KRL* 268 (Naved Ashraf 78, Intikhab Alam 42, Asif Mahmood 33, Yasir Arafat 50 not out; Iftikhar Anjum four for 94, Fahad Khan five for 57); ADBP 312 for five (Zahoor Elahi 145 not out, Mansoor Rana 49, Ijaz Mahmood 54). *ADBP 3 pts.*

At Sheikhupura Stadium, Sheikhupura, March 26, 27, 28, 29. Drawn. Habib Bank 323 (Taufeeq Umar 71, Asadullah Butt 60, Farhan Adil 40, Atiq-uz-Zaman 60; Aqib Javed three for 41, Tanvir Ahmed five for 127) and 295 (Mujahid Jamshed 54, Farhan Adil 34, Atiq-uz-Zaman 104 not out, Akram Raza 39; Tanvir Ahmed six for 81); Allied Bank* 256 (Mohammad Nawaz 35, Wajahatullah Wasti 40, Manzoor Akhtar 44, Ata-ur-Rehman 35, Extras 42; Asadullah Butt five for 67) and 76 for two (Mohammad Nawaz 35). *Habib Bank 3 pts.*

At Arbab Niaz Stadium, Peshawar, March 26, 27, 28, 29. Drawn. National Bank 210 (Sajid Ali 77; Mohammad Zahid, jun. seven for 71) and 262 for six (Sajid Ali 33, Qaiser Abbas 43, Akhtar Sarfraz 115); PIA* 95 (Athar Laeeq three for 40, Aleem Moosa seven for 39). *National Bank 3 pts.*

Mohammad Zahid, jun. took a hat-trick in National Bank's first innings. The third and fourth days were washed out.

At Iqbal Stadium, Faisalabad, March 26, 27, 28, 29. Drawn. Pakistan Customs 375 (Ali Naqvi 31, Naved Latif 133, Naved-ul-Hasan 70, Extras 61; Kamran Hussain five for 126, Faisal Irfan three for 47) and 34 for one; WAPDA* 208 (Zahid Umar 42, Adil Nisar 36; Nadeem Iqbal three for 82, Naved-ul-Hasan three for 49) and 377 (Tariq Aziz 32, Adil Nisar 171 not out, Hasan Adnan 99, Extras 35; Naved-ul-Hasan three for 79). *Pakistan Customs 3 pts.*

At Saga Cricket Ground, Sialkot, March 31, April 1, 2. National Bank won by seven wickets. ADBP 240 (Majid Jahangir 48, Zahoor Elahi 31, Extras 47; Shabbir Ahmed three for 96, Aleem Moosa three for 41, Zahid Saeed four for 70) and 146 (Shabbir Ahmed four for 58, Aleem Moosa three for 32, Zahid Saeed three for 40); National Bank* 231 (Akhtar Sarfraz 46, Kamran Akmal 59; Mubashir Nazir three for 80, Iftikhar Anjum three for 91, Fahad Masood three for 39) and 157 for three (Sajid Ali 50, Akhtar Sarfraz 35 not out). *National Bank 9 pts.*

Saga Cricket Ground became the 72nd first-class ground in Pakistan and the second in Sialkot.

At Iqbal Stadium, Faisalabad, March 31, April 1, 2. Pakistan Customs won by an innings and 108 runs. Allied Bank 146 (Iqbal Saleem 34; Stephen John three for 50, Naved-ul-Hasan four for 53) and 171 (Ata-ur-Rehman 71; Naved-ul-Hasan three for 66); Pakistan Customs* 425 (Azhar Shafiq 33, Aamer Bashir 97, Aamer Iqbal 129, Mohtashim Rasheed 38, Naved-ul-Hasan 30; Aqib Javed five for 139). *Pakistan Customs 12 pts.*

At Sheikhupura Stadium, Sheikhupura, March 31, April 1, 2. WAPDA won by three wickets. Habib Bank 126 (Kamran Hussain three for 30, Faisal Irfan four for 43) and 174 (Asadullah Butt 34, Farhan Adil 32; Faisal Irfan six for 19); WAPDA* 181 (Adil Nisar 30, Hasan Adnan 45; Danish Kaneria three for 46) and 120 for seven (Hasan Adnan 38 not out; Danish Kaneria four for 47). *WAPDA 12 pts.*

At KRL Cricket Ground, Rawalpindi, March 31, April 1, 2, 3. Drawn. KRL 295 (Saeed Anwar 35, Mohammad Wasim 63, Saeed Bin Nasir 124; Shoaib Malik four for 40) and 199 for nine dec. (Naved Ashraf 61, Saeed Bin Nasir 44; Mohammad Zahid, jun. three for 33); PIA* 212 (Ghulam Ali 44, Yasir Hameed 57; Yasir Arafat three for 59, Saeed Anwar three for 20) and 65 for one (Ghulam Ali 32 not out). *KRL 3 pts.*

FINAL

NATIONAL BANK v PAKISTAN CUSTOMS

At Gaddafi Stadium, Lahore, April 7, 8, 9, 10. Pakistan Customs won by four wickets. Toss: Pakistan Customs.

A third-day collapse cost National Bank much good work earlier in the game and handed Pakistan Customs their first first-class trophy. Whereas the Bank openers alone had raised 113 on the first morning, their entire second innings totalled just 110. Akhtar Sarfraz and Naumanullah had built on that healthy start with a stand of 134, helping National Bank to a convincing 365. Customs captain Ali Naqvi claimed five wickets with his off-spin, then saw 55 on the board. A century stand between Nasim Khan and Aamer Bashir established the innings and, despite a middle-order collapse of three for five in four overs, a fine fifty from Wasim Yousufi, plus 57 extras, kept the first-innings deficit to 44. Nadeem Iqbal led the demolition of National Bank's second attempt, with five for 27 in 16 overs. To win, Pakistan Customs needed 155; they lost Azhar Shafiq first ball, and looked shaky on the fourth morning, slipping to 111 for six. But Naqvi, who had dropped himself down the order, hit 41 in 47 balls to steer his side to victory.

Close of play: First day, National Bank 324-7 (Naumanullah 83*, Zahid Saeed 0*); Second day, Pakistan Customs 245-7 (Naved-ul-Hasan 8*, Wasim Yousufi 9*); Third day, Pakistan Customs 51-2 (Nasim Khan 12*, Aamer Bashir 14*).

National Bank

Shahid Anwar c Naved Latif b Ali Naqvi	46	– lbw b Stephen John	19
*Sajid Ali c Wasim Yousufi b Azhar Shafiq	59	– c sub (Nisar Abbas) b Nadeem Iqbal	23
Qaiser Abbas b Ali Naqvi	0	– c sub (Nisar Abbas) b Nadeem Iqbal	2
Akhtar Sarfraz c Wasim Yousufi b Naved-ul-Hasan	74	– (7) lbw b Nadeem Iqbal	0
Naumanullah c Naved-ul-Hasan b Ali Naqvi	91	– lbw b Nadeem Iqbal	2
Saeed Azad c Aamer Bashir b Naved-ul-Hasan	2	– (4) c Wasim Yousufi b Azhar Shafiq	7
Mohammad Javed b Ali Naqvi	9	– (6) c Aamer Bashir b Ali Naqvi	26
†Kamran Akmal c Wasim Yousufi b Nadeem Iqbal	24	– c Wasim Yousufi b Stephen John	3
Zahid Saeed c Wasim Yousufi b Ali Naqvi	13	– (10) not out	8
Shabbir Ahmed c Azam Khan b Stephen John	4	– (9) c Stephen John b Nadeem Iqbal	5
Aleem Moosa not out	2	– c Aamer Bashir b Naved-ul-Hasan	1
B 9, l-b 10, w 6, n-b 16	41	L-b 4, n-b 10	14
1/113 2/114 3/117 4/251 5/259 6/282 7/322 8/358 9/363	365	1/15 2/31 3/41 4/57 5/62 6/62 7/80 8/93 9/109	110

In the second innings Sajid Ali, when 4, retired hurt at 9 and resumed at 41.

Bowling: *First Innings*—Nadeem Iqbal 29–7–59–1; Stephen John 21.1–4–70–1; Naved-ul-Hasan 23–4–91–2; Azhar Shafiq 15–5–52–1; Ali Naqvi 16–4–65–5; Nasim Khan 2–0–9–0. *Second Innings*—Nadeem Iqbal 16–6–27–5; Naved-ul-Hasan 7.2–0–23–1; Azhar Shafiq 10–3–20–1; Stephen John 12–1–34–2; Ali Naqvi 1–0–2–1.

Pakistan Customs

*Ali Naqvi c Kamran Akmal b Aleem Moosa	10	– (6) not out	41
Azhar Shafiq c Kamran Akmal b Aleem Moosa	1	– (1) lbw b Shabbir Ahmed	0
Nasim Khan c Kamran Akmal b Shabbir Ahmed	76	– lbw b Zahid Saeed	14
Aamer Bashir lbw b Mohammad Javed	70	– b Shabbir Ahmed	37
Naved Latif lbw b Shabbir Ahmed	0	– c Kamran Akmal b Shabbir Ahmed	12
Azam Khan c Kamran Akmal b Shabbir Ahmed	1	– (2) lbw b Zahid Saeed	16
Aamer Iqbal lbw b Mohammad Javed	22	– c Akhtar Sarfraz b Zahid Saeed	0
Naved-ul-Hasan c Kamran Akmal b Mohammad Javed	12		
†Wasim Yousufi c Naumanullah b Zahid Saeed	54	– (8) not out	6
Stephen John b Zahid Saeed	16		
Nadeem Iqbal not out	2		
L-b 20, w 4, n-b 33	57	B 5, l-b 3, w 5, n-b 16	29
1/12 2/55 3/173 4/173 5/178 6/219 7/234 8/251 9/316	321	1/0 2/32 3/68 4/95 5/102 6/111 (6 wkts)	155

Bowling: *First Innings*—Shabbir Ahmed 30–5–103–3; Aleem Moosa 23–2–90–2; Mohammad Javed 21–1–51–3; Zahid Saeed 14.5–2–44–2; Shahid Anwar 5–1–13–0; Qaiser Abbas 1–1–0–0. *Second Innings*—Shabbir Ahmed 17–4–42–3; Aleem Moosa 2–0–8–0; Zahid Saeed 16.4–3–85–3; Mohammad Javed 3–1–12–0.

Umpires: Mian Mohammad Aslam and Riazuddin.
Referee: Shafiq Ahmed.

WINNERS

Ayub Trophy		1973-74	Railways	1988-89	Karachi
1960-61	Railways-Quetta	1974-75	National Bank	1989-90	Karachi Whites
1961-62	Karachi	1975-76	National Bank	1990-91	ADBP
1962-63	Karachi	1976-77	Habib Bank	1991-92	Habib Bank
1964-65	Karachi	1977-78	Habib Bank	1992-93	Habib Bank
1965-66	Karachi Blues	1978-79	National Bank	1993-94	ADBP
1967-68	Karachi Blues	†1979-80	IDBP	1994-95	Allied Bank
1969-70	PIA	†1980-81	Rawalpindi		
		†1981-82	Allied Bank	*PCB Patron's Trophy*	
BCCP Trophy		†1982-83	PACO	1995-96	ADBP
1970-71	PIA	1983-84	Karachi Blues	1996-97	United Bank
1971-72	PIA	1984-85	Karachi Whites	1997-98	Habib Bank
		1985-86	Karachi Whites	1998-99	Habib Bank
BCCP Patron's Trophy		1986-87	National Bank	†1999-2000	Lahore City Blues
1972-73	Karachi Blues	1987-88	Habib Bank	2000-01	Pakistan Customs

† *The Patron's Trophy was not first-class between 1979-80 and 1982-83, when it served as a qualifying competition for the Quaid-e-Azam Trophy, or in 1999-2000.*

Note: Matches in the following competitions were not first-class.

NATIONAL ONE-DAY TOURNAMENT FOR ASSOCIATIONS, 2000-01

Semi-finals

At National Stadium, Karachi, May 10. Karachi Whites won by seven runs. Karachi Whites 216 (49.1 overs) (Shadab Kabir 61, Naumanullah 54, Saeed Bin Nasir 30; Irfanuddin three for 33); Karachi Blues* 209 (48.1 overs) (Tariq Haroon 65, Mansoor Baig 41, Extras 32; Tabish Nawab four for 28, Adnan Malik three for 46).

At Gaddafi Stadium, Lahore, May 10. Sheikhupura won by 68 runs. Sheikhupura 250 for seven (50 overs) (Imran Nazir 37, Mohammad Ayub 58, Mohammad Haroon 40, Sarfraz Kazmi 45 not out; Naeem Akhtar three for 56); Rawalpindi* 182 (44.1 overs) (Tasawwar Hussain 34, Nadeem Abbasi 49; Kashif Raza four for 37).

Final

At Gaddafi Stadium, Lahore, May 13. Karachi Whites won by 79 runs. Karachi Whites* 278 for five (50 overs) (Saeed Bin Nasir 49, Naumanullah 74, Moin Khan 67 not out, Arif Mahmood 43 not out); Sheikhupura 199 (45.4 overs) (Qaiser Abbas 106 not out; Adnan Malik three for 48).

NATIONAL ONE-DAY TOURNAMENT FOR DEPARTMENTS, 2000-01

Final

At Sheikhupura Stadium, Sheikhupura, April 27. Habib Bank won by eight wickets. National Bank 192 (48.5 overs) (Imran Nazir 46, Mohammad Javed 49, Mushtaq Ahmed 32; Kabir Khan three for 38, Sajid Shah three for 44); Habib Bank* 196 for two (29.2 overs) (Taufeeq Umar 71 not out, Salim Elahi 61, Younis Khan 51 not out).

CRICKET IN SRI LANKA, 2000-01

By SA'ADI THAWFEEQ and GERRY VAIDYASEKERA

Hashan Tillekeratne

Sri Lanka enjoyed mixed fortunes during the season, losing Test series in South Africa and at home to England, who came from behind, though they compensated by beating India 2–1 in August. In limited-overs cricket, they won three trophies, two in Sharjah and one at home – where they also made a clean sweep of three one-day internationals against England.

Even as England were leaving, however, Sri Lanka's cricket administration was hit by politics, again. For the second time in two years, the Thilanga Sumathipala regime running the board was dissolved by the sports minister and replaced by an interim committee, headed by Vijay Malalasekera. Chief executive Dhammika Ranatunga, brother of former Test captain Arjuna, was also removed. Sumathipala had been back in office for nine months, and a few days earlier Sri Lanka had beaten England in the inaugural senior game at the Rangiri International Stadium at Dambulla. This project, the brainchild of Sumathipala, provided a magnificent setting for cricket, but absorbed large sums of money. The administration was accused of misappropriating funds during its construction, and there was confusion surrounding the ownership of the ground on which it was built.

On the domestic front, Nondescripts became champions for the first time in seven years. Unbeaten in 12 Premier Trophy matches, they thrived on first-innings points, completing only three outright wins. The most important was in their final game in the Super League. Nondescripts needed only a first-innings win for the title, and had led on first innings in every match so far; this time, they were bowled out an agonising single short of Colombo's 246. They rallied magnificently. Off-spinner Ruwan Kalpage snatched seven wickets to dismiss Colombo for 141 – leaving a target of 143 in 27 overs – and vice-captain Naveed Nawaz launched the assault, with four sixes in a 45-ball 57. But by the 21st over, Nondescripts were six down for 117. Kalpage's experience proved invaluable; scoring 31 in 36 balls, he steered them to a thrilling three-wicket victory with 15 balls to spare.

It was a complete turnaround for Nondescripts – the previous season, they had to be content with second place in the Plate Championship, for teams not qualifying for the Super League. It was also a personal triumph for captain Hashan Tillekeratne. Shedding the heavy responsibilities he had imposed on himself in the past, the 33-year-old left-hander played his normal game, rattling up 665 runs at 110.83 in the competition, including three centuries. He was supported by opener Pradeep Hewage, who accumulated 784 at 60.30 and scored the only double-century of the domestic season, against Panadura. But it was Tillekeratne's fighting unbeaten 185 that rescued Nondescripts from a perilous 14 for five against Burgher; he shared century partnerships for the eighth and ninth wickets and saw them to 372. That almost brought them victory. Burgher were forced to follow on, after Aravinda de Silva's fast off-breaks claimed five victims, and finished at 79 for seven. Tillekeratne's performances earned him a Test recall after two years, and he justified it with a magnificent 136 not out against India. It enabled him to head the overall averages with 954 runs at 68.14. No one reached 1,000 first-class runs, a disappointment given the number of batsmen playing at least 18 innings. Poor pitch preparation and an over-emphasis on limited-overs cricket at school level seemed to be having a dismal effect; unless curbed, these trends could lead to a paucity of quality batsmen for the national side.

Burgher recorded six outright wins, more than any other team, and harboured hopes of the title if they could take full points from their final match, against Tamil Union. But they had to settle for the Super League runners-up spot, despite a Herculean effort from left-arm spinner Sajeewa Weerakoon, who took a dozen wickets – the third time in the season he had claimed a match haul of ten or more. Weerakoon's devastating form made him the leading first-class wicket-taker, with 86 at 15.68, and earned him a place in the national training squad.

Defending champions Colombo Colts, like Nondescripts unbeaten throughout the tournament, finished third, followed by Sinhalese, whose captain, Hemantha Wickremaratne, was in prolific form – he accumulated 830 runs at 51.87, and scored five hundreds, the most by any batsman. These four teams went into a Super Group, guaranteed Super League qualification, for 2001-02.

The Plate champions were Sebastianites, who had won the Under-23 title earlier in the season. Their path to success was not rosy. After failing to qualify for the Super League by two points, they forfeited eight for not producing a suitable venue for their first Plate match, and suffered a two-wicket defeat by Matara in the next round. However, they came back strongly and finished 14 points ahead of Moors. Captain Nimesh Perera led from the front. His leg-spin claimed the season's best figures, eight for 24 against Nondescripts in the qualifying rounds, while opening bowler Dinusha Fernando took 68 wickets. Moors were kept in the hunt by slow left-armer Rangana Herath, who finished with 72 at 13.54.

The Navy and Air Force clubs had been promoted to the Premier Trophy after leading the non-first-class Sara Trophy in 1999-2000. Singha and Matara, who had finished at the bottom of the Plate, should have been relegated, but the rules were waived, and all four played. To return the Trophy to 16 teams, the bottom four from the Plate were asked to play off against the 2000-01 Sara group leaders, Chilaw Marians and Ragama; both won promotion. Navy went straight down again, having started life in the Premier Trophy with seven successive defeats. With them went Singha and Police, and Matara, who had been fourth in the Plate until they were retrospectively disqualified, for the second year running. They were accused of violating transfer regulations in signing five cricketers who had played one-day cricket for Moors earlier in the season. In protest, Matara boycotted the play-offs.

September 2000 saw the revival of the Gopalan Trophy, a traditional fixture against Sri Lanka's Indian neighbours, Tamil Nadu. It was first contested by Madras and Ceylon in 1952-53, but discontinued after 1982-83. Now played between Tamil Nadu and Colombo District Cricket Association, the game was badly affected by rain.

In minor cricket, Tharanga Paranawitharana hit 309 not out, including ten sixes and 55 fours, in 265 minutes for Saracens against Petersons in an Under-23 match. In schools cricket, he amassed 1,291 for St Mary's, Kegalla, averaging 107.58, and scored seven centuries, five in successive innings. Suranga de Silva, of St Sebastian's in Moratuwa, reached 1,000 for the third year running. There was some remarkable hitting from Nalin Roshan of Tissa Madhya Maha Vidyalaya, who smashed 11 sixes and ten fours against Kalutara Maha Vidyalaya. Of the bowlers, K. D. Asanka Premkumara of Devapathiraja College collected 40 wickets in four games, with best figures of eight for 69. Cathura Darshana of Dharmapala returned the best match analysis, 14 for 75 against Richmond. But there was a worrying incident at the Sara Stadium after Ananda Sastralaya defeated St John's of Nugegoda; some of the crowd attacked the umpires, who luckily escaped unhurt.

FIRST-CLASS AVERAGES, 2000-01

BATTING

(Qualification: 500 runs, average 30.00)

	M	*I*	*NO*	*R*	*HS*	*100s*	*Avge*
H. P. Tillekeratne (*Nondescripts*)	16	18	4	954	185*	4	68.14
D. P. M. D. Jayawardene (*Sinhalese*)	7	10	0	615	139	3	61.50
R. P. Hewage (*Nondescripts*)	11	15	2	784	200*	1	60.30
S. K. L. de Silva (*Colombo*)	9	11	1	603	164*	2	60.30
T. T. Samaraweera (*Sinhalese*)	15	20	7	687	103*	1	52.84
R. P. A. H. Wickremaratne (*Sinhalese*)	11	16	0	830	139	5	51.87
D. P. Samaraweera (*Colts*)	9	12	2	512	177*	1	51.20
H. G. J. M. Kulatunga (*Colts*)	11	16	1	738	175	2	49.20
J. S. K. Peiris (*Panadura*)	11	20	3	797	136	3	46.88
D. N. Hunukumbura (*Colombo*)	10	13	0	550	116	2	42.30
W. M. G. Ramyakumara (*Tamil Union*)	11	18	3	629	108	1	41.93
M. G. van Dort (*Colombo*)	12	18	1	685	116	2	40.29
R. H. S. Silva (*Burgher*)	12	19	2	671	155	1	39.47
A. Rideegammanagedera (*Tamil Union*)	11	17	1	611	120	1	38.18
M. N. Nawaz (*Nondescripts*)	12	17	3	530	97	0	37.85
S. D. Abeynayake (*Bloomfield*)	11	17	2	545	152	1	36.33
K. Sangakkara (*Nondescripts*)	10	15	1	506	105*	1	36.14
S. Kalawithigoda (*Colts*)	12	17	1	578	119	1	36.12
W. N. de Silva (*Sebastianites*)	11	15	0	524	107	1	34.93
G. A. S. Perera (*Panadura*)	11	18	1	586	115*	1	34.47
H. S. S. M. K. Weerasiri (*Navy*)	13	25	2	785	107	1	34.13
H. M. Maduwantha (*Kurunegala Youth*)	13	25	4	701	93	0	33.38
M. D. K. Perera (*Panadura*)	9	16	0	503	105	1	31.43
P. K. Siriwardene (*Antonians*)	13	23	0	718	87	0	31.21
W. M. S. M. Perera (*Sinhalese*)	12	22	3	589	129	1	31.00
B. S. M. Warnapura (*Burgher*)	12	19	2	514	138	2	30.23

* *Signifies not out.*

BOWLING

(Qualification: 35 wickets)

	O	*M*	*R*	*W*	*BB*	*5W/i*	*Avge*
A. W. Ekanayake (*Kurunegala Youth*)	441.1	146	891	67	8-93	7	13.29
H. M. R. K. B. Herath (*Moors*)	530	200	975	72	6-32	5	13.54
M. M. Perera (*Navy*)	231.3	37	681	48	6-40	1	14.18
S. Weerakoon (*Burgher*)	559.4	163	1,349	86	7-51	7	15.68
M. M. D. P. V. Perera (*Galle*)	202.1	46	588	37	6-46	3	15.89
K. L. S. L. Dias (*Tamil Union*)	233.1	55	606	38	6-47	2	15.94
S. H. S. M. K. Silva (*Sinhalese*)	332.4	98	706	43	7-52	2	16.41
H. S. H. Alles (*Bloomfield*)	267.5	67	762	46	5-23	2	16.56
K. S. C. de Silva (*Burgher*)	289.4	82	692	41	5-16	3	16.87
M. M. D. N. R. G. Perera (*Sebastianites*)	242.1	25	830	45	8-24	2	18.44
W. C. A. Ganegama (*Nondescripts*)	275.4	49	856	46	5-34	3	18.60
K. A. D. M. Fernando (*Sebastianites*)	399.1	64	1,289	68	7-67	5	18.95
S. I. Fernando (*Colts*)	365.1	97	820	42	7-37	2	19.52
M. C. R. Fernando (*Moors*)	436	115	1,023	52	5-86	2	19.67
T. T. Samaraweera (*Sinhalese*)	416.4	93	1,197	60	6-55	3	19.95
K. G. Perera (*Galle*)	509.3	162	1,058	53	6-14	3	19.96
C. M. Bandara (*Nondescripts*)	334.4	76	964	48	5-58	3	20.08
M. K. G. C. P. Lakshitha (*Air Force*)	287.5	62	851	42	6-41	2	20.26

	O	*M*	*R*	*W*	*BB*	*5W/i*	*Avge*
N. S. Rupasinghe (*Colombo*)	373.1	108	792	39	5-50	1	20.30
M. K. D. I. Amerasinghe (*Nondescripts*)	287.4	65	781	37	5-34	1	21.10
D. K. Liyanage (*Colts*)	271.3	68	836	38	5-34	2	22.00
P. D. R. L. Perera (*Sinhalese*)	279.4	52	848	38	7-40	1	22.31
S. Chandana (*Antonians*)	544.4	118	1,590	71	8-85	6	22.39
G. A. S. Perera (*Panadura*)	349.1	84	967	42	7-45	2	23.02
M. Muralitharan (*Tamil Union*)	413.3	117	865	37	8-87	2	23.37
B. A. R. S. Priyadarshana (*Matara*)	275.3	51	916	36	5-30	2	25.44

Note: Averages include India's tour in August to September 2001.

PREMIER TROPHY, 2000-01

SUPER LEAGUE

	Played	*Won*	*Lost*	*Drawn*	*1st-inns Lead*	*Points*
Nondescripts CC	7	1	0	6	6	83.580
Burgher RC	7	3	0	4	1	67.805
Colts CC	7	1	0	6	3	55.050
Sinhalese SC	7	2	1	4	1	53.580
Colombo CC	7	0	1	6	3	45.090
Tamil Union C and AC	7	1	1	5	1	40.530
Bloomfield C and AC	7	1	3	3	1	39.070
Panadura SC	7	0	3	4	0	21.965

Super League teams carried forward results and points gained against fellow-qualifiers in the first round, but not those gained against the teams eliminated.

PLATE CHAMPIONSHIP

	Played	*Won*	*Lost*	*Drawn*	*1st-inns Lead*	*Points*
Sebastianites C and AC	9	3	1	5	5	97.485
Moors SC	9	3	1	5	2	83.120
Antonians SC	9	3	2	4	2	79.490
Galle CC	9	2	0	7	2	70.220
Air Force SC	9	1	3	5	3	61.235
Kurunegala Youth CC	9	2	2	5	1	60.485
Singha SC	9	1	5	3	2	58.245
Police SC	9	2	1	6	2	56.865
Navy SC	9	2	4	3	0	52.295
Matara SC*	9	2	2	5	3	00.000

** Matara SC were disqualified from the tournament for violating regulations on the transfer of players; all points from their fixtures were excluded from the table.*

Teams carried forward results and points gained against fellow group members in the first round, but not those gained against the teams who qualified for the Super League.

*In the following scores, * by the name of a team indicates that they won the toss.*

Group A

At Air Force Ground, Katunayake, January 5, 6, 7. Drawn. Matara 293 (H. A. H. U. Tillekeratne 55, E. F. M. U. Fernando 45, M. A. P. Salgado 42, C. I. Bandaratilleke 64 not out; M. K. G. C. P. Lakshitha four for 72, P. T. S. Fernando four for 77) and 40 for no wkt; Air Force* 402 for eight dec. (S. E. D. R. Fernando 93, R. C. Galappathy 48, W. R. D. Dissanayake 85, K. A. Kumara 34; S. M. Ramzan four for 100).

At Reid Avenue, Colombo, January 5, 6, 7. Bloomfield won by an innings and 158 runs. Police 120 (H. S. H. Alles five for 23) and 100 (H. G. D. Nayanakantha five for 38, H. D. P. K. Dharmasena three for 15); Bloomfield* 378 (H. D. P. K. Dharmasena 157, P. B. Dassanayake 36, K. K. K. Gangodawila 37, P. P. Wickremasinghe 42 not out, Extras 34; W. N. M. Soysa three for 83).

At Havelock Park, Colombo (BRC), January 5, 6, 7. Kurunegala Youth won by three wickets. Burgher 120 (J. A. M. W. Kumara three for 25, H. M. Maduwantha three for 32) and 154 (G. S. T. Perera 30, B. de Silva 34; A. W. Ekanayake three for four); Kurunegala Youth* 154 (R. H. Sureshchandra 44, H. M. S. Jayawardene 38; S. Weerakoon three for 22, W. C. Labrooy three for 38) and 124 for seven (S. Weerakoon four for 35).

Ekanayake's second-innings analysis was 12.1–8–4–3.

At Maitland Crescent, Colombo (CCC), January 5, 6, 7. Drawn. Colts 130 (A. S. S. P. A. Attanayake 33 not out; M. S. Villavarayen five for 35) and 283 for seven (S. Kalawithigoda 32, D. P. Samaraweera 79, H. G. J. M. Kulatunga 67; B. M. T. T. Mendis three for 52); Colombo* 403 for eight dec. (P. B. Ediriweera 36, M. G. van Dort 75, S. K. L. de Silva 96, J. W. H. D. Boteju 61, B. M. T. T. Mendis 46, Extras 39; D. Hettiarachchi three for 94).

At Air Force Ground, Katunayake, January 12, 13, 14. Burgher won by an innings and 151 runs. Burgher 380 (C. P. Handunnettige 80, R. H. S. Silva 155, C. U. Jayasinghe 32; M. K. G. C. P. Lakshitha three for 78, W. R. D. Dissanayake three for 93); Air Force* 130 (W. R. D. Dissanayake 50; S. Weerakoon six for 31) and 99 (B. de Silva three for 30, S. Weerakoon four for 15).

At P. Saravanamuttu Stadium, Colombo, January 12, 13, 14. Drawn. Matara 153 (N. H. V. Chinthaka 34; H. S. H. Alles four for 32, R. S. A. Palliyaguruge four for 41) and 225 (B. A. R. S. Priyadarshana 71, S. M. Ramzan 39, Extras 30; H. S. H. Alles five for 38, P. P. Wickremasinghe three for 72); Bloomfield* 267 (S. D. Abeynayake 65, R. S. A. Palliyaguruge 81; K. G. A. S. Kalum eight for 76) and 88 for nine (M. A. P. Salgado six for 24).

At Havelock Park, Colombo (Colts), January 12, 13, 14. Drawn. Galle* 194 (C. P. H. Ramanayake 31; S. I. Fernando seven for 37) and 294 (I. C. D. Perera 52, H. S. S. Fonseka 97, C. P. H. Ramanayake 51; M. H. R. M. Fernando four for 101); Colts 405 for nine dec. (S. Kalawithigoda 61, S. I. Fernando 54, H. G. J. M. Kulatunga 175, A. S. S. P. A. Attanayake 62; M. H. R. M. Fernando three for 50).

At Welagedera Stadium, Kurunegala, January 12, 13, 14. Colombo won by nine wickets. Colombo* 372 (P. B. Ediriweera 46, D. N. Hunukumbura 106, A. S. Polonowita 77; J. A. M. W. Kumara four for 60) and 21 for one; Kurunegala Youth 159 (M. I. Thahir 40; J. W. H. D. Boteju three for 33, C. R. B. Mudalige five for 48) and 233 (H. M. Maduwantha 61, R. P. Mapatuna 33, M. I. Thahir 47; N. S. Rupasinghe three for 33).

At Havelock Park, Colombo (BRC), January 19, 20, 21. Drawn. Air Force* 181 (W. C. R. Tissera 31; I. D. Gunawardene three for 49, H. P. A. Priyantha three for 35) and 284 (R. C. Galappathy 31, W. R. D. Dissanayake 48, S. C. Gunasekera 35, W. C. R. Tissera 39, A. Rizan 45; W. T. Abeyratne five for 76); Police 172 (S. A. Wijeratne 31, H. M. N. C. Silva 30, I. D. Gunawardene 31; M. K. G. C. P. Lakshitha three for 48) and 132 for five (W. N. M. Soysa 38, S. A. Wijeratne 34).

At Reid Avenue, Colombo, January 19, 20, 21. Bloomfield won by an innings and seven runs. Bloomfield* 304 (S. Rodrigo 68, W. D. D. S. Perera 57, H. S. H. Alles 61, Extras 30; K. G. Perera four for 62); Galle 146 (C. M. Withanage 49, H. S. S. Fonseka 31; D. M. G. S. Dissanayake five for 16) and 151 (H. S. H. Alles three for 50, S. D. Dissanayake six for 51).

At Maitland Crescent, Colombo (CCC), January 19, 20, 21. Drawn. Burgher 341 (B. C. M. S. Mendis 42, G. S. T. Perera 82, B. S. M. Warnapura 59, C. U. Jayasinghe 56; M. S. Villavarayen four for 95) and 328 for seven (B. C. M. S. Mendis 126, R. H. S. Silva 64, W. C. Labrooy 66 not out; N. S. Rajan three for 54, C. R. B. Mudalige three for 89); Colombo* 320 (D. N. Hunukumbura 36, J. W. H. D. Boteju 51, A. S. Polonowita 64, M. S. Villavarayen 30, N. S. Rupasinghe 32 not out; K. S. C. de Silva four for 70).

At Havelock Park, Colombo (Colts), January 19, 20, 21. Colts won by seven wickets. Kurunegala Youth 238 (H. M. S. Jayawardene 74, H. M. Maduwantha 45; K. E. A. Upashantha three for 58, M. J. Sigera three for 62) and 162 (W. T. M. C. Boteju 59; K. E. A. Upashantha three for 50, D. K. Liyanage five for 34); Colts* 348 (G. N. Abeyratne 59, D. P. Samaraweera 51, H. G. J. M. Kulatunga 53, K. E. A. Upashantha 39, D. K. Liyanage 48; A. W. Ekanayake six for 113) and 55 for three.

At Reid Avenue, Colombo, January 26, 27, 28. Burgher won by an innings and ten runs. Bloomfield 108 (K. S. C. de Silva five for 28, S. Weerakoon three for 16) and 112 (S. Weerakoon five for 17, B. de Silva three for 28); Burgher* 230 for seven dec. (B. C. M. S. Mendis 101, C. U. Jayasinghe 41, D. F. Arnolda 39).

At Maitland Crescent, Colombo (CCC), January 26, 27, 28. Drawn. Colombo* 273 (D. K. Ranaweera 43, D. N. Hunukumbura 116; I. C. D. Perera three for 62, K. G. Perera three for 41, M. H. Wijesinghe three for 47) and 113 for five dec. (A. S. Polonowita 36 not out); Galle 134 (I. C. D. Perera 33; J. W. H. D. Boteju five for 35) and 150 for eight (N. S. Rupasinghe three for 47, C. R. B. Mudalige three for 28).

At Havelock Park, Colombo (Colts), January 26, 27, 28. Colts won by nine wickets. Air Force* 207 (M. K. G. C. P. Lakshitha 45, W. R. Fernando 76; M. J. Sigera three for 58, S. Alexander three for 36, P. C. L. Perera three for 48) and 199 (W. R. D. Dissanayake 47; S. I. Fernando three for 63, D. P. Samaraweera three for 19); Colts 353 for nine dec. (S. Kalawithigoda 50, D. P. Samaraweera 177 not out, G. V. S. Janaka 49) and 54 for one.

At Uyanwatte Stadium, Matara, January 26, 27, 28. Drawn. Police 248 (C. N. Liyanage 46, H. M. N. C. Silva 75 not out, H. P. A. Priyantha 40; B. A. R. S. Priyadarshana four for 84); Matara* 374 (E. F. M. U. Fernando 164, N. P. Wickramasekera 30, B. A. R. S. Priyadarshana 99; H. P. A. Priyantha three for 86).

At Air Force Ground, Katunayake, February 2, 3, 4. Drawn. Kurunegala Youth 208 (W. T. de Silva 49, H. M. Maduwantha 41, R. P. Mapatuna 30, M. I. Thahir 33 not out; M. K. G. C. P. Lakshitha four for 71, H. K. Karunaratne three for 18) and 48 for no wkt (G. V. K. C. Dissanayake 31 not out); Air Force* 283 (W. C. R. Tissera 32, W. R. D. Dissanayake 45, S. C. Gunasekera 71, A. Rizan 38; A. W. Ekanayake five for 59).

At Reid Avenue, Colombo, February 2, 3, 4. Drawn. Bloomfield 272 (C. R. Kumarage 44, R. S. A. Palliyaguruge 43, D. M. G. S. Dissanayake 56, H. S. H. Alles 43; B. M. T. T. Mendis three for 29, N. S. Rajan three for 30); Colombo* 225 for eight (M. G. van Dort 38, S. K. L. de Silva 32, B. M. T. T. Mendis 66 not out; D. M. G. S. Dissanayake four for 73).

At Police Park, Colombo, February 2, 3. Burgher won by an innings and 164 runs. Burgher 355 for seven dec. (R. H. S. Silva 33, G. S. T. Perera 62, B. S. M. Warnapura 111, C. U. Jayasinghe 107 not out; I. D. Gunawardene three for 53); Police* 92 (I. D. Gunawardene 55; K. S. C. de Silva five for 16) and 99 (H. M. N. C. Silva 40).

At Reid Avenue, Colombo, February 9, 10, 11. Drawn. Kurunegala Youth 297 (H. M. S. Jayawardene 58, H. P. K. Rajapakse 44, H. M. Maduwantha 56, M. I. Thahir 71; H. G. D. Nayanakantha three for 80) and 177 for eight (H. M. Maduwantha 46; H. S. H. Alles three for 37, S. D. Dissanayake four for 47); Bloomfield* 411 for nine dec. (S. D. Abeynayake 152, W. D. D. S. Perera 64, D. M. G. S. Dissanayake 53, R. S. A. Palliyaguruge 32, K. K. K. Gangodawila 61 not out; W. T. M. C. Boteju three for 88, H. M. Maduwantha five for 98).

Bloomfield wicket-keeper Y. S. S. Mendis took seven catches and a stumping in Kurunegala Youth's first innings, and eight catches and two stumpings in the match.

At Maitland Crescent, Colombo (CCC), February 9, 10, 11. Drawn. Air Force* 214 (S. E. D. R. Fernando 37, W. R. Fernando 61 not out, M. K. G. C. P. Lakshitha 37; N. S. Rupasinghe five for

50) and 208 for nine (A. Rizan 45, W. R. D. Dissanayake 34, S. C. Gunasekera 55, W. R. Fernando 34; J. W. H. D. Boteju three for 30, N. S. Rupasinghe four for 58); Colombo 246 (D. N. Hunukumbura 37, S. K. L. de Silva 55, J. W. H. D. Boteju 30; W. R. D. Dissanayake four for 50).

At Havelock Park, Colombo (Colts), February 9, 10, 11. Colts won by an innings and 37 runs. Matara 220 (N. H. V. Chinthaka 36, B. A. R. S. Priyadarshana 56, S. W. K. Shantha 40; J. T. Samaratunga three for 44) and 217 (S. W. N. D. Chinthaka 46, M. A. P. Salgado 44, H. A. H. U. Tillekeratne 33, Extras 31; D. K. Liyanage five for 49, S. I. Fernando three for 85); Colts* 474 for eight dec. (S. Kalawithigoda 89, S. I. Fernando 56, D. P. Samaraweera 34, H. G. J. M. Kulatunga 152, G. V. S. Janaka 58 not out).

At Police Park, Colombo, February 9, 10, 11. Drawn. Police* 490 for eight dec. (P. N. Udawatta 38, P. R. T. Fernando 46, H. M. N. C. Silva 62, C. N. Liyanage 108, W. N. M. Soysa 155; M. H. Wijesinghe four for 72); Galle 224 (I. C. D. Perera 46, D. D. Wickremasinghe 67 not out; V. N. Algama four for 64) and 186 for two (H. S. S. Fonseka 89 not out, C. M. Withanage 41, W. M. P. N. Wanasinghe 32 not out).

Liyanage and Soysa added 240 for the sixth wicket.

At Air Force Ground, Katunayake, February 16, 17, 18. Drawn. Air Force 265 (S. E. D. R. Fernando 36, R. de Silva 40, W. P. A. Ariyadasa 53, P. T. S. Fernando 52; D. M. G. S. Dissanayake four for 60) and 110 for five (W. R. D. Dissanayake 41; D. M. G. S. Dissanayake three for 29); Bloomfield* 301 (Y. S. S. Mendis 76, D. M. G. S. Dissanayake 108, R. S. A. Palliyaguruge 44; W. C. R. Tissera seven for 89).

At Maitland Crescent, Colombo (CCC), February 16, 17, 18. Colombo won by an innings and 112 runs. Police* 170 (H. P. A. Priyantha 38, C. N. Liyanage 64; N. S. Rupasinghe three for 35, C. R. B. Mudalige three for 34) and 96 (N. S. Rupasinghe four for 42, C. R. B. Mudalige four for 19); Colombo 378 for eight dec. (J. Mubarak 36, D. N. Hunukumbura 56, S. K. L. de Silva 51, P. B. Ediriweera 112 not out, I. S. Gallage 44; W. T. Abeyratne five for 116).

At Havelock Park, Colombo (Colts), February 16, 17, 18. Drawn. Burgher 280 (B. S. M. Warnapura 138, B. de Silva 48; S. I. Fernando three for 60) and 292 for seven (R. H. S. Silva 58, D. F. Arnolda 79, B. S. M. Warnapura 55 not out, Extras 31; D. Hettiarachchi four for 131); Colts* 320 (S. I. Fernando 140, G. V. S. Janaka 30; S. Weerakoon four for 103, B. S. M. Warnapura four for 40).

At Reid Avenue, Colombo, February 23, 24, 25. Colts won by six wickets. Bloomfield* 240 (C. R. Kumarage 54, S. D. Abeynayake 97; S. I. Fernando six for 53) and 177 (S. D. Abeynayake 36; K. E. A. Upashantha three for 28, J. T. Samaratunga four for 33); Colts 270 (S. Kalawithigoda 119, G. V. S. Janaka 38; T. M. M. K. Abeywickreme five for 100) and 148 for four (S. I. Fernando 70 not out, D. P. Samaraweera 48).

At Havelock Park, Colombo (BRC), February 23, 24, 25. Drawn. Galle 295 (W. M. P. N. Wanasinghe 35, D. D. Wickremasinghe 44, M. M. D. P. V. Perera 72 not out, M. K. P. B. Kularatne 44; E. J. P. R. Sampath four for 63) and 257 for two (C. M. Withanage 108 not out, T. K. D. Sudarshana 39, W. M. P. N. Wanasinghe 101 not out); Burgher* 293 (B. C. M. S. Mendis 35, N. S. Bopage 75, R. H. S. Silva 48, C. U. Jayasinghe 44, K. S. C. de Silva 34; K. G. Perera five for 95).

At Police Park, Colombo, February 23, 24, 25. Drawn. Police* 233 (P. R. T. Fernando 99 not out, W. N. M. Soysa 44; J. A. M. W. Kumara three for 30) and 111 for nine dec. (A. W. Ekanayake five for 22); Kurunegala Youth 190 (W. T. de Silva 79; W. T. Abeyratne three for 51, V. N. Algama three for 55) and 94 for seven (H. M. Maduwantha 32 not out; N. H. Tennekoon four for 38, W. N. M. Soysa three for 22).

At Air Force Ground, Katunayake, March 2, 3, 4. Galle won by six wickets. Galle* 269 (W. M. P. N. Wanasinghe 49, D. D. Wickremasinghe 51, M. M. D. P. V. Perera 48; W. C. R. Tissera three for 33) and 76 for four (M. M. D. P. V. Perera 33 not out); Air Force 116 (M. H. R. M. Fernando three for 35, K. G. Perera six for 14) and 228 (S. E. D. R. Fernando 45, W. R. Fernando 79, R. de Silva 41; K. G. Perera three for 49).

At Havelock Park, Colombo (Colts), March 2, 3, 4. Colts won by an innings and 21 runs. Police* 187 (P. R. T. Fernando 72, C. N. Liyanage 37; D. K. Liyanage three for 60, M. J. Sigera three for 31, S. I. Fernando four for 32) and 122 (C. N. Liyanage 31; D. K. Liyanage three for 47, J. T. Samaratunga three for 12); Colts 330 (S. Kalawithigoda 63, S. I. Fernando 38, A. S. S. P. A. Attanayake 38, D. K. Liyanage 73 not out, P. C. L. Perera 32; H. P. A. Priyantha three for 61, W. T. Abeyratne three for 107).

At Uyanwatte Stadium, Matara, March 2, 3, 4. Drawn. Kurunegala Youth* 238 (R. H. Sureshchandra 47, H. M. S. Jayawardene 34, W. T. M. C. Boteju 33, Extras 34; P. I. W. Jayasekera six for 85, M. A. P. Salgado three for 34) and 142 for five dec. (R. H. Sureshchandra 35, H. M. Maduwantha 31 not out; P. I. W. Jayasekera five for 36); Matara 243 (H. A. H. U. Tillekeratne 39, N. H. V. Chinthaka 48, S. W. N. D. Chinthaka 39, E. F. M. U. Fernando 36; A. W. Ekanayake six for 73) and 38 for one.

At Havelock Park, Colombo (BRC), March 10, 11, 12. Burgher won by 120 runs. Burgher* 245 (N. S. Bopage 38, R. H. S. Silva 72; S. M. Ramzan three for 35) and 96 (B. A. R. S. Priyadarshana five for 38, M. A. P. Salgado four for 21); Matara 99 (K. S. C. de Silva five for 40, S. Weerakoon three for 16) and 122 (S. Weerakoon five for 43, B. de Silva four for 28).

At Maitland Crescent, Colombo (CCC), March 16, 17, 18. Drawn. Matara* 273 (N. H. V. Chinthaka 58, B. A. R. S. Priyadarshana 31, M. A. P. Salgado 39, S. M. Ramzan 55; R. M. A. R. Ratnayake four for 42, N. S. Rupasinghe four for 110) and 253 (N. H. V. Chinthaka 38, E. F. M. U. Fernando 36, S. M. Ramzan 66; N. S. Rupasinghe four for 95); Colombo 348 (D. N. Hunukumbura 59, J. Mubarak 77, M. G. van Dort 32, S. K. L. de Silva 64, P. B. Ediriweera 31, A. S. Polonowita 35; M. A. P. Salgado three for 79, S. M. Ramzan four for 72) and 91 for four (J. Mubarak 50 not out).

At Braybrooke Place, Colombo (Moors), March 16, 17, 18. Galle won by 198 runs. Galle* 163 (H. S. S. Fonseka 42; A. W. Ekanayake five for 48, H. M. Maduwantha four for 34) and 240 for nine dec. (T. K. D. Sudarshana 102, I. C. D. Perera 33; A. W. Ekanayake three for 74, N. M. Ramzi four for 48); Kurunegala Youth 74 (K. G. Perera four for 15, W. M. P. N. Wanasinghe four for 24) and 131 (K. G. Perera four for 58, W. M. P. N. Wanasinghe five for 29).

At Reid Avenue, Colombo, March 23, 24, 25. Drawn. Galle* 185 (H. S. S. Fonseka 36; N. C. Komasaru five for 45, S. M. Ramzan three for 28) and 124 for three (H. S. S. Fonseka 46, W. M. P. N. Wanasinghe 63 not out); Matara 223 (N. H. V. Chinthaka 40, K. A. S. Jayasinghe 91; C. P. H. Ramanayake three for 44, M. M. D. P. V. Perera three for 66).

Colts, Burgher, Colombo and Bloomfield qualified for the Super League.

Group B

At Braybrooke Place, Colombo (Moors), January 5, 6, 7. Drawn. Sebastianites 205 (N. G. Peiris 37, K. A. D. J. Siriwardene 32, K. A. D. M. Fernando 40; M. C. R. Fernando four for 54, W. M. B. Perera four for 41) and 233 (R. R. Jaymon 100; H. M. R. K. B. Herath three for 57); Moors* 180 (W. M. B. Perera 47, M. N. R. Cooray 60, Extras 32; M. M. D. N. R. G. Perera four for 31) and 91 for four (D. W. A. N. D. Vitharana 36).

At Maitland Place, Colombo (NCC), January 5, 6, 7. Nondescripts won by an innings and five runs. Nondescripts 400 for nine dec. (R. P. Hewage 58, P. A. de Silva 49, H. P. Tillekeratne 157; A. K. I. N. Perera three for 99); Navy* 216 (A. A. I. Dinuka 36, G. L. Hewage 68; W. C. A. Ganegama four for 42) and 179 (A. A. I. Dinuka 64; M. K. D. I. Amerasinghe four for 41, H. P. Tillekeratne three for 54).

Seven batsmen were lbw in Navy's second innings.

At Panadura Esplanade, Panadura, January 5, 6, 7. Drawn. Panadura 245 (W. P. Wickrama 47, L. P. C. Silva 60, K. R. R. K. Wimalasena 35; M. T. T. Mirando three for 60, R. A. D. C. Perera four for 47) and 330 for nine dec. (W. S. P. Jayawardene 34, J. S. K. Peiris 129, G. A. S. Perera

115 not out; I. C. Soysa three for 54, R. A. D. C. Perera three for 75); Singha* 196 (M. T. T. Mirando 47 not out, Extras 38; K. C. A. Weerasinghe three for 35) and 222 for seven (S. Jayantha 44, Y. M. W. B. Ekanayake 77; M. M. P. Silva three for 42).

In Panadura's second innings, Peiris and Perera added 153 for the eighth wicket.

At P. Saravanamuttu Stadium, Colombo, January 5, 6, 7. Drawn. Sinhalese 315 (W. M. S. M. Perera 43, U. A. Fernando 70, A. Ranatunga 86, P. H. M. G. Fernando 31 not out; M. R. C. N. Bandaratilleke six for 97) and 141 for five dec. (G. I. Daniel 50 not out, A. Ranatunga 42); Tamil Union* 147 (A. Rideegammanagedera 50; M. A. M. Aslam three for 24, S. H. S. M. K. Silva four for 40) and 244 for six (P. S. A. N. Shiroman 93, E. M. I. Galagoda 59 not out).

At Braybrooke Place, Colombo (Moors), January 12, 13, 14. Drawn. Tamil Union* 246 (P. S. A. N. Shiroman 40, W. M. G. Ramyakumara 70, M. K. Gajanayake 54, O. C. Warnapura 56; H. M. R. K. B. Herath six for 67) and 251 (A. Rideegammanagedera 95, D. P. S. Jayaratne 53; H. M. R. K. B. Herath four for 68, W. M. B. Perera three for 32); Moors 242 (W. M. B. Perera 80, M. C. R. Fernando 37; A. Rideegammanagedera three for 61, K. L. S. L. Dias three for 71) and 94 for two (M. S. Sampan 33 not out, M. N. R. Cooray 41).

At Maitland Place, Colombo (NCC), January 12, 13, 14. Nondescripts won by nine wickets. Antonians 294 (P. R. L. Peiris 86, W. A. L. Chaturanga 45, P. K. Siriwardene 35, H. L. D. I. P. Hittatiya 31, S. Chandana 32; W. C. A. Ganegama three for 62, M. K. D. I. Amerasinghe three for 68) and 112 (K. A. D. C. Silva 42; W. C. A. Ganegama five for 34, C. M. Bandara three for 42); Nondescripts* 304 (R. P. Hewage 45, M. N. Nawaz 30, C. P. Mapatuna 104, C. M. Bandara 61; S. Chandana seven for 116) and 103 for one (R. P. Hewage 48 not out, M. N. Nawaz 40 not out).

At Panadura Esplanade, Panadura, January 12, 13, 14. Panadura won by an innings and 55 runs. Panadura* 386 (W. S. P. Jayawardene 84, W. P. Wickrama 53, J. S. K. Peiris 136, K. R. R. K. Wimalasena 37, G. A. S. Perera 38; A. R. M. S. Ranaweera four for 110); Navy 159 (A. K. I. N. Perera 74, H. S. S. M. K. Weerasiri 35; T. C. B. Fernando three for 38, M. D. K. Perera four for 30) and 172 (A. R. M. S. Ranaweera 31, H. S. S. M. K. Weerasiri 45 not out, G. L. Hewage 37; G. A. S. Perera seven for 45).

At Maitland Place, Colombo (SSC), January 12, 13, 14. Drawn. Sinhalese* 400 for eight dec. (W. M. S. M. Perera 129, R. P. A. H. Wickremaratne 123, T. T. Samaraweera 32; K. A. D. M. Fernando three for 118, M. N. T. H. Kumara four for 81) and 140 for three (W. M. S. M. Perera 40, S. Ranatunga 55 not out, R. P. A. H. Wickremaratne 32); Sebastianites 231 (K. A. D. J. Siriwardene 38, S. A. L. J. Fernando 62, M. N. T. H. Kumara 31; A. S. A. Perera three for 54, M. A. M. Aslam four for 63, T. T. Samaraweera three for 67).

At Braybrooke Place, Colombo (Moors), January 19, 20, 21. Moors won by 217 runs. Moors 279 (M. S. Sampan 59, W. M. B. Perera 64, M. F. A. Farhath 67; A. R. M. S. Ranaweera three for 74, B. W. D. M. M. Dissanayake three for 53) and 191 for five dec. (E. D. I. L. de Silva 56 not out, W. M. B. Perera 63, R. G. D. Sanjeewa 32; M. M. Perera three for 44); Navy* 137 (A. K. I. N. Perera 45; H. M. R. K. B. Herath five for 46, W. M. B. Perera three for 31) and 116 (P. C. V. B. de Silva 39; H. M. R. K. B. Herath six for 32, M. C. R. Fernando four for 42).

At Maitland Place, Colombo (NCC), January 19, 20, 21. Drawn. Singha 287 (H. S. G. S. Silva 75, H. W. M. Kumara 32, A. S. Wewalwala 66, I. C. Soysa 34, Y. M. W. B. Ekanayake 36; H. P. Tillekeratne three for 54) and 255 for eight (H. W. M. Kumara 30, S. Jayantha 47, I. C. Soysa 100 not out; C. M. Bandara five for 69); Nondescripts* 308 for five dec. (R. R. Tissera 44, R. P. Hewage 73, M. N. Nawaz 31, H. P. Tillekeratne 69 not out, C. P. Mapatuna 33, Extras 36; S. Jayantha three for 36).

At Maitland Place, Colombo (SSC), January 19, 20, 21. Sinhalese won by ten wickets. Antonians 190 (W. A. L. Chaturanga 71; A. S. A. Perera three for 36, D. G. R. Dhammika three for 30) and 218 (W. A. L. Chaturanga 39, P. K. Siriwardene 44, C. K. Hewamanne 44; D. G. R. Dhammika five for 47, S. H. S. M. K. Silva three for 15); Sinhalese* 400 for five dec. (G. I. Daniel 106, R. P. A. H. Wickremaratne 139, A. Ranatunga 46, T. T. Samaraweera 32 not out, A. S. A. Perera 38 not out) and nine for no wkt.

At P. Saravanamuttu Stadium, Colombo, January 19, 20, 21. Drawn. Sebastianites* 365 (W. N. de Silva 96, K. A. D. J. Siriwardene 89, S. A. L. J. Fernando 58, K. A. D. M. Fernando 30, Extras 34; A. Rideegammanagedera three for 121, K. L. S. L. Dias three for 77); Tamil Union 394 (P. S. A. N. Shiroman 64, M. K. Gajanayake 45, A. Rideegammanagedera 87, O. C. Warnapura 30, B. C. Jeganathan 58; K. A. D. M. Fernando five for 127, M. N. T. H. Kumara five for 66).

At Kadirana Cricket Grounds, Gampaha, January 26, 27, 28. Drawn. Antonians 282 (P. R. L. Peiris 32, P. K. Siriwardene 87, W. J. U. Perera 52, K. D. D. H. N. Perera 58; K. C. A. Weerasinghe four for 52, M. D. K. Perera four for 97) and 210 (K. A. D. C. Silva 81, K. D. D. H. N. Perera 69; K. C. A. Weerasinghe four for 55, M. D. K. Perera four for 60); Panadura* 329 (M. D. K. Perera 31, K. R. R. K. Wimalasena 97, J. S. K. Peiris 84, G. A. S. Perera 69; P. K. Siriwardene five for 49) and 29 for one.

At Maitland Place, Colombo (NCC), January 26, 27, 28. Drawn. Nondescripts* 326 for seven dec. (R. P. Hewage 33, M. N. Nawaz 70, H. P. Tillekeratne 107 not out, D. H. S. Pradeep 56; M. C. R. Fernando three for 97, H. M. R. K. B. Herath three for 104) and 205 for five (R. R. Tissera 56, R. P. Hewage 94; H. M. R. K. B. Herath four for 39); Moors 187 (R. G. D. Sanjeewa 37, M. N. R. Cooray 86; M. K. D. I. Amerasinghe three for 22, C. M. Bandara five for 58).

Umpire Pathirana called Moors opening bowler P. N. Ranjith for throwing.

At Maitland Place, Colombo (SSC), January 26, 27, 28. Drawn. Sinhalese 314 for five dec. (W. M. S. M. Perera 58, A. Ranatunga 46, T. T. Samaraweera 69 not out, P. H. M. G. Fernando 61 not out, Extras 37) and 353 for five (W. M. S. M. Perera 54, S. Ranatunga 131, R. P. A. H. Wickremaratne 54, A. Ranatunga 40, T. T. Samaraweera 30 not out); Singha* 191 (H. S. G. S. Silva 30, H. Rajapakse 67 not out; M. A. M. Aslam three for 53, T. T. Samaraweera six for 55).

At P. Saravanamuttu Stadium, Colombo, January 26, 27, 28. Tamil Union won by nine wickets. Navy 53 (A. Rideegammanagedera five for eight, K. L. S. L. Dias three for 16) and 190 (M. M. Perera 30, G. L. Hewage 73 not out; A. Rideegammanagedera three for 42, K. L. S. L. Dias three for 44); Tamil Union* 196 (W. M. G. Ramyakumara 32, M. K. Gajanayake 59; M. M. Perera four for 35, A. R. M. S. Ranaweera three for 60) and 48 for one (W. M. G. Ramyakumara 31 not out).

Rideegammanagedera's first-innings analysis was 9–4–8–5.

At FTZ Sports Complex, Katunayake, February 2, 3, 4. Drawn. Antonians 107 (W. R. S. de Silva six for 35) and 185 for seven (W. A. L. Chaturanga 70; P. L. U. Irandika three for 44); Sebastianites* 304 for nine dec. (W. N. de Silva 107, K. A. D. M. Fernando 59 not out; L. H. D. Dilhara three for 72, S. Chandana three for 100).

At Braybrooke Place, Colombo (Moors), February 2, 3, 4. Drawn. Singha 359 (Y. M. W. B. Ekanayake 69, S. Jayantha 66, H. W. M. Kumara 43, R. N. Weerasinghe 50, H. Rajapakse 43; H. M. R. K. B. Herath three for 91, M. C. R. Fernando five for 114) and 170 for nine (H. S. G. S. Silva 31, S. Jayantha 39, I. C. Soysa 33; M. N. R. Cooray four for nine); Moors* 223 (R. G. D. Sanjeewa 55, W. M. B. Perera 38, D. W. A. N. D. Vitharana 40; S. Jayantha four for 61, H. Rajapakse three for 36).

At Maitland Place, Colombo (NCC), February 2, 3, 4. Drawn. Panadura 305 (M. D. K. Perera 82, J. S. K. Peiris 31, K. R. R. K. Wimalasena 40, S. N. Liyanage 33, G. A. S. Perera 72; K. R. Pushpakumara three for 60, W. C. A. Ganegama three for 52, C. M. Bandara three for 55) and 68 for two (L. P. C. Silva 50 not out); Nondescripts* 413 for eight dec. (R. R. Tissera 53, R. P. Hewage 200 not out, H. P. Tillekeratne 37, C. M. Bandara 31; G. A. S. Perera three for 104).

Hewage's 200 not out lasted 495 minutes and 435 balls and included 22 fours.

At Maitland Place, Colombo (SSC), February 2, 3, 4. Sinhalese won by 147 runs. Sinhalese 310 for seven dec. (W. M. S. M. Perera 35, R. P. A. H. Wickremaratne 121, T. T. Samaraweera 74, S. H. S. M. K. Silva 30 not out; M. M. Perera four for 74) and 88 (G. I. Daniel 34; M. M. Perera four for 32, B. W. D. M. M. Dissanayake five for 29); Navy* 184 (H. S. S. M. K. Weerasiri 68; T. T. Samaraweera four for 72, D. G. R. Dhammika three for 15) and 67 (S. H. S. M. K. Silva four for 12, T. T. Samaraweera three for 16).

At Kadirana Cricket Grounds, Gampaha, February 9, 10, 11. Singha won by 32 runs. Singha 132 (Y. M. W. B. Ekanayake 34; S. Chandana four for 29) and 256 (Y. M. W. B. Ekanayake 69, S. Jayantha 86, I. C. Soysa 52; S. Chandana five for 85); Antonians* 181 (S. Jayantha three for 29, H. Rajapakse three for 52, R. A. D. C. Perera three for 48) and 175 (P. K. Siriwardene 84, W. A. L. Chaturanga 34; R. A. D. C. Perera five for 41).

At Braybrooke Place, Colombo (Moors), February 9, 10, 11. Sinhalese won by nine wickets. Moors* 133 (M. S. Sampan 40; S. H. S. M. K. Silva four for 30) and 159 (M. S. Sampan 34, W. M. B. Perera 51 not out; D. G. R. Dhammika four for 43, S. H. S. M. K. Silva four for 63); Sinhalese 252 (S. Ranatunga 66, U. A. Fernando 34, A. S. A. Perera 78; M. C. R. Fernando five for 84, H. M. R. K. B. Herath four for 72) and 41 for one.

At Maitland Place, Colombo (NCC), February 9, 10, 11. Drawn. Tamil Union* 269 (P. S. A. N. Shiroman 31, G. R. P. Peiris 30, S. I. de Saram 86, O. C. Warnapura 40 not out; W. C. A. Ganegama three for 60, C. M. Bandara four for 75) and 234 for seven (G. R. P. Peiris 54, P. S. A. N. Shiroman 32, A. Rideegammanagedera 53 not out; C. M. Bandara five for 86); Nondescripts 324 (R. R. Tissera 45, R. P. Hewage 68, C. P. Mapatuna 44, T. A. Weerappuli 63; M. R. C. N. Bandaratilleke three for 90, K. L. S. L. Dias five for 59).

At Panadura Esplanade, Panadura, February 9, 10, 11. Drawn. Sebastianites* 236 (N. G. Peiris 46, K. A. D. J. Siriwardene 73, M. M. D. N. R. G. Perera 41; T. C. B. Fernando five for 43, M. D. K. Perera three for 34) and 266 (K. A. D. J. Siriwardene 31, M. M. D. N. R. G. Perera 34, G. N. Silva 57; K. C. A. Weerasinghe three for 22, G. A. S. Perera three for 64); Panadura 307 (R. H. T. A. Perera 95, J. S. K. Peiris 69, T. C. B. Fernando 37 not out, G. A. S. Perera 37, Extras 36; K. A. D. M. Fernando four for 67, M. M. D. N. R. G. Perera three for 114) and 182 for seven (G. A. S. Perera 34; M. N. T. H. Kumara four for 48).

At Braybrooke Place, Colombo (Moors), February 16, 17, 18. Antonians won by six wickets. Navy 136 (A. K. I. N. Perera 41, D. T. Ariyadasa 50; L. H. D. Dilhara three for 43, S. Chandana three for 37) and 226 (M. M. Perera 44, H. S. S. M. K. Weerasiri 52; S. Chandana eight for 85); Antonians* 226 (P. K. Siriwardene 54, W. A. L. Chaturanga 44, L. H. D. Dilhara 43; A. R. M. S. Ranaweera four for 74) and 137 for four (P. K. Siriwardene 42, W. A. L. Chaturanga 38 not out, S. Chandana 31 not out).

At Maitland Place, Colombo (NCC), February 16, 17, 18. Drawn. Nondescripts* 231 (T. A. Weerappuli 37, K. L. S. Gamage 57, C. D. C. Rupasinghe 42 not out; W. R. S. de Silva five for 53, G. N. Silva three for 49) and 208 (R. R. Tissera 55, M. N. Nawaz 63; M. M. D. N. R. G. Perera eight for 24); Sebastianites 153 (H. G. P. Ranaweera 35; W. C. A. Ganegama five for 34) and 204 for seven (D. N. Jayakody 61, R. R. Jaymon 63).

At Panadura Esplanade, Panadura, February 16, 17, 18. Drawn. Panadura* 233 (M. D. K. Perera 45, L. V. V. Silva 50, G. A. S. Perera 39; M. I. Abdeen four for 44, H. M. R. K. B. Herath three for 37) and 221 for eight (M. D. K. Perera 105, L. P. C. Silva 35; H. M. R. K. B. Herath five for 33); Moors 220 (M. S. Sampan 60; G. A. S. Perera six for 54).

At P. Saravanamuttu Stadium, Colombo, February 16, 17, 18. Tamil Union won by 188 runs. Tamil Union* 237 (W. M. G. Ramyakumara 88, M. K. Gajanayake 34, A. Rideegammanagedera 33; R. C. R. P. Silva six for 65) and 232 (P. S. A. N. Shiroman 31, S. I. de Saram 55, E. M. I. Galagoda 33, O. C. Warnapura 31, D. P. S. Jayaratne 43; R. A. D. C. Perera five for 60); Singha 59 (W. M. G. Ramyakumara seven for 25) and 222 (H. W. M. Kumara 48, S. Jayantha 32, I. C. Soysa 41, R. N. Weerasinghe 39; W. M. G. Ramyakumara three for 61, K. L. S. L. Dias four for 48).

At Kadirana Cricket Grounds, Gampaha, February 23, 24, 25. Drawn. Tamil Union* 499 for seven dec. (W. M. G. Ramyakumara 108, G. R. P. Peiris 134, A. Rideegammanagedera 120, M. K. Gajanayake 48, Extras 36) and 214 for five (O. C. Warnapura 57, G. R. P. Peiris 114); Antonians 184 (W. A. L. Chaturanga 30, P. K. R. P. Fernando 34 not out, L. H. D. Dilhara 42; D. P. S. Jayaratne three for 20, M. R. C. N. Bandaratilleke four for 53).

Peiris scored a hundred in each innings.

At De Zoysa Stadium, Moratuwa, February 23, 24. Sebastianites won by ten wickets. Navy 110 (K. A. D. M. Fernando three for 51, W. R. S. de Silva six for 23) and 122 (A. K. I. N. Perera 43; M. M. D. N. R. G. Perera four for 46, K. A. D. M. Fernando three for five); Sebastianites* 232 for eight dec. (N. G. Peiris 38, D. N. Jayakody 62, K. A. D. J. Siriwardene 34, R. R. Jaymon 43; A. R. M. S. Ranaweera three for 77) and one for no wkt.

At Maitland Place, Colombo (SSC), February 23, 24, 25. Sinhalese won by an innings and one run. Sinhalese* 426 for five dec. (D. A. Gunawardene 69, R. P. A. H. Wickremaratne 108, U. A. Fernando 128, A. Ranatunga 53 not out); Panadura 167 (K. R. R. K. Wimalasena 56 not out; S. H. S. M. K. Silva six for 28, T. T. Samaraweera three for 53) and 258 (R. H. T. A. Perera 53, M. D. K. Perera 42, T. C. B. Fernando 81, K. R. R. K. Wimalasena 31; G. P. Wickremasinghe five for 22).

At Braybrooke Place, Colombo (Moors), March 2, 3, 4. Drawn. Antonians* 337 (W. A. L. Chaturanga 44, C. K. Hewamanne 71, R. A. T. D. Perera 32, L. H. D. Dilhara 61; M. N. R. Cooray three for 50, R. G. D. Sanjeewa three for 41) and 138 (R. G. D. Sanjeewa three for 42, M. C. R. Fernando three for 34); Moors 310 (R. G. D. Sanjeewa 77, C. Hewawitharana 37, M. C. R. Fernando 92, M. F. A. Farhath 34; S. Chandana four for 98) and 82 for two (M. N. R. Cooray 31 not out).

At Maitland Place, Colombo (NCC), March 2, 3, 4. Drawn. Sinhalese 209 (G. I. Daniel 33, H. A. P. W. Jayawardene 70, A. S. A. Perera 31; M. K. D. I. Amerasinghe three for 63, C. M. Bandara three for 42) and 250 for nine dec. (W. M. S. M. Perera 50, S. Ranatunga 75, P. H. M. G. Fernando 30; W. C. A. Ganegama five for 46); Nondescripts* 233 (R. R. Tissera 43, R. P. Hewage 41, T. A. Weerappuli 32; S. H. S. M. K. Silva seven for 52) and 174 for seven (T. A. Weerappuli 76 not out, K. L. S. Gamage 31; G. P. Wickremasinghe three for 44).

At Panadura Esplanade, Panadura, March 2, 3, 4. Tamil Union won by 195 runs. Tamil Union* 278 (P. S. A. N. Shiroman 44, W. M. G. Ramyakumara 46, A. Rideegammanagedera 30, O. C. Warnapura 36, M. R. C. N. Bandaratilleke 39; G. A. S. Perera four for 102) and 242 for eight dec. (P. S. A. N. Shiroman 43, W. M. G. Ramyakumara 80 not out; G. A. S. Perera three for 68, J. S. K. Peiris three for 45); Panadura 175 (W. P. Wickrama 44, J. S. K. Peiris 79; W. M. G. Ramyakumara three for 34, M. R. C. N. Bandaratilleke four for 52) and 150 (G. A. S. Perera 32; K. L. S. L. Dias six for 47).

At De Zoysa Stadium, Moratuwa, March 2, 3. Sebastianites won by an innings and 64 runs. Singha 123 (H. W. M. Kumara 39; K. A. D. M. Fernando five for 62) and 196 (H. S. G. S. Silva 38, M. T. T. Mirando 75; K. A. D. M. Fernando five for 74, W. R. S. de Silva three for 62); Sebastianites* 383 (N. G. Peiris 86, W. N. de Silva 85, M. M. D. N. R. G. Perera 113, Extras 39; R. A. D. C. Perera four for 106, S. Jayantha five for 74).

At Braybrooke Place, Colombo (Moors), March 9, 10, 11. Navy won by five wickets. Singha* 165 (R. N. Weerasinghe 73; A. A. I. Dinuka three for 32) and 229 (H. W. M. Kumara 39, T. J. Madanayake 56; A. R. M. S. Ranaweera seven for 70); Navy 264 (H. S. S. M. K. Weerasiri 36, G. L. Hewage 34, H. G. S. P. Fernando 82, A. R. M. S. Ranaweera 46 not out, Extras 39; I. C. Soysa three for 26, H. Rajapakse three for 31) and 131 for five (H. S. S. M. K. Weerasiri 52 not out).

Navy's first win, after seven defeats.

Nondescripts, Sinhalese, Tamil Union and Panadura qualified for the Super League.

Super League

At Maitland Crescent, Colombo (CCC), April 6, 7, 8. Drawn. Nondescripts* 376 for nine dec. (M. N. Nawaz 97, P. A. de Silva 83, T. A. Weerappuli 33, H. P. Tillekeratne 42, C. M. Bandara 37 not out, K. R. Pushpakumara 39; H. S. H. Alles three for 84, K. K. K. Gangodawila three for 50); Bloomfield 148 (R. S. Kalpage three for 38, P. A. de Silva three for 50, C. M. Bandara three for 17) and 25 for one.

At Havelock Park, Colombo (Colts), April 6, 7, 8. Burgher won by an innings and 62 runs. Panadura 101 (R. H. T. A. Perera 62; P. W. Gunaratne seven for 25, S. Weerakoon three for 23) and 104 (S. Weerakoon seven for 51); Burgher* 267 (B. C. M. S. Mendis 47, V. S. K. Waragoda 36, K. S. C. de Silva 74; T. C. B. Fernando four for 61, G. A. S. Perera three for 72).

At Maitland Place, Colombo (NCC), April 6, 7, 8. Drawn. Colombo 373 (D. N. Hunukumbura 49, S. K. L. de Silva 164 not out, A. S. Polonowita 37; P. D. R. L. Perera four for 93, M. A. M. Aslam three for 105); Sinhalese* 108 (D. A. Gunawardene 39, H. A. P. W. Jayawardene 32; M. S. Villavarayen five for 41, J. W. H. D. Boteju three for 21) and 45 for two.

At Havelock Park, Colombo (BRC), April 6, 7, 8. Drawn. Colts* 234 (D. P. Samaraweera 47, H. G. J. M. Kulatunga 98; W. M. G. Ramyakumara three for 26, K. L. S. L. Dias three for 44); Tamil Union 227 for nine (G. R. P. Peiris 61, A. Rideegammanagedera 35; D. K. Liyanage three for 36, D. Hettiarachchi six for 80).

At Maitland Place, Colombo (SSC), April 20, 21, 22. Bloomfield won by ten wickets. Tamil Union* 126 (B. C. Jeganathan 52; R. S. A. Palliyaguruge four for 25) and 160 (A. L. D. M. Deshapriya 30, P. S. A. N. Shiroman 36, M. K. Gajanayake 69; H. S. H. Alles four for 40, S. D. Dissanayake three for 30); Bloomfield 266 for eight dec. (S. Rodrigo 48, P. B. Dassanayake 72 not out, S. D. Dissanayake 33 not out) and 21 for no wkt.

At Havelock Park, Colombo (Colts), April 20, 21, 22. Burgher won by three wickets. Sinhalese 190 (G. I. Daniel 39, R. P. A. H. Wickremaratne 105; P. W. Gunaratne three for 49, S. Weerakoon four for 58) and 116 (R. P. A. H. Wickremaratne 33; S. Weerakoon six for 34); Burgher* 117 (R. H. S. Silva 46 not out, S. Weerakoon 34; P. D. R. L. Perera seven for 40) and 191 for seven (B. C. M. S. Mendis 39, N. S. Bopage 58; M. A. M. Aslam five for 50).

At P. Saravanamuttu Stadium, Colombo, April 20, 21, 22. Drawn. Panadura 152 (W. P. Wickrama 60; J. W. H. D. Boteju three for 22, N. S. Rajan four for 65) and 274 (L. P. C. Silva 61, G. A. S. Perera 55, S. N. Liyanage 36; R. M. A. R. Ratnayake three for 38, N. S. Rajan four for 70); Colombo* 158 (R. M. A. R. Ratnayake 31; T. C. B. Fernando three for 29, M. D. K. Perera three for 39) and 154 for nine (B. M. T. T. Mendis 40 not out, Extras 31; G. A. S. Perera three for 48).

At Panadura Esplanade, Panadura, April 20, 21, 22. Drawn. Colts 181 (W. C. S. Kumara 48; M. K. D. I. Amerasinghe five for 34, R. S. Kalpage three for 39) and 56 for five (M. K. D. I. Amerasinghe three for 14); Nondescripts* 229 for three dec. (R. R. Tissera 31, R. P. Hewage 89, M. N. Nawaz 65 not out).

The last two sessions of the opening day were lost because of a VIP's helicopter landing on the ground.

At P. Saravanamuttu Stadium, Colombo, April 27, 28, 29. Drawn. Bloomfield 212 (Y. S. S. Mendis 54, Extras 38; G. A. S. Perera three for 61, M. D. K. Perera three for 60) and 183 (S. D. Abeynayake 33, S. H. T. Kandamby 43, H. D. P. K. Dharmasena 38; M. D. K. Perera five for 42); Panadura* 180 (J. S. K. Peiris 62 not out; H. S. H. Alles four for 17) and 120 for nine (L. P. C. Silva 38; H. D. P. K. Dharmasena four for ten).

At Maitland Place, Colombo (SSC), April 27, 28, 29. Drawn. Nondescripts 372 (P. A. de Silva 55, H. P. Tillekeratne 185 not out, C. M. Bandara 63, K. R. Pushpakumara 43; K. S. C. de Silva four for 66, S. Weerakoon three for 105); Burgher* 125 (M. K. D. I. Amerasinghe four for 39, P. A. de Silva five for 53) and 79 for seven (C. M. Bandara three for 26).

At Reid Avenue, Colombo, April 27, 28, 29. Drawn. Colombo 301 for eight dec. (M. G. van Dort 102, S. K. L. de Silva 112; A. Rideegammanagedera three for 62); Tamil Union* 23 for two.

At Maitland Place, Colombo (NCC), April 27, 28, 29. Drawn. Sinhalese 170 (R. P. A. H. Wickremaratne 32, U. A. Fernando 38, T. T. Samaraweera 32; K. E. A. Upashantha three for 33, D. K. Liyanage three for 38); Colts* 196 for eight (K. M. H. Perera 62 not out; P. D. R. L. Perera three for 50, T. T. Samaraweera three for 34).

At Maitland Crescent, Colombo (CCC), May 4, 5, 6. Sinhalese won by ten wickets. Bloomfield 88 (T. T. Samaraweera four for 16) and 222 (S. D. Abeynayake 46, Extras 33); Sinhalese* 300 (W. M. S. M. Perera 51, D. P. M. D. Jayawardene 57, R. P. A. H. Wickremaratne 32, T. T. Samaraweera 65; R. S. A. Palliyaguruge three for 33) and 12 for no wkt.

At Panadura Esplanade, Panadura, May 4, 5, 6. Drawn. Tamil Union* 314 (S. I. de Saram 86, U. D. U. Chandana 40, B. C. Jeganathan 32, M. R. C. N. Bandaratilleke 49; K. S. C. de Silva three for 54, S. Weerakoon six for 133) and 182 (S. I. de Saram 32, U. D. U. Chandana 48; K. S. C. de Silva three for 43, S. Weerakoon six for 79); Burgher 217 (R. H. S. Silva 53, V. S. K. Waragoda 32, C. U. Jayasinghe 49, C. P. Handunnettige 38; M. R. C. N. Bandaratilleke three for 58, U. D. U. Chandana four for 31) and 98 for two (B. C. M. S. Mendis 35, R. H. S. Silva 36 not out).

Weerakoon took 12 for 212 in the match.

At Reid Avenue, Colombo, May 4, 5, 6. Nondescripts won by three wickets. Colombo* 246 (A. S. Polonowita 86, J. Mubarak 48, B. M. T. T. Mendis 43; W. C. A. Ganegama four for 70) and 141 (K. P. P. B. Seneviratne 34, A. S. Polonowita 33; R. S. Kalpage seven for 27); Nondescripts 245 (T. A. Weerappuli 44, H. P. Tillekeratne 48, R. S. Kalpage 41, C. M. Bandara 32) and 143 for seven (M. N. Nawaz 57, R. S. Kalpage 31 not out; J. W. H. D. Boteju three for 31).

Victory gave Nondescripts the Premier Trophy.

At Havelock Park, Colombo (BRC), May 4, 5, 6. Drawn. Panadura 257 (M. D. K. Perera 38, W. P. Wickrama 91, S. N. Liyanage 65; D. K. Liyanage four for 63, M. Pushpakumara four for 52) and 282 for four (M. D. K. Perera 66, L. P. C. Silva 46, J. S. K. Peiris 106 not out, K. R. R. K. Wimalasena 50 not out); Colts* 370 (S. Kalawithigoda 39, C. Mendis 80, K. M. H. Perera 44, H. G. J. M. Kulatunga 52, M. Pushpakumara 69; G. A. S. Perera four for 97, J. S. K. Peiris four for 35).

CHAMPIONS

Lakspray Trophy

1988-89	Nondescripts CC / Sinhalese SC
1989-90	Sinhalese SC

P. Saravanamuttu Trophy

1990-91	Sinhalese SC
1991-92	Colts CC
1992-93	Sinhalese SC
1993-94	Nondescripts CC
1994-95	Bloomfield C and AC / Sinhalese SC
1995-96	Colombo CC
1996-97	Bloomfield C and AC
1997-98	Sinhalese SC

Premier Trophy

1998-99	Bloomfield C and AC
1999-2000	Colts CC
2000-01	Nondescripts CC

Plate Championship

At Air Force Ground, Katunayake, April 6, 7, 8. Drawn. Air Force* 178 (W. R. D. Dissanayake 32, W. R. Fernando 31; L. H. D. Dilhara three for 34, P. K. R. P. Fernando three for 22); Antonians 32 for two.

At Braybrooke Place, Colombo (Moors), April 6, 7, 8. Drawn. Galle 111 (T. K. D. Sudarshana 50; P. N. Ranjith three for 33, H. M. R. K. B. Herath five for 18) and 121 for nine (T. K. D. Sudarshana 62; H. M. R. K. B. Herath three for 16); Moors* 255 for eight dec. (U. C. Hathurusinghe 56, M. C. R. Fernando 60 not out; W. M. P. N. Wanasinghe three for 79, M. H. A. Jabbar three for 44).

At Reid Avenue, Colombo, April 6, 7, 8. Drawn. Kurunegala Youth 264 (H. M. Maduwantha 93, R. H. Sureshchandra 43, G. S. P. Dharmapala 41; M. M. Perera three for 44) and 104 for six (W. T. de Silva 41, H. M. Maduwantha 38; M. M. Perera three for 25); Navy* 179 (H. S. S. M. K. Weerasiri 64; J. A. M. W. Kumara three for 31, A. W. Ekanayake four for 56).

At Air Force Ground, Katunayake, April 20, 21. Air Force won by an innings and 24 runs. Singha 118 (M. K. G. C. P. Lakshitha six for 51, W. R. D. Dissanayake four for 29) and 116 (M. R. Porage 38, Y. M. W. B. Ekanayake 37; W. C. R. Tissera three for 26, W. R. D. Dissanayake four for 18); Air Force* 258 (S. E. D. R. Fernando 83, K. R. P. Silva 32, Extras 33; I. Dilshan five for 71).

At Braybrooke Place, Colombo (Moors), April 20, 21, 22. Kurunegala Youth won by 167 runs. Kurunegala Youth* 180 (H. M. S. Jayawardene 90; P. N. Ranjith four for 39) and 219 (K. D. Gunawardene 47, H. M. S. Jayawardene 45; H. M. R. K. B. Herath three for 48); Moors 99 (J. A. M. W. Kumara four for 26) and 133 (J. A. M. W. Kumara three for nine, A. W. Ekanayake three for 39).

At Police Park, Colombo, April 20, 21, 22. Police won by 26 runs. Police 211 (C. N. Liyanage 43, I. D. Gunawardene 57; M. M. Perera six for 40) and 94 (S. Senadeera three for 14); Navy* 130 (H. S. S. M. K. Weerasiri 44) and 149 (H. S. S. M. K. Weerasiri 80; I. D. Gunawardene five for 28, H. P. A. Priyantha three for 38).

Navy wicket-keeper S. M. A. K. S. Kumara took eight catches in the match.

At Galle International Stadium, Galle, April 21, 22, 23. Drawn. Galle* 170 (T. K. D. Sudarshana 35, H. S. S. Fonseka 35; S. Chandana seven for 76) and 279 for seven dec. (T. K. D. Sudarshana 49, C. M. Withanage 51, I. C. D. Perera 80, D. D. Wickremasinghe 47 not out; L. H. D. Dilhara three for 67, S. Chandana four for 115); Antonians 200 (K. A. D. C. Silva 66; M. M. D. P. V. Perera six for 46) and 100 for seven (C. K. Hewamanne 36 not out; M. M. D. P. V. Perera four for 33).

At Uyanwatte Stadium, Matara, April 21, 22, 23. Matara won by two wickets. Sebastianites* 242 (G. E. Randiligama 47, M. M. D. N. R. G. Perera 55, W. S. H. Fernando 35; N. C. Komasaru four for 56) and 175 (W. N. de Silva 32; M. A. P. Salgado three for 54, P. I. W. Jayasekera three for 29); Matara 307 (N. H. V. Chinthaka 95, B. A. R. S. Priyadarshana 55, S. M. Ramzan 39, Extras 45; M. N. T. H. Kumara three for 88, P. L. U. Irandika three for 33) and 111 for eight (H. A. H. U. Tillekeratne 31, S. W. N. D. Chinthaka 32; P. L. U. Irandika six for 28).

At Air Force Ground, Katunayake, April 27, 28, 29. Drawn. Air Force 118 (T. R. Peiris 34; K. A. D. M. Fernando four for 28) and 159 for eight (P. T. S. Fernando 31, W. R. Fernando 49; M. M. D. N. R. G. Perera four for 17); Sebastianites* 182 (G. E. Randiligama 43, R. R. Jaymon 32; M. K. G. C. P. Lakshitha three for 65).

At Galle International Stadium, Galle, April 27, 28, 29. Drawn. Singha 227 (Y. M. W. B. Ekanayake 30, S. Jayantha 39, R. N. Weerasinghe 86; C. P. H. Ramanayake four for 53, K. G. Perera four for 65) and 194 (H. W. M. Kumara 30; C. P. H. Ramanayake three for 46, C. M. Withanage four for 25, M. M. D. P. V. Perera three for 54); Galle* 267 (C. M. Withanage 31, P. A. R. C. Karunasena 45, M. M. D. P. V. Perera 59, Extras 31; O. L. A. Wijesiriwardene three for 33, I. Dilshan three for 47) and two for no wkt.

At Welagedera Stadium, Kurunegala, April 27, 28, 29. Antonians won by four wickets. Kurunegala Youth* 151 (K. D. Gunawardene 34, R. H. Sureshchandra 31; P. K. R. P. Fernando three for 30, S. Chandana four for 34) and 140 for four dec.; Antonians 148 (W. M. J. Wannukuwatta 43; J. A. M. W. Kumara four for 34, A. W. Ekanayake five for 52) and 144 for six (P. K. Siriwardene 71, S. Chandana 30 not out).

At Braybrooke Place, Colombo (Moors), April 27, 28, 29. Drawn. Police* 145 (S. A. Wijeratne 46; M. C. R. Fernando four for 25) and 181 (H. P. A. Priyantha 43, S. A. Wijeratne 52; M. C. R. Fernando four for 68, M. N. R. Cooray four for 34); Moors 152 (D. W. A. N. D. Vitharana 51; T. A. V. H. K. Ranaweera five for 36, W. T. Abeyratne three for 26) and 62 for no wkt.

At R. Premadasa Stadium, Colombo, April 27, 28, 29. Drawn. Matara 195 (N. H. V. Chinthaka 32, K. A. S. Jayasinghe 31, S. M. Ramzan 37; A. A. I. Dinuka four for 64, H. G. S. P. Fernando four for 44) and 202 for eight dec. (H. A. H. U. Tillekeratne 75, S. W. N. D. Chinthaka 36, B. A. R. S. Priyadarshana 31; A. K. I. N. Perera four for 32); Navy* 99 (B. A. R. S. Priyadarshana five for 30, M. A. P. Salgado three for 20) and 133 for five (A. K. I. N. Perera 54; M. A. P. Salgado four for 41).

At De Zoysa Stadium, Moratuwa, May 3, 4, 5. Drawn. Sebastianites 307 (N. G. Peiris 53, W. S. H. Fernando 62, Extras 38; N. N. N. Nanayakkara four for 83, M. M. D. P. V. Perera four for 74) and 134 (C. P. H. Ramanayake three for 39, M. M. D. P. V. Perera five for 47); Galle* 209 (T. K. D. Sudarshana 70, P. A. R. C. Karunasena 40; K. A. D. M. Fernando seven for 67) and 66 for two (C. M. Withanage 36).

At Air Force Ground, Katunayake, May 4, 5, 6. Navy won by 131 runs. Navy 214 (H. S. S. M. K. Weerasiri 47, K. K. P. K. Anthony 46, H. G. S. P. Fernando 37; M. K. G. C. P. Lakshitha three for 54) and 220 (M. M. Perera 50, H. S. S. M. K. Weerasiri 107; M. K. G. C. P. Lakshitha six for 41, P. T. S. Fernando three for 63); Air Force* 142 (T. R. Peiris 31, Extras 30; H. G. S. P. Fernando six for 37) and 161 (W. R. D. Dissanayake 35, H. P. I. Dilhan 31; M. M. Perera three for 26, H. S. S. M. K. Weerasiri six for 25).

At Welagedera Stadium, Kurunegala, May 4, 5, 6. Kurunegala Youth won by three wickets. Singha* 123 (M. P. G. D. P. Gunatilleke four for 41) and 186 (H. W. M. Kumara 56, R. N. Weerasinghe 37); Kurunegala Youth 175 (B. M. S. N. Mendis 32; S. Jayantha five for 54, I. Dilshan four for 55) and 135 for seven (A. W. Ekanayake 57).

At Braybrooke Place, Colombo (Moors), May 4, 5, 6. Moors won by 46 runs. Moors* 148 (U. C. Hathurusinghe 34, D. W. A. N. D. Vitharana 52; S. M. Ramzan three for eight) and 229 (R. G. D. Sanjeewa 41, U. C. Hathurusinghe 56, M. N. R. Cooray 59; B. A. R. S. Priyadarshana four for 36, N. C. Komasaru four for 52); Matara 113 (K. A. S. Jayasinghe 34; P. N. Ranjith five for 42) and 218 (S. W. N. D. Chinthaka 32, S. M. Ramzan 112; P. N. Ranjith three for 42, U. C. Hathurusinghe four for 40).

At FTZ Sports Complex, Katunayake, May 11, 12, 13. Drawn. Kurunegala Youth* 252 (K. D. Gunawardene 62, H. P. K. Rajapakse 45, H. M. Maduwantha 50; K. A. D. M. Fernando three for 76, M. M. D. N. R. G. Perera five for 69) and 234 for five (H. P. K. Rajapakse 98 not out, R. H. Sureshchandra 63); Sebastianites 314 (D. N. Jayakody 42, G. E. Randiligama 41, W. N. de Silva 74, M. M. D. N. R. G. Perera 32, S. A. L. J. Fernando 35; A. W. Ekanayake eight for 93).

At Galle International Stadium, Galle, May 11, 12, 13. Drawn. Singha 179 (H. W. M. Kumara 44; N. H. Tennekoon three for 46, W. N. M. Soysa three for 22) and 250 for nine dec. (A. S. Wewalwala 125, R. N. Weerasinghe 39; W. T. Abeyratne three for 35); Police* 127 (M. T. T. Mirando three for 29, I. Dilshan four for 22) and 239 for six (H. P. A. Priyantha 59, C. N. Liyanage 65 not out, W. N. M. Soysa 33, W. T. Abeyratne 30 not out; M. T. T. Mirando three for 43).

At Air Force Ground, Katunayake, May 12, 13, 14. Moors won by nine wickets. Air Force* 117 (M. K. G. C. P. Lakshitha 44; P. N. Ranjith three for 16, H. M. R. K. B. Herath three for 35) and 112 (H. M. R. K. B. Herath four for 19, M. N. R. Cooray three for 13); Moors 182 (M. S. Sampan 61, M. C. R. Fernando 47 not out; M. K. G. C. P. Lakshitha three for 50, W. R. D. Dissanayake four for 43) and 48 for one.

At R. Premadasa Stadium, Colombo, May 12, 13, 14. Antonians won by 28 runs. Antonians* 135 (K. A. S. Jayasinghe three for 34, N. C. Komasaru four for 26) and 100 (P. K. Siriwardene 42; N. C. Komasaru five for 11); Matara 80 (K. A. S. Jayasinghe 32; R. A. T. D. Perera three for 28, S. Chandana three for 31) and 127 (H. A. H. U. Tillekeratne 35, S. W. K. Shantha 46 not out; S. Chandana five for 52).

At Reid Avenue, Colombo, May 12, 13, 14. Drawn. Galle* 285 (C. M. Withanage 30, I. C. D. Perera 41, P. A. R. C. Karunasena 48, M. K. P. B. Kularatne 35, Extras 38) and 226 for seven dec. (C. M. Withanage 68, C. P. H. Ramanayake 100; B. W. D. M. M. Dissanayake four for 42); Navy 159 (G. L. Hewage 39; K. G. Perera five for 45) and 154 for nine (A. K. I. N. Perera 37, S. M. A. K. S. Kumara 43; K. G. Perera three for 29, M. M. D. P. V. Perera five for 72).

At Uyanwatte Stadium, Matara, May 18, 19, 20. Matara won by five runs. Matara 279 (N. H. V. Chinthaka 40, H. A. H. U. Tillekeratne 35, E. F. M. U. Fernando 75 not out, Extras 36; T. J. Madanayake three for 60) and 122 (E. F. M. U. Fernando 30; M. T. T. Mirando five for 40); Singha* 204 (A. S. Wewalwala 31, H. W. M. Kumara 67; K. G. A. S. Kalum three for 45, S. M. Ramzan three for 46) and 192 (W. U. Tharanga 75, H. W. M. Kumara 32; P. I. W. Jayasekera five for 41).

At De Zoysa Stadium, Moratuwa, May 18, 19, 20. Sebastianites won by eight wickets. Police 166 (H. P. A. Priyantha 43, W. N. M. Soysa 44; K. A. D. M. Fernando four for 67, M. M. D. N. R. G. Perera three for 27) and 138 (K. A. D. M. Fernando six for 53); Sebastianites* 270 (M. M. D. N. R. G. Perera 54, W. S. H. Fernando 63, K. A. D. M. Fernando 56; W. N. M. Soysa five for 62) and 35 for two.

At Police Park, Colombo, May 23, 24, 25. Police won by four wickets. Antonians* 206 (P. K. Siriwardene 50, W. M. J. Wannukuwatta 61, L. H. D. Dilhara 42; T. A. V. H. K. Ranaweera four for 73, N. H. Tennekoon six for 65) and 167 (P. K. Siriwardene 44; W. T. Abeyratne three for 42); Police 140 (C. N. Liyanage 52; S. Chandana six for 65, K. A. D. C. Silva three for 15) and 236 for six (H. P. A. Priyantha 41, P. R. T. Fernando 72, W. N. M. Soysa 65).

Other First-Class Match

At Maitland Place, Colombo (SSC), September 27, 28, 29, 30. Gopalan Trophy: Drawn. Tamil Nadu 168 (S. Mahesh 41; P. D. R. L. Perera three for 38); Colombo District CA* 82 for two.

Play was possible only on the third day.

The first-class matches played by Pakistan A may be found in the Other A-Team Tours section.

PREMIER LIMITED-OVERS TOURNAMENT, 2000-01

Note: Matches in this section were not first-class.

Semi-finals

At R. Premadasa Stadium, Colombo, November 25 (day/night). Colts won by 44 runs. Colts* 174 (48.4 overs) (C. Mendis 35, H. G. J. M. Kulatunga 35, K. E. A. Upashantha 34; M. Muralitharan five for 15); Tamil Union 130 (46.3 overs) (G. R. P. Peiris 34; D. Hettiarachchi four for 29).

At R. Premadasa Stadium, Colombo, November 27. Sinhalese won by two runs. Sinhalese* 182 for eight (50 overs) (A. Ranatunga 36, R. P. A. H. Wickremaratne 49; J. W. H. D. Boteju three for 27); Colombo 180 for eight (50 overs) (R. S. Mahanama 42, A. S. Polonowita 46; T. T. Samaraweera three for 29).

Final

At R. Premadasa Stadium, Colombo, November 29 (day/night). Sinhalese won by eight wickets. Colts* 214 for eight (50 overs) (R. S. Kaluwitharana 49, D. P. Samaraweera 81 not out, K. Weeraratne 31 not out); Sinhalese 215 for two (35.3 overs) (M. S. Atapattu 113 not out, D. P. M. D. Jayawardene 83 not out).

CRICKET IN ZIMBABWE, 2000-01

By JOHN WARD

Hamilton Masakadza

A seemingly unending season of 11 months saw Zimbabwe play 11 Tests and 31 one-day internationals in six countries. They sometimes played dismally, sometimes fought hard but unavailingly, and now and then pulled off a superb victory. For the first time, Zimbabwe won three Tests in a season, two against Bangladesh, one against India, but there were also five defeats. They won nine and lost 22 one-day internationals.

A factor in their erratic form was the Zimbabwe Cricket Union's sacking of captain Andy Flower in August 2000. Since Alistair Campbell resigned the previous November, Flower had gradually restored discipline to a demoralised side, and scored nearly twice as many runs as anyone else on top of keeping wicket. No one in the modern game had successfully combined all three roles; Flower did, even if it did not always bring the desired results. The players believed his removal was a reprisal for his part in a threatened strike during the 2000 tour of England; the ZCU denied it.

Deeply hurt, Flower responded with his finest form ever. In nine Tests, he scored 1,066 runs at 88.83, and equalled Everton Weekes's record of seven consecutive fifties. When injury forced him out in June, it was his first break after 224 appearances – 52 Tests and 172 limited-overs internationals – since his century on debut against Sri Lanka in the 1991-92 World Cup. In July, the Federation of International Cricketers' Associations voted him Player of the Year.

Another grudge against the administrators spilled on to the field. Senior players were outraged by what they saw as political interference in selection; in September, vice-captain Guy Whittall actually withdrew from the First Test against New Zealand. In June, Heath Streak, Flower's successor as captain, briefly resigned until he and coach Carl Rackemann were added to the selectors' panel. In Zimbabwe's volatile political climate, there was much pressure for more "players of colour". Advocates failed to realise how long it could take to develop a cricket culture in the black population where none existed before 1980. The ZCU appointed a task force to investigate and eliminate discrimination; some saw it as a vehicle to fast-track on race rather than merit.

In fact, black players were emerging, suggesting patience would achieve more than quotas. Pace bowler Brighton Watambwa took 13 wickets in four Tests before limping off with a leg injury. Hamilton Masakadza began the Logan Cup season by becoming the youngest, and first black, Zimbabwean to score a first-class century. Against West Indies, he became Zimbabwe's youngest Test player and, at 17 years 354 days, briefly the youngest batsman to score a century on Test debut. In the same series, 18-year-old Tatenda Taibu kept wicket well, while his 35 first-class victims set a domestic record. Masakadza and Taibu were in their final year at Churchill High School in Harare; a schoolmate, Stuart Matsikenyeri, scored freely for Manicaland.

Two more developing players who made an impression were all-rounders Andy Blignaut and Mluleki Nkala. Blignaut, ambitious to fill a role for Zimbabwe similar to Lance Klusener's for South Africa, confounded those critics who felt he lacked the stomach for international cricket, but he did need greater consistency. Nkala, Zimbabwe's Young Sportsman of the Year, matured rapidly, but perhaps found the almost non-stop round of cricket wearing.

Of the old guard, Streak had easily his best Test season with the bat, scoring 571 to complete the double of 1,000 runs and 100 wickets; his bowling, however, declined. The attack relied heavily on him, especially with Paul Strang and Henry Olonga injured. Left-arm seamer Bryan Strang lost favour with selectors preferring pace to accuracy; he returned after Streak's protest, but "Pommie" Mbangwa was ignored. Opener Grant Flower struggled for form, was dropped to No. 6 in India – and hit a dashing hundred. Campbell finally struck his maiden Test century, in India, and made another when promoted to open against West Indies. In between, Guy Whittall opened with varying success.

The saddest event occurred in June, with the untimely death through cerebral malaria of Trevor Madondo, often described as Zimbabwe's most promising black batsman. Despite his somewhat undisciplined liftstyle, he had made encouraging progress in 2000-01, with a one-day 71 in India and 74 not out in the Wellington Test with New Zealand. And to universal regret, Rackemann, Zimbabwe's coach throughout the season, decided to return to Queensland. The ZCU lost no time in securing his former Test team-mate, Geoff Marsh, more recently Australia's coach, to replace him.

For the first time, Zimbabwe staged international cricket – against India and West Indies – during the winter months of June and July. The weather was drier than between November and March, but the cooler temperatures probably contributed to the injury rate. Moreover, the ball often swung and seamed sharply early on, giving the toss too much weight. Adult crowds were more or less as usual until the West Indian Tests, when it got colder. The ZCU regularly bused in over 1,000 children from development areas, greatly adding to the atmosphere as well as extending their horizons.

The domestic Logan Cup began in February when the national side returned after four months' touring. Heavy rains disrupted the first two rounds. Wisely, Zimbabwean cricket's main power base, Mashonaland, was allowed a second team; had there been a final, as in 1999-2000, it would have been between the two of them. The senior side, led by Grant Flower, won all five matches and undoubtedly benefited from playing four on Harare Sports Club's bowler-friendly pitches. Even so, it was a remarkable feat for Eddo Brandes and Bryan Strang to dismiss Matabeleland for 19 runs, only the second first-class total below 20 worldwide in the last 40 years. Brandes, turning 38 in probably his final season, looked as good as ever; though he was ignored by the selectors, the ZCU did award him a benefit. He took 21 wickets at an incredible 6.95 in the Logan Cup, while Strang picked up 24 at 9.62. Mashonaland's batting was sound, and they were seriously challenged only once, when a gallant Manicaland derailed their run-chase at 68 for seven but still lost by two wickets. While Mashonaland could field 11 internationals, Mashonaland A had ten. A strong attack featured the pace of Watambwa, Blignaut, David Mutendera and captain Everton Matambanadzo, backed by Dirk Viljoen's spin. Wet conditions handicapped their batsmen, but Trevor Gripper and Dion Ebrahim scored solidly.

Matabeleland began with an embarrassment of bowling riches, too: Streak, captain Mbangwa, Nkala, Olonga and John Rennie. But with Nkala losing form, Olonga injured and Rennie unavailable, their top bowler was left-arm spinner Ian Engelbrecht, the competition's leading wicket-taker with 25. Matabeleland showed their fighting spirit when, one match after collapsing for 19, they amassed 508 against the CFX Academy, including 168 from Nkala. The languid Mark Vermeulen scored 396 Logan Cup runs.

Manicaland, who lost the 1999-2000 final to Mashonaland, had a harder time; with the major provinces near full strength, their lack of depth showed. Gary Brent was outstanding, with 212 runs and 23 wickets in the competition, but wicket-keeper/opener and new captain Neil Ferreira found runs harder to score than the previous year.

Midlands also struggled, but were second to none for enthusiasm. They were led by Doug Marillier, who almost became a legend when his improvised strokeplay against Glenn McGrath so nearly won a one-day international in Perth. Marillier topped the Logan Cup aggregates with 412 runs, including two centuries, in four matches. Craig Wishart, transferred from Mashonaland, won a Test recall against West Indies, as did slow left-armer Raymond Price, also a stubborn opener. Travis Friend's bowling was limited by a stress fracture, but he made a hundred in the final game.

The CFX Academy, coached by former Test batsman Dave Houghton, lost all five matches, but this third Academy intake was younger than the first two, and plunged into first-class cricket almost at once. The Academy would benefit more if the Logan Cup could be staged in September and October; it might mean better weather, too. Their biggest success was Barney Rogers, who totalled 394 runs in the competition, and claimed eight wickets with off-spin. The uninhibited Guy Croxford also passed 200, while Ryan Butterworth scored their only century. Campbell Macmillan looked a promising pace bowler who could also bat.

In South Africa, the Zimbabwe Board XI reached the finals of both three-day and one-day UCBSA Bowl competitions. They lost the three-day game to Western Province B, whom they beat to win the one-day title.

Ground development remained a major part of the ZCU's plans, with Harare and Bulawayo due to host matches in the 2003 World Cup. Bulawayo, a ground that looked almost derelict a few years before, had been transformed, while the final phase at Harare Sports Club was to begin after England's visit in October. Indeed, cricket's continued development in a country in political and economic crisis has been remarkable. But the ZCU face a tough challenge in keeping the international players happy and running the sport free from political interference.

FIRST-CLASS AVERAGES, 2000-01

BATTING

(Qualification: 250 runs)

	M	*I*	*NO*	*R*	*HS*	*100s*	*Avge*
D. A. Marillier (*Midlands*)	5	10	1	496	132*	2	55.11
G. J. Whittall (*Manicaland*)	9	17	2	725	188*	2	48.33
B. G. Rogers (*CFX Academy*)	7	12	2	465	86	0	46.50
A. Flower (*Mashonaland*)	11	18	3	671	83	0	44.73
M. A. Vermeulen (*Matabeleland*)	7	12	1	483	180	1	43.90
H. Masakadza (*Mashonaland*)	10	15	0	554	119	2	36.93
S. V. Carlisle (*Mashonaland A*)	11	19	3	579	92	0	36.18
H. H. Streak (*Matabeleland*)	10	17	1	576	119	1	36.00
T. R. Gripper (*Mashonaland A*)	6	8	0	286	112	1	35.75
T. J. Friend (*Midlands*)	7	11	3	277	115	1	34.62
C. B. Wishart (*Midlands*)	9	17	1	552	151	1	34.50
G. W. Flower (*Mashonaland*)	13	22	1	684	86	0	32.57
G. B. Brent (*Manicaland*)	6	12	3	293	72*	0	32.55
A. D. R. Campbell (*Mashonaland*)	14	24	1	732	140	2	31.82
M. L. Nkala (*Matabeleland*)	14	21	4	508	168	1	29.88
G. M. Croxford (*CFX Academy*)	7	13	2	327	80	0	29.72
P. A. Strang (*Mashonaland*)	10	14	5	260	81*	0	28.88
D. D. Ebrahim (*Mashonaland A*)	14	21	0	560	90	0	26.66
A. M. Blignaut (*Mashonaland A*)	11	16	1	355	92	0	23.66
G. J. Rennie (*Mashonaland*)	12	21	2	404	79*	0	21.26

BOWLING

(Qualification: 10 wickets)

	O	*M*	*R*	*W*	*BB*	*5W/i*	*Avge*
E. A. Brandes (*Mashonaland*)	70.4	29	146	21	6-48	3	6.95
I. A. Engelbrecht (*Matabeleland*)	150.5	32	430	25	6-56	1	17.20
G. B. Brent (*Manicaland*)	174.2	46	461	26	5-44	1	17.73
P. A. Strang (*Mashonaland*)	288	60	698	35	8-109	1	19.94
B. T. Watambwa (*Mashonaland A*)	264.3	48	768	38	5-36	2	20.21
B. C. Strang (*Mashonaland*)	308.4	98	760	37	5-6	2	20.54
D. P. Viljoen (*Mashonaland A*)	131.4	33	409	17	4-49	0	24.05
H. H. Streak (*Matabeleland*)	373.2	110	877	36	4-38	0	24.36
M. Mbangwa (*Matabeleland*)	161.4	56	344	13	2-2	0	26.46
A. M. Blignaut (*Mashonaland A*)	300.4	78	900	31	5-73	2	29.03
R. W. Price (*Midlands*)	390.5	105	1,065	36	5-36	2	29.58
M. Kenny (*Matabeleland*)	98.1	16	358	11	4-47	0	32.54
D. A. Marillier (*Midlands*)	91	11	353	10	3-32	0	35.30
D. T. Mutendera (*Mashonaland A*)	187.3	36	681	19	3-22	0	35.84
E. Z. Matambanadzo (*Mashonaland A*)	116.5	20	451	12	3-38	0	37.58
M. L. Nkala (*Matabeleland*)	278.4	60	903	24	4-46	0	37.62
B. G. Rogers (*CFX Academy*)	126.3	12	505	13	3-49	0	38.84
B. A. Murphy (*Mashonaland A*)	150	25	501	12	4-77	0	41.75
T. J. Friend (*Midlands*)	149	36	472	11	3-30	0	42.90

Note: Averages include India and West Indies' tours in May to July 2001.

LOGAN CUP, 2000-01

					Bonus points			
	Played	*Won*	*Lost*	*Drawn*	*Batting*	*Bowling*	*Penalty*	*Points*
Mashonaland	5	5	0	0	7	12	1	78
Mashonaland A	5	2	1	2	8	19	7	50
Matabeleland	5	2	1	2	5	14	3	46
Manicaland	5	1	2	2*	5	14	3.5	33.5
Midlands	5	1	2	2*	5	10	0	33
CFX Academy	5	0	5	0	5	13	0.5	17.5

** The match between Manicaland and Midlands was abandoned.*
Outright win = 12 pts; drawn match = 3 pts.
Bonus points are awarded for the first 120 overs of each team's first innings. One batting point is awarded for the first 200 runs and for every subsequent 50, to a maximum of four points. One bowling point is awarded for the third wicket taken and for every subsequent two.
Penalty points are imposed for slow over-rates.

*In the following scores, * by the name of a team signifies that they won the toss.*

At Mutare Sports Club, Mutare, February 16, 17, 18. Manicaland v Midlands. Abandoned. *Manicaland 3 pts, Midlands 3 pts.*

At Harare Sports Club, Harare, February 16, 17, 18. Mashonaland won by 65 runs. Mashonaland 253 for three dec. (G. J. Rennie 33, H. Masakadza 100, A. Flower 69 not out, C. N. Evans 33 not out) and forfeited second innings; CFX Academy* forfeited first innings and 188 (W. T. Siziba 48, B. G. Rogers 55; E. A. Brandes six for 48). *Mashonaland 14 pts, CFX Academy 1 pt.*

Aged 17 years 191 days, Masakadza became the youngest Zimbabwean to score a first-class century. Rain prevented any play on the second day.

At Alexandra Sports Club, Harare, February 16, 17, 18. Drawn. Matabeleland 128 for eight dec. (M. A. Vermeulen 38; D. P. Viljoen three for 21) v Mashonaland A*. *Mashonaland A 3.5 pts, Matabeleland 3 pts.*

At Harare Sports Club, Harare, March 2, 3, 4. Mashonaland won by 115 runs. Mashonaland 171 (P. A. Strang 48, D. J. R. Campbell 37; A. M. Blignaut four for 44) and 66 for five dec. (A. Flower 33; D. T. Mutendera three for 22); Mashonaland A* forfeited first innings and 122 (D. D. Ebrahim 53; P. A. Strang four for 36). *Mashonaland 13 pts, Mashonaland A 1 pt.*

In Mashonaland's first innings, Brighton Watambwa was taken off after bowling 8.1 overs for persistently running on the pitch. Rain prevented any play on the second day.

At Bulawayo Athletic Club, Bulawayo, March 2, 3, 4. Drawn. Manicaland 201 for nine dec. (I. A. Engelbrecht three for 41) and 141 for nine dec. (R. W. Sims 30, S. Matsikenyeri 36; I. A. Engelbrecht four for 56, M. A. Vermeulen three for 26); Matabeleland* 122 for five dec. (M. A. Vermeulen 44) and 124 for five (C. K. Coventry 43). *Matabeleland 6.5 pts, Manicaland 6 pts.*

There was no play on the first day.

At Kwekwe Sports Club, Kwekwe, March 2, 3, 4. Midlands won by 111 runs. Midlands 200 for eight dec. (C. Delport 55, C. B. Wishart 70; I. M. Coulson three for 48) and 168 for six dec. (C. A. Grant 36, D. A. Marillier 57; B. G. Rogers three for 49); CFX Academy* 118 for three dec. (B. G. Rogers 44 not out) and 139 (B. G. Rogers 35; R. W. Price four for 51, D. A. Marillier three for 32). *Midlands 14 pts, CFX Academy 3 pts.*

This match and the following one at Alexandra Sports Club were moved from the Academy's home ground at Country Club, Harare, where the pitch was waterlogged; the first day was still washed out.

At Alexandra Sports Club, Harare, March 9, 10, 11. Mashonaland A won by an innings and 15 runs. CFX Academy* 207 (B. G. Rogers 48, G. M. Croxford 80; A. M. Blignaut three for 26) and 137 (G. M. Croxford 34; B. T. Watambwa five for 36, G. A. Lamb three for 69); Mashonaland A 359 (T. R. Gripper 112, E. Z. Matambanadzo 39, D. D. Ebrahim 71, G. A. Lamb 38; J. M. Lewis four for 40). *Mashonaland A 20 pts, CFX Academy 5 pts.*

At Harare Sports Club, Harare, March 9, 10, 11. Mashonaland won by two wickets. Manicaland 205 (P. K. Gada 41, S. Matsikenyeri 70, A. D. Soma 31 not out; P. A. Strang three for 56) and 114 (R. W. Sims 33; B. C. Strang four for 26, P. A. Strang three for 42); Mashonaland* 205 (C. N. Evans 78; G. B. Brent three for 48, M. G. Burmester three for 34) and 115 for eight (G. B. Brent five for 44). *Mashonaland 17 pts, Manicaland 2 pts.*

The match was moved from a waterlogged pitch at Mutare. Chasing 115 to win, Mashonaland were 68 for seven before Paul Strang and Donald Campbell set up victory with 44 for the eighth wicket.

At Bulawayo Athletic Club, Bulawayo, March 9, 10, 11. Matabeleland won by four wickets. Midlands* 380 for six dec. (C. A. Grant 39, C. B. Wishart 151, D. A. Marillier 100, T. J. Friend 36 not out) and 120 (D. A. Marillier 55; I. A. Engelbrecht six for 56); Matabeleland 384 (M. Kenny 33, M. A. Vermeulen 180, M. L. Nkala 51, G. M. Strydom 31, I. A. Engelbrecht 30; C. B. Wishart four for 50) and 117 for six (C. K. Coventry 35; R. W. Price five for 36). *Matabeleland 16 pts, Midlands 6 pts.*

At Alexandra Sports Club, Harare, March 23, 24, 25. Manicaland won by nine wickets. CFX Academy* 222 (W. T. Siziba 31, B. G. Rogers 69, R. E. Butterworth 34; G. B. Brent four for 50) and 134; Manicaland 250 (P. K. Gada 71, G. B. Brent 61; L. J. Soma four for 35, I. M. Coulson four for 72) and 107 for one (N. R. Ferreira 49 not out, G. B. Brent 48 not out). *Manicaland 18 pts, CFX Academy 4.5 pts.*

At Harare Sports Club, Harare, March 23, 24, 25. Mashonaland won by 285 runs. Mashonaland 194 (A. Flower 74, D. J. R. Campbell 65; I. A. Engelbrecht four for 33) and 225 for five dec. (G. J. Rennie 60, H. Masakadza 31, G. W. Flower 78, A. D. R. Campbell 34); Matabeleland* 115 (G. M. Strydom 30; B. C. Strang four for 42, A. J. Mackay three for 44) and 19 (E. A. Brandes five for 12, B. C. Strang five for six). *Mashonaland 15 pts, Matabeleland 1.5 pts.*

Matabeleland's 19 all out in 11.5 overs was the lowest first-class total in Zimbabwe, and the lowest worldwide since Surrey's 14 v Essex in 1983. Brandes's full second-innings analysis was 6–3–12–5 and Strang's 5.5–3–6–5.

At Kwekwe Sports Club, Kwekwe, March 23, 24, 25. Drawn. Mashonaland A* 248 (T. R. Gripper 44, T. Taibu 75 not out, D. T. Mutendera 53; R. W. Price three for 49) and 263 for five dec.

(D. D. Ebrahim 90, T. R. Gripper 53, S. V. Carlisle 48, A. M. Blignaut 39); Midlands 175 (D. A. Marillier 54; E. Z. Matambanadzo three for 38, D. P. Viljoen four for 51) and 274 for nine (R. W. Price 56, D. A. Marillier 132 not out; B. T. Watambwa four for 36, D. P. Viljoen three for 67). *Midlands 7 pts, Mashonaland A 7 pts.*

In Mashonaland A's first innings, Taibu and Mutendera added 122 for the ninth wicket.

At Mutare Sports Club, Mutare, March 30, 31, April 1. Mashonaland A won by 74 runs. Mashonaland A 325 (D. D. Ebrahim 33, T. R. Gripper 31, S. V. Carlisle 76, D. P. Viljoen 79; J. A. Young three for 64, G. B. Brent three for 69, R. W. Sims three for 68) and 225 for nine dec. (T. R. Gripper 30, A. Maregwede 50, T. Taibu 34; G. B. Brent three for 46); Manicaland* 244 (R. W. Sims 72, S. Matsikenyeri 36, Extras 35; B. T. Watambwa five for 76, D. P. Viljoen three for 66) and 232 (G. J. Whittall 68, J. A. Young 32; B. A. Murphy four for 77, D. P. Viljoen four for 49). *Mashonaland A 18.5 pts, Manicaland 4.5 pts.*

Manicaland's first-innings extras included five penalty runs awarded after Andy Blignaut left and re-entered the field without informing the umpires.

At Queens Sports Club, Bulawayo, March 30, 31, April 1. Matabeleland won by an innings and 62 runs. CFX Academy* 320 (T. Duffin 74, B. G. Rogers 86, R. E. Butterworth 113; M. Kenny four for 98) and 126 (B. G. Rogers 30; M. Kenny four for 47); Matabeleland 508 for nine dec. (R. J. King 54, M. A. Vermeulen 77, M. L. Nkala 168, H. H. Streak 119; J. M. Lewis three for 82). *Matabeleland 19 pts, CFX Academy 4 pts.*

Matabeleland scored 508 for nine, the highest by a first-class provincial side. Nkala and Streak added 267 for the fifth wicket in 228 minutes.

At Kwekwe Sports Club, Kwekwe, March 30, 31, April 1. Mashonaland won by an innings and 43 runs. Mashonaland 357 for seven dec. (G. J. Rennie 37, H. Masakadza 85, G. W. Flower 83, C. N. Evans 73 not out); Midlands* 92 (T. J. Friend 32; B. C. Strang five for 13) and 222 (T. J. Friend 115, C. Delport 44; E. A. Brandes five for 19, B. C. Strang three for 56). *Mashonaland 19 pts, Midlands 3 pts.*

Midlands recovered from 36 for eight in their first innings and 41 for five in their second.

LOGAN CUP WINNERS

1993-94	Mashonaland Under-24	1997-98	Mashonaland
1994-95	Mashonaland	1998-99	Matabeleland
1995-96	Matabeleland	1999-2000	Mashonaland
1996-97	Mashonaland	2000-01	Mashonaland

CRICKET IN BANGLADESH, 2000-01

By UTPAL SHUVRO

Enamul Haque

In Bangladesh's most memorable cricket season yet, the long-cherished dream came true. By making their Test debut, in November 2000, they entered a new era, and started to rub shoulders with the big boys of international cricket. Predictably, Bangladesh lost the inaugural Test against India, by nine wickets. They also lost their first two overseas Tests, when they toured Zimbabwe in April 2001, and all their four one-day internationals during the season. But there were signs of improvement, and some memorable performances. In the First Test at Bulawayo, opener Javed Omar became only the third batsman, and the first for more than a century, to carry his bat on Test debut.

Thanks to the International Cricket Council's ten-year Test Championship schedule, Bangladesh could look forward to much-needed regular doses of Test cricket. They played host to Zimbabwe and toured New Zealand by the end of the year, and also joined their neighbours in the second Asian Test Championship. Test status brought the promise of financial solvency, with television rights providing the major portion of their income. This meant that they were no longer dependent on government grants, and were able to set up a huge development programme. The salaries of contracted players rose sharply, indoor facilities were established in the major cricketing centres, and four Sri Lankan coaches, each working with a local colleague, were assigned to the age-group teams.

Sadly, the national coach had to be replaced. Former South African all-rounder Eddie Barlow, appointed in September 1999, had been determined to return to the post after suffering a stroke the following April, which left him partly paralysed. He toured Kenya and South Africa with Bangladesh in October, but was practically confined to a wheelchair. The board was in a dilemma; it was becoming clear that he was in no state to continue his duties, and at an emotional press conference, it was announced that Barlow was stepping down. He still hoped to come back, and even those who had campaigned for his removal felt a lump in the throat as he tried to convince them he was fully fit. Trevor Chappell, younger brother of Australian Test captains Ian and Greg, took up the job in March.

There was also a controversial change at the helm of the board. The government appoints the presidents of all sports federations, and Saber Hossain Chowdhury, president of the Cricket Board, was also a government deputy minister until July 2001. An interim, caretaker administration then decided to replace all presidents due to stand in October's general election. Accordingly, Chowdhury, a member of the ICC executive committee, whose dynamic leadership had helped secure Bangladesh's Test status, was replaced in August by a bureaucrat – amid vehement protests from the board's other directors.

The inaugural Test was the only senior international cricket during the home season, though the Australian Cricket Academy toured, and demonstrated their strength by winning five of their seven matches, with the other two drawn. Bangladesh also hosted the Under-17 Asia Cup, contested by ten teams, and caused an upset by beating defending champions Sri Lanka to reach the final, only to lose to India.

On the domestic front, the Green Delta National League received a huge lift when it was awarded first-class status. This tournament began in 1999-2000 as a pre-condition of the ICC elevating Bangladesh to Test rank. Initially, there were six divisional teams: Dhaka, Chittagong, Barisal, Khulna, Rajshahi and Sylhet. In 2000-01, two more sides joined. Dhaka, who had more players than any other division, split into two: Dhaka Metropolis, drawn only from the city, and Dhaka Division. The eighth team was Biman Bangladesh Airlines, who had won the National Championship, contested by 64 district and corporate teams, when it was last held in 1998-99. Biman capitalised by winning the National League to become Bangladesh's first first-class champions.

Both first-class matches and one-day games contributed to the final standings in the League. The teams were divided into two groups of four, who played each other home and away, first in a three-day first-class game, worth up to six points, and then in a 50-overs match worth two points. The top two teams from each group then played two more rounds against their opposite numbers from the other group, with the first-class matches now scheduled for four days.

Biman headed Group A from Chittagong, who had won the tournament in its inaugural, non-first-class season. Khulna and Dhaka Metropolis led Group B. Biman and Chittagong entered the final round of the tournament level on 44 points. But Chittagong faltered against Dhaka Metropolis, conceding first-innings lead as they drew their last first-class match, while Biman outclassed Khulna, first over four days to secure the championship, and then in the one-day game to widen their lead to eight points.

Biman's team was studded with stars, but the key to their success was signing left-hander Imran Farhat as their overseas player. An 18-year-old all-rounder from Lahore, Imran was virtually unknown until he broke into Pakistan's international side during the New Zealand tour later in the year. With Biman, he lost no time exploring his talent; he scored a double-century in their first match, against Chittagong, and batted with similar brilliance in five more group matches before returning to Pakistan. There was another century and four fifties as he amassed 735 runs – the next-highest aggregate in this tournament was 635 by Mehrab Hossain of Dhaka Metropolis, who played four more games. Imran averaged 91.87, but that was beaten by another Pakistani, Manzoor Akhtar, who replaced him for two matches and scored 288 runs at 96.00.

Biman's local stars shone almost as brightly. Test batsmen Habibul Bashar, Aminul Islam and Javed Omar all aggregated at least 550 runs in the League, as did Hasanuzzaman, who hit three centuries. In the final first-class game, against Khulna, he shared a 295-run partnership with Habibul, who recorded 224, the season's highest innings. On the bowling front, Biman unearthed a gem in 15-year-old seamer Mohammad Sharif, who took 49 wickets and made his Test debut in Zimbabwe. Sharif was not the tournament's leading wicket-taker, however; that honour went to Chittagong's 34-year-old left-arm spinner, Enamul Haque, who captured 57. He added 454 runs at an average of 50.44, and was easily the best all-rounder, though he could not quite ensure that Chittagong retained their crown. Still, they were an effective unit and won five of their ten first-class matches, more than anyone else. Young opener Nafis Iqbal played alongside his uncle, former Bangladesh captain Akram Khan, and promised much for the future.

Dhaka Metropolis finished third and enjoyed their moments in the sun, particularly when making 452 runs in a day to win a thriller against Biman. The chase featured brilliant hundreds by Mehrab, Al-Shahriar Rokon and Test captain Naimur Rahman, as well as 80 from all-rounder Mohammad Ashraful. An aggressive batsman and more than useful leg-break bowler, the 16-year-old Ashraful combined 585 runs with 39 wickets; he added a century against the Australian Academy, and later toured Zimbabwe.

Though Bangladesh's contracted players were not allowed to play in Dhaka's premier league, it generated the usual heated interest up to the last game, when Mohammedan beat arch-rivals Abahani by three runs to claim their first title since 1995-96. Steve Tikolo, playing for Mohammedan for the second year running, alongside fellow-Kenyan Maurice Odumbe, beat Gazi Ashraf's 1986 league record of 1,017 runs in a season; Tikolo's 1,222 included four centuries and seven fifties.

FIRST-CLASS AVERAGES, 2000-01

BATTING

(Qualification: 300 runs, average 30.00)

	M	*I*	*NO*	*R*	*HS*	*100s*	*Avge*
Imran Farhat (*Biman*)	6	10	2	735	216	2	91.87
Aminul Islam (*Biman*)	10	15	2	704	153	3	54.15
Hasanuzzaman (*Biman*)	10	14	3	575	118	3	52.27
Enamul Haque (*Chittagong*)	9	10	1	454	81	0	50.44
Sanuar Hossain (*Biman*)	10	11	2	449	116	1	49.88
Minhazul Abedin (*Chittagong*)	10	13	2	531	139	1	48.27
Habibul Bashar (*Biman*)	11	17	1	695	224	1	43.43
Javed Omar (*Biman*)	9	14	0	562	102	2	40.14
Naimur Rahman (*Dhaka Met.*)	5	9	1	317	106	1	39.62
Ehsanul Haque (*Chittagong*)	10	15	1	540	101	1	38.57
Rafiqul Islam (*Rajshahi*)	6	12	0	461	124	1	38.41
Al-Shahriar Rokon (*Dhaka Met.*)	9	16	1	575	128*	1	38.33
Safaiat Islam (*Barisal*)	6	11	2	343	105*	1	38.11
Nafis Iqbal (*Chittagong*)	10	16	1	550	147	1	36.66
Mehrab Hossain (*Dhaka Met.*)	11	18	0	641	133	2	35.61
Sajjadul Hasan (*Khulna*)	9	17	3	491	147	1	35.07
Khaled Mahmud (*Dhaka Met.*)	10	14	1	418	71	0	32.15
Jamaluddin Ahmed (*Khulna*)	10	16	3	413	50	0	31.76
Anisur Rahman (*Rajshahi*)	6	12	0	381	70	0	31.75
Mohammad Ashraful (*Dhaka Met.*)	10	19	0	585	157	2	30.78

* *Signifies not out.*

BOWLING

(Qualification: 15 wickets, average 30.00)

	O	*M*	*R*	*W*	*BB*	*5W/i*	*Avge*
Enamul Haque (*Chittagong*)	433	130	948	57	7-74	6	16.63
Mushfiqur Rehman (*Rajshahi*)	113	27	304	17	4-51	0	17.88
Mohammad Sharif (*Biman*)	312.5	67	879	49	6-31	5	17.93
Saiful Islam (*Dhaka Div.*)	135.2	48	342	19	7-62	2	18.00
Ahsanullah Hasan (*Barisal*)	143	40	405	21	8-76	2	19.28
Manjurul Islam Rana (*Khulna*)	309	81	705	35	6-24	3	20.14
Mohammad Rafiq (*Sylhet*)	213.5	63	425	21	4-16	0	20.23
Imran Farhat (*Biman*)	144.2	28	474	23	7-31	2	20.60
Jamaluddin Ahmed (*Khulna*)	259	42	636	30	5-82	1	21.20
Neeyamur Rashid (*Dhaka Met.*)	120.4	24	349	16	3-30	0	21.81
Hasibul Hussain (*Sylhet*)	120.5	23	349	16	6-41	1	21.81
Al Amin (*Khulna*)	132	37	361	16	5-39	1	22.56

	O	M	R	W	BB	5W/i	Avge
Sharafudoulla (*Dhaka Met.*)	353.4	106	713	31	6-45	2	23.00
Aminul Islam, jun. (*Rajshahi*)	139.3	31	416	17	6-57	1	24.47
Shahid Mahmood (*Chittagong*)	312	39	1,120	45	5-37	3	24.88
Mohammad Ashraful (*Dhaka Met.*)	326	75	994	39	7-99	3	25.48
Imran Parvez (*Rajshahi*)	158	29	490	18	5-82	1	27.22
Manjurul Islam (*Khulna*)	171	52	411	15	6-27	1	27.40
Sohel Islam (*Khulna*)	215.4	43	576	21	4-40	0	27.42
Shafiuddin Ahmed (*Chittagong*)	233.1	64	575	20	4-52	0	28.75

GREEN DELTA NATIONAL CRICKET LEAGUE, 2000-01

Group A	Played	Won	Lost	Drawn	1st-inns Points	1-day Wins	Points
Biman Bangladesh Airlines	6	2	0	4	12	4	32
Chittagong	6	3	0	3	8	2	30
Rajshahi	6	2	2	2	0	3	18
Dhaka Division	6	0	5	1	0	3	6

Group B	Played	Won	Lost	Drawn	1st-inns Points	1-day Wins	Points
Khulna	6	3	1	2	4	2	26
Dhaka Metropolis	6	2	0	4	8	3	26
Barisal	6	0	2	4	9	3	15
Sylhet	6	0	2	4	5	4	13

Final Stage	Played	Won	Lost	Drawn	1st-inns Points	1-day Wins	Points
Biman Bangladesh Airlines	10	4	1	5	16	6	52
Chittagong	10	5	1	4	8	3	44
Dhaka Metropolis	10	3	1	6	12	6	42
Khulna	10	4	4	2	4	4	36

The top two teams from each group advanced to the final stage, carrying forward all results and points already gained. The one-day match was played the day after the first-class match.

Win in first-class match = 6 pts; 1st-innings lead in a drawn match = 4 pts; no 1st-innings lead in a drawn match = 1 pt; win in one-day match = 2 pts. First innings in the group first-class matches closed at 100 overs.

*In the following scores, * by the name of a team indicates that they won the toss.*

Group A

At Bangladesh Krira Shikkha Protisthan Ground, Savar, November 22, 23, 24. Drawn. Biman Bangladesh Airlines* 411 for five (Imran Farhat 216, Habibul Bashar 51, Aminul Islam 57; Enamul Haque three for 93) and 170 for three (Imran Farhat 71, Habibul Bashar 41); Chittagong 397 for nine (Azam Iqbal 35, Nafis Iqbal 75, Ehsanul Haque 59, Minhazul Abedin 74, Akram Khan 56, Shahid Mahmood 34; Mohammad Sharif four for 75). *Biman Bangladesh Airlines 4 pts.*

Imran Farhat's 216 lasted 418 minutes and 301 balls and included 28 fours. He added 167 for Biman's second wicket with Habibul Bashar, and 135 for the third with Aminul Islam.

November 25: Biman Bangladesh Airlines (213 for nine) beat Chittagong (212) by one wicket. Biman Bangladesh Airlines 2 pts.

At Rajshahi Stadium, Rajshahi, November 22, 23, 24. Rajshahi won by 212 runs. Rajshahi* 190 (Mushfiqur Rehman 67, Mohammad Kalim 38; Saiful Islam five for 31) and 281 for eight dec. (Rafiqul Islam 85, Mushfiqur Rehman 71, Nuruzzaman 42, Anisur Rahman 34; Biplab Sarkar four for 75); Dhaka Division 167 (Mahbubur Rahman 42, Fahim Muntasir 34; Mushfiqur Rehman three for 54, Mohammad Mostadir three for 21) and 92 (Aminul Islam, jun. three for 23, Imran Parvez three for 33, Mushfiqur Rehman three for 11). *Rajshahi 6 pts.*

November 25: Dhaka Division (190 for nine) beat Rajshahi (55) by 135 runs. Dhaka Division 2 pts.

At Mymensingh Stadium, Mymensingh, November 27, 28, 29. Biman Bangladesh Airlines won by an innings and 129 runs. Biman Bangladesh Airlines* 383 for nine (Javed Omar 102, Imran Farhat 88, Aminul Islam 52, Hasanuzzaman 36, Sanuar Hossain 34 not out, Extras 38; Bikash Ranjan Das three for 120, Saiful Islam three for 81); Dhaka Division 119 (Imran Farhat seven for 31) and 135 (Harunur Rashid 46; Saifullah Khan three for 28). *Biman Bangladesh Airlines 6 pts.*

November 30: Dhaka Division (221 for five) beat Biman Bangladesh Airlines (220 for five) by five wickets. Dhaka Division 2 pts.

At Cricket Garden, Rangpur, November 27, 28, 29. Chittagong won by nine wickets. Chittagong* 335 for nine (Azam Iqbal 50, Minhazul Abedin 139, Akram Khan 31, Enamul Haque 36; Alamgir Kabir four for 93) and six for one; Rajshahi 175 (Mohammad Kalim 35; Enamul Haque five for 39, Shahid Mahmood three for 70) and 164 (Shafiuddin Ahmed three for 32, Enamul Haque five for 29). *Chittagong 6 pts.*

November 30: Chittagong (202 for nine) beat Rajshahi (157) by 45 runs. Chittagong 2 pts.

At Bangladesh Krira Shikkha Protisthan Ground, Savar, December 2, 3, 4. Drawn. Biman Bangladesh Airlines* 422 (Imran Farhat 97, Habibul Bashar 72, Hasanuzzaman 104, Sanuar Hossain 44; Nuruzzaman six for 135) and 185 for four dec. (Javed Omar 59, Aminul Islam 74 not out); Rajshahi 288 (Rafiqul Islam 67, Omar Sharif 42, Anisur Rahman 70; Imran Farhat three for 59, Rafiqul Islam four for 111) and 236 for eight (Rafiqul Islam 124, Anisur Rahman 60). *Biman Bangladesh Airlines 4 pts.*

December 5: Biman Bangladesh Airlines (203 for six) beat Rajshahi (200 for eight) by four wickets. Biman Bangladesh Airlines 2 pts.

At Mymensingh Stadium, Mymensingh, December 2, 3, 4. Chittagong won by an innings and 61 runs. Chittagong* 344 for seven dec. (Azam Iqbal 61, Ehsanul Haque 96, Minhazul Abedin 31, Enamul Haque 75 not out; Biplab Sarkar four for 69); Dhaka Division 132 (Shabbir Khan three for 36, Shahid Mahmood five for 37) and 151 (Rashidul Haque 38, Sajjad Kadir 45, Mazharul Haque 37 not out; Shabbir Khan three for 18, Shahid Mahmood five for 68). *Chittagong 6 pts.*

Sajjad Kadir and Shahid Mahmood were both suspended for dissent for one match.

December 5: Dhaka Division (214 for nine) beat Chittagong (169) by 45 runs. Dhaka Division 2 pts.

At Comilla Stadium, Comilla, December 8, 9, 10. Drawn. Chittagong 317 (Nafis Iqbal 147, Minhazul Abedin 63, Akram Khan 48, Extras 30; Jahangir Alam three for 56, Mohammad Sharif six for 44) and 199 for eight dec. (Shahid Mahmood 49, Golam Mortaza 43); Biman Bangladesh Airlines* 262 (Javed Omar 71, Habibul Bashar 44, Sanuar Hossain 42, Extras 40; Shafiuddin Ahmed four for 52) and 23 for four. *Chittagong 4 pts.*

December 11: Biman Bangladesh Airlines (223 for six) beat Chittagong (222 for nine) by four wickets. Biman Bangladesh Airlines 2 pts.

At Faridpur Stadium, Faridpur, December 8, 9, 10. Rajshahi won by 57 runs. Rajshahi* 230 (Nuruzzaman 80; Fahim Muntasir four for 57) and 173 (Rafiqul Islam 55, Rezwanul Islam 45; Bikash Ranjan Das three for 64, Mosaddek Hossain three for 19); Dhaka Division 153 (Biplab Sarkar 31; Mushfiqur Rehman four for 51) and 193 (Rashidul Haque 52, Fahim Muntasir 35; Mushfiqur Rehman three for 62, Mohammad Mostadir three for 42). *Rajshahi 6 pts.*

December 11: Rajshahi (143 for three) beat Dhaka Division (142) by seven wickets. Rajshahi 2 pts.

At Bangabandhu National Stadium, Dhaka, December 14, 15, 16. Drawn. Dhaka Division 216 (Sajjad Kadir 39, Sohel Hossain 50, Mazharul Haque 37; Enamul Haque four for 48, Shahid Mahmood four for 57) and 327 for six dec. (Rashidul Haque 71, Mosaddek Hossain 140, Fahim Muntasir 81; Enamul Haque four for 78); Chittagong* 359 for seven (Nafis Iqbal 45, Ehsanul Haque 64, Enamul Haque 68, Shahid Mahmood 84, Extras 33; Fahim Muntasir four for 88) and 15 for two. *Chittagong 4 pts.*

This match was originally scheduled for Comilla but switched owing to Victory Day celebrations.

December 17: Chittagong (291 for seven) beat Dhaka Division (200) by 91 runs. Chittagong 2 pts.

At Cricket Garden, Rangpur, December 14, 15, 16. Drawn. Biman Bangladesh Airlines* 256 (Faruq Ahmed 44, Ziaur Rashid 49, Atiar Rahman 38, Extras 34; Aminul Islam, jun. six for 57) and 199 for three dec. (Javed Omar 67, Habibul Bashar 53, Imran Farhat 47 not out); Rajshahi 158 (Rafiqul Islam 38; Imran Farhat six for 22) and 180 for six (Anisur Rahman 58, Mushfiqur Rehman 68 not out). *Biman Bangladesh Airlines 4 pts.*

December 17: Rajshahi (223 for nine) beat Biman Bangladesh Airlines (170) by 53 runs. Rajshahi 2 pts.

At Shahid Bulu Stadium, Noakhali, December 20, 21, 22. Chittagong won by an innings and ten runs. Rajshahi* 148 (Rafiqul Islam 33, Anisur Rahman 38; Enamul Haque three for 25, Shahid Mahmood five for 62) and 132 (Mohammad Kalim 32; Enamul Haque six for 36, Shahid Mahmood three for 54); Chittagong 290 for nine (Nafis Iqbal 52, Ehsanul Haque 34, Minhazul Abedin 50, Akram Khan 34, Rezaul Hasan 59 not out, Enamul Haque 31; Imran Parvez five for 82, Mohammad Mostadir three for 72). *Chittagong 6 pts.*

December 23: Rajshahi (134 for four) beat Chittagong (132) by six wickets. Rajshahi 2 pts.

At Faridpur Stadium, Faridpur, December 20, 21, 22. Biman Bangladesh Airlines won by eight wickets. Dhaka Division* 158 (Harunur Rashid 66; Mohammad Sharif six for 43) and 134 (Mohammad Sharif six for 31); Biman Bangladesh Airlines 160 (Imran Farhat 52; Saiful Islam seven for 62) and 133 for two (Imran Farhat 105 not out). *Biman Bangladesh Airlines 6 pts.*

Mohammad Sharif took 12 for 74 in the match.

December 23: Biman Bangladesh Airlines (209) beat Dhaka Division (179) by 30 runs. Biman Bangladesh Airlines 2 pts.

Group B

At Dhanmondi Cricket Stadium, Dhaka, November 22, 23, 24. Drawn. Dhaka Metropolis* 302 (Mohammad Ashraful 41, Khaled Mahmud 55, Neeyamur Rashid 66; Hasibul Hussain three for 64, Mohammad Rafiq three for 90) and 184 for eight dec. (Al-Shahriar Rokon 50, Halim Shah 71; Imran Rahim three for 69, Mohammad Rafiq three for 31); Sylhet 153 (Mohammad Rafiq 53; Mohammad Ashraful five for 59) and 203 for three (Parvez Ahmed 91, Rajin Saleh 78 not out). *Dhaka Metropolis 4 pts.*

November 25: Dhaka Metropolis (129 for six) beat Sylhet (126) by four wickets. Dhaka Metropolis 2 pts.

At Shamsul Huda Stadium, Jessore, November 22, 23, 24. Drawn. Barisal* 179 (Towhid Hossain 35, Extras 32; Sohel Islam three for 27) and 186 for eight (Tashriqul Islam 30, Safaiat Islam 44 not out; Manjurul Islam Rana three for 30); Khulna 292 for seven (Nahidul Haque 45, Tushar Imran 40, Sohel Islam 51, Asadullah Khan 90; Ahsanullah Hasan three for 75). *Khulna 4 pts.*

November 25: Barisal (165) beat Khulna (144) by 21 runs. Barisal 2 pts.

At Abdur Rab Serniabad Stadium, Barisal, November 27, 28, 29. Drawn. Barisal* 207 for seven (Safaiat Islam 48, Mizanur Rahman 76) v Sylhet. *Barisal 1 pt, Sylhet 1 pt.*

November 30: Sylhet (109 for seven) beat Barisal (108) by three wickets. Sylhet 2 pts.

At Dhanmondi Cricket Stadium, Dhaka, November 27, 28, 29. Drawn. Khulna* 192 (Raju Parvez 75; Ziaul Haque seven for 63) and 345 (Sajjadul Hasan 47, Mohammad Salim 150; Mohammad Ashraful three for 114, Sharafudoulla three for 35); Dhaka Metropolis 312 for eight dec. (Mohammad Ashraful 101, Sajjad Ahmed 39, Khaled Mahmud 40; Sohel Islam four for 112, Jamaluddin Ahmed three for 91) and 35 for two. *Dhaka Metropolis 4 pts.*

November 30: Dhaka Metropolis (175 for three) beat Khulna (174) by seven wickets. Dhaka Metropolis 2 pts.

At Dhanmondi Cricket Stadium, Dhaka, December 2, 3, 4. Drawn. Barisal* 277 for six (Hannan Sarkar 100, Safaiat Islam 105 not out; Sharafudoulla three for 62) and 228 (Hannan Sarkar 64, Imran Ahmed 47, Ahsanullah Hasan 37 not out; Ziaul Haque five for 87); Dhaka Metropolis 244 (Mehrab Hossain 40, Sajjad Ahmed 58, Khaled Mahmud 38, Mafizul Islam 34 not out; Ahsanullah Hasan six for 103) and 212 for eight (Al-Shahriar Rokon 74). *Barisal 4 pts.*

December 5: Dhaka Metropolis (133 for one) beat Barisal (130) by nine wickets. Dhaka Metropolis 2 pts.

At Shamsul Huda Stadium, Jessore, December 2, 3, 4. Khulna won by ten wickets. Sylhet* 115 (Manjurul Islam Rana five for 34, Jamaluddin Ahmed four for 16) and 185 (Ekrimul Hadi 68, Rajin Saleh 34; Ahmed Kamal four for 40, Jamaluddin Ahmed four for 32); Khulna 236 (Sajjadul Hasan 71, Mohammad Salim 31, Extras 37; Imran Rahim four for 51) and 65 for no wkt (Sajjadul Hasan 44 not out). *Khulna 6 pts.*

December 5: Sylhet (71 for five) beat Khulna (69) by five wickets. Sylhet 2 pts.

At Abdur Rab Serniabad Stadium, Barisal, December 8, 9, 10. Khulna won by nine wickets. Barisal 194 (Safaiat Islam 44, Ahsanullah Hasan 78; Ahmed Kamal three for 42, Manjurul Islam Rana four for 53, Sohel Islam three for 49) and 173 (Ishtiaq Ahmed 39, Towhid Hossain 51; Nahidul Haque four for 14); Khulna* 332 for nine (Sajjadul Hasan 147, Raju Parvez 84, Asadullah Khan 31; Ishtiaq Ahmed five for 53, Hannan Sarkar three for 93) and 36 for one. *Khulna 6 pts.*

December 11: Barisal (171) beat Khulna (75) by 96 runs. Barisal 2 pts.

At Sylhet Stadium, Sylhet, December 8, 9, 10. Drawn. Sylhet* 220 (Rajin Saleh 115, Nasirul Alam 33; Sharafudoulla six for 45) and 225 for six dec. (Parvez Ahmed 65, Alok Kapali 76, Rajin Saleh 34 not out); Dhaka Metropolis 167 (Mehrab Hossain 42, Khaled Mahmud 45; Mohammad Rafiq three for 33, Alok Kapali five for 33) and 26 for three. *Sylhet 4 pts.*

December 11: Sylhet (142 for eight) beat Dhaka Metropolis (80) by 62 runs. Sylhet 2 pts.

At Abdur Rab Serniabad Stadium, Barisal, December 14, 15, 16. Dhaka Metropolis won by eight wickets. Barisal* 239 (Imran Ahmed 34, Safaiat Islam 40, Mizanur Rahman 39, Ahsanullah Hasan 37; Mohammad Ashraful three for 47) and 154 (Imran Ahmed 40, Mizanur Rahman 48; Mohammad Ashraful six for 49, Khaled Mahmud three for 19); Dhaka Metropolis 322 (Zahoor Elahi 56, Sajjad Ahmed 117, Al-Shahriar Rokon 31, Khaled Mahmud 35; Ahsanullah Hasan eight for 76) and 73 for two (Zahoor Elahi 38 not out). *Dhaka Metropolis 6 pts.*

December 17: Barisal (179 for nine) beat Dhaka Metropolis (176) by one wicket. Barisal 2 pts.

At Sylhet Stadium, Sylhet, December 14, 15, 17. Khulna won by 32 runs. Khulna* 139 (Asadullah Khan 50; Hasibul Hussain four for 31) and 101 (Jamaluddin Ahmed 31; Hasibul Hussain six for 41, Mohammad Rafiq four for 16); Sylhet 112 (Iqbal Hossain 30; Tarikul Hasan three for 23, Manjurul Islam Rana five for 32) and 96 (Al Amin three for 34, Manjurul Islam Rana six for 24). *Khulna 6 pts.*

There was no play on December 16 owing to Victory Day celebrations.

December 18: Khulna (242 for six) beat Sylhet (82) by 160 runs. Khulna 2 pts.

At Sylhet Stadium, Sylhet, December 20, 21, 22. Drawn. Barisal* 199 for eight (Imran Ahmed 60, Ahsanullah Hasan 34; Alok Kapali three for 34) and 162 (Rezaul Haque three for 32, Iqbal Hossain three for 28); Sylhet 195 for nine (Parvez Ahmed 49, Iqbal Hossain 56 not out) and 48 for one. *Barisal 4 pts.*

December 23: Sylhet (177 for three) beat Barisal (175 for eight) by seven wickets. Sylhet 2 pts.

At Shamsul Huda Stadium, Jessore, December 21, 22, 23. Dhaka Metropolis won by an innings and 108 runs. Dhaka Metropolis* 359 (Mehrab Hossain 74, Zahoor Elahi 83, Sajjad Ahmed 79; Jamaluddin Ahmed four for 90, Sohel Islam four for 40); Khulna 103 (Raju Parvez 37; Sharafudoulla five for 22) and 148 (Jamaluddin Ahmed 49 not out; Khaled Mahmud three for 31, Neeyamur Rashid three for 30). *Dhaka Metropolis 6 pts.*

December 24: Khulna (203 for seven) beat Dhaka Metropolis (202) by three wickets. Khulna 2 pts.

Final Stage

At Dhanmondi Cricket Stadium, Dhaka, January 2, 3, 4, 5. Dhaka Metropolis won by six wickets. Biman Bangladesh Airlines* 354 (Javed Omar 37, Manzoor Akhtar 95, Sanuar Hossain 116, Hasanuzzaman 37; Neeyamur Rashid three for 32) and 410 for seven dec. (Habibul Bashar 39, Aminul Islam 153, Manzoor Akhtar 62, Sanuar Hossain 36, Hasanuzzaman 69 not out; Mohammad Ashraful three for 104); Dhaka Metropolis 314 (Mehrab Hossain 70, Khaled Mahmud 71, Extras 37; Mohammad Sharif three for 80, Manzoor Akhtar five for 104) and 452 for four (Mohammad Ashraful 80, Mehrab Hossain 114, Al-Shahriar Rokon 128 not out, Naimur Rahman 106). *Dhaka Metropolis 6 pts.*

The match aggregate was 1,530 runs for 31 wickets. On the final day, Dhaka Metropolis scored 452 for four in 80.3 overs to win.

January 6: Dhaka Metropolis (191) beat Biman Bangladesh Airlines (93) by 98 runs. Dhaka Metropolis 2 pts.

At Shamsul Huda Stadium, Jessore, January 2, 3, 4, 5. Khulna won by nine wickets. Chittagong* 238 (Ehsanul Haque 55, Enamul Haque 81, Golam Mortaza 33; Al Amin five for 39) and 98 (Rezaul Hasan 31; Manjurul Islam six for 27); Khulna 274 (Asadullah Khan 47, Tushar Imran 45, Jamaluddin Ahmed 35; Enamul Haque three for 58, Shahid Mahmood four for 95) and 64 for one (Sajjadul Hasan 31 not out). *Khulna 6 pts.*

January 6: Khulna (242 for nine) beat Chittagong (212) by 30 runs. Khulna 2 pts.

At Bangladesh Krira Shikkha Protisthan Ground, Savar, January 11, 12, 13, 14. Biman Bangladesh Airlines won by nine wickets. Khulna 229 (Sajjadul Hasan 33, Salahuddin Ahmed 96, Jamaluddin Ahmed 41; Mohammad Sharif five for 71) and 267 (Nahidul Haque 61, Sajjadul Hasan 40, Raju Parvez 80; Mohammad Sharif five for 75, Manzoor Akhtar five for 91); Biman Bangladesh Airlines* 416 (Habibul Bashar 38, Ziaur Rashid 47, Manzoor Akhtar 131, Sanuar Hossain 74, Hasanuzzaman 36; Sohel Islam three for 102) and 81 for one (Faruq Ahmed 43 not out). *Biman Bangladesh Airlines 6 pts.*

January 15: Khulna (186 for five) beat Biman Bangladesh Airlines (184 for seven) by five wickets. Khulna 2 pts.

At Comilla Stadium, Comilla, January 11, 12, 13. Chittagong won by seven wickets. Dhaka Metropolis* 217 (Naimur Rahman 99; Enamul Haque seven for 74) and 184 (Halim Shah 30; Enamul Haque three for 53, Shahid Mahmood four for 48); Chittagong 300 (Azam Iqbal 76, Rezaul Hasan 48, Enamul Haque 66, Golam Mortaza 33 not out) and 104 for three (Nafis Iqbal 59). *Chittagong 6 pts.*

January 14: Dhaka Metropolis (275 for nine) beat Chittagong (200) by 75 runs. Dhaka Metropolis 2 pts.

At Bangladesh Krira Shikkha Protisthan Ground, Savar, January 17, 18, 19, 20. Drawn. Biman Bangladesh Airlines 550 for nine dec. (Javed Omar 102, Faruq Ahmed 68, Aminul Islam 100, Sanuar Hossain 63, Hasanuzzaman 111, Mukhtar Siddique 36; Khaled Mahmud three for 132, Naimur Rahman three for 139); Dhaka Metropolis* 224 (Khaled Mahmud 32, Mafizul Islam 48; Ziaur Rashid three for 53, Aamer Wasim four for 53) and 222 for three (Mohammad Ashraful 53, Mehrab Hossain 133). *Biman Bangladesh Airlines 4 pts.*

January 21: Biman Bangladesh Airlines (176 for two) beat Dhaka Metropolis (172 for nine) by eight wickets. Biman Bangladesh Airlines 2 pts.

At Comilla Stadium, Comilla, January 17, 18, 19, 20. Chittagong won by eight wickets. Khulna 211 (Nahidul Haque 81, Manjurul Islam Rana 41, Tushar Imran 30; Enamul Haque six for 49, Shahid Mahmood three for 48) and 223 (Nahidul Haque 55, Raju Parvez 35, Jamaluddin Ahmed 50; Enamul Haque five for 79, Shahid Mahmood three for 79); Chittagong* 290 (Shahid Mahmood 31, Ehsanul Haque 49, Minhazul Abedin 36, Enamul Haque 78; Al Amin three for 34, Nahidul Haque three for 51) and 145 for two (Shahid Mahmood 55, Ehsanul Haque 52 not out). *Chittagong 6 pts.*

January 21: Chittagong (141 for seven) beat Khulna (140) by three wickets. Chittagong 2 pts.

At Bangabandhu National Stadium, Dhaka, January 27, 28, 29, 30. Drawn. Dhaka Metropolis 503 for nine dec. (Mohammad Ashraful 157, Mehrab Hossain 53, Al-Shahriar Rokon 95, Mafizul Islam 58, Neeyamur Rashid 69, Extras 30; Shafiuddin Ahmed four for 95) and 177 for four (Halim

Shah 41, Al-Shahriar Rokon 69); Chittagong* 374 (Nafis Iqbal 50, Ehsanul Haque 101, Akram Khan 58, Minhazul Abedin 55; Mohammad Ashraful seven for 99). *Dhaka Metropolis 4 pts.*

The captains agreed to call off play before lunch on the fourth day on hearing that Biman Bangladesh Airlines had already won their match and become champions.

January 31: Dhaka Metropolis (318 for seven) beat Chittagong (139) by 179 runs. Dhaka Metropolis 2 pts.

At Shamsul Huda Stadium, Jessore, January 27, 28, 29, 30. Biman Bangladesh Airlines won by an innings and 55 runs. Khulna 289 (Mohammad Salim 34, Manjurul Islam Rana 76, Asadullah Khan 39, Jamaluddin Ahmed 46 not out, Extras 36; Aamer Wasim three for 63) and 145 (Raju Parvez 34; Mohammad Sharif three for 38, Anwar Hossain four for 37); Biman Bangladesh Airlines* 489 (Faruq Ahmed 47, Habibul Bashar 224, Aminul Islam 31, Hasanuzzaman 118; Jamaluddin Ahmed five for 82, Manjurul Islam Rana four for 105). *Biman Bangladesh Airlines 6 pts.*

Habibul Bashar's 224 lasted 378 minutes and 310 balls and included 28 fours. He and Hasanuzzaman added 295 for Biman's fifth wicket to help secure the championship.

January 31: Biman Bangladesh Airlines (185 for seven) beat Khulna (181 for seven) by three wickets. Biman Bangladesh Airlines 2 pts.

CRICKET IN KENYA, 2001

By JASMER SINGH

After the euphoria surrounding the ICC Knockout in Nairobi in October 2000, it was generally accepted that 2001 would be a quieter year for Kenyan cricket. And, comparatively speaking, it was. It began with a visit by a strong Sri Lanka A side in January, but this promising-looking tour was spoilt by unusual wet weather and overshadowed by the discontent of Kenya's contracted players. The two three-day matches ended in draws, but Kenya lost both the one-day games; another two were abandoned. The stand-off that followed between the players and the national body over contracts was prolonged, although it was ultimately resolved amicably.

In June, Kenya presented their case for Test status to the International Cricket Council. It was well received but deferred for the time being, and once again two of Kenya's officials were elected to ICC committees – Jimmy Rayani to the executive board and Harilal Shah to the cricket committee (playing). The West Indians, who had proposed Kenya for Test status, then provided further evidence of solidarity by becoming the first Test-playing team to make an official tour of the country.

This visit, in August, was both welcome and highly successful. Coming fresh from their triumphs in Zimbabwe, the West Indians understandably proved too strong for Kenya in the three one-day internationals, but there was no disgrace in the Kenyan totals of 205, 192 and 232 for seven. And although Kenya lost the three-day match by an innings in the closing minutes, through a devastating spell of fast bowling from Marlon Black (six for 35), they did come out of the rain-affected four-day match with a draw. More significant than the results, however, was the emergence of two promising young players in David Obuya, an opening batsman/wicket-keeper, and his younger brother, Collins Obuya, a spin-bowling all-rounder.

Hard on the heels of the West Indians came two Indian state teams, Mumbai and Baroda, to contest a triangular tournament as part of Kenya's preparation for the Standard Bank international series in South Africa in October. Kenya beat them both twice, and went on to win the tournament by humbling Mumbai in the final. Having put together 276 for seven, the Kenyans bowled out the Indians for 121, with Thomas Odoyo taking four for 22 in seven overs. Kennedy Otieno Obuya hit Kenya's only century, 139 in the final, while his brother David had an excellent series with scores of 55, 72, 48 and 65. Odoyo was the most successful Kenyan bowler, with 12 wickets.

Kenya, with just 37 official one-day internationals behind them, and only two of those under lights, went south to rub shoulders ambitiously with two one-day powerhouses, hosts South Africa and India. Not unexpectedly, they were outplayed overall, but in Port Elizabeth they put up a performance that will make October 17 as much a red-letter day in Kenyan cricket as February 29, 1996, when they beat West Indies at Pune in the World Cup. This time, they caused a major upset by beating India. Joseph Angara, with three for 30, and Odoyo, three for 41, were the architects as the Indians managed only 176 in response to Kenya's 246 for six and lost by 70 runs.

The domestic season saw a complete reshaping of the teams in the Premier Division, as most of the national squad players switched clubs for financial reasons. Worst hit in this shuffle were Nairobi Gymkhana, the former champions, who lost five internationals and were eventually relegated after finishing last in the eight-team league. The championship was won by Swamibapa, who went through their 14 matches unbeaten; Steve Tikolo scored two double-centuries for them. Simba Union won Division One and so jumped back into the Premier Division after only one season out of it.

The year also saw the appointment of Nasoor Verjee, a former international, as development director, and the implementation of a four-year development programme incorporating coaching for primary and secondary schools around the country. The first African cricket academy north of Harare, at the Simba Union club in Nairobi, was expected to be operational early in 2002. Bob Woolmer, who visited Kenya in November on behalf of the ICC, had some very successful sessions with the national authorities to work out how best to prepare the Kenya team for the 2003 World Cup. This included tours, specialist coaches to assist the national coach, the provision of sports scientists from South Africa, and the supply of specialised equipment.

Kenya's year ended on a bright note when they beat a visiting Zimbabwe A side, containing eight Test players, 1–0 in their two first-class matches and 3–2 in a one-day series. Kenyan batsmen dominated to such an extent that Tikolo's aggregate for the seven games was 557 runs, including three centuries, at an average of 79.57. Ravindu Shah hit two hundreds, while Maurice Odumbe and Kennedy Otieno made one each. In the first three-day match, which Kenya won by an innings and 23 runs to record their maiden first-class victory, Odumbe returned the remarkable analysis of 20–13–17–5 in the Zimbabwean second innings of 148. Details of the first-class matches will appear in *Wisden 2003*.

CRICKET IN THE NETHERLANDS, 2001

By DAVID HARDY

The Dutch national team finally achieved a long-standing ambition by winning the ICC Trophy in Canada in July, and will join the Test countries at the 2003 World Cup in South Africa and Zimbabwe. Test status may remain a dream, but international one-day status, such as Kenya enjoy, might not be unrealistic. Cricket is now played in The Netherlands on grass (in Amstelveen, Deventer and, since 2001, in Utrecht at Kampong CC), and there is a larger pool of players than in Kenya, or even Zimbabwe. Bob Woolmer was impressed by the infrastructure when he visited the non-Test World Cup participants on behalf of the International Cricket Council.

This was the second time Holland had reached the World Cup. They were runners-up to Zimbabwe in the 1986 and 1990 ICC Trophy tournaments (when only the winner obtained a World Cup ticket) and were third in 1994, qualifying for the 1995-96 World Cup in Pakistan and India. The 2001 final against Namibia was a thriller, with Holland stealing a win off the last ball – an unlikely scenario with ten overs to go, 75 runs required and only four wickets standing. They still needed ten when the last over began, and then three from the last ball, which they got when an inside edge to fine leg was misfielded. The hero was No. 7 Jacob-Jan Esmeijer, more renowned for his left-arm spin, whose 58 not out was one of only four half-centuries in Holland's ten matches. Klaas Jan van Noortwijk also scored 50 in the final, Zulfiqar Ahmed contributed 87 to a crucial two-run win over Ireland in the Super League, and Robert van Oosterom made 52 against Fiji. Holland's real strength was their medium-pace bowling, led by their captain, 38-year-old Roland Lefebvre, who captured 20 wickets at 11.05. Tim de Leede claimed 18 wickets, and Sebastian Gokke eight at just 8.75. Van Noortwijk was the leading run-scorer with 227 and Esmeijer headed the batting averages at 34.33.

The victory was a triumph for Lefebvre and for Barbadian coach Emmerson Trotman, the culmination of a run of success including victory over Durham in the 1999 NatWest Trophy and winning the European Championship in 2000. Lefebvre intended to crown an illustrious career at the 2003 World Cup. But there was no lack of young players coming through, and a number have already made their mark, notably Gokke and batsman Henk Jan Mol. Over the years, individual Dutch cricketers have wintered in southern Test countries, and now more youngsters are doing so, often putting studies or regular employment on hold to further their cricketing ambitions. In 2000-01, 12 talented players spent three months in South Africa.

Back in Holland, the Hoofdklasse (premier league) was won for the third time in four seasons by VRA Amstelveen, who play all their home matches on grass. VRA's professional approach, which brought 14 victories in 15 completed matches, was exemplified by the acquisition of former Dutch captain Steven Lubbers to lead their second eleven, and of ex-New Zealand seamer Chris Pringle from HCC to strengthen the first team. Two more New Zealanders played a vital role: ex-Test batsman Shane Thomson and player-coach Craig Cumming, who topped the Hoofdklasse averages for the second year running, with 885 runs at 73.75. All-rounder Rashid Amin combined 334 runs at 37.11 with 36 wickets at 12.61, the most wickets and lowest average in the league. Pringle was not far behind, with 32 wickets at 13.40. The league's highest run-scorer was another New Zealander, player-coach Darron Reekers of Quick CC The Hague, who totalled 932 at 62.13.

Gandhi CC were relegated from the Hoofdklasse and replaced by Jinnah CC, who defeated Bijlmer CC in a play-off between the champions of the two Eerste Klasse (first division) pools. These three, based in Amsterdam, are essentially new clubs whose players originate almost exclusively from ethnic minority groups – the one real growth area in Dutch cricket. Jinnah have been in existence for only six years.

The 2001 season saw the restoration of the pyramid league system, with promotion and relegation at all levels. The second elevens of the larger clubs were restored to the Eerste Klasse, from which they were expelled after the infamous match-fixing day in 1994. HCC had "arranged" for their first eleven to beat the second eleven in order to prevent Gandhi's promotion – while Gandhi were busy fixing a win over another ethnic minority team, Success CC. To avoid any recurrence, the national cricket association created a separate league of second elevens in 1995.

Across the North Sea, Bas Zuiderent became the fourth Dutchman to make his mark in county cricket, and the first batsman. Zuiderent came to prominence as an 18-year-old when he scored 54 against England at the 1996 World Cup, and in 2001 he won a regular place in Sussex's first team. He chose not to join Holland for the ICC Trophy, preferring to secure his county contract, a decision respected by the Dutch coach and captain. But it was hoped that he would be available for the 2003 World Cup, when his experience should be highly valuable.

CRICKET IN DENMARK, 2001

By PETER S. HARGREAVES

Following the disappointing performances of their injury-plagued side at the European Championship in 2000, Denmark hoped to finish within the first seven at the ICC Trophy tournament at Toronto in 2001. In the event they finished sixth, which is as close as they have come to qualifying for the World Cup since winning the third-place play-off in England in 1986. They won their group in Toronto but lost all four Super League games.

Their preparations began in Cape Town in March, with 14 players being tried in seven matches against combined sides of suitable strength. With still only one turf pitch in Denmark, it was essential to gain experience of conditions similar to those that would be found in the tournament. Six games were won, and 12 of those involved later appeared in Toronto. In June, the St Augustine club from Cape Town visited Copenhagen, with Test player Paul Adams in their ranks. At that point there seemed to be grounds for optimism. In the ICC Trophy itself, the bowling was generally sufficient, although a good off-spinner was lacking, and the fielding was praised throughout. The top five bowlers all averaged less than 20, with Søren Vestergaard, now medium pace, the tournament's joint leading wicket-taker on 20 alongside Dutch captain Roland Lefebvre. He took a hat-trick against the United States. But the batting was less stable, and only Aftab Ahmed emerged with a creditable average, just below 39. Too often the innings had to be retrieved by the all-rounders after top wickets had gone cheaply.

In August, Denmark travelled to England to play Suffolk in the first round of the 2002 Cheltenham & Gloucester Trophy. The side was about two-thirds the strength of that fielded in Toronto, was without opening bowlers Thomas Hansen and Amjad Khan, and was comfortably beaten by seven wickets.

On the domestic scene, the inevitable annual question – could long-term champions Svanholm be toppled? – arose early when they were beaten by an Esbjerg side full of left-handed batsmen in the final of the knockout cup. And when they later lost to Herning and Glostrup inside a fortnight, the champions looked likely to be dethroned. However, over a single weekend, Herning went down to foot-of-the-table Ishøj and were beaten by Svanholm, who climbed back to the top of the division. Herning finished runners-up. While Svanholm celebrated their move to the new cricket stadium at Brøndby with their 11th successive championship, Ishøj had to change places with Aalborg from the division below. Husum, however, staved off the challenge from KB to remain in the top division for 2002.

Herning's Kent Jensen headed the batting with an average of 57.75, mainly through an unbeaten century, while the Husum No. 8, Gerrit Müller, recorded the highest aggregate – 442 at 36.83. Best all-rounder was Thomas Hansen of Svanholm, third in the batting averages at 43.83 and easily the most economical bowler, with 25 wickets at 10.56 apiece. Herning's Lars Hedegaard was the only other international all-rounder to impress, and it was something of an anomaly that the country's best batsman, Aftab Ahmed, managed only 24th place in the league averages.

In women's cricket, there has been a serious loss in playing strength, mostly through players in their thirties having families. A thriving teenage force is coming through in Central Jutland, but there is a danger of women's cricket withering on the eastern side of the country. Herning achieved the double, winning both the knockout competition and the championship, with Nykøbing Mors rather a poor second in each.

Finally, at veteran level, Dansk XL CC had problems fielding a full side for the annual triangular tournament of Forty Clubs, held at Oakham in Rutland. Expense was the main reason, but the Danish team is expected to be back to strength when the clubs meet again at Brøndby in July 2002. In a season when not too many things fell into place, this new stadium could be one sign that better times lie ahead.

CRICKET ROUND THE WORLD, 2001

ARGENTINA

Argentine cricket received a huge fillip when the national side did better than ever before in the ICC Trophy. Since the first tournament in 1979, when they failed to win a game, they had managed only one victory. Now they won four – all in the last over – and lost only to group winners Uganda. The previous December, Argentina A had won the fourth South American Championship when Buenos Aires hosted Brazil, Chile, Guyana Masters, Panama, Peru and Venezuela. Argentina had also won the previous three tournaments. Highlight of the home season was MCC's visit in March, even if the weather put a damper on it. The three-day fixture was rescheduled as three one-day games to give more local cricketers a chance to play the tourists, but the fixture against Rosario Athletic Club was rained off. Rain also washed out the second day of the 102nd North–South match, played at Lomas AC for the last time because the ground is to be used exclusively for hockey. On the final day, Van Steeden struck a whirlwind 68 in 47 minutes as the North chased 211, before settling for a draw. Lomas won the First Division from Belgrano, while Hurlingham took the Saturday Championship by beating Old Georgians in the final match. – David Parsons.

AZERBAIJAN

The 2001 season had a slow start. Though cricketers have use of the all-purpose playing-field at the International School in Baku, they did not begin playing until June. The school was then closed for building work in August and September, though once cricket restarted, the weather remained reasonable until November. The turnout, on the other hand, was pretty miserable. When it comes to leisure time, people here trade town life on the desert peninsula for the beautiful lushness of the countryside; only two games had 14 or more players. But for the first time there was a regular attendance of Azeri students, members of the Anglo-Azeri Society, and hopes are high that some will develop into useful cricketers. – Alum Bati.

BELGIUM

So much happened in 2001 it was a wonder Belgians spoke of anything but cricket in the cafés from Mons to Antwerp. Belgium were fifth at the 12-nation European Indoor Championship in Portugal in February, and third at the ECC Trophy in Vienna in August, after losing to eventual champions Portugal in the semi-finals. The annual two-match weekend against France, this time in Paris, was squared. But what really had Belgian cricket buzzing was the interest shown by youngsters: anyone coming upon the Saturday morning sessions, with up to 70 at each ground, would have been amazed – if only by the noise. Three age-group leagues were launched and, marking Belgium's first foray into youth internationals, a side was sent to the European Under-15 event in Berlin. There, they beat Spain by a distance in their opening game, lost by eight runs to tournament winners Germany, and ultimately finished sixth. On the domestic front, Pakistan (Greens) again swept all before them, adding the reinstated Cup to their third League title. In one 40-overs Cup game, the Greens made 335 for three (Amjad Mohammed 204 not out) and Antwerp 286 for six (Nadeem Khan 114). Optimists of Luxembourg, hopeful to the last, were relegated, making way for Mechelen CC from the heart of Flanders. The two Mechelen clubs, along with Ostende and Antwerp, fly the Belgian flag high amidst the *braais* and curries that give an international flavour to the game here, and Mechelen hosts the 2002 European indoor tournament. – Colin Wolfe.

BRUNEI DARUSSALAM

That large broken window, reported in *Wisden 2001*, and the resultant ban on cricket at the Shell Recreation Ground proved fatal to the Shell club's cricket eleven. This left only four teams to contest the League and Cup in 2001. Royal Brunei claimed the League but, for once, surrendered the Galfar Knockout Cup, which was won by Panaga. Although Panaga's ground is now the only regular venue for cricket, some fixtures, including the Borneo Cup matches with Sabah and Sarawak, were played on the No. 2 polo ground at Jerudong Park, near the capital – an encouraging development. The games were played on turf, a concrete strip being incompatible with the ground's principal use, and in the absence of specially sown grasses this brought a much wider dimension to the term "low slow pitch". The Borneo Cup was won by Sarawak, who defeated Brunei in an exciting final after both had beaten Sabah. It was their first victory since returning to regular cricket in 1996, so cricket in Borneo is once again truly a triangular affair. – Derek Thursby.

CANADA

Just when there should be so much to celebrate, Canada's successful staging of the 2001 ICC Trophy and qualification for the 2003 World Cup left cricket's future here at a crossroads. It had been expected that the cost of new facilities and hosting expenses would be covered by income from the India–Pakistan Sahara Cup series. When that was cancelled for Asian political reasons, Canada's financial position was severely compromised. The nine new turf squares and the artificial practice facilities laid on for the tournament proved a crushing expense in the absence of sponsorship, with the result that all World Cup plans have been put on hold. In addition, Canada were forced to withdraw from the 2001 Red Stripe tournament in Jamaica and an Under-19 event in Guyana – this at a time when the Under-19s, without five of their best players, had qualified for their World Cup in New Zealand in January 2002. Whatever the future holds, though, nothing can take away the fact that 2001 was the outstanding year in Canadian cricket history. The efforts of the ICC, of Canada's friends worldwide, of fans, players and volunteers would have been an unbeatable combination, even without some incredible weather: not one game was rained off. But overcoming top-seeded Scotland, to reach the World Cup for the first time since 1979, topped everything. We now pray that funding will be available so we can prepare properly. – Geoff Edwards.

CHILE

Two events gave Chilean cricket considerable impetus. In December 2000, the national team were runners-up in a field of seven at the South American Championship, losing only to hosts Argentina A in the final. Then, in March 2001, we received a visit from MCC. While Chile did not deprive them of their unbeaten record in South America, the two games, and the interaction with the MCC managers, players and umpires, provided the locals with valuable experience. These high-profile events, together with the huge enthusiasm generated by both expats and Chileans, led to the formation of the Chilean Cricket Association and an application for Affiliate membership of the ICC. We hope they will not be discouraged by the bemused reaction of an ICC official who attended the inauguration of our fourth cricket ground. It is not every day a cowboy rides round the boundary before the game, and then gets roped in as a substitute. Santiago now has four teams – the Prince of Wales, La Dehesa, La Reina and Santiago – while Valparaiso, whose field and pavilion date from the 1880s, hopes to revive the game where it began in Chile in 1829. – Anthony Adams.

CHINA

Ever since officers from HMS *Highflyer* played a Shanghai eleven in April 1858, cricket's popularity in China has been linked to the level of foreign influence. A century and a half on, the game is active again following the influx of British and Australian expats – enough to stage the inaugural Shanghai Ashes, in which a courageous England team overturned a highly fancied, typically confident Australian side. Beijing and Shanghai both have Cavaliers clubs, and in 2001 Shanghai's played a large role in promoting cricket among the Chinese population. Kanga Cricket kit and an indoor tennis court provided the wherewithal for regular games attracting players from every continent bar Antarctica. The hope is that these strongly social occasions will spawn outdoor cricket. Having survived the Hua Hin Sixes in Thailand in April, Shanghai staged their own event six weeks later, with former Australian Test cricketers Kim Hughes and Tom Hogan as guest players. Teams from Beijing, Hong Kong, Sri Lanka, India, Thailand and Australia took part, but Shanghai, urged on by their local community, reached the final and beat CBB from Thailand off the last ball. Fortunately, no one called for an ICC pitch inspector after groundstaff mowed the brand-new Astroturf wicket. Now if only we could stop them top-dressing it. – Mike Tsesmelis.

COSTA RICA

Cricket's "modest revival" in Costa Rica, reported last year, lost momentum when the ICC turned down their application for Affiliate membership, ostensibly because Argentina's sponsoring letter arrived too late. The Costa Rican association hopes to be accepted in 2002, believing that membership will facilitate the game's expansion. Meanwhile, they did become a full founder member of the Cricket Council of the Americas, and later held practice games in readiness for the tour in November by Southern California's Hollywood Golden Oldies Cricket Club. – Richard Illingworth.

ESTONIA

Although the outdoor season started in April, before the last snows, the Estonian Kriketi Klubi spent much of the year in the gyms, explaining Kwik Cricket to puzzled PE teachers and schoolchildren. However, an indoor tournament between schools in November made it all worth while. In fact, given the short Estonian summer, we continue to play inside throughout the year and hope to host an indoor event early in 2002. When we did get outdoors on to our new all-weather pitch and grass outfield, the club hosted teams from Latvia, Finland and England; Acton Trussell from Staffordshire were beaten with a six off the last ball by EKK captain Jason Barry. EKK also travelled south to Latvia and across the water to Helsinki, performing well both on and off the field. It will be some time before cricket is widely played in this part of the world, so it is an occasion when we get visitors, and we always do our best to welcome them. – Phil Marsdale.

FRANCE

The high point for France in 2001 was their *Cadets* team's triumph in the European Under-17 tournament in Corfu, with crushing wins over Greece, Italy, Germany, Austria and Gibraltar. They were well led by 15-year-old Arun Ayyavooraju, ably seconded by Sulanga Hewalandanage (16), who took 14 wickets overall and scored 135 not out against Greece. Both also impressed playing for the senior side at the ICC Trophy in Toronto where, with three French citizens declared ineligible by the ICC at the last moment, a weakened team performed creditably. Simon Hewitt, who had played in all of France's 108 official games since 1989, the last 106 as captain, retired after the ICC Trophy to become coach to the national side. He will be looking to groom younger, home-grown players. Several Frenchmen made their debuts when France played Holland and Kent at Folkestone in September in the first European Cricket Challenge. In Portugal in February, 16-year-old leg-spinner Cindy Paquin made history as the first woman to play in the European Indoor Championship. Paquin has received tips from France's patron, Richie Benaud, who in a Channel 4 documentary charted his origins and visited the village of Benaud in Auvergne. In the Club Championship, Dreux, a Pakistani team, defeated British expats Standard Athletic, from Paris, by one wicket in a thrilling final. Disappointingly, neither side fielded a native Frenchman. – Michel Cogne.

GERMANY

First-time participation in the ICC Trophy was a proud moment for the Deutscher Cricket Bund (DCB). Losing to Namibia was no disgrace, as their subsequent achievements in Toronto showed, and only a two-run defeat by Nepal prevented Germany from being runners-up in their group. Gerrit Müller continued his practice of scoring a century at each international tournament he has played in (110 not out against Gibraltar), topping Germany's averages with 56.50, while captain Hamid Bhatti headed the bowling with eight wickets at 12.50. An MCC tour, the second in the DCB's short history, had provided welcome exposure to good-class opposition before the team left for Canada. In Berlin, the national team were only 13 runs away from spoiling their visitors' unbeaten record. On the ECC stage, Germany's Colts won their title in Edinburgh, the Under-15s ran out winners in Berlin and the Under-17s were third in Corfu. With the DCB committed to seeking out and coaching youth cricketers, and schools in major cities bringing new recruits into the game, the future looks positive. The events of September 11 meant the final rounds of the 2001 German Club Championship, due to be played on the British Army grounds at Mönchengladbach on September 15, had to be postponed until May 2002. Pak Alemi Hamburg from the north league, DSSC Berlin (east), MCC Munich (south) and Frankfurt CC (west) were the Championship qualifiers. North-West beat the North in the annual championship between the five regional leagues. – Brian Fell.

GIBRALTAR

Though Gibraltar's season does not start until May, some of the Rock's cricketers were in action well before that, competing at the European Indoor Championship in Portugal in February. The squad of eight included two 16-year-olds and finished seventh out of 12, a reasonable placing given that this was Gibraltar's first international indoor tournament. Associate Members, such as Gibraltar, were restricted to Under-19 players, whereas Affiliates could select players aged up to 27. At home, Gibraltar hosted four touring teams: Morton and RAF Kinloss from Scotland, Galah CC from Western Australia, and the London Stock Exchange. All but the last lost all their games; by October, when the Stock Exchange visited, our most promising young cricketers were back at university or college in England. Grammarians CC picked up their first trophy since 1984 by winning the 30-overs Wiggins Shield competition, while the 50-overs Senior League went to UKCCC, who also won the Murto Cup. Focal point of the year was the ICC Trophy, where Gibraltar finished fourth in their section. Age-group sides went to European tournaments in Scotland, Corfu and Germany and, although results might have been better, provided further evidence that the GCA's youth development programme is succeeding in turning out teams with indigenous cricketers. – Tom Finlayson.

HONG KONG

Despite 11th place in the ICC Trophy, Hong Kong had a successful year domestically, with their development programme prospering and a significant sponsorship received from a major retail company, Wellcome. At primary-school level, teams in the Playground League doubled to 32; the elementary programme, with instruction in Cantonese, grew steadily with several eight-week courses at five outdoor and six indoor venues; and there are now leagues for age-groups from 11 to 19. Statistics show participation rose from 6,000 in 1999 to more than 10,000 in 2000. With assistance from the Auckland Cricket Association, 20 Cantonese-speaking coaches qualified at HKCA level 2 (NZ level 1). Grounds remain a major constraint, but a site at Po Kong Village in Kowloon, the first new cricket ground since 1974, will be ready in 2002, and Hong Kong are evaluating whether artificial pitches could be used at multi-purpose sports fields. They are also looking to develop indoor cricket. An innovation in the senior game was the Platypus Cup match, in which the two principal clubs, Kowloon and Hong Kong, combined to play a side comprising the best players from other teams, the Independents. This fixture, which the Independents won, will become a regular opening to the season. Hong Kong qualified for the 2002 Asia Cup by reaching the ACC Trophy final in Sharjah, although losing to the UAE, and again won the Tuanku Ja'afar Tournament, involving Malaysia, Thailand and Singapore. In April, the MCCs of Marylebone and Melbourne played in a triangular tournament to celebrate Hong Kong CC's 150th anniversary, the first time they had met outside their respective countries. – John Cribbin.

ICELAND

It was bad news for the caption writer but great publicity for Iceland when Sky Sport sent a crew in July to film the annual Icelandic Cricket Championship, in which the combined team of Kylfan and Ungmennafelagid Glaumur, from Reykjavik and Stykkisholmur respectively, beat Tryggingamidstodin by 58 runs (111 to 53). The event also attracted the attention of the local media, and players spent the better part of the day being interviewed by TV, radio and newspaper journalists. A common question was why and how the interest in cricket had taken hold of so many Icelanders. The answer may be found, in part anyway, in *Wisden 2001*, and this entry may explain why we had teams from as far away as India wanting to play here. Some diplomatic skills were needed to convince them that our level of cricket would not justify traversing half the globe. But our game is improving. ECC coach Tim Dellor came to Stykkisholmur in May to teach us the finer skills, and more youngsters were introduced to the game. Practice sessions were held during the summer on various green places in the capital, Reykjavik, and attracted not just attention but also a number of foreigners more familiar with the game. This resulted in a higher level of cricket, so who knows what the future will bring? – Benedikt Waage.

ISRAEL

After the senior side had failed to win a game at the ICC Trophy, our Under-15s did Israel proud with the silver medal at their ECC tournament in Berlin. Expectations went no further than one win and showing the flag; in the event, four games were won, including a last-over semi-final victory against Gibraltar thanks to a captain's half-century by Gal Matz, one of the tournament's leading all-rounders. The batting and keeping of Danny Hotz, coupled with the bowling of Michael Muchi, were the principal reasons for the outstanding results. Hosts Germany won the final, played in trying, rainy conditions, but Israel did beat them in an earlier round. That first game, however, was marred by a German player of Afghan origin ripping the Israeli flag from its pole: a great pity, given the significance of an Israeli team competing on German soil. On the senior team's return from Canada, the national selectors had hoped to play a new-look side against MCC, who were due in Israel in October. However, to the disappointment of cricketers and fans, MCC called off the visit, citing security concerns. After waiting ten years, Tel Aviv CC won the League when they beat Lions Lod by 20 runs in a rain-reduced 33-overs match. Danny Malyinkar hit a maiden hundred in Tel Aviv's 229 for six. Meanwhile, the youth programme continues to exceed Israel's wildest dreams, with some 500 girls and boys playing regularly in schools and at afternoon sessions. The success of the programme, along with the Under-15s' silver medal, is a deserved reward for the hard work put in by George Sheader, Steven Shein and national coach Herschel Gutman. – Stanley Perlman.

ITALY

For Italy, 2001 will long be remembered as the first and, it is hoped, the only time a country withdrew from an official ICC event in protest at what it believed to be illegitimate interference in its civil rights and national sovereignty. When the ICC prohibited Italy from playing its own citizens, albeit not Italian-born, at the ICC Trophy, the *Nazionale* withdrew from the Toronto event and an official protest was lodged by the Italian Foreign Ministry. On a happier note, Italy's three youth teams performed well in ECC events, with the Under-17s finishing second to France in Corfu. At home, Pianoro regained the EIS Cup, their sixth pennant in eight seasons, defeating Bologna 2–0 in the finals, and confirming their superiority by adding the Italian Cup. Their season was a personal triumph for 27-year-old Valerio Zuppiroli in his first year as captain; he is potentially Italy's captain at the 2002 European Championship. Pianoro's two main rivals, Capannelle and Bologna, gained some consolation by winning respectively the Under-13 and Under-15 titles, while Cirnechi Catania became Italy's first women's champions. – Simone Gambino.

IVORY COAST

Cricket is starting from scratch in Côte d'Ivoire: there is no league, just an occasional weekly game within the expat community on Abidjan's Cocody University campus. There are no facilities and no shops selling cricket gear. In fact, until we invited ICC development officer Hossain Ayob to Abidjan in June 2001, there was little likelihood the game might start up. He suggested we attempt to establish cricket in schools and, when the national sports authorities expressed interest, he held lectures and training sessions at the Ivorian National Institute of Youth and Sport (INJS), the PE student teachers' college. They appointed two of their coaches to liaise with us. The initial objective is to teach the teachers so that they can teach the children, and so establish the game. It will take time. Meanwhile, articles of federation are being drawn up for submission to the ICC, prior to applying for Affiliate membership. – Chris Frean.

JAPAN

A dream came true for the Japan Cricket Association when, in September 2001, they made their first tour of England. It was, moreover, the first time the men's and ladies' teams, all Japanese nationals, had toured together, and they provided MCC with a first when both touring teams played them at Shenley Park on the same day. Although the visitors did not win a match, they were always learning – and when you start with 11 ducks in your opening game, as the ladies did against Hitchin, things can only improve. Batting first, they managed only 14: ten extras and four by Masumi Masuyama, who made the 11th duck when Japan had a consolation "second" innings. After that, they were never bowled out again. The JCA also launched a new constitution and logo, the latter featuring a "j" surmounted by a cricket ball. With some 60 clubs and 3,000 players, including foreign nationals, cricket is making progress. A new league started in Kanto, the first with two divisions, where Friends XI beat another Pakistani team, Tokyo Giants, for the championship crown. There are also leagues in Kyushu and Kansai, and the JCA have plans for an All-Japan winter six-a-side tournament. Ambitiously, they also aim to have cricket teams in every school. Should any of the students follow the example of Tetsuo Fuji, umpires and batsmen could be in for interesting times. A few years ago, in an ACC Trophy match, Fuji took two wickets in two balls, bowled from either hand. As he demonstrated during a national training session, he can still do it, bowling one batsman three times in four balls from alternate hands. – Naoaki Saida.

KUWAIT

Participation by age-group teams in ICC events in 2000-01 offered proof that Kuwait continue to make good progress in this area. The Under-19s proved their mettle when they hit a record 387 in 40 overs against Maldives in Nepal, where they won the Plate with four victories in five games. The Under-17s picked up an award as best fielding team in a tournament in Pakistan, while finishing behind three Test-playing countries, and the Under-13s won when Kuwait hosted a tournament for Gulf countries. This brought the Under-13s an invitation to the United States to play in the first global tournament for their age-group, but unfortunately this was postponed. There are 52 teams registered with the Kuwait Cricket Association and one of them, Lanka Lions CC, made news in May when wicket-keeper Gagira Perusinghe established a local record by stumping nine Federal Express batsmen in an innings. – Asad Beig.

LIBYA

Cricket in Libya is based largely in the two major cities: Tripoli, which has seven clubs, and Benghazi, five. Competitive cricket began here in 1992, when Benghazi hosted the All-Libya Tournament, and there are now clubs in the smaller settlements of Adjabia and Misrata. In 2001, the newly formed Libyan Cricket Association applied for Affiliate membership of the ICC. – Arfat Malik.

LUXEMBOURG

Luxembourg made steady progress in 2001, with over 100 cricketers playing in leagues and many more joining in the growing programme of friendlies. While the LCF–Crosscomm League was again contested by six teams, a new club joined the LCF halfway through the season and will enter the League in either 2002 or 2003. Such is the game's growth that the only ground, Optimists CC's excellent facility at Walferdange, is in use almost every day of the season, causing the LCF to consider developing a second ground. In the meantime, a new double-bay net has been installed at the European School, which could encourage student interest and boost the rapidly expanding junior scene. New net areas are also needed at Walferdange, after the existing ones were demolished in flood-prevention works. Star CC were 2001 League champions, finishing just ahead of Optimists despite losing to them by one run, while Communities CC, who were third, won the annual six-a-side. Highlights of the year included the four-day programme of matches to celebrate Optimists' 25th anniversary, though unfortunately they went on to be relegated from the first division of the Belgian League for the first time. As disappointingly, Luxembourg's scheduled internationals – against

France at home and Switzerland away – were rained off. An interesting record, of sorts, was set in a game between Communities and Rugby Club when, in eight overs, one fielder dropped the same batsman five times in three different fielding positions. On the distaff side, Optimists Maidens continued to play with unabated enthusiasm as they approached their tenth birthday. – Bryan Rouse.

MALAYSIA

A busy year for the Malaysian Cricket Association was capped on the field by participation in the ICC Trophy and off it by hosting the ICC executive board meeting in October. Though favoured to head their group, and so enter the play-off for a place in the Super League, Malaysia managed only third. The Under-19 side performed better in the Asia Youth Cup by reaching the final, which they lost to hosts Nepal in front of 15,000 home-team supporters. However, the senior eleven could look back on some solid achievements, including winning the Stan Nagaiah Trophy match against Singapore and reaching the semi-finals of the ACC Trophy in Sharjah. The Saudara Cup fixture against Singapore in Kuala Lumpur was drawn. As part of Malaysia's preparations for Toronto, the MCA welcomed Pakistan's Under-19s in April, and the national squad later spent ten days in Bangalore. The domestic League, which ran from February to September with a five-week break for the ICC Trophy, was won by favourites Malaysian Malays, aided by Sri Lankan imports Sarath Jayawardene and Pryankara Wickramasinghe. TNB were second and Selangor third. Malays also won the five-team MCA Cup, beating Selangor in the final. – Venu Ramadass.

MALTA

No fewer than 18 touring teams took advantage of Malta's year-round season and the facilities at the Marsa Sports Club, with most booking a return visit. The strongest opposition came from the increasing number of English schools who tour, while cricketers from The Hague, a Swiss Select side and Milan CC gave the comings and goings an international flavour. Middlesex CCC were also here for outdoor practice before the start of the English season. All told, 40 games of 35 to 50 overs were played against local sides of varying ability, fitness and age, with the record being 26 wins, 13 defeats and a pulsating tie against RMA Sandhurst. Andrew Naudi, aged 19, did the double of 1,000 runs and 50 wickets for the season, a feat previously achieved by very few locals. National captain Michael Caruana continued to dominate the batting averages, and there was a welcome return to Malta by Frank Spiteri – a great asset to club and country. Highlight of the year was Malta's equal third at the ten-nation ECC Trophy in Vienna in August. By the end, the heavy schedule had told on the players' fitness, but it could not dampen their determination or team spirit. Another of the year's achievements was the inauguration of the Cricket Youth Nursery at Marsa CC. – Pierre Naudi.

MEXICO

The 2000-01 season saw the 107-year-old Mexico City club make sweeping strides towards securing cricket's future in Mexico. The club appointed a coach, set up a website, launched a monthly publication and recruited new players – as well as providing entertaining cricket in domestic and representative games. The home team won both matches when the British and Dominion club arrived from Los Angeles in November, while the spoils were shared 1–1 when old friends Houston Memorial CC came down from Texas in mid-March to play MCCC's first and second elevens. In June, former West Indies opener Faoud Bacchus warmed up for America's games in the ICC Trophy by bringing his Miami Masters side to town for a weekend. He hit an unbeaten 130 against the seconds on Saturday, but had less of the limelight next day when local all-rounder Hugo van Belle smashed six sixes on his way to a career-best 94 for MCCC's firsts. Even so, the Masters won by 41 runs. The domestic competitions – the limited and unlimited overs – had their share of thrills. Corinthians started strongly in the former, but Aztecs and Reforma pegged them back with some gutsy cricket after Christmas to force a three-way tie. The unlimited-overs competition, which ran from March to June, was won by Aztecs. However, it was the Anzacs who provided the best entertainment, with an Anzac Day match against a Rest of the World line-up. Some 200 spectators were treated to an authentic Aussie barbie, didgeridoo player and pulsating finish in which, with two wickets in hand, the Anzacs needed 12 off the last over. They managed 11 and the game was tied. – E. J. Cartledge.

NAMIBIA

Namibia went to the ICC Trophy seeded 13th, hoping at best for a place in the top ten. They came away with a ticket to the World Cup in neighbouring South Africa and Zimbabwe after taking Trophy-winners Holland to the last ball in the final. Their courage and commitment overcame a tournament structure that disadvantaged the bottom-seeded nations. The Namibia Cricket Board had set up a series of games to give their team every opportunity of being well prepared. There was a quadrangular tournament in Windhoek involving the Boland and Western Province academies and the South African Correctional Services, and Namibia also took part in South Africa's three-day Bowl matches and limited-overs competition, just failing to reach the final. An MCC side came for a ten-match programme that took them to the towns of Swakopmund, Walvis Bay and Blomfelde, and provided opposition for the ICC Trophy squad in five games. Namibia won three and lost one, and they later shared a two-game series against Scotland, the Trophy's top seeds. Of the 17 international games Namibia played in 2001, they won 13, lost three and had one no result. In addition to this fine record, Namibia's Under-19s had earlier won the ICC Associates' Youth Africa Championship in Uganda to qualify for their World Cup in New Zealand in 2002. With club cricket expected to grow over the next two years, Namibia's main concern now is to develop facilities quickly enough to accommodate the game's growing popularity. – Laurie Pieters.

NIGERIA

The West African Cricket Conference's decision in 2001 to support the Nigerian Cricket Association's bid for individual ICC membership was tangible proof of cricket's regeneration here after two decades of decline. And the NCA received another boost when the Nigerian government agreed to hand back the Tafawa Balewa cricket ground, which had been held by the Ministry of Defence for 27 years. These decisions were deserved reward for the country's former cricketers who had vowed to salvage the game from the brink of extinction. In January, ICC development officer Hossain Ayob conducted coaching and umpiring courses, and Nigeria subsequently contributed ten players to the West African Under-19 squad that contested the ICC Associates' Youth Africa Championship in Uganda. In a group game, West Africa beat eventual winners Namibia. Nigeria also sent teams to the second African Championship, in Kenya, and to a quadrangular tournament in Freetown, where they played hosts Sierra Leone, Gambia and Ghana. The Howzat Foundation, a non-profit organisation for the development and promotion of cricket, attracted more than 200 aspiring cricketers between the age of five and 22 to a holiday coaching clinic in August, offering further grounds for confidence in the game's future. The Lagos League, which has been running for more than 40 years, saw Foundation CC head off nine other clubs. – Patrick Opara.

[*Mueen ud din Hameed*

Bryan Murgatroyd top-scored for Namibia with a half-century in the ICC Trophy final against Holland.

NORWAY

The controversial changes at the top of Norwegian cricket administration late in 2000 were bound to have ramifications, but no one expected them to be quite so startling. Communication problems between the new board members and the European Cricket Council threatened to derail the game's progress in 2001. There were neither coaching classes nor improvements in playing and practice facilities. And, in the absence of any commitment by Norway's board to the ECC's development programme, there was no invitation to the ECC Trophy tournament in Vienna, where the previous year Norway had won a developing countries' festival. The upshot was another change at the top after the year-old board was voted out at an extraordinary general meeting. Before it came to that, however, a visit from an ECC officer would have been welcome; some in Norwegian cricket felt the council had not done enough to help sort out the problems. Happily for Norway's cricket-lovers, Pakistan Test cricketers Abdur Razzaq and Imran Nazir did pay a visit during the summer. They played in a limited-overs game and, more importantly, mixed freely with supporters. As for the number of times they were photographed in the day – it must have set some kind of record. Sentrum CC retained the Oslo League title, while Star CC won the Norway and Sinsen Cups. – Bob Gibb.

PANAMA

Panama failed to win a match at the inaugural Americas Affiliates tournament in Jamaica, a qualification event for the 2002 Americas Cup in Buenos Aires. They lost to unbeaten Cayman Islands, Bahamas and the Turks and Caicos Islands. A weekend visit to Colombia proved more successful; Panama won the two 40-overs games by comfortable margins. With both sides struggling for runs because of the thickly grassed outfield, the accuracy of Panama's bowlers proved decisive. In an exciting season of club cricket, Nawab, Bhattay, Dada Bhai and Muslim emerged from the 25-overs league to contest the semi-finals which, like the final, were 40-overs games. Bhattay beat Dada Bhai by two wickets in front of 500 people, and several days later, on Good Friday, 650 watched Muslim eliminate favourites Nawab by four runs. The final, however, was an anticlimax: Muslim won by five wickets after dismissing Bhattay for 85. – Saleh and Musaji Bhana.

PARAGUAY

Though it never took root, cricket in Paraguay can be traced back for a century, played mostly by the British, who were building railways, and by the Australian immigrants who set up colonies in Cosme and Nueva Australia. There was the occasional game organised by the British Community Council, and the formation of the Stragglers club in the 1980s led to games against teams from Argentina. The Turtles of Buenos Aires, in 1984, were the last international opposition. However, the establishment of the Association of Paraguayan Cricket in November 2000 has opened up new prospects. The ICC have sent Kanga Cricket kits, and we hope the 2002 schools programme will introduce the game to up to 500 youngsters, mostly the children of expats. Because our Brazilian counterparts in São Paulo have expressed interest in an international fixture, provided the games are not played on our "cabbage patches", we are trying to raise funds to purchase Astroturf pitches for Asunción and Ciudad del Este. In the capital, we play on a soccer pitch belonging to the Air Force; in Ciudad del Este, where around 80 Asian cricketers keep the game alive, facilities are possibly worse – and they have no protective equipment. – Norman M. Langer.

PORTUGAL

A busy year began when the Federação Portuguesa de Cricket hosted the ECC six-a-side Indoor Championship at Mafra. With 12 countries participating, this was the largest yet, and Portugal enhanced their administrative and playing reputations by staging a highly successful tournament and winning it in a nail-biting final against the 2000 champions, Holland. Their victory, which made local TV, significantly furthered the popularity of indoor cricket in Portugal, as renewed interest in the Lisbon Indoor League demonstrated. In the final of that competition, Amadora beat Oeiras to win the Gauntlett Trophy. April took cricket outdoors once again, with the familiar venues in Oporto and Carcavelos (Lisbon) seeing the bulk of the action. Seven teams competed in the Lisbon League, where reigning champions ACC swept all before them. ACC's Nadeem Butt scored over 1,000 runs in 12 innings, including an amazing 220 not out in 35 overs against CHP "A", and was the mainstay of Portugal's batting at the ECC Trophy in Vienna in August. Wins over Finland, Sweden, Spain, Malta and Belgium put them in the final against Austria. After the disappointment of losing the 1999 final to Greece, the Portuguese, ably led by Akbar Saiyad, made no mistake with a comfortable eight-wicket victory. In the Kendall Cup, an annual two-day match between Lisbon and Oporto dating from 1861, Lisbon were victorious for the first time in seven years, winning by an innings and 46 runs. The many visiting teams included MCC, whose short stay was unfortunately ruined by rain, and an England All-Stars side led by Graham Gooch. – Peter D. Eckersley.

ST HELENA

Cricket has been played on St Helena for more than 120 years, but for this small territory hidden in the South Atlantic 2001 was a landmark year: St Helena was admitted to Affiliate membership of the ICC, and it was hoped this would lead to the provision of coaching and other facilities. With transport dependent on the monthly visit of a ship plying between Cardiff and Cape Town, tours are not envisaged, though a regular challenge match with Ascension Island, 500 miles north, might be possible. St Helena has only one area flat enough for cricket of any proper standard, and each weekend from January to June the ground at Francis Plain stages four games: two on Saturday and two on Sunday. There is a well-contested league, followed by a knockout, and the season concludes with a district competition. In 2001, there was great excitement when Jamestown B and Jamestown Z finished the league with the same playing record (played ten, won nine, lost one) but "Z" had 176 points to their rivals' 175. "B", who usually win the League, gained revenge in the semi-finals of the knockout and then beat Western B in the final. Gavin George was in exceptional form for them, hitting six centuries while compiling 1,168 runs in 14 innings. His unbeaten 117 out of 160 in one game was 73 per cent of Jamestown B's total, and he topped 50 per cent in four others. – Fraser M. Simm.

SOLOMON ISLANDS

The last few years have been difficult ones for the Solomons, and cricket has not been high on most people's priority list. We were invited by the ICC to apply for Affiliate membership but did not qualify owing to the lack of a regular competition: we had only two games in 2001. However, the ICC have provided us with equipment and we hope that we can start a coaching programme in two of Honiara's primary schools in 2002. – Kevin Chant.

SPAIN

One of the more positive aspects of the year was the participation of more Spanish nationals in the administration of the Asociación Española de Cricket. This is already having a beneficial effect on the development of cricket in schools, although the lack of financial support and suitable venues continues to hamper progress on a broader scale. Participation at the European Indoor Championship, the ECC Trophy in Vienna and the Under-15 tournament in Berlin was possible only through sponsorship from the Andrew Copeland Group. The repossession of the Javea CC ground by the local council was a blow to cricket on the Costa Blanca, although the area remains the focus of the game's development in Spain, with Kwik Cricket included in the syllabus of several Spanish and international schools. One new club from the Alicante area joined the Asociación, but this did not offset the decline, almost to extinction, in the south of the country. Additional facilities in other areas are urgently required if young cricketers are to have an opportunity to fulfil their potential. At senior level, Sporting Alfas maintained their position as Spain's leading club when they carried off the Royal & SunAlliance Cup for a record third successive year. – Clive Woodbridge.

SURINAM

Cricket, or something resembling it, was first played in Surinam in 1880, when it was Dutch Guiana. In all probability, these first cricketers were indentured Indians. The game became organised with the establishment of Royal Scott's CC in 1885, and a national association, which today is an associate member of the West Indies board, was founded in 1931. As games were played more regularly against sides from neighbouring Guyana (British Guiana) and other West Indian countries, cricket flourished in Surinam, particularly in the 1950s and 1960s. Members of Surinam's youth teams of the 1980s went on to play for the Dutch national side. Today, there are some 25 senior clubs and the Surinamese Cricket Association have applied for membership of the Cricket Council of the Americas and for Affiliate membership of the ICC. – Ram Hiralal.

SWITZERLAND

Two sad occurrences early in 2001 cast a pall over the Swiss season. In January, Dr David Barmes, a former president of the Swiss Cricket Association and at the time president of Geneva CC, died while on holiday in Australia. Then, four days before the European Indoor Championship in Portugal, Nasir Hamirani, the SCA treasurer and former captain of the national team, died in Zurich after a short illness. These events left the SCA with gaps to fill and plans to be remade. Happily, the memory of both men lived on when Geneva, Dr Barmes's old club, became the first winners of the Nasir Hamirani Memorial Trophy, organised by one of Nasir's old clubs, Zurich Nomads. In Portugal, the Swiss Under-27s finished last, but Switzerland's national side managed slightly better at the ECC Trophy in Vienna by finishing eighth of ten. Despite a sodden summer, a full Championship programme was completed. Reigning champions Winterthur went out in the semi-finals to Berne, whom they had beaten in the previous year's final, while newcomers Zurich United beat Geneva. Storms in Zurich on the eve of the final left the outfield damp and temperatures unusually low. Put in to bat, United were dismissed for 52 in 22 overs. Berne's reply was slow and cautious in the dripping conditions, but they eventually reached their target in the 23rd over for the loss of one wicket. The Swiss circuit welcomed a new club, Fribourg CC, to its number during the summer. The playing members are mainly local Swiss, although there is a Macedonian in the line-up. – John McKillop.

VANUATU

The Mele Bulls drove all before them in 2001, winning the BDO Club Championship, Roger Strickland Shield, Independence Cup and President's seven-a-side. Their success left Mele CC president Rob Agius poorer by some 18 tickets to New Caledonia and its Club Med, the prize he had promised pre-season for a clean sweep. Off the field, the Vanuatu Cricket Association took a great step forward when they appointed national captain Pierre Chillia as their first development officer, and since then he has made a big impact at primary schools in and around Port Vila. The emphasis has been on Kanga Cricket and developing basic skills; hard-ball games for older children will be introduced in the next few years. Four years ago, we had contact with 60 youngsters; in 2001, we had brought cricket in one form or another to around 1,000. Before the domestic season started, Vanuatu sent a team to New Zealand for the inaugural Pacifica Championship, which was won by NZ Maoris (captained by a blond). Although Vanuatu finished a disappointing seventh, left-hander Richard Tatwin was selected for the Pacifica Eleven. – Mark Stafford.

VENEZUELA

With no domestic tournament and just one ground, at the Caracas Sports Club, Venezuela's cricketers look to visiting teams to give their games some spice. They are not short of cricket, just variety: after all, they play every other week throughout the year. Tourists Sports Club of Miami and a side from Queen's Park Oval, Port-of-Spain made appearances in 2001 – the latter as part of Trinidad's Independence Day celebrations – and both were expected to return in January 2002 to celebrate the Caracas club's 50th anniversary. Other opponents included teams from Belize, Colombia and Panama. In December 2000, Venezuela competed in the South American Championship in Buenos Aires. All three games, though close, were lost, partly because several leading Venezuelan players could not afford to travel. For the game against eventual winners Argentina A, Venezuela were loaned three boys aged 10, 12 and 14. – Basil Mathura.

PART SIX: ADMINISTRATION AND LAWS

INTERNATIONAL CRICKET COUNCIL

On June 15, 1909, representatives of cricket in England, Australia and South Africa met at Lord's and founded the Imperial Cricket Conference. Membership was confined to the governing bodies of cricket in countries within the British Commonwealth where Test cricket was played. India, New Zealand and West Indies were elected as members on May 31, 1926, Pakistan on July 28, 1952, Sri Lanka on July 21, 1981, Zimbabwe on July 8, 1992 and Bangladesh on June 26, 2000. South Africa ceased to be a member of the ICC on leaving the British Commonwealth in May, 1961, but was elected as a Full Member on July 10, 1991.

On July 15, 1965, the Conference was renamed the International Cricket Conference and new rules were adopted to permit the election of countries from outside the British Commonwealth. This led to the growth of the Conference, with the admission of Associate Members, who were each entitled to one vote, while the Foundation and Full Members were each entitled to two votes, on ICC resolutions. On July 12, 13, 1989, the Conference was renamed the International Cricket Council and revised rules were adopted.

On July 7, 1993, the ICC ceased to be administered by MCC and became an independent organisation with its own chief executive, the headquarters remaining at Lord's. The category of Foundation Member, with its special rights, was abolished. On October 1, 1993, Sir Clyde Walcott became the first non-British chairman of the ICC.

On June 16, 1997, the ICC became an incorporated body, with an executive board and a president instead of a chairman. Jagmohan Dalmiya became the ICC's first president.

Officers

President: M. A. Gray (2000–02). *Chief Executive:* M. W. Speed.

Chairman of Committees: Cricket – Management: M. W. Speed; *Cricket – Playing:* S. M. Gavaskar; *Development:* M. W. Speed; *Finance and Marketing:* E. Mani.

Executive Board: The president and chief executive sit on the board and all committees *ex officio*. They are joined by Ali Mohammad Asghar (Bangladesh), Sir John Anderson (New Zealand), P. Chingoka (Zimbabwe), J. Dalmiya (India), W. W. Hall (West Indies), Lord MacLaurin (England), V. P. Malalasekera (Sri Lanka), R. F. Merriman (Australia), J. Rayani (Kenya), P. H. F. Sonn (South Africa), Tauqir Zia (Pakistan), HRH Tunku Imran (Malaysia), R. van Ierschot (Netherlands).

General Manager: R. M. G. Hill. *General Manager – Cricket:* D. J. Richardson. *Cricket Operations Manager:* C. D. Hitchcock. *Development Manager:* A. Eade. *Financial/Project Manager:* D. C. Jamieson. *Communications Manager:* M. J. Harrison.

Constitution

President: Each Full Member has the right, by rotation, to appoint ICC's president. In 1997, India named J. Dalmiya to serve until June 2000, when M. A. Gray of Australia took over. Gray and subsequent presidents will serve for two years.

Chief Executive: Appointed by the Council. D. L. Richards was appointed in 1993; he stepped down in September 2001, and was succeeded by M. W. Speed.

Membership

Full Members: Australia, Bangladesh, England, India, New Zealand, Pakistan, South Africa, Sri Lanka, West Indies and Zimbabwe.

Associate Members*: Argentina (1974), Bermuda (1966), Canada (1968), Denmark (1966), East and Central Africa (1966), Fiji (1965), France (1998), Germany (1999), Gibraltar (1969), Hong Kong (1969), Ireland (1993), Israel (1974), Italy (1995), Kenya (1981), Malaysia (1967), Namibia (1992), Nepal (1996), Netherlands (1966), Papua New Guinea (1973), Scotland (1994), Singapore (1974), Tanzania (2001), Uganda (1998), United Arab Emirates (1990), USA (1965) and West Africa (1976).

Affiliate Members*: Afghanistan (2001), Austria (1992), Bahamas (1987), Bahrain (2001), Belgium (1991), Belize (1997), Bhutan (2001), Botswana (2001), Brunei (1992), Cayman Islands (1997), Cook Islands (2000), Croatia (2001), Cyprus (1999), Czech Republic (2000), Finland (2000), Greece (1995), Indonesia (2001), Japan (1989), Kuwait (1998), Lesotho (2001), Luxembourg (1998), Maldives (2001), Malta (1998), Morocco (1999), Norway (2000), Oman (2000), Philippines (2000), Portugal (1996), Qatar (1999), St Helena (2001), Samoa (2000), South Korea (2001), Spain (1992), Sweden (1997), Switzerland (1985), Thailand (1995), Tonga (2000) and Vanuatu (1995).

* *Year of election shown in parentheses.*

The following governing bodies for cricket shall be eligible for election.

Full Members: The governing body for cricket recognised by the ICC of a country, or countries associated for cricket purposes, or a geographical area, from which representative teams are qualified to play official Test matches.

Associate Members: The governing body for cricket recognised by the ICC of a country, or countries associated for cricket purposes, or a geographical area, which does not qualify as a Full Member but where cricket is firmly established and organised.

Affiliate Members: The governing body for cricket recognised by the ICC of a country, or countries associated for cricket purposes, or a geographical area (which is not part of one of those already constituted as a Full or Associate Member) where the ICC recognises that cricket is played in accordance with the Laws of Cricket. Affiliate Members have no right to vote or to propose or second resolutions at ICC meetings.

ENGLAND AND WALES CRICKET BOARD

The England and Wales Cricket Board (ECB) became responsible for the administration of all cricket – professional and recreational – in England and Wales on January 1, 1997. It took over the functions of the Cricket Council, the Test and County Cricket Board and the National Cricket Association which had run the game in England and Wales since 1968. The Management Board is answerable to the First-Class Forum on matters concerning the first-class game and to the Recreational Forum on matters concerning the non-professional game. The First-Class Forum elects five members to the Management Board and the Recreational Forum elects four.

Officers

Chairman: Lord MacLaurin of Knebworth. *Chief Executive:* T. M. Lamb.

Management Board: Lord MacLaurin (*chairman*), D. L. Acfield, P. W. Anderson, J. B. Bolus, D. G. Collier, S. P. Coverdale, P. W. Gooden, H. M. V. Gray, R. Jackson, R. D. V. Knight, F. D. Morgan, R. C. Moylan-Jones, J. B. Pickup, M. J. Soper, D. P. Stewart.

Chairmen of Committees: First-Class Forum: F. D. Morgan; *Recreational Forum:* J. B. Pickup; *Cricket Advisory Committee:* D. L. Acfield; *International Teams Management Group:* J. B. Bolus; *Finance Advisory Committee:* D. P. Stewart; *Marketing Advisory Committee:* H. M. V. Gray; *Discipline Standing Committee:* G. Elias QC; *Registration Standing Committee:* D. S. Kemp.

Finance Director: B. W. Havill; *Director of Cricket Operations:* J. D. Carr; *Commercial Director:* T. D. M. Blake; *Director of Corporate Affairs:* J. C. Read; *Performance Director:* H. Morris; *National Development Director:* K. R. Pont; *Executive Director for Women's Cricket:* G. E. McConway; *Director of Legal Affairs:* M. N. Roper-Drimie; *Cricket Operations Manager (First-Class):* A. Fordham; *Cricket Operations Manager (Recreational):* F. R. Kemp.

THE MARYLEBONE CRICKET CLUB

The Marylebone Cricket Club evolved out of the White Conduit Club in 1787, when Thomas Lord laid out his first ground in Dorset Square. Its members revised the Laws in 1788 and gradually took responsibility for cricket throughout the world. However, it relinquished control of the game in the UK in 1968 and the International Cricket Council finally established its own secretariat in 1993. MCC still owns Lord's and remains the guardian of the Laws. It calls itself "a private club with a public function" and aims to support cricket everywhere, especially at grassroots level and in countries where the game is least developed.

Patron: HER MAJESTY THE QUEEN

Officers

President: 2001–02 – E. R. Dexter.

Club Chairman: Lord Alexander of Weedon. *Chairman of Finance:* O. H. J. Stocken.

Trustees: A. C. D. Ingleby-Mackenzie, Sir Michael Jenkins, M. E. L. Melluish.

Hon. Life Vice-Presidents: Sir Alec Bedser, Lord Bramall, D. G. Clark, G. H. G. Doggart, Lord Griffiths, D. J. Insole, C. H. Palmer, D. R. W. Silk, J. J. Warr, J. C. Woodcock.

Secretary and Chief Executive: R. D. V. Knight. *Deputy Chief Executive:* D. N. Batts.

Head of Cricket: A. I. C. Dodemaide. *Assistant Secretary (Membership):* C. Maynard. *Personal Assistant to Secretary and Chief Executive:* Miss S. A. Lawrence. *Curator:* S. E. A. Green.

MCC Committee: J. A. Bailey, P. H. Edmonds, D. J. C. Faber, D. I. Gower, M. G. Griffith, W. R. Griffiths, Rt Hon. J. Major, R. G. Marlar, M. C. J. Nicholas, N. M. Peters, Sir Timothy Rice, Lt-Col. J. R. Stephenson.

Chairmen of main sub-committees: E. R. Dexter (Cricket); M. J. de Rohan (Estates); C. A. Fry (Membership); A. W. Wreford (Marketing); *Additional Member of the Cricket Committee:* G. J. Toogood.

PROFESSIONAL CRICKETERS' ASSOCIATION

The Professional Cricketers' Association was formed in 1967 (as the Cricketers' Association) to represent the first-class county playing staffs, and to promote and protect professional players' interests. During the 1970s, it succeeded in establishing pension schemes and a minimum wage. In 1995, David Graveney became the Association's general secretary and first full-time employee; in 1998, he became chief executive. In 1997, the organisation set up its own management company to raise regular revenue and fund improved benefits for members of the PCA during and after their playing careers.

President: M. W. Gatting. *Chairman:* M. V. Fleming. *Chief Executive:* D. A. Graveney. *Chairman, PCA Management:* P. M. Walker. *Managing Director:* R. H. Bevan. *Directors:* R. H. Bevan, D. A. Graveney.

EUROPEAN CRICKET COUNCIL

On June 16, 1997, the eight-year-old European Cricket Federation was superseded by the European Cricket Council, bringing together all European ICC members, plus Israel. In 2001, the Council consisted of England (Full Member); Denmark, France, Germany, Gibraltar, Ireland, Israel, Italy, Netherlands and Scotland (Associate Members); and Austria, Belgium, Croatia, Cyprus, Czech Republic, Finland, Greece, Luxembourg, Malta, Norway, Portugal, Spain, Sweden and Switzerland (Affiliate Members). The ECC also supports development initiatives in non-member countries Azerbaijan, Belarus, Bulgaria, Estonia, Hungary, Iceland, Poland, Romania, Slovenia and Ukraine.

Chairman: D. J. Insole. *European Development Manager:* I. C. D. Stuart.

ADDRESSES

INTERNATIONAL CRICKET COUNCIL

M. W. Speed, The Clock Tower, Lord's Cricket Ground, London NW8 8QN (020 7266 1818; fax 020 7266 1777; website www.icc.cricket.org; e-mail icc@icc.cricket.org).

Full Members

AUSTRALIA: Australian Cricket Board, J. Sutherland, 90 Jolimont Street, Jolimont, Victoria 3002 (00 61 3 9653 9999; fax 00 61 3 9653 9900; website www.acb.com.au).

BANGLADESH: Bangladesh Cricket Board, Syed Ashraful Huq, Bangabandhu National Stadium, Dhaka 1000 (00 880 2 966 6805; fax 00 880 2 956 3844; e-mail bcb@bangla.net).

ENGLAND: England and Wales Cricket Board, T. M. Lamb, Lord's Ground, London NW8 8QZ (020 7432 1200; fax 020 7289 5619; website www.ecb.co.uk).

INDIA: Board of Control for Cricket in India, N. Shah, Sanmitra, Anandpura, Baroda 390 001 (00 91 265 431233; fax 00 91 265 428833).

NEW ZEALAND: New Zealand Cricket Inc., M. C. Snedden, PO Box 958, 109 Cambridge Terrace, Christchurch (00 64 3 366 2964; fax 00 64 3 365 7491; website www.nzcricket.org.nz).

PAKISTAN: Pakistan Cricket Board, Brig. Munawar Rana, Gaddafi Stadium, Ferozepur Road, Lahore 54600 (00 92 42 111 22 7777; fax 00 92 42 571 1860).

SOUTH AFRICA: United Cricket Board of South Africa, M. G. Majola, PO Box 55009, North Street, Illovo, Northlands 2116 (00 27 11 880 2810; fax 00 27 11 880 6578; website www.ucbsa.cricket.org; e-mail ucbsa@ucb.co.za).

SRI LANKA: Board of Control for Cricket in Sri Lanka, A. P. B. Tennekoon, 35 Maitland Place, Colombo 7 (00 94 1 691439/689551; fax 00 94 1 697405; e-mail: cricket@sri.lanka.net).

WEST INDIES: West Indies Cricket Board, G. Shillingford, Factory Road, PO Box 616 W, Woods Centre, St John's, Antigua (00 1 268 481 2450; fax 00 1 268 481 2498; e-mail wicb@candw.ag).

ZIMBABWE: Zimbabwe Cricket Union, M. Dudhia, PO Box 2739, Josiah Tongogara Avenue, Harare (00 263 4 704616; fax 00 263 4 729370; website www.zcu.cricket.org; e-mail zcu@mweb.co.zw).

Associate and Affiliate Members

AFGHANISTAN: Afghanistan Cricket Federation, PO Box 970, Kabul (00 93 23 90017; fax 00 92 91 287 655).

ARGENTINA: Argentine Cricket Association, D. Lord, ACA Sede Central, PTE Jose E. Uriburu 1468, Piso 3-Departamento A, Buenos Aires (00 54 11 4806 7306; fax 00 54 11 4804 5389; website cricketargentina@mail.com; e-mail cricarg@hotmail.com).

AUSTRIA: Österreichischer Cricket Verband, A. Simpson-Parker, Apollogasse 3/42, A-1070 Vienna (00 43 1 924 6851; website www.austria.cricket.org; e-mail austria_cricket@yahoo.com).

BAHAMAS: Bahamas Cricket Association, S. Deveaux, Government House, PO Box N1001, Nassau (00 1 242 326 4720; fax 00 1 242 322 4659; e-mail bahamascricket@go.com).

BAHRAIN: Bahrain Cricket Association, PO Box 2400, Manma (fax 00 973 234 244).

BELGIUM: Belgian Cricket Federation, M. O'Connor, Koningin Astridlaan 98, B-2800 Mechelen (00 32 15 331 635; fax 00 32 15 331 639; e-mail paul.lariviere@almo.be).

BELIZE: Belize National Cricket Association, 1128 Baracuda Street, Belize City (00 501 2 72201; fax 00 501 2 30936).

BERMUDA: Bermuda Cricket Board of Control, R. Horton, PO Box HM992, Hamilton HM DX (00 1 441 292 8958; fax 00 1 441 292 8959; e-mail bcbc@ibl.bm).

BHUTAN: Bhutan Cricket Association, PO Box 242, Thimpu (00 975 2322 319; fax 00 972 2322 753; millia@druknet.net.bt).

BOTSWANA: Botswana Cricket Association, J. Sands, Private Bag 00379, Gaborone (00 267 309867; fax 00 267 309 881; e-mail jsands@global.bw).

BRUNEI: Persatuan Keriket Negara Brunei Darussalam, S. Langton, PO Box 931, MPC-Old Airport, Berakas-BB 3577 (00 673 223 5834; fax 00 673 243 1122; e-mail mirbash@brunet.bn).

CANADA: Canadian Cricket Association, G. Edwards, 46 Port Street East, Mississauga, Ontario L5G 1C1 (00 1 905 278 5000; fax 00 1 905 278 5005; e-mail 74253.1641@compuserve.com).

CAYMAN ISLANDS: Cayman Islands Cricket Association, C. Myles, PO Box 1201 GT, George Town, Grand Cayman (00 1 345 244 3458; fax 00 1 345 949 8487; e-mail jayke@candw.ky).

COOK ISLANDS: Cook Islands Cricket Association, G. Hoskings, PO Box 139, Rarotoonga (00 682 29 312; fax 00 682 29 314).

CROATIA: Croatia Cricket Board, Kvinticka 14B, Zagreb 10 000.

CYPRUS: Cyprus Cricket Association, G. Collins, PO Box 3293, Limassol, Cyprus CY 3301 (00 357 662 2226; fax 00 357 662 2227; e-mail guttenbergs@yahoo.com).

CZECH REPUBLIC: Czech Republic Cricket Union, J. Locke, Na Berance 7/1773, 160 00 Praha 6 (00 420 22 432 1716; e-mail locke@cmail.cz.).

DENMARK: Dansk Cricket-Forbund, C. B. S. Hansen, Idraettens Hus, 2605 Brøndby (00 45 4326 2160; fax 00 45 4326 2163; website www.cricket.dk; e-mail dcf@cricket.dk).

EAST AND CENTRAL AFRICA: East and Central African Cricket Conference, T. B. McCarthy, PO Box 34321, Lusaka 1010, Zambia (00 260 1 226 228; fax 00 260 1 224 454; e-mail acricket@zamtel.zm).

FIJI: Fiji Cricket Association, P. I. Knight, PO Box 300, Suva (00 679 301 499; fax 00 679 301 618; e-mail fijicrick@is.com.fi).

FINLAND: Finnish Cricket Association, A. Armitage, Coats Opti Oy, Ketjutie 3, Fin-04220, Kerava (00 358 927 487 327; fax 00 358 927 487 371; e-mail andrew.armitage@coats.com).

FRANCE: Fédération Française de Baseball, Softball et Cricket, O. Dubaut, 41 rue de Fécamp, 75012 Paris (00 33 1 4468 8930; fax 00 33 1 4468 9600; e-mail edcannon@club-internet.fr).

GERMANY: Deutscher Cricket Bund, B. Fell, Luragogasse 5, D-94032 Passau (00 49 851 34307; fax 00 49 851 32815; website www.dcb-cricket.de; e-mail brimarfell@t-online.de).

GIBRALTAR: Gibraltar Cricket Association, T. J. Finlayson, 23 Merlot House, Vineyards Estate (00 350 79461; also fax; website www.gca.gi; e-mail thewoods@gibnet.gi).

GREECE: Hellenic Cricket Federation, C. Evangelos, Kat. Pappa 8, Corfu 49100 (00 30 661 47753; fax 00 30 661 47754; e-mail cricketadm@otenet.gr).

HONG KONG: Hong Kong Cricket Association, J. A. Cribbin, Room 1019, Sports House, 1 Stadium Path, So Kon Po, Causeway Bay (00 852 250 48101; fax 00 852 257 78486; website www.hkabc.net; e-mail hkca@hkabc.net).

INDONESIA: Indonesia Cricket Federation, Gedung BRI II, 19th Floor, Suite 1907, II Jend Sudirman No. 44-46, Jakarta (00 62 21 251 2660; fax 00 62 21 570 9455).

IRELAND: Irish Cricket Union, J. Wright, The Diamond, Malahide, Co Dublin 18 (00 353 1 845 0710; fax 00 353 1 845 5545; website www.theicu.org; e-mail typetext@eircom.net).

ISRAEL: Israel Cricket Association, S. Perlman, PO Box 65085, Tel-Aviv 61650 (00 972 3 642 5529; fax 00 972 3 641 7271; e-mail israel@cricket.org).

ITALY: Federazione Cricket Italiana, S. Gambino, Via S. Ignazio 9, 00186 Roma (00 39 06 689 6989; fax 00 39 06 687 8684; website www.crickitalia.org).

JAPAN: Japan Cricket Association, K. Matsumura, Koshi Bidg, 5F 2-11-14, Minamiaoyama Minato-ku, Tokyo 107-0062 (00 81 3 5772 3470; fax 00 81 3 5772 3471; website www.jca@cricket.ne.jp; e-mail nao720@aol.com).

KENYA: Kenya Cricket Association, H. Shah, PO Box 45870, Nairobi (00 254 2 766447; fax 00 254 2 765057; e-mail kcricket@iconnect.co.ke).

KUWAIT: Kuwait Cricket Association, Abdul Muttaleb Ahmad, PO Box 6706, Hawalli-32042 (00 965 572 6600; fax 00 965 573 4973).

LESOTHO: Lesotho Cricket Association, PO Box 964, Maseru 100, Lioli Street, Old Industrial Area, Maseru (00 266 313 914; fax 00 266 310 252; e-mail mico@ilesotho.com).

LUXEMBOURG: Federation Luxembourgeoise de Cricket, T. Dunning, 87 rue de Gasperich, L-1617 Luxembourg-Ville (00 352 4301 32795; fax 00 352 4301 35049; e-mail lcf@cricket.lu).

MALAYSIA: Malaysian Cricket Association, K. Selveratnam, 1st Floor, Wisma OCM, Jalan Hang Jebat, 50150 Kuala Lumpur (00 60 3 201 6761; fax 00 60 3 201 3878; e-mail crickmal@tm.net.my).

MALDIVES: Cricket Control Board of Maldives, Kulhivaru Ekuveni, 1st Floor, Cricket Indoor Hall, Male, Republic of Maldives (00 960 317 886; fax 00 960 310 573; e-mail ccbm@avasmail.com).

MALTA: Malta Cricket Association, M. Sacco, c/o Marsa Sports Club, Marsa HMR 15 (00 356 233 851; fax 00 356 231 809; e-mail maltacricket@yahoo.co.uk).

MOROCCO: Moroccan Cricket Association, C. Laroussi, 6 Rue Sefrou A8, Hassan-Rabat (00 212 7 766 453; fax 00 212 7 766 742; e-mail parebrabat@megghrbenet.net.ma).

NAMIBIA: Namibia Cricket Board, L. Pieters, PO Box 457, Windhoek (00 264 61 263128/263129; fax 00 264 61 215149; e-mail rocwindk@iafrica.com.na).

NEPAL: Cricket Association of Nepal, B. R. Pandey, Heritage Plaza, 5th Floor, Kamaldi, PO Box 20291, Kathmandu (00 977 1 247485 ext. 252; fax 00 977 1 247946; e-mail bone@wlink.com.np).

NETHERLANDS: Koninklijke Nederlandse Cricket Bond, A. de la Mar, Nieuwe Kalfjeslaan 21-B, 1182 AA Amstelveen (00 31 20 645 1705; fax 00 31 20 645 1715; website www.kncb.nl; e-mail cricket@kncb.nl).

NORWAY: Norway Cricket Association, R. Gibb, Geologsvingen 11, 0380 Oslo (00 47 22 73 0653; also fax; e-mail bobgibb@enitel.no).

OMAN: Oman Cricket Association, A. M. Yousef, PO Box 3948, Ruwi 112, Muscat, Sultanate of Oman (00 968 703 142; fax 00 968 796 045; e-mail kanaksi@omantel.net.om).

PAPUA NEW GUINEA: Papua New Guinea Cricket Board of Control, W. Satchell, PO Box 83, Konedobu NCD, Port Moresby (00 675 321 1070; fax 00 675 321 7974; e-mail mahav@lands.gov.pg).

PHILIPPINES: Philippine Cricket Association, c/o Davies, Langdon & Search Philippines Inc., 4th Floor, 2129 Pasong Tamo, Makati City, Metro Manilla (00 63 2 811 2971; fax 00 632 811 2071; e-mail cjh@dls.com.ph).

PORTUGAL: Federação Portuguesa de Cricket, J. Simonson, PO Box 76, P-2766 Estoril Codex (00 351 21 444 6466; fax 00 351 21 924 3004; e-mail cricket@gauntlett.com).

QATAR: Qatar Cricket Association, F. H. Alfardan, PO Box 339, Dohar (00 974 440 8225/442 7050; fax 00 974 441 7468; e-mail afx@qatar.net.qa).

ST HELENA: St Helena Cricket Association, Nia Roo, New Bridge Road, Jamestown (fax 00 44 870 127 5517; e-mail band.niaroo@helanta.sh).

SAMOA: Samoa Cricket Association, S. Kohlhasse, Seb & Rene Sports, PO Box 9599 (00 685 22 790; fax 00 685 22 480).

SCOTLAND: Scottish Cricket Union, National Cricket Academy, MES Sports Centre, Ravelston, Edinburgh EH4 3NT (0131 313 7420; fax 0131 313 7430; website www.scu.org.uk; e-mail admin.scu@btinternet.com).

SINGAPORE: Singapore Cricket Association, A. Kalaver, 31 Stadium Crescent (South Entrance) Singapore 397639 (00 65 348 6566; fax 00 65 348 6506; e-mail cricket@singnet.co.sg).

SOUTH KOREA: Korea Cricket Association, 60-25 Hannam-Dang, Yongsam-Ku, Seoul 140 210 (00 82 2 3706 3001; e-mail dunnan@hlcl.com).

SPAIN: Asociacion Española de Cricket, K. Sainsbury, Casa Desiderata, VA 153, 03737 Javea, Alicante (00 34 96 579 4948; e-mail ksainsy@dragonet.es).

SWEDEN: Svenska Cricket Förbundet, N. Hashmi, Osbyringen 38, 163 73 Spånga, Stockholm (00 46 8 508 02053; fax 00 46 8 508 02179; e-mail naveed.hashmi@rinkeby.stockholm.se).

SWITZERLAND: Swiss Cricket Association, A. MacKay, Wingertlistrasse 22, 8405 Winterthur (00 41 1 839 4973/52 233 4601; fax 00 41 1 839 4999; e-mail alex.mackay@mackay.ch).

TANZANIA: Tanzania Cricket Association, PO Box 918, Dar es Salaam (00 255 22 213 0037; fax 00 255 22 212 3394; e-mail wizards@cats-net.com).

THAILAND: Thailand Cricket League, 12th Floor, Silom Condominium, 52/38 Soi Saladaeng 2, Silom Road, Bangkok 10500 (00 66 2 266 9040; fax 00 66 2 236 6764; e-mail ravisehgal1@hotmail.com).

TONGA: Tonga Cricket Association, 57 Hihifo Road, PO Box 297, Nuku' Alofa (00 676 25 888; fax 00 676 23 671; e-mail pmotrain@kalianet.to).

UGANDA: Uganda Cricket Association, J. Ligya, c/o National Council of Sports, Lugogo Stadium, PO Box 8346, Kampala (00 256 41 349550; fax 00 256 41 258350; e-mail ncsuga@infocom.co.ug).

UNITED ARAB EMIRATES: Emirates Cricket Board, M. Khan, Sharjah Cricket Stadium, PO Box 88, Sharjah (00 971 5 0646 3570; fax 00 971 6 533 4741; e-mail cricket@emirates.net.ae).

USA: United States of America Cricket Association, 3780 Brenner Drive, Santa Barbara, California 93105 (00 1 805 569 0503; fax 00 1 805 563 6085; e-mail president@usaca.org).

VANUATU: Vanuatu Cricket Association, M. Stafford, c/o BDO, BDO House, Lini Highway, PO Box 240, Port Vila, Vanuatu (00 678 22280; fax 00 678 22317; e-mail stafford@vanuatu.com.vu).

WEST AFRICA: West Africa Cricket Conference, Olusegun Akinlotan, Tafawa Balewa Square, Race Course, Lagos, PO Box 9309, Nigeria (00 234 6224 0931; fax 00 234 1585 0529; e-mail olusegunakinlotan@hyperia.net).

UK ADDRESSES

ENGLAND AND WALES CRICKET BOARD: T. M. Lamb, Lord's Ground, London NW8 8QZ (020 7432 1200; fax 020 7289 5619; website www.ecb.co.uk).

MARYLEBONE CRICKET CLUB: R. D. V. Knight, Lord's Ground, London NW8 8QN (020 7289 1611; fax 020 7289 9100. Tickets 020 7432 1066; fax 020 7432 1061).

First-Class Counties

DERBYSHIRE: County Ground, Nottingham Road, Derby DE21 6DA (01332 383211; fax 01332 290251; website www.dccc.org.uk; e-mail post@dccc.org.uk).
DURHAM: County Ground, Riverside, Chester-le-Street, County Durham DH3 3QR (0191 387 1717; fax 0191 387 1616; website www.durham-ccc.org.uk; e-mail marketing@durham-ccc.org.uk).
ESSEX: County Ground, New Writtle Street, Chelmsford CM2 0PG (01245 252420; fax 01245 254030; website www.essexcricket.org.uk; e-mail administration.essex@ecb.co.uk).
GLAMORGAN: Sophia Gardens, Cardiff CF11 9XR (029 2040 9380; fax 029 2040 9390; website www.glamorgancricket.com; e-mail glam@ecb.co.uk).
GLOUCESTERSHIRE: Phoenix County Ground, Nevil Road, Bristol BS7 9EJ (0117 910 8000; fax 0117 924 1193; website www.gloucestershire.cricinfo.com; e-mail suzanne.finch.glos@ecb.co.uk).
HAMPSHIRE: The Hampshire Rose Bowl, Botley Road, West End, Southampton SO30 3XH (023 8047 2002; fax 023 8047 2122; website www.hampshire.cricinfo.com; e-mail enquiries.hants@ecb.co.uk).
KENT: St Lawrence Ground, Old Dover Road, Canterbury CT1 3NZ (01227 456886; fax 01227 762168; website www.kentcountycricket.co.uk; e-mail kent@ecb.co.uk).
LANCASHIRE: County Cricket Ground, Old Trafford, Manchester M16 0PX (0161 282 4000; fax 0161 282 4100; website www.lccc.co.uk; e-mail enquiries@lccc.co.uk).
LEICESTERSHIRE: County Ground, Grace Road, Leicester LE2 8AD (0116 283 2128; fax 0116 244 0363; website www.leicestershireccc.com; e-mail kevin.hill.leics@ecb.co.uk).
MIDDLESEX: Lord's Cricket Ground, London NW8 8QN (020 7289 1300; fax 020 7289 5831; website www.middlesexccc.com; e-mail enquiries.middx@ecb.co.uk).
NORTHAMPTONSHIRE: County Ground, Wantage Road, Northampton NN1 4TJ (01604 514455; fax 01604 514488; website www.nccc.co.uk; e-mail post@nccc.co.uk).
NOTTINGHAMSHIRE: County Cricket Ground, Trent Bridge, Nottingham NG2 6AG (0115 982 3000; fax 0115 945 5730; website www.nottsccc.co.uk; e-mail administration.notts@ecb.co.uk).
SOMERSET: County Ground, St James's Street, Taunton TA1 1JT (01823 272946; fax 01823 332395; website www.somerset.cricinfo.com; e-mail somerset@ecb.co.uk).
SURREY: The Oval, Kennington, London SE11 5SS (020 7582 6660; fax 020 7735 7769; website www.surreycricket.com; e-mail jgrave@surreyccc.co.uk).
SUSSEX: County Ground, Eaton Road, Hove BN3 3AN (01273 827100; fax 01273 771549; website www.sussexcricket.co.uk; e-mail fwatson@btconnect.com).
WARWICKSHIRE: County Ground, Edgbaston, Birmingham B5 7QU (0121 446 4422; fax 0121 446 4544; website www.thebears.co.uk; e-mail info@thebears.co.uk).
WORCESTERSHIRE: County Ground, New Road, Worcester WR2 4QQ (01905 748474; fax 01905 748005; website www.wccc.co.uk; e-mail joan.grundy@wccc.co.uk).
YORKSHIRE: Headingley Cricket Ground, Leeds LS6 3BU (0113 278 7394; fax 0113 278 4099; website www.yorkshire.org.uk; e-mail cricket@yorkshireccc.org.uk).

Minor Counties

MINOR COUNTIES CRICKET ASSOCIATION: G. R. Evans, Blueberry Haven, 20 Boucher Road, Budleigh Salterton, Devon EX9 6JF (01395 445216, fax 01395 445334; e-mail evans@20boucher.freeserve.co.uk/geoff.evans@ecb.co.uk).
BEDFORDSHIRE: P. G. M. August, 5 Mill Street, Bedford MK40 3EU (01234 327935).
BERKSHIRE: R. New, 41 Holyrood Close, Caversham, Reading, Berkshire RG4 6PZ (0118 947 7959, mobile 07831 746285).
BUCKINGHAMSHIRE: M. Watts, Kempton, Vache Lane, Chalfont St Giles HP8 4SB (01494 583855).
CAMBRIDGESHIRE: P. W. Gooden, The Redlands, Oakington Road, Cottenham, Cambridge CB4 8TW (01954 250429).
CHESHIRE: J. B. Pickup, 36 Landswood Park, Hartford, Northwich, Cheshire CW8 1NF (01606 74970 home; fax 01606 79357).
CORNWALL: Mrs A. M. George, The Logan Rock Inn, Treen, St Levan, Penzance, Cornwall TR19 6LG (01736 810495, fax 01736 810177).
CUMBERLAND: K. Ion, 47 Beech Grove, Stanwix, Carlisle, Cumbria CA3 9BG (01228 528858, mobile 07970 421589; e-mail kion47bg@aol.com).
DEVON: G. R. Evans, Blueberry Haven, 20 Boucher Road, Budleigh Salterton, Devon EX9 6JF (01395 445216, fax 01395 445334; e-mail evans@20boucher.freeserve.co.uk/geoff.evans@ecb.co.uk).
DORSET: K. H. House, The Barn, Higher Farm, Bagber Common, Sturminster Newton, Dorset DT10 2HB (01258 473394, mobile 07971 245889).

HEREFORDSHIRE: P. Sykes, 5 Dale Drive, Holmer Grange, Hereford HR4 9RF (01432 264703, fax 01432 382323, mobile 07809 026484).

HERTFORDSHIRE: B. Mulholland, 16 Landford Close, Rickmansworth, Hertfordshire WD3 1NG (01923 772755, fax 01923 711683, mobile 07385 257502).

LINCOLNSHIRE: C. A. North, Lincolnshire CCC, First Floor, 27 The Forum, North Hykeham, Lincoln LN6 9HW (office/fax 01522 688073, home 01522 681636).

NORFOLK: S. J. Skinner, 27 Colkett Drive, Old Catton, Norwich NR6 7ND (01603 485940, office 01603 624236; e-mail s.skinner@barclays.net).

NORTHUMBERLAND: A. B. Stephenson, Northumberland CCC, Osborne Avenue, Jesmond, Newcastle-upon-Tyne NE2 1JS (office 0191 281 2738, home 0191 213 1152).

OXFORDSHIRE: P. R. N. O'Neill, 4 Brookside, Thame, Oxfordshire OX9 3DE (01844 260439, also fax, mobile 07411 943449).

SHROPSHIRE: N. H. Birch, Four Winds, 24 Ridgebourne Road, Shrewsbury, Shropshire SY3 9AB (01743 233650, mobile 07974 000906).

STAFFORDSHIRE: W. S. Bourne, 10 The Pavement, Brewood, Staffordshire ST19 9BZ (01902 850325).

SUFFOLK: T. J. Pound, 94 Henley Road, Ipswich IP1 4NJ (01473 213288, office 01473 232121).

WALES MINOR COUNTIES: W. Edwards, 59a King Edward Road, Swansea SA1 4LN (01792 462233; fax 01792 643931).

WILTSHIRE: C. R. Sheppard, PO Box 10, Fairford, Gloucestershire GL7 4YR (01285 810809, also fax, mobile 07831 565866; e-mail chris.sheppard@ecb.co.uk).

HUNTINGDONSHIRE (ECB 38-county) D. Swannell, 23 Popes Lane, Warboys, Huntingdon PE17 2RN (01487 823122).

Other Bodies

ASSOCIATION OF CRICKET STATISTICIANS AND HISTORIANS: P. Wynne-Thomas, 3 Radcliffe Road, West Bridgford, Nottingham NG2 5FF (0115 945 5407; website www.acs.cricket.org; e-mail acsoffice@cricket.org).

ASSOCIATION OF CRICKET UMPIRES AND SCORERS: G. J. Bullock, PO Box 399, Camberley, Surrey GU15 3JZ (01276 27962; fax 01276 62277; website www.acus.cricket.org).

BRITISH UNIVERSITIES SPORTS ASSOCIATION: J. Ellis, 8 Union Street, London SE1 1SZ (020 7357 8555; website www.busaresults.org.uk; e-mail jim@busa.org.uk).

CLUB CRICKET CONFERENCE: D. Franklin, 10 Christchurch Gardens, Epsom, Surrey KT19 8RU (020 8336 0586; fax 020 8336 0537).

ENGLISH SCHOOLS' CRICKET ASSOCIATION: K. S. Lake, 38 Mill House, Woods Lane, Cottingham, Hull HU16 4HQ.

EUROPEAN CRICKET COUNCIL: I. C. D. Stuart, Europe Office, Lord's Ground, London NW8 8QN (020 7432 1019; fax 020 7432 1091; website www.ecc.cricket.org).

LEAGUE CRICKET CONFERENCE: N. Edwards, 1 Longfield, Freshfield, Formby, Merseyside L37 3LD (01704 877103).

MIDLAND CLUB CRICKET CONFERENCE: D. Thomas, 4 Silverdale Gardens, Wordsley, Stowbridge, West Midlands DY8 5NY (01384 278107; office 01902 864685).

PROFESSIONAL CRICKETERS' ASSOCIATION/PCA MANAGEMENT: R. H. Bevan, 3rd Floor, 338 Euston Road, London NW1 3BT (020 7544 8668; fax 020 7868 1830; e-mail pcam@enta.net).

RUTLAND COUNTY CRICKET ASSOCIATION: I. H. S. Balfour, Nanjazel, 7 Nightingale Way, Oakham, Rutland LE15 6ES.

Cricket Associations and Societies

AUSTRALIAN CRICKET SOCIETY: Queensland – Mrs D. Durrand, 128 Somerset Road, Kedron, Qld 4031. Victoria – D. Manning, Ravenstone, 240-246 Oban Road, North Ringwood, Vic 3134. South Australia – Mrs M. Hilton, PO Box 646, North Adelaide, S. Australia 5006.

CHELTENHAM CRICKET SOCIETY: P. Murphy, 1 Colesbourne Road, Benhall, Cheltenham, Gloucestershire GL51 6DJ.

CHESTERFIELD CRICKET SOCIETY: J. S. Cook, 44 Morris Avenue, Newbold, Chesterfield, Derbyshire S41 7BA.

COUNCIL OF CRICKET SOCIETIES, THE: B. Rickson, 31 Grange Avenue, Cheadle Hulme, Cheshire SK8 5EN.

COUNTY CRICKET SUPPORTERS ASSOCIATION: Miss F. J. Walker, 12 Grasmere Drive, Linton Croft, Wetherby, West Yorkshire LS22 6GP.

CRICKET FAN CLUB: 1407 Qasimjan Street, Ballimaran, Delhi 110006, India.
CRICKET MEMORABILIA SOCIETY: S. Cashmore, 4 Stoke Park Court, Stoke Road, Bishops Cleeve, Cheltenham, Gloucestershire GL52 4US.
CRICKET SOCIETY, THE: PO Box 6024, Leighton Buzzard LU7 2SY.
CRICKET STATISTICIANS AND SCORERS OF INDIA, ASSOCIATION OF: PO Box 7145, Wadala Post Office, Mumbai 400-041.
DERBYSHIRE CRICKET SOCIETY: O. C. Kinselle, 27 Wilsthorpe Road, Breaston, Derby DE72 3EA.
DUNELM CRICKET SOCIETY: Mrs M. Coombs, White Lodge, Halliford Road, Shepperton, Middlesex TW17 8RU.
DURHAM AND NORTH-EAST BRANCH OF THE CRICKET SOCIETY: Prof. R. Storer, 164 Eastern Way, Darras Hall, Ponteland, Newcastle-upon-Tyne NE20 9RH.
EAST RIDING CRICKET SOCIETY: Mrs S. Forward, 121 Fairfax Avenue, Hull HU5 4QU.
ESSEX CRICKET SOCIETY: T. D. Percival, 31 Wellfield, Writtle, Chelmsford, Essex CM1 3LF.
GLOUCESTERSHIRE CRICKET LOVERS' SOCIETY: M. Simpson, 318 Canford Lane, Westbury-on-Trym, Bristol BS9 3PL.
HAMPSHIRE CRICKET SOCIETY: J. Moore, 85 Kingsway, Chandlers Ford, Hants SO53 1FD.
HEREFORDSHIRE CRICKET SOCIETY: T. R. Lowe, Hereford Cathedral Junior School, 28 Castle Street, Hereford HR1 2NW.
HERTFORDSHIRE CRICKET SOCIETY: W. A. Powell, 17 Swan Mead, The Willows, Hemel Hempstead, Hertfordshire HP3 9DQ.
HIGH PEAK CRICKET SOCIETY: R. H. Wood, 3 Orchard Avenue, Whaley Bridge, Derbyshire SK23 7AH.
LANCASHIRE AND CHESHIRE CRICKET SOCIETY: J. L. Petch, 63 Linksway, Gatley, Cheshire SK8 4LA.
LINCOLNSHIRE CRICKET LOVERS' SOCIETY: C. Kennedy, 26 Eastwood Avenue, Great Grimsby, South Humberside DN34 5BE.
MERSEYSIDE CRICKET SOCIETY: W. T. Robins, 31 Elmswood Court, Palmerston Road, Liverpool L18 8DJ.
MIDLANDS BRANCH OF THE CRICKET SOCIETY: Miss H. Allen, 14 Merrions Close, Birmingham B43 7AT.
NATIONAL CRICKET MEMBERSHIP SCHEME: 22 Grazebrook Road, London N16 0HS.
NEEDWOOD CRICKET LOVERS' SOCIETY: A. D. Campion, 45 Fallowfield Drive, Barton-under-Needwood, Staffordshire DE13 8DH.
NEW ZEALAND, CRICKET SOCIETY OF: C. Rosie, Eden Park, PO Box 2860, Auckland 1.
NORFOLK CRICKET SOCIETY: A. V. Burgess, 41 Ashby Street, Norwich, Norfolk NR1 3PT.
NORTHERN CRICKET SOCIETY: H. Jackson, 20 Foxholes Lane, Calverley, Leeds LS8 5NS.
NOTTINGHAM CRICKET LOVERS' SOCIETY: G. Blagdurn, 2 Inham Circus, Chilwell, Nottingham NG9 4FN.
PAKISTAN ASSOCIATION OF CRICKET STATISTICIANS: Abid Ali Kazi and Nauman Bader, 256-N, Model Town Ext, Lahore 54700 (e-mail naumanb@brain.net.pk).
ROTHERHAM CRICKET SOCIETY: J. A. R. Atkin, 15 Gallow Tree Road, Rotherham S65 3FE.
SCOTLAND, CRICKET SOCIETY OF: A. J. Robertson, 5 Riverside Road, Eaglesham, Glasgow G76 0DQ.
SOUTH AFRICA, CRICKET SOCIETY OF: Mrs E. Sim, PO Box 78040, Sandton, Gauteng 2146.
STOURBRIDGE AND DISTRICT CRICKET SOCIETY: M. Taylor, 26 Wrekin Walk, Stourport, Worcestershire DY13 0LR.
SUSSEX CRICKET SOCIETY: Mrs P. Brabyn, 4 Wolstonbury Walk, Shoreham-by-Sea, West Sussex BN43 5GU.
WEST LANCASHIRE CRICKET SOCIETY: G. D. Anderson, 32 Dunster Rd, Southport PR8 2EN.
WEST OF ENGLAND BRANCH OF THE CRICKET SOCIETY: F. J. Endacott, 84 Hardens Mead, Chippenham, Wiltshire SN15 3AF.
WOMBWELL CRICKET LOVERS' SOCIETY: M. Pope, 32 Louden Road, Scholes, Rotherham, South Yorkshire S61 2SU.
WORCESTER CRICKET SOCIETY: M. Niccols, 70 Park Avenue, Worcester WR3 7AQ.
YORKSHIRE CCC SOUTHERN GROUP: D. M. Wood, 15 Rothschild Road, Linslade, Leighton Buzzard, Bedfordshire LU7 7SY.
ZIMBABWE, CRICKET SOCIETY OF: J. B. Stockwell, 6 Howard Close, Mount Pleasant, Harare.

THE LAWS OF CRICKET

(2000 CODE)

INDEX OF THE LAWS

THE PREAMBLE – THE SPIRIT OF CRICKET

Cricket is a game that owes much of its unique appeal to the fact that it should be played not only within its Laws, but also within the Spirit of the Game. Any action which is seen to abuse this spirit causes injury to the game itself. The major responsibility for ensuring the spirit of fair play rests with the captains.

1. There are two Laws which place the responsibility for the team's conduct firmly on the captain.

Responsibility of captains

The captains are responsible at all times for ensuring that play is conducted within the Spirit of the Game as well as within the Laws.

Player's conduct

In the event of a player failing to comply with instructions by an umpire, or criticising by word or action the decisions of an umpire, or showing dissent, or generally behaving in a manner which might bring the game into disrepute, the umpire concerned shall in the first place report the matter to the other umpire and to the player's captain, and instruct the latter to take action.

2. Fair and unfair play

According to the Laws the umpires are the sole judges of fair and unfair play. The umpires may intervene at any time, and it is the responsibility of the captain to take action where required.

3. The umpires are authorised to intervene in cases of

- Time-wasting.
- Damaging the pitch.
- Dangerous or unfair bowling.
- Tampering with the ball.
- Any other action that they consider to be unfair.

4. The Spirit of the Game involves respect for

- Your opponents.
- Your own captain and team.
- The role of the umpires.
- The game's traditional values.

5. It is against the Spirit of the Game

- To dispute an umpire's decision by word, action or gesture.
- To direct abusive language towards an opponent or umpire.
- To indulge in cheating or any sharp practice, for instance:

  (a) To appeal knowing that the batsman is not out.

  (b) To advance towards an umpire in an aggressive manner when appealing.

  (c) To seek to distract an opponent either verbally or by harassment with persistent clapping or unnecessary noise under the guise of enthusiasm and motivation of one's own side.

6. Violence

There is no place for any act of violence on the field of play.

7. Players

Captains and umpires together set the tone for the conduct of a cricket match. Every player is expected to make an important contribution to this.

The players, umpires and scorers in a game of cricket may be of either gender and the Laws apply equally to both. The use, throughout the text, of pronouns indicating the male gender is purely for brevity. Except where specifically stated otherwise, every provision of the Laws is to be read as applying to women and girls equally as to men and boys.

LAW 1. THE PLAYERS

1. Number of players

A match is played between two sides, each of 11 players, one of whom shall be captain. By agreement a match may be played between sides of more or less than 11 players, but not more than 11 players may field at any time.

2. Nomination of players

Each captain shall nominate his players in writing to one of the umpires before the toss. No player may be changed after the nomination without the consent of the opposing captain.

3. Captain

If at any time the captain is not available, a deputy shall act for him.

(a) If a captain is not available during the period in which the toss is to take place, then the deputy must be responsible for the nomination of the players, if this has not already been done, and for the toss. See 2 above and Law 12.4 (The toss).

(b) At any time after the toss, the deputy must be one of the nominated players.

4. Responsibility of captains

The captains are responsible at all times for ensuring that play is conducted within the spirit and traditions of the game as well as within the Laws. See The Preamble – The Spirit of Cricket and Law 42.1 (Fair and unfair play – responsibility of captains).

LAW 2. SUBSTITUTES AND RUNNERS; BATSMAN OR FIELDER LEAVING THE FIELD; BATSMAN RETIRING; BATSMAN COMMENCING INNINGS

1. Substitutes and runners

(a) If the umpires are satisfied that a player has been injured or become ill after the nomination of the players, they shall allow that player to have:

(i) A substitute acting instead of him in the field.

(ii) A runner when batting.

Any injury or illness that occurs at any time after the nomination of the players until the conclusion of the match shall be allowable, irrespective of whether play is in progress or not.

(b) The umpires shall have discretion, for other wholly acceptable reasons, to allow a substitute for a fielder, or a runner for a batsman, at the start of the match or at any subsequent time.

(c) A player wishing to change his shirt, boots, etc. must leave the field to do so. No substitute shall be allowed for him.

2. Objection to substitutes

The opposing captain shall have no right of objection to any player acting as a substitute on the field, nor as to where the substitute shall field. However, no substitute shall act as wicket-keeper. See 3 below.

3. Restrictions on the role of substitutes

A substitute shall not be allowed to bat or bowl nor to act as wicket-keeper or as captain on the field of play.

4. A player for whom a substitute has acted

A player is allowed to bat, bowl or field even though a substitute has previously acted for him.

5. Fielder absent or leaving the field

If a fielder fails to take the field with his side at the start of the match or at any later time, or leaves the field during a session of play:

(a) The umpire shall be informed of the reason for his absence.

(b) He shall not thereafter come on to the field during a session of play without the consent of the umpire. See 6 below. The umpire shall give such consent as soon as is practicable.

(c) If he is absent for 15 minutes or longer, he shall not be permitted to bowl thereafter, subject to (i), (ii) or (iii) below, until he has been on the field for at least that length of playing time for which he was absent.

(i) Absence or penalty for time absent shall not be carried over into a new day's play.

(ii) If, in the case of a follow-on or forfeiture, a side fields for two consecutive innings, this restriction shall, subject to (i) above, continue as necessary into the second innings but shall not otherwise be carried over into a new innings.

(iii) The time lost for an unscheduled break in play shall be counted as time on the field for any fielder who comes on to the field at the resumption of play. See Law 15.1 (An interval).

6. Player returning without permission

If a player comes on to the field of play in contravention of 5(b) above and comes into contact with the ball while it is in play:

(i) The ball shall immediately become dead and the umpire shall award five penalty runs to the batting side. See Law 42.17 (Penalty runs).

(ii) The umpire shall inform the other umpire, the captain of the fielding side, the batsmen and, as soon as practicable, the captain of the batting side of the reason for this action.

(iii) The umpires together shall report the occurrence as soon as possible to the executive of the fielding side and any governing body responsible for the match, who shall take such action as is considered appropriate against the captain and player concerned.

7. Runner

The player acting as a runner for a batsman shall be a member of the batting side and shall, if possible, have already batted in that innings. The runner shall wear external protective equipment equivalent to that worn by the batsman for whom he runs and shall carry a bat.

8. Transgression of the Laws by a batsman who has a runner

(a) A batsman's runner is subject to the Laws. He will be regarded as a batsman except where there are specific provisions for his role as a runner. See 7 above and Law 29.2 (Which is a batsman's ground).

(b) A batsman with a runner will suffer the penalty for any infringement of the Laws by his runner as though he had been himself responsible for the infringement. In particular he will be out if his runner is out under any of Laws 33 (Handled the ball), 37 (Obstructing the field) or 38 (Run out).

(c) When a batsman with a runner is striker he remains himself subject to the Laws and will be liable to the penalties that any infringement of them demands.

Additionally, if he is out of his ground when the wicket is put down at the wicket-keeper's end, he will be out in the circumstances of Law 38 (Run out) or Law 39 (Stumped) irrespective of the position of the non-striker or of the runner. If he is thus dismissed, runs completed by the runner and the other batsman before the dismissal shall not be scored. However, the penalty for a no-ball or a wide shall stand, together with any penalties to be awarded to either side when the ball is dead. See Law 42.17 (Penalty runs).

(d) When a batsman with a runner is not the striker:

(i) He remains subject to Laws 33 (Handled the ball) and 37 (Obstructing the field) but is otherwise out of the game.

(ii) He shall stand where directed by the striker's end umpire so as not to interfere with play.

(iii) He will be liable, notwithstanding (i) above, to the penalty demanded by the Laws should he commit any act of unfair play.

9. Batsman leaving the field or retiring

A batsman may retire at any time during his innings. The umpires, before allowing play to proceed, shall be informed of the reason for a batsman retiring.

(a) If a batsman retires because of illness, injury or any other unavoidable cause, he is entitled to resume his innings subject to (c) below. If for any reason he does not do so, his innings is to be recorded as "Retired – not out".

(b) If a batsman retires for any reason other than as in (a) above, he may resume his innings only with the consent of the opposing captain. If for any reason he does not resume his innings it is to be recorded as "Retired – out".

(c) If after retiring a batsman resumes his innings, it shall be only at the fall of a wicket or the retirement of another batsman.

10. Commencement of a batsman's innings

Except at the start of a side's innings, a batsman shall be considered to have commenced his innings when he first steps on to the field of play, provided "Time" has not been called. The innings of the opening batsmen, and that of any new batsman at the resumption of play after a call of "Time", shall commence at the call of "Play".

LAW 3. THE UMPIRES

1. Appointment and attendance

Before the match, two umpires shall be appointed, one for each end to control the game as required by the Laws, with absolute impartiality. The umpires shall be present on the ground and report to the executive of the ground at least 45 minutes before the start of each day's play.

2. Change of umpire

An umpire shall not be changed during the match, other than in exceptional circumstances, unless he is injured or ill. If there has to be a change of umpire, the replacement shall act only as the striker's end umpire unless the captains agree that he should take full responsibility as an umpire.

3. Agreement with captains

Before the toss the umpires shall:

(a) Ascertain the hours of play and agree with the captains:

(i) The balls to be used during the match. See Law 5 (The ball).

(ii) Times and durations of intervals for meals and times for drinks intervals. See Law 15 (Intervals).

(iii) The boundary of the field of play and allowances for boundaries. See Law 19 (Boundaries).

(iv) Any special conditions of play affecting the conduct of the match.

(b) Inform the scorers of the agreements in (ii), (iii) and (iv) above.

4. To inform captains and scorers

Before the toss the umpires shall agree between themselves and inform both captains and both scorers:

(i) Which clock or watch and back-up timepiece is to be used during the match.

(ii) Whether or not any obstacle within the field of play is to be regarded as a boundary. See Law 19 (Boundaries).

5. The wickets, creases and boundaries

Before the toss and during the match, the umpires shall satisfy themselves that:

(i) The wickets are properly pitched. See Law 8 (The wickets).

(ii) The creases are correctly marked. See Law 9 (The bowling, popping and return creases).

(iii) The boundary of the field of play complies with the requirements of Law 19.2 (Defining the boundary – boundary marking).

6. Conduct of the game, implements and equipment

Before the toss and during the match, the umpires shall satisfy themselves that:

(a) The conduct of the game is strictly in accordance with the Laws.

(b) The implements of the game conform to the requirements of Laws 5 (The ball) and 6 (The bat), together with either Laws 8.2 (Size of stumps) and 8.3 (The bails) or, if appropriate, Law 8.4 (Junior cricket).

(c) (i) No player uses equipment other than that permitted.

(ii) The wicket-keeper's gloves comply with the requirements of Law 40.2 (Gloves).

7. Fair and unfair play

The umpires shall be the sole judges of fair and unfair play.

8. Fitness of ground, weather and light

The umpires shall be the final judges of the fitness of the ground, weather and light for play. See 9 below and Law 7.2 (Fitness of the pitch for play).

9. Suspension of play for adverse conditions of ground, weather or light

(a) (i) All references to ground include the pitch. See Law 7.1 (Area of pitch).

(ii) For the purpose of this Law the batsmen at the wicket may deputise for their captain at any appropriate time.

(b) If at any time the umpires together agree that the condition of the ground, weather or light is not suitable for play, they shall inform the captains and, unless

(i) in unsuitable ground or weather conditions both captains agree to continue, or to commence, or to restart play, or

(ii) in unsuitable light the batting side wish to continue, or to commence, or to restart play,

they shall suspend play, or not allow play to commence or to restart.

(c) (i) After agreeing to play in unsuitable ground or weather conditions, either captain may appeal against the conditions to the umpires before the next call of "Time". The umpires shall uphold the appeal only if, in their opinion, the factors taken into account when making their previous decision are the same or the conditions have further deteriorated.

(ii) After deciding to play in unsuitable light, the captain of the batting side may appeal against the light to the umpires before the next call of "Time". The umpires shall uphold the appeal only if, in their opinion, the factors taken into account when making their previous decision are the same or the condition of the light has further deteriorated.

(d) If at any time the umpires together agree that the conditions of ground, weather or light are so bad that there is obvious and foreseeable risk to the safety of any player or umpire, so that it would be unreasonable or dangerous for play to take place, then notwithstanding the provisions of 9(b)(i) and 9(b)(ii) above, they shall immediately suspend play, or not allow play to commence or to restart. The decision as to whether conditions are so bad as to warrant such action is one for the umpires alone to make.

Merely because the grass and the ball are wet and slippery does not warrant the ground conditions being regarded as unreasonable or dangerous. If the umpires consider the ground is so wet or slippery as to deprive the bowler of a reasonable foothold, the fielders of the power of free movement, or the batsmen of the ability to play their strokes or to run between the wickets, then these conditions shall be regarded as so bad that it would be unreasonable for play to take place.

(e) When there is a suspension of play it is the responsibility of the umpires to monitor the conditions. They shall make inspections as often as appropriate, unaccompanied by any of the players or officials. Immediately the umpires together agree that conditions are suitable for play they shall call upon the players to resume the game.

(f) If play is in progress up to the start of an agreed interval then it will resume after the interval unless the umpires together agree that conditions are or have become unsuitable or dangerous. If they do so agree, then they shall implement the procedure in (b) or (d) above, as appropriate, whether or not there had been any decision by the captains to continue, or any appeal against the conditions by either captain, prior to the commencement of the interval.

10. Exceptional circumstances

The umpires shall have the discretion to implement the procedures of 9 above for reasons other than ground, weather or light if they consider that exceptional circumstances warrant it.

11. Position of umpires

The umpires shall stand where they can best see any act upon which their decision may be required. Subject to this over-riding consideration the umpire at the bowler's end shall stand where he does not interfere with either the bowler's run-up or the striker's view.

The umpire at the striker's end may elect to stand on the off side instead of the on side of the pitch, provided he informs the captain of the fielding side, the striker and the other umpire of his intention to do so.

12. Umpires changing ends

The umpires shall change ends after each side has had one completed innings. See Law 14.2 (Forfeiture of an innings).

13. Consultation between umpires

All disputes shall be determined by the umpires. The umpires shall consult with each other whenever necessary. See also Law 27.6 (Consultation by umpires).

14. Signals

(a) The following code of signals shall be used by umpires.

(i) Signals made while the ball is in play:

Dead ball	– by crossing and re-crossing the wrists below the waist.
No-ball	– by extending one arm horizontally.
Out	– by raising the index finger above the head. (If not out the umpire shall call "Not out".)
Wide	– by extending both arms horizontally.

(ii) When the ball is dead, the signals above, with the exception of the signal for "Out", shall be repeated to the scorers. The signals listed below shall be made to the scorers only when the ball is dead.

Boundary 4	– by waving an arm from side to side finishing with the arm across the chest.
Boundary 6	– by raising both arms above the head.
Bye	– by raising an open hand above the head.
Commencement of last hour	– by pointing to a raised wrist with the other hand.
Five penalty runs awarded to the batting side	– by repeated tapping of one shoulder with the opposite hand.
Five penalty runs awarded to the fielding side	– by placing one hand on the opposite shoulder.
Leg-bye	– by touching a raised knee with the hand.
New ball	– by holding the ball above the head.
Revoke last signal	– by touching both shoulders, each with the opposite hand.

Short run – by bending one arm upwards and touching the nearer shoulder with the tips of the fingers.

(b) The umpires shall wait until each signal to the scorers has been separately acknowledged by a scorer before allowing play to proceed.

15. Correctness of scores

Consultation between umpires and scorers on doubtful points is essential. The umpires shall satisfy themselves as to the correctness of the number of runs scored, the wickets that have fallen and, where appropriate, the number of overs bowled. They shall agree these with the scorers at least at every interval, other than a drinks interval, and at the conclusion of the match. See Laws 4.2 (Correctness of scores), 21.8 (Correctness of result) and 21.10 (Result not to be changed).

LAW 4. THE SCORERS

1. Appointment of scorers

Two scorers shall be appointed to record all runs scored, all wickets taken and, where appropriate, number of overs bowled.

2. Correctness of scores

The scorers shall frequently check to ensure that their records agree. They shall agree with the umpires, at least at every interval, other than a drinks interval, and at the conclusion of the match, the runs scored, the wickets that have fallen and, where appropriate, the number of overs bowled. See Law 3.15 (Correctness of scores).

3. Acknowledging signals

The scorers shall accept all instructions and signals given to them by the umpires. They shall immediately acknowledge each separate signal.

LAW 5. THE BALL

1. Weight and size

The ball, when new, shall weigh not less than 5½oz/155.9g, nor more than 5¾oz/163g, and shall measure not less than 8 13/16in/22.4cm, nor more than 9in/22.9cm in circumference.

2. Approval and control of balls

(a) All balls to be used in the match, having been approved by the umpires and captains, shall be in the possession of the umpires before the toss and shall remain under their control throughout the match.

(b) The umpire shall take possession of the ball in use at the fall of each wicket, at the start of any interval and at any interruption of play.

3. New ball

Unless an agreement to the contrary has been made before the match, either captain may demand a new ball at the start of each innings.

4. New ball in match of more than one day's duration

In a match of more than one day's duration, the captain of the fielding side may demand a new ball after the prescribed number of overs has been bowled with the old one. The governing body for cricket in the country concerned shall decide the number of overs applicable in that country, which shall not be less than 75 overs.

The umpires shall indicate to the batsmen and the scorers whenever a new ball is taken into play.

5. Ball lost or becoming unfit for play

If, during play, the ball cannot be found or recovered or the umpires agree that it has become unfit for play through normal use, the umpires shall replace it with a ball which has had wear comparable with that which the previous ball had received before the need for its replacement. When the ball is replaced the umpires shall inform the batsmen and the fielding captain.

6. Specifications

The specifications as described in 1 above shall apply to men's cricket only. The following specifications will apply to:

(i) *Women's cricket*
Weight – from $4\frac{15}{16}$oz/140g to $5\frac{5}{16}$oz/151g.
Circumference – from $8\frac{1}{4}$in/21.0cm to $8\frac{7}{8}$in/22.5cm.

(ii) *Junior cricket – Under-13*
Weight – from $4\frac{11}{16}$oz/133g to $5\frac{1}{16}$oz/144g.
Circumference – from $8\frac{1}{16}$in/20.5cm to $8\frac{11}{16}$in/22.0cm.

LAW 6. THE BAT

1. Width and length

The bat overall shall not be more than 38in/96.5cm in length. The blade of the bat shall be made solely of wood and shall not exceed $4\frac{1}{4}$in/10.8cm at the widest part.

2. Covering the blade

The blade may be covered with material for protection, strengthening or repair. Such material shall not exceed $\frac{1}{16}$in/1.56mm in thickness, and shall not be likely to cause unacceptable damage to the ball.

3. Hand or glove to count as part of bat

In these Laws,

(a) Reference to the bat shall imply that the bat is held by the batsman.

(b) Contact between the ball and either

(i) the striker's bat itself, or

(ii) the striker's hand holding the bat, or

(iii) any part of a glove worn on the striker's hand holding the bat

shall be regarded as the ball striking or touching the bat, or being struck by the bat.

LAW 7. THE PITCH

1. Area of pitch

The pitch is a rectangular area of the ground 22yds/20.12m in length and 10ft/3.05m in width. It is bounded at either end by the bowling creases and on either side by imaginary lines, one each side of the imaginary line joining the centres of the two middle stumps, each parallel to it and 5ft/1.52m from it. See Laws 8.1 (Width and pitching) and 9.2 (The bowling crease).

2. Fitness of the pitch for play

The umpires shall be the final judges of the fitness of the pitch for play. See Laws 3.8 (Fitness of ground, weather and light) and 3.9 (Suspension of play for adverse conditions of ground, weather or light).

3. Selection and preparation

Before the toss the ground authority shall be responsible for the selection and preparation of the pitch. During the match the umpires shall control its use and maintenance.

4. Changing the pitch

The pitch shall not be changed during the match unless the umpires decide that it is unreasonable or dangerous for play to continue on it and then only with the consent of both captains.

5. Non-turf pitches

In the event of a non-turf pitch being used, the artificial surface shall conform to the following measurements:

Length – a minimum of 58ft/17.68m.
Width – a minimum of 6ft/1.83m.

See Law 10.8 (Non-turf pitches).

LAW 8. THE WICKETS

1. Width and pitching

Two sets of wickets shall be pitched opposite and parallel to each other at a distance of 22yds/20.12m between the centres of the two middle stumps. Each set shall be 9in/22.86cm wide and shall consist of three wooden stumps with two wooden bails on top.

2. Size of stumps

The tops of the stumps shall be 28in/71.1cm above the playing surface and shall be dome-shaped except for the bail grooves. The portion of a stump above the playing surface shall be cylindrical, apart from the domed top, with a circular section of diameter not less than $1\frac{3}{8}$in/3.49cm nor more than $1\frac{1}{2}$in/3.81cm.

3. The bails

(a) The bails, when in position on the top of the stumps:

(i) Shall not project more than $\frac{1}{2}$in/1.27cm above them.

(ii) Shall fit between the stumps without forcing them out of the vertical.

(b) Each bail shall conform to the following specifications.

Overall length	– $4\frac{5}{16}$in/10.95cm.
Length of barrel	– $2\frac{1}{8}$in/5.40cm.
Longer spigot	– $1\frac{3}{8}$in/3.49cm.
Shorter spigot	– $\frac{13}{16}$in/2.06cm.

4. Junior cricket

In junior cricket, the same definitions of the wickets shall apply subject to the following measurements being used:

Width	– 8in/20.32cm.
Pitched for Under-13	– 21yds/19.20m.
Pitched for Under-11	– 20yds/18.29m.
Pitched for Under-9	– 18yds/16.46m.
Height above playing surface	– 27in/68.58cm.

Each stump

Diameter	– not less than $1\frac{1}{4}$in/3.18cm nor more than $1\frac{3}{8}$in/3.49cm.

Each bail

Overall	– $3\frac{13}{16}$in/9.68cm.
Barrel	– $1\frac{13}{16}$in/4.60cm.
Longer Spigot	– $1\frac{1}{4}$in/3.18cm.
Shorter Spigot	– $\frac{3}{4}$in/1.91cm.

5. Dispensing with bails

The umpires may agree to dispense with the use of bails, if necessary. If they so agree then no bails shall be used at either end. The use of bails shall be resumed as soon as conditions permit. See Law 28.4 (Dispensing with bails).

LAW 9. THE BOWLING, POPPING AND RETURN CREASES

1. The creases

A bowling crease, a popping crease and two return creases shall be marked in white, as set out in 2, 3 and 4 below, at each end of the pitch.

2. The bowling crease

The bowling crease, which is the back edge of the crease marking, shall be the line through the centres of the three stumps at that end. It shall be 8ft 8in/2.64m in length, with the stumps in the centre.

3. The popping crease

The popping crease, which is the back edge of the crease marking, shall be in front of and parallel to the bowling crease and shall be 4ft/1.22m from it. The popping crease shall be marked to a minimum of 6ft/1.83m on either side of the imaginary line joining the centres of the middle stumps and shall be considered to be unlimited in length.

4. The return creases

The return creases, which are the inside edges of the crease markings, shall be at right angles to the popping crease at a distance of 4ft 4in/1.32m either side of the imaginary line joining the centres of the two middle stumps. Each return crease shall be marked from the popping crease to a minimum of 8ft/2.44m behind it and shall be considered to be unlimited in length.

LAW 10. PREPARATION AND MAINTENANCE OF THE PLAYING AREA

1. Rolling

The pitch shall not be rolled during the match except as permitted in (a) and (b) below.

(a) Frequency and duration of rolling
During the match the pitch may be rolled at the request of the captain of the batting side, for a period of not more than seven minutes, before the start of each innings, other than the first innings of the match, and before the start of each subsequent day's play. See (d) below.

(b) Rolling after a delayed start
In addition to the rolling permitted above, if, after the toss and before the first innings of the match, the start is delayed, the captain of the batting side may request to have the pitch rolled for not more than seven minutes. However, if the umpires together agree that the delay has had no significant effect on the state of the pitch, they shall refuse the request for the rolling of the pitch.

(c) Choice of rollers
If there is more than one roller available the captain of the batting side shall have the choice.

(d) Timing of permitted rolling
The rolling permitted (maximum seven minutes) before play begins on any day shall be started not more than 30 minutes before the time scheduled or rescheduled for play to begin. The captain of the batting side may, however, delay the start of such rolling until not less than ten minutes before the time scheduled or rescheduled for play to begin, should he so desire.

(e) Insufficient time to complete rolling
If a captain declares an innings closed, or forfeits an innings, or enforces the follow-on, and the other captain is prevented thereby from exercising his option of the rolling permitted (maximum seven minutes), or if he is so prevented for any other reason, the extra time required to complete the rolling shall be taken out of the normal playing time.

2. Sweeping

(a) If rolling is to take place the pitch shall first be swept to avoid any possible damage by rolling in debris. This sweeping shall be done so that the seven minutes allowed for rolling is not affected.

(b) The pitch shall be cleared of any debris at all intervals for meals, between innings and at the beginning of each day, not earlier than 30 minutes nor later than ten minutes before the time scheduled or rescheduled for play to begin. See Law 15.1 (An interval).

(c) Notwithstanding the provisions of (a) and (b) above, the umpires shall not allow sweeping to take place where they consider it may be detrimental to the surface of the pitch.

3. Mowing

(a) The pitch
The pitch shall be mown on each day of the match on which play is expected to take place, if ground and weather conditions allow.

(b) The outfield
In order to ensure that conditions are as similar as possible for both sides, the outfield shall be mown on each day of the match on which play is expected to take place, if ground and weather conditions allow.

If, for reasons other than ground and weather conditions, complete mowing of the outfield is not possible, the ground authority shall notify the captains and umpires of the procedure to be adopted for such mowing during the match.

(c) Responsibility for mowing
All mowings which are carried out before the match shall be the responsibility of the ground authority.

All subsequent mowings shall be carried out under the supervision of the umpires.

(d) Time of mowing

(i) Mowing of the pitch on any day of the match shall be completed not later than 30 minutes before the time scheduled or rescheduled for play to begin on that day.

(ii) Mowing of the outfield on any day of the match shall be completed not later than 15 minutes before the time scheduled or rescheduled for play to begin on that day.

4. Watering

The pitch shall not be watered during the match.

5. Re-marking creases

The creases shall be re-marked whenever either umpire considers it necessary.

6. Maintenance of footholes

The umpires shall ensure that the holes made by the bowlers and batsmen are cleaned out and dried whenever necessary to facilitate play. In matches of more than one day's duration, the umpires shall allow, if necessary, the re-turfing of footholes made by the bowler in his delivery stride, or the use of quick-setting fillings for the same purpose.

7. Securing of footholds and maintenance of pitch

During play, the umpires shall allow the players to secure their footholds by the use of sawdust provided that no damage to the pitch is caused and that Law 42 (Fair and unfair play) is not contravened.

8. Non-turf pitches

Wherever appropriate, the provisions set out in 1 to 7 above shall apply.

LAW 11. COVERING THE PITCH

1. Before the match

The use of covers before the match is the responsibility of the ground authority and may include full covering if required. However, the ground authority shall grant suitable facility to the captains to inspect the pitch before the nomination of their players and to the umpires to discharge their duties as laid down in Laws 3 (The umpires), 7 (The pitch), 8 (The wickets), 9 (The bowling, popping and return creases) and 10 (Preparation and maintenance of the playing area).

2. During the match

The pitch shall not be completely covered during the match unless provided otherwise by regulations or by agreement before the toss.

3. Covering bowlers' run-ups

Whenever possible, the bowlers' run-ups shall be covered in inclement weather, in order to keep them dry. Unless there is agreement for full covering under 2 above the covers so used shall not extend further than 5ft/1.52m in front of each popping crease.

4. Removal of covers

(a) If after the toss the pitch is covered overnight, the covers shall be removed in the morning at the earliest possible moment on each day that play is expected to take place.

(b) If covers are used during the day as protection from inclement weather, or if inclement weather delays the removal of overnight covers, they shall be removed promptly as soon as conditions allow.

LAW 12. INNINGS

1. Number of innings

(a) A match shall be one or two innings of each side according to agreement reached before the start of play.

(b) It may be agreed to limit any innings to a number of overs or by a period of time. If such an agreement is made then:

- (i) In a one-innings match it shall apply to both innings.
- (ii) In a two-innings match it shall apply to either
  the first innings of each side, or
  the second innings of each side, or
  both innings of each side.

2. Alternate innings

In a two-innings match each side shall take their innings alternately except in the cases provided for in Law 13 (The follow-on) or Law 14.2 (Forfeiture of an innings).

3. Completed innings

A side's innings is to be considered as completed if:

(a) The side is all out, or

(b) At the fall of a wicket, further balls remain to be bowled, but no further batsman is available to come in, or

(c) The captain declares the innings closed, or

(d) The captain forfeits the innings, or

(e) In the case of an agreement under 1(b) above, either

- (i) the prescribed number of overs has been bowled, or
- (ii) the prescribed time has expired.

4. The toss

The captains shall toss for the choice of innings on the field of play not earlier than 30 minutes, nor later than 15 minutes, before the scheduled or any rescheduled time for the match to start. Note, however, the provisions of Law 1.3 (Captain).

5. Decision to be notified

The captain of the side winning the toss shall notify the opposing captain of his decision to bat or to field, not later than ten minutes before the scheduled or any rescheduled time for the match to start. Once notified the decision may not be altered.

LAW 13. THE FOLLOW-ON

1. Lead on first innings

(a) In a two-innings match of five days or more, the side which bats first and leads by at least 200 runs shall have the option of requiring the other side to follow their innings.

(b) The same option shall be available in two-innings matches of shorter duration with the minimum required leads as follows:

(i) 150 runs in a match of three or four days.

(ii) 100 runs in a two-day match.

(iii) 75 runs in a one-day match.

2. Notification

A captain shall notify the opposing captain and the umpires of his intention to take up this option. Law 10.1 (e) (Insufficient time to complete rolling) shall apply.

3. First day's play lost

If no play takes place on the first day of a match of more than one day's duration, 1 above shall apply in accordance with the number of days remaining from the actual start of the match. The day on which play first commences shall count as a whole day for this purpose, irrespective of the time at which play starts.

Play will have taken place as soon as, after the call of "Play", the first over has started. See Law 22.2 (Start of an over).

LAW 14. DECLARATION AND FORFEITURE

1. Time of declaration

The captain of the batting side may declare an innings closed, when the ball is dead, at any time during a match.

2. Forfeiture of an innings

A captain may forfeit either of his side's innings. A forfeited innings shall be considered as a completed innings.

3. Notification

A captain shall notify the opposing captain and the umpires of his decision to declare or to forfeit an innings. Law 10.1 (e) (Insufficient time to complete rolling) shall apply.

LAW 15. INTERVALS

1. An interval

The following shall be classed as intervals:

(i) The period between close of play on one day and the start of the next day's play.

(ii) Intervals between innings.

(iii) Intervals for meals.

(iv) Intervals for drinks.

(v) Any other agreed interval.

All these intervals shall be considered as scheduled breaks for the purposes of Law 2.5 (Fielder absent or leaving the field).

2. Agreement of intervals

(a) Before the toss:

(i) The hours of play shall be established.

(ii) Except as in (b) below, the timing and duration of intervals for meals shall be agreed.

(iii) The timing and duration of any other interval under 1(v) above shall be agreed.

(b) In a one-day match no specific time need be agreed for the tea interval. It may be agreed instead to take this interval between the innings.

(c) Intervals for drinks may not be taken during the last hour of the match, as defined in Law 16.6 (Last hour of match – number of overs). Subject to this limitation the captains and umpires shall agree the times for such intervals, if any, before the toss and on each subsequent day not later than ten minutes before play is scheduled to start. See also Law 3.3 (Agreement with captains).

3. Duration of intervals

(a) An interval for lunch or for tea shall be of the duration agreed under 2(a) above, taken from the call of "Time" before the interval until the call of "Play" on resumption after the interval.

(b) An interval between innings shall be ten minutes from the close of an innings to the call of "Play" for the start of the next innings, except as in 4, 6 and 7 below.

4. No allowance for interval between innings

In addition to the provisions of 6 and 7 below:

(a) If an innings ends when ten minutes or less remain before the time agreed for close of play on any day, there will be no further play on that day. No change will be made to the time for the start of play on the following day on account of the ten minutes between innings.

(b) If a captain declares an innings closed during an interruption in play of more than ten minutes duration, no adjustment shall be made to the time for resumption of play on account of the ten minutes between innings, which shall be considered as included in the interruption. Law 10.1(e) (Insufficient time to complete rolling) shall apply.

(c) If a captain declares an innings closed during any interval other than an interval for drinks, the interval shall be of the agreed duration and shall be considered to include the ten minutes between innings. Law 10.1(e) (Insufficient time to complete rolling) shall apply.

5. Changing agreed times for intervals

If for adverse conditions of ground, weather or light, or for any other reason, playing time is lost, the umpires and captains together may alter the time of the lunch interval or of the tea interval. See also 6, 7 and 9(c) below.

6. Changing agreed time for lunch interval

(a) If an innings ends when ten minutes or less remain before the agreed time for lunch, the interval shall be taken immediately. It shall be of the agreed length and shall be considered to include the ten minutes between innings.

(b) If, because of adverse conditions of ground, weather or light, or in exceptional circumstances, a stoppage occurs when ten minutes or less remain before the agreed time for lunch then, notwithstanding 5 above, the interval shall be taken immediately. It shall be of the agreed length. Play shall resume at the end of this interval or as soon after as conditions permit.

(c) If the players have occasion to leave the field for any reason when more than ten minutes remain before the agreed time for lunch then, unless the umpires and captains together agree to alter it, lunch will be taken at the agreed time.

7. Changing agreed time for tea interval

(a) (i) If an innings ends when 30 minutes or less remain before the agreed time for tea, then the interval shall be taken immediately. It shall be of the agreed length and shall be considered to include the ten minutes between innings.

(ii) If, when 30 minutes remain before the agreed time for tea, an interval between innings is already in progress, play will resume at the end of the ten-minute interval.

(b) (i) If, because of adverse conditions of ground, weather or light, or in exceptional circumstances, a stoppage occurs when 30 minutes or less remain before the agreed time for tea, then unless

either there is an agreement to change the time for tea, as permitted in 5 above,
or the captains agree to forgo the tea interval, as permitted in 10 below,

the interval shall be taken immediately. The interval shall be of the agreed length. Play shall resume at the end of this interval or as soon after as conditions permit.

(ii) If a stoppage is already in progress when 30 minutes remain before the time agreed for tea, 5 above will apply.

8. Tea interval – nine wickets down

If nine wickets are down at the end of the over in progress when the agreed time for the tea interval has been reached, then play shall continue for a period not exceeding 30 minutes, unless the players have cause to leave the field of play, or the innings is concluded earlier.

9. Intervals for drinks

(a) If on any day the captains agree that there shall be intervals for drinks, the option to take such intervals shall be available to either side. Each interval shall be kept as short as possible and in any case shall not exceed five minutes.

(b) (i) Unless both captains agree to forgo any drinks interval, it shall be taken at the end of the over in progress when the agreed time is reached. If, however, a wicket falls within five minutes of the agreed time then drinks shall be taken immediately. No other variation in the timing of drinks intervals shall be permitted except as provided for in (c) below.

(ii) For the purpose of (i) above and Law 3.9(a)(ii) (Suspension of play for adverse conditions of ground, weather or light) only, the batsmen at the wicket may deputise for their captain.

(c) If an innings ends or the players have to leave the field of play for any other reason within 30 minutes of the agreed time for a drinks interval, the umpires and captains together may rearrange the timing of drinks intervals in that session.

10. Agreement to forgo intervals

At any time during the match, the captains may agree to forgo the tea interval or any of the drinks intervals. The umpires shall be informed of the decision.

11. Scorers to be informed

The umpires shall ensure that the scorers are informed of all agreements about hours of play and intervals, and of any changes made thereto as permitted under this Law.

LAW 16. START OF PLAY; CESSATION OF PLAY

1. Call of "Play"

The umpire at the bowler's end shall call "Play" at the start of the match and on the resumption of play after any interval or interruption.

2. Call of "Time"

The umpire at the bowler's end shall call "Time" on the cessation of play before any interval or interruption of play and at the conclusion of the match. See Law 27 (Appeals).

3. Removal of bails

After the call of "Time", the bails shall be removed from both wickets.

4. Starting a new over

Another over shall always be started at any time during the match, unless an interval is to be taken in the circumstances set out in 5 below, if the umpire, after walking at his normal pace, has arrived at his position behind the stumps at the bowler's end before the time agreed for the next interval, or for the close of play, has been reached.

5. Completion of an over

Other than at the end of the match:

(a) If the agreed time for an interval is reached during an over, the over shall be completed before the interval is taken except as provided for in (b) below.

(b) When less than two minutes remain before the time agreed for the next interval, the interval will be taken immediately if either

(i) a batsman is out or retires, or

(ii) the players have occasion to leave the field

whether this occurs during an over or at the end of an over. Except at the end of an innings, if an over is thus interrupted it shall be completed on resumption of play.

6. Last hour of match – number of overs

When one hour of playing time of the match remains, according to the agreed hours of play, the over in progress shall be completed. The next over shall be the first of a minimum of 20 overs which must be bowled, provided that a result is not reached earlier and provided that there is no interval or interruption in play.

The umpire at the bowler's end shall indicate the commencement of this 20 overs to the players and the scorers. The period of play thereafter shall be referred to as the last hour, whatever its actual duration.

7. Last hour of match – interruptions of play

If there is an interruption in play during the last hour of the match, the minimum number of overs to be bowled shall be reduced from 20 as follows:

(a) The time lost for an interruption is counted from the call of "Time" until the time for resumption of play as decided by the umpires.

(b) One over shall be deducted for every complete three minutes of time lost.

(c) In the case of more than one such interruption, the minutes lost shall not be aggregated; the calculation shall be made for each interruption separately.

(d) If, when one hour of playing time remains, an interruption is already in progress:

(i) Only the time lost after this moment shall be counted in the calculation.

(ii) The over in progress at the start of the interruption shall be completed on resumption of play and shall not count as one of the minimum number of overs to be bowled.

(e) If, after the start of the last hour, an interruption occurs during an over, the over shall be completed on resumption of play. The two part-overs shall between them count as one over of the minimum number to be bowled.

8. Last hour of match – intervals between innings

If an innings ends so that a new innings is to be started during the last hour of the match, the interval starts with the end of the innings and is to end ten minutes later.

(a) If this interval is already in progress at the start of the last hour, then to determine the number of overs to be bowled in the new innings, calculations are to be made as set out in 7 above.

(b) If the innings ends after the last hour has started, two calculations are to be made, as set out in (c) and (d) below. The greater of the numbers yielded by these two calculations is to be the minimum number of overs to be bowled in the new innings.

(c) Calculation based on overs remaining:

(i) At the conclusion of the innings, the number of overs that remain to be bowled, of the minimum in the last hour, to be noted.

(ii) If this is not a whole number it is to be rounded up to the next whole number.

(iii) Three overs to be deducted from the result for the interval.

(d) Calculation based on time remaining:

(i) At the conclusion of the innings, the time remaining until the agreed time for close of play to be noted.

(ii) Ten minutes to be deducted from this time, for the interval, to determine the playing time remaining.

(iii) A calculation to be made of one over for every complete three minutes of the playing time remaining, plus one more over for any further part of three minutes remaining.

9. Conclusion of match

The match is concluded:

(a) As soon as a result, as defined in sections 1, 2, 3 or 4 of Law 21 (The result), is reached.

(b) As soon as both

(i) the minimum number of overs for the last hour are completed, and

(ii) the agreed time for close of play is reached

unless a result has been reached earlier.

(c) If, without the match being concluded either as in (a) or in (b) above, the players leave the field, either for adverse conditions of ground, weather or light, or in exceptional circumstances, and no further play is possible thereafter.

10. Completion of last over of match

The over in progress at the close of play on the final day shall be completed unless either

(i) a result has been reached, or

(ii) the players have occasion to leave the field. In this case there shall be no resumption of play except in the circumstances of Law 21.9 (Mistakes in scoring), and the match shall be at an end.

11. Bowler unable to complete an over during last hour of match

If, for any reason, a bowler is unable to complete an over during the last hour, Law 22.8 (Bowler incapacitated or suspended during an over) shall apply.

LAW 17. PRACTICE ON THE FIELD

1. Practice on the field

(a) There shall be no bowling or batting practice on the pitch, or on the area parallel and immediately adjacent to the pitch, at any time on any day of the match.

(b) There shall be no bowling or batting practice on any other part of the square on any day of the match, except before the start of play or after the close of play on that day. Practice before the start of play:

(i) Must not continue later than 30 minutes before the scheduled time or any rescheduled time for play to start on that day.

(ii) Shall not be allowed if the umpires consider that, in the prevailing conditions of ground and weather, it will be detrimental to the surface of the square.

(c) There shall be no practice on the field of play between the call of "Play" and the call of "Time", if the umpire considers that it could result in a waste of time. See Law 42.9 (Time-wasting by the fielding side).

(d) If a player contravenes (a) or (b) above he shall not be allowed to bowl until at least five complete overs have been bowled by his side after the contravention. If an over is in progress at the contravention he shall not be allowed to complete that over nor shall the remaining part-over count towards the five overs above.

2. Trial run-up

No bowler shall have a trial run-up between the call of "Play" and the call of "Time" unless the umpire is satisfied that it will not cause any waste of time.

LAW 18. SCORING RUNS

1. A run

The score shall be reckoned by runs. A run is scored:

(a) So often as the batsmen, at any time while the ball is in play, have crossed and made good their ground from end to end.

(b) When a boundary is scored. See Law 19 (Boundaries).

(c) When penalty runs are awarded. See 6 below.

(d) When "Lost ball" is called. See Law 20 (Lost ball).

2. Runs disallowed

Notwithstanding 1 above, or any other provisions elsewhere in the Laws, the scoring of runs or awarding of penalties will be subject to any disallowance of runs provided for within the Laws that may be applicable.

3. Short runs

(a) A run is short if a batsman fails to make good his ground on turning for a further run.

(b) Although a short run shortens the succeeding one, the latter if completed shall not be regarded as short. A striker taking stance in front of his popping crease may run from that point also without penalty.

4. Unintentional short runs

Except in the circumstances of 5 below:

(a) If either batsman runs a short run, unless a boundary is scored the umpire concerned shall call and signal "Short run" as soon as the ball becomes dead and that run shall not be scored.

(b) If, after either or both batsmen run short, a boundary is scored, the umpire concerned shall disregard the short running and shall not call or signal "Short run".

(c) If both batsmen run short in one and the same run, this shall be regarded as only one short run.

(d) If more than one run is short then, subject to (b) and (c) above, all runs so called shall not be scored.

If there has been more than one short run the umpire shall inform the scorers as to the number of runs scored.

5. Deliberate short runs

Notwithstanding 4 above, if either umpire considers that either or both batsmen deliberately runs short at his end, the following procedure shall be adopted:

(a) (i) The umpire concerned shall, when the ball is dead, warn the batsman or batsmen that the practice is unfair, indicate that this is a first and final warning and inform the other umpire of what has occurred.

(ii) The batsmen shall return to their original ends.

(iii) Whether a batsman is dismissed or not, the umpire at the bowler's end shall disallow all runs to the batting side from that delivery other than the penalty for a no-ball or wide, or penalties under Laws 42.5 (Deliberate distraction or obstruction of batsman) and 42.13 (Fielders damaging the pitch), if applicable.

(iv) The umpire at the bowler's end shall inform the scorers as to the number of runs scored.

(b) If there is any further instance of deliberate short running by either of the same batsmen in that innings, when the ball is dead the umpire concerned shall inform the other umpire of what has occurred and the procedure set out in (a)(ii) and (iii) above shall be repeated. Additionally, the umpire at the bowler's end shall:

(i) Award five penalty runs to the fielding side. See Law 42.17 (Penalty runs).

(ii) Inform the scorers as to the number of runs scored.

(iii) Inform the batsmen, the captain of the fielding side and, as soon as practicable, the captain of the batting side of the reason for this action.

(iv) Report the occurrence, with the other umpire, to the executive of the batting side and any governing body responsible for the match, who shall take such action as is considered appropriate against the captain and player or players concerned.

6. Runs scored for penalties

Runs shall be scored for penalties under 5 above and Laws 2.6 (Player returning without permission), 24 (No-ball), 25 (Wide ball), 41.2 (Fielding the ball), 41.3 (Protective helmets belonging to the fielding side) and 42 (Fair and unfair play).

7. Runs scored for boundaries

Runs shall be scored for boundary allowances under Law 19 (Boundaries).

8. Runs scored for lost ball

Runs shall be scored when "Lost ball" is called under Law 20 (Lost ball).

9. Batsman dismissed

When either batsman is dismissed:

(a) Any penalties to either side that may be applicable shall stand but no other runs shall be scored, except as stated in 10 below. Note, however, Law 42.17(b) (Penalty runs).

(b) 12(a) below will apply if the method of dismissal is caught, handled the ball or obstructing the field. 12(a) will also apply if a batsman is run out, except in the circumstances of Law 2.8 (Transgression of the Laws by a batsman who has a runner) where 12(b) below will apply.

(c) The not out batsman shall return to his original end except as stated in (b) above.

10. Runs scored when a batsman is dismissed

In addition to any penalties to either side that may be applicable, if a batsman is:

(a) Dismissed handled the ball, the batting side shall score the runs completed before the offence.

(b) Dismissed obstructing the field, the batting side shall score the runs completed before the offence.

If, however, the obstruction prevents a catch from being made, no runs other than penalties shall be scored.

(c) Dismissed run out, the batting side shall score the runs completed before the dismissal. If however, a striker with a runner is himself dismissed run out, no runs other than penalties shall be scored. See Law 2.8 (Transgression of the Laws by a batsman who has a runner).

11. Runs scored when ball becomes dead

(a) When the ball becomes dead on the fall of a wicket, runs shall be scored as laid down in 9 and 10 above.

(b) When the ball becomes dead for any reason other than the fall of a wicket, or is called dead by an umpire, unless there is specific provision otherwise in the Laws, the batting side shall be credited with:

(i) All runs completed by the batsmen before the incident or call, and

(ii) the run in progress if the batsmen have crossed at the instant of the incident or call. Note specifically, however, the provisions of Law 34.4(c) (Runs permitted from a ball lawfully struck more than once) and 42.5(b)(iii) (Deliberate distraction or obstruction of batsman), and

(iii) any penalties that are applicable.

12. Batsman returning to wicket he has left

(a) If, while the ball is in play, the batsmen have crossed in running, neither shall return to the wicket he has left, except as in (b) below.

(b) The batsmen shall return to the wickets they originally left in the cases of, and only in the cases of:

(i) A boundary.

(ii) Disallowance of runs for any reason.

(iii) The dismissal of a batsman, except as in 9(b) above.

LAW 19. BOUNDARIES

1. The boundary of the field of play

(a) Before the toss, the umpires shall agree the boundary of the field of play with both captains. The boundary shall if possible be marked along its whole length.

(b) The boundary shall be agreed so that no part of any sightscreen is within the field of play.

(c) An obstacle or person within the field of play shall not be regarded as a boundary unless so decided by the umpires before the toss. See Law 3.4(ii) (To inform captains and scorers).

2. Defining the boundary – boundary marking

(a) Wherever practicable the boundary shall be marked by means of a white line or a rope laid along the ground.

(b) If the boundary is marked by a white line:

(i) The inside edge of the line shall be the boundary edge.

(ii) A flag, post or board used merely to highlight the position of a line marked on the ground must be placed outside the boundary edge and is not itself to be regarded as defining or marking the boundary. Note, however, the provisions of (c) below.

(c) If a solid object is used to mark the boundary, it must have an edge or a line to constitute the boundary edge.

(i) For a rope, which includes any similar object of curved cross section lying on the ground, the boundary edge will be the line formed by the innermost points of the rope along its length.

(ii) For a fence, which includes any similar object in contact with the ground, but with a flat surface projecting above the ground, the boundary edge will be the base line of the fence.

(d) If the boundary edge is not defined as in (b) or (c) above, the umpires and captains must agree, before the toss, what line will be the boundary edge. Where there is no physical marker for a section of boundary, the boundary edge shall be the imaginary straight line joining the two nearest marked points of the boundary edge.

(e) If a solid object used to mark the boundary is disturbed for any reason during play, then if possible it shall be restored to its original position as soon as the ball is dead. If this is not possible, then:

(i) If some part of the fence or other marker has come within the field of play, that portion is to be removed from the field of play as soon as the ball is dead.

(ii) The line where the base of the fence or marker originally stood shall define the boundary edge.

3. Scoring a boundary

(a) A boundary shall be scored and signalled by the umpire at the bowler's end whenever, while the ball is in play, in his opinion:

(i) The ball touches the boundary, or is grounded beyond the boundary.

(ii) A fielder, with some part of his person in contact with the ball, touches the boundary or has some part of his person grounded beyond the boundary.

(b) The phrases "touches the boundary" and "touching the boundary" shall mean contact with either

(i) the boundary edge as defined in 2 above, or

(ii) any person or obstacle within the field of play which has been designated a boundary by the umpires before the toss.

(c) The phrase "grounded beyond the boundary" shall mean contact with either

(i) any part of a line or a solid object marking the boundary, except its boundary edge, or

(ii) the ground outside the boundary edge, or

(iii) any object in contact with the ground outside the boundary edge.

4. Runs allowed for boundaries

(a) Before the toss, the umpires shall agree with both captains the runs to be allowed for boundaries. In deciding the allowances, the umpires and captains shall be guided by the prevailing custom of the ground.

(b) Unless agreed differently under (a) above, the allowances for boundaries shall be six runs if the ball having been struck by the bat pitches beyond the boundary, but otherwise four runs. These allowances shall still apply even though the ball has previously touched a fielder. See also (c) below.

(c) The ball shall be regarded as pitching beyond the boundary and six runs shall be scored if a fielder:

(i) Has any part of his person touching the boundary or grounded beyond the boundary when he catches the ball.

(ii) Catches the ball and subsequently touches the boundary or grounds some part of his person beyond the boundary while carrying the ball but before completing the catch. See Law 32 (Caught).

5. Runs scored

When a boundary is scored:

(a) The penalty for a no-ball or a wide, if applicable, shall stand together with any penalties under any of Laws 2.6 (Player returning without permission), 18.5(b) (Deliberate short runs) or Law 42 (Fair and unfair play) that apply before the boundary is scored.

(b) The batting side, except in the circumstances of 6 below, shall additionally be awarded whichever is the greater of:

(i) The allowance for the boundary.

(ii) The runs completed by the batsmen, together with the run in progress if they have crossed at the instant the boundary is scored. When these runs exceed the boundary allowance, they shall replace the boundary for the purposes of Law 18.12 (Batsman returning to wicket he has left).

6. Overthrow or wilful act of fielder

If the boundary results either from an overthrow or from the wilful act of a fielder the runs scored shall be:

(i) The penalty for a no-ball or a wide, if applicable, and any penalties under Laws 2.6 (Player returning without permission), 18.5(b) (Deliberate short runs) or Law 42 (Fair and unfair play) that are applicable before the boundary is scored, and

(ii) the allowance for the boundary, and

(iii) the runs completed by the batsmen, together with the run in progress if they have crossed at the instant of the throw or act.

Law 18.12(a) (Batsman returning to the wicket he has left) shall apply as from the instant of the throw or act.

LAW 20. LOST BALL

1. Fielder to call "Lost ball"

If a ball in play cannot be found or recovered, any fielder may call "Lost ball". The ball shall then become dead. See Law 23.1 (Ball is dead). Law 18.12(a) (Batsman returning to wicket he has left) shall apply as from the instant of the call.

2. Ball to be replaced

The umpires shall replace the ball with one which has had wear comparable with that which the previous ball had received before it was lost or became irrecoverable. See Law 5.5 (Ball lost or becoming unfit for play).

3. Runs scored

(a) The penalty for a no-ball or a wide, if applicable, shall stand, together with any penalties under any of Laws 2.6 (Player returning without permission), 18.5(b) (Deliberate short runs) or Law 42 (Fair and unfair play) that are applicable before the call of "Lost ball".

(b) The batting side shall additionally be awarded either

(i) the runs completed by the batsmen, together with the run in progress if they have crossed at the instant of the call, or

(ii) six runs,

whichever is the greater.

4. How scored

If there is a one-run penalty for a no-ball or for a wide, it shall be scored as a no-ball extra or as a wide as appropriate. See Laws 24.13 (Runs resulting from a no-ball – how scored) and 25.6 (Runs resulting from a wide – how scored). If any other penalties have been awarded to either side, they shall be scored as penalty extras. See Law 42.17 (Penalty runs).

Runs to the batting side in 3(b) above shall be credited to the striker if the ball has been struck by the bat, but otherwise to the total of byes, leg-byes, no-balls or wides as the case may be.

LAW 21. THE RESULT

1. A win – two-innings match

The side which has scored a total of runs in excess of that scored in the two completed innings of the opposing side shall win the match. Note also 6 below.

A forfeited innings is to count as a completed innings. See Law 14 (Declaration and forfeiture).

2. A win – one-innings match

The side which has scored in its one innings a total of runs in excess of that scored by the opposing side in its one completed innings shall win the match. Note also 6 below.

3. Umpires awarding a match

(a) A match shall be lost by a side which either

(i) concedes defeat, or

(ii) in the opinion of the umpires, refuses to play

and the umpires shall award the match to the other side.

(b) If an umpire considers that an action by any player or players might constitute a refusal by either side to play then the umpires together shall ascertain the cause of the action. If they then decide together that this action does constitute a refusal to play by one side, they shall so inform the captain of that side. If the captain persists in the action the umpires shall award the match in accordance with (a)(ii) above.

(c) If action as in (b) above takes place after play has started and does not constitute a refusal to play:

- (i) Playing time lost shall be counted from the start of the action until play recommences, subject to Law 15.5 (Changing agreed times for intervals).
- (ii) The time for close of play on that day shall be extended by this length of time, subject to Law 3.9 (Suspension of play for adverse conditions of ground, weather or light).
- (iii) If applicable, no overs shall be deducted during the last hour of the match solely on account of this time.

4. A tie

The result of a match shall be a tie when the scores are equal at the conclusion of play, but only if the side batting last has completed its innings.

5. A draw

A match which is concluded, as defined in Law 16.9 (Conclusion of a match), without being determined in any of the ways stated in 1, 2, 3 or 4 above, shall count as a draw.

6. Winning hit or extras

(a) As soon as a result is reached, as defined in 1, 2, 3 or 4 above, the match is at an end. Nothing that happens thereafter shall be regarded as part of it. Note also 9 below.

(b) The side batting last will have scored enough runs to win only if its total of runs is sufficient without including any runs completed before the dismissal of the striker by the completion of a catch or by the obstruction of a catch.

(c) If a boundary is scored before the batsmen have completed sufficient runs to win the match, then the whole of the boundary allowance shall be credited to the side's total and, in the case of a hit by the bat, to the striker's score.

7. Statement of result

If the side batting last wins the match, the result shall be stated as a win by the number of wickets still then to fall. If the other side wins the match, the result shall be stated as a win by runs.

If the match is decided by one side conceding defeat or refusing to play, the result shall be stated as "Match conceded" or "Match awarded" as the case may be.

8. Correctness of result

Any decision as to the correctness of the scores shall be the responsibility of the umpires. See Law 3.15 (Correctness of scores).

9. Mistakes in scoring

If, after the umpires and players have left the field in the belief that the match has been concluded, the umpires discover that a mistake in scoring has occurred which affects the result, then, subject to 10 below, they shall adopt the following procedure.

(a) If, when the players leave the field, the side batting last has not completed its innings, and either

- (i) the number of overs to be bowled in the last hour has not been completed, or
- (ii) the agreed finishing time has not been reached,

then unless one side concedes defeat the umpires shall order play to resume.

If conditions permit, play will then continue until the prescribed number of overs has been completed and the time remaining has elapsed, unless a result is reached earlier. The number of overs and/or the time remaining shall be taken as they were when the players left the field; no account shall be taken of the time between that moment and the resumption of play.

(b) If, when the players leave the field, the overs have been completed and time has been reached, or if the side batting last has completed its innings, the umpires shall immediately inform both captains of the necessary corrections to the scores and to the result.

10. Result not to be changed

Once the umpires have agreed with the scorers the correctness of the scores at the conclusion of the match – see Laws 3.15 (Correctness of scores) and 4.2 (Correctness of scores) – the result cannot thereafter be changed.

LAW 22. THE OVER

1. Number of balls

The ball shall be bowled from each wicket alternately in overs of six balls.

2. Start of an over

An over has started when the bowler starts his run-up or, if he has no run-up, his delivery action for the first delivery of that over.

3. Call of "Over"

When six balls have been bowled other than those which are not to count in the over and as the ball becomes dead – see Law 23 (Dead ball) – the umpire shall call "Over" before leaving the wicket.

4. Balls not to count in the over

(a) A ball shall not count as one of the six balls of the over unless it is delivered, even though a batsman may be dismissed or some other incident occurs before the ball is delivered.

(b) A ball which is delivered by the bowler shall not count as one of the six balls of the over:

(i) If it is called dead, or is to be considered dead, before the striker has had an opportunity to play it. See Law 23 (Dead ball).

(ii) If it is a no-ball. See Law 24 (No-ball).

(iii) If it is a wide. See Law 25 (Wide ball).

(iv) If it is called dead in the circumstances of either of Laws 23.3(b)(vi) (Umpire calling and signalling "Dead ball") or 42.4 (Deliberate attempt to distract striker).

5. Umpire miscounting

If an umpire miscounts the number of balls, the over as counted by the umpire shall stand.

6. Bowler changing ends

A bowler shall be allowed to change ends as often as desired, provided only that he does not bowl two overs, or parts thereof, consecutively in the same innings.

7. Finishing an over

(a) Other than at the end of an innings, a bowler shall finish an over in progress unless he is incapacitated, or he is suspended under any of Laws 17.1 (Practice on the field), 42.7 (Dangerous and unfair bowling – action by the umpire), 42.9 (Time-wasting by the fielding side), or 42.12 (Bowler running on the protected area after delivering the ball).

(b) If for any reason, other than the end of an innings, an over is left uncompleted at the start of an interval or interruption of play, it shall be completed on resumption of play.

8. Bowler incapacitated or suspended during an over

If for any reason a bowler is incapacitated while running up to bowl the first ball of an over, or is incapacitated or suspended during an over, the umpire shall call and signal "Dead ball". Another bowler shall complete the over from the same end, provided that he does not bowl two overs, or parts thereof, consecutively in one innings.

LAW 23. DEAD BALL

1. Ball is dead

(a) The ball becomes dead when:

(i) It is finally settled in the hands of the wicket-keeper or the bowler.

(ii) A boundary is scored. See Law 19.3 (Scoring a boundary).

(iii) A batsman is dismissed.

(iv) Whether played or not it becomes trapped between the bat and person of a batsman or between items of his clothing or equipment.

(v) Whether played or not it lodges in the clothing or equipment of a batsman or the clothing of an umpire.

(vi) It lodges in a protective helmet worn by a member of the fielding side.

(vii) There is a contravention of Law 41.2 (Fielding the ball) or Law 41.3 (Protective helmets belonging to the fielding side).

(viii) This is an award of penalty runs under Law 2.6 (Player returning without permission).

(ix) "Lost ball" is called. See Law 20 (Lost ball).

(x) The umpire calls "Over" or "Time".

(b) The ball shall be considered to be dead when it is clear to the umpire at the bowler's end that the fielding side and both batsmen at the wicket have ceased to regard it as in play.

2. Ball finally settled

Whether the ball is finally settled or not is a matter for the umpire alone to decide.

3. Umpire calling and signalling "Dead ball"

(a) When the ball has become dead under 1 above, the bowler's end umpire may call "Dead ball", if it is necessary to inform the players.

(b) Either umpire shall call and signal "Dead ball" when:

(i) He intervenes in a case of unfair play.

(ii) A serious injury to a player or umpire occurs.

(iii) He leaves his normal position for consultation.

(iv) One or both bails fall from the striker's wicket before he has the opportunity of playing the ball.

(v) He is satisfied that for an adequate reason the striker is not ready for the delivery of the ball and, if the ball is delivered, makes no attempt to play it.

(vi) The striker is distracted by any noise or movement or in any other way while he is preparing to receive or receiving a delivery. This shall apply whether the source of the distraction is within the game or outside it. Note, however, the provisions of Law 42.4 (Deliberate attempt to distract the striker).

The ball shall not count as one of the over.

(vii) The bowler drops the ball accidentally before delivery.

(viii) The ball does not leave the bowler's hand for any reason other than an attempt to run out the non-striker before entering his delivery stride. See Law 42.15 (Bowler attempting to run out non-striker before delivery).

(ix) He is required to do so under any of the Laws.

4. Ball ceases to be dead

The ball ceases to be dead – that is, it comes into play – when the bowler starts his run-up or, if he has no run-up, his bowling action.

5. Action on call of "Dead ball"

(a) A ball is not to count as one of the over if it becomes dead or is to be considered dead before the striker has had an opportunity to play it.

(b) If the ball becomes dead or is to be considered dead after the striker has had an opportunity to play the ball, except in the circumstances of 3(b)(vi) above and Law 42.4 (Deliberate attempt to distract striker), no additional delivery shall be allowed unless "No-ball" or "Wide" has been called.

LAW 24. NO-BALL

1. Mode of delivery

(a) The umpire shall ascertain whether the bowler intends to bowl right-handed or left-handed, and whether over or round the wicket, and shall so inform the striker.

It is unfair if the bowler fails to notify the umpire of a change in his mode of delivery. In this case the umpire shall call and signal "No-ball".

(b) Underarm bowling shall not be permitted except by special agreement before the match.

2. Fair delivery – the arm

For a delivery to be fair in respect of the arm the ball must not be thrown. See 3 below.

Although it is the primary responsibility of the striker's end umpire to ensure the fairness of a delivery in this respect, there is nothing in this Law to debar the bowler's end umpire from calling and signalling "No-ball" if he considers that the ball has been thrown.

(a) If, in the opinion of either umpire, the ball has been thrown, he shall:

- (i) Call and signal "No-ball".
- (ii) Caution the bowler, when the ball is dead. This caution shall apply throughout the innings.
- (iii) Inform the other umpire, the batsmen at the wicket, the captain of the fielding side and, as soon as practicable, the captain of the batting side of what has occurred.

(b) If either umpire considers that after such caution, a further delivery by the same bowler in that innings is thrown, the umpire concerned shall repeat the procedure set out in (a) above, indicating to the bowler that this is a final warning. This warning shall also apply throughout the innings.

(c) If either umpire considers that a further delivery by the same bowler in that innings is thrown:

- (i) The umpire concerned shall call and signal "No-ball". When the ball is dead he shall inform the other umpire, the batsmen at the wicket and, as soon as practicable, the captain of the batting side of what has occurred.
- (ii) The umpire at the bowler's end shall direct the captain of the fielding side to take the bowler off forthwith. The over shall be completed by another bowler, who shall neither have bowled the previous over nor be allowed to bowl the next over.
  The bowler thus taken off shall not bowl again in that innings.
- (iii) The umpires together shall report the occurrence as soon as possible to the executive of the fielding side and any governing body responsible for the match, who shall take such action as is considered appropriate against the captain and bowler concerned.

3. Definition of fair delivery – the arm

A ball is fairly delivered in respect of the arm if, once the bowler's arm has reached the level of the shoulder in the delivery swing, the elbow joint is not straightened partially or completely from that point until the ball has left the hand. This definition shall not debar a bowler from flexing or rotating the wrist in the delivery swing.

4. Bowler throwing towards striker's end before delivery

If the bowler throws the ball towards the striker's end before entering his delivery stride, either umpire shall instantly call and signal "No-ball". See Law 42.16 (Batsmen stealing a run). However, the procedure stated in 2 above of caution, informing, final warning, action against the bowler and reporting shall not apply.

5. Fair delivery – the feet

For a delivery to be fair in respect of the feet, in the delivery stride:

(i) The bowler's back foot must land within and not touching the return crease.

(ii) The bowler's front foot must land with some part of the foot, whether grounded or raised, behind the popping crease.

If the umpire at the bowler's end is not satisfied that both these conditions have been met, he shall call and signal "No-ball".

6. Ball bouncing more than twice or rolling along the ground

The umpire at the bowler's end shall call and signal "No-ball" if a ball which he considers to have been delivered, without having previously touched the bat or person of the striker, either

(i) bounces more than twice, or

(ii) rolls along the ground

before it reaches the popping crease.

7. Ball coming to rest in front of striker's wicket

If a ball delivered by the bowler comes to rest in front of the line of the striker's wicket, without having touched the bat or person of the striker, the umpire shall call and signal "No-ball" and immediately call and signal "Dead ball".

8. Call of "No-ball" for infringement of other Laws

In addition to the instances above, an umpire shall call and signal "No-ball" as required by the following Laws.

Law 40.3 – Position of wicket-keeper.
Law 41.5 – Limitation of on-side fielders.
Law 41.6 – Fielders not to encroach on the pitch.
Law 42.6 – Dangerous and unfair bowling.
Law 42.7 – Dangerous and unfair bowling – action by the umpire.
Law 42.8 – Deliberate bowling of high full-pitched balls.

9. Revoking a call of "No-ball"

An umpire shall revoke the call of "No-ball" if the ball does not leave the bowler's hand for any reason.

10. No-ball to over-ride wide

A call of "No-ball" shall over-ride the call of "Wide ball" at any time. See Law 25.1 (Judging a wide) and 25.3 (Call and signal of "Wide ball").

11. Ball not dead

The ball does not become dead on the call of "No-ball".

12. Penalty for a No-ball

A penalty of one run shall be awarded instantly on the call of "No-ball". Unless the call is revoked this penalty shall stand even if a batsman is dismissed. It shall be in addition to any other runs scored, any boundary allowance and any other penalties awarded.

13. Runs resulting from a no-ball – how scored

The one-run penalty for a no-ball shall be scored as a no-ball extra. If other penalty runs have been awarded to either side, these shall be scored as in Law 42.17 (Penalty runs). Any runs completed by the batsmen or a boundary allowance shall be credited to the striker if the ball has been struck by the bat; otherwise they also shall be scored as no-ball extras.

Apart from any award of a five-run penalty, all runs resulting from a no-ball, whether as no-ball extras or credited to the striker, shall be debited against the bowler.

14. No-ball not to count

A no-ball shall not count as one of the over. See Law 22.4 (Balls not to count in the over).

15. Out from a no-ball

When "No-ball" has been called, neither batsman shall be out under any of the Laws except Laws 33 (Handled the ball), 34 (Hit the ball twice), 37 (Obstructing the field) or 38 (Run out).

LAW 25. WIDE BALL

1. Judging a wide

(a) If a bowler bowls a ball, not being a no-ball, the umpire shall adjudge it a wide if, according to the definition in (b) below, in his opinion the ball passes wide of the striker where he is standing and would also have passed wide of him in a normal guard position.

(b) The ball will be considered as passing wide of the striker unless it is sufficiently within his reach for him to be able to hit it with his bat by means of a normal cricket stroke.

2. Delivery not a wide

The umpire shall not adjudge a delivery as being a wide:

(a) If the striker, by moving, either

(i) causes the ball to pass wide of him, as defined in 1(b) above, or

(ii) brings the ball sufficiently within his reach to be able to hit it with his bat by means of a normal cricket stroke.

(b) If the ball touches the striker's bat or person.

3. Call and signal of "Wide ball"

(a) If the umpire adjudges a delivery to be a wide he shall call and signal "Wide ball" as soon as the ball passes the striker's wicket. It shall, however, be considered to have been a wide from the instant of delivery, even though it cannot be called wide until it passes the striker's wicket.

(b) The umpire shall revoke the call of "Wide ball" if there is then any contact between the ball and the striker's bat or person.

(c) The umpire shall revoke the call of "Wide ball" if a delivery is called a "No-ball". See Law 24.10 (No-ball to over-ride wide).

4. Ball not dead

The ball does not become dead on the call of "Wide ball".

5. Penalty for a wide

A penalty of one run shall be awarded instantly on the call of "Wide ball". Unless the call is revoked (see 3 above), this penalty shall stand even if a batsman is dismissed, and shall be in addition to any other runs scored, any boundary allowance and any other penalties awarded.

6. Runs resulting from a wide – how scored

All runs completed by the batsmen or a boundary allowance, together with the penalty for the wide, shall be scored as wide balls. Apart from any award of a five-run penalty, all runs resulting from a wide shall be debited against the bowler.

7. Wide not to count

A wide shall not count as one of the over. See Law 22.4 (Balls not to count in the over).

8. Out from a wide

When "Wide ball" has been called, neither batsman shall be out under any of the Laws except Laws 33 (Handled the ball), 35 (Hit wicket), 37 (Obstructing the field), 38 (Run out) or 39 (Stumped).

LAW 26. BYE AND LEG-BYE

1. Byes

If the ball, not being a no-ball or a wide, passes the striker without touching his bat or person, any runs completed by the batsmen or a boundary allowance shall be credited as byes to the batting side.

2. Leg-byes

(a) If the ball, not having previously touched the striker's bat, strikes his person and the umpire is satisfied that the striker has either

(i) attempted to play the ball with his bat, or

(ii) tried to avoid being hit by the ball,

then any runs completed by the batsmen or a boundary allowance shall be credited to the batting side as leg-byes, unless "No-ball" has been called.

(b) If "No-ball" has been called, the runs in (a) above, together with the penalty for the no-ball, shall be scored as no-ball extras.

3. Leg-byes not to be awarded

If in the circumstances of 2(a) above the umpire considers that neither of the conditions (i) and (ii) therein has been met, then leg-byes will not be awarded. The batting side shall not be credited with any runs from that delivery apart from the one run penalty for a no-ball if applicable. Moreover, no other penalties shall be awarded to the batting side when the ball is dead. See Law 42.17 (Penalty runs). The following procedure shall be adopted.

(a) If no run is attempted but the ball reaches the boundary, the umpire shall call and signal "Dead ball", and disallow the boundary.

(b) If runs are attempted and if:

(i) Neither batsman is dismissed and the ball does not become dead for any other reason, the umpire shall call and signal "Dead ball" as soon as one run is completed or the ball reaches the boundary. The batsmen shall return to their original ends. The run or boundary shall be disallowed.

(ii) Before one run is completed or the ball reaches the boundary, a batsman is dismissed, or the ball becomes dead for any other reason, all the provisions of the Laws will apply, except that no runs and no penalties shall be credited to the batting side, other than the penalty for a no-ball if applicable.

LAW 27. APPEALS

1. Umpire not to give batsman out without an appeal

Neither umpire shall give a batsman out, even though he may be out under the Laws, unless appealed to by the fielding side. This shall not debar a batsman who is out under any of the Laws from leaving his wicket without an appeal having been made. Note, however, the provisions of 7 below.

2. Batsman dismissed

A batsman is dismissed if either

(a) he is given out by an umpire, on appeal, or

(b) he is out under any of the Laws and leaves his wicket as in 1 above.

3. Timing of appeals

For an appeal to be valid it must be made before the bowler begins his run-up or, if he has no run-up, his bowling action to deliver the next ball, and before "Time" has been called.

The call of "Over" does not invalidate an appeal made prior to the start of the following over provided "Time" has not been called. See Laws 16.2 (Call of "Time") and 22.2 (Start of an over).

4. Appeal "How's that?"

An appeal "How's that?" covers all ways of being out.

5. Answering appeals

The umpire at the bowler's end shall answer all appeals except those arising out of any of Laws 35 (Hit wicket), 39 (Stumped) or 38 (Run out) when this occurs at the striker's wicket. A decision "Not out" by one umpire shall not prevent the other umpire from giving a decision, provided that each is considering only matters within his jurisdiction.

When a batsman has been given not out, either umpire may, within his jurisdiction, answer a further appeal provided that it is made in accordance with 3 above.

6. Consultation by umpires

Each umpire shall answer appeals on matters within his own jurisdiction. If an umpire is doubtful about any point that the other umpire may have been in a better position to see, he shall consult the latter on this point of fact and shall then give his decision. If, after consultation, there is still doubt remaining the decision shall be "Not out".

7. Batsman leaving his wicket under a misapprehension

An umpire shall intervene if satisfied that a batsman, not having been given out, has left his wicket under a misapprehension that he is out. The umpire intervening shall call and signal "Dead ball" to prevent any further action by the fielding side and shall recall the batsman.

8. Withdrawal of an appeal

The captain of the fielding side may withdraw an appeal only with the consent of the umpire within whose jurisdiction the appeal falls and before the outgoing batsman has left the field of play. If such consent is given the umpire concerned shall, if applicable, revoke his decision and recall the batsman.

9. Umpire's decision

An umpire may alter his decision provided that such alteration is made promptly. This apart, the umpire's decision, once made, is final.

LAW 28. THE WICKET IS DOWN

1. Wicket put down

(a) The wicket is put down if a bail is completely removed from the top of the stumps, or a stump is struck out of the ground by:

- (i) The ball.
- (ii) The striker's bat, whether he is holding it or has let go of it.
- (iii) The striker's person or by any part of his clothing or equipment becoming detached from his person.
- (iv) A fielder, with his hand or arm, provided that the ball is held in the hand or hands so used, or in the hand of the arm so used.

  The wicket is also put down if a fielder pulls a stump out of the ground in the same manner.

(b) The disturbance of a bail, whether temporary or not, shall not constitute its complete removal from the top of the stumps, but if a bail in falling lodges between two of the stumps this shall be regarded as complete removal.

2. One bail off

If one bail is off, it shall be sufficient for the purpose of putting the wicket down to remove the remaining bail, or to strike or pull any of the three stumps out of the ground, in any of the ways stated in 1 above.

3. Remaking the wicket

If the wicket is broken or put down while the ball is in play, the umpire shall not remake the wicket until the ball is dead. See Law 23 (Dead ball). Any fielder, however, may:

(i) Replace a bail or bails on top of the stumps.

(ii) Put back one or more stumps into the ground where the wicket originally stood.

4. Dispensing with bails

If the umpires have agreed to dispense with bails, in accordance with Law 8.5 (Dispensing with bails), the decision as to whether the wicket has been put down is one for the umpire concerned to decide.

(a) After a decision to play without bails, the wicket has been put down if the umpire concerned is satisfied that the wicket has been struck by the ball, by the striker's bat, person, or items of his clothing or equipment separated from his person as described in 1(a)(ii) or 1(a)(iii) above, or by a fielder with the hand holding the ball or with the arm of the hand holding the ball.

(b) If the wicket has already been broken or put down, (a) above shall apply to any stump or stumps still in the ground. Any fielder may replace a stump or stumps, in accordance with 3 above, in order to have an opportunity of putting the wicket down.

LAW 29. BATSMAN OUT OF HIS GROUND

1. When out of his ground

A batsman shall be considered to be out of his ground unless his bat or some part of his person is grounded behind the popping crease at that end.

2. Which is a batsman's ground?

(a) If only one batsman is within a ground:

(i) It is his ground.

(ii) It remains his ground even if he is later joined there by the other batsman.

(b) If both batsmen are in the same ground and one of them subsequently leaves it, (a)(i) above applies.

(c) If there is no batsman in either ground, then each ground belongs to whichever of the batsmen is nearer to it, or, if the batsmen are level, to whichever was nearer to it immediately prior to their drawing level.

(d) If a ground belongs to one batsman, then, unless there is a striker with a runner, the other ground belongs to the other batsman irrespective of his position.

(e) When a batsman with a runner is striker, his ground is always that at the wicket-keeper's end. However, (a), (b), (c) and (d) above will still apply, but only to the runner and the non-striker, so that that ground will also belong to either the non-striker or the runner, as the case may be.

3. Position of non-striker

The non-striker, when standing at the bowler's end, should be positioned on the opposite side of the wicket to that from which the ball is being delivered, unless a request to do otherwise is granted by the umpire.

LAW 30. BOWLED

1. Out Bowled

(a) The striker is out *Bowled* if his wicket is put down by a ball delivered by the bowler, not being a no-ball, even if it first touches his bat or person.

(b) Notwithstanding (a) above he shall not be out bowled if before striking the wicket the ball has been in contact with any other player or with an umpire. He will, however, be subject to Laws 33 (Handled the ball), 37 (Obstructing the field), 38 (Run out) and 39 (Stumped).

2. Bowled to take precedence

The striker is out bowled if his wicket is put down as in 1 above, even though a decision against him for any other method of dismissal would be justified.

LAW 31. TIMED OUT

1. Out Timed out

(a) Unless "Time" has been called, the incoming batsman must be in position to take guard or for his partner to be ready to receive the next ball within three minutes of the fall of the previous wicket. If this requirement is not met, the incoming batsman will be out, *Timed out*.

(b) In the event of protracted delay in which no batsman comes to the wicket, the umpires shall adopt the procedure of Law 21.3 (Umpires awarding a match). For the purposes of that Law the start of the action shall be taken as the expiry of the three minutes referred to above.

2. Bowler does not get credit

The bowler does not get credit for the wicket.

LAW 32. CAUGHT

1. Out Caught

The striker is out *Caught* if a ball delivered by the bowler, not being a no-ball, touches his bat without having previously been in contact with any member of the fielding side and is subsequently held by a fielder as a fair catch before it touches the ground.

2. Caught to take precedence

If the criteria of 1 above are met and the striker is not out bowled, then he is out caught even though a decision against either batsman for another method of dismissal would be justified. Runs completed by the batsmen before the completion of the catch will not be scored. Note also Laws 21.6 (Winning hit or extras) and 42.17(b) (Penalty runs).

3. A fair catch

A catch shall be considered to have been fairly made if:

(a) Throughout the act of making the catch:

(i) Any fielder in contact with the ball is within the field of play. See 4 below.

(ii) The ball is at no time in contact with any object grounded beyond the boundary.

The act of making the catch shall start from the time when a fielder first handles the ball and shall end when a fielder obtains complete control both over the ball and over his own movement.

(b) The ball is hugged to the body of the catcher or accidentally lodges in his clothing or, in the case of the wicket-keeper, in his pads. However, it is not a fair catch if the ball lodges in a protective helmet worn by a fielder. See Law 23 (Dead ball).

(c) The ball does not touch the ground, even though the hand holding it does so in effecting the catch.

(d) A fielder catches the ball after it has been lawfully struck more than once by the striker, but only if the ball has not touched the ground since first being struck.

(e) A fielder catches the ball after it has touched an umpire, another fielder or the other batsman. However, it is not a fair catch if the ball has touched a protective helmet worn by a fielder, although the ball remains in play.

(f) A fielder catches the ball in the air after it has crossed the boundary provided that:

(i) He has no part of his person touching, or grounded beyond, the boundary at any time when he is in contact with the ball.

(ii) The ball has not been grounded beyond the boundary.

See Law 19.3 (Scoring a boundary).

(g) The ball is caught off an obstruction within the boundary, provided it has not previously been decided to regard the obstruction as a boundary.

4. Fielder within the field of play

(a) A fielder is not within the field of play if he touches the boundary or has any part of his person grounded beyond the boundary. See Law 19.3 (Scoring a boundary).

(b) Six runs shall be scored if a fielder:

(i) Has any part of his person touching, or grounded beyond, the boundary when he catches the ball.

(ii) Catches the ball and subsequently touches the boundary or grounds some part of his person over the boundary while carrying the ball but before completing the catch.

See Laws 19.3 (Scoring a boundary) and 19.4 (Runs allowed for boundaries).

5. No runs to be scored

If the striker is dismissed caught, runs from that delivery completed by the batsmen before the completion of the catch shall not be scored, but any penalties awarded to either side when the ball is dead, if applicable, will stand. Law 18.12(a) (Batsman returning to wicket he has left) shall apply from the instant of the catch.

LAW 33. HANDLED THE BALL

1. Out Handled the ball

Either batsman is out *Handled the ball* if he wilfully touches the ball while in play with a hand or hands not holding the bat unless he does so with the consent of the opposing side.

2. Not out Handled the ball

Notwithstanding 1 above, a batsman will not be out under this Law if:

(i) He handles the ball in order to avoid injury.

(ii) He uses his hand or hands to return the ball to any member of the fielding side without the consent of that side. Note, however, the provisions of Law 37.4 (Returning the ball to a member of the fielding side).

3. Runs scored

If either batsman is dismissed under this Law, any runs completed before the offence, together with any penalty extras and the penalty for a no-ball or wide, if applicable, shall be scored. See Laws 18.10 (Runs scored when a batsman is dismissed) and 42.17 (Penalty runs).

4. Bowler does not get credit

The bowler does not get credit for the wicket.

LAW 34. HIT THE BALL TWICE

1. Out Hit the ball twice

(a) The striker is out *Hit the ball twice* if, while the ball is in play and it strikes any part of his person or is struck by his bat and, before the ball has been touched by a fielder, he wilfully strikes it again with his bat or person, other than a hand not holding the bat, except for the sole purpose of guarding his wicket. See 3 below and Laws 33 (Handled the ball) and 37 (Obstructing the field).

(b) For the purpose of this Law, "struck" or "strike" shall include contact with the person of the striker.

2. Not out Hit the ball twice

Notwithstanding 1(a) above, the striker will not be out under this Law if:

(i) He makes a second or subsequent stroke in order to return the ball to any member of the fielding side. Note, however, the provisions of Law 37.4 (Returning the ball to a member of the fielding side).

(ii) He wilfully strikes the ball after it has touched a fielder. Note, however, the provisions of Law 37.1 (Out obstructing the field).

3. Ball lawfully struck more than once

Solely in order to guard his wicket and before the ball has been touched by a fielder, the striker may lawfully strike the ball more than once with his bat or with any part of his person other than a hand not holding the bat.

Notwithstanding this provision, the striker may not prevent the ball from being caught by making more than one stroke in defence of his wicket. See Law 37.3 (Obstructing a ball from being caught).

4. Runs permitted from ball lawfully struck more than once

When the ball is lawfully struck more than once, as permitted in 3 above, only the first strike is to be considered in determining whether runs are to be allowed and how they are to be scored.

(a) If on the first strike the umpire is satisfied that either

- (i) the ball first struck the bat, or
- (ii) the striker attempted to play the ball with his bat, or
- (iii) the striker tried to avoid being hit by the ball,

then any penalties to the batting side that are applicable shall be allowed.

(b) If the conditions in (a) above are met then, if they result from overthrows, and only if they result from overthrows, runs completed by the batsmen or a boundary will be allowed in addition to any penalties that are applicable. They shall be credited to the striker if the first strike was with the bat. If the first strike was on the person of the striker they shall be scored as leg-byes or no-ball extras, as appropriate. See Law 26.2 (Leg-byes).

(c) If the conditions of (a) above are met and there is no overthrow until after the batsmen have started to run, but before one run is completed:

- (i) Only subsequent completed runs or a boundary shall be allowed. The first run shall count as a completed run for this purpose only if the batsmen have not crossed at the instant of the throw.
- (ii) If in these circumstances the ball goes to the boundary from the throw then, notwithstanding the provisions of Law 19.6 (Overthrow or wilful act of fielder), only the boundary allowance shall be scored.
- (iii) If the ball goes to the boundary as the result of a further overthrow, then runs completed by the batsmen after the first throw and before this final throw shall be added to the boundary allowance. The run in progress at the first throw will count only if they have not crossed at that moment; the run in progress at the final throw shall count only if they have crossed at that moment. Law 18.12 (Batsman returning to wicket he has left) shall apply as from the moment of the final throw.

(d) If, in the opinion of the umpire, none of the conditions in (a) above has been met then, whether there is an overthrow or not, the batting side shall not be credited with any runs from that delivery apart from the penalty for a no-ball if applicable. Moreover, no other penalties shall be awarded to the batting side when the ball is dead. See Law 42.17 (Penalty runs).

5. Ball lawfully struck more than once – action by the umpire

If no runs are to be allowed, either in the circumstances of 4(d) above, or because there has been no overthrow and:

(a) If no run is attempted but the ball reaches the boundary, the umpire shall call and signal "Dead ball" and disallow the boundary.

(b) If the batsmen run and:

(i) Neither batsman is dismissed and the ball does not become dead for any other reason, the umpire shall call and signal "Dead ball" as soon as one run is completed or the ball reaches the boundary. The batsmen shall return to their original ends. The run or boundary shall be disallowed.

(ii) A batsman is dismissed, or if for any other reason the ball becomes dead before one run is completed or the ball reaches the boundary, all the provisions of the Laws will apply except that the award of penalties to the batting side shall be as laid down in 4(a) or 4(d) above as appropriate.

6. Bowler does not get credit

The bowler does not get credit for the wicket.

LAW 35. HIT WICKET

1. Out Hit wicket

The striker is out *Hit wicket* if, while the ball is in play, his wicket is put down either by the striker's bat or person as described in Law 28.1(a)(ii) and (iii) (Wicket put down) either

(i) in the course of any action taken by him in preparing to receive or in receiving a delivery, or

(ii) in setting off for his first run immediately after playing, or playing at, the ball, or

(iii) if he makes no attempt to play the ball, in setting off for his first run, provided that in the opinion of the umpire this is immediately after he has had the opportunity of playing the ball, or

(iv) in lawfully making a second or further stroke for the purpose of guarding his wicket within the provisions of Law 34.3 (Ball lawfully struck more than once).

2. Not out Hit wicket

Notwithstanding 1 above, the batsman is not out under this Law should his wicket be put down in any of the ways referred to in 1 above if:

(a) It occurs after he has completed any action in receiving the delivery, other than as in 1(ii), (iii) or (iv) above.

(b) It occurs when he is in the act of running, other than in setting off immediately for his first run.

(c) It occurs when he is trying to avoid being run out or stumped.

(d) It occurs while he is trying to avoid a throw-in at any time.

(e) The bowler after starting his run-up, or his bowling action if he has no run-up, does not deliver the ball. In this case either umpire shall immediately call and signal "Dead ball". See Law 23.3 (Umpire calling and signalling "Dead ball").

(f) The delivery is a no-ball.

LAW 36. LEG BEFORE WICKET

1. Out LBW

The striker is out *LBW* in the circumstances set out below.

(a) The bowler delivers a ball, not being a no-ball, and

(b) the ball, if it is not intercepted full pitch, pitches in line between wicket and wicket or on the off side of the striker's wicket, and

(c) the ball not having previously touched his bat, the striker intercepts the ball, either full pitch or after pitching, with any part of his person, and

(d) the point of impact, even if above the level of the bails, either

(i) is between wicket and wicket, or

(ii) is either between wicket and wicket or outside the line of the off stump, if the striker has made no genuine attempt to play the ball with his bat, and

(e) but for the interception, the ball would have hit the wicket.

2. Interception of the ball

(a) In assessing points (c), (d) and (e) in 1 above, only the first interception is to be considered.

(b) In assessing point (e) in 1 above, it is to be assumed that the path of the ball before interception would have continued after interception, irrespective of whether the ball might have pitched subsequently or not.

3. Off side of wicket

The off side of the striker's wicket shall be determined by the striker's stance at the moment the ball comes into play for that delivery.

LAW 37. OBSTRUCTING THE FIELD

1. Out Obstructing the field

Either batsman is out *Obstructing the field* if he wilfully obstructs or distracts the opposing side by word or action. It shall be regarded as obstruction if either batsman wilfully, and without the consent of the fielding side, strikes the ball with his bat or person, other than a hand not holding the bat, after the ball has touched a fielder. See 4 below.

2. Accidental obstruction

It is for either umpire to decide whether any obstruction or distraction is wilful or not. He shall consult the other umpire if he has any doubt.

3. Obstructing a ball from being caught

The striker is out should wilful obstruction or distraction by either batsman prevent a catch being made.

This shall apply even though the striker causes the obstruction in lawfully guarding his wicket under the provisions of Law 34.3 (Ball lawfully struck more than once).

4. Returning the ball to a member of the fielding side

Either batsman is out under this Law if, without the consent of the fielding side and while the ball is in play, he uses his bat or person to return the ball to any member of that side.

5. Runs scored

If a batsman is dismissed under this Law, runs completed by the batsmen before the offence shall be scored, together with the penalty for a no-ball or a wide, if applicable. Other penalties that may be awarded to either side when the ball is dead shall also stand. See Law 42.17(b) (Penalty runs).

If, however, the obstruction prevents a catch from being made, runs completed by the batsmen before the offence shall not be scored, but other penalties that may be awarded to either side when the ball is dead shall stand. See Law 42.17(b) (Penalty runs).

6. Bowler does not get credit

The bowler does not get credit for the wicket.

LAW 38. RUN OUT

1. Out Run out

(a) Either batsman is out *Run out*, except as in 2 below, if at any time while the ball is in play

(i) he is out of his ground and

(ii) his wicket is fairly put down by the opposing side.

(b) (a) above shall apply even though "No-ball" has been called and whether or not a run is being attempted, except in the circumstances of Law 39.3(b) (Not out Stumped).

2. Batsman not Run out

Notwithstanding 1 above, a batsman is not out run out if:

(a) He has been within his ground and has subsequently left it to avoid injury, when the wicket is put down.

(b) The ball has not subsequently been touched again by a fielder, after the bowler has entered his delivery stride, before the wicket is put down.

(c) The ball, having been played by the striker, or having come off his person, directly strikes a helmet worn by a fielder and without further contact with him or any other fielder rebounds directly on to the wicket. However, the ball remains in play and either batsman may be run out in the circumstances of 1 above if a wicket is subsequently put down.

(d) He is out stumped. See Law 39.1(b) (Out Stumped).

(e) He is out of his ground, not attempting a run and his wicket is fairly put down by the wicket-keeper without the intervention of another member of the fielding side, if "No-ball" has been called. See Law 39.3(b) (Not out Stumped).

3. Which batsman is out

The batsman out in the circumstances of 1 above is the one whose ground is at the end where the wicket is put down. See Laws 2.8 (Transgression of the Laws by a batsman who has a runner) and 29.2 (Which is a batsman's ground).

4. Runs scored

If a batsman is dismissed run out, the batting side shall score the runs completed before the dismissal together with the penalty for a no-ball or wide, if applicable. Other penalties to either side that may be awarded when the ball is dead shall also stand. See Law 42.17 (Penalty runs).

If, however, a striker with a runner is himself dismissed run out, runs completed by the runner and the other batsman before the dismissal shall not be scored. The penalty for a no-ball or a wide and any other penalties to either side that may be awarded when the ball is dead shall stand. See Laws 2.8 (Transgression of the Laws by a batsman who has a runner) and 42.17(b) (Penalty runs).

5. Bowler does not get credit

The bowler does not get credit for the wicket.

LAW 39. STUMPED

1. Out Stumped

(a) The striker is out *Stumped* if

(i) he is out of his ground, and

(ii) he is receiving a ball which is not a no-ball, and

(iii) he is not attempting a run, and

(iv) his wicket is fairly put down by the wicket-keeper without the intervention of another member of the fielding side. Note Law 40.3 (Position of wicket-keeper).

(b) The striker is out stumped if all the conditions of (a) above are satisfied, even though a decision of run out would be justified.

2. Ball rebounding from wicket-keeper's person

(a) If the wicket is put down by the ball, it shall be regarded as having been put down by the wicket-keeper, if the ball

(i) rebounds on to the stumps from any part of his person, other than a protective helmet, or

(ii) has been kicked or thrown on to the stumps by the wicket-keeper.

(b) If the ball touches a helmet worn by the wicket-keeper, the ball is still in play but the striker shall not be out stumped. He will, however, be liable to be run out in these circumstances if there is subsequent contact between the ball and any member of the fielding side. Note, however, 3 below.

3. Not out Stumped

(a) If the striker is not out stumped, he is liable to be out run out if the conditions of Law 38 (Run out) apply, except as set out in (b) below.

(b) The striker shall not be out run out if he is out of his ground, not attempting a run, and his wicket is fairly put down by the wicket-keeper without the intervention of another member of the fielding side, if "No-ball" has been called.

LAW 40. THE WICKET-KEEPER

1. Protective equipment

The wicket-keeper is the only member of the fielding side permitted to wear gloves and external leg guards. If he does so, these are to be regarded as part of his person for the purposes of Law 41.2 (Fielding the ball). If by his actions and positioning it is apparent to the umpires that he will not be able to discharge his duties as a wicket-keeper, he shall forfeit this right and also the right to be recognised as a wicket-keeper for the purposes of Laws 32.3 (A fair catch), 39 (Stumped), 41.1 (Protective equipment), 41.5 (Limitation of on-side fielders) and 41.6 (Fielders not to encroach on the pitch).

2. Gloves

If the wicket-keeper wears gloves as permitted under 1 above, they shall have no webbing between fingers except that a single piece of flat non-stretch material may be inserted between index finger and thumb solely as a means of support. This insert shall not form a pouch when the hand is extended.

3. Position of wicket-keeper

The wicket-keeper shall remain wholly behind the wicket at the striker's end from the moment the ball comes into play until

(a) a ball delivered by the bowler either

(i) touches the bat or person of the striker, or

(ii) passes the wicket at the striker's end, or

(b) the striker attempts a run.

In the event of the wicket-keeper contravening this Law, the umpire at the striker's end shall call and signal "No-ball" as soon as possible after the delivery of the ball.

4. Movement by wicket-keeper

It is unfair if the wicket-keeper standing back makes a significant movement towards the wicket after the ball comes into play and before it reaches the striker. In the event of such unfair movement by the wicket-keeper, either umpire shall call and signal "Dead ball". It will not be considered a significant movement if the wicket-keeper moves a few paces forward for a slower delivery.

5. Restriction on actions of wicket-keeper

If the wicket-keeper interferes with the striker's right to play the ball and to guard his wicket, the striker shall not be out, except under Laws 33 (Handled the ball), 34 (Hit the ball twice), 37 (Obstructing the field) or 38 (Run out).

6. Interference with wicket-keeper by striker

If, in playing at the ball or in the legitimate defence of his wicket, the striker interferes with the wicket-keeper, he shall not be out, except as provided for in Law 37.3 (Obstructing a ball from being caught).

LAW 41. THE FIELDER

1. Protective equipment

No member of the fielding side other than the wicket-keeper shall be permitted to wear gloves or external leg guards. In addition, protection for the hand or fingers may be worn only with the consent of the umpires.

2. Fielding the ball

A fielder may field the ball with any part of his person but if, while the ball is in play, he wilfully fields it otherwise:

(a) The ball shall become dead and five penalty runs shall be awarded to the batting side. See Law 42.17 (Penalty runs).

(b) The umpire shall inform the other umpire, the captain of the fielding side, the batsmen and, as soon as practicable, the captain of the batting side of what has occurred.

(c) The umpires together shall report the occurrence as soon as possible to the executive of the fielding side and any governing body responsible for the match who shall take such action as is considered appropriate against the captain and player concerned.

3. Protective helmets belonging to the fielding side

Protective helmets, when not in use by fielders, shall only be placed, if above the surface, on the ground behind the wicket-keeper and in line with both sets of stumps. If a helmet belonging to the fielding side is on the ground within the field of play, and the ball while in play strikes it, the ball shall become dead. Five penalty runs shall then be awarded to the batting side. See Laws 18.11 (Runs scored when ball becomes dead) and 42.17 (Penalty runs).

4. Penalty runs not to be awarded

Notwithstanding 2 and 3 above, if from the delivery by the bowler the ball first struck the person of the striker and if, in the opinion of the umpire, the striker neither

(i) attempted to play the ball with his bat, nor

(ii) tried to avoid being hit by the ball,

then no award of five penalty runs shall be made and no other runs or penalties shall be credited to the batting side except the penalty for a no-ball if applicable. See Law 26.3 (Leg-byes not to be awarded).

5. Limitation of on-side fielders

At the instant of the bowler's delivery there shall not be more than two fielders, other than the wicket-keeper, behind the popping crease on the on side. A fielder will be considered to be behind the popping crease unless the whole of his person, whether grounded or in the air, is in front of this line.

In the event of infringement of this Law by the fielding side the umpire at the striker's end shall call and signal "No-ball".

6. Fielders not to encroach on the pitch

While the ball is in play and until the ball has made contact with the bat or person of the striker, or has passed the striker's bat, no fielder, other than the bowler, may have any part of his person grounded on or extended over the pitch.

In the event of infringement of this Law by any fielder other than the wicket-keeper, the umpire at the bowler's end shall call and signal "No-ball" as soon as possible after the delivery of the ball. Note, however, Law 40.3 (Position of wicket-keeper).

7. Movement by fielders

Any significant movement by any fielder after the ball comes into play and before the ball reaches the striker is unfair. In the event of such unfair movement, either umpire shall call and signal "Dead ball". Note also the provisions of Law 42.4 (Deliberate attempt to distract striker).

8. Definition of significant movement

(a) For close fielders anything other than minor adjustments to stance or position in relation to the striker is significant.

(b) In the outfield, fielders are permitted to move in towards the striker or striker's wicket, provided that 5 above is not contravened. Anything other than slight movement off line or away from the striker is to be considered significant.

(c) For restrictions on movement by the wicket-keeper see Law 40.4 (Movement by wicket-keeper).

LAW 42. FAIR AND UNFAIR PLAY

1. Fair and unfair play – responsibility of captains

The responsibility lies with the captains for ensuring that play is conducted within the spirit and traditions of the game, as described in The Preamble – The Spirit of Cricket, as well as within the Laws.

2. Fair and unfair play – responsibility of umpires

The umpires shall be sole judges of fair and unfair play. If either umpire considers an action, not covered by the Laws, to be unfair, he shall intervene without appeal and, if the ball is in play, shall call and signal "Dead ball" and implement the procedure as set out in 18 below. Otherwise the umpires shall not interfere with the progress of play, except as required to do so by the Laws.

3. The match ball – changing its condition

(a) Any fielder may:

(i) Polish the ball provided that no artificial substance is used and that such polishing wastes no time.

(ii) Remove mud from the ball under the supervision of the umpire.

(iii) Dry a wet ball on a towel.

(b) It is unfair for anyone to rub the ball on the ground for any reason, interfere with any of the seams or the surface of the ball, use any implement, or take any other action whatsoever which is likely to alter the condition of the ball, except as permitted in (a) above.

(c) The umpires shall make frequent and irregular inspections of the ball.

(d) In the event of any fielder changing the condition of the ball unfairly, as set out in (b) above, the umpires after consultation shall:

(i) Change the ball forthwith. It shall be for the umpires to decide on the replacement ball, which shall, in their opinion, have had wear comparable with that which the previous ball had received immediately prior to the contravention.

(ii) Inform the batsmen that the ball has been changed.

(iii) Award five penalty runs to the batting side. See 17 below.

(iv) Inform the captain of the fielding side that the reason for the action was the unfair interference with the ball.

(v) Inform the captain of the batting side as soon as practicable of what has occurred.

(vi) Report the occurrence as soon as possible to the executive of the fielding side and any governing body responsible for the match, who shall take such action as is considered appropriate against the captain and team concerned.

(e) If there is any further instance of unfairly changing the condition of the ball in that innings, the umpires after consultation shall:

(i) Repeat the procedure in (d)(i), (ii) and (iii) above.

(ii) Inform the captain of the fielding side of the reason for the action taken and direct him to take off forthwith the bowler who delivered the immediately preceding ball. The bowler thus taken off shall not be allowed to bowl again in that innings.

(iii) Inform the captain of the batting side as soon as practicable of what has occurred.

(iv) Report the occurrence as soon as possible to the executive of the fielding side and any governing body responsible for the match, who shall take such action as is considered appropriate against the captain and team concerned.

4. Deliberate attempt to distract striker

It is unfair for any member of the fielding side deliberately to attempt to distract the striker while he is preparing to receive or receiving a delivery.

(a) If either umpire considers that any action by a member of the fielding side is such an attempt, at the first instance he shall:

(i) Immediately call and signal "Dead ball".

(ii) Warn the captain of the fielding side that the action is unfair and indicate that this is a first and final warning.

(iii) Inform the other umpire and the batsmen of what has occurred.

Neither batsman shall be dismissed from that delivery and the ball shall not count as one of the over.

(b) If there is any further such deliberate attempt in that innings, by any member of the fielding side, the procedures, other than warning, as set out in (a) above shall apply. Additionally, the umpire at the bowler's end shall:

(i) Award five penalty runs to the batting side. See 17 below.

(ii) Inform the captain of the fielding side of the reason for this action and, as soon as practicable, inform the captain of the batting side.

(iii) Report the occurrence, together with the other umpire, as soon as possible to the executive of the fielding side and any governing body responsible for the match, who shall take such action as is considered appropriate against the captain and player or players concerned.

5. Deliberate distraction or obstruction of batsman

In addition to 4 above, it is unfair for any member of the fielding side, by word or action, wilfully to attempt to distract or to obstruct either batsman after the striker has received the ball.

(a) It is for either one of the umpires to decide whether any distraction or obstruction is wilful or not.

(b) If either umpire considers that a member of the fielding side has wilfully caused or attempted to cause such a distraction or obstruction he shall:

(i) Immediately call and signal "Dead ball".

(ii) Inform the captain of the fielding side and the other umpire of the reason for the call.

Additionally:

(iii) Neither batsman shall be dismissed from that delivery.

(iv) Five penalty runs shall be awarded to the batting side. See 17 below. In this instance, the run in progress shall be scored, whether or not the batsmen had crossed at the instant of the call. See Law 18.11 (Runs scored when ball becomes dead).

(v) The umpire at the bowler's end shall inform the captain of the fielding side of the reason for this action and, as soon as practicable, inform the captain of the batting side.

(vi) The umpires shall report the occurrence as soon as possible to the executive of the fielding side and any governing body responsible for the match, who shall take such action as is considered appropriate against the captain and player or players concerned.

6. Dangerous and unfair bowling

(a) Bowling of fast short-pitched balls

(i) The bowling of fast short-pitched balls is dangerous and unfair if the umpire at the bowler's end considers that by their repetition and taking into account their length, height and direction they are likely to inflict physical injury on the striker, irrespective of the protective equipment he may be wearing. The relative skill of the striker shall be taken into consideration.

(ii) Any delivery which, after pitching, passes or would have passed over head height of the striker standing upright at the crease, although not threatening physical injury, is unfair and shall be considered as part of the repetition sequence in (i) above. The umpire shall call and signal "No-ball" for each such delivery.

(b) Bowling of high full-pitched balls

(i) Any delivery, other than a slow-paced one, which passes or would have passed on the full above waist height of the striker standing upright at the crease is to be deemed dangerous and unfair, whether or not it is likely to inflict physical injury on the striker.

(ii) A slow delivery which passes or would have passed on the full above shoulder height of the striker standing upright at the crease is to be deemed dangerous and unfair, whether or not it is likely to inflict physical injury on the striker.

7. Dangerous and unfair bowling – action by the umpire

(a) In the event of dangerous and/or unfair bowling, as defined in 6 above, by any bowler, except as in 8 below, at the first instance the umpire at the bowler's end shall call and signal "No-ball" and, when the ball is dead, caution the bowler, inform the other umpire, the captain of the fielding side and the batsmen of what has occurred. This caution shall continue to apply throughout the innings.

(b) If there is a second instance of such dangerous and/or unfair bowling by the same bowler in that innings, the umpire at the bowler's end shall repeat the above procedure and indicate to the bowler that this is a final warning.

Both the above caution and final warning shall continue to apply even though the bowler may later change ends.

(c) Should there be a further instance by the same bowler in that innings, the umpire shall:

(i) call and signal "No-ball".

(ii) Direct the captain, when the ball is dead, to take the bowler off forthwith. The over shall be completed by another bowler, who shall neither have bowled the previous over nor be allowed to bowl the next over.

The bowler thus taken off shall not be allowed to bowl again in that innings.

(iii) Report the occurrence to the other umpire, the batsmen and, as soon as practicable, the captain of the batting side.

(iv) Report the occurrence, with the other umpire, as soon as possible to the executive of the fielding side and to any governing body responsible for the match, who shall take such action as is considered appropriate against the captain and bowler concerned.

8. Deliberate bowling of high full-pitched balls

If the umpire considers that a high full pitch which is deemed to be dangerous and unfair, as defined in 6(b) above, was deliberately bowled, then the caution and warning prescribed in 7 above shall be dispensed with. The umpire shall:

(a) Call and signal "No-ball".

(b) Direct the captain, when the ball is dead, to take the bowler off forthwith.

(c) Implement the remainder of the procedure as laid down in 7(c) above.

9. Time-wasting by the fielding side

It is unfair for any member of the fielding side to waste time.

(a) If the captain of the fielding side wastes time, or allows any member of his side to waste time, or if the progress of an over is unnecessarily slow, at the first instance the umpire shall call and signal "Dead ball" if necessary and:

(i) Warn the captain, and indicate that this is a first and final warning.

(ii) Inform the other umpire and the batsmen of what has occurred.

(b) If there is any further waste of time in that innings, by any member of the fielding side, the umpire shall either

(i) if the waste of time is not during the course of an over, award five penalty runs to the batting side (See 17 below), or

(ii) if the waste of time is during the course of an over, when the ball is dead, direct the captain to take the bowler off forthwith. If applicable, the over shall be completed by another bowler, who shall neither have bowled the previous over nor be allowed to bowl the next over. The bowler thus taken off shall not be allowed to bowl again in that innings.

(iii) Inform the other umpire, the batsmen and, as soon as practicable, the captain of the batting side, of what has occurred.

(iv) Report the occurrence, with the other umpire, as soon as possible to the executive of the fielding side and to any governing body responsible for the match, who shall take such action as is considered appropriate against the captain and team concerned.

10. Batsman wasting time

It is unfair for a batsman to waste time. In normal circumstances the striker should always be ready to take strike when the bowler is ready to start his run-up.

(a) Should either batsman waste time by failing to meet this requirement, or in any other way, the following procedure shall be adopted. At the first instance, either before the bowler starts his run-up or when the ball is dead, as appropriate, the umpire shall:

(i) Warn the batsman and indicate that this is a first and final warning. This warning shall continue to apply throughout that innings. The umpire shall so inform each incoming batsman.

(ii) Inform the other umpire, the other batsman and the captain of the fielding side of what has occurred.

(iii) Inform the captain of the batting side as soon as practicable.

(b) If there is any further time-wasting by any batsman in that innings, the umpire shall, at the appropriate time while the ball is dead:

(i) Award five penalty runs to the fielding side. See 17 below.

(ii) Inform the other umpire, the other batsman, the captain of the fielding side and, as soon as practicable, the captain of the batting side, of what has occurred.

(iii) Report the occurrence, with the other umpire, as soon as possible to the executive of the batting side and to any governing body responsible for the match, who shall take such action as is considered appropriate against the captain and player or players, or, if appropriate, the team concerned.

11. Damaging the pitch – area to be protected

(a) It is incumbent on all players to avoid unnecessary damage to the pitch. It is unfair for any player to cause deliberate damage to the pitch.

(b) An area of the pitch, to be referred to as "the protected area", is defined as that area contained within a rectangle bounded at each end by imaginary lines parallel to the popping creases and 5ft/1.52m in front of each and on the sides by imaginary lines, one each side of the imaginary line joining the centres of the two middle stumps, each parallel to it and 1ft/30.48cm from it.

12. Bowler running on the protected area after delivering the ball

(a) If the bowler, after delivering the ball, runs on the protected area as defined in 11(b) above, the umpire shall at the first instance, and when the ball is dead:

(i) Caution the bowler. This caution shall continue to apply throughout the innings.

(ii) Inform the other umpire, the captain of the fielding side and the batsmen of what has occurred.

(b) If, in that innings, the same bowler runs on the protected area again after delivering the ball, the umpire shall repeat the above procedure, indicating that this is a final warning.

(c) If, in that innings, the same bowler runs on the protected area a third time after delivering the ball, when the ball is dead the umpire shall:

(i) Direct the captain of the fielding side to take the bowler off forthwith. If applicable, the over shall be completed by another bowler, who shall neither have bowled the previous over nor be allowed to bowl the next over. The bowler thus taken off shall not be allowed to bowl again in that innings.

(ii) Inform the other umpire, the batsmen and, as soon as practicable, the captain of the batting side of what has occurred.

(iii) Report the occurrence, with the other umpire, as soon as possible to the executive of the fielding side and to any governing body responsible for the match, who shall take such action as is considered appropriate against the captain and bowler concerned.

13. Fielders damaging the pitch

(a) If any fielder causes avoidable damage to the pitch, other than as in 12(a) above, at the first instance the umpire shall, when the ball is dead:

(i) Caution the captain of the fielding side, indicating that this is a first and final warning. This caution shall continue to apply throughout the innings.

(ii) Inform the other umpire and the batsmen of what has occurred.

(b) If there is any further avoidable damage to the pitch by any fielder in that innings, the umpire shall, when the ball is dead:

(i) Award five penalty runs to the batting side. See 17 below.

(ii) Inform the other umpire, the batsmen, the captain of the fielding side and, as soon as practicable, the captain of the batting side of what has occurred.

(iii) Report the occurrence, with the other umpire, as soon as possible to the executive of the fielding side and any governing body responsible for the match, who shall take such action as is considered appropriate against the captain and player or players concerned.

14. Batsman damaging the pitch

(a) If either batsman causes avoidable damage to the pitch, at the first instance the umpire shall, when the ball is dead:

(i) Caution the batsman. This caution shall continue to apply throughout the innings. The umpire shall so inform each incoming batsman.

(ii) Inform the other umpire, the other batsman, the captain of the fielding side and, as soon as practicable, the captain of the batting side.

(b) If there is a second instance of avoidable damage to the pitch by any batsman in that innings:

(i) The umpire shall repeat the above procedure, indicating that this is a final warning.

(ii) Additionally he shall disallow all runs to the batting side from that delivery other than the penalty for a no-ball or a wide, if applicable. The batsmen shall return to their original ends.

(c) If there is any further avoidable damage to the pitch by any batsman in that innings, the umpire shall, when the ball is dead:

(i) Disallow all runs to the batting side from that delivery other than the penalty for a no-ball or a wide, if applicable.

(ii) Additionally award five penalty runs to the fielding side. See 17 below.

(iii) Inform the other umpire, the other batsman, the captain of the fielding side and, as soon as practicable, the captain of the batting side of what has occurred.

(iv) Report the occurrence, with the other umpire, as soon as possible to the executive of the batting side and any governing body responsible for the match, who shall take such action as is considered appropriate against the captain and player or players concerned.

15. Bowler attempting to run out non-striker before delivery

The bowler is permitted, before entering his delivery stride, to attempt to run out the non-striker. The ball shall not count in the over.

The umpire shall call and signal "Dead ball" as soon as possible if the bowler fails in the attempt to run out the non-striker.

16. Batsmen stealing a run

It is unfair for the batsmen to attempt to steal a run during the bowler's run-up. Unless the bowler attempts to run out either batsman – see 15 above and Law 24.4 (Bowler throwing towards striker's end before delivery) – the umpire shall:

(i) Call and signal "Dead ball" as soon as the batsmen cross in any such attempt.

(ii) Return the batsmen to their original ends.

(iii) Award five penalty runs to the fielding side. See 17 below.

(iv) Inform the other umpire, the other batsman, the captain of the fielding side and, as soon as practicable, the captain of the batting side of the reason for the action taken.

(v) Report the occurrence, with the other umpire, as soon as possible to the executive of the batting side and any governing body responsible for the match, who shall take such action as is considered appropriate against the captain and player or players concerned.

17. Penalty runs

(a) When penalty runs are awarded to either side, when the ball is dead the umpire shall signal the penalty runs to the scorers as laid down in Law 3.14 (Signals).

(b) Notwithstanding any provisions elsewhere in the Laws, penalty runs shall not be awarded once the match is concluded as defined in Law 16.9 (Conclusion of a match).

(c) When five penalty runs are awarded to the batting side, under either Law 2.6 (Player returning without permission) or Law 41 (The fielder) or under 3, 4, 5, 9 or 13 above, then:

(i) They shall be scored as penalty extras and shall be in addition to any other penalties.

(ii) They shall not be regarded as runs scored from either the immediately preceding delivery or the following delivery and shall be in addition to any runs from those deliveries.

(iii) The batsmen shall not change ends solely by reason of the five-run penalty.

(d) When five penalty runs are awarded to the fielding side, under Law 18.5(b) (Deliberate short runs), or under 10, 14 or 16 above, they shall be added as penalty extras to that side's total of runs in its most recently completed innings. If the fielding side has not completed an innings, the five penalty extras shall be added to its next innings.

18. Players' conduct

If there is any breach of the Spirit of the Game by a player failing to comply with the instructions of an umpire, or criticising his decisions by word or action, or showing dissent, or generally behaving in a manner which might bring the game into disrepute, the umpire concerned shall immediately report the matter to the other umpire.

The umpires together shall:

(i) Inform the player's captain of the occurrence, instructing the latter to take action.

(ii) Warn him of the gravity of the offence, and tell him that it will be reported to higher authority.

(iii) Report the occurrence as soon as possible to the executive of the player's team and any governing body responsible for the match, who shall take such action as is considered appropriate against the captain and player or players, and, if appropriate, the team concerned.

REGULATIONS OF THE INTERNATIONAL CRICKET COUNCIL

Extracts

1. Standard playing conditions

In 2001, the ICC Cricket Committee amended its standard playing conditions for all Tests and one-day internationals to include the new Laws of Cricket. The following playing conditions were to apply for three years from September 1, 2001:

Duration of Test Matches

Test matches shall be of five days' scheduled duration and of two innings per side. The two participating countries may:

(a) Provide for a rest day during the match, and/or a reserve day after the scheduled days of play.

(b) Play on any scheduled rest day, conditions and circumstances permitting, should a full day's play be lost on any day prior to the rest day.

(c) Play on any scheduled reserve day, conditions and circumstances permitting, should a full day's play be lost on any day. Play shall not take place on more than five days.

(d) Make up time lost in excess of five minutes in each day's play due to circumstances outside the game, other than acts of God.

Hours of Play and Minimum Overs in the Day in Test Matches

1. Start and cessation times shall be determined by the home board, subject to there being six hours scheduled for play per day (Pakistan a minimum of five and a half hours).

(a) Play shall continue on each day until the completion of a minimum number of overs or until the scheduled or rescheduled cessation time, whichever is the later. The minimum number of overs to be completed, unless an innings ends or an interruption occurs, shall be:

(i) on days other than the last day – a minimum of 90 overs (or a minimum of 15 overs per hour).

(ii) on the last day – a minimum of 75 overs (or 15 overs per hour) for playing time other than the last hour when a minimum of 15 overs shall be bowled. All calculations with regard to suspensions of play or the start of a new innings shall be based on one over for each full four minutes. (Fractions are to be ignored in all calculations except where there is a change of innings in a day's play, when theover in progress at the conclusion shall be rounded up.) If, however, at any time after 30 minutes of the last hour have elapsed both captains (the batsmen at the wicket may act for their captain) accept that there is no prospect of a result to the match, they may agree to cease play at that time.

(iii) Subject to weather and light, except in the last hour of the match, in the event of play being suspended for any reason other than normal intervals, the playing time on that day shall be extended by the amount of time lost up to a maximum of one hour. The minimum number of overs to be bowled shall be in accordance with the provisions of this clause (i.e. a minimum of 15 overs per hour) and the cessation time shall be rescheduled accordingly.

(iv) If any time is lost and cannot be made up under (a)(iii), additional time of up to a maximum of one hour per day shall be added to the scheduled playing hours for the next day, and subsequent day(s) as required. Where appropriate, the first 30 minutes (or less) of this additional time shall be added before the scheduled start of the first session and the remainder to the last session. Where it is not possible to add this time before the scheduled start, the timing of the lunch and tea intervals will be adjusted to provide a scheduled two-and-a-half-hour session and not affect the start time. On any day's play, except the last day, when the scheduled hours have been completed but the required number of overs have not been bowled, and weather or bad light causes play to be abandoned, the remaining overs shall be made up on the next or subsequent days. On any one day, a maximum of 15 additional overs shall be permitted. When additional time is added to subsequent day(s), no scheduled day's play shall exceed seven hours. The length of each session is subject to Law 15. Timings can be altered at any time on any day if time is lost, not necessarily on that day. The captains, umpires and referee can agree different timings under those circumstances before play starts on any day.

(b) When an innings ends, a minimum number of overs shall be bowled from the start of the new innings. The number of overs to be bowled shall be calculated at the rate of one over for each full four minutes to enable a minimum of 90 overs to be bowled in a day. The last hour of the match shall be excluded from this calculation (see (a) (ii)).

Where a change of innings occurs during a day's play, in the event of the team bowling second being unable to complete its overs by the scheduled cessation time, play shall continue until the required number of overs have been completed.

2. The umpires may decide to play 30 minutes (a minimum eight overs) extra time at the end of any day (other than the last day) if requested by either captain if, in the umpires' opinion, it would bring about a definite result on that day. If the umpires do not believe a result can be achieved, no extra time shall be allowed. If it is decided to play such extra time, the whole period shall be played out even though the possibility of finishing the match may have disappeared before the full period has expired. Only the actual amount of playing time up to the maximum 30 minutes' extra time by which play is extended on any day shall be deducted from the total number of hours of play remaining and the match shall end earlier on the final day by that amount of time.

Use of Lights:

If, in the opinion of the umpires, natural light is deteriorating to an unfit level, they shall authorise the ground authorities to use the available artificial lighting so that the match can continue in acceptable conditions.

The lights are only to be used to enable a full day's play to be completed as provided for in Clause 1 above. In the event of power failure or lights malfunction, the existing provisions of Clause 1 shall apply.

Dangerous and Unfair Bowling: The Bowling of Fast, Short-Pitched Balls: Law 42.6

1. (a) A bowler shall be limited to two fast, short-pitched deliveries per over.

(b) A fast, short-pitched ball is defined as a ball which passes or would have passed above the shoulder height of the batsman standing upright at the crease, but not clearly above the batsman's head so that it is so high it prevents him from being able to hit it with his bat by means of a normal cricket stroke.

(c) The umpire at the bowler's end shall advise the bowler and the batsman on strike when each fast short-pitched ball has been bowled.

(d) For the purpose of this regulation, a ball that passes clearly above head height, other than a fast, short-pitched ball, that prevents the batsman from being able to hit it with his bat by means of a normal cricket stroke shall be a no-ball.

(e) Any fast, short-pitched delivery called no-ball under this condition shall count as one of the allowable short-pitched deliveries in that over.

2. In the event of a bowler bowling more than two fast, short-pitched deliveries in an over, the umpire at the bowler's end shall call and signal "no-ball" on each occasion. The umpire shall call and signal "no-ball" and then tap the head with the other hand.

If a bowler delivers a third fast, short-pitched ball in one over, the umpire must call no-ball and then invoke the procedures of caution, final warning, action against the bowler and reporting as set out in Law 42.7. The umpires will report the matter to the ICC referee who shall take such action as is considered appropriate against the captain and bowler concerned.

The above Regulation is not a substitute for Law 42.6 (as amended below), which umpires are able to apply at any time:

The bowling of fast, short-pitched balls is unfair if the umpire at the bowler's end considers that, by their repetition and taking into account their length, height and direction, they are likely to inflict physical injury on the striker, irrespective of the protective clothing and equipment he may be wearing. The relative skill of the striker shall also be taken into consideration.

The umpire at the bowler's end shall adopt the procedures of caution, final warning, action against the bowler and reporting as set out in Law 42.7. The ICC referee shall take any further action considered appropriate against the captain and bowler concerned.

New Ball: Law 5.4

The captain of the fielding side shall have the choice of taking a new ball any time after 80 overs have been bowled with the previous ball. The umpires shall indicate to the batsmen and the scorers whenever a new ball is taken into play.

Ball Lost or Becoming Unfit for Play: Law 5.5

The following shall apply in addition to Law 5.5

However, if the ball needs to be replaced after 110 overs for any of the reasons above, it shall be replaced by a new ball. If the ball is to be replaced, the umpires shall inform the batsmen.

Judging a Wide: Law 25.1

Law 25.1 will apply, but in addition

For bowlers attempting to utilise the rough outside a batsman's leg stump, not necessarily as a negative tactic, the strict limited-overs wide interpretation shall be applied. For bowlers whom umpires consider to be bowling down the leg side as a negative tactic, the strict limited-overs wide interpretation shall be applied.

Practice on the Field: Law 17

In addition to Law 17.1:

The use of the square for practice on any day of any match will be restricted to any netted practice area on the square set aside for that purpose.

Fieldsman Leaving the Field: Law 2.5

If a fielder fails to take the field with his side at the start of the match or at any later time, or leaves the field during a session of play, the umpire shall be informed of the reason for his absence, and he shall not thereafter come on to the field during a session without the consent of the umpire. The umpire shall give such consent as soon as practicable. If the player is absent from the field longer than eight minutes, he shall not be permitted to bowl in that innings after his return until he has been on the field for at least that length of playing time for which he was absent. In the event of a follow-on, this restriction will, if necessary, continue into the second innings. Nor shall he be permitted to bat unless or until, in the aggregate, he has returned to the field and/or his side's innings has been in progress for at least that length of playing time for which he has been absent or, if earlier, when his side has lost five wickets. The restrictions shall not apply if he has suffered an external blow (as opposed to an internal injury such as a pulled muscle) while participating earlier in the match and consequently been forced to leave the field, nor if he has been absent for exceptional and acceptable reasons (other than injury or illness).

2. Classification of first-class matches

1. Definitions

A match of three or more days' duration between two sides of 11 players played on natural turf pitches on international standard grounds and substantially conforming with standard playing conditions shall be regarded as a first-class fixture.

2. Rules

(a) Full Members of the ICC shall decide the status of matches of three or more days' duration played in their countries.

(b) In matches of three or more days' duration played in countries which are not Full Members of the ICC, except Kenya (see 2.3 (l) below):

(i) If the visiting team comes from a country which is a Full Member of the ICC, that country shall decide the status of matches.

(ii) If the visiting team does not come from a country which is a Full Member of the ICC, or is a Commonwealth team composed of players from different countries, the ICC shall decide the status of matches.

Notes

(a) Governing bodies agree that the interest of first-class cricket will be served by ensuring that first-class status is not accorded to any match in which one or other of the teams taking part cannot on a strict interpretation of the definitions be adjudged first-class.

(b) In case of any disputes arising from these Rules, the Chief Executive of the ICC shall refer the matter for decision to the Council, failing unanimous agreement by postal communication being reached.

3. First-Class Status

The following matches shall be regarded as first-class, subject to the provisions of 2.1 (Definitions) being complied with:

(a) **In Great Britain and Ireland:** (i) County Championship matches. (ii) Official representative tourist matches from Full Member countries unless specifically excluded. (iii) MCC v any first-class county. (iv) Oxford, Cambridge and Durham University Centres of Excellence against first-class counties. (v) Oxford v Cambridge. (vi) Scotland v Ireland.

(b) **In Australia:** (i) Pura Cup matches. (ii) Matches played by Australia A or an Australian XI and teams representing states of the Commonwealth of Australia between each other or against opponents adjudged first-class.

(c) **In Bangladesh:** (i) Matches between Bangladesh and a Full Member. (ii) Matches between Full Member teams adjudged first-class and Bangladesh. (iii) Matches between teams adjudged first-class and a Full Member. (iv) Matches between Bangladesh and Kenya. (v) Matches between teams adjudged first-class and Kenya. (vi) National League three-day matches between the Divisions of Barisal, Chittagong, Dhaka, Khulna, Rajshahi and Sylhet.

(d) **In India:** (i) Ranji Trophy matches. (ii) Duleep Trophy matches. (iii) Irani Trophy matches. (iv) Matches played by teams representing state or regional associations affiliated to the Board of Control between each other or against opponents adjudged first-class. (v) Matches of three days or more against representative visiting sides.

(e) **In New Zealand:** (i) State Championship matches. (ii) Matches played by teams representing major associations affiliated to New Zealand Cricket, between each other or against opponents adjudged first-class.

(f) **In Pakistan:** (i) Quaid-e-Azam Trophy (Grade 1) matches. (ii) Patron's Trophy (Grade 1) matches. (iii) Matches played by teams representing cricket associations affiliated to the Pakistan Cricket Board, between each other or against teams adjudged first-class (organised by the PCB).

(g) **In South Africa:** (i) SuperSport Series four-day matches between Boland, Border, Eastern Province, Easterns, Free State, Gauteng, Griqualand West, KwaZulu-Natal, Northerns, North West, Western Province. (ii) Matches against touring teams adjudged first-class.

(h) **In Sri Lanka:** (i) Matches of three days or more against touring sides adjudged first-class. (ii) Premier League Division I matches played over three or more days for the Premier Trophy.

(i) **In West Indies:** Matches played by teams representing Barbados, Guyana, Jamaica, the Leeward Islands, Trinidad & Tobago and the Windward Islands, either for the Busta Cup or against other opponents adjudged first-class.

(j) **In Zimbabwe:** (i) Logan Cup matches. (ii) Matches played by teams representing associations affiliated to the ZCU, between each other or against opponents adjudged first-class.

(k) **In all Full Member countries represented on the Council:** (i) Test matches and matches against teams adjudged first-class played by official touring teams. (ii) Official Test Trial matches. (iii) Special matches between teams adjudged first-class by the governing body or bodies concerned.

(l) **In Kenya:** (i) Matches between a Full Member and Kenya. (ii) Matches between teams adjudged first-class and Kenya.

3. Classification of one-day international matches

The following shall be classified as one-day internationals:

(a) All matches played in the official World Cup competition, including matches involving Associate Member countries.

(b) All matches played between the Full Member countries of the ICC as part of an official tour itinerary.

(c) All matches played as part of an official tournament between Full Member countries. These need not necessarily be held in a Full Member country.

(d) All matches between the Full Members and Kenya.

Note: Matches involving the A team of a Full Member country shall not be classified as one-day internationals.

4. Qualification rules for Test matches and one-day international matches

Qualification by Birth

A cricketer is qualified to play in Tests, one-day internationals or any other representative cricket match for the country of his birth provided he has not played in Tests, one-day internationals or, after October 1, 1994, in any other representative cricket match for any other Member country during the two immediately preceding years. However, cricketers qualified for ICC Associate and Affiliate countries can continue to represent that country without negating their eligibility or interrupting their qualification period for a Full Member country until the stage that the cricketer has played for the Full Member at Under-19 level or above.

Qualification by Residence

A cricketer is qualified to play in Tests, one-day internationals or in any other representative cricket match for any Full or Associate Member country in which he has resided for at least 183 days in each of the four immediately preceding years provided that he has not played in Tests, one-day internationals or, after October 1, 1994, in any other representative cricket match for any other Member country during that period of four years. However, cricketers qualified for ICC Associate and Affiliate countries can continue to represent that country under the same terms as given under Qualification by Birth.

Exceptional Circumstances

Should a player be deemed ineligible under the above qualifications and his Board believe that there are exceptional circumstances requiring consideration, a detailed written application shall be made to the Chief Executive of the ICC. The application will be referred to the Chairman of the Cricket Committee whose decision shall be final.

Notes: "Representative cricket match" means any cricket match in which a team representing a Member country at Under-19 level or above takes part, including Tests and one-day internationals.

The governing body for cricket of any Member country may impose more stringent qualification rules for that country.

ICC CODE OF CONDUCT

1. The captains are responsible at all times for ensuring that play is conducted within the spirit of the game as well as within the Laws.

2. Players and/or team officials shall at no time engage in conduct unbecoming to their status which could bring them or the game of cricket into disrepute.

3. Players and/or team officials must at all times accept the umpire's decision and not show dissent at the umpire's decision.

4. Players and/or team officials shall not verbally abuse, assault, intimidate or attempt to assault or intimidate any umpire, spectator, referee, player or team official. Nor shall any player or team official engage in any conduct towards or speak to any other player, umpire, spectator, referee or team official in a manner which offends, insults, humiliates, intimidates, disparages or vilifies the other person on the basis of that other person's race, religion, colour, descent or national or ethnic origin.

5. Players and/or team officials shall not use crude or abusive language nor make offensive gestures.

6. Players and/or team officials shall not disclose or comment publicly upon any alleged or actual breach of this Code, whether by themselves or any other person to whom the Code applies, or upon any hearing, report or decision arising from such an alleged or proven breach.

7. Players and/or team officials shall not at any time breach any ICC regulation which may be in force from time to time.

8. Players and/or team officials shall not make any public pronouncement or media comment which is detrimental either to the game of cricket in general; or to a particular tour whether or not they are personally involved with the tour; or to relations between the home boards of competing teams.

9. Players and/or team officials shall be required to report to the captain and/or team manager any approach made to them by a bookmaker or any other corrupt approach or knowledge of such approach made to any other player or team official.

10. Players and/or team officials shall not bet on matches nor otherwise engage in conduct of the nature described in Appendix A of the ICC Code of Conduct Commission Terms of Reference and in the paragraphs below. For conduct in breach of this rule, the penalties to be considered are set out below, for individuals who have:

- i. Bet on any match or series of matches, or on any connected event, in which such player, umpire, referee, team official or administrator took part or in which the Member country or any such individual was represented (penalty (a));
- ii. Induced or encouraged any other person to bet on any match or series of matches or on any connected event or to offer the facility for such bets to be placed (penalty (b));
- iii. Gambled or entered into any other form of financial speculation on any match or on any connected event (penalty (a));
- iv. Induced or encouraged any other person to gamble or enter into any other form of financial speculation on any match or any connected event (penalty (b));
- v. Was a party to contriving or attempting to contrive the result of any match or the occurrence of any connected event (penalty (c));
- vi. Failed to perform on his merits in any match owing to an arrangement relating to betting on the outcome of any match or on the occurrence of any connected event (penalty (c));
- vii. Induced or encouraged any other player not to perform on his merits in any match owing to any such arrangement (penalty (c));
- viii. Received from another person any money, benefit or other reward (whether financial or otherwise) for the provision of any information concerning the weather, the teams, the state of the ground, the status of, or the outcome of, any match or the occurrence of any

connected event unless such information has been provided to a newspaper or other form of media in accordance with an obligation entered into in the normal course and disclosed in advance to the cricket authority of the relevant Member country (penalty (b));

ix. Received any money, benefit or other reward (whether financial or otherwise) which could bring him or the game of cricket into disrepute (penalty (d));

x. Provided any money, benefit or other reward (whether financial or otherwise) which could bring the game of cricket into disrepute (penalty (d));

xi. Received any approaches from another person to engage in conduct such as that described above, and has failed to disclose the same to the chief executive officer of the home board of his member country or to the ICC chief executive (penalty (e)); or

xii. Is aware that any other player or individual has engaged in conduct, or received approaches, such as described above, and has failed to disclose the same to the chief executive officer of the home board of his member country or to the ICC chief executive (penalty (e));

xiii. Has received or is aware that any other person has received threats of any nature which might induce him to engage in conduct, or acquiesce in any proposal made by an approach, such as described above, and has failed to disclose the same to the chief executive officer of the home board of his member country or to the ICC chief executive (penalty (e));.

xiv. Has engaged in any conduct which, in the opinion of the Executive Board, relates directly or indirectly to any of the above paragraphs (i to xiii) and is prejudicial to the interests of the game of cricket (penalty (e)).

Penalties:

(a) Ban for a minimum of two years and a maximum of five years. In addition, a fine may be imposed, the amount to be assessed in the circumstances.

(b) Ban for a minimum of two years and a maximum of five years if a bet was placed directly or indirectly for the benefit of the individual; otherwise, a ban for a minimum of 12 months. In addition, a fine may be imposed, the amount to be assessed in the circumstances.

(c) Ban for life (a minimum of 20 years).

(d) Ban for a minimum of two years and a maximum of life. In addition, a fine may be imposed, the amount to be assessed in the circumstances.

(e) Ban for a minimum of one year and a maximum of five years. In addition, a fine may be imposed, the amount to be assessed in the circumstances.

Note: The terms of Appendix A are almost identical to paragraphs (i) to (xiv) above, except that they are stated to apply to any player, umpire, referee, team official or administrator connected with any Test, one-day international or representative match after July 1, 1993.

11. Players and/or team officials shall not use or in any way be concerned in the use or distribution of illegal drugs.

CRIME AND PUNISHMENT

ICC Code of Conduct – Breaches and Penalties in 2000-01 and 2001

A. C. Parore New Zealand v Zimbabwe, 2nd Test at Harare.
Pushed batsman who allegedly obstructed him. Severely reprimanded by C. W. Smith.

A. D. R. Campbell Zimbabwe v New Zealand, one-day international at Nairobi.
Dissent when given out lbw. Banned for one one-day international by C. W. Smith.

R. Telemachus South Africa v India, one-day international at Nairobi.
Barged into R. Dravid. Banned for one one-day international by C. W. Smith.

N. Hussain England v Pakistan, one-day international at Rawalpindi.
Broke dressing-room fridge door after given out lbw. Severely reprimanded by B. N. Jarman.

S. C. Ganguly India v Zimbabwe, one-day international at Kanpur.
Showed dissent several times towards umpire Sathe. Banned for one one-day international, with further ban for two one-day internationals suspended for six months, by B. N. Jarman.

S. M. Pollock South Africa v New Zealand, 1st Test at Bloemfontein.
Exchanged abusive language with C. D. McMillan. Fined 50 per cent of match fee by Naushad Ali.

C. D. McMillan New Zealand v South Africa, 1st Test at Bloemfontein.
Exchanged abusive language with S. M. Pollock. Fined 50 per cent of match fee by Naushad Ali.

A. D. R. Campbell Zimbabwe v Australia, one-day international at Hobart.
Commented on rejected appeal against A. Symonds in newspapers. Fined 25 per cent of match fee by D. T. Lindsay.

G. A. Hick England v Sri Lanka, 1st Test at Galle.
Questioned umpire's decision. One-match ban suspended for one month by Hanumant Singh.

R. P Arnold, D. P. M. D. Jayawardene, M. Muralitharan and K. Sangakkara
Sri Lanka v England, 1st Test at Galle.
Each ran towards umpire with an appeal; each fined 25 per cent of match fee by Hanumant Singh.

K. Sangakkara Sri Lanka v England, 2nd Test at Kandy.
Exchanged heated words and verbal abuse with M. A. Atherton. Severely reprimanded by Hanumant Singh.

M. A. Atherton England v Sri Lanka, 2nd Test at Kandy.
Exchanged heated words and verbal abuse with K. Sangakkara and had words with umpire Koertzen. Severely reprimanded by Hanumant Singh.

S. T. Jayasuriya Sri Lanka v England, 2nd Test at Kandy.
Gesticulated in dissent after given out. Fined 60 per cent of match fee, with ban for two Tests and two one-day internationals suspended for six months, by Hanumant Singh.

M. J. Slater Australia v India, 1st Test at Mumbai.
Commented on radio on an incident in the Test. Fined 50 per cent of match fee, with ban for one Test suspended for six months, by C. W. Smith.

M. Muralitharan Sri Lanka v England, one-day international at Dambulla.
Dissent at umpire's decision. Fined 65 per cent of match fee, with ban for two one-day internationals and one Test suspended for six months, by Hanumant Singh.

A. C. Gilchrist Australia v India, one-day international at Bangalore.
Dissent when umpire Sharma gave S. R. Waugh out lbw. Fined 50 per cent of match fee by C. W. Smith.

G. D. McGrath Australia v India, one-day international at Bangalore.
Used foul language to umpire Sharma after given out lbw. Fined 50 per cent of match fee by C. W. Smith.

H. H. Gibbs South Africa v West Indies, 4th Test at St John's.
Dissent when given out. Reprimanded and warned about his conduct by M. H. Denness.

L. V. Garrick West Indies v South Africa, 5th Test at Kingston.
Attempted to intimidate umpire when J. H. Kallis given not out. Severely reprimanded and warned about his conduct by M. H. Denness.

D. Ramnarine West Indies v South Africa, 5th Test at Kingston.
Dissent at umpire's decision. Severely reprimanded and warned about his conduct by M. H. Denness.

Inzamam-ul-Haq Pakistan v Australia, one-day international at Lord's.
Dissent at umpire's decision. Fined 50 per cent of match fee and banned for two one-day internationals by B. F. Hastings.

R. D. Jacobs West Indies v India, one-day international at Harare.
Broke the stumps for a stumping knowing the ball was in his other hand, and made no effort to recall the batsman. Banned for one Test by D. T. Lindsay.

D. D. Ebrahim Zimbabwe v West Indies, 2nd Test at Harare.
Remained at the wicket unnecessarily long after being given out caught behind. Severely reprimanded by D. T. Lindsay.

S. C. Ganguly India v New Zealand, one-day international at Colombo (RPS).
Raised his bat and shook his head when given out lbw. Banned for one one-day international by C. W. Smith.

S. C. Ganguly India v Sri Lanka, one-day international at Colombo (SSC).
Gestured at R. P. Arnold after dismissing him. Severely reprimanded and fined 75 per cent of match fee by C. W. Smith.

A. J. Stewart England v Australia, 5th Test at The Oval.
Stood his ground before walking off when given out caught behind. Fined 20 per cent of match fee by Talat Ali.

REGULATIONS FOR FIRST-CLASS MATCHES IN BRITAIN, 2001

Hours of play

Four-day matches:

1st, 2nd, 3rd days . . . 11.00 a.m. to 6.30 p.m.
4th day . . . . 11.00 a.m. to 6.00 p.m.

Three-day matches:

1st, 2nd days . . . . . . 11.30 a.m. to 6.30 p.m. (11.00 a.m. to 6.30 p.m. in tourist matches and Oxford v Cambridge)
3rd day . . . . 11.00 a.m. to 6.00 p.m.

Intervals

Lunch: 1.15 p.m. to 1.55 p.m. (1st, 2nd [3rd] days) in Championship and tourist matches and Oxford v Cambridge, 1.30 p.m. to 2.10 p.m. in others
1.00 p.m. to 1.40 p.m. (final day)
Where an innings concludes or there is a break in play within ten minutes of the scheduled lunch interval, the interval will commence at that time and be limited to 40 minutes.

Tea: (Championship matches) A tea interval of 20 minutes shall normally be taken at 4.10 p.m. (3.40 p.m. on final day), or at the conclusion of the over in progress at that time, provided 32 overs or less remain to be bowled (except on the final day). The over in progress shall be completed unless a batsman is out or retires either within two minutes of, or after, the scheduled time for the interval. In the event of more than 32 overs remaining, the tea interval will be delayed.

If an innings ends or there is a stoppage caused by weather within 30 minutes of the scheduled time, the tea interval shall be taken immediately. There will be no tea interval if the scheduled timing for the cessation of play is earlier than 5.30 p.m.

(Other matches) 4.10 p.m. to 4.30 p.m. (1st, 2nd [3rd] days), 3.40 p.m. to 4.00 p.m. (final day).

Note: The hours of play, including intervals, are brought forward by half an hour for matches scheduled to start in September.

(i) Play shall continue on each day until the completion of a minimum number of overs or until the scheduled cessation time, whichever is the later. The minimum number of overs, unless an innings ends or an interruption occurs, shall be 104 on days other than the last day, and 80 on the last day before the last hour.

(ii) Where there is a change of innings during a day's play (except during an interval or suspension of play or exceptional circumstances or during the last hour of domestic matches), two overs will be deducted from the minimum number, plus any over in progress at the end of the completed innings (in domestic matches).

(iii) If interruptions for weather or light occur, other than in the last hour of the match, the minimum number of overs shall be reduced by one over for each full 3¾ minutes of the aggregate playing time lost.

(iv) On the last day, if any of the minimum of 80 overs, or as recalculated, have not been bowled when one hour of scheduled playing time remains, the last hour of the match shall be the hour immediately following the completion of those overs.

(v) Law 16.6, 16.7 and 16.8 will apply except that a minimum of 16 six-ball overs shall be bowled in the last hour, and *all* calculations with regard to suspensions of play or the start of a new innings shall be based on one over for each full 3¾ minutes. If, however, at 5.30 p.m. both captains accept that there is no prospect of a result or (in Championship games) of either side gaining any further first-innings bonus points, they may agree to cease play at that time or at any time after 5.30 p.m.

(vi) (Domestic matches). The captains may agree or, in the event of disagreement, the umpires may decide to play 30 minutes (a minimum eight overs) extra time at the end of any day other than the last day if, in their opinion, it would bring about a definite result on that day. The whole period shall be played out even though the possibility of finishing the match may have disappeared before the full period has expired. The time by whichplay is extended on any day shall be deducted from the total number of hours remaining, and the match shall end earlier on the last day by the amount of time by which play was extended.

(vii) Notwithstanding any other provision, there shall be no further play on any day, other than the last day, if a wicket falls or a batsman retires, or if the players leave the field during the last minimum over within two minutes of the scheduled cessation time or thereafter.

(viii) An over completed on resumption of a new day's play shall be disregarded in calculating minimum overs for that day.

(ix) The scoreboard shall show the total number of overs bowled with the ball in use and the minimum number remaining to be bowled in a day. In Championship matches, it shall show the number of overs up to 130 in each side's first innings and subsequently the number bowled with the current ball; in addition it shall indicate the number of overs that the fielding side is ahead of or behind the over-rate.

Substitutes

(Domestic matches only) Law 2.1 will apply, but in addition:

No substitute may take the field until the player for whom he is to substitute has been absent from the field for five consecutive complete overs, with the exception that if a fieldsman sustains an obvious, serious injury or is taken ill, a substitute shall be allowed immediately. In the event of any disagreement between the two sides as to the authenticity of an injury or illness, the umpires shall adjudicate. If a player leaves the field during an over, the remainder of that over shall not count in the calculation of the five complete overs.

The umpires shall have discretion, for other wholly acceptable reasons, to allow a substitute for a fielder, or a runner for a batsman, at the start of the match or at any subsequent time subject to consent being given by the opposing captain.

A substitute shall be allowed by right immediately in the event of a cricketer currently playing in a Championship match being required to join the England team for a Test match (or one-day international). Such a substitute may be permitted to bat or bowl in that match, subject to the approval of the ECB. The cricketer who is substituted shall take no further part in the match, even though he may not be required for England. If batting at the time, he shall retire "not out" and his substitute may be permitted to bat later in that innings subject to the approval of the ECB.

Fieldsman leaving the field

ICC regulations apply (see page 1500) but, in domestic matches, it is explained that "external blow" should include, but not be restricted to, collisions with boundary boards, clashes of heads, heavy falls etc and, in the case of "exceptional and acceptable reasons", consent for a substitute must be granted by the opposing captain.

New ball

The captain of the fielding side shall have the choice of taking the new ball after 100 overs (80 in tourist matches) have been bowled with the old one.

Covering of pitches and surrounding areas

The whole pitch shall be covered:

(a) The night before the match and, if necessary, until the first ball is bowled; and whenever necessary and possible at any time prior to that during the preparation of the pitch.

(b) On each night of the match and, if necessary, throughout any rest days.

(c) In the event of play being suspended on account of bad light or rain, during the specified hours of play.

The bowler's run-up shall be covered to a distance of at least ten yards, with a width of four yards, as will the areas 20 feet either side of the length of the pitch.

Declarations

Law 14 will apply, but if, due to weather conditions, play in a County Championship match has not started when less than eight hours' playing time remains, the first innings of each side shall automatically be forfeited and a one-innings match played.

MEETINGS AND DECISIONS, 2001

ECB TEST SPONSORSHIP DEAL

On January 24, the England and Wales Cricket Board announced a three-year £11 million sponsorship arrangement with gas and electricity supplier npower, covering England's home Test Series until 2003. Npower also agreed an affinity deal to generate funds for all areas of the domestic game, including grassroots initiatives.

ELIAS REPORT

At a meeting on January 31, the ECB's management board approved a report from Gerard Elias QC, chairman of the discipline standing committee, on Don Topley's allegations that Essex and Lancashire had colluded in two matches played in August 1991. After speaking to Topley and other witnesses in 2000, Elias had advised the ECB to pass transcripts of his interviews to the police. The police reviewed the evidence and decided against action, concluding that there was insufficient corroboration of the allegations, while a substantial number of witnesses rebutted them. They suggested they should be involved without delay if similar allegations are made in future. Elias felt that the ECB lacked the resources to take this particular matter further. He recommended the establishment of a confidential hotline enabling potential whistle-blowers to communicate without fear of victimisation.

ICC EXECUTIVE BOARD MEETING

Meeting in Melbourne on February 10–11, the International Cricket Council's executive board announced a co-ordinated ten-year Test and one-day international programme, with all ten Test nations playing home and away series against each other twice, and an official ICC Test Championship, to commence with England's home series against Pakistan, starting in May. The Championship was to be a rolling league, with points for each home and away series, but would start with a table using recent results, based on that used by *Wisden* since 1996.

The ICC agreed to a new system of independent umpires and referees. By April 2002, they were to appoint two panels of international umpires: an elite group of up to eight full-time umpires contracted to the ICC, and an emerging panel of up to 30 umpires. There would be two panels of referees on similar lines.

ICC CHIEF EXECUTIVE APPOINTMENT

On March 20, the ICC confirmed the appointment of Malcolm Speed as its second chief executive, succeeding David Richards, who had held the position since 1993. Speed had been chief executive of the Australian Cricket Board for the previous four years, and was to take over in early July, initially for a three-year term.

ENGLAND SUMMER CONTRACTS

Twelve England players were awarded six-month ECB contracts on March 29. The contracts brought them under the control of the England team management, who were thus able to demand that they be rested by their counties. The players, contracted for the summer's Test series against Pakistan and Australia, were: Nasser Hussain (captain), Mike Atherton, Andrew Caddick, Dominic Cork (subject to fitness), Ashley Giles, Darren Gough, Matthew Hoggard, Alec Stewart, Graham Thorpe, Marcus Trescothick, Michael Vaughan and Craig White. Seven of them had been similarly contracted in 2000; Cork, Giles, Hoggard, Thorpe and Trescothick replaced Andrew Flintoff, Dean Headley, Graeme Hick, Mark Ramprakash and Chris Schofield from the earlier list.

ECB DOMESTIC SPONSORSHIP DEALS

On April 4, the ECB announced that Cheltenham & Gloucester, the financial services company, had signed a three-year sponsorship agreement for the Trophy, the premier one-day knockout tournament in English domestic cricket. Later, on April 19, the ECB announced that internet company CricInfo would sponsor the 2001 first-class County Championship, and also the women's Ashes Test and one-day international series during the summer. CricInfo had managed the ECB's website since June 2000.

MCC ANNUAL GENERAL MEETING

The 214th AGM of the Marylebone Cricket Club was held on May 2, with president Lord Alexander of Weedon in the chair. Ted Dexter (Cambridge, Sussex and England) was named to succeed him in October, when Lord Alexander was to become chairman. The meeting raised various administrative issues for discussion. Membership of the club on December 31, 2000, was 19,814, made up of 17,397 members, 1,972 associate members, 281 honorary members and 123 senior members with 41 out-match members. There were 9,613 candidates awaiting election. In 2000, 392 vacancies arose.

ECB DISCIPLINE STANDING COMMITTEE

On May 22, a panel of the ECB's discipline standing committee heard a complaint from Middlesex that Kent had approached their contracted player, Jamie Hewitt, without first obtaining their consent. The panel agreed there had been a technical breach of the qualification and registration regulations, cautioned Kent as to future conduct and ordered them to pay £400 towards the costs of the hearing.

ICC CRICKET COMMITTEE (PLAYING)

The ICC Cricket Committee (Playing) met on May 23–25 and agreed to a series of changes in one-day international regulations. From September 2001, bonus points were to be introduced for tournaments and series involving three or more teams. Points for a win would be doubled to four, with ties/no results counting for two, and in addition a single bonus point would be available to the winning team, the formula to be decided. A six-run penalty for each over not bowled by the scheduled cessation time – in either innings – was approved (but was later dropped). Bowlers were to be permitted one bouncer per over, and the Duckworth/Lewis method for revising targets was approved for a further three years.

For Test cricket, the committee approved the mandatory use of floodlights to allow play to continue in poor natural light. It was agreed that, in both Tests and one-day internationals, five penalty runs would be awarded for all disciplinary breaches covered by the Laws, for a trial period of 12 months. The committee discussed the use of disciplinary cards.

In view of the imminent restructuring of the international umpires panel, the committee decided to maintain the status quo on technology, allowing TV replays to assist umpires on stumpings, hit wicket, run-outs and boundaries, and whether a catch had been cleanly taken.

ECB COUNTY CRICKET ACADEMIES

On May 25, the ECB offered accreditation to seven first-class counties' cricket academies, to establish the foundations of a national network complementing the National Academy. The county academies were to identify cricketers with the potential to play at the highest level, and to help them fulfil it through a comprehensive development programme. Each academy was to support up to 12 players, aged 13 to 18, each year. Durham, Northamptonshire, Nottinghamshire, Somerset, Sussex, Warwickshire and Yorkshire were the first counties accredited. The ECB would contribute £50,000 per annum to the costs of each academy.

ICC EXECUTIVE BOARD MEETING

The ICC held an executive board meeting in London on June 17–19, which fully endorsed the findings and recommendations contained in the Condon Anti-Corruption Unit's report on corruption in international cricket. Progress on the implementation of these recommendations was to be reviewed on a regular basis.

It was announced that $US5 million in prize money would be offered at the 2003 World Cup in South Africa – five times more than for the 1999 World Cup – to address the Condon report's points about raising player remuneration. The board also confirmed the plan for elite panels of international umpires and referees, to start in April 2002. After recent pitch invasions during a one-day international tournament in England, the ICC requested that all members supply a detailed report on local regulations at international venues.

Kenya applied for promotion to Full Member status; this was deferred while a tour of inspection was arranged. Tanzania, formerly included as part of East and Central Africa, were granted Associate Member status in their own right, but the Cayman Islands were turned down for the second year running. Ten countries received Affiliate Member status: Afghanistan, Bahrain, Bhutan, Botswana, Croatia, Indonesia, Lesotho, the Maldives, St Helena and South Korea.

The board accepted recommendations from a governance review process, intended to develop the organisation into a modern and contemporary business staffed by professional managers responsible for the growth, development and revenues of the sport.

ECB NATIONAL ACADEMY DIRECTOR

On July 25, the ECB appointed former Australian wicket-keeper Rodney Marsh director of the new National Academy. Marsh had previously served as director of the Australian National Academy and coach to the Australian Under-19 team. He was to be supported by assistant coach John Abrahams and National Academy manager Nigel Laughton.

ECB DEVELOPMENT PLAN FOR PEOPLE WITH DISABILITIES

The ECB launched a five-year development plan for people with disabilities, on October 10. It aimed to increase the number of people with disabilities taking part in cricket, provide the opportunity for them to attain success at all levels up to and including international, and secure funding to support growth and development of the game. According to Roger Fuggle, the ECB's national disabilities consultant, there are over 1,000 people with disabilities participating in cricket, either playing, umpiring, scoring or coaching.

ICC EXECUTIVE BOARD MEETING

The ICC's executive board moved its October 15–19 meeting from Lahore to Kuala Lumpur because of the crisis in Afghanistan. With Pakistan's home international programme under threat for the same reason, the board approved the use of independent match venues. International fixtures could be rescheduled to the opposition's country or a neutral venue, but would still be regarded as home series for the original host in the ICC Test Championship. At the same time, penalties were introduced for cricket boards refusing to fulfil touring obligations, except in cases of *force majeure*, natural disaster, war, or where the safety of players and officials was at risk. Offenders were to pay a minimum of $US2 million to the host; with Test tours, they would lose two Championship points, while the host would be awarded two points.

Progress on the recommendations of Lord Condon's Anti-Corruption Unit report was discussed. Five security managers, each covering two Test countries, were to be employed by the ICC, rather than by individual cricket boards. Ethics committees were to be introduced; draft legislation on sports corruption was to be presented to all Full Member country governments for consideration; and an ICC anti-corruption manager was to co-ordinate the implementation of recommendations.

From April 2002, the disciplinary power of referees was to be strengthened by a system of set penalties for various stages of offending behaviour. The ICC agreed in principle to a one-day international equivalent to their Test Championship. There was to be another ICC Knockout in September 2002, later planned for Sri Lanka. Zaheer Abbas, Andy Pycroft and Allan Border were to visit Kenya to review the country's application for Test status.

INTERNATIONAL STATUS FOR COUNTY GROUNDS

On November 14, the ECB announced that Durham's Riverside Ground, at Chester-le-Street, would become a Test venue from 2003. The Riverside, which staged first-class cricket for the first time in 1995 and has been hosting one-day internationals since 1999, would be the first new Test ground in England since 1902, when Edgbaston made its debut and Sheffield's Bramall Lane held its only Test. On December 11, it was also announced that the Hampshire Rose Bowl would be awarded one-day international status from 2004. The Rose Bowl, at West End, Southampton, staged its first matches only a few months earlier, in May 2001.

ECB MANAGEMENT BOARD

At a meeting of the ECB management board on November 16, it was decided, on recommendation of the Structure Working Party, to replace the England Management Advisory Committee with a seven-strong panel to be known as the International Teams Management Group. Its remit would include all international teams and the National Academy. It was to be chaired by a non-executive elected by the First-Class Forum, with ECB chief executive Tim Lamb, director of cricket operations John Carr, performance director Hugh Morris, finance director Brian Havill, England coach Duncan Fletcher and chairman of selectors David Graveney as executive members.

ECB NATIONAL ACADEMY

On December 14, the ECB and Sport England confirmed that the permanent site of the ECB National Academy would be at Loughborough University. A budget of £4 million was approved for the project, which required the development of residential accommodation as well as the building of an indoor cricket centre. The finance was to come from Sport England and Loughborough University. Building work on the facilities would begin as soon as possible, although no time-scale was set for the completion

PART SEVEN: MISCELLANEOUS

CHRONICLE OF 2001

JANUARY

1 Herschelle Gibbs is recalled by South Africa to play Sri Lanka the day after completing a six-month ban for his role in match-fixing. **2** Gibbs is out for a duck. **4** South Africa beat Sri Lanka by an innings and 229 runs – the largest innings victory and defeat for the respective teams. **6** Australia's victory at Sydney gives them their first 5–0 whitewash over West Indies and stretches their winning Test sequence to 15; it is West Indies' seventh consecutive defeat. **11** Steve Waugh plays his 300th one-day international (v West Indies, Melbourne); crowd trouble results in 34 arrests and some 160 evictions. **22** Mark Waugh refuses to be interviewed over M. K. Gupta's allegations that he accepted money for information. **24** Australian board warn Waugh he will be dropped if he does not talk to investigators. ECB announce £11 million three-year sponsorship of home Tests by npower. **25** Mark Waugh agrees to meet match-fixing investigators. Debasis Mohanty takes all ten South Zone wickets in an innings for East Zone in the Duleep Trophy. **29** Mohammad Azharuddin petitions Hyderabad court to lift his life ban for match-fixing. Yorkshire appoint Wayne Clark of Western Australia as coach. **31** ECB to take no action over Don Topley's allegations of match-fixing in 1991 Lancashire–Essex fixtures, claiming they are impossible to prove.

FEBRUARY

5 Resumption of South Africa's King Commission postponed after Hansie Cronje's lawyers question its legal status. **7** Kenya dismiss 11 national players in pay dispute and cancel their tour to India and Bangladesh. **10** Mark Waugh meets anti-corruption investigators. **11** West Indies fast bowler Marlon Black is assaulted outside a Melbourne nightclub. ICC launch World Test Championship. **22** Judge King asks for permission to end his inquiry after the threat of action by Cronje's lawyers. **25** Sir Donald Bradman dies, aged 92. **26** England lose to Sri Lanka by an innings at Galle. **28** In Mumbai, Adam Gilchrist hits the second-fastest Test hundred by an Australian. Shoaib Akhtar's action is reported after a one-day international in Dunedin.

MARCH

1 Australia extend their winning Test sequence to 16. **2** Carl Hooper is appointed captain of West Indies. **11** At Kandy, England level their series against Sri Lanka. In Kolkata, against Australia, Harbhajan Singh takes India's first Test hat-trick. **13** India follow on. **14** V. V. S. Laxman (275 not out) beats Sunil Gavaskar's Indian Test record as he and Rahul Dravid bat all day against Australia. **15** Laxman reaches 281 and India win, ending Australia's record winning sequence. **17** England win in three days at Colombo to take the series 2–1. **19** Steve Waugh is out handled the ball in Chennai Test. In Port-of-Spain, Courtney Walsh takes his 500th Test wicket. **22** India beat Australia by two wickets to win series 2–1; Harbhajan Singh claims 15 for 217 in the match. **26** Sri Lankan board chief executive Dhammika Ranatunga is dismissed. **28** Sri Lankan sports minister Lakshman Kiriella dissolves cricket board, replacing Thilanga Sumathipala's administration with an interim committee. **30** Craig McMillan hits a Test-record 26 for a six-ball over, off Younis Khan. **31** Sachin Tendulkar is the first to reach 10,000 runs in one-day internationals.

APRIL

3 Javed Miandad is sacked as Pakistan's coach; Waqar Younis replaces the injured Moin Khan as captain for Sharjah. **4** Cheltenham & Gloucester succeed NatWest as sponsor of England's premier one-day knockout. **7** Miandad is reported as alleging that Pakistan's one-day games in New Zealand were "pre-decided". **8** Miandad denies accusing Pakistan of fixing games in New Zealand. **10** Sanath Jayasuriya takes 30 off a Chris Harris over in Sharjah to beat his own one-day international record. **11** ECB appoint Australian John Harmer to coach England's women. **19** Western Australian fast bowler Duncan Spencer is banned for 18 months after testing positive for Nandrolone, a prohibited anabolic steroid. The day before the 2001 County Championship begins, it is announced that CricInfo will sponsor the competition. West Indies opener Leon Garrick is out to the first ball of the Fifth Test against South Africa (only the second instance involving a debutant after Jimmy Cook, South Africa v India at Durban, 1992-93). **23** Courtney Walsh bows out of Test cricket with 519 wickets as West Indies beat South Africa in Kingston. **24** Shoaib Akhtar's action is cleared; Moin Khan is omitted from Pakistan's party to tour England.

MAY

1 Pakistan reappoint Richard Pybus as coach for England tour. **2** The first day's play at Hampshire's new Rose Bowl ground is washed out. **4** Condon interim report on corruption is submitted to ICC for review. Wasim Akram takes his 1,000th first-class wicket. Hampshire's Rose Bowl has its first day of play. **10** Australian board remove coach John Buchanan from England tour selection committee. **11** South African board announce that six South Africans were fined for smoking marijuana in Antigua in April. **19** Shoaib Akhtar breaks Nasser Hussain's thumb in Lord's Test. **20** Darren Gough takes his 200th Test wicket as England beat Pakistan by an innings. **23** Condon Report is released, containing 24 recommendations but no new names. **25** Pakistan board set up inquiry to investigate allegations that Pakistan threw 1999 World Cup games, and that former umpire Javed Akhtar, who stood in the 1998 Headingley Test between England and South Africa, accepted bribes. **25** West Indies board sack team manager Ricky Skerritt – by e-mail. **27** Sri Lanka's sports minister sets up an inquiry into allegations of corruption and financial mismanagement in the country's board. **29** Hampshire members agree to convert the club into a private limited company.

JUNE

2 West Indies reinstate Skerritt as team manager; board president Pat Rousseau and vice-president Clarvis Joseph resign. **4** Pakistan square the Test series against England, under Alec Stewart's captaincy, at Old Trafford; umpires under scrutiny over no-balls. **7** Pitch invasion at Edgbaston as Pakistan beat England in a day/night international. **8** ECB announce measures to prevent further crowd trouble; Steve Waugh claims the ECB are not doing enough to protect players. **9** Steve Kirby, who made his Yorkshire debut mid-match the previous day, finishes with seven for 50. In Bulawayo, India's Ashish Nehra becomes only the second Test bowler banned for running on the pitch. **10** India beat Zimbabwe – their first Test win outside Asia for 15 years. **11** Zimbabwe Test batsman Trevor Madondo dies, aged 24. **14** England blown away by Australia at Old Trafford for 86, their lowest limited-overs total. **17** ICC's Anti-Corruption Unit voices frustration at Stewart's inability to agree a date to meet over Gupta's claim he accepted money. Stewart concedes a one-day international to Pakistan at Leeds after a steward is injured in a pitch invasion. **18** ICC accept all 24 recommendations of the Condon Report. Zimbabwe square series against India. **19** Steve Waugh takes his players off the field when a firework lands near Brett Lee at Trent Bridge. **21** England lose their 11th successive one-day international. **23** Michael Bevan is hit on the face by a beer can after Australia win the NatWest Series final at Lord's. Heath Streak resigns as captain of Zimbabwe, moments before a one-day game against West Indies. **24** Streak resumes as Zimbabwe's captain. **26** Stewart meets the ACU.

JULY

1 Gupta fails to meet the ACU's deadline to provide a sworn testimony over match-fixing claims. **4** Australia are presented with the inaugural ICC Test Championship Trophy. **5** West Indies keeper Ridley Jacobs is suspended for "sharp practice" in Harare one-day international against India. **7** Australia's Karen Rolton hits a women's Test-record 209 not out at Headingley. **8** Jason Gillespie breaks Hussain's little finger as England lose to Australia by an innings at Edgbaston. England Women lose to Australia by nine wickets. **9** Malcolm Speed takes office as ICC chief executive. **10** Rain ruins an experimental inter-city tournament at Bristol. **11** Stewart is cleared of claims he accepted money from Gupta. Gloucestershire's unbeaten run of 19 knockout games is ended by Durham. **12** Mike Atherton accepts the England captaincy in Hussain's absence. **15** Holland beat Namibia in the ICC Trophy final. Arjuna Ranatunga and Aravinda de Silva cleared of match-fixing. **17** Canada beat Scotland in the ICC Trophy play-off for the third World Cup place. **21** At Lord's, Graham Thorpe's right hand is broken by Brett Lee. Wes Hall becomes president of the West Indies board. **22** Mark Waugh takes a record 158th Test catch as Australia beat England by eight wickets. **25** Australian Rod Marsh is appointed director of the ECB's new National Cricket Academy. **28** Australians bowled out for 97 by Hampshire. Fellow-Australians Mike Hussey and Darren Lehmann score 329 not out and 222 not out against Essex and Lancashire respectively. **29** Zimbabwe schoolboy Hamilton Masakadza becomes the youngest player (17 years 354 days) to hit a hundred on Test debut, against West Indies in Harare. Lehmann goes to 252, the highest score in Roses history. Phil Tufnell takes his 1,000th first-class wicket. **30** Zimbabwe declare at 563 for nine, their highest Test score. **31** New Zealand inquiry finds that Martin Crowe was "unfairly accused" by Gupta of taking money.

AUGUST

4 Australia win in three days at Trent Bridge to retain the Ashes; Steve Waugh tears a calf muscle. **7** Mark Waugh is cleared by ACB of receiving money from Gupta. **16** Hussain returns as England captain at Headingley; Gilchrist leads Australia in Steve Waugh's absence. **17** At Galle, Sri Lanka complete only their second Test win over India, who are without Tendulkar for the first time in 85 Tests. **20** Mark Butcher's 173 not out leads England to victory. **21** The Indian government refuse their team permission to play in Pakistan in the Asian Test Championship. **23** Steve Waugh returns to captain Australia at The Oval. **24** Waugh twins hit hundreds. Yorkshire win their first Championship title in 33 years. **25** Shane Warne takes his 400th Test wicket. Warwickshire's Mark Wagh reaches a triple-hundred at Lord's. **26** Darren Gough and Stewart opt out of England's Test tour of India. **27** Australia win the Ashes series 4–1. **28** Atherton announces he will retire at the end of the season. **30** Pakistan declare at 546 for three against Bangladesh, after five of their first six hit hundreds. **31** Pakistan win by an innings and 264 runs in three days.

SEPTEMBER

7 Gary Kirsten's double-hundred in Harare makes him the first batsman to score 5,000 Test runs for South Africa. In Colombo, against Bangladesh, Marvan Atapattu reaches his fifth Test double-hundred. Graeme Hick joins Sir Donald Bradman on 117 hundreds, and completes a full set home and away against the other 17 counties. **8** Mohammad Ashraful, on debut for Bangladesh, becomes the youngest player to score a Test hundred at 16 years 364 days, but Sri Lanka win by an innings and 137 runs. **10** In Harare, Andy Flower becomes the first wicket-keeper to hit a hundred in each innings of a Test. **11** Flower is stranded on 199 not out as South Africa beat Zimbabwe. Islamic terrorists attack New York and Washington. **13** New Zealand call off their tour of Pakistan and recall A team from India after Afghanistan is implicated by USA. **17** ICC move their October board meeting from Pakistan to Malaysia. **18** In Bulawayo, Jacques Kallis ends South Africa's series with Zimbabwe having spent 1,027 minutes at the crease in three unbeaten innings. **24** MPs urge England to cancel their 17-day visit to Zimbabwe. **26** Hansie Cronje appeals to Pretoria High Court against his life ban. ICC appoint Bob Woolmer to help the four Associate countries prepare for the World Cup. Yorkshire captain David Byas retires. **29** Former ICC president Jagmohan Dalmiya is elected president of the Indian board by 17 votes to 13.

OCTOBER

3 England win in Harare to end their losing streak of 11 one-day internationals; James Kirtley's action is queried by referee Naushad Ali. **5** Sri Lanka's one-day series in Pakistan is cancelled. **7** Hussain, James Foster and Andy Flower are reprimanded after heated exchanges during England's third win at Harare. **11** Kirtley's action is reported to ICC. Pakistan appoint Mudassar Nazar as coach. **12** Hussain queries players' safety in India because of war in Afghanistan. **13** England complete 5–0 win in Zimbabwe. **17** Cronje fails in appeal against his life ban. Kenya beat India by 70 runs in Port Elizabeth; ACU request a video of the game. **22** South Africa beat Kenya by 208 runs in Cape Town. Indian board clears Kapil Dev of match-fixing. **23** England players meet at Lord's and are given three days to confirm their availability for the Indian tour. Streak resigns (again) as Zimbabwe's captain and is succeeded by Brian Murphy. **24** Tendulkar and Ganguly break their own record one-day international opening partnership with 258 against Kenya at Paarl; India score 351 for three and win by 186 runs. **26** Five England players ask ECB for more time before committing to the Indian tour. **30** Caddick and Croft withdraw from the England Test party.

NOVEMBER

2 Zimbabwe issue Alistair Campbell a four-match suspended ban for comments interpreted as racist. **3** India's Virender Sehwag hits a hundred at Bloemfontein on Test debut; Tendulkar, with his 26th hundred, becomes the youngest to score 7,000 runs in Tests. **4** Shoaib Akhtar's action is reported to ICC by Sharjah tournament referee, Denis Lindsay. **5** Kallis is dismissed by Ashish Nehra after a Test record 1,241 minutes unbeaten. **12** In Dhaka, Bangladesh hold out for their first Test draw, against Zimbabwe, after five defeats. **13** England fly to India. **14** Sacked Lancashire captain John Crawley threatens legal action if the county refuse to release him. Durham's Riverside ground is awarded Test status from 2003. **19** Referee Mike Denness penalises six Indian players for offences during the Second Test at Port Elizabeth: Tendulkar for interfering with the ball (one-match ban, suspended), Ganguly for not controlling his players and conduct unbecoming of a captain (one Test and two one-day internationals, all suspended), Sehwag for abusive language, dissent and attempted intimidation of an umpire (one-Test ban), and Shiv Sunder Das, Deep Dasgupta and Harbhajan Singh for excessive appealing (one Test, suspended); fines are also levied. **20** India threaten to withdraw from the Third Test at Centurion unless Denness is removed as referee. **21** ICC back Denness; South Africa support India. **22** ICC withdraw the Test status of the Centurion match after South Africa refuse Denness access. **23** South Africa and India commence an "unofficial Test", with Sehwag omitted. **27** ICC ask India to confirm by November

30 that Sehwag will not play in the Mohali Test against England on December 3. In Centurion, the Indians lose by an innings. **28** India's selectors include Sehwag in their 14 for Mohali; England confirm they will not play in a match lacking ICC status. **29** ICC extend their deadline to India. Brian Lara's century in the Third Test at Colombo takes him past 7,000 Test runs. **30** India agree not to play Sehwag at Mohali.

DECEMBER

1 For the first time since 1938, Australia concede four hundreds in a Test innings, against New Zealand at Perth. **3** Lara follows a first-innings double-hundred with another century, but Sri Lanka still win by ten wickets to complete a 3–0 whitewash. **4** Australia and New Zealand finish 0–0 after the Third Test is drawn. **6** India beat England by ten wickets at Mohali. **7** Pakistan announce Shoaib Akhtar's action has been cleared a second time by the University of Western Australia. **8** In Colombo, Sri Lanka dismiss Zimbabwe for 38, the lowest-ever in one-day internationals; Chaminda Vaas's eight for 19, the best for any country, includes Sri Lanka's first one-day hat-trick. **11** Thorpe returns to England because of marital problems as the Second Test starts in Ahmedabad. **15** In a one-day international at Kandy, Lara fractures his arm diving to regain his ground. Lehmann becomes the highest run-maker in Australian domestic first-class cricket. **18** Australia beat South Africa in First Test at Adelaide by 246 runs. **19** Michael Vaughan is out handled the ball on the first day of the Bangalore Test. **20** Anil Kumble takes his 300th Test wicket. **23** India win series 1–0 after drawing the Third Test. **26** Zimbabwe captain Murphy stands down ahead of the Colombo Test and is replaced by Stuart Carlisle. **28** In Melbourne, Steve Waugh is fined for dissent. **29** Australia beat South Africa by nine wickets in the Second Test. New Zealand beat Bangladesh by an innings in Wellington, their eighth defeat in nine Tests. **31** Sri Lanka beat Zimbabwe by an innings and 166 runs, their biggest Test win, and sixth in succession; Muralitharan finishes with 80 Test wickets in 2001.

The following were also among items reported in the media during 2001.

Peter Hain, leader of the "Stop the '70 Tour" campaign, laid himself open to prosecution for conspiracy, according to cabinet papers newly released under the 30-year rule. James Callaghan, then home secretary in the Labour government, told one cabinet meeting of the need to separate moderate opponents of the tour by South Africa – then still under apartheid – from "more radical elements... believed to have been in touch with extremist coloured organisations". Files in the Public Record Office also suggest that the government may have placed Hain and his co-campaigners under MI5 surveillance. The tour was eventually cancelled because of the threat of disorder, and England did not play South Africa again until 1994. Hain is now himself a Labour government minister. (*Western Mail*, January 1)

Anirudh Patnayak scored 364 for GLS against Diwan Balubhai in an Indian Under-19 schools cup tie; GLS totalled 638 in 90 overs and won by 549 runs. (*Times of India*, January 24)

A fraud trial in Devon was stopped after the judge revealed that he and one of the witnesses had once played cricket together. (*Express & Echo*, Exeter, January 25)

Tom Gueterbock approached the Wisden.com website to help publicise the sale of his £495,000 home in Battersea, south London, which he thought might particularly appeal to Indian cricket fans. The address was 10 Dulka Road. (*Daily Telegraph*, January 26)

Readers of a British national newspaper voted "Ian Botham's heroics at Headingley" in 1981 as their No. 1 in a poll to find "Britain's 100 Most Memorable Sporting Moments". (*Observer Sports Monthly*, February)

Lynton and Lynmouth CC in Devon were "racking brains for fund-raising ideas to replace the roller and mower" when Christopher Ondaatje, the retired businessman who owns the nearby Glenthorne Estate, donated £100,000 to the club in addition to setting up a trust fund in its favour. The Lynton and Lynmouth players, he said, "embody everything that is good and noble about cricket in England". (*Daily Telegraph*, February 10)

Lester Allison, a 35-year-old South African PE teacher and inventor, sought sponsors to enable full-scale production of a cricket box fitted with coil springs which, he claimed, significantly lessened the impact if a player is struck by a ball in that region. He tested its effectiveness by repeatedly hitting himself in the groin with a bat. Duly emboldened, and dressed only in a jockstrap, he subsequently invited onlookers to bowl directly at the target, only to retire injured a few minutes later. (*Saturday Star*, Johannesburg, February 16)

An attempt to scale a wall and retrieve a lost ball from Arjuna Ranatunga's garden led to allegations by six students from Ahoka Vidyalaya School in Colombo that the former Sri Lanka captain, helped by his elder brother Prasanna and various aides, had beaten them up. Ranatunga later surrendered to police and was released on bail pending further investigation. (*Asian Age*, March 6)

Matthew Fleming, the Kent captain and great-nephew of author Ian Fleming, held a Bond Ball at London's Grosvenor House Hotel as part of his benefit year. An auction of 007 memorabilia raised £100,000. (*Sunday Telegraph*, March 18)

Pre-season preparations at Trent Bridge, tricky enough in the wake of recent floods, were further disrupted by frogs. Groundsman Steve Birks, hitherto distracted by ducks swimming on the square, discovered the frogs jumping out of water machines; he insisted his groundstaff put them into buckets and march them down to the Trent. They were "a bit slimy," he added, "but, then again, so are some of our players". The headline read: "I've toad you… now hoppit". (*Evening Post*, Nottingham, April 14)

Charlie Watts, the Rolling Stones drummer, nominated John Arlott's commentary of Jim Laker taking 19 wickets against Australia at Old Trafford in 1956 as one of his Desert Island Discs. (BBC Radio 4, February 25)

Jane Andrews, a former aide to the Duchess of York, was jailed for life for murdering her boyfriend, Tommy Cressman. She struck him on the head with a cricket bat and stabbed him in the chest with a kitchen knife after he said he would not marry her. (*The Guardian*, May 16)

Craig Edwards was dancing in the stands at the St John's ground, Antigua, celebrating South Africa's victory over West Indies in a one-day international, when a fellow spectator took exception, picked an argument and beat him to death. (*Gujarat Samachar*, May 4)

Stephen Speak, a teacher living in Downe, South California, carved a niche in the *Guinness Book of Records* by batting for 24 hours with only two 15-minute breaks. Sponsored by America's Junior Cricketers' Association, he faced 12,353 balls. (*Gujarat Samachar*, May 5)

A Hurstpierpoint tail-ender, Joe Andrews, sent a slow half-volley from an obliging Ardingly College bowler over long-on for what appeared to be the winning six off the final ball of a Langdale Cup tie. However, there was doubt whether the ball bounced on the line or marginally in front. The umpires admitted their confusion, and so the teams, in the interests of the game's "true spirit", agreed to a replay. (*Mid Sussex Times*, May 10)

Brothers Tom, 22, and Ben Tebbutt, 26, both claimed hat-tricks for West Bridgfordians in a South Notts League match against Farndon, the latter completing the feat when, as captain, he brought himself on for a single over. All six victims were bowled. Peter Wynne-Thomas, the Nottinghamshire CCC historian, could recall only one parallel, by the Barnard brothers in a 1954 house match at Cranleigh School, Surrey. (*Evening Post*, Nottingham, May 10)

Garnet White, a 21-year-old Jamaican making his debut for Parley CC Second XI against Puddletown in the Dorset League, hit 173 not out then took eight for one, all bowled. Ian Belt, the opposing captain, described the experience as "pretty terrifying". (*Daily Telegraph*, May 17)

Mark Nicholas, the former Hampshire captain who presents Channel 4's cricket coverage, chased a youth whom he believed to have stolen a mobile phone. Nicholas was attacked with a dog chain, and his face and head wounds required 22 stitches. It did not stop him introducing the Test match. (*Daily Telegraph*, May 18)

The Belgian Cricket Federation has appointed a child protection officer. The federation stresses that this does not imply the existence of any form of abuse within the game. (*CricInfo*, May 17)

Tom Matthews, a 15-year-old schoolboy playing for Fakenham Third XI, bowled out Snettisham's Second XI with figures of 3–2–4–10. The four, a dropped slip catch that sped to the rope, constituted Snettisham's only runs. Under West Norfolk League rules, Matthews would have been restricted to five-over spells. (*Eastern Daily Press*, May 29)

Armed robbers, wielding a gun and a machete, stole jewels and $4,000 in cash from the offices of the Guyana Cricket Board. They locked West Indies fast bowler Reon King in a toilet along with three employees, who eventually escaped when King kicked down the door. (Associated Press, May 29)

Bob Walker, 50, collapsed at the crease and died while batting for Lancaster Moor Hospital against Milnthorpe CC. Life-saving equipment in emergency ambulances across Cumbria was to be checked after a defibrillator unit failed to save him. (*Westmorland Gazette*, June 1)

Lob bowling was compulsory for one bowler on either side in a match at West Wycombe CC on June 10 between The Sherlock Holmes Society of London, and The P. G. Wodehouse Society (UK). The Sherlockians' challenge called for 1895 Laws to apply – on the grounds that Sherlock Holmes once declared: "It is always 1895." Five-ball overs and eight-inch wickets were duly restored. (*Plum Lines, The Quarterly Journal of The Wodehouse Society*, *Vol. 22 No. 3*, Autumn 2001)

Usman Tariq hit six sixes in an over for Whitefield against Tranmere Victoria in the Merseyside Competition but progress was slow. A dog in an adjacent park intercepted the first blow and returned the ball only after a lengthy debate; it was less forgiving two deliveries later, allowing a fielder to retrieve the ball, but then, as he returned to the field, nipping his hand. (*Daily Telegraph*, June 12)

Mohammad Azharuddin, the former captain of India now banned from international cricket for match-fixing, scored 39 at Ripley, Surrey, for the Bunbury XI in a charity match in aid of a children's ward at the Royal Surrey County Hospital. (*Sunday Telegraph*, June 24)

The penalties for "Unfair Play" incorporated in the 2000 Code of the Laws were first imposed, it appears, during a New South Wales second-grade competition match. When Lane Cove batted first against Roseville, the batsmen were warned repeatedly for running on the pitch; when two members of the lower order repeated the transgression in successive overs, both were penalised. Thus, before they began their innings, Roseville were already 10 runs in credit. (*The Observer*, July 1)

The Indian Test cricketer Venkatesh Prasad acted speedily when he saw a pedestrian knocked down by a hit-and-run driver in Bangalore. Picking up the comatose Nandish Rajesh from the side of the road, the Indian Test seamer waded through the crowd and then drove him to hospital, saving his life. (*The Times of India*, July 3)

Mohammad Qureshi was watching friends play cricket while perched on the parapet wall of his apartment in Ahmedabad when he dived to catch a soaring hit and plunged to his death. (*Gujarat Samachar*, July 8)

Asia's largest prison has removed the name of Manoj Prabhakar from one of its jail blocks. Cited during his heyday as a role model for inmates at Tihar jail in New Delhi, the former Indian Test all-rounder had been embroiled in the match-fixing scandal. (*Asian Age*, July 9)

Roy Higgins, the umpire, was left somewhat baffled as the identities of the principals in a match in Bradford between Yorkshire LPS and Amarmilan emerged: all 22 players, and a scorer, were named Patel. "Some of us are related," elaborated Chandu Patel, the Amarmilan secretary and medium-pacer. "We used to have a player called Mahmood, but he got married and only plays when we're very short." (*The Sun*, July 19)

A new MCC has been formed in Seattle, USA: the Microsoft Cricket Club mainly comprises Indian software engineers. (*The Guardian*, July 21)

Vicky Ball, 12, took five for 30 playing alongside the menfolk for Stone CC in a third XI match against Frampton on Severn. Asked about the England bowlers playing in the Ashes series, she said: "They bowled rubbish. They needed to pitch the ball up and bowl straighter." (*Gloucester Citizen*, July 24)

A pathologist said that Tertius Bosch, the former Natal and South Africa fast bowler, who died in 2000, aged 33, might have been poisoned. Dr Reggie Perumal examined Bosch's body after it was exhumed at the request of a private investigator hired by the family. Bosch apparently died of a rare muscular condition, Guillain-Barré syndrome, leaving a widow, Karen-Anne, and two sons. However, it was discovered that millions of rand had gone missing from Bosch's dental practice in the months while he was in hospital. Meanwhile, Henry Selzer, the attorney who helped wind up Bosch's substantial estate and later became Mrs Bosch's lover, claimed to be suffering from the symptoms Bosch endured before his death. (*Natal Witness*, August 7)

Stuart Jeffrey, who had travelled 9,000 miles from Perth to watch the Headingley Test, hired a 40ft crane to watch the game after learning that the ground was sold out. (*Yorkshire Post*, August 18)

The inaugural tussle for the Hambledon Indigenous Peoples' Cup, played at Hambledon between the Down-Unders, an Australian aboriginal side, and the LA Krickets, a team of underprivileged black American youths, culminated in a vaguely familiar ceremony.

The ball, together with a boomerang, was burnt and the base of the trophy, won by the Down-Unders, filled with the remnants. It will reside, none the less, at Hambledon. (*Sunday Telegraph*, September 9)

Howzat, an educational CD-Rom sent to hundreds of primary schools by the ECB, contained a hyperlink supposed to lead to a South African equipment manufacturer. In fact, it led to a pornography site operated by the Russian mafia. (BBC Radio 4, September 10)

Peter Roebuck, the writer and former Somerset captain, was given a suspended four-month jail sentence, and ordered to pay £820 costs, after being found guilty of assault causing actual bodily harm by caning three South African teenagers. Roebuck admitted that the incidents took place, but maintained he had never detected any unhappiness among the boys, who had come to him for coaching. "Obviously I misjudged the mood, and that was my mistake and my responsibility, and I accept that," said Roebuck. (Press Association, October 19)

Narcotics detectives intercepting a consignment of cricket bats in Ahmedabad discovered 25kg of high-grade Kashmiri charas stuffed inside the cavities. (*Times of India*, October 19)

Inspired by the thick gorse bushes surrounding their local ground at Scot Hay, Staffordshire, Ben Griffiths and Harold Stanier have trained their labradors to ferret around for lost balls: in two years, the four dogs have found every stray one – 120 this season alone. "The dogs are on their feet as soon as they hear the thwack of bat on ball," claimed Griffiths, who once took the new ball for Staffordshire. "We just shout 'fetch'." (*The Sun*, October 20)

Arjuna Ranatunga was elected to the Sri Lankan parliament for the People's Alliance, with the party's second-highest number votes in Colombo: 97,409. Reggie, Ranatunga's father and until recently a government minister, has been arrested in connection with the murder of an opposition supporter. (*Daily News*, Colombo, October 26)

Kepler Wessels demonstrated that his eye was as keen as ever by winning gold medals in tandem with his son at the South African archery championships, only eight months after taking up the sport. He said his ambition was to represent his country (presumably, South Africa) at the 2004 Olympics. (*Inside Sport*, November)

Michael Slater's discovery that he was not, after all, Australia's 356th Test player found the Australian Cricket Board in magnanimous mood, decreeing that the original miscalculation should stand. Brendon Julian, who also made his debut against England at Old Trafford in 1993 but did not take the field until the second day, remains the official No. 355. There were extenuating circumstances. Slater's car registration plate includes the number 356; and it is tattooed fetchingly on one of his ankles. (*Sydney Morning Herald*, November 9)

Victorian side Moonrooduc, known somewhat inevitably as "The Ducs", lived up to their sobriquet with a vengeance in a Mornington Peninsula sub-district firsts competition match against Tootgarook: six batsmen failed to score as they were bowled out for 10. (*The Age*, November 27)

Cricket balls have been banned on Indian internal flights as part of the post-September 11 security clampdown. British Airways have banned bats on flights to the United States. (*Wisden Cricket Monthly*, January 2002)

CRICKET BOOKS, 2001

By FRANCIS WHEEN

Many authors have been cricketers, from Lord Byron and John Keats to Samuel Beckett and Sebastian Faulks. I have myself played in sides that included Martin Amis, Julian Barnes, Ian McEwan and David Hare. Yet remarkably few of these padded-up literati have written about the game, except in all-too-brief essays such as Harold Pinter's lovely tribute to Arthur Wellard and V. S. Naipaul's account of the 1963 Lord's Test. Do they feel that it isn't a fit subject for Great Literature?

At first sight, Eric Midwinter's scholarly and enjoyable new collection of essays, **Quill on Willow: Cricket in Literature**, seemed likely to disprove my thesis. "Probably no sport has so much fictional prose and poetry based upon it as does cricket," Professor Midwinter writes in his introduction. As he quickly concedes, however, most of these works are mere schoolboy yarns or doggerel. From the groaning shelves of "cricket fiction", only one book – Hugh de Selincourt's *The Cricket Match* – has the style and literary quality to transcend the ostensible subject. The same is true of verse: "At Lord's" by Francis Thompson could justifiably be included in any anthology of English poetry, but it's hard to think of many other candidates. When cricket does appear in serious literature, it has no more than a cameo role – usually as a metaphor (John Galsworthy's *The Man of Property*) or a device for moving the plot forward (L. P. Hartley's *The Go-Between*, later turned into a screenplay by the cricket-mad Pinter). True, there are references to cricket in James Joyce, but no more than a few paragraphs. As Eric Midwinter notes, "The prospector for the gold-dust of cricketing allusions in classical literature soon learns to count his blessings in tiny specks." Drama is even more barren. Although almost all the first-rate British playwrights of the past 80 years have been passionate about the game, scarcely any has written about it, the rule-proving exception being Terence Rattigan, who wrote the script for that sadly stilted film, *The Final Test*.

Even Ramachandra Guha, editor of the latest upmarket anthology, thinks that the term "cricket literature" may be an oxymoron. "**The Picador Book of Cricket** is both homage and epitaph, a tribute to the finest days of the game and an acknowledgement that the great days of cricket literature are behind us," he writes in his melancholy introduction. "There was a time when major English novelists or poets – P. G. Wodehouse, Arthur Conan Doyle, Francis Thomson [*sic*], Alec Waugh and numerous others – took time off to play and write about cricket. Now they are more likely to celebrate football (as with Nick Hornby and Ian Hamilton) or accept commissions to report on Wimbledon (like Martin Amis)."

How odd, then, that Wodehouse and the rest are unrepresented in Guha's own book. He might argue that he wanted to make room for newer voices such as Scyld Berry on Botham, Mike Marqusee on the 1996 World Cup final and Matthew Engel on Colin Milburn. Apart from these welcome additions to the canon, however, this is a deeply traditional selection, with no fewer than seven essays by Neville Cardus. (Am I alone in finding Cardus's exaggerated stylistic flourishes indigestible these days?) Guha claims that his intention was "to challenge the self-centred chauvinism of previous collections of cricket literature, [which] have tended to underrepresent writers as well as players from lands other than England". Yet there's almost nothing from the Caribbean, except for the inevitable and admirable C. L. R. James, and very little from Guha's own Indian subcontinent: brief contributions by Suresh Menon, N. S. Ramaswami and Sujit Mukherjee are scarcely visible amid the endless acres occupied by Ray Robinson, J. H. Fingleton and Cardus.

Still, one shouldn't be too curmudgeonly about a book which ends with Rowland Ryder's evocative essay on "The Pleasures of Reading *Wisden*". Rightly arguing that *Wisden* "is as exciting as a Buchan thriller", Ryder suggests that "Sir Arthur Conan Doyle, who played for the MCC and for Sussex, who had 'W.G.' as one of his victims, and who wrote 'The Missing Three-Quarter', might well have written a cricket detective story entitled, say, 'The Missing Mid-On'." Yet the fact is that he didn't. Once again the question must be asked: why is there such a dearth of great cricket literature? If Howard Jacobson can conjure up a splendid novel about such a trifling game as table-tennis (*The Mighty Walzer*), why don't the creative impulses of Salman Rushdie and Tom Stoppard seize on cricket? Its resonant complexities ought to inspire any imaginative writer – loss and triumph, comradeship and conflict, greed and generosity, the tragic and the absurd. Add to that rich brew such geopolitical biggies as nationalism, commercialism and globalisation, and you have enough to satisfy even the most demanding Booker Prize judge.

Journalists have certainly risen to the challenge. "For sheer depth and variety, if not always accuracy and impartiality, the way the game is reported in today's newspapers could scarcely be bettered," Rob Steen writes in the fifth volume of **The New Ball**, cricket's answer to *Granta*. "Books, allegedly, are another matter. In recent years the quality and clarity of writing and ideas – particularly on the Engulf-and-Devour shelves of W. H. Smith – are perceived to have slipped, even slithered. Pot-boilers, mono-dimensional autobiographies and sepia-toned reminiscences rule, OK." Steen himself has defied this received wisdom by inviting Richie Benaud, Ted Dexter, Kevin Mitchell, Simon Wilde and many others to nominate their favourite cricket writers. Cardus, Fingleton and Robinson are there, of course, but so are Peter Roebuck and Scyld Berry. It is an impressively varied and hugely enjoyable collection: Mike Marqusee's enthusiasm for Major Rowland Bowen sent me scurrying off to re-read *Cricket: A History of its Growth and Development Throughout the World*, while R. C. Robertson-Glasgow's short profile of Lord Tennyson (chosen by David Foot) made me wonder why no one had yet written a full-length study of this irresistibly boisterous cricketer, grandson of the poet.

Lo and behold, there in my tottering pile of new books was **Lionel Tennyson, Regency Buck: The Life and Times of a Cricketing Legend** by Alan Edwards. For once, that overused word "legend" is no overstatement. Tennyson was a hard-drinking, hard-gambling womaniser who seems to have come straight from the pages of a Flashman novel: wounded three times and reported dead twice in World War I; asked to resign from White's Club over a backgammon scandal; cited as co-respondent in an aristocratic divorce. As captain of Hampshire, he employed the wicket-keeper, Walter Livsey, as his butler. When Tennyson was palpably out in a charity match, the hapless Livsey (who had been drafted in as emergency umpire) could not bring himself to utter the dread word, taking refuge instead in the phrase he had often used when answering the door to creditors and cuckolded husbands: "I regret his Lordship is not in."

Though he may have been a playboy, Tennyson was no dilettante: even when batting after an all-night session at the card tables he played with fearsome skill and pugnacity. Having injured a hand while fielding in the 1921 Headingley Test against Australia, he proceeded to bat one-handed and scored an astonishing 63. In one of his last appearances at Lord's he bet a bottle of champagne that he would score a hundred; having already reached 73 by lunchtime he claimed the bottle in advance, drank it and then returned to the crease to complete the century. But his greatest feat of Bothamesque heroics occurred at Edgbaston in 1922, when Warwickshire made a first-innings total of 223 and skittled Hampshire out for just 15 runs in 53 balls. Undaunted, Tennyson announced with sublime confidence that his men would score at least 500 following on – which they did, thus setting up perhaps the most extraordinary victory in the history of the County Championship.

Lionel Tennyson was one of the few English cricketers of his generation to earn the respect of Warwick Armstrong, another man who can fairly be described as a legend, and indeed a giant (six feet three inches, and weighing 20 stone by the time he retired). Yet, like so many legends, Armstrong is also largely forgotten. In England these days, if he is remembered at all, it is probably for the farcical rumpus at Old Trafford in 1921, when he invoked Law 54 to prevent Tennyson from declaring the England innings closed, and then managed to bowl two consecutive overs without the umpires noticing. In the eight decades since he retired, the all-rounder who was commonly known as "the W. G. Grace of Australia" has inspired only one brief monograph. He was not even considered for the Australian Team of the Century, picked a year or so ago by an allegedly expert panel; nor does he get more than a passing mention in **Bradman's Best: The World's Greatest Cricketer Selects His All-Time Best Team**, an over-hyped stew of leftovers cooked up by the Don's faithful amanuensis, Roland Perry. In a 1998 essay marking Bradman's 90th birthday (included in *The Picador Book of Cricket Writing*), Gideon Haigh observed that "Sir Donald Brandname" had become a kind of universal marketing tool, and Perry's book is a perfect example of what he meant. Haigh did not wish to belittle Bradman's achievements, merely to point out the damaging effect of his subsequent canonisation and commodification. As C. L. R. James might have said: what do they know of cricket who only Bradman know? Or, as Haigh asked, "where are the home-grown biographies of Charlie Macartney, Warwick Armstrong, Bill Woodfull, Bill Ponsford, Lindsay Hassett, Keith Miller, Neil Harvey, Alan Davidson, Richie Benaud, Bob Simpson, even Ian Chappell and Dennis Lillee, plus sundry others one could name? Such is the lava flow from the Bradman volcano, they are unlikely to see the daylight."

Not quite. Haigh has now proved himself wrong by producing **The Big Ship: Warwick Armstrong and the Making of Modern Cricket**. This is not so much a great cricket book as a great book *tout court*. Through his previous work, most notably *Mystery Spinner: The Story of Jack Iverson*, Haigh has already shown himself to be a biographer of enviable wit and sensibility, with an appetite for thorough archival research and a talent for teasing out the social, psychological and political significance of his subjects. Even those who have never heard of Warwick Armstrong will find it hard not to read on, enthralled, as Haigh brings his sleeping giant to rumbustious life. The book is unflaggingly vivid and perceptive. Better still, while restoring Armstrong to his rightful place of honour in the game's history, it is wholly free of hagiography.

This is a rarer achievement than you might think. The writers of cricket lives, by and large, have been unaffected by the progress of the art of biography over recent decades, preferring to turn out the sort of flat, reverential doxologies that went out of fashion in other fields half a century ago. For a typical specimen of the genre, look at Alan Hill's **The Bedsers: Twinning Triumphs**. Thanks to its euphemistic attempts to play down the twins' less appealing characteristics, this is a book that could be read with pleasure only by devoted Bedser-worshippers or Surrey fans – though true Surrey *aficionados* may well prefer to spend their birthday book tokens on David Sawyer's **A Century of Surrey Stumpers: The History of Surrey Wicketkeepers**, a *magnum opus* of such dementedly specialised scholarship that even an Essex man such as myself can scarce forbear to cheer. Anyone who has donned the gauntlets for even an over or two qualifies for Sawyer's hall of fame: hence the inclusion of Alex Tudor, who had a brief stint behind the stumps on the final day of the 2000 season.

Gideon Haigh, by contrast, revels in the cussedness and contrariness of his man, suggesting that there was "something compelling about him, as there often is about dictators, autocrats, those who act on their own impulses, and above all *do not care*". Flourishing in what cricket historians now call the Golden Age, supposedly the high summer of amateurism and chivalry, Armstrong "played as a professional when it suited and was not averse to overt gamesmanship, verbal aggression, intimidation of umpires, disputation over playing conditions, even cheating the odd batsman out". Sometimes he went further than any modern cricketer would dare: a nervous young batsman on his Test debut was once kept waiting 18 minutes for his first ball while Armstrong bowled practice deliveries towards the boundary. On another occasion, he proposed to the Australian Board of Control that his team should deliberately win matches more slowly to increase the gate receipts, the idea being that the players and the board would split the extra profits.

Despite his bolshiness – or, more likely, because of it – Armstrong was a very Big Ship indeed, and I hope that this book will rescue him from the ocean floor to which he has been consigned these many years. Yet even if he hadn't been such a fine player and formidable influence on the development of the modern game, Armstrong's sheer force of character would make him a fit subject for biographical study.

They also serve who only stand at third man for a couple of county matches. As readers of *Wisden* will know, the brief obituaries of obscure players can be just as riveting as, say, the account of Mark Butcher's heroics at Headingley. Ronald Mason's essay "Of The Late Frederick J. Hyland", which is Gideon Haigh's choice in the *New Ball* anthology, was provoked by just such a death notice in the 1965 Almanack: "Hyland, Frederick J., who died in February, aged 70, played as a professional in one match for Hampshire in 1924. Cricket in this match was limited by rain to two overs from which Northamptonshire scored one run without loss. Hyland later earned a reputation as a nurseryman in Cheshire." There can have been few shorter first-class careers, but it elicited from Mason a beautiful meditation on Frederick J. Hyland as an epitome of the life of man as described by the Venerable Bede – the sparrow flying into the banquet-hall, fluttering for a moment in the light and heat, and then flying forth at the far door into wintry darkness. Hyland, too, disappeared into impenetrable night (or Cheshire, which is much the same thing). But, as Mason remarked, for all his life he had one comfort that nobody could ever take away from him: he had been in a first-class match while registrable balls (all 12 of them) were bowled. "He walked the field, he played, and *Wisden*, forty years after, thought it proper to recall it. I am glad that it did."

In his preface to Mason's essay for *The New Ball*, Haigh concedes that it may not be the finest example of the game's literature. "Yet it remains to me as fresh, charming and enticing as when I first encountered it… The theme captivated me, and still does. Cricket is still wedded to the Great Man Theory of History. Yet I feel an instinctive and abiding affinity for the teeming multitudes of Frederick Hylands; now, perhaps, more than ever, as publishing houses annually spew forth such adoxographic swill as *Sir Vivian* and *Bold Warnie* in a great cloacal stream." To judge by the recent vogue in the general non-fiction market for short biographies of forgotten figures from the margins of history – obscure inventors, adventurers, loners and misfits – many readers now realise that also-rans are often more interesting than megastars. And this is certainly true of cricket. One of the most moving books I have read in the last year is **Fragments of Idolatry**, a collection of "character studies" by the veteran reporter David Foot. In earlier titles such as *Harold Gimblett: Tormented Genius of Cricket* (1982) and *Cricket's Unholy Trinity* (1985), Foot has revealed his fascination with talented but troubled personalities. "It is true," he admits in the introduction to *Fragments of Idolatry*, "that I have been inclined to study complex, unfulfilled and, in some cases, sad people. This is a different collection."

Not all that different, his admirers will be relieved to learn. R. C. "Crusoe" Robertson-Glasgow, the subject of chapter one, wrote joyously, wondrously, about the absurdities of both life and sport. But he was also a manic depressive whose "inner wretchedness" condemned him to domestic isolation or, on several occasions, lengthy stays in mental hospitals; he first tried to take his own life in the early 1930s, and eventually succeeded in the spring of 1965. Foot points out that Crusoe was a friend of Harold Gimblett, another man with a talent for bringing happiness who nevertheless found life ultimately unbearable. "Their suicides, which I suspect they mutually contemplated, when Robertson-Glasgow returned to Somerset a cricket correspondent and unfailingly hunted out Gimblett, were similar in method and medical background." There is also a sympathetic though unsparing portrait of the cricket correspondent, Alan Gibson, whose wit and erudition were all too often eclipsed by alcoholism, depression and a terrible temper. "Some nights he never came home," his first wife recalled. "Once he turned up in Manchester and said he couldn't remember how he got there. And this was in the first year of our marriage." After a prosecution for drunk-driving in 1963 he tried to kill himself with an overdose of barbiturates. Fittingly enough, he spoke at Harold Gimblett's memorial service.

Sad stories often make great literature – and nothing I read last year was sadder or more engrossing than David Frith's **Silence of the Heart: Cricket Suicides**. This is a reworked and enlarged version of *By His Own Hand*, the 1990 book in which Frith investigated the lives of no fewer than 80 cricketers who had killed themselves; 11 years on, he has discovered a further 70 case histories. Its thesis can be summarised statistically: 1.77 per cent of all English Test players have taken their own lives, as against a rate in the general UK population of 1.07 per cent. If you include Test cricketers from Australia, New Zealand and South Africa, the proportion rises to 2.7 per cent.

Behind those bleak figures are dozens of individual tragedies. Frith recalls talking in 1979 to Jim Burke, the former Australian opening batsman, who seemed his usual breezy, chirpy self; yet within a month Burke had bought a shotgun, written a farewell note and turned the gun on himself. From eminent Victorians and Edwardians (such as Drewy Stoddart, who shot himself 20 years after leading England to a famous Ashes victory) through to painfully recent examples such as David Bairstow, Danny Kelleher and Mark Saxelby, the roll call continues unabated – and apparently unaffected by changes in the game's organisation and rewards.

Why cricket? Despite his profound research, Frith isn't sure. One tentative theory he advances is that the game attracts those who are highly strung anyway – people who thrive on risk and uncertainty, which in extreme cases can dislocate the soul. "Matches, big or small, take a long time to unfold. Perhaps having endured a long journey to the ground, a batsman can stand for hours in the field envisaging what fate might await him… Is it not likely that years of this sort of apprehension have a lasting effect on personality?" Another possibility is that what in boyhood seems an alluring cocktail of sunshine and fresh air, skill and heroism, can eventually destroy its practitioners when ambition dies and fellowship comes to an end. The typical professional leaves the game – or is ejected from it – by the age of 40. How does he restart his life when contemporaries in more normal trades are already well established in their occupations? By then, the years of absence from home may also have taken their toll on his family life and sobriety.

In a foreword, Mike Brearley says he always used to believe that cricket, more than any other sport, teaches people to cope with grief. "For a batsman, getting out means leaving the arena altogether and being *hors de combat* for hours or days – a symbolic loss or death. In this way cricket helps us, I imagine, to learn to accept the pain of loss. One might have thought that such a process of emotional learning would be a source of strength to the cricketer." But, he adds, Frith's magnificent and moving study has forced him to reconsider that opinion.

Silence of the Heart is one of the very few cricket books published recently that will, I'd guess, still be discussed ten years hence, even if the forbiddingly gloomy subject ensures its permanent exclusion from the bestseller lists. These, as ever, are dominated by the "adoxographic swill" of ghosted autobiographies that may solve the perennial problem of what to give Uncle Jim for his birthday, but will never be read again beyond the end of next season. Indeed, one might ask if such memoirs can be read at all, in the normal sense of the word. Only a few pages into Darren Gough's **Dazzler** I was already exhausted by the breathless prose, and irritated beyond endurance by the ceaseless banter about "Corkie", "Chalky", "Caddie", "Stewie", "Knightie", "Oggie", "Vaughanie" and "Hickie".

The memoirs of Shane Warne – sorry, "Warnie" – are just as tiresome, and even flimsier. By page 200 he has already taken us through the story of his career, so the next 100 pages are padded out with his random thoughts on sledging, the art of captaincy and so forth. A chapter on "sponsorship" turns out to be little more than an extended free advert for the companies who have paid Warnie to endorse their products. Another has the inviting title "The art of leg spin" – one topic on which we'd expect the great spinner to have something instructive to say. But it's largely composed of platitudinous tributes to his mates and his wife.

I've always admired both Darren Gough and Shane Warne, as much for their cheerful exuberance as for their lethal talents. The characters who emerge from their autobiographies, however, are rather less endearing. Even when dealing with his acceptance of $5,000 in cash from an Asian bookie known as "John", to whom he later provided information about pitches and weather, Warne somehow contrives to present himself as an innocent victim. "I thought he was a wealthy man who liked a bet, who had won money on Australia in the past and wanted to express his thanks. I took it at face value… The idea that bookmakers might be trying to buy up cricketers could have come from a work of fiction. We also knew that there were some generous people in the sub-continent." (This feeble excuse is neatly satirised in **Warwick Todd Goes The Tonk**, Tom Gleisner's spoof diary of "Australia's most controversial Test cricketer". Explaining his own dealings with John the bookie, the imaginary Todd writes: "I thought I was being interviewed and that the bloke at the bar was a journalist. It was only when he offered to pay for the drinks that I became suspicious." Pure fiction, thank God.)

Even less convincingly, Warne claims that "in 1994 none of us imagined how aspects of the game might be corrupt. There were no whispers of anything untoward occurring in the world of cricket." This overlooks the fact that Dean Jones was offered (but refused) $45,000 from a bookie while Australia were visiting Colombo two years earlier. As Simon Wilde points out in **Caught: The full story of cricket's match-fixing scandal**, "all the Australia players had been warned to be on their guard following the approach to Dean Jones in Sri Lanka in 1992, a warning Jones believed everyone had taken 'on board'". As an avid gambler, Warne was an obvious target; yet he never suspected a thing, and seems quite indignant about all the media fuss. If nothing else, **Shane Warne: My Autobiography** should finally bury the myth that only Poms whinge.

Gough, meanwhile, feels obliged to remind us on almost every page that he is "a Yorkie", and proves it with plenty of that bellyaching for which his county is renowned the world over. Scores are settled with Ray Illingworth, David Byas and Fred Trueman ("I do not even think of him as a true Yorkshireman any more"). During one of his many moans about fellow-Yorkies, however, he adds that "I get very angry when it's claimed I don't care about Yorkshire. How many youngsters, not only in Yorkshire, have taken up cricket because they want to be Darren Gough?" A fair point, but one that ought perhaps to be made by someone other than the subject of the compliment.

When not grumbling or boasting, Gough also reveals a vicious vindictiveness far beyond the normal competitive aggression that any good player requires. He keeps a mental list of opponents against whom he will exact revenge, such as the Pakistan opener Wajahatullah Wasti. In Lahore preparing for the 1999 World Cup, Wasti took part in a practice match against England "and he got right up my nose. He behaved as if we were there for his benefit, not the other way round, strutting around as if he was Viv Richards. My response was: 'You're in the book. I'll have you one day.'" The chance came on the winter tour to Pakistan in 2000, when Wasti opened the batting for the Governor's XI in Peshawar: "I broke his hand in the third over of the match and he wasn't seen again on the cricket field... That's the way we Yorkies are." Quite so.

Though cricketing traditionalists may choose to interpret this as proof that standards of sportsmanship have declined alarmingly, Gough can at least plead in mitigation that he is actually maintaining one of the game's old (if ignoble) traditions. In his book *Back to the Mark*, published almost 30 years ago, Dennis Lillee boasted that "I bowl bouncers for one reason, and that is to hit the batsman... I try to hit a batsman in the rib cage when I bowl a purposeful bouncer, and I want it to hurt so much that the batsman doesn't want to face me any more." His fellow-warrior Jeff Thomson was even blunter: "The sound of the ball hitting the batsman's skull was music to my ears." Twenty years earlier, during MCC's tour to South Africa in 1956-57, Peter Heine was heard to snarl: "I want to hit you, Bailey... I want to hit you over the heart." Going even further back in history to the Victorian era, we ought to recall the terrifying fast bowler, Charles Kortright, who once berated a batsman for taking a stance with his left toe raised, explaining that he allowed no one but W. G. Grace to cock a toe at him. When the man refused to budge, Kortright blitzed the offending foot with yorkers until he broke it with a direct hit.

These examples are all cited in Simon Rae's lively new book, **It's Not Cricket: A History of Skulduggery, Sharp Practice and Downright Cheating in the Noble Game**, which sets out to demonstrate that many of the allegedly modern sins – sledging, ball-tampering, match-fixing, arguing with umpires, pitch invasions – are almost as old as the game itself. As W. G. Grace's biographer, Rae knows better than most that gamesmanship and commercialism have always been with us. Yet even this revisionist historian is sometimes ready to accept the received wisdom of cricket lore, notably in his account of how "in 1771 the Surrey cricketer Thomas 'Shock'

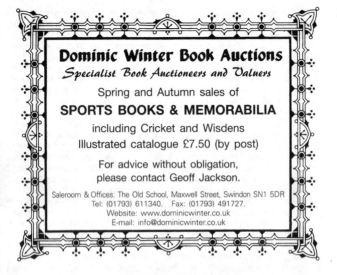

White caused shockwaves at Hambledon" by using a bat as wide as his stumps, prompting the Hambledon committee to pass a resolution limiting the width of the bat to four and a half inches.

The story has been told countless times, but it is untrue – as the awesomely diligent cricket historian John Goulstone reveals in his important new book, **Hambledon: The Men and the Myths**. The guy with the big bat was one Thomas White of Reigate and not the more famous "Shock" White of Brentford, who never played for or against Hambledon. Goulstone also demonstrates that the famous piece of paper regulating the width of the bat – signed by Richard Nyren, Thomas Brett and John Small of Hambledon – is "almost certainly a forgery". One wonders how the MCC authorities will react to this disclosure, given that the document is now one of the most treasured exhibits in the Lord's archive.

If cricket literature wishes to be taken seriously, it must aim for the same standards as other literature. This applies to cricket historians no less than cricket novelists or cricket poets: far too many of them repeat cherished old legends without bothering to check original sources. Goulstone is scathing about the new academic industry exemplified by Leicester University's "Centre for Research into Sport and Society", which, he argues, "leans too far towards an imaginative reinterpretation as opposed to factual reconstruction of the past". He is entitled to issue this rebuke, having spent years trawling through parish records, army lists, minute books, monumental inscriptions and contemporary newspapers: imaginative reconstructions are useful only if buttressed with research and evidence. An excellent example of the more scholarly approach is **Here's The Hambledon Club!: The Story of Hambledon Cricket Club 1796–2000**, Neil Jenkinson's interesting study of what happened after the classical glory days of Richard Nyren and his mates.

Hambledon was not "the Cradle of Cricket", despite the frequency with which this old cliché is still recycled. It owes its pre-eminence largely to John Nyren, author of *The Cricketers of My Time* (1833). As Jenkinson suggests, "Had Nyren chronicled Dartford or Sevenoaks Vine, both of whom boast ancient cricket grounds and long histories, they might have gained the glory, but thanks to Nyren it is the name of Hambledon which is known the world over as the place where cricket came of age." Many other "facts" about the club are exposed as fantasy by Goulstone's sleuthing. But I'm relieved to learn that even he can't challenge the authenticity of the Rev. Reynell Cotton's famous song, probably written in 1771 or 1772, celebrating the exploits of Nyren and Small. The confident message of the final stanza may be slightly dented by David Frith's ghastly chronicle of cricketing suicides, but it remains a noble aspiration:

And when the Game's o'er, and our Fate shall draw nigh,
(For the Heroes of Cricket like others must die)
Our Bats we'll resign, neither troubled or vex'd,
And give up our Wickets to those who come next.

Francis Wheen is a columnist for The Guardian.

ADDITIONAL REVIEWS

Graeme Wright writes: While cricket is rightly proud of its literary heritage, an even greater treasure is the people whose lives have been interwoven with the game. And yet, as Scyld Berry writes in his foreword to **At The Heart of English Cricket: The life and memories of Geoffrey Howard**, "We are all too good at taking things for granted." Fortunately for cricket, and happily for the reader, Stephen Chalke sat Geoffrey Howard down when he was still only 92 – and a young one at that, with his memories intact and his old letters from MCC tours to back them up. From post-war to pre-Packer, Howard saw and heard what was happening in the world of cricket: he was at The Oval as assistant-secretary and secretary, with 15 years as secretary at Old Trafford in between; witness to and victim of the conservatism and self-interest that still plague English cricket. In the 1950s, he managed MCC tours to India, Pakistan and Ceylon, Australasia and back again to Pakistan (the umpire-drenching tour). Chalke has taken Hutton's tour of Australia as the centrepiece of his tapestry and worked a wonderfully human, vital and intelligent narrative around it. After all, an England manager who signed a bill for 100 bottles of champagne when England won an Ashes series has a story to tell. Geoffrey Howard's is a gem.

Andrew Hignell's **Turnbull: A Welsh Sporting Hero** follows a more traditional biographical format. Nothing wrong with that, of course. Hignell, Glamorgan's honorary statistician and historian, is a thorough researcher and a sound writer. Heaven knows how today's generation of cricketers would cope with playing under a Maurice Turnbull, but Hignell has been careful not to go down that path. He keeps his subject in his context and his times, producing a rounded portrait of a young man true first and foremost to his family and his Catholic faith, passionate about sport, and a patriot. Turnbull captained Glamorgan throughout the 1930s, played nine Tests for England, went on MCC tours of Australasia and South Africa, and was an England selector; he was Wales's debut scrum-half in 1933 when they beat England (for the first time at Twickenham), and he also played hockey for Wales. In addition he was Glamorgan's secretary, and his fund-raising exploits to keep the club solvent were legion and legendary. But there's more to Hignell's story than Turnbull. There are the 1930s characters of cricket and the colourful lives they lived; the nights on the town and the nights in baggage cars or sleeping in luggage racks, hoping they'd bat next day. And at the last there is Turnbull's supreme sacrifice, killed in action at the age of 38. By 1944, Maurice Turnbull was more than merely a sporting hero. Andrew Hignell gets him just right.

Similarly, the publisher got **One Hundred Lord's Tests** just right. This is a celebration, not a determined history, and author Jonathan Rice has pitched the tone beautifully. Lord's can be a distracting place to watch cricket; there's so much going on in addition to the cricket. Rice captures that by letting incidentals and trivia have their time in the sun, while the generous selection of photographs, ancient and modern and handsomely reproduced, register the changes in cricketers, fashions and architecture. In keeping with a day at Lord's, there are also the time-honoured scorecards to remind you what happened – and what you missed while you were talking, or listening, or trying to put a name to the film star on the other side of the ground. The games are history, done and dust. But the magic of the old ground is timeless. This book never loses sight of that.

Two tour diaries give contrasting studies of a sub-genre. **Horan's Diary** wins by an innings, as might be expected with Frank Tyson as editor. It has a real flavour that the other lacks. In truth, the book is not a diary so much as Tyson's reconstruction from Tom Horan's scrapbook of clippings and comments on his 16 months with Australia's first "semi-representative" team, which toured Australia, New Zealand, England and America from 1877 to 1879. The language is a delight: rich in sobriquets, colourful, evocative and, in the case of W. G. Grace when he purloined Billy Midwinter at Lord's, "more pagan than parliamentary". More traditional robbery was prevented when "a dozen United States soldiers, armed to the teeth," joined the team's train at Cheyenne. "This was like the bushranging days in Australia," Horan noted with a touch of nostalgia. Dave Gregory, Charles Bannerman, Jack Blackham, Billy Murdoch, the Demon Spofforth and Harry Boyle (the "Very Devil") – they're all there, 12 in all, and they beat MCC at Lord's by nine wickets in a day.

On their return home, Gregory's side played Lord Harris's visiting Englishmen in Melbourne in January 1879. **The Diary of Vernon Royle**, a pale, slim volume compared to Horan's endeavours, gives that player's account of Harris's tour. Gerald Howat's scholarly introduction sets the cricketing scene, but Mr Royle is reluctant to paint it; on the evidence presented, the travelling interested him more than the cricket. Many a lunch and dinner are mentioned, but rarely a menu. In Adelaide, "Some of the other fellows turned up late, so the landlady calmly refused to let them have any dinner. This did not, of course, wash. I need hardly say they got it. The above will give one an idea of hotel life, at present, in Adelaide." Still, it's nice to know he went to see *Jack the Giant Killer* the evening before Tom Horan and his much travelled companions beat his Lordship's men, Royle included, by ten wickets.

Gerry Vaidyasekera, *Wisden's* Sri Lankan correspondent for many years, drew my attention to a new coaching book; in fact, a new kind of coaching book. It is by Ajith Perera, the analytical chemist and former umpire, who has been confined to a wheelchair since a horrendous accident shortly after his appointment to Sri Lanka's international panel. However, his circumstances are not why **Thinking Cricket** is an outstanding achievement. Amply illustrated, it has been carefully and thoughtfully conceived and executed to assist coaches, parents and players at all levels. Its 290 pages include 21 "subject areas" from the basic mechanics of playing, through to captaincy, discipline, physical conditioning, net practice, umpiring – choosing equipment, even. Importantly, Ajith Perera never underestimates the fact that cricket today is a mind game. As Dav Whatmore, Sri Lanka's national coach, writes in his foreword, the author's innovative, totally different approach to coaching books "provides encouragement and promotes sequential development of the required physical and mental skills, helping to turn weaknesses into strengths and potential into performance." In the hands of an English publisher, the book's design would doubtless have more style, but there would certainly be less content. *Thinking Cricket* concentrates on the content and never loses sight of what is required to make a cricketer – in every sense of the word.

BOOKS RECEIVED IN 2001

Note: The addresses for suppliers mentioned several times below are as follows:

Sportspages, Caxton Walk, 94–96 Charing Cross Road, London WC2H 0JW and Barton Square, St Ann's Square, Manchester M2 7HA.
Association of Cricket Statisticians (ACS)/Sport in Print, 3 Radcliffe Road, West Bridgford, Nottingham NG2 5FF.

GENERAL

Batty, Mike **Bill Bernau and the New Zealand Cricket Tour of England 1927** The Story of the First New Zealand Cricket Team to visit Great Britain (M. A. Batty, 49 Murville Drive, Bucklands Beach, Auckland, New Zealand, no price given, paperback. Limited edition of 99)
Blofeld, Henry **Cricket and All That** An Irreverent History Illustrations by John Ireland (Hodder & Stoughton, £14.99)
Craven, Nico **Cotswold Country Cousins** Foreword by Derek Hodgson Illustrations by Frank Fisher (published by the author, The Coach House, Ponsonby, Seascale, Cumbria CA20 1BX, £7.50, paperback)
Fine, Ron **Ashes to Ashes (1946–1987)** A Lifetime Passion (The Pentland Press, Hutton Close, South Church, Bishop Auckland, Durham DL14 6XG, £14.95)
Foot, David **Fragments of Idolatry** from 'Crusoe' to Kid Berg Twelve Character Studies (Fairfield Books, 17 George's Road, Fairfield Park, Bath BA1 6EY, £15 inc. p&p)
Frith, David **Silence of the Heart** Cricket Suicides Foreword by Mike Brearley (Mainstream, £15.99)
Goulstone, John **Hambledon: The Men and the Myths** Foreword by Robert Brooke (Roger Heavens, 2 Lowfields, Little Eversden, Cambridgeshire CB3 7HJ, £20 + £2 p&p, limited half-leather edition of 25 £150 inc. p&p)
Jenkinson, Neil **Here's the Hambledon Club!** The Story of Hambledon Cricket Club 1796–2000 (Downend Books, 20 Chilbolton Avenue, Winchester, Hampshire SO22 5HD, £14.99 inc. p&p, paperback)
MCC Cricket Library **Lord Harris's Team in Australia 1878-79** The Diary of Vernon Royle Introduction by Gerald Howat (MCC in conjunction with J. W. McKenzie, £21)
Midwinter, Eric **Quill on Willow** Cricket in Literature (Aeneas Press, £15.95)
Perry, Roland **Bradman's Best** The World's Greatest Cricketer Selects His All-Time Best Team (Bantam Press, £18.99)
Rae, Simon **It's Not Cricket** A History of Skulduggery, Sharp Practice and Downright Cheating in the Noble Game (Faber and Faber, £14.99)
Rice, Jonathan **One Hundred Lord's Tests** A Celebration of the Home of Cricket Foreword by Sir Donald Bradman (Methuen, £19.95)
Searle, Chris **Pitch of Life** Writings on Cricket Foreword by Mike Marqusee (Parrs Wood Press, £15.95)
Shuja-ud-Din and Khadim Hussain Baloch **Hussain's El Dorado** An Account of England's tour of Pakistan 2000-01 (Published by the authors, Little Court, Long Road East, Dedham, Colchester CO7 6BW, £9, paperback. Limited edition of 200)
Steen, Rob and McLellan, Alastair **500–1: The Miracle of Headingley '81** Foreword by Mike Brearley (BBC Worldwide, £16.99)
tehelka.com **Fallen Heroes** The Story that Shook the Nation Foreword by Tarun J. Tejpal (Buffalo Books, New Delhi, Rs350; in UK from Sportspages, £14.95)
Tyson, Frank ed. **Horan's Diary** The Australian Touring Team 1877–1879 (ACS, £45)
Wilde, Simon **Caught** The full story of cricket's match-fixing scandal (Aurum Press, £16.99)
Williams, Jack **Cricket and Race** (Oxford, £14.99, paperback)

ANTHOLOGY

Guha, Ramachandra ed. **The Picador Book of Cricket** (Picador, £20)
Headon, David ed. **The Best Ever Australian Sports Writing** A 200 Year Collection (Black Inc., Melbourne, no price given)

AUTOBIOGRAPHY

Gough, Darren with David Norrie **Dazzler** (Michael Joseph, £16.99)
Maynard, Matthew with Paul Rees **On the Attack** The Batsman's Story Foreword by Duncan Fletcher (Mainstream, £14.99)
Warne, Shane with Richard Hobson **My Autobiography** Foreword by Ian Botham (Hodder & Stoughton, £18.99)

BIOGRAPHY

Chalke, Stephen **At The Heart of English Cricket** The life and memories of Geoffrey Howard Foreword by Scyld Berry Illustrations by Susanna Kendall (Fairfield Books, 17 St George's Road, Fairfield Park, Bath BA1 6EY, £16).
Dhondy, Farrukh **CLR James** Cricket, the Caribbean, and World Revolution (Weidenfeld & Nicolson, £20)
Edwards, Alan **Lionel Tennyson: Regency Buck** The Life and Times of a Cricketing Legend Foreword by Mark Nicholas (Robson Books, £16.95)
Haigh, Gideon **The Big Ship: Warwick Armstrong and the Making of Modern Cricket** (Text Publishing, Melbourne, $A60)
Hignell, Andrew **Turnbull: A Welsh Sporting Hero** (Tempus Publishing, £19.99)
Hill, Alan **The Bedsers** Twinning Triumphs Foreword by Rt Hon. John Major (Mainstream, £15.99)
Lorimer, Rev. Malcolm G. ed. **Glory Lightly Worn** A Tribute to Brian Statham (Parrs Wood Press, £8.95, paperback)

REFERENCE

Couto, Marcus D. **236 Cricket Questions Answered** Foreword by Sunil Gavaskar (Ernest Publications, from Marine Sports, 63A Gokhale Road (North), Dadar, Mumbai 400 028, India, £8, paperback)
Franks, Warwick ed. **Wisden Cricketers' Almanack Australia 2001-02** Fourth edition (Hardie Grant, Melbourne, $A49.95; in UK from Sportspages and Penguin Direct, Bath Road, Harmondsworth, Middlesex UB7 0DA, tel: 020 8757 4036, £22.50)
Kazi, Abid Ali ed. **First-Class Cricket in Pakistan: Volume IV 1963-64 to 1969-70** (Pakistan Association of Cricket Statisticians and Scorers, 64/II, 20th Street, Khayaban-e-Badban, Phase 5, Defence Housing Authority, Karachi, Rs 300; in UK from Limlow Books, Blue Bell House, 2–4 Main Street, Scredington, Sleaford, Lincolnshire NG34 0AE, £30 inc. p&p)

STATISTICAL

Ambrose, Don comp. **1877: A Statistical Survey** (ACS, £6)
Bailey, Philip J. comp. **Sri Lanka First-Class Matches 1998-99** (ACS, £8.50)
Bassano, Brian **Aubrey Faulkner** His Record Innings-by-Innings (ACS, £4)
Garrod, Hugh **A. O. Jones** His Record Innings-by-Innings (ACS, £9.50)
Hudd, Gerald **Trevor Bailey** His Record Innings-by-Innings (ACS, £9.50)
Lodge, Jerry **Ken Barrington** His Record Innings-by-Innings (ACS, £7.50)
Rehmatullah, A. Aziz, ed. **Who's Who in One Day Internationals (1971–2001)** A Biographical Dictionary of One Day Internationals Cricketers (available from Ian Dyer Cricket Books, 29 High Street, Gilling West, Richmond, N. Yorkshire DL10 5JG, £13.99)
Sandiford, Keith A. P. **Wes Hall** His Record Innings-by-Innings (ACS £5.50)
Wilde, Geoff **Ernest Tyldesley** His Record Innings-by-Innings (ACS £8.50)

TECHNICAL

Hughes, Simon **Jargonbusting** The Analyst's Guide to Test Cricket Foreword by Mark Nicholas (Channel 4 Books/Macmillan, £12.99)

Perera, Ajith C. S. **Thinking Cricket** The Players' Guide to Better Cricket Foreword by Dav Whatmore Preface by Mike Brearley (Published by the author; in UK from Acumen Books, Audley, Stoke-on-Trent ST7 8DL, £12.95)

Potter, Jack and Mote, Ashley **The Winning Edge** The secrets and techniques of the world's best cricketers Foreword by Shane Warne (Parrs Wood Press, £12.95)

Roberts, David **The Cricket Coach's Guide to Man Management** (Castle Publications, £19.50)

COUNTIES

Hatton, Les **Worcestershire CCC: 100 Greats** Foreword by Tim Curtis (Tempus Publishing, £12, paperback)

Hignell, Andrew **Glamorgan CCC: Fifty of the Finest Matches** Foreword by Steve James (Tempus Publishing, £12, paperback)

Jones, Trevor **Doubling Up With Delight** Surrey's Twin Triumphs 2000 Foreword by Rt Hon. John Major (Sporting Declaration Books, PO Box 882, Sutton, Surrey SM2 5AW, £12.99 + £2 p&p, paperback)

Lambert, Dennis **Leicestershire CCC: 100 Greats** Foreword by James Whitaker (Tempus Publishing, £12, paperback)

Powell, William A. **Cricket Grounds of Surrey** (ACS, £7.50)

Sawyer, David **A Century of Surrey Stumpers** The History of Surrey Wicketkeepers Foreword by Alec Stewart (published by the author, 23 Bromley Crescent, Shortlands, Kent BR2 0HA, limited edition of 357, £18.95)

Surrey Statistics Group comp. **Surrey C. C. C. First-Class Records 1846-2000, Limited Overs Records 1963-2000** (Surrey CCC, £10.95 + £2 p&p)

Wynne-Thomas, Peter **Nottinghamshire Cricket Grounds** being a tour and survey of 463 past or present grounds in the County with a Ploughman's Lunch or two Foreword by Sir Dennis Pettitt (Nottinghamshire County Council; available from ACS, £8.50)

FICTION

Cattell, Bob **Down the Wicket** and **The Glory Ashes** in the Glory Gardens XI series (Red Fox/Random House, £3.99 each)

Coleman, Vernon **Around the Wicket** Edward Pettigrew's Diary of a Year at Little Lampton Cricket Club (Chilton Designs, Publishing House, Trinity Place, Barnstaple, Devon EX32 9HJ, £9.95, paperback)

Gleisner, Tom **Warwick Todd Goes The Tonk** (ABC Books, no price given, paperback)

Haselhurst, Alan **Eventually Cricket** More unpredictable performances from the Outcasts C.C. Illustrations by "Hoby" (Queen Anne Press, £16.99)

FIRST-CLASS COUNTY YEARBOOKS, 2001

Derbyshire £5, Durham £6, Essex £8, Glamorgan £6, Gloucestershire £5, Hampshire £8, Kent £4.99, Lancashire £8, Leicestershire £7.50, Middlesex £10, Northamptonshire £9.50, Nottinghamshire £7, Somerset £7.50, Surrey £5, Sussex £7, Warwickshire £5, Worcestershire £7, Yorkshire £14. 2002 prices may change. Some counties may add charges for p&p.

OTHER HANDBOOKS AND ANNUALS

Agnew, Jonathan ed. **Benson and Hedges Cricket Year 2001** (Bloomsbury, £20)

Bailey, Philip comp. **ACS International Cricket Year Book 2001** (ACS, £10.95)

Berry, Mike ed. **2001 Minor Counties Annual** (from Mike Berry, Idsworth, 3 Fair Close, Frankton, Nr Rugby, Warwickshire CV23 9PL, £5 + £1 p&p)

Bryden, Colin ed. **Mutual & Federal South African Cricket Annual 2001** (UCBSA/Mutual & Federal, PO Box 1120, Johannesburg 2000, no price given)

Il Cricket Italiano 2001: 20° anniversario (from Federazione Cricket Italiana, Via S. Ignazio 9, 00186 Roma)

Forty Club 2001 (from The Hon. Secretary, 133 Palace View, Bromley, Kent BR1 3EP)

Frindall, Bill ed. **Playfair Cricket Annual 2001** (Headline, £5.99)

Hatton, Les ed. **First-Class Counties Second Eleven Annual 2001** (ACS, £4.95)

Irish Cricket Annual 2001 (from Dr E. M. Power, 5 Strangford Avenue, Belfast BT9 6PG or via info@ulsterweb.com, £4 inc. p&p)

Marshall, Chris ed. **The Cricketers' Who's Who 2001** Introduction by Mark Butcher (Lennard/Queen Anne Press, £14.99)

Miller, Allan ed. **Allan's Australian Cricket Annual 2001** (from Allan Miller, PO Box 974, Busselton, WA 6280, $A45; in UK from Sport in Print, £21)

Payne, Francis and Smith, Ian ed. 2001 **New Zealand Cricket Almanack** (Hodder Moa Beckett, Auckland, no price given)

REPRINTS AND UPDATES

Arthur Haygarth's/Marylebone Club Cricket Scores and Biographies Volumes IX and X (1865–1866, 1867–1868) A continuation of Frederick Lillywhite's Scores and Biographies from 1772 to 1854. (Facsimile edition, from Roger Heavens, 2 Lowfields, Little Eversden, Cambridgeshire CB3 7HJ; limited edition of 500, £55 each inc. p&p)

John Wisden's Cricketers' Almanack for 1910, 1911 and 1912 Facsimile editions (Willows Publishing, 17 The Willows, Stone, Staffordshire ST15 0DE, fax: 01785 615867, e-mail: jenkins@willows17.fsnet.co.uk, £52 inc. p&p in UK, £2 extra overseas postage; £5 extra for facsimile of original hard cloth cover)

Lodge, Jerry **Jack Hobbs** His Record Innings-by-Innings Second edition, much expanded, of 1986 original by the late Derek Lodge (ACS, £8)

Miller, Allan ed. **Allan's Australian Cricket Annual 1987-88** First Edition (from Allan Miller, PO Box 974, Busselton, WA 6280, $A40; in UK from Sport in Print, £15)

Pollard, Jack **The Bradman Years** (The Book Company Publishing Pty Ltd, Austlink Corporate Park, 1 Minna Close, Belrose, NSW 2085, Australia, no price given)

Reminiscences of David Hunter The Genial Yorkshire Stumper Facsimile edition New introduction by Gerry Wolstenholme (Red Rose Books, 196 Belmont Road, Astley Bridge, Bolton BL1 7AR, £19.95. Limited edition of 200)

Turner, Herbert **The Life of John Briggs** Humorous and Pathetic Anecdotes, Astounding Feats with Bat and Ball in England, Scotland, Australia and Africa, Recollections of Eminent Cricketers Illustrated by "RIP" Facsimile edition New introduction by Gerry Wolstenholme (Red Rose Books, £19.95. Limited edition of 200)

P. F. Warner **Cricket Across The Seas** being an account of the tour of Lord Hawke's team in New Zealand and Australia, 1902-03 Facsimile edition New introduction and pen portraits by Gerry Wolstenholme (Red Rose Books, £23.95. Limited edition of 300)

PERIODICALS

The Cricketer International (monthly) ed. Peter Perchard (Ridge Farm, Lamberhurst, Tunbridge Wells, Kent TN3 8ER, £2.95)

The Cricketer Quarterly ed. Richard Lockwood (The Cricketer International, address as above, £3.25)

Cricket Lore (ten per volume, frequency variable) ed. Richard Hill (Cricket Lore, 22 Grazebrook Road, London N16 0HS, £35 per volume)

The Cricket Statistician (quarterly) ed. Philip J. Bailey (ACS, £2, free to ACS members)

The Journal of the Cricket Society (twice yearly) ed. Clive W. Porter (from P. Ellis, 63 Groveland Road, Beckenham, Kent BR3 3PX, £5 to non-members)

The New Ball (Volume Five): **The Right Type** ed. Rob Steen, (Sports Books Direct, 3 Luke Street, London EC2A 4PX, £9.99, paperback)

The New Ball (Volume Six): **Co-Stars** ed. Rob Steen (Sports Books Direct, £9.99, paperback)

Red Stripe Caribbean Quarterly ed. Tony Cozier (The Nation Publishing Co, Fontabelle, St Michael, Barbados; discontinued after November 2001 issue)

The Scottish Cricketer (three per year) ed. Mike McLean (36 Marywood Square, Glasgow G41 2BJ, £2)

Wisden Cricket Monthly ed. Stephen Fay (The New Boathouse, 136–142 Bramley Road, London W10 6SR, £2.95. Subscriptions: 01795 414895, e-mail: wisden@galleon.co.uk)

SELECTED LOCAL HISTORIES

Brooke, Derrick **Gone to Pott** Foreword by Peter Hancock (The Book Guild, 25 High Street, Lewes, Sussex BN7 2LU, £15.95)

Jones, Quentin **Pitch It Up** A Debut Season in Yorkshire Village Cricket (published by the author, c/o 97 Dinglederry, Olney, Buckinghamshire MK46 5EU; lurchbooks@lineone.net, £7.99 inc. p&p, paperback)

Sherlock, Harley **Villagers – Five Shillings** Sanderstead's transformation from agricultural community to London suburb, and its effect on the village cricket club Foreword by Lord Cowdrey of Tonbridge (The Bourne Society, 60 Onslow Gardens, Sanderstead, Surrey CR2 9AT, £4.50 inc. p&p, paperback)

Simm, Fraser **Saltire and Flannels** (published by the author, Stow, Borders, £5.99)

Turner, Gavin **A Century at Bath** Over One Hundred Years of Somerset County Cricket at the Rec (Broadcast Books, 4 Cotham Vale, Bristol BS6 6HR, £8.95, paperback)

THE CRICKET SOCIETY LITERARY AWARD

The Cricket Society Literary Award has been presented since 1970 to the author of the cricket book judged as best of the year. The 2001 award, sponsored by PricewaterhouseCoopers, was won by Gideon Haigh for **Mystery Spinner: The Story of Jack Iverson**. The shortlist for the 2002 award, sponsored by *The Daily Telegraph*, was: *At The Heart of English Cricket*, by Stephen Chalke; *Fragments of Idolatry*, by David Foot; *Hambledon: The Men and the Myths*, by John Goulstone; *Turnbull: A Welsh Sporting Hero*, by Andrew Hignell; *It's Not Cricket*, by Simon Rae; and *500–1: The Miracle of Headingley '81*, by Rob Steen and Alastair McLellan.

CRICKET AND THE MEDIA, 2001

By SIMON HEFFER

Having devoted itself the previous year to the untraditional subject of corruption, the press heralded the 2001 season with something more familiar: the weather. The front page of *The Times* on April 16 reported, after the wettest winter in living memory, that a plague of frogs had invaded Trent Bridge. Groundstaff were busy on the humanitarian exercise of collecting the frogs in buckets and dumping them in the River Trent. A number of ducks had also taken refuge, but at least they sounded as if they belonged there.

Barely had the season begun, though, than the media returned to business as usual: events off the field. On May 22, the *Daily Telegraph* revealed details of the inquiry into match-fixing under the banner headline, "Condon Report Exclusive". Its author, whom the *Telegraph* in a slippage of standards called "Lord Paul Condon", said: "I have spoken to people who have been threatened and others who have alleged a murder and a kidnapping linked to cricket corruption." Mihir Bose, whose exclusive it was, added that "some important figures remain fearful for their lives and investigators have had to take special precautions when interviewing them".

The next day, *The Independent* ran a leader entitled "Cricket needs to play a straighter bat". No one, it said, should be surprised. "The wages honestly earned by even top stars do not reach the stratospheric levels that make corruption in top-flight football or boxing hardly worth while." It added: "Punishment for those found guilty must be swift, sure and draconian." The paper's news story, headlined "Cricket brought to its knees by a tale of bribery, murder and match-fixing", led with the tale of Ashraf Patel, "shot in a Bombay street because of his love of betting on cricket". Derek Pringle gave a historical perspective, pointing out that cricket "only became organised in the first place as a means for wealthy 18th-century landowners to gamble". He also said that deals in the County Championship were "commonplace" when he played for Essex – usually sporting declarations followed by joke bowling in three-day matches. "But back-scratching of this sort is a very long way from the corruption within the international game that was exposed by the Hansie Cronje affair."

Maintaining his reputation for demolishing fences sooner than sit on them, the *Daily Telegraph's* Michael Henderson on May 24 branded Ali Bacher "international cricket's very own Vicar of Bray" for demanding punishment for transgressors but restoring Herschelle Gibbs, "granted the swiftest of absolutions", to the South African side. The *Telegraph* also revealed that an ICC "insider" had branded the Condon inquiry "a failure". Bose reported that inquiries will have to continue for years, and Imran Khan suggested in the same paper that "the cynic in me feels it [claims of death threats] could also be a convenient excuse to avoid answering unpleasant questions".

By early June we were back to something like cricket. "Second Test Disaster: Kicked in the No-Balls" screamed *The Sun* on June 5, with pictures of Wasim and Saqlain taking four wickets while overstepping (see page 413). Inside, the headline writer showed his form was no fluke, with "Saqcloth and Ashes". John Etheridge said, with remarkable prescience, that "if England bat like this against the Aussies, they have no flippin' chance". *The Guardian* was more restrained, running "No-ball fiasco clouds Waqar's triumph" along with the strapline "England victims of umpiring blind spot". *The Times* was somewhere between the two: "Finger of suspicion again falls on Waqar", with some seam-lifting pictures for good measure. Simon Hughes in the *Daily Telegraph* ("Waqar leads disgraceful intimidation") revealed that "as Graham Thorpe pointed out to Waqar Younis at one point: 'You can call me what you like between balls, but not when it's on its way down.' "

The one-day series, in which England failed to win a match, attracted attention for two other reasons. One was the ongoing debate about acting-captain Alec Stewart, and whether or not he would have his long-overdue meeting with Lord Condon over Indian bookmaker M. K. Gupta's allegation that he accepted his money. The other was about outbreaks of hooliganism at various grounds, notably Headingley, where steward Steve Speight was badly assaulted. This made the front page of several papers on June 19: "Cricket lunatics gave me a kicking" ran *The Sun*, in which Mr Speight described being "trampled underfoot by marauding cricket yobs". On the back page the headline was "Waugh: We're playing in fear".

On July 9, with England having been stuffed by Australia in the First Test, several papers linked it with Tim Henman's contemporaneous defeat in the semi-finals at Wimbledon when he had looked as if he was going to win. "Beaten, bruised and battered: Britain proves a lost cause" was the headline on Simon Barnes's piece in *The Times*. Adding the Lions' mauling by Australia the previous day to the cocktail of defeat, *The Sun* surpassed itself with "Crash, Bang, Wallaby". Mike Dickson asked in the *Daily Mail*, "Could it get any worse than this?" and answered his own question, "Yes, so just sit back and enjoy the tourists."

A fortnight later the story was much the same. On July 23, *The Times* referred to England's "Sunday roasting", using Wisden 20:20 graphics to show how much more frequently Australian bowlers beat the bat. *The Guardian* praised "McGrath the merciless", and all talk was of whitewash. Frank Keating was stern – "too meek, mild and bloody awful" – and Geoff Lawson called for the resignation of David Graveney. "He must surely throw himself on his sword now." Well, no.

Nor was it just on the playing field that the English seemed deficient. In the July 28 edition of *The Spectator*, Peter Oborne monstered *Test Match Special*, on the occasion of the Queen's turning up to present a cake to the programme. "It has," Oborne said, "lost the amiable inconsequence and the poetry that it used to possess." He was not the first to mourn the loss of Arlott and Johnston, whom he identified as "natural broadcasters". He praised Henry Blofeld, and rightly pointed out how the programme had suffered in 1999 when Blowers was recovering from his heart attack. Jonathan Agnew was, however, more than equal to the task in the next issue. "He might at least have done me the decency of researching the subject first," noted Aggers, in reply to Oborne's criticism that he had not extracted some laughs from Shoaib Akhtar's vomiting at the wicket. Shoaib was feared to have cancer, as Agnew pointed out. "How hilarious. What pure comedy." In fact, *TMS* had a better season than in 2000, with Graham Gooch coming on by leaps and bounds as a summariser, the Australian contingent well up to scratch, and no obsession with political correctness.

The loss of the Ashes stimulated the inevitable debate on the county system. Only Bob Woolmer, in the *Daily Telegraph* on August 7, made the sensible point about a return to three-day cricket to give Test players more chance of practice between matches. *The Sun* and the *News of the World* led the call to send MCC's priceless urn to Australia as the symbol of England's humiliation. The *Sunday Times* asked John Buchanan, the Australian coach, to write for them; he branded the county system "the true servant of mediocrity" – nothing new there – saying that each of the 18 counties had at least three "imposters" on their books. He urged an end to the benefit system and the removal of sponsored cars – though not, apparently, on the grounds that players might be fitter if they walked more often.

When England actually won a Test, the adulation of Mark Butcher, whose 173 not out was largely responsible, was unrestrained. Alison Kervin was sent by *The Times* to interview the "reformed bad boy" in an article headlined "Butcher mends his ways to carve out slice of stardom". However, none of the coverage of the victory was half so memorable as that of the various defeats; writers and sub-editors alike thrived on the mordant humour of doom and gloom.

The international unrest after the attacks on America on September 11 soon trickled down into cricket. The dodgy geographical grasp of many cricketers, who felt that India was as near to Afghanistan as Redhill is to Reigate, led to doubts about whether the England tour of India could go ahead. By October 16, panic seemed to have set in. "MacLaurin hints England tour is doomed", said the *Daily Telegraph*. *The Guardian* suggested a Caribbean tour might replace it. Ten days later, the *Telegraph* reckoned the "England tour hangs by a thread"; Mihir Bose said that Nasser Hussain would be relieved not to go. Next day the *Mail* said Croft and Caddick wouldn't tour, while the *Express* reported that Ramprakash would. On October 30, Mike Selvey in *The Guardian* wrote of a "tit for tat" mentality growing up in India. The volatile president of the Indian board, Jagmohan Dalmiya, had made it clear that if England didn't tour India, the Indians wouldn't tour England the following summer. Then Croft and Caddick confirmed their decisions not to go. Croft told the *Telegraph*: "I look forward to sleeping properly again after the most agonising few weeks of my 13 years in the first-class game." Given the excellent debut of Richard Dawson, Croft should be able to sleep for as long as he wants.

England's arrival in India did not end the uncertainty. After South Africa threw out Mike Denness for doing his job as match referee in the Centurion Test against India, the *Mail* on November 23 was apocalyptic. "It will throw the International Cricket Council into its biggest crisis since the mass defections to Kerry Packer's circus in the late seventies," wrote Graham Otway, adding that the move had been executed on the "direct orders of Thabo Mbeki," the South African president. The day before, Dicky Rutnagur in the *Daily Telegraph* had referred to "the oft-repeated argument that referees are more heavy-handed in dealing with the transgressions of Asian players and that there is racial bias in their attitudes". A day later the headline on

[*Courtesy of* The Sun

Gotcha! *The Sun's* take on cricket.

his piece was "Indian tour plunges into anarchy". Hendo went nuclear. "What a feckless, feeble bunch they really are, and how meekly they have acquiesced in the face of threats from the Indian Board of Control… the South Africans have wounded the game more than they know." Light relief came from Brigadier Munawwar Rana of the Pakistan board, who, in a magnificent flight of logic quoted in *The Times*, said that the Indians had not questioned the position of the referee, "only his decisions". Hmm.

The *Times of India*, by contrast, was remarkably sensible, and sensible in an immaculate English rarely seen in our newspapers these days. It spoke of the ICC's "sweet reasonableness backed by steely determination", and speculated that the BCCI's "fulminations" were "theatrical". With just four days to go to the Mohali Test, and an ultimatum issued to Dalmiya by the ICC about the picking of the banned Virender Sehwag, there was hardly a paper that did not have the word "brink" in its headlines. *The Times* (of London), reporting that Dalmiya had simply refused to meet the deadline, quoted Lord MacLaurin as saying that England "will not be playing against a team with a banned cricketer in it. We will not play a friendly Test match. We support the ICC." Christopher Martin-Jenkins rebuked Lord MacLaurin for getting involved "in the increasingly preposterous crisis", and criticised him for not being "shy of publicity". He contrasted MacLaurin's plain speaking with Tim Lamb's caution "in not showing his hand before he is asked to declare it". However, if anyone thought the ECB could ever have sanctioned any other course of action, then they were living in a parallel universe, and it was as well in these mealy-mouthed times that MacLaurin left no room for doubt.

In a really rather bloody year, *The Sun* had the best cricketing story. In June they doctored a number of old masters, including Rubens's *Judgment of Paris*, Titian's *Tribute Money* and Degas's *Young Spartans Exercising*, by inserting bats, balls and pads into them. They then asked Phil Tufnell to provide the commentary. On *Saint Jerome in a Landscape*, by Cima da Conegliano, the bearded saint appeared to be taking a catch low to his right. "What a fantastic catch in the slips, especially for an old fella like him!" Tuffers noted. "But it's a shame he wouldn't get an England call-up unless he had a shave."

GRANT AID FOR CRICKET, 2001

Since the National Lottery was launched in 1995, its Sports Fund has provided cricket with grants of more than £70 million towards projects costing over £119 million, money that would not have been available otherwise. Indeed, cricket has had more successful applications for grants (550) than any other sport, with clubs throughout the game receiving help to develop facilities. At first-class level, Yorkshire received a grant of £2.9 million in 2001 towards their £10 million redevelopment project at Headingley, while Nottinghamshire had a further £600,000 from the Sports Fund, plus £200,000 from the Safer Sports Grounds Programme, towards the building of the Fox Road stand. Both projects are scheduled for completion in 2002. Warwickshire and Sussex have also received the maximum £200,000 from the Safer Sports Grounds funds, available through Sport England, while MCC and six other counties obtained grants from this source in the 18 months to December 2001.

As far as the future of English cricket is concerned, the most important grant in 2001 was the £4 million from Sport England's World Class Fund for the National Cricket Academy at Loughborough University. The university already has two cricket grounds, along with sports science and sports medicine facilities; grants will help build a new indoor cricket centre and provide residential accommodation.

The Lord's Taverners, cricket's principal charity, work closely with the ECB to provide grant aid for schools and clubs with junior sections. Funding is available for non-turf pitches, netting, junior equipment bags, Kwik Cricket and Inter-cricket bags, as well as, from time to time, coaching and competitions. Application forms are available from all County Board development officers. The Taverners also fund sports equipment for young people with special needs, and each year they provide a number of specially adapted minibuses to organisations that care for young people with disabilities. Applications for these should be made directly to the Lord's Taverners.

A source of small grants, not exceeding £5,000, is Awards for All, and more than 800 cricket clubs have received £2.8 million this way. However, there are many other areas of funding, among them The Foundation for Sport and the Arts and the business-sponsorship incentive scheme, Sportsmatch, which has funded more than 300 cricket projects that focus on the grassroots. An ECB booklet, *Sources of Grant Aid for Cricket*, has recently been updated and is available to clubs looking for information on funding. It was compiled by Mike Turner, the former Leicestershire chief executive, who is available to provide clubs with free advice on grant aid. His phone number is 0116 283 1615.

CRICKET ON THE INTERNET, 2001

By LAWRENCE BOOTH

It was the best of times, it was the worst of times. The sheer breadth – and occasionally depth – of online cricket coverage continued to dazzle, but it did so against a dark backdrop of big-name dotcom bubbles bursting wherever you looked. Cricket, as usual, had taken a while to cotton on: for most websites, the year of boom and bust had been 2000; for much of the cricket community, the realities of a troubled medium only started to hit home in 2001.

The plight of CricInfo (**www.cricinfo.com**) served as the most alarming wake-up call. It remained the W.G. of its age, bestriding the internet like a colossus, and chalking up 1.5 billion page impressions in 2001 alone, which made it the most visited year-round single-sports site in the world. It also seeped further into the national consciousness by forking out £250,000 to sponsor the struggling County Championship for the summer. But the strain was starting to show. CricInfo had long since ceased to be the purely philanthropic venture of its early days, and was now a business trying to make ends meet in an unforgiving market. In August, it was forced to cut its staff by a third, from 135 to 90, and was put up for sale for £1 million, just 18 months after being valued at £100 million. The casual user wasn't overly inconvenienced – the daily e-mail newsletter disappeared briefly, while the quirky and entertaining review of cricket in its further reaches, "Beyond The Test World", made a more permanent exit – but the warning signs, like a persistent pop-up ad, refused to go away.

Channel 4's own site (**www.cricket4.com**) had problems too, despite starting the summer as the most innovative all-rounder on the web. Its refreshing novelty value was epitomised by a virtual Richie Benaud, still an icon in the commentary box, but now an icon of a different sort as well. Every time England lost another wicket or spilled another catch, a miniature Richie would stroll around your desktop, dryly uttering "Got 'im!" and "What a fiasco!" He would even open his umbrella to let you know that rain had stopped play. Elsewhere on the site, the lively chat room cemented its standing as the best-informed anywhere. But the end of the Ashes signalled a watered-down service: the budget was cut, and with it the staff.

Others weren't even as lucky as that. The best of the Australian sites, The Pavilion, dispensed with all but its outstanding editorial content, which once again became the sole property of its masthead brands, the *Sydney Morning Herald* (**www.smh.com.au**) and the *Melbourne Age* (**www.theage.com.au**). And the toast of India's online ventures, Total Cricket, fared even worse, going from diluted to completely liquidated with unnerving fluidity. It had started life as one of the most ambitious cricket projects anywhere: a huge injection of cash from businessman Mark Mascarenhas, and an array of columnists, most of whom would have been at home in an all-time World XI, promised much – and for a while delivered. But when Mascarenhas, along with Jagmohan Dalmiya, was accused of swindling India's state-owned TV company, Doordarshan, out of millions of rupees – charges which had yet to be proven – the funding dried up. Total Cricket hobbled on manfully with a staff of three, but uploaded its last page in July – another broken dotcom dream.

Throughout India, the story was only slightly better. Khel.com (**www.khel.com**) was taken over by Satyam Infoway, the first Indian internet company to be listed on the NASDAQ. Satyam had already bought a 25 per cent stake in CricInfo, and their pages now appeared with indecent regularity on Khel's once-autonomous site. Despite financial support from Kerry Packer, Cricketnext (**www.cricketnext.com**) was reduced to a skeletal staff, while a shortage of manpower meant **www.rediff.com** had to temper its ambitions too.

But if one or two ideals wilted in 2001, there was still plenty to get excited about. Doordarshan teamed up with Network of the World, an internet and digital-TV content service based in London, to form **www.ddnow.com** and broadcast live coverage of India's sensational series win over Australia. In offices all over the globe, cricket fans were able to take a few minutes – sometimes a few hours – away from their work to watch high-quality pictures on their computer screens as Harbhajan Singh and V. V. S. Laxman inspired one of the greatest comebacks in Test history. It was a massive result for India – and an even bigger breakthrough for the medium. By the time England visited India in December, Doordarshan had struck up a deal with the revamped Wisden site (**www.wisden.com**) to put together session-by-session highlights packages from the Test series. Its availability was effectively by subscription only, but that was a sign of the times. In January 2002, Wisden and ddnow went a step further by showing the one-day series between India and England live on a pay-per-view basis. It was the first time an England match had been shown live on the web.

BBC Online's cricket coverage (**www.bbc.co.uk/cricket**) pulled way ahead of its rivals at Sky (**www.skysports/sports/cricket**), largely thanks to an unrivalled package of audio interviews, a fast-reacting news service, and plenty of comment and columnists: the choice of Richard Johnson to give a behind-the-scenes account of England's tour of India proved an inspired one, but mainly because of the time Johnson found on his hands rather than the quality of his prose.

Humour was never far away. One site, Middle Stump (**www.geocities.com/middlestump1**), was exclusively tongue-in-cheek, and often rib-tickling at the same time. Another demonstrated the speed with which offline phenomena can become online institutions. The colourful TV commentary of the former Indian opener Navjot Sidhu had viewers chortling and wincing in equal measure, and spawned an internet shrine of its own (**www.setindia.com/max/sidhuisms**). Readers were invited to submit their favourite Sidhuisms, and a host of aggrieved aphorisms came flooding in. "Wickets are like wives," Sidhu informed co-commentator Martin Crowe. "You never know which way they will turn!" Had he applied his simile to cricket websites, it might just have worked.

Lawrence Booth is assistant editor of Wisden.com

CRICKET EQUIPMENT, 2001

By NORMAN HARRIS

If 2001 is anything to go by, the spotlight on cricket balls is intensifying, after several seasons of increasing criticism and conjecture. The ball going out of shape is a continuing complaint – though none had to be replaced in last summer's Ashes series, excepting the one Nasser Hussain hit out of Headingley – and they are said to soften too quickly. On the other hand, balls were thought to be too good, for the bowlers, in the previous summer's English Tests, and there was a request to the makers to soften them a little. Hindsight might suggest that the real reason for the short-lived Tests of 2000 was the fragility of West Indies' batting, if not also England's.

Whether or not the 2001 Test matches benefited from the tinkering is hard to say. Between them, Australia's bowlers and England's batsmen ensured a high incidence of early finishes. But there were complaints within the domestic game, especially in one-day matches, about soft balls needing to be changed. A significant factor, it seemed, was the desire of the fielding side to *get* the ball softer in order to put a brake on run-scoring. Accordingly, umpires sometimes warned fielding sides against persistently throwing the ball in on the bounce.

The 2001 season was the first in which the home counties were unable to use the ball of their choice, with each competition instead being allocated the ball of one or other of the two leading manufacturers, Readers and Dukes. The ECB may well have thought that, in being fair to the two makers, they were also making it easier to monitor the performances of balls. Yet, with it no longer being possible to compare the different brands side by side in the same competition, evaluation could have become more difficult.

The scenario becomes arguably more confusing in 2002, with the introduction of the Australian Kookaburra ball, which is machine-stitched. The white model will be used for all Norwich Union League games, while the traditional red Kookaburra will be used in the Second Eleven Championship. It is an interesting move, following advocacy over many years based mainly on the ball's performance in Australia. But it is also one that seems to involve a degree of contradiction. Does the ECB want balls to be a bit harder or a bit softer? Or does the answer depend on the competition?

It seems that one experiment is at an end. Last season's Second Eleven competition tried *orange* balls, which, say Dukes, were an outstanding success. Players, umpires and spectators all said they could see the ball more clearly against white clothing and backgrounds than they could a red ball (or, for that matter, a white ball against black or coloured backgrounds). The argument against using orange at higher levels seems to be that the monitor on a TV camera offers only a black-and-white picture, in which orange is less distinct than red or white.

The 2001 season demonstrated also that the search for an effective batting glove is not yet over. The limitations of existing gloves were underlined by Nasser Hussain's finger injuries, but manufacturers keen to use revolutionary materials remain frustrated. As one of them said: "As soon as you introduce something high-tech, bigger manufacturers are quick to follow, but at a lower price. The glove will be made elsewhere in the world and with cheaper foams." Many times the analogy has been made of a hammer (the ball) striking an object (the glove and fingers) against an anvil (the handle), and perhaps there will never be a complete answer. Or will it come with some lateral thinking? For example, disposable gloves that work like a crumple zone on a car?

Indeed, it was a manufacturer of protective equipment in other sports who placed some question marks against the design of helmets after players – among them Justin Langer in the Oval Test – had been hit on an unprotected area at the side or back of the head. Too much of the protection was being afforded by the visor rather than by a wrap-around helmet, as is the case in other helmet-wearing sports, explained Andrew Ainsworth, a leading manufacturer of equipment for white-water pursuits. Cricket safety standards seem more lenient than those for water sports, he said. "We wouldn't be able to use a metal visor that can be driven against the side of the head with full force. A metal visor transmits all of the shock and may even amplify it."

Wicket-keepers had to come to terms in 2001 with the new code of the Laws; this banned flaps, between thumb and first finger, that allowed catches to be "pouched". But the new Law did allow a piece of flat material as a stabilising link between the thumb and first finger. This gave rise to some uncertainty as to how big the reinforcement could be, and the lawmakers had to issue a clarification, advising that it could be any size provided the material was non-stretch and lay flat when the hand was extended.

However, no piece of individual equipment looks like having such a far-reaching impact as Channel 4's Hawk-Eye and its rival Sky Scope ball-tracking equipment. Inevitably, they caused sceptics to question some of their lbw predictions, but none of the "decisions" seemed to be obviously deviant. Can such predictions be tested? That has already happened, says the inventor of Hawk-Eye, Paul Hawkins. "We filmed thousands of balls being bowled at a set of stumps, giving us the 'evidence' of where they went. Then we tracked those balls to various points prior to reaching the stumps, and did our prediction calculations – which matched what actually happened."

The consistent feature of the devices' findings was that many more balls are passing over the stumps than might be supposed. Whether or not Hawk-Eye and its cousin eventually become an umpiring aid, their invention looks like influencing umpiring forever. As a background influence, they will probably result in fewer lbw decisions, but in the umpires' hands they're likely to produce more.

CRICKET AND THE WEATHER, 2001

By PHILIP EDEN

What was a moderately good summer, weather-wise – certainly better than 2000 – began in the most inauspicious circumstances. All parts of England and Wales had endured a record-breaking wet autumn and winter. During the six months from September 2000 to February 2001 inclusive, rainfall averaged nationally was 823mm (32.4in), some 53 per cent above normal and the highest recorded for any six-month period since rainfall recording began over 300 years ago. In Hampshire, Surrey, Sussex and Kent, more than a year's worth of rain fell in that six-month period. Flooding was widespread and long-lasting in many parts of the country. Things scarcely improved in March, which was another wet month in the southern half of England, and when county players turned up for pre-season practice most first-class grounds were still either flooded or waterlogged. April brought further rain, and the week after Easter (April 16–22) was very cold with snow and hail showers.

The weather cheered up during the first half of May, with plenty of sunshine, and temperatures soared into the high 20s Celsius between May 10 and 13, finally dissipating the last of the excessive moisture from cricket grounds. The rest of the summer was characterised by long dry periods punctuated by short unsettled spells. The dry periods were sometimes accompanied by great heat and humidity, notably between June 24 and July 6, between July 24 and August 1, and also around August 15 and August 25. The rainy episodes were generally shortlived, occurring on May 13–17, June 15–16, July 7–20, August 2–12, and August 30 to September 5.

Rain prevented any play on the opening day of the First Test between England and Pakistan on May 17, but that day's weather was exceptional for other reasons. The rain was accompanied by a strong, gusty west wind, and by temperatures rarely seen this late in spring. In fact, a search through the archives reveals that it was the coldest scheduled Test match day in England – and also in the world. But with the advent of mid-May Test matches, it was always only a matter of time.

There are no official weather records maintained at Lord's, or in the immediate vicinity. However, there are observing stations in central London and at Hampstead. The heart of London is warmer than St John's Wood by about one degree Celsius, partly because of differences in the density of the built-up area and partly because of the difference in altitude. Hampstead, where the weather station is located some 450 feet above sea level, near the summit of the Heath, is approximately one degree cooler than St John's Wood. At midday on May 17, the temperature in central London was 8.2°C, while at Hampstead it was 5.9°C. From these figures one can reasonably infer that it was close to 7°C at the same time at Lord's – a figure more appropriate to the middle of January than the middle of May.

The previous record low was at Edgbaston, where the midday temperature on the second day of the 1965 New Zealand Test (May 29) stood at 8°C. This remains the coldest day on which Test cricket was actually played. Given that the coldness of May 17 was accentuated by the windchill effect – the westerly wind was blowing at 20–25mph with gusts to 45mph – it was a relief for players and spectators alike when play was called off for the day at lunch.

The meteorological statistics, averaged over England and Wales, for the 2001 cricket season, were as follows:

	Average max temperature (°C)	*Difference from normal for 1961–90*	*Total rainfall (mm)*	*% of normal*	*Total sunshine (hours)*	*% of normal*
April (second half)	11.1	–2.2	39	138	87	110
May	17.6	+1.7	36	56	233	116
June	19.2	+0.3	40	62	204	97
July	22.3	+1.6	69	100	206	108
August	21.5	+1.1	85	99	178	98
September (first half)	17.9	–0.5	21	51	67	94
2001 season	**19.0**	**+0.6**	**290**	**82**	**975**	**107**

The following values for each county for the summer of 2001, against the average value for the standard reference period 1961–1990, are calculated using the *Wisden* summer index. This incorporates rainfall amount and frequency, sunshine, and temperature, in a single figure, and its formula may be found on page 1567 of *Wisden 2001*. Broadly speaking, an index over 650 indicates a good summer and one below 500 describes a poor summer.

	2001	*Avge*	*Variation*		*2001*	*Avge*	*Variation*
Derbyshire	590	565	+25	Middlesex	735	645	+90
Durham	581	510	+71	Northamptonshire	643	595	+48
Essex	726	620	+106	Nottinghamshire	591	575	+16
Glamorgan	590	540	+50	Somerset	692	605	+87
Gloucestershire	634	575	+59	Surrey	731	650	+81
Hampshire	735	625	+110	Sussex	746	645	+101
Kent	758	630	+128	Warwickshire	614	525	+89
Lancashire	552	515	+37	Worcestershire	674	595	+79
Leicestershire	625	570	+55	Yorkshire	665	545	+120

The *Wisden* weather index since 1991, together with the best and worst on record, are as follows:

1991	538	1995	777	1999	637
1992	556	1996	663	2000	556
1993	573	1997	601	2001	632
1994	651	1998	565		

Highest: 812 in 1976 **Lowest:** 309 in 1879

A full list of summers between 1900 and 1999 can be found in *Wisden 2000*, pages 21–24.

Philip Eden is weather expert for BBC Radio Five Live, and the Daily *and* Sunday Telegraph.

CRICKETANA, 2001

By GORDON PHILLIPS

Villainy and splendid altruism highlighted the otherwise serene and prosperous memorabilia scene in 2001. In July, the suave, plausible cricket author and former New York banker, Vijay P. Kumar, was jailed for nine months at Middlesex Crown Court on two charges of stealing cricket books and memorabilia valued at tens of thousands of pounds. None of the items, many of them taken from bookseller John McKenzie and collector Kim Baloch, and including rare editions of *Wisden*, has been recovered. Meanwhile, investigations are also under way into the disappearance of superb material from the prestigious Leslie Gutteridge collection in Canada. In Australia, however, letters touching on a disagreement between Sir Donald Bradman and Greg Chappell at the height of the Packer affair in 1977, and sold at Christie's in Melbourne for £6,970, were donated to the Bradman Foundation by a group of anonymous businessmen calling themselves SAVE (Some Australians Value Ethics). It was felt that the letters should have been cherished and not sold. Although the Foundation has been clamping down on materials relating to the Don, Australian collectors continue to make the running in this market, with UK dealers and auctioneers fielding constant entreaties from overseas callers eager to realise the healthy resale potential in Sydney, Melbourne and elsewhere, where even "struck-for-the-moment" modern souvenirs can be hot properties.

Bodyline items, enhanced by the internet's wide audience, never cease to amaze: a shipboard menu signed by Jardine's men can realise more than £2,000, while an MCC itinerary brochure/booklet, estimated at £500–£700, finished bidding at £2,300. The 1948 Australian tourists remain as rampant in the saleroom as they were on the field, but any earlier Australian tour excites, exemplified by a sheet of headed notepaper from RMS *Orontes*, signed in ink by the 1909 visitors, which sold at Phillips for £1,300.

Trumper and W.G. compel dedicated patronage and a deep pocket. The famous photogravure image of Trumper with bat held high in mid-shot, jointly signed by G. W. Beldam and the batsman, can notch £2,000, while few would blink at £550 bid for a signed sepia photograph, possibly produced for the Trumper Testimonial Fund of 1912-13. A cast-iron pub table with masks of England's champion can reach four figures, as can a twisted wooden walking stick bearing his portrait mask, dated 1881.

The memorabilia cascade of figurines, toffee containers, vestas, inkwells, tankards, benefit mementos, lapel badges, Liebig menu cards, buckles, ashtrays, flicker books and other familiars, such as anthropomorphic bulldog and rabbit cricketers, roared on unabated. Some curiosities tickled even a jaded palate: an early bowling machine became a lethal anti-intruder garden artefact; a scarce humidor of inlaid wood with a map of Jamaica, presented to the Duke of Edinburgh in 1975, made £400; and a coin-operated amusement arcade game of around 1905, entitled "The Cricket Match", earned the trustees of the Marquess of Bath £21,500, as against an estimate of £5,000.

Even mid-1960s *Wisdens* in dust wrappers are climbing, but pictures, especially framed modern specimens, lack appeal. Those popular icons of the 1990s, Chevallier Tayler and *Vanity Fair* prints – E. W. Dillon at £2,400 excepted – stagnate. Good modern coffee-table books are not sought after, whereas autographed team sheets, signed postcards and Cornhill cards make good money. Rare signatures demand attention, such as Albert Cotter shown on a postcard in full-length bowling pose (1905, £330), but pre-World War II album pages, scorecards and modern photographs are dropping behind.

The enterprising Cricket Memorabilia Society collaborated with the since defunct Sky Auctions for a second cyberspace auction, and in the process bucked the slack clothing trend by selling 18 signed county shirts for almost £2,000. Similarly, with agents increasingly alert to cash flow, the player-benefit round is growing, although much in this area hinges on the personality and his popularity. Supremely, it has been another year for fine porcelain, especially Doulton ware, rare silverware and Test caps. Allan Border's baggy green made £3,600 and Brian Booth's £1,400, while Sir Frank Worrell's West Indian cap fetched £3,000. Hansie Cronje's South African one, on the other hand, managed only £700. Clive Lloyd (£1,300), Graeme Pollock (£1,000), "Plum" Warner (£850), Wasim Akram (£800) and Doug Wright (£520) reflected market interest, as did the typically low demand for India and New Zealand: Yashpal Sharma made £850, but John Reid only £300 and Erapally Prasanna £400.

Once again the carriage trade gravitated to Christie's, Sotheby's and Phillips. Christie's hosted the widely publicised P. G. Wodehouse archive sale, comprising 75 letters (plus ancillary matter) written to S. C. "Billy" Griffith and illuminating the humorist's lifelong cricket addiction; these realised £24,000. Howard Carter's painted wooden compositions of the brothers Grace and their contemporaries, the property of actor Albert Finney, were unusual, while from the Brian Statham estate came ties, sweaters, stumps, various tankards, a lighter, cigarette box, ashtray, goblets and vases. On the first night of the F. S. Trueman sale at Sotheby's, some £57,000 changed hands, his 300th Test-wicket ball selling for £5,000. Trevor Bailey, Graham Gooch and Jack Flavell properties did less well, but the mystique attaching to Walter Hammond saw his 1938-39 MCC tour blazer fetch £5,000.

An equally discerning clientele found the right stuff at provincial auctioneers Trevor Vennett-Smith, Tim Knight, Anthemion, and Mullock Madeley, the last of which offered Hammond's masonic apron bag and a John Bratby oil portrait of Trueman resembling George Best. The provincials' expert lotting and handsome catalogues threaten to overtake those of the London houses. Over three days in March, Vennett-Smith realised £195,000 with some crown-jewel performances by a 1916 *Wisden* (£1,800), a stoneware Royal Doulton loving cup (£920) and a rarer pear-shaped Doulton jug with art nouveau designs at £700. A Miners' Welfare Institute dinner menu, signed by Harold Larwood, Bill Voce and the Nottinghamshire team, reached £880, but breathless bidding to £3,400 raised the roof for one book, *The Irish Cricketers in the United States* (1879), originally estimated at just £150. Mainstream collectors gratefully saw some important library dispersals reinvigorate the world of books and pamphlets; on offer were a clutch of true rarities from the pens of J. Goldman, Neville Weston and P. R. May, as well as R. D. Beeston's singularly scarce *St Ivo and the Ashes* (£1,500) and Ashley-Cooper limited editions including *Cricket and the Church* (£1,500). The dishevelled state of county cricket club libraries prompts anxiety, but all in all it was a very good year.

OBITUARY

Note: In *Wisden 2001*, the obituary of Lord Cottenham said he was reported to have been suffering from depression. This was not intended to imply that he took his own life; Lord Cottenham's death resulted from a subdural haemorrhage and was recorded by the coroner as an accident. *Wisden* regrets the distress to family and friends, and any misunderstanding, caused by the notice.

ARMITAGE, ROBERT LAWRENCE SUGDEN, an all-rounder for Eastern Province, died of cancer at Grahamstown on December 9, 2000, aged 45. A watchful left-handed opening bat and an off-spinner with an action of mock-balletic oddity, Robbie Armitage played for Northern Transvaal and South African Universities, as well as Eastern Province, between 1973-74 and 1987-88. Three times in 1982-83 he replaced the injured Barry Richards to represent South Africa in one-day games against the "rebel" West Indians. His 109 first-class matches produced 3,923 runs, average 23.21, with 171 not out against Northern Transvaal in 1981-82 his highest score; his 205 wickets, at 31 apiece, included a best analysis of seven for 97 for Eastern Province against Transvaal. One of his sons was recently selected for Eastern Province Under-13.

ARNSBJERG, JØRGEN, who died at Helsinge, Zealand on November 7, 2001, aged 73, had devoted more than 50 years to cricket in Denmark. Though he was best known to cricketers from outside the country as an administrator at the triangular tournaments of the Forty Clubs whenever they were held in Denmark, his outstanding role was that of promoting and watching over the game at the Sorø Akademi, Denmark's Eton. A good enough batsman to have put the West Indies bowler, Denis Atkinson, to the sword in a fighting half-century in 1968, he was respected by all as being as straight as his bat. He had an unmistakable resemblance to John Cleese, with whom his humour was also consistent.

ATKINSON, DENIS ST EVAL, seven times West Indies' captain and brother of Eric Atkinson, also a West Indian Test cricketer, died on November 9, 2001, aged 75. A useful all-rounder who had chosen life assurance as a career, he was at the centre of controversy during the Australian tour of the Caribbean in 1954-55. When West Indies' captain Jeff Stollmeyer injured a finger at slip practice before the First Test, and later damaged a collarbone in the Third, Atkinson was appointed for the first, fourth and fifth matches ahead of the black Frank Worrell. Despite the fact that Atkinson was vice-captain, the decision was interpreted as sustaining the white supremacy. It did not help him that Australia won the First Test by nine wickets, but he enjoyed a notable triumph in the Fourth on his home ground, Kensington Oval, hitting his only Test hundred and moving on to a match-saving 219; his stand with wicket-keeper Clairmonte Depeiza, a fellow-Barbadian, added a world-record 347 for the seventh wicket after West Indies had been 147 for six. They were only the second pair, after Hobbs and Sutcliffe at Melbourne in 1924-25, to bat through an entire day's play. Atkinson then took five for 56 when the Australians batted again, becoming the first to score a double-hundred and take five wickets in an innings in the same Test. The feat has since been emulated by Pakistan's Mushtaq Mohammad.

Atkinson captured most wickets and headed the home team's averages during that Australian series, and subsequently took the West Indians to New Zealand in 1955-56. Although the tourists won the series 3–1, New Zealand's first Test win possibly cost him the captaincy to England in 1957. He did tour, under John Goddard, a cousin of his wife, Betty, and began with ten for 62 at Worcester, where he was "almost unplayable with his pacy off-breaks". However, troubled later by a shoulder injury, he played in only two of the Tests. The last of his 22 appearances for West Indies came the following

[*Getty Images*

Denis Atkinson (*left*) and Alf Valentine decide on new kit after arriving in England with the 1957 West Indians. Both played in two of the Tests, but without reaching earlier heights.

year against Pakistan at Barbados, where brother Eric made his debut and Hanif Mohammad made 337. His own debut had been at Delhi in 1948-49. In Tests, Atkinson scored 922 runs at 31.79 and took 47 wickets at 35.04, with seven for 53 in the defeat by New Zealand at Auckland his best return. With limited bowling resources, he frequently took the new ball on that tour, mixing medium-pace swing with his more usual quick off-breaks and off-cutters.

A contemporary of Worrell and Clyde Walcott at Combermere School, Atkinson played for the strong Wanderers club in Barbados, and represented the island from 1946-47 until 1960-61. He also played four times for Trinidad, in both games against Gubby Allen's MCC side in 1947-48, and again in 1949-50. His 78 first-class matches realised 2,812 runs at 28.40, including five centuries, and exactly 200 wickets, which averaged an economical 26.45. His best return was eight for 58 against Essex at Ilford in 1957.

BAKER, DONALD GAY, a hard-working veteran of Philadelphia cricket, died at Warner, New Hampshire on August 25, 2000, aged 94. He had suffered from pneumonia, complicated by other ailments, and had not long survived his wife of 67 years. Born on the Haverford College campus, he toured England with the college side in 1925 and captained them in 1926, the last year of the Halifax Cup competition. For 40 years, he was a classics don at Ursinus College, where he introduced cricket and acted as coach, and he played cricket in the Philadelphia area until he was 60. According to John Lester's *A Century of Philadelphia Cricket*, Baker was one of five men who kept the game alive in the area in lean times between 1930 and 1950.

BASSANO, BRIAN STANLEY, acknowledged as the expert on South African cricket history, died at Launceston, Tasmania on July 10, 2001, aged 65. He played club cricket in England for the Sussex Martlets in the 1960s before returning to his native East London to ply his journalistic craft, as well as doing radio commentaries on first-class matches there. He was also manager of Border's Currie Cup team for a spell. In 1988, he emigrated to Tasmania. Conversations with him about South African cricket were like dipping into an encyclopaedia, as his books, such as *MCC in South Africa 1938-39, The History of South African Cricket* and *South Africa in International Cricket 1888–1970*, reveal. The last study was the basis for a 30-part TV series.

His account of the tribulations experienced by his son, Chris, in being accepted as a non-overseas player in England, made interesting listening. Happily, Chris Bassano enjoyed a sensational start to his Derbyshire career with two centuries on Championship debut, a marvellous farewell gift for his father, to whose deathbed he sadly flew a fortnight later. Modestly, Brian Bassano talked less readily about his activities in divided South Africa, where he co-founded in 1976-77 the Rainbow Cricket Club in East London with Donald Woods. The first multiracial team in the Border Premier League, it cocked a veritable snook at apartheid. He was honorary secretary of the Border Cricket Union from 1971 to 1977 and promoted cricket in the black townships as a member of the South African Cricket Union development committee. Richard Hill, founder-editor of *Cricket Lore*, said that "his knowledge and enthusiasm for the game knew no boundaries", citing as an example his compilation of a complete Who's Who of South African international cricketers – disappointingly, a project that had not been brought to published fruition.

BEARDSMORE, DAVID ARCHIBALD AUBREY, died, aged 75, on May 30, 2000. Educated at Denstone College and at Gonville and Caius College, Cambridge, he was prominent as a left-hand bat and slow left-arm bowler in war-time schools and university cricket, playing in the non-first-class Varsity Matches of 1944 and 1945. He took one wicket in the first year and did not get a chance to bat in either. Thereafter he was a captain in the RAMC and for many years a highly respected doctor in Knutsford, Cheshire.

BECKETT, DONALD GEORGE, died in August 2000, aged 64. Don Beckett had three years in the XI at St George's, Weybridge and subsequently was a dynamic strokemaker and left-arm fast bowler for the Army and Combined Services. In 1959, questions were asked in the House of Commons about his retention in the United Kingdom to play cricket for the Army, rather than proceeding overseas with his unit.

BOUSFIELD, DONALD GREENHILL, died on April 13, 2001, four days after his 87th birthday. Educated at Winchester and Trinity College, Cambridge, he had two matches for the University in 1935, when 38 runs, a highest score of 37 against Sussex at Fenner's, and no call for his leg-break bowling were insufficient to warrant further opportunities. He played for Hertfordshire in the 1930s, and with immediate success for Buckinghamshire after World War II while a housemaster at Eton.

BRADMAN, SIR DONALD GEORGE, AC, the most effective batsman in cricket's history, died in Adelaide on February 25, 2001, at the age of 92, having been ill with pneumonia. He was born on August 27, 1908, with Australia, as a nation-state, but seven years old; 25 years later, he had become and would remain its most illustrious citizen. A legion of obituarists recorded and analysed his skills, and such was his impact on the game and on society that some of their analogues – Winston Churchill, Jack Kennedy, Shakespeare, Diana, Princess of Wales, the Pope – did not appear unduly extravagant.

[*Getty Images*

Queensland's fielders carry 21-year-old Don Bradman off after his monumental world-record 452 not out for New South Wales at Sydney in January 1930. In the first innings he had scored just three; in the second he batted 415 minutes. Queensland were then bowled out for 84 and lost by 685 runs – the largest margin by runs ever.

Family and other background

Donald Bradman was the youngest of the five children of George and Emily Bradman. His father, a farmer and carpenter, was the son of Charles Bradman, who emigrated from East Anglia in 1852. Born at Cootamundra in the south-east corner of New South Wales, the young Don lived for three years on a farm at nearby Yeo Yeo, whereupon the family moved to Bowral, some 80 miles from Sydney and now the home of the Bradman Museum and Trust. These were humble beginnings. It was here that the legendary practice with golf ball and single stump was undertaken, employing the brick stand of the family water tank. A bright and quick-witted scholar, an adept pianist and an active participant in several sports, he attended primary and intermediate high school, leaving at 14 to find work in the Percy Westbrook estate agency. During his early cricketing career, he was involved, perhaps a little reluctantly, with sports goods promotion and journalism. Among his writings are four books, *Don Bradman's Book* (1930), *My Cricketing Life* (1938), *Farewell to Cricket* (1950) and a crystal-clear manual of instruction, *The Art of Cricket* (1958).

Later he would become a stockbroker with the Harry Hodgetts company in Adelaide, going on to establish his own successful stockbroking and investment concern, Don Bradman and Co., from which he retired in 1954. Over the next decades he took up directorships in a number of businesses and, having taken to golf with a will in his later years, was a long-time member of the Kooyonga Golf Club, near Adelaide. For many years, he was a strenuous worker in the field of cricket administration, serving six years as chairman of the Australian Cricket Board of Control (1960–63 and 1969–72), the first Test cricketer to hold this post, as a selector from 1936 to 1971 (apart from the 1952-53 season, when his son was ill) and, unflaggingly, as a member of the South Australia Cricket Association committee from 1935-36 to 1985-86. He did his best to offer sensible counsel on such issues as throwing, the South African ban and the Packer crisis, and he remained an unrepentant advocate of a reversion to the back-foot no-ball ruling.

In 1920, Don Bradman met Jessie Menzies of Glenquarry and, as schoolchildren, they became firm friends, eventually marrying at St Paul's Church, Burwood, Sydney on April 30, 1932. A vibrant and attractive brunette, Jessie Bradman provided him with a close and stable relationship over 65 years until her death, after severe illnesses, in 1997. Some commentators have suggested that she was his only close ally, at once his solace and his occasional good-natured goad. Having lost a baby in 1936, the Bradmans had two children, John, born in 1939, and Shirley, born in 1941. So acute did John Bradman find the stress of being his father's son that he adopted the not wildly different name of Bradsen in 1972, but, to his father's pleasure, he reverted to the family name in 2000. Bradman himself remained a warily private, if not wholly reclusive, figure, prepared to take on arduous sporting and managerial tasks but flinching a trifle at dazzling limelight or unwarranted intrusion. It was Arthur Mailey's astute conclusion that Don Bradman never made the error of confusing popularity and success. Whether, for all his triumphs, the Australian champion often pushed beyond contentment into genuine happiness is a moot point.

In the later part of his life, he lived in the fashionable Kensington district of Adelaide. He was knighted in 1949 and appointed a Companion of the Order of Australia in 1979. Following a private funeral – his family politely refused the accolade of a state funeral – a public memorial service was held in St Peter's Cathedral, Adelaide on March 25, 2001, with the proceedings shown on giant screens at the Adelaide Oval. On October 18, in the presence of family members and 60 privately invited guests, his ashes were spread at the Bradman Oval in Bowral.

Cricket: the early years

In 1920-21, the 12-year-old Bradman scored 115 not out for Bowral High School against Mittagong School, his first century, and when, a season later, one of the Bowral

[*Getty Images*

A tuck to leg keeps runs flowing from the Bradman bat at Headingley in 1930. Having gone in to face the last ball of the second over, Don Bradman was 105 at lunch, 220 at tea and 309 at the close. Next day he took his world-record Test score to 334.

club first team failed to turn up, Bradman, their scorer, played instead and made 37 not out. It was his first game with adults. After a convincingly successful flirtation with tennis, he settled down determinedly to cricket and, in 1925-26, scored a triumphant 234 for Bowral against Wingello, for whom Bill O'Reilly was bowling. He joined the St George club in Sydney for the 1926-27 season and made 110 on debut against Petersham in the more sophisticated realms of city club cricket. He had adjusted seamlessly from dirt pitch to coir matting to turf, and, in December 1927, he made his first-class debut at Adelaide for New South Wales against South Australia. Not long past his 19th birthday, Bradman made 118.

Such marked achievement quickly led to Test selection a year later, but, as Australia were trounced by England at Brisbane by 675 runs on a sticky wicket alien to his youthful experience, he made only 18 and one, and was dropped for the first and last time in his international career. Returning for the Third Test at Melbourne, he scored 79 and 112 amid tumultuous scenes as the crowd recognised the emergence of a genius and a likely upturn in Australian cricketing fortunes. They were not disappointed: Bradman hit another century at the MCG in the Fifth Test. Between these hundreds, he completed a marathon 340 not out against Victoria at Sydney; the following year, again at the SCG, he established a world first-class individual record of 452 not out in New South Wales's second innings against Queensland. Almost three-quarters of a century later, it remained the highest innings by an Australian and in Australia.

His introduction into the international arena was crowned by an astonishing first tour of England in 1930, when he assembled what remains the record sum for a series: 974 runs, with an average of 139.14, in the five Tests. This included 334 at Leeds, his highest Test score and then the highest such score ever, an innings watched by the young Len Hutton, who observed how carefully Bradman found the spaces between the fielders. But it was the 254 in his first Test at Lord's that Bradman considered his perfect innings, in that every shot, including the one when he was out, was exact in its technical assessment and operation. That fabled summer he made 2,960 runs, with a thousand before the end of May, and ten centuries. At the more material level, there was also a gift of £1,000, worth something like 40 times as much today, from the soap magnate, Arthur Whitelaw, which indicated that, although he was an amateur, his cricket was the serious key to Don Bradman's livelihood.

The West Indians were his next victims when they toured Australia in 1930-31, with 447 more Test runs flowing from his quicksilver blade. There was a national *frisson* of dismay when he was tempted by Accrington to play as its club professional in Lancashire league cricket, but a counter-offer of newspaper, radio and promotional work kept him true to his Australian roots. Against South Africa in 1931-32, he achieved his highest seasonal Test average of 201.50 from 806 runs in five innings; his four centuries included 299 not out at Adelaide. Throughout these years, he was also scoring regularly and fruitfully in club and Sheffield Shield cricket, similarly able to sustain his concentration and acumen without undue stress.

Cricket: the middle years

Then came the notorious Bodyline series against England, though before it started, on his return from touring North America with Arthur Mailey's team, he became involved in a dispute with the Australian board over his journalistic activities. That was resolved, but he still missed the First Test of 1932-33 through illness. Bill Bowes bowled him first ball in the Second, but he responded well with 103 not out in the second innings, his only hundred, as it transpired, of that controversial rubber. Douglas Jardine, the autocratic English captain, employed, as has been well rehearsed, intimidating leg-theory bowling, with Harold Larwood, along with Bill Bowes and Bill Voce, delivering short-pitched balls at high speed to a packed on-side field. There is little doubt that this ruthless campaign arose from an English despair over the ascendancy of Don Bradman. His riposte was to shift leg-wards and rap the ball through an almost deserted off side, rather after the fashion of J. T. Tyldesley's murderous approach to leg-spin bowling. England won the battle but lost the war, for Jardine's tactics were condemned as unsporting and perilous. There were unfriendly exchanges and diplomatic ramifications, followed by changes in the Laws of Cricket to restrict on-side field placements. Although Bradman's average was pared to 56.57 for the series, and this was considered a measure of containment, it is worth noting that the next best Test career average to Bradman's (from a minimum 20 innings) is the 60.97 of South Africa's Graeme Pollock. Len Hutton's Test average is 56.67.

The rancour of the Bodyline series lingered, but there was a substantive element of reconciliation on the 1934 tour of England, when Australia regained the Ashes. After a comparatively tentative beginning to the tour, Bradman scored 304 in the Headingley Test, followed by 244 at The Oval, where he shared a record second-wicket stand of 451 with Bill Ponsford. Even now, this is the third-highest Test partnership and the best in Ashes matches. Such heavy scoring sent his average for the series soaring to 94.75 from 758 runs, and he made 2,020 runs in that English summer. However, his health, which had for a year or so been troublesome, became critical when he fell victim to acute appendicitis. The cricketing world held its breath, but he recovered, although it was a year before he played first-class cricket again.

In pursuit of his business concerns, he moved to Adelaide and commenced playing for South Australia in 1935-36. Having scored a century on his last appearance for New South Wales, at Sydney in 1934, he marked his first Shield match for his new team with 117 against his old state, and captained South Australia to their first title since 1926-27. He made the sixth and last of his triple-hundreds, 369, against Tasmania at the end of the season, giving him an aggregate of 1,173 runs at 130.33, and the following season, when MCC toured under Gubby Allen, he was appointed captain of Australia. After an uneasy baptism, with two lost Tests, he rallied in characteristic fashion and saved the Ashes with spirited knocks of 270 at Melbourne (putting on 346

[*Getty Images*

Wally Hammond flips the coin, Don Bradman calls and Oval groundsman "Bosser" Martin waits to learn which side will have first use of his run-filled pitch. Hammond won the toss for the fourth consecutive time in the 1938 series and England batted until tea on the third day. By then, Len Hutton's 364 had beaten Bradman's record in England–Australia Tests, and Hammond's world record.

for the sixth wicket with Jack Fingleton after reversing Australia's batting order to counter a rain-affected pitch), 212 at Adelaide and 169, again at Melbourne. He averaged 90 from 810 runs in the series, and huge crowds cheered him on in noisy admiration.

Visiting England in 1938, he began excellently with a thousand runs by the end of May in an amazing seven innings, and overall he scored 2,429 on the tour, with 13 hundreds. In the Tests, he hit centuries at Nottingham, Lord's and Leeds and enjoyed an average of 108.50, although his exploits were overshadowed by Hutton's monumental endeavour in the final Test when he accumulated 364 to eclipse Bradman's Ashes record. Undaunted, Bradman launched into his own domestic season, 1938-39, with a stream of six consecutive centuries to equal C. B. Fry's record from 1901, and he ended it with a phenomenal average of 153.16 from seven innings in seven games. Soon, war came to rob him, as others, of manifold opportunities to add to his laurels. Statisticians may only muse over what his record might have been.

Cricket: the later years

Weary bowlers and knowledgeable critics, who had assured their readers and listeners that his genius lay in sharp eyesight, were doubtless bemused to find that, when examined during his military service, Bradman's eyes were below average, a condition ascribed to his run-down condition. Next, an excruciating back problem led him to be invalided out of the army in the June of 1941. It took him a long time to recover, and he was further dogged by the financial and legal troubles suffered by his business patron, Harry Hodgetts, a situation that led Bradman to establish, with gritty determination, his own brokerage.

Thus there were question marks over both the fitness and availability of the now 37-year-old Bradman for post-war cricket. He had an uncomfortable start to the 1946-47 MCC tour. In the First Test at Brisbane, he had laboured over 28 runs when, on the English submission, he was caught at second slip by Jack Ikin, the premier close-in fielder of his day and a chevalier among sportsmen. To Wally Hammond's chagrin, both Bradman and, more crucially, the umpire believed it was a bump ball; Bradman eschewed his ring-rustiness and flourished in what Neville Cardus termed a "Lazarus" innings of 187. In the next match, at Sydney, chiefly in a massive partnership of 405 with Sid Barnes, he scored 234, and went on to total 680 runs at an average of 97.14 for the series, a calamitous one for England.

The touring Indian party of 1947-48 was treated to even greater exercises in dominance, with Bradman notching 715 runs for an average of 178.75. It was also against these visitors, for an Australian XI at Sydney, that he completed his 100th century, all done and dusted in 295 innings. He was the first non-English batsman to reach this target, as well as the quickest to the mark before or since.

As well as nonpareil batsman, he was also now recognised as an astute and unbending captain. In 1948, he led the famed "Invincibles", a team still acknowledged by many commentators as the finest international combine ever fielded, on their unbeaten tour of England. Carping voices might have hoped for a spin bowler of the uppermost rank to complete that "ministry of all the talents", but by and large the claim remains a fair one. Don Bradman himself made 2,428 runs at an average of 89.92, while in the Tests he scored 508 runs (72.57), including the 173 not out at Headingley that enabled the Australians to speed to a winning total of 404 for three on the final day. He celebrated his 40th birthday with 150 against the Gentlemen in his *adieu* to Lord's. But a fortnight earlier, in the final Test at The Oval, Eric Hollies had bowled him second ball for "the most famous duck in history" when, to cite perhaps the best-known cricket statistic, he required only four runs to preserve an overall Test average of 100.

Apart from three more first-class games in the 1948-49 season, including a valedictory century, that was, from the straightforward cricketing angle, that. An adequate compendium of his figures is difficult to draft. The awe and the majesty of this exceptional sportsman did lie more in his serial acquisition of runs than in the manner of his doing. Other cricketers might be prettier or more regal in demeanour (although it would be unfair to hint that he was unattractive to watch, such was the balance and command of his technique), but none could realistically expect to keep the scoreboards rattling so peremptorily.

D. G. BRADMAN – TEST CAREER

	T	*I*	*NO*	*Runs*	*HS*	*Avge*	*100s*	*Runs/ Hour*	*Career Avge*
1928-29 v E. . . .	4	8	1	468	123	66.85	2	28.80	66.85
1930 v E.	5	7	0	974	334	139.14	4	40.35	103.00
1930-31 v WI. . .	5	6	0	447	223	74.50	2	47.30	94.45
1931-32 v SA. . .	5	5	1	806	299*	201.50	4	47.18	112.29
1932-33 v E. . . .	4	8	1	396	103*	56.57	1	37.53	99.70
1934 v E.	5	8	0	758	304	94.75	2	42.18	98.69
1936-37 v E. . . .	5	9	0	810	270	90.00	3	33.19	97.06
1938 v E.	4	6	2	434	144*	108.50	3	31.00	97.94
1946-47 v E. . . .	5	8	1	680	234	97.14	2	33.33	97.84
1947-48 v I	5	6	2	715	201	178.75	4	40.47	102.98
1948 v E.	5	9	2	508	173*	72.57	2	29.11	99.94
Totals	52	80	10	6,996	334	99.94	29	36.91	99.94

In the broadest of brush-strokes, he totalled 28,067 first-class runs in 234 matches and 338 innings at an average of 95.14 including 117 centuries, 37 of them double-centuries. In 62 Sheffield Shield games, he averaged 110.19 from 8,926 runs, with 36 hundreds. Of his 29 Test hundreds, there were 12 doubles including the triples at Leeds in 1930 and 1934. Within those parameters may be traced a thousand intricacies of mathematical astonishment, but in the end they all subscribe to the one fundamental truth: that a man who is able to score a century every 2.88 innings and a double-century every 9.13 innings has perfected a skill beyond normal imagining.

The cricketer

The numbers are mightily persuasive. Donald Bradman is assuredly the most efficacious batsman cricket has known. There may be mutterings about this or that batsman emulating him on damp wickets, but they scarcely affect the outcome, and it should be recalled that Bradman played all his first-class cricket in Australia or England and none, for example, on the subcontinent, where he might have found conditions to his especial liking. Another discussion relates to the alterations in the game that might have tempered his run-getting, but these, too, may be exaggerated. Certainly in comparison with other major sports, cricket has not witnessed much basic change since, about the turn of the 20th century, its institutional construct and principal techniques had been rounded and developed. The shifts have been slighter than some modern critics would claim, and may also have been self-cancelling. What, for example, Don Bradman might have lost on the swings of more consistently agile fielding, defensive field placements and dilatory over-rates, he might have gained on the roundabouts of shortened boundaries, less varied attacks and improved equipment. Visualise him in a limited-overs match, with its restrictions on bowling and fielding.

Of moderate size, some 5ft 7in tall, he was a wiry, tireless character, though beset with occasional illnesses, who seemed as unpressed at the end of a long, hot day as at its beginning. He walked slowly to the wicket, adjusting his sight to the light, always with a genial smile playing about his lips, and that measured tread was guaranteed to signal to opponents a discouraging assurance. He is said to have picked up the ball quicker than most, yet it was perhaps his ability to move rapidly into position from a stance of serene stillness that was an important key to his mastery.

From that juncture, he appeared to be ready to select shots with deceptive ease and execute them with a frightening dominance, his unusual grip always militating against him lofting the ball. Much has been written of his indomitable powers of concentration. Mortal man cannot begin to understand the degree of composed self-reliance upon which this mental vigour was based. Other cricketers, said C. L. R. James, "had inhibitions Bradman never knew". The sole tiny bow to convention lay in his rarely opening the batting, although it seldom seemed to diminish him if a wicket fell immediately and he had perforce to take centre stage. W. G. Grace would have scorned the wasted time of an inferior being permitted to replace him at the top of the order. None the less, no one has matched what Neville Cardus called Bradman's "cool deliberate murder or spifflication of the bowling".

He was a single-minded but never a selfish batsman. His compulsion, and it was as fierce in other branches of his life, was the winning of cricket matches, not the self-aggrandisement of personal run-making. Where some cricketers may have felt that making individual runs was the purpose, for Don Bradman it was a means to the end of victory. Thus he recognised that there were two foes. As well as the opposition, there was that proverbial old enemy, time. Using his unparalleled skills, he therefore conflated two extremes of batsmanship – an unrelenting tenacity in defence and a complementary resolve to score quickly. It was as if the obduracy of Richard Barlow had been wedded to the *élan* of Gilbert Jessop. He adhered to the text of the American Civil War general who believed that the spoils went to those "who get thur fustest with the mostest".

The sportsman

Charles Davis, the Melbourne author of *The Best of the Best*, demonstrated with lucid arithmetic what many cricket fans have believed as an item of faith: namely, that Bradman was not only the best cricketer but the best sportsperson of all time. Jack Nicklaus would have had to win 25 major golf titles, instead of his meagre 18, and Michael Jordan would have had to have increased his average basketball points a game from 32 to 43 to rival the great cricketer. Although the ghost of Sir Donald Bradman might occasionally glance over its ethereal shoulder to mark the progress of the phenomenal Tiger Woods, there the mathematical matter rests.

Under the pressure of such attainment, one feels forced to seek counter-arguments. It has been suggested that Bradman rarely played against what, by the statistics of wicket-taking, bowling average and strike-rate, might be regarded as England's top bowlers of all time. One statistician, Peter Hartland, has calculated that W. G. Grace, when aged 25 and having scored some 10,000 first-class runs at an average of 61, was at that moment twice as good as any contemporary batsman – a dominance not even Bradman could match. It might be cavilling to recall that Don Bradman was not a great cricketer but a great batsman. He was an unassuming leg-spinner with a mere 36 first-class wickets to his name; a highly competent out-fielder who took 131 catches, plus a solitary stumping; and a hard-nosed, shrewd captain. But this did not make him an all-round cricketer in the Garry Sobers or W.G. mould.

If one scrutinises the careers of some of his contemporaries, one finds that, because of the structure of their sport, their predominance was more comprehensive. Gordon Richards was 26 times champion jockey and, unbelievably, 4,870 of his 21,843 mounts were winners; Joe Louis held the world heavyweight title from 1937 to 1946, longer than anyone else, during which period he defended the title 25 times, more than his eight predecessors *in toto*; Joe Davis monopolised the world snooker championship from its inception in 1927 to 1946, potted 687 centuries and contrived to lose only four games on level terms between 1927 and 1964. Moreover, apart from Sir Gordon's obliging equine companions, they did it alone, whereas, a truism, Bradman depended on his fellows to dismiss the opposition twice. Of course, that is rather like criticising Stanley Matthews, Bobby Charlton and George Best for not keeping goal in addition to their other duties. Whatever the criteria, anecdotal or numerical, Donald Bradman's top-ranking place among the very highest achievers in sport is undeniable.

The legend

The young Australia was struck by three hammer-blows in its first half-century as a nation-state. Its sacrifice in World War I amounted to 14.5 per cent of its mobilised troops. That is 1.2 per cent of the entire population; close to the 1.6 per cent of the British slain. The Depression years brought unemployment to 29 per cent of the labour force, with national income dropping by 30 per cent from 1929 to 1932. Then World War II brought more perils, including the possibility of Japanese invasion of the Australian mainland. Historians are agreed that, from the late 1920s to the post-war years, Don Bradman acted as a unifier of the nation, a focus for its battered self-belief and damaged social fabric.

Of course, he was not a knowing standard-bearer: he had secular sainthood thrust upon him. At best, he was a reluctant Hereward the Wake, which makes the comparison with Churchill, an ambitious seeker after power, a little lavish. Bradman hurriedly and perhaps wisely rejected invitations to accept political or diplomatic appointments. As Charles Williams perceptively analysed in *Bradman* (1996), in cricket as well as to some extent in the nation, there was a rift in Australia. Reduced crudely to an over-simplified equation, it was Protestant-Masonic, lower middle-class English, monarchical and subdued versus Roman Catholic, working-class Irish, republican and ebullient. Naturally, some irritable envy was involved. Although Don Bradman was not over-

[*Patrick Eagar*

"Fellow here thinks he bowls fast," Sir Donald Bradman might be telling his old adversary, Harold Larwood. Whatever he said, Dennis Lillee looks amused.

gregarious, he was by no means unconvivial. But, as Australian commentator Mike Coward graphically said, he was not into "mateness": one man's *bonhomie* is another's yobbishness. However, there is no more telling tale in the Bradman canon than E. W. Swanton's recollection of the Oval press box in 1948, with Jack Fingleton and Bill O'Reilly at hazard of strokes as they choked with mirth at Bradman's downfall in his last Test.

Cricket was modified and embraced by the Muscular Christianity of the Victorian era and imbued with a genuine ethical content, and this makes it vulnerable to a gloss of religiosity. Half-consciously, mistily, the Bradman myth adopted some of this sheen. As well as the miraculous triumphs, there were in turn: his agrestic origins – "the Boy from Bowral" – which Australian historian Bernard Whimpress terms "the bush ethic"; the material temptation, with friendly Accrington in satanic garb; the torment and the trial of Bodyline, with Jardine the haughty Roman inquisitor; and the Calvary of that mortal failure at The Oval in 1948. Indeed, one might guess that the impact of that duck has, over time, been more significant than had Bradman actually scored those beggarly four runs.

That uniformly abused tag of icon may legitimately be applied, however bold the deeds of other heroes, to only two cricketers. In that cricket is transparently a cult, Grace and Bradman played the roles of founder and consolidator. Because of the initial momentum of cricket, W.G., the creature of the railway, the steamship, the telegraph and the popular newspaper, has the wider distinction of being the father of modern sport at large, while the Don, although aided by the wireless, missed out on the expansion, engendered by air travel and satellite television, that has given sport a broader global spread. Indeed, spectator sport is the nearest we have to a lingua franca, a common cultural denominator, making a very few persons into meaningful beacons. The great Brazilian footballer, Pelé (incidentally, number two to Bradman on the Davis scale of earth-shattering sports activity, with a ratio of 3.7 to the cricketer's 4.4), must take some precedence, while Muhammad Ali also must be keenly considered in such a cultural examination.

Bradman is definitely of that tiny ilk – so much so that obituarists who compared him with Shakespeare, Michelangelo and Keats were slightly missing the point that Bradman may not be exclusively captured as part of an elitist, classical culture, but glows as a bright star in the popular constellation. Much as it might offend those who admired Don Bradman in quasi-religious and high artistic terms, the logical comparisons, outside sport itself, are with the other global art-forms, such as cinema or pop music, coupling him with such names as Charlie Chaplin, Walt Disney and Elvis Presley. As both highly functional craftsman and cultural idol, he was exalted by millions.

BRAZIER, ALAN FREDERICK, who in the post-war period played 36 matches for Surrey and 20 for Kent, died on April 18, 1999, aged 74. A right-hand batsman, he made 1,366 runs for an average of 17 between 1948 and 1956, and so never realised the potential promised by his 1,212 runs at 80.80 for Surrey Second Eleven in 1949. This remains the Minor Counties record aggregate. He later coached at St George's School, Weybridge.

BULCOCK, LESLIE, who died at Colne on April 24, 2001, aged 88, was an opening batsman and medium-paced bowler of substantial success as a professional in the Lancashire, Yorkshire and Staffordshire leagues. In 1943, Corporal Les Bulcock played for the Army at Lord's with the likes of Captain Jack Robertson, Lieutenant Maurice Leyland, Sergeant Roly Jenkins and Private Leslie Compton and, in the first post-war season of 1946, he was one of scores of players who made fleeting first-class appearances. His only game was for Lancashire against Sussex at Old Trafford, when he took the wickets of Charlie Oakes and George Cox but managed no more than a single in his only innings. Although offered terms by Glamorgan, he was already 33 and decided to complete his career in the northern leagues. At the time of his death, he was Lancashire's "senior pro".

BULLUS, SIR ERIC EDWARD, died on September 8, 2001, aged 94. As MP for Wembley North for almost a quarter of a century, he was the doyen of the Lords and Commons cricket team and in 1959 published a history of its activities. Although himself a virulently right-wing Tory, it is said he mourned the electoral defeat of Labour members with cricketing prowess.

BURGE, PETER JOHN PARNELL, AM, died suddenly of a heart attack at Main Beach, Southport, Queensland on October 5, 2001, aged 69. The son of Jack Burge, an Australian team manager, he showed early signs of his ability at Brisbane Grammar School and, at 20, made his debut for Queensland in 1952-53. Two years later, at Sydney, he was playing for Australia in the last Test against Hutton's triumphant England side, scoring 17 and 18 not out. Over the next 11 years he played 42 Tests for Australia, including trips to England in 1956, 1961 and 1964; indeed, 22 of his international outings and each of his four Test hundreds were against England. One, his best Test score of 181, came in the drawn, rain-interrupted Oval Test of 1961, when Norman O'Neill also made a powerful century; another, at Leeds in 1964, was more significant. With Neil Hawke and Wally Grout in supporting roles, Burge hit a boisterous 160 to rescue Australia from an unpromising 178 for seven, enabling them to achieve the only victory of the series. In Tests, he scored 2,290 runs at an average of 38.16, while in 233 first-class games his aggregate was 14,640 at 47.53, with a highest score of 283 for Queensland against New South Wales at Brisbane in 1963-64.

Large, strong-armed and fearless, Peter Burge was a master of middle-order pugnacity, and he demonstrated some of that adamant sternness when called upon to

[*Getty Images*

"He looks a fighter; he is a fighter," *Wisden* said when naming Peter Burge among its Five Cricketers of the Year in 1965. "Big, strong and rugged in appearance… he loves a challenge and his cricketing life has been full of challenges."

act as one of the first match referees, which the ICC hoped would halt the deterioration of on-field behaviour. Amid a not always resolute bench of judges, he stood out uncompromisingly, as inflexible in resolve as when at the crease. He was the first referee to suspend a player – the Pakistani, Aqib Javed, in 1992-93 – for abuse of an umpire. He was also involved with England captain Mike Atherton over the ambiguities of the "dirt in the pocket" affair during the South African Test at Lord's in 1994. Burge, possibly feeling that matters had been snatched from his hands when England's chairman of selectors, Ray Illingworth, levied his own £2,000 fine, stalked Atherton to The Oval and fined him for dissent, like an old-fashioned schoolmaster levelling the scores. He also served as a Queensland administrator and selector, and had an interest in harness racing.

BURRELL, JOHN F., well known among cricket buffs for his research into the byways as well as the highways of the game, died in Bristol on September 28, 2001, aged 79. Jack Burrell contributed notes, letters and information to several cricket journals, including *The Cricketer* and *The Cricket Statistician*, and was especially involved with the publication of Minor Counties records. One of those cricket devotees whose endeavours go largely unsung, he also established an agency, Find-a-Pro, mainly for West Country clubs.

BUTLER, EWART BRYON, who died of cancer on April 26, 2001, aged 66, was chiefly known for his football reporting for the *Daily Telegraph* and the BBC. Bryon Butler's style was clear-cut and rational, rarely excessive or confrontational, and he brought these qualities to his affectionate writing on cricket in the late 1960s and early 1970s. His steadiness as an off-spinner, for many years with the Merrow club, near Guildford, was something he cherished.

BUTTERFIELD, Lord, DM, MD, FRCP, FACP, died on July 22, 2000, aged 80. William John Hughes Butterfield captained Oxford in the single-innings war-time Varsity Match of 1942. Having watched three wickets fall in the penultimate over, he "succumbed to the seventh ball of the last over possible", for 22, and Cambridge won by 77 runs. He had a dozen matches for Oxford, playing as the Authentics, and later played at Lord's in an Oxford and Cambridge (Past and Present) fixture. As a physician of some renown, he rose to be Vice-Chancellor of the University of Nottingham, Master of Downing College, Cambridge and Vice-Chancellor of Cambridge.

CAMA, SPEN, a former president of and indefatigable enthusiast for Sussex, died on May 22, 2001, aged 82, after a long illness. A wealthy lawyer and businessman, he founded the Preston Nomads, establishing them successfully in Fulking village amidst the beauty of the South Downs.

CARNARVON, 7TH EARL OF (Henry George Reginald Molyneux Herbert), the celebrated horse-racing manager, died on September 11, 2001, aged 77. He was president of Hampshire from 1966 to 1968. Lord Carnarvon offered the highest standard of country-house cricket at Highclere, in the middle of a park landscaped by Capability Brown, and, as Lord Porchester, captained his own eleven for many years. In 1994, the South Africans, on their first visit to England after the years of isolation, opened their tour there in the presence of the Queen. The occasion raised £30,000 for the National Playing Fields Association, with South African township cricket among the beneficiaries.

CAWTHRAY, GEORGE, who died on January 5, 2001, after a brief illness, aged 87, was groundsman at Headingley from 1964 until his retirement in 1978, after which he remained in an advisory capacity throughout the 1980s. He was very much at the centre of the controversies attached to the Leeds ground on successive Australian tours. In 1972, England won in three days, and so retained the Ashes, after the pitch had taken spin from the first morning; a freak storm had prevented use of the heavy roller and an attack of the fungus *Fusarium oxysporum* had left the pitch grassless. Three years later, the Test match was abandoned as a draw after the pitch had been damaged overnight, with knives and oil, by vandals campaigning for the release from prison of an armed robber, George Davis. Years earlier, as left-hand batsman and right-arm medium-pace bowler, George Cawthray had played two first-class matches for Yorkshire in 1939 and two in 1952 when, at the age of 38, he opened the bowling at Swansea in the absence of Fred Trueman, who was announcing himself in Test cricket with seven wickets against India at Headingley. These four games brought him 114 runs and four wickets. However, his record in Yorkshire club cricket was prodigious, and it is estimated he made more than 30,000 runs and took more than 3,000 wickets. He was professional and groundsman at the Hull club from 1946 to 1964, and later played for the Leeds club.

COLLINS, DALKEITH VALENTINE, died in Cape Town on January 7, 2001, aged 93. He umpired in ten Tests in South Africa between 1949 and 1962, and there was a fraternal moment – a Test-match first – in the 1953-54 Newlands match between South Africa and New Zealand when the other umpire was his brother, Stanley.

COX, DENNIS FRANK, a cricketer from Surrey's purple patch of the post-war era, died at Chislehurst on February 22, 2001, aged 75. Born not far from The Oval, at Bermondsey, he played 42 first-class matches for the county from 1949 to 1957, scoring 660 runs, with a highest score of 57 and an average of just under 19, and taking 68 wickets, average 34, with his quickish right-arm bowling. His seven for 22 against Cambridge University in 1952 was the highlight of his rather mixed career, which also saw him play for Cheshire between 1961 and 1967. It was his misfortune to find himself on a Surrey staff awash with world-class bowlers. His county captain, Stuart Surridge, said of him that he "was a fine cricketer, but we were so strong that he spent his time in the Second Eleven and grew old with the rest of the team". In 1992, when the Surrey president, W. D. Wickson, died suddenly just days into his incumbency, Dennis Cox took over the office, serving with civility and good humour.

CROUCH, MAURICE ALFRED, who died in Morocco on March 19, 2001, aged 83, played in four first-class matches: three for MCC and one for the Minor Counties, against Kent in 1951. Of his 205 first-class runs (average 29.28), 81 came in a two-hour partnership of 157 with Harry Halliday, the Yorkshire professional, for MCC against Oxford University at Lord's in 1952. Otherwise, his representative cricket was for Cambridgeshire over a lengthy period from 1936 to 1963 – he captained the side from 1952 onwards – and it was only in 2000 that his record aggregate for them, 8,474 runs, was overtaken by Nigel Gadsby.

DAVIS, CHARLES PERCY, died at Leicester on July 4, 2001, aged 86. Between 1935 and 1952, Percy Davis played 169 games for Northamptonshire, sometimes, post-war, in the company of his younger brother, Eddie. He was later on the county's coaching staff, and he also coached at Dale College in South Africa and Harrow School. A small, sturdy batsman – he often opened with the redoubtable Dennis Brookes – and an occasional wicket-keeper, he made 6,363 first-class runs at an average of 22.64, including three thousands for the season and ten centuries. One of these was converted into a double: 237 against Somerset at Northampton in 1947, after being missed at slip in Arthur Wellard's opening over. In personality, he appears to have veered between a gloomy pessimism and a cheerful mien, which may have been attributable to persevering in what was usually a struggling side.

DENNING, BYRON THOMAS, died at Abergavenny on November 19, 2001, after a short illness, aged 73. He had been Glamorgan's scorer since 1984 and was a popular figure on the county circuit with his fellow-scorers and the many journalists who shared his sense of humour and legendary tales. In May 2001, he made his "Test debut" when he scored for England in the Lord's match against Pakistan. Before being elected to the Glamorgan committee in the early 1970s, Byron Denning spent many years as player, committeeman and umpire with Ebbw Vale and – during the winter months – was secretary of Cross Keys rugby club. Nicknamed "Dasher" after the Somerset opener, Peter Denning, he was also Glamorgan's PA announcer. On one occasion, after Worcestershire had amassed a total over 500 at the small but delightful Abergavenny ground, he warned spectators, "I am about to read the Glamorgan bowling figures and I suggest small boys or anyone of nervous disposition cover their ears." "Byron was part of the furniture of the club," said Glamorgan captain Steve James, and there were players, umpires and scorers from around the counties at his funeral to pay tribute to a delightful character and offer condolences to his widow, Olwen, who accompanied him at every Glamorgan game, home and away.

DEWDNEY, NORMAN FOSTER, who died on December 5, 2000, aged 59, was a stalwart of umpiring administration, holding senior posts in the Army Cricket Umpires Association and the Association of Cricket Umpires and Scorers. Some of his quality is demonstrated by his rise from a boy soldier of 15 to a major in REME – he took up umpiring as a corporal in Benghazi – and, after retirement from the Army in 1991, his advance with Trinity House to the point of promotion to head of maintenance, with oversight of the nation's coastal and waterways navigational aids. He had recently been nominated by the General Council of the ACU&S for election as its general secretary.

DODDS, THOMAS CARTER, died in Huntingdon on September 17, 2001, aged 82. A Wellingborough and Warwick schoolboy and a wartime soldier, reaching the rank of captain, "Dickie" Dodds had played a little pre-war Second Eleven cricket with Warwickshire and Middlesex, and services cricket in India, some of it under Douglas Jardine, before he joined Essex as an amateur in 1946. This was also the year in which he was converted to the ideology of Moral Re-Armament, and what appeared to MRA's critics as a simplistic doctrine was, for Dickie Dodds, a burning conviction all of a piece with his venturesome batting. The post-war years were noted for county opening pairs – Robertson and Brown, Fagg and Todd, Alderman and Townsend – who were as prudent as the firms of solicitors for which they might have been mistaken. Dodds, however, opened the batting like a fiery Viking, smiting and walloping in the Essex cause until 1959. He played his last first-class match, for MCC, in 1961. In 396 games, 380 of them for Essex, he scored 19,407 belligerent runs at an average of 28.75, including 17 hundreds. His highest was 157 in a rally with Tom Pearce at Leicester in 1947. That season, his first in the professional ranks, also produced his best return of 2,147 runs, the second of 13 instances when he passed his thousand. Many of his runs were scored in fruitful alliance with "Sonny" Avery, with whom he established an Essex first-wicket record of 270 while making his maiden hundred at The Oval in 1946. Dodds scored 103, Avery went on to 210, and Surrey were beaten by an innings and 179 runs. In addition, he took 36 wickets, either with leg-breaks or at medium pace, and held 186 catches.

Dodds dedicated his life during and after his cricket career to MRA, and gave the entire proceeds of his 1957 benefit match (£2,325, more than £30,000 at today's valuation) to the movement. This commitment – he often worked in partnership with an even more famous opener, Conrad Hunte, the former West Indian vice-captain – was reflected in his 1976 autobiography, *Hit Hard and Enjoy It*, as much as his breezy cricket was.

DURIE, SIR ALEXANDER CHARLES, died in Surrey, after a short illness, on January 5, 2001, aged 85. A brisk moderniser of the Automobile Association while its director-

[*Getty Images*

Dickie Dodds was "in grand driving and hooking form" when Essex met the 1951 South Africans at Valentines Park, Ilford, hitting 18 boundaries in his first-innings 138.

general, he brought some of this acumen to the affairs of the Surrey club when, through connections with the Bedser twins, he joined the general committee in 1970, becoming a vice-president in 1980. In 1983 he was prominent in raising funds for the Bedser Stand and the Barrington indoor cricket centre at The Oval, while as a sagacious negotiator he chaired a special general meeting when Surrey members were waxing ireful about the club's administration. He was president in 1984 and 1985, and also a vice-president of Hampshire.

FERRIS, STEWART WESLEY, founder and president of the Mid-Ulster cricket group, died on May 28, 2001, aged 74. A fast-medium bowler, he played three times for Ireland, twice in first-class matches in 1956. In the first, against Scotland at Edinburgh, he took all of his four first-class wickets, but at a cost of 106 runs; in the other, against MCC at Dublin, he had only ten overs while the spoils went to off-spinner Frank Fee, who on his first-class debut claimed 14 for 100 to equal the Irish record for wickets in a match.

FORD, GEOFFREY, MC, who died on September 14, 2001, aged 85, joined the Hampshire committee in 1956 and served as a stalwart chairman from 1969 to 1986. "I'm glad to hear that at last Hampshire have come to their senses in making a Yorkshireman chairman," former Yorkshire captain Brian Sellers wrote in congratulating the Dewsbury-born Ford on his appointment. His father, Percy, had been a vice-chairman in the 1940s and 1950s, and his son Brian took the chair from 1995 to 2000. A useful fast bowler in club cricket, as well as a hockey enthusiast, Geoffrey Ford was closely involved with the Club Cricket Conference, of which he was elected president in 1979, and served on various TCCB committees, including finance: he was a chartered accountant. The day before he died, his son was able to tell him that Hampshire had been promoted to Division One of the County Championship.

GARTHWAITE, PETER FAWCITT, OBE, the last surviving Oxford cricket Blue of the 1920s, died at Hovingham, Yorkshire on May 13, 2001, aged 91. His twin brother, Clive, played first-class cricket for the Army in 1930. From Wellington College, Peter Garthwaite went up to Brasenose College and won his Blue as a freshman in 1929. He was also a hockey Blue. Though he played 11 first-class matches that year and in 1930, scoring 99 runs and taking 23 wickets at 39.86 with his leg-breaks, he did not play in the Varsity Match again. He subsequently devoted his career to forestry.

GILCHRIST, ROY, died at Portmore, St Catherine, in his native Jamaica on July 18, 2001, aged 67. The image of a bowler of genuinely high pace stricken with Parkinson's disease is a dolorous one, but such was Roy Gilchrist's fate. Following his brief but dramatic Test career, he had lived in England for many years, marrying and, not always in peaceful accord, rearing seven children before returning to the West Indies in 1985. He was accorded a ready welcome, but he was troubled by his health and by persistent hard times. His childhood on a sugar plantation had been impoverished and rough, and, in Michael Manley's sympathetic analysis, he was "burdened by those tensions which so often run like scars across the landscape of the personalities of people who come from poverty".

[*Getty Images*

Roy Gilchrist limbers up on a two-sweater April day at Eastbourne, where the 1957 West Indians opened their tour with a two-day friendly against E. W. Swanton's XI.

Certainly he was awkward to manage, insufferably so at times, and his Test career came to a precipitate termination in 1958-59 when his hard-pressed captain, Gerry Alexander, with the support of the senior players, dispatched "Gilly" home from India before the Pakistan leg of West Indies' tour of the subcontinent. Constant friction with Alexander off the field, coupled with over-aggressive bowling on it, including the unacceptable use of the beamer, was the cause. Banished from the international scene, he found professional slots in England, where he had toured in 1957 with mixed fortune. He played in the Lancashire leagues for a variety of clubs, including Middleton (for whom he took a total of 280 wickets in 1958 and 1959), going on to take 100 wickets every year until 1979. However, tales of atrocity, some perhaps arising from the proverbial tendency to give a dog a bad name, continued to emerge about his violently over-reactive attitude to batsmen and his unsparing use of the bouncer. Even charity matches were not free from his ferocious assaults: on one such occasion, at Werneth, that resolute Australian Cec Pepper luridly but successfully remonstrated with Gilchrist in terms not suitable to print.

Gilchrist's venomous bowling was the expression of a fiery, hostile personality. Of medium height, but long-armed and strong, he spearheaded, along with the young Wes Hall, the late 20th-century West Indian phalanx of unremittingly fast bowlers. Not since the heady days of Learie Constantine and Manny Martindale had they enjoyed so forceful an attack. Although Gilchrist's 21 wickets had cost almost 31 each when Pakistan toured the Caribbean in 1957-58, he was demonic in India, taking 26 in his four Tests at 16.11. In his best Test figures of six for 55, at Calcutta, five were bowled. All told, his 57 Test wickets in 13 outings averaged 26.68, while in 42 first-class matches his haul was 167 at 26, including one astonishing return of six for 16 at Nagpur when the West Indians bowled out a Combined Universities XI for 49. Roy Gilchrist played only five times for Jamaica, between 1956-57 and 1961-62, and he also had six games for Indian sides in 1962-63, when a number of West Indians were recruited to harden Indian batsmen to pace bowling.

GOVER, ALFRED RICHARD, MBE, the Mr Chips of cricket teachers, died in south London on October 7, 2001, at the age of 93. With his death, the mantle of being England's oldest living Test player passed to Norman Mitchell-Innes, born in 1914, while G. L. (Lindsay) Weir of New Zealand, born like Gover in 1908, became the oldest Test cricketer worldwide. During the 1939–45 war, Alf Gover served as a company sergeant major with the Army Physical Training Corps, before rising to the rank of major in the Pioneer Corps. As well as cricketer and coach, he was also a journalist, although whether he would wish to be remembered as the technical adviser to the leaden-footed 1953 film, *The Final Test*, is a moot point. He was president of the Lord's Taverners in 1974 and of Surrey in 1980, and manager of two Commonwealth cricket tours to the subcontinent in the 1960s.

After a spell on the Essex groundstaff, 19-year-old Alf moved to The Oval in 1927, making his debut for Surrey at Horsham against Sussex in 1928. These were the summers of "Bosser" Martin's impeccably groomed Oval wickets and of Surrey batting graced by Jack Hobbs, Andrew Sandham and others; bowling resources, not surprisingly in the circumstances, were scarce. Born on the same leap year day (February 29) as Frederic in *The Pirates of Penzance*, he was, like that ambivalent buccaneer, "a Slave to Duty", forced to act both as shock and stock bowler, galloping up his inordinately lengthy and somewhat ungainly run and hurling his thunderbolts hour after hour and over after over. Yet when he was opening the bowling in harness with Eddie Watts, his brother-in-law, Surrey were a formidable proposition for any county line-up in the second half of the 1930s.

Of Gover's 362 first-class matches, 336 were for Surrey in a career lasting until 1947. By the time he had put in 27 overs for an All England XI against Glamorgan in 1948, he had bowled a prodigious 77,269 deliveries and taken 1,555 wickets (1,437 for Surrey) at an average of 23.63. He took 100 wickets eight times, going on to 200 in 1936 and 201 in 1937 – the first fast bowler to reach 200 since Surrey's Tom

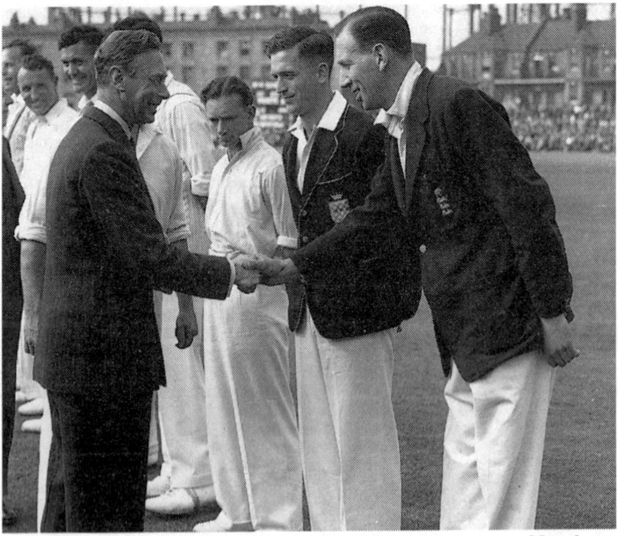

[Getty Images

King George VI, patron of Surrey, has a word with Alf Gover while meeting players and officials who participated in the one-day match between Surrey and Old England in 1946, to celebrate the centenary of the county club and of The Oval as a cricket ground.

Richardson in 1897. At Worcester in 1935, he had taken four in four balls to complete his best analysis of eight for 34, having conceded 22 runs before getting a wicket. He scored only 2,312 runs, never made a fifty and held 171 catches. Catches, however, were regularly dropped off his own luckless bowling, so that he seemed doomed, like an Ovalite Flying Dutchman, to bowl eternally, the hand of foe and butter-fingered friend alike against him. He played only four Tests: all were at home, against India in 1936 and 1946, and two against New Zealand in 1937. He was not too successful, managing no more than eight wickets for 359 runs, but he found some consolation in being the joint leading wicket-taker with Lord Tennyson's team in India in 1937-38. It was on this trip that, stricken with dysentery in an up-country match, he continued his long run-up beyond both wickets, over the boundary and into the safety of the pavilion lavatory.

For many years, Alf Gover was the proprietor of a legendary indoor cricket school in Wandsworth, south London, whither came for tuition not only the lowly but the mighty, including Tom Graveney, Ken Barrington, Viv Richards, Frank Tyson, Sunil Gavaskar, Andy Roberts and Brian Lara. It had been financed in 1928 by his future father-in-law, Bill Brooke, with Andy Sandham and Bert Strudwick as the active partners. Gover married Marjorie Brooke in 1932, and one of their sons, John, later ran the cricket retail side of the school. Alf's real interest began in 1938, and by 1954 he had obtained sole control of the premises, with its four low-slung nets. He was shrewd in his choice of fellow-tutors, employing coaches like Arthur Wellard, and he continued to bowl there until he was over 80. He finally retired in 1989, still kindly, smartly attired and upstanding. His coaching ensured that his fame was less dimmed in middle and older age than that of his peers, some of whom, without such a focus, faded from memory. At the last, none the less, it is as part of the Surrey scene of the 1930s that he will and should be remembered.

GREGORY, KENNETH, a freelance writer on cricketing and other matters, died on January 13, 2001, aged 79. His compilation *From Grace to Botham: 50 Master Cricketers from The Times* (1989), taking that newspaper's cricket reports, followed the pattern of his chief work, which consisted of letters from *The Times,* while *In Celebration of Cricket* (1978) sought "to remind the connoisseur of players and moments he has long cherished... and small boys of whatever age that there were giants before they were born".

HAMMOND-CHAMBERS-BORGNIS, RICHARD PETER, who played his one first-class game as R. P. Borgnis, died in France on May 28, 2001, aged 90. Few can have enjoyed a sole first-class appearance of such dream-like quality. A relative of Sir H. D. G. Leveson Gower, Peter Borgnis was a Royal Navy lieutenant when, in 1937, he played for the Combined Services at Portsmouth against the New Zealand tourists. He entered the fray with the score 18 for four and, in two and a half hours, struck a bold 101 out of 180. He then opened the bowling and took three for 38 in the visitors' first innings. The New Zealanders won easily by nine wickets, and that, as far as his first-class cricket was concerned, was that.

HARE, PETER MACDUFF CHRISTIAN, died in hospital at Shaftesbury on June 14, 2001, aged 81. After three years in the Canford XI, as captain in his last season, and having also appeared for Dorset, he played in the 1940 Freshmen's Trial at Oxford, but with little success. Then the war intervened. On his return to the university he was given a trial, keeping wicket against Leicestershire in The Parks in 1947. Going in at No. 9, he scored a useful 39, but his work behind the stumps – he held a catch in each innings – failed to persuade Martin Donnelly he was the keeper Oxford needed. It was his only first-class match. Hare became a schoolmaster at Rugby for many years and later at Hanford School, Childe Okeford.

HART, THOMAS MURE, who died on January 16, 2001, aged 91, had already represented Scotland twice at rugby when he went up to Brasenose College, Oxford and won a cricket Blue as a freshman in 1931 on account of his "brilliant fielding on the off side". He was kept busy as Alan Ratcliffe scored 201 in Cambridge's first innings of 385 but, not required to bat until No. 9, could enjoy the Nawab of Pataudi's riposte of 238 not out in Oxford's 453 for eight, as well as celebrate their eight-wicket win. At the time, these were the two highest individual scores in the University Match. Hart was back at Lord's the following year to observe another Ratcliffe hundred at close quarters, though was perhaps a little fortunate. He had not played for the University until they went on tour and owed his place as much to Oxford's need for an opening bowler as to his fielding. Two matches for Scotland, in 1933 and 1934, took his first-class record to 318 runs and nine wickets.

HAYNES, JOHN PERIGOE, who died in London on March 27, 2001, aged 74, was a right-hand bat and medium-fast bowler whose solitary first-class match, at Fenner's in 1946, was a discomforting experience. He made two ducks and failed to take a wicket in ten overs as Cambridge were outplayed by a formidable Yorkshire side. Last man in, he was a fifth wicket for left-arm spinner Arthur Booth, who would go on to take 111 in his first Championship season since his Yorkshire trial back in 1931. John Haynes later taught at Cranfield Prep School and in New Zealand (which qualified him to play some of his wandering cricket for the London New Zealand club); for 20 and more years he was master in charge of cricket at Highgate School.

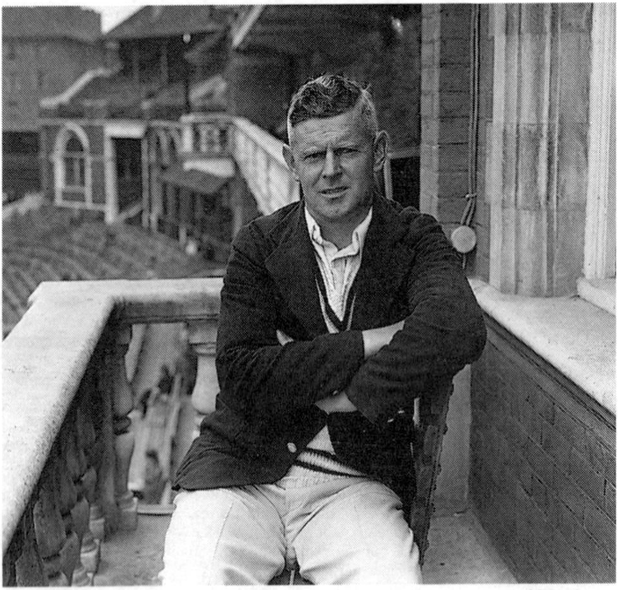

[*Getty Images*

George Heath – solid and reliable as an opening bowler for Hampshire either side of World War II. Talk of him playing for England in 1938 came to nothing more than that.

HEATH, GEORGE EDWARD MANSELL, died in Fareham, Hampshire on March 6, 1994, aged 81. Born in Hong Kong, he played 132 games for Hampshire, making his debut in 1937 after two years with the club and ground side. Indeed, he was chosen "almost as a last resort" because of injuries to other bowlers, but he soon established himself as "Lofty" Herman's opening partner, swinging the ball away at a lively pace and disconcerting batsmen with his ability to swerve it in late. In 1938, he took 97 wickets at 23.77 and would have gone past 100 had injury not cost him four games; he was also talked about by the England selectors as a possible to play against Australia. The war interrupted his progress, and afterwards he was something of a veteran as a fast-medium bowler. Not that this prevented him bowling unchanged for 26 overs when he recorded his best figures, seven for 49 against Derbyshire at Portsmouth in 1947, or following up with a further 37 overs in their second innings to finish with a match return of 13 for 152. All told, he took 404 wickets at an average of 28.11. A dedicated No. 11, he managed 586 runs in 188 innings, one of which, against Somerset in 1947, was immortalised by John Arlott in *Gone to the Cricket*: "And never let any man who saw or heard it forget George Heath's record innings of an hour and twenty minutes on three consecutive days at Bournemouth, an innings which grew slower and slower, until it stopped altogether when George had attained double figures." Along with Herman, he did not seek re-engagement after 1949, but he was awarded a deserved testimonial in 1951; like Herman also, he took up the tenancy of a pub.

HEWITT, FRANCIS STANLEY ARNOT, died suddenly on August 14, 2001, aged 65. Capped three times for Ireland, he played one first-class match, against Scotland in 1966, scoring 36 and 17 middle-order runs but, as an opening bowler, going without a wicket.

HOLT, RICHARD ANTHONY APPLEBY, died in London on May 18, 2001, aged 81. Despite glowing form for Harrow, especially in 1938 when as captain he averaged more than 100, "Bimby" Holt never, having gone up to King's College, Cambridge, represented the University at first-class level. However, he did play five times for Sussex in 1938 and 1939, and another first-class match for the Free Foresters in 1947. He made 60 runs in his nine first-class innings. He was for many years a governor of Harrow, including eight as chairman, and a vice-president of the All-England Lawn Tennis and Croquet Club.

HOLT, VESEY MARTIN EDWARD, a deputy Lord Lieutenant of Shropshire, president of that county's cricket club for more than 20 years and president of the Minor Counties Cricket Association from 1983 to 1996, died in hospital in Telford on July 14, 2001, aged 74. He was the great-great-great-great-grandson of that famous child of Shropshire, Robert Clive. The MCCA presidency had normally gone to a fairly distinguished cricketer, but Vesey Holt, of no more than village-green standard, proved a tactful and able appointment.

IRWIN, ESME ROSEMARY, died at Ickenham, Middlesex on August 18, 2001, aged 70. She opened the bowling for England in all four Tests on their tour of South Africa in 1960-61, and went on to umpire at representative level. In those matches against South Africa she took ten for 250, including four for 46 from 33 overs in the drawn game at The Wanderers.

KALAUGHER, WILFRID GEORGE, died in Newcastle upon Tyne on August 12, 1999, aged 94. From New Zealand originally, he attracted attention as a fast bowler while at Balliol College, Oxford, and played eight first-class games for the University between 1928 and 1931, taking 20 wickets at 32.05. He was considered for a Blue in 1929, but the final place went to E. M. Wellings, who subsequently played a few games for Surrey and became a well-known cricket writer. Kalaugher did, however, enjoy the consolation of an athletics Blue. He played for Oxfordshire in 1931 and 1932.

LANGLEY, GILBERT ROCHE ANDREWS, OAM, died in Adelaide on May 14, 2001, aged 81, having for several years suffered from Alzheimer's disease. Though his renown as a cricketer, and his 26 Test appearances for Australia, resulted from his wicket-keeping, Gil Langley first came to notice as a free-scoring batsman with the Sturt club in Adelaide, where he was coached by Vic Richardson, the former Australian captain. He also played Australian Rules football for Sturt, going on to represent and captain South Australia, and in later life he was a successful lawn bowler with the club.

After war-work on munitions in Melbourne – by trade he was an electrician – Langley made his first-class debut for South Australia in 1945-46 as a batsman, and it was 1947-48 before he donned the gloves for the state, with such success that next season he was the country's leading wicket-keeper, with 31 dismissals. He went on to play 55 matches for South Australia, his last in 1956-57. It was an exceptional time for Australian wicket-keeping, with both Don Tallon and Ron Saggers available, and Langley was 32 when he won his first cap, against West Indies at Brisbane in 1951-52. He had gone to South Africa as Saggers's understudy in 1949-50, and now, given his chance, he claimed 16 catches and five stumpings to equal the world Test record for a series.

[*Getty Images*

Gil Langley, in hat and coat, looks ready for the English climate as the 1953 Australians wait to disembark at Southampton. *From left:* Jack Hill, Keith Miller, Alan Davidson, Colin McDonald, Ian Craig, Gil Langley, Don Tallon, physio Arthur James and Neil Harvey.

Between then and 1956-57, he played 26 Tests. In his three against England in 1956 – he missed the other two through injury – Langley dismissed 19 of the 44 batsmen to fall, including nine at Lord's, then a Test record. All in all, he played 122 first-class matches, hitting 3,236 runs (374 in Tests) at an average of 25.68 and with a highest score of 160 not out for South Australia against the 1953-54 New Zealanders on their way home from South Africa. He closed his first-class career with a fourth century. Langley's best Test effort was 53, batting at No. 10, in an Australian total of 668 at Bridgetown in 1954-55. He caught 292 and stumped 77 batsmen, including 83 caught and 15 stumped in Tests. His average of 3.76 dismissals per Test compares favourably with the 3.66 of Wally Grout or – England's best – Jack Russell's 3.05.

Compact, a shade tubby, balding, not very agile and *déshabillé* in dress, Gil Langley was no cynosure of elegance. Ray Robinson described his stance as akin to "a boy scout grilling a chop at a barbecue". However, unshowy and solid, he brought to the exacting task of wicket-keeping the inestimable virtue of safety, day in, day out. Always a most genial and popular figure, he made what seemed a natural career move when he forsook the gauntlets for the hustings and became Labor member for Unley in the South Australia House of Assembly. There, effective and well liked, he enjoyed another kind of quiet success and eventually found himself umpiring the House as its much respected Speaker from 1977 to 1979. He also served in South Australian cricket administration from 1978 to 1989.

LAVINE, MARK JOHN, died in Coventry on May 12, 2001, after suffering a heart attack while playing for Coventry & North Warwicks against Barnt Green in a Birmingham League match. He was just 28 and left his wife, Patricia, and a two-year-old daughter, Nikita. A tall, imposing all-rounder, and a cousin of Gordon Greenidge, Mark Lavine was already a much travelled cricketer. He played first-class cricket for his native Barbados in 1992-93 but soon moved to South Africa, where he represented

North West and became a naturalised citizen. In all, he played 33 first-class matches, and there were two centuries among his 1,522 runs. His 100 wickets included a best return of six for 53, with match figures of ten for 124, against Boland in November 2000. Lavine had been recommended to Coventry by the former Warwickshire player, Andy Moles, and was playing only his third game for the club. He had struck a fine hundred to rescue them from a poor position, before collapsing later when bowling.

LUFF, JOHN, who died at home near Bath on May 4, 2001, aged 77, was Somerset's president from 1991 to 1996. However, his lifelong Somerset allegiance did not prevent him switching one of the county's sponsors (John Wainwright's quarrying company, of which he was managing director) from the Weston festival to Gloucestershire, after the festival folded in 1996. With Cedric Dickens, a grandson of Charles Dickens, he was joint founder of the Pickwick Cricket Club in Somerset.

LYGHT, ANDREW AUGUSTUS, died in his native Georgetown on April 16, 2001, aged 44, after a 15-year fight against cancer. An ebullient opening batsman, often against extremely quick bowling, he played 38 first-class games between 1976-77 and 1987-88 for Demerara, Guyana and Young West Indies, with whom he toured Zimbabwe in October 1983. In all, he scored 2,112 runs at an average of 32.00, with a top score of 122 for Guyana against Jamaica at Kingston in 1983-84, one of his six centuries. His best season was 1982-83, when, under Clive Lloyd's command, Guyana were unbeaten in winning the Shell Shield and Andrew Lyght averaged 61.62. Rather as Jack Robertson's international aspirations were thwarted by the longevity of Len Hutton and Cyril Washbrook, there was little chance for openers in the West Indies while the Haynes–Greenidge duumvirate reigned, and he never won a Test place. Lyght was professional for Crook Town in the north-east of England for six years. He earned many plaudits and insisted on playing despite the onset of his illness. To their credit, and as a mark of the respect in which he was held, Crook Town paid his hospital and allied expenses until such time as Lyght's sickness forced him to retire and return to Guyana in 1988.

McMAHON, JOHN WILLIAM JOSEPH, died suddenly in north London on May 8, 2001, aged 83. Born at Balaklava in South Australia, John McMahon was bowling left-arm spin for the Southgate club when he was spotted by Surrey. He played 84 games for them between 1947 and 1953, when he left the bustling environs of Kennington for the bucolic flavours of Taunton to replace the legendary Horace Hazell; over the next four seasons he played a further 115 first-class matches, all for Somerset. In all, he took 590 wickets, mostly in his sound, orthodox fashion, but from time to time with deliveries bowled out of the back of the hand. Unusually, he contrived to double up on his best performance, twice taking eight for 46: the first time was at The Oval in 1948, when, by way of celebrating his county cap, he took six of his eight wickets for seven runs in 6.3 overs to derail Northamptonshire's first innings; the second instance was for Somerset against Kent at Yeovil in 1955. The following season, when fellow-Australian Colin McCool headed Somerset's batting, McMahon passed 100 wickets for the only time. Not a strong batsman, he made 989 runs, averaging just over six.

John McMahon, a man who embraced the antipodean virtues of candour and conviviality, was loved more by his colleagues and the spectators than by the staid committeemen of Somerset. Legend tells of a night at the Flying Horse in Nottingham when he beheaded the gladioli with an ornamental sword, crying "When Mac drinks, everybody drinks!" Roy Virgin, a teenage apprentice batsman for Somerset at the time, tells of a Second Eleven game at Midsomer Norton, with the players billeted at a temperance hotel – and checked in at the door by the landlord for a 10.30 p.m. curfew. McMahon organised a POW-type loop, with his team-mates escaping through a ground-storey window and then presenting themselves again. But Virgin also recalled how

[*Getty Images*

Surrey spinners John McMahon (*left*) and Jim Laker, who in 1948 took 85 and 74 Championship wickets respectively as Surrey challenged Glamorgan for the title. Next season, McMahon was displaced by 20-year-old Tony Lock.

willingly he tutored young players who were prepared to listen keenly and work hard. According to David Foot, John McMahon's involvement in an embarrassing episode at Swansea's Grand Hotel led to his dismissal from Somerset, along with that of Jimmy Hilton, brother of Lancashire's better-known Malcolm. His fellow-players and members protested and petitioned – he had, after all, taken 86 wickets that 1957 season – but their pleas went unheeded and McMahon returned to London. He took an office job, but his interest in the game never diminished; in later years, he was an occasional contributor to *Wisden Cricket Monthly*.

MADONDO, TREVOR NYASHA, died in Harare of cerebral malaria on June 11, 2001, aged 24, scarcely old enough to realise his promise as his country's first black specialist batsman. He had played in three Tests, making his debut against Pakistan in Bulawayo in March 1998, 13 one-day internationals and 21 first-class matches. As a schoolboy at Falcon College, Matabeleland, Trevor Madondo had also shown prowess at hockey and rugby, but he chose to concentrate on cricket and, to this end, gave up his studies at Rhodes University, South Africa. He made his debut in 1994-95 for Matabeleland and later played for Mashonaland. A confident young man, he had some disciplinary troubles, being cast out of the Zimbabwean squad in December 1999 for alleged unpunctuality at practice sessions. There were counter-charges of racial motivation and, after an inquiry, it was recommended that the Zimbabwe Cricket Union pay him the going rate for the one-day series against the visiting Sri Lankans, in which he had already played two games. Madondo then battled hard to settle himself back in the side and, a year on, provided evidence of his talent and commitment with an unbeaten 74 against New Zealand at Wellington. It was his highest Test score and lifted his aggregate to 90 runs; in one-day internationals he made 191 runs, with a top score of 71 against India.

MAGUIRE, AIR MARSHAL SIR HAROLD JOHN, KCB, DSO, OBE, at one time Director-General of Intelligence at the Ministry of Defence, died on February 1, 2001, aged 88. In 1959, after flying a Spitfire over Whitehall as part of the Battle of Britain commemorations, he was forced to come down at Bromley. Showing commendable discernment, he avoided *The Times's* sports ground and elected to crash-land instead on the OXO cricket pitch, splintering the stumps. Fortunately, the players were having tea in the pavilion, where the intrepid pilot joined them for a reviving cuppa.

MANN, FRANCIS GEORGE, CBE, DSO, MC, died on August 8, 2001, aged 83. The elder son of Frank Mann, who captained England in South Africa in 1922-23, George Mann similarly led an MCC side there, in 1948-49. He continued another family achievement by captaining England in each of his seven Tests: five in South Africa and two at home against New Zealand the following summer. Three years in the Eton XI, and captain in 1936, he won Blues in 1938 and 1939 while at Pembroke College, Cambridge. His younger brother, John Pelham Mann, also captained Eton and played a handful of games for Middlesex. George himself made his first-class debut for Middlesex in 1937 and played several games for them in those pre-war seasons. However, before he could prosecute either a cricketing or a business career, war intervened. He would have an outstanding war, rising to the rank of major with the Scots Guards. His resourceful courage and cheerful leadership, particularly in the Italian campaign, won him great acclaim and much-merited decoration. In one judgment he was assessed as "the best regimental officer in the British Army".

He brought much of the same spirit to captaincy. Needing time to recuperate from wounds, he did not return to cricket seriously until 1947, when he played in the majority of Middlesex's usually victorious matches of that resplendent summer. He occasionally deputised as captain for Walter Robins, and took on the role full-time in 1948 and 1949 with consummate style, leading Middlesex to third and then a shared first place. Such were his personal appeal and practical skills that he was invited to take MCC to South Africa in the winter of 1948-49. Mann's success was twofold. First, the tourists were unbeaten in 23 games, and won the rubber 2–0 with Mann contributing above expectation, especially with his 136 not out at a critical point in the Fifth Test at Port Elizabeth. Secondly, the captain's gladdening temper ensured that the tour was, on and off the field, probably as unstressful as any. When South African captain Dudley Nourse was pressing for a win at Port Elizabeth to square the series, it was Mann who urged England to chase victory, rather than play for a draw. Set 172 in 95 minutes, they won with a minute to spare.

He then led England in the first two New Zealand Tests of 1949. But because he was unable to make himself available as far ahead as Australia in 1950-51, his Test career was abruptly halted and Freddie Brown appointed in his place. He also resigned the Middlesex captaincy after that summer, turning his perceptive attention to that ready adjunct of both the soldier and the cricketer, namely, beer from then on, most of his cricket was at a minor level. He played his last first-class match in 1958 for the Free Foresters. A compact, dark-haired figure at the crease, he scored quickly and freely and, in all his 166 first-class matches, made 6,350 runs at an average of 25.91; in Tests, he scored 376 at 37.60. His Port Elizabeth Test century was his highest first-class score.

That pleasing South African tour ended on a joyful note with a shipboard romance on the homebound journey with a South African, Margaret Marshall Clark, whom he married later in 1949. Family matters, both in a personal and professional sense, began to occupy him more, and for 30 years he helped manage the family brewing concern, Mann, Crossman and Paulin; from 1977 to 1987, he was involved with the Extel press agency. However, he remained close to the first-class game in a number of administrative capacities. He was honorary secretary of Middlesex from 1951 to 1965, their chairman from 1980 to 1983, and president from 1983 to 1990. Additionally, he was president of MCC in 1984-85, chairman of the Cricket Council in 1983, chairman of the TCCB

[*Patrick Eagar*

George Mann's qualities of leadership were recognised on and off the field. "Those who knew him best," Jim Swanton wrote of his election as chairman of the TCCB in 1978, "were thankful he was at hand to fill a post of such importance and responsibility."

from 1978 to 1983, and a life vice-president of MCC from 1990. He was appointed CBE in 1983.

These were not decorative jobs. The tangle of relationships among MCC, Middlesex and the TCCB meant the number of hats he wore was numerous and infinitely changeable, not unlike the Tommy Cooper sketch with its monologue of myriad characters and its skip full of headgear. But George Mann handled his assorted millinery with more aplomb than that frenetic clown, and his diplomacy and charm were often notably effective. For example, one may only applaud, in one of his background and interests, the firm decision to impose a three-year exclusion from England selection on the first "rebel" tourists to South Africa. Bob Bennett, a Lancashire chairman and an England tour manager, said simply that George Mann was "a very nice, nice, nice man," emphasising the triple application of that decent epithet. Another Lancastrian, Ken Cranston, born a month after George Mann and, with Mann's death, England's senior captain by age as well as service (he temporarily captained England in the West Indies in 1947-48), remembered his friend, contemporary and sometime Middlesex adversary as "a charming, gentlemanly figure from the old-world tradition of cricket".

MARRIOTT, SIR JOHN BROOK, the Keeper of the Royal Philatelic Collection from 1969 to 1995, died on July 3, 2001, aged 78. Having provided many a solid opening to the Merchant Taylors' innings, excelling especially in 1940, he played in wartime fixtures while at St John's College, Cambridge, including the two trials in 1942. Towards the end of World War II, his mathematical skills were put to decoding use at Bletchley Park. Thereafter, he taught his subject in the less stressful climes of Charterhouse, where he was in charge of cricket coaching for many years. Peter May was his outstanding protégé.

MASON, RONALD CHARLES, died on August 5, 2001, aged 89. After working for many years in the estate-duty office of the Inland Revenue, he became a well-respected adult educator and non-fiction writer. *Batsman's Paradise*, in 1955, was the first of several cricket books marked by a genuine affection for the subject as well as a flowing style. Others included *Sing All a Green Willow, Plum Warner's Last Season, Ashes in the Mouth* (a balanced account of the Bodyline tour) and excellent biographies of Jack Hobbs and Wally Hammond. There is some poignancy in the fact that the author of *Warwick Armstrong's Australians*, whitewash victors of 1920-21, died the day after Steve Waugh's successors retained the Ashes 80 years on.

MAY, ALLEN REGINALD, the Cambridge University, Combined and British Universities, and Cambridgeshire scorer, died on August 30, 2001, aged 78. Amiable and helpful, providing great assistance over the years to *Wisden*, Reg May took up scoring in 1983 following his retirement as a meteorologist from the London Weather Centre.

MAYLES, PETER, who died suddenly on January 13, 2001, was editor of the umpires' magazine, *How's That?*, having embarked upon umpiring in 1982 after many years of club cricket.

MENDL, DEREK FRANCIS, died in New South Wales on July 18, 2001, aged 86. Born in Argentina, he was three years in the XI at Repton, captaining them in 1933 when he also played for the Public Schools at Lord's. A hard-hitting batsman and wicket-keeper, he subsequently had two first-class games in 1951, for Free Foresters and for MCC against Oxford and Cambridge respectively. In the Cambridge match at Lord's, he caught David Sheppard, before he had scored, and Raman Subba Row, both off the 1947 England fast bowler, Jack Martin.

MENDL, JACK FRANCIS, died in Edinburgh on October 27, 2001, aged 89. Like his younger brother, who died earlier in the year, he was born in Hurlingham, Argentina, and had three years in the Repton XI, topping the batting with a highest score of 173 in 1928, his first season. A skiing accident put paid to his winning soccer and cricket Blues at Oxford, and he was in his mid-30s before he first played regularly for Oxfordshire in 1946. Although his teaching duties, first at the Dragon School, Oxford, and then at the Edinburgh Academy, delayed his Minor Counties cricket until halfway through the summer, he made 5,541 runs over ten seasons, at the fine average of 50.83. His 20 Minor Counties centuries were a (shared) record until exceeded by Lincolnshire's Steve Plumb on the last day of the 2001 Championship season. Two of these were double-hundreds. But, as John Woodcock recalled, Jack Mendl will be remembered as much for his "infectious, unaffected, almost boyish enthusiasm" for the game as for the resolute but aggressive approach he brought to opening an innings. He played seven first-class matches, one each for the Minor Counties and MCC and five for Scotland; at Buxton against Derbyshire in 1954, at the age of 42, he batted throughout Scotland's second innings for a first-class best score of 65 in a total of 100; no one else reached double figures.

MOORE, BRIAN BADEN, "the voice of soccer", died on September 1, 2001, aged 69, after some years of heart trouble. Born of humble rural stock in Kent, he won a scholarship to Cranbrook School, where, in 1950, he was a successful captain of cricket and hockey. *Wisden* described him as "a steady opener".

OATES, WILLIAM FARRAND, died on holiday in Canada on May 15, 2001, aged 71. An attractive, attacking right-hand bat, Billy Oates played three times for Yorkshire in 1956, including the Australian match at his home town, Sheffield, and afterwards made the short trip to Derbyshire. He first appeared for them in 1959. It took him a while to settle, but in 1961, playing his strokes "with refreshing freedom", he sailed past 1,000 runs. He did so again the following year – one of seven, a Derbyshire record, to reach that landmark – and was capped. However, his form began to fall away and by 1965 he could no longer command a regular place. In all, he scored 4,588 first-class runs, for an average of 22.94, but only two centuries, the better being his 148 not out in the win over Sussex at Worthing in 1961. He occupied his post-cricket years in clerical duties at a Sheffield steelworks.

O'MEARA, JOSEPH ANTHONY, died in Dublin on May 4, 2001, aged 57. He had been ill for a long time. Joey O'Meara played twice for Ireland in 1963: in the first-class international against Scotland at Londonderry, his contribution was one wicket, two ducks and three catches. Hockey was really his strong point and he won 52 caps between 1970 and 1977, as well as captaining Ireland. He was later team manager of the Irish cricket and hockey teams.

ORD, JAMES SIMPSON, died at Solihull after a brief illness on January 14, 2001, aged 88. In 273 appearances for Warwickshire, stretching from 1933 to 1953 – he was capped in 1935 – Jimmy Ord scored 11,788 runs at an average of 27.80, including 16 centuries and a top score of 187 not out against Cambridge University in 1952. Of the six seasons in which he reached his thousand, his most productive was 1948, with 1,577 runs for an average of 39.42. That was also the summer in which he hit a hundred in each innings, 107 not out and 101, against Nottinghamshire at Trent Bridge.

As for so many pre-war professionals, his career was rendered intermittent, first by the incursion of amateurs returning from university or schoolmastering, and then by the outbreak of hostilities. But like others of his patient ilk, he made a little hay when the sun shone in the immediate post-war era. Cricket fans, ever alert to the perky quality of a diminutive cricketer in the Jimmy Clitheroe mould, rewarded him in 1950 with a benefit of £4,834 18s 4d, a goodly amount for the times. A year later, he was ever present when Tom Dollery's team captured the Championship pennant. At Maidstone in 1953, his farewell season, he joined Dollery when Warwickshire were 95 for six, and inside three hours they added 250, a county record for the seventh wicket until 2000, when it was surpassed by Dougie Brown and Ashley Giles.

Jimmy Ord coached briefly at Edgbaston but soon removed himself almost totally from the Warwickshire scene. It was somehow fitting that he chose to establish a delicatessen in the Perry Bar district of Birmingham, for his batting had reflected the pungent tastiness of such ventures. He lived long enough to see another James Ord, his grandson, awarded his Warwickshire Under-13 colours in 2000.

PALWANKAR, YESHWANT BALOO, who played for clubs, notably Lancaster, in the Lancashire leagues, died in Pune on June 19, 2001, aged 75, following a short illness. He played 11 Ranji Trophy matches for Bombay from 1944-45 to 1954-55, scoring 319 runs at an average of 26.58 and taking ten wickets. In October 1948, "Antoo" Palwankar scored 53 when captaining All-India Universities in the drawn two-day game against the West Indians at the Brabourne Stadium.

RAVEN, SIMON ARTHUR NOËL, the novelist and television scriptwriter, who died in London on May 12, 2001, at the age of 73, had included cricketing references in

[*Getty Images*

Jimmy Ord – ever present and worth 1,311 runs at 31.21 when Tom Dollery's all-professional team won the County Championship for Warwickshire in 1951.

his *oeuvre*, although he himself registered no special claim to cricketing competence. His critique of public school life, *The Old School*, and his somewhat *louche* memoir, *Shadows on the Grass* (famously apostrophised by E. W. Swanton as "the filthiest book on cricket ever written") provide examples. Simon Raven's own schooldays were a paradigm of the upward mobility of trade and, like A. N. Hornby or R. G. Hargreaves (the Hampshire amateur who married Alice "in Wonderland" Liddell), he was borne upwards on the proceeds of Victorian commercial enterprise. In his case, it was his grandfather's sock-making concern that financed his education at Charterhouse, where he partnered Peter May at cricket and also attempted to embarrass the shyer, more withdrawn but infinitely more talented schoolboy cricketer.

RIST, FRANK HENRY, who died at Leytonstone on September 8, 2001, aged 87, played all his 65 first-class matches for Essex between 1934 and 1953. He was appointed the county coach in 1949, a role he performed with great dedication, and enjoyed a £1,274 testimonial in 1954. He made 1,496 runs, averaging 15.11, with a best score of 62 against Kent in 1953, and, partly as a stop-gap wicket-keeper, he caught 35 and stumped five. When the 1948 Australians rattled up a record 721 in a day at Southend, Frank Rist had the good fortune to be behind the stumps rather than chasing the ball. Something of a cricketing handyman, he also acted on occasion as emergency opening bat, and did so in the sensation of the 1935 season, when majestic Yorkshire were humbled at Huddersfield, swept aside for 31 (in less than an hour) and 99 – against the 334 (Rist 35) of the Essex giant-killers. Rist was also a sturdy centre-half for Leyton Orient, Charlton Athletic and Colchester United, and later managed West Ham United reserves.

[*John Woodcock*

Sunday best: *The Observer's* Alan Ross (*left*) and Ian Peebles of the *Sunday Times* take a little lighter refreshment as they follow England's fortunes against West Indies in 1959-60.

ROBINSON, HARRY BERTHOLF, who died on October 29, 2001, aged 71, was a much respected and kindly American jazz saxophonist. He took to playing and watching cricket with the zeal of the convert, and became a familiar Lord's figure, tootling away on the alto sax with the John Barnes' Outswingers at major matches.

ROBINSON, RAYMOND THOMAS, died at Taunton on November 13, 2001, aged 61, after suffering for 26 years from multiple sclerosis. A hard-hitting batsman in club cricket, Ray Robinson had one game for Somerset, at Taunton in 1964, and, despite failing to score in either innings, was able to enjoy their six-wicket win over Nottinghamshire. He was also a celebrated rugby scrum-half in the West Country, and for the British Police, and had the pleasure in later life of seeing his son, Andy, become head coach of the England rugby team.

ROPER, DONALD GEORGE BEAUMONT, better known as a winger for Southampton and Arsenal, died at the age of 78 on June 8, 2001, having been a sufferer from Alzheimer's disease. A useful middle-order batsman, notably for the Southgate club, he had one first-class match as an amateur for his native Hampshire in 1947. He made 30 and a duck at Portsmouth against Cambridge University.

ROSS, ALAN, CBE, cricket writer and littérateur, died suddenly of a heart attack on February 14, 2001, aged 78. He was born in Calcutta, whence he was dispatched to private schools in Falmouth and East Grinstead, and on to Haileybury, where his medium-paced bowling served the XI well. His time at Oxford was fleeting, but he did play in the hastily arranged one-day game with Cambridge in 1941; some 7,000 turned up at Lord's, and £120 in gate money was donated to the Red Cross. Then it was off to the Royal Navy and convoy duties in the Arctic. His cricket writing stemmed chiefly from his spell as cricket correspondent of *The Observer* from 1950 to 1971, and was in direct line of descent from R. C. Robertson-Glasgow. His account of the 1954-55 antipodean tour, *Australia 55,* and his 1983 biography, *Ranji: Prince of Cricketers*, are perhaps the best of his cricket books, along with the tasty pickings of *The Cricketer's Companion,* the anthology of prose and verse he first edited in 1960. From 1961, he took on the lifelong, spirited if rarely trouble-free editorship of the influential *London Magazine.*

Much as Ross enjoyed the bohemian and metropolitan life, Sussex, and in particular the Hove ground, also played host to his spirit. With Bert Wensley, the Sussex professional, having been rich in anecdote as his coach at Haileybury, his poetry and prose were both redolent of that county's pre-war flavours, as in these lines from *Cricket at Brighton:*

> Today Langridge pushes the ball for unfussed
> Singles; ladies clap from check rugs, talk to retired colonels;
> On tomato-red verandas the scoring rate is discussed.

Romanticist and averse to the trite arithmetic of the game, Alan Ross might well have chosen St Valentine's Day as an apt moment for his widely mourned demise.

ROY, PANKAJ, died in Calcutta on February 4, 2001, aged 72. He had suffered from cardiovascular problems. His son Pranab and nephew Ambar each played a few Tests for India, but Pankaj Roy had 43 to his credit; once, in 1959 at Lord's when Datta Gaekwad was poorly with bronchitis, he captained India. Cricket buffs recall him easily and affectionately for his great opening partnership with Vinoo Mankad when, against New Zealand at the Corporation Stadium, Madras in January 1956, they raised the world Test record for the first wicket to 413 runs. Mankad made 231 and Roy 173. They were the first Indians to bat together through a whole day's play in Test cricket – and only the third pair at the time. This was the highest, and also the last, of Roy's five Test centuries that went towards a Test aggregate of 2,442 runs at 32.56. The first two had been made against England in 1951-52 in his debut series. However, Roy found the pace of English bowlers and pitches too lively for him when he toured in 1952 – he managed just 54 in the four Tests – and as vice-captain in 1959. He had a happier time in the West Indies in 1952-53, averaging 47.87 in his four Tests and finishing with 150 at Kingston as he and Vijay Manjrekar put on an Indian-record 237 for the second wicket to save the match.

From 1946-47, when he hit a hundred on debut, to 1967-68, the stockily built, patient Roy was the anchor of the Bengal side in the Ranji Trophy. His highest score was 202 not out for Bengal against Orissa at Cuttack in 1963-64, and in all first-class matches he made 11,868 runs at an average of 42.38. Pankaj Roy's business life was occupied with the fisher-trawler trade and he was a figure of considerable prestige in Calcutta. He played a vital role in the development of cricket in Bengal and India, when both were coping with the political and social fall-out of World War II and the country's independence. Although he never forgot the humiliation, as he saw it, of his failures in England, he was well entitled to enjoy the compensation of that important opening partnership, still the world record at the time of his death.

SCINDIA, MADHAV RAO, the former Maharaja of Gwalior and president of India's board of control from 1990 to 1993, died on September 30, 2001, aged 56, when the private plane in which he was travelling, with seven others, crashed in the Mainpuri district of Uttar Pradesh. It was during his presidency that allegations of malpractice

[*Getty Images*

Pankaj Roy.

[*Getty Images*

Barry Shepherd.

in Sharjah first surfaced, and for almost two and a half years India, upset at what they considered was biased umpiring, boycotted cricket's desert outpost. Scindia also worked hard for women's cricket in his country.

SHAKOOR RANA, who found his few minutes of fame in an unedifying spat with Mike Gatting in the 1987-88 Faisalabad Test, died of a heart attack in Lahore on April 9, 2001, aged 65. As much as three-quarters of his press obituaries were consumed by the squabble after he halted play because, Shakoor Rana alleged, Gatting had moved a fielder without the batsman's knowledge. Umpire and England captain had a toe-to-toe, finger-jabbing confrontation, there were reciprocal charges of cheating and swearing, and the third day's play was lost, helping Pakistan escape with a draw. The match did not resume until an apology was forthcoming from the English camp.

A right-hand batsman and medium-fast bowler in his playing days, Shakoor Rana made his first-class debut for Punjab in 1957-58, and between then and 1972-73 he also played for Lahore, Khairpur and Pakistan Railways, with whom he held a post as a sports officer. In 11 first-class games, he scored 226 runs, took a dozen wickets and held 11 catches. Three of his brothers, Shafqat, Azmat and Sultan, also played first-class cricket (the first two at Test level), and two of his sons, Mansoor and Maqsood, played one-day cricket for Pakistan. Burly of frame and jocose by nature, he stood in 18 Tests and 22 one-day internationals from 1974-75 to 1996-97, and was reckoned to be upright and bold in his decision-making. It seems he could be self-important, too. In the 1984-85 Test at Karachi, he quarrelled with the New Zealand captain, Jeremy Coney, when he ignored an appeal for a catch at the wicket against Javed

Miandad, and the outraged New Zealander threatened to lead his team from the arena. But former Sussex captain John Barclay remembered a much friendlier character from the 1981 summer, when Shakoor Rana was umpiring in England. Barclay had been told by an Indian taxi-driver to ask "Where's Allah?" (rather than the customary "Howzat?") when appealing; the response would be a finger pointing to the sky. Shakoor Rana was having none of it. "Not that silly trick again," he said *sotto voce* as Barclay walked back to his mark.

SHEPHERD, BARRY KENNETH, OAM, died in Perth, Western Australia, on September 17, 2001, aged 64. Ill for some time with diabetes and an eating disorder, he had had both legs amputated. Since making a hundred on debut for Western Australia at 18, Barry Shepherd had forged a reputation as a belligerent and ruggedly forcing left-hand batsman, and in another generation he might have played more than nine Tests. Certainly, his debut 103 not out at the WACA in 1955-56, after Queensland's Ray Lindwall and Ron Archer had sent the home side tumbling to 87 for six, demonstrated that he would not be lacking in temperament or technique for the big time. Before long he was the linchpin of Western Australia's batting, but it was January 1963 before he played his first Test. Two months earlier he had made a career-best 219 against Victoria, at almost a run a minute, and now at Sydney his unbeaten 71 against Dexter's side turned the English tide and helped square the series. However, Australia brought Peter Burge back for the final Test, he hit a century and a half-century, and – despite scores of 96, 70 and 78 against South Africa the following season – Shepherd was passed over for the England tour of 1964. His only overseas trip was to the West Indies in 1964-65, when the second of his two Tests there proved to be his last. A year later, aged 28 and with a young family to support, he retired from first-class cricket to concentrate on a career with the Rothman tobacco company, ending up as chief executive. In 110 first-class matches, he scored 6,834 runs at the admirable average of 41.16, with three doubles among his 13 centuries. A Test average of 41.83 suggests he was unlucky not to have received more opportunities, but Australia's batting strength at the time meant the competition for places was intense.

He captained Western Australia from 1961-62 to 1965-66, always with the utmost verve and energy, and then served for 20 or so years on the state's executive committee. In addition, he represented Western Australia for 12 years on the Australian board. He brought much the same air of resolute command to his administrative responsibilities as he had to his cricket. Australian commentators have marked Barry Shepherd as the key to Western Australia's transformation from the gnomes to the Titans of the domestic game in Australia.

SMITH, RAYMOND CHARLES, died on December 12, 2001, aged 66, after a heart attack while playing the 14th hole on holiday in St Lucia. A tall orthodox left-arm spinner, Ray Smith had joined Leicestershire in 1952, straight from Stamford School, as a possible replacement for Jack Walsh. When, on debut in 1956, he made Warwickshire follow on with a return of 11.2–8–6–4, such a prospect seemed likely. In his last three years at Stamford, two under M. J. K. Smith's captaincy, he had taken 145 wickets at ten apiece, and in 1952 he had played for the Rest in the Lord's schools trial as an all-rounder – though with a career top score of 36 his right-hand batting counted little in the professional game. His bowling after that memorable debut tended to be fitful, depending unduly on sympathetic conditions, but he was a useful foil for John Savage's off-breaks. At Trent Bridge at the end of 1957 he took seven for 54, his best-ever figures. But only once, with 54 at 32.25 in 1959, did he take 50 wickets in a season, and at the end of 1960 Leicestershire released him. That would have been it had Grace Road not become a spinners' paradise in 1963. Invited back in mid-season, Smith had four golden games in which he took 34 wickets at nine each. Not one of them, however, brought as much pleasure, or was as much a future conversation piece, as the ball that bowled Garry Sobers for 17 when the West Indians visited Leicester. He had another summer, giving him a career aggregate of 203 wickets at 27.16, then went off to build up the haulage business, Ray C. Smith, that kept his name in the public eye.

SUTCLIFFE, BERT, MBE, who died of emphysema on April 20, 2001, aged 77, was the outstanding New Zealand batsman of the immediate post-war period, though many in England who watched that other New Zealand left-hander, Martin Donnelly, in The Parks for Oxford might pursue counter-claims. Perhaps, as R. C. Robertson-Glasgow noted, "Sutcliffe had a more powerful case in his strokes to leg" whereas "in defence, Donnelly always looked the surer". The splendour of their off-side strokes was, needless to say, a given, and their brilliant fielding never ceased to excite attention, with Sutcliffe in his element whether at short leg, in the slips or at cover. Both made manifest again in that austere era some of the more charming cricketing images of the inter-war years.

Tall and good-looking, fair-haired and enviably fit, batting in the classic manner, Bert Sutcliffe – his given name the homely choice of parents who had emigrated from Lancashire – might well have graced the pages of a novel featuring country-house cricket, not least in that he ever remained an affable man of steady temper. His blondness made him instantly recognisable, while, for the enthusiast, there was much that was identifiable in the shapely, clean-cut dispatch of his shot-making. When Walter Hadlee's New Zealanders visited England in 1949, determined to prosecute their case for an end to the insult of three-day Tests, it was in large degree thanks to Bert Sutcliffe that, with four sound draws, the slur was removed. He scored 2,627 runs in that pleasantly dry summer, including 423 at a marvellous 60.42 in the Tests; only Bradman, with 2,960 in 1930, had a higher aggregate on a tour of England. Patsy Hendren, observing Sutcliffe as he warmed up at Lord's in pre-tour nets, is reported to have said, "2,500 in a season if ever I saw 'em."

He made his first-class debut at 18, for Auckland against Wellington in 1941-42 and then spent two years at teacher training college before joining the army. Overseas service in North Africa and Italy found him playing cricket with English spinners Jim Laker and Peter Smith, and the experience would stand him in good stead when peace returned. His teaching career took him to Dunedin, where his 197 and 128 for Otago against the 1946-47 MCC tourists guaranteed his first Test cap a week later, in Christchurch. Putting on 133 for the first wicket with Hadlee, playing majestically until caught behind off Bedser for 58, he launched an illustrious career just as another was drawing to an end, for this would be the final Test of his boyhood hero, Walter Hammond.

From then until 1965, when he made his third tour of England, Sutcliffe played 42 Tests, making 2,727 runs with an average of 40.10 and a highest score of 230 not out against India at Delhi in 1955-56. He captained New Zealand in both Tests against the visiting West Indians in 1951-52, and again for the last two Tests in South Africa in 1953-54, having assumed charge of the touring side when Geoff Rabone was injured. If his form on this tour dipped below that expected of such a gifted player, there were still times, *Wisden* noted, "when he played in a manner to live in the memory of spectators". The Second Test at Ellis Park was one of them. Struck on the head by a bumper from Neil Adcock, he gallantly returned, heavily bandaged and pale, to score 80 not out in a total of 187, adding 33 for the last wicket with fast bowler Bob Blair in a partnership charged with emotion and sympathy for the New Zealanders. Two days earlier, on Christmas Eve, Blair's 19-year-old fiancée had been one of 151 people killed in a rail accident in New Zealand. A month later Sutcliffe pasted the Border bowling for 196, his only century in South Africa, but there were hundreds against Western Australia, South Australia and Victoria on the way home.

It has been suggested that his head injury at Johannesburg subsequently affected his Test batting. But he remained a genuine force in New Zealand cricket. Though he had been absent from Tests for five seasons, at the age of 41 he was included in the

[Getty Images

New Zealand openers Verdun Scott and Bert Sutcliffe (*right*) make their way to the wicket at the start of the 1949 Oval Test: they put on 121 in 80 minutes.

1965 side to tour India, Pakistan and England. His unbeaten 151 at Eden Gardens was his fifth and last Test hundred.

In all first-class cricket, he hit 44 centuries in a total of 17,447 runs at a fine average of 47.41. His highest innings, among a series of heavy scores, was 385 for Otago against Canterbury at Christchurch in 1952-53 – at the time the sixth-highest score ever and, until the advent of Brian Lara, the highest by a left-hander in first-class cricket. He had previously made 355 for Otago against Auckland in 1949-50. Six more scores over 200 included 243, followed by 100 not out in the second innings, against Essex in 1949. He also took 160 catches and claimed a stumping. Bert Sutcliffe was New Zealand's first Sportsman of the Year, in 1949, and in 1990 was selected in the inaugural list for the New Zealand Sports Hall of Fame. The decision to name the country's new cricket academy ground at Lincoln the Bert Sutcliffe Oval was a deeply felt tribute to his heroic part in their cricket history.

TAYLOR, FREDERICK, died at his birthplace, Leek, on June 18, 1999, aged 83. He had rarely strayed far from his native heath. Taken on the Warwickshire staff in 1939, he managed to portmanteau his debut and farewell game for them into one when he played against Cambridge University. Came the war and a first-class career was denied him. His father, C. J. Taylor, had had three matches for Warwickshire in 1908 and 1909. Both were fast-medium bowlers and both played with great heart for Staffordshire. In 1953, Fred Taylor was granted a second crack at first-class cricket when he represented the Minor Counties against the Australians at Stoke. The pitch was a shocker – "some balls rose chest high... others scurried through low" – and Taylor emerged with five for 71 from 39 overs. Meanwhile, Neil Harvey had been blazing away for a thrilling 109. Sensibly, given the circumstances, Taylor waited till the end before batting, though in neither innings did he wait long. Ray Lindwall took seven for 20 in 11 overs as Minor Counties disintegrated for 56, and Richie Benaud five for 13 in seven when they mustered 62. Each claimed Taylor as his final wicket.

THOMPSON, ALEXANDER WILLIAM, died, after a brief illness, in Illinois on January 13, 2001, aged 84. Sandwiched between the cultural extremes of the Mersey estuary – he was born in Liverpool – and the Prairie State could be found 195 first-class games for Middlesex between 1939 and 1955. Consequently, Alec Thompson shared in some of Middlesex's finest hours, notably their Championship triumphs of 1947 and 1949, though it would be fair to say that he was the least praised and possibly least remembered of these sides. Then again, as David Lemmon observed in his history of Middlesex, "No one would have found it easy to take centre stage after Edrich and Compton, but when the responsibility was thrust upon him... he accepted it." A vigorous right-hand batsman, he scored 7,915 first-class runs at an average of 26.47, usually in the middle order. However, his highest score of 158, against Worcestershire at Dudley in 1952, came after opening the innings and adding 315 for the second wicket with Bill Edrich. He hit five centuries in all and reached 1,000 runs in three seasons. He was a capable outfield and held 68 catches; he also took 12 wickets. In 1955, he shared a benefit with Harry Sharp, and subsequently moved to the United States, where he worked as a chemist.

TRUBSHAW, ERNEST BRIAN, CBE, died quietly in his sleep, without prior illness, at Tetbury on March 24, 2001, aged 77. After RAF service as a bomber pilot and later in The King's Flight, he joined Vickers-Armstrong in 1950 as an experimental test pilot and, in that role, flew Concorde, the first supersonic passenger jet, on its initial test flights in 1969. As a schoolboy cricketer, in H. S. Altham's house at Winchester, he played for the XI in 1941, and captained the side in 1942. Winchester were particularly strong in 1941, defeating Eton, Harrow, Bradfield and Wellington, and Brian Trubshaw, an uncomplicated opening bat, had an excellent season, including a forthright 58 in partnership with Hubert Doggart in Winchester's first defeat of Eton for 21 years. He was inducted into the RAF via a medical in the Long Room at Lord's, when the Pavilion was part of the Air Crew Reception Centre, and returned there more conventionally in 1946 to play for the RAF against the Navy and Marines. He and Dick Altham, son of H. S., held out for 40 minutes at the end to secure a draw. His sole first-class appearance, for Combined Services earlier that summer at Worcester, was not so distinguished: he managed a run in each innings and, stumped in the first off Dick Howorth, was one of seven victims for Hugo Yarnold.

TUKE, SIR ANTHONY FAVILL, MCC president in 1982-83 at the time of the Gleneagles agreement, which called for a ban on sporting connections with South Africa, died on March 6, 2001, aged 80. He rose, like his father and grandfather before him, to be chairman of Barclays Bank, and later he was chairman of the RTZ mining company and the Savoy Hotels group. In business he advocated the continuation of commercial links with the unreconstructed South Africa, while attempting to sustain the role of liberal employer in that country. On July 13, 1983, he chaired the rather stormy MCC debate at Westminster's Central Hall about the possibility of the club "implementing the selection of an MCC touring party to tour South Africa in 1983-84". The motion was defeated.

WAKLEY, BERTRAM JOSEPH, MBE, who died on September 11, 2001, aged 84, was a remarkable cricket researcher. His *Bradman the Great* (1959), a detailed and contextual analysis of each of Don Bradman's first-class innings, was a seminal and much praised study, while his *Classic Centuries in England–Australia Test Matches* (1964) was a similarly comprehensive record. He enjoyed a legal career of some eminence and acted as a judge on the south-eastern circuit from 1973 to 1992.

WEIDEMAN, IZAK FRANCOIS NEL, who represented South African Universities, Transvaal and Northern Transvaal as a medium-fast bowler in the 1980s, was murdered on June 4, 2001, aged 40, during an armed robbery at Maraisburg golf course, Johannesburg, where he was employed as a green-keeper. Until his playing career was ended by a motor-driven roller running over his foot, Francois Weideman had appeared in 40 first-class matches, scoring 662 runs at 15.39 and taking 135 wickets, with an average of 22.34 and a best return of six for 43 for Northern Transvaal against Eastern Province at Port Elizabeth in 1984-85. He later coached, and co-authored a coaching manual in Afrikaans.

WHEATLEY, GARTH ANGUS, died at Uppingham on September 4, 2001, aged 78, having been both pupil and long-while master at the school, where, late in life and to general surprise, he married one of the matrons. He played for Oxford in the war-time Varsity Matches from 1943 to 1945, the last two as captain, and won his Blue when, holding the office of secretary, he kept wicket at Lord's in 1946. Oxford, set up by Donnelly's 142, won by six wickets. The summer after, he played five times for Surrey, including their last four Championship fixtures, while the last of his 18 first-class games was for Free Foresters in 1950. In addition to his 20 catches and eight stumpings, Garth Wheatley scored 478 first-class runs, average 17.07, with a top score of 66 for Oxford against Sussex at Chichester.

WHITTLE, CHARLES JAMES RICHARDSON, died on July 4, 2001, aged 79. He played in Oxford's first two county games in 1947, but, scoring only 23 runs in his four innings, had no further opportunities once Donnelly decided to switch himself from opener back into the middle order. He had been in the Sedbergh XI before his war service in the Royal Navy.

WOODS, DONALD, CBE, the progressive South African journalist and anti-apartheid campaigner, died in Sutton, Surrey, on August 19, 2001, aged 67. He had been suffering from cancer. Placed under house arrest in 1977 for his anti-apartheid views after 12 years as editor of the East London *Daily Dispatch*, he fled South Africa in 1978 disguised as a priest and was thereafter based chiefly in London. Daringly, he had used a pair of cricket pads to hide from the South African police the typescript of his book on the murdered black consciousness leader, Steve Biko. This would form the basis of the film, *Cry Freedom*.

While a pupil at the Christian Brothers' College in Kimberley, he had represented Griqualand West in the South African Nuffield schoolboy championships. But it was as a co-founder – indeed, he was instrumental in obtaining permission for it to play – of the mixed-race Rainbow Cricket Club that Woods made his most important contribution to cricket. At the time of his arrest, he was the only white member of the governing council of the South African Cricket Board. In the 1993 *Wisden*, he wrote a thoughtful piece, "African Sunrise", on his homeland's return to the global cricketing fraternity, and he had other cricketing pieces to his name. Former South African president Nelson Mandela had telephoned with his good wishes only days before Donald Woods's death, while the South African High Commissioner in London, Cheryl Carolus, described him as "a truly great son of South Africa", and said that "A great life of courage has ended, but his spirit lives on with his people."

WYATT, GERALD, died, following a heart attack, in Stepping Hill Hospital, Stockport on June 19, 2001, aged 68. Unlucky to be reserve wicket-keeper to George Dawkes, who was immediately followed by Bob Taylor, he played but 11 games for Derbyshire between 1954 and 1960, scoring 184 runs and taking seven catches.

DIRECTORY OF BOOKSELLERS AND AUCTIONEERS

BOOKSELLERS

AARDVARK BOOKS, Larwood, 47 Melbourne Way, Lincoln, Lincolnshire LN5 9XJ. Tel/fax: 01522 722671. Peter Taylor specialises in *Wisdens*. Send SAE for list. *Wisdens* purchased and restoration service available.

ACUMEN BOOKS, Nantwich Road, Audley, Staffordshire ST7 8DL. Tel: 01782 720753; fax: 01782 720798; e-mail: wca@acumenbooks.co.uk; website: www.acumenbooks.co.uk. Everything for umpires, scorers, coaches and others, including standard text-books, all for worldwide import or export.

TIM BEDDOW, 66 Oak Road, Oldbury, West Midlands B68 0BD. Tel: 0121 421 7117; fax: 0121 422 0077; e-mail: timbeddowsports@btinternet.com; website: www.edgbastonbooks.co.uk. Large stock of cricket/football books, programmes and signed material. Items purchased. Send SAE for catalogue. Stall at Thwaite Gate, Edgbaston, every first-team match.

BODYLINE BOOKS, 150a Harbord Street, London SW6 6PH. Tel: 020 7385 2176; fax: 020 7610 3314; e-mail: cricket@dircon.co.uk. London's only specialist cricket book dealer. *Wisden* specialist.

CRICKET BOOKS DIRECT, 3 Luke Street, London EC2A 4PX. Tel: 020 7739 7173; fax: 020 7729 2305; website: www.sportsbooksdirect.co.uk. A comprehensive selection of the latest and best new cricket books, especially imports from Australia. Regular catalogues issued.

IAN DYER CRICKET BOOKS, 29 High Street, Gilling West, Richmond, North Yorkshire DL10 5JG. Tel/fax: 01748 822786; e-mail: iandyer@cricketbooks.co.uk; website: www.cricketbooks.co.uk (search/buy on a secure site). *Wisden*, second-hand/antiquarian book specialist.

BRIAN FAULKNER, 62 Friars Moor, Sturminster Newton, Dorset DT10 1BH. Tel: 01258 473974 (evenings and weekends only); e-mail: brianfaulkner@cwcom.net. Second-hand and antiquarian books, autograph material. Catalogue quarterly and on request.

K. FAULKNER, 65 Brookside, Wokingham, Berkshire RG41 2ST. Tel: 0118 978 5255; e-mail: kfaulkner@bowmore.demon.co.uk; website: www.bowmore.demon.co.uk. Cricket books, *Wisdens*, memorabilia bought and sold. Catalogues issued. Also at Gloucestershire CCC shop, Nevil Road, Bristol BS7 9EJ.

GOLD CRICKET BOOKS, 15 Bodiam Avenue, Bexhill, East Sussex TN40 2LS. Tel: 01424 217156. Antiquarian, rare, fine and second-hand cricket books and memorabilia. Catalogue available quarterly. Please send SAE to above address.

JUST CRICKET BOOKS, 16 Wordsworth Drive, Kenilworth CV8 2TB. Tel 01926 850389; e-mail: jshaw50691@aol.com. Extensive range of *Wisdens*, modern and antiquarian cricket books – send for comprehensive catalogue or indicate requirements.

E. O. KIRWAN, 3 Pine Tree Garden, Oadby, Leicestershire LE2 5UT. Tel: 0116 271 4267 (evenings and weekends only). Second-hand and antiquarian cricket books, *Wisdens*, autograph material and cricket ephemera of all kinds.

***J. W. McKENZIE, 12 Stoneleigh Park Road, Ewell, Epsom, Surrey KT19 0QT. Tel: 020 8393 7700; fax: 020 8393 1694; e-mail: jwmck@netcomuk.co.uk; website: www.mckenzie-cricket.co.uk.** Specialists in antiquarian second-hand books, particularly *Wisdens*, and memorabilia. Established 1969. Catalogues sent on request. Publishers of cricket books. Shop premises open regular business hours.

ROGER PAGE, 10 Ekari Court, Yallambie, Victoria 3085, Australia. Tel: (03) 9435 6332; fax: (03) 9432 2050; e-mail: rpcricketbooks@unite.com.au. Dealer in new and second-hand cricket books. Distributor of overseas cricket annuals and magazines. Agent for Cricket Statisticians and Cricket Memorabilia Society.

***THE PARRS WOOD PRESS, Freepost, Manchester M15 9PW. Tel: 0161 226 4466; e-mail: sport@parrswoodpress.com; website: www.parrswoodpress.com**. The Parrs Wood Press is a publisher of quality new cricket books. Contact us for a free catalogue.

***PENGUIN DIRECT. Tel: 0208 8757 4036.** New *Wisdens* for 1996–2002 and the first four editions of *Wisden Cricketers' Almanack Australia* available from Wisden's mail-order supplier. Prices from £12.50, including p&p.

RED ROSE BOOKS, 196 Belmont Road, Bolton BL1 7AR. Tel: 01204 596118; fax: 01204 597070; e-mail: redrosebooks@btinternet.com; website: www.cricketsupplies.com/books. Specialist dealer in second-hand and antiquarian cricket books. Catalogue sent on request.

WILLIAM H. ROBERTS, The Crease, 113 Hill Grove, Salendine Nook, Huddersfield, West Yorkshire HD3 3TL. Tel/fax: 01484 654463; e-mail: william.roberts2@virgin.net; website: www.williamroberts-cricket.com. Second-hand/antiquarian cricket books, *Wisdens*, autograph material and memorabilia bought and sold. Catalogues sent on request.

ST MARY'S BOOKS & PRINTS, 9 St Mary's Hill, Stamford, Lincolnshire PE9 2DP. Tel: 01780 763033; e-mail: cricket@stmarysbooks.com; website: www.stmarysbooks.com. Dealers in *Wisdens*, second-hand, rare cricket books and *Vanity Fair* prints. Also search service offered.

CHRISTOPHER SAUNDERS, Orchard Books, Kingston House, High Street, Newnham-on-Severn, Gloucestershire GL14 1BB. Tel: 01594 516030; fax: 01594 517273; e-mail: chrisbooks@aol.com. Office/bookroom by appointment. Second-hand/antiquarian cricket books and memorabilia bought and sold. Regular catalogues issued containing selections from over 10,000 items in stock.

SPORTING DECLARATIONS BOOKS, PO Box 882, Sutton SM2 5AW. Tel: 020 8643 8828; e-mail: sportdecbk@aol.com; website: www.sportingdeclarations.co.uk. Publishers/suppliers of Trevor Jones's highly acclaimed books about Surrey's recent County Championship triumphs.

***SPORTSPAGES, Caxton Walk, 94–96 Charing Cross Road, London WC2H 0JW. Tel: 020 7240 9604; fax: 020 7836 0104. Barton Square, St Ann's Square, Manchester M2 7HA. Tel: 0161 832 8530; fax: 0161 832 9391; website: www.sportspages.co.uk**. New cricket books, audio and video tapes, including imports, especially from Australasia; retail and mail-order service.

STUART TOPPS, 40 Boundary Avenue, Wheatley Hills, Doncaster, South Yorkshire DN2 5QU. Tel: 01302 366044. Our 120-page plus catalogue of cricket books, *Wisdens*, booklets, brochures and county yearbooks is always available.

***WILLOWS PUBLISHING CO., 17 The Willows, Stone, Staffordshire ST15 0DE. Tel: 01785 814700.** *Wisden* reprints 1879, 1885, 1900–1913, 1916–1919 and 1941–1945. Send SAE for prices.

MARTIN WOOD CRICKET BOOKS, 1c Wickenden Road, Sevenoaks, Kent TN13 3PJ. Tel/fax: 01732 457205. Send first-class stamp for annual catalogue listing by subject: *Wisdens*, Annuals, Biographies, Tours, Histories, Counties, Fiction and also Autographs. Established 1970.

AUCTIONEERS

***CHRISTIE'S, 85 Old Brompton Road, South Kensington, London SW7 3LD. Tel: 020 7321 3402; e-mail: lmclark@christies.com**. Christie's successful auctions devoted to cricket memorabilia have been held on a regular basis since the inaugural MCC Bicentenary sale in 1987. For enquiries, please contact Lucy Clark.

MULLOCK MADELEY, The Old Shippon, Wall-under-Heywood, Church Stretton, Shropshire SY6 7DS. Tel: 01694 771771; website: www.mullockmadeley.co.uk. Mullock Madeley hold specialist sporting memorabilia auctions. For details, please visit either our website or our offices.

***T. VENNETT-SMITH, 11 Nottingham Road, Gotham, Nottinghamshire NG11 0HE. Tel: 0115 983 0541.** Auctioneers and valuers. Twice-yearly auctions of cricket and sports memorabilia. The cricket auction is run by cricketers for cricket-lovers worldwide.

***DOMINIC WINTER BOOK AUCTIONS, Specialist Book Auctioneers & Valuers, The Old School, Maxwell Street, Swindon, Wiltshire SN1 5DR. Tel: 01793 611340; fax: 01793 491727; e-mail: info@dominicwinter.co.uk; website: www.dominicwinter.co.uk**. Twice-yearly auction sales of sports books and memorabilia, including *Wisdens*.

Asterisks indicate businesses that have display advertisements elsewhere in the Almanack. See Index of Advertisements for details.

DIRECTORY OF CRICKET SUPPLIERS

COMPUTER DATABASES

FBSS LTD, Windsor, Little Stambridge Hall Lane, Rochford, Essex SS4 1EN. Tel: 01702 530060; fax: 01702 542988; e-mail: info@e-cricket4all.com; website: www.e-cricket4all.com. Cricket Organiser for Windows™. The ideal PC software package for secretaries and managers at clubs and schools of all sizes.

GORDON VINCE, 5 Chaucer Grove, Camberley, Surrey GU15 2XZ. E-mail: gordon@gvince.demon.co.uk. The Cricket Statistics System is used worldwide to produce the widest range of averages and statistics, from Test to village level. Also available with an extensive range of up-to-date databases of matches from around the world.

CRICKET COACHING/COURSES

DURHAM SCHOOL, Durham DH1 4SZ. Tel: 0191 386 4783. E-mail: enquiries@durhamschool1.fsnet.co.uk. Professional cricket coaching for young people aged 8–18 years. Residential and non-residential courses run during Easter and summer. Course director: Mike Hirsch.

QUANTUM COACHING, Hill House, 39 Bondgate Within, Alnwick, Northumberland NE66 1SX. Tel: 01665 606551; fax: 01665 606552; e-mail: enquiries@quantumcoaching.co.uk; website: www.quantumcoaching.co.uk. Sport training and development specialists; successful, proven, practical distance-learning programmes for coaches worldwide, all levels.

CRICKET EQUIPMENT

AJ SPORTS, Unit 72, Rosemary Road, London SW17 0BA. Tel: 020 8879 7866; fax: 020 8944 1414; e-mail: ajlhr@hotmail.com. Stockist of all leading Asian brands; sole distributor of CA and BDM; Vampire (bats) also available. Top-quality clothing. Official supplier of Pakistan, Sri Lanka, Bangladesh and UAE kits. Free colour catalogue; visitors welcome; free parking; mail order; 500+ bats in stock.

DUKE SPORTSWEAR, Unit 4, Magdalene Road, Torquay, Devon TQ1 4AF. Tel/fax: 01803 292012. Test-standard sweaters to order in your club colours, using the finest yarns.

EXITO SPORTS COMPANY, Griffiths House, Griffiths Avenue, Birchwood Park, Cheshire WA3 6GH. Tel: 01925 818900; fax: 01925 657688; e-mail: info@exitosports.com; website: www.exitosports.com. Manufacturers and suppliers of top-quality cricket clothing to first-class counties, amateur clubs and schools.

FORDHAM SPORTS, 81 Robin Hood Way, Kingston Vale, London SW15 3PW. Tel: 020 8974 5654; e-mail: fordham@fordhamsports.co.uk; website: www.fordhamsports.co.uk. Cricket equipment specialist with largest range of branded stock in London at discount prices. Mail order worldwide. Free catalogue.

GUNN & MOORE, 119/121 Stanstead Road, Forest Hill, London SE23 1HJ. Tel: 020 8291 3344; fax: 020 8699 4008; e-mail: assist@unicorngroup.com. Gunn & Moore, established in 1885, is the world's most comprehensive provider of cricket bats, equipment, footwear and clothing.

NOMAD PLC. Tel: 01858 464878. Nomad manufacture coffins to suit all levels. The new "International" range has aluminium edging on all sides, wheels, and is available in ten different colours.

STUART & WILLIAMS (BOLA), 6 Brookfield Road, Cotham, Bristol BS6 5PQ. E-mail: info@bola.co.uk; website: www.bola.co.uk. Manufacturer of bowling machines and ball-throwing machines for all sports. Machines for recreational and commercial application for sale to the UK and overseas.

CRICKET TOURS

ALL WAYS SPORTS TRAVEL, 7 Whielden Street, Old Amersham, Buckinghamshire HP7 0HT. Tel: 01494 432747; fax: 01494 432767; e-mail: sales@all-ways.co.uk; website: www.all-ways.co.uk. Specialist tour operators to the South Pacific. Cricket supporters' tours to Australia and New Zealand.

BLADE, 34 Barton Gate, Barton-under-Needwood, Staffordshire DE13 8AG. Tel: 01283 711111; fax: 01283 711700; e-mail: enquiries@blade.uk.com; website: www.blade.uk.com. Specialists in tailor-made travel. Supporters tours to all major sporting events worldwide. Annual Pro-am Cricket Festivals in Barbados. PCA official travel company. ATOL bonded.

GREAT CENTRAL SPORTS & LEISURE. Tel/fax: 01788 542441; e-mail: enquiries@gcleisure.co.uk. Specialists in cricket tours to all regions throughout the UK and Ireland. Advisory bureau to assist with all local attractions.

SUN LIVING, 10 Milton Court, Ravenshead, Nottingham NG15 9BD. Tel: 01623 795365; fax: 01623 797421. Worldwide specialists in cricket tours for all levels and ages, plus our ever-popular supporters' tours. ABTA and ATOL bonded.

GIFTS, MEMORABILIA AND LIMITED-EDITION PRINTS

DD DESIGNS, 62 St Catherine's Grove, Lincoln, Lincolnshire LN5 8NA. E-mail: ddprints@aol.com. Specialists in signed limited-edition prints. Official producer of *Wisden's* "Cricketers of the Year" sets, and other art portfolios.

JOCELYN GALSWORTHY, 237 Chelsea Cloisters, Sloane Avenue, London SW3 3DT. Tel: 020 7591 0698. Limited-edition prints signed and numbered by the artist. Original cricket paintings for sale. Free brochure.

NICK POTTER LTD, 34 Sackville Street, London W1S 3ED. Tel: 020 7439 4029; fax: 020 7439 4027; e-mail: art@nickpotter.com; website: www.nickpotter.com. Specialists in fine cricket pictures, prints and memorabilia dating from the 19th century to the present day. Large stock held in our London gallery.

TONY SHELDON COLLECTIBLES PROMOTIONS, 29 Highclere Road, Higher Crumpsall, Manchester M8 4WH. Tel/fax: 0161 740 3714. Sets of trade (cigarette) cards designed, produced and supplied to your specifications.

SPORTING-GIFTS.COM LTD, 6 Arundel Close, Chippenham, Wiltshire SN14 0PR. Tel: 01249 464975; website www.sporting-gifts.com. For a wide selection of cricket and sports gifts, figures, prints, games, books and videos. Free catalogue.

PAVILION AND GROUND EQUIPMENT

AUTOGUIDE EQUIPMENT LTD, Stockley Road, Heddington, Wiltshire SN11 0PS. Tel: 01380 850885; fax: 01380 850010; e-mail: sales@autoguide.co.uk. Manufacturers of the world-famous Auto-Roller cricket wicket roller.

E. A. COMBS LIMITED, Quantum House, London E18 1BY. Tel: 020 8530 4216. Pavilion clocks for permanent and temporary siting. Wide choice of sizes and styles to suit any ground.

EUROPEAN TIMING SYSTEMS, Oldbury-on-Severn, Bristol BS35 1PL. Tel: 01454 413606; fax: 01454 415139. ETS manufacture electronic scoreboards using high-visibility 9″/12″/18″ displays. Types available to suit small clubs up to county standard. Recent installations at Old Trafford and Glamorgan.

FSL SCOREBOARDS, Sandholes Road, Cookstown, Co. Tyrone, N. Ireland BT80 9AR. Tel: 028 8676 6131; fax: 028 8676 2414; website: www.fsl.ltd.uk. Complete range of electronic scoreboards including: portable, indoor, stand-alone, and kits for modifying manual scoreboards.

HUCK NETS (UK) LTD, Gore Cross Business Park, Bridport, Dorset DT6 3UX. Tel: 01308 425100; fax: 01308 458109; e-mail: sales@hucknet.com. Quality knotless nets and cages, sightscreens, scoreboxes, synthetic pitches and covers, boundary ropes, etc.

JMS CRICKET LTD, Byeways, East Parade, Steeton, Keighley, West Yorkshire BD20 6RP. Tel: 01535 654520; fax: 01535 657309; e-mail: admin@jmscricket.com; website: www.jmscricket.com. Buy direct from the manufacturer. Mobile and flat covers, sightscreens and practice frames.

POWEROLL ROLLERS by Power Precision & Fabrication Ltd, Greenhill, Gunnislake, Cornwall PL18 9AS. Tel: 01822 832608; website: www.poweroll.com. Manufacturers of a comprehensive range of grass rollers to suit different budgets and applications.

STADIA SPORTS INTERNATIONAL LTD, 19/20 Lancaster Way Business Park, Ely, Cambridgeshire CB6 3NW. Tel: 01353 668686; fax: 01353 669444; e-mail: sales@stadia-sports.co.uk. Sightscreens, scoreboards (manual and electronic), cages, synthetic wickets and wicket covers.

STUART CANVAS PRODUCTS, Warren Works, Hardwick Grange, Warrington, Cheshire WA1 4RF. Tel: 01925 814525; fax: 01925 831709. Designers, manufacturers and suppliers of flat sheets, mobiles, roller & hover covers – sold throughout the world, including Test and county grounds.

TILDENET LTD, Hartcliffe Way, Bristol BS3 5RJ. Tel: 0117 966 9684; fax: 0117 923 1251; e-mail: enquiries@tildenet.co.uk; website: www.tildenet.co.uk. Tildenet offer a wide range of cricket equipment, including covers, practice nets, sightscreens and perimeter fencing.

PITCHES (TURF AND NON-TURF)

C. H. BINDER LTD, Moreton, Ongar, Essex CM5 0HY. Tel: 01277 890246; fax: 01277 890105; website: www.binderloams.co.uk; e-mail: sales@binderloams.co.uk. Sole producers of Ongar Loam™ top-dressing for cricket pitches, grass seed, fertilisers etc. Catalogues and quotations on request. Collections available.

BOUGHTON LOAM LTD, Telford Way, Kettering NN16 8UN. Tel: 01536 510515; fax: 01536 510691; e-mail: enquiries@boughton-loam.co.uk; website: www.boughton-loam.co.uk. Producers of nationally known "County", "Club" and "Kettering" loam for cricket pitches. Also end-of-season renovations with koro together with supplies of grass seed fertiliser and all other turf-care products.

CLUB SURFACES LIMITED, The Barn, Bisham Grange, Marlow, Buckinghamshire SL7 1RS. Tel: 01628 485969; fax: 01628 471944. ClubTurf, world-leading non-turf pitch since 1978, with over 5,500 installations; top in independent Sports Council tests. Clients include ECB, ICC, National Cricket Boards worldwide. Contact Derek Underwood for information pack.

JMS CRICKET LTD, Byeways, East Parade, Steeton, Keighley, West Yorkshire BD20 6RP. Tel: 01535 654520; fax: 01535 657309; e-mail: admin@jmscricket.com; website: www.jmscricket.com. Buy direct from the manufacturer. Mobile and flat covers, sightscreens and practice frames.

NOTTS SPORT®, Premier House, 18 Mandervell Road, Oadby, Leicester LE2 5LQ. Tel: 0116 272 0222; fax: 0116 272 0617; e-mail: info@nottssport.com; website: www.nottssport.com. World-renowned pitch systems. Clients include ICC, MCC, ECB and many other national and regional bodies.

PEAK SPORTS, Unit 4, Ford Street, Brinksway, Stockport SK3 0BT. Tel: 0161 480 2502; fax: 0161 480 1652. Agents for Wimbledon Unreal Grass pitches. Simply glue to concrete, nail to tarmac or roll out on the gym floor. Guaranteed ten years. Write for a brochure. Installed at Radley, Winchester, Manchester GS, Ipswich, Wellington, Merchiston Castle, etc.

SPORTS LAWN LTD, The Venture Park, Westcott, Buckinghamshire HP18 0XB; Tel: 01296 658255; e-mail: sales@sportslawn.com. Revolutionary non-turf pitch design, true and consistent performance, excellent value for money.

SOCIETIES

CRICKET MEMORABILIA SOCIETY. Honorary Secretary: Steve Cashmore, 4 Stoke Park Court, Stoke Road, Bishops Cleeve, Cheltenham, Gloucestershire GL52 8US. E-mail: cms87@btinternet.com. For collectors worldwide – magazines, meetings, auctions, speakers, and – most of all – friendship.

TROPHIES AND AWARDS

COLBORNE TROPHIES LTD. Tel: 01225 764101; fax: 01225 762009; e-mail: sales@awards.org.uk. Long-established and reliable suppliers of trophies and awards. Fast mail-order service and discounts available. Free catalogue.

TEST MATCHES, 2001-02

Full details of these Tests, and others too late for inclusion, will appear in *Wisden 2003*.

ASIAN TEST CHAMPIONSHIP

First Test: At Multan, August 29, 30, 31. Pakistan won by an innings and 264 runs. Toss: Bangladesh. Bangladesh 134 (Danish Kaneria six for 42) and 148 (Habibul Bashar 56 not out, Hasibul Hussain 31; Waqar Younis four for 19, Danish Kaneria six for 52); Pakistan 546 for three dec. (Saeed Anwar 101, Taufeeq Umar 104, Inzamam-ul-Haq 105 retired hurt, Yousuf Youhana 102 not out, Abdur Razzaq 110 not out).

Multan Cricket Stadium became Test cricket's 81st ground. Five Pakistanis scored hundreds in one innings (to equal Australia's record against West Indies at Kingston in 1954-55), including Taufeeq Umar on Test debut. Three shared an unbroken stand of 288 for the fourth wicket: Inzamam-ul-Haq retired hurt after adding 123 with Yousuf Youhana, who added a further 165 with Abdur Razzaq. In Bangladesh's second innings, substitute Younis Khan held four catches, equalling the match record and setting an innings record for a substitute.

Second Test: At Sinhalese Sports Club, Colombo, September 6, 7, 8. Sri Lanka won by an innings and 137 runs. Toss: Sri Lanka. Bangladesh 90 (W. P. U. J. C. Vaas three for 47, M. Muralitharan five for 13) and 328 (Javed Omar 40, Aminul Islam 56, Mohammad Ashraful 114, Naimur Rahman 48; M. Muralitharan five for 98, P. D. R. L. Perera three for 40); Sri Lanka 555 for five dec. (M. S. Atapattu 201, S. T. Jayasuriya 89, K. Sangakkara 54, D. P. M. D. Jayawardene 150, M. G. van Dort 36).

Bangladesh's 90 was their lowest Test total to date. Atapattu and Jayawardene became the first batsmen to retire out in Tests, Atapattu after scoring his fifth Test double-hundred; only Don Bradman (12), Wally Hammond (7) and Javed Miandad (6) have scored more. Debutant Mohammad Ashraful became the youngest player to score a Test hundred at 16 years 364 days, beating Mushtaq Mohammad's 17 years 82 days. Muralitharan's ten wickets took him to 350 in a record 66 Tests. Sri Lanka completed what was then their biggest Test win. With India having withdrawn from the Championship for political reasons, Pakistan and Sri Lanka did not need to play a qualifying match to reach the final, which was due to be played in early March.

ZIMBABWE v SOUTH AFRICA

First Test: At Harare, September 7, 8, 9, 10, 11. South Africa won by nine wickets. Toss: South Africa. South Africa 600 for three dec. (H. H. Gibbs 147, G. Kirsten 220, J. H. Kallis 157 not out, N. D. McKenzie 52) and 79 for one (G. Kirsten 31 not out, J. H. Kallis 42 not out); Zimbabwe 286 (D. D. Ebrahim 71, A. Flower 142, T. J. Friend 30; A. Nel four for 53) and 391 (H. Masakadza 85, A. Flower 199 not out; S. M. Pollock three for 67).

South Africa made 414 for one on the opening day, when Kirsten completed a set of centuries against the eight Test sides he had played and became South Africa's first player to reach 5,000 Test runs, in his 74th Test. Andy Flower was the first to score 4,000 for Zimbabwe, in his 53rd, and later became the first wicket-keeper to score a hundred in each innings of a Test. His aggregate of 341 was then the highest by any player losing a Test, and he scored more than half the runs off the bat in both Zimbabwe's innings.

Second Test: At Bulawayo, September 14, 15, 16, 17, 18. Drawn. Toss: Zimbabwe. Zimbabwe 419 for nine dec. (A. D. R. Campbell 77, D. D. Ebrahim 71, S. V. Carlisle 49, A. Flower 67, G. W. Flower 44, H. H. Streak 31, P. A. Strang 38 not out; C. W. Henderson four for 143) and 96 for three (H. Masakadza 42 not out; C. W. Henderson three for 33); South Africa 519 for eight dec. (H. H. Gibbs 74, G. Kirsten 65, J. H. Kallis 189 not out, N. D. McKenzie 88, S. M. Pollock 41; T. J. Friend three for 87, R. W. Price five for 181).

Kallis batted for a record 1,027 minutes in the series without being dismissed, scoring 388 runs. Price bowled 79 overs in South Africa's innings. South Africa took the series 1–0.

SOUTH AFRICA v INDIA

First Test: At Bloemfontein, November 3, 4, 5, 6. South Africa won by nine wickets. Toss: South Africa. India 379 (V. V. S. Laxman 32, S. R. Tendulkar 155, V. Sehwag 105, D. Dasgupta 34; S. M. Pollock four for 91, M. Hayward three for 70) and 237 (S. S. Das 62, S. C. Ganguly 30, V. Sehwag 31; S. M. Pollock six for 56); South Africa 563 (H. H. Gibbs 107, G. Kirsten 73, J. H. Kallis 68, N. D. McKenzie 68, L. Klusener 108, M. V. Boucher 47, Extras 43; J. Srinath five for 140, A. Kumble three for 132) and 54 for one (G. Kirsten 30 not out).

In his 85th Test, Tendulkar reached his 26th Test hundred and became the youngest player to score 7,000 Test runs, at 28 years 193 days. He added 220 with Sehwag, who scored a hundred on debut, to rescue India from 68 for four. Kallis was dismissed for the first time in 1,241 minutes, a Test record.

Second Test: At Port Elizabeth, November 16, 17, 18, 19, 20. Drawn. Toss: India. South Africa 362 (H. H. Gibbs 196, M. V. Boucher 68 not out; J. Srinath six for 76) and 233 for five dec. (J. H. Kallis 89 not out, S. M. Pollock 55 not out); India 201 (S. C. Ganguly 42, V. V. S. Laxman 89; S. M. Pollock five for 40) and 206 for three (D. Dasgupta 63, R. Dravid 87).

ICC referee Mike Denness imposed a one-Test ban (plus fine) on Sehwag, for abusive language, dissent and attempted intimidation of an umpire, and fines and suspended bans on five other Indian players: Tendulkar for interfering with the ball, Ganguly for not controlling his players and conduct unbecoming of a captain, and Das, Dasgupta and Harbhajan Singh for excessive appealing. India threatened to withdraw from the Third Test at Centurion if Denness was not replaced; when South Africa supported them, the ICC withdrew the Centurion game's Test status. In the unofficial match, played on November 23–27, South Africa won by an innings and 73 runs (India 232 and 261; South Africa 566 for eight dec.). India omitted Sehwag and argued that he had thus served his one-Test ban. Officially, South Africa won the series 1–0.

AUSTRALIA v NEW ZEALAND

First Test: At Brisbane, November 8, 9, 10, 11, 12. Drawn. Toss: New Zealand. Australia 486 for nine dec. (J. L. Langer 104, M. L. Hayden 136, A. C. Gilchrist 118, B. Lee 61; C. L. Cairns five for 146, C. D. McMillan three for 65) and 84 for two dec. (R. T. Ponting 32 not out); New Zealand 287 for eight dec. (N. J. Astle 66, C. D. McMillan 45, C. L. Cairns 61, Extras 41; J. N. Gillespie three for 56, B. Lee five for 67) and 274 for six (M. H. Richardson 57, S. P. Fleming 57, N. J. Astle 49, C. L. Cairns 43; S. K. Warne three for 89).

This was Australia's first Test draw since October 1999, after 20 wins and three defeats. New Zealand were ten short of inflicting their first home Test defeat in 13 Tests since England won at Melbourne in December 1998.

Second Test: At Hobart, November 22, 23, 24, 25, 26. Drawn. Toss: New Zealand. Australia 558 for eight dec. (J. L. Langer 123, M. L. Hayden 91, R. T. Ponting 157 not out, A. C. Gilchrist 39, S. K. Warne 70, B. Lee 41; D. L. Vettori five for 138); New Zealand 243 for seven (M. H. Richardson 30, S. P. Fleming 71, C. D. McMillan 55; J. N. Gillespie three for 45).

Langer and Hayden shared their second successive double-century opening stand (Langer did not open in the second innings at Brisbane).

Third Test: At Perth, November 30, December 1, 2, 3, 4. Drawn. Toss: New Zealand. New Zealand 534 for nine dec. (L. Vincent 104, S. P. Fleming 105, N. J. Astle 156 not out, A. C. Parore 110, Extras 34; J. N. Gillespie three for 112, B. Lee four for 125) and 256 for nine dec. (M. H. Richardson 30, L. Vincent 54, C. L. Cairns 42, N. J. Astle 40; B. Lee four for 56); Australia 351 (J. L. Langer 75, R. T. Ponting 31, M. E. Waugh 42, D. R. Martyn 60, S. K. Warne 99; D. L. Vettori six for 87) and 381 for seven (M. L. Hayden 57, M. E. Waugh 86, S. R. Waugh 67, D. R. Martyn 30, A. C. Gilchrist 83 not out).

Only four players reached double figures in New Zealand's first innings. All went on to hundreds, including debutant Lou Vincent, the first time New Zealand had scored four centuries in an innings, and only the second time Australia had conceded four, after Nottingham 1938. Astle and Parore added 253, the second-highest eighth-wicket partnership in Tests. The series was drawn 0–0.

BANGLADESH v ZIMBABWE

First Test: At Dhaka, November 8, 9, 10, 11, 12. Drawn. Toss: Zimbabwe. Bangladesh 107 (T. J. Friend five for 31, H. K. Olonga three for 18) and 125 for three (Javed Omar 35, Habibul Bashar 65); Zimbabwe 431 (S. V. Carlisle 33, C. B. Wishart 94, D. A. Marillier 73, H. H. Streak 65, T. J. Friend 81; Mashrafe bin Mortaza four for 106, Enamul Haque three for 74).

Bangladesh, in their sixth Test, avoided defeat for the first time when rain prevented play on the last two days. Earlier, 18-year-old debutant Mortaza helped reduce Zimbabwe to 89 for five.

Second Test: At Chittagong, November 15, 16, 17, 18, 19. Zimbabwe won by eight wickets. Toss: Bangladesh. Zimbabwe 542 for seven dec. (D. D. Ebrahim 41, T. R. Gripper 112, G. W. Flower 33, A. Flower 114 not out, C. B. Wishart 114, D. A. Marillier 52) and 11 for two; Bangladesh 251 (Habibul Bashar 108, Mohammad Ashraful 33; G. W. Flower four for 41) and 301 (Javed Omar 80, Al-Shahriar Rokon 40, Habibul Bashar 76; G. W. Flower four for 63, D. A. Marillier four for 57).

The M. A. Aziz Stadium became Test cricket's 82nd ground. Zimbabwe's new captain, Brian Murphy, stepped down after one Test, with a wrist injury, handing over to Stuart Carlisle. Afterwards, Bangladesh sacked captain Naimur Rahman, replacing him with Khaled Masud. Zimbabwe won the series 1–0.

SRI LANKA v WEST INDIES

First Test: At Galle, November 13, 14, 15, 16, 17. Sri Lanka won by ten wickets. Toss: West Indies. West Indies 448 (D. Ganga 47, R. R. Sarwan 88, B. C. Lara 178, C. L. Hooper 69; W. P. U. J. C. Vaas four for 95, M. Muralitharan six for 126) and 144 (D. Ganga 33, R. R. Sarwan 30, B. C. Lara 40; M. Muralitharan five for 44); Sri Lanka 590 for nine dec. (M. S. Atapattu 61, K. Sangakkara 140, D. P. M. D. Jayawardene 99, R. P. Arnold 33, H. P. Tillekeratne 105 not out, T. T. Samaraweera 77; D. Ramnarine three for 158) and six for no wkt.

West Indies lost their last six wickets for 25 in the first innings, and their last five for 13 in the second, to lose to Sri Lanka for the first time. Muralitharan took ten or more wickets for the third successive Test to equal Clarrie Grimmett's record for Australia against South Africa in 1935-36.

Second Test: At Kandy, November 21, 22, 23, 24, 25. Sri Lanka won by 131 runs. Toss: Sri Lanka. Sri Lanka 288 (D. P. M. D. Jayawardene 88, H. P. Tillekeratne 87; M. Dillon three for 55, P. T. Collins four for 78, D. Ramnarine three for 81) and 224 for six dec. (M. S. Atapattu 84, S. T. Jayasuriya 55, K. Sangakkara 45; D. Ramnarine four for 66); West Indies 191 (C. H. Gayle 44, B. C. Lara 74; W. P. U. J. C. Vaas four for 56, M. Muralitharan four for 54) and 190 (R. R. Sarwan 48, B. C. Lara 45, M. N. Samuels 54; M. Muralitharan six for 81).

In Sri Lanka's first innings, three bowlers shared the fifth over; Dillon was injured after two balls, Colin Stuart bowled two beamers (called no-ball) in three deliveries and was ordered out of the attack by umpire Hampshire, and Gayle eventually completed it. Muralitharan took ten wickets for a record fourth consecutive Test, and for the ninth time overall, equalling Richard Hadlee's record.

Third Test: At Sinhalese Sports Club, Colombo, November 29, 30, December 1, 2, 3. Sri Lanka won by ten wickets. Toss: West Indies. West Indies 390 (R. R. Sarwan 69, B. C. Lara 221, C. L. Hooper 56; W. P. U. J. C. Vaas seven for 120) and 262 (R. R. Sarwan 66, B. C. Lara 130, R. D. Jacobs 31 not out; W. P. U. J. C. Vaas seven for 71); Sri Lanka 627 for nine dec. (S. T. Jayasuriya 85, K. Sangakkara 55, D. P. M. D. Jayawardene 39, R. P. Arnold 65, H. P. Tillekeratne 204 not out, T. T. Samaraweera 87; P. T. Collins three for 156) and 27 for no wkt.

In his 83rd Test, Lara's fourth double-hundred took him past 7,000 runs. His 221 was the highest score by a player losing a Test; when he added 130 in the second innings, he beat Andy Flower's record losing match aggregate of 341 against South Africa in September. Like Flower, he scored more than half West Indies' runs off the bat in both innings. His aggregate of 688 in a three-Test series was second only to Graham Gooch's 752 for England v India in 1990. Tillekeratne scored 403 in the series for one dismissal, Vaas took 14 for 191 in the match, and Sri Lanka completed a 3–0 whitewash.

INDIA v ENGLAND

First Test Match

At Mohali, December 3, 4, 5, 6. India won by ten wickets. Toss: India.

Close of play: First day, India 24-1 (Dasgupta 19*, Kumble 1*); Second day, India 262-3 (Dravid 78*, Tendulkar 31*); Third day, England 34-0 (Butcher 11*, Trescothick 16*).

England

M. A. Butcher c Laxman b Yohannan	4	– c sub (J. J. Martin) b Yohannan	18
M. E. Trescothick b Yohannan	66	– c Iqbal Siddiqui b Yohannan	46
*N. Hussain c Laxman b Kumble	85	– b Kumble	12
G. P. Thorpe c Laxman b Iqbal Siddiqui	23	– c and b Kumble	62
M. R. Ramprakash c Das b Harbhajan Singh	17	– lbw b Kumble	28
A. Flintoff c Kumble b Harbhajan Singh	18	– c Ganguly b Kumble	4
C. White c Dravid b Kumble	5	– c Dasgupta b Harbhajan Singh	22
†J. S. Foster lbw b Harbhajan Singh	0	– lbw b Harbhajan Singh	5
J. Ormond not out	3	– b Kumble	0
R. K. J. Dawson c Laxman b Harbhajan Singh	5	b Kumble	11
M. J. Hoggard c sub (C. C. Williams) b Harbhajan Singh	0	– not out	0
L-b 7, n-b 5	12	B 10, l-b 13, w 1, n-b 3	27
1/4 (1) 2/129 (2) 3/172 (4) 4/200 (3) 5/224 (5) 6/227 (6) 7/229 (8) 8/229 (7) 9/238 (10) 10/238 (11)	238	1/68 (1) 2/82 (2) 3/87 (3) 4/159 (5) 5/163 (6) 6/196 (7) 7/206 (8) 8/207 (9) 9/224 (4) 10/235 (10)	235

Bowling: *First Innings*—Yohannan 18–3–75–2; Iqbal Siddiqui 11–2–32–1; Bangar 5–2–17–0; Kumble 19–6–52–2; Tendulkar 4–3–4–0; Harbhajan Singh 19.3–4–51–5. *Second Innings*—Yohannan 17–3–56–2; Iqbal Siddiqui 8–3–16–0; Kumble 28.4–6–81–6; Harbhajan Singh 24–9–59–2.

India

S. S. Das b Butcher	2		
†D. Dasgupta b White	100	– not out	0
A. Kumble c Foster b Dawson	37		
R. Dravid lbw b Ormond	86		
S. R. Tendulkar c Foster b Hoggard	88		
*S. C. Ganguly c Thorpe b Hoggard	47		
V. V. S. Laxman c Hussain b Dawson	28		
S. B. Bangar c and b Dawson	36		
Harbhajan Singh lbw b Dawson	1		
Iqbal Siddiqui b Hoggard	24	– (1) not out	5
T. Yohannan not out	2		
L-b 12, w 2, n-b 4	18		
1/23 (1) 2/76 (3) 3/212 (2) 4/290 (4) 5/370 (5) 6/378 (6) 7/430 (7) 8/436 (9) 9/449 (8) 10/469 (10)	469	(no wkt)	5

Bowling: *First Innings*—Hoggard 32–9–98–3; Ormond 28–8–70–1; Butcher 7–1–19–1; Flintoff 34–11–80–0; White 25–8–56–1; Dawson 43–6–134–4. *Second Innings*—Hoggard 0.2–0–5–0.

Umpires: S. A. Bucknor (West Indies) and S. Venkataraghavan.
Third umpire: K. Murali. Referee: D. T. Lindsay (South Africa).

The Test went ahead after India agreed three days before to omit Virender Sehwag, officially banned for one match after the Port Elizabeth Test. India replaced their entire pace attack from the South African series with three debutants (Bangar, Iqbal Siddiqui and Yohannan. In the first innings, Harbhajan Singh took five for six in 7.3 overs as England collapsed from 224 for four.

INDIA v ENGLAND

Second Test Match

At Ahmedabad, December 11, 12, 13, 14, 15. Drawn. Toss: England.

Close of play: First day, England 277-6 (White 42*, Foster 15*); Second day, India 71-2 (Dravid 5*, Tendulkar 2*); Third day, England 15-0 (Butcher 5*, Trescothick 10*); Fourth day, India 17-0 (Das 11*, Dasgupta 6*).

England

M. A. Butcher c Dasgupta b Kumble	51	– c Dravid b Harbhajan Singh	92
M. E. Trescothick c Dasgupta b Kumble	99	– c Das b Srinath	12
*N. Hussain lbw b Kumble	1	– c Sehwag b Harbhajan Singh	50
M. P. Vaughan c Sehwag b Kumble	11	– (7) not out	31
M. R. Ramprakash b Tendulkar	37	– (4) c Tendulkar b Harbhajan Singh	19
A. Flintoff c Laxman b Kumble	0	– (5) b Kumble	4
C. White b Harbhajan Singh	121	– (6) run out	18
†J. S. Foster c Tendulkar b Kumble	40	– c Yohannan b Kumble	3
A. F. Giles b Kumble	7	– c Das b Harbhajan Singh	8
R. K. J. Dawson c Dasgupta b Srinath	9	– c Tendulkar b Kumble	2
M. J. Hoggard not out	4	– c Das b Harbhajan Singh	1
B 6, l-b 15, w 1, n-b 5	27	B 6, l-b 8, n-b 3	17
1/124 (1) 2/144 (3) 3/172 (4) 4/176 (2) 5/180 (6) 6/239 (5) 7/344 (8) 8/360 (9) 9/391 (10) 10/407 (7)	407	1/21 (2) 2/133 (3) 3/178 (4) 4/183 (5) 5/183 (1) 6/225 (6) 7/231 (8) 8/247 (9) 9/253 (10) 10/257 (11)	257

Bowling: *First Innings*—Srinath 29–7–105–1; Yohannan 17–2–57–0; Harbhajan Singh 35.3–9–78–1; Kumble 51–13–115–7; Tendulkar 10–0–27–1; Sehwag 2–1–4–0. *Second Innings*—Srinath 9–2–24–1; Yohannan 4–0–25–0; Kumble 38–5–118–3; Harbhajan Singh 30.2–6–71–5; Sehwag 2–0–5–0.

India

S. S. Das c Butcher b Flintoff	41	– run out	58
†D. Dasgupta c Hussain b Giles	17	– c Butcher b Dawson	60
R. Dravid c Foster b Hoggard	7	– not out	26
S. R. Tendulkar c Hussain b Hoggard	103	– c Vaughan b Dawson	26
*S. C. Ganguly c sub (M. C. J. Ball) b Flintoff	5	– not out	16
V. V. S. Laxman c Butcher b Giles	75		
V. Sehwag lbw b White	20		
A. Kumble b Giles	5		
Harbhajan Singh c Flintoff b Giles	0		
J. Srinath c Butcher b Giles	0		
T. Yohannan not out	3		
B 6, l-b 5, w 1, n-b 3	15	B 12	12
1/54 (2) 2/64 (1) 3/86 (3) 4/93 (5) 5/211 (4) 6/248 (7) 7/268 (8) 8/272 (9) 9/274 (10) 10/291 (6)	291	1/119 (1) 2/124 (2) 3/168 (4)	(3 wkts) 198

Bowling: *First Innings*—Hoggard 28–7–65–2; Flintoff 22–7–42–2; Giles 43.3–16–67–5; Dawson 15–0–73–0; White 12–2–33–1. *Second Innings*—Hoggard 17–6–33–0; Giles 31–12–57–0; Dawson 32–9–72–2; Flintoff 8–4–17–0; White 9–5–7–0.

Umpires: I. D. Robinson (Zimbabwe) and A. V. Jayaprakash.
Third umpire: Jasbir Singh. Referee: D. T. Lindsay (South Africa).

Hussain won the toss for England for only the second time in 17 Tests since May 2000. Tendulkar's 27th Test hundred brought him level with Allan Border and Steve Waugh; only Sunil Gavaskar (34) and Don Bradman (29) had more.

INDIA v ENGLAND

Third Test Match

At Bangalore, December 19, 20, 21, 22, 23. Drawn. Toss: England.

Close of play: First day, England 255-6 (White 30*, Foster 14*); Second day, India 99-3 (Tendulkar 50*, Dravid 1*); Third day, India 218-7 (Kumble 10*, Harbhajan Singh 0*); Fourth day, England 33-0 (Butcher 23*, Trescothick 9*).

England

M. A. Butcher run out	27	– not out	23
M. E. Trescothick c Laxman b Srinath	8	– not out	9
*N. Hussain c Dasgupta b Srinath	43		
M. P. Vaughan handled the ball	64		
M. R. Ramprakash c Dravid b Sarandeep Singh	58		
A. Flintoff c Tendulkar b Sarandeep Singh	0		
C. White c Das b Srinath	39		
†J. S. Foster c Dasgupta b Srinath	48		
A. F. Giles lbw b Sarandeep Singh	28		
R. K. J. Dawson not out	0		
M. J. Hoggard lbw b Kumble	1		
B 8, l-b 9, n-b 3	20	B 1	1
1/21 (2) 2/68 (1) 3/93 (3) 4/206 (4) 5/206 (6) 6/219 (5) 7/271 (7) 8/334 (8) 9/334 (9) 10/336 (11)	336		(no wkt) 33

Bowling: *First Innings*—Srinath 29–9–73–4; Ganguly 13–3–39–0; Kumble 29.3–6–74–1; Harbhajan Singh 27–7–59–0; Sarandeep Singh 21–5–54–3; Tendulkar 3–0–19–0; Sehwag 1–0–1–0. *Second Innings*—Srinath 4–0–19–0; Ganguly 3–0–12–0; Harbhajan Singh 0.1–0–1–0.

India

S. S. Das b Flintoff	28
†D. Dasgupta c Trescothick b Flintoff	0
V. V. S. Laxman b Flintoff	12
S. R. Tendulkar st Foster b Giles	90
R. Dravid c Foster b Hoggard	3
*S. C. Ganguly c Butcher b Hoggard	0
V. Sehwag c Foster b Hoggard	66
A. Kumble c Trescothick b Flintoff	14
Harbhajan Singh c Hussain b Hoggard	8
Sarandeep Singh run out	4
J. Srinath not out	2
B 4, l-b 4, n-b 3	11
1/8 (2) 2/22 (3) 3/88 (1) 4/121 (5) 5/121 (6) 6/173 (4) 7/218 (7) 8/228 (8) 9/235 (9) 10/238 (10)	238

Bowling: Hoggard 24.3–7–80–4; Flintoff 28–9–50–4; Giles 34–18–74–1; White 8–2–26–0.

Umpires: E. A. R. de Silva (Sri Lanka) and A. V. Jayaprakash.
Third umpire: F. Gomes. Referee: D. T. Lindsay (South Africa).

Floodlights were used throughout the match, but most of the last two days was lost to bad weather. Vaughan was the seventh player in Test cricket, and the second in 2001 (after Steve Waugh at Chennai in March), to be out handled the ball. In his 66th Test and on his home ground, Kumble became the second Indian, after Kapil Dev, to take 300 Test wickets. Tendulkar was stumped for the first time in his 89 Tests, after England persistently bowled into the rough outside his leg stump. India won the series 1–0.

AUSTRALIA v SOUTH AFRICA

First Test: At Adelaide, December 14, 15, 16, 17, 18. Australia won by 246 runs. Toss: Australia. Australia 439 (J. L. Langer 116, M. L. Hayden 31, R. T. Ponting 54, D. R. Martyn 124 not out, S. K. Warne 41, B. Lee 32; M. Hayward three for 108, C. W. Henderson four for 116) and 309 for seven dec. (M. L. Hayden 131, M. E. Waugh 74, Extras 31; C. W. Henderson three for 130, J. H. Kallis three for 45); South Africa 374 (H. H. Gibbs 78, G. Kirsten 47, C. W. Henderson 30, N. D. McKenzie 87, M. V. Boucher 64; G. D. McGrath three for 94, S. K. Warne five for 113) and 128 (J. H. Kallis 65 not out; G. D. McGrath three for 13, S. K. Warne three for 57).

Mark and Steve Waugh became the first brothers to appear in 100 Tests together.

Second Test: At Melbourne, December 26, 27, 28, 29. Australia won by nine wickets. Toss: Australia. South Africa 277 (J. H. Kallis 38, N. D. McKenzie 67, M. V. Boucher 43, S. M. Pollock 42 not out; B. Lee three for 77, A. J. Bichel three for 44) and 219 (J. H. Kallis 99; S. K. Warne three for 68); Australia 487 (J. L. Langer 85, M. L. Hayden 138, M. E. Waugh 34, S. R. Waugh 90, D. R. Martyn 52, A. C. Gilchrist 30 not out; A. A. Donald three for 103, S. M. Pollock three for 84) and ten for one.

Mark Waugh played his 100th consecutive Test. Langer and Hayden opened with 202. Steve Waugh made a record tenth Test score in the 90s, but was fined half his fee for dissent when run out. Hayden finished the calendar year with an aggregate of 1,391 runs, beating Bob Simpson's Australian record of 1,381.

Third Test: At Sydney, January 2, 3, 4, 5. Australia won by ten wickets. Toss: Australia. Australia 554 (J. L. Langer 126, M. L. Hayden 105, S. R. Waugh 30, D. R. Martyn 117, A. C. Gilchrist 34, S. K. Warne 37; S. M. Pollock three for 109, N. Boje four for 63) and 54 for no wkt (J. L. Langer 30 not out); South Africa 154 (H. H. Gibbs 32, M. V. Boucher 35; G. D. McGrath three for 35, S. C. G. MacGill three for 51, S. K. Warne three for 47) and 452 (G. Kirsten 153, H. H. Dippenaar 74, J. H. Kallis 34, N. D. McKenzie 38, J. L. Ontong 32, S. M. Pollock 61 not out; S. K. Warne three for 132, S. C. G. MacGill four for 123).

South African board president Percy Sonn insisted on the inclusion of Justin Ontong, a "player of colour", rather than Jacques Rudolph, originally selected to replace Lance Klusener. Langer and Hayden shared their fourth double-century first-wicket stand, equalling the record of Gordon Greenidge and Desmond Haynes, in their seventh Test as opening partners. Australia won the series 3–0.

NEW ZEALAND v BANGLADESH

First Test: At Hamilton, December 18, 19, 20, 21, 22. New Zealand won by an innings and 52 runs. Toss: Bangladesh. New Zealand 365 for nine dec. (M. H. Richardson 143, C. D. McMillan 106, C. L. Cairns 48; Mashrafe bin Mortaza three for 100, Mohammad Sharif three for 114); Bangladesh 205 (Habibul Bashar 61, Sanuar Hossain 45, Khaled Mahmud 45; S. E. Bond four for 47) and 108 (Al-Shahriar Rokon 53; C. L. Cairns seven for 53).

Rain washed out the first two days, but New Zealand won an hour into the fifth. Richardson and McMillan added 190 for their fifth wicket after they were 51 for four.

Second Test: At Wellington, December 26, 27, 28, 29. New Zealand won by an innings and 74 runs. Toss: New Zealand. Bangladesh 132 (Aminul Islam 42; C. L. Cairns three for 24) and 135 (Habibul Bashar 32; S. E. Bond four for 54); New Zealand 341 for six dec. (M. H. Richardson 83, M. J. Horne 38, S. P. Fleming 61, C. D. McMillan 70, C. L. Cairns 36; Manjurul Islam three for 99).

The second day was washed out, but New Zealand won an hour into the fourth to take the series 2–0.

SRI LANKA v ZIMBABWE

First Test: At Sinhalese Sports Club, Colombo, December 27, 28, 29, 31. Sri Lanka won by an innings and 166 runs. Toss: Zimbabwe. Sri Lanka 586 for six dec. (S. T. Jayasuriya 92, K. Sangakkara 128, H. P. Tillekeratne 96, T. T. Samaraweera 123 not out, W. P. U. J. C. Vaas 74 not out; H. H. Streak three for 113); Zimbabwe 184 (T. R. Gripper 30, G. J. Rennie 35, A. Flower 42; M. Muralitharan four for 53) and 236 (S. V. Carlisle 32, T. J. Friend 44, H. H. Streak 36 not out; M. Muralitharan four for 35).

This was the first Test to have a rest day (a poya day in Sri Lanka) since West Indies v India at Bridgetown, played over Easter 1997. Sri Lanka's win was their biggest in Tests. Muralitharan finished 2001 with 80 Test wickets in the calendar year.

Second Test: At Kandy, January 4, 5, 6, 7. Sri Lanka won by an innings and 94 runs. Toss: Zimbabwe. Zimbabwe 236 (G. W. Flower 72; M. Muralitharan nine for 51) and 175 (G. J. Rennie 68; M. Muralitharan four for 64, T. C. B. Fernando four for 27); Sri Lanka 505 (S. T. Jayasuriya 139, K. Sangakkara 42, D. P. M. D. Jayawardene 56, R. P. Arnold 71, H. P. Tillekeratne 37, W. P. U. J. C. Vaas 72 not out, T. C. B. Fernando 45; T. J. Friend three for 97, G. W. Flower three for 66).

Muralitharan took nine wickets on the first day, dislocated a finger trying to catch the No. 11 off Tilan Samaraweera's bowling, and next morning had a catch dropped in his first over before Vaas took the tenth wicket, depriving him of the best Test analysis in history. He took ten in the match for a record tenth time, finishing with 13 for 115.

Third Test: At Galle, January 12, 13, 14, 15. Sri Lanka won by 315 runs. Toss: Sri Lanka. Sri Lanka 418 (M. S. Atapattu 50, D. P. M. D. Jayawardene 76, R. P. Arnold 40, T. T. Samaraweera 76, U. D. U. Chandana 92; D. A. Marillier four for 101) and 212 for two dec. (M. S. Atapattu 100 not out, S. T. Jayasuriya 36, K. Sangakkara 56); Zimbabwe 236 (S. V. Carlisle 64, T. R. Gripper 83, H. H. Streak 33; M. Muralitharan five for 67, S. T. Jayasuriya five for 43) and 79 (S. T. Jayasuriya four for 31, M. Muralitharan four for 24).

Muralitharan reached 400 wickets in his 72nd Test, beating the previous record of 80 by Richard Hadlee. He took 30 in the three-match series. Samaraweera, who finished his eighth Test with a career batting average of 103.00, and Chandana added 146, a Sri Lankan eighth-wicket record. Sri Lanka's eighth consecutive Test win (all at home) gave them the series 3–0.

BANGLADESH v PAKISTAN

First Test: At Dhaka, January 9, 10, 11. Pakistan won by an innings and 178 runs. Toss: Pakistan. Bangladesh 160 (Habibul Bashar 53; Waqar Younis six for 55) and 152 (Fahim Muntasir 33; Danish Kaneria seven for 77); Pakistan 490 for nine dec. (Taufeeq Umar 53, Shadab Kabir 55, Yousuf Youhana 72, Abdur Razzaq 134, Rashid Latif 94, Inzamam-ul-Haq 43; Enamul Haque four for 136).

Waqar Younis took six wickets in 29 balls to wrap up Bangladesh's first innings. Danish Kaneria took nine for 113 in the match, to follow 12 for 94 in his previous Test against Bangladesh in August.

Second Test: At Chittagong, January 16, 17, 18. Pakistan won by an innings and 169 runs. Toss: Bangladesh. Bangladesh 148 (Danish Kaneria four for 62, Saqlain Mushtaq five for 35) and 148 (Habibul Bashar 51, Sanuar Hossain 30; Waqar Younis four for 36, Shoaib Akhtar four for 48); Pakistan 465 for nine dec. (Taufeeq Umar 47, Younis Khan 119, Inzamam-ul-Haq 30, Yousuf Youhana 204 not out; Mohammad Sharif four for 98, Fahim Muntasir three for 131).

Pakistan completed their third three-day innings defeat of Bangladesh, who had now lost ten of their first 11 Tests, seven by an innings. Pakistan won the series 2–0.

PAKISTAN v WEST INDIES

First Test: At Sharjah, January 31, February 1, 2, 3, 4. Pakistan won by 170 runs. Toss: Pakistan. Pakistan 493 (Younis Khan 53, Yousuf Youhana 146, Abdur Razzaq 34, Rashid Latif 150; M. Dillon three for 141, C. H. Gayle three for 26) and 214 for six dec. (Younis Khan 32, Inzamam-ul-Haq 48, Rashid Latif 47 not out); West Indies 366 (C. H. Gayle 68, W. W. Hinds 59, C. L. Hooper 56, S. Chanderpaul 66, R. O. Hinds 62; Waqar Younis four for 93) and 171 (D. Ganga 34, C. H. Gayle 66; Shoaib Akhtar five for 24, Abdur Razzaq four for 24).

This series was transferred from Pakistan because of security fears during the Afghanistan crisis. Sharjah provided the 83rd Test ground, and the fifth neutral venue to host a Test, following Manchester, Lord's and Nottingham (Australia v South Africa, 1912) and Dhaka (Pakistan v Sri Lanka, 1998-99). West Indies lost their final nine wickets for 56 runs.

Second Test: At Sharjah, February 7, 8, 9, 10. Pakistan won by 244 runs. Toss: West Indies. Pakistan 472 (Shahid Afridi 107, Younis Khan 153, Inzamam-ul-Haq 36, Yousuf Youhana 60, Abdur Razzaq 64 not out; C. E. Cuffy four for 82, D. Ramnarine three for 137) and 225 for five dec. (Taufeeq Umar 69, Younis Khan 71, Yousuf Youhana 52 not out; M. Dillon three for 57); West Indies 264 (D. Ganga 65, C. L. Hooper 84 not out, R. D. Jacobs 31; Shoaib Akhtar four for 63, Saqlain Mushtaq three for 75) and 189 (W. W. Hinds 34, R. O. Hinds 46, R. D. Jacobs 35 not out; Waqar Younis four for 44, Abdur Razzaq three for 33).

On the first day, Shahid Afridi and Younis Khan added 190, a Pakistan second-wicket record against West Indies. Hooper passed 5,000 Test runs in his 92nd Test, and Waqar Younis passed 350 wickets in his 78th. Pakistan won their sixth successive Test to take the series 2–0. It was West Indies' fifth successive defeat, and their 23rd in 27 overseas Tests.

ERRATA

WISDEN 1988

Page 939 In the Third One-Day International between India and Australia at Hyderabad on September 24, Azharuddin scored 8 not out, not 9 not out; there were three leg-byes and one wide, and Davis conceded 17.

WISDEN 1994

Page 975 The stand of 278 between Wickremaratne and Atapattu was a national fourth-wicket record, not a world record as indicated by the dagger.

WISDEN 2000

Page 29 The list in *Finnegans Wake* is not James Joyce's only mention of cricket. In Chapter 16 of *Ulysses*, "he pawed the journal open and pored upon Lord only knows what, found drowned or the exploits of King Willow, Iremonger having made a hundred and something second wicket not out for Notts..." This is correct; on June 16, 1904, J. Iremonger scored a century against Kent at Nottingham, going on to 272. Earlier, Bloom appeals to Mary Driscoll's sense of justice by urging her to "Play cricket." And in *A Portrait of the Artist as a Young Man*, "In the silence of the soft grey air, he heard the cricketbats from here and from there: pock. That was a sound to hear but if you were hit then you would feel a pain."

Page 575 The dagger denoting a Test match should be next to D. C. S. Compton and A. R. Morris at Adelaide in 1946-47, not M. L. Hayden and P. C. Nobes at Adelaide in 1993-94. V. M. Merchant scored 143 and 156 for Bombay v Maharashtra in 1948-49.

Page 1344 Highest totals by losing teams should include 587-9 dec., Lancashire lost to Derbyshire by two wickets at Manchester, 1996.

Page 1475 B. K. V. Prasad, not M. S. K. Prasad, was cautioned in the Taupo one-day international.

WISDEN 2001

Page 42 Sam Mendes did attend Cambridge University, but did not play for them.

Page 652 J. Cox scored 7 not 17 in Somerset's first innings v Oxford Universities.

Page 764 In the Benson and Hedges Cup, net run-rate was calculated using runs scored/conceded per over (though the Norwich Union National League retained the earlier system of runs scored/conceded per 100 balls).

Page 906 R. J. Harden held 189 catches in his first-class career.

Page 938 Herefordshire lost their Championship match with Dorset, despite John Shaw's hat-trick.

Page 1593 David Jowett did finish on the winning side in one of his 50 first-class matches; he helped MCC beat Oxford University in 1956.

THE ICC TEST CHAMPIONSHIP

In 2001, the International Cricket Council established a Test Championship, modelled on the unofficial Wisden World Championship of 1996–2001. The ICC Championship runs in conjunction with a ten-year programme requiring Test countries to play each other in home and away series during each five-year period. The programme was launched in May 2001 with the series between England and Pakistan, though the initial table was based on results dating back to May 1996.

Only series of at least two Tests are counted (whereas *Wisden's* table included one-off Tests); the Asian Test Championship is excluded. The table is calculated on the most recent series between each two sides, home and away, with two points for winning a series and one each for a draw. Each series result is superseded as the countries concerned play again. At present, because not all countries have played each other home and away, places are decided on the average number of points per series played. Once every side has played the full 18 series (scheduled to occur by 2005), the table will revert to a straight points system. Bangladesh will not be allocated an average score before completing nine series.

The table below shows the ICC Test Championship after the completion of the series between Pakistan and West Indies at Sharjah on February 10, 2002. Because of the crisis in Afghanistan, this was played at Sharjah, rather than in Pakistan, though the ICC ruled it should count as a home series for Pakistan.

Australia have headed the table since the official Championship was introduced. At Birmingham in July 2001, they were presented with the ICC Test Championship Trophy, to be held by the country at the head of the table. Australia were due to visit second-placed South Africa for a series beginning on February 22, 2002. They had to win to retain their position; a drawn series would reduce their average to 1.46 and raise South Africa's to 1.56, while a South African win would give them 1.63 and Australia 1.38. South Africa's strong position owed much to their record on the subcontinent, where they had beaten India and drawn with Sri Lanka on recent visits; Australia had lost both equivalent series, emphasising the league system's demand for consistency against all opponents.

THE ICC TEST CHAMPIONSHIP TABLE

(as at February 10, 2001)

		Series played	*Won*	*Lost*	*Drawn*	*Points*	*Average*
1	Australia	13	9	2	2	20	1.54
2	South Africa	16	11	3	2	24	1.50
3	Sri Lanka	14	7	5	2	16	1.14
4	England	15	7	6	2	16	1.07
5	New Zealand	16	7	6	3	17	1.06
6	West Indies	14	6	7	1	13	0.93
7	Pakistan	16	4	7	5	13	0.81
8	India	14	4	7	3	11	0.79
9	Zimbabwe	16	3	11	2	8	0.50
	Bangladesh	4	0	4	0	–	–

Updated standings and the Championship results grid may be found at the ICC website, www.icc.cricket.org.

INTERNATIONAL SCHEDULE, 2002–2009

At an executive board meeting in Melbourne, in February 2001, the International Cricket Council unveiled a ten-year schedule of Tests and one-day internationals. The schedule initially runs from May 2001 to April 2011; all of the ICC's ten Test-playing members are to play each other in home and away Test series (with a minimum of two matches to a series) during each five-year period.

The programme is based around Test matches, but in most cases there will be associated one-day internationals. Countries may revise dates as long as they do not disrupt other series. The following table shows the schedule from April 2002 to February 2009.

	Australia	Bangladesh	England	India	New Zealand	Pakistan	South Africa	Sri Lanka	West Indies	Zimbabwe
Australia	–	9/05	11/02 12/06	12/03 12/07	11/06	12/04 11/08	12/05	12/02 11/07	11/04 12/08	11/03
Bangladesh	10/03 4/06	–	12/03 2/07	4/04 10/06	10/04 10/07	*	4/03 4/08	11/04 2/08	12/02	1/09
England	6/05	5/05	–	7/02 6/07	5/04	7/06	7/03 6/08	5/02 5/06	7/04	5/03 5/08
India	9/04	4/05	2/06	–	10/03	2/04 1/06	11/04 10/08	11/05	10/02 2/08	10/07
New Zealand	2/05 2/09	12/06	2/08	12/02 2/07	–	12/03 12/08	2/04	12/04 12/07	2/06	12/05
Pakistan	9/02 2/08	9/03	11/05	4/03 2/05	4/02 10/08	–	10/03 10/07	3/05	12/06	10/04 10/06
South Africa	2/06	4/02	12/04 12/08	12/06 1/09	10/05	12/02 2/07	–	10/02	12/03 12/07	2/05 2/08
Sri Lanka	2/04 9/08	7/02 2/06	11/03 10/07	7/08	5/03 8/07	3/06	8/04 10/06	–	7/05	2/07
West Indies	4/03 2/07	5/04 11/08	2/04 2/09	4/02 5/06	6/02 4/08	5/05	3/05	7/03 5/08	–	4/06
Zimbabwe	4/02 9/06	1/04 12/07	11/04	10/05	9/05	11/02 9/07	8/06	4/04 12/08	10/03 9/08	–

Home teams listed on left, away teams across top.
** Bangladesh are scheduled to host Pakistan next in January 2010.*

ENGLAND'S INTERNATIONAL SCHEDULE, 2002–2007

Home

2002 Tests and ODIs v Sri Lanka and India
2003 Tests and ODIs v Zimbabwe and South Africa
2004 Tests and ODIs v New Zealand and West Indies
2005 Tests and ODIs v Bangladesh and Australia
2006 Tests and ODIs v Sri Lanka and Pakistan
2007 Tests and ODIs v India

Away

2002-03 Tests and ODIs v Australia
WORLD CUP in South Africa
2003-04 Tests and ODIs v Sri Lanka, Bangladesh and West Indies
2004-05 Tests and ODIs v Zimbabwe and South Africa
2005-06 Tests and ODIs v Pakistan and India
2006-07 Tests and ODIs v Australia and Bangladesh
WORLD CUP in the West Indies

All tours subject to confirmation.

FIXTURES, 2002

All County Championship matches are of four days' duration; tourist matches are four days unless stated; UCCE matches are of three days; and other first-class matches are three days unless stated.
† Not first-class. ‡ Venue unconfirmed. § Fixture unconfirmed.

Saturday, April 13

Cambridge	Cambridge UCCE v Middx
Chester-le-Street	Durham v Durham UCCE
Canterbury	†Kent v Loughborough UCCE
Leicester	†Leics v Bradford/Leeds UCCE
Oxford	Oxford UCCE v Worcs
Millfield School	†Somerset v Cardiff UCCE

Thursday, April 18

Oxford	Oxford UCCE v Northants

Friday, April 19

County Championship, Division One

Canterbury	Kent v Hants
Manchester	Lancs v Leics
The Oval	Surrey v Sussex

County Championship, Division Two

Chester-le-Street	Durham v Middx
Cardiff	Glam v Derbys
Worcester	Worcs v Glos

Saturday, April 20

Cambridge	Cambridge UCCE v Essex
Nottingham	Notts v Durham UCCE
Birmingham	†Warwicks v Cardiff UCCE
Leeds	†Yorks v Bradford/Leeds UCCE

Wednesday, April 24

County Championship, Division One

Southampton	Hants v Leics
Hove	Sussex v Somerset
Birmingham	Warwicks v Lancs
Leeds	Yorks v Surrey

County Championship, Division Two

Derby	Derbys v Durham
Chelmsford	Essex v Glos
Lord's	Middx v Notts
Northampton	Northants v Worcs

Cardiff	†Glam v Cardiff UCCE

Friday, April 26

Canterbury	Kent v Sri Lankans (3 days)

Sunday, April 28

†Benson and Hedges Cup (1 day)

Derby	Derbys v Lancs
Chelmsford	Essex v Sussex
Lord's	Middx v Surrey
Northampton	Northants v Glam
Nottingham	Notts v Yorks
Birmingham	Warwicks v Somerset

Monday, April 29

†Benson and Hedges Cup (1 day)

Southampton	Hants v Kent
Leicester	Leics v Durham
Worcester	Worcs v Glos

Tuesday, April 30

†Benson and Hedges Cup (1 day)

Lord's	Middx v Essex
Nottingham	Notts v Derbys
Taunton	Somerset v Glam

Wednesday, May 1

†Benson and Hedges Cup (1 day)

Chester-le-Street	Durham v Lancs
Bristol	Glos v Warwicks
Canterbury	Kent v Sussex
Northampton	Northants v Worcs
The Oval	Surrey v Hants
Leeds	Yorks v Leics

Thursday, May 2

Northampton	British Universities v Sri Lankans (3 days)

†Benson and Hedges Cup (1 day)

Chester-le-Street	Durham v Yorks
Chelmsford	Essex v Surrey
Canterbury	Kent v Middlesex

Friday, May 3

†Benson and Hedges Cup (1 day)

Derby	Derbys v Leics
Cardiff	Glam v Glos
Manchester	Lancs v Notts
Taunton	Somerset v Northants
Hove	Sussex v Hants
Birmingham	Warwicks v Worcs

Saturday, May 4

†Benson and Hedges Cup (1 day)

Derby	Derbys v Yorks
Nottingham	Notts v Durham
The Oval	Surrey v Kent

Sunday, May 5

†Benson and Hedges Cup (1 day)

Chelmsford	Essex v Hants
Bristol	Glos v Somerset
Manchester	Lancs v Leics
Lord's	Middx v Sussex
Birmingham	Warwicks v Northants
Worcester	Worcs v Glam

Monday, May 6

†Benson and Hedges Cup (1 day)

Chester-le-Street	Durham v Derbys
Cardiff	Glam v Warwicks
Southampton	Hants v Middx
Canterbury	Kent v Essex
Leicester	Leics v Notts
Northampton	Northants v Glos
Taunton	Somerset v Worcs
Hove	Sussex v Surrey
Leeds	Yorks v Lancs

Tuesday, May 7

Chester-le-Street	Durham v Sri Lankans (3 days)

Wednesday, May 8

County Championship, Division One

Southampton	Hants v Kent
Leicester	Leics v Warwicks
Taunton	Somerset v Yorks
The Oval	Surrey v Lancs

County Championship, Division Two

Derby	Derbys v Northants
Nottingham	Notts v Essex
Worcester	Worcs v Glam
Hastings	†Sussex v Bradford/Leeds UCCE
Oxford	Oxford UCCE v Glos

Saturday, May 11

Shenley Park	Middx v Sri Lankans (3 days)

Sunday, May 12

†Norwich Union League, Division One (1 day)

Chester-le-Street	Durham v Warwicks
Leicester	Leics v Notts
Taunton	Somerset v Yorks

Division Two (1 day)

Derby	Derbys v Sussex
Southampton	Hants v Glos
The Oval	Surrey v Lancs

Wednesday, May 15

County Championship, Division One

Canterbury	Kent v Yorks
Manchester	Lancs v Sussex
Taunton	Somerset v Leics
Birmingham	Warwicks v Hants

County Championship, Division Two

Cardiff	Glam v Durham
Bristol	Glos v Notts
Northampton	Northants v Middx
Worcester	Worcs v Essex
Cambridge	Cambridge UCCE v Surrey
Derby	†Derbys v Loughborough UCCE

Thursday, May 16

Lord's	ENGLAND v SRI LANKA (1st npower Test, 5 days)

Sunday, May 19

†Norwich Union League, Division One (1 day)

Cardiff	Glam v Durham
Canterbury	Kent v Yorks
Nottingham	Notts v Warwicks
Worcester	Worcs v Somerset

Division Two (1 day)

Chelmsford	Essex v Derbys
Bristol	Glos v Surrey

Manchester	Lancs v Sussex
Northampton	Northants v Middx

Tuesday, May 21

†Benson and Hedges Cup – Quarter-final (1 day)

Wednesday, May 22

†Benson and Hedges Cup – Quarter-finals (1 day)

Thursday, May 23

Cardiff	Glam v Sri Lankans

Friday, May 24

County Championship, Division One

The Oval	Surrey v Somerset
Horsham	Sussex v Leics
Leeds	Yorks v Hants

County Championship, Division Two

Chester-le-Street	Durham v Glos
Nottingham	Notts v Northants

†Cheltenham & Gloucester Trophy – Third Round (1 day)

Chelmsford	Essex v Middx
Manchester	Lancs v Derbys

Saturday, May 25

Lord's	†Eton v Harrow (1 day)

Sunday, May 26

County Championship, Division Two

Chelmsford	Essex v Derbys

†Norwich Union League – Division Two (1 day)

Manchester	Lancs v Middx

Wednesday, May 29

†Cheltenham & Gloucester Trophy – Third Round (1 day)

Exmouth	Devon v Yorks
Bury St Edmunds	Suffolk v Northants
Telford	Salop v Glos
Beaconsfield	Bucks v Sussex
Norwich	Norfolk v Kent
Sleaford	Lincs v Glam
Coventry & NW	Warwicks Board XI v Leics
Clontarf	Ireland v Notts
Stone	Staffs v Warwicks
St Austell	Cornwall v Worcs
Grange	Scotland v Surrey
Scarborough	Yorks Board XI v Somerset
Folkestone	Kent Board XI v Hants
Cardiff	Wales v Durham

Thursday, May 30

Birmingham	ENGLAND v SRI LANKA (2nd npower Test, 5 days)

Friday, May 31

County Championship, Division One

Southampton	Hants v Warwicks
Tunbridge Wells	Kent v Sussex
Manchester	Lancs v Surrey
Leicester	Leics v Yorks

County Championship, Division Two

Derby	Derbys v Glam
Bristol	Glos v Worcs
Lord's	Middx v Durham
Northampton	Northants v Essex

Tuesday, June 4

†Norwich Union League, Division One (1 day)

Tunbridge Wells	Kent v Notts
Leicester	Leics v Glam
Birmingham	Warwicks v Durham
Leeds	Yorks v Worcs

Division Two (1 day)

Manchester	Lancs v Glos (day/night)
Lord's	Middx v Hants
Northampton	Northants v Surrey
Horsham	Sussex v Essex

Thursday, June 6

Chesterfield	MCC v Sri Lankans

†Benson and Hedges Cup – 1st Semi-final (1 day)

Friday, June 7

†Benson and Hedges Cup – 2nd Semi-final (1 day)

Sunday, June 9

†Norwich Union League, Division One (1 day)

Cardiff	Glam v Kent

Oakham School	Leics v Worcs
Nottingham	Notts v Yorks
Birmingham	Warwicks v Somerset

Division Two (1 day)

Southampton	Hants v Derbys
Lord's	Middx v Sussex
Northampton	Northants v Glos

Wednesday, June 12

County Championship, Division One

Bath	Somerset v Hants
The Oval	Surrey v Kent
Birmingham	Warwicks v Leics
Leeds	Yorks v Sussex

County Championship, Division Two

Chester-le-Street	Durham v Worcs
Ilford‡	Essex v Northants
Lord's	Middx v Glam
Nottingham	Notts v Derbys

Durham	Durham UCCE v Lancs

Thursday, June 13

Manchester	ENGLAND v SRI LANKA (3rd npower Test, 5 days)

Sunday, June 16

†Norwich Union League, Division One (1 day)

Chester-le-Street	Durham v Worcs
Bath	Somerset v Leics
Nottingham	Notts v Kent
Leeds	Yorks v Warwicks

Division Two (1 day)

Derby	Derbys v Northants
Ilford‡	Essex v Lancs
Bristol	Glos v Middx
Southampton	Hants v Surrey

Monday, June 17

Oxford	†British Universities v West Indies A (1 day)

Wednesday, June 19

†Cheltenham & Gloucester Trophy – Fourth Round (1 day)

Hove	†Sri Lankans v West Indies A (1 day, day/night)

Friday, June 21

Taunton or Cardiff or Bristol	†Somerset or Glam or Glos v Sri Lankans (1 day)
Hove or Chelmsford or The Oval	†Sussex or Essex or Surrey v West Indies A (1 day)
Birmingham	†Zone6 City Cricket (1 day)

Saturday, June 22

Lord's	†BENSON AND HEDGES CUP FINAL (1 day)

Hove or Southampton or Canterbury§	†Sussex (day/night) or Hants or Kent v Indians (1 day)

Sunday, June 23

†Norwich Union League, Division One (1 day)

Chester-le-Street	Durham v Yorks
Worcester	Worcs v Warwicks

Division Two (1 day)

Derby	Derbys v Lancs
The Oval	Surrey v Sussex

Bristol or Taunton or Cardiff	†Glos or Somerset or Glam v Sri Lankans (1 day)
Canterbury or Southampton or Chelmsford	†Kent or Hants or Essex v West Indies A (1 day)

Monday, June 24

Canterbury§	†Kent v Indians (1 day)
Northampton	†Northants v Sri Lankans (1 day, day/night)

Cardiff	†Wales v England Board XI (International Challenge, 1 day)

Tuesday, June 25

Southampton	†Hants v Loughborough UCCE

Lord's	†Oxford U v Cambridge U (1 day)

Wednesday, June 26

County Championship, Division One

Liverpool	Lancs v Kent
Arundel	Sussex v Yorks
Birmingham	Warwicks v Somerset

County Championship, Division Two

Cardiff	Glam v Middx
Gloucester	Glos v Essex
Northampton	Northants v Notts
Worcester	Worcs v Durham
Leicester§	†Leics v Indians (1 day)
Derby	Derbys v West Indies A
Oxford	Oxford U v Cambridge U (4 days)

Thursday, June 27

Nottingham	†ENGLAND v SRI LANKA (NatWest Series, 1 day, day/night)

Saturday, June 29

Lord's	†ENGLAND v INDIA (NatWest Series, 1 day)

Sunday June 30

The Oval	†INDIA v SRI LANKA (NatWest Series, 1 day)

†Norwich Union League, Division One (1 day)

Nottingham	Notts v Leics
Taunton	Somerset v Glam
Birmingham	Warwicks v Kent
Worcester	Worcs v Durham

Division Two (1 day)

Gloucester	Glos v Essex
Manchester	Lancs v Surrey
Arundel	Sussex v Middx

Tuesday, July 2

Leeds	†ENGLAND v SRI LANKA (NatWest Series, 1 day)
Lord's	†UCCE Challenge (1 day)

Wednesday, July 3

County Championship, Division One

Southampton	Hants v Sussex
Maidstone	Kent v Warwicks
Leicester	Leics v Lancs
Taunton	Somerset v Surrey

County Championship, Division Two

Derby	Derbys v Glos
Swansea	Glam v Essex
Lord's	Middx v Worcs
Northampton	Northants v Durham
Nottingham	Notts v West Indies A

Thursday, July 4

Chester-le-Street	†ENGLAND v INDIA (NatWest Series, 1 day, day/night)

Saturday, July 6

Birmingham	†INDIA v SRI LANKA (NatWest Series, 1 day)

Sunday, July 7

Manchester	†ENGLAND v SRI LANKA (NatWest Series, 1 day)

†Norwich Union League, Division One (1 day)

Swansea	Glam v Leics
Maidstone	Kent v Durham
Taunton	Somerset v Worcs

Division Two (1 day)

Derby	Derbys v Glos
Southampton	Hants v Sussex
Southgate	Middx v Surrey
Northampton	Northants v Lancs
Leeds	†Yorks v West Indies A (1 day)

Tuesday, July 9

The Oval	†ENGLAND v INDIA (NatWest Series, 1 day)

Wednesday, July 10

County Championship, Division One

Leicester	Leics v Hants

The Oval Surrey v Warwicks
Hove Sussex v Kent
Scarborough Yorks v Somerset

County Championship, Division Two

Darlington Durham v Derbys
Southend Essex v Worcs
Southgate Middx v Glos
Nottingham Notts v Glam

Manchester Lancs v West Indies A

Thursday, July 11

Bristol †INDIA v SRI LANKA (NatWest Series, 1 day, day/night)

Saturday, July 13

Lord's †NATWEST SERIES FINAL (1 day)

Sunday, July 14

†Norwich Union League, Division One (1 day)

Canterbury Kent v Worcs
Leicester Leics v Warwicks
Nottingham Notts v Glam
Scarborough Yorks v Somerset

Division Two (1 day)

Southend Essex v Hants
Southgate Middx v Glos
Hove Sussex v Northants

Monday, July 15

†Norwich Union League, Division Two (1 day)

Manchester Lancs v Derbys (day/night)

Tuesday, July 16

†Cheltenham & Gloucester Trophy – Quarter-finals (1 day)

Arundel§ Indians v West Indies A (3 days)

Wednesday, July 17

†Cheltenham & Gloucester Trophy – Quarter-finals (1 day)

Thursday, July 18

County Championship, Division Two

Southgate Middx v Essex

†Norwich Union League, Division Two (1 day)

Cheltenham Glos v Hants

Friday, July 19

County Championship, Division One

Canterbury Kent v Surrey
Taunton Somerset v Sussex
Leeds Yorks v Lancs

County Championship, Division Two

Derby Derbys v Notts
Cheltenham Glos v Glam
Worcester Worcs v Northants

Saturday, July 20

Southampton§ Hants v Indians (3 days)
Birmingham Warwicks v West Indies A (3 days)

Sunday, July 21

†Norwich Union League, Division One (1 day)

Chester-le-Street Durham v Leics

Monday, July 22

†Norwich Union League, Division Two (1 day)

Chelmsford Essex v Middx (day/night)

Tuesday, July 23

†Norwich Union League, Division Two (1 day)

Southampton Hants v Lancs (day/night)

Wednesday, July 24

County Championship, Division One

Leicester Leics v Kent
Guildford Surrey v Yorks
Birmingham Warwicks v Sussex

County Championship, Division Two

Chester-le-Street	Durham v Notts
Chelmsford	Essex v Glam
Cheltenham	Glos v Middx

†Norwich Union League, Division Two (1 day)

Northampton	Northants v Derbys (day/night)
Taunton	Somerset v West Indies A

Thursday, July 25

Lord's	ENGLAND v INDIA (1st npower Test, 5 days)

County Championship, Division One

Southampton	Hants v Lancs

County Championship, Division Two

Northampton	Northants v Derbys

Saturday, July 27

Cardiff	†England Under-19 v India Under-19 (1st Test, 4 days)

Sunday, July 28

†Norwich Union League, Division One (1 day)

Chester-le-Street	Durham v Notts
Leicester	Leics v Kent
Birmingham	Warwicks v Glam
Worcester	Worcs v Yorks

Division Two (1 day)

Cheltenham	Glos v Sussex
Guildford	Surrey v Essex

Monday, July 29

Cheltenham	†Glos v West Indies A (1 day)

Tuesday, July 30

†Norwich Union League, Division One (1 day)

Canterbury	Kent v Warwicks (day/night)

Wednesday, July 31

†Cheltenham & Gloucester Trophy – 1st Semi-final (1 day)

Worcester or Leicester or Hove§	Worcs or Leics or Sussex v Indians

Thursday, August 1

†Cheltenham & Gloucester Trophy – 2nd Semi-final (1 day)

Saturday, August 3

†Norwich Union League, Division One (1 day)

Chester-le-Street	Durham v Kent
Cardiff	Glam v Somerset
Leeds	Yorks v Notts

Division Two (1 day)

Derby	Derbys v Hants
Bristol	Glos v Lancs
Whitgift School	Surrey v Northants

Sunday, August 4

†Norwich Union League, Division One (1 day)

Birmingham	Warwicks v Leics
Worcester	Worcs v Glam

Division Two (1 day)

Lord's	Middx v Essex
Northampton	Northants v Hants

Monday, August 5

†Norwich Union League, Division One (1 day)

Leeds	Yorks v Durham (day/night)

Division Two (1 day)

Hove	Sussex v Glos (day/night)

Tuesday, August 6

†Norwich Union League, Division Two (1 day)

Manchester	Lancs v Hants (day/night)
Whitgift School, Croydon	Surrey v Middx

Wednesday, August 7

County Championship, Division One

Canterbury	Kent v Somerset
Leeds	Yorks v Warwicks

County Championship, Division Two

Derby	Derbys v Essex
Cardiff	Glam v Glos
Lord's	Middx v Northants

†Norwich Union League, Division One (1 day)

Worcester	Worcs v Notts (day/night)

Division Two (1 day)

Hove	Sussex v Surrey (day/night)

Southampton	†England Under-19 v India Under-19 (2nd Test, 4 days)

Thursday, August 8

Nottingham	ENGLAND v INDIA (2nd npower Test, 5 days)

County Championship, Division One

Manchester	Lancs v Hants
Hove	Sussex v Surrey

County Championship, Division Two

Kidderminster	Worcs v Notts

Sunday, August 11

†Norwich Union League, Division One (1 day)

Cardiff	Glam v Yorks
Canterbury	Kent v Somerset
Leicester	Leics v Durham

Division Two (1 day)

Derby	Derbys v Essex
Lord's	Middx v Northants

Tuesday, August 13

†Norwich Union League, Division Two (1 day)

Bristol	Glos v Northants (day/night)

Northampton	†England Under-19 v India Under-19 (3rd Test, 4 days)

Wednesday, August 14

Chelmsford§	Essex v Indians

County Championship, Division One

Southampton	Hants v Somerset
Manchester	Lancs v Yorks
Leicester	Leics v Surrey
Birmingham	Warwicks v Kent

County Championship, Division Two

Derby	Derbys v Worcs
Nottingham	Notts v Middx

†Norwich Union League, Division One (1 day)

Chester-le-Street	Durham v Glam (day/night)

Thursday, August 15

County Championship, Division Two

Bristol	Glos v Northants

Friday, August 16

County Championship, Division Two

Chester-le-Street	Durham v Glam

Sunday, August 18

†Norwich Union League, Division One (1 day)

Leicester	Leics v Yorks
Nottingham	Notts v Somerset

Division Two (1 day)

Southampton	Hants v Essex
The Oval	Surrey v Derbys

Monday, August 19

†Norwich Union League, Division One (1 day)

Taunton	Somerset v Notts (day/night)
Birmingham	Warwicks v Worcs (day/night)

Tuesday, August 20

†Norwich Union League, Division Two (1 day)

Hove	Sussex v Lancs (day/night)

Wednesday, August 21

County Championship, Division One

Taunton	Somerset v Warwicks

County Championship, Division Two

Colchester	Essex v Durham
Lord's	Middx v Derbys
Northampton	Northants v Glam
Nottingham	Notts v Glos

†Norwich Union League, Division One (1 day)

Canterbury	Kent v Leics (day/night)

Division Two (1 day)

The Oval	Surrey v Hants (day/night)

Thursday, August 22

Leeds	ENGLAND v INDIA (3rd npower Test, 5 days)

County Championship, Division One

Canterbury	Kent v Leics
The Oval	Surrey v Hants
Hove	Sussex v Lancs

Sunday, August 25

†Norwich Union League, Division One (1 day)

Taunton	Somerset v Warwicks

Division Two (1 day)

Colchester	Essex v Northants
Lord's	Middx v Derbys

Monday, August 26

†Norwich Union League, Division One (1 day)

Colwyn Bay	Glam v Notts

Tuesday, August 27

County Championship, Division One

Southampton	Hants v Yorks
Blackpool	Lancs v Somerset
Leicester	Leics v Sussex
Birmingham	Warwicks v Surrey

County Championship, Division Two

Chester-le-Street	Durham v Northants
Colwyn Bay	Glam v Notts
Worcester	Worcs v Middx

†Norwich Union League, Division Two (1 day)

Colchester	Essex v Glos (day/night)
Bristol	†England Under-19 v India Under-19 (1st 1-day)

Wednesday, August 28

Derby§	Derbys v Indians (3 days)

Thursday, August 29

†Cheltenham & Gloucester Trophy, 2003 – First Round (1 day) (see page 1623)

Taunton	†England Under-19 v India Under-19 (2nd 1-day)

Friday, August 30

Taunton	†England Under-19 v India Under-19 (3rd 1-day)

Saturday, August 31

Lord's	†CHELTENHAM & GLOUCESTER TROPHY FINAL (1 day)

Sunday, September 1

†Norwich Union League, Division One (1 day)

Chester-le-Street	Durham v Somerset
Birmingham	Warwicks v Notts
Worcester	Worcs v Kent
Leeds	Yorks v Glam

Division Two (1 day)

Southampton	Hants v Middx
Manchester	Lancs v Essex
Northampton	Northants v Sussex

Monday, September 2

†Norwich Union League, Division Two (1 day)

Derby	Derbys v Surrey (day/night)

Tuesday, September 3

†Norwich Union League, Division One (1 day)

Cardiff — Glam v Worcs (day/night)

Division Two (1 day)

Hove — Sussex v Hants (day/night)

Wednesday, September 4

County Championship, Division One

Manchester — Lancs v Warwicks
Taunton — Somerset v Kent
Scarborough — Yorks v Leics

County Championship, Division Two

Chelmsford — Essex v Middx
Bristol — Glos v Derbys

†Norwich Union League, Division One (1 day)

Nottingham — Notts v Durham (day/night)

Thursday, September 5

The Oval — ENGLAND v INDIA (4th npower Test, 5 days)

County Championship, Division One

Hove — Sussex v Hants

County Championship, Division Two

Cardiff — Glam v Worcs

Friday, September 6

County Championship, Division Two

Nottingham — Notts v Durham

Sunday, September 8

†Norwich Union League, Division One (1 day)

Taunton — Somerset v Kent
Scarborough — Yorks v Leics

Division Two (1 day)

Chelmsford — Essex v Surrey
Bristol — Glos v Derbys
Manchester — Lancs v Northants

Tuesday, September 10

†Norwich Union League, Division One (1 day)

Birmingham — Warwicks v Yorks (day/night)

Wednesday, September 11

County Championship, Division One

Southampton — Hants v Surrey
Canterbury — Kent v Lancs

County Championship, Division Two

Derby — Derbys v Middx
Chester-le-Street — Durham v Essex
Northampton — Northants v Glos
Nottingham — Notts v Worcs

†Norwich Union League, Division One (1 day)

Leicester — Leics v Somerset (day/night)

Thursday, September 12

County Championship, Division One

Leicester — Leics v Somerset
Birmingham — Warwicks v Yorks

†Cheltenham & Gloucester Trophy, 2003 – Second Round (1 day)
(see page 1623)

Sunday, September 15

†Norwich Union League, Division One (1 day)

Canterbury — Kent v Glam
Nottingham — Notts v Worcs

†Norwich Union League, Division Two (1 day)

Shenley Park — Middx v Lancs
Northampton — Northants v Essex
Hove — Sussex v Derbys

Wednesday, September 18

County Championship, Division One

Taunton — Somerset v Lancs
The Oval — Surrey v Leics
Hove — Sussex v Warwicks
Leeds — Yorks v Kent

County Championship, Division Two

Chelmsford — Essex v Notts

Cardiff	Glam v Northants
Bristol	Glos v Durham
Worcester	Worcs v Derbys

Sunday, September 22

†Norwich Union League, Division One (1 day)

Cardiff	Glam v Warwicks
Taunton	Somerset v Durham
Worcester	Worcs v Leics
Leeds	Yorks v Kent

Division Two (1 day)

Derby	Derbys v Middx
Chelmsford	Essex v Sussex
Southampton	Hants v Northants
The Oval	Surrey v Glos

†CHELTENHAM & GLOUCESTER TROPHY, 2003

All matches are of one day's duration.

First Round – Thursday, August 29, 2002

1	Banbury	Oxon v Lancs Board XI
2	Finchampstead	Berks v Ireland
3	Kidderminster	Worcs Board XI v Dorset
4	Ratcliffe College	Denmark v Leics Board XI
5	Camborne	Cornwall v Somerset Board XI
6	Southgate	Middx Board XI v Derbys Board XI
7	Coventry & NW	Warwicks Board XI v Herefordshire
8	Bristol	Glos Board XI v Surrey Board XI
9	Dinton	Bucks v Suffolk
10	Hursley Park	Hants Board XI v Wilts
11	Luton Town	Beds v Herts
12	Keswick	Cumberland v Notts Board XI
13	Toft	Cheshire v Hunts Board XI
14	Northampton	Northants Board XI v Yorks Board XI

Second Round – Thursday, September 12, 2002

15	Scotland v Match 1 winner
16	Match 2 winner v Norfolk
17	Match 3 winner v Sussex Board XI
18	Kent Board XI v Match 4 winner
19	Wales v Match 5 winner
20	Match 6 winner v Cambs
21	Durham Board XI v Match 7 winner
22	Essex Board XI v Match 8 winner
23	Match 9 winner v Salop
24	Match 10 winner v Staffs
25	Match 11 winner v Holland
26	Devon v Match 12 winner
27	Match 13 winner v Lincs
28	Northumberland v Match 14 winner.

†MINOR COUNTIES CHAMPIONSHIP, 2002

Unless otherwise indicated, all matches are of three days' duration.

JUNE

2–Beds v Cambs (Dunstable); Berks v Cornwall (Falkland); Bucks v Norfolk (Ascott Park, Wing); Cheshire v Oxon (Cheadle Hulme); Devon v Salop (Exmouth); Herefordshire v Wales (Colwall); Lincs v Staffs (Grantham); Wilts v Dorset (Corsham).

4–Cumberland v Northumberland (Carlisle).

23–Herts v Norfolk (Hertford); Northumberland v Suffolk (Jesmond); Oxon v Berks (Challow & Childrey); Salop v Wilts (Shrewsbury).

30–Dorset v Cornwall (Bournemouth); Herefordshire v Cheshire (Luctonians CC, Kingsland); Herts v Cambs (Welwyn Garden City); Lincs v Bucks (Grantham); Staffs v Beds (Tamworth); Wales v Berks (Lamphey); Wilts v Devon (South Wilts CC, Salisbury).

JULY

1–Suffolk v Cumberland (Bury St Edmunds).

14–Cambs v Staffs (March); Cornwall v Wales (Falmouth); Devon v Cheshire (Sidmouth); Dorset v Oxon (Bournemouth); Northumberland v Lincs (Jesmond); Salop v Herefordshire (Shifnal); Suffolk v Herts (Ransomes, Ipswich).

15–Cumberland v Bucks (Barrow).

21–Norfolk v Beds (Manor Park, Norwich).

28–Beds v Lincs (Bedford Town); Berks v Herefordshire (Finchampstead); Bucks v Cambs (Marlow); Dorset v Devon (Bournemouth); Herts v Cumberland (Long Marston); Norfolk v Suffolk (Manor Park, Norwich); Oxon v Wilts (Thame); Staffs v Northumberland (Stone); Wales v Salop (Swansea).

29–Cheshire v Cornwall (Alderley Edge).

AUGUST

4–Beds v Suffolk (Luton Town); Berks v Wilts (Reading CC); Bucks v Staffs (Beaconsfield); Cambs v Northumberland (Cambridge); Cheshire v Wales (Oxton); Herefordshire v Dorset (Luctonians CC, Kingsland); Lincs v Herts (Grantham); Oxon v Devon (Banbury).

5–Cornwall v Salop (St Austell); Norfolk v Cumberland (Manor Park, Norwich).

18–Cambs v Lincs (March); Cornwall v Herefordshire (Truro); Cumberland v Beds (Netherfield); Devon v Berks (Torquay); Northumberland v Norfolk (Jesmond); Salop v Oxon (Whitchurch); Staffs v Herts (Walsall); Suffolk v Bucks (Mildenhall); Wales v Dorset (Abergavenny); Wilts v Cheshire (Westbury).

SEPTEMBER

8–Final.

†ECB 38-COUNTY CUP, 2002

All matches are of one day's duration.

Teams are County Board XIs and do not include first-class counties.

MAY

5–Berks v Middx (Slough); Glos v Worcs (Bristol University); Herts v Suffolk (Bishop's Stortford); Notts v Hunts (Boots, Nottingham); Wilts v Somerset (Chippenham).

9–Yorks v Northumberland (York).

19–Berks v Oxon (Thatcham); Bucks v Northants (Ascott Park, Wing); Cambs v Beds (March); Cornwall v Wilts (St Just); Devon v Dorset (Bovey Tracey); Durham v Northumberland (South Shields); Hants v Channel Islands (Southampton); Herts v Essex (Harpenden); Leics v Norfolk (Hinckley Town); Notts v Lincs (Boots, Nottingham); Salop v Cheshire (Oswestry); Staffs v Lancs (Longton); Wales v Worcs (Pontarddulais); Warwicks v Glos (Stratford-upon-Avon).

21–Cumberland v Yorks (Millom).

26–Somerset v Devon (Taunton); Suffolk v Cambs (Exning).

30–Surrey v Sussex (Metropolitan Police).

JUNE

4–Surrey v Kent (Metropolitan Police).

9–Beds v Herts (Southill Park); Channel Islands v Sussex (Jersey); Cornwall v Devon (Camborne); Derbys v Salop (Lullington Park); Dorset v Somerset (Bournemouth); Essex v Suffolk (Chelmsford); Herefordshire v Wales (Leominster); Hunts v Lincs (Peterborough Town); Norfolk v Notts (Manor Park, Norwich); Northants v Berks (TBA); Northumberland v Cumberland (South Northumberland); Oxon v Bucks (Challow & Childrey); Worcs v Warwicks (Kidderminster).

12–Middx v Bucks (Ealing).

13–Lancs v Cheshire (Blackpool); Yorks v Durham (Stamford Bridge).

16–Beds v Essex (Flitwick); Cheshire v Staffs (Nantwich); Glos v Herefordshire (Bristol University); Hants v Surrey (Havant Park); Leics v Notts (Hinckley Town); Lincs v Norfolk (Lincoln Lindum); Northumberland v Yorks (Tynemouth); Oxon v Northants

(Banbury); Salop v Lancs (Wellington); Somerset v Cornwall (North Perrott); Sussex v Kent (Hastings); Warwicks v Wales (Coventry and NW); Wilts v Dorset (Swindon).

18–Durham v Cumberland (Hartlepool).

23–Derbys v Staffs (Alvaston & Boulton); Essex v Cambs (Chelmsford); Hunts v Leics (Kimbolton); Kent v Channel Islands (Ashford); Northants v Middx (Old Northamptonians); Sussex v Hants (Stirlands); Worcs v Herefordshire (Kidderminster).

25–Cheshire v Derbys (New Brighton).

27–Lancs v Derbys (Middleton).

JULY

3–Middx v Oxon (Richmond).

7–Bucks v Berks (Wormsley); Cambs v Herts (Wisbech); Channel Islands v Surrey (Jersey); Devon v Wilts (Torquay); Dorset v Cornwall (Bournemouth SC); Herefordshire v Warwicks (Brockhampton); Kent v Hants (Ashford); Lincs v Leics (Cleethorpes); Norfolk v Hunts (Manor Park, Norwich); Staffs v Salop (Porthill Park); Suffolk v Beds (Woodbridge School); Wales v Glos (Penarth).

9–Cumb v Durham (Furness).

Quarter-finals to be played on August 1.

Semi-finals to be played on August 15.

Final to be played on September 3 at Lord's.

†SECOND ELEVEN CHAMPIONSHIP, 2002

Unless otherwise stated, all matches are of three days' duration.

APRIL

23–Glos v Warwicks (Bristol; 4 days).

24–Durham v Yorks (Chester-le-Street); Worcs v Northants (Kidderminster).

MAY

1–Derbys v Surrey (Chesterfield); Leics v Kent (Hinckley); Middx v Sussex (Vine Lane, Uxbridge).

7–Glam v Glos (Pontarddulais; 4 days); Lancs v Notts (Manchester; 4 days).

8–Kent v Essex (Maidstone); Somerset v Worcs (North Perrott); Warwicks v Northants (Moseley CC); Yorks v Derbys (Stamford Bridge).

14–Lancs v Northants (Crosby); Leics v Glam (Leicester); Notts v Derbys (Notts Unity Casuals CC; 4 days); Surrey v Hants (The Oval; 4 days); Sussex v Kent (Hove; 4 days).

15–Durham v Middx (Chester-le-Street CC); Worcs v Yorks (Barnt Green).

20–Lancs v Yorks (Liverpool; 4 days); Warwicks v Durham (Coventry & NW).

21–Leics v Derbys (Hinckley; 4 days).

22–Somerset v Northants (North Perrott); Surrey v Notts (Cheam).

27–Northants v Kent (Milton Keynes).

28–Durham v Lancs (Stockton; 4 days); Middx v Essex (Southgate); Somerset v Glam (Taunton; 4 days); Sussex v Glos (Hove; 4 days).

29–Notts v Leics (Nottingham).

JUNE

4–Durham v Worcs (Hartlepool); Notts v Warwicks (Boots, Nottingham); Yorks v Lancs (Scarborough; 4 days).

5–Derbys v Leics (Dunstall); Essex v Sussex (Halstead); Glam v Northants (Abergavenny); Middx v Glos (Uxbridge).

10–Glos v Somerset (Bristol; 4 days); Lancs v Durham (Grappenhall).

11–Glam v Yorks (Cardiff; 4 days); Hants v Essex (Southampton; 4 days); Leics v Notts (Hinckley; 4 days).

12–Kent v Surrey (Canterbury); Northants v Warwicks (Northampton).

18–Derbys v Notts (Denby; 4 days); Hants v Middx (Southampton); Lancs v Somerset (Blackpool; 4 days); Worcs v Warwicks (Ombersley; 4 days).

JULY

9–Derbys v Warwicks (Sandiacre; 4 days); Essex v Notts (Coggeshall); Hants v Surrey (Southampton; 4 days); Northants v Sussex (Northampton; 4 days); Worcs v Glam (Worcester; 4 days).

10–Somerset v Glos (Taunton).

16–Sussex v Surrey (Stirlands CC; 4 days).

17–Notts v Yorks (Boots, Nottingham); Warwicks v Somerset (Knowle & Dorridge).

23–Glam v Somerset (Usk; 4 days); Leics v Essex (Oakham School); Notts v Durham (Nottingham; 4 days); Sussex v Hants (Hove; 4 days).

24–Derbys v Lancs (Repton School); Glos v Worcs (Bristol); Kent v Middx (Canterbury); Yorks v Surrey (Todmorden).

30–Durham v Northants (Seaton Carew); Glos v Hants (Bristol University; 4 days); Surrey v Sussex (Banstead; 4 days).

31–Middx v Kent (Merchant Taylors' School, Northwood); Notts v Lancs (Worksop College); Warwicks v Essex (Walmley).

AUGUST

6–Essex v Kent (Chelmsford; 4 days); Northants v Hants (Northampton; 4 days); Warwicks v Worcs (Stratford-upon-Avon; 4 days).

7–Durham v Derbys (South Northumberland); Somerset v Yorks (Taunton); Surrey v Lancs (The Oval); Sussex v Glam (Horsham).

13–Derbys v Hants (Denby; 4 days); Sussex v Northants (Hastings).

14–Middx v Notts (Ealing); Surrey v Durham (Whitgift School, Croydon); Yorks v Leics (Harrogate).

19–Glos v Leics (Bristol).

20–Glam v Warwicks (Panteg; 4 days); Hants v Notts (Southampton; 4 days); Surrey v Middx (Wimbledon); Worcs v Lancs (Worcester).

21–Kent v Somerset (Beckenham); Northants v Derbys (Stowe School).

26–Northants v Worcs (Northampton).

27–Essex v Middx (Chelmsford; 4 days); Glos v Glam (Bristol University; 4 days); Kent v Hants (Canterbury); Notts v Sussex (Nottingham; 4 days); Warwicks v Leics (Kenilworth Wardens); Yorks v Durham (Middlesbrough; 4 days).

28–Lancs v Surrey (Manchester).

SEPTEMBER

2–Yorks v Notts (Stamford Bridge).

3–Glam v Lancs (Abergavenny); Worcs v Leics (Halesowen).

4–Essex v Surrey (Colchester); Hants v Sussex (Southampton); Middx v Derbys (Shenley Park); Northants v Glos (Northampton).

11–Leics v Northants (Hinckley).

†SECOND ELEVEN TROPHY, 2002

All matches are of one day's duration.

MAY

7–Yorks v Derbys (Bradford & Bingley CC).

20–Hants v Glam (Southampton).

27–Hants v Somerset (Southampton).

29–Hants v Worcs (Southampton).

JUNE

3–Hants v Glos (Southampton).

5–Surrey v MCC Young Cricketers (Sutton).

10–Notts v Yorks (Nottingham).

17–Surrey v Kent (Sutton).

20–Essex v Sussex (Bishop's Stortford); Kent v Surrey (Beckenham); Leics v Minor Counties (Hinckley).

24–Essex v Surrey (Old Brentwoods); Lancs v Derbys (Southport); MCC Young Cricketers v Sussex (RAF Vine Lane, Uxbridge); Somerset v Worcs (Taunton); Warwicks v Middx (Stratford-upon-Avon); Yorks v Notts (Leeds).

25–Durham v Notts (Tynemouth); Glos v Somerset (Bristol); Northants v Leics (Milton Keynes).

26–Glos v Worcs (Bristol); Kent v MCC Young Cricketers (Canterbury); Minor Counties v Warwicks (Wellington); Somerset v Glam (Taunton); Surrey v Sussex (Sutton); Yorks v Lancs (Castleford).

27–Durham v Lancs (Sunderland); Kent v Sussex (Sutton Valence); Leics v Middx (Hinckley).

28–Durham v Yorks (Darlington); Glam v Worcs (Usk); Glos v Hants (Bristol); Surrey v Essex (Banstead).

JULY

1–Derbys v Notts (Ilkeston); Lancs v Durham (Nelson); MCC Young Cricketers v Surrey (Wormsley); Middx v Northants (Uxbridge); Somerset v Hants (Taunton); Sussex v Essex (Hove); Worcs v Glos (Worcester).

2–Lancs v Yorks (Wigan); Notts v Durham (Notts Unity Casuals CC); Warwicks v Northants (Studley).

3–Derbys v Yorks (Glossop); Glam v Glos (Neath CC); Leics v Warwicks (Oakham School); Sussex v Kent (Hove).

4–Sussex v Surrey (Hove); Warwicks v Minor Counties (Studley).

5–Derbys v Lancs (Chesterfield); Glam v Hants (Newport); Kent v Essex (Canterbury); Middx v Leics (Finchley); Northants v Minor Counties (Isham); Sussex v MCC Young Cricketers (Hove); Worcs v Somerset (Worcester); Yorks v Durham (York).

8–Northants v Middx (Northampton); Notts v Derbys (Welbeck); Warwicks v Leics (Harborne).

9–Somerset v Glos (Taunton).

11–MCC Young Cricketers v Kent (RAF Vine Lane, Uxbridge); Minor Counties v Middx (High Wycombe).

12–Essex v Kent (Coggeshall); Minor Counties v Leics (Milton Keynes).

15–Derbys v Durham (Dunstall); Leics v Northants (Oakham School); MCC Young Cricketers v Essex (RAF Vine Lane, Uxbridge); Middx v Warwicks (Richmond).

16–Notts v Lancs (Farnsfield); Worcs v Hants (Old Hill).

17–Middx v Minor Counties (RAF Vine Lane, Uxbridge); Worcs v Glam (Old Hill).

18–Durham v Derbys (South Shields); Glos v Glam (Cheltenham College or Bristol); Minor Counties v Northants (Luton).

19–Essex v MCC Young Cricketers (Billericay).

22–Glam v Somerset (Cardiff); Lancs v Notts (Manchester); Northants v Warwicks (Northampton).

Semi-finals to be played on August 12 (reserve day August 13).

Final to be played on September 9 (reserve day September 10).

†WOMEN'S CRICKET, 2002

JULY

10–Grainville, Jersey	ENGLAND v INDIA (Triangular Series, 1 day)
11–Grainville, Jersey	INDIA v NEW ZEALAND (Triangular Series, 1 day)
12–Grainville, Jersey	ENGLAND v NEW ZEALAND (Triangular Series, 1 day)
16–Durham	NEW ZEALAND v INDIA (Triangular Series, 1 day)
17–Durham	ENGLAND v NEW ZEALAND (Triangular Series, 1 day)
19–Chester-le-Street	ENGLAND v INDIA (Triangular Series, 1 day)
20–Chester-le-Street	TRIANGULAR SERIES FINAL (1 day)
27–Cambridge	County Championship (5 days)

AUGUST

8–Shenley Park	ENGLAND v INDIA (1st Test, 4 days)
11–Colwall	Cricket Week (6 days)
14–Taunton	ENGLAND v INDIA (2nd Test, 4 days)

SEPTEMBER

7–King's College, Taunton	National Club Knockout Plate and Cup finals

THE WORLD CUP IN SOUTH AFRICA, ZIMBABWE AND KENYA, 2003

Pool A

FEBRUARY

10	Harare	Zimbabwe v Namibia
11	Johannesburg	Australia v Pakistan
12	Paarl	Holland v India
13	Harare	Zimbabwe v England
15	Centurion	Australia v India
16	East London	England v Holland
16	Kimberley	Namibia v Pakistan
19	Port Elizabeth	England v Namibia
19	Harare	Zimbabwe v India
20	Potchefstroom	Australia v Holland
22	Cape Town*	England v Pakistan
23	Pietermaritzburg	India v Namibia
24	Bulawayo	Zimbabwe v Australia
25	Paarl	Holland v Pakistan
26	Durban*	England v India
27	Potchefstroom	Australia v Namibia
28	Bulawayo	Zimbabwe v Holland

MARCH

1	Centurion	India v Pakistan
2	Port Elizabeth	Australia v England
3	Bloemfontein	Holland v Namibia
4	Bulawayo	Zimbabwe v Pakistan

Pool B

FEBRUARY

9	Cape Town*	South Africa v West Indies
10	Bloemfontein	New Zealand v Sri Lanka
11	Durban*	Bangladesh v Canada
12	Potchefstroom	South Africa v Kenya
13	Port Elizabeth	New Zealand v West Indies
14	Pietermaritzburg	Bangladesh v Sri Lanka
15	Cape Town*	Canada v Kenya
16	Johannesburg	South Africa v New Zealand
18	Benoni	Bangladesh v West Indies
19	Paarl	Canada v Sri Lanka
21	Nairobi	Kenya v New Zealand
22	Bloemfontein	South Africa v Bangladesh
23	Centurion	Canada v West Indies
24	Nairobi	Kenya v Sri Lanka
26	Kimberley	Bangladesh v New Zealand
27	East London	South Africa v Canada
28	Cape Town*	Sri Lanka v West Indies

MARCH

1	Johannesburg	Bangladesh v Kenya
3	Benoni	Canada v New Zealand
3	Durban*	South Africa v Sri Lanka
4	Kimberley	Kenya v West Indies

The top three teams from each pool will advance to the Super Six round, carrying forward results and points gained against fellow-qualifiers, but not those against the teams eliminated. Each of them will then play the three teams from the other pool.

SUPER SIX

MARCH

7	Centurion	Pool A 1st v Pool B 1st
7	Cape Town*	Pool A 2nd v Pool B 2nd
8	Bloemfontein	Pool A 3rd v Pool B 3rd
10	Johannesburg	Pool A 2nd v Pool B 1st
11	Port Elizabeth	Pool A 1st v Pool B 3rd
12	Bloemfontein	Pool A 3rd v Pool B 2nd
14	Centurion	Pool A 2nd v Pool B 3rd
15	East London	Pool A 3rd v Pool B 1st
15	Durban*	Pool A 1st v Pool B 2nd

SEMI-FINALS

Tuesday, March 18

Port Elizabeth First v Fourth of Super Six

Thursday, March 20

Durban* Second v Third of Super Six

The World Cup Final will be played on Sunday, March 23, 2003, at Johannesburg.

* *Day/night matches.*

INDEX OF TEST MATCHES

INDEX OF FILLERS AND INSERTS

INDEX OF ADVERTISEMENTS

Roman numerals refer to the colour section between pages 48 and 49.

INDEX OF UNUSUAL OCCURRENCES